PROFESSIONAL EDITION

J.K. LASSER'S™

YOUR INCOME TAX

2024

Prepared by the

J.K. LASSER INSTITUTE™

WILEY

Staff for This Book

J.K. Lasser Editorial

J.T. Eagan, MBA, EA, *Contributing Editor*
Jaclyn Barkow, DBA, EA, *Contributing Editor*
Jason Woolwine, *Contributing Editor*
Danielle R. Page, Macc, EA, *Contributing Editor*
Mackenna R. Evans, EA, *Contributing Editor*
Angelo C. Jack, *Production Manager*
William Hamill, *Copyediting and Proofreading*
Index by WordCo Indexing Services

John Wiley & Sons, Inc.

For general information on our other products and services or for technical support, please contact our Customer Care Department within the United States at (800) 762-2974, outside the United States at (317) 572-3993 or fax (317) 572-4002.

Wiley also publishes its books in a variety of electronic formats. Some content that appears in print may not be available in electronic formats. For more information about Wiley products, visit our web site at www.wiley.com.

Library of Congress Cataloging-in-Publication Data:

ISBN   978-1-394-22352-7 (Print)
ISBN   978-1-394-22353-4 (ePub)
ISBN   978-1-394-22354-1 (ePDF)

Eighty-Seventh Edition

SKY10061706_120523

How To Use *Your Income Tax 2024*

Tax alert symbols. Throughout the text of *Your Income Tax*, these special symbols alert you to advisory tips about filing your federal tax return and tax planning opportunities:

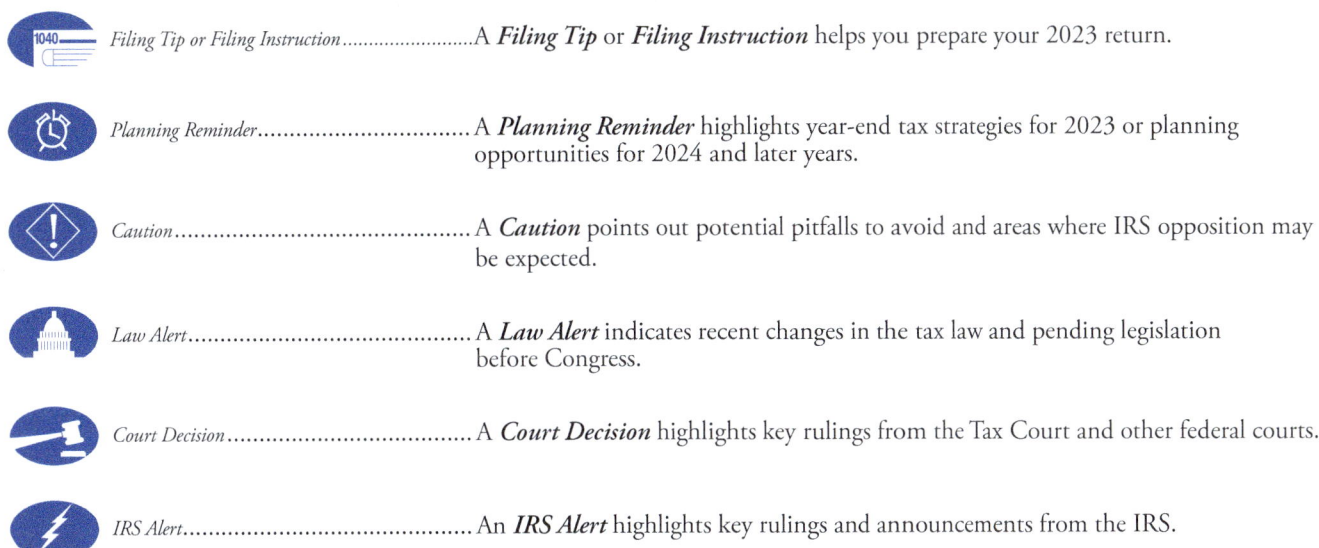

Filing Tip or Filing Instruction .... A ***Filing Tip*** or ***Filing Instruction*** helps you prepare your 2023 return.

Planning Reminder .... A ***Planning Reminder*** highlights year-end tax strategies for 2023 or planning opportunities for 2024 and later years.

Caution .... A ***Caution*** points out potential pitfalls to avoid and areas where IRS opposition may be expected.

Law Alert .... A ***Law Alert*** indicates recent changes in the tax law and pending legislation before Congress.

Court Decision .... A ***Court Decision*** highlights key rulings from the Tax Court and other federal courts.

IRS Alert .... An ***IRS Alert*** highlights key rulings and announcements from the IRS.

Visit *jklasser.com* for FREE download of *e-Supplement*

You can download a free *e-Supplement* to *Your Income Tax 2024* at *jklasser.com*. The *e-Supplement* will provide an update on tax developments from the IRS and Congress, including a look ahead to 2024.

On the homepage at *jklasser.com*, you will find free tax news, tax tips and tax planning articles.

The federal income tax law, despite efforts at simplification, remains a maze of statutes, regulations, rulings, and court decisions written in technical language covering thousands and thousands of pages. For 87 years, *J.K. Lasser's™ Your Income Tax* has aided and guided millions of taxpayers through this complex law. Every effort has been made to provide a direct and easy-to-understand explanation that shows how to comply with the law and at the same time take advantage of tax-saving options and plans.

The 2024 edition of *Your Income Tax*—our 87th edition—continues this tradition. To make maximum use of this tax guide, we suggest that you use these aids:

Contents Chapter by Chapter. The contents, on pages *v–xxv*, lists the chapters in Your Income Tax. References direct you to sections within a particular chapter. Thus a reference to *21.1* directs you to *Chapter 21* and then to section 1 within that chapter. Section and page references are provided in the index at the back of the book.

What's New for 2023. Pages *xxvii–xxix* alert you to tax developments that may affect your 2023 tax return.

Key Tax Numbers for 2023. Pages *xxx–xxxi*.

Tax-Saving Opportunities. Page *xxxii*.

Expiring Provisions. Page *xxxiii*.

Pending Tax Rule Changes. Congress may pass retroactive tax provisions which would modify certain aspects of your tax return; check the *e-Supplement* at *jklasser.com* for an explanation of any changes enacted that will impact 2023 returns and affect tax planning for 2024.

Contents | Chapter by Chapter

FILING BASICS　　　　　　　　　　　　　　　　　　　　　　　　　　　1

Filing Status　　　　　　　　　　　　　　　　　　　　　　　　　　　　9

REPORTING YOUR INCOME 35

Wages, Salary, and Other Compensation 37

Fringe Benefits 56

Dividend and Interest Income · 81

Reporting Property Sales · 109

Tax-Free Exchanges of Property

158

Retirement and Annuity Income

172

IRAs 209

Income From Real Estate Rentals and Royalties 262

Loss Restrictions: Passive Activities and At-Risk Limits — 282

Other Income — **312**

CLAIMING DEDUCTIONS — **337**

Deductions Allowed in Figuring Adjusted Gross Income — **339**

Claiming the Standard Deduction or Itemized Deductions — **345**

Charitable Contribution Deductions   352

Itemized Deduction for Interest Expenses   379

Deductions for Taxes   397

Medical and Dental Expense Deductions   406

Casualty and Theft Losses and Involuntary Conversions   426

Other Itemized Deductions   451

Travel and Meal Expense Deductions   454

Tax Withholdings — 534

Estimated Tax Payments — 542

Tax Rules for Investors in Mutual Funds   606

Educational Tax Benefits   615

Special Tax Rules for Senior Citizens and the Disabled — 634

Members of the Armed Forces — 649

How To Treat Foreign Earned Income — 657

Retirement and Medical Plans for Self-Employed   721

Claiming Depreciation Deductions   734

Deducting Car and Truck Expenses 751

Sales of Business Property 766

Figuring Self-Employment Tax

FILING YOUR RETURN AND THE PROCESS AFTER YOU FILE

Filing Your Return

Filing Refund Claims, and Amended Returns

If the IRS Examines Your Return

2023 TAX FORMS — 811

TAX LAW AUTHORITIES — 857

CITATIONS OF AUTHORITY — 863

PRACTICE BEFORE THE IRS — 977

GLOSSARY — 1017

INDEX — 1023

What's New for 2023

Some of the tax changes for 2023 noted below were provided by the Inflation Reduction Act and SECURE 2.0 Act (SECURE 2.0), such as new rules for the credit for certain home energy improvements. For an update on tax developments and a free download of the *e-Supplement* to this book, visit us online at *jklasser.com*.

Tax News for 2023

Item—	Highlight—
Filing status name change from "qualifying widow/widower" to "qualifying surviving spouse"	The IRS has renamed the filing status formerly called "qualifying widow/widower" as "qualifying surviving spouse." The rules for this filing status have not changed; the only change is to the name of the filing status.
Tax rate brackets and preferential rates for capital gains/qualified dividends	The rate brackets for 2023 ordinary income remain at 10%, 12%, 22%, 24%, 32%, 35% and 37%, but the taxable income amounts in each bracket have changed. The top bracket of 37% for 2023 applies if taxable income exceeds $578,125 for single taxpayers and heads of households, $693,750 for married persons filing jointly and qualifying widows/widowers, and $346,875 for married taxpayers filing separate returns *(1.2)*. Qualified dividends *(4.2)* and long-term capital gains *(5.3)* may escape tax entirely under the 0% rate, or be subject to capital gain rates of 15% or 20% depending on filing status, taxable income, and how much of the taxable income consists of qualified dividends and eligible long-term gains *(5.3)*. The 20% capital gain rate applies in 2023 when taxable income exceeds $492,300 for singles, $523,050 for heads of households, $553,850 for married persons filing jointly and qualifying widows/widowers, and $276,900 for married persons filing separately. The 0%, 15%, and 20% rates do not apply to long-term gains subject to the 28% rate (collectibles and taxed portion of small business stock) or the 25% rate for unrecaptured real estate depreciation *(5.3)*.
Retirement plan distributions	The SECURE Act raised the age to 72 for IRA owners who reached age 70½ after 2019, meaning those born on or after July 1, 1949. SECURE 2.0 raised the age again; anyone attaining age 72 after 2022 does not have to begin receiving RMDs until the year they reach age 73 *(8.13)*.
Education-related tax breaks	Educator expenses of up to $300 are deductible for 2023 *(12.2)*.
Standard deductions	The basic standard deduction for 2023 *(13.1)* is $27,700 for married persons filing jointly and qualifying surviving spouse, $20,800 for heads of households, or $13,850 for single taxpayers or married persons filing separately. The additional standard deduction *(13.4)* for being 65 or older or blind increases to $1,850 if single or head of household ($3,700 if 65 and blind). If married filing jointly, the additional standard deduction increases to $1,500 if one spouse is 65 or older or blind, $3,000 if both spouses are at least 65 (or one is 65 and blind, or both are blind and under age 65).
Self-employment tax and deduction for portion of self-employment tax; Social Security wage base	For 2023, the tax rate on the employee portion of Social Security is 6.2% on wages up to $160,200, so Social Security tax withholdings should not exceed $9,932. Medicare tax of 1.45% is withheld from all wages regardless of amount. On Schedule SE for 2023, self-employment tax applies to earnings of up to $160,200; only 92.35% of earnings are taken into account. The 15.3% rate equals 12.4% for Social Security (6.2% employee share and 6.2% employer share) plus 2.9% for Medicare. If net earnings exceed $160,200 (after the reduction), the 2.9% Medicare rate applies to the entire amount *(45.3–45.4)*. One-half of the self-employment tax may be claimed as an above-the-line deduction on Schedule 1 of Form 1040 or 1040-SR *(45.3–45.4)*.

Tax News for 2023 (continued)

Item—	Highlight—
IRA and Roth IRA contributions	The age cap on contributing to a traditional IRA has been repealed. Contributions to a traditional IRA for 2023 can be made as long as you have earned income (or other eligible income). You may make contributions to a traditional IRA for 2023 of up to $6,500, or $7,500 if you are age 50 or older at the end of 2023, provided that you have at least $6,500/$7,500 of earned income *(8.2)*.
Qualified business income deduction	If you are a sole proprietor or have an interest in a partnership, limited liability company, or S corporation, you may be eligible for a deduction of up to 20% of qualified business income *(40.24)*. This deduction is a personal deduction, not a business deduction, and can be claimed whether you itemize or take the standard deduction. The taxable income amounts used to figure the deduction for 2023 have been increased for inflation.
First-year expensing	For qualifying property placed in service in 2023, first-year expensing *(42.3)* is allowed up to a limit of $1,160,000, and the limit begins to phase out if the total cost of qualifying property exceeds $2,890,000 *(42.3)*.
IRS mileage allowance	The IRS standard business mileage rate for 2023 is 65.5 cents a mile *(43.1)*. The rate for medical expense *(17.9)* and moving expense for certain military personnel *(12.3)* deductions is 22 cents a mile for 2023. For charitable volunteers *(14.4)*, the mileage rate is unchanged at 14 cents a mile.
Vehicle depreciation limit	For a vehicle placed in service in 2023 and used over 50% for business, the first-year depreciation limit using bonus depreciation is $19,200. However, if you elect not to have bonus depreciation apply, or you are not eligible for the bonus, the first-year depreciation limit is $11,200 *(43.5)*.
Clean vehicle credit	Credit of up to $7,500 for eligible new clean vehicles and up to $4,000 for eligible previously owned clean vehicles. Specific criteria must be met *(25.16)*.
Health savings accounts (HSAs)	The definition of a high-deductible health plan, which is a prerequisite to funding an HSA, means a policy with a minimum deductible for 2023 of $1,500 for self-only coverage and a maximum out-of-pocket cap on co-payments and other amounts of $7,500. These limits are doubled for family coverage ($3,000/$15,000) *(41.10)*. The contribution limit for 2023 is $3,850 for self-only coverage and $7,750 for family coverage *(41.11)*. Those age 55 or older and not yet on Medicare can add an additional $1,000.
Adoption expenses	For 2023, the limit on the adoption credit as well as the exclusion for employer-paid adoption assistance is $15,950 *(3.6)*. The benefit phaseout range is modified adjusted gross income between $239,230 to $279,230 *(25.9)*.
Child tax credit	For 2023, the maximum child tax credit for a child under age 17 is $2,000 *(25.2)*. The credit begins to phase out when modified adjusted gross income exceeds $400,000 on a joint return or $200,000 for all other filers. There is an additional child tax credit that can be claimed if the child tax credit otherwise allowed is limited by tax liability; the refundable amount may not exceed $1,600 per qualifying child *(25.3)*. The credit for other dependents is unchanged (i.e., not refundable and limited to $500 per dependent) *(25.4)*.
Dependent care credit and exclusion	For 2023, the child and dependent care credit is nonrefundable *(25.5)*. Qualifying expenses taken into account in figuring the credit are $3,000 for one qualifying individual and $6,000 for two or more qualifying individuals. The credit ranges from 35% down to 20%, depending on adjusted gross income. The exclusion for dependent care under an employer's dependent care assistance plan is $5,000 ($2,500 if married filing separately).
Earned income tax credit	For 2023, the maximum credit amount is $3,995 for one qualifying child, $6,604 for two qualifying children, $7,430 for three or more qualifying children, and $560 for taxpayers who have no qualifying child *(25.7)*. The phaseout ranges for the credit have been adjusted for inflation *(25.8)*. The excessive investment income limit is $11,000.

Tax News for 2023 (continued)

Item—	Highlight—
Premium tax credit	For 2023, the premium tax credit is allowed even if household income exceeds 400% of the federal poverty line. The required contribution percentages are reduced *(25.13)*.
Alternative minimum tax (AMT) exemption and tax brackets	The AMT exemptions, exemption phaseout thresholds, and the dividing line between the 26% and 28% AMT brackets are adjusted for inflation. The 2023 AMT exemptions (prior to any phaseout) are $126,500 for married couples filing jointly and qualifying widows/widowers, $81,300 for single persons and heads of households, and $63,250 for married persons filing separately. *See 23.1* for exemption phaseout rules and AMT calculation details. All nonrefundable personal credits may be claimed against the AMT as well as the regular tax *(23.3)*.
Eligibility for saver's credit	The adjusted gross income brackets for the 10%, 20%, and 50% credits are increased for 2023. No credit is allowed when AGI exceeds $36,500 for single taxpayers, $54,750 for heads of households, and $73,000 for married persons filing jointly. ABLE account contributions can qualify for the credit *(25.12)*.
Residential energy efficient property credit	The credit for installing solar energy in your residence is 30% for 2023 *(25.15)*.
Deduction limits for long-term care premiums	The maximum amount of age-based long-term care premiums that can be included as deductible medical expenses for 2023 (subject to the AGI floor; *see 17.1*) is $480 if you are age 40 or younger at the end of 2023; $890 for those age 41 through 50; $1,790 for those age 51 through 60; $4,770 for those age 61 through 70; and $5,960 for those over age 70 *(17.15)*.
Foreign earned income and housing exclusions	The maximum foreign earned income exclusion for 2023 is $120,000 *(36.1)*. The limit on housing expenses that may be taken into account in figuring the housing exclusion is generally $36,000, but the limit is increased by the IRS for high cost localities *(36.4)*.
Annual gift tax exclusion; gift tax and estate tax exemption	The annual gift tax exclusion is increased to $17,000 per donee for 2023 gifts of cash or present interests *(39.2)*. The basic exemption amount for 2023 gift tax and estate tax purposes increases to $12,920,000 *(39.4, 39.9)*. The top tax rate remains at 40% *(39.9)*.

Key Tax Numbers for 2023

Standard Deduction *(13.2)*

Joint return/Surviving Spouse	$27,700
Head of Household	$ 20,800
Single	$13,850
Married filing separately	$13,850
Dependents—minimum deduction *(13.5)*	$ 1,250
Additional deduction if age 65 or older, or blind *(13.4)*	
Married-per spouse, filing jointly or separately	$ 1,500 ($3,000 for age and blindness)
Surviving Spouse	$ 1,500 ($3,000 for age and blindness)
Single or head of household	$ 1,850 ($3,600 for age and blindness)

Long-term Care Premiums *(17.15)*

Limit on premium allowed as medical expense	
Age 40 or under	$ 480
Over 40 but not over 50	$ 890
Over 50 but not over 60	$ 1,790
Over 60 but not over 70	$ 4,770
Over 70	$ 5,960

IRA Contributions

Traditional IRA contribution limit *(8.2)*	$ 6,500
Additional contribution if age 50 or older	$ 1,000
Deduction phaseout for active plan participant *(8.4)*	
Single or head of household	$ 73,000 – $ 83,000
Married filing jointly, two participants	$ 116,000 – $ 136,000
Married filing jointly, one participant	
Participant spouse	$ 116,000 – $ 136,000
Non-participant spouse	$ 218,000 – $ 228,000
Married filing separately, live together, either participates	$ 0 – $ 10,000
Married filing separately, live apart all year	
Participant spouse	$ 68,000 – $ 78,000
Non-participant spouse	no phaseout
Roth IRA contribution limit *(8.21)*	$ 6,500
Additional contribution if age 50 or older	$ 1,000
Roth IRA contribution limit phaseout range	
Single, head of household	$ 138,000–$ 153,000
Married filing separately, live apart all year	$ 138,000–$ 153,000
Married filing jointly, or qualifying widow/widower	$ 218,000–$ 228,000
Married filing separately, live together at any time	$ 0–$ 10,000

Elective deferral limits

401(k), 403(b), 457 plans *(7.15)*	$ 22,500
Salary-reduction SEP *(8.17)*	$ 22,500
SIMPLE IRA *(8.18)*	$ 15,500
Additional contribution if age 50 or older ("catch-up" contributions)	
401(k), 403(b), governmental 457 and SEP plans *(7.15, 8.17)*	$ 7,500
SIMPLE IRA *(8.18)*	$ 3,500

Key Tax Numbers for 2023 (continued)

Education

American opportunity credit limit-per student *(33.8)*	$2,500
Lifetime learning credit limit-per taxpayer *(33.9)*	$2,000
Phaseout of American opportunity credit *(33.8)*	
Married filing jointly	$160,000–$ 180,000
Single, head of household, or qualifying widow/widower	$80,000–$ 90,000
Phaseout of lifetime learning credit *(33.9)*	
Married filing jointly	$160,000–$ 180,000
Single, head of household, or qualifying widow/widower	$80,000–$ 90,000
Student loan interest deduction limit *(33.13)*	$2,500
Phaseout of deduction limit	
Married filing jointly	$155,000–$185,000
Single, head of household, or qualifying widow/widower	$75,000–$90,000
Coverdell ESA limit *(33.10)*	$2,000
Phaseout of limit	
Married filing jointly	$190,000–$220,000
All others	$95,000–$110,000

Capital gain rates—assets held over one year *(5.3)*

If taxable income is no more than $89,250 for married filing jointly and surviving spouses, $59,750 for heads of households, or $44,625 for singles and married filing separately:	0%
If taxable income is more than the endpoint for the zero rate shown above but no more than the threshold shown below for the 20% rate	15%
If taxable income exceeds $553,850 for married filing jointly and surviving spouses, $523,050 for heads of households, $492,300 for singles, and $276,900 for married filing separately:	20%
Collectibles gain-maximum rate	28%
Unrecaptured Section 1250 gain on depreciated real estate-maximum rate	25%

Qualified dividends tax rate *(4.2)*

See the taxable income breakpoints for capital gain rates above	0%, 15%, or 20%

IRS mileage rates

Business *(43.1)*	65.5 cents/mile
Medical *(17.9)* and moving for military personnel *(12.3)*	22 cents/mile
Charitable volunteers *(14.4)*	14 cents/mile

Exclusion for employer provided transportation *(3.8)*

Free parking, transit passes, and van pooling	$300/month

Tax-Saving Opportunities for 2023 and Beyond

Objective—	Explanation—
Realizing long-term capital gains	Long-term capital gains are taxed at lower rates than short-term gains and regular income. *See Chapter 5* for basic capital gain rules. *See Chapters 30* and *31* for discussions of special investment situations.
Earning qualifying dividends	Qualified dividends *(4.2)* are subject to the reduced tax rates for long-term capital gains.
Earning tax-free income	You can earn tax-free income by— 1. Investing in tax-exempt securities. However, before you invest, determine whether the tax-free return will exceed the after-tax return of taxed income *(30.10)*. 2. Taking a position in a company that pays tax-free fringe benefits, such as health and life insurance protection. For a complete discussion of tax-free fringe benefits, *see Chapter 3*. 3. Seeking tax-free education benefits with scholarship arrangements, qualified tuition programs, and Coverdell ESAs; *see Chapter 33*. 4. Taking a position overseas to earn excludable foreign earned income; *see Chapter 36*. 5. Investing in Roth IRAs; *see Chapter 8*. 6. Selling a principal residence for tax-free gain up to $250,000 ($500,000 on a joint return; *see Chapter 29)*.
Deferring income	You can defer income to years when you will pay less tax through— 1. Deferred pay plans, which are discussed in *Chapter 2*. 2. Qualified retirement plans such as 401(k) plans *(Chapter 7)*, self-employed plan *(Chapter 41)*, and traditional IRA and Roth IRA plans *(Chapter 8)*. 3. Transacting installment sales when you sell property; *see 5.21*. 4. Investing in U.S. Savings EE bonds or I-bonds *(4.28–4.29, 30.12–30.13)*.
Income splitting	Through income splitting you divide your income among several persons or taxpaying entities that will pay an aggregate tax lower than the tax that you would pay if you reported all of the income. Although the tax law limits income-splitting opportunities, certain business and family income planning through the use of trusts and custodian accounts can provide tax savings; *see Chapters 24* and *39*.
Tax-free exchanges	You can defer tax on appreciated property by transacting tax-free exchanges of realty *(6.1, 31.3)*.
Buying a personal residence	Homeowners are favored by the tax law. 1. Paying premiums on mortgage interest may result in deductible interest if you itemize deductions *(15.5)*. 2. Homeowners can borrow on their home equity and deduct interest expenses within limits, provided the loan qualifies as home acquisition debt *(15.3)*.
Take advantage of special personal tax breaks for education	The tax law provides several breaks for education expenses; *see Chapter 33*, which discusses scholarships, grants, tuition plans, savings bonds redeemed to pay higher education costs, a deduction or education credits, Coverdell Education Savings Accounts, and student loan interest deduction.
Take advantage of special tax breaks for health care expenses	The tax law provides several breaks for health care expenses. Employer-provided health and accident plans, including flexible spending arrangements, are discussed in *Chapter 3*. Health savings accounts (HSAs) can be used to save for health care expenses on a tax-free basis *(3.2, 41.10)*. ABLE accounts can be set up for individuals who become disabled before age 26 and be used to build up a fund from which tax-free distributions for qualified expenses can be made *(34.12)*. You may be able to qualify for the premium tax credit to help offset the cost of premiums for coverage obtained through the government Marketplace *(25.13)*.
Take advantage of personal tax credits	*See Chapter 25* for personal tax credits such as the premium tax credit, child tax credit, dependent care credit, saver's credit, tax credit for certain green energy improvements to your home, and adoption credit that can reduce your tax liability.
Energy Efficient Home Improvements.	The Inflation Reduction Act (IRA) added many credits for energy efficient home improvements and clean energy upgrades. Lifetime credits are removed through 2032 *(25.15)*.

Expiring Provisions

The following is a list of some tax breaks and reportion procedures that expired at the end of 2022 and no longer apply to 2023 returns unless Congress extends them. If there is legislation extending some or all of these provision, it will be included in the *e-Supplement* at *jklasser.com*.

- Full deduction for restaurant business meals
- 100% Bonus Depreciation is now 80%
- The deferral of the Form 1099-K issuance to 2023

PART 1

Filing Basics

In this part, you will learn these income tax basics:

- Whether you must file a return
- When and where to file your return
- Which tax form to file
- What filing status you qualify for
- When filing separately is an advantage for married persons
- How to qualify as head of household
- How filing rules for resident aliens and nonresident aliens differ

Do You Have to File a 2023 Tax Return?

If you are—	You must file if gross income for 2023 is at least
Single	
Under age 65 (on January 1, 2024)	$ 13,850
Age 65 or older (on or before January 1, 2024)	15,700
Married and living together at the end of 2023	
Filing a joint return—both spouses under age 65 (on January 1, 2024)	$27,700
Filing a joint return—one spouse age 65 or older (on or before January 1, 2024)	29,200
Filing a joint return—both spouses age 65 or older (on or before January 1, 2024)	30,700
Filing a separate return for 2023 (regardless of age)	$5
Married and living apart at the end of 2023	
Filing a joint or separate return for 2023 (regardless of age)	$5
Head of a household maintained for a child or other relative *(1.12)*	
Under age 65 (on January 1, 2024)	$20,800
Age 65 or older (on or before January 1, 2024)	22,650
Widowed in 2021 or 2022 and have a dependent child *(1.11)*	
Under age 65 (on January 1, 2024)	27,700
Age 65 or older (on or before January 1, 2024)	29,200

Age 65. Whether you are age 65 or older is generally determined as of the end of the year, but if your 65th birthday is on January 1, 2024, you are treated as being age 65 at the end of 2023.

Marital status. For 2023 returns, marital status is generally determined as of December 31, 2023. Thus, if you were divorced or legally separated during 2023, you are not considered married for 2023 tax purposes, and you must use the filing threshold for single persons unless you qualify as a head of household *(1.12)*, or you remarried in 2023 and are filing a joint return with your new spouse. If you remarry in 2023 and file separately from your new spouse, you must file a 2023 return if you have gross income of at least $5.

If your spouse died in 2023 and you were living together on the date of death, use the filing threshold shown above for married persons living together at the end of 2023. If you were not living together on the date of death, you must file a 2023 return if you have gross income of at least $5, unless you remarried during 2023 and are filing jointly with your new spouse.

Same-sex marriages. Lawfully married same-sex couples are treated as married for all federal tax purposes. The IRS recognizes your marriage to a same-sex spouse if the marriage was legally entered into in one of the 50 States, the District of Columbia, Puerto Rico, U.S. territory or possession, or foreign country *(1.1)*.

Gross income. Gross income is generally all the income that you received in 2023, except for items specifically exempt from tax.

Include wages and tips *(Chapter 2)*, self-employment income *(Chapter 45)*, taxable scholarships *(Chapter 33)*, taxable interest and dividends *(Chapter 4)*, capital gains *(Chapter 5)*, taxable pensions and annuities *(Chapter 7)*, rents *(Chapter 9)*, and taxable alimony *(Chapter 37)*, trust distributions *(Chapter 11)*. For purposes of the filing test, you must include as gross income sales home sale proceeds even if they are partly or completely excludable from income *(Chapter 29)* and you also must include tax-free foreign earned income *(Chapter 36)*.

Exclude tax-exempt interest *(Chapter 4)*, tax-free fringe benefits *(Chapter 3)*, qualifying scholarships *(Chapter 33)*, tax-free alimony *(Chapter 37)*, and life insurance *(Chapter 11)*. For purposes of the filing thresholds above, exclude Social Security benefits unless (1) you are married filing separately and you lived with your spouse at any time during 2023, or (2) 50% of net Social Security benefits plus other gross income and any tax-exempt interest exceeds $25,000 ($32,000 if married filing jointly). If (1) or (2) applies, the taxable part of Social Security benefits (as determined in *34.3*) is included in your gross income.

Other situations when you must file. Even if you are not required to file under the gross income tests, you must file a 2023 return if:

- You are self-employed and you owe self-employment tax because your net self-employment earnings for 2023 are $600 or more *(Chapter 45)*, or
- You (or your spouse if filing jointly) received HSA or Archer MSA distributions *(Chapter 41)*, or
- You are entitled to a refund of taxes withheld from your wages *(Chapter 26)* or a refund based on any of these credits: the additional child tax credit, the premium tax credit, the Earned Income Credit for working families, *(Chapter 25)*, or the American opportunity credit *(Chapter 33)*, or
- You received advance payments of the premium tax credit *(25.12)*, or
- You owe any special tax such as alternative minimum tax *(Chapter 23)*, the Additional Medicare Tax or the Net Investment Income Tax *(Chapter 28)*, IRA penalties *(Chapter 8)*, household employment taxes *(Chapter 38)*, and FICA on tips *(Chapter 26)*.

Filing Tests for Dependents: 2023 Returns

The income threshold for filing a tax return is generally lower for an individual who may be claimed as a dependent than for a nondependent. You are a "dependent" if you are the qualifying child or qualifying relative of another taxpayer, and the other tests for dependents at *21.2* are met. If you are the parent of a dependent child who had only investment income subject to the "kiddie tax" *(24.3)*, you may elect to report the child's income on your own return for 2023 instead of filing a separate return for the child; *see* *24.4* for the election rules.

If, under the tests at *21.2*, you may be claimed as a dependent by someone else, use the chart below to determine if you must file a 2023 return. Generally, a married person who files a joint return may not be claimed as a dependent by a third party, but *see* the exception at *21.2*. Include as unearned income taxable interest and dividends, capital gains, pensions, annuities, unemployment compensation, taxable Social Security benefits, and distributions of unearned income from a trust. Earned income includes wages, tips, self-employment income, and taxable scholarships or fellowships *(Chapter 33)*. Gross income is the total of unearned and earned income.

For married dependents, the filing requirements in the chart assume that the dependent is filing a separate return and not a joint return *(Chapter 1)*. Generally, a married person who files a joint return may not be claimed as a dependent by a third party who provides support.

For purposes of the following chart, a person is treated as being age 65 (or older) if his or her 65th birthday is on or before January 1, 2024. Blindness is determined as of December 31, 2023.

 *Filing Instruction*

File for Refund of Withholdings

Even if you are not required to file a return under the income tests on this page, you should file to obtain a refund of federal tax withholdings.

File a Return for 2023 If You Are a—

Single dependent. Were you *either* age 65 or older or blind?

❏ **No.** You must file a return if *any* of the following apply.
- Your unearned income was over $1,250.
- Your earned income was over $13,850.
- Your gross income was more than the *larger* of—
  - $1,250, or
  - Your earned income (up to $13,450) plus $400.

❏ **Yes.** You must file a return if *any* of the following apply.
- Your unearned income was over $3,100 ($4,950 if 65 or older *and* blind).
- Your earned income was over $15,700 ($17,550 if 65 or older *and* blind).
- Your gross income was more than the *larger* of—
  - $3,100 ($4,950 if 65 or older *and* blind), or
  - Your earned income (up to $13,450) plus $2,250 ($4,100 if 65 or older *and* blind).

Married dependent. Were you *either* age 65 or older or blind?

❏ **No.** You must file a return if *any* of the following apply.
- Your unearned income was over $1,250.
- Your earned income was over $13,850.
- Your gross income was at least $5 and your spouse files a separate return and itemizes deductions.
- Your gross income was more than the *larger* of—
  - $1,250, or
  - Your earned income (up to $13,450) plus $400.

❏ **Yes.** You must file a return if *any* of the following apply.
- Your unearned income was over $2,750 ($4,250 if 65 or older *and* blind).
- Your earned income was over $15,300 ($16,800 if 65 or older *and* blind).
- Your gross income was at least $5 and your spouse files a separate return and itemizes deductions.
- Your gross income was more than the *larger* of—
  - $2,750 ($4,250 if 65 or older *and* blind), or
  - Your earned income (up to $13,450) plus $1,850 ($3,350 if 65 or older *and* blind).

Where to File Your 2023 Form 1040 or 1040-SR

If you filed a paper Form 1040 or 1040-SR for 2022 and are filing a paper return for 2023, check the table below to see if the IRS filing address for your residence has changed. If the IRS makes late changes to the table below, the changes will be in the *e-Supplement* at *jklasser.com*.

When you file, include your complete return address and if you are enclosing numerous attachments with your return, make sure that you include enough postage.

You can use a private delivery service designated by the IRS to meet the "timely mailing is timely filing/paying" rule *(46.2)*. Only the specific services from FedEx, DHL Express, and UPS that the IRS has designated qualify; the instructions to the return has a list of these services.

Where Do You File Form 1040 or 1040-SR?

IF you live in...	THEN use this address if you:	
	Are requesting a refund or are not enclosing a check or money order...	Are enclosing a check or money order...
Alabama, Georgia, North Carolina, South Carolina, Tennessee	Department of the Treasury Internal Revenue Service Austin, TX 73301-0002	Internal Revenue Service P.O. Box 1214 Charlotte, NC 28201-1214
Alaska, California, Colorado, Hawaii, Idaho, Kansas, Michigan, Montana, Nebraska, Nevada, North Dakota, Ohio, Oregon, South Dakota, Utah, Washington, Wyoming	Department of the Treasury Internal Revenue Service Ogden, UT 84201-0002	Internal Revenue Service P.O. Box 802501 Cincinnati, OH 45280-2501
Arizona, New Mexico	Department of the Treasury Internal Revenue Service Austin, TX 73301-0002	Internal Revenue Service P.O. Box 802501 Cincinnati, OH 45280-2501
Arkansas, Oklahoma	Department of the Treasury Internal Revenue Service Austin, TX 73301-0002	Internal Revenue Service P.O. Box 931000 Louisville, KY 40293-1000
Connecticut, Delaware, District of Columbia, Illinois, Indiana, Iowa, Kentucky, Maine, Maryland, Massachusetts, Minnesota, Missouri, New Hampshire, New Jersey, New York, Rhode Island, Vermont, Virginia, West Virginia, Wisconsin	Department of the Treasury Internal Revenue Service Kansas City, MO 64999-0002	Internal Revenue Service P.O. Box 931000 Louisville, KY 40293-1000
Florida, Louisiana, Mississippi, Texas	Department of the Treasury Internal Revenue Service Austin, TX 73301-0002	Internal Revenue Service P.O. Box 1214 Charlotte, NC 28201-1214
Pennsylvania	Department of the Treasury Internal Revenue Service Kansas City, MO 64999-0002	Internal Revenue Service P.O. Box 802501 Cincinnati, OH 45280-2501
A foreign country, U.S. territory*, or use an APO or FPO address, or file Form 2555 or 4563, or are a dual-status alien	Department of the Treasury Internal Revenue Service Austin, TX 73301-0215	Internal Revenue Service P.O. Box 1303 Charlotte, NC 28201-1303

*If you live in American Samoa, Puerto Rico, Guam, the U.S. Virgin Islands, or the Northern Mariana Islands, see Pub. 570.

Filing Deadlines (on or before)

JANUARY 16, 2024—
Pay the balance of your 2023 estimated tax. If you do not meet this date, you may avoid an estimated tax penalty for the last quarter by filing your 2023 return and paying the balance due by January 31, 2024.

Farmers and fishermen: File your single 2023 estimated tax payment by January 16, 2024. If you do not, you may still avoid an estimated tax penalty by filing a final tax return and paying the full tax by March 1, 2024.

JANUARY 31, 2024—
Make sure you have received a Form W-2 from each employer for whom you worked in 2023 and Form 1099-NEC from each business for whom you worked and received at least $600 in payment.

APRIL 15, 2024—
You have until Monday, April 15, 2024, to file your 2023 return and pay the balance of your 2023 tax liability.

If you cannot meet the April 15, 2024, deadline for your 2023 return, you may obtain an automatic six-month filing extension to October 15, 2024, by filing Form 4868 (electronically or on paper). However, even if you get an extension, interest will still be charged for taxes not paid by the original April 15 deadline and late payment penalties will be imposed unless at least 90% of your tax liability is paid by the original deadline or you otherwise show reasonable cause. If you cannot pay the full amount of tax you owe when you file your return, you can file Form 9465 to request an installment payment arrangement.

If on the April 15 deadline you are a U.S. citizen or resident alien living and working outside the U.S. or Puerto Rico, or in military service outside the U.S. or Puerto Rico, you have an automatic two-month extension (you don't have to request an extension), until June 17, 2024, for filing your 2023 return and paying any balance due. However, despite the extension to June 17, interest is still charged on payments made after the original due date.

Pay the first installment of your 2024 estimated tax on or before April 15, 2024.

JUNE 17, 2024—
Pay the second installment of your 2024 estimated tax. You may amend an earlier estimate at this time.

You have until this date to file your 2023 return and pay any balance due if on April 15 you were a U.S. citizen or resident living and working outside the U.S. or Puerto Rico, or in military service outside the U.S. or Puerto Rico; however, interest will be charged on payments made after April 15. If you qualify for this out- of- the-country extension but cannot file by June 17, you may obtain an additional four-month filing extension until October 15, 2024, by filing Form 4868; this additional extension to October 15, 2024, is for filing but not for payment, so interest will be charged for taxes not paid by June 17 and late payment penalties could be imposed.

If you are a nonresident alien who did not have tax withheld from your wages, file Form 1040-NR by this date and pay the balance due.

SEPTEMBER 16, 2024—
Pay the third installment of your 2024 estimated tax. You may amend an earlier estimate at this time.

OCTOBER 15, 2024—
File your 2023 return if you received an automatic six-month filing extension using Form 4868. Also file your 2023 return and pay the balance due if on April 15 you were a U.S. citizen or resident living and working outside the U.S. or Puerto Rico, or in military service outside the U.S. or Puerto Rico, and by June 17 you obtained an additional four-month filing extension by filing Form 4868.

JANUARY 15, 2025—
Pay the balance of your 2024 estimated tax.

APRIL 15, 2025 (April 17 for residents of Maine or Massachusetts)—
File your 2024 return and pay the balance of your tax. Pay the first installment of your 2025 estimated tax by this date.

15th day of the 4th month after the fiscal year ends—
File your fiscal year return and pay the balance of the tax due. If you cannot meet the filing deadline, apply for an automatic four-month filing extension on Form 4868.

2024

January
S	M	T	W	T	F	S
	1	2	3	4	5	6
7	8	9	10	11	12	13
14	15	16	17	18	19	20
21	22	23	24	25	26	27
28	29	30	31			

February
S	M	T	W	T	F	S
				1	2	3
4	5	6	7	8	9	10
11	12	13	14	15	16	17
18	19	20	21	22	23	24
25	26	27	28	29		

March
S	M	T	W	T	F	S
					1	2
3	4	5	6	7	8	9
10	11	12	13	14	15	16
17	18	19	20	21	22	23
24	25	26	27	28	29	30
31						

April
S	M	T	W	T	F	S
	1	2	3	4	5	6
7	8	9	10	11	12	13
14	15	16	17	18	19	20
21	22	23	24	25	26	27
28	29	30				

May
S	M	T	W	T	F	S
			1	2	3	4
5	6	7	8	9	10	11
12	13	14	15	16	17	18
19	20	21	22	23	24	25
26	27	28	29	30	31	

June
S	M	T	W	T	F	S
						1
2	3	4	5	6	7	8
9	10	11	12	13	14	15
16	17	18	19	20	21	22
23	24	25	26	27	28	29
30						

July
S	M	T	W	T	F	S
	1	2	3	4	5	6
7	8	9	10	11	12	13
14	15	16	17	18	19	20
21	22	23	24	25	26	27
28	29	30	31			

August
S	M	T	W	T	F	S
				1	2	3
4	5	6	7	8	9	10
11	12	13	14	15	16	17
18	19	20	21	22	23	24
25	26	27	28	29	30	31

September
S	M	T	W	T	F	S
1	2	3	4	5	6	7
8	9	10	11	12	13	14
15	16	17	18	19	20	21
22	23	24	25	26	27	28
29	30					

October
S	M	T	W	T	F	S
		1	2	3	4	5
6	7	8	9	10	11	12
13	14	15	16	17	18	19
20	21	22	23	24	25	26
27	28	29	30	31		

November
S	M	T	W	T	F	S
					1	2
3	4	5	6	7	8	9
10	11	12	13	14	15	16
17	18	19	20	21	22	23
24	25	26	27	28	29	30

December
S	M	T	W	T	F	S
1	2	3	4	5	6	7
8	9	10	11	12	13	14
15	16	17	18	19	20	21
22	23	24	25	26	27	28
29	30	31				

2025

January
S	M	T	W	T	F	S
			1	2	3	4
5	6	7	8	9	10	11
12	13	14	15	16	17	18
19	20	21	22	23	24	25
26	27	28	29	30	31	

February
S	M	T	W	T	F	S
						1
2	3	4	5	6	7	8
9	10	11	12	13	14	15
16	17	18	19	20	21	22
23	24	25	26	27	28	

March
S	M	T	W	T	F	S
						1
2	3	4	5	6	7	8
9	10	11	12	13	14	15
16	17	18	19	20	21	22
23	24	25	26	27	28	29
30	31					

April
S	M	T	W	T	F	S
		1	2	3	4	5
6	7	8	9	10	11	12
13	14	15	16	17	18	19
20	21	22	23	24	25	26
27	28	29	30			

May
S	M	T	W	T	F	S
				1	2	3
4	5	6	7	8	9	10
11	12	13	14	15	16	17
18	19	20	21	22	23	24
25	26	27	28	29	30	31

June
S	M	T	W	T	F	S
1	2	3	4	5	6	7
8	9	10	11	12	13	14
15	16	17	18	19	20	21
22	23	24	25	26	27	28
29	30					

July
S	M	T	W	T	F	S
		1	2	3	4	5
6	7	8	9	10	11	12
13	14	15	16	17	18	19
20	21	22	23	24	25	26
27	28	29	30	31		

August
S	M	T	W	T	F	S
					1	2
3	4	5	6	7	8	9
10	11	12	13	14	15	16
17	18	19	20	21	22	23
24	25	26	27	28	29	30
31						

September
S	M	T	W	T	F	S
	1	2	3	4	5	6
7	8	9	10	11	12	13
14	15	16	17	18	19	20
21	22	23	24	25	26	27
28	29	30				

October
S	M	T	W	T	F	S
			1	2	3	4
5	6	7	8	9	10	11
12	13	14	15	16	17	18
19	20	21	22	23	24	25
26	27	28	29	30	31	

November
S	M	T	W	T	F	S
						1
2	3	4	5	6	7	8
9	10	11	12	13	14	15
16	17	18	19	20	21	22
23	24	25	26	27	28	29
30						

December
S	M	T	W	T	F	S
	1	2	3	4	5	6
7	8	9	10	11	12	13
14	15	16	17	18	19	20
21	22	23	24	25	26	27
28	29	30	31			

What Forms Do You Need to File?

All taxpayers who are required to file a return for 2023 *(pages 2–4)* must file Form 1040 or 1040-SR, and in many cases, one or more schedules and supplemental forms. Anyone can file Form 1040. If you are age 65 or older on January 1, 2024, you can use Form 1040-SR, which mirrors Form 1040 and can be used to report any type of income, deduction, credit, payment, or tax liability, the same as on Form 1040.

You likely need to complete Schedules 1, 2, and/or 3 to report various types of income or loss, above-the-line deductions, certain nonrefundable credits, certain refundable credits, tax payments, and tax liabilities for which there is no unique line on the return. In many cases, you need to complete one or more of the "lettered" schedules (such as Schedules A, B, C, D, E, or SE) or numbered forms (such as Forms 2106, 4797, 8812, 8863, or 8962) and then transfer that result to the applicable Schedule 1–3; *see* the description of Schedules 1–3 below. Totals from Schedules 1–3 are then entered on Form 1040 or 1040-SR.

Schedules 1–3

The following table shows many, but not all, of the items that must be reported on Schedules 1–3. *See* the instructions for the schedules for further details.

Use—	To Report—
Schedule 1	Various types of income, including business income or loss (from Schedule C), income from rental real estate, partnerships, S corporations, estates or trusts (from Schedule E), unemployment compensation, alimony received (under pre-2019 decrees and agreements), sales of business property (from Form 4797), taxable refunds of state or local taxes, gambling winnings, prizes and awards, and taxable distributions from an HSA, Coverdell ESA, QTP, or ABLE account.
	Above-the-line deductions ("adjustments to income") such as for traditional IRA contributions, self-employed retirement plan contributions, student loan interest, alimony paid (under pre-2019 decrees and agreements), educator expenses, HSA contributions (from Form 8889), deductible part of self-employment tax (from Schedule SE), self-employed health insurance, or employee business expenses if you are a qualifying reservist, performing artist, or fee-basis government official (from Form 2106).
Schedule 2	AMT liability (from Form 6251), required repayment of excess advance payments of the premium tax credit (from Form 8962), self-employment tax (from Schedule SE), household employment taxes (from Schedule H), early distribution penalties from IRAs and qualified retirement plans (from Form 5329), Additional Medicare Tax (from Form 8959), Net Investment Income Tax (from Form 8960).
Schedule 3	Nonrefundable credits such as the child and dependent care (from Form 2441), nonrefundable part of the American opportunity credit and the lifetime learning credit (from Form 8863), saver's credit (from Form 8880), adoption credit (from Form 8839), general business credit (from Form 3800), or foreign tax credit (from Form 1116 if required).
	Payments made with a filing extension, and the net premium tax credit (from Form 8962).

CHAPTER 1

Filing Status

Your filing status determines the tax rates that will apply *(1.2)* to your taxable income when you file your return. Filing status also determines the standard deduction you may claim *(13.1)* if you do not itemize deductions and your ability to claim certain other deductions, credits, and exclusions.

This chapter explains the five different filing statuses: single, married filing jointly, married filing separately, head of household, and qualifying widow/widower. If you are married, filing a joint return is generally advantageous, but there are exceptions discussed in *(1.3)*. If you are unmarried and are supporting a child who lives with you, you may qualify as a head of household *(1.12)*, which will enable you to use more favorable tax rates than those allowed for single taxpayers. If you were a surviving spouse in either 2022 or 2021 and in 2023 a dependent child lived with you, you may be able to file as a qualifying widow/widower for 2023, which allows you to use joint return rates *(1.11)*.

Special filing situations, such as for children, nonresident aliens, and deceased individuals, are also discussed in this chapter.

Planning Reminder

Getting Married Can Raise Your Taxes

The so-called marriage penalty is faced by couples whose joint return tax liability exceeds the combined tax they would pay if they had remained single. This is generally the case where each spouse earns a substantial share of the total income. Legislation has substantially reduced the marriage penalty by allowing married couples filing jointly a standard deduction *(13.1)* that is double the amount allowed to a single person, and by making the first five tax brackets (up to 32%) *(1.2)* twice as wide as the brackets for a single person.

On the other hand, if one spouse has little or no income, there generally is a marriage bonus or singles penalty, as the couple's tax on a joint return is less than the sum of the tax liabilities that would be owed if they were single.

1.1 Which Filing Status Should You Use?

Your filing status generally depends on whether you are married at the end of the year, and, if unmarried, whether you maintain a household for a qualifying dependent. The five filing statuses are: single, married filing jointly, married filing separately, head of household, and qualifying widow or widower. The filing status you use determines the tax rates that apply to your taxable income *(1.2)*, as well as the standard deduction you may claim *(13.1)* if you do not itemize deductions. Certain other deductions, credits, or exclusions are also affected by filing status. For example, if you are married, certain tax benefits are only allowed if you file jointly, but in certain cases, more deductions overall may be allowed if you file separately *(1.3)*.

If you are married at the end of the year, you may file jointly *(1.4)* or separately *(1.3)*. If you lived apart from your spouse for the last half of 2023 and your child lived with you, you may qualify as an "unmarried" head of household *(1.12)* for 2023, which allows you to apply more favorable tax rates than you could as a married person filing separately.

If you are unmarried at the end of the year, your filing status is single unless you meet the tests for a head of household or qualifying widow/widower. Generally, you are a head of household *(1.12)* if you pay more than 50% of the household costs for a dependent child or relative who lives with you, or for a dependent parent, whether or not he or she lives with you. For 2023, you generally are a qualifying widow/widower *(1.11)* if you were widowed in 2022 or 2021 and in 2023 you paid more than 50% of the household costs for you and your dependent child. The tax rates for heads of household and for qualifying widows/widowers are more favorable than those for single taxpayers *(1.2)*.

Marital status determined at the end of the year. If you are divorced or legally separated during the year under a final decree of divorce or separate maintenance, you are treated as unmarried for that whole year, assuming you have not remarried before the end of the year. For the year of the divorce or legal separation, file as a single person unless you care for a child or parent and qualify as a head of household *(1.12)*.

If at the end of the year you are living apart from your spouse, or you are separated under a provisional decree that has not yet been finalized, you are not considered divorced. If you care for a child and meet the other head of household tests *(1.12)*, you may file as an unmarried head of household. Otherwise, you must file a joint return or as a married person filing separately.

If at the end of the year you live together in a common law marriage that is recognized by the law of the state in which you live or the state where the marriage began, you are treated as married.

If your spouse dies during the year, you are treated as married for that entire year and may file a joint return for you and your deceased spouse, assuming you have not remarried before year's end *(1.10)*.

Same-sex marriage. Lawfully married same-sex couples are treated as married for all federal tax purposes. The IRS recognizes your marriage to a same-sex spouse if the marriage was legally entered into in one of the 50 states, the District of Columbia, Puerto Rico, U.S. territory or possession, or foreign country. However, registered domestic partnerships, civil unions, and similar relationships that are recognized by state law (or foreign law) but that are not treated as marriages under state law are not treated as marriages for federal tax purposes.

As a married couple, you and your spouse must file your federal return using a filing status of married filing jointly *(1.4)* or married filing separately *(1.3)*. However, if you lived apart for the last six months of 2023 and one of you maintained a home for a child or other qualifying relative, that spouse may be able to file as a head of household *(1.12)*.

1.2 Tax Rates Based on Filing Status

The most favorable tax brackets apply to married persons filing jointly and qualifying widows/widowers *(1.11)*, who also use the joint return rates. The least favorable brackets are those for married persons filing separately, but filing separately is still advisable for married couples in certain situations *(1.3)*. *See Table 1-1* for a comparison of the 2023 tax rate brackets that apply to ordinary income (such as salary, interest income, or short-term capital gains).

If you have children and are unmarried at the end of the year, do not assume that your filing status is single. If your child lives with you in a home you maintain, you generally may file as a head of household *(1.12)*, which allows you to use more favorable tax rates than a single person. If you were widowed in either of the two prior years and maintain a household for your dependent child, you generally may file as a qualified widow/widower, which allows you to use favorable joint return rates *(1.11)*.

If you are married at the end of the year but for the second half of the year you lived with your child apart from your spouse, and you and your spouse agree not to file jointly, you may use head of household tax rates, which are more favorable than those for married persons filing separately.

What is your top tax bracket and effective tax rate? Depending on your taxable income *(22.1)*, ordinary income such as salary, interest income, short-term capital gains, or retirement plan distributions (IRA, 401(k), etc.) can be subject to one or more of the following tax rates: 10%, 12%, 22%, 24%, 32%, 35% or 37%. Rates on qualified dividends *(4.2)* and net capital gain *(5.3)* can be either 0%, 15%, 20%, 25%, or 28%, depending on the amount of your other income and type of asset sold; *see* below.

The 2023 rate brackets that apply to income other than net capital gain or qualified dividends are shown below in *Table 1-1*. If your top bracket is 22%, for example, this means that each additional dollar of ordinary income will be taxed at 22% for regular income tax purposes; 22% is your "marginal" tax rate. However, because the rate brackets are graduated, your effective tax rate may be significantly lower than your top (marginal) rate. For example, if in 2023 you are single with taxable income of $49,315, all of which is ordinary income, your marginal rate is 22%, but the first $11,000 is taxed at 10% (tax of $1,100.00), the next $33,725.00 ($44,725 – $11,000) is taxed at 12% (tax of $4,047.00), and only the last $4,590.00 ($49,315 – $44,725) is taxed at 22% (tax of $1,009.80). The total tax on the taxable income of $49,315.00 is $6,156.80 which represents an "effective rate" of 12.49% ($6,156.80/$49,315 taxable income), reflecting the fact that most of your taxable income is taxed in the 10% and (especially) the 12% brackets, and only a small amount at your top (marginal) rate of 22%.

If you have substantial employee compensation and/or self-employment net earnings in excess of the applicable threshold for your filing status *(28.2)*, you are subject to an additional 0.9% Medicare tax on the excess earnings.

The tax rate on qualified dividends *(4.2)* and net capital gain *(5.3)* is generally lower than your top bracket rate on ordinary income. Depending on your top rate bracket for ordinary income *(Table 1-1)*, the rate applied to your net capital gain *(5.3)* and to most qualified dividends is either 0%, 15%, or 20% *(5.3)*. This does not include 28% rate gains or unrecaptured Section 1250 gains *(5.3)*, which are not eligible for the 0%, 15% and 20% rates. For unrecaptured Section 1250 gains, the rate cannot exceed 25%; for 28% rate gains the maximum rate is 28%.

If your taxable income *(22.1)* does not exceed the endpoint for the 10% bracket shown in *Table 1-1* and you do not have 28% or unrecaptured Section 1250 gains, you do not owe any tax on any of your net capital gain *(5.3)* or on your qualified dividends *(4.2)*; the rate is zero (0%). For the most part, this is also true if your taxable income is within the 12% bracket *(Table 1-1)*, except that a small amount of income that would otherwise be taxed near the top of the 12% bracket does not qualify for the 0% rate. Specifically, the 0% rate on net capital gain and qualified dividends applies for 2023 if taxable income is no more than $89,250 if you are married filing jointly or a qualifying widow or widower, $44,625 if you are single or married filing separately, or $59,750 if you are a head of household *(5.3)*. Note that the $89,250, $44,625, and $59,750 endpoints for the 0% rate are $100 less for heads of household and singles, and $200 less for joint returns and qualifying widows or widowers, than the endpoints for the 12% ordinary income bracket as shown in *Table 1-1*. For taxpayers whose taxable income exceeds the above ceiling for the 0% rate ($89,250 $44,625, or $59,750), some net capital gains (except for 28%/unrecaptured Section 1250 gains) and qualified dividends may still escape tax under the 0% rate, with the remainder subject to the 15% or 20% rate *(5.3)*.

If you are subject to the additional Medicare tax on net investment income because your modified adjusted gross income exceeds the threshold for your filing status, you will have to pay an additional 3.8% tax on some or all of the net investment income *(28.3)*.

Use the proper table or worksheet to compute regular income tax liability. To actually compute your 2023 regular income tax, look up your tax in the Tax Table *(22.2)* or use the Tax Computation Worksheet *(22.3)* only if you do not have net capital gains or qualified dividends. If you have 2023 net capital gain or qualified dividends, use the Qualified Dividends and Capital Gain Tax Worksheet or the Schedule D Tax Worksheet *(5.3)*. Depending on your income, you may also be liable for the additional 0.9% Medicare tax or the 3.8% net investment income tax *(22.8)*.

AMT. If you are subject to alternative minimum tax (AMT) on Form 6251, you generally apply either a 26% or 28% rate to your AMT taxable income (reduced by the applicable AMT exemption), but the favorable regular tax rates for net capital gains and qualified dividends also apply for AMT purposes *(23.1)*.

Table 1-1 Taxable Income Brackets for 2023 Assuming You Have Only Ordinary Income*

	Married filing jointly and qualifying widow/widower	Single	Head of Household	Married filing separately
10% bracket for 2023 applies if taxable income is:	Up to $22,000	Up to $11,000	Up to $15,700	Up to $11,000
12% bracket for 2023 applies if taxable income is:	$22,001 through $89,450	$11,001 through $44,725	$15,701 through $59,850	$11,001 through $44,725
22% bracket for 2023 applies if taxable income is:	$89,451 through $190,750	$44,726 through $95,375	$59,851 through $95,350	$44,726 through $95,375
24% bracket for 2023 applies if taxable income is:	$190,751 through $364,200	$95,376 through $182,100	$95,351 through $182,100	$95,376 through $182,100
32% bracket for 2023 applies if taxable income is:	$364,201 through $462,500	$182,101 through $231,250	$182,101 through $231,250	$182,101 through $231,250
35% bracket for 2023 applies if taxable income is:	$462,501 through $693,750	$231,251 through $578,125	$231,251 through $578,100	$231,251 through $346,875
37% bracket for 2023 applies if taxable income is:	Over $693,750	Over $578,125	Over $578,100	Over $346,875

*If you have qualified dividends and/or net capital gain, you must use the Qualified Dividends and Capital Gain Tax Worksheet, or the Schedule D Tax Worksheet to figure your tax liability; *see 5.3*.

1.3 Filing Separately Instead of Jointly

Filing a joint return saves taxes for a married couple where one spouse earns all, or substantially all, of the taxable income. If both you and your spouse earn taxable income, you should figure your tax on joint and separate returns to determine which method provides the lower tax.

Although your tax rate *(1.2)* will generally be higher on a separate return, filing separately may provide an overall tax savings (for both of you together) where filing separately allows you to claim more deductions. On separate returns, larger amounts of medical expenses or casualty losses may be deductible because lower adjusted gross income floors apply. Unless one spouse earns substantially more than the other, separate and joint tax rates are likely to be the same, regardless of the type of returns filed. The Mike & Fran Palmer Example below illustrates how filing separately can save a married couple taxes in some cases.

EXAMPLE

Mike and Fran Palmer are both under age 65. For 2023, Mike's adjusted gross income (AGI) is $84,775, and Fran's AGI is $60,000. All of their income is ordinary income (no qualified dividends or net capital gain; *1.2*). Fran has unreimbursed medical expenses of $16,605 *(17.2)* before taking into account the 7.5% of AGI floor *(17.1)*; Mike's unreimbursed medical expenses are $1,000. Personal property that Mike owned in his own name was damaged in a storm that was designated as a federal disaster *(18.1)*, and he has a disaster loss of $20,078 prior to taking into account the $100 floor and the 10% of AGI floor *(18.13)*. Mike has deductible mortgage interest expenses of $5,000 and Fran has $1,900. Mike's deductible state and local taxes are $2,399; Fran's are $1,000. Mike and Fran both made deductible charitable contributions of $3,000.

As the example worksheet below shows, filing separate returns for 2023 saves Mike and Fran an overall $2,502, because together they can deduct more on separate returns than on a joint return. They can each itemize deductions on a separate return because their deductions (*see* Line 7 below) exceed the $13,850 basic standard deduction allowed to a married person filing separately *(13.2)*. If they filed jointly, their deductible medical expenses and casualty loss would be substantially lower than the total they can claim on separate returns.

Item	Mike (Separately)	Fran (Separately)	Joint Return
1. AGI	$ 84,775	$ 60,000	$ 144,775
2. Medical expenses	1,000	16,605	17,605
Less 7.5% of AGI *(17.1)*	6,358	4,500	10,858
Allowable medical	0	12,105	6,747
3. Taxes	2,399	1,000	3,399
4. Mortgage interest	5,000	1,900	6,900
5. Disaster loss	20,078	0	20,078
Less $100 and 10% of AGI *(18.8)*	8,578		14,578
Allowable casualty loss deduction	11,500		5,500
6. Charitable contributions	3,000	3,000	6,000
7. Total itemized (Lines 2–6)	21,899	18,005	28,546
8. Taxable income (Line 1 minus Line 7)	62,876	41,995	116,229
9. Income tax for 2023 (Tax on Line 8)	9,140	4,819	16,185
Total tax filing separately (Line 9)	13,959		
Savings from filing separately ($16.185 – $13,959	$ 2,226		

Planning Reminder

Changing From Separate to Joint Return

If you and your spouse file separate returns (including a return as a head of household if eligible; *see 1.12*), you can file an amended return (Form 1040-X) to change to a joint return. You generally have three years from the original due date (without extensions) of the separate returns to file the amended return.

However, if you file separate returns and either of you has received a notice of deficiency from the IRS, you cannot file a Tax Court petition in order to switch from separate returns to a joint return. The IRS and Tax Court have held that this rule applies not just to spouses who filed as married filing separately, but also where one of the spouses mistakenly files as head of household. The Eighth Circuit Court of Appeals, as well as the Fifth and Eleventh Circuits take a more favorable view. For example, the Eighth Circuit in 2015 reversed the Tax Court and held that the prohibition against changing to a joint return after a notice of deficiency and Tax Court petition applies to married persons filing separately, but not to a spouse who has filed as head of household.

Suspicious of your spouse's tax reporting? If you suspect that your spouse is evading taxes and may be liable on a joint return, you may want to file a separate return. By filing separately, you avoid liability for unpaid taxes due on a joint return, plus interest and penalties.

If you do file jointly and the IRS tries to collect tax due on the joint return from you personally, you may be able to avoid liability under the innocent spouse rules *(1.7)*. If you are no longer married to or are separated from the person with whom you jointly filed, you may be able to elect separate liability treatment *(1.8)*.

Standard deduction restriction on separate returns. Keep in mind that if you and your spouse file separately, both of you must either itemize or claim the standard deduction, which for 2023 is $13,850 for married persons filing separately who are under age 65 and not blind *(13.3)*. Thus, if you and your spouse are both under age 65, you file separate returns for 2023 and your spouse itemizes deductions on Schedule A of Form 1040 or 1040-SR, your standard deduction is zero; you do not have the option of claiming the $13,850 standard deduction and must itemize your deductions on your separate Schedule A even if they are much less than $13,850.

Certain benefits require joint return and some benefits harder to claim if filing separately. If married, you must file jointly to claim certain tax benefits, and other tax breaks are much harder to claim on separate returns. For example, you must file jointly to claim the American opportunity credit or lifetime learning credit *(33.7)*, the premium tax credit (unless a spouse is a victim of domestic violence) *(25.13)*, and the deduction for student loan interest *(33.13)*. You also must file jointly to deduct a contribution to an IRA for a nonworking spouse *(8.3)*.

Some benefits are allowed on separate returns only if you live apart from your spouse for all or part of the year. The adoption credit, dependent care credit and the Earned Income Credit *(Chapter 25)*, must be claimed on a joint return unless you live apart for the last six months of the year. If you want to take advantage of the $25,000 rental loss allowance *(10.2)* or the credit for the elderly and disabled *(Chapter 34)*, you must file jointly unless you live apart for the whole year.

IRA contributions are restricted on separate returns. Roth IRA contributions generally may not be made by a married person filing separately because of an extremely low phase-out range *(8.21)*. Similarly, deductions for traditional IRA contributions are restricted on separate returns where the spouses live together at any time during the year and either is an active plan participant *(8.4)*.

In figuring whether you are subject to alternative minimum tax (AMT), your exemption amount is half that allowed to a joint return filer *(23.1)*.

If you receive Social Security benefits, 85% of your benefits generally are subject to tax on a separate return unless you live apart the entire year *(34.3)*. Similarly, for purposes of figuring Medicare Part B and Part D premiums, harsher premium surcharge rules apply to married persons filing separately who live together at any time during the year *(34.10)*.

1.4   Filing a Joint Return

If you are married *(1.1)* at the end of the year, you may file a joint return with your spouse. Same-sex marriages that are legally entered into are recognized for all federal tax purposes; *see 1.1*.

You may not file a 2023 joint return if you were divorced or legally separated under a decree of divorce or separate maintenance that is final by the end of the year. You may file jointly for 2023 if you separated during the year under an interlocutory (temporary or provisional) decree or order, so long as a final divorce decree was not entered by the end of the year. If during the period that a divorce decree is interlocutory you are permitted to remarry in another state, the IRS recognizes the new marriage and allows a joint return to be filed with the new spouse. However, courts have refused to allow a joint return where a new marriage took place in Mexico during the interlocutory period in violation of California law.

Would you be better off filing separately instead of jointly? Filing jointly saves taxes for many married couples, but if you and your spouse both earn taxable income, in some cases overall tax liability is reduced by filing separately. This is particularly true where one spouse has deductible expenses that could be claimed on a separate return but not on a joint return because of floors based on adjusted gross income *(1.3)*.

Once you file jointly, you cannot switch to separate returns for that year after the due date for the return has passed. The only exception is for the executor of a deceased spouse, who has one year from the due date (plus extensions) to change to a separate return for the deceased *(1.14)*. Once you file separately, you generally may file an amended return to change to a joint return; *see* the Planning Reminder in *(1.3)*.

Both spouses generally liable on joint return but "innocent" spouse may be relieved of liability. When you and your spouse file jointly, each of you may generally be held individually liable for the entire tax due, plus interest and any penalties. The IRS may try to collect the entire amount due from you even if your spouse earned all of the income reported on the joint return, or even if you have divorced under an agreement that holds your former spouse responsible for the taxes on the joint returns you filed together. However, there are exceptions to this joint liability rule for "innocent" spouses and for divorced or separated persons.

You may be able to obtain innocent spouse relief where tax on your joint return was understated without your knowledge because your spouse omitted income or claimed erroneous deductions or tax credits. In such a case, you may claim innocent spouse relief on Form 8857 within two years from the time the IRS begins a collection effort from you for taxes due on the return *(1.7)*.

If you are divorced, legally separated, living apart or the spouse with whom you filed jointly has died, you may be able to avoid tax on the portion of a joint return deficiency that is allocable to your ex-spouse by claiming separate liability relief on Form 8857 *(1.8)* within two years of the time the IRS begins collection efforts against you. In some cases, it may be easier to qualify for relief under the separate liability rules than under the innocent spouse rules because innocent spouse relief may be denied if you had "reason to know" that tax was understated on the joint return, whereas the IRS must show that you had "actual knowledge" of the omitted income or erroneous deductions or credits to deny a separate liability election.

Signing the joint return. Both you and your spouse must sign the joint return. Under the following rules, if your spouse is unable to sign, you may sign for him or her.

If, because of illness, your spouse is physically unable to sign the joint return, you may, with the oral consent of your spouse, sign his or her name on the return followed by the words "By _____, Husband (or Wife)" (The IRS continues to use husband and wife in its instructions.). You then sign the return again in your own right and attach a signed and dated statement with the following information: (1) the type of form being filed, (2) the tax year, (3) the reason for the inability of the sick spouse to sign, and (4) that the sick spouse has consented to your signing.

To sign for your spouse in other situations, you need authorization in the form of a power of attorney, which must be attached to the return. IRS Form 2848 may be used.

If your spouse does not file, you may be able to prove you filed a joint return even if your spouse did not sign and you did not sign as your spouse's agent where:

- You intended it to be a joint return—your spouse's income was included (or the spouse had no income).
- Your spouse agreed to have you handle tax matters and you filed a joint return.
- Your answers to the questions on the tax return indicate you intended to file a joint return.
- Your spouse's failure to sign can be explained.

Filing Tip

Spouse in Combat Zone

If your spouse is in a combat zone or a qualified hazardous duty area *(35.4)*, you can sign a joint return for your spouse. Attach a signed explanation to the return.

> **EXAMPLE**
>
> The Hills generally filed joint returns. In one year, Mr. Hill claimed joint return filing status and reported his wife's income as well as his own; in place of her signature on the return, he indicated that she was out of town caring for her sick mother. She did not file a separate return. The IRS refused to treat the return as joint. The Tax Court disagreed. Since Mrs. Hill testified that she would have signed had she been available, her failure to do so does not bar joint return status. The couple intended to make a joint return at the time of filing.

1.5   Nonresident Alien Spouse

If you are married and at the end of the year one of you is a U.S. citizen or resident alien *(1.18)* and the other spouse is a nonresident alien *(1.16)*, a joint return may be filed only if both of you make a special election to treat the nonresident alien spouse as a U.S. resident, which means you will both be taxed on your worldwide income. The same rule applies if one spouse is a "dual status" taxpayer for the year. Thus, if you are a U.S. citizen and your spouse is a nonresident alien at the beginning of the year who becomes a resident during the year, the special election must be made to file jointly. The election is made by attaching a signed statement to the joint return, indicating your intent to be treated as full-year U.S. residents. If you and your spouse make the election, you must keep books and records of your worldwide income and give the IRS access to such books and records.

If the election is not made, you may be able to claim your nonresident alien spouse as an exemption on a return filed as married filing separately, but only if the spouse had no income and could not be claimed as a dependent by another taxpayer *(21.2)*.

Once the election is made to treat a nonresident alien spouse as a U.S. resident, the election applies to later years unless you revoke it, or it is suspended or terminated under IRS rules. A revocation before the due date of the return is effective for that return. An election is suspended if neither spouse is a citizen or resident for any part of the taxable year. If an election is suspended it may again become effective if either spouse becomes a U.S. citizen or resident. If either spouse does not keep adequate records or provide the necessary information on world-wide income to the IRS, the election is terminated. An election also terminates if you legally separate under a decree of divorce or separate maintenance; the termination applies as of the beginning of the year in which the separation occurs. The election automatically terminates in the year following the year of the death of either spouse. However, if the survivor is a U.S. citizen or resident and has a qualifying child, he or she may be able to use joint return rates as a qualifying widow or widower *(1.11)* in the two years following the year of the spouse's death. Once the election is terminated, neither spouse may ever again make the election to file jointly.

1.6   Community Property Rules

If you live in Arizona, California, Idaho, Louisiana, Nevada, New Mexico, Texas, Washington, or Wisconsin, the income and property you and your spouse acquire during the marriage is generally regarded as community property. Community property means that each of you owns half of the community income and community property, even if legal title is held by only one spouse. But note that there are some instances in which community property rules are disregarded for tax purposes; these instances are clearly highlighted in the pertinent sections of this book.

Form 8958 required if filing separately. If the community property rules apply for tax purposes and you and your spouse file separate returns instead of filing jointly, then on your separate returns each of you must report half of your combined community income and deductions in addition to your separate income and deductions. You must attach Form 8958 to your separate Form 1040 or 1040-SR to show how the allocations between you were made.

Separate property may still be owned. Property owned before marriage generally remains separate property; it does not become community property when you marry. Property received during the marriage by one spouse as a gift or an inheritance from a third party is generally separate property. In some states, if the nature of ownership cannot be fixed, the property is presumed to be community property.

In some states, income from separate property may be treated as community property income. In other states, income from separate property remains the separate property of the individual owner.

Divorce or separation. If you and your spouse divorce, your community property automatically becomes separate property. A separation agreement or a decree of legal separation or of separate maintenance may or may not end the marital community, depending on state law.

Community income rules may not apply to separated couples. If spouses in a community property state file separate returns, each spouse must generally report one-half of the community income. However, a spouse may be able to avoid reporting income earned by his or her spouse if they live apart during the entire calendar year and do not file a joint return.

To qualify, one or both spouses must have earned income for the year and none of that earned income may be transferred, directly or indirectly, between the spouses during the year. One spouse's payment to the other spouse solely to support the couple's dependent children is not a disqualifying transfer. If the separated couple qualifies under these tests, community income is allocated as follows:

- Earned income (excluding business or partnership income) is taxed to the spouse who performed the personal services.
- Business income (other than partnership income) is treated as the income of the spouse carrying on the business.
- Partnership income is taxed to the spouse entitled to a distributive share of partnership profits.

Innocent spouse rules apply to community property. As discussed above, community property rules may not apply to earned income where spouses live apart for the entire year and file separate returns. In addition, a spouse who files a separate return may be relieved of tax liability on community income that is attributable to the other spouse if he or she does not know (or have reason to know) about the income and if it would be inequitable under the circumstances for him or her to be taxed on such income. Even if you fail to qualify for such relief because you knew (or had reason to know) about the income, the IRS may relieve you of liability if it would be inequitable to hold you liable.

The IRS may disregard community property rules and tax income to a spouse who treats such income as if it were solely his or hers and who fails to notify the other spouse of the income before the due date of the return (including extensions).

Relief from liability on joint return. If you file jointly, you may elect to avoid liability under the innocent spouse rules *(1.7)* and the separate liability rules *(1.8)*. In applying those rules, items that would otherwise be allocable solely to your spouse will not be partly allocated to you merely because of the community property laws.

Death of spouse. The death of a spouse dissolves the community property relationship, but income earned and accrued from community property before death is community income.

Moving from a community property to a common law (separate property) state. Most common law states (those which do not have community property laws) recognize that both spouses have an interest in property accumulated while residing in a community property state. If the property is not sold or reinvested, it may continue to be treated as community property. If you and your spouse sell community property after moving to a common law state and reinvest the proceeds, the reinvested proceeds are generally separate property, which you may hold as joint tenants or in another form of ownership recognized by common law states.

Moving from a common law to a community property state. Separate property brought into a community property state generally retains its character as separately owned property. However, property acquired by a couple after moving to a community property state is generally owned as community property. In at least one state (California), personal property that qualifies as community property is treated as such, even though it was acquired when the couple lived in a common law state.

1.7   Innocent Spouse Rules

Unless you qualify for relief, you are personally liable for any tax due on a joint return you have filed, whether you are still married to the spouse with whom you filed the joint return or you have since divorced or separated.

 *IRS Alert*

Registered Domestic Partners Must Split Income

Registered domestic partners in California, Nevada, and Washington are subject to the federal income tax community property rules. Each registered domestic partner must report half of the combined community property income (as determined by state law) on his or her federal tax return, whether from earnings for personal services or income from property.

For federal tax purposes, registered domestic partners are not considered married *(1.1)* and may not file joint returns. They must file as single taxpayers unless eligible for head of household status. Each registered domestic partner must file Form 8958 showing how income and deductions are allocated between the partners.

Legally married same-sex couples are treated as married for all federal tax purposes; *see 1.1*.

Knowledge May Bar Innocent Spouse Relief

The IRS may try to defeat your claim for innocent spouse relief on the grounds that you knew, or should have known, that tax was understated on the joint return.

Law Alert

IRS Must Notify Non-Electing Spouse

After the filing of Form 8857, the IRS is required to notify the non-electing spouse (or former spouse) of an electing spouse's request for relief and allow the non-electing spouse an opportunity to participate in the determination. If the IRS makes a preliminary determination granting full or partial relief to the electing spouse, the non-electing spouse may file a written protest and obtain an Appeals Office conference.

If you are still married and living with the same spouse, the only way to avoid personal liability on the joint return is to qualify as an innocent spouse under the rules in this section, or to apply for equitable relief from the IRS *(1.9)*.

If you are divorced, legally separated, living apart, or your spouse has died, you may either seek relief under the innocent spouse rules below or you may be able to claim separate liability treatment *(1.8)* or seek equitable relief *(1.9)* from the IRS.

Qualifying tests for innocent spouse relief. You must satisfy all of the following conditions to qualify for innocent spouse relief:

1. The tax shown on the joint return was understated due to the omission of income by your spouse, or erroneous deductions or credits claimed by your spouse. This means that your actual tax liability is more than the amount shown on the joint return. Innocent spouse relief is not available if the right amount of tax was reported on the return but it was not paid. However, where tax was underpaid, you may request equitable relief *(1.9)*.

2. When signing the joint return, you did not know and had no reason to know that tax on the return was understated.

    In considering whether you had "reason to know" of the tax understatement, the IRS and Tax Court will ask whether a reasonable person in similar circumstances would have known of it. All facts and circumstances will be taken into account including your education level, business experience, involvement in the activity that gave rise to the understatement, and whether you failed to ask about items on the joint return or about omissions from the return that a reasonable person would have questioned.

    Although the "knowledge" test can be a significant hurdle, partial relief may be available. If you knew or had reason to know that there was "some" tax understatement on the return but were unaware of the extent of the understatement, innocent spouse relief is available for the liability attributable to the portion of the understatement that you did not know about or have reason to know about.

3. Taking all the circumstances into account, it would be inequitable to hold you liable for the tax. The IRS and courts will consider the extent to which you benefitted from the tax underpayment, beyond receiving normal support. Thus, it is possible to be held liable for a tax understatement that you did not know about or have reason to know about, on the grounds that you benefitted from the underpayment in the form of a high standard of living. The IRS will also consider whether you later divorced or were deserted by your spouse.

4. You file Form 8857 to request innocent spouse relief.

Request for relief must be filed on Form 8857. You must file Form 8857 to request innocent spouse relief. You must provide details concerning your finances and your involvement in preparing the joint returns for which relief from liability is sought. The request must be made no later than two years from the date that the IRS first begins collection activity against you for tax due on the joint return, such as (1) by reducing a current refund by an amount the IRS says you owe on the prior joint return, or (2) garnishing your wages to recover tax the IRS says you owe on the joint return. If the request is not made by the end of that two-year period, you will not be granted innocent spouse relief even if you meet the above qualification tests. However, for equitable relief, the two-year deadline for filing a request is extended to 10 years from the date that the tax liability was assessed *(1.9)*.

The final determination on whether innocent spouse relief is granted is made by the IRS Office of Chief Counsel and not the Cinninnati Centralized Innocent Spouse Office (CCISO) that first reviews all requests.

Tax Court appeal. If the IRS denies your request for innocent spouse relief, you have 90 days to petition the Tax Court for review. If you petition the Tax Court, the non-electing spouse has the right to intervene in the proceeding.

1.8   Separate Liability Relief for Former Spouses

If the IRS attempts to collect the taxes due on a joint return from you and you have since divorced or separated, you may be able to avoid or at least limit your liability by filing Form 8857 to request separate liability relief. If you qualify, you will be liable only for the part of the tax liability (plus interest and any penalties) that is allocable to you. If a tax deficiency is entirely allocable to your former spouse under the rules discussed below, you will not have to pay any part of it. However, you may not avoid liability for any part of a tax deficiency allocable to the other spouse if you had actual knowledge of the income or expense item that gave rise to the tax deficiency that the IRS is trying to collect. *See* below for details of the knowledge test.

Furthermore, you may not avoid liability to the extent that certain disqualified property transfers were made between you and the other spouse. Relief may be completely denied for both spouses if transfers were made as part of a fraudulent scheme.

As with innocent spouse relief *(1.7)*, separate liability relief applies only to tax understatements where the proper tax liability was not shown on the joint return. If the proper liability was shown but not paid, equitable relief *(1.9)* may be requested.

Are you eligible for separate liability relief? You may request separate liability relief on Form 8857 if, at the time of filing:

1. You are divorced or legally separated from the spouse with whom you filed the joint return, or
2. You have not lived with your spouse (with whom you filed the return) at any time in the 12-month period ending on the date you file the election, or
3. The spouse with whom you filed the joint return has died.

You must be prepared to explain to the IRS which items giving rise to the tax understatement are allocable to you and which are allocable to the other spouse. However, you do not have to actually compute your separate liability on Form 8857.

Deadline for relief request. To request separate liability relief, you must file Form 8857 no later than two years after the IRS begins collection activities against you.

Actual knowledge of the item allocable to the other spouse bars relief. If you request separate liability treatment and the IRS shows that at the time you signed the joint return you had actual knowledge of an erroneous item (omitted income or improper deduction or credit) that would otherwise be allocated to the other spouse, you may not avoid liability for the portion of a deficiency attributable to that item. However, if you signed the return under duress, separate liability is not barred despite your knowledge because a return signed under duress is not considered to be a joint return. You are not liable for tax due on that return and you will be treated as filing separately.

The actual knowledge test is intended by Congress to be more favorable to the taxpayer than the "had reason to know" test under the innocent spouse rules *(1.7)*. Congressional committee reports state that the IRS is required to prove that an electing spouse had actual knowledge of an erroneous item and may not infer such knowledge. According to the Tax Court, the IRS must prove actual knowledge by a "preponderance of the evidence." If the IRS proves actual knowledge of an erroneous item, that item is treated as allocable to both spouses, so the IRS can collect that portion of the deficiency from either spouse.

Where income attributable to your spouse was omitted from your joint return, you will be considered to have "actual knowledge" of it, and separate liability relief will not be allowed, if you knew your spouse received the income, even if you did not know whether the correct taxable amount was reported on the return; *see* Example 1 below.

In the case of a disallowed deduction, the Tax Court requires the IRS to prove that you had actual knowledge of the "factual circumstances" that made the item nondeductible in order for relief to be denied. In one case, the Tax Court denied relief to a spouse who prepared the joint returns on which unsubstantiated Schedule C deductions attributable to her former husband's business were claimed. She had "actual knowledge" because she had access to the business records and knew the extent of the substantiation available for the deductions when she prepared the returns.

 *Caution*

Actual Knowledge Bars Relief

Separate liability relief generally allows you to avoid liability for the portion of a tax deficiency that is allocable to the other spouse. Such relief is unavailable, however, to the extent that you had actual knowledge of the omitted income or deducted item that gave rise to the tax deficiency.

In cases involving limited partnership tax-shelter deductions, the IRS may be unable to prove that the spouse claiming relief had disqualifying knowledge, but relief may still be partially denied if he or she received a tax benefit from the deductions; *see* Example 3 below.

> ### EXAMPLES
>
> 1. Cheshire knew that her husband had received an early retirement distribution. She knew that the distribution had been deposited into their joint account and used to pay off a mortgage, buy a truck, pay other family expenses and provide start-up capital for the husband's business. Cheshire's husband falsely told her that a CPA had determined that most of his retirement distribution was not taxable. After they divorced, Cheshire requested separate liability election to avoid tax on the unreported income. She claimed that she was entitled to relief because she did not know that the taxable amount of the retirement distribution had been misstated on their joint return. The Tax Court held that she could not obtain relief because she knew about the retirement distribution. It is immaterial that she did not know that the reporting of the distribution on the tax return was incorrect. The Court of Appeals for the Fifth Circuit affirmed. The District of Columbia Circuit has also denied a wife's claim for relief because she had actual knowledge of her husband's retirement income.
>
> 2. You file a joint return on which you report wages of $150,000 and your husband reports $30,000 of self-employment income. The IRS examines your return and determines that your husband failed to report $20,000 of income, resulting in a $9,000 deficiency. You file a claim for separate liability relief with the IRS after obtaining a divorce.
>
>   Assume that the IRS proves that you had actual knowledge of $5,000 of the unreported income but not the other $15,000. You are liable for 25% of the deficiency, or $2,250, allocable to the $5,000 of income that you knew about ($2,250 = $5,000 ÷ $20,000 × $9,000). Your former spouse is liable for the entire deficiency since the unreported income was his. The IRS can collect the entire deficiency from him, or can collect $2,250 from you and the balance from him.
>
> 3. Mora's husband arranged an investment in a cattle-breeding tax shelter partnership. He put the partnership in both of their names, although Mora did not sign any of the partnership papers. On their joint returns, they claimed partnership losses which turned out to be inflated; deductions were based on overvalued cattle. After their divorce, the IRS disallowed the partnership losses and Mora elected separate liability relief. The IRS refused, claiming that she participated in making the investment so the claimed losses were allocable to her as well as her husband. The Tax Court held that Mora was not involved in making the investment and so the partnership losses are allocable to the husband unless Mora knew the factual basis for the denial of the deductions or she received a tax benefit from the deductions. She did not know about the overvaluation of the cattle, which was the factual basis for the IRS' denial of the deductions. In fact, the IRS conceded that neither spouse understood the nature of their investment or the basis of the deductions. This may often be the case where passive investors claim deductions passed through to them by a limited partnership. For this reason, the IRS argued that the "knowledge of the factual basis" test makes it too easy for limited partnership investors to obtain relief. The Tax Court responded that the law does not distinguish between passive and active investments and there is no policy reason for the courts to create a distinction. Furthermore, although the husband also lacked knowledge of the factual basis for the disallowance of the losses, he cannot avoid liability for the deficiency since the erroneous deductions would be allocable to him on a separate return.
>
>   Despite Mora's "win" on the actual knowledge issue, she remained partially liable for the deficiency because she received a tax benefit from the erroneous deductions. Under the tax benefit rule discussed below, the deductions first offset the income that would have been reported by the husband had he filed a separate return. The balance of the deductions benefitted Mora by reducing her separate return income. If she benefitted from 25% of the deductions, she would remain liable for 25% of the deficiency.

Allocating tax liability between spouses. Generally, if you claim separate liability relief, you are liable only for the portion of the tax due on the joint return that is allocable to you, determined as if you had filed a separate return. If erroneous items (omitted income or improper deductions or credits) are allocable to the other spouse but you had actual knowledge of the items as discussed above, you cannot avoid liability and the IRS remains able to collect the tax due from either of you. Where deductions are allocable to the other spouse and you are not barred from relief by the actual knowledge test, you can still be held partially liable if you received a tax benefit from the deductions; *see* the discussion of the tax benefit rule below.

In general, the allocation of a tax deficiency depends on which spouse's "items" gave rise to the deficiency. The items may be omitted income or disallowed deductions or credits. Items are generally allocated to the spouse who would have reported them on a separate return. If a deficiency is based on unreported income, the deficiency is allocated to the spouse who earned the income. Income from a jointly owned business is allocated equally unless you provide evidence that more should be allocated to the other spouse. Similarly, if a deficiency is based on the denial of personal deductions, the deficiency is allocated equally between you unless you show that a different allocation is appropriate. A deficiency based on the denial of business deductions is allocated according to your respective ownership shares in the business. If the IRS can show fraud, it can reallocate joint return items.

On Form 8857, you do not have to figure the portion of the deficiency for which you are liable. The IRS will figure your separate liability (and any related interest and penalties).

EXAMPLES

1. After you obtain a divorce, the IRS examines a joint return you filed with your former husband and assesses a tax deficiency attributable to income he failed to report. If you did not know about the omitted income and timely elect separate liability treatment, you are not liable for any part of the tax deficiency, which is entirely allocable to your former husband who earned the income. You are not liable even if the IRS is unable to collect the tax from your former husband and you have substantial assets from which the tax could be paid.

2. The IRS assesses a joint return deficiency attributable to $35,000 of income that your former spouse failed to report and $15,000 of disallowed deductions that you claimed. Both of you may make the separate liability election and limit your respective liabilities.

   If you claim relief, your liability will be limited to 30% of the deficiency, as your disallowed deductions of $15,000 are 30% of the $50,000 of items causing the deficiency. If your former husband makes the claim, he will be liable for the remaining 70% of the deficiency (his $35,000 of unreported income is 70% of the $50,000 of items causing the deficiency).

   If either of you does not make a relief claim, the non-requesting person could be held liable for 100% of the deficiency unless innocent spouse relief is available or the IRS grants equitable relief.

Tax benefit rule limits relief based on erroneous deductions or credits. The tax benefit limitation is an exception to the general rule that allocates items between the spouses as if separate returns had been filed. If you received a tax benefit from an erroneous deduction or credit that is allocable to the other spouse, you remain liable for the proportionate part of the deficiency. You are treated as having received a tax benefit if the disallowed deduction exceeded the income that would have been reported by the other spouse on a hypothetical separate return.

Transfers intended to avoid tax. You may be held liable for more than your allocable share of a deficiency if a disqualified asset transfer was made to you by your spouse with a principal purpose of avoiding tax. Transfers made to you within the one-year period preceding the date on which the IRS sends the first letter of proposed deficiency are presumed to have a tax avoidance purpose unless they are pursuant to a divorce decree or decree of separate maintenance. You may rebut the presumption by showing that tax avoidance was not the principal purpose of the transfer. If the tax avoidance presumption is not rebutted, the transfer is considered a disqualified transfer and the value of the transferred asset adds to your share of the liability as otherwise determined under the above election rules.

Court Decision

Equitable Relief for Interest and Penalties Based on Own Income

The Tax Court held that a business owner was entitled to equitable relief for late-filing and late-payment penalties and most of the interest assessed by the IRS although the underlying tax liability was attributable to his own income. The taxpayer had relied on his spouse to handle the books for the business and deal with their accountant. She had the accountant prepare their 2003 joint return and the taxpayer signed it, but she never mailed the return, for reasons unknown. After she died in 2005, the taxpayer discovered that the return had not been filed, and in September 2006 he filed a 2003 return reporting his income (the wife had no 2003 income) but did not pay the tax due on the return.

The taxpayer asked the Tax Court for equitable relief from the IRS' interest charges and penalties but not for the tax on the underpayment itself, which he had the legal obligation to pay. The Court noted that the IRS' own guidelines (Revenue Procedure 2013-34) allow equitable relief to be granted where the other spouse's fraud was responsible for the nonpayment of tax, even though the liability was attributable to the requesting spouse (threshold condition 6; *see 1.9*). Here, the taxpayer's wife misled him into thinking that the return had been filed and the tax paid. It would be inequitable to hold him liable for the late filing and payment penalties and for the portion of interest that accrued while he reasonably believed that the tax had been paid (the interest from the due date of the 2003 return until he signed and filed the return in September 2006).

> **EXAMPLE**
>
> On a joint return, you report wages of $100,000 and your husband reports $15,000 of self-employment income. You divorce the following year. The IRS examines the return and disallows a $20,000 business expense deduction claimed by your former husband, resulting in a $5,600 tax deficiency. You elect separate liability relief. Of the $20,000 deduction, $15,000 is allocable to your former husband as that amount offset his entire income. The $5,000 balance offset your separate income and thereby gave you a tax benefit. Your former husband will be liable for 75% of the deficiency ($4,200) and you will be liable for the 25% balance ($1,400).
>
> If your former husband had reported income of $30,000 instead of $15,000, you would not be liable for any part of the deficiency under the tax benefit rule. The deduction is attributed entirely to his income, so the entire deficiency is allocated to him.
>
> These allocations assume that the IRS does not show that you had "actual knowledge" *(see above)* of the deductions attributable to your former husband. To the extent you had such knowledge, the deductions are allocable to both of you, so both of you remain liable for that part of the deficiency.

If the IRS proves that you and your former spouse transferred assets between you as part of a fraudulent scheme, neither of you will be allowed to claim separate liability relief; both of you will remain individually liable for the entire joint return deficiency.

Appeal to Tax Court. You may petition the Tax Court if the IRS disputes your claim or your allocation of liability. The petition must be filed within 90 days of the date on which the IRS mails a determination to you by registered or certified mail if the IRS mailing is within six months of the filing of the election. If an IRS notice is not mailed within the six-month period, a Tax Court petition may be filed without waiting for an IRS response or, if you do wait, you have until 90 days after the date the IRS mails the notice to file the petition.

The IRS may not take any collection action against you during the 90-day period and if the Tax Court petition is filed, the suspension lasts until a final court decision is made.

1.9   Equitable Relief

The IRS may grant equitable relief for liability on a joint return where innocent spouse relief *(1.7)* and separate liability *(1.8)* are not available. For example, separate liability relief and innocent spouse relief are not available where the proper amount of tax was reported on a joint return but your spouse failed to pay the tax owed. If you signed a correct return on which tax was owed and, without your knowledge, your spouse used the funds intended for payment of the tax for other purposes, the IRS may grant you equitable relief. A request for equitable relief is made on Form 8857. The IRS may also grant equitable relief in cases where the proper amount of tax was understated on the joint return if it would be inequitable to hold you liable.

Threshold conditions you must meet for relief. Each of the following conditions must be met before the IRS will even consider granting you equitable relief:

1. You filed a joint return for the year that relief is sought.

2. Relief is not available under the innocent spouse *(1.7)* or separate liability *(1.8)* rules.

3. No assets were transferred between you and your spouse as part of a fraudulent scheme.

4. Your spouse did not transfer assets to you for the purpose of tax avoidance. If there was such a transfer, relief can be granted only to the extent income tax liability exceeds the value of these assets.

5. You did not file or fail to file the return with fraudulent intent.

6. The income tax liability for which you are seeking relief is attributable to the other spouse (with whom the joint return was filed). There are exceptions to this requirement if community property law applies, you have nominal ownership of property subject to a deficiency, the other spouse misappropriated funds intended for payment of the tax without your knowledge, or you did not challenge the treatment of items on the joint return because of prior abuse that made you fear retaliation by the other spouse.

Deadline for requesting equitable relief. If the IRS claims that you are liable for unpaid tax on the joint return, you may submit a claim for equitable relief until the statute of limitations on IRS collections expires, which generally is 10 years after the tax has been assessed.

Relief granted in streamlined determination. If you meet the threshold requirements (shown above) for obtaining equitable relief, the IRS will grant relief in a streamlined determination if you are no longer married, you would face economic hardship if relief were not granted, and you did not know or have reason to know that tax was understated on the joint return or that the tax shown would not be paid. Streamlined relief will not be denied even if you had such knowledge or reason to know, if you were subjected to abuse by the other spouse or you were unable to challenge how items were treated on the joint return or why the tax due was not paid because the other spouse controlled the household finances. If the conditions for streamlined relief are met, the other factors normally taken into account (discussed below) will not be considered.

Factors the IRS will consider. If the threshold conditions are satisfied and you do not qualify for streamlined relief as just discussed, you must convince the IRS that equitable relief is appropriate. The IRS will consider all the facts and circumstances.

The following is a nonexclusive list of factors that the IRS will take into account (Revenue Procedure 2013-34) in determining whether to grant equitable relief: whether you are separated or divorced from the spouse with whom you filed the joint return, whether you would suffer economic hardship (i.e., be unable to meet basic living expenses), whether you received any significant benefit from the unpaid tax or item giving rise to the deficiency (beyond normal support), whether you knew or had reason to know that tax was understated on the joint return or that the tax would not be paid, whether you were obligated to pay the outstanding tax liability by a divorce decree or other legally binding agreement, whether you have made a good faith effort to comply with the tax laws in later years, and whether you were in poor health (physical or mental) when you signed the joint return or you requested relief.

In considering whether to grant equitable relief, the IRS has expanded the weight that it gives to abuse of the spouse seeking relief by the other spouse (with whom the joint return was filed), or the other spouse's financial control. If you are requesting equitable relief and were the victim of physical or psychological abuse, or were unable to challenge how items were treated on the joint return or why taxes were not paid because the other spouse controlled the family finances, the abuse or lack of financial control may mitigate other factors that might otherwise weigh against granting equitable relief (Revenue Procedure 2013-34). For example, ordinarily, if you knew or had reason to know that income was omitted from the joint return, or that the other spouse would not or could not pay the tax due on the return, such "knowledge or reason to know" would be a factor weighing against your request for equitable relief. However, if you were abused or unable to challenge the tax treatment or nonpayment because the other spouse controlled the finances, this will favor the granting of relief even if you knew or had reason to know that there was a tax understatement or that the tax would not be paid.

Appeal to Tax Court. If the IRS denies your request for equitable relief, you may petition the Tax Court for review of the IRS decision. The petition must be filed with the Tax Court no later than the 90th day after the date that the IRS mails its final determination notice to you.

 *Legislative Alert*

Taxpayer First Act Allows Tax Court to Consider Equitable Relief Requests De Novo

The standard of review by the court is "de novo," meaning it can take a new look at the case without being restricted to the administrative proceedings.

1.10 Death of Your Spouse in 2023

If your spouse died in 2023, you are considered married for the whole year. If you did not remarry in 2023, you may file a 2023 joint return for you and your deceased spouse. Generally, you file a joint return with the executor or administrator. But you alone may file a joint return if you are otherwise entitled to file jointly and:

1. The deceased did not file a separate return, and
2. Someone other than yourself has not been appointed as executor or administrator before the due date for filing the return. An executor or administrator appointed after the joint return is filed may revoke the joint return within the one-year period following the due date.

Filing Instruction

Reporting Income of Deceased Spouse

If your spouse died during the year and you are filing a joint return, include his or her income earned through the date of death.

Planning Reminder

Possible Estate Insolvency

If you will be appointed executor or administrator and are concerned about estate insolvency, it may be advisable to hedge as follows: (1) File separate returns. If it is later seen that a joint return is preferable, you have three years to change to a joint return. (2) File jointly but postpone being appointed executor or administrator until after the due date of the joint return. In this way, the joint return may be disaffirmed if the estate cannot cover its share of the taxes.

Filing Tip

Dependent Child

In determining whether a child, stepchild, or adopted child is your dependent for purposes of qualifying window/widower status, you can include someone who does not meet all of the regular dependent tests *(21.2)*. You may include a child who cannot be treated as your dependent for one of the following reasons: (1) the child has gross income equal to or more than the annual limit for qualifying relatives ($4,700 for 2023), (2) the child is married and files a joint return with their spouse, or (3) you could be claimed as the dependent of another taxpayer. Enter the child's name in the filing status area at the top of your return.

If you do file jointly, you include on the return all of your income and deductions for the full year and your deceased spouse's income and deductions up to the date of death *(1.14)*.

For 2024 and 2025, you may be able to file as a qualifying widow/widower if a dependent child lives with you *(1.11)*.

Joint return barred. As a surviving spouse, you may not file a joint return for you and your deceased spouse if:

1. You remarry before the end of the year of your spouse's death. In this case you may file jointly with your new spouse. A final return for the deceased spouse must be filed by the executor or administrator using the filing status of married filing separately.

2. You or your deceased spouse has a short year because of a change in annual accounting period.

3. Either of you was a nonresident alien at any time during the tax year; but *see 1.5*.

Executor or administrator may revoke joint return. If an executor or administrator is later appointed, he or she may revoke a joint return that you alone have filed by filing a separate return for the decedent. Even if you have properly filed a joint return for you and the deceased spouse (as just discussed), the executor or administrator is given the right to revoke the joint return. But a state court held that a co-executrix could not refuse to sign a joint return where it would save the estate money.

To revoke the joint return, the executor must file a separate return within one year of the due date (including extensions). The executor's separate return is treated as a late return; interest charges and a late filing penalty apply. The joint return that you filed is deemed to be your separate return. Tax on that return is recalculated by excluding items belonging to your deceased spouse.

Signing the return. A joint return reporting your deceased spouse's income should list both of your names. Where there is an executor or administrator, the return is signed by you as the surviving spouse and the executor or administrator in his or her official capacity. If you are the executor or administrator, sign once as surviving spouse and again as the executor or administrator. Where there is no executor or administrator, you sign the return, followed by the words "filing as surviving spouse."

Surviving spouse's liability. If a joint return is filed and the estate cannot pay its share of the joint income tax liability, you, as the surviving spouse, may be liable for the full amount. Once the return is filed and the filing date passes, you can no longer change the joint return election and file a separate return unless an administrator or executor is appointed after the due date of the return.

In that case, as previously discussed, the executor may disaffirm the joint return.

1.11 Qualifying Widow/Widower Status for 2023 If Your Spouse Died in 2022 or 2021

See the first item on page xxvii for IRS renaming of this filing status.

For the two years after the year of your spouse's death, you may be able to file as a qualifying widow or widower. If your spouse died in either 2022 or 2021 and you meet the following three requirements, your 2023 filing status is qualifying widow or widower, which allows you to use the same tax rate brackets as married persons filing jointly.

1. You have not remarried as of the end of 2023. If you did remarry in 2023, you file a 2023 joint return with your new spouse unless you choose to file as married filing separately.

2. You are entitled to claim as your dependent *(21.2)* for 2023 a child, stepchild, or adopted child who lived with you during 2023 and you paid over half the cost of maintaining your home. The child must live with you for the entire year, not counting temporary absences such as to attend school or take a vacation. A foster child is not considered your child for purposes of these rules.

3. You were entitled to file jointly in the year of your spouse's death, even if you did not do so.

If you meet all these tests and do not itemize deductions (Schedule A, Form 1040, or 1040-SR), use the standard deduction for married couples filing jointly *(13.1)*. To figure your regular income tax liability, you generally use the IRS Tax Table or Tax Computation Worksheet *(22.2)* for qualifying widows or widowers, the same one used by married couples filing jointly.

Spouse's death before 2021. If your spouse died before 2021 and you did not remarry by the end of 2023, you may be able to use head of household rates for 2023 if you maintain a home for a child or other qualified person under the rules discussed in *1.12*.

1.12 Qualifying as Head of Household

You can file as "head of household" for 2023 if you are unmarried at the end of 2023 and you maintained a household for your child, parent, or other qualifying person. You must be a U.S. citizen or resident for the entire year. Tax rates are lower for a head of household than for a person filing as single *(1.2)* and the standard deduction is higher *(13.1)*. If you are married but for the last half of 2023 you lived apart from your spouse, you may be treated as unmarried and able to qualify for head of household tax rates and standard deduction, which are more favorable than those for a married person filing separately; *see* Test 1 below.

Head of household tests. You must meet both of these tests to qualify as a head of household:

1. You were unmarried at the end of the year or you are treated as unmarried (Test 1 below).

2. You paid more than half of the year's maintenance costs for the home of a qualifying person (Test 2 below). A qualifying person other than your parent must live with you in that same house for over half the year, disregarding temporary absences. A qualifying parent does not have to live with you.

Test 1: Are you unmarried? You are "unmarried" for 2023 head of household purposes if you are any one of the following:

- Single as of the end of 2023.
- A widow or widower and your spouse died before 2023. If a dependent child lives with you, *see 1.11* to determine if you may use the even more advantageous filing status of qualifying widow/widower. If your spouse died in 2023, you are treated as married for the entire year and cannot qualify as a 2023 head of household, but a joint return may be filed *(1.10)*.
- Legally separated or divorced under a final court decree as of the end of 2023. A custody and support order does not qualify as a legal separation. A provisional decree (not final), such as a support order pendente lite (while action is pending) or a temporary order, has no effect for tax purposes until the decree is made final.
- Married but living apart from your spouse. You are considered unmarried for 2023 head of household purposes if your spouse was not a member of your household during the last six months of 2023, you file separate 2023 returns, and in 2023 you maintained a household for more than half the year for a dependent child, stepchild, or adopted child. A foster child qualifies if he or she was placed with you by an authorized placement agency, or by a court judgment, decree, or order. You must be able to claim the child as your dependent *(21.2)*, but you are treated as meeting this test if you are the custodial parent and you waive the right to claim the child as your dependent in favor of the noncustodial parent *(21.7)*. You are not considered to be "living apart" if you and your spouse lived under the same roof during the last six months of the year.
- Married to an individual who was a nonresident alien during any part of 2023 and you do not elect to file a joint return reporting your joint worldwide income *(1.5)*.

Filing Tip

Advantages of Head of Household Status

Tax rate brackets are more favorable for a head of household than for a person filing as single. The standard deduction is also higher. For a married person who lived apart from his or her spouse during the last half of the year, qualifying as a head of household allows use of tax rate brackets that are more favorable than those for married persons filing separately *(1.2)*.

Planning Reminder

Special Separate Household Rule for Parent

If your dependent parent is the qualifying person, you may claim head of household status even if he or she does not live with you. You must pay over half of your parent's household expenses, whether your parent lives alone, with someone else, or in a senior citizens' residence.

Caution

Meeting Member-of-Household Test Insufficient

Under the qualifying relative rules, you may be able to treat as your dependent a friend or distant relative that you support in your home under the "member of household" test (21.4). Even if the "member of household" test is met, head of household status is not allowed; a person who qualifies as your dependent under the "member of household" test is not a qualifying person for head of household purposes.

Test 2: Did you maintain a home for a qualifying person? You must pay more than half the costs of maintaining a home for a qualifying person.

Qualifying person. A child or relative can be your qualifying person for head of household purposes only if he or she is a qualifying child or a qualifying relative under the rules for dependents (21.2). However, you may be eligible for head of household status even if you are unable to actually claim the person as your dependent. For example, an unmarried child who meets the definition of a qualifying child (21.2) but who cannot be claimed as your dependent because of one of the additional tests (21.2) is nonetheless a qualifying person for head of household purposes. If, under the special rules for divorced or separated parents (21.7), you are the custodial parent and you waive your right to treat your child as a dependent in favor of the other parent, you may claim head of household status; the other parent may not.

A married child must be your dependent to be a qualifying person for head of household purposes unless the only reason you cannot treat the child as your dependent is that you are the dependent of another taxpayer (21.2).

Your parent or any other qualifying relative can be your qualifying person for head of household purposes only if you can treat that person as your dependent (21.2). However, you are not eligible for head of household status if the relative is your dependent only because (1) you have a multiple support agreement granting you the right to claim the person as your dependent (21.6) or (2) he or she is your qualifying relative under the member-of-household test (21.4).

Maintaining a household. For a qualifying person other than your parent, the home that you maintain must be the principal residence for both of you for more than half the year, disregarding temporary absences; *see* Example 2 below. If the qualifying person is your parent, it does not matter where he or she lives, so long as you pay more than half of the household costs.

You must pay for more than half of the rent, property taxes, mortgage interest, utilities, repairs, property insurance, domestic help, and food eaten in the home. Do not consider the rental value of the lodgings provided to the qualifying person or the cost of clothing, medical expenses, education, vacation costs, life insurance, or transportation you provide, or the value of your work around the house.

Temporary absences disregarded. In determining whether you and a qualifying person lived in the same home for more than half the year, temporary absences are ignored if the absence is due to illness, or being away at school, on a business trip, on vacation, serving in the military, or staying with a parent under a child custody agreement. The IRS requires that it be reasonable to expect your qualifying child or relative to return to your household after such a temporary absence, and that you continue to maintain the household during the temporary absence. Under this rule, you would lose the right to file as head of household if your qualifying person moved into his or her own permanent residence before the end of the year.

> **EXAMPLES**
>
> 1. Your mother lived with your sister in your sister's apartment, which cost $12,000 to maintain in 2023. Of this amount, you contributed $7,000 and your sister $5,000. Your mother's only income is from Social Security and she did not contribute any funds to the household. You qualify as head of household for 2023 because you paid over half the cost of maintaining the home for your mother, who qualifies as your dependent (she is a "qualifying relative"; 21.4). A child or dependent relative other than your parent would have to live with you to enable you to file as head of household.
>
> 2. Doctors advised McDonald that her mentally ill son might become self-sufficient if he lived in a separate residence, but one nearby enough for her to provide supervision. She took the advice and kept up a separate home for her son that was about a mile from her own home. She frequently spent nights at his home and he at hers. The Tax Court agreed with the IRS that McDonald could not file as head of household since her principal residence was not the same as her son's.

1.13 Filing for Your Child

The income of your minor child is not included on your return unless you make a special election to report a child's investment income *(24.4)*. A minor is considered a taxpayer in his or her own right. If the child is required to file a return but is unable to do so because of age or for any other reason, the parent or guardian is responsible for filing the return.

A tax return must be filed for a dependent child who had more than $1,250 of investment income and no earned income (for personal services) for 2023. If your child had only earned income (for personal services) and no investment income, a tax return must be filed if the earned income exceeded $13,850. *See* page 4 for further filing threshold rules.

If the child is unable to sign the return, the parent or guardian should sign the child's name in the proper place, followed by the words, "by [signature], parent [or guardian] for minor child." A parent is liable for tax due on pay earned by the child for services, but not on investment income.

A child who is not required to file a return should still do so for a refund of taxes withheld.

Social Security numbers. A parent or guardian must obtain a Social Security number for a child before filing the child's first income tax return. The child's Social Security number must also be provided to banks, brokers, and other payers of interest and dividends to avoid penalties and backup withholding *(26.10)*. To obtain a Social Security number, file Form SS-5 with your local Social Security office. If you have applied for a Social Security number but not yet received it by the filing due date, write "applied for" on the tax return in the space provided for the number.

Whether or not you are filing a return for a child, you must obtain and report on your return a Social Security number for a child whom you are claiming as a dependent *(21.1)*.

Wages you pay your children. You may deduct wages paid to your children in your business. Keep records showing that their activities are of a business rather than personal nature.

Withholding for children. Children with wages are generally subject to withholding and should file Form W-4 with their employer. An exemption from withholding may be claimed only in limited cases. The child must certify on Form W-4 that he or she had no federal tax liability in the prior year and expects no liability in the current year for which the withholding exemption is sought. For example, a child who had no tax liability for 2022 and who expected to qualify as another taxpayer's dependent for 2023 could not claim an exemption from withholding on Form W-4 for 2023 if he or she expected to have investment income exceeding $400 and total income (expected investment income plus wages) of more than $1,250; *see* IRS Publication 505 for further exemption details. The $400 and $1,250 amounts could be increased by an inflation adjustment for 2024.

Wages you pay to your own children under age 18 for working in your unincorporated business are not subject to FICA taxes (Social Security and Medicare) *(26.8)*.

1.14 Return for Deceased

When a person dies, another tax-paying entity is created—the decedent's estate. Until the estate is fully distributed, it will generally earn income for which a return must be filed. For example, Carlos Perez's only income is salary and bank interest. He dies on June 30, 2023. The wages and bank interest he earned through June 30 are reported on his final income tax return, which is due by April 15, 2024. Interest earned on his bank account after June 30 is attributed to the estate, or to the account beneficiary if the right to the account passes by law directly to the account beneficiary. Income received by the estate is reported on Form 1041, the income tax return for the estate, if the estate has gross income of $600 or more. If Carlos was married, his surviving spouse could file a joint return *(1.10)* for 2022 and include all of Carlos's earnings through June 30. If she jointly owned the bank account with Carlos, the interest after as well as before June 30 could be reported on their joint return.

Caution

Kiddie Tax May Apply to Investment Income

If your child has 2023 investment income exceeding $2,500, the excess is subject to the "kiddie tax" rules if (1) the child is under age 18, or (2) at the end of the year is either age 18 or a full-time student under age 24, and did not have earned income exceeding 50% of his or her total support for the year. *See Chapter 24* for kiddie tax details.

Planning Reminder

Promptly Closing the Estate

To expedite the closing of the decedent's estate, an executor or other personal representative of the decedent may file Form 4810 for a prompt assessment. Once filed, the IRS has 18 months to assess additional taxes. The request does not extend the assessment period beyond the regular limit, which is three years from the date the return was filed. Form 4810 must be filed separately from the final return.

What income tax returns must be filed on behalf of the deceased? If the individual died after the close of the taxable year but before the income tax return was filed, the following must be filed:

1. Income tax return for the prior year;
2. Final income tax return, covering earnings in the period from the beginning of the taxable year to the date of death; and
3. Estate income tax return, covering earnings in the period after the decedent's death.

If the individual died after filing a return for the prior tax year, then only 2 and 3 are filed.

> **EXAMPLE**
>
> Steven Jones, a resident of New York, died on January 31, 2024, before he could file his 2023 tax return. His 2023 income tax return must be filed by April 15, 2024 unless an extension is obtained. A final income tax return to report earnings from January 1, 2024, through January 31, 2024 (date of death), will have to be filed by April15, 2024. Jones's estate will have to file an income tax return on Form 1041 to report earnings and other income that were not earned by Jones before February 1, 2024, unless the gross income of the estate is under $600.

Who is responsible for filing? The executor, administrator, or other legal representative is responsible for filing all returns. For purposes of determining whether a final income tax return for the decedent is due, the annual gross income test at page 3 is considered in full. You do not prorate it according to the part of the year the decedent lived. A surviving spouse may assume responsibility for filing a joint return for the year of death if no executor or administrator has been appointed and other tests are met *(1.10)*. However, if a legal representative has been appointed, he or she must give the surviving spouse consent to file a joint return for the year of the decedent's death. In one case, a state court held that a co-executrix could not refuse consent and was required to sign a joint return where it would save the estate money.

How do you report the decedent's income and deductions? You follow the method used by the decedent during his or her life, either the cash method or the accrual method, to account for the income up to the date of death. The income does not have to be put on an annual basis. Each item is taxed in the same manner as it would have been taxed had the decedent lived for the entire year.

If the decedent owned U.S. Savings Bonds, *see 4.29*.

When one spouse dies in a community property state *(1.6)*, how should the income from the community property be reported during the administration of the estate? The IRS says that half the income is the estate's and the other half belongs to the surviving spouse.

Deductible expenses paid (or accrued under the accrual method) by the decedent before death are claimed on the final return.

Medical expenses of the decedent. If the estate pays the decedent's personal medical expenses (not those for the decedent's dependents) within one year of the date of death, the expenses can be deducted on the decedent's final return, subject to the adjusted gross income floor *(17.7)*. However, the expenses are not deductible for income tax purposes if they are deducted for estate tax purposes. To deduct such medical expenses on the decedent's final return, a statement must be attached to the final return affirming that no estate tax deduction has been taken and that the rights to the deduction have been waived.

Partnership income. The death of a partner closes the partnership tax year for that partner. The final return for the partner must include his or her distributive share of partnership income and deductions for the part of the partnership's tax year ending on the date of death. Thus, if a partner dies on July 26, 2023, and the partnership's taxable year ends December 31, 2023, the partner's final 2023 return must include partnership items for January 1, 2023, through July 26, 2023. Partnership items for the balance of 2023 must be reported by the partner's executor or other successor in interest on the estate's income tax return.

Filing Instruction

IRD Not Included on Decedent's Final Return

Do not report on the decedent's final return income that is received after his or her death, or accrues after or because of death if the decedent used the accrual method. This income is considered "income in respect of a decedent," or IRD *(11.16)*. IRD is taxed to the estate or beneficiary receiving the income in the year of the receipt. On the decedent's final return, only deductible expenses paid up to and including the date of death may be claimed. If the decedent reported on the accrual basis, those deductions accruable up to and including the date of death are deductible. If the decedent mailed or delivered a check for payment of a deductible item, a deduction is allowable on the decedent's last return, even though the check was not cashed or deposited by the recipient until after the decedent's death. If the check was not honored by the bank, the item is not deductible.

Dependents allowed on a final return. If the dependent could have claimed dependents *(21.2)* had he or she had not died, the final return may include those same claims.

Estimated taxes. No estimated tax need be paid by the executor after the death of an unmarried individual; the entire tax is paid when filing the final tax return. But where the deceased and a surviving spouse paid estimated tax jointly, the rule is different. The surviving spouse is still liable for the balance of the estimated tax unless an amended estimated tax voucher is filed. Further, if the surviving spouse plans to file a joint return *(1.10)* that includes the decedent's income, estimated tax payments may be required; *see Chapter 27.*

Where the estate has gross income, estimated tax installments are not required on Form 1041-ES for the first two years after the decedent's death.

Signing the return. An executor or administrator of the estate signs the return. If it is a joint return; *see 1.10.*

When a refund is due on a final return. The decedent's final return may also be used as a claim for a refund of an overpayment of withheld or estimated taxes. Form 1310 may be used to get the refund, but the form is not required if you are a surviving spouse filing a joint return for the year your spouse died. If you are an executor or administrator of the estate and you are filing Form 1040 or 1040-SR for the decedent, you do not need Form 1310, but you must attach to the return a copy of the court certificate showing your appointment as personal representative.

Itemized deduction for IRD subject to estate tax. Items of gross income that the decedent had a right to receive but did not receive before death (or accrue if under the accrual method) are subject to income tax when received by the estate or beneficiary. This "income in respect of a decedent," or IRD, is also included in the decedent's estate for estate tax purposes. If estate tax is paid, an individual beneficiary may claim an itemized deduction for an allocable share of the estate tax paid on IRD items; *see 11.17* for deduction details.

1.15 Return for an Incompetent Person

A legal guardian of an incompetent person files a return for an incompetent whose gross income meets the filing tests on pages 2 and 3. Where a spouse becomes incompetent, the IRS says the other spouse may file a return for the incompetent without a power of attorney, if no legal guardian has been appointed. For example, during the period an individual was in a mental hospital, and before he was adjudged legally incompetent, his spouse continued to operate his business. She filed an income tax return for him and signed it for him although she had no power of attorney. The IRS accepted the return as properly filed. Until a legal guardian was appointed, she was charged with the care of her husband and his property.

The IRS has accepted a joint return filed by a wife in her capacity as legal guardian for her missing husband. However, the Tax Court has held that where one spouse is mentally incompetent, a joint return may not be filed because the incompetent spouse was unable to consent to a joint return; an appeals court agreed.

1.16 How a Nonresident Alien Is Taxed

A nonresident alien is generally taxed only on income from U.S. sources. A nonresident alien's income that is effectively connected with a U.S. business and capital gains from the sale of U.S. real property interests are subject to tax at regular graduated U.S. rates, the same as for a U.S. citizen *(1.2)*. Other capital gains are not taxed unless a nonresident alien has a U.S. business or is in the U.S. for 183 days during the year. Generally, investment income of a nonresident alien from U.S. sources that is not effectively connected with a U.S. business is subject to a 30% tax rate (or lower rate if provided by treaty).

Nonresident aliens who are required to file must do so on Form 1040-NR. If you are a nonresident alien, get a copy of IRS Publication 519, U.S. Tax Guide for Aliens. It explains how nonresident aliens pay U.S. tax.

 *Caution*

Who Is a Resident?

An alien's mere presence in the U.S. does not make him or her a "resident." An alien is generally treated as a "resident" only if he or she is a lawful permanent resident who has a "green card" or meets a substantial presence test *(1.18)*.

Dual status. In the year a person arrives in or departs from the U.S., both resident and nonresident status may apply.

Certain restrictions apply to dual status taxpayers. For example, a joint return may not be filed, unless you and your spouse agree to be taxed as U.S. residents for the entire year.

For details on filing a return for a dual status year, *see* IRS Publication 519 and the instructions to Form 1040-NR.

> ### EXAMPLE
>
> On May 14, 2023, Leon Marchand arrived on a non-immigrant visa and was present in the U.S. for the rest of the year. From January 1 to May 13, 2023, he is a nonresident; from May 14 to the end of the year, he is a resident, under the 183-day test *(1.18)*. Since he is a U.S. resident on the last day of the year, he files Form 1040 or 1040-SR and reports on it the income received during the period he was a resident, as well as income received during the period of nonresidency that was effectively connected with a U.S. business. He writes "Dual-Status Return" across the top of the Form 1040 or 1040-SR. The income for the nonresident portion of the year should be shown on a statement attached to the Form 1040 or 1040-SR. Form 1040-NR (or, if eligible, Form 1040-NR-EZ) can be used as the statement; mark "Dual-Status Statement" across the top of the Form 1040-NR (or 1040-NR-EZ).

1.17 How a Resident Alien Is Taxed

A resident alien *(1.18)* is taxed on worldwide income from all sources, just like a U.S. citizen. The exclusion for foreign earned income may be claimed if the foreign physical presence test is satisfied or if the bona fide residence test is met by an individual residing in a treaty country *(36.11)*. A resident alien may generally claim a foreign tax credit *(36.13)*. A resident alien's pension from a foreign government is subject to regular U.S. tax. A resident alien working in the United States for a foreign government is not taxed on the wages if the foreign government allows a similar exemption to U.S. citizens.

1.18 Who Is a Resident Alien?

The following tests determine whether an alien is taxed as a U.S. resident. Intent to remain in the U.S. is not considered.

You are treated as a resident alien and taxed as a U.S. resident for 2023 tax purposes if you meet either of the following tests:

1. You have been issued a "green card," which grants you the status of lawful permanent resident. If you were outside the U.S. for part of 2023 and then became a lawful permanent resident, *see* the rules below for dual tax status.

2. You meet a 183-day substantial presence test. Under this test, you are treated as a U.S. resident if you were in the U.S. for at least 31 days during the calendar year and have been in the U.S. for at least 183 days within the last three years (the current year and the two preceding calendar years). The 183-day test is complicated and there are several exceptions, as discussed below.

Substantial presence test. To determine if you meet the 183-day substantial presence test for 2023, the following cumulative times are totaled. Each day in the U.S. during 2023 is counted as a full day. Each day in 2022 counts as ⅓ of a day; each day in 2021 counts as ⅙ of a day. Note that you must be physically present in the U.S. for at least 31 days in the current year. If you are not, the 183-day test does not apply.

Other exceptions to the substantial presence test are: commuting from Canada or Mexico; keeping a tax home and close contacts or connections in a foreign country; having a diplomat, teacher, trainee, or student status; being a professional athlete temporarily in the U.S. to compete in a charitable sports event; or being confined in the U.S. for certain medical reasons. These exceptions are explained in the following paragraphs.

Commute from Mexico or Canada. If you regularly commute to work in the U.S. from Mexico or Canada, commuting days do not count as days of physical presence for the 183-day test.

Planning Reminder

Is 2023 Your First Year of Residency?

If you were not a U.S. resident during 2022 but in 2023 you satisfy both the lawful resident (green card) test and the 183-day presence test, your residence begins on the earlier of the first day you are in the U.S. while a lawful permanent resident or the first day of physical presence.

Medical exception. If you plan to leave but cannot physically leave the U.S. because of a medical condition that arose in the U.S., you may be treated as a nonresident, even if present here for more than 183 days during the year. You must file Form 8843 to claim the medical exception.

Tax home/closer connection exception. If you are in the United States for less than 183 days during 2023, show that you had a closer connection with a foreign country than with the U.S., and keep a tax home there for the year, you generally will not be subject to tax as a U.S. resident even if you meet the substantial presence test. Under this exception, it is possible to have a U.S. abode and a tax home in a foreign country. A tax home is usually where a person has his or her principal place of business; if there is no principal place of business, it is the place of regular abode. Proving a tax home alone is not sufficient; the closer connection relationship must also be shown.

To claim the closer connection exception, you must file Form 8840 explaining the basis of your claim. The tax home/closer connection exception does not apply to an alien who is present for 183 days or more during a year or who has applied for a "green card." A relative's application is not considered as the alien's application.

Exempt-person exception. Days of presence in the U.S. are not counted under the 183- day test if you are considered an exempt person such as a teacher, trainee, student, foreign-government-related person, or professional athlete temporarily in the U.S. to compete in a charitable sports event.

To exclude days of presence as a teacher, trainee, student, or professional athlete, you must file Form 8843 with the IRS.

A foreign-government-related person is any individual temporarily present in the U.S. who (1) has diplomatic status or a visa that the Secretary of the Treasury (after consultation with the Secretary of State) determined represents full-time diplomatic or consular status; or (2) is a full-time employee of an international organization; or (3) is a member of the immediate family of a diplomat or international organization employee.

A teacher or trainee is any individual other than a student who is temporarily present in the U.S. under a "J" or "Q" visa and who substantially complies with the requirements for being so present.

A student is any individual who is temporarily present in the U.S. under either an "F," "J," "M," or "Q" visa and who substantially complies with the requirements for being so present.

The exception generally does not apply to a teacher or trainee who has been exempt as a teacher, trainee, or student for any part of two of the six preceding calendar years. However, if during the period you are temporarily present in the U.S. under an "F," "J," "M," or "Q" visa and all of your compensation is received from outside the U.S., you may qualify for the exception if you were exempt as a teacher, trainee, or student for less than four years in the six preceding calendar years. The exception also does not apply to a student who has been exempt as a teacher, trainee, or student for more than five calendar years, unless you show that you do not intend to reside permanently in the U.S. and that you have substantially complied with the requirements of the student visa providing for temporary presence in the U.S.

Medical exception. If you plan to leave but cannot physically leave the U.S. because of a medical condition that arose in the U.S., you may be treated as a nonresident, even if present here for more than 183 days during the year. You must file Form 8843 to claim the medical exception.

Tax treaty exceptions. The lawful permanent residence test and the substantial physical presence test do not override tax treaty definitions of residence. Thus, you may be protected by a tax treaty from being treated as a U.S. resident even if you would be treated as a resident under either test.

Dual tax status in first year of residency. If you first became a lawful permanent resident of the U.S. (received a green card) during 2023 and were not a U.S. resident during 2022, your period of U.S. residency begins with the first day in 2023 that you are present in the U.S. with the status of lawful permanent resident. Before that date, you are a nonresident alien. This means that if you become a lawful permanent resident during 2023 and remain a resident at the end of the year, you have a dual status tax year. On Form 1040 or 1040-SR, you attach a separate statement showing the income for the part of the year you are a nonresident. Form 1040-NR (or 1040-NR-EZ) may be used as the statement. Write "Dual-Status Return" across the top of the Form 1040 or 1040-SR and "Dual-Status Statement" across the top of the Form 1040-NR (or 1040-NR-EZ).

To figure tax for a dual status year, *see* IRS Publication 519 and the instructions to Form 1040-NR.

You also may have a dual status year if you were not a U.S. resident in 2022, and in 2023 you are a U.S. resident under the 183-day presence test. Your period of U.S. residency starts on the first day in 2023 for which you were physically present; before that date you are treated as a nonresident alien. However, if you meet the 183-day presence test (but not the green card test) and also spent 10 or fewer days in the U.S. during a period in which you had a closer connection to a foreign country than to the U.S., you may disregard the 10-day period. The purpose of this exception is to allow a brief presence in the U.S. for business trips or house hunting before the U.S. residency period starts.

If you are married at the end of the year to a U.S. citizen or resident alien, you and your spouse may elect to be treated as U.S. residents for the entire year by reporting your worldwide income on a joint return. You must attach to the joint return a statement signed by both of you that you are choosing to be treated as full-year U.S. residents.

> ### EXAMPLES
>
> 1. Manuel Riveras, who has never before been a U.S. resident, lives in Spain until May 18, 2023, when he moves to the U.S. He remains in the U.S. through the end of the year, thereby satisfying the physical presence test. On May 18, he is a U.S. resident. However, for the period before May 18, he is taxed as a nonresident *(1.16)*.
>
> 2. Same facts as in Example 1, but Riveras attends a meeting in the U.S. on February 2 through 8. On May 18, he moves to the U.S.; May 18, not February 2, is the starting date of the residency. During February, he had closer connection to Spain than to the U.S. Thus, his short stay in February is an exempt period.

First-year choice. If you do not meet either the green card test or the 183-day substantial presence test for the year of your arrival in the U.S. or for the immediately preceding year, but you do meet the substantial presence test for the year immediately following the year of your arrival, you may elect to be treated as a U.S. resident for part of the year of your arrival. To do this, you must (1) be present in the U.S. for at least 31 consecutive days in the year of your arrival; and (2) be present in the U.S. for at least 75% of the number of days beginning with the first day of the 31-consecutive-day period and ending with the last day of the year of arrival. For purposes of this 75% requirement, you may treat up to five days of absence from the U.S. as days of presence within the U.S.

Do not count as days of presence in the U.S. days for which you are an exempt individual as discussed earlier.

You make the first-year election to be treated as a U.S. resident by attaching a statement to Form 1040 or 1040-SR for the year of your arrival. A first-year election, once made, may not be revoked without the consent of the IRS.

If you make the election, your residence starting date for the year of your arrival is the first day of the earliest 31-consecutive-day period of presence that you use to qualify for the choice. You are treated as a U.S. resident for the remainder of the year.

Last year of residence. You are no longer treated as a U.S. resident as of your residency termination date. If you do not have a green card but are a U.S. resident for the year under the 183-day presence test, and you leave the U.S. during that year, your residency termination date is the last day you are present in the U.S., provided that: (1) after leaving the U.S. you had a closer connection to a foreign country than to the U.S. and had your tax home in that foreign country for the rest of the year, and (2) you are not treated as a U.S. resident for any part of the next calendar year.

If during the year you give up your green card (lawful permanent resident status) and meet tests (1) and (2), your residency termination date is the first day that you are no longer a lawful permanent resident. If during the year you meet both the green card test and the 183-day presence test and meet tests (1) and (2), your residency termination date is the later of the last day of U.S. presence or the first day you are no longer a lawful permanent resident. If tests (1) and (2) are not met, the residency termination date is the last day of the calendar year. In the year of your residency termination date, the filing rules for dual status taxpayers in this section apply.

For the year you give up your residence in the United States, you must file Form 1040-NR (or Form 1040-NR-EZ if eligible) and write "Dual-Status Return" across the top. Attach Form 1040, Form 1040-SR, or other statement to show the income for the part of the year you are a resident; across the top write "Dual-Status Statement." *See* the instructions to Form 1040-NR and IRS Publication 519 for filing the dual status return.

1.19 Certificate of Tax Compliance for Alien Leaving the United States

Current law generally requires an alien who plans on leaving the U.S. to go to an IRS office before departure to obtain a "sailing" or "departure" permit, technically known as a "certificate of compliance." Diplomats, employees of international organizations or foreign governments, students, industrial trainees and exchange visitors are generally exempt from the permit requirement; *see* Publication 519 for other exceptions. If an exception does not apply, Form 1040-C must be filed to report the income received and expected to be received for the year. In some cases, a shorter Form 2063 may be filed instead of Form 1040-C. If the Form 1040-C (or Form 2063) shows that there will be a tax due, the IRS will generally issue a certificate of compliance without requiring you to pay the tax or posting a bond for it so long as the IRS determines that your departure will not jeopardize collection of the tax. *See* Publication 519 for further details.

Planning Reminder

Departure Permit

An alien planning to leave the U.S. may have to obtain a "certificate of compliance" on Form 1040-C (or Form 2063) from the IRS to certify that his or her U.S. tax obligations have been satisfied; *see* Publication 519 for exceptions and further details.

1.20 Expatriation Tax

U.S. citizens who have renounced their citizenship and long-term U.S. residents who end their residency are considered expatriates subject to special tax rules. You are considered a long-term resident for purposes of these rules if you give up lawful permanent residency ("green card") after holding it for at least eight of the prior 15 years. Form 8854 must be filed to establish that you have expatriated for tax purposes. The IRS warns that until Form 8854 is filed and the appropriate actions are taken to notify the State Department or Department of Homeland Security of the expatriation, you are not relieved of the obligation to file U.S. tax returns and report your worldwide income as a citizen or resident of the United States.

Expatriation in 2023 or before 2023 but after June 16, 2008. If you expatriated in 2023, you are generally subject to a "mark-to-market" tax (under Code Section 877A) on Form 8854 if any of the following is true: (1) your average annual net income tax liability for the five years ending before the date of expatriation exceeds $178,000 or (2) your net worth on the date of expatriation was $2 million or more, or (3) you fail to certify on Form 8854 under penalty of perjury that you complied with all U.S. federal tax obligations for the five years preceding the expatriation date. The $178,000 threshold is subject to an inflation adjustment for expatriations after 2023.

Under the "mark-to market" tax, you are treated as if you had sold all of your assets (but *see* below for deferred compensation items and interests in nongrantor trusts) for their fair market value on the day before the expatriation date, and the net gain on the deemed sale is taxable for 2023 to the extent it exceeds $767,000. Losses are taken into account and the wash sale rules do not apply. The $767,000 floor may be increased by an inflation adjustment for expatriations after 2023.

An irrevocable election can be made on Form 8854 (in Part II, Section D) to defer payment of the tax on the deemed sales until the assets are sold (or death, if sooner) provided a bond or other security is provided to the IRS. The election is made on a property-by-property basis. Interest will be charged for the deferral period. If the deferral election is made, Form 8854 must be filed annually.

Deferred compensation items and interests in nongrantor trusts are not subject to the mark-to-market tax, but are generally subject to a withholding tax of 30% when distributed to you. IRAs and certain other tax-deferred accounts are treated as if they were completely distributed on the day before the expatriation date, but early distribution penalties do not apply.

See the Form 8854 instructions for further details.

Expatriation after June 3, 2004, and before June 17, 2008. In general, special tax rules that applied under Code Section 877 to individuals who expatriated after June 3, 2004, and before June 17, 2008, no longer apply. Individuals who expatriated during this period were subject to tax on their U.S. source income (as determined under Code Section 877) for a 10-year period if (1) their average annual net income tax liability for the five years ending before the date of expatriation exceeded a specified amount that depended on the year of expatriation, or (2) their net worth on the date of expatriation was $2 million or more, or (3) they failed to certify on Form 8854 under penalty of perjury that they complied with all U.S. federal tax obligations for the five years preceding the expatriation date. Form 8854 had to be filed for the 10-year period.

If you expatriated after June 3, 2004, and before June 17, 2008, and you complied with the annual Form 8854 filing requirements, you are no longer subject to the Section 877 tax rules because the 10-year period for which the Section 877 rules applied ended by 2018. However, if you never filed a Form 8854, you continue to be treated as a U.S. citizen or U.S. permanent resident for income tax purposes until Form 8854 is filed. The 10-year period for which you are subject to the special tax rules of Section 877 begins after the Form 8854 is filed. Use the 2018 Form 8854 and the 2018 instructions for your initial filing but modify the year on the form by crossing out 2018 at the top and entering the actual year of filing. Also use the 2018 form and enter the current year (crossing out 2018) for subsequent annual filings within the 10-year period.

PART 2

Reporting Your Income

In this part, you will learn what income is taxable, what income is tax free, and how to report income on your tax return.

Pay special attention to—

- Form W-2, which shows your taxable wages and provides other important information on fringe benefits received (*Chapter 2*).
- Tax-free fringe benefit plans available from your employer (*Chapter 3*).
- Reporting rules for interest and dividend income (*Chapter 4*).
- Reporting gains and losses from sales of property (*Chapter 5*).
- Rules for tax-free exchanges of like-kind property (*Chapter 6*).
- Planning for retirement distributions. Lump-sum distributions from employer plans may qualify for special averaging or tax-free rollover (*Chapter 7*).
- IRA contributions and distributions. Penalties for distributions before age 59½ and for not taking required minimum distributions may be avoided by advance planning (*Chapter 8*).
- Restrictions on rental losses where a rented residence is used personally by you or by family members during the year (*Chapter 9*).
- Passive activity restrictions. Losses from rentals or passive business operations are generally not allowed, but certain real estate professionals are exempt from the loss restrictions, and for others, a special rental loss allowance of up to $25,000 may be available (*Chapter 10*).
- Reporting refunds of state and local taxes. A refund of previously deducted taxes is generally taxable unless you had no benefit from the deduction (*Chapter 11*).
- Cancellation of debts. When your creditor cancels debts you owe, you generally have taxable income, but there are exceptions for debts discharged while you are bankrupt or insolvent or under a government forgiveness program (*Chapter 11*).
- Damages received in court proceedings. Learn when these are tax free and when taxable (*Chapter 11*).
- How life insurance proceeds are taxed (*Chapter 11*).

This list of income items is not exclusive. Other types of income, such as Social Security benefits (*34.2*), taxable alimony (*37.2*), and business income (*Chapter 40*), are discussed throughout the book.

CHAPTER 2

Wages, Salary, and Other Compensation

Except for tax-free fringe benefits *(Chapter 3)*, tax-free foreign earned income *(Chapter 36)* and tax-free armed forces and veterans' benefits *(Chapter 35)*, practically everything you receive for your work or services is taxed, whether paid in cash, property, or services. Your employer will generally report your taxable compensation on Form W-2 and other information returns, such as Form 1099-R for certain retirement payments. Do not reduce the amount you report as taxable compensation on your return by withholdings for income taxes, Social Security taxes, union dues, or U.S. Savings Bond purchases. Your Form W-2 excludes from taxable pay your qualifying salary-reduction contributions to a retirement plan, although the amount may be shown on the form.

If you file a paper return, attach Copy B of Form W-2; do not attach Forms 1099 unless there are withholdings.

Unemployment benefits are fully taxable. The benefits are reported to the IRS on Form 1099-G. You do not have to attach your copy of Form 1099-G to your return.

Income and expenses from self-employment are discussed in *Chapter 40*.

Table 2-1 Understanding Your Form W-2 for 2023 Wages and Tips

Amount in—	What You Should Know—
Box 1	**Taxable wages and tips.** Your taxable wages, tips, and other forms of taxable compensation *(2.1)* are listed in Box 1. Taxable fringe benefits will also be included in Box 1 and may be shown in Box 14.
Box 2	**Federal income tax withholdings.** Enter the amount of federal income tax withheld from your pay on Line 25a of Form 1040 or 1040-SR.
Boxes 3, 4, and 7	**Social Security withholdings.** Wages subject to Social Security withholding are shown in Box 3. Tips you reported to your employer are shown separately in Box 7. The total of Boxes 3 and 7 should not exceed $160,200, the maximum Social Security wage base for 2023. Social Security taxes withheld from wages and tips are shown in Box 4 and should not exceed the maximum 2023 Social Security tax of $9,932.40 ($160,200 × 6.2% rate). If you worked for more than one employer in 2023 and total Social Security tax withholdings exceeded $9,932, you claim the excess as a tax payment on your tax return; *see 26.8.* Elective salary deferrals to a 401(k), SIMPLE, salary-reduction SEP, or 403(b) plan, as well as employer payments of qualified adoption expenses, are included in Box 3 and subject to Social Security withholding even though these amounts are not includible in Box 1 taxable wages. Amounts deferred under a nonqualified plan or a 457 plan are included in Box 3 in the year that the deferred amounts are no longer subject to a substantial risk of forfeiture.
Boxes 5–6	**Medicare tax withholdings.** Wages, tips, elective salary deferrals, and other compensation subject to Social Security tax (Boxes 3 and 7) are also subject to a 1.45% Medicare tax, except that there is no wage base limit for Medicare tax. Thus, the Medicare wages shown in Box 5 are not limited to the $160,200 maximum for Boxes 3 and 7. In Box 6, total Medicare withholdings are reported. For employees with wages and tips over $200,000, the Box 6 total includes the 0.9% Additional Medicare Tax *(28.2).*
Box 8	**Allocated tips.** If you worked in a restaurant employing at least 10 people, your employer will report in Box 8 your share of 8% of gross receipts unless you reported tips at least equal to that share *(26.6).* The amount shown here is not included in Boxes 1, 3, 5, or 7, but you must add it to wages on Line 1 of Form 1040 or 1040-SR.
Box 10	**Dependent care benefits.** Reimbursements from your employer for dependent care expenses and the value of employer-provided care services under a qualifying plan *(3.5)* are included in Box 10. Amounts in excess of $5,000 are also included as taxable wages for 2023 in Boxes 1, 3, and 5. Generally, amounts up to $5,000 are tax free, but you must determine the amount of the exclusion on Form 2441. The tax-free amount reduces expenses eligible for the dependent care credit; *see Chapter 25.*
Box 11	**Nonqualified plan distributions.** Distributions shown in Box 11 are from a nonqualified deferred compensation plan, or a nongovernmental Section 457 plan *(7.20).* Do not report these distributions separately since they have already been included as taxable wages in Box 1.

Box 12	**Elective deferrals to retirement plans.** Elective salary deferrals to a 401(k) plan or SIMPLE 401(k) (including any excess over the annual deferral limit; *see 7.15*) are shown in Box 12 with Code D. For example, if you made elective pre-tax salary deferrals of $4,500 to a 401(k) plan, your employer would enter D 4500.00 in Box 12. Code E is used for deferrals to a 403(b) plan *(7.19),* Code F for deferrals to a salary-reduction simplified employee pension *(8.17),* Code G for deferrals (including non-elective as well as elective) to a governmental or nongovernmental Section 457 plan *(7.20),* Code H for elective deferrals to a pension plan created before June 25, 1959, and funded only by employee contributions, and Code S for salary-reduction deferrals to a SIMPLE IRA *(8.19).*
	
	  Designated Roth contributions *(7.18)* to a 401(k) plan are reported in Box 12 with Code AA. If the designated Roth contributions are to a 403(b) plan, they will be reported with Code BB, and if they are to a governmental Section 457 plan, Code EE will be used.
	
	Cost of employer-sponsored health coverage. Your employer may show in Box 12, using Code DD, the total cost of your 2023 health plan coverage. Reporting is optional for certain employers and certain contributions, such as salary-reduction FSA contributions *(3.3)* and HSA contributions *(3.2),* are not reportable. Any amount reported here is not taxable; it is provided for informational purposes only.
	
	Reimbursements under qualified small employer health reimbursement arrangements (QSEHRAs). If you were reimbursed for health costs under a QSEHRA *(3.3),* your employer will show the total amount of permitted reimbursements in Box 12 using Code FF.
	
	Travel allowance reimbursements. If you received a flat mileage allowance from your employer for business trips *(20.20);* or a per diem travel allowance to cover meals, lodging, and incidentals *(20.19);* and the allowance exceeded the IRS rate, the amount up to the IRS rate (the nontaxable portion) is shown in Box 12 using Code L. The excess is included as taxable wages in Box 1.
	
	Group-term life insurance over $50,000. The cost of taxable coverage over $50,000 is shown in Box 12 using Code C. It is also included in Box 1 wages, Box 3 Social Security wages, and Box 5 Medicare wages and tips.
	
	  If you are a retiree or other former employee who received group-term coverage over $50,000, any uncollected Social Security tax is shown using Code M and uncollected Medicare tax using Code N. The uncollected amount must be reported as an "Other Tax" on Line 8 of Schedule 2 (Form 1040 or 1040-SR); check box c and write "UT" next to it.
	
	Nontaxable sick pay. If you contributed to a sick pay plan, an allocable portion of benefits received is tax free and is shown using Code J.

Table 2-1	Understanding Your Form W-2 for 2023 Wages and Tips (continued)

Amount in—	What You Should Know—
Box 12	**Uncollected Social Security and Medicare taxes on tips.** If your employer could not withhold sufficient Social Security on tips, the uncollected amount is shown using Code A. For uncollected Medicare tax, Code B is used. This amount must be reported as an "Other tax" on Line 8 of Schedule 2 (Form 1040 or 1040-SR); check box c and next to it write the amount and label it as "UT".

Excess golden parachute payments. If you received an "excess parachute payment as wages," Code K identifies the 20% penalty tax on the excess payment that was withheld by the employer. This withheld amount is included in Box 2 (federal income tax withheld), but you also must add it as an additional tax on Line 8 of Schedule 2 of Form 1040 or 1040-SR; identify as "EPP".

Moving expense reimbursements. For members of the U.S. Armed Services, reimbursements of qualifying moving expenses are excludable from income *(2.1)*; the excludable reimbursements are shown with Code P. For all others, employer reimbursements of moving expenses are taxable *(2.1)* and are included in Box 1 wages, and subject to Social Security (Box 3) and Medicare tax (Box 5) withholdings.

Employer contributions to health savings account (HSA) or Archer MSA. Total employer contributions to an HSA are shown with Code W; this includes any contributions you elected to make under a Section 125 cafeteria plan *(3.2, 3.15)*. Total employer contributions to an MSA are shown with Code R. Contributions exceeding the excludable limit *(3.2)* are included as taxable wages in Boxes 1, 3, and 5.

Employer-financed adoption benefits. Total qualified adoption expenses paid or reimbursed by your employer *(3.6)* plus any pre-tax contributions you made to an adoption plan account under a cafeteria plan *(3.15)* are shown with Code T.

Nonstatutory stock option exercised. If you exercised a nonstatutory stock option, Code V shows the taxable "spread" (excess of fair market value of stock over exercise price). The income should be included in Boxes 1, 3 (up to the $160,200 Social Security wage ceiling), and 5.

Deferrals and income under Section 409A nonqualified deferred compensation plan. Current year deferrals plus all earnings under a 409A plan may be shown (its optional) with Code Y. Code Z shows amounts included as income in Box 1; this income is subject to a penalty plus interest on Schedule 2 of Form 1040 or 1040-SR *(2.7)*. |
| Box 13 | **Statutory employee.** If this box is checked you report your wage income and deductible job expenses on Schedule C *(40.6)*. Your earnings are not subject to income tax withholding, but are subject to Social Security and Medicare taxes.
  Retirement plan. This box is checked if you were an active participant in an employer plan at some point during the year. As an active participant, you are subject to the phaseout rules for IRA deductions) *(8.4)*. |
| Box 14 | **Taxable fringe benefits and miscellaneous payments.** Your employer may use Box 14 to report fringe benefits or deductions from your pay, such as state disability insurance taxes, union dues, educational assistance, health insurance premiums, or voluntary after-tax contributions to profit-sharing or pension plans. If your employer included in Box 1 the lease value of a car *(3.7)* provided to you, this value must also be shown in Box 14 or on a separate statement. |
| Boxes 17 and 19 | **State and local taxes.** State and local tax withholdings shown in Boxes 17 and 19 may be deductible as itemized deductions *(16.3)*. |

22222	**a** Employee's social security number 08-X1X0X1X	OMB No. 1545-0008		
b Employer identification number (EIN)			**1** Wages, tips, other compensation 57,800.00	**2** Federal income tax withheld 10,000.00
c Employer's name, address, and ZIP code Finkle Construction Company 5532 Glasgow Plaza City, State XX111			**3** Social security wages 63,580.00	**4** Social security tax withheld 3,941.96
			5 Medicare wages and tips 63,580.00	**6** Medicare tax withheld 921.91
			7 Social security tips	**8** Allocated tips
d Control number 0X1-XX-1X00			**9**	**10** Dependent care benefits
e Employee's first name and initial Mary Last name Moll Suff.			**11** Nonqualified plans	**12a** 5,780.00
			13 ☐ Statutory employee ☒ Retirement plan ☐ Third-party sick pay	**12b**
176 Garden Road City, State 1XXX1			**14** Other	**12c**
				12d
f Employee's address and ZIP code				
15 State Employer's state ID number State 11-X1X0X1X	**16** State wages, tips, etc. 57,800.00	**17** State income tax 2,980.00	**18** Local wages, tips, etc. 57,800.00	**19** Local income tax 1,734.00 **20** Locality name City

Form **W-2** Wage and Tax Statement   **2023**   Department of the Treasury—Internal Revenue Service
Copy 1—For State, City, or Local Tax Department

Law Alert

Reimbursed Moving Expenses Taxable

The exclusion for reimbursements of qualified moving expenses applies only to certain members of the U.S. Armed Forces; *see* the text on this page for details *(2.1)*.

Caution

Severance Pay Taxable

Severance pay received upon losing a job is treated as taxable wages subject to income tax withholding and also withholdings for Social Security and Medicare taxes *(26.8)*. The severance pay is taxable even if you signed a waiver releasing your former employer from potential future damage claims. The waiver does not change the nature of the payments from taxable pay to tax-free personal injury damages *(11.7)*.

Filing Instruction

Tips Must Be Reported

Tips you receive are taxable income. You must report tips to your employer so your employer can withhold FICA and income tax from your regular pay to cover the tips *(26.6)*.

2.1 Salary and Wage Income

The key to reporting your pay is Form W-2 ("Wage and Tax Statement") sent to you by your employer. It lists your taxable wages, which may include not only your regular pay, but also other taxable items, such as taxable fringe benefits. *Table 2-1* explains how employee pay benefits and tax withholdings are reported on Form W-2.

Your employer reports your taxable pay under a simple rule. Unless the item is specifically exempt from tax, you are taxed on practically everything you receive for your work whether paid in cash, property, or services. Benefits that the law specifically excludes from tax are discussed in *Chapter 3*. The most common tax-free benefits are employer-paid premiums for health and accident plans, medical expense reimbursements, and group-term life insurance coverage up to $50,000.

Your employer will include in Box 1 of your Form W-2 the total wages, tips, commissions, and other compensation, before payroll deductions, that were paid to you during the year. Box 1 may include, in addition to regular wages and tips, the following types of taxable compensation:

- Bonuses (including signing bonuses)
- Taxable fringe benefits *(Chapter 3)*
- Per diem or mileage allowances exceeding the IRS rate *(20.19–20.20)*
- Expense allowances or business expense reimbursements under a non-accountable plan *(20.21)*
- Moving expense reimbursements, unless you are a qualifying member of the U.S. Armed Forces; *see* below.
- Awards or prizes not exempt under *3.11*
- Cost of group-term life insurance over $50,000 *(3.4)*
- Cost of accident and health insurance premiums paid by an S corporation for 2%-or-more shareholder-employees
- Deferred income that is currently taxable under a Section 409A nonqualified deferred compensation plan *(2.7)*
- Severance pay

Compensation reported in Box 1 of Form W-2 must be reported as wages on Line 1 of Form 1040 or 1040-SR. Other types of income must also be reported as wages on your return although they are not included in Box 1 of Form W-2, such as non-excludable dependent care *(3.5)* or adoption *(3.6)* benefits, tips not reported to your employer or allocated tips *(26.6)*, disability pension shown on Form 1099-R if you are under your employer's minimum retirement age, or excess salary deferrals to an employer retirement plan *(7.16)*.

Reimbursed moving expenses. All employees other than qualifying members of the U.S. Armed Forces are taxed on reimbursements of moving expenses, effective for 2018 through 2025 (under the Tax Cuts and Jobs Act).

Members of the U.S. Armed Forces on active duty can exclude reimbursed moving expenses from income if the move is pursuant to a military order and incident to a permanent change of station. The moving expenses must be reimbursed under an accountable plan, and must be expenses that the Armed Forces member could claim as an above-the-line deduction had the member not been reimbursed *(12.3)*. The excludable moving expense reimbursements are shown in Box 12 of Form W-2 with Code P. *See 12.3* for details on deductible moving expenses for Armed Forces members and reimbursements.

Qualifying members of the U.S. Armed Forces are also the only taxpayers allowed to deduct unreimbursed moving expenses under the new law *(12.3)*.

Withholdings for retirement plans. Amounts withheld from wages as your contribution to your pension or profit-sharing account are generally taxable as compensation unless they are tax-deferred elective deferrals under the limits allowed for Section 401(k) plans *(7.16)*, simplified employee pension plans *(8.17)*, SIMPLE IRAs *(8.19)*, or tax-sheltered annuity plans *(7.19)*. Elective deferrals are reported in Box 12 of Form W-2.

Wages withheld for compulsory forfeitable contributions to a nonqualified pension plan are not taxable if these conditions exist:

1. The contribution is forfeited if employment is terminated prior to death or retirement.
2. The plan does not provide for a refund of employee contributions and, in the administration of the plan, no refund will be made. Where only part of the contribution is subject to forfeiture, the amount of withheld contribution not subject to forfeiture is taxable income.

You should check with your employer to determine the status of your contributions.

Assigning pay. You may not avoid tax on income you earned by assigning the right to payment to another person. For example, you must report earnings that you donate to charity, even if they are paid directly by your employer to a charity. If you claim itemized deductions, you may claim a contribution deduction for the donation; *see Chapter 14*. Assignments of income-generating intellectual property are held taxable to the assignee. However, if the assignor retained power or control of the property, the assignor could be held liable for the tax according to the 8th Circuit.

The IRS allowed an exception for doctors working in a clinic. The doctors were not taxed on fees for treating patients with limited income (teaching cases) where they were required to assign the fees to a foundation.

Gifts from employers. A payment may be called a gift but still be taxable income. Any payment made in recognition of past services or in anticipation of future services or benefits is taxable as wages even if the employer is not obligated to make the payment. However, there are exceptions for employee achievement awards *(3.11)*.

To prove a gift is tax free, you must show that the employer acted with pure and unselfish motives of affection, admiration, or charity. This is difficult to do, given the employer-employee relationship. A gift of stock by majority stockholders to key employees has been held to be taxable.

Employer leave sharing programs. Under employer leave sharing programs, employees can elect to forgo vacation, sick, or personal leave so that other employees can use this paid time. Usually, donated leave is still taxable wages to the employee who donates it; it is included in wages reported on Form W-2. "Golden parachute" payments. Golden parachute arrangements are agreements to pay key employees additional compensation upon a change in company control. If you receive such a payment, part of it may be deemed to be an "excess payment" under a complex formula in the law. You must pay a 20% penalty tax on the "excess" amount in addition to regular income tax on the total. The 20% penalty should be identified on Form W-2 with Code K in Box 12; *see Table 2-1*.

If the golden parachute payment is made to a non-employee, the company will report it in Box 7 (non-employee compensation) of Form 1099-MISC. If you are self-employed, report the total compensation on Schedule C *(40.6)* and compute self-employment tax on Schedule SE *(45.3)*. Any "excess parachute payment" should be separately labeled in Box 13 of Form 1099-MISC. Multiply the Box 13 amount by 20% and report it as an "other tax" on Line 17k of Schedule 2 (Form 1040 or 1040-SR); label it "EPP."

2.2 Constructive Receipt of Year-End Paychecks

As an employee, you use the cash-basis method of accounting. This means that you report all income items in the year they are actually received and deduct expenses in the year you pay them. You are also subject to the "constructive receipt rule," which requires you to report income not actually received but which has been credited to your account, subject to your control, or put aside for you. Thus, if you received a paycheck at the end of 2023, you must report the pay on your 2023 return, even though you do not cash or deposit it to your account until 2024, even if you receive the check after banking hours on the last business day of the year and cannot cash or deposit it until the next year. The Tax Court has also ruled that receipt by an agent (e.g., an attorney) is constructive receipt by the principal.

Court Decision

Tax on Assigned Contingent Fee

An attorney who took a medical malpractice case on a contingent fee basis agreed to split the net fee with his ex-wife pursuant to their divorce agreement. After a favorable settlement, the attorney's take was approximately $40,000 after expenses, half of which went to his ex-wife. Each paid tax on his or her share. The attorney argued that his partial assignment of the fee could shift the tax liability because collection was contingent on the outcome of the lawsuit. However, the IRS and the Tax Court held that the attorney was liable for the tax on the entire contingent fee, and an appeals court agreed. The attorney transferred only the right to receive income. Although his fee was contingent upon the successful outcome of the case, once the fee materialized, it was indisputably compensation for his personal services.

If your employer does not have funds in the bank and asks you to hold the check before depositing it, you do not have taxable income until the check is cashed. If services rendered in 2023 are paid for by check dated for 2024, the pay is taxable for 2024.

The IRS has ruled that an employee who is not at home on December 31 to take delivery of a check sent by certified mail must still report the check in that year. However, where an employee was not at home to take certified mail delivery of a year-end check that was unexpected until the next year, the Tax Court held that the funds were taxable when received in the following year.

2.3 Pay Received in Property Is Taxed

Your employer may pay you with property instead of cash. You report the fair market value of the property as wages.

> **EXAMPLE**
>
> For consulting services rendered, Kate Chong receives a check for $10,000 and property with a fair market value of $5,000. She reports $15,000 as wages.

If you receive an unrestricted company stock as payment for your services, you include the value of the stock on the date of transfer as pay in the year you receive it. However, if the stock is nontransferable or subject to substantial risk of forfeiture, you do not have to include its value as pay until the restrictions no longer apply *(2.17)*. You must report dividends on the restricted stock in the year it is received as income. If you receive your employer's note that has a fair market value, you are taxed on the value of the note less what it would cost you to discount it. If the note bears interest, report the full face value. It is not necessary to report income if the note has no fair market value. Report income on the note only when payments are made on it.

A debt canceled by an employer is taxable income.

Salespeople employed by a dealer have taxable income on receipt of "prize points" redeemable for merchandise from a distributor.

2.4 Commissions Taxable When Credited

Earned commissions are taxable in the year they are credited to your account and subject to your drawing, whether or not you actually draw them.

Do not report commissions that were earned in 2023 on your 2023 return if they cannot be computed or collected until a later year.

> **EXAMPLE**
>
> Arno Jeffers earns commissions based on a percentage of the profits from realty sales. In 2023 he draws $20,000 from his account. However, at the end of 2023 the full amount of his commissions is unknown because profits for the year have not been figured. In January 2024, his 2023 commissions are computed to be $25,000, and the $5,000 balance is paid to him. The $5,000 is taxable in 2024 even though earned in 2023.

Advances against unearned commissions. Under standard insurance industry practice, an agent who sells a policy does not earn commissions until premiums are received by the insurance company. However, the company may issue a cash advance on the commissions before the premiums are received. Agents have claimed that they may defer reporting the income until the year the premiums are earned. The IRS, recognizing that in practice companies rarely demand repayment, requires that advances be included in income in the year received if the agent has full control over the advanced funds. If a repayment of unearned commissions in a later year exceeds $3,000, you may claim a tax credit for the repayment or deduct it as an "other" itemized deduction on Schedule A, provided you itemize deductions for that year *(2.8)*.

Salespeople have been taxed on commissions received on property bought for their personal use. In one case, an insurance agent was taxed on commissions paid to him

Caution

Earned Commissions Credited to Your Account

You may not postpone tax on earned commissions credited to your account in 2023 by not drawing them until 2024 or a later year. However, where a portion of earned commissions is not withdrawn because your employer is holding it to cover future expenses, you are not taxed on the amount withheld.

on his purchase of an insurance policy. In another case, a real estate agent was taxed on commissions he received on his purchase of land. A salesman was also taxed for commissions waived on policies he sold to friends, relatives, and employees.

Kickback of commissions. An insurance agent's kickback of his or her commission is taxable where agents may not under local law give rebates or kickbacks of premiums to their clients. The commissions are income and may not be offset with a business expense deduction; illegal kickbacks may not be deducted.

However, in one case, a federal appeals court allowed an insurance broker to avoid tax when he did not charge clients the basic first-year commission. The clients paid the broker the net premium (gross premium less the commission), which he remitted to the insurance company. The IRS and Tax Court held that the commissions were taxable despite the broker's voluntary waiver of his right to them. He could not deduct them because his discount scheme violated state anti-rebate law (Oklahoma). On appeal, the broker won. The Tenth Circuit Court of Appeals held that since the broker never had any right to commissions under the terms of the contracts he structured with his clients, he was not taxed on the commissions. The court cautioned that if the broker had remitted the full premium (including commission) to the insurance company and then reimbursed the client after having received the commission from the company, the commission probably would have been taxable.

2.5 Unemployment Benefits

All unemployment benefits received in 2023 are taxable. You should receive Form 1099-G, showing the amount of the payments. Report the payments on Line 7 of Schedule 1 (Form 1040 or 1040-SR). Supplemental unemployment benefits paid from company-financed funds are taxable as wages and not reported as unemployment compensation. Such benefits are usually paid under guaranteed annual wage plans made between unions and employers.

Unemployment benefits from a private or union fund to which you voluntarily contribute dues are reportable as "other" income on Schedule 1 (Form 1040 or 1040-SR), but only to the extent the benefits exceed your contributions to the fund. Your contributions to the fund are not deductible.

Workers' compensation payments *(2.13)* are not taxable.

Taxable unemployment benefits include federal trade readjustment allowances (1974 Trade Act), airline deregulation benefits (1978 Airline Deregulation Act), and disaster unemployment assistance (1974 Disaster Relief Act).

Repaid supplemental unemployment benefits. If you had to repay supplemental unemployment benefits to receive trade readjustment allowances (1974 Trade Act), taxable unemployment benefits are reduced by repayments made in the same year. If you repay the benefits in a later year, the benefits are taxed in the year of receipt and a deduction may be claimed in the later year. If the repayment is $3,000 or less, an "above-the-line" deduction is allowed; enter it as an adjustment to income on Line 24e of Schedule 1 (Form 1040 or 1040-SR). If the repayment exceeds $3,000, you have the choice between the above-the-line deduction or a credit *(2.8)*.

2.6 Strike Pay Benefits and Penalties

Strike and lockout benefits paid out of regular union dues are taxable as wages unless the payment qualifies as a gift, as discussed below. However, if you have made voluntary contributions to a strike fund, benefits you receive from the fund are tax free up to the amount of your contributions and are taxable to the extent they exceed your contributions.

Strike benefits as tax-free gifts. Factors indicating that benefits are gifts include: Payments are based on individual need; payments are paid to both union and non-union members; and no conditions are imposed on the strikers who receive benefits.

Law Violation Not Deductible

No deduction is allowed for a fine or penalty paid to a government for the violation of a law.

Penalty and Interest on Nonqualified Deferred Compensation

If deferred pay is currently taxable under the rules of Code Section 409A, you must also pay a 20% penalty and interest at a rate 1% higher than the regular underpayment rate.

If you receive benefits under conditions by which you are to participate in the strike and the payments are tied to your scale of wages, the benefits are taxable.

Strike pay penalties. Pay penalties charged to striking teachers are not deductible. State law may prohibit public school teachers from striking and charge a penalty equal to one day's pay for each day spent on strike. For example, when striking teachers returned to work after a one-week strike, a penalty of one week's salary was deducted from their pay. Although they did not actually receive pay for the week they worked after the strike, they earned taxable wages. Furthermore, the penalty is not deductible. No deduction is allowed for a fine or penalty paid to a government for the violation of a law.

> **EXAMPLE**
>
> A striking union pilot claimed that strike benefits were tax-free gifts because they were funded by assessments paid by other union pilots who were not on strike. The IRS and Tax Court held that the benefits were taxable. They were not gifts because they were not motivated by a "detached and disinterested generosity." The union was promoting its own self-interest by giving pilots an incentive to support the strike. The non-striking pilots contributed to the strike fund as an obligation of union membership. The strikers were eligible for benefits only if they agreed to perform any strike activities requested by the union, did not fly for airlines in dispute with the union, and did not take actions that could adversely affect the outcome of the dispute.

2.7 Nonqualified Deferred Compensation

The rules for determining whether tax may be deferred under a nonqualified deferred compensation plan are governed by Code Section 409A. Section 409A applies generally to amounts deferred after 2004. Amounts deferred before 2005 are "grandfathered," and thus generally exempt, but they become subject to Section 409A (unless excluded under IRS rules) if the plan is materially modified after October 3, 2004.

Plans subject to and excluded from Section 409A. Unless an exception applies, Code Section 409A applies to all nonqualified deferred plans, including arrangements between an independent contractor and a service recipient, and a partner and partnership. Under Code Section 409A, the service provider has a legally binding right during a year to compensation that is not actually or constructively received, and which is payable in a later year. The law does not apply to qualified retirement plans (such as 401(k) plans), Section 403(b) tax-deferred annuities, SIMPLE accounts, simplified employee pensions, and Section 457 plans; these are excluded from the definition of "nonqualified deferred compensation plans." Also excluded are welfare benefit plans such as vacation, sick leave, and disability programs.

The IRS has allowed exceptions for short-term deferrals, incentive stock options, employee stock purchase plan options, and certain stock appreciation rights, tax equalization payments, separation payments, reimbursement arrangements, and fringe benefits. For details, *see* the IRS final regulations (T.D. 9321, 2007-19 IRB 1123).

Section 409A requirements. Plans subject to Section 409A must meet detailed requirements pertaining to the timing of deferral elections and the availability of distributions. For example, a deferral election generally must be made prior to the beginning of the year during which the services will be provided, but special rules apply to short-term deferrals and deferrals with respect to forfeitable rights. Distributions before separation from service are generally allowed only if the participant is disabled or has an unforeseeable emergency, the distribution is used to satisfy a domestic relations order, the distribution is on a specific date or under a fixed schedule specified in the plan, or there has been a change in the ownership or effective control of the corporation or in the ownership of a substantial portion of the assets.

If the Section 409A requirements are not met at any time during a taxable year, all amounts deferred under the plan for all years are currently includible in a participant's gross income to the extent that the amounts are not subject to a substantial risk of forfeiture and were not previously included in gross income.

Reporting of Section 409A plan deferrals and earnings on your tax return. Your employer may include 2023 plan deferrals in Box 12 of your Form W-2 using Code Y (reporting is optional). If deferrals are reported, Code Y should also be used to show earnings in 2023 on all deferrals, whether for 2023 or prior years. If any amounts are taxable because the Section 409A requirements have not been met, the taxable amount should be reported as taxable wages in Box 1 of Form W-2, and also shown in Box 12 using Code Z.

If you are not an employee, current year Section 409A deferrals of at least $600 and earnings on current and prior year deferrals may be reported in Box 12 of Form 1099-MISC. If any amounts are taxable because the Section 409A requirements have not been met, the taxable amount is reported in Box 14 of Form 1099-MISC and also included as non-employee compensation in Box 1 of Form 1099-NEC; this amount is generally subject to self-employment tax.

If there is a taxable amount, a penalty also must be paid equal to 20% of the includible compensation, plus interest at a rate that is 1% higher than the regular underpayment rate. The penalty and interest must be added to Line 8 of Schedule 2 (Form 1040 or 1040-SR), and identified as "NQDC".

Financial health triggers and offshore rabbi trusts. Section 409A blocks the benefit of two funding arrangements that set aside assets to secure the payment of promised deferred compensation. If a nonqualified deferred compensation plan provides that assets will be restricted to payment of deferrals if the employer's financial condition deteriorates, the setting aside of the assets will be considered a transfer of restricted property to the participants, taxable under the Section 83 rules *(2.17)*. This is so even if the assets nominally remain available to satisfy the claims of the employer's general creditors.

Also, a Section 83 transfer *(2.17)* is generally deemed to occur when assets to pay nonqualified deferred compensation are set aside in an offshore rabbi trust. Section 409A treats the funding of an offshore trust as a transfer of property to the participants, taxable under the Section 83 rules *(2.17)*, unless substantially all of the services relating to the deferred compensation were performed in the foreign jurisdiction where the assets are held. A Section 83 transfer is deemed to occur whether or not the offshore assets are nominally available to satisfy the claims of the employer's general creditors.

If deferrals are includible in a participant's income because of the financial health trigger or offshore trust provisions, there is an additional 20% penalty plus interest at 1% more than the regular rate.

Rabbi trusts. If IRS tests are met, employer contributions to a domestic "rabbi trust" are not taxed until distributions from the trust are received or made available. The trust must be irrevocable and the trust assets must be subject to the claims of the employer's creditors in the event of insolvency or bankruptcy. Employees and their beneficiaries must have no preferred claim on the trust assets.

Offshore rabbi trusts are subject to Section 409A, as discussed above.

2.8 Did You Return Wages Received in a Prior Year?

Did you return income in 2023 such as salary or commissions that you reported in a prior taxable year under a "claim of right," meaning that it appeared you had an unrestricted right to the income in the earlier year? If the repayment of wages exceeds $3,000, you may claim a tax credit, based upon a recomputation of the prior year's tax *(see below)*, or, if you itemize deductions on Schedule A (Form 1040 or 1040-SR), you can claim the repayment as an "other" itemized deduction *(19.1)*.

However, if the repayment is $3,000 or less, you are not allowed to claim the tax credit or any deduction. For years before 2018, a repayment of $3,000 or less was deductible as a miscellaneous itemized deduction that was subject to the 2% of adjusted gross income floor, but under the Tax Cuts and Jobs Act, miscellaneous expenses that had been subject to the 2% floor are not deductible in 2018 through 2025.

Option of tax credit or deduction for repayments over $3,000. If your repayment of wages exceeded $3,000, you may either (1) claim the repayment as an "other itemized deduction" (Line 16 of Schedule A) *(19.1)*, assuming you itemize deductions on Schedule

Filing Instruction

Repayment of Wages Exceeding $3,000

If you repay wages of more than $3,000, a special law (Code Section 1341) allows you to recompute your tax for the prior year as if the wages had not been reported. The difference between the actual tax paid in the prior year and the recomputed tax may be claimed as a tax credit for 2023 on Line 13d of Schedule 3 (Form 1040 or 1040-SR). In some cases, you might pay less tax for the year of repayment if you claim the repayment as an "other" itemized deduction (Line 16, Schedule A, Form 1040 or 1040-SR), rather than claiming the credit. Choose either the credit or the itemized deduction, whichever gives you the larger tax reduction.

A rather than claim the standard deduction *(13.1)* or (2) claim a tax credit, based upon a recomputation of the prior year's tax.

Repayment of supplemental unemployment benefits. Where repayment is required to qualify for trade readjustment allowances, you may deduct the repayment from gross income. Claim the deduction as an "above-the-line" deduction on Line 24e of Schedule 1 (Form 1040 or 1040-SR). The deduction is allowed even if you do not itemize. If repayment exceeds $3,000, you have the choice of a deduction or claiming a tax credit based on a recomputation of your tax for the year supplemental unemployment benefits were received.

Repayment of disallowed travel expenses. If a "hedge" agreement between you and your company requires you to repay salary or travel expenses if they are disallowed to the company by the IRS, you may claim a deduction in the year of repayment. According to the IRS, you may not recalculate your tax for the prior year and claim a tax credit under the rules of Section 1341. However, an appeals court rejected the position taken by the IRS and allowed a tax recomputation under Section 1341 to an executive who returned part of a disallowed salary under the terms of a corporate by-law.

2.9　Waiver of Executor's and Trustee's Commissions

Commissions received by an executor for services performed are taxable as compensation. An executor may waive commissions without income or gift tax consequences by giving a principal legatee or devisee a formal waiver of the executor's right to commissions within six months after the initial appointment or by not claiming commissions at the time of filing the usual accountings.

The waiver may not be recognized if the executor takes any action that is inconsistent with the waiver. An example of an inconsistent action would be the claiming of an executor's fee as a deduction on an estate, inheritance, or income tax return.

A bequest received by an executor from an estate is tax free if it is not compensation for services.

2.10　Life Insurance Benefits

Company-financed insurance gives employees benefits at low or no tax cost.

Group life insurance. Group insurance plans may furnish not only life insurance protection but also accident and health benefits. Premium costs are low and tax deductible to the company while tax free to you unless you have nonforfeitable rights to permanent life insurance, or, in the case of group-term life insurance, your coverage exceeds $50,000 *(3.4)*. Even where your coverage exceeds $50,000, the tax incurred on your employer's premium payment is generally less than what you would have to pay privately for similar insurance.

It may be possible to avoid estate tax on the group policy proceeds if you assign all of your ownership rights in the policy, including the right to convert the policy, and if the beneficiary is other than your estate. Where the policy allows assignment of the conversion right, in addition to all other rights, and state law does not bar the assignment, you are considered to have made a complete assignment of the group insurance for estate tax purposes.

The IRS has ruled that where an employee assigns a group life policy and the value of the employee's interest in the policy cannot be ascertained, there is no taxable gift. This is so where the employer could simply have stopped making payments. However, there is a gift by the employee to the assignee to the extent of premiums paid by the employer. The gift may be a present interest qualifying for the annual gift tax exclusion *(39.2)*.

Split-dollar insurance. Where you want more insurance than is provided by a group plan, your company may be able to help you get additional protection through a split-dollar insurance plan. Under the basic split-dollar plan, your employer purchases permanent cash value life insurance on your life and pays all or part of the annual premium. At your death, your employer is entitled to part of the proceeds equal to the premiums he or she paid. You have the right to name a beneficiary to receive the remaining proceeds which, under most policies, are substantial compared with the employer's share. Equity split-dollar arrangements allow employees to retain the right to the cash surrender value in excess of the premiums paid by the employer.

In final regulations applicable to split-dollar arrangements entered into or materially modified after September 17, 2003, the IRS has provided two sets of rules, depending on whether the employee or the employer owns the insurance policy (T.D. 9092, 2003-46 IRB 1055). If the employee is the owner, the employer's premium payments will be treated as loans and the imputed interest will be taxed to the employee. If the employer owns the policy, the employee will be taxed on the value of the life insurance protection, the policy cash value that the employee has access to, and the value of any other economic benefits received from the policy.

In addition, the Section 409A rules for nonqualified deferred compensation plans *(2.7)* may also apply to certain types of split-dollar arrangements. Notice 2007-34 contains IRS guidance on applying the Section 409A rules and explaining the effect of modifications to a split-dollar arrangement.

2.11 Educational Benefits for Employees' Children

Private foundations. The IRS has published guidelines for determining whether educational grants made by a private foundation established by an employer to children of employees constitute scholarships. An objective, nondiscriminatory program must be adopted. If the guidelines are satisfied, employees are not taxed on the benefits provided to their children. Advance approval of the grant program must be obtained from the IRS.

IRS guidelines require that:

- Grant recipients must be selected by a scholarship committee that is independent of the employer and the foundation. Former employees of the employer or the foundation are not considered independent.
- Eligibility for the grants may be restricted to children of employees who have been employed for a minimum of up to three years, but eligibility may not be related to the employee's position, services, or duties.
- Once awarded, a grant may not be terminated if the parent leaves his job with the employer, regardless of the reason for the termination of employment. If a one-year grant is awarded or a multi-year grant is awarded subject to renewal, a child who reapplies for a later grant may not be considered ineligible because his parent no longer works for the employer.
- Grant decisions must be based solely upon objective standards unrelated to the employer's business and the parent's employment such as prior academic performance, aptitude tests, recommendations from instructors, financial needs, and conclusions drawn from personal interviews.
- Recipients must be free to use the grants for courses that are not of particular benefit to the employer or the foundation.
- The grant program must not be used by the foundation or employer to recruit employees or induce employees to continue employment.
- There must be no requirement or suggestion that the child or parent is expected to render future employment services.
- A percentage test generally must be met. The number of grants awarded in a given year to children of employees must not exceed (1) 25% of the number of employees' children who were eligible, applied for the grants, and were considered by the selection committee in that year; or (2) 10% of the number of employees' children who were eligible during that year, whether or not they applied. Renewals of grants are not considered in determining the number of grants awarded.

If all of the above tests other than the percentage test are met, the educational grant program can still qualify if the facts and circumstances indicate that the primary purpose of the program is to provide educational benefits rather than to compensate the employees.

Educational benefit trusts and other plans. An educational benefit plan can be set up and used to pay for college costs for children of "key employees." Children enrolled in a degree program within two years of graduating high school may participate in the plan. If

 *Caution*

Charitable Split-Dollar Insurance

In a charitable split-dollar insurance plan, you give money to a charity, which invests in a life insurance policy and splits the proceeds with your beneficiaries. Taxpayers have attempted to deduct the initial "donations," but the tax law was changed to disallow the deduction.

 *Caution*

Primary Purpose Determination

If all guidelines other than the percentage test are satisfied, the IRS will determine whether the primary purpose of the program is to educate the children. If it is, the grants will be considered scholarships or fellowships; if it is not, the grants are taxed to the parent-employees as extra compensation.

an eligible employee quits for any reason other than death or permanent disability, his or her children may no longer receive benefits except for expenses incurred from termination. According to the IRS, any amount contributed to a trust is a form of pay to a qualified employee because contributions are made on the basis of the parents' employment, not the child's needs, merit, or motivation. Tax is not incurred until a person has vested the right to receive benefits. Once the child's right to receive a distribution from the plan has been vested, the parent of the child could be taxed on the amount of the distribution. The company offering the benefits can deduct the same amount.

2.12 Sick Pay Is Taxable

Sick pay received from an employer is generally taxable as wages unless it qualifies as workers' compensation *(2.13)*. Reimbursed medical expenses under an accident or health plan are generally tax free *(3.3)*, unless they constitute excess reimbursements *(17.4)*. Payments from your employer's plan for permanent physical injuries are tax free *(3.3)*.

Disability pensions are discussed in *2.14*.

Sick pay received from your employer is subject to income tax withholding as if it were wages. Sick pay from a third party such as an insurance company is not subject to withholdings unless you request withholding on Form W-4S.

2.13 Workers' Compensation Is Tax Free

You do not pay tax on workers' compensation payments for job-related injuries or illness. However, your employer might continue paying your regular salary but require you to turn over your workers' compensation payments. Then you are taxed on the difference between what was paid to you and what you returned.

> **EXAMPLE**
>
> John Wright was injured while at work and was out of work for two months. His company continues to pay his weekly salary of $775. He also receives workers' compensation of $200 a week from the state, which is tax free. He gives the $200 weekly payments to his employer. The balance of $575 a week is considered taxable wages.

To qualify as tax-free workers' compensation, the payments must be made under the authority of a law (or regulation having the force of a law) that provides compensation for on-the-job injury or illness. Payments made under a labor agreement do not qualify as tax-free workers' compensation.

A retirement pension or annuity does not qualify for tax-free treatment if benefits are based on age, length of service, or prior plan contributions. Such benefits are taxable even if retirement was triggered by a work-related injury or sickness.

State law may impose a penalty for unreasonable delay in paying a worker's compensation award. If the penalty is considered to have the remedial purpose of facilitating the injured employee's return to work, the IRS may treat the penalty as part of the original tax-free compensation award.

Survivors of fallen state and federal public safety officers. Survivor benefits paid to families of police officers, firefighters, paramedics, and other public safety workers killed in the line of duty are excluded from gross income. The exclusion applies to (1) survivor benefits paid by the federal Bureau of Justice Assistance to families of fallen public safety officers, and (2) state-paid benefits to survivors of public safety officers who died as a result of injuries sustained in the line of duty, but the exclusion does not apply to state benefits that would have been paid even if the death had not been sustained in the line of duty.

Effect of workers' compensation on Social Security. In figuring whether Social Security benefits are taxable *(34.2)*, workers' compensation that reduces Social Security or equivalent Railroad Retirement benefits is treated as a Social Security (or Railroad Retirement) benefit received during the year. Thus, the workers' compensation may be indirectly subject to tax *(34.2)*.

Court Decision

Is Sick Leave Tax-Free Workers' Compensation?

According to the Tax Court, sick leave may qualify as tax-free workers' compensation if it is paid under a specific workers' compensation statute or similar government regulation that authorizes the sick leave payment for job-related injuries or illness; *see* Examples 2, 3, and 4 *(2.13)*.

Caution

Job-Related Injury or Illness

Not all payments for job-related illness or injury qualify as tax-free workers' compensation. Unless the statute or regulation authorizing your disability payment restricts awards to on-the-job injury or illness, your payment is taxable. Even if your payments are in fact based upon job-related injury or illness, they are taxed if other individuals can receive payments from the plan for disabilities that are not work related; *see* Example 1 *(2.13)*.

EXAMPLES

1. Kane, a federal district judge, suffered from sleep apnea, a condition characterized by a cessation of breathing during sleep, which was aggravated by the stress of his judicial work. He received a retirement disability payment of $65,135.

   A federal appeals court held that the payment was taxable because it was paid under a statute which did not specifically require that the payments be for work-related injuries. Here, the federal law under which the judge received his payments provided benefits for all permanent disabilities, whether or not job related.

2. A teacher, injured while working, received full salary during a two-year sick leave. She argued that the payments, made under board of education regulations, were similar to workers' compensation and thus tax free. The IRS disagreed, arguing that the regulations were not the same as a workers' compensation statute. The Tax Court supported the teacher. The payments were made because of job-related injuries and were authorized by regulations having the force of law.

3. The IRS claimed that a police officer in Lynbrook, N.Y., was subject to tax on line-of-duty disability pay because the payment was under a labor agreement with the Police Benevolent Association (PBA). The Tax Court supported the police officer's claim that the payments were authorized by a specific New York State law requiring full salary for job-related police injuries. The PBA agreement did not affect the officer's rights to those state law payments. Lynbrook treated the case as a workers' compensation claim and in fact received reimbursement from the state workers' compensation board for the payments made to the officer.

4. A Los Angeles sheriff injured on the job retired on disability and, under the Los Angeles workers' compensation law, was allowed to elect sick pay in lieu of the regular workers' compensation amount because the sick pay was larger. The IRS argued that the sheriff had merely received taxable sick pay because he would have received the same amount as sick pay if his injuries had been suffered in a personal accident. However, the Tax Court allowed tax-free treatment. The sick leave was paid under a workers' compensation law that applied solely to work-related injuries. The fact that sick leave may also have been available to other employees under other laws does not mean that it may not be included as an option under a workers' compensation statute.

   The IRS announced that it does not agree with the Tax Court's decision allowing full tax-free treatment. According to the IRS, benefits up to the regular workers' compensation amount should be tax free but excess amounts should be taxed.

2.14 Disability Pay and Pensions

Disability pensions financed by your employer are taxable wages unless they are for severe permanent physical injuries that qualify for tax-free treatment *(3.3)*, they are tax-free workers' compensation *(2.13)*, or they are tax-free government payments as discussed in this section.

Taxable disability pensions are reported as wages until you reach the minimum retirement age under the employer's plan. After reaching minimum retirement age, payments are reported as a pension *(7.24)*.

If you receive little or no Social Security and your other income is low, you may be eligible to claim a tax credit for disability payments received while you are under the age of 65 and permanently and totally disabled *(34.7)*.

State short-term disability payments. Some states provide or require employers to provide short-term disability pay to workers who are temporarily unable to work due to a non-work related illness or injury, or pregnancy. For federal tax purposes, payments from such plans are taxable to the extent they were financed by your employer or are a substitute for unemployment benefits. For example, payments from the Rhode Island program are not taxable, and payments from California are not taxable unless they are a substitute for unemployment benefits. State disability payments from New York, New Jersey, and Hawaii are taxable to the extent of employer contributions.

Injury or sickness resulting from active military service. Disability pensions for personal injuries or sickness resulting from active service in the armed forces are taxable if you joined the service after September 24, 1975.

Military disability payments are tax free if before September 25, 1975, you were entitled to military disability benefits or if on that date you were a member of the armed forces (or reserve unit) of the U.S. or any other country or were under a binding written commitment to become a member. A similar tax-free rule applies to disability pensions from the following government agencies if you were entitled to the payments before September 25, 1975, or were a member of the service (or committed to joining) on that date: The Foreign Service, Public Health Service, or National Oceanic and Atmospheric Administration. The exclusion for pre–September 25, 1975, service applies to disability pensions based upon percentage of disability. However, if a disability pension was based upon years of service, you do not pay tax on the amount that would be received based upon percentage of disability.

VA pensions. Disability pensions from the Department of Veterans Affairs (VA) are tax free. If you retire from the military and are later given a retroactive award of VA disability benefits, the retirement pay received prior to the award (other than a lump-sum readjustment payment upon retirement) is retroactively made tax free to the extent of the VA disability determination. You may have more than the normal three-year period *(47.2)* to file a refund claim for any tax you paid on the amount that was retroactively determined to be a VA disability benefit. The refund deadline is extended for one year beginning on the date of the VA determination. However, a refund claim within the extended one-year period cannot be made for tax years that began more than five years before the date of the VA determination.

Social Security disability benefits. Disability benefits from the Social Security Administration (SSA) are treated as regular Social Security retirement benefits that may be taxable *(34.2)*.

In one case, a veteran who received disability benefits from the SSA as well as a disability pension from the Department of Veterans Affairs (VA) for cancer caused by exposure to Agent Orange during the Vietnam War tried to exclude both benefits from income. The IRS did not dispute the exclusion for the VA payments, but it held that the SSA disability benefits were subject to tax as if they were Social Security retirement benefits. The Tax Court and the Second Circuit Court of Appeals rejected the taxpayer's argument that his SSA disability benefits were excludable as amounts received for personal injuries/sickness resulting from active military service. The Second Circuit held that the military service exclusion is not applicable for SSA disability payments because they are a wage-replacement benefit based on the number of quarters of Social Security coverage, and are payable whether or not the disability arose from military service.

Disability pay of federal public safety officers. Disability benefits paid to federal public safety officers by the federal Bureau of Justice Assistance are tax free.

Severance payments to disabled combat veterans. Lump-sum severance payments to veterans who separate from service because of combat-related injuries are tax free and should not be reported on Form W-2.

Pension based on combat-related injuries. Tax-free treatment applies to payments for combat-related injury or sickness that is incurred as a result of any one of the following activities: (1) as a direct result of armed conflict; (2) while engaged in extra-hazardous service, even if not directly engaged in combat; (3) under conditions simulating war, including maneuvers or training; or (4) that is caused by an instrumentality of war, such as weapons.

Terrorist attacks or United States military actions. Tax-free treatment applies to disability payments received by any individual for injuries incurred as the direct result of a terrorist attack against the United States or its allies. The exclusion also applies to disability income received as a direct result of a military action involving U.S. Armed Forces in response to aggression against the United States or its allies.

2.15 Stock Appreciation Rights (SARs)

Stock appreciation rights, or SARs, enable employees to receive the benefit of an increase in value of the employer's stock between the date the SARs are granted and the date they are exercised. When the SARs are exercised, cash or stock may be delivered as payment for the post-grant appreciation. For example, when your employer's stock is worth $30 a share, you

Law Alert

Terrorist Attacks

Tax-free treatment applies to disability payments resulting from terrorist attacks inside as well as outside the United States.

get 100 SARs exercisable within five years. Two years later, when the stock price has increased to $50 a share, you exercise the SARs and receive $2,000 ($5,000 value at exercise minus $3,000 value at grant). SARs that remains unexercised have no tax consequence to you.For example, if the value of yourstock declines, you recognizeno income or loss. If IRS tests are satisfied, you are not taxed until you exercise the SARs and the post-grant appreciation is received. The enactment of Code Section 409A further complicates the situation *(2.7)*, because it restricts deferrals of income under nonqualified deferred compensation plans. However, the IRS has provided an exception to the Section 409A rules for SARs issued with an exercise price equal to the stock's fair market value when the rights are granted.

2.16 Stock Options

Employees receiving statutory stock options do not incur regular income tax liability either at the time the option is granted or when the option is exercised. However, the option spread is generally subject to AMT *(23.2)*. Statutory options include incentive stock options (ISOs) and options under an employee stock purchase plan (ESPP). Employees receiving nonstatutory (nonqualified) stock options generally must include the option spread in income for the year the option is exercised unless the stock does not become vested until a later year.

Incentive stock options (ISOs). A corporation may provide its employees with incentive stock options to acquire its stock (or the stock of its parent or subsidiaries). For regular income tax purposes, ISOs meeting tax law tests are not taxed when granted or exercised. Income or loss is not reported until you sell the stock acquired from exercising the ISO. However, for purposes of the alternative minimum tax (AMT), the excess of the fair market value of the stock at exercise over the option price is treated as an adjustment that may substantially increase AMT income. The AMT adjustment applies for the year of exercise or if later, the year in which your rights to the stock are transferrable or no longer subject to a substantial risk of forfeiture; *see* the Caution on this page.

To qualify as an ISO, the option must be exercisable within 10 years of the date it is granted and the option price must be at least equal to the fair market value of the stock when the option is granted. If the fair market value of stock for which ISOs may first be exercised in a particular year by an employee exceeds $100,000 (valued at date of grant), the excess is not considered a qualifying ISO. An ISO may be exercised by a former employee within three months of the termination of employment; if exercised after three months, income is realized under the rules for nonqualified options, discussed later in this section.

AMT consequences of exercising ISO. Although you do not realize taxable income for regular tax purposes when you exercise an ISO, the "bargain element" could subject you to the alternative minimum tax (AMT) *(23.2)*. *See* the Caution on this page.

Form 3921 for ISO. You should receive Form 3921 (or equivalent statement) from the corporation for the year you exercise an ISO. Form 3921 shows the dates on which the ISO was granted and exercised, the exercise price per share, the fair market value per share on the exercise date, and the number of shares acquired when the option was exercised. Keep the Form 3921 in your records and use it to figure the gain or loss when you sell the shares; *see* "Gain or loss on sale of ISO stock," below. The Form 3921 entries can also be used to figure the AMT adjustment; *see* the Form 6251 instructions.

Gain or loss on sale of ISO stock. If the stock acquired by the exercise of the ISO is held for more than one year after acquisition and more than two years after the ISO was granted, you have long-term capital gain or loss *(5.3)* on the sale, equal to the difference between the selling price of the stock and the option price you paid when you exercised the ISO. If you sell to comply with conflict-of-interest requirements, the holding period rules are considered satisfied.

If you sell before meeting the one-year and two-year holding period tests, a gain on the sale is generally treated as ordinary wage income to the extent of the option spread (bargain element)—the excess of the value of the stock when you exercised the ISO over the option price. Any gain in excess of the spread is reported as capital gain. In figuring the capital gain, cost basis for the stock is increased by the amount treated as wages. If the fair market value of the stock declines between the date the option was exercised and the date the stock is sold,

 *Caution*

Possible AMT Liability for ISO

If you exercise an incentive stock option and your rights in the acquired stock are transferable and not subject to a substantial risk of forfeiture, then on your tax return for the year of exercise you must treat the "bargain element" as an adjustment for alternative minimum tax purposes *(23.2)* unless you sell the stock by the end of that year. The bargain element is the excess of the fair-market value of the stock when the option was exercised over the option price. You must report an AMT adjustment based on the value of the stock when the option was exercised, even if the value later declines substantially. You avoid the AMT adjustment if you sell the stock in the same year the option was exercised. If your rights in the stock are restricted in the year you exercise the option, the AMT adjustment applies for the year the restrictions are lifted. *See 23.2* for further details.

the amount that must be treated as wages is generally reduced. The ordinary income (wages) is limited to the actual gain on the stock sale where the gain is less than the option spread at exercise. However, the reduction to ordinary income does not apply on a sale of the stock to a related person or if replacement shares are purchased within the wash sale period *(30.6)* because the reduction applies only if a loss "would be" recognized if sustained (actual loss is not required for limitation to apply so long as a loss "would be" recognized).

If you have a loss on the sale of stock acquired by exercising an ISO, it is a capital loss and there is no ordinary wage income to report.

EXAMPLE

You were granted an incentive stock option (ISO) on March 14, 2021, to buy 1,000 shares of your employer company's stock at its then fair market value of $10 a share. You exercised the option on January 17, 2022, when the market price for the stock was $15 a share. You sold the stock on January 25, 2023, for $20 a share. Although you held the stock for more than one year, you did not sell more than two years after the date the option was granted. Therefore, part of your gain on the sale in 2023 is ordinary wage income. You have ordinary wage income of $5,000, equal to the option spread ($15,000 value on January 17, 2022, minus $10,000 option price) and $5,000 of long-term capital gain.

Selling price ($20 × 1,000 shares)	$20,000
Less: Cost of stock ($10 exercise price × 1,000 shares)	10,000
Gain	10,000
Less: Ordinary wage income ($15,000 value at exercise – $10,000 option price)	5,000
Capital gain ($20,000 sales price – basis of $15,000 ($10,000 cost + $5,000 treated as wages))	$5,000

Employee stock purchase plans (ESPPs). These plans allow employees to buy their company's stock, usually at a discount. A discount cannot exceed 15% (option price must be at least 85% of fair market value). The plan must be nondiscriminatory and meet tax law tests on option terms. Options granted under qualified plans are not taxed until you sell the shares acquired from exercising the option.

If you sell the stock more than one year after exercising the option and also more than two years after the option was granted, gain on the sale is capital gain unless the option was granted at a discount. If at the time the option was granted the fair market value of the stock exceeded the option price (which must be no less than 85% of fair market value), then when you sell the stock, gain is ordinary wage income to the extent of that discount. Any excess gain is long-term capital gain. A loss on the sale is long-term capital loss.

If you sell the acquired stock before meeting the one-year and two-year holding period tests, you must report as ordinary wage income the option spread—the excess of the value of the stock when you exercised the option over the option price. This amount must be reported as ordinary income even if it exceeds the gain on the sale (which would occur if the sale price were lower than the exercise price). Add the ordinary income amount to your cost basis for the stock. If the increased basis is less than the selling price, the difference is capital gain. You have a capital loss if the increased basis exceeds the selling price.

For the year that you sell stock acquired at a discount under an ESPP, you should receive Form 3922 (or equivalent statement from the corporation). Form 3922 shows the dates the option was granted and exercised, the fair market value per share on the grant date and also the exercise date, the exercise price per share, and the number of shares sold.

Nonstatutory (nonqualified) stock options. A nonstatutory stock option (also called a nonqualified option) can in some cases be considered nonqualified deferred compensation subject to the requirements of Code Section 409A *(2.7)*. Under IRS regulations, the Section 409A rules apply if the exercise price can be less than the value of the underlying stock when the option is granted or the option permits any other deferral feature.

If the Section 409A rules do not apply, the amount of income to include and the time to include it depends on whether the option has a readily ascertainable fair market value when the option is granted. It is very rare for a nonstatutory option to be actively traded on an established securities market or to meet the other tests in IRS regulations for having a readily ascertainable fair market value.

In the usual case where there is no readily ascertainable fair market value for the option at the time it is granted, no income is realized on the receipt of the option. Income will not be realized until the year the option is exercised, or if later, the year your rights to the stock become vested. If the stock is not vested when you exercise the option, income is deferred until the vesting year under the restricted property rules *(2.18)*. In the year that you become vested in the stock, you must report as ordinary wage income the value of the stock (as of the vesting date), minus the amount you paid.

EXAMPLES

1. You are granted an option to buy 1,000 shares from your employer's ESPP for $20 a share at a time when the market price is $22 a share. You exercise the option 14 months later when the value of the stock is $23 a share. You sell the stock for $30 a share 18 months after exercising the option. You meet the one-year and two-year holding period tests but because the option was granted at a discount, part of the gain on the sale is treated as ordinary income.

Selling price ($30 × 1,000 shares)	$30,000
Less: Cost of stock ($20 × 1,000 shares)	20,000
Gain	10,000
Less: Ordinary wage income ($22,000 value at grant – $20,000 option price)	2,000
Capital gain ($30,000 sales price – basis of $22,000 ($20,000 cost + $2,000 treated as wages))	$8,000

2. Same facts as in Example 1, except that you sold the stock only six months after you exercised the ESPP option. Since the one-year holding period test was not met, $3,000 of your $10,000 gain is taxed as ordinary wage income. The $3,000 ordinary income equals the option spread between the $23,000 value of the stock when you exercised the option and the $20,000 option price. You also have a $7,000 short-term capital gain: $30,000 sales price – $23,000 basis ($20,000 cost + $3,000 treated as wages).

If you receive vested stock when the option is exercised, you are taxed on the difference between the fair market value of the stock when you exercise the option and the option price. For example, in 2023, you exercise a nonstatutory stock option to buy 1,000 shares of your employer's stock at $10 a share when the stock has a value of $30 a share. Your rights to the stock are vested when you buy it. When you exercise the option you are treated as receiving wages of $20,000, equal to the option spread ($30,000 value – $10,000 cost). This income is subject to withholding taxes that you will have to pay out-of-pocket at the time of exercise unless the withholding can be taken from regular cash wages. The taxable spread will be reported as wages on Form W-2 and will be separately identified in Box 12, using Code V. Your cost basis for the shares is increased by the ordinary income reported for exercising the option. If you hold the shares for more than one year after exercising the option and then sell them for $35,000 ($35 a share × 1,000 shares), you will have a $5,000 long-term capital gain ($35,000 – $30,000 basis ($10,000 cost plus $20,000 taxed as wages at exercise)).

If in a rare case a nonstatutory stock option has an ascertainable fair market value, the value of the option less any amount you paid is taxable under the restricted property rules *(2.18)* as ordinary wage income in the first year that your right to the option is freely transferable or not subject to a substantial risk of forfeiture. However, a Section 83(b) election *(2.18)* may not be made for the nonstatutory option. For other details and requirements, *see* IRS Regulation Section 1.83-7.

Caution

Tax Due on Option Exercise

Determine the amount of cash you will need to make the purchases and meet your tax liability before you exercise a nonqualified option and receive vested stock. If you receive vested stock when you exercise the option, you will realize wage income equal to the excess of the value of the stock over the option price. In addition to the cash to buy the stock, you will need cash to pay the tax on the wage income. The tax is due even if you plan to hold onto the stock before selling.

Nonstatutory stock options may be granted in addition to or in place of incentive stock options. There are no restrictions on the amount of nonstatutory stock options that may be granted.

2.17 Election to Defer Income on Qualified Equity Grants from Private Companies (Section 83(i) election)

If an employee works for a privately held corporation that adopts a "qualified equity grant" program, he or she may be able elect to defer ordinary income for up to five years on stock acquired pursuant to exercising stock options or upon settlement of restricted stock units (RSUs) (Code Section 83(i)). The corporation is not eligible if it had any readily traded stock on an established securities market during any preceding year. Deferral elections are allowed only if the corporation has a written plan under which at least 80% of all U.S. employees are given stock options or RSUs with the same rights.

The deferral election may not be made by any of the following: more-than-1% owners (currently or at any point in the 10 prior years) and their family members, one of the four highest compensated officers (currently or at any point in the 10 prior years), or the current or former CEO or CFO and their family members.

An eligible employee must make a Section 83(i) election within 30 days after the first date his or her rights in the stock become substantially vested—when the rights become transferable or are no longer subject to a substantial risk of forfeiture. The election is made by filing a statement with the IRS that is similar to the statement required for a Section 83(b) election, discussed in *2.18*.

If the election is made, the income to be reported at the end of the deferral period is determined by the value of the stock when the rights of the employee first become substantially vested. The deferral period generally ends five years from the date the stock is substantially vested, but it may end sooner if you become ineligible or the corporation becomes ineligible because some of its stock becomes tradable on an established securities market. For the year that the income is includible, the employer must withhold income tax at the highest marginal rate, currently 37%. To ensure the corporation meets its withholding obligation on the income, the deferral stock must be held in escrow.

For further details on the Section 83(i) election rules, *see* IRS Publication 525 and Notice 2018-97.

2.18 Restricted Stock

If in return for performing services you buy or receive company stock (or other property) subject to restrictions, special tax rules apply. Unless you make the Section 83(b) election discussed below, you do not have to pay tax on the stock until the first year in which it is substantially vested, which is the year that the stock either becomes transferable or is not subject to a substantial risk of forfeiture. A risk of forfeiture exists where your rights are conditioned upon the future performance of substantial services. In the year the property becomes substantially vested, you must report as compensation (wages) the difference between the amount, if any, that you paid for the stock and its value at the time the risk of forfeiture is removed. The valuation at the time the forfeiture restrictions lapse is not reduced because of restrictions imposed on the right to sell the property. However, restrictions that will never lapse do affect valuation.

SEC restrictions on insider trading are considered a substantial risk of forfeiture, so there is no tax on the receipt of stock subject to such restrictions. However, the SEC permits insiders to immediately resell stock acquired through exercise of an option granted at least six months earlier. As the stock acquired through such options is not subject to SEC restrictions, the executive is subject to immediate tax upon exercise of an option held for at least six months.

If the stock is subject to a restriction on transfer to comply with SEC pooling-of-interests accounting rules, the stock is considered to be subject to a substantial restriction.

Non-employees. The tax rules for restricted property are not limited to employees. They also apply to independent contractors who are compensated for services with restricted stock or other property.

Caution

Likelihood of Enforcement Required for Substantial Risk of Forfeiture

The IRS will take into account both the likelihood that a forfeiture event will occur and the likelihood that the forfeiture will be enforced in determining if there is a "substantial risk of forfeiture" under the restricted property rules.

Sale of property that is not substantially vested. If you sell restricted property in an arm's-length transaction before it has become substantially vested and you did not make the Section 83(b) election discussed below, gain on the sale (amount realized minus what you paid) must be reported as compensation income for the year of the sale. If the sale is to a related person or is otherwise not at arm's length, compensation must be reported not only for the year of sale but also for the year the original property becomes substantially vested, as if you still held it. In the later year, the compensation income equals the fair market reported on the earlier sale.

Election to include value of restricted stock in taxable pay when stock is received (Section 83(b) election). Restricted stock is generally not taxable until the year in which it is substantially vested, but you may elect to be taxed in the year you receive it on the unrestricted value (as of the date the stock is received), less any payment you made by using the Section 83(b) election. The Section 83(b) election must be made by filing a signed statement with the IRS (at the Service Center where you file your return) no later than 30 days after the date the stock is transferred to you. Also give a copy of the statement to the employer or other party for whom you provided the services.

The statement must specify that you are making the election under Section 83(b) and include the following: your name, address, Social Security number, the year for which you are making the election, a description of the stock and the restrictions on the stock, the date you received the stock, the fair market value of the stock at receipt (ignoring restrictions unless they never lapse), your cost, if any, for the stock, and a statement that you have provided a copy of the statement to your employer or other party for whom the services were provided. The IRS has provided a sample election statement in Revenue Procedure 2012-29 you may use to make the election.

You do not have to attach a copy of the statement to your tax return for the year in which the stock was transferred to you; this was required for pre-2015 transfers, but the IRS deleted the requirement because it prevented the return from being e-filed.

If you make the election, you recognize ordinary income (wages) based on the value of the stock when it is received, but thereafter you are treated as an investor and later appreciation in value is not taxed as pay when your rights to the stock become vested. When you sell the stock, your basis for figuring capital gain or loss is your cost basis increased by the amount of income you reported as pay under the Section 83 (b) election. If you forfeit the stock after the election is made, a capital loss *(5.4)* is allowed for your cost minus any amount realized on the forfeiture. The election may not be revoked without the consent of the IRS.

Planning Reminder

Electing Immediate Tax on Restricted Stock

If you expect restricted stock to appreciate, consider making an election (Section 83(b) election) to be immediately taxed on the value of the restricted stock, minus your cost. If you make the election, any appreciation in value that has accrued since the election was made will not be taxable when the stock becomes substantially vested. Tax on appreciation will not be due until the stock is sold.

CHAPTER 3

Fringe Benefits

Employer-furnished fringe benefits are exempt from tax if the tests discussed in this chapter are met.

The most common tax-free benefits are accident and health plan coverage, including employer contributions to health savings accounts (HSAs), group-term life insurance plans, dependent care plans, education assistance plans, tuition reduction plans, adoption benefit plans, cafeteria plans, and plans providing employees with discounts, no-additional-cost services, or employer-subsidized meal facilities.

Highly compensated individuals may be taxed on certain benefits from such plans if nondiscrimination rules are not met.

Table 3-1   Are Your Fringe Benefits Tax Free?

Fringe benefit—	Tax Pointer—
Adoption benefits	Employer payments to a third party or reimbursements to you in 2023 for qualified adoption expenses are generally tax free up to a limit of $15,950. The exclusion for 2023 starts to phase out if modified adjusted gross income (MAGI) exceeds $239,230 and is completely phased out if MAGI is $279,230 or more *(3.6)*.
Athletic facilities	The fair market value of athletic facilities, such as gyms, swimming pools, golf courses, and tennis courts, is tax free if the facilities are on property owned or leased by the employer (not necessarily the main business premises) and substantially all of the use of the facilities is by employees, their spouses, and dependent children. Such facilities must be open to all employees on a nondiscriminatory basis in order for the company to deduct related expenses.
Child or dependent care plans	The value of day-care services provided or reimbursed by an employer under a written, nondiscriminatory plan is tax free for 2023 up to a limit of $5,000, or $2,500 for married persons filing separately *(3.5)*. Expenses are excludable if they would qualify for the dependent care credit; *see Chapter 25*. On Form 2441, you must report employer-provided benefits to figure the tax-free exclusion; excludable benefits reduce expenses eligible for the dependent care tax credit *(3.5)*.
De minimis (minor) fringe benefits	These are small benefits that are administratively impractical to tax, such as occasional supper money and taxi fares for overtime work, company parties or picnics, and occasional theater or sporting event tickets *(3.10)*.
Discounts on company products and services	Services from your employer that are usually sold to customers are tax free if your employer does not incur additional costs in providing them to you *(3.17)*. Merchandise discounts and other discounted services are also eligible for a tax-free exclusion *(3.18)*.
Education plans	An exclusion of up to $5,250 applies to employer-financed undergraduate and graduate courses, whether or not job-related, as well as assistance with student loan debt for 2023 *(3.7)*.
Employee achievement awards	Achievement awards are taxable unless they qualify under special rules for length of service or safety achievement *(3.12)*.
Group-term life insurance	Premiums paid by employers are not taxed if policy coverage is $50,000 or less *(3.4)*.
Health and accident plans including HSAs	Premiums paid by an employer are tax free. For 2023, employer contributions to a health savings account, or HSA, on behalf of an eligible employee are generally not taxed up to $3,850 for self-only coverage or $7,750 for family coverage *(3.2)*. Health benefits paid from an employer plan are also generally tax free *(3.1–3.4)*.
Interest-free or low-interest loans	Interest-free loans received from your employer may be taxed *(4.31)*.
Moving expense reimbursements	Employer reimbursements of moving expenses to an employee are taxable, with one exception: reimbursements of qualifying moving costs are tax free to members of the U.S. Armed Forces on active duty who move pursuant to a military order and incident to a permanent change of station *(2.1, 12.3)*.
Retirement planning advice	Employer-provided retirement income planning advice and information are tax free to employees (and their spouses) so long as the employer maintains a qualified retirement plan. The exclusion does not apply to tax preparation, accounting, legal, or brokerage services.
Transportation benefits	Employer-provided parking benefits and transit passes in 2023 are tax free up to $300 per month; *see 3.8*.
Tuition reductions	Tuition reductions for courses below the graduate level are generally tax free. Graduate students who are teaching or research assistants are not taxed on tuition reduction unless the reduction is compensation for teaching services *(3.7)*.
Working condition benefits	Benefits provided by your employer that would be deductible if you paid the expenses yourself are a tax-free working condition fringe benefit. These include business use of a company car, employer-provided cell phone, and education assistance (with no dollar limit) to maintain or improve job skills or required by law to keep job status *(3.9)*.
Volunteer firefighter and emergency medical responder benefits	Volunteer firefighters and emergency medical responders are not taxed on the following benefits received from a state or local government: (1) property tax rebates or reductions, or (2) payments or reimbursements of up to $50 per month *(3.19)*.

3.1 Tax-Free Health and Accident Coverage Under Employer Plans

You are not taxed on contributions or insurance premiums your employer makes to a health, hospitalization, or accident plan to cover you, your spouse, your dependents, and your children under age 27 (as of the end of the year) whether or not they can be claimed as your dependents. Tax-free treatment for a spouse applies to same-sex as well as opposite sex spouses. A domestic partner is not a spouse; you must pay tax on employer-paid coverage for a domestic partner.

If you obtain coverage by making pre-tax salary-reduction contributions under your employer's cafeteria plan *(3.15)*, the salary reductions are treated as employer contributions that are tax free to you. If you are temporarily laid off and continue to receive health coverage, the employer's contributions during this layoff period are tax free. If you are retired, you do not pay tax on insurance paid by your former employer. Medical coverage provided to the family of a deceased employee is tax free since it is treated as a continuation of the employee's fringe-benefit package. If you are age 65 or older, Medicare premiums paid by your employer are not taxed. If you retire and have the option of receiving continued coverage under the medical plan or a lump-sum payment covering unused accumulated sick leave instead of coverage, the lump-sum amount is reported as income at the time you have the option to receive it. If you elect continued coverage, the amount reported as income may be deductible as medical insurance if you itemize deductions *(17.2)*.

Disability coverage. If your employer pays the premiums for your disability coverage (short term or long term) and does not report the payment as compensation income on your Form W-2, or if you pay the premiums with pre-tax salary-reduction contributions, your coverage is tax free but any benefits you subsequently receive from the plan upon becoming disabled is includible in your gross income *(3.3)*. If you pay the premiums with after-tax contributions or your employer makes contributions that are included on your Form W-2, any disability benefits you receive from the plan will not be taxable to you.

Health Reimbursement Arrangements (HRAs). Employer contributions to health reimbursement arrangements (HRAs) are not taxed to the employees. The contributions must be paid by the employer and not provided by salary reduction. HRA contributions can be used to reimburse the medical costs of employees, their spouses, and their dependents, and unused expenses may be carried forward to later years *(3.3)*.

Long-term care coverage. You are not taxed on contributions your employer makes for long-term care coverage that would pay you benefits in the event you become chronically ill *(17.15)*. However, long-term care coverage may not be offered to you through a cafeteria plan *(3.15)* and reimbursements of long-term care expenses may not be made through a flexible spending arrangement *(3.16)*.

Continuing coverage for group health plans (COBRA coverage). Employers are subject to daily penalties unless the employer offers continuing group health and accident coverage to employees who leave the company voluntarily or involuntarily (unless for gross misconduct). This also applies to spouses and dependent children who would lose coverage in the case of divorce or the death of the employee. Federal COBRA continuing coverage rules apply to employers with 20 or more employees but smaller employers may be required under state law to provide comparable continuing coverage under "mini-COBRA" laws.

Generally, an employer may charge you premiums for continuing coverage that are as much as 102% of the regular plan premium for the applicable (family or individual) coverage.

3.2 Health Savings Accounts (HSAs) and Archer MSAs

If you are covered by a qualifying high-deductible health plan (HDHP), your employer may make tax-free contributions to a health savings account (HSA) on your behalf. Earnings accumulate tax free within an HSA and distributions are tax free if used to pay your qualified medical expenses, or those of your spouse or dependents. If your employer does not make the maximum tax-free contribution to your HSA, you can make a deductible contribution, so long as the total does not exceed the annual contribution limit *(see below)*.

Archer MSAs are an older type of medical savings plan that HSAs are intended to replace. If your employer set up an Archer MSA on your behalf before 2008, or you became eligible to participate after 2007 in a pre-2008 plan, your employer may continue to contribute to the account. If you work for an eligible small employer with a high-deductible plan, your employer may make tax-free contributions to an Archer MSA on your behalf. A rollover can be made from an Archer MSA to a new health savings account (HSA) that accepts rollovers. If the Archer MSA is retained, withdrawals will be tax free if used to pay qualified medical expenses for you, your spouse, or your dependents.

Health Savings Account (HSA)

You may set up an HSA only if you are covered by a qualifying high-deductible health plan (HDHP, *see* details below), you are not enrolled in Medicare, and you are not the dependent of another taxpayer. Generally, you must have no coverage other than HDHP coverage; however, there are exceptions. You are allowed to have separate coverage for vision, dental, or long-term care, accidents, disability, per diem insurance while hospitalized, insurance for a specific disease or illness, car insurance (or similar insurance for owning or using property), or insurance for workers' compensation or tort liabilities. Also, as discussed below, the HDHP minimum annual deductible does not apply to preventive care.

As an eligible employee, you, your employer, or both may contribute to your HSA. The same maximum annual contribution limit applies *(see below)* regardless of the number of contributors. Your employer may allow you to make pre-tax salary-reduction contributions to an HDHP and HSA as an option under a cafeteria plan *(3.13)*.

High-deductible health plan (HDHP). An HDHP must have a minimum annual deductible and an annual out-of-pocket maximum. For 2023, the minimum plan deductible is $1,500 for self-only coverage and $3,000 for family coverage. Out-of-pocket costs for 2023 are limited to $7,500 for self-only coverage and $15,000 for family coverage The limit for out-of-pocket costs covers plan deductibles, co-payments and other out-of-pocket expenses, but not premiums.

In the case of family coverage, the terms of the HDHP must deny payments to all family members until the family as a unit incurs annual covered expenses in excess of the minimum annual deductible ($3,000 for 2023). Thus, a plan is not a qualified HDHP for 2023 if it allows payment of an individual family member's medical expenses exceeding $1,400 (the minimum deductible for self-only coverage) but the family as a whole does not have expenses over $3,000. However, preventive care benefits are not subject to the minimum annual HDHP deductible. The plan can qualify as an HDHP even if it pays for preventive care without a deductible or after a small deductible (below the regular HDHP minimum). The IRS has provided a safe harbor list of preventive care benefits, including annual physicals, routine prenatal and well-child care, immunizations, tobacco cessation and obesity programs, and screening services for a broad range of conditions including cancer (such as breast, cervical, prostate, ovarian, and colorectal cancer) and cardiovascular disease. Prescription drugs qualify for the preventive care safe harbor if taken by asymptomatic patients with risk factors for a disease, or by recovering patients to prevent the recurrence of a disease. For individuals diagnosed with specified chronic conditions (such as hypertension, heart disease, diabetes, asthma, liver disease), the IRS recognizes specified medical services and prescription drugs as being preventive care.

By law, prescription drug coverage, other than coverage meeting the preventive care safe harbor, is not a permitted exception to the high-deductible requirement. This is a problem for employees whose employers offer separate prescription drug plans that provide first-dollar drug coverage with either a flat dollar or percentage co-payment. HSA contributions cannot be made for individuals with an HDHP and such a prescription drug plan because the prescription drug benefits are not subject to the HDHP minimum annual deductible.

Maximum annual HSA contribution for employees. For 2023, the maximum HSA contribution for an employee with self coverage is $3,850. For an employee with family coverage, the maximum contribution for 2023 is $7,750. For employees who are of age 55 or older by the end of 2023 and are not enrolled in Medicare, an additional

 *Filing Tip*

Above-the-Line Deduction for HSA Contributions

If you are an eligible employee, contributions made to your HSA are reported on Form 8889 and deducted on Line 13 of Schedule 1 (Form 1040 or 1040-SR); *see 3.2* for contribution limits. The deduction is "above the line," so it is allowed even if you claim the standard deduction.

If self-employed, you may claim the "above-the-line" HSA deduction subject to the same limits; *see Chapter 41* for further details.

Planning Reminder

One-Time Transfer From IRA to HSA

You can make a one-time tax-free transfer from your IRA or Roth IRA to your HSA. A qualifying transfer is not taxable or subject to the 10% penalty for distributions before age 59½. Generally, only one IRA/Roth IRA transfer to an HSA is allowed during your lifetime, but if a transfer is made to a self-only HDHP, and later in the same year you obtain family HDHP coverage, a second transfer from an IRA or Roth IRA may be made in that year. The transfer (or transfers) count towards the annual HSA contribution limit for that year, so if the transfer exceeds the annual HSA contribution limit, the excess is taxable (and possibly subject to the pre-59½ penalty). If you want to transfer amounts from more than one IRA or Roth IRA to an HSA, you have to first roll the funds into a single IRA/Roth IRA and then make the transfer from that account.

To be tax free, the transfer must be directly to the HSA trustee or custodian. Furthermore, you must remain HSA-eligible (have qualifying HDHP coverage) for 12 months following the date of the distribution; otherwise, the distribution is taxable (and possibly subject to the pre-59½ penalty) in the year that you cease to be eligible. Changing from family-HDHP coverage to a self-only HDHP during the 12-month testing period is not considered a cessation of HSA eligibility.

"catch-up" contribution of $1,000 may be made. The $1,000 catch-up is fixed by statute. The applicable limit must be reduced by any contributions to an Archer MSA.

If you become eligible under an HDHP, contributions are allowed for the months prior to your enrollment in the HDHP, provided you are eligible in December of that year. However, the contributions for the months prior to your enrollment will be included in your income and subject to a 10% penalty if you do not remain eligible for the 12 months following the end of the first eligibility year, unless you are disabled (or die).

All employer contributions must be reported on Form 8889. Contributions by your employer up to the limit are tax free and are not subject to withholding for income tax or FICA (Social Security and Medicare) purposes. All employer contributions to an HSA are reported in Box 12 of Form W-2 with Code W. Contributions exceeding the excludable limit are also reported in Box 1 of Form W-2 as taxable wages. If you do not remove an excess contribution (and any net income) by the due date for your return (including extensions), the excess is subject to a 6% penalty; *see* the instructions to Forms 8889 and 5329.

If your employer contributes less than the limit, you may contribute to your HSA but the same overall limit applies to the aggregate contributions. Contributions you make are reported on Form 8889 and deductible "above the line" from gross income on Line 13 of Schedule 1 (Form 1040 or 1040-SR). You must attach Form 8889 to your Form 1040 or 1040-SR.

Archer MSAs

Most employers have replaced Archer MSAs (medical savings accounts) with HSAs. However, an Archer MSA that is not rolled over to a new HSA may continue to be funded.

To contribute, you must have coverage under a high-deductible health plan and must work for a "small employer," one that had an average of 50 or fewer employees during either of the two preceding years. For 2023, self-only coverage under a high-deductible health plan, the minimum deductible is $2,650 the maximum deductible is $3,950, and the plan limit on out-of-pocket expenses (other than premiums) is $5,300. For 2023 family coverage, the deductible must be at least $5,300 and no more than $7,900, and the limit on out-of-pocket expenses (other than premiums) is $9,650. All of these limits are subject to an inflation adjustment for 2024 *see* the *e-Supplement* at *jklasser.com*.

Generally, you are not eligible for an Archer MSA if you have any other health insurance in addition to the high-deductible plan coverage, except for policies covering only disability, vision or dental care, long-term care, or accidental injuries, or plans that pay a flat amount during hospitalization.

Employer contribution limits. Your employer's contributions to your Archer MSA are tax free up to an annual limit of 65% of the plan deductible if you have individual coverage and 75% of the deductible for family coverage. The limit is reduced on a monthly basis if you are not covered for the entire year. For example, if for all of 2023 you were covered by a qualifying family coverage high-deductible plan with a $7,900 annual deductible (the maximum deductible for 2023), the maximum tax-free contribution is $5,925 (75% of $7,900). If you had coverage for only 10 months, the limit would be $4,937 ($10/_{12} × $5,925). All employer contributions to your Archer MSA are reported in Box 12 of Form W-2 (Code R). If the contributions exceed the tax-free limit, the excess is reported in Box 1 of Form W-2 as taxable wages. You must report all employer contributions on Form 8853, which you attach to your Form 1040 or 1040-SR.

If your employer makes any contributions to your account, you may not make any contributions for that year. In addition, if you and your spouse have family coverage under a high-deductible plan and your spouse's employer contributes to his or her Archer MSA, you cannot contribute to your Archer MSA. If your employer (or spouse's employer) does not contribute, you may make deductible contributions up to the above employer contribution limits. You report your contributions on Form 8853 and claim your deduction on Line 23 of Schedule 1 (Form 1040 or 1040-SR). Contributions exceeding the annual limit are subject to a 6% penalty.

3.3 Reimbursements and Other Tax-Free Payments From Employer Health and Accident Plans

Several types of payments from a health or accident plan are tax free to you even if your employer paid the entire cost of your coverage:

1. Reimbursements of your medical expenses; *see* below.

2. Payments for permanent physical injuries; *see* below.

3. Distributions from a health savings account (HSA) or Archer MSA if they are used to pay for qualified medical expenses; *see* below.

4. Payments you receive when you are chronically ill from a qualifying long-term-care insurance contract; but if payments are made on a per diem or other periodic basis, the exclusion may be limited. For 2023, payments of up to $390 per day are tax free regardless of actual expenses. If the payments exceed $390 per day, you are only taxed to the extent that the payments exceed your qualifying long-term-care expenses. See *17.15* for further details.

The use of COVID 19 home-testing is an eligible medical expense that can be paid or reimbursed under a health-FSA, HSA, HRA or Archer MSA.

Payments that are not within the above tax-free categories, such as disability benefits, are not taxable to you if you paid all of the premiums with after-tax contributions. If your contributions were made on a pre-tax basis, benefits received from the plan are taxable. For example, disability benefits are taxable if you paid premiums paid under a cafeteria plan *(3.15)* with pre-tax contributions that were excluded from your income. If your employer paid all the premiums and you were not taxed on your employer's payment, any benefits you receive from the plan are fully taxable. If both you (with after-tax contributions) and your employer contributed to the plan, only the amount received that is attributable to your employer's payments is taxable.

Tax-Free Reimbursements for Medical Expenses

Reimbursements of qualified medical expenses *(17.2)* that you paid for yourself, your spouse, or any dependents and your children under age 27 are tax free, provided you incurred the expenses after the plan was established. Payment does not have to come directly to you to be tax free; it may go directly to your medical care providers.

Tax-free reimbursements may be from a health-care flexible spending arrangement (FSA) *(3.16)*. Reimbursements made under a qualifying health reimbursement arrangement (HRA) also qualify for tax-free treatment; *see* below.

Tax-free treatment applies only for reimbursed expenses, not amounts you would have received anyway, such as sick leave that is not dependent on actual medical expenses. If your employer reimburses you for premiums you paid, the reimbursement is tax free so long as your payment was from after-tax funds. If you paid premiums with pre-tax salary reductions, a "reimbursement" from the employer will be taxable to you because the salary reductions are treated as your employer's payment, not yours.

Reimbursements for your dependents' medical expenses are tax free. This exclusion only applies to reimbursesd expenses of individuals claimed as a dependent on your tax return. The exclusion also applies to qualifying children or relatives who cannot be claimed as a dependent for the following reasons: (1) they are claimed by the other parent due to divorce/seperation, *(21.7)* (2) their gross income exceeds the limit for qualifying relatives, (3) they file a joint return with their spouse, or (4) you are the dependent of another taxpayer and thus are barred from claiming any dependents on your return.

A qualifying dependent does not include a live-in mate where the relationship violates the local law.

If the reimbursement is for medical expenses you deducted in a previous year, the reimbursement may be taxable. See *17.4* for the rules on reimbursements of deducted medical expenses.

If you receive payments from more than one policy and the total exceeds your actual medical expenses, the excess is taxable if your employer paid the entire premium; *see* the Examples in *17.4*.

 *Caution*

Reimbursed Cosmetic Surgery

An employer's reimbursement of expenses for cosmetic surgery is taxable unless the employee had surgery to correct disfigurement from an accident, disease, or congenital deformity.

Health Reimbursement Arrangements (HRAs). Employers can set up health reimbursement arrangements (HRAs) that are integrated with a group health plan. The HRA reimburses out-of-pocket medical expenses of employees, their spouses, children under age 27 and their dependents. Former employees including retired employees, and spouses and dependents of deceased employees can be covered. Self-employed individuals are not eligible. An HRA must be funded solely by employer contributions and not by salary reductions or after-tax contributions from employees.

Employees are not taxed on HRA reimbursements for medical expenses that may be claimed as itemized deductions *(17.2)*, including premiums. Qualifying medical expenses include over-the-counter medicines or drugs and menstrual products.

For contributions and reimbursements *(3.1)* to be tax free, employees must not receive cash or any benefit (taxable or nontaxable) from an HRA other than reimbursement for qualifying medical expenses. If the reimbursement limit is not fully used up by the end of a coverage year, the unused limit can be carried forward to a subsequent year. Nondiscrimination rules apply to self-insured HRAs.

Qualified Small Employer Health Reimbursement Arrangements (QSEHRAs). If your employer is a "small employer" (no more than 49 full-time and full-time-equivalent employees) that does not offer a group health plan, you may be offered reimbursements of your premiums for personally obtained health coverage and other out-of-pocket medical expenses (that may be claimed as itemized deductions; *see 17.2*) through a qualified small employer health reimbursement arrangement (QSEHRA). A QSEHRA is funded solely by the employer (no salary reductions permitted) and must meet certain nondiscrimination requirements. Reimbursements are tax-free up to an annual limit. For 2023, the maximum amount of excludable reimbursements under a QSEHRA is $5,850 for self-only coverage, or $11,800 for family coverage; these amounts may get an inflation increase for 2024; *see* the *e-Supplement* at *jklasser.com*. The dollar limit is prorated for your period of coverage. For example, if you obtained family coverage starting July 1, 2023, your excludable reimbursement for 2023 is limited to $5,900 ($^{6}/_{12}$^{th} of $11,800. You must provide proof of coverage to your employer. On Form W-2, the employer will report in Box 12, using Code FF, the reimbursable limit you are entitled to under the plan, without regard to the actual reimbursements made.

A QSEHRA is not treated as a group health plan. If you obtain health coverage through a government marketplace and are eligible for the premium tax credit *(25.13)*, the credit amount is reduced by reimbursements through a QSEHRA; you must disclose to the marketplace the amount that you could be reimbursed for under a QSEHRA if you are applying for advance payment of the credit.

Your employer must provide you with a written notice about your eligibility for reimbursement and the terms of your employer's QSEHRA. The notice generally must be provided at least 90 days before the start of the year for which the QSEHRA is provided, or 90 days before the first eligibility date for employees not eligible at the beginning of the year. The notice must include the requirement (noted above) that you disclose your QSEHRA coverage to a government marketplace when applying for advance payment of the premium tax credit.

Self-employed health plan that includes spouse. If a self-employed person hires his or her spouse and provides family coverage under a health plan purchased in the name of the business, the employee-spouse may be reimbursed tax free for medical expenses incurred by both spouses and their dependent children.

Executives taxed in discriminatory self-insured medical reimbursement plans. Although reimbursements from an employer plan for medical expenses of an employee, his or her spouse, and dependents are generally tax free, this exclusion does not apply to certain highly compensated employees and stockholders if the plan is self-insured and it discriminates on their behalf. A plan is self-insured if reimbursement is not provided by an unrelated insurance company. If coverage is provided by an unrelated insurer, these discrimination rules do not apply. If a self-insured plan is deemed discriminatory, rank-and-file employees are not affected; only highly compensated employees are subject to tax.

 *Law Alert*

Qualified Small Employer Health Reimburement Arrangements (QSEHRAs)

Employers with less than 50 employees and without a group health plan may offer tax-free reimbursements of premiums and other medical costs to employees under a qualified small employer health reimbursement arrangement (QSEHRA). *See* the nearby text for details.

Highly compensated participants subject to these rules include employees owning more than 10% of the employer's stock, the highest paid 25% of all employees (other than employees who do not have to be covered under the law), and the five highest paid officers.

If highly compensated employees are entitled to reimbursement for expenses not available to other plan participants, any such reimbursements are taxable to them. For example, if only the five highest paid officers are entitled to dental benefits, any dental reimbursements they receive are taxable. However, routine physical exams may be provided to highly compensated employees (but not their dependents) on a discriminatory basis. This exception does not apply to testing for, or treatment of, a specific complaint.

If highly compensated participants are entitled to a higher reimbursement limit than other participants, any excess reimbursement over the lower limit is taxable to the highly compensated participant. For example, if highly compensated employees are entitled to reimbursements up to $5,000 while all others have a $1,000 limit, a highly compensated employee who receives a $4,000 reimbursement must report $3,000 ($4,000 received minus the $1,000 lower limit) as income.

A separate nondiscrimination test applies to plan eligibility. The eligibility test requires that the plan benefit: (1) 70% or more of all employees or (2) 80% or more of employees eligible to participate, provided that at least 70% of all employees are eligible. A plan not meeting either test is considered discriminatory unless proven otherwise. In applying these tests, employees may be excluded if they have less than three years of service, are under age 25, do part-time or seasonal work, or are covered by a union collective bargaining agreement. A fraction of the benefits received by a highly compensated individual from a nonqualifying plan is taxable. The fraction equals the total reimbursements to highly compensated participants divided by total plan reimbursements; benefits available only to highly compensated employees are disregarded. For example, assume that a plan failing the eligibility tests pays total reimbursements of $50,000, of which $30,000 is to highly compensated participants. A highly compensated executive who is reimbursed $4,500 for medical expenses must include $2,700 in income:

$$\frac{30,000}{50,000} \times 4,500 = 2,700$$

Taxable reimbursements are reported in the year during which the applicable plan year ends. For example, in early 2024 you are reimbursed for a 2023 expense from a calendar-year plan. If under plan provisions the expenses are allocated to the 2023 plan year, the taxable amount should be reported as 2023 income. If the plan does not specify the plan year to which the reimbursement relates, the reimbursement is attributed to the plan year in which payment is made.

Individual Coverage HRAs. Like a QSEHRA explained above, employers can use an Individual Coverage HRA (ICHRA) to reimburse you for your individually-obtained health coverage. The coverage may be obtained on or off the government Exchange; it can include Medicare. Reimbursements cannot be used for short-term, limited-duration insurance (STLDI) or coverage consisting solely of dental, vision, or similar "excepted benefits" (explained below).

The amount of the reimbursement is at the discretion of the employer; it may cover only some of your personal premiums. Employers may choose to combine an ICHRA with a salary reduction arrangement under a cafeteria plan to allow you to pay the unreimbursed premiums on a pre-tax basis. Employer reimbursements under an ICHRA are tax free to you.

To obtain reimbursement, you must attest to your employer that you use the reimbursements to pay the premiums for coverage. This can be individual coverage, or family coverage for you and a spouse and/or a dependent.

Excepted Benefit HRAs. Some insurance coverage does not pay for certain medical costs, such as certain vision, dental, or hearing needs. There may be other similar "excepted benefits" that will not be covered, such as your cost-sharing responsibility (co-payments and deductibles) and premiums for long-term care insurance. Your employer can choose to reimburse you for these costs if there is an Excepted Benefit HRA (EBHRA). The EBHRA is a supplement to traditional group health coverage, but you may be eligible for benefits from the EBHRA even if you are not enrolled in your employer's group plan.

The dollar limit on reimbursement is up to $1,950 in 2023. The EBHRA can allow for unused amounts to be rolled over to the following year. Employers are not required to permit rollovers, so check with the plan administrator.

Tax-Free Payments for Permanent Physical Injuries

Payments from an employer plan are tax free if they are for the permanent loss of part of the body, permanent loss of use of part of the body, or for permanent disfigurement of yourself, your spouse, your children under age 27 (as of the end of the year), or your dependent. An appeals court held that severe hypertension does not involve loss of a bodily part or function and thus does not qualify for the exclusion.

To be tax free, the payments must be based on the kind of injury and have no relation to the length of time you are out of work or prior years of service. If the employer's plan does not specifically allocate benefits according to the nature of the injury, the benefits are taxable even if an employee is in fact permanently disabled.

Disability payments from profit-sharing plan. The Tax Court has held that a profit-sharing plan may provide benefits that qualify for the exclusion for permanent disfigurement or permanent loss of bodily function. The plan must clearly state that its purpose is to provide qualifying tax-free benefits, and a specific payment schedule must be provided for different types of injuries. Without such provisions, payments from the plan are treated as taxable retirement distributions.

> **EXAMPLE**
>
> After he lost a foot in an accident, Marc Jones receives $50,000 as specified in his employer's plan. The payment is tax free as it does not depend on how long Jones is out from work.

HSA or Archer MSA Payments

Tax-free distributions from a health savings account (HSA). Distributions from an HSA *(3.2)* are tax free if used to pay qualified medical expenses for you, your spouse, or your dependents. Qualified medical expenses are unreimbursed costs eligible for the itemized deduction *(17.2)* on Schedule A (Form 1040 or 1040-SR). Over-the-counter medicines and menstrual care products are qualifying expenses for HSA purposes although they are not eligible for an itemized deduction *(17.2)*.

Medical expenses are qualified only if incurred after the HSA has been established. A distribution is taxable to the extent it is not used to pay qualified medical expenses. A taxable distribution is also subject to a 20% penalty unless you are disabled or are age 65 or older. Distributions will be reported to you on Form 1099-SA and you must report them on Form 8889, which you attach to Form 1040 or 1040-SR. On Form 8889, you determine if any part of the distribution is taxable and, if it is, that amount must be included as "Other income" on Line 8f of Schedule 1 (Form 1040 or 1040-SR). The 20% penalty from Form 8889, if any, is entered as an "Other Tax" on Line 17c of Schedule 2 (Form 1040 or 1040-SR).

A non-spouse beneficiary who inherits an HSA after the death of the account owner generally must include in income the fair market value of the assets as of the date of death. However, the beneficiary is not subject to the 20% penalty for taxable distributions. If the beneficiary is the account owner's spouse, he or she becomes the owner of the HSA and will be taxed only on distributions that are not used for qualified medical expenses.

Tax-free distributions from Archer MSA. If you work for a small-business employer and have a qualifying Archer MSA *(3.2)*, earnings accumulate in the account tax free. Withdrawals are tax free if used to pay deductible medical costs *(17.2)*, over-the-counter

Filing Tip

Permanent Physical Injuries

An employer's payment for permanent disfigurement or permanent loss of bodily function is tax free if the payment is based solely on the nature of the injury. Whether or not you qualify for this exclusion, you may deduct as an itemized deduction any unreimbursed medical expense you have in connection with these injuries subject to the adjusted gross income floor if you don't claim the standard deduction *(17.1)*.

medications, and menstrual products, for you, your spouse, or dependents. Withdrawals used for a non-qualifying purpose are taxable and a taxable distribution before age 65 or becoming disabled is also subject to a 20% penalty. *See 41.13* for further details.

3.4 Group-Term Life Insurance Premiums

You are not taxed on your employer's payments of premiums of up to $50,000 on your life under a group-term insurance policy. You are taxed only on the cost of premiums for coverage of over $50,000 as determined by the IRS rates shown in the table below. On Form W-2 your employer should include the taxable amount as wages in Box 1 and separately label the amount in Box 12 with Code C. You may not avoid tax by assigning the policy to another person.

If two or more employers provide you with group-term insurance coverage, you get only one $50,000 exclusion. You must figure the taxable cost for coverage over $50,000 by using the IRS rates shown in *Table 3-2* below.

Regardless of the amount of the policy, you are not taxed if, for your entire tax year, the beneficiary of the policy is a tax-exempt charitable organization or your employer.

Your payments reduce taxable amount. If you pay part of the cost of the insurance, your payment reduces dollar for dollar the amount includible as pay on Form W-2.

Retirees. If your former employer provides you with over $50,000 of group-term life insurance coverage, the cost of the coverage over $50,000 is generally taxable to you as if you were an employee. However, if you retired because of a total and permanent disability and remain covered by your company's plan, you are not taxed even if coverage exceeds $50,000.

The entire cost of your coverage is tax free if it is provided under a plan in existence on January 1, 1984, if you retired on or before that date (normal retirement or disability), were covered by the plan when you retired, and are still covered by it. If you were age 55 or older on January 1, 1984, and retired after that date, and were employed during 1983 by the employer providing the current coverage or a predecessor employer, you are not taxed on the cost of your current coverage.

However, even if the above tests for tax-free coverage are met, you may be taxed under the rule below for discriminatory plans if you retired after 1986 and were a key employee.

Key employees taxed under discriminatory plans. The $50,000 exclusion is not available to key employees unless the group plan meets nondiscrimination tests for eligibility and benefits. For 2023, key employees include those who during the year were: (1) more-than-5% owners; (2) more-than-1% owners earning over $150,000; and (3) officers with compensation over $215,000. If the plan discriminates, a key employee's taxable benefit is based on the larger of (1) the actual cost of coverage or (2) the amount for coverage using the IRS rate table below.

The nondiscrimination rules also apply to former employees who were key employees when they separated from service. The discrimination tests are applied separately with respect to active and former employees. A former employee who was a key employee after retirement or separation from service is also considered a key employee. This exception doesn't apply to church plans. *See* Section 416 (i) of the Internal Revenue Code for further details.

Group-term life insurance for dependents. Employer-paid coverage for your spouse or dependents is a tax-free *de minimis* fringe benefit *(3.10)* if the policy is $2,000 or less. Even for coverage over $2,000, the *de minimis* exception may apply *(3.10)*, but if it does not, you are taxed on the excess of the cost (determined under *Table 3-2* below) over your after-tax payments for the insurance, if any.

Permanent life insurance. If your employer pays premiums on your behalf for permanent nonforfeitable life insurance, you report as taxable wages the cost of the benefit, less any amount you paid. A permanent benefit is an economic value that extends beyond one year and includes paid-up insurance or cash surrender value, but does not include, for example, the right to convert or continue life insurance coverage after group coverage is terminated. Where permanent benefits are combined with term insurance, the permanent benefits are taxed under formulas found in IRS regulations.

Filing Instruction

Uncollected Social Security and Medicare of Former Employees

If you receive coverage as a former employee, you must pay with Form 1040 or 1040-SR your share of Social Security and Medicare taxes on group-term life insurance over $50,000. The taxable amounts are shown in Box 12 of Form W-2, with Codes M (Uncollected Social Security tax) and N (Uncollected Medicare tax).

EXAMPLE

In 2023, Lynda Jackson's company pays all the premiums on $200,000 of group-term life insurance it provides for her for the entire year. Lynda is age 52 at the end of 2023. The taxable value of the coverage is based on the $150,000 coverage in excess of the $50,000 exclusion. As shown in *Table 3-2*, the premium used to determine the taxable coverage is $0.23 for every $1,000 of coverage over $50,000. The taxable amount for the year is $414 ($0.23 × 12 months × 150).

If Lynda had paid $120 towards the coverage, the taxable amount would be reduced to $294 ($414 − $120).

Table 3-2 Taxable Premiums for Group-Term Insurance Coverage Over $50,000

Age—*	Monthly cost for each $1,000 of coverage over $50,000—
Under 25	$0.05
25–29	0.06
30–34	0.08
35–39	0.09
40–44	0.10
45–49	0.15
50–54	0.23
55–59	0.43
60–64	0.66
65–69	1.27
70 and over	2.06

*Age is determined at end of year.

 *Caution*

Tax-Free Exclusion for Employer-Provided Dependent Care

You cannot assume that your employer-provided dependent care benefit is completely tax free merely because your employer has not included any part of it in Box 1 of Form W-2 as taxable wages. Although up to $5,000 of benefits are generally tax free for 2023 *(3.5)*, the tax-free amount is reduced where you or your spouse earn less than $5,000 or where you file separately from your spouse. You must show the amount of your qualifying dependent care expenses and figure the tax-free exclusion on Form 2441.

3.5 Dependent Care Assistance

The exclusion limit for 2023 is $5,000 ($2,500 if married filing separately). The $5,000/$2,500 limit for 2023 applies whether your employer provides the day care services directly under a written, nondiscriminatory plan, or you make pre-tax salary deferrals to a flexible spending account (FSA) for reimbursing dependent care expenses and you then receive reimbursements from the FSA for your expenses *(3.15)*.

Note that the maximum exclusion (plus carryover if applicable, *see 3.16*) applies regardless of the number of dependents for whom care is provided. However, you may not exclude from income more than your earned income. If you are married and your spouse earns less than you do, your tax-free benefit is limited to his or her earned income. If your spouse does not work, all of your benefits are taxable unless he or she is a full-time student or is disabled. If a full-time student or disabled, your spouse is treated as earning $250 a month if your dependent care expenses are for one dependent, or $500 a month if the expenses are for two or more dependents.

Expenses are excludable from income only if they are for the dependent care credit; *see 25.6*. If you are being reimbursed by your employer, the exclusion is not allowed if dependent care is provided by a relative who is your dependent (or your spouse's dependent) or by your child under the age of 19. You must give your employer a record of the care provider's name, address, and tax identification number. The identifying information also must be listed on your return.

If the plan does not meet nondiscriminatory tests, benefits provided for highly-compensated employees are not excludable from their income.

Reporting employer benefits on your return. Your employer will show the total amount of your dependent care benefits in Box 10 of your Form W-2. Any benefits over the excludable limit will also be included as taxable wages in Box 1 of Form W-2 and as Social Security wages (Box 3) and Medicare wages (Box 5).

You must report the benefits on Part III of Form 2441, where you determine both the tax-free and taxable (if any) portions of the employer-provided benefits. If any part is taxable, that amount must be included on Line 1e of Form 1040 or 1040-SR as wages and labeled "DCB."

Follow IRS instructions for identifying the care provider (employer, babysitter, etc.) on Part I of Form 2441.

The tax-free portion of employer benefits reduces expenses eligible for the dependent care credit *(Chapter 25)*.

3.6 Adoption Benefits

If your employer pays or reimburses you in 2023 for qualifying adoption expenses under a written, nondiscriminatory plan, up to $15,950 per qualifying child may be tax free. Employer-provided adoption assistance may be for any child under age 18, or a person physically or mentally incapable of self-care. The exclusion applies to adoption fees, attorney fees, court costs, travel expenses, and other expenses directly related to a legal adoption. Expenses for adopting your spouse's child and the costs of a surrogate-parenting arrangement do not qualify. If you have other qualifying adoption expenses, you may also be able to claim a tax credit up to a separate $15,950 limit; both the exclusion and the credit may be claimed for the same adoption if they are not for the same expenses. The exclusion and the credit are subject to similar limitations, including a phaseout based on income. *See Chapter 25* for a full discussion of the credit.

The full $15,950 exclusion limit is available for the adoption of a "special needs" child even if actual adoption expenses are less than $15,950. A "special needs" designation is made when a state determines that adoption assistance is required to place a child (U.S. citizen or resident) with adoptive parents because of special factors, such as the child's physical condition or ethnicity.

If you are adopting a child who is not a U.S. citizen or resident when the adoption effort begins, the exclusion is available only in the year the adoption becomes final. For example, if in 2023 your employer pays for expenses of adopting a foreign child but the adoption has not become final by the end of the year, you must report the employer's payment as wage income for 2023. You will claim the exclusion on Form 8839 in the year the adoption is final.

Reporting employer benefits and claiming the exclusion on your return. You must file Form 8839 to report your employer's payments and to figure the tax-free and taxable portions of the benefits. The employer's payments will be included in Box 12 of Form W-2 (Code T). This total includes pre-tax salary reduction contributions that you made to a cafeteria plan *(3.14)* to cover such expenses.

If you are married, you generally must file a joint return to exclude the benefits as income. However, if you are legally separated or if you lived apart from your spouse for the last six months of the year, the exclusion may be available on a separate return; *see* Form 8839 for details.

On 2023 tax returns, the allowable exclusion begins to phase out if your modified adjusted gross income (MAGI) exceeds $239,230. If MAGI is $279,230 or more (including the employer's adoption assistance and adding back certain tax-free income from foreign sources), the phaseout is complete and all of the employer-paid adoption assistance is taxable. Figure the tax-free amount on Form 8839.

 *Filing Tip*

Claiming Credit and Exclusion

If you paid adoption expenses that were not reimbursed by your employer, and the adoption was final by the end of the year, you may be able to claim the adoption credit; *see 25.10*.

3.7 Education Assistance Plans

If your employer pays for job-related courses, the payment is tax free to you provided that the courses do not satisfy the employer's minimum education standards and do not qualify you for a new profession. If these tests are met, the employer's education assistance is a tax-free working condition fringe benefit *(3.9)*.

Even if not job related, your employer's payment for courses is tax free up to $5,250, provided the assistance is under a qualifying Section 127 plan meeting nondiscriminatory tests. Graduate courses qualify for the exclusion as well as undergraduate courses. The Section 127 exclusion covers tuition, fees, books, and equipment, plus supplies that you cannot keep at the end of the course. Lodging, meals, and transportation are not covered by the exclusion. Sports or hobby-type courses qualify only if the courses are related to your business or are required as part of a degree program.

For 2020 through 2025, employer reimbursements to employees or payments directly to lenders to cover student loan principal or interest payments are considered educational assistance eligible up to the $5,250 exclusion.

Tuition reductions. Employees and retired employees of educational institutions, their spouses, and their dependent children are not taxed on tuition reductions for undergraduate courses provided the reduction is not payment for teaching or other services. However, an exclusion is allowed for tuition reductions under the National Health Services Corps Scholarship Program and the Armed Forces Health Professions Scholarship Program despite the recipient's service obligation. Widows or widowers of deceased employees or of former employees also qualify. Officers and highly paid employees may claim the exclusion only if the employer plan does not discriminate on their behalf. The exclusion applies to tuition for undergraduate education at any educational institution, not only the employer's school.

Graduate students who are teaching or research assistants at an educational institution are not taxed on tuition reductions for courses at that school if the tuition reduction is in addition to regular pay for the teaching or research services or the reduction is provided under the National Health Services Corps Scholarship Program or the Armed Forces Health Professions Scholarship Program. The graduate student exclusion for tuition reductions applies only to teaching and research assistants, and not to faculty or other staff members (or their spouses and dependents) who take graduate courses and also do research for or teach at the school. However, if the graduate courses are work related, a tuition reduction for faculty and staff may qualify as a tax-free working condition fringe benefit *(3.9)*.

3.8 Company Cars, Parking, and Transit Passes

The costs of commuting to a regular job site are not deductible *(20.2)*, but employees who receive transit passes or travel to work on an employer-financed van get a tax break by not having to pay tax on some or all of such benefits. Where a company car is provided, the value of personal use is generally taxable, as discussed below. The same rules apply to the use of a company van or pickup truck.

Company cars. The use of a company car is tax free under the working condition fringe benefit rule *(3.9)* to the extent you use the car for business. If you use the car for personal driving, your company has the responsibility of calculating taxable income, which generally is based on IRS tables that specify the annual lease value of various priced cars. You are also required to keep for your employer a mileage log or similar record to substantiate your business use; your employer should specify what you need to provide.

Regardless of personal use, you are not subject to tax for a company vehicle that the IRS considers to be of limited personal value. These are ambulances or hearses; flatbed trucks; dump, garbage, or refrigerated trucks; one-passenger delivery trucks (including trucks with folding jump seats); tractors, combines, and other farm equipment; or forklifts. Also not taxable is personal use of school buses, passenger buses (seating at least 20), and moving vans where such personal use is restricted. Exclusions are also allowed for commuting use of a clearly marked police, fire, or public safety officer vehicle by officers required to be on call at all times, and for officially authorized uses of unmarked vehicles by law enforcement officers.

Demonstration cars. The value of a demonstration car used by a full-time auto salesperson is tax free as a working condition fringe benefit if the use of the car facilitates job performance and if there are substantial personal-use restrictions, including a prohibition on use by family members and for vacation trips. Furthermore, mileage outside of normal working hours must be limited and personal driving must generally be restricted to a 75-mile radius around the dealer's sales office.

Chauffeur services. If chauffeur services are provided for both business and personal purposes, you must report as income the value of the personal services. For example, if the full value of the chauffeur services is $30,000 and 30% of the chauffeur's workday is spent driving on personal trips, then $9,000 is taxable (30% of $30,000) and $21,000 is tax free.

If an employer provides a bodyguard-chauffeur for business security reasons, the entire value of the chauffeur services is considered a tax-free working condition fringe benefit if: (1) the automobile is specially equipped for security and (2) the bodyguard is trained in evasive driving techniques and is provided as part of an overall 24-hour-a-day security program. If the value of the bodyguard-chauffeur services is tax free, the employee is still taxable on the value of using the vehicle for commuting or other personal travel.

How your employer reports taxable automobile benefits. Social Security and Medicare tax must be withheld. Income tax withholding is not required, but your employer may choose to withhold income tax. If income tax is not withheld, you must be notified of this fact so that you may consider the taxable benefits when determining whether to make estimated tax installments; *see Chapter 27*. Whether or not withholdings are taken, the taxable value of the benefits is entered on your Form W-2 in Box 14 or on a separate Form W-2 for fringe benefits.

A special IRS rule allows your employer to include 100% of the lease value of using the car as income on your Form W-2, even if you used the car primarily for business. Your employer must specifically indicate on Form W-2 (Box 14) or on a separate statement if 100% of the lease value has been included as income on your Form W-2. If your employer does this on your Form W-2, you may not claim an offsetting deduction for the value of your business use of the car. For years before 2018, a deduction for the business value of the car, plus any unreimbursed car operating expenses, may have been available as a miscellaneous itemized deduction on Schedule A, but it was subject to the 2% of AGI floor. However, the deduction for employee job expenses subject to the 2% floor has been suspended for 2018 through 2025 *(19.1)*.

Company planes. Under rules similar to those for company cars, employees who use a company airplane for personal trips are taxable on the value of the flights, as determined by the employer using IRS tables.

Qualified Transportation Benefits

Your employer may provide you with transportation benefits that are tax free within certain limits. There are two categories of qualified benefits: (1) transit passes and commuter transportation in a van, bus, or similar highway vehicle are considered together, and (2) parking. For years before 2018, qualifying bicycle commuting reimbursements were tax free up to $20 per month, but this exclusion is suspended for tax years 2018 through 2025.

For 2023, benefits from each category are excludable from your income so long as the $300 monthly limit *(see below)* is not exceeded. If the benefits exceed the $300 monthly limit, the excess is treated as wages subject to income tax, Social Security, and Medicare tax.

Transit pass/commuter transportation benefits and parking benefits may be provided through a salary-reduction arrangement. An irrevocable salary-reduction election may be made prospectively for a monthly amount of benefits. The salary reduction for any month may not exceed the total limit for both categories. Unused salary reductions may be carried over to later months and from year to year. However, if you leave the company before using the carryover, the unused amount is forfeited; you cannot get a refund.

Exclusion limit. The same monthly exclusion limit applies to (1) the combined value of qualified employer-provided transit passes plus commuting in an employer's van or bus,

 *Law Alert*

Employer Deductions for Transportation Fringe Benefits Disallowed

The Tax Cuts and Jobs Act amended the Tax Code to disallow deductions by employers for the expense of any qualified transportation fringe benefit, effective January 1, 2018. Employees may continue to receive these benefits tax free, or as a pre-tax benefit made available by an employer.

 *Law Alert*

Bicycle Commuting Reimbursements Now Taxable

The Tax Cuts and Jobs Act suspended (for 2018 through 2025) the prior law exclusion for up to $20 of qualified bicycle reimbursements per month.

and (2) qualified parking benefits. For 2023, the maximum monthly exclusion for each of these categories is $300 per month. If the value of benefits for any month does not equal the exclusion limit, the unused amount is lost and may not be carried over to other months. For 2024, the monthly cap for each benefit may be increased above $300 by an inflation adjustment; *see* the *e-Supplement* at *jklasser.com*.

Details on what constitutes qualified transit pass/van pool, and parking benefits are in the following paragraphs.

Qualified transit passes and van/bus transportation. For purposes of the exclusion, qualifying transit passes include tokens, fare cards, or vouchers for mass transit or private transportation businesses using highway vehicles seating at least six passengers. A cash reimbursement for a transit pass is taxable if vouchers (or similar items) are readily available to the employer for distribution to employees. "Ready availability" is determined under tests in IRS regulations. Cash advances are taxable.

Qualifying van or bus pool vehicles must seat at least six passengers and be used at least 80% of the time for employee commuting; on average, the number of employees must be at least half the seating capacity.

The exclusion applies only to regular employees. For partners, more than 2% S corporation shareholders, and independent contractors who are provided transit passes, the IRS allows up to $21 per month as a tax-free *de minimis* benefit. If the monthly value exceeds $21, the full value is taxable and not just the excess over $21.

Qualified parking benefits. The value of employer-provided parking spots or subsidized parking qualifies for the exclusion (up to the monthly limit) if the parking is on or near the employer's premises, or at a mass transit facility such as a train station or car pooling center. For purposes of determining if the value of the parking exceeds the monthly limit ($300 per month in 2023), the IRS tells employers to value parking benefits according to the regular commercial price for parking at the same or nearby locations. For example, if an employer in a rural or suburban location provides free parking for employees and there are no commercial parking lots in the area, the employee parking is tax free. Where free parking is available to both business customers and employees, the employee parking is considered to have "zero" value unless the employee has a reserved parking space that is closer to the business entrance than the spaces allotted to customers.

If the value of the right of access to a parking space for a month exceeds the monthly exclusion limit ($300 per month in 2023), an employee will be taxed on the excess even if he or she actually uses the space for only a few days during the month.

If the employee pays a reduced monthly price for parking, there is a taxable benefit for that month only if the price paid plus the monthly exclusion amount is less than the value of the parking.

Commuter parking benefits for self-employed partners, independent contractors, or more-than-2% S corporation shareholders do not qualify for the $300 per month exclusion but qualify as a tax-free *de minimis* benefit if the monthly value does not exceed $21 *(3.10)*.

3.9 Working Condition Fringe Benefits

An employer-provided benefit is a tax-free working condition fringe benefit if it would be deductible by you as a job expense if you had paid for it yourself, assuming that the miscellaneous itemized deduction subject to the 2% of adjusted gross income floor had not been suspended for 2018 through 2025; *see 19.2*. These benefits include:

Company car or plane. The value of a company car or plane is tax free to the extent that you use it for business; *see 3.8* for more on company cars.

Employer-provided cell phone. The cost of an employer-provided cell phone is a tax-free working condition benefit if your employer has substantial business reasons for giving you the phone. The phone qualifies if the employer needs to reach you at all times for work-related emergencies or you need to call clients when away from the office or outside of normal business hours. On the other hand, the value of the phone is taxable if it is

Planning Reminder

Transportation Benefits

If your employer offers you the choice of receiving parking, transit pass, or van pooling benefits instead of cash salary as part of a "cafeteria" plan *(3.13)* and you elect the benefits rather than the cash, you are not taxed, provided the value does not exceed the monthly tax-free limit.

a goodwill gesture or intended as additional compensation; these are not considered substantial business reasons.

Employer-paid subscriptions or memberships. For example, if your employer pays for your subscriptions to business-related publications or online services, or reimburses you for membership dues in professional associations, these are tax-free working condition benefits.

Product testing. This is a limited exclusion for employees who test and evaluate company manufactured goods away from company premises.

Employer-provided education assistance. Employer-paid undergraduate and graduate courses may be a tax-free working condition fringe benefit if the courses maintain or improve your job skills but are not needed to meet your employer's minimum educational requirements and do not prepare you for a new profession.

Job-placement assistance. Job placement services are tax free as long as they are geared to helping you find a job in the same line of work and you do not have an option to take cash instead of the benefits. The employer must also have a business purpose for providing assistance, such as maintaining employee morale or promoting a positive business image.

For tax-free treatment, there is no nondiscrimination requirement; different types of job placement assistance may be offered, or no assistance at all, in the case of discharged employees with readily transferable skills. Tax-free benefits include the value of counseling on interviewing skills and resume preparation. Executives may be given secretarial support and the use of a private office during the job search.

Job placement benefits that you receive as part of a severance pay arrangement are taxable to the extent that you could have elected to receive cash. If your severance benefits are reduced because you get job placement assistance, you are taxed on the difference between the reduced and unreduced severance amounts.

3.10 *De Minimis* Fringe Benefits

Small benefits that would be administratively impractical to tax are considered tax-free *de minimis* (minor) fringe benefits. Examples are personal use of an employer-provided cell phone *(see below)*, occasional meal money or local transportation fares given to employees working overtime, employer-provided coffee, tea, doughnuts, or soft drinks, personal use of company copying machines, company parties, holiday or birthday gifts other than cash (e.g., flowers) or tickets for the theater or sporting events.

Personal use of employer-provided cell phone. If your employer gives you a phone for substantial business reasons, the value of the phone is a tax-free working condition fringe benefit *(3.9)*. In such a case, your personal use of the phone is tax free as a *de minimis* benefit.

Company eating facility. The value of meals provided to employees on workdays at a subsidized eating facility is a tax-free *de minimis* fringe benefit if the facility is located on or near the business premises and the annual revenue from meal charges equals or exceeds the facility's direct operating costs. Revenue is treated as equal to operating costs for meals that are tax-free to employees under the employer convenience test *(3.13)*.

Highly compensated employees or owners with special access to executive dining rooms may not exclude the value of their meals as a *de minimis* fringe benefit; however, the meals may be tax free if meals must be taken on company premises for business reasons *(3.13)*.

Group-term life insurance coverage for dependents. If your employer provides group-term coverage *(3.4)* for your dependents of up to $2,000, the coverage is a tax-free *de minimis* fringe benefit for you. If the coverage exceeds $2,000, the coverage is a tax-free *de minimis* fringe benefit if the employer's cost exceeds what you paid for it by so little that it would be impractical to account for it.

Commuting under unsafe circumstances. If you are asked to work outside your normal working hours and due to unsafe conditions your employer provides transportation such as taxi fare, the first $1.50 per one-way commute is taxable but the excess over $1.50 is a tax-free *de minimis* benefit. This exclusion is not available to certain highly compensated employees and officers, corporate directors, or owners of 1% or more of the company.

Occasional Overtime Meal Money or Cab Fare

If you work overtime and occasionally receive meal money or cab fare home, the amount is tax free. The IRS has not provided a numerical standard for determining when payments are "occasional."

Caution

Underpriced Award Items

If the value of an achievement award item is disproportionately high compared to the employer's cost, the IRS may conclude that the award is disguised compensation, in which case the entire value would be taxable.

Court Decision

House One Block Away

Two federal courts held that a school superintendent received tax-free lodging where the home was one block away from the school and separated by a row of other houses. This met the business premises test. The IRS announced that it would continue to litigate similar cases arising outside the Eighth Circuit in which the case arose. The Eighth Circuit includes the states of Arkansas, Iowa, Minnesota, Missouri, Nebraska, and North and South Dakota.

Even when working their regular shift, hourly employees eligible for overtime who are not considered highly compensated are taxed on only $1.50 per one-way commute if their employer pays for car service or taxi fare because walking or taking public transportation to or from work would be unsafe. The excess value of the transportation over $1.50 is tax free. These rules can apply to day-shift employees who work overtime as well as night-shift employees working regular hours so long as transportation is provided because of unsafe conditions.

3.11 Employer-Provided Retirement Advice

If your employer maintains a qualified retirement plan, the value of retirement planning information and advice provided to you by the employer is not taxable. The exclusion is not limited to information pertaining to the employer's particular retirement plan. It applies to information for you and your spouse on general retirement income planning, as well as information on how the employer's plan fits within your overall plan.

Highly compensated employees qualify for the exclusion if similar services are provided to all employees who normally receive information updates on the employer's retirement plan.

The exclusion does not apply to related services that may be provided by the employer, such as brokerage services, tax preparation, accounting, or legal services; the value of such services is taxable.

3.12 Employee Achievement Awards

Achievement awards are taxable unless they meet special rules for awards of tangible personal property (such as a watch, television, or golf clubs) given to you in recognition of length of service or safety achievement. The Tax Cuts and Jobs Act specifies that the following items are not "tangible personal property" and thus are taxable: cash awards, gift cards, gift certificates (unless they entitle the employee to select from an approved employer list of items of tangible personal property), vacations, meals, lodging, tickets to sports or theater events, stocks, bonds, other securities, or similar items.

As a general rule, if your employer is allowed to deduct the cost of a tangible personal property award, you are not taxed. The employer's deduction limit, and therefore the excludable limit for you, is $400 for awards from nonqualified plans and $1,600 for awards from qualified plans or from a combination of qualified and nonqualified plans. If your employer's deduction is less than the item's cost, you are taxed on the greater of: (1) the difference between the cost and your employer's deduction, but no more than the award's fair market value; or (2) the excess of the item's fair market value over your employer's deduction. Deduction tests for achievement awards are discussed in *40.6*. Your employer must tell you if the award qualifies for full or partial tax-free treatment.

An award will not be treated as a tax-free safety achievement award if employee safety achievement awards (other than those of *de minimis* value) during the year have already been granted to more than 10% of employees (not counting managers, administrators, clerical employees, or other professional employees). An award made to a manager, administrator, clerical employee, or other professional employee for safety achievement does not qualify for tax-free treatment.

Tax-free treatment also does not apply when you receive an award for length of service during your first five years of employment or when you previously received such an award during the current year or in the four preceding years, unless the prior award qualified as a *de minimis* fringe benefit.

3.13 Employer-Furnished Meals or Lodging

The value of employer-furnished meals is not taxable if furnished on your employer's business premises for the employer's convenience. The value of lodging is not taxable if, as a condition of your employment, you must accept the lodging on the employer's business premises for the employer's convenience.

Business premises test. The IRS generally defines business premises as the place of employment, such as a company cafeteria in a factory for a cook or an employer's home for a household employee. The Tax Court has a more liberal view, extending the area of business premises beyond the actual place of business in such cases as these:

- A house provided a hotel manager, although located across the street from the hotel. The IRS has agreed to the decision.
- A house provided a motel manager, two blocks from the motel. However, a court of appeals reversed the decision and held in the IRS' favor.
- A rented hotel suite that is used daily by executives for a luncheon conference.

Remote camp in foreign country. Lodging in certain foreign "camps" is considered to be furnished on the business premises of the employer. To qualify, lodging must be provided to employees working in remote foreign areas where satisfactory housing is not available on the open market, it must be located as near as practicable to where they work, and it must be in a common area or enclave that is not available to the public and which normally accommodates at least 10 employees.

Convenience of employer test. The employer convenience test requires proof that an employer provides the free meals or lodging for a business purpose other than providing extra pay. In the case of meals, the employer convenience test is deemed to be satisfied for all meals provided on employer premises if a qualifying business purpose is shown for more than 50% of the meals. If meals and lodging are described in a contract or state statute as extra pay, this does not bar tax-free treatment provided they are also furnished for other substantial, noncompensatory business reasons; for example, you are required to be on call 24 hours a day, or there are inadequate eating facilities near the business premises.

> **EXAMPLE**
>
> Tyrone Jones is employed at a construction project at a remote job site. His pay is $1,500 a week. Because there are no accessible places near the site for food and lodging, the employer furnishes meals and lodging for which it charges $400 a week, which is taken out of Jones's pay. Jones reports only the net amount he receives—$1,100 a week. The value of the meals and lodging is a tax-free benefit.

Meal charges. Your company may charge for meals on company premises and give you an option to accept or decline the meals. However, by law, the IRS must disregard the charge and option factors in determining whether meals that you buy are furnished for noncompensatory business reasons. If such business reasons exist, the convenience-of-employer test is satisfied. If such reasons do not exist, the value of the meals may be tax free as a *de minimis* benefit *(3.10)*; otherwise, the value of the meal subsidy provided by the employer is taxable.

Where your employer provides meals on business premises at a fixed charge that is subtracted from your pay whether you accept the meals or not, the amount of the charge is excluded from your taxable pay. If the meal is provided for the employer's convenience, as in the following Examples, the value of the meals received is also tax free. If it is not provided for the employer's convenience, the value is taxable whether it exceeds or is less than the amount charged.

> **EXAMPLES**
>
> 1. A Las Vegas casino operator provided free cafeteria meals to employees, who were required to remain on casino premises during their entire shift. A federal appeals court (Ninth Circuit) held that the casino's "stay-on-premises" requirement constituted a legitimate business reason for the meals and thus all of the employee meals were tax free under the employer convenience test. The court refused to second guess the casino's business decision that a "stay-on-premises" policy was necessary for security and logistics reasons. Once that policy was adopted, the casino employees had no choice but to eat on the premises. The IRS responded to the decision by announcing that it would not challenge "employer convenience" treatment in similar cases where employees are precluded from obtaining a meal off-premises within a normal meal period.

 *Planning Reminder*

Meal Exclusion

You may be able to avoid tax on meals that you receive on your employer's premises even if your meals do not satisfy the employer convenience test. If more than half of the employees to whom meals are furnished on the employer's business premises are furnished the meals for the employer's convenience, all of the on-premises meals are treated as being furnished for the employer's convenience.

2. A waitress who works from 7 a.m. to 4 p.m. is furnished two meals a day without charge. Her employer encourages her to have her breakfast at the restaurant before working, but she is required to have her lunch there. The value of her breakfast and lunch is not taxable under IRS regulations because it is furnished during her work period or immediately before or after the period. But say she is also allowed to have free meals on her days off and a free supper on the days she works. The value of these meals is taxable; they are not furnished during or immediately before or after her work period.

3. A hospital maintains a cafeteria on its premises where all of its employees may eat during their working hours. No charge is made for these meals. The hospital furnishes meals to have the employees available for emergencies. The employees are not required to eat there. Since the hospital furnishes the meals in order to have employees available for emergency call during meal periods, the meals are not income to any of the hospital employees who obtain their meals at the hospital cafeteria.

4. To assure bank teller service during the busy lunch period, a bank limits tellers to 30 minutes for lunch and provides them with free meals in a cafeteria on the premises so they can eat within this time period. The value of the meals is tax free.

Lodging must be condition of employment. This test requires evidence that the lodging is necessary for you to perform your job properly, as where you are required to be available for duty at all times. The IRS may question the claim that you are required to be on 24-hour duty. For example, at one college, rent-free lodgings were provided to teaching and administrative staff members, maintenance workers, dormitory parents who supervised and resided with students, and an evening nurse. The IRS ruled that only the lodgings provided to the dorm parents and the nurse met the tax-free lodging tests because, for the convenience of the college, they had to be available after regular school hours to respond to emergencies.

If you are given the choice of free lodging at your place of employment or a cash allowance, the lodging is not considered to be a condition of employment, and its value is taxable.

If the lodging qualifies as tax free, so does the value of employer-paid utilities such as heat, electricity, gas, water, sewerage, and other utilities. Where these services are furnished by the employer and their value is deducted from your salary, the amount deducted is excluded from taxable wages on Form W-2. But if you pay for the utilities yourself, you may not exclude their cost from your income.

Groceries. An employer may furnish unprepared food, such as groceries, rather than prepared meals. Courts are divided on whether the value of the groceries is excludable from income. One court allowed an exclusion for the value of nonfood items, such as napkins and soap—as well as for groceries—furnished to a doctor who ate at his home on the hospital grounds so that he would be available for emergencies.

Cash allowances. A cash allowance for meals and lodging is taxable.

Faculty lodging. Teachers and other employees (and their spouses and dependents) of an educational institution, including a state university system or academic health center, do not have to pay tax on the value of school-provided lodging if they pay a minimal rent. The lodging must be on or near the campus. The minimal required rent is the smaller of: (1) 5% of the appraised value of the lodging; or (2) the average rental paid for comparable school housing by persons who are neither employees nor students. Appraised value must be determined by an independent appraiser and the appraisal must be reviewed annually.

For purposes of the 5% minimum rent rule, academic health centers include medical teaching hospitals and medical research organizations with regular faculties and curricula in basic and clinical medical science and research.

> **EXAMPLE**
>
> Carol Eng, a professor, pays annual rent of $12,000 for university housing appraised at $200,000. The average annual rent for comparable university housing paid by non-employees and non-students is $14,000. She does not have to pay any tax on the housing since her rental payments are at least 5% of the appraised housing value (5% of $200,000, or $10,000). If her rent was $9,000, she would have to report income of $1,000 ($10,000 minimum required rent – $9,000).

Caution

Housing as Job Requirement

If housing is provided to some employees with a certain job and not others, the IRS may hold that the lodging is not a condition of employment. For example, the IRS taxed medical residents on the value of hospital lodging where other residents lived in their own apartments.

Caution

Partners Are Not Employees

The IRS does not consider partners or self-employed persons as employees and so does not allow them to exclude the value of partnership-provided meals and lodging.

Table 3-3   Are Your Meals and Lodging Tax Free?

Yes—	No—
• Hotel executives, managers, housekeepers, and auditors who are required to live at the hotel.	• Your employer gives you a cash allowance for your meals or lodgings.
• Domestics, farm laborers, fishermen, canners, seamen, servicemen, building superintendents, and hospital and sanitarium employees who are required to have meals and lodging on employer premises.	• You have a choice of accepting cash or getting the meals or lodging. For example, under a union contract you get meals, but you may refuse to take them and get an automatic pay increase.
• Restaurant and other food service employees who have meals furnished during or immediately before or after working hours.	• A state hospital employee is given a choice. He or she may live at the institution rent free or live elsewhere and get extra pay each month. Whether he or she stays at the institution or lives outside, the extra pay is included in his or her income.
• Employees who must be available during meal periods for emergencies.	
• Employees who, because of the nature of the business, must be given short meal periods.	• A waitress, on her days off, is allowed to eat free meals at the restaurant where she works.
• Workers who must use company-supplied facilities in remote areas.	
• Park employees who voluntarily live in rent-free apartments provided by a park department in order to protect the park from vandalism.	

Peace Corps and VISTA volunteers. Peace Corps volunteers working overseas may exclude subsistence allowances from income under a specific code provision. The law does not provide a similar exclusion for the small living expense allowances received by VISTA volunteers.

3.14   Minister's Housing or Housing Allowance

By statute, a duly ordained minister pays no tax on the rental value of a home provided as part of his or her pay. If a minister is provided with a cash allowance rather than a home itself, the allowance is generally tax free if used to pay rent, to make a down payment to buy a house, to pay mortgage installments, or for utilities, interest, tax, and repair expenses of the house. However, the exclusion for a cash allowance is limited to the fair rental value of the home, including furnishings and appurtenances such as a garage, plus the cost of utilities. A rabbi or cantor is treated the same as a minister for purposes of the allowance or in-kind housing exclusion.

The Tax Court has held that the parsonage exclusion is allowed for expenses of a second home as well as for a principal residence. However, the Eleventh Circuit appeals court reversed the Tax Court, concluding that the exclusion can apply only to one home.

The church or local congregation must officially designate the part of the minister's compensation that is a rental or housing allowance. To qualify for tax-free treatment, the designation must be made in advance of the payments. Official action may be shown by an employment contract, minutes, a resolution, or a budget allowance.

Who qualifies for the exclusion? Tax-free treatment is allowed to ordained ministers, rabbis, and cantors who receive in-kind housing or housing allowances as part of their compensation for ministerial duties. Retired ministers qualify if the housing or allowance is furnished in recognition of past services.

Filing Tip

Mortgage Interest and Taxes

If you itemize deductions on Schedule A (Form 1040 or 1040-SR), deduct payments for qualifying home mortgage interest *(15.1)* and real estate taxes *(16.6)* on your home even if you use a tax-free housing allowance to finance the payments.

Court Decision

Appeals Court Upholds Constitutionality of Cash Housing Allowance

The Seventh Circuit Court of Appeals upheld the constitutionality of the law allowing ministers and other religious leaders to exclude from income cash housing allowances (Code Section 107(2)). The Seventh Circuit reversed a Wisconsin federal district court that had held that the housing allowance exclusion violates the Establishment Clause of the U.S. Constitution. According to the Seventh Circuit, Code Section 107(2) is constitutional because it has a secular legislative purpose, does not primarily endorse religion, and does not foster excessive entanglement of government and religion.

The IRS has allowed the exclusion to ministers working as teachers or administrators for a parochial school, college, or theological seminary which is an integral part of a church organization. A traveling evangelist was allowed to exclude rental allowances from out-of-town churches to maintain his permanent home. Church officers who are not ordained, such as a "minister" of music (music director) or "minister" of education (Sunday School director), do not qualify.

The IRS has generally barred an exclusion to ordained ministers working as executives of nonreligious organizations even where services or religious functions are performed as part of the job. The Tax Court has focused on the duties performed. A minister employed as a chaplain by a municipal police department under church supervision was allowed a housing exclusion, but the exclusion was denied to a minister-administrator of an old-age home that was not under the authority of a church and a rabbi who worked for a religious organization as director of inter-religious affairs.

Allowance subject to self-employment tax. Although a qualifying housing allowance is not treated as taxable income, the exempt amount is included as self-employment income for Social Security and Medicare purposes; *see Chapter 45*. If you do not receive a cash allowance, report the rental value of the parsonage as self-employment income. Rental value is usually equal to what you would pay for similar quarters in your locality. Also include as self-employment income the value of house furnishings, utilities, appurtenances supplied—such as a garage—and the value of meals furnished that meet the rules in *3.13*.

Business expenses allocable to tax-free housing not deductible. A minister may deduct business expenses allocable to taxable compensation, but not expenses allocable to a tax-free housing allowance or in-kind housing. If part of a minister's salary is designated as a housing allowance, and the minister also has self-employment earnings from the exercise of his ministry, a double allocation is required, first between salary income and self-employment income, and then between the taxable and tax free parts of salary.

For example, in one case a minister had self-employment income comprising 21.56% of his annual income. Of the rest, 53.85% was a tax-free housing allowance and 46.15% was taxable salary. The Tax Court agreed with the double allocation required by the IRS. Since the minister did not provide evidence as to which expenses were generated by which type of income, the Court allocated expenses on a pro rata basis, applying the ratio of salary and self-employment income to total income. Since the self-employment income was 21.56% of total income (including the allowance), 21.56% of the expenses were deductible on Schedule C. The remaining expenses were treated as job-related costs deductible, if at all, as miscellaneous itemized expenses on Schedule A. However, because 53.85% of the minister's salary was a tax-free housing allowance, 53.85% of the expenses were nondeductible. The balance (46.15% of the expenses) is treated as a miscellaneous itemized deduction subject to the 2% of adjusted gross income floor, which is not deductible in 2018 through 2025 *(19.3)*.

3.15   Cafeteria Plans Provide Choice of Benefits

"Cafeteria plans" is a nickname for plans that give an employee a choice of selecting either cash or at least one qualifying nontaxable benefit. You are not taxed when you elect qualifying nontaxable benefits, although cash could have been chosen instead. A cafeteria plan may offer tax-free benefits such as group health insurance or life insurance coverage, long-term disability coverage, dependent care or adoption assistance, medical expense reimbursements, or group legal services. However, long-term care insurance may not be offered through a cafeteria plan under current law.

Under a flexible spending arrangement (FSA), employees may be allowed to make pre-tax salary-reduction contributions to a medical or dependent care reimbursement plan *(3.16)*.

Employees may be offered a premium-only plan (POP), which allows them to purchase group health insurance coverage or life insurance on a pre-tax basis using salary-reduction contributions.

Health savings accounts (HSAs) and their related high-deductible health plans (HDHPs) may be offered as options by a cafeteria plan *(3.2)*. If so, employees may elect to have contributions made to an HSA and an HDHP on a pre-tax salary-reduction basis.

A cafeteria plan may also offer benefits that are nontaxable because they are attributable to after-tax employee contributions. For example, employees may be offered the opportunity to purchase disability benefits (short term or long term) with after-tax contributions. If a covered employee subsequently receives disability benefits that are attributable to after-tax contributions, the benefits will be tax free. On the other hand, the plan may allow employees to elect paying for disability coverage on a pre-tax basis and, in this case, any benefits from the plan attributable to the pre-tax contributions will be taxable when received.

A qualified cafeteria plan must be written and not discriminate in favor of highly compensated employees and stockholders. If the plan provides for health benefits, a special rule applies to determine whether the plan is discriminatory. If a plan is held to be discriminatory, the highly compensated participants are taxed to the extent they could have elected cash. Furthermore, if key employees *(3.4)* receive more than 25% of the "tax-free" benefits under the plan, they are taxed on the benefits. Employers averaging 100 or fewer employees who agree to contribute a fixed amount towards benefits are treated as meeting the nondiscrimination tests under special rules for "simple" cafeteria plans.

Wellness program's cash rewards and reimbursements of premiums are taxable. A cafeteria plan may allow employees to make pre-tax salary-reduction contributions to a wellness program that provides health benefits such as screenings, as well as benefits that are not qualifying medical expenses, such as gym memberships or other cash rewards. In a legal memorandum, IRS Chief Counsel concluded that the coverage purchased with the salary reduction is tax free, assuming there are screenings and other health benefits sufficient for the wellness program to be treated as a health and accident plan *(3.1)*, and the health screenings and similar benefits are tax-free reimbursements of medical expenses *(3.2)*. However, any cash rewards or other benefits received from the program that are not medical care are includible in the employee's income as wages, unless they are excludable as *de minimis* benefits *(3.10)*. A T-shirt qualifies as a tax-free *de minimis* benefit, but payment or reimbursement of gym membership fees is a cash benefit that is not excludable as a *de minimis* fringe benefit. The gym fees and any other benefits or rewards not otherwise excludable from income are treated as wages subject to employment taxes. Similarly, any reimbursement of an employee's salary-reduction contributions to the wellness program are includible in the employee's income as wages subject to employment taxes.

3.16 Flexible Spending Arrangements

A flexible spending arrangement (FSA) allows employees to get reimbursed for medical or dependent care expenses from an account they set up with pre-tax dollars. Under a typical FSA, you agree to a salary reduction that is deducted from each paycheck and deposited in a separate account. Salary-reduction contributions within the annual limit are not included in your taxable wages reported on Form W-2. As expenses are incurred, you are reimbursed from the account. Reimbursements used to pay qualified medical or dependent care expenses are excluded from your income even though the contributions to your account were also not taxed to you.

The tax advantage of an FSA is that your salary-reduction contributions are not subject to federal income tax or Social Security taxes, allowing your medical or dependent care expenses to be paid with pre-tax rather than after-tax income. The salary deferrals are also exempt from most state and local taxes; check with the administrator of your employer's plan.

In the case of a health FSA, paying medical expenses with pre-tax dollars allows you to avoid the adjusted gross income (AGI) floor *(17.1)* that limits itemized deductions for medical costs.

To get these tax advantages, you must assume some risk. If your qualifying out-of-pocket expenses for the year are less than your contributions, the balance of the contributions will be forfeited unless your employer allows a carryover or grace period for using the leftover funds, as discussed below.

Making an FSA election. An election to contribute to a FSA is generally irrevocable. An election to set up an FSA for a given year must be made before the start of that year. You elect how much you want to contribute during the coming year and that amount will be withheld from your pay in monthly installments. *See* below for the contribution limits for health FSAs or dependent care FSAs.

Once the election for a particular year takes effect, you may not discontinue contributions to your account or increase or decrease a coverage election unless there is a change in family or work status that qualifies under IRS regulations.

Employers have discretion to offer carryover or grace period. In general, if your qualifying out-of-pocket expenses for the year are less than your contributions, the balance of the contributions will be forfeited unless your employer allows a carryover of the unused contributions in the case of a health FSA (carryover is not allowed for a dependent care FSA), or the plan allows a grace period (can be for a health FSA or a dependent care FSA). The tax law does not require employers to provide a carryover or grace period; it is up to the employer. A health FSA may not offer both a grace period and a carryover; it's one or the other, or neither, at the discretion of the employer.

If your employer offers a grace period for unused 2023 health FSA or dependent care FSA funds, the maximum grace period is 2½ months. A 2½ month grace period would allow FSA funds that were not used by the end of 2023 to reimburse expenses you incur during the grace period beginning January 1, 2024 and ending March 15, 2024. If the expenses incurred by March 15, 2024 do not cover the unused amount from 2023, the balance is forfeited to the employer.

The maximum carryover of unused health FSA amounts from 2023 to 2024 is $610. The health FSA carryover limit is subject to inflation adjustments; *see* the *e-Supplement* at *jklasser.com* for the 2024-to-2025 carryover limit.

Health FSAs. There is an annual limit on salary-reduction contributions to a health FSA. The maximum salary-reduction contribution that could be made to a health FSA for 2022 was $2,850. For 2023, the maximum contribution level is $3,050. The maximum carryover amount from 2023 to 2024 is $610. For 2024, the $3,050 limit and the $610 carryover limit may get an inflation increase; *see* the *e-Supplement* at *jklasser.com*. A plan must apply the annual dollar limit to remain a qualified cafeteria plan; otherwise, all plan benefits are includible in the employees' gross income. The annual limit is the maximum salary-reduction contribution that the plan can allow, but employers may set a lower limit.

The annual limit applies per person and not per household. If you and your spouse each work and both of you are offered health FSA coverage, you may each elect to make salary-reduction contributions up to the annual limit, provided the employer allows that much. This is true even if you and your spouse work for the same employer.

Funds from a health FSA may generally be used to reimburse you for expenses that you could claim as a medical expense deduction *(17.2)* such as the annual deductible under your employer's regular health plan, co-payments you must make to physicians or for prescriptions, and any other expenses that your health plan does not cover. These may include eye examinations, eyeglasses, routine physicals, and orthodontia work for you and your dependents. In addition, a health FSA may reimburse (1) over-the-counter medications such as cold remedies, pain relievers, and allergy medications, regardless of whether the medication was prescribed by a physician, and (2) menstrual care products.

A health FSA may not be used to reimburse you for premiums paid for other health plan coverage, including premiums for coverage under a plan of your spouse or dependent. Premiums are not reimbursable under a FSA regardless of whether the premiums were paid with pre-tax or after-tax funds. In addition, expenses for long-term care services cannot be reimbursed under a health FSA. You may not receive tax-free reimbursements for cosmetic surgery expenses unless the surgery is necessary to correct a deformity existing since birth or resulting from a disease or from injury caused by an accident. Nonqualifying reimbursements are taxable.

At any time during the year, you may receive reimbursements up to your designated limit, even though your payments into the FSA account up to that point may add up to less. For example, if you elect to make salary-reduction contributions of $100 per

Law Alert

O-T-C Drugs Can Be Reimbursed From Health FSA

For years, the law prohibited health FSAs from reimbursing over-the-counter medications unless a physician provided a prescription for the medication. The CARES Act eliminated this restriction. Starting with 2020 expenses, over-the-counter medications qualify for health FSA reimbursement.

month to a health-care FSA and you incur $500 of qualifying medical expenses in January, you may get the full $500 reimbursement even though you have paid only $100 into the plan. Your employer may not require you to accelerate contributions to match reimbursement claims.

Your employer may allow a grace period of up to 2½ months or a carryover for unused health FSA expenses, but not both, as discussed earlier.

Employees on medical or family leave. Employees who take unpaid leave under the Family and Medical Leave Act (FMLA) to deal with medical emergencies or care for a newborn child may either continue or revoke their coverage during FMLA leave. If the coverage continues, the maximum reimbursement selected by such an employee must be available at all times during the leave period. If the coverage is terminated, the employee must be reinstated under the FSA after returning from the leave, but no reimbursement claims may be made for expenses incurred during the leave.

Dependent Care FSAs. You may contribute to a dependent care FSA if you expect to pay expenses for a qualifying child under the dependent care tax credit *(25.4)*, but if you contribute to a dependent care FSA, any tax-free reimbursement from the account reduces the expenses eligible for the credit *(25.5)*. If you are married, both you and your spouse must work in order for you to receive tax-free reimbursements from an FSA, unless your spouse is disabled or a full-time student *(3.5)*. You must use Part III of Form 2441 to figure how much of your reimbursement is tax free and how much must be included in your income *(3.5)*.

The maximum tax-free reimbursement under a dependent care FSA in 2023 is $5,000, or $2,500 if married filing separately. Unlike health FSAs, an employer may limit reimbursements from a dependent care FSA to your account balance. For example, if you contribute $400 a month to the FSA and in January you pay $1,500 to a day-care center for your child, your employer may choose to reimburse you $400 a month as contributions are made to your account.

Your employer may allow a grace period of up to 2½ months (but not a carryover) for unused dependent care FSA expenses, as discussed earlier.s

3.17 Company Services Provided at No Additional Cost

Employees are not taxed on the receipt of services usually sold by their employer to customers where the employer does not incur additional costs in providing them to the employees. Examples are free or low-cost flights provided by an airline to its employees; free or discount lodging for employees of a hotel; and telephone service provided to employees of telephone companies. These tax-free fringes also may be provided to the employee's spouse and dependent children; retired employees, including employees retired on disability; and widows or widowers of deceased or retired employees. Tax-free treatment also applies to free or discount flights provided to parents of airline employees. Benefits provided by another company under a reciprocal arrangement, such as standby tickets on another airline, may also qualify as tax free.

The employer must have excess service capacity to provide the service and not forego potential revenue from regular customers. For example, airline employees who receive free reserved seating on company planes must pay tax on the benefit because the airline is foregoing potential revenue by reserving seating that could otherwise be sold. In addition, the Tax Court sees a difference between (1) standby tickets exempt when issued to employees, spouses, and dependent children and (2) those issued to adult friends and family.

Line of business limitations. If a company has two lines of business, such as an airline and a hotel, an employee of the airline may not receive tax-free benefits provided by the hotel. However, there are exceptions. An employee who provides services to both business lines may receive benefits from both business lines. Benefits from more than one line in existence before 1984 may also be available under a special election made by the company for 1985 and later years. Your employer should notify you of this tax benefit.

 *Filing Instruction*

Dependent Care Reimbursements Affect Credit

Reimbursements received tax free from your dependent care FSA reduce the expense base for figuring the dependent care credit; *see Chapter 25.*

Your employer may allow a 2½ month grace period for unused dependent care FSA contributions (but not a carryover), as discussed earlier.

 *Caution*

Highly Compensated Employees

Highly compensated employees can receive tax-free company services *(3.17)* or tax-free discounts on company products or services *(3.18)* only if the same benefits are available to other employees on a nondiscriminatory basis. For 2023, highly compensated employees include employees owning more than a 5% interest in 2023 or 2022, and employees who in 2022 (prior year) had compensation over $130,000. Employers have the option of including only the top-paid 20% for 2022 in the over-$130,000 category for determining 2023 highly compensated employees.

3.18   Discounts on Company Products or Services

The value of discounts on company products is a tax-free benefit if the discount does not exceed the employer's gross profit percentage. For example, if a company's profit percentage is 40%, the maximum tax-free employee discount for merchandise is 40% of the regular selling price. If you received a 50% discount, then 10% of the price charged customers would be taxable income. The employer has a choice of methods for figuring profit percentage.

Discounts on services that are not tax free under *3.17* for no-additional-cost services qualify for an exclusion, limited to 20% of the selling price charged customers. Discounts above 20% are taxable. An insurance policy is treated as a service. Thus, insurance company employees are not taxed on a discount of up to 20% of the policy's price.

Some company products do not qualify for the exclusion. Discounts on real estate and investment property such as securities, commodities, currency, or bullion are taxable. Interest-free or low-interest loans given by banks or other financial institutions to employees are not excludable. Such loans are subject to tax under the rules discussed at *4.31*.

CHAPTER 4

Dividend and Interest Income

Dividends and interest that are paid to you are reported by the payer to the IRS on Forms 1099.

You will receive copies of:

- Forms 1099-DIV, for dividends
- Forms 1099-INT, for interest
- Forms 1099-OID, for original issue discount

Dividends paid by most domestic corporations and many foreign corporations are subject to the same preferential tax rates as net long-term capital gains (4.2).

Report the amounts shown on the Forms 1099 on your tax return. The IRS uses the Forms 1099 to check the income you report. If you fail to report income reported on Forms 1099, you will receive a statement asking for an explanation and a bill for the tax deficiency. If you receive a Form 1099 that you believe is incorrect, contact the payer for a corrected form.

Do not attach your copies of Forms 1099 to your return. Keep them with a copy of your tax return.

 *Filing Instruction*

So-Called Dividends That Are Really Interest

Distributions from the following financial institutions are called "dividends," but are actually interest reported on Form 1099-INT: dividends from credit unions, cooperative banks, savings and loan associations, building and loan associations, and mutual savings banks.

4.1   Reporting Dividends and Mutual Fund Distributions

Dividends paid to you out of a corporation's earnings and profits are taxable as ordinary income. The corporation will report dividends on Form 1099-DIV (or equivalent statement). Mutual fund dividends and distributions are also reported on Form 1099-DIV (or similar form). Corporate dividends and mutual fund distributions of $10 or more are reported on Form 1099-DIV (or equivalent) whether you receive them in cash or they have been reinvested at your request.

Form 1099-DIV. Form 1099-DIV gives you a breakdown of the dividends and distributions paid to you during the year. If you were a shareholder of record in a mutual fund or real estate investment trust (REIT) during October, November, or December of 2023 and entitled to a dividend declared in one of those months, but the dividend was not paid to you until January 2024, it will be reported to you on the 2023 Form 1099-DIV, as if it had been paid before the end of the year *(4.10)*. The company or fund may send a statement that is similar to Form 1099-DIV. You do not have to attach the Form 1099-DIV (or similar statement) to your tax return.

Box 1a. Ordinary dividends taxed to you are shown in Box 1a. These are the most common type of distribution, payable out of a corporation's earnings and profits. Your share of a mutual fund's ordinary dividends is also shown on Form 1099-DIV; short-term capital gain distributions are included in the Box 1a total.

Box 1b. Part of the Box 1a amount may be qualified dividends. Qualified dividends reported in Box 1b are generally taxed at the same favorable rates (zero, 15% or 20%) as net capital gains. Any net capital losses, however, do not directly offset qualified dividends despite their sharing the same rate structure. See *4.2* for further details on qualified dividends.

Boxes 2a–2d. Capital gain distributions (long term) from a mutual fund (or real estate investment trust) are shown in Box 2a. Box 2b shows the portion of the Box 2a amount, if any, that is unrecaptured Section 1250 gain from the sale of depreciable real estate. Box 2c shows the part of Box 2a that is Section 1202 gain from small business stock eligible for an exclusion *(5.7)*. Box 2d shows the amount from Box 2a that is 28% rate gain from the sale of collectibles. If any amount is reported in Box 2b, 2c, or 2d, you must file Schedule D with Form 1040 or 1040-SR *(5.3)*.

Box 3. Nondividend distributions that are a nontaxable return of your investment are shown in Box 3; *see* "Return of capital distributions" below.

Box 4. If you did not give your taxpayer identification number to the payer, backup withholding at a 24% rate *(26.10)* is shown in Box 4.

Box 5. The portion of ordinary dividends (Box 1a) that is eligible for the QBI (qualified business income) deduction *(40.24)* is shown in Box 5.

PAYER'S name, street address, city or town, state or province, country, ZIP or foreign postal code, and telephone no.		1a Total ordinary dividends $ 500	OMB No. 1545-0110 Form **1099-DIV** (Rev. January 2022)	Dividends and Distributions
Very Mutual Fund 155 East 38th Street City, State, 010X0		1b Qualified dividends $ 435	For calendar year 20 ___	
		2a Total capital gain distr. $ 375	2b Unrecap. Sec. 1250 gain $	Copy B For Recipient
PAYER'S TIN 0X-01X0110	RECIPIENT'S TIN 00X-1X-0X00	2c Section 1202 gain $	2d Collectibles (28%) gain $	
		2e Section 897 ordinary dividends $	2f Section 897 capital gain $	
RECIPIENT'S name Noelle Ballesteros		3 Nondividend distributions $	4 Federal income tax withheld $	This is important tax information and is being furnished to the IRS. If you are required to file a return, a negligence penalty or other sanction may be imposed on you if this income is taxable and the IRS determines that it has not been reported.
Street address (including apt. no.) 21 Chauncy Street		5 Section 199A dividends $	6 Investment expenses $	
		7 Foreign tax paid $	8 Foreign country or U.S. possession	
City or town, state or province, country, and ZIP or foreign postal code City, State 1X011		9 Cash liquidation distributions $	10 Noncash liquidation distributions $	
	11 FATCA filing requirement ☐	12 Exempt-interest dividends $	13 Specified private activity bond interest dividends $	
Account number (see instructions)		14 State	15 State identification no.	16 State tax withheld $ $

☐ CORRECTED (if checked)

Form **1099-DIV** (Rev. 1-2022)   (keep for your records)   www.irs.gov/Form1099DIV   Department of the Treasury - Internal Revenue Service

Box 6. Your share of expenses from a non–publicly offered mutual fund is shown in Box 6, which is included in Box 1a. Due to the suspension of miscellaneous itemized deductions subject to the 2%-of-adjusted-gross income floor, they are not deductible.

Boxes 7 and 8. The foreign tax shown in Box 7 (imposed by the country shown in Box 8) may be claimed as a tax credit on Form 1116 or as an itemized deduction on Schedule A, Form 1040 or 1040-SR *(36.13)*.

Boxes 9 and 10. Cash and noncash liquidation distributions are shown in these boxes.

Nominee distribution—joint accounts. If you receive dividends on stock held as a nominee for someone else, or you receive a Form 1099-DIV that includes dividends belonging to another person, such as a joint owner of the account, you are considered to be a "nominee recipient." If the other owner is someone other than your spouse, you should file a separate Form 1099-DIV showing you as the payer and the other owner as the recipient of the allocable income. For 2023 dividends, give the owner a copy of Form 1099-DIV by January 31, 2024, so the dividends can be reported on his or her 2023 return. File the Form 1099-DIV, together with a Form 1096 ("Transmittal of Information Return"), with the IRS by February 29, 2024; the deadline is March 31, 2024, if filing electronically.

On your Schedule B (Form 1040 or 1040-SR), you enter on Line 5 the ordinary dividends reported to you on Form 1099-DIV, including the nominee distribution (the amount allocable to the other owner). Enter a subtotal for the dividends, and then subtract the nominee distribution from the subtotal; label the subtraction "Nominee Distribution." That way, the nominee distribution is not included in the taxable dividends shown on Line 6 of Schedule B.

Return of capital distributions. A distribution that is not paid out of earnings is a nontaxable return of capital, that is, a partial payback of your investment. The company will report the distribution in Box 3 of Form 1099-DIV as a nondividend distribution. You must reduce the cost basis of your stock by the nondividend distribution. If your basis is reduced to zero by such return of capital distributions, any further distributions are taxable as capital gains, which you report on Schedule D of Form 1040 or 1040-SR.

Planning Reminder

Dividends on Life Insurance Policies
Dividends on a life insurance policy (other than a modified endowment contract) are actually a refund of your premiums and are not taxed until they exceed the total premiums paid.

4.2 Qualified Corporate Dividends Taxed at Favorable Capital Gain Rates

Dividends paid out of current or accumulated earnings of a corporation are taxable *(4.5)*. Stock dividends on common stock *(4.6)* are generally not taxable, but other types of stock dividends are taxed *(4.8)*.

Dividends from most domestic corporations and many foreign corporations are treated as "qualified dividends," which are subject to the same favorable rates as net capital gain (the excess of net long-term capital gains over net short-term losses; *see 5.3*). The rate on your qualified dividends is either zero, 15% or 20%, depending on your taxable income *(5.3)*. More than one of these favorable rates may apply to your qualified dividends depending on their amount and your other income. Although the zero rate is intended to benefit taxpayers with modest incomes, taxpayers with substantial dividends/gains whose top bracket would be 22% or higher (assuming there were no capital gain rates) may pay no tax (zero rate) on a portion of their qualified dividends/net capital gains, provided their ordinary income (such as salary and interest) is low; *see* the Examples in *5.3*.

The benefit of the reduced rates is obtained as part of the computation of tax liability on the "Qualified Dividends and Capital Gain Tax Worksheet" in the instructions for Form 1040 and 1040-SR, or, if required, on the Schedule D Tax Worksheet *(5.3)*.

On Form 1099-DIV for 2023, the amount of qualified dividends eligible for the capital gain rate will be shown in Box 1b. To be eligible, the dividend must be received on stock you held at least 61 days during the 121-day period beginning 60 days before the ex-dividend date. The ex-dividend date is the first date following the declaration of a dividend on which the purchaser of the stock is not entitled to receive the dividend *(4.9)*. When counting the number of days you held the stock, include the day you disposed of the stock but not the day you acquired it. You cannot count towards the 61-day test any days on which your position in the securities was hedged, thereby diminishing your risk of loss.

Some dividends from a mutual fund or exchange-traded fund (ETF) may be reported as qualified distributions on Form 1099 although they are not actually qualified distributions and cannot be reported as such on your return. Both you and the fund must hold the underlying security for the required 61-day period. The fund may report a dividend as qualifying without taking into account whether you purchased or sold your shares during the year, so you must determine whether you have met the 61-day holding period test for the shares on which the dividends were paid. When counting the number of days you held the shares, include the day you disposed of the shares but not the day you acquired them.

Generally, distributions on preferred stock instruments do not qualify for qualified dividend treatment because the instruments are hybrid securities that are treated as debt and not stock. Payments on such hybrid instruments are considered interest rather than dividends and thus are not eligible for the reduced tax rate. If the preferred instrument is treated as stock, the reduced rate does not apply to dividends attributable to periods totaling less than 367 days unless the 61-day holding period (discussed above) is met. If the dividends are attributable to periods of more than 366 days, the stock must be held at least 91 days in the 181-day period starting 90 days before the ex-dividend date.

Some dividends are actually interest. Distributions that are called dividends but are actually interest income, such as payments from credit unions and mutual savings banks, are not eligible for the reduced dividend rate. Similarly, certain dividends from exchange-traded funds (ETFs) and from mutual funds represent interest earnings and are not eligible for the reduced rate. Dividends paid by a real estate investment trust (REIT) generally are not eligible, but the reduced rate does apply to REIT distributions that are attributable to corporate tax at the REIT level or which represent qualified dividends received by the REIT and passed through to shareholders.

Dividends from foreign corporations qualify for the reduced rate if the corporation is traded on an established U.S. securities market, incorporated in a U.S. possession, or certain treaty requirements are met.

If your broker loans out your shares as part of a short sale, substitute payments in lieu of dividends may be received on your behalf while the short sale is open. Such substitute payments are not considered dividends and should be included in Box 8 of Form 1099-MISC and reported by you as "Other income" on Line 8z of Schedule 1 (Form 1040-1040-SR).

Tax-deferred retirement accounts such as traditional IRAs and 401(k) plans do not benefit from the reduced dividend rate. Distributions from such retirement plans are taxable as ordinary income even if the distribution is attributable to dividends that otherwise meet the tests for qualified dividends.

4.3 Dividends From a Partnership, S Corporation, Estate, or Trust

Dividends you receive as a member of a partnership, stockholder in an S corporation, or as a beneficiary of an estate or trust may be qualified dividends eligible for the reduced capital gain rate of zero, 15%, or 20% (4.2).

A distribution from a partnership or S corporation is reported as a dividend only if it is portfolio income derived from nonbusiness activities. Your allowable share of the dividend will be shown on the Schedule K-1 you receive from the partnership or S corporation.

4.4 Real Estate Investment Trust (REIT) Dividends

Dividends from a real estate investment trust (REIT) are shown on Form 1099-DIV. Ordinary dividends reported in Box 1a are taxable at ordinary income rates except for the portion, if any, shown in Box 1b that qualifies for the zero, 15% or 20% capital gain rate. Dividends reported in Box 2a as capital gain distributions are reported by you as long-term capital gains regardless of how long you have held your trust shares. A loss on the sale of REIT shares held for six months or less is treated as a long-term capital loss to the extent of any capital gain distribution received before the sale plus any undistributed capital gains. However, this long-term loss rule does not apply to sales under periodic redemption plans.

Filing Tip

REIT Dividends May Create a QBI Deduction

You may be able to claim a deduction of up to 20% of qualified REIT dividends. This is a component of the qualified business income (QBI) deduction. *See 40.24.*

4.5 Taxable Dividends of Earnings and Profits

You pay tax on dividends only when the corporation distributing the dividends has earnings and profits. Publicly held corporations will tell you whether their distributions are taxable. If you hold stock in a close corporation, you may have to determine the tax status of its distribution. You need to know earnings and profits at two different periods:

1. Current earnings and profits as of the end of the current taxable year. A dividend is considered to have been made from earnings most recently accumulated.

2. Accumulated earnings and profits as of the beginning of the current year. However, when current earnings and profits are large enough to meet the dividend, you do not have to make this computation. It is only when the dividends exceed current earnings (or there are no current earnings) that you match accumulated earnings against the dividend.

The tax term "accumulated earnings and profits" is similar in meaning to the accounting term "retained earnings." Both stand for the net profits of the company after deducting distributions to stockholders. However, "tax" earnings may differ from "retained earnings" for the following reason: Reserve accounts, the additions to which are not deductible for income tax purposes, are ordinarily included as tax earnings.

EXAMPLES

1. During 2023, Corporation A paid dividends of $25,000. At the beginning of 2023 it had accumulated earnings of $50,000. It lost $25,000 during 2023. You are taxed on your dividend income in 2023 because the corporation's net accumulated earnings and profits exceed its dividends.

2. At the end of 2022, Corporation B had a deficit of $200,000. Earnings for 2023 were $100,000. In 2023, it paid stockholders dividends of $25,000. The dividends are taxed in 2023; earnings in 2023 exceeded the dividends.

4.6 Stock Dividends on Common Stock

If you own common stock in a company and receive additional shares of the same company as a dividend, the dividend is generally not taxable *(Chapter 30)* for the method of computing cost basis of stock dividends *(30.3)* and rights and sales of such stock *(30.4)*.

Exceptions to tax-free rule. A stock dividend on common stock is taxable *(4.8)* when (1) you may elect to take either stock or cash; (2) there are different classes of common stock, one class receiving cash dividends and another class receiving stock; or (3) the dividend is of convertible preferred stock.

Fractional shares. If a stock dividend is declared and you are only entitled to a fractional share, you may be given cash instead. To save the trouble and expense of issuing fractional shares, many companies directly issue cash in lieu of fractional shares or they set up a plan, with shareholder approval, for the fractional shares to be sold and the cash proceeds distributed to the shareholders. Your company should tell you how to report the cash payment. According to the IRS, you are generally treated as receiving a tax-free dividend of fractional shares, followed by a taxable redemption of the shares by the company. You report on Form 8949 and Schedule D *(5.8)* capital gain or loss equal to the excess of the cash over the basis of the fractional share; long- or short-term treatment depends on the holding period of the original stock. In certain cases, a cash distribution may be taxed as an ordinary dividend and not as a sale reported on Form 8949 (and Schedule D); your company should tell you if this is the case.

Stock rights. The rules that apply to stock dividends also apply to distributions of stock rights. If you, as a common stockholder, receive rights to subscribe to additional common stock, the receipt of the rights is not taxable provided the terms of the distribution do not fall within the taxable distribution rules *(4.8)*.

Planning Reminder

Dividend Reinvestment in Company Stock

Your company may allow you either to take cash dividends or automatically reinvest the dividends in company stock. If you elect the stock plan, and pay fair market value for the stock, the full cash dividend is taxable.

If the plan lets you buy the stock at a discount, the amount of the taxable dividend is the fair market value of the stock on the dividend payment date plus any service fee charged for the acquisition. The basis of the stock is also the fair market value at the dividend payment date. Any service charges you pay are not deductible *(19.2)*. If at the same time you also have the option to buy additional stock at a discount and you exercise the option, you have additional dividend income for the difference between the fair market value (as of the dividend payment date) of the optional shares and the discounted amount you paid for the shares.

Filing Tip

Stock Splits Are Not Taxed

The receipt of stock under a stock split is not taxable. Stock splits resemble the receipt of stock dividends, but they are not dividends. They do not represent a distribution of surplus as in the case of stock dividends. Although you own more shares, your ownership percentage has not changed. The purpose of a stock split is generally to reduce the price of individual shares in order to increase their marketability. The basis of the old holding is divided among all the shares in order to find the basis for the new shares *(30.3)*.

4.7　Dividends Paid in Property

A dividend may be paid in property such as securities of another corporation or merchandise. You report as income the fair market value of the property. A dividend paid in property is sometimes called a dividend in kind.

Corporate benefit may be treated as constructive dividend. On an audit, the IRS may charge that a benefit given to a shareholder-employee should be taxed as a constructive dividend. For example, the Tax Court agreed with the IRS that a corporation's payment for a license that gave the sole shareholder the right to buy season tickets to Houston Texans football games was a constructive dividend to the shareholder.

> **EXAMPLE**
>
> You receive one share of X corporation stock as a dividend from the G company of which you are a stockholder. You received the X stock when it had a market value of $25; you report $25, the value of the property received. The $25 value is also your basis for the stock.

4.8　Taxable Stock Dividends

The most frequent type of stock dividend is not taxable: the receipt by a common stockholder of a corporation's own common stock as a dividend *(4.6)*.

Taxable stock dividends. The following stock dividends are taxable:
- Stock dividends paid to holders of preferred stock. However, no taxable income is realized where the conversion ratio of convertible preferred stock is increased only to take account of a stock dividend or split involving the stock into which the convertible stock is convertible.
- Stock dividends elected by a shareholder of common stock who had the choice of taking stock, property, or cash. A distribution of stock that was immediately redeemable for cash at the stockholder's option was treated as a taxable dividend.
- Stock dividends paid in a distribution where some shareholders receive property or cash and other shareholders' proportionate interests in the assets or earnings and profits of the corporation are increased.
- Distributions of preferred stock to some common shareholders and common stock to other common shareholders.
- Distributions of convertible preferred stock to holders of common stock, unless it can be shown that the distribution will not result in the creation of disproportionate stock interests.

Constructive stock dividends. You may not actually receive a stock dividend, but under certain circumstances, the IRS may treat you as having received a taxable distribution. This may happen when a company increases the ratio of convertible preferred stock.

4.9　Who Reports the Dividends

Stock held by broker in street name. If your broker holds stock for you in a street name, dividends earned on this stock are received by the broker and credited to your account. You report on your 2023 return all dividends credited to your account in 2023. The broker is required to file an information return on Form 1099-DIV (or similar form) showing all such dividends. The information may be included in a consolidated Form 1099-B that you receive from your broker.

If your statement shows only a gross amount of dividends, check with your broker if any of the dividends represented nontaxable returns of capital.

Dividends on stock sold or bought between ex-dividend date and record date. Record date is the date set by a company on which you must be listed as a stockholder on its records to receive the dividend. However, in the case of publicly traded stock, an ex-dividend date, which usually precedes the record date by several business days, is fixed by the exchange to determine who is entitled to the dividend.

If you buy stock before the ex-dividend date, the dividend belongs to you and is reported by you. If you buy on or after the ex-dividend date, the dividend belongs to the seller.

If you sell stock before the ex-dividend date, you do not have a right to the dividend. If you sell on or after the ex-dividend date, you receive the dividend and report it as income.

The dividend declaration date and date of payment do not determine who receives the dividend.

Nominees or joint owners. If you receive ordinary dividends on stock held as a nominee for another person, other than your spouse, give that owner a Form 1099-DIV and file a copy of that return with the IRS, along with a Form 1096 ("Transmittal of U.S. Information Return"). The actual owner then reports the income. List the nominee dividends on Schedule B (Form 1040 or 1040-SR) along with your other dividends, and then subtract the nominee dividends from the total.

EXAMPLE

You receive Form 1099-DIV showing dividends of $960 including a $200 nominee distribution. You prepare a Form 1099-DIV for the actual owner showing the $200 distribution, and file a copy of the form with the IRS, plus Form 1096. When you file your Form 1040 or 1040-SR, report the nominee distribution along with other ordinary dividends on Schedule B and then subtract it from the total.

Dividend Income	Amount
Mutual Fund	$ 310
Computer Inc.	450
Utility Inc.	200
Subtotal	$ 960
Less: Nominee distribution	(200)
Net dividends	$ 760

Follow the same procedure if you receive a Form 1099-DIV for an account owned jointly with someone other than your spouse. Give the other owner a Form 1099-DIV, and file a copy with the IRS, along with a Form 1096. The other owner then reports his or her share of the joint income. On your return, you list the total dividends shown on Forms 1099-DIV and subtract from the total the nominee dividends reported to the other owner.

4.10 Year Dividends Are Reported

Dividends are generally reported on the tax return for the year in which the dividend is credited to your account or when you receive the dividend if paid by check.

Dividends received from a corporation in a year after the one in which they were declared, when you held the stock on the record date, are taxed in the year they are received; *see* Example 4 below.

EXAMPLES

1. A corporation declares a dividend payable on December 29, 2023. It follows a practice of paying dividends by checks that are mailed so that stockholders do not receive them until January 2024. You report this dividend on your 2024 return.

2. On December 27, 2023, a mutual fund declares a dividend payable to shareholders of record as of that date. You receive it in January 2024. The dividend is taxable in 2023, when declared, and not 2024, when received, under the special rule for dividends declared by a mutual fund in the last three months of the year.

3. On December 28, 2023, a dividend is credited by a corporation to a stockholder's account and made immediately available. The dividend is taxable in 2023 as the crediting is considered constructive receipt by you in 2023, even if you do not receive it until 2024.

4. You own stock in a corporation. In April 2023, the corporation declared a dividend, but it provided that the dividend will be paid when it gets the cash. It finally pays the dividend in September 2024; the dividend is taxable in 2024.

 *Caution*

Year-End Dividend From Mutual Fund

A dividend declared in October through December by a mutual fund or REIT that is payable to shareholders of record on a date within those three months is taxable in the year it is declared, even if it is not paid until January of the following year.

Filing Tip

Insurance Premium Refund

Dividends on insurance policies are actually returns of premiums you previously paid. They are not subject to tax until they exceed the net premiums paid for the contract.

Caution

Reporting Foreign Accounts

If in 2023 you had a financial interest in or signature authority over a financial account in a foreign country, you must file Schedule B (Form 1040 or 1040-SR) even if you are not otherwise required to file it. In Part III of Schedule B, you must disclose your interest in the foreign account and are directed to the instructions for FinCEN Form 114 (FBAR) to determine if you must file that form (if yes, it must be filed electronically), and to indicate in Part III of Schedule B if the FBAR is required. There are substantial penalties for not filing a required FBAR. Regardless of whether you must file a FBAR, you may have to file Form 8938 to disclose your ownership of specified foreign financial assets. Penalties also apply for failure to file a required Form 8938. *See 48.7* for details on the FBAR and Form 8938 filing requirements.

4.11 Distribution Not Out of Earnings: Return of Capital

A return of capital or "nontaxable distribution" reduces the cost basis of the stock. If your shares were purchased at different times, reduce the basis of the oldest shares first. When the cost basis is reduced to zero, further returns of capital are taxed as capital gains on Schedule D. Whether the gain is short term or long term depends on the length of time you have held the stock. The company paying the dividend will usually inform you of the tax treatment of the payment.

Life insurance dividends. Dividends on insurance policies are not true dividends. They are returns of premiums you previously paid. They reduce the cost of the policy and are not subject to tax until they exceed the net premiums paid for the contract. Interest paid or credited on dividends left with the insurance company is taxable. Dividends on VA insurance are tax free, as is interest on dividends left with the VA.

Where insurance premiums were deducted as a business expense in prior years, receipts of insurance dividends are included as business income. Dividends on capital stock of an insurance company are taxable.

4.12 Reporting Interest on Your Tax Return

You must report all taxable interest. Forms 1099-INT, sent by payers of interest income, give you the amount of interest to enter on your tax return. Although they are generally correct, you should check for mistakes, notify payers of any error, and request a new form marked "corrected." If tax was withheld *(26.10)*, claim this tax as a payment on your tax return. The IRS will check interest reported on your return against the Forms 1099-INT sent by banks and other payers. If you earn over $1,500 of taxable interest, you list the payers of interest on Part I of Schedule B (Form 1040 or Form 1040-SR). You must also list tax-exempt interest on your Form 1040 or Form 1040-SR even though it is not taxable.

You must report interest that has been shown on a Form 1099-INT in your name although it may not be taxable to you. For example, you may have received interest as a nominee or as accrued interest on bonds bought between interest dates. In these cases, list the amounts reported on Form 1099 along with your other interest income on Schedule B (Form 1040 or Form 1040-SR). On a separate line, label the amount as "Nominee distribution," or "Accrued interest" *(4.15)*, and subtract it from the total interest shown. Accrued interest is discussed below. Nominee distributions are discussed below under "Joint Accounts."

If you received interest on a frozen account *(4.13)*, include the interest from Form 1099 on Schedule B (Form 1040 or 1040-SR). On a separate line, write "frozen deposits" and subtract the amount from the total interest reported.

You generally do not have to list the payers of interest if your interest receipts are $1,500 or less. However, complete Part I of Schedule B (Form 1040 or 1040-SR) if you have to reduce the interest shown on Form 1099 by nontaxable amounts such as accrued interest, tax-exempt interest, nominee distributions, frozen deposit interest, amortized bond premium, or excludable interest on savings bonds used for tuition.

Joint accounts. Form 1099-INT will be sent to the joint owner whose name and Social Security number was reported to the bank (or other payer) on Form W-9 when the account was opened. If you receive a Form 1099-INT for interest on an account you own with someone other than your spouse, you should file a nominee Form 1099-INT with the IRS to indicate that person's share of the interest, together with Form 1096 ("Transmittal of Information Return"). Give a copy of the Form 1099-INT to the other person. When you file your own return, you report the total interest shown on Form 1099-INT and then subtract the other person's share so you are taxed only on your portion of the interest; *see* the Example below.

Do not follow this procedure if you contributed all of the funds and set up the joint account merely as a "convenience" account to allow the other person to automatically inherit the account when you die. In this case, you report all of the interest income.

EXAMPLE

Your Social Security number is listed on a bank account owned jointly with your sister. You each invested 50% of the account principal and have agreed to share the interest income. You receive a Form 1099-INT for 2023 reporting total interest of $1,700 on the account. By January 31, 2024, prepare and give to your sister another Form 1099-INT that identifies you as the payer and her as the recipient of her share, or $850 interest. Send a copy of the Form 1099-INT and a Form 1096 to the IRS no later than February 28, 2024 (March 31, if filing electronically). Your sister will report the $850 interest on her return. On your Form 1040, report the full $1,700 interest on Line 1 of Schedule B (Form 1040 or 1040-SR), along with your other interest income. Above Line 2, subtract the $850 belonging to your sister to avoid being taxed on that amount; label the subtraction "Nominee distribution."

Savings certificates, deferred interest. The interest element on certificates of deposit and similar plans of more than one year is treated as deferred interest original issue discount (OID) and is taxable on an annual basis. The bank notifies you of the taxable OID amount on Form 1099-OID. If you discontinue a savings plan before maturity, you may have a loss deduction for forfeited interest, which is listed on Form 1099-INT or Form 1099-OID *(4.16)*.

Tax on interest can be deferred in some cases on a savings certificate with a term of one year or less. Interest is taxable in the year it is available for withdrawal without substantial penalty. Where you invest in a six-month certificate before July 1, the entire amount of interest is paid by the end of the year and is taxable in that year (the year of payment). However, when you invest in a six-month certificate after June 30, only interest actually paid or made available for withdrawal before the end of the year without substantial penalty is taxable in the year of issuance. The balance is taxable in the year of maturity. You can defer interest to the following year by investing in a six-month certificate after June 30, provided the payment of interest is specifically deferred to the year of maturity by the terms of the certificate. Similarly, interest may be deferred to the following year by investing in certificates of up to one year, provided that the crediting of interest is specifically deferred until the year of maturity.

Accrued interest on a bond bought between interest payment dates. Interest accrued between interest payment dates is part of the purchase price of the bond. This amount is taxable to the seller as explained in *4.15*. If you purchased a bond and received a Form 1099-INT that includes accrued interest on a bond, include the interest on Line 1 of Schedule B (Form 1040 or 1040-SR), and then on a separate line above Line 2 subtract the accrued interest from the Line 1 total.

Custodian account of a minor (Uniform Transfers to Minors Act). The interest is taxable to the child if his or her name and Social Security number were provided to the payer on Form W-9. However, if the child has net investment income for 2022 over $2,300, the "kiddie tax" likely applies; *see 24.2*.

4.13 Interest on Frozen Accounts Not Taxed

If you have funds in a bankrupt or insolvent financial institution that freezes your account by limiting withdrawals, you do not pay tax on interest allocable to the frozen deposits. The interest is taxable when withdrawals are permitted. Officers and owners of at least a 1% interest in the financial institution, or their relatives, may not take advantage of this rule and must still report interest on frozen deposits.

On Part I of Schedule B (Form 1040 or 1040-SR), report the full amount shown on Form 1099-INT, even if the interest is on a "frozen" deposit. Then, on a separate line, subtract the amount allocable to the frozen deposit from the total interest shown on the Schedule; label the subtraction "frozen deposits." Thus, the interest on the frozen deposit is not included on the line of your return showing taxable interest.

Refund opportunity. If you reported interest on a frozen deposit on a tax return for a prior year, you generally have three years to file a refund claim for the tax paid on the interest *(47.2)*.

 *Filing Instruction*

Tax-Exempt Interest

Tax-exempt interest, such as from municipal bonds, must be reported on your return although it is not subject to regular income tax. Tax-exempt interest is shown in Box 8 of Form 1099-INT and any portion that is subject to AMT *(23.3)* is shown in Box 9. Report the Box 8 amount on Line 2a of Form 1040 or 1040-SR.

4.14   Interest Income on Debts Owed to You

You report interest earned on money that you loan to another person. If you are on the cash basis, you report interest in the year you actually receive it or when it is considered received under the "constructive receipt rule." If you are on the accrual basis, you report interest when it is earned, whether or not you have received it.

See *4.31* for minimum interest rates required for loans and *4.18* when OID rules apply.

Where partial payment is being made on a debt, or when a debt is being compromised, the parties may agree in advance which part of the payment covers interest and which covers principal. If a payment is not identified as either principal or interest, the payment is first applied against interest due and reported as interest income to the extent of the interest due.

Interest income is not realized when a debtor gives you a new note for an old note where the new note includes the interest due on the old note.

If you give away a debtor's note, you report as income the collectible interest due at the date of the gift. To avoid tax on the interest, the note must be transferred before interest becomes due.

4.15   Reporting Interest on Bonds Bought or Sold

When you buy or sell bonds between interest dates, interest is included in the price of the bonds. If you are the buyer, you do not report as income the interest that accrued before your date of purchase. The seller reports the accrued interest. Reduce the basis of the bond by the accrued interest reported by the seller. The following Examples illustrate these rules.

EXAMPLES

1. Purchase. On April 30, you buy for $5,200 a $5,000 corporate bond bearing interest at 2.5% per year, payable January 1 and July 1. The purchase price of the bond included accrued interest of $41.67 for the period January 1–April 30.

Interest received on 7/1	$62.50
Less: Accrued interest	$41.67
Taxable interest	$20.83

Form 1099 sent to you includes the $41.67 of accrued interest. On Schedule B (Form 1040 or 1040-SR), you report the total interest of $62.50 received on July 1 and then on a separate line subtract the accrued interest of $41.67. Write "Accrued Interest" on the line where you show the subtraction.

Your basis for the bond is $5,158 ($5,200 – $41.67) for purposes of figuring gain or loss on a later sale of the bond.

2. Sale. On April 30, you sell for $5,200 a $5,000 2.5% bond with interest payable January 1 and July 1. The sales price included interest of $41.67 accrued from January 1–April 30. Your cost for the bond was $5,000. On your return, you report interest of $41.67 and capital gain of $158.

You receive	$ 5,200.00
Less: Accrued interest	$41.67
Sales proceeds	$ 5,158.33
Less: Your cost	$5000.00
Capital gain	$ 158.33, or $158

Redemptions, bankruptcy, reorganizations. On a redemption, interest received in excess of the amount due at that time is not treated as interest income but as capital gain.

EXAMPLE

You hold a $5,000 9% bond with interest payable January 1 and July 1. The company can call the bonds for redemption on any interest date. In May, the company announces it will redeem the bonds on July 1. But you may present the bond for redemption beginning with June 1 and it will be redeemed with interest to July 1. On June 1 you present the bond and receive $5,225: $5,000 principal, $187.50 interest to June 1, and $37.50 extra interest to July 1. The $37.50 is treated as a capital gain; the $187.50 is interest.

Taxable interest may continue on bonds after the issuer becomes bankrupt, if a guarantor continues to pay the interest when due. The loss on the bonds will occur only when they mature and are not redeemed or when they are sold below your cost. In the meantime, the interest received from the guarantor is taxed.

Bondholders exchanging their bonds for stock, securities, or other property in a tax-free reorganization, including a reorganization in bankruptcy, have interest income to the extent the property received is attributable to accrued but unpaid interest; *see* Internal Revenue Code Section 354(a)(2)(B).

Bonds selling at a flat price. When you buy bonds with defaulted interest at a "flat" price, a later payment of the defaulted interest is not taxed. It is a tax-free return of capital that reduces your cost of the bond. This rule applies only to interest in default at the time the bond is purchased. Interest that accrues after the date of your purchase is taxed as ordinary income.

4.16 Forfeiture of Interest on Premature Withdrawals

Banks usually impose an interest penalty if you withdraw funds from a savings certificate before the specified maturity date. You may lose interest if you prematurely withdraw funds in order to switch to higher paying investments, or if you need the funds for personal use. In some cases, the penalty may exceed the interest earned so that principal is also forfeited to make up the difference.

If you are penalized, you must still report the full amount of interest credited to your account. However, on Form 1040 or 1040-SR, you may deduct the full amount of the penalty, forfeited principal as well as interest. The deductible penalty amount is shown in Box 2 of Form 1099-INT sent to you. You may claim the deduction even if you do not itemize deductions. On Schedule 1 (Form 1040 or 1040-SR), enter the deduction on Line 18, marked "Penalty on early withdrawal of savings."

Loss on redemption before maturity of a savings certificate. If you redeem a long-term (more than one year) savings certificate for a price less than the stated redemption price at maturity, you are allowed a loss deduction for the amount of original issue discount (OID) reported as income but not received. The deductible amount is shown in Box 3 of Form 1099-OID. Claim the deduction on Line 18 of Schedule 1 (Form 1040 or 1040-SR). The basis of the obligation is reduced by the amount of the deductible loss.

Do not include in the computation any amount based on a fixed rate of simple or compound interest that is actually payable or is treated as constructively received at fixed periodic intervals of one year or less.

4.17 Amortization of Bond Premium

Bond premium is the extra amount paid for a bond in excess of its principal or face amount when the value of the bond has increased due to falling interest rates. The premium is included in your basis in the bond but if the bond pays taxable interest, you may elect to amortize the premium by deducting it over the life of the bond. Amortizing the premium annually is usually advantageous because it gives an annual deduction to offset the interest income from the bond. Basis of the bond is reduced by the amortized premium. If you claim amortization deductions and hold the bond to maturity, basis is reduced by the entire amortized premium and you have neither gain nor loss at redemption.

 *Caution*

CD Early Withdrawal

If you are penalized for making an early withdrawal from a certificate of deposit, you may lose part of your interest or principal. You must report the full amount of interest credited to your account, but you may deduct the full amount of the penalty (whether forfeited principal or interest) on Line 18 of Schedule 1 (Form 1040 or 1040-SR).

 *Filing Tip*

How To Deduct Amortized Premium

You may not have to deduct the amortized premium because you are reporting the net amount of interest income (interest income reduced by the allocable premium amortization), as shown by the payer on Form 1099-INT. If you are reporting the total interest income and want to offset it by the amortizable premium, you must show the reduction on Schedule B (Form 1040 or 1040-SR). Report the full interest from the bond on Line 1 of Schedule B, along with the rest of your interest income. On a separate line, subtract the amortized premium from a subtotal of the other interest. Label the subtraction "ABP Adjustment."

You may not claim a deduction for a premium paid on a tax-exempt bond. However, you must still reduce your basis in the bond by the annual amortization amount. The amortized amount also reduces the amount of tax-exempt interest that you report on your return *(4.24)*.

Dealers in bonds may not deduct amortization but must include the premium as part of cost.

Capital loss alternative to amortizing premium. If you do not elect to amortize the premium on a taxable bond, you will realize a capital loss when the bond is redeemed at par or you sell it for less than you paid for it. For example, you bought a $1,000 corporate bond for $1,300 and did not amortize the $300 premium; you will realize a $300 capital loss when the bond is redeemed at par: $1,000 proceeds less $1,300 cost basis ($1,000 face value plus $300 premium). You could realize a capital gain if you sell the bond for more than the premium price you paid.

Determining the amortizable amount for the year. For a taxable "covered" bond issued by a corporation, the amount of premium amortization allocable to the interest payments will be reported by the payer in Box 11 of Form 1099-INT unless (1) the interest reported in Box 1 has been reduced to reflect the offset of the interest by the allocable premium amortization, or (2) you provided written notice to the payer that you did not want to amortize the bond premium. For example, if the taxable interest from a "covered" corporate bond is $40 and the amount of bond premium amortization allocable to the interest is $4, the payer may either report the net interest of $36 in Box 1 and $0 in Box 11, or report the $40 of interest income in Box 1 and the $4 of allocable premium amortization in Box 11.

For a U.S. Treasury bond that is "covered," Box 12 of Form 1099-INT will show the amount of bond premium amortization allocable to the interest paid during the year, unless the net amount of interest is reported in Box 3 to reflect the offset of the interest by the allocable amortization.

If a taxable bond is "noncovered," the payer is required to report only the gross amount of interest in Box 1 of Form 1099-INT.

The annual amortizable premium is based on the constant yield method (this has been the method for all bonds issued after September 27, 1985). The constant yield method is also an option for reporting market discount *(4.20)*. *See* IRS Publication 550 for details on figuring the amortizable premium or consult a tax professional for making the complex computations.

For taxable bonds subject to a call before maturity, the amortization computation is based on the earlier call date if that results in a smaller amortization deduction.

Electing amortization—either in or after the year you acquire a bond. An election to amortize premium on a taxable bond does not have to be made in the year you acquire the bond. Attach a statement to the tax return for the first year to which you want the election to apply. If the election is made after the year of acquisition, the premium allocable to the years prior to the year of election is not amortizable; the unamortized amount is included in your cost basis for the bond and will result in a capital loss when the bond is redeemed at par or sold prior to maturity for less than basis.

How to deduct amortized premium on taxable bonds. The premium amortization for the year offsets your interest income from the bonds; *see* the adjacent Filing Tip. If the allocable premium exceeds the interest income, and you claim itemized deductions (rather than the standard deduction), the excess of the allocable premium over interest income may be deducted as an "Other" itemized deduction on Line 16 of Schedule A (Form 1040 or 1040-SR). However, the itemized deduction is limited to the excess of total interest inclusions on the bonds in prior years over total bond premium deductions in the prior years.

Effect of amortization election on other taxable bonds you acquire. If you elect to amortize the premium for one bond, you must also amortize the premium on all similar bonds owned by you at the beginning of the tax year, and also to all similar bonds acquired thereafter. An election to amortize may not be revoked without IRS permission. If you file your return without claiming the deduction, you may not change your mind and make the election for that year by filing an amended return or refund claim.

Planning Reminder

Amortized Premium Reduces Basis

You reduce the cost basis of the bond by the amount of the premium taken as a deduction.

If you hold the bond to maturity, the entire premium is amortized and you have neither gain nor loss on redemption of the bond. If before maturity you sell the bond at a gain (selling price exceeds your basis for the bond), you realize long-term capital gain if you held the bond long term. A sale of the bond for less than its adjusted basis gives a capital loss.

Callable bonds. On taxable bonds, amortization is based either on the maturity or earlier call date, depending on which date gives a smaller yearly deduction. This rule applies regardless of the issue date of the bond. If the bond is called before maturity, you may deduct as an ordinary loss the unamortized bond premium in the year the bond is redeemed.

Convertible bonds. A premium paid for a convertible bond that is allocated to the conversion feature may not be amortized; the value of the conversion option reduces basis in the bond.

Premium on tax-exempt bonds. You may not take a deduction for the amortization of a premium paid on a tax-exempt bond. However, you must still reduce your basis in the bond each year by the amortized amount. The amortization for the year also reduces the amount of tax-exempt interest otherwise reportable on Line 2a of Form 1040 or 1040-SR. If the tax-exempt bond is a "covered" security, the payer of the bond must report in Box 13 of Form 1099-INT the amount of premium amortization that is allocable to the annual interest payments, unless the tax-exempt interest reported in Box 8 of the Form 1099-INT is the net amount (Box 9 if the tax-exempt interest is subject to alternative minimum tax), reflecting the offset of the interest paid by the allocable premium.

When you dispose of the bond, you reduce the basis of the bond by the amortized premium for the period you held the bond amount. If the bond has call dates, the IRS may require the premium to be amortized to the earliest call date.

4.18 Discount on Bonds

There are two types of bond discounts: original issue discount and market discount.

Market discount. Market discount arises when the price of a bond declines because its interest rate is less than the current interest rate. For example, a bond originally issued at its face amount of $1,000 declines in value to $900 because the interest payable on the bond is less than the current interest rate. The difference of $100 is called market discount. The tax treatment of market discount is explained in *4.20*.

Original issue discount (OID). OID arises when a bond is issued for a price less than its face or principal amount. OID is the difference between the principal amount (redemption price at maturity) and the issue price. For publicly offered obligations, the issue price is the initial offering price to the public at which a substantial amount of such obligations were sold. All obligations that pay no interest before maturity, such as zero coupon bonds, are considered to be issued at a discount. For example, a bond with a face amount of $1,000 is issued at an offering price of $900. The $100 difference is OID.

Generally, part of the OID must be reported as interest income each year you hold the bond, whether or not you receive any payment from the bond issuer. This is also true for certificates of deposit (CDs), time deposits, and similar savings arrangements with a term of more than one year, provided payment of interest is deferred until maturity. OID is reported to you by the issuer (or by your broker if you bought the obligation on a secondary market) on Form 1099-OID *(4.19)*.

Exceptions to OID. OID rules do not apply to: (1) obligations with a term of one year or less held by cash-basis taxpayers *(4.21)*; (2) tax-exempt obligations, except for certain stripped tax-exempts *(4.26)*; (3) U.S. Savings Bonds; (4) an obligation issued by an individual before March 2, 1984; and (5) loans of $10,000 or less from individuals who are not professional money lenders, provided the loans do not have a tax avoidance motivation.

 *Filing Tip*

When OID May Be Ignored

You may disregard OID that is less than one-fourth of one percent (.0025) of the principal amount multiplied by the number of full years from the date of original issue to maturity. On most long-term bonds, the OID will exceed this amount and must be reported.

EXAMPLES

1. A 10-year bond with a face amount of $1,000 is issued at $980. One-fourth of one percent (.0025) of $1,000 times 10 is $25. As the $20 OID is less than $25, it may be ignored for tax purposes.
2. Same facts as in Example 1, except that the bond is issued at $950. As OID of $50 is more than the $25, OID must be reported under the rules explained at *4.19*.

Bond bought at premium or acquisition premium. You do not report OID as ordinary income if you buy a bond at a premium. You buy at a premium where you pay more than the total amount payable on the bond after your purchase, not including qualified stated interest. When you dispose of a bond bought at a premium, the difference between the sale or redemption price and your basis is a capital gain or loss *(4.17)*.

If you do not pay more than the total due at maturity, you do not have a premium, but there is "acquisition premium" if you pay more than the adjusted issue price. This is the issue price plus previously accrued OID but minus previous payments on the bond other than qualified stated interest. The acquisition premium reduces the amount of OID you must report as income; *see 4.19*.

4.19 Reporting Original Issue Discount on Your Return

The issuer of the bond (or your broker) will make the Original Issue Discount (OID) computation and report in Box 1 of Form 1099-OID the OID for the actual dates of your ownership during the calendar year. In most cases, the entire OID must be reported as interest income on your return. However, the amount shown in Box 1 of Form 1099-OID may have to be adjusted if you bought the bond at an acquisition premium and generally must be adjusted if you bought the bond at a premium, the bond is indexed for inflation, the obligation is a stripped bond or stripped coupon (including zero coupon instruments backed by U.S. Treasury securities), or if you received Form 1099-OID as a nominee for someone else. Your basis in the bond is increased by the OID included in income.

If you did not receive a Form 1099-OID, contact the issuer or *see* IRS Publication 1212 for OID amounts.

Treasury inflation-indexed securities. You must report as OID any increase in the inflation-adjusted principal amount of a Treasury inflation-indexed security that occurs while you held the bond during the tax year. This amount should be reported to you in Box 1 of Form 1099-OID, but this amount must be adjusted if during the year you bought the bond after original issue or sold it. The adjusted amount of OID must be computed using the coupon bond method discussed in IRS Publication 1212.

Periodic interest (non-OID) paid to you during the year on a Treasury inflation-indexed security may be reported to you either in Box 2 of Form 1099-OID or in Box 3 of Form 1099-INT.

Premium. If you paid a premium *(4.18)* for a bond originally issued at discount, you do not have to report any OID as income. Report the amount shown on Form 1099-OID and then subtract it as discussed in the Filing Tip in this section.

Acquisition premium. If you pay an acquisition premium *(4.18)* and the payer reports the gross amount of OID in Box 1 of Form 1099-OID, that amount will not be correct because such premium reduces the amount of OID you must report as interest income. However, for a newly acquired bond, the payer may either (1) report in Box 1 a net amount of OID that reflects the offset of OID by the amortized acquisition premium for the year, or (2) report the gross amount of OID in Box 1 and show in Box 6 the acquisition premium amortization for the year; the Box 6 amount reduces the OID that you must report as interest income.

If you are reporting less than the full Box 1 amount of OID, report the full amount and then reduce it, as discussed in the Filing Tip on this page.

Stripped bonds or coupons. The amount that is shown in Box 1 of Form 1099-OID may not be correct for a stripped bond or coupon *(4.22)*. If the amount is incorrect, adjust it following the rules in Publication 1212.

Nominee. If you receive a Form 1099-OID for an obligation owned by someone else, other than your spouse, you must file another Form 1099-OID for that owner. The OID computation rules shown in IRS Publication 1212 should be used to compute the other owner's share of OID. You file the other owner's Form 1099-OID and a transmittal Form 1096 with the IRS, and give the other owner a copy of the Form 1099-OID. On your own tax return, report the amount shown on the Form 1099-OID you received and then reduce it, as discussed in the Filing Tip in this section.

Filing Tip

Reporting OID and Recomputed OID

If you are reporting the full amount of OID from Box 1 of Form 1099-OID, include the amount as interest on Form 1040. However, if you are reporting less OID than the amount shown in Box 1 of Form 1099-OID, you must adjust the reportable amount on Schedule B (Form 1040 or 1040-SR). Include the full amount shown in Box 1 of Form 1099-OID on Line 1 of Schedule B, along with other interest income. Make a subtotal of the Line 1 amounts and subtract from it the OID you are not required to report. Write "OID Adjustment" on the line where you show the subtraction. Label the subtraction "Nominee Distribution" if that is the reason for the reduction.

Your basis for the obligation is increased by the taxable OID for purposes of figuring gain on a sale or redemption *(4.23)*.

Periodic interest reported on Form 1099-OID. If in addition to OID there is regular interest payable on the bond, such interest will be reported in Box 2 of Form 1099-OID. However, for a Treasury inflation-indexed security, the interest may be reported in Box 3 of Form 1099-INT. Report the full amount as interest income if you held the bond for the entire year. If you acquired the bond or disposed of it during the year, figure the interest allocable to your ownership period *(4.15)*.

REMICS. If you are a regular interest holder in a REMIC (real estate mortgage investment conduit), Box 1 of Form 1099-OID shows the amount of OID you must report on your return and Box 2 includes periodic interest other than OID. If you bought the regular interest at a premium or acquisition, the OID shown on Form 1099-OID must be adjusted as discussed above.

4.20 Reporting Income on Market Discount Bonds

Market discount arises where the price of a bond declines below its face amount because it carries an interest rate that is below the current rate of interest.

When you realize a profit on the sale of a market discount bond, the portion of the profit equal to the accrued discount must be reported as ordinary interest income rather than as capital gain. Alternatively, an election may be made to report the accrued market discount annually instead of in the year of disposition; *see* below for "Reporting discount annually".

These tax reporting rules do not apply to the following bonds, which are excluded from the "market discount bond" category: (1) bonds with a maturity date of up to one year from date of issuance; (2) certain installment obligations, (3) U.S. Savings Bonds, and (4) tax-exempt bonds bought before May 1, 1993; at disposition, all the gain on these older tax-exempts is capital gain.

Furthermore, you may treat as zero any market discount that is less than one-fourth of one percent (.0025) of the redemption price multiplied by the number of full years after you acquire the bond to maturity. Such minimal discount will not affect capital gain on a sale.

Deferral of interest deduction and ordinary income at disposition if you borrow to buy or carry market discount bonds. If you do not elect to report the accrued market discount annually as interest income (see below for "Reporting discount annually"), and you took a loan to buy or carry a market discount bond, your interest deductions may be limited. If your interest expense exceeds the income earned on the bond (including OID income, if any), the excess may not be currently deducted to the extent of the market discount allocated to the days you held the bond during the year. The allocation of market discount is based on either the ratable accrual method or constant yield method; *see* below.

In the year you dispose of the bond, you may deduct the interest expenses that were disallowed in prior years because of the above limitations.

You may choose to deduct disallowed interest in a year before the year of disposition if you have net interest income from the bond. Net interest income is interest income for the year (including OID) less the interest expense incurred during the year to purchase or carry the bond. This election lets you deduct any disallowed interest expense to the extent it does not exceed the net interest income of that year. The balance of the disallowed interest expense is deductible in the year of disposition.

How to figure accrued market discount. If the election to report market discount annually is not made, gain on a market discount bond is taxed as ordinary interest income to the extent of the market discount accrued to the date of sale. There are two methods for figuring the accrued market discount. The basic method, called the ratable accrual method, is figured by dividing market discount by the number of days in the period from the date you bought the bond until the date of maturity. This daily amount is then multiplied by the number of days you held the bond to determine your accrued market discount; *see* Example 1 below.

Instead of using the ratable accrual method to compute accrual of market discount, you may elect to figure the accrued discount for any bond under an optional constant yield (economic accrual) method. If you make the election, you may not change it. The constant yield method initially provides a smaller accrual of market discount than the ratable method, but it is more complicated to figure. It is generally the same as the constant yield method used in IRS Publication 1212 to compute taxable OID *(4.19)*. For accruing market discount, treat your acquisition date as the original issue date and your basis for the market discount bond (immediately after you acquire it) as the issue price when applying the formula in Publication 1212.

Reporting discount annually. Rather than report market discount in the year you sell the bond, you may elect, in the year you acquire the bond, to report market discount currently as interest income. You may use either the ratable accrual method, as in Example 3 below, or the elective constant yield method discussed earlier. If you notified the payer that you are electing to report the market discount currently, the payer may include the annual accrued discount in Box 5 of Form 1099-OID. Attach to your timely filed return a statement that you are making the election and describe the method used to figure the accrued market discount. Your election to report annually applies to all market discount bonds that you later acquire. You may not revoke the election without IRS consent. If the election is made, the interest deduction deferral rule discussed earlier does not apply. Furthermore, the election could provide a tax advantage if you sell the bond at a profit and you can benefit from lower tax rates applied to net long-term capital gains.

Filing Instruction

Discount Bonds Held to Maturity

If you do not report the discount annually and hold a bond until maturity, the discount is reported as interest income in the year of redemption. However, you have the option of reporting the market discount annually instead of at sale.

EXAMPLES

1. You buy a taxable bond at a market discount of $200. There are 1,000 days between the date of your purchase and the maturity date. The daily accrual rate is 20 cents. You hold the bond for 600 days before selling it for a price exceeding what you paid for the bond. Under the ratable accrual method, up to $120 of your profit is market discount taxable as interest income (600 × $0.20).

2. You paid $9,100 for a $10,000 bond maturing in 2024. If you hold the bond to maturity, you will receive $10,000, giving you a gain of $900, equal to the market discount. The entire $900 market discount will be taxable as interest income in 2024 when the bond is redeemed.

3. In 2023, you buy a bond at a $200 discount. There are 1,000 days between the date of your purchase and the maturity date, so that daily accrual is 20 cents. You elect to report the market discount currently using the ratable accrual method. If you held the bond for 112 days in 2023, on your 2023 return you report $22 as interest income (112 × $0.20).

Partial principal payments. If the issuer of a bond (acquired by you after October 22, 1986) makes a partial payment of the principal (face amount) and you did not elect to report the discount annually, you must include the payment as ordinary interest income to the extent it does not exceed the accrued market discount on the bond. *See* IRS Publication 550 for options on determining accrued market discount. A taxable partial principal payment reduces the amount of remaining accrued market discount when figuring your tax on a later sale or receipt of another partial principal payment.

Market discount on a bond originally issued at a discount. A bond issued at original issue discount may later be acquired at a market discount because of an increase in interest rates. If you acquire at a market discount a bond with OID, the market discount is the excess of: (1) the issue price of the bond plus the total original issue discount includible in the gross income of all prior holders of the bond over (2) what you paid for the bond.

Exchanging a market discount bond in corporate mergers or reorganizations. If you hold a market discount bond and exchange it for another bond as part of a merger or other reorganization, the new bond is subject to the market discount rules when you sell it. However, under an exception, market discount rules will not apply to the new bond if the old market discount bond was issued before July 19, 1984, and the terms and interest rates of both bonds are identical.

4.21 Discount on Short-Term Obligations

Short-term obligations (maturity of a year or less from date of issue) may be purchased at a discount from face value. If you are on the cash basis, the discount on short-term obligations other than tax-exempt obligations must be reported as interest income in the year the obligations are sold or redeemed unless you elect to include the accrued discount in income currently.

EXAMPLE

In July 2022, you paid $970 for a short-term note with a face amount of $1,000. In January 2023, you received payment of $1,000 on the note. On your 2023 tax return, you report $30 as interest.

Discount must be currently reported by dealers and accrual-basis taxpayers. Discount allocable to the current year must be reported as income by accrual-basis taxpayers, dealers who sell short-term obligations in the course of business, banks, regulated investment companies, common trust funds, certain pass-through entities, and for obligations identified as part of a hedging transaction. Current reporting also applies to persons who separate or strip interest coupons from a bond and then retain the stripped bond or stripped coupon; the accrual rule applies to the retained obligation.

For short-term nongovernmental obligations, OID is generally taken into account instead of acquisition discount, but an election may be made to report the accrued acquisition discount. *See* IRS Publication 550 for details.

Basis in the obligation is increased by the amount of acquisition discount (or OID for nongovernmental obligations) that is currently reported as income.

Interest deduction limitation for cash-basis investors. A cash-basis investor who borrows funds to buy a short-term discount obligation may not fully deduct interest on the loan unless an election is made to report the accrued acquisition discount as income. If the election is not made, the interest you paid during the year is deductible only to the extent it exceeds (1) the portion of the discount allocated to the days you held the bond during the year, plus (2) the portion of interest not taxable for the year under your method of accounting. Any interest expense disallowed under this limitation is deductible in the year in which the obligation is disposed of.

The interest deduction limitation does not apply if you elect to include in income the accruable discount under the ratable accrual method or constant yield method *(4.20)*. The election applies to all short-term obligations acquired during the year and also in all later years.

Gain or loss on disposition of short-term obligations for cash-basis investors. If you have a gain on the sale or exchange of a discounted short-term governmental obligation (other than tax-exempt local obligations), the gain is ordinary income to the extent of the ratable share of the acquisition discount received when you bought the obligation. Follow the computation shown in the discussion of Treasury bills *(4.27)* to figure this ordinary income portion. Any gain over this ordinary income portion is short-term capital gain; a loss would be a short-term capital loss.

Gain on short-term nongovernmental obligations is treated as ordinary income up to the ratable share of OID. The formula for figuring this ordinary income portion is similar to the formula for short-term governmental obligations *(4.27)*, except that the denominator of the fraction is days from original issue to maturity, rather than days from acquisition. A constant yield method may also be elected to figure the ordinary income portion. Gain above the computed ordinary income amount is short-term capital gain *(Chapter 5)*. For more information, *see* IRS Publication 550.

4.22 Stripped Coupon Bonds and Stock

Brokers holding coupon bonds may separate or strip the coupons from the bonds and sell the bonds or coupons to investors. Examples include zero-coupon instruments sold by brokerage houses that are backed by U.S. Treasury bonds.

The U.S. Treasury also offers its version of zero coupon instruments, with the name STRIPS, which are available from brokers and banks.

Brokers holding preferred stock may strip the dividend rights from the stock and sell the stripped stock to investors.

If you buy a stripped bond or coupon, the spread between the cost of the bond or coupon and its higher face amount is treated as original issue discount (OID). This means that you annually report a part of the spread as interest income. For a stripped bond, the

Filing Tip

Discount on Short-Term Government Obligations

For short-term governmental obligations (other than tax-exempts), the acquisition discount is accrued in daily installments under the ratable method, unless an election is made to use the constant yield method.

Caution

Recomputing Form 1099-OID Amount

Do not report the amount shown in Box 1 of Form 1099-OID for a stripped bond or coupon; that amount must be recomputed under complicated rules described in IRS Publication 1212. *See 4.19* for reporting the recomputed OID on your return.

Caution

Reporting Zero Coupon Bond Discount

Zero coupon bond discount is reported annually as interest over the life of the bond, even though interest is not received. This tax cost tends to make zero coupon bonds unattractive to investors, unless the bonds can be bought for IRA and other retirement plans that defer tax on income until distributions are made.

The value of zero coupon bonds fluctuates sharply with interest rate changes. This fact should be considered before investing in long-term zero coupon bonds. If you sell zero coupon bonds before the maturity term at a time when interest rates rise, you may lose part of your investment.

amount of the original issue discount is the difference between the stated redemption price of the bond at maturity and the cost of the bond. For a stripped coupon, the amount of the discount is the difference between the amount payable on the due date of the coupon and the cost of the coupon. The rules for figuring the amount of OID *(4.19)* to be reported annually are in IRS Publication 1212.

If you strip a coupon bond, interest accrual and allocation rules prevent you from creating a tax loss on a sale of the bond or coupons. You are required to report interest accrued up to the date of the sale and also add the amount to the basis of the bond. If you acquired the obligation after October 22, 1986, you must also include in income any market discount that accrued before the date you sold the stripped bond or coupons. The method of accrual depends on the date you bought the obligation; *see* IRS Publication 1212. The accrued market discount is also added to the basis of the bond. You then allocate this basis between the bond and the coupons. The allocation is based on the relative fair market values of the bond and coupons at the date of sale. Gain or loss on the sale is the difference between the sales price of the stripped item (bond or coupons) and its allocated basis. Furthermore, the original issue discount rules apply to the stripped item which you keep (bond or coupon). Original issue discount for this purpose is the difference between the basis allocated to the retained item and the redemption price of the bond (if retained) or the amount payable on the coupons (if retained). You must annually report a ratable portion of the discount.

4.23 Sale or Retirement of Bonds and Notes

Gain or loss on the sale, redemption, or retirement of debt obligations issued by a government or corporation is generally capital gain or loss.

A redemption or retirement of a bond at maturity must be reported as a sale on Form 8949 and Schedule D of Form 1040 or 1040-SR *(5.8)* although there may be no gain or loss realized.

The accrued amount of OID is reported annually as interest income *(4.19)* and added to basis; this includes the accrued OID for the year the bond is sold. If the bonds are sold or redeemed before maturity, you realize capital gain for the proceeds over the adjusted basis (as increased by accrued OID) of the bond, provided there was no intention to call the bond before maturity. If at the time of original issue there was an intention to call the obligation before maturity, the entire OID that has not yet been included in your income is taxable as ordinary income; the balance is capital gain.

Market discount on bonds is taxable under the rules in *4.20*.

> **EXAMPLE**
>
> On February 6, 2021, you bought a 10-year, 5% corporate bond at original issue for $7,600. If you hold the bond to maturity, you will receive $10,000 (the stated redemption price). At the time of original issue, there was no intention to call the bond before maturity. You sold the bond for $9,040 on February 10, 2023. Assume that for 2021, 2022, and the period in 2023 prior to the sale, you accrue $334 of OID, which you report as interest income on your 2021–2023 returns. Your basis in the bond is increased by the accrued OID to $7,934 ($7,600 + $334). On the sale, you have a long-term capital gain of $1,106 ($9,040 − $7,934).
>
> If at original issue there had been an intention to call the bond before maturity, a gain of up to $2,066 (total OID of $2,400 ($10,000 − $7,600) minus $334 of OID reported as interest income) would be taxed as ordinary income. Since this is more than the actual gain of $1,106, the entire $1,106 is ordinary income.

Tax-exempts. *See 4.26* for discount on tax-exempt bonds.

Obligations issued by individuals. If you hold an individual's note for over $10,000, accrued OID must be reported annually *(4.19)* and added to basis, unless the note was issued before March 2, 1984. Gain on your sale of the note is subject to the rules discussed above for corporate and government OID bonds.

If the note is $10,000 or less (when combined with other prior outstanding loans from the same individual), OID is not reported annually provided you are not a professional lender and tax avoidance was not a principal purpose of the loan. On a sale of the note at a gain, your ratable share of the OID is taxed as ordinary income; any balance is capital gain. A loss is a capital loss.

4.24   State and City Interest Generally Tax Exempt

Generally, you pay no federal tax on interest on bonds or notes of states, cities, counties, the District of Columbia, or a possession of the United States. This includes bonds or notes of port authorities, toll road commissions, utility services activities, community redevelopment agencies, and similar bodies created for public purposes. Bonds issued after June 30, 1983, must be in registered form for the interest to be tax exempt. Interest on federally guaranteed obligations is generally taxable, but *see* exceptions in *4.25*.

Check with the issuer of the bond to verify the tax-exempt status of the interest.

Tax-exempt interest must be reported on your return. If you are required to file a federal return, you must report the amount of your tax-exempt interest although it is not taxable. On Form 1040 or 1040-SR, you list the tax-exempt interest on Line 2a.

Private activity bonds. Interest on so-called private activity bonds is generally taxable *(4.25)*, but there are certain exceptions. For example, interest on the following "qualified bonds" is tax exempt even if the bond may technically be in the category of private activity bonds: qualified student loan bonds; exempt facility bonds, including New York Liberty bonds, Gulf Opportunity Zone bonds, Midwestern disaster and Hurricane Ike area bonds, and enterprise zone facility bonds; qualified small issue bonds; qualified mortgage bonds and qualified veterans' mortgage bonds; qualified redevelopment bonds; and qualified 501(c)(3) bonds issued by charitable organizations and hospitals. Check with the issuer for the tax status of a private activity bond.

AMT treatment. Tax-exempt interest on qualified private activity bonds issued after August 7, 1986 and before 2009, or on bonds issued after 2010, is generally treated as a tax preference item subject to alternative minimum tax (AMT, *23.2*), but there are exceptions. The AMT does not apply to interest on qualified 501(c)(3) bonds, New York Liberty bonds, Gulf Opportunity Zone bonds, Midwestern disaster and Hurricane Ike disaster area bonds, and exempt facility, qualified mortgage, and qualified veterans' bonds issued after July 30, 2008.

4.25   Taxable State and City Interest

Interest on certain state and city obligations is taxable. These taxable obligations include federally guaranteed obligations, mortgage subsidy bonds, private activity bonds, and arbitrage bonds.

Federally guaranteed obligations. Interest on state and local obligations issued after April 14, 1983, is generally taxable if the obligation is federally guaranteed, but there are exceptions allowing tax exemptions for obligations guaranteed by the Federal Housing Administration, Department of Veterans Affairs, Bonneville Power Authority, Federal Home Loan Mortgage Corporation, Federal National Mortgage Association, Government National Mortgage Corporation, Resolution Funding Corporation, and Student Loan Marketing Association.

Mortgage revenue bonds. Interest on bonds issued by a state or local government after April 24, 1979, may not be tax exempt if funds raised by the bonds are used to finance home mortgages. There are exceptions for certain qualified mortgage bonds and veterans' bonds. Check on the tax-exempt status of mortgage bonds with the issuing authority.

Private activity bonds. Generally, a private activity bond is any bond where more than 10% of the issue's proceeds are used by a private business whose property secures the issue, or if at least 5% of the proceeds (or $5 million if less) are used for loans to parties other than governmental units. Interest on such bonds is generally taxable, but there are exceptions *(4.24)*. Check on the tax status of the bonds with the issuing authority.

 *Filing Tip*

Private Activity Bond Interest Exempt from AMT

The interest on any qualified private activity bond issued in 2009 or 2010 is not subject to AMT *(23.2)*.

4.26   Tax-Exempt Bonds Bought at a Discount

Original issue discount (OID) on tax-exempt obligations is not taxable, and on a sale or redemption, gain attributed to OID is tax exempt. Gain attributed to market discount is capital gain or ordinary income depending on whether the bond was purchased before May 1, 1993, or on or after that date; *see* below.

Original issue discount tax-exempt bond. This arises when a bond is issued for a price less than the face amount of the bond. The discount is considered tax-exempt interest. Thus, if you are the original buyer and hold the bond to maturity, the entire amount of the discount is tax free. On a disposition of a tax-exempt bond issued after September 3, 1982, and acquired after March 1, 1984, you must add to basis accrued OID before determining gain or loss. OID must generally be accrued using a constant yield method; *see* IRS Publication 1212.

Market discount tax-exempts. A market discount arises when a bond originally issued at not less than par is bought at below par because its market value has declined. If before May 1, 1993, you bought at a market discount a tax-exempt bond which you sell for a price exceeding your purchase price, the excess is capital gain. If the bond was held long term, the gain is long term. A redemption of the bond at a price exceeding your purchase price is similarly treated.

However, for market discount tax-exempt bonds purchased after April 30, 1993, market discount is treated as ordinary income *(4.20)*. If you do not report the accrued market discount as taxable interest income each year you own the bond, any gain when you sell the bond is treated as interest income to the extent of the market discount *(4.20)*.

Stripped tax-exempt obligations. OID is not currently taxed on a stripped tax-exempt bond or stripped coupon from the bond if you bought it before June 11, 1987. However, for any stripped bond or coupon you bought or sold after October 22, 1986, OID must be accrued and added to basis for purposes of figuring gain or loss on a disposition. Furthermore, if you bought the stripped bond or coupon after June 10, 1987, part of the OID may be taxable; *see* Publication 1212 for figuring the tax-free portion.

4.27   Treasury Bills, Notes, and Bonds

Interest on securities issued by the federal government is fully taxable on your federal return. However, interest on federal obligations is not subject to state or local income taxes. Interest on Treasury bills, notes, and bonds is reported on Form 1099-INT.

Treasury bonds and notes. Treasury notes have maturities of two, three, five, seven or 10 years. Treasury bonds have maturities of 30 years. Interest on notes and bonds is paid every six months and is taxable when received on your federal return. Treasury bonds and notes are capital assets; gain or loss on their sale, exchange, or redemption is reported as capital gain or loss on Form 8949 and Schedule D *(Chapter 5)*. If you purchased a federal obligation below par (at a discount), *see 4.19* for the rules on reporting original issue discount. If you purchased a Treasury bond or note above par (at a premium), you may elect to amortize the premium *(4.17)*. If you do not elect to amortize and you hold the bond or note to maturity, you have a capital loss.

Treasury inflation-protected securities (TIPS). These pay interest semiannually at a fixed rate on a principal amount that is adjusted to take into account inflation or deflation. The interest is taxable when received and any increase in the inflation-adjusted principal amount while you hold the bond must be reported as original issue discount (OID) *(4.19)*. Your basis in the bond is increased by the OID included in income. On a sale or redemption before maturity, any gain is generally capital gain, but if there was an intention to call before maturity, gain is ordinary income to the extent of the previously unreported OID *(4.23)*.

Treasury bills. These are short-term U.S. obligations with maturities of four weeks, 13 weeks, 26 weeks, or 52 weeks. On a bill held to maturity, you report as interest income the difference between the discounted price and the amount you receive on a redemption of the bills at maturity.

Interest on United States Savings Bonds

Treasury bills are capital assets and a loss on a disposition before maturity is taxed as a capital loss. If you are a cash-basis taxpayer and have a gain on a sale or exchange, ordinary income is realized up to the amount of the ratable share of the discount received when you bought the obligation. This amount is treated as interest income and is figured as follows:

$$\frac{\text{Days T-bill was held}}{\text{Days from acquisition to maturity}} \times \begin{array}{c}\text{Acquisition discount (redemption value}\\\text{at maturity } \textit{minus} \text{ your cost)}\end{array}$$

Any gain over this amount is capital gain; *see* the Example below. Instead of using the above fractional computation for figuring the ordinary income portion of the gain, an election may be made to apply the constant yield method. This method follows the OID computation rules shown in IRS Publication 1212 for obligations issued after 1984, except that the acquisition cost of the Treasury bill would be treated as the issue price in applying the Publication 1212 formula.

Planning Reminder

Tax Deferral: T-Bill Maturing Next Year

If you are a cash-basis taxpayer, you may postpone the tax on Treasury bill interest by selecting a Treasury bill maturing next year. Income is not recognized until the date on which the Treasury bill is paid at maturity, unless it has been sold or otherwise disposed of earlier.

> **EXAMPLE**
>
> You buy at original issue a 26-week $10,000 Treasury bill (182-day maturity) for $9,900. You sell it 95 days later for $9,950. Your entire $50 gain ($9,950 – $9,900) is taxed as interest income as it is less than the $52 treated as interest income under the ratable daily formula:
>
> $$\frac{95 \text{ days held}}{182 \text{ days from acquisition to maturity}} \times \quad \$100 \text{ discount} = \$52$$

Accrual-basis taxpayers and dealers who are required to currently report the acquisition discount element of Treasury bills using either the ratable accrual method or the constant yield method *(4.20)* do not apply the above formula on a sale before maturity. In figuring gain or loss, the discount included as income is added to basis.

Interest deduction limitation. Interest incurred on loans used to buy Treasury bills is deductible by a cash-basis investor only to the extent that interest expenses exceed the following: (1) the portion of the acquisition discount allocated to the days you held the bond during the year; and (2) the portion of interest not taxable for the year under your method of accounting. The deferred interest expense is deductible in the year the bill is disposed of. If an election is made to report the acquisition discount as current income under the rules for governmental obligations *(4.21)*, the interest expense may also be deducted currently. The election applies to all future acquisitions.

4.28 Interest on United States Savings Bonds

Savings Bond Tables: The *e-Supplement* at *jklasser.com* will contain redemption tables showing the 2023 year-end values of Series EE bonds and Series I bonds.

EE Bonds. Series EE bonds may be cashed for what you paid for them plus an increase in their value over their 30-year maturity period. *See* the discussion of the interest accrual and redemption rules for Series EE Savings Bonds *(30.12)*.

The increase in redemption value is taxable as interest, but you do not have to report the increase in value each year on your federal return. You may defer *(4.29)* the interest income until the year in which you cash the bond or the year in which the bond finally matures, whichever is earlier. But if you want, you may report the annual increase by merely including it on your tax return. If you use the accrual method of reporting, you must include the interest each year as it accrues. Savings bond interest is not subject to state or local taxes.

If you initially choose to defer the reporting of interest and later want to switch to annual reporting, you may do so. You may also change from the annual reporting method to the deferral method. *See 4.29* for rules on changing reporting methods.

Dividend and Interest Income | **101**

Election for Children Not Subject to Kiddie Tax

If your child has net investment income under the annual threshold ($2,500 for 2023) for the kiddie tax *(24.2)*, making the election to report the interest annually may be advisable. For example, a dependent child may claim a standard deduction for 2023 of at least $1,250 *(13.5)*. If the election to report the savings bond interest currently was made for 2023, up to $1,250 of the interest would be offset by the standard deduction, assuming the child had no other income.

Filing Tip

Form 1099-INT When Savings Bond Is Cashed

When you cash in an EE or I bond, you receive Form 1099-INT that lists as interest the difference between the amount received and the amount paid for the bond. The form may show more taxable interest than you are required to report because you have regularly reported the interest or a prior owner reported the interest. Report the full amount shown on Form 1099-INT on Schedule B (Form 1040 or 1040-SR), along with your other interest income. Enter a subtotal of the total interest and then, on a separate line, reduce the subtotal by the savings bond interest that was previously reported and identify the reduction as "Previously Reported U.S. Savings Bond Interest." The interest is exempt from state and local taxes.

Series I bonds. "I bonds" are inflation-indexed bonds issued at face amount *(30.13)*. As with EE bonds, you may defer the interest income (the increase in redemption value each year is interest) until the year in which the bond is redeemed or matures in 30 years, whichever is earlier *(4.29)*.

Education funding. If you buy EE or I bonds to pay for educational expenses and you defer the reporting of interest *(4.29)*, you may be able to exclude the accumulated interest from income when you redeem the bonds to pay for higher education *(33.4)*.

Bonds registered only in name of child. Interest on U.S. savings bonds bought for and registered in the name of a child will be taxed to the child, even if the parent paid for the bonds and is named as beneficiary. Unless an election is made to report the increases in redemption value annually, the accumulated interest will be taxable to the child in the year he or she redeems the bond, or if earlier, when the bond finally matures. The kiddie tax *(24.2)* may apply to a portion of the annually reported interest or to interest on redeemed bonds. For example, if a child under age 18 has 2023 investment income over $2,500, the kiddie tax applies *(24.2)*. To avoid kiddie tax, savings bond interest may be deferred *(4.29)*.

Bonds must be reissued to make gift. Assume you have bought I or EE bonds and had them registered in joint names of yourself and your daughter. The law of your state provides that jointly owned property may be transferred to a co-owner by delivery or possession. You deliver the bonds to your daughter and tell her they now belong to her alone. According to Treasury regulations, this is not a valid gift of the bonds. The bonds must be surrendered and reissued in your daughter's name. For the year of reissue, you must include in your income all of the interest earned on the bonds other than interest you previously reported.

If you do not have the bonds reissued and you die, the bonds are taxable to your estate. Ownership of the bonds is a matter of contract between the United States and the bond purchaser. The bonds are nontransferable. A valid gift cannot be accomplished by manual delivery to a donee unless the bonds also are surrendered and registered in the donee's name in accordance with Treasury regulations.

Series E bonds. There are no Series E bonds still earning interest. The last E bonds, those issued in June 1980, reached final maturity in June 2010, 30 years from the date of issue.

Series HH. These bonds were available after 1979 and before September 1, 2004, in exchange for E or EE bonds, or for Freedom Shares. They were issued at face value and pay semiannual interest that is taxable when received. They mature in 20 years.

Series H. These bonds were available before 1980 and they reached final maturity 30 years later. If you obtained Series H bonds in an exchange for Series E bonds, and you did not report the E bond interest annually, the accumulated interest on the E bonds became taxable when the H bonds were redeemed or, if earlier, when the H bonds reached final maturity 30 years from issue.

4.29 Deferring United States Savings Bond Interest

You do not have to make a special election on your tax return in order to defer the interest on Series EE or I savings bonds. You may simply postpone reporting the interest until the year you redeem the bond or the year in which it reaches final maturity, whichever is earlier. If you choose to defer the interest, you may decide in a later year to begin reporting the increase in redemption value each year as interest, but this election applies to all the EE and I bonds you own. You may also switch from annual reporting to the deferral method. You must use the same method—deferral or annual reporting—for all of your EE and I bonds. These options are discussed in this section.

Changing from deferral to annual reporting. If you have deferred reporting of interest (the annual increases in redemption value) and want to change to annual reporting starting with your 2023 return, you must report on your 2023 return all interest accrued through 2023 on all your EE and I bonds. Then, starting in 2024, you report the interest accruing each year on all of your bonds, including bonds you acquired after the 2023 election.

Suppose you do not change from the deferral method to the annual method on your 2023 return and later wish you had. If the due date of the return has passed, it is too late to make the election. You may not file an amended return for 2023 to report the accrued interest. You have to wait until next year's return to make the election.

Changing from annual reporting to deferral. If you have been reporting annual increases in redemption value as interest income, you may change your method and elect to defer interest reporting until the bonds mature or are redeemed. You make the election by attaching a statement to your federal income tax return for the year of the change; *see* IRS Publication 550 for details.

Co-Owners. How to report interest on a Series EE or I bond depends on how it was bought or issued:

1. You paid for the entire bond: Either you or the co-owner may redeem it. You are taxed on all the interest, even though the co-owner cashes the bond and you receive no proceeds. If the other co-owner does cash in the bond, he or she will receive a Form 1099-INT reporting the accumulated interest. However, since that interest is taxable to you, the co-owner should give you a nominee Form 1099-INT, as explained in the rules for joint accounts in *4.12*.

2. You paid for only part of the bond: Either of you may redeem it. You are taxed on that part of the interest which is in proportion to your share of the purchase price. This is so even though you do not receive the proceeds.

3. You paid for part of the bond, and then had it reissued in another's name. You pay tax only on the interest accrued while you held the bond. The new co-owner picks up his or her share of the interest accruing afterwards.

Changing the form of registration. Changing the form of registration of an I or EE bond may result in tax. Assume you use your own funds to purchase a bond issued in your name, payable on your death to your son. Later, at your request, a new bond is issued in your son's name only. The increased value of the original bond up to the date it was redeemed and reissued in your son's name is taxed to you as interest income.

As shown in the Examples below, certain changes in registration do not result in an immediate tax.

Transfer to a spouse. If you have been deferring interest on U.S. Savings Bonds, and then you transfer them to your spouse or ex-spouse as part of a divorce-related property settlement, you will be taxed on the interest deferred before the transfer date *(6.7)*.

Transfer to a trust. If you transfer U.S. Savings Bonds to a trust giving up all rights of ownership, you are taxed on the accumulated interest to date of transfer. If, however, you are considered to be the owner of the trust and the interest earned before and after the transfer is taxable to you, you may continue to defer reporting the interest.

Transfer to a charity. Tax on the accumulated interest is not avoided by having the bonds reissued to a philanthropy. The IRS held that by having the bonds reissued in the philanthropy's name, the owner realized taxable income on the accumulated bond interest.

 *Caution*

E Bonds and Certain EE Bonds No Longer Earn Interest

All E bonds have reached final maturity and no longer earn interest. EE bonds stop earning interest when they reach final maturity, 30 years from their issue date *(30.12)*. All deferred interest is taxable in the year of final maturity.

 *Filing Tip*

Deduction for Estate Tax Paid on Interest

Where federal estate tax has been paid on bond interest accrued during the owner's lifetime, the new bondholder may claim the allocable estate tax as an "other" itemized deduction in the year that he or she reports the accumulated interest (depending on whether the election to defer reporting is made or it is reported annually) *(19.1)*.

EXAMPLES

1. Jones buys an EE bond and has it registered in his name and in the name of his son as co-owner. Jones has the bonds reissued solely in his own name; he is not required to report the accumulated interest at that time.

2. You and your spouse each contributed an equal amount toward the purchase of a $1,000 EE bond, which was issued to you as co-owners. You later have the bond reissued as two $500 bonds, one in your name and one in your spouse's name. Neither of you has to report the interest earned to the date of reissue. But if you bought the $1,000 bond entirely with your own funds, you report half the interest earned to the date of reissue.

3. You add another person's name as co-owner to facilitate a transfer of the bond on death. The change in registration does not result in a tax.

Transfer of savings bond at death. If an owner does not report the bond interest annually and dies before redeeming the bond, the income tax liability on the interest accumulated during the deceased's lifetime becomes the liability of the person who acquires the bond, unless an election is made to report the accrued interest in the decedent's final income tax return *(1.14)*. If the election is not made on the decedent's final return, the new owner may choose to report the accumulated interest annually, or defer reporting it until the bond is redeemed or reaches final maturity, whichever is earlier. If the election is made on the decedent's final return, the new owner is taxable only on interest earned after the date of death.

4.30 Minimum Interest Rules

The law requires a minimum rate of interest to be charged on loan transactions unless a specific exception covers the transaction. Where minimum interest is not charged, the law imputes interest as if the parties agreed to the charge.

The rules are complicated and have been subject to several revisions. There are different minimum interest rates and reporting rules depending on the nature of the transaction. The following discussion provides the important details for understanding the rules. For specific cases and computations, we suggest that you consult IRS regulations for details not covered in this book.

There are two broad classes of transactions:

Loans. These are generally covered by Internal Revenue Code Section 7872. Below-market or low-rate interest loans are discussed in *4.31*.

Seller-financed sales of property. These are covered by either Internal Revenue Code Section 1274 or Section 483. Seller-financed sales are discussed in *4.32*. If parties fail to charge the minimum required interest rate, the same minimum rate is imputed by law.

4.31 Interest-Free or Below-Market-Interest Loans

For many years, the IRS tried to tax interest-free or below-market-interest loans. However, court decisions had supported taxpayers who argued that such loans did not result in taxable income or gifts. To reverse these decisions, the IRS convinced Congress to pass a law imposing tax on interest-free or low-interest loans made by individuals and businesses. If you make an interest-free or low-interest loan to a relative, you may have to report imputed interest income that you do not actually receive ("phantom income"), and also be subject to gift tax, although there are exceptions that shield many gift loans from the imputed interest rules; *see* below for the $10,000 and $100,000 gift loan exceptions.

How the imputed interest rules work. If interest at least equal to the applicable federal rate set by the IRS is not charged, the law generally treats a below-market-interest loan as two transactions:

1. The law assumes that the lender has transferred to the borrower an amount equal to the "foregone" interest element of the loan. In the case of a loan between individuals, such as a parent and child, the lender is. technically subject to gift tax on this interest element, but it is unlikely the tax will apply because of the annual gift tax exclusion. In the case of a stockholder borrowing from a company, the element is a taxable dividend. In the case of a loan made to an employee, it is taxable pay.

   Note: For gift tax purposes *(39.2)*, a term loan is treated as if the lender gave the borrower the excess of the amount of the loan over the present value of payments due during the loan term. Demand loans are treated as if the lender gave the borrower annually the amount of the foregone interest.

2. The law assumes that imputed interest equal to the applicable federal rate is paid by the borrower to the lender, who must report it as interest income. In other words, the lender must report as income an amount (the imputed interest) that is not actually received. Until recently the applicable federal rate had been very low, so the taxable imputed interest was generally minimal. This may change if inflation continues to rise. Also, the borrower may be able to claim a deduction for the interest if the loan is used to buy a home and the loan is secured by the residence *(15.1)*, or the loan is used to buy investment property *(15.9)*.

With gift loans and demand loans between individuals, the above transfers between the lender and borrower are treated as made on the last day of the borrower's taxable year.

An IRS "blended annual rate" may be used to figure the imputed interest on certain demand loans; *see* below.

Blended annual rate for demand loans. Where a demand loan is in effect for the entire calendar year, a "blended annual rate" issued by the IRS to simplify reporting may be used to compute the imputed interest. For 2023, the blended rate is 4.65%. The blended rate may be used for a gift loan to an individual or for a business loan, such as an interest-free loan to an employee, so long as it is payable on demand and is of a fixed principal amount that remains outstanding for the entire calendar year. If the loan was not outstanding for the entire year or if the loan balance fluctuated, the regular imputed interest rules apply, as the blended rate is not available.

Charging the applicable federal rate avoids the imputed interest rules. Gift loans qualifying for the $10,000 and $100,000 exceptions (below) are not subject to imputed interest rules. For other loans, the rules imputing income to you as the lender may be avoided by charging interest at least equal to the applicable federal rate. Applicable federal rates are set by the IRS monthly and published in the Internal Revenue Bulletin; you can also get the rates from your local IRS office. For a term loan, the applicable federal rate is the one in effect as of the day on which the loan is made, compounded semiannually. The short-term rate applies to loans of three years or less; the mid-term rate to loans over three and up to nine years; the long-term rate applies to loans over nine years. These are the same rates as for seller-financed sales; *see Table 4-1* below.

For a demand loan, the applicable federal rate is the short-term rate in effect at the start of each semiannual period (January and July).

Different computations for different types of loans. There are two general classes of loans: (1) Gift loans, whether term or demand, and nongift demand loans, and (2) nongift term loans.

The distinction is important for figuring and reporting imputed interest. For example, in the case of nongift term loans, the imputed interest element is treated as original issue discount *(4.19)*.

Gift loans and nongift loans payable on demand. As a lender, you are taxable on the "foregone interest," that is, the interest that you would have received had you charged interest at the applicable federal rate *(see above)* over any interest actually charged. The borrower may be able to claim an interest deduction if the funds are used to buy investment property *(15.9)*.

Nongift term loans. A term loan is any loan not payable on demand. As a lender of a nongift term loan, you are taxable on any excess of the loan principal over the present value of all payments due under the loan. The excess is treated as original issue (OID) which you report annually as interest income *(4.19)*.

Reporting imputed interest. Imputed interest is generally treated as transferred by the lender to the borrower and retransferred by the borrower to the lender on December 31 in the calendar year of imputation and is reported under the regular accounting method of the borrower and lender.

> **EXAMPLE**
>
> On January 1, 2023, Jones Company makes a $200,000 interest-free demand loan to Frank, an executive. The loan remains outstanding for the entire 2023 calendar year. Jones Company has a taxable year ending September 30. Frank is a calendar year taxpayer. For 2023 the imputed compensation payment to Frank and the imputed interest payment to the corporation are treated as made on December 31, 2023.

Certain Loans Are Exempt From Imputed Interest Rules

The $10,000 exception for gift loans. In the case of a gift loan to an individual, no interest is imputed to any day on which the aggregate outstanding amount of all loans between the parties is $10,000 or less, provided the loan is not attributed to the purchase or carrying of income-producing assets. If the exception applies, there are no income tax or gift tax consequences to the loan.

 *Planning Reminder*

Gift Loans up to $100,000

If you give a child or other individual an interest-free or below-market-interest loan, such as to buy a home or start a business, the amount of interest imputed to you may be limited or completely avoided provided (1) the total outstanding loan balance owed to you by the borrower at all times during the year does not exceed $100,000, and (2) avoidance of federal tax is not a principal purpose of the interest arrangement.

If the above tests are met, and the borrower's net investment income is $1,000 or less, there is no imputed interest. The imputed amount cannot exceed the borrower's net investment income and net investment income of $1,000 or less is treated as zero.

The $100,000 gift loan exception. No interest is imputed on an interest-free or low-interest loan to an individual of up to $100,000 if the borrower's net investment income is $1,000 or less. Under the exception, imputed interest cannot exceed the borrower's net investment income, and net investment income of $1,000 or less is treated as zero; *see* the following Example. The exception applies only if avoiding federal tax is not a main purpose of the interest arrangement.

> **EXAMPLE**
>
> On January 1, 2023, you make a $100,000 interest-free loan to your son, payable on demand, which he uses for a down payment on a home. This is the only outstanding loan between you and your son. Your son's net investment income for 2023 is $650. Since the loan does not exceed $100,000, and your son's net investment income does not exceed $1,000, you do not have to report the "foregone interest" as interest income. Under the $100,000 gift loan exception, imputed interest is limited to the borrower's net investment income and net investment income of $1,000 or less is treated as zero.
>
> If your son's net investment income were $2,650 instead of $650, you would have to report the foregone interest as imputed interest income. Using the IRS blended annual rate for 2023 of 4.65%, the imputed interest would be $4,650 ($100,000 × 4.65%), which you must report as interest income for 2023 since it is well below your son's net investment income of $2,650.
>
> For gift tax purposes, the foregone interest is a taxable gift. Using the IRS blended annual rate, the foregone interest of $4,650 ($100,000 × 4.65%) is a taxable gift, but if this was your only gift to your son in 2023, there would be no gift tax, and you would not have to file a gift tax return because of the annual gift tax exclusion of $17,000 per donee *(39.2)*.

Exceptions for compensation-related loans. For compensation-related and corporate-shareholder loans, the imputed interest rules do not apply to any day on which the total amount of outstanding loans between the parties is $10,000 or less, provided the principal purpose of the loan is not tax avoidance. Certain low-interest loans given to employees by employers to buy a new residence in a new job location are exempt from the imputed interest requirements.

Exception for loans to continuing care facilities. If you pay a refundable fee when moving into a qualified continuing care facility under a continuing care contract (as defined in Code Section 7872(h)), the fee is not treated as a "loan" subject to the imputed interest rules if you or your spouse is age 62 or older at the end of the year.

4.32 Minimum Interest on Seller-Financed Sales

The law requires minimum interest charges for seller-financed sales. Generally, interest at the applicable federal rate (AFR) must be charged; *see Table 4-1* for AFR rules. If the AFR is not charged, the IRS imputes interest based on the AFR, requiring both buyer and seller to treat part of the purchase price as interest even though it is not called interest in the sales contract. For example, investment property is sold on the installment basis for $100,000 and the parties fail to charge adequate interest. Assume the IRS imputes interest of $2,000. For tax purposes, $98,000 is allocated to the sale of the property and the principal amount of the debt; the balance is imputed interest of $2,000, taxable to the seller and deductible by the buyer if allowed under the rules of *Chapter 15*.

Two statute classes. The minimum or imputed interest rules are covered by two Internal Revenue Code statutes: Sections 1274 and 483. Under both, the same minimum interest rates apply but the timing of interest reporting is different, as discussed below.

Section 483 applies to any payment due more than six months after the date of sale under a contract which calls for some or all payments more than one year after the date of sale. If the sales price cannot exceed $3,000, Section 483 does not apply. Transactions within Section 483 are sales or exchanges of: (1) principal residences; (2) any property if

 *Caution*

Buyer's Personal-Use Property

If adequate interest is not charged on an installment sale of personal-use property, such as a residence to be used by the buyer, imputed interest rules do not apply to the buyer. Thus, the buyer may not deduct the imputed interest. The buyer's deduction is limited to the payment of interest stated in the contract if a deduction is allowed under the home mortgage interest rules in *Chapter 15*.

total payments, including interest and any other consideration to be received by the seller, cannot exceed $250,000; (3) farms if the total price is $1 million or less; and (4) sales of land between family members to the extent the aggregate sales price of all sales between the same parties in the same year is $500,000 or less.

If the selling price exceeds the respective $250,000, $1 million, or $500,000 amount listed in (2) through (4) above, the sale is subject to Section 1274 reporting rules provided some or all payments are due more than six months after the date of sale. Section 1274 also applies to all other transactions where neither the debt instrument nor the property being sold is publicly traded as long as some payments are deferred more than six months.

Timing of interest reporting. One important practical difference between the two statutes covering minimum interest involves the timing of the reporting and deducting of interest.

Under Section 483, a seller and lender use their regular reporting method for imputed interest. For a cash-basis seller, interest is taxed when received; a cash-basis buyer deducts interest when paid if a deduction is allowable. However, if too much interest is allocated to a payment period, the excess interest is treated as prepaid interest, and the deduction is postponed to the year or years interest is earned. Section 483 also describes imputed interest as unstated interest.

Under Section 1274, the interest element is generally reported by both buyer and seller according to the OID accrual rules, even if they otherwise report on the cash basis. Where the seller financing does not exceed an annual threshold ($4,810,600 for a 2023 sale), the parties can elect the cash method to report the interest regardless of the OID and accrual rules if: (1) the seller-lender is on a cash-basis method and is not a dealer of the property sold and (2) the seller and buyer jointly elect to use the cash method. The cash-basis election binds any cash-basis successor of the buyer or seller. If the lender transfers his interest to an accrual-basis taxpayer, the election no longer applies; interest is thereafter taxed under the accrual method rules. The OID rules also do not apply to a cash basis buyer of personal-use property; here, the cash basis debtor deducts only payments of interest required by the contract, assuming a deduction is allowed under the home mortgage rules discussed in *Chapter 15*.

Figuring applicable federal rate (AFR). There is no imputed interest if the sales contract provides for interest that is at least equal to the AFR. *See Table 4-1* above for determining the AFR.

Assumptions of loans. The imputed interest rules of Sections 1274 and 483 do not generally apply to debt instruments assumed as part of a sale or exchange, or if the property is taken subject to the debt, provided that neither the terms of the debt instrument nor the nature of the transactions are changed.

Important: In planning deferred or installment sales, review Treasury regulations to the Internal Revenue Code Sections 483 and 1274 for further examples and details.

Table 4-1   Minimum Interest Rate for Seller Financing

Type—	Description—
Applicable federal rates	The IRS determines applicable federal rates (AFRs) and publishes them in a Revenue Ruling at the beginning of each month in the Internal Revenue Bulletin; an index of AFRs by month can be found at https://apps.irs.gov/app/picklist/list/federalRates.html. There are three AFRs depending on the length of the contract: • Short-term AFR—A term of three years or less. • Mid-term AFR—A term of over three years but not over nine years. • Long-term AFR—A term of over nine years. The imputed interest rules do not apply if the interest rate provided for in the sales contract is at least the lesser of (1) the lowest AFR in effect during the three-month period ending with the month in which a binding written sales contract is entered into, or (2) the lowest AFR in effect during the three-month period ending with the month of sale. Prior to 2023, the AFRs were extremely low but they have increased with inflation. If insufficient interest is charged, the total unstated interest is allocated to payments under an OID computation.
9% safe harbor rate	If seller financing does not exceed an annual limit, the minimum required interest is the lower of 9% compounded semiannually and the applicable federal rate (AFR; *see* above for the term-based AFRs). For sales in 2023, the seller financing limit is $6,734,800; this limit is indexed annually for inflation. The amount of seller financing is the stated principal amount under the contract. If the seller-financed amount exceeds the annual limit, the minimum interest rate is 100% of the AFR. The 9% safe harbor provides a benefit only if it is less than the AFR, and in recent years the AFRs have been much lower than 9%. Although the AFRs steadily increased throughout 2023 and this could continue, it is likely that they will remain well below 9% for the forseeable future. Thus, charging interest at the AFR will be sufficient to avoid application of the minimum interest rules. IRS regulations allow the parties to use an interest rate lower than the AFR if it is shown that the borrower could obtain a loan on an arm's-length basis at lower interest.
Seller-financed sale-leaseback transactions	Interest equal to 110% of AFR must be charged.
Sales of land between family members	To the extent that the sales price does not exceed $500,000 during a calendar year, the minimum required interest rate is the lower of 6% compounded semiannually and the applicable federal rate (AFR). As with the 9% safe harbor discussed above, the 6% rate safe harbor has not been an advantage in recent years since the AFR has been much lower than 6%, and even with increasing inflation this is likely to continue for the forseeable future. To prevent multiple sales from being used to avoid the $500,000 limit, the $500,000 ceiling applies to all land sales between family members during the same year. To the extent that the $500,000 sales price limit is exceeded, the general 9% or 100% of AFR rules apply.

CHAPTER 5

Reporting Property Sales

Long-term capital gains are generally taxed at lower rates than those imposed on ordinary income. Depending on your taxable income, some or all of your long-term capital gains may qualify for a 0% rate and thus completely avoid tax *(5.3)*. If the 0% rate does not apply, your long-term gains are subject to maximum rates of 15% or 20% depending on your income, or, for certain assets, a maximum rate of 25% or 28% *(5.3)*, but regular tax rates apply if they result in a lower tax than the maximum rate.

If you sell property and will receive payments in a year (or years) after the year of sale, you may report the sale as an installment sale on Form 6252 and spread the tax on your gain over the installment period *(5.21)*.

Sales of business assets and depreciable rental property are reported on Form 4797. Most assets used in a business are considered Section 1231 assets, and capital gain or ordinary loss treatment may apply depending upon the result of a netting computation made on Form 4797 for all such assets sold during the year *(44.8)*.

Special types of sale situations are detailed in other chapters.

See Chapter 29 for the exclusion of gain on the sale of a principal residence.

See Chapter 32 for figuring gain or loss on the sale of mutual fund shares.

See Chapter 6 for tax-free exchanges of property.

See Chapter 30 for sales of stock dividends, stock rights, wash sales, short sales, and sales by traders in securities.

5.1 General Tax Rules for Property Sales

1. Property is classified according to its nature and your purpose for holding it; *see 5.2, Table 5-1*, and holding period rules at *5.3* and *5.9–5.12*.

2. Sales of capital assets must generally be reported on Form 8949, with Part I used for short-term gains and losses and Part II for long-term gains and losses *(5.8)*. However, in some cases you do not need Form 8949 and may report your transactions directly on Schedule D; *see 5.8*. If you file Form 8949, you must check a box to indicate whether you received a Form 1099-B from a broker showing your basis in securities sold. If you are reporting more than one sale of securities, you may need to file multiple Forms 8949 depending on how basis was reported on Form 1099-B. Total amounts for sales price and basis are transferred from Form 8949 to Schedule D of Form 1040 or 1040-SR. On Schedule D you net short-term and long-term transactions to figure your net gain or loss for the year and, if you have net long-term gain, you are directed to the appropriate IRS worksheet for computing your tax liability taking into account the favorable capital gain rates, as discussed in the next paragraph. Filing Form 8949 or Schedule D may not be necessary if your only capital gains are from a mutual fund or REIT *(32.7)*.

3. If you sell property at a gain, the applicable tax rate depends on the classification of the property *(Table 5-1)* and, in the case of capital assets, the period you held the property before sale. A capital gain is long term if you held the asset for more than one year, short-term if you held it for one year or less. Short-term capital gains that are not offset by short- or long-term losses are subject to regular income tax rates.

   If you have net capital gain for the year (net long-term gain over net short-term loss if any), your gains are subject to favorable capital gain rates. Depending on your taxable income and the amount and source of your long-term gains, the gains may be completely tax free under the 0% rate or subject to a maximum rate of 15%, 20%, 25%, or 28% where that maximum rate is less than the otherwise applicable regular tax rate *(5.3)*. In some cases when the 15% rate applies, and in all cases when the 20% capital gain rate applies, the 3.8% net investment income also applies, effectively increasing the rate by 3.8% *(28.3)*.

   If you do not have 28% rate gains or unrecaptured Section 1250 gains subject to a maximum 25% rate, you compute your tax liability taking into account the 0%, 15% and 20% capital gain rates on the Qualified Dividends and Capital Gain Tax Worksheet in the Form 1040 instructions. If you have either 28% gain or unrecaptured Section 1250 gain, use the Schedule D Tax Worksheet in the Schedule D instructions to compute your tax liability.

4. Loss deductions are allowed on the sale of investment and business property but losses are not deductible on the sale of personal assets; *see Table 5-1*. Capital loss deductions in excess of capital gains are limited to $3,000 annually, $1,500 if married filing separately; *see* the details on the capital loss limitations later in this *Chapter (5.4– 5.5)*.

5.2 How Property Sales Are Classified and Taxed

The tax treatment of gains and losses is not the same for all types of property sales. Tax reporting generally depends on your purpose in holding the property, as shown in *Table 5-1*.

When capital gain or loss treatment does not apply. Certain sales do not qualify for capital gain or loss treatment. Business inventory and property held for sale to customers are not capital assets. Depreciable business and rental property are not capital assets, but you may still realize capital gain after following a netting computation for Section 1231 assets *(44.8)*.

Although assets held for personal use, such as a car or home, are technically capital assets, you may not deduct a capital loss on their sale.

Certain other assets held for investment or personal use are excluded by law from the capital asset category. These include copyrights, literary or musical compositions, letters, memoranda, or similar property that: (1) you created by your personal efforts or (2) you acquired as a gift from the person who created the property or for whom the property was prepared or produced.

Although musical compositions and copyrights in musical works that you personally created (or you acquired as a gift from the creator) are generally excluded from the capital asset category, you can make an election on a timely filed (including extensions) Form 8949 for the year the musical composition or copyright is sold to treat the sale as a sale of a capital asset.

⚠ Caution

Loss on Sale of Personal-Use Assets

You may not deduct a capital loss on the sale of property held for personal use, such as a car or vacation home. The loss is not deductible.

Losses on the sale of property held for investment, such as stock or mutual fund shares, are fully deductible against capital gains but any excess loss is subject to the $3,000 limit *(5.4)*.

Table 5-1 Capital or Ordinary Gains and Losses From Sales and Exchanges of Property

If you sell—	Your gain is—	Your loss is—	Reported on—
Stocks, mutual funds, bonds, land, art, gems, stamps, and coins held for investment are capital assets.	Capital gain. Holding period determines short-term or long-term gain treatment *(5.3)*. Security traders may report ordinary income and loss under a mark-to-market election *(30.15)*.	Capital loss. Capital losses are deductible from capital gains. If the losses exceed the gains, only $3,000 of the excess is deductible from ordinary income; $1,500 if married filing separately *(5.4)*.	Form 8949 and Schedule D *(5.8)*. However, if the only amounts you have to report on these forms are mutual fund capital gain distributions, then you may report the distributions directly on Form 1040 or 1040-SR *(Table 32-1*, "Reporting Mutual Fund Distributions for 2023" in *Chapter 32)*. Form 4797 for gains and losses of a trader in securities who makes the mark-to-market election *(30.15)*.
Business inventory held for sale to customers. Also, accounts or notes receivable acquired in the ordinary course of business or from the sale of inventory or property held for sale to customers, or acquired for services as an employee.	Ordinary income. Such property is excluded by law from the definition of capital assets.	Ordinary loss. Ordinary loss is not subject to the $3,000 deduction limit imposed on capital losses. However, passive loss restrictions, discussed in *Chapter 10*, may defer the time when certain ordinary losses are deductible.	Schedule C if self-employed; Schedule F if a farmer; Form 1065 for a business operated as a partnership or multi-member limited liability company; Form 1120 or 1120-S for an incorporated business.
Depreciable residential rental property, or trucks, autos, computers, machinery, fixtures, or equipment used in your business.	Capital gain or ordinary income. Section 1231 determines whether gain is taxable as ordinary income or capital gain *(44.8)*. Where an asset such as an auto or residence is used partly for personal purposes and partly for business or rental purposes, the asset is treated as two separate assets for purposes of figuring gain or loss *(44.9)*.	Ordinary loss if there is a net Section 1231 loss *(44.8)*. However, if you are considered to be an investor in a passive activity, see *10.12* and *10.13*.	Form 4797 for Section 1231 transactions.
Personal residence, car, jewelry, furniture, art objects, and collectibles held for personal use.	Capital gain. *See* the holding period rules that determine short-term or long-term gain treatment and the preferential tax rates applied to net long-term capital gains *(5.3)*. Where an asset such as an auto or residence is used partly for personal purposes and partly for business or rental purposes, the asset is treated as two separate assets for purposes of figuring gain or loss *(44.9)*. All or part of a profit from a sale of a principal residence may be excludable from income; *see Chapter 29*.	Not deductible. Losses on sales of assets held for personal use are not deductible although profits are taxable. The losses do not offset the profits.	Form 8949 and Schedule D

 *Filing Tip*

Holding Periods for Capital Assets

The time you own a capital asset determines short-term or long-term treatment when you sell. The short-term holding period is a year or less. The long-term holding period more than one year *(5.9–5.12)*.

Also excluded from the capital asset category are letters, memoranda, or similar property prepared or produced for you by someone else. U.S. government publications obtained from the government for free or for less than the normal sales price do not qualify as capital assets.

A patent, invention, model or design, secret formula or process is excluded from the capital asset category if held by: (1) the person whose personal efforts created the property, or (2) a person who acquired it as a gift from the person who created the property.

Stock is generally treated as a capital asset, but losses on Section 1244 stock of qualifying small businesses may be claimed as ordinary losses on Form 4797, rather than on Schedule D as capital losses, which are subject to the $3,000 deduction limit ($1,500 if married filing separately) *(30.11)*.

Traders in securities may elect to report their sales as ordinary income or loss rather than as capital gain or loss *(30.14)*.

Small business/empowerment zone business stock exclusion. Gains on the sale of qualifying small business stock held for more than five years may be excluded from income *(5.7)*.

Deferral of gains reinvested in qualified Opportunity Zones. Taxable gain from the sale of any property can be deferred if the gain is reinvested in a qualified Opportunity Zone within 180 days of the sale *(5.7)*.

Like-kind exchanges of business or investment real property. Exchanges of like-kind business or investment real estate are subject to special rules that allow gain to be deferred, generally until you sell the property received in the exchange *(6.1)*. When property received in a like-kind exchange is held until death, the unrecognized gain escapes income tax forever because the basis of property in the hands of an heir is generally the fair market value of the property at the date of death *(5.17)*. A loss on a like-kind exchange is not deductible.

Stock redemption allocation to covenant not to compete. If you sell company stock back to your employer and you are subject to a covenant not to compete with the company for a period of time, any portion of the purchase price for the stock that is allocated to the covenant in the contract is taxed to you as ordinary income and not capital gain.

5.3 Capital Gains Rates and Holding Periods

Form 8949 is used for reporting sales of capital assets. On Form 8949, you separate your sales into short-term and long-term categories. Assets held for one year or less are in the short-term category and assets held for more than one year are in the long-term category *(5.9–5.12)*. The totals from Form 8949 are entered on Schedule D (Form 1040 or 1040-SR). *See* the Example in *5.8*, which includes filled-in samples of Form 8949 and Schedule D.

The computation of tax liability using the favorable long-term capital gain rates is not made directly on Schedule D, but on worksheets in the IRS instructions. Mutual fund and REIT investors may be able to apply the favorable rates on the "Qualified Dividends and Capital Gain Tax Worksheet" included in the Form 1040 and 1040-SR instructions, without having to file Form 8949 or Schedule D *(see Table 32-1,* "Reporting Mutual Fund Distributions for 2023," in *Chapter 32)*.

Held for a year or less. Details for sales of capital assets held for a year or less are reported in Part I of Form 8949 unless you are able to report them directly on Schedule D and you choose to do so. The total sales prices and total cost basis shown on Form 8949 for short-term transactions, along with any adjustments for such transactions, are transferred to Part I of Schedule D, where the net short-term gain or loss for the year is determined. A net short-term capital gain is subject to the regular tax rates on ordinary income. On Part III of Schedule D, a net short-term loss from Part I offsets a net long-term gain, if any, from Part II of Schedule D. A net short-term loss in excess of net long-term gain is deductible up to the $3,000 ($1,500 if married filing separately) capital loss limit *(5.4)*.

Held for more than a year. Details for sales of capital assets held for more than a year are reported in Part II of Form 8949, unless you are able to report them directly on Schedule D and you choose to do so. The total sales prices and total cost basis for all the long-term transactions shown on form 8949, along with any adjustments for such transactions, are transferred to Part II of Schedule D, where the net long-term gain or loss for the year is determined. A net long-term capital loss offsets a net short-term gain, if any, from Part I of Schedule D. If you have a net long-term capital gain on Part II and also a net short-term capital loss on Part I of Schedule D, the short-term loss offsets the net long-term gain. The offsets are made on Part III of Schedule D. If the net short-term loss exceeds the net long-term gain, the excess short-term loss is deductible up to the $3,000 ($1,500 if married filing separately) capital loss limit *(5.4)*. If you have a net long-term gain in excess of a net short-term capital loss (if any), the excess is called net capital gain and it is this amount to which the favorable capital gain rates may apply, as discussed below.

Reduced Rates on Net Capital Gain

Net capital gain is the excess of your net long-term capital gain over your net short-term capital loss. The net capital gain is subject to maximum tax rates that are generally lower than the rates that would apply if it were ordinary income. Qualified dividends *(4.2)* are subject to the same favorable rates as net capital gain. To get the benefit of the favorable rates for net capital gain and qualified dividends, you must compute your regular income tax liability on IRS worksheets, as discussed in the following paragraphs.

If you have a net capital gain for 2023 that does *not* include a 28% rate gain or unrecaptured Section 1250 gain *(see below)*, you should compute your 2023 regular tax liability on the "Qualified Dividends and Capital Gain Tax Worksheet" in the Form 1040 and 1040-SR instructions. On the "Qualified Dividends and Capital Gain Tax Worksheet," take into account the favorable capital gain rates, as applicable, and the regular tax rates on the rest of your taxable income. This worksheet must be used to figure your regular income tax liability instead of the IRS Tax Table *(22.2)* or Tax Computation Worksheet *(22.3)* in order to benefit from the maximum capital gain rates.

If you have a net capital gain that includes either a net 28% rate gain or unrecaptured Section 1250 gain, you must compute your regular income tax liability on the "Schedule D Tax Worksheet" in the Schedule D instructions.

You also must use the Schedule D Tax Worksheet if you file Form 4952 to figure the itemized deduction for investment interest *(15.10)* and on Line 4g, you elect to include some (or all) of your qualified dividends or net capital gain from investment property as investment income for purposes of figuring the deduction on Form 4952.

The 0%, 15%, and 20% rates. Your qualified dividends *(4.2)* and net capital gain (net long-term gains in excess of net short-term losses) are generally subject to a 0%, 15%, or 20% rate, or a combination of these rates, depending on your taxable income, filing status, and the amount of your ordinary income. *Table 5-2* below shows the 2023 brackets for the 0%, 15%, and 20% rates.

The 0%, 15% and 20% rates do *not* apply to any portion of net capital gain that is 28% rate gain (from collectibles and Section 1202 exclusion) or unrecaptured Section 1250 gain (from post-1986 real estate depreciation); these gains are subject, respectively, to maximum rates of 28% and 25%. The 28% and 25% rates are discussed below. Also keep in mind that if your MAGI exceeds the threshold for the 3.8% tax on net investment income *(28.3)*, the effective rate on some or all of your gains (depending on MAGI) will be increased by 3.8%.

Note that for joint filers and qualifying widows/widowers), the 0% rate bracket for 2023 net capital gain and qualified dividends ends $200 below the endpoint of the 12% ordinary income bracket *(see Table 1-1* in *1.2)*. For single taxpayers, heads of households and married persons filing separately, the endpoint of the 0% rate bracket is $100 below the endpoint of the 12% ordinary income bracket.

 *Law Alert*

0%,15%, and 20% Rates Apply to Most Long-term Gains

If you have a net capital gain (net long-term gain over net short-term loss if any), the net gain may avoid tax under the 0% rate or be taxed at 15% or 20%, depending on your income. However, the 0%, 15%, and 20% rates do not apply to 28% rate gains from collectibles or 25% unrecaptured Section 1250 gains (real estate depreciation); see *5.3*. Qualified dividends *(4.2)* may also be tax free under the 0% rate, and if the 0% rate does not apply, they are taxed at either 15% or 20%, depending on your income.

The effective tax rate on capital gains and qualified dividends, as well as on other investment income, increases by 3.8% for higher-income taxpayers subject to the additional tax on net investment income *(28.3)*.

Table 5-2   Rates and Brackets for 2023 Net Capital Gain and Qualified Dividends

	Married filing jointly and qualifying widow/widower	Single	Head of Household	Married filing separately
0% rate applies if taxable income is:	$1 through $89,250	$1 through $44,625	$1 through $59,750	$1 through $44,625
15% rate applies if taxable income is:	$89,251 through $553,850	$44,626 through $492,300	$59,751 through $523,050	$44,626 through $276,900
20% rate applies if taxable income is:	$553,851 and over	$4592,301 and over	$523,501 and over	$276,901 and over

Do your qualified dividends and net capital gain fall within the 0% rate bracket?

If your 2023 taxable income (Line 15 of Form 1040 or 1040-SR), including your qualified dividends and net capital gain, is entirely within the 0% rate bracket shown in *Table 5-2*, and none of your net capital gain is 28% rate gain or 25% rate unrecaptured Section 1250 gain, then all of your net capital gain and qualified dividend income is tax free. Perhaps surprisingly, you may be able to benefit from the 0% rate even if your total taxable income is above the endpoint of the 0% rate bracket and it appears, at least at first glance, that you are subject to the 15% or even the 20% rate on your qualified dividends and net capital gain.

The extent to which you can benefit from the 0% rate depends on your taxable income, your filing status, which determines the top of your 0% rate bracket, and the amount of your qualified dividends and net capital gain, which in turn determines the amount of your "ordinary income." On the IRS worksheets used to figure tax liability (the "Qualified Dividends and Capital Gain Tax Worksheet," or the "Schedule D Tax Worksheet," as applicable), your taxable income is reduced by your qualified dividends and net capital gain (other than 28% rate gain and unrecaptured Section 1250 gain). The resulting amount is treated as ordinary income on the worksheets and if it is less than the top of the 0% rate bracket for your filing status *(Table 5-2)*, your qualified dividends and net capital gain (other than 28% rate gain and unrecaptured Section 1250 gain) are tax free under the 0% rate to the extent that they "fill up" the rest of the 0% rate bracket.

For example, if you are single and for 2023 you have taxable income of $50,925, including $2,000 of qualified dividends and $12,000 of eligible net capital gain, your ordinary income for purposes of the 2023 worksheet computation is $36,925 ($50,925 − $14,000), and since the top of the 0% rate bracket for single taxpayers is taxable income of $44,625 *(Table 5-2)*, there is still $7,700 left within the 0% rate bracket ($44,625 − $36,925 ordinary income). The 0% rate applies to $7,700 of your $14,000 in gains/dividends, and the $6,300 balance ($14,000 − $7,700) is taxed at 15%.

If the ordinary income (taxable income minus the qualified dividends and net capital gain other than 28% rate gain and unrecaptured Section 1250 gain) is equal to or more than the top of your 0% rate bracket ($44,625, $59,750, or $89,250, as shown in *Table 5-2*), the 0% rate will not apply to any of your qualified dividends and eligible gains; *see* Example 3 below.

28% rate gains from sales of collectibles and small business or empowerment zone business stock eligible for exclusion. Long-term gains on the sale of collectibles such as art, antiques, precious metals, gems, stamps, and coins are considered "28% rate gains." If you sell qualified small business stock eligible for an exclusion (Section 1202 exclusion *(5.7)*), the taxable portion of the gain is also treated as a 28% rate gain. The 28% rate transactions are reported first in Part II (long-term capital gains and losses) of Form 8949 and then transferred to Schedule D, unless you are able to directly report them on Schedule D. If taking into account all your transactions you have both a net long-term capital gain for the year and a net capital gain (excess of net long-term gain over net short-term loss if there is one), you have to complete the "28% Rate Gain Worksheet" in the Schedule D instructions. On the Worksheet, 28% rate gains are reduced by any long-term collectibles losses and net short-term capital loss for the current year, and any long-term capital loss carryover from the previous year.

A net 28% rate gain from the 28% Rate Gain Worksheet is entered on Line 18 of Schedule D and then on the "Schedule D Tax Worksheet" in the Schedule D instructions. The Schedule D Tax Worksheet is used to figure the regular tax on all of your taxable income (not just on your net capital gain and qualified dividends). The effect of the worksheet computation is to tax 28% rate gain as if it were ordinary income, but the rate is capped at 28%. The 28% rate is a "maximum" rate, so it does not apply if your top ordinary income rate is 24% or less. If the ordinary income rate for the 28% rate gain would otherwise be 32%, 35%, or 37%, the gain is taxed at the 28% rate. Note that in applying ordinary income rates, the Worksheet takes into account 28% rate gains last; if you have any "unrecaptured Section 1250 gain" *(see below)*, those are taken into account before the 28% rate gains.

EXAMPLES

1. Arlen and Alice Able file a joint return for 2023 and report taxable income of $65,428. This includes qualified dividends of $3,298 and a long-term gain of $6,702 from the sale of stock. The 0% rate applies to the qualified dividends and long-term gain to the extent that they fit within the 0% rate bracket after taking into account the Ables' "ordinary" income. On the Qualified Dividends and Capital Gain Tax Worksheet, their ordinary income is considered to be $55,428 ($65,428 taxable income – $10,000 ($3,298 qualified dividends + $6,702 long-term gain)). Since the top, or end-point, of the 0% rate bracket for 2023 joint returns is taxable income of $89,250 *(Table 5-2)*, the 0% rate can apply to dividends/gains of up to $33,822 ($89,250 – $55,428 ordinary income) and as $33,822 exceeds the Ables' $10,000 of qualified dividends and long-term gain, the entire $10,000 is tax free under the 0% rate.

2. Same facts as in Example 1, except Arlen and Alice have taxable income of $89,650. On the Qualified Dividends and Capital Gain Tax Worksheet, ordinary income is $79,650 ($89,650 taxable income – $10,000 qualified dividends and long-term gain). After taking into account the ordinary income, there is still room for another $9,600 before the endpoint of the 0% rate bracket is reached ($89,250 endpoint of the 0% rate bracket – $79,650 ordinary income = $9,600). Thus, $9,600 of their dividends/gain are tax free under the 0% rate. The $400 balance of dividends/gain ($10,000 – $9,600) is taxed at the 15% capital gain rate on the Qualified Dividends and Capital Gain Tax Worksheet.

3. Same facts as in Example 1, except Arlen and Alice's taxable income is $99,450. Since the ordinary income of $89,450 ($99,450 taxable income – $10,000 qualified dividends and long-term gain) exceeds the $89,250 endpoint of the 0% rate bracket, none of the dividends/gains are eligible for the 0% rate. The entire $10,000 is taxed at 15%.

Unrecaptured Section 1250 gain on sale of real estate. Long-term gain that is attributable to real estate depreciation is not taxable at the 0%, 15% or 20% capital gain rate. Gain attributable to pre-1987 depreciation may be recaptured as ordinary income *(44.2)*. To the extent your gain is attributable to post-1986 depreciation, the gain is considered "unrecaptured Section 1250 gain." Unrecaptured Section 1250 gain is figured on the "Unrecaptured Section 1250 Gain Worksheet" in the Schedule D instructions. The worksheet computation reduces unrecaptured Section 1250 gain by a net loss, if any, from the 28% rate group.

The net unrecaptured Section 1250 gain from the worksheet is entered on Line 19 of Schedule D and then on the Schedule D Tax Worksheet, where tax liability on all of your taxable income is computed. The effect of the computation on the Schedule D Tax Worksheet is to tax unrecaptured Section 1250 gain at as if it were ordinary income, but the rate is capped at 25%. This means that the 25% rate applies to the unrecaptured Section 1250 gain only if your ordinary income rate would otherwise be higher than 25%; that is, the rate would otherwise be 32%, 35%, or 37%.

Capital gain distributions from mutual funds. Your fund will report long-term capital gain distributions on Form 1099-DIV. *See Chapter 32* for details on how to report the distributions.

Capital gain from Schedule K-1. Net capital gain or loss from a pass-through entity such as a partnership, S corporation, estate, or trust is reported to you on a Schedule K-1. Report net short-term gain or loss in Part I of Schedule D and net long-term gain or loss in Part II of Schedule D.

5.4 Capital Losses and Carryovers

Capital losses are fully deductible against capital gains on Schedule D, and if losses exceed gains, you may deduct the excess from up to $3,000 of ordinary income on Form 1040 or 1040-SR. Net losses over $3,000 are carried over to future years. On a joint return, the $3,000 limit applies to the combined losses of both spouses *(5.5)*. The $3,000 limit is reduced to $1,500 for married persons filing separately.

Although qualified dividends *(4.1)* are subject to the same rates as net capital gain, the dividends are not reported as long-term gains on Part II of Form 8949 or Schedule D and thus are not offset by capital losses in determining whether you have a net capital gain or loss for the year.

In preparing your 2023 Schedule D, remember to include any capital loss carryovers from your 2022 return. Use the carryover worksheet in the 2023 Schedule D instructions for figuring your short-term and long-term loss carryovers from 2022 to 2023. On Schedule D, short-term carryover losses are entered on Line 6 of Part I and long-term carryover losses are entered on Line 14, Part II.

Losses from wash sales not deductible. You cannot deduct a loss from a wash sale of stock or securities unless you are a dealer in those securities. A wash sale occurs if within 30 days before or after your sale at a loss, you acquire substantially identical securities or purchase an option to acquire such securities *(30.6)*. A disallowed wash sale loss should be reported in Box 1g of Form 1099-B.

Report a wash sale on Part 1 (short-term) or Part II (long-term) of Form 8949 and enter code "W" in column (f) to identify the wash sale loss. In column (g) enter the disallowed loss as a positive amount.

Death of taxpayer cuts off carryover. If an individual dies and on his or her final income tax return net capital losses, including prior year carryovers, exceed the $3,000 or $1,500 limit, the excess may not be deducted by the individual's estate. If the deceased individual was married, his or her unused individual losses may not be carried over by the surviving spouse *(5.5)*.

5.5 Capital Losses of Married Couples

On a joint return, the capital asset transactions of both spouses are combined and reported on one Schedule D. A carryover loss of one spouse may offset capital gains of the other spouse on a jointly filed Schedule D. Where you and your spouse separately incur net capital losses, $3,000 is the maximum capital loss deduction that may be claimed for the combined losses on your joint return. This limitation may not be avoided by filing separate returns. If you file separately, the deduction limit for each return is $1,500. Neither of you may deduct any of the other's losses on a separate return.

> **EXAMPLE**
>
> In 2023, you individually incurred net long-term capital losses of $5,000 and your spouse individually incurred net long-term capital losses of $4,000. If you file jointly, the maximum amount deductible from ordinary income on your 2023 joint return is $3,000. The balance must be carried forward to 2024.
>
> If you file separately for 2023, the maximum amount deductible from ordinary income on each return is $1,500. The balance must be carried forward to 2024. If you had net losses below the $1,500 limit, you could not claim any part of your spouse's losses on your separate return.

 *Filing Tip*

Keep Records of Loss Carryovers

If you have capital losses for 2023 in excess of the deductible limit, keep a copy of your 2023 Form 1040 or 1040-SR and Schedule D. The excess can be claimed as a capital loss carryover on your 2024 return (Schedule D for 2024); there will be a carryover worksheet in the 2024 Schedule D instructions. IRS Publication 550 for 2023 also has a worksheet you can use to figure your loss carryovers from 2023 to 2024.

Death of a spouse. The IRS holds that if a capital loss is incurred by a spouse on his or her own property and that spouse dies, the loss may be deducted only on the final return for the spouse (which may be a joint return). The surviving spouse may not claim any unused loss carryover on a separate return and the decedent's estate may not deduct the unused carryover.

 *Filing Tip*

Carryovers From Joint or Separate Returns

If you or your spouse has a capital loss carryover from a year in which separate returns were filed, and you are now filing a joint return, the carryovers from the separate returns may be combined on the joint return. If you previously filed jointly and are now filing separately, any loss carryover from the joint return may be claimed only on the separate return of the spouse who originally incurred the loss *(5.5)*.

> **EXAMPLE**
>
> In 2021, Alex Smith realized a substantial net long-term capital loss on separately owned property, which was reported on a 2021 joint return filed with his wife, Anne. Part of the excess loss (over the $3,000 limit) was carried over to the couple's 2022 joint return. In 2023, before the carryover loss was used up, Alex died. Anne can claim the unused carryover, up to the $3,000 limit, on a joint return filed for 2023, the year of Alex's death. However, there is no loss carryover for 2024 or later years for the balance. Although the loss was originally reported on a joint return, Anne may claim only her allocable share of the loss on her individual returns for years after 2023, the year of Alex's death. However, since the 2021 loss was on property owned solely by Alex, no part of the loss is allocable to Anne after 2023.

5.6 Losses May Be Disallowed on Sales to Related Persons

A loss on a sale to certain related taxpayers may not be deductible, even though you make the sale at an arm's-length price, the sale is involuntary (for example, a member of your family forecloses a mortgage on your property), or you sell through a public stock exchange and related persons buy the equivalent property; *see* Examples 1 and 2 in this section.

If you have a nondeductible related party loss, identify it by entering code "L" in column (f) of Form 8949 (Part I or Part II as appropriate), and enter it as a positive amount in column (g).

Related parties. Losses are not allowed on sales between you and your brothers or sisters (whether by the whole or half blood), parents, grandparents, great-grandparents, children, grandchildren, or great-grandchildren. Furthermore, no loss may be claimed on a sale to your spouse; the tax-free exchange rules discussed in *Chapter 6* apply *(6.7)*.

A loss is disallowed where the sale is made to your sister-in-law, as nominee of your brother. This sale is deemed to be between you and your brother. But you may deduct the loss on sales to your spouse's relative (for example, your brother-in-law or spouse's step-parent) even if you and your spouse file a joint return.

The Tax Court has allowed a loss on a direct sale to a son-in-law. In a private ruling, the IRS allowed a loss on a sale of a business to a son-in-law where it was shown that his wife (the seller's daughter) did not own an interest in the company. Losses have been disallowed upon withdrawal from a joint venture and from a partnership conducted by members of a family. Family members have argued that losses should be allowed where the sales were motivated by family hostility. The Tax Court ruled that family hostility may not be considered; losses between proscribed family members are disallowed in all cases. See IRS Publication 544 for details.

Losses are barred on sales between an individual and a controlled partnership or controlled corporation (where that individual owns more than 50% in value of the outstanding stock or capital interests). In calculating the stock owned, not only must the stock held in your own name be taken into account, but also that owned by your family. You also add (1) the proportionate share of any stock held by a corporation, estate, trust, or partnership in which you have an interest as a shareholder, beneficiary, or partner; and (2) any other stock owned individually by your partner.

Losses may also be disallowed in sales between controlled companies, a trust and its creator, a trust and a beneficiary, a partnership and a corporation controlled by the same person (more than 50% ownership), or a tax-exempt organization and its founder. An estate and a beneficiary of that estate are also treated as related parties, except where a sale is in satisfaction of a pecuniary bequest. Check with your tax professional whenever you plan to sell property at a loss to a buyer who may fit one of these descriptions.

Related buyer's resale at profit. Sometimes, the disallowed loss may be saved. When you sell to a related party who resells the property at a profit, he or she gets the benefit of your disallowed loss. Your purchaser's gain is not taxed to the extent of your disallowed loss; *see* Example 4 above.

EXAMPLES

1. You sell 100 shares of A Co. stock to your brother for $1,000. They cost you $5,000. You may not deduct your $4,000 loss.

2. The stock investments of a mother and son were managed by the same investment counselor. But neither the son nor mother had any right or control over the other's securities. The counselor followed separate and independent policies for each. Without the son's or his mother's prior approval, the counselor carried out the following transactions: (1) on the same day, he sold at a loss the son's stock in four companies and bought the same stock for the mother's account; and (2) he sold at a loss the son's stock in a copper company, and 28 days later bought the same stock for his mother. The losses of the first sale were disallowed, but not the losses of the copper stock sale because of the time break of 28 days. However, the court did not say how much of a minimum time break is needed to remove a sale-purchase transaction from the rule disallowing losses between related parties.

3. You own 30% of the stock of a company. A trust in which you have a one-half beneficial interest owns 30%. Your partner owns 10% of the stock of the same company. You are deemed the owner of 55% of the stock of that company (30%, plus one-half of 30%, plus 10%) and may not deduct a loss on the sale of property to that company since your deemed ownership exceeds 50%.

4. Smith bought securities in 2010 that cost $10,000. In 2013, he sold them to his sister for $8,000. The $2,000 loss was not deductible by Smith. His sister's basis for the securities is $8,000. In 2023, she sells them for $9,000. The $1,000 gain is not taxed because it is washed out by part of the brother's disallowed loss. If she sold the securities for $11,000, then only $1,000 of the $3,000 gain would be taxed.

5.7 Special Treatment of Gain on Sale of Small Business Stock or Qualified Opportunity Zone Investment

To encourage investments in certain "small" businesses and businesses in distressed areas, the tax law provides special tax benefits. On a sale at a gain of qualified small business stock held more than five years, you can avoid tax on some or all of your gain under the Section 1202 exclusion. Capital gain from a property sale can be deferred by investing in a "Qualified Opportunity Fund (QOF)," and depending on how long the QOF investment is held, a potential exclusion may be available when the QOF investment is sold.

Section 1202 Exclusion on Sale of Small Business Stock

If you sell qualified small business stock (QSB stock) after holding it more than five years, 50%, 75% or even 100% of the gain is excludable from your income, depending on when you acquired it. To qualify as QSB stock, the stock must be stock in a C corporation (not an S corporation) that was originally issued after August 10, 1993. The gross assets of the corporation must have been no more than $50 million at all times after August 9, 1993, and before issuance of the stock, as well as immediately after issuance of the stock. You must have acquired the stock at its original issue by purchase or as compensation for services rendered to the corporation, as a gift or inheritance from a qualifying transferor, or in a conversion of other qualified stock. The C corporation must have met an active business requirement for substantially the entire time you held the stock. The active business test generally requires that the C corporation used at least 80% of its assets (by value) in the active conduct of at least one qualified trade or business, which is any business not specifically excluded by the law. However, many types of businesses are excluded from the "qualified" category. These are: (1) service businesses in the fields of health, law, accounting, financial services, brokerage, consulting, actuarial science, engineering, architecture, performing arts, or sports, (2) any business whose principal asset is the skill or reputation of one or more of its employees, (3) restaurants, hotels, motels or similar businesses, (4) insurance, banking, financing, leasing or similar businesses, (5) farming, and (6) oil, gas, and extraction businesses that can use percentage depletion.

If you acquired the QSB stock before February 18, 2009, 50% of the gain is excludable from income. The exclusion increases to 60% for sales of QSB stock that qualify as empowerment zone business stock, but only for gain attributable to 2018 and earlier years.

If you acquired the QSB stock after February 17, 2009, and before September 28, 2010, the exclusion is 75%. The 100% exclusion applies to the gain on a sale of QSB stock acquired after September 27, 2010, if the over-five-year holding period was met.

If you qualify for the exclusion, report the sale in Part II of Form 8949. Enter code "Q" in column (f) and enter the excluded amount as a negative adjustment in column (g). If you have a net capital gain (net long-term gain in excess of net short-term loss, if any) on Schedule D, include the taxable portion (the non-excluded part) of the QSB stock gain on the 28% Rate Gain Worksheet in the Schedule D instructions *(5.3)*.

There is an annual and lifetime limit on the Section 1202 exclusion for QSB stock from any one issuer. The amount of gain from any one issuer that is eligible for the exclusion in 2023 is limited to the greater of (1) 10 times your basis in the qualified stock that you disposed of during 2023, or (2) $10 million ($5 million if married filing separately) minus any gain on stock from the same issuer that you excluded in prior years.

Deferral of Gain Reinvested in a Qualified Opportunity Fund (QOF)

If you realize capital gain on the sale of any property (wherever located), including Section 1231 gains, to an unrelated party, you may defer the gain (called "eligible gain") if, within 180 days of the sale, you reinvest the gain in a Qualified Opportunity Fund (QOF). Eligible gain includes gain from Section 1231 property, including gains from installment sales and like-kind exchanges. The QOF investment can be used to defer long-term gain, short-term gain, or a combination of short-term and long-term gain. The deferral lasts until you dispose of your QOF interest (sell, exchange, or gift the interest) or December 31, 2026, whichever is earlier. The election to defer tax on eligible gain invested in a QOF is made on Form 8949; *see* the Filing Instruction on this page. For the year of your QOF investment and for each later year, you must report details of your QOF holdings on Form 8997. When you sell or exchange your QOF investment, you may be able to permanently exclude some or all of your gain, depending on how long you held the investment; *see* "Gain or loss on the sale or disposition of a QOF investment," below.

A QOF is an interest in a corporation or partnership organized to invest in a designated Qualified Opportunity Zone (QOZ) and which holds at least 90% of its assets in QOZ property (QOZ stock, partnership interest, or property used in a QOZ business). Thousands of areas have been designated as Opportunity Zones.

The 180-day period for investing in a QOF usually begins on the date the gain would be recognized had not deferral been elected. However, if you have gain that's passed through to you from a partnership, S corporation, estate, or non-grantor trust and reported on Schedule K-1, you have the option to start the 180-day period on any of the following:

- The last day of the K-1 issuer's taxable year
- The same date as the entity's 180-day period begins
- The due date of the entity's tax return, without extensions, for the year in which the gain was realized.

Example

A partnership, which reports on a calendar year, sold assets on June 30, 2023. You receive Schedule K-1 for the 2023 tax year on May 1, 2024. Your 180-day period can begin on December 31, 2023 (the last day of the partnership's tax year), June 30, 2023 (the date that gain would be recognized but for your deferral election), or March 15, 2024 (the original due date of the partnership's return). The date of receiving Schedule K-1 is irrelevant.

 *Planning Reminder*

Rollover of Gain From Sale of QSB Stock

If you sell qualifying small business stock (QSB stock) that you held more than six months and do not qualify for the 100% Section 1202 exclusion, you may elect to defer gain by buying other QSB stock within the 60-day period starting on the date of sale. If the sale proceeds exceed the cost of the replacement stock, your gain is taxable to the extent of the difference. You must reduce the basis of the replacement stock by the deferred gain.

The election to defer gain generally must be made by the due date (including extensions) for filing your return for the year of the sale. If you timely file your original return without making the election, you may make the election on an amended return filed no later than six months after the original due date (disregarding extensions). To elect deferral, report the sale on Part I (short-term gain) or Part II (long-term gain) of Form 8949. Enter code "R" in column (f) and enter the deferred gain as a negative adjustment in column (g). *See* the Schedule D instructions and IRS Publication 550 for further election details.

 *Filing Instruction*

Deferring Gain by Investing in a Qualified Opportunity Fund (QOF)

To elect deferral of eligible gain that has been reinvested in a QOF, report the gain on Form 8949. Enter code "Z" in column (f) and enter the deferred gain as a negative adjustment in column (g). *See* the Form 8949 instructions for further election details. You also must complete Form 8997 for the year of the election, and also for later years in which you hold your QOF interest; *see* the Form 8997 instructions.

Gain or loss on the sale or disposition of a QOF. Tax treatment on the sale or disposition of a QOF depends on how long you hold the investment. Basis in the QOF investment is treated as zero ($0) if the investment is held under five years, so in this case, all of the originally deferred gain will have to be reported as income in the year the QOF investment is sold, plus the appreciation if any (excess of the sales price over the investment in the QOF). If the QOF investment is sold after being held at least five years but under seven years, the zero basis is increased by 10% of the originally deferred gain, so only 90% of the deferred gain will have to be included in income for the year the investment is sold, plus the appreciation if any. If the QOF investment is held at least seven but under 10 years before it is sold, the basis is increased by 15% of the deferred gain and 85% of the deferred gain will have to be includible in income. If the QOF investment is held for at least 10 years, you can adjust the basis in the QOF to its fair market value at that time, effectively allowing you to permanently exclude gain on the appreciation of the investment to that point. *See* IRS Publication 544 for further information on QOF investments.

Exclusion for gain from DC Zone assets. If you sold or exchanged a District of Columbia Enterprise Zone (DC Zone) asset acquired after 1997 and before 2012 and held for more than 5 years, you may be able to exclude the amount of qualified capital gain. The exclusion applies to an interest in, or property of, certain businesses operating in the District of Columbia. Report the sale or exchange on Form 8949, Part II, as you would if you were not taking the exclusion. Enter "X" in column (f) and enter the amount of the exclusion as a negative number in column (g). Put the amount in parentheses to show it is negative. For more details, *see* IRS Publication 550.

5.8 Reporting Capital Asset Sales on Form 8949 and on Schedule D

You generally must report sales and other dispositions of capital assets on Form 8949, but in some cases *(see below)*, you can report your transactions directly on Schedule D without having to report them on Form 8949. You report on Form 8949/Schedule D sales of securities, redemptions of mutual fund shares, worthless personal loans, sales of stock rights and warrants, sales of land held for investment, and sales of personal residences where part of the gain does not qualify for the home sale exclusion *(29.1)*.

Although capital gain distributions from mutual funds and REITs are generally reported as long-term capital gains on Line 13 of Schedule D, investors who receive such distributions but have no other capital gains or losses to report may report the distributions directly on Form 1040 or 1040-SR without having to file Schedule D; *see Table 32-1* in *32.8* for details.

The favorable maximum capital gain rates *(5.3)* apply to net capital gain (net long-term capital gain in excess of net short-term capital loss) from Schedule D, and also to qualified dividends *(4.2)*. Although qualified dividends are subject to the same favorable maximum rates as net capital gain, they are not entered as long-term gains in Part II of Schedule D. The favorable rates are applied to qualified dividends when tax liability is computed on either the Qualified Dividends and Capital Gain Tax Worksheet or the Schedule D Tax Worksheet. You must use the applicable worksheet to obtain the benefit of the favorable maximum capital gain rates for your net capital gain and qualified dividends. The Schedule D Tax Worksheet in the Schedule D instructions is used only if you have a net 28% rate gain or unrecaptured Section 1250 gain *(5.3)*. If you do not have a net 28% rate gain or unrecaptured Section 1250 gain, use the Qualified Dividends and Capital Gain Tax Worksheet in the Form 1040 and 1040-SR instructions.

Basis of "covered" securities reported on Form 1099-B. When you sell a "covered" security, the broker must report your basis in the security in Box 1e of the Form 1099-B sent to you and the IRS. Box 12 should be checked where the basis is being reported to the IRS. In general, a covered security is stock acquired after 2010, mutual fund shares acquired after 2011, stock acquired after 2011 in a dividend reinvestment plan eligible for the average basis method, futures contracts entered into after 2013, certain bonds acquired after 2013 (described in the Form 1099-B instructions) and certain bonds acquired after 2015, including variable rate and inflation-indexed bonds (see further details in the Form 1099-B instructions).

Even if you sell a "noncovered" security, the broker may report basis in Box 1e and if so, Box 12 should be checked to indicate that basis is being reported to the IRS. For a noncovered security, Box 5 should have been checked whether or not basis is reported. If the broker does not check Box 5 for a noncovered security, penalties can be assessed against the broker for not correctly completing Boxes 1b (date acquired), 1e (basis), 1f (accrued market discount), 1g (disallowed wash sale loss) and 2 (short-term or long-term gain or loss or ordinary income).

If during the year you have sold more than one security with the same broker, each transaction is generally reported on a separate Form 1099-B (or equivalent statement); there is an exception for futures, option and foreign currency contracts that may be reported on an aggregate basis.

If in the same transaction both covered and noncovered securities were sold, each type should be reported on a separate Form 1099-B (or equivalent statement). If some covered securities were held short term and others long term (over a year), the short-term transactions should be reported separately from the long-term transactions.

Can you report directly on Schedule D?
You do not need to report certain transactions on Form 8949. You can aggregate the transactions reported on Forms 1099-B that show (in Box 12) that basis was reported to the IRS and report them directly on Schedule D if you do not have to adjust the basis, the amount of gain or loss, or the type of capital gain or loss (short-term or long-term). Check the Form 8949 instructions for other requirements. You may choose to report the transactions separately on Form 8949 even if direct reporting on Schedule D is allowed. If you qualify for direct reporting and choose to do so, the aggregated short-term transactions are entered on Line 1a of Schedule D and the aggregated long-term transactions are reported on Line 8a of Schedule D.

Reporting transactions first on Form 8949 and then entering totals on Schedule D.
Use Part I of Form 8949 for short-term capital gains and losses (assets held one year or less) and Part II for long-term capital gains and losses (assets held more than one year). You may have to file more than one Part I or Part II, or multiple copies of both, depending on whether and how your transactions were reported on Form 1099-B ("Proceeds From Broker and Barter Exchange Transactions"). In Parts I and II of Form 8949, you must check a box to indicate whether your basis for sold securities was reported to the IRS by your broker on Form 1099-B. When reporting short-term transactions in Part I, check Box A if Form 1099-B shows that basis was reported to the IRS; check Box B if Form 1099-B shows that basis was not reported to the IRS; and check Box C if you did not receive Form 1099-B for the transactions. In Part II of Form 8949 for long-term transactions, you check Box D if Form 1099-B shows that basis was reported to the IRS, Box E if Form 1099-B shows that basis was not reported to the IRS; and Box F if you did not receive Form 1099-B for the transaction. If you need to check more than one type of box in either Part I or Part II, as when you have some Box A and some Box B or C transactions in Part I, or some Box D and some Box E or F transactions in Part II, you must complete a separate Part I or Part II for each type of box.

In the columns of Form 8949, you report transaction details. You report the sale proceeds in column (d) and your basis in column (e). Report your gain or loss in column (h).

If you did not receive a Form 1099-B (or substitute statement) for a securities transaction, enter in column (d) of Form 8949 the net proceeds. That is, reduce the gross proceeds by your selling expenses such as broker fees, commissions and state and local transfer taxes. Similarly, if you sold real estate and did not receive a Form 1099-S (or substitute statement), you should enter the net proceeds (gross proceeds minus your selling expenses) in column (d) of Form 8949.

If you received a Form 1099-B for a securities transaction, the net proceeds (gross proceeds minus commissions, fees and transfer taxes) should have been reported in Box 1d, but in Box 6 ("Reported to the IRS"), the "gross proceeds" box should be checked. If securities were sold because of the exercise of an option, the broker may report in Box 1d of Form 1099-B either the gross proceeds or reduce the proceeds by any option premiums; a box in Box 6 will be checked to indicate if the gross proceeds or net proceeds have been reported.

Caution

Sale Details Reported to IRS by Brokers on Form 1099-B

If you sold stocks, bonds, commodities, regulated futures contracts or other financial instruments through a broker in 2023, or you exchanged property or services through a barter exchange, the sale is reported to the IRS on Form 1099-B. You are sent Copy B of Form 1099-B or a substitute statement. In Box 1e of Form 1099-B, the broker must report your basis for "covered" securities, which includes stock acquired after 2010, mutual fund shares acquired after 2011, and certain bonds acquired after 2013 (or after 2015 in some cases). If basis is shown in Box 1e, Box 12 should be checked, indicating that the basis has been reported to the IRS. For a "noncovered" security, such as stock acquired before 2011, the broker may omit basis from Box 1e if Box 5 is checked, indicating that a "noncovered" security was sold. Alternatively, the broker may report basis for a noncovered security in Box 1e even though Box 5 is checked, and in this case Box 12 (basis reported to IRS) will also be checked.

You report basis for the asset in column (e) of Form 8949 and Schedule D. The IRS can use the basis information from Box 1e of Form 1099-B to check your computation of gain or loss on Form 8949 and Schedule D.

Caution

Loss on the sale of a personal residence.

You cannot deduct a loss on the sale (or exchange) of a capital asset held for personal use, such as a loss on the sale of your principal residence or a vacation home. Although the loss is not deductible, you must report the transaction on Form 8949 and Schedule D if you received a Form 1099-S. On Form 8949, enter code "L" (the code for a nondeductible loss) in column (f), and then enter the loss as a positive adjustment in column (g). In column (h), the gain or loss will be "0," since the adjustment in column (g) offsets the loss.

If a "covered" security was sold, the basis will be reported in Box 1e of Form 1099-B, and even if a "noncovered" security was sold (if so, Box 5 will be checked), basis may be shown in Box 1e.

On Form 8949, report the sales proceeds and basis as shown on Form 1099-B, and if you have to adjust the amounts shown, follow the Form 8949 instructions for entering the adjustment in column (g) and the adjustment code in column (f).

If you received a Form 1099-S for a real estate sale, the gross proceeds are shown in Box 2. Selling expenses are not taken into account on the form and neither is basis. On Form 8949, enter in column (d) the gross proceeds shown on the Form 1099-S and enter your basis in column (e). You must enter your selling expenses as a negative adjustment in column (g) of Form 8949, with code "E" entered in column (f).

Form 8949 must be attached to Schedule D. The totals from columns (d), (e), (g) and (h) of Form 8949 are transferred to the appropriate lines of Schedule D, depending on which Box was checked on Form 8949 (Box A, B, C, D, E, or F).

The Example below for John and Keisha Taylor and accompanying worksheets illustrate how transactions are entered on Form 8949 and Schedule D.

EXAMPLE

For 2023, John and Keisha Taylor file jointly on Form 1040. They report two short-term transactions in Part I of Form 8949 and three long-term transactions in Part II of Form 8949. On Part I, they check Box A to indicate that for each transaction they received a Form 1099-B that reported their basis. In Part II, they check Box E, indicating that the Forms 1099-B they received did not report basis. For each sale, the broker reported on Form 1099-B the net proceeds (gross sales price minus broker's commissions on the sale and state and local transfer taxes, if any), and the Taylors report that net sales price in column (d) of Form 8949. The totals from columns (d), (e), and (h) of John and Keisha's Form 8949 are transferred to the applicable lines of their Schedule D, as shown below. They also report on Schedule D capital gain distributions received in 2023 from their mutual funds as well as a long-term loss carryover from 2022.

1. Sale of stock (short-term gain)—The Taylors bought 200 shares of XL Research Co. stock on July 26, 2022, for $2,400. They sold the stock on May 12, 2023, for $3,360.

2. Sale of mutual fund shares (short-term loss)—The Taylors bought 100 shares of the XYZ Mutual Fund on November 16, 2022, for $3,500. They sold the shares on February 9, 2023, for $2,500.

3. Sale of stock (long-term gain)—The Taylors bought 100 shares of Acme Steel Co. stock on October 20, 2009, for $6,000. On April 27, 2023, they sold the 100 shares for $13,100.

4. Sale of stock (long-term loss)—The Taylors bought 200 shares of Zero Computer Co. stock for $5,000 on July 10, 2007. On March 18, 2023, they sold the shares for $2,000.

5. Sale of mutual fund shares (long-term gain)—The Taylors bought 1,435 shares of the ABC Mutual Fund between 2010 and 2016. On July 25, 2023, they sold 500 of the shares for $22,500. The average basis *(32.9)* for their shares, shown on their sale confirmation from the Fund, is $24.50 per share. Thus, their basis for the 500 sold shares is $12,250 (500 × $24.50).

6. Capital gain distributions—The Taylors received capital gain distributions of $1,050 in December 2023 from mutual funds *(32.4, 32.8)*.

7. Long-term capital loss carryover—The Taylors had a long-term capital loss carryover of $950 from their 2022 return.

John and Keisha's tax computation on the Qualified Dividends and Capital Gain Tax Worksheet. In the following pages, we show how John and Keisha report their transactions on Form 8949 and Schedule D, and how their 2023 tax liability is figured on the Qualified Dividends and Capital Gain Tax Worksheet (*see* page 128). Because the Taylors do not have a net 28% rate gain or unrecaptured Section 1250 gain, they are directed by Line 20 of Schedule D to use the Qualified Dividends and Capital Gain Tax Worksheet in the Form 1040 instructions to compute their regular income tax liability. If they did have a net 28% rate gain or unrecaptured Section 1250 gain, the Taylors would use the Schedule D Tax Worksheet in the Schedule D instructions, rather than the Qualified Dividends and Capital Gain Tax Worksheet, to figure their tax.

On the Qualified Dividends and Capital Gain Tax Worksheet, John and Keisha will figure the tax on their entire 2023 taxable income, applying the regular tax rates to their ordinary income *(1.2, Table 1-1)*, and the favorable capital gain rates *(5.3, Table 5-2)* to their net capital gain and qualified dividends. Assume that John and Keisha's adjusted gross income (AGI; *12.1*) is $121,450 and they claim the basic standard deduction of $27,700 *(13.2)*, so their taxable income is $93,750 ($121,450 - $27,700). Based on the seven transactions for 2023 shown above, their net capital gain is $14,310; *see* Line 16 of the filled-in Schedule D below (net long-term gain of $14,350 less net short term loss of $40). Also assume that the Taylors have $5,750 of qualified dividends *(4.2)* from Line 3a of Form 1040 that are eligible for the favorable capital gain rates *(5.3)*. The qualified dividends are added to their net capital gain on Lines 2-4 of the Qualified Dividends and Capital Gain Tax Worksheet.

On Lines 6-10 of the Worksheet, the Taylors determine that they are not taxed at all on $15,560 of their $20,060 in combined qualified dividends ($5,750) and net capital gain ($14,310). Since their taxable income of $93,750 exceeds their $20,060 of net capital gain/qualified dividends by $73,690 is treated as their "ordinary income". The 0% rate bracket for net capital gain/qualified dividends ends at $89,250 for 2023 joint filers *(5.3, Table 5-2 and Line 6 of the Worksheet)*, so after taking into account the $73,690 of ordinary income, there is room in the 0% bracket for $15,560 of qualifying dividends and net capital gain ($89,250 − $73,690 = $15,560). The balance of their qualifying dividends and net capital gain, or $4,500 ($20,060 − $15,560 untaxed amount), is taxed at the 15% capital gain rate, for a tax of $675 (Line 18 of the Worksheet). The tax on the ordinary income of $73,690 is $8,403 (using the IRS 2023 Tax Table). The Taylors' total tax liability of $9,078 ($675 plus $8,403; Line 25 of the Worksheet) is $2,162 less than the liability of $11,240 that would apply (shown on Line 24 of the Worksheet) if the law did not provide favorable rates for net capital gain and qualified dividends.

Sample Form 8949—Sales and Other Dispositions of Capital Assets

(This sample is subject to change; see the e-Supplement at jklasser.com)

Form **8949**	**Sales and Other Dispositions of Capital Assets**	OMB No. 1545-0074
Department of the Treasury Internal Revenue Service	File with your Schedule D to list your transactions for lines 1b, 2, 3, 8b, 9, and 10 of Schedule D. Go to *www.irs.gov/Form8949* for instructions and the latest information.	**2023** Attachment Sequence No. **12A**

Name(s) shown on return	Social security number or taxpayer identification number
John and Keisha Taylor	

Before you check Box A, B, or C below, see whether you received any Form(s) 1099-B or substitute statement(s) from your broker. A substitute statement will have the same information as Form 1099-B. Either will show whether your basis (usually your cost) was reported to the IRS by your broker and may even tell you which box to check.

Part I — **Short-Term.** Transactions involving capital assets you held 1 year or less are generally short-term (see instructions). For long-term transactions, see page 2.

Note: You may aggregate all short-term transactions reported on Form(s) 1099-B showing basis was reported to the IRS and for which no adjustments or codes are required. Enter the totals directly on Schedule D, line 1a; you aren't required to report these transactions on Form 8949 (see instructions).

You *must* check Box A, B, or C below. Check only one box. If more than one box applies for your short-term transactions, complete a separate Form 8949, page 1, for each applicable box. If you have more short-term transactions than will fit on this page for one or more of the boxes, complete as many forms with the same box checked as you need.

- ☑ **(A)** Short-term transactions reported on Form(s) 1099-B showing basis was reported to the IRS (see **Note** above)
- ☐ **(B)** Short-term transactions reported on Form(s) 1099-B showing basis **wasn't** reported to the IRS
- ☐ **(C)** Short-term transactions not reported to you on Form 1099-B

1 **(a)** Description of property (Example: 100 sh. XYZ Co.)	**(b)** Date acquired (Mo., day, yr.)	**(c)** Date sold or disposed of (Mo., day, yr.)	**(d)** Proceeds (sales price) (see instructions)	**(e)** Cost or other basis See the **Note** below and see *Column (e)* in the separate instructions.	**(f)** Code(s) from instructions	**(g)** Amount of adjustment	**(h)** Gain or (loss) Subtract column (e) from column (d) and combine the result with column (g).
200 Shares—XL Research Company	7-26-2022	5-12-2023	3,360	2,400			960
100 Shares—XYZ Mutual Funds	11-16-2022	2-9-2023	2,500	3,500			(1,000)
2 Totals. Add the amounts in columns (d), (e), (g), and (h) (subtract negative amounts). Enter each total here and include on your Schedule D, **line 1b** (if **Box A** above is checked), **line 2** (if **Box B** above is checked), or **line 3** (if **Box C** above is checked) . .			5,860	5,900			(40)

Note: If you checked Box A above but the basis reported to the IRS was incorrect, enter in column (e) the basis as reported to the IRS, and enter an adjustment in column (g) to correct the basis. See *Column (g)* in the separate instructions for how to figure the amount of the adjustment.

For Paperwork Reduction Act Notice, see your tax return instructions.   Cat. No. 37768Z   Form **8949** (2023)

Sample Form 8949—Sales and Other Dispositions of Capital Assets

(This sample is subject to change; see the e-Supplement at jklasser.com)

Form 8949 (2023)	Attachment Sequence No. **12A** Page **2**
Name(s) shown on return. Name and SSN or taxpayer identification no. not required if shown on other side	**Social security number or taxpayer identification number**

Before you check Box D, E, or F below, see whether you received any Form(s) 1099-B or substitute statement(s) from your broker. A substitute statement will have the same information as Form 1099-B. Either will show whether your basis (usually your cost) was reported to the IRS by your broker and may even tell you which box to check.

Part II **Long-Term.** Transactions involving capital assets you held more than 1 year are generally long-term (see instructions). For short-term transactions, see page 1.

Note: You may aggregate all long-term transactions reported on Form(s) 1099-B showing basis was reported to the IRS and for which no adjustments or codes are required. Enter the totals directly on Schedule D, line 8a; you aren't required to report these transactions on Form 8949 (see instructions).

You **must** check Box D, E, *or* F below. **Check only one box.** If more than one box applies for your long-term transactions, complete a separate Form 8949, page 2, for each applicable box. If you have more long-term transactions than will fit on this page for one or more of the boxes, complete as many forms with the same box checked as you need.

- ☐ **(D)** Long-term transactions reported on Form(s) 1099-B showing basis was reported to the IRS (see **Note** above)
- ☑ **(E)** Long-term transactions reported on Form(s) 1099-B showing basis **wasn't** reported to the IRS
- ☐ **(F)** Long-term transactions not reported to you on Form 1099-B

1

(a) Description of property (Example: 100 sh. XYZ Co.)	(b) Date acquired (Mo., day, yr.)	(c) Date sold or disposed of (Mo., day, yr.)	(d) Proceeds (sales price) (see instructions)	(e) Cost or other basis See the **Note** below and see *Column (e)* in the separate instructions.	(f) Code(s) from instructions	(g) Amount of adjustment	(h) Gain or (loss) Subtract column (e) from column (d) and combine the result with column (g).
100 Shares—ACME Steel Company	10-20-2009	4-27-2023	13,100	6,000			7,100
200 Shares—ZERO Computer Company	7-10-2007	3-18-2023	2,000	5,000			(3,000)
500 Shares—ABC Mutuals Funds	"Various"	7-25-2023	22,500	12,250			10,250
2 Totals. Add the amounts in columns (d), (e), (g), and (h) (subtract negative amounts). Enter each total here and include on your Schedule D, **line 8b** (if **Box D** above is checked), **line 9** (if **Box E** above is checked), or **line 10** (if **Box F** above is checked) .			37,600	23,250			14,350

Note: If you checked Box D above but the basis reported to the IRS was incorrect, enter in column (e) the basis as reported to the IRS, and enter an adjustment in column (g) to correct the basis. See *Column (g)* in the separate instructions for how to figure the amount of the adjustment.

Form **8949** (2023)

Sample Schedule D—Capital Gains and Losses
(This sample is subject to change; see the e-Supplement at jklasser.com)

SCHEDULE D (Form 1040) Department of the Treasury Internal Revenue Service	**Capital Gains and Losses** Attach to Form 1040, 1040-SR, or 1040-NR. Use Form 8949 to list your transactions for lines 1b, 2, 3, 8b, 9, and 10. Go to *www.irs.gov/ScheduleD* for instructions and the latest information.	OMB No. 1545-0074 2023 Attachment Sequence No. 12

Name(s) shown on return	Your social security number
John and Keisha Taylor	X11-01-11X0

Did you dispose of any investment(s) in a qualified opportunity fund during the tax year? ☐ Yes ☑ No
If "Yes," attach Form 8949 and see its instructions for additional requirements for reporting your gain or loss.

Part I — Short-Term Capital Gains and Losses—Generally Assets Held One Year or Less (see instructions)

See instructions for how to figure the amounts to enter on the lines below. This form may be easier to complete if you round off cents to whole dollars.	(d) Proceeds (sales price)	(e) Cost (or other basis)	(g) Adjustments to gain or loss from Form(s) 8949, Part I, line 2, column (g)	(h) Gain or (loss) Subtract column (e) from column (d) and combine the result with column (g)
1a Totals for all short-term transactions reported on Form 1099-B for which basis was reported to the IRS and for which you have no adjustments (see instructions). However, if you choose to report all these transactions on Form 8949, leave this line blank and go to line 1b .	5,860	5,900		(40)
1b Totals for all transactions reported on Form(s) 8949 with **Box A** checked				
2 Totals for all transactions reported on Form(s) 8949 with **Box B** checked				
3 Totals for all transactions reported on Form(s) 8949 with **Box C** checked				

4 Short-term gain from Form 6252 and short-term gain or (loss) from Forms 4684, 6781, and 8824 . .	**4**	
5 Net short-term gain or (loss) from partnerships, S corporations, estates, and trusts from Schedule(s) K-1	**5**	
6 Short-term capital loss carryover. Enter the amount, if any, from line 8 of your **Capital Loss Carryover Worksheet** in the instructions	**6**	( )
7 **Net short-term capital gain or (loss).** Combine lines 1a through 6 in column (h). If you have any long-term capital gains or losses, go to Part II below. Otherwise, go to Part III on the back	**7**	(40)

Part II — Long-Term Capital Gains and Losses—Generally Assets Held More Than One Year (see instructions)

See instructions for how to figure the amounts to enter on the lines below. This form may be easier to complete if you round off cents to whole dollars.	(d) Proceeds (sales price)	(e) Cost (or other basis)	(g) Adjustments to gain or loss from Form(s) 8949, Part II, line 2, column (g)	(h) Gain or (loss) Subtract column (e) from column (d) and combine the result with column (g)
8a Totals for all long-term transactions reported on Form 1099-B for which basis was reported to the IRS and for which you have no adjustments (see instructions). However, if you choose to report all these transactions on Form 8949, leave this line blank and go to line 8b .	37,600	23,250		14,350
8b Totals for all transactions reported on Form(s) 8949 with **Box D** checked				
9 Totals for all transactions reported on Form(s) 8949 with **Box E** checked				
10 Totals for all transactions reported on Form(s) 8949 with **Box F** checked.				

11 Gain from Form 4797, Part I; long-term gain from Forms 2439 and 6252; and long-term gain or (loss) from Forms 4684, 6781, and 8824	**11**	
12 Net long-term gain or (loss) from partnerships, S corporations, estates, and trusts from Schedule(s) K-1	**12**	
13 Capital gain distributions. See the instructions	**13**	
14 Long-term capital loss carryover. Enter the amount, if any, from line 13 of your **Capital Loss Carryover Worksheet** in the instructions	**14**	( )
15 **Net long-term capital gain or (loss).** Combine lines 8a through 14 in column (h). Then, go to Part III on the back	**15**	14,350

For Paperwork Reduction Act Notice, see your tax return instructions. Cat. No. 11338H Schedule D (Form 1040) 2023

Sample Schedule D—Capital Gains and Losses
(This sample is subject to change; see the e-Supplement at jklasser.com)

Part III	**Summary**

16	Combine lines 7 and 15 and enter the result	**16**	14,310

- If line 16 is a **gain**, enter the amount from line 16 on Form 1040, 1040-SR, or 1040-NR, line 7. Then, go to line 17 below.
- If line 16 is a **loss**, skip lines 17 through 20 below. Then, go to line 21. Also be sure to complete line 22.
- If line 16 is **zero**, skip lines 17 through 21 below and enter -0- on Form 1040, 1040-SR, or 1040-NR, line 7. Then, go to line 22.

17   Are lines 15 and 16 **both** gains?

     ☐ **Yes.** Go to line 18.

     ☐ **No.** Skip lines 18 through 21, and go to line 22.

18   If you are required to complete the **28% Rate Gain Worksheet** (see instructions), enter the amount, if any, from line 7 of that worksheet **18**

19   If you are required to complete the **Unrecaptured Section 1250 Gain Worksheet** (see instructions), enter the amount, if any, from line 18 of that worksheet **19**

20   Are lines 18 and 19 both zero or blank and you are not filing Form 4952?

     ☐ **Yes.** Complete the **Qualified Dividends and Capital Gain Tax Worksheet** in the instructions for Form 1040, line 16. **Don't** complete lines 21 and 22 below.

     ☐ **No.** Complete the **Schedule D Tax Worksheet** in the instructions. **Don't** complete lines 21 and 22 below.

21   If line 16 is a loss, enter here and on Form 1040, 1040-SR, or 1040-NR, line 7, the **smaller** of:

- The loss on line 16; or
- ($3,000), or if married filing separately, ($1,500)   . . . . **21** (   )

Note: When figuring which amount is smaller, treat both amounts as positive numbers.

22   Do you have qualified dividends on Form 1040, 1040-SR, or 1040-NR, line 3a?

     ☐ **Yes.** Complete the **Qualified Dividends and Capital Gain Tax Worksheet** in the instructions for Form 1040, line 16.

     ☐ **No.** Complete the rest of Form 1040, 1040-SR, or 1040-NR.

Schedule D (Form 1040) 2023

Qualified Dividends and Capital Gain Tax Worksheet—Line 16

Keep for Your Records

Before you begin:	✓ See the earlier instructions for line 16 to see if you can use this worksheet to figure your tax.	
	✓ Before completing this worksheet, complete Form 1040 or 1040-SR through line 15.	
	✓ If you don't have to file Schedule D and you received capital gain distributions, be sure you checked the box on Form 1040 or 1040-SR, line 7.	

1.	Enter the amount from Form 1040 or 1040-SR, line 15. However, if you are filing Form 2555 (relating to foreign earned income), enter the amount from line 3 of the Foreign Earned Income Tax Worksheet	1.	93,750
2.	Enter the amount from Form 1040 or 1040-SR, line 3a*	2.	5,750
3.	Are you filing Schedule D?*	3.	14,310
	■ **Yes.** Enter the **smaller** of line 15 or line 16 of Schedule D. If either line 15 or line 16 is blank or a loss, enter -0-.		
	☐ **No.** Enter the amount from Form 1040 or 1040-SR, line 7.		
4.	Add lines 2 and 3	4.	20,060
5.	Subtract line 4 from line 1. If zero or less, enter -0-	5.	73,690
6.	Enter: $44,625 if single or married filing separately, $89,250 if married filing jointly or qualifying surviving spouse, $59,750 if head of household.	6.	89,250
7.	Enter the smaller of line 1 or line 6	7.	89,250
8.	Enter the smaller of line 5 or line 7	8.	73,690
9.	Subtract line 8 from line 7. This amount is taxed at 0%	9.	15,560
10.	Enter the smaller of line 1 or line 4	10.	20,060
11.	Enter the amount from line 9	11.	15,560
12.	Subtract line 11 from line 10	12.	4,500
13.	Enter: $492,300 if single, $276,900 if married filing separately, $553,850 if married filing jointly or qualifying surviving spouse, $523,050 if head of household.	13.	553,850
14.	Enter the smaller of line 1 or line 13	14.	93,750
15.	Add lines 5 and 9	15.	89,250
16.	Subtract line 15 from line 14. If zero or less, enter -0-	16.	4,500
17.	Enter the smaller of line 12 or line 16	17.	4,500
18.	Multiply line 17 by 15% (0.15)	18.	675
19.	Add lines 9 and 17	19.	20,060
20.	Subtract line 19 from line 10	20.	– 0 –
21.	Multiply line 20 by 20% (0.20)	21.	– 0 –
22.	Figure the tax on the amount on line 5. If the amount on line 5 is less than $100,000, use the Tax Table to figure the tax. If the amount on line 5 is $100,000 or more, use the Tax Computation Worksheet	22.	8,403
23.	Add lines 18, 21, and 22	23.	9,078
24.	Figure the tax on the amount on line 1. If the amount on line 1 is less than $100,000, use the Tax Table to figure the tax. If the amount on line 1 is $100,000 or more, use the Tax Computation Worksheet	24.	11,240
25.	**Tax on all taxable income.** Enter the **smaller** of line 23 or line 24. Also include this amount on the entry space on Form 1040 or 1040-SR, line 16. If you are filing Form 2555, don't enter this amount on the entry space on Form 1040 or 1040-SR, line 16. Instead, enter it on line 4 of the Foreign Earned Income Tax Worksheet	25.	9,078

* If you are filing Form 2555, see the footnote in the Foreign Earned Income Tax Worksheet before completing this line.

5.9   Counting the Months in Your Holding Period

The period of time you own a capital asset before its sale or exchange determines whether capital gain or loss is short term or long term.

These are the rules for counting the holding period:

1. A holding period is figured in months and fractions of months.

2. The beginning date of a holding month is generally the day after the asset was acquired. The same numerical date of each following month starts a new holding month regardless of the number of days in the preceding month. If you acquire an asset on the last day of a month, a holding month ends on the last day of a following calendar month, regardless of the number of days in each month.

3. The last day of the holding period is the day on which the asset is sold.

EXAMPLES

1. On September 20, 2023, you buy stock. The holding months begin on September 21, October 21, November 21, and December 21, etc., and end on October 20, November 20, December 20, etc. A sale on or after September 21, 2024, would result in long-term gain or loss.

2. You buy stock on June 30, 2023. A holding month ends on July 31, August 31, September 30, October 31, November 30, and December 31, 2023, and in 2024, January 31, February 28, etc.

5.10   Holding Period for Securities

Rules for counting your holding period for various securities transactions are as follows:

Stock sold on a public exchange. The holding period starts on the day after your purchase order is executed (trade date). The day your sale order is executed (trade date) is the last day of the holding period, even if delivery and payment are not made until several days after the actual sale (settlement date).

EXAMPLES

1. On June 3, you sell a stock at a profit. Your holding period ends on June 3, although proceeds are not received until June 6.

2. You sell stock at a gain on a public exchange on Friday, December 29, 2023. The gain must be reported on your 2023 return even though the proceeds are received in 2024. The installment sale rule does not apply; *see 5.21.*

Stock subscriptions. If you are bound by your subscription but the corporation is not, the holding period begins the day after the date on which the stock is issued. If both you and the company are bound, the date the subscription is accepted by the corporation is the date of acquisition, and your holding period begins the day after.

Tax-free stock rights. When you exercise rights to acquire corporate stock from the issuing corporation, your holding period for the stock begins on the day of exercise, not on the day after. You are deemed to exercise stock rights when you assent to the terms of the rights in the manner requested or authorized by the corporation. An option to acquire stock is not a stock right.

FIFO method for stock sold from different lots. If you purchased shares of the same stock on different dates and cannot determine which shares you are selling, the shares purchased at the earliest time are considered the stock sold first; this is called the FIFO (first-in, first-out) method *(30.2)*.

Commodities. If you acquired a commodity futures contract, the holding period of a commodity accepted in satisfaction of the contract includes your holding period of the contract, unless you are a dealer in commodities.

Planning Reminder

Long-Term Holding Period of More Than a Year

To obtain the benefit of favorable long-term capital gains rates *(5.3)*, you must hold an asset more than a year before selling it.

Employee stock options. When an employee exercises a stock option, the holding period of the acquired stock begins on the day after the option is exercised. If an employee option plan allows the exercise of an option by giving notes, the terms of the plan should be reviewed to determine when ownership rights to the stock are transferred. The terms may affect the start of the holding period for the stock.

Wash sales. After a wash sale, the holding period of the new stock includes the holding period of the old stock for which a loss has been disallowed *(30.6)*.

Other references. For the holding period of stock dividends, *see 30.3*; for short sales, *see 30.5*; and for convertible securities, *see 30.7*.

> **EXAMPLE**
>
> You purchased 100 shares of ABC stock on May 3, 1995, 100 shares of ABC stock on May 1, 1997, and 300 shares of ABC stock on September 2, 1998. In 2023, you sell 250 shares of ABC stock, and are unable to determine when those particular shares were bought. Using the "first-in, first-out" method, 100 shares are from May 3, 1995, 100 shares from May 1, 1997, and 50 shares are from September 2, 1998 *(30.2)*.

5.11 Holding Period for Real Estate

Your holding period starts on the day after the date of acquisition. The acquisition date is the earlier of: (1) the date title passes to you or (2) the date you take possession and you assume the burdens and privileges of ownership under the contract of sale; taking possession under an option agreement does not start your holding period. In disputes involving the starting and closing dates of a holding period, you may refer to the state law that applies to your sale or purchase agreement. State law determines when title to property passes.

If you convert a residence to rental property and later sell the home, the holding period includes the time you held the home for personal purposes.

Year-end sale. The date of sale is the last day of your holding period even if you do not receive the sale proceeds until the following year. For example, you sell land held for investment at a gain on December 30, 2023, receiving payment in January 2024. Your holding period ends on December 30, although the sale is reported in 2024 when the proceeds are received. Note that the December 30 gain transaction can be reported on your 2023 return by making an election to "elect out" of installment reporting *(5.23)*. If you had a loss on the sale, it is reported as a loss for 2024, when the proceeds are received.

5.12 Holding Period: Gifts, Inheritances, and Other Property

Gift property. If, in figuring a gain or loss, your basis for the property under *5.17* is the same as the donor's basis, you add the donor's holding period to the period you held the property. If you sell the property at a loss using as your basis the fair market value at the date of the gift *(5.17)*, your holding period begins on the day after the date of the gift.

Inherited property. The law gives an automatic holding period of more than one year for property inherited from someone who died before or after 2010. Report the transaction in Part II of Form 8949 ("Long-Term") and enter "INHERITED" in column (b) as the date of acquisition.

If property was inherited from someone who died in 2010 and the executor elected on Form 8939 to apply modified carryover basis rules *(5.17)*, the holding period for property subject to those rules includes the period that the deceased held it; *see* Publication 4895 (Rev. October 2011) and Revenue Procedure 2011-41.

Where property is purchased by the executor or trustee and distributed to you, your holding period begins the day after the date on which the property was purchased.

Partnership property. When you receive property as a distribution in kind from your partnership, the period your partnership held the property is added to your holding period. But there is no adding on of holding periods if the partnership property distributed was inventory and was sold by you within five years of distribution.

Planning Reminder

Year-End Sales

Tax reporting for year-end sales of real estate is different from that for publicly traded securities. Gain on a sale of realty at the end of 2023 may be deferred under the installment sale rules *(5.22)* if payments will be received in 2024 or later years. Gain on a sale of publicly traded securities at the end of 2023 must be reported on your 2023 return although you receive payment in 2024.

Filing Tip

Selling Inherited Property

When you sell property that you inherited from someone who died before or after 2010 (and usually in 2010 as well, *see 5.17*), report the sale as long-term gain or loss on Form 8949 and Schedule D even if you actually held the property for less than one year. The law automatically treats inherited property as if it were held for more than one year.

Involuntary conversions. When you have an involuntary conversion and elect to defer tax on gain, the holding period for the qualified replacement property generally includes the period you held the converted property. A new holding period begins for new property if you do not make an election to defer tax.

5.13 Calculating Gain or Loss

In most cases, you know if you have realized an economic profit or loss on the sale or exchange of property. You know your cost and selling price. The difference between the two is your profit or loss. The computation of gain or loss for tax purposes is similarly figured, except that the basis adjustment rules may require you to increase or decrease your cost and the amount-realized rules may require you to increase the selling price. As a result, your gain or loss for tax purposes may differ from your initial calculation.

When reporting a sale on Form 8949, follow the form instructions for reporting sale proceeds, basis, and selling expenses (5.8).

 *Planning Reminder*

Records for Rental Property Improvements

Keep records of permanent improvements and legal fees for rental property. These increase your basis and lower any potential gain when you sell the property.

EXAMPLE

You sell rental property to a buyer who pays you cash of $150,000 and assumes your $135,000 mortgage. You bought the property for $55,000 and made $12,000 of permanent improvements. You deducted depreciation of $7,250. Selling expenses were $6,000. Your gain on the sale is $219,250, figured as follows:

1.	Amount realized (5.14)		
	Cash	$150,000	
	Mortgage assumed by buyer	135,000	
		$285,000	
2.	Minus selling expenses*	6,000	
3.	Net proceeds	279,000	
4.	Original cost	55,000	
5.	Plus improvements	12,000	
		$67,000	
6.	Minus depreciation	7,250	
7.	Adjusted basis	59,750	
8.	Gain: Subtract Line 7 from Line 3	$219,250	

Table 5-3   Figuring Gain or Loss on Form 8949 and Schedule D

1.	Amount realized or total selling price (5.14), minus selling expenses*.		$ _____
2.	Cost or other unadjusted basis (5.16).	$ _____	
3.	Plus: Improvements; certain legal fees (5.20).	$ _____	
4.	Minus: Depreciation, casualty losses (5.20).	$ _____	
5.	Adjusted basis: 2 plus 3 minus 4 (5.20).	$ _____	
6.	Gain or loss: Subtract 5 from 1.		$ _____

*Selling expenses on Form 8949 and Schedule D. As discussed in 5.8, the Form 8949 instructions require you to report the net proceeds (gross proceeds minus your selling expenses) if you did not receive a Form 1099-B or Form 1099-S for your transaction. If you sold securities and received a Form 1099-B on which the net proceeds shown does not include all of your selling expenses, you enter on Form 8949/Schedule D the proceeds shown on Form 1099-B and then enter the additional selling expenses as a negative adjustment. If you sold real estate for which you received a Form 1099-S, selling expenses are not shown on that form; enter on Form 8949/Schedule D the proceeds shown on Form 1099-S and then enter the additional selling expenses as a negative adjustment.

5.14 Amount Realized Is the Total Selling Price

Amount realized is the tax term for the total selling price. It includes cash, the fair market value of additional property received, and any of your liabilities that the buyer agrees to pay. The buyer's note is included in the selling price at fair market value. This is generally the discounted amount that a bank or other party will pay for the note.

Sale of mortgaged property. The selling price includes the amount of the unpaid mortgage. This is true whether or not you are personally liable on the debt, and whether or not the buyer assumes the mortgage or merely takes the property subject to the mortgage. The full amount of the unpaid mortgage is included, even where the value of the property is less than the unpaid mortgage. Computing amount realized on foreclosure sales is discussed in *Chapter 31 (31.9)*.

If, at the time of the sale, the buyer pays off the existing mortgage or your other liabilities, you include the payment as part of the sales proceeds.

Caution

Mortgaged Property

When you sell mortgaged property, you must include the unpaid balance of the mortgage as part of the sales price received, in addition to any cash.

EXAMPLES

1. You sell property subject to a mortgage of $60,000. The seller pays you cash of $30,000 and takes the property subject to the mortgage. The sales price or "amount realized" is $90,000.

2. A partnership receives a nonrecourse mortgage of $1,851,500 from a bank to build an apartment project. Several years later, the partnership sells the project for the buyer's agreement to assume the unpaid mortgage. At the time, the value of the project is $1,400,000 and the partnership basis in the project is $1,455,740. The partnership figures a loss of $55,740, the difference between basis and the value of the project. The IRS figures a gain of $395,760, the difference between the unpaid mortgage and basis. The partnership claims the selling price is limited to the lower fair market value and is supported by an appeals court. The Supreme Court reverses, supporting the IRS position. That the value of property is less than the amount of the mortgage has no effect on the rule requiring the unpaid mortgage to be part of the selling price. A mortgagor realizes value to the extent that his or her obligation to repay is relieved by a third party's assumption of the mortgage debt.

5.15 Finding Your Cost

In figuring gain or loss, you need to know the "unadjusted basis" of the property sold. This term refers to the original cost of your property if you purchased it. The general rules for determining your unadjusted basis are in *5.16*. Basis for property received by gift or inheritance is in *5.17*; rules for surviving joint tenants are in *5.18*. Keep in mind that you have to adjust this figure for improvements to the property, depreciation, or losses *(5.20)*.

5.16 Unadjusted Basis of Your Property

To determine your tax cost for property, first find in the following section the unadjusted basis of the property, and then increase or decrease that basis *(5.20)*.

Property you bought. Unadjusted basis is your cash cost plus the value of any property you gave to the seller. If you assumed a mortgage or bought property subject to a mortgage, the amount of the mortgage is part of your unadjusted basis.

Purchase expenses are included in your cost, such as commissions, title insurance, recording fees, survey costs, and transfer taxes.

If you buy real estate and reimburse the seller for property taxes he or she paid that cover the period after you took title, and you include the payment in your itemized deduction for real estate taxes *(16.4)*, do not add the reimbursement to your basis. However, if you did not reimburse the seller, you must reduce your basis by the seller's payment.

Filing Tip

Basis of Mutual Fund Shares

To figure gain or loss on the sale of mutual fund shares where purchases are made at various times, you may use an averaging method to determine the cost basis of the shares sold *(32.9, 32.10)*.

EXAMPLE

You bought a building for $120,000 in cash and a purchase money mortgage of $60,000. The unadjusted basis of the building is $180,000.

If at the closing you also paid property taxes attributable to the time the seller held the property, you add such taxes to basis.

Property obtained for services. If you paid for the property by providing services, the value of the property, which is taxable compensation, is also your adjusted basis.

Property received in taxable exchange. Your unadjusted basis for the new property is generally equal to the fair market value of the property received. *See* below for tax-free exchanges.

> ### EXAMPLE
>
> You acquire real estate for $135,000. When the property has a fair market value of $140,000, you exchange it for machinery also worth $140,000. You have a gain of $5,000 and the basis of the machinery is $140,000.

Real property held for investment or business received in a tax-free like-kind exchange. The computation of basis is made on Form 8824. If the exchange is completely tax free *(6.2)*, your basis for the new property will be your basis for the property you gave up in the exchange, plus any additional cash and exchange expenses you paid. If the exchange is partly nontaxable and partly taxable because you received "boot" *(6.2)*, your basis for the new property will be your basis for the property given up in the exchange, decreased by any cash received and by any liabilities on the property you gave up, and increased by any cash and exchange expenses you paid, liabilities on the property you received, and gain taxed to you on the exchange. Gain is taxed to the extent you receive "boot," in the form of cash or a transfer of liabilities that exceeds the liabilities assumed in the exchange; *see 6.2* for a discussion on taxable boot. The Example in *6.2* illustrates the basis computation.

Property received from a spouse or former spouse. Tax-free exchange rules apply to transfers of property to a spouse, or to a former spouse where the transfer is incident to a divorce *(6.6)*. The spouse receiving the property takes a basis equal to that of the transferor. Certain adjustments may be required where a transfer of mortgaged property is made in trust. The tax-free exchange rule applies to transfers between spouses after July 18, 1984.

If you received property before July 19, 1984, under a prenuptial agreement in exchange for your release of your dower and marital rights, your basis is the fair market value at the time you received it.

 *Planning Reminder*

Carryover Basis From Spouse or Ex-Spouse

If you receive a gift of property from your spouse or you receive property from a former spouse in a divorce settlement, your basis for the property is generally the same as the spouse's basis *(6.6)*.

> ### EXAMPLES
>
> 1. You exchange investment real estate, which cost you $100,000, for other investment real estate. Both properties have a fair market value of $125,000 and neither property is mortgaged. You pay no tax on the exchange. The unadjusted basis of the new property received in the exchange is $100,000.
>
> 2. Same facts as in Example 1, but you receive real estate worth $115,000 and cash of $10,000. On this transaction, you realize gain of $25,000 (amount realized of $125,000 less your basis of $100,000), but only $10,000 of the gain is taxable, equal to the cash "boot" received. Your basis for the new property is $100,000, figured this way:
>
> | | |
> |---|---:|
> | Basis of old property | $100,000 |
> | Less: Cash received | 10,000 |
> | | 90,000 |
> | Plus: Gain recognized | 10,000 |
> | Basis of new property | $100,000 |

New residence purchased under tax deferral rule of prior law. If you sold your old principal residence and bought a qualifying replacement under the prior law deferral rules, your basis for the new house is what you paid for it, less any gain that was not taxed on the sale of the old residence.

Property received as a trust beneficiary. Generally, you take the same basis the trust had for the property. But if the distribution is made to settle a claim you had against the trust, your basis for the property is the amount of the settled claim.

If you received a distribution in kind for your share of trust income after June 1, 1984, your basis is the basis of the property in the hands of the trust. If the trust elects to treat the distribution as a taxable sale, your basis is generally fair market value. For distributions before June 2, 1984, the basis of the distribution is generally the value of the property to the extent allocated to distributable net income.

> **EXAMPLE**
>
> A building with an adjusted basis of $100,000 is destroyed by fire. The owner receives an insurance award of $200,000, realizing a gain of $100,000. He buys a building as a replacement for $150,000. Of the $100,000 gain, $50,000 is taxable, while the remaining $50,000 is deferred. Taxable gain is limited to the portion of the insurance award not used to buy replacement property ($200,000 − $150,000). The basis of the new building is $100,000:
>
> | | |
> |---|---|
> | Cost of the new building | $150,000 |
> | Less: deferred gain | 50,000 |
> | Basis | $100,000 |

Property acquired with involuntary conversion proceeds. If you acquire replacement property *(18.17)* with insurance proceeds from destroyed property, or a government payment for condemned property, basis is the cost of the new property decreased by the amount of the gain that is deferred *(18.16)*. If the replacement property consists of more than one piece of property, basis is allocated to each piece in proportion to its respective cost.

5.17 Basis of Property You Inherited or Received as a Gift

Special basis rules apply to property you received as a gift or that you inherited. Gifts from a spouse are subject to the rules discussed in *6.7*. If you are a surviving joint tenant who received full title to property upon the death of the other joint tenant, *see 5.18*.

Basis of Property Received as Gift

If the fair market value of the property equaled or exceeded the donor's adjusted basis *(5.20)* at the time you received the gift, your basis for figuring gain or loss when you sell it is the donor's adjusted basis plus all or part of any gift tax paid; *see* the gift tax rule below. Additional adjustments to basis (plus or minus) may be required for the period you held the property *(5.20)*.

If on the date of the gift the fair market value of the property was less than the donor's adjusted basis, there are two basis rules, one for determining if you have a gain, and another for determining if you have a loss. For purposes of figuring gain when you sell the property, your basis is the donor's adjusted basis, and your basis for figuring loss is the fair market value on the date of the gift. Additional adjustments to basis (plus or minus) may be required for the period you held the property *(5.20)*.

Depending on your selling price, it is possible that you will have neither gain nor loss when you sell. This happens when you figure a loss when using the donor's basis as your basis (the basis rule for determining if you have a gain), and you figure a gain when using the fair market value of the property at the time of the gift as your basis (the basis rule for determining if you have a loss); *see* Line 3 of Example 1 below.

Did the donor pay gift tax? If the donor paid a gift tax *(39.2)* on the gift to you, your basis for the property is increased under these rules:

1. For property received after December 31, 1976, the basis is increased by an amount that bears the same ratio to the amount of gift tax paid by the donor as the net appreciation in the value of the gift bears to the amount of the gift after taking into account the annual gift tax exclusion *(39.2)* that applied in the year of the gift. The

Caution

Basis for Gift

The basis of gift property you receive generally depends on the donor's basis. Make sure you get this information from the donor.

increase may not exceed the tax paid. Net appreciation in the value of any gift is the amount by which the fair market value of the gift exceeds the donor's adjusted basis immediately before the gift. *See* Example 3 below.

2. For property received after September 1, 1958, but before 1977, basis is increased by the gift tax paid on the property but not above the fair market value of the property at the time of the gift.

EXAMPLES

1. Assume that in 2008 you received a gift of stock from your father that you sold in 2023. Your father's adjusted basis for the stock was $1,000.

   The basis you use to determine your gain or loss on your 2023 sale depends on whether the fair market value of the stock on the date of the gift equaled or exceeded your father's $1,000 adjusted basis. If it did, your basis is your father's $1,000 basis and you will realize a gain if your selling price exceeds $1,000, as on Line 1 below, or a loss if the selling price is below $1,000, as on Line 4.

   If the value of the stock on the date of the gift was less than $1,000 (father's basis) then you use your father's basis to figure if you have a gain and the date-of-gift value to figure if you have a loss. Thus, you have a gain if you sell for more than $1,000, as on Line 5 below; a loss if you sell for less than the date-of-gift value, as on Line 2; or neither gain nor loss if you sell for more than the date-of-gift value but no more than $1,000 (father's basis), as on Line 3.

	If value of the gift at receipt was—	And you sold it for—	Your basis is—	Your gain is—	Your loss is—
1.	$3,000	$2,000	$1,000	$1,000	none
2.	700	500	700	none	$ 200
3.	300	500	*	none	none
4.	1,500	500	1,000	none	500
5.	500	1,200	1,000	200	none

   *On Line 3 of the Example, where you sell for more than the date-of-gift value but for no more than the donor's basis, there is neither gain nor loss. To see if you have a gain, you use the donor's $1,000 basis as your basis, but on a sale for $500, you have a loss ($500) and not a gain. To see if you have a loss, you use the $300 date-of-gift value of the stock as your basis, but on a sale for $500, you have a gain ($200) and not a loss. Thus, you have neither gain nor loss under the basis rules, which require you to use the donor's basis for determining if you have a gain and the date-of-gift value for determining if you have a loss.

2. In 1975, your father gave you rental property with a fair market value of $78,000. The basis of the property in his hands was $60,000. He paid a gift tax of $15,000 on the gift. The basis of the property in your hands is $75,000 ($60,000 + $15,000).

3. In 2001, your father gave you rental property with a fair market value of $178,000. His basis in the property was $160,000. He paid a gift tax of $44,560 on a taxable gift of $168,000, after claiming the $10,000 annual exclusion. The basis of the property in your hands is your father's basis increased by the gift tax attributable to the appreciation. Gift tax attributable to the appreciation is:

$$\frac{\text{Appreciation}}{\text{Gift minus annual exclusion}} \times \text{Gift tax paid}$$

$$\frac{\$18,000}{\$168,000} \times \$44,560 = \$4,774$$

   Your basis for figuring gain or loss or depreciation is $164,774 ($4,774 + $160,000 father's basis).

Filing Tip

No Gain or Loss

When you sell property that you received as a gift, it is possible that you may realize neither gain nor loss. You have neither gain nor loss if you sell for more than the date-of-gift value but not more than the donor's adjusted basis.

Depreciation on property received as a gift. If the property is depreciable *(Chapter 42)*, your basis for computing depreciation deductions is the donor's adjusted basis *(5.20)*, plus all or part of the gift tax paid by the donors as previously discussed.

To figure gain or loss when you sell the property, you must adjust basis for depreciation you claimed and make other adjustments required for the period you hold the property *(5.20)*. If accelerated depreciation is claimed and you sell at a gain, you are subject to the ordinary income recapture rules *(44.1)*.

Basis of Inherited Property

Your basis for property inherited from someone who died before or after 2010 is generally the fair market value of the property on the date of the decedent's death. If the executor of the decedent's estate elected to use an alternate valuation date (within six months after the date of death), your basis is the fair market value on the alternate valuation date. If the decedent died in 2010, your basis may be the fair market value, but *see* below for the exception where the executor filed Form 8939.

If the property increased in value while the decedent owned the property, the "step-up" in basis to its fair market value on the date of death can provide a substantial tax break. If your basis is the value at the decedent's death or at the alternate valuation date, then, when you sell the property, you completely avoid income tax on the appreciation in value that occurred while the decedent owned it.

If you inherit property that was reported on an estate tax return (Form 706) filed after July 31, 2015, the executor is generally required to report the value of the estate assets to the IRS on Form 8971 and Schedule A, and if the property you inherit increased estate tax liability, you will face a penalty if you claim a basis for the property that exceeds the value shown on your copy of Schedule A. *See* below for details of this basis consistency rule.

If you owned the property jointly with the deceased, *see 5.18*.

If you inherit appreciated property that you (or your spouse) gave to the deceased person within one year of his or her death, your basis is the decedent's basis immediately before death, not its fair market value.

If the inherited property is subject to a mortgage, your basis is the value of the property, and not its equity at the date of death. If the property is subject to a lease under which no income is to be received for years, the basis is the value of the property—not the equity.

You might be given the right to buy the deceased person's property under his or her will. This is not the same as inheriting that property. Your basis is what you pay—not what the property is worth on the date of the deceased's death.

If property was inherited from an individual who died after 1976 and before November 7, 1978, and the executor elected to apply a carryover basis to all estate property, your basis is figured with reference to the decedent's basis. The executor must inform you of the basis of such property.

Community property. Upon the death of a spouse in a community property state, one-half of the fair market value of the community property is generally included in the deceased spouse's estate for estate tax purposes. The surviving spouse's basis for his or her half of the property is 50% of the total fair market value. For the other half, the surviving spouse, if he/she receives the asset, or the other heirs of the deceased spouse have a basis equal to 50% of the fair market value.

Did executor of decedent who died in 2010 elect modified carryover basis rules on Form 8939? If you inherited property from a person who died in 2010, you get a full stepped-up basis (to fair market value on date of death or alternate valuation date), provided the executor did not elect to file Form 8939. Under the Tax Relief, Unemployment Insurance Reauthorization, and Job Creation Act of 2010, the executors of estates of individuals dying in 2010 were allowed to opt out of estate tax entirely (no estate tax at all applied even if the gross estate exceeded the $5 million exemption) provided an election was made on Form 8939 to apply modified carryover basis rules under which the heirs generally received a stepped-up basis only for the first $1.3 million in assets, plus an additional $3 million for property passing to a surviving spouse. Executors had to make the modified carryover basis election on Form 8939 by January 17, 2012. Further details on the modified carryover basis rules are in Publication 4895 (Rev. October 2011) and Revenue Procedure 2011-41.

If the executor of a 2010 estate did not elect on Form 8939 to apply the modified carryover basis rules, the regular stepped-up basis rules apply.

Farm or closely-held business property. If for estate tax purposes the executor of the estate valued qualifying real estate based on its use as a farm or use in a closely-held business, rather than at its fair market value, that farm or business value is the basis for the heirs. If you inherit such property, contact the executor for the special valuation.

Basis consistency requirement may apply to you if you inherit property reported on estate tax return filed after July 31, 2015. Legislation was enacted in 2015 in an attempt to ensure that the values reported for property on a federal estate tax return (Form 706) are used by the estate beneficiaries as their basis for the assets they inherit. Congress was concerned that some beneficiaries understate their gain when they sell inherited property, or overstate a loss (for investment property), by claiming a basis for the property that is more than the fair market value reported by the executor on the estate tax return. Similarly, deductions for depreciation or amortization could be inflated by using a basis higher than the estate tax value of the property.

Reporting by executor to the IRS and beneficiaries on Form 8971 and Schedule A. An executor who files an estate tax return generally must report the value of the property included in the gross estate to the IRS on Form 8971 and Schedule A no later than 30 days after the date the estate tax return is filed, or if earlier, 30 days after the filing due date with extensions. Executors are subject to penalties for failure to file timely and correct Forms 8971 and Schedules A. The penalty amounts generally depend on how late the filing is; details are in the Form 8971/Schedule A instructions.

However, the Form 8971 and Schedule A requirements do not apply if the gross estate (plus adjusted gifts) was under the filing threshold for Form 706 and the sole reason for filing the estate tax return was to make a portability election that allows the decedent's unused estate tax exemption to be preserved for the decedent's surviving spouse *(39.9)*. Also, the reporting requirements do not apply if the estate tax return is filed solely to make a generation-skipping transfer election.

Certain property included in the gross estate is exempt from reporting. This includes (1) cash bequests, but not coins or bills with numismatic value, (2) income in respect of a decedent *(11.16)*, (3) small items of tangible personal property (generally household and personal effects) that do not require an estate tax appraisal, and (4) property sold by the estate and therefore not distributed to a beneficiary.

Where reporting is required, the executor must submit to the IRS a separate Schedule A for each beneficiary receiving property from the estate, and give each beneficiary (within the above 30-day deadline) a copy of his/her Schedule A. Schedule A provides information about the beneficiary and the property he or she has inherited (e.g., the beneficiary's name and tax identification number, description of the property, and its valuation). If the executor has not yet determined which beneficiary will receive an item of property as of the due date of the Form 8971 and Schedule(s) A, that property must be reported on a Schedule A for each beneficiary who might receive it. In this case, the same property will be reported on multiple Schedules A, and when the property is actually distributed, or the property is used to fund the distributions of multiple beneficiaries, the executor may (but is not required to) file a supplemental Form 8971 and corresponding Schedules A to each of the affected beneficiaries.

Potential penalty for beneficiary. You will receive a copy of your Schedule A from the executor, but not a copy of the Form 8971 and Schedules A prepared for other beneficiaries. Column C of Schedule A will indicate if the property you inherited increased the estate tax liability payable by the estate. If it did ("Y" will be entered in this column), there is a notice on your Schedule A warning you that you are subject to the basis consistency requirement. This means that you are required to use as your basis the estate tax value for that property, which is shown in Column E of the Schedule A. If you claim a basis that exceeds the estate tax value when reporting a sale or other taxable event (such as depreciation), you are subject to a 20% "accuracy-related" penalty *(48.6)*. If the value reported to you in Column E subsequently changes (such as when a valuation dispute is settled), the executor must send you (and the IRS) an updated Schedule A within 30 days after the adjustment.

 *Law Alert*

Beneficiary Can Be Penalized for Claiming Basis Higher Than Estate Tax Value

A beneficiary who sells inherited property and understates the tax due on the sale may be subject to a 20% penalty if the understatement results from claiming a basis for the property that exceeds the value reported by the executor on the estate tax return. The penalty applies to property included in an estate tax return filed after July 31, 2015, provided that inclusion of the property in the estate increased the estate tax liability.

If you are a surviving spouse and received property that qualified for the marital deduction, that property did not increase the estate tax liability ("N" should be entered in Column C) and the basis consistency rule and potential penalty do not apply.

5.18 Joint Tenancy Basis Rules for Surviving Tenants

If you are a surviving joint tenant, your basis for the property you inherit depends on (1) how much of the value was includible in the deceased tenant's gross estate, and this depends on whether the joint tenant was your spouse or someone other than your spouse, and (2) how much of the tax basis of the property is treated as your contribution, and this amount also depends on whether the joint tenant was your spouse or someone other than your spouse.

These rules apply only to jointly owned real estate or other physical property and jointly owned investment accounts, and not to inherited retirement accounts (inherited IRA, or inherited account from a 401(k) plan or other qualified retirement plan).

Caution: If you inherited property from a person who died in 2010 and the executor elected on Form 8939 to apply the modified carryover basis rules *(5.17)*, basis will be determined under that election.

Qualified joint interest rule for survivor of spouse who died after 1981. A "qualified joint interest" rule applies to a joint tenancy with right of survivorship where the spouses are the only joint tenants, and to a tenancy by the entirety between a husband and wife.

Where the surviving spouse is a U.S. citizen, the qualified joint interest rules provide that one-half of the fair market value of the property is includible in the decedent's gross estate. This "one-half" rule applies *regardless* of how much each spouse contributed to the purchase price and improvements. Fair market value is fixed at the date of death, or six months later if an estate tax return is filed and the optional alternate valuation date is elected.

The qualified joint interest rules do not apply if the surviving spouse is not a U.S. citizen on the due date of the estate tax return. In this case, the basis rule is generally the same as the rule discussed below for unmarried joint tenants.

Surviving spouse's basis. Under the qualified joint interest rules, the surviving spouse's basis equals the total of these two amounts: (1) 50% of the amount includible in the decedent's gross estate (either 50% of the date-of-death value, or 50% of the alternate valuation date value if an estate tax return was filed for the decedent and alternate valuation was elected), plus (2) 50% of the adjusted basis *(5.20)* for the property; *see* Example 1 below.

In the typical case, no estate tax return is due because the value of the estate is below the filing threshold, so under (1) above, the surviving spouse always takes into account 50% of the fair market value of the property at the date of death, since alternate valuation is not available where no estate tax return is filed.

If depreciation deductions for the property were claimed before the date of death, the surviving spouse must reduce basis by his or her share (under local law) of the depreciation; *see* Example 2 below.

EXAMPLES

1. John and his spouse Jennifer jointly bought a house for $50,000 in 1979. John paid $45,000 of the purchase price and Jennifer, $5,000. Over the years, they made $60,000 in improvements to the house. In 2023, John died when the house was worth $300,000. One-half of the date-of-death value, or $150,000, is includible in John's estate tax return (or would be if an estate tax return were due) although he contributed 90% of the purchase price. Under the qualified joint interest rule, Jennifer's basis for the house is $205,000 figured as follows:

One-half of adjusted basis ($50,000 cost plus $60,000 improvements × 50%)	$55,000
Inherited portion (50% of $300,000 date-of-death value)	150,000
Jennifer's basis	$205,000

2. Same facts as in Example 1 except that the home was rental property for which $30,000 of depreciation deductions had been allowed before John's death. Under local law, Jennifer had a right to 50% of the income from the property and, thus, a right to 50% of the depreciation. Her basis for the property is $190,000: $205,000 as shown in Example 1, reduced by $15,000, her share of the depreciation.

3. Assume that in addition to their jointly owned home, John and Jennifer also jointly owned an investment account holding mutual funds and stocks. When John dies in 2023, their cost basis for the investments, including reinvested dividends, is $100,000, and the value of the investments on the date of his death is $250,000. Jennifer's basis for the investment account is $175,000, equal to (1) 50% of the $250,000 value of the account on the date of John's death, plus (2) 50% of their $100,000 basis in the account.

4. The Gallensteins purchased farm property in 1955 as joint tenants; Mr. Gallenstein provided all the funds. When he died in 1987, Mrs. Gallenstein claimed that 100% of the property was includible in her husband's gross estate and she had a stepped-up basis for that full amount. The IRS argued that under the rules for estates of spouses dying after 1981, she received a stepped-up basis for only 50% of the date-of-death value. The federal appeals court for the Sixth Circuit (Kentucky, Michigan, Ohio, and Tennessee) agreed with Mrs. Gallenstein. The appeals court held that pre-1977 spousal joint tenancies were not affected when the law was changed to provide a 50% estate tax inclusion and 50% stepped-up basis for spousal deaths after 1981. For pre-1977 spousal joint tenancies, the prior law rule continues to apply: 100% of the date-of-death value of jointly held property is included in the estate of the first spouse to die unless it is shown that the survivor contributed towards the purchase. In this case, where Mrs. Gallenstein's deceased husband had paid the entire purchase price, her basis was 100% of the value of the property and she realized no taxable gain when she sold the property at a price equal to that stepped-up basis.

   The Tax Court and the Fourth Circuit Appeals Court (Maryland, North Carolina, South Carolina, Virginia, and West Virginia) agreed with the Sixth Circuit's approach of allowing a 100% stepped-up basis for a pre-1977 spousal joint interest where the deceased spouse had paid the entire purchase price. The IRS acquiesced to the Tax Court decision and no longer litigates the issue.

Unmarried joint tenants. If you are a surviving joint tenant who owned property with someone other than your spouse, your basis for the inherited property depends on how much you contributed to the adjusted basis *(5.20)* for the property. Specifically, your basis equals (1) what you paid toward the original price, capital improvements and other additions to basis *(5.20)* before the joint owner died, plus (2) the decedent's share of the fair market value of the property at the date of death (or on the alternate valuation date if an estate tax return was filed and the alternate valuation method was elected).

The decedent's share under (2) above depends on the percentage of the adjusted basis *(5.20)* which he or she contributed. For example, if the decedent paid 75% of the cost, 75% of the fair market value at the date-of-death is includible in his or her estate and treated as passing to you at the date of death, which is why it is included in your basis under (2) above. You include the decedent's share of the date-of-death value in your basis even if, as is usually the case, the estate is too small to require the filing of an estate tax return.

If the jointly owned property was business or investment property for which depreciation deductions were claimed before the other owner's death, your basis as figured under (1) and (2) above is reduced by your share of the depreciation.

EXAMPLES

1. You and your sister lived in a home which you bought together in 1990 for $120,000. Capital improvements of $20,000 were made over the years. She paid $84,000 of the costs, and you paid $56,000. Title to the house was held by both of you as joint tenants with right of survivorship. Your sister died in 2023 when the house was worth $275,000. Since your sister paid 60% of the costs (60% of $140,000, or $84,000), 60% of the value at her death, $165,000 (60% of $275,000), is includible in her estate (or would be included if an estate tax return was due). Your basis for the house is now $221,000, equal to the $56,000 you paid plus the $165,000 fair market value of your sister's 60% share at her death.

> 2. Same as Example 1 except that your sister paid for the entire purchase price and improvements. 100% of the fair market value at the date of death, or $275,000, would be includible in your sister's estate (or would be included if an estate tax return was due), and that becomes your basis for the property after her death.

Survivor of spouse who died before 1982. The basis rule for a surviving spouse who held property jointly (or as tenancy by the entirety) with a spouse who died before 1982 is generally the same as the above rule for unmarried joint tenants. However, special rules applied to qualified joint interests and eligible joint interests are discussed below.

EXAMPLE

Spouses owned rental property as tenants by the entirety that they purchased for $30,000. One spouse furnished two-thirds of the purchase price ($20,000) and the other spouse furnished one-third ($10,000). Depreciation deductions taken before the death of the first spouse were $12,000. On the date of his death in 1979, the property had a fair market value of $60,000. Under the law of the state in which the property is located, as tenants by the entirety, each had a half interest in the property. The surviving spouse's basis in the property at the date of the deceased spouse's death was $44,000, computed as follows:

Interest acquired with surviving spouse's own funds	$ 10,000
Interest acquired from deceased spouse (²/₃ of $60,000)	40,000
	$50,000
Less: Depreciation of ½ interest not acquired by reason of death (½ of $12,000)	6,000
Surviving spouse's basis at date of deceased spouse's death	$ 44,000

If the surviving spouse had not contributed any part of the purchase price, the basis at the date of deceased spouse's death would be $54,000 ($60,000 fair market value less $6,000 depreciation). This basis would be increased by any additions or improvements made to the property by the surviving spouse after the other spouse's death, and reduced by any depreciation *(5.20)*.

Qualified joint interest and eligible joint interest where spouse died before 1982. Where, after 1976, a spouse dying before 1982 elected to treat realty as a "qualified joint interest" subject to gift tax, such joint property was treated as owned 50–50 by each spouse, and 50% of the value was included in the decedent's estate. Thus, for income tax purposes, the survivor's basis for the inherited 50% half of the property is the estate tax value; the basis for the other half is determined under the gift rules *(5.17)*. Personal property is treated as a "qualified joint interest" only if it was created or deemed to have been created after 1976 by a husband and wife and was subject to gift tax.

Where death occurred before 1982 and a surviving spouse materially participated in the operation of a farm or other business, the estate could have elected to treat the farm or business property as an "eligible joint interest," which means that part of the investment in the property was attributed to the surviving spouse's services and that part was not included in the deceased spouse's estate. Where such an election was made, the survivor's basis for income tax purposes includes the estate tax value of property included in the decedent's estate.

5.19 Allocating Cost Among Several Assets

Allocation of basis is generally required in these cases: when the property includes land and building; the land is to be divided into lots; securities or mutual fund shares are purchased at different times; stock splits; and in the purchase of a business.

Purchase of land and building. To figure depreciation on the building, part of the purchase price must be allocated to the building. The allocation is made according to the fair market values of the building and land. The amount allocated to land is not depreciated.

Purchase of land to be divided into lots. The purchase price of the tract is allocated to each lot, so that the gain or loss from the sale of each lot may be reported in the year of its sale. Allocation is not made ratably, that is, with an equal share to each lot or parcel. It is based on the relative value of each piece of property. Comparable sales, competent appraisals, or assessed values may be used as guides.

Securities. *See 30.2* for details on methods of identifying securities bought at different dates. *See 30.3* for allocating basis of stock dividends and stock splits and *see 30.4* for allocating the basis of stock rights.

Mutual fund shares. *See 32.9* for determining the basis of mutual fund shares where purchases were made at different times.

Purchase price of a business. *See 44.9* for allocation rule.

5.20 How To Find Adjusted Basis

After determining the unadjusted cost basis for property *(5.16–5.19)*, you may have to increase it or decrease it to find your adjusted basis, which is the amount used to figure your gain or loss on a sale *(5.13)*.

Additions to basis. You add to unadjusted basis the cost of these items:

- All permanent improvements and additions to the property and other capital costs. Increase basis for capital improvements such as adding a room or a fence, putting in new plumbing or wiring, and paving a driveway. Also include capital costs such as the cost of extending utility service lines, assessments for local improvements such as streets, sidewalks, or water connections, and repairing your property after a casualty (for example, repair costs after a fire or storm).
- *Legal fees.* Increase basis by legal fees incurred for defending or perfecting title, or for obtaining a reduction of an assessment levied against property to pay for local benefits.
- *Sale of unharvested land.* If you sell land with unharvested crops, add the cost of producing the crops to the basis of the property sold.

Decreases to basis. You reduce cost basis for these items:

- Return of capital, such as dividends on stock paid out of capital or out of a depletion reserve when the company has no available earnings or surplus *(4.11)*.
- *Losses from casualties and thefts.* Decrease basis by insurance awards, by payments in settlement of damages to your property, and by deductible casualty/theft losses not covered by insurance.
- Depletion allowances *(9.15)*.
- Depreciation, first-year expensing deduction, amortization, and obsolescence on property used in business or for the production of income. In some years, you may have taken more or less depreciation than was allowable.
- If you claim less than what was allowable, you must deduct from basis the allowable amount rather than what was actually claimed. You may be able to file an amended return to claim the full allowable depreciation for a year. If IRS rules do not allow the correction on an amended return, you can change your accounting method in order to claim the correct amount of depreciation; *see* IRS Publication 946 for details.
- If you took more depreciation than was allowable, you may have to make the following adjustments: If you have deducted more than what was allowable and you received a tax benefit from the deduction, you deduct from basis the full amount of the depreciation. But if the excess depreciation did not give you a tax benefit, because income was eliminated by other deductions, the excess is not deducted from basis.
- Amortized bond premium *(4.17)*.
- *Canceled debt excluded from income.* If you did not pay tax on certain cancellations of debt because of bankruptcy or insolvency, or on qualifying farm debt or business real property, you reduce basis of your property for the amount forgiven *(11.8)*.
- *Investment credit.* Where the full investment credit was claimed in 1983 or later years, basis is reduced by one-half the credit.

Court Decision

Improvements Covered by Note

In an unusual case, the owner of office condominiums financed substantial improvements to the units by giving promissory notes to a contracting company that he controlled. Before paying off the notes he sold the units. He included the cost of the improvements in basis to figure his gain on the sale, but the IRS, with the approval of a federal district court, held that this was improper. The court held that as a cash-basis taxpayer, he could not include the face amount of the notes in the basis of the condominiums until the notes were paid.

5.21 Tax Advantage of Installment Sales

Filing Instruction

Payments from Prior Installment Sales

If you reported a pre-2023 sale on the installment method, use Form 6252 to report any 2023 payments on the sale.

If you sell property at a gain in 2023 and you will receive one or more payments in a later year or years, you may use the installment method to defer tax unless the property is publicly traded securities or you are a dealer of the property sold. If you report the sale as an installment sale on Form 6252, your profit is taxed as installments are received. You may elect not to use the installment method if you want to report the entire profit in the year of sale; *see* Example 1 below and *5.22.* Losses may not be deferred under the installment method.

How the installment method works. For each year you receive installment payments, report the allocable gain for that year on Form 6252. Installment income from the sale of a capital asset is then transferred to Schedule D. If your gain in the year of sale is long-term capital gain, gain in later years is also long term; short-term treatment in the year of sale applies also to later years. Interest payments you receive on the deferred sale installments are reported with your other interest income on Form 1040 or 1040-SR, not on Form 6252.

Installment income from the sale of business or rental property is figured on Form 6252 and then entered on Form 4797. If you make an installment sale of depreciable property, any depreciation recapture *(44.1)* is reported as income in the year of disposition. The recaptured amount is first figured on Form 4797 and then entered on Form 6252. On Form 6252, recaptured income is added to basis of the property for purposes of figuring the gross profit ratio for the balance of gain to be reported, if any, over the installment period *(44.6)*.

Installment sales of business or rental property for over $150,000 may be subject to a special tax if deferred payments exceed $5 million *(5.31)*.

Caution

Year-End Sales of Securities

Gain on a 2023 year-end sale of publicly traded securities cannot be deferred to 2024, even if you do not receive payment until early January 2024.

Year-end sales of publicly traded stock or securities. You have no choice about when to report the gain from a sale of publicly traded stock or securities made at the end of 2023. Any gain must be reported on your 2023 Form 1040 or 1040-SR, even if the proceeds are not received until early 2024. The sale is not considered an installment sale.

Farm property. A farmer may use the installment method to report gain from the sale of property that does not have to be inventoried under his method of accounting. This is true even though such property is held for regular sale.

Dealer sales. Generally, dealers must report gain in the year of sale for personal property regularly sold on an installment plan or real estate held for resale to customers. However, the installment method may be used by dealers of certain time share units (generally time shares of up to six weeks per year) and residential lots, but only if an election is made to pay interest on the tax deferred by using the installment method. The rules for computing the interest are in Code Section 453(l)(3). The interest is reported as "453(l)(3)" on Line 8c of Schedule 2 (Form 1040 or 1040-SR).

expenses). For installment sale purposes, your gross profit percentage, which is the percentage of each payment that you must report, is 50% ($50,000 profit ÷ $100,000 contract price). When the buyer makes the installment note payments, you report the following:

In	You report	
	Payment of:	Income of:
2023	$20,000	$10,000
2024	20,000	10,000
2025	20,000	10,000
2026	40,000	20,000
Total	$100,000	$50,000

With your 2023 return, you file Form 6252 on which you figure your gross profit and gross profit percentage. You report only $10,000 as long-term gain on Line 11 of Schedule D; *see* the sample Schedule D at *5.8*. If you do not want to use the installment method, make an election to report the entire gain of $50,000 on Form 8949 for 2022 *(5.23)*.

The buyer's interest payments are separately reported as interest income on Form 1040 or 1040-SR.

2. On November 16, 2023, you sell a building for $150,000, realizing a profit of $25,000. You take a note payable in January 2024. You report the gain on Form 6252 with your 2024 return. Receiving a lump-sum payment in a taxable year after the year of sale is considered an installment sale.

5.22 Figuring the Taxable Part of Installment Payments

On the installment method, a portion of each payment other than interest represents part of your gain and is taxable. The interest (including imputed interest *(5.27)* if any) is reported as interest income on your return and does not enter into the calculation of taxable installment payments on Form 6252.

On Form 6252, the taxable part of your installments payments is based on the gross profit percentage or ratio, which is figured by dividing gross profit by the contract price. The contract price is the same as the selling price unless an adjustment is made for an existing mortgage assumed or "taken subject to" by the buyer; *see* below for the mortgage adjustment to contract price. By following the line-by-line instructions to Form 6252, you get the gross profit percentage. Selling price, gross profit, and contract price are explained in the following paragraphs.

Interest equal to the applicable federal rate must generally be charged on a deferred payment sale. Otherwise, the IRS treats part of the sale price as interest *(4.32)*.

Selling price. Include cash, fair market value of property received from the buyer, the buyer's notes (at face value), and any outstanding mortgage on the property that the buyer assumes or takes subject to. If, under the contract of sale, the buyer pays off an existing mortgage or assumes liability for any other liens on the property, such as taxes you owe, or pays the sales commissions, such payments are also included in the selling price. Notes of a third party given to you by the buyer are valued at fair market value. Interest, including minimum interest imputed under the rules in *4.32*, is not included in the selling price.

Installment sale basis. You need to know your installment sale basis to figure your gross profit. Installment sale basis is the total of the adjusted basis of the property *(5.20)*, selling expenses, such as brokers' commissions and legal fees, and recaptured depreciation income, if any *(44.1)*.

 *Caution*

Foreclosures

If your property is foreclosed, the amount of the mortgage is treated as sales proceeds even if you do not receive anything on the sale.

Caution

Recapture of Depreciation or First-Year Expensing Deduction

The entire amount of ordinary income recapture (44.1–44.3) is reported in the year of sale on Form 4797, even though you report the sale on the installment basis. An installment sale does not defer the reporting of the recaptured depreciation. You also add the recaptured amount to the basis of the sold asset on Line 12 of Form 6252 to compute the amount of the remaining gain to be reported on each installment. *See* the instructions to Form 6252.

Gross profit and gross profit percentage. Gross profit is the selling price minus your installment sale basis. Divide the gross profit by the contract price (see next paragraph) to get the gross profit percentage. Each year, you multiply this percentage by your payments to determine the taxable amount under the installment method.

Contract price where the buyer takes subject to or assumes an existing mortgage. The selling price includes the amount of your existing mortgages that the buyer assumes or takes the property subject to. To figure the gross profit percentage, first reduce the selling price by the mortgages. The reduced amount is the contract price. You then divide your gross profit by the contract price to get the gross profit percentage.

However, if the mortgage exceeds your installment sale basis (total of adjusted basis of the property, selling expenses, and depreciation recapture), you are required to report the excess as a payment received in the year of sale and also increase the contract price by that excess amount. Where the mortgage equals or exceeds your installment sale basis, the contract price will be the same as the gross profit, and the gross profit percentage will be 100%; *see* Example 3 next.

> **EXAMPLE**
>
> On December 14, 2023, you sell unmortgaged real estate for $100,000. The property had an adjusted basis of $56,000. Selling expenses are $4,000. You receive installment payments of $25,000 in 2023, 2024, 2025, and 2026, plus interest at 2%, compounded semiannually. The gross profit percentage of 40% is figured as follows:
>
> | | |
> |---|---:|
> | Selling price (contract price) | $100,000 |
> | Less: Installment sale basis | |
> | (adjusted basis plus selling expenses) | 60,000 |
> | Gross profit | $40,000 |
>
> $$\frac{\text{Gross profit}}{\text{Contract price}} = \frac{\$40{,}000}{\$100{,}000} = 40\% \text{ (gross profit percentage)}$$
>
> In 2023 (year of sale), you report a profit of $10,000 (40% of $25,000 payment) on Form 6252. Interest received with the payment is separately reported as interest income on your Form 1040 or 1040-SR. Similarly, in each of the following three years, a profit of $10,000 is reported so that by the end of four years, the entire $40,000 profit will have been reported.

In a wraparound mortgage transaction, the buyer does not assume the seller's mortgage or take the property subject to it, but instead makes payments that cover the seller's outstanding mortgage liability. At one time, the IRS treated a wraparound mortgage transaction as an assumption of a mortgage by the buyer and required a reduction of the selling price by the mortgage to compute the contract price. The Tax Court rejected the IRS position, and the IRS acquiesced in the decision. Currently, the IRS does not require a reduction of selling price for a wraparound mortgage in the Form 6252 instructions or in Publication 537; *see* Example 4 below.

> **EXAMPLES**
>
> 1. You sell a building for $300,000. The building was secured by an existing mortgage of $50,000 that you pay off at the sale closing from the buyer's initial payment. The contract price is $300,000.
> 2. Same facts as in Example 1, but the buyer will pay $250,000 and assume the mortgage of $50,000. The contract price is $250,000 ($300,000 – $50,000).
> 3. You sell a building for $90,000. The buyer will pay you $10,000 annually for three years (plus 5% interest) and assume an existing mortgage of $60,000. The adjusted basis of the property is $45,000. Selling expenses are $5,000. The total installment

sale basis is $50,000 ($45,000 plus $5,000). The mortgage exceeds this basis by $10,000 ($60,000 − $50,000). This $10,000 excess is included in the contract price and treated as a payment made in the year of sale. The contract price is $40,000:

Selling price (including $60,000 mortgage)	$90,000
Less: Mortgage	60,000
Total amount to be received from buyer (other than interest)	$30,000
Add: Excess of mortgage ($60,000) over installment sale basis ($50,000)	10,000
Contract price	$40,000
Selling price	$90,000
Less: Installment sale basis	50,000
Gross profit	$40,000
Gross profit percentage ($40,000 gross profit ÷ $40,000 contract price)	100%

Since the gross profit percentage is 100%, 100% of each annual payment must be reported as taxable gain from the sale. The $10,000 excess of the mortgage over installment basis is treated as a payment in the year of sale, and so 100% (the gross profit percentage) of it must be reported as taxable gain for that year.

4. Abel sells real property, encumbered by a mortgage of $900,000, for $2 million. Installment sale basis (adjusted basis plus selling costs) is $700,000. The buyer pays $200,000 cash and gives an interest-bearing wraparound mortgage note for $1.8 million. Abel remains obligated to pay off the $900,000 mortgage. The gross profit ratio is 65% ($1,300,000 gross profit ÷ $2,000,000 contract price). In the year of sale, Abel reports the $200,000 cash, of which 65%, or $130,000, is taxable income.

Change of selling price. If the selling price is changed during the period payments are outstanding, the gross profit percentage is refigured on the new selling price. The adjusted profit ratio is then applied to payments received after the adjustment.

EXAMPLE

Jones sold real estate in 2021 for $100,000. His basis, including selling expenses, was $40,000, so his gross profit was $60,000. The buyer agreed to pay, starting in 2021 (year of sale), five annual installments of $20,000 plus 5% interest. As the gross profit percentage was 60% ($60,000 ÷ $100,000), Jones reported profit of $12,000 (60% of $20,000) on the installments received in 2021 and 2022.

In early 2023 (year 3 of 5 scheduled installments), the parties renegotiated the sales price, reducing it from $100,000 to $85,000, and lowering the last three payments—the payments for 2023, 2024 and 2025—to $15,000 each. Jones's original profit of $60,000 is reduced to $45,000 ($85,000 revised sales price less $40,000 basis). Of the $45,000 profit, $24,000 has already been reported: $12,000 was reported in 2021 and an additional $12,000 in 2022. To get the revised profit percentage, Jones must divide the $21,000 of profit not yet received ($45,000 less $24,000) by the remaining sales price of $45,000 ($85,000 revised price less $40,000 in total installments received in 2021 and 2022). The revised profit percentage is 46.67% ($21,000 ÷ $45,000). In 2023, 2024, and 2025, Jones reports profit of $7,000 on each $15,000 installment (46.67% of $15,000).

Payments received during the year. Payments include cash, the fair market value of property or services received, and payments on the buyer's notes. Payments do not include receipt of the buyer's notes or other evidence of indebtedness, unless payable on demand or readily tradable. "Readily tradable" means registered bonds, bonds with coupons attached, debentures, and other evidences of indebtedness of the buyer that are readily tradable in an established securities market. This rule is directed mainly at corporate acquisitions. A third-party guarantee (including a standby letter of credit) is not treated as a payment received on an installment obligation.

Caution

Extension of Pledge Rule

If a loan arrangement gives you the right to repay the debt by transferring an installment obligation, you are treated as if you had directly pledged the obligation as security for the debt. As a result, the loan proceeds are treated as a payment on the installment obligation, which will increase installment income for the year of the "deemed pledge."

If the buyer has assumed or taken property subject to a mortgage that exceeds your installment sale basis (adjusted basis plus selling expenses plus depreciation recapture, if any), you include as a payment in the year of the sale the excess of the mortgage over the installment basis; *see* the Johnson Example below.

> **EXAMPLE**
>
> Johnson sells a building for $160,000, subject to a mortgage of $60,000. Installments plus interest are to be paid over five years. His adjusted basis in the building was $30,000 and his selling expenses were $10,000, so his installment sale basis is $40,000 and his gross profit is $120,000 ($160,000 − $40,000). The contract price is also $120,000, the selling price of $160,000 less $40,000, the part of the mortgage that did not exceed the installment sale basis.
>
> The $20,000 excess of the $60,000 mortgage over the installment sale basis of $40,000 is part of the contract price and is also treated as a payment received in the year of sale. Since the mortgage exceeds Johnson's installment sale basis, he is treated as having recovered his entire basis in the year of sale, and all installment payments will be taxable, as his gross profit ratio is 100%: gross profit of $120,000 ÷ contract price of $120,000. In the year of sale, Johnson must report as taxable gain 100% of the installment payment received, plus the $20,000 difference between the mortgage and his installment sale basis.

Pledging installment obligation as security. If, as security for a loan, you pledge an installment obligation from a sale of property of more than $150,000 (excluding farm property, personal-use property and timeshares and residential lots), the net loan proceeds must be treated as a payment on the installment obligation. The net loan proceeds are treated as received on the later of the date the loan is secured and the date you receive the loan proceeds. These pledging rules do not apply if the debt refinances a debt that was outstanding on December 17, 1987, and secured by the installment obligation until the refinancing. If the refinancing exceeds the loan principal owed immediately before the refinancing, the excess is treated as a payment on the installment obligation. *See* the Form 6252 instructions.

5.23 Electing Not To Report on the Installment Method

If any sale proceeds are to be received after the year of sale, you must file Form 6252 and use the installment method unless you "elect out" by making a timely election to report the entire gain in the year of sale. If you want to report the entire gain in the year of sale, do not file Form 6252. Include the entire gain on Form 8949 or Form 4797 by the due date for filing your return (plus extensions) for the year of sale. If you timely file your return without making the election, you can do so on an amended return filed no later than six months after the original due date (without extensions); write "Filed pursuant to section 301.9100-2" at the top of the amended return.

Election out is generally irrevocable. If you "elect out" of the installment method by reporting the entire gain in the year of sale, you may change to the installment method on an amended return only with the consent of the IRS. In private rulings, the IRS has granted permission to revoke an election out that was inadvertent, such as where the taxpayer's accountant was instructed to use the installment method but the accountant mistakenly reported the entire gain in the year of sale.

In one case on October 1, 2014, where the sales price was payable over 12 years, the accountant who was preparing the taxpayers' joint return erroneously determined that the installment method would not be beneficial to them, so he "elected out" of the installment method by reporting the entire gain as income in the year of the sale. The taxpayers were not aware that the accountant did this. When the accountant prepared their return for the following year, he realized he made a mistake and that installment sale reporting would have been beneficial. On behalf of the taxpayers, the accountant filed a request with the IRS to revoke the "election out," and the IRS agreed in a private ruling. The election out was based on the accountant's erroneous computation and the taxpayers were unaware of the error. See IRS Code 15A.453-1(d) of the Temporary Income Tax Regulations for more details on case PLR-118950-14.

If the IRS is not convinced that the election out was inadvertent, it will likely refuse permission to retroactively allow the change to the installment method, on the grounds that a revocation of the election would involve hindsight and result in tax avoidance. For example, if a seller "elects out" in a year in which he plans to deduct a net operating loss carryforward from an installment sale gain. In a later year, the IRS substantially reduces the loss. The seller then asks the IRS to allow him to revoke the "election out" so he can use the installment method. The IRS then would refuse in a private ruling, claiming that the seller asked for the revocation to avoid tax. The installment sale would defer gain to a later year, which is a tax avoidance purpose.

5.24 Restriction on Installment Sales to Relatives

The installment sale method is not allowed where you sell depreciable property to a controlled business, or to a trust in which you or your spouse is a beneficiary. All payments to be received over the installment period are considered received in the year of sale.

Further, if you sell property to a relative on the installment basis, and the relative later resells the property, you could lose the benefit of installment reporting. Generally, you are taxed on your relative's sale if it is within two years of the original sale.

Two-year resale rule for property. If you make an installment sale of property to a related party, you are taxed on a second sale by the related party only if it occurs within two years of the initial installment sale and before all payments from the first installment sale are made. However, the two-year limitation does not apply if the property is marketable securities.

Related parties include a spouse, child, grandchild, parent, grandparent, brother or sister, controlled corporation (50% or more direct or indirect ownership), any S corporation in which you own stock or partnership in which you are a partner, a trust in which you are a beneficiary, or a grantor trust of which you are treated as the owner. You are treated as owning stock held by your spouse, brothers, sisters, children, grandchildren, parents, and grandparents.

For the year of the related party sale, you must report as additional installment sale income: (1) the proceeds from the related party's sale or the contract price from the initial installment sale, whichever is less, minus (2) installment payments received from the related party as of the end of the year. The computation is made in Part III of Form 6252.

The two-year period is extended during any period in which the buyer's risk is lessened by a put on the property, an option by another person to acquire the property, or a short sale or other transaction lessening the risk of loss.

Exceptions to related-party rule. There are exceptions to the related-party rule. Second dispositions resulting from an involuntary conversion of the property will not be subject to the related-party rule so long as the first disposition occurred before the threat or imminence of conversion. Similarly, transfers after the death of the person making the first disposition or the death of the related person (who acquired the property in the first disposition) are not treated as second dispositions. Also, a sale or exchange of stock to the issuing corporation is not treated as a first disposition. Finally, you may avoid tax on a related party's second sale by satisfying the IRS that neither the initial nor the second sale was made for tax avoidance purposes. The non-tax-avoidance exception is considered met if the second disposition by the related party is an installment sale with payment terms that are substantially equal to or longer than those for the original installment sale; there must not be significant deferral of gain from the original sale.

Sales of depreciable property to related party. Installment reporting is not allowed for sales of depreciable property made to a controlled corporation or partnership (50% control by seller) and between such controlled corporations and partnerships. In figuring control of a corporation, you are considered to own stock held by your spouse, children, grandchildren, brothers or sisters, parents, and grandparents. Installment reporting is also disallowed on a sale to a trust in which you or a spouse is a beneficiary unless your interest is considered a remote contingent interest whose actuarial value is 5% or less of the trust property's value. On these related-party sales, the entire gain is reported in the year of sale, unless the seller convinces the IRS that the transfer was not motivated by tax avoidance purposes.

 *Caution*

Installment Sale to Relative

If you sell property on the installment basis to a relative who later resells the property, you could lose the benefit of installment reporting.

 *Caution*

IRS Notice of Related Party Transfer

Where you transfer property to a related party, the IRS has two years from the date you notify it that there has been a second disposition to assess a deficiency with respect to your transfer.

On a sale of depreciable property to a related party, if the amounts of payments are contingent (for example, payments are tied to profits), the seller must make a special calculation. He or she must treat as received in the year of sale all noncontingent payments plus the fair market value of the contingent payments if such value may be reasonably ascertained. If the fair market value of the contingent payments may not be reasonably calculated, the seller recovers basis ratably. The purchaser's basis for the acquired property includes only amounts that the seller has included in income under the basis recovery rule. Thus, the purchaser's basis is increased annually as the seller recovers basis.

EXAMPLE

In 2023, Jones Sr. sells unmortgaged land to his son for $300,000, payable in five equal annual installments starting that year, plus 3% interest. The father's installment sale basis is $120,000, so his gross profit is $180,000 and his gross profit percentage is 60% ($180,000 profit / $300,000 contract price). In 2023 (the year of sale), Jones Sr. receives the first $60,000 payment and reports on his 2023 return $36,000 ($60,000 × 60%) as installment sale income. The next year, in 2024, the son makes the required $60,000 payment to his father and then sells the land to a third party for $400,000. Under the two-year resale rule, the father must report additional income for 2024. The father is considered to have received $180,000 on the son's resale, and he must report a total of $144,000 as installment sale income for 2024:

Lesser of sale proceeds from son's resale ($400,000) or original contract price ($300,000)	$300,000
Minus: total payments from son by end of 2024	120,000
Treated as received by father from resale	180,000
Plus: payment from son in 2024 (resale year)	60,000
Total amount treated as received by father for 2024	240,000
Multiply by 60% gross profit percentage	.60
Father's total installment sale income for 2024	$144,000

The father will not be taxed on payments from the son after 2024, apart from interest, since he has already reported all of the payments ($300,000) due on the initial sale ($60,000 payment was reported for 2023 and $240,000 for 2024).

5.25 Contingent Payment Sales

Where the final selling price or payment period of an installment sale is not fixed at the end of the taxable year of sale, you are considered to have transacted a "contingent payment sale." Special rules apply where a maximum selling price may be figured under the terms of the agreement or there is no fixed price but there is a fixed payment period, or there is neither a fixed price nor a fixed payment period.

Stated maximum selling price. Under IRS regulations, a stated maximum selling price may be determined by assuming that all of the contingencies contemplated under the agreement are met. When the maximum amount is later reduced, the gross profit ratio is recomputed.

Fixed period. When a stated maximum selling price is not determinable but the maximum payment period is fixed, basis—including selling expenses—is allocated equally to the taxable years in which payment may be received under the agreement. If, in any year, no payment is received or the amount of payment received is less than the basis allocated to that taxable year, no loss is allowed unless the taxable year is the final payment year or the agreement has become worthless. When no loss is allowed in a year, the basis allocated to the taxable year is carried forward to the next succeeding taxable year.

Smith sells stock in Acme Co. for a down payment of $100,000 plus an amount equal to 5% of the net profits of Acme for the next nine years. Smith's basis for the stock is $200,000. The contract provides that the maximum amount payable, including the $100,000 down payment but exclusive of interest, is $2,000,000. The selling price and contract price is $2,000,000. Gross profit is $1,800,000. The gross profit ratio is 90% ($1,800,000 ÷ $2,000,000). Thus, $90,000 of the first payment is reportable as gain and $10,000 as a recovery of basis.

No stated maximum selling price or fixed period. If the agreement fails to specify a maximum selling price and payment period, the IRS may view the agreement as a rent or royalty income agreement. However, if the arrangement qualifies as a sale, basis (including selling expenses) is recovered in equal annual increments over a 15-year period commencing with the date of sale. If in any taxable year no payment is received or the amount of payment received (exclusive of interest) is less than basis allocated to the year, no loss is allowed unless the agreement has become worthless. Excess basis not recovered in one year is reallocated in level amounts over the balance of the 15-year term. Any basis not recovered at the end of the 15th year is carried forward to the next succeeding year, and to the extent unrecovered, carried forward from year to year until basis has been recovered or the agreement is determined to be worthless. The rule requiring initial level allocation of basis over 15 years may not apply if you prove to the IRS that a 15-year general rule will substantially and inappropriately defer recovery of basis.

In some cases, basis recovery under an income forecast type of method may also be allowed.

Caution

Contingent Sales

An example of a contingent sale in which the selling price cannot be determined by the end of the year of the sale is a sale of your business where the selling price includes a percentage of future profits. You and your tax advisor should consult the technical rules in IRS Regulation Section 15A.453-1(c) for details on reporting such sales.

EXAMPLE

Brown sells property for 10% of the property's gross rents over a five-year period. Brown's basis is $5,000,000. The sales price is indefinite and the maximum selling price is not fixed under the terms of the contract; basis is recovered ratably over the five-year period.

Year	Payment	Basis recovered	Gain
First	$ 1,300,000	$ 1,000,000	$ 300,000
Second	1,500,000	1,000,000	500,000
Third	1,400,000	1,000,000	400,000
Fourth	1,800,000	1,000,000	800,000
Fifth	2,100,000	1,000,000	1,100,000

5.26 Using Escrow and Other Security Arrangements

When you sell property on the installment basis, the remaining sales proceeds (plus interest) may be placed in an escrow account pending the possible occurrence of an event such as the approval of title or your performance of certain contractual conditions. If the escrow account is irrevocable or there are no escrow restrictions preventing you from receiving immediate payment, the IRS does not allow installment reporting. It considers the buyer's obligation paid in full when the balance of the proceeds is deposited into the unrestricted escrow account. If in a year after the year of the installment sale an escrow account is set up as a substitute for unpaid notes or deeds of trust, the IRS considers the escrow funds as payment in full, assuming there are no substantial restrictions on your right to the proceeds.

EXAMPLES

1. Anderson sold stock and mining property for almost $5 million. He agreed to place $500,000 in escrow to protect the buyer against his possible breaches of warranty and to provide security for certain liabilities. The escrow agreement called for Anderson to direct the investments of the escrow fund and receive income from the fund in excess of $500,000.

The IRS claimed that in the year of sale Anderson was taxable on the $500,000 held in escrow on the ground that Anderson's control of the fund rendered the fund taxable immediately. Anderson argued he was only taxable as the funds were released to him, and the Tax Court agreed. The fund was not under his unqualified control. He might never get the fund if the liabilities materialized. Although Anderson had a free hand with investment of the money, he still lacked ultimate ownership.

2. Rhodes sold a tract to a buyer who was willing to pay at once the entire purchase price of $157,000. But Rhodes wanted to report the sale on the installment basis over a period of years. The buyer refused to execute a purchase money mortgage on the property to allow the installment sale election (required under prior law) because he wanted clear and unencumbered title to the tract. As a solution, Rhodes asked the buyer to turn over the purchase price to a bank, as escrow agent, which would pay the sum over a five-year period.

   The escrow arrangement failed to support an installment sale. Rhodes was fully taxable on the entire price in the year of the sale. The buyer's payment was unconditional and irrevocable. The escrow arrangement involved no genuine conditions that could defeat Rhodes's right to payment, as the buyer could not revoke, alter, or end the arrangement.

3. In January, an investor sold real estate for $100,000. He received $10,000 as a down payment and six notes, each for $15,000, secured by a deed of trust on the property. The notes, together with interest, were due annually over the next six years. In July, the buyer deposited the remainder of the purchase price with an escrow agent and got the seller to cancel the deed of trust.

   The agreement provides that the escrow agent will pay off the buyer's notes as they fall due. The buyer remains liable for the installment payments. The escrow deposit is irrevocable, and the payment schedule may not be accelerated by any party under any circumstances. According to the IRS, the sale, which initially qualified as an installment sale, is disqualified by the escrow account.

Caution

Charging Minimum Interest

If you do not charge a minimum interest rate, the IRS may do so. This would require you and the buyer to treat part of the purchase price as interest.

5.27 Minimum Interest on Deferred Payment Sales

The tax law requires a minimum amount of interest to be charged on deferred payment sales. The rules for imputing interest on sales are discussed in *4.32*. Imputed interest is included in the taxable income of the seller. Imputed interest is deductible by the buyer if the property is business or investment property, but not if it is used substantially all the time for personal purposes.

5.28 Dispositions of Installment Notes

A sale, a gift, an exchange or other transfer or cancellation of mortgage notes or other obligations received in an installment sale has tax consequences. If you sell or exchange the notes or if you accept less than face value in satisfaction of the obligation, gain or loss results to the extent of the difference between the basis of the notes and the amount realized. For example, if in satisfaction of an installment note, the buyer gives you other property worth less than the face value of the note, you have gain (or loss) to the extent your amount realized exceeds (or is less than) your basis in the installment note. The basis of an installment note or obligation is the face value of the note less the income that would be reported if the obligation were paid in full; *see* Example 2 below.

Gain or loss is long term if the original sale was entitled to long-term capital gain treatment. This is true even if the notes were held short term. If the original sale resulted in short-term gain or ordinary income, the sale of the notes gives short-term gain or ordinary income, regardless of the holding period of the notes.

Suppose you make an installment sale of your real estate, taking back a land contract. Later a mortgage is substituted for the unpaid balance of the land contract. The IRS has ruled that the substitution is not the same as a disposition of the unpaid installment obligations. There is no tax on the substitution.

Gift of installment obligation. If the installment obligations are disposed of other than by sale or exchange, such as when you make a gift of the installment obligations to someone else, gain or loss is the difference between the basis of the obligations and their fair market

Filing Tip

Transfer of Installment Notes to Former Spouse

A transfer of installment obligations to your spouse or a transfer to a former spouse that is incident to a divorce is treated as a tax-free exchange (*6.7*) unless the transfer is in trust.

value at the time of the disposition. If an installment obligation is canceled or otherwise becomes unenforceable, the same rule for determining gain or loss applies. However, no gain or loss is recognized on a gift to a spouse *(6.7)*.

A gift of installment obligations to a person other than a spouse or to a charitable organization is treated as a taxable disposition. Gain or loss is the difference between the basis of the obligations and their fair market value at the time of the gift. If the notes are donated to a qualified charity, you may claim a contribution deduction for the fair market value of the obligations at the time of the gift.

EXAMPLES

1. You sell a lot for $200,000 that cost you $100,000. In the year of the sale, you received $50,000 in cash and the purchaser's notes for the remainder of the selling price, or $150,000. A year later, before the buyer makes a payment on the notes, you sell them for $130,000 cash:

Selling price of property	$200,000
Cost of property	100,000
Total profit	$100,000
Profit percentage, or proportion of each payment returnable as income, is 50% ($100,000 total profit ÷ $200,000 contract price)	
Unpaid balance of notes	$150,000
Amount of income reportable if notes were paid in full (50% of $150,000)	75,000
Adjusted basis of the notes	$75,000

   Your profit on the sale of the notes is $55,000 ($130,000 – $75,000). It is capital gain if the sale of the lot was taxable as capital gain.

2. You sell a lot on the installment basis for $200,000 that cost you $120,000. In the year of sale, you received $20,000 in cash and the buyer's note for $180,000. Your gross profit percentage is 40% ($80,000 total profit ÷ $200,000 contract price).

   Two years later, the buyer is facing financial difficulties and is unable to make payments on the $180,000 note. In satisfaction of the installment note, the buyer agrees to give you two other parcels of real estate, each worth $50,000. By accepting less than the $180,000 face value of the note in satisfaction of the obligation, you realize an $8,000 capital loss; the difference between the amount you realize and your basis in the installment obligation is figured as follows:

Amount realized ($50,000 for each parcel)	$100,000
Face value of note	180,000
Less: Amount of income reportable if note was paid in full given 40% profit percentage (40% of $180,000 = $72,000)	72,000
Basis in installment note	$108,000

   The difference between the $100,000 amount realized and $108,000 basis gives you an $8,000 loss. Assuming your profit on the original sale was long-term capital gain, the loss would be deducted as a long-term capital loss.

Transfer at death. A transfer of installment obligations at the death of the holder of the obligation is not taxed as a disposition. As the notes are paid, the estate or beneficiaries report income in the same proportion as the decedent would have, had he or she lived. A transfer of installment obligations to a revocable trust is also not taxed. However, the estate is subject to tax if the obligation is canceled, becomes unenforceable, or is transferred to the buyer because of the death of the obligation holder.

5.29 Repossession of Personal Property Sold on Installment

When a buyer defaults and you repossess personal property, either by a voluntary surrender or a foreclosure, you may realize gain or loss. The method of calculating gain or loss is similar to the method used for disposition of installment notes *(5.28)*. Gain or loss is the difference between the fair market value of the repossessed property and your basis for the installment obligations satisfied by the repossession. This rule is followed whether or not title was kept by you or transferred to the buyer. The amount realized is reduced by costs incurred during the repossession. The basis of the obligation is face value less unreported profit.

If the property repossessed is bid in at a lawful public auction or judicial sale, the fair market value of the property is presumed to be the purchase or bid price, in the absence of proof to the contrary. Gain or loss in the repossession is reported in the year of the repossession.

Repossession gain or loss keeps the same character as the gain or loss realized on the original sale. If the sale originally resulted in a capital gain, the repossession gain is also a capital gain. Your basis in the repossessed property is its fair market value at the time of repossession.

Real property. Repossessions of real property are discussed in *Chapter 31 (31.12)*.

EXAMPLE

In December 2022, you sell home furniture for $4,500—$900 down and $300 a month plus 2% interest beginning January 2023. You reported the installment sale on your 2022 tax return. The buyer defaulted after making three monthly payments. You foreclosed and repossessed the property in 2023; the fair market value on the repossession date was $4,200. The legal costs of foreclosure and the cost of moving the furniture back to your home was $400. The gain on the repossession in 2023 is computed as follows:

Fair market value of property repossessed		$ 4,200
Basis of the buyer's notes at time of repossession:		
Selling price	$ 4,500	
Less: Payments made	1,800	
Unpaid balance of notes at repossession	$ 2,700	
Less: Unrealized profit (assume gross profit percentage of $33\frac{1}{3} \times \$2,700$)	$ 900	
Basis of obligation ($2,700 unpaid balance of notes − $900 unrealized profit)		1,800
Gain on repossession ($4,200 value of repossessed property − $1,800 basis of obligation)		$ 2,400
Less: Repossession costs		400
Taxable gain on repossession		$ 2,000

5.30 Boot in Like-Kind Exchange Payable in Installments

An exchange of like-kind real property held for investment or business is tax free unless boot is received. "Boot" may be cash or notes. If the transferred real property is subject to a mortgage and the amount of the mortgage you give up exceeds the mortgage you assume on the property received, that excess is boot *(6.2)*. Boot is taxable, and if payable in installments, the following rules apply. Contract price is reduced by the fair market value of like-kind property received. Gross profit is reduced by gain not recognized. "Payment" does not include like-kind property.

The same treatment applies to certain tax-free reorganizations that are not treated as dividends, to exchanges of certain insurance policies, exchanges of the stock of the same corporation, and exchanges of United States obligations.

 *Planning Reminder*

Taxable Boot Received in Exchange

If you make an exchange of like-kind real property and also receive cash or other property that is payable in one or more future years, you may report the gain using the installment method.

> **EXAMPLE**
>
> In 2023, investment real estate with an installment sale basis (basis plus selling expenses) of $400,000 is exchanged for like-kind property worth $200,000, plus installment obligations of $800,000, of which $100,000 is payable in 2024, plus interest. The balance of $700,000 plus interest will be paid in 2025. The contract price is $800,000 ($1 million selling price less $200,000 like-kind property received). The gross profit is $600,000 ($1 million less $400,000 installment sale basis). The gross profit ratio is 75% (gross profit of $600,000 ÷ contract price of $800,000). Like-kind property is not treated as a payment received in the year of exchange, so no gain is reported in 2023. In 2024, gain of $75,000 will have to be reported (75% gross profit ratio × $100,000 payment), and in 2025 there will be a gain of $525,000 (75% of $700,000 payment).

5.31 "Interest" Taxed if Sales Price Exceeds $150,000 With Over $5 Million Debt

If property is sold on the installment basis for more than $150,000, and the balance of installment obligations outstanding at the end of the year exceeds $5 million, an interest charge is imposed on the tax-deferred amount. The special tax applies to non-dealer sales of business or rental property (real estate or personal property) for over $150,000. Farm property and personal-use property, such as a residence, are exempt from the tax.

How to report interest tax. The interest charge is an additional tax. The method of computing the interest tax is complicated; the rules are in Internal Revenue Code Section 453A. In general, you compute the ratio of the face amount of outstanding installment obligations in excess of $5 million to the face amount of all outstanding installment obligations. This ratio is multiplied by the year-end unrecognized gain on the obligation, your top tax rate (ordinary income or capital gain) for the year, and also by the IRS interest rate for the last month of the year.

The interest is not deductible. It is reported on Line 15 of Schedule 2 (Form 1040 or 1040-SR).

Dealer sale of time shares and residential lots. The installment method can be used to report income from sales of certain time-share rights (generally time shares of up to six weeks per year) or residential lots if the seller elects to pay interest on the tax deferred under the installment method. The rules for computing the interest are in Code Section 453(l)(3). The interest is reported on Line 14 of Schedule 2 (Form 1040 or 1040-SR).

5.32 Worthless Securities

If you owned stock or a bond as an investor (not as a securities dealer) that became completely worthless in 2023, you may deduct your cost basis for the security as a capital loss, subject to the deduction limit of $3,000 ($1,500 if married filing separately) in excess of capital gains *(5.4)*. The worthless security is treated as sold on the last day of the year, which determines whether the loss is a short-term or long-term capital loss. Report the worthless security in the short-term or long-term section of Form 8949, as applicable *(see below)*. Capital loss treatment applies unless ordinary loss treatment is available for worthless Section 1244 stock *(30.11)*.

A loss of worthless securities is deductible only in the year the securities become completely worthless. If you abandon the securities, the securities are treated as completely worthless under an IRS regulation; *see* below. The loss may not be deducted in any other year. You may not claim a loss for a partially worthless security. However, if there is a market for it, sell the security and deduct the capital loss.

Filing Tip

Refund Deadline for Worthless Stock

You can take advantage of a special seven-year statute of limitations to claim a refund due to a worthless security or bad debt. An amended return for the year the security or debt became worthless can be filed within seven years from the date your original return for that year had to be filed, or, if later, within two years from the date you paid the tax.

For example, if you have been holding securities that you learn became worthless in 2016, you still have until April 15, 2024, to file for a refund of 2016 taxes by claiming a deduction for the worthless securities on an amended return (Form 1040-X) for 2016.

Planning Reminder

Selling Before the Security Becomes Worthless

To claim a deduction for worthless stock or bonds, you must be able to prove that the security became completely worthless in the year for which you are claiming the deduction. Sometimes you can avoid the problem of proving worthlessness by selling while there is still a market for the security. For example, a company you own stock in is on the verge of bankruptcy in 2024, but there is some doubt about the complete worthlessness of its securities. You might sell the securities for whatever you can get for them and claim the loss on the sale as a capital loss on your 2024 return. Sell to an unrelated buyer to avoid the loss disallowance rule (5.6). If there is no market for the security, you can abandon it to claim a deduction for worthlessness; *see 5.32* for the abandonment rule.

Because it is sometimes difficult to determine the year in which a security becomes completely worthless, the law allows you to file a refund claim within seven years from the due date of the return for the proper year (the year the security actually became completely worthless), or, if later, within two years from the date you paid the tax for that year.

To support a deduction for 2023, you must show:

1. The security had some value at the end of 2022. That is, you must be ready to show that the stock did not become worthless in a year prior to 2023. If you learn that the security did become worthless in a prior year, file an amended return for that year; *see* the Filing Tip on this page.
2. The security became totally worthless in 2023. You must be able to present facts fixing the time of loss during this year. For example, the company went bankrupt, stopped doing business, and is insolvent. Despite evidence of worthlessness, such as insolvency, the stock may be considered to have some value if the company continues to do business, or there are plans to reorganize the company. No deduction may be claimed for a partially worthless corporate bond or stock.

If you are making payments on a negotiable note you used to buy the stock that became worthless and you are on the cash-basis method, your payments are deductible losses in the years the payments are made, rather than in the year the stock became worthless.

If the security is a bond, note, certificate, or other evidence of a debt incurred by a corporation, the loss is deducted as a capital loss, provided the obligation is in registered form or has attached interest coupons. A loss on a worthless corporate obligation is always deemed sustained on the last day of the year, regardless of when the company failed during the year.

If the obligation is not issued with interest coupons or in registered form, or if it is issued by an individual, the loss is treated as a bad debt. If you received the obligation in a business transaction, the loss is fully deductible. You may also make a claim for a partially worthless business bad debt. If it is a nonbusiness debt, the loss is a capital loss and no claim may be made for partial worthlessness (5.33).

When to deduct worthless stock. If at the end of 2023 a company is in financial trouble but you are not sure whether its condition is hopeless, it is advisable to claim the deduction on your 2023 return to protect your claim. If you claim the deduction for 2023 and it turns out that complete worthlessness did not occur until a later year, you can claim the deduction for the proper year and then file an amended return for 2023 to eliminate the deduction.

Another option in fixing the timing of your loss deduction is to abandon the securities, as discussed below.

Abandoned securities treated as worthless. The IRS treats abandoned securities as totally worthless under a regulation that took effect for abandonments after March 12, 2008. To abandon a security, you must permanently surrender and relinquish all rights in the security and receive no payment in exchange for the security. Make sure that the security is removed from your account. The IRS will determine whether there has been an abandonment based on all the facts and circumstances. Under the general timing rule for worthless securities, the loss on abandonment is treated as resulting from a sale of a capital asset on the last day of the year in which the abandonment occurs.

Report a worthless security as a long-term or short-term loss on Form 8949. If securities became worthless during 2023, they are treated as if they were sold on the last day of the year for purposes of determining your holding period, regardless of when in the year worthlessness actually occurred. If a sale on the last day of the year provides you with a short-term (one year or less) holding period, report the loss as a short-term capital loss in Part I of Form 8949. Use Part II of Form 8949 for a long-term loss.

Ordinary loss on Small Business Investment Company (SBIC) stock. On Form 4797, investors may take ordinary loss deductions for losses on the worthlessness or sale of SBIC stock. The loss may also be treated as a business loss for net operating loss purposes. However, a loss realized on a short sale of SBIC stock is deductible as a capital loss. A Small Business Investment Company is a company authorized to provide small businesses with equity capital. Do not confuse investments in these companies with investments in small business stock (Section 1244 stock) *(30.11)*.

S corporation stock. If an S corporation's stock becomes worthless during the taxable year, the basis in the stock is adjusted for the stockholder's share of corporate items of income, loss, and deductions before a deduction for worthlessness is claimed.

> **EXAMPLE**
>
> You bought 100 shares of Z Co. stock on July 1, 1999. On March 23, 2023, the stock is considered wholly worthless. The loss is deemed to have been incurred on December 31, 2023. The loss is reported as a long-term capital loss on Form 8949; the holding period is from July 2, 1999 to December 31, 2023. Label the loss as "Worthless" across the columns for date sold and sales price. The long-term loss from Form 8949 will be transferred to Schedule D, where net capital gain or loss for the year is determined.

5.33 Tax Consequences of Bad Debts

When you lend money or sell on credit and your debtor does not repay, you may deduct your loss. The type of deduction depends on whether the debt was incurred in a business or personal transaction. This distinction is important because business bad debts receive favored tax treatment.

Business bad debt. You may deduct partially or totally worthless business debts. A business bad debt is fully deductible from gross income on Schedule C if you are self-employed, or on Schedule F if your business is farming; *see* IRS Publication 535 for details.

Nonbusiness bad debt. To be deductible, a nonbusiness bad debt must be totally worthless; you may not deduct a partially worthless nonbusiness debt. A nonbusiness bad debt for 2023 is reported as a short-term capital loss on Part 1 of Form 8949 with Box C checked (to indicate that you did not receive a Form 1099-B). On Line 1, column (a), enter the name of the debtor and write "bad debt statement attached". Enter "0" as the proceeds in column (d). Enter your basis in the debt in column (e). On the attached statement, you must describe the debt, your relationship to the debtor, your efforts to collect the debt, and your reasons for concluding that it had become worthless in 2023. As a short-term capital loss, a nonbusiness bad debt is deductible only from capital gains, if any, and $3,000 of ordinary income ($1,500 if married filing separately). Any excess is deductible as a capital loss carryover to 2024 and later years *(5.4)*.

Examples of nonbusiness bad debts:

- You enter into a deal for profit that is not connected with your business; for example, debts arising from investments are nonbusiness bad debts.
- You make a personal loan to a family member or friend with a reasonable hope of recovery and you are not in the business of making loans. You must be able to show that this is a bona fide loan and not a gift. Put the loan in writing and spell out repayment terms.
- You are assigned a debt that arose in the assignor's business. The fact that he or she could have deducted it as a business bad debt does not make it your business debt. A business debt must arise in your business.
- You pay liens filed against your property by mechanics or suppliers who have not been paid by your builder or contractor. Your payment is considered a deductible bad debt when there is no possibility of recovering reimbursement from the contractor and a judgment obtained against him or her is uncollectible.
- You lose a deposit on a house when the contractor becomes insolvent.
- You loan money to a corporation in which you are a shareholder, and your primary motivation is to protect your investment rather than your job; *see* below.
- You had an uninsured savings account in a financial institution that went into default.
- You are held secondarily liable on a mortgage debt assumed but not paid by a buyer of your home. Your payment to the bank or other holder of the mortgage is deductible as a bad debt if you cannot collect it from the buyer of the home.

Caution

Accounts and Notes Receivable

If you report income and expenses using the cash method, you may not claim a bad debt deduction for accounts and notes receivable on unpaid goods or services that you have not included as gross income *(40.6)*. If your client or customer fails to pay your bill for services rendered, you do not have a deductible bad debt because you do not have a "basis" in the debt to deduct.

Filing Instruction

Nonbusiness Bad Debt

If a nonbusiness bad debt became totally worthless in 2023, claim it as a short-term capital loss in Part I of Form 8949. Attach a statement describing the loan, your relationship to the debtor, how you tried to collect it, and why you decided it was worthless.

Refund claim for nonbusiness bad debt. If you do not claim a deduction on your original return for the year your nonbusiness debt becomes worthless, you can file a refund claim on Form 1040-X to amend your return for that year. You can file a refund claim for the year the debt became worthless within 7 years from the date your original return for that year had to be filed, or 2 years from the date you paid the tax, whichever is later; *see* the Filing Tip on page 154.

Guarantor or endorsement losses as bad debts. If you guarantee a loan and must pay it off after the principal debtor defaults, your payment is deductible as a business bad debt if you had a business reason for the guarantee. For example, to protect a business relationship with a major client, you guarantee the client's loan. Your payment on the guarantee qualifies as a business bad debt. If, as a result of your payment, you have a legal right to recover the amount from the client (right of subrogation or similar right), you may not claim a bad debt deduction unless that right is partially or totally worthless.

A loss on a guarantee may be a nonbusiness bad debt if you made the guarantee to protect an investment, such as where you are a main shareholder of a corporation and guarantee a bank loan to the company. No deduction is allowed if you guaranteed the loan as a favor to a relative or friend.

Loans by shareholders. It is a common practice for stockholders to make loans to their corporations or to guarantee loans made to the company by banks or other lenders. If the corporation fails and the stockholder is not repaid or has to make good on the guarantee, tax treatment of the bad debt depends on whether the stockholder is an employee who made the loan to protect his or her job.

If the dominant motivation for the loan was to maintain employment, the bad debt is not deductible; because this makes it an employee business expense, which is not deductible for 2018 through 2025 under the Tax Cuts and Jobs Act *(19.2)*.

If the dominant motivation for the loan was to protect the stockholder's investment in the company and not his or her job, the bad debt is generally a nonbusiness bad debt deductible on Form 8949/Schedule D as a short-term capital loss.

If the stockholder is in the business of lending money and the loan was made in that capacity, the bad debt would be a business bad debt, deductible on Schedule C by a sole proprietor.

5.34 Four Rules To Prove a Bad Debt Deduction

To determine whether you have a bad debt deduction, read the four rules explained below. Pay close attention to the fourth rule, which requires proof that the debt became worthless in the year the deduction is claimed. Your belief that your debt is bad, or the mere refusal of the debtor to pay, is not sufficient evidence. There must be an event, such as the debtor's bankruptcy, to fix the debt as worthless.

Rule 1. You must have a valid debt. There must be a valid loan and not a gift, as in the case of an informal loan to a friend or relative. You have no loss if your right to repayment is not fixed or depends upon some event that may not happen. Thus, advances to a corporation already insolvent are not valid debts. Nor are advances that are to be repaid only if the corporation has a profit. Voluntary payment of another's debt is also nondeductible. If usurious interest was charged on a worthless debt, and under state law the debt was void or voidable, the debt is not deductible as a bad debt. However, where the lender was in the business of lending money, a court allowed him to deduct the unpaid amounts as business losses.

If advances are made to a company that has lost outside borrowing sources and is thinly capitalized, with heavy debt-to-equity ratio, this indicates that the advances are actually capital contributions and not loans.

Rule 2. A debtor-creditor relationship must exist at the time the debt arose. You have a loss if there was a promise to repay at the time the debt was created and you had the right to enforce it. If the advance was a gift and you did not expect to be repaid, you may not take a deduction.

Planning Reminder

Debt Worthless Before Due

You do not have to wait until the debt is due in order to deduct a bad debt. Claim the deduction for the year that you can prove worthlessness occurred.

Rule 3. The funds providing the loan or credit were previously reported as income or part of your capital. If you are on the cash basis, you may not deduct salary, rent, or fees that have not been paid to you as a bad debt. On the cash basis, you do not include these items in income until you are paid.

Rule 4. You must show that the debt became worthless during the year for which you are claiming the deduction. To prove that a debt became worthless in 2023, you must show:

First, that the debt had some value at the end of the previous year (2022), and that there was a reasonable hope and expectation of recovering something on the debt. Your personal belief unsupported by other facts is not enough.

Second, that an identifiable event occurred in 2023—such as a bankruptcy proceeding—that caused you to conclude the debt was worthless. In the case of a business debt that has become partially worthless, you need evidence that the debt has declined in value. Additionally, reasonable collection steps must have been undertaken. That you cancel a debt does not make it worthless. You must still show that the debt was worthless when you canceled it. You do not have to go to court to try to collect the debt if you can show that a court judgment would be uncollectible.

Third, that there is no reasonable hope the debt may have some value in a later year. You are not required to prove that there is no possibility of ever receiving some payment on your debt.

Effect of statute of limitations. A debt is not deductible merely because a statute of limitations has run against the debt. Although the debtor has a legal defense against your demand for payment, he or she may still recognize the obligation to pay. A debt is deductible only in the year it becomes worthless. What if your debtor recognized his or her moral obligation to pay in spite of the expiration of the statute of limitations, but dies before paying? Your claim would be defeated if the executor raises the statute of limitations. You have a bad debt deduction in the year you made the claim against the estate.

5.35 Family Bad Debts

The IRS views loans to relatives, especially to children and parents, as gifts, so that it is rather difficult to deduct family bad debts.

To overcome the presumption of a gift when you advance money to a relative, take the same steps you would in making a business loan. Take a note, set a definite payment date, and require interest and collateral. If the relative fails to pay, make an attempt to collect. Failure to enforce collection of a family debt is viewed by the courts as evidence of a gift, despite the taking of notes and the receipt of interest.

Is a former spouse's default on child support a basis for a bad debt deduction? If you pay support for your children when your former spouse defaults on court-ordered support payments, can you claim your expenses as a nonbusiness bad debt deduction on the grounds that your position is similar to a guarantor who pays a creditor when the principal debtor defaults? The IRS does not agree with such a claim and will disallow the deduction; its position is supported by the Tax Court.

The federal appeals court for the Ninth Circuit left open the possibility that such a claim may have merit if the spouse who did not receive the required child support can show: (1) what she or he spent on the children; and (2) that the former spouse's obligation to support was worthless in the year the deduction is claimed.

The Tax Court has subsequently reiterated its position that defaulted child support payments are not a basis for a bad debt deduction. Following these Tax Court decisions, the IRS also announced its continuing opposition to the Ninth Circuit's suggestion that a deduction may be possible. The IRS holds that since the support obligation of the defaulting spouse is imposed directly by the divorce court, the other parent who pays support to make up for the arrearage has no "basis" to support a bad debt deduction.

Periodically, legislation has been proposed to allow a bad debt deduction for unpaid child support, but none of the proposals have been enacted into law.

 *Caution*

Formalize Loan With Relative

To protect against a possible IRS claim that your loan was a gift and not a loan, put the loan in writing with repayment terms as if the debtor were a third party.

CHAPTER 6

Tax-Free Exchanges of Property

You may exchange investment or business real property for "like-kind" real property without incurring a tax in the year of exchange if you meet the rules detailed in this chapter. Gain may be taxed upon a later disposition of the replacement property because the basis of the replacement property is usually the same as the basis of the property surrendered in the exchange. Thus, if you exchange property with a tax basis of $50,000 for property worth $250,000, the basis of the property received in exchange is fixed at $50,000, even though its fair market value is $250,000. The gain of $200,000 ($250,000 – $50,000), which is not taxed at the time of the exchange, is technically called "unrecognized gain." If you later sell the new property for $350,000, you will realize a taxable gain of $300,000 ($350,000 – $50,000).

Where property received in a tax-free exchange is held until death, the unrecognized gain escapes income tax forever because basis of the property in the hands of an heir is generally the value of the property at the date of death. If the exchange involves the transfer of boot, such as cash or other property, gain on the exchange is taxable to the extent of the value of boot.

You may not make a tax-free exchange of U.S. real estate for foreign real estate.

Tax-free exchanges between related parties may become taxable if either party disposes of the exchanged property within a two-year period.

6.1 Like-Kind Exchanges of Real Property Used for Investment or Business

You do not realize gain or loss on the "like-kind" exchange of business or investment real property (Code Section 1031). By making a qualifying exchange, you can defer the gain. On the other hand, a loss is also generally deferred; a loss on a qualifying exchange is not deductible unless you give up "unlike" property (not like-kind); *see* below.

For tax-free gain treatment, you must trade real property held for business use or investment for like-kind business or investment real property. Under IRS final regulations, real property includes land and improvements to land, unsevered crops and other natural products of land, and water and air space superjacent to land. Improvements to land include inherently permanent structures (e.g., buildings) and the structural components of inherently permanent structures.

The regulations also include an incidental rule under which personal property may be treated as part of real property qualifying for like-kind exchange treatment. Personal property is incidental to real property acquired in an exchange if, in standard commercial transactions, the personal property is typically transferred together with the real property, and the aggregate fair market value of the incidental personal property transferred with the real property does not exceed 15% of the aggregate fair market value of the replacement real property.

If the properties are not simultaneously exchanged, the time limits for deferred exchanges *(6.3)* must be satisfied. The entire gain is deferred only if you do not receive any "boot"; gain is taxed to the extent of boot received *(6.2)*. Where gain on a qualifying exchange is deferred and not immediately taxed, it may be taxable in a later year when you sell the property because your basis for the new property (called "replacement property") is generally the same as the basis for the property you traded (called "relinquished property") *(5.16–5.20)*.

If you make a qualifying like-kind exchange with certain related parties, tax-free treatment may be lost unless both of you keep the exchanged properties for at least two years *(6.5)*.

What is "like-kind" real property? The term like-kind refers to the nature or character of the property, that is, whether real estate is traded for real estate. It does not refer to grade or quality, that is, whether the properties traded are new or used, improved or unimproved. This means that land may be traded for a building, farm land for city lots, commercial property for residential rental property, or a leasehold interest of 30 years or more for an outright ownership in realty. These are all considered like-kind exchanges of real estate. However, real property in the United States and foreign real property are not (by statute) like-kind.

Personal use safe harbor for rental residence. An IRS safe harbor (Revenue Procedure 2008-16) allows rental real estate used occasionally as a vacation home to be treated as investment property so that it can be exchanged without endangering tax-deferred treatment.

To qualify, the relinquished residence has to be owned for at least 24 months immediately before the exchange, and, in each of the two 12-month periods immediately preceding the exchange, the residence must be rented at a fair rental for at least 14 days and personal use by the owner and his or her relatives cannot exceed the greater of 14 days or 10% of the days for which the residence is rented at a fair rental in the 12-month period.

Parallel requirements apply to the replacement residence. The replacement residence must be owned for at least 24 months after the exchange and, within each of the two 12-month periods following the exchange, it must be rented at a fair rental for 14 days or more and the taxpayer's personal use (including use by relatives) cannot exceed the greater of 14 days or 10% of the fair rental days during the 12-month period.

If a taxpayer expects to meet the fair rental and personal use tests for the replacement residence and based on that expectation reports the exchange on his or her return as a tax-deferred exchange, but it turns out that the tests are not met, an amended return must be filed to report the exchange as a taxable sale.

Losses. If a loss is incurred on a like-kind exchange, the loss is not deductible, whether you receive only like-kind property or "unlike" property together with like-kind property. However, a deductible loss may be incurred if you give up unlike property as part of the exchange; the loss equals any excess of the adjusted basis of the unlike property over its fair market value.

 *Law Alert*

Tax Deferral for Like-Kind Exchanges Continues to be Questioned

Over the years there have been numerous proposals to limit or eliminate like-kind exchange treatment. Current law allows like-kind exchange treatment only for real property held for investment or business. Deferral is not allowed for exchanges of personal property after 2017. There have been proposals to cap the amount of gain that can be deferred. For example, one proposal would allow deferral for up to $500,000 of gain ($1 million if married filing jointly) per year for like-kind real property exchanges. Developments, if any, will be in the *e-Supplement* at *jklasser.com*.

 *Caution*

Exchanging Depreciable Realty May Be Subject to Depreciation Recapture

Recapture provisions supersede tax-free exchange rules. Thus, if you exchange a depreciable building placed in service before 1987, depreciation may be recaptured as ordinary income, so check the consequences of any "recapture" element. For example, if you exchange the building for land, the recaptured amount is fully taxable as ordinary income; *see 44.2*.

EXAMPLES

1. Jones, a real estate investor, purchased Parcel A for investment in 1999 for $5,000. In 2011, he exchanged it for another parcel, Parcel B, which had a fair market value of $50,000. The gain of $45,000 was not taxed in 2011.

2. Same facts as above, except that in 2023 Parcel B still has a fair market value of $50,000 and Jones sells it for that price. His taxable gain in 2023 is $45,000. The "tax-free" exchange rules have the effect of deferring tax on the appreciation on Parcel A until the property received in exchange for it is sold.

3. Same facts as in 1 above, but the value of Parcel B was $3,000 in 2011. Jones could not deduct the loss in 2011. Jones' basis in Parcel B is $5,000, the same as the basis of Parcel A. If Jones sells Parcel B in 2023 for $3,000, he may deduct a loss of $2,000.

Reporting an exchange. You must file Form 8824 to report an exchange of like-kind property. If you figure a recognized gain on Form 8824, you also must report the gain on Schedule D (investment property) or on Form 4797 (business property).

If in addition to the like-kind property you gave up "unlike" property (other than cash), you figure the gain or loss on the unlike property on Lines 12-14 of Form 8824 and report it as if it were from a regular sale. If the fair market value of the unlike property exceeds its adjusted basis, the gain should be reported on Form 8949 and Schedule D (if investment property) or Form 4797 (business property). If the adjusted basis of the unlike property exceeds its fair market value, the loss is deductible on Form 8949/Schedule D or Form 4797 as if the exchange were a regular sale.

If your exchange is with a related party *(6.6)*, Form 8824 must be filed not only for the year of the exchange but also for the two years following the year of the exchange.

Property not within the tax-free trade rules. In addition to exchanges of personal property (other than incidental personal property treated as part of a real property exchange as explained on the prior page), which do not qualify for like-kind treatment after 2017 (see the Law Alert on the preceding page), the following exchanges are ineligible:

- Real property used for personal purposes (but exchanges of principal residences may qualify as tax free under different rules; *see Chapter 29*)
- Foreign real estate
- Property held for sale
- Inventory or stock-in-trade
- Securities
- Notes
- Partnership interest; *see* below

See also *31.3* for tax-free exchanges of realty and *6.11* for tax-free exchanges of insurance policies.

Exchange of partnership interests. Exchanges of partnership interests in different partnerships are not within the tax-free exchange rules. If you have an interest in a partnership that has elected to be excluded from the application of partnership rules, your interest is treated as an interest in each partnership asset, not as an interest in the partnership.

Real estate or personal property in foreign countries. You may not make a tax-free exchange of U.S. real estate for foreign real estate; by law they are not considered like-kind property. However, if your real estate is condemned, foreign and U.S. real estate are treated as like-kind property for purposes of making a tax-free reinvestment.

6.2   Receipt of Cash and Other Property—"Boot"

If, in addition to like-kind *(6.1)* property, you receive cash or other property (unlike kind), gain is taxable up to the amount of the cash and the fair market value of any unlike property received. The additional cash or unlike property is called "boot." If a loss was incurred on the exchange, the receipt of boot does not permit you to deduct the loss unless it is attributable to unlike-kind property you gave up in the exchange.

EXAMPLE

Jones owns an apartment house held for investment that has a fair market value of $220,000, subject to an $80,000 mortgage. His adjusted basis is $100,000. In 2023, Jones exchanges his building for Smith's apartment building (also held for investment), which has a fair market value of $250,000, is subject to a $150,000 mortgage, and has an adjusted basis of $175,000. Jones and Smith each assume the mortgage on the building received. Jones also receives $40,000 in cash from Smith. Smith and Jones each pay $5,000 in exchange expenses.

The Sample Forms 8824 for Jones and Smith on the following page show how they report the exchange. On Line 15, they show the boot received; their taxable gain on Line 22 is limited to this boot.

For Jones, the Line 15 boot is $35,000:

Cash received from Smith	$40,000
Less: Exchange expenses	(5,000)
Boot received by Jones	35,000

Jones does not have to include the $80,000 in mortgage liabilities transferred to Smith as boot on Line 15 because it does not exceed the $150,000 of mortgage liabilities he assumed from Smith; see "Assumption of mortgages" on page 163.

For Smith, the Line 15 boot is $25,000:

Mortgage transferred to Jones	$150,000
Less: Mortgage assumed from Jones	(80,000)
Less: Cash paid to Jones	(40,000)
Net amount received by Smith	30,000
Less: Exchange expenses	(5,000)
Boot received by Smith	$25,000

On Line 18, Jones and Smith increase their basis for the buildings they gave up by the net amount paid to the other party, if any.

For Jones, the Line 18 total of $170,000 includes:

Adjusted basis of building transferred		$100,000
Plus: Net mortgage assumed:		
Mortgage assumed	$150,000	
Less: Mortgage transferred	(80,000)	70,000
	70,000	$170,000

For Smith, the Line 18 total of $175,000 includes:

Adjusted basis of building transferred		$175,000
Plus: Net amount paid:		
Mortgage assumed	$80,000	
Plus: Cash paid	40,000	
Less: Mortgage transferred	(150,000)	0
	(30,000)	$175,000

The liabilities Smith assumed and the cash he paid are not included on Line 18 as an adjustment to basis because their total of $120,000 does not exceed the $150,000 of liabilities he transferred to Jones.

Line 22 of the Sample Forms 8824 shows the taxable gain Jones and Smith must report for 2023 on Schedule D. Line 24 shows the amount of deferred gain (not taxable for 2023). Line 25 shows the basis of the like-kind buildings Jones and Smith received in the exchange.

Receipt of Cash and Other Property—"Boot"

Name(s) shown on tax return. Do not enter name and social security number if shown on other side.	Your social security number
John Jones	X00-01-XX11

Part III Realized Gain or (Loss), Recognized Gain, and Basis of Like-Kind Property Received

Caution: If you transferred **and** received (**a**) more than one group of like-kind properties, or (**b**) cash or other (not like-kind) property, see *Reporting of multi-asset exchanges* in the instructions.

Note: Complete lines 12 through 14 **only** if you gave up property that was not like-kind. Otherwise, go to line 15.

12	Fair market value (FMV) of other property given up. See instructions	12	
a	Description of other property given up		
13	Adjusted basis of other property given up	13	
14	Gain or (loss) recognized on other property given up. Subtract line 13 from line 12. Report the gain or (loss) in the same manner as if the exchange had been a sale	14	
	Caution: If the property given up was used previously or partly as a home, see *Property used as home* in the instructions.		
15	Cash received, FMV of other property received, plus net liabilities assumed by other party, reduced (but not below zero) by any exchange expenses you incurred. See instructions	15	35,000
a	Description of other property received		
16	FMV of like-kind property you received	16	250,000
17	Add lines 15 and 16	17	285,000
18	Adjusted basis of like-kind property you gave up, net amounts paid to other party, plus any exchange expenses **not** used on line 15. See instructions	18	170,000
19	**Realized gain or (loss).** Subtract line 18 from line 17	19	115,000
20	Enter the smaller of line 15 or line 19, but not less than zero	20	35,000
21	Ordinary income under recapture rules. Enter here and on Form 4797, line 16. See instructions	21	- 0 -
22	Subtract line 21 from line 20. If zero or less, enter -0-. If more than zero, enter here and on Schedule D or Form 4797, unless the installment method applies. See instructions	22	35,000
23	**Recognized gain.** Add lines 21 and 22	23	35,000
24	Deferred gain or (loss). Subtract line 23 from line 19. If a related party exchange, see instructions	24	80,000
25	**Basis of like-kind property received.** Subtract line 15 from the sum of lines 18 and 23. See instructions		
	Note: Complete lines 25a, 25b, and 25c if you received like-kind section 1250 property, like-kind section 1245 property, or like-kind intangible property in the exchange.	25	170,000
a	Basis of like-kind section 1250 property received	25a	
b	Basis of like-kind section 1245 property received	25b	
c	Basis of like-kind intangible property received	25c	

Name(s) shown on tax return. Do not enter name and social security number if shown on other side.	Your social security number
Al Smith	X00-1X-XX11

Part III Realized Gain or (Loss), Recognized Gain, and Basis of Like-Kind Property Received

Caution: If you transferred **and** received (**a**) more than one group of like-kind properties, or (**b**) cash or other (not like-kind) property, see *Reporting of multi-asset exchanges* in the instructions.

Note: Complete lines 12 through 14 **only** if you gave up property that was not like-kind. Otherwise, go to line 15.

12	Fair market value (FMV) of other property given up. See instructions	12	
a	Description of other property given up		
13	Adjusted basis of other property given up	13	
14	Gain or (loss) recognized on other property given up. Subtract line 13 from line 12. Report the gain or (loss) in the same manner as if the exchange had been a sale	14	
	Caution: If the property given up was used previously or partly as a home, see *Property used as home* in the instructions.		
15	Cash received, FMV of other property received, plus net liabilities assumed by other party, reduced (but not below zero) by any exchange expenses you incurred. See instructions	15	25,000
a	Description of other property received		
16	FMV of like-kind property you received	16	220,000
17	Add lines 15 and 16	17	245,000
18	Adjusted basis of like-kind property you gave up, net amounts paid to other party, plus any exchange expenses **not** used on line 15. See instructions	18	175,000
19	**Realized gain or (loss).** Subtract line 18 from line 17	19	70,000
20	Enter the smaller of line 15 or line 19, but not less than zero	20	25,000
21	Ordinary income under recapture rules. Enter here and on Form 4797, line 16. See instructions	21	- 0 -
22	Subtract line 21 from line 20. If zero or less, enter -0-. If more than zero, enter here and on Schedule D or Form 4797, unless the installment method applies. See instructions	22	25,000
23	**Recognized gain.** Add lines 21 and 22	23	25,000
24	Deferred gain or (loss). Subtract line 23 from line 19. If a related party exchange, see instructions	24	45,000
25	**Basis of like-kind property received.** Subtract line 15 from the sum of lines 18 and 23. See instructions		
	Note: Complete lines 25a, 25b, and 25c if you received like-kind section 1250 property, like-kind section 1245 property, or like-kind intangible property in the exchange.	25	175,000
a	Basis of like-kind section 1250 property received	25a	
b	Basis of like-kind section 1245 property received	25b	
c	Basis of like-kind intangible property received	25c	

Assumption of mortgages. If you transfer mortgaged property and the other party assumes the mortgage, the amount of the assumed mortgage is part of your boot, as if you had received cash equal to the liability. If both you and the other party assume mortgages on the exchanged properties, the party giving up the larger debt treats the excess as taxable boot. The party giving up the smaller debt does not have boot; *see also* *31.3*. If you pay cash to the other party, or give up unlike-kind property, add this to the mortgage you assume in figuring which party has given up the larger debt.

Form 8824. The computation of boot, gain (or loss), and basis of the property received is made on Form 8824. Form 8824 must be filed for the year in which you transfer like-kind property. If the other party to the exchange is related to you, Form 8824 must also be filed for each of the two years following your transfer *(6.5)*.

6.3 Time Limits and Security Arrangements for Deferred Exchanges

Assume you own investment or business real property that has appreciated in value. You want to sell it and reinvest the proceeds in other property, but you would like to avoid having to pay tax on the appreciation. You can defer the tax on the gain if you are able to arrange an exchange for like-kind *(6.1)* property.

The problem is that it may be difficult to find a buyer who has property you want in exchange, and the time for closing the exchange is restricted. If IRS tests are met, intermediaries and security arrangements may be used without running afoul of constructive receipt rules that could trigger an immediate tax.

Deferred exchange distinguished from a reverse exchange. A deferred exchange is one in which you first transfer investment or business real property and then later receive like-kind investment or business real property *(6.1)*. If before you receive the replacement property you actually or constructively receive money or unlike property as full payment for the property you have transferred, the transaction will be treated as a sale rather than a deferred exchange. In that case, you must recognize gain (or loss) on the transaction even if you later receive like-kind replacement property. In determining whether you have received money or unlike property, you may take advantage of certain safe harbor security arrangements that allow you to ensure that the replacement property will be provided to you without jeopardizing like-kind exchange treatment; *see* below for the safe harbor security tests.

A reverse exchange is one in which you acquire replacement property before you transfer the relinquished property. The like-kind exchange rules generally do not apply to reverse exchanges. However, the IRS has provided safe harbor rules that allow like-kind exchange treatment to be obtained if either the replacement property or the relinquished property is held in a qualified exchange accommodation arrangement (QEAA) *(6.4)*.

Time limits for completing deferred exchanges. There is a time limit for identifying the replacement property that you will receive and a time limit within which you must receive it:

1. The property to be received must be identified in writing within 45 days after the date on which you transferred your property; *see* "How to identify replacement property", below.

2. You generally have up to 180 days to receive the replacement property, but the period may be shorter. Specifically, you must receive the like-kind property by whichever of these dates is earlier: (a) the 180th day after the date you transferred the property you are relinquishing or (b) the due date of your return (including extensions) for the year in which you made the transfer.

If the transaction involves more than one property, the 45-day identification period and the 180-day exchange period are determined by the earliest date on which any property is transferred. When the identification or exchange period ends on a Saturday, Sunday, or legal holiday, the deadline is not advanced to the next business day (as it is when the deadline for filing a tax return is on a weekend or holiday).

How to identify replacement property. You must identify replacement property in a written document signed by you and delivered before the end of the 45-day identification period to the person handling the transfer of the replacement property or to any other person involved in the exchange other than yourself or a related party. The identification

Caution

Deducting a Loss

You may deduct a loss incurred on an exchange if it is attributable to unlike property transferred in the exchange. The loss is recognized to the extent that the basis of the unlike property (other than cash) transferred exceeds its fair market value. However, a loss is not recognized if the unlike property is received together with the like-kind property in the exchange. Such a loss is not deductible.

Caution

Strict Time Limits

No extensions of time are allowed if the 45-day or 180-day statutory deadline for a deferred exchange cannot be met. If extra time is needed for finding suitable replacement property, it is advisable to delay the date of your property transfer because the transfer date starts the 45-day identification period.

may also be made in a written agreement. The property must be unambiguously described by a legal description or street address.

You may identify more than one property as replacement property. However, the maximum number of replacement properties that you may identify without regard to the fair market value is three properties. You may identify any number of properties provided the aggregate fair market value at the end of the 45-day identification period does not exceed 200% of the aggregate fair market value of all the relinquished properties as of the date you transferred them. If, as of the end of the identification period, you have identified more than the allowable number of properties, you are generally treated as if no replacement property has been identified.

If property is valued at no more than 15% of the total value of a larger item of property that it is transferred with, the smaller property is considered "incidental" and does not have to be separately identified.

Avoiding constructive receipt. In a deferred exchange, you want financial security for the buyer's performance and compensation for delay in receiving property. To avoid immediate tax, you must not make a security arrangement that gives you an unrestricted right to funds before the deal is closed. As discussed next, certain safe harbor security arrangements may be used without endangering like-kind exchange treatment.

Safe harbor tests for deferred exchange security arrangements. If any one of the four following safe harbors applies to your security arrangement, you are not treated by the IRS as having actually or constructively received cash or unlike property prior to receiving the like-kind replacement, so tax-deferred exchange treatment may be obtained.

The first two "safe harbors" cover escrow accounts, mortgages and other security arrangements with your transferee. The third allows the use of a "qualified intermediary", an unrelated professional who, for a fee, arrange the details of the deferred exchange. The fourth allows you to earn interest on an escrow account.

1. The transferee may give you a mortgage, deed of trust, or other security interest in property (other than cash or a cash equivalent), or a third-party guarantee. A standby letter of credit may be given if you are not allowed to draw on such standby letter except upon a default of the transferee's obligation to transfer like-kind replacement property.

2. The transferee may put cash or a cash equivalent in a qualified escrow account or a qualified trust. The escrow holder or trustee must not be related to you. Your rights to receive, pledge, borrow, or otherwise obtain the cash must be limited. For example, you may obtain the cash after all of the replacement property to which you are entitled is received. After you identify replacement property, you may obtain the cash after the later of (1) the end of the identification period and (2) the occurrence of a contingency beyond your control that you have specified in writing. You may receive the funds after the end of the identification period if within that period you do not identify replacement property. In other cases, there can be no right to the funds until the exchange period ends.

3. You may use a qualified intermediary if your right to receive money or other property is limited (as discussed in safe harbor rule 2, above). A qualified intermediary (QI) is an unrelated party who, for a fee, acts to facilitate a deferred exchange by entering into an agreement with you for the exchange of properties pursuant to which the intermediary acquires your property from you and transfers it to the other party, acquires the replacement property, and transfers the replacement property to you. Typically, the QI transfers your property to the buyer in exchange for cash and uses the cash to purchase the replacement property that will be transferred to you.

   There are restrictions on who may act as an intermediary. You may not employ any person as an intermediary who is your employee or is related to you or your agent or has generally acted as your professional adviser, such as an attorney, accountant, investment broker, real estate agent, or banker, in a two-year period preceding the exchange. Related parties include family members and controlled businesses or trusts *(5.6)*, except that for purposes of control, a 10% interest is sufficient under the intermediary rule. The performance of routine financial, escrow, trust, or title insurance services by a financial institution or title company within the two-year period is not taken into account. State laws that may be interpreted as fixing an agency relationship between the transferor and transferee or fixing the transferor's right to security funds are ignored.

   In a simultaneous exchange, the intermediary is not considered the transferor's agent.

4. You are permitted to receive interest or a "growth factor" on escrowed funds if your right to receive the amount is limited as discussed under safe harbor rule 2.

IRS Alert

Safe Harbor If Exchange Fails Due to Qualified Intermediary's Default

The IRS has provided relief if you hire a qualified intermediary (QI) to facilitate an exchange but are unable to meet the deadlines for relinquishing or receiving replacement property solely because the QI defaults on its obligations due to bankruptcy or receivership proceedings. By meeting the requirements of Revenue Procedure 2010-14, you can use a safe harbor that allows you to avoid having to report gain from the failed exchange until payments attributable to the relinquished property are received. A safe harbor gross profits ratio method is provided for reporting the gain.

EXAMPLE

You and Jones agree to enter a deferred exchange under the following terms and conditions. On May 19, 2023, you transfer to Jones real estate that has been held for investment; it is unencumbered and has a fair market value of $100,000. On or before July 3, 2023 (the last day of the 45-day identification period), you must identify like-kind replacement property. On or before November 15, 2023 (the last day of the 180-day exchange period), Jones is required to buy the property and transfer it to you. At any time after May 19, 2023, and before Jones has purchased the replacement property, you have the right, upon notice, to demand that Jones pay you $100,000 instead of acquiring and transferring the replacement property. However, you identify replacement property, and Jones purchases and transfers it to you. According to the regulations, you have an unrestricted right to demand the payment of $100,000 as of May 19, 2023. You are therefore in constructive receipt of $100,000 on that date. Thus, the transaction is treated as a taxable sale, and the transfer of the real property does not qualify as a tax-free exchange. You are treated as if you received the $100,000 for the sale of your property and then purchased replacement property.

Escrow account earnings are generally exempt from imputed interest rules. Under final IRS regulations, it is possible for a taxpayer who has an escrow arrangement with a qualified intermediary to be taxed on imputed interest, but there is a $2 million exemption that allows the majority of exchange arrangements with small business exchange facilitators to avoid the imputed interest. Under the regulations, when a qualified intermediary holds exchange funds (cash, cash equivalents, or relinquished property) in escrow for a taxpayer under a deferred exchange agreement prior to the acquisition of replacement property, the exchange funds are treated as a loan from the taxpayer to the qualified intermediary unless the agreement provides that all of the earnings (such as bank interest) on the exchange funds will be paid to the taxpayer.

However, even when the intermediary retains the escrow earnings, as is typically the case with small nonbank exchange facilitators, the imputed interest rules do not apply if the deemed loan does not exceed $2 million and the loan does not extend beyond six months. If the loan exceeds $2 million or lasts more than six months, the taxpayer must report imputed interest. For example, a taxpayer transfers property to a qualified intermediary who transfers it to a purchaser in exchange for $2.1 million cash, which the intermediary deposits in a money market account for three months until the intermediary withdraws the funds and purchases replacement property identified by the taxpayer. Assuming that the taxpayer is not entitled to the earnings under the exchange agreement, the taxpayer is treated as having made a $2.1 million loan to the intermediary. The amount of the imputed interest taxable to the taxpayer is based on the lower of (1) the short-term applicable federal rate in effect on the day the deemed loan was made, compounded semiannually, or (2) the rate on a 91-day Treasury bill issued on or before the date of the deemed loan. The IRS could increase the $2 million exempt amount in future guidance.

6.4 Qualified Exchange Accommodation Arrangements (QEAAs) for Reverse Exchanges

The like-kind exchange rules (6.1) generally do not apply to a so-called reverse exchange in which you acquire replacement property before you transfer relinquished property. However, if you use a qualified exchange accommodation arrangement (QEAA), the transfer may qualify as a like-kind exchange.

Under a QEAA, either the replacement property or the relinquished property is transferred to an exchange accommodation titleholder (EAT) who is treated as the beneficial owner of the property for federal income tax purposes. If the property is held in a QEAA, the IRS will accept the qualification of property as either replacement property or relinquished property, and the treatment of an EAT as the beneficial owner of the property for federal income tax purposes.

Caution

Parking Transactions

Property transferred to you by the exchange accommodation titleholder (EAT) cannot be treated as property received in an exchange if you previously owned it within 180 days of its transfer to the EAT.

The QEAA rules allow taxpayers to structure "parking transactions" in which the replacement property is acquired by the EAT before the transfer of the relinquished property. However, a QEAA safe harbor does not apply if the taxpayer transfers property to an EAT and receives that same property back as replacement property for other property of the taxpayer.

The IRS has set numerous technical requirements for QEAAs. Property is held in a QEAA only if you have a written agreement with the EAT, the time limits for identifying and transferring the property are met, and the qualified indicia of ownership of property are transferred to the EAT.

The EAT must meet all the following requirements: (1) Hold qualified indicia of ownership *(see below)* at all times from the date of acquisition of the property until the property is transferred within the 180-day period *(see below)*; (2) be someone other than you, your agent, or a person related to you or your agent; (3) be subject to federal income tax. If the EAT is treated as a partnership or S corporation, more than 90% of its interests or stock must be owned by partners or shareholders who are subject to federal income tax.

The IRS defines qualified indicia of ownership as either legal title to the property, other indicia of ownership of the property that are treated as beneficial ownership of the property under principles of commercial law (for example, a contract for deed), or interests in an entity that is disregarded as an entity separate from its owner for federal income tax purposes (for example, a single member limited liability company) and that holds either legal title to the property or other indicia of ownership.

There are time limits for identifying and transferring property under a QEAA. No later than 45 days after the transfer of qualified indicia of ownership of the replacement property to the EAT, you must identify the relinquished property in a manner consistent with the principles for deferred exchanges *(6.3)*. If qualified indicia of ownership in replacement property have been transferred to the EAT, then no later than 180 days after that transfer, the replacement property must be transferred to you either directly or indirectly through a qualified intermediary *(6.3)*. If the EAT receives qualified indicia of ownership in the relinquished property, then no later than 180 days after that transfer, the relinquished property must be transferred to a person other than you, your agent at the time of the transaction, or a person who is related to you or your agent.

Note: For further details on the IRS' guidelines for QEAAs, *see* Revenue Procedure 2000-37, as modified by Revenue Procedure 2004-51 (parking transactions).

6.5 Exchanges Between Related Parties

A like-kind exchange between related persons may be disqualified if either party disposes of the property received in the exchange within two years after the date of the last transfer that was part of the exchange. Unless an exception applies, any gain deferred on the original exchange becomes taxable when the original like-kind property is disposed of by either party within the two-year period. If a loss was deferred on the original exchange, the loss becomes deductible if allowed under the rules in *5.6*.

Indirect dispositions of the property within the two-year period, such as transfer of stock of a corporation or interests in a partnership that owns the property, may also be treated as taxable dispositions.

Related parties. Related persons falling within the two-year rule include your children, grandchildren, parent, brother, or sister, controlled corporations or partnerships (more than 50% ownership), and a trust in which you are a beneficiary. A transfer to a spouse is not subject to the two-year rule unless he or she is a nonresident alien.

Plan to avoid two-year rule. If you set up a prearranged plan under which you first transfer property to an unrelated party who within two years makes an exchange with a party related to you, the related party will not qualify for tax-free treatment on that exchange.

Exceptions. No tax will be incurred on a disposition made after the death of either related party; in an involuntary conversion provided the original exchange occurred before the threat of the conversion; or if you can prove that neither the exchange nor the later disposition was for a tax avoidance purpose.

Filing Instruction

Filing Form 8824

The IRS requires related parties who exchange property to file Form 8824 for the year of the exchange and also for the two years following the exchange. If either party disposes of the property received in the original exchange in any of these years, the gain deferred on the original exchange must be reported in the year of disposition.

The two-year period is suspended for a holder of exchanged property who has substantially diminished his or her risk of loss, such as by use of a put or short sale.

6.6   Property Transfers Between Spouses and Ex-Spouses

Under Section 1041, all transfers of property between spouses are treated as tax-free exchanges, other than transfers to a nonresident alien spouse, certain trust transfers of mortgaged property, and transfers of U.S. Savings Bonds; these exceptions are discussed below. Section 1041 applies to transfers during marriage as well as to property settlements incident to a divorce. In a Section 1041 transfer, there is no taxable gain or deductible loss to the transferor spouse. The transferee-spouse takes the transferor's basis in the property, and so appreciation in value will be taxed to the recipient on a later sale. This basis rule applies to all property received after July 18, 1984, under divorce or separation instruments in effect after that date.

A transfer is "incident to the divorce" if it occurs either within one year after the date the marriage ceases or, if later, is related to the cessation of the marriage, such as a transfer authorized by a divorce decree. A Treasury regulation provides that any transfer pursuant to a divorce or separation instrument occurring within six years of the end of the marriage is considered to be "related to the cessation of the marriage," and therefore as "incident to a divorce." Transfers made pursuant to the divorce or separation instrument that are more than six years after the end of the marriage, or transfers made within the six-year period that are not pursuant to the divorce or separation instrument, are generally presumed to be unrelated to the cessation of the marriage, but this negative presumption does not apply, and therefore the transfer will be considered to be related to the cessation of the marriage, if it was made to effect the division of property owned by the spouses when the marriage ended. For example, a transfer not made within the six-year period qualifies if it is shown that an earlier sale was hampered by legal or business disputes such as a fight over the property value.

 *Planning Reminder*

Recipient Spouse Bears Tax Consequences of Transferred Property

Under the tax-free exchange rules, the transferor-spouse does not have taxable gain or deductible loss on the transfer of property, even if cash is received for the property or the other spouse (or former spouse) assumes liabilities or gives up marital rights as part of a property settlement. The spouse who receives property may incur tax on a later sale because his or her basis in the property is the same as the transferor-spouse's basis; *see* the Examples in 6.6. Because the transferee bears the tax consequences of a later sale, he or she should consider the potential tax on the appreciation in negotiating a marital settlement. In a marital settlement, the transferee spouse can lessen the tax burden by negotiating for assets that have little or no unrealized appreciation.

EXAMPLES

1. In a property settlement accompanying a divorce, a husband plans to transfer to his wife stock worth $250,000 that cost him $50,000. In deciding whether to agree to the transfer, the wife should be aware that her basis for the stock will be $50,000. If she sells the stock for $250,000, she will have to pay tax on a $200,000 gain. This tax cost should be accounted for in arriving at the settlement.

2. Basis of the property in the hands of the transferee-spouse is not increased even if cash is paid as part of the transfer. For example, a husband received a house originally owned by the wife as part of a marital settlement. Her basis for the house was $32,200. He paid her $18,000 cash as part of the settlement and when he later sold the house for $64,000, he argued that his basis for purposes of computing profit was $50,200—the wife's $32,200 basis plus his $18,000 cash payment. The IRS refused to consider the cash payment as part of basis, and the Tax Court agreed that the carryover basis rule applies.

Nonresident alien. The tax-free exchange rule does not apply to transfers to a nonresident alien spouse or former spouse.

Transfers of U.S. Savings Bonds. The IRS has ruled that the tax-free exchange rules do not apply to transfers of U.S. Savings Bonds. For example, if a spouse has deferred the reporting of interest on EE bonds and transfers the bonds to his former spouse as part of a divorce settlement, the deferred interest is taxed to him on the transfer. The former spouse's basis for the bonds is the spouse's basis plus the income realized on the transfer. When the former spouse redeems the bonds, that former spouse will be taxed on the interest accrued from the date of the transfer to the redemption date.

Payment for release of community property interest in retirement pay. The Tax Court allowed tax-free treatment for a payment made to a wife for releasing her community property claim to her husband's military retirement pay. The IRS had argued that the tax-free exchange rules discussed in this section did not apply to the release of rights to retirement pay that would otherwise be subject to ordinary income tax. The Tax Court disagreed, holding that the tax-free exchange rule applies whether the transfer is for relinquishment of marital rights, cash, or other property.

Transfers in trust. The tax-free exchange rules generally apply to transfers in trust for the benefit of a spouse or a former spouse if incident to a divorce. However, gain cannot be avoided on a trust transfer of heavily mortgaged property. If the trust property is mortgaged, the transferor spouse must report a taxable gain to the extent that the liabilities assumed by the transferee spouse plus the liabilities to which the property is subject (even if not assumed) exceed the transferor's adjusted basis for the property. If the transferor realizes a taxable gain under this rule, the transferee's basis for the property is increased by the gain.

Sole proprietorship sale to spouse. Tax-free exchange rules may apply to a sale of business property by a sole proprietor to a spouse. The buyer spouse assumes a carryover basis even if fair market value is paid. The transferor is not required to recapture previously claimed depreciation deductions or investment credits. However, the transferee is subject to the recapture rules on premature dispositions or if the property ceases to be used for business purposes.

Transfer of nonstatutory options or nonqualified deferred compensation. According to the IRS, if a vested interest in nonstatutory (nonqualified) stock options or nonqualified deferred compensation is transferred to a former spouse as part of a property settlement, the transferor-spouse (the employee) does not have to report any income; the Section 1041 tax-free exchange rules apply. When the transferee-spouse later exercises the options or receives the deferred compensation, he or she will be taxed on the option spread *(2.17)* or the deferred compensation as if he or she was the employee. Income tax withholding and FICA tax withholding (Social Security and Medicare taxes) is generally required from the payments made to the transferee-spouse.

Divorce-related redemptions of stock in closely held corporation. When a married couple own all (or most) of the stock in a closely held corporation, the corporation may redeem the stock of one of the spouses as part of an overall divorce settlement. Does the transferring spouse avoid tax on the redemption under the Section 1041 tax-free exchange rules?

If the redemption of one of the spouses' stock is treated as a transfer to a third party on behalf of the other spouse, Section 1041 applies and the transferor-spouse would escape tax on the redemption. However, there has been much confusion and litigation as to the standards for determining whether a redemption is "on behalf of" the non-transferor spouse, and whether different tests should apply for determining the tax treatment of each spouse. Court decisions have generally supported tax-free treatment for a spouse whose stock is redeemed under the terms of the couple's divorce or separation instrument, or where the other (non-transferring) spouse requests or consents to the redemption. However, the courts are divided on the issue of whether the non-transferor spouse, who is left in control of the corporation, has realized a constructive dividend as a result of the redemption. *See* Example 2 below for the disputed positions taken by Tax Court judges in the *Read* case.

In response to the inconsistent standards used by the courts (see the Examples below), the IRS amended its regulations to provide a specific rule for determining which spouse will be taxed on the redemption. The regulation allows tax-free exchange treatment under Section 1041 to the transferor-spouse (whose stock was redeemed) only if under applicable law the redemption is treated as resulting in a constructive dividend to the nontransferor-spouse. If constructive dividend treatment does not apply to the nontransferor-spouse, the form of the redemption transaction is followed and the transferor-spouse is taxed on the redemption. The IRS regulation adopts the position of some of the dissenting judges in the *Read* case; *see* Example 2 below. The spouses are allowed to provide in a divorce or separation agreement that the redemption will be taxable to the nontransferor-spouse even if the redemption would not result in a constructive dividend to that spouse under applicable law. Alternatively, they can provide that the transferor will be taxed on the redemption although the redemption would otherwise be treated as a constructive dividend to the nontransferor-spouse.

Basis of property received before July 19, 1984, or under instruments in effect before that date. The tax-free exchange rules do not apply to property received before July 19, 1984, from your spouse (or former spouse if the transfer was incident to divorce). Your

Court Decision

Interest on Marital Property Settlements

Parties may agree to pay interest on property transfers relating to divorce settlements when payments are to be made over time. The actual property transfer is generally a tax-free exchange. According to the Tax Court, the interest is separate and apart from the property transferred. The deductibility of the interest paid depends on the nature of the property transferred. Interest allocated to residential property, for instance, is deductible as residential mortgage interest; interest allocated to investment property is deductible as investment interest subject to the net investment income limit. *See Chapter 15*.

Planning Reminder

Transfers to Third Parties

If you transfer property to a third party on behalf of your spouse or former spouse where the transfer is required by a divorce or separation instrument, or if you have your spouse's or former spouse's written request or consent for the transfer, the transfer is tax free to you under Section 1041. The transfer is treated as if made to your spouse or former spouse, who then retransfers the property to the third party. A written request or consent must specifically state that the tax-free exchange rules of Code Section 1041 are intended, and you must receive it before filing the tax return for the year of the transfer. As discussed in the Examples in *6.6*, a divorce-related stock redemption may qualify for Section 1041 treatment as a transfer "on behalf of" the other spouse.

basis for determining gain or loss when you sell such property is its fair market value when you received it. The same fair market value basis rule applies to property received after June 18, 1984, under an instrument in effect on or before that date unless a Section 1041 election was made to have the tax-free exchange rules apply. For property subject to such an election, your basis is the same as the transferor-spouse's adjusted basis.

EXAMPLES

1. A federal district court and the Ninth Circuit Court of Appeals held that, under Section 1041, a wife was not taxable on the redemption of her stock by the couple's closely held corporation where the redemption was pursuant to their divorce agreement and incorporated into the divorce decree. The Ninth Circuit viewed the transfer as if the husband had received the stock directly from the wife and then transferred it to the company.

   After the Ninth Circuit held that the redemption was not taxable to the wife, the IRS argued in a separate case against the nonredeeming husband that he received a taxable constructive dividend. However, the Tax Court disagreed, holding that there was no dividend to the husband because under state law he was merely a guarantor; he was not primarily and unconditionally obligated to buy the stock. The IRS did not appeal the Tax Court decision.

   In this unusual situation, the IRS is in the position of being unable to collect tax on the redemption proceeds from either the transferor or transferee spouse.

2. After William and Carol Read divorced, William, pursuant to their divorce decree, elected to have their controlled corporation purchase all of Carol's stock. A Tax Court majority held that Carol was not taxed on her transfer to the corporation; the transfer was on behalf of William and thus qualified for Section 1041 non-recognition treatment.

   The Tax Court majority also held that William realized a constructive dividend on the corporation's redemption of Carol's stock. However, the majority relied on a concession by William and did not specify a legal standard for determining whether he should be taxed. Concurring judges suggested that constructive dividend treatment for William followed automatically from the holding that Carol's stock transfer was on his behalf and thus within Section 1041. There were four dissenting opinions, all of which held that under traditional law for constructive dividends, there is no constructive dividend unless William had a "primary and unconditional obligation" to buy the shares, an obligation the corporation satisfied by making the redemption. Most of the dissenters argued that William did not have such an obligation and should not be taxed. They further argued that if William was not obligated to buy the shares, Section 1041 does not apply and thus Carol realized capital gain on the redemption of her shares. Other dissenting judges held that a spouse can never avoid taxable gain under Section 1041 on a redemption incident to divorce.

3. The Eleventh Circuit Court of Appeals allowed tax-free treatment to a redemption of a wife's stock, following the reasoning of the Tax Court majority in *Read* (Example 2 above). The redemption was on behalf of her ex-husband. The redemption was required by their divorce decree and it left him in control of 98% of the corporation's stock. He had guaranteed the corporation's 10-year promissory note to her, and the terms of the note specifically said that the guarantee was in his interests.

   Furthermore, although the corporation's note did not provide for interest, interest income was not imputed to the wife. Imputed interest does not apply where the underlying transfer is not taxable under Section 1041.

6.7 Tax-Free Exchanges of Stock in Same Corporation

Gain on the exchange of common stock for other common stock of the same corporation is not taxable. The same rule generally applies to an exchange of preferred stock of the same corporation, but not if "nonqualified" preferred with special redemption rights or a varying dividend rate is received. Loss realized on a qualifying exchange is not deductible. The exchange may take place between the stockholder and the company or between two stockholders.

An exchange of preferred stock for common, or common for preferred, in the same company is generally not tax free, unless the exchange is part of a tax-free recapitalization. In such exchanges, the company should inform you of the tax consequences.

Convertible securities. A conversion of securities under a conversion privilege is tax free *(30.7)*.

6.8   Joint Ownership Interests

The change to a tenancy in common from a joint tenancy is tax free. You may convert a joint tenancy in corporate stock to a tenancy in common without income-tax consequences. The transfer is tax free even though survivorship rights are eliminated. Similarly, a partition and issuance of separate certificates in the names of each joint tenant is also tax free.

A joint tenancy and a tenancy in common differ in this respect. On the death of a joint tenant, ownership passes to the surviving joint tenant or tenants. But on the death of a tenant holding property in common, ownership passes to his or her heirs, not to the other tenant or tenants with whom the property was held.

A tenancy by the entirety is a form of joint ownership recognized in some states and can be only between a husband and wife.

Dividing properties held in common. A division of properties held as tenants in common may qualify as tax-free exchanges.

For example, three men owned three pieces of real estate as tenants in common. Each man wanted to be the sole owner of one of the pieces of property. They disentangled themselves by exchanging interests in a three-way exchange. No money or property other than the three pieces of real estate changed hands, and none of the men assumed the others' liability. The transactions qualified as tax-free exchanges and no gain or loss was recognized.

Receipt of boot. Exchanges of jointly owned property are tax free as long as no "boot," such as cash or other property, passes between the parties *(6.2)*.

6.9   Setting up Closely Held Corporations

Tax-free exchange rules facilitate the organization of a corporation. When you transfer property to a corporation that you control solely in exchange for corporate stock in that corporation (but not nonqualified preferred stock), no gain or loss is recognized on the transfer. For control, you alone or together with other transferors (such as partners, where a partnership is being incorporated) must own at least 80% of the combined voting power of the corporation and 80% of all other classes of stock immediately after the transfer to the corporation. If you receive securities in addition to stock, the securities are treated as taxable "boot." The corporation takes your basis in the property, and your basis in the stock received in the exchange is the same as your basis in the property. Gain not recognized on the organization of the corporation may be taxed when you sell your stock, or the corporation disposes of the property.

Transfer of liabilities. When assets subject to liabilities are transferred to the corporation, the liability assumed by the corporation is not treated as taxable "boot," but your stock basis is reduced by the amount of liability. The transfer of liabilities may be taxable when the transfer is part of a tax avoidance scheme, or the liabilities exceed the basis of the property transferred to the corporation.

 *Caution*

Consider Taxable Transfer

Before making a property transfer to a closely held corporation, consult an accountant or an attorney on the tax consequences. There may be instances when you have potential losses or you desire the corporation to take a stepped-up basis that would make tax-free treatment undesirable.

> **EXAMPLE**
>
> You transfer a building worth $500,000, which cost you $100,000, to your newly organized corporation in exchange for all of its outstanding stock. You realize a $400,000 gain ($500,000 – $100,000) that is not recognized. Your basis in the stock is $100,000 (same as your basis in the building); the corporation's basis in the building also is $100,000. The following year, you sell all of your stock to a third party for $500,000. The $400,000 gain that had been deferred is now recognized.

6.10 Tax-Free Exchanges of Insurance Policies

Certain types of insurance policies can be exchanged tax free.

These exchanges are tax free:

- Life insurance policy for another life insurance policy, endowment policy, or an annuity contract.
- Life insurance policy, an endowment policy, or an annuity contract for a qualified long-term care policy.
- Endowment policy for another endowment policy that provides for regular payments beginning no later than the date payments would have started under the old policy, or in exchange for an annuity contract.
- Annuity contract for another annuity contract with identical annuitants.

These exchanges are not tax free:

- Endowment policy for a life insurance policy, or for another endowment policy that provides for payments beginning at a date later than payments would have started under the old policy.
- Annuity contract for a life insurance or endowment policy.
- Transfers of life insurance contracts where the insured is not the same person in both contracts. The IRS held that a company could not make a tax-free exchange of a key executive policy where the company could change insured executives as they leave or join the firm.

Endorsement of annuity check for another annuity is taxable. Cashing out a commercial annuity or nonqualified employee contract and investing it in another annuity does not qualify as a tax-free exchange. The IRS denied tax-free exchange treatment to a taxpayer who tried to complete a direct exchange of a non-qualified annuity contract but was foiled by the insurance company holding the contract. The taxpayer had asked the insurance company to issue a check directly to another insurer as consideration for a new annuity contract, intending the transaction to be treated as a tax-free exchange under Section 1035. The insurer refused and instead issued a check to the taxpayer. The taxpayer did not deposit the check, but instead endorsed it to the second insurance company to obtain the new annuity contract.

The IRS ruled that endorsing the check over to the second insurance company as consideration for the new contract was not a tax-free exchange. Instead, the taxpayer had to include in gross income the portion of the check that was allocable to income on the contract. If this had been a tax-sheltered 403(b) annuity or a qualified employee annuity, a distribution from the policy could have been rolled over tax-free to another such annuity, or even to another eligible retirement plan such as an IRA or qualified employer trust. However, in the case of a non-qualified annuity, there is no rollover provision for amounts distributed from the contract.

Note: Tax-free exchange treatment may be allowed if you surrender an annuity contract or insurance policy of an insurer in serious financial difficulty, and roll over the proceeds in a new policy or contract with a different insurer; *see* the Planning Reminder in this section *(6.10)*.

Direct transfer of a portion of the cash surrender value of an existing annuity contract for another annuity. The IRS has guidelines for determining whether the direct transfer of a portion of the cash surrender value of an existing annuity contract to another contract is a tax-free exchange. The rules apply whether or not the two contracts are issued by the same or different companies. Revenue Procedure 2011-38 allows tax-free exchange treatment for a direct transfer of a portion of the cash surrender value of an existing annuity contract for a second annuity contract if no amount, other than an amount received as an annuity for 10 or more years or during one or more lives, is received under either the original or new contract during the 180-day period starting on the transfer date. If tax-free exchange treatment is allowed under these guidelines, the two annuity contracts will be treated separately and the IRS will not require that they be aggregated even if the same insurance company issued both. If the 180-day test is not met, the IRS will determine if the amount received under either contract within the 180 days should be treated as a distribution taxable to the extent of earnings, or as boot *(6.2)* in a tax-free exchange.

 *Planning Reminder*

Reinvesting Cash Proceeds Received from Financially Troubled Insurer

If your annuity contract or insurance policy is with an insurance company that is in a rehabilitation, conservatorship, insolvency, or a similar state proceeding, you may surrender the policy and make a tax-free reinvestment of the cash proceeds in a new policy with a different insurance company. The transfer must be completed within 60 days. If a government agency does not allow you to withdraw your entire balance from the troubled insurance company, you must assign all rights to any future distributions to the issuer of the new contract or policy. *See* IRS Revenue Procedure 92-44.

CHAPTER 7

Retirement and Annuity Income

For employees, coverage in a qualified employer retirement plan is a valuable fringe benefit, as employer contributions are tax-free within specified limits. Certain salary-reduction plans allow you to make elective deferrals of salary not subject to income tax. An advantage of all qualified retirement plans is that earnings accumulate tax free until withdrawal.

Along with tax savings opportunities come technical restrictions and pitfalls. For example, retirement plan distributions eligible for rollover are subject to a mandatory 20% withholding tax if you receive the distribution instead of asking your employer to make a direct trustee-to-trustee transfer of the distribution to an IRA or another qualified employer plan.

This chapter discusses tax treatment of annuities and employer plan distributions, including how to avoid tax penalties, such as for distributions before age 59½.

The distribution rules in this chapter also generally apply to plans for self-employed individuals; retirement plans for self-employed individuals are discussed further in *Chapter 41*.

IRAs are discussed in *Chapter 8*.

A tax credit is available to low-to-moderate income taxpayers who make traditional or Roth IRA contributions, electives deferrals to a 401(k) or other employer plan, and voluntary after-tax contributions to a qualified plan. The credit is discussed in *Chapter 25*.

Table 7-1   Key to Tax-Favored Retirement Plans

Type—	General Tax Considerations—	Tax Treatment of Distributions—
Company qualified plan	A company qualified pension or profit-sharing plan offers these benefits: 1. You do not realize current income on your employer's contributions to the plan on your behalf. 2. Income earned on funds contributed to your account compounds tax-free. 3. Your employer may allow you to make voluntary after-tax contributions. Although these contributions may not be deducted, income earned on the voluntary contributions is not taxed until withdrawn.	If you collect your retirement benefits as an annuity over a period of years, the part of each payment allocable to your investment is tax-free and the rest is taxable *(7.25)*. If you receive a lump-sum payment from the plan, the distribution is generally taxable except to the extent of after-tax contributions you made. Taxable distributions before age 59½ are generally subject to penalties, but there are exceptions *(7.13)*. However, you can avoid immediate tax by making a rollover to a traditional IRA or to another company plan *(7.5)*. If the lump-sum distribution includes company securities, unrealized appreciation on those securities is not taxed until you finally sell the stock *(7.8)*. If you were born before January 2, 1936, and receive a lump sum, tax on employer contributions and plan earnings may be reduced by a special averaging rule *(7.3)*. When you reach your "required beginning date," you must start to receive minimum annual distributions from the plan *(7.11)*.
Plans for self-employed	You may set up a qualified self-employed retirement plan if you earn self-employment income through your performance of personal services. You may deduct contributions up to limits discussed in *Chapter 41*; income earned on assets held by the plan is not taxed. You must include employees in your plan under rules explained in *Chapter 41*. Other retirement plan options, such as a SEP or SIMPLE plan, are also discussed in *Chapter 41*.	You may not withdraw plan funds until age 59½ unless you are disabled or meet other exceptions at *7.13*. Qualified distributions to self-employed persons or to beneficiaries at death may qualify for favored lump-sum treatment *(7.2)*. Distributions from a SEP are subject to traditional IRA rules *(8.8)*. Distributions from a SIMPLE-IRA also are subject to traditional IRA rules, but a 25% penalty (instead of 10%) applies to pre-age-59½ distributions in the first two years *(8.19)*.
IRA and Roth IRA	Anyone who has earned income may contribute to a traditional IRA, but the contribution is deductible only if certain requirements are met. Your status as a participant in an employer retirement plan and your income determine whether you may claim a deduction up to the annual contribution limit (for 2023, $6,500, or $7,500 if age 50 or older), a partial deduction, or no deduction at all. *See Chapter 8* for these deduction limitations. Incomes earned on IRA accounts are not taxed until the funds are withdrawn. This tax-free buildup of earnings also applies where you make nondeductible contributions to a Roth IRA under the rules in *Chapter 8*.	Traditional IRA distributions are fully taxable unless you have previously made nondeductible contributions *(8.9)*. A taxable withdrawal before age 59½ is subject to a 10% penalty, but there are exceptions if you are disabled, have substantial medical expenses, pay medical premiums while unemployed, or receive payments in a series of substantially equal installments; *see* the details on these and other exceptions *(8.12)*. Starting at age 73, you must receive minimum annual distributions from your IRA to avoid a 25% penalty *(8.13)*. Distributions from a Roth IRA of contributions are tax-free. Distributions of earnings are also tax-free after you are over age 59½ and have held the account for at least five years *(8.25)*.
Simplified Employee Plan (SEP)	Your employer may set up a SEP and contribute to an IRA more than you can under regular IRA rules *(8.16)*. You are not taxed on employer contributions of up to 25% of your compensation (but no more than $66,000 for 2023). Elective deferrals of salary may be made to qualifying plans set up before 1997 *(8.17)*.	Withdrawals from a SEP are taxable under the rules explained above for IRAs.
Deferred salary or 401(k) plans	If your company has a profit-sharing or stock bonus plan, the tax law allows the company to add a cash or deferred pay plan which can operate in one of two ways: (1) Your employer contributes an amount for your benefit to your trust account, or (2) You agree to take a salary reduction or to forego a salary increase. The reduction is placed in a trust account for your benefit and is treated as your employer's contribution, which is tax-free within an annual limit *(7.15)*. Income earned on your trust account accumulates tax free until it is withdrawn.	Withdrawals are penalized unless you have reached age 59½, become disabled, or meet other exceptions *(7.13)*. If you were born before January 2, 1936, and receive a qualifying lump sum *(7.3)*, or you receive a qualifying lump sum as the beneficiary of a plan participant born before January 2, 1936 *(7.4)*, tax on the lump sum may be computed using a special averaging rule.

7.1 Retirement Distributions on Form 1099-R

On Form 1099-R, payments from pensions, annuities, IRAs, Roth IRAs, SIMPLE IRAs, insurance contracts, profit-sharing, and other qualified corporate and self-employed plans are reported to you and the IRS. Social Security benefits are reported on Form SSA-1099; *see Chapter 34* for the special rules to apply in determining the taxable portion of Social Security benefits.

Here is a guide to the information reported on Form 1099-R. A sample form is on the next page.

Box 1. The total amount received from the payer is shown here without taking any withholdings into account.

If an exchange of insurance contracts was made, the value of the contract will be shown in Box 1, but if the exchange qualified as tax-free, a zero taxable amount will be shown in Box 2a and Code 6 will be entered in Box 7.

Boxes 2a and 2b. The taxable portion of distributions from employer plans and insurance contracts may be shown in Box 2a. The taxable portion does not include your after-tax contributions to an employer plan or insurance premium payments.

If the payer cannot figure the taxable portion, the first box in 2b should be checked ("Taxable amount not determined"); Box 2a should be blank. You will then have to figure the taxable amount yourself. A 2023 payment from a pension or an annuity is only partially taxed if you contributed to the cost and you did not recover your entire cost investment before 2023. *See* the discussion of commercial annuities *(7.21)* or employee annuities *(7.25)* for details on computing the taxable portion if you have an unrecovered investment.

The payer of a traditional IRA distribution will probably not compute the taxable portion, and in this case, the total distribution from Box 1 should be entered as the taxable portion in Box 2a, with a check in Box 2b for "Taxable amount not determined". The total distribution amount is fully taxable unless you have made nondeductible contributions, in which case Form 8606 is used to figure the taxable portion of the distribution *(8.9)*. Form 8606 is also used to figure the taxable part, if any, of a nonqualified distribution from a Roth IRA *(8.25)*.

If the payment is from an employer plan and the "total distribution" box has been checked in 2b, *see* the discussion of possible rollover options *(7.2, 7.5)*. The taxable amount in Box 2a should not include net unrealized appreciation (NUA; *see 7.8*) in any employer securities included in the lump sum or the value of an annuity contract included in the distribution.

Box 3. If the payment is a lump-sum distribution, you were born before January 2, 1936, and you participated in the plan before 1974, or if you are the beneficiary of such a person, you may treat the amount shown in Box 3 as capital gain subject to a 20% rate *(7.3, 7.4)*.

Box 4. Any federal income tax withheld is shown here. Do not forget to include it along with your other income tax withholdings on Form 1040 or 1040-SR. If Box 4 shows any withholdings of federal tax, attach Copy B of Form 1099-R to your Form 1040 or 1040-SR.

Box 5. If you made after-tax contributions to your employer's plan, or paid premiums for a commercial annuity or insurance contract, your contribution is shown here, less any such contributions previously distributed. IRA or SEP contributions *(Chapter 8)* are not shown here.

Box 6. If you received a qualifying lump-sum distribution which includes securities of your employer's company, the total net unrealized appreciation (NUA) is shown here. Unless you elect to pay tax on it currently *(7.8)*, this amount is not taxed until you sell the securities. If you did not receive a qualifying lump sum, the amount shown here is the net unrealized appreciation attributable to your after-tax employee contributions, which are also not taxed until you sell the securities *(7.8)*.

Box 7. In Box 7, the payer will indicate if the distribution is from a Traditional IRA, SEP, or SIMPLE and enter codes that are used by the IRS to check whether you have reported the distribution correctly, including the penalty for distributions before age 59½.

If you are at least age 59½, Code 7 should be entered; this indicates you received a "normal" distribution not subject to the 10% early distribution penalty *(7.13)*. If Code 1 is entered, this indicates you were under age 59½ at the time of the distribution and, as far as the payer knows, no exception to the early distribution penalty applies. However, the fact that Code 1 is entered does not mean a penalty exception applies. For example,

Filing Instruction

Conversion or Direct Rollover to Roth IRA

If you converted a SEP or SIMPLE IRA to a Roth IRA, the total amount converted will be included in Box 1 and Box 2a of Form 1099-R, but in Box 2b, the "Taxable amount not determined" box will be checked. A conversion to a Roth IRA is fully taxable except for any portion allocable to nondeductible contributions *(8.23)*.

If you made a direct rollover from a designated Roth account *(7.18)* to a Roth IRA, the amount rolled over will be reported in Box 1 of Form 1099-R, but "0" (zero) will be entered as the taxable amount in Box 2a.

Filing Instruction

Rules for Qualified Charitable Distributions

If you made a qualified charitable distribution from an IRA to a eligible charity *(8.8)*, it is reported on Form 1099-R as a taxable distribution in Box 2a. It is up to you to correctly report the QDC as nontaxable on line 4b of Form 1040 or 1040-SR, with a QCD notation.

you may qualify for the medical expense exception *(7.13)* or you may have made a tax-free 60-day rollover instead of having your employer make a direct rollover *(7.5)*.

Code 2 will be entered in Box 7 if you are under age 59½ and the payer knows you do qualify for an exception to the early distribution penalty, such as the exception for separation of service after age 55 for an employer-plan distribution, or the distribution is part of a series of substantially equal payments. Code 3 will be used if the disability exception applies. If you are the beneficiary of a deceased employee, the early distribution penalty does not apply to your distribution; Code 4 should be entered to indicate the exception for beneficiaries applies.

If the employer made a direct rollover to another eligible plan *(7.6)*, the distribution is not taxable and Code G will be entered; however, Code H is used for a direct rollover from a designated Roth account to a Roth IRA.

If an annual IRA contribution was recharacterized from one type of IRA to another *(8.22)*, either Code N or R will be entered. For example, on Form 1099-R for 2023, Code N is entered if the original contribution and recharacterization were both made in 2023, and Code R is entered if the original contribution was for 2022 and the recharacterization was in 2023.

If you contributed to a 401(k) plan and are a highly compensated employee, your employer may have made a corrective distribution to you in 2022 of contributions (and allocable income) that exceed allowable nondiscrimination ceilings. In this case, the employer will enter Code 8 if the corrective distribution is taxable in 2022, Code P if taxable in 2021.

If you receive a lump-sum distribution that qualifies for special averaging, Code A will be entered. *See* the sample Form 1099-R below and the discussion of the special averaging rules *(7.3)*.

Box 8. If the value of an annuity contract was included as part of a lump sum you received, the value of the contract is shown here. It is not taxable when you receive it and should not be included in Boxes 1 and 2a. For purposes of computing averaging on Form 4972, this amount is added to the ordinary income portion of the distribution *(7.3)*.

Box 9. If several beneficiaries are receiving payment from an employer plan total distribution, the amount shown in Box 9a is your share of the distribution. Box 9b may show your after-tax contributions to your employer's plan

Box 10. A distribution from a designated Roth account allocable to an in-plan Roth rollover is reported here.

Box 11. If you have made contributions to a designated Roth account, the year of your first contribution will be shown here.

Box 12. If you received a 1099-R with this box checked you may be required to file Form 8938 (Statement of Specified Foreign Financial Assets). *(48.7)*

Box 13. The date of payment will be listed here to the extent the payment was made for reportable death benefits.

Boxes 14–19. The payer may make entries in these boxes to show state or local income tax withholdings.

 *Filing Tip*

Lump-Sum Distribution

If you are paid a distribution which qualifies for lump-sum averaging *(7.3)*, Code A will be entered in Box 7 of Form 1099-R.

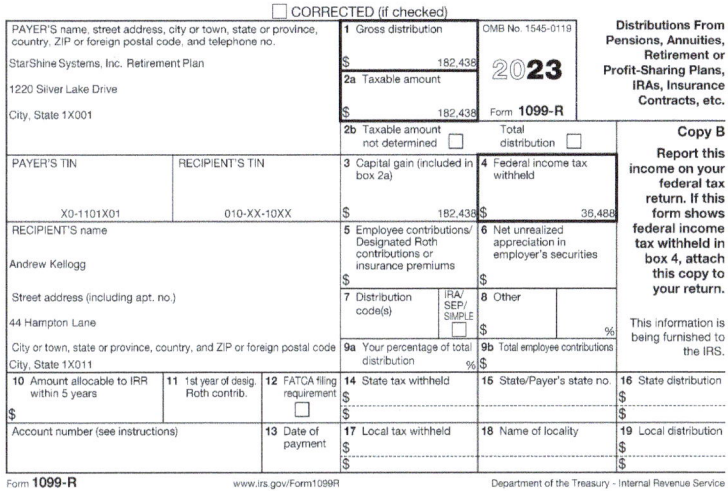

7.2 Lump-Sum Distributions

If you are entitled to a lump-sum distribution from a qualified company or self-employed retirement plan, you may avoid current tax by asking your employer to make a direct rollover of your account to an IRA or another qualified employer plan. If the distribution is made to you, 20% will be withheld, but it may still be possible to make a tax-free rollover within 60 days *(7.5)*.

If you receive a lump-sum and do not make a rollover, the taxable part of the distribution (shown in Box 2a of Form 1099-R) must be reported as ordinary pension income on your return. There is one rare exception: if you were born before January 2, 1936, you may qualify for special averaging, as discussed in *7.3*.

Your after-tax contributions and any net unrealized appreciation (NUA *see 7.8*) in employer securities included in the lump-sum are recovered tax-free; they are not part of the taxable distribution.

A taxable distribution before age 59½ is subject to a 10% penalty in addition to regular income tax, unless you qualify for an exception *(7.13)*.

Spousal consent to lump-sum distribution. If you are married, you may have to obtain your spouse's consent to elect a lump-sum distribution *(7.9)*.

Withholding tax. An employer must withhold a 20% tax from a lump-sum distribution paid to you and not rolled over directly by the employer to a traditional IRA or another employer plan *(7.5)*.

Beneficiaries. If you are the surviving spouse of a deceased plan participant (employee or self-employed) and receive a lump-sum distribution from his or her account, you can roll over the distribution to another qualified employer plan or to your own IRA. If you are a nonspouse beneficiary of a lump-sum distribution, you may instruct the plan to make a direct trustee-to-trustee transfer to an IRA which must be treated as an inherited IRA *(7.6)*.

If you are the beneficiary of a deceased employee who was born before January 2, 1936, you may elect special averaging or capital gain treatment for a lump-sum distribution of the account *(7.4)*, unless the distribution is disqualified.

Court ordered lump-sum distribution to a spouse or former spouse. If you are the spouse or former spouse of an employee and you receive a distribution under a Qualified Domestic Relations Order (QDRO), you may be eligible for a tax-free rollover or, in some cases, special averaging treatment *(7.10)*.

7.3 Lump-Sum Options If You Were Born Before January 2, 1936

Averaging for a lump-sum distribution is available to very few taxpayers. Because of the age requirement—you had to be born before January 2, 1936, fewer and fewer taxpayers have been able to benefit from the averaging method. The same is true for the special 20% capital gain rate option, which allows taxpayers who were born before January 2, 1936, and who participated in the plan before 1974, to apply a 20% capital gain rate to the pre-1974 portion of a lump-sum distribution.

Even if you meet the age test, you may be *disqualified* from making the averaging and capital gain elections for a lump-sum distribution. You are disqualified if you did not participate in the plan for at least five years prior to the year of the lunp-sum distribution. You are barred from electing averaging currently if at any time after 1986 you used averaging (10-year or prior law 5-year averaging) for a prior lump-sum distribution as the plan participant (not as beneficiary of someone else). You also may be disqualified because rollovers were made in prior years to or from the same employer plan from which the current lump-sum distribution is paid. *See* the Form 4972 instructions for the full list of disqualified distributions.

Note: If you receive a lump-sum distribution as the beneficiary of a deceased plan participant who was born before January 2, 1936, you generally may elect averaging or capital gain treatment for the distribution unless it is disqualified; *see 7.4* for the beneficiary rules.

Caution

Averaging Not Allowed for Those Born After January 1, 1936

If you were born after January 1, 1936, a lump-sum distribution from your plan is not eligible for averaging.

Electing averaging and capital gain treatment. If your lump-sum distribution is not disqualified *(see above)*, you may elect on Form 4972 to compute the tax on the taxable portion of the distribution (Box 2a of Form 1099-R) using a 10-year averaging method based on 1986 tax rates for single persons. Note: If you rolled over *(7.6)* any part of the distribution to another qualified plan or IRA, you may not use special averaging or capital gain treatment for the part not rolled over.

If part of an eligible lump sum is attributable to pre-1974 participation (shown in Box 3 of Form 1099-R), you may (1) elect to treat the pre-1974 portion as ordinary income eligible for averaging (Part III of Form 4972), or (2) elect in Part II of Form 4972 to treat the pre-1974 portion as capital gain subject to a flat rate of 20%. If option (2) is chosen, the tax on the balance of the distribution (the Box 2a taxable amount minus the Box 3 capital gain portion) may be figured under the averaging method, or it may be reported as regular pension income on Form 1040 or 1040-SR, Line 5b. The 20% rate for the capital gain portion is fixed by law, and applies regardless of the tax rate imposed on your other capital gains. You may not elect to report any portion of the pre-1974 portion of the lump-sum distribution as long-term capital gain on Schedule D.

Follow the IRS instructions to Form 4972 for applying the 10-year averaging method and the 20% rate.

7.4 Lump-Sum Payments Received by Beneficiary

If you receive a qualifying lump-sum distribution as the beneficiary of a deceased employee or self-employed plan participant who was not your spouse, you may instruct the plan to make a direct trustee-to-trustee transfer to an IRA that must be treated as an inherited IRA. If you are the surviving spouse, you can roll over the distribution to another qualified employer plan or to your own IRA. *See 7.6* for the beneficiary rollover rules.

Was the plan participant born before January 2, 1936? If you are the beneficiary of a deceased employee who was born before January 2, 1936, and receive a qualifying lump-sum distribution of that person's account, you generally may elect special averaging or capital gain treatment for the lump-sum *unless* the distribution is disqualified as discussed in *7.3*. Your age is irrelevant. The five-year participation rule which applies to plan participants does not apply to beneficiaries. Thus, if the deceased employee was in the plan for less than five years, you may still elect averaging as his or her beneficiary, although less than five years of participation would have disqualified *(7.3)* the distribution from lump-sum treatment had the distribution been received by the employee.

An election may be made on Form 4972 only once as the beneficiary of a particular plan participant after 1986. For example, if in 2022 you received a lump-sum distribution as the beneficiary of a plan participant and used Form 4972 for the 2022 distribution, you may not use Form 4972 for a distribution you received in 2023 from a different plan for the same participant. If you receive more than one lump-sum distribution as beneficiary for the same participant in the same year, you must treat them all the same way. Averaging must be elected for all of the distributions on a single Form 4972 or for none of them.

If the participant was born before January 2, 1936, and had participated in the plan before 1974, you may elect a 20% capital gain rate for the pre-1974 portion of the distribution and apply the averaging method to the balance *(7.3)*. You may not claim averaging or capital gain treatment for a lump-sum distribution if the plan participant was born after January 1, 1936.

See the Form 4972 instructions for computing tax under the averaging method or to make the 20% capital gain election *(7.3)*. Any federal estate tax attributable to the distribution reduces the taxable amount on Form 4972.

7.5 Tax-Free Rollovers From Qualified Plans

A rollover allows you to make a tax-free transfer of a distribution from a qualified retirement plan to another qualified plan which accepts rollovers or to a traditional IRA. For rollover purposes, a 403(b) plan *(7.19)*, or a state or local government 457 plan *(7.20)* is treated as a qualified retirement plan. If a rollover is made to a traditional IRA, later distributions received from the IRA are taxable under the IRA rules *(8.8)*. A tax-free

 *Filing Tip*

Pre-1974 Capital Gain Portion of Distribution

If you were born before January 2, 1936, and a portion of your lump-sum distribution is attributable to plan participation before 1974 *(7.3)*, you may treat it as ordinary income eligible for averaging, or you may elect to treat it as capital gain taxable at a flat 20% rate; choose the method on Form 4972 that gives the lower overall tax.

 *Filing Tip*

Lump Sums to Multiple Beneficiaries

A lump-sum distribution to two or more beneficiaries may qualify for averaging and capital gain treatment, so long as the plan participant was born before January 2, 1936. Each beneficiary may separately elect the averaging method for the ordinary income portion, even though other beneficiaries do not so elect. Follow the Form 4972 instructions for multiple recipients.

rollover can be made from a qualified retirement plan to a SIMPLE IRA after the first two years of participation in the SIMPLE IRA *(8.19)*.

The rollover rules below and in *7.6* apply whether you are an employee or are self-employed.

Eligible rollover distributions. Almost all taxable distributions received from a qualified corporate or self-employed pension, profit-sharing, stock bonus, or annuity plan are eligible for tax-free rollover. Exceptions include substantially equal periodic payments over your lifetime or over a period of at least 10 years, hardship distributions, and required minimum distributions *(7.11)* ; *see* below for the list of ineligible distributions.

Rollover of after-tax contributions. When you are entitled to take distributions, after-tax contributions that you have made to the plan may be rolled over to a traditional IRA or to a Roth IRA. A trustee-to-trustee transfer of after-tax contributions may also be made to a qualified defined contribution plan, a defined benefit plan, or a 403(b) tax-sheltered annuity that separately accounts for the after-tax amount.

The IRS has provided a method for making a direct rollover of after-tax contributions to a Roth IRA while directly rolling the pre-tax portion of the account (pre-tax contributions plus the earnings on all contributions) to a traditional IRA; *see* "Allocating a direct rollover between pre-tax and after-tax contributions" in *7.6*.

Rollover options: direct rollover or personal rollover. If you want to make a tax-free rollover of an eligible rollover distribution, you should instruct your employer to directly roll over the funds to a traditional IRA you designate or to the plan of your new employer. You could also choose to have the distribution paid to you, and within 60 days you could make a tax-free rollover yourself. However, to avoid the 20% mandatory withholding tax, you must elect to have the plan make a direct rollover. If an eligible rollover distribution is paid to you, the 20% withholding tax applies. Before a distribution is made, your plan administrator must provide you with written notice concerning the rollover options and the withholding tax rules. See *7.6* for further details on the direct rollover and personal rollover alternatives.

Rollover of distribution from designated Roth account. An eligible rollover distribution from a designated Roth account may be rolled over to a Roth IRA. A qualified (nontaxable) distribution from a designated Roth account may be rolled over to another designated Roth account in a different plan, but only in a direct rollover *(7.6)*. For further details on distributions from designated Roth accounts, including rollovers, see *7.18*.

Rollover from qualified retirement plan to traditional IRA. If you expect to receive an eligible rollover distribution from your employer's plan (including a plan for self-employed participants), you may avoid immediate tax on the distribution by instructing your plan administrator to make a direct rollover of the distribution to a traditional IRA *(7.6)*. If you receive the distribution from the employer, a 20% tax will be withheld. You may then make a tax-free rollover within 60 days of the distribution; *see* the discussion of "personal rollovers" *(7.6)*. After the year of the rollover, you are subject to the required minimum distribution rules from the IRA *(8.13)*.

Beneficiaries. *See* "Rollover by Beneficiary" in *7.6* for rollover options open to beneficiaries *(7.6)*.

Distributions that are not eligible for rollover. Any lump-sum or partial distribution from your account is eligible for rollover except for the following:

- Hardship distributions from a 401(k) plan or 403(b) plan *(7.17)*.
- Payments that are part of a series of substantially equal payments made at least annually over a period of 10 years or more or over your life or life expectancy (or the joint lives or joint life and last survivor expectancies of you and your designated beneficiary).
- Minimum required distributions after reaching the required beginning date *(7.11)*.
- Corrective distributions of excess 401(k) plan contributions and deferrals.
- Dividends on employer stock.
- Life insurance coverage costs.
- Loans that are deemed to be taxable distributions because they exceed the limits discussed in *7.14*.

Planning Reminder

Direct Rollover to Roth IRA

A distribution from a qualified employer plan, 403(b) plan, or governmental 457 plan can be rolled over to a Roth IRA, but the rollover is a taxable distribution except to the extent it is allocable to after-tax contributions *(8.23)*.

For all of the above taxable distributions that are ineligible for rollover, you may elect to completely avoid withholding on Form W-4P *(26.9)*.

7.6   Direct Rollover or Personal Rollover

If you are an employee or a self-employed person entitled to an eligible rollover distribution *(7.5)* from a qualified plan, you may choose a direct rollover, or if you actually receive the distribution you may make a personal rollover within 60 days. To avoid withholding, choose a direct rollover. You must receive a written explanation of your rollover rights from your plan administrator before an eligible rollover distribution is made.

Rollover to Roth IRA. An eligible rollover distribution from a qualified employer plan, 403(b) plan, or governmental 457 plan may be rolled over to a Roth IRA, but the rollover is not tax free. A rollover to a Roth IRA, like a conversion from a traditional IRA, is a taxable distribution except to the extent it is allocable to after-tax contributions *(8.23)*.

Direct Rollover From Employer Plan

If you choose to have your plan administrator make a direct rollover of an eligible rollover distribution to a traditional IRA or another eligible employer plan, you avoid tax on the payment and no tax will be withheld. If you are changing jobs and want a direct rollover to the plan of the new employer, make sure that the plan accepts rollovers; if it does not, choose a direct rollover to a traditional IRA.

When you select the direct rollover option, your plan administrator may transfer the funds directly by check or electronically to the new plan, or you may be given a check payable to the new plan that you must deliver to the new plan.

In choosing a direct rollover to a traditional IRA, the terms of the plan making the payment will determine whether you may divide the distribution among several IRAs or whether you will be restricted to one IRA. For example, if you are entitled to receive a lump-sum distribution from your employer's plan, you may want to split up your distribution into several traditional IRAs, but the employer may force you to select only one. After the direct rollover is made, you may then diversify your holdings by making tax-free trustee-to-trustee transfers to other traditional IRAs.

You may elect to make a direct rollover of part of your distribution and to receive the balance. The portion paid to you will be subject to 20% withholding. Withholding is generally not required on distributions of less than $200.

A direct rollover will be reported by the payer plan to the IRS and to you on Form 1099-R, although the transfer is not taxable. The direct rollover will be reported in Box 1 of Form 1099-R, but zero will be entered as the taxable amount in Box 2a. In Box 7, Code G should be entered.

Allocating a direct rollover between pre-tax and after-tax contributions. If you have made after-tax contributions as well as pre-tax elective deferrals to the plan, the IRS has provided guidelines that allow you to transfer only the after-tax contributions to a Roth IRA, in what amounts to a tax-free conversion, while moving the pre-tax portion of the account to a traditional IRA in a tax-free rollover. These rules, in IRS Notice 2014-54 (2014-41 IRB 670), apply to distributions from 401(k) plans, 403(b) plans, and governmental Section 457 plans. Regulations apply the Notice 2014-54 allocation rules to distributions from designated Roth accounts (T.D. 9769, 2016-23 IRB 1020).

> #### EXAMPLE
>
> When Tom retires, he has a 401(k) plan account with a $200,000 balance, $40,000 of which is from after-tax contributions and $160,000 of which is pre-tax, consisting of pre-tax contributions, employer matching contributions, and earnings on all contributions including the after-tax contributions. Tom wants to make a tax-free rollover of his after-tax contributions to a Roth IRA and a tax-free rollover of the balance to a traditional IRA. He can do this by specifically instructing the 401(k) plan administrator to directly roll over the $160,000 pre-tax amount to a traditional IRA and the $40,000 after-tax amount to a Roth IRA.

The guidelines allow you to make a direct rollover to more than one plan and to select which funds (pre-tax or after-tax) are going into which plan, provided both of these conditions are met: (1) all the transfers are scheduled to be made at the same time, apart from reasonable delays to facilitate plan administration, and (2) you inform the plan administrator of your allocation prior to the time of the direct rollovers.

Personal Rollover After Receiving a Distribution

If you do not tell your plan administrator to make a direct rollover of an eligible rollover distribution, and you instead receive the distribution yourself, you will receive only 80% of the taxable portion (generally the entire distribution unless you made after-tax contributions); 20% will be withheld. Withholding does not apply to the portion of the distribution consisting of net unrealized appreciation from employer securities that is tax-free *(7.8)*. Remember to include the withheld 20% on your tax return as federal income tax withheld (on Line 25b of Form 1040 or 1040-SR), so that it can be treated as a credit against the tax otherwise owed.

Although you receive only 80% of the taxable eligible rollover distribution, the full amount before withholding will be reported as the gross distribution in Box 1 of Form 1099-R. To avoid tax you must roll over the full amount within 60 days to a traditional IRA or another eligible employer plan. However, to roll over 100% of the distribution you will have to use other funds to replace the 20% withheld. If you roll over only the 80% received, the 20% balance will be taxable; *see* the John Anderson Example below. In addition, if the distribution was made to you before you reached age 59½, the taxable amount will be subject to a 10% penalty unless you are disabled, separating from service after reaching age 55, or have substantial medical expenses; *see* the full list of exceptions below *(7.13)*.

If a distribution includes your voluntary after-tax contributions to the qualified plan, they are tax free to you if you keep them. However, after-tax contributions may be rolled over to a qualified plan or a 403(b) plan that separately accounts for the after-tax amounts.

A rollover may include salary deferral contributions that were excludable from income when made, such as qualifying deferrals to a 401(k) plan. The rollover may also include accumulated deductible employee contributions (and allocable income) made after 1981 and before 1987. If a qualified retirement plan has invested in a life insurance contract that is distributed to you as part of a lump-sum retirement distribution, you may be able to roll over the life insurance contract to the qualified plan of a new employer, but not to a traditional IRA. The law bars investment of IRA funds in life insurance contracts.

You may not claim a deduction for your rollover.

Multiple rollover accounts allowed. You may wish to diversify a distribution in different investments. There is no limit on the number of rollover accounts you may have. A lump-sum distribution from a qualified plan may be rolled over to several traditional IRAs.

Reporting a personal rollover on your return. When you receive a distribution that could have been rolled over, the payer will report on Form 1099-R the full taxable amount before withholding, although 20% has been withheld. However, if you make a rollover yourself within the 60-day period, the rollover reduces the taxable amount on your tax return. For example, if in 2023 you were entitled to a $100,000 lump-sum distribution and received $80,000 after mandatory 20% withholding and then within 60 days you rolled over the full $100,000 into a traditional IRA, report $100,000 as a pension payment on line 5a of Form 1040 or 1040-SR, but enter zero as the taxable amount on line 5b (assuming this is your only taxable pension payment for the year) and write "Rollover" next to the line. If you roll over only part of the distribution, the amount of the lump sum not rolled over is entered as the taxable amount. Remember to include the 20% withholding as federal income tax withheld on Line 25b of Form 1040 or 1040-SR.

IRS may waive 60-day deadline for personal rollover on equitable grounds. Generally, a personal rollover must be completed by the 60th day following the day on which you receive a distribution from the qualified plan. However, the IRS has discretion to waive the 60-day deadline and permit more time for a rollover where failure to complete a timely rollover was due to events beyond your reasonable control.

Planning Reminder

Pre-Age-59½ Distributions

If you are under age 59½ and do not roll over an eligible distribution, you will generally be subject to a 10% penalty in addition to regular income tax. However, penalty exceptions apply if you separate from service and are age 55 or older, you are disabled, or you pay substantial medical expenses; *see* the full list of penalty exceptions in *7.13*.

Caution

Mandatory 20% Withholding Unless Direct Rollover Made

If you are entitled to an eligible rollover distribution and it is directly rolled over to a traditional IRA or to a qualified employer plan, no tax is withheld and the directly rolled over amount is not taxed. If a direct rollover is not made and the distribution is paid to you, 20% of the taxable portion will be withheld. You will receive only 80% but will be taxed on 100% unless the entire amount is rolled over within 60 days; *see* the John Anderson Example on the following page.

You may be able to use a self-certification procedure provided by the IRS to obtain a waiver of the 60-day deadline if you have one or more of 11 acceptable reasons for being late. The self-certification guidelines, which also apply to rollovers from traditional IRAs, as well as the other IRS waiver guidelines, are discussed in *8.10*.

Extension of 60-day rollover period for frozen deposits. If you receive a qualifying distribution from a retirement plan and deposit the funds in a financial institution that becomes bankrupt or insolvent, you may be prevented from withdrawing the funds in time to complete a rollover within 60 days. If this happens, the 60-day period is extended while your account is "frozen." The 60-day rollover period does not include days on which your account is frozen. Further, you have a minimum of 10 days after the release of the funds to complete the rollover.

> **EXAMPLE**
>
> John Anderson plans to retire in June 2024 at age 52. Assume that at retirement he is eligible to receive a lump-sum distribution of $100,000 from his employer's qualified plan. If he instructs his plan administrator to make a direct rollover of the entire amount to a traditional IRA or to an eligible employer plan, there is no tax withholding, and the $100,000 will be transferred to the IRA tax free.
>
> Now assume that prior to retirement, a business opportunity presents itself and John decides not to choose a direct rollover so he can use the funds to invest in the business. The plan will pay him $80,000 and withhold a tax of $20,000 (20% of $100,000) that John will apply to his tax liability when he files his 2023 return (by reporting the $20,000 as federal income tax withheld). But, say, a month after receiving the $80,000, John has a change of heart. He changes his mind about the investment and now wants to roll over his benefits to a traditional IRA. He must make the rollover within 30 days because 30 days of the 60-day rollover period have already passed. Furthermore, to avoid tax on the entire distribution, he must deposit $100,000 in the traditional IRA, even though $20,000 tax has been withheld. If he does not have the $20,000, he must borrow the $20,000 and deposit it in the IRA. If he rolls over only $80,000, he must report $20,000 as a taxable distribution on his 2023 return and since the distribution was made before he reached age 59½, the 10% penalty for early withdrawals will apply; based on these facts, John does not qualify for a penalty exception *(7.13)*.

Rollover by Beneficiary

Surviving spouse. If you are your deceased spouse's beneficiary, you have the same rollover options that your spouse would have had for a distribution. You may choose to have the plan make a direct rollover to your own traditional IRA. The advantage of choosing the direct rollover is to avoid a 20% withholding tax. If the distribution is paid to you, 20% will be withheld. You may make a rollover within 60 days, but to completely avoid tax, you must include in the rollover the withheld amount, as illustrated in the John Anderson Example above. If you receive the distribution but do not make the rollover, you will be taxed on the distribution, except for any amount allocable to after-tax contributions. If your spouse was born before January 2, 1936, you may be able to use special averaging *(7.4)* to compute the tax on the distribution. You are not subject to the 10% penalty for early distributions *(7.13)* even if you are under age 59½.

You can roll over the distribution to a Roth IRA but the rollover is taxable under the rules for conversions from traditional IRAs *(8.23)*.

You may also roll over a distribution from your deceased spouse's account to your own qualified plan, 403(a) qualified annuity, 403(b) tax-sheltered annuity, or governmental section 457 plan. In the unlikely event that you were born before January 2, 1936, are still working, and want to preserve the option of electing averaging or capital gain treatment (for pre-1974 participation) for a later distribution from your employer's qualified plan *(7.3)*, you should not roll over your deceased spouse's account to your employer's qualified plan. If the rollover is made to your employer's qualified plan, a lump-sum distribution from the plan will not be eligible for averaging or capital gains treatment.

 *Law Alert*

Nonspouse Beneficiary Rollover to Inherited IRA

A qualified plan must allow a nonspouse beneficiary to make a trustee-to-trustee transfer to an IRA that is treated as an inherited IRA.

Rollover of distribution received under a divorce or support proceeding. In a qualified domestic relations order (QDRO) meeting special tax law tests, a state court may give you the right to receive all or part of your spouse's or former spouse's retirement benefits. If you are entitled to receive an eligible rollover distribution, you can instruct the plan to make a direct rollover *(see above)* to a traditional IRA or to your employer's qualified plan if it accepts rollovers. If the distribution is paid to you, 20% withholding will apply. You may complete a rollover within 60 days under the rules for personal rollovers discussed earlier. If you do not make the rollover, the distribution you receive is taxable. If only part of the distribution is rolled over, the balance is taxed as ordinary income in the year of receipt. In figuring your tax, you are allowed a prorated share of your former spouse's cost investment, if any. If your spouse or former spouse was born before January 2, 1936, and you receive a lump-sum distribution that would have been eligible for special averaging *(7.3)* had he or she received it, you may use the averaging method to figure the tax on the distribution. You are not subject to the 10% penalty for early distributions *(7.13)* even if you are under age 59½.

Nonspouse beneficiaries. If you are entitled as a nonspouse beneficiary to receive a distribution from a deceased participant's qualified plan, 403(b) plan, or governmental 457 plan account, the plan must allow you to roll it over to an IRA in a trustee-to-trustee transfer. The IRA must be treated as an inherited IRA subject to the required minimum distribution (RMD) rules for nonspouse beneficiaries *(8.15)*.

7.7 Rollover of Proceeds From Sale of Property

A lump-sum distribution from a qualified plan may include property, such as non-employer stock; *see 7.8* for employer securities. If you plan to roll over the distribution, you may find that a bank or other plan trustee does not want to take the property. You cannot get tax-free rollover treatment by keeping the property and rolling over cash to the new plan. If you sell the property, you may roll over the sale proceeds to a traditional IRA as long as the sale and rollover occur within 60 days of receipt of the distribution. If you roll over all of the proceeds, you do not recognize a gain or loss from the sale; the proceeds are treated as part of the distribution. If you make a partial rollover of sale proceeds, you must report as capital gain the portion of the gain that is allocable to the retained sale proceeds.

If you receive cash and property, and you sell the property but only make a partial rollover, you must designate how much of the rolled-over cash is from the employer distribution and how much from the sale proceeds. The designation must be made by the time for filing your return (plus any extensions) and is irrevocable. If you do not make a timely designation, the IRS will allocate the rollover between cash and sales proceeds on a ratable basis; the allocation will determine tax on the retained amount.

7.8 Distribution of Employer Stock or Other Securities

If you are entitled to a distribution from a qualified plan that includes employer stock (or other employer securities), you may be able to take advantage of a special exclusion rule. If you withdraw the stock from the plan as part of a lump-sum distribution and invest the stock in a taxable brokerage account instead of rolling it over to a traditional IRA, tax on the "net unrealized appreciation," or NUA, may be deferred until you sell the stock. To defer tax on the full NUA, the employer stock must be received in a lump-sum distribution, as discussed below. If the distribution is not a lump sum, a less favorable NUA exclusion is available, but only if you made after-tax contributions to buy the shares; *see* below.

Lump-sum distribution. If you receive appreciated stock or securities as part of a lump-sum distribution, net unrealized appreciation (increase in value since purchase of securities) is not subject to tax at the time of distribution unless you elect to treat it as taxable.

For purposes of the NUA exclusion, a lump-sum distribution is the payment within a single year of the plan participant's entire balance from all of the employer's qualified plans of the same kind (all of the employer's profit-sharing plans, or all pension or stock bonus plans). The distribution must be paid to: (1) a participant after reaching age 59½, (2) an employee-participant who separates from service (by retiring, resigning,

Court Decision

Stock Purchased With Cash Withdrawal Cannot Be Rolled Over

A taxpayer withdrew cash from his qualified self-employment retirement accounts and used most of the net distribution (after withholdings) to buy stock, which was then transferred to an IRA within 60 days of the withdrawal. He treated the entire distribution as a tax-free rollover but the IRS and Tax Court held it was taxable. The transfer of stock to the IRA was not a tax-free rollover; only the cash distribution itself could be rolled over. A negligence penalty was also imposed.

A direct rollover from the accounts to an IRA would have been tax free; the stock could then have been purchased through the new IRA.

Planning Reminder

Deferring Tax on NUA

If you receive a lump-sum distribution that includes appreciated employer securities, you may defer the tax on the net unrealized appreciation (NUA) in the securities.

changing employers, or being fired), (3) a self-employed participant who becomes totally and permanently disabled, or (4) a beneficiary of a deceased plan participant. If there is any plan balance at the end of the year, there is no lump sum and the NUA exclusion is not available.

Assuming you do not waive the NUA exclusion, you are taxed (at ordinary income rates) only on the original cost of the stock when contributed to the plan. Tax on the appreciation is delayed until the shares are later sold by you at a price exceeding cost basis and the gain attributable to the NUA will be taxed at long-term capital gain rates *(5.3)*.

The NUA in employer's securities is shown in Box 6 of the Form 1099-R received from the payer. It is not included in the taxable amount in Box 2a.

If, when distributed, the shares are valued at below the cost contribution to the plan, the fair market value of the shares is subject to tax. If you contributed to the purchase of the shares and their value is less than your contribution, you do not realize a loss deduction on the distribution. You realize a loss only when the stock is sold for less than your cost or becomes worthless *(5.32)* at a later date. If a plan distributes worthless stock, you may not deduct your contributions to the stock; the prior law miscellaneous itemized deduction for expenses subject to the 2% of adjusted gross income floor is suspended for 2018 through 2025.

EXAMPLES

1. Shares valued below your cost contribution. You contributed $500 and your employer contributed $300 to buy 10 shares of company stock having at the time a fair market value of $80 per share. When you retire, the fair market value of the stock is $40 per share, or a total of $400. You do not realize income on the distribution, and you do not have a deductible loss for the difference between your cost contribution and the lower fair market value. Your contribution to the stock is its basis. This is $50 per share. If you sell the stock for $40 per share, you have a capital loss of $10 per share. However, if you sell the stock for $60 per share, you have gain of $10 per share.

2. Appreciated shares. You receive 10 shares of company stock that was purchased entirely with the employer's funds. Your employer's cost was $50 a share. At the time of a lump-sum distribution, the shares are valued at $80 a share. Your employer's contribution of $50 a share, or $500, is included as part of your taxable distribution. The appreciation of $300 (the NUA) is not included, assuming you do not elect to be taxed currently on the appreciation. The cost basis of the shares in your hands is $500 (the amount currently taxable to you). The holding period of the stock starts from the date of distribution. However, if you sell the shares for any amount exceeding $500 and up to $800, your profit is long-term capital gain regardless of how long you held the shares. If you sell for more than $800, the gain exceeding the original NUA of $300 is subject to long-term capital gain treatment only if the sale is long term from the date of distribution. Thus, if within a month of the distribution you sold the shares for $900, $300 would be long-term gain; $100 would be short-term gain.

Election to waive tax-free treatment. You may elect to include the NUA in employer stock or securities as ordinary income. You might consider making this election when the NUA is not substantial or you want to accelerate income to the current year by taking into account the entire lump-sum distribution. Make the election to include the unrealized appreciation as ordinary income by reporting it on Line 5b (taxable pensions and annuities) of Form 1040 or 1040-SR. If you were born before January 2, 1936, and are claiming averaging or capital gain treatment on Form 4972 *(7.3)*, follow the form instructions for adding the unrealized appreciation to the taxable distribution.

Distribution not a lump sum. If you receive appreciated employer securities in a distribution that does not meet the lump-sum tests above, you report as ordinary income the amount of the employer's contribution to the purchase of the shares and the appreciation allocated to the employer's cost contribution. You do not report the amount of appreciation allocated to your own after-tax contribution to the purchase. In other words, tax is deferred only on the NUA attributable to your after-tax employee contributions. Net unrealized appreciation is shown in Box 6 of Form 1099-R. Cost contributions must be supplied by the company distributing the stock.

7.9   Survivor Annuity for Spouse

If you have been married for at least a year as of the annuity starting date, the law generally requires that payments to you of vested benefits be in a specific annuity form to protect your surviving spouse. All defined benefit and money purchase pension plans must provide benefits in the form of a qualified joint and survivor annuity (QJSA) unless you, with the written consent of your spouse, elect a different form of benefit. A qualified joint and survivor annuity must also be provided by profit-sharing or stock bonus plans if you elect a life annuity payout or the plan does not provide that your nonforfeitable benefit is payable in full upon your death either to your surviving spouse, or to another beneficiary if there is no surviving spouse or your spouse consents to the naming of the non-spouse beneficiary.

Under a QJSA, you receive an annuity for your life and then your surviving spouse receives an annuity for his or her life that is at least 50% of the amount payable during your joint lives. Most plans allow you to choose among several options that will provide your surviving spouse with more than 50% of your lifetime benefit after your death. You may waive the QJSA only with your spouse's consent. Without the consent, you may not take a lump-sum distribution or a single life annuity ending when you die. A single life annuity pays higher monthly benefits during your lifetime than the qualified joint and survivor annuity, and a larger QJSA benefit for your surviving spouse means a greater reduction to your lifetime benefit. If benefits begin under a QJSA and you divorce the spouse to whom you were married as of the annuity starting date, that former spouse will be entitled to the QJSA survivor benefits if you die unless there is a contrary provision in a QDRO *(7.10)*.

The law also requires that a qualified pre-retirement survivor annuity (QPSA) be paid to your surviving spouse if you die before the date vested benefits first become payable or if you die after the earliest payment date but before retiring. The QPSA is automatic unless you, with your spouse's consent, agree to a different benefit. Your plan should provide you with a written explanation of these annuity rules within a reasonable period before the annuity starting date, as well as the rules for electing to waive the joint and survivor annuity benefit and the pre-retirement survivor annuity.

Plan may provide exception for marriages of less than one year. The terms of a plan may provide that a QJSA or QPSA will not be provided to a spouse of the plan participant if the couple has been married for less than one year as of the participant's annuity starting date (QJSA) or, if earlier, the date of the participant's death (QPSA).

Cash out of annuity. If the present value of the QJSA is $5,000 or less, your employer may "cash out" your interest without your consent or your spouse's consent by making a lump-sum distribution of the present value of the annuity before the annuity starting date. After the annuity starting date, you and your spouse must consent to a cash-out. Written consent is required for a cash-out if the present value of the annuity exceeds $5,000. Similar cash-out rules apply to a QPSA.

7.10   Court Distributions to Former Spouse Under a QDRO

As a part of a divorce-related property settlement, or to cover alimony or support obligations, a state domestic relations court can require that all or part of a plan participant's retirement benefits be paid to a spouse, former spouse, child, or other dependent. Administrators of

pension, profit-sharing, or stock bonus plans are required to honor a qualified domestic relations order (QDRO) that meets specific tax law tests. For example, the QDRO generally may not alter the amount or form of benefits provided by the plan, but it may authorize payments after the participant reaches the earliest retirement age, even if he or she continues working. A QDRO may provide that a spouse is entitled to all, some, or none of the spousal survivor benefits payable under the plan.

QDRO distributions to spouse or former spouse. If you are the spouse or former spouse of an employee or self-employed plan participant and you receive a distribution pursuant to a QDRO, the distribution is generally taxable to you. However, if the distribution would have been eligible for rollover by your spouse or former spouse, you may make a tax-free rollover to a traditional IRA or to a qualified plan *(7.5)*.

To create a valid QDRO, the court order must contain specific language. The recipient spouse (or former spouse) must be assigned rights to the plan participant's retirement benefits plan, and must be referred to as an "alternate payee" in the court decree. The decree must identify the retirement plan and indicate the amount and number of payments subject to the QDRO. Both spouses must be identified by name and address. If the required information is not clearly provided in the decree, QDRO treatment may be denied and the plan participant taxed on the retirement plan distributions, rather than the spouse who actually receives payments.

If you do not make a rollover, and your spouse or former spouse (the plan participant) was born before January 2, 1936, a distribution to you of your entire share of the benefits may be eligible on Form 4972 for special averaging, and possibly the 20% capital gain election, provided the distribution, if received by your spouse (or former spouse), would be a qualifying lump-sum distribution *(7.3)*.

Distributions to a child or other dependent. Payments from a QDRO are taxed to the plan participant, not to the dependent who actually receives them, where the recipient is not a spouse or former spouse.

7.11 When You Must Begin Receiving Required Minimum Distributions (RMDs)

The longer you can delay taking retirement distributions from your company plan or self-employed plan, the greater will be the tax-deferred buildup of your retirement fund. To cut off this tax deferral, the law requires minimum distributions (RMDs) to begin no later than a specified date in order to avoid an IRS penalty. The required beginning date rules apply to distributions from all qualified corporate and self-employed qualified retirement plans, qualified annuity plans, and Section 457 plans of tax-exempt organizations and state and local government employers. The rules also apply to distributions from tax-sheltered annuities *(7.19)* but only for benefits accrued after 1986; there is no mandatory beginning date for tax-sheltered annuity benefits accrued before 1987.

You do not have to figure your required minimum distributions (RMDs). If you are not receiving an annuity, your plan administrator will determine the minimum amount that must be distributed to you each year from your account balance, based upon IRS regulations. The rules for figuring the minimum amount (the RMD) are similar to the rules for traditional IRAs *(8.13)*.

If you do not receive your RMD for a year, a penalty tax applies unless the IRS waives it. The penalty is 25% of the difference between what was received and what should have been received. The IRS may reduce the penalty tax to 10% if you file Form 5329 and on an attached statement explain that a reasonable error caused the underpayment and the shortfall was or will be corrected.

Required beginning date. Under current law (SECURE 2.0), you must begin to receive required minimum distributions (RMDs) when you reach age 73. For those born before July 1, 1949, RMDs generally had to begin at age 70½.

Despite the general age 73 rule (or prior law 70½ rule), many plans allow a delayed beginning date for those who are still working when they reach the RMD age, provided

Caution

RMD Cannot Be Rolled Over

If an RMD from your employer's plan is due, you cannot avoid tax on the RMD by rolling it over to an IRA or directly transferring it (trustee-to-trustee) to an IRA. Under the IRS' "first-dollars-out" rule, the first funds distributed from the plan in a year in which an RMD is required is treated as part of the RMD, and that amount is not eligible for rollover or direct transfer. The RMD must be taken first, and then a rollover or transfer can be made from the balance of the account. If an erroneous rollover/transfer of RMD amounts is made to an IRA, it is treated as an excess IRA contribution, subject to a 6% penalty unless timely withdrawn *(8.7)*.

Caution

RMDs from Multiple Accounts Generally Cannot Be Combined

If you have more than one qualified employee retirement plan account, such as 401(k) plan accounts with two employers, you must take a required minimum distribution (RMD) from each plan; you cannot combine the separate RMDs and take the total from one of the accounts. Similarly, if you have a 401(k) plan and a tax-sheltered annuity account (403(b) plan *(7.19)*, you must take the RMD from each plan. However, if you have more than one tax-sheltered annuity account, these accounts can be combined for RMD purposes; the total RMD for all the accounts can be taken from any one of the tax-sheltered annuities, or from more than one as you choose.

If you also have traditional IRAs, the IRA RMDs *(8.13)* cannot be combined with your employer plan RMDs. That is, RMDs from your employer retirement plans cannot be taken from the IRAs, and your IRA RMDs *(8.13)* cannot be taken from the employer plans. However, if you must receive RMDs from multiple traditional IRAs, the separately determined IRA RMDs may be combined and taken from any one of the IRAs or from more than one of the IRAs in any combination; *see* Step 3 at *8.13*.

they are not more than 5% owners (*see* the last paragraph in this section). For example, if you were born in 1948, so your RMD age was 70½, you were still working in 2018 when you reached 70½, you were not a more-than-5% owner, and your plan allowed the delay to the year of retirement, your required beginning date is April 1 of the year after the year in which you retire. If you retire in 2023, your first RMD, the RMD for 2023, may be received at any time in 2023, or you may take it in 2024 by April 1. Your RMD for 2024 (the second RMD) must be received by December 31, 2024.

If your RMD age is 73 (you were born after June 30, 1950), you are not a more than 5% owner, and the plan allows the delay until retirement, your required beginning date will be the later of (1) April 1 following the year of your 73rd birthday, or (2) April 1 following the year in which you retire. If you retire before the year in which you reach age 73, your required beginning date is April 1 of the year after the year in which you reach age 73. If you continue working past age 73, your required beginning date is April 1 of the year after the year in which you retire. For example, assume you turn age 73 in 2023 but do not retire until 2026. Your first RMD will be for 2026, and may be received any time in 2026 or in early 2027 but no later than April 1, 2027. Your second RMD, the RMD for 2027, must be received by December 31, 2027. Thus, delaying the first RMD until early 2027 (no later than April 1) would mean that you would have to take two distributions in 2027, which could substantially increase your taxable income for that year. As noted, this example assumes that the plan allows a delay of the first RMD until you retire. However, an IRS regulation allows a plan to apply the rule for more than 5% owners (see the next paragraph) to all employees. If the plan does this and you reach age 73 in 2023, you would have to receive an RMD for 2024 no later than April 1, 2025, even if you do not retire until 2026.

A more-than-5% owner must begin RMDs by April 1 following the year in which he or she reaches the RMD age, even if still working. Being a more-than-5% owner means that you own over 5% of the capital or profits interest in the business. As noted in the preceding paragraph, the IRS permits plans to require all employees, and not just more-than-5% owners, to begin RMDs by April 1 of the year after the year in which age 72 is attained, even if they are still working.

7.12 Payouts to Beneficiaries

As the beneficiary of a qualified plan account (corporate or self-employed plan), including a 403(b) tax-sheltered annuity or Section 457 plan, your distribution options depend on the terms of the plan, whether you are a surviving spouse, and if you are a nonspouse beneficiary, your status under the SECURE Act, which applies to beneficiaries of plan participants who die after 2019. Under the SECURE Act, "eligible designated beneficiaries" *(8.15)* may receive beneficiaries distributions over their life expectancies, but beneficiaries who are not "eligible designated beneficiaries" must withdraw the entire account balance by the end of the 10th year after the year of the participant's death; *see 8.15* for details on these rules (the same rules apply to IRA beneficiaries under the SECURE Act). A surviving spouse may make a tax-free rollover, or, as an eligible designated beneficiary under the SECURE Act, may use the life expectancy method; *see* below.

Even if a life expectancy distribution method is allowed under the SECURE Act, the plan may require that you receive a lump-sum distribution or allow installment payments over only a limited number of years.

If you receive a lump-sum distribution, you generally may make a tax-free rollover to another plan, but the rollover options are more restricted for nonspouse beneficiaries than for surviving spouses as discussed below. In the rare case where the plan participant was born before January 2, 1936, and you receive a qualifying lump sum, you may be able to claim special averaging *(7.4)*.

Surviving spouse. If you are a surviving spouse and receive a distribution that would have been eligible for rollover had your spouse received it, you may make a tax-free rollover to the qualified plan of your employer or to your own traditional IRA. If you make a rollover to a traditional IRA, your subsequent withdrawals are subject to the regular IRA distribution rules *(8.8)*.

If you do not make a rollover and the payer plan gives you the option of taking distributions over your life expectancy as allowed by the SECURE Act, you may be able to delay the commencement of distributions for several years. If your spouse died before the year he or she would have reached age 72 *(7.11)*, and you are the sole designated beneficiary of the account as of September 30 of the year following the year of death, you do not have to begin receiving required minimum distributions (RMDs) until the end of the year in which your spouse would have reached age 72. This is an exception to the general rule that requires RMDs under the life expectancy method (for eligible designated beneficiaries) to begin by the end of the year following the year in which the plan participant died *(8.15)*.

Nonspouse beneficiary. If you are the designated beneficiary of a deceased plan participant who was not your spouse, you are allowed to roll over a distribution, but only by means of a direct trustee-to-trustee transfer to an IRA that is set up as an inherited IRA *(8.15)*. If you make the trustee-to-trustee transfer to an inherited IRA, the distribution method depends on whether you are an "eligible designated beneficiary," which would allow you to receive distributions over your life expectancy, or a "non-eligible designated beneficiary," in which case you must withdraw the entire IRA balance by the end of the 10th year following the year of plan participant's death *(8.15)*.

If a trustee-to-trustee transfer is made to a Roth IRA, you are taxed as if you made a conversion from a traditional IRA *(8.23)*.

If you do not make such a trustee-to-trustee transfer, you must receive distributions as required under the terms of the deceased participant's plan.

7.13 Penalty for Distributions Before Age 59½

A 10% penalty (the IRS calls this an "additional tax") generally applies to taxable distributions made to you before you reach age 59½ from a qualified corporate or self-employed retirement plan, qualified annuity plan, or tax-sheltered annuity plan (403(b) plan; *see 7.19*), but there are several exceptions. For example, the penalty does not apply to distributions made to you after separation from service if the separation occurs during or after the year in which you reach age 55. A full list of exceptions is shown below.

If no exception applies, the penalty is 10% of the taxable distribution. If you make a tax-free rollover *(7.5)*, the distribution is not taxable and not subject to the penalty. If a partial rollover is made, the part not rolled over is taxable and subject to the penalty.

The penalty generally does not apply to Section 457 plans of tax-exempt employers or state or local governments *(7.20)*. However, if a direct transfer or rollover is made to a governmental Section 457 plan from a qualified plan, 403(b) annuity, or IRA, a later distribution from the Section 457 plan is subject to the penalty to the extent of the direct transfer or rollover.

If you make an in-plan rollover to a designated Roth account *(7.18)* from your 401(k) plan, 403(b) plan or governmental 457 plan, the 10% penalty may apply to a distribution received from the designated Roth account within five years of the rollover.

A similar 10% penalty applies to IRA distributions before age 59½ *(8.12)*. The penalty is 25% if a distribution before age 59½ is made from a SIMPLE IRA in the first two years of plan participation *(8.19)*. The 10% penalty generally applies to pre–age 59½ distributions from nonqualified annuities *(7.21)*.

There are a few differences between the penalty exceptions shown below for qualified corporate and self-employed plan distributions and the exceptions for IRA distributions *(8.12)*. There is no qualified plan exception for higher education expenses as there is for IRAs. On the other hand, the exception for distributions after separation from service at age 55 (or over) applies only to qualified plans and not to IRAs.

Caution

Penalty Exception for Substantially Equal Payments

The substantially equal payments exception to the 10% early distribution penalty is generally revoked if qualifying payments are not received for at least five years. For example, you separate from service when you are age 57 and you begin to receive a series of qualifying substantially equal payments. When you are age 61, you stop the payments or modify the payment schedule so that it no longer qualifies. Unless the IRS permits an exception, the 10% penalty applies to the payments received before age 59½ because the five-year test was not met.

Exceptions to the penalty. The following distributions from a qualified employer plan are exempt from the 10% penalty, even if made to you before age 59½. If the plan administrator knows that an exception applies, a code for the exception will be entered in Box 7 of Form 1099-R on which the distribution is reported.

- *Rollovers.* Distributions that you roll over tax free under the "direct rollover" or "personal rollover" rules *(7.6)* are not subject to the early distribution penalty.

- *Disability.* Distributions made on account of your total disability do not subject you to the early distribution penalty.

- *Separation from service at age 55 or older.* The early distribution penalty does not apply to distributions after separation from service if you are age 55 or over in the year you retire or leave the company. If you reach age 55 in the same year you separate from service, the distribution must be received after the separation from service but you do not have to turn age 55 before receiving the distribution; the exception applies so long as the distribution is received after the separation from service and you reach age 55 before the end of the same year. You cannot separate from service before the year you reach age 55, wait until the year you reach age 55, and then take a distribution; the penalty will apply because in the year of separation you were not at least age 55.

  As discussed below, the age test is reduced from 55 to 50 for qualified public safety employees (police, fire fighting, emergency medical services).

  Note that the age 55 separation from service exception does not apply to IRA distributions. If you separate from service after age 55 and rollover a distribution to an IRA, the penalty exception will not apply to a distribution received before age 59½ from that IRA. This happened to an attorney who left his law firm at age 56 and rolled over funds from the law firm's pension plan to an IRA. The next year he withdrew about $240,000 from the IRA and was hit with the 10% penalty by the IRS. The Tax Court upheld the 10% penalty and also imposed a penalty for substantially understating tax *(48.6)*. The Seventh Circuit affirmed. The appeals court was sympathetic to the taxpayer's argument that it made no sense to impose the 10% early distribution penalty on the IRA distribution when he could have taken the distribution from his law firm's plan at age 56 with no penalty, but that is how Congress wrote the law. The Courts cannot change the rules that allow the age 55 exception only for qualified plan distributions and not IRAs. The Seventh Circuit also upheld the substantial understatement penalty; the taxpayer had no authority for claiming that the penalty exception applied to his IRA distribution.

- *Public safety employees separated from service at age 50 or later.* The early distribution penalty does not apply to distributions received by public safety officers who separate from service in or after the year of reaching age 50. The penalty exception applies to state and local public safety officers (police, fire, emergency medical), as well as to federal law enforcement officers, customs and border protection officers, federal firefighters, and air traffic controllers. The exception applies whether the distribution is from a defined benefit pension plan or a defined contribution plan such as the federal Thrift Savings Plan (TSP).

- *Medical costs.* Distributions are not subject to the early distribution penalty to the extent that you pay deductible medical expenses exceeding the threshold for medical expense deductions *(17.1)*, whether or not an itemized deduction for medical expenses is actually claimed for the year.

- *Qualified birth or adoption distributions.* Your employer's plan has the option of allowing in-service qualified birth or adoption distributions (Notice 2020-68). A distribution of up to $5,000 that is made within one year of the birth of your child, or a distribution of up to $5,000 that is within one year from the date you finalize the adoption of someone under age 18 or a person who is physically or mentally incapable of self-support (regardless of age), is not subject to the early distribution penalty. However, your spouse's child is not an eligible adoptee. Each parent may receive a qualified birth or adoption distribution of up to $5,000 with respect to the same child or eligible adoptee. If there are multiple births (twins, triplets, etc.) or multiple adoptions, a separate $5,000 distribution limit applies to each birth or adoption, provided the distributions are within the one-year period following the date on which the children are born or the adoptions are finalized. On your return for the year of the distribution, you must include the name, age and taxpayer identification number of the child or adoptee. Qualified birth or adoption distributions may be repaid to the plan.

- *Substantially equal payments.* The early distribution penalty does not apply to distributions received after your separation from service that are part of a series of substantially equal payments (at least annually) over your life expectancy, or over the joint life expectancy of yourself and your designated beneficiary. The IRS allows three methods of structuring payments that can satisfy the penalty exception: the required minimum distribution method, the fixed amortization method, and the fixed annuitization method. If you claim the exception and begin to receive such a series of payments but then before age 59½ you receive a lump sum or change the distribution method and you are not totally disabled, a recapture penalty tax will generally apply. The recapture tax also applies to payments received before age 59½ if substantially equal payments are not received for at least five years. The recapture tax applies the 10% penalty to all amounts received before age 59½, as if the exception had never been allowed, plus interest for that period. However, the IRS allows taxpayers who have been receiving substantially equal payments under the fixed amortization or fixed annuitization method to switch without penalty to the required minimum distribution method. *See 8.12* for details on the three payment methods.

- *Beneficiaries.* If you are the beneficiary of a deceased plan participant, you are not subject to the 10% penalty, regardless of your age or the participant's age.

- *Qualified reservist distribution.* If you are a member of the reserves called to active military duty for over 179 days, or indefinitely, distributions received during the active duty period that are attributable to elective deferrals (401(k) or 403(b) plan) are not subject to the early distribution penalty. Furthermore, a qualified reservist distribution may be recontributed to an IRA within two years after the end of the active duty period; a recontribution is not deductible.

- *IRS levy.* Involuntary distributions that result from an IRS levy on your plan account are not subject to the early distribution penalty.

- *QDRO.* Distributions paid to an alternate payee pursuant to a qualified domestic relations court order (QDRO) are not subject to the early distribution penalty.

Financial hardship distributions or distributions used for college or home-buying costs are subject to the penalty. The 10% penalty generally applies to a hardship distribution that you receive before age 59½ from a 401(k) plan *(7.17)* or 403(b) tax-sheltered annuity plan *(7.19)*. For example, there is no penalty exception for distributions you take to deal with a casualty loss, to pay tuition costs, or to buy a principal residence. However, as noted above, a distribution used to pay medical costs may qualify for an exception if your medical expenses exceed the floor for claiming an itemized deduction *(17.1)*.

Note that for IRA distributions, a penalty exception may apply for a distribution used to pay tuition costs or buy a principal residence *(8.12)*.

Corrective distributions from 401(k) plans. If you are considered a highly compensated employee and excess elective deferrals or excess contributions are made on your behalf, a distribution of the excess to you is not subject to the penalty.

Filing Form 5329 for exceptions. If your employer correctly entered a penalty exception code in Box 7 of Form 1099-R, you do not have to file Form 5329 to claim the exception. You also do not have to file Form 5329 if you made a tax-free rollover of the entire taxable distribution. You must file Form 5329 if you qualify for an exception, other than the rollover exception, that is not indicated in Box 7 of Form 1099-R.

7.14 Restrictions on Loans From Company Plans

Within limits, you may receive a loan from a qualified company plan, annuity plan, 403(b) plan, or government plan without triggering tax consequences. The maximum loan you can receive without tax is generally the lesser of 50% of your vested account balance or $50,000, but the $50,000 limit is subject to reductions where there are other loans outstanding; *see* below. Congress temporarily doubled the 50%/$50,000 loan limit to the lesser of $100,000 (minus other outstanding loans) or 100% of the account balance, for certain 2020 loans to employees eligible for coronavirus-related distributions, and for loans made from December 27, 2020, through June 24, 2021, to employees living in a qualified disaster area.

Loans within the applicable limit must be repayable within five years, unless they are used for buying your principal residence. If loan repayments were suspended for a year under the CARES Act *(see above)*, the suspension period is disregarded for purposes of determining the five-year repayment period. Loans that do not meet these guidelines are treated as taxable distributions from the plan. If the plan treats a loan as a taxable distribution, you should receive a Form 1099-R with Code L marked in Box 7.

Did you borrow from the plan within the one-year period ending on the day before the new loan? If you did not borrow within the year, you are not taxed on a loan that does not exceed the lesser of $50,000 or 50% of the vested benefit (or if applicable, the $100,000/100% limit allowed under the special legislation discussed in the Law Alert).

If there were loans within the one-year period, the dollar limit must be further reduced. The loan, when added to the outstanding loan balance, may not exceed the dollar limit less the excess of (1) the highest outstanding loan balance during the one-year period (ending the day before the new loan) over (2) the outstanding balance on the date of the new loan. Assuming the limit is $50,000, the reduction under (1) and (2) is the maximum tax-free loan where it is less than 50% of the vested benefit; if 50% of the vested benefit is the smaller amount, that would be the maximum tax-free loan.

Repayment period. Generally, loans within the previously discussed limits must be repayable within five years to avoid being treated as a taxable distribution. However, if you use the loan to purchase a principal residence for yourself, the repayment period may be longer than five years; any reasonable period is allowed. This exception does not apply if the plan loan is used to improve your existing principal residence, to buy a second home, or to finance the purchase of a home or home improvements for other family members; such loans are subject to the five-year repayment rule.

Level loan amortization required. To avoid tax consequences on a plan loan, you must be required to repay using a level amortization schedule, with payments at least quarterly. According to Congressional committee reports, you may accelerate repayment, and the employer may use a variable interest rate and require full repayment if you leave the company.

Giving a demand note does not satisfy the repayment requirements. The IRS and Tax Court held the entire amount of an employee's loan to be a taxable distribution since his demand loan did not require level amortization of principal and interest with at least quarterly payments. It did not matter that the employee had paid interest quarterly and actually repaid the loan within five years.

If required installments are not made, the entire loan balance must be treated as a "deemed distribution" from the plan under IRS regulations. However, the IRS allows the plan administrator to permit a grace period of up to one calendar quarter. If the missed installment is not paid by the end of the grace period, there is at that time a deemed distribution in the amount of the outstanding loan balance.

Under IRS regulations, loan repayments may be suspended for up to one year (or longer if you are in the uniformed services) if you take a leave of absence during which you are paid less than the installments due. However, the installments after the leave must at least equal the original required amount and the loan must be repaid by the end of the allowable repayment period (five years if not used to buy a principal residence). For example, on July 1, 2023, when his vested account balance is $80,000, Joe Smith takes out a $40,000 non–principal residence loan, to be repaid with interest in level monthly installments of $825 over five years. He makes nine payments and then takes a year of unpaid leave. When he returns to work he can either increase his monthly payment to make up for the missed payments or resume paying $825 a month and on June 30, 2028, repay the entire balance owed in a lump sum.

> **EXAMPLE**
>
> Your vested plan benefit is $200,000. Assume that in August 2023 you borrow $30,000 from the plan. On July 1, 2024, when the outstanding balance on the first loan is $20,000, you want to take another loan without incurring tax.

You may borrow an additional $20,000 without incurring tax: The $50,000 limit is first reduced by the outstanding loan balance of $20,000—leaving $30,000. The reduced $30,000 limit is in turn reduced by $10,000, the excess of $30,000 (the highest loan balance within one year of the new loan) over $20,000 (the loan balance as of November 1).

If loan payments are suspended while you are serving in the uniformed services, the loan payments must resume upon returning to work and the loan repayment period (five years from the date of the loan unless the loan was used to buy your principal residence) is extended by the period of suspension.

Spousal consent generally required to get a loan. All plans subject to the joint and survivor rules *(7.11)* must require spousal consent in order to use your account balance as security for the loan in case you default. Check with your plan administrator for consent requirements.

Interest deduction limitations. If you want to borrow from your account to buy a first or second residence and you are not a "key" employee *(3.4)*, you can generally obtain a full interest deduction by using the residence as collateral for the loan *(15.2)*. Your account balance may not be used to secure the loan. Key employees are not allowed any interest deduction for plan loans.

If you use a plan loan for investment purposes and are not a key employee, and the loan is not secured by your elective deferrals (or allocable income) to a 401(k) plan or tax-sheltered annuity, the loan account interest is deductible up to investment income *(15.10)*. Interest on loans used for personal purposes is not deductible, unless your residence is the security for the loan.

7.15 Tax Benefits of 401(k) Plans

If your company has a profit-sharing or stock bonus plan, it has the opportunity of giving you additional tax-sheltered pay. The tax law allows the company to add a cash or deferred pay plan, called a 401(k) plan.

Your company may offer to contribute to a 401(k) plan trust account on your behalf if you forego a salary increase, but in most plans, contributions take the form of salary-reduction deferrals. Under a salary-reduction agreement, you elect to contribute a specified percentage of your wages to the 401(k) plan instead of receiving it as regular salary. In addition, your company may match a portion of your contribution. A salary-reduction deferral is treated as a contribution by your employer that is not taxable to you if the annual contribution limits are not exceeded.

Employers have the option of amending their 401(k) plans to allow employees to designate part or all of their elective contributions as Roth contributions *(7.18)*.

Salary-reduction deferrals. Making elective salary deferrals allows you to defer tax on salary and get a tax-free buildup of earnings within your 401(k) plan account until withdrawals are made.

The tax law sets a maximum annual limit on salary deferrals to a 401(k) plan. For 2023, the maximum deferral was $22,500, plus an additional $7,500 for plan participants age 50 or older if the plan permitted the extra "catch-up" contribution. If these limits are increased for 2024, the adjusted amounts will be reported in the *e-Supplement* at *jklasser.com*. The maximum annual deferral is lower for employees of "small" employers who adopt a SIMPLE 401(k); *see* below. Note that the terms of your employer's plan may limit your maximum deferral to a percentage of your compensation, so you may be unable to defer the maximum annual limit allowed by the tax law.

Elective deferrals within the annual limit are generally pre-tax contributions, so they are not subject to income tax withholding. However, pre-tax contributions are subject to Social Security and Medicare withholdings. If the plan allows, you may apply part or all of the annual deferral limit (including catch-up amount if applicable) to after-tax Roth contributions in a designated Roth account *(7.18)*.

Planning Reminder

Rolling Over Unpaid Loan When Leaving Job

If you leave your company before your loan is paid off, the company will reduce your vested account balance by the outstanding debt and report the defaulted amount (the "loan offset") as a taxable distribution on Form 1099-R. However, tax on the loan offset can be deferred if you can come up with the funds to make a timely rollover *(7.6)* of the amount to an IRA or another eligible employer retirement plan.

For example, if your vested account balance is $100,000, and the outstanding loan is $25,000 when your employment ends, your account balance is reduced to $75,000. You could choose a direct rollover *(7.6)* of the $75,000 balance, deferring tax on that amount. The $25,000 loan offset will be reported on Form 1099-R as a taxable distribution.

Tax on the loan offset can be deferred by rolling it over by the due date, including extensions, for filing the tax return for the year the loan offset occurred (the year for which it is treated as a distribution), provided the loan offset results from a termination of employment or the employer's termination of the plan.

In the above example, note that if you elected to receive the account balance following the loan offset, rather than choosing a direct rollover to another eligible plan, $20,000 would be withheld (20% of the full $100,000) and you would receive only $55,000 ($100,000 – $25,000 loan offset – $20,000 withheld), but the full $100,000 would be treated as a taxable distribution *(7.6)*. In that case, if the entire $100,000 were not rolled over by the due date, including extensions, for filing the return for the year of the loan offset, you would be taxed on the portion not rolled over.

Also note that to the extent a rollover is not made, the 10% early distribution penalty would apply if you were under age 59½ at the time of the loan offset, unless a penalty exception were available *(7.13)*.

Law Alert

Automatic 401(k) Plan Coverage

Employers are encouraged to automatically enroll employees in a 401(k) plan. Unless employees affirmatively opt out, a specified percentage of their pay is contributed to the plan. Even though the employees do not make affirmative elections to contribute, such plans are qualified provided that the employees are given advance notice of their right either to receive cash or have the designated amount contributed by the employer to the plan.

Employers are granted protection from nondiscrimination restrictions if they have automatic enrollment plans that include mandatory matching or non-elective employer contributions.

Caution

Reduced Deferral Limit for Highly Compensated Employees

To avoid discrimination problems an employer may set a lower limit for elective salary deferrals by highly compensated employees than the generally applicable ceiling.

If, after contributions are made, the plan fails to meet the nondiscrimination tests, the excess contributions will either be returned to the highly compensated employees or kept in the plan but recharacterized as after-tax contributions. In either case, the excess contribution is taxable. Form 1099-R will indicate the excess contribution.

Your employer may not require you to make elective deferrals in order to obtain any other benefits, apart from matching contributions. For example, benefits provided under health plans or other compensation plans may not be conditioned on your making salary deferrals to a 401(k) plan.

Distributions. Withdrawals from a 401(k) plan before age 59½ are restricted *(7.13)*. Mandatory 20% withholding applies to a lump sum as well as other distributions that are eligible for rollover if the distribution is paid to you and not directly rolled over to another plan *(7.6)*. For those born before January 2, 1936, a lump-sum distribution may be eligible for averaging *(7.3)*. After you reach the required beginning date, you must begin to receive required minimum distributions *(7.11)*

Nondiscrimination rules. The law imposes strict contribution percentage tests to prevent discrimination in favor of employees who are highly compensated. If these tests are violated, the employer is subject to penalties and the plan could be disqualified unless the excess contributions (plus allocable income) are distributed back to the highly compensated employees within specified time limits.

SIMPLE 401(k). Nondiscrimination tests are eased for employers who adopt a 401(k) plan with SIMPLE contribution provisions. A SIMPLE 401(k) may be set up only by employers who in the preceding year had no more than 100 employees with compensation of at least $5,000. An employer who contributes to a SIMPLE 401(k) must report on a calendar-year basis and may not maintain another qualified plan for employees eligible to participate in the SIMPLE plan.

If the SIMPLE contribution requirements are met, the plan is considered to meet 401(k) nondiscrimination requirements. Employee elective deferrals may not exceed an annual limitation, which was $15,500 for 2023. The plan may also allow additional contributions by participants who are age 50 or older by the end of the year. The limit on the additional contribution was $3,500 for 2023. The limits for 2024 will be reported in the *e-Supplement* at *jklasser.com*.

The employer must either match the employee deferral, up to 3% of compensation, or contribute 2% of compensation for all eligible employees, whether or not they make elective deferrals. All contributions are nonforfeitable. No other type of contribution is allowed. In figuring the 3% or 2% employer contribution, compensation is subject to an annual compensation ceiling; for 2023, the compensation limit was $330,000.

Partnership plans. Partnership plans that allow partners to vary annual contributions are treated as 401(k) plans by the IRS. Thus, elective deferrals are subject to the annual limit *(7.16)* and the special 401(k) plan nondiscrimination rules apply.

7.16 Limit on Salary-Reduction Deferrals

Elective deferrals to a 401(k) plan must not exceed the annual tax-free ceiling *(7.15)*; otherwise, the plan could be disqualified. If you also participate in a 403(b) tax-sheltered annuity plan *(7.19)*, a salary-reduction SEP established before 1997 *(8.17)*, or you have a self-employed 401(k) plan to which elective deferrals can be made *(41.4)*, the annual limit applies to the total salary reductions for all the plans and any excess deferral should be withdrawn as discussed below. Because of percentage-of-compensation limitations in your employer's plan, you may be unable to make deferrals up to the annual tax-free ceiling. Also, certain highly compensated employees may be unable to take advantage of the maximum annual tax-free ceiling because of restrictions imposed by nondiscrimination tests.

Both the regular annual deferral limit ($22,500 for 2023) and, if permitted by the plan, the "catch-up" contribution limit for those age 50 or older ($7,500 for 2023), are subject to cost-of-living increases; *see* the *e-Supplement* at *jklasser.com* for whether the limits will be increased for 2024.

To avoid the strict nondiscrimination tests for employee elective deferrals and employer matching contributions, an employer may make contributions to a SIMPLE 401(k) *(7.15)*.

An employer may make matching or other contributions, provided the total contribution for the year, including the employee's pre-tax salary deferral and any employee after-tax contributions, does not exceed the annual limit for defined contribution plans, which for 2023 was the lesser of 100% of compensation or $66,000.

Withdrawing excess deferrals. A single plan must apply the annual limit on salary deferrals to maintain qualified status. If your deferrals to the plan for a year exceed the annual limit, the excess, plus allocable earnings, must be distributed to you or the plan risks disqualification. If you participated in more than one plan and the deferrals to all of the plans exceeded the limit, you should withdraw the excess, plus the allocable income, from any of the plans, by April 15 of the year following the year of the excess deferral.

Whether the excess deferrals were made to one or several plans, you must report the excess as wages (Line 1, Form 1040 or 1040-SR) for the year of the deferral. If you withdraw the excess by April 15 of the following year, it is not taxable again when you receive it. However, if the withdrawal of the excess is not received by the April 15 date, the excess is taxed again when received. The withdrawal of allocable earnings is always taxable in the year of the distribution. If a withdrawal of an excess deferral to a salary-reduction SEP (set up before 1997 *(8.17)*) is not withdrawn by the April 15 date, it is treated as a regular IRA contribution that could be subject to the penalty for excess IRA contributions *(8.7)*.

Excess deferrals (and earnings) distributed by the April 15 date are not subject to the 10% early distribution penalty *(7.13)* even if you are under age 59½.

For the year in which the excess deferral and allocable earnings are distributed to you, the plan will send you a Form 1099-R. Box 7 will include a code designating the year for which the excess is taxable.

7.17 Withdrawals From 401(k) Plans Restricted

By law, you may not withdraw funds attributable to elective salary-reduction contributions to a 401(k) plan unless (1) you no longer work for the employer maintaining the plan; (2) you have reached age 59½; (3) you have become totally disabled; (4) you can show financial hardship; (5) you are eligible for a qualified reservist distribution *(7.13)*; (6) you are the beneficiary of a deceased employee; or (7) the plan is terminated and no successor defined contribution plan (other than an employee stock ownership plan) is maintained by the employer. If a distribution is allowed and all of your plan contributions were pre-tax elective salary deferrals, the entire distribution is taxable unless it is rolled over to an eligible plan *(7.5)*.

Under IRS rules, it is difficult to qualify for hardship withdrawals; *see* below. If you do qualify, the withdrawal is taxable, and if you are under age 59½, it is subject to the 10% early distribution penalty unless you meet a penalty exception *(7.13)*.

The hardship provision and age 59½ withdrawal allowance do not apply to certain "pre-ERISA" money purchase pension plans (in existence June 27, 1974).

An "involuntary" distribution resulting from an IRS levy on a 401(k) plan account is taxable to the employee (assuming only "pre-tax" contributions) but is not subject to the 10% penalty on pre-age 59½ distributions *(7.13)*.

Withdrawals before age 59½. Withdrawals for medical disability, financial hardship, or separation from service are subject to the 10% penalty for early distributions unless you meet one of the exceptions *(7.13)*.

Loans. If you are allowed to borrow from the plan, loan restrictions *(7.14)* apply.

Qualifying for hardship withdrawals. IRS regulations restrict hardship withdrawals. If you qualify, you may withdraw your elective deferrals, employer nonelective contributions and matching contributions, and earnings on these amounts regardless of when contributed or earned. Keep in mind that any hardship distribution you are allowed to take is a taxable distribution, and if you are under age 59½, it is subject to the 10% early distribution penalty unless you meet a penalty exception *(7.13)*.

The IRS requires you to show an immediate and heavy financial need that cannot be met with other resources.

Law Alert

In-Plan Conversion From 401(k) to Roth 401(k) May Be Permitted

Employers with 401(k), 403(b), or governmental 457 plans have the option of allowing employees to roll over distributions of vested amounts to a designated Roth account within the same plan. An in-plan Roth rollover is taxable unless attributable to after-tax contributions.

Law Alert

Repayment of a Wrongful Levy

If there is an IRS levy on a 401(k) plan account that turns out to be wrongful, an individual can recontribute the amount returned (the amount levied plus interest).

Avoiding Withholding on Hardship Distribution

A hardship distribution from a 401(k) plan is not eligible for rollover *(7.5)* to an IRA or an eligible employer plan. Your employer will not apply 20% withholding to the distribution, as mandatory withholding applies only to rollover-eligible distributions *(7.5)*. However, the withholding rules for nonperiodic distributions apply. You can completely avoid withholding on Form W-4R; if you do not do this, 10% will be withheld *(26.9)*.

Contributions Permitted for Those Taking a Hardship Distribution

You are not required to exhaust plan loans before a hardship distribution can be made, but the plan may require that all available nontaxable loans be taken first.

Financial need includes the following expenses under final IRS regulations (this list may be expanded by the IRS in rulings):

- Purchase of a principal residence for yourself (but not mortgage payments);
- Tuition, related fees and room and board for the next 12 months of post-secondary education for yourself, your spouse, children, or other dependents, or for a named beneficiary under the plan;
- Medical expenses previously incurred for yourself, your spouse, your dependents or named beneficiaries under the plan, or expenses incurred to obtain medical care for such persons;
- Repair costs to your principal residence due to damage from a casualty (without regard to whether the costs are a deductible casualty loss under *18.1*);
- Expenses or losses incurred on account of a federally-declared disaster if your home or place of employment at the time of the disaster was in an area designated by FEMA for assistance;
- Preventing your eviction or mortgage foreclosure; and
- Paying funeral expenses for a family member or named beneficiary under the plan.

Even if you can show financial need, you may not make a hardship withdrawal if you have other resources to pay the expenses. You do not have to provide your employer with a detailed financial statement, but you must provide a statement to your employer that you do not have readily available cash or other liquid assets to pay the expenses. You must have received all currently available nonhardship distributions under the plan and all of the employer's other qualified and nonqualified deferred compensation plans. The plan may provide that before a hardship distribution can be made, you must take all nontaxable loans available under the plan. However, the plan may not provide for a suspension of contributions as a condition of obtaining a hardship distribution.

7.18 Designated Roth Account Within 401(k), 403(b), or Governmental 457 Plans

Employers with a 401(k) plan may allow employees to irrevocably designate all or part of their elective salary deferrals (including catch-up contributions if age 50 or older) as after-tax Roth contributions. Similarly, a 403(b) plan *(7.19)* or a governmental 457 plan *(7.20)* may allow employees to make elective deferrals to a designated Roth account. The plan must be amended to allow for designated Roth contributions. The annual tax-free ceiling on elective salary-reduction deferrals, including the additional catch-up amount for those age 50 or older *(7.16)*, applies to the combined total of pre-tax elective deferrals and designated Roth contributions. The Roth contributions, being after-tax, are treated as taxable wages subject to withholding.

The major incentive for employees to choose designated Roth contributions is to obtain tax-free treatment for distributions under the qualified distribution rules applicable to Roth IRAs; *see* below for details of the "qualified" and "nonqualified" distribution rules.

The option to make designated Roth contributions can benefit employees who might otherwise be unable to make annual contributions to a Roth IRA. Subject to 401(k) nondiscrimination tests, there are no income limitations on the right to make Roth 401(k) contributions, whereas contributions to a Roth IRA are barred if adjusted gross income exceeds an annual threshold *(8.21)*.

Plans must segregate designated Roth contributions from regular pre-tax 401(k), 403(b), or governmental 457 plan elective deferrals and maintain separate accounts for employees with both types of contributions. Only Roth elective deferrals may be contributed to the designated Roth account. If the employer makes matching contributions, they may not be made to the designated Roth account. Gains, losses, and other credits or charges, as well as contribution and withdrawals, must be allocated between the accounts on a reasonable and consistent basis. Designated Roth contributions are subject to the 401(k) nonforfeitability and distribution restrictions and also to the nondiscrimination tests for pre-tax elective contributions.

In-plan Roth rollovers. Employers may (but do not have to) allow employees to roll over amounts from their 401(k), 403(b), or governmental 457(b) plan to a designated Roth account within the same plan. An in-plan Roth rollover is taxable except to the extent attributable to after-tax contributions; this is the same rule as for a conversion of a traditional IRA to a Roth IRA. The taxable amount will be reported on Form 1099-R in Box 2a. If a direct rollover was made, Code G will be entered in Box 7.

Qualified distributions from designated Roth account are tax free. The rules for determining tax treatment of distributions from designated Roth accounts generally follow the rules for Roth IRA distributions *(8.25)*. There is a two-part test for determining if a distribution from a designated Roth account is a qualified distribution, and therefore totally tax free:

(1.) it is received at least five years after the year in which the employee's first designated Roth contribution was made, and

(2.) one of the following is true: (a) the distribution is made to an employee age 59½ or older, (b) the distribution is made because the employee is disabled, or (c) the distribution is made to a beneficiary after the employee's death.

If these tests are met, the distribution is a completely tax-free qualified distribution; you are not taxed on the earnings part of the distribution or the part attributable to your investment (your designated Roth contributions). For purposes of the five-year participation test (Test 1 above), the five-year period begins on the first day of the year for which the first designated Roth contribution is made. For example, if you made your first designated Roth contribution in 2019, then 2019 was year one of the five-year period, which ends December 31, 2023. A distribution in 2024 or later will be a qualified distribution if you are age 59½ or older or you are disabled when you receive it, or if the distribution is paid to your beneficiary after your death.

Nonqualified distributions from designated Roth account are partly tax free, partly taxable. A distribution from a designated Roth account that is not a qualified distribution under the above tests is taxable to the extent it is allocable to earnings. For example, assume you receive a nonqualified distribution of $10,000 from your designated Roth account when the account balance is $20,000, consisting of $18,800 of designated Roth contributions and $1,200 of earnings. Of the $10,000 distribution, $600 is allocable to earnings and is taxable ($1,200 total earnings/$20,000 account balance × $10,000 distribution = $600). The $9,400 balance is allocable to your designated Roth contributions (basis) and is nontaxable ($18,800 designated Roth contributions/$20,000 account balance × $10,000 distribution = $9,400).

Required minimum distributions. The required minimum distribution rules apply to designated Roth accounts and thus you generally must begin to receive minimum annual distributions from the account by your required beginning date; *see 7.11* for details. However, if before your required beginning date you make a rollover *(7.5)* from your designated Roth account to a Roth IRA, you will not have to take any required minimum distributions from the Roth IRA *(8.20)*.

Rollovers from designated Roth account. If you have a designated Roth account within your employer's plan, an eligible rollover distribution *(7.5)* from the designated Roth account may be rolled over to a Roth IRA *(8.23)*. The nontaxable portion of a distribution (*see* the above discussion of qualified and nonqualified distributions) may be rolled over to another designated Roth account with a different employer, but the rollover must be made by means of a direct rollover *(7.6)*, rather than a personal rollover within 60 days of receiving the distribution. If a direct rollover is not made and you receive the distribution, you may roll over the entire amount to a Roth IRA within the 60-day period, but you cannot roll over the nontaxable portion allocable to your designated Roth contributions (your basis) to another designated Roth account.

If an employee receives a nonqualified distribution (*see above*) and part of it is rolled over, the rollover is allocated first to the earnings portion of the distribution. For example, assume you receive a nonqualified distribution of $28,000 that is eligible for rollover from your designated Roth account. Also assume that of the $28,000 distribution, $22,000 is allocable to your designated Roth contributions and the other $6,000 is earnings on the account. You can avoid tax on the earnings by rolling over at least $6,000 within 60 days of receipt. If $14,000 is rolled over to a Roth IRA within 60 days, the $14,000 is treated as consisting of the $6,000 of earnings and $8,000 of designated Roth contributions (basis). The entire distribution of $28,000 is tax free because the only part of it that could be taxed is the $6,000 of earnings (the rest is your investment), and that $6,000 is treated as having been rolled over.

7.19 403(b) Plans (Tax-Sheltered Annuity Plans) for Employees of Tax-Exempts and Schools and Ministers

If you are employed by a state or local government public school, or by a tax-exempt (501(c)(3)) religious, charitable, scientific, or educational organization, or are on the civilian staff or faculty of the Uniformed Services University of the Health Sciences (Department of Defense), you may be able to participate in a 403(b) plan, also known as a tax-sheltered annuity plan, that is set up by your employer. A 403(b) plan may invest funds for employees in mutual fund shares as well as in annuity contracts. A 403(b) account may also be made available to ministers employed by Section 501(c)(3) tax-exempt organizations, self-employed ministers who are treated as employed by a tax-exempt organization, and ministers or chaplains employed by organizations that are not tax-exempt.

The purchase of an annuity contract or mutual fund shares is generally made through pre-tax elective deferrals made through salary-reduction contributions. Your plan may allow you to allocate some of your elective deferral limit to Roth contributions or to make non-Roth after-tax contributions, and the employer may make non-elective contributions.

Caution: As the following contribution rules for 403(b) plans have been stated in general terms, we suggest that you also consult your employer or the issuer of the contract. IRS Publication 571 has detailed examples.

Limit on tax-free contributions. Tax-free salary reductions are limited to the annual ceiling for elective deferrals, and the plan may permit additional deferrals for participants who are age 50 or older *(7.16)*.

If, you make salary deferrals to a 403(b) plan as well as to a 401(k) plan, SIMPLE plan, or simplified employee pension plan, the annual salary-reduction limit applies to the total deferrals *(7.16)*. If you defer more than the annual limit, the excess is taxable. Further, if a salary-reduction deferral in excess of the annual limit is made and the excess is not distributed to you by April 15 of the following year, the excess will be taxed twice—not only in the year of deferral but again in the year it is actually distributed. To avoid the double tax, any excess deferral plus the income attributable to such excess should be distributed no later than April 15 of the year following the year in which the excess deferral is made *(7.16)*.

The annual salary-reduction ceiling is generally increased by $3,000 for employees of educational organizations, hospitals, churches, home health service agencies, and health and welfare service agencies who have completed 15 years of service. However, the extra $3,000 annual deferral may not be claimed indefinitely. There is a lifetime limit of $15,000 on the amount of extra deferrals allowed. Furthermore, the extra deferrals may not be claimed after lifetime elective deferrals to the plan exceed $5,000 multiplied by your years of service, minus prior-year elective deferrals. Publication 571 has a worksheet for figuring the limit on elective deferrals, including the extra amount under the 15-year rule.

The employee's salary reduction plus any after-tax contributions and any non-elective contributions made by the employer for the year are tax free only if they do not exceed the annual limit on contributions to a defined contribution plan, which for 2023 was the lesser of 100% of compensation or $66,000.

Roth contributions and in-plan rollover to designated Roth account. Your plan may allow you to contribute some of the elective deferral limit to a designated Roth account *(7.18)*. These Roth contributions are part of your taxable pay and not excludable from income (they are after-tax contributions). In addition, as noted in *7.18*, your employer may allow you to make an in-plan rollover from your 403(b) plan to a designated Roth IRA within the same plan.

Distributions from 403(b) plans. Distributions attributable to salary reduction 403(b) plan contributions are allowed only when an employee reaches age 59½, has experienced a severance from employment, becomes disabled, suffers financial hardship, becomes eligible for a qualified reservist distribution *(7.13)*, or dies. The hardship distribution rules are the same as for 401(k) plans *(7.17)*. Annuity payments are taxed under the general rules for employees *(7.24)*. Payments are fully taxable if the only contributions to the plan were salary reduction contributions excluded from income (pre-tax contributions) under the annual limits discussed earlier in this section.

Non-annuity distributions from a 403(b) plan may be rolled over tax free to another 403(b) plan or traditional IRA unless the distribution is not eligible under the rollover rules *(7.5)*. An eligible rollover distribution *(7.5)* from a 403(b) plan may also be rolled over to a qualified plan or governmental Section 527 plan. If you do not choose to have the payer of the distribution make a direct rollover, mandatory 20% withholding will be applied. You may then personally make a rollover within 60 days, but you would have to include the withheld amount in the rolled-over amount to avoid tax on the entire distribution. *See 7.6* for further rollover and withholding details. A 403(b) distribution is not eligible for special averaging *(7.3)*.

Required minimum distributions (RMDs). Benefits accruing after 1986 in a 403(b) account are subject to the required beginning date rules and a penalty may be imposed for failure to take required minimum distributions *(7.11)*. Benefits accrued before 1987 are not subject to the required minimum distribution rules until the year you reach age 75.

7.20 Government and Exempt Organization Deferred Pay Plans

Federal government civilian employees may make salary-reduction contributions to the Federal Thrift Savings Plan. Employees of state and local governments and of tax-exempt organizations may be able to make salary-reduction contributions to a Section 457(b) deferred compensation plan.

Federal Thrift Savings Plan (TSP). Federal employees may elect to make salary-reduction deferrals (pre-tax contributions) to the Thrift Savings Plan (TSP) up to the elective deferral limit for 401(k) plans *(7.15)*. Deferrals are not taxed until distributed from the plan. The deferred amount is counted as wages for purposes of computing Social Security taxes and benefits.

The TSP offers employees a Roth option. This allows employees to contribute part or all of the regular deferral limit to a designated Roth account, instead of to the basic pre-tax deferral account. Roth TSP contributions are after-tax contributions, so they are included in taxable pay. Qualified distributions from the Roth TSP are tax free *(7.18)*. The government does not allow employees to roll over funds from their traditional (pre-tax) TSP account into a Roth TSP.

Distributions from the Thrift Savings Plan that are attributable to pre-tax deferrals are generally fully taxable. However, lump-sum distributions are eligible for tax-free rollover treatment *(7.5)*. If you receive a distribution before age 59½, you are subject to the 10% penalty for early distributions unless an exception applies *(7.13)*. As noted above, employees with a Roth TSP are not taxed on qualified distributions from the account *(7.18)*.

Section 457(b) plan contributions. State and local governments and tax-exempt organizations other than churches may set up Section 457(b) deferred compensation plans. Non-governmental 457(b) plans are sometimes referred to as "Top Hat" plans, because they are only open to highly-compensated employees, managers and executives; rank-and-file employees may not participate.

Employees eligible to participate in a 457(b) plan may annually defer compensation up to the elective deferral limit, which for 2023 was $22,500 *(7.15)*. Generally, deferrals from all your plans must be aggregated to stay within the annual limit *(7.16)*, but the deferral limit for a 457(b) plan is separate from the deferral limit for other plans. Thus, if you participate in a 457(b) plan and also a 403(b) or 401(k) plan, you do not aggregate the 457(b) deferrals with the deferrals from the other plan. In addition to the annual deferral limit ($22,500 for 2023), employees in state and local government 457(b) plans who are 50 years of age or older may be permitted by the plan to defer an additional "catch-up" amount, which for 2023 was $7,000. The age-50-or-older catch-up is not allowed in non-governmental 457(b) plans.

As discussed in *7.18*, a governmental 457(b) plan may allow you to designate some or all of your salary-deferral limit as after-tax Roth contributions, or to make an in-plan rollover to a designated Roth IRA account within the same plan.

A Section 457(b) plan (whether governmental or non-governmental) may also provide for another type of "catch-up" increase for employees in the last three years before the year in which they reach normal retirement age under the terms of the plan. However, this catch-up increase only applies if the employee has "unused deferral limits" from prior years, so employees who deferred the maximum amount into their plan for every prior year that they were eligible cannot take advantage of it. For employees within three years of normal retirement age who have unused deferral limits from prior years, this catch-up provision allows them to increase the regular deferral limit by the unused deferral limits, up to the regular deferral limit for the current year, which means that it may be possible to double the regular deferral limit for a given year (which for 2023 was $22,500 × 2 = $45,000), depending on the amount of the prior unused deferrals. For employees in a governmental 457(b) plan that allows both the age-50-or -older catch-up and the last-three-years catch-up, the catch-up providing the larger deferral may be used, but not both.

Deferred compensation (and allocable income) under a non-governmental (tax-exempt organization) 457(b) plan is not taxed until paid or otherwise made available under the terms of the plan. Amounts deferred (and earnings) under state or local government 457(b) plans are taxed only when paid. All distributions are taxed as ordinary income.

Distributions from Section 457(b) plans. Distributions of deferred amounts to employees or beneficiaries generally may not be made before the employee stops working for the employer, retires, reaches the required beginning date for required minimum distributions, or dies. The plan may (but does not have to) permit a distribution to an employee or beneficiary who faces an "unforeseeable" emergency. Under IRS regulations, an unforeseeable emergency means severe financial hardship resulting from a sudden illness or accident of the employee or a dependent, the loss of property due to a casualty, or other extraordinary and unforseeable event beyond the employee's control, such as imminent foreclosure or eviction from a primary residence, or having to pay medical costs or funeral expenses. The regulations specifically prohibit payments from the plan to purchase a home or pay for a child's college tuition. If the employee can obtain funds by ceasing deferrals to the plan or by liquidating assets without causing himself or herself severe financial hardship, payment from the plan is not allowed. In one case, an employee covered by a state governmental 457 plan wanted to take a withdrawal from the plan to help pay off substantial credit card debt. IRS Chief Counsel concluded that credit card debt is usually not an unforeseeable emergency, but it would qualify if the debt was incurred to pay medical costs or similar expense beyond the employee's control.

Eligible rollover distributions *(7.5)* from a governmental 457(b) plan may be rolled over tax free to a traditional IRA, another governmental 457(b) plan, a qualified plan (such as a 401(k)plan), or a 403(b) plan. An eligible distribution from a governmental 457(b) plan may also be rolled over to a Roth IRA, subject to the rules for a taxable conversion *(7.6)*. Rollovers of eligible distributions from other plans may also be made to governmental 457(b) plans.

A distribution from a non-governmental 457(b) plan may not be rolled over tax free to a traditional IRA, a qualified plan, or a 403(b) plan. The only rollover option is to roll it over to a new employer with a non-governmental 457(b) plan, assuming that the plan accepts rollovers. Because rollovers from non-governmental 457(b) plans generally may not be made, employees who anticipate a separation from service should carefully review the terms of their employer's plan to determine their distribution options in order to avoid unintended tax consequences.

See *7.11* for required minimum distribution (RMD) rules.

Note: Check with your employer for other details on Section 457(b) contributions and distribution rules.

Caution

Unforeseen Emergency Distributions

If you can show severe financial hardship arising from a sudden illness or accident, or loss of property due to events beyond your control, and you are unable to obtain funds elsewhere, you may make a withdrawal from your employer's Section 457 plan. However, the need to buy a home or pay college expenses does not qualify as an unforeseeable emergency.

7.21 Figuring the Taxable Part of Commercial Annuities

A purchased commercial annuity is a nonqualified annuity contract. Tax treatment of a distribution from a commercial annuity depends on whether you receive it before or after the annuity starting date, and on the amount of your investment. A cash withdrawal before age 59½ from an annuity contract is generally subject to a 10% penalty, but there are exceptions; the penalty is discussed on page 202. If your annuity is from an employer plan, *see 7.24*.

Annuity starting date. The annuity starting date is the later of (1) the first day of the first period for which you receive a payment, or (2) the date on which the obligation under the contract becomes fixed. For example, if your right to an annuity is fixed on June 1, 2023, and your monthly payments start on December 1, 2023, for the period starting November 1, 2023, then November 1, 2023, is your annuity starting date.

Payments before the annuity starting date. Withdrawals from a commercial annuity contract before the annuity starting date are taxable to the extent that the cash value of the contract (ignoring any surrender charge), immediately before the distribution, exceeds your investment in the contract at that time. This is a LIFO (last-in, first-out) rule, since payments are taxed first on the growth in the contract's value before you can recover your investment tax free. Loans under the contract or pledges are treated as cash withdrawals.

Payments on or after the annuity starting date. If the withdrawal is a regular (not variable) annuity payment, the part of the annuity payment that is allocated to your cost investment is treated as a nontaxable return of the cost; the balance is taxable income earned on the investment. The payer of the annuity probably will tell you on Form 1099-R (Box 2a) what the taxable amount is, but if not, you can compute the taxable part of your annuity payment by following the six steps listed below under "Taxable Portion of Commercial Annuity Payments." If you have a variable annuity, the computation of the tax-free portion is discussed following Step 6.

Payments on or after the annuity starting date that are not part of the annuity, such as dividends, are generally taxable, but there are exceptions. If the contract is a life insurance or endowment contract, withdrawals of earnings are tax free to the extent of your investment, unless the contract is a modified endowment contract.

Filing Tip

Surrender of Contract

Payments on a complete surrender of the annuity contract or at maturity are taxable only to the extent they exceed your investment.

If your annuity is—	Your investment is—
Single premium annuity contract	The single premium paid.
Deferred annuity contract	The total premiums paid.
A gift	Your donor's cost.
An employee annuity for which the rules for commercial annuities apply because you cannot use the simplified method at *7.24*	The total of your after-tax contributions to the plan plus your employer's contributions that you were required to report as income
With a refund feature	The value of the refund feature; *see* "Value of refund feature" below.

Taxable Portion of Commercial Annuity Payments

The payer of your annuity will generally enter the taxable amount in Box 2a of Form 1099-R, but Box 2a will be left blank if the payer lacks the data needed to compute the amount. You can compute the taxable amount yourself using Steps 1-6 below. However, if you have a variable annuity, *see* the text and the Andrew Taylor Examples below Step 6.

If your annuity began before 2023, keep in mind that the tax-free percentage determined for the first year of your annuity remains the same every year; *see* Step 3 below.

Step 1: Figure your investment in the annuity contract as of the annuity starting date. You must know your investment in the contract to figure the tax-free and taxable portions of your annuity payments. If you have no investment in the contract, annuity income is fully taxable; therefore, ignore Steps 2 through 6.

Determine the above investment amounts as of the annuity starting date (defined on page 199). From that total investment, subtract the following items, if any:

- Any premiums refunded, and rebates or dividends received on or before the annuity starting date, or, if later, the date you received your first payment.
- Additional premiums for double indemnity or disability benefits.
- Any other tax-free amounts received under the contract before the later of the two dates in bullet #1.
- Value of refund feature; *see* below.

Value of refund feature. Your investment in the contract is reduced by the value, if any, of a refund feature. Your annuity has a refund feature when these three requirements are present: (1) the refund under the contract depends, even in part, on the life expectancy of at least one person; (2) the contract provides for payments to a beneficiary or the annuitant's estate after the annuitant's death; and (3) the payments to the estate or beneficiary are a refund of the amount paid for the annuity.

The refund feature is considered to be zero if (1) for a joint and survivor annuity, both annuitants are age 74 or younger, the payments are guaranteed for less than 2½ years, and the survivor's annuity is at least 50% of the first annuitant's (retiree's) annuity or (2) for a single life annuity without survivor benefits, the payments are guaranteed for less than 2½ years and you are age 57 or younger.

If the value of the refund feature is not zero, it must be figured using a life expectancy multiple from Table VII in IRS Publication 939; the multiple depends on the number of years for which payment is guaranteed; *see* Publication 939 for an example.

Step 2: Find your expected return. This is the total of all the payments you and other eligible annuitants (if any) are expected to receive under the contract.

If your annuity is for a specific number of years not tied to your life expectancy, such as a three-year annuity (36 months), your expected return is 36 months multiplied by the contractual monthly payment.

For annuities tied to life expectancy, the computation of expected return depends on the type of annuity you have, as this determines the IRS life expectancy table you must use. For example, if you are to receive annuity payments for the rest of your life, your expected return is figured by multiplying the amount of the annual payment by a multiple based on your life expectancy as of your birthday nearest to the annuity starting date *(see above)*. Your life expectancy is the single life multiple found in IRS Table V from Publication 939, shown in *Table 7-2* on page 203. The multiple from the table assumes monthly payments and must be adjusted slightly (*Table 7-3* on page 203) if payments are made quarterly, semiannually or annually. The Bill Jones Example on page 204 shows how expected return for a single life annuity is figured, as well as the computation of the tax-free and taxable portions of the annuity.

Different life expectancy tables are used to determine expected return if your annuity is a joint and survivor annuity or an annuity for the shorter of a fixed number of years or the rest of your life. These rules are discussed in *7.22*.

Step 3: Figure your tax-free percentage. Divide the investment in the contract (Step 1) by the expected return (Step 2) and round to three decimal places. The result is the tax-free percentage (also called exclusion percentage) of each annuity payment. A different computation of the tax-free percentage applies to variable annuities; *see* page 202.

The tax-free percentage determined for the first year of your annuity stays the same in future years; *see* Step 5.

Step 4: Total your annuity payments for the year. For example, you received 10 monthly payments of $1,000 as your annuity began in March. Your total payments are $10,000 ($1,000 × 10).

Step 5: Nontaxable portion—multiply the tax-free percentage in Step 3 by the number of payments from Step 4. The result is the nontaxable portion (or excludable amount) of your annuity payments for the year.

The tax-free percentage determined for the first year under Step 3 remains the same in future years; *see* the Bill Jones Example on page 204. If the annuity payments increase due to a cost-of-living adjustment, the tax-free amount does not change; the tax-free percentage from the first year applies only to the original payments (as of the annuity starting date) and the extra amount (due to the cost-of-living increase) is fully taxable.

There is a limit on the total amount you can exclude from income over the years. Your lifetime exclusion may not exceed your net cost, which is your unrecovered investment as of the annuity starting date, without reduction for any refund feature. Once you have recovered your net cost, further payments are fully taxable. If you die before recovering your net cost, an itemized deduction is allowed on your final income tax return for the unrecovered cost; the deduction may be claimed as an "Other" itemized deduction on Schedule A of Form 1040 or 1040-SR *(19.1)*. If the contract has a refund feature and a refund of the unrecovered investment is made under the contract to your beneficiary, the beneficiary is allowed the "other" itemized deduction.

The rule is different if your annuity starting date was before 1987. There is no lifetime limit on your total exclusion. Regardless of your age, you apply the same tax-free percentage to each payment you receive, so you can exclude more than your investment.

Step 6: Taxable portion for the year—subtract the amount in Step 5 from the amount in Step 4. The result is the portion of your annuity payments that is subject to tax for the year.

Note: See the Bill Jones Example on page 204, which shows how to figure the taxable and nontaxable portions for a single life annuity.

EXAMPLES of Variable Annuities (see text below the examples)

1. In April 2023, Andrew Taylor invested $12,000 in a variable annuity with a starting date of June 1, 2023. Starting July 1, 2023, he is to receive variable annual installments for life. Andrew's age (nearest birthday) on the June 1 annuity starting date was 65. To figure the tax-free part of each annual payment, he uses a life expectancy multiple of 20.0, the amount shown in *Table 7-2* for a person age 65. The amount of each payment excluded from tax is:

Investment in the contract	$12,000
Multiple (from *Table 7-2*)	20.0
Amount of each payment excluded from tax ($12,000 ÷ 20)	$600

   If the first annual payment is $920, then $320 ($920 – $600) will be included in Andrew's 2023 income.

2. Assume that, after receiving the 2023 payment of $920 in Example 1, Andrew receives $500 in 2024 and $1,200 in 2025. None of the $500 received in 2024 is taxable, as $600 is excludable from each annual payment (Example 1). Andrew may also elect to recompute his annual exclusion starting with the 2025 payment. The exclusion is recomputed as follows:

Amount excludable in 2024	$600
Amount received in 2024	500
Difference	$100
Multiple as of 1/1/25 (*see Table 7-2* for age 67)	18.4
Amount added to previously determined annual exclusion ($100 ÷ 18.4 = $5.43)	$5.00
Revised annual exclusion for 2025 and later years ($600 + $5)	$605
Amount taxable in 2025 ($1,200 – $605)	$595

Variable annuities. If you have a variable annuity that pays different benefits depending on cost-of-living indexes, profits earned by the annuity fund, or similar fluctuating standards, the tax-free portion of each payment is computed by dividing your investment in the contract (Step 1 above) by the total number of payments you expect to receive. If the annuity is for a definite period, the total number of payments equals the number of payments to be made each year multiplied by the number of years you will receive payments. If the annuity is for life, you divide the amount you invested in the contract by a multiple obtained from the appropriate life expectancy table; *see* Step 2 and *7.22*. The result is the tax-free amount of your annual annuity income; *see* the Andrew Taylor Example above.

If you receive a payment for a year that is less than the nontaxable amount, you may elect when you receive the next payment to recalculate the nontaxable portion. The amount by which the prior nontaxable portion exceeded the payment you received is divided by the number of payments you expect as of the time of the next payment. The result is added to the previously calculated nontaxable portion, and the sum is the amount of each future payment to be excluded from tax. A statement must be attached to your return explaining the recomputation; *see* Andrew Taylor, Example 2 above.

Penalty on Premature Withdrawals From Deferred Annuities

Withdrawals before the annuity starting date may be taxable or tax free, depending on whether the cash value of the contract exceeds your investment, as discussed at the beginning of *7.21*.

Withdrawals before age 59½ are also generally subject to a penalty of 10% of the amount includible in income. A withdrawal from an annuity contract is penalized unless:

1. You have reached age 59½ or have become totally disabled.

2. The distribution is part of a series of substantially equal payments, made at least annually over your life expectancy or over the joint life expectancies of you and a beneficiary. If you can avoid the penalty under this exception and you change to a nonqualifying distribution method within five years or before age 59½, such as where you receive a lump sum, a recapture tax will apply to the payments received before age 59½.

3. The payment is received by a beneficiary or estate after the policyholder's death.

4. Payment is from a qualified retirement plan, tax-sheltered annuity, or IRA; in this case the penalty rules for qualified plans *(7.13)* or IRAs *(8.8)* apply.

5. Payment is from an annuity contract under a qualified personal injury settlement.

6. Payment is from a single-premium annuity where the starting date is no more than one year from the date of purchase (an "immediate" annuity).

7. Payment is from an annuity purchased by an employer upon the termination of a qualified retirement plan and held until you separated from service.

Filing Tip

Form 5329 for Early Distribution Penalty

See the nearby text for exceptions to the penalty for pre-age 59½ distributions. If no exception to the early withdrawal penalty applies, you compute the 10% penalty in Part I of Form 5329.

7.22 Life Expectancy Tables for Figuring Expected Return for Commercial Annuities

Depending on what kind of annuity you have, IRS tables provide an age-based multiple which is used to figure your expected return (Step 2 in *7.21*). The table for single life annuities, IRS Table V, is shown at *Table 7-2* on the following page. The other IRS tables referred to below (as well as Table V) are in IRS Publication 939.

Annuity for life. If the annuity is for your life, you use the multiple shown in *Table 7-2* (next page) for your age as of your birthday nearest to annuity starting date; *see* the Bill Jones Example on page 204.

Joint and survivor annuity. If you have a joint and survivor annuity that after your death will pay a second annuitant (spouse or anyone else) the same lifetime payments that you are receiving, the expected return is based on your joint life expectancies, as shown in IRS Table VI in Publication 939. *See* Example 3 on page 204.

Table 7-2 Life Expectancy for Single Life Annuity

TABLE V From IRS Publication 939

Age	Multiple	Age	Multiple	Age	Multiple
5	76.6	42	40.6	79	10.0
6	75.6	43	39.6	80	9.5
7	74.7	44	38.7	81	8.9
8	73.7	45	37.7	82	8.4
9	72.7	46	36.8	83	7.9
10	71.7	47	35.9	84	7.4
11	70.7	48	34.9	85	6.9
12	69.7	49	34.0	86	6.5
13	68.8	50	33.1	87	6.1
14	67.8	51	32.2	88	5.7
15	66.8	52	31.3	89	5.3
16	65.8	53	30.4	90	5.0
17	64.8	54	29.5	91	4.7
18	63.9	55	28.6	92	4.4
19	62.9	56	27.7	93	4.1
20	61.9	57	26.8	94	3.9
21	60.9	58	25.9	95	3.7
22	59.9	59	25.0	96	3.4
23	59.0	60	24.2	97	3.2
24	58.0	61	23.3	98	3.0
25	57.0	62	22.5	99	2.8
26	56.0	63	21.6	100	2.7
27	55.1	64	20.8	101	2.5
28	54.1	65	20.0	102	2.3
29	53.1	66	19.2	103	2.1
30	52.2	67	18.4	104	1.9
31	51.2	68	17.6	105	1.8
32	50.2	69	16.8	106	1.6
33	49.3	70	16.0	107	1.4
34	48.3	71	15.3	108	1.3
35	47.3	72	14.6	109	1.1
36	46.4	73	13.9	110	1.0
37	45.4	74	13.2	111	0.9
38	44.4	75	12.5	112	0.8
39	43.5	76	11.9	113	0.7
40	42.5	77	11.2	114	0.6
41	41.5	78	10.6	115	0.5

Table 7-3 Multiple Adjustment Table

If the number of whole months from the annuity starting date to the first payment date is—	0–1	2	3	4	5	6	7	8	9	10	11	12
And payments under the contract are to be made:												
Annually	+0.5	+0.4	+0.3	+0.2	+0.1	0.0	0.0	−0.1	−0.2	−0.3	−0.4	−0.5
Semiannually	+0.2	+0.1	0.0	0.0	−0.1	−0.2						
Quarterly	+0.1	0.0	−0.1									

If your joint and survivor annuity provides for a different payment amount to the survivor, you must separately compute the expected return for each of you and add them together; *see* Example 4 below.

Annuity is for a fixed number of years or for life, whichever is shorter. With this type of annuity, you use the multiple shown in IRS Table VIII for temporary life annuities; *see* Example 5 on page 205.

Birthday nearest annuity starting date. In looking up single life or joint life expectancy in the applicable table, use your age (and the age of a joint annuitant) at the birthday nearest to the annuity starting date. The number in the table next to this age is the life expectancy multiple used to figure your expected return; *see* Examples 1-5 below.

Adjustments for nonmonthly payments. An adjustment is required when your annuity payments are received quarterly, semiannually, or annually, rather than monthly; *see* Example 2 below and *Table 7-3* on page 203.

EXAMPLES

1. In March 2023, Bill Jones bought an annuity that will pay him $1,000 a month for life. Bill had his 66th birthday on April 14, 2023. He received his first monthly check on May 1, 2023, which covered the annuity payment for April. Bill's annuity starting date was April 1, 2023. He uses *Table 7-2* (page 203) to get his life expectancy multiple. For age 66, Bill finds the multiple 19.2. He multiplies 19.2 by his annual payment of $12,000 ($1,000 a month × 12 months) to get his expected return (Step 2 at *7.21*) of $230,400. Assume there is no refund feature and Bill's net investment (Step 1 at *7.21*) is $129,600. He divides his expected return into the net investment to get an exclusion percentage (Step 3 at *7.21*) of 56.3% ($129,600 ÷ $230,400 = 56.25, rounded to 56.3%). In 2023, Bill receives $8,000 in annuity payments ($1,000 in May through December) and reports $3,496 as taxable on his 2023 return:

Amount received	$8,000
Tax-free amount (56.3% exclusion percentage × $8,000)	4,504
Taxable portion	$3,496

   For 2024, $12,000 will be received ($1,000 a month). The amount excludable from income will be $6,756 (56.3% × $12,000), and the taxable portion, $5,244 ($12,000 – $6,756). The tax-free and taxable amounts for 2024 will apply in later years until Bill has excluded his net investment of $129,600. Thereafter, all payments will be fully taxable. If Bill dies before his total exclusions equal $129,600, the unrecovered amount is an allowable itemized deduction on his final income tax return.

2. Same facts as Example 1 except Bill receives quarterly annuity payments, with the first payment on July 1, 2023. Since the number of whole months from the annuity starting date of April 1 to the first payment date of July 1 is three full months, Bill adjusts the 19.2 multiple by -0.1, as shown in *Table 7-3* (page 203), reducing the multiple to 19.1. His expected return would then be $229,200 (19.1 x annual payment of $12,000).

3. Margo Smith buys a joint and survivor annuity in 2024 that will pay her $500 a month for her life ($6,000 a year), and after her death, the same $500 will be paid to her husband Joseph for the rest of his life. Margo is age 70 on her birthday nearest the annuity starting date and Joseph is age 67. IRS Table VI in Publication 936 provides a multiple of 22.0 for ages 70 and 67. The expected return (Step 2 at *7.21*) is $132,000, the annual payment of $6,000 multiplied by 22.00.

4. Same facts as Example 3 except that after Margo's death, Joseph will receive monthly payments of $350 ($4,200 a year). To figure the total expected return under the contract, Margo and Joseph must figure separate expected returns. Margo must reduce their combined multiple of 22.0 from Table VI (*see* Example 3), by her single life multiple from *Table 7-2* (page 203) to determine the multiple attributable to Joseph. Based on her age of 70, *Table 7-2* shows a multiple of 16.0, so the multiple attributable to Joseph is 6.0 (22.00 – 16.00). Margo's expected return is $96,000, equal to 16.0 (her multiple) x $6,000 (her annual payment, $500 x 12). Joseph's expected return is $25,200, equal to 6.0 (his multiple) x $4,200 (his annual payment, $350 × 12). The combined amount of $121,200 ($96,000 + $25,200) is the total expected return used in Step 2 (*7.21*).

5. Sofia buys an annuity that will pay her $500 a month ($6,000 a year) for five years or until she dies if sooner. She is 65 on her birthday nearest the annuity starting date. IRS Table VIII in Publication 939 provides a multiple of 4.9 for a person age 65 with a maximum 5-year annuity term. Sofia's expected return (Step 2 at *7.21*) is $29,400 ($6,000 annual payment × 4.9).

7.23 When You Convert Your Endowment Policy

When an endowment policy matures, you may elect to receive a lump sum, an annuity, an interest option, or a paid-up life insurance policy. If you elect—

A lump sum. You report the difference between your cost (premium payments less dividends) and what you receive.

An annuity before the policy matures or within 60 days after maturity. You report income in the years you receive your annuity *(7.21)*. Use as your investment in the annuity contract the cost of the endowment policy less premiums paid for other benefits such as double indemnity or disability income. If you elect the annuity option more than 60 days after maturity, you report income on the matured policy as if you received the lump sum; *see* above rule. The lump sum is treated as the cost investment in the annuity contract.

An interest option before the policy matures. You report only the interest as it is received, provided you do not have the right to withdraw the policy proceeds. If you have the right to withdraw the proceeds, you are treated as in constructive receipt; the difference between your cost and what you receive would be taxed as if you had received a lump sum.

Paid-up insurance. You report the difference between the present value of the paid-up life insurance policy and the premium paid for the endowment policy. In figuring the value of the insurance policy, you do not use its cash surrender value, but the amount you would have to pay for a similar policy with the company at the date of exchange. Your insurance company can give you this figure. The difference is taxed at ordinary income tax rates.

Tax-free exchange rules apply to the policy exchanges listed in *6.12*.

Gain on the sale of a life insurance policy is partly ordinary income and partly capital gain; *see 11.20*.

The proceeds of a veteran's endowment policy paid before the veteran's death are not taxable.

7.24 Reporting Employee Annuities

Tax treatment of employee annuity payments from a qualified employee plan, qualified employee annuity, or 403(b) plan *(7.19)* depends on the amount of your contributions and your annuity starting date. These rules are discussed in *7.25–7.26*. If payments are from a nonqualified employee plan, you must use the rules for commercial annuities *(7.21)*.

Fully taxable payments if you have no investment in the plan. If you did not contribute to the cost of a pension or employee annuity, and you did not report as income your employer's contributions, you are fully taxed on payments after the annuity starting date.

An employee is taxed on the full value of a nonforfeitable annuity contract that the employer buys him or her if the employer does not have a qualified pension plan. Tax is imposed in the year the policy is purchased. A qualified plan is one approved by the IRS for special tax benefits.

Disability pension before minimum retirement age. Disability payments received before you reach the minimum retirement age (at which you would be entitled under the plan to a regular retirement annuity) are fully taxable as wages. After minimum retirement age, payments are treated as an annuity *(7.25)*.

Partially taxable payments if you have an investment in the plan. If you and your employer both contributed to the cost of your annuity, the part of each payment allocable to your investment is tax free and the balance is taxable. You generally must use the simplified method to figure the tax-free portion allocable to your investment *(7.25)*. For withdrawals before the annuity starting date, *see 7.26*.

 *Filing Tip*

Credit or Deduction for Repaying Pension Overpayment Over $3,000

If you pay tax on a pension distribution and in the next year the plan determines that there was an overpayment, which you repay, and the repayment exceeds $3,000, you may claim whichever of the following would provide a lower tax for the year of repayment: (1) an "Other" itemized deduction, assuming you itemize deductions on Schedule A of Form 1040 or 1040-SR rather than taking the standard deduction *(13.1)*, or (2) a tax credit based on a recomputation of the prior year's tax *(2.8)*.

No deduction or credit is allowed if the repayment is $3,000 or less. For years before 2018, a repayment of $3,000 or less was potentially deductible as a miscellaneous itemized deduction subject to the 2% AGI floor, but the Tax Cuts and Jobs Act has suspended the itemized deduction for miscellaneous expenses subject to the 2% AGI floor for 2018 through 2025 *(19.2)*.

7.25 Simplified Method for Calculating Taxable Employee Annuity

If you have an investment in the plan and your annuity starting date was in 2023, you must use the simplified method explained below to figure the tax-free portion of your 2023 annuity payments from a qualified employer plan, qualified employee annuity, or 403(b) tax-sheltered annuity. The only exception is if you are age 75 or older on your annuity starting date and are entitled to guaranteed annuity payments for at least five years; in that case you must use the six-step method *(7.21)* for commercial annuities rather than the simplified method.

A beneficiary receiving a survivor annuity may use the simplified method.

If your annuity started in 2023. If your annuity started in 2023, figure the tax-free and taxable portions of your annuity by using Steps 1–4 below.

If you have a monthly annuity for your life only, the tax-free portion of each payment under Step 2 is based on the "number of expected monthly payments" shown for your age in Table 1 (from IRS Publication 575) shown below.

Use Table 2 (from IRS Publication 575) if your annuity benefits are payable for the lives of more than one annuitant, such as where you started to receive payments in 2023 under a joint and survivor annuity for you and your spouse. Combine your age with the age of your survivor annuitant. If you are the primary annuitant and there is more than one survivor annuitant, combine your age and the youngest survivor annuitant's age when using Table 2. If there is no primary annuitant and the annuity is payable to you and other survivor annuitants, the ages of the oldest and youngest are combined. Disregard a survivor annuitant whose entitlement to payment is contingent on something other than the primary annuitant's death.

If your annuity started before 2023. If your annuity started before 2023 and you have been using the simplified method to report your annuity payments, continue to do so, using the applicable number of expected monthly payments from either Table 1 or Table 2, as discussed in Step 2.

Figuring taxable and tax-free payments under the simplified method. Under the simplified method, a level tax-free portion is determined for each monthly payment with the following steps:

Step 1. Figure your investment in the contract as of the annuity starting date. Include premiums you paid and any after-tax contributions you made to the employer's pension plan, plus employer contributions that were included in your pay. Reduce the total by any refunded premiums that you received by the annuity starting date, or, if later, the date of your first payment.

Step 2. Divide the investment from Step 1 by the number of expected monthly payments shown in Table 1 or Table 2 below, using your age on the annuity starting date. The result is the tax-free recovery portion of each monthly payment (monthly exclusion). However, multiply this amount by three (3 months) to get the tax-free portion if payments are made quarterly rather than monthly. The tax-free portion remains the same after the employee's death if a spouse or other beneficiary receives payments under a joint and survivor annuity.

Use Table 1 if your annuity is based on your life only. Also use Table 1 for a multiple-lives annuity with a starting date before 1998, taking into account only the primary annuitant's age as of the starting date.

Use Table 2 if your annuity benefits are payable for the lives of more than one annuitant and the annuity starting date was after December 31, 1997. The ages of the annuitants are combined as discussed earlier under "If your annuity started in 2023".

Step 3. Multiply the monthly exclusion amount from Step 2 by the number of monthly payments received during the year; this is the total tax-free payment for the year (your annual exclusion).

Unless your annuity starting date was before 1987, you need to keep track of your annual tax-free cost recoveries because your total tax-free

Filing Instruction

Simplified Method Mandatory

If your annuity starting date was in 2023, you must use the simplified method *(7.25)* to figure the taxable part of your 2023 payments, unless on the annuity starting date you were age 75 or older and your payments are guaranteed for at least five years.

recovery under the simplified method for all years is limited to your investment in the plan from Step 1. Once you, or you and your survivor annuitant, have recovered the full investment, further payments will be fully taxable. The tax-free amount for any year under the Step 3 computation cannot exceed the excess of your investment from Step 1 over the prior year cost recoveries. If the full investment has not been recovered when the last annuitant dies, the unrecovered investment is allowed on his or her final income tax return as an "Other" itemized deduction if deductions are itemized on Schedule A (rather than taking the standard deduction) on that return *(19.1)*.

If the annuity starting date was before 1987, the total exclusion for all years is not limited to the investment. You may continue to take your monthly exclusion (the Step 2 amount) for life, and if there is a survivor annuitant, he or she can continue to take the exclusion for as long as annuity payments are received.

Step 4. Step 4. Subtract the Step 3 tax-free payment from the total annuity received this year; this is the taxable annuity you must report on Form 1040 or Form 1040-SR. If the payer of the annuity shows a higher taxable amount on Form 1099-R, use the amount figured here.

Table 1 (from IRS Publication 575)

Age of primary annuitant at annuity starting date	Number of expected monthly payments	
	Annuity starting date before November 19, 1996	Annuity starting date after November 18, 1996
55 and under	300	360
56–60	260	310
61–65	240	260
66–70	170	210
71 and over	120	160

Table 2 (from IRS Publication 575)

Combined ages of annuitants at annuity starting date	Number of expected monthly payments
110 and under	410
111–120	360
121–130	310
131–140	260
141 and over	210

EXAMPLE

Fred Smith, age 57, retires and receives his first employee annuity payment August 1, 2023. The annuity is a joint and 50% survivor annuity with his wife Betty, also age 57. Fred receives an annuity of $1,500 per month and Betty will receive a survivor annuity of $750 per month after Fred's death. Fred's investment in the plan was $29,000. To figure the tax-free portion of each payment, Fred divides his $29,000 investment by 360, the number of expected monthly payments shown in Table 2 for two annuitants with a combined age of 114 years; the result is $80.56. Thus, the tax-free portion of each $1,500 payment is $81 and the balance of each payment, or $1,419 ($1,500 − $81), is taxable. On his 2023 return, Fred reports $7,095 as taxable annuity payments (5 payments × $1,419). In 2024, Fred will receive 12 monthly payments of $1,500, a total of $18,000, of which $972 will be excludable (12 × $81) and $17,028 will be taxable ($18,000 − $972).

In subsequent years, Fred will continue to exclude $81 of each monthly payment from income and report the rest as taxable until the full $29,000 investment is recovered. If Fred dies before the monthly exclusions total $29,000, Betty will also exclude $81 from each of her payments of $750 until the total plan investment of $29,000 is recovered. Once the $29,000 investment is recovered, all subsequent payments will be fully taxable to Betty. If Betty dies before the full investment is recovered, and itemized deductions are claimed on her final income tax return, an "Other" itemized deduction will be allowed on the final return for the unrecovered investment *(19.1)*.

7.26 Withdrawals From Employer's Qualified Retirement Plan Before Annuity Starting Date

You generally may not make completely tax-free withdrawals from your employer's qualified retirement plan, qualified employee annuity plan, or 403(b) plan before the annuity starting date, even if your withdrawals are less than your investment. On a withdrawal before the annuity starting date, you must pay tax on the portion of the withdrawal that is allocable to employer contributions (that were not reported as additional pay) and income earned on the contract; the portion of the withdrawal allocable to your investment is recovered tax free. However, if one of the exceptions below applies, the tax-free recovery may be increased.

To compute the tax-free recovery under the general rule, multiply the withdrawal by this fraction:

$$\frac{\text{Your total investment}}{\text{Your vested (nonforfeitable) account balance or accrued benefit}}$$

Your investment and vested benefit are determined as of the date of distribution.

Exceptions. More favorable investment recovery rules are allowed in the following cases:

1. Employer plans in effect on May 5, 1986. If on May 5, 1986, your employer's plan allowed distributions of employee contributions before separation from service, the above pro-rata recovery rule applies only to the extent that the withdrawal exceeds the total investment in the contract on December 31, 1986.

   For example, assume that as of December 31, 1986, you had an account balance of $9,750, which included $4,000 of your own contributions. If the plan on May 5, 1986, allowed pre-retirement distributions of employee contributions, you may receive prior to your annuity starting date withdrawals up to your $4,000 investment without incurring tax.

2. Separate accounts for employee contributions. A defined contribution plan (such as a profit-sharing plan) is allowed to account for after-tax employee contributions (and earnings on the contributions) separately from employer contributions (and earnings on the employer contributions). If separate accounting is maintained, the tax-free part of the withdrawal is increased because the account balance used as the denominator in the fractional computation includes only the employee's after-tax contributions and allocable earnings, without regard to the employer contributions (and allocable earnings).

Caution

Favorable Recovery Rules

Both of the favorable cost recovery rules discussed under "Exceptions" in this section *(7.26)* are complicated and you should consult your plan administrator to determine if the exceptions apply and how to make the required calculations.

CHAPTER 8

IRAs

There are several types of IRAs: Traditional IRAs, Roth IRAs, SIMPLE IRAs, and SEPs. You may personally set up a traditional or Roth IRA with your bank or broker. SIMPLE IRAs *(8.19)* and SEPs *(8.16)* are available only if your employer offers such plans. For 2023, the contribution limit for both traditional *(8.2)* and Roth IRAs *(8.21)* is $6,500, or $7,500 for individuals who are age 50 or older at the end of the year. There is no deduction for Roth IRA contributions, which are allowed only if you have earned income and only if your modified adjusted gross income (MAGI) is within specified limits *(8.21)*. If you have earnings, you may make traditional IRA contributions, which are either fully deductible, partly deductible, or not deductible at all, depending on whether you (and your spouse) have retirement coverage where you work and if so, whether your MAGI subjects you to the deduction phaseout rules *(8.4)*.

Traditional IRA distributions are generally fully taxable and, if made before age 59½, subject to a penalty; *see 8.12* for penalty exceptions. Minimum annual distributions from a traditional IRA must begin after you reach the required beginning date *(8.13)*.

Although annual contributions to a Roth IRA are not deductible *(8.21)*, the Roth IRA has a major tax advantage: tax-free withdrawals of earnings may be made after a five-year waiting period if you are over age 59½ *(8.25)*. Tax-free withdrawals of contributions may be made at any time. A traditional IRA may also be converted to a Roth IRA; conversions are taxable *(8.23)*.

Low-to-moderate-income taxpayers may be able to claim a tax credit on Form 8880 for contributions to a traditional IRA, Roth IRA, SIMPLE IRA, or salary-reduction SEP *(25.11)*.

Caution

IRA Fees and Brokerage Commissions

Broker's commissions, if any, that are paid when you make investments for your IRA are considered IRA contributions subject to the annual contribution limit ($6,500, or $7,500 if age 50 or older for 2023). However, fees paid to set up or manage an IRA, and annual account maintenance fees, are not considered IRA contributions if they are separately billed. Currently, there is no deduction for the fees. For 2018 through 2025, the Tax Cuts and Jobs Act has suspended the deduction for investment fees and all other miscellaneous expenses that for years before 2018 were allowable as a miscellaneous itemized deduction subject to the 2% of adjusted gross income floor *(19.1).*

Planning Reminder

Do You Have to File a Form When You Contribute to a Traditional IRA?

You do not have to file any forms with your tax return when you set up or make deductible contributions to a traditional IRA. Form 8606 must be attached to Form 1040 or Form 1040-SR if you make nondeductible contributions to a traditional IRA *(8.6).* The trustee or issuer of your IRA will report your contribution to the IRS on Form 5498, and you should receive a copy.

Caution

Restrictions on Collectibles Investments

If you have a self-directed traditional IRA and you invest in collectibles, such as art works, gems, stamps, antiques, rugs, metals, guns, or certain coins, you will have to pay a tax on your investment. The investment is treated as a taxable distribution to you in the year you make it. Coins are treated as collectibles, except for state-issued coins or certain U.S. minted gold, silver, and platinum coins. There is also an exception for gold, silver, platinum, or palladium bullion held by the IRA trustee, provided the fineness of the metal meets commodity market standards. If bullion is stored with a company other than the IRA trustee, the investment is subject to the deemed distribution rule for collectibles. To date, the IRS has not ruled on whether Bitcoin or other digital currency can be held in an IRA.

8.1 Starting a Traditional IRA

If you have earnings, you may contribute to a traditional IRA up to an annual limit *(8.2).* The contribution may be deductible *(8.4)* or nondeductible *(8.6).* Earnings within the IRA accumulate tax free until withdrawals are made *(8.8).*

You also may set up a traditional IRA by rolling over a distribution received from a qualified employer plan. For example, if you receive a lump-sum payment from a qualified employer plan upon retirement, changing jobs, or becoming totally disabled, you may make a tax-free rollover to a traditional IRA *(7.8).* If you have a traditional IRA, you can roll it over or make a direct transfer to a different traditional IRA *(8.10).*

Your employer can set up a "deemed IRA" as a separate account under a qualified retirement plan. As long as the separate account otherwise meets IRA requirements, you can make voluntary employee contributions that will be treated as IRA contributions subject to the regular IRA rules. The separate account can be treated as a traditional IRA or Roth IRA *(8.20).*

Roth IRAs. A Roth IRA is an alternative to a traditional IRA. Roth IRA contributions are never deductible, but there are tax advantages for withdrawals. Annual contributions to a Roth IRA and conversions of traditional IRAs to Roth IRAs are discussed at *8.20–8.23.*

Restrictions on traditional IRAs. Excess contributions *(8.7)* are penalized. You may withdraw funds from a traditional IRA at any time, but if you take money out before the date you reach age 59½ or become disabled, you are subject to a penalty unless an exception applies *(8.12).* Pledging the account as collateral is treated as a taxable distribution from the account *(8.8).* All traditional IRA withdrawals are fully taxable except for amounts allocable to nondeductible contributions *(8.8–8.9).* When you reach your "required beginning date" *(8.13),* you must start receiving required minimum distributions annually from the account.

If your IRA loses value because of poor investments, you may not deduct the loss.

Types of traditional IRAs. You may set up an IRA as:

1. An individual retirement account with a bank, savings and loan association, federally insured credit union, or other qualified person or instituion as trustee or custodian. An individual retirement account is technically a trust or custodial account. Your contribution may be invested in vehicles such as certificates of deposit, mutual funds, and certain limited partnerships.

2. An individual retirement annuity by purchasing an annuity contract (including a joint and survivor contract for the benefit of you and your spouse) issued by an insurance company; no trustee or custodian is required. The contract, endorsed to meet the terms of an IRA, is all that is required. It must provide for flexible premiums up to the annual contribution limit, so that if your compensation changes, your payment may also change. As borrowing or pledging of the contract is not allowed under an IRA, the contracts will not contain loan provisions. Endowment contracts that provide life insurance protection may not be used as individual retirement annuities.

You may set up one type of IRA one year and choose another form the next year. You also may split your contribution between two or more investment vehicles. For example, you are eligible to contribute $6,500 for 2023 if under age 50. You may choose to put $3,000 into an individual retirement annuity and $3,500 into an individual retirement account with a bank, mutual fund, or brokerage firm.

Self-directed IRA. If you wish to take a more active role in managing your IRA investments, you may set up a "self-directed" IRA using an IRS model form. The model trust (Form 5305) and the model custodial account agreement (Form 5305-A) meet the requirements of an exempt individual retirement account and so do not require a ruling or determination letter approving the exemption of the account and the deductibility of contributions made to the account. If you use this method, you still have to find a bank or other institution or trustee to handle your account or investment. Investments in a self-directed IRA are subject to restrictions; *see* the Caution in *8.1.*

SIMPLE IRA. If you work for a company with 100 or fewer workers, your employer may set up a SIMPLE IRA to which you may make salary reduction contributions *(8.18)*.

Contributions are allowed up to the filing due date. To make deductible or nondeductible IRA contributions for a year, you have until the regular filing due date (without extensions) of the return for that year. Since the deadline for 2023 returns is April 15, 2024 (page 6), you have until the April 15 due date to make your contribution for 2023. For a contribution to count as a 2023 contribution, it must be made by the April 15 due date, even if you get an extension to file your 2023 return *(46.3)*. If you make a contribution between January 1 and April 15, 2024, make sure the IRA trustee or custodian designates it as a 2023 contribution (and not as a 2024 contribution) if that is what you intend.

8.2 Contribution Limit for Traditional IRAs

You may make contributions to a traditional IRA for 2023 of up to $6,500, or $7,500 if you are age 50 or older at the end of 2023, provided that you have at least $6,500/$7,500 of earned income (compensation; *see* below) in 2023, such as wages, salary, or net self-employment earnings. If your earned income is less than $6,500 ($7,500 if age 50 or older), the contribution limit is 100% of your pay or net earned income if self-employed. If you have more than one traditional IRA, the limit applies to total contributions to all of the IRAs for the year.

There is no age limit for contributions; *see* the nearby Law Alert. Also, there is no minimum age for contributing to an IRA. So, for example, if a 16-year old has a summer job, he or she may contribute up to their earnings (but no more than $6,500).

If you are married filing jointly, you may each contribute up to $6,500 (or $7,500 if age 50 or older) to an IRA for 2023, as long as your combined earned income covers the contributions *(8.3)*.

Contributions for 2023 may be made up to the filing deadline of April 15, 2024; this is the deadline even if you obtain a filing extension for your 2023 return.

Are contributions deductible? Contributions up to the $6,500 or $7,500 limit (or up to your compensation if less) may or may not be deductible. Your contributions for 2023 are fully deductible if neither you nor your spouse is an active participant in an employer plan or self-employed retirement plan. The deduction limit is phased out for active plan participants with modified adjusted gross income (MAGI) over an annual threshold. For 2023, the MAGI phaseout threshold for single persons is $73,000. The phaseout threshold on a 2023 joint return is generally $116,000 *(8.3, 8.4)*, but a more favorable $218,000 phaseout threshold applies to a jointly filing spouse who is not a plan participant *(8.4)*. *See* *8.4* for details on the deduction phaseout rules for active plan participants.

> **EXAMPLE**
>
> A trader whose sole income was derived from stock dividends and gains in buying and selling stocks contributed to an IRA. The IRS disallowed the deduction on the grounds that his income was not earned income.
>
> If you live in a community property state, the fact that one-half of your spouse's income is considered your income does not entitle you to make contributions to an IRA. Your contribution must either be based on pay earned through your services or, if you file jointly, it must be allowed under the spousal IRA rules *(8.3)*.

Contributions must be based on compensation. Traditional IRA contributions, whether deductible or nondeductible, must generally be based on taxable compensation received for rendering personal services, such as salary, wages, commissions, tips, fees, bonuses, jury fees, or net earnings from self-employment (less retirement plan contributions on behalf of the self-employed). If you elect the foreign earned income exclusion *(36.1)*, the excluded income may not be the basis of an IRA contribution. There is one type of pay that may be counted as compensation for IRA purposes although it is not taxable, and that is nontaxable combat pay *(35.4)*. Although it is not pay for services, taxable alimony *(37.1)* may be treated as compensation for IRA purposes; *see* below.

 *Law Alert*

There Is No Age Limit for Traditional IRA Contributions

You may make traditional IRA contributions (deductible or nondeductible) regardless of how high your age, provided you have compensation for the year *(8.2)*. This rule took effect with 2020 returns. The SECURE Act repealed the prior-law rule that for 2019 and earlier years barred contributions to a traditional IRA if you were age 70½ or older at the end of the year.

There has never been an age limit for Roth IRA contributions. Contributions to a Roth IRA may be made regardless of your age, provided you have compensation *(8.2)* to support the contribution and your income is within the annual limit allowed under the Roth IRA contribution rules *(8.21)*.

 *Planning Reminder*

IRA Contribution Based on Tax-Free Combat Pay

Members of the armed services serving in a combat zone *(35.4)* can contribute to either a traditional IRA or a Roth IRA *(8.21)* based on their tax-free combat pay. Without this law, members of the military who did not have any earnings apart from the combat zone pay could not make IRA contributions, which otherwise must be based on taxable compensation.

An IRA contribution (deductible or nondeductible) may not be based upon:
1. Investment income such as interest, dividends, or profits from sales of property;
2. Deferred compensation, pensions, or annuities;
3. Income earned abroad for which the foreign earned income exclusion is claimed; or
4. Social Security benefits, disability benefits, workers' compensation, or unemployment compensation.

Working for spouse. If you work for your spouse, you may make an IRA contribution provided you actually perform services and receive an actual payment of wages. In one situation, a wife who worked as a receptionist and assistant to her husband, a veterinarian, failed to meet the second test. Her husband did not pay her a salary. Instead, he deposited all income from his business into a joint bank account held with his wife. In addition, no federal income tax was withheld from her wages. The IRS ruled that the wife could not set up her own IRA, even though she performed services; she failed to receive actual payment. Depositing business income into a joint account is neither actual nor constructive payment of the wife's salary. Furthermore, any deduction claimed for the wife's wages was disallowed.

Self-employed may make IRA contributions. IRA contributions may be based on net self-employment earnings *(45.1)*. For IRA purposes, net earnings from Schedule C are reduced by deductible contributions made on your behalf to qualified plans and SEPs *(41.5)* and by the deductible portion of self-employment tax liability *(45.3)*. If you have a net loss for the year, you may not make an IRA contribution unless you also have wages.

If you have more than one self-employed activity, you must aggregate profits and losses from all of your self-employed businesses to determine if you have net income on which to base an IRA contribution. For example, if one self-employed business produces a net profit of $15,000 but another a net loss of $20,000, you may not make an IRA contribution based on the net profit of $15,000 as you have an overall loss. This netting rule does not apply to salary or wage income. If you are an employee who also has an unprofitable business, you may make an IRA contribution based on your salary.

If you have a self-employed retirement plan from your business, you are considered an active participant in a retirement plan for purposes of the adjusted gross income phaseout rules *(8.4)*.

Taxable alimony treated as compensation. A divorced spouse with little or no earnings may treat taxable alimony as compensation for IRA purposes. Alimony is taxable only if received under a pre-2019 decree that meets the tests at *37.2*. If your alimony is taxable, you generally may make an IRA contribution for 2023 equal to 100% of the taxable alimony you received in 2023, up to the $6,500 limit ($7,500 if age 50 or older). However, if you are an active participant in an employer plan and your adjusted gross income exceeds the $73,000 phaseout threshold for unmarried individuals, *see 8.4* for the phaseout of the deduction limit. Alimony received under a post-2018 divorce or separation agreement is not taxable and is not treated as compensation for IRA purposes *(37.1)*.

Stipends and non-tuition fellowship payments. Such payments received by graduate and postdoctoral students after 2019 can be treated as compensation for purposes of making an IRA contribution as long as such amounts are includible in gross income.

Qualified reservist repayments. If you were called to active duty as a member of the reserves for over 179 days, or indefinitely, and took a distribution from your IRA during your active duty period, the distribution may be repaid to an IRA within the two-year period beginning on the day after the end of the active duty period. The repayment is allowed regardless of the regular IRA contribution limit for the year of repayment. The repaid amount is not deductible. The qualified reservist repayment must be reported as a nondeductible IRA contribution *(8.6)* on Line 1 of Form 8606.

8.3 Contributions to a Traditional IRA If You Are Married

If both you and your spouse earned compensation *(8.2)* in 2023 of at least $6,500 and you are both under age 50 at the end of the year, each of you may make a contribution of up to $6,500 to a traditional IRA for 2023 by April 15, 2024. Under the spousal IRA rule *(see below)*, the $6,500 per spouse contribution limit applies even if only one of you has compensation, provided you file jointly and your combined taxable compensation is at least $13,000. An additional contribution of up to $1,000 can be made for each spouse who is age 50 or older by the end of 2023. There is no upper age limit for making contributions; *see* the Law Alert at the beginning of *8.2*.

Contributions for 2023 are fully deductible up to the $6,500 limit ($7,500, if applicable) if neither you nor your spouse was covered by an employer retirement plan during the year. If either one of you was an active plan participant *(8.5)*, you are both considered active participants, and a deduction may be limited or disallowed *(8.4)* depending on your modified adjusted gross income (MAGI). However, if you file jointly and only one of you was an active plan participant, a more favorable MAGI phaseout rule applies to the nonparticipant spouse, so that the spouse without coverage may be able to claim a deduction even if the participant spouse may not. The deduction phaseout rules are discussed below.

Spousal IRA contribution on joint return for nonworking or low-earning spouse. If you file a joint return for 2023, and you and your spouse are both under age 50 at the end of the year, you may each contribute up to $6,500 to a traditional IRA as long as your combined taxable compensation *(8.2)* is at least $13,000. If you are both age 50 or older by the end of 2023, the contribution limit for each of you is raised to $7,500, so long as your combined taxable compensation is at least $15,000. If one spouse is under age 50 and one is age 50 or older at the end of 2023, the total contribution limit is $14,000 ($6,500 for the spouse under age 50 plus $7,500 for the spouse age 50 or more), provided your combined taxable compensation is at least $14,000. This spousal IRA rule allows a spouse with minimal earnings to "borrow" compensation from his or her spouse in order to reach the maximum contribution limit. In figuring a couple's combined compensation for purposes of the "borrowing" rule, the higher earning spouse's compensation is reduced by his or her deductible IRA contribution and by any regular contributions made by the higher earning spouse to a Roth IRA for the year.

Deduction phaseout rule for spouses filing jointly for 2023. If neither you nor your spouse is an active participant in an employer plan *(8.5)* in 2023, the phaseout rules do not apply and each of you may deduct contributions up to the $6,500 or $7,500 (if age 50 or older) limit if you each have compensation *(8.2)* of at least that much.

If either you or your spouse was an active participant *(8.4)* in an employer retirement plan during 2023, the phaseout rule may limit or completely disallow an IRA deduction. However, even if one or both of you were active participants in an employer plan, the phaseout rule does not apply and you may each deduct contributions up to the $6,500/$7,500 limit (or compensation if less) if your 2023 joint return modified adjusted gross income (MAGI) *(8.4)* is $116,000 or less.

If both of you were active plan participants for 2023, the deduction limit is phased out over a $20,000 range once your joint return MAGI exceeds $116,000. Thus, no deduction is allowed for either of you if your 2023 joint return MAGI is $136,000 or more.

If you were not an active plan participant in 2023 but your spouse was, a different phaseout rule applies to each of you. Your spouse, as an active plan participant, is subject to the deduction phaseout if MAGI on the joint return is between $116,000 and $136,000; your spouse gets no deduction if joint MAGI is $136,000 or more. However, as the nonparticipant spouse, your deduction limit is not subject to phaseout unless MAGI on the joint return is over $218,000. Your deduction is phased out if joint MAGI is between $218,000 and $228,000, and no deduction is allowed if MAGI is $228,000 or more.

See 8.4 for an Example of how the reduced deduction limit is figured if MAGI is within the above phaseout ranges.

Deduction phaseout rule for married persons filing separately for 2023. If you are married, live together at any time during 2023, file separate returns for 2023, and either of you was an active participant in an employer plan, the other spouse is also considered an active participant. Both of you are subject to the $0 to $10,000 MAGI deduction phaseout range *(8.4)*.

Planning Reminder

Phaseout Rule for Nonparticipant Spouses

If you are not covered by an employer retirement plan but your spouse is, and you file a joint return for 2023, your individual deduction limit is not subject to the phaseout rule unless modified adjusted gross income (MAGI) on the joint return exceeds $218,000 (phaseout complete at $228,000 or more). For your spouse, who is covered by an employer plan, a deduction for 2023 is phased out if MAGI on the joint return is between $116,000 and $136,000.

If you live apart for all of 2023, you each figure IRA deductions as if single. Thus, the more favorable deduction phaseout range of $73,000 to $83,000 applies if you are covered by an employer retirement plan *(8.4)*. If you are not covered, you may claim a full deduction on your separate return.

EXAMPLE

Rhonda and Elliot Richards, both under age 50, file a joint return for 2023. Rhonda had salary income of $78,000 in 2023. Elliot was a full-time student and had no compensation. Rhonda may contribute up to $6,500 to her own traditional IRA for 2023. Even though Elliot did not work in 2023, a contribution of up to $6,500 may also be made to his traditional IRA for 2023. Given Rhonda's earnings exceeded $13,000, $6,500 of her earnings may be credited to Elliot for contribution purposes.

If Rhonda and Elliot's modified adjusted gross income (MAGI) *(8.4)* for 2023 does not exceed $116,000, contributions for each of them up to the $6,500 limit are fully deductible on their joint return. If MAGI on their 2023 joint return exceeded $116,000 and if Rhonda was an active participant in her employer's retirement plan during 2023, her deduction would be phased out over a MAGI range of $116,000–$136,000. Under the special rule for spouses who are not active participants, Elliot would be allowed a full $6,500 deduction for 2023 so long as the joint return MAGI was $218,000 or less. *See* the phaseout rules in *8.4*.

8.4 Restrictions on Traditional IRA Deduction for Active Participants in Employer Plans

If you are covered by an employer retirement plan, including a self-employed plan, you may be unable to make deductible IRA contributions to a traditional IRA. When you have coverage, your right to claim a full deduction, a limited deduction, or no deduction at all depends on your modified adjusted gross income (MAGI). If you are married, and your spouse has employer plan coverage for 2023 you are also considered to have coverage in most cases. However, if you file jointly and do not individually have employer plan coverage, a special MAGI phaseout rule may allow you to deduct IRA contributions even if a deduction for your spouse is limited or barred.

The deduction phaseout rules do not apply, regardless of your income, if you are unmarried and do not have employer plan coverage, or if you are married and neither of you has coverage. An IRA deduction of up to $6,500 ($7,500 if age 50 or older at end of year) is allowed for 2023 as long as you have compensation *(8.2)* of at least $6,500 ($7,500 if age 50 or older).

Are you an active plan participant? Generally, you are considered to be "covered" by a retirement plan if you are an active participant in the plan for any part of the plan year ending within your taxable year. If you are an employee, your Form W-2 for 2023 should indicate whether you are covered for the year; if you are, the "Retirement plan" box within Box 13 of Form W-2 should be checked. Active participation *(8.5)* in a self-employed qualified plan or SEP *(Chapter 41)* is treated as employer plan coverage for purposes of the IRA deduction phaseout rules.

EXAMPLE

Sara Wartes, a college teacher, quit her job in 1988 and withdrew all of the contributions she had made to her employee pension plan. The Tax Court held that Sara could not claim an IRA deduction in that year. Sara was an active participant in the college plan during 1988 and under the phaseout rules based upon adjusted gross income, no IRA deduction was allowed. The court noted that the active participation test is not applied at the end of the year. Participation in a company plan at any time during the year triggers the deduction phaseout rules. This is true even where a person has forfeitable benefits.

Table 8-1 Can You Deduct Traditional IRA Contributions for 2023?

If you are—	MAGI phaseout threshold is—	MAGI phaseout range is—	No deduction (100% phaseout) if MAGI is—
Single, head of household, or qualifying widow/widower and you are NOT an active plan participant, or Married filing jointly or separately and NEITHER you nor your spouse are active plan participants	There is no phaseout regardless of your income. You may deduct contributions up to the full deduction limit *(8.2)*. If married filing jointly, *see* the spousal contribution rule at *8.3* if one spouse has little or no compensation		
Single or head of household and you are an active plan participant	$73,000	over $73,000 and under $83,000	$83,000 or more
Married filing jointly and both you and your spouse are active plan participants. The same phaseout threshold and phaseout range applies to each of you.	$116,000	over $116,000 and under $136,000	$136,000 or more
Married filing jointly and one of you is an active plan participant and one of you is not. Although you file jointly, you and your spouse have different phaseout thresholds and phaseout ranges.	Plan-participant spouse: $116,000	over $116,000 and under $136,000	$136,000 or more
	Non-participant spouse: $218,000	over $218,000 and under $228,000	$228,000 or more
Qualifying widow or widower and you are an active plan participant	$116,000	over $116,000 and under $136,000	$136,000 or more
Married filing separately, you lived with your spouse at any time during the year and either one of you is an active plan participant. The same unfavorable phaseout rule applies to each of you on your separate returns.	$0	over $0 and under $10,000	$10,000 or more
Married filing separately, you lived apart from your spouse for the entire year and one of you is an active plan participant and the other is not. You are each treated as if you were single for IRA deduction purposes.	Plan-participant spouse: $73,000	over $73,000 and under $83,000	$83,000 or more
	Non-participant spouse: There is no phaseout regardless of your income. On your separate return, you may deduct contributions up to the full deduction limit *(8.3)*.		

Worksheet 8-1 Figuring Your MAGI for Purposes of the Phaseout of the Traditional IRA Deduction Limit for 2023

In most cases, your modified adjusted gross income (MAGI) will be the same as the actual AGI reported on your tax return, but it may be higher because certain deductions and exclusions allowed in figuring AGI must be added back when figuring MAGI. You can use the following steps to figure your MAGI.

1. Enter the AGI reported on your return, assuming no deduction for traditional IRA contributions is claimed 1. _____

2. Enter any deductions claimed for:

    a. student loan interest *(33.13)* 2a. _____

    b. foreign housing expenses if self-employed *(36.4)*; 2b. _____

    c. Total of (a)—(b) 2c. _____

3. Enter any exclusions claimed for:

    a. employer-provided adoption assistance *(3.6)* 3a. _____

    b. interest on U.S. Savings Bonds used for tuition *(33.4)* 3b. _____

    c. foreign earned income *(36.1)* 3c. _____

    d. employer-provided foreign housing expenses *(36.4)* 3d. _____

    e. Total of (a)—(d) 3e. _____

4. Add Lines 1, 2c and 3e. This is your MAGI for 2023 traditional IRA deduction purposes. 4. _____

Worksheet 8-2 Phaseout of IRA Deduction Limit for 2023*

1. Enter your MAGI for 2023; *see* Line 4 of *Worksheet 8-1*. If MAGI equals or exceeds the phaseout endpoint for your status—either $10,000, $83,000, $136,000, or $228,000, as shown in the right-hand column of *Table 8-1*, STOP. You are not allowed any deduction; 100% of the deduction limit is phased out. Do not enter the MAGI here and do not complete the rest of this Worksheet. 1. _____

2. Enter your phaseout threshold—either $0, $73,000, $116,000, or $228,000, as shown in the second column of *Table 8-1*. 2. _____

3. Does your MAGI exceed your phaseout threshold?
Yes—If Line 1 exceeds Line 2, subtract Line 2 from Line 1. This is your excess MAGI. Go to Line 4.
No—If Line 2 equals or exceeds Line 1, you are not subject to any phaseout.
    Enter "0" here and also on Lines 4 and Line 5. Go to Line 6. 3. _____

4. If Line 2 (your phaseout threshold) is:
$0, $73,000, or $218,000—
    Your phaseout percentage is 60% if you were under age 50 at the end of 2023, or 70% if you were age 50 or older at the end of 2023. Enter it here and go to Line 5.
$116,000—
    Your phaseout percentage is 30% if you were under age 50 at the end of 2023, or 35% if you were age 50 or older at the end of 2023. Enter it here and go to Line 5. 4. _____

5. Multiply your excess MAGI on Line 3 by your phaseout percentage on Line 4. This is the phased out portion of your deduction limit. 5. _____

6. Subtract Line 5 from the lesser of:
(1) the maximum deduction limit of $6,500 if you were under age 50 at the end of 2023, or $7,500 if you were age 50 or older at the end of 2023, or
(2) your taxable compensation *(8.2, 8.3)* for 2023. 6. _____

7. If Line 6 is not a multiple of $10, round it up to the next highest multiple of $10. If this amount is under $200, increase it to $200. This is your deductible limit for 2023 traditional IRA contributions. 7. _____

Note: Use this Worksheet if you were an active participant in an employer retirement plan for 2023 *(8.5)*, or if you were married at the end of 2023 and either one of you was an active plan participant for 2023. If you were married and you and your spouse both contributed to a traditional IRA in 2023, or you will both contribute for 2023 by the filing due date, you should separately complete this Worksheet, as you may have different phaseout thresholds and phaseout percentages.

You are not an active plan participant but your spouse is. Even if you were not an active participant in an employer retirement plan at any time in 2023, your IRA deduction limit for 2023 may be phased out because of your spouse's coverage. However, if you file jointly, your own deduction is not limited unless modified adjusted gross income (MAGI) on the 2023 joint return exceeds $218,000. For your spouse who has employer plan coverage, the rule is different: the phaseout threshold for his or her 2023 deduction is joint MAGI of $116,000, assuming you file jointly.

As a nonparticipant, you are not allowed any deduction if MAGI on your joint return is $228,000 or more. A deduction for your spouse as an active participant is completely phased out if joint return MAGI for 2023 is $136,000 or more.

Harsher phaseout rules apply to married persons filing separately if they live together at any time during the year. If you lived with your spouse at any time during 2023 and either of you was an active plan participant in 2023, you are both subject to the $0 – $10,000 MAGI phaseout range on separate returns. Neither of you may claim an IRA deduction if the MAGI on your separate return is $10,000 or more.

If you are married filing separately and you lived apart for all of 2023, your spouse's plan participation does not affect your IRA deduction. Take into account only your own participation, if any, and if you are an active participant, your IRA deduction under the phaseout rules is figured as if you were single, so for 2023, the deduction limit is phased out if MAGI on your separate return is between $73,000 and $83,000; *see Table 8-1*. If you are not an active participant, you may claim the full deduction limit of $6,500, or $7,500 if age 50 or older, assuming you have compensation *(8.2)* of at least that much.

See *Table 8-1* for the 2023 phaseout ranges for you and your spouse.

Figuring Your 2023 IRA Deduction Under the Phaseout Rules

If you are an active plan participant for 2023, or you file a joint return for 2023 and your spouse is an active participant for 2023, the full deduction limit (lesser of $6,500/$7,500 (age 50 or older at end of year) or your compensation; *see 8.2*) is available to you only if your modified adjusted gross income (MAGI) does not exceed the applicable phaseout threshold for your status. Use *Worksheet 8-1* to figure your MAGI and then *see Table 8-1* for the 2023 phaseout thresholds and phaseout ranges. As shown in *Table 8-1*, the deduction limit for active plan participants is phased out over the first $10,000 of MAGI exceeding the threshold unless you are married filing jointly or a qualifying widow/widower who is an active plan participant, in which case the phaseout range doubles to $20,000.

If your MAGI exceeds your phaseout threshold but does not exceed the phaseout endpoint (shown in the right-hand column of *Table 8-1*), you can figure your deduction limit by applying the steps of *Worksheet 8-2*. If you are married and both you and your spouse are contributing to traditional IRAs for 2023, you should separately figure your deduction limits, as your phaseout threshold and phaseout range may be different from that of your spouse. The Examples 1-4 below illustrate the computation of the deduction limit.

Nondeductible contributions. Any contributions exceeding the amount allowed under the above rules may be treated as nondeductible IRA contributions *(8.6)*. Alternatively, the excess may be contributed to a Roth IRA if allowed under the Roth IRA rules *(8.21)*.

Figuring your IRA deduction if you receive Social Security benefits. If you or your spouse *(8.3)* is an active participant in an employer plan and either of you receives Social Security benefits, you need to make an extra computation before you can figure whether an IRA deduction is allowed. First follow the rules discussed in *34.3* to determine if part of your Social Security benefits would be subject to tax, assuming no IRA deduction were claimed. If none of your benefits would be taxable, you follow the regular rules above for determining IRA deductions. If part of your Social Security benefits would be taxable, MAGI for IRA purposes is increased by the taxable benefits. The allowable IRA deduction is then taken into account to determine the actual amount of taxable Social Security. IRS Publication 590-A has worksheets for making these computations.

 *Planning Reminder*

Roth IRA vs. Deductible IRA

Even if you qualify for a full IRA deduction, you may want to consider making a nondeductible contribution to a Roth IRA *(8.21)*. For example, you may be willing to give up the current tax deduction in order to create a Roth IRA from which distributions will be completely tax free after you reach age 59½ and a five-year waiting period has passed. If you choose to make a deductible contribution to a traditional IRA, distributions from the traditional IRA will be taxable. You may also prefer the Roth IRA advantage of not having to take required minimum distributions, as you must do with traditional IRAs *(8.13)*.

EXAMPLES

1. Rob Porter is single and under age 50 at the end of 2023. He is an active participant in an employer retirement plan. His salary for 2023 is $66,865 and his MAGI for 2022 is $74,343. His MAGI exceeds the $73,000 phaseout threshold for single persons *(Table 8-1)* by $1,343. Following the steps of *Worksheet 8-2*, the maximum deductible contribution Rob can make to a traditional IRA for 2023 is $5,200, figured as follows:

1.	MAGI for 2023	$74,343.00
2.	Phaseout threshold for single taxpayer	73,000.00
3.	Excess MAGI (Line 1– Line 2)	1,343.00
4.	60% phaseout percentage for single taxpayer under age 50 (Step 4 of *Worksheet 8-2*)	.60
5.	$1,343 (Line 3) x .60 (Line 4). This amount is phased out.	805.80
6.	$6,000 deduction limit -$805.80 phased out amount (Line 5)	5,194.20
7.	Since $5,194.20 on Line 6 is not a multiple of $10, round it up to the next highest multiple of $10. This is Rob's deductible limit for 2023.	5,200.00

2. Ted and Lynn Baker are both under age 50 at the end of 2023 and they file a 2023 joint return. They report wages of $58,770 for Ted and $60,250 for Lynn. Their modified adjusted gross income (MAGI) for 2023 is $119,020. Ted and Lynn are both active participants in employer retirement plans in 2023 and so they are both subject to the $116,000 phaseout threshold *(Table 8-1)*. Following the steps of *Worksheet 8-2*, each of them may make a deductible contribution of up to $5,600 to a traditional IRA for 2023, figured as follows:

1.	MAGI for 2022	$119,020.00
2.	Phaseout threshold for married person filing jointly	116,000.00
3.	Excess MAGI (Line 1 – Line 2)	3,020.00
4.	30% phaseout percentage for married person filing jointly under age 50 (Step 4 of *Worksheet 8-2*)	.30
5.	$3,020 (Line 3) x .30 (Line 4). This amount is phased out.	906.00
6.	$6,500 deduction limit -$906 phased out amount (Line 5)	5,594
7.	Given $5,594 on Line 6 is not a multiple of $10, round it up to $5,600, the next highest multiple of $10. This is the deductible limit for both Ted and Lynn. On their 2023 joint return, they can each deduct IRA contributions of up to $5,600, for a total maximum deduction of $11,200 on their joint return.	$5,600

3. Assume the same facts as in Example 2 except that only Lynn was an active participant in an employer plan. Ted and Lynn must figure their deduction limitations separately using different phaseout thresholds.

    For Lynn, the same $5,600 deduction limit applies as in Example 2. The $116,000 phaseout threshold applies, her excess MAGI is $3,020 ($119,020 MAGI on joint return – $116,000 threshold), and her deduction limit as shown in Example 2 is $5,600.

    For Ted, the special $218,000 threshold for nonparticipant spouses applies. Given the joint return MAGI is well below the $218,000 threshold, he is not affected by the phaseout rules and may deduct IRA contributions up to the $6,500 ceiling for 2023.

    On their 2023 joint return, they may deduct IRA contributions of $12,100: $5,600 for Lynn and $6,500 for Ted.

4. Assume the same facts as in Example 2 except that Lynn was age 51 at the end of 2023. Ted and Lynn will have different deduction limitations. They are both subject to the $116,000 phaseout threshold because both are active plan participants in 2023. However, since Lynn is at least age 50 at the end of 2023, her maximum deduction limit prior to any phaseout is $7,500, while the limit for Ted (under age 50) is $6,500. This means that both the phaseout percentage and phased out amount on Lines 4 and 5 are different for Lynn, as well as the deduction limit on Line 7.

For Ted, the deduction limit is $5,600 as shown in Example 2.
For Lynn, the deduction limit is $5,950, figured as follows:

1.	MAGI for 2022	$119,020.00
2.	Phaseout threshold for married person filing jointly	116,000.00
3.	Excess MAGI (Line 1-Line 2)	3,020.00
4.	35% phaseout percentage for married person filing jointly age 50 or older (Step 4 of *Worksheet 8-2*)	.35
5.	$3,020 (Line 3) x .35 (Line 4). This amount is phased out.	1,057
6.	$7,500 deduction limit - $1,057 phased out amount (Line 5)	6,443
7.	Given $6,443 on Line 6 is not a multiple of $10, round it up to $6,450, the next highest multiple of $10. This is Lynn's deductible limit for 2023.	$6,450

On their 2023 joint return, they may deduct IRA contributions of $12,050: $5,600 for Ted and $6,450 for Lynn.

8.5   Active Participation in an Employer Plan

Active participants in an employer retirement plan are subject to the phaseout rules for deducting contributions *(8.4)*. When a married couple files jointly and only one of the spouses was an active plan participant for the taxable year, a more favorable phaseout range applies to the non-participant spouse than to the spouse who was an active participant *(8.4)*.

An employer retirement plan means:

1. A qualified pension, profit-sharing, or stock bonus plan, including a qualified self-employed retirement plan, SIMPLE IRA, or simplified employee pension (SEP) plan;

2. A qualified annuity plan;

3. A tax-sheltered annuity; and

4. A plan established for its employees by the United States, by a state or political subdivision, or by any agency or instrumentality of the United States or a state or political subdivision, but not eligible state Section 457 plans.

Form W-2. If your employer checks the "Retirement plan" box within Box 13 of your 2023 Form W-2, this indicates that you were an active participant in your employer's retirement plan during the year. If you want to make a contribution before you receive your Form W-2, check the following guidelines and consult your plan administrator for your status.

Type of plan. Under any type of plan, if you are considered an active participant for any part of the plan year ending with or within your taxable year, you are treated as an active participant for the entire taxable year. Due to this plan year rule, you may be treated as an active participant even if you worked for the employer only part of the year. Under IRS guidelines, it is possible to be treated as an active participant in the year of retirement and even in the year after retirement if your employer maintains a fiscal year plan.

The plan year rule works differently for defined benefit pension plans than for defined contribution plans such as profit-sharing plans, 401(k) plans, money purchase pension plans, and stock bonus plans. These rules are discussed below.

If you are married, and either you or your spouse is treated as an active participant for 2023, *see 8.3* for the effect on the other spouse.

Defined benefit pension plans. You are treated as an active participant in a defined benefit pension plan if, for the plan year ending with or within your taxable year, you are eligible to participate in the plan. Under this rule, as long as you are eligible, you are treated as an active participant, even if you decline participation in the plan or you fail to make a mandatory contribution specified in the plan. Furthermore, you are treated as an active participant even if your rights to benefits are not vested.

 *Caution*

Active Participant Status

You are treated as an active participant in a 401(k) plan, profit-sharing plan, stock bonus plan, or money-purchase pension plan if contributions are made or allocated to your account for the plan year that ends with or within your tax year. Under this rule, you may be considered an active participant for a year during which no contributions by you or your employer are made to your account; *see* the Examples in this section.

Defined contribution plan. For a defined contribution plan, you are generally considered an active participant if "with respect to" the plan year ending with or within your taxable year (1) you make elective deferrals to the plan; (2) your employer contributes to your account; or (3) forfeitures are allocated to your account. If any of these events occur, you are treated as an active participant for that taxable year, even if you do not have a vested right to receive benefits from your account.

8.6 Nondeductible Contributions to Traditional IRAs

If you are not allowed to deduct any traditional IRA contributions for 2023 because of the phaseout rule for active participants *(8.4)*, you may make nondeductible contributions of up to $6,500 ($7,500 if age 50 or over at the end of 2023) where you have compensation of at least that much *(8.2)*. If the deduction limit is reduced under the phaseout rules *(8.4)*, you may make a nondeductible contribution to the extent the maximum contribution limit of $6,500 or $7,500 (where compensation is at least that much) exceeds the reduced deductible limit *(8.4)*.

However, because the phaseout endpoint for a Roth IRA contribution is so much higher *(8.21)* than the phaseout endpoint for a traditional IRA, a Roth IRA contribution can in many cases be an alternative to a nondeductible traditional IRA contribution, and the Roth option may be preferable for several reasons; *see* "Roth IRA alternative" below.

If you make contributions to a traditional IRA during the year, you may not know whether your active participation status *(8.5)* and modified adjusted gross income (MAGI) will permit you to claim a deduction under the phaseout rules in *(8.4)*. You can make your contribution and wait until you prepare your return to determine if you are eligible for a deduction. Assume that you make a contribution in 2023 and after the end of the year you determine that you are eligible for only a portion of the deductible amount under the phaseout rule *(8.4)*. In that case, you can leave the nondeductible portion in a nondeductible traditional IRA (reporting it on Form 8606), or you may recharacterize *(8.22)* the nondeductible contribution as a Roth IRA contribution assuming you qualify to contribute to a Roth IRA *(8.21)*. On the other hand, you may decide to withdraw the nondeductible contribution as discussed below.

Difficulty of care payments. If you have taxable compensation below the $6,500 or $7,500 limit and are a foster care provider who receives "difficulty of care" payments that are excluded from income (Section 131 exclusion), then a nondeductible traditional IRA contribution is allowed up to the lesser of the exclusion or the difference between the $6,500/$7,500 limit and your compensation.

Planning Reminder

Roth IRA Alternative

A Roth IRA is a nondeductible IRA that offers significant tax and retirement planning advantages. Contributions up to the annual limit for a Roth IRA may be made if modified adjusted gross income is below the annual phaseout threshold *(8.21)*. In general, after the five-year period beginning with the first taxable year for which a Roth IRA contribution was made, tax-free withdrawals may be made if you are age 59½ or older, you are disabled or you have qualifying first-time homebuyer expenses. If you have a traditional IRA, you can also obtain the advantages of a Roth IRA by making a conversion to a Roth IRA. The conversion is taxable except to the extent that it is attributable to nondeductible contributions *(8.23)*.

Roth IRA alternative. If you are not barred from making Roth IRA contributions *(8.21)* because of your income level, the Roth IRA has advantages over the nondeductible traditional IRA. Although both types of plans allow earnings to accumulate tax-free until withdrawal, the Roth IRA has advantages at withdrawal. After a five-year period, completely tax-free withdrawals of earnings as well as contributions may be made from a Roth IRA if you are age 59½ or older, you are disabled, or you withdraw no more than $10,000 for first-time homebuyer expenses *(8.25)*. Even within the first five-year period, contributions (but not earnings) may be withdrawn tax free from a Roth IRA. On the other hand, withdrawals from a nondeductible traditional IRA are partially taxed if any deductible contributions to any traditional IRA were previously made *(8.9)*. Furthermore, mandatory required minimum distributions (RMDs) are required from a traditional IRA when you reach your required beginning date *(8.13)*, but there is no RMD requirement for a Roth IRA that you set up, regardless of your age. Roth IRAs are discussed in *8.20–8.26*.

Form 8606. You must file Form 8606 for any year for which you make a nondeductible contribution to a traditional IRA, unless you withdraw the contribution as discussed below. You must list on Form 8606 the value of all of your IRAs as of the end of the year, including amounts based on deductible contributions. If you are married and you and your spouse both make nondeductible contributions, you must each file a separate Form 8606. A $50 penalty may be imposed for not filing Form 8606 unless there is reasonable cause. Furthermore, if you overstate the amount of designated nondeductible contributions made for any taxable year, you are subject to a $100 penalty for each such overstatement unless you can demonstrate that the overstatement was due to reasonable cause. You may file an amended return for a taxable year and change the designation of IRA contributions from deductible to nondeductible or nondeductible to deductible.

Withdrawing nondeductible contributions. If you make a contribution to a traditional IRA contribution for 2023 and later realize it is not deductible, you may recharacterize the contribution by transferring it (plus allocable income if any) to a Roth IRA, assuming your income is within the annual Roth IRA contribution limit *(8.22)*.

If you do not want (or are ineligible) to recharacterize the traditional IRA contribution to a Roth IRA, you may make a tax-free withdrawal of the contribution by the filing due date (plus extensions), instead of designating the contribution as nondeductible on Form 8606. To do this, you must also withdraw the earnings allocable to the withdrawn contribution and include the earnings as income on your 2023 return. You might want to make the withdrawal if you incorrectly determined that a contribution would be deductible and you do not want to leave nondeductible contributions in your account. However, making the withdrawal could subject you to bank penalties for premature withdrawals, or other withdrawal penalties imposed by the IRA trustee. Furthermore, if you are under age 59½, the 10% premature withdrawal penalty applies to the withdrawn earnings unless one of the exceptions *(8.12)* is available.

8.7 Penalty for Excess Contributions to Traditional IRAs

If you contribute more than the allowable amount to a traditional IRA, whether deductible or nondeductible, the excess contribution may be subject to a penalty tax of 6%. The penalty tax is cumulative. That is, unless you correct the excess, you will be subject to another penalty on the excess contribution in the following year. The penalty tax is not deductible. The penalty is figured in Part III of Form 5329, which must be attached to Form 1040 or 1040-SR.

The 6% penalty may be avoided by withdrawing the excess contribution by the due date for your return, including extensions, plus any income earned on it. The withdrawn excess contribution is not taxable provided no deduction was allowed for it. The withdrawn earnings must be reported as income on your return for the year in which the excess contribution was made. The earnings should be reported to you as a taxable distribution on Form 1099-R. If you are under age 59½ (and not disabled) when you receive the income, the 10% premature withdrawal penalty applies to the income. Similar rules apply to withdrawals of excess employer contributions to a simplified employee pension plan *(8.16)* made by the due date for your return.

 *Planning Reminder*

Distributions Allocable to Nondeductible Traditional IRA Contributions

Keep a copy of each Form 8606 filed showing nondeductible contributions and keep a separate record of deductible contributions. Once you make nondeductible contributions to any traditional IRA, a withdrawal from any of the IRAs will be tax free to the extent the withdrawal is allocable to nondeductible contributions; the balance will be taxed. You may not completely avoid tax even if you withdraw an amount equal to your non-deductible contributions. The tax-free and taxable portions of the withdrawal are figured on Form 8606; *see 8.9*.

If an excess contribution for 2023 is not withdrawn by the due date (plus extensions) for your 2023 return, but you filed by the due date (with extensions), the IRS allows the withdrawal to be made no later than October 15, 2024, provided the related earnings are reported on an amended return that explains the withdrawal; *see* the Form 5329 instructions for details. If the withdrawal is not made, the 6% penalty will apply to your 2023 return but it may be avoided for 2024 by withdrawing the excess by the end of 2024. Instead of withdrawing the excess contribution during 2024, you may also avoid or at least reduce a penalty for 2024 by making an IRA contribution for 2024 that is less than the maximum allowable amount for 2024. That is, you reduce the 2024 IRA contribution by the excess contribution for the prior year; *see* IRS Publication 590-A and Form 5329 for details.

If you deducted an excess contribution in an earlier year for which total contributions were no more than the maximum deductible amount for that year, you may make a tax-free withdrawal of the excess by filing an amended return by the deadline *(47.2)* to correct the excess deduction. However, the 6% penalty tax applies for each year that the excess was still in the account at the end of the year.

See IRS Publication 590-A for further information on correcting excess contributions made in a prior year.

Roth IRAs. A similar 6% penalty applies on Form 5329 to excess contributions to a Roth IRA; *see* Form 5329 and IRS Publication 590-A for further details.

8.8 Distributions From Traditional IRAs

If all of your contributions to all of your traditional IRAs were deductible, any distribution from any of your traditional IRAs will be taxable unless you roll it over or redeposit it within 60 days *(8.10)*. If you made both deductible and nondeductible contributions to your traditional IRAs (any of them), withdrawals allocable to the deductible contributions plus earnings are taxable and the balance allocable to the nondeductible contributions is tax free *(8.9)*.

In addition to regular income tax, taxable distributions are also subject to these age-related restrictions:

- Distributions before age 59½ are subject to a 10% tax penalty, unless you are totally disabled, meet exceptions for paying medical costs, receive annual payments under an annuity-type schedule or you qualify for another exception *(8.12)*.
- You must start taking required minimum distributions (RMDs) from your traditional IRAs when you are age 73. RMDs are annual distributions based on IRS life-expectancy tables. Failure to take the annual required minimum distribution can subject you to a substantial penalty. The RMD rules are explained at *8.13*.

QCDs are not taxable distributions. If you are age 70½ or older and you tell your IRA trustee to directly transfer up to $100,000 of deductible contributions and earnings from your IRA to a qualified charitable organization, this is treated as a qualified charitable distribution (QCD) that is not taxable to you and it offsets the required minimum distribution *(8.13)* you must receive for the year; *see* below for QCD details.

Conversion to Roth IRA. A conversion of a traditional IRA to a Roth IRA is generally treated as a fully taxed distribution from the traditional IRA *(8.23)*.

Loan treated as distribution. If you borrow from your IRA account or use it as security for a loan, you generally are considered to have received your entire interest. Borrowing will subject the account or the fair market value of the contract to tax at ordinary income rates as of the first day of the taxable year of the borrowing. Your IRA account loses its tax-exempt status. If you use the account or part of it as security for a loan, the portion that is pledged is treated as a distribution. However, under the rollover rules, a short-term loan may be made by withdrawing IRA funds and redepositing them in an IRA within 60 days, subject to the once-a-year rollover rule *(8.10)*.

IRS seizure of IRA treated as distribution. The Tax Court has held that an IRS levy of an IRA to cover back taxes is a taxable distribution to the account owner, even though the funds are transferred directly from the account to the IRS and not actually received by the owner. Where the owner is under age 59½, the 10% penalty for early withdrawals *(8.12)* does not apply to involuntary distributions attributable to an IRS levy.

How to report IRA distributions on your 2023 return. All IRA distributions are reported to you and to the IRS on Form 1099-R *(7.1)*. Form 1099-R must be attached to your return only if federal tax has been withheld. You can avoid withholding by instructing the payer not to withhold using Form W-4P or a substitute form *(26.9)*.

If you have never made nondeductible contributions, your IRA withdrawals are fully taxable and should be reported on Line 4b of Form 1040 or 1040-SR. If you have made deductible and nondeductible contributions, complete Form 8606 to figure the nontaxable and taxable portions *(8.9)*. Then you report the total IRA withdrawal on Line 4a of Form 1040 or 1040-SR and enter only the taxable portion on Line 4b.

If you have an individual retirement annuity, your investment in the contract is treated as zero so all payments are fully taxable. Distributions from an endowment policy due to death are taxed as ordinary income to the extent allocable to retirement savings; to the extent allocable to life insurance, they are considered insurance proceeds.

See below for reporting qualified charitable distributions (QCDs).

Qualified Charitable Distribution by IRA Owner Age 70½ or Older

If you are at least age 70½, a qualified charitable distribution (QCD) allows you to avoid tax on a transfer made directly from your traditional IRA to an eligible charity, up to an annual exclusion limit of $100,000. You can also make a QCD from a SEP or SIMPLE plan, but only if no employer contributions are made for the plan year that ends with or within the year in which the QCD occurs. In addition to getting the exclusion from income, a QCD can lower or eliminate the required minimum distribution *(8.13)* that you otherwise must receive for the year. If you claim a deduction *(8.4)* for a traditional IRA contribution, the exclusion limit is reduced; *see* below. The $100,000 QCD limit is now indexed for inflation starting in 2024.

If you are the beneficiary of an inherited IRA *(8.14–8.15)*, you can do a QCD; QCDs are not limited to IRA owners. Provided you are at least age 70½, you can make a QCD from your inherited IRA, subject to the other QCD rules in this section.

Because a QCD is not included in adjusted gross income (up to the $100,00 exclusion limit), the exclusion may help you limit the taxability of Social Security benefits *(34.3)*, limit exposure to the 3.8% tax on net investment income *(28.3)*, increase deductibility of unreimbursed medical expenses *(17.1)*, and preserve eligibility for the $25,000 loss allowance under the passive loss rules *(10.2)*.

QCD requirements. To be a qualified charitable distribution (QCD) eligible for the exclusion, the transfer must be made on or after the date you reach 70½; it does not qualify if you make the transfer in the same year you turn 70½ but before you actually are 70½. If your spouse is also at least age 70½ and instructs the trustee of his or her traditional IRA to make a qualifying direct transfer, you can each claim the up-to-$100,000 exclusion; thus, on a joint return, up to $200,000 is potentially excludable. Although the age for starting required minimum distributions (RMDs) has been raised from age 72 to 73 *(8.13)*, the age at which a QCD may be made is still 70½. The QCD rules apply only to traditional IRAs, and not to distributions from SIMPLE IRAs, qualified employer plans, 403(b) plans, or SEPs (including salary-reduction SEPs set up before 1997).

To be a QCD, the transfer must be made directly by the trustee of your traditional IRA to a qualifying charity that is eligible to receive tax-deductible donations (this excludes a "supporting organization" or donor-advised fund). If your IRA trustee gives you a check that is payable to the charity (not to you), and you deliver the check to the charity, this qualifies as a direct transfer. To count as a QCD for a given year, the transfer must be completed by December 31 of that year; it must be withdrawn from your account and on the books of the charity's custodian by the end of the year. You cannot claim a charitable deduction for the amount of the QCD excluded from your income. Note, there is a one-time opportunity to transfer up to $50,000 to a split interest arrangement, which includes a charitable remainder trust, a charitable annuity trust, or a charitable gift annuity. If these transfers are made, the IRA owner and spouse must treat all distributions from the split interest arrangement as ordinary income.

QCD offsets your RMD. If you are age 73 or older, a QCD counts towards the required minimum distribution *(8.13)* that you must receive from your IRAs for the year. For

Caution

Form 1099-R Does Not Identify a QCD

If a QCD is made from your traditional IRA, it will reported as a "regular" distribution on Form 1099-R. There is no code or box on the Form 1099-R that indicates that the transfer was a QCD. It is up to you to follow the instructions for Line 4 of Form 1040 to report the QCD and exclude it from your income. *See* "How to report a QCD" at the end of *8.8*.

example, if you would otherwise have to receive a $20,000 RMD, a QCD of $20,000 or more completely eliminates the RMD and so long as it does not exceed the $100,000 limit, the entire QCD is excluded from your income. If your RMD is $40,000 and a $20,000 QCD is made, you must take the remaining $20,000 RMD and pay tax on it.

You must obtain a timely acknowledgment. Make sure that you get a timely written acknowledgment from the charity. You need the same type of acknowledgment that you have to get to substantiate a donation exceeding $250 under the charitable contribution deduction rules *(14.14)*.

Exclusion limit reduced by deductible IRA contributions made after age 70½. You can contribute to a traditional IRA regardless of your age so long as you have compensation *(8.2–8.4)*, but if you claim an IRA deduction for a year in which you are age 70½ or older, and you make a QCD transfer in the same year or in a later year, the QCD exclusion is reduced by the aggregate deductions for the post-age 70½ IRA contributions.

For example, Tom Taxpayer, who is age 72 and still working in 2023, makes a $7,000 deductible contribution to his traditional IRA for 2023; this is his first IRA contribution since turning age 70½. He also authorizes a $10,000 QCD from his IRA to a charity during 2023; this is his first QCD. Tom's potential QCD exclusion of $10,000 is reduced by his $7,000 IRA deduction, so Tom's exclusion is reduced to $3,000 and $7,000 of the transfer to charity is treated as a taxable IRA distribution rather than a nontaxable QCD on his 2023 return. If Tom is able to itemize deductions *(13.1)* on Schedule A (Form 1040 or 1040-SR), the non-excludable $7,000 can be claimed as a charitable contribution. No charitable deduction is allowed for the excludable $3,000 part of the transfer.

What if Tom had also made a $7,000 deductible IRA contribution in 2022 (when he turned age 71)? In that case, Tom would have no exclusion at all for the 2023 QCD; the $14,000 of deductible post-age 70½ IRA contributions ($7,000 for each of 2022 and 2023) would reduce the potential exclusion for 2023 to zero ($10,000 QCD - $14,000 deductible contributions). In addition, if Tom were to make a $10,000 QCD in 2024, the exclusion for 2024 would be reduced by the remaining $4,000 of post-age 70½ IRA contributions that did not reduce the 2023 QCD, so the exclusion for the 2024 QCD would be reduced to $6,000 ($10,000 – $4,000).

Have you made nondeductible IRA contributions? If you authorize a QCD and there were any nondeductible contributions to any of your traditional IRAs, the transfer is deemed to come first out of the part of the distribution that otherwise would be taxable (without the QCD rules)—that is, the amount equal to your deductible contributions plus earnings. The part of the distribution equal to the deductible contributions plus earnings is the amount eligible for the QCD exclusion, up to the $100,000 limit; anything over $100,000 is includible in income, as would any other traditional IRA distribution. Any balance of the transfer (above the amount allocable to deductible contributions plus earnings) is deemed to be a transfer of nondeductible contributions and is nontaxable, but it is not part of the QCD. You must file Form 8606 *(8.9)* to report a distribution of nondeductible contributions and to figure your remaining basis in the IRAs: your pre-distribution basis is reduced by the portion of the distribution that is not considered part of the QCD because it is allocable to nondeductible contributions.

How to report a QCD. A QCD must be reported on your return as an IRA distribution on Line 4 of Form 1040 or 1040-SR. The total transfer is shown on Line 4a. If the entire transfer is a QCD excludable from income, enter "0" on Line 4b as the taxable amount. A transfer in excess of the $100,000 QCD exclusion limit must be included on Line 4b as a taxable IRA distribution. If the exclusion is reduced because you made a deductible IRA contribution *(see above)*, the nonexcludable transfer must be included on Line 4b as a taxable IRA distribution. If part of the transfer was allocable to nondeductible contributions reported on Form 8606, that part is not taxable and is not entered on Line 4b. Enter "QCD" next to Line 4b to indicate that you are claiming the QCD exclusion.

If you are able to itemize deductions *(13.1)* on Schedule A (Form 1040 or 1040-SR), any portion of the transfer allocable to nondeductible contributions can be claimed as a charitable contribution. No charitable deduction is allowed for the excludable part of the QCD (deductible contributions plus earnings).

8.9 Partially Tax-Free Traditional IRA Distributions Allocable to Nondeductible Contributions

If you ever made a nondeductible contribution to a traditional IRA, you must file Form 8606 to report a 2023 distribution from any of your traditional IRAs, even if the distribution is from an IRA to which only nondeductible contributions were made. All of your traditional IRAs are treated as one contract. If you receive distributions from more than one traditional IRA in the same year, they are combined for reporting purposes on Form 8606. Roth IRA distributions are also reported on Form 8606, but do not combine your traditional and Roth IRAs. Roth IRAs are treated separately. After a five-year period, withdrawals after age 59½ from a Roth IRA are completely tax free *(8.25)*.

Part of your distribution will be taxed under the "pro rata" rule. When you have made nondeductible as well as deductible contributions to traditional IRAs, any distribution from any of the traditional IRAs will be treated partly as a tax-free return of cost basis in the nondeductible contributions, and partly as a taxable distribution of deductible contributions and earnings. This is the "pro-rata rule". The part of your withdrawal that is allocable to your nondeductible contributions is tax-free; any balance is taxable. You may not claim that you are withdrawing only your tax-free contributions, even if your withdrawal is less than your nondeductible contributions. You can use the six steps below ("Figuring the taxable portion of a traditional IRA distribution") to figure the nontaxable and taxable portions of the IRA distribution.

The payer of the distribution will not indicate on Form 1099-R whether any part of a distribution is a tax-free return of basis allocable to nondeductible contributions. It is up to you to keep records that show the nondeductible contributions you have made. IRS instructions require you to keep copies of all Forms 8606 on which nondeductible contributions have been designated, as well as copies of (1) your tax returns for years you made nondeductible contributions to traditional IRAs; (2) Forms 5498 showing all IRA contributions and showing the value of your IRAs for each year you received a distribution; and (3) Form 1099-R (or previously used Form W-2P) showing IRA distributions. According to the IRS, you should keep such records until you have withdrawn all IRA funds.

Figuring the taxable portion of a traditional IRA distribution. If you received a distribution from a traditional IRA in 2023 and have ever made nondeductible contributions to any of your traditional IRAs, follow Steps 1–6 to determine the tax-free and taxable portions of the 2023 distribution. These steps reflect the IRS method used on Form 8606, but assume that you did not convert a traditional IRA to a Roth IRA during 2023. If you did convert a traditional IRA to a Roth IRA, follow the instructions to Form 8606.

1. Total traditional IRA withdrawals during 2023.

2. Total nondeductible contributions to all traditional IRAs made by the end of 2023. Tax-free withdrawals of nondeductible contributions in prior years reduce the total. If you made any contributions to traditional IRAs for 2023 (including a contribution for 2023 made between January 1 and April 15, 2024) that may be partly nondeductible because your modified adjusted gross income is within the deduction phaseout range shown in *8.4* for active plan participants, you should include the contributions in the Step 2 total.

3. Add Step 1 to the value of all your traditional IRAs (and if any, the value of all SIMPLE IRAs and SEP IRAs) as of the end of 2023. If you received an IRA distribution within the last 60 days of 2023 that was rolled over to another IRA within the 60-day rollover period *(8.10)* but not until 2024, add the 2024 rollover to the 2023 year-end balance.

4. Divide Step 2 by Step 3. This is the tax-free percentage of your IRA withdrawal.

5. Multiply the Step 4 percentage by Step 1. This amount is tax free.

6. Subtract Step 5 from Step 1. This amount must be reported as a taxable IRA distribution on your 2023 return.

No deduction allowed for IRA loss based on unrecovered nondeductible contributions. You suffer a loss if all of your IRA funds have been withdrawn and you have not recovered your basis in nondeductible contributions. However, a deduction for such a loss is not allowed under current law. Before 2018, the loss could have been deducted as a miscellaneous itemized deduction subject to the 2% of adjusted gross income floor, but this deduction has been suspended for 2018 through 2025.

EXAMPLE

Nick James has one traditional IRA. His only contributions were from 2002 through 2008, when he made deductible IRA contributions of $8,000 and nondeductible contributions of $6,000 as follows

Year	Deductible	Nondeductible
2002	$2,000	0
2003	2,000	0
2004	2,000	0
2005	1,000	$1,000
2006	1,000	1,000
2007	0	2,000
2008	0	2,000
	$8,000	$6,000

On November 21, 2023, Nick withdraws $5,000 from the traditional IRA. Assume that on December 31, 2023, Nick's total IRA account balance, including earnings, is $27,500, and that the November withdrawal was his first ever IRA withdrawal. On Form 8606 for 2023, Nick figures that $923 of the $5,000 IRA withdrawal is tax free and $4,077 is taxable.

Step 1.	IRA withdrawal in November 2023	$5,000
Step 2.	Nondeductible contributions for all years	6,000
Step 3.	IRA balance at end of 2023 ($27,500) plus Step 1 withdrawal ($5,000)	32,500
Step 4.	Tax-free percentage:$6,000 (Step 2) ÷ $32,500 (Step 3)	18.46%
Step 5.	Tax-free withdrawal:18.46% (Step 4) × $5,000 (Step 1)	923
Step 6.	Taxable withdrawal: $5,000 (Step 1) − $923 (Step 5)	$4,077

The total $5,000 withdrawal should be reported on Line 4a of Form 1040 or 1040-SR, and the taxable $4,077 portion should be entered on Line 4b (Form 1040 or 1040-SR).

8.10 Tax-Free Direct Transfer or Rollover From One Traditional IRA to Another

You may switch how your traditional IRA funds are invested without incurring tax on a distribution by rolling over a distribution to another IRA within 60 days of receiving it, although another option, a direct transfer, is a more advantageous way of changing IRA investments, as discussed below.

Distributions from inherited IRAs are subject to separate rules. A surviving spouse beneficiary who withdraws funds from an inherited IRA can do a 60-day rollover *(see below)*, provided it is not a required minimum distribution (RMD) *(8.14, 8.15)*. A nonspouse beneficiary cannot roll over a withdrawal. However, a nonspouse beneficiary as well as a surviving spouse beneficiary can make a direct trustee-to-trustee transfer to another traditional IRA *(8.14, 8.15)*.

Direct transfer from one IRA to another. A direct transfer is made by instructing the trustee (or custodian) of a traditional IRA to transfer all or part of your account to another IRA trustee (or custodian). Direct transfers are tax free because you do not directly receive the funds. With a direct transfer, there is no risk of missing the 60-day deadline for rolling over a withdrawal into a new IRA. There is also no need to worry about making multiple transfers within the same 12-month period if you use direct transfers. The tax law does not require a waiting period between direct transfers, whereas rollovers are subject to a once-a-year limitation, as discussed below.

For example, assume you have a traditional IRA at Brokerage Firm "ABC" and decide to switch your account to Mutual Fund "XYZ." The mutual fund provides you with transfer request forms that you complete and return to the fund, which will then forward the forms to the brokerage firm, which will process the request and then transfer the funds to the fund to complete the direct transfer. You are not taxed on the transfer from the brokerage firm to the mutual fund because the IRA funds were not paid to you, and the direct transfer is not considered a rollover subject to the once-a-year rollover limitation. This means that if within one year you become unhappy with the performance of Mutual Fund "XYZ," you may make another tax-free direct transfer of your IRA to Fund "123", or to Bank "B", or any other IRA trustee or custodian.

In some cases, the old IRA trustee may issue you a check payable to the new trustee that you must give to the new trustee. As long as the check is payable to the new trustee for your benefit and not payable to you, this is considered a direct transfer and not a rollover.

Rollover within 60 days. If you withdraw funds from your traditional IRA, you can make a tax-free rollover within 60 days to another traditional IRA, provided (1) it is not a required minimum distribution (RMD) *(8.13)*, and (2) you did not previously do a 60-day rollover in the prior 12 months; *see* "Only One IRA Rollover is Allowed Within Any 12-Month Period" on page 229. The amount you receive from your old IRA must be transferred to the new plan by the 60th day after the day you received it. Amounts not rolled over within the 60-day period must be treated as a taxable distribution for the year you received the distribution (not the year in which the 60-day period expired, if that is later) unless the IRS waives the 60-day deadline *(see below)*. If the distribution is taxed and you were under age 59½ when the distribution was made, the 10% penalty for an "early" distribution applies unless a penalty exception *(8.12)* is available.

The IRS may waive the 60-day rollover deadline on equitable grounds if a distribution cannot be rolled over on time because of events beyond your reasonable control, such as illness, natural disaster, or a financial institution's error; *see* the IRS waiver guidelines below.

There are two other possible grounds for an extension of the 60-day rollover deadline. An extension is allowed if your distribution is "frozen" and cannot be withdrawn from an insolvent or bankrupt financial institution. The deadline is extended to 120 days if a distribution is taken to buy or build a qualifying "first home" and the deal falls through. These extensions are discussed below.

> **Caution:** There is a one-year waiting period between rollovers. Once you complete a rollover between traditional IRAs, you must wait one year before you can make another tax-free rollover; *see* page 229.

IRS may waive 60-day rollover deadline on equitable grounds. You may be able to obtain a waiver of the 60-day rollover deadline in one of three ways:

1. You qualify for an automatic waiver. The IRS will automatically waive the deadline if: (a) you deposited the rollover funds with a financial institution within the 60-day period, (b) you followed all of the institution's rollover procedures but the rollover account was not established on time solely because of the institution's error, and (c) the funds were actually deposited in a valid rollover account within one year of the start of the 60-day period.

2. You use the self-certification procedure for a waiver where you missed the 60-day deadline because of one or more of 11 reasons recognized by the IRS, as described below.

3. You apply for a waiver by requesting a private letter ruling and showing that your failure to meet the 60-day deadline was due to reasons beyond your reasonable control. However, a $10,000 user fee must be submitted with the ruling request.

Self-certification procedure for getting waiver of 60-day deadline. The IRS has provided rules (Revenue Procedure 2020-46) that extend the time for completing a rollover if you "self-certify" that you meet specified conditions. The IRS could later question your eligibility, but the procedure allows you and the IRA trustee that receives your transfer after the 60-day period to treat it as a valid rollover.

 *Planning Reminder*

60-Day Loan From IRA

You can take advantage of the rollover rule to borrow funds from your IRA if you need a short-term loan to pay your taxes or other expenses. As long as you redeposit the amount in an IRA within 60 days you are not taxed on the withdrawal; the redeposit is considered a tax-free rollover. You may roll over the funds to a different IRA from the one from which the withdrawal was made. Keep in mind that only one tax-free rollover can be made within a 12-month period. Thus, if you use a 60-day rollover for a short-term loan (or any other reason), a second withdrawal from the same IRA or from any of your other traditional IRAs within one year would be taxable; *see* "Only One IRA Rollover is Allowed Within Any 12-Month Period".

Conditions for self-certification. You can use this procedure if you give a written certification *(see below)* to the IRA trustee that you meet all of the following three conditions:

1. You were not previously denied a waiver request for a rollover of this distribution by the IRS.

2. You have a good reason for missing the 60-day deadline. There are 12 acceptable reasons:

   - An error was made by the financial institution making the distribution or receiving the rollover transfer.
   - You misplaced and never cashed the distribution check.
   - You deposited the distribution in an account you mistakenly thought was an eligible retirement plan.
   - Your principal residence was severely damaged.
   - A member of your family died.
   - You or a member of your family was seriously ill.
   - You were incarcerated.
   - You were subject to restrictions imposed by a foreign country.
   - There was a postal error.
   - The distribution was made on account of an IRS levy and the proceeds have been returned to you.
   - The party making the distribution delayed providing information required by the receiving IRA despite your efforts to obtain it.
   - The distribution was made to a state unclaimed property fund.

3. You completed the rollover as soon as practicable. This test is considered met if you satisfy a 30-day safe harbor, which applies when the funds are rolled over within 30 days after you are no longer subject to the condition that prevented a timely rollover.

Written self-certification must be given to the new IRA trustee. To make the self-certification, you must give the IRA trustee (the trustee of the IRA to which you are making the late transfer) a signed letter stating that you intended to make the rollover within 60 days of receiving the distribution but were unable to do so because of one or more of the reasons shown above (condition 2), and that conditions 1 and 3 were also met. You can use the model letter in the Appendix to Rev. Proc. 2020-46, or a letter that is substantially similar. Keep a copy of the certification with your records.

Unless the IRA trustee has actual knowledge that you are not eligible for the self-certification, the trustee may rely on your written notification for purposes of accepting the late transfer as a timely rollover and reporting it as a rollover on Form 5498 ("IRA Contribution Information"). On Form 5498, the IRA trustee will report the amount of the late rollover for which self-certification was made in Box 13a ("Postponed/Late Contribution"), and in Box 13c ("Code"), code "SC" will be entered.

> **Caution:** The IRS may question your self-certification. This self-certification process does not require you to provide documentation to the IRA trustee about the circumstance that made you eligible for the waiver. You may report the transfer on your return as a valid rollover (therefore not taxable) unless the IRS has informed you otherwise. However, if you are audited and the IRS questions the waiver, then it is up to you to prove that you met the conditions for the self-certification.

Note that even if you do not self-certify, the IRS could grant a waiver for equitable reasons on an audit of your return.

Frozen deposits in insolvent financial institutions. The 60-day limit for completing a rollover is extended if the funds are "frozen" and may not be withdrawn from a bankrupt or insolvent financial institution. The 60-day period is extended while the account is frozen and you have a minimum of 10 days after the release of the funds to complete the rollover.

If a government agency takes control of an insolvent bank, you might receive an "involuntary" distribution of your IRA account from the agency. According to the IRS and Tax Court, such a payment is subject to the regular IRA distribution rules. For example, a couple received payment for their $11,000 IRA balance from the Maryland Deposit Insurance Fund after the bank in which the funds were invested became insolvent. The Tax

Court held that the payment was taxable, even though the distribution was from a state insurance fund and not from the bank itself. Furthermore, since they were under age 59½, the 10% penalty for early distributions *(8.12)* was imposed, even though the distribution was involuntary. The tax and penalty could have been avoided by making a rollover of the distribution within 60 days, but this was not done.

120-day rollover period after failure to acquire "first-time" home. A "first-time" homebuyer may be able to limit or avoid a 10% penalty for a distribution before age 59½ by using the funds within 120 days to help buy, build, or rebuild a principal residence *(8.12)*. If the requirements of the exception cannot be met because the planned purchase or construction of the home falls through, the law allows the taxpayer to return the distribution to an IRA within 120 days after receiving the distribution. The recontribution is not taken into account for purposes of the once-a-year rollover limit discussed above. The extension of the tax-free rollover period from 60 days to 120 days is automatic if the requirements are met; a waiver of the 60-day deadline (as discussed above) from the IRS is not required. For example, a taxpayer withdrew IRA funds to buy a home and would have qualified as a "first-time" homebuyer, but his offer was rejected by the seller and approximately 72 days after the IRA withdrawal he put the amount of the distribution back into his IRA. The IRS in a private ruling held that the recontribution to the IRA was timely under the special 120-day rollover rule.

Only One IRA Rollover is Allowed Within Any 12-Month Period

If you receive an IRA distribution and within 60 days of receiving it you rolled it over to the same IRA or to another IRA, you cannot roll over another distribution from any of your IRAs within the 12-month period starting on the date you received the first distribution. A second tax-free rollover within the 12-month period is not allowed even if the proceeds of the second distribution are redeposited into the same IRA from which the distribution was made. Note that if you receive a distribution and roll it over at a later date within the 60-day rollover period, the 12-month period begins on the date that the distribution was received, not the later rollover date; *see* the Example below.

For purposes of the one-rollover-per year limitation, all of your traditional IRAs, Roth IRAs, SEPs and SIMPLE IRAs are aggregated as if they were one IRA. Only one rollover from any of these accounts is allowed within a 12-month period. Thus, if you make a rollover from one traditional IRA to another, you cannot make a rollover between Roth IRAs within the same 12-month period. Similarly, if a rollover is made from one Roth IRA to another, you cannot make a rollover from one traditional IRA to another within the same 12-month period. However, conversions from a traditional IRA to a Roth IRA are not limited; *see* below.

If within 12 months of making an IRA-to-IRA rollover you receive an IRA distribution and attempt to roll it over, the distribution will be taxable to the extent it is allocable to pre-tax contributions plus earnings (there is no tax on any portion allocable to after-tax contributions), and if you are under age 59½, the 10% early distribution penalty will apply unless you qualify for a penalty exception *(8.12)*. Furthermore, the failed rollover will be treated as an excess contribution subject to a 6% penalty unless it is withdrawn *(8.7)*.

Conversions to Roth IRAs are not limited. A rollover or a direct transfer from a traditional IRA to a Roth IRA is treated as a taxable distribution *(8.23)* and thus it is not subject to the one-per-year limit on tax-free rollovers. Within the same 12-month period, you can make one or several taxable conversions of traditional IRAs to Roth IRAs and still make one tax-free IRA rollover.

Direct transfers are not limited. You can make a trustee-to-trustee transfer from one IRA to another in order to change your IRA investment as often as you would like without limitation. Since the funds do not pass through your hands, a trustee-to-trustee transfer is not a "rollover" and therefore is not subject to the one-rollover-per year limitation. If you receive a check for a distribution from the transferring IRA trustee that is payable to the receiving IRA trustee (not payable to you) and you deliver the check to the new trustee, this is considered a trustee-to-trustee transfer.

Recharacterizations of annual contributions not counted as rollovers. If you make a timely recharacterization of a traditional IRA contribution to a Roth IRA, or a Roth IRA contribution to a traditional IRA, the recharacterization is not treated as a rollover for purposes of the one-rollover-a-year limit *(8.22)*.

> **EXAMPLE**
>
> On July 20, 2023, you received a distribution from traditional IRA-1. You rolled it over to traditional IRA-2 on August 30, 2023 (within the 60-day rollover period). Under the one-rollover-per-year rule, you cannot make a tax-free rollover of any other IRA distribution (whether from a traditional, Roth, SEP, or SIMPLE IRA) in the 12-month period starting on July 20, 2023 and ending on July 19, 2024. The one-year period starts on July 20, 2023, the date you received the distribution from traditional IRA-1, not on August 30 when you rolled it over.
>
> If you want to change IRA investments in the 12-month period ending July 19, 2024, you can do so by authorizing a direct transfer between IRA trustees, as direct transfers are not limited. In addition, a conversion of a traditional IRA to a Roth IRA is not affected by the rollover limitation and can be made at any time; *see* above.

8.11 Transfer of Traditional IRA to Spouse at Divorce

If you receive your former spouse's IRA pursuant to a divorce decree or written instrument incident to the decree, the transfer is not taxable to either of you. From the date of transfer the account is treated as your IRA. If you are legally separated, a transfer of your spouse's IRA to you is tax free if made under a decree of separate maintenance or written instrument incident to the decree. The transferred account is then treated as your IRA.

How to make a divorce-related transfer. If you are required to transfer IRA assets from your account to your spouse or former spouse by a decree of divorce or separate maintenance, or a written instrument incident to such a decree, use one of these transfer methods to avoid being taxed on the transfer: (1) change the name on the IRA from your name to the name of your spouse or former spouse if you are transferring your entire interest in the IRA, or (2) direct your IRA trustee to transfer the IRA assets directly to the trustee of a new or existing IRA in the name of your spouse or former spouse.

If you simply withdraw money from your IRA and pay it to your spouse, you will be treated as having received a taxable distribution from your IRA. If you are under age 59½, you will be subject to the 10% early distribution penalty (unless an exception applies; *see 8.12*) as well as regular tax on the withdrawal.

QDRO transfer of spouse's employer plan benefits to your IRA. If you receive your share of your spouse's or former spouse's benefits from an employer plan under a qualified domestic relations order (QDRO), you can make a tax-free rollover to a traditional IRA or another eligible retirement plan so long as it would have been eligible for rollover had your spouse received it *(7.12)*. If you roll over only part of a qualifying QDRO distribution, you figure the tax on the retained portion by taking into account a prorated share of your former spouse's cost investment.

8.12 Penalty for Traditional IRA Withdrawals Before Age 59½

If you receive a taxable distribution from a traditional IRA *(8.8)* before you are age 59½, you have to pay a 10% penalty in addition to regular tax on the distribution, unless you qualify for a penalty exception specified in the tax law. There is no general exception for financial hardship. Although you may be forced in tough economic times to tap your IRA to cover living expenses, or you face a family emergency, you will be able to avoid the early distribution penalty only if you fit within one of the designated penalty exceptions, such as for the birth or adoption of a child, disability, paying substantial medical expenses, or higher education expenses.

Here is the list of allowable penalty exceptions: (1) you receive a distribution of up to $5,000 within a year of the birth of your child or an adoption, (2) you take the distribution because you are totally disabled or terminally ill, (3) you pay medical expenses exceeding

Court Decision

No Penalty Exception for Financial Hardship

The Tax Court would not let a taxpayer under age 59½ avoid the early withdrawal penalty despite her financial hardship. She did not meet any other penalty exception.

the applicable percentage of adjusted gross income *(17.1)*, (4) you receive unemployment compensation for at least 12 consecutive weeks and pay medical insurance premiums, (5) you pay qualified higher education expenses, (6) the distribution is $10,000 or less and used for qualified first-time homebuyer expenses, (7) you receive a qualified reservist distribution, (8) the distribution is one of a series of payments being made under one of several annuity-type methods, (9) the distributions are made to you as a beneficiary of a deceased IRA owner, or (10) the distribution was due to an IRS levy on your IRA. These exceptions are further discussed below.

Also note that a qualifying rollover *(8.10)* of an IRA distribution is not subject to tax and therefore not subject to the 10% penalty even if you are under age 59½.

The penalty is 10% of the taxable IRA distribution. For example, if before age 59½ you withdraw $3,000 from your traditional IRA, you must include the $3,000 as part of your taxable income and, in addition, pay a $300 penalty tax. If part of a pre-59½ distribution is tax free because it is allocable to nondeductible contributions *(8.9)* or rolled over to another IRA *(8.10)*, the 10% penalty applies only to the taxable portion of the distribution.

If you do not owe the penalty because you qualify for an exception, you may have to file Form 5329, depending on whether the payer of the distribution correctly marked the exception in Box 7 of Form 1099-R. If the plan administrator knows that you qualify for an exception and indicates this by entering a code in Box 7 of Form 1099-R, you do not have to file Form 5329. For example, if the distribution was made to you as the beneficiary of a deceased IRA owner and the payer has correctly entered Code 4 ("Death") in Box 7, you do not have to file Form 5329 to claim the beneficiary exception. Similarly, if the plan administrator knows that you qualify for the annuity-method exception and enters Code 2 in Box 7 ("Early distribution, exception applies"), you do not have to file Form 5329. If the annuity method or beneficiary exception applies but Code 2 is not entered in Box 7 of Form 1099-R, you must file Form 5329 to claim the penalty exception.

If you qualify for the disability exception, the medical expenses exception, or the higher education expenses exception *(see below)*, it is unlikely that the payer will know of that fact and thus Code 2 ("Early distribution, exception applies") will probably not be marked in Box 7 of Form 1099-R. In this case, you must file Form 5329 to claim the exception: On Line 2 of Part I (Form 5329), you would enter exception number 3 for the disability exception, number 5 for the medical expenses exception, or number 8 for the higher education expenses exception; *see* the Form 5329 instructions for any changes to these exception numbers.

If part of your distribution is eligible for a penalty exception, you must enter on Form 5329 the exception number (from the instructions) and figure the 10% penalty on the nonqualifying part. The penalty is entered on Schedule 2 of Form 1040 or 1040-SR ("Additional Tax on IRAs, Other Qualified Plans, etc.").

Birth or adoption of child.
A distribution of up to $5,000 is not subject to the pre–age 59½ penalty if the distribution is received within one year from the date of birth of your child, or within one year after an adoption is finalized. An adoptee qualifies if he or she is under age 18, or any age if incapable of self support; however, a child of your spouse does not qualify. The distribution can be repaid to an IRA or to an employer plan that accepts rollovers; under current law there is no time limit on repayment. *See 7.13* for further details on this penalty exception.

Beneficiaries are not subject to the penalty.
Beneficiaries are exempt from the pre–age 59½ penalty. If the IRA owner was not your spouse and you liquidate the account and receive the proceeds, or if you receive annual payments as a beneficiary under the inherited IRA rules *(8.14)*, any distributions you receive before age 59½ are not subject to the early distribution penalty, although they are subject to regular income tax.

If you inherit an IRA from your deceased spouse and elect to treat it as your own IRA as discussed in *8.14*, you are not eligible for the beneficiary exception; distributions from the account before you reach age 59½ will be subject to the penalty unless another exception applies. The beneficiary exception applies if the account is maintained in the name of your deceased spouse and you are receiving the distribution according to the rules for a spousal beneficiary *(8.14)*.

 *Law Alert*

Repayment of a Wrongful Levy

If there is an IRS levy on a 401(k) plan account that turns out to be wrongful, an individual can recontribute the amount returned (the amount levied plus interest).

Caution

Medical Expenses Exception

The medical expense exception to the early distribution penalty applies only to the extent that in the year you receive the distribution, you pay deductible medical costs *(17.2)* in excess of the AGI floor for claiming itemized medical expenses *(17.1)*. If the deductible medical expenses are not paid in the year the distribution is received, the exception is not available.

Disability & Terminally ill exception. To qualify for the disability exception, you must be able to show that you have a physical or mental condition that can be expected to last indefinitely or result in death and that prevents you from engaging in "substantial gainful activity" similar to the type of work you were doing before the condition arose. The terminally ill exception is effective for distributions made after December 29, 2022.

In one case, a 53-year-old stockbroker claimed that his IRA withdrawal of over $200,000 should be exempt from the 10% penalty because he suffered from mental depression. However, the Tax Court upheld the IRS imposition of the penalty because he continued to work as a stockbroker.

Medical expense exception. If you withdraw IRA funds in a year in which you pay deductible medical costs *(17.1)*, part of the distribution may avoid the pre–age 59½ penalty. The penalty does not apply to the part of the distribution equal to the expenses over your AGI floor; *see 17.1* . The distribution must be received in the same year that the medical expenses are paid. The medical costs must be eligible for the itemized medical deduction *(17.2)*, but the IRA penalty exception applies whether you itemize or claim the standard deduction.

Unemployed person's medical insurance exceptions. There is no general penalty exception for being unemployed. However, if you are unemployed and received unemployment benefits under Federal or state law for at least 12 consecutive weeks, you may make penalty-free IRA withdrawals to the extent of medical insurance premiums paid during the year for you, your spouse, and your dependents. The withdrawals may be made in the year the 12-week unemployment test is met, or in the following year. However, the penalty exception does not apply to distributions made more than 60 days after you return to the work force.

Self-employed persons who are ineligible by law for unemployment benefits may be treated as meeting the 12-week test, and thus eligible for the exception, under regulations to be issued by the IRS.

Higher education expenses exception. A penalty exception is allowed for IRA distributions that do not exceed higher education expenses, including graduate school costs, for you, your spouse, your or your spouse's children, or your or your spouse's grandchildren that you paid during the year of the IRA distribution. Eligible expenses include tuition, fees, books, supplies, and equipment that are required for enrollment or attendance, plus room and board for a person who is at least a half-time student.

The penalty exception applies only if the withdrawal from the IRA and the payment of the qualified higher education expenses occur within the same year. For example, in one case, a taxpayer under age 59½ took IRA distributions in 2001 to pay credit card debt incurred in 1999 and 2000 to pay qualified higher education expenses for those years. Another taxpayer under age 59½ took IRA distributions in 2002 and used them to pay qualified expenses incurred in 2003 and 2004. In both cases, the Tax Court agreed with the IRS that the penalty exception was not available because the IRA withdrawals were not made in the same year that the qualified higher education expenses were incurred.

Caution

Timing Problem for Higher Education Costs

Qualified higher education expenses must be paid in the same year that the distribution is received for the penalty exception to apply. This timing rule turns the penalty exception into a tax trap when a tuition payment made at the end of the year is "reimbursed" by an IRA withdrawal at the beginning of the following year, or an IRA distribution is taken at the end of the year to cover a tuition payment due at the start of the next year.

First-time homebuyer expense exception. A penalty exception is allowed for up to $10,000 of qualifying "first-time" homebuyer expenses. You are a qualifying first-time homebuyer if you did not have a present ownership interest in a principal residence in the two-year period ending on the acquisition date of the new home. If you are married, your spouse also must have had no such ownership interest within the two-year period. The penalty does not apply to IRA distributions that are used within 120 days to buy, construct, or reconstruct a principal residence for you, your spouse, child, grandchild, or ancestor of you or your spouse. Qualifying home acquisition costs include reasonable settlement, financing, or other closing costs. If you qualify, the exception applies only for $10,000 of homebuyer expenses. This is a lifetime cap per IRA owner and not an annual limit.

If you take a distribution, intending to use it for home acquisition costs that would qualify for the first-time buyer exception, but the transaction falls through, you have 120 days from the date you receive the distribution to roll it back to an IRA *(8.10)*.

IRS levy. The 10% penalty does not apply to an "involuntary" distribution due to an IRS levy on your IRA.

Qualified reservist distribution. If you are a member of the reserves called to active military duty for over 179 days, or indefinitely, distributions received during the active duty period are not subject to the early distribution penalty. Furthermore, a qualified reservist distribution may be recontributed to the plan within two years after the end of your active duty period without regard to the regular limits on IRA contributions *(8.2)*. A recontribution is not deductible.

Substantially Equal Periodic Payments Avoid 10% Penalty

The exception for substantially equal periodic payments allows you to avoid the 10% penalty if you are willing to receive annual distributions that are within one of the three IRS-approved methods discussed in this section. Before arranging such a schedule of payments, consider these points: all of the payments will be taxable (unless allocable to nondeductible contributions; *see 8.9*), and if you do not continue the payments for a minimum number of years, the IRS will impose the 10% penalty for all taxable payments received before age 59½, plus interest charges. The minimum payout period rules do not apply to totally disabled individuals or to beneficiaries of deceased IRA owners.

Payments must continue for minimum period. The payments must continue for at least five years, or until you reach age 59½, whichever period is longer. Thus, if you are in your 40s, you would have to continue the scheduled payments until you are age 59½. If you are in your mid-50s, the minimum payout period is not as serious a burden, as you only need to continue the scheduled payments for at least five years, starting with the date of the first distribution, provided that the period ends after you reach age 59½.

During this minimum period, the arranged annuity-type schedule generally may not be changed unless you become disabled. For example, taking a lump-sum distribution of your account balance before the end of the minimum payout period would trigger the retroactive penalty, plus interest charges. The penalty is triggered even if the change in distribution methods is made after you reach age 59½. However, the IRS may allow a reduction in payments during the minimum period, such as where part of an IRA has been transferred to an ex-spouse following a divorce. Also, as noted below, the IRS allows a one-time irrevocable switch from the fixed amortization method or fixed annuitization method to the required minimum distribution method. After the minimum payout period, you can discontinue the payments or change the method without penalty.

Three approved payment methods. If you would like to take advantage of this penalty exception, you may apply one of the following three payout methods that have been approved by the IRS. With each method, you must receive at least one distribution annually. Method 1(the required minimum distribution method) is the easiest method to figure but provides smaller annual payments than the other methods. Methods 2(fixed amortization method) and 3 (fixed annuitization method) require the assistance of a tax professional and financial advisor to plan the series of payments. Under Method 1, the payment changes annually based on the value of the account. Under Methods 2 and 3, the annual payment determined for the first distribution year stays the same in succeeding years. However, after the first year, you can switch without penalty from Method 2 or 3 to Method 1.

The IRS revised the interest rate rules used to apply Methods 2 and 3 for payment schedules starting in 2023 or later (Notice 2022-6); the new rules were optional for payment schedules starting in 2022. Under Notice 2022-6, the interest rate used can be up to 5%, but if that is less than 120% of the federal mid-term rate for either of the two months immediately preceding the month distributions begin, then up to the 120% rate can be used. This is more favorable than the prior rules (Revenue Ruling 2002-62), under which the interest rate could not exceed 120% of the federal mid-term rate. Being able to use an interest rate up to the greater of 5% or the 120% rate allows IRA owners to receive higher annual payments under Methods 2 and 3.

IRS Alert

Division of IRA in Divorce

The IRS in private rulings has allowed a reduction in the scheduled payments from an IRA if part of the IRA is transferred to an ex-spouse as part of a divorce settlement. The reduction in payments is not treated by the IRS as a "modification" that triggers the penalty.

Planning Reminder

Substantially Equal Payments Exception

If you are planning a series of payments to avoid the 10% early distribution penalty, keep in mind that payments under this exception must continue for at least five years, or until you reach age 59½, whichever is the longer period.

Under Notice 2022-6, the life expectancy tables to be used for Methods 1, 2, and 3 are the Single Life Expectancy Table *(Table 8-5 at 8.15)*, the Joint Life Expectancy Table *(see Table 8-2 below)*, and a Uniform Lifetime Table included in the Appendix to Notice 2022-6. If you began a series of payments under the RMD method using the "old" life expectancy table that applied before 2022, you may switch to the new table and the switch will not be considered a "modification" that voids the penalty exception and triggers the 10% penalty on all payments received before age 59½.

1. *Required minimum distribution method.* Figure the annual withdrawal by dividing your account balance by the life expectancy from the table you choose to use. For example, assume that in 2023 you are age 50 on your birthday and need to begin receiving distributions from your IRA, which has a balance of $100,000 at the beginning of the year. If you use your single life expectancy, you may take a penalty-free payment of $2,762 in 2023 ($100,000 account balance ÷ 36.2 life expectancy for a 50-year old from *Table 8-5 (8.15)*). If instead of using your single life expectancy you used the joint life and last survivor expectancy of you and your beneficiary, the penalty-free amount would be smaller given the longer joint life expectancy. If your beneficiary was age 45 (on his or birthday in 2023), your joint life and last survivor life expectancy, as shown in *Table 8-2* below, would be 45.1 years (using ages 50 and 45), and the penalty-free withdrawal would be $2,217 ($100,000 account balance ÷ 45.1). Using the Uniform Lifetime Table from the Appendix in Notice 2022-6, the life expectancy (for a 50-year old) would be 48.5 years, and the penalty-free amount would be $2,062 ($100,000 account balance ÷ 48.5). After 2023, you must continue to use the same life expectancy table.

2. *Fixed amortization method.* Under this method, you amortize your IRA account balance like a mortgage, using one of the life expectancy tables discussed under Method 1 *(see above)*, and an interest rate that can be up to the greater of 5% or 120% of the federal mid-term rate for either of the two months immediately preceding the month in which distributions begin. Once the payment for the first distribution year is determined, the payment must stay the same in each succeeding year. *See* Notice 2022-6 and consult a professional advisor if you are considering using this method.

3. *Fixed annuitization method.* This method figures the annual payment by dividing the account balance by an annuity factor that is the present value of an annuity of $1 per year starting at your current age and continuing for your life or the joint lives of you and your designated beneficiary. The annuity factor is derived from the mortality rates used to calculate the IRS life expectancy tables and an interest rate that can be up to the greater of 5% or 120% of the federal mid-term rate for either of the two months immediately preceding the month in which distributions begin. Once the payment for the first distribution year is determined, the payment must stay the same in each succeeding year. *See* Notice 2022-6 and consult a professional advisor if you are considering using this method.

Table 8-2 Joint Life and Last Survivor Life Expectancy*—*See* "Three approved payment methods" on page 233

Beneficiary \ Self	30	31	32	33	34	35	36	37	38	39	40	41	42	43	44	45	46	47	48	49	50	51	52	53	54	55	56	57	58	59
30	62.0	61.6	61.1	60.7	60.3	59.9	59.5	59.2	58.9	58.6	58.4	58.1	57.9	57.7	57.5	57.3	57.2	57	56.9	56.7	56.6	56.5	56.4	56.3	56.2	56.2	56.1	56	56	55.9
31	61.6	61.1	60.6	60.1	59.7	59.3	58.9	58.6	58.2	57.9	57.6	57.4	57.1	56.9	56.7	56.5	56.3	56.2	56	55.9	55.8	55.6	55.5	55.4	55.3	55.3	55.2	55.1	55	55
32	61.1	60.6	60.1	59.6	59.1	58.7	58.3	57.9	57.6	57.2	56.9	56.7	56.4	56.2	55.9	55.7	55.5	55.4	55.2	55	54.9	54.8	54.7	54.6	54.5	54.4	54.3	54.2	54.1	54.1
33	60.7	60.1	59.6	59.1	58.6	58.1	57.7	57.3	56.9	56.6	56.3	56	55.7	55.4	55.2	54.9	54.7	54.5	54.4	54.2	54.1	53.9	53.8	53.7	53.6	53.5	53.4	53.3	53.2	53.2
34	60.3	59.7	59.1	58.6	58.1	57.6	57.2	56.7	56.3	55.9	55.6	55.3	55	54.7	54.4	54.2	54	53.7	53.6	53.4	53.2	53.1	52.9	52.8	52.7	52.6	52.5	52.4	52.3	52.2
35	59.9	59.3	58.7	58.1	57.6	57.1	56.6	56.2	55.7	55.3	55	54.6	54.3	54	53.7	53.4	53.2	53	52.8	52.6	52.4	52.2	52.1	52	51.8	51.7	51.6	51.5	51.4	51.3
36	59.5	58.9	58.3	57.7	57.2	56.6	56.1	55.6	55.2	54.7	54.3	54	53.6	53.3	53	52.7	52.4	52.2	52	51.8	51.6	51.4	51.3	51.1	51	50.9	50.7	50.6	50.5	50.5
37	59.2	58.6	57.9	57.3	56.7	56.2	55.6	55.1	54.6	54.2	53.8	53.4	53	52.6	52.3	52	51.7	51.5	51.2	51	50.8	50.6	50.4	50.3	50.1	50	49.9	49.8	49.7	49.6
38	58.9	58.2	57.6	56.9	56.3	55.7	55.2	54.6	54.1	53.6	53.2	52.8	52.4	52	51.6	51.3	51	50.7	50.5	50.2	50	49.8	49.6	49.5	49.3	49.1	49	48.9	48.8	48.7
39	58.6	57.9	57.2	56.6	55.9	55.3	54.7	54.2	53.6	53.1	52.7	52.2	51.8	51.4	51	50.7	50.3	50	49.7	49.5	49.2	49	48.8	48.6	48.5	48.3	48.2	48	47.9	47.8
40	58.4	57.6	56.9	56.3	55.6	55	54.3	53.8	53.2	52.7	52.2	51.7	51.2	50.8	50.4	50	49.7	49.3	49	48.8	48.5	48.3	48	47.8	47.7	47.5	47.3	47.2	47.1	46.9
41	58.1	57.4	56.7	56.0	55.3	54.6	54	53.4	52.8	52.2	51.7	51.2	50.7	50.2	49.8	49.4	49	48.7	48.4	48.1	47.8	47.5	47.3	47.1	46.9	46.7	46.5	46.3	46.2	46.1
42	57.9	57.1	56.4	55.7	55	54.3	53.6	53	52.4	51.8	51.2	50.7	50.2	49.7	49.2	48.8	48.4	48	47.7	47.4	47.1	46.8	46.5	46.3	46.1	45.9	45.7	45.5	45.4	45.2
43	57.7	56.9	56.2	55.4	54.7	54	53.3	52.6	52	51.4	50.8	50.2	49.7	49.2	48.7	48.3	47.8	47.4	47.1	46.7	46.4	46.1	45.8	45.6	45.3	45.1	44.9	44.7	44.5	44.4
44	57.5	56.7	55.9	55.2	54.4	53.7	53	52.3	51.6	51	50.4	49.8	49.2	48.7	48.2	47.7	47.3	46.8	46.4	46.1	45.7	45.4	45.1	44.8	44.6	44.3	44.1	43.9	43.7	43.6
45	57.3	56.5	55.7	54.9	54.2	53.4	52.7	52	51.3	50.7	50	49.4	48.8	48.3	47.7	47.2	46.7	46.3	45.9	45.5	45.1	44.7	44.4	44.1	43.8	43.6	43.4	43.1	42.9	42.8
46	57.2	56.3	55.5	54.7	54	53.2	52.4	51.7	51	50.3	49.7	49	48.4	47.8	47.3	46.7	46.2	45.7	45.3	44.9	44.5	44.1	43.8	43.4	43.1	42.9	42.6	42.4	42.2	42
47	57.0	56.2	55.4	54.5	53.7	53	52.2	51.5	50.7	50	49.3	48.7	48	47.4	46.8	46.3	45.7	45.2	44.8	44.3	43.9	43.5	43.1	42.8	42.5	42.2	41.9	41.6	41.4	41.2
48	56.9	56	55.2	54.4	53.6	52.8	52	51.2	50.5	49.7	49	48.4	47.7	47.1	46.4	45.9	45.3	44.8	44.3	43.8	43.3	42.9	42.5	42.1	41.8	41.5	41.2	40.9	40.7	40.4
49	56.7	55.9	55	54.2	53.4	52.6	51.8	51	50.2	49.5	48.8	48.1	47.4	46.7	46.1	45.5	44.9	44.3	43.8	43.3	42.8	42.3	41.9	41.5	41.2	40.8	40.5	40.2	39.9	39.7
50	56.6	55.8	54.9	54.1	53.2	52.4	51.6	50.8	50	49.2	48.5	47.8	47.1	46.4	45.7	45.1	44.5	43.9	43.3	42.8	42.3	41.8	41.4	40.9	40.6	40.2	39.8	39.5	39.2	39
51	56.5	55.6	54.8	53.9	53.1	52.2	51.4	50.6	49.8	49	48.3	47.5	46.8	46.1	45.4	44.7	44.1	43.5	42.9	42.3	41.8	41.3	40.8	40.4	40	39.6	39.2	38.9	38.6	38.3
52	56.4	55.5	54.7	53.8	52.9	52.1	51.3	50.4	49.6	48.8	48	47.3	46.5	45.8	45.1	44.4	43.8	43.1	42.5	41.9	41.4	40.8	40.3	39.9	39.4	39	38.6	38.2	37.9	37.6
53	56.3	55.4	54.6	53.7	52.8	52	51.1	50.3	49.5	48.6	47.8	47.1	46.3	45.6	44.8	44.1	43.4	42.8	42.1	41.5	40.9	40.4	39.9	39.4	38.9	38.4	38	37.6	37.3	36.9
54	56.2	55.3	54.5	53.6	52.7	51.8	51	50.1	49.3	48.5	47.7	46.9	46.1	45.3	44.6	43.8	43.1	42.5	41.8	41.2	40.6	40	39.4	38.9	38.4	37.9	37.5	37.1	36.7	36.3
55	56.2	55.3	54.4	53.5	52.6	51.7	50.9	50	49.1	48.3	47.5	46.7	45.9	45.1	44.3	43.6	42.9	42.2	41.5	40.8	40.2	39.6	39	38.4	37.9	37.4	36.9	36.5	36.1	35.7
56	56.1	55.2	54.3	53.4	52.5	51.6	50.7	49.9	49	48.2	47.3	46.5	45.7	44.9	44.1	43.4	42.6	41.9	41.2	40.5	39.8	39.2	38.6	38	37.5	36.9	36.5	36	35.5	35.1
57	56.0	55.1	54.2	53.3	52.4	51.5	50.6	49.8	48.9	48	47.2	46.3	45.5	44.7	43.9	43.1	42.4	41.6	40.9	40.2	39.5	38.9	38.2	37.6	37.1	36.5	36	35.5	35	34.6
58	56.0	55	54.1	53.2	52.3	51.4	50.5	49.7	48.8	47.9	47.1	46.2	45.4	44.5	43.7	42.9	42.2	41.4	40.7	39.9	39.2	38.6	37.9	37.3	36.7	36.1	35.5	35	34.5	34.1
59	55.9	55	54.1	53.2	52.2	51.3	50.5	49.6	48.7	47.8	46.9	46.1	45.2	44.4	43.6	42.8	42	41.2	40.4	39.7	39	38.3	37.6	36.9	36.3	35.7	35.1	34.6	34.1	33.6

* This table is a section from the IRS' Joint Life and Last Survivor Expectancy Table included in IRS Publication 590-B.

8.13 Required Minimum Distributions (RMDs) From a Traditional IRA

You must start receiving annual required minimum distributions (RMDs) from your traditional IRAs by your "required beginning date". If you also have Roth IRAs *(8.25)*, you do not have to receive any RMDs from those accounts regardless of your age. The RMD rules in this section apply only to traditional IRA owners, not to beneficiaries. Upon the death of the account owner, separate distribution rules apply to beneficiaries of traditional IRAs *(8.14, 8.15)* as well as to Roth IRA beneficiaries *(8.26)*.

As discussed in *8.8*, you can satisfy your RMD requirement while avoiding tax on the distribution by authorizing the trustee of your traditional IRA to make a qualified charitable distribution (QCD).

Failing to take an RMD can result in a 25% penalty; *see* "How much must you receive?" below.

What is your required beginning date? Your required beginning date for starting RMDs is April 1 of the year following the year in which you reach age 73. The rule was different for those who were born before July 1, 1949; for them the required beginning date was April 1 of the year following the year in which they reached age 70½. The SECURE Act raised the age to 72 for IRA owners who reached age 70½ after 2019, meaning those born on or after July 1, 1949. SECURE 2.0 raised the age again; anyone attaining age 72 after 2022 does not have to begin receiving RMDs until the year they reach age 73.

If you were born in 1950, you reach age 73 in 2023 and must receive your first RMD for 2023. You can take the RMD at any time in 2023, or you can delay it until 2024 but no later than April 1, 2024, your required beginning date. However, keep in mind that your second RMD, and the RMD for each year after that, must be received by December 31 of the applicable year. This means that if you delay the first RMD until 2024 (but no later than April 1), you will have to take two distributions in 2024, one by April 1 (the RMD for 2023) and the other by December 31 (the RMD for 2024). This could substantially increase your 2024 taxable income. *See* "How much must you receive", below, for figuring the amount of the 2023 RMD.

If you were born in 1951 or later, you do not have to take an RMD for 2023. If you were born in 1951, you will reach age 73 on your birthday in 2024, and thus your first RMD will be for 2024.

How much must you receive? If an RMD from your traditional IRA is required for 2023, the trustee or custodian of the IRA should have sent you a notice by January 31, 2023, telling you what the RMD for 2023 is or offering to calculate it for you upon your request. You can use Steps 1-3 on below to figure the RMD for 2023 or a later year.

If you do not receive the RMD, a 25% penalty tax applies. If you are subject to a penalty, you should report it on Form 5329, which must be attached to Form 1040 or 1040-SR. You can request a waiver of the penalty on Form 5329 if the failure to receive the proper amount was due to reasonable error and you have or will make up for the shortfall; follow the Form 5329 instructions.

Keep in mind that the RMD rules only determine the minimum amount you must receive each year. You are not limited to that amount; you may withdraw more than the RMD or the entire account if you wish. Whatever you receive will be taxable except to the extent that it is allocable to nondeductible contributions *(8.9)*.

Caution: You cannot avoid tax on an RMD by rolling it over to another account. If you are due an RMD for a year, and a distribution is paid to you before the entire RMD is received, the distribution will be allocated to the RMD, so the amount received cannot be rolled over to the same or different IRA within 60 days *(8.10)*. If erroneously rolled over, the RMD would be treated as an excess contribution, subject to a 6% penalty unless the excess is withdrawn *(8.7)*. However, you may do a tax-free direct transfer of your IRA (where the transfer is direct from your IRA trustee or custodian to another; *see 8.10*) prior to receiving your RMD for the year, so long as the RMD is received from the new IRA.

IRS Alert

Limited Relief for RMDs

IRS Notice 2023-54, released July 14, 2023, provides numerous points of guidance and relief on RMDs. Namely, the IRS will not impose an excise tax for failure to take *specified RMDs*, which the Notice defined as any RMD that would have been required for 2021–2023 under the proposed regulations for (1) an account holder who died after their required beginning date or (2) the beneficiary of an eligible designated beneficiary who died in 2020–2022. For 2021–2023, the IRS will not impose an excise tax for failures to take specified RMDs in the correct amount. If you paid an excise tax for a missed specified RMD, you may request a refund of the excise tax.

As previously noted, you can satisfy your RMD requirement, avoid tax on the distribution and benefit a favored charity by authorizing a qualified charitable distribution (QCD) that goes directly from your account to the charity; *see 8.8* for details.

Figuring Your Required Minimum Distribution (RMD)

As noted earlier, the trustee or custodian of your traditional IRA must calculate the amount of your required minimum distribution or offer to do so. If you are required to receive an RMD for 2023 (see discussion above), the IRA trustee or custodian must tell you what your RMD is by January 31, 2023, or offer to calculate it for you upon your request. The calculation is based on final IRS regulations.

To calculate the RMD for yourself, you can use Steps 1–3 below, which are based on the final IRS regulations.

If the IRA trustee or custodian calculates your RMD, the calculation may be based on the Uniform Lifetime Table *(Table 8-3)*, which assumes that your beneficiary is 10 years younger than you are. However, if your sole beneficiary is your spouse who is more than 10 years younger than you, your RMD can be reduced by using the Joint Life and Last Survivor Expectancy Table *(Table 8-4)*. If this more-than-10-years-younger spousal exception applies and your IRA trustee or custodian does not use the Joint Life and Last Survivor Expectancy Table in calculating your RMD, you can do so yourself by calculating the RMD under Steps 1–3 below.

Steps for figuring your required minimum distribution (RMD). For each of your traditional IRAs, figure the required minimum distribution (RMD) you must receive using Steps 1-3 below. Once you have separately determined the RMD for each IRA, the IRS allows you to aggregate them, so you can withdraw the total RMD for the year from any of the accounts in any combination you choose; *see* Step 3 below. However, keep in mind that these rules apply only to traditional IRAs that you own; they do not apply to IRAs that you have inherited. RMDs from inherited IRAs are figured separately *(see 8.14* or *8.15)*. You may not aggregate the RMDs from your inherited IRAs with the RMDs from your own IRAs.

Step 1: Find the account balance of your traditional IRA as of the previous December 31. The account balance to be used for figuring a required minimum distribution (RMD) is the account balance as of the end of the year before the year for which you are figuring the RMD. Thus, if you are figuring your required minimum distribution (RMD) for 2023, the applicable account balance is the account balance as of December 31, 2022.

The year-end account balance must be adjusted if toward the end of the year there is an outstanding rollover. For example, assume that you withdrew funds from your IRA towards the end of 2022 and you rolled the funds back to the same IRA or a different one within 60 days *(8.10)* but not until early in 2023. To figure your RMDs for 2023, the December 31, 2022 account balance of the receiving IRA must be increased by the rollover amount valued on the date of receipt, even though the rolled over amount was not actually in either account on that date.

Step 2: Divide the account balance (Step 1) by the applicable life expectancy. Under the IRS rules, your life expectancy is taken from the Uniform Lifetime Table *(Table 8-3*, page 240) unless your sole beneficiary is your spouse who is more than 10 years younger than you are. If your spouse is your sole beneficiary and is more than 10 years younger than you are, use the Joint Life and Last Survivor Expectancy Table *(Table 8-4*, page 240); *see* "Exception for younger spouses" below.

The Uniform Lifetime Table provides a distribution period that is different than your single life expectancy; it is based upon a joint life expectancy for you and a "deemed" beneficiary who is exactly 10 years younger than you are. Your beneficiary's actual age does not matter; *see* the Joe Blake Example below. The life expectancy period from the Uniform Lifetime Table applies even if you have not named a beneficiary as of your required beginning date. Furthermore, you continue to use the Uniform Lifetime Table even if you change your beneficiary or beneficiaries after starting to receive RMDs, unless the change results in the naming of your spouse as sole beneficiary for the entire year and you qualify to use the Joint Life and Last Survivor Expectancy Table *(Table 8-4)* because your spouse is more than 10 years younger than you are.

Law Alert

Which Life Expectancy Table to Use

To figure your required minimum distribution (RMD) for any year, use the Uniform Lifetime Table unless the exception for younger spouses applies, in which case you should use the Joint Life and Last Survivor Expectancy Table. *See* Step 2 in *8.13* for details on these tables.

Your distribution period from the Uniform Lifetime Table is the number of years listed next to your age on your birthday in the year for which you are making the computation. For example, if you turn age 73 in 2023 and thus you must receive your first RMD, the distribution period from the Uniform Lifetime Table, based on age 73, is 26.5 years *(Table 8-3*, page 239*)*. Your 2023 RMD is your account balance on December 31, 2022, divided by 26.5. When you figure your RMD for 2024, you will use the distribution period of 25.5 years from the Uniform Lifetime Table for someone age 74.

Exception for younger spouses. If the sole beneficiary of your IRA is your spouse and he or she is more than 10 years younger than you are, do not use the Uniform Lifetime Table *(Table 8-3)* to get your life expectancy for Step 2. Instead, use the actual joint life expectancy of you and your spouse, which will allow you to spread out RMDs over an even longer period. *See Table 8-4* below, which has a sample section of the Joint Life and Last Survivor Expectancy Table. *Table 8-4*, like *Table 8-3*, has been revised by the IRS to reflect longer life expectancies, as noted above.

This exception applies only if your spouse meets the more-than-ten-years-younger test and is the sole beneficiary of your entire interest in the IRA at all times during the calendar year for which the RMD is being figured. If your spouse is named beneficiary during the year or he or she is one of several beneficiaries on the account, the Uniform Lifetime Table must be used for that year. Your spouse would not meet the sole beneficiary test. However, if you are married on January 1 of a year and during the year you divorce or your spouse dies, you are considered married for the entire year and may use the spousal exception to figure that year's RMD using the joint life table *(Table 8-4)*.

If this exception for younger spouse beneficiaries applies, find your joint life expectancy from the IRS table corresponding to both of your ages on your birthdays for the year of the computation. For example, if you are age 73 on your birthday in 2023 and your spouse on his or her birthday in 2023 is age 58, use a joint life expectancy of 30.1 years *(see Table 8-4)* to figure your RMD for 2023. This is longer than the 26.5-year distribution period provided by the Uniform Lifetime Table *(Table 8-3)* for a 72-year-old, which means that your RMD will be somewhat lower using this exception.

Step 3: If you have more than one traditional IRA, total the required minimum distributions (RMDs) for all the accounts. After separately figuring the required minimum distribution (RMD) for each of your IRAs under Step 2, total the amounts. This is the minimum you must receive for the year; you are, of course, free to withdraw more than that. Although you must calculate the RMD separately for each account, you do not have to make withdrawals from each of them. The total RMD from all accounts may be taken from any one account, or more than one account if you prefer. For example, if you have five mutual fund IRAs, you may take the entire RMD from the fund in which you have the largest balance, or from any other combination of funds; *see* Example 3 below. The entire distribution is taxable unless part is allocable to nondeductible IRA contributions *(8.9)*.

EXAMPLES—

1. Joe Blake turned 73 on his birthday in September 2023 and received his first RMD in December 2023. He has one traditional IRA. Joe's beneficiary is his wife Natalia, who is five years younger than he is. To figure his RMD for 2023, Joe divides his account balance at the end of 2023 by the life expectancy from the Uniform Lifetime Table *(Table 8-3)*; the Uniform Lifetime Table is used because Natalia is not more than 10 years younger than he is. As of December 31, 2022, Joe's IRA balance was $300,000. Here is how Joe figures his required minimum distribution (RMD) for 2023:

   Step 1. Account balance of $300,000 as of December 31, 2022.

   Step 2. Based on Joe's age of 73 (as of his birthday in 2023), the applicable life expectancy from the Uniform Lifetime Table *(Table 8-3)* is 26.5 years. The table assumes that Joe has a beneficiary who is age 63 (10 years younger than he is). The fact that Natalia is age 68 in 2023 does not matter.

   Step 3. Divide Step 1 by Step 2: $300,000 ÷ 26.5 = $11,321. This is the RMD for 2023 that Joe must receive by April 1, 2024.

2. Same facts as Example 1, except that Natalia is age 60 on her birthday in 2023. Because she is more than 10 years younger than Joe is, Joe uses the joint life and last survivor expectancy table *(Table 8-4) to figure his 2023 RMD.* Based on their ages of 73 and 60 (on their birthdays in 2023), the joint life expectancy from *Table 8-4* is 28.6 years. Joe's RMD for 2023 is $10,490 ($300,000 ÷ 28.6).

3. Cynthia Lowell has two traditional IRAs. She is 75 on her birthday in 2023. The beneficiary of IRA-1 is Cynthia's brother, who is age 62 on his birthday in 2023. The account balance of IRA-1 as of December 31, 2022 is $200,000. The beneficiary of IRA-2 is Cynthia's husband, who is age 76 on his birthday in 2023. The account balance of IRA-2 at the end of 2021 is $150,000.

   To figure her RMD for 2023, Cynthia finds the applicable life expectancy under the IRS' Uniform Lifetime Table *(Table 8-3)*, using her age of 75 (as of her birthday in 2023). The table assumes that Cynthia has a beneficiary who is 10 years younger than she is; the actual ages of her beneficiaries do not matter.

   IRA-1: The RMD is $8,130. This is the 2022 year-end account balance of $200,000 divided by 24.6, the life expectancy from the Uniform Lifetime Table for a person age 75.

   IRA-2: The RMD is $6,098, the 2022 year-end account balance of $150,000 divided by 24.6, the life expectancy from the Uniform Lifetime Table, using age 75.

   Cynthia's total RMD for 2023 from both IRAs is $14,228, which may be withdrawn from either one of the IRAs or taken partly from both, by Decmber 31, 2023.

Table 8-3   Uniform Lifetime Table*—see Step 2 on page 237

IRA Owner's Age	Distribution Period	IRA Owner's Age	Distribution Period	IRA Owner's Age	Distribution Period
72	27.4	88	13.7	104	4.9
73	26.5	89	12.9	105	4.6
74	25.5	90	12.2	106	4.3
75	24.6	91	11.5	107	4.1
76	23.7	92	10.8	108	3.9
77	22.9	93	10.1	109	3.7
78	22.0	94	9.5	110	3.5
79	21.1	95	8.9	111	3.4
80	20.2	96	8.4	112	3.3
81	19.4	97	7.8	113	3.1
82	18.5	98	7.3	114	3.0
83	17.7	99	6.8	115	2.9
84	16.8	100	6.4	116	2.8
85	16.0	101	6.0	117	2.7
86	15.2	102	5.6	118	2.5
87	14.4	103	5.2	119	2.3
				120+	2.0

*Use this table unless your spouse is your sole IRA beneficiary and he or she is more than 10 years younger than you are. If the exception for younger spouse beneficiaries applies, use the IRS' joint life and last survivor expectancy table with the actual ages of both spouses; *see Table 8-4*, which will provide a longer life expectancy distribution period than the above table provides).

Table 8-4 Joint Life and Last Survivor Expectancy Table—*See* Step 2 on page 237
(for use by owners whose spouses are more than 10 years younger)*

Spouse \ Self	72	73	74	75	76	77	78	79	80	81	82	83	84	85	86	87	88	89	90	91	92
35	50.8	50.7	50.7	50.7	50.7	50.7	50.6	50.6	50.6	50.6	50.6	50.6	50.6	50.6	50.6	50.6	50.6	50.6	50.6	50.6	50.6
36	49.8	49.8	49.8	49.7	49.7	49.7	49.7	49.7	49.7	49.7	49.7	49.6	49.6	49.6	49.6	49.6	49.6	49.6	49.6	49.6	49.6
37	48.9	48.8	48.8	48.8	48.8	48.8	48.7	48.7	48.7	48.7	48.7	48.7	48.7	48.7	48.7	48.7	48.7	48.7	48.6	48.6	48.6
38	47.9	47.9	47.9	47.8	47.8	47.8	47.8	47.8	47.8	47.7	47.7	47.7	47.7	47.7	47.7	47.7	47.7	47.7	47.7	47.7	47.7
39	47.0	46.9	46.9	46.9	46.9	46.9	46.8	46.8	46.8	46.8	46.8	46.8	46.8	46.8	46.7	46.7	46.7	46.7	46.7	46.7	46.7
40	46.0	46.0	46.0	45.9	45.9	45.9	45.9	45.9	45.9	45.8	45.8	45.8	45.8	45.8	45.8	45.8	45.8	45.8	45.8	45.8	45.8
41	45.1	45.1	45.0	45.0	45.0	45.0	44.9	44.9	44.9	44.9	44.9	44.9	44.9	44.8	44.8	44.8	44.8	44.8	44.8	44.8	44.8
42	44.2	44.1	44.1	44.1	44.0	44.0	44.0	44.0	43.9	43.9	43.9	43.9	43.9	43.9	43.9	43.9	43.9	43.9	43.9	43.9	43.8
43	43.2	43.2	43.2	43.1	43.1	43.1	43	43	43	43	43	43	42.9	42.9	42.9	42.9	42.9	42.9	42.9	42.9	42.9
44	42.3	42.3	42.2	42.2	42.2	42.1	42.1	42.1	42.1	42	42	42	42	42	42	42	42	41.9	41.9	41.9	41.9
45	41.4	41.4	41.3	41.3	41.2	41.2	41.2	41.1	41.1	41.1	41.1	41.1	41	41	41	41	41	41	41	41	41
46	40.5	40.4	40.4	40.3	40.3	40.3	40.2	40.2	40.2	40.1	40.1	40.1	40.1	40.1	40.1	40.1	40	40	40	40	40
47	39.6	39.5	39.5	39.4	39.4	39.3	39.3	39.3	39.2	39.2	39.2	39.2	39.2	39.1	39.1	39.1	39.1	39.1	39.1	39.1	39.1
48	38.7	38.6	38.6	38.5	38.5	38.4	38.4	38.3	38.3	38.3	38.3	38.2	38.2	38.2	38.2	38.2	38.2	38.1	38.1	38.1	38.1
49	37.8	37.7	37.7	37.6	37.5	37.5	37.5	37.4	37.4	37.3	37.3	37.3	37.3	37.3	37.2	37.2	37.2	37.2	37.2	37.2	37.2
50	36.9	36.8	36.8	36.7	36.6	36.6	36.5	36.5	36.5	36.4	36.4	36.4	36.3	36.3	36.3	36.3	36.3	36.3	36.3	36.2	36.2
51	36	36	35.9	35.8	35.7	35.7	35.6	35.6	35.5	35.5	35.5	35.4	35.4	35.4	35.4	35.4	35.3	35.3	35.3	35.3	35.3
52	35.2	35.1	35	34.9	34.9	34.8	34.7	34.7	34.6	34.6	34.6	34.5	34.5	34.5	34.5	34.4	34.4	34.4	34.4	34.4	34.4
53	34.3	34.2	34.1	34.1	34	33.9	33.9	33.8	33.7	33.7	33.7	33.6	33.6	33.6	33.5	33.5	33.5	33.5	33.5	33.5	33.5
54	33.5	33.4	33.3	33.2	33.1	33	33	32.9	32.9	32.8	32.8	32.7	32.7	32.7	32.6	32.6	32.6	32.6	32.6	32.5	32.5
55	32.7	32.6	32.4	32.4	32.3	32.2	32.1	32	32	31.9	31.9	31.8	31.8	31.8	31.7	31.7	31.7	31.7	31.7	31.6	31.6
56	31.9	31.7	31.6	31.5	31.4	31.3	31.2	31.2	31.1	31.1	31	31	30.9	30.9	30.9	30.8	30.8	30.8	30.8	30.7	30.7
57	31.1	30.9	30.8	30.7	30.6	30.5	30.4	30.3	30.3	30.2	30.1	30.1	30	30	30	29.9	29.9	29.9	29.9	29.9	29.8
58	30.3	30.1	30	29.9	29.8	29.7	29.6	29.5	29.4	29.3	29.3	29.2	29.2	29.1	29.1	29.1	29	29	29	29	29
59	29.5	29.4	29.2	29.1	29	28.8	28.7	28.7	28.6	28.5	28.4	28.4	28.3	28.3	28.2	28.2	28.2	28.2	28.1	28.1	28.1
60	28.8	28.6	28.4	28.3	28.2	28	27.9	27.8	27.8	27.7	27.6	27.5	27.5	27.4	27.4	27.4	27.3	27.3	27.3	27.3	27.2
61	28.1	27.9	27.7	27.5	27.4	27.3	27.1	27	26.9	26.9	26.8	26.7	26.7	26.6	26.6	26.5	26.5	26.4	26.4	26.4	26.4
62		27.2	27	26.8	26.6	26.5	26.4	26.2	26.1	26	26	25.9	25.8	25.8	25.7	25.7	25.6	25.6	25.6	25.6	25.5
63			26.2	26.1	25.9	25.7	25.6	25.5	25.3	25.2	25.2	25.1	25	25	24.9	24.9	24.8	24.8	24.7	24.7	24.7
64				25.3	25.2	25	24.8	24.7	24.6	24.5	24.4	24.3	24.2	24.1	24.1	24	24	24	23.9	23.9	23.9
65					24.4	24.3	24.1	23.9	23.8	23.7	23.6	23.5	23.4	23.3	23.3	23.2	23.2	23.1	23.1	23.1	23
66						23.5	23.4	23.2	23.1	22.9	22.8	22.7	22.6	22.6	22.5	22.4	22.4	22.3	22.3	22.3	22.2
67							22.7	22.5	22.3	22.2	22.1	22	21.9	21.8	21.7	21.6	21.6	21.5	21.5	21.5	21.4
68								21.8	21.6	21.5	21.3	21.2	21.1	21	20.9	20.9	20.8	20.7	20.7	20.7	20.6
69									20.9	20.7	20.6	20.5	20.4	20.3	20.2	20.1	20	20	19.9	19.9	19.8
70										20	19.9	19.7	19.6	19.5	19.4	19.3	19.2	19.2	19.1	19.1	19
71											19.2	19	18.9	18.8	18.7	18.6	18.5	18.4	18.4	18.3	18.3
72												18.3	18.2	18.1	17.9	17.8	17.7	17.7	17.6	17.5	17.5
73													17.5	17.4	17.2	17.1	17	16.9	16.9	16.8	16.7
74														16.7	16.5	16.4	16.3	16.2	16.1	16.1	16
75															15.9	15.7	15.6	15.5	15.4	15.3	15.3
76																15.1	14.9	14.8	14.7	14.6	14.6
77																	14.3	14.2	14.1	14	13.9
78																		13.5	13.4	13.3	13.2
79																			12.8	12.7	12.6
80																				12.1	11.9
81																					11.4

* This is a section from the IRS' Joint Life and Last Survivor Expectancy Table. Use this table to figure your required minimum distribution only if your spouse is your sole beneficiary and he or she is more than 10 years younger than you are; see "Exception for younger spouses" in Step 2 on page 238. Find your age (as of your birthday for the year you are making the computation) on the horizontal line and your spousal beneficiary's age in the vertical column. For example, if you are age 74 and your spousal beneficiary is 63, the life expectancy factor is 26.2 years. If your age or your spouse's age is not shown here, refer to the full Joint Life and Last Survivor Expectancy Table in IRS Publication 590-B.

8.14 Beneficiaries of Traditional IRA Owners Who Died Before 2020

The major changes for IRA beneficiaries introduced by the SECURE Act *(8.15)* do not apply to you if you are the designated beneficiary of an IRA owner who died before 2020. You may continue to receive required minimum distributions (RMDs) over your life expectancy under pre-SECURE Act rules, taking into account the life expectancy "reset" that took effect starting with 2022 RMDs, as explained below and in the Fred Johnson Example on page 244.

Keep in mind that if the RMD for a year is not received, a penalty tax applies unless the IRS waives it, equal to 25% of the difference between the RMD that should have been received and the amount actually received.

Nonspouse beneficiaries had to reset life expectancy for 2022 and later years. In order to transition to the IRS' new IRS Single Life Expectancy Table *(Table 8-5)* that took effect in 2022, you were required to "reset" the life expectancy that had been used to figure your pre-2022 RMDs, unless you were the surviving spouse of the IRA owner and the sole designated beneficiary of the IRA; *see* "Surviving spouse who is sole designated beneficiary" below.

The new Single Life Expectancy Table *(Table 8-5)* reflects slightly longer life expectancies compared to the pre-2022 table, and the effect of the reset rule was to figure what your life expectancy would have been for 2022 had your initial life expectancy (the life expectancy used to figure your first RMD) been determined under the new table, rather than under the old (pre-2022) table. That redetermined initial life expectancy was then reduced by one (1) for each year that had passed from the initial year until 2022; the result was the reset life expectancy for 2022. Your RMD for 2022 was the account balance at the end of 2021 divided by the reset life expectancy for 2022. The life expectancy used to figure your RMD for 2023 is one year less than the reset life expectancy for 2022, and this "minus one" reduction of life expectancy will continue for each year after 2023. *See* the Fred Johnson Example on page 244 for a step-by-step explanation of the reset rule for 2022 and how it affects your post-2022 RMDs.

> **Note:** If you were older than the IRA owner (not your spouse) and the owner died on or after his or her required beginning date (April 1 of the year after the year in which age 70½ was reached; *see 8.13*), you were allowed to figure your RMDs using the owner's remaining life expectancy, which was longer than your own life expectancy. To reset life expectancy for 2022, the starting point was the life expectancy shown in *Table 8-5* next to the owner's age (on birthday) in the year he or she died, and that number was reduced by one for each subsequent year through 2022.

Surviving spouse who is sole designated beneficiary. If you were the surviving spouse of an IRA owner who died before 2020, and were the sole designated beneficiary of the IRA, you may have elected to treat the IRA as your own, either by retitling the IRA in your name or by making a spousal IRA to an IRA in your name. If you did this, you are subject to the distribution rules for IRA owners *(8.8)*. If your required beginning date age for RMDs was 70½ (because you were born before July 1, 1949), you have been subject to the RMD rules for owners for several years and you must continue taking RMDs under the rules at *8.13*. If you were born on or after July 1, 1949, you will have to begin RMDs for the year in which you reach age 72, at which time your RMDs will be based on the Uniform Lifetime Table for IRA owners, unless you remarry and the exception for younger spouses applies *(8.13)*.

If you did not elect to treat the IRA as your own, you must receive RMDs as a beneficiary over your life expectancy. As the surviving spouse and sole IRA beneficiary, the "reset" rule (discussed earlier) for refiguring life expectancy for 2022 and later years does not apply for you. Your life expectancy is recalculated each year based on your attained age in that year. For example, if you have been receiving RMD's from your spouse's IRA and you are age 63 on your birthday in 2023, your life expectancy for figuring your 2023 RMD is 24.5 years, shown in *Table 8-5* (for a 63-year old, page 243). For 2024, your life expectancy from *Table 8-5* will be 23.7 years, based on age 64, and for 2025, it will be 22.9 years, based on age 65. Recalculating life expectancy this way results in a slightly lower RMD compared to that of nonspouse beneficiaries of the same age, because nonspouse beneficiaries must reduce their initial life expectancy (for the first RMD year), as adjusted by the "reset" rule for 2022, by one year for each succeeding year.

Caution

Nonspouse Beneficiaries Cannot Make a Rollover

If you inherited a traditional IRA before 2020 from someone other than your spouse, and receive a distribution from the account, you are not allowed to roll it over within 60 days. Once a distribution is paid to you, tax on it cannot be avoided. If you want to change investments without incurring tax, you can use a trustee-to-trustee transfer to send all or some of the funds in the inherited IRA to another investment firm. A trustee-to-trustee transfer is not treated as a taxable distribution and is not a prohibited rollover because you do not take possession of the funds *(8.10)*. Make sure that the transferred funds remain in the name of the deceased account owner; *see* the Caution on page 245.

Planning Reminder

Surviving Spouse Can Roll Over a Distribution That Is Not an RMD

If you receive a distribution from your deceased spouse's IRA and it is not an RMD, you can roll that distribution over to your own IRA within the 60-day limit *(8.10)*, even if you are not the sole beneficiary of your deceased spouse's IRA.

Successor beneficiaries. If you are the designated beneficiary of an IRA owner dying before 2020, and you die before receiving the entire account balance, your successor beneficiary may have to receive RMDs for up to nine years after your death, and whether or not the 1–9 year RMD rule applies, your successor must receive the remaining balance by the end of the 10th year after the year of your death. These rules apply regardless of who the successor beneficiary is. The Fred Johnson Example illustrates the rules for successor beneficiaries.

IRS Alert

New Single Life Expectancy Table Took Effect in 2022

Table 8-5 is the Single Life Expectancy Table used to figure RMDs under the life expectancy method. It took effect in 2022 and reflects slightly longer life expectancies than the prior version of the table that applied for 2021 and earlier years. To transition from the old table to the new table, a nonspouse beneficiary who used the prior version of the table to determine his or her initial life expectancy before 2022 had to "reset" life expectancy for 2022, as explained in *8.14*.

Table 8-5 Beneficiary's Single Life Expectancy Table for 2022 and Later Years

Age	Life expectancy	Age	Life expectancy
0	84.6	56	30.6
1	83.7	57	29.8
2	82.8	58	28.9
3	81.8	59	28.0
4	80.8	60	27.1
5	79.8	61	26.2
6	78.8	62	25.4
7	77.9	63	24.5
8	76.9	64	23.7
9	75.9	65	22.9
10	74.9	66	22.0
11	73.9	67	21.2
12	72.9	68	20.4
13	71.9	69	19.6
14	70.9	70	18.8
15	69.9	71	18.0
16	69.0	72	17.2
17	68.0	73	16.4
18	67.0	74	15.6
19	66.0	75	14.8
20	65.0	76	14.1
21	64.1	77	13.3
22	63.1	78	12.6
23	62.1	79	11.9
24	61.1	80	11.2
25	60.2	81	10.5
26	59.2	82	9.9
27	58.2	83	9.3
28	57.3	84	8.7
29	56.3	85	8.1
30	55.3	86	7.6
31	54.4	87	7.1
32	53.4	88	6.6
33	52.5	89	6.1
34	51.5	90	5.7
35	50.5	91	5.3
36	49.6	92	4.9
37	48.6	93	4.6
38	47.7	94	4.3
39	46.7	95	4.0
40	45.7	96	3.7
41	44.8	97	3.4
42	43.8	98	3.2
43	42.9	99	3.0
44	41.9	100	2.8
45	41.0	101	2.6
46	40.0	102	2.5
47	39.0	103	2.3
48	38.1	104	2.2
49	37.1	105	2.1
50	36.2	106	2.1
51	35.3	107	2.1
52	34.3	108	2.0
53	33.4	109	2.0
54	32.5	110	2.0
55	31.6	111+	2.0

EXAMPLE—

Fred Johnson inherited the traditional IRA of his father Todd, who died in 2018 at age 75 after receiving his 2018 required minimum distribution (RMD). As the designated beneficiary, Fred had to begin receiving RMDs from the IRA starting in 2019, the year after the year of Todd's death. To figure his RMD for 2019, Fred divided the account balance as of the end of 2018 (year of Todd's death) by his life expectancy on his birthday in 2019. On his birthday in 2019, Fred was age 50, and under the then-applicable IRS Single Life Expectancy Table, the life expectancy of a 50-year old was 34.2 years. The account balance at the end of 2018 was $400,000, so Fred's RMD for 2019 was $11,696 ($400,000/34.2), which he received by the end of 2019.

To figure his RMD for 2020 (which Fred decided to take although the CARES Act waived RMDs for 2020) and for 2021, Fred continued to decrease his initial life expectancy of 34.2 years by one for each year, and he divided that reduced life expectancy into the account balance as of the end of the prior year. Thus, for the 2020 RMD, Fred's applicable life expectancy was 33.2 years (the initial 34.2 years, minus one), and for the 2021 RMD, life expectancy was reduced to 32.2 years (33.2 for 2020, minus one).

If the IRS had not released a new Single Life Expectancy Table, Fred's applicable life expectancy for figuring his 2022 RMD would have been 31.2 years (one less than the life expectancy of 32.2 years he used to figure his 2021 RMD). However, to transition to the new Table, which took effect with RMDs for 2022 *(Table 8-5* on page 243*)* Fred must refigure his life expectancy for 2022, using the special "reset rule" discussed earlier.

Under the reset rule, Fred's initial life expectancy of 34.2 years for 2019 (his first RMD year; *see* above) is refigured, as if the new Single Life Expectancy Table had applied starting in 2019, when he was age 50. In the new Single Life Expectancy Table *(see* page 243), the life expectancy of a 50-year-old is 36.2 years. This was Fred's refigured initial life expectancy for 2019, which then was reduced by one for each of 2020, 2021, and 2022. Thus, to figure his 2022 RMD, Fred used a "reset" life expectancy of 33.2 years (36.2 years reduced by 3 years). The account balance at the end of 2021 was $525,000, so Fred's RMD for 2022 was $15,813 ($525,000/33.2).

If the old life expectancy table still applied (31.2 years life expectancy for 2022; *see* above), Fred's RMD for 2022 would have been $16,827($525,000/31.2).

To figure his 2023 RMD, Fred will use a life expectancy of 32.2 years (reset life expectancy for 2022 of 33.2, minus 1), and this "minus 1" rule will continue for the rest of his life while there are still funds in the IRA. Thus, to figure his 2024 RMD, Fred's life expectancy will be 31.2 years, for 2025 it will be 30.2 years, and so on. Each year, the applicable life expectancy will be divided into the prior year-end balance to determine the RMD. Of course, Fred may withdraw more than the RMD in any year, which is simply the minimum needed to avoid an IRS penalty. All withdrawals will be taxable unless allocable to nondeductible contributions made by Todd *(8.9)*.

What happens if Fred dies with money still in the account? Under the SECURE Act, Fred's successor beneficiary will have to empty the entire account by the end of the 10th year following the year of Fred's death. However, IRS proposed regulations *(see 8.15)* impose an additional requirement when the account owner died after his or her required beginning date for RMDs *(8.13)*, as was true for Todd here. Since Todd died after his required beginning date, Fred's successor must "step into the shoes" of Fred and for the first nine years after his death continue to receive the same RMDs that Fred would have received had he lived. For example, assume that Fred dies in 2040 after receiving the RMD for the year. His daughter Joan is the beneficiary of his IRA. Under the proposed regulation, Joan must receive the RMDs that Fred would have received for 2041 through 2049, dividing Fred's reduced life expectancy for that year into the account balance at the end of the prior year, as described above. Of course, Joan could withdraw more than the RMD or empty the account at any point during the nine-year period. If anything remains in the account after 2049, Joan must withdraw the balance by the end of 2050, the 10th year after the year of Fred's death.

On the other hand, if Todd had died before his required beginning date, Joan would still have to empty the account by December 31, 2050 under the 10-year rule, but she would not have to receive any distributions before 2050. The proposed regulation requiring RMDs for years 1–9 would not apply so Joan would have flexibility during the 10-year period to decide whether she wants to take distributions (and pay tax on them) in one or more years before 2050.

 *Caution*

Successor Beneficiaries

Where the IRA owner died before 2020 and the designated beneficiary dies after 2019 with money still in the IRA, the SECURE Act requires the successor beneficiary to withdraw all funds from the account by the end of the 10th year following the year of the designated beneficiary's death. However, IRS proposed regulations treat the successor beneficiary as inheriting from an eligible designated beneficiary (EDB, *see 8.15*) and therefore, as in the Fred Johnson example, where the IRA owner died after his or her required beginning date, the successor beneficiary (Joan in this example) must receive annual RMDs for up to nine years after the death of the designated beneficiary (Fred), and then withdraw any balance by the end of the tenth year.

> If Joan were to die with money still in the account during the nine-year RMD period following Fred's death, Joan's successor beneficiary would step into her shoes and continue RMDs for the remainder of the nine-year period, and then withdraw any balance by the end of 2050 under the 10-year rule.

8.15 Beneficiaries of Traditional IRA Owners Who Die After 2019

Unless you are a surviving spouse or other "eligible designated beneficiary" (EDB, defined below), you may not stretch distributions over your life expectancy if you are the beneficiary of an IRA owner dying after 2019. Under the SECURE Act, a designated beneficiary who is not an eligible designated beneficiary (a non-EDB) must receive the entire balance of the inherited IRA by the end of the 10th year following the year of the IRA owner's death. Proposed regulations released in February 2022 (REG-105954-20, 2022-11 IRB 828) add another layer to the 10-year rule by also requiring some non-EDBs to receive required minimum distributions (RMDs) prior to the tenth year, as discussed below. The proposed regulations are comprehensive; some provisions, such as those dealing with trusts as beneficiaries, are beyond the scope of this book. In response to public comments, some of the proposed regulations could be delayed or changed.

Keep in mind that if a beneficiary does not receive an RMD, a penalty generally applies, equal to 25% of the excess of the RMD that should have been received over the amount actually received, although the IRS may waive the penalty if failure to take the required amount was due to reasonable error and the failure is being corrected; an automatic waiver allows a beneficiary more time to take the owner's RMD for the year of death; *see* Example 5 below.

Proposed regulations treat non-EDBs differently depending on when the account owner dies. For non-eligible designated beneficiaries (non-EDBs), the 10-year rule applies regardless of the age of the IRA owner on the date of death; that is, whether the IRA owner died before, on, or after his or her required beginning date for RMDs *(8.13)*. Prior to the release of the proposed regulations, the general consensus among tax practitioners was that under the 10-year rule, there were no annual RMDs prior to the 10th year. That is, the non-EDB could receive distributions in some years and not others so long as the entire IRA was emptied by the end of the 10th year after the year of the owner's death. However, the proposed regulations unexpectedly applied this interpretation of the 10-year rule only to non-EDBs who inherit from account owners who died **before** their required beginning date *(8.13)*. Such non-EDBs do not have to receive anything before the 10th. On the other hand, if the account owner died **on or after** the required beginning date, then the non-EDB must receive RMDs in each of the first nine years after the account owner's death (assuming the account has not been emptied), and also empty the account by the end of the 10th year after the year of the owner's death. In effect, where the owner dies on or after the required beginning date, there is a mandatory "mini-stretch" for years 1-through-9 under which RMDs are figured under the life expectancy method *(see below)*, and if any account balance remains after 9 years, a complete distribution of the balance is required by the end of the 10th year. Examples 3–5 below illustrate these two different versions of the 10-year rule for non-EDBs.

NOTE: The proposed regulation requiring RMDs in the first nine years of the 10-year period (if owner died on/after required beginning date) was strongly criticized by tax practitioners for adding complexity and not being required by the text of the SECURE Act. Shortly before this book was completed, the IRS announced in *Notice 2022-53* (2022-45 IRB 437) that final RMD regulations will apply "no earlier than the 2023 distribution calendar year", and that transition relief for failure to take an RMD for 2021 or 2022 is being provided. No penalty will be imposed if an RMD was required for 2021 or 2022 under the interpretation taken in the proposed regulations but it was not taken by (1) a non-EDB of an IRA owner who died in 2020 or 2021, or (2) a successor beneficiary of an EDB taking life expectancy RMDs if the EDB died in 2020 or 2021.

The following text and the Examples assume that the proposed regulation provisions will be adopted in the forthcoming final regulations. *See* the *e-Supplement* at *jklasser.com* for any update on the regulations.

Caution

Nonspouse Beneficiaries

If you inherit an IRA from someone other than your spouse, you may not treat the inherited IRA as your own IRA, rollover the account, or convert it to a Roth IRA. The deceased IRA owner's name must remain on the account. For example, if you inherit an IRA from your sister, Ann Jones, who died on May 9, 2023, the account should be retitled to indicate that your sister has died and that the IRA is now being held for you, John Jones, as her beneficiary. It could be worded something like this: "Ann Jones, deceased May 9, 2023, IRA FBO John Jones, Beneficiary." Do not put the account in your name. Doing so would be treated by the IRS as a prohibited rollover, resulting in a taxable distribution, as if you had received a total distribution. Although you may not rollover the account, you can authorize a trustee-to-trustee transfer to another IRA custodian if you want to change where your IRA is invested.

As discussed in *8.15*, the distribution rules for a nonspouse beneficiary depend on whether he or she is an eligible designated beneficiary (EDB) or a non-eligible designated beneficiary (non-EDB).

Eligible designated beneficiaries (EDBs). The following beneficiaries are treated as "eligible designated beneficiaries" who can stretch required minimum distributions (RMDs) over their life expectancy (*see* "RMDs figured under life expectancy method" below):

1. *Surviving spouse of the IRA owner.* However, if the surviving spouse is the sole beneficiary of the IRA, he or she can elect to treat the IRA as his or her own (by retitling the IRA or transferring it to an IRA in own name) and be treated as an IRA owner (subject to the owner RMD rules at *8.13*). If the election is not made, the surviving spouse may delay RMDs until the year their spouse would have reached age 72; *see* Example 7 below. A surviving spouse may do a 60-day rollover *(8.10)* of a distribution that is not an RMD, even if he or she is not the sole beneficiary of the IRA.

2. *IRA owner's minor child (grandchildren do not qualify).* EDB status lasts only until the age of majority is reached. Under the proposed regulations, a child is treated as reaching the age of majority on his or her 21st birthday, regardless of whether state law provides a different majority age for other purposes. Starting in the year after the year in which age 21 is reached, the child is treated as a non-eligible designated beneficiary and becomes subject to the 10-year rule. *See* Example 6 below.

3. *Disabled individual.* Under the proposed regulations, if the Social Security Administration has determined, as of the account owner's date of death, that an individual is disabled, that individual is treated as disabled for EDB purposes. If there has not been a Social Security determination, an individual age 18 or older must be unable to engage in any substantial gainful activity because of an impairment (physical or mental) that is expected to result in death or be of " long continued and indefinite duration". If under age 18 when the owner dies, the individual must have an impairment that results in "marked and severe functional limitations" expected to be long continued and of indefinite duration. Documentation of disability must be provided to the IRA custodian by October 31st of the year after the year of the owner's death.

4. *Chronically ill individual.* To qualify as chronically ill for EDB purposes, an individual must provide the IRA custodian with a certification from a licensed health care practitioner by October 31st of the year after the year of the owner's death that the individual is unable to complete at least two activities of daily living (dressing, grooming, eating, ambulating or transferring) without substantial assistance for an indefinite period expected to be lengthy, and not merely for 90 days as under the general tax definition of chronically ill.

5. *Individual who is not more than 10 years younger than the IRA owner.* This category includes anyone who is older than the IRA owner or is 10 years younger or less, taking into account the dates of birth of the account owner and the beneficiary. *See* Example 1 below.

Plan may provide option for EDB. Although an EDB may stretch RMDs over his or her life expectancy and is not subject to the 10-year rule, the proposed regulations allow (but not require) the IRA plan to give an EDB the option to elect the 10-year rule if the IRA owner died before reaching his or her required beginning date; *see* Example 1 below.

RMDs figured under life expectancy method. An EDB generally must begin RMDs under the life expectancy method in the year after the year of the IRA owner's death. Thus, if you are an EDB of an IRA owner who died in 2023, your first RMD is for 2024. However, if the IRA owner died before the year in which he or she would have reached age 72, and you are the owner's surviving spouse and the sole beneficiary of the IRA, you may delay the start of RMDs until the year in which your spouse would have reached age 72; *see* Example 7 below. Under the proposed regulations, a non-EDB of an IRA owner who dies on or after his or her required beginning date also uses the life expectancy method to figure RMDs, but only for up to nine years after the year of the IRA owner's death, with a full distribution required by the end of the 10th year.

The RMD for a year is generally figured by dividing the account balance as of the end of the prior year by your life expectancy from the Single Life Expectancy Table *(Table 8-5)*. If you are not the IRA owner's surviving spouse, the initial life expectancy used for the first RMD year is reduced by one year for each subsequent year, as shown in Example 1 below. If you are the EDB of an IRA owner who died on or after the required beginning date, and you were older than the owner, you figure your RMDs using the owner's life expectancy

 *Law Alert*

An Estate Is Not a Designated Beneficiary

The rules in *8.15* apply only to eligible designated beneficiaries, or non-eligible designated beneficiaries. A designated beneficiary is an individual named by the IRA owner on the IRA beneficiary form, or an individual designated as a beneficiary by the terms of the plan. An estate is not a designated beneficiary, so IRS regulations apply different distribution rules where the owner's estate is the IRA beneficiary and you inherit through the estate. These rules were **not** changed by the SECURE Act.

If the IRA owner dies on or after his or her required beginning date *(8.13)*, distributions may be spread over the IRA owner's remaining life expectancy; the life expectancy as of the year of death is reduced by one for each subsequent year when figuring RMDs. Note that the remaining life expectancy may be longer than the 10-year period over which non-eligible designated beneficiaries must empty the account under the SECURE Act *(8.15)*.

If the IRA owner dies before his or her required beginning date *(8.13)*, the 5-year rule applies, and the entire account must be distributed by the end of the fifth year following the year of the owner's death; nothing has to be distributed before the fifth year. For example, if a 68-year old IRA owner dies in 2022, leaving his IRA to his estate, the entire account must be paid out by the end of 2027.

(longer than your own life expectancy) as of the year of death *(Table 8-5)*, reduced by one for each subsequent year.

If you are the owner's surviving spouse and sole IRA beneficiary, your life expectancy is recalculated each year based on your attained age in that year, as shown in *Table 8-5*, so the" minus one" rule does not apply. For example, if your first RMD is for 2024 and you are age 63 on your birthday in 2024, your life expectancy for figuring your 2024 RMD is 24.5 years, shown in *Table 8-5* (for a 63-year old). For 2025, your life expectancy from *Table 8-5* will be 23.7 years, based on age 64, and for 2026, it will be 22.9 years, the life expectancy from *Table 8-5* for a 65-year old.

If you are a nonspouse EDB who began RMDs in 2021, your life expectancy had to be "reset" for 2022 and future years in order to transition to the new IRS Single Life Expectancy Table *(Table 8-5)*; *see* the explanation of the reset rule in *8.14*.

Co-beneficiaries can split IRA into separate accounts. If there is more than one individual beneficiary on the IRA as of September 30 of the year after the year of the owner's death, and there is not a timely split of the IRA into separate accounts, the IRS requires the life expectancy of the oldest beneficiary (the shortest life expectancy) to be used by all the beneficiaries when figuring RMDs. The IRS deadline for co-beneficiaries to split the IRA into separate accounts is December 31 of the year following the year of the IRA owner's death. If one of the IRA beneficiaries is an EDB and one or more beneficiaries are non-EDBs, such as where one beneficiary is the owner's adult child (non- EDB) and another is the owner's minor child (EDB), they are subject to different rules and the account should be split. Similarly, a surviving spouse can treat the IRA as his or her own only if the surviving spouse is the sole IRA beneficiary, so if there is a co-beneficiary, separate accounts should be created to allow the surviving spouse to use that rule. If all beneficiaries are EDBs, the IRA should be split into separate accounts so they can each take RMDs from separate accounts based on their own life expectancy. Even if all of the co-beneficiaries are non-EDBs subject to the 10-year rule, splitting the IRA into separate accounts allows each beneficiary to decide how to invest their account and how to time distributions within the 10-year period, and if the non-EDBs are also required by the proposed regulations to take RMDs for up to nine years after the year of the owner's death, splitting the IRA into separate accounts allows each of them to figure the RMDs using their own life expectancy.

Successor beneficiaries. If an EDB receiving RMDs under the life expectancy method dies with money remaining in the account, the successor beneficiary must empty the account by the end of the 10th year following the year of the EDB's death, but under the proposed regulations, the successor may also have to take annual RMDs for up to nine years after the year of the EDB's death; *see* Example 2 below.

A non-EDB is always subject to the 10-year rule and may also be required by the proposed regulations to receive RMDs for up to nine years after the year of the owner's death. If the non-EDB dies before the end of the 10-year period with money still in the account, the successor beneficiary is subject to the same 10-year rule that applied to the non-EDB, and if the non-EDB was required to take RMDs for the first nine years and dies within the nine-year period, the successor must continue those RMDs in addition to taking a full distribution of the balance by the end of the 10th year; *see* Examples 4 and 5 below.

EXAMPLES

1. Steven dies in 2024 at age 68. His IRA beneficiary is his brother Peter, age 63. Peter is an eligible designated beneficiary (EDB) because he was not more than 10 years younger than Steven. As an EDB, Peter can take required minimum distributions (RMDs) under the life expectancy method starting in 2025 (the year after Steven's death). Peter's RMD for 2025 will equal the account balance as of the end of 2024 divided by 23.7, the life expectancy of a 64-year-old (Peter's age on his birthday in 2025) from *Table 8-5.* If the 2024 year-end balance is $500,000, the 2025 RMD will be $21,097 ($500,000/23.7). For 2026, Peter will reduce the initial 23.7-year life expectancy by one year to 22.7-years, and continue this "minus one" reduction for years after 2026. Of course, Peter may take more than the RMD in any year.

Under the proposed regulations, the plan may, but is not required to, allow an EDB of an owner who dies before the required beginning date to "elect out" of the life expectancy method and use the 10-year rule instead. Steven was born in 1956 and his death in 2024 at age 68 was before his required beginning date (he died before April 1 of the year after the year age 72 would have been reached, 8.13), so if the plan allows it, Peter could elect the 10-year rule instead of taking RMDs annually over his life expectancy. Peter might consider making the election if he prefers the flexibility of the 10-year rule, which would allow him to take distributions in some years but not others prior to the 10th year; however, the entire IRA would have to be emptied by the end of 2034, the 10th year after the year Steven died.

2. Same facts as Example 1, but Peter dies in 2041 after receiving his RMD for the year. His IRA successor beneficiary is his daughter Kathy. Kathy is subject to the 10-year rule and must empty the account by December 31, 2051. Because Steven died before his required beginning date, Kathy may but does not have to take any distributions before 2051.

   What if Steven had died after his required beginning date? For example, assume Steven is age 74 when he dies in 2024, and Peter is 69. Peter would still take RMDs as an EDB (he was not more than 10 years younger than Steven) under the life expectancy method. However, because Steven died after his required beginning date, when Peter dies in 2041, his successor beneficiary Kathy will be subject to both the 10-year rule and the proposed regulation requirement that she take annual RMDs for the first nine year's after Peter's death. Kathy would "step into" Peter's shoes and continue his RMDs for 2042 through 2050 (using the same method Peter would have had he lived), and she must empty the account by December 31, 2051.

3. Kristen dies in 2024 at age 67. The beneficiary of her IRA is her 45-year-old daughter, Carla. Carla is not disabled or chronically ill and thus she is a non-EDB. Carla is subject to the 10-year rule and must empty the account by December 31, 2034. Under the IRS proposed regulations, Carla is not required to take annual distributions from the IRA before 2034 because Kristen died before her required beginning date (8.13). This provides Carla tax-planning flexibility, as she can take distributions in some years and not others to minimize the tax liability on the distributions. The only requirement is that the account must be completely distributed by the end of 2034 (the 10th year after the year of Kristen's death).

4. Same facts as Example 3, but Carla dies in 2030, four years before her 10-year deadline of December 31, 2034, with money still in the account. Carla's son Jonathan is the successor beneficiary of the IRA. Jonathan must empty the account by Carla's deadline of December 31, 2034; he does not get a new 10-year period. He does not have to take annual distributions before 2034.

5. Same facts as in Examples 3 and 4, but Kristen is age 77 when she dies in 2024. Because Kristen dies after her required beginning date, the proposed regulations require Carla to take RMDs (figured under the life expectancy method; see Example 1) for nine years, for 2025 (year after Kristen's death) through 2033. Of course, Carla may take more than the RMD in any year. If there is an account balance at the end of 2033, Carla must receive it by December 31, 2034 under the 10-year rule.

   What if Kristen had not received her RMD for 2024 before she died, or she had received only part of the RMD? Generally, if an IRA owner dies before receiving the RMD for the year, the beneficiary must do so by the end of that year or be subject to a penalty. However, the proposed regulations automatically waive the penalty for the year of the owner's death if the beneficiary receives the RMD by the beneficiary's tax filing deadline (including extensions). Here, the penalty would be waived if Carla receives the RMD by the deadline for her 2024 return, April 15, 2025 (plus any extensions).

   If Carla dies in 2030, her successor beneficiary Jonathan "steps into" Carla's shoes and must continue to receive the same RMDs that Carla would have received for the remainder of the 9-year period. Assume Carla received her 2030 RMD before she died. Jonathan would have to receive the RMDs that Carla would have received for 2031 through 2033, and then, if there is a balance, take it by the end of 2034.

6. James dies in 2024 at age 51. His daughter Marla, age 11, is the beneficiary of his IRA. As James' minor child, Marla is an eligible designated beneficiary (EDB) through the year in which she turns age 21. Starting in 2025 (year after James' death), when she is 12, through 2034, the year in which she turns age 21, Marla receives RMDs under the life expectancy method. Starting in 2035 (the year after reaching age 21), Marla is considered a non-EDB subject to the 10-year rule. She

Caution

Inherited IRAs Not Exempt in Bankruptcy

The Supreme Court unanimously held that funds held in an inherited IRA are not "retirement funds", and thus are not exempt from creditors under the federal bankruptcy law. Although contributory IRAs (traditional and Roth) are exempt from creditors up to a limit, and IRAs set up by rollovers from 401(k) plans are fully exempt, similar bankruptcy protection does not apply to inherited IRAs. Although the beneficiary seeking the bankruptcy exemption might invest the funds and preserve the account for his or her own future retirement, the beneficiary did not set aside the funds for retirement. In support of its conclusion that inherited IRAs are not "retirement funds," the Court pointed out that the beneficiary may not add contributions to the inherited account, required minimum distributions must be taken based on life expectancy without regard to retirement, and withdrawals can be taken at any time for any purpose without penalty, as there is no pre-age 59½ penalty for beneficiaries (Clark, U.S. Supreme Court, 6/12/14). But check state law because some states do exempt all inherited IRAs from creditor claims in bankruptcy; this overrides the Court's decision where applicable.

must empty the balance of the IRA by the end of 2044, the year in which she turns age 31, but annual distributions are not required in 2035 through 2043.

In most cases, as here with James and Marla, when a minor child inherits an IRA from a parent, the parent will have died before his or her required beginning date. But if James had died after his required beginning date, say at age 74, then under the proposed regulations, Marla would continue to receive annual RMDs under the life expectancy method for the nine years after the year in which she turned age 21 (2035 through 2043), with a full distribution of the account required by the end of 2044, the year she turns age 31.

7. Jana's husband Luis dies in 2023 at age 66. Jana is the sole beneficiary of Luis' IRA. Since Luis died before 2029, the year in which he would have reached age 72, Jana may delay the start of RMDs from the IRA until 2029, assuming she did not elect to treat the IRA as her own. On her birthday in 2029, Jana will be 65. To figure her RMD for 2029, she will use a life expectancy of 22.9 years, the life expectancy for a 65-year-old in *Table 8-5*. If the account balance at the end of 2028 is $450,000, Jana's RMD for 2029 will be $19,651 ($450,000/22.9). For each subsequent year, Jana will use the life expectancy from *Table 8-5* for her attained age. Thus, for 2030, her life expectancy from *Table 8-5*, based on age 66, will be 22 years, and for 2031, based on age 67, it will be 21.2 years.

8.16 SEP Basics

A simplified employee pension plan (SEP) set up by an employer allows the employer to contribute to an employee's IRA account more money than is allowed under regular IRA rules. For 2023, your employer generally could contribute and deduct up to 25% of your compensation or $66,000, whichever is less. Your employer's SEP contributions are excluded from your pay and are not included on Form W-2 unless they exceed the limit. If contributions exceed the limit, the excess is included in your gross income and a 6% penalty tax may be imposed unless the excess (plus allocable income) is withdrawn by the due date of the return, plus extensions *(8.7)*. If you are under age 59½, the 10% early distribution penalty may apply to the withdrawal of income earned on the excess contributions *(8.12)*. Self-employed individuals may set up a SEP as an alternative to a self-employed retirement plan; *see Chapter 41*.

Eligibility. A SEP must cover all employees who are at least age 21, earn over $750, and who have worked for the employer at any time during at least three of the past five years. Union employees covered by union agreements may generally be excluded.

SEP salary-reduction arrangements. If a qualifying small employer set up a salary-reduction SEP before 1997, employees may contribute a portion of their pay to the plan instead of receiving it in cash *(8.17)*.

SEP distributions. Distributions from a SEP, including salary-reduction SEPs established before 1997, are subject to the regular distribution rules for traditional IRAs *(8.8)*.

8.17 Salary-Reduction SEP Set Up Before 1997

Qualifying small employers may offer employees the option of deferring a portion of their salary to an IRA. There are two types of salary-reduction IRAs, with different eligibility and contribution rules: (1) salary-reduction SEPs established before 1997 and (2) "SIMPLE" IRA accounts established after 1996.

After 1996, an employer may establish a SIMPLE plan but not a salary-reduction SEP. Rules for SIMPLE IRAs established after 1996 are at *8.17–8.18*. A salary-reduction SEP that was established before 1997 may continue to receive contributions under the prior law rules discussed below, and employees hired after 1996 may participate in the plan, subject to those rules.

Salary-reduction SEPs established before 1997. Salary reductions are allowed for a year only if the employer had no more than 25 employees eligible to participate in the SEP at any time during the prior taxable year. Furthermore, at least 50% of the eligible employees must elect the salary-reduction option, and the deferral percentage for highly compensated employees may not exceed 125% of the average contribution of regular employees.

Assuming salary reductions were allowed, the maximum salary-reduction contribution for 2023 was $22,500 ($30,000 for participants age 50 or older if the plan permitted the extra $7,500 "catch-up" deferral), although a lower limit may be imposed by the plan terms. These are the same limits as for 401(k) plans *(7.16)*. Deferrals over $22,500 ($30,000 if extra deferral for participants age 50 or older was allowed) are taxable, and if not timely distributed to the employee, can be taxed again when distributed from the plan.

If an employee contributes to both a SEP and a 401(k) plan, the annual limit applies to the total salary reductions from both plans. If an employee makes salary-reduction contributions to a SEP and also to a tax-sheltered annuity plan *(7.21)*, the annual limit generally applies to the total salary reductions to both plans. In some cases, employees with at least 15 years of service may be able to defer an additional $3,000 to the tax-sheltered annuity plan *(7.21)*.

8.18 Who Is Eligible for a SIMPLE IRA?

A SIMPLE IRA is a salary-reduction retirement plan that qualifying small employers may offer their employees. For 2023, the maximum salary-reduction contribution was $15,500, or $19,000 for participants age 50 or older (by the end of 2023) if the plan allowed the additional contributions. Employers are required to make matching contributions or a flat contribution *(8.19)*.

Qualifying employers. A SIMPLE IRA may be maintained only by an employer that (1) in the previous calendar year had no more than 100 employees who earned compensation of $5,000 or more and (2) does not maintain any other retirement plan (unless the other plan is for collective bargaining employees). A self-employed individual who meets these tests may set up a SIMPLE IRA, as discussed in *Chapter 41*. A simple IRA must be maintained on a calendar-year basis.

In determining whether the 100-employee test is met for the prior year, all employees under the common control of the employer must be counted. For example, Joe Smith owned two businesses in 2022, a computer rental company with 80 employees and a computer repair company with 60 employees. If they all earned at least $5,000, they all count towards the 100 limit, so if Joe decides in 2023 to set up a retirement plan for his businesses, a different type of plan must be used. He may not establish a SIMPLE IRA for either business under the 100-employee limit.

If a SIMPLE IRA is established but the employer in a later year grows beyond the 100-employee limit, the employer generally has a two-year "grace period" during which contributions may continue to be made.

Eligible employees. In general, an employee must be allowed to contribute to a SIMPLE IRA for a year in which he or she is reasonably expected to earn $5,000 or more, provided at least $5,000 of compensation was received in any two prior years, whether or not consecutive. If the employer owns more than one business (under common control rules) and sets up a SIMPLE IRA for one of them, employees of the other business must also be allowed to participate if they meet the $5,000 compensation tests. Employees who are covered by a collective bargaining agreement may be excluded if retirement benefits were the subject of good-faith negotiations.

The employer may lower or eliminate the $5,000 compensation requirement in order to broaden participation in the plan. No other conditions on eligibility, such as age or hours of work, are permitted.

Deadline for setting up a SIMPLE IRA. An employer generally may establish a SIMPLE IRA effective on any date between January 1 and October 1 of a year. If the employer (or a predecessor employer) previously maintained a SIMPLE IRA, a new SIMPLE IRA may be effective only on January 1 of a year. A new employer that comes into existence after October 1 of a year may establish a SIMPLE IRA for that year if the plan is established as soon as administratively feasible after the start of the business.

 *Planning Reminder*

401(k) SIMPLE Plans

An employer with a 401(k) plan that reports on the calendar year may avoid the regular 401(k) nondiscrimination tests by following the contribution rules for SIMPLE IRAs *(7.17)*.

Planning Reminder

Employer's Intended Contributions

The IRS model notification included with Form 5304-SIMPLE or 5305-SIMPLE requires the employer to tell employees how much the employer will be contributing for the upcoming year.

Planning Reminder

Rollover to SIMPLE IRA from Other Retirement Plans

A tax-free rollover contribution may not be made to a SIMPLE IRA from a qualified employer plan or traditional IRA until after the end of the two-year period starting with the date the employee initially participates in the SIMPLE IRA. There is no such waiting period for a rollover from one SIMPLE IRA to another SIMPLE IRA; the rollover can be made in the initial two years of participation, as well as afterwards.

Planning Reminder

Deciding on Your Elective Deferrals

You must be given time—from November 1 through December 31—to decide on your elective deferrals for the coming year.

The employer may use a model SIMPLE IRA approved by the IRS to set up a SIMPLE IRA. Form 5304-SIMPLE allows employees to select a financial institution to which the contributions will be made. With Form 5305-SIMPLE, the employer selects the financial institution to which contributions are initially deposited, but employees have the right to subsequently transfer their account balances without cost or penalty to another SIMPLE-IRA at a financial institution of their own choosing. Use of the IRS model forms is optional; other documents satisfying the statutory requirements for a SIMPLE IRA may be used.

SIMPLE IRA contributions and distributions. Contributions and distributions to SIMPLE IRAs are subject to limitations *(8.19)*.

8.19   SIMPLE IRA Contributions and Distributions

The only contributions that may be made to a SIMPLE IRA are elective salary-reduction contributions by employees and matching or non-elective contributions by employers. All contributions are fully vested and nonforfeitable when made.

Regardless of compensation, eligible employees *(8.18)* may elect each year to make salary-reduction contributions to the plan up to the annual SIMPLE IRA limit *(8.18)*. Salary-reduction contributions are excluded from the employee's taxable pay on Form W-2 and not subject to federal tax withholding. They are subject to FICA withholding for Social Security and Medicare tax.

Eligible employees must be given notice by the employer of their right to elect salary-reduction contributions and at least 60 days to make the election. After the first year of eligibility, the election to defer for the upcoming year is made during the last 60 days (at minimum) of the prior calendar year. If the employer uses model IRS Form 5304-SIMPLE or 5305-SIMPLE, a notification document is included.

If an employee contributes to a SIMPLE IRA and also to a 401(k) plan, 403(b) or salary-reduction SEP of another employer for the same year, the salary-reduction contributions to the SIMPLE IRA count toward the overall annual limit on tax-free salary-reduction deferrals *(7.17)*. Deferrals over the annual limit are taxable and must be removed to avoid being taxed again when distributed from the plan *(7.18)*.

Employer contributions. Each year, the employer must make either a matching contribution or a fixed "non-elective" contribution. If the employer chooses matching contributions, the employee's elective salary-reduction contribution generally must be matched, up to a limit of 3% of the employee's compensation. For up to two years in any five-year period, the 3% matching limit may be reduced to as low as 1% for each eligible employee.

Instead of making either the 3% or reduced (between 1% and 3%) limit matching contribution, the employer may make a "non-elective" contribution equal to 2% of each eligible employee's compensation. If this option is chosen, the 2% contribution must be made for eligible employees whether or not they elect to make salary-reduction contributions for the year. The 2% contribution is subject to an annual compensation limit, which for 2023 was $330,000. Thus, for 2023, the maximum 2% non-elective contribution was $6,600 (2% of $330,000) even if an employee earned more than $330,000. The 3% matching contribution is not subject to the annual compensation limit, but only to the annual salary-reduction limit *(8.18)*. The employer must notify eligible employees of the type of contribution it will be making for the upcoming year prior to the employees' 60-day election period for making elective salary-reduction contributions. The employer must make the matching or non-elective contributions by the due date for filing the employer's tax return (plus extensions) for the year.

Distributions from a SIMPLE IRA. A distribution from a SIMPLE IRA is fully taxable unless a tax-free rollover or trustee-to-trustee transfer is made. The penalty for distributions before age 59½ *(8.12)* is increased to 25% from 10%, assuming no penalty exception applies, if the distribution is received during the two-year period starting with the employee's initial participation in the plan. After the first two years, the regular 10% penalty applies.

In the initial two-year period, a tax-free rollover or direct trustee-to-trustee transfer *(8.10)* of a SIMPLE IRA may be made to another SIMPLE IRA. After two years of participation, a tax-free rollover or direct transfer may be made to a traditional IRA, qualified plan, 403(b) plan, or state or local government 457 plan, as well as to a SIMPLE IRA. The required minimum distribution rules that apply to regular IRAs also apply to SIMPLE IRAs *(8.13)*.

8.20 Roth IRA Advantages

As with traditional IRAs, earnings accumulate within a Roth IRA tax free until distributions are made. The key benefit of the Roth IRA is that tax-free withdrawals of contributions may be made at any time and earnings may be withdrawn tax free after a five-year holding period by an individual who is age 59½ or older, is disabled, or who pays qualifying first-time homebuyer expenses *(8.25)*.

A Roth IRA can provide attractive retirement planning and estate planning opportunities. Roth IRA contributions can be made at any age, provided you have taxable compensation for the year and your modified adjusted gross income does not exceed the annual limitation under the Roth IRA phaseout rule *(8.21)*. Also, the minimum required distribution (RMD) rules that apply to traditional IRA owners *(8.13)* do not apply to Roth IRA owners; a Roth IRA owner does not have to take any distributions from the account, regardless of age. The balance of a Roth IRA that is not withdrawn during the owner's lifetime generally may be paid out to the beneficiaries tax free *(8.26)*.

A Roth IRA is funded by making annual nondeductible contributions (subject to the income phaseout rule at *8.21*), by converting a traditional IRA, SEP or SIMPLE IRA, or rolling over a distribution from an employer plan, but the conversion or rollover to the Roth IRA is treated as a taxable transfer, as discussed at *(8.22)*.

Your employer can set up a "deemed Roth IRA" as a separate account under a qualified retirement plan. As long as the separate account otherwise meets the Roth IRA rules, you can make voluntary employee contributions that will be subject only to the Roth IRA rules. A deemed IRA can also be set up as a traditional IRA *(8.1)*.

8.21 Annual Contributions to a Roth IRA

You may make a nondeductible Roth IRA contribution, regardless of your age, for a year in which you have taxable compensation for personal services and your modified adjusted gross income (MAGI) does not exceed the upper end of the phaseout range for your filing status. An annual Roth IRA contribution is not reported on your tax return.

The maximum contribution to a Roth IRA, prior to any phaseout, is the same as the traditional IRA limit *(8.2)*. For 2023, the pre-phaseout limit is $6,500 if you are under age 50, or $7,500 if you are age 50 or older at the end of the year, assuming taxable compensation is at least much. The 2023 phaseout rules for Roth IRA contributions are explained below.

If you decide to contribute to a traditional IRA to get a tax deduction, you can in a later year transfer the funds to a Roth IRA by making a taxable conversion *(8.23)*. If you initially contribute to a traditional IRA, you have until the filing deadline to "recharacterize" the contribution as a Roth IRA contribution, and similarly, if you initially contribute to a Roth IRA, you can recharacterize it as a traditional IRA contribution; *see 8.22* for the recharacterization rules. You can contribute to both a Roth IRA and a traditional IRA for the same year, but the annual contribution limit ($6,500/$7,500 for 2023) applies to the combined contributions, as discussed further below.

The Roth IRA rules do not replace the traditional IRA nondeductible contribution rules *(8.6)*. For an individual who is unable to contribute to a Roth IRA because the contribution limit is phased out, and who is unable to make deductible traditional IRA contributions because of the phaseout rules for active plan participants *(8.4)*, nondeductible contributions may still be made to a traditional IRA *(8.6)*.

Contributing to Roth IRA and traditional IRA for the same year. If you contribute to both a traditional IRA and Roth IRA for the same year, total contributions for the year to both types of IRAs may not exceed the lesser of (1) the annual limit ($6,500/$7,500 for 2023), or (2) your taxable compensation. This overall limit is applied first to the traditional IRA contributions and then to the Roth IRA contributions. Thus, the maximum contribution limit for 2023 to a Roth IRA is: (1) $6,500, or $7,500 if you are age 50 or older, or,

Caution

Increased Pre–Age 59½ Penalty

In the first two years of SIMPLE IRA participation, the penalty for distributions before age 59½ is increased from 10% to 25%.

Caution

Roth IRA Contribution Deadline

The deadline for making Roth IRA contributions for 2023 is April 15, 2024, the regular due date for your 2023 return. This is the contribution deadline even if you obtain a filing extension for your 2023 return.

No Age Limit for Roth IRA Contributions

You can contribute to a Roth IRA regardless of age, provided you have taxable compensation and are not subject to the MAGI phaseout.

if less, your taxable compensation, minus (2) deductible *(8.4)* or nondeductible *(8.6)* contributions to traditional IRAs. However, this maximum contribution limit may be reduced, as discussed below, by the MAGI phaseout rule for annual Roth IRA contributions.

Contribution deadline. Contributions to a Roth IRA for a year may be made by the filing due date, without extensions. For 2023 contributions, the deadline is April 15, 2024.

Spousal contribution on joint return for nonworking or low-earning spouse. If you are married filing jointly, you generally may contribute to a Roth IRA for each spouse up to the annual limit ($6,500 for spouse under age 50 or $7,500 for spouse age 50 or older at end of 2023) so long as your combined taxable compensation is at least $13,000 if both of you are under age 50 at the end of 2023, $14,000 if one of you is age 50 or older at the end of 2023, or $15,000 if both of you are age 50 or older at the end of 2023. This is the same spousal contribution rule as for traditional IRAs *(8.3)*; the lower-earning spouse is allowed to "borrow" compensation of the higher-earning spouse for contribution purposes. However, the Roth IRA contribution limit may be reduced because of the MAGI phaseout rules, discussed below.

Excess contributions. If Roth IRA contributions exceed the allowable limit, the excess contribution is subject to a 6% penalty tax unless you withdraw the excess, plus any earnings on the excess contribution, by the filing due date including extensions. The earnings must be reported as income for the year the contribution was made. If you timely file your 2023 return (by April 15, 2024) without withdrawing an excess contribution made in 2023, the IRS will give you until October 15, 2024 to make the withdrawal, and an amended return must be filed for 2023 to report the earnings on the withdrawn contributions; *see* the instructions to Form 5329.

Phaseout of Roth IRA Contribution Limit for 2023

The 2023 Roth IRA contribution limit of $6,500 or $7,500 (or if less, your taxable compensation) is phased out if your 2023 modified adjusted gross income (MAGI) falls within the phaseout range shown in *Table 8-6*. If your MAGI for 2023 is over the phaseout threshold but less than the phaseout endpoint in *Table 8-6*, part or most of the full contribution limit ($6,500 or $7,500, or if less, taxable compensation) will be phased out, depending on how close MAGI is to the endpoint. If MAGI equals or exceeds the applicable phaseout endpoint, the phaseout is 100% and no Roth IRA contribution for 2023 is allowed.

The MAGI phaseout rule applies to Roth IRA contributions regardless of whether you are covered by an employer retirement plan, unlike the deductible traditional IRA phaseout rules *(8.4)*, which apply only to active plan participants.

Note that the Roth IRA phaseout ranges in *Table 8-6* are considerably higher than the phaseout ranges for deductible contributions to a traditional IRA *(8.4)*, unless you are married filing separately and lived with your spouse at any time during the year. If you could claim a deduction for a traditional IRA contribution, consider whether the present tax benefit from the deduction is outweighed by the value of being able to obtain tax-free distributions from a Roth IRA in the future (*see 8.25* for the Roth IRA distribution rules).

MAGI. For purposes of determining if your Roth IRA contribution limit is reduced by the phaseout rule, MAGI may be higher than the actual AGI reported on your return because certain deductions and exclusions that you claim must be added back to AGI. On the other hand, if you convert a traditional IRA to a Roth IRA (or rollover funds from employer plan to a Roth IRA), the transfer is generally fully taxable *(8.23)*, but the amount included in AGI from the conversion is subtracted from AGI to figure MAGI for Roth IRA contribution purposes. The specific steps for computing MAGI for Roth IRA purposes are in *Worksheet 8-3* below.

After computing your MAGI using *Worksheet 8-3*, you can use *Worksheet 8-4* to figure if your Roth IRA contribution limit is reduced for 2023 under the phaseout rules, The Examples below *Worksheet 8-4* illustrates how the phaseout rule works.

Worksheet 8-3   Figuring MAGI for 2023 Roth IRA Purposes

1. Enter the adjusted gross income (AGI); *12.1* reported on Line 11 of your 2023 Form 1040 or 1040-SR. _____

2. If you converted a traditional IRA to a Roth IRA or rolled over an employer plan distribution to a Roth IRA in 2023, enter the conversion or rollover amount here. If only part of the conversion or rollover is includible in 2023 income *(8.23)*, enter the taxable amount here. _____

3. Subtract Line 2, if any, from Line 1, and enter the result here. _____

4. If you claimed any of the following deductions or exclusions on your 2023 return, enter the amount here:
   Deductions for:
   traditional IRA contributions *(8.4)* _____
   student loan interest *(33.14)* _____
   self-employed foreign housing expenses *(36.4)* _____
   Exclusions for:
   employer-provided adoption assistance *(3.6)* _____
   interest on U.S. Savings Bonds used for tuition *(33.4)* _____
   foreign-earned income *(36.1)* _____
   employer-provided foreign housing expenses *(36.4)* _____
   Total of above deductions and exclusions _____

5. If there is no entry on Line 4, enter the amount from Line 3 here. If there is an entry on Line 4,
   add Line 4 to Line 3 and enter the total here.
   This is your MAGI for 2023 Roth IRA purposes. Enter this Line 5 amount on Line 1
   of *Worksheet 8-4* to figure if your 2023 contribution limit is reduced under the phaseout rules. _____

Worksheet 8-4   Phaseout of Roth IRA Contribution Limit for 2023

1. Enter your 2023 MAGI from Line 5 of *Worksheet 8-3*. _____

2. Enter the phaseout threshold for your status from *Table 8-6*. _____

3. Subtract Line 2 from Line 1. This is your excess MAGI. _____

4. Enter the following phaseout range for your status:
   - $10,000 if married filing jointly, or a qualifying widow or widower, or married filing separately and you lived with your spouse at any time in 2023, or
   - $15,000 if you are single, head of household, or married filing separately and you lived apart from your spouse for all of 2023 _____

5. Divide Line 3 by Line 4 and enter the result as a decimal rounded to at least three places. This is your phaseout percentage. If the phaseout percentage (decimal) here is under 100%, go to Line 6.
   If Line 3 equals or exceeds Line 4 (phaseout percentage here on Line 5 is 1.000 or more), the phaseout is 100% and you are not allowed any Roth IRA contribution for 2023; do not complete Lines 6-11. _____

6. Enter the annual contribution limit of $6,500, or $7,500 if you are age 50 or older at the end of 2023. However, if your 2023 taxable compensation from work is less than the $6,500/$7,500 limit, enter that lesser amount.
   If married filing jointly, and your own taxable compensation is under the annual $6,500 or $7,500 limit, you can enter the $6,500 or $7,500 limit here if the combined taxable compensation for you and your spouse is at least $13,000 if both of you are under age 50 at the end of 2023, $14,000 if one of you is age 50 or older at the end of 2023, or $15,000 if both of you are age 50 or older at the end of 2023; *see* the spousal contribution rule discussed earlier in *8.21*. _____

7. Multiply Line 5 by Line 6. This is the phased out part of the contribution limit. _____

8. Subtract Line 7 from Line 6. If the result is not a multiple of $10, round it up to the next highest multiple of $10. If the result is under $200, increase it to $200. _____

9. Enter any contributions made to your traditional IRAs for 2023. These reduce the Roth IRA contribution limit. _____

10. Subtract Line 9 from Line 6 _____

11. Enter the lesser of Line 8 or Line 10. This is your maximum 2023 Roth IRA contribution. _____

TABLE 8-6   MAGI Limits for 2023 Roth IRA Contributions

If you are—	Phaseout threshold is—	Phaseout Range—	Phaseout endpoint; no contribution if MAGI is—
Single, head of household, or married filing separately and you lived apart from spouse for all of 2023	$138,000	over $138,000 and under $153,000	$153,000 or more
Married filing jointly or qualifying widow/widower	$218,000	over $218,000 and under $228,000	$228,000 or more
Married filing separately and you lived with your spouse at any time in 2023	$0	over $0 and under $10,000	$10,000 or more

EXAMPLES

1. In 2023, Mark Davis is under age 50 and single. His 2023 salary is $136,000 and his modified adjusted gross income (MAGI) is $141,000, $3,000 more than the $138,000 phaseout threshold for a single person's 2023 Roth IRA contribution. Mark did not make any contributions to a traditional IRA for 2023.

   Following the steps of *Worksheet 8-4*, Mark determines that he can contribute up to $5,200 to a Roth IRA for 2023. Of the $6,500 contribution limit, 20% is phased out ($3,000 excess MAGI divided by the $15,000 phaseout range for single persons). Thus, the $6,500 contribution limit is reduced by 20%, or $1,300. Mark may contribute $5,200 ($6,500 − $1,300) to a Roth IRA for 2023. Here are Lines 1–11 of Mark's *Worksheet 8-4*.

1.	MAGI	$ 141,000
2.	Phaseout threshold	138,000
3.	Excess MAGI	3,000
4.	Phaseout range for single person	15,000
5.	Phaseout percentage (Line 3 / Line 4)	.20
6.	$6,500 annual contribution limit (under age 50)	6,500
7.	20% (Line 5) × $6,500 (Line 6) is phased out	1,300
8.	Line 6 minus Line 7	5,200
9.	Contributions to traditional IRA for 2023	0
10.	Line 6 minus Line 9	6,500
11.	Lesser of Line 8 or Line 10. This is Mark's Roth IRA contribution limit for 2023	5,200

   If Mark was age 50 or over at the end of 2023, the contribution limit on Line 6 would be $7,500. The phaseout on Line 7 would be $1,500 (20% phaseout percentage × $7,500 limit = $1,500 reduction), reducing his allowable contribution limit on Lines 8 and 11 to $6,000.

2. In 2023, Simon and Kallie Vickers are both age 57. They file a 2023 joint return reporting Simon's salary of $83,000 and Kallie's salary of $118,000. Their modified adjusted gross income (MAGI) for 2023 is $222,480, $4,480 more than the $218,000 phaseout threshold for married couples filing jointly.

   Following the steps of *Worksheet 8-4*, Simon and Kallie determine that they can each contribute up to $3,360 to a Roth IRA for 2023. Prior to phaseout, the contribution limit for each of them is $7,500, as they both are at least age 50 at the end of the year and each has taxable compensation of at least $7,500 (step 6 of Worksheet). Given the contribution limit for each of them is the same, and they file jointly, the computation on Worksheet 8-4 gives the same contribution limit for each of them.

Here are Lines 1-11 of their Worksheet 8-4.

1.	MAGI	$ 222,480
2.	Phaseout threshold	218,000
3.	Excess MAGI	4,480
4.	Phaseout range for married filing jointly	10,000
5.	Phaseout percentage (Line 3 / Line 4 rounded to 3 places)	.448
6.	$7,500 annual contribution limit (age 50 or more)	7,500
7.	44.8% (Line 5) × $7,500 (Line 6) is phased out	3,360
8.	Line 6 minus Line 7 = 4,140. Note, 3,360 is a multiple of $10, there is no need to round.	4,140
9.	Contributions to traditional IRA for 2023	0
10.	Line 6 minus Line 9	7,500
11.	Lesser of Line 8 or Line 10. This is the Roth IRA contribution limit for both Simon and Kallie for 2023	$4,140

If only Kallie, or only Simon, was at least age 50 at the end of 2022, they would have to figure their contribution limit separately, because they would have different contribution limits on Line 6 of the Worksheet ($7,000 for the spouse at least age 50, $6,000 for the spouse under age 50), and this would give them different results on Lines 7–11.

8.22 Recharacterizing a Traditional IRA Contribution to a Roth IRA and Vice Versa

You cannot "recharacterize" (undo) a conversion of a traditional IRA to a Roth IRA made after 2017 (8.24). However, you may be able to change an annual contribution from a traditional IRA contribution to a Roth IRA contribution, or an annual Roth IRA contribution to a traditional IRA contribution, by making a trustee-to-trustee transfer. This is called a recharacterization.

For example, you make a contribution to a traditional IRA early in the year with the expectation of being able to claim a deduction for your contribution (8.4), but it turns out that your MAGI is much higher than expected, such as when you receive large year-end capital gain distributions, and you realize that no deduction would be allowed under the phaseout rule, or that only part of your contribution would be deductible. In this situation, you could recharacterize all or part of the contribution (the part that would not be deductible) by transferring it (plus allocable income) to a Roth IRA, provided the contribution is not barred by the Roth IRA phaseout rule (8.21). For example, if you are single, a 2023 deduction for a traditional IRA contribution (up to $6,500 if under age 50 or $7,500 if age 50 or older at end of year) begins to phase out when your 2023 MAGI exceeds $73,000 and is completely phased out if MAGI is $83,000 or more (8.4), but the limit for a 2023 Roth IRA contribution does not begin to phase out until MAGI reaches $138,000, with a complete phaseout at $153,000 or more (8.21).

On the other hand, if you initially contribute to a Roth IRA, you could decide to recharacterize and switch the contribution to a traditional IRA. This could be the case if you initially contribute to a Roth IRA and it turns out that your MAGI for the year would allow you to claim a full traditional IRA deduction (8.4).

Effect of a recharacterization. When you recharacterize a contribution, the IRA which receives the recharacterized amount is treated as if it had received the original contribution (and the earnings transferred over in the recharacterization) on the date of the original contribution. A recharacterization is not counted as a rollover for purposes of the one-rollover-per-year limit (8.10).

How to recharacterize and deadline for completing transfer. You make an election to recharacterize a contribution by notifying the trustees of both IRAs of your intention. If you are changing trustees, you authorize a trustee-to-trustee transfer from the first IRA (to which the contribution was originally made) to the second IRA (the transferee IRA). If the account is remaining with the same trustee, instruct the trustee that you are electing to treat the contribution as having been made to the second IRA rather than the first. The transfer must include any net income allocable to the original contribution; an allocable loss would reduce the amount that must be transferred.

The election and the transfer itself must be completed on or before the due date, including extensions, for filing your tax return for the year of the original contribution. If you miss this deadline, but you timely filed the return, the IRS allows you six months from the original due date (without extensions) to complete a recharacterization, which in the case of a 2023 return, would allow until October 15, 2024. If you take advantage of this extension and recharacterize after a timely filing, you must file an amended return *(47.1)* to report the recharacterization.

When you recharacterize an IRA contribution (traditional to Roth or Roth to traditional), you must attach a statement to your return to explain the recharacterization. *See* the instructions to Form 8606 for the details to be included in the statement. Form 8606 does not have to be filed unless you recharacterized only part of a traditional IRA contribution and some of the contribution left in the traditional IRA is nondeductible, or you partially recharacterized a Roth IRA contribution and a portion of the contribution transferred to the traditional IRA is nondeductible.

8.23 Converting a Traditional IRA to a Roth IRA

A conversion of a traditional IRA to a Roth IRA is a taxable transfer, unlike a tax-free direct transfer or rollover *(8.10)* to a traditional IRA. If you converted a traditional IRA to a Roth IRA in 2023, the entire transfer must be reported as 2023 income unless after-tax contributions were made to any of your traditional IRAs (see "How to report a 2023 conversion to a Roth IRA," below).

You can convert a traditional IRA to a Roth IRA regardless of your income or filing status. A conversion may be made by directing the trustee of your traditional IRA to make a trustee-to-trustee transfer of your IRA to a new Roth IRA trustee, or by keeping the account with the same trustee but instructing the trustee to change the registration of the account from a traditional IRA to a Roth IRA. You may also make a conversion by receiving a distribution from your traditional IRA and rolling it over to a Roth IRA; the rollover must be completed within 60 days from the time you receive the distribution. A conversion to a Roth IRA is not treated as a rollover for purposes of the one-rollover-per-year rule *(8.10)*.

There is no time limit for making a conversion to a Roth IRA. It is taxable in the year in which the conversion is made.

Conversion from SEP or SIMPLE IRA. You may also convert a SEP *(8.16)* to a Roth IRA. A SIMPLE IRA *(8.19)* may be converted to a Roth IRA if more than two years have passed since you began participation in the SIMPLE IRA.

Rollover from employer plan to Roth IRA. The tax treatment of a rollover to a Roth IRA from a 401(k) plan or other qualified employer plan, a 403(b) plan, or a governmental 457 plan, is similar to that of a conversion from a traditional IRA. That is, the rollover is a taxable distribution except to the extent that it is a return of your after-tax contributions, if any.

Required minimum distributions (RMDs) may not be converted to a Roth IRA. If you are required to receive a required minimum distribution (RMD) from your traditional IRA, you may not convert to a Roth IRA the amount of that RMD *(8.13)*. Similarly, the RMD from an employer plan *(7.11)* may not be rolled over to a Roth IRA. Only an amount exceeding the RMD is eligible for conversion or rollover. For 2020 only, this "take the RMD first" rule had no effect, since the CARES Act waived RMDs for 2020; the entire amount of a 2020 conversion from a traditional IRA or rollover from an employer plan to a Roth IRA was allowed. However, the no-rollover rule for RMDs went back into effect for 2021 and later years.

How to report a 2023 conversion to a Roth IRA. If you converted a traditional IRA, SEP, or SIMPLE IRA to a Roth IRA in 2023, you have to report the conversion on Form 8606 and the entire amount must be reported as a taxable distribution on your 2023 return, except to the extent that it is allocable to after-tax contributions in all of your traditional IRAs. If you converted all of your traditional, SEP and SIMPLE IRAs to Roth IRAs in 2023, report the conversions on Part II of Form 8606; after-tax contributions in all your traditional

Law Alert

Conversions Are Generally Fully Taxable

A conversion from a traditional IRA to a Roth IRA is treated as a fully taxable distribution except to the extent it includes an amount allocable to nondeductible traditional IRA contributions.

If you are planning a conversion, you may need to substantially increase your tax withholding or make estimated tax installments in order to avoid an estimated tax penalty *(27.1)*.

Law Alert

Rollover From Employer Plan

A distribution from a qualified employer plan, a 403(b) plan, or a governmental 457 plan may be rolled over to a Roth IRA under the same rules as for converting a traditional IRA to a Roth IRA. This means that a rollover is treated as a taxable distribution except to the extent it is allocable to after-tax contributions.

IRAs, if any, reduce the taxable amount to be reported on your 2023 return. If you made after-tax contributions to any of your traditional IRAs and in 2023 you converted only part of your traditional IRAs, SEPs and SIMPLE IRAs to Roth IRAs, a prorated portion of the converted amount is treated as allocable to the after-tax contributions and that is the nontaxable portion of the conversion. You figure the tax-free percentage on Part 1 of Form 8606 by dividing the after-tax contributions by the sum of the year-end value of all the IRAs plus the conversion amount. Multiplying the resulting percentage by the conversion amount gives you the tax-free part of the conversion. The balance is the taxable part of the conversion. The 10% penalty for pre-age-59½ distributions *(8.12)* does not apply to the taxable part of the conversion. *See* the instructions to Parts I and II of Form 8606 for details on reporting conversions to Roth IRAs.

If you withdrew funds from a traditional IRA towards the end of 2023 and complete a rollover to a Roth IRA in early 2024 within 60 days of withdrawal, this is treated as a 2023 conversion (and thus generally fully taxable on your 2023 return) and not a 2024 conversion.

8.24 Conversions Made After 2017 to a Roth IRA Cannot Be Recharacterized

The Tax Cuts and Jobs Act ended a valuable planning opportunity: the ability to convert a traditional IRA to a Roth IRA *(8.23)* and still have an opportunity to reconsider the move. For conversions made before 2018, you could recharacterize, or undo the conversion, if the value of the Roth IRA dropped substantially after the date of the conversion and you did not want to have to include the conversion date value in income, or you simply were unable to pay the tax due on the conversion *(8.23)*.

This option is no longer available. The ability to in effect "undo" the conversion by recharacterizing all or part of it back to a traditional IRA is no longer allowed for a conversion made after 2017. In other words, a conversion is now irrevocable. Similarly, a rollover made after 2017 from an employer retirement plan *(8.23)* to a Roth IRA cannot be recharacterized.

8.25 Distributions From a Roth IRA

A distribution from a Roth IRA is tax free if it is a qualified distribution, as discussed below. Even if a distribution is not a qualified distribution, it is tax-free to the extent it does not exceed your regular Roth IRA contributions *(8.21)* and conversion contributions *(8.23)*. The part of a nonqualified distribution allocable to earnings is taxable, but distributions are considered to be from contributions first and then from earnings; *see* the "Ordering rules for nonqualified distributions" below for the allocation between contributions and earnings. You must report Roth IRA distributions on Form 8606.

You may make a tax-free direct transfer (trustee-to-trustee) from one Roth IRA to another. If you receive a Roth IRA distribution, a tax-free rollover may be made to another Roth IRA if you complete the rollover within 60 days, but the rollover is subject to the one-rollover-per-year limit *(8.10)*.

You do not have to take RMDs. You do not have to receive required minimum distributions from your Roth IRA. No Roth IRA distributions at all are required during your lifetime. After your death, your beneficiaries will be subject to a minimum distribution requirement *(8.26)*.

Qualified Roth IRA distributions are tax free. Two tests must be met for a Roth IRA distribution to be "qualified," and thus completely tax free: (1) the distribution must be made after the end of the five-year period beginning with the first day of the first taxable year for which any Roth IRA contribution was made and (2) one of the following conditions must be met:

- you are age 59½ or older when the distribution is made,
- you are disabled,
- you use the distribution to pay up to $10,000 of qualifying first-time homebuyer expenses as discussed below, or
- you are a beneficiary receiving distributions following the death of the account owner *(8.26)*.

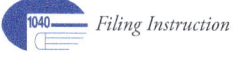
Filing Instruction

File Form 8606 to Report a Nonqualified Distribution

If you receive a nonqualified Roth IRA distribution, you must file Form 8606. On Part III of Form 8606, you report the nonqualified distribution and figure the taxable portion. A qualified distribution is not reported on Form 8606.

Five-year holding period for qualified distributions. In order to receive tax-free withdrawals of earnings from your Roth IRA, you must satisfy the five-year holding period and also be at least age 59½, be disabled, or pay qualifying first-time homebuyer expenses. The five-year holding period begins with January 1 (assuming you are a calendar-year taxpayer) of the first year for which any Roth IRA contribution is made. After the five-year period, distributions to a beneficiary are tax free *(8.26)*.

For purposes of determining qualified distributions, you have only one five-year period regardless of the number of Roth IRAs you have. Once you satisfy the five-year test for one Roth IRA, you also meet it for all subsequently established Roth IRAs. For example, if you converted a traditional IRA to a Roth IRA during 1998 (the first year Roth IRA contributions were allowed), or made a regular Roth IRA contribution for 1998 at any time between January 1, 1998, and April 15, 1999, your five-year holding period began January 1, 1998. If in a later year you converted *(8.23)* a traditional IRA to a Roth IRA, or made a regular Roth IRA contribution to a different account *(8.21)*, that new Roth IRA does not get its own five-year holding period. In this case, the five-year period for all your Roth IRAs began January 1, 1998, and ended December 31, 2002.

If you receive a Roth IRA distribution after the end of your five-year holding period, and you also meet one of the other qualified distribution requirements such as being age 59½ or older, the distribution is completely tax free. For example, if your first Roth IRA contribution was a regular contribution for 2018 (made by April 16, 2019) or a conversion made during 2018, the five-year period for all your Roth IRAs ended December 31, 2022, and thus any distribution you receive from any of your Roth IRAs in 2023 or in a later year is tax free if you are at least age 59½ when the distribution is made.

If you receive a distribution before satisfying both the five-year holding period requirement and one of the other qualified distribution requirements, and the withdrawal exceeds your contributions, the excess (i.e., earnings) is taxable and possibly subject to the 10% penalty for pre–age 59½ distributions *(8.12)*. Under the ordering rules discussed below, Roth IRA distributions are treated as being made first from contributions and then from earnings.

Ordering rules for nonqualified distributions. Even if a distribution does not meet the above tests for a qualified distribution and thus is not automatically completely tax free, such as where the distribution is made before you are age 59½, it may still be fully or partly tax free because a nonqualified distribution is not taxable to the extent of your Roth IRA contributions. All of your Roth IRAs are treated as one account for purposes of determining if contributions or earnings have been withdrawn. If a distribution does not exceed total contributions to all of your Roth IRAs, it is not taxable. The taxable part of a nonqualified distribution is figured on Part III of Form 8606.

Where you have made regular annual contributions and also conversion contributions from a traditional IRA or rollover contributions from an employer plan to a Roth IRA, the regular contributions are considered to be withdrawn first. Allocate a distribution to your contributions and then to earnings in this order:

1. *Regular Roth IRA contributions.* This is the total of all of your annual contributions for all years.

2. *Conversion contributions and rollover contributions.* Conversion contributions and rollover contributions are considered to be withdrawn in the order in which they were made. For example, if you made a conversion in 2009 to one Roth IRA and in 2010 you made another conversion to the same account or to a different Roth IRA, and you receive a distribution from any of your Roth IRAs, you allocate the distribution first to the 2009 conversion and then to the 2010 conversion. If part of a conversion or rollover contribution was not taxable (because it was allocable to nondeductible or after-tax contributions in the converted or rolled-over account), the taxable part of the conversion or rollover is deemed withdrawn before the nontaxable part. Assume that the 2009 conversion was partly taxable and partly nontaxable, and the same was true for the 2010 conversion. You would first allocate the distribution to the taxable part of the 2009 conversion, then to the nontaxable part of the 2009 conversion, then to the taxable part of the 2010 conversion, and finally, to the nontaxable part of the 2010 conversion.

Planning Reminder

Meeting the Five-Year Holding Test

For a withdrawal of earnings from a Roth IRA to be tax free, the five-year holding period test must be met and the taxpayer must be at least age 59½ or meet one of the other conditions for a qualified distribution. For example, a taxpayer whose first Roth IRA contribution was for 2018 satisfied the five-year test at the end of 2022, so a distribution received after age 59½ in 2023 (or later) is a tax-free qualified distribution.

Taking into account the taxable part of a conversion or rollover contribution before the nontaxable part (if any) of the contribution may be important for purposes of determining whether the 10% early distribution penalty applies to the withdrawal before age 59½ of a conversion or rollover contribution within five years of the conversion/rollover *(see below)*.

3. ***Earnings.*** Earnings on Roth IRA contributions are considered to be withdrawn last, after all contributions are taken into account. If a distribution is not a qualified distribution, and it exceeds the contributions under (1) and (2) above, the withdrawn earnings are subject to tax and, if you are under age 59½, to the 10% early distribution penalty, unless a penalty exception applies *(8.12)*.

Potential 10% early distribution penalty on withdrawal within five years of conversion or rollover. If you receive a Roth IRA distribution before age 59½ and within the prior five years you made a conversion from a traditional IRA or rollover from an employer plan, you may be subject to the regular 10% early distribution penalty *(8.12)*. Do not confuse this potential 10% penalty on conversions or rollovers with the 10% penalty that applies before age 59½ to a nonqualified distribution that is allocable to taxable earnings (category 3 under the "Ordering rules" above).

The 10% penalty applies only if all of the following are true: (1) you are under age 59½ when you receive the Roth IRA distribution, (2) you converted or rolled over an amount to a Roth IRA within the five-year period preceding the current Roth IRA distribution, (3) the Roth IRA distribution is allocable to the taxable portion of any conversion or rollover made within the five-year period, and (4) you do not qualify for a penalty exception, such as for first-time homebuyer expenses or higher education costs, or being disabled *(8.12)*.

For purposes of determining the five-year period under test 2, every conversion or rollover is considered made on January 1 of the year in which it occurred, regardless of its actual date. Thus, there is a separate five-year period for each conversion or rollover you have made. For any conversion (or rollover) made in 2017, the five-year period began January 1, 2018, and ended December 31, 2022, so a 2023 Roth IRA distribution cannot be penalized on account of a 2018 conversion (or rollover), even if the 2023 distribution is before age 59½. The 10% penalty could apply to a 2023 distribution if it is allocable to a conversion or rollover made in 2019 through 2023.

Even if there were conversions or rollovers within the five-year period, the penalty applies only to the extent that the current distribution from the Roth IRA is allocable to the taxable portion of any of those conversions or rollovers, as determined by the ordering rules above; *see* category 2 of the ordering rules. Note that under the ordering rules, the entire Roth IRA distribution may be tax free because it is allocable to your contributions- either regular annual contributions (category 1) or your conversion or rollover contributions (category 2). But even if the distribution is entirely tax free, the 10% penalty applies to an early distribution that is allocable to the category 2 conversions or rollovers that were taxable when made, assuming a penalty exception *(8.12)* is not available. Follow the instructions to Form 5329 to figure whether you owe the penalty on any of your Roth conversions or rollovers.

Distribution used for up to $10,000 of first-time homebuyer expenses. A Roth IRA distribution is "qualified", and therefore tax free, if you meet the five-year holding period and the distribution is used for up to $10,000 of qualifying "first-time" homebuyer expenses. The $10,000 limit is a lifetime cap per IRA owner, not an annual limitation. Expenses qualify if they are used within 120 days of the distribution to pay the acquisition costs of a principal residence for you, your spouse, your child, or your grandchild, or an ancestor of you or your spouse. The residence does not have to be your "first" home. A qualifying first-time homebuyer is considered to be someone who did not have a present ownership interest in a principal residence in the two-year period ending on the acquisition date of the new home. If the homebuyer is married, both spouses must satisfy the two-year test. Eligible acquisition costs include buying, constructing, or reconstructing the principal residence, including reasonable settlement, financing, and closing costs.

 *Caution*

Early Withdrawal Within 5 Years of Conversion to Roth IRA

The 10% penalty *(8.12)* for pre–age 59½ distributions may apply if within five years of making a conversion to a Roth IRA, a distribution from any Roth IRA is received. The penalty applies to the portion of the withdrawal allocable to the conversion amount that was taxable in the year of the conversion. This is so even if the withdrawal is tax free under the ordering rule for Roth IRA distributions.

Planning Reminder

Distributions to Roth IRA Beneficiary May Be Completely or Partially Tax Free

If you inherit a Roth IRA and receive a distribution before the end of the owner's five-year holding period for qualified distributions *(8.25)*, the part of the distribution that represents a return of the owner's contributions under the ordering rules *(8.25)* is tax free, but the part of the distribution that is allocable to earnings must be included in your taxable income. However, even if you receive a taxable distribution and are under age 59½, you are not subject to the 10% early distribution penalty.

After the end of the owner's five-year holding period, all distributions you receive from the account are tax free.

IRS Alert

Non-EDB Does Not Have to Receive Distributions Before 10th Year

If you are a non-EDB of an inherited Roth IRA, you must empty the account by the end of the 10th year after the year of the owner's death, but you do not have to receive annual RMDs before the 10th year. Proposed regulations *(8.15)* require non-EDBs of traditional IRAs to receive annual RMDs in years 1-through-9 if the IRA owner died on or after the required beginning date, but this rule does not apply to Roth IRA beneficiaries because Roth IRA owners are not subject to RMDs *(8.25)*, and so Roth IRA owners are always considered to have died before their required beginning date, regardless of their age at death.

8.26 Distributions to Roth IRA Beneficiaries

If you inherited a Roth IRA before 2020 and you have been receiving annual required minimum distributions (RMDs) over your life expectancy, you must continue to do so. However, under the SECURE Act, where a Roth IRA owner dies after 2019, the RMD life expectancy method may be used only by surviving spouses who do not elect to treat the account as their own *(see below)*, and by nonspouse beneficiaries who are treated as "eligible designated beneficiaries" (EDBs). Other nonspouse beneficiaries (non-EDBs) must receive the entire balance of the account by the end of the 10th year following the year of the owner's death; there are no RMDs before the 10th year; *see* below.

Whether you are subject to the 10-year rule or the life expectancy method, distributions you receive are tax free so long as the Roth IRA owner had satisfied the five-year holding period rule for qualified distributions; *see* below and the adjacent Planning Reminder.

Failure to take an RMD will result in a penalty. The penalty is 25% of the difference between the RMD and the amount you received. Of course, you are not limited to the RMD, which is just the minimum you must receive for the year to avoid a penalty.

Surviving spouse who is sole designated beneficiary. If the Roth IRA owner was your spouse, and you are the sole designated beneficiary of the IRA, you may treat the account as your own Roth IRA by retitling the account or rolling it over to a Roth IRA in your name. If you treat the account as your own, you do not have to take distributions at any time, since a Roth IRA owner is not subject to minimum distribution (RMD) requirements *(8.25)*. If you take some distributions, you are not locked into a specific distribution schedule unless you agree to that schedule.

If your spouse was born after June 30, 1949, and died before the year in which he or she would have reached age 72, and you did not elect to treat the Roth IRA as your own, you do not have to start your RMDs until the year your spouse would have reached age 72. As a surviving spouse, you are an EDB under the SECURE Act and may take RMDs over your life expectancy, which is recalculated each year based on your attained age in that year; *see* Example 7 in *8.15*.

Nonspouse beneficiaries—if Roth IRA owner died before 2020. As the account owner's designated beneficiary, you must continue to receive RMDs over your life expectancy. To figure the RMD for each year, divide the account balance as of the end of the preceding year by your life expectancy in that year; *see* the required reset of life expectancy for 2023 and the Fred Johnson Example in *8.14*.

If you die while there is money remaining in the account, your successor beneficiary will have to empty the account by the end of the 10th year following the year of your death.

Nonspouse beneficiaries—if Roth IRA owner died after 2019. If the Roth IRA owner died after 2019 and you are the designated beneficiary, the SECURE Act requires that you empty the account by the end of the 10th year following the year of the owner's death unless you are an "eligible designated beneficiary" (EDB). You are an EDB only if: you have a disability, you are chronically ill, or you were no more than 10 years younger than the owner was on the date of death. A minor child of the account owner (but not a grandchild), is also an EDB, but only until the age of majority is reached; after that, the 10-year rule applies. *See 8.15* for further EDB details.

If you are an EDB, you generally must receive RMDs over your life expectancy. Under the life expectancy method, divide the account balance as of the end of the preceding year by your life expectancy in the year for which the RMD is being determined; *see* "RMDs figured under life expectancy method" in *8.15* and Example 1 on page 247. If you die while there is money remaining in the account, your successor beneficiary will have to empty the account by the end of the 10th year following the year of your death (*see* the Law Alert regarding Successor Roth IRA Beneficiaries on the next page). Under IRS proposed regulations, the terms of the Roth IRA may allow an EDB to elect the 10-year rule (*see* the next paragraph) if the Roth IRA owner was born after June 30, 1949, and died before April 1 of the year after the year age 72 would have been reached.

If you are a non-EDB and thus are subject to the 10-year rule, there are no RMDs before the 10th year (*see* the IRS Alert on this page). You may take distributions in some years and not others, so long as the entire Roth IRA is emptied by the end of the 10th year after the year of the owner's death. If the Roth IRA owner met the five-year holding period test *(see below)*, all distributions you receive will be tax free, so if you choose, you can allow the account to grow tax-free and then withdraw all the funds with no tax due in the 10th year following the year of the owner's death. If you die before the end of the 10-year period with money still in the account, your successor beneficiary is subject to the same 10-year deadline as you were and must empty the account by the same deadline (*see* the Law Alert regarding Successor Roth IRA Beneficiaries on this page).

Co-beneficiaries. Co-beneficiaries of a Roth IRA should split the IRA into separate accounts by December 31 of the year following the year of the owner's death. Otherwise, the life expectancy of the oldest beneficiary must be used by all the beneficiaries when figuring RMDs. If there are two EDBs, splitting the IRA into separate accounts allows each of you to figure RMDs using your own life expectancy. If one of you is an EDB, splitting the IRA allows the EDB to take life expectancy RMDs from a separate account; the non-EDB is subject to the 10-year rule. If neither of you is an EDB, splitting the IRA into separate accounts allows you to separately decide how to invest your accounts and how to time distributions within the 10-year period.

A surviving spouse can treat the IRA as his or her own only if the surviving spouse is the sole IRA beneficiary, so if there is a co-beneficiary, a separate account should be created to allow the surviving spouse to use the "treat as own" rule.

Tax-free treatment depends on whether owner met five-year holding period. The same five-year holding period for receiving fully tax-free distributions that applied to the Roth IRA owner *(8.25)* also applies to you as the beneficiary. The five-year holding period began on January 1 of the year for which the owner's first Roth IRA contribution was made.

If you receive distributions after the end of the owner's five-year holding period, all of the distributions are "qualified" *(8.25)* and thus are completely tax free.

If you receive distributions before the end of the five-year holding period, the distributions are "nonqualified," which means that they will be tax free to the extent that they are a recovery of the owner's Roth IRA contributions and taxable to the extent they are earnings under the "ordering rules" at *8.25*. If you receive a nonqualified distribution, you must report it and figure the taxable portion, if any, on Part III of Form 8606.

 *Law Alert*

Successor Roth IRA Beneficiaries Subject to 10-Year Rule

If the Roth IRA owner died before 2020 and the designated beneficiary dies after 2019 with money still in the account, the successor beneficiary must empty the Roth IRA by the end of the 10th year after the year of the designated beneficiary's death.

If the Roth IRA owner died after 2019, and the designated beneficiary dies with money still in the account, the deadline for the successor beneficiary to empty the account depends on whether the designated beneficiary was an EDB or a non-EDB.

If the designated beneficiary was a non-EDB and he or she did not empty the account by the end of the 10th year after the year of the owner's death, the successor beneficiary must do so; the successor is subject to the non-EDB's 10-year deadline.

If the designated beneficiary was an EDB taking RMDs under the life expectancy method, the successor beneficiary must empty the account by the end of the 10th year following the year of the EDB's death.

If the successor beneficiary dies before the end of the applicable 10-year period, with money still in the account, subsequent successor beneficiaries must empty the account by the end of that same 10-year period.

CHAPTER 9

Income From Real Estate Rentals and Royalties

Use Schedule E of Form 1040 to report real estate rental income and expenses. The same form is used if you file Form 1040-SR. You must also file Form 4562 with your 2023 return to claim depreciation deductions for buildings you placed in service during the year.

Use Schedule C instead of Schedule E if you provide substantial services for the convenience of the tenants, such as maid service. That is, Schedule C is used to report payments received for the use and occupancy of rooms or other areas in a hotel, motel, boarding house, apartment, tourist home, or trailer court where services are provided primarily for the occupant.

If you rent out an apartment or room in the same building in which you live, you report the rent income less expenses allocated to the rental property (9.4).

The law prevents most homeowners from deducting losses (expenses in excess of income) on the rental of a personal vacation home or personal residence if the owner or close relatives personally use the premises during the year. Tests based on days of personal and rental use determine whether you may deduct losses (9.7).

Rental losses may also be limited by the passive activity rules discussed in *Chapter 10*. Real estate professionals may avoid the passive restrictions on rental income. An investor who actively manages property may deduct rental losses of up to $25,000 under an exception to the passive activity loss restrictions.

Use Schedule E to report royalties, but if you are a self-employed author, artist, or inventor, report royalty income and expenses on Schedule C.

Business rentals of equipment, vehicles, or similar personal property are reported on Schedule C, not Schedule E.

9.1   Reporting Rental Real Estate Income and Expenses

On the cash basis, you report rent income on your tax return for the year in which you receive payment or in which you "constructively" receive it, such as where payment is credited to your bank account.

On the accrual basis, you report income on your tax return for the year in which you are entitled to receive payment, even if it is not actually paid. However, you do not report accrued income if the financial condition of the tenant makes collection doubtful. If you sue for payment, you do not report income until you win a collectible judgment.

Schedule E reporting. Use Schedule E (Form 1040 or 1040-SR) to report rental real estate income and expenses unless you are providing substantial services for tenants that go beyond the provision of utilities, trash collection, and cleaning of public areas. For example, if you operate a hotel or motel, and provide cleaning services such as maid service and changing linens, you should use Schedule C (Profit or Loss from Business; *see 40.6*) rather than Schedule E.

Advance rentals. Advance rentals or bonuses are reported in the year received, whether you are on the cash or accrual basis.

Tenant's payment of landlord's expenses. The tenant's payment of your taxes, interest, insurance, mortgage amortization (even if you are not personally liable on the mortgage), repairs, or other expenses is considered additional rental income to you. If your tenant pays your utility bills or your emergency repairs and deducts the amount from the rent payment, you must include as rental income the full rental amount, not the actual net payment. However, you can claim an offsetting deduction for expenses, such as repairs, that would have been deductible had you paid them.

Tenant's payment to cancel lease. A tenant's payment for canceling a lease or modifying its terms is considered rental income in the year you receive it regardless of your method of accounting. You may deduct expenses incurred because of the cancellation or modification and any unamortized balance of expenses paid in negotiating the lease.

Insurance. Insurance proceeds for loss of rental income because of fire or other casualty are rental income.

Improvements by tenants. You do not realize taxable income when your tenant improves the leased premises, provided the improvements are not substitute rent payments. Furthermore, when you take possession of the improvements at the time the lease ends, you do not realize income. However, you may not depreciate the value of the improvements as the basis to you is considered zero.

Property or services. If you receive property or services instead of money, include the fair market value of such property or services as rental income.

If you agree upon a specified price for services rendered, that price is generally treated as the fair market value.

Rental losses. Rental income may be offset by deductions claimed for depreciation, mortgage interest, and repair and maintenance costs. However, if these expenses exceed rental income, the resulting loss is subject to the passive activity loss restrictions. If you do not qualify as a real estate professional *(10.3)*, you generally may not deduct rental losses from other income (nonpassive income such as salary, interest, and dividends) under the passive loss rules. Rental losses may offset only other rental and passive activity income; excess losses are carried forward to later years until there is passive income to offset or the property is disposed of *(10.13)*. However, if you perform some management role, you may deduct from other income real estate rental losses of up to $25,000, provided your adjusted gross income does not exceed $100,000 *(10.2)*. These restrictions on passive losses make rental income attractive, since the rental income can be offset by the passive losses. *See Chapter 10* for details on the passive loss restrictions.

Application of the passive activity loss rules and exceptions assumes that the property is not considered a residence under the personal-use rules *(9.7)*. If a rented property is treated as a residence, rental expenses are deductible from rental income *(9.9)* but a loss is not allowed for that property.

Filing Tip

Married Owners Can File Schedule E for Qualified Joint Venture

If you and your spouse are sole owners of a rental real estate business that you both materially participate in, and you file jointly, you can elect to be treated as a qualified joint venture (QJV) on Schedule E; *see 40.6*. You do not each file a separate Schedule E to report your respective share of the income and expenses. Instead, on Line 1 of Schedule E, each of your individual QJV interests is reported as a separate property, and on Line 2 you check the QJV box for each of the QJV property interests. For each separate property interest, enter on Lines 3-22 (income and expenses) the applicable share of the QJV income, deductions or loss.

Electing QJV status does not change the rule that exempts rental real estate income from self-employment tax *(45.1)*. The passive loss rules *(10.1)* also continue to apply.

Caution

Security Deposits

Distinguish advance rentals, which are income, from security deposits, which are not. Security deposits are amounts deposited with you solely as security for the tenant's performance of the terms of the lease, and as such are usually not taxed, particularly where local law treats security deposits as trust funds. If the tenant breaches the lease, you are entitled to apply the sum as rent, at which time you report it as income. If both you and your tenant agree that a security deposit is to be used as a final rent payment, it is advance rent. Include it in your income when you receive it.

Law Alert

Qualified Business Income (QBI) Deduction for Certain Rental Activities

If your rental activities are considered to be a trade or business, you may be eligible for a deduction of up to 20% of your qualified business income (QBI). An IRS safe harbor may allow you to treat a "rental real estate enterprise" as a business for purposes of qualifying for the QBI deduction. The deduction does not reduce rental income; the deduction is subtracted from adjusted gross income on Form 1040 or 1040-SR. The QBI deduction and the safe harbor is explained in *9.17*.

Court Decision

Co-Tenant's Deduction for Real Estate Taxes

The Tax Court may allow a co-tenant to deduct more than his or her proportionate share of real estate taxes. According to the court, the deduction test for real estate taxes is whether the payment satisfies a personal liability or protects a beneficial interest in the property. In the case of co-tenants, nonpayment of taxes by the other co-tenants could result in the property being lost or foreclosed. To prevent this, a co-tenant who pays the tax is protecting his or her beneficial interest and, therefore, is entitled to deduct the payment of the full tax, provided the payment is from his or her own funds.

In several cases, the Tax Court limited the taxpayer's deduction for taxes to his or her proportionate share, despite payment of the entire amount of taxes, because the taxpayer could not prove that the payment came from his own separate funds. Similarly, where a joint obligor on a mortgage pays more than his or her share of the mortgage interest in order to avoid default, the Tax Court has limited the taxpayer's deduction to his or her proportionate share where it could not be proven that the taxpayer's own separate funds were used to make the payment.

9.2 Checklist of Rental Deductions

The expenses in this section are deductible from rental income on Schedule E of Form 1040 or 1040-SR in determining your profit.

Real estate taxes but not assessments for local improvements. Deductible real estate taxes do not include special assessments for paving, sewer systems, or other local improvements; these assessments are added to the cost of the land. However, you can deduct as real estate taxes assessments that merely maintain or repair local benefits, and which do not increase the value of your property. See *16.4* through *16.7* for details on real estate tax deductions.

Construction period interest and taxes. These expenses generally have to be capitalized and depreciated *(16.4)*.

Depreciation of a rental building. You may start claiming depreciation in the month the building is ready for tenants. For example, you bought a house in May 2023 and spent June and July making repairs. The house was ready to rent in August and you began advertising for tenants. On your 2023 return you can begin depreciation as of August, even if a tenant did not move in until September or some later month. The month the building is ready for tenants is the month that determines the first-year depreciation write-off under the mid-month convention. See *9.5* for the monthly depreciation rates for residential rental property. Rates for nonresidential buildings are at *42.13*.

Depreciation for furniture and appliances. Furniture, carpeting, and appliances such as stoves and refrigerators used in residential rental property are considered five-year property for MACRS depreciation purposes. Furniture used in office buildings is considered seven-year property. See *42.5* for MACRS rates.

Management expenses. Include fees paid to a company for collecting the rent.

Maintenance expenses. Include heating, repairs, lighting, water, electricity, gas, telephone, coal, and other service costs *(9.3)*.

Salaries and wages. Include payments to superintendents, janitors, elevator operators, and service and maintenance personnel.

Traveling expenses to look after the properties. If you travel "away from home" to inspect or repair rental property, be prepared to show that this was the primary purpose of your trip, rather than vacationing or other personal purposes. Otherwise, the IRS may disallow deductions for round-trip travel costs.

Legal expenses for dispossessing tenants. Expenses of long-term leases are capital expenditures deductible over the term of the lease.

Interest paid on mortgages and other indebtedness. Deductible interest does not include expenses paid to obtain a mortgage such as mortgage commissions and abstract or recording fees. Such costs are capital expenses that can be amortized over the life of the mortgage. For a mortgage obtained in 2023, amortization is claimed on Part VI of Form 4562 ("Depreciation and Amortization") and amortization for expenses of pre-2023 mortgages is claimed on Schedule E as an "Other" expense.

Commissions paid to collect rentals. Commissions paid to secure long-term rentals must be deducted over the life of the lease. Commissions paid to acquire the property are capitalized as an addition to basis.

Premiums for fire, liability, and plate glass insurance. If payment is made in one year for insurance covering a period longer than one year, you amortize and deduct the premium over the life of the policy, even though you are on a cash basis.

Tax return preparation. You may deduct as a rental expense the part of a tax preparation fee allocable to Part 1 of Schedule E (income or loss from rentals or royalties). You may also deduct, as a rental expense, a fee paid to a tax consultant to resolve a tax underpayment related to your rental activities.

Charging below fair market rent. If you rent your property to a friend or relative for less than the fair rental value, you may deduct expenses and depreciation only to the extent of the rental income *(9.8)*.

Co-tenants. One of two tenants-in-common may deduct only half of the maintenance expenses even if he or she pays the entire bill. A tenant-in-common who pays all of the maintenance expenses of the common property is entitled to reimbursement from the other co-tenant, so one-half of the bill is not his or her ordinary and necessary expense. Each co-tenant owns a separate property interest in the common property that produces separate income for each. Each tenant's deductible expense is that portion of the entire expense that each separate interest bears to the whole, and no more.

Costs of canceling lease. A landlord may pay a tenant to cancel an unfavorable lease. The way the landlord treats the payment depends on the reason for the cancellation. If the purpose of the cancellation is to enable the landlord to construct a new building in place of the old, the cancellation payment is added to the basis of the new building. If the purpose is to sell the property, the payment is added to the cost of the property. If the landlord wants the premises for his or her own use, the payment is deducted over the remaining term of the old lease. If the landlord gets a new tenant to replace the old one, the cancellation payment is also generally deductible over the remaining term of the old lease.

> **EXAMPLE**
>
> Handlery Hotels, Inc., had to pay its lessee $85,000 to terminate a lease on a building three years before the lease term expired. Handlery entered into a new 20-year lease on more favorable terms with another lessee. Handlery amortized the $85,000 cancellation payment over the three-year unexpired term of the old lease. The IRS claimed that the payment had to be amortized over the 20-year term of the new lease because it was part of the cost of obtaining the new lease. A federal district court agreed with the IRS, but an appeals court sided with Handlery. Since the unexpired lease term was the major factor in determining the amount of the cancellation payment, the cost of cancellation should be amortized over that unexpired term.

9.3   Distinguishing Between a Repair and an Improvement

Maintenance and repair expenses are not treated in the same way as expenses for improvements and replacements. Only maintenance and incidental repair costs are deductible against rental income. Improvements that add to the value or prolong the life of the property or adapt it to new uses are capital improvements. Capital improvements may not be deducted currently but may be depreciated *(42.14)*. If you make improvements to property before renting it out, add the cost of the improvements to your basis in the property. A safe harbor under final IRS regulations *(see below)* may allow you to claim a current deduction for an expense that would otherwise have to be treated as an improvement.

A repair keeps your property in good operating condition. For example, repairs include painting, fixing gutters or floors, fixing leaks, plastering, and replacing broken windows. Adding a recreation room in an unfinished basement, paneling a den, putting up a fence, putting in new plumbing or wiring, and paving a driveway are all examples of depreciable capital improvements *(42.14)*. Putting on a new roof is generally a depreciable capital improvement; however, the Tax Court has allowed current deductions for roof replacements intended to prevent leaks; *see* Example 2 below.

Repairs may not be separated from capital expenditures when both are part of an improvement program; *see* Example 3 below.

Distinguishing repairs from improvements. Under final IRS regulations issued in 2013, an expense that results in the betterment, restoration, or adaptation to a new and different use of property is treated as an improvement that must be capitalized (and depreciated) unless a special safe harbor *(see below)* allows a current deduction. For example, the regulations affirm the long-held IRS position that replacing a roof is a restoration that is treated as an improvement to the building structure and as such it must be capitalized. An example of a betterment is the installation of bolts to a building located in an earthquake prone area to add structural support and resistance to seismic forces. An example of an adaptation is making modifications to a manufacturing building so it can be used as a showroom.

 *Planning Reminder*

Repairs and Improvements

What if repairs and improvements are unconnected and not part of an overall improvement program? Assume you repair the floors of one story and improve another story by putting in new windows. You probably may deduct the cost of repairing the floors provided you have separate bills for the jobs. To safeguard the deduction for repairs, schedule the work at separate times so that the two jobs are not lumped together as an overall improvement program.

The regulations also identify specific building systems, called "units of property" or UOPs, and require that an improvement to a particular UOP must be depreciated rather than deducted currently. These UOPs include the HVAC (heating, ventilation, air conditioning), plumbing, electrical, fire protection, security and gas distribution systems.

Safe harbors under the IRS regulations. The final regulations provide safe harbors that may allow a current deduction. There are three safe harbors: a *de minimis* safe harbor, a safe harbor for small taxpayers, and a safe harbor for routine maintenance. To the extent that a safe harbor applies, a current deduction is allowed, although the expense might otherwise be considered a depreciable improvement. The *de minimis* safe harbor and small taxpayer safe harbor are annual elections made on a statement attached to your return; they are not a change in accounting method.

1. *De minimis safe harbor.* This safe harbor, updated for increased amounts by Notice 2015-82 allows you to deduct amounts up to $2,500 per item or invoice. Thus, a low-cost purchase (such as a small appliance or window replacement) is fully deductible if it costs $2,500 or less. To elect the *de minimis* safe harbor, the IRS requires that you attach a statement to your return and you must apply the safe harbor to all items purchased during the year that are within the $2,500 limit.

   There is also a $5,000 *de minimis* safe harbor (per item or invoice), but this applies only to taxpayers that have an applicable financial statement (AFS), which generally applies to companies required to file financial statements with the SEC or obtain certified audited financial statements.

2. *Safe harbor for small taxpayers.* This safe harbor allows small taxpayers (average annual gross receipts of no more than $10 million in the three prior years) to elect an overall exemption from the capitalization rules for repairs, maintenance, and improvements, but the benefit is limited. The safe harbor applies separately to each building you own, but only buildings with an unadjusted basis of up to $1 million qualify. For each such building, the safe harbor allows a current deduction only if your expenses do not exceed the lesser of $10,000 or 2% of the unadjusted basis of the building. This limit applies to the total expenses during the year for repairs, maintenance, and improvements to that building. Thus, for a building with a $250,000 unadjusted basis, the expense limit is $5,000 (2% × $250,000).

   To the extent that the annual expenses fall within the $10,000/2% ceiling, a deduction is allowed for amounts that would otherwise be considered improvements. To claim the safe harbor, you must file an election on a timely filed original tax return for that year, including extensions. For a building owned by a partnership or S corporation, the election must be made by the entity and not by the shareholders or partners.

   If the total expenses for the year for repairs, maintenance, and improvements exceed the $10,000/2% limit, the safe harbor is not allowed for any of the expenses, and the general rules for determining whether an item is a repair or an improvement apply. This means that a low-cost item may be deductible under the *de minimis* safe harbor, or an expense may be allowed under the routine maintenance safe harbor.

3. *Safe harbor for routine maintenance.* This safe harbor allows you to deduct an expense that is for keeping the property in efficient operating condition if it is reasonably expected that the expense will have to be performed more than once over a 10-year period. An IRS example of a qualifying expense is maintenance of an HVAC system at the manufacturer's recommended schedule of once every four years, including inspection, cleaning, and repair or replacement of component parts.

> **EXAMPLES**
>
> 1. The cost of painting the outside of a rental building and the cost of papering and painting the inside are repair costs and may be deducted. A change in the plumbing system is generally a capital expenditure that must be depreciated under MACRS *(42.12),* unless a current deduction is allowed under the small taxpayer safe harbor of the final regulations *(see above).*

2. Campbell owned a one-story house that she rented to a tenant. She paid $8,000 to repair the roof after the tenant complained of leaks. The contractor she employed removed the existing layers of roof and replaced them with fiberglass and asphalt; no structural changes were made. The Tax Court allowed Campbell to deduct the full amount of the payment to the contractor as an ordinary and necessary repair because the roof replacement merely restored the property to a leak-free condition and did not add to the value of the home.

    The Tax Court also allowed an owner of a commercial building with a leaky roof to fully deduct the $52,000 cost of stripping the roof layers, replacing them, and spraying the new ones with foam to prevent future leaks. These were repairs intended to keep the property in working condition and did not extend the life of the building.

3. You buy a dilapidated business building and have it renovated and repaired before renting it to commercial tenants. The total cost comes to about $130,000, of which $17,800 is allocable to the repairs. The cost of the repairs is generally not deductible because the entire project is a capital expenditure. According to the IRS, when a general improvement program is undertaken, you may not separate repairs from improvements. Both become an integral part of the overall betterment and are a capital investment, although a portion could be characterized as repairs when viewed independently.

9.4   Reporting Rents From a Multi-Unit Residence

If you rent out an apartment or room in a multi-unit residence in which you also live, you report rent receipts and deduct expenses allocated to the rented part of the property on Schedule E (Form 1040 or 1040-SR) whether or not you itemize deductions. You deduct interest and taxes on your personal share of the property as itemized deductions on Schedule A (Form 1040 or 1040-SR) if you itemize deductions. If you or close relatives personally use the rented portion during the year and expenses exceed income, loss deductions may be barred under the personal-use rules *(9.7)*.

EXAMPLE

You buy a three-family house in March 2023. You occupy one floor as your personal residence and starting in June 2023, when the other two floors are ready for tenants, you rent out the two floors. The house cost you $300,000 ($270,000 for the building and $30,000 for the land). Two-thirds of the basis of the building is subject to depreciation, or $180,000 ($2/3$ of $270,000). For a building placed in service in June, the depreciation rate is 1.970%, as shown in *Table 9-1*, so your depreciation deduction is $3,546 (1.970% $180,000). Assuming you paid property taxes of $6,000, mortgage interest of $3,900, and repairs of $3,000, this is how you deduct expenses for 2023:

	Total	Personal portion deductible as itemized deductions	Rental portion deductible on Schedule E	Not deductible
Taxes	$ 6,000	$ 2,000	$ 4,000	
Interest	3,900	1,300	2,600	
Repairs	3,000		2,000	$ 1,000
Depreciation	3,546		3,546	
	$ 16,446	$ 3,300	$ 12,146	$ 1,000

    The taxes and interest allocated to personal use are deductible on Schedule A (Form 1040 or 1040-SR) if you itemize deductions. The taxes are subject to the overall limit of $10,000 that can be claimed for state and local property taxes plus state income or sales taxes *(16.1)*. Repairs allocated to your apartment are nondeductible personal expenses.

Court Decision

Rented Rooms That Are Not Separate Dwelling Units

A rental loss was denied to an owner of a two-story, four-bedroom house when he rented out two bedrooms to separate tenants after he lost his job. Although individual locks were placed on the doors of the rented bedrooms, the tenants and the owner shared access to the kitchen, bathroom, and other parts of the house. The Tax Court held that the rented rooms were not separate and distinct from the rest of the house that the owner used. The house was a single dwelling unit shared by the owner and tenants and under the personal-use rules *(9.7)*, the owner could not claim a rental loss.

Even if a loss is not barred by the personal-use rules *(9.7)*, a loss shown on Schedule E is subject to the passive loss restrictions discussed in *Chapter 10*. The loss, if it comes within the $25,000 allowance *(10.2)* or the exception for real estate professionals *(10.3)*, may be deducted from any type of income. If your only passive activity losses are rental losses of $25,000 or less from actively managed rental real estate and your modified adjusted gross income is $100,000 or less, you do not have to use Form 8582 to deduct losses under the $25,000 allowance *(10.12)*. If you are not a qualifying real estate professional and cannot claim the allowance, the loss may be deducted only from passive activity income.

9.5   Depreciation on Converting a Home to Rental Property

When you convert your residence to rental property, you may depreciate the building. You figure depreciation on the lower of:

- Fair market value of the building at the time you convert it to rental property; or
- Your adjusted basis at the time of the conversion. This is your original cost for the building, exclusive of land, plus permanent improvements and other capital costs, and minus items that represent a return of your cost, such as casualty or theft loss or home-office deductions claimed on prior tax returns.

You claim MACRS depreciation based on a 27½-year recovery period, which extends to 28 or 29 years due to the mid-month convention. The specific rate for the year of conversion is the rate for the month in which the property is ready for tenants. For example, you move out of your home in May and make some minor repairs. You advertise the house for rent in June. Depreciation starts in June because that is when the home is ready for rental, even if you do not actually obtain a tenant until a later month. Under a mid-month convention, the house is treated as placed in service during the middle of the month. This means that one-half of a full month's depreciation is allowed for that month. In *Table 9-1*, the monthly depreciation rates for the year the property is placed in service and later years are shown. The table incorporates the mid-month convention.

Planning Reminder

Obtain Appraisal

Have an appraiser estimate the fair market value of the house when it is rented. The appraisal will help support your basis for depreciation or a loss deduction on a sale if your return is examined.

> ### EXAMPLE
>
> In 2016, you bought a house for $125,000, of which $100,000 is allocated to the house; the $25,000 balance is allocated to the land. In June 2023, you move out of the house and rent it to tenants. At that time, the fair market value of the house exclusive of the land is $150,000. The depreciable basis of the house is the adjusted basis of $100,000, as it is less than the $150,000 value. The depreciation rate for placing the house in service in June is 1.970%, as shown in *Table 9-1*. Thus, your 2023 depreciation deduction is $1,970 ($100,000 × 1.970%). Your 2024 depreciation deduction (your second year of depreciation) will be $3,636 ($100,000 × 3.636% rate for year 2).

Depreciating a rented cooperative apartment. If you rent out a co-op apartment, you may deduct your share of the total depreciation claimed by the cooperative corporation. The method for computing your share depends on whether you bought your co-op shares as part of the first offering. If you did, follow these steps: (1) Ask the co-op corporation officials for the total real estate depreciation deduction of the corporation, not counting depreciation for office space that cannot be lived in by tenant-shareholders. (2) Multiply Step 1 by the following fraction: number of your co-op shares divided by total shares outstanding. The result is your share of the co-op's depreciation, but you may not deduct more than your adjusted basis.

The computation is more complicated if you bought your co-op shares after the first offering. You must compute your depreciable basis as follows: Increase your cost for the co-op shares by your share of the co-op's total mortgage. Reduce this amount by your share of the value of the co-op's land and your share of the commercial space not available for occupancy by tenant-stockholders. Your "share" of the co-op's mortgage, land value, or commercial space is the co-op's total amount for such items multiplied by the fraction in Step 2 above, that is, the number of your shares divided by the total shares outstanding. After computing your depreciable basis, multiply that basis by the depreciation percentage for the month your apartment is ready for rental.

Basis to use when you sell a rented residence. For purposes of figuring gain, you use adjusted basis at the time of the conversion, plus subsequent capital improvements, and minus depreciation and casualty loss deductions. For purposes of figuring loss, you use the lower of adjusted basis and fair market value at the time of the conversion, plus subsequent improvements and minus depreciation and casualty losses. You may have neither gain nor loss to report; this would happen if you figure a loss when using the above basis rule for gains and you figure a gain when using the basis rule for losses.

Depreciation on a vacant residence. If you move from your house before it is sold, you generally may not deduct depreciation on the vacant residence while it is held for sale. The IRS will not allow the deduction, and, according to the Tax Court, a deduction is possible only if you can show that you held the house expecting to make a profit on an increase in value over and above the value of the house when you moved from it. That is, you held the house for sale on the expectation of profiting on a future increase in value after abandoning the house as a residence.

Table 9-1 Depreciation for Residential Rental Property: Use the Row for the Month the Residence Is Ready for Rental in the First Rental Year (*see* IRS Pub. 527)

Month property placed in service

Year	1	2	3	4	5	6	7	8	9	10	11	12
1	3.485%	3.182%	2.879%	2.576%	2.273%	1.970%	1.667%	1.364%	1.061%	0.758%	0.455%	0.152%
2–9	3.636	3.636	3.636	3.636	3.636	3.636	3.636	3.636	3.636	3.636	3.636	3.636
10	3.637	3.637	3.637	3.637	3.637	3.637	3.636	3.636	3.636	3.636	3.636	3.636
11	3.636	3.636	3.636	3.636	3.636	3.636	3.637	3.637	3.637	3.637	3.637	3.637
12	3.637	3.637	3.637	3.637	3.637	3.637	3.636	3.636	3.636	3.636	3.636	3.636
13	3.636	3.636	3.636	3.636	3.636	3.636	3.637	3.637	3.637	3.637	3.637	3.637
14	3.637	3.637	3.637	3.637	3.637	3.637	3.636	3.636	3.636	3.636	3.636	3.636
15	3.636	3.636	3.636	3.636	3.636	3.636	3.637	3.637	3.637	3.637	3.637	3.637
16	3.637	3.637	3.637	3.637	3.637	3.637	3.636	3.636	3.636	3.636	3.636	3.636
17	3.636	3.636	3.636	3.636	3.636	3.636	3.637	3.637	3.637	3.637	3.637	3.637
18	3.637	3.637	3.637	3.637	3.637	3.637	3.636	3.636	3.636	3.636	3.636	3.636
19	3.636	3.636	3.636	3.636	3.636	3.636	3.637	3.637	3.637	3.637	3.637	3.637
20	3.637	3.637	3.637	3.637	3.637	3.637	3.636	3.636	3.636	3.636	3.636	3.636
21	3.636	3.636	3.636	3.636	3.636	3.636	3.637	3.637	3.637	3.637	3.637	3.637
22	3.637	3.637	3.637	3.637	3.637	3.637	3.636	3.636	3.636	3.636	3.636	3.636
23	3.636	3.636	3.636	3.636	3.636	3.636	3.637	3.637	3.637	3.637	3.637	3.637
24	3.637	3.637	3.637	3.637	3.637	3.637	3.636	3.636	3.636	3.636	3.636	3.636
25	3.636	3.636	3.636	3.636	3.636	3.636	3.637	3.637	3.637	3.637	3.637	3.637
26	3.637	3.637	3.637	3.637	3.637	3.637	3.636	3.636	3.636	3.636	3.636	3.636
27	3.636	3.636	3.636	3.636	3.636	3.636	3.637	3.637	3.637	3.637	3.637	3.637
28	1.97	2.273	2.576	2.879	3.182	3.485	3.636	3.636	3.636	3.636	3.636	3.636
29							0.152	0.455	0.758	1.061	1.364	1.667

9.6 Renting a Residence to a Relative

The tax law distinguishes between a rental of a unit used by a close relative as a principal residence and a rental of a unit that is not the relative's principal residence, such as a second home or vacation home. It is easier to deduct a rental loss on the principal residence rental.

If you rent a unit at a fair market rental price to a close relative who uses it as his or her principal residence, your relative's use is not considered personal use by you that could bar a loss deduction under the personal-use test *(9.7)*. A relative's use of the unit as a second or vacation home is attributed to you in applying the personal-use test *(9.7)*, even if you receive a fair market value rent.

Close relatives who come within these rules are: brothers and sisters, half-brothers and half-sisters, spouses, parents, grandparents, children, and grandchildren.

Fair market rental is the amount a person who is not related to you would be willing to pay. The most direct way to determine fair market rental is to ask a real estate agent in your neighborhood for comparative rentals.

EXAMPLE

Barranti inherited a residence from her grandmother. The house was in a state of disrepair. A real estate agent estimated the fair market rental rate for the house to be between $700 and $750 per month. Barranti rented the house to her brother for $500 a month while he repaired the structure. After a year, he moved out and Barranti sold the house and claimed a rental loss and a loss on the sale. The Tax Court disallowed both losses. The below-market rental to Barranti's brother was treated as her own personal use of the house, preventing the rental loss deduction. The below-market rental was also treated as evidence that Barranti held the property for personal purposes and therefore she could not deduct the loss on the sale either.

9.7 Personal Use and Rental of a Residence During the Year

The number of personal-use days and fair-market-rental days for your residential unit determines how you must report rental income and expenses. If you rent the property for 15 or more days and your personal use of the unit exceeds the 14-day/10% test described below, the unit is treated as a residence rather than rental property, and in this case, some of your rental expenses are deductible only to the extent of the rental income from the property; *see* Rule 2 below. *(9.9)*. If personal use exceeds the 14-day/10% test but you rent the property for under 15 days, you do not report the rental income or deduct rental expenses; *see* Rule 3 below.

Personal-use days include not only your days of personal use but may also include rental days to family members listed at *9.6* and use days under co-ownership agreements. *See 9.8* for details on personal-use days.

Dwelling units subject to the 14-day/10% test. The daily-use tests apply to any "dwelling unit" you rent out that is also used as a residence during the year by yourself or other family members. A dwelling unit may be a house, apartment, condominium, cooperative, house trailer, mini motor home, boat, or similar property with basic living accommodations, including any appurtenant structure such as a garage. A dwelling unit does not include property used exclusively as a hotel, motel, inn, or similar establishment.

The hotel/motel/inn exception applies only to property that is used exclusively in such a business. The exception does not apply to the dual-use portion of a hotel, inn, or bed and breakfast. In one case, the Tax Court agreed with the IRS that the owners of a three-floor bed-and-breakfast could not claim business expense deductions for depreciation or interest on the areas that were used both in the B&B business as well as by them personally. The lobby, registration area, office, kitchen, and laundry room were used 75% of the time for the business and 25% of the time for personal purposes. Because these areas were not used solely for operating the B&B, they could not qualify for the hotel exception. The dual-use areas were treated as part of the owners' dwelling unit for purposes of the 14-day/10% personal-use test.

14-day/10% personal-use test determines if unit is treated as a residence. A daily-use test determines whether your use of the unit during the taxable year is treated as residential use.

You are considered to have used the unit as a residence if your personal-use days during the year, determined according to the rules for counting personal-use and rental days *(9.8)*, exceeded 14 days, or, if greater, 10% of the days on which the unit was rented to others at a fair market rental price.

If the property is treated as used as a residence because your personal use exceeds the greater of 14 days or 10% of the fair market rental days, and you have a rental loss, a deduction for some of your allocable rental deductions will be limited, as the expenses are offset against rental income following a specific order; *see* Rule 2 below and Steps 1-3 in *9.9*.

EXAMPLES

1. In 2023, you rented out your condominium unit in Florida at a fair market rental for 260 days. The property is considered used as a residence if your personal use exceeds the greater of 14 days or 10% of the days it is rented to others at a fair market value. Here, under the "greater of" test, 10% of the 260 fair market value days, or 26 days, exceeds 14 days, so if your personal use exceeds 26 days, the condominium is considered a residence subject to the deduction limitation rules under Rule 2 below and Steps 1–3 in *9.9*.

   If you only used the unit for 26 days (10% of the rental days) or less than that, you are not treated as using the property as a residence under the 14-day/10% test. You may treat the unit for the taxable year as rental property and your expenses are not limited to rental income (under Steps 1–3 in *9.9*). You may deduct a loss, if any, subject to the passive activity rules *(10.1)*. However, if personal use did not exceed 26 days, the mortgage interest allocable to the personal-use days would be nondeductible personal interest.

2. Assume the same unit as in Example 1 but you rented the unit for 130 days. The unit would be treated as a residence if your personal use exceeded 14 days, since under the "greater of" test, 14 days is greater than 10% of the rental days (10% of 130 days or 13 days). If you used the unit personally for 14 days or less, you may treat the unit as a rental property.

Rule 1: If your personal use does not meet the 14-day/10% test. If your personal-use days do not exceed 14 days or 10% of the fair market rental days, whichever is more, the property is treated as rental property and not property used as a residence. You report the rental income and expenses on Schedule E (Form 1040 or 1040-SR) and the rental deductions are not limited to rental income by the personal-use test. However, a loss deduction is subject to the passive activity loss restrictions *(10.1)*. The passive loss rules generally prevent you from deducting a passive rental loss against nonpassive income, but if you are an "active participant" with modified adjusted gross income of no more than $100,000, you may deduct expenses up to $25,000 *(10.2)*; and if you qualify as a real estate professional and materially participate *(10.3)*, a full loss is allowed against nonpassive income.

Another consequence of not meeting the 14-day/10% personal use test is that you lose part of the mortgage interest deduction because the unit is not a qualified second home for mortgage interest purposes if personal use does not exceed the greater of 14 days or 10% of the fair market rental days. The mortgage interest allocable to the rental use *(9.9)* is deductible against rental income on Schedule E, but the balance is nondeductible personal interest.

Rule 2: If your personal use exceeds the 14-day/10% test and you rent the unit for 15 or more days during the year. If you are considered to have used the unit as a residence because your personal use of the property exceeds the greater of 14 days or 10% of the fair market rental days, and you rent the property for at least 15 days during the year, you cannot deduct a rental loss on Schedule E. Your rental expenses and depreciation are deductible on Schedule E only to the extent of rental income, following the allocation rules of Steps 1–3 in *9.9*. Expenses that are not deductible in the current year under this limitation may be carried forward and will be deductible up to rental income in the following year. The deduction limit is irrelevant if your rental income exceeds expenses. When you have a profit, you report the rental income and claim all of the deductible rental expenses on Schedule E.

Planning Reminder

Rentals of 14 Days or Less

Where your personal use of a home exceeds the greater of 14 days or 10% of the fair market rental days, and you rent it out for less than 15 days, you do not have to report the rental income on your tax return, and no rental expenses are deductible. If you itemize deductions on Schedule A (Form 1040 or 1040-SR), you may claim the deductions allowed to you as a homeowner for qualified mortgage interest, property taxes, and casualty losses if any.

Planning Reminder

Shared-Equity Financing Agreements

As an investor, you can help finance the purchase of a principal residence for a family member or other individual. The rental income you receive for your ownership share in the property may be offset by deductions for your share of the mortgage interest, taxes, and operating expenses you pay under the terms of the agreement, as well as depreciation deductions for your percentage share. Rental losses are subject to the passive loss restrictions in *Chapter 10*.

The other co-owner living in the house may claim itemized deductions for payment of his or her share of the mortgage interest and taxes, subject to applicable limits explained on the next page.

Rule 3: If your personal use exceeds the 14-day/10% test but you rent the unit for fewer than 15 days during the taxable year. If your personal use of the property exceeds the greater of 14 days or 10% of the fair market rental days, and you rent it for fewer than 15 days in the taxable year, do not report the rental income on your tax return (it is not gross income) and the only deductions allowed are those you would be allowed anyway as a homeowner. That is, if you itemize deductions on Schedule A, you deduct allowable mortgage interest *(15.1)*, real estate taxes *(16.4)*, and casualty losses if allowed *(18.1)*. No other rental expenses such as depreciation and maintenance expenses are deductible.

9.8 Counting Personal-Use Days and Rental Days for a Residence

In applying the 14-day/10% personal-use test *(9.7)*, personal-use days are:

- Days you used the residence for personal purposes other than days primarily spent making repairs or getting the property ready for tenants. If you use a residence for personal purposes on a day you rent it at fair market value, count that day as a personal day, not a rental day, in applying the 14-day/10% test.
- Days on which the residence is used by your spouse, children, grandchildren or great-grandchildren, parents, brothers, sisters, grandparents, or great-grandparents. However, if such a relative pays you a fair rental value to use the home as a principal residence, the relative's use is not considered personal use by you. If you rent a vacation home to such relatives, their use is considered personal use by you even if they pay a fair rental value amount; *see* Example 1 below. The same rules apply if the use of the residence is by a family member of a co-owner of the property.
- Days on which the residence is used by any person under a reciprocal arrangement that allows you to use some other dwelling during the year.
- Days on which you rent the residence to any person for less than fair market value.
- Days that a co-owner of the property uses the residence, unless the co-owner's use is under a shared-equity financing agreement discussed later in this section.

An owner is not considered to have personally used a home that is used by an employee if the value of such use is tax-free lodging required as a condition of employment *(3.13)*.

Shared-equity financing agreements for co-owners. Use by a co-owner is not considered personal use by you if you have a shared-equity financing agreement under which: (1) the co-owner pays you a fair rent for using the home as his or her principal residence; and (2) you and your co-owner each have undivided interests for more than 50 years in the entire home and in any appurtenant land acquired with the residence.

Any use by a co-owner that does not meet these two tests is considered personal use by you if, for any part of the day, the home is used by a co-owner or a holder of any interest in the home (other than a security interest or an interest under a lease for fair rental) for personal purposes. For this purpose, any other ownership interest existing at the time you have an interest in the home is counted, even if there are no immediate rights to possession and enjoyment of the home under such other interest. For example, you have a life estate in the home and your friend owns the remainder interest. Use by either of you is personal use.

Moving back in after rental of principal residence or renting it prior to sale. When you move out of your principal residence and rent it at a fair rental (or try to rent it) and then move back in, or rent it for a period and then sell it, the days that you use the house as your principal residence before or after the rental period are not counted as personal-use days if (1) you rent it (or try to) for a consecutive period of 12 months or more, or (2) you rent it (or try to) for a period of less than 12 months that ends with the sale or exchange of the residence. For example, you move out of your principal residence on May 21, 2023, offering it for rental as of June 1. You rent it from June 15 until mid-November, when you sell the house. Under the special rental period rule, your use of the house from January 1 until May 21, 2023, is not counted as personal use. This means that deductions for the rental period are not subject to the rental income limitation (Steps 1-3 in *9.9*).

1. A son rented a condominium in Florida to his parents, who split their time between the Florida apartment and the home they owned in Illinois. Although the parents paid a fair amount for the Florida condo, the son's rental deductions were limited by the IRS and the Tax Court to interest and real estate taxes that did not exceed the rental income. The parents' rental days were attributed to the son under the 14 day/10% rental day limit since the home in Illinois, and not the Florida apartment, was their principal residence.

2. You and your neighbor Joe are co-owners of a vacation condominium. You rent the unit out whenever possible; Joe uses the unit for two weeks every year. As Joe owns an interest in the unit, both of you are considered to have used the unit for personal purposes during those weeks.

3. You and your neighbor Tom are co-owners of a house under a shared-equity financing agreement. Tom lives in the house and pays you a fair rental price. Even though Tom has an interest in the house, the days he lives there are not counted as days of personal use by you because Tom rents the house as a main home under a shared-equity financing agreement.

4. You rent a beach house to Jane. Jane rents her house in the mountains to you. You each pay a fair rental price. You are using your house for personal purposes on the days that Jane uses it because your house is used by Jane under an arrangement that allows you to use her house.

9.9 Allocating Expenses of a Residence to Rental Days

When you rent out your home or other dwelling unit *(9.7)* for part of the year at fair market value and also use it personally on some days during the taxable year, expenses are allocated between personal and rental use. The deductible rental portion equals your total expenses for the year multiplied by this fraction:

$$\frac{\text{Days unit is rented for fair market rental price}}{\text{Total days of rental and personal use}}$$

The days a unit is held out for rent but not actually rented are not counted as rental days in the numerator of the fraction. Any day for which the unit is rented at a fair rental price is counted as a rental day for allocation purposes even if in fact you use it for personal purposes on that day.

Mortgage interest and real estate taxes. There is a conflict of opinion between the IRS and some courts over the issue of whether the above fractional formula applies also to interest and taxes. According to the IRS, it does. According to the Tax Court and two federal appeals courts, it does not; interest and taxes are allocated on a daily basis. Thus, if a house is rented for 61 days in 2023, 16.71% (61/365) of the deductible interest and taxes is deducted first from the rental income under the Tax Court rule. This Tax Court rule in most cases will allocate less of the interest and taxes against the rental income than the IRS method, thereby allowing a larger amount of other expenses to be deducted from rental income than is allowed under the IRS application of the formula; *see* the Examples below. However, where you are subject to the $10,000 overall limitation on the itemized deduction for state and local taxes (the so-called SALT deduction limit; *see 16.1*), then the IRS method may be more favorable.

Claiming expenses on Schedule E if personal use limits a loss deduction. If your personal use of a residence exceeds the 14-day /10% test *(9.7)*, the residence was rented for at least 15 days during the year, and the allocable rental expenses (including depreciation) exceed rental income, you cannot deduct the net loss from other income. Some of the expenses will not be currently deductible. The allocable rental expenses are deducted from rental income in a specific order:

1. The rental portion of the following expenses is fully deductible on Schedule E of Form 1040 or 1040-SR, even if the total exceeds rental income: deductible home mortgage interest *(15.1)*, real estate taxes *(16.4)*, deductible casualty and theft losses *(Chapter 18)*, and directly related rental expenses. Directly related rental expenses are rental expenses not related to the use or maintenance of the residence itself, such as

office supplies, rental agency fees, advertising, and depreciation on office equipment used in the rental activity. If you claim the standard deduction, the rental portion of your home mortgage interest and the rental portion of your real estate taxes are not taken into account here in Step 1; they are taken into account in Step 2 below. If you itemize deductions on Schedule A, and the SALT limitation applies to your deduction for state and local taxes *(16.1)*, a special computation must be made to figure the amount of real estate taxes to enter here in Step 1 and the amount to enter in Step 2; the IRS has a worksheet in Publication 527 for figuring these amounts.

2. If there is any rental income remaining after the income is reduced by the expenses in Step 1, the balance is next offset by the rental portion of operating expenses for the residence itself, such as utilities, repairs, and insurance. If you claim the standard deduction, the rental portion of your home mortgage interest and the rental portion of your real estate taxes is added to to the operating expenses here in Step 2. If you claim itemized deductions and the SALT limitation applies to your deduction for state and local taxes *(16.1)*, the real estate taxes which are not taken into account in Step 1 are added here; *see* the IRS worksheet in Publication 527. Do not include depreciation on the rental part of the home in this group.

3. If any rental income remains after Step 2, depreciation on the rental portion of the residence may be deducted from the balance.

Step 1 expenses, as well as the expenses from Steps 2 and 3 that offset rental income, are deducted on the applicable lines of Schedule E. Operating expenses from Step 2 and depreciation from Step 3 that exceed the balance of rental income are carried forward to the next year as rental expenses for the same property. In the next year, the carried-over expenses are deductible only to the extent of rental income from the property for that year, following Steps 1–3, whether or not your personal use of the residence exceeds the 14-day/10% test *(9.7)* for that carryover year.

If you itemize deductions (rather than claim the standard deduction), you claim the personal-use portion of deductible mortgage interest, real estate taxes, and disaster-related casualty and theft losses on Schedule A (Form 1040 or 1040-SR). Business casualty losses for the rental portion are not limited to those sustained in disaster areas.

Filing Tip

Carryover of Disallowed Expenses

If your deductions for operating expenses and depreciation are limited by the personal-use rules, the disallowed amounts may be carried over to the following year.

EXAMPLES

1. You rent out your vacation home for July and August of 2023 (62 days), receiving rent of $4,000 (a fair market rental). You use the home yourself for 124 days during the year. Your annual expenses are mortgage interest of $4,200, real estate taxes of $3,900, and maintenance costs (including utilities and insurance) of $4,500. Depreciation (based on 100% rental use) is $3,940. Since your personal use (124 days) exceeds 14 days (the greater of 14 days or 10% of the 62 fair market rental days *(9.7)*) and your rental expenses exceed the rental income, you may deduct expenses only up to the amount of rental income under Steps 1-3 above. Assume the vacation home is a qualifying second home *(15.1)*, so that all the interest is deductible under the mortgage interest rules. Under the IRS allocation method, one-third of all the expenses (62 rental days divided by 186 total days of use), including the interest and taxes, are deducted on Schedule E in this order:

Rental income		$ 4,000
Less Step 1 expenses:		
Interest ($\frac{1}{3}$ of $4,200)	$1,400	
Taxes ($\frac{1}{3}$ of $3,900)	1,300	2,700
		$ 1,300
Less Step 2 expenses:		
Maintenance ($\frac{1}{3}$ of $4,500, or $1,500, but the offset cannot exceed the $1,300 balance of rental income)		1,300
		$ 0

Step 3 Depreciation:
$\frac{1}{3}$ of $3,940, or $1,313, is allocable to the rental, but none is deductible because there is no remaining rental income.

The $200 of maintenance expenses and the $1,313 of depreciation that are not deductible for 2023 because of the rental income limitation may be carried forward to 2024.

Under the Tax Court's method of allocating interest and taxes, 16.99% (62/365) of the interest and taxes, or $1,376 (16.99% × $8,100) is deductible from rental income, rather than the $2,700 (one-third) required by the IRS method, so more rental income is left that can be offset by maintenance expenses and depreciation.

The interest and taxes allocable to your personal use are deductible as itemized deductions provided you claim itemized deductions on Schedule A of Form 1040 or 1040-SR; the taxes are subject to the overall $10,000 limit for state and local taxes.

If the vacation home were not a qualifying second residence *(15.1)*, the interest would not be deducted with taxes from the $4,000 of rental income, but would be treated as an operating expense and deducted along with the maintenance expenses.

2. The Boltons paid interest and property taxes totaling $3,475 on their vacation home. Maintenance expenses (not including depreciation) totaled $2,693. The Boltons stayed at the home 30 days and rented it for 91 days, receiving rents of $2,700. Because the personal use for 30 days exceeded the 14-day limit *(9.7)*, the Boltons could deduct rental expenses only up to the gross rental income of $2,700, reduced by interest and taxes allocable to rental. In figuring the amount of interest and taxes deductible from rents, they divided the number of rental days, or 91, by 365, the number of days in the year. This gave them an allocation of 25%. After subtracting $869 for interest and taxes (25% of $3,475) from rental income, they deducted $1,831 ($2,700 − $869) of maintenance expenses from rental income.

The IRS argued that 75% of the Boltons' interest and tax payments had to be allocated to the rental income. The IRS used an allocation fraction with a denominator of 121 days, the total days of use (30 personal and 91 rental days). Thus, the IRS allocated 75% (91/121) of the interest and taxes, or $2,606, to gross rental income of $2,700. This allocation allowed only $94 maintenance expenses to be deducted ($2,700 − $2,606).

The Tax Court sided with the Boltons and an appeals court (the Ninth Circuit) agreed. The IRS method of allocating interest and taxes to rental use is bizarre, according to the Tax Court. Interest and taxes are expenses that accrue ratably over the year and are deductible even if a vacation home is not rented for a single day. Thus, the allocation to rental use should be based on a ratable portion of the annual expense by dividing the number of rental days by the number of days in a year.

The Tenth Circuit appeals court also supports the Tax Court allocation method. The IRS, however, had not yet acquiesced to this view.

Court Decision

Allocation of Taxes and Interest

The IRS position on allocating mortgage interest and real estate taxes to rental income is not as favorable as the position adopted by the Tax Court and several appeals courts if overall state and local taxes are below the $10,000 SALT limitation *(16.1)*. But the IRS position may be more favorable for those with state and local taxes exceeding this limitation.

Interest expenses. If you personally use a rental vacation home for more than the greater of 14 days or 10% of the fair market rental days *(9.7)*, the residence may be treated as a qualifying second residence under the mortgage interest rules *(15.1)*. The interest on a qualifying second home is not subject to disallowance under the passive activity restrictions; the rental is not treated as a passive activity *(10.1)*. As shown in Step 1 above, the portion of the deductible mortgage interest allocable to the rental portion is deducted from rental income (along with taxes) before other expenses.

9.10 IRS May Challenge Loss Claimed on Temporary Rental of Residence Before Sale

If you are unable to sell your home and must move, it may be advisable to put it up for rent. This way you may be able to deduct maintenance expenses and depreciation on the unit even if it remains vacant. However, the IRS has disallowed loss deductions for some rentals preceding a sale on the ground that there was no "profit motive" for the rental *(40.10)*. For example, where minimal efforts are made to rent out a vacation home in anticipation of an eventual sale, the IRS may claim, as in Example 1 below, that the home was not converted to rental property held for the production of income. Where the IRS determines that you lacked a profit motive for renting the property, it will limit your deduction for rental expenses to the amount of the rental income, and the expenses in excess of rental income cannot be carried forward to a later year. Courts have allowed loss deductions in certain cases.

EXAMPLES

1. A married couple bought an oceanfront condominium in 2004 for $875,000, planning to use it as a seasonal home. After the tragic death of their daughter in 2006, they stopped staying at the property and in 2008 they removed most of their belongings from the unit and entered into a one-year contract with a realty company located in their oceanfront community, intending to rent out the condo and eventually sell it at a profit. However, they could not rent out the property and because of the collapsing real estate market in Florida in 2009, they could not sell the property. They changed realtors and sold the home for a $160,000 loss in 2010. The taxpayers claimed rental expenses on their 2009 and 2010 returns and claimed that the loss on the 2010 sale was a fully deductible ordinary loss.

   The IRS disallowed deductions for the rental expenses and disallowed any loss deduction on the sale. The Tax Court agreed with the IRS. Although the couple clearly abandoned personal use of the condo in 2008, they did not convert it to a profit-motivated rental property. The realty company's efforts were limited to featuring the condo in an office portfolio and telling prospective buyers that it was available for rent. The taxpayers did change realtors, but beyond putting it on a multiple listing service, there is no evidence that the second agent did anything to rent out the condo. Nor is there evidence that they took any other steps to rent it. The minimal efforts taken did not constitute a bona fide attempt to rent out the condo and therefore did not convert it to property held for the production of income. Thus, "rental" expenses are not allowed, and the loss on the sale was a nondeductible personal loss.

2. The IRS and Tax Court disallowed a loss deduction for rental expenses under the "profit-motive rules" *(40.10)* where a principal residence was rented for 10 months until it could be sold. According to the Tax Court, the temporary rental did not convert the residence to rental property. Since the sales effort was primary, there was no profit motive for the rental. Thus, no loss could be claimed; rental expenses were deductible only to the extent of rental income. The favorable side of the Tax Court position: Since the residence was not converted to rental property, the owners could under prior law rules defer tax on the gain from the sale by buying a new home. An appeals court reversed the Tax Court and allowed both tax deferral and a loss deduction. The rental loss was allowed since the old home was rented almost continuously until sold for a fair rental price.

3. In 1976, a couple bought a condo apartment in Pompano Beach, Florida. In 1983, they decided to move and listed the unit for either sale or rent with a local real estate broker. Sale of the unit was difficult because of the saturation of the Florida real estate market. Rental of the unit was also difficult because the condominium association's rules barred the rental of condominium units on a seasonal basis. The unit remained unrented until it was sold in 1986 for a substantial gain. In 1984, the couple deducted a $9,576 rental loss ($7,596 for maintenance expenses and $1,980 for depreciation). The IRS disallowed the deduction as not incurred in a bona fide rental activity. The Tax Court allowed the deduction, under a rationale that appears to continue to apply. The couple made an honest and reasonable effort to rent the condominium. Lack of rental income was caused by a slack rental market and the condominium association rules prohibiting short-term rentals.

9.11 Reporting Royalty Income

Royalties are payment for use of patents or copyrights or for the use and exhaustion of mineral properties. Royalties are taxable as ordinary income and are reported on Schedule E (Form 1040 or 1040-SR). Depletion deductions relating to the royalties are also reported on Schedule E. If you own an operating oil, gas, or mineral interest, or are a self-employed writer, investor, or artist, you report royalty income, expenses, and depletion on Schedule C.

Examples of Royalty Income

- License fees received for use, manufacture, or sale of a patented article.
- Renting fees received from patents, copyrights, and depletable assets (such as oil wells).
- Authors' royalties including advance royalties if not a loan.
- Royalties for musical compositions, works of art, etc.

- Proceeds of sale of part of your rights in an artistic composition or book, for example, sale of motion picture or television rights.
- Royalties from oil, gas, or other similar interests *(9.16)*. To have a royalty, you must retain an economic interest in the minerals deposited in the land you have leased to the producer. You usually have a royalty when payments are based on the amount of minerals produced. However, if you are paid regardless of the minerals produced, you have a sale that is taxed as capital gain if the proceeds exceed the basis of the transferred property interest. Bonuses and advance royalties that are paid to you before the production of minerals are taxable as royalty income and are entitled to an allowance for depletion. However, bonuses and advance royalties for gas and oil wells and geothermal deposits are not treated as gross income for purposes of calculating percentage depletion. If the lease is terminated without production and you received a bonus or advance royalty, you report as income previously claimed depletion deductions. You increase the basis of your property by the restored depletion deductions.

Planning Reminder

Passive Income Exception

Certain working oil and gas interests are exempt from the passive activity loss restrictions *(10.10)*.

9.12 Production Costs of Books and Creative Properties

Freelance authors, artists, and photographers may deduct their costs of producing original works in the years that the expenses are paid or incurred. If you qualify, the uniform capitalization rules that generally apply to property that you produce for resale *(40.3)* do not apply to the expenses.

You qualify for current expense deductions if you are self-employed and you personally create literary manuscripts, musical or dance scores, paintings, pictures, sculptures, drawings, cartoons, graphic designs, original print editions, photographs, or photographic negatives or transparencies. However, the exception to the uniform capitalization rules does not apply to, and thus current deductions are not allowed for, expenses relating to motion picture films, videotapes, printing, photographic plates, or similar items.

If you conduct business as an owner-employee of a personal service corporation and you are a qualifying author, artist, or photographer, the corporation may claim current deductions related to your expenses in producing books or other eligible creative works. You and your relatives must own substantially all of the corporation's stock.

9.13 Deducting the Cost of Patents or Copyrights

If you create an artistic work or invention for which you get a government patent or copyright, you may depreciate your costs over the life of the patent or copyright. Basis for depreciation includes all expenses that you are required to capitalize in connection with creating the work, such as the cost of drawings, experimental models, stationery, and supplies; travel expenses to obtain material for a book; fees to counsel; government charges for patent or copyright; and litigation costs in protecting or perfecting title.

If you purchased the patent or artistic creation, depreciate your cost over the remaining life of the patent or copyright. If your cost for a patent is payable annually as a fixed percentage of the revenue derived from use of the patent, the depreciation deduction equals the royalty paid or incurred for that year. However, if a copyright or patent is acquired in connection with the acquisition of a business, the cost is amortizable over a 15-year period as a Section 197 intangible *(42.18)*.

If you inherited the patent or rights to an artistic creation, your cost is the fair market value either at the time of death of the person from whom you inherited it *(5.17)* or the alternate valuation date if elected by the executor. You get this cost basis even if the decedent paid nothing for it. Figure your depreciation by dividing the fair market value by the number of years of remaining life.

If your patent or copyright becomes valueless, you may deduct your unrecovered cost or other basis in the year it became worthless.

9.14 Intangible Drilling Costs

Intangible drilling and development costs (IDCs) refer to drilling and development costs of items with no salvage value, including wages, fuel, repairs, hauling, and supplies incident to and necessary for the preparation and drilling of wells for the production of oil or gas, and geothermal wells. For wells you are developing in the United States, you can elect to deduct the costs currently as business expenses or treat them as capital expenses subject to depreciation or depletion.

Electing current business deduction. The election to deduct IDCs as a current business expense must be made on your income tax return for the first tax year in which you pay or incur the costs. As a sole proprietor, you deduct the IDCs as "other expenses" on Schedule C (Form 1040 or 1040-SR).

Prepayments. Tax-shelter investors may deduct prepayments of drilling expenses only if the well is "spudded" within 90 days after the close of the taxable year in which the prepayment is made. The prepayment must also have a business purpose, not be a deposit, and not materially distort income. The investor's deduction is limited to his or her cash investment in the tax shelter. For purposes of this limitation, an investor's cash investment includes loans that are not secured by his or her shelter interest or the shelter's assets and loans that are not arranged by the organizer or promoter. If the above tests are not met, a deduction may be claimed only as actual drilling services are provided.

Amortizing intangible drilling costs. If you do not elect to deduct IDCs as current business expenses, you may amortize them on Form 4562, Depreciation and Amortization, over a 60-month period, beginning with the month they were paid or incurred. If you elect 60-month amortization, there is no AMT adjustment; *see* below.

Recapture of intangible drilling costs for oil, gas, geothermal, or mineral property. Upon the disposition of oil, gas, geothermal, or other mineral property placed in service after 1986, ordinary income treatment applies to previously claimed deductions for intangible drilling and development costs for oil, gas, and geothermal wells, and to mineral development and exploration costs. Depletion deductions *(9.15)* are also generally subject to this ordinary income treatment upon disposition of the property.

AMT and intangible drilling costs. If you are an independent producer or royalty owner and elect to deduct IDCs as a current business expense on Schedule C, you may qualify for an exception to the AMT preference rules for IDCs, but the exception is limited. If your IDC preference (figured under the regular AMT rules) exceeds 40% of your alternative minimum taxable income, figured without regard to the AMT net operating loss deduction, the excess over 40% must be included as a preference item; *see* the instructions on Form 6251. The AMT adjustment can be completely avoided by electing 60-month amortization for the IDCs.

9.15 Depletion Deduction

Properties subject to depletion deductions are mines, oil and gas wells, timber, and exhaustible natural deposits.

Two methods of computing depletion are: (1) cost depletion and (2) percentage depletion. If you are allowed to compute under either method, you must use the one that produces the larger deduction. In most cases, this will be percentage depletion. For timber, you must use cost depletion.

Cost depletion. The cost depletion of minerals is computed as follows: (1) divide the total number of units (such as tons or barrels) remaining in the deposit to be mined into the adjusted basis of the property; and (2) multiply the unit rate found in Step 1 by the number of units for which payment is received during the taxable year if you are on the cash basis, or by the number of units sold if you are on the accrual basis.

Adjusted basis is the original cost of the property, less depletion allowed, whether computed under the percentage or cost depletion method. It does not include nonmineral property such as mining equipment. Adjusted basis may not be less than zero.

Timber depletion is based on the cost of timber (or other basis in the owner's hands) and does not include any part of the cost of land. Depletion takes place when standing timber is cut. Depletion must be computed by the cost method, not by the percentage method. However, instead of claiming the cost depletion method, you may elect to treat the cutting of timber as a sale subject to capital gain or loss treatment. For further details, *see* IRS Publication 535.

Caution

Drilling Expense Prepayments

Prepayments of drilling expenses are deductible by tax-shelter investors only if the well is "spudded" within 90 days after the close of the taxable year in which the prepayment was made, and the deduction is limited to the original amount of the investment.

Percentage depletion. Percentage depletion is based on a certain percentage rate applied to annual gross income derived from the resource. In determining gross income for percentage depletion, do not include any lease bonuses, advance royalties, or any other amount payable without regard to production. A deduction for percentage depletion is allowed even if the basis of the property is already fully recovered by prior depletion deductions. The percentage to be applied depends upon the mineral involved; the range is from 5% up to 22%. For example, the maximum 22% depletion deduction applies to sulfur, uranium, and U.S. deposits of lead, zinc, nickel, mica, and asbestos. A 15% depletion percentage applies to U.S. deposits of gold, silver, copper, iron ore, and shale.

Taxable income limit. For properties other than oil and gas, the percentage depletion deduction may not exceed 50% of taxable income from the property computed without the depletion deduction. In computing the 50% limitation, a net operating loss deduction is not deducted from gross income. A 100% taxable income limit applies to oil and gas properties *(9.16)*.

Oil and gas property. Percentage depletion for oil and gas wells was repealed as of January 1, 1975, except for small independent producers and royalty owners *(9.16)*.

9.16 Oil and Gas Percentage Depletion

Small independent producers and royalty owners generally are allowed to deduct percentage depletion at a 15% rate for domestic oil and gas production. The deduction is subject to a taxable income limit.

The 15% rate applies to a small producer exemption that equals the gross income from a maximum daily average of 1,000 barrels of oil or 6 million cubic feet of natural gas, or a combination of both. Gross income from the property does not include advance royalties or lease bonuses that are payable without regard to the actual production.

The depletable natural gas quantity depends on an election made annually by independent producers or royalty owners to apply part of their 1,000-barrel-per-day oil limitation to natural gas. The depletable quantity of natural gas is 6,000 cubic feet times the barrels of depletable oil for which an election has been made. The election is made on an original or amended return or on a claim for credit or refund. For example, if your average daily production is 1,200 barrels of oil and 6.2 million cubic feet of natural gas, your maximum depletable limit is 1,000 barrels of oil, which you may split between the oil and gas. You could claim depletion for 500 barrels of oil per day and for 3 million cubic feet of gas per day: 3 million cubic feet of gas is the equivalent of the remaining 500 barrels of oil limit (500 barrels × 6,000 cubic feet depletable gas quantity equals 3 million cubic feet of gas).

Ineligible retailers and refiners. Percentage depletion cannot be claimed by a producer who owns or controls a retail outlet for the sale of oil, natural gas, or petroleum products unless gross sales of oil and gas products are $5 million or less for the tax year, or if all sales of oil or natural gas products occur outside the United States and none of the taxpayer's domestic production is exported. Bulk sales of oil or natural gas to industrial or utility customers are not to be treated as retail sales.

Percentage depletion also is not allowed to a refiner who refines (directly or through a related person) more than 75,000 barrels of crude oil on any day during the year. The limit is based on average (rather than actual) daily refinery runs for the tax year.

Figuring average daily domestic production. Average daily production is figured by dividing your aggregate production during the taxable year by the number of days in the taxable year. If you hold a partial interest in the production (including a partnership interest), production rate is found by multiplying total production of such property by your income percentage participation in such property.

The production over the entire year is averaged regardless of when production actually occurred. If average daily production for the year exceeds the 1,000-barrel or 6-million-cubic-feet limit, the exemption must be allocated among all the properties in which you have an interest.

Taxable income limits on percentage depletion. The percentage depletion deduction for a small producer or royalty owner may not exceed the lesser of (1) 100% of the taxable income from the property before the depletion allowance or the deduction for production activities, or (2) 65% of your taxable income from all sources computed without regard to the depletion deduction allowed under the small producer's exemption, the deduction for production activities, any net operating loss carryback, and any capital loss carryback. Any amount not deductible because of the 65% limit can be carried over and added to the next year's depletion allowance.

Limitations where family members or related businesses own interests. The daily exemption rate is allocated among members of the same family in proportion to their respective production of oil. Similar allocation is required where business entities are under common control. This affects interests owned by you, your spouse, and minor children; by corporations, estates, and trusts in which 50% of the beneficial interest is owned by the same or related persons; and by a corporation that is a member of the same controled group.

Depletion for marginal production. For independent producers and royalty owners with production from "marginal" wells, the 15% depletion rate could be increased by 1% for each whole dollar that the "reference price" (the average annual wellhead price as estimated by the IRS) of domestic crude oil for the previous year was below $20 per barrel. However, despite relatively low oil prices in recent years, the reference price has been substantially over $20 per barrel (for example, according to IRS Notice 2023-50, the reference price for 2022 was $93.97), and therefore the basic 15% rate has applied for marginal production every year from 2001 through 2023. See IRS Section 45K(d)(2)(C) for reference price updates.

9.17 Qualified Business Income Deduction for Real Estate Activities

If your real estate activities constitute a trade or business, you may be eligible for a deduction of up to 20% of qualified business income (QBI) (*see* below and *40.24* for QBI deduction details). To deal with the confusion about when real estate activities constitute a trade or business, the IRS has created a safe harbor for a "rental real estate enterprise". If you meet the safe harbor conditions *(see below)* for a rental real estate enterprise, your real estate activities are treated as a trade or business for purposes of the QBI deduction, and only for purposes of this deduction. Thus, self-employment tax does not apply to the rental income although the safe harbor allows you to claim the QBI deduction.

Even if you do not meet all of the safe harbor conditions, you can still try to demonstrate that you have a profit motive and other indices of being in a trade or business. For example, if you are actively engaged in the real estate activity (e.g., you make decisions about leases, collect rents, coordinate maintenance and repairs, and hire contractors), you may be considered to be in a trade or business for purposes of the QBI deduction. Owning even a single property can constitute a trade or business, although renting out your vacation home may not rise to the level of a trade or business. The determination of trade or business is made on a case by case basis. Being a real estate professional for purposes of the passive activity loss rules *(10.3)* does not impact this determination.

Safe harbor for rental real estate enterprises. The IRS safe harbor (see requirements below) applies to a "rental real estate enterprise," which is defined as an interest in real property held for the production of rents and may consist of an interest in multiple properties. The interest may be owned directly or through a passthrough entity. If you have interests in multiple rent-producing properties, each is a separate enterprise, but you may treat (aggregate) all similar properties as a single enterprise. However, commercial and residential real estate cannot be combined in the same enterprise.

Certain rental real estate interests are not eligible for the safe harbor. Property that you use as a residence (under the 14-day/10% personal use test in *9.7*) is not eligible for the safe harbor. In addition, real estate rented or leased under a "triple net lease" is not eligible. A triple net lease refers to an agreement that requires the tenant or lessee to pay taxes, fees, and insurance, and to pay for maintenance activities of the property in addition to rent and utilities.

All of the following requirements must be met for a rental real estate enterprise to be treated as a business under the safe harbor:

1. You maintain separate books and records to reflect income and expenses for each rental real estate enterprise;

2. You perform 250 or more hours of rental services per year with respect to the rental real estate enterprise. For rental real estate enterprises in existence for at least 4 years, the hours of rental services requirement can be met by performing 250 or more hours of rental services in at least 3 of the 5 consecutive taxable years that end with the current taxable year. The services must be performed by you, or by your employees, agents, and/or independent contractors. Time spent on investor-type activities does not count.

3. You maintain contemporaneous records, including time reports, logs, or similar documents, regarding the following: (i) hours of all services performed; (ii) description of all services performed; (iii) dates on which such services were performed; and (iv) who performed the services. Such records are to be made available for inspection at the request of the IRS.

4. You must attach a statement to your return for each year that you are relying on the safe harbor. The statement must describe all properties being treated as a rental real estate enterprise and any rental real estate properties acquired or disposed of during the year. It also must state that you have satisfied the safe harbor requirements of Revenue Procedure 2019-38.

Limitation on QBI deduction. The QBI deduction income threshold changes annually depending on your filing status. For married filing jointly, the 2023 income threshold starts limiting your deduction at $364,200 with a complete phase out at $464,200. For all other filing statuses, the 2023 income threshold starts limiting at $182,100 and completely phases out at $232,100. For purposes of the limitation explained in *40.24*, a key component for real estate trades or businesses is the unadjusted basis immediately after acquisition (UBIA) of qualified tangible property; 2.5% of UBIA of qualified tangible property is part of the limitation. UBIA is tangible property subject to depreciation held by a business at the end of the year and used during the year for the production of QBI. The unadjusted basis means the original cost of the property, without any depreciation. For the property to be taken into account, it must still be in use by the business and the depreciable period of the property must not have ended. The depreciable period begins with the first year the property is placed in service and ends on the later of:

- 10 years after it was placed in service, or
- The last day of the applicable recovery period (e.g., 39 years for commercial property; 27.5 years for residential rental property; *see 42.12*).

 *Law Alert*

Qualified Business Income (QBI) Deduction for Real Estate Businesses

Because many real estate businesses do not entail wages, a special rule was added by the Tax Cuts and Jobs Act to the limitation on the QBI deduction for real estate activities, based on the cost of property. In other words, high-income owners may qualify for a QBI deduction based on a percentage of the cost of their property.

EXAMPLE

Harold built a 10-unit apartment building in 2008 at a cost of $1 million, and it constitutes a trade or business for him. In figuring his QBI deduction for 2023, he can take $25,000 into account ($1 million UBIA × 2.5%). Although the building was placed in service more than 10 years ago, Harold is still using and depreciating the building, and the 27.5-year recovery period has not ended.

CHAPTER 10

Loss Restrictions: Passive Activities and At-Risk Limits

The passive activity laws were intended to discourage tax-shelter investments, but their reach extends beyond tax shelters to cover all real estate investors and persons who invest in businesses as "silent partners" or who are not involved full time in the business. The passive activity rules prevent an investor from deducting what the law defines as a passive loss from salary, self-employment income, interest, dividends, sales of investment property, or retirement income. Such losses are deductible only from income from other passive activities. Losses disallowed by the passive activity rules are suspended and carried forward to later taxable years and become deductible only when passive income is realized or substantially all of the activity is sold.

Casualty and theft losses are not passive losses unless they are of the type usually occurring in a business, such as shoplifting theft losses.

On your tax return, passive income items and allowable deductible items are reported as regular income and deductions. For example, rental income and allowable deductions are reported on Schedule E. However, before you make these entries, you may have to prepare Form 8582, which identifies your passive income and losses and helps you to determine whether passive loss items are deductible.

At-risk rules generally limit losses for an activity to your cash investment and loans for which you are personally liable, as well as certain nonrecourse financing for real estate investments. You must apply the at-risk rules before the passive activity rules in determining your allowable losses from any activity. *See 10.17.*

10.1   Rental Activities Generally Treated as Passive

Rental activities (real estate or personal property) are automatically treated as passive unless you qualify as a real estate professional *(10.3)* or the rentals by law are excluded from the rental category and are instead considered to be business activity *(see below)*. If "automatic" passive activity treatment applies, you may not deduct a rental loss against nonpassive income such as salary, dividends, or interest income unless you can take advantage of the up-to-$25,000 allowance that applies to rental real estate losses *(10.2)*. Even where rental income or loss is not automatically treated as passive because you qualify as a real estate professional or because the activity is excluded from the rental category and treated as a business *(see* the list, items 1–6, below), income or loss will still be "passive" unless you materially participate *(10.6)* in the business activity.

A loss that is not currently deductible due to the passive loss restrictions is suspended and carried forward indefinitely until there is passive income to offset, or until you dispose of your entire interest in the activity *(10.13)*.

If the at-risk rules apply *(10.17)*, the at-risk limits are applied before the passive loss limits. If you have a business loss after applying the at-risk and the passive loss limits, the allowable loss could be further reduced under the "excess business loss" limitation *(40.20)*.

What is a rental activity? Except for activities specifically excluded from the rental category (see the list of rentals treated as businesses below), rentals include all activities in which a customer pays for the use of tangible property (real estate or personal property). Such activities include rentals of apartments and commercial office space (whether long- or short-term); long-term rentals of office equipment, vehicles, and/or a vessel under a bareboat charter or a plane under a dry lease (no pilot or captain and no fuel); and net-leased property. A property is under a net lease if the deductions (other than rents and reimbursed amounts) are less than 15% of rental income or where the lessor is guaranteed a specific return or is guaranteed against loss of income.

Rentals treated as business activity. Although rental activities are generally treated as "passive," the following six activities are excluded from the category of rental activity and thus losses from these activities are not deductible under the $25,000 rental real estate loss allowance *(10.2)*. The fact that these activities are not treated as rentals does not mean that the passive activity rules are inapplicable. Income or loss from these activities will still be treated as passive income or loss if you fail to meet one of the business material participation tests *(10.6)*.

> ### EXAMPLE
>
> The Toups purchased a cottage in Callaway Gardens, a vacation resort south of Atlanta, Georgia. The unit was rented for short-term periods of seven days or less during the year to resort guests. The resort's operator was the sole managing and rental agent. Over a three-year period, they deducted net losses of $46,848. Under the seven-days-or-less rule, the activity was not a rental activity. It was treated as a business activity subject to the material participation tests. The IRS disallowed the losses as passive activity losses because the Toups were passive investors who did not materially participate in the activity. The Toups argued that they materially participated, spending more than 300 hours each year preparing an annual budget and cash flow analysis and meeting with other owners to set rental fees and inspect the grounds.
>
> The Tax Court sided with the IRS. The losses were passive because the Toups did not materially participate in the resort operation. They had nothing to do with running the resort on a day-to-day basis. Their activity was merely that of investors.

1. **The average period of customer use of the property is seven days or less.** Short-term rentals of vacation units, autos, hotel and motel rooms, DVDs, and tuxedos or other clothes are not considered rental activities if the average period of customer use is seven days or less. You figure the average period of customer use for the year by dividing the aggregate number of days in all rental periods that end during the tax year by the number of rentals. Each period during which a customer has a continuous or recurring right to use the property is treated as a separate rental.

Planning Reminder

Short-Term Vacation Home Rentals

If you rent out a vacation unit for an average rental period of seven days or less at a loss, the loss is treated as a business (not rental) loss that you can deduct from nonpassive income if you meet one of the material participation tests *(10.6)*. If you do not materially participate, the loss is treated as a passive loss, deductible only from passive income. The loss does not qualify for the up-to-$25,000 rental loss allowance *(10.2)* because the property is not treated as rental property.

A loss from a seven-day-or-less real estate rental activity is *not* eligible for the up-to-$25,000 loss allowance *(10.2)*. Since it is not treated as a real estate rental activity, it may not be included in the election to aggregate rental real estate activities under the real estate professional rules *(10.3)*.

2. **The average period of customer use of the property is more than seven days but is 30 days or less, and you provide significant personal services.** Personal services include only services performed by individuals and do not include (a) services necessary to permit the lawful use of the property; (b) construction or repair services that extend the useful life of the property for a period substantially longer than the average period of customer use; and (c) services that are provided with long-term rentals of high-grade commercial or residential real property such as cleaning and maintenance of common areas, routine repairs, trash collection, elevator service, and security guards.

   Note: For purposes of Exceptions 1 and 2, if more than one class of property is rented as part of the same activity, average period of customer use is figured separately for each class. The average period of customer use (as explained in Exception 1) is multiplied by the ratio of gross rental income from that class to the total rental income from the activity; *see* the Form 8582 instructions.

3. **Regardless of the average period of customer use, extraordinary personal services are provided so that rental is incidental.** In a rare case, it may be possible to avoid the passive loss disallowance rule by showing that "extraordinary personal services" were provided to tenants who rented the space primarily to obtain these services. IRS regulations give as examples the use by patients of a hospital's room and board facilities, which is incidental to the medical services provided, and the use by students of school dormitories, which is incidental to the teaching services provided.

   In one case, an attorney and her husband, a medical doctor, convinced the Tax Court that they met the "personal services" exception by providing legal support services to law firms who leased office space from their LLC. The attorney supervised three clerical employees in providing legal support services to the tenant firms, which included client intake, answering phones and taking messages, conducting legal research, typing briefs and memoranda, binding briefs, photocopying, taking dictation, express mailing, process serving, filing documents at the courthouse and state capital, maintaining a file room, law library, and conference facilities, and providing coffee service. Her husband provided consulting services to the attorneys, reviewing medical malpractice cases, serving as an expert medical witness, helping the attorneys prepare for accreditation reviews of health-care organizations, and providing quality assurance trainings.

   Before the Tax Court, the tenant firms testified that these support services, particularly the legal research, were unique and that they would not have moved into the LLC's building without them. The Tax Court held that the LLC's leasing activity was not a rental activity under the extraordinary services exception, but the taxpayers still had to prove that they "materially participated" in the leasing/support activities to avoid passive loss disallowance for the rental losses. They did so by showing that at least 500 hours were spent working on the activity *(10.6)*.

4. **Rental is incidental to a nonrental activity.** A rental of property is excluded from the rental activity category if the property is held mainly for investment or for use in a business. A rental is considered incidental to an investment activity if the principal purpose of holding the property is to realize gain from its appreciation and the gross rental income from the property for the year is less than 2% of the unadjusted basis or fair market value of the property, whichever is less; *see* the Example below (Kyle Gail).

   A rental is incidental to a business activity if (1) you own an interest in the business during the year, (2) the rented property was predominately used in that business during the current year or during at least two of the immediately preceding five tax years, and (3) gross rental income from the property is less than 2% of the lower of the unadjusted basis of the property or its fair market value. Under test (2), a rental may qualify for the exception although it is not rented to the related business in the current year, so long as it was used in the business in two or more of the preceding five years.

5. **Providing property to a partnership or S corporation that is not engaged in rentals.** If you own an interest in a partnership or S corporation and you contributed property to it as an owner, the contributed property is not considered a rental activity. For example, if as a partner you contribute property to a partnership, your distributive share of partnership income will not be considered as income from a rental activity. However, this exception will not apply if the partnership is engaged in a rental activity.

6. **The property is generally allowed for the non-exclusive use of customers during fixed business hours, such as operating a golf course.** The customers are treated as licensees, not lessees.

> **EXAMPLE**
>
> Kyle Gail owns unimproved land with a fair market value of $400,000 and an unadjusted basis of $300,000. He holds it for the principal purpose of realizing gain from its appreciation. To help reduce the cost of holding the land, he leases it to a rancher for grazing purposes at an annual rental of $5,000. The gross rental income of $5,000 is less than 2% of the lower of the fair market value or the unadjusted basis of the land. The rental of the land is not a rental activity.

Rental of dwelling unit meeting personal use test is not a passive activity. If you rented out a residential unit that you personally used as a home during the year for more than the greater of 14 days or 10% of the number of days that it was rented to others at a fair market rental price *(9.7)*, the rental is not a passive activity. However, if you had a net loss from the rental, some rental expenses are not deductible on Schedule E under the allocation rules of *9.9*.

Grouping rental and nonrental business activities. Where you conduct rental as well as nonrental business activities, you may not group a rental activity with a nonrental activity, unless they form an appropriate economic unit and one of the activities is considered insubstantial in relation to the other. No guidelines are provided for determining what is "substantial" or "insubstantial."

Under an exception, a rental of property to a business may be grouped together with the business, although one activity is not insubstantial to the other, provided each business owner has the same proportionate ownership in the rental activity and the activities are an appropriate economic unit.

Real property rentals and personal property rentals. An activity involving the rental of realty and one involving the rental of personal property may not be treated as a single activity, unless the personal property is provided in connection with the real property or the realty is provided in connection with the personal property.

10.2 Rental Real Estate Loss Allowance of up to $25,000

If you are not a real estate professional *(10.3)* but you actively participate by performing some management role in a real estate rental venture, you may deduct up to $25,000 of a real estate rental loss against your regular, nonpassive income such as wages. Your rental loss is still "passive," but the allowance lets you deduct the loss (up to $25,000) as if it were a nonpassive loss. The allowance is phased out if your modified adjusted gross income (MAGI) is between $100,000 and $150,000. You generally take the allowance into account on Schedule E, but Form 8582 is sometimes required *(10.12)*.

If you are married filing separately, you are not eligible for the special loss allowance unless you lived apart for the entire year, and in that case, the allowance is limited to $12,500; *see* below. The allowance applies only to real estate rentals not excluded from the rental category by the rules at *10.1*. For example, short-term vacation home rentals averaging seven days or less do not qualify for the allowance. The allowance applies only to real estate rentals, not to any rentals of equipment or other personal property.

A trust may not qualify for the $25,000 allowance. Thus, you may not circumvent the $25,000 ceiling or multiply the number of $25,000 allowances by transferring rental real properties to one or more trusts.

Married filing separately. If you file separately and at any time during the taxable year live with your spouse, you are not allowed to claim any allowance. If you are married but live apart from your spouse for the entire year and file a separate return, the $25,000 allowance and the adjusted gross income phaseout range are reduced by 50%. Thus, the maximum allowance on your separate return is $12,500 and this amount is phased out by 50% of MAGI over $50,000. Therefore, if your MAGI exceeds $75,000, no allowance is allowed.

Active participation test must be met. To qualify for the allowance, you must meet an active participation test. Having an agent manage your property does not prevent you from meeting the test, but you must show that you or your spouse participates in management decisions, such as selecting tenants, setting rental terms, and reviewing expenses. The IRS may not recognize your activity as meeting the test if you merely ratify your manager's decisions. You

Planning Reminder

Rental of Personal Residence

Renting a personal residence is not treated as a passive rental activity if you personally use the home for more than the greater of (1) 14 days or (2) 10% of the days the home is rented for a fair market rental amount *(9.7)*. On Schedule E, you generally may claim a full deduction for the rental portion of real estate taxes and mortgage interest, assuming the home is a principal residence or qualifying second home under the mortgage interest rules *(15.1)*. See *9.9* for how these and other rental expenses are allocated against rental income.

Planning Reminder

Proving Management Activities

To take advantage of the $25,000 loss allowance, make sure you have proof of active management, such as approving leases and repairs.

(together with your spouse) must also have at least a 10% interest in the property. Limited partners are not considered active participants and do not qualify for the allowance.

If a decedent actively participated in property held by an estate, the estate is deemed to actively participate for the two years following the death of the taxpayer.

EXAMPLES

1. You live in New York and own a condominium in Florida that you rent through an agent. You set the rental terms and give final approval to any rental arrangement. You also have final approval over any repairs ordered by the agent. You are an active participant and may claim the $25,000 rental loss allowance.

2. A married couple who owned a time-share interest in an ocean-front condominium rented the condo during their allotted period to vacationers. They claimed a rental loss that the IRS held did not qualify for the up-to-$25,000 allowance. Since the average rental period for their unit was seven days or less, the rentals were excluded from the category of rental activity; *see 10.1.*

Figuring the $25,000 allowance. First match income and loss from all of your passive rental real estate activities in which you actively participate. A net loss from these activities is then applied against net passive income (if any) from other activities and if there is a remaining loss, that loss is deductible under the $25,000 allowance. Keep in mind that rental income or loss from renting a personal residence is disregarded in figuring the $25,000 allowance if the rental is not a passive activity, and it is not a passive activity if your personal use of the home during the year exceeds the greater of 14 days or 10% of the days the home is rented at a fair market rental amount *(9.7).* The allowance may not be used against carryover losses from prior taxable years when you were not an active participant.

EXAMPLE

David Chung is single and has a $90,000 salary, $15,000 income from a limited partnership, and a $26,000 loss from rental real estate in which he actively participated. The $26,000 loss is first reduced by the $15,000 of passive income from the partnership. Since he actively participated in the rental real estate activities, the remaining balance of the $11,000 rental loss can be deducted from his nonpassive salary income. David's loss allowance is not subject to phaseout *(see below)* because his modified adjusted gross income (MAGI) is under $100,000. The partnership income and rental loss, which are passive, are disregarded in figuring MAGI.

Phaseout of the allowance. The maximum loss allowance of $25,000 ($12,500 if married filing separately and living apart for the entire year) is reduced by 50 cents for every dollar of modified adjusted gross income (MAGI) over $100,000 (or $50,000 if married filing separately).

Modified adjusted gross income (MAGI). For purposes of the allowance phaseout, MAGI is adjusted gross income shown on your return, but you should disregard:

- Any passive activity income or loss.
- Any loss allowed for real estate professionals *(10.3).*
- Taxable Social Security and railroad retirement payments *(34.3).* For example, if your adjusted gross income on Form 1040 or 1040-SR is $90,000, and that includes $5,000 of taxable Social Security benefits, your modified adjusted gross income is $85,000 for purposes of the allowance phaseout.
- Deductible IRA contributions *(Chapter 8).*
- The deduction for one-half of self-employment tax liability *(45.3).*
- Deductible student loan interest *(33.13).*
- Overall loss from a publicly traded partnership (PTP) *(see* instructions to Form 8582).
- Excluded interest on U.S. savings bonds used for paying tuition in the year the bonds are redeemed. If you are allowed to exclude the interest from income for regular tax purposes *(33.4),* the interest must still be included for purposes of the allowance phaseout.
- Employer-provided adoption assistance that is a tax-free fringe benefit *(Chapter 3).* The assistance must be included in MAGI for purposes of applying the allowance phaseout rule.

A rental loss that is carried over because it exceeds the allowance may be deductible in a later year if you continue to meet the active participation test.

 *Filing Tip*

EXAMPLES

1. In 2023, Liz Blake had $120,000 in salary, $5,000 of partnership income from a limited partnership, and a $31,000 loss from a rental building in which she actively participates. For purposes of the phaseout rule, the $5,000 limited partnership income and the $31,000 rental loss are disregarded in figuring MAGI because they are passive. The $31,000 rental loss is reduced by the $5,000 of passive partnership income, and of the $26,000 balance, only $15,000 is deductible under the rental loss allowance; $10,000 of the allowance is phased out. The remaining $11,000 loss ($26,000 − $15,000) must be carried over to 2024. Her deduction and carryover are computed as follows:

Modified adjusted gross income for 2023	$ 120,000
Less: phaseout threshold (MAGI not subject to phaseout)	$ 100,000
Amount subject to phaseout	$ 20,000
Phaseout percentage	50%
Portion of allowance phased out	$ 10,000
Maximum rental allowance	$ 25,000
Less: Phased out part of allowance	$ 10,000
Deductible rental loss for 2023 under the allowance after phaseout	$ 15,000
Passive loss from rental real estate	$ 31,000
Less: Passive income from partnership	$ 5,000
Passive activity loss	$ 26,000
Less: Deductible rental loss allowance for 2023	$ 15,000
Carryover loss to 2024	$ 11,000

2. Assume the facts of Example 1, and then assume that in 2024 Liz's modified adjusted gross income is below the phaseout range for the loss allowance, that she continues to actively participate in the rental building, and that she has a loss from the rental building of $5,000. Under the allowance, she may deduct a rental loss of $16,000 for 2024 (the $5,000 loss for 2024 plus the $11,000 carryover loss from 2023 under Example 1).

Rental Allowance Based on Income

If you are single or married filing jointly, the rental loss allowance is phased out when your modified adjusted gross income is over $100,000. For every dollar of income over $100,000, the loss allowance is reduced by 50 cents. When your modified adjusted gross income reaches $150,000, the allowance is completely phased out.

If modified AGI is—	Loss allowance is—
Up to $100,000	$25,000
110,000	20,000
120,000	15,000
130,000	10,000
140,000	5,000
150,000 or more	0

Real estate allowance for tax credits. On Form 8582-CR, a deduction equivalent of up to $25,000 may allow a credit that otherwise would be disallowed. You must meet the active participation test in the year the credit arose. The $25,000 allowance is generally subject to the regular MAGI phaseout rule. The special allowance applies to low-income housing and rehabilitation credits even if you do not meet the active participation test.

The deduction equivalent of a credit is the amount which, if allowed as a deduction, would reduce your tax by an amount equal to the credit. For example, a tax credit of $1,200 for a taxpayer in the 24% bracket equals a deduction of $5,000 and would come within the $25,000 allowance provided you actively participated. In the 24% bracket, the equivalent of a $25,000 allowance is a tax credit of $6,000 ($25,000 × 24%). Thus, if you have a rehabilitation credit of $7,000 and you are in the 24% bracket, the $25,000 allowance may allow you to claim $6,000 of the credit, while the balance of the credit would be carried forward to the following year.

If in one year you have both losses and tax credits, the $25,000 allowance applies first to the losses, then to tax credits from rental real estate with active participation, then to tax credits for rehabilitation or low-income housing placed in service before 1990, and finally to tax credits for low-income housing placed in service after 1989.

The allowance and net operating losses. If losses are allowed by the $25,000 allowance but your nonpassive income and other income are less than the loss, the balance of the loss may be treated as a net operating loss and may be carried back and forward; *see 40.18* for further details.

10.3   Real Estate Professionals

Real estate rental activities are automatically passive *(10.1)* for all taxpayers except qualifying real estate professionals. You qualify as a real estate professional if you meet both parts of Test 1 below. If you qualify under Test 1, any rental real estate activity in which you materially participate (Test 2) is not a passive activity. Income or loss from the rental real estate is reported as nonpassive on Schedule E (Form 1040 or 1040-SR).

You need reliable records to substantiate your hours worked in real property businesses in order to qualify as a real estate professional (Test 1 below), as well as to substantiate your participation in your rental real estate activities (Test 2).

Test 1: Qualifying as a real estate professional. There are two parts to Test 1, and you must meet both of them for the tax year for you to qualify:

1. More than 50% of your personal services in all of your businesses must be performed in real property businesses in which you materially participate *(10.6)*. For this purpose, a real property business means any real property development, redevelopment, construction, reconstruction, acquisition, conversion, rental operation, management, leasing, or brokerage trade or business. Real estate financing is not included. Personal services performed as an employee are not treated as performed in a real estate business unless you are considered a "more than 5% owner" in the employer. That is, you must own more than 5% of the outstanding stock or more than 5% of total combined voting powers of all stock issued by the corporation. In a noncorporate employer such as a partnership, you must own more than a 5% capital or profit interest.

2. More than 750 hours of your services are in real property businesses in which you materially participate *(10.6)*. You must be able to establish that you materially participate (under the tests at *10.6*) in a real property business in order to count your work in that business towards the 750-hour threshold.

   In one case, a taxpayer claimed that when he was not at his full-time job he was "on call" for working on his four rental properties because he could have been called to do work at any time on the properties, and he argued that the "on call" hours should count towards the 750-hour test. Without the "on call" hours, he could substantiate only 645.5 hours of work on the rentals. The Tax Court held that even if the taxpayer was "on call," on call hours do not count towards the 750-hour test, since the law requires that the taxpayer actually perform over 750 hours of service.

For purposes of determining hours of material participation under (1) and (2) above, each interest in rental real estate property is treated as a separate activity unless you elect to treat all of your interests as one rental activity. The election to aggregate can make it easier to prove material participation as discussed below. If, under the rules in *10.1*, you group a rental real estate activity with a business activity, that rental activity is not treated as rental real estate for purposes of the real estate professional rules.

For a married couple filing jointly, both the "50% of services test" and the "750 hours test" must be met by one of the spouses individually, without regard to the other spouse's services.

Attorneys who specialize in real estate practice while participating in a rental business may not treat the legal practice as material participation for purposes of qualifying as real estate professionals.

A closely held C corporation qualifies under the real estate professional rules if in a taxable year more than 50% of the gross receipts of the corporation are from a real property business in which the corporation materially participates *(10.15)*.

Test 2: Rental real estate activity material participation. If you qualify as a real estate professional under Test 1 above, you must still show that you materially participate *(10.6)* in your rental real estate activity/activities to avoid passive activity treatment. If you have more than one rental real estate activity and elect to aggregate *(see below)*, total participation in all of the activities is combined in applying the material participation tests in *10.6*. If an election to aggregate has not been made, material participation must be determined separately for each rental property.

Planning Reminder

Tax Break for Real Estate Professionals

Proving professional status and material participation allows you to avoid passive loss limitations. You may improve your ability to meet the material participation tests in *10.6* by aggregating your rental real estate activities. However, you may not want to aggregate activities if you have passive losses from non–real estate activities and have rental income from an operation that, if treated as passive income, could be offset by the losses.

Also be aware that if you elect to aggregate your rental real estate activities as one activity and later sell one of the rental properties, you will probably be unable to deduct suspended losses from that property because of the rule that requires "substantially all" of your interest in an activity (here, the combined activity) to be disposed of in order to deduct suspended losses *(10.13)*.

Election to aggregate rental real estate activities. For purposes of Test 2 (rental real estate material participation), you may elect to aggregate all of your rental real estate activities for any year you qualify under Test 1 as a real estate professional. You elect to aggregate by attaching a statement to your original tax return for the year. The required election statement must contain a declaration that you are a qualifying real estate professional and are treating all of your rental real estate activities as a single activity under Internal Revenue Code Section 469(c)(7)(A). The election is binding for all future years in which you qualify as a real estate professional, even if there are intervening years in which you do not qualify. In the nonqualifying years, the election has no effect. You may not revoke the election in a later year unless there has been a material change in circumstances that you explain in a statement attached to your original return for the year of revocation. That the election no longer gives you a tax advantage is not a basis for a revocation.

If the election to aggregate is made and there is net income for the aggregated activity, the income may be offset by prior-year suspended losses from any of the aggregated rental real estate activities regardless of which of the rental activities produced the income.

 *Caution*

Consistent Treatment Required

Once you treat activities separately or group them together as a single activity, the IRS generally requires you to continue the same treatment in later taxable years. You can re-group activities only if the original treatment was "clearly inappropriate" or has become clearly inappropriate because of a material change in circumstances.

EXAMPLE

Kosonen owned seven rental properties. In the tax year under consideration, he worked on all his properties a total of 877 hours, which qualified him as a real estate professional. But he could not meet the material participation test for each of the individual properties. If he could aggregate the activities, the material participation test would be met for the combined activity, which would be treated as nonpassive, allowing him to deduct his net rental losses against nonpassive income.

On his return for that year, he reported the losses from all the activities as an aggregate deduction and treated it as nonpassive. The IRS disallowed the deduction because he had not made a specific election to aggregate. Kosonen argued that by claiming on his return the total of his losses, he had put the IRS on notice that he was aggregating his rental activities.

The Tax Court disagreed. A specific election is required to put the IRS on notice that a taxpayer is a qualifying real estate professional making the election to aggregate rental activities. Reporting the net losses on his return as an aggregate active (nonpassive) loss was not enough because Kosonen could also have reported his net losses as active if he had materially participated in each of the seven activities and had not elected to aggregate.

Late elections. If you do not make the election to aggregate on your original return, Revenue Procedure 2011-34 allows you to make a late election on an amended return if you (1) had reasonable cause for not meeting the original deadline; (2) took positions on your tax returns as if the election to aggregate had been timely made—consistent filing is required for all years including and following the year the requested aggregation is to be effective; and (3) timely filed all the returns that would have been affected by the election had it been timely made. Returns filed within six months of the original due date (without extensions) are treated as timely filed for this purpose.

If you meet tests 1–3, you should attach a statement to an amended return for the most recent tax year and mail it to the IRS service center where your current year return will be filed. The statement must include the required aggregation declaration that you are a qualified real estate professional and are making the election to aggregate pursuant to Code Section 469(c)(7)(A). It must also declare that tests 1–3 have been met and explain what the reasonable cause was for not making a timely election. The statement must be dated and signed under penalties of perjury. At the top, write "FILED PURSUANT TO REV. PROC. 2011-34." Even if the IRS grants relief to make the late election, the IRS can later challenge whether you met the real estate professional and material participation tests, or whether the eligibility requirements of Revenue Procedure 2011-34 were met.

Rental loss allowance may apply to nonqualifying rental activity. A real estate professional may also be able to claim all or part of the $25,000 rental loss allowance *(10.2)*. For example, you are a real estate professional and meet the material participation test for one rental real estate activity but not for another and do not elect to aggregate. Losses from the nonqualifying activity can qualify for the rental allowance. Furthermore, suspended prior year losses from the qualifying activity may also be deductible under the rental loss allowance, as illustrated in the Example below.

Interests in S corporations and partnerships. Your interest in rental real estate held by a partnership or an S corporation is treated as a single interest in rental real estate if the entity grouped its rental real estate as one rental activity. If not, each rental real estate activity of the entity is treated as a separate interest in rental real estate. However, you may elect to treat all interests in rental real estate, including the rental real estate interests held by an S corporation or partnership, as a single rental real estate activity.

If you hold a 50% or greater interest in the capital, income, gain, loss, deduction, or credit in a partnership or S corporation for the taxable year, each interest in rental real estate held by the entity is treated as a separate interest in rental real estate, regardless of the entity's grouping of activities. However, you may elect to treat all interests in rental real estate, including your share of the rental real estate interests held by the entities, as a single rental real estate activity.

> **EXAMPLE**
>
> Jane Morton owns a rental building in Manhattan and a rental building in Newark. In 2023, she qualifies as a real estate professional. She has not previously elected to treat the two buildings as one activity (such an election would be binding for 2023), and does not make an election to aggregate on her 2023 return. She materially participates in the operations of the Manhattan building, which has $100,000 of disallowed passive losses from prior years and a $20,000 loss for 2023. She does not materially participate in the operation of the Newark building, which has $40,000 of rental income for 2023. Jane also has $50,000 of 2023 income from other nonpassive sources.
>
> Because Jane materially participates in operating the Manhattan building, the $20,000 loss from the building for 2023 is treated as nonpassive and offsets $20,000 of the $50,000 nonpassive income from other sources.
>
> Jane can also use $40,000 of the $100,000 prior year suspended losses from the Manhattan building to offset the $40,000 of passive rental income for 2023 from the Newark building. Of the $60,000 remaining suspended loss, $25,000 may be deducted under the rental loss allowance provided Jane's MAGI is under $100,000, the phaseout threshold for the allowance *(10.2)*. Assuming she qualifies for the full $25,000 allowance, the rental loss allowance is deducted from the $30,000 of remaining nonpassive income ($50,000 nonpassive income − $20,000 offset by nonpassive loss from Manhattan building), leaving Jane with $5,000 of nonpassive income for 2023 ($30,000 nonpassive income − $25,000 allowance). The balance of suspended losses from the Manhattan building of $35,000 ($60,000 − $25,000 rental allowance) may be carried forward and used in 2024 to offset income from the Newark building or passive income from other sources.

Limited partners. Generally, a person who has a limited partnership interest *(10.11)* in rental real estate must establish material participation by participating for more than 500 hours during the year; Test 1 *(10.6)*, or meeting Test 5 or Test 6 in *10.6*. These material participation tests also generally apply if an election is made to aggregate limited partnership interests in rental real estate with other rental real estate interests. However, the requirement that material participation can be established only under Tests 1, 5, or 6 may be avoided under a *de minimis* exception, which applies if the election to aggregate is made and less than 10% of the gross rental income for the taxable year from all rental real estate activities is attributed to limited partnership interests. In such a case, you may make the election to aggregate all rental real estate activities and determine material participation for the aggregated activity under any of the seven material participation tests *(10.6)*.

10.4 Business Participation May Avoid Passive Loss Restrictions

To avoid passive activity treatment of income and loss from a business investment, you must show material participation in that activity. The word "activity" does not necessarily relate to one specific business. If you invest in several businesses, you may be able to treat all or some of those activities as one activity or treat each separately.

Determining aggregate or separate treatment for your activities is discussed in *10.5* and material participation tests are discussed in *10.6*.

For a rental activity, material participation tests apply only if you are trying to qualify for the passive activity exception for real estate professionals *(10.3)*. For other rental real estate operators or investors, an "active" participation test that requires only certain management duties may allow you to deduct rental losses of up to $25,000 *(10.2)*.

10.5 Classifying Business Activities as One or Several

If you are in more than one activity, determining aggregate or separate treatment is important for:

- Deducting suspended losses when you dispose of an activity. If the activity is considered separate from the others, you may deduct a suspended loss incurred from that activity when you dispose of it. If it is not separate from the others, the suspended loss is deductible only if you dispose of substantially all of your investment *(10.13)*.

- Applying the material participation rules *(10.6)*. If activities are separate and apart from each other, the material participation tests are applied to each activity separately. If the activities are aggregated as one activity, material participation in one activity applies to all.

- Determining if you meet the 10% interest requirement for active participation *(10.2)*.

Grouping activities together. You may use any reasonable method under the facts and circumstances of your situation to determine if several business activities should be grouped together or treated separately. To be grouped together, the IRS says that the activities should be "an appropriate economic unit" for measuring gain or loss. For making this determination, the IRS sets these general guidelines: (1) similarities and differences in types of business; (2) the extent of common control; (3) geographic location; (4) the extent of common ownership; and (5) interdependencies among the activities. Interdependency is measured by the extent to which several business activities buy or sell among themselves, use the same products or services, have the same customers and employees, or use a single set of books and records.

> **EXAMPLE**
>
> Lance Jones has a significant interest in a bakery and a movie theater at a shopping mall in Baltimore and in a bakery and a movie theater in Philadelphia. The IRS does not explain what constitutes a significant interest. In grouping his activities into appropriate economic units based on the relevant facts and circumstances, Jones could: (1) group the theaters and bakeries into a single activity; (2) place the two theaters into one group and the two bakeries into a second group; (3) put his Baltimore businesses into one group and his Philadelphia businesses in another group; or (4) treat the two bakeries and two movie theaters as four separate activities.
>
> Once he chooses a grouping, he must consistently use that grouping for all future years unless a material change makes the grouping inappropriate. His decision is also subject to IRS review and, if questioned, he must show the factual basis for his grouping.

Final regulations control. Certain technical rules on grouping and the definition of real property in a trade or business were made optional when first released in earlier IRS regulations to give impacted taxpayers time to adjust. These rules (see T.D. 9943) are now mandatory, applicable to tax years beginning on or after March 22, 2021. They involve limitations on the deduction for business interest expense as well as applicable definitions governing real property operations, management, development, and redevelopment.

You must report new groupings and regroupings to the IRS. You must file a statement with your return for the first year in which you originally group two or more activities together. The statement must identify the activities (including, if applicable, the employer identification number (EIN)) and must specifically state that the grouped activities are an appropriate economic unit as discussed in the previous paragraph. You also must file

IRS Alert

Regrouping Due to Net Investment Income Tax (NII Tax)

The IRS may allow a one-time election to regroup your activities for the first taxable year that you become subject to the 3.8% NII tax *(28.3)*. This regrouping is also binding for all future tax years. *See* the instructions to Form 8582 for the eligibility requirements and other election details.

a statement with your return for any year in which you add a new activity to an existing group, or for any year in which you regroup activities. When activities are regrouped, the statement must explain how a material change in the facts and circumstances has made the original grouping "clearly inappropriate." *See* the instructions to Form 8582 and Revenue Procedure 2010-13 for further details on these disclosure requirements.

Rental activities. Rental activities may not be grouped with business activities unless one of the exceptions discussed in *10.1* applies.

IRS may regroup activities. The IRS may regroup your activities if your grouping does not reflect one or more appropriate economic units and a primary purpose of the grouping is to circumvent the passive loss rules.

> **EXAMPLE**
>
> Five doctors operate separate medical practices and also invest in tax shelters that generate passive losses. They form a partnership to operate X-ray equipment. In exchange for the equipment contributed to the partnership, each doctor receives limited partnership interests. The partnership is managed by a general partner selected by the doctors. Partnership services are provided to the doctors in proportion to their interests in the partnership and service fees are set at a level to offset the income generated by the partnership against individual passive losses. Under these facts, the IRS will not allow the medical practices and the partnership to be treated as separate activities as this would circumvent the passive loss limitations by generating passive income from the partnership to offset the tax-shelter losses. The IRS will require each doctor to treat his or her medical practice and interests in the partnership as a single activity.

Partnerships and S corporations. A partnership or S corporation must group its activities under the facts and circumstances test. Once a partnership or S corporation determines its activities, the partners or shareholders are bound by that decision and may not regroup them. The partners and shareholders then apply the facts and circumstances test to combine the partnership or S corporation activities with, or separate them from, their other activities.

Caution

Overcoming Investor Status

The IRS will not recognize time spent as an investor as "participation" unless you can show you are involved in daily operations or management of the activity. According to the IRS, this requires you to be at the business site on a regular basis. Even if you do appear daily, the IRS may ignore such evidence if there is an on-site manager or you have full-time business obligations at another site. Activity of an investor includes the studying and reviewing of financial reports for your own use that are considered unrelated to management decisions. If you invest in a business that is out of state or a distance from your home, you may also find it difficult to prove material participation.

Special rule for certain limited partners and limited entrepreneurs. A limited entrepreneur is a person with an ownership interest who does not actively participate in management. A limited entrepreneur or limited partner in films, videotapes, farming, oil and gas, or the renting of depreciable property generally may combine each such activity only with another of such activities in the same type of business, and only if he or she is a limited entrepreneur or partner in both. Grouping of such activities with other activities in the same type of business in which he or she is not a limited partner or entrepreneur is allowed if the grouping is appropriate under the general facts and circumstances test.

10.6　Material Participation in a Business

The IRS has seven tests for determining material participation in a business. Some tests require only a minimum amount of work, such as 500 hours a year, and others only 100 hours. You need to meet only one of the seven tests to qualify as a material participant. If you do, then the income and loss from that business is treated as nonpassive.

The tests apply whether you do business as a sole proprietor or in an S corporation or partnership. Losses and credits passed through S corporations and partnerships are subject to passive activity rules.

If you are a limited partner, the law presumes that you are not a material participant in the activities of the limited partnership, but IRS regulations provide a limited opportunity to show that you materially participate. Only three of the seven material participation tests are available to you; *see 10.11*.

The impact of the IRS participation rules on your tax position will depend on whether the particular activity produces income or loss. If you have passive activity losses from other activities, you may prefer to have a profitable business activity treated as a passive activity in order to offset the income by the losses from passive activities.

On the other hand, if the business activity operates at a loss and you do not have passive income from other sources, you may want to meet the material participation test for that business activity in order to claim current loss deductions. IRS strategy in reviewing your activities would be the opposite. If your return were under audit, an agent would attempt to prevent you from treating income from a business activity as passive. For example, the IRS, by applying Tests 5 and 6, can prevent a retired person from treating post-retirement income from a prior business or profession as passive income that could offset passive losses from another activity. If you realize a loss in one passive activity, Test 4 may prevent you from generating passive income by merely reducing your participation in another activity.

Material participation results in nonpassive treatment. If you materially participate by meeting one of the seven IRS tests, your activity is not a passive activity. For example, under Test 1, working during a year for more than 500 hours in an activity is considered material participation.

If you work for more than 100 hours but less than 500 hours at an activity in which you do not otherwise materially participate, the activity is considered a "significant participation activity," and under Test 4, if you have several of such activities and your total participation in all of them exceeds 500 hours, you are treated as materially participating in all of the activities. Further, if you significantly participate but do not materially participate in one or more activities, what would otherwise be passive income from the significant participation activities may be recharacterized by the IRS as nonpassive income; *see 10.9*.

IRS Tests for Material Participation

If you meet one of the following tests for the year in question, you are considered to have materially participated in that activity, and therefore the activity is considered nonpassive for that year. Tests 5 and 6 prevent retired individuals from treating post-retirement income as passive income.

Rules for limited partners and members of LLCs and LLPs are at *10.11*. For participation rules for personal service and closely held corporations, *see 10.15*.

Work by you or your spouse that counts as participation. Apart from the exceptions listed below, any work you do in a business in which you have an ownership interest is treated as "participation." If you are married, work by your spouse in the activity during the tax year is generally treated as your participation. This is true even if your spouse does not own an interest in the business or if you file separately. However, this favorable spousal participation rule does not apply if you and your spouse elect to treat your jointly owned business as a qualified joint venture, thereby requiring each of you to report your respective shares of the business income, deductions, credits, gains, and losses on Schedule E; *see 9.1* and the Schedule E instructions.

Do not count the following types of work as participation:

1. Work that is not of a type customarily done by an owner of an activity, if one of the principal reasons for the performance of the work is to avoid the passive loss rules (*see* the Example below).

2. An investor's review of financial statements or analysis that is unrelated to day-to-day management or operation of the activity.

> **EXAMPLE**
>
> An attorney owns an interest in a professional football team for which he performs no services. He anticipates a net loss from the football activity and to qualify as a material participant, he hires his wife to work 15 hours a week as an office receptionist for the team. Although a spouse's participation in an activity generally qualifies as participation by both spouses, the receptionist work here does not qualify as participation because (1) it is not the type of work customarily done by an owner of a football team and (2) the attorney hired his spouse to avoid disallowance of a passive loss.

Test 1. You participate in the activity for more than 500 hours during the tax year.

Test 2. Your participation in the activity for the tax year constitutes substantially all of the participation in the activity of all individuals including non-owners for the year.

Test 3. You participate in the activity for more than 100 hours during the tax year, and your participation is at least as great as that of any other person including non-owners for that year.

> **EXAMPLE**
>
> Joan Brown and Pat Collins are partners in a moving van business that they conduct entirely on weekends with the help of two employees. They both work for eight hours each weekend. Although neither partner participates for more than 500 hours (Test 1) and do not meet Test 2, they are both treated as material participants under Test 3 because they each participate for more than 100 hours and no one else participates more.

Test 4. Any business activity in which you participate for more than 100 hours during the year and for which you do not meet any of the other material participation tests (other than this Test 4 as explained next) is considered a "significant participation activity". If you participate in several significant participation activities during the year and your total participation in all of the activities exceeds 500 hours, you are treated as a material participant in each of these activities.

Test 5. You materially participated in the activity (under any of the other tests) for any five tax years during the 10 tax years preceding the tax year in question. The five tax years do not have to be consecutive. Thus, if you are retired but meet the five-out-of-10-year participation test, you are currently considered a material participant, with the result that net income from the activity is treated as nonpassive, rather than passive. If you retired from a personal service profession, an even stricter rule applies; *see* Test 6.

Test 6. In a personal service activity, you materially participated for any three tax years preceding the tax year in question. The three years do not have to be consecutive. Examples of personal services within this test are the professions of health, law, engineering, architecture, accounting, actuarial science, the performing arts, consulting, or any other trade or business in which capital is not a material income-producing factor.

Test 7. Under the facts and circumstances test, you participate in the activity on a regular, continuous, and substantial basis. According to the IRS, you do not come within this test if you participated 100 hours or less in the activity during the year.

> **EXAMPLES**
>
> 1. Mike Smith is a full-time accountant with ownership interests in a restaurant and shoe store. He works 150 hours in the shoe store and 360 hours in the restaurant. Under the significant participation test (Test 4), Smith is considered a material participant in both activities, as the total hours of both exceed 500.
> 2. Carl Young invests in five businesses. He works 110 hours in activity (a); 100 hours in activity (b); 125 hours in activity (c); 120 hours in activity (d); and 140 hours in activity (e). He does not qualify under the significant participation test (Test 4). Although his total hours in the five activities exceed 500, activity (b) is ignored in the total count because the hours did not exceed 100. The total of the four other activities is 495.
> 3. Assume that Young worked one hour more for activity (b). It and all of the other activities would be considered as meeting the significant material participation test. The total hours are 596. Assuming that activity (a) totaled 125 hours and activity (b) remained at 100 hours or less, he would meet the test for all of the activities except for activity (b), which did not exceed 100 hours. The total of the four qualified activities is 510 hours.

Caution

Retired Farmers

Retired or disabled farmers are treated as materially participating in a farming activity if they materially participated for five of the eight years preceding their retirement or disability. A surviving spouse is also treated as materially participating in a farming activity if the real property used in the activity meets the estate tax rules for special valuation of farm property passed from a qualified decedent and the surviving spouse actively manages the farm.

10.7 Tax Credits of Passive Activities Limited

You may generally not claim a tax credit from a passive activity unless you report and pay taxes on income from a passive activity. Furthermore, the tax allocated to that income must be at least as much as the credit. If the tax credit exceeds your tax liability on income allocable to passive activities, the excess credit is not allowed. Use Form 8582-CR to figure the allowable credit. Suspended credits are not allowed when property is disposed of. The credits may be used only when passive income is earned.

EXAMPLE

Ben Wall has a $1,000 credit from a passive activity. He does not report income from any passive activity. He may not claim the credit because no part of his tax is attributed to passive activity income. The credit is suspended until he has income from a passive activity and he incurs tax on that income. All or part of the credit may then be claimed to offset the tax. If he disposed of his interest before using a suspended credit, the credit may no longer be claimed but the election to reduce basis, discussed below, could be made.

Credits for real estate activities. More favorable tax credit rules apply to real estate activities *(10.2)*.

Basis adjustment for suspended credits. If the basis of property was reduced by tax credits, you may elect on Form 8582-CR to add back a suspended credit to the basis when your entire interest in an activity is disposed of. If the property is disposed of in a transaction that is not treated as a fully taxable disposition *(10.13)*, then no basis adjustment is allowed.

EXAMPLE

Mark places in service rehabilitation credit property and claims an allowable credit of $50, which also reduces basis by $50. However, under the passive loss rule, he is prevented from claiming the credit. In a later year, he disposes of his entire interest in the activity, including the property whose basis was reduced. He may elect to increase basis of the property by the amount of the original basis adjustment.

10.8 Determining Passive or Nonpassive Income and Loss

The purpose of the passive loss rules is to prevent you from deducting passive losses from nonpassive income. Passive losses are losses from business activities in which you do not materially participate *(10.6)* or losses from rental activities that are not deductible under the $25,000 allowance *(10.2)* or which do not qualify you as a real estate professional *(10.3)*. In some cases passive income may be recharacterized as nonpassive income *(10.9)*.

Where you do not materially participate in a business activity, passive income or loss is determined on Form 8582 by matching income and expenses of that activity. Portfolio income *(see below)* earned by the activity or any pay that you earn is not included to determine passive income or loss.

Portfolio income. Portfolio income is nonpassive income and broadly defined as income that is not derived in the ordinary course of business of the activity. Portfolio income includes interest, dividends, annuities, and royalties from property held for investment. However, interest income on loans and investments made in the business of lending money or received on business accounts receivable is generally not treated as portfolio income; *see 10.9* for special recharacterization rules. Similarly, royalties derived from a business of licensing property are not portfolio income to the person who created the property or performed substantial services or incurred substantial costs.

Portfolio income also includes gains from the sale of properties that produce portfolio income or are held for investment.

Expenses allocable to portfolio income, including interest expenses, do not enter into the computation of passive income or loss.

 *Filing Tip*

Portfolio Income Accounting

You cannot deduct passive losses from portfolio income. The tax law broadly defines "portfolio income" to include nonbusiness types of income including interest, dividends, and profits on the sale of investment property.

Sale of property used in activity. Gain or loss realized on the sale of property used in the activity is generally treated as passive income/loss if at the time of disposition the activity was passive. Under this rule, if you have a gain that you are reporting on the installment method, the treatment of installment payments depends on your status at the time of the initial sale. If you were not a material participant in the year of sale, installment payments in a later year are treated as passive income, even if you become a material participant in the later year. However, an exception to the year-of-sale status rule applies to certain sales of property formerly used in a passive activity *(10.16)*.

Although gain on the sale of property is generally passive income if the activity is passive at the time of sale, there is an exception that could recharacterize the gain as nonpassive income if the property was formerly used in a nonpassive activity *(10.16)*.

Compensation for personal services is not passive activity income. The term "compensation for personal services" includes only (1) wages, salaries and other earned income, including certain payments made by a partnership to a partner and representing compensation for the services of the partner; (2) amounts included in gross income involving the transfer of property in exchange for the performance of services; (3) amounts distributed under qualified plans; (4) amounts distributed under retirement, pension, and other arrangements for deferred compensation of services; and (5) Social Security benefits includible in gross income.

Passive activity gross income also does not include (1) income from patent, copyright, or literary, musical, or artistic compositions, if your personal efforts significantly contributed to the creation of the property; (2) income from a qualified low-income housing project; (3) income tax refunds; and (4) payments on a covenant not to compete.

Passive activity deductions. On Form 8582, you can offset passive income of an activity with deductible expenses that are related to the activity, such as real property taxes. Deductible expenses from prior years that were disallowed by the passive loss rules and carried forward to the current year are added to the current year deductions. The following are not considered passive activity deductions:

- Casualty and theft losses if similar losses do not recur regularly in the activity.
- Charitable deductions.
- State, local, and foreign income taxes.
- Carryovers of net operating losses or capital losses.
- Expenses clearly and directly allocable to portfolio income.
- Loss on the sale of property producing portfolio income.
- Loss on the sale of your entire interest in a passive activity to an unrelated party; the loss is allowed in full *(10.13)*.

Interest deductions. Interest expenses attributable to passive activities are treated as passive activity deductions and are not subject to the investment interest limitations. For example, if you have a net passive loss of $100, of which $40 is attributable to interest expenses, the entire $100 is a passive loss; the $40 is not subject to the investment interest limitation *(15.10)*. Similarly, income and loss from a passive activity is generally not treated as investment income or loss in figuring the investment interest limitation.

If you rent out a vacation home that you personally use for more than the greater of 14 days or 10% of the fair market rental days *(9.7)*, you may treat the residence as a qualified second residence under the mortgage interest rules *(15.1)*. Interest on such a qualifying second home is generally fully deductible, and the deductible interest *(15.1)* is not treated as a passive activity deduction. The rental portion of the interest is deducted on Schedule E and the personal-use portion on Schedule A if itemized deductions are claimed *(9.9)*.

Self-charged management fees or interest. For an individual with interests in several business entities, the payment of management fees by one of the entities to another is in effect a payment by the owner to himself. However, if the taxpayer materially participates in the entity providing the management services but not in the entity that pays the fees, the passive loss rules prevent the "self-charged" expense from offsetting the nonpassive fee income. IRS final regulations allow a netting deduction only for self-charged interest but not for any other self-charged expense.

EXAMPLE

As an employee of his S corporation, Hillman provided real estate management services to rental real estate partnerships in which he had invested. On his personal return, he reported the management fees as passed-through S corporation income and deducted his allocable share of the fee payments by the partnership. The IRS disallowed the deduction: Since Hillman materially participated in the S corporation but not the partnerships, the fee payments by the partnerships were passive activity expenses that could not be deducted against the S corporation's nonpassive fee income. The fact that IRS regulations allow a deduction for self-charged interest does not mean that other self-charged passive expenses should also be deductible.

The Tax Court agreed with Hillman that there is no difference between interest and other self-charged expenses. The legislative history indicates a Congressional intent to allow deductions for self-charged expenses because they do not result in a net accretion to the taxpayer's wealth.

However, the Fourth Circuit, while sympathetic to Hillman's situation, reversed the Tax Court. Nothing in the tax law allows self-charged expenses to be deducted against nonpassive income. Although there is no reason why management fees should be distinguished from interest, the legislative history on self-charged expenses specifically mentioned only interest as an exception to the general statutory rule. The Congressional Committee reports that gave the IRS discretion to provide a deduction for other self-charged expenses did not limit that discretion. Unless the IRS changes its regulations, relief must come from Congress. The Fourth Circuit noted that while the denial of a deduction in this situation appears harsh, the deduction is not completely lost; the fee payments may be carried forward to later years as a passive expense.

After the Fourth Circuit ruled against him, Hillman went back to the Tax Court and tried an alternative argument in an attempt to deduct the management fees paid by the partnerships. He argued that the fees were nonpassive deductions that could offset the nonpassive income from the S corporation because the payment of the fees, by itself, constituted a separate business distinguishable from the passive rental activities of the partnerships. The Tax Court disagreed. The management fees were incurred in connection with the rental activities and thus were passive deductions. The Tax Court again acknowledged the unfairness of denying a deduction for the "self-charged" fees. Hillman's plight is lamentable, but as the Fourth Circuit ruled, relief can only come from Congress if the IRS does not liberalize its regulation on self-charged expenses.

10.9 Passive Income Recharacterized as Nonpassive Income

There is an advantage in treating income as passive income when you have passive losses that may offset the income. However, the law may prevent you from treating certain income as passive income. The conversion of passive income to nonpassive income is technically called "recharacterization." This may occur when you do not materially participate in the business activity, but are sufficiently active for the IRS to consider your participation as significant. Recharacterization may also occur when you rent property to a business in which you materially participate, rent nondepreciable property, or sell development rental property.

Significant participation. The IRS combines net income and net losses from your significant participation activities (defined at Test 4 in *10.6*). If you have aggregate net income from all of the activities, part of the net income is treated as nonpassive income according to the computation illustrated in the Carol Warren Example.

Net interest income from passive equity-financed lending. Gross income from "equity-financed lending activity" is treated as nonpassive income to the extent of the lesser of the equity-financed interest income or net passive income. An activity is an "equity-financed lending activity" for a tax year if (1) the activity involves a trade or business of lending money and (2) the average outstanding balance of the liabilities incurred in the activity for the tax year does not exceed 80% of the average outstanding balance of the interest-bearing assets held in the activity.

 *Caution*

"Recharacterization" of Passive Income

Gain on the sale of property used in a passive activity may be recharacterized as nonpassive income if the property was formerly used in a nonpassive activity *(10.16)*.

Incidental rental of property by development activity. Where gains on the sale of rental property are attributable to recent development, passive income treatment may be lost if the sale comes within the following tests: (1) the rental started less than 12 months before the date of disposition; and (2) you materially participated or significantly participated in the performance of services enhancing the value of the property. The 12-month period starts at the completion of the development services that increased the property's value.

> **EXAMPLE**
>
> Carol Warren invests in three business activities—A, B, and C. She does not materially participate in any of the activities during the year but participates in Activity A for 105 hours, in Activity B for 160 hours, and in Activity C for 125 hours. Her net passive income or loss from the three activities is:
>
> | | A | B | C | Total |
> |---|---|---|---|---|
> | Passive activity gross income | $600 | $700 | $900 | $2,200 |
> | Passive activity deductions | (200) | (1,000) | (300) | (1,500) |
> | Net passive activity income | $400 | ($300) | $600 | $700 |
>
> Carol's passive activity gross income from significant participation passive activities of $2,200 exceeds passive activity deductions of $1,500 by $700. A ratable portion of her gross income from significant participation activities with net passive income for the tax year (Activities A and C) is treated as gross income that is not from a passive activity. The ratable portion is figured by dividing:
>
> 1. The excess of her passive activity gross income from significant participation over passive activity deductions from such activities (here $700) by
>
> 2. The net passive income of only the significant participation passive activities having net passive income (here $1,000). The ratable portion is 70%.
>
> Thus, $280 of gross income from Activity A ($400 × 70%) and $420 of gross income from Activity C ($600 × 70%) is treated as nonpassive gross income. This adjustment prevents $700 from being offset by passive losses from another activity.

Caution

Property Rented to Nonpassive Activity (Self-Rental Property)

You may not generate passive income by renting property to a business in which you materially participate. *See* "Self-rental rule: Renting to your business" in this section.

Self-rental rule: Renting to your business. If you rent a building to your business, the rental income, normally treated as passive income, may be recharacterized by the IRS as nonpassive income where you also have losses from other rentals. Recharacterization prevents you from deducting the rental losses against the net rental income. Although not specifically written into the law, the recharacterization rules are incorporated in IRS regulations. For the recharacterization rule to apply, you must "materially participate" in the business that rents the property from you; *see* the following Examples. The Tax Court and several federal appeals courts have upheld the IRS recharacterization rule.

> **EXAMPLE**
>
> Krukowski, an attorney who operated two businesses through wholly owned C corporations, claimed that the IRS' recharacterization regulations were arbitrary and capricious. He rented personally owned buildings to the corporations, one of which ran a health club and the other the attorney's law firm. He reported net income of $175,149 from the rental to the law firm and a $69,100 net loss from the rental to the health club. He deducted the loss from the income and reported net rental income of $106,049. The IRS disallowed the loss offset by recharacterizing the rental income he received from the law firm as nonpassive income. Recharacterization could be applied under the regulations because the time spent by the attorney in the law firm was material participation. The attorney had to report rental income of $175,149; the health club rental loss was treated as a "suspended" passive loss.

Before the Tax Court, the attorney claimed that the recharacterization rule was arbitrary and contrary to the passive loss statute. The Court disagreed. The law authorizes the IRS to write regulations interpreting the law. Further, Congressional committee reports contemplate that the IRS would define nonpassive income in such a way as to prevent a taxpayer from offsetting active business income with passive business losses.

The Seventh Circuit Court of Appeals affirmed the Tax Court. The IRS was given authority by Congress to enact the self-rental rule as a way of eliminating tax shelters. Three other appeals courts, the First, Fifth, and Ninth Circuits, have also upheld the IRS regulation.

Rental of property with an insubstantial depreciable basis. This rule prevents you from generating passive rental income with vacant land or land on which a unit is constructed that has a value substantially less than the land. If less than 30% of the unadjusted basis *(5.16)* of rental property is depreciable, and you have net passive income from rentals (taking into account carried-over passive losses from prior years), the net passive income is treated as nonpassive income.

EXAMPLES

1. A limited partnership buys vacant land for $300,000, constructs improvements on the land at a cost of $100,000, and leases the entire property. After the rental period, the partnership sells the property for $600,000, realizing a gain. The unadjusted basis of the depreciable improvements of $100,000 is only 25% of the basis of the property of $400,000. The rent and the gain allocated to the improvements are treated as nonpassive income.
2. Shirley offset a passive rental loss from an investment in a limited partnership, LP, which was a substantial owner of a general partnership, GP, against rental income from an investment in a joint venture, JV. JV had leased to GP land on which GP constructed a shopping center. The IRS held that the rental income from JV was nonpassive rental income within the 30% test and could not be offset by the passive rental loss. The Tax Court agreed and also rejected Shirley's attempt to aggregate her investment activities in JV and LP as one activity. The operations of each group, JV, LP, and GP, were separate and not owned by the same person. She was not the direct owner of any of the units. Further, the aggregation rule does not apply to property falling within the 30% test.

Licensing of intangible property. Your share of royalty income in a partnership, S corporation, estate, or trust is treated as nonpassive income if you invested after the organization created the intangible property, performed substantial services, or incurred substantial costs in the development or marketing of it. *See* Publication 925 for further details.

10.10 Working Interests in Oil and Gas Wells

Working interests are not treated as passive activities provided your liability is not limited. This is true whether you hold your interest directly or through an entity. As long as you have unlimited liability, the working interest is not a passive activity even if you do not materially participate in the activity. A working interest is one burdened with the financial risk of developing and operating the property, such as a share in tort liability (for example, uninsured losses from a fire); some responsibility to share in additional costs; responsibility for authorizing expenses; receiving periodic reports about drilling, completion, and expected production; and the possession of voting rights and rights to continue operations if the present operator steps out.

Limited liability. If you hold a working interest through any of the following entities, the entity is considered to limit your liability and you are subject to the passive loss rules: (1) a limited partnership interest in a partnership in which you are not a general partner; (2) stock in a corporation; or (3) an interest in any entity other than a limited partnership or corporation that, under applicable state law, limits the liability of a holder of such interest for all obligations of the entity to a determinable fixed amount.

Working interests are considered on a well-by-well basis. Rights to overriding royalties or production payments, and contract rights to extract or share in oil and gas profits without liability for a share of production costs, are not working interests.

 *Planning Reminder*

Limited Liability for Oil or Gas Well

A working interest in an oil or gas well is exempt from the passive activity restrictions if your liability is unlimited. The following forms of loss protection are disregarded and, thus, are not treated as limiting your liability: protection against loss by an indemnification agreement; a stop-loss agreement; insurance; or any similar arrangement or combination of agreements.

Planning Reminder

Publicly Traded Partnerships (PTPs)

A PTP is a partnership whose interests are traded on established securities exchanges or are readily tradable in secondary markets. PTPs that are not treated as corporations for tax purposes are subject to special rules that allow losses to be used only to offset income from the same PTP. *See* the instructions to Form 8582.

10.11 Partners and Members of LLCs and LLPs

As a general partner, your share of partnership income or loss during the partnership year ending within your tax year is passive or nonpassive, depending on whether you materially participated under any of the seven IRS tests *(10.6)* in the partnership activities during the year. Limited partners have a reduced ability to show material participation as discussed below. On Schedule K-1 of Form 1065, the partnership will identify each activity it conducts and specify the income, loss, deductions, and credits from each activity.

> **EXAMPLE**
>
> Don Bailey is a general partner of a fiscal year partnership that ends on March 31, 2023. During that fiscal year he was inactive. Since he did not materially participate, his share of partnership income or loss for 2023 is passive activity income or loss, even if he becomes active from April 1, 2023, to the end of 2023.

Not treated as passive income are payments for services and certain guaranteed payments made in liquidation of a retiring or deceased partner's interest unless attributed to unrealized receivables and goodwill at a time the partner was passive.

Gain or loss on the disposition of a partnership interest may be attributed to different trade, investment, or rental activities of the partnership. The allocation is made according to a complicated formula included in IRS regulations.

Payments to a retired partner. Gain or loss is treated as passive only to the extent that it would be treated as such at the start of the liquidation of the partner's interest.

Limited partners. Under IRS regulations, a limited partner has only a limited opportunity to establish material participation. A limited partner may use only three of the seven tests to establish material participation and thereby avoid passive treatment for the partnership income or loss:

1. The limited partner participates for more than 500 hours during the tax year; *see* Test 1 *(10.6)*, or
2. The limited partner materially participated in the partnership during prior years under either Test 5 or Test 6 *(10.6)*.

To determine material participation in rental real estate activities under the special rules for real estate professionals, a limited partner must meet Test 1, Test 5, or Test 6 *(10.6)*, but *see* the *de minimis* exception at *10.3*.

A limited partner is not considered to be an "active participant" and thus does not qualify for the $25,000 rental loss allowance *(10.2)*.

Who is a limited partner? The current regulations treat a partner other than a general partner as a limited partner if his or her liability is limited under state law. However, the focus in determining who is a limited partner has shifted from limited liability to management rights, based upon regulations that the IRS proposed in 2011. Although still not finalized, likely because of general lack of IRS resources allocated to the regulation process in general, the IRS has acknowledged that a new test for determining limited partner status is necessary given the emergence of LLCs and changes in state law that allow limited partners to make management decisions while retaining limited liability. Under the proposed regulations, a taxpayer's interest in an entity that is classified as a partnership is treated as a limited partnership interest if the taxpayer does not have rights to manage the partnership under both the governing agreement and under the law of the jurisdiction in which the partnership was organized. A taxpayer who is treated as a limited partner under this definition would have to establish material participation under Test 1, 5, or 6 as noted above. A taxpayer who has management rights and who is not treated as a limited partner would be able to establish material participation under any of the seven material participation tests described in *10.6*. The *e-Supplement* at *jklasser.com* will report any change in the status of the proposed regulations.

LLC and LLP members. The Tax Court and the Court of Federal Claims rejected IRS attempts to treat LLC and LLP members as limited partners under the regulations that focus on limited liability. These court decisions allowed an LLC or LLP member to apply any of the IRS' seven tests for material participation *(10.6)*.

The IRS acquiesced after the result in the Court of Federal Claims case and announced that it would no longer litigate similar cases. This was followed by the release of the 2011 proposed regulations discussed above.

10.12 Form 8582 and Other Tax Forms

The purpose of Form 8582 is to assemble in one place items of income and expenses from passive activities in order to determine the effect of the passive loss rules on these items. Note that if you actively participate in a rental real estate activity and therefore qualify for the special loss allowance of up to $25,000, you may not have to complete Form 8582; *see* the conditions under "Schedule E" below.

After Form 8582 is completed, the income and allowable deductions are reported as regular income and deductions in appropriate schedules attached to your tax return. For example, net profits of a self-employed person who is not active in the business are reported on Schedule C, sales of capital assets of a passive activity are reported on Form 8949 and Schedule D, your share of partnership income and allowable deductions is reported on Schedule E, and rental income and allowable deductions are reported on Schedule E.

Forms 8949 & Schedule D or Form 4797. Gains or losses from the sale of assets from a passive activity or from the sale of a partial interest that is less than "substantially all" of your entire interest in a passive activity are reported on Form 8949/Schedule D (capital assets) or on Form 4797 (business property). The gain is also entered on Form 8582. Losses must first be entered on Form 8582 to see how much, if any, is allowable under the passive loss restrictions before an amount can be entered as a loss on Form 8949/Schedule D or Form 4797.

Partial dispositions. A disposition of an insubstantial part of your interest in the activity does not allow a deduction of suspended passive losses from prior years. When you dispose of your entire interest in a passive activity to a nonrelated party in a fully taxable transaction, your losses for the year plus prior year suspended losses from the activity are fully deductible. The same rule applies to a partial disposition only if you are disposing of substantially all of the activity and you have proof of the current year and prior year suspended losses allocable to the disposed-of portion. You net the gain or loss from the disposition with the net income or loss from current year operations and any prior year suspended passive losses. If the netting gives you an overall gain, you enter the gain from the sale, the current year income or loss, and any prior year unallowed losses on the appropriate lines of the Worksheets attached to Form 8582; *see* the Form 8582 instructions. If you have an overall loss after the netting, you do not file Form 8582; all losses including prior year unallowed losses are reported on the normally used forms and schedules (Schedule E, Form 8949 and Schedule D, or Form 4797).

Schedule E. If you have a net profit from rental real estate or other passive activity reported on Schedule E and you also have losses from other passive activities, the income reported on Schedule E is also entered on Form 8582.

If you have a net loss on Schedule E (on Line 21) from a rental real estate activity subject to the passive activity rules, the loss generally must be entered on Form 8582. If a loss is allowable after application of the passive loss limits, the allowable amount from Form 8582 is entered on Line 22 of Schedule E as your deductible rental loss.

You do not have to complete Form 8582 if you qualify for the rental real estate loss allowance of up to $25,000 (you actively participated in the rental activity; *see 10.2*) and you meet all of these conditions:

- Your only passive activities are rental real estate activities and you have no suspended prior year passive losses from these or any other passive activities;
- You have no credits related to passive activities;
- Your overall net loss from the rental real estate activities is $25,000 or less ($12,500 or less if married filing separately and you lived apart from your spouse all year);
- Your modified adjusted gross income is $100,000 or less ($50,000 or less if married filing separately and you lived apart from your spouse all year); and
- You do not own any interest in a rental real estate activity as a limited partner or beneficiary of a trust or estate.

If you meet the above conditions, your rental real estate losses are not limited by the passive activity rules and you do not need to complete Form 8582. Enter the loss from Line 21 of Schedule E as the deductible rental real estate loss on Line 22.

If you have a loss from a passive interest in a partnership, trust, estate, or S corporation, you first determine on Form 8582 whether the loss is deductible on Schedule E.

Schedule F. A passive activity farm loss is entered on Form 8582 to determine the deductible loss. If only part of the loss is allowed, only that portion is claimed on Schedule F. A net profit from passive farm activities is also entered on Form 8582 to offset losses from other passive activities.

Other tax forms. Other forms tied to Form 8582 are Form 4797 (sale of business assets or equipment), Form 4835 (farm rental income), and Form 4952 (investment interest deductions). For further details *see* Form 8582 and its instructions.

10.13 Suspended Losses Allowed on Disposition of Your Interest

Losses and credits that may not be claimed in one year because of the passive activity limitations are suspended and carried forward to later years. The carryover lasts indefinitely, until you have passive income against which to claim the losses and credits. No carryback is allowed. What if you have suspended losses from a business and in a later year you materially participate in the business so it is no longer a passive activity? If the activity is not passive in the current year, and you have net income from the activity for the year, you can offset that income with the suspended losses. Any remaining suspended losses continue to be carried forward to future years. Generally, you may deduct in full your remaining suspended losses when you sell your entire interest in the activity; *see* below.

> **EXAMPLE**
>
> In 2022, Nick Milo was not a material participant in a business activity and his share of losses was $10,000, which was suspended because he had no passive income. In 2023, he becomes a material participant in the business and his share of income is $1,000. He may apply $1,000 of the suspended loss to offset that income and the remaining $9,000 will be carried over to 2024 as a suspended passive loss.

Allocation of suspended loss. If your suspended loss is incurred from several activities, you allocate the loss among the activities using the worksheets accompanying Form 8582. The loss is allocated among the activities in proportion to the total loss. If you have net income from significant participation activities *(see* Test 4 *(10.6))*, such activities may be treated as one single activity in making the allocation; *see* the instructions to Form 8582.

Disposition of entire interest in passive activity. If you sell your entire interest in an activity to a nonrelated person in a fully taxable transaction, you can claim any suspended passive losses from the activity. On a qualifying disposition, the suspended losses plus any current year income or loss from the activity are combined with the gain or loss from the sale; *see* the Examples below and follow the instructions to Form 8582 for reporting the net gain or loss.

A "fully taxable transaction" is one in which you recognize all the realized gain or loss. In some cases, it may be unclear if a fully taxable transaction has occurred. The IRS treats an abandonment of property as a qualifying disposition that releases suspended losses.

IRS Chief Counsel has held that there is a fully taxable disposition when you sell at a gain rental property that previously had been your principal residence and the gain is not taxable under the home sale exclusion *(29.1)*. A taxpayer had $30,000 in suspended passive losses from three years of rentals when the home was sold to an unrelated party for a $100,000 gain. Since gain or loss on a disposition must be "recognized" for there to be a "fully taxable transaction," the issue before the IRS was whether tax-free home sale gain is "recognized." Chief Counsel concluded that the taxpayer's home sale gain was realized and recognized; it was simply excluded from income because of the specific exclusion provision. The $30,000 in suspended losses were deductible in the year of sale. Since the $100,000 home sale gain was excluded from income, it was not considered passive income from the rental property and did not offset the $30,000 of suspended losses.

IRS Chief Counsel has also said that a foreclosure on rental real estate subject to recourse debt is a fully taxable transaction, even though the taxpayer avoids tax on the cancellation of his debt because he is insolvent *(11.8)*. A foreclosure is treated as a sale for tax purposes *(31.9)*; here, the taxpayer realized a $25,000 gain on the foreclosure. He also had cancellation of debt income of $75,000, which was not taxed because of the insolvency exclusion. Chief Counsel concluded that since a foreclosure is a taxable sale, a foreclosure of property constituting the taxpayer's interest in the rental property qualifies as a fully taxable transaction under the passive activity disposition rules. This is so whether or not the taxpayer avoids tax on cancellation of debt income due to the insolvency exclusion.

EXAMPLES

1. Jill Stein has a 5% interest in a limited partnership with an adjusted basis of $42,000. In 2023, she sells her interest in the partnership to an unrelated person for $50,000. For 2022, she had a current year passive loss from the partnership (shown on Schedule K-1) of $3,000. She also has $2,000 of suspended passive losses from prior years that have been carried forward to 2023. Jill's $8,000 gain from the sale of her interest is combined on Form 8582 with the current year loss and suspended losses giving her an overall gain of $3,000, figured as follows:

Sales price	$50,000
Less: Adjusted basis	$42,000
Gain	$8,000
Less: Current year loss	$3,000
Less: Suspended losses	$2,000
Overall gain	$3,000

2. Assume that Jill's suspended losses from prior years were $10,000 instead of $2,000. She has an overall loss of $5,000 after combining the gain from the sale of $8,000, the current year loss of $3,000, and the suspended losses of $10,000.

   Since there is an overall loss after combining the gain and losses, Jill does not file Form 8582. The current year loss plus the suspended losses are reported as nonpassive losses on Schedule E and the gain from the disposition on Form 8949 and Schedule D.

3. Assume in Example 1 that Jill sold her interest for $30,000 instead of $50,000. She would have a $12,000 loss on the sale ($42,000 adjusted basis less $30,000 sales price). Combining the loss with the current year loss of $3,000 and the $2,000 of suspended losses, she has an overall loss of $17,000.

   Since there is an overall loss, Jill does not file Form 8582. The current year loss plus the suspended losses are reported as nonpassive losses on Schedule E. The $12,000 loss on the sale is reported on Form 8949 and Schedule D as a capital loss. Under the regular rules for capital losses, the loss will offset capital gains for 2023 and any excess will be deductible only up to $3,000 *(5.4)*. Assuming the $3,000 limit applies to her 2023 loss, Jill has a $9,000 capital loss carryover to 2024.

Partial disposition. If you dispose of substantially all of your interest in an activity, you may treat the part disposed of as a separate activity, thereby allowing the deduction of suspended losses. You must show: (1) the amount of prior year suspended deductions and credits allocable to that part of the activity, and (2) the amount of gross income and any other deductions and credits allocable to that part of the activity for the year of disposition.

If the part disposed of is less than substantially all of your interest, suspended losses are not allowed. Gain or loss will be treated as part of the net income or loss from the activity for the year.

Gifts. When a passive activity interest is given away, you may not deduct suspended passive losses. The donee's basis in the property is increased by the suspended loss if he or she sells the property at a gain. If a loss is realized by the donee on a sale of the interest, the donee's basis may not exceed fair market value of the gift at the time of the donation.

Death. On the death of an investor in a passive interest, suspended losses are deductible on the decedent's final tax return, to the extent the suspended loss exceeds the amount by which the basis of the interest in the hands of the heir is increased.

> **EXAMPLE**
>
> An owner dies holding an interest in a passive activity with a suspended loss of $8,000. After the owner's death, the heir's stepped-up basis for the property (equal to fair market value) is $6,000 greater than the decedent's basis. On the decedent's final return, $2,000 of the loss is deductible ($8,000 − $6,000).

Installment sales. If you sell your entire interest in a passive activity at a profit on the installment basis, suspended losses are deducted over the installment period in the same ratio as the gain recognized each year bears to the gain remaining to be recognized as of the start of the year. For example, if you realize a gain of $10,000 and report $2,000 of gain each year for five years, in the year of sale you report 20% of your total gain under the installment method, and 20% of your suspended losses are also allowed. In the second year, you report $2,000 of the remaining $8,000 gain and 25% of the remaining losses ($2,000 ÷ $8,000) are allowed.

Filing Tip

Installment Sale of Your Interest

If you sell your passive activity interest at a profit and have suspended losses, you may deduct a percentage of the losses each year during the installment period *(10.13)*.

10.14 Suspended Tax Credits

If you have tax credits that were barred under the passive activity rules, they may be claimed only in future years when you have tax liability attributable to passive income. However, in the year you dispose of your interest, a special election may be available to decrease your gain by the amount of your suspended credit; *see* below.

> **EXAMPLE**
>
> Dan Brown places in service rehabilitated credit property qualifying for a $50 credit, but the credit is not allowed under the passive loss rules. However, his basis is still reduced by $50. In a later year, Brown makes a taxable disposition of his entire interest in the activity and in the rehabilitation property. Assuming that no part of the suspended $50 credit has been used, Brown may elect on Form 8582-CR to increase his basis in the property by the unused $50 credit.

Basis election for suspended credits. If you qualify for an investment credit (under transition rules) or a rehabilitation credit, you are required to reduce the basis of the property even if you are unable to claim the credit because of the passive activity rules. If this occurs and you later dispose of your entire interest in the passive activity, including the property whose basis was reduced, your gain will be increased by virtue of the basis reduction although you never benefitted from the credit. To prevent this, you may reduce the taxable gain by electing to increase the pre-transfer basis of the property by the amount of the unused credit. The election is made on Form 8582-CR.

10.15 Personal Service and Closely Held Corporations

To prevent avoidance of the passive activity rules through use of corporations, the law imposes restrictions on income and loss offsets in closely held C corporations and personal service corporations.

Unless the material participation tests discussed in this section are met, the activities of a personal service corporation or a closely held corporation are considered passive activities, subject to the restrictions on loss deductions and tax credits. For purposes of these passive activity rules, a closely held C corporation is a corporation in which more than 50% in value of the stock is owned by five or fewer persons during the last half of the tax year.

A personal service corporation is a C corporation the principal activity of which is the performance of personal services by the employee-owners. Personal services in a personal service corporation are services in the fields of health, law, engineering, architecture, accounting, actuarial sciences, performing arts, or consulting. An employee-owner is any employee who on any day in the tax year owns any stock in the corporation. If an individual owns any stock in a corporation which in turn owns stock in another corporation, the individual is deemed to own a proportionate part of the stock in the other corporation. Further, more than 10% of the corporation's stock by value must be owned by owner-employees for the corporation to be a personal service corporation.

Form 8810 must be used. Personal service corporations and closely held corporations use Form 8810 to figure the amount of the passive activity loss or credit that is allowed on the corporation's tax return for the year.

Material participation. A personal service corporation or closely held corporation is treated as materially participating in an activity during a tax year only if either:

1. One or more stockholders are treated as materially participating in the activity and they directly or indirectly hold in the aggregate more than 50% of the value of the corporation's outstanding shares; or

2. The corporation is a closely held corporation and in the 12-month period ending on the last day of the tax year, the corporation had at least one full-time manager, three full-time employees, none of whom own more than 5% of the stock, and business deductions exceeded 15% of gross income from the activity.

A stockholder is treated as materially participating or significantly participating in the activity of a corporation if he or she satisfies one of the seven tests for material participation *(10.6)*. For purposes of applying the significant participation test *(Test 4* at *10.6)*, an activity of a personal service or closely held corporation will be treated as a significant participation activity for a tax year only if:

1. The corporation is not treated as materially participating in the activity for the tax year; and

2. One or more individuals, each of whom is treated as significantly participating in the activity directly or indirectly, hold in the aggregate more than 50% of the value of the outstanding stock of the corporation. Furthermore, in applying the seven participation tests, all activities of the corporation are treated as activities in which the individual holds an interest in determining whether the individual participates in an activity of the corporation; and the individual's participation in all activities other than activities of the corporation is disregarded in determining whether his or her participation in an activity of the corporation is treated as material participation under the significant participation test *(see Test 4* in *10.6)*.

Closely held corporation's computation of passive loss. Even if a closely held corporation does not meet the material participation tests above, it still qualifies for a slight break from the passive loss restrictions. On Form 8810, a closely held corporation may use passive activity deductions to offset not only passive activity gross income but also net active income. Generally, net active income is taxable income from business operations, disregarding passive activity income and expenses, and also disregarding portfolio income and expenses *(10.8)*. Passive activity losses cannot offset portfolio income.

If a corporation stops being closely held, its passive losses and credits from prior years are not allowable against portfolio income but continue to be allowable only against passive income and net active income.

Tax liability on net active income may be offset by passive activity credits.

10.16 Sales of Property and Passive Activity Interests

Gain on the sale or disposition of property is generally passive or nonpassive, depending on whether your activity is passive or nonpassive in the year of sale or disposition. Thus, gain on the sale of property used in a rental activity is generally treated as passive income, as is the gain on property used in a nonrental business if you did not materially participate in the business in the year of sale. On the other hand, gain on the sale of property is generally nonpassive if the property was used in a business that you materially participated in during the year of sale. However, exceptions described below may change this treatment.

In situations under which you transact an installment sale, treatment of gain in later years depends on your status in the year of sale. For example, if you were considered a material participant in a business, all gain is treated as nonpassive income, including gain for later installments. If you were in a rental activity or were not a material participant in a nonrental business, the gain is treated as passive income, unless the exceptions in this section apply.

Gain on substantially appreciated property formerly used in nonpassive activity. Even if an activity is passive in the year that you sell substantially appreciated property, gain on the sale is treated as nonpassive unless the property was used in a passive activity for either 20% of its holding period or the entire 24-month period ending on the date of the disposition. Property is substantially appreciated if fair market value exceeds 120% of its adjusted basis.

Property used in more than one activity in a 12-month period preceding disposition. You are required to allocate the amount realized on the disposition and the adjusted basis of the property among the activities in which the property was used during a 12-month period preceding the disposition. For purposes of this rule, the term "activity" includes personal use and holding for investment. The allocation may be based on the period for which the property is used in each activity during the 12-month period. However, if during the 12-month period the value of the property does not exceed the lesser of $10,000 or 10% of the value of all property used in the activity at the time of disposition, gain may be allocated to the predominant use.

> ### EXAMPLE
> Joe Smith sells equipment for $8,000. During the 12-month period that ended on the date of the sale, 70% of Smith's use of the equipment was in a passive activity. Immediately before the sale, the fair market value of all property used in the passive activity, including the equipment, was $200,000. The equipment was predominantly used in the passive activity during the 12-month period ending on the date of the sale. The value of the equipment, $8,000, did not exceed the lesser of $10,000 or 10% of the $200,000 value of all property used in the activity immediately before the sale. Thus, the amount realized and the adjusted basis are allocated to the passive activity.

Disposition of partnership and S corporation interests. Gain or loss from the disposition of an interest in a partnership and S corporation is generally allocated among the entity's activities in proportion to the amount that the entity would have allocated to the partner or shareholder for each of its activities if the entity had sold its interest in the activities on the "applicable valuation date" chosen by the entity, either the date of the disposition or the beginning of the entity's taxable year in which the disposition occurs.

Gain is allocated only to appreciated activities. Loss is allocated only to depreciated activities. The entity may select either the beginning of its tax year in which the holder's disposition occurs or the date of the disposition as the applicable valuation date.

Claiming suspended loss on disposition of interest in passive activity. A fully taxable sale of your entire interest or of substantially all of your interest to a nonrelated person will allow you to claim suspended loss deductions from the activity (10.13).

Dealer's sale of property similar to property sold in the ordinary course of business. IRS regulations set down complex tests that determine whether the result of the sale is treated as passive or nonpassive income or loss.

10.17 At-Risk Limits

The at-risk rules prevent investors from claiming losses in excess of their actual tax investment by barring them from including nonrecourse liabilities as part of the tax basis for their interest. Almost all ventures are subject to the at-risk limits. Real estate placed in service after 1986 is subject to the at-risk rules as well, but most real estate nonrecourse financing can qualify for an exception (10.18).

> **EXAMPLE**
>
> Crystal Parker invests cash of $1,000 in a venture and signs a nonrecourse note for $8,000. In 2023, her share of the venture's loss is $1,200. The at-risk rules limit her deduction to $1,000, the amount of her cash investment; as she is not personally liable on the note, the amount of the liability is not included as part of her basis for loss purposes.

Losses disallowed under the at-risk rules are carried over to the following year (10.21).

Form 6198. If you have amounts that are not at risk, you must file Form 6198 (At Risk Limitations), to figure your deductible loss. A separate form must be filed for each activity. However, if you have an interest in a partnership or S corporation that has more than one investment in any of the following four categories, the IRS allows you to aggregate all of the partnership or S corporation activities within each category. For example, all partnership or S corporation films and videotapes may be treated as one activity in determining amounts at risk; *see* the instructions to Form 6198.

1. Holding, producing, or distributing motion picture films or videotapes;

2. Exploring for or exploiting oil or gas properties;

3. Exploring for, or exploiting, geothermal deposits (for wells commenced on or after October 1, 1978); and

4. Farming. For this purpose, farming is defined as the cultivation of land and the raising or harvesting of any agricultural or horticultural commodity— including raising, shearing, breeding, caring for, or management of animals. Forestry and timber activities are not included, but orchards bearing fruits and nuts are within the definition of farming. Certain activities carried on within the physical boundaries of the farm may not necessarily be treated as farming.

In addition to the previous categories, the law treats as a single activity all leased depreciable business equipment (Section 1245 property) that is placed in service during any year by a partnership or S corporation.

Exempt from the at-risk rules are C corporations which meet active business tests and are not in the equipment leasing business or any business involving master sound recording, films, videotapes, or other artistic, literary, or musical property. For details on the active business tests, as well as a special at-risk exception for equipment leasing activities of closely held corporations, *see* IRS Publication 925.

The at-risk limitation applies only to tax losses produced by expense deductions that are not disallowed by reason of another provision of the law. For example, if a prepaid interest expense is deferred under the prepaid interest limitation (15.14), the interest will not be included in the loss subject to the risk limitation. When the interest accrues and becomes deductible, the expense may be considered within the at-risk provision. Similarly, if a deduction is deferred because of farming syndicate rules, that deduction will enter into the computation of the tax loss subject to the risk limitation only when it becomes deductible under the farming syndicate rules.

Effect of passive loss rules. Where a loss is also subject to the at-risk rules, you apply the at-risk rules first. If the loss is deductible under the at-risk rules, the passive activity rules then apply. On Form 6198 (At Risk Limitations), you figure the deductible loss allowed as at risk and then carry the loss over to Form 8582 to determine the passive activity loss.

 *Caution*

At-Risk Rules Limit Loss Deductions

The purpose of at-risk rules is to keep you from deducting losses from investments in which you have little cash invested and no personal liability for debts.

 *Filing Tip*

Form 6198

If you have invested an amount for which you are not at risk, such as a nonrecourse loan, you generally must file Form 6198 to figure a deductible loss. However, nonrecourse financing for real estate that secures the loan is treated as an at-risk investment in most cases (10.18).

 *Filing Tip*

Note Amount Not At Risk on Schedule E

Partners and S corporation shareholders must check a box in Part II of Schedule E to indicate if they have any amount that is not at risk.

10.18 What Is At Risk?

The following amounts are considered at risk in determining your tax position in a business or investment:

- Cash;
- Adjusted basis of property that you contribute; and
- Borrowed funds for which you are personally liable for repayment.

Personal liability alone does not assure that the borrowed funds are considered at risk. The lender generally must have no interest in the venture other than as a creditor and must not be related to a person (other than the borrower) with an interest in the activity other than that of a creditor. Under final IRS regulations, a lender or person related to the lender is considered to have an interest other than that of a creditor only if the person has a capital interest in the activity or an interest in the net profits of the activity. However, even if the lender has such an interest, a loan after May 3, 2004, for which you are personally liable is treated as at risk if: (1) the loan is secured by real estate used in the activity and (2) the loan, were it nonrecourse, would be qualified nonrecourse financing, as discussed below.

At-risk basis is figured as of the end of the year. Any loss allowed for a year reduces the at-risk amount as of the start of the next year. Therefore, if a loss exceeds your at-risk investment, the excess loss will not be deductible in later years unless you increase your at-risk investment; *see* the Example below and *10.21*.

> **EXAMPLE**
>
> Julie Kahn, an investor, pays a promoter of a book purchase plan $45,000 for a limited partnership interest. The promoter is the general partner. Kahn pays $30,000 cash and gives a note for $15,000 on which she is personally liable. Her amount at risk is $30,000; the $15,000 personal liability note is not counted because it is owed to the general partner.

Qualified nonrecourse financing for real estate considered at risk. Generally, you are not considered at risk for nonrecourse financing, that is, loans for which you are not personally liable, unless the loan is secured by property not used in the activity. However, you are considered to be at risk for qualified nonrecourse financing. This is financing from an unrelated commercial lender or government agency for which no one is personally liable and which is secured by real estate used in the activity. The debt obligation must not be convertible to an ownership interest. In determining whether the financing is secured only by real property used in the activity, you can ignore security that is property valued at less than 10% of the total value of all property securing the financing, as well as property that is incidental to the activity of holding real property. Loans from the seller or promoter do not qualify. Third-party nonrecourse debt from a related lender, other than the seller or promoter, may also be treated as at risk, providing the terms of the loan are commercially reasonable and on substantially the same terms as loans involving unrelated persons.

Pledges of other property. If you pledge personally owned real estate used outside the activity to secure a nonrecourse debt and invest the proceeds in an at-risk activity, the proceeds may be considered part of your at-risk investment. The proceeds included in basis are limited by the fair market value of the property used as collateral (determined as of the date the property is pledged as security) less any prior (or superior) claims to which the collateral is subject.

Partners. A partner is treated as at-risk to the extent that basis in the partnership is increased by the share of partnership income. That partnership income is then used to reduce the partnership's nonrecourse indebtedness will have no effect on a partner's amount at risk. If the partnership makes actual distributions of the income in the taxable year, the amount distributed reduces the partner's amount at risk. A buy-sell agreement, effective at a partner's death or retirement, is not considered for at-risk purposes.

10.19 Amounts Not At Risk

The following may not be treated as part of basis for at-risk purposes in determining your tax position in a business or investment:

- Liabilities for which you have no personal liability, but an exception applies to certain real estate financing *(10.18)*.
- Liabilities for which you have personal liability, but the lender also has a capital or profit-sharing interest in the venture; but *see* the exception in *10.18*.
- Recourse liabilities convertible to a nonrecourse basis.
- Money borrowed from a relative listed in *5.6* who has an interest in the venture, other than as a creditor, or from a partnership in which you own more than a 10% interest.
- Funds borrowed from a person whose recourse is solely your interest in the activity or property used in the activity.
- Amounts for which your economic loss is limited by a nonrecourse financing guarantee, stop-loss agreement, or other similar arrangement.
- Investments protected by insurance or loss reimbursement agreement between you and another person. If you are personally liable on a mortgage but you separately obtain insurance to compensate you for any mortgage payments, you are at risk only to the extent of the uninsured portion of the personal liability. You may, however, include as at risk any amount of premium paid from your personal assets. Taking out casualty insurance or insurance protecting you against tort liability is not considered within the at-risk provisions, and such insurance does not affect your investment basis.

 *Caution*

Lender Has Interest

Even if you are personally liable for a debt, you may not be considered at risk if the lender has an interest in the activity other than as a creditor *(10.18)*.

Limited partner's potential cash call. Under the terms of a partnership agreement, limited partners may be required to make additional capital contributions under specified circumstances. Whether such a potential cash call increases the limited partner's at-risk amount has been a matter of dispute.

In one case, the IRS and Tax Court held that a limited partner was not at risk with respect to a partnership note where, under the terms of the partnership agreement, he could be required to make additional capital contributions if the general partners did not pay off the note at maturity. The possibility of such a potential cash call was too uncertain; the partnership might earn profits to pay off the note and even if there were losses, the general partners might not demand additional contributions from the limited partners.

However, a federal appeals court reversed, holding that the limited partner was at risk because his obligation was mandatory and "economic reality" insured that the general partners would insure their rights by requiring the additional capital contribution.

In another case, limited partners relied upon the earlier favorable federal appeals court decision to argue that they were at risk where they could be required by the general partners to make additional cash contributions, but only in order to cover liabilities or expenses that could not be paid out of partnership assets. So long as the partnership was solvent, the limited partners could "elect out" of the call provision. Because of this election, the Tax Court held that the limited partners' obligation was contingent, rather than unavoidable as in the earlier federal appeals court case. Thus, the cash call provision did not increase their at-risk amount.

> **EXAMPLES**
>
> 1. Some commercial feedlots in livestock feeding operations may reimburse investors against any loss sustained on sales of the livestock above a stated dollar amount per head. Under such "stop-loss" orders, an investor is at risk only to the extent of the portion of his or her capital against which he or she is not entitled to reimbursement. Where a limited partnership makes an agreement with a limited partner that, at the partner's election, his or her partnership interest will be bought at a stated minimum dollar amount (usually less than the investor's original capital contribution), the partner is considered at risk only to the extent of his or her investment exceeding the guaranteed repurchase price.

2. A TV film promoter sold half-hour TV series programs to individual investors. Each investor gave a cash down payment and a note for which he or she was personally liable for the balance. Each investor's note, which was identical in face amount, terms, and maturity date, was payable out of the distribution proceeds from the film. Each investor also bought from the promoter the right to the unpaid balance on another investor's note. The promoter arranged the distribution of the films as a unit and was to apportion the sales proceeds equally among the investors.

   The IRS held that each investor is not at risk on the investment evidenced by the note. Upon maturity, each may receive a payment from another investor equal to the one that he or she owes.

3. A gold mine investment offered tax write-offs of four times the cash invested. For $10,000 cash, an investor bought from a foreign mining company a seven-year mineral claim lease to a gold reserve. Under the lease, he could develop and extract all of the gold in the reserve. At the same time, he agreed to spend $40,000 to develop the lease before the end of the year. To fund this commitment, the investor authorized the promoter to sell an option for $30,000 to a third party who was to buy all the gold to be extracted. The $30,000 along with the $10,000 down payment was to be used to develop the reserve. The promoter advised the investor that he could claim a $40,000 deduction for certain development costs.

   The IRS ruled that $30,000 was not deductible because the amount was not "risk capital." The investor got $30,000 by selling an option that could be exercised only if gold were found. If no gold were found, he would be under no obligation to the option holder. The investor's risk position for the $30,000 was substantially the same as if he had borrowed from the option holder on a nonrecourse basis repayable only from his interest in the activity.

   The Tax Court struck down a similar plan on different grounds. Without deciding the question of what was at risk, the court held that the option was only a right of first refusal. Thus, $30,000 was taxable income to the investor in the year of the arranged sale.

4. David Krepp, an investor, purchases cattle from a rancher for $10,000 cash and a $30,000 note payable to the rancher. Krepp is personally liable on the note. In a separate agreement, the rancher agrees to care for the cattle for 6% of Krepp's net profits from the cattle activity. Krepp is considered at risk for $10,000; he may not increase the amount at risk by the $30,000 borrowed from the rancher.

10.20 At-Risk Investment in Several Activities

If you invest in several activities, each is generally treated separately when applying the at-risk limitation on Form 6198. You generally may not aggregate basis, gains, and losses from the activities for purposes of at-risk limitations. Thus, income from one activity may not be offset by losses from another; the income from one must be reported while the losses from the other may be nondeductible because of at-risk limitations.

However, you may aggregate activities that are part of a business you actively manage. Activities of a business carried on by a partnership or S corporation qualify if 65% or more of losses for the year are allocable to persons who actively participate in management.

The law allows partnerships and S corporations to treat as a single activity all depreciable equipment (Section 1245 property) that is leased or held for lease and placed in service in any tax year. Furthermore, you may aggregate all partnership or S corporation activities within the four categories of films and videotapes, oil and gas properties, geothermal properties, and farms *(10.17)*.

10.21 Carryover of Disallowed Losses

A loss disallowed in a current year by the at-risk limitation may be carried over and deducted in the next taxable year, provided it does not fall within the at-risk limits or the passive loss limits in that year. The loss is subject to an unlimited carryover period until there is an at-risk basis to support the deduction. This may occur when additional contributions are made to the business or when there is income from the business which has not been distributed.

Gain from the disposition of property used in an at-risk activity is treated as income from the activity. In general, the reporting of gain will allow a deduction for losses disallowed in previous years to be claimed in the year of disposition.

10.22 Recapture of Losses Where At Risk Is Less Than Zero

To prevent manipulation of at-risk basis after a loss is claimed, there is a special recapture rule. If the amount at risk in an activity is reduced to below zero because of a distribution or a change in the status of a loan from recourse to nonrecourse, income may be realized to the extent of the negative at-risk amount. The taxable amount may not exceed the amount of losses previously deducted.

The recaptured amount is not treated as income from the activity for purposes of determining whether current or suspended losses are allowable. Instead, the recaptured amount is treated as a deduction allocable to that activity in the following year. *See* IRS Publication 925 for further details.

 *Filing Tip*

Carryover Losses

Losses disallowed by at-risk rules are carried over and may be deductible in a later year.

CHAPTER 11

Other Income

This chapter discusses various types of payments you may receive; some are taxable and others are not taxable. Examples of taxable items include:

- State or local tax refunds if the tax was claimed as an itemized deduction and the refunded amount provided a tax benefit *(11.5)*.
- Prizes, gambling winnings, and awards *(11.2–11.3)*.
- Cancellations of debt, but there are several exceptions, such as for debts discharged in a bankruptcy proceeding or while you are insolvent *(11.8)*.
- Your share of partnership, S corporation, trust, or estate income or loss, as reported on Schedules K-1 *(11.9–11.15)*.

Examples of nontaxable items include:

- Gifts and inheritances *(11.4)*.
- Compensatory damages for physical injury or sickness *(11.7)*.
- Life insurance proceeds *(11.18)*.
- Economic impact payment *(25.19)*.

11.1 Prizes and Awards

Prizes and awards are taxable income except for an award or prize that meets all these four tests:

1. It is primarily in recognition of religious, charitable, scientific, educational, artistic, literary, or civic achievement.

2. You were selected without any action on your part.

3. You do not have to perform services.

4. You assign the prize or award to a government unit or tax-exempt charitable organization. You must make the assignment before you use or benefit from the award. You may not claim a charitable deduction for the assignment.

Prize taxed at fair market value. A prize of merchandise is taxable at fair market value. For example, where a prize of first-class steamship tickets was exchanged for tourist-class tickets for a winner's family, the taxable value of the prize was the price of the tourist tickets. What is the taxable fair market value of an automobile won as a prize? In one case, the Tax Court held that the taxable value was what the recipient could realize on an immediate resale of the car.

Employee achievement awards. Awards from an employer are generally taxable (as part of regular pay on form W-2) but there is an exception for certain awards of tangible personal property given for length of service or safety achievement. An award in the form of cash, a gift certificate or equivalent item does not qualify for the exclusion, but other types of tangible personal property, such as a watch, or golf clubs are generally not taxable up to a limit of $1,600 for a qualified plan award or $400 for a non-qualified plan award *(3.12)*.

Olympic medals. Cash awards paid by the U.S. Olympic Committee to athletes winnings medals at the Olympic and Paralympic games are tax free, as well as the value of the medal itself (value of gold, silver or bronze content). However, the exclusion does not apply to athletes with adjusted gross income exceeding $1 million, $500,000 if married filing separately. If the exclusion applies, the nontaxable amount must still be reported as income, but an offsetting deduction is allowed *(12.2)*.

11.2 Lottery and Sweepstake Winnings

Sweepstake, lottery, and raffle winnings are reportable as gambling income on Schedule 1 (Form 1040 or 1040-SR), Line 8b. The cost of tickets is deductible only to the extent you report winnings, and only if you itemize deductions rather than claim the standard deduction. If you itemize on Schedule A (Form 1040 or 1040-SR), a deduction for the cost of tickets may be claimed as an "other" itemized deduction *(11.3, 19.1)*. For example, if you buy state lottery tickets and win a 2023 drawing, you may deduct on Schedule A the cost of your losing tickets in 2023 up to the amount of the winnings reported as income on Schedule 1.

When a minor wins a state lottery and the prize is held by his or her parents as custodians under the Uniform Transfers to Minors Act, the prize is taxed to the minor in the year the prize is won.

Installment payments. If lottery or sweepstakes winnings or casino jackpots are payable in installments, you pay tax only as installments are received. If within 60 days of winning a prize you have an option to choose a discounted lump-sum payment instead of an annuity, and you elect the annuity, you are taxed as the annuity payments are received. Merely having the cash option does not make the present value of the annuity taxable in the year the prize is won.

11.3 Gambling Winnings and Losses

Gambling winnings are taxable but losses are limited. If you are not a professional gambler, gambling winnings in 2023 must be reported as "other income" on Line 8b of Schedule 1 of Form 1040 (or 1040-SR). According to the IRS and Tax Court, you cannot reduce the winnings by your losses for the year and report only the net win (if any) as income on your tax return. Slot machine players determine if they have a win or loss at the end of a playing session; *see* below.

Court Decision

Assignment of Future Lottery Payments

Courts have agreed with the IRS that a lump sum received for assigning the rights to future state lottery payments is taxed as ordinary income, not capital gain. The right to receive annual lottery payments is not a capital asset.

Filing Tip

Winnings Paid in Installments

If you received lottery installments in 2023, these are treated as gambling winnings that you must report as "other income" on Schedule 1 (Form 1040 or 1040-SR). If you itemize deductions, you may deduct any gambling losses incurred in 2023 up to the amount of the reported installments as an "other" itemized deduction on Schedule A (Form 1040 or 1040-SR).

To deduct losses from gambling, you must itemize deductions on Schedule A (not claim the standard deduction). Even if you itemize, the losses are deductible only up to the amount of your gambling winnings. The deduction, not to exceed the gambling income reported on Schedule 1, is claimed as an "other" itemized deduction on Line 16 of Schedule A; *see 19.1*. Keep records that document your gambling losses in case your itemized deduction is questioned by the IRS.

You may not deduct a net gambling loss for the year (losses exceeding gains) even though a particular state says gambling is legal. Nor does it matter that your business is gambling. You may not deduct a net loss from wagering transactions even if you are a professional gambler *(see below)*.

Professional gamblers. According to the Supreme Court, a gambler is engaged in the business of gambling if he or she gambles full time to earn a livelihood and not merely as a hobby.

A professional gambler reports winnings and expenses (wagers and other gambling-related expenses) on Schedule C (Form 1040 or 1040-SR). However, the Tax Court and federal appeals courts have consistently held that wagers on gambling transactions are deductible only to the extent of wagering gains even if the gambling activity is a business. The statute that specifically bars a deduction of gambling losses in excess of gambling winnings trumps the general statute allowing full deductibility for ordinary and necessary business expenses.

For 2017 and earlier years, a professional's gambling-related expenses other than the cost of actual wagers were not limited to gambling winnings under a Tax Court decision that held that expenses such as transportation and lodging costs (casino gambling), tournament entry fees and gambling-related publications were fully deductible business expenses on Schedule C. However, for 2018 and later years, transportation and other gambling-related expenses are treated as "losses from wagering transactions," and thus they, together with the cost of wagers, are deductible by a professional gambler only to the extent of gambling winnings.

> **EXAMPLE**
>
> Tschetschot, a professional gambler, argued that her losses from poker tournaments should not be limited to her winnings because tournament poker, unlike traditional poker, is not "gambling" but a sports and entertainment activity like a golf or tennis tournament. Her tournaments were distinguishable from "wagering activities," she argued, because tournament players have a limited monetary stake in the form of a buy-in entrance fee, they receive the same number of chips, and the highest-place finishers receive cash prizes in predetermined amounts. The Tax Court, however, held that despite the differences between tournament play and other types of poker, the basic nature of the game remains a wagering activity, as bets are still played on each hand and each betting round has consequences. The Court also held that it is not unconstitutional to treat gambling losses differently from losses in sports tournaments, but it implied that Congress might want to reconsider the restriction on gambling losses given the increased acceptance of gambling in our society and improvements in the IRS' ability to accurately track winnings and losses.

Certain winnings reported to the IRS on Form W-2G. A payer must report a win from slot machine play or bingo of $1,200 or more (not reduced by the wager) to you and the IRS on Form W-2G. For keno the threshold is $1,500 (reduced by the wager), and for poker tournament winnings the threshold is winnings over $5,000 (reduced by the wager or buy-in). For lotteries, sweepstakes, horse racing, and other wagers, a Form W-2G is required for winnings of $600 or more that are at least 300 times the amount of the wager *(26.7)*.

If you have more than one reportable win from slot machines, bingo, or keno on the same calendar day or "gaming day," the gaming establishment may (this is optional) combine the winnings on one Form W-2G instead of reporting each win separately. A "gaming day" is the 24-hour period ending when business is slowest or the establishment closes down.

Slot machine win or loss determined on a session by session basis. The IRS and Tax Court have followed a "per session" rule for determining whether a slot machine player has realized a win or a loss. That is, whether a player has a win or loss is determined for each "session" of play at the end of that session. A session win is taxable income, which a recreational gambler must include as "other income" on Schedule 1 (Form 1040 or 1040-SR). A session loss is only deductible as an "other itemized deduction" on Schedule A (Form 1040 or 1040-SR, if you itemize rather than claim the standard deduction), and the itemized deduction for total session losses cannot exceed the total winnings and other gambling income that you report as income.

However, there has been no single standard for determining what a "session" of slot machine play is. In the absence of a specific standard, the IRS uses a facts and circumstances test to determine a session.

In 2015, the IRS proposed an optional safe harbor that taxpayers could use to define a "session of play" for purposes of calculating wins or losses from electronically tracked slot play (Notice 2015-21). If finalized, the safe harbor could help eliminate disputes with the IRS but the IRS has not finalized it so it is not in effect. Nevertheless, here are the major components of the proposed safe harbor in Notice 2015-21, which gives an indication as to the IRS' general approach:

1. A taxpayer determines gain or loss from electronically tracked slot machines at the end of each session of play, which begins when the first wager on an electronically tracked slot machine is placed and ends when the last wager on an electronically tracked slot machine is made at the same casino by the end of the same calendar day (12:00 a.m. to 11:59 p.m.).

2. The taxpayer has a gain if the payouts from a session of play exceed the amount wagered during that session. A taxpayer has a loss if the amount wagered is more than the payouts during that session.

3. The session of play does not end if the taxpayer stops and resumes play within the same gaming establishment during the calendar day. However, moving to a new gaming establishment during the same calendar day begins a new session.

Any update on the status of the safe harbor will be in the *e-Supplement* at *jklasser.com*.

11.4 Gifts and Inheritances

Gifts and inheritances you receive are not taxable. However, distributions taken from an inherited traditional IRA *(8.14, 8.15)*, and distributions from inherited qualified plan accounts such as 401(k) and profit-sharing plan accounts *(7.12)*, are taxable, except for amounts attributable to nondeductible contributions made by the deceased account owner. Income earned from gift or inherited property after you receive it is taxable.

Describing a payment as a gift or inheritance will not necessarily shield it from tax if it is, in fact, a payment for your services *(2.1)*.

A sale of an expected inheritance from a living person is taxable as ordinary income.

 *Planning Reminder*

Gifts You Make

You may have to file a gift tax return if your gifts to an individual within the year exceed the annual gift tax exclusion, which for 2023 is $17,000 *(39.2)*.

EXAMPLES

1. An employee is promised by his employer that he will be remembered in his will if he continues to work for him. The employer dies but fails to mention the employee in his will. The employee sues the estate, which settles his claim. The settlement is taxable.

2. A nephew left his uncle a bequest of $200,000. In another clause of the will, the uncle was appointed executor, and the bequest of the $200,000 was described as being made in lieu of all commissions to which he would otherwise be entitled as executor. The bequest is considered tax-free income. It was not conditioned upon the uncle performing as executor. If the will had made the bequest contingent upon the uncle's acting as executor, the $200,000 would have been taxed.

3. An attorney performed services for a friend without expectation of pay. The friend died and in his will left the attorney a bequest in appreciation for his services. The payment was considered a tax-free bequest. The amount was not bargained for.

4. A lawyer agreed to handle a client's legal affairs without charge; she promised to leave him securities. Twenty years later, under her will, the lawyer inherited the securities. The IRS taxed the bequest as pay. Both he and the client expected that he would be paid for legal services. If the client meant to make a bequest from their agreement, she should have said so in her will.

11.5   Refunds of State and Local Tax Deductions

A refund of state or local tax is not taxable if you did not previously claim the tax as an itemized deduction (Schedule A) in a prior year. For example, assume you claimed the standard deduction on your 2022 Form 1040 and when you filed your 2022 state return in 2023 you received a refund of state income tax withheld from your 2022 wages, or a refund of state estimated tax payments made in 2022. The state refund for 2022, regardless of the amount, is not taxable on your 2023 Form 1040 or 1040-SR.

Tax benefit rule. If you claimed an itemized deduction (on Schedule A) for state/local tax in a prior year, you generally must include a refund of that tax in income to the extent that the refunded amount lowered your tax in the earlier year; this is the "tax benefit" rule. The taxable part of the refund is reported on Line 1 of Schedule 1 (Form 1040 or 1040-SR). Determining the tax benefit from a deduction of state or local tax has been complicated by the SALT deduction limit, which, for 2018 through 2025, limits the total deduction for state and local taxes to $10,000 ($5,000 if married filing separately), whether state or local income tax or general sales tax, state or local real estate tax, or state or local personal property tax *(16.1)*.

The IRS in Revenue Ruling 2019-11 has clarified how to determine how much of a refund of state or local tax is taxable, and provided examples that show how to apply the long-standing tax benefit rule in light of the SALT limit; *see* the next paragraph.

Determining how much of your refund of state or local tax is taxable. If your deduction of the refunded state or local tax increased your itemized deductions, or allowed you to itemize instead of claiming the standard deduction, you received a tax benefit from your deduction. Under Revenue Ruling 2019-11, the tax benefit from the refunded amount, and thus the portion of the refund that must be included in income, is the lesser of:

1. the difference between the actual itemized deductions you claimed in the prior year and the amount of itemized deductions that would have been claimed had you paid only the "proper" amount of state or local tax (ie.your actual libility), OR

2. the difference between the actual itemized deductions you claimed in the prior year and the standard deduction you could have claimed for the prior year. This would not apply if you were precluded from taking the standard deduction, as where you were married filing separately in the prior year and your spouse claimed itemized deductions on his or her separate return.

See Examples 1–4 below, which are based upon examples in Revenue Ruling 2019-11 and illustrate the application of the tax benefit rule in various situations. Note that although Examples 1–4 involve refunds received in 2023 of state income tax deducted on the taxpayer's 2022 Form 1040 or 1040-SR, the result would be the same if the refund was for state or local general sales tax, state or local real estate tax, or state or local personal property tax that had been claimed as an itemized deduction for 2021.

If your itemized deductions for 2022 would have been less had you not deducted the refunded amount, the entire refunded amount gave you a tax benefit for 2022 by increasing your itemized deductions, so the entire refund is taxable on your 2023 return, as in Example 1. If your 2022 deduction was capped by the $10,000/$5,000 SALT limit and you would have been subject to the SALT limit even if you had not paid and deducted the refunded amount (ie. had you paid and deducted the "proper" amount), you did not receive any tax benefit from the refunded amount, so none of the refund received in 2023 is taxable; this is Example 2. The refund may be partially taxable, as in Example 3, where the refund exceeded the tax benefit received, or as in Example 4, where your itemized deductions would have been below the standard deduction without the refunded amount.

If AMT applied in year of deduction. If the refunded state tax was claimed as an itemized deduction but you were subject to the alternative minimum tax (AMT) for that year, the deduction was not allowable for AMT purposes *(23.2)*. The refund is taxable only if the deduction gave you a tax benefit in the prior year. To determine if there was a tax benefit, you must recompute regular tax liability and AMT for the prior year after increasing your income by the refunded amount. If the recomputation does not increase your total tax, there was no tax benefit and the refund is not taxable. If your total tax increases by any amount, the deduction gave you a tax benefit and the refund is taxable to the extent that the deduction reduced your tax in the prior year.

Table 11-1 2022 Standard Deduction for Non-Dependents**
(For Determining Whether Recovery in 2023 of 2022 Itemized Deductions Is Taxable on Your 2023 Form 1040 or 1040-SR; *see 11.5, 11.6*)

If on 2022 return you were—	2022 standard deduction was—
Married filing jointly	$ 25,900
Single	12,950
Head of household	19,400
Married filing separately	12,950
Qualifying widow or widower	25,900
Single age 65 or over	14,700
Single and blind	14,700
Single age 65 or over and also blind	16,450
Married filing jointly with:	
• One spouse age 65 or over	27,300
• Both spouses age 65 or over	28,700
• One spouse blind under age 65	27,300
• Both spouses blind under age 65	28,700
• One spouse age 65 or over and also blind	28,700
• One spouse age 65 or over and other spouse blind and under age 65	28,700
• One spouse age 65 or over and also blind; other spouse blind and under age 65	30,100
• Both spouses age 65 or over and also blind	31,500
Qualifying widow or widower age 65 or over	27,300
Qualifying widow or widower and blind	27,300
Qualifying widow or widower age 65 or over and also blind	28,700
Head of household age 65 or over	21,150
Head of household and blind	21,150
Head of household age 65 or over and also blind	22,900
Married filing separately age 65 or over*	14,350
Married filing separately and blind*	14,350
Married filing separately age 65 or over and also blind*	15,750

*If you filed separately from your spouse who had no income and did not file a 2022 return, and he or she could not be claimed as another taxpayer's dependent for 2022, add $1,400 if your spouse was either blind or age 65 or older; add $2,800 if he or she was both blind and age 65 or older.

**If you could be claimed as a dependent by another taxpayer for 2022 (or your spouse could if you filed jointly), your 2022 standard deduction was the larger of (1) your earned income for 2022 plus $350, or (2) $1,100, but no more than the basic $12,950, $19,400, or $25,900 standard deduction. If you were age 65 or blind, the standard deduction was increased by $1,750, or by $1,400 if you were married ($3,500 or $2,800 if both age 65 or older and blind).

EXAMPLES

Assume in all the Examples that for 2022 the taxpayer was single, under age 65, and not blind. Itemized deductions were claimed on Schedule A (Form 1040) because the itemized deductions exceeded $12,950, the allowable standard deduction for 2022; *see Table 11-1*.

1. **State income tax refund fully includible on 2023 federal return—entire refunded amount provided a tax benefit.** Taxpayer A claimed itemized deductions of $16,000 on his 2022 Form 1040, of which $5,000 was for state income taxes and $4,000 for local real estate taxes paid in 2022. The entire $9,000 of state and local tax paid in 2022 was deductible because it was under the $10,000 SALT deduction limit *(16.1)*. In 2023, A received a $1,500 refund from the state for overpaying state income tax in 2022.

   The entire $1,500 refund must be reported as income on A's 2023 federal return. If A had paid only the "proper" amount (actual liability) of state income tax in 2022, or $3,500 ($5,000 paid − $1,500 refunded), A's total itemized deductions would have been reduced by $1,500, from $16,000 to $14,500. The entire $1,500 overpayment of state income tax gave A a tax benefit by increasing 2022 itemized deductions by $1,500, so the entire $1,500 refund must be included by A as "additional income" for 2023 on Line 1, Schedule 1 (Form 1040 or 1040-SR).

2. **State income tax refund not includible at all on 2023 federal return—no tax benefit from overpayment.** Taxpayer B paid $5,000 of state income taxes and $7,000 of local real estate taxes in 2022, but only $10,000 of the $12,000 could be deducted on her 2022 Form 1040 because of the SALT deduction limit *(16.1)*. In addition, B claimed $5,000 of other itemized deductions, so total itemized deductions for 2022 were $15,000. In 2023, B received a $750 refund from the state for overpaying state income tax during 2022.

   None of the $750 refund is includible on B's 2023 Form 1040. The refunded $750 did not provide a tax benefit on B's 2022 return because even if the $750 had not been paid in 2022, B's itemized deductions for 2022 would have remained the same, at $15,000. Without the $750 overpayment, B's payments of state and local taxes would have been $11,250 instead of $12,000, and the SALT limit would have capped the deduction at $10,000, the same as what was actually claimed.

3. **Part of state income tax refund includible on 2023 federal return—refund exceeds tax benefit from overpayment.** Taxpayer C paid $6,000 of state income taxes and $5,000 of local real estate taxes in 2022, but only $10,000 of the $11,000 could be deducted because of the SALT deduction limit *(16.1)*. B also claimed $5,000 of other itemized deductions, so total itemized deductions claimed for 2022 were $15,000. In 2023, C received a $1,500 refund from the state for overpaying state income tax in 2022.

   Of the $1,500 refund, only $500 is includible on C's 2023 Form 1040. Had the $1,500 not been paid in 2022, C's state and local tax deduction would only have been reduced by $500, from $10,000 (the SALT limit) to $9,500 ($5,000 local real estate taxes plus $4,500 for state income tax, the "proper" amount of income tax liability), and total itemized deductions would also have been reduced by $500, from $15,000 to $14,500. The tax benefit received from the overpayment was $500, so $500 of the $1,500 refund is includible in C's 2023 gross income on Line 1, Schedule 1 (Form 1040 or 1040-SR). The $1,000 balance is not taxable.

4. **Part of state income tax refund includible on 2023 federal return—tax benefit from overpayment limited by standard deduction rule.** Taxpayer D paid $6,000 of state income taxes and $4,250 of local real estate taxes in 2022, but only $10,000 of the $10,250 could be deducted because of the SALT deduction limit *(16.1)*. D also claimed $3,050 of other itemized deductions, so total itemized deductions claimed for 2022 were $13,050. In 2023, D received a $1,200 refund from the state for overpaying state income tax in 2022.

   Only $500 of the $1,200 refund is includible on D's 2023 Form 1040. If D had not made the $1,200 overpayment of state income tax in 2022, the deduction for state and local taxes would have been reduced from $10,000 (the SALT deduction limit) to $9,050 ($10,250 state and local taxes actually paid − $1,200). Combining the reduced state and local tax deduction of $9,050 with the $3,050 of other itemized deductions would have given D only $12,100 in total itemized deductions, so D would have claimed the $12,950 standard deduction instead of itemizing for 2021.

   The tax benefit from the $1,200 overpayment was $500, the difference between the $13,050 of itemized deductions actually claimed for 2022 and the $12,950 standard deduction that would have been claimed had the overpayment not been made. Thus, $500 of the $1,200 refund is includible in D's 2023 gross income on Line 1, Schedule 1 (Form 1040 or 1040-SR); the other $700 is not taxable.

Refund of state tax paid in installments over two tax years. If you pay estimated state or local income taxes, your last tax installment may be in the year you receive a refund. In this case, you allocate the refund between the two years; *see* the following Example.

EXAMPLE

Your estimated state income tax for 2022 was $4,000, which you paid in four equal installments. You made your fourth payment in January 2023. No state income tax was withheld during 2022. You did not pay any other deductible state or local tax in 2022. You included the state estimated tax payments made in 2022 ($3,000) in the itemized deductions claimed on your 2022 Form 1040. In 2023, when you filed your 2022 state income tax return, you received a state income tax refund of $400.

You must allocate the $400 refund between 2022 and 2023. As you paid 75% ($3,000 ÷ $4,000) of the estimated tax in 2022, 75% of the $400 refund, or $300, is treated as a recovery of taxes paid in 2022. Use the rules discussed above ("Determining how much of your refund of state or local tax is taxable") to figure the tax benefit received for 2022 from the refunded $300; the tax benefit is reported as 2023 income on Line 1 of Schedule 1 (Form 1040 or 1040-SR).

If you itemize deductions for 2023, then in figuring your 2023 deduction for state and local taxes *(16.1)*, you reduce the $1,000 paid in January 2023 by $100 (25% of $400 refund), which is the portion of the refund attributed to your January 2023 payment of estimated state income tax. Your 2023 deduction for state income taxes will include the January net amount of $900 plus any estimated state income taxes paid in 2023 for 2023, any state income tax withheld during 2023, and any state income tax for 2022 that you paid in 2023 when you filed your 2022 state return.

11.6   Other Recovered Deductions

The rules in the preceding section *(11.5)* for determining whether a refund of state or local taxes is taxable also apply to the recovery of other items for which you claimed a tax deduction, such as a refund of adjustable rate mortgage interest *(15.1)*, reimbursement of a deducted medical expense *(17.4)*, a reimbursed casualty loss *(18.1)*, a return of donated property that was claimed as a charitable deduction *(14.1)*, and a payment of debt previously claimed as a bad debt *(5.33)*.

In determining how much of the recovered deduction gave you a tax benefit in the prior year, keep in mind the standard deduction rule *(11.5)*. The taxable portion of a recovered deduction cannot exceed the lesser of the refund or the excess of your itemized deductions for the prior year over the standard deduction that could have been claimed.

Allocating a refund recovery. If in 2023 you received a refund of state or local taxes and also a recovery of other deductions, and only part of the total recovery gave you a tax benefit in the year of the deduction, you allocate the taxable amount of the recovery according to the ratio between the state tax refund and the other recovery. You do this by first dividing the refund of state or local taxes by the total of all itemized deductions recovered. The resulting percentage is then applied to the taxable recovery to find the amount to report as the taxable state tax refund on Line 1 of Schedule 1 (Form 1040 or 1040-SR); other taxable recoveries are reported as "other income" on Line 8z of Schedule 1 (Form 1040 or 1040-SR).

Unused tax credit in prior year. If you recover an item deducted in a prior year in which tax credits exceeded your tax, you refigure the prior year tax to determine if the recovery is taxable. Add the amount of the recovery to taxable income of the prior year and refigure the earlier year tax based on the increased taxable income. If the recomputed tax, after application of the tax credits, exceeds the actual tax for the earlier year, include the recovery in income to the extent the recovery reduced your tax in the prior year. The recovery may reduce an available credit carryforward to the current year.

Alternative minimum tax in the prior year. If you were subject to the alternative minimum tax (AMT) in the year the recovered deduction was claimed, recompute your regular and AMT tax for the prior year based on the taxable income you reported plus the recovered amount. If inclusion of the recovery does not change your total tax, you do not include

Filing Instruction

Negative Taxable Income

If your taxable income was a negative amount in the year in which the recovered item was deducted, you reduce the recovery includible in income by the negative amount. For example, if the taxable recovery would be $1,700 but you had a negative taxable income of $500 for the year the deduction was claimed, only $1,200 is taxable.

the recovery in income. If your total tax increases by any amount, the recovered deduction gave you a tax benefit and you must include the recovery in income to the extent the deduction reduced your tax in the prior year. The recovery may reduce a carryforward of a tax credit based on prior year AMT.

11.7 How Legal Damages Are Taxed

By statute, compensatory damages for personal physical injury or physical sickness are tax free, whether fixed by a court or in a negotiated settlement. Damages for nonphysical personal injuries, such as for discrimination, back pay, or injury to reputation, are taxable; a limited exception for certain emotional distress damages may be available as discussed below. Damages for lost profits, breach of contract, or interference with business operations are taxable.

These are the general rules, but damages that would otherwise be taxable can be tax free if received as part of a judgment or settlement relating to a physical injury or sickness. The law excludes from income compensatory damages received "on account of" physical injuries or sickness, so if this "account of" test is met, all compensatory damages are tax free, including amounts for lost wages or emotional distress *(see below)*. Interest added to an award is taxable, even if the award is tax-free damages for physical injury or sickness.

Emotional distress. The law that provides an exclusion for damages received on account of a physical illness or sickness specifically provides that emotional distress by itself is not treated as a physical injury or sickness. To be tax free, damages for emotional distress must be attributable to a physical injury or sickness. For example, if you are injured in an accident and receive damages for emotional distress, or damages for emotional distress are included in the damages received in a wrongful death action, the emotional distress damages are tax free because they are deemed to be received "on account of" a physical injury; *see* Example 1 below.

If emotional distress damages are due to an injury other than a physical injury or sickness, as in a discrimination action, the damages are taxable with one exception: Damages up to the amount of actual medical care expenses attributable to emotional distress are tax free. That is, if you can prove actual expenditures for medical care to deal with emotional distress, that portion of the damages is tax free.

Apart from the medical expenses exception, damages for emotional distress are taxable when received for a personal injury other than a physical injury or sickness. Keep in mind that emotional distress, including its physical symptoms, is not treated as a physical injury or sickness, and so in an action for wrongful termination of employment or discrimination, emotional distress damages are taxable, even where the damages cover physical symptoms of emotional distress such as insomnia, headaches, and stomach disorders, although no tax would be due on actual medical costs incurred to deal with those physical symptoms. The Tax Court has held that depression falls within the category of emotional distress; *see* Example 2 below.

The National Taxpayer Advocate has argued that it is confusing and unfair to allow tax-free treatment for emotional distress damages that are attributable to physical injury or sickness while imposing tax on emotional distress damages for non-physical injuries such as employer discrimination. She has urged Congress to change the law and allow tax-free treatment for all awards for emotional distress, mental anguish, and pain and suffering.

Damages for wrongful termination. If damages are received from a former employer for wrongful termination, the damages are usually taxable as compensation, but any amount for a workplace-related physical injury or illness are excludable from income. Unless the terms of a settlement or verdict specifically allocate damages to a physical illness or injury, it may be difficult to show that you are entitled to the exclusion. But the Tax Court was convinced in the following case.

Domeny was working as a fund-raiser for nonprofit organizations when she was diagnosed with multiple sclerosis (MS) in 1996. She managed her symptoms without medication but in 2000 she took a job with an autism center where she could spend less time on her feet. The position involved fund-raising, grant writing and community

Caution

Deducting Legal Fees

You may not deduct legal fees incurred in obtaining tax-free damages for physical injury or physical sickness. If you recover taxable damages, you may be able to deduct legal fees, as discussed in this section *(11.7)*.

development. Domeny had a strained relationship with her supervisor, who restricted her duties. The stress caused her MS symptoms to flare up. In November 2004 she discovered that her supervisor was embezzling funds and she reported this to the center's board of directors, who promised her that they would take action but did not. She felt uncomfortable about having to raise funds from parents while knowing that her supervisor was embezzling funds. This situation continued for months, during which time her distress increased and her MS symptoms intensified. In March 2005, she went to her physician, complaining of vertigo, leg pain, numbness in both feet, burning behind her eyes and extreme fatigue. Her physician told her to stay home from work for two weeks but when Domeny notified the center, she was fired.

Domeny sued the center, alleging numerous discrimination and civil rights violations. The center agreed to settle and paid her a total of $33,308 of which $8,187.50 was treated as Form W-2 wages and $8,187.50 as attorney fees. The $16,933 balance was reported on Form 1099-MISC as nonemployee compensation. Domeny did not include the $16,933 on her 2005 return on the grounds that it was to compensate her for the worsening of her physical condition caused by working in a hostile work environment, and the fact that her condition prevented her from returning to work until more than a year after her termination.

The Tax Court agreed that the $16,933 payment was excludable from Domeny's income. Even though the settlement agreement did not specify why the payment was made, the inference was clear that the center was recognizing Domeny's complaint that a hostile and stressful work environment aggravated her physical illness. The fact that the settlement was segregated into three portions suggested that the center knew that part of the settlement was to compensate for physical illness. The center knew about Domeny's illness before her termination, and her only claim was that she was fired after her work environment had caused the flareup in her MS symptoms.

Punitive damages. Punitive damages are taxable, even if they relate to a physical injury or sickness. An exception in the law allows an exclusion from income for punitive damages awarded under a state wrongful death statute if the punitive damages are the only damages that may be awarded.

Restitution for wrongful incarceration. Wrongfully incarcerated individuals may exclude from income any civil damages, restitution, or other monetary awards received in connection with the incarceration. There is no cap on the exclusion. The IRS has a set of frequently asked questions and answers on the exclusion and refund claim rules at https://www.irs.gov/individuals/wrongful-incarceration-faqs.

Holocaust restitution payments. There is a broad exclusion from gross income for Holocaust restitution payments. Tax-free treatment applies to payments received by persons persecuted by Nazi Germany or any Nazi-controlled or allied country, as well as to payments received by heirs or estates of such persecuted persons. Persecution on the basis of race, religion, physical or mental disability, or sexual orientation is covered.

Excludable restitution includes compensation for assets that were stolen or lost before, during, or immediately after World War II and to life insurance issued by European insurers immediately before and during the war. Tax-free treatment also applies to interest earned on escrow accounts and funds established in settlement of Holocaust victim claims against European banks or corporations.

Legal fees. If your damages are tax free, you may not deduct your litigation costs. If your damages are taxable, including the contingency fee portion of a taxable recovery *(see below)* you may be able to deduct your legal fees. A business expense deduction may be claimed on Schedule C for legal fees to recover taxable business income. An above-the-line deduction (claimed directly from gross income) is allowed on Line 24h of Schedule 1 (Form 1040 or 1040-SR) for legal fees in employment discrimination suits, certain other unlawful discrimination cases, and federal False Claims Act cases paid in connection with a court judgment or settlement after October 22, 2004. The deduction cannot exceed the amount of the judgment or settlement you are including in income for the year *(12.2)*. On Line 24i of Schedule 1, an above-the-line deduction is allowed for attorney fees and court costs you paid in connection with receiving a whistleblower's award from the IRS, up to the amount of the award included in income.

EXAMPLES

1. A wrongful death recovery clearly is attributable to a physical injury. The IRS in several private rulings held that where a claim for intentional infliction of emotional distress is part of a wrongful death action, any recovery of compensatory damages is excludable from gross income. In these rulings, the estates of individuals killed in an accident initially brought claims for wrongful death and intentional infliction of emotional distress and a court awarded compensatory damages, prejudgment interest and punitive damages. The exact nature of the accident was not disclosed in the rulings, but it was apparently severe enough that local legislators passed a law to provide compensation to claimants for all their wrongful death and physical injury claims, including emotional distress. The law voided all prior court proceedings. The original defendant paid into a government fund from which damages to the claimants were paid.

   The IRS ruled that all recoveries of compensatory damages from the government fund were for wrongful death, including amounts for emotional distress, and thus excludable as being received on account of a personal physical injury. The only exception is for amounts equal to medical expenses incurred to treat emotional distress that were previously deducted in prior years. Any damages reimbursing the previously deducted expenses are taxable.

2. The Tax Court has held that depression and physical symptoms of depression are a form of emotional distress. In one case, a taxpayer received a settlement after she was fired and brought a wrongful termination case against her former employer. She had suffered from depression, and her symptoms got worse after she lost her job, including insomnia and sleeping too much, migraines, nausea, vomiting, weight gain, acne and pain in her back, shoulder, and neck. In the Tax Court, the taxpayer argued that the exacerbation of her depression symptoms as a result of her termination was a physical injury or sickness, and so her damages should not be taxed. The Tax Court disagreed, reiterating prior holdings that depression falls within the category of emotional distress, which by itself is not considered a physical injury or sickness for which the exclusion from income is allowed.

   The Court rejected the taxpayer's claim that her depression symptoms should be treated like the multiple sclerosis symptoms in the Domeny case discussed in the next paragraph. Unlike in Domeny, the taxpayer here was not determined to be too ill to work by a physician and she did not show that the physical symptoms of her depression were severe enough to rise to the level of a physical disorder.

If you pay legal fees to recover taxable damages and the fees are not eligible for the above-the-line deduction or allowed as a Schedule C deduction, there is no way to deduct them under current law. For years before 2018, a taxpayer who itemized deductions could include the legal fee as a miscellaneous itemized deductions on Schedule A subject to the 2% of adjusted gross income floor, this miscellaneous itemized deduction is suspended for 2018 through 2025 *(19.2)*.

Attorney's contingent fee paid from taxable award. If you receive taxable damages, such as back pay in an employment dispute, and a percentage goes directly to your attorney under a contingent fee agreement, can you exclude from your income the contingent fee payment, so that you are only taxed on the net amount you receive?

The answer from the Supreme Court is no. The Supreme Court held in its 2005 *Banks* decision that the contingency-fee portion of a taxable damages award or settlement generally must be included in the litigant's gross income. The Court's decision did not resolve whether attorney fees paid pursuant to a statutory fee-shifting provision must be included in income, but it suggested that such statutory fees might in some cases be excludable. However, a subsequent Tax Court decision held that the attorney-fee portion of a taxable settlement was includible in the litigant's income where attorney fees were awarded under a California fee-shifting statute. Since the Supreme Court had not decided that issue, the Tax Court relied on its own prior decisions and precedent of the Ninth Circuit (where appeal would lie), which required inclusion of the fee portion of a settlement where a contingency-fee obligation was satisfied by a fee-shifting statute.

Note: If the contingency-fee portion of a taxable award in an unlawful employment discrimination case must be included in gross income under the Supreme Court decision, you may be able to offset the inclusion of the fees by an above-the-line deduction, as discussed above.

11.8 Cancellation of Debts You Owe

If a debt is canceled or forgiven other than as a gift or a bequest, a debtor who is personally liable on the loan (recourse debt) generally must include the canceled amount in gross income. Exclusions are allowed for discharges of qualified principal residence indebtedness, farm or business real estate debt and debts of insolvent and bankrupt persons.

Details on the various exclusions are provided below. If you qualify for one of the exclusions, you generally must reduce certain "tax attributes" (such as the basis of property) by the amount excluded. The reduction of tax attributes is made on Form 982.

Form 1099-C. You should receive Form 1099-C from a federal government agency, credit union, or bank that cancels or forgives a debt you owe of $600 or more. The IRS receives a copy of the form. Generally, the amount of canceled debt shown in Box 2 of Form 1099-C must be reported as "other income" on Line 8c of Schedule 1 (Form 1040 or 1040-SR), unless one of the exclusions discussed below applies.

Exclusion for discharges of qualified principal residence indebtedness. If you have qualified principal residence indebtedness that is discharged as part of a mortgage restructuring or foreclosure, some or all of the discharge may be excludable from income. An exclusion is allowed for discharges up to $750,000 ($375,000 if married filing separately). The $750,000/375,000 exclusion limit is a cumulative limit for all discharges in 2021 through 2025 of qualified principal residence indebtedness. The exclusion is scheduled to expire at the end of 2025 (except for discharges entered into in writing before 2026).

Qualified principal residence indebtedness is debt incurred in acquiring, constructing, or substantially improving your principal residence and which is secured by the residence. A refinancing of such debt also qualifies to the extent of the refinanced amount. If only part of the debt prior to discharge was qualified debt, the exclusion applies only to the extent the discharged debt exceeds the non-qualified amount. For example, assume the total debt securing the principal residence is $1 million, of which $800,000 is qualified debt and $200,000 is not. In 2023, the house is sold for $700,000 and $300,000 of the debt is discharged. The exclusion is limited to $100,000, the excess of $300,000 (debt discharge) over $200,000 (non-qualified debt prior to discharge).

Mortgage loan "workouts" and repayment discounts. If your lender agrees to a "workout" that restructures your loan and reduces the principal balance of your debt, or you are allowed a discount for paying off your loan early, the debt reduction or discount is generally considered cancellation of debt income if you retain the collateral (31.10). If it is considered a cancellation of debt, report it as "other income" on Line 8c of Schedule 1 (Form 1040 or 1040-SR) unless you can exclude the debt from income under the exclusion for qualified principal residence indebtedness or one of the other exclusions. As noted below, some states treat a loan used to buy a principal residence as nonrecourse debt, and in that case, any forgiveness of the loan does not give rise to cancellation of debt income.

Foreclosure, repossession, or voluntary conveyance. If a lender forecloses on a loan secured by your property (such as your home mortgage) or repossesses the property secured by the loan (such as your car), or you voluntarily convey the property to the lender, the transaction is treated as a sale on which you realize gain or loss, as explained in 31.9.

Apart from the gain or loss on the deemed sale, if you are personally liable on the loan (recourse debt) and the amount of the debt canceled by the lender exceeds the fair market value of the property, you have cancellation of debt income that must be reported as ordinary income unless one of the exclusions discussed below applies. The lender will report fair market value of the property in Box 7 Form 1099-C.

State law may treat home mortgage debt as nonrecourse. Some states have "anti-deficiency" statutes that treat a loan used to purchase a principal residence as a "nonrecourse" loan. In these states, a lender has no recourse against a homeowner for a deficiency judgment following a foreclosure or lender-approved short sale. Where a mortgage debt subject to one of these state laws is forgiven, the taxpayer does not realize cancellation of debt income, as the income rule applies only to the cancellation of recourse debts for which there is personal liability.

Caution

Cancellation of Credit Card Debt

If debt on your personal (non-business) credit card was canceled, you must report the canceled amount as income unless you were insolvent immediately before the cancellation or the cancellation occurred in a Title 11 bankruptcy case.

Court Decision

Credit Card Insurance Payments Taxable

Insurance can be purchased to cover a portion of credit card debt in the event you become unemployed or disabled, or you die. The Tax Court held that insurance payments of an unemployed credit card holder's debt were a taxable cancellation of debt to the extent the payments exceeded the premiums paid.

Cancellation of student loans. The American Rescue Plan Act allows an exclusion from income for most cancellations of student loans from 2021 through 2025. The exclusion applies to the discharge of (1) any loan for post-secondary educational expenses made, insured or guaranteed by the federal, state or local government, or by a higher educational institution, (2) qualifying private education loans, (3) loans from tax-exempt education organizations that were made under an agreement with a government or higher educational institution, or under a program designed to encourage students to serve in occupations or areas with unmet needs, and (4) refinancings of loans from tax-exempt education organizations under programs designed to recipients. The exclusions under (2)–(4) do not apply if the loan discharge is made because of services provided to the private lender or educational lender.

Debts canceled in bankruptcy. Debt canceled in a Title 11 bankruptcy case is not included in your gross income if the cancellation is granted by the court or under a plan approved by the court. Instead, certain losses, credits, and basis of property must be reduced by the amount excluded from income. These losses, credits, and basis of property are called "tax attributes." The amount of canceled debt is used to reduce the tax attributes in the order listed below:

1. Net operating losses and carryovers—dollar for dollar of debt discharge;
2. Carryovers of the general business credit—33⅓ cents for each dollar of debt discharge;
3. AMT minimum tax credit as of the beginning of the year immediately after the taxable year of the discharge—33⅓ cents for each dollar of debt discharge;
4. Net capital losses and carryovers—dollar for dollar of debt discharge;
5. Basis of depreciable and nondepreciable assets—dollar for dollar of debt discharge (but not below the amount of your total undischarged liabilities). Basis of property held at the beginning of the year is reduced in a specific order and within each category, in proportion to adjusted basis. *See* Publication 4681 for details.
6. Passive activity loss and credit carryovers—dollar for dollar of debt discharge for passive losses; 33⅓ cents for each dollar of debt discharge in the case of passive credits; and
7. Foreign tax credit carryovers—33⅓ cents for each dollar of debt discharge.

After these reductions, any remaining balance of the debt discharge is disregarded. On Line 5 of Form 982, you may make a special election to first reduce the basis of any depreciable assets before reducing other tax attributes in the order above. Realty held for sale to customers may be treated as depreciable assets for purposes of the election. The election allows you to preserve your current deductions, such as a net operating loss carryover or capital loss carryover, for use in the following year. The election also will have the effect of reducing your depreciation deductions for years following the year of debt cancellation. If you later sell the depreciable property at a gain, the gain attributable to the basis reduction will be taxable as ordinary income under the depreciation recapture rules *(44.1)*.

Debts discharged while you are insolvent. If your debt is canceled outside of bankruptcy while you are insolvent, the cancellation does not result in taxable income to the extent of the insolvency. Insolvency means that liabilities exceed the fair market value of your assets immediately before the discharge of the debt. IRS Publication 4681 has a worksheet you can use to determine whether you were insolvent immediately before the debt discharge and the extent of the insolvency. The IRS and Tax Court hold that in determining whether liabilities exceed the value of assets at the time of a debt discharge, a taxpayer must include assets that are shielded from creditors under state law. This is true even though for federal bankruptcy purposes creditor-exempt assets do not have to be counted in determining whether an individual seeking bankruptcy protection is insolvent.

If liabilities do exceed the value of assets, the discharged debt is not taxed to the extent of your insolvency and is applied to the reduction of tax attributes on Form 982 in the same manner as to a bankrupt individual. If the canceled debt exceeds the insolvency, any remaining balance is treated as if it were a debt cancellation of a solvent person and, thus, it is taxable unless another exclusion is available as discussed in this section. *See* the Example below for the IRS approach to figuring insolvency upon a debt cancellation.

Paycheck Protection Program loans. Forgiveness of these loans to owners of pass-through entities and self-employed individuals is not taxable.

Partnership debts. When a partnership's debt is discharged because of bankruptcy, insolvency, or if it is qualified farm debt or business real estate debt that is canceled, the discharged amount is allocated among the partners. Bankruptcy or insolvency is tested not at the partnership level, but separately for each partner. Thus, a bankrupt or insolvent partner applies the allocated amount to reduce the specified tax attributes as previously discussed. A solvent partner may not take advantage of the rules applied to insolvent or bankrupt partners, even if the partnership is insolvent or bankrupt.

S corporation debts. The tax consequences of a debt discharge are determined at the corporate level. A debt discharge that is excludable from the S corporation's income because of insolvency or bankruptcy does not pass through to the shareholders and thus does not increase the shareholders' basis.

Purchase price adjustment for solvent debtors. If you buy property on credit and the seller reduces or cancels the debt arising out of the purchase, the reduction is generally treated as a purchase price adjustment (reducing your basis in the property). Since the reduction is not treated as a debt cancellation, you do not realize taxable income on the price adjustment. This favorable price adjustment rule applies only if you are solvent and not in bankruptcy, you have not transferred the property to a third party, and the seller has not transferred the debt to a third party, such as with the sale of your installment contract to a collection company.

Qualified farm debt. A solvent farmer may avoid tax from a discharge of indebtedness by an unrelated lender, including any federal, state, or local government agency, if the debt was incurred in operating a farm business. This relief is available only if 50% or more of your total gross receipts for the preceding three taxable years was derived from farming. The excluded amount first reduces tax attributes such as net operating loss carryovers and business tax credits, next reduces basis in all property other than farmland, and then reduces the basis in land used in the farming business. *See* IRS Publication 4681 for details.

Filing Instruction

Price Adjustments Not Taxed

If you bought property on credit and the seller cancels or reduces your purchase-related debt, this is a price adjustment, not a taxable cancellation of debt.

> ### EXAMPLE
>
> In 2018, Jones borrowed $1,000,000 from Chester and signed a note payable for that amount. Jones was not personally liable on the note, which was secured by an office building valued at $1,000,000 that he bought from Baker with the proceeds of Chester's loan. In 2023, when the value of the building declined to $800,000, Chester agreed to reduce the principal of the loan to $825,000. At the time, Jones held other assets valued at $100,000 and owed another person $50,000.
>
> To determine the extent of Jones's insolvency, the IRS compares the value of Jones's assets and liabilities immediately before the discharge. According to the IRS, his assets total $900,000: the building valued at $800,000 plus other assets of $100,000. His liabilities total $1,025,000: the other debt of $50,000 plus the liability on the note, which the IRS considered to be $975,000, equal to the $800,000 value of the building and the discharged debt of $175,000. Jones is insolvent by $125,000 ($1,025,000 in liabilities less $900,000 in assets). As $175,000 was the amount of the discharged debt and Jones was insolvent to the extent of $125,000, only $50,000 is treated as taxable income in 2023.
>
> Jones claims the insolvency exception on Form 982 by checking the box on Line 1b and entering the excludable $125,000 on Line 2. In Part II of Form 982, Jones must reduce his "tax attributes," as discussed above under the bankruptcy rules. The $50,000 debt cancellation that is not excludable under the insolvency rule must be reported as "other" income on Line 8c of Schedule 1 (Form 1040 or 1040-SR).

Business real estate debt. A solvent taxpayer may elect on Form 982 to avoid tax on a discharge of qualifying real property business debt. Such a discharge may occur where the fair market value of the property securing the debt has fallen in value. The debt must have been incurred or assumed in connection with business real property and must be secured by such property. A debt incurred or assumed after 1992 must be incurred or assumed to buy, construct, or substantially improve real property used in a business, or to refinance such acquisition debt (up to the refinanced amount). Debt incurred after 1992 to refinance a pre-1993 business real property debt (up to the refinanced amount) also qualifies. The debt must be secured by the property. Discharges of farm indebtedness do not qualify but may be tax free under the separate rules discussed earlier.

The maximum amount that can be excluded from income is the excess of the outstanding loan principal (immediately before the discharge) over the fair market value (immediately before the discharge) of the real property securing the debt, less any other outstanding qualifying real property business debts secured by the property. The excludable amount also may not exceed the taxpayer's adjusted basis for all depreciable real property held before the discharge. On Form 982, you reduce your basis in all your depreciable real property by the excluded amount.

Effect of basis reduction on later disposition of property. A reduction of basis is treated as a depreciation deduction so that a profitable sale of the property at a later date may be subject to the rules of recapture of depreciation *(44.1)*.

11.9 Schedule K-1

Although partnerships, S corporations, trusts, and estates are different types of tax entities, they share a common tax-reporting characteristic. The entity itself generally does not pay income taxes (with some exceptions). As a partner, shareholder, or beneficiary, you report your share of the entity's income or loss. The entity files a Schedule K-1 with the IRS that indicates your share of the income, deductions, and credits passed through from the entity. You will receive a copy of the Schedule K-1, which you should keep for your records; it does not have to be attached to your tax return.

To ensure that Schedule K-1 income is being reported, IRS computers match the information shown on the schedules with the tax returns of partners, S corporation shareholders, and beneficiaries.

If the entity has foreign activities, you also receive a copy of Schedule K-3. The reporting rules for Schedule K-1 in *11.10*, *11.13*, and *11.15* apply to Schedule K-3.

11.10 How Partners Report Partnership Profit and Loss

A partnership files Form 1065, which informs the IRS of partnership profit or loss and each partner's share on Schedule K-1. The partnership pays no tax on partnership income; each partner reports his or her share of partnership net profit or loss and special deductions and credits, whether or not distributions are received from the partnership, as shown on Schedule K-1. Income that is not distributed or withdrawn increases the basis of a partner's partnership interest.

Your share reported to you on Schedule K-1 (Form 1065) is generally based on your proportionate capital interest in the partnership, unless the partnership agreement provides for another allocation.

Your partnership must give you a copy of Schedule K-1 (Form 1065), which lists your share of income, loss, deduction, and credit items, and where to report them on your return. For example, your share of income or loss from a business or real estate activity is reported on Schedule E and is subject to passive activity adjustments, if any. Interest and dividends are reported on Schedule B, royalties on Schedule E, and capital gains and losses on Schedule D. Your share of charitable donations is claimed on Schedule A if you itemize deductions. Tax preference items for alternative minimum tax purposes are also listed.

Health insurance premiums. A partnership that pays premiums for health insurance for partners has a choice. It may treat the premium as a reduction in distributions to the partners. Alternatively, it may deduct the premium as an expense and charge each partner's share as a guaranteed salary payment taxable to the partner. The partner reports the guaranteed payment shown on Schedule K-1 as nonpassive income on Schedule E and may deduct 100% of the premium as an adjustment to income (above-the-line deduction) on Line 17 of Schedule 1 (Form 1040 or 1040-SR) *(12.2)*.

Filing Tip

Schedule K-3 for Foreign Activities

If a partnership or S corporation (not a trust or estate) engages in certain foreign activities, the entity must issue Schedule K-3 to owners. The reporting rules applicable to Schedule K-1 apply to Schedule K-3.

Filing Instruction

Partnership Elections

The partnership, not the individual partners, makes elections affecting the computation of partnership income such as the election to defer involuntary conversion gains, to amortize organization and start-up costs, and to choose depreciation methods, including first-year expensing. An election to claim a foreign tax credit is made by the partners.

Guaranteed salary and interest. A guaranteed salary that is fixed without regard to partnership income is taxable as ordinary wages and not as partnership earnings. If you receive a percentage of the partnership income with a stipulated minimum payment, the guaranteed payment is the amount by which the minimum guarantee exceeds your share of the partnership income before taking into account the minimum guarantee. Interest on capital is reported as interest income.

Self-employment tax. As a general partner, you pay self-employment tax on your net partnership income, including guaranteed salary and other guaranteed payments. The self-employment tax is explained in *Chapter 45*. Limited partners do not pay self-employment tax, unless guaranteed payments are received *(45.2)*.

Special allocations. Partners may agree to special allocations of gain, income, loss, deductions, or credits disproportionate to their capital contributions. The allocation should have a substantial economic effect to avoid an IRS disallowance. The IRS will not issue an advance ruling on whether an allocation has a substantial economic effect. If the allocation is rejected, a partner's share is determined by his or her partnership interest.

To have substantial economic effect, a special allocation must be reflected by adjustments to the partners' capital accounts; liquidation proceeds must be distributed in accordance with the partners' capital accounts, and following a liquidating distribution, the partners must be liable to the partnership to restore any deficit in their capital.

If there is a change of partnership interests during the year, items are allocated to a partner for that part of the year he or she is a member of the partnership. Thus, a partner who acquires an interest late in the year is barred from deducting partnership expenses incurred prior to his entry into the partnership. If the partners agree to give an incoming partner a disproportionate share of partnership losses for the period after he or she becomes a member, the allocation must meet the substantial economic effect test to avoid IRS disallowance.

See IRS regulations to Code Section 704 and Form 1065 instructions for further details.

Reporting transfers of interest to IRS. If you transfer a partnership interest that includes an interest in partnership receivables and appreciated inventory, you must report the disposition to the partnership within 30 days, or, if earlier, by January 15 of the calendar year after the year of the transfer. The partnership in turn files a report with the IRS on Form 8308. You must also attach a statement to your income tax return describing the transaction and allocating basis to the receivables and inventory items. The IRS wants to keep track of such dispositions because partners have to pay ordinary income tax on the portion of profit attributable to the receivables and inventory.

Within 30 days of your transfer, provide the partnership with a statement that includes the date of the exchange and identifies the transferee (include Social Security number if known). You can be penalized for failure to notify the partnership. You and your transferee should receive a copy of the Form 8308 that the partnership will send to the IRS along with its Form 1065.

11.11 When a Partner Reports Income or Loss

You report your share of the partnership gain or loss for the partnership year that ends in your tax reporting year. If you and the partnership are on a calendar-year basis, you report your share of the 2023 partnership income on your 2023 income tax return. If the partnership is on a fiscal year ending March 31, for example, and you report on a calendar year, you report on your 2023 return your share of the partnership income for the whole fiscal year ending March 31, 2023—that is, partnership income for the fiscal year April 1, 2022, through March 31, 2023.

If a Section 444 election of a fiscal year is made on Form 8716, a special tax payment must be computed for each fiscal year and if the computed payment exceeds $500, it must be paid to the IRS. The tax payment is figured and reported on Form 8752. The tax does not apply to the first tax year of a partnership's existence but Form 8752 must still be filed. In later years, a refund of prior payments is available to the extent the prior payments exceed the payment required for the current fiscal year. For example, if the required payment was $12,000 for the fiscal year July 1, 2022–June 30, 2023, and the

Law Alert

Qualified Business Income (QBI) Deduction for Partnership Income

If you receive income from a partnership, you may be eligible for a deduction of up to 20% of qualified business income (QBI); *see 40.24*. If the partnership is on a fiscal year, you take into account all items for the fiscal year ending in 2023; an allocation for the portion of the fiscal year beginning January 1, 2023, is not required.

required payment for the fiscal year starting July 1, 2023 is $10,000, a $2,000 refund may be claimed on Form 8752. Refunds of prior year payments also are available if the fiscal-year election is terminated and a calendar year adopted or if the partnership liquidates.

11.12 Partnership Loss Limitations

Your share of partnership losses may not exceed the adjusted basis of your partnership interest. If the loss exceeds basis, the excess loss may not be deducted until you have partnership earnings to cover the loss or contribute capital to cover the loss. The basis of your partnership interest is generally the amount paid for the interest (either through contribution or purchase) less withdrawals plus accumulated taxed earnings that have not been withdrawn. You also have a basis in loans to the partnership for which you are personally liable.

A partner's basis is not increased by accrued but unpaid expenses such as interest costs and accounts payable unless the partnership uses the accrual accounting method. However, basis is increased by capitalized items allocable to future periods such as organization and construction period expenses.

Partners are subject to the "at-risk" loss limitation rules. These rules limit the amount of loss that may be deducted to the amount each partner personally has at stake in the partnership, such as contributions of property and loans for which the partner is personally liable. *See* the discussion of the "at-risk" rules in *Chapter 10 (10.17)*. Furthermore, if the IRS determines that a tax-shelter partnership is not operated to make a profit, deductions may be disallowed even where there is an "at-risk" investment. Finally, any loss not barred by these limitations may be disallowed under the passive activity rules discussed in *Chapter 10*.

11.13 Tax Audits of Partnerships

For audits of partnership returns for tax years beginning after December 31, 2017, the Bipartisan Budget Act of 2015 (BBA) provides a "centralized audit system" that allows the IRS to audit partnerships at the partnership level. Any adjustments to the partnership return are handled at the partnership level, unless the partnership opts to "push out" a deficiency to its partners (certain notices are required and revised Schedule K-1s will be issued for this purpose). Partnerships with up to 100 "eligible partners" may elect out of the BBA rules (T.D. 9829, 2018-4 IRB 307).

Under the BBA, the partnership must annually name a partnership representative on the partnership return. The representative has the sole power to bind the partnership in an audit. IRS regulations specify who is eligible to serve as the partnership representative and provide rules on the timing and mechanics for designating, appointing, and changing a partnership representative (T.D. 9839, 2018-35 IRB 325).

The BBA replaces the prior-law rules, commonly referred to as the TEFRA audit rules, under which audits (for tax years beginning before 2018) were conducted at the partnership level for partnerships with over 10 partners but any additional tax resulting from the partnership-level audit was assessed and collected against the individual partners. The 10-partner TEFRA exception applied if all the partners were individuals (but not nonresident aliens), estates of deceased partners, or C corporations. A husband and wife (and their estates) were treated as one partner.

11.14 Stockholder Reporting of S Corporation Income or Loss

S corporations are subject to tax reporting rules similar to those applied to partnerships. However, shareholders who work for the corporation are treated as employees for payroll tax purposes. The IRS and the courts require that S corporation shareholders receive reasonable compensation on which Social Security and Medicare taxes (FICA) must be paid. Self-employment tax does not apply to a shareholder's salary or similar receipts from the S corporation.

Your company must give you a copy of Schedule K-1 (Form 1120-S), which lists your share of income or loss, deductions, and credits that must be reported on your return. It also includes information needed to figure the qualified business income (QBI) deduction, which is a personal deduction of up to 20% of QBI.

Filing Tip

Child of S Corporation Owner Treated Like Owner

If an S corporation provides health coverage to a child who is an employee who's parent is a more-than-2% owner, the child is treated the same as the parent. This means the amount of group health plan premiums for the child are included in his or her income on Form W-2; the child can claim the self-employed health insurance deduction (*see* IRS Memorandum 201912001).

Your share of business income or loss is reported on Schedule E and is subject to passive activity adjustments, if any. Interest and dividends from other corporations are reported on Schedule B, capital gains and losses on Schedule D, Section 1231 gains or losses on Form 4797, and charitable donations on Schedule A. Tax preference items for alternative minimum tax purposes are also listed.

Health insurance premiums paid by an S corporation for more-than-2% stockholders are treated as wages, deductible on Form 1120-S by the corporation and reported to the stockholder on Form W-2. A more-than-2% shareholder who reports premiums as wages may deduct the premiums as an adjustment to income (above-the-line deduction) on Line 17 of Schedule 1 (Form 1040 or 1040-SR) *(12.2)*.

Allocation to shareholders. The following items are allocated to and pass through to the shareholders based on the proportion of stock held in the corporation:

- Gains and losses from the sale and exchange of capital assets and Section 1231 property, as well as interest and dividends on corporate investments and losses. Investment interest expenses subject to the rules discussed in *Chapter 15 (15.10)* also pass through.

- Tax-exempt interest. Tax-exempt interest remains tax free in the hands of the stockholders but increases the basis of their stock. Dividends from other companies may qualify for the exclusion.

- First-year expense deduction (Section 179 deduction).

- Charitable contributions made by the corporation.

- Foreign income or loss.

- Foreign taxes paid by the corporation. Each stockholder elects whether to claim these as a credit or deduction.

- Tax preference items.

- Recovery of bad debts and prior taxes.

If your interest changed during the year, your pro rata share must reflect the time you held the stock.

Passive activity rules limit loss deductions. Losses allocated to you may be disallowed under the passive activity rules discussed in *Chapter 10*.

Basis adjustments. Because of the nature of S corporation reporting, the basis of each shareholder's stock is subject to change. Basis is increased by the pass-through of income items and by loans to the S corporation for which the shareholder is personally liable. Basis is reduced by the pass-through of loss items and the receipt of certain distributions. Because income and loss items pass through to stockholders, an S corporation has no current earnings and profits. An income item will not increase basis, unless you actually report the amount on your tax return.

EXAMPLES

1. A calendar-year corporation incurs a loss of $10,000. Smith and Jones each own 50% of the stock. On May 1, Smith sells all of his stock to Harris. For the year, Smith was a shareholder for 120 days, Jones for 365 days, and Harris for 245 days. The loss is allocated on a daily basis; the daily basis of the loss is $27.3973 ($10,000 divided by 365 days). The allocation is as follows:

   Smith: $1,644 ($27.3973 × 120 days × 50% interest)
   Jones: $5,000 ($27.3973 × 365 days × 50% interest)
   Harris: $3,356 ($27.3973 × 245 days × 50% interest)

2. Same facts as in Example 1, except that on May 1, Smith sells only 50% of his stock to Harris. The allocation for Smith accounts for his 50% interest for 120 days and his 25% interest for the remainder of the year.

   Smith: $3,322 ($27.3973 × 120 days × 50% plus $27.3973 × 245 days × 25%)
   Jones: $5,000 (as above)
   Harris: $1,678 ($27.3973 × 245 days × 25%)

Schedule K-3 for Foreign Activities

If an S corporation engages in certain foreign activities, the entity must issue Schedule K-3 to owners. The reporting rules applicable to Schedule K-1 apply to Schedule K-3.

Qualified Business Income (QBI) Deduction for S Corporation Shareholders

You may be eligible for the qualified business income (QBI) deduction for your share of items from the S corporation. See *(40.24)*.

Basis Limits Loss Deductions

Deductible losses may not exceed your basis in S corporation stock and loans to the corporation. If losses exceed basis, the excess loss is carried over and becomes deductible when you invest or lend an equivalent amount of money to the corporation. This rule may allow for timing a loss deduction. In a year in which you want to deduct the loss, you may contribute capital or make an additional loan to the corporation. If a carryover loss exists when an S election terminates, a limited loss deduction may be allowed.

Form 7203 (S Corporation Shareholder Stock and Debt Basis Limitations) has replaced the worksheet that previously was in the shareholder's instructions for Schedule K-1 (Form 1120-S) to figure a shareholder's basis in stock and debt. Use Form 7203 and its instructions to figure any limitations on the share of the S corporation's deductions, credits, and other items that can be deducted on your return.

11.15 How Beneficiaries Report Estate or Trust Income

Trust or estate income is treated as if you had received the income directly from the original source instead of from the estate or trust. This means your share of the trust's capital gain income remains capital gain to you, ordinary income is fully taxed, and tax-exempt income remains tax free. Tax preference items of a trust or estate are apportioned between the estate or trust and beneficiaries, according to allocation of income.

Your share of the trust or estate income, deductions and credits is reported to you (and the IRS) by the fiduciary on Schedule K-1 of Form 1041. You do not file Schedule K-1 with your return; keep it for your records. The instructions to Schedule K-1 indicate the schedules on which to report the trust or estate items. For example, you report capital gains from Schedule K-1 on Schedule D, along with your other capital gains. You report Schedule K-1 income or loss from real estate or business activities) on Schedule E, subject to the passive activity restrictions discussed in *Chapter 10*.

Excess deductions passed through by estates and non-grantor trusts. If an estate or non-grantor trust has deductions exceeding its income, the excess deductions are passed through to the beneficiaries. In response to the Tax Cuts and Jobs Act provision that bars individuals from claiming miscellaneous itemized deductions subject to the 2% of adjusted gross income floor from 2018 through 2025, the IRS released proposed regulations that require executors and trustees to tell beneficiaries how to treat the passed through deductions. Specifically, executors and trustees must state whether the passed through deductions are adjustments to gross income (above-the-line deductions) *(12.2)*, miscellaneous itemized deductions subject to the 2% floor (not deductible for 2018 through 2025) or "other" itemized deductions not subject to the 2% floor (allowable itemized deduction on Schedule A). The tax character of the deduction is determined at the estate or trust level and preserved when passed through to beneficiaries.

Reporting rule for revocable grantor trusts. A grantor who sets up a revocable trust or keeps certain powers over trust income or corpus must report all of the trust income, deductions, and credits. This rule applies if a grantor retains a reversionary interest in the trust that is valued at more than 5% of the trust (valued at the time the trust is set up) *(39.6)*. If a grantor is also a trustee of a revocable trust and all the trust assets are in the United States, filing Form 1041 is not necessary. The grantor simply reports the trust income, deductions, and credits on his or her Form 1040 or 1040-SR. *See* the Form 1041 instructions for reporting requirements.

11.16 Reporting Income in Respect of a Decedent (IRD)

If you receive income that was earned by but not paid to a decedent before death, such as wages, IRA and qualified plan distributions, accrued savings bond interest, lottery prize winnings, or installment sale proceeds, you are said to have "income in respect of a decedent," or IRD. You report the IRD on your return. Where the purchaser of a deferred annuity contract dies before the annuity starting date, payments to a beneficiary in excess of the purchaser's investment are IRD that the beneficiary must report as income, whether payable in a lump sum or as periodic payments.

If the decedent's estate paid federal estate tax that was attributable to the IRD you received, you may claim an itemized deduction for the estate tax paid on that income *(11.17)*.

11.17 Deduction for Estate Tax Attributable to IRD

A beneficiary who receives income in respect of a decedent (IRD) on which federal estate tax was paid can claim an itemized deduction for the amount of the allocable federal estate tax. The deduction is allowed to the IRD recipient only for the year in which the recipient

Law Alert

Qualified Business Income (QBI) Deduction for Beneficiaries

You may be eligible for the qualified business income (QBI) deduction for your share of items from a trust or estate. *See 40.24*.

Filing Instruction

Consistent Reporting by Beneficiaries

Beneficiaries of trusts and estates must report items consistently with the Schedule K-1 provided by the trust or estate. If an item is treated inconsistently and a statement identifying the inconsistency is not attached to the beneficiary's return, the IRS may make a summary assessment for additional tax without issuing a deficiency notice.

reports the IRD income, assuming the beneficiary claims itemized deductions (and not the standard deduction) for that year. No deduction is allowed for state death taxes paid on IRD. If you receive IRD, ask the executor of the decedent's estate for the amount of federal estate tax paid and the portion of the estate that the IRD represented to help you compute the deduction. The deduction is claimed as an "other itemized deduction" on Schedule A (Form 1040 or 1040-SR).

However, if the IRD you receive is long-term capital gain, such as an installment payment on a sale transacted before a decedent's death, the estate tax attributed to the capital gain item is not claimed as an itemized deduction. The deductible amount is treated as if it were an expense of sale and, thus, reduces the amount of gain, but not below zero.

> **EXAMPLE**
>
> When Jim Bennett died, he was owed a fee of $10,000. He also had not collected accrued bond interest of $5,000. Ed Bennett, Jim's nephew and the sole heir, will collect both items and pay income tax on them. These items are called "income in respect of a decedent." Assume that Jim left a substantial taxable estate and that estate tax of $6,000 was paid on the $15,000 *(39.9)*. Ed collects the $10,000 fee, which he reports on his income tax return. If Ed itemizes deductions, he may deduct $4,000, computed as follows:
>
> $$\frac{\$10,000}{\$15,000} \times \$6,000 = \$4,000$$
>
> When Ed collects the $5,000, he may deduct the balance, or $2,000 ($6,000 − $4,000), if he itemizes deductions for that year.

11.18 How Life Insurance Proceeds Are Taxed to a Beneficiary

Life insurance proceeds received upon the death of the insured are generally tax free. However, in some cases, life insurance proceeds may be includible in a decedent's taxable estate, and if the taxable estate is substantial enough to be subject to estate tax, the beneficiary may actually receive a reduced amount *(39.8)*. Interest paid on proceeds left with the insurer is taxable.

Read the following cases to find how your insurance receipts are taxed.

A lump-sum payment of the full face value of a life insurance policy: The proceeds are generally tax free. The tax-free exclusion also covers death benefit payments made under endowment contracts, workers' compensation insurance contracts, employers' group insurance plans, or accident and health insurance contracts.

Insurance proceeds may be taxable where the policy was transferred for valuable consideration. Exceptions to this rule are made for transfers among partners and corporations and their stockholders and officers.

Installment payments spread over your life under a policy that could have been paid in a lump sum: Part of each installment attributed to interest may be taxed. Divide the face amount of the policy by the number of years the installments are to be paid. The result is the amount that is received tax free each year.

If the policy guarantees payments to a secondary beneficiary if you should die before receiving a specified number of payments, the tax-free amount is reduced by the present value of the secondary beneficiary's interest in the policy. The insurance company can give you this figure.

Installment payments for a fixed number of years under a policy that could have been paid in a lump sum. Divide the full face amount of the policy by the number of years you are to receive the installments. The result is the amount that is received tax free each year.

> **EXAMPLE**
>
> Korinna is the beneficiary of her husband's $100,000 life insurance policy. She elects to take installment payments for 10 years. Each year she may receive tax-free principal of $10,000 ($100,000 ÷ 10).

 *Planning Reminder*

Accelerated Death Benefits

A person who is terminally ill may withdraw without tax life insurance proceeds to pay medical bills and other living expenses. For policies lacking an accelerated benefits clause, a terminally ill individual may sell a life insurance policy to a viatical settlement company without incurring tax *(17.16)*.

Installment payments when there is no lump-sum option in the policy. You must find the discounted value of the policy at the date of the insured's death and use that as the principal amount. The insurance company can give you that figure. After you find the discounted value, you divide it by the number of years you are to receive installments. The result is the amount that is tax free. The remainder is taxed.

> **EXAMPLE**
>
> Ena is the beneficiary of her husband's life insurance policy. She is entitled to $10,000 a year for life. Her life expectancy is 20 years. There is no lump sum stated in the policy. Say the discounted value of the wife's rights is $120,000. The principal amount spread to each year for the wife is $6,000 ($120,000 ÷ 20). Subtracting $6,000 from each annual $10,000 payment gives her taxable income of $4,000.

Payments to you along with other beneficiaries under the same policy, by lump-sum or varying installments. *See* the following Example for the way multiple beneficiaries may be taxed.

> **EXAMPLE**
>
> The beneficiaries of an insured's life insurance policy are his surviving wife, daughter, and nephew. The wife is entitled to a lump sum of $120,000. The daughter and nephew are each entitled to a lump sum of $70,000. Under the installment options, the wife chooses to receive $10,000 a year for the rest of her life. (She has a 20-year life expectancy.) The daughter and the nephew each choose a yearly payment of $10,000 for 10 years. This is how each yearly installment is taxed:
>
> Wife: The principal amount spread to each year is $6,000 ($120,000 ÷ 20-year life expectancy). Subtracting $6,000 from the yearly $10,000 payment gives the wife taxable income of $4,000.
>
> Daughter and Nephew: For both of them, the principal amount spread to each of the 10 years is $7,000 ($70,000 ÷ 10-year installment period). Subtracting this $7,000 from the yearly $10,000 installment gives the daughter and the nephew taxable income of $3,000 each.

11.19 A Policy with a Family Income Rider

Payments received under a family income rider are taxed under a special rule. A family income rider provides additional term insurance coverage for a fixed number of years from the date of the basic policy. Under the terms of a rider, if the insured dies at any time during the term period, the beneficiary receives monthly payments during the balance of the term period, and then at the end of the term period, receives the lump-sum proceeds of the basic policy. If the insured dies after the end of the term period, the beneficiary receives only the lump sum from the basic policy.

When the insured dies during the term period, part of each monthly payment received during the term period includes interest on the lump-sum proceeds of the basic policy (which is held by the company until the end of the term period). That interest is fully taxed. The balance of the monthly payment consists of an installment (principal plus interest) of the proceeds from the term insurance purchased under the family income rider. You may exclude from this balance a prorated portion of the present value of the lump sum under the basic policy. The lump sum under the basic policy is tax free when you eventually receive it.

The rules here also apply to an integrated family income policy and to family maintenance policies, whether integrated or with an attached rider.

In figuring your taxable portions, ask the insurance company for its interest rate and the present value of term payments.

11.20 Selling or Surrendering Life Insurance Policy

Surrendering or selling a life insurance policy can result in ordinary income, long-term gain, or a combination of both, or in a loss, depending on the type of policy and type of

 *Caution*

Surrender of Policy for Cash

If the cash received on the surrender of a policy exceeds the premiums paid less dividends received, the excess is taxed as ordinary income (not capital gain). If you take, instead, a paid-up policy, you may avoid tax *(6.12)*. You get no deduction if there is a loss on the surrender of a policy.

Tax may be avoided by a terminally ill individual on the surrender of a policy under an accelerated death benefit clause or on a sale of the policy to a viatical settlement company *(17.16)*.

transaction. The IRS has issued rulings that explain the tax consequences of surrendering or selling a whole life or term insurance contract; *see* Situations 1-4 below.

Situation 1 — insured policyholder surrenders whole life insurance contract (Revenue Ruling 2009-13).

On January 1 of Year 1, Tom Taxpayer bought a whole life insurance policy on his life, with the proceeds payable to a family member. Tom retained the right to change the beneficiary, take out a policy loan, or surrender the contract for its cash surrender value.

After 89½ months, on June 15 of Year 8, Tom surrenders the contract for its cash surrender value of $78,000. As of the surrender date, Tom had paid total premiums of $64,000, $10,000 of which was the cost of the insurance protection received as of that date. The $78,000 cash surrender value reflected the subtraction of the $10,000 insurance cost.

On the surrender, Tom recognizes income of $14,000, the $78,000 received minus the total premiums paid of $64,000.

The Tax Code does not specify whether income recognized upon the surrender of a life insurance contract, as opposed to a sale, is treated as ordinary income or as capital gain. However, relying on a 1964 ruling (Revenue Ruling 64-51), the IRS holds that the proceeds received by an insured upon the surrender of a life insurance policy constitute ordinary income to the extent such proceeds exceed the cost of the policy. Thus here the $14,000 of income recognized on the surrender of the insurance contract is ordinary income and not capital gain.

Situation 2 — insured policyholder sells whole life insurance contract to investor (Revenue Ruling 2020-05).

Same facts as in Situation 1 except that on June 15 of Year 8, Tom sold the contract for $80,000 to Jones, an unrelated person (an investor). To figure gain on the sale, Tom must reduce the $80,000 amount realized by his adjusted basis in the insurance contract. Under the Tax Cuts and Jobs Act (amending Section 1016(a) of the Code), basis is not reduced by the cost of insurance. Thus Tom's basis is the $64,000 of total premiums he paid as of the date of sale (with no reduction for the $10,000 cost of insurance) and his gain on the sale of the contract is $16,000 ($80,000 proceeds minus $64,000 basis).

Part of Tom's $16,000 gain is ordinary income and part is capital gain. The Supreme Court has held that under the "substitute for ordinary income" doctrine, income that has been earned but not yet recognized by a taxpayer cannot be converted into capital gain by a sale or exchange. In the case of a sale of a life insurance policy, the portion of the gain that would have been ordinary income if the policy had been surrendered (i.e., the inside buildup under the contract) is ordinary income. However, any income over that amount can qualify for capital gain treatment.

Here, $14,000 of the $16,000 gain is ordinary income representing the inside buildup under the contract ($78,000 cash surrender value minus $64,000 total premiums paid). The remaining $2,000 of income is long-term capital gain.

Situation 3 — insured policyholder sells term life insurance contract to investor (Revenue Ruling 2020-05).

Assume that Tom had entered into a 15-year level premium term life insurance contract with no cash surrender value, rather than the whole life contract in Situation 2 above. Monthly premiums were $500 and total premiums paid were $45,000 when Tom sold the policy after 89.5 months to Jones, an unrelated party (an investor) for $20,000.

In this case, as in Situation 2, the adjusted basis of the contract for purposes of determining gain or loss on the sale is the total premiums paid before the sale. Therefore, Tom's adjusted basis is $45,000 (total premiums). On the sale, Tom has a $25,000 loss ($20,000 sale proceeds minus $45,000 adjusted basis). The loss is a nondeductible personal loss, assuming the insurance contract was not an investment or business asset for Tom.

Situation 4 — investor who buys term life insurance contract from insured policyholder sells the contract to another investor (Revenue Ruling 2020-05).

After buying Tom's term-life contract in Situation 3, Jones pays $9,000 in premiums and more than one year after buying the contract from Tom, Jones sells the contract to Smith, an investor unrelated to either Jones or to Tom, for $30,000.

On the sale, Jones has a $1,000 long-term capital gain. Jones' adjusted basis is $29,000, equal to the $20,000 he paid for the contract from Tom, plus $9,000, the premiums he paid. Thus, on the sale to Smith, the long-term capital gain is $1,000, the $30,000 sales price minus the $29,000 adjusted basis.

11.21 Jury Duty Fees

Fees that you receive for serving on a jury must be reported as "other income" on Line 8h of Schedule 1 (Form 1040 or 1040-SR).

If you are an employee and are required to turn over the jury duty fees to your employer because you continue to receive your regular salary while serving on the jury, you can offset the "other income" with a deduction. The deduction is claimed as an adjustment to income (above-the-line deduction) on Line 24a of Schedule 1 (Form 1040 or 1040-SR).

11.22 Foster Care Payments

You may generally exclude from gross income payments received from a state or local government or a certified placement agency for providing foster care services in your home. However, payments are taxable to the extent they are received for the care of more than five individuals age 19 or older.

In one case, taxpayers who owned two homes were denied the exclusion for payments they received under a state program on the grounds that the home where they provided the foster care services to disabled adults was not "their home." The Tax Court held that a taxpayer's home for purposes of the exclusion is where the taxpayer resides and experiences the routines of private life such as sharing meals, time, and holidays with family. The taxpayers worked in the home where they provided the services but they did not "live" there and so the exclusion was not allowed.

Exclusion for difficulty-of-care payments. The exclusion also generally applies to difficulty-of-care payments, which are designated by a state as extra compensation for providing additional care required by handicapped foster individuals in your home. However, difficulty-of-care payments must be reported as income to the extent they are for more than 10 qualified foster individuals under age 19, or more than 5 qualified foster individuals age 19 or older.

Exclusion for difficulty-of-care payments applies to qualified Medicaid waiver payments. States provide payments to care givers as additional compensation for providing nonmedical support services to a handicapped Medicaid recipient in the care giver's home. Such payments are considered "Medicaid waiver payments." The IRS allows care providers to exclude Medicaid waiver payments as difficulty-of care payments even if the provider is related to the care recipient (Notice 2014-7). In several letter rulings, the IRS concluded that Notice 2014-7 allows states to treat payments made to individual care providers under in-home supportive care programs as excludable difficulty-of-care payments. Thus, the state did not have to report the payments to the care providers as wages subject to tax.

11.23 Virtual Currency

The IRS treats virtual currency, also referred to as digital currency or cryptocurrency, as property for federal tax purposes. All other tax rules for virtual currency flow from this "property" characterization. Holding virtual currency for investment results in capital gain or loss when you sell it or use it as payment for purchases. The gain or loss may be long or short term, depending upon how long you hold the virtual currency. Accepting virtual currency in the ordinary course of business generally results in ordinary income. Receiving virtual currency as payment for services generally results in reportable wage income.

Basic structure of virtual currency. Although virtual currencies are not issued or backed by the U.S. government or any other government or central bank, their conversion into sovereign currency, particularly U.S. dollars, is a key feature of most digital currencies now on the marketplace. The IRS defines "convertible virtual currency" as virtual currency that has an equivalent value in real currency, or that acts as a substitute for real currency. Bitcoin is an example of a convertible virtual currency.

 *Planning Reminder*

IRA Contributions Based on Difficulty-of-Care Payments

Even though difficulty-of-care payments are not taxable wages, they may be the basis for contributing to an IRA *(8.2)*.

Virtual currencies do not provide for a physical token to count and hold. Rather, exchanges usually provide custodial accounts to hold an investor's funds and track them on an internal ledger to permit trading and exchanges. All transactions are written into the blockchain. An investor has a record of their virtual currency amounts and trades in a "wallet," in which a private key is stored to sign transactions. Each digital wallet contains encrypted information, called public and private keys, that is used to send and receive the digital currency.

Virtually currency itself is created by "miners" who use complex algorithms and computing power to create "tokens." The resources put into this mining is in large part what gives each coin its initial value. "Miners" are considered wage earners or manufacturers, and as such are taxed on the initial value of their mined coins as earning ordinary income.

How virtual currency is taxed.
The IRS applies the general principles governing property transactions to determine the taxation of transactions using convertible virtual currency. This property treatment applies to investment use of virtual currency and use in sales or exchanges, as well as estate and gift tax transfers.

Gain or loss.
If you exchange virtual currency for other property, you have a taxable gain or loss:

- Gain, if the fair market value of the property received in exchange for the virtual currency exceeds your adjusted basis of the virtual currency; and
- Loss, if the fair market value of the property received is less than the adjusted basis of the virtual currency.

Capital or ordinary gain or loss?
The character of your gain or loss – whether capital or ordinary—on the exchange of virtual currency generally depends on whether you held the virtual currency as a capital asset. If held as an investment, you realize a capital gain or loss. If held as inventory or property held mainly for sale to customers in a trade or business, your gain or loss is taxed as ordinary income or loss.

A sale or other disposition of virtual currency that is a capital asset through a sale, exchange or transfer is reported on Form 8949. The net amount of capital gain or loss is then reported on Schedule D (Form 1040 or Form 1040-SR).

If you receive virtual currency as payment for your goods or services, you must include, in computing gross income, the fair market value of the virtual currency, measured in U.S. dollars, as of the date the virtual currency was received.

- Virtual currency received by an independent contractor is self-employment income and is subject to self-employment tax. You pay self-employment tax on Schedule SE (Form 1040 or Form 1040-SR). The payor from whom you receive the virtual currency reports the value of that payment on Form 1099-NEC if it is $600 or more for the year.
- Your basis in the virtual currency received in a goods-or-services transaction is the fair market value of the virtual currency, in U.S. dollars, on the date of receipt.
- If you pay for goods or services with virtual currency you are deemed to have liquidated your position in the virtual currency on the date of payment. As a result, capital gain or loss is computed based upon the value of the virtual currency when acquired and its value when transferred. Again, you must report capital gains on Form 1040, Schedule D.

Hard or soft forks.
In the course of owning virtual currency, a hard or soft fork may occur. A hard fork in which your virtual currency undergoes a protocol change does not result in taxable income as long as no new cryptocurrency is distributed, whether through an "airdrop" or other type of transfer. If you do receive new cryptocurrency in a hard fork, you report as original income an amount equal to the fair market value of the new cryptocurrency. On the other hand, a soft fork, which takes place when a distributed ledger only undergoes a protocol change, does not result in a diversion of the ledger and, therefore, will not result in any income or other reportable transaction for tax purposes.

Filing Tip

Capital Losses

Losses on cryptocurrency held for investment are treated as capital losses, which can offset capital gains and then up to $3,000 in ordinary income. Any excess losses are carried forward (*5.4*).

Form 1040's virtual currency question. There is a virtual currency question on page 1 of Form 1040 or 1040-SR: "At any time during 2023, did you: (a) receive (as a reward, award, or payment for property or services); or (b) sell, exchange, gift, or otherwise dispose of a digital asset (or a financial interest in a digital asset)? (See instructions.)" You must answer the question by checking yes or no; do not leave this blank.

- A "No" is the appropriate answer if you merely owned virtual currency at any time during the tax year but did not engage in any transactions involving virtual currency during the year, or your activities were limited to holding or transferring virtual currency in your wallet or purchasing virtual currency using real currency.
- A "Yes" is appropriate in a wide variety of circumstances. You must respond "Yes" if during the past year you received virtual currency as payment or in exchange for property, goods or services, from mining, in a transfer not qualifying as a bona fide gift, as the result of a hard fork, in exchange for another virtual currency, from the sale of virtual currency, or from any other disposition of a financial interest in virtual currency.

Information reporting. Virtual currency is subject to information reporting at a minimum to the same extent as would be triggered by a cash payment. As a result, a person who in the course of their trade or business makes a payment of fixed and determinable income using virtual currency with a value of $600 or more to a U.S. non-exempt recipient in a taxable year is required to report the payment to the IRS and to the payee. Examples of these payments include rent, salaries, wages, premium annuities, and compensation, reported on Form W-2 or Form 1099, as applicable.

Law Alert

New law adds to information-reporting requirements

The Infrastructure Investment and Jobs Act requires information reporting to the IRS with respect to virtual currency and other digital assets under broker-to-broker rules for transactions beginning in 2023 (and reported in 2024). In addition, businesses must report payments in digital assets over $10,000.

Claiming Deductions

In this part, you'll learn how you may be able to reduce your tax liability by claiming deductions directly from gross income, and whether you should use the standard or itemized deductions. Your tax liability may be lowered by—

- "Above-the-line" deductions, or adjusted gross income (AGI) deductions that is, amounts deducted directly from gross income in arriving at adjusted gross income. For AGI, deductions are allowed even if you claim the standard deduction. *See Chapter 12.*

- The standard deduction or itemized deductions, or from AGI, deductions reduce AGI to taxable income. For most taxpayers, increases to the standard deduction and the cutback or elimination of previously allowed itemized deductions means the standard deduction *(Chapter 13)* is more advantageous than itemizing. However, read the chapters on itemized deductions *(Chapters 14–20)* to verify you have not overlooked itemized deductions for charitable donations, interest expenses, state and local taxes, medical expenses, casualty and theft losses from a federally declared disaster, and miscellaneous expenses. Each itemized deduction is subject to specific restrictions and limitations.

- The qualified business income (QBI) deduction *(40.24)*.

- Other deductions are discussed in the following chapters:
  Chapter 40 Business expenses
  Chapter 9 Rental expenses
  Chapter 43 Automobile expenses

CHAPTER 12

Deductions Allowed in Figuring Adjusted Gross Income

Adjusted Gross Income ("AGI") is the amount used in figuring the 7.5% adjusted gross income floor for medical expense deductions *(17.1)*, the 10% floor for personal casualty and theft losses from a federally declared disaster *(18.8)*, and the charitable contribution percentage limitations *(14.17)*.

AGI generally determines the thresholds for the phaseouts of the child tax credit, the credit for other dependents, and the child and dependent care credit *(Chapter 25)*.

If you follow the instructions and order of the tax return, you will arrive at adjusted gross income automatically. However, if you are planning the tax consequences of a transaction in advance of preparing your return, *see* the explanation of how to figure adjusted gross income (AGI) *(12.1)*.

For AGI, deductions are allowed regardless of whether you take the standard deduction or itemize your deductions on Schedule A (Form 1040 or 1040-SR). If the state in which you reside computes tax based on Federal AGI, the state tax may be reduced by taking advantage of "above-the-line" deductions. This chapter will explain the deductions which qualify for the direct deduction from gross income.

12.1 Determining Adjusted Gross Income (AGI)

Adjusted gross income is the difference between gross income in Step 1 and the deductions listed in Step 2. The items listed in Step 2 are called "For AGI" deductions or "above-the-line" deductions because the AGI tends to be the line item used to determine the limitations for certain other deductions and credits.

Step 1. Figure gross income. Gross income is all income received by you from any source, such as wages, salary, tips, gross business income, income from sales and exchanges of property, interest and dividends, rents, royalties, annuities, pensions, etc. Gross income does not include those items specifically excluded by law such as tax-free interest from state or local bonds *(4.24)*, tax-free parsonage allowance *(3.13)*, tax-free insurance proceeds *(11.18–11.20)*, gifts and inheritances *(11.4)*, certain home sale gains *(29.1)*, Social Security benefits below the threshold for being taxed *(34.3)*, Supplemental Security Income (SSI) *(21.5, 34.2)*, tax-free scholarship grants *(33.1)*, tax-free meals and lodging *(3.13)*, and other tax-free fringe benefits *(Chapter 3)*.

Step 2. Deduct from your 2023 gross income the following items as applicable:

- Repayment of supplemental unemployment benefits required because of receipt of trade readjustment allowances *(2.9)*
- Forfeiture-of-interest penalties because of premature withdrawals *(4.16)*
- Capital loss deduction up to $3,000 *(5.4)*
- Traditional IRA contributions *(8.4)*
- Rent and royalty expenses *(9.2)*
- Educator expenses *(12.2)*
- 50% of self-employment tax liability *(12.2)*
- Health savings account (HSA) contributions *(12.2)*
- Health insurance premiums if self-employed or treated as such *(12.2)*
- Jury duty pay turned over to your employer *(12.2)*
- Performing artist's qualifying expenses *(12.2)*
- Reforestation expenses *(12.2)*
- Reservists' travel costs *(12.2)*
- State and local official expenses *(12.2)*
- Moving expenses for certain military personnel *(12.3)*
- Student loan interest *(33.6)*
- Alimony payments under a divorce decree or agreement entered into before 2019 *(37.1)*
- Business expenses *(40.7)*
- Net operating losses *(40.19)*
- Self-employed retirement plan contributions for yourself *(41.5)*
- Archer MSA contributions *(41.13)*

Step 3. The difference between Steps 1 and 2 is adjusted gross income.

12.2 Claiming Deductions from Gross Income

Many deductions taken directly from gross income in arriving at adjusted gross income are first claimed on Form 1040 or 1040-SR schedules devoted to a specific activity, and then the net gain or loss amount for that activity is entered on Form 1040 or 1040-SR. This includes business deductions claimed on Schedule C *(Chapter 40)*, capital losses claimed on Schedule D *(Chapter 5)*, and real estate rental expenses claimed on Schedule E *(Chapter 9)*.

Adjustments to income (above-the-line deductions). Various expenses are claimed as "adjustments to income" on Schedule 1 (Form 1040 or 1040-SR), and then entered on Form 1040 or 1040-SR as a reduction to gross income. These adjustments are sometimes referred to as "above the line" or "For AGI" deductions and they reduce gross (total) income whether you claim the standard deduction or you itemize on Schedule A. Here are the adjustments to income (above-the-line deductions) that may be available on your 2023 tax return:

Educator expenses. If you were a teacher, instructor, counselor, principal, or aide in a private or public elementary or secondary school (kindergarten through grade 12) for at least 900 hours during the school year in 2023, you may deduct up to $300 of qualifying costs on Line 11 of Schedule 1 (Form 1040 or 1040-SR). Qualified costs include (1) books, classroom supplies, computer equipment (including related software and services), and other materials used in the classroom, (2) professional development courses related to the curriculum you teach, and (3) items that protect against the spread of COVID-19 in the classroom, such as masks, hand sanitizer, and gloves. For courses in health or physical education, supplies must be related to athletics to qualify. Home schooling expenses do not qualify.

If you are married filing jointly and you and your spouse both qualify as educators, each of you may deduct up to $300 of your respective qualified costs, for a $600 maximum on your joint return. The limit is $300 of expenses per spouse, so if you have $600 of qualified expenses and your spouse has $150, the maximum deduction on your joint return is $450 ($300 + $150).

If eligible expenses exceed the $300 limit, the excess is not deductible even if you itemize deductions, as job expenses are not deductible in 2018 through 2025 under the Tax Cuts and Jobs Act *(19.2)*.

The $300 deduction limit may have to be reduced or eliminated completely if certain tax-free amounts are received during the year. The deduction is reduced by tax-free interest on savings bonds used for tuition *(33.4)*, as well as by tax-free distributions from qualified tuition programs *(33.5)*, and Coverdell education savings accounts *(33.12)*.

For 2024, the deduction limit may be raised above $300 by an inflation adjustment; *see* the *e-Supplement* at *jklasser.com*.

Overnight travel costs of Reservists and National Guard members. If you are an Armed Forces Reservist or National Guard member who traveled over 100 miles and stay overnight to attend Reserve and Guard meetings, you may deduct unreimbursed travel expenses as an above-the-line-deduction to the extent of the Federal Government per diem rate for that locality (for lodging, meals, and incidental expenses), plus any parking fees, tolls, and ferry fees. Qualifying expenses are reported on Form 2106 and the deductible amount is entered on Line 12 of Schedule 1 (Form 1040 or 1040-SR).

Expenses of performing artists. If you are a performing artist, you may be able to deduct job expenses from gross income, depending on your income. To qualify, you must have:

1. Two or more employers during the year in the performing arts with at least $200 of earnings from at least two of them.
2. Expenses from acting or other services in the performing arts that exceed 10% of gross income from such work; and
3. Adjusted gross income (before deducting these expenses) that does not exceed $16,000.

If you are married, a joint return must be filed to claim the deduction, unless you lived apart from your spouse during the whole year. The $16,000 adjusted gross income limitation (AGI) applies to your combined incomes. If both spouses are performing artists, the $16,000 adjusted income limit applies to the combined incomes, but each spouse must separately meet the two-employer test and 10% expense test for his or her job expenses to be deductible on the joint return.

The $16,000 AGI limit has been in the law since 1986. If you qualify, you report the performing artist expenses on Form 2106 and enter the unreimbursed amount on Line 12 of Schedule 1 (Form 1040 or 1040-SR).

If you do not meet tests 1-3 above, the expenses are not deductible even if you itemize deductions, as job expenses are not deductible from 2018 through 2025 *(19.2)*.

State and local officials. State and local officials paid on a fee basis may deduct their unreimbursed business expenses on Line 12 of Schedule 1 (Form 1040 or 1040-SR) *(20.1)*.

Health savings account (HSA) deduction. If you are self-employed and have coverage under a high-deductible health plan, are not entitled to Medicare benefits, and are not the dependent of another taxpayer, you generally can deduct contributions to an HSA within the limits discussed in *41.10*. The deduction is claimed on Schedule 1. If you are an employee, and your employer has contributed less than the applicable limit to an HSA on your behalf, you may contribute the balance and deduct it on Line 13 of Schedule 1 *(3.2)*. If your contributions are made through your employer, you will not deduct again on Schedule 1; the amount is already deducted from income. For 2023, individuals may contribute up to $3,850 for self-only coverage and $7,750 for family coverage. Individuals over the age of 55 may contribute up to $1,000 additional each year.

Moving expenses of an Armed Forces member. Moving expenses are deductible by active-duty members of the U.S. Armed Forces who move pursuant to a military order that is incident to a permanent change of station; *see* details at *12.3*.

Deductible part of self-employment tax. After you figure your self-employment tax liability on Schedule SE, the deductible portion shown on Schedule SE is an adjustment to income on Line 15 of Schedule 1 (Form 1040 or 1040-SR); *see 45.3–45.4, 45.7*.

Contributions to self-employed SEP, SIMPLE, and qualified plans. *See Chapter 41* for details on deducting these retirement plan contributions.

Self-employed health insurance deduction. The self-employed health insurance deduction includes costs for medical, dental, and qualified long-term care insurance for yourself, your spouse, dependents, and children, regardless of dependency status if under 27. The instructions for Schedule 1 (Form 1040 or 1040-SR) and IRS Publication 535 (Business Expenses) have worksheets for figuring the self-employed health insurance deduction. The deduction is available in each of the following situations.

If you were self-employed with a net profit in 2023, you may deduct from gross income 100% of premiums you paid in 2023 for medical and dental insurance, and qualified *(see below)* long-term-care insurance for qualified individuals. As a sole proprietor, you may claim the 100% above-the-line deduction whether the policy is purchased in your own name or the name of the business.

If you are a general partner with net earnings, or a limited partner receiving guaranteed payments, premiums may be paid by yourself or by the partnership. The partnership must reimburse self-named policies and include on the Partnership's Schedule K-1. If you are a partner, a health plan in your name is considered "established" by the partnership if (1) the partnership pays the premiums or you pay them and are reimbursed by the partnership, and (2) the partnership reports the premiums as guaranteed payments on Schedule K-1 (Form 1065) and you include the payments as income on your tax return.

If you are a more than 2% shareholder-employee of an S corporation, the IRS position is that the S corporation must "establish" the health plan, but the plan can be considered "established" by the S corporation even if you obtain the policy in your own name, so long as (1) the corporation makes the premium payments to the insurance company or the corporation reimburses you for premiums you pay, and (2) the premiums are reported as wages on your Form W-2 and on your tax return. Similarly, Medicare premiums qualify for the 100% deduction, since they provide insurance that constitutes medical care. As with other health insurance premiums, premiums paid for Medicare coverage of your spouse, dependents, and children who at the end of the year are under age 27 may be included in the 100% deduction.

If you have a qualified long-term-care policy, the 100% deduction applies to the premiums that would be deductible as an itemized deduction under the medical expense rules. This amount depends on the age of each person covered, as shown in *17.15*. For example, if in 2023 you paid long-term care premiums for yourself and your spouse, and both of you are age 57 at the end of 2023, premiums of up to $1,690 for each of you are includible in the 100% deduction, assuming the policy is a qualifying long-term care policy *(17.15)*.

Restrictions on the 100% deduction. The 100% deduction may not exceed your net profit from the business under which the health premiums are paid, minus the deductible part of your self-employment tax liability and your deductible contributions to self-employed, SEP, or SIMPLE, and qualified retirement plans.

The 100% health insurance deduction may not be claimed for any month that you were eligible to participate in an employer's subsidized health plan, including a plan of your spouse's employer or a plan of the employer of your dependent or child under age 27 at the end of the year. If the deduction would be barred for any month because of such eligibility and you have long-term-care coverage that is not employer subsidized, you may claim the 100% deduction for the portion of the long-term-care premiums that is deductible for your age *(17.15)*.

Are you entitled to the premium tax credit? If you are entitled to the premium tax credit for purchasing health insurance on a government exchange, the worksheets provided in Publication 974 should be used to determine the allowable deduction *(25.13)*. The computations are interrelated because the amount of the credit affects the computation of the above-the-line deduction and the credit is based in part on adjusted gross income, which reflects the allowable deduction. If you or your professional tax preparer use tax preparation software, the software will make the circular computations to figure the deduction and the credit.

Penalty on early savings withdrawals *(4.16)*. If you lost interest because you made an early redemption of a savings certificate, the penalty shown on Form 1099-INT or 1099-OID is an above-the-line deduction on Line 18 of Schedule 1 (Form 1040 or 1040-SR).

Alimony paid. You can deduct alimony that you paid to your former spouse under a pre-2019 divorce or separation agreement provided that he or she reports the payments as taxable income; *see Chapter 37*.

Traditional IRA contribution. You can deduct contributions to a Traditional IRA. The deductible limits, including the phaseout rules for individuals covered by employer retirement plans, are explained in *8.3–8.4*.

Student loan interest. You may be able to deduct interest you pay on a qualified student loan, up to a $2,500 limit, subject to a phaseout based on modified adjusted gross income *(33.13)*.

Attorney fees in employment discrimination cases. You may deduct attorney fees and court costs in actions involving unlawful discrimination claims as an adjustment to income, but only to the extent of the amount included in income as a result of the judgment or settlement *(11.7)*. The deduction is claimed on Line 24h of Schedule 1 (Form 1040 or 1040-SR).

Archer MSA contribution. If you are self-employed or employed by a qualifying small business and have high-deductible health coverage, a deduction for contributions to an Archer MSA account may be deductible. The deduction is figured on Form 8853 and then entered on Line 23 of Schedule 1 (Form 1040 or 1040-SR).

Jury duty pay turned over to employer. If you receive your regular pay while on jury duty and turn over your jury duty fees to your employer, report the fees as "other income" on Line 8h of Schedule 1 (Form 1040 or 1040-SR) and claim an offsetting adjustment to income on Line 24a of Schedule 1.

Repayment of supplemental unemployment benefits. You may claim a deduction from gross income for the repayment or in some cases a tax credit *(2.9)*. Claim the deduction as an adjustment to income on Line 24e of Schedule 1 (Form 1040 or 1040-SR).

Reforestation amortization. If you do not have to file Schedule C or F to report income from a timber activity, an amortization deduction for qualifying reforestation expenses may be claimed over an 84-month period; *see* Publication 535 for details. Any deduction allowed is claimed on Line 24d of Schedule 1 (Form 1040 or 1040-SR).

Costs incurred in obtaining whistleblower award from the IRS. You may claim an above-the-line deduction for costs you incurred, including attorneys' fees, in connection with obtaining a whistleblower award from the IRS as an informant, up to the amount of the award reported as income. Claim the deduction on Line 24i of Schedule 1 (Form 1040 or 1040-SR).

Nontaxable Olympic and Paralympic medals and prize money. If you are an Olympic or Paralympic athlete who won medals or prize money, you are not taxed on the value of the medals won and prize money received from the U.S. Olympic Committee unless you have adjusted gross income exceeding $1,000,000, or $500,000 if married filing separately *(11.1)*. You must report the prize money and the value of medals as "Other income" on Line 8m of Schedule 1 (Form 1040 or 1040-SR) even if you qualify for the exclusion. However, where the exclusion applies, the reported income is offset by an adjustment to income claimed on Line 24c of Schedule 1 (Form 1040 or 1040-SR).

12.3 Moving Costs Are Deductible Only by Qualifying Members of the U.S. Armed Forces

The only taxpayers who may deduct unreimbursed moving expenses for 2018 through 2025 are members of the U.S. Armed Forces on active duty who move pursuant to a military order and incident to a permanent change of station, or whose spouse or dependent moves because of a permanent change in station pursuant to a military order. These qualifying Armed Forces members are also the only taxpayers who may exclude employer allowances or reimbursements for eligible moving expenses *(2.1)*.

Qualifying Armed Forces members report deductible moving expenses on Form 3903. The excess of deductible moving expenses over excludable government allowances or reimbursements, as shown on Form 3903, is entered as an adjustment to income (above-the-line deduction on Line 14 of Schedule 1 (Form 1040 or 1040-SR).

If you are a qualifying member of the U.S. Armed Forces, you may claim the following unreimbursed moving expenses on Form 3903:

1. Traveling costs of yourself and members of your household en route from your old to the new locality. Travel costs include the costs of transportation and lodging for yourself and household members while traveling to your new residence. Lodging costs may also include lodging one day before departure and for lodging costs for one day before departure after the old residence is unusable and lodging for the day of arrival at the new locality.

   If you use your own car, you may either deduct your actual costs of gas, oil, and repairs (but not depreciation) during the trip or take a deduction based on the IRS standard mileage rate. For 2023, the IRS standard mileage was 22 cents per mile. Also add parking fees and tolls. Meal expenses are not a deductible moving expense. The rate for 2024 will be in the *e-Supplement* at *jklasser.com*.

2. The actual cost of moving your personal effects and household goods. This includes the cost of packing, crating, and transporting furniture and household belongings, in-transit storage up to 30 consecutive days, insurance costs for the goods, and the cost of moving a pet or shipping an automobile to your new residence. You may also deduct expenses of moving your personal effects from a place other than your former home, but only up to the estimated cost of such a move from your former home.

Nondeductible moving expenses. Meal expenses while traveling to your new residence are not deductible.

You may not deduct the cost of pre-move house-hunting trips, temporary living expenses, or expenses of selling, purchasing, or leasing the old or new residence, such as attorneys' fees, real estate fees, mortgage penalties, expenses for trips to sell your old house, a loss on the sale of the house, or costs of settling an unexpired lease. If you have to pay a fee to get out of your apartment lease when you move, the fee is not a deductible moving expense. If you have self-employment income and part of your apartment was a qualifying home office, you may be able to claim an allocable part of the lease cancellation fee as a home office deduction; *see 40.12*. Certain expenses that go into selling your home and buying a new home may be relevant in determining the selling price of your old home or the adjusted basis of your new residence for capital gain purposes; *see 29.5*.

Other nondeductible costs include the cost of travel incurred for a maid, nurse, chauffeur, or similar domestic help (unless the person is also your dependent), the cost of transporting furniture that you purchased en route from your old home, expenses of refitting rugs and drapes, forfeited tuition, car tags or driver's license for the state you move to, or forfeited club membership fees.

Planning Reminder

Retiring from the Military

You may deduct moving expenses from your last post of duty to your home as long as the move occurs within one year of ending your active duty; *see* the instructions to Form 3903.

CHAPTER 13

Claiming the Standard Deduction or Itemized Deductions

For most taxpayers, the standard deduction provides a larger deduction than itemizing deductions does, given the large increase in the standard deduction and reductions to or elimination of certain itemized deductions *(13.2)* for years after 2017.

The basic 2023 standard deduction amount is $27,700 for married filing jointly or a qualifying surviving spouse, $13,850 for a single person and a married person filing separately, and $20,800 for a head of household. Larger standard deductions are allowed to individuals who are age 65 or older or blind *(13.4)*, and lower standard deductions are allowed to dependents with only investment income *(13.5)*.

In deciding between the standard or itemized deductions, the higher of all allowed itemized deductions or the applicable standard deduction should be selected. If filing as married filing separately, both spouses must select the same deduction. For example, if one spouse itemizes deductions, the other must also itemize deductions regardless of the potential lost tax benefits. Itemized deductions include deductions for mortgage interest, state income tax and property taxes, medical costs, charitable donations, and "other" itemized deductions, as explained in *Chapters 14* through *19*. If the total of these itemized deductions does not exceed the standard deduction, the standard deduction should be selected.

Table 13-1   Itemized Deductions and the Standard Deduction for 2023

Item—	Basic Rule—	Limitations—
Standard deduction	The basic standard deduction depends on your filing status and is adjusted annually for inflation. For 2023, the basic standard deduction is: • $27,700 if you are married filing jointly or • a qualifying surviving spouse. • $13,850 if you are single. • $20,800 if you are a head of household. • $13,850 if you are married filing separately. An additional standard deduction is allowed for being age 65 or older or blind (13.4).	A married person filing separately may not use the standard deduction if his or her spouse itemizes deductions (13.3). The standard deduction may not be claimed by a nonresident or dual-status alien or on a return filed for a short taxable year caused by a change in accounting period. For a dependent with only unearned income in 2023, the standard deduction is limited to $1,250; this amount is increased for dependents with earned income (13.5).
Itemized deductions	You should itemize deductions on Schedule A of Form 1040 or 1040-SR if your allowable deductions exceed the standard deduction for your filing status.	Each separate itemized deduction is subject to limitations. For example, the total deduction for state and local taxes (including income taxes as well as real estate taxes) is limited to $10,000. Medical expenses are deductible only to the extent they exceed 7.5% of your AGI. Casualty and theft losses are deductible only if they are attributable to a federally declared disaster. See Chapters 14 through 19 for details on the itemized deduction limitations. There is no overall reduction to itemized deductions for higher-income taxpayers, as there was for pre-2018 years; this phaseout has been suspended through 2025.
Charitable Contributions	If you itemize deductions on Schedule A, you may deduct donations to religious, charitable, educational, and other philanthropic organizations that have been approved to receive deductible contributions (14.1).	If you itemize, the deduction for cash donations is generally 60% of adjusted gross income (14.17). Lower ceilings apply to most property donations and contributions to foundations. See Chapter 14 for details on charitable contributions.
Interest expenses	If you itemize, you may deduct interest on qualified home acquisition mortgages, points, and interest on loans to carry investments. Interest on student loans are deductible as an adjustment to gross income (33.13)	Interest on investment loans is deductible only to the extent of net investment income (15.10). Interest on personal and consumer loans is not deductible. Interest on home mortgages is deductible if certain tests are met (15.1). See Chapter 15 for details on interest deductions.
Taxes	If you itemize, you can deduct real estate taxes and state and local income taxes, or you may be able to elect to deduct general sales taxes in lieu of the income taxes (16.3).	The amount of state and local taxes that can be claimed as an itemized deduction on Schedule A is capped at $10,000 ($5,000 if married filing separately). The $10,000/$5,000 limit applies to the combined total of state and local income taxes or sales taxes, and property taxes (16.1).
Medical and dental expenses	If you itemize, you may be able to deduct medical and dental expenses you paid for yourself, your spouse, and your dependents (17.1). A checklist of deductible medical items is provided in (17.2). With the exception of insulin, drugs are deductible only if they require a prescription by a physician.	Qualified medical and dental expenses are deductible for 2023 only to the extent they exceed 7.5% of your 2023 adjusted gross income; the 7.5% floor applies regardless of your age (17.1).
Casualty and theft losses	You may deduct personal casualty and theft losses only if they are attributable to a federal-declared disaster (18.1).	Each individual disaster-related loss generally must exceed $100 and the total of all losses during the year must exceed 10% of adjusted gross income (18.12). However, for a "qualified" disaster loss (18.8), the per-event floor is $500 and the loss is not subject to the 10% of adjusted gross income floor. See Chapter 18 for casualty and theft loss details.

13.1 Does Your Standard Deduction for 2023 Exceed Your Itemized Deductions?

The standard deduction is an "automatic" deduction based on your filing status that you may claim regardless of your actual expenses. If your standard deduction exceeds your allowable itemized deductions, you should claim the standard deduction. The standard deduction reduces adjusted gross income (AGI: *see 12.1*).

The basic standard amounts for 2023 returns are shown in *13.2*. Taxpayers who are age 65 or older, or who are blind, are allowed an additional standard deduction in addition to the basic standard deduction *(13.4)*. For taxpayers who may be claimed as a dependent by another person, the basic standard deduction generally is reduced *(13.5)*.

The number of taxpayers who claim the standard deduction has increased since the passage of the Tax Cuts and Jobs Act. The Tax Cuts and Jobs Act either reduced or eliminated a variety of itemized deductions leading to fewer taxpayers qualifying. The standard deduction also increased significantly under the Tax Cuts and Jobs Act. Depending on your individual circumstances, your allowable itemized deductions for medical/dental expenses, state and local taxes, home mortgage interest, charitable contributions, casualty and theft losses from federally declared disasters and certain miscellaneous expenses may exceed your standard deduction, in which case you can claim those itemized deductions on Schedule A of Form 1040 or 1040-SR.

Read *Chapters 14* through *19* for details on allowable itemized deductions, so you can compare the total to your allowable standard deduction.

If you are married filing separately and your spouse itemizes deductions on his or her return, you must itemize on your return, even if the standard deduction exceeds your itemized deductions *(13.3)*.

13.2 Basic Standard Deduction

You can claim the basic standard deduction if you are under age 65 and not blind. For 2023, the basic standard deduction is:

- $27,700 if married filing jointly or a qualifying surviving spouse (also referred to as qualifying widow/widower);
- $20,800 if filing as a head of household; and
- $13,850 if single or married filing separately.

If you are married filing separately, you must itemize deductions and may not claim any standard deduction if your spouse itemizes on a separate return *(13.3)*. Likewise, if your spouse uses the standard deduction, you must also claim the standard deduction even if itemizing your deductions would be more tax advantageous.

The above 2023 basic standard deduction amounts will be subject to an inflation adjustment for 2024; *see* the *e-Supplement* at *jklasser.com* for updates on the 2024 amounts.

Additional standard deduction if age 65 or older or blind. For taxpayers age 65 or over, or taxpayers of any age who are blind, the basic standard deduction is increased by an additional amount *(13.4)*.

Dependents. Individuals under age 65 (or who are blind) who may be treated as dependents by other taxpayers are limited to a standard deduction for 2023 equal to the greater of (1) $1,250, or (2) earned income plus $400, but no more than the basic standard deduction for your filing status shown in the bulleted list above *(13.5)*.

Dual-status alien. You are generally not entitled to any standard deduction if for part of the year you are a nonresident and part of the year a resident alien. However, a standard deduction may be claimed on a joint return if your spouse is a U.S. citizen or resident and you elect to be taxed on your worldwide income *(1.5)*.

EXAMPLE

Ben Green is age 25, single, and a U.S. citizen. His only income in 2023 is salary income of $58,125 and interest income of $298. He made a tax deductible contribution of $6,000 to a traditional IRA for 2023 *(8.2)*. To figure his taxable income for 2023, Ben reduces his adjusted gross income of $52,423 by the $13,850 standard deduction because it exceeds his itemized deductions. Note that no personal exemption is allowed in calculating taxable income; the deduction for personal exemptions has been suspended *(21.1)*.

Gross income:		
Salary	$58,125	
Interest income	298	$58,423
Deductions from gross income:		
IRA contribution *(8.4)*		6,000
Adjusted gross income		$52,423
Less:		
Standard deduction		13,850
Taxable income for 2023		$38,573

13.3 Spouses Filing Separate Returns

If you and your spouse file separate returns *(1.3)* for 2023, and neither of you is a qualifying head of household *(1.12)*, both of you must either itemize deductions or claim the standard deduction. You must both make the same election; when one of you itemizes the other is not entitled to any standard deduction. That is, if your spouse has itemized deductions exceeding the 2023 basic standard deduction of $13,850 *(13.2)* and elects to itemize on his or her separate return, you must also itemize on your separate return, even if your itemized deductions are less than $13,850 and you would be better off claiming the standard deduction.

On married filing separate returns, each spouse may deduct only those itemized expenses for which he or she is liable and pays. This is true even if one spouse pays expenses for the other. For example, if a wife owns property, the interest and taxes imposed on the property are her deductions, not her husband's. If he pays the interest and taxes, neither spouse may deduct them on separate returns. The husband may not because the expenses were not his liability. The wife may not because she did not pay them. This is also true for casualty or theft losses where the property was owned by only one of the spouses.

No restrictions if divorced or legally separated. Following a divorce or legal separation under a decree of divorce or separate maintenance, you and your former spouse are free to compute your tax without reference to the way the other files. Both of you are treated as single. If you have itemized deductions, you may elect to claim them, and your former spouse is not required to itemize. Head of household tax rates may be available if certain requirements are met *(1.12)*.

Head of household possibility if you live apart from your spouse. If you are separated but do not have a decree of divorce or separate maintenance at the end of 2023, and you file separately from your spouse, then as stated above, both of you must either itemize or claim the basic standard deduction of $13,850, plus the additional standard deduction if you are age 65 or older or blind *(13.4)*). An exception to this rule applies if you qualify as head of household by meeting the following conditions:.

- Your spouse was not a member of your household during the last six months of 2023.
- You paid over half of the costs of maintaining a home that for more than half of 2023 was the principal residence for you and a qualifying dependent. *See* Test 2 at *1.12* for details.

If you meet these tests and file as a head of household, you may claim the standard deduction or itemize deductions regardless of what your spouse does. If you elect not to itemize, your 2023 standard deduction as a head of household is $20,800 if you are under age 65 and not blind. If you are age 65 or over or blind, your standard deduction is increased by $1,850 *(13.4)*. The filing status of your spouse remains married filing separately. He or she must itemize deductions if you itemize. If you claim the $20,800 standard deduction for a head of household (or $22,650 if age 65 or older, or blind), your spouse can either itemize or claim the $13,850 standard deduction for married persons filing separately, or $15,350 if he or she is age 65 or older, or blind *(13.4)*.

13.4 Standard Deduction If 65 or Older or Blind

A larger standard deduction is provided for persons who are age 65 or over or who are blind. The larger deduction for blindness is allowed regardless of age.

For purposes of the 2023 standard deduction, blindness and age are determined as of December 31, 2023. If your 65th birthday is January 1, 2023, the IRS treats you as reaching age 65 on the last day of 2023, allowing you to claim the additional standard deduction for those 65 and older on your 2023 return.

If you are age 65 or older or blind for 2023, you may claim an additional standard deduction of $1,850 if you file as a single person or head of household, or $1,500 if your filing status is married filing jointly, married filing separately, or qualifying surviving spouse. Keep in mind that if you are married filing separately, you are only allowed to claim the standard deduction if your spouse also claims the standard deduction on his or her own return *(13.3)*.

You can use *Worksheet 13-1* to figure your standard deduction for 2023.

13.5 Standard Deduction for Dependents

If you are considered a dependent for 2023 under the tests at *21.2*, your standard deduction is determined under the following rules. You may elect to itemize deductions if these exceed the allowable standard deduction. If you are married and your spouse itemizes on a separate return, you must itemize *(13.3)*.

Dependent under age 65 and not blind. Your standard deduction for 2023 is the greater of (1) $1,250, or (2) your earned income plus $400, but no more than the basic standard deduction for your filing status *(13.1)*. Thus, if you can be treated as a dependent for 2023 and you do not have earned income or your earned income is $850 or less, you may claim a standard deduction of $1,250 for 2023.

EXAMPLES

1. Susan, age 17, qualifies as a dependent of her parents for 2023 (Susan is a qualifying child; *21.2*). For 2023, she has earned income of $695 and interest income of $80. Her standard deduction is $1,250 because $1,250 is more than the total of her earned income ($695) and $400, or $1,095.

2. Assume Susan's earned income is $2,000 rather than $695. Her standard deduction for 2023 is $2,400, the total of her earned income ($2,000) and $400, because that total exceeds the $1,250 minimum amount.

3. Assume Susan's earned income is $14,000 rather than $695. Her standard deduction for 2023 is $13,850. Although the rules specify her standard deduction is the greater of $1,250 and $14,400 (earned income plus $400), Susan's standard deduction may not exceed the 2023 standard deduction for her filing status of $13,850. Thus, her standard deduction is limited to the single standard deduction for 2023 of $13,850.

Dependents age 65 or older or blind. Your standard deduction for 2023 consists of two parts. First, you can deduct the greater of (1) $1,250, or (2) your earned income plus $400, but no more than the basic standard deduction for your filing status *(13.1)*. You then add $1,500 if you are married filing jointly or married filing separately, or $1,850 if single or head of household. The $1,500 or $1,850 amount is doubled for dependents who are age 65 or older and also blind.

Filing Instruction

Total or Partial Blindness

For 2023, an additional standard deduction of $1,500 or $1,850 *(13.4)* is allowed to a person who is completely blind as of December 31, 2023. If you are partially blind at the end of the year, you may claim the additional deduction if you obtain a letter from an ophthalmologist or optometrist certifying that you cannot see better than 20/200 in your better eye with lenses or that your field of vision is 20 degrees or less. Keep a copy of this letter. If your eye doctor believes your vision will never improve beyond these limits, the certification should state that fact.

Caution

Determine Dependency Status First

The reduced standard deduction rules apply to you if you may be treated as a dependent on another tax return, such as by your parents. If you can be treated as a dependent (under the rules at *21.2*), it does not matter whether or not you actually are claimed as a dependent by that other taxpayer.

EXAMPLE

For 2023, Beth, a 67-year old widow, has interest income of $400, wages of $2,000, and Social Security benefits of $14,000 that are exempt from tax under the rules discussed at *34.3*. Beth can be treated as a dependent of her daughter Jane under the qualifying relative rules *(21.2)*. Beth's standard deduction is $4,250: $2,400 plus $1,850. Under Step 1 of *Worksheet 13-2* below, Beth has a deduction of $2,400, equal to her wages of $2,000 plus $400, as this exceeds the $1,250 minimum. In Step 4 of *Worksheet 13-2*, the deduction is increased by $1,250, the additional deduction for a single person over age 65. Beth's taxable income is zero. Although her gross income of $2,400 is below the filing threshold (*see* filing tests for dependents on page 4), she should file a tax return to obtain a refund of income tax withheld from her wages.

Worksheet 13-1   Standard Deduction for 2023 if 65 or Older or Blind

Check applicable boxes

	65 or older	Blind
Yourself	☐	☐
Your spouse if you file a joint return	☐	☐
Your spouse if you file separately, provided your spouse has no income, does not file a return, and cannot be claimed as a dependent by another taxpayer (21.2)	☐	☐

Total checks _____

1. Enter your basic standard deduction for 2023:
    - Married filing jointly or qualifying surviving spouse—$27,700
    - Head of household—$20,800
    - Single or married filing separately—$13,850 $ _____

2. Multiply the number of checks above by:
    - $1,850 if you are single or head of household
    - $1,500 if you are married filing jointly, married filing separately, or a qualifying surviving spouse   _____

3. Add Lines 1 and 2. This is your standard deduction for 2023.   _____

Worksheet 13-2 Standard Deduction if a Dependent for 2023

1. Enter the larger of:
   - $1,250, or
   - Your earned income* in 2023 plus $400 $ _____

2. Enter your basic standard deduction:
   - Married filing jointly — $27,700
   - Head of household — $20,800
   - Single or married filing separately — $13,850 $ _____

3. Enter the smaller of Line 1 or 2 $ _____

4. If you are age 65 or older or blind *(13.4)*, enter:
   - $1,850 if you are single $1,500 if you are married filing jointly
     or separately
   - If both age 65 or older and blind, the $1,850 or $1,500
     amount is doubled to $3,700 or $3,000, respectively. $ _____

5. Add Lines 3 and 4. This is your standard deduction for 2023. $ _____

*Earned income. Include pay for services and taxable scholarships *(33.1).* Include net earnings from self-employment and then subtract the deductible part of self-employment tax liability *(45.3)* when figuring earned income.

13.6 Prepaying or Postponing Itemized Expenses

Before the end of the year, check your records for payments of deductible itemized expenses. If you find your payments up to that time are slightly less than the allowable standard deduction *(13.2–13.5)* for the year, accelerating payment of an expense you would otherwise pay in the following year could allow you to itemize. For example, at the end of 2023, you may make an additional charitable contribution, or pay a state or local tax bill that is not due until 2024 but which would be deductible for 2023 under the overall $10,000 limit (or $5,000 if married filing separately) for state and local taxes *(16.1).* There is no tax advantage to prepaying state or local taxes if your payments earlier in the year already exceed the overall $10,000/$5,000 itemized deduction limit, or if you are either subject to AMT or a deduction for the prepayment will make you subject to AMT for 2023 *(23.2).*

If making a year-end payment would not increase your deductions enough to itemize, you would get no tax benefit from the payment. By postponing the payment until the next year, you may make it easier to itemize on that year's return. You may also find no tax benefit to prepaying or postponing, as your standard deduction *(13.1),* may in either case exceed the expenses that could be itemized.

13.7 Itemized Deductions No Longer Reduced for Higher-Income Taxpayers

For years before 2018, taxpayers with adjusted gross income (AGI) exceeding an annual threshold had to reduce their overall itemized deductions. This reduction no longer applies; the Tax Cuts and Jobs Act suspended the reduction for 2018 through 2025.

Planning Reminder

Prepaying Deductible Expenses May Allow You To Itemize

As the end of the year approaches, check your records for payments of deductible itemized expenses. If these payments are slightly less than the allowable standard deduction for the year, making a year-end payment of a deductible expense you would otherwise pay in the following year might allow you to itemize.

CHAPTER 14

Charitable Contribution Deductions

You can help your favorite philanthropy and at the same time receive a tax benefit for 2023 if you itemize deductions *(13.1)* and make contributions that are deductible within the rules discussed in this chapter. The tax benefit from your donation depends on your marginal tax bracket. For example, if you are in the 24% tax bracket and itemize deductions, a donation of $1,000 reduces your taxes by $240.

For cash donations of any amount, your deduction will be disallowed if you do not have a canceled check or account statement, or a written receipt from the charity, to substantiate your contribution.

For donations of $250 or more, you must receive a written acknowledgment from the organization that indicates whether you received goods or services in return for your donation. You need the acknowledgment as well as a canceled check for a cash donation of $250 or more *(14.14)*.

If you claim deductions for property valued at more than $500, you must substantiate the contribution on Form 8283 and attach it to Form 1040 or 1040-SR. If the value you claimed for the property exceeds $5,000, you generally must obtain a written appraisal *(14.15)*.

If you donated a car (or other vehicle) valued at over $500, you also must attach Copy B of Form 1098-C to your return. Your deduction is generally limited to the gross sales proceeds received by the charity on a sale of the vehicle, even if you could substantiate a higher fair market value *(14.7)*.

Deduction ceilings may apply, depending on the type of donation and the nature of the charity *(14.17)*.

14.1 Deductible Contributions

To be deductible, donations must be to religious, charitable, educational, and other philanthropic organizations approved by the IRS to receive deductible contributions; *see* the listing below. If you are unsure of the tax status of a philanthropy, ask the organization about its status, or check the IRS list of tax-exempt organizations (irs.gov/eoselectcheck). Donations to the federal, state, and local government are also deductible.

Substantiating your donations. Keep a canceled check or receipt from the charity as proof of your donations. For donations of $250 or more, you need to obtain a written acknowledgment that notes any benefits or goods that you received in exchange *(14.14)*.

For a donated car, other motor vehicle, boat, or airplane valued at over $500, you must obtain an acknowledgment on Form 1098-C (or equivalent substitute) that you must attach to your return *(14.7)*.

Year-end donations. You deduct donations on the tax return filed for the year in which you paid them in cash or property. A contribution by check is deductible in the year you give the check, even if it is cashed in the following year. A check mailed and dated at the end of 2023 is deductible for 2023. A check postdated until 2024 is not deductible until 2024. A pledge or a note is not deductible until paid. Donations made through a credit card are deductible in the year the charge is made, so if you donate online or by phone towards the end of 2023, the donation is deductible on your 2023 return, even though you do not pay the credit card bill until 2024. Donations made through a pay-by-phone bank account are not deductible until the payment date shown on the bank statement.

Delivering securities. If you are planning to donate appreciated securities near the end of the year, make sure that you consider the following delivery rules in timing the donation. If you unconditionally deliver or mail a properly endorsed stock certificate to the donee or its agent, the gift is considered completed on the date of delivery or mailing, provided it is received in the ordinary course of the mails. If you deliver the certificate to your bank or broker as your agent, or to the issuing corporation or its agent, your gift is not complete until the stock is transferred to the donee's name on the corporation's books. This transfer may take several weeks, so, if possible, make the delivery at least three weeks before the end of the year to assure a current deduction. If you plan to donate mutual fund shares to a charity towards the end of the year, contact the fund company to ensure that the transfer of shares to the name of the charity can be completed by the end of the year.

Debts. You may assign to a charity a debt payable to you. A deductible contribution may be claimed in the year your debtor pays the charity.

Limits on deduction. Depending on the nature of the organization and the donated property, a deduction ceiling of 100%, 60%, 50%, 30%, or 20% of adjusted gross income applies. For details on the ceilings, *see 14.17*. Where donations in one year exceed the percentage limits, a five-year carryover of the excess may be allowed *(14.18)*.

Organizations Qualifying for Deductible Donations

The following types of organizations may qualify to receive deductible contributions:
- A domestic nonprofit organization, trust, community chest, fund, or foundation that is operated exclusively for one of the following purposes:
  - *Religious.* Payments for pew rents, assessments, and dues to churches and synagogues are deductible.
  - *Charitable.* In this class are organizations such as Boy Scouts, Girl Scouts, American Red Cross, Community Funds, Cancer Societies, CARE, Salvation Army, Y.M.C.A., and Y.W.C.A.
  - *Scientific, literary, and educational.* Included in this group are hospitals, research organizations, colleges, universities, and other schools that do not maintain racially discriminatory policies; and leagues or associations set up for education or to combat crime, improve public morals, and aid public welfare.

- Prevention of cruelty to children or animals.
- Fostering amateur sports competition. However, the organization's activities may not provide athletic facilities or equipment.
- Domestic nonprofit veterans' organizations or auxiliary units.

A domestic fraternal group operating under the lodge system. The contributions must be used exclusively for religious, charitable, scientific, literary, or educational purposes; or for the prevention of cruelty to children or animals.

Nonprofit cemetery and burial companies. Contributions must benefit the whole cemetery, not only your plot.

Legal services corporations established under the Legal Services Corporation Act. Such corporations provide legal assistance to financially needy people in noncriminal proceedings.

The United States, a U.S. possession, Puerto Rico, a state, city, or town or Indian tribal government. The gift must be for public purposes. The gift may be directed to a government unit, or it may be to a government agency such as a state university, a fire department, a civil defense group, or a committee to raise funds to develop land into a public park. Donations may be made to the Social Security system (Federal Old Age and Survivors Insurance Trust Fund). Donations may be made to the federal government to help reduce the national debt; checks should be made payable to "Bureau of the Public Debt."

14.2 Nondeductible Contributions

The following types of contributions are not deductible:

1. Donations to or on behalf of specific individuals, even if needy or worthy. Generally, scholarships for specific students, or gifts to organizations to benefit only certain groups, are not deductible. However, the IRS in private rulings has allowed deductions for scholarship funds that are limited to (1) members of a particular religion, so long as that religion is open to all on a racially nondiscriminatory basis, or (2) are open only to male students.
2. Payments to political campaign committees or political action committees.
3. Payments to an organization that devotes a substantial part of its activities to lobbying, trying to influence legislation, or carrying on propaganda or whose lobbying activities exceed certain limits set by the law, causing the organization to lose its tax-exempt status. The IRS has disallowed contributions to a civic group opposing saloons, nightclubs, and gambling places, although the group also aided libraries, churches, and other public programs.
4. Gifts to organizations such as:

   Fraternal groups—except when they set up special organizations exclusively devoted to charitable, educational, or other approved purposes.

   Professional groups such as those organized by accountants, lawyers, and physicians—except when they are specially created for exclusive charitable, educational, or other philanthropic purposes. The IRS will disallow unrestricted gifts made to state bar associations, although such organizations may have some public purposes. Some courts have allowed deductions for donations to bar associations on the grounds that their activities benefit the general public. However, an appeals court disallowed deductible donations to a bar association that rates candidates for judicial office.

   Clubs for social purposes—fraternities and sororities are generally in this class. Unless an organization is exclusively operated for a charitable, religious, or other approved purpose, you may not deduct your contribution, even though your funds are used for a charitable or religious purpose.
5. Donations to civic leagues, chambers of commerce, business leagues, or labor unions.
6. Contributions to a hospital or school operated for profit.
7. Purchase price of church building bond. To claim a deduction, you must donate the bond to the church. The amount of the deduction is the fair market value of the bond when you make the donation. Interest on the bond is income each year, under the original issue discount rules *(4.19)*, where no interest will be paid until the bond matures.
8. Donations of blood to the Red Cross or other blood banks.
9. Contributions to foreign charitable organizations or directly to foreign governments. Thus, a contribution to the State of Israel was disallowed.

Law Alert

Contributions to Donor-Advised Funds

No deduction can be claimed for a contribution to a donor-advised fund if the sponsoring organization is a war veteran's organization, fraternal society, veteran's organization, or a non-functionally integrated Type III supporting organization.

Contributions that provide you with benefits. In general, you cannot deduct a contribution to a charity to the extent that you receive benefits *(14.3)*.

Donation of services. You may not deduct the value of your time when you provide volunteer services for charity. But you can deduct unreimbursed expenses incurred during such work *(14.4)*.

Free use of property. You may not deduct the rental value of property you allow a charity to use without charge. If you allow a charity rent-free use of an office in your building, you may not deduct the fair rental value. You also have no deduction when you lend money to a charity without charging interest. Supporters of the organization may donate rental time for their vacation home to be auctioned off to the public. However, no deduction is allowed for donating the rental time *(14.10)*.

Tickets or seating rights at college sports events. Payments to a college or university for tickets to a sporting event are not deductible. Also nondeductible are payments that give you the right to purchase tickets to athletic events; *see* the nearby Law Alert.

Parents' support payments of children serving as Mormon missionaries. According to the Supreme Court, support payments made by parents directly to their children who serve as missionaries are not deductible because the church does not control the funds.

14.3 Contributions That Provide You With Benefits

A contribution to a qualifying organization *(14.1)* is generally deductible only to the extent that you intend to give more than the value of benefits you receive and actually do so. In other words, to the extent that you receive a quid pro quo, your deduction must be reduced.

If you contribute $75 or less and receive benefits, the organization may tell you the value of the benefits. If your contribution exceeds $75, the organization by law must give you a written statement that estimates the value of the benefits provided to you and instructs you to deduct only the portion of your contribution that exceeds the benefits. However, the disclosure statement does not have to be provided to you if you receive only token benefits, or if you receive from a religious organization only "intangible religious benefits."

> **EXAMPLES**
> 1. You contribute $200 to a philanthropy and receive a book that you have seen on sale for prices ranging between $18 and $25. The charity estimates the value at $20. As the estimate is between the typical retail prices, it is acceptable to the IRS. Although the book sold at a price as high as $25, you may treat the $20 estimate as fair market value and claim a deduction of $180.
> 2. A charitable organization sponsors an art auction and provides a catalogue that lists the items being auctioned and estimates of fair market value. The catalogue lists the value of a vase at $1,000. At the auction, you bid and pay $5,000 for the vase. Because you were aware of the estimate before the auction and paid more for the vase, you may deduct $4,000.

Dues. Dues paid to a qualified tax-exempt organization are deductible to the extent they exceed the value of benefits from the organization, such as monthly journals, use of a library, or the right to attend luncheons and lectures. As discussed above, you generally must be provided with an estimate of any benefits you received if your donation exceeds $75.

If dues are paid to a social club with the understanding that a specified part goes to a qualifying charity *(14.1)*, you may claim a charitable deduction for dues earmarked for the charity. If the treasurer of your club is actually the agent of the charity, you take the deduction in the year you give him or her the money. If the treasurer is merely your agent, you may take the deduction only in the year the money is remitted to the charity.

Benefit tickets. Tickets to theater events, tours, concerts, and other entertainments are often sold by charitable organizations at prices higher than the regular admission charge. The difference between the regular admission and the higher amount you pay is deductible as a charitable contribution. If you decline to accept the ticket or return it to the charity for resale, your deduction is the price you paid.

 *Law Alert*

Payments Giving Right To Buy Athletic Stadium Tickets No Longer Deductible

You may not deduct payments to a public or nonprofit college or university that give you the right to buy tickets at the school's athletic events or the right to buy seating in stadium skyboxes, suites, or special viewing areas. Prior law allowed a deduction for 80% of a contribution paid in exchange for sports seating rights; the nondeductible 20% was considered to be the fair market value of the right to purchase tickets. Payments for actual tickets have always been nondeductible.

 *Caution*

Foreign Charities

You may deduct donations to domestic organizations that distribute funds to charities in foreign countries, as long as the U.S. organization controls the distribution of the funds overseas. An outright contribution to a foreign charitable organization is not deductible. Some exceptions to this ban are provided by international treaties. For example, if you have income from Canadian, Mexican, or Israeli sources, contributions to certain organizations in those countries are deductible subject to limitations. For details, *see* IRS Publication 526

Caution

Bingo and Lotteries

You may not deduct the cost of raffle tickets, bingo games, or tickets for other types of lotteries organized by charities.

The charity should explain to you how much is deductible. The charity must provide an explanation if you paid more than $75; *see* the discussion above. If the ticket is at or below its normal cost, no deduction is allowed unless you decline the ticket or return it to the charity. If tickets were purchased for a charity-sponsored series of events and the average cost of a single event is equal to or less than the cost of an individual performance, then a deduction for a returned ticket is based upon the time the ticket was held. Generally, you may deduct only your cost. However, if you have held the ticket for more than a year, you may deduct the price the charity will charge on resale of the ticket.

> **EXAMPLE**
>
> A couple claimed a full deduction for regular-price tickets to a high-school fund-raising event that they did not attend. They argued that they were entitled to the deduction because they received no benefit from their ticket purchase. The IRS disallowed the deduction and the Tax Court agreed, holding that a donor receives a benefit by merely having the right to attend the event. To claim a deduction for the price of the tickets the couple should have returned them to the charity.

No deduction for donation that gives the right to buy athletic stadium tickets. If you contribute to a public or nonprofit college or university and receive the right to buy preferential seating at the school's athletic complexes, you may not deduct any part of the contribution; *see 14.2.*

Deduction must be reduced when state and local tax credits are received. In an effort to allow their residents to continue to enjoy a federal tax benefit from the payment of state and local taxes (SALT) in excess of the $10,000 ($5,000 if married filing separately) deduction cap *(16.1)*, some states have enacted "workaround" programs that allow a state and local tax credit for payments to an entity that is eligible to receive tax deductible contributions. However, final IRS regulations require the federal charitable contribution deduction to be reduced by the amount of the state and local tax credit that the taxpayer receives or expects to receive (unless it is *de minimis*, as explained below). In effect, the IRS views the tax credit offset as a nondeductible quid pro quo. Under the *de minimis* exception, no reduction in the federal charitable contribution deduction is required if the state or local tax credit received (or expected to be received) is no more than 15% of the payment amount or fair market value of the property transferred to the entity.

> **EXAMPLE**
>
> A state has a program under which it gives a 70% state tax credit to taxpayers who make payments to an eligible entity (to which deductible charitable contributions can be made). Thus, a taxpayer who pays $1,000 to an eligible entity receives a $700 state tax credit. Under the IRS regulations, the taxpayer must reduce the $1,000 contribution by the $700 state tax credit, leaving an allowable charitable contribution deduction of $300 on the taxpayer's federal income tax return.
>
> Under the *de minimis* rule, no reduction in the federal charitable contribution deduction would be required if the state tax credit percentage was 15% or less.

The rules requiring a reduction in the charitable deduction if a state or local tax credit of over 15% is received applies to all itemizers, whether or not their deduction for state or local taxes is subject to the SALT deduction limit. However, for taxpayers with state and local taxes under the SALT limit, the IRS provides a safe harbor, which allows the amount disallowed as a charitable deduction (due to the receipt of state or local tax credits) to be treated as a payment of state or local tax for purposes of figuring the allowable deduction for state and local taxes; *see 16.1* for details on the safe harbor.

Note: The IRS treats state or local tax deductions differently than tax credits. If a taxpayer receives a state or local tax deduction rather than a tax credit for making the charitable contribution, the taxpayer's federal charitable contribution deduction does not have to be reduced to account for the state or local deduction. However, if the state or local tax deduction exceeds the payment or the fair market value of property transferred to the eligible entity, the excess reduces the deductible charitable contribution.

No deduction for house donated to fire department. If a taxpayer contributed the right to use property for training purposes, no deduction is allowed because the contribution of the right to use the property is less than the taxpayers's interest in the property. Some homeowners who tore down their homes to make way for constructing new ones donated the homes to a fire department and claimed a charitable contribution deduction. The fire department uses the home for training exercises in extinguishing fires. The homeowner's goal was to avoid the costs of demolishing the house while claiming a charitable deduction for the value of the home. However, the IRS and Tax Court have held in such cases that the donated homes have minimal value and disallowed the claimed deductions. A federal appeals court sided with the IRS and Tax Court in barring a charitable deduction where a couple donated their house but not the land, with the understanding that the fire department would use it for training exercises and burn it down within a short period of time. The demolition of the home by the fire department was a benefit to the taxpayers and under the "quid-pro-quo" test, no deduction could be claimed because they could not show that the fair market value of the house exceeded the estimated $10,000 in demolition and debris removal costs that would have been incurred had there been no donation. The donated home had only a minimal value because it could not be used by the fire department for residential purposes but only for training exercises.

> **EXAMPLE**
>
> A taxpayer who makes a $1,000 contribution to an eligible entity is not required to reduce the $1,000 deduction on the taxpayer's federal income tax return if the state or local tax credit received or expected to be received is no more than $150.

Token Items/Membership Benefits That Do Not Reduce Your Deduction

Token items. Popular fund-raising campaigns, such as those for museums, zoos, and public TV, offer token items such as calendars, tote bags, tee shirts, and other items carrying the organization's logo. You are allowed a full deduction for your contribution if the item is considered to be of insubstantial value under IRS guidelines.

The charity must tell you how much of your contribution is deductible in the solicitation that offers the token item. If the items are insubstantial in value, the charity should tell you that your payment is fully deductible. For example, if in 2023 you contributed at least $62.50, and the offered items cost the charity no more than $12.50, the value of the benefits is ignored and a full 2023 deduction is allowed. A full deduction for 2023 is also allowed if the items were worth no more than 2% of the contribution or $125, whichever is less. The $62.50, $12.50, and $125 amounts change annually for inflation.

Newsletters or program guides that are not of commercial quality are treated as token items having no fair market value or cost if their primary purpose is to inform members about the organization's activities, and they are not available to nonmembers by paid subscription or through newsstand sales.

Publications with articles written for compensation and advertising are treated as commercial-quality publications for which the organization must figure value to determine if a full deduction is allowed under the "insubstantial value" test. Professional journals, whether or not they have such articles and advertising, will generally be treated as commercial-quality publications that must be valued.

Membership benefits. If you contribute $75 or less for an annual membership in a qualified charity *(14.1)* and you receive only the following benefits, the benefits can be disregarded and you may deduct your entire payment:

1. Privileges that can be exercised frequently, such as free or discounted parking or admission to organization events, or discounts on gift shop or online merchandise, or

2. Admission to events that are open only to members and the organization's reasonably projected cost per person for each event excluding overhead (as of the time the membership package is offered) is no more than the annual limit for "low cost articles." For 2023, the "low cost article" limit is $12.50.

 *Filing Tip*

Estimated Value of Benefits

You may rely on a written estimate from the organization of the value of any benefits given to you unless it seems unreasonable. Although the value of benefits received generally reduces your deductible contribution, certain token items and membership benefits do not reduce the amount of your deduction.

14.4 Unreimbursed Expenses of Volunteer Workers

If you work without pay for an organization listed at *14.1*, and you itemize deductions, you may deduct as a charitable contribution your unreimbursed expenses in providing the services, such as the out-of-pocket costs of driving your car (gas, oil, parking, tolls) to and from the place of charitable operations. On a trip away from home *(20.6)* for the organization, you can deduct your unreimbursed travel expenses, including transportation (air, rail, bus, taxi and car costs), meals and lodging.

To qualify for the deduction, the expenses must be incurred for a domestic organization that authorizes you to travel. You may not deduct the value of your donated services. In general, you may be able to deduct amounts paid in giving services to a qualified organization as long as the amounts are: unreimbursed, directly part of the service, only expenses as a result of the services, and not considered personal, living, or family expenses.

Substantiating expenses under $250. The IRS does not have a recordkeeping regulation that is specific to unreimbursed volunteer expenses under $250. The Tax Court held in a 2011 case that volunteer expenses of under $250 are subject to the rules for cash gifts of less than $250 *(14.14)*, even though the terms of the cash gift regulation are a bad fit for volunteer expenses. The regulation requires a cash donor *(14.14)* to have canceled checks or receipts from the charity, or in lieu of either, other reliable written records showing the name of the charity and the date and amount of the contribution. These requirements were not written with volunteer expenses in mind, as a volunteer's out-of-pocket expenses (supplies, for example) will generally be paid to third parties rather than to the charity itself. In the case before it, the Tax Court held that a volunteer was in substantial compliance with the IRS rules for expenses of less than $250 because she had records showing the name of the payees, and the dates and amounts of payment, the same information that would be on canceled checks from the charity.

Substantiating expenses of $250 or more. To deduct an unreimbursed expense of $250 or more, such as for a plane ticket or a luncheon you hosted on behalf of the organization, you need, in addition to records substantiating the amount of the expense, a written acknowledgment from the charity *(14.14)*. The acknowledgment must describe your services, and state whether you were provided any goods or services by the charity. If so, an estimate of their value must be given unless the benefits are "intangible religious benefits." The acknowledgment must be obtained by the date you file your return, but if you file after the due date (or extended due date if you get an extension), the acknowledgment must be obtained by the filing due date, including extensions. For 2023 returns, the due date (without an extension) is April 15, 2024; *see* page 6.

Car expenses. If you used your car (or other motor vehicle) to provide volunteer services for a charity, you may deduct either the actual vehicle operating costs (such as gas and oil) that are directly related to your volunteer services, or you may claim a flat mileage rate of 14 cents per mile. The 14-cents-per-mile rate is set by statute and not subject to annual cost-of-living increases. Parking fees and tolls are deductible whether you claim actual expenses or the flat mileage rate. This amount is unchanged from 2022 tax year. Any update will be in the *e-Supplement* at *jklasser.com*.

Other deductible volunteer expenses. In addition to car expenses, you may claim the following unreimbursed expenses:

- Uniform costs required in serving the organization.
- Cost of telephone calls, and cost of materials and supplies you furnished such as stamps or stationery.
- Travel expenses, including meals and lodging on overnight trips away from home as an official delegate to a convention of a church, charitable, veteran, or other similar organization. If you are a member but not a delegate, you may not deduct travel costs, but you may deduct expenses paid for the benefit of your organization at the convention.
- All related expenses in hosting a fund-raiser are deductible, from the invitations to the food and drink.

EXAMPLE

In the course of doing volunteer work for a charity in 2023, Jill Patton drove her car 1,000 miles. If Jill itemizes deductions on her 2023 return, she may include a charitable contribution deduction of $140 (14 cents a mile), plus tolls and parking.

The IRS does not allow a deduction for "babysitting" expenses of charity volunteer workers. Although incurred to make the volunteer work possible, babysitting costs are a nondeductible personal expense. This would be considered a personal or family expense and is therefore not a charitable contribution deduction.

Recreational purposes may bar travel expense deduction. To claim a charitable deduction for travel expenses of a research project for a charitable organization, you must show that you had substantial duties and that the trip had no significant element of personal pleasure, recreation, or vacation.

EXAMPLES

1. Al Jones sails from one Caribbean island to another and spends eight hours a day counting whales and other forms of marine life as part of a project sponsored by a charitable organization. According to the IRS, he may not claim a charitable deduction for the cost of the trip.

2. Sara Smith works on an archaeological excavation sponsored by a charitable organization for several hours each morning, with the rest of the day free for recreation and sightseeing. According to the IRS, she may not deduct the cost of the trip.

3. Myra Scott, a member of a chapter of a local charitable organization, travels to New York City and spends the entire day at the required regional meeting. According to the IRS, she may deduct her travel expenses as a charitable donation, even if she attends a theater in the evening.

14.5 Support of a Student in Your Home

A limited charitable deduction is allowed for support of a full-time elementary or high-school student in your home under an educational program arranged by a charitable organization. If the student is not a relative or your dependent, you may deduct as a charitable contribution your support payments up to $50 for each month the student stays in your home. For this purpose, 15 days or more of a calendar month is considered a full month. You may not deduct any payments received from the charitable organization if any reimbursements are received for the student's maintenance. The only exception is that if you prepay a "one-time" expense such as a hospital bill or vacation for the child at the request of the child's parents or the sponsoring charity, and you are later reimbursed for part of your payment, you may deduct your unreimbursed expenses.

To support the deduction, be prepared to show a written agreement between you and the organization relating to the support arrangement. Keep records of amounts spent for such items as food, clothing, medical and dental care, tuition, books, and recreation in order to substantiate your deduction. No deduction is allowed for depreciation on your house.

14.6 What Kind of Property Are You Donating?

If you itemize deductions, a deduction for the fair market value of donated property may generally be claimed, but the tax law does not treat all donations of appreciated property in the same way. Whether the full amount of the fair market value of the property is deductible depends on the type of property donated, your holding period, the nature of the philanthropy, and the use to which the property is put by the philanthropy. For donations of motor vehicles, boats, or airplanes valued at over $500, special deduction restrictions and substantiation restrictions apply *(14.7)*.

Save records to support the market value and cost of donated property. Get a receipt or letter from the charitable organization acknowledging and describing the gift. You must get a receipt for donations of property valued at $250 or more *(14.14)*. Lack of substantiation may disqualify an otherwise valid deduction.

Law Alert

Appraisal Fees not Deductible

A fee paid for an appraisal of donated real estate or art is not deductible as a charitable contribution and no other deduction is available. For years before 2018, appraisal fees could be claimed as a miscellaneous itemized deduction subject to the 2% floor, but the deduction is suspended for 2018–2025 *(19.2)*.

If the total claimed value for all of your property donations exceeds $500, you must report the donations on Form 8283 *(14.15)*, which you attach to Schedule A (Form 1040 or 1040-SR). If the claimed value of a donated item (or group of similar items) exceeds $5,000, you generally must base the valuation on a written appraisal from a qualified appraiser; *see 14.15* for details on the appraisal requirements.

Figuring value. When donating securities listed on a public exchange, fair market value is readily ascertainable from newspaper listings of stock prices. It is the average of the high and low sales price on the date of the donation.

To value other property, such as real estate or works of art, you will need the services of an experienced appraiser. Fees paid to an appraiser are not deductible as a charitable contribution, nor are they deductible under any other provision of the tax law for 2018-2025; *see* the nearby Law Alert.

Fair market value deductible for appreciated intangible personal property (such as securities) and real estate held long term. Fair market value is deductible where you have held such property long term (longer than one year) and you give it to a publicly supported charity or to a private foundation that qualifies as a 50% limit organization, but you may not deduct more than 30% of adjusted gross income *(14.17)*. A five-year carryover for the excess is allowed *(14.18)*. If the donation exceeds the 30% ceiling, you may consider a special election that allows you to apply the 50% ceiling *(14.19)*.

A contribution of appreciated securities or real estate held long term has two tax advantages that reduce the real cost of making the contribution:

1. Your taxes are reduced by the deduction for the fair market value of the property. For example, you donate appreciated stock that is selling at $1,000. You are in the 24% federal tax bracket. The deduction for the donation reduces your taxes by $240.

2. You avoid the tax you would have paid on a sale of the stock. Assume that your cost for the stock was $400, that your regular top bracket is 24%, and that gain on the sale would be taxed at the 15% capital gain rate *(5.3)*. On a sale at $1,000, you would pay tax of $90 (15% capital gain rate on $600 profit). By donating the stock, you save that $90 plus $240 from the $1,000 charitable deduction ($1,000 × 24% bracket), for a total tax savings of $330. Your "cost" for donating the $1,000 asset is $670 ($1,000 – $330).

The IRS ruled that you may not claim a deduction on donated stock if you retain the voting rights, even though the charity has the right to receive dividends and sell the stock. The right to vote is considered a substantial interest and is crucial in protecting a stockholder's investment.

If you are planning a year-end donation of securities, keep in mind that the gift is generally not considered complete until the properly endorsed securities are mailed or otherwise delivered to the charity or its agent *(14.1)*.

Deduction limited to cost for appreciated property not held long term and ordinary income property. This is property that, if sold by you at its fair market value, would not result in long-term capital gain. The deduction for donations of this kind is restricted to your cost for the property. Examples include: stock and other capital assets held by you for one year or less, inventory items donated by business, farm crops, Section 306 stock (preferred stock received as a tax-free stock dividend, usually in a closely held corporation), and works of art *(14.9)*, books, letters, and memoranda donated by the person who prepared or created them. For example, a former Congressman claimed a charitable deduction for the donation of his papers. His deduction was disallowed. His papers were ordinary income property, and since his cost basis in the papers was zero, he could claim no deduction. Depreciable business property is considered ordinary income property to the extent that depreciation would be recaptured as ordinary income on a sale *(44.1–44.3)*. If the cost of the property was fully deducted under first-year expensing *(42.3)*, you have no cost basis and you may not claim a deduction.

Caution

Tangible Personal Property

When you donate appreciated collectibles and artwork (other than taxidermy property) held long term, you get a full deduction for the fair market value of the property if the items are used in connection with the charity's main activity or tax-exempt purpose.

If the charity sells your property, your deduction is limited to your basis in the property (what you paid for it, rather than its appreciated value). Protect a deduction for fair market value by obtaining a letter from the charity stating that it intends to use your gift in connection with its tax-exempt purposes.

EXAMPLE

Bob James holds stock that cost him $1,000. It is now worth $1,500. If he holds it for one year or less and donates it to a philanthropy, his deduction would be limited to $1,000. He would get no tax benefit for the appreciation of $500. On the other hand, if he holds the stock over a year before donating it, he could claim a deduction for the full market value of the stock.

Use of property by charity determines whether fair market value or cost is deductible for appreciated tangible personal property held long term. If you donate appreciated tangible personal property held long term, such as works of art *(14.9)*, jewelry, furniture, books, equipment, fixtures (severed from realty), and antique cars, the deduction limit depends on how the charitable organization uses the property. If the property is used by the organization for purposes related to its tax-exempt purpose or function, you may deduct the fair market value.

If the organization puts the property to a use that is unrelated to its tax-exempt purpose or function, the deduction is limited to your cost basis because the fair market value must be reduced by the amount of long-term capital gain that would have been realized if the property had been sold at fair market value. If the charity sells your gift to obtain cash for its exempt purposes, your donation is treated as being put to an unrelated use by the charity, and your deduction must be reduced by the long-term gain element unless on the date of the donation you could reasonably anticipate that the property would not be sold (or put to another nonrelated use). A certification of exempt use from the charity is required if you claim a deduction exceeding $5,000 and the charity sells the property within three years; *see* below.

If the donation of tangible personal property is to a 50% deduction limit organization such as a church or college, and you must reduce the deduction as an unrelated gift, the reduced gift is then subject to the 50% annual deduction ceiling discussed in *14.17*. If the organization's use of the property is related to its tax-exempt charitable purposes, and it is a 50% limit organization, you may deduct the property's fair market value subject to the 30% of adjusted gross income deduction ceiling *(14.17)*. Alternatively, you may elect to deduct up to 50% of adjusted gross income by reducing the deduction by the long-term gain *(14.19)*.

Deductions of appreciated tangible personal property exceeding $5,000 may be reduced or recaptured on sale by charity within three years. Special certification rules apply to donations of appreciated tangible personal property for which you claim a deduction of more than $5,000:

1. If the charity sells or otherwise disposes of the property during the year that you donated it, your deduction is limited to your cost basis unless the charity provides a written certification of exempt use to the IRS on Form 8282, and gives you a copy. The certification, signed by an officer under penalty of perjury, must either state (1) that the charity's use of the property was substantial and furthered its tax-exempt purpose or function, or (2) that a related and substantial use of the property was intended at the time of the donation but it became impossible or unfeasible to implement such intent.

2. If you deduct more than your basis in the property and the charity sells it (or otherwise disposes of it) after the year of contribution but within three years of the contribution, and the charity does not provide the IRS and you with the required certification described in 1. above, you must recapture part of your original deduction. In the year of the sale, you must report as ordinary income the excess of the deduction claimed over your cost basis for the property at the time of the donation. Report the recaptured amount as "other income" on Line 8z of Schedule 1 (Form 1040 or 1040-SR).

EXAMPLE

On October 19, 2023, you contribute to a college a painting worth $27,500 that you held long term. The college displays it in a library where art students may study it. The college's use of the painting is related to its tax-exempt educational purposes and you may deduct fair market value.

Caution

Recapture of Deduction for Property Sold Within Three Years

If you donate appreciated tangible personal property held long term, for which you claim a deduction exceeding $5,000, and it is sold by the charity by the end of the year of the contribution, the deduction is limited to your cost basis (you may not deduct fair market value) unless the charity makes a qualifying written certification (*see* adjacent text) to the IRS and gives you a copy.

If you deduct more than your basis for the property and the charity sells the property after the year of the contribution but within three years of the contribution, and the charity does not provide the required certification, you must recapture part of the previously claimed deduction.

However, assume that the college sells the painting in 2024 and uses the proceeds for its educational purposes. Because you claimed a value for the painting that exceeded $5,000, the college must report the sale to the IRS on Form 8282 and give you a copy. There is no effect on your deduction if the college on Form 8282 certifies its exempt use or its intended exempt use. Without the required certification, the recapture rule would apply (rule 2 above) and you would have to report the excess of your $27,500 deduction over your cost basis for the paintings as income for 2024. The same result would apply if the college disposed of the painting in 2025 or in 2026 by October 18, 2026, the end of the three-year recapture period.

Donating mortgaged property. A donation of mortgaged property may produce a taxable gain as well as a deduction. Have an attorney review the transaction before donating mortgaged property. You may deduct the excess of fair market value over the amount of the outstanding mortgage but you may also realize a taxable gain. The IRS and Tax Court treat the transferred mortgage debt as cash received in a part-gift, part-sale, subject to the rules for bargain sales of appreciated property *(14.8)*. You will realize a taxable gain if the transferred mortgage exceeds the portion of basis allocated to the sale part of the transaction. This is true even if the charity does not assume the mortgage.

EXAMPLE

John Hill donates land to a college held over a year that is worth $250,000 and subject to a $100,000 mortgage. His basis for the land is $150,000. Hill's charitable contribution deduction is $150,000 ($250,000 − $100,000). He also is considered to have made a bargain sale for $100,000 (transferred mortgage debt) on which he realized $40,000 long-term capital gain.

$$\frac{\$100,000 \text{ (amount of mortgage)}}{\$250,000 \text{ (fair market value)}} = 40\%$$

Basis allocated to sale: 40% of John's $150,000 basis, or $60,000

Amount realized	$100,000
Allocated basis	60,000
Gain	$ 40,000

Donating capital gain property to private non-operating foundations. You usually may not deduct the full fair market value of gifts of capital gain property to private non-operating foundations that are subject to the 20% deduction ceiling for non–50% limit organizations *(14.17)*. Capital gain property is property that, if sold by you at fair market value, would result in long-term capital gain *(5.3)*. The deduction must be reduced by the long-term gain that would have been realized if the property had been sold at fair market value. In other words, your deduction is limited to your cost basis.

An exception is available for certain contributions of stock to a private non-operating foundation; *see* below.

Stock donation to private non-operating foundation. A deduction for fair market value is allowed on a donation to a non-operating private foundation of appreciated publicly traded stock held long term. To qualify, there must be readily available market quotations on an established securities market for the stock on the date of the contribution. If you or family members donated more than 10% of a corporation's stock, the fair market value deduction is allowed only for the first 10%. Under the family aggregation rule, your contributions of stock in a particular publicly traded corporation are aggregated with those of your spouse, brothers, sisters, parents and grandparents, children, grandchildren, and great-grandchildren to all private non-operating foundations, whether the foundations are related or not. If the 10% limit is exceeded, the excess contributions are subject to the cost basis deduction limitation.

The IRS has ruled that for purposes of applying the 10% limit, you must take into account previous stock contributions the private foundation sold before the new contributions were made. Once publicly traded stock is donated to a private foundation, it must be counted toward the 10% limit, even if it is later disposed of. Furthermore, the value of each stock contribution at the time of contribution is taken into account for applying the 10% limitation; prior contributions are not revalued each time there is a new contribution.

Patents and other intellectual property. If you donate patents or other intellectual property to charity, such as trademarks, trade names, trade secrets, know-how, and certain copyrights and software, you can claim an initial charitable contribution deduction for your cost basis in the property (assuming that is less than its fair market value). Additional deductions may be claimed in the year of the donation and in later years, based on a percentage of the income that the charity realizes from the property.

The additional deductions are allowed on a sliding scale percentage basis for the 10-year period beginning on the date of the contribution. In order to obtain the additional deductions, you must accompany the donation with a written statement to the charity that includes your name, address, and taxpayer identification number, a description of the intellectual property, and the date of the contribution. The statement must specify that you intend to treat the contribution as a qualified intellectual property contribution and will claim additional deductions for the allowable annual percentage of the charity's income from the property.

For each year that the charity realizes net income from the property in the 10-year period beginning on the date of the contribution, the charity must report the income to the IRS on Form 8899. A copy of Form 8899 is sent to you and the income shown may be used as the basis for claiming an additional contribution deduction.

For further details, *see* the instructions to Form 8899 and IRS Publication 526.

U.S. Savings Bonds. You may not donate U.S. Saving Bonds, such as EE bonds or I bonds, because you may not transfer them. They are nonnegotiable. You must first cash the bonds and then give the proceeds to the charity, or surrender the bonds and have new ones registered in the donee's name. When cashed in, the accrued interest must be reported on your income tax return, and you may claim a charitable deduction for the cash gift if you itemize deductions for that year.

Gift of installment obligations. You may deduct your donation of installment notes to a qualified philanthropy. However, if you received them on your sale of property that you reported on the installment basis, you may realize gain or loss on the gift of the notes *(5.28)*. The amount of the contribution is the fair market value of the obligation, not the face amount of the notes.

14.7   Cars, Clothing, and Other Property Valued Below Cost

If you donate property whose value has declined below your cost, your deduction generally is limited to the fair market value. However, the rules for cars, trucks, boats, and airplanes are more complicated. Strict substantiation requirements apply to prevent donors from claiming inflated deductions for donated vehicles where the charity actually received much less on a sale to raise cash; *see* below.

If you are planning a donation of stock or other investment or business property worth less than your basis *(5.20)*, consider selling the property and then donating the proceeds. If you donate the property, your deduction is limited to the fair market value and you cannot deduct a loss. If you first sell the property, you can claim a loss on the sale and then claim a charitable contribution on your donation of the sale proceeds; *see* the Example below.

> **EXAMPLE**
>
> Betty Dunn owns securities that cost $20,000 several years ago but have declined in value to $5,000. A donation of these securities gives a charitable contribution deduction of $5,000. If Betty sold the securities for $5,000, she could claim a long-term capital loss *(5.3)* of $15,000. She could then donate the sales proceeds and claim a $5,000 charitable deduction for the cash contribution.

Clothing or household items. You can claim a deduction for used clothing or household items only if they are in good used condition or better. Household items include furniture or furnishings, linens, appliances or electronics, but not antiques, art, collections, or jewelry. Your deduction for "good condition" clothing or household items is limited to their fair market value, which is usually much less than your original cost. Prices paid in thrift shops for similar items are an indication of fair market value. If the IRS questions your charitable donations of clothing or household items, photographs of the donated items or a statement describing the items helps support the valuation. Without valuation, the IRS may disallow your deduction. If an item is valued at over $500 in a qualified appraisal that you attach to your return, a deduction is allowed even if the item is not in good used condition or better.

Cars, other motor vehicles, boats, and airplanes. You must obtain a timely written acknowledgment from the charity to substantiate a deduction for a car or other motor vehicle, boat, or airplane with a claimed value of over $500. The required acknowledgment must be on Form 1098-C or an equivalent statement from the charity. Copy B of the Form 1098-C (or equivalent acknowledgment) must be attached to your return; if you do not attach the form to your return, the IRS will disallow your deduction. If you e-file your return, attach the Copy B as a PDF attachment if your software program allows; otherwise, attach Copy B of Form 1098-C to Form 8453 and mail the forms to the IRS. You also must attach Form 8283 if your total deduction for all property donations exceeds $500 *(14.15)*. Vehicles held primarily for sale, such as dealer inventory, are not subject to the acknowledgment rules or the deduction restrictions in the following paragraphs *(14.12)*.

If the charity sells the vehicle for more than $500 to a buyer other than a needy individual *(see below)* without having put it to a significant intervening use, or without materially improving it, your deduction is limited to the gross sales proceeds. You must be sent the Form 1098-C (or equivalent substitute) within 30 days of the sale. The charity must certify in Box 4a that the sale was made in an arm's-length transaction to an unrelated party. The amount of the gross proceeds (not reduced by expenses or fees) will be shown in Box 4c.

If the charity intends to significantly use the vehicle in furtherance of its regularly conducted activities or to materially improve it before selling it, Form 1098-C (or other acknowledgment) must be provided to you within 30 days of the donation. In Box 5a, the charity must certify its intent and in Box 5c it must certify a detailed description of the planned use or improvement, including the intended duration of such use or improvement. If Box 5a is checked, you may take a deduction equal to the fair market value of the vehicle on the date of contribution.

Fair market value is also deductible if the charity checks Box 5b to certify that the donated vehicle will be given to a needy individual, or sold to such to an individual for significantly less than fair market value, in furtherance of the organization's charitable purpose. You must be given Form 1098-C (or equivalent acknowledgment) with Box 5b checked within 30 days of the donation.

Copy B of Form 1098-C states that the deduction may not exceed the gross sales proceeds unless Box 5a or 5b is checked. If fair market value is deductible because Box 5a or 5b is checked, value may be based on an established used-vehicle-pricing guide, provided the amount is for a comparable model in similar condition and sold in the same area.

In Boxes 6a–6c of Form 1098-C, the charity indicates whether any goods or services were provided to the donor and, if so, they are described and a good faith estimate of their fair market value is shown. The deduction must be reduced by the value of the goods/services provided, with one exception. If the only benefits provided to the donor are intangible religious benefits (such as admission to a religious ceremony), Box 6c will be checked and the deduction does not have to be reduced by such benefits.

If the claimed value of the vehicle is at least $250 but not over $500. If the claimed value of a car, other motor vehicle, boat, or airplane (but not dealer property) is at least $250 but not over $500, the contribution is not acknowledged on Form 1098-C (or equivalent), but you must obtain a written acknowledgment meeting the general substantiation rules *(14.14)* by the due date for filing.

If the charity sells the donated vehicle (other than a sale to a needy person in furtherance of charitable purposes) without a significant intervening use or material improvement, and the gross sale proceeds are $500 or less, IRS guidelines allow a deduction to be claimed for fair market value if that exceeds the proceeds, but no more than $500 can be deducted. For example, if the gross sale proceeds are $400 but the donor can substantiate a fair market value of $450, a deduction of $450 would be allowed, provided a qualified acknowledgment *(14.14)* is obtained. If the donor could substantiate a fair market value exceeding $500, the deduction would be limited to $500.

14.8 Bargain Sales of Appreciated Property

A sale of appreciated property to a charity for less than fair market value allows you to claim a charitable deduction while receiving proceeds from the sale. However, the sale is divided into two parts—the sale and the gift—and you must pay a tax on the part of the gain attributed to the sale.

To compute gain on the sale, you allocate the adjusted basis of the property between the sale and the gift following these steps:

1. Divide the sales proceeds by the fair market value of the property. If the property is mortgaged, include the outstanding debt as sale proceeds; *see* the John Hill Example in *14.6*.

2. Apply the Step 1 percentage to the adjusted basis of the property. This is the portion of basis allocated to the sale.

3. Deduct the resulting basis of Step 2 from the sales proceeds to find the gain.

   You may deduct the excess of the fair market value over the sales proceeds if the property is capital gain property (gain is long-term capital gain) for which full market value would be deductible on a straight donation (no sale) under the rules in *14.6*. Thus, if the property is securities or real estate held long term or long-term tangible personal property related to the charity's exempt function, you may deduct the excess of the fair market value over the sale proceeds; *see* Example 1 below. However, if a deduction for the property (assuming no sale) would be reduced to cost basis as discussed in *14.6*, your charitable deduction on the bargain sale is also reduced; *see* Example 2 below. This reduction affects sales of capital assets held short term; ordinary income property; tangible personal property not related to the charity's exempt function; depreciable personal property subject to recapture; and sales of capital gain property to private non-operating foundations.

EXAMPLES

1. Lana Briggs sells stock she held over a year to a university for $12,000 when the fair market value is $20,000. The $12,000 sales price equals Lana's adjusted basis in the stock. On the sale, she recouped her investment and donated the appreciation in value of $8,000 ($20,000 value – $12,000 basis), which she may deduct. At the same time, she realized taxable gain of $4,800 computed as follows: The percentage of basis applied to the sale is 60% ($12,000 sale proceeds ÷ $20,000 fair market value). Thus, 60% of the $12,000 basis, or $7,200, is allocated to the sale. Gain on the sale equals the $12,000 sale proceeds less the $7,200 allocated basis, or $4,800.

2. Joel Marx sells to his church stock that he held short term for his basis of $4,000. At the time of the sale, the stock is worth $10,000. Using Steps 1-3 above and the allocation method in Example 1, 40% ($4,000 sale proceeds ÷ $10,000 fair market value) of his $4,000 basis, or $1,600, is allocated to the sale. Thus, he has a short-term capital gain of $2,400 ($4,000 sale proceeds – $1,600 allocated basis). Furthermore, his deductible charitable contribution is also $2,400, equal to the 60% of basis allocated to the gift (60% of $4,000 = $2,400).

Basis allocation applies even if a deduction is barred by the annual ceiling. The basis allocation rules for determining gain on a bargain sale apply even if the annual deduction ceilings *(14.17)* bar a deduction in the year of the donation and in the five-year carryover period.

EXAMPLE

The Hodgdons contributed real estate valued at $3.9 million but subject to mortgage debt of $2.6 million. The IRS treated the mortgage debt as sales proceeds and figured gain based on the difference between the debt and the portion of basis allocated to the sale element. The Hodgdons claimed that the basis allocation rule, which increased the amount of their gain, should not apply. Earlier in the year, they had made another donation that used up their charitable deduction ceiling for that year as well as for the following five-year carryover period. The Tax Court held that the basis allocation rule applied because a charitable deduction was "allowable," even if the contribution did not actually result in a deduction in the carryover period.

14.9 Art Objects

You may claim a charitable deduction for a painting or other art object donated to a charity. The amount of the deduction depends on (1) whether you are the artist (*see* the Caution on this page); (2) if you are not the artist, how long you owned it; and (3) the type of organization receiving the gift.

If you owned the art work short term, your deduction is limited to cost, under the rules applying to donations of ordinary income property *(14.6)*.

If you owned the art work long term *(14.6)*, your deduction depends on the way the charity uses the property. If the charity uses it for its exempt purposes, you may deduct the fair market value. However, if the charity's use is unrelated to its exempt purposes, your deduction is reduced by 100% of the appreciation. A donation of art work to a general fund-raising agency would be reduced because the agency would have no direct use for it. It would have to sell the art work and use the cash for its exempt purposes.

Deductions of over $5,000 for art donations (as well as other types of appreciated tangible personal property) may be limited or recaptured if the charity disposes of the property within three years *(14.6)*.

EXAMPLES

1. You give your college a painting that you have owned for many years. Its cost was $1,000 but it is now worth $10,000. The school displays the painting in its library for study by students. This use is related to the school's educational purposes. Your donation is deductible at fair market value. If, however, the school told you it was going to sell the painting and use the proceeds for general education purposes, its use would not be considered related. Your deduction would be reduced by the $9,000 appreciation to $1,000.

   If a deduction for fair market value is allowed, a sale by the charity within three years of the donation will trigger a recapture of a deduction, unless the charity makes a qualifying certification *(14.6)*.

2. You donate to the Community Fund a collection of first edition books held for many years and worth $5,000. Your cost is $1,000. Since the charity is a general fund-raising organization, its use of your gift is not related. Your deduction would be $1,000 ($5,000 less $4,000).

3. You contribute to a charity antique furnishings you owned for years. The antiques cost you $500 and are now worth $5,000. The charity uses the furnishings in its office in the course of carrying on its functions. This is a related use. Your contribution deduction is $5,000.

Appraisals. Be prepared to support your deduction with detailed proof of cost, the date of acquisition, and how value was appraised. *See* the discussion of appraisal requirements later in this chapter *(14.15)*.

The IRS has its own art advisory panel to assess whether the fair market value claimed for donated art works is reasonable. The appraisal fee is not deductible for 2018 through 2025; *see* the Law Alert in *14.6*.

Requesting advance valuation of art from the IRS. To avoid a later dispute, you may ask the IRS for an advance valuation of art that you have had appraised at $50,000 or

Caution

Donations of Personal Creative Works

If you are the artist, your deduction is limited to cost regardless of how long you held the art work or to what use the charity puts it. In the case of a painting, the deduction would be the lower of the cost for canvas and paints and the fair market value.

Filing Instruction

Appraisal Required

To claim a deduction of over $5,000 for any type of property, including art, you must have a written appraisal from a qualified appraiser and the donation must be described on Form 8283, which you file with your return *(14.15)*. If you claim a deduction for art of $20,000 or more you must attach to Form 8283 a copy of the signed appraisal.

more. A request for an IRS Statement of Value (SOV) may be submitted for income tax, gift tax, or estate tax purposes. The IRS has the discretion to value items appraised at less than $50,000 if the SOV request includes at least one item appraised at $50,000 or more, and the IRS determines that the valuation is in the best interest of efficient tax administration.

A request for an SOV must be submitted to the IRS before filing the tax return reporting the donation. The request must include a copy of an appraisal for the item of art and a $7,500 fee, which pays for an SOV for up to three items of art. There is an additional charge of $400 for each item of art over three. It takes the IRS between six and 12 months to issue an SOV.

If the IRS agrees with the value reported on the appraisal, the IRS will issue an SOV approving the appraisal. If the IRS disagrees, the IRS will issue an SOV indicating its own valuation and stating the reasons it disagrees with the appraised amount. Regardless of whether you agree with the IRS appraisal, the SOV must be attached to and filed with the return reporting the donation. If you file the return before the SOV is issued, a copy of your request for the SOV must be attached to your return and on receipt of the SOV, an amended return must be filed with the SOV attached. For further SOV details, *see* IRS Publication 561 and Revenue Procedure 96-15, as well as the "Art Appraisal Services" page at IRS.gov.

Donating a fractional interest in an art collection. You may deduct the value of a donated partial interest in an art collection, such as where you give a museum the right to exhibit the works for a specific period during the year. The deduction is allowed even if the museum does not take possession of the art works, provided it has the right to take possession. However, if you made a fractional donation after August 17, 2006, and later donate an additional fractional interest in the same property, the deduction for the later contribution is based on the fair market value of the property at the time of the initial fractional contribution where that is less than the value at the time of the later contribution. Furthermore, if you do not transfer your entire remaining interest to the same charity or the charity does not take possession within 10 years of the initial fractional donation, or, if earlier, the date of your death, your charitable contributions will have to be recaptured as "other income" (Line 8z of Schedule 1(Form 1040 or 1040-SR), plus interest and a penalty equal to 10% of the recaptured amount will be imposed ("additional tax" on Line 17g of Schedule 2 (Form 1040 or 1040-SR)). *See* Publication 526 for further details.

Keeping a reversionary interest. The IRS may challenge a charitable deduction where you retain some control over the donated property. However, if the possibility of the property reverting back to you is considered to be remote, a deduction may be allowed. For example, a taxpayer who donated her art collection to a museum was allowed to claim a charitable deduction even though she retained the right to decide where and how the art would be displayed. The parties agreed that if there were disputes concerning the art displays, they would be settled by a mutually acceptable museum curator. If the museum breached a condition, it had a period of time to cure the violation. If the museum did not timely cure a violation, ownership of the art collection would revert back to the donor. The IRS allowed the deduction; the retained rights were fiduciary in nature and the possibility of the art reverting to the donor was so remote as to be negligible.

14.10 Interests in Real Estate

No deduction is allowed for the rental value of property you allow a charity to use free of charge. This is the case even if the property is used directly in furtherance of the organization's charitable purpose; *see* the Example on the following page.

If you donate an undivided fractional part of your entire interest, a deduction will be allowed for the fair market value of the proportionate interest donated.

A donation of an option is not deductible until the year the option to buy the property is exercised.

Law Alert

Recapture of Deductions for Certain Fractional Interests

If, within 10 years of a contribution of a fractional interest in art or other tangible personal property *(14.6)*, or earlier if the owner dies, the charity does not receive complete ownership of the item, or does not take substantial physical possession of the item and use it for its tax-exempt purposes, all prior charitable deductions for the property will have to be recaptured, and interest charges plus a 10% penalty will be imposed.

Caution

Donating Vacation Home Use Not Advisable

To raise funds, a charitable organization may ask contributors who own vacation homes to donate use of the property, which the charity then auctions off to the public. Be warned that if you offer your home in this way you will not only be denied a charitable deduction for your generosity, but you may jeopardize your deduction for rental expenses. A deduction is not allowed for giving a charity the free use of your property; *see* the Example below.

Caution

IRS Scrutiny of Easement Deductions

In Notice 2017-10, the IRS designated certain syndicated conservation easement promotions offered to investors in pass-through entities as tax-avoidance transactions. In these transactions, the promoters tell the investors that they can claim charitable deductions that are at least two-and-a-half times their investment. Because of the questionable nature of these promotions, the IRS is treating them as "listed transactions," which means that participating taxpayers must disclose them each year on Form 8886 *(48.6)*; *see* Notice 2017-10 for further details.

The IRS issued a proposed regulation in December 2022 that requires certain syndicated conservation easement transactions and similar transactions to be reportable. The IRS has been challenging deductions claimed for conservation easements and has won court support in several court cases. If you are considering making such a donation, consult with an experienced tax practitioner to make sure you meet the stringent deduction requirements.

Law Alert

Higher Deduction Limit for Conservation Contributions

The deduction for qualified conservation contributions is allowed up to 50% of adjusted gross income, or up to 100% of adjusted gross income for a qualified farmer or rancher *(14.17)*.

> ## EXAMPLE
>
> To help a charity raise money, one owner allowed the charity to auction off a week's stay in his vacation home, and the highest bidder paid the charity a fair rental. The IRS ruled that not only was the owner's donation not deductible, but the one week stay by the bidder was considered personal use by the owner for purposes of figuring deductions for rental expenses. True, if the owner had directly rented the property to the bidder, the bidder's payment of a fair rental value would have been counted as a rental day and not a personal use day. However, the donation for charitable use is not a business rental, and the bidder's rental payment to the charity is not considered a payment to the owner.
>
> Furthermore, the bidder's use of the home pushed the owner over the personal-use ceiling, which in turn prevented him from deducting a rental loss. A rental loss may not be claimed if personal use of a home exceeds the greater of 14 days and 10% of the number of days the home is rented at fair rental value *(9.7)*. Here, the owner personally used the home for 14 days and rented the home for 80 days. The rental expenses exceeded rental income. If the bidder's use of the home was not considered his personal use, the owner could have deducted the loss because his personal use did not exceed the 14-day limit (which was more than 10% of the 80 rental days). However, by adding the bidder's seven days of use to the owner's 14 days, the resulting 21 days of personal use exceeded the 14-day ceiling.

Remainder interest in home or farm. You may claim a charitable deduction for a gift of the remainder value of a residence or farm donated to a charity, even though you reserve the use of the property for yourself and your spouse for a term of years or life. Remainder gifts generally must be made in trust. However, where a residence or farm is donated, the remainder interest must be conveyed outright, not in trust. A remainder interest in a vacation home or in a "hobby" farm is also deductible. There is no requirement that the home be your principal residence or that the farm be profitable.

Qualified conservation contributions. A deduction may be claimed for the contribution of certain partial interests in real property to government agencies or publicly supported charities for exclusively conservational purposes. Qualified conservation contributions include: (1) your entire interest in real property other than retained rights to subsurface oil, gas, or other minerals; (2) a remainder interest; or (3) an easement, restrictive covenant, or similar property restriction granted in perpetuity. The contribution must be in perpetuity and further at least one of the following "conservation purposes"—preservation of land areas for the general public's outdoor recreation, education, or scenic enjoyment; preservation of historically important land areas or structures; or the protection of plant, fish, or wildlife habitats or similar natural ecosystems.

If an easement is donated and the property is subject to a mortgage, the mortgagee's interest must be subordinated to the charity's conservation easement at the time it was granted. In one case, the Tenth Circuit Court of Appeals agreed with the Tax Court and the IRS that a land conservancy's easement rights on mortgaged property were not protected in perpetuity when the prior owner's deed of trust was not subordinated to the easement at the time it was granted. A deduction was disallowed although the prior owner signed a subordination agreement two years after the donation. If the donors had defaulted on their promissory note between the time of the donation and the signing of the subordination agreement, the prior owner could have brought foreclosure proceedings and eliminated the conservation easement. The Appeals Court held that failure to meet the subordination requirement when the easement was granted could not be excused; the likelihood of a default by the donor was not so remote as to be negligible.

To meet the requirement that the conservation purpose of the easement be protected "in perpetuity", there must be legally enforceable restrictions that prevent you from using your retained interest in the property in a way contrary to the intended conservation purpose. The donee organization must be prohibited from transferring the contributed interest except to other organizations that will hold the property for exclusively conservational purposes.

The Fourth Circuit Court of Appeals agreed with the Tax Court and the IRS that the "in perpetuity" test was not met where a donation agreement allowed the donor to substitute other property to be subject to the easement. A deduction was denied even though the charity would have to agree to any substitution and the conservation purposes of the easement would have to be protected after the substitution. IRS regulations allow a change in the property subject to the easement only where continued use of the original property for conservation purposes becomes impossible or impractical.

If you retain an interest in subsurface oil, gas, or minerals, surface mining must generally be specifically prohibited. However, where the mineral rights and surface interests are separately owned, a deduction will be allowed if the probability of surface mining is so remote as to be considered negligible. The exception does not apply if you are related to the owner of the surface interest or if you received the mineral interest (directly or indirectly) from the surface owner.

The Tax Court has held that the written acknowledgment requirement for donations of $250 or more *(14.14)* can be met by the written agreement conveying a conservation easement, "taken as a whole." Thus, even where the easement agreement does not specifically state whether the donor received goods or services in exchange as required by the acknowledgment rule *(14.14)*, the overall terms of the agreement can indicate that no goods or services were received.

Contributions valued at over $5,000 must be supported by a written appraisal from a qualified appraiser *(14.15)*.

Historic building façade easements. A donation of a façade easement with respect to a certified historic structure in a registered historic district, other than one listed in the National Register, is allowed only if the easement preserves the entire exterior, including the space above as well as the front, rear, and sides of the building. The easement must bar exterior changes inconsistent with the historical character of the building. A written agreement between the donor and the donee must certify that the donee is a qualifying historic preservation organization with the resources and commitment to enforce the easement.

The donor must attach to his or her tax return a qualified appraisal of the easement, photographs of the building exterior, and a description of all zoning laws and similar restrictions on development.

If a deduction of over $10,000 is claimed for a façade easement, a $500 fee must be paid or no deduction will be allowed. The fee may be paid electronically or sent to the IRS with Form 8283-V. The $500 fee is not deductible under the Tax Cuts and Jobs Act, which has suspended miscellaneous itemized deductions (subject to the 2% of adjusted gross income floor) for 2018–2025 *(19.2)*.

Reduction for prior rehabilitation credit. The deduction for a historic building easement must be reduced if a rehabilitation tax credit *(31.8)* was claimed for the building in the five years preceding the donation.

14.11 Life Insurance

You may deduct the value of a life insurance policy if the charity is irrevocably named as beneficiary and you make both a legal assignment and a complete delivery of the policy. A deduction may be disallowed where you reserve the right to change the beneficiary.

The amount of your deduction generally depends on the type of policy donated. Your insurance company can furnish you with the information necessary to calculate your deduction. In addition, you may deduct premiums you pay after you assign the policy.

Deducting premium payments on donated policy. If you assign a life insurance policy to a charity and continue to pay the premiums, you generally may deduct your premium payments as a charitable contribution. However, in states where charities do not have an "insurable interest" in the donor's life, the IRS may challenge income tax and gift tax deductions for the premium payments. The IRS took this position in a private ruling interpreting New York law. In response, New York amended its insurance code to allow individuals to buy a life insurance policy and immediately transfer it to a charity. The IRS then revoked the earlier ruling but it did not announce a change in its position. Thus, the IRS may challenge premium deductions of donors in other states where a charity's insurable interest is not clearly provided by state law.

 *Caution*

Split-Dollar Insurance Arrangements

No deduction is allowed for giving a charitable organization money with the understanding that it will be used to pay premiums on life insurance, annuities, or endowment contracts for your benefit or that of a beneficiary designated by you.

14.12 Business Inventory

Self-employed business owners generally may not deduct more than cost for donations of inventory. If a charitable deduction is claimed, costs incurred in a year prior to the year of donation must be removed from opening inventory and excluded from the cost of goods sold when figuring business gross profit for the year of the contribution.

If inventory was treated as non-incidental materials and supplies because owners were "small businesses" exempt from inventory rules, the deduction is limited to the cost of the items. This assumes the cost has not already been deducted because the items have been used by the business (e.g., in manufacturing).

No contribution deduction is allowed for a gift of merchandise that was produced or acquired in the year donated. Instead, the cost is added to the cost of goods sold to figure gross profit for the year of the contribution. Business deductions are not subject to the percentage limitation applied to donations.

Special rules apply to donated food inventory. If you donate food from your trade or business, the food must be donated to a qualified organization and meet certain conditions. For a list of the food inventory specifications, *see* Pub. 526.

14.13 Donations Through Trusts

Outright gifts are not the only way to make deductible gifts to charities. You may transfer property to a charitable lead trust or a charitable remainder trust to provide funds for charity.

A charitable lead trust involves your transfer of property to a trust directed to pay income to a charity you name, for the term of the trust, and then to return the property to you or to someone else. A charitable remainder trust is one that provides income for you or another beneficiary for life, after which the property passes to a charity.

Trust arrangements require the services of an experienced attorney who will draft the trust in appropriate form and advise you of the tax consequences.

Deductions for gifts of income interests in trust. Current law is designed to prevent a donor from claiming an immediate deduction for the present value of trust income payable to a charity for a term of years. In limited situations, you may claim a deduction if either: (1) You give away all of your interests in the property to qualifying *(14.1)* organizations. For example, you put your property in trust, giving an income interest for 20 years to a church and the remainder to a college. A deduction is allowed for the value of the property. Or (2) you create a unitrust or annuity trust, and are taxed on the income. A unitrust for this purpose provides that a fixed percentage of trust assets is payable to the charitable income beneficiary each year. An annuity trust provides for payment of a guaranteed dollar amount to the charitable income beneficiary each year. A deduction is allowed for the present value of the unitrust or annuity trust interest.

Because income remains taxable to the grantor, alternative (2) will probably not be chosen, unless the income of the trust is from tax-exempt securities. If such a trust is created, a tax may be due if the donor dies before the trust ends or is no longer the taxable owner of trust income. The law provides for recapture of part of the tax deduction, even where the income was tax exempt.

Charitable remainder trusts. A charitable deduction is allowable for transfers of property to charitable remainder trusts only if the trust meets these requirements: The income payable for a noncharitable income beneficiary's life or a term of up to 20 years must be guaranteed under a unitrust or annuity trust. If a donor gives all of his or her interests in the property to the charities, the annuity or unitrust requirements need not be satisfied. IRS tables determine the value of the allowable charitable deduction for a gift in trust.

14.14 Records Needed To Substantiate Your Contributions

The type of records you must keep to substantiate your donations generally depends on their amount and whether you are contributing cash or property.

Cash contributions. A deduction is not allowed for a cash contribution, regardless of amount, without a receipt or bank record to substantiate the amount and donee. This

Planning Reminder

Life Income Plans

A charitable organization may offer a life income plan (pooled income fund) to which you transfer property or money in return for a guaranteed income for life. After your death, the charity has full control over the property. If you enter such a plan, ask the organization for the amount of the deduction that you may claim for the value of your gift.

includes donations made by check, credit card, electronic fund transfer, or gift card redeemable for cash. You need an e-mail or other written receipt, a canceled check, bank copy of both sides of a canceled check, electronic fund transfer receipt, monthly account statement, or credit card statement that shows the name of the organization and the date and amount of the contribution. Maintaining a diary or log is not sufficient substantiation. If you volunteer your services to a charity, you need similar records to substantiate a deduction for your out-of-pocket expenses of under $250 *(14.4)*.

For a contribution of $250 or more, a canceled check, e-mail, or receipt showing the name of the organization and the date and amount of your contribution is not enough. You must timely obtain a written acknowledgment from the charity, as described below.

For a contribution made by payroll deduction, you need to keep a pay stub, Form W-2, or other employer-furnished document showing the amount withheld as a donation, along with a pledge card or similar document from the charity. If the amount withheld from a single paycheck is $250 or more, the pledge card must include a statement to the effect that no goods or services were provided in return for the contribution.

Noncash contributions under $250. As proof of your donation, you need a dated receipt from the organization that provides a reasonably detailed description of the property. However, if it is impractical to obtain a receipt, as where you deposit canned food at a charity's drop site, you can satisfy the recordkeeping requirement with a contemporaneous notation that documents the contribution.

You need a written acknowledgment from the charity for cash or noncash contributions of $250 or more. A written acknowledgment is mandatory to prove cash or noncash contributions of $250 or more; *see* below for content details. The acknowledgment requirement does not apply if the donation is less than $250, but if the contribution exceeds $75, you must be given a disclosure statement *(see below)* from the charity estimating the value of any benefits you received in return for the donation.

The IRS exempts from the acknowledgment requirement grantors of a charitable lead trust, charitable remainder annuity trust, or charitable remainder unitrust. Since a specific charity does not have to be designated as beneficiary at the time the trust transfer is made, there may be no organization available to provide an acknowledgment.

A separate acknowledgment rule applies if you are deducting over $500 for a motor vehicle, boat, or airplane. You must attach Copy B of Form 1098-C to your return *(14.7)*.

Content of acknowledgment. An acknowledgment for a donation of $250 or more may be a letter, e-mail, computer-generated form, or postcard. If you gave cash, the amount of the donation must be shown. If you gave property, the property must be described in the acknowledgment, but the charity does not have to value it. If the acknowledgment does not show the date of the contribution, you need a dated bank record or receipt.

The acknowledgment must state whether or not you have received any goods or services from the charity in exchange for the contribution. If you have, the receipt must include a statement describing such benefits and estimating their value. However, "token" items and certain membership benefits, as described in *14.3*, do not have to be described or valued. There is also an exception if the contribution is to a religious organization and the only benefits received are "intangible" religious benefits, such as admission to religious ceremonies; these do not have to be described or valued, but the statement must indicate that they are the sole benefits provided.

Deadline for 2023 donation acknowledgments. For a 2023 contribution, the deadline for obtaining an acknowledgment is the earlier of (1) the date you file your 2023 return, or (2) the filing due date of April 15, 2024, or, if you obtain a filing extension *(46.3)*, the extended due date. Keep the acknowledgment with your records; it does not have to be attached to your return.

Payments throughout the year. For purposes of the $250 threshold for an acknowledgment, each contribution made during the year is separately considered. Thus, for small donations (each under $250) made during the year, you do not have to obtain an acknowledgment even if they total $250 or more.

If contributions are made by payroll deductions from your wages, the amount withheld from each paycheck is treated separately. An acknowledgment is not required unless withholding on a single paycheck is at least $250. A pay stub or Form W-2 from the employer indicating the amount of a single withholding over $249 is considered a valid "acknowledgment"; a pledge card or other document from the charity must state that you have not received benefits in exchange for the payroll deduction contribution.

A charity must provide a disclosure statement if you contribute more than $75 and receive benefits. If you contribute more than $75 but less than $250 to a charity, the charity is required to give you a "disclosure" statement that estimates the value of any benefits you received, such as concert tickets or books. The statement must instruct you to deduct only the excess of your contribution over the value of the benefits. Certain "token" items and membership benefits, and "intangible" religious benefits, can be disregarded; *see Table 14-1*. If a required disclosure statement is not provided when contributions are solicited, it must be provided when you make a contribution exceeding $75.

Noncash contributions. For donations of property, the amount of the deduction claimed determines the records you must keep. For a noncash contribution of under $250, you need as proof of your donation a dated receipt from the organization that provides a reasonably detailed description of the property. However, if it is impractical to obtain a receipt, as where you deposit canned food at a charity's drop site, you can satisfy the recordkeeping requirement with a contemporaneous notation that documents the contribution.

For a noncash contribution of $250 or more, you must obtain a written acknowledgment from the charity as described above. The acknowledgment must indicate if you received benefits in exchange for your contribution; *see* the above discussion for acknowledgment details.

To claim a deduction for more than $500 but no more than $5,000, you need, in addition to the written acknowledgment, records that show when and how you got the property (purchase, gift, inheritance), your cost or other basis for the property, and the fair market value; you must report this information on Form 8283 *(14.15)*.

For a deduction over $5,000, you need the written acknowledgment and in most cases you also need an appraisal from a qualified appraiser. You must summarize the appraisal on Form 8283 but generally do not have to attach it to your return. *see 14.15*.

14.15 Form 8283 and Written Appraisal Requirements for Property Donations

You must attach Form 8283 to your Schedule A (Form 1040 or 1040-SR) if you claim a total deduction of over $500 for all of your donations of property. The IRS may disallow your deduction if you fail to attach Form 8283.

Use Section A of Form 8283 to provide details for an item, or a group of similar items, for which you claimed a deduction of under $5,000. You must identify the charity, describe the donated property, provide the value of the property on the date of the donation and indicate how you valued it (such as by appraisal, catalog for a collectible, or thrift shop value for clothing or household furniture). For each item valued at over $500, you also have to indicate how and when you acquired the property, and your cost or other basis.

Complete Section B of Form 8283 if you are claiming a deduction exceeding $5,000 for an item, or for a group of similar items (such as paintings, buildings, coins, stamps, or books). You generally need a written appraisal from a qualified appraiser for such items. The appraiser must sign a declaration in Part IV of Section B that he or she is unrelated to you and meets the other requirements for qualified appraisers. The appraisal must be made no earlier than 60 days before your donation, and you must receive it by the due date (including extensions) of the return on which you claim the deduction.

Failure to obtain a qualified appraisal can cost you a deduction even if the value you claim for the property on Form 8283 is a fair value. In one case, the Tax Court sided with the IRS in completely disallowing deductions for property worth about $18.5 million because the donor (a real estate broker and certified real estate appraiser) appraised the properties himself. The Tax Court, although sympathetic to the donor, held that even though the contributions were not overvalued on Form 8283, and may well have been

Table 14-1   What You Need To Substantiate Your Donations

For each individual contribution of—	You need—
Cash	Regardless of amount, you need a canceled check, bank copy of a canceled check, account statement, electronic fund transfer receipt, credit card statement, e-mail, or written receipt from the charity showing the name of the organization and the date and amount of the contribution. In addition, for a donation of $250 or more, you need a written acknowledgment as described below.

Less than $250	For a cash donation, you need a bank record, e-mail, or receipt as described above. For a noncash donation, you need a receipt from the charity unless it is impractical to obtain one, as when you have deposited canned food in an organization's drop site. The receipt must show the name of the organization and the date and amount of the contribution and provide a reasonably detailed description of the property, which for securities includes their type and whether they are publicly traded.
	    In addition, if you contributed over $75 and received benefits, the charity is required to give you a "disclosure" statement that estimates the value of any benefits you received, such as concert tickets or books. The statement will tell you to deduct only the excess of your contribution over the value of the benefits. If a required disclosure statement is not provided when contributions are solicited, it must be provided when you make a contribution exceeding $75.
	    The disclosure statement is not required if the only benefits you receive are "token items" or membership benefits that can be disregarded *(14.3)*. Nor is it required where you contribute to a religious organization and the only benefits you receive are "intangible religious benefits." An example of an intangible religious benefit would be admission to religious ceremonies. A Congressional committee report also suggests that tuition for wholly religious education that does not lead to a recognized degree would qualify.

$250 or more	You need a written acknowledgment for all donations of $250 or more. For each cash donation of $250 or more, you need a written acknowledgment from the charity that indicates whether you were given any goods or services in exchange for your contribution *(14.14)*. You may not rely on a canceled check, a receipt (including e-mail) or credit card statement to document a cash contribution of $250 or more. A written acknowledgment is also required for a donation of property if you are claiming a deduction of $250 or more, but the charity does not have to value the property, just describe it. If you received any goods or services from the charity in exchange for the contribution, the acknowledgment must estimate their value unless you receive only "token" items or "intangible religious benefits" as discussed in the preceding paragraph. The deadline for obtaining acknowledgments is the date you file your return. If you file after the filing due date or extended due date, get the acknowledgment by the due date or extended due date. Keep the acknowledgment from the charity with your tax records; do not attach it to your tax return.
	    If your total deduction for all property donations exceeds $500, you must report each of the contributions on Form 8283 (not just those valued over $500). If you are not allowed to deduct fair market value for a property donation under the rules at *14.6*, you must attach a statement to Form 8283 explaining the reduction for the appreciation.
	    For each deduction of property for which you are claiming a value over $5,000, you need a written appraisal from a qualified appraiser *(14.15)*.

More than $500 in the case of a donated car, other motor vehicle, boat, or airplane	Special acknowledgment rules apply where the claimed value of the vehicle exceeds $500 *(14.7)*.

Caution

Charity Reports Transfer Within Three Years

If you reported a property donation exceeding $5,000 on Form 8283 and the charity sells or otherwise disposes of the property within three years after your gift, it must notify the IRS on Form 8283 and send you a copy. The sale might trigger the recapture of a deduction claimed for a contribution of tangible personal property exceeding $5,000 *(14.6)*. Reporting on Form 8283 is not required by the charity for a particular item if in Section B, Part III, of Form 8283 you indicated that the appraised value of that item was not more than $500. Similar items such as a collection of books by the same author, stereo components, or place settings of silverware may be treated as one item. Reporting is also not required on Form 8283 for donated property that the organization uses or distributes without consideration, if this use furthers the organization's tax-exempt function or purpose.

undervalued, the deductions had to be completely disallowed because a timely appraisal from an independent qualified appraiser had not been obtained.

You do not need an appraisal for a car, boat, or airplane if your deduction is limited to the gross proceeds from its sale *(14.17)*, or for publicly traded securities, non-publicly-traded securities of $10,000 or less, intellectual property *(14.6)*, or business inventory.

Whether or not a written appraisal is required for property valued at over $5,000, you must describe the property, value it, and provide your cost and other acquisition details on Form 8283 in Section B, Part I.

The appraisal itself should be kept with your records and does not have to be attached to your return except in two situations: If you are claiming a deduction of $20,000 or more for art, you must attach a complete copy of the appraisal to Form 8283 and you may be asked by the IRS to submit a high-resolution digital image or color photograph (8" × 10") of the art. If the claimed deduction exceeds $500,000, the qualified appraisal must be attached to your return (assuming no exception to the appraisal requirement).

See the Form 8283 instructions for further details on the appraisal requirements.

Donee acknowledgment. For property donations exceeding $5,000, the donee organization must acknowledge the receipt of the property in Section B, Part V of Form 8283. If the organization sells or otherwise disposes of the property within three years of the donation, it must file Form 8282 with the IRS and give you a copy.

Penalty for overvaluation. You may be penalized for a substantial overvaluation of donated property *(14.16)*.

Appraisal fees. A fee paid to an appraiser is not considered a charitable deduction, and no other itemized deduction is allowed for 2018 through 2025 *(14.6, 14.9)*.

14.16 Penalty for Substantial Overvaluation of Property

If the IRS disallows a portion of your claimed deduction for appreciated property on the grounds that you overvalued the property, you may be subject to a 20% or 40% penalty, depending on the extent of the overvaluation. No penalty is imposed unless the overvaluation results in a tax underpayment exceeding $5,000.

20% penalty. If the claimed value of donated property is 150% or more of the correct value, the penalty is 20% of the tax underpayment resulting from the overvaluation, provided the underpayment exceeds $5,000.

40% penalty. If the claimed value of donated property is 200% or more of the correct value, the penalty is 40% of the tax underpayment resulting from the overvaluation, provided the underpayment exceeds $5,000.

Reasonable cause exception for relying on appraisal. The 20% penalty (but not the 40%) may be avoided under a reasonable cause exception if you relied on a qualified appraisal prepared by a qualified appraiser and, in addition, you made a good faith investigation of the value of the property.

14.17 Ceiling on Charitable Contributions

Unless you make donations that are very substantial in relation to your adjusted gross income (Line 11, Form 1040 or 1040-SR), you do not have to be concerned with the deduction ceilings discussed in this section. For cash contributions you made in 2023 to churches, colleges, and other 50% limit organizations (see the list below in "Contributions to 50% Limit Organizations"), the deduction ceiling is 60% of adjusted gross income. A 30% limit applies to cash contributions to organizations that are not 50% limit organizations such as veterans' organizations (see "Contributions to Non-50% Limit Organizations" below).

For property donations, the deduction limit is generally 30% of adjusted gross income, although it sometimes is 50% or even 20%. As discussed below, the specific limit depends whether the property donation is made to a "50% limit organization," whether it is capital gain property, and whether the special 50% or 100% limit for qualified conservation contributions applies.

Where you have made contributions subject to different ceilings, the ceilings are applied in a specific order, and the amount deductible under a particular ceiling may be reduced by contributions subject to other ceilings; *see* "Applying the Deduction Ceilings" below.

If your deduction is limited by any of the ceilings, a five-year carryover is allowed for the excess, but the carryover period is extended to 15 years for qualified conservation contributions *(14.18)*.

Volunteer expenses. The deduction ceiling for unreimbursed expenses you incur doing volunteer work for a charity *(14.4)* is 50% of adjusted gross income if your services were for a 50% limit organization such as a church or college (see the list below), or 30% of adjusted gross income if the services were on behalf of an organization other than a 50% limit organization.

Contributions "for the use of" an organization. If a donation is treated as "for the use of," rather than directly "to," any organization, it is deductible under a 30% or 20% of adjusted gross income ceiling. A contribution is "for the use of" an organization if it is held in a legally enforceable trust or similar arrangement. Such contributions include a deductible charitable unitrust or annuity trust income interest, as well as a charitable remainder trust transfer if the trust provides that after the death of the income beneficiary, the property is to be held in the trust for the benefit of the charity, rather than distributed to the charity *(14.13)*.

The 20% ceiling applies to contributions of capital gain property (capital assets held over one year) that are for the use of any organization, including 50% limit organizations.

The 30% ceiling applies to contributions of non-capital gain property, such as cash, ordinary income property, and capital assets held short term, that are for the use of any organization, including 50% limit organizations.

Deductible expenses for supporting a student in your home *(14.5)* are considered to be for the use of a charitable organization and thus subject to the 30% ceiling.

Contributions to 50% Limit Organizations

Organizations in the 50% limit category include churches, schools, publicly supported charities, and certain private foundations; *see* the list below. In addition, the United States, any state or political subdivision of a state, the District of Columbia, Puerto Rico, a U.S. possession or political subdivision of a U.S. possession, or an Indian tribal government or any of its subdivisions is treated as a 50% limit organization.

The following charitable organizations are 50% limit organizations:

- Churches, synagogues, mosques, and other religious organizations.
- Schools, colleges, and other educational organizations that normally have regular faculties and student bodies in attendance on site.
- Hospitals and medical research organizations associated with hospitals.
- Government-supported or publicly supported foundations for state and municipal universities and colleges.
- Religious, charitable, educational, scientific, or literary organizations that receive a substantial part of their financial support from the general public or a government unit. Libraries, museums, drama, opera, ballet and orchestral societies, community funds, and numerous familiar charities (such as the American Red Cross and the United Way) are in this category. Also included are organizations to prevent cruelty to children or animals, or to foster amateur sports (provided they do not provide athletic facilities or equipment).
- Private operating foundations.
- Private non-operating foundations that distribute their contributions annually to qualified charities within 2½ months after the end of their taxable year.
- Private non-operating foundations that pool donations and allow donors to designate the charities to receive their gifts, if the foundation pays out all income within 2½ months after the end of the tax year.
- Organizations that normally receive more than one-third of their support from the general public or governmental units.

Filing Instruction

Appreciated Securities and Real Estate

When you contribute appreciated securities or real estate that you have held for more than a year to a church, college, or other organization treated as a 50% limit organization, your deduction for the property donation is limited to 30% of your adjusted gross income unless you elect to reduce the fair market value of the property by the appreciation. This election lets you elect the 50% ceiling *(14.19)*.

60% ceiling for cash contributions. Cash contributions made in 2023 to 50% limit organizations are deductible up to 60% of adjusted gross income.

100% ceiling for qualified conservation contribution by a farmer or rancher. The deduction limit for a qualified conservation contribution *(14.10)* by a qualified farmer or rancher is 100% of adjusted gross income. The 100% ceiling applies instead of the usual 30% or 20% limit for capital gain property. The 100% limit applies if over 50% of gross income is from farming or ranching. For farmers and ranchers donating land used in, or available for, agriculture or livestock production, there must be a requirement that the property remain available for such production.

If you are not a qualified farmer or rancher, the deduction limit for a qualified conservation contribution is 50% rather than 100% of adjusted gross income; *see* below.

The 100% limit for qualified conservation contributions is applied after other contributions are taken into account; *see* Step 7 under "Applying the Deduction Ceilings" below.

50% ceiling. Contributions to 50% limit organizations of clothing or household items valued at below cost, and ordinary income property (such as inventory or a work of art you created), including capital assets held short term, are deductible up to 50% of adjusted gross income. If you make contributions subject to this 50% ceiling and in the same year you make cash contributions subject to the above 100% or 60% ceiling, *see* Step 2 under "Applying the Deduction Ceilings" below for how the ceilings interact.

50% ceiling for qualified conservation contributions if you are not a farmer or rancher. If you are not a qualified farmer or rancher, the deduction limit for a qualified conservation contribution is 50% of adjusted gross income; *see* Step 6 under "Applying the Deduction Ceilings" below.

30% ceiling for capital gain property held long term. If you donate property to a 50% limit organization and you would have realized long-term capital gain had you sold it at fair market value, the deduction ceiling is generally 30% of adjusted gross income.

The 30% ceiling applies where the fair market value of the property is deductible under the rules discussed in *14.6*. This includes donations of appreciated securities and real estate held long term. It also includes donations of appreciated tangible personal property (such as furniture or art) held long term where the organization's use of your gift is directly related to its tax-exempt charitable purposes.

You may elect to apply the 50% ceiling instead of the 30% ceiling to such property donations if you reduce the fair market value of the property by the appreciation *(14.19)*.

If you donate tangible personal property held long term that is not used by the organization for its tax-exempt charitable purposes, so that your deduction must be reduced for the appreciation *(14.6)*, the reduced amount is deductible under the 50% ceiling, not the 30% ceiling.

Note that for qualified conservation contributions, the deduction ceiling is 100% or 50% of adjusted gross income *(see above)*, not 30%.

If you make contributions subject to the 30% ceiling for long-term capital gain property and in the same year you make contributions subject to any of the other ceilings *(see above)*, *see* Step 4 under "Applying the Deduction Ceilings" below.

30% or 20% ceiling for contribution "for the use of" a 50% limit organization. A cash contribution "for the use of" a 50% limit organization *(see* "Contributions for the use of an organization" near the beginning of *14.17)*, rather than "to" the organization, is deductible up to 30% of adjusted gross income; *see* Step 3 under "Applying the Deduction Ceilings" below.

If a contribution of capital gain property is made "for the use of" a 50% limit organization, the deduction limit is 20% of adjusted gross income; *see* Step 5 under "Applying the Deduction Ceilings" below.

Contributions to Non–50% Limit Organizations

If a contribution is made to a qualifying organization that is not in the above list of 50% limit organizations, a deduction ceiling of 30% or 20% of adjusted gross income applies. Organizations in this category include veterans' organizations, fraternal societies, nonprofit cemeteries and private non-operating foundations that do not meet the payout requirements for 50% limit organizations.

The 30% limit applies to contributions of cash, ordinary income property, and capital gain property held short term. The 20% limit applies to contributions of capital gain property held long term (more than one year). However, the actual ceiling may be less than 30% or 20% of adjusted gross income where in the same year you have made contributions to 50% limit organizations; *see* Steps 3 and 5 under "Applying the Deduction Ceilings" below.

Applying the Deduction Ceilings

The various deduction ceilings are applied in a specific order. Check above for the ceilings that apply to your donations and then use the following steps to figure your total deduction for the year. If a portion of your donations is not deductible under the ceilings, *see* the carryover rules *(14.18)*.

1. 60% of adjusted gross income ceiling for cash contributions to 50% limit organizations made in 2023.

2. 50% of adjusted gross income ceiling for contributions of clothing or household items or ordinary income property (including capital assets held short term) to 50% limit organizations. If you also made contributions eligible for the 60% ceiling (Step 1), your Step 2 deduction is 50% of adjusted gross income minus the cash contributions.

3. 30% of adjusted gross income ceiling for contributions of cash or ordinary income property (including capital gain property held short term) that are (1) to non-50% limit organizations, or (2) "for the use of" any organization, including 50% limit organizations.

    If you made contributions to 50% limit organizations subject to Steps 1, 2, 4, or 5, this Step 3 ceiling is the lesser of (1) 30% of adjusted gross income, or (2) 50% of adjusted gross income minus the contributions to the 50% limit organizations. The "minus" in (2) does not include qualified conservation contributions under Steps 6 or 7.

4. 30% of adjusted gross income ceiling for contributions of capital gain property held long term to 50% limit organizations.

    If contributions eligible for the 60% (Step 1) or 50% (Step 2) ceilings were also made, the limit here under Step 4 is the lesser of (1) 30% of adjusted gross income, or (2) 50% of adjusted gross income minus the contributions claimed under Steps 1 and 2.

5. 20% of adjusted gross income ceiling for contributions of capital gain property that are (1) to non-50% limit organizations, or (2) "for the use of" any organization.

    If contributions subject to any of the previous steps were made (Steps 1–4), the limit under this Step 5 is whichever of these amounts is smallest: (1) 20% of adjusted gross income, (2) 30% of adjusted gross income minus contributions of capital gain property taken into account under Step 4, (3) 30% of adjusted gross income minus contributions (cash and ordinary income property) taken into account under Step 3, or (4) 50% of adjusted gross income minus all contributions taken into account under Steps 1–4.

6. 50% of adjusted gross income ceiling for qualified conservation contributions (other than by farmers or ranchers). If any other contributions were made, the limit for these qualified conservation contributions is 50% of adjusted gross income minus all contributions taken into account under Steps 1–5.

7. 100% of adjusted gross income ceiling for qualified conservation contributions by farmers and ranchers. If any other contributions were made, the limit for these qualified conservation contributions is 100% of adjusted gross income minus all contributions taken into account under Steps 1–6.

> **EXAMPLE**
>
> Linda Jones made two contributions to her church in 2023: $22,000 in cash and land held long term with a fair market value of $45,000. The cash donation of $22,000 is considered first and is fully deductible as it is within the 60% of adjusted gross income limit (Step 1 above).
>
> The deduction for the land is subject to the 30% of adjusted gross income limit in Step 4 above. Under Step 4, the deduction is limited to $28,000, the lesser of (1) $30,000, which is 30% of $100,000 adjusted gross income, or (2) $28,000, which is $50,000 (50% of adjusted gross income) minus the $22,000 cash contribution from Step 1.
>
> Linda's total charitable contribution for 2023 is $50,000 ($22,000 + $28,000). Linda may carry over to 2024 $17,000, the excess of the land's $45,000 fair market value over the $28,000 deduction allowed for 2023 under the 30% limit.

14.18 Carryover for Excess Donations

If you make donations that are not deductible because they exceed the 100%, 60%, 50%, 30%, or 20% of adjusted gross income ceilings *(14.17)*, you may carry the excess over the next five years. A 15-year carryforward applies for donations of qualified conservation contributions subject to the special 50% and 100% of adjusted gross income ceilings *(14.17)*.

In each carryover year, the original percentage ceiling applies. For example, where contributions of appreciated long-term intangible personal property or real estate (or tangible personal property put to a related use by the charity) exceed the 30% ceiling for capital gain property *(14.17)*, the excess remains subject to the 30% ceiling in the carryover years.

Where you have both current year contributions and carried-over deductions from a prior year, you must first figure your deduction for contributions in the current year under the applicable ceilings *(14.17)*, before taking into account the carried-over contributions. However, a carryover of a contribution to a 50% limit organization must be used before contributions in the current year to non-50% limit organizations. *See* IRS Publication 526 for further details on carryovers.

14.19 Election To Reduce Fair Market Value by Appreciation

Although the 30% ceiling generally applies to long-term capital gain property (such as securities and real estate) contributed to 50% limit organizations *(14.17)*, you may elect the 50% ceiling, provided you reduce the fair market value of the property by 100% of the appreciation on all such donations during the year. The reduction also applies to donations of tangible personal property related in use to the organization's charitable function. In most cases, this election should be made only where the amount of appreciation is negligible. Where there is substantial appreciation, the increase in the deduction may not make up or exceed the required 100% reduction, which allows you to claim a deduction only for your cost basis in the property. If the election is made in a year in which there are carryovers of capital gain property subject to the 30% ceiling, the carryovers are subject to reduction; *see* IRS Publication 526.

The election of the 50% ceiling is made by attaching a statement to your original return or amended return filed by the original due date. Even where no formal electing statement is made, claiming a deduction without the appreciation in order to come within the 50% ceiling is treated as an election. A formal or "informal" election is not revocable unless a material mistake is shown. A revocation based on a reconsideration of tax consequences is not considered sufficient grounds.

Caution

Tax Court Bars Surviving Spouse form Using Carryover

A carryover of an unused charitable contribution expires on the death of the taxpayer who made the donation (other than on a joint return for the year of death). The surviving spouse may not continue to use the remaining carryover for years after the year of death.

CHAPTER 15

Itemized Deduction for Interest Expenses

On Schedule A (Form 1040 or 1040-SR), you may deduct three types of interest charges:

- Interest on qualifying home acquisition loans *(15.2)* and home equity loans that qualify as home acquisition loans *(15.3)*
- Points *(15.7)*
- Investment interest, but only up to the amount of net investment income *(15.9)*.

Premiums paid in 2023 for qualified mortgage insurance on a principal or second residence are no longer deductible as interest. Such premiums were qualified deductions for interest in years 2021 and earlier *(15.5)*.

Interest on personal loans (such as loans to buy autos and other personal items and credit card finance charges) is not deductible with the exception of qualifying student loan interest; *see Chapter 33*.

Interest on loans for business purposes is fully deductible on Schedule C. Interest on loans related to rental property is fully deductible from rental income on Schedule E. Whether interest is a business, investment, or a personal expense generally depends upon the use made of the money borrowed, not on the kind of property used to secure the loan. However, interest on a loan secured by a first or second home may be deductible as home equity mortgage interest regardless of the way you use the loan.

Interest on a loan used to finance an investment in a passive activity is subject to the limitations discussed in *Chapter 10*. However, if you rent out a second home that qualifies as a second residence, the portion of mortgage interest allocable to rental use is deductible as qualified mortgage interest and is not treated as a passive activity expense.

15.1 Deduction for Home Mortgage Interest

If you itemize deductions, you generally may deduct on Schedule A (Form 1040 or 1040-SR) interest on home acquisition debt that is secured by a first or second home (see two-residence limit, below). This includes interest on home equity debt that also qualifies as home acquisition debt. However, there are limits on the amount of acquisition debt that can support an interest deduction. Home acquisition debt is debt used to buy, construct, or substantially improve the residence that secures the loan *(15.2)*.

For 2018 through 2025, the Tax Cuts and Jobs Act made two changes to the mortgage interest deduction rules: (1) the limit on home acquisition debt is lowered except for debt that is "grandfathered," and (2) no deduction is allowed for interest on home equity debt that does not otherwise qualify as acquisition debt.

Mortgage interest is deductible on up to $750,000 ($375,000 if married filing separately) of home acquisition debt taken out after December 15, 2017. Acquisition debt incurred on or before December 15, 2017, is "grandfathered." Therefore, the prior law limit of $1 million ($500,000 if married filing separately) still applies to these loans for purposes of deducting interest on your returns for 2018 through 2025.

If you refinance grandfathered debt (debt obtained before 12/16/17), the refinanced debt remains grandfathered to the extent of the loan balance at the time of refinancing; *see 15.2*.

Examples showing how to apply the grandfather rules and the $750,000 ($375,000) limit for non-grandfathered acquisition debt are in *15.2*.

Although current law generally prohibits a deduction for interest on a home equity loan for 2018 through 2025, this does not mean that interest on a home equity loan or home equity line of credit is never deductible. As discussed in *15.3*, if a home equity loan is used to buy, construct, or substantially improve a first or second residence that the loan is secured by, the loan falls within the definition of home acquisition debt, so if the applicable limit on acquisition debt has not been reached, the interest on the home equity loan falling within the limit can still be deducted. The Examples in *15.3* illustrate how the new law rules for home equity debt work, including how the grandfather rules apply to some home equity loans but not others.

Acquisition loan must be secured by residence. To deduct interest on a home acquisition debt *(15.2)* or a home equity loan that qualifies as home acquisition debt *(15.3)*, the loan must be secured by your main home or a second home, and the home that secures the loan must be the home that you use the loan to buy, construct, or substantially improve. For the loan to be "secured," it must be recorded or satisfy similar requirements under state law. For example, if a relative gives you a loan to help you purchase a home, the relative must take the legal steps required to record the loan with local authorities; otherwise, you may not deduct interest that you pay on the loan. The IRS held in a private ruling that interest paid by a homeowners' association on a loan to rebuild the common area is not deductible by the individual homeowners where their residences are not pledged as collateral.

Two-residence limit for qualifying mortgage debt. The rules for deducting interest on qualifying home acquisition debt or home equity debt apply to loans secured by your principal residence and one other residence. A residence may be a condominium or cooperative unit, houseboat, mobile home, or house trailer that has sleeping, cooking, and toilet facilities. If you own more than two houses, you decide which residence will be considered your second residence. You do not have to live in the second residence to designate it as a qualifying home. However, a home that you rent out during the year may be designated as a second residence only if your personal use exceeds the greater of 14 days or 10% of the rental days. In counting rental days, include days that the home is held out for rental or listed for resale. In counting days of personal use, use by close relatives generally qualifies as your personal use *(9.6)*.

A married couple filing jointly may designate as a second residence a home owned by either spouse.

If a married couple files separately, each spouse may generally deduct interest on debt secured by one residence. However, both spouses may agree in writing to allow one of them to deduct the interest on a principal residence plus a designated second residence.

Law Alert

Limit on Home Acquisition Debt

The maximum amount of home acquisition debt on which mortgage interest may be deducted for 2018 through 2025 is $750,000 ($375,000 if married filing separately). This limit applies only to loans obtained after December 15, 2017. For loans obtained on or before December 15, 2017, the prior-law limit of $1 million ($500,000 if married filing separately) continues to apply.

Caution

Mortgage Interest Reported on Form 1098

Banks and other lending institutions report mortgage interest payments of $600 or more to the IRS on Form 1098 or a similar statement. You should receive a copy of Form 1098 (or similar statement) for 2023 by January 31, 2024. The lender will report in Box 1 of Form 1098 the mortgage interest it received from you in 2023. Deductible points *(15.7)* paid on the purchase of a principal home are included in Box 6 of Form 1098.

Interest on debt secured by a residence other than your principal or second home may still be deductible, but only if you use the proceeds for investment or business purposes *(15.11)*.

Mortgage interest paid on your principal residence with assistance from Hardest Hit Fund. An IRS safe harbor (Revenue Procedure 2021-47) allows you to claim an itemized deduction for mortgage interest and for real estate taxes *(16.4)* even though some of the interest and taxes were paid by your State using funds from the Homeowner Assistance Fund (HAF), which was established by Congress in response to the COVID-19 pandemic. The HAF payments are not taxable income, but you cannot claim a deduction for expenses paid with those funds. For 2021 through 2025, the safe harbor allows you to claim a deduction for mortgage interest and/or real estate taxes to the extent you make payments to the mortgage servicer from your own sources; that is, they are out-of-pocket payments not made from the HAF or any other federal, state or local government program.

Interest on mortgage credit certificates. Under special state and local programs, you may be able to obtain a "mortgage credit certificate" to finance the purchase of a principal residence or to borrow funds for certain home improvements. A nonrefundable tax credit for interest paid on the mortgage may be claimed. The credit is computed on Form 8396 and claimed on Line 6g of Schedule 3 (Form 1040 or 1040-SR). The credit equals the interest paid multiplied by the certificate rate set by the governmental authority, but the maximum annual credit is $2,000. If you claim the credit, your home mortgage interest deduction is reduced by the amount of the current year credit claimed on Form 8396. If you buy a home using a qualifying mortgage credit certificate and sell that home within nine years, you may have to recapture part of the tax credit on Form 8828 and report this on Line 17b of Schedule 2 (Form 1040 or 1040-SR).

Planning Reminder

No Deduction for Postponed Mortgage Interest

If your lender agreed to forbearance on your home mortgage, which means your payments were postponed, you cannot deduct the interest that would have been paid during this time. Only interest payments actually made are deductible.

> **EXAMPLE**
>
> You pay $5,000 interest for a mortgage issued under a qualifying mortgage credit certificate. Under its terms, you are allowed a tax credit of $750. You may claim the balance of your mortgage interest, or $4,250 ($5,000 − $750), as home mortgage interest if you itemize deductions. If the allowable credit exceeds tax liability, a three-year carryover is allowed for the excess credit.

15.2 Home Acquisition Loans

A qualifying "home acquisition loan" is a loan used to buy, build, or substantially improve your principal residence or second home (*see 15.1* for the two-residence limit), and that is secured by the home being bought, constructed, or substantially improved. To be considered a substantial improvement, an improvement must add to the value of the home or prolong its useful life. Repairs do not qualify. You may deduct the interest paid on all your home acquisition debt, provided the total debt does not exceed the limit as discussed in the next paragraph.

Limit on home acquisition debt. If you have home acquisition debt that you incurred before December 16, 2017, you may deduct the interest you pay on the entire amount so long as the total acquisition debt does not exceed $1 million ($500,000 if you are married filing separately). Such debts are "grandfathered" by the Tax Cuts and Jobs Act, and the pre-Act $1 million limit (or $500,000 if married filing separately) continues to apply to the grandfathered debt *(15.1)*.

For home acquisition debt incurred after December 15, 2017, the debt ceiling for purposes of figuring mortgage interest deductions for 2018 through 2025 is $750,000 ($375,000 if married filing separately). However, two "grandfather" rules allow the prior-law loan limit of $1 million limit (or $500,000 if married filing separately) to apply to debt obtained after December 15, 2017:

1. The first exception is a transition rule for acquisition debt taken out to buy a home under a binding written contract that was in effect before December 16, 2017, provided the home purchase closing was on or before April 1, 2018.

Law Alert

Higher Loan Limit on "Grandfathered" Loans

Interest is deductible on home acquisition loans obtained before December 16, 2017, of up to $1 million ($500,000 if married filing separately). The prior-law $1 million (or $500,000) acquisition debt limit is "grandfathered", allowing the interest on such loans, and on a refinancing of such loans to be deducted currently. For home acquisition debt obtained after December 15, 2017, other than a refinancing of grandfathered debt, interest is deductible on loans up to $750,000 ($375,000 if married filing separately). *See 15.2* for details and Examples.

Court Decision

Family Financing of Residence

The Tax Court allowed a taxpayer to deduct mortgage interest payments on a loan that his brother obtained when the taxpayer's poor credit rating prevented him from obtaining a mortgage loan. The taxpayer's brother bought the house but allowed the taxpayer and his wife to live there on the condition that they make the mortgage payments directly to the bank.

The IRS disallowed the taxpayer's deduction for the mortgage interest on the grounds that he was not liable for the mortgage debt; his brother was. However, the Tax Court allowed the deduction, holding that the taxpayer was the beneficial (equitable) owner of the home and that he was legally obligated to his brother to pay off the mortgage.

As discussed in *15.2*, the Tax Court has taken a similar approach in other cases to allow a mortgage interest deduction to a family member who could show that he or she was the beneficial owner of the home.

2. The second grandfather exception applies if, after December 15, 2017, you refinance acquisition debt that was originally obtained by that date. The $1 million debt limit (or $500,000 if married filing separately) continues to apply to the loan balance on the date of refinancing; *see* Example 2 on the next page. This refinancing exception lasts until the end of the term of the original loan. If the original loan is not being amortized over its term, the refinancing exception lasts until the first refinancing term ends, but no more than 30 years from the first date of refinancing.

When you have grandfathered home acquisition debt from before December 16, 2017 (no more than $1 million, or $500,000 if married filing separately), and you take out new loans subject to the $750,000 limit ($375,000 if married filing separately), the grandfathered debt reduces the $750,000 (or $375,000) limit available for the new loans. In other words, interest is only deductible on the new debt to the extent that the grandfathered debt has not used up the entire $750,000 (or $375,000) limit; *see* Example 2 (Tom and Traci) on the next page.

Use IRS worksheets if debt limit exceeded. If your total debt exceeds the home acquisition debt limit (grandfathered limit or new law limit), you must use IRS worksheets included in Publication 936 to figure the amount of your deductible interest. You need to divide the debt limit by the average mortgage balance to get the deductible percentage of interest paid. See Publication 936 for options on figuring your average balance.

Unmarried co-owners. Unmarried co-owners do not have to allocate the applicable acquisition debt limit *(see above)* between them. For example, you and a co-owner (not your spouse) buy a principal residence in 2023 using a $500,000 home acquisition loan for which you are both liable and that is secured by the residence. On your individual returns, you may each deduct your share of the total interest paid on the $500,000 debt. If the loan were for more than $750,000, each of your deductions would be based on the $750,000 limit for home acquisition debt obtained after December 15, 2017; the allowable deduction must be figured using the IRS worksheets in Publication 936. Prior to a 2015 Ninth Circuit Appeals Court decision, the IRS had taken the position, and the Tax Court agreed, that unmarried co-owners had to allocate the debt limit between them (at that time the limit was $1.1 million, $1 million for acquisition debt and $100,000 for home equity debt). The Ninth Circuit disagreed and allowed each co-owner to deduct interest on the full debt limit. The IRS announced in 2016 that it would follow the Ninth Circuit opinion (2016-31 IRB 193; acquiescence to Voss v. Commissioner, 796 F.3d 1051 (9th Cir. 2015).

Family member may be treated as beneficial/equitable owner entitled to deduction. A taxpayer who is not a legal owner of the property on the deed and who has no legal obligation to make mortgage payments may be allowed a deduction for payments of mortgage interest if he or she can show a beneficial or equitable ownership interest in the residence. This requires a showing that the taxpayer has assumed the benefits and burdens of ownership. The Tax Court considers the following factors as evidence that the benefits and burdens of ownership have been assumed:

1. The right to possess the property and enjoy its use, rents, or profits;
2. A duty to maintain the property;
3. Being responsible for insuring the property;
4. Bearing the property's risk of loss;
5. Being obligated to pay the property's taxes, assessments, or charges;
6. Having the right to improve the property without the legal owner's consent;
7. Having the right to obtain legal title at any time by paying the balance of the purchase price.

In several cases, the Tax Court concluded that a family member who was not a legal owner had assumed the benefits and burdens of ownership and thus became an equitable owner who could deduct mortgage interest payments; *see* the adjacent Court Decision sidebar for an example.

In one case, the Tax Court allowed an interest deduction to a son who moved in with his mother on her California ranch after her divorce. She was unable to pay the mortgage and property taxes, and he agreed to pay them in exchange for her oral agreement to give him an ownership interest in the property. In 2010, the son paid $35,880 in interest on the mortgage, which he deducted. In 2013, his name was added to the legal title of the property. The IRS disallowed the 2010 deduction on the grounds that the son was not a legal owner obligated to make the payments until 2013. The Tax Court, however, allowed the deduction. Under California law, it is presumed that the legal owner, here the mother, is the sole beneficial owner, but the son was able to overcome this presumption by testifying credibly that they had an agreement that indicated an intent contrary to what was reflected in the deed. Moreover, he assumed the benefits and burdens of ownership by paying the mortgage and property taxes, as well as the insurance, cable bill, maintenance costs, and property improvements. He also bore a substantial risk of loss for his payments. Based on all the facts and circumstances, the Tax Court concluded that the son was an equitable owner of the property in 2010, and thereby entitled to a deduction for his mortgage interest payments.

EXAMPLES

1. Tom and Traci are married and file joint returns. Prior to December 16, 2017, they obtained an $875,000 first mortgage to buy their principal residence. They have not taken out any new debt or refinanced their mortgage. Because their loan was obtained before December 16, 2017, their debt is "grandfathered," and the $1 million home acquisition debt limit that applied to pre-12/16/17 loans continues to apply to their loan. On their 2023 joint return, Tom and Traci may deduct all of their mortgage interest payments, as their loan is under the grandfathered loan limit of $1 million.

2. In 2023, when the loan in Example 1 has a balance of $825,000, Tom and Traci refinance the debt, taking out a new first mortgage for the same amount. The refinanced debt is treated as grandfathered acquisition debt, subject to the $1 million limit, and thus interest on the entire $825,000 refinanced debt is deductible.

   However, if they had refinanced the debt for $900,000, the refinanced debt would be treated as grandfathered acquisition debt only to the extent of the loan balance at the time of refinancing, or $825,000. For 2023, interest may be deducted on up to $825,000 of the debt. Interest on the excess $75,000 debt ($900,000 - $825,000) cannot be deducted because, even if the debt was used for substantial home improvements, thereby qualifying it as home acquisition debt, it is subject to the $750,000 limit for acquisition debt incurred after December 15, 2017 that is not grandfathered, and the $750,000 limit is reduced to zero by the $825,000 of grandfathered debt.

3. Andrew obtains a first mortgage of $850,000 in 2023 to buy his principal residence. Andrew may deduct interest on only $750,000 of the debt for 2023 through 2025. Because the debt was taken out after December 15, 2017, and it is not used to refinance grandfathered debt, the $750,000 limit applies. The interest deduction allowed must be figured using the IRS worksheets in Publication 936.

Was your debt incurred in buying, constructing, or substantially improving a qualifying first or second residence? In some cases, you may treat a loan as home acquisition debt even though you do not actually use the loan proceeds to buy, build, or substantially improve the home. For example, if you buy a home for cash and within 90 days you take out a mortgage secured by the home, the mortgage is treated as home acquisition debt to the extent it does not exceed the home's cost; it does not matter how you use the mortgage loan proceeds.

When you build a home, construction expenses incurred before the loan may qualify as home acquisition debt for a 24-month period; *see 15.4*. If substantial improvements to a home are begun but not completed before a loan is obtained, the loan will be treated as acquisition debt (assuming the debt is secured by the home) to the extent of improvement expenses made within 24 months before the loan. If the loan is obtained within 90 days after an improvement is completed, the loan is treated as acquisition debt (assuming the debt is secured by the home) to the extent of improvement expenses made within the period starting 24 months before completion of the improvement and ending on the date of the loan.

Interest on a mortgage to buy or build a home other than your principal residence or qualifying second home *(15.1)* is treated as nondeductible personal interest. If a nonqualifying home is rented out, the part of the mortgage interest that is allocable to the rental activity is treated as passive activity interest subject to the limitations discussed in *Chapter 10*; the interest allocable to your personal use is nondeductible personal interest.

Cooperatives. In the case of housing cooperatives, debt secured by stock as a tenant-stockholder is treated as secured by a residence. The cooperative should provide you with the proper amount of your deductible interest. If the stock cannot be used to secure the debt because of restrictions under local law or the cooperative agreement, the debt is still considered to be secured by the stock if the loan was used to buy the stock. For further details on allocation rules, *see* IRS Publication 936.

Mortgage interest paid after house destroyed. If your principal residence or second home *(15.1)* is destroyed and the land is sold within a reasonable period of time following the destruction, the IRS treats the property as a residence for purposes of deducting interest payments on the mortgage during the period between the destruction of the residence and the sale of the land. In one case, the IRS allowed the interest deduction where a sale of land took place 26 months after the destruction of a home by a tornado.

If the destroyed residence is reconstructed and reoccupied within a reasonable period of time following the destruction, the property will continue to be treated as a residence during that period, and the interest payments on the mortgage on the property will be deductible. The IRS allowed an interest deduction where reconstruction began 18 months after, and was completed 34 months after, destruction of the home.

15.3 Home Equity Loans

Interest paid on home equity debt may be deducted as home mortgage interest for 2018 through 2025 only if the loan otherwise qualifies as home acquisition debt. If the debt is "only" home equity debt but not home acquisition debt, a mortgage interest deduction is not allowed.

As discussed in *15.2*, home acquisition debt is debt that is secured by your principal residence or second home and used to buy, build, or substantially improve that residence. If a home acquisition loan was taken out before December 16, 2017, the loan is treated as "grandfathered" debt subject to a loan limit of $1 million ($500,000 if married filing separately). If the loan was taken out after December 15, 2017, and it is not used to refinance a grandfathered debt, it is subject to an acquisition debt limit of $750,000 ($375,000 if married filing separately).

It is the use of the loan proceeds that determines if the loan qualifies and not how the loan is labeled. If a home equity loan or home equity line of credit (HELOC) is used to renovate a room in your main home or build an addition to the home, or to buy a second residence, the loan qualifies as home acquisition debt, assuming the loan is secured by the residence (first or second home) that is improved or purchased. If home equity debt qualifies as acquisition debt and the limit on acquisition debt has not already been reached, interest on the home equity debt falling within the limit is deductible; *see* the Examples next.

However, if the loan is not used to buy, build, or substantially improve your principal residence or second home, the interest is not deductible (for 2018-2025) as home mortgage interest regardless of the amount of the loan, because the loan does not qualify as home acquisition debt. For example, if you take a home equity loan in 2023 and use it to pay credit card debt, student loans, college tuition, medical bills, or other personal expenses, none of your interest payments in 2023-2025 on the loan will be deductible as home mortgage interest. For 2017 and prior years, the rule was different: interest on home equity loans used for personal expenses was generally deductible up to a debt limit of $100,000 ($50,000 if married filing separately), but the limit could not exceed the excess of the fair market value of your principal residence and second home (if any) over the amount of acquisition debt. However, for 2018 through 2025, no deduction is allowed for home equity loans used to pay personal living expenses.

Law Alert

Interest on Certain Home Equity Loans Is Deductible

Interest on a home equity loan or equity line of credit is deductible as home mortgage interest only if the loan is used to buy, build, or substantially improve a residence (first or second home) that secures the loan. Such loans qualify as home acquisition loans and the interest paid is deductible subject to the acquisition loan limits *(15.2)*.

Interest on a home equity loan used to pay personal living expenses, such as a loan used to pay off credit cards or student debt, is not deductible.

See 15.3 for details and Examples.

Loans used for investment or business purposes. The mortgage interest restrictions on home equity loans do not apply to loan proceeds used to buy or improve investment or business property. For example, if you use a home equity loan secured by your principal residence to buy investment securities, the interest deduction is figured on Form 4562 and claimed on Schedule A as investment interest *(15.9)*, not as mortgage interest. If you use a mortgage secured by your home to buy rental real estate, the interest paid is a rental expense deductible on Schedule E *(9.2)*. If you are self-employed and use the mortgage loan proceeds to buy property used in your business, the interest is deductible on Schedule C *(40.6)*.

EXAMPLES

1. Jim and Joni are married and file joint returns. In 2016, they took out an $825,000 first mortgage to buy their principal residence; the loan was secured by the residence. Prior to December 16, 2017, they took out a home equity line of credit (HELOC) secured by the residence and borrowed $70,000 which they used to renovate their kitchen and bathrooms. The HELOC qualified as home acquisition debt because it was secured by the principal residence and used to substantially improve it. Since both the first mortgage and the HELOC were incurred before December 16, 2017, both loans are treated as "grandfathered" acquisition debt subject to the $1 million debt limit, and as the total grandfathered debt is less than the $1 million limit, Jim and Joni may deduct the interest paid in 2023 on both loans.

2. Same facts as Example 1 except that Jim and Joni open the HELOC and use the $70,000 loan in 2022 to renovate their home. Assume the balance of the first mortgage is $800,000 as of January 1, 2022. The $800,000 balance is grandfathered debt as it was incurred before December 16, 2017, and as it is under the $1 million debt limit, interest is fully deductible on that loan. However, none of the interest paid on the HELOC loan is deductible. The HELOC loan qualifies as acquisition debt, as it was secured by their principal residence and used in 2023 to substantially improve it (renovating the kitchen and bathrooms). However, it is not grandfathered debt because it was not incurred before December 16, 2017, and therefore it cannot count towards the $1 million grandfathered limit. As acquisition debt incurred after December 15, 2017, the $70,000 loan is subject to the $750,000 limit, and since the $800,000 mortgage "uses up" the entire $750,000 limit, Jim and Joni cannot deduct any of the interest they pay on the HELOC loan in 2023.

3. Same facts as Example 2, except that the balance of the first mortgage has been reduced to $660,000 as of January 1, 2023. In this case, Jim and Joni may deduct the interest paid in 2023 on both loans. Although the HELOC debt is not grandfathered (because it was incurred after December 15, 2017), it qualifies as home acquisition debt subject to the $750,000 limit and since the total acquisition debt of $730,000 ($660,000 + $70,000) is below $750,000, Jim and Joni may deduct the interest they pay in 2023 on both loans.

4. Same facts as Example 1 except that Jim and Joni used the $70,000 HELOC loan to pay their son's college tuition and some medical bills, instead of renovating their home. Although the $70,000 loan was incurred before December 16, 2017, it is not grandfathered debt because it does not qualify as home acquisition debt; Jim and Joni did not use it to buy, build, or substantially improve their residence. Since the HELOC loan does not qualify as home acquisition debt, it is treated only as home equity debt, and interest on home equity debt that is not home acquisition debt is not deductible for 2018 through 2025. *See 33.13* for rules governing student loan interest deduction.

5. Karl and Kathryn are married and file jointly. In March 2023 they take out a first mortgage of $550,000 to buy their principal residence. In November 2023, they take a $100,000 home equity loan, secured by their principal residence, and use it to buy a vacation home. Although the home equity loan was used to buy a second home, the loan does not qualify as home acquisition debt because it was secured by the principal residence and not by the vacation home it was used to buy. Karl and Kathryn can deduct the interest paid in 2023 on the $550,000 mortgage, as it is well under the $750,000 limit, but none of the interest on the $100,000 home equity loan is deductible.

6. Assume that in Example 5, Karl and Kathryn had purchased their vacation home using a $300,000 first mortgage loan that was secured by the vacation home. The $300,000 loan now qualifies as home acquisition debt (because the loan was secured by the vacation home being purchased) subject to the $750,000 loan limit. Because the $300,000 vacation home loan and the $550,000 principal residence loan total more than $750,000, some of the interest paid by Karl and Kathryn in 2023 is not deductible; they should use the worksheets in IRS Publication 936 to figure their average balance and deductible home mortgage interest for 2023, based on a loan limit of $750,000.

15.4 Home Construction Loans

Interest on a home construction loan may be fully deductible for a period of up to 24 months while the home is under construction. For the 24-month period starting with the commencement of construction, the loan is considered home acquisition debt subject to the $1 million ceiling or the $750,000 ceiling, depending on when the loan was obtained *(15.2)*, provided that the loan is secured by the lot on which construction is taking place and the home is a principal residence or second home when it is actually ready for occupancy. In one case, the Tax Court allowed an interest deduction under the 24-month construction period rule even though the home was never built; *see* the case of the Roses in the text below.

According to the IRS, if construction begins before a loan is obtained, the loan is treated as acquisition debt to the extent of construction expenses within the 24-month period before the date of the loan. In determining the date of the loan for purposes of this 24-month rule, you can treat the date of a written loan application as the loan date, provided you receive the loan proceeds within 30 days after loan approval.

Interest incurred on the loan before construction begins is treated as nondeductible personal interest *(see* Example 1 in this section). If construction lasts more than 24 months, interest after the 24-month period also is treated as nondeductible personal interest.

Interest on loans taken out within 90 days after construction is completed may qualify for a full deduction. The loan is treated as acquisition debt to the extent of construction expenses within the last 24 months before the residence was completed, plus expenses through the date of the loan *(see* Example 2 below). For purposes of the 90-day rule, the loan proceeds generally are treated as received on the loan closing date. However, the date of a written loan application is treated as the loan date if the loan proceeds are actually received within 30 days after loan approval. If a loan application is made within the 90-day period and it is rejected, and a new application with another lender is made within a reasonable time after the rejection, a loan from the second lender will be considered timely even if more than 90 days have passed since the end of construction.

In one Tax Court case, Rose and his wife took out a $1.2 million loan and, in March 2006, bought beach-front property in Fort Myers, Florida. The loan was secured by the property. They tore down the existing home, intending to build a new vacation home on the site. However, they needed a construction permit from the Florida Department of Environmental Protection, and to obtain the permit they had to submit plans, surveys, and drilling samples to show their proposed home would meet hurricane and flood standards and not harm turtle habitats. By the time they obtained the construction permit in February 2008, the Florida real estate market was in decline, and they could not get financing to start constructing a building. In June 2009, they sold the property at a loss of $825,000.

The Roses claimed that their mortgage interest payments in 2006 and 2007 were deductible under the 24-month construction period rule. They argued that their demolition of the old house, clearing of the site and their preparatory work for the intended home in surveying and drawing up plans as part of the permit process should be treated as "construction." The IRS countered that there was no construction since the physical building process never began.

The Tax Court allowed the deductions. The demolition and site clearing work, and the planning and preparation work as part of the permit process, were necessary components of the overall process of construction. The deductions are not barred by the fact that the Roses sold the property before completing a residence that was ready for occupancy. The IRS regulation does not specifically address the situation where the residence under construction never becomes ready for occupancy. Each tax year must stand on its own; as things stood in 2006 and 2007, it was impossible for the Roses to know that they would be unable to complete the planned residence because of events beyond their control.

EXAMPLES

1. On October 19, 2022, you borrow $100,000 to buy a residential lot. The loan is secured by the lot. You begin construction of a principal residence on April 12, 2023, and use $250,000 of your own funds for construction expenses. The residence is completed November 21, 2024.

   The interest paid before the 24-month qualifying construction period began on April 12, 2023, is nondeductible personal interest. The $100,000 loan is treated as acquisition debt for the construction period (April 12, 2023–November 21, 2024), and the interest paid during that period is fully deductible *(15.2)*.

2. Same facts as in Example 1, but on February 13, 2024, you take out a $300,000 mortgage on the completed house to raise funds. You use $100,000 of the loan proceeds to pay off the $100,000 loan on the lot and keep the balance.

   All of the interest on the $300,000 loan is fully deductible because the loan qualifies as acquisition debt; $100,000 of the debt is treated as acquisition debt used for construction, since it was used to refinance the original 2022 debt to purchase the lot. The $200,000 balance is also treated as a construction loan under the 90-day rule. It was borrowed within 90 days after the residence was completed (November 21, 2024), and it reimbursed construction expenses of at least $200,000 incurred within 24 months before the completion date.

3. On January 11, 2023, you purchased a residential lot and began building a home on the lot using $90,000 of your personal funds. The home was completed on October 28, 2023. On November 30, 2023, you took out a loan of $72,000 that was secured by the home. The debt may be treated as acquisition debt taken out to build the home since it was taken out no later than 90 days after the home was completed, and expenditures of at least $72,000 were made within the period of 24 months before the home was completed.

 *Law Alert*

Deduction for Mortgage Insurance Premiums Expired at End of 2021

The law authorizing the deduction for mortgage insurance premiums expired at the end of 2021, as a result, no deduction is allowed for premiums paid in 2023.

15.5 Mortgage Insurance Premiums and Other Payment Rules

Payments to the bank or lending institution holding your mortgage may include interest, principal payments, taxes, and insurance premiums. If you itemize deductions, you may deduct eligible home mortgage interest *(15.2, 15.3)* and real estate taxes *(16.4)*. *See* below for mortgage insurance premiums.

In the year you sell your home, check your settlement papers for interest charged up to the date of sale; this amount is deductible.

Mortgage insurance premiums. The law authorizing a deduction for mortgage insurance premiums expired at the end of 2021 and was not extended. Therefore, after 2021, no deduction is allowed for mortgage insurance premiums paid in 2023.

Mortgage interest paid on your principal residence with assistance from the Homeowner Assistance Fund (HAF). As discussed in *15.1*, an IRS safe harbor (Revenue Procedure 2021-47) allows you to claim a deduction for mortgage interest and for real estate taxes *(16.4)* paid with out-of-pocket funds even though tax-free assistance has been received from the Homeowner Assistance Fund (HAF).

Interest on mortgage credit certificates. Under special state and local programs, you may be able to obtain a "mortgage credit certificate" to finance the purchase of a principal residence or to borrow funds for certain home improvements. A tax credit for interest paid on the mortgage may be claimed; *see 15.1*.

Prepayment penalty. A penalty for prepayment of a home mortgage is deductible as home mortgage interest provided the penalty is not for specific services provided by the mortgage holder.

 *Filing Tip*

Joint Liability on Mortgage

If you do not personally receive a Form 1098 but a person (other than your spouse with whom you file a joint return) who is also liable for and paid interest on the mortgage received a Form 1098, you deduct your share of the interest and attach a statement to your Schedule A showing the name and address of the person who received the form. If you are the payer of record on a mortgage on which there are other borrowers entitled to a deduction for the interest shown on the Form 1098 you received, provide them with information on their share of the deductible amount.

The Tax Court has allowed a joint obligor to deduct his or her payment of another obligor's share of the mortgage interest if the payment is made to avoid the loss of the property, and payment is made with his or her separate funds.

Mortgage assistance payments. You may not deduct interest paid on your behalf under Section 235 of the National Housing Act.

Delinquency charges for late payment. According to the IRS, a late payment charge is deductible as mortgage interest if it was not for a specific service provided by the mortgage holder. In one case, the Tax Court agreed with the IRS that delinquency charges imposed by a bank were not interest where they were a flat percentage of the installment due, regardless of how late payment was. The late charges were primarily imposed by the bank to recoup costs related to collection efforts, such as telephone calls, letters, and supervisory reviews. They were also intended to discourage untimely payments by imposing a penalty.

Graduated payment mortgages. Monthly payments are initially smaller than under the standard mortgage on the same amount of principal, but payments increase each year over the first five- or 10-year period and continue at the increased monthly amount for the balance of the mortgage term. As a cash-basis taxpayer, you deduct the amount of interest actually paid even though, during the early years of the mortgage, payments are less than the interest owed on the loan. The unpaid interest is added to the loan principal, and future interest is figured on the increased unpaid mortgage loan balance. The bank, in a year-end statement, will identify the amount of interest actually paid. (An accrual-basis taxpayer may deduct the accrued interest each year.)

Reverse mortgage loan. Homeowners who own their homes outright may in certain states cash in on their equity by taking a "reverse mortgage loan." Typically, 80% of the value of the home is paid by a bank to a homeowner in a lump sum or in installments. Principal is due when the home is sold or when the homeowner dies; interest is added to the loan and is payable when the principal is paid. The IRS has ruled that an interest deduction may be claimed by a cash-basis home-owner only when the interest is paid, not when the interest is added to the outstanding loan balance. A deduction is subject to the limits for interest on home equity loans *(15.3)*.

Redeemable ground rents. In a ground rent arrangement, you lease rather than buy the land on which your home is located. Ground rent is deductible as mortgage interest if: (1) the land you lease is for a term exceeding 15 years (including renewal periods) and is freely assignable; (2) you have a present or future right to end the lease and buy the entire interest; and (3) the lessor's interest in the land is primarily a security interest. Payments to end the lease and buy the lessor's interest are not deductible ground rents.

15.6 Interest on Refinanced Loans

When you refinance home acquisition debt *(15.2)* for the same amount as the remaining principal balance on the old loan, there is no change in the tax treatment of interest. In other words, if interest was fully deductible on the old loan, then it is fully deductible on the new loan.

As discussed in *15.2*, if you took out home acquisition debt before December 16, 2017, and you refinance that debt for more than the existing balance, the refinanced debt is considered "grandfathered" acquisition debt to the extent of the loan balance at the time of refinancing, and as "grandfathered" debt, that amount is subject to the $1 million limit for acquisition debt. The refinanced amount in excess of the existing balance is considered acquisition debt only if it is used to buy, build, or substantially improve your first or second home *(15.2)*, and interest on that debt is deductible for 2018 through 2025 only if the debt falls within the $750,000 limit for non-grandfathered loans incurred after December 15, 2017.

Interest paid on home acquisition loans in excess of the applicable ceiling (either $1 million or $750,000; *(15.2)*) is generally treated as nondeductible personal interest unless the proceeds are used for business or investment purposes *(15.3, 15.11)*.

Points Paid on Refinancing

The IRS does not allow a current deduction for points on a refinanced mortgage. According to the IRS, the points must be deducted ratably over the loan period, unless part of the new loan is used for improvements to a principal residence. Thus, if you pay points of

$2,400 when refinancing a 20-year loan on your principal residence, the IRS allows you to deduct only $10 a month, or $120 each full year.

A federal appeals court rejected the IRS allocation rule where points are paid on a long-term mortgage that replaces a short-term loan; *see* the Court Decision in this section *(15.7)*.

If part of a refinancing is used for home improvements to a principal residence, the IRS allows a deduction for a portion of the points allocable to the home improvements, as in the following Example.

> **EXAMPLE**
>
> In June 2023, Craig Smith refinances the mortgage on his principal residence when the loan balance is $80,000. The new loan is for $100,000, payable over 15 years starting in July 2023. He uses $80,000 to pay off the old $80,000 balance and the remaining $20,000 is used for home improvements. Assume that at the closing of the new loan, Smith pays points of $2,000 from his separate funds. In 2023, the year of payment, he may deduct 20% of the points, or $400, the amount allocable to the 20% of the loan used for home improvements. He may also deduct the ratable portion of the $1,600 balance of the points, which must be deducted over the period of the new loan. The ratable portion is $53 ($1,600 ÷ 180-month loan term × 6 months in 2023). Thus, Craig's total deduction for points in 2023 is $453 ($400 + $53).

Mortgage ends early. If you are ratably deducting points on a refinanced loan and you refinance again with a different lender, or the mortgage ends early because you prepay it or the lender forecloses, you can deduct the remaining points in the year the mortgage ends *(15.7)*.

15.7 "Points"

Lenders sometimes charge "points" in addition to the stated interest rate. The points increase the lender's upfront fees, but in return borrowers generally are charged a lower interest rate over the loan term. Points are either treated as a type of prepaid interest *(15.13)* or as a nondeductible service fee, depending on what the charge covers. If the points qualify as interest, they are deductible over the term of the loan unless they are paid on the purchase or improvement of your principal residence, in which case they are deductible in the year they are paid, as discussed below. If you pay points on a loan to purchase or improve a second home, you must deduct the points ratably over the term of the loan.

Points are treated as interest if your payment is solely for your use of the money and is not for specific services performed by the lender that are separately charged. Whether a payment is called "points" or a "loan origination fee" does not affect its deductibility if it is actually a charge for the use of money. The purpose of the charge—that is, for the use of the money or the services rendered—will be controlling. For example, you may not deduct points that are fees for services, such as appraisal fees, preparation of a mortgage note or deed of trust, settlement fees, notary fees, abstract fees, commissions, and recording fees.

If you are selling property and you assume the buyer's liability for points, do not deduct the payment as interest but include it as a selling expense that reduces the amount realized on the sale.

Deduction for Points on Purchase or Improvement of Principal Residence

Points are generally treated as prepaid interest *(15.13)* that must be deducted over the period of the loan. However, there is an exception for points you pay on a loan to buy, build, or improve your principal residence. The points on such loans are deductible in the year paid if these tests are met: (1) the loan is secured by your principal residence; (2) the charging of points is an established business practice in the geographic area in which the loan is made; (3) the points charged do not exceed the points generally charged in the area; (4) the amount of points is computed as a percentage of the loan and specifically earmarked on the loan closing statement as "points," "loan origination fees," or "loan discount"; and (5) you pay the points directly to the lender; *see* "Points withheld from the principal," below.

Court Decision

Current Deduction for Points on Refinancing

Huntsman replaced a three-year loan used to purchase his principal residence with a 30-year mortgage. He deducted $4,400 of points paid on the new mortgage. The IRS and the Tax Court held that the points had to be deducted over the 30-year loan term.

The Federal Appeals Court for the Eighth Circuit disagreed and allowed a full deduction in the year the points were paid. The first loan was temporary and merely a step in obtaining permanent financing for the purchase of the principal residence.

The IRS has announced that in areas outside of the Eighth Circuit, it will continue to disallow full deductions in the year of payment for points paid on refinancings. The Eighth Circuit includes only these states: Minnesota, Iowa, North and South Dakota, Nebraska, Missouri, and Arkansas. In these states, the IRS will not challenge deductions for points on refinancing agreements similar to Huntsman's that replace short-term financing with long-term permanent financing.

In a later case, the Tax Court held that the Huntsman exception does not apply where a borrower refinances a long-term mortgage to take advantage of lower interest rates; the points must be deducted over the term of the new mortgage.

Caution

Service Fees Are Not Deductible Points

You may not deduct as points amounts that are for specific lender services. To be deductible, points on the purchase of a principal residence must be prepaid interest for the use of the loan money.

Filing Tip

Amortize Points Starting in Second Year

A married couple purchased a principal residence and paid points late in the year. For the year of the purchase, their standard deduction exceeded their itemized deductions. The IRS ruled that claiming the standard deduction for the year the points are paid would not entirely forfeit the deduction for points. The points may be amortized starting in the second year. Assuming that they itemize deductions starting in the second year, the allocable portion of the points may be deducted each year over the remaining loan term.

Caution

Points Reported to the IRS

Points you paid in 2023 on the purchase of your principal residence will be reported to the IRS by the lender on Form 1098 if they meet the five tests for a deduction listed in *15.7*. Seller-paid points are also included on Form 1098. Form 1098 is used by the IRS to check on the deduction you claim for points on Schedule A. Points paid on an improvement loan for your principal residence also are deductible if they meet the tests; they are not shown on Form 1098.

Points paid by seller are deductible by buyer. The seller's payment is treated as an adjustment to the purchase price that the seller gives to you as the buyer and that you then turn over to the lender to pay off the points. You may fully deduct the points in the year paid if you meet the tests in the preceding paragraph. Otherwise, deduct them over the term of the loan. You must reduce your cost basis for the home by the seller-paid points.

Points withheld from the principal. Points withheld from the principal of a loan used to buy, build, or improve your principal residence are deductible as if you paid them directly to the lender if, at or before closing, you have made a down payment, escrow deposit, or earnest money payment that is at least equal to the amount of points withheld. These payments must have been from your own funds and not from funds that have been borrowed from the lender as part of the overall transaction.

Points on second home. If you pay points on a mortgage secured by a second home or a vacation home, the points are not fully deductible in the year of payment; you must claim the deduction ratably over the loan term.

Points paid on refinancing. The IRS does not allow a current deduction for points on a refinanced mortgage *(15.6)*.

Deduct balance of points if mortgage ends early. If you are deducting points over the term of the loan because a full first-year deduction is not allowed, you are allowed to deduct the balance in the year the mortgage ends, such as when you prepay the loan, or the lender forecloses. If the mortgage ends early because you refinance the mortgage with a different lender, you may deduct the balance of the points. For example, if you refinanced your mortgage in 2012 and paid points, those points had to be amortized over the loan term *(15.6)*. If in 2023 you refinance again with a different lender and pay points again, the balance of the points from the 2012 loan are deductible on your 2023 return, and the points on the new loan must be amortized over the loan term. If you refinanced with the same lender, the balance of the points from the 2012 loan must be deducted over the term of the new loan.

15.8 Cooperative and Condominium Apartments

Cooperative apartments. If you are a tenant-stockholder of a cooperative apartment, you may deduct your portion of:

- Mortgage interest paid by the cooperative on its debts to buy the land, or buy, build or improve the housing complex, provided the apartment is your first or second home *(15.1)*. This includes your pro rata share of the permanent financing expenses (points) of the cooperative on its mortgage covering the housing project.
- Real estate taxes paid by the cooperative *(16.6)*. However, if the cooperative does not own the land and building but merely leases them and is required to pay real estate taxes under the terms of the lease, you may not deduct your share of the tax payment.

In some localities, such as New York City, rent control rules allow tenants of a building converted to a cooperative to remain in their apartments even if they do not buy into the co-op. A holdover tenant may prevent some co-op purchasers from occupying an apartment. The IRS ruled that the fact that a holdover tenant stays in the apartment will not bar the owner from deducting his or her share of the co-op's interest and taxes.

Condominiums. If you own an apartment in a condominium, you have a direct ownership interest in the property and are treated, for tax purposes, just as any other property owner. You may deduct your payments of real estate taxes and mortgage interest. You may also deduct taxes and interest paid on the mortgage debt of the project allocable to your share of the property. The deduction of interest from condominium ownership is also subject to the two-residence limit *(15.1)*. If your condominium is used part of the time for rental purposes, you may deduct expenses of maintenance and repairs and claim depreciation deductions subject to certain limitations *(9.7)*.

15.9 Investment Interest Limitations

Interest paid on margin accounts and debts to buy or carry other investments is deductible on Schedule A up to the amount of net investment income. If you do not have investment income such as interest, you may not deduct investment interest. Investment income for purposes of the deduction generally does not include net capital gains or qualified dividends, but you may elect to include them in order to increase your investment interest deduction. If you make the election, the elected amount will not be eligible for the favorable capital gain rates; *see* "Computing the Deduction" below. Investment interest in excess of net investment income may be carried forward and deducted from next year's net investment income.

You compute the deduction for investment interest on Form 4952, which must be attached along with Schedule A (Form 1040 or 1040-SR).

What is investment interest? It is all interest paid or accrued on debts incurred or continued to buy or carry investment property such as interest on securities in a margin account. However, interest on loans to buy tax-exempt securities is not deductible *(15.10)*.

Investment interest does not include interest on qualifying home acquisition debt *(15.2)* or home equity debt *(15.3)*, construction period interest that is capitalized *(16.4)*, or interest related to a passive activity *(10.8)*.

Investment property includes property producing portfolio income (interest, dividends, or royalties not realized in the ordinary course of business) under the passive activity rules discussed in *Chapter 10*, and property in activities that are not treated as passive activities, even if you do not materially participate, such as working interests in oil and gas wells.

Passive activity interest is not investment interest. Interest expenses incurred in a passive activity such as rental real estate *(10.1)*, or a limited partnership or S corporation in which you do not materially participate *(10.6)*, are taken into account on Form 8582 when figuring net passive income or loss. This includes interest incurred on loans used to finance your investment in a passive activity. Do not treat passive activity interest as investment interest on Form 4952.

However, interest expenses allocable to portfolio income (non–business activity interest, dividends, or royalties) from a limited partnership or S corporation are investment interest and not passive interest. The investment interest will be listed separately on Schedule K-1 received from the partnership or S corporation.

Computing the Deduction

Deductible investment interest is limited to net investment income. Net investment income is the excess of investment income over investment expenses. The key terms investment income and investment expenses are defined below.

Investment income. Investment income is generally gross income from property held for investment, such as interest, dividends (but not qualified dividends unless you elect to include them; *see* next paragraph), annuities, and royalties. Income or expenses considered in figuring profit or loss of a passive activity *(10.8)* is not considered investment income or expenses. Property subject to a net lease is not treated as investment property, as it is within the passive activity rules.

Do you have net capital gain or qualified dividends? If you have net capital gain (net long-term capital gains exceeding net short-term losses) from the sale of investment property such as stocks or mutual fund shares, or capital gain distributions from mutual funds, such gains and distributions are not treated as investment income unless you specifically elect to include them in investment income on Form 4952. You may elect to include all or part of them. The same election rule applies to qualified dividends *(4.1)* that are subject to net capital gain tax rates. An election must be made on Form 4952 to include qualified dividends in investment income. If you make this election, you may not apply preferential capital gain rates *(5.3)* to the amount of the capital gains (and capital gain distributions) or qualified dividends treated as investment interest on Form 4952. If you make the election on Form 4952, the elected amount is not counted as net capital gains when applying the capital gain tax rates on the IRS worksheets *(5.3)*.

 *Filing Tip*

Investment Interest Deduction Reduces NII Tax

The amount of deductible investment interest reduces investment income for purposes of the net investment income (NII) tax. *See 28.3*.

 *Planning Reminder*

Deductible Investment Interest Cuts NII Tax

The net investment income tax *(28.3)* is imposed on investment income minus investment deductions. Thus, deductible investment interest reduces the amount of investment income subject to the NII tax.

 *Caution*

Interest on Loans To Buy Market Discount Bonds and Treasury Bills

Limits apply to the deduction for interest on loans used to buy or carry market discount bonds *(4.20)* and Treasury bills *(4.27)*.

Investment expenses. If you have deductible expenses, other than interest, directly connected with the production of investment income, they reduce investment income on Form 4952; *see* the form instructions.

Net investment income. Reducing investment income by investment expenses gives you net investment income. Your deduction for investment interest expenses is limited to this amount. If your 2022 investment interest exceeded your 2022 net investment income, the disallowed interest expense from 2022 may be carried over to 2023 and added to your investment interest (if any) for 2023. Similarly, disallowed investment interest expense for 2023 may be carried forward to 2024; *see* the Larry Jones Example.

Where to enter the deduction on your return. The deduction figured on Form 4952 is generally entered on Schedule A (Form 1040 or 1040-SR) as investment interest. However, if the interest is attributable to royalties, you may have to enter the interest on Schedule E; follow the Form 4952 instructions. Furthermore, there is an additional complication if you have investment interest for an activity for which you are not "at risk" *(10.18)*. After figuring the investment interest deduction on Form 4952, you must enter the portion of the interest that is attributable to the at-risk activity on Form 6198. The amount carried over to Form 6198 is subtracted from the investment interest deduction claimed on Form 4952.

Carryover of disallowed investment interest expense. Investment interest in excess of net investment income may be carried forward to future years until it can be claimed. On Form 4952 for 2023, any carried-over amount from 2022 is added to the amount of 2023 investment interest expense and the total is deductible to the extent it does not exceed net investment income for 2023. Any disallowed investment interest expense from Form 4952 for 2023 is carried over to Form 4952 for 2024 and will be deductible to the extent the total does not exceed 2024 net investment income.

> *EXAMPLE*
>
> For 2023, Larry Jones has $10,000 of investment income from interest and annuities. He has investment expenses, other than interest, of $3,200. In 2023 he paid $8,000 of investment interest expense on securities margin account loans. He also has $1,200 of disallowed investment interest expense from 2022 (excess of 2022 investment interest expense over 2022 net investment income). Jones also has income of $2,000 from a passive partnership investment.
>
> On his Form 4952 for 2023, Jones reports total investment interest expense of $9,200 ($8,000 plus the carried over $1,200 from 2022). His net investment income for 2023 is $6,800: $10,000 of investment income less $3,200 of non-interest investment expenses. The passive activity income from the partnership is not included in investment income.
>
> Jones's investment interest deduction for 2023 is limited to the $6,800 of net investment income. The $2,400 of investment interest expense in excess of net investment income ($9,200 − $6,800) is carried forward to 2024.

15.10 Debts To Carry Tax-Exempt Obligations

When you borrow money in order to buy or carry tax-exempt bonds, you may not deduct any interest paid on your loan. Application of this disallowance rule is clear where there is actual evidence that loan proceeds were used to buy tax-exempts or that tax-exempts were used as collateral. Sometimes the relationship between a loan and the purchase of tax-exempts is less obvious, as where you hold tax-exempts and borrow to carry other securities or investments. IRS guidelines explain when a direct relationship between the debt and an investment in tax-exempts will be inferred so that no interest deduction is allowed. The IRS will not infer a direct relationship between a debt and an investment in tax-exempts in these cases:

1. The investment in tax-exempts is not substantial. That is, it is not more than 2% of the adjusted basis of the investment portfolio and any assets held in an actively conducted business.
2. The debt is incurred for a personal purpose. For example, an investor may take out a home mortgage instead of selling his tax-exempts and using the proceeds to finance the home purchase. Interest on the mortgage is deductible subject to certain limitations *(15.1)*.
3. The debt is incurred in connection with the active conduct of a business and does not exceed business needs. But if a person reasonably could have foreseen when the tax-exempts were purchased that he or she would have to borrow funds to meet ordinary and recurrent business needs, the interest expenses are not deductible.

The guidelines infer a direct relationship between the debt and an investment in tax-exempts in this type of case: An investor in tax-exempts has outstanding debts not directly related to personal expenses or to his or her business. The interest will be disallowed even if the debt appears to have been incurred to purchase other portfolio investments. Portfolio investments include transactions entered into for profit, including investments in real estate, that are not connected with the active conduct of a business; *see* the Example below.

EXAMPLE

An investor owning $360,000 in tax-exempt bonds purchased real estate in a joint venture, giving a purchase money mortgage and cash for the price. He deducted interest on the mortgage. The IRS disallowed the deduction, claiming the debt was incurred to carry tax-exempts. A court allowed the deduction. A mortgage is the customary manner of financing such a purchase. Furthermore, since the purchase was part of a joint venture, the other parties' desires in the manner of financing had to be considered.

15.11 Earmarking Use of Loan Proceeds For Investment or Business

The IRS has set down complex record keeping and allocation rules for claiming interest deductions on loans used for business or investment purposes, or for passive activities. The rules deal primarily with the use of loan proceeds for more than one purpose and the commingling of loan proceeds in an account with unborrowed funds. The thrust of the rules is to base deductibility of interest on the use of the borrowed funds. The allocation rules do not affect mortgage interest deductions on loans secured by a qualifying first or second home *(15.1)*.

Keep separate accounts for business, personal, and investment borrowing. For example, if you borrow for investment purposes, keep the proceeds of the loan in a separate account and use the proceeds only for investment purposes. Do not use the funds to pay for personal expenses; interest is not deductible on personal loans other than qualifying student loans *(33.13)*. Furthermore, do not deposit loan proceeds in an account funded with unborrowed money, unless you intend to use the proceeds within 30 days of the deposit. By following these directions, you can identify your use of the proceeds with a specific expenditure, such as for investment, personal, or business purposes, and the interest on the loan may be treated as incurred for that purpose. See the 30-day rule discussed below.

The IRS treats undisbursed loan proceeds deposited in an account as investment property, even though the account does not bear interest. When proceeds are disbursed from the account, the use of the proceeds determines how interest is treated; *see* Examples 1 and 2.

 *Caution*

Tax-Exempt Income From Mutual Fund

You may not deduct interest on loans used to buy or carry tax-exempt securities. If you receive exempt-interest dividends from a mutual fund during the year, you may deduct interest on a loan used to buy or carry the mutual fund shares only to the extent that the proceeds can be allocated to taxable dividends you also receive.

 *Planning Reminder*

Keep Loans Separate

To safeguard your investment and business interest deductions, you must earmark and keep a record of your loans. You should avoid using loan proceeds to fund different types of expenditures.

30-day disbursement rule. If you deposit borrowed funds in an account with unborrowed funds, a special 30-day rule allows you to treat payments from the account as made from the loan proceeds. Where you make more than one disbursement from such an account, you may treat any expenses paid within 30 days before or after deposit of the loan proceeds as if made from the loan proceeds. Thus, you may allocate interest on the loan to that disbursement, even if earlier payments from the account have been made; *see* Example 3. If you make the disbursement after 30 days, the IRS requires you to allocate interest on the loan to the first disbursement; *see* Example 4. Furthermore, if an account includes only loan proceeds and interest earned on the proceeds, disbursements may be allocated first to the interest income and then to the loan proceeds.

Allocation period. Interest is allocated to an expenditure for the period beginning on the date the loan proceeds are used or treated as used and ending on the earlier of either the date the debt is repaid or the date it is reallocated.

Accrued interest is treated as a debt until it is paid, and any interest accruing on unpaid interest is allocated in the same manner as the unpaid interest is allocated. Compound interest accruing on such debt, other than compound interest accruing on interest that accrued before the beginning of the year, may be allocated between the original expenditure and any new expenditure from the same account on a straight-line basis. That is done by allocating an equal amount of such interest expense to each day during the taxable year. In addition, you may treat a year as twelve 30-day months for purposes of allocating interest on a straight-line basis.

Payments from a checking account. A disbursement from a checking account is treated as made at the time the check is written on the account, provided the check is delivered or mailed to the payee within a reasonable period after the writing of the check. You may treat checks written on the same day as written in any order. A check is presumed to be written on the date appearing on the check and to be delivered or mailed to the payee within a reasonable period thereafter. However, the presumption may not apply if the check does not clear within a reasonable period after the date appearing on the check.

Change in use of property. You must reallocate interest if you convert debt-financed property to a different use; for example, when you buy a business auto with an installment loan, interest paid on the auto is business interest, but if during the year you convert the auto to personal use, interest paid after the conversion is personal interest.

Order of repayment. If you used loan proceeds to repay several different kinds of debt, the debts being repaid are assumed to be repaid in the following order: (1) personal debt; (2) investment debt and passive activity debt other than active real estate debt; (3) debt from a real estate activity in which you actively participate; (4) former passive activity debt; and (5) business debt. *See* Example 5 below. Payments made on the same day may be treated as made in any order.

Planning Reminder

Using Borrowed Funds to Pay Investment or Business Interest

To get an interest deduction you must pay the interest; you may not claim a deduction by having the creditor add the interest to the debt. If you do not have funds to pay the interest, you may borrow money to pay the interest. The borrowed funds must be from a different creditor. The IRS disallows deductions where a debtor borrows from the same creditor to make interest payments on an earlier loan. The second loan is considered a device for getting an interest expense deduction without actually making payments. The Tax Court and several federal appeals courts have sided with the IRS.

EXAMPLES

1. On January 1, you borrow $10,000 and deposit the proceeds in a non–interest-bearing checking account. No other amounts are deposited in the account during the year and no part of the loan is repaid during the year. On April 1, you invest $2,000 of the proceeds in a real estate venture. On September 1, you use $4,000 to buy furniture.

    From January 1 through March 31, interest on the entire undisbursed $10,000 is treated as investment interest. From April 1 through August 31, interest on $2,000 of the debt is treated as passive activity interest and interest on $8,000 of the debt is treated as investment interest. From September 1 through December 31, interest on $4,000 of the debt is treated as personal interest; interest on $2,000 is treated as passive activity interest; and interest on $4,000 is treated as investment interest.

2. On September 1, you borrow money for business purposes and deposit it in a checking account. On October 15, you disburse the proceeds for business purposes. Interest incurred on the loan before the disbursement of the funds is

treated as investment interest expense. Interest starting on October 15 is treated as business interest. However, you may elect to treat the starting date for business interest as of the first of the month in which the disbursement was made—that is, October 1—provided all other disbursements from the account during the same month are similarly treated.

3. On September 1, you borrow $5,000 to invest in stock and deposit the proceeds in your regular checking account. On September 10, you buy a TV and sound system for $2,500 and on September 14 invest $5,000 in stock, using funds from the account. As the stock investment was made within 30 days of depositing the loan proceeds in the account, interest on the entire loan is treated as incurred for investment purposes.

4. Same facts as in Example 3, but the TV and sound system were bought on October 1 and the stock on October 31. As the stock investment was not made within 30 days, the IRS requires you to treat the purchase of the TV and the stereo for $2,500 as the first purchase made with the loan proceeds of $5,000. Thus, the 50% of loan interest that is allocated to the TV and sound system is nondeductible.

5. On July 12, Smith borrows $100,000 and immediately deposits the proceeds in an account. He uses the proceeds as follows:

August 31	$40,000 for passive activity
October 5	$20,000 for rental activity
December 24	$40,000 for personal use

On January 19 of the following year, Smith repays $90,000. Of the repayment, $40,000 is allocated as a repayment of the personal expenditure, $40,000 of the passive activity, and $10,000 of the rental activity. The outstanding $10,000 is treated as debt incurred in a rental activity.

15.12 Year To Claim an Interest Deduction

As a cash-basis taxpayer, you deduct interest in the year of payment except for prepayments of interest *(15.13)*. Giving a promissory note is not considered payment. Increasing the amount of a loan by interest owed, as with insurance loans, is also not considered payment and will not support a deduction. However, an accrual-basis taxpayer generally deducts interest in the year the interest accrues *(40.3)*.

Here is how a cash-basis taxpayer treats interest in the following situations:

On a life insurance loan, where proceeds are used for a deductible (nonpersonal) purpose, you claim a deduction in the year in which the interest is paid. You may not claim a deduction when the insurance company adds the interest to your debt. You may not deduct your payment of interest on an insurance loan after you assign the policy.

On a margin account with a broker, interest is deductible in the year in which it is paid or your account is credited after the interest has been charged. But an interest charge to your account is not payment if you do not pay it in cash or the broker has not collected dividends, interest, or security sales proceeds that may be applied against the interest due. Note that the interest deduction on margin accounts is subject to investment interest limitations *(15.9)*.

For partial payment of a loan used for a deductible (nonpersonal) purpose, interest is deductible in the year the payment is credited against interest due. When a loan has no provision for allocating payments between principal and income, the law presumes that a partial payment is applied first to interest and then to principal, unless you agree otherwise. Where the payment is in full settlement of the debt, the payment is applied first to principal, unless you agree otherwise. Where there is an involuntary payment, such as that following a foreclosure sale of collateral, sales proceeds are applied first to principal, unless you agree to the contrary. *See* also *15.11* for the effect of payments on the allocation of debt proceeds.

Note renewed. You may not deduct interest by merely giving a new note. You claim a deduction in the year the renewed note is paid. The giving of a new note or increasing the amount due is not payment. The same is true when past due interest is deducted from the proceeds of a new loan; this is not a payment of the interest.

15.13 Prepaid Interest

If you prepay interest on a loan used for investment or business purposes you may not deduct interest allocable to any period falling in a later taxable year. The prepaid interest must be deducted over the period of the loan, whether you are a cash-basis or accrual-basis taxpayer.

Points paid on the purchase of a principal residence are generally fully deductible in the year paid *(15.7)*. Points paid on refinancing generally are not deductible *(15.6)*. With the exception of deductible points *(15.7)*, prepayments of mortgage interest are not deductible; interest must be spread to the years to which it applies. You can only deduct the interest that qualifies as home mortgage interest *(15.1)* for that particular year.

Treatment of interest included in a level payment schedule. Where payments of principal and interest are equal, a large amount of interest allocated to the payments made in early years of a loan will generally not be considered prepaid interest. However, if the loan calls for a variable interest rate, the IRS may treat interest payments as consisting partly of interest, computed under an average level effective rate, and partly of prepaid interest allocable to later years of the loan. An interest rate that varies with the "prime rate" does not necessarily indicate a prepaid interest element.

When you borrow money for a deductible purpose and give a note to the lender, the amount of your loan proceeds may be less than the face value of the note. The difference between the proceeds and the face amount is interest discount. For loans that do not fall within the OID rules *(4.18)*, such as loans of a year or less, interest is deductible in the year of payment if you are on the cash basis. If you use the accrual basis, the interest is deductible as it accrues. For loans that fall within OID rules, your lender should provide a statement showing the interest element and the tax treatment of the interest.

Planning Reminder

Business or Investment Loans

If you prepay business or investment loan interest, you must spread the interest deduction over the period of the loan. In the year of payment, you may deduct only the interest allocable to that year.

CHAPTER 16

Deductions for Taxes

If you itemize deductions on Schedule A (Form 1040 or 1040-SR), you may deduct your payments of state and local income taxes (or state and local general sales taxes in lieu of state and local income taxes), state and local real property taxes, and state and local personal property taxes, but your total deduction for all of such taxes may not exceed $10,000 ($5,000 if you are married filing separately) *(16.1)*.

Subject to the $10,000 (or $5,000) limit, you can increase your deduction for state and local taxes by making a year-end prepayment of estimated tax liability. You also may be able to increase withholdings from your pay to increase your deduction.

If you pay transfer taxes on the sale of securities or investment real estate, the taxes are not deductible. However, transfer taxes on the sale may reduce the sales price when figuring your profit or loss.

Taxes paid in operating a business are generally deductible, except for sales taxes, which are added to the cost of the property.

Foreign real property taxes are no longer deductible, but an itemized deduction for foreign income taxes is allowed on Schedule A. Alternatively, you can opt to claim a tax credit for foreign taxes *(16.10, 36.13)*.

IRS Disallows Charitable Deduction Received in Exchange for State or Local Tax Credit under State Workarounds

As a way of trying to offset the effect of the $10,000 SALT deduction limit, some states enacted programs which provide residents with state or local tax credits if they make contributions to charitable organizations. However, the IRS treats the state or local tax credit as a quid pro quo if the credit exceeds 15% of the charitable payment, and thus no charitable contribution deduction is allowed for the amount of the credit; *see 14.3*.

You may be able to benefit from an IRS safe harbor that allows you to include the disallowed charitable deduction as a payment of state and local taxes, as discussed in *16.1*.

Law Alert

State and Local Taxes Deduction Limited

Your itemized deduction for state and local taxes cannot exceed $10,000 ($5,000 if married filing separately). The $10,000/$5,000 SALT limit is an overall limit that applies to the total of your state and local property taxes (real estate or personal property) and state and local income taxes, or general sales taxes in lieu of income taxes.

Several states challenged the consitutionality of the SALT deduction limit, but the Second Circuit Court of Appeals held that Congress had the constitutional authority to impose the limit, and the Supreme Court declined review, letting the Second Circuit decision stand.

16.1 Overall Limit on Deduction for State and Local Taxes

There is an overall limit on the amount of state and local taxes (referred to as SALT) that can be claimed as an itemized deduction on Schedule A (Form 1040 or 1040-SR). For 2018 through 2025, you cannot deduct more than $10,000 ($5,000 if you are married filing separately) for the following taxes, in any combination:

- State and local income taxes. You have the option to deduct state and local general sales taxes in lieu of state and local income taxes *(16.3)*.
- State and local real property taxes *(16.4)*, and
- State and local personal property taxes.

Note that if you are married filing jointly, your deduction limit for total state and local taxes in (1) through (3) above is the same $10,000 limit allowed to a single taxpayer.

There is no dollar limit for state and local real property and personal property taxes that you pay or incur with respect to property used in your business or investment property, such as residential rental property. These business/investment property taxes are not claimed as itemized deductions and therefore are not subject to the $10,000 limit ($5,000 if married filing separately). State and local real estate taxes imposed on business property are deductible on your Schedule C *(40.6)*, and property taxes imposed on residential rental property are deductible on Schedule E *(9.2)*.

Foreign real property taxes are not deductible for 2018 through 2025. Foreign income taxes are deductible under "Other taxes" (Line 6 of Schedule A) and they are not subject to the $10,000 limit ($5,000 if married filing separately). However, a tax credit may be a better alternative to the deduction *(16.10)*.

Safe harbor may allow increased deduction if you made charitable contribution in exchange for a state or local tax credit. As discussed in *14.3*, the IRS will not allow a charitable contribution deduction for amounts paid under a state program to an eligible charity to the extent that you receive state or local tax credits in exchange for the contribution (disregarding tax credits of 15% or less that are considered *de minimis*). However, where your charitable contribution must be reduced by the amount of the state or local tax credit received, a safe harbor allows the disallowed charitable amount to be added to the state and local tax payments you claim on your Schedule A, but only to the extent the credit offsets the current year's state or local tax liability.

This safe harbor is intended to benefit taxpayers who have a total state and local tax liability that is less than the SALT deduction limit, as such taxpayers would have been able to deduct their payment as state or local tax had a tax payment been made to the state or local government rather than making the contribution to the charity. Since the total deduction remains subject to the $10,000 SALT deduction limit ($5,000 if you are married filing separately), you get no benefit from the safe harbor if you are already over the limit even before adding the disallowed charitable amount.

> **EXAMPLE**
>
> In 2023, you make a $500 payment to a charitable organization and in return you receive a dollar-for-dollar state income tax credit. Assume your 2023 state income tax liability prior to the credit exceeds $500, so you are able to apply the entire $500 credit against the 2023 state liability. The $500 contribution may not be claimed as a charitable contribution under the IRS quid-pro-quo rule, *(14.3)*, but under the safe harbor, you can include the $500 disallowed charitable payment as a payment of state income tax on Schedule A for 2023, subject to the overall $10,000 SALT deduction limit ($5,000 if you are married filing separately).
>
> If your 2023 state tax income tax liability prior to the credit had been only $300, only $300 could be treated as a payment of state income tax on your 2023 Schedule A, and $200 would be carried over to 2024, assuming state law allows a carryover for unused credits. If you apply the $200 carryover credit against your 2024 state income tax liability, and you itemize deductions on your 2023 return, you can include the $200 as a payment of state or local income tax for 2023, subject to the overall $10,000 SALT deduction limit ($5,000 if you are married filing separately).

If the state or local tax credit exceeds the current year's state/local tax liability, only the amount of the current liability can be added to your state and local taxes on Schedule A; you can carry over the excess amount to next year and add it to next year's payments of state and local taxes. The above Example illustrates the carryover.

Workaround for owners of pass-through entities. Some states have created a way for owners of pass-through entities (PTEs) to avoid the SALT cap with respect to state income taxes on their share of business income. The PTEs elect to pay tax at the entity level and owners then get a tax credit on their state income tax returns for their share of the PTEs' tax payment. The IRS has allowed this "workaround" treatment; check state law for availability of this type of workaround.

16.2   Nondeductible Taxes

Transfer taxes. Transfer taxes paid on the sale of securities or investment real estate are not separately deductible; but when you report the sale on Form 8949, transfer taxes along with other selling expenses will decrease your gain or increases your loss; *see 5.8*.

A transfer tax (may be called an excise tax in some states) on the sale of a personal residence is not deductible as a real estate tax; it is imposed on the transaction and not on the value of the property. Transfer taxes are added to cost basis by the buyer or treated as an expense of sale by the seller.

Gasoline taxes. State and local taxes on gasoline used for personal purposes are not deductible. If you travel for business, the taxes are deductible as part of your expenses on Schedule C. If the standard mileage rate set by the IRS is not used, actual costs, including gasoline taxes, may be deducted.

Federal taxes. You cannot deduct federal income taxes or FICA taxes you pay on taxable compensation.

16.3   State and Local Income Taxes or General Sales Taxes

On Schedule A (Form 1040 or 1040-SR), you may deduct either your payments of state and local income taxes or your payments of state and local general sales taxes, but whichever you choose, the deduction is subject to the overall $10,000/$5,000 limit on state and local taxes discussed in *16.1*. On Line 5a of Schedule A, you may claim state and local income taxes or general sales taxes but not both; check the box on Line 5a if you elect to include state and local general sales taxes instead of income taxes. If your state and local income tax payments exceed the general sales tax, you should select the state and local income tax option. If your general sales tax amount exceeds the state and local income tax payments, you should select the general sales tax option

State and local income taxes. Subject to the overall $10,000/$5,000 limit on state and local taxes *(16.1)*, you may deduct on Schedule A (Form 1040 or 1040-SR) for 2023 state and local income taxes withheld from your pay during 2023 and estimated state and local taxes you paid in 2023, including the last installment of state and local estimated tax for 2022 if you paid it in January 2023. Also deduct any balance of your 2022 state and local taxes that you may have paid in 2023 when you filed your 2022 state/local tax return. If you pay additional state/local income tax in 2024 on your 2023 income (such as paying the last 2023 installment of state/local estimated tax in January 2024, or paying the balance due on your 2023 state/local return when you file the 2023 state return in 2024), that payment will be deductible on Schedule A for 2024 if you itemize deductions.

State income taxes may be claimed only as itemized deductions, even if attributed solely to business income. That is, state income taxes are not a deductible business expense on Schedule C *(40.6)*.

To increase your itemized deductions, consider prepaying state income taxes before the end of the year. The prepayment is deductible provided the state tax authority accepts prepayments and state law recognizes them as tax payments. The IRS has ruled, however,

 *Filing Tip*

State Income Tax Paid in 2023 For 2022

When you filed your 2022 state and local tax return in 2023, did you pay a balance due? If so, add the state/local tax paid with your return to your other 2023 payments of state and local tax (withholdings, estimated tax) when figuring your deduction on Schedule A for 2023.

that prepayments are not deductible if you do not reasonably believe that you owe additional state tax. Do not make prepayments if you expect to be subject to alternative minimum tax, since state and local taxes are not deductible for AMT purposes *(23.2)*.

If you report on the accrual basis and you contest a tax liability, claim the deduction in the year of payment.

You may deduct on your federal return state and local income taxes allocable to interest income that is exempt from federal tax but not from state and local income tax. However, state and local taxes that are allocated to other federal exempt income are not deductible. For example, state income tax allocated to a cost-of-living allowance exempt from federal income tax is not deductible as a state tax.

The IRS has held that mandatory employee contributions to state disability or worker's compensation funds in California, Massachusetts (as of October 1, 2019), New Jersey, New York, Rhode Island and Washington, and mandatory contributions to the Alaska, California, New Jersey, and Pennsylvania state unemployment funds, are deductible as state income taxes. In addition, mandatory contributions to state family leave programs, such as in New Jersey and California, are deductible as state income taxes.

However, employee contributions to a private or voluntary disability plan in California, New Jersey, or New York have been held by the IRS to be nondeductible.

Note: If you get a refund of state income taxes that you claimed as an itemized deduction, you may have to report it as income *(11.5)*.

State and local general sales taxes option. If you elect to deduct state and local general sales taxes in lieu of state and local income taxes, you have two ways to figure the sales tax deduction. You can figure deductible state and local general sales taxes using your credit card receipts and other records of non-business purchases for the year. Otherwise, you can use the IRS' optional tables and worksheet in the Schedule A instructions or the Sales Tax Deduction Calculator at IRS.gov.

Generally, you can only deduct sales taxes to the extent that the rate is the same as the general sales tax rate. However, sales taxes on food, clothing, medical supplies, and motor vehicles are deductible as general sales taxes even if the rate paid is less than the general sales tax rate.

If you paid sales taxes on the purchase or lease of a motor vehicle used for personal purposes (car, motorcycle, SUV, truck, van, or off-road vehicle) at a rate that is higher than the general sales tax rate, you may only include up to the general sales tax rate.

You may also include sales taxes paid at the general sales tax rate on the purchase of (1) a home, including a mobile or prefabricated home, or on a substantial addition to a home or a major home renovation, (2) a boat, or (3) an aircraft. *See* the Schedule A instructions for restrictions on taxes paid on the purchase of a home or major home renovation.

16.4 Deducting Real Estate Taxes

Your payments of state and local real estate taxes on your non-business property are deductible on Schedule A (Form 1040 or 1040-SR), subject to the overall $10,000/$5,000 limit on state and local taxes *(16.1)*. The tax must be based on the assessed value of the property and the assessment must be based on a uniform rate imposed for public purposes. *See 16.5* for deductible and nondeductible assessments for local benefits. Foreign real estate taxes are not deductible for 2018 through 2025.

The monthly mortgage payment to a bank or other mortgage holder generally includes amounts allocated to real estate taxes, which are paid to the taxing authority on their due date. Mortgage payments allocated to real estate taxes are deductible in the year you make the payments only if the mortgage holder actually pays the taxes to the tax authority by the end of that year. Typically, banks will furnish you with a year-end statement of disbursements to taxing authorities, indicating dates of payment. *See 16.5–16.7* for further details on real estate taxes.

Who may deduct real property taxes. A person who pays a property tax must have an ownership interest in the property to deduct the payment. *Table 16-2* summarizes who may deduct payments of real property taxes.

Real estate tax paid on your principal residence with assistance from the Homeowner Assistance Fund. As discussed in *15.1*, for 2021 through 2025, an IRS safe harbor (Revenue Procedure 2021-47) allows you to claim an itemized deduction for mortgage interest and for real estate taxes even though some of the interest and taxes were paid by your State using funds from the Homeowner Assistance Fund (HAF), which was established by Congress in response to the COVID-19 pandemic. You cannot claim a deduction for expenses paid with those funds, since the assistance was tax free, but the safe harbor allows you to claim a deduction for mortgage interest and/or real estate taxes to the extent you make payments to the mortgage servicer that are out-of-pocket: that is, they are not from the HAF or any other federal, state or local government program.

Table 16-1   Checklist of Taxes

Type of tax—	Deductible as itemized deduction for 2023—
Admission	No
Alcoholic beverage	No
Assessments for local benefits	No
Automobile license fees not qualifying as personal property tax	No
Cigarette	No
Customs duties	No
Driver's license	No
Estate—federal or state	No*
Excise—federal or state, for example, on telephone service	No
Foreign income tax	Yes *(16.10)*
Gasoline—federal	No
Gasoline and other motor fuel—state and local	No
Gift taxes—federal and state	No
Income—federal (including alternative minimum tax)	No
Income—state or local	Yes *(but see limit in 16.1)*
Inheritance tax	No
Mortgage tax	No
Personal property—state or local	Yes *(but see limit in 16.1)*
Poll	No
Real estate (state, local)	Yes *(but see limit in 16.1)*
Regulatory license fees (dog licenses, parking meter fees, hunting and fishing licenses)	No
Social Security	No
Tolls	No
Transfer taxes on securities and real estate	No

* But *see* the exception for miscellaneous itemized deduction for estate tax paid on "income in respect of a decedent" *(11.17)*.

Table 16-2 Who Claims the Deduction for Real Estate Taxes?

If the tax is paid by—	Then it is deductible by—
You, for your spouse	You may deduct if you file a joint return. But neither of you may deduct if your spouse has title to the property, and you each file a separate return. This is true even if the mortgage requires you to pay the taxes.
You, as owner of a condominium	You deduct real estate tax paid on your separate unit. You also deduct your share of the tax paid on the common property.
Your cooperative apartment or corporation	You deduct your share of real estate tax paid on the property; *see 15.9*. But if the organization leases the land and building and pays the tax under the terms of the lease, you may not deduct your share.
A life tenant	The life tenant may deduct the taxes. A court allowed the deduction to a widow required to pay the taxes under a will for the privilege of occupying the house during her life.
A tenant	The tenant of a business lease may deduct the payment of tax as additional rent, not tax. The tenant of a personal residence may not deduct the payment as either a tax or rent expense, unless placed on the real estate assessment rolls so that the tax is assessed directly against him or her; *see 16.6*.
You, where the tax is to maintain or repair an existing public facility, or meet interest costs on the maintenance	You deduct only that part of the tax that you can show is for maintenance, repair, or interest on maintenance expenses. If you cannot make the allocation, no deduction is allowed. If the benefit increases the value of the property, you add the non-deductible assessment to the basis of the property.
You, where your property was foreclosed for failure to pay taxes	You may not deduct the taxes paid out of the proceeds of the foreclosure sale if your interest in the property ended with the foreclosure.
Tenant by the entirety or joint tenant	A tenant who is jointly and severally liable for the tax may deduct it if it is paid with his or her separate funds. If a husband and wife own real estate as joint tenants or as tenants by the entirety, taxes paid by either of them may be deducted on their joint return, or if they file separately, by the spouse who pays the tax from his or her own funds.
Tenant in common	When property is owned as a tenancy in common, the IRS allows a tenant to deduct only his or her share of the tax, even if the tenant paid the entire tax. However, the Tax Court may allow a co-tenant to deduct the full amount if the tax is paid from his or her separate funds and the payment protects against the possibility of foreclosure in the event the other co-tenants failed to pay their share of the taxes *(9.2)*.
A mortgagee	No deduction. If tax is paid before the foreclosure, it is added to the loan. If paid after the foreclosure, it is added to the cost of property.

16.5   Assessments

Assessments by homeowner's association not deductible as taxes. Assessments paid to a local homeowner's association for the purpose of maintaining the common areas of the residential project and for promoting the recreation, health, and safety of the residents are not deductible as real property taxes because they are not imposed by a state or local government.

Assessments for government services. If property is used solely as your residence, you may not deduct charges for municipal water bills (even if described as a "tax"), sewer assessments, assessments for sanitation service, or title registration fees. A permit fee to build or improve a personal residence is added to the cost basis of the house.

Assessments for local benefits are deductible if they cover maintenance or repairs of streets, sidewalks, or water or sewer systems, or interest costs on such maintenance. However, assessments for construction of streets, sidewalks, or other local improvements that tend to increase the value of your property are not deductible as real estate taxes. Such assessments are added to your cost basis for the property.

If you are billed a single amount, you may deduct the portion allocable to assessments for government services maintenance or repairs. The burden is on you to support the allocation.

16.6   Tenants' Payment of Taxes

You generally may not deduct on Schedule A (Form 1040 or 1040-SR) a portion of your rent as property taxes. This is so even where state or local law identifies a portion of the rent as being tied to tax increases.

Tenants have been allowed a deduction for property taxes in the following cases: In Hawaii tenants with leases of 15 years or more were allowed to deduct the portion of the rent representing taxes. In California, homeowners on leased land who placed their names on the county tax rolls and who paid the taxes directly to the county were allowed to claim a deduction.

A locality may place liability for property tax directly on the tenant but the landlord is a collecting agent for paying over the tax to the taxing authorities. Where the landlord also remains liable for the tax, the IRS has ruled that the tenant's payment is in reality rent that cannot be deducted as a payment of real estate tax.

> **EXAMPLE**
>
> A municipal rent control ordinance allowed landlords to charge real property tax increases to the tenants as a monthly "tax surcharge." The ordinance stated that the surcharge was not to be considered rent for purposes of computing cost-of-living rental increases. The IRS ruled that the tenant may not deduct the "tax surcharge" as a property tax. The tax is imposed on the landlord, not on the tenant. The city ordinance, which permitted the landlord to pass on the tax increases to a tenant, did not shift liability for the property taxes from the landlord to the tenant. For federal tax purposes, the surcharge is merely an additional rental payment by the tenant. Similarly, "rates tax" or "renters' tax" imposed on tenants was ruled to be nondeductible because the tax is imposed on the person using the property rather than the property itself.

16.7   Allocating Taxes When You Sell or Buy Realty

When property is sold, the buyer and seller apportion the real estate taxes imposed on the property during the "real property year." A "real property year" is the period that a real estate tax covers. This allocation is provided for you in a settlement statement at the time of closing. If you want to figure your own allocations, your local tax authority can give you the "real property year" of the taxes you plan to apportion. If you are the seller and itemize deductions, you can claim on Schedule A the portion of the tax covering the beginning of the real property year through the day before the sale. If you are the buyer and itemize deductions, you can claim on Schedule A the part of the tax covering the date of the sale through the end of the real property year, even if the seller paid the entire tax prior to your purchase. Keep in mind that the deduction is subject to the overall $10,000/$5,000 limit on state and local taxes (16.1).

 *IRS Alert*

Form 1099-S for Sale of Principal Residence

The lender or real estate agent responsible for the closing does not have to report the sale of your principal residence on Form 1099-S if (1) the sales price is $250,000 or less, or $500,000 or less if you are married filing jointly, and (2) you certify in writing under penalty of perjury that you have met the tests for excluding from income the full gain on the sale *(29.1)*.

 *Filing Instruction*

Buyer's Share of Real Estate Tax

If you sold a house in 2023 and received Form 1099-S, check Box 6 for the amount of real estate tax that you paid in advance and that is allocable to the buyer. The buyer may deduct this amount. You subtract it from the amount you paid when claiming your 2023 itemized deduction for real estate taxes.

EXAMPLE

Your home is located in East County, which has a real property year starting April 1 and ending the following March 31. On May 1, 2023, you pay the $1,000 tax for the real property year that began April 1, 2023, and which ends March 31, 2024. You sell your home on July 12, 2023. You deduct $279 (102/365 of $1,000) as real estate tax for 2023, since there are 102 days in the period beginning April 1, 2023, and ending July 11, 2023 (day before sale). The buyer deducts $721 (263/365 of $1,000), since there are 263 days in the period beginning with the date of sale on July 12, 2023, and ending March 31, 2024 (the end of the real property year).

The allocation of taxes between the buyer and seller is mandatory for a property year during which both the seller and buyer own the property, whether or not your contract provides for an allocation. However, you do not allocate taxes for a real property year that begins after the date of sale. The buyer gets the deduction for all of the tax for that year because he or she owns the property for the entire real property year. There also is no allocation for a real property year that ends before the date of sale. The seller gets the deduction for that year's tax because the seller owned the property for that entire real property year.

Form 1099-S. If Form 1099-S is filed by the mortgage lender or real estate broker responsible for the closing, Box 6 will show the buyer's share of the real estate tax paid in advance by the seller. For example, Smith sells her house in Green County, where the real estate tax is paid annually in advance. In the year of sale she paid $1,200 in real estate taxes. Assuming that the home is sold at the end of the ninth month of the real property tax year, the amount of the real estate tax allocable to the buyer is $300 ($100 per month × 3 months). This amount, which is shown as paid by the seller in advance on an HUD-1 ("Settlement Statement") form provided at the closing, is reported as the buyer's share of the real estate tax in Box 6 of Form 1099-S.

Seller's deduction in excess of the allocated amount is taxed. If, in the year before the sale, the seller deducts an amount for taxes in excess of the allocated amount, the seller must report the excess as income in the year of the sale. This may happen when the seller is on the cash basis and pays the tax in the year before the sale.

EXAMPLE

A real property tax of $1,000 is due and payable by November 30 for the following calendar year. On November 23, 2022, Keith Jones, who uses the cash basis and reports on a calendar year, pays the 2023 tax. Jones deducts the payment on his 2022 Form 1040. On June 25, 2023, he sells the real property. Under the apportionment rule, Jones is allowed to deduct only $480 of the tax for the 2023 real property tax year ($480 = 175/365 of $1,000, since there are 175 days in the period from January 1 through June 24, 2023, the day before the sale). But Jones has already deducted the full amount on his 2022 return. Therefore, he must report as "Other income" for 2023 (Line 8z of Schedule 1, Form 1040 or 1040-SR), that part of the tax deduction that he was not entitled to under the apportionment.

Buyer may not deduct payment of seller's back taxes. If you agree to pay the seller's delinquent taxes as part of your purchase, the back taxes paid are added to your cost of the property. The amount realized on the sale by the seller is increased by your payment of the back taxes.

Seller's payment upon buyer's failure to pay. If a buyer is obligated to pay taxes under a land contract but fails to pay, the owner who pays the tax may deduct the payment if the tax is assessed to him or her.

Buyer of foreclosed property. If you buy realty at a tax sale and you do not receive immediate title to the property under state law until after a redemption period, you may not be able to deduct payment of realty taxes for several years.

16.8   Automobile License Fees

You may not deduct an auto license fee based on weight, model, year, or horsepower. However, you may include a fee based on the value of the car as a state or local personal property tax (Line 5c of Schedule A) if these three tests are met: (1) the fee is an ad valorem tax, based on a percentage of value of the property; (2) it is imposed on an annual basis, even though it is collected more or less frequently; and (3) it is imposed on personal property. This third test is met even though the tax is imposed on the exercise of a privilege of registering a car or for using a car on the road. A deduction for state/local personal property tax is subject to the overall limit of $10,000/$5,000 for state and local taxes *(16.1)*.

The majority of state motor vehicle registration fees are not ad valorem taxes and do not qualify for the deduction. Various states and localities impose ad valorem or personal property taxes on motor vehicles that may qualify for the deduction. Contact a state or local authority to determine whether a license fee qualifies.

Filing Tip

Value Portion of Auto License Fee

If an automobile license fee is based partly on value and partly on weight or other tests, the tax attributed to the value is deductible as an ad valorem tax and is deductible as a personal property tax on Line 5c of Schedule A.

16.9   Taxes Deductible as Business Expenses

If a tax may not be deducted as an itemized deduction, you may be able to deduct it elsewhere on your return. For example, you may generally deduct property taxes incurred as a cost of doing business on Schedule C. Here are some other examples:

If you pay excise taxes on merchandise you sell in your business, you deduct the tax as a business expense. If you pay Social Security taxes (FICA) on your employees' wages, you deduct the tax as a business expense on Schedule C. If you pay sales tax on business property, you add the tax to the cost of the property for depreciation purposes. If the tax is paid on nondepreciable property, the tax is included in the currently deductible cost. If you pay sales tax on a deductible business meal, the tax is deductible as part of the meal costs, subject to the allowable cost limit *(20.15)*.

Note: If you are not a material participant in the business, your Schedule C expenses are subject to passive activity limitations; *see Chapter 10.*

Above-the-line deduction for portion of self-employment tax.   Part of the self-employment tax figured on Schedule SE is deductible as an above-the-line adjustment to gross income on Line 15 of Schedule 1 (Form 1040 or 1040-SR) *(45.3)*. This is not a business expense and is not deductible on Schedule C.

16.10   Foreign Taxes

If you itemize deductions on Schedule A (Form 1040 or 1040-SR), you may include your payment of foreign income taxes and excess profits taxes on Line 6. Where you pay foreign income or excess profits tax, you have an election of either claiming the tax as an itemized deduction or as a tax credit. Claiming the credit may provide a larger tax savings *(36.13)*.

CHAPTER 17

Medical and Dental Expense Deductions

If you have unreimbursed medical expenses that exceed 7.5% of your adjusted gross income *(17.1)*, you may be able to deduct some of your expenses, assuming that you are able to claim itemized deductions that exceed your standard deduction *(13.1)*.

A different rule applies if you are self-employed and paid health insurance premiums. As a self-employed person, you do not have to itemize deductions to claim your premiums; you can claim 100% of the premiums as an above-the-line deduction directly from gross income *(12.2)*.

Carefully review the list of deductible expenses in this chapter so that you do not overlook any deductible expenses. Include payments of doctors' fees, health-care premiums, prescription medicines, travel costs for obtaining medical care, and eligible home improvements. COVID-19-related personal protective equipment is also deductible *(17.2)*.

If you are married, both you and your spouse work, and one of you has substantial medical expenses, filing separate returns may result in a lower overall tax.

Qualifying long-term-care expenses may be treated as medical expenses subject to the AGI floor, including a specified deductible amount of premiums paid for a qualifying long-term-care contract *(17.15)*.

Deductible contributions to health savings accounts (HSAs) and Archer MSAs may be available to individuals covered by high deductible health plans; *see Chapters 12 and 41*.

17.1 Medical and Dental Expenses Must Exceed AGI Threshold

The tax law provides only a limited opportunity to deduct unreimbursed medical and dental costs for you, your spouse *(17.5)*, and your dependents *(17.6)*. Although a wide range of expenses are potentially deductible *(Table 17-1)* if you itemize expenses on Schedule A of Form 1040 or 1040-SR (rather than claiming the standard deduction), your deduction may be completely disallowed or severely limited because of the 7.5% of adjusted gross income (AGI) floor. Only expenses that exceed 7.5% of your AGI may be claimed. The 7.5% floor applies regardless of your age. AGI is the amount shown on Line 11 of your Form 1040 or 1040-SR *(12.1)*.

Caution

Only Unreimbursed Expenses Are Deductible

You may not deduct medical expenses for which you have been reimbursed by insurance or other awards *(17.4)*. Furthermore, a reimbursement of medical expenses that you deducted in prior tax years may be taxable income in the year of the reimbursement *(11.6)*.

EXAMPLES

1. Frank Ryan's adjusted gross income (AGI) *(12.1)* for 2023 is $80,000. His unreimbursed expenses in 2023 are $6,875 for doctor and dentist visits, $1,845 for prescribed *(17.2)* drugs and medicines, and $3,750 for medical insurance premiums. Assuming that Frank itemizes deductions for 2023 on Schedule A (Form 1040 or 1040-SR), he may deduct medical/dental expenses of $6,470 after taking into account the 7.5% AGI floor:

Doctor and dentist fees	$ 6,875
Premiums	3,750
Drugs	1,845
Total	$ 12,470
Less: 7.5% of adjusted gross income (7.5% of $80,000)	6,000
Medical and dental expense deduction for 2023	$6,470

2. Same facts as in Example 1 except that Frank's AGI for 2023 is $170,000, not $80,000. Here, Frank may not claim any medical/dental deduction because his expenses of $12,470 do not exceed $12,750 (7.5% × $170,000 AGI).

Do your expenses count as paid in 2023? On your 2023 return, you may deduct allowable expenses *(17.2)* paid in 2023 in cash or by a check you mail in 2023 (unless the check is postdated to 2024) for yourself, your spouse *(17.6)*, or your dependents *(17.7)*. The 2023 deduction includes payments made in 2023 for allowable services provided before 2023. If you paid medical or dental expenses by credit card in 2023, the deduction is allowed for 2023, even if you do not pay the charge bill until 2024. If you pay expenses online, the payment date shown on your online bank statement governs. If you borrow to pay medical or dental expenses, you claim the deduction in the year you use the loan proceeds to pay the bill, even if you do not repay the loan until a later year.

17.2 Allowable Medical and Dental Care Costs

In determining whether you have paid deductible medical expenses exceeding the 7.5% AGI floor *(17.1)*, include the cost of diagnosis, cure, mitigation, treatment, or prevention of disease, or any treatment that affects a part or function of your body; *see* the text below and *Table 17-1*. Qualifying costs include those for yourself, your spouse *(17.5)*, and your dependents *(17.6)*.

Expenses incurred solely for cosmetic reasons are not deductible. Expenses incurred to benefit your general health are not deductible even if recommended by a physician *(17.3)*.

Over-the-Counter Drugs and Menstrual Products

The cost of OTC drugs is not deductible on Schedule A, even if a doctor gave you a prescription for it. Medicine must be obtainable only through a prescription to be deductible. The only exception is for insulin, which is deductible regardless of whether it is obtained over the counter or with a prescription. Although the CARES Act removed restrictions on reimbursements for OTC drugs and menstrual products from HSAs *(3.3, 41.12)*, Archer MSAs *(3.3, 41.13)*, health FSAs *(31.6)*, and HRAs *(3.3)*, the rule barring an itemized deduction for products that are obtainable without a prescription still stands.

Medicine and drugs. To be deductible, medicines and drugs other than insulin must be obtainable solely through a prescription by a doctor. Insulin is deductible even though a prescription may not be required. You may not deduct the cost of over-the-counter (OTC) medicines and drugs, such as aspirin and other cold remedies, even if you have a doctor's prescription for them.

Marijuana is not deductible even if prescribed by a doctor in a state allowing the prescription.

A prescribed drug brought in or shipped into the U.S. from another country is not deductible unless the FDA (Food and Drug Administration) allows that drug to be legally imported by individuals.

Diagnostic tests. The IRS treats unreimbursed diagnostic procedures as deductible medical expenses (subject to the AGI floor), even if you had no symptoms of illness and you underwent the test without a physician's recommendation. For example, the cost of an annual physical performed by a doctor and related laboratory tests is a medical expense, whether or not you were feeling ill. Similarly, a full body scan is a deductible diagnostic procedure, whether or not a physician recommended it. Where a procedure does not have a nonmedical function, a physician's recommendation is not necessary. It also does not matter if a less expensive alternative to the full body scan is available. Finally, a home pregnancy test qualifies as a medical expense even though its purpose is not to detect disease but to test for the healthy functioning of the body.

Health insurance premiums. Premiums you pay for health insurance covering yourself, your spouse *(17.5)* and your dependents *(17.6)* generally qualify for a deduction, *see 17.8* for limitations.

Covid-19-related personal protective equipment. The IRS announced that the costs of masks, hand sanitizers, sanitizing wipes, or other personal protective equipment purchased to prevent the spread of COVID-19 are deductible medical expenses.

Vitamins and nutritional or herbal supplements. The IRS does not allow a deduction for the cost of vitamins, nutritional or herbal supplements, or "natural" medicines unless a medical practitioner recommends them as treatment for a specific medical condition diagnosed by a physician. Otherwise, they are considered to be for maintaining your general health rather than for medical care.

Stop-smoking programs. The cost of smoking cessation programs is a deductible medical expense, as well as nicotine withdrawal drugs that require a physician's prescription. Over-the-counter nicotine patches and gums are not deductible.

Exercise and weight-reduction programs. If you incur costs for such programs to improve your general health, the costs are not deductible even if your doctor has recommended them. However, if your doctor has recommended a program as treatment for a specific condition, such as heart disease or hypertension, the IRS allows a deduction for the cost.

The IRS considers obesity a disease. If a physician has made a diagnosis of obesity, the costs of joining a weight-loss program and additional fees for meetings are eligible medical expenses. However, reduced-calorie diet foods that are substitutes for foods normally consumed are not deductible even if they are part of the program; *see* "Special foods" below.

Special foods. The IRS position on deducting the cost of "special foods" is unclear. The IRS states you may deduct the cost of special food in medical expenses if all of the following conditions exist: (1) the food does not satisfy normal nutritional needs, (2) an illness is treated or alleviated by the food, and (3) the need for the special food is substantiated by a physician. If all three conditions are met, the amount deductible is limited to the excess of the amount over what would normally be paid for a normal diet. This IRS position not only bars a deduction for low-calorie foods, on the grounds that they replace a "normal" diet, but it could also block a deduction for diets required to deal with conditions such as Celiac disease. Although gluten-free foods may have a clear medical purpose as diagnosed by a physician, such foods obviously "satisfy normal nutritional needs"; therefore, the IRS could deny a deduction for the excess cost.

Deducting Costs of Health Improvement Programs

Exercise and weight-reduction programs are deductible as treatments for specific conditions, but not as ways to improve your general health, even if your doctor has recommended them *(17.2)*.

EXAMPLES

1. To alleviate an ulcer, your doctor puts you on a special diet. According to the IRS, the cost of your food and beverages is not deductible. The special diet replaces the food you normally eat.

   Under the Tax Court test, the extra costs of the special diet would be deductible given the medical purpose of the diet.

2. Anna Von Kalb suffered from hypoglycemia and her physician prescribed a special high protein diet, which required her to consume twice as much protein as an average person and exclude all processed foods and carbohydrates. She spent $3,483 for food, and deducted 30%, or $1,045, as the extra cost of her high protein diet. The IRS disallowed the deduction, claiming that the protein supplements were a substitute for foods normally consumed. The Tax Court disagreed. The high protein food did not substitute for her usual diet but helped alleviate her hypoglycemia. Thus, she may deduct its additional expense.

3. The Bechers suffered from allergies and were advised by a physician to eat organically grown food to avoid the chemicals in commercial food. The Bechers claimed a medical expense deduction of $2,255, the extra cost of buying organic food.

   The IRS disallowed the deduction and the Tax Court agreed. They did not present evidence that their allergies could be cured by limiting their diet to organic food. That the food was beneficial to their general health and was prescribed by a doctor is not sufficient for a deduction.

Infant formula. Applying its "nutritional needs" test, the IRS in a private ruling denied a mother's deduction for the cost of infant formula for her healthy child. Although the mother had a medical reason for buying the formula—she was unable to breastfeed her baby following a double mastectomy—the formula was food satisfying the child's ordinary nutritional needs, and therefore was a nondeductible personal expense.

Portion of monthly service fees paid to retirement community. The portion of the monthly fees that is allocable to medical care is a deductible medical expense *(34.9)*.

Advance payment for lifetime care in retirement community. If you pay a life-care fee or "founder's fee" either monthly or in a lump sum to a retirement community, the portion allocable to future medical care may be included as a current medical expense *(34.9)*.

Advance payments for lifetime care of disabled dependent. You can treat as a current medical expense a nonrefundable advance payment to a private institution for the lifetime care and treatment of your physically or mentally impaired child upon your death or when you become unable to provide care. The nonrefundable payment must be a condition for the institution's future acceptance of your child.

EXAMPLE

Parents contracted with an institution to care for their handicapped child after their death. The contract provided for payments as follows: 20% on signing, 10% within 12 months, 10% within 24 months, and the balance when the child enters. Payment of specified amounts at specified intervals was a condition imposed by the institution for its agreement to accept the child for lifetime care. Since the obligation to pay was incurred at the time payments were made, the IRS held that they were deductible as medical expenses, although the medical services were not to be performed until a future time, if at all.

 *Filing Tip*

Childbirth Classes

A mother-to-be may deduct the cost of classes instructing her in Lamaze breathing and relaxation techniques, stages of labor, and delivery procedures. If her husband or other childbirth "coach" also attends the classes, the portion of the fee allocable to the coach is not deductible. Costs of classes on early pregnancy, fetal development, or caring for newborns also are not deductible.

 *Filing Tip*

DNA Collection Kits

The IRS has ruled informally that, for a DNA collection kit purchased to obtain health care information, the portion of the cost related to this feature can be treated as a deductible medical expense.

 *Court Decision*

Sex Reassignment Surgery Is Deductible Expense

The IRS has agreed to follow a 2010 decision in which a Tax Court majority held, over a rigorous dissent, that Gender Identity Disorder (GID) is a disease for medical deduction purposes. A taxpayer, born male, was allowed to deduct expenses for cross-gender hormone therapy and sex reassignment surgery (SRS). Expert testimony confirmed that the taxpayer suffered from severe GID, and hormone therapy and SRS are essential elements of a widely accepted treatment protocol for that condition. The cost of breast augmentation surgery was potentially deductible, but under the facts here, the procedure was not shown to be medically necessary under accepted treatment protocols.

The IRS acquiescence to the decision means that it will no longer dispute that GID is a disease and that expenses for its treatment, including sex reassignment surgery and hormone therapy, are deductible medical expenses where there is medical documentation of GID.

Table 17-1   Deductible Medical Expenses

Professional Services

Chiropodist	Optician	Practical or other nonprofessional nurse for medical services only, not for care of a healthy person or a child who is not ill. Costs for medical care of elderly person unable to get about or person subject to spells are deductible (17.12).	Psychoanalyst
Chiropractor	Optometrist		Psychologist
Christian Science practitioner	Orthopedist		Registered nurse
Dermatologist	Osteopath		Surgeon
Dentist	Pediatrician		Unlicensed practitioner services are deductible if the type and quality of the services are not illegal.
Gynecologist	Physician		
Neurologist	Physiotherapist		
Obstetrician	Plastic surgeon; but see 17.3.	Psychiatrist	
Ophthalmologist	Podiatrist		

Dental Services

Artificial teeth	Dental X-rays	Filling teeth	Oral surgery
Cleaning teeth	Extracting teeth	Gum treatment	Straightening teeth

Equipment and Supplies

Abdominal supports	Breast pumps and lactation supplies	Hearing aids	Repair of special telephone equipment for the deaf
Air conditioner where necessary for relief from an allergy or for relieving difficulty in breathing (17.13).	Contact lenses and solutions	Heating devices	Sacroiliac belt
	Cost of installing stair-seat elevator for person with heart condition (17.13).	Invalid chair	Special mattress and plywood bed boards for relief of arthritis or spine
Ambulance hire		Iron lung	
Arches	COVID-19-related personal protective equipment (17.2).	Orthopedic shoes—excess cost over cost of regular shoes	Splints
Artificial eyes, limb	Crutches	Oxygen or oxygen equipment to relieve breathing problems caused by a medical condition	Truss
Autoette (auto device for handicapped person)	Elastic hosiery		Wheelchair
Back supports	Eyeglasses	Reclining chair if prescribed by doctor	Wig advised by doctor as essential to mental health of person who lost all hair from disease
Braces	Fluoridation unit in home		

Medical Treatments

Abortion	Hydrotherapy (water treatments)	Navajo healing ceremonies ("sings")	Radial keratotomy
Acupuncture	In vitro fertilization for a female otherwise unable to conceive	Nursing	Radium therapy
Blood transfusion	Injections	Organ transplant	Ultraviolet ray treatments
Childbirth delivery	Insulin treatments	Prenatal and postnatal treatments	Vasectomy
Diathermy	Laser eye surgery or radial keratotomy to improve vision	Psychotherapy	Whirlpool baths
Electric shock treatments		Sterilization	X-ray treatments
Hearing services			

Medicines and Drugs

Cost of prescriptions only; over-the-counter medicine is not deductible.

Laboratory Examinations and Tests

Blood tests	Sputum tests	Hospital Services	Use of operating room
Cardiographs	Stool examinations	Anesthetist	Vaccines
Metabolism tests	Urine analyses	Hospital bills	X-ray technician
Spinal fluid tests	X-ray examinations	Oxygen mask, tent	

Premiums for Medical Care Policies (17.5)

Blue Cross and Blue Shield	supplemental insurance, and Medicare D prescription drug coverage	Health insurance covering hospital, surgical, and other medical expenses	Membership in medical service cooperative
Contact lens replacement insurance			
Medicare A (if not covered by Social Security), Medicare B			

Table 17-1   Deductible Medical Expenses (continued)

Miscellaneous

Alcoholic inpatient care costs

Birth control pills or other birth control items prescribed by your doctor

Braille books—excess cost of Braille works over cost of regular editions

Childbirth classes for expectant mother

Convalescent home—for medical treatment only

Drug treatment center—inpatient care costs

Fees paid to health institute where the exercises, massages, etc., taken there are prescribed

by a physician as treatments necessary to alleviate a physical or mental defect or illness

Kidney donor's or possible kidney donor's expenses

Lead-based paint removal to prevent a child who has had lead poisoning from eating the paint. Repainting the scraped area is not deductible.

Legal fees for guardianship of mentally ill spouse where commitment was necessary for medical treatment

Lifetime care—advance payments made either monthly or as a lump

sum under an agreement with a retirement home *(34.10)*.

Long-term care costs for chronically ill *(17.15)*.

Nurse's board and wages, including Social Security taxes paid on wages

Pregnancy test kit

Remedial reading for child suffering from dyslexia

School—payments to a special school for a mentally or physically impaired person if the main reason for using the school is its resources for relieving the disability *(17.10)*.

"Seeing-eye" dog and its maintenance

Smoking cessation programs

Special school costs for physically and mentally handicapped children *(17.10)*.

Telephone-teletype costs and television adapter for closed caption service for deaf person

Travel to obtain medical care *(17.9)*.

Wages of guide for a blind person

Weight-loss program to treat obesity or other specific disease *(17.2)*.

Table 17-2   Nondeductible Medical Expenses

Antiseptic diaper service

Athletic club expenses

Babysitting fees to enable you to make doctor's visits

Boarding school fees paid for healthy child while parent is recuperating from illness

Bottled water bought to avoid drinking fluoridated city water

Cost of divorce recommended by a psychiatrist

Cost of hotel room suggested for sex therapy

Cost of moving away from airport noise by person suffering a nervous breakdown

Cost of trips prescribed by a doctor for a "change of environment" to boost an ailing person's morale

Dance lessons advised by a doctor as general physical and mental therapy

Divorced spouse's medical bills

Domestic help; but *see 17.12* if nursing duties are performed.

Ear piercing

Funeral, cremation, burial, cemetery plot, monument, or mausoleum

Health programs offered by resort hotels, health clubs, and gyms

Illegal operations and drugs

Marijuana, even if prescribed by a physician in a state permitting the prescription (but this may change, so check the *e-Supplement* at *jklasser.com* for any update)

Marriage counseling fees

Massages recommended by physician for general stress reduction

Maternity clothes

Premiums on policies guaranteeing you a specified amount of money each week in the event hospitalization

Scientology fees

Special food or beverage substitutes; but *see 17.2*.

Tattooing

Teeth whitening to reverse age-related discoloration

Toothpaste

Transportation costs of a disabled person to and from work

Travel costs to favorable climate when you can live there permanently

Travel costs to look for a new place to live—on a doctor's advice

Tuition and travel expenses to send a problem child to a particular school for a beneficial change in environment *(17.10)*.

Weight-loss program to improve general health *(17.2)*.

17.3   Nondeductible Medical Expenses

The most common nondeductible medical expense is the cost of over-the-counter medicines and drugs, such as aspirin and other cold remedies. A deduction for over-the-counter medicines is disallowed even if you have a doctor's prescription *(17.2)*. Expenses incurred to improve your general health, such as exercise programs not related to a specific condition, are not deductible *(17.2 and Table 17-2)*.

Cosmetic procedures. A medical expense deduction is allowed for cosmetic surgery if it is necessary to improve a disfigurement related to a congenital abnormality, disfiguring disease, or an accidental injury. For example, a deduction is allowed for breast reconstruction surgery, as well as breast prosthesis, following a mastectomy as part of a treatment for cancer.

You may not deduct the cost of cosmetic surgery or other procedures that do not have a medical purpose. Thus, face lifts, hair transplants, electrolysis, teeth-whitening procedures, and liposuction intended to improve appearance are generally not deductible. However, in one case, the Tax Court allowed an exotic dancer to claim a depreciation deduction for breast implants essential for her business *(19.10)*.

Future medical care. Generally, you cannot include as a current medical expense payment for medical care that is to be provided substantially beyond the end of the year. However, advance payments for the care of a disabled dependent or the portion of a life-care fee or "founder's fee" to a retirement community that is allocable to future medical care is a currently deductible expense *(17.2)*.

17.4 Reimbursements Reduce Deductible Expenses

Insurance or other reimbursements of your medical costs reduce your potential medical deduction. Reimbursements for loss of earnings or damages for personal injuries and mental suffering do not have to be taken into account. A reimbursement first reduces the medical expense for which it is paid. The excess is then applied to your other deductible medical costs. *See* Example 1 below.

Personal injury settlements or awards. Generally, a cash settlement recovered in a personal injury suit does not reduce your medical expense deduction. The settlement is not treated as reimbursement of your medical bills. But when part of the settlement is specifically earmarked by a court or by law for payment of hospital bills, the medical expense deduction is reduced.

If you receive a settlement for a personal injury that is partly allocable to future medical expenses, you reduce medical expenses for these injuries by the allocated amount until it is used up.

Fake claims. Medical reimbursements for fake injury claims are treated as taxable income; *see* Example 2 below.

EXAMPLES

1. In 2023, Gail Hurz paid $3,600 in medical insurance premiums, $4,800 for doctor and hospital bills and $750 for prescription drugs. She received reimbursements of $1,175 from group hospitalization insurance ($800 for the doctor and hospital bills and $375 for the drugs.) Her adjusted gross income for 2023 is $63,000. If Gail itemizes deductions on Schedule A, she can claim a medical expense deduction of $3,250, after taking into account the 7.5% AGI floor.

Prescription drugs	$750
Medical care expenses	4,800
Premiums	3,600
Total	$9,150
Less reimbursement	1,175
Unreimbursed costs	$7,975
Less: 7.5% of $63,000	4,725
Medical expense deduction for 2023	$3,250

2. Dodge, with the aid of a "friendly" doctor, arranged to be hospitalized for alleged back injuries and realized over $200,000 from HIP policies. The IRS charged that the insurance proceeds were taxable income. Dodge argued they were tax-free reimbursements of medical costs.

   The Tax Court sided with the IRS. The tax-free rules cover the payment of legitimate medical costs. Here there were no legitimate medical costs of actual injuries. Dodge took out the policies in a scam arrangement with the doctor.

Reimbursements in excess of your medical expenses. If you paid the entire premium for health insurance, you are not taxed on payments from the plan even if they exceed your medical expenses for the year. If you and your employer each contributed to the policy, you generally have to include in income that part of the excess reimbursement that is attributable to employer premium contributions not included in your gross income; *see* Examples 2–4. The taxable excess reimbursement must be reported as "Other income" on Line 8z of Schedule 1 (Form 1040 or 1040-SR).

You do not have to report any excess reimbursements that are tax-free payments for permanent disfigurement or loss of bodily functions *(3.2)*.

If your employer paid the total cost of the policy and the contributions were not taxed to you, you report as income all of your excess reimbursement, unless it covers payment for permanent injury or disfigurement *(3.2)*.

For the treatment of insurance reimbursements of long-term care costs, *see 17.15*.

 *Caution*

Reimbursements Exceeding Expenses

If you have more than one policy and receive reimbursements that exceed your total medical expenses for the year, you must pay tax on all or part of the reimbursement where your employer paid premiums on the policies; *see* Examples 1–4 in this section.

EXAMPLES

1. Henry Knight pays the premiums for two personal health insurance policies. His total medical expenses are $900. He receives $700 from one insurance company and $500 from the other. The excess reimbursement of $300 ($1,200 − $900) is not taxable because he paid the entire premiums on the policies.

2. Lionel Guest's employer paid premiums of $1,800 for two employee health insurance policies covering medical expenses. Guest's medical expenses in one year are $900. He receives $1,200 from the two companies. The entire $300 excess is taxable because Guest's employer paid the total cost of the policies and the contributions were not taxed to him.

3. Kay Brown's employer paid a premium of $1,000 for a group health policy covering Brown, and Brown herself paid $300 for a personal health policy. Her medical expenses are $900. She receives reimbursements of $1,200, $700 under her employer's policy and $500 under her own policy. Brown's reimbursements exceed expenses by $300, but the taxable portion attributed to her employer's premium contribution is $175, computed this way:

Reimbursement allocated to Brown's policy ($500 ÷ $1,200) × $900	$375
Reimbursement allocated to employer's policy ($700 ÷ $1,200) × $900	$525
Taxable excess allocated to employer's policy ($700 − $525)	$175

4. Mike Green's employer paid $1,200 for a health insurance policy but contributed only $450 and deducted $750 from Green's wages. Green also paid $300 for a personal health insurance policy. His medical expenses are $900. He recovered $700 from the employer's policy and $500 from his personal policy. The excess attributable to the employer's policy is $175 (computed as in Example 3 above). However, the taxable portion is only $65.63. Both Green and his employer contributed to the cost of the employer's policy and a further allocation is necessary:

Green's contribution	$750
Employer's contribution	450
Total cost of policy	$1,200
Ratio of employer's contribution to annual cost of policy (450 ÷ 1,200, or 37.50%)	
Taxable portion: 37.50% of excess reimbursement of $175	$65.63

Reimbursement in a later year may be taxed. If you took a medical expense deduction in one year and are reimbursed for all or part of the expense in a later year, the reimbursement may be taxed in the year received. The reimbursement is generally taxable income to the extent the deduction reduced your tax in the prior year. *See* the details for figuring taxable income on a recovery of a prior deduction in *Chapter 11 (11.6)*.

EXAMPLES

1. In 2022, Anna Gurchani had adjusted gross income of $32,000. On Schedule A, she claimed itemized deductions that exceeded her allowable standard deduction by $1,000. Gurchani listed medical expenses of $3,800 before taking into account the 7.5% AGI floor. She claimed $1,400 as her medical expenses deduction for 2022:

Medical expenses	$3,800
Less: 7.5% of $32,000	2,400
Allowable deduction	$1,400

   In 2023, she collects $300 from insurance, reimbursing part of her 2022 medical expenses. If she had collected that amount in 2022, her medical expenses would have been $3,500 and her deduction would have been $1,100. The entire reimbursement of $300 is includible as taxable income for 2023. It is the amount by which the 2022 deduction of $1,400 exceeds the deduction of $1,100 that would have been allowed if the reimbursement had been received in 2022.

2. Same facts as in Example 1 above, but Anna did not deduct medical expenses for 2022 because she claimed the standard deduction. The reimbursement in 2023 is not taxable.

17.5 Expenses of Your Spouse

Subject to the 7.5% AGI floor *(17.1)*, you may deduct as medical expenses your payments of medical bills for your spouse if you were married either when your spouse received the medical services or at the time you paid the expenses. That is, you may deduct your payment of your spouse's medical bills even though you are divorced or widowed, if, at the time the expenses were incurred, you were married. Furthermore, if your spouse incurred medical expenses before you married and you pay the bills after you marry, you may deduct the expense.

EXAMPLES

1. You got married in 2023. After the marriage, you pay your spouse's outstanding medical bills from 2022. You may claim the payment as a medical expense for 2023 (subject to the 7.5% AGI floor) if you itemize expenses on a joint return or on your own return if you and your spouse file separately.

2. In October 2022, your spouse had dental work done. In February 2023, you are divorced and in April 2023, you pay your former spouse's dental bills. If you itemize expenses on your 2023 tax return, you may include the payment in figuring your deductible medical expenses (subject to the 7.5% AGI floor).

3. In 2023, you pay medical expenses for your spouse who died in 2022. In 2023 you remarry and file a joint 2023 return with your new spouse. If you itemize expenses on the 2023 joint return, you may include your payment of your deceased spouse's medical expenses in figuring your deductible medical expenses (subject to the 7.5% AGI floor).

Filing separately in community property states. If you and your spouse file separately and live in a community property state, any medical expenses paid out of community funds are treated as paid 50% by each of you. Medical expenses paid out of separate funds of one spouse can be deducted only by that spouse.

Filing Tip

Should Spouses File Separately?

If you are married and both you and your spouse have separate incomes, and one of you has substantial unreimbursed medical expenses for 2023, consider filing separate returns. This way the 7.5% AGI floor *(17.1)* will apply separately to your individual incomes, not to the higher joint income. To make sure which option to take—filing jointly or separately—you compute your tax on both types of returns and choose the one giving the lower overall tax *(1.3)*.

On a separate return, only include the expenses you paid. If you paid medical expenses out of a joint checking account in which you and your spouse have an equal interest, then each of you are considered to have paid half of the medical expenses unless you show otherwise.

17.6   Expenses of Your Dependents

You may deduct your payment of medical bills for your children or other dependents, subject to the 7.5% AGI floor *(17.1)*. You may deduct the expenses of a person who was your dependent (your qualifying child or qualifying relative; *21.2*) either at the time the medical services were provided or at the time you paid the expenses. That person must have been a U.S. citizen or national, or a resident of the United States, Canada, or Mexico, but this test does not apply to an adopted child who lived with you.

In determining whether a person is your "dependent" for medical expense purposes, you may be able to claim the expenses of someone who does not meet all of the regular tests for being your qualifying child or qualifying relative *(21.2)*. Specifically, you may deduct your payment of medical costs for a person who cannot be treated as your dependent for one of the following reasons: (1) the person is your child who is treated as a dependent of the other parent under the special rules *(21.7)* for divorced/separated parents; *see* below, (2) the person has gross income equal to or more than the annual limit for qualifying relatives ($4,700 for 2023), (3) the person files a joint return with their spouse, or (4) you (or your spouse if filing jointly) are the dependent of another taxpayer and thus are barred from claiming any dependents on your return.

The other dependent tests for a qualifying child or a qualifying relative must be met. For example, to claim your payment of medical expenses for your parent, or for your child who is not your qualifying child *(21.3)*, you must pay over 50% of his or her support under the qualifying relative rules *(21.4)*. *See* Examples 1–3 below. A child may not deduct medical expenses paid with his or her parent's welfare payments; *see* Example 4 below.

Divorced and separated parents.   You may be able to deduct your payment of your child's medical costs, even though your ex-spouse is entitled to treat the child as a dependent *(21.7)*. For purposes of a 2023 medical deduction, the child is considered to be the dependent of both you and the child's other parent if (1) you are divorced or legally separated under a court agreement, separated under a written agreement, or married but living apart during the last six months of 2023; (2) the child was in the custody of one or both of you for more than half of 2023; and (3) together you provided more than half of the child's 2023 support.

EXAMPLES

1. You contribute more than half of your married 19-year-old son's support in 2023, including a payment of a medical expense of $800. Because your son filed a joint return with his wife for 2023, he is not your "qualifying relative" for purposes of the $500 credit for other dependents *(21.4, 25.4)*. But if you claim itemized deductions for 2023, you may include your $800 payment for your son with your other qualifying medical expenses since you contributed more than half of his support.

2. Your mother, a U.S. citizen, underwent an operation in November 2022. You paid for the operation in February 2023. You may deduct the cost of the operation in 2023 (subject to the 7.5% AGI floor) if you furnished more than one-half of your mother's support in either 2023 or 2022.

3. Same facts as Example 2, except your mother is a citizen and resident of Italy. You may not deduct the cost of the operation. She is not a U.S. citizen or a resident of the United States, Canada, or Mexico and thus does not qualify as a dependent for medical deduction purposes. She also does not qualify for other tax purposes under the general tests for dependents *(21.2)*.

4. A son is the legal guardian of his mother who is mentally incompetent. As guardian, he received his mother's state welfare and Social Security benefits, which he deposited in his personal bank account and used to pay part of his mother's medical expenses. On his tax return, he claimed a deduction for the total medical expenses paid on behalf of his mother. The court held that he could deduct only medical expenses in excess of the amounts received as welfare and Social Security payments. The benefits, to the extent used to pay medical expenses, represented the mother's payments in her own behalf.

Adopted children. You may deduct medical expenses of an adopted child if you may claim the child as a dependent either when the medical services are rendered or when you pay the expenses. An adopted child is treated as your child for dependent purposes when a court has approved the adoption or the child is lawfully placed with you for legal adoption.

If you reimburse an adoption agency for medical expenses it paid under an agreement with you, you are considered to have paid the expenses. But if the reimbursement is for medical services that were provided and paid for before you began your adoption negotiations, you may not deduct your payment.

You may not deduct medical expenses for services rendered to the natural mother of the child you adopt.

Multiple support agreements. If you have the right to treat a person as your dependent under a multiple support agreement *(21.6)*, you may claim your unreimbursed payments of that person's medical expenses. Even if the person has a gross income of $4,700 or more in 2023, and therefore cannot be considered your qualifying relative for other tax purposes *(21.4)*, you may still deduct your 2023 payments of his or her medical expenses (subject to the 7.5% AGI floor) provided the other multiple support agreement tests *(21.6)* are met.

> **EXAMPLE**
>
> Ingrid Fromm and her brother and sister share equally in the support of their mother. Part of their mother's support includes medical expenses. Should the three of them share in the payment of the medical bills or should only one of them pay the bills? The answer: The siblings should agree to a multiple support agreement *(21.6)* that gives one of them the right to claim the mother as a dependent (qualifying relative *(21.4)*, and that person should pay the mother's medical bills, since only that person may deduct the payment as a medical expense. If the multiple support agreement allows Ingrid to claim her mother as a dependent, Ingrid should pay the mother's medical bills. Assuming Ingrid claims itemized deductions, she can include the payment of her mother's medical expenses as her own in figuring her medical expense deduction. If her brother and sister reimburse her for part of the bill, Ingrid may include only the unreimbursed portion in her medical expenses. Neither Ingrid's brother nor her sister may deduct this share. Thus, a deduction is lost for these amounts.

17.7 Decedent's Medical Expenses

If you pay the medical expenses of your deceased spouse or dependent *(17.6)*, you may claim the payment as a medical expense in the year you pay the expenses, whether that is before or after the person's death.

If the executor or administrator of the estate pays the decedent's medical expenses within one year after the date of death, an election may be made to treat the expenses as if the deceased had paid them in the year the medical services were provided. The executor or administrator may file an amended return for the year the services were provided and claim them as a medical deduction for that year, assuming the period for filing the amended return *(47.2)* has not passed.

If the election is made by the executor to claim the expenses as an income tax deduction, and an estate tax return is filed, the expenses may not also be claimed as a deduction on the estate tax return. The executor must file a statement with the decedent's income tax return that the expenses have not been deducted on the estate tax return and the estate waives its right to deduct them for estate tax purposes.

> **EXAMPLE**
>
> Oscar Reyes incurred medical expenses of $5,000 in 2022 and $3,000 in 2023. He timely filed (by April 15, 2024) his 2023 return and died June 1, 2024, without having paid the $8,000 of medical expenses. In October 2024 his executor pays the medical expenses. The executor may file an amended return (in Oscar's name) for 2022, claim a medical expense deduction for the $5,000 of 2022 expenses, and get a refund for the increased deductions. The executor may claim the remaining $3,000 as a medical expense deduction on an amended final return for 2023.

Filing Instruction

Multiple Support Agreement

If you may claim a person as your dependent under a multiple support agreement, include with your medical expenses only the amount you actually pay for the dependent's medical expenses. If you are reimbursed by others who signed the multiple support agreement, you must reduce your deduction by the amount of reimbursement.

If medical expenses are claimed as an income tax deduction, the portion of the expenses that are not allowed because they are below the 7.5% AGI floor *(17.1)* may not be claimed as an estate tax deduction if an estate tax return is filed. Although the expenses were not actually deducted, the IRS considers them to be part of the overall income tax deduction.

17.8 Premiums for Health Insurance

Unless you are self-employed and qualify for the 100% above-the-line deduction (discussed below), health insurance premiums are deductible only as an itemized medical expense on Schedule A (Form 1040 or 1040-SR), subject to the 7.5% AGI floor *(17.1)*. Include premiums you paid for health insurance that covers hospital, surgical, drug costs, and other medical expenses for you, your spouse *(17.6)*, and your dependents *(17.7)*. Deductions may be claimed for premiums paid for contact lens replacement insurance, membership payments in associations furnishing cooperative or free-choice medical services, group hospitalization, or clinical care policies, including HMOs (health maintenance organizations) and medical care premiums paid to colleges as part of a tuition bill, if the amount is separately stated in the bill.

You may deduct premiums for Medicare Part B supplemental insurance and Medicare Part D prescription drug insurance. Payroll withholdings for Medicare Part A are not medical expenses. Premiums for voluntary coverage under Medicare (Part A) are deductible by those over age 65 who are not covered by Social Security.

Premiums paid before you reach age 65 for medical care insurance for protection after you reach age 65 are deductible in the year paid if they are payable on a level payment basis under the contract (1) for a period of 10 years or more or (2) until the year you reach age 65 (but in no case for a period of less than five years).

Premiums for qualifying long-term care policies are deductible subject to limitations *(17.15)*.

Nondeductible premiums. You may not deduct premiums for a policy guaranteeing you a specified amount each week (not to exceed a specified number of weeks) in the event you are hospitalized. Also, no deduction may be claimed for premiums paid for a policy that compensates you for loss of earnings while ill or injured, or for loss of life, limb, or sight. If your policy covers both medical care and loss of income or loss of life, limb, or sight, no part of the premium is deductible unless (1) the contract or separate statement from the insurance company states what part of the premium is allocated to medical care and (2) the premium allocated to medical care is reasonable.

You may not deduct part of the car insurance premiums for medical insurance coverage for persons injured by or in your car where the premium covering you, your spouse *(17.6)*, or your dependents *(17.7)* is not stated separately from the premium covering medical care for others.

You generally cannot deduct premiums you pay for covering someone who is not your dependent, even if that person is your child (such as your non-dependent child under age 27 who is included on your policy). However, if that person is not your dependent only for the reasons specified in *17.7*, you may deduct the premiums paid for that person.

Self-employed deduction. If you were self-employed in 2023 you may claim a deduction on Line 17 of Schedule 1 (Form 1040 or 1040-SR) for 100% of health insurance premiums you paid for yourself, your spouse, and your dependents. The deduction is also allowed if you received wages from an S corporation in which you were more than a 2% shareholder, you were a general partner, or you were a limited partner who received guaranteed payments.

The above-the-line deduction *(12.2)* may not be claimed for any month that you were eligible for coverage under an employer's subsidized health plan, including a plan of your spouse's employer. Also, the deduction may not exceed your net earnings from the business under which the health premiums are paid.

Any balance of premiums not deductible because you had coverage under a subsidized employer health plan may be claimed as an itemized medical expense subject to the 7.5% AGI floor *(17.1)*.

Filing Instruction

Long-Term Care Premiums

The amount of deductible premiums for a qualifying long-term care policy depends on your age *(17.15)*.

Filing Instruction

Above-the-Line Deduction for Relatives Employed by 2% S Corporation Owners

Relatives who are treated as owners under attribution rules—spouses, children, and some others—who work for the S corporation and whose health insurance coverage is reported on their W-2s as compensation can deduct the cost as an above-the-line deduction.

17.9 Travel Costs May Be Medical Deductions

Travel costs to a doctor's office, hospital, or clinic where you, your spouse, or your dependents receive medical care are deductible medical expenses, subject to the 7.5% AGI floor *(17.1)*. Commuting to work is not a medical expense, even if your condition requires you to make special travel arrangements.

Deductible travel includes fares for buses, taxis or trains, and the costs of hiring a car service or ambulance to obtain medical care. Plane fares to another city are allowed by the IRS so long as obtaining medical care is the primary purpose of the trip; *see* below for lodging expense rule.

If you used your automobile in 2023 to obtain medical care, you may include in your medical expenses a flat IRS rate (standard mileage rate) of 22 cents per mile. You may also deduct parking fees and tolls. However, if auto expenses exceed the standard mileage rate, you may deduct your actual out-of-pocket costs for gas, oil, repairs, tolls, and parking fees. Do not include depreciation, general maintenance, or car insurance. The cost, as well as the operating and repair costs, of a wheelchair, autoette, or special auto device for a person with a disability is deductible if not used mainly for commuting.

Filing Tip

Deductible Travel Costs

The costs of trips to receive medical treatment are deductible as medical expenses subject to the 7.5% AGI floor. The costs of a trip to a conference to learn about medical treatment may be deductible if recommended by a doctor.

> **EXAMPLE**
>
> In 2023, you drove your car to a doctor's office for treatment 40 times throughout the year. Each round trip was 25 miles, so the mileage for the year was 1,000 miles (40 trips x 25 miles). If you use the IRS' flat mileage rate, you may include $220 for the doctor visits (1,000 miles × 22 cents), plus parking fees or tolls you paid on the doctor visits, as 2023 medical expenses.

Medical conferences. Travel costs and admission fees to a medical conference are deductible medical expenses if an illness suffered by you, your spouse, or your dependents is the subject of the conference. For example, the IRS allowed a parent to deduct the registration fees and cost of traveling to a medical conference dealing with treatment options for a disease suffered by her dependent child. The child's doctor had recommended the conference. During the conference, most of the parent's time was spent attending sessions on her child's condition. Any recreational activities were secondary. If the parent had attended the conference because of her own condition the same deductions would have been allowed.

Lodging and meals while attending the conference are not deductible medical expenses; these are allowed only if treatment is received at a licensed hospital or similar facility, as discussed below.

Lodging expenses. If you are receiving inpatient care at a hospital or similar facility, your expenses, including lodging and meals, are deductible medical expenses subject to the AGI floor. If you are not an inpatient, lodging expenses while away from home are deductible as medical expenses if the trip is primarily to receive treatment from a doctor in a licensed hospital, hospital-related outpatient facility, or a facility equivalent to a hospital. Meal expenses are not deductible unless they are paid as part of inpatient care.

The deduction for lodging while receiving treatment as an outpatient at a licensed hospital, clinic, or hospital-equivalent facility is limited to $50 per night per person. For example, the limit is $100 if a parent travels with a sick child. The IRS ruled that the $50 allowance could be claimed by a parent for a six-week hotel stay while her eight-year-old daughter was treated in a nearby hospital for serious injuries received in an automobile accident. The mother's presence was necessary so that she could sign release forms.

Caution

Meal Costs of Medical Trip

While transportation to receive medical care is a deductible medical expense subject to the AGI floor, meals while on a trip for medical treatment are not deductible. They simply replace the meals you normally would eat. However, if you are hospitalized, the cost of meals while an inpatient is a deductible expense.

Deductible Transportation Costs

Examples of travel costs that have been treated as medical expenses by IRS rulings or court decisions are:

- Nurse's fare if the nurse is required on the trip
- Parent's fare if parent is needed to accompany child who requires medical care
- Parent's fare to visit his child at an institution where the visits are prescribed by a doctor

- Trip to visit specialist in another city
- Airplane fare to a distant city in which a patient used to live to have a checkup by a family doctor living there. That he could have received the same examination in the city in which he presently lived did not bar his deduction.
- Trip to escape a climate that is bad for a specific condition. For example, the cost of a trip from a northern state to Florida during the winter on the advice of a doctor to relieve a chronic heart condition is deductible. The cost of a trip made solely to improve a post-operative condition by a person recovering from a throat operation was ruled deductible.
- Travel to an Alcoholics Anonymous club meeting if membership in the group has been advised by a doctor
- Disabled veteran's commuting expenses where a doctor prescribed work and driving as therapy
- Wife's trip to provide nursing care for an ailing husband in a distant city. The trip was ordered by her husband's doctor as a necessity.
- Driving prescribed as therapy
- Travel costs of a kidney transplant donor or prospective donor

Nondeductible Transportation Costs

- Commuting to work
- Trip for the general improvement of your health
- Traveling to areas of favorable climates during the year for general health reasons, rather than living permanently in a locality suitable for your health Meals while on a trip for outpatient medical treatment—even if cost of transportation is a valid medical cost. However, a court has allowed the deduction of the extra cost of specially prepared food.
- Trip to get "spiritual" rather than medical aid. For example, the cost of a trip to the Shrine of Our Lady of Lourdes is not deductible.
- Moving a family to a climate more suitable to an ill mother's condition. Only the mother's travel costs are deductible.
- Moving household furnishings to area advised by physician
- Operating an auto or special vehicle to go to work because of a disability (but costs may be a deductible business expense); *see 17.14*
- Convalescence cruise advised by a doctor for a patient recovering from pneumonia
- Loss on sale of car bought for medical travel
- Medical seminar cruise taken by patient whose condition was reviewed by physicians taking the cruise

EXAMPLE

Polyak spent the winter in Florida on the advice of her doctor to alleviate a chronic heart and lung condition. While in Florida, she stayed in a rented trailer that cost $1,426. She saw a physician for treatment of an infection and to renew medications. She deducted the trailer costs as a medical deduction, which the IRS and Tax Court disallowed. Although her Florida trip was primarily for mitigating her condition, she did not travel to receive medical care from a physician in a licensed hospital or related outpatient facility. The medical care was routine and incidental to her travel to Florida. Her deduction for transportation costs to Florida was not contested by the IRS, which conceded that the trip was primarily for and essential to her health.

17.10 Schooling for the Mentally or Physically Disabled

You may include as medical expenses subject to the AGI floor *(17.1)* the costs of sending on a doctor's recommendation a mentally or physically disabled dependent to a school or institution with special programs to overcome or alleviate his or her disability. Such costs may cover:

- Teaching of Braille or lip reading
- Training, caring for, supervising, and treating a mentally retarded person
- Training for a child with dyslexia
- Cost of meals and lodgings, if boarding is required at the school
- Costs of regular education courses also taught at the school, provided they are incidental to the special courses and services provided to overcome the disability

Caution

Counseling at a Private School

The parent of a child with psychological problems may deduct only that part of a private school fee directly related to psychological aid given to the child.

The school must have professional staff competent to design and supervise a program for helping your dependent overcome his or her disability. The fact that a particular school or camp is recommended for an emotionally disturbed child by a psychiatrist will not qualify the tuition as a deduction if the school or camp has no special program geared to the child's specific personal problem. The IRS allows a deduction for the costs of maintaining a mentally handicapped person in a home specially selected to meet the standards set by a psychiatrist to aid in an adjustment from life in a mental hospital to community living.

Payment for future medical care expenses is deductible if immediate payment is required by contract.

> **EXAMPLES**
>
> 1. An emotionally disturbed child was sent to a private school maintaining a staff of three psychologists. His father deducted the school fee of $6,270 as a medical expense. The IRS disallowed the amount, claiming that the child, who was neither mentally impaired nor handicapped, was sent to school primarily for an education. The Tax Court allowed the father to deduct $3,000 covering the psychological treatment.
>
> 2. A mentally handicapped boy had been excluded from several schools for the mentally handicapped because he needed close attention. The director of a military academy had extensive experience in training young boys. Although it was not the usual practice of the academy to enroll mentally handicapped children, the director accepted the boy on a day-to-day basis as a personal challenge. The Tax Court held that the cost of both tuition and transportation to bring the boy to and from the school were deductible medical expenses. The primary purpose of the training given the boy was not ordinary education but remedial training designed to overcome his handicap. But note that, in other cases, a deduction for tuition of a military school to which a child was sent in order to remove him from a tense family environment, and the cost of a blind boy's attendance at a regular private school that made a special effort to accommodate his Braille equipment, were disallowed.

17.11 Nursing Homes

Your payment for medical services, meals, and lodging to a nursing home, convalescent home, home for the aged, or similar facility is treated as a medical expense subject to the 7.5% AGI floor *(17.1)* if you, your spouse, or dependent is confined for medical treatment.

If obtaining medical care is not the main reason for admission, but you can show the part of the cost covering actual medical and nursing care, that amount is deductible, but not the cost of meals and lodging.

Establishing medical purpose. The following facts are helpful in establishing the full deductibility of payments to a nursing home, convalescent home, home for the aged, or sanitarium:

- The patient entered the institution on the direction or suggestion of a doctor.
- Attendance or treatment at the institution had a direct therapeutic effect on the condition suffered by the patient.
- The attendance at the institution was for a specific ailment rather than for a "general" health condition. Simply showing that the patient suffers from an ailment is not sufficient proof that he or she is in the home for treatment.

In an unusual case, a court allowed a medical expense deduction for apartment rent of an aged parent; *see* the following Example.

Assisted living facilities. The same deductible treatment applies if an individual is resident in an assisted living facility because of chronic illness that requires assistance with at least two activities of daily living (eating, toileting, transferring, bathing, dressing, or incontinence) or requires supervision due to a cognitive impairment (e.g., Alzheimer's disease).

Filing Tip

Meal Costs at a Nursing Home

If the patient entered a nursing home to receive medical care, a deduction may be taken for meals and lodging while there, in addition to medical care costs.

> **EXAMPLE**
>
> A doctor recommended to Ungar that his 90-year-old mother, convalescing from a brain hemorrhage, could receive better care at less expense in accommodations away from a hospital. A two-room apartment was rented, hospital equipment installed, and nurses engaged for seven months. The rent totaled $1,400. Ungar's

sister, who worked in her husband's shoe store, nursed her mother for six weeks. Ungar paid the wages of a clerk who was hired to substitute for his sister in the store. Ungar deducted both the rent and wages as medical expenses. The IRS disallowed them; a Tax Court reversed the IRS' decision. The apartment rent was no less a medical expense than the cost of a hospital room. As for the clerk's wages, they too were deductible medical costs. The clerk was hired specifically to allow the daughter to nurse her mother, thereby avoiding the larger, though more direct, medical expense of hiring a nurse.

17.12 Nurses' Wages

Wages or fees paid for nursing services are medical expenses subject to the 7.5% AGI floor *(17.1)*. Include any Social Security or Medicare (FICA) tax, federal unemployment (FUTA), and state unemployment tax that you pay for the nurse. A nurse does not have to be registered or licensed so long as he or she provides nursing services. Nursing services include giving medications, changing dressings, and bathing and grooming the patient. If the nurse also performs personal or household services, you generally can deduct only that part of the pay attributable to nursing services for the patient. However, if the patient is considered chronically ill, certain maintenance or personal care services are deductible as long-term care services *(17.15)*.

The cost of an attendant's meals that you provide is included in your medical expenses. Divide total food costs among the household members to determine the attendant's share.

The salary of a clerk hired specifically to relieve a wife from working in her husband's store in order to care for her ill mother was allowed as a medical expense; *see* the Ungar Example *(17.11)*.

 *Caution*

Nurse's Services
The cost of a nurse's services is a deductible medical expense, even if the nurse is not licensed or registered, so long as he or she provides the patient with nursing services. If household services are also provided, only the portion of the nurse's pay attributable to the provision of nursing services qualifies.

EXAMPLE

Dodge's wife was arthritic. He was advised by her doctor to have someone take care of her to prevent her from falling. He moved her to his daughter's home and paid the daughter to care for her mother. He deducted the payments to his daughter. The IRS disallowed the deduction, claiming that the daughter was not a trained nurse. The Tax Court allowed that part of the deduction specifically attributed to nursing aid. Whether a medical service has been rendered depends on the nature of the services rendered, not on the qualifications or title of the person who renders them. Here, the daughter's services, following the doctor's advice, qualified as medical care.

Costs eligible for dependent tax credit. If, in order to work, you pay a nurse to look after a physically or mentally disabled dependent, you may be able to claim a credit for all or part of the nurse's wages as a dependent care expense *(25.4)*. You may not, however, claim both a credit and a medical expense deduction. First, you claim the nurse's wages as a dependent care cost. If not all of the wages are allowed as dependent care costs because of the expense limits *(25.5)*, the remaining balance is deductible as a medical expense.

17.13 Home Improvements as Medical Expenses

A disease or ailment may require the construction or installation of special equipment or facilities in a home: A heart patient may need an elevator to carry him or her upstairs; a polio patient, a pool; and an asthmatic patient, an air cleaning system.

Subject to the 7.5% AGI floor *(17.1)*, you may deduct the full cost of equipment installed for a medical reason if it does not increase the value of your property, as, for example, the cost of a detachable window air conditioner. Where equipment or home improvement increases the value of your property, only the cost in excess of the increase in value to the home may be treated as a medical expense. This increased-value test does not apply to certain structural changes to a residence made to accommodate a disabling condition, as discussed below. If the equipment does not increase the value of the property, its entire cost is deductible, even though it is permanently fixed to the property.

The expense of maintaining and operating equipment installed for medical reasons may be claimed as a medical expense even if some or all of the cost does not qualify for a

 *Caution*

Does Equipment Increase Value of Home?

When special equipment is installed in your home to alleviate a disease or ailment, you must determine if it increases the value of your home. You generally may claim a medical deduction only to the extent that the cost of the equipment exceeds the increase in value. However, if you install a ramp or railing, widen doorways or hallways, or add similar improvements to cope with a disability, these are usually treated by the IRS as not adding to the value of the home.

deduction because it must be reduced by the increase in value to your home. For example, if a heart patient installs an elevator in his home on the advice of his doctor, but an appraisal shows that the elevator increased the value of the home by more than the cost of the elevator, the cost would not be a medical expense. However, the cost of electricity to operate it and any maintenance costs are medical expenses as long as the medical reason for the elevator continues.

> **EXAMPLE**
>
> Mike Gerard's daughter suffered from cystic fibrosis. While there is no known cure for the disease, doctors attempt to prolong life by preventing pulmonary infection. One approach is to maintain a constant temperature and high humidity. A doctor recommended that Gerard install a central air-conditioning unit in his home for his daughter. It cost $1,300 and increased the value of his home by $800. The $500 balance was a deductible medical expense.

Certain structural improvements to accommodate disability fully taken into account. The increased-value test does not apply to structural changes made to a residence to accommodate your disabled condition, or the condition of your spouse or dependents who live with you. Eligible expenses include adding ramps, modifying doorways and stairways, installing railings and support bars, and altering cabinets, outlets, fixtures, and warning systems. Lifts, but not elevators, are also in this category. Such improvements are treated for medical deduction purposes as not increasing the value of the home. The full cost of such improvements is added to other deductible expenses and the total is deductible to the extent that it exceeds the 7.5% AGI floor.

Prepaid home construction costs. Zipkin suffered from multiple chemical sensitivity syndrome and built a house with special filtering and ventilation systems. The cost of the special features exceeded the fair market value of the home by $645,000. She claimed a deduction for the full amount when the house was completed. The IRS disallowed the deduction for the construction costs incurred in the years before the home was completed. Zipkin successfully argued before a federal district court that the construction costs should be treated as prepaid medical expenses that are deductible in the year medical benefits are received. The federal court allowed Zipkin to deduct the full amount in the year the home became habitable.

Deducting the cost of a swimming pool. If swimming is prescribed as physical therapy, the cost of constructing a home swimming pool may be partly deductible as a medical expense but only to the extent the cost exceeds the increase in value to the house. However, the IRS is likely to question any deduction because of the possibility that the pool may be used for recreation. If you can show that the pool is specially equipped to alleviate your condition and is not generally suited for recreation, the IRS will allow the deduction unless the expense is considered to be "lavish or extravagant." For example, the IRS allowed a deduction for a pool constructed by an osteoarthritis patient. His physician prescribed swimming several times a day as treatment. He built an indoor lap pool with specially designed stairs and a hydrotherapy device. Given these features, the IRS concluded that the pool was specially designed to provide medical treatment.

In one case the IRS tried to limit the cost of a luxury indoor pool built for therapeutic reasons to the least expensive construction. The Tax Court rejected the IRS position, holding that a medical expense is not to be limited to the cheapest form of treatment; on appeal, the IRS position was adopted.

If, instead of building a pool, you buy a home with a pool, can you deduct the part of the purchase price allocated to the pool? The Tax Court said no. The purchase price of the house includes the fair market value of the pool. Therefore, there is no extra cost above the increase in the home's value that would support a medical expense deduction.

The operating costs of an indoor pool were allowed by the Tax Court as a deduction to an emphysema sufferer.

A deduction is barred where the primary purpose of the improvement is for personal convenience rather than medical necessity.

EXAMPLES

1. Ken Cherry was advised by his doctor to swim to relieve his severe emphysema and bronchitis. He could not swim at local health spas; they did not open early enough or stay open late enough to allow him to swim before or after work. His home was too small for a pool. He bought a lot and built a new house with an indoor pool. He used the pool several times a day, and swimming improved his condition; if he did not swim, his symptoms returned. Cherry deducted pool operating costs of $4,000 for fuel, electricity, insurance, and repairs. The IRS disallowed the deductions, claiming that the pool was used for personal recreation. Besides, it did not have special medical equipment. The Tax Court allowed the deduction. Cherry built the pool to swim in order to exercise his lungs. That there was no special equipment is irrelevant; Cherry did not need special ramps, railings, a shallow floor, or whirlpool. Finally, his family rarely used the pool.

2. Doug Haines broke his leg in a skiing accident and underwent various forms of physical therapy, including swimming. To aid his recovery, his physician recommended that he install a swimming pool at his home. The Tax Court agreed with the IRS that the cost of the pool was not deductible. Although swimming was beneficial to his condition, he needed special therapy only for a limited period of time, and he could have gotten it at less cost at a nearby public pool. Finally, because of weather conditions, the pool could not be used for about half of the year.

17.14 Costs Deductible as Business Expenses

In some cases, expenses may be deductible as business expenses rather than as medical expenses. Claiming a business deduction is preferable because the deduction is not subject to the 7.5% adjusted gross income floor *(17.1)*. However, under the Tax Cuts and Jobs Act, the cost of a checkup required by your employer is not deductible as a miscellaneous itemized deduction for 2018 through 2025 *(19.2)*.

The Tax Court allowed a licensed social worker working as a therapist to deduct psychoanalysis costs as an education expense; *see 33.15*.

EXAMPLE

In 2023, an airline pilot is required by his company to take a semi-annual physical exam at his own expense. If he fails to produce a resultant certificate of good health, he is subject to discharge. The cost of such checkups certifying physical fitness for a job is an ordinary and necessary business expense but employee job costs are not deductible as a miscellaneous itemized deduction for 2018 through 2025 *(19.2)*. If the doctor prescribes a treatment or further examinations to maintain the pilot's physical condition, the cost of these subsequent treatments or examinations may be deducted only as medical expenses, even though they are needed to maintain the physical standards required by the job. Similarly, a self-employed professional singer who consults a throat specialist may not deduct the fee as a business expense. The fee is a medical expense subject to the 7.5% AGI floor.

Impairment-related work expenses. Some expenses incurred by a person with a physical or mental disability may be deductible as business expenses rather than as medical expenses. A business expense deduction may be allowed if the expense is necessary for you to satisfactorily perform your job and is not required or used, except incidentally, for personal purposes. If you are self-employed, claim the deduction on Schedule C *(40.6)*. If you are an employee, the expenses are listed on Form 2106 and if not reimbursed, entered on Line 16 of Schedule A as an "Other" itemized deduction; *see 19.1*.

EXAMPLES

1. A professor is paralyzed from the waist down and confined to a wheelchair. When he attends out-of-town business meetings, he has his wife, a friend, or a colleague accompany him to help him with baggage, stairs, narrow doors, and to sit with him on airplanes when airlines will not allow wheelchair passengers without an attendant. While he does not pay them a salary, he does pay their travel costs. He may deduct these costs as business expenses. They are incurred solely because of his occupation.

 *Filing Tip*

Disability-Related Job Costs

If you are an individual with a disability and incur costs to enable you to work, the payments may be treated as a deductible business expense rather than as a medical expense.

> 2. An attorney uses prostheses due to bilateral amputation of his legs and takes medication several times a day for other ailments. On both personal and business trips, his wife or a neighbor accompanies him to help him travel and receive medication. He may deduct the out-of-town expenses paid for his neighbor only as a medical expense. The neighbor's services are not business expenses because assistance in personal activities is regularly provided. When his wife accompanies him, he may deduct her transportation costs as a medical expense; her food and lodging are nondeductible ordinary living expenses.

17.15 Long-Term Care Premiums and Services

A qualified long-term care policy provides only for long-term-care services for the "chronically ill" *(see below)*. If you pay premiums for a qualified long-term care policy, you may treat a fixed amount that depends on your age as medical expenses (subject to the 7.5% AGI floor); *see 17.1*.

If you, your spouse, or your dependent is chronically ill, you may include as medical expenses your unreimbursed expenses for qualifying long-term-care services.

Did you pay qualifying long-term care services for a chronically ill individual? A chronically ill person is someone who has been certified by a licensed health-care practitioner within the preceding 12 months as being unable to perform for a period of at least 90 days at least two of the following activities without substantial assistance: eating, toileting, dressing, bathing, continence, or transferring. Also qualifying as chronically ill is someone who requires substantial supervision because of severe cognitive impairment, such as from Alzheimer's disease.

Qualifying long-term-care services for a chronically ill individual are broadly defined as necessary diagnostic, preventive, therapeutic, curing, treating, mitigation, and rehabilitative services, and also maintenance or personal care services. The services must be provided under a plan of care prescribed by a licensed health-care practitioner, who may be a physician, a registered nurse, a licensed social worker, or other individual meeting Treasury requirements. Services provided by a spouse or relative are deductible only if that person is a licensed professional; services provided by a related corporation or partnership do not qualify.

Deductible premium costs of long-term-care policies. Depending on your age at the end of the year, all or part of your premium payments for a qualified long-term-care policy may be included as deductible medical expenses, subject to the 7.5% AGI floor *(17.1)*.

For 2023, the maximum deductible premium for each person covered under a qualifying policy is: $480 for covered persons age 40 or younger at the end of 2023; $890 for those age 41 through 50; $1,790 for those age 51 through 60; $4,770 for those age 61 through 70; and $5,960 for those over age 70. These limits will likely be increased for 2024 by an inflation factor; *see* the *e-Supplement* at *jklasser.com*.

If you are considering purchase of a long-term-care insurance policy, make sure that it qualifies for the tax treatment explained in this section. A qualified contract must provide only for coverage of qualified long-term-care services for the chronically ill *(see above)* and be guaranteed renewable; it may not provide for a cash surrender value or money that can be assigned, pledged, or borrowed; it may not reimburse expenses covered by Medicare except where Medicare is a secondary payer or the contract makes per diem payments without regard to expenses.

Benefits paid by qualified long-term-care policies. Benefits from a qualified long-term-care insurance contract (other than dividends) are generally excludable from income. If payments are made on a per diem or other periodic basis, meaning that they are made without regard to actual expenses incurred, there is an annual limitation on the amount that can be excluded. For 2023, per diem payments of up to $420 per day are tax free. If per diem payments exceed the $420 limit, the excess is tax free only to the extent of unreimbursed expenses for qualified long-term-care services. The per diem limit must be allocated among all policyholders who own qualified long-term-care insurance contracts for the same insured.

Filing Tip

Long-Term Care Insurance

Unreimbursed expenses for long-term care services to care for a chronically ill patient are deductible medical expenses subject to the 7.5% AGI floor. Premiums paid for a qualifying policy are includible in your medical expenses subject to a limit based on your age; *see 17.15*.

You should receive a Form 1099-LTC showing any payments to you from a long-term-care insurance contract. Box 3 of Form 1099-LTC should indicate whether the payments were made on a per diem basis or were reimbursements of actual long-term-care expenses. Per diem payments and reimbursements must be reported on Form 8853 to determine if any of the per diem payments are taxable.

17.16 Life Insurance Used by Chronically ill or Terminally ill Person

A person who is terminally ill may be forced to cash in a life insurance policy to pay medical bills and other living expenses. Insurance companies have developed life insurance policies with accelerated death benefit clauses to help terminally ill patients meet the high cost of medical care. Where a policy lacks an accelerated payment clause, it is also possible to sell a life insurance policy to a viatical settlement company that specializes in buying policies from ill persons who require funds to pay expenses.

Accelerated death benefits and viatical settlement proceeds received by terminally ill individuals are not taxed.

Accelerated benefits from chronically ill person's life insurance contract. A chronically ill *(17.15)* individual may sell a life insurance policy to a viatical settlement company to pay for long-term-care costs. However, if accelerated benefits are received on a per diem (or other periodic basis), the rules for long-term-care policies *(17.15)* determine if the proceeds are taxed. Thus, if the proceeds exceed the $420 per diem limit for 2023 and also exceed actual long-term care costs, the excess is taxable on Form 8853. Accelerated life insurance proceeds paid under a long-term-care rider are also subject to these rules *(17.15)*.

Filing Instruction

Form 8853

If you received payments in 2023 from a qualified long-term care policy, you must figure the amount of taxable payments, if any, on Form 8853.

CHAPTER 18

Casualty and Theft Losses and Involuntary Conversions

An itemized deduction for casualty and theft losses of personal-use property is allowed for 2018 through 2025 only if the losses are attributed to federally declared disasters. An eligible loss is deductible for the year it is "sustained" *(18.2)*. The loss is claimed on Form 4684 and the allowable amount is entered on Schedule A (Form 1040 or 1040-SR). If you have a "qualified disaster loss" that was "sustained" in 2023 *(18.8)* and you do not itemize deductions on Schedule A for 2023, you can increase your 2023 standard deduction by the loss *(18.8, 13.2)*.

A loss of property held for:

- Personal purposes must be attributable to a federally declared disaster *(18.1)* and the loss is subject to a dollar floor that reduces the deduction by $100, or by $500 for a qualified disaster loss *(18.8)*. In addition, net losses for personal-use assets are reduced by 10% of your adjusted gross income on Form 4684, unless the loss is a qualified disaster loss *(18.8)*.
- Income-producing purposes, such as negotiable securities, should be claimed on Form 4684 and then entered on Line 16 of Schedule A as an "other itemized deduction" *(19.1)*.
- Business or rental purposes is claimed on Form 4684 and then as a loss on Form 4797. It is not subject to any floor. Follow the instructions to Form 4684.

If you have realized a gain, you may defer tax by replacing or repairing the property *(18.14)*.

18.1 Casualty or Theft Losses for Personal-Use Property Must Be Due to a Federally Declared Disaster

A casualty is damage to or destruction of property due to a sudden event such as a flood, storm (including hurricanes and tornadoes), or wildfire. The itemized deduction for personal casualty and theft losses has been restricted for 2018 through 2025: only losses that are attributable to a federally declared disaster are deductible. For example, if in 2023 a tree fell on your home during a local storm, causing significant damage, and the storm was not a federally declared disaster, your unreimbursed casualty loss is not deductible. However, if you also had a casualty gain from other personal-use property, an exception allows you to offset the gain with the otherwise nondeductible loss; *see* the Law Alert below on this page.

Technically, there are three types of federally declared disasters and each has different rules for deductibility explained throughout this chapter:

1. *Federal casualty loss* attributable to a federally declared disaster (explained below) where a state receives a federal disaster declaration. This type of loss is limited to a casualty or theft loss of personal-use property.

2. *Disaster loss* attributable to a federally declared disaster occurring in an area eligible for assistance pursuant to a Presidential declaration. This type of loss is applicable to personal-use property as well as business or investment property.

3. *Qualified disaster loss* attributable to a major federal disaster declared by the President under authority of special legislation (*see* "Qualified disaster losses" below). This type of loss applies solely to casualty or theft losses of personal-use property.

Federally declared disasters. A federally declared disaster is a disaster in an area determined by the President as warranting federal assistance (under the Robert T. Stafford Disaster Relief and Emergency Assistance Act or successor law); the declaration can be a "major" disaster declaration or an "emergency" declaration.

The IRS provides a list of federally declared disasters at FEMA.gov/disaster. For links to tax relief information for disaster victims by year, check, https://www.irs.gov/newsroom/tax-relief-in-disaster-situations.

Generally, a loss that is "attributable to" a federally declared disaster will also occur in a disaster area, but the IRS has said that the loss does not have to occur "in" a disaster area to be deductible. Since declarations of federally declared disasters are issued on a state-wide basis, the loss must occur in the state receiving the federal disaster declaration. If the loss occurs in the state receiving the federal disaster declaration, a loss that is attributable to the disaster is deductible even if the property is not located in one of the counties that are designated as eligible for assistance under the disaster declaration. If the loss did occur in a county eligible for assistance under the disaster declaration, and the loss was attributable to the disaster, it is considered a "disaster loss" which may be claimed either for the year in which the loss was sustained or for the preceding year *(18.3)*.

Claiming a personal or casualty theft loss. Although a deduction generally is not allowed for personal casualty or theft losses that are not attributable to a federally declared disaster, such losses offset any gains you realize from casualties or thefts of personal-use property. Thus, if you have losses such as damage to or destruction of your home in a fire, flood, or storm that is not a federally declared disaster, or your car is destroyed in an accident, or your property is stolen and the theft is unrelated to a federally declared disaster, and you also have personal casualty gains, the losses offset the gains; *see* Step 7 in *18.9*. You have a gain from a casualty or theft if you receive an insurance reimbursement that exceeds your adjusted basis for the property *(18.2, 18.9)*.

Gains and losses from casualties and thefts of personal-use property are reported on Section A of Form 4684 (Personal Use Property). Each casualty or theft loss of personal-use property (figured under the steps at *18.9*) must be reduced by insurance or other reimbursements *(18.2, 18.9)*. If the loss is not a "qualified disaster loss" *(see below)*, the loss (after reimbursements) is reduced by a $100 floor and then further reduced by 10% of your adjusted gross income *(18.8)*. All or a substantial part of your potential deduction may be eliminated by the 10% AGI floor; *see* *18.8* and *18.9* for details on the $100 and 10% floors. For a qualified disaster loss *(see below)*, the floor is $500 instead of $100, but the 10% AGI floor does not apply.

 *Law Alert*

Deductions for Personal Casualties and Thefts Are Limited

For 2018 through 2025, a casualty or theft loss for personal-use property is allowed only if the loss is attributable to a federally declared disaster. However, if you have gains from personal casualties (because of generous insurance settlements or otherwise), losses from personal casualties and thefts that are not otherwise deductible (because they are not attributable to a federally declared disaster) can offset the gains on Form 4684 (see Step 7 in *18.9*).

Gains (if any) from casualties and thefts of personal-use property are reduced by losses attributable to federally declared disasters (after the $100 or $500 floor) on Section A of Form 4684; *see* Steps 6-7 in *18.9*. A net loss, if any, is reduced by 10% of your adjusted gross income unless it is attributable to a qualified disaster loss *(see below)*.

An allowable loss from Form 4684 is entered as your casualty or theft loss deduction on Line 15 of Schedule A (Form 1040 or 1040-SR), unless it is a net qualified disaster loss, as discussed in the next paragraph.

Qualified disaster losses. Congress has provided special rules for "qualified disaster losses." A qualified disaster loss is a loss of personal-use property (casualty or theft) that is attributable to a "major disaster" declared by the President (an "emergency declaration" does not qualify), but only if Congress has designated the disaster as qualified in specific legislation. On Form 4684, each qualified disaster loss is subject to a $500 floor (instead of a $100 floor) but the 10% AGI floor does not apply, which is a major advantage. You can claim a qualified disaster loss even if you do not itemize deductions; the allowable loss is added to your standard deduction.

As noted above, a loss can be a "qualified disaster loss" only if Congress designates the disaster as qualified in specific legislation. In some years, legislation provided qualified disaster loss status for certain major storms, such as Hurricanes Harvey, Irma, or Maria, or California wildfires. At other times, Congress has provided qualified disaster loss status to all major disasters declared within a specified time period. The most recent example is the Taxpayer Certainty and Disaster Tax Relief Act of 2020 (the 2020 Act), which provided qualified disaster loss treatment to any casualty or theft loss of personal-use property that was attributable to a major disaster declared by the President from January 1, 2020, through February 25, 2021, provided the disaster began after December 27, 2019, but no later than December 27, 2020, and which ended no later than January 26, 2021 *(18.8)*.

The only way to have a qualified disaster loss for 2023 is if your personal-use property was damaged in a major disaster that was qualified under the 2020 Act or earlier legislation, and the loss was not "sustained" *(18.2)* until 2023. This would be the case if your insurance claim attributable to a 2020 Act disaster was settled in 2023 or litigation concerning your claim was resolved in 2023. If you were left with an unreimbursed loss, the loss was sustained in 2023.

A net qualified disaster loss, if allowed for 2023, is entered on Line 16 of Schedule A as an "Other" itemized deduction. If you claim the standard deduction, a qualified disaster loss is combined with your regular standard deduction on Line 16 of Schedule A, and the total is then entered as your standard deduction on Form 1040 or 1040-SR *(13.2)*.

Disaster relief payments are not taxable. If you receive qualified disaster relief payments, the payments are not taxable so long as you have not otherwise been reimbursed for the expenses covered. Tax-free treatment applies to (1) payments for reasonable and necessary personal, family, living, or funeral expenses incurred as a result of a federally declared disaster, (2) the costs of repairing your personal residence (whether you rent or own it), or repairing or replacing the contents of the home due to a federally declared disaster, or (3) payments from a federal, state or local government fund that are based on your individual or family need as the result of a federally declared disaster.

Disaster relief grants and loan cancellations. Cancellation of part of a federal disaster loan under the Robert T. Stafford Disaster Relief and Emergency Assistance Act is treated as a reimbursement that reduces your loss *(18.2, 18.9)*. If you receive a post-disaster grant under the Disaster Relief Act to help you meet medical, dental, housing, transportation, personal property, or funeral expenses, the grant is excludable from income. However, to the extent the grant specifically reimburses a medical expense, the payment is treated as a reimbursement that offsets the expense *(17.4)*. Similarly, if a casualty loss is specifically reimbursed by a grant, treat the grant as a reimbursement in figuring your disaster loss *(18.2, 18.9)*. Unemployment assistance payments under the Disaster Relief Act are taxable unemployment benefits *(2.5)*.

Casualty or theft gains and losses for business and investment property. Casualty and theft losses for business or income-producing property are figured in Section B of Form

4684. A gain is reported on Form 4684 only if you do not elect to defer it under the involuntary conversion rules *(18.14)*.

Losses do not have to be attributable to a federally declared disaster to be deductible (as do losses to personal-use property for 2018 through 2025). Business and investment property losses (following steps 1–4) *(18.9)* are not subject to the $100 and 10% of adjusted gross income floors. For investment property, a loss from Form 4684 is entered as an "other itemized deduction" on Line 16 of Schedule A (Form 1040 or 1040-SR), not on Line 15 for "casualty and theft losses." For business property, a loss from Form 4684 is entered as a loss on Form 4797. Follow the Form 4684 instructions.

Disaster grants for business property losses. Payments by the federal government or a state or local government to a business for property losses may not be excluded from business gross income. The IRS has ruled that the disaster relief exclusion that applies to government payments made to individuals to promote the general welfare does not apply to business property losses. The business realizes a taxable gain to the extent the grant exceeds the adjusted basis in the damaged or destroyed property, but that gain can be deferred under the involuntary conversion rules *(18.14)* by making a timely reinvestment of the payments in qualified replacement property. The replacement period for damaged or destroyed business property is two years *(18.18)*.

IRS may extend filing and payment deadlines and abate interest charges. If you live or work in a federally declared disaster area, or your tax records are in a disaster area, the IRS will abate interest on taxes due for the period covered by an extension to file tax returns and pay taxes.

18.2 When To Deduct a Casualty or Theft Loss

A casualty or theft loss attributable to a federally declared disaster *(18.1)*. is deductible for the year the loss is "sustained." Usually, a loss is "sustained" in the year in which the disaster occurs, but the situation is more complicated when you have a pending claim for insurance or other reimbursement. According to the IRS, when a claim for reimbursement exists and there is a reasonable prospect of recovery as of the end of the year in which the disaster occurs, the loss is considered sustained in the year that the reimbursement claim is settled or in which there is no longer a reasonable prospect that reimbursement will be received. The Examples in *18.3* illustrate how a loss can be sustained in a year after the year in which a federally declared disaster occurs.

Determining the year in which the loss is sustained is crucial for the "prior-year election" that can be made for disaster losses, discussed in *18.3*. You can elect to deduct a disaster loss either for the year in which it is sustained or for the year immediately preceding the year in which the loss is sustained; *see 18.3* for examples and election details.

Note that you must file a timely insurance claim if your property is covered by insurance. Otherwise, the amount covered by the insurance cannot be taken into account when figuring your deductible casualty loss; *see 18.9*. In addition to insurance, the IRS says that if you have a reasonable prospect of receiving federal or state benefits to restore your property, you must take those benefits into account as potential reimbursements.

If you reasonably expect partial or complete reimbursement in a later year. For the year the disaster occurred, you should deduct only that part of your loss, after applying the personal property floors *(18.8)* for which you do not expect reimbursement. For example, if your property was damaged in a 2023 federally declared disaster but you expect a full insurance recovery in 2024, you should not take any deduction on your 2023 return. If you are not sure if part of your loss will be reimbursed, the IRS advises you not to claim a deduction for that part until the year you become reasonably certain that it will not be reimbursed.

If you deduct a loss and then are reimbursed for it. If you deduct a loss attributable to a federally declared disaster occurring in 2023 on your 2023 return because you do not expect any reimbursement, but you receive an insurance settlement or other reimbursement in 2024, the reimbursement is taxable in 2024 to the extent that the 2023 deduction gave you a tax benefit by reducing your 2023 taxable income *(11.6)*. You cannot avoid this

Planning Reminder

IRS Interest Abatement

If the IRS extends the due date to file tax returns and pay taxes for a person in an area declared to be a disaster area by the President, the IRS will abate interest on past-due taxes for the period covered by the extension.

Caution

Are You Uncertain About Whether You Will Be Reimbursed?

If you think you might be reimbursed for part of your casualty loss in a later year but are not sure, the IRS says to delay taking the deduction for that part until the year you become reasonably certain that it will not be reimbursed.

income for 2024 by amending your 2023 tax return to reduce or eliminate the 2023 loss by the 2024 reimbursement.

Theft losses. A theft loss attributable to a federally declared disaster is deductible for the year the theft is discovered *(18.7)*.

You have a gain if reimbursements exceed your adjusted basis for the property. Receiving reimbursements in excess of adjusted basis generally results in a gain that you must report on your return. The gain may be minimized by special rules where your principal residence is damaged or destroyed in a federally declared disaster *(18.4)*. The recognized gain must be reported unless you acquire qualifying replacement property and elect to defer the gain, or, if the gain is due to reimbursements for a destroyed principal residence, the gain is not taxable under the home sale exclusion *(18.14)*.

If a loss is claimed in one year and in a later year you receive reimbursements that exceed your adjusted basis, the gain is included in income for the later year to the extent the original deduction reduced your taxable income *(11.6)*. The remainder of the gain is taxable unless you buy replacement property that enables you to defer the gain *(18.14)*.

18.3 Prior-Year Election for Disaster Losses

A disaster loss is a loss attributable to a federally declared disaster which occurs in a county eligible for assistance pursuant to a Presidential declaration; *see* "Federally declared disasters" in *18.1*. You may deduct a disaster loss (figured on Form 4684 under the steps at *18.9*) either on your return for the year in which the loss is sustained or on the return for the year immediately preceding the year in which the loss is sustained. As discussed in *18.2*, if there is a pending claim for reimbursement as of the end of the year in which the disaster occurs, the loss is not considered sustained until the year in which it can be ascertained with reasonable certainty whether the reimbursement will be received. In the Form 4684 instructions, the IRS also refers to the year in which the loss is sustained as "the disaster year." Thus, the "prior year" for which the prior-year election may be made is the year preceding the disaster year.

Disaster loss treatment if you are forced to relocate because your home was made unsafe by a federally declared disaster. If your home was located in a federally declared disaster area, your state or local government may order you to demolish it or relocate it because it was rendered unsafe by the disaster, even though the actual damage from the disaster itself was minor. This could happen, for example, if a severe storm created a danger of mudslides to area homes. In this situation, the loss in value to your home is treated as a disaster loss, provided the order to demolish or relocate the home was issued within 120 days of the President's determination that the area warranted federal disaster assistance. You may elect to deduct the disaster loss either for the year the loss was sustained (the year of the demolition or relocation order) or for the prior taxable year, as discussed below. The home could be your principal residence, vacation home, or rental property. In figuring the amount of the loss *(18.9)*, compare the fair market value of the home immediately before the disaster with the value after the disaster and prior to the demolition or relocation.

How and when to make the prior-year election. You have time to decide whether it is more advantageous for you to deduct a disaster loss for the disaster year (the year in which the loss is sustained) or make the election to deduct it for the year preceding the disaster year. The deadline for making the prior-year election is the date that is six months after the original due date (without extensions) for your return for the disaster year. Thus, if the disaster year for a federally declared disaster is 2023 (meaning you sustain the loss in 2023), you have until October 15, 2024, to elect to claim the loss for 2022 (the year before 2023, the disaster year). The prior-year election is made on Part 1 of Section D on the 2022 Form 4684. By October 15, 2024, complete the Section D and attach it with the rest of Form 4684 to an amended return (Form 1040-X) for 2022, assuming you have filed an original 2022 return, or with an original 2022 return if you have not yet filed it.

Filing Tip

File Form 1040-X Electronically

Filing electronically rather than by mail will expedite your refund resulting from the prior-year election.

If the disaster year is 2024, the prior-year election to claim the loss for 2023 is made on Part 1 of Section D on the 2023 Form 4684. Attach it to an original or amended return for 2023 by October 15, 2025.

Revoking prior-year election. If you make the prior-year election for a disaster loss, you may revoke it in order to deduct the loss on your return for the disaster year (the year in which the loss is sustained). You must file the revocation with an amended return for the prior year to remove the disaster loss deduction. Your amended return eliminating the election must be filed (1) on or before the date that is 90 days after the due date for making the prior-year election *(see above)*, and also (2) on or before the date on which you file the return or amended return for the disaster year on which you are going to claim the loss.

If 2023 is the disaster year and you made the prior-year election (by October 15, 2024; *see* above) to deduct the loss on your 2022 return, you revoke the election by completing Part II of Section D and attaching it to an amended return for 2022 (the prior year for which the election was made). As a result of the revocation, the amended return will show a higher tax liability for 2022. The amended return for 2022 must be filed by January 15, 2025; the 90th day after October 15, 2024. You also must file the amended return for 2022 before you file an original or amended return for 2023 (the disaster year) that includes the loss.

EXAMPLES

1. In 2023, severe flooding destroyed your car and caused major damage to your home in a county that the President determined warranted federal disaster assistance. You filed a reimbursement claim with your insurance company but at the end of 2023, it was not clear how much reimbursement you would receive. In January 2024, your insurance company settles your claim and reimburses you for only half of your loss. For deduction purposes, the unreimbursed disaster loss is "sustained" in 2024, not 2023, because 2024 is when it became reasonably certain how much you would be reimbursed for. You can deduct the unreimbursed loss, subject to the personal property floors *(18.8)*, on your return for 2024, the year in which the loss is sustained, or you can make the prior-year election and claim the deduction on your 2023 return; *see* "How and when to make the prior-year election", above.

2. Same facts as in Example 1 but in 2024 the insurance company completely denies your claim. You sue the insurance company and at the end of 2024, the case is still pending and you have a reasonable prospect of winning your claim. However, in 2025, the court rules against you. Your unreimbursed loss is considered sustained in 2025. You can deduct the unreimbursed loss, subject to the personal property floors *(18.8)*, on your return for 2025, the year in which the loss is sustained, or you can make the prior-year election and claim the deduction on your 2024 return; *see* "How and when to make the prior-year election", above.

18.4 Gain Realized From Insurance Proceeds for Damaged or Destroyed Principal Residence

Generally, you have a taxable gain if you receive insurance proceeds in excess of your adjusted basis for damaged or destroyed property *(18.2, 18.14)*. However, if a principal residence is destroyed, the home sale exclusion may be available. Other special rules may allow you to avoid or minimize the gain, or make it easier to defer gain by purchasing replacement property, when the insurance proceeds are for a principal residence damaged or destroyed in a federally declared disaster area.

Destruction of principal residence and contents. If your principal residence is destroyed, and you receive insurance proceeds that exceed your adjusted basis in the property, you may be able to exclude the gain from your gross income under the $250,000 ($500,000 if married filing jointly) home sale exclusion *(29.1)*. The destruction does not have to be attributable to a federally declared disaster; thus, destruction of a home due to a fire that is not a federally declared disaster could qualify. For the exclusion to apply, you generally must have owned and lived in the home for at least two out of the five years ending on the date of destruction, the same ownership and use test that applies to a sale *(29.2)*.

IRS Alert

IRS Deadline for Election to Claim Disaster Loss in Prior Year

An election to deduct a disaster loss for the year preceding the year in which the loss is sustained can accelerate your loss deduction, generating an immediate tax refund for the prior year that you can use to recover from the disaster. The IRS gives you time to consider whether to claim the disaster loss for the year in which the loss is sustained or for the preceding year. The deadline for making the prior-year election is six months after the original due date (without extensions) for the return for the year in which the loss is sustained, generally October 15. If you make the election, you may revoke it on or before the date that is 90 days after the due date for making the election).

Filing Tip

Nontaxable Disaster Mitigation Payments

Property owners are not taxed on qualified disaster mitigation payments from FEMA (Federal Emergency Management Agency) to elevate or relocate flood-prone homes and businesses or build hurricane shelters.

According to the IRS, a principal residence must be completely destroyed to qualify for the home sale exclusion; a partial destruction does not qualify. If a residence is damaged to the extent that the remaining structure must be deconstructed in order to rebuild, or the costs of repair substantially exceed the pre-disaster value of the home, the home is considered to have been completely destroyed, allowing the gain to be excluded from income subject to the $250,000/$500,000 exclusion limit. If the home sale exclusion is not available to you or if the gain exceeds your exclusion, the nonexcludable gain may be reduced under the gain minimization rules discussed next, and the balance deferred under the involuntary conversion rules if you buy a replacement residence *(18.14)*.

Gain may be minimized by special computation rules. Where your principal residence is damaged or destroyed in a federally declared disaster, favorable involuntary conversion rules eliminate tax on some of the gain and make it easier to defer the balance. These rules apply to renters as well as home owners.

1. Any gain on insurance proceeds received for "unscheduled" personal property in your principal residence (rented or owned) is not "recognized" by the tax law, so it is not taxable. Personal property is unscheduled if it is not separately listed on a schedule or rider to the basic insurance policy.

2. Insurance proceeds received for the home itself or for scheduled property are treated as received for a single item of property. Gain on this combined insurance pool may be deferred by reinvesting in replacement property that is similar or related in service or use to either the damaged residence or its contents *(18.14)*. If the cost of a new principal residence and/or contents equals or exceeds the combined insurance pool, you may elect to defer any gain attributable to the insurance recovery *(18.19)*. The deferred gain reduces your basis in the replacement property. The period for purchasing replacement property ends four years after the end of the first tax year in which any part of your gain is realized *(18.18)*. If the cost of the replacement property is less than the combined insurance pool, your gain is taxed to the extent of the unspent reimbursement *(18.19)*.

> **EXAMPLE**
>
> You rent an apartment as your principal residence. Your apartment and its contents were completely destroyed by a hurricane in 2023; the county in which your apartment was located was in a federally declared disaster area. Later in 2023, you received insurance proceeds of $25,000 for unscheduled personal property in your apartment. The $25,000 proceeds for the unscheduled property are not taxable. Assume that in addition to the $25,000 for unscheduled property, you received in 2023 insurance proceeds of $200,000 for the home itself, and also $10,000 for jewelry and $5,000 for a stamp collection that were listed on a rider to your policy. If you invest the combined $215,000 of proceeds (for the home, jewelry, and stamps) in a replacement residence, scheduled or unscheduled property, or any combination thereof, you can elect to defer any gain ($215,000 minus adjusted basis) realized from the $215,000 of insurance proceeds. If you reinvest less than $215,000, your gain is taxable only to the extent that $215,000 exceeds the reinvestment (whether in a home or in scheduled or unscheduled property). To defer gain, you must buy replacement property by the end of 2027, four years after the end of 2023, the year in which gain was realized on the receipt of the insurance. If gain is deferred, basis in the replacement property equals its cost minus the deferred gain.

Sale of land underlying destroyed principal residence or second home. If your principal residence is destroyed in a federally declared disaster, and you decide to relocate elsewhere and sell the underlying land, the IRS treats the sale and the destruction as a single involuntary conversion. If you have a gain that is not excludable under the home sale exclusion rules *(Chapter 29)*, the land sale proceeds are combined with your insurance recovery for purposes of figuring deferrable gain under the involuntary conversion replacement rules *(18.14)*. All of the gain resulting from the insurance recovery may be deferred if a new principal residence is purchased within the four-year replacement period and it costs at least as much as the combined insurance and sales proceeds. The replacement period ends four years after the close of the first year in which any part of your gain is realized.

The destroyed home does not have to be your principal residence or even be located in a federal disaster area for the above "single conversion" rule to apply. The rule applies to the destruction of a second residence such as a vacation home that qualifies for a mortgage interest deduction *(15.1)*, However, the replacement period *(18.18)* for a second home is two years, whether or not it was in a federal disaster area. The two-year replacement period also applies for principal residences that were not located in a federal disaster area (rather than the four-year period allowed for principal residences within federal disaster areas).

18.5 Who May Deduct a Casualty or Theft Loss

A casualty loss deduction may be claimed only by the owner of the property. For example, in 2023 a federally declared disaster destroys a car owned solely by one spouse. If the spouses file separate returns for 2023, the other spouse may not deduct the loss because he or she does not have an ownership interest; only the spouse who owned the car may deduct the loss on a separate return.

On jointly owned property, the loss is divided among the owners. If you and your spouse own the property jointly, you can deduct the entire loss on a joint return. If you file separately, each owner deducts his or her share of the loss on each separate return.

If you have a legal life estate in the property, the loss is apportioned between yourself and those who will get the property after your death. The apportionment may be based on actuarial tables that consider your life expectancy.

Lessee. A person leasing property may be allowed to deduct payments to a lessor that are required under the lease to compensate for a casualty loss.

> ### EXAMPLE
> You buy or lease a lot on which to build a cottage. Along with your purchase or lease, you have the privilege of using a nearby lake. The lake is later destroyed by a storm that is declared to be a federal disaster and the value of your property drops. You may not deduct the loss. The lake is not your property. You only had a privilege to use it, and this is not an ownership right that supports a casualty loss deduction.

18.6 Proving a Casualty Loss

If your return is audited, you will have to prove that the casualty occurred and the amount of the loss. For personal-use property, you must be prepared to show that your claimed loss is attributable to a federally declared disaster *(18.1)*. The time to collect your evidence is as soon after the casualty as possible. *Table 18-1*, Proving a Casualty Loss, indicates the information that you will need when computing your loss *(18.9)*.

18.7 Theft Losses

For 2018 through 2025, a theft of personal-use property (not used in a business or held for investment) can be deducted only if the theft is attributable to a federally declared disaster *(18.1)*. This may be difficult to prove. For example, if you are forced to leave your home during a federally declared disaster and later find that property is missing, this by itself is not sufficient evidence that there was a theft, which requires that the taking of your property was illegal under state law; nor is it evidence that the theft, if there was one, was attributable to the disaster. There may be police records or news reports that could document that there were break-ins in your area following the disaster.

If you can establish that a theft of your personal-use property was attributable to a federally declared disaster, take into account expected and actual reimbursements in determining the timing *(18.2)* and amount *(18.9)* of the deductible loss.

If personal-use property, such as your car, is stolen, and the theft is unrelated to a federally declared disaster, your loss is not deductible, but there is an exception if you also have any gains from personal casualties or thefts. In this case, you may reduce the gain (or gains) by theft or casualty losses that are not attributable to a federally declared disaster; *see* Step 7 at *18.9* for making this offset.

Caution

Damage to Nearby Property

The casualty must have caused damage to your property. Damage to a nearby area that lowered the value of your property does not give you a loss deduction.

Filing Instruction

If Stolen Property Is Recovered

If you claim a theft loss and in a later year the property is returned to you, you must refigure your loss deduction. If the refigured deduction is lower than the amount you claimed, the difference must be reported as income in the year of the recovery. To recalculate the loss, follow the steps for figuring deductible losses *(18.9)*, but in Step 1, compute the loss in fair market value from the time the property was stolen until you recovered it. The lower of this loss in value, if any, or your adjusted basis for the property, is then reduced by insurance reimbursements and the personal-use floors *(18.8)* to get the recalculated loss.

Stock Devaluation Due to Corporate Misconduct

The IRS has warned shareholders who suffer a loss in the value of their stock due to the fraud, misappropriation, or other misconduct of corporate officers or directors that their loss is not a deductible theft loss. A decline in stock value is not a theft if the stock was purchased on the open market rather than directly from the corporate officials accused of misconduct. The loss for stock bought on the open market is deductible only as a capital loss when the stock is sold or becomes worthless (*5.4*).

The Tax Court took the same approach in holding that a taxpayer who bought stock on the open market could not support a theft loss under California law because there was no "privity" relationship between the taxpayer and the corporate officers accused of wrongdoing, and so it could not be shown that there was intent to obtain the taxpayer's property.

> **EXAMPLE**
>
> Your jewelry was stolen from your home in 2023. Assume that the loss (figured under the steps of *18.9*) is $15,000. Also assume that your vehicle was destroyed by a lightning strike, and that after taking into account insurance reimbursement, you have a $22,000 gain *(18.14)*. The jewelry loss was not attributable to a federally declared disaster, so the loss would generally not be deductible, but since you have a personal casualty gain, the $15,000 loss can offset $15,000 of the gain on Form 4684; *see Step 7 at 18.9 and* the Form 4684 instructions.

Theft of business or investment property. A theft of property used in your business or which you held for investment may be claimed in Section B of Form 4684. A loss for the unreimbursed value of the property is allowed; *see* steps 1-4 at *18.9* and follow the instructions to Section B of Form 4684.

An embezzlement from a business or investment account qualifies as a theft, but if you report on the cash basis, you may not take a deduction for the embezzlement of income you have not reported. For example, an agent embezzled royalties of $46,000 due an author. The author's theft deduction was disallowed. The author had not previously reported the royalties as income; therefore, she could not get the deduction. *See* below for special rules that apply to fraudulent Ponzi-type investment schemes.

Stock bought on the open market. The IRS does not allow a theft loss deduction if you buy stock on the open market and some or all of your investment is lost because of the fraudulent activities of corporate officers or directors. Your loss is a capital loss (*5.4*), not a theft loss. There is no theft in this situation because there is no direct connection between the corporate wrongdoers and the investors, and the officers and directors lacked a specific criminal intent to take the shareholders' funds.

The IRS contrasts such open market transactions with Ponzi-type fraudulent schemes, in which it holds there is a criminal intent to target the investors, and thus a theft loss is allowed for such Ponzi-scheme losses; *see* below.

Deduction allowed to victims of Ponzi schemes and similar fraudulent schemes. The IRS allows investors who fall victim to fraudulent investment arrangements, including Ponzi schemes, to claim a theft loss deduction under special rule (see Revenue Ruling 2009-9). A theft loss is deductible for the year the loss is discovered. The loss is considered a "theft," not a capital loss, as it is the result of a criminal fraudulent scheme intended to deprive investors of the funds they invested. Since the loss is to their investment account (transaction entered into for profit), the floors for personal-use property in *18.8* do not apply. The deductible theft loss includes the investments made in the fraudulent arrangement and any interest, dividends and capital gains from the scheme that were reported on prior-year tax returns and reinvested, minus any withdrawals. If in the year the loss is discovered the investor has a reasonable prospect of reimbursement, the deductible amount is reduced by the expected reimbursement.

Recognizing that it could be difficult to determine when and how much to deduct as a Ponzi-scheme loss, the IRS provides certain taxpayers with an optional safe harbor method, discussed below, for computing and reporting the theft loss (see Revenue Procedure 2009-20).

If you are eligible for and choose to use the IRS safe harbor, first complete Section C of Form 4684, and then enter the deductible amount from Section C on Section B. If you cannot use the safe harbor, or choose not to, just complete Section B of Form 4684.

Safe harbor. The safe harbor allows eligible investors to deduct either 75% or 95% of their "qualified investment," less any actual or projected recovery from insurance, loss-protection arrangement, or the SIPC (Securities Investor Protection Corporation). The 75% deduction applies if the investor intends to pursue a third-party recovery, and the 95% deduction applies if a third-party recovery will not be pursued. If in a later year there is a recovery that exceeds the non-deducted 5% or 25% portion of the loss, the recovery is taxable under the tax benefit rule *(11.6)* to the extent of the safe harbor deduction (see Revenue Procedure 2009-20).

Eligibility for the safe harbor is limited to investors who had a taxable investment account in the fraudulent arrangement and the investment must have been made directly, not through a fund, partnership, or other entity. Losses in IRAs or other tax-deferred retirement plans invested with the scheme do not qualify for the safe harbor.

A loss is eligible for safe harbor relief only if (1) the "lead figure" in the scheme was charged under federal or state law (by way of indictment or information) with fraud, embezzlement, or a similar crime, or (2) in response to a federal or state criminal complaint, the lead figure admitted guilt or a receiver or trustee was appointed or the assets were frozen, or (3) the assets of the investment scheme were frozen or a receiver or trustee was appointed after a state or federal agency filed a civil complaint in a court or administrative proceeding alleging a fraudulent arrangement conducted by the lead figure, and the lead figure died before being charged with criminal theft.

The loss is deductible for the taxable year in which the theft was discovered (the "discovery year"). Generally, this is the year in which the indictment, information, or complaint against the lead figure was filed. However, if the lead figure died before being charged with criminal theft and a civil complaint under (3) above was filed, the discovery year is the year of the lead figure's death where that is later than the year that the civil complaint was filed (see Revenue Procedure 2011-58). In one case, a civil complaint under (3) above was filed against several lead figures, and in that same year, a receiver was appointed and one of the lead figures died before being criminally charged. In the following year, criminal charges were brought against another lead figure. The IRS ruled that the "year of discovery" for claiming the safe harbor loss was the first year, the year in which the civil complaint was filed, one of the lead figures died before being criminally charged, and a receiver was appointed, rather than in the second year in which criminal charges were brought against one of the lead figures.

Table 18-1   Proving a Casualty Loss

To prove—	You need this information—
That a casualty actually occurred	With a federally declared disaster, you will have no difficulty proving the disaster occurred, but you must prove it affected your property. On Form 4684, you must enter the FEMA disaster declaration number for the disaster. Videos or photographs of the area where your property was located, before and after, and newspaper or online stories placing the damage in your neighborhood are helpful.
The cost of repairing the property	Cost of repairs is allowed as a measure of loss of repairing the property if the cost is not excessive and the repair merely restored your property to its condition immediately before the casualty. Save canceled checks, bills, receipts, and vouchers for expenses of clearing debris and restoring the property to its condition before the casualty.
The value immediately before and after the casualty	Appraisals by a competent expert are important. Get them in writing—in the form of an affidavit, deposition, estimate, appraisal, etc. The expert—an appraiser, engineer, or architect—should be qualified to judge local values. Any records of offers to buy your property, either before or after the casualty, are helpful. Automobile "blue books" may be used as guides in fixing the value of a car. But an amount offered for your car as a trade-in on a new car is not usually an acceptable measure of value.
Cost or other basis of your property—the deductible loss cannot be more than that	A deed, contract, bill of sale, or other document probably shows your original cost. Bills, receipts, and canceled checks probably show the cost of improvements. One court refused to allow a deduction because an owner failed to prove the original cost of a destroyed house and its value before the fire. In another case, estimates were allowed where a fire destroyed records of cost. A court held that the homeowner could not be expected to prove cost by documents lost in the fire that destroyed her property. She made inventories after the fire and again at a later date. Her reliance on memory to establish cost, even though inflated, was no bar to the deduction. The court estimated the market value based on her inventories. If you acquired the property by gift or inheritance, you must establish an adjusted basis in the property from records of the donor or the executor of the estate; see 5.17 and 5.18.

18.8 Floors for Personal-Use Property Losses

A casualty or theft loss of personal-use property is deductible for 2018 through 2025 only if the loss is attributable to a federally declared disaster *(18.1)*. Allowable losses are subject to "floors" that will reduce, and in some cases eliminate, your deduction on Form 4684. Each casualty or theft loss for personal-use property, after taking into account reimbursements (Steps 1–4 at *18.9*), must be reduced by $100, or $500 for a "qualified disaster loss" (*see* the adjacent Law Alert). Your net loss for the year on all items of personal-use property is further reduced by 10% of your adjusted gross income, but the 10% floor does not apply to qualified disaster losses. These reductions are further discussed in Steps 5–7 of *18.9*.

Each loss is reduced by a $100 floor; $500 floor for qualified disaster losses. Generally, each casualty or theft loss of property used for personal purposes is reduced by $100 on Form 4684. The $100 floor is applied after taking into account insurance proceeds received and insurance you expect to receive in a later year *(18.2)*. However, for a "qualified disaster loss," the floor is $500 instead of $100; *see* the nearby Law Alert on Qualified Disaster Losses.

The $100 (or $500) floor does not apply to losses of business property or property held for the production of income such as securities. If property used in personal activities as well as for business or investment is damaged, the offset applies only to the loss allocated to personal use.

For each personal casualty or theft, a separate reduction applies. For example, if you suffer losses to personal-use property in two different federally declared disasters during 2023, there will be a separate $100 offset applied to each of the losses. But when two or more items of property are destroyed in one event, only one $100 offset is applied to the total loss. For example, a severe storm (designated as a federally declared disaster) damages your residence and also your car parked in the driveway. You figure the loss on the residence and car separately on Form 4684, but only one $100 offset applies to the total loss (*see* Example 1 in *18.9*).

Where a federally declared disaster damages property owned by two or more individuals, the $100 floor applies separately to the loss of each co-owner. The only exception is for a married couple filing jointly who apply only one $100 floor to their losses from a single casualty.

See the instructions to Form 4684 for applying the $500 floor if you have a qualified disaster loss.

> **EXAMPLES**
>
> 1. Two sisters own and occupy a house that in 2023 is damaged in a federally declared disaster. Each sister applies the $100 floor to figure her separate deduction on Form 4684 for 2023.
> 2. In 2023, a federally declared disaster damages your house and also the personal property of a houseguest. You are subject to one $100 floor and the houseguest is subject to a separate $100 floor.

10% AGI floor. The 10% adjusted gross income (AGI) floor reduces your deduction for net casualty and theft losses realized during the year on personal-use property. However, the 10% floor does not apply to qualified disaster losses; *see* the Law Alert on this page.

For losses that are not qualified disaster losses, the potential deduction can be substantially reduced or completely eliminated by the 10% of AGI floor. The Example below illustrates the application of the $100 and 10% AGI floors.

If you have gains from casualties and thefts on personal-use property and also have losses that are attributable to federally declared disasters, and the total loss (after the $100 floor reduces each casualty/theft loss) exceeds the total gain, the net loss is reduced by 10% of your AGI; *see* Step 6 in *18.9*.

Qualified disaster losses. As noted above, the per-event floor for a qualified disaster loss is $500 (instead of $100), but the 10% adjusted gross income (AGI) floor does not apply. Unlike other casualty or theft losses, a qualified disaster loss can be claimed even if you claim the standard deduction rather than itemizing deductions. *See* the Law Alert on this page for details on qualified disaster losses.

EXAMPLE

In June 2023, your car, which was worth $28,000, was completely destroyed by a severe flood that was a federally declared disaster. You received insurance reimbursement of $14,000, so your unreimbursed loss was $14,000. In October 2023, another federally declared disaster floods your basement and causes $5,000 of damage to appliances and furniture stored there. You received insurance reimbursement of $2,700 so your loss was $2,300. Your adjusted gross income is $85,000. If you itemize deductions for 2023, use a separate Form 4684 to figure the allowable loss for each casualty. Assume that neither of the floods was a major disaster allowing qualified disaster loss treatment. On the separate Forms 4684, calculate each loss through Line 10. On Line 11, you enter the $100 floor and on Line 12 you subtract the $100 floor from the loss on Line 10. Then combine the two losses (from Line 12 of each form) on a single Form 4684 and apply the 10% AGI floor on Line 17. Your deductible loss for 2023 is $7,600, figured as follows:

Loss on car (after reimbursement)	$14,000	
Less $100 floor	100	$13,900
Loss on basement (after reimbursement)	$2,300	
Less $100 floor	100	2,200
Total loss ($13,900 + $2,200)		16,100
Less 10% of $85,000 AGI		8,500
Deductible loss		$7,600

18.9   Figuring Your Loss on Form 4684

Form 4684 is used to report casualties or thefts of personal-use property, business property, or income-producing property. For 2018 through 2025, a loss to personal-use property is deductible only if the loss is attributable to a federally declared disaster *(18.1)*. However, if you have casualty or theft losses of personal-use property that are not attributable to federally declared disasters, and also have gains from casualties and thefts of personal-use property, whether or not the gains are attributable to federally declared disasters, the gains are offset by the losses, but a deduction for an excess loss is not allowed. *See* Step 7 below and the Form 4684 instructions on offsetting the losses against the gains.

On Form 4684, a deductible loss is usually the difference between the fair market value of the property before the casualty or theft and the fair market value after the casualty or theft but this loss in value must be reduced by (1) reimbursements received for the loss and (2) if the property was used for personal purposes, by the $100 floor ($500 if a qualified disaster loss; *see* the Law Alert on page 436). However, the loss may not exceed your adjusted basis *(5.20)* for the property, which for many items will be your cost. If your adjusted basis is less than the loss in value, your deduction is limited to basis, less reimbursements and the $100 (or $500) floor for each personal-use asset. After figuring all allowable casualty and theft losses and gains for personal-use property, the net loss (losses in excess of gains if any) is deductible as an itemized deduction on Schedule A (Form 1040 or 1040-SR) only to the extent it exceeds the 10% adjusted gross income (AGI) floor *(18.8)*. However, the 10% AGI floor does not apply to qualified disaster losses. A net loss from business property is not claimed as an itemized deduction; the loss from Form 4684 is entered on Form 4797.

Steps for calculating your deductible loss for 2023. The following steps reflect the procedure on Form 4684 for computing a casualty or theft loss. If your loss is to business inventory, you do not have to use Form 4684, but may take the loss into account when figuring the cost of goods sold; *see* "Inventory losses" later in this section.

To figure your deductible loss, follow these seven steps:

1. Step 1. Compute the loss in fair market value of the property. This is the difference between the fair market value immediately before and immediately after the casualty. You do not have to compute the loss in fair market value for business or income-producing property (such as a rental property) that has been completely destroyed or stolen; go to Step 2. *See* the IRS Alert on the following page for safe harbors that can be used to determine the loss in value of personal residential property.

 *Caution*

Failure To Make an Insurance Claim

If you have insurance coverage but do not file a claim because you do not want to risk cancellation of your policy, you may not claim a deduction for the part of your loss that is covered by the policy. The instructions to Form 4684 require you to report as a reimbursement the amount that would have been covered by insurance after taking into account the "deductible" under your policy. This means that the only part of the loss that is potentially deductible on your return (subject to the floors for personal-use property losses,) is the part not covered by the insurance. For example, assume your car worth $30,000 is completely destroyed in a federally declared disaster and your car insurance policy has a $2,500 deductible. If you do not file an insurance claim, you must report $27,500, the loss covered by the policy, as a reimbursement on Form 4684. The $2,500 not covered under the insurance policy, the amount equal to the plan deductible, is reduced by the $100 floor and the $2,400 balance is deductible only to the extent it exceeds 10% of your adjusted gross income, which means no deduction at all is allowed if AGI is $24,000 or more; *see* Step 5 in *18.9*.

IRS Alert

Safe Harbors for Figuring Loss in Value to Home

The IRS has provided an optional safe harbor method in Revenue Procedure 2018-8 that taxpayers can use to determine the decrease in fair market value of personal-use residential property and personal belongings as the result of a casualty or theft. If the taxpayer qualifies for and uses one of the safe harbors, that would establish the decrease in fair market value required under Step 1 of *18.9*; the IRS will not challenge that amount. Revenue Procedure 2018-9 provides an additional safe harbor based on cost indexes that can be used to determine the amount of loss to a home resulting from Hurricane and Tropical Storm Harvey, Hurricane Irma and Hurricane Maria. *See* the instructions to Form 4684 and Publication 547 for further details.

Filing Tip

Business or Income-Producing Property

If you are claiming a loss for property used in your business or income-producing activity, use Section B on page 2 of Form 4684 to figure the allowable loss. Losses from income-producing property are entered on Line 16 of Schedule A as "other itemized deductions". Losses from business property are entered on Form 4797.

You will need written appraisals to support your claim for loss of value. You may not claim sentimental or aesthetic values or a fluctuation in property values caused by a casualty; you must deal with cost or market values of what has been lost. If the value of your property has been lowered because of damage to a nearby area, you do not have a deductible loss since your own property has not been damaged. No deduction may be claimed for estimated decline in value based on buyer resistance in an area subject to landslides.

For household items, the Tax Court has allowed losses based on cost less depreciation, rather than on the decrease in fair market value.

2. Step 2. Compute your adjusted basis *(5.20)* for the property. This is usually the cost of the property plus the cost of improvements, less previous casualty loss deductions and depreciation if the property is used in business or for income-producing purposes. Unadjusted basis of property acquired other than by purchase is explained at *5.16*.

3. Step 3. Take the lower amount of Step 1 or 2. For business or income-producing property that was stolen or completely destroyed, reduce adjusted basis from Step 2 by any salvage value.

4. Step 4. Reduce the loss in Step 3 by the insurance proceeds or other reimbursements you receive for the loss. This is your deductible loss for business or income-producing property. If the loss was on property used for personal purposes, apply the reductions in Step 5.

   In addition to insurance proceeds, reimbursement includes property cleanup, repair, and restoration services you receive from relief agencies such as the Red Cross. However, cash gifts, donations, or grants you receive from relatives, friends, or organizations to help you recover are not treated as reimbursements if there are no conditions on your use of the money. Even if you actually use the money for repairs, it is not considered a reimbursement unless you were required to use it to repair or replace the property. If you successfully sue for damages for your loss, the net award you collect (after lawyer's fees and other expenses) is included as a reimbursement. If part of a disaster loan is canceled, the canceled part is a reimbursement. If your employer has an emergency disaster fund and you receive amounts from that fund that must be used to repair or replace your property, the amount you use is treated as a reimbursement.

   Insurance payments for the cost of additional living expenses you incur because of damage to your home are not treated as reimbursements. The payments are treated as separate and apart from payments for property damage. Insurance payments for excess living costs are not taxable if they are qualified disaster relief payments *(18.1)*; in other cases, some payments may be taxed *(18.12)*.

   If the insurance or other compensation exceeds your adjusted basis for the property, you have a taxable gain rather than a deductible loss. You may be able to defer the gain by buying replacement property *(18.14)*. If you have purchased replacement property or plan to do so within the replacement period, you elect deferral by filing a statement with your return; *see 18.16* for the required statement. If the election to defer is made, do not report the gain on Form 4684.

5. Step 5. If you had only one 2023 casualty or theft loss and the property was used for personal purposes, the loss from Step 4 must be reduced by the $100 floor and any balance is deductible only to the extent it exceeds 10% of your adjusted gross income. If you have more than one casualty or theft loss of personal-use property, you must reduce each loss by the $100 floor and then the total loss (after the $100 floor reduces each casualty/theft loss) is deductible only to the extent it exceeds the 10% AGI floor.

   However, for a "qualified disaster loss," the floor is $500 instead of $100, but the regular 10% AGI floor does not apply; *see* the Law Alert in *18.8* and the Form 4684 instructions.

6. Step 6. If you report gains from casualties and thefts on personal-use property (you do not elect deferral *(18.14)*) and also have losses for personal-use property (after the $100 or $500 floor reduces each casualty/theft loss) that are attributable to federally declared disasters, combine the gains and losses. If the total loss exceeds the total gain, and there are no qualified disaster losses, the net loss is reduced by 10% of your AGI and the excess if any is the deductible loss. For example, if you have a $12,700 loss (after reimbursements and the $100 floor) attributable to a federally declared disaster that is not a qualified disaster loss, and also have a $6,700 casualty gain for a personal-use asset, the net loss of $6,000 ($12,700 − $6,700) is deductible only to the extent it exceeds the 10% AGI floor. If the gain was $12,700

and the loss $6,700, the net gain of $6,000 is reported as capital gain income (either short-term or long-term) on Schedule D (Form 1040 or 1040-SR).

7. Step 7. If you had casualty or theft gains on personal-use property (that are not deferred (18.14) and also casualty or theft losses on personal-use property that are not attributable to federally declared disasters, the losses are allowed to the extent of the gains. There is a worksheet in the instructions to Line 14 of Form 4684 for offsetting the gains by the losses that are not attributable to federally declared disasters.

You also use the Line 14 worksheet in the instructions if some losses are attributable to federally declared disasters and some losses are not attributable to federally declared disasters. On the worksheet, the losses that are not attributable to federally declared disasters are allowed to the extent of the gains, and that amount (losses up to gains) is added to the losses that are attributable to federally declared disasters. For example, assume the facts in the Example in Step 6, except that in addition to the $12,700 loss that is attributable to a federally declared disaster and the $6,700 casualty gain, you also have a $4,300 loss (after reimbursements and the $100 floor) that is not attributable to a federally declared disaster. Since the $4,300 loss that is not attributable to a federally declared disaster does not exceed the $6,700 gain, the entire $4,300 loss is added to the $12,700 loss on the worksheet in the Line 14 instructions, for a total loss of $17,000.

The losses from the Line 14 worksheet are then netted against your gains on Line 15 of Form 4684. A net gain is reported as capital gain income (either short-term or long-term) on Schedule D (Form 1040 or 1040-SR). If there is a net loss, it is deductible only to the extent it exceeds the 10% AGI floor on Line 17 of Form 4684. However, a net qualified disaster loss is not subject to the 10% floor.

Using the amounts from the above Example, the $6,700 gain will reduce the total loss of $17,000 ($4,300 + $12,700) from the Line 14 worksheet, and the net loss of $10,300 ($17,000 − $6,700) will be deductible only to the extent that it exceeds the 10% AGI floor on Line 17 of Form 4684.

EXAMPLES

1. Your home, which cost $76,000 in 1979, and to which you made $20,000 of improvements in 2004, was damaged by a storm that was declared a federal disaster in August 2023. The value of the house before the storm was $247,500, but afterwards, $202,500. Furniture that cost $5,000 in 1995 and was valued at $2,500 before the storm was totally destroyed. In September 2023, the insurance company reimbursed you $25,000 for your house damage and $1,000 for your furnishings. This was the only casualty for the year. Your adjusted gross income for 2023 is $88,000. Assuming that the losses are not qualified disaster losses, the $100 floor and 10% AGI floor apply. You figure your loss for the furniture separately from the loss on the house but apply only one $100 floor because the damage was from a single casualty.

1.	Decrease in home's fair market value:	
	Value of house before storm	$247,500
	Value of house after storm	202,500
	Decrease in value	$45,000
2.	Adjusted basis of house:	$96,000
3.	Loss sustained on house (lower of 1 or 2)	$45,000
	Less: Insurance reimbursement	25,000
	Loss on house	$20,000
4.	Loss on furnishings (decreased value)*	$2,500
	Less: Insurance reimbursement	1,000
	Loss on furnishings	$1,500
5.	Total loss ($20,000 and $1,500)	$21,500
	Less: $100 floor	100
	Casualty loss (subject to 10% floor)	$21,400
6.	10% AGI floor (10% of $88,000 AGI)	$8,800
7.	Deductible casualty loss ($21,400 − $8,800)	$12,600

*The loss for the furnishings on Line 4 is $2,500, the decrease in fair market value, as this is lower than the $5,000 basis.

2. Your depreciable business property with a fair market value of $3,500 and an adjusted basis of $4,000 is totally destroyed in a federally declared disaster. Because property used in your business was totally destroyed (*see* Step 3) *(18.9)*, your loss is measured by your adjusted basis of $4,000, which is larger than the $3,500 loss in fair market value. Salvage value, if any, reduces your deduction, but you disregard the $100 floor and 10% AGI floor, which apply only to casualty losses on personal property. If the property was used for personal purposes, the loss would have been limited to the $3,500 loss in market value less $100, leaving a loss of $3,400 before applying the 10% adjusted gross income floor.

Business losses. Losses from business property are generally netted against gains from casualties or thefts on Form 4684 and the net gain or loss is entered on Form 4797. Follow the instructions to Form 4684.

Inventory losses. A casualty or theft loss of inventory is automatically reflected on Schedule C in the cost of goods sold, which includes the lost items as part of your opening inventory. Any insurance or other reimbursement received for the loss must be included as sales income.

You may separately claim the inventory loss as a casualty or theft loss on Form 4684 instead of automatically claiming it as part of the cost of goods sold. If you do this, you must eliminate the items from inventory by lowering either opening inventory or purchases when figuring the cost of goods sold.

18.10 Personal and Business Use of Property

For property held partly for personal use and partly for business or income-producing purposes, a casualty or theft loss deduction is computed as if two separate pieces of property were damaged, destroyed, or stolen. Follow the steps for figuring the allowable loss *(18.9)*, but apply the per-event floor of $100 (or $500 if a qualified disaster loss) and the 10% of adjusted gross income floor (if not a qualified disater loss) only to the personal part of the loss.

Caution

Incidental Expenses

Expenses that are incidental to a casualty or theft, such as medical treatment for personal injury, temporary housing, fuel, moving, or rentals for temporary living quarters, are not deductible as casualty losses.

EXAMPLE

A building with two apartments, one used by the owner as his home and the other rented to a tenant, is damaged by a flood that is a federally declared disaster. The fair market value of the building before the flood was $369,000 and it was $309,000 after the flood, which damaged both apartments equally. Assume that the losses were not qualified disaster losses. Cost basis of the building was $120,000. Depreciation taken before the fire was $14,000. The insurance company paid $30,000. The owner has adjusted gross income of $80,000. This is his only loss this year. He has a business casualty loss of $15,000 and a deductible personal casualty loss of $6,900 figured as follows:

	Business	Personal
1. Decrease in value of building:		
Value before flood ($369,000)	$184,500	$184,500
Value after flood ($309,000)	(154,500)	(154,500)
Decrease in value	$30,000	$30,000
2. Adjusted basis of building:	$60,000	$60,000
Less: Depreciation	(14,000)	
Adjusted basis	$46,000	$60,000
3. Loss sustained (lower of 1 or 2)	$30,000	$30,000
Less: Insurance (total $30,000)	($15,000)	($15,000)
4. Loss	$15,000	$15,000
Less: $100 floor and 10% of adjusted gross income ($8,000) for personal loss	—	(8,100)
Deductible casualty loss	$15,000	$6,900

18.11 Repairs May Be a "Measure of Loss"

The cost of repairs may be treated as evidence of the loss of value (Step 1) *(18.9)*, if the amount is not excessive and the repairs do nothing more than restore the property to its condition before the casualty. An estimate for repairs will not suffice; only actual repairs may be used as a measure of loss. However, where you measure your loss by comparing appraisals of value for before and after the casualty, repairs may be considered in arriving at a post-casualty value even though no actual repairs are made.

Deduction not limited to repairs. A casualty loss deduction is not limited to repair expenses where the decline in market value is greater, according to a federal appeals court; *see* the following Example.

Planning Reminder

Keep Records of Deductible Losses

If your property is damaged, you must reduce the basis of the damaged property by the casualty loss deduction and compensation received for the loss *(5.20)*. When you later sell the property, gain or loss is the difference between the selling price and the reduced basis.

EXAMPLE

Connor claimed that the market value of his house dropped $93,000 after it was damaged by fire. His $52,000 cash outlay in repairing the house was reimbursed by insurance. He claimed a casualty loss of approximately $40,000, the uncompensated drop in market value. The IRS barred the deduction. The house was restored to pre-casualty condition. The cost of the repairs is a realistic measure of the loss, and, as the expense was fully compensated by insurance, Connor suffered no loss. A federal appeals court disagreed. The house dropped $70,000 in market value, of which $20,000 was uncompensated by insurance. The deduction is measured by the uncompensated difference in value before and after the casualty. It is not limited to the cost of repairs, even where the repair expense is less than the difference in fair market values. Had the repairs cost more than this difference, the IRS would not have allowed a larger deduction.

18.12 Excess Living Costs Paid by Insurance Are Not Taxable

Your insurance contract may reimburse you for excess living costs when a casualty or a threat of casualty forces you to vacate your house. The insurance payments are completely tax free if the temporary increase in your living costs was due to a casualty (storm, flood, wildfire) in a federal disaster area; they are treated as qualified disaster area relief payments *(18.1)*.

If the casualty that forces you to vacate your home is not a federally declared disaster, some of the insurance payments may be taxable. These rules apply if:

1. Your principal residence is damaged or destroyed by fire, storm, or other casualty that is not a federally declared disaster or you are denied access to your home by a governmental order because of the occurrence or threat of the casualty.

2. You are paid under an insurance contract for living expenses resulting from the loss of occupancy or use of the residence.

Tax-free reimbursements. Whether you have a taxable or tax-free reimbursement is figured at the end of the period you were unable to use your residence. Thus, if the dislocation covers more than one taxable year, the taxable income, if any, will be reported in the taxable year in which the dislocation ended.

The tax-free amount is limited to the excess living costs paid by the insurance company. The excess is the difference between (1) the actual living expenses incurred during the time you could not use or occupy your house and (2) the normal living expenses that you would have incurred for yourself and members of your household during the period. Insurance payments that exceed (1) minus (2) are generally taxable; *see* the Examples below.

Living expenses during the period may include the cost of renting suitable housing and extraordinary expenses for transportation, food, utilities, and miscellaneous services. The expenses must be incurred for items and services (such as laundry) needed to maintain your standard of living that you enjoyed before the loss and must be covered by the policy.

Where a lump-sum settlement does not identify the amount covering living expenses, an allocation is required to determine the tax-free portion. In the case of uncontested claims, the tax-free portion is that part of the settlement that bears the same ratio to total recovery as increased living expense bears to total loss and expense. If your claim is contested, you must show the amount reasonably allocable to increased living expenses consistent with the terms of the insurance contract, but not in excess of coverage limitations specified in the contract.

The exclusion from income does not cover insurance reimbursements for loss of rental income or for loss of or damage to real or personal property; such reimbursements for property damage reduce your casualty loss *(18.9)*.

If your home is used for both residential and business purposes, the exclusion does not apply to insurance proceeds and expenses attributable to the nonresidential portion of the house. There is no exclusion for insurance recovered for expenses resulting from governmental condemnation or order unrelated to a casualty or threat of casualty.

The insurance reimbursement may cover part of your normal living expenses as well as the excess expenses due to the casualty. The part covering normal expenses is income; it does not reduce your casualty loss.

EXAMPLES

1. On March 1, your home was damaged by a fire (not a federally declared disaster). While it was being repaired, you and your spouse lived at a motel for a month and ate meals at restaurants. Costs for the month are $2,400 for the motel, $2,000 for meals, and $150 for laundry services. You make the required March payment of $1,580 on your home mortgage. Your customary monthly commuting expense of $80 is cut in half to $40 because the motel is closer to your work. Furthermore, you do not incur your customary monthly expenses when at home of $1,000 for food, $175 for utilities, and $100 for laundry. Your insurance company pays you $4,000 for expenses. The tax-free exclusion for insurance payments is limited to $3,235, computed in the third column below. On Line 8z of Schedule 1 (Form 1040 or 1040-SR) you must report $765 ($4,000 insurance – $3,235 exclusion) as "Other income."

	Expenses from casualty	Expenses not incurred	Increase (Decrease)
Housing	$2,400		$2,400
Utilities		$175	(175)
Meals	2,000	1,000	1,000
Transportation	40	80	(40)
Laundry	150	100	50
Total	$4,590	$1,355	$3,235

2. Same facts as in Example 1 except that you rented the residence for $2,000 per month and the risk of loss was to the landlord. You did not pay the March rent. The excludable amount is $1,235 ($3,235 less $2,000 normal rent not incurred). You would have to report as income the excess of the insurance received over the $1,235 exclusion.

Filing Tip

Involuntary Conversion of Personal Residence

Gain on the destruction or condemnation of your principal residence may escape tax under the home sale exclusion rules discussed in *Chapter 29*. If the exclusion is not available or the gain exceeds the excludable amount, but you buy a replacement residence, gain may be deferred under the involuntary conversion replacement rules *(18.14)*. Special rules apply if your principal residence was damaged or destroyed in a federally declared disaster: gain on insurance proceeds received for unscheduled personal property in the home is not taxable, and insurance proceeds for the home itself and scheduled personal property are combined for purposes of making a reinvestment in replacement property that qualifies for deferral *(18.4)*.

18.13 Do Your Casualty or Theft Losses Exceed Your Income?

If your 2023 casualty or theft losses exceed your income for the year, you pay no tax for 2023. Under the net operating loss (NOL) rules *(40.18)*, you may carry forward any unused amount until it is used up by offseting 80% of your taxable income in those future years.

The $100 floor *(18.8)* and the 10% of adjusted gross income floor *(18.8)* for personal casualty or theft losses apply only in the year of the loss; you do not again reduce your loss in the carryforward years.

18.14 Defer Gain from Involuntary Conversion by Replacing Property

If your property is destroyed, damaged, stolen, or seized or condemned by a government authority, this is considered to be an involuntary conversion for tax purposes *(18.15)*. If upon an involuntary conversion you receive insurance or other compensation (reduced by expenses in obtaining reimbursement) that exceeds the adjusted basis of the property, you realize a gain that is taxable unless you elect to defer (postpone) the gain or, in the case of a principal residence, it is gain that you may exclude from income under the rules in *Chapter 29*.

You may elect to postpone tax on the full gain provided you invest the proceeds in replacement property the cost of which is equal to or exceeds the net proceeds from the conversion *(18.19)*. Buying a replacement from a related party generally qualifies only if your gains from involuntary conversions are $100,000 or less *(18.17)*. Gain realized on a destroyed or condemned principal residence that exceeds the allowable exclusion under the rules in *Chapter 29* may be postponed if the cost of a replacement residence at least equals the conversion proceeds minus the excluded gain *(18.19)*.

The replacement period *(18.18)* is two years for personal-use property; for business and investment property it is two or three years depending on the type of involuntary conversion; for a principal residence and its contents involuntarily converted due to a federally declared disaster it is four years. If you find that you cannot buy a replacement by the end of the period, ask the IRS for an extension of time. *See 18.18* for replacement period details.

Insurance proceeds may have to be allocated to determine if you have a gain. If property used in your business is involuntarily converted, make a distinction between insurance proceeds compensating you for the loss of your property and any insurance that compensates you for loss of profits because of business interruption. Business interruption proceeds are fully taxed as ordinary income and may not be treated as proceeds of an involuntary conversion. Only take into account the insurance for the loss of property in figuring if you have a gain from the involuntary conversion.

A single standard fire insurance policy may cover several assets. Assume a fire occurs, and in a settlement the proceeds are allocated to each destroyed item according to its fair market value before the fire. In comparing the allocated proceeds to the adjusted basis of each item, you find that on some items, you have realized a gain; that is, the proceeds exceed basis. On the other items, you have a loss; the proceeds are less than basis. According to the IRS, you may elect to defer tax on the gain items by buying replacement property. You do not treat the proceeds paid under the single policy as a unit, but as separate payments made for each covered item.

Election to defer reporting of a gain. To defer reporting of your gain, do not report the gain on your return for the year it is realized. Make the election to defer on a statement attached to your return that provides details of the involuntary conversion and computation of the gain, and which describes the replacement property if you have already acquired it or states your intention to buy a replacement if you have not yet done so. Details on the required statement or statements you must file are at *18.16*.

Basis of replacement property. Your basis for the replacement property is its replacement cost, minus any postponed gain. This is the actual mechanism of deferral. By reducing basis of the replacement property by the amount of the deferred gain, tax on that gain is postponed until the replacement property is disposed of.

Should you elect to postpone gain? An election to defer your gain gives an immediate advantage: tax on gain is postponed and the funds that would have been spent to pay the tax may be used for other investments.

However, as a condition of deferring the gain, your basis for the replacement property equals its cost minus the deferred gain. If your reinvestment matches the insurance or other compensation, your basis for the new property will be the same as the basis for the converted property. If your reinvestment exceeds the compensation, the excess increases the basis of the replacement property. As long as the value of the replacement property does not decline, tax on the original gain is finally incurred when the property is sold.

 *Planning Reminder*

Basis Reduction

Consider whether postponement of gain at the expense of a reduced basis for property is advisable, compared with the tax consequences of reporting the gain in the year it is realized.

> **EXAMPLE**
>
> Your rental building is destroyed by fire and after taking into account insurance payments, you have a gain (excess of insurance over adjusted basis for building) that is taxable as capital gain if you do not elect to defer the gain. Assume that you reinvest the reimbursement in replacement property so you qualify to make the election. Should you do so? An election to defer the gain is generally not advisable if you have capital losses to offset the gain. However, even if you have no capital losses, you may still decide to pay tax on the gain now and not make the election to defer. Reporting the gain now would allow you treat the purchase price of the new building as its basis for depreciation purposes. This can be an advantage if you anticipate that future depreciation deductions will offset income that will be taxed at a higher rate than the rate you are subject to currently. Of course, it may turn out that there will be little or no difference between your current tax rate and your future rate, so that a net after-tax benefit from the depreciation would not arise.
>
> Ultimately, projecting future consequences may not be your key concern. You may decide to elect to defer the gain simply because you want to postpone the payment of tax.

18.15 Involuntary Conversions Qualifying for Tax Deferral

For purposes of an election to defer tax on gains, "involuntary conversion" is broadly defined. You have an involuntary conversion when your property is:

Damaged or destroyed by some outside force, such as a storm, fire, or car accident, or it is stolen.

Seized, requisitioned, or condemned by a governmental authority. If you voluntarily sell land made useless to you by the condemnation of your adjacent land, the sale may also qualify as a conversion. Condemnation of property as unfit for human habitation does not qualify. Condemnation, as used by the tax law, refers to the taking of private property for public use, not to the condemnation of property for noncompliance with housing and health regulations. Similarly, a tax sale to pay delinquent taxes is not an involuntary conversion. *See* condemnation awards below.

Sold under a threat of seizure, condemnation, or requisition. The threat must be made by an authority qualified to take property for public use. A sale following a threat of condemnation made by a government employee is a conversion if you reasonably believe he or she speaks with authority and could and would carry out the threat to have your property condemned. If you learn of the plan of an imminent condemnation from the news media, the IRS requires you to confirm the report from a government official before you act on the news.

Condemnation awards. You have a gain if your net condemnation award exceeds your adjusted basis in the condemned property. The net award is the total award reduced by expenses of getting the award such as legal, engineering, and appraisal fees. The treatment of special assessments and severance damages received when part of your property is condemned is explained in *18.20*.

Payments made directly by the condemning authority to your mortgagee do not reduce the gross award. For example, your condemnation award is set at $200,000 but you are paid only $148,000 because $52,000 was paid to your mortgage holder, including $2,000 to cover accrued real estate taxes. The entire $200,000 is treated as your condemnation award.

Do not include as part of the award interest paid on the award for delay in its payment; you separately report the interest as interest income. The IRS may treat as interest part of an award paid late, even though the award does not make any allocation for interest.

Caution

Loss on Condemned Residence Not Deductible

If your principal residence or vacation home is condemned and the net condemnation award is less than your adjusted basis in the residence, you have a loss. The loss is not deductible, but if you received a Form 1099-S, you must report the condemnation on Form 8949 and Schedule D; *see 5.8*.

Filing Tip

Sale of Property Under Hazard Mitigation Program

A sale or other transfer of vulnerable property to federal, state, or local authorities (or Indian tribal governments) under a hazard mitigation program is treated as an involuntary conversion, thereby allowing a gain to be deferred if a qualifying replacement *(18.17, 18.19)* is made.

Relocation payments are not considered part of the condemnation award and are not treated as taxable income to the extent that they are spent for purposes of relocation. Such payments increase basis of the newly acquired property.

Farmers. In addition to the above types of involuntary conversions, farmers also have involuntary conversions when:

- Land is sold within an irrigation project to meet federal acreage limitations;
- Cattle are destroyed by disease or sold because of disease; or
- Draft, breeding, or dairy livestock is sold because of drought in counties identified by the IRS. The election to treat the sale as a conversion is limited to livestock sold over the number that would have been sold but for the drought.

If there is a gain from the involuntary conversion of livestock and it is not feasible to replace the proceeds because of soil contamination or other environmental contamination, then other property (including real property) used for farming purposes is treated as "similar or related in service or use" *(18.17)* and qualifies as replacement property.

18.16 How to Elect to Defer Gain

To defer reporting a gain, include your election on a statement attached to your return for the year the gain is realized. For example, for a gain realized in 2023 from an involuntary conversion *(18.15)*, attach a statement to your 2023 return that provides details of the involuntary conversion, including reimbursements you received and how you figured the gain. If you have purchased replacement property *(18.17)* by the time you file your 2023 return, your statement should describe:

- The replacement property and its cost,
- The amount of gain that can be deferred, which depends on the cost of the replacement *(18.19)*,
- The basis of the replacement property (cost minus deferred gain), and
- If not all of the gain is deferred, the gain being reported as income.

If you intend to purchase the replacement property after you file your 2023 return, the statement filed with the 2023 return should describe the conversion and the computation of gain and indicate that you intend to buy a replacement within the replacement period *(18.18)*. Then, when you file your return for the year you buy the replacement property, attach a statement to that return giving the details of the replacement property. Providing this statement starts the running of the three-year period of limitations during which the IRS can assess tax on the gain. Failure to give notice keeps the period open. Similarly, a failure to give notice of an intention not to replace also keeps the period open.

If you make an election to postpone the gain but do not buy replacement property within the replacement period (plus extensions if any; *see 18.18*), you must file an amended return for the year in which gain was realized to report the gain and pay the tax (if any) on the gain. Similarly, if you elect to defer gain and buy replacement property that costs less than the amount realized from the conversion *(18.19)*, you must file an amended return to report the gain that cannot be deferred and pay any additional tax due. Also *see* the Caution titled "Nullifying Deferral Election on Amended Return."

If you have a gain from an involuntary conversion and do not expect to reinvest the proceeds, you report the gain and pay the tax due. In a later year, but within the prescribed time limits, you buy qualifying replacement property. On an amended return for the year of the conversion, you may make an election to defer the gain and claim a refund for the tax paid in the earlier year on the gain.

Deferring a gain from condemnation. To defer reporting a gain from a condemnation, the replacement rules and required statement requirements discussed in the preceding paragraph generally apply.

However, if your property is condemned and the government authority gives you property that is similar or related in use to the condemned property, no election is necessary. You do not have to report the gain on your return; postponement of tax on the

Attach Statement to Your Return to Defer Gain

To defer reporting a gain when you receive reimbursements that exceed your adjusted basis for the involuntarily converted property, you must attach a statement to your return that provides details of the involuntary conversion and that describes replacement property that you have already acquired or which states your intention to buy a replacement within the replacement period; *see 18.16* for details.

Nullifying Deferral Election on Amended Return

If you elect to defer a gain, intending to buy replacement property, but you fail to make a replacement within the time limit, you must file an amended return for the year of the gain and pay the tax that you had elected to defer. You also must file an amended return and report the gain not eligible for deferral if you invest in property that does not qualify as a replacement, or which costs less than the amount realized from the involuntary conversion *(18.19)*.

However, if you elect to defer and make a timely qualifying replacement, you may not change your mind and pay tax on the gain in order to obtain a higher basis *(18.14)* for the replacement property. The Tax Court has agreed with the IRS that the election to defer is irrevocable once a qualified replacement is made within the time limits. Similarly, once you acquire qualified replacement property and designate it as such in a statement attached to your tax return, you may not substitute other replacement property, even if the replacement period has not yet expired.

Reporting a Condemnation Gain On Your Return

Gain from a condemnation of personal-use property is reported on Forms 8949 and Schedule D *(5.8)* if it cannot be excluded from income (if a principal residence); *see 18.14* or you do not elect to defer the gain. Gain from a condemnation of business property or investment property that is not deferred is generally reported on Form 4797.

Note: A loss on condemned business or investment property (net condemnation award is less than adjusted basis) is also reported on Form 4797.

gain is required. For example, your local government condemns the building in which you operate your retail business and gives you a similar building, the value of which exceeds the adjusted basis of the old one. The gain is not taxed, and your basis for the new building is the same as your basis in the condemned building.

Partnerships. The election to defer gain must be made at the partnership level. Individual partners may not make separate elections unless the partnership has terminated, with all partnership affairs wound up. Dissolution under state law is not a termination for tax purposes.

18.17 Types of Qualifying Replacement Property

Under the deferral rules *(18.14)* for destroyed, damaged, or stolen property, or for condemned personal-use property, replacement property must be similar or related in service or use to the property that was involuntarily converted in order to defer tax. Where real property held for productive use in a business or for investment is converted through a condemnation or threat of condemnation, "like-kind" property is treated as similar or related in service or use; *see* "Similar or related in service use test for condemned property" below.

Under the "similar or related in service or use" test, the replacement of unimproved land for improved land does not qualify. A replacement generally must be closely related in function to the destroyed property. For example, a destroyed principal residence must be replaced with another principal residence. If the destroyed residence is replaced with a home that is rented to tenants, or with a retail store, the replacement does not qualify, as it is not being used for the same purpose as the destroyed residence.

This functional test, however, is not strictly applied where destroyed or damaged rental property is replaced with other rental property. Here, the role of the owner toward the properties, rather than the functional use of the buildings, is reviewed. If an owner held both properties as investments and offered similar services and took similar business risks in both, the replacement may qualify, as in the following IRS Example:

> **EXAMPLE**
>
> A tornado destroys a building that was rented to a manufacturing company. The owner has another building constructed, and rents it out as a wholesale grocery warehouse. Because both properties are rental properties, they are considered to be similar or related in use if there is a similarity in all of the following areas: (1) the owner's management activities, (2) the amount and kind of services provided to tenants, and (3) the nature of the business risks connected with the properties.

Similar or related in service use test for condemned property. The "similar or related in service or use" test discussed above generally applies to condemned property, but there is a more liberal replacement test where the condemned property is real property held for investment or for productive use in the owner's business (provided it was not inventory held mainly for sale). In this case, regardless of its function, a replacement is treated as similar or related in service or use where it is "like-kind" property to be held either for productive use in business or for investment. Under the like-kind test, condemned investment or business real estate can be replaced with other investment or business real estate. Improved real property may be replaced by unimproved real property *(6.1)*. Foreign and U.S. real property are considered to be of like kind for purposes of replacing the condemned property, even though under the like-kind exchange rules *(6.1)*, U.S. real estate and foreign real estate are not considered like-kind property.

Where both the condemned property and the replacement property are held for rental, and there is similarity in management, services offered to tenants and business risks taken, the replacement can also qualify under the rule discussed above for destroyed or damaged property. Thus, in the above Example, if the building rented to a manufacturing company had been condemned rather than destroyed by a tornado, the IRS would take the same approach in deciding if the replacement rental warehouse was "similar or related in service or use."

You may own several parcels of property, one of which is condemned. You may want to use the condemnation award to make improvements on the other land, such as drainage and grading. The IRS generally will not accept the improvements as a qualified replacement. However, an appeals court has rejected the IRS approach in one case.

Deferral may be barred when buying a replacement from a relative. The gain deferral rules do not apply if you buy a replacement from a close relative or a related business organization unless the total gain you realized for the year on all involuntary conversions on which there are realized gains is $100,000 or less. In determining whether gains exceed $100,000, gains are not offset by losses. Affected related parties are the same as defined for loss transactions discussed in *5.6*.

Buying controlling interest in a corporation. The replacement test is satisfied by purchasing a controlling interest (80%) in a corporation owning property that is similar or related in service or use to the converted property.

Business and investment property in a disaster area. The similar or related-use tests do not have to be met when replacing business or investment property damaged or destroyed in a federally declared disaster area, provided you use the new property for business. You may make a qualified replacement by buying any tangible property held for business use; the replacement does not have to be in the federally declared disaster area.

Caution

Buying Replacement From Relative

Buying a replacement from a relative or related business organization will not defer gain unless total gains from involuntary conversions for the year are $100,000 or less.

18.18 Time Period for Buying Replacement Property

To defer tax, you generally must buy property similar or related in use *(18.17)* to the converted property within a fixed time period. The replacement period is either two, three, or four years:

1. A two-year replacement period applies for destroyed, damaged, or stolen property, whether used for business, investment, or personal purposes, but there is a four-year period for principal residences in federally declared disaster areas *(18.3)*; *see* below. The two-year period for damaged, destroyed, and stolen property starts on the date the property was destroyed, damaged, or stolen, and ends two years after the end of the first year in which any part of your gain is realized. A two-year period also applies to a condemned residence.

2. A three-year replacement period applies for condemned business or investment real estate, excluding inventory. However, the two-year and not the three-year period applies if you replace the condemned business or investment real estate by acquiring control of a corporation that owns the replacement property.

3. A four-year replacement period applies for a principal residence or its contents involuntarily converted as a result of a federally declared disaster *(18.3)*. The four-year replacement period starts on the date the residence is involuntarily converted and ends four years after the end of the first taxable year in which any part of the gain is realized.

4. A four-year replacement period for farmers and ranchers who are forced to sell livestock due to drought, flooding, or other weather conditions in areas eligible for federal assistance. Gain on such a forced sale may be deferred by buying replacement livestock within four years after the end of the first taxable year in which any part of the gain is realized. The IRS may extend the four-year replacement period on a regional basis if the severe weather conditions persist for more than three years. Each year in September, the IRS releases a Notice that provides an extension of the replacement period for farmers and ranchers who have sold livestock in specified counties suffering severe drought; *see* the Filing Tip on this page.

Filing Tip

Extended Replacement Period for Livestock Sales Due to Drought

The regular 4-year period for drought-related livestock sales can be extended in areas of persistent drought until the end of the taxpayer's first taxable year ending after the first drought-free year for the applicable region. The IRS announced an extended replacement period for farmers and ranchers whose 4-year replacement period was scheduled to expire at the end of 2022, provided their county is listed in IRS Notice 2022-43.

Giving IRS notice of replacement. On your return for the year you realize the gain, you must attach a statement that describes the involuntary conversion and notifies the IRS either that you have acquired replacement property, or that you plan to do so within the replacement period, in which case another statement must be filed with your return for the year of the replacement. Details on these required statements are in *18.16*.

Replacing condemned property. For condemnations, the replacement period starts on the earlier of (1) the date you receive notification of the condemnation threat or (2) the date you dispose of the condemned property. Depending on the replacement period *(see above)*, the period ends two, three, or four years after the end of the first year in which any part of the gain on the condemnation is realized. You may make a replacement after a threat of condemnation. If you buy property before the actual threat, it will not qualify as a replacement even though you still own it at the time of the actual condemnation.

Advance payment of award. Gain is realized in the year compensation for the converted property exceeds the basis of the converted property. An advance payment of an award that exceeds the adjusted basis of the property starts the running of the replacement period.

An award is treated as received in the year that it is made available to you without restrictions, even if you contest the amount.

Replacement by an estate. A person whose property was involuntarily converted may die before he or she makes a replacement. According to the IRS, his or her estate may not reinvest the proceeds within the allowed time and postpone tax on the gain. The Tax Court rejects the IRS position and has allowed tax deferral where the replacement was made by the deceased owner's estate. However, the Tax Court agreed with the IRS that a surviving spouse's investment in land did not defer tax on gain realized by her deceased husband on an involuntary conversion of his land. She had received his property as survivor of joint tenancy and could not, in making the investment, be considered as acting for his estate.

EXAMPLES

1. On January 13, 2023, your parcel of investment real estate is condemned; the parcel cost $150,000. On March 28, 2023, you received a check for $230,500 from the state. Your expenses in obtaining the award were $10,000, so the net condemnation award is $220,500. You may defer the tax on the gain of $70,500 ($220,500 − $150,000 basis) if you invest at least the net award *(18.19)*, or $220,500, in other real estate not later than December 31, 2026, the end of the three-year replacement period.

2. Business property was contaminated by dangerous chemicals, and after the Environmental Protection Agency ordered businesses and residents to relocate, the property was sold to the local government under a threat of condemnation. The owner was paid the full pre-contamination fair market value for the property. The owner wanted to defer gain under the three-year replacement rule for condemnations. However, the IRS said that part of the gain was deferrable under the two-year rule and part under the three-year rule. There were two conversions: (1) the contamination, subject to the two-year replacement rule; and (2) the later condemnation, subject to the three-year rule.

   To determine the amount eligible for deferral for each period, an allocation must be made between the proceeds allocable to the destruction of the property and the proceeds allocable to the condemnation.

   According to the IRS, the burden for making the allocation between the two conversions rests with the owner. The government's payments are allocable to the condemnation and, therefore, eligible for the three-year replacement rule, only to the extent of the post-contamination value. Practically speaking, it may be advisable in a case like this to make the replacement within the two-year period, as it may be difficult to show the contaminated land had any value after the contamination.

18.19 Cost of Replacement Property Determines Postponed Gain

To defer tax on the full gain realized on an involuntary conversion *(18.15)*, the cost of replacement property *(18.17)* must be equal to or exceed the net proceeds from the conversion (amount received minus your expenses). If replacement cost is no more than the adjusted basis of the converted property, you must include the entire gain in your income. If replacement cost is less than the net proceeds on the conversion but more than the basis of the converted property, the difference between the net proceeds and the cost of the replacement must be reported as a taxable gain; you may elect to postpone tax on the balance of the gain. *See* Examples 1–4 below.

EXAMPLES

1. The adjusted basis of the apartment house that you rent out to tenants is $175,000. It is condemned to make way for a new street. You receive a condemnation award from the state of $305,000. Your legal expenses in obtaining the award were $5,000, so the net award is $300,000. Your gain is $125,000 ($300,000 net award – $175,000 adjusted basis). If you buy a similar apartment house for $175,000 or less, you must report the entire $125,000 gain.

2. Same facts as in Example 1, except that you buy an apartment house for $250,000. Of the gain of $125,000, you must report $50,000 as taxable gain ($300,000 net award – $250,000 replacement cost). You may elect to postpone the tax on the balance of the gain, or $75,000. If you elect deferral, your basis for the new building is $175,000 ($250,000 cost – $75,000 postponed gain).

3. Same facts as in Example 1, but you buy an apartment house for $300,000 or more. You may elect to postpone tax on the entire gain because you have invested the entire net award in replacement property. If the cost of the new building is $325,000 and you elect deferral, your basis for the new building is $200,000 ($325,000 cost – $125,000 postponed gain).

4. You bought a vacation home 20 years ago for $150,000 and over the years made capital improvements of $30,000, giving you an adjusted basis of $180,000. In January 2023, when the home was worth $350,000, it was destroyed in a storm. In May 2023, you received $284,000 from the insurance company. You have a gain of $104,000 ($284,000 insurance – $180,000 basis). In October 2023, you bought a new vacation home for $250,000. Since the cost of the replacement property ($250,000) was less than the $284,000 insurance proceeds, you must include in your income the unspent amount, or $34,000 ($284,000 – $250,000).

18.20 Special Assessments and Severance Damages from Condemnation

When only part of a property parcel is condemned for a public improvement, the condemning authority may:

1. Levy a special assessment against the remaining property, claiming that it is benefited by the improvement. The authority usually deducts the assessment from the condemnation award.

2. Grant an award for severance damages if the condemnation of part of your property causes a loss in value or damage to the remaining property that you keep.

A special assessment that is taken out of the award reduces the amount of the gross condemnation award. An assessment levied after the award is made may not be deducted from the award.

When both the condemnation award and severance damages are received, the condemnation is treated as two separate involuntary conversions: (1) A conversion of the condemned land. Here, the condemnation award is applied against the basis of the condemned land to determine gain or loss on its conversion; and (2) a conversion of part of the remaining land in the sense that its utility has been reduced by condemnation, for which severance damages are paid.

Net severance damages reduce the basis of the retained property. Net severance damages are the total severance damages, reduced by expenses in obtaining the damages and by any special assessment withheld from the condemnation award. If the damages exceed basis, gain is realized. Tax may be deferred on the gain through the purchase of replacement property under the "similar or related in service or use" test *(18.17)*, such as adjacent land or restoration of the property to its original condition.

Allocating the proceeds between the condemnation award and severance damages will either reduce the gain or increase the loss realized on the condemned land. The IRS will allow such a division only when the condemnation authority specifically identifies part of the award as severance damage in the contract or in an itemized statement or closing sheet. The Tax Court, however, has allowed an allocation in the absence of earmarking where the state considered severance damages, and the value of the condemned land was small in comparison to the damages suffered by the remaining property. To avoid a dispute with the IRS, make sure the authority makes this breakdown. Without such identification, the IRS will treat the entire proceeds as consideration for the condemned property.

EXAMPLE

Two acres of a 10-acre tract are condemned for a new highway. The adjusted basis of the land is $30,000, or $3,000 per acre. The condemnation award is $11,000; you incurred expenses of $1,000 to get the award. A special assessment against the remaining eight acres of $2,500 is withheld from the award. The net gain on the condemnation is $1,500:

Condemnation award minus your expenses ($11,000 award − $1,000 expenses)	$10,000
Less:	
Special assessment withheld from award	2,500
Net condemnation award	7,500
Basis of two condemned acres	6,000
Net gain (net award minus basis)	$1,500

CHAPTER 19

Other Itemized Deductions

Apart from the expenses listed in Chapters 14 through 18, only a few expenses can be claimed as itemized deductions on Schedule A (Form 1040 or 1040-SR). These include net qualified disaster losses, casualty and theft losses of income-producing property, gambling losses to the extent of reported gambling winnings, and impairment-related job expenses *(19.1)*.

A wide-ranging list of expenses that were deductible before 2018 to the extent the total exceeded 2% of adjusted gross income are not deductible for 2018 through 2025. These include unreimbursed employee expenses (employee travel expenses, work clothes, union and professional dues, education expenses, and home office expenses), investment expenses, legal expenses, and tax preparation expenses *(19.2)*.

19.1 Only a Few Expenses Are Allowed as "Other" Itemized Deductions

If you itemize deductions on Schedule A, the following expenses may be claimed on Line 16 as "Other Itemized Deductions":

Impairment-related work expenses. If you have a physical or mental disability that substantially limits your ability to walk, speak, breathe, or perform manual tasks and which limits your ability to work, you can deduct unreimbursed ordinary and necessary expenses that enable you to work. This includes attendant care services at your place of work and similar expenses.

Where to deduct the impairment-related work expenses depends upon employee status. If you are an employee, enter the impairment-related work expenses as well as any employer reimbursements on Form 2106. Then enter the unreimbursed amount on Line 16 (Other Itemized Deductions) of Schedule A. If you are self-employed, the impairment-related expenses are reported as business expenses on Schedule C *(40.6)* and not as an itemized deduction.

Casualty and theft losses of property held for investment. If your investment property (work of art, rental property, stocks, bonds, precious metals) was stolen or damaged in a storm or other casualty, figure your allowable loss on Section B of Form 4684 *(18.7, 18.9)*. If you are a victim of a Ponzi or Ponzi-type scheme, your loss is treated as a theft loss of investment property; *see 18.7*.

Net qualified disaster loss. A net qualified disaster loss from Form 4684 *(18.8)* is added to any other "other itemized deductions" on Line 16 of Schedule A. If you claim the standard deduction rather than itemizing, the net qualified disaster loss is still reported on Line 16 of Schedule A. You combine your regular standard deduction with the net qualified disaster loss and show the increased standard deduction amount on Line 16; the combined amount is entered on Form 1040 or 1040-SR as your standard deduction.

Gambling losses up to reported gambling winnings. As discussed in *11.3*, gambling losses are deductible only up to the amount of gambling winnings reported as "other income" on Schedule 1 (1040 or 1040-SR).

Repayment of more than $3,000 that you previously included in income under a claim of right. Instead of claiming the repayment as an "other" itemized deduction, you may recompute your tax for the year you reported the income and claim a tax credit for the year you repay it *(2.8)*.

Estate tax attributable to income in respect of a decedent (IRD). If federal estate tax was paid on IRD you include on your return, the estate tax attributable to that IRD is deductible *(11.17)*.

Amortizable bond premium in excess of interest on taxable bond. If the allocable amortizable premium exceeds the interest income for the year, the excess premium is deductible *(4.17)*.

Unrecovered investment in employee annuity. If the last surviving annuitant of an employee annuity dies before the retiree's entire investment is recovered tax-free, the balance is deductible on the final income tax return of the last annuitant; *see* the Example in *7.25*.

Ordinary loss attributable to a contingent debt instrument or an inflation-indexed debt instrument. The ordinary loss on a Treasury Inflation-Protected Security (TIPS) is reported here.

Unrecovered investment in annuity. If a person dies before recovering the investment in an annuity with a starting date before 1986, the unrecovered amount is treated as an itemized deduction on the decedent's final income tax return. For an annuity that started later, the unrecovered cost is not deductible.

19.2 Deductions for Job Costs and Other Miscellaneous Expenses No Longer Allowed

For 2018 through 2025, all the miscellaneous itemized deductions that were deductible in 2017 and prior years to the extent they exceeded 2% of adjusted gross income are not deductible. The 2% floor had the effect of substantially reducing or eliminating the deduction for these expenses, but now an itemized deduction for these expenses is completely disallowed regardless of amount.

In general, three categories of expenses are no longer deductible: (1) unreimbursed employee expenses, (2) tax preparation expenses and practitioner fees for representing you in a tax dispute before the IRS or a court, and (3) fees to produce or collect taxable income and costs of managing or protecting investment property.

Here is a more specific list of expenses that are no longer deductible itemized deductions:

- Unreimbursed employee expenses. This includes employee travel and meals expenses on trips away from home *(20.6)*, local transportation costs to see clients or customers, union dues, professional and business association dues, uniforms and work clothes, costs of looking for a new job in the same line of work, employee home office expenses, job-related education costs, and business bad debt on a loan made to your employer to protect your job.

  However, the non-deduction rule for unreimbursed employee expenses does not apply to a few expenses that are allowed as an above-the-line deduction (an "adjustment to income" *(12.2)* allowed whether you claim the standard deduction or itemized deductions). This includes educator expenses up to $300 per taxpayer, qualifying travel costs of Armed Forces Reservists, expenses of state or local government officials paid on a fee basis, and expenses of qualifying performing artists.

- General tax advice and tax return preparation fees. An exception exists for self-employment, farming, rental, and royalty income. If you are self-employed, a tax practitioner's fee for preparing your Schedule C and related schedules, or Schedule F and related schedules, is a business expense deductible on the Schedule C or F. A tax preparation fee allocable to reporting rental or royalty income on Schedule E is deduced on that form.

- Fees to a tax practitioner to represent you at an IRS examination, trial, or hearing involving any tax.

- Appraisal fees related to casualty losses and charitable property contributions.

- Investment costs, such as IRA custodial fees, safe-deposit rentals, subscriptions to investment services, fees to investment counselors, and travel costs of a trip away from home *(20.6)* to look after investment property or confer with an attorney, accountant, or financial advisor about managing your investments.

- Legal fees for recovering taxable job-related damages or personal damages. An exception exists for discrimination and business related legal fees. Certain discrimination suits are deductible from gross income *(12.2)*. If you are self-employed, legal fees relating to your business are deductible on Schedule C (Schedule F for farming) *(40.6)*.

CHAPTER 20

Travel and Meal Expense Deductions

Unreimbursed employee travel expenses are not deductible, except for a very limited number of employees who may claim their expenses on Form 2106 and deduct them as an above-the-line adjustment to income *(20.1)*.

Under an "accountable plan" arrangement, an expense allowance from an employer for travel costs is not reported as income on Form W-2 if you substantiated the expenses to your employer and returned any unsubstantiated portion of the allowance *(20.18)*. If you are self-employed, travel expenses are claimed on Schedule C *(40.6)*.

The types of deductible travel expenses are highlighted in *Table 20-1*. You must be away from home to deduct travel expenses on overnight business trips. Meal costs on overnight trips away from home are subject to restrictions, including a 50% deduction limit (80% for certain transportation workers) unless they are provided at restaurants *(20.15)*. On one-day business trips within the general area of your employment, only transportation costs may be deducted; meals may not, unless taken as part of a business meal with current or potential customers/clients.

To support your travel expense deductions, keep records that comply with IRS rules *(20.16)*.

You may no longer deduct entertainment expenses. Although deductions for entertainment have been eliminated, business meals may still be fully or 50% deductible, provided that IRS requirements are satisfied *(20.13, 20.14)*.

20.1 Who May Deduct Travel and Transportation Expenses

Due to the suspension of miscellaneous itemized deductions subject to the 2% floor *(19.2)*, the only employees who may deduct unreimbursed travel and transportation costs for 2018 through 2025 are those in the following limited categories: (1) Armed Forces reservists who have reserves-related expenses for trips away from home *(20.6)* of more than 100 miles *(35.8)*, (2) fee-basis state or local government officials *(12.2)*, and (3) qualifying performing artists; *see* requirements at *12.2*.

Employees in these three categories use Form 2106 to report their eligible business expenses and employer reimbursements if any. Meals on business trips away from home are 50% deductible on Form 2106. The qualifying portion of unreimbursed expenses from Form 2106 is entered as an above-the-line deduction ("adjustment to income") on Line 12 of Schedule 1 (Form 1040 or 1040-SR), so it is allowed whether the employee claims the standard deduction or deductions are itemized on Schedule A *(12.2)*. In priors years 2021 and 2022, the IRS granted a temporary 100% deduction, which expired as of January 1, 2023.

Employees who are not within categories (1) through (3) may not use Form 2106 and may not deduct unreimbursed travel and transportation costs for 2018 through 2025. For reimbursement under an accountable plan; *see 20.18*.

Self-employed individuals, as well as employees in categories (1) through (3), should *see Table 20-1*, which summarizes the rules for deducting local business transportation costs and travel expenses while "away from home" *(20.6)* on business trips. Generally, commuting expenses from your home to your place of business when you are not away from home are not deductible *(20.2)*. However, you may be able to claim a deduction for daily transportation expenses incurred in commuting *(20.2)* to a temporary job location; *see Table 20-1*.

If you are self-employed, claim your deductible transportation and travel costs on Schedule C *(40.6)*.

20.2 Commuting Expenses

The cost of travel between your home and place of work is generally not deductible, even if the work location is in a remote area not serviced by public transportation. Nor can you justify the deduction by showing you need a car for faster trips to work or for emergency trips. Travel from a union hall to an assigned job is also considered commuting. If you join a car pool, you may not deduct expenses of gasoline, repairs, or other costs of driving you and your passengers to work.

According to the IRS, if you use your cell phone to make calls to clients or business associates while driving to your office, you are still commuting and your expenses are not deductible. Similarly, the deduction is not allowed if you drive passengers to work and discuss business.

Deductible commuting expenses. The IRS allows these exceptions to its blanket ban on commuting expense deductions.

If you are on a business trip out of town, you may deduct taxi fares or other transportation costs from your hotel to the first business call of the day and all other transportation costs between business calls. If you use your car to carry tools to work, you may deduct transportation costs where you can prove that they were incurred in addition to the ordinary, nondeductible commuting expenses. The deduction will be allowed even if you would use a car in any event to commute; *see* the Examples below.

Commuting to a temporary place of work. Whether you can deduct commuting expenses to a temporary place of work may depend on the location of the temporary assignment and whether you have a regular place of business or a home office that is your principal place of business. According to the IRS, if you have a regular place of work outside of your home, or you have a home office that is your principal place of business, you may deduct the cost of commuting between your home and a temporary *(see below)* work location, regardless of where the temporary location is.

If you do not have a regular place of work but normally work at several locations in the metropolitan area where you live, you may deduct the costs of commuting to a temporary location that is outside that metropolitan area, but not to a temporary location within

Court Decision

Self-Employed Person's Office at Home

If you are self-employed and your regular office is outside your home, you may not deduct the cost of commuting to the office or from that office to your home even if you work at home at a second job. However, if your home office is your principal place of business *(40.12)*, you can deduct travel costs between the home office and the offices or worksites of your clients or customers.

Planning Reminder

Qualified Transportation Benefits

A tax-free exclusion from wages (up to $300/month for 2023) is allowed for transit passes and employer-provided transportation in a "commuter highway vehicle", and also for at-work vehicle parking. Alternatively, an employer may provide these commuter benefits to employees on a pre-tax basis *(3.8)*.

the metropolitan area. If you do not have a regular place of work and all of your work assignments are outside the metropolitan area where you live, none of your commuting costs are deductible under the IRS rule.

What is a temporary place of work? A temporary work location is one at which your assignment is realistically expected to last, and actually does last, for one year or less. If at first you realistically expect an assignment to last for no more than one year but that expectation changes, the IRS will generally treat the assignment as temporary until the date that it became realistic to expect that the work would exceed one year.

Accountants, architects, engineers, and other professionals often have to travel to job sites of their clients. If such work at the site is temporary and they can show they also have a regular work office, they may deduct commuting expenses from their homes to their work sites.

 *Caution*

IRS Definition of "Temporary"

The IRS considers a work location temporary if the period of work is realistically expected to last, and actually does last, one year or less. If you take an assignment expected to last more than a year but it actually lasts less than a year, your assignment is not considered temporary and commuting costs are not deductible.

EXAMPLES

1. Jones commuted to and from work by public transportation before he had to carry tools. Public transportation cost $5 per day to commute to and from work. When he had to use the car to carry the tools, the cost of driving was $12 a day and $35 a day to rent a trailer to carry the tools. Jones may deduct only the cost of renting the trailer. The IRS does not allow a deduction for the additional $7 a day cost of operating the car. It is not considered related to the carrying of the tools. It is treated as part of the cost of commuting, which is not deductible.

2. Same facts as above, but Jones does not rent a trailer. He uses the car trunk to store his tools. He may not claim a deduction because he incurs no additional cost for carrying the tools.

3. Smith uses his car regardless of the need to transport tools. He rents a trailer for $35 a day to carry tools. He may deduct $35 a day under the "additional-cost" rule.

20.3 Overnight-Sleep Test Limits Deduction of Meal Costs

The overnight-sleep rule prevents the deduction of meal costs on one-day business trips. To be deductible, meal costs must be incurred while "away from home" and this test requires that they be on a business trip that lasts longer than a regular working day (but not necessarily 24 hours) and requires time off to sleep (not just to eat or rest) before returning home. Non-restaurant meals while away from home are subject to the 50% deduction limit *(20.15)*. Taking a nap in a parked car off the road does not meet the overnight-sleep test.

EXAMPLES

1. A New York business owner flies to Washington, D.C., which is about 250 miles away, to see a client. He arrives at noon, eats lunch, and then visits the client. He flies back to New York that evening. He may deduct the cost of the plane fare, but not the cost of his lunch. He was not away overnight nor was he required to take time out to sleep before returning home.

2. Same facts as above except the business owner sleeps overnight in a Washington hotel. He eats breakfast there, and then sees another client and returns home to New York in the afternoon. He may deduct not only the cost of the plane fare but also the cost of his meals while on the trip and the cost of the hotel, since he was away overnight.

Several courts held that the IRS rule was unreasonable and outdated in the world of jet travel, and they would have allowed the New Yorker on the one-day trip to Washington, D.C., to deduct the cost of his lunch. In 1968, the Supreme Court disagreed and upheld the IRS rule as a fair administrative approach; there have been no additional decisions on this point.

Meal costs during overtime. Such costs are not deductible if you are not away from your place of business. Thus, for example, a resident physician could not deduct the cost of meals and sleeping quarters at the hospital during overnight or weekend duty.

Table 20-1   Deductible Travel and Transportation Expenses

Caution: If you are an employee, you may not deduct any unreimbursed employee travel and transportation costs for 2018 through 2025 unless you are (1) a fee-basis state or local government official, (2) an Armed Forces reservist who travels over 100 miles from home to attend reservist meetings or trainings, or (3) a qualifying performing artist; *see 20.1*.

Your Travel Status—	Tax Rule—
Local trips to see customers and client	You may deduct your transportation expenses but not the cost of personal meals on one-day business trips within the general area of your tax home.
Overnight trips away from home	On business trips "away from home," you may deduct the cost of travel between your home and business destination, meals and lodging while away, as well as local transportation expenses at the destination *(20.5)*.
Work in an area other than where you have your residence EXAMPLE: You live with your family in Chicago, but work in Milwaukee where your business is located. During the week, you stay in a hotel in Milwaukee and eat meals in a restaurant. You return to your family in Chicago every weekend.	Milwaukee is your "home" for tax purposes; *see 20.6*. Thus, your expenses for traveling to Milwaukee and your meals and lodging there are personal, nondeductible expenses.
Temporary assignment in an area other than where you have your residence EXAMPLE: You live in and operate your business in Kansas City. To supervise a project in Omaha, you travel to Omaha where you stay for 60 days. Occasionally, you return to Kansas City on your days off, and the rest of the time you stay in Omaha.	You may deduct the necessary expenses for traveling away from home from Kansas City to Omaha and returning to Kansas City after your temporary assignment is completed. You may also deduct expenses for meals and lodging (even for your days off) while you are in Omaha. As discussed at *20.8*, deductions are not allowed on temporary assignments that are expected to last more than one year.
Weekend trip home from temporary assignment EXAMPLE: Same facts as in the Example above except that you return home to Kansas City on weekends.	You are not "away from home" while you are in Kansas City on your days off and your meals and lodging while you are there are not deductible. However, you may deduct your traveling expenses (including meals and lodging, if any) from Omaha to Kansas City and back if they are no more than the amount it would have cost you for your meals and lodging if you had stayed in Omaha. If they are more, your deduction is limited to the amount you would have spent in Omaha. If you retain your room in Omaha while in Kansas City, your expenses of returning to Kansas City on days off are deductible only to the extent of the amount you would have spent for your meals had you stayed in Omaha.
Seasonal work in different areas EXAMPLE: You live in Cincinnati, where you work for eight months each year. You earn the greater share of your annual income from that work. For the remaining four months of the year, you work in Miami. When in Miami, you eat and sleep in a hotel. You have been working in both of these cities for several years and expect to continue to do so.	You have two recurring seasonal places of business. Cincinnati is your principal place of business. You may deduct the costs of your traveling expenses while away from Cincinnati working at your minor place of business in Miami, including meals and lodging in Miami.
Convention trip	You may deduct the costs of travel to a business convention under the rules in *20.11*. If you are a delegate to a charitable or veterans' convention, you may claim a charitable deduction for the travel costs *(14.4)*.
Trip for health reasons	If you claim itemized expenses on Schedule A, you may deduct the cost of the trip as a medical expense if you meet the rules at *17.9*.

20.4 IRS Meal Allowance

If you find it difficult to keep records of meal costs while away from home *(20.3)* on business trips, you may prefer to claim an IRS meal allowance. In government tables, the allowance is referred to as the "M&IE" rate (rate for meals and incidental expenses), the amount of which depends on where you travel. In addition to meals and tips for food servers, the allowance (M&IE rate) covers a limited amount of "incidental" expenses such as fees and tips for porters, baggage carriers, hotel maids, or room stewards. Self-employed individuals may claim the M&IE allowance *(40.6)*, as well as employees listed in *20.1* who have qualifying expenses that are not reimbursed under an "accountable" plan *(20.18)*. You must keep a record of the time, place, and business purpose of the trips. As long as you have this proof, you may claim the allowance even if your actual costs for meals and incidental expenses are less than the allowance.

If you are self-employed, the allowance is claimed on Schedule C, where the cost must be reduced by 50%, (80% deduction for transportation workers subject to the Department of Transportation hours of service limits applies) *(20.15)*.

Employees eligible to deduct travel costs (only if they are listed at *20.1*) claim the meal allowance, reduced by 50%, on Form 2106; *see 20.1*.

Meal allowance on 2023 tax returns. For 2023 business travel through September 30, 2023, within the lower 48 continental U.S. (referred to as CONUS locations), the standard meal allowance (M&IE) for most locations is $59 per day, but higher rates of $64, $69, $74, or $79 apply in major cities and other high-cost locations (such as resort areas), as determined by the federal government's General Services Administration (GSA). These amounts are unchanged from 2022. The location-specific CONUS M&IE rates can be obtained from the GSA website at gsa.gov/perdiem. The GSA website lists M&IE rates by reference to the federal government's fiscal year, which begins October 1, and the per-locality rate is the same for that entire fiscal year.

If you travel to more than one area on a given day, use the M&IE rate for the area where you stop for sleep. A special M&IE rule applies to workers in the transportation industry, as discussed below.

Travel outside the continental United States. Different rates apply for travel in Alaska, Hawaii, Puerto Rico, and U.S. possessions, as well as for travel to foreign countries. These rates (OCONUS) are set by the Defense Department and there is a link to the DoD site from the GSA website at gsa.gov/perdiem.

Transportation industry workers. Self-employed persons in the transportation industry may elect to claim a special M&IE rate. The special rate avoids the need to apply the CONUS or OCONUS M&IE rates on a locality-by-locality basis. You cannot combine the two methods. If the special rate is used for one trip, it must be used for all trips during the same year.

For the first nine months of 2023, the special transportation industry M&IE rate was $69 per day for any CONUS location and $74 per day for any OCONUS location. The rate was unchanged from 2022. At the time of writing, the October 1, 2023, rates were not available. See the *e-Supplement* at *jklasser.com* for any update.

Allowance for first and last day must be reduced. The M&IE allowance is prorated for the first and last day of a trip. You may claim 75% of the allowance for the days you depart and return. Alternatively, you may claim 100% of the allowance if you are away for a regular "9-to-5" business day.

20.5 Business Trip Deductions

If you are self employed or an employee listed in *20.1*, the following expenses of a business trip away from home *(20.6)* are deductible:

- Plane, railroad, taxi, ride-share, and other transportation fares between your home and your business destination
- Hotel and other lodging expenses. You need receipts or similar evidence for lodging expenses; there is no IRS standard lodging allowance as there is for meals *(20.4)*.

- Meal costs. You may claim your actual meal costs if you maintain records to substantiate the expense *(20.16)*. and the amount is not "lavish or extravagant," which, according to the IRS, means it is reasonable under the circumstances. Alternatively, you may use the standard meal allowance *(20.4)*. Whichever method you use, only 50% of the non-restaurant meal costs are deductible unless the 80% limit for workers subject to Department of transportation limits applies *(20.15)*.
- Tips, telephone, and telegraph costs
- Laundry and cleaning expenses
- Baggage charges (including insurance)
- Cab fares or other costs of transportation to and from the airport or station and your hotel. Also deductible are cab fares or other transportation costs, beginning with your first business call of the day, of getting from one customer to another, or from one place of business to another.

Travel costs of a spouse, dependent, or business associate. Travel costs of a spouse, dependent, or any other individual who accompanies you on a business trip are not deductible unless that person is also your employee or your business associate (partner, agent, advisor, client, customer, supplier) who has a bona fide business reason for taking the trip that would justify claiming a deduction if the person took the trip on his or her own.

Filing Tip

How Much To Deduct for Spouse

If your spouse accompanied you on a business trip, your bills will probably show costs for both of you. These usually are less than twice the cost for a single person. To find what you may deduct where your spouse's presence is for personal and not qualifying business reasons, do not divide the bill in half. Figure what accommodations and transportation would have cost you alone and deduct that. The excess over the single person's costs is not deductible.

EXAMPLES

1. You and your spouse travel by car to a business convention in another city. You pay $200 a day for a double room. A single room would have cost $150 a day. Your spouse's presence at the convention was for social reasons. You may deduct the total cost of operating your car to and from the convention city. You may deduct $150 a day for your room. If you traveled by plane or railroad, you would deduct only your own fare. You may deduct your own meal expenses to the extent allowed *(20.15)*. during the trip, assuming the costs were not lavish or extravagant, but your spouse's meal costs are not deductible.

2. Connie worked with her husband operating a home improvement contracting business. With him, she attended trade shows and conventions, where they ran a display booth. There, she talked about their company's services and solicited new business. The IRS disallowed the company's deduction of her travel expenses as having no business purpose. The Tax Court disagreed. Both Connie and her husband were officers and employees of the company. They attended the conferences together. As the IRS allowed her husband's expenses, it should have also allowed expenses attributed to her participation, especially as they were incurred together as employees.

Cruise ship. If you travel by cruise ship on a business trip, your deductible cruise costs are limited to twice the highest federal per diem rate for travel in the United States on that date multiplied by the number of days in transit.

EXAMPLE

You sail to Europe on business. While you are away, the highest per diem federal rate is $288 and the trip lasts six days. The maximum deduction for the cost of the trip is $3,456 (2 × $288 × 6). The double per diem rule applies without regard to the 50% limit on meal costs if meals are not separately stated in your bill. If a separate amount for meals or entertainment is included, such amount must be reduced by 50% (the 100% limit does not apply to meals on luxury vessels).

The double per diem rule does not apply to cruise ship convention costs that are deductible up to $2,000 a year if all the ports of call are in the U.S. or U.S. possessions and if the ship is registered in the United States *(20.19)*.

Important: Recordkeeping requirements. See the sections for recordkeeping rules to support a deduction for unreimbursed travel expenses or to avoid being taxed on employer reimbursements *(20.16–20.18)*.

Law Alert

Tax Home Defined

For travel expense purposes, your home is your place of business, employment, or post of duty, regardless of where you maintain your family residence. This tax home includes the entire city or general area of your business premises or place of employment. The area of your residence may be your tax home if your job requires you to work at widely scattered locations, you have no fixed place of work, and your residence is in a location economically suited to your work.

Planning Reminder

Determining Your Principal Place of Business

If you have more than one regular place of business, your tax home is your principal place of business. Your principal place of business or employment is determined by comparing: (1) the time ordinarily spent working in each area; (2) the degree of your business activity in each area; (3) the amount of your income from each area; (4) the taxpayer's permanent residence; and (5) whether employment at one location is temporary or indefinite.

No single factor is determinative. The relative importance of each factor will vary depending on the facts of a particular case. For example, where there are no substantial differences between incomes earned in two places of employment, your tax home is probably the area in which you spend more of your time. Where there are substantial income differences, your tax home is probably the area in which you earn more of your income.

20.6 When Are You Away From Home?

You have to meet the "away from home" test to deduct the cost of meals and lodging while traveling *(20.5)*. You have to be away from your tax home and satisfy the overnight-sleep rule *(20.3)* to be "away from home." In general, your tax home is the city or general area in which your regular place of business or post of duty is located, regardless of where your family is.

Do you regularly work at more than one location? If you regularly work in two or more separate locations, your tax home is the area of your principal place of business or employment. You are away from home when you are away from the area of your principal place of business or employment. Therefore, you may deduct your transportation costs to and from your minor place of business and your living costs there.

> **EXAMPLES**
>
> 1. Sherman lived in Worcester, Mass., where he managed a factory. He opened his own sales agency in New York. He continued to manage the factory and spent considerable time in Worcester. The larger part of his income came from the New York business. However, he was allowed to treat New York as his minor place of business and to deduct his travel expenses to New York and his living expenses there because he spent most of his time in Worcester and his income there was substantial.
>
> 2. Benson, a consulting engineer, maintained a combination residence-business office in a home he owned in New York. He also taught four days a week at a Technological Institute in West Virginia under a temporary nine-month appointment. He spent three-day weekends, holidays, and part of the summer at his New York address. At the Institute, he rented a room in the student union building. The IRS disallowed transportation expenses between New York and West Virginia and meals and lodging there as not incurred while away from home. The Tax Court disagreed. A taxpayer may have more than one occupation in more than one city. When his occupations require him to spend a substantial amount of time in each place, he may deduct his travel expenses, including meals and lodging, at the place away from his permanent residence. That Benson's teaching salary happened to exceed his income from his private practice does not change the result.

Are you constantly on the road? If you do not work within any particular locality, an IRS agent may disallow your travel deductions on the grounds that your tax home is wherever you work; thus, you are never "away from home." You are considered a transient worker.

If your deduction is questioned because you have no regular or main place of business, you may be able to show that your tax home is the area of your residence. If you meet the following three tests, the IRS will treat your residence as your tax home: (1) you do some work in the vicinity of your residence, house, apartment, or room and live there while performing services in the area; (2) you have mortgage expenses or pay rent for the residence while away on the road; and (3) the residence is in an area where you were raised or lived for a long time, or a member of your immediate family such as your parent or child lives in the residence, or you frequently return there.

According to the IRS, if you meet only two of these three tests, it will decide on a case-by-case basis if your residence is your tax home. If you meet less than two of the tests, the IRS will not allow a deduction; each of your work locations is treated as your tax home.

If you live in a trailer at each work location and have no other home, each location is your principal place of business and you are not "away from home."

Permanent duty station of service members. The Supreme Court held that a member of the Armed Forces is not away from home when he or she is at a permanent duty station. This is true even if the service member has to maintain a separate home for family members who are not permitted to live at the duty station.

> **EXAMPLES**
>
> 1. Your residence is in a suburb within commuting distance of New York City where you do freelance work full time. Your personal home and tax home are the same, that is,

within the metropolitan area of New York City. You are away from home when you leave this area, say, for Philadelphia. Meals and lodging are deductible only if you meet the overnight-sleep test *(20.3)*.

2. Your residence is in New York City, but you work in Baltimore. Your tax home is Baltimore; you may not deduct living expenses there. But you may deduct travel expenses on a temporary assignment to New York City even while living at your home there.

20.7 Tax Home of Married Couple Working in Different Cities

When spouses work and live in different cities during the week, one of them may seek to deduct travel expenses away from home. Such deductions have generally been disallowed, but courts have allowed some exceptions. Each spouse may have a separate tax home.

EXAMPLES

1. Robert worked in Wilmington, Delaware; his wife, Margaret, worked in New York City. During the weekend, she traveled to Wilmington and deducted, as travel expenses away from home, her living costs in New York and weekend travel expenses to Wilmington. She argued that because she and her husband filed a joint return, they were a single taxable unit, and the tax home of this unit was Wilmington where her husband lived. The deduction was disallowed. That a couple can file a joint return does not give them deductions that are not otherwise available to them as individuals. Margaret's tax home was New York, where she worked. Therefore, her expenses there are not deductible. And, as the weekend trips to Wilmington had no relationship to her job, they, too, were not deductible.

2. Hundt and his wife lived in Arlington, Va., but he wrote and directed films in various parts of the country. He wrote screenplays either at his Arlington home or on location, but most of his business came from New York City, where he lived in hotels. One year, he spent 175 days in New York City on business and rented an apartment for $1,200 because it was cheaper than a hotel. He deducted half the annual rent for the New York apartment, the costs of traveling between Arlington and New York, and the cost of meals in New York. The IRS disallowed the expenses, finding New York to be his tax home. The Tax Court disagreed. Arlington was Hundt's tax home because (1) part of his income came from his creative writing in Arlington; and (2) his travel to other parts of the country was temporary. The fact that most of his income came from New York did not make New York his tax home.

20.8 Deducting Living Costs on Temporary Assignment

A business trip away from home *(20.6)* at a single location may last a few days, weeks, or months. If your assignment is considered temporary, you may deduct travel costs *(see below)* while there because your tax home has not changed. The IRS considers an assignment to be temporary if you realistically expect it to last for one year or less and it actually does last no more than one year. If an assignment is realistically expected to last more than a year, it is considered indefinite, and you cannot deduct your living costs at the area of the assignment because that location becomes your tax home. This is true even if the assignment actually lasts only a year or less. That is, you can be away for a year or less and still be barred from claiming a deduction if at the time you started the assignment you realistically expected it to last for more than a year. Likewise, employment that is initially temporary may become indefinite due to changed circumstances; *see* the Examples below.

EXAMPLES

1. You are on an assignment away from home in a single location that is expected to last (and it does in fact last) for one year or less. The IRS will treat the assignment as temporary, unless facts and circumstances indicate otherwise. Expenses are deductible.

2. You are on an assignment away from home at a single location. You expect that the job will last 18 months. However, due to financial difficulties the assignment ends after 11 months. Even though your assignment actually lasted for less than one year the IRS treats it as indefinite because you realistically expected it to last more than one year. Thus, your travel and living expenses while away from home are not deductible.

3. You are on an assignment away from home at a single location. You expect that it will last only nine months. However, due to changed circumstances occurring after eight months, you remain on the assignment for six more months. The IRS treats the assignment as temporary for eight months, and indefinite for the remaining time you are away from home. Thus, travel and living expenses you pay or incur during the first eight months are deductible; expenses paid or incurred thereafter are not.

Caution

Taking Your Family With You

If you take your family with you to a temporary job site, an IRS agent may argue that this is evidence that you considered the assignment to be indefinite. In the Michaels Example in this section, however, such a move was not considered detrimental to a deduction of living expenses at the job location.

Deductible travel costs on temporary trip. While on a temporary assignment expected to last a year or less, you may deduct the cost of meals (*see 20.15* for limits, if any), and lodging at the temporary location, even for your days off. If you return home, say for weekends, your living expenses at home are not deductible. You may deduct travel expenses, meals, and lodging en route between your home and your assignment location provided they do not exceed your living expenses had you stayed at the temporary location. If you keep a hotel room at the temporary location while you return home, you may deduct your round-trip expenses for the trip home only up to the amount you would have spent had you stayed at the temporary workplace.

EXAMPLE

Michaels, a cost analyst for Boeing, lived in Seattle. He traveled for Boeing, but was generally not away from home for more than five weeks. Michaels agreed to go to Los Angeles for a year to service Boeing's suppliers in that area. He rented his Seattle house and brought his family with him to Los Angeles. Ten months later, Boeing opened a permanent office in Los Angeles and asked Michaels to remain there permanently. Michaels argued that his expenses for food and lodging during the 10-month period were deductible as "away from home" expenses. The IRS contended that the Los Angeles assignment was for an indefinite period.

The Tax Court sided with Michaels. He was told that the stay was for a year only. He leased his Seattle house to a tenant for one year, planning to return to it. He regarded his work in Los Angeles as temporary until Boeing changed its plans. The one-year period justified his taking the family but did not alter the temporary nature of the assignment.

Separate assignments over a period over a year. Where over a period of years you work on several separate assignments for one client, the IRS may attempt to treat the separate assignments as amounting to a permanent assignment and disallow living costs away from home, as in the Mitchell Example below.

EXAMPLE

Mitchell, a publishing consultant who lived and worked out of his home in Illinois, advised a publisher of a magazine with offices in California. Over a five-year period, from 1991 to 1995, he worked on short job assignments that averaged 130 days a year for the magazine. Some assignments arose because of unforeseen events, such as the abrupt firing of a novice editor, the hiring of a new editor, and the editor's later absence because of cancer and her death. In 1994 and 1995, when working in California, he rented an apartment because it was cheaper than a hotel. He claimed lodging and meal expenses in California that the IRS disallowed on the grounds that his employment in California was not temporary; it lasted more than one year.

The Tax Court disagreed. Just because an independent contractor returns to the same general location in more than one year does not mean that he is working there on an indefinite basis. Mitchell's work followed an on again, off again pattern. Each job assignment that lasted less than a year ended with no expectation of future assignments. Throughout the five-year period, his consultancy services were required by unexpected events.

20.9   Business-Vacation Trips Within the United States

On a business trip to a resort area, you may also spend time vacationing. If the primary purpose of the trip is to transact business and the area is within the United States (50 states and the District of Columbia) you may deduct all of the costs of your transportation to and from the area, lodging, and meal expenses *(20.6)*, even if you do spend time vacationing. If the main purpose of the trip is personal, you may not deduct any part of your travel costs to and from the area. The amount of time spent on business as opposed to sightseeing or personal visits is the most important issue in determining your primary purpose. Regardless of the primary purpose of your trip, you are allowed to deduct expenses related to the business you transacted while in the area.

No deductions will be allowed if you attend a convention or seminar where you are given videotapes to view at your own convenience and no other business-related activities or lectures occur during the convention. The trip is considered a vacation.

If your trip is primarily for business, and while at the business destination you extend your stay for a few days for nonbusiness reasons, such as to visit relatives, you deduct travel expenses to and from the business destination.

> **EXAMPLE**
>
> You work in Atlanta and make a business trip to New Orleans. You stay in New Orleans for six days and your total costs, including round-trip transportation to and from New Orleans, meals at restaurants (50% of the cost), and lodging, is $1,800, which you may deduct. If, on your way home, you spend three days in Mobile visiting relatives and incur an additional $600 in travel costs, your deduction is limited to the $1,800 you would have spent had you gone home directly from New Orleans.

20.10   Business-Vacation Trips Outside the United States

If your travel expenses are otherwise deductible *(20.1, 20.5–20.6)*, expenses are allowed for a business trip abroad, even though you take time out to vacation, provided you can prove: (1) the primary purpose of the trip was business and (2) you did not have control over arranging the trip.

If you are an employee, selecting the date of the trip does not mean that you had control over the assignment. IRS regulations assume that when you travel for your company under a reimbursement or allowance arrangement, you do not control the trip arrangements, provided also that you are not: (1) a managing executive of the company; (2) related to your employer; or (3) have more than a 10% stock interest in the company. You are considered a managing executive if you are authorized without effective veto procedures to decide on the necessity of the trip. You are related to your employer if the employer is your spouse, parent, child, brother, sister, grandparent, or grandchild *(20.19)*.

Rule for managing executives and self-employed persons. If you are a managing executive, self-employed, related to your employer, or have a more-than-10% stock interest, you are treated as having control over arranging the trip and your deduction for transportation costs to and from your business destination may be limited. However, a full deduction for transportation costs is allowed if:

1. The trip outside the United States took a week (7 consecutive days) or less, not counting the day you left the U.S. but counting the day you returned,

2. If the trip abroad lasted more than a week, you spent less than 25% of your time, counting the days your trip began and ended, on vacation or other personal activities, or

3. In planning the trip you did not place a major emphasis on taking a vacation.

If the vacationing and other personal activities took up 25% or more of your time on a trip lasting more than one week, and you cannot prove that the vacation was a minor consideration in planning the trip, you must allocate travel expenses between the time spent on business and that spent on personal affairs. The part allocated to business is deductible; the balance is not. To allocate, count the number of days spent on the trip

Primary Business Purpose

If your return is examined, proving the business purpose of your trip depends on presenting evidence to convince an examining agent that the trip, despite your vacationing, was planned primarily to transact business. Keep a log or diary to substantiate business activities.

Vacation Areas

If the IRS determines that you were primarily on vacation, it will disallow all travel costs except for costs directly related to your business in the area such as registration fees at a foreign business convention *(20.12)*.

outside the United States, including the day you leave the U.S. and the day you return. Then divide this total into the number of days on which you had business activities; include days of travel to and from a business destination.

If you vacation at, near, or beyond the city in which you do business, the expense subject to allocation is the cost of travel from the place of departure to the business destination and back. For example, you travel from New York to London on business and then vacation in Paris before returning to New York. The expense subject to allocation is the cost of traveling from New York to London and back; *see* Example 2 below. However, if from London you vacationed in Dublin before returning to New York, you would allocate the round-trip fare between New York and Dublin and also deduct the difference between that round-trip fare and the fare between New York and London; *see* Example 3 below.

EXAMPLES

1. You fly from New York to Paris to attend a business meeting for one day. You spend the next two days sightseeing and then fly back to New York. The entire trip, including two days for travel en route, took five days. The plane fare is deductible. The trip did not exceed one week.

2. You fly from Chicago to New York, where you spend six days on business. You then fly to London, where you conduct business for two days. You then fly to Paris for a five-day vacation after which you fly back to Chicago. You would not have made the trip except for the business that you had to transact in London. The nine days of travel outside the United States away from home, including two days for travel en route, exceeded a week, and the five days devoted to vacationing were not less than 25% of the total travel time outside the U.S. The two days spent traveling between Chicago and New York, and the six days spent in New York, are not counted in determining whether the travel outside the United States exceeded a week and whether the time devoted to personal activities was less than 25%.

   Assume you are unable to prove either that you did not have substantial control over the arrangements of the trip or that an opportunity for taking a personal vacation was not a major consideration in your decision to take the trip. Thus, 5/9 (five nonbusiness days out of nine days outside the U.S.) of the plane fare from New York to London and from London to New York is not deductible. You may deduct 4/9 of the New-York-to-London round-trip fare, plus lodging, 50% of meals (100% if provided at restaurants), and other allowable travel costs while in London. No deduction is allowed for any part of the costs of the trip from London to Paris.

3. Same facts as in Example 2, except that the vacation is in Dublin, which is closer to the U.S. than London. The allocation is based on the round-trip fare between New York and Dublin. Thus, 4/9 of the New York to Dublin fare is deductible and 5/9 is not deductible. Further, the IRS allows a deduction for the excess of the New-York-to-London fare over the New-York-to-Dublin fare.

Filing Tip

Weekend Expenses

If your business trip is extended over a weekend to take advantage of reduced airfares, the additional cost of meals, lodging, and other incidental expenses is deductible.

Weekends, holidays, and business standby days. If you have business meetings scheduled before and after a weekend or holiday, the days in between the meetings are treated as days spent on business for purposes of the 25% business test discussed above. This is true although you spend the days for sightseeing or other personal travel. A similar rule applies if you have business meetings on Friday and the next scheduled meeting is the following Tuesday; Saturday through Monday are treated as business days. If your trip is extended over a weekend to take advantage of reduced airfares, the additional expense of meals, lodging, and other incidental expenses is deductible *(20.10)*.

20.11 Deducting Expenses of Business Conventions

Conventions and seminars at resort areas usually combine business with pleasure. Therefore, the IRS scrutinizes deductions claimed for attending a business convention where opportunities exist for vacationing. Especially questioned are trips where you are accompanied by your spouse and other members of your family. Deducting expenses of foreign conventions is subject to restrictions *(20.12)*.

You may not deduct expenses of attending investment conventions and seminars *(19.2)*. You also may not deduct the costs of business conventions or seminars where you merely receive a video or download of business lectures to be viewed at your convenience and no other business-related activities occur during the event.

In claiming a deduction for convention expenses, be prepared to show that your attendance at the convention benefitted your business. Cases and IRS rulings have upheld deductions for doctors, lawyers, and dentists attending professional conventions. One case allowed a deduction to a legal secretary for her costs at a secretaries' convention. If you are a delegate to a business convention, make sure you prove you attended to serve primarily your own business interests, not those of the association. However, it is not necessary for you to show that the convention dealt specifically with your business. It is sufficient that attendance at the convention may advance or benefit your business. If you fail to prove business purpose, the IRS will allocate your expenses between the time spent on your business and the time spent as a delegate. You then deduct only the expenses attributed to your business activities.

> **EXAMPLE**
>
> An attorney with a general law practice was interested in international law and relations. He was appointed a delegate to represent the American branch of the International Law Association at a convention in Paris. The attorney deducted the cost of the trip and convention as business expenses which the IRS and a court disallowed. He failed to prove that attending the conference on international law helped his general practice. He did not get any business referrals as a result of his attendance at the convention. Nor did he prove the chance of getting any potential business from the conference.

What expenses are deductible? If the convention trip is primarily for business, you may deduct travel costs both to and from the convention, food costs, tips, display expenses (such as sample room costs), and hotel bills. If you entertain business clients or customers, you may deduct these amounts too.

Food and beverage costs are subject to the 50% cost limitation rule *(20.15)*.

Keep records of your payments identifying expenses directly connected with your business dealings at the convention and those that are part of your personal activity, such as sightseeing, social visiting, and entertaining. Recreation costs are not deductible even though a part of your overall convention costs.

> **EXAMPLE**
>
> You attend a business convention held in a coastal resort city primarily for business reasons. During the convention period, you do some local sightseeing, social entertaining, and visiting—all unrelated to your business. You may deduct your traveling expenses to and from the resort, your living expenses at the resort, and other expenses such as business entertaining, sample displays, etc. But you may not deduct the cost of sightseeing, personal entertaining, and social visiting.

Fraternal organizations. You may not deduct expenses at conventions held by fraternal organizations, such as the American Legion, Shriners, etc., even though incidental business was carried on. However, delegates to fraternal conventions may in some instances deduct expenses as charitable contributions *(14.4)*.

20.12 Restrictions on Foreign Conventions and Cruises

You may not deduct expenses at a foreign convention outside the North American area unless you satisfy the general deduction rules *(20.10)* and also can show the convention is directly related to your business and it was as reasonable for the meeting to be held outside the North American area as within it.

Apart from the United States, the North American area includes Mexico, Canada, Puerto Rico, U.S. Virgin Islands, American Samoa, Northern Mariana Islands, Guam, Marshall and Midway Islands, Micronesia, Palau and U.S. island possessions.

 *Caution*

Substantiate Convention Business

Keep a copy of the convention program and a record of the business sessions you attend. If the convention provides a sign-in book, sign it. In addition, keep a record of all of your business expenses *(20.16)*.

Conventions may also be held in eligible Caribbean countries that agree to exchange certain data with the U.S. and do not discriminate against conventions held in the United States. Antigua and Barbuda, Aruba, Bahamas, Barbados, Bermuda, Costa Rica, Curacao, Dominica, Dominican Republic, Grenada, Guyana, Honduras, Jamaica, Panama, Saint Lucia, and Trinidad and Tobago have qualified and are considered to be within the North American area.

Check with the convention operator about whether the country in which your convention is being held has qualified.

Limited cruise ship deduction. Up to $2,000 a year is allowed for attending cruise ship conventions if all the ports of call are in the U.S. or U.S. possessions and if the ship is registered in the United States. A deduction is allowed only if you attach to your return statements signed by you and by an officer of the convention sponsor that detail the daily schedule of business activities, the number of hours you attended these activities, and the total days of the trip. Do not confuse the $2,000 limitation with the per diem limitation for cruise ship costs (20.5). The per diem limitation does not apply to cruises that meet the tests for the up-to-$2,000 deduction.

20.13 Entertainment Expenses Generally Not Deductible

A business expense deduction is not allowed for the cost of attending entertainment events, such as tickets to theaters and sporting events. Also nondeductible are club dues and membership fees, and the costs of owning, renting, or using an entertainment facility; *see* below.

Business meal costs are generally deductible. Before 2018, deductions were allowed for meal expenses that were "directly related to" or "associated with" the active conduct of a business, but these rules were repealed for years after 2017. The repeal of the "directly related to" or "associated with" tests caused confusion as to whether business meals for clients, customers, vendors, and other business associates would still be deductible, but the IRS has provided guidelines that allow a deduction for such business meals, provided the tests at *20.14* are met. Employers may deduct 100% for certain meal costs, such as those reimbursed expenses that are treated as taxable compensation, and recreational expenses for employees such as holiday parties and picnics (20.15).

Club dues and membership fees. No deduction is allowed for dues or membership fees for country clubs, golf and athletic clubs, airline clubs, hotel clubs, business luncheon clubs, and other clubs organized for business, pleasure, recreation, or other social purposes. However, an IRS regulation allows a deduction for dues paid to (1) civic or public service organizations such as Kiwanis, Lions, and Rotary clubs; (2) professional organizations such as medical or bar associations; and (3) chambers of commerce, trade associations, business leagues, real estate boards, and boards of trade. The regulation allows the deduction for dues provided that the organization in (1)–(3) does not have a principal purpose of providing entertainment for members or their guests.

Costs of using entertainment facilities. No deduction is allowed for the expenses of using, maintaining and operating facilities used to entertain clients and customers. Examples of entertainment facilities include country clubs, golf clubs, yachts, hunting lodges, fishing camps, swimming pools, tennis courts, bowling alleys, automobiles, airplanes, apartments, hotel suites, or homes in a vacation area. The disallowance rule applies to operating expenses such as rent, utilities, and security, and also to depreciation, but not to such expenses as interest, taxes, and casualty losses that may be deductible without having to show business purpose.

20.14 Business Meals Are Generally Deductible

In general, IRS guidelines allow businesses to deduct the cost of business meals provided at restaurants, so long as the taxpayer (or an employee) is present during the meal, the cost of the food and beverages is not lavish or extravagant, and, when food and beverages is provided during an entertainment event, the cost is separately billed. Food or beverages provided by a restaurant are 50% deductible for 2023. The temporary legislation allowing for 100% meal deductions in 2021 and 2022 was not extended.

In Tax Tip 2022-91, the IRS reminds businesses that the cost of a meal can include taxes and tips, but that transportation costs to and from the meal isn't part of the cost of the business meal. In Notice 2018-76, the IRS provided rules for distinguishing deductible business meal expenses from nondeductible entertainment expenses. These rules were incorporated into final regulations (T.D. 9925), which are discussed below.

Meals during or at an entertainment activity. Although the cost of attending an entertainment event is not deductible *(20.13)*, the cost of food and beverages during or at an entertainment event is not treated as an entertainment expense, and thus the cost (including tips and sales tax) is deductible, if all of the following conditions from the final regulations are met:

1. The expense is an ordinary and necessary business expense paid or incurred during the taxable year;
2. The expense is not lavish or extravagant under the circumstances;
3. The taxpayer, or an employee of the taxpayer, is present at the furnishing of the food or beverages;
4. The food and beverages are provided to a *business associate* (see below for the IRS definition); and
5. The food and beverages are purchased separately from the entertainment, or the cost of the food and beverages is stated separately from the cost of the entertainment on a bill, invoice, or receipt. The bill, invoice, or receipt must reflect the venue's usual selling price for separately purchased food and beverages, or must approximate their reasonable value. If the food and beverages are included in the cost of the entertainment event, the IRS does not allow you to allocate part of the cost to the food and beverages; the entire amount is treated as a nondeductible entertainment expense (Example 2 below).

> ### *EXAMPLES*
> In these examples, assume that the food and beverages are ordinary and necessary business expenses and the cost is not lavish or extravagant.
>
> 1. You take a business client to a baseball game to discuss a proposed business deal. The game is entertainment so the cost of the tickets is not deductible. However, your business may deduct the cost of hot dogs and drinks purchased during the game, as they are purchased separately from the tickets and therefore not considered an entertainment expense.
>
> 2. You take a business customer to a basketball game. You watch the game in a suite that provides food and beverages. The invoice for the tickets includes the food and beverages. Your business cannot deduct either the cost of the tickets or the cost of the food and beverages. The tickets are a nondeductible entertainment expense, and the food and beverages are also treated as entertainment and thus not deductible because they were not purchased separately or stated separately on the invoice.
>
> 3. Same facts as Example 2 except that the cost of food and beverages is stated separately on the invoice. As in Example 2, the cost of the game tickets themselves is a nondeductible entertainment expense. However, since the food and beverages are stated separately on the invoice, their cost is deductible.

Meals with business associates. You may deduct the cost of meals with a business associate, provided (1) the expense is an ordinary and necessary business expense, (2) the expense is not lavish or extravagant under the circumstances, and (3) you or your employee is present when the food or beverages are furnished at restaurants. The cost of the meal includes tips, sales tax, and delivery charges if any.

The IRS broadly defines a business associate as any person with whom you could reasonably expect to engage or deal in the active conduct of your business, such as an established or prospective customer, client, supplier, employee, agent, partner or professional adviser.

As discussed above, the cost of food and beverages from a restaurant is 100% deductible in 2021 and 2022. Other meal costs may be 50% or 100% deductible; *see 20.15*.

20.15 Limitation on Some Deductible Meals

You may deduct 50% of meal expenses not provided by restaurants while on business trips away from home *(20.5)*. However, the deductible percentage for workers subject to the Department of Transportation's "hours of service" limits is 80% rather than 50%. If you are self-employed and claim expenses for business travel while away from home, the percentage limitation, if applicable, is taken into account on Line 24b of Schedule C *(40.6)*, whether you claim the IRS meal allowance *(20.4)* or actual meal expenses (including taxes and tips).

As discussed at *20.1*, most employees are no longer able to deduct business travel expenses, including meals away from home, because miscellaneous itemized deductions are no longer allowed. Only employees listed at *20.1* can deduct business travel expenses, subject to any deduction limit on meals. Employees who are reimbursed by their employers under "accountable plans" *(20.18)* do not have to report the reimbursements as taxable wages; their employers take the tax deduction.

50% limit for food and beverages from restaurants, convenience stores, and groceries. The 50% limit applies to food or beverages from restaurants; grocery stores; convenience stores; specialty food stores; beer, wine or liquor stores; newsstands, vending machines or kiosks. This limit of 50% applies to business meals with clients; food items for the office (see exceptions for 100% deductibility below); meals while traveling for work; and meals at conferences.

As discussed below, a 100% deduction is allowed for certain reimbursed meal costs and for certain food and beverages provided to employees or the general public.

80% limit for certain transportation workers. The deductible percentage for non-restaurant meals on business trips away from home *(20.6)* is 80% instead of 50% where the meals are consumed "during or incident to" any period of duty for which the Department of Transportation (DOT) hours of service limits are in effect and are not provided by restaurants. Individuals subject to the DOT hours of service limits include interstate truck and bus drivers, pilots, crew and other air transportation workers such as mechanics and control tower operators, and certain merchant mariners.

Food or beverages provided on premises to employees. If you are an employer, the 50% deduction limit applies for food or beverages provided to your employees as a tax-free *de minimis* fringe benefit *(3.10)*. This includes free drinks and snacks you provide in a pantry or "break room" for your employees. This 50% limit also applies to food and beverages you provide to employees in an on-premises cafeteria (even if the facility is operated by a third party under contract with the employer) if the meals are tax free to employees because they are furnished for your convenience (you have a substantial noncompensatory business purpose; *see 3.13*).

However, if on-premises meals do not qualify as a tax-free *de minimis* fringe benefit, and you treat the value of the food and beverages as taxable wages, you as the business owner may deduct 100% of the food and beverage costs.

100% deduction for reimbursed meals treated as taxable compensation. If you reimburse employees for food or beverage costs that they do not adequately account for *(20.18)*, the reimbursement is treated as taxable wages, which you can fully deduct. A similar rule applies if you reimburse an independent contractor for meal costs he or she incurs on your behalf, but the contractor does not give you an adequate accounting for the expenses. You should report the reimbursements as compensation to the contractor (Form 1099), and you may fully deduct the reimbursement.

Final regulations (T.D. 9925) have further details and examples of meal reimbursement arrangements that involve independent contractors.

100% deduction for food and beverages at recreational or social activities for employees. You may deduct 100% of the cost of food and beverages you provide at a recreational, social, or similar activity that is primarily for the benefit of your non-highly compensated employees. This includes holiday parties, annual picnics, summer outings, and similar events.

If only highly compensated employees are invited, the 100% deduction for non-highly compensated employees does not apply, but if the cost of the food and beverages is separately stated and the other tests for meals at an entertainment event are met *(20.14)*, you may deduct 50% of the food and beverage costs.

An example in the final regulations (T.D. 9925) indicates that the 100% deduction does not apply for snacks and drinks provided in a break room for employees. Although it could be argued that employees may socialize while in the break room, the break room is not a recreational, social, or similar activity according to the IRS, so the employer's deduction for the food and beverages is limited to 50%.

Another IRS example holds that the 100% deduction does not apply for meals provided in an on-premises cafeteria where the meals are tax free to the employees because they are provided for the "convenience of the employer" *(3.10)*. Since the food and beverages are provided for the employer's convenience, they cannot be primarily for the benefit of employees, so the employer's deduction for them is limited to 50%, even if there is some socializing between employees while in the cafeteria.

100% deduction for food or beverages provided to the general public. If you provide food or beverages to the general public for advertising or goodwill purposes, the cost is 100% deductible. This includes refreshments in your office lobby or waiting room, or at a promotional open house. Where the food or beverages are available to employees as well the general public, the entire cost is 100% deductible if more than 50% is consumed by the general public. For example, if refreshments in your waiting room are available to employees as well as customers, and over 50% of the actual or reasonably estimated food and beverage consumption is by customers, the entire cost of the food and beverages is deductible. If the over 50% test is not met, only the costs attributable to the food and beverages for the customers qualifies for the 100% deduction.

100% deduction for food or beverages sold to customers. A restaurant or catering business may deduct 100% of its costs for food and beverages that are purchased for sale to customers, even if employees are allowed to eat for free before, during, and after their shifts.

20.16 Substantiating Travel Expenses

To meet IRS substantiation requirements for costs of business trips "away from home," *(20.5)*, you need two types of records in the event of an audit:

1. A computer log, diary, account book, or similar record to list the time, place, and business purpose of your travel expenses; and

2. Receipts, itemized paid bills, or similar statements for lodging regardless of the amount, and for other expenses of $75 or more. But note these exceptions:

   - A receipt for transportation expenses of $75 or more is required only when it is readily obtainable.

   - A canceled check by itself is not an acceptable voucher. If you cannot produce a bill or voucher, you may have to present other evidence such as a statement in writing from witnesses to prove business purpose of the expense.

   - A receipted bill or voucher must show (1) the amount of the expense; (2) the date the expense was incurred; (3) where the expense was incurred; and (4) the nature of the expense.

   - A receipt for meals or lodging is not needed if its cost is covered by a per diem allowance under an accountable plan *(20.19)*.

A hotel bill must show the name, location, date, and separate amounts for charges such as lodgings, meals, and telephone calls. The IRS will not allow a credit card statement to substitute for a lodging receipt. The IRS wants detailed receipts to catch personal items such as personal phone calls or the purchase of gifts.

A restaurant bill must show the restaurant's name and location, the date and amount of the expense, and, when a charge is made for items other than meals or beverages, a description of the charge.

 *Planning Reminder*

Credit Cards

Credit card charge statements for travel costs meet the IRS tests, provided the business purpose of the expense is also shown. Note on the credit card statements the names of people entertained, their business relationship, the business purpose of the expense, and the portion of the expense to be allocated to business and personal purposes. These statements generally meet the IRS requirements of accounting to your employer for reimbursed expenses *(20.18)*, provided a responsible company official reviews them. However, you need a receipt for lodging; the IRS will not accept a credit card statement as substantiation of a lodging expense.

Account book or computer entries. Your records do not have to duplicate data recorded on a receipt, provided that a notation in your record is connected to the receipt. You are also not required to record amounts your company pays directly for any ticket or fare. Credit card charges should be recorded.

Excuses for Inadequate Records

Substantial compliance. If you have made a "good faith" effort to comply with the IRS rules, you will not be penalized if your records do not satisfy every requirement. For example, you would not automatically be denied a deduction merely because you did not keep a receipt.

Accidental destruction of records. If receipts or records are lost or destroyed through circumstances beyond your control, such as in a flood or fire, you may substantiate deductions by reasonable reconstruction of your expenditures.

Exceptional circumstances. If, by reason of the "inherent nature of the situation," you are unable to keep adequate records, you may substantially comply by presenting the best evidence possible given the circumstances. IRS regulations do not explain the meaning of "inherent nature of the situation."

20.17 Employee Reporting of Unreimbursed Expenses

If you are paid a salary with the understanding that you will pay all of your travel expenses without reimbursement, you report all of your salary or commission income as shown on Form W-2. Under current law, you may not claim a deduction for the expenses, because the itemized deduction for unreimbursed job expenses is suspended *(19.2)*. However, if you are an employee within one of the limited employee categories discussed at *20.1*, you may be able to deduct travel costs.

The result is the same if your employer has a reimbursement plan but the rules for accountable plans *(20.18)* are not met; the non-accountable reimbursements are treated as part of your taxable pay and you may not claim an offsetting deduction *(20.21)*.

20.18 Are You Reimbursed Under an Accountable Plan?

An employer's reimbursement or allowance arrangement is an accountable plan if you must:

- Adequately account to your employer for your job expenses; and
- Return to your employer any excess reimbursement or allowance that you do not show was spent for ordinary and necessary business expenses.

If these requirements are not met, the plan is treated as a nonaccountable plan, and all reimbursements are reported as wages on your Form W-2 *(20.21)*.

If these requirements are met, the plan is treated as an accountable plan, and reimbursements made to you by the plan are not reported as taxable wages on your Form W-2. However, if the reimbursement is less than your expenses, you may not claim a deduction for the difference, except in the unlikely case that you are an employee listed at *20.1*. Under prior law, employees who itemized deductions could use Form 2106 to report their expenses and the reimbursement, and then enter the unreimbursed amount on Schedule A, where a deduction was limited by the 2% of AGI floor applicable to total miscellaneous itemized deductions. However, this limited deduction opportunity is not an option for 2018 through 2025, as the deduction for unreimbursed job expenses, as well as other miscellaneous deductions, has been suspended for these years *(19.2)*.

For employees listed at *20.1*, Form 2106 may be used to report unreimbursed job expenses (meals on business trips away from home not provided at restaurants are subject to a 50% reduction), and an above-the-line deduction for eligible amounts may be claimed; *see 20.1*.

What is an adequate accounting? You adequately account to your employer by submitting receipts and an account book, diary, or similar record in which you entered each expense at or near the time you had it. You must account to your employer for all amounts received as advances, reimbursements, or allowances, including amounts charged on a company

Planning Reminder

Sampling Can Support Deduction

If an adequate record of expenses is kept for part of a tax year, and that period is representative of the whole year, the IRS will accept those records as proof of expenses for the entire year. For example, if you keep records for the first week of each month that show that 75% of the use of your car is for business purposes, and your invoices and bills show the same business pattern for the rest of each month, the IRS will treat your partial record as proof of 75% business use for the whole year.

credit card. Your records and supporting information must meet IRS rules *(20.16)*. You must also pay back reimbursements or allowances that exceed the expenses that you adequately accounted for, or the nonreturned excess will be taxable under the rules for non-accountable plans *(20.21)*.

The accounting requirements are eased if you are reimbursed under a per diem arrangement covering meals, lodging, and incidental expenses *(20.19)* or you receive a flat mileage allowance *(20.20)*.

Planning Reminder

Importance of Adequate Accounting

If you adequately report expenses to your employer and return excess reimbursements, you are treated as being reimbursed under an accountable plan and generally do not have to report the reimbursed amount as income on your return.

> **EXAMPLE**
>
> Your adjusted gross income is $85,000, and you incur travel expenses of $1,600, all of which are reimbursed by your company. If your reimbursement arrangement qualified as an accountable plan, and you made an adequate reporting to your employer, the $1,600 would not be reported as income on your Form W-2. You receive the equivalent of a full deduction by substantiating the expenses to your employer and not having the reimbursement included as income on your Form W-2.

Time limits for receiving advances, substantiating expenses, and returning excess payments. The general rule is that these events must occur within a reasonable time. Under an IRS "safe harbor," the following payments are considered to be within a reasonable time:

- Advance payments—if given to you within 30 days before you reasonably anticipate to pay or incur expenses;
- Substantiation of expenses—if provided to your employer within 60 days after the expense is paid or incurred; and
- Return of excess—if done within 120 days after you pay or incur expense.

An employer may set up a "periodic statement method" to meet IRS rules. Here, an employer gives each employee periodic statements (at least quarterly) that list the amounts paid in excess of expenses substantiated by the employee and request substantiation of the additional amounts paid, or a return of the excess, within 120 days of the date of the statement. Substantiation or return within the 120-day period satisfies the reasonable time test.

Filing Tip

Failure To Timely Return Excess

If you fail to return excess payments within a reasonable time but you meet all of the other tests applied to an accountable plan, such as providing proof of the expenses, only the retained excess is taxed to you as if paid outside of an accountable plan.

20.19 *Per Diem* Travel Allowance Under Accountable Plans

Instead of providing a straight reimbursement for substantiated out-of-pocket travel expenses, an employer may use a per diem allowance to cover meals, lodging, and incidental *(20.4)* expenses of employees on business trips away from home. If you are not related to the employer, you do not have to give your employer proof of your actual expenses if you receive a per diem allowance or reimbursement that is equal to or less than the federal travel rate for the particular area. You do have to account for the time, place, and business purpose of your travel. If you do not provide such an accounting for some travel days, you must be required to return the per diem allowance received for such days in order for the employer's plan to qualify. If these tests are met, the allowance satisfies the accountable plan *(20.18)* requirements and it does not have to be reported as income on your Form W-2.

Federal travel rate. Tables published by the government show the federal travel rate for areas within the continental U.S. (called CONUS locations) and for areas outside the continental U.S., including Hawaii and Alaska (called OCONUS locations). New CONUS tables released annually are effective for the government's October 1–September 30 fiscal year *(20.4)*. You can obtain the CONUS per diem rates from the General Services Administration at www.gsa.gov. The OCONUS rates can also be accessed from the GSA website.

If an employer uses the CONUS per diem rates to reimburse employees in the first nine months of the year, the CONUS per diem method must also be used for those employees for the last three months of the year; the "high-low" method *(see below)* may not be used for those employees until the following calendar year. Where employees are reimbursed in the first nine months using the CONUS per diem rates, the employer may reimburse their travel during the last three months using the per diem rates for the first nine months, or may use the new per diem rates taking effect October 1.

High-low method. For business trips within the continental United States (CONUS), employers may use the IRS' "high-low" method to reimburse employees for lodging, meals, and incidental expenses instead of using the locality-by-locality per diem CONUS rates set by the General Services Administration (GSA) for federal government workers. For each employee, either the federal per diem rates or the high-low method has to be used for the entire year.

There is a high-cost area rate and a rate for all other areas within CONUS. The rates are announced by the IRS in an annual notice that lists the areas qualifying for the high-cost rate, as well as the months for which the high-cost rate may be used if the area qualifies for less than the full year. For the period October 1, 2022, through September 30, 2023, the rates are $297 for high-cost areas and $204 for other areas (IRS Notice 2022-44). At the time of writing, the October 1, 2023 - September 30, 2024, rates were not available; *see* the *e-Supplement* at *jklasser.com* for updates.

For employer deduction purposes, $74 of the $297 or $296 high-cost area rate is allocable to meals, and $64 of the $204 or $202 low-cost area rate is allocable to meals. The allocated meals portion may be subject to a deduction limitation; *see 20.15*.

Transition rules require employers that used the high-low rates for a particular employee during the first nine months of a year to continue to use the high-low method for that employee for the remainder of that calendar year. If an employer used the high-low method for business trips during the first nine months of 2023, then for the last three months, the employer may either (1) use the new high-low rates and list of high-cost localities that took effect October 1, 2023, or (2) use the pre-October 2023 high-low rates and pre-October high-cost localities (from Notice 2022-44) for the last three months provided that those pre-October rates and localities are used for all employees who are reimbursed under the high-low method. An employer may not use the high-low method until 2024 for an employee whose expenses within CONUS for January through September 2023 were reimbursed using the locality-by-locality per diem CONUS rates set by the General Services Administration (GSA) for federal government workers.

Employees related to the employer. The IRS per diem rules that allow you to avoid accounting for actual expenses do not apply if you work for a brother, sister, spouse, parent, child, grandparent, or grandchild. They also do not apply if you are an employee-stockholder who owns more than 10% of the company's stock.

Reporting a per diem allowance. If the allowance does not exceed the federal travel rate or IRS high-low rate, the reimbursement is not reported on Form W-2. You do not have to report the expenses or the reimbursement on your tax return; *see* Example 1 below. If your expenses exceed the allowance, you may not deduct the excess by reporting the expenses and reimbursement on Form 2106, unless you are an eligible employee listed at *20.1*; *see* Examples 2 and 3 below.

If the allowance exceeds the federal rate, the allowance up to the federal rate is reported by the employer in Box 12 of your Form W-2, using Code L. This amount is not taxable. However, the excess allowance will be included as wages in Box 1 of your Form W-2; *see* Example 4 below.

Allowance covering only meals and incidentals. If your employer gives you a per diem allowance covering only meals and incidental expenses, it is not taxable to you if you are not related to the employer and the allowance does not exceed the IRS meal allowance rate for that locality (M&IE rate; *see 20.4*). Alternatively, for travel within CONUS, your employer may use the meals rate under the high-low method to substantiate the allowance. An allowance that does not exceed the applicable IRS high-low meals rate is not taxable to you.

For the first nine months of 2023, the amount allocable by employers to meals under the high-low method is $74 for high-cost localities and $64 for other areas (Notice 2022-44).

Caution

Excess Per Diem Allowances

If a per diem allowance exceeds the federal travel rate or the IRS high-low rate, the excess will be reported as income on your Form W-2, unless you return the excess. The excess reportable on Form W-2 is also subject to income tax and FICA tax withholding.

EXAMPLES

1. You take a three-day business trip to a locality at a time when the federal travel rate for the area is $202 per day. You account for the date, place, and business purpose of the trip. Your employer reimburses you at the federal rate of $202 a day for lodging, meals, and incidental expenses, for a total of $606. Your actual expenses do not exceed this amount. Your employer does not report the reimbursement on your Form W-2. You do not have to report the reimbursement on your return.

2. Same facts as in Example 1, except that the reimbursement is less than your actual expenses of $700. Even if you have records that substantiate your expenses, you cannot claim a deduction for any part of the nonreimbursed amount, because of the suspension of the miscellaneous itemized deduction for unreimbursed job expenses *(20.1)*.

3. Same facts as in Example 2, except that you are a fee-basis state or local government official eligible to file Form 2106 *(20.1)*. On Form 2106, you report the $606 reimbursement and your $700 of expenses and also must allocate part of the allowance to your meals expenses to apply the 50% deduction limit for meals not provided at restaurants *(20.15)*. The instructions to Form 2106 have a worksheet for making the allocation. The net amount from Form 2106 is deductible as an above-the-line deduction on Line 12 of Schedule 1 (Form 1040 or 1040-SR).

4. Same facts as in Example 1, except that you receive a per diem allowance of $222 per day, or $20 per day more than the federal travel rate. If you do not return the excess of $60 ($20 × 3 days) within a reasonable time *(20.18)*, your employer must report the $60 as income in Box 1 of your Form W-2. The amount up to the federal travel rate, or $606, will be reported in Box 12 of Form W-2 with Code L, but not included as income.

20.20 Automobile Mileage Allowance

If your employer paid you a fixed mileage allowance for business miles driven in 2023 of up to 65.5 cents per mile through December 31, 2023 (the IRS standard mileage rate), the amount of your driving costs is treated as substantiated under the accountable plan rules *(20.18)*, provided you show the time, place, and business purpose of your travel. If the allowance is in the form of an advance, it must be given within a reasonable period before the anticipated travel and you must also be required to return within a reasonable period *(20.18)* any portion of the allowance that covers mileage that you have not substantiated.

If these tests are met, the allowance will not be reported as income on Form W-2, and you will not have to report the allowance or expenses on your return; *see* Example 1 below. If you do not prove to your employer the time, place, and purpose of your travel, the entire reimbursement is treated as paid from a non-accountable plan and will be reported as income on your Form W-2 *(20.21)*.

Your employer may reimburse you for any parking fees and tolls in addition to the mileage allowance.

If you are not reimbursed for your business driving costs, or you are given a mileage allowance that is less than the expenses that you can substantiate, you may not use the cents-per-mile allowance to claim a deduction for the unreimbursed costs unless you are an eligible employee described in *20.1*.

Fixed and variable rate allowance (FAVR). In lieu of setting the allowance at the IRS standard mileage rate, an employer may use a fixed and variable rate allowance, called a FAVR, that gives employees a cents-per-mile rate to cover gas and other operating costs, plus a flat amount to cover fixed costs such as depreciation or lease payments, insurance, and registration. A FAVR allowance must reflect local driving costs and allows employers to set reimbursements at a rate that more closely approximates employee expenses. If your employer sets up a qualifying FAVR under IRS guidelines, you will be required to provide records substantiating your mileage and certain car ownership information. Expenses up to the FAVR limits are deemed substantiated and will not be reported as wages on your Form W-2.

EXAMPLES

1. In 2023 you drove 12,000 miles for business. You accounted to your employer for the time, place, and business purpose of each trip. Your employer reimbursed you at the IRS rate of 65.5 cents per mile for the 12,000 miles driven throughout 2023 ($7,860 reimbursement). None of the reimbursement will be reported as income on your 2023 Form W-2, and you do not have to report the reimbursements on your return.

2. Same facts as in Example 1, except that your employer reimbursed you at a rate of 70 cents per mile for the entire year. The amount using the IRS rates, or $7,860 (under the 65.5 cents per mile rates), is $540 less than the reimbursement of $8,400 (.70 × 12,000) The $540 excess reimbursement over the IRS rate will be reported as wages on your 2023 Form W-2.

   Even if you, as an employee, have records substantiating expenses over the IRS rate per mile, you cannot claim the excess costs on Form 2106 because the miscellaneous itemized deduction for unreimbursed job costs has been suspended *(20.1)*.

3. Same facts as in Example 1, except that you were reimbursed only 50 cents per mile for all your business driving, for a total reimbursement of $6,000 (.50 × 12,000 miles). The reimbursement will not be reported as income on your Form W-2. You may not use the standard mileage rate for 2023 to claim a deduction for expenses up to the IRS rate of *65.5* cents per mile because the miscellaneous itemized deduction for unreimbursed job costs has been suspended *(20.1)*.

4. Same facts as Example 3, except you are a fee-basis state or local government official eligible to file Form 2106 *(20.1)*. The amount allowed by the IRS rate, or $7,860 (.655 × 12,000 miles), is $1,860 more than your $6,000 reimbursement (.50 × 12,000 miles). You report the excess $1,860 on Form 2106 and claim it as an as an above-the-line deduction on Line 12 of Schedule 1 (Form 1040 or 1040-SR).

20.21 Reimbursements Under Non-Accountable Plans

A non-accountable plan is one that either does not require you to adequately account to your employer for your expenses or allows you to keep any excess reimbursement or allowances over the expenses for which you did adequately account *(20.18)*.

Your employer reports allowances or reimbursements for a non-accountable plan as part of your salary income in Box 1 of your Form W-2. The allowance or reimbursement is also subject to income tax and FICA tax (Social Security and Medicare) withholding. You cannot deduct your expenses to offset the reimbursement (or allowance) included in your income, unless you are eligible to file Form 2106 and claim an above-the-line deduction as explained at *20.1*.

PART 4

Personal Tax Computations

In this part, you will learn how to:

- Figure your regular tax. After reducing adjusted gross income *(12.1)* by the standard deduction or itemized deductions *(13.1)* and, if applicable, the qualified business income deduction *(40.24)*, you figure your 2023 regular tax by looking up the tax in the Tax Table or by figuring the tax using the Tax Computation Worksheet or special capital gain worksheets *(22.1)*.

- Apply the alternative minimum tax. If you have reduced your taxable income by certain deductions and tax benefits, you may be subject to the AMT *(23.1)*.

- Reduce your tax liability with tax credits. You may be entitled to tax credits *(22.7)* that lower your regular tax as well as any AMT.

- Figure estimated tax payments. If you have investment and self-employment income, you generally have to pay quarterly estimated tax *(27.1)*.

- Compute the "kiddie tax." If your child under age 18 has investment income for 2023 exceeding $2,500, you must compute tax on it using the tax rates applicable to the parent's marginal tax rate. The "kiddie tax" rules also apply if at the end of 2023 your child is age 18 or a full-time student under age 24, unless the child's earned income for 2023 exceeds 50% of his or her total support for the year *(24.2)*.

- Apply the Additional Medicare Tax and the Net Investment Income Tax. There is an 0.9% additional Medicare tax on earnings exceeding $200,000 if you are single or $250,000 if married filing jointly. Also, if modified adjusted gross income exceeds the $200,000 or $250,000 threshold, a 3.8% tax applies to the lesser of your net investment income or MAGI exceeding the threshold. *See Chapter 28* for details on these additional taxes.

Dependents

Although the deduction for personal exemptions has been suspended for 2018 through 2025, the definition of a dependent is still important for purposes of claiming the child tax credit *(25.2)*, the credit for other dependents *(25.4)*, claiming medical expenses of a dependent *(17.6)*, and qualifying for head of household status *(1.12)*.

To treat someone as your dependent, that person must be your qualifying child or qualifying relative, as explained in this chapter.

21.1   No Exemption Deductions Are Allowed

You cannot claim exemptions for yourself, your spouse (on a joint return), or your dependents. The Tax Cuts and Jobs Act suspended the deduction for exemptions for 2018 through 2025.

Definition of dependent still important. Although you can no longer deduct exemptions for your dependents, being able to treat someone as your dependent is still important for purposes of qualifying for several tax benefits, such as the child tax credit *(25.2)*, the credit for other dependents *(25.4)*, the child and dependent care credit *(25.5)*, the Earned Income Credit *(25.7)*, and eligibility to file as a head of household *(1.12)* or surviving spouse *(1.11)*. If you choose to take advantage of the itemize deductions option and are claiming medical expenses, you may include expenses you pay for your dependents *(17.6)*.

21.2   How Many Dependents Do You Have?

You claim someone as your dependent by naming that person and providing his or her Social Security number in the "Dependents" section on Form 1040 or 1040-SR. To claim someone as your dependent, he or she must be either your qualifying child or your qualifying relative. You must have a qualifying child under the age of 17 to claim the child tax credit or the additional child tax credit on your 2023 return *(25.2)*. You must have a qualifying child over the age of 16 or a qualifying relative to claim the credit for "other" dependents on your 2023 return *(25.4)*. To file as a head of household, you must maintain a home for a dependent (qualifying child or qualifying relative; *see 1.12* for relaxation of some of the dependent tests). Similarly, for surviving spouse status, you must maintain a home for a dependent child who lives with you *(1.11)*.

In addition to meeting the tests for a qualifying child or qualifying relative, a child/relative can be your dependent only if he or she meets a citizen or resident test, and if married, he or she generally must file separately. Finally, a dependent cannot claim someone else as a dependent. This means that even if a person meets the tests for being your dependent, you cannot claim that person as your dependent if you, or your spouse if filing jointly, can be claimed as a dependent by another taxpayer. *See* "Additional tests for treating someone as your dependent" below for further details.

Do you have a qualifying child for 2023? In addition to a biological child, a qualifying child can include your stepchild, adopted child, foster child, sibling, half-sibling, or step-sibling, and the descendants of any of these, such as your grandchild, niece, or nephew, provided all of the following tests are met:

1. The child had the same principal place of abode (residence) as you did for more than half of 2023. Temporary absences are disregarded.
2. The child is under age 19 at the end of 2023, or under age 24 at the end of 2023 if a full-time student during any part of at least five months during the year. In addition, the child must be younger than you are, or younger than your spouse if you file jointly. However, there is no age limit if the child is permanently and totally disabled at any time during the year.

    Keep in mind that a lower age limit applies for purposes of the child tax credit and the additional child tax credit *(25.2, 25.3)*. For 2023, your child is a "qualifying" child for purposes of these credits only if he or she is under age 17, although for other dependent rules, the under age 19 or under age 24 test in the previous paragraph applies.
3. The child did not provide more than half of his or her own support *(21.3)* for 2023.
4. If married, the child does not file a joint return for 2023, unless the joint return is filed only to claim a refund of income tax withholdings or of estimated tax payments.

See 21.3 for further details on the qualifying child rules, including the tie-breaker rules that determine who can claim the child as a dependent when the child is a qualifying child of more than one person.

Do you have a qualifying relative for 2023? An individual is your qualified relative for 2023 if the following three tests are met:

1. The individual is your relative or member of your household *(21.4)*, but that person must not be your qualifying child or the qualifying child of any other taxpayer. That person also cannot be your spouse, as a spouse cannot be your dependent for tax purposes.

2. The individual's gross income for 2023 is less than $4,700.

3. You contributed over half of the individual's support for 2023, or you contributed more than 10% of his or her support and the other contributors of more than 10% agree to let you claim the individual as your dependent under the multiple support agreement rules *(21.6)*.

See *21.4* for the broad category of relatives that can meet the relationship test, and for further details on the other qualifying relative tests.

For each of your qualifying relatives, you may claim the credit allowed for "other dependents," provided the tests at *25.4* are satisfied.

Additional tests for treating someone as your dependent. Even if a person is your qualifying child or relative, you cannot claim that person as your dependent if any of the following apply:

1. You, or your spouse if filing jointly, could be claimed as a dependent by another taxpayer for the taxable year. You are not considered another person's dependent if that person is not required to file a return and either does not file or files solely to claim a refund for withheld income taxes or estimated tax payments.

2. The child/relative is not a U.S. citizen or U.S. national, a U.S. resident alien, or a resident of Canada or Mexico for at least some part of the year; *see* below for an exception for certain adopted children. A U.S. national is one who owes permanent allegiance to the U.S., principally, a person born in American Samoa or the Northern Mariana Islands who has not become a naturalized American citizen.

   However, a stricter test applies for purposes of the child tax credit and additional child tax credit *(25.1)*. You cannot claim theses credits for an otherwise qualifying child who is a resident of Canada or Mexico. Similarly, for purposes of the credit for other dependents (dependents who do not qualify for the child tax credit *(25.4)*), a qualifying dependent does not include a resident of Canada or Mexico.

   If you are a U.S. citizen or U.S. national, and you legally adopted a child who is not a U.S. citizen, U.S. resident alien, or U.S. national, or the child was placed with you for legal adoption, your adopted child is treated as a U.S. citizen if the child lived with you as a member of your household for the entire year.

3. The child/relative is married and files a joint return. However, there is a limited exception. You are not barred from claiming the child/relative as your dependent if he or she files the joint return only to claim a refund of withheld income taxes or of estimated tax payments

Special rules for divorced or separated parents. The custodial parent generally may claim the child tax credit, additional child tax credit, and in some cases the credit for other dependents for the children, but special rules allow the custodial parent to waive the right to these benefits in favor of the noncustodial parent *(21.7)*.

Death of dependent during the year. If a dependent who otherwise met the tests for a qualifying child or relative died during the year, you can claim that dependent.

21.3 Qualifying Children

Qualifying children include your children, siblings, and their descendants (*see* the relationship test below) if a residence test and age or student test are also met. If the relationship, residence, and age/student tests are met, you do not have to show that you provided more than half of the child's support, as is required for a qualifying relative *(21.4)*. However, a child is not a qualifying child if he or she provides over half of his or her

Caution

Should Married Dependents File Separately?

When a married dependent files a joint return, the dependent's parent cannot claim him or her. This may cost the parent more than the joint return saves the couple. In such a case, it may be advisable for the couple to file separate returns so that the parent may benefit from the larger tax saving.

If the couple decides to revoke their election to file jointly and then file separately in order to preserve the parent's claim, they must do so before the filing date for the return. Once a joint return is filed, the couple may not, after the filing deadline, file separate returns for the same year.

Planning Reminder

Qualifying Children

There is no gross income test for your child or your sibling (or descendant of your child or sibling) if the qualifying child rules under *21.3* are met. Nor do you have to provide over half of the child's support. However, *see* the "Additional tests for treating someone as your dependent" in *21.2*.

own support. A married child who files a joint return also cannot be your qualifying child, unless the joint return is filed solely to obtain a refund. For a qualifying child, there is no gross income test; he or she may earn any amount and still be claimed as your dependent. Even if a child is not your qualifying child, as where the age/student test or place of abode test is not met, you may still treat the child as your "qualifying relative," provided he or she has little or no income (under $4,700 for 2023) and you meet the support test *(21.4)*.

Relationship test. Your children, stepchildren, and their descendants (your grandchildren and great-grandchildren), and your siblings, including step- and half-brothers and -sisters and their descendants (your nieces and nephews), meet the relationship test. A legally adopted child or a child lawfully placed with you for adoption is treated as your child, as is a foster child placed with you by a court order or by an authorized placement agency.

Residence test (abode test). The qualifying child must have the same principal place of abode as you for more than half the year. You do not have to own the home or pay the maintenance costs, but the child must live with you for over half the year.

Temporary absences disregarded. In applying the residence test, your child is considered to be living with you while either of you is temporarily absent (or you both are) due to special circumstances. This includes temporary absences while away at school or on business, while obtaining medical treatment or institutional care, taking vacations, serving in the military, or while incarcerated.

Kidnapped child. The principal place of abode test is considered met for a child under age 18 who met the test prior to being kidnapped by a non–family member.

Birth or death of child during the year. The principal place of abode test is considered met for a child who died during the year if the child lived with you while alive. Similarly, the principal place of abode test is considered met for a newborn child who lives with you after birth for over half of the rest of the year, apart from required hospital stays. A child born alive but who dies shortly thereafter is considered your dependent.

Age or student test. Your qualifying child must either be: (1) under age 19 at the end of the year, (2) a full-time student under age 24 at the end of the year, or (3) permanently and totally disabled, regardless of age.

In addition, to qualify under Test 1 or 2, a child who is not permanently and totally disabled must be younger than you. If you are married and file jointly, the child must be younger than you or your spouse. For example, you are age 21 and you file jointly with your 25-year-old spouse. Your 23-year-old brother, a non-disabled full-time student, lives with you and your spouse. On your joint return, you can claim your brother as a qualifying child because he is younger than your spouse although older than you.

As noted in *21.2*, a different age test applies for purposes of the child tax credit and the additional child tax credit; for these 2023 credits, the child must be under age 17 *(25.2, 25.3)*.

Qualifying as a full-time student. A full-time student is one who attends school full time during at least five calendar months in the tax year. For example: attendance from February through some part of June—or from February through May and then at least one month from September through December—qualifies. The five months do not have to run consecutively. Attendance at a vocational, trade, or technical school for the five-month period qualifies, but not correspondence schools or on-the-job training courses. Your child who attends school at night is considered a full-time student only if he or she is enrolled for the number of hours or classes that is considered full-time attendance.

Child's self-support test. You do not have to contribute over 50% of a qualifying child's support. This is required for a qualifying relative *(21.4)* but not for a qualifying child. However, if a child contributes over half of his or her own support, he or she cannot be claimed as your qualifying child, even if the other tests are met (the relationship, residence, and age/student tests). See *21.5* for a list of items (such as food, lodging and clothing) that count as support.

Tie-breaker rules. The law provides tie-breaker rules to determine who can treat a child as a qualifying child when the qualifying child tests are met by more than one taxpayer.

If only one of the eligible taxpayers is the parent of the child, the child is treated as the qualifying child of that parent. This situation could arise, for example, where a parent and infant child live with the child's grandparent for more than half the year. Both the child's parent and grandparent would meet the principal place of abode test and relationship test with respect to the child, but under the tie-breaker rule, the child is treated as the qualifying child of the parent. However, the parent can choose not to claim the child, and allow the grandparent to claim the child, provided the grandparent's adjusted gross income (AGI) exceeds his or her own AGI. If the parent's AGI equals or is higher than the grandparent's AGI, the grandparent cannot claim the child as a qualifying child; only the parent can. If the parent or grandparent files a joint return, the total AGI on the joint return is taken into account in determining which of them has the higher AGI.

If the parents file separate returns and both meet the tests for treating the child as a qualifying child, they may be unable to agree on which of them should claim the child. If they each claim the child on a separate return, the IRS will first determine if the noncustodial parent can claim the child as his/her qualifying child under the special rule for divorced or separated parents *(21.7)*. If the special rule applies, the tie-breaker rules do not apply. If the special rule does not apply and the child is a qualifying child of both parents under the above tests, the tie-breaker rule deems the child to be the qualifying child of the parent with whom the child has resided for the longer period during the year. If the residency period with both parents is the same, the parent with the higher adjusted gross income is entitled to treat the child as a qualifying child.

If no parent meets the tests for claiming the child and more than one non-parent meets the tests, the non-parent with the highest adjusted gross income is entitled to claim the child as a qualifying child.

21.4 Qualifying Relatives

You may claim a person as your qualifying relative if:

1. the relationship, gross income, and support tests described below are met, and
2. the individual is not your qualifying child *(21.3)* nor the qualifying child of any other taxpayer, and
3. the individual meets the citizenship/resident test and joint return test required of all dependents (see "Additional tests for treating someone as your dependent", in *21.2*), and
4. you cannot be claimed as a dependent (nor your spouse if you file jointly) by another taxpayer (see "Additional tests for treating someone as your dependent", in *21.2*),

If the member-of-household test described below is met, it may be possible to claim an individual as your qualifying relative even if he or she is "technically" the qualifying child of another taxpayer.

Relationship test. Relatives listed below meet the relationship test; they do not have to live with you. Unrelated or distantly related persons not on this list meet the relationship test if they live with you as discussed below under the member-of-household test. Your spouse cannot be your qualifying relative; nor can your former spouse be your qualifying relative for the year in which you get divorced or legally separated.

Children, grandchildren, and great-grandchildren who are not qualifying children. Your children, grandchildren, and great-grandchildren can meet the relationship test for a qualifying relative only if they are not your qualifying children or the qualifying children of any other taxpayer under the rules for qualifying children *(21.3)*. For example, if your child is not your qualifying child for 2023 because he or she does not meet the age/student test or the principal place of abode test *(21.3)*, that child may be treated as your qualifying relative, but only if his or her gross income for 2023 is under $4,700 and you provide over 50% of his or her support for the year.

Brothers, sisters, and their children. The same considerations discussed above for children, grandchildren, and great-grandchildren apply for your siblings (including half- or step-siblings) and their children (your nieces and nephews). They can be your qualifying

Filing Tip

Nephew, Niece, Uncle, and Aunt

Nephews, nieces, uncles, and aunts must be your blood relatives to qualify under the relationship test. For example, the brother or sister of your father or mother qualifies as your relative; their spouses do not. You may not claim your spouse's nephews, nieces, uncles, or aunts as your qualifying relatives unless you file a joint return.

relatives only if they are not your qualifying children *(21.3)* or the qualifying children of anyone else.

Parents, grandparents, and other relatives. The following individuals also meet the relationship test: your parent, grandparent, great-grandparent, step-parent, son- or daughter-in-law, father- or mother-in-law, and brother- or sister-in-law. If related by blood, aunts and uncles also qualify.

Stepchild's husband or wife or child. Your stepchild's spouse does not meet the relationship test. Nor may you treat a step-grandchild as your qualifying relative if you file a separate return. But you may treat them on a joint return as qualifying relatives if the other tests are met. On a joint return, it is not necessary that the close relationship exist between the dependent and the spouse who furnishes the support. It is sufficient that the relationship exists with either spouse.

> **EXAMPLE**
>
> You contribute more than half of the support of the sister of your wife's mother (your wife's aunt). If you and your wife file a joint return, her aunt meets the relationship test. But your wife's aunt's husband is not related by blood to you or your wife. You cannot claim him, even on a joint return, unless he is a member of your household under the rules discussed below and other qualifying relative tests are met.

In-laws. Brother-in-law, sister-in-law, father-in-law, mother-in-law, son-in-law, and daughter-in-law are relatives by marriage. They meet the relationship test and you may claim them as qualifying relatives if the other tests are satisfied. An in-law who was related to you by marriage and whom you continue to support after divorce or the death of your spouse meets the relationship test.

> **EXAMPLE**
>
> For many years, Allen has contributed all the support of his father-in-law, Jerry, who has no gross income. Allen's wife died in 2014. Allen has continued to be Jerry's sole source of support. Allen may claim Jerry as a qualifying relative for 2023.

Death during the year. If a person who meets the relationship test died during 2023 but was supported by you while alive, and the other tests are met, you may claim that person as your qualifying relative for 2023.

> **EXAMPLE**
>
> On January 21, 2023, your father died. Until that date, you contributed all of his support. He had no gross income for 2023. You may treat him as your qualifying relative for 2023.

Member-of-household test for unrelated or distantly related dependents living with you. A relative not listed above, such as a cousin, meets the relationship test if he or she lives with you all year as a member of your household, except for temporary absences due to schooling, vacationing, being away on business, serving in the military, or being confined to a hospital. A friend or live-in mate can also qualify, except in those few states where cohabitation is illegal. Your spouse cannot qualify; under the tax law, one spouse is not considered a dependent of the other. If you are divorced or legally separated during the year, your former spouse cannot be your qualifying relative for that year even if he or she is a member of your household for the whole year.

The "all-year" test can prevent you from treating someone as your qualifying relative, despite the level of your support. For example, in one case, a taxpayer let his cousin and her children move in with him in May because the cousin feared her estranged husband. The Tax Court held that he could not claim the children as dependents under the member-of-household test because they did not live with him for the whole year, but only from May through December.

Special exception for child of unmarried cohabitant. If a taxpayer lives with and supports a mate and the mate's child, dependent treatment for the child may or may not be allowed to the taxpayer under the member-of-household test. For example,

Caution

Qualifying Relationship Not Enough

Assuming a person meets the relationship test *(21.4)*, you must provide over 50% of his or her support and his or her gross income for 2023 must be under $4,700 for you to claim that person as your qualifying relative for 2023.

if a taxpayer supports his girlfriend and her child as members of his household, he "technically" cannot claim the child as his qualifying relative because the child is the mother's qualifying child *(21.3)* and a qualifying child cannot be the qualifying relative of someone else. However, the IRS allows a limited exception. The child can be claimed if the child's mother (for whom the child is a qualifying child) is not required to file a tax return because of low income, and she does not file a return or files solely to get a refund of withheld income taxes. If the mother files a return to claim the Earned Income Credit as well as to obtain a refund for withheld income taxes, the exception does not apply and the taxpayer cannot treat the child as his qualifying relative.

The mother can also be the qualifying relative of the taxpayer under the member-of-household test, provided that their relationship is not illegal under local law.

Gross income limit. A person meeting the above relationship test cannot be claimed as your qualifying relative for 2023 if he or she had gross income of $4,700 or more; gross income must be under $4,700. This gross income test applies even if you provide most or all of that person's support.

Keep in mind that the gross income test does not apply to children who meet the tests for a qualifying child *(21.3)*. However, if a child does not meet the age/student test or principal place of abode test, and thus is not a qualifying child *(21.3)*, he or she must have gross income under the annual limit ($4,700 for 2023) to be claimed as a dependent under the qualifying relative rules.

Gross income here means taxable income items includible in the dependent's tax return. It does not include nontaxable items such as gifts and tax-exempt bond interest. Gross income for a service-type business is gross receipts without deductions of expenses and for a manufacturing or merchandising business is total sales less cost of goods sold. A partner's share of partnership gross income, not the share of net income, is treated as gross income.

Social Security benefits are treated as gross income only to the extent they are taxable *(34.3)*.

Exception for disabled student working at sheltered workshop. For purposes of the gross income test, gross income does not include income earned by a totally and permanently disabled individual at a school operated by a government agency or tax-exempt organization, if the school provides special instruction for alleviating the disability and the income is incidental to medical care received.

Support test. A person cannot be your qualifying relative unless you provide over half of his or her total support for the year. The support test applies to a child who does not meet the tests for a qualifying child *(21.3)*. See *21.5* for how to count total support and your contribution to the total.

21.5 Meeting the Support Test for a Qualifying Relative

To claim a dependent as your qualifying relative *(21.4)*, you must contribute more than 50% of the dependent's total support for the year. You do not have to meet this support test to claim a child as your dependent under the qualifying child rules *(21.3)*, but qualifying child status is denied if a child provides over half of his or her own support, and the support items listed below count when making that determination.

Meeting the support test. Follow these steps to figure support: (1) Total the value of the support contributed by you, by the dependent, and by others for the dependent. *See* the "Checklist of Support Items" on page 484 and the "Checklist of Items Not Counted as Support of Dependent" on page 486 for determining what to include in total support and what to exclude. (2) Determine your share of the total. If your share is more than 50% of the dependent's total support, you meet the support test. It does not matter how many months or days you provided the support; only the total cost of the support is considered. You do not meet the support test if the dependent contributed 50% or more of his or her own support or 50% or more was contributed by others, including government sources.

Multiple support agreement. If the dependent or someone else did not contribute 50% or more of the support, and you contributed more than 10% of the total support, you may be able to claim the dependent under a multiple support agreement *(21.6)*.

Divorced or separated parents contributing to support of their children should follow a special rule (21.7).

> **EXAMPLE**
>
> Eric Hill receives $300 in bank interest in 2023 and Social Security benefits of $13,000, which are not subject to tax *(34.3)*. He has no other income, so the gross income test *(21.4)* for qualifying relatives is satisfied. Eric spends $8,800 on food, clothes, transportation, and recreation. The $8,800 spent is his contribution to his own support. Eric's rent, utilities, unreimbursed medical expenses, and other necessities are paid by his son, Mike. If Mike's payments exceed $8,800, and no one else contributes to Eric's support, Mike may claim Eric as a dependent.

Checklist of Support Items

- Food and lodging; *see* below.
- Clothing
- Medical and dental expenses, including premiums paid for health insurance policies and Medicare coverage (premiums paid for Medicare Parts A (if any), B, C, or D).
- Education expenses such as tuition, books, and supplies. If your child receives a student loan and is the primary obligor, the loan proceeds are considered his or her own support contribution. This is true even if you are a guarantor of the loan. Scholarships received by full-time students are not treated as support; *see* the checklist of nonsupport items in this section.
- Cars and transportation expenses. Include the cost of a car bought for a dependent as support. If you buy a car but register it in your own name, the cost of the car is not support provided by you, but any out-of-pocket expenses you have for operating the car are part of your support contribution.
- Recreation, travel and entertainment. A computer, cell phone or TV bought for your child or other dependent is support. Also include costs such as vacations, summer camp, singing and dancing lessons, musical instruments, and wedding expenses.

Planning Reminder

Savings and Investments as Support

Income that is invested is not treated as support. However, personal savings are treated as support if they are used for food, clothing, lodging, or other support items.

Dependent's income and personal savings may be support. In figuring a person's total support, include his or her taxable and tax-exempt income and personal savings if actually used for support items such as food, lodging, or clothing. Also include support items that are financed by loans. Income that is invested and not actually spent for support is not included in the earner's total support.

Social Security. Social Security benefits (whether taxable or tax-exempt) received by your dependent are included in his or her total support only if they are actually spent on support items and not invested.

Social Security benefits paid to children of deceased workers that are used for their support are treated as the children's contribution to their own support. Follow this rule even though benefits are paid to you as the child's parent or custodian. If the Social Security benefits used for a child's support are more than half of the child's total support, no one may claim the child as a dependent.

Where spouses are paid Social Security benefits in one check made out in their joint names, 50% is considered to be used by each spouse unless shown otherwise.

Government benefits. In figuring whether you have provided more than 50% of the dependent's support, you have to consider certain government benefits as support provided by a third party to the dependent. For example, Supplemental Security Income (SSI), welfare, food stamps, or housing payments based on need are support payments from the government if they are used for support of the dependent. G.I. Bill education assistance is support provided by the government.

Foster care payments by a child placement agency to parents are support provided by the agency and not by the parents. The value of board, lodging, and education provided to a child in a state juvenile home is treated as support provided by the state.

When a person joins the Armed Forces, the value of board, lodging, and clothing he or she receives is treated as the government's support contribution. However, if you are in the Armed Forces, dependency allotments withheld from your pay and used to support your dependents are included in your support contributions for them. Also included in your support contribution is a military quarters allowance covering a dependent.

Lodging and food as support. The dependent's total support includes the fair rental value of a room, apartment, or house in which the dependent lives. In your estimate of fair retail value, include a reasonable allowance for the rental value of furnishings and appliances, and for heat and other utilities. You do not add payments of rent, taxes, interest, depreciation, paint, insurance, and utilities. These are presumed to be accounted for in the fair rental estimate. The fair rental value of lodging you furnish a dependent is the amount you could reasonably expect to receive from a stranger for the lodging.

Does dependent live in his or her own home? If a dependent lives in his or her own home, treat the total fair rental value as his or her own contribution to support. However, if you help maintain the home by giving cash, or you directly pay such expenses as the mortgage, real estate taxes, fire insurance premiums, and repairs, you reduce the total fair rental value of the home by the amount you contributed when figuring his or her own support contributions; *see* the Example below.

If you lived with your dependent rent-free in his or her home, the fair rental value of lodging furnished to you must be offset against the amounts you spent for your dependent in determining the net amount of your contribution to the dependent's support.

Planning Reminder

Dependents in the Armed Forces

If your dependent joins the military, the value of food, lodging, clothing, and educational assistance provided by the government constitutes government support.

Planning Reminder

Lump-Sum Payment to Care Facilities

A lump-sum contribution covering a relative's lifetime care in a long-term care facility is prorated over the relative's life expectancy to determine your current support contribution.

> **EXAMPLE**
>
> You contribute $9,000 as support to your father who lives in his own home, which has a fair rental value of $10,000 a year. He uses $6,600 of the money you give him to pay real estate taxes and $2,400 for food. His Social Security benefits are $14,000, of which he spends $5,000 for recreation and invests the rest. He has no other income. The Social Security benefits are not taxable *(34.3)*. Your father has no gross income for the year *(21.4)* and receives no other support. Your father's contribution to his own support is $8,400:
>
> | | |
> |---|---:|
> | Fair rental value of house | |
> | ($10,000 less $6,600 you gave for taxes) | 3,400 |
> | Social Security spent by father for recreation | 5,000 |
> | Father's contribution to his own support | $8,400 |
>
> You may claim your father as a dependent because your contribution of $9,000 exceeds $8,700, which is half of his total support of $17,400 (your $9,000 contribution and his $8,400 contribution).

Food and other similar household expenses. If the dependent lives with you, you divide your total food expenses equally among all the members of your household, unless you have records showing the exact amount spent on the dependent; *see* the Examples at the end of this section. If he or she does not live with you, you count the actual amount of food expenses spent by or for that dependent.

Do you pay for a relative's care in a health facility? If you pay part of a relative's expenses for care in a nursing home or other facility, your payment is a support contribution. If you make a lump-sum contribution covering a relative's stay in an old-age home or other care facility, you prorate your payment over the relative's life expectancy to determine the current support contribution.

Checklist of Items Not Counted as Support of Dependent

- Federal, state, and local income taxes and Social Security taxes paid by the dependent from his or her own income
- Funeral expenses
- Life insurance premiums
- Medicare benefits or proceeds under Medicare Parts A, B, C, or D. Note that the rule is different for Medicare premiums: Medicare premiums are treated as support, but Medicare benefits are disregarded in determining a person's support. In one case the IRS argued that Medicaid benefits were includible in total support but the Tax Court disagreed, holding that Medicaid is similar to excludable Medicare benefits.
- Medical insurance benefits received by the dependent
- Scholarships received by your child, stepchild, or legally adopted child who is a full-time student for at least five calendar months during the year. Scholarship aid is counted as support contributed by the child if he or she is not a full-time student for at least five months. Naval R.O.T.C. payments and payments made under the War Orphans Educational Assistance Act are scholarships that are not counted as support. State aid to a disabled child for education or training, including room and board, is a scholarship.
- Survivors' and Dependents' Educational Assistance payments used for the support of a child who receives them.

Allocating Support

The Examples below illustrate how you should allocate various support items when your contributions benefit more than one person or when your dependent provides part of his or her own support.

EXAMPLES

1. Your father lives in your home with you, your spouse, and your three children. He receives Social Security benefits of $9,800, which are not subject to tax *(34.3)* and half of which ($4,900) he spends for his own clothing, travel, and recreation. You spend $7,800 for food during the year. You also paid his dental bill of $500. You estimate the annual fair rental value of the room furnished him as $6,000. Your father's total support is $12,700:

Social Security used for support	$4,900
Share of food costs (1/6 of $7,800)	1,300
Dental bill paid by you	500
Rental value of room	6,000
	$12,700

   You meet the support test. Your support contribution for your father of $7,800 ($6,000 for lodging, $500 for the dental bill, and $1,300 for food), is more than half of his total support of $12,700.

2. Your parents live with you, your spouse, and your two children in a house you rent. The annual fair rental value of their room is $6,000. Your father receives a tax-free government pension of $10,400, half of which he spent equally for your mother and himself for clothing and recreation. Your parents' only other income was $500 of tax-exempt interest. They did not make any other contributions toward their own support. Your total expense in providing food for the household is $7,800. You pay heat and utility bills of $2,400. You paid your mother's medical expenses of $1,600. Your father's total support from all sources is $9,500 and your mother's is $11,100, figured as follows:

	Father	Mother
Fair rental value of their room	$3,000	$3,000
Father's pension used for their support	5,200	5,200
Share of food costs (1/6 of $7,800)	1,300	1,300
Medical expenses for mother		1,600
	$9,500	$11,100

In figuring your parents' total support, you do not include the cost of heat and utilities, because these are presumed to be included in the fair rental value of the room ($6,000). The support you furnish your father, $4,300 (lodging, $3,000; food, $1,300), is not over half of his total support of $9,500. The support you furnish your mother, $5,900 (lodging, $3,000; food, $1,300; medical, $1,600), is over half of her total support of $11,100. You meet the support test for your mother but not your father. Since she did not have taxable income, the gross income test *(21.4)* is satisfied.

Earmarking support to one dependent. If you are contributing funds to a household consisting of several persons and the amount you contribute does not exceed 50% of the total household support, you may be able to claim at least one dependent by earmarking your support to his or her use. Your earmarked contributions must exceed 50% of this dependent's support costs. Mark your checks for the benefit of the dependent, or provide the dependents with a written statement of your support arrangement at the time you start your payments. If you do not designate for whom you are providing support, your contribution is allocated equally among all members of a household.

21.6 Multiple Support Agreements

Are you and others sharing the support of one person, but with no one individual providing more than 50% *(21.5)* of the person's total support? You are treated as meeting the support test for a person who otherwise could be claimed as your qualifying relative *(21.4)* if all of the following apply:

1. You gave more than 10% of the person's support;
2. No one individual contributed over 50% of the person's support;
3. More than 50% of the person's support was provided by you together with other eligible contributors (anyone who could have claimed the person as his/her qualifying relative had they paid over 50% of the person's support);
4. Each of the other eligible contributors who gave more than 10% of the support agrees to let you claim the dependent. They must each sign a statement waiving his or her right to claim the dependent for the particular year. On Form 2120 (Multiple Support Declaration), you identify the individuals who have given you the signed waiver statements; attach the Form 2120 to your Form 1040 or 1040-SR. Do not file the signed waiver statements with your return; keep them with your records in case the IRS later questions your right to claim the dependent.

Planning Reminder

Households with Several Dependents

If your contribution does not exceed 50% of total household support, earmark contributions to at least one of the dependents. This will allow you to claim at least one dependent. Without proper records, however, the IRS treats your contributions as divided among the members of the household.

Filing Instruction

Multiple Support Agreement

If you contribute more than 10% of a person's support and all other more-than-10% contributors agree to let you claim the dependent, each of them should give you a signed statement waiving his or her right to claim the person as a qualifying relative. You identify each of those consenting individuals on a Form 2120 that you attach to your return.

EXAMPLES

1. You and your two brothers contribute $3,000 each toward the support of your mother. She contributes $4,000 of her own to support herself. Your two sisters contribute $1,000 each. Thus, the total support comes to $15,000. Of this, you and your brothers each gave 20% ($3,000 ÷ $15,000), for a total of 60%. Each sister gave 6 2/3% ($1,000 ÷ $15,000). You or one of your brothers may claim your mother as a dependent, assuming the other tests for a qualifying relative *(21.4)* are met. Since each of you contributed more than 10% and the total of your contributions is more than half of your mother's support, you may decide among yourselves which of the three of you will claim her. If it is agreed that you will claim your mother, your brothers must sign statements waiving their right to claim her. You identify your brothers on Form 2120, which you attach to your return. If it is agreed that one of your brothers will claim your mother, he must obtain from you and your other brother signed statements waiving your right to claim her, and he will attach Form 2120 to his return. Since neither of your sisters furnished more than 10%, neither can claim your mother as a dependent, and so neither of them has to provide a signed waiver.

2. Your mother's support totals $10,000; you contribute $2,500; your brother, $2,000; your father, $2,100; and your mother from her savings contributes $3,400. You and your brother cannot use your father's contribution to meet the more than 50% test required by Rule 3 above. Your father may not join in a multiple support agreement because your mother cannot be his qualifying relative *(21.4)*. Since you and your brother did not contribute over 50% of your mother's support, neither of you can benefit from the multiple support agreement rule.

21.7 Special Rule for Divorced or Separated Parents

Although a deduction for exemptions is not allowed for 2018 through 2025 (*21.1*), the right to claim an exemption still matters to divorced or separated parents because the right to claim the exemption for a child also determines which parent may claim the child tax credit and additional child tax credit (*25.2–25.3*), and for some children, the credit for other dependents (*25.4*). Due to the residence test, a child is generally treated as the qualifying child of the custodial parent, the parent with whom the child lives for the greater part of the year (*21.3*).

For the tax years of 2018 through 2025, a waiver on Form 8332 (or similar statement) by the custodial parent for a child has the effect of allowing the noncustodial parent to claim the child tax credit and additional child tax credit, or if applicable, the credit for other dependents, for that child. The custodial parent must attach the release of claim Form 8332 to their tax filing, and the noncustodial parent must receive a copy of the completed and signed release form, and also attach the form to their tax filing.

For the waiver rule to apply, the threshold conditions listed below must be present.

Note: Even if the custodial parent agrees to waive the right to claim the child on Form 8332, this waiver does not apply to the Earned Income Credit (*25.7*), child and dependent care credit (*25.5*), or the exclusion for dependent care benefits (*3.5*), which may be claimed, if at all, only by the custodial parent. Similarly, only a custodial parent can file as a head of household (*1.12*).

Threshold conditions for special rule. The waiver rule applies only if all of the following threshold conditions are met: (1) the child receives over one-half of his or her total support for the year from one or both parents, (2) the parents are divorced or legally separated under a decree of divorce or separate maintenance, separated under a written separation agreement, or live apart at all times during the last six months of the year (this includes parents who were never married to each other), and (3) the child is in the custody of one or both parents for more than half the year. If all of these conditions are not met, the child is treated as the qualifying child, or, if applicable, qualifying relative, of the custodial parent, and a waiver in favor of the noncustodial parent is not allowed.

The first condition is not met, and the waiver rule does not apply, if a parent and other individuals contributing more than 10% of the child's support enter into a multiple support agreement (*21.6*) authorizing the parent to claim the child.

Custodial parent and noncustodial parent. For purposes of the waiver rule, the custodial parent is the parent with whom the child resides for the greater number of nights during the year. The other parent is the noncustodial parent. A child who is temporarily absent is treated as residing with the parent with whom the child would otherwise have resided on that night. If during the year the child resides with both parents for an equal number of nights, the parent with the higher adjusted gross income is treated as the custodial parent.

Custodial parent's waiver on Form 8332 or similar statement. If the above threshold conditions are met, the custodial parent may provide a written waiver on Form 8332 (or similar statement) that releases his or her right to claim a named child as a dependent for one or more years. If the noncustodial parent attaches the waiver to his or her return, the child is treated as the qualifying child or qualifying relative of the noncustodial parent for purposes of the child tax credit, the additional child tax credit, and the credit for other dependents (*25.2–25.4*).

Under proposed regulations, the noncustodial parent can attach the waiver to an original or amended return, but a waiver attached to an amended return will not qualify if (1) the custodial parent filed a return claiming the child as a dependent before signing the waiver, and (2) the custodial parent has not filed an amended return to remove his or her claim.

A waiver on Form 8332 (or similar written release) by the custodial parent must specify the year or years for which it is effective. Part I of Form 8332 is completed to waive the right to claim a child for the current tax year, and Part II is used for waivers that apply to specific future years or all future years. If Part II provides a release for "all future years," IRS regulations treat this as referring to the first taxable year after the year of execution

---

Planning Reminder

Form 8332 Waiver Applies to Child Tax Credit

If a custodial parent releases the right to claim as a dependent his or her child on Form 8332 (or substitute statement), the release gives the noncustodial parent the right to claim the child tax credit and the additional child tax credit, assuming the credits are not phased out; see *25.2*.

---

and all taxable years after that. The waiver cannot be conditioned on the payment of support, or the meeting of some other obligation, by the noncustodial parent.

If a post-1984 decree or agreement executed before 2009 states that the noncustodial parent has the unconditional right to claim the child as a dependent, and that the custodial parent is waiving his/her right to claim the child as a dependent for a specified year or years, the noncustodial parent can attach to his or her return the relevant pages from the decree or agreement instead of attaching Form 8332. The attachment must include the page that gives the noncustodial parent the unconditional right to claim the child, the page showing the custodial parent's waiver, the cover page, on which the custodial parent's Social Security number should be written, and the signature page showing the custodial parent's signature and date of the agreement.

The option to attach pages from a decree or agreement is not available if the decree/agreement was executed after 2008. The noncustodial parent must obtain the custodial parent's waiver on Form 8332 (or similar written release) and attach it to his or her return.

Note: If a pre-1985 agreement gives a noncustodial parent the right to claim a disabled child who has reached the age of majority as a dependent, the noncustodial parent may continue to treat the child as a dependent by providing at least $600 of the child's support for the year; *see* Publication 501 for details.

Custodial parent may revoke waiver. A custodial parent who has signed a waiver in favor of the noncustodial parent can revoke the waiver. The revocation can be made in Part III of Form 8332.

However, a revocation has a delayed effect. It does not apply until the year after the year in which you give a copy of it to the noncustodial parent or make a reasonable attempt to do so. For example, you are the custodial parent of your daughter and on Form 8332 you waived your right to claim your daughter as your dependent for the years 2016 through 2024. In 2021 you revoked your waiver on Form 8332 and gave a copy of it to the noncustodial parent. You can treat your daughter as your dependent on your 2022 return, assuming the other qualifying child *(21.3)* or qualifying relative *(21.4)* tests are met, as well as on your 2023 and 2024 returns. However, if you did not give the copy of the revocation to the noncustodial parent until 2022, the revocation is not effective until 2023. You must attach a copy of the revocation to your return for each year that you claim the child as your dependent.

21.8 Reporting Social Security Numbers of Dependents

You must enter the Social Security number (SSN) of each dependent you list in the "Dependents" section on page 1 of Form 1040 or 1040-SR. Include the SSNs of parents or other adults you claim as dependents, as well as those of children.

An SSN may be obtained from the Social Security Administration for U.S. citizens and aliens who have been lawfully admitted for permanent residence or employment. If a dependent is a resident alien or nonresident alien ineligible to obtain an SSN, an individual taxpayer identification number (ITIN) must be obtained from the IRS by filing Form W-7.

If you are in the process of legally adopting a U.S. citizen or resident child who has been placed in your home by an authorized placement agency, and you cannot obtain a Social Security number for the child in time to file your tax return, you may use Form W-7A to apply to the IRS for a temporary adoption taxpayer identification number (ATIN).

If you fail to include a correct SSN or ITIN for a dependent claimed on your return, the IRS may disallow dependent treatment, although it may contact you and give you an opportunity to provide the number. If your claim is disallowed, the IRS may assess the extra tax using a summary assessment procedure if you fail to request abatement of the assessment within 60 days of receiving notice; this procedure does not require issuance of a deficiency notice, so there is no appeal to the Tax Court.

To obtain a Social Security number for a dependent child, file Form SS-5 with your local Social Security Administration office. Parents of newborn children may request a number when filling out hospital birth-registration records.

Caution

Child Must Have SSN for You to Claim Child Tax Credit

You cannot claim the child tax credit or the additional child tax credit for a qualified child unless the child has been issued a Social Security number by the due date of your return *(25.2)*.

Religious beliefs. Religious beliefs against applying for and using SSN numbers for their children do not excuse taxpayers from the obligation to provide them. That's what the Tax Court told the Millers, who had refused to use SSN numbers for claiming their two children as dependents. They argued that SSNs are universal numerical identifiers equal to the "mark of the Beast," as described in the New Testament, and that the requirement to use SSNs "substantially burdened" their First Amendment right to free exercise of religion. However, they were willing to use Individual Taxpayer Identification Numbers (ITINs).

The Tax Court held that the IRS properly refused to issue ITINs in this case because ITINs are issued only to taxpayers who are ineligible to receive SSNs. The Tax Court held that it did not have to decide the "burden-on-religion" issue because the IRS was able to show that the SSN requirement furthers a compelling governmental interest in effectively tracking dependency claims,enabling the IRS to detect improper and fraudulent claims.

CHAPTER 22

Figuring Your Regular Income Tax Liability

There are two types of income tax rates: (1) regular tax rates, which apply to all taxpayers, and (2) alternative minimum tax (AMT) rates, which apply only if certain tax benefits, when added back to your income, result in an AMT liability that exceeds your regular tax liability.

Most taxpayers with taxable income less than $100,000 will use the IRS Tax Table to find their tax liability, by locating the table that correlates with their filing status and income *(22.2)*. The Tax Computation Worksheet must be used by taxpayers to figure their regular income tax if taxable income is $100,000 or more *(22.3)*. However, if a taxpayer has net capital gain or qualified dividends, they do not use the Tax Table or the Tax Computation Worksheet. Instead, the taxpayer figures their regular tax liability on the applicable capital gains worksheet in the IRS instructions *(22.4)*. A taxpayer will use the Foreign Earned Income Tax Worksheet to figure their regular tax if they are claiming the foreign earned income exclusion or foreign housing exclusion *(22.5)*.

To determine if a taxpayer owes alternative minimum tax *(23.1)*, Form 6251 will need to be completed.

22.1   Taxable Income and Regular Income Tax Liability

The way you calculate your regular tax liability depends on the amount of your taxable income and in some cases the type of income you have. Your taxable income is your adjusted gross income *(12.1)* minus: (1) your standard deduction or itemized deductions, whichever is more beneficial *(13.1)*, and (2) the deduction for qualified business income *(40.24)*. If your taxable income is less than $100,000, you generally use the IRS Tax Table to look up your tax *(22.2)*. If your taxable income is $100,000 or more, you use the Tax Computation Worksheet to determine your tax *(22.3)*. However, if you have net capital gain or qualified dividends, you generally figure your tax on the Qualified Dividends and Capital Gain Tax Worksheet in the IRS instructions for Form 1040 or Form 1040-SR *(22.4)*. The Foreign Earned Income Tax Worksheet is used if you claim the foreign earned income or housing exclusion, or on Form 8615 if the "kiddie tax" computation *(24.3)* must be made.

Separate self-employment tax computation. If you have net self-employment earnings, figure your self-employment tax under the rules at *45.3*. Half of the self-employment tax is deductible as an above-the-line deduction from gross income when figuring your regular tax *(12.2, 45.3)*. The self-employment tax figured on Schedule SE (Form 1040 or 1040-SR) is entered as an "other tax" on Part II of Schedule 2 (Form 1040 or 1040-SR), and then the "total other taxes" from Schedule 2 are entered on Form 1040 or 1040-SR where they are added to your regular income tax liability.

AMT computation. Regardless of how your regular tax liability is determined, you may also be liable for alternative minimum tax (AMT), which is figured on Form 6251 *(23.1)*. If the tentative AMT figured on Form 6251 exceeds your regular tax (less any foreign tax credit and special averaging tax *(7.3)* on a lump-sum distribution if born before January 1, 1936), the excess is your AMT liability, and must be reported as an additional tax on Schedule 2 (Form 1040 or 1040-SR).

22.2   Using the Tax Table

You must use the Tax Table (shown in Part 8 of this book) to look up your regular income tax liability unless you have taxable income of $100,000 or more, you have net capital gain or qualified dividends *(22.4)*, or you are claiming the foreign earned income or housing exclusion *(22.5)*.   In the Tax Table, the tax for your taxable income amount will be shown in the column corresponding to your filing status. Filing status (single, married filing jointly, head of household, married filing separately, or qualifying widow/widower) is discussed in *Chapter 1*.

Filing Tip

Total Tax Is Line 24 (Form 1040 or 1040-SR)

Total tax includes regular tax and other taxes (e.g., self-employment tax and household employment taxes); *(38.1)*. Additional taxes are listed on Schedule 2 (Form 1040 or 1040-SR) and are added to regular tax to arrive at your total tax.

EXAMPLES

1. You are single, under age 65, and have adjusted gross income for 2023 of $60,345, consisting solely of salary and interest income. You claim the standard deduction *(13.2)*.

Adjusted gross income	$60,345
Less: Standard deduction	$13,850
Taxable income	$46,495

   Your 2023 tax liability from the Tax Table is $5,536, as shown in the column for single persons with taxable income of at least $44,725 but less than $95,375.

2. You are married filing jointly and have 2023 adjusted gross income of $87,590, consisting of salary, pensions and interest. You are over age 65 and your spouse is under age 65. Your standard deduction for 2023 is $29,200 *(13.4)*, but this is less than your itemized deductions of $29,800, so you claim the itemized deductions.

Adjusted gross income	$87,590
Less: Itemized deductions	$29,800
Taxable income	$57,790

   Your 2023 tax liability from the Tax Table is $6,495, as shown in the column for taxpayers who are married filing jointly with taxable income of at least $22,000 but less than $89,450.

22.3 Tax Computation Worksheet

If your taxable income is $100,000 or more and you do not have net capital gain or qualified dividends *(22.4)*, or claim the foreign earned income or housing exclusion *(22.5)*, you must figure your 2023 regular tax liability on Form 1040 or Form 1040-SR using the IRS' Tax Computation Worksheet, which is shown in Part 8 of this book.

Since the Tax Computation Worksheet is used only by taxpayers with taxable incomes of $100,000 or more, the Worksheet only shows the tax rate brackets that a taxpayer with taxable income of at least $100,000. The Worksheet has four sections (A, B, C, D), one for each filing status. To figure your regular income tax liability using the Tax Computation Worksheet, follow the column-by-column instructions in the section for your filing status. The following Example and *Table 22-1* illustrates the computation for a married couple filing jointly for 2023.

EXAMPLE

You and your spouse file a joint return reporting taxable income of $142,274 for 2023. You do not have qualified dividends or capital gains or losses to report, so your regular tax liability is figured on the Tax Computation Worksheet. Following the column instructions for Section B of the Worksheet (for joint filers), as shown in *Table 22-1*, you figure a tax of $21,915.28.

$142,274 × 22% rate from column (b)	$ 31,300.28
Less: subtraction amount from column (d)	9,385.00
Tax	$ 21,915.28

Table 22-1 Sample Section from 2023 Tax Computation Worksheet for Married Filing Jointly or Qualifying Surviving Spouse
(Complete the row below that applies to you, based on your 2023 taxable income.)

If Taxable Income is—	(a) Enter taxable income—	(b) Multiplication amount—	(c) Multiply (a) by (b)—	(d) Subtraction Amount—	Tax Subtract (d) from (c)—
At least $100,000 but not over $190,750	$142,274.00	× 22% (.22)	$ 31,300.28	$ 9,385.00	$21,915.28
Over $190,750 but not over $364,200		× 24% (.24)		13,200.00	
Over $364,200 but not over $462,500		× 32% (.32)		42,336.00	
Over $462,500 but not over $693,750		× 35% (.35)		56,211.00	
Over $693,750		× 37% (.37)		70,086.00	

22.4   Tax Calculation If You Have Net Capital Gain or Qualified Dividends

If a portion of your taxable income consists of net capital gain (net long-term capital gain in excess of net short-term capital loss; *see 5.3*) or qualified dividends *(4.1)*, you should figure your regular tax liability on the Qualified Dividends and Capital Gain Tax Worksheet in the IRS instructions for Form 1040 and Form 1040-SR. On the Worksheet, you can apply the favorable capital gain rates *(5.3)* to your net capital gain and qualified dividends. An Example of how to report transactions on Form 8949 and Schedule D (Form 1040 or 1040-SR) and a filled-in sample of the Qualified Dividends and Capital Gain Tax Worksheet is shown in *5.8*. You may be able to figure your liability on the Qualified Dividends and Capital Gain Tax Worksheet without having to file form 8949 and Schedule D if you have capital gain distributions from Box 2a of Form 1099-DIV *(32.3)* and/or qualified dividends from Box 1b of Form 1099-DIV and no other capital gains or losses.

However, you use a different worksheet if you report any 28% rate gains or unrecaptured Section 1250 gain on Schedule D. In this case, you must use the Schedule D Tax Worksheet *(5.3)* in the Schedule D instructions to figure tax liability.

22.5   Foreign Earned Income Tax Worksheet

If you claim the foreign earned income exclusion *(36.1)* or the foreign housing exclusion on Form 2555, you must figure your regular tax liability using the Foreign Earned Income Tax Worksheet in the Form 1040 and Form 1040-SR instructions. The worksheet computation must be used due to the rule requiring non-excluded income to be "stacked" on top of the excluded income, so the non-excluded income is subject to the same tax rate or rates that would have applied if the foreign exclusions had not been elected.

22.6   Income Averaging for Farmers and Fishermen

A farmer or fisherman may elect to average 2023 farm or fishing income over three years on Schedule J of Form 1040 or 1040-SR. On Schedule J, one-third of elected farm or fishing income is allocated to each of 2020, 2021, and 2022. The tax for 2023 equals the tax liability figured without elected farm or fishing income plus the increase in tax for each of the three prior years after including allocated elected farm or fishing income to the income of those years. Income averaging is available only to individual farmers or fishermen and may not be elected by estates or trusts engaged in the farming or fishing business. When computing potential AMT on Form 6251 *(23.1)*, regular tax liability is determined without regard to Schedule J averaging. Since AMT liability is based on the excess of tentative AMT over regular tax, ignoring the Schedule J reduction to the regular tax limits or eliminates the AMT.

Elected farm or fishing income is taxable income attributable to a farming or fishing business. A farming business is generally any business that involves cultivating land or raising or harvesting agricultural or horticultural commodities. A fishing business is generally any business involving the actual or attempted catching, taking, or harvesting of fish. *See* the Schedule J instructions.

A previous election to average farm income may by revoked or the elected farm income may be changed by filing an amended return within the period of limitations for a refund claim *(47.2)*.

22.7   Tax Credits

After figuring your 2023 regular tax liability, you may be able to reduce that liability as well as AMT liability *(23.1)* by claiming tax credits. The child tax credit, credit for other dependents, credit for child and dependent care, Earned Income Credit, adoption credit, credit for retirement savings contributions, residential energy credits, plug-in electric drive motor vehicle credit, mortgage interest credit, premium tax credit, and health coverage credit are discussed in *Chapter 25*. The education tax credits are discussed in *Chapter 33*. The credit for the elderly is discussed in *Chapter 34* and the foreign tax credit in *Chapter 36*. The business tax credits are discussed in *Chapter 40*. The credit for prior year AMT liability is discussed at *23.4*. If you worked for more than one employer in 2023 and had Social Security taxes of more than $9,932 withheld from your wages, the excess may be claimed as a credit on Part II of Schedule 3 (Form 1040 or 1040-SR) *(26.8)*.

22.8 Additional Medicare Tax and Net Investment Income Tax

There is a 0.9% additional Medicare tax on wages and self-employment income exceeding $250,000 if married filing jointly; $200,000, if single, head of household, or a surviving spouse; or $125,000, if married filing separately. To the extent the tax was not withheld *(26.8)* from your wages, you will have to pay it when you file Form 1040 or 1040-SR *(28.2)*.

If you have net investment income (NII), some or all of it will be subject to a 3.8% tax if you have modified adjusted gross income (MAGI) exceeding the applicable threshold. The same $250,000, $200,000 or $125,000 threshold shown above for the 0.9% tax also applies to the tax on NII except for surviving spouse, who are treated as married persons filing jointly for purposes of the 3.8% tax. If MAGI exceeds the threshold, the 3.8% tax applies to the lesser of your NII or the MAGI exceeding the threshold *(28.3)*.

Court Decision

NII Tax Not Offset by Foreign Tax Credit

The Tax Court said that the NII tax may not be offset by the foreign tax credit. The reason: The NII tax is in a different part of the Internal Revenue Code than the regular and alternative minimum tax for which credits may be used as reductions to tax liability.

CHAPTER 23

Alternative Minimum Tax (AMT)

The purpose of AMT is to effectively take back some of the tax breaks allowed for regular tax purposes. The AMT is an additional tax that you may owe if for regular tax purposes you claimed:

- Itemized deductions for taxes or investment expenses.
- Certain tax-exempt interest, accelerated depreciation, and incentive stock option benefits.

There are no specific tests to determine whether or not you are liable for AMT. You must first figure your regular income tax and then *see* whether tax benefit items must be added back to taxable income to figure alternative minimum taxable income, on which the AMT is figured. If after claiming the AMT exemption and applying the AMT rates of 26% and 28%, the tentative alternative minimum tax exceeds your regular income tax, the excess is your AMT liability, which is added to the regular tax on your return. In other words, your tax liability for the year will be the greater of your regular tax or your AMT.

AMT liability is figured on Form 6251 and is attached to Form 1040 or 1040-SR.

Table 23-1 Key to AMT Rules for 2023

Item—	AMT Rule—
AMT exemptions and tax rates	The exemption shields an equivalent amount of alternative minimum taxable income (AMTI) from the AMT. For 2023, the AMT exemption amounts are $126,500 for married couples filing jointly and qualifying widows/widowers, $81,300 for single taxpayers and heads of households, and $63,250 for married persons filing separately. The exemption amounts are subject to a phaseout, but only if AMTI exceeds $1,156,300 for joint filers and qualifying widows/widowers, or $578,150 for all others *(23.1)*. AMTI in excess of the exemption (after phaseout if any) is subject to an AMT tax rate of 26% or 28% on Form 6251. For 2023, the 26% rate applies to a balance of $220,700 or less, $110,350 or less if married filing separately. A 28% rate applies to amounts exceeding the $220,700 or $110,350 ceiling for the 26% rate. However, net capital gain and qualified dividends are taxable on Form 6251 at the same capital gain rates (0%, 15%, and 20%) used to figure regular income tax liability *(5.3)*. The resulting tax, reduced by any AMT foreign tax credit, is your tentative AMT liability, but you will have to pay it only to the extent that it exceeds your regular income tax liability
AMT taxable income (AMTI)	On Form 6251, you start with your regular taxable income on Form 1040 or 1040-SR and then increase (or sometimes decrease) that amount by AMT adjustments and preferences to figure alternative minimum taxable income (AMTI).
AMT adjustments and preference items	Itemized deductions for taxes, and in some cases investment interest deductions, are not allowed. The standard deduction is not an allowable AMT deduction. Tax-exempt interest from certain private activity bonds is taxable for the AMT. MACRS depreciation is figured under the alternative MACRS system for real estate using 40-year straight-line recovery, and, for personal property, the 150% declining balance method. For incentive stock options; *see 23.2*. If you sell qualified small business stock that qualifies for an exclusion *(5.7)*, 7% of the exclusion is a preference item. Mining exploration and development costs are allowable costs amortized over 10 years. For long-term contracts, income is generally figured under the percentage-of-completion method. Pollution control facilities amortization is figured under alternate MACRS. Alternative tax net operating loss is allowed with adjustments. Circulation expenditures must be amortized ratably over three years. Research and experimental expenditures must be amortized ratably over 10 years. Passive activity losses are recomputed; certain tax-shelter farm losses may not be allowed.
Adjusted gross income	In making AMT computations involving adjusted gross income limitations, use adjusted gross income as computed for regular tax purposes.
Partnership AMT	If you are a partner, include for AMT your distributive share of the partnership's adjustments and tax preference items. These are reported on Schedule K-1 (Form 1065). The partnership itself does not pay alternative minimum tax.
Trust or estate AMT	If you are a beneficiary of an estate or trust, consider for AMT your share of distributable net alternative minimum taxable income shown on Schedule K-1 (Form 1041). The estate or trust must pay tax on any remaining alternative minimum taxable income.
S corporation stockholder	If you are a shareholder, consider for AMT your share of the adjustments and tax preference items reported on Schedule K-1 (Form 1120-S).
Children subject to "kiddie tax"	Children under age 24 who are subject to the "kiddie tax" *(24.3)* may have to compute AMT liability on Form 6251. The AMT exemption for a child subject to the "kiddie tax" is figured the same way as for any other taxpayer.

23.1   Computing Alternative Minimum Tax on Form 6251

In addition to regular income tax, you might have to pay alternative minimum tax (AMT). To the extent that your tentative AMT figured on Form 6251 exceeds your regular tax liability, the excess is the AMT that you are liable for.

Fewer taxpayers are likely to be subject to the AMT because of the increases to the exemption amount and the phaseout threshold enacted by the Tax Cuts and Jobs Act; *see* below.

If you claim any of the items on the list below, you should complete Form 6251 to determine if you are liable for AMT. The starting point for calculating alternative minimum taxable income (AMTI) on Form 6251 is generally taxable income. Note: the standard deduction is not allowed for AMT purposes; it must be added back to regular taxable income when figuring AMTI. Similarly, the other items on the list below are AMT adjustments and preferences and, generally, some or all of the amount allowed for regular tax purposes must be added back to regular taxable income to calculate AMTI. The item that most commonly gets added back to income when calculating AMTI is state and local taxes. *See 23.2* for details on the AMT adjustments and preference items.

Items subject to AMT:	Check: √
1. Standard deduction	❏
2. Itemized deductions for taxes and investment interest	❏
3. Accelerated depreciation in excess of straight line	❏
4. Income from the exercise of incentive stock options	❏
5. Tax-exempt interest from private activity bonds	❏
6. Intangible drilling costs	❏
7. Depletion	❏
8. Circulation expenses	❏
9. Mining exploration and development costs	❏
10. Research and experimental costs	❏
11. Pollution control facility amortization	❏
12. Tax-shelter farm income or loss	❏
13. Passive income or loss	❏
14. Certain installment sale income	❏
15. Income from long-term contracts computed under percentage-of-income method	❏
16. Net operating loss deduction	❏
17. Foreign tax credit	❏
18. Gain on small business stock qualifying for exclusion	❏

AMT exemption amounts for 2023. The 2023 exemptions are $126,500 for married couples filing jointly and qualifying widows/widowers, $81,300 for single persons and heads of households, and $63,250 for married persons filing separately.

The exemption amounts may be reduced under the phaseout rule, but only for taxpayers with very high AMTI as discussed next.

For 2024, the exemption amounts will likely be increased for inflation; *see* the *e-Supplement* at *jklasser.com*.

Exemption phaseout rules for 2023. The AMT exemptions are subject to a phaseout rule. For 2023, the phaseout threshold is $1,156,300 for married couples filing jointly and qualifying widows/widowers and for all others, the threshold is $578,150.

For 2024, the phaseout thresholds will likely be increased for inflation; *see* the *e-Supplement* at *jklasser.com*.

Under the phaseout formula, the exemption amount is phased out by 25 cents for every dollar of AMTI in excess of the phaseout threshold. This means that the exemption for 2023 is completely phased out when AMTI equals or exceeds: $1,662,300 for married couples filing jointly and qualifying widows/widowers, $903,350 for single taxpayers and heads of household, and $831,150 for married persons filing separately. The Form 6251 instructions have a worksheet for figuring the phaseout.

If a married person filing separately for 2023 has AMTI exceeding the $831,150 phaseout endpoint, 25% of the excess over $831,150, but no more than $63,250 (the full exemption amount), must be added to the AMTI before applying the 26%/28% AMT rates.

AMT calculation. After reducing AMTI by the allowable exemption, the 26% and possibly 28% AMT rate is applied. For 2023, the 26% AMT rate generally applies to the first $220,700 of AMTI, or $110,350 if married filing separately. The 28% rate applies to any balance of the AMTI over $220,700 or $110,350. However, if you had net capital gain or qualified dividends that qualify for reduced capital gains rates *(5.3)*, you apply the same capital gains rate for AMT purposes as for regular income tax purposes; the capital gains calculation is made on page 2 of Form 6251. The boundary between the 26% and 28% brackets will likely be increased for 2024 by an inflation adjustment; *see* the *e-Supplement* at *jklasser.com*.

The resulting tax, less any AMT foreign tax credit, is the tentative AMT, which applies only to the extent it *exceeds* your regular income tax. For this purpose, regular income tax is the tax on Line 16 of Form 1040 or 1040-SR, *plus* any repayment of advances of the premium tax credit *(25.13)*, with no reduction for tax credits other than the foreign tax credit, *minus* any special averaging tax on a lump-sum distribution (available only if you were born before January 2, 1936; *see 7.3*). If income averaging was used on Schedule J to figure the regular tax for farm or fishing income *(22.6)*, that tax must be refigured without using averaging for purposes of determining AMT.

The excess, if any, of tentative AMT over the regular tax (modified as required by the Form 6251 instructions) is the AMT liability that you must report as an additional tax on Line 1 of Schedule 2 (Form 1040 or 1040-SR). You do not have to pay the AMT if your regular tax (adjusted as required) equals or exceeds the tentative AMT.

Follow the line-by-line instructions to Form 6251 to figure your AMT liability, if any.

23.2 Adjustments and Preferences for AMT

You have to add back to your income certain tax breaks allowed for regular tax purposes. This includes the standard deduction *(23.1)*, as well as the items described below. In some cases, a negative adjustment reduces AMTI. Some of the items discussed below are technically "preference items" under the Internal Revenue Code (such as interest from private activity bonds), rather than "adjustments", but the IRS lists them together on Part I of Form 6251 as items that increase or decrease AMTI.

Taxes. State, local, and foreign taxes deducted on Schedule A *(16.1)* must be added back to income in figuring alternative minimum taxable income (AMTI).

If you received in 2023 a refund of state or local taxes deducted in a prior year and the refund is reported as income on your 2023 Form 1040 or 1040-SR *(11.5–11.6)*, you enter the refund on Form 6251 as a *negative* adjustment that reduces AMTI.

Investment interest. If for regular tax purposes you claimed an itemized deduction (Schedule A) for investment interest on Form 4952, or if you deducted investment interest for rental property on Schedule E, you must complete a second Form 4952 to determine if your allowable deduction for AMT is more or less than the itemized deduction, taking into account AMT adjustments and preferences. The difference between the regular tax deduction and the allowable AMT deduction is entered on Form 6251 as a positive adjustment if the regular tax deduction is more, or as a negative adjustment if the AMT amount is more.

Net operating losses. A net operating loss (NOL) claimed for regular tax purposes must be recomputed for AMT. The recomputed loss, or ATNOLD (alternative tax net operating loss deduction), is generally the excess of the deductions allowed in figuring AMTI (alternative minimum taxable income) over the income included in AMTI. For example, the nonbusiness deduction adjustment *(40.19)* must be separately figured for the ATNOLD, taking into account only nonbusiness income and deductions included in AMTI. Thus, state and local taxes that are not allowable AMT deductions *(23.2)* do not reduce nonbusiness income in figuring the ATNOLD.

The ATNOLD generally is limited to 90% of AMTI but certain losses (such as qualified disaster losses) are not subject to the 90% limit; *see* the instructions to Form 6251 for further details.

Tax-exempt interest on private activity bonds. You generally must increase alternative minimum taxable income (AMTI) by tax-exempt interest on private activity bonds issued after August 7, 1986 and before 2009, and on such bonds issued after 2010, but this does not include qualified 501(3) bonds, New York Liberty bonds, Gulf Opportunity Zone bonds, and Midwestern disaster area bonds. Also, if issued after July 30, 2008, qualified mortgage bonds, veterans' mortgage bonds, and exempt-facility bonds that have at least 95% of the net proceeds going to fund qualified residential rental projects are not treated as private activity bonds for AMT purposes.

Any bonds issued in 2009 and 2010 that would otherwise be treated as private activity bonds are not considered private activity bonds, so the interest on the 2009/2010 bonds does not get added back to AMTI.

Exclusion on qualifying small business stock. If you claim an exclusion for gain on the sale of qualified small business stock that was issued to you before September 28, 2010 *(5.7)*, 7% of the excluded gain must be added as a positive adjustment to AMTI.

Incentive stock option (ISO) exercised. For regular tax purposes, you are not taxed when you exercise an incentive stock option (ISO) *(2.16)*. If you acquire stock by exercising an ISO and you dispose of that stock in the same year, the tax treatment under the regular tax and the AMT is the same. No AMT adjustment is required. However, if you do not sell the stock in the same year that the option is exercised, the exercise of an ISO can result in a substantial AMT liability. You generally must increase AMT income by including on Form 6251 the excess, if any, of:

1. The fair market value of the stock acquired through exercise of the option (determined without regard to any lapse restriction) when your rights in the acquired stock first become transferable or when these rights are no longer subject to a substantial risk of forfeiture, over
2. The amount you paid for the stock, including any amount you paid for the ISO used to acquire the stock.

You should have received a Form 3921 from your employer that indicates the number of shares you acquired when you exercised the ISO, the exercise price you paid for each acquired share, and the fair market value of each share on the exercise date. You can use these Form 3921 entries to figure the AMT adjustment (fair market value of acquired shares minus the amount you paid).

Filing Instruction

Private Activity Bond Interest

Private activity bond interest that is subject to AMT is reported in Box 9 of Form 1099-INT.

If in the year you exercise the ISO your rights in the acquired ISO stock are *not* transferable and *are* subject to a substantial risk of forfeiture, you do not report the AMT adjustment until the year your rights become transferable or are no longer forfeitable. However, within 30 days of the transfer to you of the stock acquired through exercise of the ISO, you may elect to include in AMT income for that year the excess of the stock's fair market value (determined without regard to any lapse restriction) over the exercise price; *see* the discussion of the Section 83(b) election at *2.17*.

If you report an AMT adjustment for stock acquired through the exercise of an ISO, increase the AMT basis of the stock by the amount of the adjustment. Since the AMT basis in stock acquired through an ISO is likely to be significantly higher than your regular tax basis, you may have a larger gain for regular tax purposes and a larger loss for AMT purposes in the year you sell the stock. This would produce a negative adjustment for AMT. Follow the Form 6251 instructions to the line for "Dispositions of Property".

MACRS depreciation. Depreciation allowed for AMT may differ from that allowed for regular tax purposes. For example, if for regular tax purposes you use the 200% declining balance method to depreciate business equipment with a recovery period of three, five, seven, or 10 years *(42.5)*, the difference between the regular depreciation and the 150% declining balance rate method allowed for AMT is generally an adjustment that increases alternative minimum taxable income, but there is an exception for property eligible for bonus depreciation *(42.18)*; *see* the Form 6251 instructions.

There is no AMT adjustment for real estate placed in service after 1998. For real estate placed in service before 1999, the adjustment is the difference between the straight-line depreciation claimed for regular tax purposes using the recovery period discussed in *42.12* and the straight-line recovery over the AMT 40-year recovery period.

The adjustment for MACRS may result in providing more depreciation for AMT purposes where the AMT depreciation computation towards the latter part of the useful life of the property provides larger deductions than the regular MACRS deduction. If the AMT deduction exceeds the regular tax deduction, the difference is entered as a negative adjustment that reduces alternative minimum taxable income.

Basis adjustment affects AMT gain or loss. When post-1986 depreciable assets are sold, gain for AMT purposes is figured on the basis of the property as adjusted by depreciation claimed for AMT purposes. This gain or loss will be different from the gain or loss figured for regular tax purposes where regular MACRS depreciation was used.

Oil and gas costs. Independent oil and gas producers and royalty owners do not have to refigure depletion deductions for the AMT. Excess intangible drilling costs (IDC) are generally not treated as a preference item unless they exceed 40% of AMT income; *see* the instructions to Form 6251.

Mining exploration and development costs. Unless the optional 10-year deduction was elected for regular tax purposes for mining exploration and development costs, the costs must be amortized ratably over a 10-year period for AMT purposes. The difference between the regular tax deduction and AMT deduction is entered on Form 6251 as an adjustment (positive or negative).

If a mine is abandoned as worthless, all mining exploration and development costs that have not been written off are deductible in the year of abandonment.

Circulation costs. If circulation costs were deducted in full for regular tax purposes (instead of using the optional three-year write-off), they must be amortized over three years for the AMT. The difference between the two allowable deductions must be reported as an adjustment on Form 6251, as either a positive or negative amount.

Long-term contracts. The use of the completed contract method of accounting or certain other methods of accounting for long-term contracts is generally not allowable for AMT. The percentage of completion method must be used to figure the AMT income from a long-term contract. However, there is an exception for home construction contracts. The difference between the regular tax and AMT income is an AMT adjustment, either positive or negative.

Caution

Gain on Sale of Incentive Stock Option Stock

Your AMT basis in stock acquired through the exercise of an ISO is increased by the amount of the required AMT adjustment. Keep basis records for both AMT and regular tax purposes, since in the year the stock is sold, the higher AMT basis will reduce (or even eliminate in some cases) the gain reportable for AMT purposes.

Research and experimental expenditures. Costs must be amortized over 10 years for AMT purposes if incurred in a business in which you are not a material participant. The difference between the regular tax and AMT deductions must be entered as an adjustment (positive or negative) on Form 6251.

Passive tax-shelter farm losses. Generally, no AMT loss is deductible for any tax-shelter farm activity. A tax-shelter farm activity is any farming syndicate or any farming activity in which you do not materially participate. You may be treated as a material participant if a member of your family materially participates or you meet certain retirement or disability tests discussed at *10.6*.

Gains and losses reported for regular tax purposes from tax-shelter farm activities must be refigured by taking into account any AMT adjustments and preferences. However, a refigured loss is not allowed for AMT purposes except to the extent that you are insolvent at the end of the year, which means that you deduct the loss to the extent of your insolvency. Insolvency is the excess of liabilities over fair market value of assets. Any AMT-disallowed loss is carried forward to later years in which there is gain from that same activity, or until you dispose of the activity.

Passive losses from nonfarming activities. The passive losses are reduced by preference or adjustment items not allowed for AMT purposes. For example, an adjustment for MACRS depreciation is made directly against the passive loss and is not treated as a separate AMT adjustment item. The loss allowed for AMT purposes is increased by the amount by which you are insolvent at the end of the year. *See* the instructions to Form 6251, which suggest that you figure the AMT adjustment of passive losses on a separate Form 8582 that you do not file.

23.3 Tax Credits Allowed Against AMT

The only tax credit allowed in computing tentative alternative minimum tax liability on Form 6251 is a revised version of the foreign tax credit allowed for regular tax purposes. The allowable credit is generally based on foreign source AMT income. If the AMT foreign tax credit exceeds the limits detailed in the Form 6251 instructions, the unused amount generally may be carried back or forward; follow the Form 6251 instructions.

The AMT foreign tax credit reduces the tentative AMT figured on Form 6251 before comparing it to your regular tax liability. You subtract your regular tax from the tentative AMT, and if the result is more than zero, that is your actual AMT liability.

If there is an AMT liability on Form 6251, you enter the AMT as a separate tax on Schedule 2 of Form 1040 or 1040-SR. If you are entitled to any nonrefundable personal tax credits (including the education credits, adoption credit, saver's credit; *see 25.1*), you may use them to offset your AMT as well as your regular tax liability.

23.4 Regular Tax Credit for Prior-Year AMT

You may be able to reduce your regular 2023 tax liability by a tax credit based on AMT incurred in prior years. The prior-year AMT had to be attributable to "deferral items" such as the ISO adjustment or depreciation that provide only a temporary difference to taxable income. Use Form 8801 to figure the credit. The credit is not allowed for 2023 unless your regular tax liability (as reduced by allowable tax credits) for 2023 exceeds your tentative alternative minimum tax liability for 2023 as shown on Form 6251.

23.5 Avoiding AMT

If you are within the range of the AMT tax, review periodically your income and expenses to determine whether to postpone or accelerate income, defer the payment of expenses, and/or make certain tax elections.

There are elections, such as the election of alternative straight-line MACRS depreciation, that may avoid AMT adjustments. However, such elections will increase your regular tax. Similarly, adjustment treatment for mining exploration and development costs, circulation expenses, and research expenses can be avoided by elections to amortize *(23.2)*.

If you are on the verge of becoming subject to the AMT, or are already subject to the AMT, and the 26% or 28% AMT rate exceeds your top rate for regular tax purposes you might want to consider the following steps:

- Postpone income that could trigger AMT by pushing your income over the AMT exemption. On a sale of property, an installment sale *(5.21)* can spread gain over a number of years.
- Do not prepay state or local income taxes or property taxes, as these are not deductible under the AMT.
- Spread out the exercise of incentive stock options (ISOs) over more than one year to limit the AMT adjustment for the bargain element (the difference between the option price and the fair market value of the stock on the date of exercise). If you exercise an ISO and hold the acquired stock beyond the end of the year, the bargain element is subject to AMT *(23.2)*. You may find yourself with an unexpected tax liability and if the stock has depreciated in value since the date of exercise, you may find yourself short of funds to pay the liability even after selling the stock. To limit the AMT adjustment, you can stagger the exercise of options over more than one year. You can avoid the adjustment completely by selling the stock in the same year that the option was exercised, but if you do, any gain on the sale will be taxed as ordinary income and not at the favorable rate for long-term capital gains.

Accelerating income. If you are generally in a tax bracket higher than the 26% or 28% AMT rate and project that you will be subject to AMT in a current year, you may want to subject additional income in the current year to the 26% or 28% AMT tax rate. In such a case, consider accelerating the receipt of income to the current tax year. If you are in business, you might ask for earlier payments from customers or clients. If you control a small corporation, you might prepay your salary or pay yourself a larger bonus, but be careful in the subsequent year not to run afoul of the reasonable compensation rule.

CHAPTER 24

Computing the "Kiddie Tax" on Your Child's Unearned Income

If the "kiddie tax" applies to a child, the child's 2023 investment income in excess of $2,500 is taxed at the parent's marginal tax rate *(24.3)*.

The kiddie tax applies not only to children under age 18, but also to children who are age 18 or full-time students age 19–23 who do not have earned income exceeding half of their support *(24.2)*. Only investment income of a child over $2,500 is subject to the kiddie tax, not wages or self-employment earnings.

The kiddie tax is generally figured on Form 8615 as part of the computation of the child's regular tax liability for the year. The liability from Form 8615 is then entered on the child's Form 1040 tax return, and Form 8615 is attached. Instead of completing Form 8615, the parent of a child under age 19 (or under 24 if a full-time student) may elect on Form 8814 to report the child's investment income on the parent's own return, provided the child received only interest and dividend income. If the parent elects on Form 8814 to report the child's investment income, the tax on the child's income could be higher than if a separate return for the child was filed *(24.4)*.

24.1 Filing Your Child's Return

To discourage substantial income splitting of investment income between parents and minor children, the tax law has complicated income reporting for parents and children by:

1. Imposing a "kiddie tax" that taxes a child's investment income over an annual floor ($2,500 for 2023) at the parent's marginal tax rate *(24.3)*. The kiddie tax applies not only to children under age 18, but also to most 18-year-olds and students under age 24 *(24.2)*.

2. Barring a child who is treated as another taxpayer's dependent *(21.1)* from treating some other person as a dependent on his or her own tax return.

3. Limiting the standard deduction for a dependent child who has only investment income. For 2023, the deduction is $1,250 *(13.5)*.

Does your child have to file? For a child who can be claimed as a dependent either as a qualifying child or a qualifying relative *(21.1)*, the income filing threshold for 2023 is generally $1,250. If your dependent child has gross income (earned and investment income) of $1,250 or less for 2023, he or she is not subject to tax and does not have to file a tax return.

A 2023 return must be filed for a dependent child with investment income exceeding $400 and gross income of more than $1,150. If a dependent child has salary or other earned income but no investment income, a return does not have to be filed unless such earned income exceeds $13,850 for 2023. If your child's only income is from interest and dividends, you may be able to make an election to report the income on your own return, but this generally is not advisable *(24.4)*.

A dependent child is allowed to claim at least a $1,250 standard deduction. A dependent child with earned income may claim a standard deduction up to those earnings plus an additional $400 (if this total is greater than $1,250), but no more than the basic standard deduction, which is generally $13,850 *(13.1)*.

EXAMPLES

1. Your 14-year-old son, whom you claim as your dependent, has interest and dividend income of $480 and no other income for 2023. He has no income tax liability and does not have to file a return.

Interest and dividend income	$480
Less: standard deduction *(13.5)*	1,250
Tax liability	0

2. In 2023, your 17-year-old daughter, whom you claim as your dependent, has interest income of $1,750 and qualified dividends *(4.2)* of $500. Her taxable income is $1,000.

Interest income	$1,750
Qualified dividends	500
	$2,250
Less: standard deduction	1,250
Taxable income	$1,000

   You must file a 2023 Form 1040 for your daughter because she has taxable income, but the kiddie tax computation does not apply because her investment income does not exceed $2,500. On the Qualified Dividends and Capital Gain Tax Worksheet in the Form 1040 instructions (see sample on page 128), the $1,000 of taxable income is reduced by the $500 of qualified dividends and the $600 balance is treated as ordinary income subject to a tax of $50 (from the Tax Table). The $500 of qualified dividends are not taxed as they are eligible for the 0% rate for qualified dividends and capital gains *(4.2)*.

How to file a 2023 return for your child. If your child is not subject to the "kiddie tax" under the rules at *24.2*, follow the regular filing rules and report the child's income and deductions on the child's Form 1040. Since the "kiddie tax" computation does not apply, all of the child's income will be taxed at his or her own tax rate. If your child is unable to sign his or her tax return, you must do so *(1.13)*.

If the kiddie tax computation applies *(24.2)*, Form 8615 must be filed to compute the kiddie tax unless your child's only income is interest and dividends and you elect to report your child's investment earnings on your own return *(24.4)*. On Form 8615 you must provide your Social Security number and taxable income. Form 8615 is attached to the child's tax return *(24.3)*.

Child's AMT liability. A child who has substantial tax-exempt interest, tax preferences, or tax adjustments subject to the alternative minimum tax must compute tentative AMT liability on Form 6251; *see Chapter 23*.

24.2 Children Subject to "Kiddie Tax" for 2023

Form 8615 for 2023 must be filed for your child if all of the following conditions are met:

- Your child either (1) was under age 18 at the end of 2023, (2) was age 18 at the end of 2023 and did not have earned income exceeding half of his or her support for the year, or (3) was a full-time student during 2023 who at the end of the year was age 19 through 23 and did not have earned income exceeding half of his or her support for the year.
- For children born on January 1, the IRS treats the child's birthday as being on the last day of the prior year. Thus, a child who attains age 24 on January 1, 2024, is considered to be age 24, not 23, on December 31, 2023, and so the kiddie tax does not apply to the child's 2023 investment income under test (3) above even if he or she is a full-time student at the end of 2023.
- For purposes of determining if the kiddie tax applies under tests (2) or (3) above, use the dependent rules for figuring full-time student status *(21.3)* and support *(21.5)*.
- Your child had more than $2,500 of investment income for 2023.
- If married, your child files a separate 2023 return from his or her spouse.

If both of a child's parents were deceased at the end of 2023, the kiddie tax computation does not apply regardless of the above tests, and the child's tax is figured under the regular rules.

Exceptions for children filing jointly and distributions from qualified disability trusts. A married child can be subject to the kiddie tax only if he or she files separately; kiddie tax does not apply if a joint return is filed.

If a child is a beneficiary of a qualified disability trust (see the Form 8615 instructions), distributions of investment income from the trust are treated as earned income and thus not subject to the kiddie tax rules.

Reporting child's unearned income on child's or parent's return. The kiddie tax computation is generally made on Form 8615, which must be attached to your child's return. However, if your child is under age 19 or a full-time student under age 24 and his or her only income is interest and dividends and other tests are met, you may elect on Form 8814 to include your child's unearned income on your own tax return, instead of computing the kiddie tax on Form 8615 *(24.4)*.

Kiddie tax on Form 8615 applies to investment income exceeding $2,500 floor. If your child files his or her own 2023 return, the "kiddie tax" computation on Form 8615 applies to the child's net unearned income. For purposes of this rule, net unearned income equals gross unearned income minus $2,500. Thus, the first $2,500 of unearned income is exempt from the kiddie tax. Unearned income exceeding $2,500 is considered net unearned income subject to the kiddie tax.

Unearned income includes all taxable income that is not earned income (compensation for personal services). Include taxable interest income (but not tax-exempt interest), dividends, capital gain distributions and capital gains on the sale of property, royalties, rents, and taxable pension payments. Payments from a trust are generally included to the extent of distributable net income, but, as noted earlier, there is an exception for distributions from qualified disability trusts, which are treated as earned income and thus not subject to the kiddie tax. Income in custodial accounts is treated as the child's income and is subject to the kiddie tax computation. Capital losses first offset capital gains, and any excess loss offsets up to $3,000 of other investment income.

Unearned income on all of your child's property must be considered, even if the property was a gift from you or someone else, or if the property was produced from your child's wages, such as a bank account into which the wages were deposited. The wages themselves, or self-employment earnings, are not considered.

24.3 Computing "Kiddie Tax" on Child's Return

If your child is subject to the "kiddie tax" (24.2) for 2023, your child's regular income tax liability is computed on Form 8615, which is attached to his or her return, unless you make the parent's election to report the child's dividends and interest income on your own return (24.4).

Before you can complete Form 8615 (see sample below) for your child, you have to figure your own taxable income and regular tax on Form 1040 (or 1040-SR).

In general, your child's unearned income over the $2,500 floor (24.2) is taxed at your marginal tax rate on Form 8615. In Part II of Form 8615, the excess over the $2,500 floor is added to your own taxable income, and you figure the tax on the combined amount based on your filing status. If the combined amount includes net capital gain or qualified dividends, the tax is figured on the Qualified Dividends and Capital Gain Tax Worksheet, or if applicable, the Schedule D Tax Worksheet (5.3). The "kiddie tax" for your child is the excess of (1) the tax figured on your combined incomes, over (2) your separate tax liability (from your Form 1040 or 1040-SR). In Part III of Form 8615, you add the kiddie tax figured in Part II to the child's tax on the part of his or her taxable income that is not subject to the kiddie tax; the total is entered on the child's Form 1040 as his or her tax liability.

If you have more than one child with unearned income over the $2,500 floor, you must figure the kiddie tax for each child on a separate Form 8615. On each Form 8615, the excess unearned income for all of the children is combined with your own taxable income. Follow the steps of Form 8615 to figure the kiddie tax allocable to each of the children.

Do parents file jointly or separately? If you and your spouse file a joint return, the taxable income from the joint return is used on Form 8615 to figure the kiddie tax for your child or children. If you are married filing separately, the larger of your taxable incomes is used on Form 8615. If you are divorced or separated, the taxable income of the parent with custody of the child for most of the year is generally used; see the Form 8615 instructions for details.

Estimating the kiddie tax in case of filing delay. If the child's taxable income, net unearned income, or filing status for 2023 is not known by the filing due date of April 15, 2024, or your own taxable income or filing status is unknown by the due date, reasonable estimates may be used on a timely filed Form 8615. When the correct details become available, an amended return for the child should be filed on Form 1040-X.

Instead of estimating the kiddie tax, you may file Form 4868 to get a six-month extension (46.3) for the child's return on which the kiddie tax is included. However, interest will be charged on any tax due that was not paid by the original filing date, and late payment penalties may also apply (46.3).

24.4 Parent's Election To Report Child's Dividends and Interest

Instead of filing a separate return for your child (24.3) whose income is subject to the "kiddie tax," you may elect on Form 8814 to report your child's income and compute the kiddie tax on your own 2023 return if all of the following tests are met:

- The child was under age 19, or under age 24 if a full-time student (24.2) at the end of 2023;
- The child's only 2023 income is from interest and dividends (including mutual fund capital gain distributions and Alaska Permanent Fund dividends);
- The total interest, dividends, and capital gain distributions are over $1,250 but less than $11,500;
- Estimated tax payments were not made in the child's name and Social Security number for 2023 and there was no overpayment from the child's 2022 return applied to his or her 2023 estimated tax; and
- The child was not subject to 2023 backup withholding.

On Form 8814, you determine the portion of the child's qualified dividends and capital gain distributions that you report on your own return, where they are eligible for the preferential rates *(5.3)* for qualified dividends/net capital gains. You report the balance of the child's investment income over $2,500 as "other income" on Line 8z of Schedule 1 (Form 1040 or 1040-SR). You also figure an additional tax equal to the smaller of $125 or 10% of your child's income over $1,250, which is included in the regular income tax liability you enter on Line 16 of your Form 1040 or 1040-SR.

If the parents are married filing separately, or are divorced, separated, or living apart for the last six months of the year, the custodial parent (with whom child lived with most of the year) is the parent who may make the election on Form 8814. If unmarried parents lived together with the child, the parent with the higher taxable income may make the election.

The election can have major disadvantages. For most taxpayers, the only advantage in making the election is to skip the paperwork involved in preparing a return in the child's name or returns in the children's names. This could save you money in the form of reduced tax preparation costs. In some cases, the increase in your income could allow you to deduct more charitable contributions *(14.17)*. Reporting your child's interest or dividends increases your net investment income, which may allow you to claim a larger deduction for investment interest *(15.10)*, but if you are close to or already over the threshold for the additional 3.8% tax on net investment income *(28.3)*, making the election could subject you to or increase your liability for the 3.8% tax.

There is a distinct disadvantage to the election if your child's investment income consists of qualified dividends or capital gain distributions. With the election, there is a 10% tax on the child's income between $1,250 and $2,500 (the income not subject to kiddie tax), whereas if a separate return is filed for the child, it is highly likely that the qualified dividends and capital gain distributions will escape tax entirely under the zero percent rate *(5.3, 24.3)*.

If you elect to report the child's interest and dividends on your own return, you may not claim any deductions that your child would have been able to claim on his or her own return such as the additional standard deduction for blindness, itemized deductions such as charitable donations or investment interest, or the above-the-line deduction for the penalty on premature withdrawals from a savings account.

Finally, including the child's investment income as your own may create these disadvantages by increasing your AGI:

- Make it more difficult to deduct medical deductions because of the AGI floor *(17.1)*.
- Reduce tax credits subject to income limits, such as the child tax credit *(25.2)*, the dependent care credit *(25.5)*, or the education tax credits *(33.7)*.
- Limit a deduction for IRA contributions under the phaseout rules *(8.4)*.
- Limit a deduction for student loan interest *(33.13)*.
- Limit your ability to claim the special $25,000 rental loss allowance under the passive activity rules *(10.2)*.
- Increase local and state tax liability.
- As noted earlier, subject you to or increase your liability for the additional 3.8% tax on net investment income *(28.3)*.
- Increase liability for the alternative minimum tax. In figuring whether you owe alternative minimum tax (AMT) on Form 6251, you must include, as a tax preference item, interest income your child receives from specified private activity bonds *(23.3)*; *see* the Form 6251 instructions.
- Subject you to an estimated tax penalty *(27.1)*. If you did not account for the child's income when planning your 2023 withholdings or estimated tax installments, you could face an estimated tax penalty if you make the election on Form 8814 for 2023. If you plan to report your child's income on your 2024 return, provide for the tax in your estimated tax payments or withholdings during 2024.

Caution

Reporting Child's Income on Your Return

Including the child's income on your return could be disadvantageous not only by subjecting the income to a higher tax rate (than on the child's own return), but also by making it more difficult for you to claim certain deductions and tax credits and raising your state and local taxes.

Sample Form 8615—Tax for Certain Children Who Have Unearned Income

Form **8615**

Department of the Treasury
Internal Revenue Service

Tax for Certain Children Who Have Unearned Income

Attach only to the child's Form 1040 or 1040-NR.
Go to *www.irs.gov/Form8615* for instructions and the latest information.

OMB No. 1545-0074

2023

Attachment
Sequence No. **33**

Child's name shown on return

Child's social security number

A Parent's name (first, initial, and last). **Caution:** See instructions before completing.

B Parent's social security number

C Parent's filing status (check one):
☐ Single   ☐ Married filing jointly   ☐ Married filing separately   ☐ Head of household   ☐ Qualifying surviving spouse

Part I   Child's Net Unearned Income

1	Enter the child's unearned income. See instructions	**1**	
2	If the child **did not** itemize deductions on **Schedule A** (Form 1040) or **Schedule A** (Form 1040-NR), enter $2,500. Otherwise, see instructions	**2**	
3	Subtract line 2 from line 1. If zero or less, **stop**; do not complete the rest of this form but **do** attach it to the child's return	**3**	
4	Enter the child's **taxable income** from Form 1040 or 1040-NR, line 15. If the child files Form 2555, see the instructions	**4**	
5	Enter the **smaller** of line 3 or line 4. If zero, **stop**; do not complete the rest of this form but **do** attach it to the child's return	**5**	

Part II   Tentative Tax Based on the Tax Rate of the Parent

6	Enter the parent's **taxable income** from Form 1040 or 1040-NR, line 15. If zero or less, enter -0-. If the parent files Form 2555, see the instructions	**6**	
7	Enter the total, if any, from Forms 8615, line 5, of **all other** children of the parent named above. **Do not** include the amount from line 5 above	**7**	
8	Add lines 5, 6, and 7. See instructions	**8**	
9	Enter the tax on the amount on line 8 based on the **parent's** filing status above. See instructions. If the Qualified Dividends and Capital Gain Tax Worksheet, Schedule D Tax Worksheet, or Schedule J (Form 1040) is used to figure the tax, check here ☐	**9**	
10	Enter the parent's tax from Form 1040 or 1040-NR, line 16, minus any alternative minimum tax. **Do not** include any tax from **Form 4972** or **Form 8814**, or any tax from the recapture of an education credit. If the parent files Form 2555, see the instructions. If the Qualified Dividends and Capital Gain Tax Worksheet, Schedule D Tax Worksheet, or Schedule J (Form 1040) was used to figure the tax, check here ☐	**10**	
11	Subtract line 10 from line 9 and enter the result. If line 7 is blank, also enter this amount on line 13 and go to **Part III**	**11**	
12a	Add lines 5 and 7 ... **12a**		
b	Divide line 5 by line 12a. Enter the result as a decimal (rounded to at least three places)	**12b**	× .
13	Multiply line 11 by line 12b	**13**	

Part III   Child's Tax—If lines 4 and 5 above are the same, enter -0- on line 15 and go to line 16.

14	Subtract line 5 from line 4 ... **14**		
15	Enter the tax on the amount on line 14 based on the **child's** filing status. See instructions. If the Qualified Dividends and Capital Gain Tax Worksheet, Schedule D Tax Worksheet, or Schedule J (Form 1040) is used to figure the tax, check here ☐	**15**	
16	Add lines 13 and 15	**16**	
17	Enter the tax on the amount on line 4 based on the **child's** filing status. See instructions. If the Qualified Dividends and Capital Gain Tax Worksheet, Schedule D Tax Worksheet, or Schedule J (Form 1040) is used to figure the tax, check here ☐	**17**	
18	Enter the **larger** of line 16 or line 17 here and on the **child's** Form 1040 or 1040-NR, line 16. If the child files Form 2555, see the instructions	**18**	

For Paperwork Reduction Act Notice, see your tax return instructions.   Cat. No. 64113U   Form **8615** (2023)

CHAPTER 25

Personal Tax Credits Reduce Your Tax Liability

In this chapter you will find discussions of the child tax credit, dependent care credit, Earned Income Credit (EIC), adoption credit, retirement savings credit, mortgage interest credit, credit for plug-in electric vehicles, and the premium tax credit, the residential energy credits. Education tax credits are discussed in *Chapter 33*.

The child tax credit is $2,000 for each qualifying dependent child under age 17. There is also a $500 credit for other dependents. Both credits are subject to the same phaseout rule *(25.3, 25.4)*. If the child tax credit exceeds your tax liability, you may be entitled to a refundable credit called the "additional child tax credit" *(25.3)*.

Depending on your income, the child and dependent care credit is 20% to 35% of up to $3,000 of care expenses for one dependent and up to $6,000 of expenses for two or more dependents. If your adjusted gross income exceeds $43,000, the maximum credit is $600 for one dependent and $1,200 for two or more dependents *(25.5)*.

The Earned Income Credit (EIC) is provided to low-income workers who support children, and a limited credit is allowed to certain workers without qualifying children *(25.6)*.

An adoption credit of up to $15,950 may be claimed on your 2023 return for costs of adopting a child under the age of 18 or a disabled person incapable of self-care *(25.8)*.

The premium tax credit applies to taxpayers with income within specified limits who obtain health coverage through a government Marketplace (also called exchange). Taxpayers who received an advance of the credit during 2023 to help pay their premiums must reconcile, on Form 8962, the advanced amount with the actual credit allowed for the year *(25.13)*.

There are credits for making green energy improvements to your home *(25.16)* and for buying a "clean" vehicle *(25.17)*.

25.1 Overview of Personal Tax Credits

After you determine your regular tax liability using the tax table *(22.2)*, Tax Computation Worksheet *(22.3)*, or capital gain worksheets *(22.4)*, and your AMT liability if any *(23.1)*, you may be able to reduce that liability by one or more tax credits. Most tax credits are nonrefundable, meaning that they are limited by your tax liability. All nonrefundable personal credits, including the child tax credit, dependent care credit, education credits, saver's credit and the adoption credit, may be claimed to the full extent of regular tax liability plus alternative minimum tax (AMT) liability.

Eligibility rules and credit limitations for many of the personal credits are discussed in this chapter, while some are discussed in other chapters as shown below. Business tax credits are in *Chapter 40*.

Child tax credit and additional child tax credit *(25.2–25.3)*.

Credit for other dependents *(25.4)*

Child and dependent care credit *(25.5–25.6)*.

Earned income credit *(25.7–25.8)*.

Adoption credit *(25.9–25.10)*.

Qualified retirement savings contributions credit *(25.11–25.12)*.

Premium tax credit *(25.13)*.

Mortgage interest credit *(25.14)*.

Residential energy tax credits *(25.15)*.

Plug-in electric ("clean") vehicle credit *(25.16)*.

Repayment of the first-time homebuyer credit *(25.17)*.

Education credits (American opportunity and lifetime learning credits) *(33.7–33.9)*.

Credit for elderly or disabled *(34.7–34.9)*.

Foreign tax credit *(36.13)*.

Prior-year AMT credit *(23.4)*.

Credit for excess Social Security or Railroad Retirement withholdings *(26.8)*.

Credit for tax on mutual fund undistributed capital gain *(32.6)*.

25.2 Child Tax Credit for Children Under Age 17

For 2023, the child tax credit is $2,000 per qualifying child under the age of 17 at the end of the year (*see* "qualifying child" below) for those with modified adjusted gross income below set limits. The credit begins to phase out when modified adjusted gross income (MAGI) exceeds $400,000 if married filing jointly, or $200,000 for all others *(25.3)*.

To figure the exact amount of your child tax credit on your 2023 return, you must complete Schedule 8812 (Form 1040 or 1040-SR). On Schedule 8812, you determine if the potential credit ($2,000 × number of qualifying children) is limited by the phaseout rule *(25.3)*. Whether or not the phaseout applies, the tentative credit (either full credit or reduced amount after phaseout) is compared with your tax liability (regular tax plus AMT minus specified credits), and the smaller amount is the allowable child tax credit. However, if your child tax credit is limited to your tax liability, part or all of the excess credit may be refundable as an additional credit (ACTC) if your earned income exceeds $2,500 or you have three or more children *(25.3)*.

If you are eligible for the credit for other dependents *(25.4)* as well as for the child tax credit, both credits are combined on Schedule 8812 and the same phaseout rule and liability limitation applies to both credits.

Qualifying child. You can claim the child tax credit (and, if applicable, the ACTC) for a child who is under age 17 at the end of 2023 if the child is your "qualifying child" under the rules for dependents *(21.2 and 21.3)*, and you are not disqualified from claiming that child as your dependent (*see* "Additional tests for treating someone as your dependent") *(21.2)*. Note that the age test for the child tax credit is lower than the age test under the

Filing Tip

Credits Reported on Schedule 3

While some personal tax credits are entered directly on Form 1040 or 1040-SR, some credits are first entered on Schedule 3 of Form 1040 or 1040-SR.

Law Alert

Valid SSN for Child Needed by Due Date of Return

You (and your spouse if filing jointly) must have a valid Social Security number (SSN) by the due date for filing your 2023 return (plus extensions if any) to claim the child tax credit or the additional child tax credit (ACTC) *(25.3)* for 2023. If you are not eligible for a SSN, you must have an ITIN by the return due date (with extensions). If the SSN or ITIN has not been issued by the due date (with extensions), you cannot claim the child tax credit or the ACTC on your original return, or on an amended return if you get the number later.

In addition, each qualifying child must have a SSN (that is valid for employment) issued before the due date of your return (with extensions). If the required SSN is not obtained by the due date (with extensions), you cannot claim the child tax credit or ACTC for that child, either on your original return, or on an amended return if you get the number later. However, if a qualifying child does not have the required SSN by your filing due date, you may be able to treat that child as your dependent for purposes of claiming the credit for other dependents *(25.4)*.

general definition of qualifying child *(21.2 and 21.3)*. If the child is age 17 or older at the end of 2023, you cannot claim the child tax credit (or ACTC) for that child, even if he or she is your qualifying child for other purposes *(21.2)*, such as to claim head of household status or the itemized deduction for medical expenses of dependents.

The qualifying child rules require the child to live with you for over half the year and not provide over half of his or her own support *(21.2)*. The child may be your child, stepchild, grandchild, great-grandchild, brother, sister, stepbrother, stepsister, half-brother or -sister, or the descendant of any of these. An adopted child qualifies for a 2023 credit if placed with you by an authorized agency for legal adoption, even if the adoption is not final by the end of 2023. A foster child placed with you by a court or an authorized agency qualifies.

For purposes of the child tax credit and the ACTC *(25.3)*, the child must be a U.S. citizen, U.S. resident alien *(1.18)*, or U.S. national. An adopted child who would not otherwise meet this test is treated as a U.S. citizen if you are a U.S. citizen or national and he or she lived with you all year.

The child must have a Social Security number (SSN) that was issued before the due date of your return (including extensions). The SSN must be valid for employment; this test is automatically met if the child was a U.S. citizen when receiving the SSN. If the child is a qualifying child but lacks the required SSN, you cannot claim the child tax credit or the additional child tax credit (ACTC) for that child, but you may be able to claim the credit for other dependents for the child *(25.4)*.

Did the IRS reduce or deny your 2020, 2021, or 2022 credit? If the IRS reduced or disallowed your 2022 child tax credit or additional child tax credit *(25.3)* for any reason other than a math or clerical error on your part, you must complete and attach Form 8862 to your 2023 return to document your eligibility to claim a credit for 2023. If your 2020 or 2021 credit was reduced or disallowed, file Form 8862 with your 2023 return unless you filed it with your 2022 return and the IRS allowed your 2022 credit.

If the child tax credit or ACTC is disallowed because you recklessly or intentionally disregarded the rules, you will not be allowed to claim the credit for the next two years, and if you fraudulently claimed it, the disallowance period increases to 10 years.

25.3 Figuring the Child Tax Credit and Additional Child Tax Credit

You use Schedule 8812 (Form 1040 or 1040-SR to figure the child tax credit and if applicable, the additional child tax credit for 2023.

Phaseout formula for child tax credit. On Part I of Schedule 8812, the $2,000 per qualifying child credit for 2023 is phased out if your modified adjusted gross income (MAGI) exceeds the phaseout threshold, which is:

- $200,000 if your filing status is single, head of household, qualifying widow/ widower, or married filing separately, or
- $400,000 if you are married filing jointly

The maximum credit of $2,000 per qualifying child is reduced by 5%, or $50 for each $1,000 (or fraction of $1,000) that your MAGI exceeds the phaseout threshold. In most cases, MAGI is the same as the AGI reported on Line 11 of Form 1040 or 1040-SR. However, if you claim the foreign earned income exclusion, foreign housing exclusion or deduction, or possession exclusion for American Samoa residents, these amounts must be added back to AGI to get MAGI for credit purposes.

Since the phaseout percentage is 5%, one $2,000 credit is generally completely phased out when MAGI exceeds the phaseout threshold by $40,000 ($2,000 credit/.05 = $40,000 phaseout range). However, because of the "round up" rule for excess amounts that are not a multiple of $1,000, any excess of more than $39,000 but less than $40,000 ($39,001 through $39,999) will be rounded up to $40,000 and the $2,000 credit will be completely phased out. Thus, for a parent who is single, the phaseout of one $2,000 credit will be complete when MAGI is $239,001 or more. For married persons filing jointly, the phaseout of one $2,000 credit will be complete when MAGI is $439,001 or more.

If there are two qualifying children, both $2,000 credits ($4,000 total) are completely phased out when MAGI exceeds the phaseout threshold by $80,000 (2 × $40,000), but because of the "round up" rule, an excess of $79,001 through $79,999 is treated the same as an excess of $80,000. Thus, if you are married filing jointly with two qualifying children, the credits for both of them are completely phased out when MAGI is $479,001 or more.

If your MAGI exceeds your phaseout threshold, follow the steps of Schedule 8812 to figure how much of your credit is phased out. *See* Examples 2 and 3 below.

After applying the phaseout rule, you must apply the liability limitation discussed next.

Liability limitation. On Part I of Schedule 8812, the child tax credit is limited to your tax liability where the liability is less than the otherwise allowable credit (either the full credit or reduced credit if part is phased out). Your tax liability is the regular tax plus alternative minimum tax and repayment of excess advance payment of the premium tax credit, if any, reduced on the worksheet by certain other credits that you claim. If your liability equals or exceeds the otherwise allowable credit, the liability limit does not reduce the allowable credit. If your child tax credit is limited to your tax liability, you may be able to claim the "additional child tax credit" (ACTC), which is refundable up to a limit of $1,600 per qualifying child; *see* below.

The allowable child tax credit from Part I of Schedule 8812 is entered on Line 19 of Form 1040 or 1040-SR.

EXAMPLES—
Assume that MAGI is the same as the taxpayer's AGI in these Examples

1. Carl and Abby's only children, twin daughters, were born in 2023. Carl and Abby file a joint return for 2023. Their MAGI is $88,000, and they claim the standard deduction. Their MAGI is well below the $400,000 phaseout threshold for the child tax credit *(25.3)*. They may claim the full child tax credit of $4,000 ($2,000 per child), as the $4,000 credit does not exceed their tax liability.

2. Same as Example 1, except that Carl and Abby's MAGI for 2023 is $438,650. Their potential child tax credit of $4,000 is partially phased out since MAGI exceeds the $400,000 phaseout threshold. The excess AGI of $38,650 ($438,650 – $400,000) is rounded up to $39,000 (next multiple of $1,000) and that is multiplied by 5% (the phaseout percentage), resulting in a phaseout of $1,950 ($39,000 × 5%). The non-phased portion of the credit is $2,050 ($4,000 – $1,950), and this is Carl and Abby's allowable child tax credit for 2023, as $2,050 is much lower than their tax liability.

3. Jane is single and has two dependent children, ages six and three. She files her 2023 return as head of household and claims the standard deduction. Her 2023 MAGI is $217,500. Because her AGI exceeds the $200,000 phaseout threshold for a head of household, her child tax credit for 2023 is reduced. The excess MAGI of $17,500 is rounded up to $18,000 (next multiple of $1,000) and that is multiplied by the phaseout percentage of 5%, resulting in a $900 phaseout ($18,000 × 5%). Jane may claim a child tax credit of $3,100 ($4,000 – $900) on her 2023 return, as the $3,100 credit is well below her tax liability.

The additional child tax credit (ACTC) on Schedule 8812. If the full amount of the child tax credit cannot be claimed on Part I of Schedule 8812, you may be able to obtain a refund for the balance in the form of the additional child tax credit (ACTC). For 2023, the child tax credit is refundable to the extent of 15% of your taxable earned income plus tax-free combat pay *(35.4)* in excess of $2,500, but the refundable amount cannot exceed $1,600 per qualifying child. There is an alternative formula for figuring the ACTC if you have three or more qualifying children and you paid Social Security and Medicare taxes that exceed your Earned Income Credit, if any. Follow the IRS instructions to Schedule 8812 for figuring the ACTC. Any portion of the credit that is phased out as discussed above is "lost" and is not eligible for the ACTC on Schedule 8812. The allowable ACTC from Schedule 8812 is entered on Line 28 of Form 1040 or 1040-SR.

Law Alert

ACTC Is a Refundable Credit

For 2023, the refundable portion of the child tax credit (called the "Additional Child Tax Credit", or ACTC, on Schedule 8812) is 15% of taxable earned income in excess of $2,500, but no more than $1,600 per qualifying child. Combat pay that is otherwise excluded from income *(35.4)* is treated as taxable earned income for purposes of figuring the refundable amount.

The ACTC is not allowed if you claim the exclusion for foreign earned income *(36.1)* or employer-financed foreign housing costs *(36.4)*, or if self-employed, the deduction for foreign housing costs *(36.4)*.

If the ACTC is claimed on a return filed at the very beginning of the tax filing season in late January, your anticipated refund may be delayed. The IRS cannot issue a refund before February 15 if the return includes the AOTC. The same rule applies to the Earned Income Credit *(25.6)*. The entire refund must be withheld until February 15 and not just the portion of the refund attributable to the refundable child tax credit. The delay in issuing these very early refund claims is intended to give the IRS some extra time to review the returns and reduce improper refund payments.

25.4 Credit for Other Dependents

You generally can claim a $500 nonrefundable credit for each eligible dependent for whom the child tax credit *(25.2)* cannot be claimed. The credit for "other" dependents is figured together with the child tax credit on Schedule 8812.

You can claim the credit for each of the following dependents:

1. Your qualifying relative (meeting the tests) *(21.4)*, provided he or she is a U.S. citizen, U.S. national, or U.S. resident alien, and has a Social Security number (SSN), an ITIN (if a resident alien not eligible for a SSN), or adoption taxpayer identification number (ATIN) that is issued on or before the due date of your 2023 return (including extensions). If you apply for an ITIN or ATIN by the return due date (with extensions), the number is considered issued by the due date. Note that for other tax purposes, such as claiming head of household status, a qualifying relative can be a resident of Canada or Mexico, but to claim the credit for other dependents, the qualifying relative must be a U.S. citizen, U.S. national, or U.S. resident alien.

2. Your qualifying child for whom the child tax credit cannot be claimed (*see* "Qualifying child") *(25.2)* because the child is (a) age 17 or older at the end of 2023 or (b) under age 17 at the end of 2023 but did not have a SSN valid for employment issued before the due date of your 2023 return (including extensions). In either case, the child must be a U.S. citizen, U.S. national, or U.S. resident alien, and must have a SSN, ITIN, or ATIN as discussed in 1 above.

For each of the above dependents, figure your credit on Part I of Schedule 8812. The $500 credit per qualifying dependent may be reduced under the same phaseout rule and liability limitation discussed above for the child tax credit *(25.3)*. If you can claim both credits, the computation of both is combined on Schedule 8812. The allowable credit for other dependents is entered on Line 19 of Form 1040 or 1040-SR (together with the child tax credit if any).

25.5 Qualifying for the Child and Dependent Care Credit

For 2023, if you hired someone to care for your children under age 13 or other dependents while you work, you may qualify for a tax credit for the expenses. The credit is generally available to the extent you have earnings from employment. You may claim the credit even if you work part time. You may claim the credit if you work from home and pay someone to care for your child while you are there. Your employer may have a plan qualifying for tax-free child care and, if you are covered, you may be unable to claim a tax credit *(25.6)*.

Credit requirements. To qualify for the child and dependent care credit, you must:

1. Incur qualifying expenses to care for a qualifying person *(see below)*, so that you can work. Expenses that you incur while looking for work qualify for the credit, but you must have earnings for the year; *see* Test 2 below. Qualifying expenses must be reduced by tax-free reimbursements received from your employer. Qualifying care expenses and dollar limits are discussed in *25.6*.

2. Have earned income for the year. If married, both you and your spouse generally must work, but there is an exception if one of you is a full-time student or is incapacitated; *see 25.6* for the exception details ("Earned income rule for married couples").

3. File jointly if you are married, unless you are separated under the rules discussed below.

4. Hire a care provider other than a person you may claim as your dependent *(21.1)*. Thus, if you pay your mother to care for your child and you cannot claim your mother as a dependent, such payments qualify for the credit, but if you can claim her as your dependent you cannot claim the credit. In addition, no credit may be claimed for payments made to (1) your child who is under 19 years of age at the close of the tax year, whether or not you may claim the child as a dependent, (2) your spouse, or (3) the other parent (who is not your spouse) of your child under age 13 whom you are claiming as your qualifying person.

5. Report on your tax return the name, address, and taxpayer identification number (Social Security number for individuals) of the child-care provider; *see* below.

Where to claim the credit. The credit is claimed on Form 2441 and entered on line 2 of Schedule 3 (Form 1040 or 1040-SR). The size of the credit depends on the amount of your care expenses, number of dependents, and income. Depending on your adjusted gross income, the credit is 20% to 35% of up to $3,000 of care expenses for one dependent and up to $6,000 of expenses for two or more dependents. The minimum credit percentage of 20% applies if your adjusted gross income exceeds $43,000; there is no maximum income for the credit. *See Table 25-1 (25.6)*.

Identifying care provider on your return. On Form 2441, you must list the name, address, and taxpayer identification number of the person you paid to care for your dependent. If the care provider is an individual, his or her Social Security number is required. If the provider is a business, enter its employer identification number (EIN), but you do need to enter a taxpayer identification number if the care provider is a tax-exempt organization. Failure to list the correct name, address, and identifying number may result in a disallowance of the credit. To avoid this possibility, ask the provider to fill out Form W-10 or get the identifying information from a Social Security card, driver's license, or business letterhead or invoice. If a household employee has filled out Form W-4 for you, this may act as a backup record.

Withholding tax for a housekeeper. Where you employ help to care for your dependent in your home, you may be liable for FICA (Social Security) and FUTA (unemployment) taxes *(38.3)*.

Are you married but separated from your spouse? If you are married at the end of the year, you generally must file a joint return to claim the dependent care credit, but you are treated as unmarried and may claim the credit when you file as married filing separately, provided you meet all of the following tests:

1. You lived apart from your spouse during the last six months of the year;

2. Your home was the home of the qualifying person *(see below)* for more than half the year, and

3. You paid over half the cost of maintaining the household for the entire year.

If you satisfy these three tests, you do not have to take your spouse's income into account when applying the credit percentage shown at *25.6*.

If you are divorced or separated and are the custodial parent. If you are the custodial parent of your child who was under age 13 or physically or mentally incapable of caring for himself or herself, you may claim the credit even though you waived the right to claim your child as a dependent in favor of the noncustodial parent on Form 8332 (or equivalent) under the special rules for divorced or separated parents at *21.7*. You are the custodial parent if your child lived with you for more nights during the year than with his or her other parent. If your child stayed with each of you an equal number of nights, you are treated as the custodial parent if your adjusted gross income is higher than the other parent's adjusted gross income *(21.7)*. The noncustodial parent cannot treat the child as a qualifying person even though he or she claims the exemption under the special rules.

Caution

Nonrefundable Credit

The dependent care credit in 2023 is limited to your tax liability. In other words, if the credit amount exceeds the tax that you owe, you will not be given a refund of the difference.

Who is a Qualifying Person for Credit Purposes?

To claim the dependent care credit, you must incur employment-related expenses *(25.6)* for at least one of the following qualifying persons who lives with you more than half the year:

1. A dependent under the age of 13 who is your "qualifying child" under *21.3*. If you are divorced or separated, and you resided with the child for a longer time during the year than the other parent, you may be able to claim the credit even if the other parent is entitled to claim the child as a dependent; *see* above.

   If your child becomes age 13 during the year, take into account expenses incurred for his or her care prior to the 13th birthday. However, you do not prorate the $3,000 limitation on expenses *(25.6)*. For example, if your child had her 13th birthday on May 1, 2023, and you incurred $3,000 or more in care expenses between January 1 and April 30, the entire $3,000 qualifies for the 2023 credit.

2. Your spouse, if physically or mentally incapable of caring for him- or herself.

3. A dependent, regardless of age, who is physically or mentally incapable of caring for himself or herself. For example, he or she needs help to dress or to take care of personal hygiene or nutritional needs, or requires constant attention to avoid hurting him- or herself or others. Generally, you must be able to claim the person as a dependent, either as your qualifying child *(21.3)* or qualifying relative *(21.4)*, but even if the person cannot be claimed as your qualifying relative because he or she has gross income of $4,700 or more for 2023, you may still claim a credit for his or her care costs. Also, if you cannot treat a person as your dependent because he or she filed a joint return, or because you (or your spouse if you file jointly) can be claimed as a dependent by another taxpayer *(21.2)*, you can still claim the credit for care costs that otherwise qualify.

> **EXAMPLE**
>
> You live with your mother, who is physically incapable of caring for herself. You hire a practical nurse to care for her in the home while you are at work. Payments to the nurse qualify as care costs. However, if you placed her in a nursing home, the cost of the nursing home would not qualify as a dependent care cost, but a medical expense deduction may be available *(17.11)*.

25.6 Figuring the Child and Dependent Care Credit

In figuring the credit on Form 2441, you may take into account up to $3,000 of the following types of expenses when figuring the credit for one dependent, or up to $6,000 for two or more dependents. If you receive employer-financed dependent care, tax-free reimbursements reduce the $3,000 or $6,000 base.

1. Costs of caring for your qualifying child under age 13, incapacitated spouse, or incapacitated dependent (of any age) in your home *(25.5)*. If you pay FICA or FUTA taxes on your housekeeper's wages *(38.3)*, you may include your share of the tax (employer) as part of the wages when entering your qualifying expenses. Also include your housekeeper's share of FICA tax if you pay it. Note that these taxes may more than offset your allowable credit.

   The manner of care need not be the least expensive alternative. For example, where a grandparent resides with you and may provide adequate care for your child to enable you to work, the cost of hiring someone to care for the child is still eligible for the credit.

2. Ordinary domestic services in your home, such as laundry, cleaning, and cooking (but not payments to a gardener or chauffeur) that are partly for the care of the qualifying person. Expenses for the dependent's food, clothing, or entertainment do not qualify. Food costs for a housekeeper who eats in your home may be added to qualifying expenses. Extra expenses for a housekeeper's lodging (extra rent or utilities) also qualify.

3. Outside-the-home care costs for a child under age 13, as in a day-care center (must meet all state and local regulations and provide care services for over 6 persons), a day camp (including a specialty camp such as a computer or soccer camp), nursery school, or in the home of a babysitter. Outside-the-home care costs also qualify if incurred for a handicapped dependent, regardless of age, provided he or she regularly spends at least eight hours per day in your home. However, the cost

of schooling in kindergarten or higher does not qualify for the credit. Costs for sleep-away camp also do not qualify for the credit.

You may not take into account your transportation costs in taking your qualifying person to and from a care center, or your payment of a care provider's transportation to and from your home.

Limits on Eligible Expenses

In figuring the credit for 2023, you take into account qualifying expenses up to a limit of $3,000 for one qualifying person, or $6,000 for two or more qualifying persons. The $3,000 or $6,000 limit applies even if your actual expenses are much greater. Further, the $3,000 or $6,000 limit must be reduced by tax-free benefits received from an employer's dependent care plan, as discussed below. Finally, if your earned income is less than the $3,000 or $6,000 limit, your credit is figured on the lower income amount; *see* the earned income rule for married couples below.

Earned income rule for married couples. Generally, both spouses must work (wages, salary, or self-employment) at least part time to claim the credit, unless one is incapable of self-care or is a full-time student. If either you or your spouse earns less than the maximum $3,000 or $6,000 credit base, the base is limited to the smaller earned income. However, for each month you or your spouse is a full-time student or is disabled, that spouse is considered to have earned income of $250 if care expenses are incurred for one dependent, or $500 for two or more dependents, even if the spouse had no earnings or earnings under $250/$500 for the month. A full-time student is one who attends school full time during each of five calendar months during the year, whether or not the months are consecutive. A spouse who is incapable of self-care is considered disabled for purposes of the $250/$500 rule.

> ### EXAMPLES
>
> 1. John and Mary are married. In 2023, John earns $5,300. Mary earns $33,000. They incur care costs of $6,200 for their two children, ages 5 and 7. Their adjusted gross income including interest earnings is $38,575. As shown in *Table 25-1* below, the credit percentage for their adjusted gross income is 23%. The maximum $6,000 credit base (for two or more dependents) is limited to John's lower income of $5,300. They may claim a credit of $1,219 ($5,300 × 23%).
>
> 2. Same facts as in Example 1, except John was a full-time student for nine months and earned no income for the year. John is considered to have earned income of $500 for each month he was a full-time student since he and Mary had care costs for more than one qualifying child. The credit base is limited to $4,500 ($500 × 9 months). Their credit is $1,035 ($4,500 × 23%).

Employer-financed dependent care reduces credit base. Tax-free reimbursements under an employer's dependent care program *(3.5)* reduce the $3,000 or $6,000 credit base. For example, if you have one child and you receive a $1,500 reimbursement of child-care costs from your company's plan, the amount eligible for the tax credit is reduced to $1,500 ($3,000 – $1,500). A reimbursement of $3,000 or more would bar any credit. The $6,000 credit expense limit for two or more dependents is similarly reduced by dependent care benefits from your employer. On your Form W-2, your employer will report the amount of tax-free reimbursement *(3.4)*.

If your employer's plan allows you to fund a reimbursement account with salary-reduction contributions that are excluded from taxable pay *(3.14)*, reimbursements from the account are considered employer-financed payments that reduce the $3,000 or $6,000 credit base. In deciding whether to make salary reduction contributions, you should determine whether the tax-free salary reduction will provide a larger tax savings than that provided by the credit. You may find that the salary reduction provides the larger tax savings, taking into consideration not only the decrease in federal income tax, but also the Social Security tax and state and local taxes avoided by using the salary reduction. Further, by lowering your adjusted gross income, a salary reduction may enable you to claim a larger IRA deduction if you are subject to the deduction phaseout rule *(8.4)*.

Filing Tip

Day-Care Center or Nursery School

The amount you pay to a day-care center or nursery school for a dependent child under age 13 is eligible for the credit, even if it covers such incidental benefits as lunch. However, tuition for a child in kindergarten or higher is not taken into account. If the dependent is not your child, costs for care outside the home qualify only if the dependent regularly spends at least eight hours per day in your home. Up to $3,000 a year of outside-the-home care expenses may be taken into account in figuring the credit for one dependent, and up to $6,000 for two or more.

Filing Instruction

Credit Limited if One Spouse Is a Student or Disabled

If one spouse works and the other is a full-time student and has no earned income for the year, the student-spouse is considered to have earned income of $250 ($500 if caring for more than one qualified person) for each month he or she is a student. Their credit base is limited to the deemed income amount for the student, assuming that is less than the working spouse's earnings. The same $250/$500 rule applies for each month one of the spouses is incapable of self-care.

Filing Tip

Employer Reimbursements Reduce Credit

Expenses qualifying for the dependent care credit are reduced by any tax-free reimbursements under a qualified employer dependent care program. That is, the reimbursements reduce the expense limit of $3,000 for one dependent, or the $6,000 expense limit for two or more qualifying dependents. Your employer will report reimbursements in Box 10 of your Form W-2. On Form 2441, you figure the tax-free portion of the reimbursement and any reduction to the credit expense base.

Filing Tip

Care Costs Qualifying as Medical Expenses

Care costs, such as a nurse's wages, may also qualify as medical expenses, but you may not claim both the dependent care credit and the medical expense deduction. If you use the expenses to figure the credit and your care costs exceed the amount allowed as dependent care costs, the excess, to the extent it qualifies as a medical expense *(17.12)*, may be added to other deductible medical costs.

How to treat prepayments and payments of prior year expenses. Your credit for 2023 generally must be based on payments you made in 2023 for qualifying care services provided in 2023. There is an exception if in 2022 you prepaid for 2023 qualifying services; claim the 2022 prepayment as a qualifying expense paid in 2023 when you figure your 2023 credit on Form 2441.

If you paid for 2022 services in 2023, you may be able to claim an additional credit on your 2023 return, but only in limited circumstances. Specifically, payments made in 2023 for 2022 services may be eligible for an additional credit on your 2023 return but only if you did not use up the expense limit that applied for the 2022 credit. Follow the instructions for Form 2441 to figure the additional credit.

If in 2023 you prepaid for 2024 services, you must allocate your payment. Only 2023 payments for 2023 services should be counted toward the $3,000 or $6,000 limit when figuring your 2023 credit; the prepayment for 2024 services will count as a 2024 expense in figuring the credit for 2024.

Allocating expenses when employed less than an entire year. If your dependent care expenses covered a period in which you worked or looked for work only part of the time, you must allocate the expenses on a daily basis to determine the work-related portion. However, if you were away on vacation or missed work due to illness for a short period, this is treated as a temporary absence from work and the expenses incurred during the absence qualify for the credit. The IRS considers an absence from work of two weeks or less as temporary; an absence of more than two weeks may be temporary depending on the facts and circumstances.

> **EXAMPLE**
>
> For the year, you are employed or look for work for only two months and 10 days. Monthly care expenses are $300. Eligible care expenses amount to $700 ($300 × 2 months, plus 1/3 of $300).

Allocation if expenses cover noncare services. If a portion of expenses is for other than dependent care or household services, only the portion allocable to dependent care or household services qualifies. No allocation is required if the non–dependent care services are minimal.

> **EXAMPLES**
>
> 1. A person accepts a full-time position and sends his 12-year-old child to boarding school. The expenses paid to the school must be allocated. The part representing care of the child qualifies; the part representing tuition does not.
> 2. A full-time housekeeper is hired to care for two children, ages 9 and 12. The housekeeper also drives the mother to and from work each day. The driving takes no longer than 30 minutes. No allocation is required because the non–dependent care driving services are minimal.

Credit percentage

Depending on your adjusted gross income (AGI), a credit percentage of 20% to 35% applies to your expenses up to the $3,000 (one dependent) or $6,000 (two or more dependents) limit. The maximum credit is 35% for families with AGI of $15,000 or less. The 35% maximum credit percentage is reduced by 1% for each $2,000 of AGI or fraction of $2,000 over $15,000, but not below 20%. The minimum credit percentage of 20% applies where AGI exceeds $43,000, regardless of how high AGI is.

The dependent care credit is nonrefundable. It is limited to your tax liability; follow the IRS instructions.

> **EXAMPLES**
>
> 1. You pay $6,500 in 2023 to a neighbor to care for your two children while you work. Your adjusted gross income is $34,824. The credit percentage of 25% is applied to the maximum expense limit of $6,000, giving you a credit of $1,500.

2. Same facts as in Example 1, except you receive a tax-free reimbursement of $2,500 from your employer's plan. The reimbursement reduces the $6,000 expense limit to $3,500 ($6,000 − $2,500). Your credit is $875 (25% of $3,500). If the tax-free reimbursement was $5,000 ($5,000 is the maximum allowable exclusion; *see 3.5*), the credit would be $250 (25% × $1,000 ($6,000 − $5,000)).

Table 25-1   Allowable Dependent Care Credit*

Adjusted gross income	Credit percentage	Maximum credit for one dependent*	Maximum credit for two or more dependents*
$15,000 or less	35%	$1,050	$2,100
15,001–17,000	34	1,020	2,040
17,001–19,000	33	990	1,980
19,001–21,000	32	960	1,920
21,001–23,000	31	930	1,860
23,001–25,000	30	900	1,800
25,001–27,000	29	870	1,740
27,001–29,000	28	840	1,680
29,001–31,000	27	810	1,620
31,001–33,000	26	780	1,560
33,001–35,000	25	750	1,500
35,001–37,000	24	720	1,440
37,001–39,000	23	690	1,380
39,001–41,000	22	660	1,320
41,001–43,000	21	630	1,260
43,001 and over	20	600	1,200

*Maximum credit assumes qualifying expenses are at least $3,000 for one dependent, or $6,000 for two or more dependents. If qualifying expenses are less than the $3,000/$6,000 maximum, your credit is the credit percentage multiplied by the expenses.

25.7   Qualifying Tests for EIC

The Earned Income Credit (EIC) is generally claimed by workers with qualifying children who meet the tests below, but in limited cases the credit is allowed to childless workers. Taxpayers with three or more qualifying children get a higher credit rate than taxpayers with fewer children. Also, a more favorable phaseout range is allowed for married couples filing jointly. Married persons may be treated as unmarried for purposes of claiming the Earned Income Credit if a qualifying child lives with them for more than half the year and they (1) live apart from their spouse for the last six months of the year or (2) have a support decree, instrument, or separation agreement and are not living with their spouse by the end of the year.

For 2023, the maximum EIC is $3,995 if you have one qualifying child, $6,604 if you have two qualifying children, $7,430 if you have three or more qualifying children, and $600 if you do not have a qualifying child. However, the maximum credit is subject to a phaseout based on income *(25.8)*. The allowable credit is "refundable," meaning that you will receive a refund from the IRS if the credit exceeds your tax liability.

Earliest refund claims delayed until February 15. Taxpayers who claim the Earned Income Credit and file their returns as soon as the tax filing season begins in January may face a slight delay in getting a refund. The IRS cannot issue a refund before February 15 if the return includes the Earned Income Credit. The same rule applies to returns claiming the refundable child tax credit *(25.3)*. The entire refund must be withheld until February 15 and not just the portion of the refund attributable to the Earned Income Credit or the refundable child tax credit. The delay in issuing these very early refund claims is intended to give the IRS some extra time to review the returns and reduce improper refund payments.

Claiming the EIC for 2023 if You Have One or More Qualifying Children

You may be eligible to claim the EIC on a 2023 return if you:

- Are single, head of household, or a qualifying widow/widower with earned income, such as wages and self-employment earnings, and also adjusted gross income (AGI), under $46,560 if you have one qualifying child, $52,918 if you have two qualifying children, $56,838 if you have three or more qualifying children, or $17,640 if you have no qualifying children. Investment income must not exceed $11,000 *(25.8)*.
- Are married filing jointly, with earned income and AGI under $53,120 if you have one qualifying child, $59,478 if you have two qualifying children, $63,398 if you have three or more qualifying children, or $24,210 if you have no qualifying children. Investment income must not exceed $11,000 *(25.8)*.
- If both your earned income and AGI equals or exceeds the applicable amount shown above, the credit is completely phased out, so if your income is close to the applicable amount your credit will be low. The credit begins to phase out at much lower income levels *(25.8)*.
- Have a qualifying child who lived with you in your main home in the U.S. for more than six months in 2023; *see* below. If you meet the income criteria as an individual with no dependents, you may still be entitled to claim EIC; *see* "Claiming the Childless EIC for 2023 if You Have No Qualifying Children" below.
- File a joint return if married. Married persons filing separately may not claim the EIC. If you lived apart from your spouse for the last half of the year, you may be able to claim the credit as a head of household.
- File Schedule EIC with your Form 1040 or 1040-SR. On Schedule EIC, you identify and provide information about a qualifying child. Your child's Social Security number must be entered on Schedule EIC.
- Are not a qualifying child of another person.
- Include on your return your Social Security number and, if married, that of your spouse.

To claim the credit, your Social Security number (and if married, your spouse's) and the Social Security numbers of your qualifying children must be obtained by the due date of your return, including any extension; *see* the Law Alert in this section. Individuals with a qualifying child who does not have a Social Security number may claim the Earned Income Credit as if they were without a qualifying child.

A qualifying child. A qualifying child is your son, daughter, adopted child, stepchild, grandchild or other descendent of any of these (your great-grandchild) who at the end of the year is under age 19 or under age 24 and a full-time student (enrolled full time during any five months), or any age if permanently and totally disabled. The qualifying person must live with you for over half the year. Your brother, sister, step- or half-brother or step- or half-sister, or their descendants (your niece or nephew), who meets the age 19 or 24 test and lives with you more than half the year also qualifies if he/she is younger than you (or your spouse if you file jointly) or is permanently and totally disabled. A foster child who lives with you for more than half the year qualifies if the child was placed with you by a court order or by an authorized placement agency.

The child must have a valid Social Security number to be treated as a qualifying child; *see* the Law Alert in this section.

Household requirement. The qualifying child must have lived with you in your main home in the U.S. for more than six months. Temporary absences for school, vacation, medical care, or detention in a juvenile facility count as time lived at home.

A person in the U.S. Armed Forces who is stationed outside the U.S. on extended active duty is treated as maintaining a main residence within the U.S.

If you are married, you must file a joint return with your spouse to claim the credit. However, if your spouse did not live in your household for the last six months of the year, and you maintained a home for a child who lived with you for more than half of the year, you may claim the credit as a head of household *(1.12)*.

Law Alert

Valid SSN Needed by Due Date of Return to Claim EIC

You (and if married your spouse) must have a valid Social Security number (SSN) by the due date for your 2023 return (April 15, 2024), plus extensions if any) to claim the EIC for 2024. If you claim the EIC for qualifying children, they also must have a valid SSN by the return due date (including extensions). If you do not have a SSN by the return due date (with extensions), you cannot claim the credit on your original return and you cannot claim it on an amended return if you later obtain a SSN. Similarly, you cannot treat a child as a qualifying child on either your original return or on an amended return if that child did not have a SSN by the return due date (with extensions), even if the child later obtains the SSN.

Permanently and totally disabled. A person is permanently and totally disabled if: (1) he or she cannot engage in any substantial gainful activity because of a physical or mental condition and (2) a physician determines that the condition has lasted or is expected to last for at least a year or lead to death.

Qualifying child of two or more people. "Tie-breaking" rules determine who can take the EIC if a child is a qualifying child of more than one person.

If both parents are eligible to claim the credit for the same qualifying child and they do not file a joint return, the custodial parent, the parent with whom the child resided for the longer period during the year, may claim the child. If the child lived with each parent for the same amount of time, the child will be treated as the qualifying child of the parent who had the higher adjusted gross income (AGI).

If a parent and one or more nonparents, such as a grandparent, are otherwise entitled to claim the child as a qualifying child, only the parent may claim the credit for the child. However, in this situation the parent can decline to claim the child as a qualifying child in order to allow the grandparent to claim the child, but only if the grandparent's AGI is more than the parent's AGI. If none of the persons otherwise entitled to treat the child as a qualifying child are the child's parent, the child will be treated as the qualifying child of the person who had the highest AGI for the year.

A taxpayer who "loses" under the tie-breaker rule, and who thus cannot claim a child as his or her qualifying child for EIC purposes, may still be allowed to claim the EIC under the rules below for taxpayers without a qualifying child (the childless EIC). The IRS instructions follow a 2017 proposed regulation that allows the childless EIC to be claimed by a taxpayer who otherwise qualifies; this reverses an earlier IRS position that prevented the childless EIC to be claimed in this situation. For example, a baby lives with her mother and grandmother in the grandmother's home. The baby "could be" the qualifying child of both the mother and the grandmother, but under the tie-breaker rule, the mother is entitled to treat the baby as her qualifying child, so she can claim the EIC for one qualifying child. Under the new IRS rule, the grandmother can claim the childless EIC if she meets the tests below ("Claiming the Childless EIC if You Have No Qualifying Children").

Married child. If your child was married at the end of the year, he or she is your qualifying child only if your child is your dependent under the rules at *21.3*, or the custodial parent waived the dependency exemption under the rules at *21.7*. However, if your child files a joint return, he or she is not your qualifying child unless the joint return is filed only as a refund claim.

Nonresident aliens. An individual who is a nonresident alien for any part of the year is not eligible for the credit unless he or she is married and an election is made by the couple to have all of their worldwide income subject to U.S. tax.

Claiming the Childless EIC for 2023 if You Have No Qualifying Children

If you do not have a qualifying child, you may claim the childless EIC on a 2023 return if you:

- Have earned income, such as wages and self-employment earnings and also adjusted gross income under $17,640 ($24,210 if married filing jointly). These are the amounts at which the credit is completely phased out. The phaseout threshold is considerably lower *(25.8)*.
- Have your main home in the U.S. for more than six months in 2023.
- Are at least 25 but under age 65 at the end of 2023. If filing a joint return, either you or your spouse must satisfy this age test.
- File a joint return if married, unless you lived apart for the last six months and qualify to file as a head of household.
- Are not a dependent of another taxpayer. If filing jointly, your spouse also must not be another taxpayer's dependent.
- Are not a qualifying child of another taxpayer. If filing jointly, your spouse also must not be another taxpayer's qualifying child.
- Include your Social Security number on your return, and, if married, that of your spouse. You must have the Social Security number by the due date of your return, including extensions; *see* the Law Alert on page 520.

Denial of Future Credits for Recklessness or Fraud

A taxpayer who negligently or fraudulently claims the EIC is prohibited from claiming future credits over a period of several years. The credit is disallowed for two years from the tax year for which it is determined that the EIC claim was claimed with reckless or intentional disregard of the rules. The disallowance period increases to 10 years from the most recent tax year for which it is found that the EIC was claimed fraudulently.

Recertification Required if EIC Denied

If the IRS denies an EIC by issuing a deficiency notice, the credit may not be claimed in a future tax year unless you show on Form 8862 that you are eligible to take the credit. If the IRS recertifies eligibility, Form 8862 does not have to be filed again in subsequent tax years unless the IRS again denies the EIC in a deficiency proceeding.

25.8 Income Tests for Earned Income Credit (EIC)

For purposes of the credit, earned income includes wages, salary, tips, commissions, jury duty pay, union strike benefits, and net earnings from self-employment. If you retired on disability and you receive payments from the employer's plan that are reported as taxable wages, such disability benefits are considered earned income for EIC purposes until you reach minimum retirement age under the employer's plan. Once you reach minimum retirement age, the payments are treated as a pension and not earned income.

An election may be made to include combat pay that is otherwise excluded from income *(35.4)* as earned income for EIC purposes. The IRS cautions that electing to include combat pay may sometimes decrease, rather than increase, the allowable EIC; you can figure the credit with and without the combat pay on the IRS worksheet *(see below)* before deciding whether to make the election. Apart from such combat pay, nontaxable employee compensation, such as salary deferrals, or excludable dependent care benefits, is not considered when computing the credit.

Figure the EIC on IRS worksheet. A worksheet in the instructions to Form 1040 or 1040-SR is used to figure the EIC. Self-employed individuals have a separate worksheet. On the worksheet, you first look up the credit allowed based on your earned income *(see* above for combat pay election) in the EIC Table (shown in Part 8 of this book). If your earned income and adjusted gross income (AGI) are the same, the credit based on earned income is the allowable EIC. That amount (credit based on earned income) is also the allowable EIC if AGI is different than earned income and the AGI is under the phaseout threshold *(see below)*. However, if AGI is at least as much as the phaseout threshold, you look up the credit based on the AGI in the EIC Table and the smaller of that amount and the amount based on earned income is the allowable EIC, which you enter on Line 27 of Form 1040 or 1040-SR.

Investment income limit. For 2023, an individual is not eligible for the Earned Income Credit if he or she has investment income exceeding $11,000. This includes interest (taxable and tax-exempt), dividends, net rent and royalty income, net capital gain income, and net passive income that is not self-employment income.

Credit phases out with income. The phaseout range for married couples filing jointly is different from single taxpayers, heads of household, or qualifying widows/widowers.

If your filing status is single, head of household, or qualifying widow/widower, and you have qualifying children, your 2023 credit begins to phase out in the EIC Table if either earned income or adjusted gross income is at least $21,560, regardless of the number of children. The phaseout endpoint depends on the number of children. The credit is completely phased out if earned income or adjusted gross income is at least $46,560 for one child, $52,918 for two children, and $56,838 for three or more children.

If you are married filing jointly and have qualifying children, the 2023 credit begins to phase out in the EIC Table if either earned income or adjusted gross income is at least $28,120, regardless of the number of children. The phaseout endpoint depends on the number of children. The credit is completely phased out if earned income or adjusted gross income is at least $53,120 for one child, $59,478 for two children, and $63,398 for three or more children.

If you do not have any qualifying children, the phaseout of the childless EIC begins in the EIC Table when either earned income or AGI is at least $9,800, or $16,370 if married filing jointly, and the credit is completely phased out if either amount is $17,640 or more, or $24,210 or more if married filing jointly.

Self-employed. If you were self-employed in 2023, you figure your earned income for EIC purposes on the worksheet in the IRS instructions. Generally, your earned income for EIC purposes is the net earnings shown on Schedule SE, less the income tax deduction for 50% of self-employment tax. If your net earnings were less than $400, the net amount is your earned income for purposes of the credit. If you had a net loss, the loss is subtracted from any wages or other employee earned income. If you are a statutory employee, the income reported on Schedule C qualifies for the credit.

Foreign earned income. If you work abroad and claim the foreign earned income exclusion, you may not take the EIC.

25.9   Qualifying for the Adoption Credit

A tax credit of up to $15,950 may be available on your 2023 return for the qualifying costs of adopting an eligible child. An eligible child is a child under age 18, or any person who is physically and mentally incapable of self-care. The credit is phased out ratably for those with modified adjusted gross income between $239,230 and $279,230.

The credit is claimed on Form 8839. Special credit timing rules apply. If you paid qualifying adoption costs in 2023 but the adoption was not final at the end of the year, the credit may not be claimed on your 2023 return *(25.10)*.

If you are married, you generally must file a joint return to take the adoption credit or exclusion, even if only one spouse is adopting the child. You may take the credit or exclusion on a separate return if you are legally separated under a decree of divorce or separate maintenance, or if you lived apart from your spouse for the last six months of the tax year and (1) your home is the eligible child's home for more than half the year and (2) you pay more than half the cost of keeping up your home for the year.

Qualified adoption expenses. Qualifying adoption expenses are reasonable and necessary adoption fees, court costs, attorney fees, travel expenses away from home, and other expenses directly related to, and whose principal purpose is for, the legal adoption of an eligible child. Do not include expenses paid or reimbursed by your employer or any other person or organization. You may not claim a credit for the costs of a surrogate parenting arrangement or for adopting your spouse's child.

Employer plans. As discussed in *3.6*, an exclusion from income is also available to employees if adoption expenses are paid through a qualifying employer program, subject to rules similar to that of the credit. If you receive employer adoption benefits that are less than your qualifying adoption expenses, you may be able to claim the credit on Form 8839.

 *Law Alert*

Adoption Credit Limited by Tax Liability with Carryover for Excess

The maximum 2023 credit is $15,950, but even if you would be entitled to the full amount, you may be unable to claim it because it is nonrefundable, meaning that it is limited to your tax liability. If the allowable credit exceeds your tax liability, the excess can be carried forward for up to five years.

25.10   Claiming the Adoption Credit on Form 8839

The fact that you paid qualified adoption expenses during 2023 does not mean that you can claim a credit for those costs on your 2023 return. A 2023 credit is not allowed for 2023 expenses unless the adoption was finalized by the end of the year. Under the credit timing rules discussed below, you may claim a 2023 credit for expenses incurred in 2022 if the eligible child was a U.S. citizen or resident when the adoption effort began, even if the adoption is still not final at the end of 2023. If the child was not a U.S. citizen or resident when the adoption effort began, a credit is not allowed until the year the adoption is finalized even if you incurred expenses in one or more previous years.

If a credit is allowed for 2023, figure it on Form 8839 and attach the form to your Form 1040 or 1040-SR. You must enter an identification number for the child on Form 8839. Generally this is a Social Security number (SSN), but if you are in the process of adopting a child who is U.S. citizen or resident and you cannot get an SSN for the child before you file your return, you should apply for an adoption taxpayer identification number (ATIN) on IRS Form W-7A. If the child is not eligible for an SSN, apply for an individual identification number (ITIN) on Form W-7.

When to claim the adoption credit for a child who is a U.S. citizen or resident (U.S. child). If at the time the adoption effort begins the child is a U.S. citizen or resident and you pay qualifying expenses in any year before the year the adoption becomes final, the credit is delayed one year. The credit is allowed in the year after the year of the payment, whether or not the adoption is final in that year. If you pay qualifying expenses in the year the adoption becomes final, the credit for those expenses is claimed in that year. If qualifying expenses are paid in any year after the year in which the adoption becomes final, the credit is claimed in the year of payment.

When to claim the adoption credit for a child who is not a U.S. citizen or resident (foreign child). If you pay qualifying expenses to adopt a child who is not a U.S. citizen or resident at the time the adoption effort begins, a credit may not be claimed until the year the adoption becomes final. If adoption expenses are paid after the tax year in which the adoption became finalized, a credit for such expenses is allowed for the tax year of payment.

The IRS has released safe harbors for determining the finality of an adoption of a foreign-born child and thereby the timing of a credit. These safe harbors apply only to adoptions of foreign-born children who receive an "immediate relative" (IR) visa from the State Department. IR visas are issued to a foreign-born child entering the U.S. after a foreign court or government agency (with authority over child welfare) has granted an adoption or guardianship decree.

If there is an adoption proceeding in a foreign country that is not a party to the Hague Adoption Convention, and the adopting parents bring a foreign-born child into the U.S. with an IR-2 visa, an IR-3 visa, or an IR-4 visa (if a "simple" adoption), the parents may treat the adoption as final in either (1) the taxable year in which the foreign court or agency enters the adoption decree or, (2) the taxable year in which a court in the parents' home state enters a decree of "re-adoption" or the home state otherwise recognizes the foreign adoption decree, provided this occurs in one of the two years after the year in which the foreign court or agency enters its decree. If the child receives an IR-4 visa under a guardianship or legal custody arrangement, the adoption may not be treated as final for tax purposes until the year in which a court in the parents' home state enters a decree of adoption (Rev. Proc. 2005-31, 2005-26 IRB 1374).

For a foreign adoption finalized abroad that is governed by the Hague Adoption Convention, the adoption may be treated as final in either the year the foreign country entered the final decree of adoption, or the year the U.S. Secretary of State issued a Hague Adoption Certificate (IHAC) (Rev. Proc. 2010-31, 2010-40 IRB 413).

Credit limit and phaseout. The maximum adoption credit on a 2023 return is $15,950 per child, before application of the phaseout rule. The limit is per child, not per taxpayer. If the parents are not spouses filing a joint return, and, to adopt the same child, each parent paid expenses that are allowed in 2023 under the credit timing rules, the parents must divide the $15,950 limit between them.

If under the credit timing rules you are claiming adoption expenses for a child on Form 8839 for 2023, but you claimed expenses for the same child in an earlier year, the earlier expenses reduce the $15,950 maximum credit for 2023. If under the credit timing rules you are allowed a 2023 credit for more than one child, a separate $15,950 limit applies for each. However, if an adoption of a child with special needs is finalized in 2023, the maximum $15,950 credit is allowed even if this amount exceeds your qualified adoption expenses; *see* below.

The credit may be reduced or eliminated on Form 8839 by a phaseout rule based on modified adjusted gross income (MAGI). For 2023, the phaseout applies if MAGI exceeds $239,230. The phaseout range is $40,000, so the credit for 2023 is completely phased out if MAGI is $279,230 or more.

After application of the phaseout rule, you also must apply the liability limit. The credit cannot exceed your tax liability (regular tax plus AMT if any), reduced by various other tax credits. There is a worksheet in the instructions to Form 8839 for figuring the liability limit. If you are unable to use the full credit because it exceeds the liability limit, the excess credit can be carried forward for up to five years.

The allowable credit for 2023 from Form 8839 is entered on Line 6c of Schedule 3 (Form 1040 or 1040-SR).

Special needs adoption. A special rule allows qualifying expenses to be grossed up to the maximum credit in the year the adoption is finalized where the aggregate of qualifying expenses for that year and all prior years is under the maximum. For example, if a special needs adoption is initiated in 2022 and finalized in 2023 and actual qualifying expenses for both years are $11,020, a $15,950 credit may be claimed for 2023, subject to the phaseout rule and liability limit. Total expenses are deemed to be the $15,950 maximum, so the credit for 2023 includes not only the $11,020 of actual expenses, but also an additional $4,930, the excess of $15,950 over the actual expenses. This special rule applies only to finalized special needs adoptions.

An adoption is considered a "special needs" adoption if the child is a U.S. citizen or resident when the adoption process begins, and a state (or District of Columbia) determines that the child cannot or should not be returned to his or her parents and that because of special factors, assistance is required to place the child with adoptive parents.

Without a formal determination by the state that the child has special needs that justify providing financial assistance to the adoptive parents, the adoption is not treated as a special needs adoption. In one case, adoptive parents claimed that the fact that they had adopted a biracial child automatically entitled them to use the full credit amount allowed for finalized special needs adoptions, but a federal district court disagreed. There was no state determination of special needs, so the special needs credit rule did not apply.

25.11 Eligibility for the Saver's Credit

You may be able to claim the retirement savings contributions credit (saver's credit) on your 2023 return if you, or your spouse if filing jointly, made contributions (25.12) to a retirement plan for 2023. This includes a contribution made to a traditional IRA or Roth IRA for 2023 by April 15, 2024.

Eligibility for the saver's credit is restricted. You cannot claim the credit for 2023 contributions you made if any of the following are true:

1. Your adjusted gross income exceeds $73,000 if married filing jointly, $54,750 if a head of household, or $36,500 if single, married filing separately, or a qualifying widow or widower. Adjusted gross income is increased by any exclusion for foreign earned income or income from Puerto Rico or American Samoa, or the foreign housing exclusion or deduction.

2. You were born after January 1, 2006. That is, you must be age 18 or older on January 1, 2024, to claim the credit for 2023.

3. You are claimed as a dependent on another taxpayer's 2023 return.

4. You were a full-time student during any part of five or more months in 2023.

If you are not disqualified from claiming the credit under tests 1-4 above, you generally may claim a credit on Form 8880 based on the first $2,000 of your retirement contributions, but only after contributions are reduced by recent retirement plan withdrawals (25.12). As shown in Table 25-2, the credit percentage declines from 50% to 20% to 10% as income approaches the applicable $73,000, $54,750, or $36,500 limit.

Details on figuring the credit are in 25.12. Any allowable credit is in addition to s tax breaks you may receive for making the contribution, such as the exclusion for elective salary deferrals to a 401(k) plan, or a deduction for a traditional IRA contribution.

25.12 Figuring the Saver's Credit

You figure your saver's credit on Form 8880. The maximum credit for 2023 equals the applicable income-dependent rate shown in Table 25-2 (50%, 20%, or 10%) multiplied by the first $2,000 of eligible retirement contributions made for the year. If you are married filing jointly, you and your spouse may each take into account up to $2,000 of eligible contributions. Eligible contributions include: (1) contributions to a traditional IRA or Roth IRA, (2) salary-reduction contributions to a 401(k) plan (including a SIMPLE 401(k)), 403(b) plan, SIMPLE IRA, governmental Section 457 plan, or salary-reduction SEP, (3) contributions to your ABLE account (34.12), or (4) voluntary after-tax contributions to a qualified plan or 403(b) plan.

Note in Table 25-2 that the 20% credit bracket is extremely narrow, so as a practical matter, most eligible taxpayers will qualify for either the 50% or 10% credit percentage.

Withdrawals can eliminate the credit. A credit can be lost because you have withdrawn money from a retirement plan. In figuring a credit for 2023, your eligible contributions for 2023 must be reduced by the total of distributions you received (and also your spouse if filing jointly) after 2020 and before the due date of your 2023 return (including extensions) from traditional IRAs and Roth IRAs, ABLE accounts, 401(k) plans, SEPs, SIMPLE plans, 403(b) plans, governmental 457(b) plans, the Federal Thrift Savings Plan, and other qualified retirement plans. Do not count tax-free rollovers, direct transfers (trustee-to-trustee), conversions of a traditional IRA to a Roth IRA, in-plan rollovers from a 401(k) plan to a designated Roth account, distributions of excess contributions or deferrals, IRA contributions returned by the due date; see the instructions to Form 8880 for other disregarded distributions.

Filing Tip

IRS Tool on Eligibility for Saver's Credit

You can use an online interactive IRS tool to determine if you're eligible to claim the retirement savings contribution credit at www.irs.gov/help/ita/do-i-qualify-for-the-retirement-savings-contributions-credit.

Table 25-2 Saver's Credit Based on AGI for 2023			
Credit Rate	Married Filing Jointly	Head of Household	Single, Married Filing Separately, or Qualifying Widow/Widower
50%	up to $43,500	up to $32,625	up to $21,750
20%	$ 43,501 – $47,500	$32,626– $35,625	$21,751 – $23,750
10%	$ 47,501 – $73,000	$35,626 – $54,750	$23,751 – $36,500
0%	over $73,000	over $54,750	over $36,500

For 2024, the income limits may be increased by an inflation adjustment; *see* the *e-Supplement* at *jklasser. com* for an update.

Law Alert

ABLE Account Beneficiaries

The designated beneficiary of an ABLE account *(34.12)* may base the saver's credit on contributions he or she makes to that ABLE account.

Caution

Report Changes to Marketplace That Could Affect Credit for 2024

If you obtain coverage for 2024 through the Marketplace, your right to advance payments of the premium tax credit for 2024 will be based on the information you provide concerning your family composition and projected income. When you file your 2024 return, your actual credit will be based on the income and family size reported on Form 8962. If the advance payments are too high, you will have to make a repayment to the government. This could substantially reduce your expected refund or increase the balance due on your 2024 return. If you want to reduce the chances of having to make a repayment when you file, notify the Marketplace about increases in your household income or decreases in your family size. Also notify the Marketplace if you become eligible for employer-sponsored coverage or government sponsored coverage, as this will usually make you ineligible for the credit.

Similarly, notify the Marketplace about changed circumstances that could increase your advance payments, such as where you get married, have a child, or your household income drops below your initial estimate. If your advance payments are not adjusted to account for such changes, you will be entitled to a larger credit when you file.

Tax liability limit. The credit is not refundable. It is limited to your tax liability (regular tax plus AMT, if any), reduced by certain other nonrefundable credits such as the child and dependent care credit or the American Opportunity or Lifetime Learning credits.

25.13 Premium Tax Credit

Although the penalty for failing to carry minimum essential health coverage no longer applies, eligible individuals can still receive government help in paying health care premiums via the premium tax credit. If you bought health care coverage in 2023 through a government exchange (also called "The Health Insurance Marketplace") and your household income is at least 100% of the federal poverty line (FPL), you may be able to claim a tax credit on Form 8962 when you file your 2023 return. Those with household income above 400% of the FPL could not claim the credit before 2021, but for 2021 through 2025 the 400% limit does not apply. If, like most Marketplace applicants, you received an advance of the credit that went right to your insurance company and was applied to your monthly premiums, you will have to reconcile the advance payments you received with the actual credit that you are entitled to on Form 8962. The advance payments may have been too much or too little, depending on changes to your income or family composition between the time you received the advance payments and when you file your 2023 return.

If your allowable credit on Form 8962 exceeds the advance payments, the excess, called the "Net Premium Tax Credit," can be claimed as a refundable credit on Line 9 of Schedule 3 (Form 1040 or 1040-SR). As a refundable credit, it will be paid to you even if it exceeds your tax liability.

However, if your advance payments exceed the allowable credit, you must pay back the excess, but there is a limit on the required repayment (shown below). The repayment is an additional tax that must be reported on Line 2 of Schedule 2 (Form 1040 or 1040-SR).

To complete Form 8962, you will need to enter amounts shown on Form 1095-A, which you will receive from the Marketplace through which you obtained coverage. Form 1095-A will provide a month-by-month breakdown of the coverage premiums for you and your family and show the advance payments you received.

Eligibility for the premium tax credit. You must have purchased health coverage through the Marketplace and must meet these requirements to be eligible for a 2023 premium tax credit:

1. Your household income for 2023 is at least 100% of the poverty level for your family size. Household income is the modified adjusted gross income (MAGI) for you, your spouse, (if filing jointly) and your dependents who are required to file a tax return. MAGI is regular AGI increased by tax-exempt interest, the nontaxable part of Social Security benefits, and excluded foreign earned income. The Form 8962 instructions have worksheets for figuring MAGI and federal poverty tables that show the federal poverty line for your family size, depending on whether you live in the 48 contiguous states (and Washington DC), Alaska, or Hawaii.

2. You are not eligible for coverage from an employer plan or from a government plan (including Medicaid or Medicare). If you were offered employer plan coverage, but it was unaffordable or did not provide minimum value, the offered coverage does not block eligibility for the credit. The employer coverage is considered "unaffordable" for 2023 if the premium for self-only coverage exceeds 9.12% of your household income. You also remain eligible if the employer plan does not cover at least 60% of the cost of covered services; your employer must provide you with a plan summary that indicates if the plan meets the 60% test.

3. If married, you must file jointly. However, if you have been the victim of domestic abuse or abandoned by your spouse, and you live apart when you file your 2023 return, you can claim the credit as a married person filing separately. Alternatively, you can claim the credit if you lived apart for the last six months of 2023 and can file as a head of household *(1.12)*.

4. You cannot be claimed as a dependent by another taxpayer.

5. You bought your coverage through the Marketplace. Purchasing identical coverage directly from the insurer disqualifies you from claiming the credit.

Figuring the credit on Form 8962. In Part I of Form 8962 (*see* the Sample form later in this chapter), you compare your household income to the applicable federal poverty line (FPL). If eligible, you figure your credit based on the premiums for your policy, your contribution amount, and the Marketplace premium for the second lowest cost silver plan (SLCSP) for your family in your local area.

Contribution amount. Your contribution amount is the amount you are required by law to contribute toward your coverage. Your annual contribution amount is your household income multiplied by the "applicable percentage" for your income level, shown in the "applicable figure" table in the Form 8962 instructions. As the percentage of household income to the federal poverty line increases (from 100% of the federal poverty line to 400%), your contribution percentage increases. For 2023, the contribution percentages range from 1.92% to 9.12%, depending on household income. There is a 1.92% required contribution for those with household income up to 150% of the FPL; those with household income of 400% of the FPL or higher have a 9.12% expected contribution.

Premium amount for SLCSP. The Form 1095-A you get from the Marketplace will give you the monthly premium for the second lowest cost silver plan (SLCSP) for your family in your local area. The SLCSP is referred to as the "reference" or "benchmark" plan and the SLCSP premium is used to calculate the monthly advance payments as well as the allowable credit on Form 8962, regardless of what coverage plan you actually have.

Credit figured on annual or monthly basis. In Part II of Form 8962, the maximum full-year credit is the lesser of (1) the annual premium for your policy, or (2) the excess of the annual SLCSP premium over your annual contribution amount. However, if Form 1095-A shows that you did not have Marketplace coverage for the whole year, or there were monthly changes to your premiums or to the SLCSP premiums, you have to figure your credit on a monthly basis. That is, for each month, you get a credit equal to the lesser of (1) the monthly premium amount for your coverage, or (2) the excess of the monthly SLCSP premium over your monthly contribution amount (1/12 of the annual contribution amount described above). Your Form 1095-A has the annual and monthly premium and SLCSP amounts; you enter these on Part II of your Form 8962.

You must then compare the allowable credit, either the annual amount or the total of the monthly amounts, to your advance payments. The advance payments, which are shown on Form 1095-A, must be entered in Part II of Form 8962. If the credit exceeds the advance payments, the excess is the "net premium tax credit" you are entitled to claim on Line 9 of Schedule 3 (Form 1040 or 1040-SR). However, if the advance payments exceed the credit, you must make a repayment; *see* the section "Repayment of excess advance payments" and *Table 25-3* on the following page.

Table 25-3 Repayment Limit on Excess Advances for 2023		
Household income as a percentage of federal poverty line	Repayment limit for filing status of single	Repayment limit for any other filing status
Under 200%	$ 350	$ 700
At least 200%, but under 300%	900	1,800
At least 300%, but under 400%	1,500	3,000
400% or more	Repay entire excess	Repay entire excess

Repayment of excess advance payments. If the advance payments you received in 2023 exceed your allowable credit for 2023, the excess must be repaid with your 2023 Form 1040 or 1040-SR; report the repayment as an additional tax on Line 2 of Schedule 2 (Form 1040 or 1040-SR). There is a cap on the required repayment based on filing status and income; *see Table 25-3.*

If you are married at the end of 2023 but your filing status is married filing separately, you are allowed a credit only if you are a victim of spousal abuse or abandonment (see requirement 3 under "Eligibility for the premium tax credit" above). In that case, the repayment limitation in *Table 25-3* applies separately to you and your spouse based on the household income reported on your respective returns. If you are not a victim of spousal abuse or abandonment, you are not allowed any credit and must repay all or half of the advance payments you received, depending on who was covered by the policy; *see* the Form 8962 repayment instructions.

For 2024, the repayment limits may be increased by an inflation adjustment; *see* the *e-Supplement* at *jklasser.com.*

25.14 Mortgage Interest Credit

Under special state and local programs, you may obtain a "mortgage credit certificate" to finance the purchase of a principal residence or to borrow funds for certain home improvements. Generally, a qualifying principal residence may not cost more than 90% of the average area purchase price, 110% in certain targeted areas. A tax credit for interest paid on the mortgage may be claimed. The credit is computed on Form 8396. The credit equals the interest paid multiplied by the certificate rate set by the governmental authority, but if the credit rate is over 20%, the credit is limited to $2,000.

Liability limit and carryover. The mortgage interest credit is subject to a tax liability limit and any excess is nonrefundable. The tax liability limitation is figured on Form 8396. The allowable credit from Form 8396 is entered on Line 6g of Schedule 3 (Form 1040 or 1040-SR). However, if your allowable credit exceeds the liability limitation, the unused credit can be carried forward for up to three years; *see* Part II of Form 8396.

Mortgage interest deduction must be reduced. If you itemize deductions, you must reduce your home mortgage interest deduction *(15.1)* by the tentative (prior to liability limit) mortgage interest credit shown on Line 3 of Form 8396 (certificate credit rate multiplied by interest paid, subject to the $2,000 limit). The reduction to the mortgage interest deduction applies even if part of the Line 3 credit is carried forward to the next tax year.

25.15 Residential Energy Credits

Beginning in January 2023, new credits for energy-efficient improvements replace or expand previous credits. From January 2023 through December 2032, qualified energy-efficient home improvements may qualify you for either the energy-efficient home improvement credit or the residential clean energy credit. Both are nonrefundable credits but unused credits may carryforward to future years, depending upon the credit you claim. Credits are claimed on Form 5695, Residential Energy Credits. Special rules may apply if the home is used for business use as well as residence.

Caution

Recapture of Mortgage Subsidy

If within nine years of receiving a mortgage credit certificate you sell or dispose of your home at a gain, the mortgage subsidy you received generally must be recaptured as income. *See* Form 8828 for details.

Table 25-4 Qualified Energy Efficient Home Improvement Expenses and limits

Type of home improvement	Qualifications	Credit Limit
Envelope Components		
Exterior Doors	Must meet applicable Energy Star Qualifications	$250 per door and $500 total
Exterior Windows and Skylights	Must meet Energy Star Most efficient certification requirements	$600 total
Insulation and Air Sealing materials or systems	Must meet International Energy Conservation Code (IECC) standards at the start of the year 2 years before installation	No specific credit limit other than the total $1,200
Home Energy Audits	Must be conducted by a home energy auditor and include a written report and inspection identifying significant and cost-effective energy efficient improvements	up to $150
Residential Energy Property		
Air Conditioners	Must meet Consortium for Energy Efficiency (CEE) highest efficiency tier at the beginning of the year when property is installed. Costs may include labor	Up to $600 per item
Natural gas, propane, oil water heaters		
Natural gas, propane, oil furnaces and hot water boilers		
Heat pumps and Biomass Stoves and Boilers		
Electric or natural gas heat pumps	Must have thermal efficiency rating of at least 75%	up to $2,000 per year
Electric or natural gas heat pump water heaters		
Biomass stoves and boilers		

Energy-efficient home improvement credit. If you make qualified energy-efficient improvements in 2023, you may qualify for a credit up to $3,200. In order to qualify, the home being updated must be an existing home (not new construction) in the United States and must be your primary residence in most cases. The credit may be up to 30% of qualified expenses including: qualified energy efficiency improvements installed during the year, residential property expenses, and home energy audits. Prior energy-efficient credits had lifetime dollar limits. However, beginning in 2023, the maximum credit each year is $1,200 for energy property costs and energy-efficient home improvements (see specific limits in Table 25.4 below) and $2,000 per year for qualified heat pumps, biomass stoves or biomass boilers. While prior energy-efficient credits had lifetime dollar limits, no lifetime dollar limit exists through 2032. That is, you may potentially claim the full $3,200 credit, if qualified, each year from 2023 through 2032. Any costs incurred must be reduced by any subsidies, rebates, or other incentives received. State energy efficiency incentives generally do not have to be subtracted from costs unless they qualify as a rebate or purchase-price adjustment. This credit is nonrefundable, and any unused credits may not carry forward to future years.

Residential clean energy credit. The Residential Clean Energy Credit is 30% of the cost of new, qualified clean energy property for your home between 2022 and 2032. After January 1, 2033, the credit begins phasing down from 30%. You may claim the credit for improvements to your principal residence, even if you do not own it. Qualified expenses for the residential clean energy credit include; solar panels, solar water heaters, fuel cell property expenditures, wind turbines, geothermal heat pumps, and battery storage technology. Qualified expenditures include not only the property but the labor and assembly associated with installation and support. All property installed must be new. Unlike the energy-efficient home improvement credit, the residential clean energy credit has no annual limit. The only exception is for fuel cell property, which has a limit of $500 for each half kilowatt of capacity up to $1,667 for each half kilowatt of capacity of qualified fuel cell property in the case of residences occupied by two or more individuals. Like the energy-efficient home improvement credit, the clean energy credit is nonrefundable, but unused credits may carry forward to future years.

25.16 Clean Vehicle Credits

The Inflation Reduction Act of 2022 (IRA) updated the existing credit for clean vehicles and added fuel cell vehicles. For 2022, you could claim a credit for certain clean vehicles, which included electric vehicles (EVs), plug-in hybrids, and hydrogen fuel cell vehicles. For 2023, under the IRA, you may still claim the credit for these vehicles, but the credit now includes previously owned clean vehicles.

New Clean Vehicle Credit. In order to qualify, the vehicle must meet the following requirements:
- Be manufactured by a qualified manufacturer
- Meet the definition of a motor vehicle under Title II of the Clean Air Act
- Have gross vehicle weight rating of less than 14,000 pounds
- Be powered by an electric motor with a battery capacity of 7 kilowatt hours or more
- Final assembly was in North America.

The credit for eligible vehicles in 2023 is up to $7,500 depending upon when the new vehicle was placed in service and whether the vehicle meets the criteria for full or partial credit. The credit for vehicles placed in service between January 1, 2023, and April 17, 2023, is a $2,500 base with additional credit up to $5,000 based on $417 for a battery with at least 7 kilowatt hours plus an additional $417 for each kilowatt hour of battery capacity exceeding 5 kilowatt hours. The credit for vehicles placed in service after April 17, 2023, is $3,750 if it meets the critical minerals requirement and $3,750 if it meets the battery components requirement. For details about vehicles and the qualifications, view https://www.fueleconomy.gov/feg/taxcenter.shtml. The vehicle's MSRP may not exceed $80,000 for vans, SUVs or Pickup trucks or $55,000 for other vehicle types. If your MAGI exceeds the following thresholds, you may not claim the New Clean Vehicle Credit. MAGI for the purpose of this credit includes AGI plus any foreign earned income and any income from Puerto Rico or Samoa excluded from AGI. Income thresholds are $300,000 for married filing joint or qualifying surviving spouse; $225,000 for Head of Household; and $150,000 for single or married filing separately.

Previously owned Clean Vehicles Credit. If you purchased a used clean vehicle in 2023, you may be eligible for a credit up to $4,000. To qualify, the previously owned vehicle must be a model year at least two years earlier, the taxpayer may not be the original owner, original sales price was $25,000 or less and the purchasing taxpayer must be the first eligible individual to claim the credit since August 16, 2022, other than the original owner. You may not have claimed another clean vehicle credit for the past three years. To check for eligibility *see* https://www.fueleconomy.gov/feg/taxused.shtml. If your MAGI exceeds the following thresholds, you may not claim the Previously owned clean vehicle credit. MAGI for the purpose of this credit includes AGI plus any foreign earned income and any income from Puerto Rico or Samoa excluded from AGI. Income thresholds are $150,000 for married filing joint or qualifying surviving spouse; $112,500 for Head of Household; and $75,000 for single or married filing separately.

Final assembly requirement. Effective August 16, 2022, only vehicles meeting a final assembly requirement, which means final assembly occurred in North American, can qualify for the credit. The Department of Energy has a list at https://afdc.energy.gov/laws/inflation-reduction-act of Model Year 2022 and Model Year 2023 vehicles that may meet the final assembly requirement.

25.17 Repayment of the First-Time Homebuyer Credit

For 2023 there is a repayment requirement only if a credit was claimed for a home purchased in 2008. The repayment requirement has expired for homes purchased after 2008.

If you claimed the credit for a 2008 home purchase and you continued to own and use it as your principal residence for all of 2023, continue to repay at least $\frac{1}{15}^{th}$ of the credit with your 2023 return, as you have been required to do starting with your 2010 return. Your repayment installment for 2023 should be entered on Line 10 of Schedule 2 (Form 1040 or 1040-SR). You do not have to attach Form 5405 to report the repayment.

However, if you sold your home or converted your entire residence to rental or business use during 2023, repayment of the rest of the 2008 credit is generally accelerated, meaning that the balance must be reported on Form 5405 and repaid with your 2023 return. But there are exceptions that limit or eliminate the accelerated repayment requirement. For example, if you sold the home in 2023 to an unrelated party at a loss, no repayment of the credit is required. If you sold the home in 2023 for a gain to an unrelated party and the gain is less than the credit balance (the 2008 credit minus repayments made for 2010 through 2022), the 2023 repayment is limited to the gain.

If in 2023 your home was destroyed, condemned, or sold to an unrelated person through condemnation or threat of condemnation and you had a loss on the disposition, you do not have to repay any of the credit. If there was a gain on the 2023 disposition, repayment over the rest of the 15-year period is limited to the gain if the gain is less than the un-repaid balance of the credit. In that case, the minimum repayment for 2023 is one-half of the total gain, as there are two years left (including 2023) on the original 15-year repayment period that started with 2010 and which will end with 2024. But if you do not acquire a new principal residence within two years of the 2023 home destruction, condemnation, or condemnation-related sale, then in 2023 you will have to repay all of the remaining gain. *See* the Form 5405 instructions for details on the exceptions to the accelerated repayment rule.

Form **8962**	**Premium Tax Credit (PTC)**	OMB No. 1545-0074
Department of the Treasury Internal Revenue Service	Attach to Form 1040, 1040-SR, or 1040-NR. Go to *www.irs.gov/Form8962* for instructions and the latest information.	**2023** Attachment Sequence No. **73**

Name shown on your return	Your social security number

A. You cannot take the PTC if your filing status is married filing separately unless you qualify for an exception. See instructions. If you qualify, check the box ☐

Part I — Annual and Monthly Contribution Amount

1	Tax family size. Enter your tax family size. See instructions	**1**
2a	Modified AGI. Enter your modified AGI. See instructions **2a**	
b	Enter the total of your dependents' modified AGI. See instructions **2b**	
3	Household income. Add the amounts on lines 2a and 2b. See instructions	**3**
4	Federal poverty line. Enter the federal poverty line amount from Table 1-1, 1-2, or 1-3. See instructions. Check the appropriate box for the federal poverty table used. **a** ☐ Alaska **b** ☐ Hawaii **c** ☐ Other 48 states and DC	**4**
5	Household income as a percentage of federal poverty line (see instructions)	**5** %
6	Reserved for future use	
7	Applicable figure. Using your line 5 percentage, locate your "applicable figure" on the table in the instructions . .	**7**
8a	Annual contribution amount. Multiply line 3 by line 7. Round to nearest whole dollar amount **8a**	**b** Monthly contribution amount. Divide line 8a by 12. Round to nearest whole dollar amount **8b**

Part II — Premium Tax Credit Claim and Reconciliation of Advance Payment of Premium Tax Credit

9 Are you allocating policy amounts with another taxpayer or do you want to use the alternative calculation for year of marriage? See instructions.

☐ **Yes.** Skip to Part IV, Allocation of Policy Amounts, or Part V, Alternative Calculation for Year of Marriage. ☐ **No.** Continue to line 10.

10 See the instructions to determine if you can use line 11 or must complete lines 12 through 23.

☐ **Yes.** Continue to line 11. Compute your annual PTC. Then skip lines 12–23 and continue to line 24. ☐ **No.** Continue to lines 12–23. Compute your monthly PTC and continue to line 24.

Annual Calculation	(a) Annual enrollment premiums (Form(s) 1095-A, line 33A)	(b) Annual applicable SLCSP premium (Form(s) 1095-A, line 33B)	(c) Annual contribution amount (line 8a)	(d) Annual maximum premium assistance (subtract (c) from (b); if zero or less, enter -0-)	(e) Annual premium tax credit allowed (smaller of (a) or (d))	(f) Annual advance payment of PTC (Form(s) 1095-A, line 33C)
11 Annual Totals						

Monthly Calculation	(a) Monthly enrollment premiums (Form(s) 1095-A, lines 21–32, column A)	(b) Monthly applicable SLCSP premium (Form(s) 1095-A, lines 21–32, column B)	(c) Monthly contribution amount (amount from line 8b or alternative marriage monthly calculation)	(d) Monthly maximum premium assistance (subtract (c) from (b); if zero or less, enter -0-)	(e) Monthly premium tax credit allowed (smaller of (a) or (d))	(f) Monthly advance payment of PTC (Form(s) 1095-A, lines 21–32, column C)
12 January						
13 February						
14 March						
15 April						
16 May						
17 June						
18 July						
19 August						
20 September						
21 October						
22 November						
23 December						

24	Total premium tax credit. Enter the amount from line 11(e) or add lines 12(e) through 23(e) and enter the total here	**24**
25	Advance payment of PTC. Enter the amount from line 11(f) or add lines 12(f) through 23(f) and enter the total here	**25**
26	Net premium tax credit. If line 24 is greater than line 25, subtract line 25 from line 24. Enter the difference here and on Schedule 3 (Form 1040), line 9. If line 24 equals line 25, enter -0-. Stop here. If line 25 is greater than line 24, leave this line blank and continue to line 27	**26**

Part III — Repayment of Excess Advance Payment of the Premium Tax Credit

27	Excess advance payment of PTC. If line 25 is greater than line 24, subtract line 24 from line 25. Enter the difference here	**27**
28	Repayment limitation (see instructions)	**28**
29	Excess advance premium tax credit repayment. Enter the smaller of line 27 or line 28 here and on Schedule 2 (Form 1040), line 2	**29**

For Paperwork Reduction Act Notice, see your tax return instructions. Cat. No. 37784Z Form **8962** (2023)

Sample Form 8962—Premium Tax Credit (PTC)
(This sample is subject to change; *see* the *e-Supplement* at *jklasser.com*)

Form 8962 (2023)　　　　　　　　　　　　　　　　　　　　　　　　　　　　　　　　　　　　　　　Page **2**

Part IV　Allocation of Policy Amounts
Complete the following information for up to four policy amount allocations. See instructions for allocation details.

Allocation 1

30	**(a)** Policy Number (Form 1095-A, line 2)	**(b)** SSN of other taxpayer	**(c)** Allocation start month	**(d)** Allocation stop month
	Allocation percentage applied to monthly amounts	**(e)** Premium Percentage	**(f)** SLCSP Percentage	**(g)** Advance Payment of the PTC Percentage

Allocation 2

31	**(a)** Policy Number (Form 1095-A, line 2)	**(b)** SSN of other taxpayer	**(c)** Allocation start month	**(d)** Allocation stop month
	Allocation percentage applied to monthly amounts	**(e)** Premium Percentage	**(f)** SLCSP Percentage	**(g)** Advance Payment of the PTC Percentage

Allocation 3

32	**(a)** Policy Number (Form 1095-A, line 2)	**(b)** SSN of other taxpayer	**(c)** Allocation start month	**(d)** Allocation stop month
	Allocation percentage applied to monthly amounts	**(e)** Premium Percentage	**(f)** SLCSP Percentage	**(g)** Advance Payment of the PTC Percentage

Allocation 4

33	**(a)** Policy Number (Form 1095-A, line 2)	**(b)** SSN of other taxpayer	**(c)** Allocation start month	**(d)** Allocation stop month
	Allocation percentage applied to monthly amounts	**(e)** Premium Percentage	**(f)** SLCSP Percentage	**(g)** Advance Payment of the PTC Percentage

34　Have you completed all policy amount allocations?

　　☐ **Yes.** Multiply the amounts on Form 1095-A by the allocation percentages entered by policy. Add all allocated policy amounts and non-allocated policy amounts from Forms 1095-A, if any, to compute a combined total for each month. Enter the combined total for each month on lines 12–23, columns (a), (b), and (f). Compute the amounts for lines 12–23, columns (c)–(e), and continue to line 24.

　　☐ **No.** See the instructions to report additional policy amount allocations.

Part V　Alternative Calculation for Year of Marriage
Complete line(s) 35 and/or 36 to elect the alternative calculation for year of marriage. For eligibility to make the election, see the instructions for line 9. To complete line(s) 35 and/or 36 and compute the amounts for lines 12–23, see the instructions for this Part V.

		(a) Alternative family size	**(b)** Alternative monthly contribution amount	**(c)** Alternative start month	**(d)** Alternative stop month
35	Alternative entries for your SSN				
36	Alternative entries for your spouse's SSN				

Form **8962** (2023)

CHAPTER 26

Tax Withholdings

Withholding taxes gives the Government part of your income before you may have a chance to use it. Withholding tax is imposed on salary and wage income, tip income, certain gambling winnings, pensions, and retirement distributions, but you may avoid withholding on retirement payments *(26.10)*. Withholding is also imposed on interest and dividends if you do not give your taxpayer identification number to a payer of interest or dividend income.

You may increase or decrease withholdings on your wages by submitting a new Form W-4 to your employer.

Make sure that tax withholdings meet or help you meet the estimated tax rules that require withholdings plus estimated tax payments to equal 90% of your current year liability or the required percentage of the prior year's liability; *see Chapter 27*.

A mandatory 20% withholding rate applies to eligible rollover distributions that are paid to you from an employer retirement plan. You may avoid the withholding by instructing your employer to directly transfer the funds to an IRA or the plan of a new employer *(26.9)*.

26.1 Withholdings Should Cover Estimated Tax

In fixing the rate of withholding on your wages, pay attention to the tests for determining whether sufficient income taxes have been withheld from your pay. A penalty will apply if your wage withholdings plus estimated tax payments (including prior year overpayment credited to current estimated tax) do not equal the lesser of 90% of your current tax liability or the required percentage of the prior year's tax *(27.1)*.

Taxes are withheld from payments made to you for services that you perform as an employee, subject to certain exceptions *(26.2)*. Use Form W-4 to figure the proper withholding amount. If you have multiple jobs or a spouse who works, you can figure withholding for Steps 2 through 4 of Form W-4 by using one of the following:

- The IRS estimator at www.irs.gov/W4App.
- The Multiple Jobs Worksheet, which is part of Form W-4.
- Checking the box in Step 2 if there are two jobs total with similar pay (you do the same on the Form W-4 for each job); your employer will withhold accordingly. Because of privacy concerns, however, the IRS makes this Step optional; an employee can go directly to Step 4(c) "Extra withholding" and add an amount for each pay period without any further details needed to be disclosed to the employer. Or an employee can go directly for the signature line and not have any additional withholding taken out of a paycheck. Choosing instead to make estimated tax payments or additional amounts taken out by another employer. If your income for the year will be $200,000 or less ($400,000 or less if married filing jointly) and you have dependents, you can adjust withholding to account for the child tax credit. The adjustments are made in Step 3 on line 3 of Form W-4; or, again, if privacy is a concern, the adjustment may be made in Step/line 4(c).

If you have other income, such as from investments, and you want additional withholding from your paycheck, you can enter the amount to be withhold on line 4a, Step 4, of Form W-4. If you expect to itemize deductions instead of taking the standard deduction and want to reduce your withholding, figure the reduction on the Deductions Worksheet, which is part of Form W-4. Enter the results on line 4b in Step 4 of Form W-4.

You can change your withholdings, either increasing or decreasing them, if your financial or family situation changes *(26.4)*.

26.2 Income Taxes Withheld on Wages

The amount of income tax withheld for your wage bracket depends on your marital status. You file a withholding certificate, Form W-4, with your employer, indicating your status and any adjustments to increase or decrease withholding. Without a Form W-4, your employer must withhold tax as if you are a single person with no special adjustments.

Cash payments or the cash value of benefits paid to an employee by an employer are subject to withholding, unless the payments are specifically excluded.

Income Taxes Are Withheld on:

- Payments by your employer for salaries, wages, fees, commissions, vacation allowances, severance pay, and other payments for services performed (whether paid in cash or goods). You generally may elect to avoid withholding on pensions and retirement annuities *(26.9)*. If supplemental wages (payments that are not regular wages) such as bonuses, commissions, overtime pay, accumulated leave, or taxable expense allowances (under nonaccountable plans) are separately identified from regular wages, an employer may withhold at a flat rate of 22% for the supplemental wages instead of using the regular withholding tables.
- Sick pay paid by your employer. If a third party pays you sick pay on a plan funded by your employer, you may request withholding by filing Form W-4S.
- Taxable group insurance coverage over $50,000.

Planning Reminder

Adjust Withholdings

If you do not expect withholdings to meet your final tax liability, ask your employer to withhold a greater amount of tax *(26.1)*. On the other hand, if the withholding rate applied to your wages results in overwithholding, you can reduce withholding during the year *(26.4–26.5)*.

Law Alert

Differential Wages Paid to Workers Joining Military

Employees who enlist or are called up to active military service may receive "differential wages" from their former employer to cover the difference between their military pay and the wages that were being received prior to joining the military. Income tax must be withheld from the differential wages, but not FICA tax (Social Security and Medicare).

- Reimbursements of expenses that do not meet qualifying rules of accountable plans discussed in *20.18*. Also, reimbursements from accountable plans that exceed federal travel rates *(20.19)* if the employee does not return the reimbursement or show that it is substantiated by proof of expenses.
- Pay to members of the U.S. Armed Forces. Differential wages paid by an employer to a former employee while on active military duty are subject to withholding.
- Prize awarded to a salesperson in a contest run by his or her employer.
- Retroactive pay and overtime under the Fair Labor Standards Act.
- Taxable supplemental unemployment compensation benefits.

Income Taxes Are Not Withheld on:

- Earnings of self-employed persons; they may pay estimated tax installments throughout the year *(27.2)*.
- Payments to household workers. However, although income tax withholding is not required, the worker and the employer may make a voluntary withholding agreement; *see Chapter 38*.
- Value of tax-free board and lodging furnished by an employer.
- Fringe benefits not subject to tax (although there are limits on some benefits).
- Substantiated reimbursements for deductible moving expenses or medical care benefits under a self-insured medical reimbursement plan.
- Advances for traveling expenses if the employee substantiates expenses to the employer and if the employee returns any unsubstantiated amount *(20.18)*.
- Pay for U.S. citizen working abroad or in U.S. possessions to the extent that the pay is tax free *(36.1)*.
- Payments to agricultural workers, ministers of the gospel (except chaplains in the Armed Forces), nonresident aliens, public officials who receive fees directly from the public, notaries, jurors, witnesses, precinct workers, etc.
- Pay for newspaper home delivery by children under age 18.
- Death benefit payments to beneficiary of employee; wages due but unpaid at employee's death and paid to estate or beneficiary.

Form W-2. By January 31, 2024, your employer must give you duplicate copies of your 2023 Form W-2, which is a record of your pay and the withheld income tax, Social Security and Medicare taxes. If you leave your job or your employment is terminated and you request a Form W-2 from the employer, you should receive it within 30 days of the request or, if later, within 30 days of your final wage payment.

26.3   Low Earners May Be Exempt From Withholding

If you had no income tax liability in 2023 and expect none for 2024, you may be exempt from income tax withholdings on your 2024 wages. If eligible for an exemption, students working for the summer, retired persons working part time, and other part-time workers do not have to wait for a refund of withheld taxes they do not owe. The exemption applies only to income tax withholding, not to withholdings for Social Security and Medicare *(26.8)*.

If you are not another taxpayer's dependent, you can claim the exemption from withholding if last year you had no tax liability and this year your total income is expected to be no more than the standard deduction for your filing status. However, if you are the dependent of another taxpayer and are under age 65, the exemption from withholding is not allowed if your expected total income (wages and investments) and investment income exceeds annual limits. For 2023, the total income limit was $1,250 and the investment income limit was $400. These amounts may be increased by an inflation adjustment for 2024; if so, the revised amounts will be on the Form W-4 or in IRS Publication 505 for 2024.

Planning Reminder

When to Change Withholdings

Adjust the withholdings in effect during 2023 if you expect there to be a significant change in the tax you will owe for 2024. For example, if you have a child entitling you to the child tax credit, you can reduce your withholdings to increase your take home pay. On the other hand, a withholding increase in 2024 may be advisable if you itemized in 2023 but expect to claim the standard deduction in 2024, or if you expect an increase in nonwage income such as capital gains. Check the instructions to Forms W-4 and 1040-ES for 2024 to help you adjust your withholdings for 2024.

To claim an exemption for 2024, you must file Form W-4 with your employer and certify that you owed no federal income tax in 2023 and expect to owe no federal income tax in 2024 (write "exempt" in the space below Step 4(c) and complete Steps 1 and 5 of Form W-4). If you will file a joint return for 2024, do not claim an exemption on Form W-4 if the joint return will show a tax liability. An exemption claimed during 2023 expires February 15, 2024.

26.4 Are You Withholding the Right Amount?

You do not want to withhold too little from your pay and you do not want to withhold too much. You may need to withhold more to avoid a large tax payment or an estimated tax penalty *(26.1)* when you file your return, especially if you have substantial income from investments or a business.

On the other hand, if you have been receiving large refunds from the IRS, you may want to re-visit your withholding (use the IRS Tax Withholding Estimator at https://www.irs.gov/individuals/tax-withholding-estimator). Balance the loss of the use of your earnings during the year against the value of receiving a substantial refund check from the IRS after you file your return.

If you are starting a new job or if you have not changed your withholding in several years, review the 2024 Form W-4 or the IRS Tax Withholding Estimator to help you determine if you are withholding the right amount.

If you have more than one job at time or you are married filing jointly and your spouse also works, you may want to adjust withholding so that the correct amount is taken from your paycheck(s). Use the Tax Withholding Estimator at irs.gov/W4App for the most accurate withholding. Alternatively, use the Multiple Jobs Worksheet or simply check the box on line 2c of Form W-4.

File a new Form W-4 each year for withholding if there is a change in marital status, a change in the number of your dependents, deciding whether or not to itemize, having additional income, or other factors impacting the correct amount of withholding.

IRS review of Form W-4. Employers are not required to submit Forms W-4 to the IRS for review unless the IRS sends written notice directing the employer to provide the W-4 forms of specified employees. The IRS uses the information on Form W-2 wage statements to spot employees who are not withholding enough federal income tax from their income. If the IRS determines that too many withholding reductions have been claimed on your Form W-4, the IRS can issue a "lock-in letter" requiring your employer to limit the reductions. You will receive a copy of the "lock-in letter" and be given an opportunity to dispute the IRS determination before your employer adjusts your withholding.

The IRS may impose a $500 civil penalty if you did not have a reasonable basis for statements made on Form W-4 that reduce your withholding. There is also a criminal penalty for willfully supplying false information on Form W-4. Upon conviction, there could be a fine of up to $1,000, a jail sentence of up to a year, or both.

When to file a new Form W-4. You should file a new Form W-4 any time the facts and circumstances surrounding your withholding increase or decrease, such as when a child is born or adopted, you marry, you get a divorce, or your deductible expenses change. Nevertheless, filing a new Form W-4 is not mandatory.

Your employer may make the new Form W-4 effective with the next payment of wages. However, an employer may postpone the new withholding rate until the start of the first payroll period ending on or after the 30th day from the day you submit the revised form.

26.5 Voluntary Withholding on Government Payments

You can choose to have federal income tax withheld from Social Security benefits (and equivalent tier 1 Railroad Retirement benefits), unemployment compensation, crop disaster payments, distributions from Alaska Native Corporations, and Commodity

 *Planning Reminder*

Part-Year Employees May Avoid Over-withholding

Starting a new job in the middle of a year presents a withholding problem. The amount of tax withheld from your paycheck is figured by taking your weekly pay and multiplying this by a 52-week pay period. For example, if as a recent graduate, you start a job on July 1 and your weekly pay is $1,000 for 26 weeks (July 1–December 31), your withholding will be based on an annual income of $52,000 ($1,000 × 52 weeks) and not the $26,000 you will actually earn that year. This will result in over-withholding. To alleviate this problem, you may ask your employer to calculate withholdings on what is known as the "part year" method if your work days during the year are expected to be 245 or fewer. This formula calculates withholding based on actual earnings rather than expected earnings over a full year of employment. As an alternative, use the Tax Withholding Estimator at irs.gov/W4App to calculate the appropriate withholding amount.

Credit Corporation loans. The withholding request is made on Form W-4V. Electing to have tax withheld may eliminate the need to make estimated tax installments *(27.2)*.

For unemployment compensation you may have withholding at the rate of 10%; this is the only rate you can choose. For Social Security and the other payments, you may select a withholding rate of 7%, 10%, 12%, or 22%. If you elect withholding and later decide to stop it, you can do so on a new Form W-4V.

26.6 When Tips Are Subject to Withholding

Tips are subject to income tax and FICA (Social Security and Medicare) withholdings. If you receive cash tips amounting to $20 or more in a month, you must report the total amount of tips received during the month to your employer on Form 4070 (or a similar written report). Include cash tips paid to you in your own behalf. If you "split" or share tips with others, you include in your report only your share. You do not include tips received in the form of merchandise or your share of service charges turned over to you by your employer. Make the report on or before the 10th day after the end of the month in which the tips are received. (If the 10th day is a Saturday, Sunday, or legal holiday, you must submit the report by the next business day.) For example, tips amounting to $20 or more that are received during January 2024 are reported by February 10, 2024. Your employer may require more frequent reporting.

You are considered to have income from tips when you receive the tips, even if they are not reported to the employer.

Your employer withholds the Social Security, Medicare, and income tax due on the tips from your wages or from funds you give him or her for withholding purposes. If the taxes due cannot be collected on the tips, either from your wages or from voluntary contributions, by the 10th day after the end of the month in which tips are reported, you have to pay the tax when you file your income tax return.

Penalty for failure to report tips. Failure to report tip income of $20 or more received during the month to your employer may subject you to a penalty of 50% of the Social Security and Medicare tax due on the unreported tips, unless your failure was due to reasonable cause rather than to willful neglect.

Tips of less than $20 per month are taxable but not subject to withholding.

Tip allocation reporting by large restaurants. To help the IRS audit the reporting of tip income, restaurants employing more than 10 people on a typical business day must make a special report of income and allocate tips based on gross receipts. For purposes of the allocation, the law assumes tip income of at least 8%. If you voluntarily report tips equal to your allocable share of 8% of the restaurant's gross receipts, no allocation will be made to you. However, if the total tips reported by all employees is less than 8% of gross receipts and you do not report your share of the 8%, your employer must make an allocation based on the difference between the amount you reported and your share of the 8% amount. The allocated amount is shown in Box 8 of your Form W-2. However, taxes are not withheld on the allocated amount. Taxes are withheld only on amounts actually reported by employees. An employer or majority of employees may ask the IRS to apply a tip percentage of less than 8%, but no lower than 2%.

Reporting allocated tips. Your employer will show allocated tips in Box 8 of your Form W-2. However, this amount will not be included in Box 1 wages and you must add it to income yourself by reporting it on Line 1 of Form 1040 or 1040 -SR. You also must compute Social Security and Medicare tax on the allocated tips on Form 4137 and enter the tax from Form 4137 on Schedule 2 of Form 1040 or 1040-SR.

26.7 Withholding on Gambling Winnings

Gambling winnings are generally reported by the payer to the IRS and to the winner on Form W-2G if the amount paid is $600 or more and at least 300 times the amount of the wager. The payer has the option of reducing the amount paid by the wager in applying the $600 test.

Filing Instruction

Tip Reporting

If you have not reported tips of $20 or more in any month, or tips are allocated to you under the special tip allocation rules, you must compute Social Security and Medicare tax on that amount on Form 4137 and enter it as a tax due on Line 5 of Schedule 2 (Form 1040 or 1040-SR); attach Form 4137 to Form 1040 or 1040-SR. The unreported tips must be included as wages on Line 1 of Form 1040 or 1040-SR.

Filing Instruction

Uncollected Social Security and Medicare Taxes on Tips

If your employer is unable to collect enough money from your wages during the year to cover the Social Security or Medicare tax on the tips you reported, the uncollected amount is shown on your Form W-2 in Box 12 with Code A next to it for Social Security or Code B for Medicare. You must report the uncollected amount on Line 13 of Schedule 2 (Form 1040 or 1040-SR) as an additional tax due.

Different reporting rules apply to winnings from poker tournaments, keno, bingo, and slot machines. Winnings from slot machines or bingo games of $1,200 or more, *not* reduced by the wager, are reported on Form W-2G. Poker tournament winnings are reported on Form W-2G if they exceed $5,000, *reduced* by the wager or buy-in. Keno winnings are reported on Form W-2G if they are $1,500 or more, *reduced* by the wager.

Withholding. Your winnings from gambling are subject to 24% withholding if your winnings minus the wager exceed:

1. $5,000 from lotteries, sweepstakes, and wagering pools, whether or not state-conducted, including church raffles and charity drawings, or

2. $5,000 from pari-mutuel pool wagers on horse races, dog races, or jai alai if the proceeds are at least 300 times as large as the amount wagered.

Winnings from slot machines, bingo, keno, or poker tournaments are exempt from the 24% withholding rule. However, "backup" withholding at 24% applies to reportable slot, keno, bingo, or tournament poker winnings if you do not provide a taxpayer identification number (TIN) to the payer; *see* the *Caution* on this page.

If your winnings exceed the $5,000 threshold, 24% withholding applies to your gross winnings less your wagers, and not just the amounts over $5,000. Any withholdings will be shown on Form W-2G.

The IRS requires you to tell the payers of gambling winnings if you are also receiving winnings from identical wagers; winnings from identical wagers must be added together to determine if withholding is required.

If you have agreed to share your winnings with another person, give the payer a Form 5754. The payer will then prepare separate Forms W-2G for each of you.

26.8 FICA Withholdings

FICA withholdings are employee contributions for Social Security and Medicare coverage. Your employer is liable for the tax if he or she fails to make proper withholdings. The amount withheld is figured on your wages and is not affected by your marital status, number of exemptions, or the fact that you may be collecting Social Security benefits. On Form W-2, Social Security withholdings are shown in Box 4 and Medicare withholdings in Box 6.

Subject to FICA tax are your regular salary, commissions, bonuses, vacation pay, cash tips, group-term insurance coverage over $50,000, the first six months of sick pay, and contributions to cash or deferred (401(k)) pay plans or salary-reduction contributions to a simplified employee pension (SEP), SIMPLE IRA, or tax-sheltered annuity. Severance pay to laid-off employees is also subject to FICA tax (the U.S. Supreme Court held this in 2014).

FICA tax does not apply to the value of tax-free meals and lodgings *(3.12)* or to reimbursements for substantiated travel or entertainment expenses or moving expenses.

Excess Social Security and Railroad Retirement withholding. If you have worked for more than one employer during 2023, attach all Copies B of Form W-2 to your return. Withholdings for Social Security taxes are shown in Box 4 of Form W-2. Check to see that the total withheld in 2023 by all your employers does not exceed the annual limit for Social Security taxes. The maximum 2023 liability for Social Security is $9,932, 6.2% of the first $160,200 of salary income. If too much was withheld for 2023, claim the excess as a credit against the tax you owe on Line 11 of Schedule 3 (Form 1040 or 1040-SR).

Employees covered by the Railroad Retirement Tax Act (RRTA) receive Form W-2, which lists total wages paid and withholdings of income and Railroad Retirement taxes. Follow tax form instructions for claiming a credit for excess Railroad Retirement withholding.

If any one employer withheld too much Social Security or Railroad Retirement tax, you cannot claim the excess on your income tax return. You must ask that employer for a refund of the excess and if the employer refuses, get a record of the overpayment and file for a refund on Form 843.

Caution

Backup Gambling Withholding

Winnings from bingo, keno, and slot machines are not subject to 24% income tax withholding. However, if your slots or bingo winnings are $1,200 or more, keno winnings are $1,500 or more, or tournament poker winnings are over $5,000, and you do not provide a taxpayer identification number, the payer will withhold tax at the 24% backup withholding rate *(26.10)* on the winnings reduced, at the payer's option, by the wager.

Law Alert

Additional Medicare Tax May Be Shown on W-2

Your employer must withhold the 0.9% Additional Medicare from your wages once the total exceeds $200,000 in a calendar year, regardless of your filing status. Any withheld Additional Medicare Tax on the excess over $200,000 will be reported in Box 6 of your Form W-2, along with the regular 1.45% Medicare tax withholding on all the wages. Even if the Additional Medicare tax is not withheld from your pay, you must pay it when you file your Form 1040 or 1040-SR if your wages for the year exceeded $200,000 if single, $250,000 if married filing jointly, or $125,000 if married filing separately. Self-employed individuals are also subject to the additional 0.9% Medicare tax. *See 28.2* for further details.

Planning Reminder

Wages Paid to Household Employees

See Chapter 38 for FICA withholding on wages paid to household employees.

Medicare tax withholding. Medicare tax is withheld at a rate of 1.45% on all salary and wage income; the amount is shown in Box 6 of Form W-2. In addition, if you had wages exceeding $200,000, your employer withheld the 0.9% Additional Medicare Tax on the excess, and this withholding is included in Box 6. *See 28.2* for further details on the 0.9% Additional Medicare Tax.

Wages you pay to your spouse or child. Wages you pay to your spouse for working in your business are subject to FICA tax and income tax withholding. Wages you pay to your child are subject to income tax withholding but if your child is under age 18 and your business is a sole proprietorship or a partnership in which the only partners are you and the child's other parent, the wages are exempt from FICA taxes. Wages you pay to your child under age 21 or to your spouse for domestic work or child care in your own home are exempt from FICA.

26.9 Withholding on Distributions from Retirement Plans and Commercial Annuities

Retirement plan and annuity distributions are subject to income tax withholding, but you may be able to choose to avoid withholding or have flexibility as to the withholding rate, depending on the type of payment. Form W-4P is used only for periodic payments from a pension, annuity, or IRA, and Form W-4R is used for nonperiodic payments and in some cases, eligible rollover distributions, as discussed below.

Form W-4P for periodic payments. Periodic payments are payments from a pension or annuity (employee annuity or commercial annuity), or from an IRA, that are made in regular installments over more than one year; installments could be monthly, quarterly, semi-annual, or annual. Withholding is required on the taxable portion of periodic payments unless you elect to avoid withholding on Form W-4P or on a substitute form furnished by the payer.

On Form W-4P, you choose to avoid withholding by writing "No Withholding" in the space below Step 4(c). You then only need complete Steps 1a and 1b (name, address, Social Security number), and 5 (signature and date).

If you are a U.S. citizen or resident alien, withholding may not be avoided on periodic payments delivered outside the U.S. or U.S. possessions. Payment must be to a home address within the U.S. (or within a U.S. possession) to avoid withholding.

Planning Reminder

Section 401(k) Plan RMDs

Distributions from Section 401(k) plans that are required minimum distributions (RMDs) are not considered rollovers subject to withholding; *see 7.11*. However, account holders may request that a plan fiduciary withhold on required minimum distributions. Some taxpayers, in fact, use such permitted higher withholding on year-end required minimum distributions as "catch-up" payments on shortfalls from other withholding or estimated tax payments for the year. Form 1099-R is used by the plan to report these distributions.

To have tax withheld from your payments, indicate in Step 1 (c) your anticipated filing status, which will determine the standard deduction and tax rates the payer will use to compute the withholding on your distribution. If you have multiple pensions or annuities, or income from a job, or you file jointly with your spouse who has income from a job or pension/annuity income, you must complete Step 2 of Form W-4P. The payer will use the Step 2 entries to assign to this pension or annuity the marginal tax associated with it, after taking into account income from other jobs and other pensions or annuities that pay less (annually) than this one.

If you expect to claim tax credits and/or deductions other than the basic standard deduction when you file your return, you may be able to take these into account to reduce the withholding on your payments; *see* Steps 3 and 4 of Form W-4P.

If you do not give Form W-4P to your payer, do not provide a Social Security number, or the IRS notifies the payer that you provided an incorrect SSN, the payer will withhold tax from your payments as if you were single with no adjustments.

Form W-4R for nonperiodic payments. Nonperiodic payments from an employer plan or commercial annuity that are not eligible rollover distributions (see the next paragraph) are subject to withholding at a default rate of 10% unless you elect to avoid withholding or choose a different rate on Form W-4R (or substitute form). IRA distributions that are payable on demand are considered nonperiodic payments.

You can choose to avoid withholding by entering "0" on Line 2 of Form W-4R. You can also pick a withholding rate between 1% and 10% on Line 2, or you can choose a higher rate if you want more than 10% withheld, up to 100%. However, you cannot avoid withholding or pick a rate below 10% if you are a U.S. citizen or resident alien and the payments are to be delivered outside the U.S. or U.S. possessions.

If you do not give Form W-4R to your payer, do not provide a Social Security number, or the IRS notifies the payer that you provided an incorrect SSN, the payer must withhold 10% of your nonperiodic payment.

Eligible rollover distributions from qualified employer plans. Employers must withhold 20% from nonperiodic payments, such as lump-sum distributions, that are eligible for tax-free rollover but which are paid directly to you. To avoid withholding you must direct your employer to make a direct rollover *(7.6)* of the funds to an IRA or to a qualified plan of your new employer. If you do not instruct your employer to make the direct transfer and elect to personally receive the distribution, 20% will be withheld before payment is made to you. The 20% withholding rule does not apply to required minimum distributions (RMDs), qualifying hardship distributions or payments that are part of a series of substantially equal payments, as these are not eligible for rollover *(7.5)*

You can file Form W-4R with the payer if you want to have more than 20% withheld from an eligible rollover distribution; enter the higher rate on Line 2. You cannot choose a withholding rate that is less than 20%. Apart from choosing a withholding rate of more than 20%, there is no reason to give the payer of an eligible rollover distribution a Form W-4R.

See 7.6 for a further explanation and the "John Anderson" Example showing the effects of the withholding rule where you receive the distribution and then decide to make a rollover yourself.

26.10 Backup Withholding

Backup withholding is designed to pressure taxpayers to report interest and dividend income. You may be subject to backup withholding if you do not give your taxpayer identification number to parties paying you interest or dividend income, you give an incorrect number, or you ignore IRS notices stating that you have underreported interest or dividends. Your taxpayer identification number generally is your Social Security number or your employer identification number. The backup withholding rate is 24%.

Backup withholding applies to fees of $600 or more reported on Form 1099-NEC for work you did as an independent contractor, payments from brokers (Form 1099-B), royalty payments (Form 1099-MISC), and certain gambling winnings *(26.7)* if you did not give the payer your taxpayer identification number.

If you provide false information to avoid backup withholding, you could face a civil penalty of $500 or, if convicted of a willful violation, a criminal penalty of up to a $1,000 fine or imprisonment of up to one year or both.

 *Planning Reminder*

Direct Rollover from Employer Plan Avoids Withholding

Your employer must withhold 20% from a distribution paid to you if the distribution was eligible for tax-free rollover *(7.6)*. You can choose to withhold more than 20% (but not less) on Form W4-R. Withholding does not apply if you have the employer make a direct rollover to a qualified plan or IRA.

CHAPTER 27

Estimated Tax Payments

Income taxes are collected on a pay-as-you-go basis through withholding on wages and pensions, as well as quarterly estimated tax payments on other income. Where all or most of your income is from wages, pensions, and annuities, you will generally not have to pay estimated tax, because your estimated tax liability has been satisfied by withholding. But do not assume you are not required to pay simply because taxes have been withheld from your wages. Always check your estimated tax liability. Withholding may not cover your tax; the withholding tax rate may be below your actual tax rate when considering other income such as interest, dividends, business income, and capital gains.

Your withholdings and estimated tax payments must also cover any liability for self-employment tax, alternative minimum tax (AMT), the additional 0.9% Medicare tax on earnings, the 3.8% tax on net investment income, and FICA withholding tax for household employees.

If you expect your 2024 tax liability to be $1,000 or more after taking into account withheld taxes and refundable credits, you should make quarterly estimated tax payments unless you expect the withholdings and credits to be at least 90% of your 2024 total tax, or, if less, 100% or 110% of your total tax for 2023. The 100% test applies if your adjusted gross income (AGI) was $150,000 or less in 2023, or $75,000 or less in 2023 if you will file your 2024 return as married filing separately. The 110% test applies for 2024 if your 2023 AGI exceeded the $150,000 or $75,000 threshold.

Failure to pay a required estimated tax installment will subject you to a penalty based on the prevailing IRS interest rate applied to tax deficiencies, unless the IRS waives the penalty.

27.1   Do You Owe an Estimated Tax Penalty for 2023?

When you have computed the exact amount of your tax liability on your 2023 return, you can determine whether you are subject to an estimated tax penalty. If you owe less than $1,000 on your 2023 return after taking into account withheld taxes and refundable credits, you are not subject to a penalty. If the tax owed after withholdings is $1,000 or more, you will not owe a penalty if your 2023 withholdings plus refundable credits and estimated tax installments were at least 90% (66 $^2/_3$ % for farmers and fishermen) of your 2023 total tax.

Total tax here means not only your 2023 regular income tax and alternative minimum tax (AMT) liability after credits, but also other taxes such as self-employment tax, the additional 0.9% Medicare tax on earnings *(28.2)*, the 3.8% tax on net investment income *(28.3)*, household employment taxes, penalty taxes (such as penalties on early retirement plan distributions and on distributions from qualified tuition programs not used for education), and taxes from recaptured credits. The total tax also includes any excess advanced premium tax credit that you received in 2023 and have to repay with your 2023 return when you reconcile your advanced credit with the credit you are actually entitled to *(25.13)*.

Even if the 90% test was not met, you may be able to avoid a penalty if your 2023 withholdings, refundable credits and estimated tax installments were at least 100% of the total tax *(see above)* shown on your 2022 return. This exception requires that the 2022 return covered all 12 months. However, if your 2022 adjusted gross income exceeded $150,000 ($75,000 if you are married filing separately for 2023), your withholdings plus estimated tax installments for 2023 had to be at least 110% of your 2022 total tax (not 100%) to qualify for this prior-year liability exception. The 110% rule does not apply to farmers and fishermen.

Note that to completely avoid a penalty for 2023 under either the 90% current year exception or the 100%/110% prior-year exception, you must have paid at least 25% of the amount required under the applicable exception by each of the four payment dates in 2023. The penalty is figured separately for each payment period; *see* below.

You are not subject to an estimated tax penalty for 2023 if you did not have to file a 2022 return or your 2022 total tax was zero. This is so even if you owe $1,000 or more (after withholdings) on your 2023 return and you do not qualify for either the 90% current-year exception, or the 100%/110% prior-year exception. This exception applies only if you were a U.S. citizen or resident for all of 2022 and your 2022 tax year included 12 full months.

If you underestimated your 2023 liability because of an unexpected increase in income during 2023, or if you did not earn income evenly throughout 2023, such as where you operated a seasonal business, you may be able to lower or eliminate the penalty by using the annualized income installment method. Under this exception, your required installment for one or more payment periods could be reduced below 25% of the required annual payment by figuring the installment that would be due if the income (and deductions) earned before the date for the installment were annualized. The computation is quite complicated; *see* the Form 2210 instructions and the worksheets in IRS Publication 505 for the details of applying the annualized income exception.

Penalties are figured separately for each payment period.   Separate penalty determinations must be made for each of the four 2023 estimated tax payment periods, as of the applicable installment dates: April 18, 2023, June 15, 2023, September 15, 2023, and January 16, 2024. This means that if, after taking into account withholdings from your pay, you underpaid an installment, you may owe a penalty for that period even though you overpaid later installments to make up the difference. However, withholdings towards the end of the year can eliminate an underpayment for an earlier period. In applying withholdings, the total withholdings of the year are divided equally between each installment period unless you elect on Form 2210 to apply them to the periods in which they were actually withheld. An overpayment for a period carries over to the next period.

Planning Reminder

Withholdings Cover Prior Underpayment

You have a choice in allocating withholdings from pay or other income that is subject to withholding: (1) You may treat your entire year's withholdings as having been withheld in equal amounts for each of the four payment periods or (2) you may allocate to each payment period the actual withholdings paid for that period. If toward the end of the year you find that you have underestimated for an earlier period, ask your employer to withhold an extra amount that may be allocated equally over the four periods. This way, you may eliminate the underestimate for the earlier periods under the equal allocation method.

The penalty for each period, which is based on the prevailing IRS interest rate for deficiencies *(46.8)*, runs from the installment due date until the amount is paid or until the regular filing date for the final tax return, whichever is earlier.

Figure the 2023 penalty for yourself on Form 2210 or let the IRS do it. In most cases you do not have to file Form 2210 to figure an estimated tax penalty; the IRS prefers to figure it and send you a bill if a penalty is due. However, you must figure your penalty and file Form 2210 if (1) you request a partial waiver of your penalty (see below for waiver rules), (2) you use the annualized income method (Schedule AI of Form 2210) to reduce or eliminate your penalty, or (3) you elect to treat your withholdings as paid on the dates withheld rather than in equal amounts on the four installment dates.

In the following situations, the IRS requires you to file only page 1 of Form 2210 but not the rest of the form (Parts III and IV) on which the penalty computation is made: (1) you request a waiver for your entire penalty, or (2) you filed a joint return for either 2022 or 2023 (not both) and your required annual payment for 2023 was based on the 100% or 110% prior-year safe harbor (because it was less than the amount required by the 90% current-year test). If you are requesting a waiver, attach a statement to page 1 of Form 2210 that explains the grounds for the request (*see* the waiver rules below). For situations (1) or (2), you must file only page 1 (Parts I and II) of Form 2210 and are not required to figure your penalty, but you may use Part III or Part IV of Form 2210 as a worksheet to figure the penalty and enter it on your return.

If you use Part IV to figure the penalty under the regular method, an underpayment for any payment period reduces the payments made in the following period. That is, an underpayment of one period is carried over to succeeding periods on Form 2210. If you underpay for a period, any payment you make after that installment date will be applied first to the earlier underpayment. Thus, even if you make the required payment for a period, you could still be subject to a penalty for that period because your payment is applied to a prior underpayment.

If you overpaid for any period, the excess carries over to the next period. The excess cannot be used to make up for an underpayment of the prior period if the earlier payments were made online, by phone, or with Form 1040-ES vouchers. However, withholdings are allocated equally over the year so that withholdings late in the year can reduce an underpayment for an earlier payment period.

Waiver of penalty for hardship, retirement, or disability. The IRS may waive the penalty if you can show you failed to pay the estimated tax because of casualty, disaster, or other unusual circumstances.

The IRS may also waive a penalty for a 2023 underpayment if in 2022 or 2023 you retired after reaching age 62 or became disabled, and you failed to make a payment due to reasonable cause and not due to willful neglect.

To apply for the waiver, attach an explanation to Form 2210 that documents the circumstances supporting your waiver request. For a waiver due to retirement or disability, show your retirement date and age or disability date. If an underpayment was due to a federally declared disaster, you do not have to request a waiver on Form 2210 because the IRS allows an automatic postponement following such a disaster. When you file your return, the IRS should identify your residence as being in a federally declared disaster area and if you still owe a penalty following the end of the disaster waiver period, the IRS will send you a bill. If you are requesting a waiver due to a disaster other than a federally declared disaster, other casualty, or unusual circumstance, attach documentation of the event, including police and insurance company reports, and an explanation as to how it prevented you from making estimated tax payments.

Farmers and fishermen. Farmers or fishermen who earned at least ⅔ of their 2022 or 2023 gross income from farming or fishing can use Form 2210-F to determine whether they owe an estimated penalty for 2023, but generally the form does not have to be filed because the IRS will figure any penalty; *see* the Form 2210-F instructions.

27.2 Planning Estimated Tax Payments for 2024

In planning your payments for 2024, you may not want to pay any more than is necessary to avoid a penalty. You can avoid a penalty for 2024 by planning payments in 2024 that meet the 90% current-year test or the 100%/110% prior-year safe harbor.

90% current-year test. If you expect your income, deductions, and tax credits for 2024 to be about the same as they were for 2023, and you will not have any additional liabilities for 2024 that you did not have for 2023, you can base your 2023 withholdings and quarterly estimated tax installments on 90% of your projected 2024 total tax. In projecting your tax liability for 2024, take into account possible liability for the alternative minimum tax (AMT), self-employment tax, the 0.9% additional Medicare tax on earnings, the 3.8% tax on net investment income, household employee taxes, penalty taxes, and recapture taxes, including a repayment of advance payments of the premium tax credit.

If you expect your 2024 total tax to be lower than your 2023 total tax, such as where your income has dropped, you can base your 2024 withholdings and estimated tax installments on 90% of the estimated 2024 total tax.

You can use the 2024 Estimated Tax Worksheet in the instructions to Form 1040-ES for 2024 to figure the required annual payment under the 90% test, as well as under the prior-year safe harbor test discussed next.

Safe harbor for 2024 based on 2023 tax. If you cannot make a precise projection of your 2024 income and deductions, you can play it safe and avoid a possible penalty for 2024 by planning withholdings and quarterly estimated tax installments in 2024 that equal your 2023 total tax if your 2023 adjusted gross income is $150,000 or less ($75,000 or less if married filing separately for 2023), provided you filed a 2023 return covering a full 12 months. If your 2023 AGI exceeds the $150,000 (or $75,000) threshold, your payments for 2024 must be at least 110% of your 2023 tax under the prior-year safe harbor.

If an accurate estimate for 2024 is possible, it is generally advantageous to base your estimated payments on the 90% current year test rather than the 100%/110% prior year test, as using this prior year test will probably result in an overestimation of your liability unless the 2024 tax turns out to be substantially larger than the 2023 tax.

You may use the worksheet and the tax rate schedule included in the 2024 Form 1040-ES to figure your estimated tax liability and the required annual payment to avoid a penalty under either the 90% current-year or the 100%/110% prior-year liability tests.

Making estimated tax payments. Reduce your 2024 estimated tax liability by expected withholdings from wages, pensions, and annuities. If after withholdings and expected refundable credits your estimated tax is $1,000 or more, you must make estimated tax payments unless the withholdings and refundable credits will cover at least 90% of your estimated 2024 liability or 100%/110% of your 2023 liability. If the projected withholdings and credits will not cover the amount required under the 90% or 100%/110% tests, you may pay the balance of the estimated tax with Form 1040-ES vouchers, by credit card or debit card (online or by phone), online by direct transfer from your bank account ("Direct Pay"), or by scheduling payments from your bank account using the Electronic Federal Tax Payment System (EFTPS). *See* www.irs.gov/payments for details on the electronic payment options.

Crediting 2023 refund to 2024 estimated tax. If you are due a refund when you file your 2023 return, it may be credited to your 2024 estimated tax. You may also split up the amount due you. You may take part of the overpayment as a refund. The other part may be credited to your estimate of 2024 taxes. The IRS will credit the refund to the April installment of 2024 estimated tax unless you attach a statement to your return instructing the IRS to apply the refund to later installments.

Check your arithmetic before you apply an overpayment as a credit on your next year's estimate. If you apply too much, the amount credited may not be used to offset any additional tax due that the IRS determines you owe. For example, your 2023 return shows a $500 refund due, and you apply it towards your 2024 estimated tax. However, the IRS

Planning Reminder

Take COLAs and Law Changes into Account

Numerous Cost-of-Living Adjustments (COLAs) are made annually to specified provisions in the tax law, including the tax brackets, standard deduction amounts, and the earned income tax credit. Be sure to review all the new amounts in estimating taxes for 2024. *See* the *e-Supplement* at *jklasser.com* for the 2024 COLAs.

Planning Reminder

Annualized Income Method

If your income typically fluctuates throughout the year, or if your income unexpectedly changes during the year, you may base installment payments on the annualized income method. This method allows you to avoid a penalty for installment periods during which less income is earned by reducing the required estimated tax payment for such periods. To figure your installment payments, use the Annualized Estimated Tax Worksheet in IRS Publication 505. If you base installment payments on the annualized method, you must file Form 2210 with your return to determine if you are subject to an estimated tax penalty.

Planning Reminder

Estimate May Have to Include Additional Medicare Tax and NII Tax

In planning your estimated tax payments, take into account possible liability for the 0.9% additional Medicare tax on wages and self-employment earnings in excess of the threshold amount for your filing status *(28.2)*. Also project possible liability for the 3.8% tax on net investment income (NII) tax if modified adjusted gross income exceeds the threshold amount *(28.3)*.

Planning Reminder

Credit Card or Electronic Payments

You can make estimated tax payments by check or money order with the Form 1040-ES vouchers, use a credit card, authorize withdrawals from your checking or savings account, or schedule payments through EFTPS (Electronic Federal Tax Payment System); *see* www.irs.gov/payments.

determines that you overpaid only $200 for 2023, not $500. You will be billed for the additional $300 tax, plus interest due; you may not offset the extra tax with the amount credited to 2024.

Farmers or fishermen. In figuring the required annual payment to avoid a penalty for 2024, a farmer or fisherman has to pay only 66⅔% of the 2024 estimated liability, rather than 90%. A penalty may also be avoided by paying 100% of the 2023 tax, provided a tax return covering a 12-month period was filed for 2023; the 110% test for higher-income taxpayers does not apply to a farmer or fisherman. To qualify as a farmer or fisherman for 2024 under these rules, at least two-thirds of gross income for 2023 or 2024 must be from farming or fishing.

27.3 Dates for Paying Estimated Tax Installments for 2024

The four installment dates for 2024 estimated tax are: April 15, 2024; June 17, 2024; September 16, 2024; and January 15, 2025. Later installments may be used to amend earlier ones *(27.1)*. You do not have to make the payment due January 15, 2025, if you file your 2024 tax return and pay the balance of tax due by January 31, 2025.

If you use a fiscal year. A fiscal year is any year other than the calendar year. If you file using a fiscal year, your first estimated installment is due on or before the 15th day of the fourth month of your fiscal year, assuming the 15th day. The second and third installments are due on or before the 15th day of the sixth and ninth months of your fiscal year with the final installment due by the 15th day of the first month of your next fiscal year. If any of these days are on the weekend or a legal holiday, the due date is the next business day.

Farmers and fishermen. Farmers only have to make one installment payment, generally by January 15 of the following year. Instead of making the estimated tax payment for 2024 by January 15, 2025, farmers may file their 2024 returns and pay the total tax due by March 1, 2025. To qualify under these rules, a farmer must receive two-thirds of his or her 2023 or 2024 gross income from farming.

Fishermen who expect to receive at least two-thirds of their gross income from fishing pay estimated taxes as farmers do.

Caution

Estimated Tax Paid by One Spouse May not Be Credited to a Joint Return

Because of the way in which IRS computers are set up, if a spouse makes a separate estimated tax payment and then files jointly, the payment is recognized only if that spouse is listed first on the joint return. While the estimated tax payment can eventually be properly credited to the joint return, it can slow down a refund.

27.4 Estimates by Married Taxpayers

A married couple may pay joint or separate estimated taxes. The joint or separate nature of the estimated tax does not control the kind of final return you can file.

Where a joint estimated tax is paid but separate tax returns are filed, you and your spouse can decide on how to divide the estimated payments between you. Either one of you can claim the whole amount, or you can agree to divide it in any way you choose. If you cannot agree, the IRS will allocate the estimated taxes proportionally according to the percentage of total tax each spouse owes.

If separate estimated taxes are paid, overpayment by one spouse is not applied against an underpayment by the other when separate final returns are filed.

Spouses may make joint estimated tax payments only if they are both citizens or residents of the United States. Both must have the same taxable year. A joint estimate may not be made if they are divorced or legally separated under a decree. If a joint estimate is made and the spouses are divorced or legally separated later in that year, they may divide the joint payments between them under the above rule for spouses who file separately.

Prior-year safe harbor. If you and your spouse file separately for 2023 (as single, head of household, or married filing separately) but expect to file a joint 2024 return, your 2023 total tax for purposes of determining the required 2024 annual payment under the prior-year safe harbor *(27.2)* is the total tax for both of you on the 2023 separate returns.

If you and your spouse file jointly for 2023 but expect to file separately for 2024, you must figure your share of the 2023 joint return tax to apply the prior-year safe harbor. Figure the tax that each of you would have paid on separate returns for 2023 using your 2024 filing status (single, head of household, or married filing separately). Then divide your separate return tax by the total tax for both separate returns. For example, if you would have paid tax of $7,000 on a separate 2023 return and your spouse would have paid $3,000 on a separate return, your 70% share ($7,000/$10,000) is the share of the 2023 joint return tax that you take into account in applying the prior-year safe harbor. Your spouse's share of the 2023 joint return tax is 30%.

27.5 Adjusting Your Payments During the Year

If, during the year, your income, expenses, or exemptions change, refigure your estimated tax liability and adjust your payment schedule as shown in the following Examples. Increasing an installment payment cannot make up for an underpayment in a prior period; *see* Example 2 below. However, withholdings from pay, pensions, and IRA withdrawals can be allocated equally over all four periods; so if you increase withholding at the end of the year, you may apply it to earlier periods.

If taxes paid in the previous installments total more than your revised estimate, you cannot obtain a refund at that time. You must wait until you file your final return showing that a refund is due.

EXAMPLES

1. Ben, who is self-employed, figures that to avoid a penalty for 2024 under the rules at *27.2*, he must make estimated tax installments of $6,000. By April 16, 2024, he pays an installment of $1,500. In June, he amends his estimate, showing a tax of $3,000 instead of $6,000. He refigures the installment schedule by dividing $3,000 by 4, which gives a payment rate of $750 for each period. As he paid $1,500 in April, the $750 overpayment covers his June obligation. By September 16, 2024, he pays $750; by January 15, 2025, he makes the last $750 payment.

2. In August 2024, Kate realizes that her estimated 2024 tax liability should be $25,000 rather than her original estimate of $20,000. She paid $5,000 as her April and June installments ($10,000 total). Under the amended schedule, she should have paid $6,250 per period ($25,000 ÷ 4), $6,250 by April 16 and $6,250 by June 17. Thus, there is a $2,500 underpayment ($12,500 – 10,000) for the first two periods.

   To cover the underpayment of $2,500, which carries over to the third payment period (June 1 through August 31), Kate's installment by September 16, 2024, must be at least $8,750 ($6,250 + $2,500). If less than $8,750 is paid, there will be an underpayment for the third payment period, as payments in that period are applied first to the carried-over underpayment of $2,500. If at least $8,750 is paid by September 16, there is no third period underpayment to be carried over, so the required installment for the fourth period (September 1 through December 31), due by January 15, 2025, will be $6,250. Unless an exception *(27.1)* applies, the underpayments for the first two periods will be subject to a penalty.

CHAPTER 28

Additional Medicare Tax and Net Investment Income Tax

An Additional Medicare Tax of 0.9% applies to wages, other employee compensation, and self-employment income to the extent such income exceeds a threshold of $250,000 for married persons filing jointly, $200,000 if single, head of household, or a qualifying widow/widower, or $125,000 if married filing separately. Figure liability for the additional tax on Form 8959. If the tax was withheld from your 2023 wages, you show the amount on Form 8959 and add it to your regular withholdings on Form 1040 or 1040-SR. *See 28.2* for details on the 0.9% tax.

A 3.8% tax (Net Investment Income Tax) applies to some or all of your net investment income if your modified adjusted gross income exceeds the applicable threshold of $250,000 for joint filers and qualifying widows/widowers, $200,000 if single or head of household, or $125,000 if married filing separately. The 3.8% tax is figured on Form 8960. *See 28.3* for details on the 3.8% tax.

In your planning for 2024, you may need to increase your withholdings or estimated tax installments to account for these taxes. Also, in light of legislative proposals, check the *e-Supplement* at *jklasser.com* for any update on changes to the applicable thresholds.

28.1 Higher-Income Taxpayers May be Subject to Additional Taxes

Higher-income taxpayers may be subject to one or both of two additional taxes, one on earned income and the other on investment income.

If you have wages and/or self-employed earnings over $200,000 if single, or $250,000 if married filing jointly, you are subject to the 0.9% Additional Medicare Tax on the earnings over the threshold. If you have modified adjusted gross income over the $200,000 or $250,000 thresholds, you are subject to a 3.8% tax on some or all of your net investment income (Net Investment Income Tax (NIIT)). The 0.9% Additional Medicare Tax is computed on Form 8959 and the 3.8% NIIT tax is computed on Form 8960.

Details on the thresholds and tax computations are in *28.2* for the 0.9% Additional Medicare Tax and in *28.3* for the 3.8% NIIT. Note that the thresholds for both of these taxes are fixed by statute; there is no annual cost-of-living adjustment for the thresholds. Take this into account in estimating your tax liability for 2024. The lack of an inflation adjustment means that taxpayers who are now slightly below the thresholds may become subject to the taxes in upcoming years.

If withholdings or estimated tax payments were not made in 2023 to cover these taxes, you could be subject to an estimated tax penalty *(27.1)*. The 0.9% tax may have been withheld from your 2023 wages, but as discussed in *28.2*, you may not be subject to the tax even though the tax was withheld, or you may not have been subject to withholding but may still owe the tax when you file your 2023 return.

28.2 Additional 0.9% Medicare Tax on Earnings

Wages, other employee compensation (tips, taxable fringe benefits), and net earnings from self-employment are combined to determine if you exceed the threshold for the 0.9% Additional Medicare Tax. The 0.9% tax, if applicable, is on top of the basic Medicare tax otherwise due (1.45% on all wages and salary; 2.90% on net self-employment earnings). Liability for the 0.9% tax does not depend on your adjusted gross income but only on your earnings. The 0.9% tax applies only to earnings above the following thresholds:

- $250,000 for married persons filing jointly
- $200,000 for single persons, heads of households and qualifying widows/widowers
- $125,000 for married persons filing separately

The tax is figured on Form 8959. If in 2023 you had wages (and tips or other taxable employee compensation treated as wages) but not self-employment earnings, the 0.9% tax applies on Part 1 of Form 8959 to the excess of the wages over your filing threshold. For example, if your 2023 wages are $225,000 and you are single, the tax applies to the $25,000 of wages over the $200,000 threshold, for a tax of $225 ($25,000 excess wages × 0.9% (0.009)). The $225 tax must be entered on Line 11 of Schedule 2 (Form 1040 or 1040-SR). Even if withholdings were taken from your pay to cover the 0.9% tax, they do not reduce liability for the tax on Form 8959. In the previous example, the $225 tax is reported as an additional tax on Schedule 2 whether or not your employer withheld the 0.9% tax. Withholdings for the 0.9% tax are separated out from regular Medicare withholdings on Part V of Form 8959 and then added to your federal income tax withholdings on Line 25c of Form 1040 or 1040-SR.

If you had only self-employment earnings in 2023, and no wages, you would figure liability for the 0.9% tax on Part II of Form 8959. If you had wages and also net self-employment earnings in 2023, you first determine if the 0.9% tax applies to your wages (Part I of Form 8959), and then you reduce your threshold amount by your wages to get a reduced threshold that is used to determine if the tax applies to the self-employment income; *see* the Examples below. A net loss from self-employment does not offset wages. The above-the-line deduction for one half of self-employment tax liability *(45.3–45.4)* does not apply to the 0.9% Additional Medicare Tax.

 *Caution*

Additional Medicare Tax Not Deductible

While self-employed individuals deduct one-half of their self-employment tax from gross income *(12.2)*, they cannot increase their deduction by any portion of the 0.9% additional Medicare tax.

Employer withholding for the 0.9% tax. Although the additional tax applies to the portion of earnings over the threshold ($250,000, $200,000, or $125,000), an employer will only withhold the Additional Medicare Tax once wages for the year (including tips, bonuses, and other taxable compensation) exceed $200,000. This means that some taxpayers will be subject to withholding but not owe the tax, while others will owe the tax but not be subject to withholding.

For example, assume that the combined wages of a married couple filing jointly do not exceed the $250,000 threshold, but one of the spouses has wages from one employer exceeding $200,000, In that case, the employer of the higher-earning spouse will withhold the 0.9% tax from the wages over $200,000. On Form 8959, there will be no liability for the tax because total wages do not exceed the threshold, but Form 8959 will have to be filed to show the additional withholding so it can be claimed on Form 1040 or 1040-SR.

On the other hand, an unmarried employee with several jobs could have wages well over the $200,000 threshold but not have the tax withheld by any employer because the wages from each job do not exceed $200,000. Similarly, for a married couple filing jointly, combined wages may exceed the $250,000 threshold but unless one spouse has wages exceeding $200,000 from a single employer, the additional tax will not be withheld from either spouse's pay. Thus, if one spouse has wages of $180,000 and the other has wages of $170,000, the 0.9% tax will not be withheld from either of them although their combined wages are $100,000 over the $250,000 threshold and they will owe additional tax of $900 (0.9% × $100,000 excess) on Form 8959. Finally, a married person filing separately with wages between $125,000 and $200,000 will not have the 0.9% tax withheld from his or her pay, but the tax will apply on Form 8959 to the wages over $125,000, the threshold for married persons filing separately.

If you (or you and your spouse on a joint return) owe the 0.9% but it is not withheld from your wages, you could face an estimated tax penalty *(27.2)* if the liability is not covered by regular income tax withholdings (Form W-4) or estimated tax installments.

Caution

Withholdings May Not Cover 0.9% Additional Medicare Tax

Employees who have more than one job and married couples where both spouses have wages may be subject to the 0.9% Additional Medicare Tax because the combined wages exceed the floor for the tax, but the tax will not be withheld from their pay because an employer will not withhold it unless the employee's wages exceed $200,000. *See 28.2* for withholding rule details. If you expect to have wages exceeding the tax threshold but not to have the tax withheld, you may need to increase your regular income tax withholding or make estimated tax installments to avoid an estimated tax penalty when you file your return.

EXAMPLES

1. For 2023, you have wages of $150,000 and your spouse has $175,000 of net self-employment earnings (as reported on Schedule SE, Line 4). You file a 2023 joint return. Your threshold for figuring the 0.9% tax is $250,000. Because you and spouse do not have wages over $250,000, the 0.9% tax does not apply to your wages on Part I of Form 8959. On Part II of Form 8959, the $250,000 threshold is reduced by your $150,000 of wages, giving you a reduced self-employment income threshold of $100,000. Since the self-employment earnings of $175,000 exceed the reduced threshold of $100,000 by $75,000, there is a Part II tax of $675 on the excess self-employment income (0.9% (.009) × $75,000 = $675).

2. For 2023, you file as a head of household. You have wages of $235,000 from one employer, and net self-employment earnings of $50,000. In addition to regular Medicare withholding, your employer withheld an additional $315, the amount of the 0.9% tax on the $35,000 of wages exceeding $200,000 ($235,000 wages – $200,000 threshold). On Part I of Form 8959, you figure the $315 Additional Medicare Tax on the excess $35,000 of wages (0.9% × $35,000). On Part II of Form 8959, the total wages are subtracted from the threshold, leaving you with a zero threshold ($200,000 threshold – $235,000 wages). Since the threshold is zero, the 0.9% tax applies to the entire $50,000 of self-employment income ($50,000 – $0 reduced threshold), for a tax of $450 (0.9% × $50,000). The total tax on Form 8959 is $765 ($315 + $450). Add the $315 of additional Medicare tax withheld by your employer to your federal income tax withholdings on Line 25c of Form 1040 or 1040-SR. In other words, the $315 withheld to cover the 0.9% tax does not directly offset the $765 liability for the tax on Form 8959, but rather is applied against all of the taxes you are liable for on Form 1040 or 1040-SR, including the 0.9% tax.

28.3 Additional 3.8% Tax on Net Investment Income

If you have net investment income and you have modified adjusted gross income (MAGI) exceeding the applicable threshold for your filing status, some or all of the net investment income will be subject to a 3.8% tax on Form 8960. The tax is called the Net Investment Income Tax (NIIT) on Form 8960. The thresholds for the tax are:

- $250,000 for married persons filing jointly and qualifying widows/widowers
- $200,000 for single persons and heads of households
- $125,000 for married persons filing separately

If your MAGI exceeds the applicable threshold, the 3.8% tax applies to the lesser of (1) your net investment income, or (2) your MAGI exceeding the threshold. Thus, if you have net investment income of $50,000, but your MAGI exceeds your threshold by only $20,000, the 3.8% tax applies to the lesser amount of $20,000. Also *see* the Examples below.

Estates and trusts may also be subject to the net investment income tax; *see* below.

MAGI thresholds. The thresholds are based on modified adjusted gross income, which, for calculating this specific tax, is the same as adjusted gross income (AGI) unless the foreign earned income exclusion *(36.1)* is claimed. If the foreign earned income exclusion is claimed, add back the excluded income (minus any above-the-line deductions or exclusions that were disallowed as allocable to the excluded foreign earned income) to get modified adjusted gross income.

Investment income and net investment income. Investment income subject to the 3.8% tax is entered on Part I of Form 8960. Investment income includes taxable interest, dividends, payments from commercial annuities (but not employee annuities), rents and royalties, capital gains from sales of stocks, bonds, mutual funds, or investment real estate including a vacation home, capital gain distributions from mutual funds, and passive income from partnerships and S corporations, including gain from the sale of a partnership or S corporation interest if you were a passive owner.

Do not count as investment income the following: tax-exempt interest, distributions from traditional IRAs, Roth IRAs, 401(k) plans and other qualified retirement plans such as pension plans, 403(b) plans and qualified annuity plans, and income from businesses, including partnerships and S corporations, in which you materially participate. Do not count excludable gain on qualified small business stock *(5.7)*. Also excluded are Social Security benefits, life insurance, taxable alimony and nontaxable veterans benefits.

A homeowner who sells his or her principal residence at a gain treats the gain as investment income for purposes of the 3.8% tax only to the extent that it exceeds the applicable home sale exclusion (usually $250,000 for singles and $500,000 for joint filers; *see 29.1*). If the gain is excluded from income, it is not subject to the 3.8% tax; *see* Examples 2 and 3 below.

Check the instructions to Form 8960 for further exceptions to the investment income category and details on items includible as investment income.

Note that a taxable distribution from a traditional IRA *(8.8)* or a qualified retirement plan, although excluded from the investment income category, is part of your MAGI, and the distribution, by increasing your MAGI, could push you over the threshold for the 3.8% tax or increase the tax if you are already over the threshold. This would not be true for a qualified Roth IRA distribution *(8.25)*, tax-exempt interest, or other item excluded from MAGI.

Investment expenses that are allocable to investment income are entered on Part II of Form 8960 and subtracted from investment income in Part III to arrive at net investment income. Allocable investment expenses include investment interest, depreciation or depletion, investment expenses reported on Schedule K-1 from a partnership or S corporation if not already included in Part I, and state and local income taxes allocable to items included as investment income: *see* the Form 8960 instructions for details on qualifying investment expenses.

Filing Tip

Excludable Home Sale Gain Not Subject to 3.8% Tax

Gain on the sale of a principal residence is not treated as investment income subject to the 3.8% tax to the extent it is tax free under the home sale exclusion rules *(29.1)*. See Examples 2 and 3 in *28.3*.

Caution

NIIT May Not Be Offset by Foreign Tax Credit

If you have a foreign tax credit, it may not be used to reduce or eliminate your NIIT, says the Tax Court.

EXAMPLES

1. John Smith, who is single, has $180,000 of wages in 2023, $20,000 of interest and dividends, and $80,000 of income from a passive partnership interest. John's MAGI is $280,000. His investment income is $100,000, which he reports on Part I of Form 8960. John's MAGI exceeds the $200,000 threshold for the 3.8% tax by $80,000, so in Part III of Form 8960, he figures the tax on the $80,000 excess MAGI, as it is less than the $100,000 of net investment income. John is liable for a tax of $3,040 ($80,000 × 3.8%). He must add the $3,040 to his other tax liability on Schedule 2 of Form 1040 or 1040-SR.

2. Donna Jones, who is single, earns wages of $45,000 in 2023. She also sells her principal residence, which she has owned and lived in since 2005, for $1 million. The home cost her $600,000, so her gain is $400,000. After claiming the $250,000 home sale exclusion (29.1), her taxable gain on the sale is $150,000 ($400,000 – $250,000). The $150,000 gain is net investment income. However, since her MAGI of $195,000 ($45,000 wages plus $150,000 taxed gain) is under the $200,000 threshold amount for the 3.8% tax, Donna does not owe the tax.

3. Bob and Carol Wilson file a joint return. Together they have $75,000 of wages, and $125,000 of interest, dividends, and capital gains in 2023. They also sell their principal residence, which they owned and lived in since 2002, for $1.3 million. The house cost them $700,000, so their profit is $600,000. After claiming the $500,000 home sale exclusion (29.3), their taxable gain from the sale is $100,000. Adding the $100,000 gain to the other $125,000 of investment income in Part I of Form 8960, Bob and Carol's net investment income is $225,000. Their MAGI is $300,000 ($75,000 wages plus $225,000 net investment income), $50,000 over the $250,000 threshold for the 3.8% tax. The tax applies to the $50,000 of excess MAGI, as it is less than the net investment income of $225,000. Bob and Carol's tax on Form 8960 is $1,900 ($50,000 × 3.8%).

Law Alert

QBI Deduction Does not Impact the 3.8% Tax

The qualified business income (QBI) deduction (40.24) does not reduce net investment income for purposes of the 3.8% net investment income tax. And because the QBI deduction is subtracted from adjusted gross income, it has no impact on MAGI for purposes of figuring whether the threshold for the 3.8% tax is exceeded.

Estates and trusts may also be subject to the 3.8% tax. For an estate or trust, the 3.8% tax generally applies to the lesser of its undistributed net investment income for the year or the excess of its AGI over the annual threshold for the 37% bracket for an estate or trust. For 2023, the 37% bracket threshold is $14,451. Grantor trusts and certain charitable trusts are exempt from the 3.8% tax. *See* the Form 8960 instructions for details.

Sample Form 8959—Additional Medicare Tax
(This sample is subject to change; see the e-Supplement at jklasser.com)

Form 8959

Department of the Treasury
Internal Revenue Service

Additional Medicare Tax

If any line does not apply to you, leave it blank. See separate instructions.
Attach to Form 1040, 1040-SR, 1040-NR, or 1040-SS.
Go to www.irs.gov/Form8959 for instructions and the latest information.

OMB No. 1545-0074

2023
Attachment Sequence No. **71**

Name(s) shown on return

Your social security number

Part I — Additional Medicare Tax on Medicare Wages

1	Medicare wages and tips from Form W-2, box 5. If you have more than one Form W-2, enter the total of the amounts from box 5	1	
2	Unreported tips from Form 4137, line 6	2	
3	Wages from Form 8919, line 6	3	
4	Add lines 1 through 3	4	
5	Enter the following amount for your filing status:		
	Married filing jointly $250,000		
	Married filing separately $125,000		
	Single, Head of household, or Qualifying surviving spouse $200,000	5	
6	Subtract line 5 from line 4. If zero or less, enter -0-		6
7	Additional Medicare Tax on Medicare wages. Multiply line 6 by 0.9% (0.009). Enter here and go to Part II		7

Part II — Additional Medicare Tax on Self-Employment Income

8	Self-employment income from Schedule SE (Form 1040), Part I, line 6. If you had a loss, enter -0-	8	
9	Enter the following amount for your filing status:		
	Married filing jointly $250,000		
	Married filing separately $125,000		
	Single, Head of household, or Qualifying surviving spouse $200,000	9	
10	Enter the amount from line 4	10	
11	Subtract line 10 from line 9. If zero or less, enter -0-	11	
12	Subtract line 11 from line 8. If zero or less, enter -0-		12
13	Additional Medicare Tax on self-employment income. Multiply line 12 by 0.9% (0.009). Enter here and go to Part III		13

Part III — Additional Medicare Tax on Railroad Retirement Tax Act (RRTA) Compensation

14	Railroad retirement (RRTA) compensation and tips from Form(s) W-2, box 14 (see instructions)	14	
15	Enter the following amount for your filing status:		
	Married filing jointly $250,000		
	Married filing separately $125,000		
	Single, Head of household, or Qualifying surviving spouse $200,000	15	
16	Subtract line 15 from line 14. If zero or less, enter -0-		16
17	Additional Medicare Tax on railroad retirement (RRTA) compensation. Multiply line 16 by 0.9% (0.009). Enter here and go to Part IV		17

Part IV — Total Additional Medicare Tax

18	Add lines 7, 13, and 17. Also include this amount on Schedule 2 (Form 1040), line 11 (Form 1040-SS filers, see instructions), and go to Part V		18

Part V — Withholding Reconciliation

19	Medicare tax withheld from Form W-2, box 6. If you have more than one Form W-2, enter the total of the amounts from box 6	19	
20	Enter the amount from line 1	20	
21	Multiply line 20 by 1.45% (0.0145). This is your regular Medicare tax withholding on Medicare wages	21	
22	Subtract line 21 from line 19. If zero or less, enter -0-. This is your Additional Medicare Tax withholding on Medicare wages		22
23	Additional Medicare Tax withholding on railroad retirement (RRTA) compensation from Form W-2, box 14 (see instructions)		23
24	**Total Additional Medicare Tax withholding.** Add lines 22 and 23. Also include this amount with federal income tax withholding on Form 1040, 1040-SR, or 1040-NR, line 25c (Form 1040-SS filers, see instructions)		24

For Paperwork Reduction Act Notice, see your tax return instructions.　　Cat. No. 59475X　　Form **8959** (2023)

Form **8960**	**Net Investment Income Tax—**	OMB No. 1545-2227
Department of the Treasury Internal Revenue Service	**Individuals, Estates, and Trusts** **Attach to your tax return.** **Go to *www.irs.gov/Form8960* for instructions and the latest information.**	**2023** Attachment Sequence No. **72**

Name(s) shown on your tax return | Your social security number or EIN

Part I **Investment Income**
☐ Section 6013(g) election (see instructions)
☐ Section 6013(h) election (see instructions)
☐ Regulations section 1.1411-10(g) election (see instructions)

1	Taxable interest (see instructions)	**1**	
2	Ordinary dividends (see instructions)	**2**	
3	Annuities (see instructions)	**3**	
4a	Rental real estate, royalties, partnerships, S corporations, trusts, trades or businesses, etc. (see instructions)	**4a**	
b	Adjustment for net income or loss derived in the ordinary course of a non-section 1411 trade or business (see instructions)	**4b**	
c	Combine lines 4a and 4b	**4c**	
5a	Net gain or loss from disposition of property (see instructions)	**5a**	
b	Net gain or loss from disposition of property that is not subject to net investment income tax (see instructions)	**5b**	
c	Adjustment from disposition of partnership interest or S corporation stock (see instructions)	**5c**	
d	Combine lines 5a through 5c	**5d**	
6	Adjustments to investment income for certain CFCs and PFICs (see instructions)	**6**	
7	Other modifications to investment income (see instructions)	**7**	
8	Total investment income. Combine lines 1, 2, 3, 4c, 5d, 6, and 7	**8**	

Part II **Investment Expenses Allocable to Investment Income and Modifications**

9a	Investment interest expenses (see instructions)	**9a**	
b	State, local, and foreign income tax (see instructions)	**9b**	
c	Miscellaneous investment expenses (see instructions)	**9c**	
d	Add lines 9a, 9b, and 9c	**9d**	
10	Additional modifications (see instructions)	**10**	
11	Total deductions and modifications. Add lines 9d and 10	**11**	

Part III **Tax Computation**

12	Net investment income. Subtract Part II, line 11, from Part I, line 8. Individuals, complete lines 13–17. Estates and trusts, complete lines 18a–21. If zero or less, enter -0-	**12**	
	Individuals:		
13	Modified adjusted gross income (see instructions)	**13**	
14	Threshold based on filing status (see instructions)	**14**	
15	Subtract line 14 from line 13. If zero or less, enter -0-	**15**	
16	Enter the smaller of line 12 or line 15	**16**	
17	Net investment income tax for individuals. Multiply line 16 by 3.8% (0.038). **Enter here and include on your tax return** (see instructions)	**17**	
	Estates and Trusts:		
18a	Net investment income (line 12 above)	**18a**	
b	Deductions for distributions of net investment income and charitable deductions (see instructions)	**18b**	
c	Undistributed net investment income. Subtract line 18b from line 18a (see instructions). If zero or less, enter -0-	**18c**	
19a	Adjusted gross income (see instructions)	**19a**	
b	Highest tax bracket for estates and trusts for the year (see instructions)	**19b**	
c	Subtract line 19b from line 19a. If zero or less, enter -0-	**19c**	
20	Enter the smaller of line 18c or line 19c	**20**	
21	Net investment income tax for estates and trusts. Multiply line 20 by 3.8% (0.038). **Enter here and include on your tax return** (see instructions)	**21**	

For Paperwork Reduction Act Notice, see your tax return instructions. Cat. No. 59474M Form **8960** (2023)

PART 5

Tax Planning

The chapters in this part will alert you to special tax situations. They will point out tax-saving opportunities and show you how to take advantage of tax-saving ideas and planning strategies.

CHAPTER 29

Tax Savings for Residence Sales

You may avoid tax on gain on the sale of a principal residence if you owned and used it as your principal residence for at least two years during the five-year ownership period ending on the date of sale. If you are single, you may avoid tax on up to $250,000 of gain, $500,000 if you are married and file jointly. However, gain attributable to nonqualified use after 2008 is not excludable *(29.2)*.

If you used the residence as your principal residence for less than two years, you may avoid tax if you sold because of a change of job location, poor health or unforeseen circumstance *(29.4)*.

You may not deduct a loss on the sale of a personal residence. Losses on the sale of property devoted to personal use in general are nondeductible *(29.8)*. However, there are circumstances under which you may claim a loss deduction on the sale of a residence *(29.9–29.10)*.

If you rent out a residential property and you or family members also use the residence during the year, rental expenses are subject to special restrictions *(9.7)*.

Reporting Home Sale Gain or Loss on Your Return

If you have a gain on the sale of your principal residence and the entire gain is excludable from income under the rules discussed in this chapter *(29.1–29.7)*, you do not have to report the sale at all on your return unless you received a Form 1099-S from the settlement agent reporting the sale, in which case the sale must be reported on Form 8949 *(5.8)*. Form 8949 is also used to report the sale if you have a taxable gain and did not receive Form 1099-S, or you received Form 1099-S and have any gain that cannot be excluded, or you decide not to claim the exclusion for excludable gain. If you can exclude all or part of your gain, you claim the allowable exclusion by entering code "H" in column (f) of Form 8949 and entering the exclusion as a negative adjustment in column (g). *See* the IRS instructions for Form 8949 for further details.

If you have gain that cannot be excluded, the taxable gain is subject to the 3.8% Net Investment Income Tax (NIIT), provided your income exceeds the applicable threshold for the NIIT *(28.3)*.

If you had a loss on the sale of your home, the loss is not deductible, but if you received a Form 1099-S, you must report the sale on Form 8949 *(29.8)*.

Planning Reminder

Form 1099-S

The settlement agent responsible for closing the sale of your principal residence must report the sale to the IRS on Form 1099-S if the sales price exceeded $250,000, or $500,000 if you are married filing jointly. If the price was $250,000/$500,000 or less and you provide a written, signed certification that the full amount of your gain qualifies for the exclusion, the settlement agent may rely on the certification and not file the Form 1099-S or may choose to file the form anyway. IRS Revenue Procedure 2007-12 has a sample certification form, but certain required assurances that are not included in Revenue Procedure 2007-12 must be added to your certification; *see* the Form 1099-S instructions.

29.1 Avoiding Tax on Sale of Principal Residence

If you sell (or exchange) your principal residence at a gain *(29.5)*, up to $250,000 of the gain may be excluded from income if you owned and occupied it as a principal residence for an aggregate of at least two years in the five-year period ending on the date of sale and did not claim an exclusion on another sale within the prior two years. *See* the discussion of the two-out-of-five-year ownership and use tests in the following section *(29.2)*. If you are married filing jointly, you may be able to exclude up to $500,000 of gain *(29.3)*. Even if you do not meet the two-out-of-five-year ownership and use tests, you are entitled to a reduced maximum exclusion limit if the primary reason for your sale was a change in the place of employment, health reasons, or unforeseen circumstances *(29.4)*.

No indexing. The $250,000/$500,000 exclusion, which was first enacted in 1997, is not indexed for inflation, in contrast to individual income tax rate brackets. Several attempts in Congress since then to raise this ceiling, either across the board or for older homeowners, have failed.

Caution: If you use a residence as a vacation home or rental property after 2008, an allocable part of your gain may not qualify for the exclusion, even if you meet the two-out-of-five-year ownership and use tests; see "No Exclusion for Nonqualified Use After 2008", in 29.2.

Frequency of exclusion. If you meet the ownership and use tests for a principal residence *(29.2)*, you may claim the exclusion when you sell the residence although you previously claimed the exclusion for another residence, provided that the sales are more than two years apart. If you claim the exclusion on a sale and within two years of the first sale you sell another principal residence, an exclusion may not be claimed on the second sale even if you meet the ownership and use tests for that residence. There is an exception if the second sale was due to a change in employment, health reasons, or unforeseen circumstances. In that case, a prorated exclusion limit is allowed *(29.4)*.

Principal residence. A principal residence is not restricted to one-family houses but includes a mobile home, trailer, houseboat, and condominium apartment used as a principal residence. An investment in a retirement community does not qualify as a principal residence unless you receive equity in the property. In the case of a tenant-stockholder of a cooperative housing corporation, the residence ownership requirement applies to the ownership of the stock and the use requirement applies to the house or apartment that the stockholder occupies *(29.2)*.

If you have multiple homes. If you have more than one home, you may exclude gain only on the sale of your principal residence and only if you meet the ownership and use tests *(29.2)* for that residence. Your "principal residence" is determined on a year-to-year basis, based primarily on where you live most of the time. However, the IRS may also consider such factors as the primary residence of your family members, your place of employment, mailing address, the address listed on your tax returns, driver's license and automobile and voter registration, and the location of your bank.

Vacant land. Vacant land owned and used as part of a taxpayer's principal residence may qualify for the exclusion. The vacant land must be adjacent to the residence and the sale of the residence must be within two years before or after the sale of the land. Qualifying sales of land and residence are treated as one sale, so the $250,000 exclusion limit ($500,000 for qualifying joint filers) applies to the combined sales. If the sales occur in different years, the exclusion limit applies first to the residence sale.

Business or rental use. If part of your home was rented out or used for business, *see* the rules for determining whether you can exclude all or some of the gain on a sale *(29.7)*. Also *see* the rules for deducting a loss where your residence was converted to rental property *(29.9)*.

Home destroyed or condemned. If your home is destroyed or condemned, this is treated as a sale, so any gain realized on the conversion may qualify for the exclusion. If vacant land used as part of your home is sold within two years of the conversion, the sale of the land may be combined with the sale of the residence for exclusion purposes; *see* the vacant land rule earlier. Any part of the gain that may not be excluded (because it exceeds the limit) may be postponed under the rules explained in *18.15*.

Sale of remainder interest. You may choose to exclude gain from the sale of a remainder interest in your home. If you do, you may not choose to exclude gain from your sale of any other interest in the home that you sell separately. Also, you may not exclude gain from the sale of a remainder interest to a related party. Related parties include your brothers and sisters, half-brothers and half-sisters, spouse, ancestors (parents, grandparents, etc.), and lineal descendants (children, grandchildren, etc.). Related parties also include certain corporations, partnerships, trusts, and exempt organizations.

Ownership by trust. Ownership of the residence by a trust may be considered owned by the individual taxpayer who benefits under the "grantor trust rules" explained at *39.6*. Likewise, any sale by such a trust is considered made by the taxpayer who benefits for purposes of qualifying for the home-sale exclusion under the tests at *29.2*. Similar rules apply to single-owner estates disassociated for tax purposes from its underlying owner.

Expatriates. You cannot claim the home sale exclusion if the expatriation tax *(1.20)* applies to you. The expatriation tax applies to U.S. citizens who have renounced their citizenship (and long-term residents who have ended their residency) if one of their principal purposes was to avoid U.S. taxes.

The exclusion is not mandatory. You do not have to apply the exclusion to a particular qualifying sale. For example, you are unable to sell a residence when you acquire a new residence. When you finally are able to find a buyer for the first home, you also decide to sell the second residence. Assume both sales may qualify for the exclusion, but the potential gain on the first house will be less than the potential gain on the sale of the second home. You will not want to apply the exclusion to the sale of the first home if doing so will prevent you from applying the exclusion to the second sale because of the rule allowing an exclusion for only one sale every two years.

Federal subsidy recapture. If your home was financed with the proceeds of a tax-exempt bond or a qualified mortgage credit certificate *(15.1)* and you sell or dispose of the home within nine years of the financing, you may have to recapture the federal subsidy received even if the sale qualifies for the home sale exclusion. Use Form 8828 to figure the amount of the recapture tax, which is reported on Form 1040 or 1040-SR as a separate tax.

29.2 Meeting the Ownership and Use Tests for Exclusion

To qualify for the exclusion of up-to-$250,000, you must have owned and occupied a home as your principal residence for at least two years during the five-year period ending on the date of sale. If you are married and file a joint return, you may claim an exclusion of up to $500,000 if one of you meets the ownership test and both of you meet the use test *(29.3)*. If you are a joint owner of the residence and file a separate return, the up-to-$250,000 exclusion applies to your share of the gain, assuming you meet the ownership and use tests.

A sale generally is considered to take place when title passes (usually at the "closing"), rather than when the contract of sale is executed. An installment sale of a residence under normal circumstances does not change the date for determining ownership and use but may impact when any gain must be recognized by the seller *(5.21)*.

The periods of ownership and use do not have to be continuous. The ownership and use tests may be met in different two-year periods, provided both tests are met within the five-year period ending on the date of sale (as in Example 3 below). You qualify if you can show that you owned the home and lived in it as your principal residence for 24 full months or for 730 days (365 × 2) during the five-year period ending on the date of sale. "Short temporary absences" can count as periods of residential use. The IRS has allowed a two-month summer vacation away from the residence as temporary. It also considers such absences as counting toward the 24-month rule even if the home was rented out in the taxpayer's absence.

Filing Tip

Short Absences

Short temporary absences for vacations count as time you used the residence for purposes of the two-out-of-five year tests *(29.2)*.

Court Decision

Co-Owner Can Claim Full $250,000 Exclusion

A single taxpayer who sells her home at a gain after owning and using it for at least two of the five years preceding the date of sale can exclude up to $250,000 of gain from income. What if there are two co-owners: do they have to split the $250,000 exclusion? The IRS argued, in a 2010 case, that the $250,000 exclusion has to be shared. The taxpayer owned a 50% interest in a home she used as her principal residence since February 1997. When the home was sold in 2005, her share of the gain was $264,644.50 (half of the $529,289 total gain, which she excluded). The IRS said she was only entitled to half of the full exclusion, or $125,000.

The Tax Court allowed the full $250,000 exclusion. The statute (Code Section 121) does not limit the exclusion for partial owners of a principal residence. In fact, an example in the IRS regulations specifically allows unmarried joint owners holding 50% interests in a home to each exclude up to the full $250,000 limit for their shares of the gain on a sale so long as they each meet the ownership and use tests and have not excluded gain from another home sale within the prior two-year period.

If the ownership and use tests are not met but the primary reason for the sale was a change in the place of employment, health reasons, or unforeseen circumstances, an exclusion is allowed under the reduced maximum exclusion rules *(29.4)*. If the ownership and use tests are met, but within the two-year period ending on the date of sale you sold another principal residence for which you claimed the exclusion, you cannot claim an exclusion unless the reduced maximum exclusion rules apply *(29.4)*.

Further, even if you meet the two-out-of-five-year ownership and use tests, some of your gain will be taxable if you use the residence after 2008 as a second home or rental property, unless an exception applies; *see* the discussion of the nonqualified use rule at the end of this section.

> **EXAMPLES**
>
> 1. From 2008 through August 2023 Janet lives with her parents in a house that her parents owned. In September 2023, she buys this house from her parents. She continues to live there until December 18, 2024, when she sells it at a gain. Although Janet lived in the home for more than two years, she did not own it for at least two years. She may not exclude any part of her gain on the sale, unless she sells because of a change in her place of employment, health reasons, or unforeseen circumstances *(29.4)*.
>
> 2. John buys and moves into a house on July 9, 2022. He lives in it as his principal residence continuously until October 1, 2023, when he goes abroad for a one-year sabbatical leave. After returning from the leave, he sells the house on November 6, 2024. He does not meet the two-year use test. Because his sabbatical was not a short, temporary absence, he may not include the period of leave in his period of use in order to meet the two-year use test. He may avoid tax on gain if he sells because of a changed job location unforeseen circumstances, or poor health *(29.4)*.
>
> 3. Since 1997, Jonah has lived in an apartment building that was changed to a condominium. He bought the apartment on December 3, 2020. In February 2022, he becomes ill and on April 16, 2022, he moves into his son's home. On July 16, 2024, while still living with his son, he sells the apartment.
>
>   He may exclude gain on the sale of the apartment because he met the ownership and use tests. The five-year period is from July 17, 2019, to July 16, 2024, the date of the sale of the apartment. He owned the apartment from December 3, 2020, to July 16, 2024 (over two years). He lived in the apartment from July 17, 2019 (the beginning of the five-year period) to April 16, 2022, a period of use of over two years.
>
> 4. In 2012, Carol buys a house and lives in it until January 31, 2021, when she moves out. She rents the house to a tenant from March 1, 2021, until May 31, 2024. Carol moves back into the house on June 1, 2024, and lives there until she sells it on October 30, 2024. During the five-year period ending on the date of the sale (November 1, 2019 – October 30, 2024), Carol lived in the house for less than two years.
>
> | Five-year period— | Home use (months)— | Rental use (months)— |
> |---|---|---|
> | 11/1/19–1/31/21 | 15 | |
> | 3/1/21–5/31/24 | | 39 |
> | 6/1/24–10/30/24 | 5 | |
> | Total | 20 | 39 |
>
> Carol may not exclude any of the gain on the sale, unless she sells the house for health or employment reasons or due to unforeseen circumstances *(29.4)*.

Military and Foreign Service personnel, intelligence officers, and Peace Corps workers can suspend five-year period. You may elect to suspend the running of the five-year ownership and use period while you or your spouse is on qualified official extended duty as a member of the uniformed services or Foreign Service of the United States. The suspension can be for up to 10 years. It is allowed for only one residence at a time. By making the election and disregarding up to 10 years of qualifying service, you can claim an exclusion where the two-year use test is met before you began the qualifying service and after your return; *see* the Example below. Qualified official extended duty means active duty for over 90 days or for an indefinite period with a branch of the U.S. Armed Forces at a duty station at least 50 miles from your principal residence or in Government-mandated quarters. Members of the Foreign Service, commissioned corps of the National Oceanic and Atmospheric Administration, and commissioned corps of the Public Health Service who meet the active duty tests also qualify.

Similarly, the five-year testing period is suspended for up to 10 years for intelligence community employees (specified national agencies and departments) and Peace Corps workers. The suspension rule for Peace Corps workers applies to Peace Corps employees, enrolled volunteers, or volunteer leaders for periods during which they are on qualified official extended duty outside the United States.

Caution

Residence Acquired in Like-Kind Exchange

A residence acquired in a like-kind exchange must be owned for at least five years before gain on its sale can qualify for the exclusion.

> **EXAMPLE**
>
> Michael bought a home in Maryland in March 2011 that he lived in before moving to Brazil in November 2015 as a member of the Foreign Service of the United States. He served there on qualified official extended duty for eight years, until the end of 2023. In January 2024, he sells the Maryland home at a gain. He did not use the home as his principal residence for two out of the five years preceding the sale and so does not qualify for an exclusion under the regular rule. However, Michael can exclude gain of up to $250,000 by electing to suspend the running of the five-year test period while he was abroad with the Foreign Service. Under the election, his eight years of service are disregarded and his years of use from March 2011—November 2015 are considered to be within the five-year period preceding the sale. He thus meets the two-out-of-five-year test and can claim the exclusion.

Cooperative apartments. If you sell your stock in a cooperative housing corporation, you meet the ownership and use tests if, during the five-year period ending on the date of sale, you:

1. Owned stock for at least two years, and
2. Used the house or apartment that the stock entitles you to occupy as your principal residence for at least two years.

Incapacitated homeowner. A homeowner who becomes physically or mentally incapable of self-care is deemed to use a residence as a principal residence during the time in which the individual owns the residence and resides in a licensed care facility. For this rule to apply, the homeowner must have owned and used the residence as a principal residence for an aggregate period of at least one year during the five years preceding the sale.

If you meet this disability exception, you still have to meet the two-out-of-five-year ownership test to claim the exclusion.

Previous home destroyed or condemned. For the ownership and use tests, you may add time you owned and lived in a previous home that was destroyed or condemned if any part of the basis of the current home sold depended on the basis of the destroyed or condemned home under the involuntary conversion rules *(18.15)*.

No Exclusion for Nonqualified Use After 2008

Even if the two-out-of-five-year test for an exclusion is met, gain attributable to "nonqualified" use after 2008 is not eligible for the exclusion. The primary intent of the rule is to deny an exclusion for some of the gain realized by taxpayers who convert a vacation home or rented residence to their principal residence and live in it for a few years before selling. However, the law as written is broader, generally treating any period after 2008 in which the home is not used as a principal residence by you, your spouse, or former spouse as "nonqualified use." Despite the broad wording of the law, there are exceptions (below) that lessen the potential impact of the nonqualified use rule. In particular, exception 1 allows many home sellers to avoid nonqualified use treatment where they move out and rent the home before selling it; *see* Example 2 below.

Exceptions to nonqualified use. There are exceptions that limit the impact of the nonqualified use rule. The law specifically exempts the following from the definition of post-2008 "nonqualified use": (1) the period after you, or your spouse, last use the home as your principal residence, so long as it is within the five years ending on the date of sale; *see* Example 2 below, (2) temporary absences from the residence, not to exceed two years in total, due to a change in employment, health reasons (such as time in a hospital or nursing home), or other unforeseen circumstances to be specified by the IRS, and (3) periods of up to 10 years (in aggregate) during which you, or your spouse, are on qualified official extended duty (duty station at least 50 miles from residence) as a member of the uniformed services, as a Foreign Service officer, or as an employee of the intelligence community.

The IRS has not released formal guidelines on "nonqualified use," including any other possible exceptions, such as whether short-term rental periods will be disregarded. However, in Publication 523 it takes the position that where rental or business space is physically part of the living area of your home, such as a home office or a spare bedroom that you rent out as part of a bed-and-breakfast business, that use is treated as residential use. Although the IRS does not specifically say so, such home office or rental space within the home is not considered "nonqualified use" in applying the fractional computation below.

Figuring the excludable and nonexcludable gain. To figure the exclusion on a sale where there is nonqualified use after 2008, the gain equal to post–May 6, 1997 depreciation (allowed or allowable) *(29.7)* is taken into account first. No exclusion is allowed for this depreciation amount *(29.7)*; this is a long-standing rule that is not changed by the nonqualified use calculation.

After taking into account post-May 6, 1997 depreciation, the portion of the remaining gain that is allocable to nonqualified use must be figured; this amount also is not eligible for the exclusion. The allocation is made by multiplying the gain by the following fraction:

$$\frac{\text{Total days of nonqualified use after 2008}}{\text{Total days of ownership of the home}}$$

You can use *Worksheet 29-3* later in this chapter to make the allocation and figure your excludable and taxable gain.

EXAMPLES

1. Martin bought his home on April 23, 2018, and lived in it until June 30, 2020, when he moved out. He rented the home from July 1, 2020, to June 30, 2022, and claimed depreciation deductions of $10,000 for that period. Martin moves back into the house July 1, 2022, and lives there until he sells it on January 31, 2024, for a gain of $310,000. In the five-year period ending on the date of sale (February 1, 2019–January 31, 2024), Martin met the ownership and use test for an exclusion: he owned the home and used it for more than two years in the five-year period. He owned it for the entire five years and used it as his home for 36 months (17 months from February 1, 2019–June 30, 2020, and 19 months from July 1, 2022–January 31, 2024), while renting it for the other 24 months (July 1, 2020–June 30, 2022). The rental period is nonqualified use.

    Using *Worksheet 29-3*, Martin figures his exclusion and taxable gain. The $10,000 of gain allocable to depreciation cannot be excluded. Of the remaining $300,000 gain ($310,000 gain -$10,000 depreciation), Martin figures that $104,100 is allocable to nonqualified use and thus not eligible for an exclusion. Martin owned the home for 2,109 days (beginning with April 24, 2018, the day after he bought it, and ending on January 31, 2024, the date of sale). Of his 2,109 ownership days, 731 days (the rental days, July 1, 2020 through June 30, 2022) were nonqualified use. The allocation to nonqualified use is 731/ 2,109, or 34.7%, and 34.7% × $300,000 is $104,100. Martin may exclude $195,900 of the gain from his 2024 income ($300,000–$104,100).

    On Form 8949 and Schedule D *(5.8)* for 2023, Martin will report taxable gain of $114,100 ($10,000 gain allocable to depreciation + $104,100 gain allocable to nonqualified use), and also will report the exclusion of $195,900. The $10,000 gain from depreciation is unrecaptured Section 1250 gain, which Martin will enter on the Unrecaptured Section 1250 Gain Worksheet in the Schedule D instructions *(5.3)*.

Keep in mind that even without the nonqualified use rule, only $250,000 of Martin's $300,000 gain (after depreciation is subtracted) would have been excludable. The effect of the nonqualified use rule under these facts is to increase the taxed (nonexcludable) gain by an additional $54,100, from $50,000 ($300,000 − $250,000) to $104,100 under the allocation formula.

2. Andrea owned and lived in her principal residence from 2018 through 2021 and then moved to another state. She rents the home from January 1, 2022, until April 30, 2024, when she sells it. Andrea has met the ownership and use test: she owned and lived in the house for more than two years in the five-year period ending on the date of sale (May 1, 2019–April 30, 2024). Although Andrea rented out the home after 2008, the rental period (January 1, 2022–April 30, 2024) is not considered nonqualified use because it was after she moved out of the home and was within the five-year period ending on the sale date (Exception 1 under "Exceptions to nonqualified use" on pages 561-562). Andrea may exclude gain of up to $250,000, but not gain equal to the depreciation she claimed (or could have claimed) while the house was rented. Because the property was rented at the time of sale, the IRS requires the sale to be reported and the exclusion claimed on Form 4797.

29.3 Home Sales by Married Persons

Where a married couple owned and lived in their principal residence for at least two years during the five-year period ending on the date of sale, they may claim an exclusion of up to $500,000 of gain on a joint return. Under the law, the up-to-$500,000 exclusion may be claimed on a joint return provided that during the five-year period ending on the date of sale: (1) either spouse owned the residence for at least two years, (2) both spouses lived in the house as their principal residence for at least two years, and (3) neither spouse is ineligible to claim the exclusion because an exclusion was previously claimed on a sale of a principal residence within the two-year period ending on the date of this sale. If Tests 1 and 3 are met but only one of you meets Test 2, your exclusion limit on a joint return is $250,000. However, even if the two-out-of-five-year use test is met, "nonqualified use" after 2008 may limit the exclusion you can claim; *see 29.2*.

Death of spouse before sale. If your spouse died and you inherit the house and later sell it, you are considered to have owned and used the property during any period of time when your spouse owned and used it as a principal home, provided you did not remarry before your sale. This rule can enable you to satisfy the two-out-of-five-year ownership and use tests where your spouse met the tests but you on your own did not. It may also enable you to claim the $500,000 exclusion if you sell the house in the year your spouse died or within the next two years, as discussed in the next two paragraphs.

If you and your spouse each met the use test and at least one of you met the ownership test as of the date of your spouse's death, and you sell the residence in the year he or she dies, you may use the $500,000 exclusion limit, assuming you file a joint return for the year of your spouse's death and neither of you claimed the exclusion for another home sale in the two years before your spouse died.

You are also entitled to use the $500,000 exclusion limit on a sale that is within two years of your spouse's death, provided you have not remarried and you and your spouse would have qualified for the $500,000 limit on a sale immediately before his or her death under Tests 1–3 at the beginning of *29.3*.

Caution

Exclusion for Married Couple

For a recently married couple, the exclusion limit on a joint return is $250,000, not $500,000, where one of the spouses has satisfied both the ownership test and the use test before a sale and the other spouse has not met the use test. Gain in excess of the $250,000 exclusion is reported on Form 8949 *(5.8)*.

EXAMPLES

1. You and your spouse have owned and occupied your principal residence for 20 years. In December 2024, you sell the house for a gain of $450,000. If you file jointly, none of the gain is taxable as the up-to-$500,000 exclusion applies.

2. After your spouse dies, you own and live in your principal residence from June 2019 through the end of 2023. In January 2024, you remarry and you and your wife live in the house for nine months. In October 2024, you sell the house and realize a gain of $350,000. On a joint return for 2024, you may claim an exclusion of $250,000; the balance of $100,000 is taxable. You meet the exclusion tests, but your wife does not. Thus, the exclusion is limited to $250,000.

Step-up basis. Under the Internal Revenue Code, most assets owned by a decedent receive a step-up in basis to its date of death market value. For joint ownership prior to death, that allows half the residence to receive a basis of half its fair market value at death. In community property states, a surviving spouse may be entitled to a stepped-up basis equal to the entire value of the residence at date of death *(5.17)*.

Divorce or separation. If a residence is transferred to you incident to divorce, the time during which your former spouse owned the residence is added to your period of ownership. If pursuant to a divorce or separation decree or agreement you move out of a home that you own or jointly own with your spouse or former spouse, you are treated as having used the home for any period that you retain an ownership interest in the residence while the other spouse or former spouse continues to use it as a principal residence under the terms of the divorce or separation agreement.

Separate residences. Where a husband and wife own and live in separate residences, each spouse is entitled to a separate exclusion limit of $250,000 on the sale of his or her residence. If both residences are sold in the same year and each spouse met the ownership and use test for his or her separate residence, two exclusions may be claimed (up to $250,000 each), either on a joint return or on separate returns.

29.4 Reduced Maximum Exclusion

Generally, no exclusion is allowed on a sale of a principal residence if you owned or used the home for less than two of the five years preceding the sale *(29.2)*. Similarly, an exclusion is generally disallowed if within the two-year period ending on the date of sale, you sold another home at a gain that was wholly or partially excluded from your income.

However, even if a sale of a principal residence is made before meeting the ownership and use tests or it is within two years of a prior sale for which an exclusion was claimed, a partial exclusion is available if the primary reason for the sale is: (1) a change in the place of employment, (2) health, or (3) unforeseen circumstances. If the sale is for one of these qualifying reasons, you are entitled to a prorated portion of the regular $250,000 or $500,000 exclusion limit. The employment change, health problem, or unforeseen circumstance can be attributable to you or another "qualified individual," as defined below.

You automatically qualify for the reduced exclusion if your sale is within a safe harbor established by the IRS. If a safe harbor is not available, you may qualify by showing that the "facts and circumstances" of your situation establish that the primary reason for the sale was a change in the place of employment, health problem or unforeseen circumstances.

When you fall within a safe harbor or meet the primary reason test, you are allowed an allocable percentage of the regular $250,000 or $500,000 exclusion limit, depending on how much of the regular two-year ownership and use test was satisfied, or the time between this sale and a sale within the prior two years. For example, if you owned and lived in your home for 438 days before selling it to take a new job, you are entitled to 60% of the regular exclusion limit, which is based on 730 qualifying days (438/730 = 60%). Use *Worksheet 29-1* to figure your reduced exclusion limit. Although the maximum exclusion is reduced, this may not be a disadvantage. If the reduced exclusion limit equals or exceeds your gain, none of your gain is subject to tax.

Qualified individual. In addition to yourself, the following persons are considered qualified individuals for purposes of qualifying for the reduced maximum exclusion: your spouse, a co-owner of the residence, or any person whose main home was your principal residence.

For purposes of the "health reasons" category, qualified individuals include not only the above individuals but also their family members: parents or step-parents, grandparents, children, stepchildren, adopted children, grandchildren, siblings (including step- or half-siblings), in-laws (mother/father, brother/sister, son/daughter), uncles, aunts, nephews, or nieces.

IRS Alert

Amended Return to Claim Reduced Maximum Exclusion

If you reported gain on a sale that can be avoided under the reduced maximum exclusion rules for sales due to a change in place of employment, health, or unforeseen circumstances, a refund claim can be made on an amended return, provided the prior year is not closed by the statute of limitations *(47.2)*.

Worksheet 29-1   Reduced Maximum Exclusion

Caution: *Complete this worksheet only if you qualify for a reduced maximum exclusion (under the rules at 29.4).*

			(a) You	(b) Your Spouse
1.	Maximum amount	**1.**	$250,000	$250,000
2a.	Enter the number of days (or months) that you used the property as a main home during the 5-year period* ending on the date of sale	**2a.**		
b.	Enter the number of days (or months) that you owned the property during the 5-year period* ending on the date of sale. If you used days on line 2a, you also must use days on this line and on lines 3 and 5. If you used months on line 2a, you also must use months on this line and on lines 3 and 5. (If married filing jointly and one spouse owned the property longer than the other spouse, both spouses are treated as owning the property for the longer period.)	**b.**		
c.	Enter the smaller of line 2a or 2b	**c.**		
3.	Have you (or your spouse, if filing jointly) excluded gain from the sale of another home during the 2-year period ending on the date of this sale? ☐ **No.** Skip line 3 and enter the number of days (or months) from line 2c on line 4. ☐ **Yes.** Enter the number of days (or months) between the date of the most recent sale of another home on which you excluded gain and the date of sale of this home	**3.**		
4.	Enter the smaller of line 2c or 3	**4.**		
5.	Divide the amount on line 4 by 730 days (or 24 months). Enter the result as a decimal (rounded to at least 3 places). But do not enter an amount greater than 1.000	**5.**		
6.	Multiply the amount on line 1 by the decimal amount on line 5	**6.**		
7.	**Reduced maximum exclusion.** Add the amounts in columns (a) and (b) of line 6. Enter it here and on Worksheet 29-3, Line 13	**7.**		

*If you were a member of the uniformed services or Foreign Service, an employee of the intelligence community, or an employee or volunteer of the Peace Corps during the time you owned the home, see 29.2 to determine your 5-year period.

EXAMPLE

You buy and move into your residence on April 4, 2023, so your holding period begins on April 5, 2023. In 2024 you move to a new job location in another state and sell your house at a gain of $50,000 on April 4, 2024. Since you owned and used your home for 12 months (365 days), your exclusion limit is reduced by 50% (365/730 days). You are single. Your reduced exclusion limit is $125,000 (50% of $250,000) and since the gain of $50,000 is totally covered by the $125,000 exclusion it is not taxable.

Sale due to change in place of employment. The reduced exclusion limit applies if the primary reason for your sale is a change in the location of a qualified individual's employment; *see* the above definition of qualified individual. "Employment" includes working for the same employer at a different location or starting with a new employer. It also includes the commencement of self-employment or the continuation of self-employment at a new location.

The IRS provides a safe harbor based on distance. If a qualified individual's new place of employment is at least 50 miles farther from the sold home than the old place of employment was, the reduced exclusion limit is allowed so long as the change in employment occurred while you owned and used the home as your principal residence. If an unemployed qualified person obtains employment, the safe harbor applies if the sold home is at least 50 miles from the place of employment.

If the 50-mile safe harbor cannot be met, the facts and circumstances may indicate that a change in the place of employment was the primary reason for the sale, thereby allowing the reduced exclusion limit.

> **EXAMPLE**
>
> An emergency room physician buys a condominium in March 2024 that is five miles from the hospital where she works. In November 2024, she takes a new job at a hospital 51 miles away from her home. She sells her home in December 2024 and buys a townhouse that is four miles away from the new hospital. The sale does not qualify for the 50-mile safe harbor since the new hospital is only 46 miles further from the old home than the first hospital was. However, given the doctor's need to work unscheduled hours and to get to work quickly, the IRS allows the reduced exclusion limit; the facts show that her change in place of employment was the primary reason for the home sale.

Sale due to health problems. The reduced exclusion limit applies if a principal residence is sold primarily to obtain or facilitate the diagnosis, treatment, or mitigation of a qualified person's disease, illness or injury, or to obtain or provide medical or personal care for a qualified individual suffering from a disease, illness, or injury. A sale does not qualify if it is merely to improve general health. Note that for "health sales," the definition of qualified individual is broadened to include family members; *see* above.

A physician's recommendation of a change in residence for health reasons automatically qualifies under an IRS safe harbor.

> **EXAMPLES**
>
> 1. One year after purchasing a home in Michigan, Smith is told by his doctor that moving to a warm, dry climate would mitigate his chronic asthma symptoms. Smith takes the advice, selling the house and moving to a desert location in Arizona. The sale is within the doctor recommendation safe harbor and Smith may claim a reduced maximum exclusion for gain on the sale of the Michigan home.
> 2. In 2024, Mike and Kathy Anderson sell the house they bought in 2023 so they can move in with Kathy's father, who is chronically ill and unable to care for himself. The IRS allows the Andersons to claim a reduced maximum exclusion, as the primary reason for the sale is to provide care for Kathy's father, a qualified individual.

Sale due to unforeseen circumstances. A sale of a principal residence due to any of the following events fits within an IRS safe harbor for unforeseen circumstances and automatically qualifies for a reduced maximum exclusion:

1. The involuntary conversion of the home (condemnation or destruction of house in a storm or fire);
2. Damage to the residence from a natural or man-made disaster, war, or act of terrorism;
3. Any of the following events involving a qualified individual *(see above)*: death, divorce or legal separation, becoming eligible for unemployment compensation, a change in employment or self-employment status that left the qualified individual unable to pay housing costs and reasonable basic household expenses, or multiple births resulting from the same pregnancy.

The IRS may expand the list of safe harbors in generally applicable revenue rulings or in private rulings requested by individual taxpayers.

Sales not covered by a safe harbor can qualify if the facts and circumstances indicate that the home was sold primarily because of an event that could not have been reasonably anticipated before the residence was purchased and occupied. The IRS in private letter rulings has been quite liberal in allowing the reduced maximum exclusion for unforeseen sales; *see* the examples below. Even the birth of a second child has been held to be an unforeseen circumstance (Example 5). However, an improvement in financial circumstances does not qualify under IRS regulations, even if the improvement is the result of unforeseen events, such as receiving a promotion and a large salary increase that would allow the purchase of a bigger home.

EXAMPLES

1. Three months after Jones buys a condominium as his principal residence, the condominium association replaces the roof and heating system and a few months later the monthly condominium fees are doubled. If Jones sells the condo because he cannot pay the higher fees and his monthly mortgage payment, the sale is considered to be due to unforeseen circumstances and Jones may claim a reduced maximum exclusion.

2. Tom and his fiancée, Alice, buy a house and live in it as their principal residence. The next year they break up and Tom moves out. The house is sold because Alice cannot afford to make the monthly payments alone. According to the IRS, the sale is due to unforeseen circumstances and Alice and Tom may each claim a reduced maximum exclusion.

3. A married couple purchased a home in a retirement community that had minimum age requirements for residents. Shortly after they moved in, their daughter lost her job and was in the process of getting a divorce. The daughter and her child wanted to move in but could not because of the community's age requirements. The couple sold the home and bought a new one in which their daughter and grandchild lived while the daughter looked for full-time employment. The IRS privately ruled that the sale of the retirement community home was due to unforeseen circumstances and the reduced maximum exclusion could be claimed.

4. A single mother bought a home and lived in it with her two daughters as their principal residence. One of the daughters was subjected to unruly behavior, verbal abuse, and sexual assault on the school bus. As a result, the daughter suffered from persistent fear and her school performance seriously declined. Her behavior was noticed by the school and brought to the mother's attention. She tried to work with the school district to resolve the problem, but when attempts failed, she sold her home and moved. The mother had not owned the home for two full years and asked the IRS whether she qualified for a partial exclusion. The IRS said yes. The primary reason for the sale prior to satisfying the two-year test was an unforeseen circumstance—the extreme bullying suffered by her daughter. Therefore, she can prorate the home sale exclusion for the part of the two years that she owned and lived in the home.

5. A married couple with one child bought a condominium with two small bedrooms and two baths. The child's bedroom was also used as the husband's home office and a guest room. After the wife gave birth to a second child, they moved out of the condo and later sold it at a gain. The IRS in a private ruling concluded that the birth of a second child was an unforeseen circumstance that rendered the condo unsuitable as a residence. Therefore, the couple could claim the reduced maximum exclusion.

29.5 Figuring Gain or Loss

To figure the gain or loss on the sale of your principal residence, you must determine the selling price, the amount realized, and the adjusted basis. *Worksheet 29-3* may be used to figure gain or loss on the sale of a principal residence.

Gain or loss. The difference between the amount realized and adjusted basis is your gain or loss. If the amount realized exceeds the adjusted basis, the difference is a gain that may be excluded *(29.1)*. If amount realized is less than adjusted basis, the difference is a loss. A loss on the sale of your main home may not be deducted. Any dual-purpose purchase of a home as a residence and an investment in a "hot" real estate market will not transform any unexpected loss due to market downturn into a deductible loss *(29.8)*.

Foreclosure or repossession. If your home was foreclosed on or repossessed, you have a sale. *See Chapter 31*.

Selling price. This is the total amount received for your home. It includes money, all notes, mortgages, or other debts assumed by the buyer as part of the sale, and the fair market value of any other property or any services received. The selling price does not include receipts for personal property sold with your home. Personal property is property that is not a permanent part of the home, such as furniture, draperies, and lawn equipment.

If your employer pays you for a loss on the sale or for your selling expenses, do not include the payment as part of the selling price. Include the payment as wages on Line 1 of

Filing Tip

Form 1099-S

If you received Form 1099-S, Box 2 should show the gross proceeds from the sale of your home. However, Box 2 does not include the fair market value of any property other than cash or notes, or any services you received or will receive. For these, Box 4 will be checked. If the sales price of your home does not exceed $250,000 or $500,000 (if filing jointly) and you certify to the person responsible for closing the sale that your entire gain is excludable from your gross income, that person does not have to report the sale on Form 1099-S but may choose to do so.

Filing Tip

Jointly Owned Home

If you and your spouse sell your jointly owned home and file a joint return, you figure your gain or loss as one taxpayer. If you file separate returns, each of you must figure your own gain or loss according to your ownership interest in the home. Your ownership interest is determined by state law.

If you and a joint owner other than your spouse sell your jointly owned home, each of you must figure your own gain or loss according to your ownership interest in the home.

Form 1040 or 1040-SR. (Your employer includes the payment with the rest of your wages in Box 1 of your Form W-2.)

If you grant an option to buy your home and the option is exercised, add the amount received for the option to the selling price of your home. If the option is not exercised, you report the amount as ordinary income in the year the option expires. Report the amount on Line 8z ("other income") of Schedule 1(Form 1040 or 1040-SR).

Amount realized. This is the selling price minus selling expenses, including broker commissions, advertising fees, legal fees, and loan charges paid by the seller (e.g., loan placement fees or "points").

Adjusted basis. This is the cost basis of your home increased by the cost of improvements and decreased by deducted casualty losses, if any *(29.6)*. "Fix-up"expenses, such as minor repairs, painting, and cleaning services to help sell the home are not deductible, specifically excluded since enactment of the Taxpayer Relief Act of 1997. However, the cost of "staging" furniture and other removable items from the home may be considered a separate expense. Cost basis is generally what you paid for the residence. If you obtained possession through other means, such as a gift or inheritance, *see* the special basis rules for gifts and inheritances *(5.17)*. Pre-1997 gain that was postponed under prior law "rollover" rules reduces adjusted basis *(29.6)*.

Seller-paid points. If the person who sold you your residence paid points on your loan, you may have to reduce your basis in the home by the amount of the points. If you bought your residence after 1990 but before April 4, 1994, you reduce basis by the points only if you chose to deduct them as home mortgage interest in the year paid. If you bought the residence after April 3, 1994, you reduce basis by the points even if you did not deduct the points.

Settlement fees or closing costs. When buying your home, you may have to pay settlement fees or closing costs in addition to the contract price of the property. You may include in basis fees and closing costs that are for buying the home. You may not include in your basis the fees and costs of getting a mortgage loan. Settlement fees also do not include amounts placed in escrow for the future payment of items such as taxes and insurance.

Examples of the settlement fees or closing costs that you may include in the basis of your property are: (1) abstract fees (sometimes called abstract of title fees), (2) charges for installing utility services, (3) legal fees (including fees for the title search and preparing the sales contract and deed), (4) recording fees, (5) survey fees, (6) transfer taxes, (7) owner's title insurance, and (8) any amounts the seller owes that you agree to pay, such as certain real estate taxes, back interest, recording or mortgage fees, charges for improvements or repairs, and sales commissions.

Examples of settlement fees and closing costs not included in your basis are: (1) fire insurance premiums, (2) rent for occupancy of the home before closing, (3) charges for utilities or other services relating to occupancy of the home before closing, (4) any fee or cost that you deducted as a moving expense before 1994, (5) charges connected with getting a mortgage loan, such as mortgage insurance premiums (including VA funding fees), loan assumption fees, cost of a credit report, and fee for an appraisal required by a lender, and (6) fees for refinancing a mortgage.

Construction. If you contracted to have your residence built on land you own, your basis is the cost of the land plus the cost of building the home, including the cost of labor and materials, payments to a contractor, architect's fees, building permit charges, utility meter and connection charges, and legal fees directly connected with building the home. Likewise, the cost of demolishing an existing structure is included, whether or not you have lived in that structure.

Cooperative apartment. Your basis in the apartment is usually the cost of your stock in the co-op housing corporation, which may include your share of a mortgage on the apartment building.

29.6 Figuring Adjusted Basis

Adjusted basis in your home is cost basis *(29.5)* adjusted for items discussed below. *Worksheet 29-2* may be used to figure adjusted basis.

Increases to cost basis include: improvements with a useful life of more than one year, special assessments for local improvements, and amounts spent after a casualty to restore damaged property.

Decreases to cost basis include: gain you postponed from the sale of a previous home before May 7, 1997, deductible casualty losses not covered by insurance, insurance payments you received or expect to receive for casualty losses, itemized deductions claimed for general sales taxes on the purchase of a houseboat or a mobile home, payments you received for granting an easement or right-of-way, depreciation allowed or allowable if you used your home for business or rental purposes, any allowable tax credit after 2005 for a home energy improvement *(25.15)* that increases the basis of the home, residential energy credit (generally allowed from 1977 through 1987 and 2009 through 2021) claimed for the cost of energy improvements added to the basis of your home, adoption credit you claimed for improvements added to the basis of your home, nontaxable payments from an adoption assistance program of your employer that you used for improvements added to the basis of your home, District of Columbia first-time homebuyers credit (allowed to qualifying first-time homebuyers for purchase after August 4, 1997 and before 2012), and an energy conservation subsidy excluded from your gross income because you received it (directly or indirectly) from a public utility after 1992 to buy or install any energy conservation measure. An energy conservation measure is an installation or modification that is primarily designed either to reduce consumption of electricity or natural gas or to improve the management of energy demand for a home.

Improvements. Improvements add to the value of your home, prolong its useful life, or adapt it to new uses. You add the cost of improvements to the basis of your property.

Examples of improvements include: bedroom, bathroom, deck, garage, porch, and patio additions, landscaping, paving driveway, walkway, fencing, retaining wall, sprinkler system, swimming pool, storm windows and doors, new roof, wiring upgrades, satellite dish, security system, heating system, central air conditioning, furnace, duct work, central humidifier, filtration system, septic system, water heater, soft water system, built-in appliances, kitchen modernization, flooring, wall-to-wall carpeting, attic, walls, and pipes.

Adjusted basis does not include the cost of any improvements that are no longer part of the home.

> **EXAMPLE**
>
> You installed wall-to-wall carpeting in your home 15 years ago. In 2024, you replace that carpeting with new wall-to-wall carpeting. The cost of the new carpeting increases your basis, but the cost of the old carpeting is no longer part of adjusted basis.

"Sweat equity." A homeowner's time and effort in making improvements do not add to his or her cost basis, although the cost of the materials that are used do. Further, as long as a taxpayer can prove that he or she meets the use and ownership tests, periodically making improvements to realize a profit that is sheltered by the home sale rules appears to be allowed.

Recordkeeping. Ordinarily, you must keep records for three years after the due date for filing your return for the tax year in which you sold your home. But you should keep home records as long as they are needed for tax purposes to prove adjusted basis. These include: (1) proof of the home's purchase price and purchase expenses, (2) receipts and other records for all improvements, additions, and other items that affect the home's adjusted basis, (3) any worksheets you used to figure the adjusted basis of the home you sold, the gain or loss on the sale, the exclusion, and the taxable gain, and (4) any Form 2119 that you filed to postpone gain from a home sale before May 7, 1997.

 *Caution*

Repairs

These maintain your home in good condition but are not considered by the IRS to add to its value or prolong its life. You do not add their cost to the basis of your property. Examples of repairs include repainting your house inside or outside, fixing gutters or floors, repairing leaks or plastering, and replacing broken window panes. However, repairs made as part of a larger remodeling or restoration project are treated by the IRS as capital improvements that increase basis *(9.3)*.

 *Planning Reminder*

Gains Postponed Under Prior Law Rules

Gain on a previous home sale that you postponed under the prior law rollover rules reduces the basis of your current home if your current home was a qualifying replacement residence for the previous home. Postponed gains on several earlier sales may have to be taken into account under the basis reduction rule. The basis reduction will increase the gain on the sale of your current home.

29.7 Personal and Business Use of a Home

If you sell a home that you used for business or rental as well as residential purposes, you may be able to exclude part or all of any gain realized on the sale. The excludable amount depends on whether the non-residential and residential areas were part of the same dwelling unit, whether the ownership and use tests *(29.2)* were met, whether depreciation was allowable after May 6, 1997, and whether the non-residential use was before 2009 or after 2008.

Nonqualified use after 2008. Gain allocable to periods of "nonqualified" use (not used as principal residence) after 2008 is not excludable from income *(29.2)*, but certain nonresidential periods are excluded from the definition of nonqualified use. For example, renting your home after you (and your spouse) move out is not nonqualified use if the rental occurs within the five-year period ending on the date of sale *(see* Example 2 (Andrea) at the end of *29.2)*.

The IRS does not treat home office use or rental of a spare room after 2008 as nonqualified use; *see* below.

Home office or rental space within your principal residence. The IRS takes the position that gain does not have to be allocated between the residential and business use portions of your home where both are within the same dwelling unit. This rule allows a home office to be considered part of your residential property for purposes of the home sale exclusion. Similarly, the IRS considers renting a spare room as a bed-and-breakfast bedroom to be residential use. If the two-out-of-five-year ownership and use test *(29.2)* is met for the regular residential portion, you are also treated as meeting the two-year residential use test for the home office or rental space, even if you used the area as a business office or rented room for your entire period of ownership. As a result, the gain on the entire residence is eligible for the exclusion, except for the gain equal to depreciation for periods after May 6, 1997. The gain equal to post–May 6, 1997, depreciation is never excludable; it must be reported on Schedule D (Form 1040 or 1040-SR) as unrecaptured Section 1250 gain *(5.3)*.

Depreciation allowed or allowable. Under IRS rules, you must reduce your basis *(29.6)* in the home for purposes of figuring gain on a sale by any depreciation you were entitled to deduct, even if you did not deduct it. Furthermore, you cannot exclude the gain equal to the depreciation allowed or allowable for periods after May 6, 1997. This means that if you were entitled to take depreciation deductions for periods after May 6, 1997, but did not do so, the gain equal to the allowable depreciation is generally not excludable. However, if you have records showing that you claimed less depreciation than was allowable, the IRS will reduce the excludable gain only by the claimed (allowed) depreciation.

> **EXAMPLE**
>
> Alice bought a house in March 2018 that she lived in as her principal residence. She used one room as a law office from May 2020 until September 2023, and claimed depreciation deductions of $2,500 for the office space during that period. She sells the home in 2024. Assume that gain on the sale is $24,000. Since the office and residential area were in the same dwelling unit, Alice does not have to allocate gain to the office. Since she meets the ownership and use tests for the residential part, the tests are also considered met for the office space, She may exclude $21,500 of the $24,000 gain from her 2024 income. The $2,500 of gain equal to depreciation cannot be excluded. Alice reports her $24,000 gain and the $21,500 exclusion in Part II of Form 8949 *(5.8)*. The $2,500 gain attributable to the depreciation is unrecaptured Section 1250 gain, which Alice enters on the Unrecaptured Section 1250 Gain Worksheet in the Schedule D instructions *(5.3)*.

Business or rental area separate from your dwelling unit. If you sell property that was partly your home and partly business or rental property separate from your dwelling unit, and the business/rental use of the separate part exceeded three years during the five years before the sale, the gain allocable to the separate part is not eligible for an exclusion (since the two-year use test *(29.2)* has not been met for that part) and must be reported as taxable income on Form 4797. This could be the case if you lived in one apartment and

Law Alert

Nonqualified Use After 2008 May Limit Exclusion

Unless an exception applies *(29.7)*, any period after 2008 that a home is not used as your principal residence is considered a period of "nonqualified use," and gain allocable to the nonqualified use is taxable, even if the two-year residential use test for an exclusion is otherwise met *(29.2)*.

rented out other apartments in the same building, you rented out an unattached garage or building elsewhere on your property, your apartment was upstairs from your business, you operated a business from a barn or other structure separate from your business, or your home was located on a working farm. The gain allocable to the part used as your home and any exclusion allowed for that part is reported on Form 8949 and Schedule D *(29.2)*. *See* IRS Publication 523 for reporting details.

29.8 No Loss Allowed on Personal Residence

A loss on the sale of your principal residence is not deductible. You do not have to report the sale on your return unless you received a Form 1099-S. If you received Form 1099-S, you must report the sale on Form 8949 *(5.8)* even though the loss is not deductible. Code "L" must be entered in column (f) of Form 8949 to indicate that the loss is not deductible, and the nondeductible loss must be entered as a positive adjustment in column (g). These are the same reporting rules as for a second home or vacation home discussed below.

If part of the sold property was a business or rental area separate from your principal residence and you did not meet the two-year residential use test *(29.2)* for that separate part, treat the sale as if two pieces of property were sold (*see* last paragraph of *29.7*). Report the personal part on Form 8949 and the business part on Form 4797. A loss is deductible only on the business part.

Second home or vacation home. If you sell at a loss a second home or vacation home that was used entirely for personal purposes and the sale was reported on Form 1099-S, you report the sale on Form 8949 and Schedule D, even though the loss is not deductible. On Form 8949 *(5.8)*, report the proceeds in column (d) and your basis in column (e). The loss (excess of basis over proceeds) is not deductible, so code "L" must be entered in column (f) and the amount of the loss entered as a positive amount in column (g). The positive adjustment in column (g) negates the loss, so the gain or loss in column (h) will be "0" *(5.8)*. If in the year of sale part of the home was rented out or used for business, allocate the sale between the personal part and the rental or business part; report the personal part on Form 8949 *(5.8)* and the rental or business part on Form 4797.

29.9 Loss on Residence Converted to Rental Property

You are not allowed to deduct a loss on the sale of your personal residence. If you convert the house from personal use to rental use you may claim a loss on a sale if the value has declined below the basis fixed for the residence as rental property.

To determine if you have a loss for tax purposes, you need to know the conversion date basis. This is the lower of (1) your adjusted basis *(29.6)* for the house at the time of conversion or (2) the fair market value at the time of conversion. Add to the lower amount the cost of capital improvements made after the conversion, and subtract depreciation and casualty loss deductions claimed after the conversion. To deduct a loss, you have to be able to show that this basis exceeds the sales price. For example, if you paid $200,000 for your home and convert it to rental property when the value has declined to $150,000, your conversion date basis for the rental property is $150,000. If the property continues to decline in value, and you sell for $125,000 after having deducted $10,000 for depreciation, you may claim a loss of $15,000 ($140,000 (conversion date basis of $150,000 reduced by $10,000 depreciation) – $125,000 sales price). Your loss deduction will not reflect the $50,000 loss occurring before the conversion.

Filing Tip

Loss Allowed

If you sell a house that has been converted from personal to rental use, and the sales price is less than the conversion date basis, a loss on the sale is deductible *(29.9)*.

Caution

Temporary Rental Before Sale

A rental loss may be barred on a temporary rental before sale. The IRS and Tax Court held that where a principal residence was rented for several months while being offered for sale, the rental did not convert the home to rental property. Deductions for rental expenses were limited to rental income; no loss could be claimed. A federal appeals court disagreed and allowed a rental loss deduction; also *see 9.7*.

> **EXAMPLE**
>
> In 1988, Adams bought a house in Fort Worth, Texas. He paid $124,000, put in capital improvements, and lived there until he was forced to put it on the market when he lost his job. In 1989, he listed the house with a broker for $145,000. After receiving no offers, he decided to lease the house through 1990. By October of 1990 Adams owed $4,551 in property taxes and was three months behind on his mortgage payments. Fearing foreclosure, he sold the house for $130,000.

For purposes of figuring a loss, Adams assumed that the fair market value at the time of conversion was equal to the $145,000 list price. The adjusted basis of the house was $141,026. As this was less than the estimated fair market value of $145,000, he used the $141,026 adjusted basis to figure a loss of $11,026 ($130,000 – $141,026). The IRS claimed the fair market value at the time of conversion was equal to the actual sale price of $130,000. Since basis for the converted property is the lesser of fair market value ($130,000) or adjusted basis ($141,026), Adams had no loss on the sale.

However, the Tax Court allowed a $5,000 loss by fixing the fair market value at the time of conversion at $135,000. It held that Adams sold at a lower price because of his weak financial position of which the buyer took advantage. The court figured the $135,000 as follows: $129,000 fair market value in 1988 (based on an appraisal report, which both parties agree was correct), plus $6,000 of appreciation attributable to the capital improvements made to the property after it was converted.

Partially rented home. If you rented part of your home for over three years during the five years preceding the sale, you must allocate the basis and amount realized between the portion used as your home and the rented portion *(29.7)*. A loss on a sale is allowable on the rented portion, which is reported on Form 4797.

Profit-making purposes. Renting a residence is a changeover from personal to profit-making purposes. If a house is merely put up for rent such as by listing it with a realty company but little else is done to obtain tenants and the property is in fact not rented, the IRS is likely to conclude that it was not converted to property held for the production of income and a loss on the sale will be treated as a nondeductible personal loss; *see* Example 1 in *9.10*.

Similarly, where a house is only rented for several months prior to a sale, the IRS may not treat this as a conversion to rental property and may disallow a loss deduction claimed on the sale.

Loss allowed on house bought for resale. A loss deduction may also be allowed where you acquired the house as an investment with the intention of selling it at a profit, even though you occupied it incidentally as a residence prior to sale. In an unusual case, an owner bought a house with the intention of selling it. He lived in it for six years, but during that period it was for sale. The Tax Court allowed him to deduct the loss on its sale by proving he lived in it to protect it from vandalism and to keep it in good condition so that it would attract possible buyers.

In another case, an architect and builder built a house and offered it for sale through an agent and advertisements. He had a home and no intention to occupy the new house. On a realtor's advice, he moved into the house to make it more saleable. Ten months later, he sold the house at a loss of $4,065 and promptly moved out. The loss was allowed on proof that his main purpose in building and occupying the house was to realize a profit by a sale; the residential use was incidental.

Gain on rented residence. You have a gain on the sale of rental property if you sell for more than your adjusted basis at the time of conversion, plus subsequent capital improvements, and minus depreciation and casualty loss deductions. The sale is subject to the rules in *Chapter 44* for depreciable property.

29.10 Loss on Residence Acquired by Gift or Inheritance

You may deduct a loss on the sale of a house received as an inheritance or gift if you personally did not use it and offered it for sale or rental immediately or within a few weeks after acquisition.

EXAMPLES

1. A couple owned a winter vacation home in Florida. When the husband died, his wife immediately put the house up for sale and never lived in it. It was sold at a loss. The IRS disallowed her capital loss deduction, claiming it was personal and nondeductible. The wife argued that her case was no different from the case of an heir inheriting and selling a home, since at the death of her husband her interest in the property was increased. The Tax Court agreed with her reasoning and allowed the capital loss deduction.

Planning Reminder

Inherited Residence

If you inherit a residence in which you do not intend to live, it may be advisable to put it up for rent to allow for an ordinary loss deduction on a later sale. If you merely try to sell, and you finally do so at a loss, you are limited to a capital loss.

2. A widow inherited a house owned by her late husband and rented out by his estate. Shortly after getting title to the house, she sold it at a loss that she deducted as an ordinary loss. The IRS limited her to a capital loss deduction. The Tax Court agreed. She could not show any business activity. She did not negotiate the lease with the tenant who was in the house when she received title. She never arranged any maintenance or repairs for the building. Moreover, she sold the property shortly after receiving title, which indicates she viewed the house as investment, not rental, property.

3. An inherited residence was rented out by the owner to her brother for $500 a month when the fair market rental value was $700 to $750 per month. When she sold the residence at a loss, the IRS disallowed the loss, and the Tax Court agreed. The below-market rental was treated as evidence that she held the property for personal purposes, not as rental property or as investment property held for appreciation in value.

Worksheet 29-2   Adjusted Basis of Home Sold

Caution: *See 29.6 before you use this worksheet.*

1. Enter the purchase price of the home sold. (If you filed Form 2119 when you originally acquired that home to postpone gain on the sale of a previous home before May 7, 1997, enter the adjusted basis of the new home from that Form 2119.) . . . .   **1.** _____

2. Seller-paid points for home bought after 1990 (see 29.5). Do not include any seller-paid points you already subtracted to arrive at the amount entered on line 1 . . . .   **2.** _____

3. Subtract line 2 from line 1 . . . .   **3.** _____

4. Settlement fees or closing costs (see 29.5). If line 1 includes the adjusted basis of the new home from Form 2119, skip lines 4a–4g and 5; go to line 6.

   a. Abstract and recording fees . . . .   **4a.** _____
   b. Legal fees (including fees for title search and preparing documents) . . . .   **4b.** _____
   c. Survey fees . . . .   **4c.** _____
   d. Title insurance . . . .   **4d.** _____
   e. Transfer or stamp taxes . . . .   **4e.** _____
   f. Amounts that the seller owed that you agreed to pay (back taxes or interest, recording or mortgage fees, and sales commissions) . . . .   **4f.** _____
   g. Other . . . .   **4g.** _____

5. Add lines 4a through 4g . . . .   **5.** _____

6. Cost of additions and improvements. Do not include any additions and improvements included on line 1 . . . .   **6.** _____

7. Special tax assessments paid for local improvements, such as streets and sidewalks . . . .   **7.** _____

8. Other increases to basis . . . .   **8.** _____

9. Add lines 3, 5, 6, 7, and 8 . . . .   **9.** _____

10. Depreciation allowed or allowable, related to the business use or rental of the home . . . .   **10.** _____

11. Other decreases to basis (see 29.6) . . . .   **11.** _____

12. Add lines 10 and 11 . . . .   **12.** _____

13. **Adjusted basis of home sold**. Subtract line 12 from line 9. Enter here and on Worksheet 29-3, line 4 . . . .   **13.** _____

Worksheet 29-3   Gain (or Loss), Exclusion, and Taxable Gain

Part 1. Gain or (Loss) on Sale

1. Selling price of home . . . .   **1.** _____

2. Selling expenses (including commissions, advertising and legal fees, and seller-paid loan charges) . . . .   **2.** _____

3. Subtract line 2 from line 1. This is the amount realized . . . .   **3.** _____

4. Adjusted basis of home sold (from Worksheet 29-2, line 13) . . . .   **4.** _____

5. **Gain or (loss)** on the sale. Subtract line 4 from line 3. If this is a loss, stop here . . . .   **5.** _____

Part 2. Exclusion and Taxable Gain

6. Enter any depreciation allowed or allowable on the property for periods after May 6, 1997. If none, enter -0- . . . .   **6.** _____

7. Subtract line 6 from line 5. If the result is less than zero, enter -0- . . . .   **7.** _____

8. Aggregate number of days of nonqualified use after 12/31/2008 . . . .   **8.** _____

9. Number of days taxpayer owned the property . . . .   **9.** _____

10. Divide the amount on line 8 by the amount on line 9. Enter the result as a decimal (rounded to at least 3 places). But do not enter an amount greater than 1.00 . . . .   **10.** _____

11. Gain allocated to nonqualified use. (Line 7 multiplied by line 10) . . . .   **11.** _____

12. Gain eligible for exclusion. Subtract line 11 from line 7. . . . .   **12.** _____

13. If you qualify to exclude gain on the sale, enter your maximum exclusion (see 29.2 – 29.4). If you qualify for a reduced maximum exclusion, enter the amount from Worksheet 29-1, line 7. If you do not qualify to exclude gain, enter -0- . . . .   **13.** _____

14. **Exclusion**. Enter the smaller of line 12 or line 13 . . . .   **14.** _____

15. **Taxable gain**. Subtract line 14 from line 5. Report this taxable gain and the exclusion from line 14 on Form 8949 and Schedule D as required by the instructions for those forms. Use Form 6252 if reporting the gain on the installment sale method (5.21) and enter the exclusion from line 14 on line 15 of Form 6252. . . . .   **15.** _____

16. Enter the **smaller** of line 6 or line 15. Enter this amount on line 12 of the Unrecaptured Section 1250 Gain Worksheet in the instructions for Schedule D (Form 1040) . . . .   **16.** _____

CHAPTER 30

Tax Rules for Investors in Securities

You have the opportunity to control the taxable year in which to realize gains and losses. Gains and losses are realized when you sell, and if there are no market pressures, you can time sales to your advantage.

If you sell securities at a gain in 2023, and you held the securities more than one year, you can benefit from the 0%, 15% or 20% rate for long-term capital gains. You may also owe the additional Medicare tax on net investment income (NII) *(22.8)*.

The $3,000 limitation ($1,500 if married filing separately) on deducting capital losses from other types of income is a substantial restriction. If you have capital losses exceeding the $3,000 (or $1,500) limit, it is advisable to realize capital gains income that can be offset by the losses.

Investors who have multiple or numerous transactions throughout the year generally need not manually enter each transaction on self-prepared returns or provide details to a tax return preparer. Tax return preparation software allows transactions through brokerage firms and mutual fund companies to be imported to your tax return by a simple keystroke. The information contained in this chapter is intended to provide general information on the underlying tax implications of securities.

Planning Reminder

December 29 Deadline for 2023 Gains and Losses

If you want to realize gains on publicly traded securities for 2023, you have until Friday, December 29, 2023, to transact the sale. Gain is reported in 2023, although payment is not received until the settlement date in 2024. If you do not want to realize the gain in 2023, delay the trade date until 2024.

Losses are also realized as of the trade date; a loss on a sale made by December 29, 2023, is reported on your 2023 return.

30.1 Planning Year-End Securities Transactions

First establish your current gain and loss position for the year. List gains and losses already realized from completed transactions. Then review the records of earlier years to find any carryover capital losses. Include nonbusiness bad debts as short-term capital losses. Then review your paper gains and losses and determine what losses might now be realized to offset realized gains or what gains might be realized to be offset by realized losses.

If you have already realized net capital losses exceeding $3,000 ($1,500 if married filing separately), you may want to realize capital gains that will be absorbed by the excess loss. Remember, only up to $3,000 (or $1,500) of capital losses exceeding net capital gain may be deducted from other income such as salary, interest, and dividends.

Planning for losses. Realizing losses may pose a problem if you believe the security is due to increase in value sometime in the near future. Although the wash sale rule *(30.6)* prevents you from taking the loss if you buy the security 30 days before or after the sale, the following possibilities are open to you.

- If you believe the security will go up, but not immediately, you can sell now, realize your loss, wait 31 days, and then recover your position by repurchasing before the expected rise.
- You can hedge by repurchasing similar securities immediately after the sale provided they are not substantially identical. They can be in the same industry and of the same quality without being considered substantially identical. Check with your broker to see if you can use a loss and still maintain your position. Some brokerage firms maintain recommended "switch" lists and suggest a practice of "doubling up"—that is, buying the stock of the same company and then 31 days later selling the original shares. Doubling up has disadvantages: It requires additional funds for the purchase of the second lot, exposes you to additional risks should the stock price fall, and the new shares take a new holding period.

> **EXAMPLE**
>
> You own 100 shares of Steel Co. stock that cost you $10,000. In mid-November 2023, the stock is selling at $6,000 ($60 a share × 100 shares). You would like to realize the $4,000 loss but, at the same time, you want to hold on to the investment. You buy 100 shares at a market price of $60 a share (total investment $6,000) and 31 days later sell your original 100 shares, realizing a loss for 2023 so long as the sales price is under $100 a share. You retain your investment in the new lot.

30.2 Earmarking Stock Lots

Keep a record of all your stock transactions, especially when you buy the stock of one company at varying prices. By keeping a record of each stock lot, you may control the amount of gain or loss on a sale of a part of your holdings. If you do not make an adequate identification, the IRS will treat the shares you bought first as the shares being sold under a first-in, first-out (FIFO) rule.

You may not average the cost of stock lots; averaging is generally allowed only for mutual fund shares *(32.10)*. However, under the basis reporting rules *(5.8)* for "covered" securities acquired after 2011, averaging is allowed for most ETFs structured as regulated investment companies, and for shares acquired through a qualifying dividend reinvestment plan (DRIP).

If your stock is held by your broker, the IRS considers that an adequate identification is made if you give instructions to your broker about which particular shares are to be sold, and you receive a written confirmation of your instructions from the broker or transfer agent within a reasonable time.

> **EXAMPLE**
>
> Over a three-year period, you bought the following shares of Acme Steel stock: In 2017, 100 shares at $77 per share; in 2018, 200 shares at $84 per share; and in 2019, 100 shares at $105 per share. When the stock is selling at $90, you plan to sell 100 shares. You may use the cost of your 2019 lot and get a $1,500 loss if, for example, you want to offset some gains or other income you have already earned this year. Or you may get capital gains by selling the 2017 lot or part of the 2018 lot.

You must clearly identify the lot you want to sell. Say you want a loss and sell the 2019 lot. Unless you identify it as the lot sold, the IRS will hold that you sold the 2017 lot under the "first-in, first-out" rule. This rule assumes that, when you have a number of identical items that you bought at different times, your sale of any of them is automatically the sale of the first you bought. So the cost of your first purchase is what you match against your selling price to find your gain or loss. Here is what to do to counteract the first-in, first-out rule: If you have stock certificates registered in your name, show that you delivered the 2019 stock certificates. If the broker is holding the stock, specifically identify the 2018 lot in your selling instructions and get a written confirmation.

On the sale of mutual fund shares, you have the option of using an average cost basis *(32.10)*.

30.3 Sale of Stock Dividends

A sale of stock originally received as a dividend is treated as any other sale of stock. The holding period of a taxable stock dividend *(4.8)* begins on the date of distribution. The holding period of a tax-free stock dividend or stock received in a split *(4.6)* begins on the same date as the holding period of the original stock.

EXAMPLE

You bought 100 shares of X Co. stock on December 4, 2019. On August 4, 2023, you receive 10 shares of X Co. stock as a tax-free stock dividend. On December 15, 2023, you sell the 10 shares at a profit. You report the sale as long-term capital gain because the holding period of the 10 shares begins December 5, 2019 (day after original purchase), not August 4, 2023.

Basis of tax-free dividend in the same class of stock. Assume you receive a common stock dividend on common stock. You divide the original cost by the total number of old shares and new shares to find the new basis per share.

EXAMPLE

You bought 100 shares of common stock for $1,000, so that each share has a basis of $10. You receive 100 shares of common stock as a tax-free stock dividend. The basis of your 200 shares remains $1,000. The new cost basis of each share is now $5 ($1,000 ÷ 200 shares). You sell 50 shares for $560. Your profit is $310 ($560 − $250).

Basis of tax-free dividend in a different class of stock. Assume you receive preferred stock dividends on common stock. You divide the basis of the old shares over the two classes in the ratio of their values at the time the stock dividend was distributed.

EXAMPLE

You bought 100 shares of common stock for $1,000. You receive a tax-free dividend of 10 shares of preferred stock. On the date of distribution, the market value of the common stock is $9 a share and that of the preferred stock is $30. That makes the market value of your common stock $900 and your preferred stock $300. So you allocate 75% ($900 ÷ $1,200) of your $1,000 original cost, or $750, to your common stock and 25% ($300 ÷ $1,200) of your cost to the preferred stock.

Basis of taxable stock dividend. The basis of a taxable stock dividend *(4.6)* is its fair market value at the time of the distribution. Its holding period begins on the date of distribution. The basis of the old stock remains unchanged.

EXAMPLE

You bought 1,000 shares of stock for $10,000. The company gives you a choice of a cash dividend or stock (one share for every hundred held). You elect the stock. On the date of the distribution, its market value was $15 a share. The basis of the new stock is $150 (10 shares × $15), the amount of the taxable dividend. The basis of the old stock remains $10,000.

30.4 Stock Rights

The tax consequences of the receipt of stock rights are discussed at *4.6*. The following is an explanation of how to treat the sale, exercise, or expiration of nontaxable stock rights. The basis of taxable rights is their fair market value at the time of distribution.

Expiration of nontaxable distributed stock rights. When you allow nontaxable rights to expire, you do not have a deductible loss; you have no basis in the rights.

Sale of nontaxable distributed stock rights. If you sell stock rights distributed on your stock, you treat the sale as the sale of a capital asset. The holding period begins from the date you acquired the original stock on which the rights were distributed.

Purchased rights. If you buy stock rights, your holding period starts the day after the date of the purchase. Your basis for the rights is the price paid; this basis is used in computing your capital gain or loss on the sale.

If you allow purchased rights to expire without sale or exercise, you realize a capital loss. The rights are treated as having been sold on the day of expiration. When purchased rights become worthless during the year prior to the year they lapse, you have a capital loss that is treated as having occurred on the last day of the year in which they became worthless.

Figuring the basis of nontaxable stock rights. Whether rights received by you as a stockholder have a basis depends on their fair market value when distributed. If the market value of rights is less than 15% of the market value of your old stock, the basis of your rights is zero, unless you elect to allocate the basis between the rights and your original stock. You make the election on your tax return for the year the rights are received by attaching to your return a statement that you are electing to divide basis. Keep a copy of the election and the return.

If the market value of the rights is 15% or more of the market value of your old stock, you must divide the basis of the stock between the old stock and the rights, according to their respective values on the date of distribution.

No basis adjustment is required for stock rights that become worthless during the year of issue.

30.5 Short Sales of Stock

A short sale is a sale of stock borrowed from a broker. The short sale is closed when you replace the borrowed stock by buying substantially identical stock and delivering it to the broker or by delivering stock that you held at the time of the short sale. One objective of a short sale is to profit from an anticipated drop in the market price of the stock; another objective may be to use the short sale as a hedge.

Tax rules applied to short sales are designed to prevent you from:

- Postponing gain to a later year when you sell short while holding an appreciated position in the same or substantially identical stock. This type of short sale is called "a sale against the box."
- Converting short-term gains to long-term gains.
- Converting long-term losses to short-term losses.

Year in which gain on short sale is realized. Generally, you report gain on a short sale on Form 8949 and Schedule D for the year in which you close the short sale by delivering replacement stock. However, if you execute a short sale while holding an appreciated position in the same stock (short sale against the box) or substantially identical stock is acquired to close an appreciated short position, the short sale or acquisition of substantially identical stock is treated as a constructive sale of an appreciated financial position *(30.9)* and you must report the transaction in the year of the constructive sale, even though delivery of replacement stock is made in a later year; *see* Examples below.

There is this exception to the constructive sale rule: The short sale is reported in the year of delivery of the replacement stock if (1) you close the short sale before the end of the 30th day of the next year, (2) you continue to hold a similar position in the stock for at least 60 days after the closing of the short sale, and (3) your risk of loss during the 60-day period was not reduced by other positions. *See* Example 3 below and *30.9* for further details on constructive sales.

Planning Reminder

Exercise of Stock Rights

You realize no taxable income on the exercise of stock rights. Capital gain or loss on the new stock is recognized when you later sell the stock. The holding period of the new stock begins on the date you exercised the rights. Your basis for the new stock is the subscription price you paid plus your basis for the rights exercised.

If the stock sold short becomes worthless before you close the short sale, you recognize taxable gain in the year the shares became worthless.

EXAMPLES

1. On May 3, 2023, you buy 100 shares of Auto Corp. stock for $1,000. On September 7, 2023, you borrow 100 shares of Auto Corp. from your broker and sell them short for $1,600. You make no subsequent transactions involving Auto Corp. stock. The short sale is treated as a constructive sale of an appreciated financial position because a sale of your Auto Corp. stock on September 7, the date of the short sale, would have resulted in a gain. You have a $600 short-term capital gain from the constructive sale and you have a new holding period for your Auto Corp. stock that begins on September 7, 2023.

2. In January 2023 you buy 100 shares of Steel Co. stock for $1,000 (100 × $10). In November 2023 when the stock is selling at $50, you execute a short sale of 100 shares (100 × $50 = $5,000). In February 2024, you deliver your shares to close the short sale. The tax law treats the short sale as a constructive sale of an appreciated financial position because a sale of your Steel Co. stock on the date of the short sale would have resulted in a gain. You report the gain of $4,000 ($5,000 − $1,000) in 2023, the year of the short sale, not in 2024 when you close the sale. To shift tax reporting to 2024, you would have had to close the short sale by the 30th of January and obtain similar stock, which you would have had to hold for at least 60 days after the closing of the short sale; *see* Example 3.

3. On October 3, 2023, you buy 100 shares of Oil Co. for $60 a share. On December 12, 2023, you sell short 100 shares of Oil Co. for $80 a share. On January 18, 2024, you buy 100 shares of Oil Co. for $75 a share to close the short sale. You hold the October lot for over 60 days after January 18, 2024. The December 2023 short sale is not treated as a constructive sale in 2023 because you closed the short sale by January 30th and you held the October lot for at least 60 days after the short sale was closed. You have a gain of $5 per share when you close the short sale in January 2024.

4. A taxpayer who does not own any shares of XYZ stock directs his broker in January of Year 1 to sell short borrowed XYZ shares. On December 31 of Year 1, when the value of XYZ shares has decreased, the taxpayer directs the broker to close the short sale by purchasing XYZ shares in a "regular-way" sale, with actual delivery of the shares taking place at the beginning of Year 2. The IRS ruled that the short position is an appreciated financial position as of December 31, given the decrease in the stock price since the short sale. The purchase of replacement shares on December 31 is a constructive sale of the appreciated position. Gain is taxable in Year 1, not in Year 2 when the shares were delivered.

Short-term or long-term gain or loss. Whether you have short-term or long-term capital gain or loss generally depends on your holding period for the property delivered to the broker to close the short sale. Furthermore, you must apply Rules 1 and 2 below if you answer "yes" to either of the following questions:

- When you sold short, did you or your spouse hold for one year or less securities substantially identical to the securities sold short? (Substantially identical securities are described at *30.6*.)
- After the short sale, did you or your spouse acquire substantially identical securities on or before the date of the closing of the short sale?

Rule 1. Gain realized on the closing of the short sale is short term. The gain is short term regardless of the period of time you have held the securities as of the closing date of the short sale.

Rule 2. The beginning date of the holding period of substantially identical stock is suspended. The holding period of substantially identical securities owned or bought under the facts of question (1) or (2) does not begin until the date of the closing of the short sale (or the date of the sale, gift, or other disposition of the securities, whichever date occurs first). But note that this rule applies only to the number of securities that do not exceed the quantity sold short.

Losses. A loss on a short sale is not deductible until shares closing the short sale are delivered to the broker. You may not realize a short-term loss on the closing of a short sale if you held substantially identical securities long term (that is, for more than a year) on the date of the short sale. The loss is long term even if the securities used to close the sale were held for one year or less. This rule prevents you from creating short-term losses when you held the covering stock long term. Loss deductions on short sales may be disallowed under the wash sale rules in *30.6*.

EXAMPLES

1. On February 3, 2023, the stock of Oil Co., which you do not own, is selling at $90 per share. You expect the price to fall over the next year and sell short 500 shares borrowed from your broker for $45,000 (500 × $ 90). However, 13 months later, on March 15, 2024, after the price has risen to $110, you close the short sale by buying 500 shares of Oil Co. stock ($500 × $110 = $55,000 cost) and immediately delivering them to your broker. Your loss of $10,000 ($55,000 − $45,000) is treated as a short-term capital loss because your holding period for the delivered stock is less than one day.

2. On February 10, 2023, you buy 100 shares of Tech Corp. stock for $1,000. On July 14, 2023, you sell short 100 shares of Tech Corp. for $1,600. You close the short sale on November 9, 2023, by buying 100 shares for $1,800 and delivering them to your broker. On the short sale, you realize a $200 short-term capital loss.

   On February 23, 2024, you sell for $1,900 your original lot of Tech Corp. stock bought on February 10, 2023. Although you have held these shares for more than one year, the $900 gain realized on the sale is treated as a short-term capital gain under Rule 2 above. Rule 2 applies because on the date of the short sale (July 14, 2023), the February 10 shares were held short term (one year or less). Under Rule 2, the holding period of the February 10 lot is considered to begin on November 9, 2023, the date the short sale was closed.

Expenses of short sales. Before you buy stock to close out a short sale, you pay the broker for dividends paid on stock you have sold short. If you itemize deductions, you may treat your payment as investment interest *(15.9)*, provided the short sale is held open at least 46 days, or more than a year in the case of extraordinary dividends. If the 46-day (or one-year) test is not met, the payment is generally not deductible and is added to basis; in counting the short-sale period, do not count any period during which you have an option to buy or are obligated to buy substantially identical securities, or are protected from the risk of loss from the short sale by a substantially similar position.

Under an exception to the 46-day test, if you receive compensation from the lender of the stock for the use of collateral and you report the compensation as ordinary income, your payment for dividends is deductible to the extent of the compensation; only the excess of your payment over the compensation is disallowed. This exception does not apply to payments with respect to extraordinary dividends.

An extraordinary dividend is generally a dividend that equals or exceeds the amount realized on the short sale by 10% for any common stock or by 5% for any preferred stock dividends. For purposes of this test, dividends on stock received within an 85-day period are aggregated; a one-year aggregation period applies if dividends exceed 20% of the adjusted basis in the stock.

30.6   Wash Sales

The objective of the wash sale rule is to disallow a loss deduction where you recover your market position in a security within a short period of time after the sale. Under the wash sale rule, which applies to investors and traders (but not dealers), your loss deduction is barred if within 30 days of the sale you buy substantially identical stock or securities, you buy a "call" option on such securities, or you sell a "put" option on the securities that is "deep-in-the-money". The wash sale period is 61 days—running from 30 days before to 30 days after the date of sale. The end of a taxable year during this 61-day period does not affect the wash sale rule. The loss is still denied. If you sell at a loss and your spouse buys substantially identical stock within this period, the loss is also barred. The disallowed loss is added to the basis of the replacement stock.

The wash sale rule does not apply to gains. It also does not apply to acquisitions by gift, inheritance, or tax-free exchange.

 *Caution*

Wash Sale Rule Applies If Replacement Bought in IRA

The IRS has ruled that a loss on the sale of stock is disallowed by the wash sale rule if within 30 days before or after the sale replacement shares are bought through a traditional IRA or Roth IRA.

EXAMPLES

1. You bought common stock of Appliance Co. for $10,000 in 2021. On June 23, 2023, you sold the stock for $8,000, incurring a $2,000 loss. A week later, you repurchased the same number of shares of Appliance stock for $9,000. Your loss of $2,000 on the sale is disallowed because of the wash sale rule. The basis of the new lot becomes $11,000, equal to the cost of the new shares ($9,000) plus the disallowed loss ($2,000).

2. Assume the same facts as in Example 1, except that you repurchase the stock for $7,000. The basis of the new lot is $9,000, the cost of the new shares ($7,000) plus the disallowed loss ($2,000).

3. Assume that in February 2024 you sell the new lot of stock acquired in Example 1 above for $9,000 and do not run afoul of the wash sale rule. On the sale, you realize a loss of $2,000 ($11,000 basis – $9,000 sales price).

Buying replacement shares through IRA. The IRS has ruled that buying replacement shares in a traditional IRA or Roth IRA triggers the wash sale rule. Some commentators had suggested that the wash sale rule should not apply because the seller and the IRA, although "related," are different entities for tax purposes. The IRS disagrees. Although the IRA is a separate tax-exempt trust, the seller of the loss shares is treated as acquiring the replacement shares through the IRA.

There is an additional penalty for using an IRA to acquire replacement shares. The increase to basis that would have applied if the replacement shares had been bought in a taxable account is lost. When the replacement is made in a taxable account, the basis increase preserves for future use the economic value of the disallowed loss by allowing gain to be reduced, or loss to be increased, on a later sale of the replacement shares. However, there is no basis increase for the shares held in the IRA and the wash sale loss is permanently disallowed, making this a worse result than if the replacement had been made in a taxable account.

Loss on the sale of part of a stock lot bought less than 30 days ago. If you buy stock and then, within 30 days, sell some of those shares, a loss on the sale is deductible; the wash sale disallowance rule does not apply.

EXAMPLE

You buy 200 shares of stock. Within 30 days, you sell 100 shares at a loss. The loss is not disallowed by the wash sale rule. The wash sale rule does not apply to a loss sustained in a bona fide sale made to reduce your market position. It does apply when you sustain a loss for tax purposes with the intent of recovering your position in the security within a short period. Thus if, after selling the 100 shares, you repurchase 100 shares of the same stock within 30 days after the sale, the loss is disallowed.

Oral sale-repurchase agreement. The wash sale rule applies to an oral sale-repurchase agreement between business associates.

Defining "substantially identical." What is substantially identical stock or securities? Buying and selling Facebook stock is dealing in an identical security. Selling Facebook and buying Twitter stock is not dealing in substantially identical securities.

Bonds of the same obligor are substantially identical if they carry the same rate of interest; that they have different issue dates and interest payment dates will not remove them from the wash sale provisions. Different maturity dates will have no effect, unless the difference is economically significant. Where there is a long time span between the purchase date and the maturity date, a difference of several years between maturity dates may be considered insignificant. A difference of three years between maturity dates was held to be insignificant where the maturity dates of the bonds, measured from the time of purchase, were 45 and 48 years away. There was no significant difference where the maturity dates differed by less than one year, and the remaining life, measured from the time of purchase, was more than 15 years.

The wash sale rules do not apply if you buy bonds of the same company with substantially different interest rates, buy bonds of a different company, or buy substantially identical bonds outside of the wash sale period.

 *Planning Reminder*

Tax Advantage of Wash Sale Rule

Sometimes the wash sale rule can work to your advantage. Assume that during December you are negotiating a sale of real estate that will bring you a large capital gain. You want to offset a part of that gain by selling certain securities at a loss. You are unsure just when the gain transaction will go through. It may be on the last day of the year, at which point it may be too late to sell the loss securities before the end of the same year.

You can do this: Sell the loss securities during the last week of December. If the profitable deal goes through before the end of the year, you need not do anything further. If it does not, buy back the loss securities early in January. The December sale will be a wash sale and the loss disallowed. When the profitable real estate sale occurs next year, you can sell the loss securities again. This time the loss will be allowed and will offset the gain.

 *Planning Reminder*

Basis Adjusted for New Stock

Although the loss deduction is barred if the wash-sale rule applies, the economic loss is not forfeited for tax purposes. The loss might be realized at a later date when the repurchased stock is sold, because after the disallowance of the loss, the cost basis of the new lot is increased by the disallowed loss. However, the basis increase is not allowed by the IRS if the shares are purchased by your IRA rather than by you individually.

Warrants. A warrant falls within the wash sale rule if it is an option to buy substantially identical stock. Consequently, a loss on the sale of common stocks of a corporation is disallowed when warrants for the common stock of the same corporation are bought within the period 30 days before or after the sale. But if the timing is reversed—that is, you sell warrants at a loss and simultaneously buy common stock of the same corporation—the wash sale rules may or may not apply depending on whether the warrants are substantially identical to the purchased stock. This is determined by comparing the relative values of the stock and warrants. The wash sale rule will apply only if the relative values and price changes are so similar that the warrants become fully convertible securities.

Repurchasing fewer shares. If the number of shares of stock reacquired in a wash sale is less than the amount sold, only a proportionate part of the loss is disallowed.

> **EXAMPLE**
>
> On August 18, 2023, you bought 100 shares of Stock A for $10,000. On December 8, 2023, you sell the lot for $8,000, incurring a loss of $2,000. On January 12, 2024, you repurchase 75 shares of Stock A for $6,000. Three-quarters (75/100) of your loss is disallowed, or $1,500 (¾ of $2,000). You deduct the remaining loss of $500 on your return for 2023. The basis of the new shares is $7,500 ($6,000 cost plus $1,500 disallowed loss).

Holding period of new stock. After a wash sale, the holding period of the new stock includes the holding period of the old lots. If you sold more than one old lot in wash sales, you add the holding periods of all the old lots to the holding period of the new lot. You do this even if your holding periods overlapped as you purchased another lot before you sold the first. You do not count the periods between the sale and purchase when you have no stock.

Losses on short sales. Losses incurred on short sales are subject to the wash sale rules. A loss on the closing of a short sale is denied if you sell the stock or enter into a second short sale within the period beginning 30 days before and ending 30 days after the closing of the short sale. Furthermore, you cannot deduct a loss on the closing of a short sale if within 30 days of the short sale you bought substantially identical stock.

30.7 Convertible Stocks and Bonds

You realize no gain or loss when you convert a bond into stock, or preferred stock into common stock of the same corporation, provided the conversion privilege was allowed by the bond or preferred stock certificate.

> **EXAMPLES**
>
> 1. On January 5, you paid $100 for a bond of A Co. Your holding period for the bond begins on January 6 *(5.9)*. The bond provides that the holder may receive one share of A Co. common stock upon surrender of the bond and the payment of $50. On October 19, you convert the bond to stock on payment of $50. For tax purposes, you realize no gain or loss upon the conversion regardless of whether the fair market value of the stock is more or less than $150 on the date of the conversion. The basis and holding period for the stock is as follows: $100 basis for the portion attributed to the ownership of the bond with the holding period beginning January 6; and $50 basis attributed to the cash payment with the holding period for this portion beginning October 20.
> 2. Same facts as in the above Example, but you acquired the bond on January 5 through the exercise of rights on that date. Since the holding period for the bond includes the date of exercise of the rights *(5.10)*, the portion of the stock allocable to the bond takes a holding period beginning on January 5.

Holding period. Stock acquired through the conversion of bonds or preferred stock takes the same holding period as the securities exchanged. However, where the new stock is acquired partly for cash and partly by tax-free exchange, each new share of stock has a split holding period. The portion of each new share allocable to the ownership of the converted bonds (or preferred stock) includes the holding period of the bonds (or preferred stock). The portion of the new stock allocable to the cash purchase takes a holding period beginning with the day after acquisition of the stock.

Basis. Securities acquired through the conversion of bonds or preferred stock into common take the same basis as the securities exchanged. Where there is a partial cash payment, the basis of the portion of the stock attributable to the cash is the amount of cash paid; *see* Examples 1 and 2 below.

If you paid a premium for a convertible bond, you may not amortize the amount of the premium that is attributable to the conversion feature.

30.8 Stock Options

Stock options are contracts to buy or sell a fixed number of shares by a set date (called the expiration date). Stock options are purchased from public exchanges. If you are buying an option, you are a holder; if you are selling an option, you are a writer. Writers receive a cash premium from the holder. While there are numerous variations on how stock options can be used as investment strategies, the basic ones include the following.

Calls. Buying a call gives the holder the right to buy a specified number of shares of the underlying stock at a given exercise price on or before the option expiration date. Selling a call gives the seller, called the writer, the obligation to sell shares to the holder at the agreed upon price on or before the option expiration date. The holder pays a premium to the writer for the right to buy the shares. If the price of the stock rises above the agreed-upon price (the strike or exercise price), the holder exercises the buy option and acquires the shares. If not, the holder lets the options expire. The holder can sell the call prior to the expiration date.

Puts. Buying a put gives the holder the right, but not the obligation, to sell a specified number of shares of the underlying stock at the given exercise price on or before the option expiration date. Selling a put gives the seller, called the writer, the obligation to buy shares from the holder at the agreed upon price (the strike or exercise price). The writer receives a premium for this obligation. If the stock price rises above the strike price, the holder does not exercise the put option. The holder may sell the put option before the expiration date.

Planning Pointer

Employee Stock Options

Different tax rules apply to incentive stock options and nonqualified stock options obtained in connection with employment *(2.16)*.

Planning Reminder

Speculate with Puts and Calls

Puts and calls allow you to speculate at the expense of a small investment—a call by the holder, for expected price rises, and a put by the holder, for expected price declines. They may also be used to protect paper profits or fix the amount of your losses on securities you own.

Table 30-1 Tax results from calls:

The call—	The holder—	The writer—
Is exercised	Add the cost of the call to your basis in the stock	Increase the amount realized on the sale of the stock by the amount you received for the call
Expires	Report the cost of the call as a capital loss on the date it expires	Report the amount you received for the call as a short-term capital gain
Is sold by the holder	Report as capital gain or loss the difference between the cost of the call and the amount you receive for it	N/A

Table 30-2 Tax results from puts:

The put—	The holder—	The writer—
Is exercised	Reduce the amount realized from the sale of the underlying stock by the cost of the put	Reduce your basis in the stock that you acquire as a result of the put by the amount you received for the put
Expires	Report the cost of the put as a capital loss on the date it expires	Report the amount you received for the call as a short-term capital gain
Is sold by the holder	Report as capital gain or loss the difference between the cost of the put and the amount you receive for it	N/A

Caution

Get Professional Help

Anyone engaging in any sophisticated financial transaction should fully understand the nature of the transaction and the risk, and would be well advised to work with a financial adviser and a tax professional.

Planning Reminder

Avoiding Constructive Sale Treatment

Certain actions (e.g., closing a transaction before a set time; holding a position through a set time) can be employed to avoid the constructive sale rules.

30.9 Sophisticated Financial Transactions

Some individuals may engage in certain complicated and risky financial transactions in the stock market. These activities are not for the average investor, and the tax treatment of these transactions can be complex. The following is a brief overview of some of these transactions and where you can find more information if necessary.

Arbitrage transactions. These are transactions in which an investor simultaneously buys and sells securities, currency, or commodities in different markets to benefit from differing prices for the same asset. Special holding period rules apply to short sales involved in identifying arbitrage transactions in convertible securities and stocks into which the securities are convertible (*see* Treasury regulations under Internal Revenue Code 1233).

Constructive sales of appreciated financial positions. You have made a constructive sale of an appreciated financial position if you:

1. Enter into a short sale of the same or substantially identical property *(30.5)*,
2. Enter into an offsetting notional principal contract relating to the same or substantially identical property,
3. Enter into a futures or forward contract to deliver the same or substantially identical property, or
4. Acquire the same or substantially identical property (if the appreciated financial position is a short sale, an offsetting notional principal contract, or a futures or forward contract).

You are also treated as having made a constructive sale of an appreciated financial position if a person related to you enters into any of the above transactions.

A contract for sale of any stock, debt instrument, or partnership interest that is not a marketable security is not a constructive sale if it settles within one year of the date you enter into it.

If you are considered to have transacted a constructive sale, you must report as taxable income gain on the financial position as if the position was sold at its fair market value on the date of the constructive sale. The property held by you receives a new holding period starting on the date of the constructive sale and its basis is the fair market value at that date. Thus, under the constructive sale rule you are also treated as immediately repurchasing the position as of the date of the constructive sale.

Straddle losses. Commodities and stock options can be used to straddle positions that an investor holds to effectively hedge his or her bets against future price changes. Generally, under tax accounting rules, losses are used to match unrealized gains. Find more information in the instructions to Form 6781 and in IRS Publication 550.

Regulated futures contracts. These are contracts to buy or sell commodities or currency on a futures exchange (e.g., the Chicago Board of Trade). Gain or loss is reported annually under the marked-to-market accounting system. Find more information in the instructions to Form 6781 and in IRS Publication 550.

Conversion transactions. A conversion transaction is one involving two or more positions taken with regard to the same or similar property. The investor is in the economic position of a lender who expects to receive income while undertaking no significant risks other than those of a lender. Conversion transactions are reported on Form 6781. However, the ordinary income element from a conversion transaction is not reported as interest; it is treated as ordinary gain on Form 4797.

30.10 Investing in Tax-Exempts

Interest on state and local obligations is not subject to federal income tax. It is also exempt from the tax of the state in which the obligations are issued. In comparing the interest return of a tax-exempt with that of a taxable bond, you figure the taxable return that is equivalent to the tax-free yield of the tax-exempt. This amount depends on your marginal tax bracket (your top tax rate). For example, a tax-exempt municipal bond yielding 3% is the equivalent of a taxable yield of 3.95% subject to a marginal tax rate of 24%.

You can compare the value of tax-exempt interest to taxable interest for your tax bracket by using this formula:

$$\frac{\text{Tax-exempt interest rate}}{\text{1 minus your marginal tax bracket}}$$

The denominator of the above fraction is:

0.88 if your marginal tax bracket is 12%
0.78 if your marginal tax bracket is 22%
0.76 if your marginal tax bracket is 24%
0.68 if your marginal tax bracket is 32%
0.65 if your marginal tax bracket is 35%
0.63 if your marginal tax bracket is 37%

EXAMPLE

You are deciding between a tax-exempt bond and a taxable bond. You want to find which will give you more income after taxes. You have a choice between a tax-exempt bond paying 2.5% and a taxable bond paying 3.25%. Your marginal tax bracket is 32%.

You find that the tax-exempt bond is a slightly better buy in your tax bracket as it is the equivalent of a taxable bond paying nearly 3.68%.

$$\text{Taxable Equivalent Rate (T)} = \frac{0.025}{0.68\,(1.00 - 0.32)}$$

$$T = .03676, \text{ or } 3.676\%$$

AMT and other restrictions. In buying state or local bonds, check the prospectus for the issue date and tax status of the bond. The tax law treats bonds issued after August 7, 1986, as follows:

1. "Public-purpose" bonds. These include bonds issued directly by state or local governments or their agencies to meet essential government functions, such as highway construction and school financing. These bonds are generally tax exempt.

2. "Qualified private activity" bonds. Interest on private activity bonds is taxable unless the bond is a qualified bond. Qualified bonds generally finance housing, student loans, or redevelopment, or they benefit tax-exempt organizations. Interest on qualified private activity bonds issued after August 7, 1986, although tax free for regular income tax purposes, is a tax preference item for purposes of computing alternative minimum tax *(23.3)* unless an exception applies. Because of the AMT, these private activity bonds may pay slightly higher interest than public-purpose bonds.

    Several types of bonds have been excluded from private activity bond treatment so the interest is not treated as an AMT preference item, including qualified Section 501(c)(3) bonds, Gulf Opportunity Zone bonds, Midwestern disaster area bonds, most New York Liberty bonds, and qualified mortgage bonds issued after July 30, 2008. In addition, any bonds issued in 2009 and 2010 that would otherwise be considered private activity bonds are not treated as private activity bonds, so the interest on the 2009/2010 bonds is not a tax preference item.

    Your broker can help you identify bonds subject to and exempt from AMT preference item treatment.

3. "Taxable" municipals. These are bonds issued for nonqualifying private purposes. They are subject to federal income tax, but may be exempt from state and local taxes in the states in which they are issued.

30.11 Ordinary Loss for Small Business Stock (Section 1244)

Shareholders of qualifying "small" corporations may claim within limits an ordinary loss, rather than a capital loss, on the sale or worthlessness of Section 1244 stock. An ordinary loss up to $50,000, or $100,000 on a joint return, may be claimed on Form 4797. On a joint return, the $100,000 limit applies even if only one spouse has a Section 1244 loss. Losses in excess of these limits are deductible as capital losses on Form 8949. Any gains on Section 1244 stock are reported as capital gain on Form 8949.

Planning Reminder

Municipal Bond Funds

Instead of purchasing tax-exempts directly, you may consider investing in municipal bond funds. The funds invest in various municipal bonds and, thus, offer the safety of diversity. The value of fund shares will fluctuate with the bond markets. Also, an investment in the fund may be as small as $1,000 compared with the typical $5,000 municipal bond. Check on fees and other restrictions in municipal bond funds.

Filing Instruction

Interest Subject to AMT

Interest on qualified private activity bonds issued after August 7, 1986, is tax free for regular tax purposes but may be a tax preference item for alternative minimum tax (AMT) purposes *(23.2)*.

Planning Reminder

Recordkeeping for Section 1244 Stock

You must keep records that distinguish between Section 1244 stock and other stock interests. Your records must show that the corporation qualified as a small business corporation when the stock was issued, you are the original holder of the Section 1244 stock, and it was issued for money or property. Stock issued for services does not qualify. In addition, the records should also show the amount paid for the stock, information relating to any property transferred for the stock, any tax-free stock dividends issued on the stock, and the corporation's gross receipts data for the most recent five-year period.

You do not attach the records to the return, but should attach a computation of the loss to Form 4797. However, the failure to keep these records will be grounds for disallowing a loss that is claimed on Section 1244 stock.

Caution

Timing Redemptions of Older EE Bonds

In the year you cash in a Series EE savings bond you could lose interest by cashing it in too soon. Interest accrues only twice a year on EE bonds issued prior to May 1, 1997. The accrual months depend on the month of issue. If you cash pre–May 1997 bonds before the accrual month that applies to your bond, you will lose interest, as explained in *30.12*.

An ordinary loss may be claimed only by the original owner of the stock. If a partnership sells Section 1244 stock at a loss, an ordinary loss deduction may be claimed by individuals who were partners when the stock was issued. If a partnership distributes the Section 1244 stock to the partners, the partners may not claim an ordinary loss on their disposition of the stock.

If an S corporation sells Section 1244 stock at a loss, S corporation shareholders may not claim an ordinary loss deduction. The IRS with Tax Court approval limits shareholders' deductions to capital losses, which are deductible only against capital gains plus $3,000 ($1,500 if married filing separately) *(5.4)*.

To qualify as Section 1244 stock:

1. The corporation's equity may not exceed $1,000,000 at the time the stock is issued, including amounts received for the stock to be issued. Thus, if the corporation already has $600,000 equity from stock previously issued, it may not designate more than $400,000 worth of additional stock as Section 1244 stock.

   If the $1,000,000 equity limit is exceeded, the corporation follows an IRS procedure for designating which shares qualify as Section 1244 stock.

   Preferred stock issued after July 18, 1984, may qualify for Section 1244 loss treatment, as well as common stock.

2. The stock must be issued for money or property (other than stock and securities).

3. The corporation for the five years preceding your loss must generally have derived more than half of its gross receipts from business operations and not from passive income such as rents, royalties, dividends, interest, annuities, or gains from the sales or exchanges of stock or securities. The five-year requirement is waived if the corporation's deductions (other than for dividends received or net operating losses) exceed gross income. If the corporation has not been in existence for the five years before your loss, then generally the period for which the corporation has been in existence is examined for the gross receipts test.

30.12 Series EE Bonds

Series EE savings bonds give you an opportunity to defer tax; *see* below. EE bonds may only be purchased online from Treasury Direct at www.treasurydirect.gov. They must be held 12 months from the issue date before they can be redeemed. Bonds cashed in any time before five years are subject to a three-month interest penalty; *see* the Example below.

Series EE savings bonds with an issue date on or after May 1, 2005, earn a fixed rate of interest. The Treasury announces the fixed rate that will apply to new bonds every May 1 and November 1. Interest accrues monthly and is compounded semiannually. EE bonds issued from May 1997 through April 2005 continue to earn market-based interest rates set at 90% of the average five-year Treasury securities yields for the preceding six months; these rates change every May 1 and November 1. EE bonds issued before May 1997 earn various rates depending on the date of issue.

> **EXAMPLE**
>
> You purchased series EE bonds in March 2022. If you redeem them 24 months later, in March 2024, you get your original investment back plus 21 months of interest (instead of 24 months of interest). You lose the last three months of interest. The three-month penalty applies to redemptions within the first five years of ownership.

Deferring tax on savings bond interest. Unless you report the interest annually, Series EE bond interest is deferred *(4.29)* until the year you redeem the bond or it reaches final maturity. When you redeem the bond, the accumulated interest is taxable on your federal return but not taxable on your state and local income tax return. If in the year of redemption you use the proceeds to pay for higher education or vocational school costs, the accumulated interest may be tax free for federal tax purposes *(33.4)*.

Interest accrual dates for Series EE savings bonds. For EE bonds issued after April 1997, interest accrues on the first day of every month. For EE bonds issued before May 1, 1997, interest generally accrues twice a year: on the first day of the issue month and first day of the sixth month after the issue month. For example, if you own an EE bond issued in August 1995, interest accrues every August 1 (month of issue) and every February 1 (six months after the August issue month). There is an exception for EE bonds issued from March 1993 through April 1995; these bonds accrue interest monthly (not just twice-a-year) to guarantee a 4% return.

When you cash a bond, you receive the value of the bond as of the last date that interest was added. If you cash a bond in between accrual months, you will not receive interest for the partial period. For example, if interest on a bond issued before May 1, 1997, accrues in February and August, and you cash a bond in during July, you would earn interest only through February. By waiting until August 1 to cash the bond, you would earn another six months of interest.

Final maturity for savings bonds. Do not neglect the final maturity date for older bonds. After the final maturity date, no further interest will accrue. No E bonds are still accruing interest. The last issued E bonds, those from June 1980, reached final maturity after 30 years in June 2010 and thus they, as well as all older E bonds, have ceased earning interest.

EE bonds issued in 1980 (the first year available) reached final maturity in 2010, 30 years after issue, after which no further interest has accrued. All EE bonds have 30-year maturities, so EE bonds issued in 1993 stopped earning interest in 2023 after they earned interest for 30 years, and EE bonds issued in 1994 will stop earning interest after the month in 2024 that is 30 years after issue.

Series HH bonds. HH bonds obtained before September 1, 2004, in exchange for savings bonds or savings notes pay taxable interest every six months at a fixed rate. Currently, all HH bonds are paying 1.5% per year. Interest is paid until final maturity is reached 20 years after issue.

30.13 I Bonds

Treasury "I bonds" provide a return that rises and falls with inflation. I bonds may only be purchased online from TreasuryDirect at www.treasurydirect.gov. An individual is limited to a purchase of up to $10,000 per year. In addition, however, you can ask the IRS on Form 8888 to use your federal tax refund, up to $5,000, to buy I bonds, either by directly depositing the refund into your TreasuryDirect account if you have one, or to buy paper bonds if you do not have a TreasuryDirect account; *see* the Form 8888 instructions.

I bonds earn interest for 30 years. Interest is credited to a bond on the first day of every month and paid when the bond is redeemed.

I bonds are not redeemable within the first 12 months. You forfeit the last three months of interest if you redeem an I bond within the first five years, the same rule as for EE bonds *(30.12)*.

Rates. Interest on an I bond is determined by two rates. One rate, set by the Treasury Department, remains constant for the life of the bond. The second rate is a variable inflation rate announced each May 1 and November 1 by the Treasury Department to reflect changes reported by the Bureau of Labor Statistics in the Consumer Price Index. The variable rate on an I bond changes on the first day of the issue month and the first day of the sixth month after the issue month. For example, if you own an I bond issued in September, the inflation rate on your bond changes every September 1 to the rate announced on the previous May 1 and then changes six months later on March 1 to the rate announced on the previous November 1. If deflation sets in, the variable rate will be negative for a six-month period and the negative rate will reduce the fixed rate, but not below zero, so, even if the negative variable rate exceeds the fixed rate, the redemption value of the bond is not reduced.

Income tax reporting. Investors may defer paying federal income taxes on I bond interest, which is automatically reinvested and added to the principal. Deferral applies to the fixed rate interest as well as the variable inflation rate interest. You may defer federal tax on the interest until you redeem the bond or the bond reaches maturity in 30 years *(4.29)*. You may report the interest each year as it accrues instead of deferring the interest. I bond interest is exempt from state and local income taxes.

If an I bond is redeemed to pay for college tuition or other college fees, all or part of the interest may be excludable from income under the rules discussed in *33.4*.

 *Caution*

All E Bonds and Some EE Bonds Have Reached Final Maturity

The last outstanding E bonds reached their 30-year final maturity by June 2010 and are no longer earning additional interest. If you are still holding any E bonds, you can redeem them for their value as of the final maturity date.

EE bonds that have reached final maturity after 30 years have also stopped earning interest *(30.12)*.

Table 30-3	Savings Bond Maturity Dates	
Bond	**Issue Date**	**Final Maturity**
Series E	May 1941–November 1965	40 years after issue
	December 1965–June 1980	30 years after issue
Series EE	January 1980 or later	30 years after issue
Savings notes (Freedom Shares)	May 1967–October 1970	30 years after issue
H bonds	February 1957–December 1979	30 years after issue
HH bonds	January 1980–August 2004	20 years after issue
I bonds	September 1998 or later	30 years after issue

30.14 Trader, Dealer, or Investor?

The tax law recognizes three types of individuals who may sell and buy securities. They are:

Investor. You are an investor if you buy and sell securities for long-term capital gains and to earn dividends and interest.

Trader. You may be a trader if you buy and sell securities to profit from daily market movements in the prices of securities and not from dividends, interest, or capital appreciation. Your buy and sell orders must be frequent, continuous, and substantial. There are at present no clear-cut tests to determine the amount of sales volume that qualifies a person as a trader. The term "trader" is not defined in the Internal Revenue Code or Treasury regulations. The IRS has not issued rulings for determining trader status. The Tax Court has held that sporadic trading does not qualify; *see* the Examples below.

Dealer. You are a dealer if you hold an inventory of securities to sell to others. Dealers report their profits and losses as business income and losses under special tax rules not discussed in this book.

Tax treatment of traders. The tax rules applied to traders are a hybrid of tax rules applied to investors and business persons, as discussed in the following paragraphs.

Reporting trader gains and losses. Unless a trader previously made a mark-to-market election, gains and losses are reported as capital gains and losses on Form 8949 and Schedule D. As almost all or substantially all of a trader's sales are short-term, such gains are reported as short-term gains and losses as short-term losses. A net profit from Schedule D is not subject to self-employment tax *(45.1)*. Substantial losses subject to capital loss treatment are a tax disadvantage because capital losses in excess of capital gains are deductible only up to $3,000 of ordinary income in one tax year. True, carryover capital losses may offset capital gains in the next year, but your inability to deduct them immediately may subject you to paying a tax liability that might have been reduced or eliminated if the losses had been deductible for the year of the sale. If you are concerned about incurring substantial short-term capital losses that would be limited by capital loss treatment, you may consider a mark-to-market election *(30.15)*, which would allow you to treat your security gains and losses as ordinary income and loss.

Deducting trader expenses. Although a trader does not sell to customers but for his or her own account, a trader is considered to be in business. Expenses such as subscriptions and margin interest may be deducted as ordinary business losses on Schedule C of Form 1040 or 1040-SR. Home office expenses are deductible if the office is regularly and exclusively used as the principal place of conducting the trading business *(40.12)*.

An investor, on the other hand, may deduct margin interest only as an itemized deduction to the extent of net investment income *(15.10)*. Other investment expenses are not deductible in 2018 through 2025 due to the suspension of miscellaneous itemized costs in excess of the 2% of adjusted gross income floor *(19.2)*. An investor may not deduct home office expenses since investment activities, no matter how extensive, are not considered a business; *see* the *Moller* decision discussed in *40.16*.

EXAMPLES

1. After he retired, Holsinger began buying and selling stocks. In 2001, he made 289 trades over 63 days, and had losses of almost $179,000, which he reported as ordinary losses. In 2002, he made 372 trades over 110 days, and reported trading losses of just over $11,000 as an ordinary loss.

   The Tax Court held that Holsinger was an investor, not a trader. His trading losses were capital losses, and as such they could be deducted only to the extent of capital gains and then $3,000 of ordinary income. The Court held that the level of Holsinger's trading activities was not substantial enough to constitute a business. In addition, his trades were not aimed at catching the swings in daily market movements and profiting from these short-term changes, as evidenced by the fact that a significant amount of his positions were held more than 31 days. Since Holsinger failed to establish that he was in business as a trader, he could not make a mark-to-market election.

2. While holding a full-time job as a computer chip engineer in 1999, Chen made 323 transactions, 94 percent of which occurred in February, March, and April; he did no trading in June or August through December. Most of the securities were held for less than a month. He had losses of nearly $85,000, which he reported as ordinary losses.

   The Tax Court held that Chen was not a trader in securities and was limited to deducting $3,000 of his net 1999 loss against ordinary income. To be considered a trader, the purchases and sales of securities must amount to a trade or business. There is no exact number of trades or other clear standard used to make this determination. Rather, it is based on the taxpayer's intent, the nature of the income derived from trading, and the frequency, extent, and regularity of the transactions. During three months of the year, Chen bought and sold with frequency, but he failed to achieve trader status because, overall, his activities were not frequent, regular, and continuous. In prior cases, trader status has been found where such activities usually were frequent, regular, and continuous for a period of more than a single year. Because Chen could not claim trader status, he was ineligible to make a mark-to-market election.

30.15 Mark-to-Market Election for Traders

A trader in securities may elect to have his gains and losses treated as ordinary gains and losses by making a mark-to-market election. As explained below, it is too late to make an election for 2023. In the absence of an election, gains and losses of a trader are treated as capital gains and losses on Form 8949 and Schedule D.

If the mark-to-market election is made, you report trading gains and losses on closed transactions plus unrealized gains and losses on securities held in your trading business at the end of your taxable year as ordinary gains and losses on Form 4797. Trader profits are not subject to self-employment tax *(45.1)*, whether or not the mark-to-market election is made. The unrealized gain or loss on a security that is reported on Form 4797 increases or reduces the basis of the security. For example, if you report an unrealized gain of $50 on stock with a cost of $100, you increase the basis of the stock to $150. If you later sell the stock for $90, you report a loss of $60 in the year of the sale. The requirement to report unrealized gains and losses at the end of the year and to adjust basis of shares is an automatic change in accounting method that requires you to file Form 3115 with the IRS National Office. On Form 3115, use code #64 (the designated automatic accounting method change number), and report required adjustments; *see* IRS Publication 550 for details. The failure to file Form 3115 does not invalidate a timely and valid election.

Once the mark-to-market election is made, it applies to all future years unless the IRS agrees in writing to a revocation.

Planning Reminder

Wash Sale Rule Does Not Apply

If you make a mark-to-market election, the wash sale rule does not apply; all losses are reported as ordinary losses under the mark-to-market rules

Making the election is not proof that you are actually a trader in securities. If you are audited by the IRS, you must be able to prove that your activities are such that you are in the business of making money by buying and selling over short periods of time. As mentioned in *30.14*, there are no hard and fast rules that specify how many daily or short-term trades qualify you as a trader.

The mark-to-market election does not apply to the securities you hold for investment. Sales of your investment securities are reported on Form 8949 and Schedule D, not Form 4797.

When to make the mark-to-market election. The IRS requires you to make the election by the due date (without extensions) of the tax return for the year prior to the year for which the election is to be effective. Under this due date rule, it is too late to make an election for 2023, as this had to be done by April 18, 2023, the due date for your 2022 return. The election for 2024 must be filed by April 15, 2024, the due date of the 2023 return; *see* "How to make the mark-to-market election" below.

A regulation gives the IRS authority to grant an extension of time to file the mark-to-market election if the taxpayer has acted reasonably and in good faith and allowing relief does not prejudice the interests of the government. However, the IRS has refused to allow such extensions, claiming that a late election invariably results in prejudice to the interests of the government.

The Tax Court has supported the IRS in cases where the taxpayers, in filing their elections several years late, were relying on hindsight to try to gain a tax advantage from ordinary loss treatment.

The Ninth Circuit Court of Appeals has also refused to allow a late election where the taxpayer was relying on hindsight to try to gain a tax advantage. On his 1999 return, Acar reported over $954,041 in losses from trading securities, treating them as capital losses. In early 2002, he filed an amended return and tried to make a retroactive mark-to-market election beginning with 1999 so he could treat his 1999 losses as ordinary losses and claim a refund. The IRS disallowed the late election and a federal district court and the Ninth Circuit affirmed. Allowing the late election would give Acar an advantage that was not available on April 15, 1999, the due date for making the election for 1999 under Revenue Procedure 99-17. When the late election was made, Acar knew that he had incurred losses and, with that hindsight, was trying to convert what had been capital losses on his original return into ordinary losses. It does not matter that any advantage from a late election for 1999 could be outweighed if Acar in later years realized trading gains that under the irrevocable election would have to be treated as ordinary rather than capital gains. That a taxpayer might come to regret an election in later years does not mean that hindsight was not used to gain an advantage at the time of the retroactive election.

In another case, the Tax Court was more sympathetic, allowing an extension to a taxpayer who filed his election for 2000 on July 21, 2000, three months after the IRS deadline of April 17, 2000. He had left his law practice and became a trader in January 2000. The accountant who prepared his 1999 return did not know about the mark-to-mark election but a friend told him about it in June 2000 and in July the taxpayer hired a law firm, which filed the election for him and asked the IRS to allow the extension. The taxpayer did not conduct any trading activities between the date he should have filed the election and the date he actually filed it. Over IRS objection, the Tax Court allowed the late election on the grounds that the taxpayer had acted reasonably and in good faith by promptly employing the law firm after learning about the availability of the election. Since the taxpayer did not realize any further gains or losses between the date he should have filed the election and when he actually did so, the Court held that the interests of the government were not prejudiced.

How to make the mark-to-market election. The election for 2024 is made by attaching a statement to your 2023 return by April 15, 2024, and by filing Form 3115 for an accounting method change with the return; enter code #64 (the designated automatic accounting method change number) on the Form 3115 (Section 24.01 of Revenue Procedure 2019-43). The statement with your return must specify that effective for the taxable year starting January 1, 2024, you are electing to report gains and losses from your trading business under the mark-to-market rules of Section 475(f). However, if you are not required to file a 2023 return, make the election for 2024 by placing a statement of election in your books and records no later than March 15, 2024. A copy of the statement must be attached to your original 2024 return.

One of the conditions of the election is that you must clearly distinguish between securities held for investment and trading purposes. The election applies only to the securities held in your trading business, not to the securities held for investment. Holding investment securities in a separate account is advisable.

See IRS Revenue Procedure 99-17 and the instructions to Form 3115 for further details on making the mark-to-market election. In light of the accounting requirements and the overall effect of reporting unrealized gains and losses, before making the election you should consult a professional experienced in the use of mark-to-market accounting.

Revoking the election. An election can only be revoked as an automatic change in accounting method (code #218 is the designated automatic accounting method change number). Details about the revocation procedure are in Revenue Procedure 2019-43(Section 24.02).

30.16 Cryptocurrency Transactions

If you invest in digital currency, also referred to as virtual currency or cryptocurrency, you figure your gain or loss as you would on any asset you hold. Holding cryptocurrency for investment results in capital gain or loss when you sell it or use it to pay for purchases. Gain or loss may be long term or short term, depending on how long you held the cryptocurrency (*see 11.23* for further developments governing cryptocurrency/virtual currency).

Hard fork. A hard fork occurs when a cryptocurrency undergoes a protocol change resulting in a permanent diversion from the legacy distributed ledger. This may result in the creation of a new cryptocurrency on a new distributed ledger in addition to the legacy cryptocurrency on the legacy distributed ledger. If your cryptocurrency went through a hard fork, but you did not receive any new cryptocurrency, whether through an airdrop (a distribution of cryptocurrency to multiple taxpayers' distributed ledger addresses) or some other kind of transfer, you don't have taxable income.

If a hard fork is followed by an airdrop but you receive new cryptocurrency, you have taxable income in the year you receive that cryptocurrency. When you receive cryptocurrency from an airdrop following a hard fork, you have ordinary income equal to the fair market value of the new cryptocurrency when it is received (i.e., when the transaction is recorded on the distributed ledger), provided you have dominion and control over the cryptocurrency so that you can transfer, sell, exchange, or otherwise dispose of the cryptocurrency.

If you receive cryptocurrency in a transaction facilitated by a cryptocurrency exchange, the value of the cryptocurrency is the amount that is recorded by the cryptocurrency exchange for that transaction in U.S. dollars. If the transaction is facilitated by a centralized or decentralized cryptocurrency exchange but is not recorded on a distributed ledger or is otherwise an off-chain transaction, then the fair market value is the amount the cryptocurrency was trading for on the exchange at the date and time the transaction would have been recorded on the ledger if it had been an on-chain transaction.

Soft fork. A soft fork occurs when a distributed ledger undergoes a protocol change that does not result in a diversion of the ledger and thus does not result in the creation of a new cryptocurrency. Because soft forks do not result in you receiving new cryptocurrency, you are in the same position you were in prior to the soft fork, meaning that the soft fork does not result in any income to you.

Reporting cryptocurrency. Gain or loss on the sale or exchange of virtual currency is reported on Form 8949 and Schedule D of Form 1040 or 1040-SR. If you bought or sold any cryptocurrency in 2023, you are required to check the "Digital Assets" box on page 1 of Form 1040 or 1040-SR, which asks: "At any time during 2023, did you: (a) receive (as a reward, award, or payment for property or services); or (b) sell, exchange, gift, or otherwise dispose of a digital asset (or a financial interest in a digital asset)?"

 *Filing Tip*

Classifying Cryptocurrency Income

If you mine for virtual currency, this is not investment income. Instead, it is treated as self-employment income *(40.1)*. If you earn interest on cryptocurrency sitting in a wallet, you have interest income *(4.12)*.

CHAPTER 31

Tax Savings for Investors in Real Estate

Real estate investors may take advantage of the following tax benefits:

- Gains on the sale of investment property may be taxed at capital gain rates.
- Depreciation can provide a source of temporary tax-free income *(31.1)*.
- Rental income can be used to offset passive losses *Chapter 10*.
- Tax-free exchanges make it possible to defer tax on exchanges of real estate held for investment *(31.3)*.

However, rental income and real estate gains usually are subject to the 3.8% net investment income tax *(28.3)*.

Losses on real estate transactions may be subject to the following disadvantages:

- Rental losses may not be deductible from other income such as salary, interest, and dividends unless you qualify as a real estate professional or for the special $25,000 rental loss allowance under the passive loss rules *Chapter 10*.
- Compromises of mortgage liability may subject you to tax *(31.10)*.
- A foreclosure or repossession is treated as a sale on which you realize gain or loss. In addition, if you are personally liable on the loan and the amount of debt canceled in the foreclosure exceeds the fair market value of the transferred property, you will owe tax on cancellation of debt income unless an exception is available *(31.9)*.
- Certain dividends from REITs are eligible for the qualified business income (QBI) deduction *(31.16)*.

31.1 Real Estate Ventures

A real estate investment should provide a current income return and an appreciation in the value of the original investment. As an additional incentive, a real estate investment may return income subject to little or no tax in the early years of the investment. Such occurrennce may be from depreciation and other expense deductions reducing taxable income without reducing the amount of cash available for distribution. This tax savings is temporary and limited by the terms and the amount of the mortgage debt on the property. Payments allocated to amortization of mortgage principal reduce the amount of cash available to investors without an offsetting tax deduction. Thus, the amount of tax-free return depends on the extent to which depreciation deductions exceed the amortization payments.

To provide a higher return of tax-free income, at least during the early years of its operations, a venture must obtain a constant payment mortgage that provides for the payment of fixed annual amounts that are allocated to continually decreasing amounts of interest and increasing amounts of amortization payments. Consequently, in the early years, a tax-free return of income is high while the amortization payments are low, but as the amortization payments increase, nontaxable income decreases. When this tax-free return has been substantially reduced, a partnership must refinance the mortgage to reduce the amortization payments and once again increase the tax-free return; *see* Examples 1 and 2 below.

In the case of a building, the tax-free return is based on the assumption that the building does not actually depreciate at as fast a rate as the tax depreciation rate being claimed by the investors. If the building is depreciating physically at a faster rate, the so-called tax-free return on investment is illusory. There is no tax-free return because the distributions to investors (over and above current income return) are, in fact, a return of the investor's own capital.

 *Caution*

NII Tax on Rental Income

Rental income and expenses are taken into account in figuring the 3.8% net investment income tax for high-income taxpayers *(28.3)*.

EXAMPLES

1. A limited partnership of 100 investors owns a building that returns an annual income of $100,000 after a deduction of operating expenses, but before a depreciation deduction of $80,000. Thus, taxable income is $20,000 ($100,000 – $80,000). Assuming that there is no mortgage on the building, all of the $100,000 is available for distribution. (Since the depreciation requires no cash outlay, it does not reduce the cash available for distribution.) Each investor receives $1,000. Taxable income being $20,000, only 20% ($20,000 ÷ $100,000) of the distribution is taxable. Thus, each investor reports as income only $200 of his or her $1,000 distribution; $800 is tax free.

2. Same facts as in Example 1, except that the building is mortgaged, and an annual amortization payment of $40,000 is being made. Consequently, only $60,000 is available for distribution, of which $20,000 is taxable. Each investor receives $600, of which 1/3 ($20,000 ÷ $60,000), or $200, is taxed, and $400 is tax free. In other words, the $60,000 distribution is tax free to the extent that the depreciation deduction of $80,000 exceeds the amortization of $40,000—namely $40,000. If the amortization payment were increased to $50,000, only $30,000 of the distribution would be tax free ($80,000 – $50,000).

Real estate investment trusts (REITs). The tax treatment of real estate investment trusts resembles that of open-end mutual funds. Distributions generally are reported to the investors on Form 1099-DIV as dividend income. However, distributions generally do not qualify for the reduced tax rate on qualified dividends *(4.2)* but may be eligible for the qualified business income (QBI) deduction *(31.16)*. A distribution qualifies for the reduced rate (but not the QBI deduction) only to the extent it represents previously taxed undistributed income or qualifying dividends received by the REIT (from stock investments) that are passed through to the investors. Capital gain distributions reported on Form 1099-DIV must be reported as long-term capital gains regardless of how long the REIT shares have been held *(4.4)*. If the trust operates at a loss, the loss may not be passed on to the investors.

REMICs. A real estate mortgage investment company (REMIC) holds a fixed pool of mortgages. Investors are treated as holding a regular or residual interest. A REMIC is not a taxable entity for federal income tax purposes. It is generally treated as a partnership, with the residual interest holders as partners.

Investors with regular REMIC interests are treated as holding debt obligations. Interest income is reported to them by the REMIC on Form 1099-INT and original issue discount (OID) on Form 1099-OID.

The net income of the REMIC, after payments to regular interest holders, is passed through to the holders of residual interests. A residual interest holder's share of the REMIC's taxable income or loss is reported by the REMIC to the interest holder each quarter on Schedule Q of Form 1066, and the investor reports his or her total share of the year in Part IV of Schedule E.

31.2   Sales of Subdivided Land—Dealer or Investor?

An investor faces a degree of uncertainty in determining the tax treatment of sales of subdivided realty. In some situations, investor status may be preferred, and in others, dealer status.

Capital gain on sale. Investor status allows capital gain treatment. Capital losses may offset the gains. For capital gain, an investor generally has to show that his or her activities were not those of a dealer but were steps taken in a liquidation of the investment. To convince an IRS agent or a court of investment activity, this type of evidence may present a favorable argument for capital gain treatment:

- The property was bought as an investment, to build a residence, or received as a gift or inheritance.
- No substantial improvements were added to the tract.
- The property was subdivided to liquidate the investment.
- Sales came through unsolicited offers. There was no advertising or agents.
- Sales were infrequent.
- There were no previous activities as a real estate dealer.
- The seller was in a business unrelated to real estate.
- The property was held for a long period of time.
- Sales proceeds were invested in other investment property.

Planning Reminder

Installment Sales

The distinction between an investor and dealer is significant if land is sold on the installment basis. Investor status is preferable if you want to elect the installment method. Dealers may not elect installment sale treatment *(5.21)*.

EXAMPLE

Morley was interested in buying farm acreage to resell at a profit. Two and a half million dollars was set as the purchase price. To swing the deal, Morley borrowed $600,000. His attempts to resell the property quickly failed, and he allowed the property to be foreclosed. While he held the property he incurred interest costs of over $400,000, which he deducted. The IRS held the interest was not fully deductible. It claimed the interest was investment interest subject to investment interest restrictions. That is, the debt was incurred to purchase and carry investment property. The IRS position was based on the so-called "one-bite" rule, which holds that a taxpayer who engages in only one venture may not under any circumstances be held to be in a business as to that venture. Morley argued that he bought the property not as an investment property but as business property for immediate resale.

The Tax Court sided with Morley, holding that he held the acreage as ordinary business property. The court rejected the "one-bite" rule. The fact that he had not previously sold business property did not mean that he could not prove that he held acreage for resale. Here, he intended promptly to resell it, and the facts supported his intention.

Section 1237 capital gain opportunity. Section 1237 is a limited tax provision that provides a capital gain opportunity for subdivided lots only if arbitrary holding period rules and restrictions on substantial improvements are complied with. For example, the lots must generally be held at least five years before sale unless they were inherited. If the lots were previously held for sale to customers, or if other lots are so held in the year of sale, Section 1237 does not apply. Furthermore, substantial improvements must not have been made to the lots. According to the IRS, a disqualifying substantial improvement is one that increases the value of the property by more than 10%. The IRS considers buildings, hard surface roads, or utilities, such as sewers, water, gas, or electric lines, as substantial improvements.

Interest expense deductions. The distinction between an investor in land and a dealer is also important in the case of interest expenses. Dealer status is usually preferable here. Interest expenses incurred by an investor are subject to investment interest deduction limitations; *see Chapter 15*. On the other hand, interest expenses of a dealer in the course of business activities are fully deductible (subject to the limitation for large dealers *see 40.6*); *see* the Morley Example below.

Passive activity. Income from sales of lots is not considered passive activity income. Thus, losses from sales of land may offset salary and other investment income. If you hold rental property and also sell land, make sure that your accounts distinguish between and separate each type of income. This way income and losses from land sales will not be commingled with rent income subject to the passive activity restrictions discussed in *Chapter 10*. Your activity in real property development counts towards qualifying you as a real estate professional who may deduct rental losses from nonpassive income if material participation tests are met *(10.3)*.

31.3 Exchanging Real Estate Without Tax

You may exchange real estate held for investment for other investment real estate and incur no immediate tax consequences. On a fully tax-free exchange of "like-kind" property, you do not recognize any gain realized on the exchange and you cannot deduct any loss. If you had a gain, the potential tax on the gain is postponed until you sell the new property for more than your basis. A tax-free exchange may also defer a potential tax due on gain from depreciation recapture and might be considered where the depreciable basis of a building has been substantially written off. Here, the building may be exchanged for other property that will give larger tax deductions.

Like-kind exchanges apply only to real property. The Tax Code does not define the term "real property", but final regulations (T.D. 9935, 2020-52 IRB 1746) specify the meaning. Real property includes land, improvements to land, natural products of land (e.g., crops, timber, minerals), and water and air space superjacent to land. Intangible interests in real property such as fee ownership, co-ownership, a leasehold, an easement, and stock in a cooperative housing corporation are considered real property. Improvements to land include "inherently permanent structures" (i.e., buildings affixed to the land) as well as structural components of such inherently permanent structures. Generally, property is considered real property if it is treated as such under state or local law on the date of the exchange, but the regulations provide exceptions. The regulations include a rule that the receipt of personal property that is incidental to real property does not disqualify like-kind treatment. Personal property transferred with real property is incidental if (1) in a standard commercial transaction, it is typical for such personal property to be transferred with the real property (such as furniture acquired with an office building), and (2) the aggregate fair market value of the personal property does not exceed 15% of the aggregate fair market value of the replacement real property received in the exchange. Keep in mind that the value of the personal property received in the exchange is taxable "boot" (as it is not like-kind); *see* "Partially tax-free exchanges" below. For examples and further details on the rules defining real property; *see* T.D. 9935.

Fully tax-free exchanges. To transact a fully tax-free exchange, you must satisfy these conditions:

- The property traded must be solely for property of a "like kind." The words like kind are liberally interpreted. They refer to the nature or character of the property, not its grade, quality, or use. Some examples of like-kind exchanges are: farm or ranch for city property; unimproved land for improved real estate; rental house for a store building; and fee in business property for 30-year or more leasehold in the same type of property *(6.1)*. However, you may not make a tax-free exchange of U.S. real estate for real estate in foreign countries; your gain or loss on the exchange must be recognized.

- The property exchanged must have been held for productive use in your business or for investment and traded for property to be held for productive use in business or investment. Therefore, trades of property used, or to be used, for personal purposes, such as exchanging a residence for rental property, cannot receive tax-free treatment. However, if you rent out your vacation home and meet the conditions of an IRS safe

Planning Reminder

Exchanging a Building for Land

A tax-free exchange may be advantageous in the case of land. Land is not depreciable, but it may be exchanged for a depreciable rental building. The exchange is tax free and depreciation may be claimed on the building. However, be aware of a possible tax trap if you exchange rental property for land because the building is subject to depreciation recapture. The recapture provisions override the tax-free exchange rules. The "recapture element" will be taxable as ordinary income.

harbor *(6.1)*, the residence is treated as investment property rather than personal-use property, so it can be part of a like-kind exchange for other investment property.

- If you trade your principal residence for another principal residence, gain may be tax free under the home sale exclusion rules *(29.2)*.
- The like-kind trade must generally occur within a 180-day period, and property identification must occur within 45 days of the first transfer *(6.4)*.

A real estate dealer cannot transact a tax-free exchange of property held for sale to customers. Also, an exchange is not tax free if the property received is held for immediate resale.

Tax-free exchanges between related parties are subject to tax if either party disposes of the exchanged property within a two-year period *(6.6)*.

Disadvantage of tax-free exchange. Although the postponement of tax on gain from a tax-free exchange is equivalent to an interest-free loan from the government equal to the amount you would have owed in taxes had you sold the property, this tax advantage is offset by a disadvantage in the case of an exchange of depreciable real estate. You must carry over the basis of the old property to the new property; *see* the following Example.

EXAMPLE

You have property with a basis of $25,000, now valued at $50,000, that you exchange for another property worth $50,000. Your basis for depreciation for the new property is $25,000.

If—instead of making an exchange—you sell the old property and use the proceeds to buy similarly valued property, the tax basis for depreciation would be $50,000, giving you larger depreciation deductions than you would get in the exchange transaction. If increased depreciation deductions are desirable, then it may pay to sell the property and purchase new property. Tax may be spread by transacting an installment sale. Project the tax consequences of a sale and an exchange and choose the one giving the greater overall tax benefits. You may find it preferable to sell the property and purchase new property on which MACRS depreciation may be claimed.

Partially tax-free exchanges. To be completely tax free, the exchange must be solely an exchange of like-kind properties. If you receive "boot," such as cash or property that is not of like kind, gain is taxed up to the amount of the boot.

If you trade mortgaged property, the mortgage released is treated as boot *(6.3)*. When there are mortgages on both properties, the mortgages are netted. The party giving up the larger mortgage and getting the smaller mortgage treats the excess as boot. Taxable boot cannot exceed the amount of your gain. *See* the Example below and also the Example in *6.2*, which illustrates how to report an exchange on Form 8824.

EXAMPLE

You own a small office building with a fair market value of $170,000, and an adjusted basis of $150,000. There is a $130,000 mortgage on the building. You exchange it for Low's building valued at $155,000, having a $120,000 mortgage, and you also get $5,000 in cash. You compute your gain in this way:

What you received		
Fair market value of Low's property		$155,000
Cash		5,000
Mortgage assumed by Low on building you traded		130,000
Total received		$290,000
Less:		
Adjusted basis of building you traded	$150,000	
Mortgage assumed by you	120,000	270,000
Actual gain on the exchange		$20,000

However, your actual gain of $20,000 is taxed only up to the amount of boot, $15,000.

Figuring boot		
Cash received		$5,000
Mortgage assumed by Low on building you traded	$130,000	
Less:		
Mortgage you assumed on Low's property	$120,000	$10,000
Gain taxed to the extent of boot		$15,000

31.4 Timing Your Real Property Sales

Generally, a taxable transaction occurs in the year in which title or possession to property passes to the buyer. By controlling the year title and possession pass, you may select the year in which to report profit or loss. For example, you intend to sell property this year, but you estimate that reporting the sale next year will incur less in taxes. You can postpone the transfer of title and possession to next year. Alternatively, you can transact an installment sale, giving title and possession this year but delaying the receipt of all or most of the sale proceeds until next year *(5.21)*.

31.5 Cancellation of a Lease

Payments received by the tenant on the cancellation of a business lease held long term are treated as proceeds received in a Section 1231 transaction *(44.8)*. Payments received by the tenant on cancellation of a lease on a personal residence or apartment are treated as proceeds of a capital asset transaction. Gain is long-term capital gain if the lease was held long term; losses are not deductible.

Payments received by a landlord from a tenant for canceling a lease or modifying lease terms are reported as rental income when received *(9.1)*.

Cancellation of a distributor's agreement is treated as a sale if you made a substantial capital investment in the distributorship. For example, you own facilities for storage, transporting, processing, or dealing with the physical product covered by the franchise. If you have an office mainly for clerical work, or where you handle just a small part of the goods covered by the franchise, the cancellation is not treated as a sale. Your gain or loss is ordinary income or loss. If the cancellation is treated as a sale, the sale is subject to Section 1231 treatment *(44.8)*.

31.6 Sale of an Option

The tax treatment of the sale of an option to buy property depends on the tax classification of the property to which the option relates.

If the option is for the purchase of property that would be a capital asset in your hands, profit on the sale of the option is treated as capital gain. A loss is treated as a capital loss if the property subject to the option was investment property; if the property was personal property, the loss is not deductible. Whether the gain or loss is long term or short term depends on your holding period.

EXAMPLES

1. You pay $500 for an option to purchase a house. After holding the option for five months, you sell the option for $750. Your profit of $250 is short-term capital gain.

2. The same facts as in Example 1 above, except that you sell the option for $300. The loss is not deductible because the option is related to a sale of a personal residence.

If the option is for a "Section 1231 asset" *(44.8)*, gain or loss on the sale of the option is combined with other Section 1231 asset transactions to determine if there is capital gain or ordinary loss.

If the option relates to an ordinary income asset in your hands, then gain or loss would be ordinary income or loss.

If you fail to exercise an option and allow it to lapse, the option is considered to have been sold on the expiration date. Gain or loss is computed according to the rules just discussed.

The party granting the option realizes ordinary income on its expiration, regardless of the nature of the underlying property. If the option is exercised, the option payment is added to the selling price of the property when figuring gain or loss.

31.7 Granting of an Easement

Granting an easement presents a practical problem of determining whether all or part of the basis of the property is allocable to the easement proceeds. This requires an opinion as to whether the easement affects the entire property or just a part of the property. There is no hard and fast rule to determine whether an easement affects all or part of the property. The issue is factual. For example, an easement for electric lines will generally affect only the area over which the lines are suspended and for which the right of way is granted. In such a case, an allocation may be required; *see* Example 1 below. If the entire property is affected, no allocation is required and the proceeds reduce the basis of the property. If only part of the property is affected, then the proceeds are applied to the cost allocated to the area affected by the easement. If the proceeds exceed the amount allocated to basis, a gain is realized. Capital gain treatment generally applies to grants of easements. The granting of a perpetual easement that requires you to give up all or substantially all of a beneficial use of the area affected by the easement is treated as a sale. The contribution to a government body of a scenic easement in perpetuity is a charitable contribution *(14.10)*, not a sale.

Condemnation. If you realize a gain on a grant of an easement under a condemnation or threat of condemnation, you may defer tax by investing in replacement property *(18.19)*.

Planning Reminder

Basis Allocation

In reviewing an easement, the IRS will generally try to find grounds for allocating part of a property owner's basis to easement proceeds, especially where the allocation will result in a taxable gain. In opposition, a property owner will generally argue that the easement affects the entire property or that it is impossible to make an allocation because of the nature of the easement or the particular nature of the property. If he or she can sustain that argument, the proceeds for granting the easement reduce the basis of the entire property; *see* the Examples in *31.7*.

EXAMPLES

1. The owner of a 600-acre farm was paid $5,000 by a power company for the right to put up poles and power lines. The right of way covered 20 acres along one boundary that the owner continued to farm. The cost basis of the farm was $60,000, or $100 an acre. The IRS ruled that he had to allocate the basis. At $100 an acre, the allocated basis for the 20 acres was $2,000. Thus, a gain of $3,000 was realized ($5,000 − $2,000).

2. The owner of a tract of unimproved land gave a state highway department a perpetual easement affecting only part of the land. He wanted to treat the payment as a reduction of the basis of the entire tract and so report no gain. The IRS ruled that he had to allocate basis to the portion affected by the road.

3. The owner of farmland gave a transmission company a 50-foot right of way for an underground pipeline that did not interfere with farming. During construction, the right of way was 150 feet. The owner received payments for damages covering loss of rental income during construction and for the 50-foot permanent right of way. The IRS ruled that the damage payment was taxable as ordinary income; the payment for the right of way was a taxable gain to the extent that it exceeded the basis allocated to the acreage within the 50-foot strip.

Release of a restrictive covenant. A payment received for a release of a restrictive covenant is treated as a capital gain if the release involves property held for investment.

EXAMPLE

You sell several acres of land held for investment to a construction company subject to a covenant that restricts construction to residential dwellings. Later, the company wants to erect structures other than individual homes and pays you for the release of the restrictive covenant in the deed. You realize capital gain on receipt of the payment. The restrictive covenant is a property interest and a capital asset in your hands.

31.8 Special Tax Credits for Real Estate Investments

To encourage certain real estate investments, the tax law offers the following tax credits:

Low-income housing credit. Qualifying investors are allowed to claim a tax credit in annual installments over 10 years for qualifying newly constructed low-income housing and certain existing structures that are substantially rehabilitated. The amount of the credit depends on whether the building is new and whether federal subsidies are received. If you are the building owner, you must receive a certification from an authorized housing credit agency on Form 8609. Individual investors who get their share of the credit from a pass-through entity (from a partnership, S corporation, estate, or trust) may claim their credit directly on Form 3800 (General Business Credit) and do not have to complete Form 8586, which otherwise must be used; *see* the Form 8586 instructions.

Building owners are subject to a 15-year compliance period during which recapture of the credit may be required (on Form 8611) if the building is disposed of or the qualified basis of the building is reduced. Owners must file Form 8609-A for each year of the compliance period.

Rehabilitation credit for certified historic structures. On Form 3468, you may claim a 20% credit for rehabilitating certified historic structures. To claim the credit, you must generally incur rehabilitation expenses that exceed the greater of $5,000 or your adjusted basis in the building. For purposes of figuring depreciation deductions, you must reduce basis by the full amount of the rehabilitation credit.

The credit is subject to recapture if you dispose of the property within five years after it was placed in service or you change use of the property within the five-year period so it no longer qualifies for the credit; *see* Form 4255 for recapture details.

Certified historic structure. A certified historic structure may be used for residential or nonresidential purposes. The National Park Service must certify that a planned rehabilitation is in keeping with the building's historic status designation for the credit to be available.

In one case, a developer who rehabilitated a certified historic structure and donated a conservation easement to a historic society in the same year was required to base the credit computation on the rehabilitation expenses minus the charitable deduction claimed. If the donation had been made in a later year, a portion of the original credit claimed would be subject to recapture.

Tax credit limitations. Tax credits for low-income housing and rehabilitating historic structures may be limited by passive activity restrictions on Form 8582-CR *(Chapter 10)* and by tax liability limits for the general business credit on Form 3800 *(Chapter 40)*.

31.9 Foreclosures, Repossessions, Short Sales, and Voluntary Conveyances to Creditors

If you are unable to meet payments on a debt secured by property, the creditor may foreclose on the loan or repossess the property. A foreclosure sale or repossession, including a voluntary return by you of the property to the creditor, is treated as a sale of the property on which you must figure gain or loss. Similarly, if the lender agrees to a "short sale" for less than the outstanding mortgage balance in which it accepts the sales proceeds in satisfaction of the mortgage, you must figure gain or loss. A loss on a principal residence or other personal real estate is not deductible. If you were personally liable on the debt, then in addition to realizing gain or loss on the transfer, you also have debt forgiveness income from the cancellation of the debt to the extent the canceled debt exceeds the value of the property, unless an exception *(11.8)* applies. For example, if you were insolvent at the time of the debt discharge, the debt forgiveness is not taxable. In the case of a principal residence, a special exclusion for up to $750,000 ($375,000 for married filing separately) of forgiven debt *(11.8)* is allowed for tax years 2021 through 2025 under the Mortgage Debt Relief Act.

Filing Instruction

Donating Easement After Claiming Rehabilitation Credit

The charitable deduction for a historic building easement *(14.10)* must be reduced if a rehabilitation credit was claimed for the building in the five years preceding the donation.

Caution

Form 1099-A Notifies IRS

If your mortgaged property is foreclosed or repossessed, and the bank or other lender reacquires it, or if the lender knows that you have abandoned the property, you should receive from the lender Form 1099-A, which indicates the fair market value of the property (generally the foreclosure bid price), the amount of your unpaid debt, and whether you were personally liable. The IRS may compare its copy of Form 1099-A with your return to check whether you have reported income from the foreclosure or abandonment.

If the lender also cancels your debt of $600 or more, you may instead receive Form 1099-C, on which the information about the foreclosure or repossession will be included.

Figuring gain or loss and income from cancellation of debt on a foreclosure, short sale, or repossession. You have gain or loss equal to the difference between your adjusted basis *(5.20)* in the property and the amount realized on the foreclosure, short sale, or repossession. The amount realized depends on whether or not you are personally liable for the debt that secures the property, as discussed below. Note that if the property was your home or other personal-use property and a loss is realized on the foreclosure or repossession, the loss is nondeductible. If the property was your principal residence and you realize a gain on a foreclosure, short sale, or repossession, you may be able to exclude from income up to $250,000 of the gain, or $500,000 on a joint return, under the home sale exclusion rules *(29.1)*.

In addition to realizing gain or loss on the transfer of the property to the lender, you may also have to report income from the cancellation of the debt if you are personally liable for the debt *(11.8)*.

Amount realized if you are not personally liable (nonrecourse debt). If you are not personally liable on the debt secured by the property, the amount realized on the foreclosure, short sale, or repossession includes, in addition to any sale proceeds you receive, the full amount of the debt that is canceled as part of the transfer to the lender, even if the fair market value of the property is less than the canceled debt.

You do not realize income from the cancellation of nonrecourse debt upon a foreclosure, short sale, or repossession. However, if in lieu of foreclosure (or repossession) the lender offers a discount for early repayment or agrees to a loan modification ("workout") in which the principal balance of the nonrecourse loan is reduced, and you retain the collateral, the debt reduction results in income from the cancellation of debt even where you are not personally liable on the loan *(31.10)*.

Amount realized if you are personally liable (recourse debt). If you are personally liable on the debt secured by the property, the amount realized includes the smaller of the canceled debt or the fair market value of the property transferred to the lender. This is in addition to any sale proceeds received.

Where the canceled debt exceeds the fair market value of the transferred property, the excess must be reported as ordinary income from the cancellation of debt, unless the law allows it to be excluded. Exclusions that may be available are the exclusions for insolvency, bankruptcy, qualified principal residence indebtedness, or qualified farm debt, discussed in *11.8*, or the exclusion for qualified business real estate debt discussed in *31.10*.

Filing Instruction

Reporting a Foreclosure or Voluntary Conveyance

You generally report a foreclosure sale or voluntary conveyance in 2023 to a creditor on Form 8949 and Schedule D if the property was held for personal or investment purposes. However, if the property was your principal residence and you have a gain, the foreclosure or voluntary conveyance does not have to be reported at all if you can exclude all of it under the home sale exclusion rules *(29.1)*.

Foreclosures and reconveyances of business assets are reported on Form 4797.

If income from cancellation of indebtedness is realized and it is not excludable under the rules discussed at *11.8*, you report the taxable amount on Schedule 1 (Form 1040 or 1040-SR).

> **EXAMPLE**
>
> Jones could not meet the mortgage payments on a vacation home that cost him $185,000. He had paid cash of $20,000 and taken a mortgage loan of $165,000 on which he was personally liable. In 2023, when the remaining balance of the loan was $162,000, he defaulted, and the bank accepted his voluntary conveyance of the unit, canceling the loan. Similar units at the time were selling for $150,000. Because Jones was personally liable for the debt, he is deemed to have an amount realized of $150,000, the fair market value of the property, as this is less than the $162,000 canceled loan. Jones incurred a loss of $35,000: the difference between his adjusted basis of $185,000 and the $150,000 fair market value of the unit. The loss is not deductible because the unit was held for personal purposes. Jones also recognizes income on the cancellation of the loan because the amount of the debt ($162,000) exceeded the fair market value of the unit ($150,000) by $12,000. This amount is taxable, unless Jones can show he was insolvent at the time of the transfer to the bank; *see 11.8*.

31.10 Restructuring Mortgage Debt

Rather than foreclose on a mortgage, a lender (mortgagee) may be willing to restructure the mortgage debt by canceling either all or part of the debt. As a borrower (mortgagor), do not overlook the tax consequences of the new debt arrangement. If the lender agrees to a "workout," under which part of your loan principal is reduced as part of a loan modification, or if you pay off the loan early in return for a "discount" that reduces the debt, and you keep the collateral, the reduction or discount is canceled debt, reportable as ordinary income (cancellation of debt income) unless an exception applies. This is true whether or not you are personally liable for the debt. However, if you were not personally liable (nonrecourse debt) and do not keep the collateral, there is no cancellation of debt income.

You may be able to avoid the ordinary income from the cancellation of the debt by taking advantage of one of the exclusions in the law, such as the exclusions for insolvency, bankruptcy, qualified business real estate debt *(see below)*, or qualified farm debt. Details of these exclusions are discussed in *11.8*. The Jones Example in *11.8* illustrates the IRS approach to figuring insolvency upon a reduction of a nonrecourse debt.

In the case of partnership property, tax consequences of the restructuring of a third-party loan are determined at the partner level. This means that if you are a partner and are solvent *(11.8)*, you may not avoid tax on the transaction, even if the partnership is insolvent.

Restructuring debt on business real estate. A solvent taxpayer may avoid tax on a restructuring of qualifying business real estate debt *(11.8)* by electing to reduce the basis of depreciable real property by the amount of the tax-free debt discharge. The election to reduce basis is made on Form 982.

Caution

Form 1099-C

If your lender agrees to a "workout" that reduces the principal balance of your loan, the canceled debt will be reported on Form 1099-C in Box 2. This amount must be included in your income unless one of the exclusion rules *(11.8)* applies.

EXAMPLE

Grant, who is solvent, owns a building worth $150,000 used in his business. It is subject to a first mortgage of $110,000 and a second mortgage of $90,000. Grant's basis in the building is $120,000. On July 15, 2023, the second mortgagee agrees to reduce the second mortgage to $30,000. This results in debt discharge of $60,000 ($90,000 − $30,000). The $60,000 is considered debt discharge income. But Grant may elect to exclude $50,000. He reports the remaining $10,000 of discharged debt as taxable income. The exclusion limit is the excess of (1) the pre-discharge mortgage balance, over (2) the pre-discharge fair market value of the building, minus the pre-discharge balance of the other mortgage *(11.8)*, calculated as follows:

2nd mortgage before discharge	$90,000
Less: Fair market value of building reduced by first mortgage ($150,000 − $110,000)	$40,000
Excludable amount	$50,000

On Form 982, Grant may elect to exclude $50,000 from income because the basis of the building is sufficient to absorb a basis reduction of $50,000.

31.11 Abandonments

To abandon property, you must terminate your ownership by voluntarily and permanently giving up possession and use of the property without passing it on to someone else. On an abandonment of mortgaged real estate (whether held for business, investment, or personal use), the type of debt determines if there is gain or loss on the abandonment. If you are personally liable for the debt (recourse debt), there is no gain or loss until a later foreclosure or repossession. If you are not personally liable (nonrecourse debt), the IRS treats the abandonment itself as a sale on which gain or loss is realized.

For example, if in 2023 you abandon investment real estate that secures your recourse debt, you do not have gain or loss for 2023, but if the lender forecloses on the loan in 2024, you will have a gain or loss in 2024. Under the foreclosure sale rules for recourse debt property *(31.9)*, the amount realized in 2024 will include the smaller of the canceled debt or the fair market value of the property. In addition, if the canceled recourse debt exceeds the fair market value, the excess is ordinary income from cancellation of debt *(31.9)*. On the other hand, if you were not personally liable for the debt securing the property (nonrecourse debt), then an abandonment in 2023 would be treated by the IRS as a 2023 sale, and the full outstanding debt would be treated as the amount realized in figuring gain or loss; there would not be any cancellation of debt income *(31.9)*.

If the abandoned property was held for personal use, any loss on the abandonment or on a foreclosure or repossession is not deductible. If recourse debt is canceled in a foreclosure or repossession, you will realize ordinary income from cancellation of the debt if the canceled amount exceeds the value of the transferred property *(31.9)*.

Abandoning a partnership interest. Where real estate values have sharply declined, partnerships may be holding realty subject to mortgage debt that exceeds the current value of the property. Some investors in such partnerships have claimed they can abandon their partnership interests and claim abandonment losses. In one case, an investor in a partnership holding land in Houston, Texas, argued he abandoned his partnership interest by making an abandonment declaration at a meeting of partners, and also declaring he would make no further payments. He offered his interest to the others, who refused his offer. The IRS held that he failed to prove abandonment of his partnership interest or that the partnership abandoned the land. The Tax Court sided with the IRS, emphasizing his failure to show that the partnership abandoned the land. However, the appeals court for the Fifth Circuit reversed and allowed the abandonment loss. It held that the emphasis should be on the partner's actions, not the actions of the partnership. Although neither state law nor the IRS regulations described how a partnership interest is to be abandoned, the appeals court held that the partner's acts and declaration were sufficient to effect an abandonment of his partnership interest. The appeals court also held that the loss on the partnership interest could have been sustained on the basis of the worthlessness of his interest. The partnership was insolvent beyond hope of rehabilitation: (1) the partnership's only asset was land with a fair market value less than the mortgage debt; (2) the partnership had no source of income; and (3) the partners refused to contribute more funds to keep the partnership afloat.

In a subsequent case, the Tax Court held that a doctor had abandoned a movie production partnership interest when he refused to advance any more money or to participate in the venture because he disapproved of the content of the film being produced and feared it might jeopardize his position at a hospital operated by a religious organization. Also, the limited partners had voted to dissolve.

31.12 Seller's Repossession After Buyer's Default on Mortgage

When you, as a seller, repossess realty on the buyer's default of a debt that the realty secures, you may realize gain or loss. (If the realty was a personal residence, the loss is not deductible.) A debt is secured by real property whenever you have the right to take title or possession or both in the event the buyer defaults on his or her obligation under the contract.

Figuring gain on the repossession. Gain on the repossession is the excess of: (1) payments received on the original sales contract prior to and on the repossession, including payments made by the buyer for your benefit to another party, over (2) the amount of taxable gain previously reported prior to the repossession.

Gain computed under these two steps may not be fully taxable. Taxable gain is limited to (1) the amount of original profit less gain on the sale already reported as income for periods prior to the repossession, plus (2) your repossession costs.

The limitation on gain does not apply if the selling price cannot be computed at the time of sale as, for example, where the selling price is stated as a percentage of the profits to be realized from the development of the property sold.

These repossession gain rules do not apply if you repurchase the property by paying the buyer a sum in addition to the discharge of the debt, unless the repurchase and payment was provided for in the original sale contract, or the buyer has defaulted on his or her obligation, or default is imminent. In such cases, gain or loss on the repossession, and basis in the repossessed property, must be determined under the different rules for personal property; *see* IRS Publication 537 for details.

The basis of repossessed property. This is the adjusted basis of the debt (face value of the debt less the unreported profits) secured by the property, figured as of the date of repossession, increased by (1) the taxable gain on repossession and (2) the legal fees and other repossession costs you paid.

 *Caution*

Character of Gain

The gain limitation rules *(31.12)* do not affect the character of the gain. Thus, if you repossess property as a dealer, the gain is subject to ordinary income rates. If you, as an investor, repossess a tract originally held long term whose gain was reported on the installment method, the gain is capital gain.

If you treated the debt as having become worthless or partially worthless before repossession, you are considered to receive, upon the repossession of the property securing the debt, an amount equal to the amount of the debt treated as worthless. You report as income the amount of any prior bad debt deduction and increase the basis of the debt by an amount equal to the amount reported as income.

If your debt is not fully discharged as a result of the repossession, the basis of the undischarged debt is zero. No loss may be claimed if the obligations subsequently become worthless. This rule applies to undischarged debts on the original obligation of the purchaser, a substituted obligation of the purchaser, a deficiency judgment entered in a court of law into which the purchaser's obligation was merged, and any other obligations arising from the transaction.

EXAMPLE

Assume you sell land for $25,000. You take a $5,000 down payment plus a $20,000 mortgage, secured by the property, from the buyer, with principal payable at the rate of $4,000 annually plus 9% interest. The adjusted basis of the land was $20,000 and you elected to report the transaction on the installment basis. Your gross profit percentage is 20% ($5,000 profit divided by $25,000 selling price). In the year of sale, you include $1,000 in your income on the installment basis (20% of $5,000 down payment). The next year you reported profit of $800 (20% of $4,000 annual installment). In the third year, the buyer defaults, and you repossess the property. Your repossession costs are $500. The amount of gain on repossession is computed as follows:

1. Compute gain:

Amount of money received before repossession ($5,000 plus $4,000)	$9,000
Less: Amount of gain taxed in prior years ($1,000 plus $800)	1,800
Gain	$7,200

2. Compute limit on taxable gain:

Original profit		$5,000
Less:		
Gain reported as income	$1,800	
Repossession costs	500	2,300
Taxable gain on repossession		$2,700

Principal residence. Special rules apply to repossessions and resales of a principal residence if you excluded all or part of the gain on your original sale of the residence *(29.1)*, and you resell it within a year after you repossess it.

The original sale and resale is treated as one transaction. You refigure the amount realized on the sale. You combine the selling price of the resale with the selling price of the original sale. From this total, you subtract selling expenses for both sales, the part of the original installment obligation that remains unpaid at the time of repossession, and repossession costs. The net is the amount realized on the combined sale-resale. Subtracting basis in the home from the amount realized gives the gain on the combined sale-resale before taking into account the home sale exclusion *(29.1)* rules. *See* Treasury Regulation Section 1.1038-2 for further details.

If the repossessed principal residence is not sold within one year, the combined sale-resale rule does not apply. The seller must report as income previously received payments that were not taxed (they were excluded under the home sale exclusion).

EXAMPLE

Same facts as in the previous Example. The basis of the repossessed property is computed as follows:

1.	Unpaid debt ($20,000 note less $4,000 payment)		$16,000
2.	*Less:* Unreported profit (20% of the $16,000 still due on the note)		3,200
3.	Adjusted basis in installment obligation at date of repossession		$12,800
4.	*Plus:* Gain on repossession	$2,700	
	Repossession costs	500	3,200
5.	Basis of repossessed property		$16,000

31.13 Foreclosure on Mortgages Other Than Purchase Money

If you, as a mortgagee (lender), bid in on a foreclosure sale to pay off a mortgage that is not a purchase money mortgage, your actual financial loss is the difference between the unpaid mortgage debt and the value of the property. For tax purposes, however, you may realize a capital gain or loss and a bad debt loss that are reportable in the year of the foreclosure sale.

Your bid is treated as consisting of two distinct transactions:

1. The repayment of your loan. To determine whether this results in a bad debt, the bid price is matched against the face amount of the mortgage.

2. A taxable exchange of your mortgage note for the foreclosed property, which may result in a capital gain or loss. This is determined by matching the bid price against the fair market value of the property.

Where the bid price equals the mortgage debt plus unreported but accrued interest, you report the interest as income. But where the accrued interest has been reported, the unpaid amount is added to the collection expenses.

EXAMPLES

1. Mortgagee's bid less than market value. You hold a $40,000 mortgage on property having a fair market value of $30,000. You bid on the property at the foreclosure sale at $28,000. The expenses of the sale are $2,000, reducing the bid price to $26,000. The mortgagor is insolvent, so you have a bad debt loss of $14,000 ($40,000 − $26,000). You also have a $4,000 capital gain (the fair market value of the property of $30,000 − $26,000 net bid price).

2. Mortgagee's bid equal to market value. Suppose your bid was $32,000, and you had $2,000 in expenses. The difference between the net bid price of $30,000 and the mortgage of $40,000 is $10,000. As the mortgagor is insolvent, there is a bad debt loss of $10,000. Since the net bid price equals the fair market value, there is neither capital gain nor loss.

3. Mortgagee's bid greater than market value. Suppose your bid was $36,000 and you had $2,000 in expenses. Your bad debt deduction is $6,000—the difference between the mortgage debt of $40,000 and the net bid price of $34,000. You also had a capital loss of $4,000 (the difference between the net bid price of $34,000 and the fair market value of $30,000).

31.14 Foreclosure Sale to Third Party

When a third party buys the property in a foreclosure, you, as the mortgagee, receive the purchase price to apply against the mortgage debt. If it is less than the debt, and the mortgagor was personally liable, you may proceed against the mortgagor for the difference. Foreclosure expenses are treated as offsets against the foreclosure proceeds and increase the loss.

Planning Reminder

Voluntary Conveyance

Instead of forcing you to foreclose, the mortgagor may voluntarily convey the property to you in consideration for your canceling the mortgage debt. Your loss is the amount by which the mortgage debt plus accrued interest exceeds the fair market value of the property. If, however, the fair market value exceeds the mortgage debt plus accrued interest, the difference is taxable gain. The gain or loss is reportable in the year you receive the property. Your basis in the property is its fair market value when you receive it.

EXAMPLE

You hold a $30,000 note and mortgage that are in default. You foreclose, and a third party buys the property for $20,000. Foreclosure expenses amount to $2,000. The deficiency is uncollectible. Your $12,000 loss is figured as follows:

Unpaid mortgage debt		$30,000
Foreclosure proceeds	$20,000	
Less: Expenses	2,000	
Net proceeds		18,000
Bad debt loss		$12,000

You deduct your loss as a bad debt. The law distinguishes between two types of bad debt deductions: business bad debts and nonbusiness bad debts. A business bad debt is fully deductible. A nonbusiness bad debt is a short-term capital loss that can be offset only against capital gains, plus a limited amount of ordinary income (5.33). In addition, you may deduct a partially worthless business bad debt, but you may not deduct a partially worthless nonbusiness bad debt. Remember this distinction if you are thinking of forgiving part of the mortgage debt as a settlement. If the debt is a nonbusiness bad debt, you will not be able to take a deduction until the entire debt proves to be worthless. But whether you are deducting a business or a nonbusiness bad debt, your deduction will be allowed only if you show the debt to be uncollectible—for example, because a deficiency judgment is worthless or because the mortgagor is declared bankrupt.

31.15 Transferring Mortgaged Realty

Mortgaging realty that has appreciated in value is one way of realizing cash on the appreciation without current tax consequences. The receipt of cash by mortgaging the property is not taxed; tax will generally be imposed only when the property is sold. However, there is a possible tax where the mortgage exceeds the adjusted basis of the property and the property is given away or transferred to a controlled corporation. Where the property is transferred to a controlled corporation, the excess is taxable gain. Further, if the IRS successfully charges that the transfer is part of a tax avoidance scheme, the taxable gain may be as high as the amount of the mortgage liability.

Charitable donations. The IRS holds that a donation of mortgaged property to a charity is a part-sale, part-gift, and the donor has taxable gain to the extent the mortgage liability exceeds the portion of the donor's basis allocable to the sale part of the transaction (14.8).

31.16 QBI Deduction for REIT Dividends

If you own an interest in a real estate investment trust (REIT), you can take a deduction (a subtraction from adjusted gross income) of up to 20% of combined qualified REIT dividends and publicly-traded partnership (PTP) income. This deduction applies whether you hold the interest directly or through a pass-through entity (including a trust).

Qualified REIT dividends for purposes of the QBI deduction means dividends from REITs that do not qualify for preferential tax rates (i.e., ordinary dividends).

The qualified REIT dividend component of the qualified business income (QBI) deduction (40.24) is not limited by W-2 wages or the unadjusted basis immediately after acquisition (UBIA) of qualified property. But the total QBI deduction is the lesser of the sum of combined amounts of the deduction from pass-through businesses plus amounts from REITs and PTPs, or 20% of the excess of taxable income over net capital gains for the year.

If your taxable income in 2023 is not more than $364,200 for married couples filing jointly and $182,100 for all other filers, you figure this deduction on the Form 8995, *Qualified Business Income Deduction Simplified Computation*. If your taxable income is higher, use Form 8995-A, *Qualified Business Income Deduction* and accompanying schedules.

 *Planning Reminder*

Keep Records

Preserve evidence of the property's fair market value. At a later date, the IRS may claim that the property was worth more than your bid and may tax you for the difference. Furthermore, be prepared to prove the worthlessness of the debt in order to support the bad debt deduction.

CHAPTER 32

Tax Rules for Investors in Mutual Funds

As a mutual fund shareholder, you may receive several types of distributions, such as ordinary dividends, capital gain distributions, exempt-interest dividends, and return of capital distributions. The rules for reporting the different types of distributions are discussed in this chapter.

The tax law provides different methods of identifying the particular shares being sold when you sell a portion of your mutual fund holdings and of determining the cost basis of those shares. You may be able to use these methods to obtain a preferred tax result on the sale.

32.1   Timing of Your Investment Can Affect Your Taxes

You may buy a tax liability if you invest in a mutual fund that has already realized significant capital gains during the year. For example, if a fund is about to make a year-end capital gain distribution and you invest shortly before that, you will in effect have to pay tax on the return of your recently invested money.

You will be eligible to receive a forthcoming dividend or capital gain distribution if you are a shareholder of record on the "record date" set by the fund. On the "ex-dividend date," the net asset value per share will be reduced by the distribution amount per share. If you buy before the record date, the higher cost for your shares will be offset by the distributions you receive, but you will have to pay tax on the distributions. On the other hand, because you paid the higher pre-distribution price, your higher basis will reduce any capital gain on a later sale, or increase any capital loss.

If you want to limit your current tax and forego the basis increase, postpone your investment until after the record date for distributions. By that time, the value per share that determines the price will have been reduced by the distribution. Before investing, you may be able to find out from the fund when distributions for the year are expected; call the fund or check the fund's website for an estimate of projected distributions.

32.2   Reinvestment Plans

A mutual fund will allow you to reinvest dividends and capital gain distributions from the fund in new fund shares instead of receiving cash. You report reinvested distributions as if you received them in cash. Form 1099-DIV sent to you by a fund reports the gross amount of taxable distributions that you must report on your return *(32.3)*.

Keep track of reinvested distributions. If you reinvest your mutual fund distributions instead of taking them in cash, you will need a record of the distributions and of the shares purchased with the reinvestment; your fund can likely provide you with a history of your reinvestments. The reinvested distributions are considered your cost basis for the acquired shares. You need a record of reinvestments to figure your cost when you sell your shares; *see* below *(32.8)* for calculating gain on the sale of mutual fund shares.

Reinvested distribution can trigger wash sale. If you redeem fund shares at a loss within 30 days before or after a dividend distribution is reinvested into your account, a "wash sale" results, and the portion of the loss allocable to the reinvestment is not deductible *(30.6)*. The allocable loss is disallowed even though the wash sale was inadvertently caused by the reinvestment. The disallowed loss is actually deferred, as it is added to the cost basis of the replacement shares and will affect the computation of gain or loss on a later sale.

32.3   Mutual Fund Distributions Reported on Form 1099-DIV

Mutual fund distributions are reported to you and the IRS by the fund on Form 1099-DIV or substitute statement. Distributions that you reinvested to acquire additional shares are reported and taxed in the same way as distributions that are actually paid out to you.

Types of distributions. The Form 1099-DIV (or substitute statement) from your fund for 2023 may show several kinds of distributions. Distributions that you reinvested *(32.2)* instead of receiving in cash are included on the Form 1099-DIV.

- Ordinary dividends—are the most common type of dividend, payable out of the fund's earnings and profits. They are shown in Box 1a of Form 1099-DIV. Short-term capital gain distributions are reported as ordinary dividends.
- Qualified dividends—shown in Box 1b, are your share of the ordinary dividends (Box 1a) that are qualified dividends *(4.2)* from the fund's investments in U.S. corporations and qualified foreign corporations. This amount is eligible for the zero, 15%, or 20% capital gain rate *(5.3)*, but only if you held your fund shares for at least 61 days during the 121-day period beginning 60 days before the ex-dividend date *(4.2)*.
- Capital gain distributions—shown in Box 2a of Form 1099-DIV, are your share of the net long-term capital gains realized by the fund on sales of securities in its portfolio. These are taxable to you as long-term capital gain *(5.3)* regardless of how long you have owned your fund shares.

Caution

Reinvested Dividends Subject to NII Tax

Even though you don't receive the dividends reinvested in stock or mutual funds, they still count as investment income for purposes of the additional Medicare tax on net investment income (NII) *(see 22.8)*.

Filing Tip

Reduced Rate Qualified Dividends

Box 1b of Form 1099-DIV for 2023 shows your qualified dividends, the portion of the amount in Box 1a (total ordinary dividends) that is eligible for the 0%, 15% or 20% capital gain rate.

- If the fund retained long-term capital gains and paid tax on them, your share will be reported to you on Form 2439, rather than Form 1099-DIV *(32.6)*.
- Return of capital (nontaxable) distributions—shown in Box 3 of Form 1099-DIV, are a return of your investment that reduce your basis in your shares and are not taxed until basis has been reduced to zero. If basis has been reduced to zero, you report the excess amount on Form 8949 as either short-term or long-term gain (depending on your holding period for the shares) by reporting the excess as the sales price in column (d), and reporting a zero basis in column (f). *See* the Form 8949 instructions for further details.

See Table 32-1 for details on how to report these and other distributions on your tax return.

Year-end dividends. Mutual funds sometimes declare dividends at the end of a calendar year but do not pay them until January of the following year. If the dividend is declared in October, November, or December, and paid in the following January, the fund will report the distribution as taxable in the year it is declared.

32.4 Tax-Exempt Bond Funds

Dividends from a bond fund that represent tax-exempt interest earned by the fund are not subject to regular income tax, but capital gain distributions are taxable. The exempt-interest dividends are shown by the fund in Box 12 of Form 1099-DIV. You report exempt-interest dividends along with your other tax-exempt interest on Line 2a of Form 1040 or 1040-SR. The amount on Line 2a is not taxable, but if you receive Social Security benefits, it could increase the amount of taxable benefits *(34.3)*. If part of the exempt-interest dividends is attributable to private activity bonds, that amount may be a preference item subject to alternative minimum tax (AMT) *(23.2)*. The amount subject to AMT is shown in Box 13 of Form 1099-DIV.

Capital gain distributions are shown on Form 1099-DIV and must be reported on your return; *see Table 32-1*.

When you redeem your shares in a tax-exempt bond fund or exchange the fund shares for other shares in a different fund, you realize taxable capital gain or deductible loss.

If you received exempt-interest dividends on mutual fund shares held for six months or less and sold those shares at a loss, the amount of your loss is reduced by the exempt-interest dividend. To reflect this adjustment, on Part I (short-term gains and losses) of Form 8949, you increase the sales price in column (d) by the exempt-interest dividend.

> **EXAMPLE**
>
> In January 2023, you bought a mutual fund share for $40. In February 2023, the mutual fund paid a $5 dividend from tax-exempt interest, which is not taxable to you. In March 2023, you sold the share for $34. If it were not for the tax-exempt dividend, your loss would be $6 ($40 − 34). However, you may deduct only $1, the part of the loss that exceeds the exempt-interest dividend ($6 − 5). On Form 8949, increase the sales price in column (d) of Part I by $5 (the $5 nondeductible loss), to $39 from $34, thereby reducing your short-term capital loss to $1 ($40 − 39).

32.5 Fund Expenses

If you own shares in a publicly offered mutual fund, you do not pay tax on your share of the fund expenses. There should be no entry in Box 6 of your Form 1099-DIV. However, expenses of a non–publicly offered fund are included in Box 6 of Form 1099-DIV and must be reported as a taxable dividend, even though the amount has not actually been distributed to you. This amount is included as a fully taxable ordinary dividend in Box 1 of Form 1099-DIV. Because of the suspension of miscellaneous itemized deductions subject to the 2% of adjusted gross income floor for 2018 through 2025 *(19.2)*, an offsetting deduction is not permissible.

Filing Tip

Mutual Funds Held in Variable Annuities

Distributions from variable annuities holding mutual fund shares are reported on Form 1099-R and not on Form 1099-D.

Filing Tip

Tax-exempt Interest Impacts Premium Tax Credit

Tax-exempt interest is taken into account in determining household income, which is the amount on which eligibility for the premium tax credit hinges. *See 25.13*.

32.6 Tax Credits From Mutual Funds

Undistributed capital gains. Some mutual funds retain their long-term capital gains and pay capital gains tax on those amounts. Even though not actually received by you, include the amount of the undistributed capital gain allocated to you by the fund as a capital gain distribution on your return. If the mutual fund paid a tax on the undistributed capital gain, you are entitled to a tax credit.

To claim the credit, check Form 2439 sent to you by your fund, which lists your share of undistributed capital gain and the amount of tax paid on it by the fund. Enter your share of the tax the fund paid on this gain as a tax payment on Line 13a of Schedule 3 (Form 1040 or 1040-SR). Attach Copy B of Form 2439 to your return to support your tax credit. Increase the basis of your shares by the excess of the undistributed capital gain over the amount of tax paid by the mutual fund, as reported on Form 2439.

Foreign tax credit or deduction. You may be able to claim a foreign tax credit (on Form 1116) or a deduction on Schedule A for your share of the fund's foreign taxes. In Box 7 of Form 1099-DIV, the fund will report your share of the foreign taxes paid by the fund. The fund should give you instructions for claiming the foreign tax credit or deduction (36.13).

32.7 How to Report Mutual Fund Distributions

Report an undistributed capital gain on Schedule D or a return of capital distribution on Form 8949 and Schedule D because your basis in your fund shares has been reduced to zero.

Check *Table 32-1* below for details on reporting distributions on your return.

32.8 Redemptions and Exchanges of Fund Shares

When you ask the fund to redeem all or part of your shares, you have transacted a sale subject to capital gain or loss rules explained in *Chapter 5*. Exchanges of shares of one fund for shares of another fund within the same fund "family" are treated as sales. If you owned the shares for more than one year, your gain or loss is long term; if you held them for a year or less, your gain or loss is short term. However, if you received a capital gain distribution before selling shares held six months or less at a loss, your loss must be reported as a long-term capital loss to the extent of the capital gain distribution attributable to the sold shares. Any excess loss is reported as a short-term capital loss. This restriction does not apply to dispositions under periodic redemption plans.

> **EXAMPLE**
>
> In June 2023, you bought mutual fund shares for $1,000. In August, you received a capital gain distribution of $50, and in September you sold the shares for $850. Instead of reporting a $150 short-term capital loss ($1,000 cost − $850 proceeds), you must report a long-term capital loss of $50, the amount of the capital gain distribution; the remaining $100 of the loss is a short-term capital loss.

Identifying the shares you sell. Determining which mutual funds shares are being sold is necessary to figure your gain or loss and whether the gain or loss is short term or long term (32.9).

Holding period of fund shares. You determine your holding period by using the trade dates. The trade date is the date you buy or redeem the mutual fund shares. Do not confuse the trade date with the settlement date, which is the date the mutual fund shares must be delivered and payment must be made. Most mutual funds will show the trade date on your purchase and redemption confirmation statements.

Your holding period starts on the day after the day you bought the shares (the trade date). This same date of each succeeding month is the start of a new month regardless of the number of days in the month before. The day you dispose of the shares (trade date) is also part of your holding period.

Filing Tip

Undistributed Capital Gains From REITs

The capital gain reporting and credit rules for mutual funds (32.6) also apply if you own shares in a REIT that has retained its long-term capital gains.

Planning Reminder

Keeping Track of Cost Basis

Keep confirmation statements for purchases of shares as well as a record of distributions that are automatically reinvested in your account. These will show the cost basis for your shares. Your basis is increased by amounts reported to you by the fund on Form 2439, representing the difference between your share of undistributed capital gains that you were required to report as income and your share of the tax paid by the fund on undistributed gains. Your basis is reduced by nontaxable dividends that are a return of your investment. Keep copies of Form 2439 and information returns showing nontaxable dividends.

Table 32-1 Reporting Mutual Fund Distributions for 2023

Type of Distribution	Shown by the Fund in	How To Report
Ordinary dividends and short-term capital gain distributions.	Box 1a, Form 1099-DIV	Box 1a of Form 1099-DIV shows taxable ordinary dividends. The total includes ordinary dividends and short-term capital gain distributions, which are taxed as ordinary income, and also qualified dividends, if any, which are taxable at the applicable capital gain rate *(5.3)*. The Box 1a total must be entered on Line 3b of Form 1040 or 1040-SR. If your total ordinary dividends from all sources exceed $1,500 or if you received as a nominee ordinary dividends on behalf of another taxpayer, you must itemize the ordinary dividends on Line 5 of Schedule B (Form 1040 or 1040-SR).
Qualified dividends (eligible for capital gain rate if you held shares at least 61 days during the 121-day period beginning 60 days before the ex-dividend date)	Box 1b, Form 1099-DIV	Box 1b shows the portion of the Box 1a amount that is eligible for the 0%, 15% or 20% capital gain rate *(5.3)*. Report these qualified dividends on Line 3a of Form 1040 or 1040-SR. Unless you have 28% rate gains or unrecaptured Section 1250 gains that have to be reported on the "Schedule D Tax Worksheet" in the Schedule D instructions, you may use the "Qualified Dividends and Capital Gain Tax Worksheet'" in the Form 1040 or 1040-SR instructions to figure your regular tax liability using the capital gain rates.
Capital gain distributions. (your share of net long-term gains realized by a fund on sales made from its portfolio)	Boxes 2a–2d, Form 1099-DIV	Box 2a of Form 1099-DIV shows your total capital gain distributions. If you are not deferring capital gain due to an investment in a qualified opportunity zone fund *(5.7)*, your only capital gains are capital gain distributions, you do not have capital losses, and no amount is shown in Boxes 2b–2d of all your Forms 1099-DIV, you generally do not have to complete Schedule D (Form 1040 or 1040-SR) and may report the capital gain distributions from Box 2a directly on Line 7 of Form 1040 or Form 1040-SR. In that case, you use the Qualified Dividends and Capital Gain Tax Worksheet in the Form 1040 or 1040-SR instructions to figure your tax using the capital gain rates. If Schedule D is required, the total capital gain distributions from Box 2a must be reported on Line 13 of Schedule D and the rest of Schedule D completed. Box 2b shows the part of Box 2a that is unrecaptured Section 1250 gain from the sale of depreciable buildings. Box 2c shows the part of Box 2a that is Section 1202 gain eligible for an exclusion *(5.7)*. Box 2d shows the amount of Box 2a that is 28% rate gain from sales of collectibles. If you have an amount in Box 2b, 2c, or 2d, you must complete Schedule D.
Return of capital distributions (nontaxable)	Box 3, Form 1099-DIV	A return of capital distribution is not taxable income. However, if your basis for your shares has been reduced to zero by return of capital gain distributions, report additional nontaxable distributions as either long-term or short-term capital gain on Form 8949, depending on how long you held the shares *(32.3)*.
Exempt-interest dividends	Box 11, Form 1099-DIV	Report along with other tax-exempt interest on Line 2a of Form 1040. The portion of the exempt-interest dividends that is attributable to private activity bonds subject to AMT *(23.3)* is shown in Box 12 of Form 1099-DIV
Undistributed capital gains	Undistributed long-term gains shown on Form 2439, Box 1a; Tax paid by fund shown on Form 2439, Box 2	Box 1a of Form 2439 shows your total share of undistributed long-term capital gains. The undistributed gains are reported on Line 11 of Schedule D. To get a tax credit for the tax paid by the fund, enter the tax as a payment on Line 13a of Schedule 3 (Form 1040 or 1040-SR). Increase the basis of your mutual fund shares by the excess of the undistributed gains included on Schedule D over the tax credit claimed on Form 1040 or 1040-SR.
Foreign taxes	Box 7, Form 1099-DIV.	The foreign taxes may be claimed as a tax credit on Form 1116 or as an itemized deduction on Schedule A (Form 1040 or 1040-SR) *(36.13)*.
Federal income tax withheld	Box 4, Form 1099-DIV. Box 4 Form 1099-INT.	If you are subject to back-up withholding, the amount of federal income tax withheld should be included on Line 25b of Form 1040 or 1040-SR.

32.9 Basis of Redeemed Shares

To figure gain or loss, you need to know the basis per share. Generally, your basis is the purchase price of the shares, including shares acquired by reinvesting distributions back into the fund, plus commission or load charges.

Load charges. Basis does not include load charges (acquisition fees) on the purchase of mutual fund shares if you held the shares for 90 days or less and then exchanged them for shares in a different fund in the same family of funds for which the load charge is reduced or waived.

> **EXAMPLE**
>
> You pay a $200 load charge on purchasing shares for $10,000 in Fund A. Within 90 days, you exchange the Fund A shares for Fund B shares. Because Fund A and Fund B are in the same family of funds, the $200 load charge that would otherwise be due on the purchase of the Fund B shares is waived. For purposes of figuring your gain or loss on the exchange of Fund A shares, your basis is $10,000, not $10,200. The disallowed $200 is added to the basis of the new Fund B shares, provided those shares are held more than 90 days. If the waived load charge on Fund B shares had been $100, basis for the original Fund A shares would be increased by $100, the excess of the original $200 load charge over the amount waived on the reinvestment.

Cost basis of sold shares. If you are selling your entire mutual fund account, you need to know your total basis for all the shares. If your shares in the fund were acquired at different times, and you are selling only some of the shares in your account, you need to know which shares are being sold and the basis of those shares to determine gain or loss. In general, you can choose between at least three basis methods: the average cost method, the specific identification method, and the first- in, first-out method. These methods are discussed below. When you sell shares that you acquired after 2011, your cost basis for those shares will be reported to both you and the IRS; *see* below.

Basis will be reported to the IRS when you sell shares acquired after 2011. Mutual fund shares acquired after 2011 are considered "covered shares." When you sell covered shares, the fund will report your cost basis for the shares in Box 1e of Form 1099-B sent to both you and the IRS.

When you sell shares acquired before 2012, or "noncovered shares," your mutual fund will generally not report cost basis on the Form 1099-B it sends to the IRS. On the Form 1099-B it sends to you, the fund will probably report basis using the average cost method, but this does not require you to use the average cost method on your tax return.

If you acquired shares both before 2012 and after 2011, a sale may involve noncovered shares, covered shares, or both, depending on the basis method you select and the number of shares sold. For example, if you use the average cost method, noncovered shares will be considered redeemed first in the order you acquired them, before covered shares are considered sold. The fund will separately figure the average cost for your noncovered and covered shares.

Whether the sold shares are covered or noncovered, you are responsible for reporting your cost basis and calculating your gain or loss on Form 8949 and Schedule D (Form 1040 or 1040-SR). For covered shares, the IRS can match the basis reported by the fund on Form 1099-B with the basis you report on your return.

Basis methods you can select. To identify the shares you are selling, you can choose between the average cost method, the specific identification method, the first in, first out method, or some other variation of the specification method. Check with the fund for its rules on selecting a preferred basis method for covered shares and its rules for changing the basis method.

If you sell covered shares without having designated a cost basis method, the fund will likely use average cost as its "default" method for reporting basis on the Forms 1099-B (in Box 1e, with Box 12 checked) it sends to you and the IRS. If average cost is the fund's default method, and you want to use another basis method for your first sale of covered shares, such as the specific identification method, you must select that method online or on a paper form you mail to the fund before the fund will complete your transaction. Once specific identification is selected, you can identify the specific shares you want to sell by phone (if

Wash Sale Loss Disallowance

A loss on the redemption of fund shares is disallowed to the extent that within 30 days before or after the sale, you buy shares in the same fund. The wash sale rule *(30.6)* is triggered even when the acquisition of new shares occurs automatically (within the 61-day period) under a dividend reinvestment plan.

Inherited Shares

If you inherit shares of a decedent and an estate tax return was filed after July 31, 2015, the executor of the estate must provide you with a statement that shows the date-of-death value of the property you received, and if the property increased the estate tax liability, you are required to use that value as your basis when you sell. For further inherited property basis rules, *see 5.17*.

Basis of Shares Acquired After 2011 Reported to the IRS

When you sell mutual fund shares that you acquired after 2011 in a nonretirement account, the fund will report the cost basis of the shares to both the IRS and you on Form 1099-B.

allowed by the fund), online, or in writing. If you initially use the average cost method, either as the default or because you selected it, and you want to change to another method, or you initially choose another method and want to change to average cost, you must make the change from or to average cost online or in writing, not by phone. If you sell covered shares using the average cost method and then elect another basis method, the new method will apply only to shares purchased after the date that the change request is processed.

If you plan to sell noncovered shares and want to use the specific identification method when you report basis on Form 8949 and Schedule D, you must select that method prior to the sale (online or in writing) and must keep for your records a confirmation from the fund showing that you selected specific shares to be sold. You will need purchase records to substantiate the basis you report on your return for the specifically identified shares.

Here is a summary of the basis methods for noncovered shares.

- *Average Cost Method*—averages your cost for all shares in the fund regardless of when they were acquired. You do not have to identify the exact shares being sold. The average cost for each share is the total cost for all shares, including those acquired by reinvesting dividends and capital gain distributions, divided by the number of shares. For holding period purposes when you file your return (long- or short-term treatment on Form 8949/Schedule D), shares sold under the average cost method are considered sold in the order you acquired them (FIFO). Your fund will calculate average cost separately for your covered and noncovered shares.
- *Specific Identification Method*—allows you to select exactly which shares are being sold, enabling you to determine your gain or loss and achieve a desired tax result. Check with your fund for its procedures in selecting the specific identification method and for identifying the shares to be sold using the method.
- *First-in, first-out (FIFO) Method*—treats shares as sold in the order that they were acquired.

Your fund may also offer variations of the above methods, such as highest in, first out (HIFO), which treats the highest cost shares as sold first, or last in, first out (LIFO), which treats the most recently acquired shares as sold first. Check with your fund for the available methods and selection procedures.

Planning Reminder

Shares Received as Gift

To determine your original basis of mutual fund shares you acquired by gift, you must know the donor's adjusted basis, the date of the gift, the fair market value of the shares at the time of the gift, and whether any gift tax was paid on the shares *(5.17)*.

EXAMPLE

You bought 160 shares of the XYZ Mutual Fund on February 4, 2011, for $4,000. On August 12, 2011, you bought another 240 shares for $4,800. You obtained an additional 10 shares on December 16, 2011, when you reinvested a $300 dividend. On December 21, 2012, you obtained an additional 20 shares when you reinvested a $750 dividend. This was your last investment in the fund. Since then, you have taken distributions in cash rather than reinvesting them. You sell 200 shares of the fund on September 23, 2023, for $8,000.

For holding period purposes, shares sold under the average cost method are deemed sold in the order they were acquired (FIFO). Thus, you are deemed to have sold the 160 shares bought on February 4, 2011, and 40 of the 240 shares bought on August 12, 2011. As all of the sold shares were acquired before 2012, they are considered noncovered shares. The XYZ Fund provides your average cost basis on the Form 1099-B it sends to you but it does not include basis on the Form 1099-B sent to the IRS.

Using the average cost method, your average basis is $22.91 per share. Your total cost basis for all 430 shares is $9,850. Dividing $9,850 by 430 gives you an average basis per share of $22.91. Thus, your basis for the 200 sold shares is $4,582 (200 × $22.91 = $4,582).

The sold shares were held long term on the sale date of September 23, 2023. You have a $3,418 long-term capital gain on the sale: $8,000 proceeds less $4,582 basis figured under the average cost method.

32.10 Comparison of Basis Methods

Your choice of basis method can have a significant effect on the computation of capital gains and losses when you sell a portion of your noncovered shares in a mutual fund *(32.9)*. The following Example compares the average cost method to the specific identification and FIFO methods.

Transaction history. Assume that on February 5, 2010, you made an initial investment of $4,500 for 375 shares in ABC Mutual Fund at $12 per share. Under the dividend reinvestment plan, you received a $400 dividend on December 17, 2010, that you reinvested for an additional 40 shares at $10 per share. On June 13, 2011, you bought 350 shares at $15 per share. On December 22, 2011, you reinvested your dividend, this time for 25 shares at $12 per share. On September 7, 2012, you bought 200 shares at $16 per share. On August 17, 2021, you bought 200 shares at $25 per share. You did not reinvest your dividends received after 2011 and did not buy any more shares after August 17, 2021, or sell any of the shares.

Now assume that you are planning to redeem some of your shares in October of 2023 and are trying to decide whether to use the average cost, specific identification, or FIFO method for figuring basis. Since all of your shares have been held long term, capital gain or loss will be long term regardless of which basis method is used.

You decide to redeem 200 shares on October 17, 2023, when shares are selling at $20 per share. The table below shows your transaction history and following that is a comparison of how the three basis methods would work given these facts.

Specific identification method. If you identify the particular shares you are selling, you can use the basis of those shares to figure your gain or loss. You must specifically tell the funds the particular shares you want to be redeemed prior to the time of the sale, and must receive a written confirmation of your specification within a reasonable time. Depending on your situation, you may want to either maximize or minimize your gain or loss on the sale.

Assume that under the transaction facts above, you want to realize a loss on the redemption that can be used to offset other gains. You would specify the 200 shares purchased at $25 per share on August 17, 2021, as the shares sold. Since the sales price on October 17, 2023, was $20 per share, the loss would be $5 per share, for an overall long-term capital loss of $1,000 ($4,000 – $5,000).

On the other hand, if you realized a gain, you could offset some capital losses that you realized earlier in the year, but you want to minimize the gain. You would specify the 200 shares bought at $16 per share on September 7, 2012, as the shares sold. Since the shares were sold for $20 per share, the gain would be $4 per share, for an overall $800 long-term capital gain ($4,000 – $3,200).

FIFO (first-in, first-out). Under the FIFO method, the oldest shares, the February 5, 2010, shares, are considered sold first. Thus, the basis of the 200 shares sold would be $12 per share. Your long-term capital gain is $1,600 ($4,000 – $2,400).

Average cost. Assume that the ABC Mutual Fund has calculated your average basis and provides it on your account statements. Your average cost is $15.67. This is your total investment of $18,650 divided by the 1,190 total shares. At $15.67 per share, the total cost is $3,134 for the 200 redeemed shares. Your long-term capital gain is $866 ($4,000 – $3,134). The shares sold are considered to be from the earliest lot in 2010.

Conclusion. Given this transaction history and preferred gain or loss objective, the specific identification method is advantageous. It allows you to realize a loss if that is your preferred tax result, or to realize the lowest capital gain if that is your preferred tax result.

 *Caution*

Get Written Confirmation for Specific Identification Method

If you want to take advantage of the specific identification method, make sure the fund sends you a written confirmation of your selling instructions.

The specific identification method allows you to designate specific shares as the shares sold, allowing you to minimize a gain on the sale or to select shares that, because of their basis, would give you a loss.

Transaction History				
Date	Action	Share Price	No. of Shares	Shares Owned
2/5/2010	Invest $4,500	$12	375	375
12/17/2010	Reinvest $400 dividend	$10	40	415
6/13/2011	Invest $5,250	$15	350	765
12/22/2011	Reinvest $300 dividend	$12	25	790
9/7/2012	Invest $3,200	$16	200	990
8/17/2021	Invest $5,000	$25	200	1,190
10/17/2023	Redeem $4,000	$20	200	990

32.11 Mutual Funds Compared to Exchange-Traded Funds

From an investment perspective, mutual funds are similar to exchange traded funds (ETFs); both offer a bundle of underlying investments providing diversity that reduces the risk of loss. If there are any dividends from these investments, both permit dividend reinvestment in most cases. However, there are significant differences in tax treatment.

Tax efficiency. Mutual funds may generate tax consequences for investors because fund managers trade and re-balance the funds' holdings to satisfy shareholder redemptions. In effect, there may be capital gains for shareholders even though such shareholders have unrealized losses on their holdings (i.e., the value of their investment may have declined even though they are required to report gains). In contrast, ETFs generally do not generate gains from underlying investments while shareholders hold their positions; shareholders only realize gain or loss when they sell their ETF shares. However, certain ETFs offer less tax efficiency (check with a financial/tax advisor for guidance on the tax ramifications of a particular ETF).

Dividends. Dividends paid from ETFs may be treated as qualified dividends, which are subject to favorable tax treatment *(4.2)*. These dividends cannot offset capital losses. Capital gain distributions from mutual funds are considered long-term capital gains; they are taxed at favorable capital gain rates *(32.3)*. They can also be used to offset capital losses and a limited amount of ordinary income *(5.4)*.

Identifying shares sold. If you acquire shares at different times and sell less than your entire holdings, you may take action to minimize gain or maximize loss (depending on your overall tax position for the year). If no action is taken, you are treated as selling the first shares acquired (first-in, first-out). For ETFs, which are treated like stock, you can choose to use the specific identification method *(32.10)* to select those shares that produce the desired tax results. For mutual fund shares, you can use the specific identification method or an averaging method *(32.10)*. You cannot use the averaging method for shares in ETFs.

CHAPTER 33

Educational Tax Benefits

The tax law provides several tax benefits for people attending school. If you can take advantage of them, you are in effect receiving a government subsidy lowering the cost of education.

Qualified tuition programs (529 plans), which are designed primarily to cover higher education costs, can also be used to pay tuition up to $10,000 for elementary and secondary school, student loans up to $10,000 for the beneficiary and each sibling, and expenses related to apprenticeship programs.

The American opportunity tax credit, the lifetime learning credit, the student loan interest deduction, and Coverdell ESAs can also provide substantial tax savings. However, these tax benefit provisions are hedged with restrictions, such as income-based limitations, which may bar or limit their availability.

Law Alert

HEERF Grants Are Tax Free

If you received a grant under the Higher Education Emergency Relief Fund (HEERF) for expenses related to the disruption of campus operations due to COVID-19, you are not taxed on the money. The funds are designed to cover food, housing, course materials, technology, health care, and childcare.

Law Alert

IRA Contributions Based on Certain Tuition Fellowships and Stipends

Non-tuition fellowships and stipends received by graduate and postdoctoral students includible in gross income can be the basis on which to make IRA contributions *(8.2)*.

Caution

Graduate Teaching and Research Assistants

If you must teach, do research, or provide other services to obtain a tuition reduction for graduate studies, a tuition reduction from the school is tax free if it is in addition to regular pay for the services. If the tuition reduction is your compensation, it is taxable, unless it is paid under the National Health Services Corps Scholarship Program or the Armed Forces Health Professions Scholarship and Financial Assistance Program.

33.1 Scholarships and Grants

Scholarships and fellowships of a degree candidate are tax-free to the extent the grants pay for tuition and course-related fees, books, supplies, and equipment required for courses. Amounts for room, board, travel, and incidental expenses do not qualify and must be reported as income. If you are not a candidate for a degree (*see* the degree test below), your entire grant is taxable.

Generally, you must pay tax on grants or tuition reductions that pay for teaching, research, or other services required as a condition of receiving the grant. This is true even if all degree candidates are required to perform the services. Thus, if you are a graduate student and receive a stipend for teaching, those payments are taxable, subject to withholding, and reported by the school on Form W-2. Similarly, no tax-free exclusion is allowed for federal grants where the recipient agrees to do future work with the federal government. However, a grant or tuition reduction representing payment for teaching, research, or other services is not taxable if it is paid under the National Health Services Corps Scholarship Program or the Armed Forces Health Professions Scholarship and Financial Assistance Program.

Degree test. Scholarships given to students attending a primary or secondary school, or to those pursuing a degree at a college or university, meet the degree test. Also qualifying are full-time or part-time scholarships for study at an educational institution that (1) provides an educational program acceptable for full-time credit towards a higher degree or offers a program of training to prepare students for gainful employment in a recognized occupation and (2) is authorized under federal or state law to provide such a program and is accredited by a nationally recognized accreditation agency.

Pell grants. Pell grants are need-based grants subject to the above rules for scholarships. Thus, they are tax-free to the extent they are used for tuition and course-related fees, books, supplies, and equipment required for courses.

33.2 Tuition Reductions for College Employees

Free or partially free tuition for undergraduate studies provided to a faculty member or school employee is generally not taxable. The tuition reduction may be for education at his or her own school or at another school. Tuition benefits may be taxable to highly compensated employees if the tuition plan discriminates in their favor. Tuition reductions representing compensation for services are taxable unless paid under the National Health Services Corps Scholarship Program or the Armed Forces Health Professions Scholarship and Financial Assistance Program.

Tax-free tuition benefits may also be provided to the employee's spouse, dependent child, a former employee who retired or left on disability, a widow or widower of an individual who died while employed by the school, or a widow or widower of a retired or disabled employee.

A child under the age of 25 qualifies for a tax-free tuition reduction if both parents have died and one of the parents qualified for tax-free tuition benefits. If the child is age 25 or over, tuition reductions are taxed even if both parents are deceased.

A tuition reduction for graduate studies may also be tax free; *see* the Caution on this page.

33.3 How Fulbright Awards Are Taxed

Most Fulbright awards are treated as taxable wages for teaching, lecturing, or research. If you are abroad over a year, you may be able to claim the foreign earned income exclusion to avoid tax on the grant *(Chapter 36)*. Foreign income taxes paid on taxable Fulbright wages are eligible for the foreign tax credit *(36.12)*.

33.4 United States Savings Bond Tuition Plans

Consider the use of Series EE bonds *(30.12)* or I bonds *(30.13)* to fund part of a college savings program. You can defer the interest income until final maturity (30 years) or report the interest annually. At redemption, the interest is not subject to state or local tax. For bonds purchased in your child's name, having your child report the interest annually may be advisable where it can be offset by the child's standard deduction or itemized deductions. To the extent interest is offset each year, the interest escapes tax *(4.29)*.

Interest exclusion may be available if you redeem EE bonds issued in your own name after 1989 or I bonds. If you purchased I bonds *(30.13)* or post-1989 EE bonds *(30.12)* in your own name or jointly with your spouse and have been deferring the reporting of interest income, you may be able to exclude accumulated interest from federal tax in the year you redeem the bonds if in that year you pay tuition and enrollment education fees or you contribute to a Coverdell ESA *(33.11)* or qualified tuition program (QTP) *(33.5)*. The exclusion, claimed on Form 8815, is subject to several limitations as discussed in the following paragraphs.

Who qualifies for the exclusion. You must have been age 24 or over before the month in which the qualified bonds were purchased, and the bonds must have been issued solely in your name or in the joint names of you and your spouse. You may not claim the exclusion for bonds bought in your child's name or owned jointly with your child. In the year the bonds are redeemed you must pay tuition and enrollment fees or contribute to a Coverdell ESA or QTP for yourself, your spouse, or your dependents *(21.2)*. Thus, grandparents who redeem bonds they bought to fund the college education of their grandchildren may not claim the exclusion unless the grandchildren are their dependents in the year the bonds are redeemed. If you are married, you must file a joint return for the year you redeem the bonds; married persons filing separately are not eligible for the exclusion.

If these tests are met, and your income does not exceed the annual limit for the exclusion, you may claim a full or partial exclusion, depending on whether your qualified education expenses exceed the bond redemption proceeds, as discussed in the following paragraphs.

Excludable amount and phaseout rule. The tax-free amount of EE or I bond interest is figured on Form 8815. Even if you pay qualified higher educational expenses in the year you redeem the bond, your potential interest exclusion may be limited or barred because: (1) the qualified expenses must be reduced by nontaxable educational benefits received in the year the bond is redeemed, (2) your potential exclusion is reduced or eliminated under the phaseout rule based on modified adjusted gross income (MAGI), or (3) you are married filing separately, in which case you are not allowed an exclusion regardless of your income or amount of expenses.

Qualified higher education expenses include the following expenses that you pay in the year of redemption for yourself, your spouse, or your dependents *(21.2)*: (1) tuition and fees required for enrollment at a college, university, or vocational school that meets federal financial aid standards, and (2) contributions to a Coverdell. ESA or QTP. Room and board are not eligible expenses.

On Form 8815, qualified expenses must be reduced by the amount of any nontaxable scholarship or fellowship grant, tax-free employer-provided educational assistance, educational expenses taken into account when figuring the American opportunity credit or Lifetime learning credit *(33.7)*, and educational expenses taken into account when figuring the tax-free portion of a distribution from a qualified tuition plan *(33.6)* or a Coverdell ESA *(33.11)*.

If after the required reductions, qualified expenses equal or exceed the redemption proceeds, 100% of the interest is potentially excludable, subject to the phaseout based on MAGI. If the redeemed amount exceeds the amount of educational expenses (after any required reduction), the excludable amount is based on the ratio of expenses to the redemption amount and the phaseout computation.

A full interest exclusion is allowed only to persons with MAGI below a phaseout threshold which changes annually. For 2023, the MAGI phaseout ranges are:

- $91,850 to $106,850 for single persons, heads of household, and qualifying widows/widowers
- $137,800 to $167,800 for married persons filing jointly

No exclusion is allowed if MAGI equals or exceeds the $106,850 or $167,800 limit. For purposes of applying the phaseout, MAGI is generally your regular adjusted gross income plus the interest on the redeemed EE or I bonds and student loan interest *(33.13)* that you deduct, and foreign income items and employer-provided adoption assistance that you excluded from income. *See* the Form 8815 instructions.

> **EXAMPLE**
>
> In November 2023, you redeem a $10,000 (face value) I bond that you purchased in September 2004. On the redemption you receive $19,512 of which $10,000 is the return of your investment and $9,512 is interest. In 2023, you paid qualified higher education expenses of $19,250 for your daughter, who is your dependent. She did not receive any scholarships or grants. After taking into account $4,000 of expenses used to figure an American opportunity credit *(33.8)*, you show $15,250 of qualified higher education expenses ($19,250-$4,000) on Line 2 of Form 8815. Prior to application of the phaseout rule, the excludable percentage of interest is 78.2% ($15,250 education expenses divided by $19,512 redemption proceeds, rounded to 3 places). Thus, $7,438 of the interest (78.2% × $9,512 interest) is potentially excludable from income, pending application of the phaseout rule.
>
> Assume you are married filing jointly and have MAGI for 2023 of $158,652, which exceeds the phaseout threshold of $167,800 by $9,148. On Form 8815, you divide your excess MAGI of $9,148 by the $30,000 phaseout range (for joint return) to get a phaseout percentage of 30.5% (rounded to 3 places). Thus, 30.5% of the potential $7,438 exclusion, or $2,269, is phased out. The balance, or $5,169 ($7,438– $2,269), is the excludable I bond interest. The $5,169 exclusion is entered on Line 3 of Schedule B, where it reduces the taxable interest you must include on your return.

33.5 Contributing to a Qualified Tuition Program (Section 529 Plan)

Qualified tuition programs (QTPs), also known as Section 529 plans, allow you to either prepay a designated beneficiary's future qualified higher education expenses or to establish a savings plan from which such expenses can be paid. States can sponsor savings plans and prepayment plans and often provide a state tax credit or state deduction. Private colleges, universities, and vocational schools can set up prepayment plans only. Distributions are generally tax-free to the extent of qualified higher education expenses, and distributions of up to $10,000 to pay tuition for elementary or secondary school also qualify *(33.6)*.

In a college prepayment plan, a parent or other relative can purchase tuition credits or certificates as a prepayment of a child's future college costs. Where the child will not start college for many years, prepaying tuition according to a set schedule can avoid higher inflation-based tuition costs down the road. In a state-sponsored savings plan, annual contributions are made to an account for the benefit of the designated beneficiary, earnings accumulate tax-free, and withdrawals can later be made to pay the beneficiary's qualified higher education costs.

Contribution details and other plan terms including investment options can vary greatly from plan to plan. If you are considering an investment, you should contact the state or educational institution maintaining the plan for details.

Contributions are not deductible for federal tax purposes. However, a state income tax deduction may be available or a state tax credit may be generated for residents who contribute to a state-sponsored QTP.

You may contribute to both a QTP and a Coverdell ESA *(33.11)* in the same year on behalf of the same beneficiary.

Gift tax consequences. A contribution to a QTP is treated as a completed gift of a present interest passed from the contributor to the beneficiary at the time of contribution. Contributions are eligible for the annual gift tax exclusion, which applies separately to each individual to whom you make gifts during a year. For 2023, you can make gifts of up to $17,000 per person that are free from gift tax under the annual exclusion, but if you are married and your spouse elects to split your gift on Form 709, the per-donee exclusion doubles to $34,000 *(39.2)*. If your gift exceeds the annual exclusion, a special gift tax rule allows you to elect on Form 709 (annual gift tax and generation-skipping transfer tax return) to treat contributions of up to five times the annual exclusion as if they were made over five years. Thus, for 2023, you can elect to treat QTP contributions of up to $85,000 (five times the $17,000 exclusion) as if the contributions were made ratably over five years, and this is doubled to $170,000 if your spouse elects to split your gifts. If the election is made, the reportable gift on Form 709 for 2023 is (1) 20% of the QTP contributions up to the $85,000/$170,000 limit, allowing that amount to be offset by the annual exclusion, plus (2) the amount of any contribution exceeding the $85,000/$170,000 limit.

33.6 Distributions From Qualified Tuition Programs (Section 529 Plans)

The portion of a QTP distribution allocable to a recovery of contributions to the plan (basis) is not taxable. This is true whether the plan is a state QTP or a private educational institution QTP. A beneficiary who receives a distribution of earnings from a state or private QTP to pay qualified education costs does not have to include the earnings in income if the total distribution does not exceed "adjusted qualified education expenses" (AQEE) for the year, as discussed below in "Figuring the taxable portion of a distribution from a QTP."

On Form 1099-Q, which is sent by the plan paying the distribution to the recipient, the gross distribution in Box 1 is divided between earnings in Box 2 and the return of investment (or basis) in Box 3.

Qualified higher education expenses. For purposes of figuring if part of a distribution from a QTP is taxable *(see below)*, qualified higher education costs are tuition, fees, books, supplies, and equipment required for enrollment or attendance at an eligible educational institution, which is any college, university, vocational school, or other postsecondary school eligible to participate in federal student aid programs. Qualified expenses also include the purchase of computer or peripheral equipment, software, and internet access.

Reasonable room and board costs for a designated beneficiary who is at least a half-time student also qualify. The limit considered reasonable for room and board expenses is the greater of the room and board allowance determined by the eligible institution for federal financial aid purposes or the actual amount charged for a student residing in housing owned and operated by the eligible educational institution. In the case of a special needs beneficiary, the definition of qualifying expenses includes all expenses necessary for that person's enrollment or attendance at an eligible institution.

Qualified elementary and secondary school tuition. A distribution from a QTP of up to $10,000 for tuition at a public, private, or religious elementary or secondary school (K-12) is a qualified expense. The $10,000 cap applies per year, per beneficiary, not per account. So if a child is a beneficiary of more than one 529 plan from which distributions are made in 2023, only a maximum of $10,000 can be excluded from 2023 gross income (assuming the tuition is at least equal to the distribution).

Student loan repayment. Qualified distributions include student loan repayments up to a lifetime cap of $10,000 per beneficiary, plus another $10,000 for each sibling. A sibling includes a brother, sister, stepbrother, and stepsister. For example, if a 529 plan beneficiary has one sibling, a total of $20,000 can be distributed tax-free to make student loan repayments.

Apprenticeship programs. The expenses of an apprenticeship program are treated as qualified expenses, even though they are not viewed as being for higher education. To be eligible for this treatment, the apprenticeship program must be certified by the U.S. Department of Labor under the National Apprenticeship Act. Eligible expenses include fees, books, supplies, and equipment (e.g., tools of the trade).

Figuring the taxable portion of a distribution from a QTP. Whether or not a distribution of earnings from a QTP is taxable depends on whether the distribution exceeds the adjusted qualified education expenses (AQEE), which equals the qualified education expenses paid during the year minus any tax-free assistance such as scholarships, Pell grants, veterans' assistance, and employer-paid expenses. If an American opportunity or lifetime learning

Filing Tip

Tuition for Elementary and Secondary School

A distribution from a 529 plan to pay tuition up to $10,000 per beneficiary for public, private, or religious elementary or secondary school is tax free.

credit is claimed for the year of the distribution, the expenses taken into account in determining the credit also reduce qualified education expenses. If after the reductions the resulting AQEE equal or exceed the total QTP distribution, the entire distribution is tax-free. If after the reductions the resulting AQEE are less than the total QTP distribution, part of the earnings (shown in Box 2 of Form 1099-Q) is taxable. The Example below illustrates the computation of the taxable amount.

If earnings are taxable, a 10% "additional tax" may also be due, but there are exceptions for distributions that are taxable merely because qualified expenses had to be reduced by tax-free education assistance or expenses taken into account in figuring an American opportunity or lifetime learning credit. The additional tax is figured on Form 5329.

Coordination with Coverdell ESA distributions. If distributions from both a QTP and a Coverdell ESA *(33.11)* are received in the same year and the total distributions exceed the adjusted qualified education expenses, the expenses must be allocated between the distributions. Assume in the Example below Marta had withdrawn $3,000 from her QTP and $600 from her Coverdell ESA instead of taking the entire amount from her QTP. Marta would allocate $1,250 of the expenses to the QTP distribution ($3,000 QTP / $3,600 total distribution × $1,500 expenses = $1,250), and $250 of the expenses to the ESA ($600 ESA/$3,600 distribution × $1,500 expenses = $250). She would then figure the taxable portion of earnings from each distribution based on the allocable $1,250 or $250 of expenses.

Contributor's loss on QTP investment. If the entire account is distributed and the total investment in the account has not been recovered, the contributor cannot claim a loss because of the suspension of the miscellaneous itemized deduction subject to the 2% of AGI floor for 2018 through 2025.

Planning Reminder

Rollover to ABLE Account Barred

You can make a tax-free rollover from a 529 plan to an ABLE account if the ABLE account is owned by the same designated beneficiary of the 529 plan.

EXAMPLE

In 2013, Marta's parents opened a QTP for her with the savings plan maintained by their state government. Over the years they contributed $18,000 to the account. In June 2023, when the total balance in the account is $27,000, a $3,600 distribution from the plan is made to Marta. In the summer of 2023, Marta enrolled in college and had $8,500 of qualified education expenses for the rest of the year. Marta was awarded a $3,000 scholarship. On their 2023 return, Marta's parents claimed an American opportunity tax credit of $2,500 (the maximum credit per student) *(33.8)*.

Before Marta can determine the taxable portion of her QTP withdrawal, she must reduce her total qualified education expenses. Note that the reduction for the American opportunity tax credit is $4,000, as $4,000 of expenses are taken into account in figuring a $2,500 credit *(33.8)*.

Total qualified education expenses	$8,500
Less: Tax-free scholarship	− 3,000
Less: Expenses taken into account in figuring American opportunity credit	− 4,000
Equals: Adjusted qualified education expenses (AQEE)	$1,500

Given Marta's adjusted qualified expenses (AQEE) of $1,500 are less than the $3,600 QTP distribution, she must pay tax on the part of the distributed earnings that is not allocable to the expenses. She received a Form 1099-Q that showed that $2,400 of the QTP distribution was a recovery of basis and $1,200 was earnings. Marta figures the taxable part of distributed earnings as follows:

1. The tax-free portion of the earnings is $500: $1,200 distributed earnings × $1,500 (AQEE)/ $3,600 distribution.

2. The balance of the earnings, or $700 ($1,200 − $500), is taxable. Marta must report it as "other income" on Schedule 1 (Form 1040 or 1040-SR).

Changing the designated beneficiary or rolling over a QTP distribution. The QTP owner can instruct the trustee of the account to change the designated beneficiary to a member of the beneficiary's family with no tax consequences. Similarly, a distribution from a 529 plan can be rolled over tax-free to a different plan for the same beneficiary within 60 days after receipt of the distribution, or the rollover can be to a QTP for a member of the original beneficiary's family. For purposes of these rules, family members include the beneficiary's spouse, his or her siblings, children and grandchildren, parents, aunts, uncles, nieces, nephews, in-laws, the spouse of any of these relatives, or a first cousin. For each beneficiary, only one rollover is allowed within a 12-month period.

529 Plan Rollover to Roth IRA. SECURE 2.0 provides a rollover mechanism for 529 plans to a Roth IRA. Beginning in 2024, 529 plans may roll over up to $6,500 annually to a Roth IRA with a total lifetime limit of $35,000. The 529 plan must have been established for at least 15 years before the conversion, and any contributions made within the last five years are ineligible for rollover. Further, State benefits may require a deduction/credit recapture.

33.7 Education Tax Credits

There are two tax credits for higher education tuition and qualified fees: The American opportunity tax credit and the Lifetime learning credit. Both credits are figured on Form 8863. You may not claim both credits for the same student for the same year.

The maximum American opportunity tax credit is $2,500 per eligible student per year for qualified expenses in the first four years of post-secondary education. And 40% of the credit is generally refundable, meaning that it is allowed even if it exceeds your tax liability. *See 33.8* for details on the American opportunity tax credit.

Unlike the American opportunity tax credit, the Lifetime learning credit may be claimed for higher education costs beyond the fourth year of post-secondary education and for non-degree courses which enable the student to acquire or improve job skills. Only tuition and fees/expenses required for enrollment or attendance qualify. The maximum Lifetime learning credit is $2,000 annually, regardless of how many students you pay expenses for. *See 33.9* for details on the lifetime learning credit.

A phaseout rule based on modified adjusted gross income (MAGI), may limit or even eliminate both credits. The phaseout rule for the Lifetime learning credit *(33.9)* is the same as for the American opportunity tax credit *(33.8)*.

Some of the qualification rules for the American opportunity tax credit and Lifetime learning credit are the same and these are discussed below.

Rules Applicable to Both the American opportunity tax credit and Lifetime learning credit

Married persons filing separately are not eligible. If you are married at the end of the year, you must file jointly to claim either the American opportunity tax credit or the Lifetime learning credit.

Borrowed funds used to pay expenses. You can claim either the American opportunity tax credit or the Lifetime learning credit for eligible expenses paid with loan proceeds. If loan proceeds are sent directly to the educational institution, they are not considered paid until the institution credits the student's account.

Prepaid expenses. Your American opportunity tax credit or Lifetime learning credit for 2023 is based on qualified expenses you paid in 2023 for academic periods beginning in 2023, as well as 2023 payments of qualified expenses for academic periods beginning in the first three months of 2024. If you made a payment in 2023 for academic periods beginning after March 2024, the payment is not eligible for a 2023 credit and it also will not be eligible for a 2024 credit.

Eligible students at eligible educational institutions. To claim an American opportunity tax credit or a Lifetime learning credit you must pay qualified expenses for yourself, your spouse, or dependents you claim on your return. The expenses must be for courses at

Law Alert

Form 1098-T Needed to Claim Education Credit

Form 1098-T is required to support any claim for the American Opportunity credit *(33.8)* or Lifetime Learning Credit (c), unless the IRS provides an exception; *see* the Form 8863 instructions and "Form 1098-T" in the text on the next page.

Filing Instruction

Prepaid Tuition Payments Not Creditable for the Next Year

If you prepay 2023 tuition in 2022, you may not choose to treat the payments as eligible for an education credit in 2023. The payments may only be taken into account for 2022 education credits if eligible in 2022.

eligible educational institutions. Specific student eligibility requirements for the American opportunity tax credit are discussed at *33.8*. An eligible educational institution is any accredited public, nonprofit, or proprietary college, university, vocational school, or other postsecondary institution eligible to participate in the student aid programs administered by the U.S. Department of Education.

Qualified expenses. For both credits, qualified expenses include tuition, student activity fees required of all students for enrollment or attendance, and course-related books, supplies, and equipment that must be purchased from the educational institution as a condition of enrollment or attendance. Other required course materials, such as books or equipment bought privately, qualify for the American opportunity tax credit but not the Lifetime learning credit. Expenses for sports or hobby-related courses not part of the student's degree program do not qualify for the American opportunity tax credit but such non-degree courses qualify for the Lifetime learning credit if they help the student acquire or improve job skills. Room and board, insurance, medical expenses, transportation, and other personal expenses are not qualified expenses for either credit.

For purposes of figuring either credit, qualified expenses must be reduced by tax-free scholarships, Pell grants, educational assistance from the VA (Department of Veterans Affairs) or employer-provided educational assistance *(3.7)*.

Form 1098-T. On Form 1098-T for 2023, the educational institution must report to the enrolled student the total payments received in 2023 for qualified tuition and related expenses (Box 1). The Box 1 amount is after any reduction for reimbursements or refunds made in 2023. Any scholarships or grants that could reduce the allowable credit are shown in Box 5. Your credit for 2023 must be based on payments you actually made in 2023, or payments made by your child or a third party that you are deemed to have paid (*see* next paragraph), which could be different than the amount shown on Form 1098-T.

Who can claim a credit for expenses paid by your child or by a third party? If you claim an eligible student as your dependent *(21.2)*, all of the student's qualified expenses are treated as having been paid by you. For example, if your child is an eligible student and he or she pays qualified expenses in 2023 or the expenses are paid by a third party (such as by the child's grandparent or under a court-approved divorce decree) you are treated as paying the expenses if you claim the student as your dependent and only you can claim a credit for those expenses. If no one claims the student as a dependent, only the student can claim the credit.

Double benefits not allowed. You may not claim an American opportunity tax credit and the Lifetime learning credit for the same student for the same year. If you claim either credit, you may not claim the above-the-line tuition and fees deduction *(33.12)* for the same student for the same year.

You may be able to receive a tax-free distribution from either a Coverdell ESA or a state qualified tuition program (QTP) in the same year in which you claim an American opportunity tax credit or Lifetime learning credit. The expenses taken into account as the basis of an American opportunity tax credit or Lifetime learning credit reduce eligible expenses for purposes of figuring the tax-free part of an ESA or state QTP distribution.

Recapture of credit. If you claim a credit and after you file your return for that year you receive tax-free educational assistance for the prior year or receive a refund of an expense used to figure the prior-year credit, you have to refigure the original credit. If the refund or assistance would have reduced the original credit, the amount of the reduction must be added to your tax liability for the year you receive the refund or assistance; *see* the Form 8863 instructions.

33.8 American opportunity tax credit

You may claim an American opportunity tax credit on Form 8863 if you pay qualified tuition and fees for an eligible student in the first four years of college or other post-secondary institution and the credit is not barred by the phaseout rule *(see below)*.

A student is an eligible student for purposes of the credit only if all of the following requirements are met: (1) the student must be enrolled in one of the first four years of postsecondary education, (2) the student is enrolled in a program that leads to a degree, certificate, or other recognized educational credential, (3) the student is taking at least one-half of the normal full-time workload for his or her course of study for at least one academic period beginning during the calendar year, (4) both the taxpayer claiming the credit and the student have a TIN by the due date of the return (*see* the Law Alert on this page), and (5) the student does not have any felony conviction (state or federal) for possessing or distributing a controlled substance as of the end of the tax year.

Even if the above five requirements are met, a student is not eligible for the American opportunity tax credit if the credit, together with its predecessor the Hope Scholarship credit, was claimed for any four years preceding the current year. This means a 2023 American opportunity tax credit cannot be claimed by anyone for a student if the American opportunity tax credit and/or the Hope Scholarship was claimed for that student for any four tax years before 2023.

To claim the maximum credit of $2,500 for an eligible student, you must pay at least $4,000 in qualified expenses for that student. For each eligible student, the American opportunity tax credit is 100% of the first $2,000 and 25% of the next $2,000 (for a maximum of $2,500) of tuition, student-activity fees that are required as a condition of enrollment or attendance, and books, supplies, and equipment needed for courses. The books, supplies, and equipment qualify for the credit whether or not they had to be purchased from the educational institution.

Keep in mind the qualified expenses eligible for the credit are reduced by tax-free educational assistance, including the tax-free part of a Pell grant or other scholarship or fellowship, tax-free employer-provided assistance *(3.7)*, and VA educational assistance. The reduction of the expenses by the tax-free educational assistance could eliminate much or all of the credit. You have the option of allocating part of a Pell grant to room and board, or other education costs which do not qualify for the credit. The amount allocated to the room and board would be included in the student's gross income rather than be a tax-free scholarship, but the allocated amount would not reduce the expenses eligible for the credit. *See* the instructions to Form 8863 for further details.

Phaseout of credit based on MAGI. The phaseout of the tentative credit (100% of the first $2,000 and 25% of the next $2,000 of qualified expenses) begins when MAGI exceeds a phaseout threshold of $80,000 if you are single, head of household, or a qualifying widow/widower, or $160,000 if married filing jointly. These thresholds are fixed by law and are not subject to inflation adjustments.

The phaseout range is narrow: only $10,000 for non-joint return filers and $20,000 for joint return filers. Thus, if you are single, head of household, or a qualifying widow/widower, the credit is completely phased out if your MAGI is $90,000 or more. If you are married filing jointly, the credit is completely phased out if your joint return MAGI is $180,000 or more. The Example below illustrates the application of the phaseout rule.

Modified adjusted gross income is the same as adjusted gross income (AGI) unless you are claiming the foreign earned income exclusion *(36.3)* or foreign housing exclusion or deduction *(36.4)*, or the exclusions for income from Puerto Rico *(36.10)* or American Samoa *(36.9)*. If so, adjusted gross income is increased by such amounts on Form 8863.

Refundable and nonrefundable parts of the credit. After applying the phaseout rule, 40% of the allowable credit is refundable, meaning you claim it on your return as if it were a tax payment, and like withholding, you get it back even if it exceeds your tax liability for the year. However, none of the credit is refundable if you are under age 24 with investment income subject to the kiddie tax *(24.2)*.

The balance of the credit (60% unless the kiddie tax applies) is a nonrefundable credit that offsets your regular tax plus AMT (minus certain credits). The Form 8863 instructions have a credit limit worksheet for applying the tax liability limitation.

For example, assume after applying the phaseout rule, you are allowed a $2,500 credit. 40% of the $2,500, or $1,000, is a refundable credit. The $1,500 balance is a nonrefundable credit which offsets your total tax liability but may not exceed the liability. Assume your

Law Alert

TIN Needed by Filer and Student by Return Due Date

The American opportunity credit cannot be claimed by a taxpayer who does not have a taxpayer identification number (TIN) by the due date of the return including extensions. This is your Social Security number, or an ITIN if not eligible for a Social Security number. The student also must have a TIN by the due date of the return (with extensions).

Law Alert

Credit Denial Could Lead to Future Disallowance

If the American opportunity credit is denied by the IRS, you may have to recertify on Form 8862 your eligibility for future credits. However, if the credit is denied because you recklessly or intentionally disregarded the rules, you will not be allowed to claim the credit for the next two years, and if you fraudulently claimed it, the disallowance period increases to 10 years.

Law Alert

Preparer's Due Diligence Requirement

Paid preparers must complete Form 8867, which is a due diligence checklist, to ensure a taxpayer is eligible for the American Opportunity Tax Credit.

regular tax plus AMT liabilities total $1,300. Your nonrefundable credit is reduced from $1,500 to $1,300. You may claim a $1,000 refundable credit and a $1,300 nonrefundable credit. Also *see* the following Example for how the refundable and nonrefundable portions of the credit are figured after application of the phaseout rule.

EXAMPLE

Ron and Jackie are married and file jointly. In 2023, they pay $7,000 in qualifying college tuition and fees for their son Leo, and $8,500 for their daughter Ally. Leo and Ally both meet the tests for eligible students, and both are claimed as dependents on Ron and Jackie's joint return for 2023. Their joint return MAGI for 2023 is $163,000. A tentative American opportunity credit of $5,000, $2,500 for each child *(33.8)*, is allowed on Line 1 of Form 8863 prior to application of the phaseout rule. The phaseout rule reduces their credit to $4,250. Their excess MAGI of $3,000 ($163,000 MAGI − $160,000 phaseout threshold on joint return) is 15% of the $20,000 phaseout range, so 15% of the tentative $5,000 credit, or $750, is phased out, and 85%, or $4,250 (85% of $5,000), is allowed.

Of the $4,250 allowed by the phaseout rule, 40%, or $1,700, is a refundable credit, which Ron and Jackie enter on Line 29 of Form 1040 or 1040-SR. The $2,550 credit balance ($4,250 − $1,700) is allowed as a nonrefundable credit on Line 3 of Schedule 3 (Form 1040 or 1040-SR), assuming their tax liability is at least much, as figured in the credit limit worksheet in the Form 8863 instructions.

33.9 Lifetime learning credit

You may claim on Form 8863 a Lifetime learning credit of up to $2,000 for the total qualified expenses paid for yourself, your spouse, or your dependents enrolled in eligible educational institutions *(33.7)* during the year, subject to the income phaseout *(see below)*. The credit is nonrefundable, meaning it cannot exceed your regular tax plus AMT liability. In addition to tuition, the only qualified expenses are student activity fees and course-related books, supplies, and equipment which must be paid to the educational institution as a condition of enrollment or attendance.

In contrast to the American opportunity tax credit, the Lifetime learning credit does not have a degree requirement or a workload requirement. The credit may be claimed for one or more courses at an eligible educational institution which are either part of a post-secondary degree program or part of a nondegree program taken to acquire or improve job skills. The Lifetime learning credit is not limited to students in the first four years of postsecondary education, as is the American opportunity tax credit. There is no limit on the number of years for which the Lifetime learning credit can be claimed.

The Lifetime learning credit for any year is 20% of the first $10,000 paid in that year for qualified expenses for all eligible students. Thus, the maximum lifetime learning credit you may claim for 2023 is $2,000 (20% of $10,000), even if you paid qualified expenses for more than one eligible student. The $2,000 maximum may be reduced because of the income-based phaseout or because the allowable credit (after the phaseout) exceeds your tax liability. Under current law, both the credit percentage (20%) and the expense limit ($10,000) are fixed and not eligible for an inflation adjustment.

For students within the first four years of post-secondary education, both the Lifetime learning credit and the American opportunity tax credit are potentially available, but you cannot elect both credits for the same student and the American opportunity tax credit is more advantageous. For one student, the maximum Lifetime learning credit is $2,000 and the maximum American opportunity tax credit is $2,500, and if you paid qualified expenses for more than one eligible student, the overall lifetime learning credit you may claim remains $2,000 regardless of the number of students, whereas the American opportunity tax credit is up to $2,500 per eligible student *(33.8)*. In addition, 40% of the American opportunity tax credit may be refundable *(33.8)*, whereas the Lifetime learning credit is nonrefundable.

Phaseout of credit. The Lifetime learning credit is phased out over the same MAGI range as is the American opportunity tax credit *(33.8)*. Thus, there is no phaseout of the tentative

Lifetime learning credit (20% of the first $10,000 of qualified expenses) if your modified adjusted gross income (MAGI; same definition as at *33.8*) is $80,000 or less and you are single, head of household, or a qualifying widow/widower, or, if you are married filing jointly, MAGI is $160,000 or less. The credit begins to phase out when MAGI exceeds the $80,000 or $160,000 threshold and it is completely phased out if your MAGI is $90,000 or more and you are single, head of household, or a qualifying widow/widower, or MAGI is $180,000 or more and you are married filing jointly. The Example below illustrates the application of the phaseout.

EXAMPLE

John, unmarried, pays $6,400 in qualified tuition and fees in 2023 for courses to improve his job skills. His MAGI for 2023 is $84,600. His tentative lifetime learning credit *(33.9)* before taking into account the phaseout is $1,280 (20% of $6,400). After applying the phaseout rule on Form 8863, John is allowed a lifetime learning credit of $691. His excess MAGI of $4,600 ($84,600 MAGI − $80,000 phaseout threshold for single filer) is 46% of the $10,000 phaseout range, so 46% of the tentative $1,280 credit, or $589, is phased out. The other 54%, or $691, is allowed as a nonrefundable credit on Line 3 of Schedule 3 (Form 1040 or 1040-SR), assuming it is less than his tax liability as figured in the credit limit worksheet in the Form 8863 instructions.

Tax liability limitation. The Lifetime learning credit allowed after applying the phaseout rule is a nonrefundable credit and is allowed only to the extent of your regular tax and AMT liability (minus certain credits). The Form 8863 instructions have a credit limit worksheet for applying the tax liability limitation.

33.10 Contributing to a Coverdell Education Savings Account (ESA)

A Coverdell Education Savings Account, or ESA, is a trust or custodial account set up specifically for the purpose of paying the qualified education expenses of the designated beneficiary of the account. A contribution cannot be made for a beneficiary after he or she reaches age 18 unless the beneficiary is a special needs beneficiary, as discussed below. Contributions must be in cash. Coverdell Education Savings Accounts were formerly known as Education IRAs.

Contribution deadline. The deadline for making a contribution for any year is the due date of your return for that year (not including extensions). You can make a contribution to a Coverdell ESA up until April 15, 2024, and designate it as a contribution for 2023.

Two annual contribution limits. The maximum annual cash contribution that can be made for a designated beneficiary is $2,000. The $2,000 limit applies to the total contributions for each designated beneficiary for the year. For example, if you and several family members would each like to contribute to a Coverdell ESA for your child, the total amount of 2023 contributions that can be made for your child is $2,000, no matter how many Coverdell ESAs have been set up or how many persons contribute.

Each contributor is also subject to a $2,000 annual contribution limit for each beneficiary, but the $2,000 limit can be reduced by the phaseout rule. The $2,000 per beneficiary limit is reduced if your modified adjusted gross income (MAGI) is between $95,000 and $110,000, or between $190,000 and $220,000 if you are married filing jointly. You may not contribute to any beneficiary's Coverdell ESA if your MAGI is $110,000 or more, or $220,000 or more if filing a joint return. These phaseout ranges are not adjusted for inflation. For most individuals, MAGI is the same as adjusted gross income (AGI), but if the foreign earned income exclusion or an exclusion of income from Puerto Rico or American Samoa is claimed, the exclusion is added back to AGI.

The Coverdell ESA beneficiary must pay a 6% excise tax on Form 5329 if total contributions to his or her ESAs for the year exceed $2,000, or the contributions exceed the reduced limits allowed to contributors under the phaseout rule. The penalty is imposed on the beneficiary and not the contributors. The excise tax does not apply if the excess contributions (and any earnings) are withdrawn before the first day of the sixth month (June 1) of the following year. The withdrawn earnings are taxable to the beneficiary for the year in which the excess contribution was made.

> **EXAMPLE**
>
> Assume you are single and have MAGI of $96,500 for 2023. Given your MAGI exceeds the phaseout threshold of $95,000 by $1,500 and the phaseout range is $15,000, 10% ($1,500/$15,000) of your contribution limit or $200 (10% of $2,000) is phased out. For 2023, you may contribute up to $1,800 for each Coverdell ESA beneficiary. If you contribute $1,800 for a beneficiary, others can contribute no more than $200 for that beneficiary for that year, as contributions for a beneficiary may not exceed $2,000 from all sources.

Special needs beneficiary. Contributions to a Coverdell ESA for a special needs beneficiary may be made even if he or she is over age 18.

33.11 Distributions From Coverdell ESAs

A designated beneficiary of a Coverdell ESA is not taxed on withdrawals which do not exceed qualified education expenses for that year. If withdrawals in a year exceed the qualified education expenses *(see below)* for that year, a portion of the withdrawals is taxable to the beneficiary. The distribution will be reported to the beneficiary and the IRS on Form 1099-Q. The taxable portion is the amount of the excess withdrawal allocable to earnings; *see* the Example below and the worksheet in IRS Publication 970.

Qualified education expenses. In addition to qualified higher education expenses (as defined at *33.6* for QTPs), qualified expenses for ESA distribution purposes include contributions to a QTP *(33.5)* on behalf of the ESA beneficiary. Also qualifying are elementary and secondary education expenses, kindergarten through grade 12. The elementary or secondary school may be a public, private, or religious school. Eligible expenses for elementary and secondary school students include tuition, fees, academic tutoring, books, supplies, special services for special needs beneficiaries, computers and peripheral equipment, internet access, and software. Software designed for sports or hobbies must be predominately educational in nature. Qualified expenses also include room and board, uniforms, transportation, and supplementary items and services including extended day programs required or provided by the school.

Coordination with education credits. If an American opportunity tax credit or Lifetime learning credit is claimed for 2023, then in figuring the tax-free portion of a 2023 Coverdell ESA distribution, qualified Coverdell ESA expenses must be reduced by the expenses taken into account when figuring the credit.

Figuring the tax-free and taxable part of a distribution. If the adjusted qualified education expenses (AQEE) of the beneficiary equal or exceed the distribution, the entire distribution is tax-free. If a distribution exceeds the AQEE, then part of the earnings included in the distribution is taxable. To determine the amount of AQEE, reduce the total qualified education expenses (defined above) by any tax-free educational assistance such as excludable scholarships, Pell grants, Veteran's educational assistance or employer-provided educational assistance. Any expenses taken into account when figuring an American opportunity tax credit or Lifetime learning credit further reduce qualified expenses. The balance of qualifying expenses after subtracting tax-free educational assistance and credit-related expenses is the beneficiary's AQEE. The Example below shows how the taxable portion of the distribution is determined when the total distribution exceeds the AQEE.

Additional tax on taxable distributions. Generally, a taxable distribution is subject to a 10% additional tax, which is figured on Form 5329. However, the 10% additional tax does not apply to distributions that are: (1) made to a beneficiary (or to the estate of the designated beneficiary) on or after the death of the designated beneficiary,

Filing Tip

Coordination with Education Credits

An American Opportunity Tax Credit or Lifetime Learning Credit may be claimed even if for the same year you exclude a Coverdell ESA distribution from income, as long as the distribution does not cover the same expenses for which a credit is claimed.

(2) made because the designated beneficiary is disabled, (3) taxable because the designated beneficiary received a tax-free scholarship or educational assistance allowance equal to or exceeding the distribution, or (4) taxable only because the qualified ESA education expenses were reduced by expenses used in figuring an American opportunity tax credit or the Lifetime learning credit.

The 10% additional tax also does not apply to the withdrawal of an excess contribution and allocable earnings before June 1 of the following year.

Age 30 duration rule. If there are assets remaining in a Coverdell ESA when the designated beneficiary reaches age 30, the beneficiary must withdraw the assets within 30 days, unless he or she is a special needs beneficiary. The duration of the account can be extended by changing the designated beneficiary or rolling over the account to a member of the beneficiary's family who is under age 30; *see* below.

Rollovers and other transfers. Withdrawn assets may be rolled over tax-free from one Coverdell ESA to another for the benefit of the same beneficiary or a member of the beneficiary's family if the recipient is under age 30. For example, if a beneficiary still has money in his or her account upon graduation from college, the Coverdell ESA can be rolled over tax-free to the Coverdell ESA of a younger sibling. The withdrawal is considered rolled over if it is paid to another Coverdell ESA within 60 days. Only one rollover per Coverdell ESA is allowed during the 12-month period ending on the date of the payment or withdrawal. For rollover purposes, members of the beneficiary's family include the beneficiary's spouse, child, grandchild, stepchild, brother, sister (and a sibling's son or daughter), half-sister, half-brother, stepbrother, stepsister, father, mother (and siblings of parents), grandfather, grandmother, stepfather, stepmother, in-laws, the spouses of any of the above, and first cousins.

Filing Tip

Additional Tax Exception for Service Academy Appointees

If a designated beneficiary is appointed to the U.S. Military Academy, Naval Academy, Air Force Academy, Coast Guard Academy, or Merchant Marine Academy, a distribution is not subject to the 10% additional tax to the extent of the costs of "advanced education" at such academy (as defined by Section 2005(d)(3) of Title 10, United States Code).

EXAMPLE

Bianca Jane had $6,200 of qualified higher education expenses in 2023, her first year of college. She paid her college expenses from a variety of sources: a partial scholarship (excluded from gross income) of $1,500, a $1,000 Coverdell ESA withdrawal, a $1,500 gift from her parents, and $2,200 of earnings from a part-time job.

Of her $6,200 of qualified expenses, $4,300 was tuition and required fees that also qualified for an American opportunity tax credit. Bianca Jane's parents claimed the maximum $2,500 American opportunity tax credit on their 2023 tax return *(33.8)*.

Before Bianca Jane can determine the taxable portion of her ESA withdrawal, she must reduce her total qualified higher education expenses. Note that the reduction for the American opportunity credit is $4,000, as $4,000 of expenses are taken into account in figuring a $2,500 credit *(33.8)*.

Total qualified higher education expenses	$6,200
Less: Tax-free education benefits	− 1,500
Less: Expenses taken into account in figuring American opportunity credit	− 4,000
Equals: Adjusted qualified education expenses (AQEE)	$700

Given Bianca Jane's AQEE of $700 are less than the $1,000 Coverdell ESA withdrawal, part of the withdrawal will be taxable. At the end of 2023 (year of distribution), the balance in Bianca Jane's ESA account was $1,800; total contributions were $2,500. The Form 1099-Q sent to Bianca Jane shows that $893 of the $1,000 withdrawal is allocable to contributions (basis) and $107 to earnings. She must include $32 of the $107 earnings in her income, figured as follows:

1. The tax-free portion of the earnings used for qualified expenses is $75: $107 earnings × ($700 AQEE ÷ $1,000 distribution).
2. The balance of the earnings, or $32 ($107 − $75), is taxable, and must be reported as "other income" on Schedule 1 of Form 1040.

> If Form 1099-Q had not provided Bianca with the breakdown between earnings and basis, she would need to rely on records showing her unrecovered contributions (basis) in order to figure the taxable part of the distribution. For example, Bianca's records show that total contributions to her account (none of which have previously been distributed) were $2,500. Dividing the $2,500 contributions by $2,800 (the $1,800 year-end account balance plus the $1,000 distribution) and multiplying the result by the $1,000 distribution gives the $893 basis portion of the distribution ($1,000 × $2,500 ÷ $2,800 = $893). The balance of the distribution, or $107 ($1,000 − $893), is the earnings portion of the distribution.

The designated beneficiary can be changed to a member of the beneficiary's family (included in the above list) with no tax consequences if the new beneficiary is under age 30. The new beneficiary will have to withdraw the account balance no later than 30 days after reaching age 30, unless he or she is a special needs beneficiary.

If the beneficiary dies before age 30, the account balance generally must be distributed to the beneficiary's estate within 30 days of the date of death. However, if the Coverdell ESA is transferred to a surviving spouse or other family member (*see* the list in "Rollovers and other transfers"above) who is under age 30, the account may be maintained until he or she reaches age 30. The age 30 limitation will not apply if the new beneficiary is a special needs beneficiary.

33.12 Tuition and Fees Deduction No Longer Allowed

For years before 2021, the tuition and fees deduction (Form 8917) allowed an "above-the-line" adjustment from gross income (whether or not itemized deductions were claimed) for up to $2,000 or $4,000 of qualifying higher education tuition and fees, subject to an income limitation. The deduction was repealed for years after 2020.

33.13 Student Loan Interest Deduction

Depending on your income, you may be able to claim an above-the-line (directly from gross income) deduction of up to $2,500. You should receive a Form 1098-E (or substitute statement) from each lender that received interest payments of $600 or more from you during the year.

Eligibility for the deduction is phased out for 2023 if you have modified adjusted gross income (MAGI, *see* below) between $75,000 and $90,000, or between $155,000 and $185,000 if married filing a joint return. On a joint return, the deduction limit remains $2,500 even if you and your spouse each pay interest on a qualified student loan. The $2,500 deduction limit is set by statute and is not subject to annual inflation adjustments. If you are claimed as a dependent by another taxpayer, or you are married filing separately, you may not claim the deduction regardless of your income. The deduction is claimed on Line 21 of Schedule 1 (Form 1040 or 1040-SR) as an above-the-line deduction available even if you do not claim itemized deductions.

Qualified loans and expenses. A qualified student loan is one taken out to pay qualified higher education expenses (defined below) for you, your spouse, or a person who was your dependent when you took out the loan. The education expenses must be paid or incurred within a reasonable time before or after the loan was taken out, and the funds obtained must be used toward education furnished while the student is enrolled at least half-time in a program leading to a degree or other recognized educational credential at an eligible educational institution. Eligible institutions are colleges, universities, vocational schools, and other post-secondary educational institutions eligible to participate in Department of Education student aid programs. Graduate school programs are included. Also included are medical internships or residency programs leading to a degree or certificate from an educational institution or hospital offering postgraduate training.

Law Alert

No Double Dipping on Student Loan Interest

Student loan repayment may be made by an employer as a tax-free benefit up to $5,250 (3.7). And tax-free distributions for student loan repayment up to $10,000 can be made from a 529 plan (33.6). To the extent these other benefits are used, no deduction can be claimed for interest on student loans.

Law Alert

Suspension of Student Loan Interest Payments

Due to COVID-19, interest payments for certain (but not all) federal student loans were suspended from March 13, 2020, through December 31, 2022. No interest accrued during this period; it was set at 0% during this period. However, only actual interest payments are taken into account in figuring the deduction for student loan interest.

Qualified higher education expenses include tuition, fees, room and board (within the limits at *33.6*), books, equipment, and other necessary expenses such as transportation. These costs must be reduced by:

1. Nontaxable employer-provided educational assistance benefits.
2. Nontaxable Coverdell ESA or QTP distributions.
3. U.S. Savings Bond interest excluded from income because it is used to pay higher education expenses.
4. Qualified tax-free scholarships.
5. Veterans' educational assistance benefits.

Loan origination fees and capitalized interest (unpaid interest that accrues and is added by the lender to the outstanding balance of the loan principal) can be counted as interest. In general, a payment, regardless of its label, is treated first as a payment of interest to the extent accrued interest remains unpaid, second as a payment of any loan origination fees or capitalized interest, until such amounts are reduced to zero, and, third as a payment of principal.

Voluntary interest payments are deductible. You can deduct voluntary payments of interest made before your loan has entered repayment status or while you have a repayment deferment.

Dependents and married persons filing separately are ineligible. You may not claim a student loan interest deduction during any year in which someone claims you as a dependent. However, you may deduct interest payments made in a later year when you are no longer claimed as a dependent.

You may not claim a student loan interest deduction for any year in which you are married and file a separate tax return.

Loans that do not qualify for deduction. You may not deduct interest paid on a loan from a relative as student loan interest *(5.6)*.

You may not deduct interest on a loan from a qualified employer plan.

You may not treat interest paid on a revolving line of credit as qualified student loan debt unless you use the funds solely to pay qualified higher education costs.

You may not claim a student loan interest deduction for any amount you may deduct under any other tax law provision, for example home mortgage interest. You also cannot use the deduction if you use part of the borrowed money for purposes other than education, for instance to make improvements to your house.

Phaseout for 2023. The student loan interest deduction is reduced or eliminated if your modified adjusted gross income (MAGI) exceeds phaseout limits. For 2023, the reduction applies if your MAGI is more than $75,000, or more than $155,000 on a joint return. If MAGI is $90,000 or more, or $185,000 or more on a joint return, you may not claim any deduction for 2023; the deduction is completely phased out. For 2024, the phaseout ranges could be raised by an inflation adjustment; *see* the *e-Supplement* at *jklasser.com*. For purposes of the phaseout limits, MAGI is the same as the adjusted gross income shown on your return (disregarding student loan interest) unless you claim the exclusion for foreign earned income *(Chapter 36)*, or certain other items of foreign income or expenses were excluded or deducted from your income. Such items generally must be added back to adjusted gross income.

If your MAGI is within the phaseout range, the phased out amount is figured by multiplying your deductible interest (up to the $2,500 limit) by a fraction, the numerator of which is your MAGI minus the phaseout threshold ($75,000, or $155,000 if married filing jointly), and the denominator of which is the phaseout range of $15,000, or $30,000 if married filing jointly. The result is subtracted from the qualifying student loan interest to get the deductible amount; *see* the Examples above for the computation.

The student loan deduction worksheet in the Form 1040 or 1040-SR instructions can be used to figure the phaseout reduction and the amount of your deduction.

 *Filing Tip*

Forgiveness of Student Loans

Federal student loan debt may be forgiven after 20 or 25 years, depending on when the loan was taken. Public service workers (e.g., teachers, nurses, police) may receive loan forgiveness after 10 years. Loan forgiveness in general is taxable unless a special exception applies; the American Rescue Plan allows exclusion from income of cancellation of student loans from 2021 through 2025, including any student loan forgiveness that may take place through Executive Order: *see 11.8*.

 *Caution*

Deduction Lost for Student Dependent's Loan

If your parent or someone else claims you as a dependent on his or her return, you may not deduct interest on your return for student loan interest you paid. Furthermore, the person who claims you as a dependent may not deduct the interest where you are the borrower legally obligated to repay the loan.

EXAMPLES

1. In 2023 you paid $900 interest on a qualified student loan. You are married and file a 2023 joint return with MAGI of $160,000. Your deduction for 2023 is reduced by $150 under the phaseout rule. You can deduct $750 ($900 − $150).

$$\$900 \times \frac{\$160,000 \text{ MAGI} - \$155,000 \text{ phaseout threshold}}{\$30,000 \text{ phaseout range}} = \$150 \text{ reduction}$$

2. The same facts as in Example 1, except you paid $2,600 interest. The maximum deduction of $2,500 is reduced by $417. You can deduct $2,083 ($2,500 − $417).

$$\$2,500 \times \frac{\$160,000 \text{ MAGI} - \$155,000 \text{ phaseout threshold}}{\$30,000 \text{ phaseout range}} = \$417 \text{ reduction}$$

33.14 Types of Deductible Education Costs Related to Work

If you improve your professional skills by attending continuing education or refresher classes, advanced academic courses, or vocational training, you may be able to treat your expenses as a business expense deduction. As a self-employed business owner or professional, allowable expenses are deductible on Schedule C and reduce income subject to self-employment tax (45.1) as well as income tax liability. However, as an employee, for 2018 through 2025, no deduction can be claimed for work-related education costs because of the suspension of the miscellaneous itemized deduction for costs exceeding 2% of your adjusted gross income; see 19.2.

Keep in mind tuition and fees (but not transportation and usually not books or supplies) for work-related educational courses may also qualify for the lifetime learning credit (33.9) The lifetime learning credit, by reducing tax liability rather than taxable income, is generally more valuable than a Schedule C deduction for education costs. However, you may be unable to claim the credit because your income exceeds the phaseout limit for the credit (33.9).

To deduct education costs on Schedule C (self-employed), you must show the following conditions are met:

1. You are self-employed;
2. You already meet the minimum requirements of your business or profession;
3. The course maintains or improves your professional skills, or you are required by law to take the course to keep your present salary or position; and
4. The course does not lead to qualification for a new profession or business. The cost of courses preparing you for a new profession is not deductible, even if you take them to improve your skills. This rule prevents the deduction of law school costs. Furthermore, the cost of a bar review course or CPA review course is not deductible because it leads to a new profession as an attorney or CPA. If courses lead to qualification for a new business or profession, no deduction is allowed even if you keep your current position.

If your courses meet the above requirements you may deduct the following education costs on Schedule C if self-employed:

1. Tuition, textbooks, fees, equipment, and supplies required by the courses.
2. Local transportation costs (33.16).
3. Travel to and from a school away from home, and lodging and 50% of meals while at school away from home (33.16). The IRS will not disallow traveling expenses to attend a school away from home or in a foreign country merely because you could have taken the course in a local school. However, it may disallow your board and lodging and expenses at the school if your stay lasts longer than a year.

Further details of the deduction requirements are provided in 33.15.

 *Filing Tip*

Check Availability of Lifetime Learning Credit

If you have qualifying work-related education costs, you should determine whether you can claim the Lifetime Learning Credit (33.9). The credit may be more valuable to you than a business deduction.

33.15 Work-Related Tests for Education Costs

Educational costs are not deductible on Schedule C (self-employed) if you are inactive in a business or profession. The cost of "brush-up" courses taken in anticipation of resuming work is also not deductible.

You are not considered unemployed when you take courses during a temporary leave of absence lasting one year or less.

Course must not meet minimum standards. You may not deduct the cost of courses taken to meet the minimum requirements of your work. The minimum requirements of a position are based on a review of the laws and regulations of the state you live in and the standards of your profession or business.

If minimum standards change after you enter a profession, courses you take to meet the new standards are deductible.

Course must maintain or improve work skills. To be deductible, the education must maintain or improve your current work skills. That you are established in your position and that persons in similar positions usually pursue such education indicates whether the courses are taken to maintain and improve work skills. However, the IRS may not allow a deduction for a general education course which is a prerequisite for a work-related course.

If the courses lead to a change of your line of work within the same occupation, a deduction for their cost will usually be allowed if your new duties involve the same general type of work. However, if the course leads to qualification for a new profession, the IRS will disallow a deduction even if the course also improves current work skills.

Courses must not lead to qualification for a new profession. If a course improves your current work skills but leads to qualification for a new profession, the course is not deductible, even if you have no intention of entering that business or profession. For example, a deduction is not allowed for the cost of law school or medical school courses as they prepare you for a new profession. This is true even if you do not intend to practice medicine or law. The IRS with Tax Court approval has also held a deduction is not allowed for the cost of college courses which are part of a degree program, such as a bachelor of arts or science degree.

If you are practicing your profession, the cost of courses leading to a specialty within that profession is deductible. For example, a practicing attorney may deduct the cost of a master's of law degree program (LLM).

> ### EXAMPLES
>
> 1. A practicing dentist returned to school full time to study orthodontics while continuing his practice on a part-time basis. When he finished his training, he limited his work to orthodontics. The IRS ruled he could deduct the cost of his studies. His post-graduate schooling improved his professional skills as a dentist. It did not qualify him for a new profession.
>
> 2. A practicing psychiatrist may deduct the cost of attending an accredited psychoanalytic institute to qualify to practice psychoanalysis. A social worker has also been allowed a deduction for the cost of learning psychoanalysis. In one case, the Tax Court allowed a psychiatrist to deduct the cost of personal therapy sessions conducted through telephone conversations and tape cassettes. The court was convinced the therapy improved his job skills by eliminating psychological blind spots that prevented him from understanding his patients' problems.
>
> 3. A licensed practical nurse may not deduct the costs of a college program that qualifies him or her as a "physician's assistant," which is a new business/profession. Physicians' assistants and practical nurses are subject to different registration and certification requirements under state law, and, more importantly, the physician's assistant may perform duties, such as physical examinations and minor surgery, which go beyond practical nursing duties.

4. Edward, a self-employed golf instructor without an undergraduate degree, earned an associate's degree in business from the Golf Academy of the South. The IRS and Tax Court disallowed his deduction for tuition and fees. It does not matter the courses may have improved his skills as a golf instructor. No deduction was allowed because completing the associate's program was a first step in acquiring a basic undergraduate degree that would qualify Edward for a variety of trades or businesses other than that of a golf instructor.

33.16 Local Transportation and Travel Away From Home To Take Courses

If you are self-employed and your courses meet the requirements in the preceding two sections *(33.14, 33.15)*, costs of local transportation and travel away from home may be included in the business expense deduction.

Local transportation expenses. If your courses qualify for a deduction under *33.15*, you may deduct transportation costs of going from work directly to school. Transportation costs include the actual costs of bus, subway, cab, or other fares, as well as the costs of using your car. According to the IRS, the return trip from school to home is also deductible if you are regularly employed and going to school on a temporary basis. According to the IRS, you are going to school on a temporary basis if your courses are realistically expected to last for one year or less and actually do last no more than one year. This is the same one-year test for determining whether you can deduct the cost of commuting to a "temporary" work location *(20.2)* or living costs while away from home on a "temporary" assignment *(20.9)*. The IRS position is illustrated in the following Examples.

Using your car. If you use your own car for transportation to school, you may deduct your actual expenses or use the standard business mileage rate to figure the deductible amount. The standard mileage rate is 65.5 cents per mile in 2023. Whether you deduct the standard mileage rate or actual expenses, you may also deduct parking fees and tolls.

EXAMPLES

1. You drive home from work, and two nights a week for one month you drive from home to attend a refresher course. The course is considered temporary. You may deduct the round-trip transportation costs between home and school. The deduction is allowed regardless of how far you travel.

    If you went directly from work to the school, you may deduct transportation from work to school, and from school to home.

2. On six consecutive Saturdays, which are nonworkdays for you, you drive from home to attend a qualifying course. This is considered a temporary course. You are allowed a deduction for round-trip transportation between home and school, even though you are traveling on a nonworkday.

3. Assume that in Example 1, you took classes twice a week for 15 months instead of one month. The IRS does not consider the course to be temporary. You may deduct the cost of going directly from work to school, but the costs of going between home and school are nondeductible to the extent they exceed the cost of going to school directly from work.

Travel and living expenses away from home. "Away from home" has a special tax meaning *(20.7)*. You are not away from home unless you are away overnight. If you are away from home to attend a qualifying course, you may deduct the cost of travel to and from the site of the course, plus lodging and 50% of meals while you are there.

Expenses of sightseeing, social visiting, and entertaining while taking courses are not deductible. If personal reasons are your main purpose in going to the vicinity of the school, such as to take a vacation, you may deduct only the cost of the courses and your living expenses while attending school. You may not deduct the rest of your travel costs.

To determine the purpose of your trip, an IRS agent will pay close attention to the amount of time devoted to personal activities relative to the time devoted to the courses using data such as social media posts.

Is travel itself a form of education? You generally may not deduct the cost of an "educational" trip to another state or country. Although a trip may have educational value, the IRS position is a specific statute, Code Section 274(m)(2), baring a deduction for travel as a form of education. For example, an architect who travels to Rome to look at buildings usually cannot deduct travel costs as an education expense.

There may be exceptions where specific research can only be accomplished at a particular location, but a trip for "general" educational purposes does not qualify according to the IRS. For example, if the architect takes a course on architecture at a university in Rome (and otherwise meets the requirements outlined earlier in *33.14* and *33.15*), then education costs (e.g., tuition, travel costs) may be deductible.

CHAPTER 34

Special Tax Rules for Senior Citizens and the Disabled

All of your Social Security benefits are tax free if your "provisional income," explained in *34.3*, is $25,000 or less if you are single, or $32,000 or less if you are married and file a joint return. No more than 50% of your benefits are subject to tax if you file a joint return and your provisional income is over $32,000 but no more than $44,000, or if you are single and your provisional income is over $25,000 but no more than $34,000. When provisional income exceeds $34,000 or $44,000 (depending on your filing status), no more than 85% of your benefits are subject to tax. If you are married and filing separately, and did not live apart for the whole year, you must apply the 85% rate without considering the base amounts. If you are married filing separately and you lived apart the entire year, are a head of household, or are a qualifying widow/widower, use the $25,000 and $34,000 amounts for single persons.

If you are receiving Social Security benefits but continue to earn wages or self-employed income, you must pay FICA taxes or self-employment tax on that income regardless of your age.

If you are on Medicare, be sure you understand the impact of adjusted gross income on your premiums *(34.10)*.

If you are disabled, you may be receiving Social Security and other benefits. The tax rules for Social Security disability payments are the same as for Social Security retirement payments. Other government benefits may be tax free *(34.11)*.

Those who become disabled at a young age may be able to have a special savings account, called an ABLE account, which does not prevent eligibility for government programs, such as Medicaid *(34.12)*.

34.1 Senior Citizens Get Certain Filing Breaks

The following special tax rules favor senior citizens:

- **Special tax form.** If you are age 65 or older, you can use Form 1040-SR as your income tax return. The form has a larger type size and includes a table of the standard deduction amounts, including additional amounts for age and/or blindness. Otherwise, Form 1040-SR is identical to Form 1040; the line entries are the same. Use of the form is optional; you can choose to file Form 1040 instead (although if you self-prepare your return using tax preparation software, it will default to Form 1040-SR based on your age).

- **Higher filing thresholds.** If you are single and age 65 or older on or before January 1, 2024, you do not have to file a 2023 return unless your gross income is over $15,700. This is $1,850 more than for younger taxpayers. If you are married and you and your spouse are both age 65 or older, a joint return does not have to be filed unless your gross income is over $30,700, or $29,200 or over if only one of you is age 65 or older; *see* the chart on page 2 for further details.

- **Higher standard deduction.** If you are age 65 or older on or before January 1, 2024, you receive an additional standard deduction for 2023 if you do not itemize deductions. If you are single, your 2023 standard deduction is increased by $1,850, or by $1,500 if you are married or a qualifying widow/widower *(13.4)*. Your 2023 standard deduction is $15,700 if you are single. If married filing jointly, it is $29,200 if one of you is age 65 or over, or $30,700 if both of you are *(13.4)*.

- **Social Security benefits may be exempt from tax.** The taxable portion of your Social Security benefits may vary from year to year because it depends on an amount called "provisional income" *(34.3)*. If you are married and file jointly, none of your net Social Security benefits are taxable if your provisional income is not more than a base amount of $32,000. The base amount is $25,000 if your filing status is single, head of household, qualifying widow/widower, or you are married filing separately and did not live with your spouse at any time during the year. Married persons who file separately and live together at any time during the year are not allowed any base amount; *see 34.3* for computing taxable Social Security benefits.

- **Tax credit if age 65 or older.** This is a minimal tax credit for taxpayers age 65 or older who receive little or no Social Security or Railroad Retirement benefits and for individuals under age 65 who are totally disabled with extremely low incomes *(34.7)*. If you are single, or married but only you are eligible, and receive more than $416 each month from Social Security, you may not claim the credit. If you are married and both you and your spouse are eligible for the credit and file a joint return, you may not claim the credit if you receive more than $625 each month from Social Security.

34.2 Social Security Benefits Subject to Tax

If you received or repaid Social Security benefits in 2023, you will receive Form SSA-1099 from the Social Security Administration, showing the total benefits paid to you and any benefits you repaid to the government in 2023. Box 3 of Form SSA-1099 shows the total benefits paid to you in 2023. This may include, in addition to Social Security retirement benefits, survivor and disability benefits, which are subject to the same tax rules as retirement benefits. Also included in the Box 3 total are amounts withheld from your benefits for Medicare premiums, workers' compensation offset, or attorneys' fees for handling your Social Security claim; these and other withholdings are itemized in the "description" section below Box 3. However, Box 3 does not include Supplemental Security Income (SSI), which is not taxable.

The net benefit shown in Box 5 of Form SSA-1099 (benefits paid from Box 3 less benefits repaid, if any, from Box 4) is the benefit amount used to determine the taxable portion of your benefits (if any) *(34.3)*. Keep Form SSA-1099 for your records; do not attach it to your return.

Railroad Retirement benefits. The portion of your Tier 1 Railroad Retirement benefits that is equivalent to Social Security retirement benefits is subject to the computation for determining taxable benefits *(34.3)*. If any part of your 2023 Tier 1 benefits is equivalent to Social Security benefits, you will receive Form RRB-1099 from the government. The net Social Security Equivalent Benefit shown on Form RRB-1099 is the amount used to determine taxable benefits *(34.3)*. Other Tier 1 Railroad Retirement benefits, as well as Tier 2 benefits, are treated as pension income and not as Social Security benefits for tax purposes.

Planning Reminder

Voluntary Withholding on Social Security Benefits

You can use your Social Security benefits to meet your estimated and final tax liability by electing on Form W-4V to have tax withheld from benefits at a 7%, 10%, 12%, or 22% rate.

Benefits paid on behalf of child or incompetent. If a child is entitled to Social Security benefits, such as after the death of a parent, the benefit is considered to be the child's regardless of who actually receives the payment. Whether the child's benefit is subject to tax will depend on the amount of the child's income.

Medicare premiums deducted from benefits. The Medicare premiums deducted from your benefits are included in the total for benefits paid in Box 3 of Form SSA-1099. This includes premiums for Medicare Parts B, C, and D. The premiums do not reduce the net benefits in Box 5 used to figure taxable benefits *(34.3)*.

Workers' compensation. If you are receiving Social Security disability payments and workers' compensation for the same disability, your Social Security benefits may be reduced in order for the total benefits to stay within an overall limit. The combined monthly total of the workers' compensation and Social Security disability cannot exceed 80% of your "average current earnings" before you became disabled. If the total exceeds 80%, your Social Security disability benefits are reduced by the excess amount. The reduction continues until you reach your full retirement age *(34.5)*.

However, when your Social Security disability benefits are reduced under the 80% rule, the amount reported to you in Box 3 of Form SSA-1099 as "benefits paid" includes the reduction. Box 3 will include the reduction (it will be labeled as "workers' compensation offset" in the description section below Box 3) as a "benefit paid" to you although you did not receive it. For purposes of the computation steps to determine taxability of benefits *(34.3)*, you treat the full amount shown in Box 3 as your Social Security benefits.

In several cases, disabled workers whose Social Security disability benefits were reduced because they received workers' compensation argued that since the workers' compensation payments are tax free *(2.13)*, the portion of Social Security benefits not paid to them because of the overall limit should also be tax free. The Tax Court however agreed with the IRS that for purposes of figuring the tax on Social Security benefits *(34.3)*, the specific terms of the tax code include the reduction for workers' compensation as a Social Security benefit that must be taken into account.

Net benefits. The net benefit shown in Box 5 of Form SSA-1099 is the amount used to determine the taxable portion of your benefits. If Box 5 shows a negative amount (a figure in parentheses), none of your benefits are taxable. If the negative amount is related to Social Security benefits included in gross income in a prior year, you may be entitled to a deduction or a credit; *see* IRS Publication 915 for further instructions on how to figure the deduction or credit when your repayments exceed your gross benefits.

Taxable Social Security benefits are not considered earnings and therefore may not be the basis of an IRA contribution *(8.2)*, Earned Income Credit *(25.6)*, or foreign earned income exclusion *(36.2)*.

Nonresident aliens. Unless provided otherwise by tax treaty, 85% of a nonresident alien's Social Security benefits will be subject to the 30% withholding tax imposed on U.S. source income that is not connected with a U.S. trade or business. *See* IRS Publication 915 for further details.

34.3 Computing Taxable Social Security Benefits

To calculate the taxable part of your Social Security benefits you must determine your provisional income *(see Worksheet 34-1)* and compare it to the base amount and adjusted base amount allowed for your filing status *(see Table 34-1)*. Provisional income is not an amount you find on your tax return; it is only relevant to the computation of your Social Security benefits. As detailed below in *Worksheet 34-1*, provisional income will always be more than the "total income" reported on your return because you have to increase your reported income by 50% of your net Social Security benefits, tax-exempt interest if any, and certain other fringe benefits and above-the-line adjustments claimed on your return.

Overview of rules for taxation of Social Security benefits

The benefits that are potentially subject to tax are your net benefits, shown in Box 5 of Form SSA-1099 (or Form RRB-1099). If your provisional income (figured on *Worksheet 34-1* below) does not exceed your base amount (from *Table 34-1* below), none of your benefits are taxable. Thus, if you are single and your provisional income does not exceed $25,000, or you are married filing jointly and your provisional income does not exceed $32,000, you are not taxed on any of your Social Security benefits. However, you cannot avoid tax on your benefits if you are married filing separately and you lived with your spouse at any time during the year, because the law does not allow you any base amount or adjusted base amount.

If you are subject to the $25,000 or $32,000 base amount *(Table 34-1* below*).* If you are subject to the $25,000 or $32,000 base amount *(Table 34-1* below*)*, and your provisional income exceeds your base amount but does not exceed your $34,000 or $44,000 adjusted base amount *(Table 34-1)*, the taxable amount of benefits will generally equal 50% of the excess of your provisional income over the base amount, and in no event can the taxable amount be more than 50% of your net benefits. Use *Worksheet 34-2* to figure the exact amount of your taxable benefits. Example 3 illustrates the computation.

If your provisional income exceeds your $34,000 or $44,000 adjusted base amount, the taxable portion of your benefits depends on the excess, but in no event can the taxable amount exceed 85% of your net benefits. Use *Worksheet 34-3* to figure the exact amount of your taxable benefits. Examples 2 and 4 illustrate the computation.

If you are married filing separately with no base amount. If you are married filing separately and you lived with your spouse at any time during the year, your base amount and adjusted base amount is $0 *(Table 34-1* below*)*, and you are subject to the most disadvantageous rule for figuring taxable benefits. You must include in your taxable income the lesser of (1) 85% of your net Social Security benefits, or (2) 85% of your provisional income. Use *Worksheet 34-4* to figure the exact amount of taxable benefits.

Publication 590-Worksheets and IRA contributions. Do not use *Worksheet 34-2*, *Worksheet 34-3* or *Worksheet 34-4* to figure your taxable Social Security benefits for 2023 if (1) you made or are planning to make a contribution to a traditional IRA *(8.4)* for 2023, and (2) you or your spouse is an active participant *(8.5)* in an employer plan for 2023. In that case, you must use three worksheets in Appendix B of IRS Publication 590-A. The first worksheet is used to determine the amount of Social Security benefits that would be subject to tax if no IRA deduction were claimed. That taxable Social Security amount (if any) is included in MAGI on the second worksheet in order to figure if your IRA deduction is affected by the deduction phaseout rules *(8.4)* for active plan participants. Finally, the allowable IRA deduction from the second worksheet is included in the third worksheet to compute the taxable portion of your Social Security benefits.

Caution

Married Filing Separately

If you are married filing separately and you lived with your spouse at any time during the year, you must include in your taxable income the lesser of (1) 85% of your net Social Security benefits, or (2) 85% of your provisional income.

Table 34-1 Base Amount and Adjusted Base Amount*

Filing Status	Base Amount	Adjusted Base Amount
Single, head of household, qualifying widow/widower, or married filing separately and you lived apart from your spouse for the entire year	$25,000	$34,000
Married filing jointly	$32,000	$44,000
Married filing separately and you lived with your spouse at any time during the year	$0	$0

*NOTE: The base amounts and adjusted base amounts are fixed by statute and are not adjusted for inflation.

Worksheet 34-1 Figure Your Provisional Income

1. Enter your net Social Security benefits, the amount shown in Box 5 of all of your Forms SSA-1099 and RRB-1099. If married filing jointly, total the Box 5 amounts for you and your spouse. Enter the net benefits on Line 6a of your Form 1040 or 1040-SR.   1. _____

2. Enter one-half of the net benefits on Line 1 (50% × Line 1).   2. _____

3. Enter the "total income" from your return, without taking into account any Social Security benefits. In other words, enter the total shown on Line 9 of your Form 1040 or 1040-SR, disregarding net Social Security benefits reported on Line 6a of your return.   3. _____

4. Enter the tax-exempt interest received for the year, if any (should be included on Line 2a of Form 1040 or 1040-SR).   4. _____

5. Enter the total of the following amounts, if any: adoption benefits excluded from income (Form 8839), Series EE or I Savings Bond interest excluded from income (Form 8815), foreign earned income exclusion, foreign housing exclusion, foreign housing deduction (from Form 2555), excludable income from Puerto Rico or American Samoa (Form 4563).   5. _____

6. Add Lines 2, 3, 4 and 5. The total is your provisional income if you did not claim any above-the-line deductions on your return (deductions that reduce total income to arrive at adjusted gross income (12.2). If you claimed such deductions on Schedule 1 of Form 1040 or 1040-SR, go to Line 7.   6. _____

7. Enter the total of the above-the-line deductions that you reported on Schedule 1 and entered on Line 10 of Form 1040 or 1040-SR, but do NOT include the student loan interest deduction.   7. _____

8. If there is an amount on Line 7, subtract Line 7 from Line 6. If Line 7 is blank, enter the amount from Line 6. This is your provisional income.   8. _____

Worksheet 34-2 Figure Your Taxable Benefits if Your Provisional Income Exceeds the $25,000 or $32,000 Base Amount But Not the $34,000 or $44,000 Adjusted Base Amount

1. Excess provisional income:
   a. Enter your provisional income from Line 8 of *Worksheet 34-1*   _____
   b. Enter your base amount ($25,000 or $32,000; *see Table 34-1*)   _____
   c. Subtract b from a and enter your excess provisional income here   1c. _____

2. Multiply Line 1c by 50%.   2. _____

3. Enter 50% of your net Social Security benefits (Line 2 of *Worksheet 34-1*).   3. _____

4. The smaller of Line 2 or Line 3 is taxable. Enter the smaller amount as your taxable Social Security benefits here and on Line 6b of Form 1040 or 1040-SR.   4. _____

Worksheet 34-3 Figure Your Taxable Benefits if Your Provisional Income Exceeds the $34,000 or $44,000 Adjusted Base Amount

1. Excess provisional income:
   a. Enter your provisional income from Line 8 of *Worksheet 34-1*   _____
   b. Enter your adjusted base amount ($34,000 or $44,000; *see Table 34-1*)   _____
   c. Subtract b from a and enter your excess provisional income here   _____   1c. _____

2. Multiply Line 1c by 85%.   2. _____

3. Enter your net Social Security benefits (Line 1 of *Worksheet 34-1*).   3. _____

4. Multiply Line 3 by 85%.   4. _____

5. If Line 4 is more than Line 2, leave this line blank and complete Lines 6-8. If Line 4 is less than Line 2, or if Line 4 is equal to Line 2, 85% of your net Social Security benefits, shown on Line 4, is taxable. This is the maximum amount of benefits that can be taxed under the law. Enter the Line 4 amount as your taxable Social Security benefits here and on Line 6b of Form 1040 or 1040-SR. Do not complete Lines 6–8.   5. _____

6. If Line 5 is blank, enter the smaller of (a) or (b):
   (a) $6,000 if your adjusted base amount is $44,000, or $4,500 if your adjusted base amount is $34,000 (*see Table 34-1*), OR
   (b) 50% of Line 3 (i.e., 50% of your net Social Security benefits)   6. _____

7. Add Line 2 and Line 6.   7. _____

8. The smaller of Line 4 or Line 7 is taxable. Enter the smaller amount as your taxable Social Security benefits here and on Line 6b of Form 1040 or 1040-SR.   8. _____

Worksheet 34-4 Figure Your Taxable Benefits if You Are Married Filing Separately and You Lived With Your Spouse at Any Time During the Year

1. Enter your net Social Security benefits (Line 1 of *Worksheet 34-1*).   1. _____

2. Multiply Line 1 by 85%.   2. _____

3. Enter your provisional income (Line 8 of *Worksheet 34-1*).   3. _____

4. Multiply Line 3 by 85%.   4. _____

5. The smaller of Line 2 or Line 4 is taxable. Enter the smaller amount as your taxable Social Security benefits here and on Line 6b of Form 1040 or 1040-SR.   5. _____

EXAMPLES

1. Frank Adams, who is single and age 68, has 2023 earnings of $14,000 from a part-time job, $500 of interest income, and $1,700 of dividends. He also receives $15,800 of net Social Security benefits (Box 5 of Form SSA-1099). Frank's provisional income, figured on *Worksheet 34-1*, is $24,100 ($14,000 + $500 + $1,700 + $7,900 [50% of the $15,800 net Social Security benefits]). Since provisional income of $24,100 does not exceed the base amount of $25,000 for single taxpayers *(Table 34-1)*, none of Frank's Social Security benefits are taxable.

2. Same facts as Example 1 except that Frank also has a pension of $24,950. This raises his provisional income from $24,100 to $49,050 ($24,950 + $14,000 + $500 + $1,700 + $7,900 [50% of the $15,800 net Social Security benefits]). His provisional income exceeds the adjusted base amount for single taxpayers of $34,000 *(Table 34-1)*. On *Worksheet 34-3*, he figures that $13,430 of his $15,800 of net benefits are subject to tax. Here are Frank's line entries on *Worksheet 34-3*:

1.	Provisional income in excess of $34,000 adjusted base amount ($49,050 – $34,000)	$ 15,050
2.	85% of Line 1	12,793
3.	Net Social Security benefits	15,800
4.	85% of Line 3	13,430
5.	Leave blank because Line 4 is more than Line 2	
6.	Smaller of (a) $4,500 (because adjusted base amount is $34,000), or (b) $7,900 (50% of $15,800 net benefits)	4,500
7.	Add Lines 2 and 6	17,293
8.	Smaller of Line 4 or Line 7 is taxable	$13,430

Given these facts, 85% of Frank's net Social Security benefits, or $13,430, is taxable. Since 85% is the maximum taxable percentage under the law, the result would be the same even if Frank's provisional income was much higher than $49,050. The taxable amount of benefits would still be $13,430, equal to 85% of Frank's net benefits.

3. Sam and Fran Baker are both retired. In 2023, they receive net Social Security benefits (Box 5 of Form SSA-1099) of $27,600 between them. They have taxable pensions of $24,000, interest income of $300, dividends of $750 and tax-exempt interest of $1,200. They file a joint return on Form 1040. Their provisional income, figured on *Worksheet 34-1*, is $40,050 ($24,000 + $300 + 750 + $1,200 + $13,800 [50% of the $27,600 net Social Security benefits]). Their provisional income exceeds the base amount of $32,000 for married persons filing jointly *(Table 34-1)*, but not the adjusted base amount of $44,000 *(Table 34-1)*. On *Worksheet 34-2*, Sam and Fran determine that $4,025 of their benefits are subject to tax. Here are Sam and Fran's line entries on *Worksheet 34-2*:

1.	Provisional income in excess of $32,000 base amount ($40,050 – $32,000)	$ 8,050
2.	50% of Line 1	4,025
3.	50% of net Social Security benefits	13,800
4.	Smaller of Line 2 or Line 3 is taxable	4,025

Note that the taxable amount of $4,025 represents only 14.58% of Sam and Fran's net benefits ($4,025/$27,600); the other 85.42% of net benefits are not taxable.

4. Same facts as Example 3 except that Sam and Fran have taxable pensions of $60,000 instead of $24,000. This raises their provisional income by $36,000 to $76,050 ($60,000 + $300 + 750 + $1,200 + $13,800 [50% of the $27,600 net Social Security benefits]). Since their provisional income exceeds their adjusted base amount of $44,000 *(Table 34-1)*, they use *Worksheet 34-3* to figure the amount of their taxable benefits and determine that 85% of their $27,600 net benefits, or $23,460, is subject to tax. 85% is the maximum taxable percentage under the law.

Here are Sam and Fran's line entries on *Worksheet 34-3*:

1.	Provisional income in excess of $44,000 adjusted base amount ($76,050–$44,000)	$ 32,050
2.	85% of Line 1	27,243
3.	Net Social Security benefits	27,600
4.	85% of Line 3	23,460
5.	Line 4 is taxable because it is less than Line 2. Lines 6-8 of *Worksheet 34-3* do not have to be completed	23,460

Given these facts, 85% of Sam and Fran's net Social Security benefits, or $23,460, is taxable. Since 85% is the maximum taxable percentage under the law, the result would be the same even if Sam and Fran's provisional income was much higher than $76,050. The taxable amount of benefits would still be $23,460, equal to 85% of their net benefits.

34.4 Election for Lump-Sum Social Security Benefit Payment

If in 2023 you receive a lump-sum payment of Social Security benefits (whether retirement or disability benefits) covering prior years, you have a choice as to how to determine the taxable portion of the benefits: (1) You may treat the entire payment as a 2023 benefit taxable under the regular rules *(34.3)*, or (2) you may allocate the benefits between 2023 and the earlier years. Choose the method that provides the lowest required increase to income in the current year. For example, if you receive a 2023 lump-sum payment that includes benefits for 2022, you may find that an allocation of benefits is advantageous where your income over the two-year period has fluctuated and benefits allocated to 2022 would be subject to a lower taxable percentage than if they were treated as 2023 benefits.

When you elect to allocate benefits to a prior year, you do not amend the return for that year. You compute the increase in income (if any) that would have resulted if the Social Security benefits had been received in that prior year. You then add that amount to the income of the current year.

See IRS Publication 915 for instructions and worksheets for making the allocation and figuring the amount to be reported on your return.

34.5 Retiring on Social Security Benefits

Retirement benefits are not paid automatically. You should file for Social Security retirement benefits three months before you want to start receiving benefits. The age for receiving full Social Security benefits depends on the year you were born, as shown in the Law Alert on page 642. For example, if you were born in 1957, your full Social Security retirement age is 66 and six months, which you will reach in 2023 if your birthday is in January through June, or in 2024 if your birthday is in July through December. Reduced benefits may be elected if you are at least age 62. The reduction for starting benefits early depends on the number of months between the start date and your full Social Security retirement age. For example, if you were born in 1961 and elect benefits at age 62 in 2023, your benefit will be 70% of what it would have been at your full retirement age of 67. Even though your full Social Security retirement age is over 65, you should register with the Social Security Administration three months before the month in which you turn age 65 to ensure Medicare coverage.

If you delay benefits beyond full Social Security retirement age, your Social Security benefit increases 8% for each year you delay retirement. The increase for delaying benefits no longer applies once you reach age 70.

Benefits before reaching full retirement age may be reduced because of earnings. If you are under full retirement age and are receiving benefits, $1 of benefits will be deducted for each $2 earned above an annual limit. In 2023, the limit was $21,240. The 2024 limit will be listed in the *e-Supplement* at *jklasser.com*. For the year you reach full retirement age, $1 of benefits is deducted for each $3 earned over a different limit. For example, if in 2023 you reached your full Social Security retirement age of 66 and five months, benefits were reduced $1 for every $3 of earnings over $56,520, but only earnings before the month in which you

Law Alert

Social Security Retirement Age

The retirement age for receiving full Social Security benefits has gradually increased over the years. For those born in 1943 through 1954 it was age 66. It was 66 and two months if born in 1955 and 66 and four months if born in 1956. Thus, if you were born in 1956 before September, you reached full retirement age in 2022, or if born in September through December, you reached full retirement age of 66 and four months in early 2023. Full retirement age will continue to increase to 67, as shown below. If you were born on the first of the month, Social Security treats your birthday as if it were in the previous month.

Birth year—	Full Social Security retirement age—
1957	66 and 6 months
1958	66 and 8 months
1959	66 and 10 months
1960 and after	67

reached age 66 and four months are counted. Starting with the month in which you reach full retirement age, you are entitled to full benefits with no limit on how much you may earn.

There is also a favorable rule for the first year of retirement. A full benefit may be received for any month in which your earnings do not exceed 1/12 of the annual limit, even if the yearly limit is exceeded. However, this special rule does not apply for any month in which you are self-employed and devote over 45 hours to the business, or between 15 and 45 hours if your business involves a highly skilled profession.

So long as you continue to work, you pay Social Security taxes on your earnings, regardless of your age, so the additional earnings can increase your benefits if the year is one of your top-35 years of earnings. In addition, after you reach full retirement age, you will be given credit for any months in which you did not receive a benefit because of your earnings.

Regardless of your age, you may receive any amount of income from sources other than work—for example, pensions or investments—without affecting the amount of Social Security retirement benefits.

EXAMPLES

1. Jones retires and begins receiving reduced Social Security benefits in January 2023 at age 62. Without regard to earnings, he is entitled to receive $975 a month ($11,700 annually). He takes a part time job in May and for the year earns $26,480, which is $5,240 over the $21,240 limit for 2023. Under the regular benefit reduction rule, Jones would lose $2,620 of benefits ($1 for every $2 of earnings over $21,240). However, since this is his first year of retirement, a full benefit is paid for any month in which earnings were $1,770 (1/12 of $21,240) or less.

2. Smith, who was born in April 1957 and began receiving benefits at age 62, reaches full retirement age of 66 and four months in August 2023. Without regard to earnings, he would be entitled to monthly benefits of $1,850. He was fully employed during the year, earning $58,480 before August and $22,500 for the remainder of the year. The benefit reduction applies to his pre-August benefits. He earned $1960 over the $56,520 limit and loses $653 of benefits ($1 for every $3 earned over $56,520). Starting with his benefit for August, his monthly benefit is not reduced regardless of the amount of his earnings.

34.6 How Tax on Social Security Reduces Your Earnings

There is an added tax cost of earning income if the earnings will subject your Social Security benefits to tax. Therefore, if your benefits are not currently exposed to tax, you have to figure not only the tax on the extra income but also the amount of Social Security benefits subjected to tax by those earnings. If the additional earnings will put you over the base amount (34.3), then you will not only have to pay tax on the additional earnings but also on the Social Security benefits that will be subject to tax.

EXAMPLES

1. You are over full Social Security retirement age (34.5) and you and your spouse receive net Social Security benefits of $18,000. You file jointly. You have pension income of $21,900, taxable interest of $500 and $400 in tax-exempt interest. Your provisional income (34.3) is $31,800. No part of your Social Security benefits is taxable because your provisional income of $31,800 does not exceed the $32,000 base amount for married persons filing jointly.

2. Same facts as in Example 1, except that you take a part-time job paying $7,000. This increases your provisional income to $38,800 and subjects $3,400 of Social Security benefits to tax, following the steps of Worksheet 34-2 on page 638.

Provisional income	$38,800
Less: Base amount	32,000
Excess	$6,800
Taxable Social Security benefits: 50% of $6,800 excess (see Worksheet 34-2)	$3,400

> The $7,000 of additional earnings increases your taxable income by $10,400, which is the $7,000 of earnings plus the $3,400 of Social Security benefits made taxable because of the increase in provisional income.

34.7 Eligibility for the Credit for the Elderly or the Disabled

The tax credit for the elderly or disabled can be claimed by very few taxpayers. You can qualify for a 2023 credit only if your income is extremely low and you meet one of the following conditions:

- Your 65th birthday is on or before January 1, 2024; or
- You were under age 65 at the end of 2023, you retired before the end of 2023 because of permanent and total disability, you received taxable disability income in 2023 from your former employer's disability plan, and you had not reached mandatory retirement age from the employer plan as of January 1, 2023. Disability income is taxable wages or payments in lieu of wages paid to you while you are absent from work because of permanent and total disability.

You will not be able to claim any credit if your Social Security benefits or adjusted gross income is "too high," or if you have no tax liability *(34.8)*.

Disabled. You must be considered permanently and totally disabled, which means you are unable to engage in any substantial gainful activity by reason of any medically determinable physical or mental impairment that can be expected to result in death or that has lasted or can be expected to last for a continuous period of not less than 12 months.

For the first year you claim the credit, you need a physician's certification of your disability. For later years, new certifications are generally not required.

Married couples. If you are married, the credit generally may be claimed only if you file jointly. However, if you and your spouse live apart at all times during the taxable year, a qualifying spouse may claim the credit on a separate return.

Nonresident aliens. You may not claim the credit if you are a nonresident alien at any time during the year, unless you are married to a citizen or resident and you have elected to be treated as a resident *(1.5)*.

34.8 Figuring the Credit for the Elderly or Disabled

The credit is figured on Schedule R, which you attach to Form 1040 or 1040-SR if any amount is allowed. The law specifies an initial base amount for figuring the credit. This base amount is reduced by nontaxable Social Security and other tax-free pensions, as well as by adjusted gross income exceeding specific limits. The 15% credit amount applies to the reduced base amount, but the resulting credit is allowed only to the extent it does not exceed your tax liability. These limitations are discussed below.

The initial base amount is:

- $5,000, if you are single, head of household, or are a qualifying widow/widower age 65 or over. If you are under age 65 and retired on permanent and total disability, the base amount is the lower of your taxable disability income or $5,000.
- $5,000, if you file a joint return and only one spouse is eligible for the credit (the eligible spouse is either age 65 or older or under 65 but retired on permanent and total disability).
- $7,500, if you file a joint return and both spouses are 65 or over. The credit is figured solely on this base; a separate computation is not made for each spouse. If one of you is age 65 or over and the other is under age 65 and retired on total disability, the initial base amount is the lesser of (1) $7,500 or (2) $5,000 plus the taxable disability income of the spouse under age 65. If both of you are under age 65 and retired on permanent and total disability, the initial base amount is the lower of your combined taxable disability income or $7,500.
- $3,750, if you are married filing a separate return and you lived apart from your spouse the entire year, and you are either age 65 or older or under 65 but retired on permanent and total disability.

Law Alert

Lack of Inflation Adjustment Severely Limits Credit

Since 1983, the base amounts and AGI phaseout thresholds *(34.8)* for figuring the credit for the elderly or disabled have remained the same while inflation adjustments and tax law changes have reduced tax liability. Since the credit cannot exceed tax liability, the number of taxpayers able to claim the credit has dropped drastically and continues to decline annually.

Caution

Low Social Security Benefits Required for Credit

The tax credit for the elderly or disabled is not available to an unmarried individual who receives $5,000 or more of nontaxable Social Security benefits or nontaxable federal pensions such as from the Veterans Administration. The $5,000 limit also applies if you are married filing jointly and only one spouse qualifies for the credit. The limit is $7,500 if you file a joint return and both spouses qualify for the credit.

Nontaxable Social Security and pensions reduce the base amount. The base amount is reduced by:

- Social Security and Railroad Retirement benefits that are not taxable *(34.3)*; and
- Tax-free pension, annuity, or disability income paid under a law administered by the Veterans Administration (but not military disability pensions) or under other federal laws.

The base amount is not reduced by military disability pensions received for active service in the armed forces of any country, disability pensions for active service in the National Oceanic and Atmospheric Administration or Public Health Service, certain disability annuities paid under the Foreign Service Act of 1980, and workers' compensation benefits. But if Social Security benefits are reduced by workers' compensation benefits, the amount of workers' compensation benefits is treated as Social Security benefits that reduce the base.

Excess adjusted gross income reduces the base amount. You reduce the base amount by one-half of adjusted gross income (AGI) exceeding: $7,500 if you are single, head of household, or a qualifying widow/widower; $10,000 if you are married filing a joint return; or $5,000 if you are married, live apart from your spouse for the entire year, and file a separate return. Because of these income reductions, the credit is not available to a single person (or head of household or qualifying widow/widower) when AGI reaches $17,500, $20,000 on a joint return where one spouse is eligible for the credit, $25,000 on a joint return where both spouses are eligible for the credit, and $12,500 where a married person files separately.

15% credit limited by tax liability. After reducing the credit base amount as just discussed for nontaxable Social Security and pensions and excess AGI, the remaining credit base is multiplied by 15%. This is the maximum credit but where this amount exceeds tax liability, the credit is limited to the lesser liability, as in the Example below.

EXAMPLE

John Andrews is 58 years old and single. In 2015, he retired on permanent and total disability. In 2023, he receives a taxable disability pension of $13,800, nontaxable Social Security disability benefits of $1,400, and taxable interest of $300. Adjusted gross income (AGI) is $14,100 ($13,800 + $300). His taxable income after claiming the standard deduction ($13,850) is only $250 ($14,100 − $13,850). As shown below, the credit formula would allow a credit of $45, but the credit cannot exceed John's 2023 tax liability, which is $25 ($25 liability from Tax Table based on taxable income of $250).

Initial base amount	$5,000
Less: nontaxable Social Security disability	1,400
Less: 50% of AGI over $7,500 (50% of $6,600 [$14,100 AGI minus $7,500])	3,300
Credit base amount	$300
Credit (15% of $300 credit base amount)	$45
Tax liability limitation	$25

34.9 Tax Effects of Moving to a Continuing Care Facility

Senior citizens moving into "continuing care" or "life-care" facilities pay large upfront entrance fees upon admittance, and monthly fees thereafter in return for a residence, meals, and lifetime health care, including long-term skilled nursing care, should that become necessary.

Portion of monthly fees deductible as medical expense. Part of the monthly fees to a life-care community are allocable to health care. If you itemize deductions on Schedule A (Form 1040 or 1040-SR), you may include the allocable fee in your medical expenses (subject to the AGI floor), *(17.1)*. Continuing care facilities generally send a statement to the residents specifying the portion of their monthly service fees that went towards health care.

The IRS and Tax Court have approved the use of a "percentage method" for allocating the community's medical expenses among the residents. In general, the annual medical expenses of the community are divided by total operating expenses to get the medical care allocation percentage. In a particular case, the IRS could contest how the allocation is figured or how the allocated amount is divided among the residents.

For example, in a 2004 case (Baker, 122 TC 143), the IRS contested a couple's medical expense deduction for a portion of the monthly service fees paid for their two-bedroom duplex apartment, categorized as an "independent living unit" (ILU). Using a percentage method computation supplied by the resident council of their continuing care retirement community, the Bakers deducted $6,557 of their 1997 monthly service fees and $9,891 of their 1998 monthly fees as medical expenses. The IRS initially allowed a deduction for $4,488 of the 1997 fees and $5,142 of the 1998 fees using a different percentage method. Then, when the Bakers appealed to the Tax Court, the IRS argued that the deductible part of the service fees should be figured using an "actuarial method," which would increase the Bakers' two-year deduction by a few hundred dollars over what the examining agent had allowed.

However, the Tax Court refused to require use of the actuarial method, which requires projections of longevity and lifetime utilization of health-care services, and is so complicated that the IRS could not fully explain the method to the Court. The Court held that the percentage method is appropriate, noting that the IRS has approved use of the percentage method in rulings since 1967. However, in applying the percentage method to determine the Bakers' deductions, the Court had to resolve disputes over how certain expenses should be treated and how the allocated medical care percentage, once determined, should be split among the residents. For example, the Court held that the community's interest expenses, depreciation and amortization allowances should be included in both the numerator and denominator when dividing medical costs by operating costs to determine the medical care allocation percentage.

The Court calculated that 27.93% of the community's 1997 total costs and 30.07% of the 1998 costs were allocable to medical care. The Court then held that the Bakers could not simply multiply these percentages by the fees they paid to get their deductions. The same medical expense amount must be allocated to each ILU resident by multiplying the allocation percentage by a weighted average of the service fees paid each year by the ILU residents. The weighted average annual service fee for 1997 paid by the ILU residents was $13,902, which when multiplied by the allocation percentage of 27.93%, gave a medical care allocation of $3,883 per resident. For 1998, the weighted average annual service fee for ILU residents was $14,093, which when multiplied by the allocation percentage of 30.07%, gave a medical care allocation of $4,238 per resident. On their joint returns, the Bakers could treat double the per resident amounts as medical expenses; that is, $7,766 for 1997 and $8,476 for 1998.

Portion of nonrefundable entrance fee deductible as medical expense.

What about the upfront payments required by life-care communities? If an entrance fee or founder's fee for lifetime care is nonrefundable, part may be treated as a medical expense *(17.1)* if you can prove what part of the lump sum is allocable to future medical coverage. The IRS recognizes that a deduction may be based on a showing that the life-care facility historically allocates a specified percentage of the fee to future medical care. With such proof there is a current obligation to pay and the allocable amount is treated as a deductible medical expense when the lump sum is paid. The same rules apply if the life-care or founder's fee is paid monthly rather than as a lump sum.

Separate sponsorship gift.

In one case, an individual was allowed by the Tax Court and an appeals court to claim a charitable contribution deduction for a "sponsorship gift" paid to a life-care retirement facility where she and her husband were residents. The sponsorship gift was entirely separate from her entrance fee; it was not required for admission and did not entitle her to reduced monthly payments. She did not receive any extra benefit from her gift and was not entitled to a refund of any part of it.

 *Caution*

Charitable Contribution Deductions

Payments you make to a tax-exempt organization that operates a life-care community are generally not deductible as a charitable contribution if you are a resident receiving services in exchange for the payments. If you donate amounts over and above your regular monthly fees and do not receive any extra benefit as a result, you may deduct the excess payment as a charitable contribution *(14.3)*.

34.10 Medicare Part B and Part D Premiums for 2024

The standard monthly Medicare Part B premium for 2024 is $174.70, an increase of $9.80 per month from $164.90 in 2023. Individuals whose modified adjusted gross income for 2022 exceeded $103,000, or $206,000 if married filing jointly, must generally pay a surcharge for 2024 in addition to the standard premium. There are five surcharge brackets. Those subject to the Part B surcharge must also pay a surcharge with their Part D prescription drug plan premiums. *See* the *e-Supplement* at *jklasser.com* for a table showing the 2024 Part B premiums and surcharge amounts, and the Part D surcharges.

34.11 Special Tax Rules for Individuals with a Disability

The following special tax rules apply for individuals with a disability:

- *Higher standard deduction for the blind.* If you are completely blind, or partially blind with a note from an ophthalmologist or optometrist that vision is no better than $20/200$ in the better eye with corrective lenses or that the field of vision is 20 degrees or less, you can claim an additional standard deduction amount if you do not itemize personal deductions *(13.4)*. The additional amount for 2023 is $1,850 if you are single or head of household, or $1,500 if you are married filing jointly, married filing separately, or a qualifying widow(er).

- *Workers' compensation.* This benefit, which is paid because of an injury or illness sustained on a job, is usually tax free *(2.13)*.

- *Social Security disability benefits.* If you are a worker receiving Social Security benefits on account of disability, the benefits are taxed in the same way as benefits received by retirees *(34.3)*. If you also receive workers' compensation that reduces Social Security benefits, all of the benefits are treated as Social Security benefits, which may be partially includible in gross income.

- *Tax credit for the permanently disabled.* This is an extremely limited tax credit for seniors (age 65 and older) who receive little or no Social Security or Railroad Retirement benefits or who are under age 65 and who receive disability income for being permanently and totally disabled *(34.7)*.

- *ABLE accounts.* A special savings account can be used to pay for an array of qualified disability expenses *(34.12)*.

- *Impairment-related work expenses.* Unreimbursed work-related expenses incurred because of a disability are deductible on Schedule A (Form 1040 or 1040-SR) if you itemize deductions *(19.1)*.

- *Penalty-free distributions from qualified retirement plans and IRAs.* The 10% early distribution penalty does not apply for withdrawals made by someone who has a disability *(7.13, 8.12)*.

- *Extended period for refund claims.* The usual period for claiming a tax refund is suspended for someone unable to manage his or her financial affairs due to a disability *(47.2)*.

  Those who care for a disabled individual may qualify for special tax rules:

- *Dependent care credit.* Those who work and care for a spouse or child of any age who is physically or mentally incapable of self care may claim a dependent care credit *(25.4)*.

- *Earned income credit.* When claiming an Earned Income Credit, a disabled child is a qualifying child, regardless of age *(25.6)*.

- *Medical expenses.* Various costs for the care of a disabled person may qualify as a deductible medical expense *(17.1)*, including special schooling for a physically or mentally handicapped child.

34.12 ABLE Accounts

ABLE accounts (authorized by the Stephen Beck Jr. Achieving a Better Life Experience Act of 2014) allow contributions (nondeductible) to be made to tax-favored accounts for certain disabled individuals without causing them to lose eligibility for government programs, such as Medicaid. Earnings in an ABLE account are not taxed unless a distribution exceeds the beneficiary's qualified disability expenses for that year.

Setting up an ABLE account. Each state can establish ABLE accounts for its residents or for nonresidents. The person holding the disabled individual's power of attorney may establish an ABLE account if the beneficiary cannot do so, or the beneficiary's parent or guardian may do so if no one has power of attorney.

At the time an ABLE account is set up, evidence must be presented to the state that the beneficiary became blind or disabled before age 26 and is entitled to Social Security disability benefits; otherwise a disability certification, signed under penalties of perjury, and accompanied by a physician's diagnosis, must be submitted. Annual recertifications of disability must be made; check with the plan administrator for details because "deemed recertifications" may be permissible.

A beneficiary can have only one ABLE account, and when establishing an ABLE account, the beneficiary must check a box or otherwise verify, under penalties of perjury, that the account being established is his or her only ABLE account.

If a beneficiary establishes an ABLE account in a state and then moves to another state, the ABLE account can remain with the state in which the account was created although the beneficiary is no longer a resident. However, a program-to-program transfer or a 60-day rollover of a distribution to another state program is allowed; such transfers do not violate the rule prohibiting multiple ABLE accounts. A program-to-program transfer is not treated as a taxable distribution; a rollover is not taxable unless it is within 12 months of a prior ABLE account rollover.

Contributions. Nondeductible cash contributions can be made to an ABLE account by anyone, but the combined contributions for the year (not counting rollovers or program-to-program transfers) from all contributors generally may not exceed the annual gift tax exclusion, which for 2023 was $17,000. However, an additional annual contribution can be made for working beneficiaries, provided no contribution has been made for the beneficiary to a qualified retirement plan (401(k) plan, 403(a) qualified annuity plan, 403(b) plan, or 457(b) deferred compensation plan) for the year. The additional contribution can be up to the lesser of (1) the beneficiary's compensation for the year, or (2) the amount of the federal poverty line for a one-person household for the preceding year. The designated beneficiary, or a person acting on behalf of the designated beneficiary, is responsible for maintaining records regarding the beneficiary's compensation to ensure that the limit on the additional contribution is not exceeded.

A rollover may be made to an ABLE account from a Section 529 qualified tuition plan *(33.5)*, so long as the designated beneficiary of both accounts is the same, or the ABLE account owner is a family member of the Section 529 account designated beneficiary. However, the rollover is subject to the regular annual ABLE contribution limit, equal to the annual gift tax exclusion ($17,000 for 2023).

Contributions in excess of the annual contribution limit, plus earnings on the excess, must be returned by the administrator of the ABLE program to the contributors by the beneficiary's filing due date (including extensions) in order for the contributors to avoid a 6% penalty; the penalty is figured on Form 5329.

Contributions will be reported to the beneficiary and to the IRS on Form 5498-QA. Form 5498-QA will be issued even for years for which no contributions are made; the fair market value of the account as of the end of the year will be reported, and a code showing the basis of the beneficiary's eligibility will be included.

There is also an overall limit on contributions: aggregate contributions on behalf of an ABLE account beneficiary cannot exceed the state's limit for a Section 529 qualified tuition program *(33.5)*.

Distributions. ABLE account distributions are reported to the beneficiary (and the IRS) on Form 1099-QA. If the distributions for a year do not exceed the beneficiary's annual qualified disability expenses, they are not taxed. If the distributions exceed the qualifying expenses, the portion of the distributions allocable to earnings that are not attributable to qualifying expenses are taxable and also subject to a 10% penalty figured on Form 5329.

Caution

Disabled Person Must Be the Account Owner

A person other than the beneficiary who has signature authority over the ABLE account cannot have any interest in the account and must administer it for the benefit of the beneficiary.

Filing Tip

ABLE Contribution Qualifies for Tax Credit

If a beneficiary contributes to an ABLE account in 2023, the retirement savers credit may apply to the contribution. *See 25.11.*

Law Alert

Beneficiaries With Compensation

The contribution limit is increased for ABLE account beneficiaries with compensation, but only if they are not covered by a qualified employer retirement plan. For eligible beneficiaries, the regular contribution limit, equal to the annual gift tax exclusion ($17,000 in 2023), may be increased by up to the lesser of (1) the beneficiary's compensation for the year, or (2) the prior year federal poverty line amount for a one-person household.

For example, if the qualified disability expenses for the year are 70% of the ABLE account distributions, then 70% of the earnings portion of the distribution will be tax free and 30% of the earnings portion will be taxable and subject to the 10% penalty.

Form 1099-QA will show the gross distribution, the earnings portion of the distribution, and the basis (total contributions) allocable to the distribution. A box will be checked if a program-to-program transfer was made or if the ABLE account was terminated.

The IRS broadly defines the term "qualified disability expenses" in order to carry out Congress's intent to assist the beneficiaries in maintaining or improving their "health, independence, or quality of life." Thus, qualified disability expenses are not limited to medically necessary items, but may also include basic living costs. This includes education, housing, transportation, employment training and support, assistive technology, personal support services, wellness programs, financial management, and legal fees. An IRS example indicates that buying and maintaining a smart phone would be a qualified expense for a child with autism where it helps the child navigate and communicate more safely and effectively.

CHAPTER 35

Members of the Armed Forces

Special tax benefits are provided to Armed Forces personnel. A major tax-free benefit is the combat pay exclusion. Under this exclusion, members of the Armed Forces, including active duty reservists, may exclude from gross income all compensation for active service received for any month in which they served in a combat zone or were hospitalized as a result of any wound, injury, or disease incurred while serving in a combat zone. Commissioned officers are allowed an exclusion equal to the highest rate of basic pay at the top pay level for enlisted personnel, plus any hostile fire/imminent danger pay received for the month.

Other pay benefits may be tax free, and you may be able to get filing extensions and time extensions for home residence replacements. A list of tax-free benefits may be found in *35.2*. Filing extensions are discussed in *35.5*.

Combat zone designations apply to the following locations (and the airspace above, as well as designated "direct support" areas): The Sinai Peninsula, Iraq and neighboring areas in the "Arabian Peninsula," Afghanistan, and the Balkans Kosovo area *(35.4)*. From time to time, there are qualified hazardous duty areas which are treated the same as a combat zone. *See* the *e-Supplement* at *jklasser.com* for any later official designation(s).

35.1 Taxable Armed Forces Pay and Benefits

Armed Forces personnel report as taxable pay the following items:

- Basic pay for active duty, attendance at a designated service school, back wages, drills, reserve training, and training duty.
- Special pay for hazardous duty, hostile fire or imminent danger, aviation career incentives, diving duty, foreign duty (for serving outside the 48 contiguous states and the District of Columbia), medical and dental officers, nuclear-qualified officers, and special duty assignments.
- Enlistment and reenlistment bonuses.
- Payments for accrued leave, and personal money allowances paid to high-ranking officers.
- Student loan repayment from programs such as the Department of Defense Educational Loan Repayment Program when year's service is not attributable to a combat zone.

State income tax withholding. A state that makes a withholding agreement with the Secretary of the Treasury may subject members of the Armed Forces regularly stationed within that state to its payroll withholding provisions. National Guard members and reservists are not considered to be members of the Armed Forces for purposes of this section.

Where and when to file. If you file a paper return, mail it to the Internal Revenue Service Center for the place you are stationed. For example, you are stationed in Arizona but have a permanent home address in Missouri; you send your return to the Service Center for Arizona. For filing extensions on entering the service (35.7).

35.2 Tax Breaks for Armed Forces Members

Military personnel and their families may qualify for numerous tax benefits. Here is a summary of some key tax breaks. For further details, *see* IRS Publication 3 (Armed Forces' Tax Guide).

The following payments or allowances are not subject to tax:

- Combat pay (35.4). Although qualifying combat pay is not taxed, an election may be made to treat nontaxable combat pay (35.4) as earned income for purposes of the earned income tax credit (25.8).
- Living allowances for BAH (Basic Allowance for Housing). You may deduct mortgage interest and real estate taxes on your home even if you pay these expenses with BAH funds.
- BAS (Basic Allowance for Subsistence) living allowances.
- Housing and cost-of-living allowances abroad, whether paid by the U.S. Government or by a foreign government.
- VHA (Variable Housing Allowance).
- Family allowances for educational expenses for dependents, emergencies, evacuation to a place of safety, and separation.
- Death allowances for burial services, death gratuity payments to eligible survivors, and travel of dependents to burial site.
- Dislocation allowance, intended to partially reimburse expenses such as lease forfeitures, temporary living charges in hotels, and other expenses incurred in relocating a household.
- Temporary lodging expense allowance intended to partially offset the added living expenses of temporary lodging within the United States for up to 10 days and up to 60 days abroad.
- A moving-in housing allowance, intended to defray costs, such as for rental agent fees, home-security improvements, and supplemental heating equipment, associated with occupying leased space outside the United States.
- Travel allowances for annual round trip for dependent students, leave between consecutive overseas tours, reassignment in a dependent-restricted status, and transportation for you or your dependents during ship overhaul or inactivation.

Caution

Community Property

If you are married and your domicile (permanent home to which you intend to return) is in one of the following states, your military pay is subject to community property laws of that state: Arizona, California, Idaho, Louisiana, Nevada, New Mexico, Texas, Washington, and Wisconsin (and Alaska, Florida, Kentucky, Tennessee, and South Dakota for couples who opt in by law or through a trust to make their property community property). See *1.6* for community property reporting rules.

- Defense counseling payments.
- ROTC educational and subsistence allowances.
- Survivor and retirement protection plan premium payments.
- Uniform allowances paid to officers and uniforms furnished to enlisted personnel.
- Medical or hospital treatment provided by the United States in government hospitals.
- Pay forfeited on order of a court martial.
- Education, training, or subsistence allowances paid under any law administered by the Department of Veterans Affairs (VA). However, deductible education costs must be reduced by the VA allowance.
- Adjustments in pay to compensate for losses resulting from inflated foreign currency.
- Payments to former prisoners of war from the U.S. Government in compensation for inhumane treatment suffered at the hands of an enemy government.
- Benefits under Servicemembers' Group Life Insurance.
- Dividends on GI insurance. These are a tax-free return of premiums paid.
- Interest on dividends left on deposit with the Department of Veterans Affairs (VA).

Distributions to reservists. Reservists called to active duty for at least 180 days are not subject to the general 10% penalty for distributions before age 59½ from retirement plans and IRAs. They also are allowed in some cases to make withdrawals of unused benefits from a health flexible spending account. These rules are discussed further at *35.8*.

State and local bonuses may be tax free. Some states and municipalities pay bonuses to active or former military personnel or their dependents because of service in a combat zone. Such payments may be excludable from gross income under the combat pay rules at *35.4*.

Extended statute of limitations for disability determinations. Usually, a taxpayer must file for a refund claim *(47.2)* within three years of the due date of the return on which the income was reported. Payments from the government based on a service-connected disability are tax free, while payments based on length of service are taxable. The Department of Veterans Affairs may take a long time to make a disability determination, with the result that taxpayers may include the payments as income. Then, when they receive a favorable determination, they can file an amended return to receive a tax refund. A law allows the refund claim to be filed until one year after the date of a disability determination to file a refund claim if this date is later than the end of the three-year period of limitation.

Death benefits. Beneficiaries who receive military death gratuities or payments from the Servicemembers' Group Life Insurance (SGLI) program can roll these amounts over to a Roth IRA or Coverdell education savings account (ESA) within one year of receipt. The usual limits on contribution amounts and income limitations for Roth IRAs *(8.21)* and Coverdell ESAs *(33.11)* do not apply to these rollovers.

Veterans not taxed on payments from Compensated Work Therapy program. In response to a 2007 Tax Court decision that held payments made by the U.S. Department of Veterans Affairs (VA) to disabled veterans under the Compensated Work Therapy (CWT) program are tax-free veterans' benefits, the IRS reversed position and announced that it no longer treats CWT payments as taxable pay for services. Under the CWT program, the VA provides vocational rehabilitation services to veterans who have been unable to work and support themselves. The VA contracts with private industry and government agencies to provide these veterans with therapeutic work that emphasizes work skills training.

Disability retirement pay. Your disability retirement pay may be tax free if you are a former member of the Armed Forces of any country, the Foreign Service, the Coast Guard, the National Oceanic and Atmospheric Administration, or the Public Health Service *(2.14)*. Tax-free treatment of disability retirement pay is retroactive to the date of the application for benefits. But Social Security disability payments made on account of a combat-related injury are taxable to the same extent as Social Security retirement payments *(34.3)*.

 *Caution*

Withholding on Differential Wages Paid to Workers Joining Military

Employees who enlist or are called up to active military service for over 30 days may receive "differential wages" from their former employer to cover some or all of the difference between their military pay and the wages that were being received prior to joining the military. The differential wages are taxable and cannot be excluded as combat pay *(35.4)*. Income tax must be withheld from the differential wages, but not FICA tax (Social Security and Medicare). If the active duty is for 30 days or less, differential wages are subject to FICA tax withholding as well as to income tax withholding

35.3 Deductions for Armed Forces Personnel

For 2018 through 2025, members of the Armed Forces cannot deduct certain unreimbursed business expenses as miscellaneous itemized deductions subject to the 2% of adjusted gross income (AGI) floor because of the suspension of this deduction *(19.2)*. Expenses subject to the suspension include:

- Board and lodging costs over those paid to you by the government while on temporary duty away from your home base.
- Costs of rank insignia, collar devices, gold braids, etc., and the cost of altering rank insignia when promoted or demoted.
- Contributions to a "Company" fund made according to Service regulations. But personal contributions made to stimulate interest and morale in a unit are not deductible.
- Court martial legal expenses in successfully defending against the charge of conduct unbecoming an officer.
- Dues to professional societies.
- Expense of obtaining increased retirement pay.
- Subscriptions to professional journals.
- Transportation, food, and lodging expenses while on official travel status. But you are taxed on mileage and per diem subsistence allowance.
- Uniforms. The cost and cleaning of uniforms were deductible for years before 2018 if: (1) the uniform had to be worn on duty; (2) the uniform could not under military regulations be worn off duty; and (3) the cost exceeded any tax-free clothing allowance.

However, on Schedule 1 of Form 1040 or 1040-SR, there are two types of expenses you may deduct from gross income (no itemizing is required):

- Moving expenses. If you are on active duty and move pursuant to a military order and incident to a permanent change of station, you can deduct your moving expenses; report the expenses on Form 3903 and enter the allowable amount as an adjustment to income on Schedule 1 *(12.3)*. This includes a deduction for driving your vehicle at the rate of 22¢ per mile for all of 2023. You can also exclude from your income any in-kind moving and storage expenses you receive.
- Reservists expenses. If you travel overnight more than 100 miles from home in connection with your performance of services as a member of the reserves, and you use your vehicle for this travel, you can deduct your mileage at the rate of 65.5¢ per mile for all of 2023. You can also deduct the cost of lodging and meal costs up to the regular federal per diem rate. (Meal costs furnished at restaurants are 50% deductible in 2023.) Report the allowable travel costs on Form 2106 and enter the amount as an adjustment to income on Schedule 1 *(20.1, 35.8)*.

35.4 Tax-Free Pay for Service in Combat Zone

If your grade is below commissioned officer (you are an enlisted member, warrant officer or commissioned warrant officer) and you serve in a designated combat zone during any part of a month, all of your qualifying military pay *(see below)* for that month is excluded from your taxable income. You may also exclude military pay earned during any part of a month that you are hospitalized as a result of wounds, disease, or injury incurred in a combat zone. The exclusion for military pay while hospitalized does not apply to any month that begins more than two years after the end of combat activities in that combat zone. Your hospitalization does not have to be in the combat zone.

Officers. If you are a commissioned officer, you may exclude up to the highest rate of basic pay at the highest pay grade that enlisted personnel receive per month plus any hostile fire/imminent danger pay received for each month during any part of which you served in a combat zone or were hospitalized as a result of the combat zone service.

If you are a commissioned warrant officer, you are considered an enlisted person.

Filing Tip

Who Qualifies for Exclusion?

Members of the U.S. Armed Forces qualifying for the exclusion include commissioned officers and enlisted personnel in all regular and reserve units under control of the Secretaries of Defense, Army, Navy, Air Force, and Space Force, and the Coast Guard. Members of the U.S. Merchant Marines or the American Red Cross are not included.

What is included as tax-free combat pay? The following pay received as a member of the U.S. Armed Forces qualifies for tax-free treatment: (1) active duty pay earned in any month you served in a combat zone; (2) imminent danger / hostile fire pay; (3) a reenlistment bonus if the voluntary extension or reenlistment occurs in a month you served in a combat zone; (4) pay for accrued leave earned in any month you served in a combat zone (the Department of Defense must determine that the unused leave was earned during that period); (5) pay received for duties as a member of the Armed Forces in clubs, messes, post and station theaters, and other nonappropriated fund activities. The pay must be earned in a month you served in a combat zone; (6) awards for suggestions, inventions, or scientific achievements you are entitled to because of a submission you made in a month you served in a combat zone; and (7) student loan repayments earned for military service. For each month of combat zone service during the year, $\frac{1}{12}$ of the repayment for that year is considered tax-free combat zone pay.

Service in the combat zone includes any periods you are absent from duty because of sickness, wounds, or leave. If, as a result of serving in a combat zone, you become a prisoner of war or missing in action, you are considered to be serving in the combat zone as long as you keep that status for military pay purposes.

Retirement pay and pensions do not qualify for the combat zone exclusion. According to a Fourth Circuit Court of Appeals decision, a Navy severance pay package was taxable although the recipient became entitled to the payment while on active duty in the Persian Gulf. The court differentiated the package, which was provided in order to entice the man to leave the service, from a reenlistment bonus provided as compensation for active service.

Combat zones. A combat zone is any area the President of the United States designates by Executive Order as an area in which the U.S. Armed Forces are or have engaged in combat. An area becomes and ceases to be a combat zone on the dates designated by the President. When this book was completed, there were three designated combat zones: (1) the Afghanistan area, including countries in which military service has been certified by the Defense Department as in direct support of the operations in Afghanistan, (2) the Arabian Peninsula area (including part of Turkey), and (3) the Kosovo area. The Sinai Peninsula in Egypt is a qualified hazardous duty area that is effectively treated the same as a combat zone. IRS Publication 3 has the full list of countries in each of these areas.

Qualifying service outside a combat zone considered combat zone service. Military service outside a combat zone is considered to be performed in a combat zone if: (1) the service is designated by the Defense Department to be in direct support of military operations in the combat zone, and (2) the service qualifies you for special military pay for duty subject to hostile fire or imminent danger. Military pay received for this service will qualify for the combat zone exclusion if the other requirements are met.

Nonqualifying service. The following military service does not qualify as service in a combat zone: (1) presence in a combat zone while on leave from a duty station located outside the combat zone; (2) passage over or through a combat zone during a trip between two points that are outside a combat zone; and (3) presence in a combat zone solely for your personal convenience. Such service will not qualify you for the pay exclusion.

 *Law Alert*

IRA Contributions Based on Tax-Free Combat Pay

Members of the armed services serving in a combat zone may base contributions to either a traditional IRA *(8.2)* or a Roth IRA *(8.21)* on their tax-free combat pay.

EXAMPLES

1. You are hospitalized for a specific disease after serving in a combat zone for three weeks, and the disease for which you are hospitalized has an incubation period of two to four weeks. The disease is presumed to have been incurred while you were serving in the combat zone. On the other hand, if the incubation period of the disease is one year, the disease would not have been incurred while you were serving in the combat zone.

2. You were hospitalized for a specific disease three weeks after you left the combat zone. The incubation period of the disease is from two to four weeks. The disease is considered to have been incurred while serving in the combat zone.

Hospitalized while serving in a combat zone or after leaving a combat zone. If you are hospitalized while serving in a combat zone, the wound, disease, or injury that is the reason for the hospitalization will be presumed to have been incurred while serving in the combat zone unless there is clear evidence to the contrary. The presumption may also apply if you were hospitalized after leaving a combat zone.

Form W-2. The wages shown in Box 1 of your Form W-2 should not include combat pay. Retirement pay is not combat pay.

Filing Tip

Spouses of Combat Zone Personnel

If your spouse serves in a combat zone or contingency operation, you are generally entitled to the same deadline extension as he or she is. However, any extra extension for your spouse's hospitalization within the United States is not available to you. Further, a spouse's extension does not apply to any year beginning more than two years after the area ceases to be a combat zone or the operation ceases to be a contingency operation.

35.5 Tax Deadlines Extended for Combat Zone or Contingency Operation Service

You are allowed an extension of at least 180 days *(see below)* to take care of tax matters if you are a member of the Armed Forces who served in a combat zone or in a contingency operation. The extension applies to filing tax returns, paying taxes, filing a Tax Court petition, filing refund claims, and making an IRA contribution. The time allowed for the IRS to begin an audit or take collection actions is also extended. *See* IRS Publication 3 for details on the extension rules.

Support personnel. The deadline extension also applies if you are serving in a combat zone or contingency operation in support of the Armed Forces. This includes Red Cross personnel, accredited correspondents, and civilian personnel acting under the direction of the Armed Forces in support of those forces.

Extension is a minimum of 180 days. Your deadline for taking actions with the IRS is extended for at least 180 days after the later of: (1) the last day you are in a combat zone or serving in a contingency operation (or the last day the area qualifies as a combat zone or the operation qualifies as a contingency operation), or (2) the last day of any continuous qualified hospitalization for injury from service in the combat zone or contingency operation. Hospitalization may be outside the United States, or up to five years of hospitalization in the United States.

Time in a missing status (missing in action or prisoner of war) counts as time in a combat zone or contingency operation.

In addition to the 180 days, a filing deadline is also extended by the number of days you had left to file with the IRS when you entered a combat zone or began serving in a contingency operation. If you entered the combat zone or began contingency operation service before the time to file began, the deadline is extended by the entire filing time.

35.6 Tax Forgiveness for Combat Zone or Terrorist or Military Action Deaths

If a member of the Armed Forces is killed in a combat zone or dies from wounds or disease incurred while actively serving in a combat zone, any income tax liability for the year of death and any earlier year in which he or she actively served in a combat zone is waived. In addition, the service member's estate is entitled to a refund for income tax paid while serving there.

If a member of the Armed Forces was a resident of a community property state and his or her spouse reported half of the military pay on a separate return, the spouse may get a refund of taxes paid on his or her share of the combat zone pay.

Forgiveness benefits apply to an Armed Forces member serving outside the zone if service: (1) was in direct support of military operations there, and (2) qualified the member for special military pay for duty subject to hostile fire or imminent danger.

Missing status. The date of death for a member of the Armed Forces who was in a missing status (missing in action or prisoner of war) is the date his or her name is removed from missing status for military pay purposes. This is true even if death occurred earlier.

Tax forgiveness for civilian or military personnel killed in terroristic or military action. Tax liability is waived for civilian or military U.S. government employees killed in terroristic or military actions, even if the President has not designated the area as a combat zone. The individual must be a U.S. government employee both on the date of injury and date of death. Tax liability is waived for the period beginning with the taxable year before the year in which the injuries were incurred and ending with the year of death. Refund claims for prior years must generally be filed on Form 1040-X by the later of three years from the time the original return was filed or two years from the time the tax was paid. However, if death occurred in a combat zone, the filing period is extended by the time served in the combat zone, plus the period of continuous hospitalization outside the U.S., plus an additional 180 days.

How tax forgiveness is claimed. If the individual died in a combat zone or in a terroristic or military action, you file as the individual's representative: (1) Form 1040 or 1040-SR if a U.S. individual income tax return has not been filed for the tax year. Form W-2, Wage and Tax Statement, must accompany the return. (2) Form 1040-X if a U.S. individual income tax return has been filed. A separate Form 1040-X must be filed for each year in question. *See* IRS Publication 3 for how to identify the military or terrorist action in which the death occurred.

An attachment should accompany any return or claim and should include a computation of the decedent's tax liability before any amount is forgiven and the amount that is to be forgiven.

The following documents must also accompany all returns and claims for refund: (1) Form 1310, "Statement of Person Claiming Refund Due a Deceased Taxpayer"; and (2) a certification from the Department of Defense. Department of State certification is required if the decedent was a civilian employee of an agency other than the Department of Defense. *See* IRS Publication 3 for the IRS address where the tax forgiveness claim and documents must be filed.

Caution

Training Exercises
Tax forgiveness for personnel killed in a "military action" does not apply to a U.S. civilian or military employee who dies as a result of a training exercise.

35.7 Extension To Pay Your Tax When Entering the Service

If you are unable to pay your income taxes when you enter the Armed Forces (whether they became due before or during your military service), you may get an extension until 180 days after leaving the military to pay the tax, provided that you apply for the extension after receiving a notice from the IRS asking for payment. Your request must show that your ability to pay has been materially affected because of your military service. If the request is granted and you pay the entire tax due by the end of the postponement period, no interest or penalties will be charged for that period.

The extension does not cover your spouse, who must file a separate return and pay the tax due. But you and your spouse may file a joint return before the postponement period expires even though your spouse filed a separate return for that particular year.

Automatic extension of time to file your 2023 return. If you are on duty outside the U.S. or Puerto Rico on April 15, 2024, you get an automatic two-month extension to file your 2023 return; *see* page 6.

Interest charged on back taxes. If you do not show hardship qualifying you for the above interest-free payment extension, the maximum interest rate the IRS may charge while you are on active duty for taxes incurred prior to your entry into active service is 6%, provided your service affected your ability to pay. Since 6% is the maximum interest rate, this rule does not provide a benefit when the regular interest rate is lower *(46.8)*.

35.8 Tax Information for Reservists

Due to the suspension of miscellaneous itemized deductions subject to the 2% of adjusted gross income (AGI) floor from 2018 through 2025, no deduction is allowed for reserves-related travel costs unless you travel overnight more than 100 miles away from your tax home to a meeting or training camp.

If you travel overnight more than 100 miles away from your tax home *(20.6)* to a reservist meeting or training camp, report the related travel expenses on Form 2106 and enter the allowable amount on Line 12 of Schedule 1 (Form 1040 or 1040-SR) as an adjustment to income (above-the-line deduction). You can deduct your lodging costs, and 50% of meal costs furnished at restaurants in 2023, provided they do not exceed the regular federal per diem rate *(20.19)*. If you use your vehicle for this travel, you may claim the IRS' standard mileage rate (65.5¢ cents per mile for 2023) plus any parking fees, tolls, or ferry fees.

Deferring tax payments and reduction of IRS interest rate. If you owed a tax deficiency to the IRS before being called to active duty, the IRS may defer payment, without interest, if your ability to pay has been severely impaired by your call-up *(35.7)*.

Penalty-free withdrawal and repayment of qualified reservist retirement distribution. If you are called to active military duty for over 179 days or indefinitely, and during the active duty period you receive a distribution from a traditional IRA or a distribution attributable to elective deferrals (from a 401(k) or 403(b) plan), the distribution is considered a qualified reservist distribution. If you are under age 59½ when you receive a qualified reservist distribution, you are not subject to the 10% penalty for early distributions *(7.13, 8.12)*.

Furthermore, you can recontribute a qualified reservist distribution to a traditional IRA within two years after the end of the active duty period. Repayment must be made to a traditional IRA even if the distribution was from a 401(k) or 403(b) plan. The repayment should be reported on Form 8606 (Line 1) as a nondeductible contribution to the traditional IRA.s

Distributions of unused balance from health flexible spending arrangement (HFSA). If you contribute to a health flexible spending arrangement *(3.16)*, but before you can use up your HFSA balance to reimburse your medical expenses you are called to active military duty for over 179 days, or indefinitely, you can withdraw the funds and use them for any purpose if your employer allows "qualified reservist distributions" and you withdraw the balance by the regular plan deadline for receiving reimbursements. If your employer allows employees to obtain reimbursements of medical expenses within a 2½-month grace period after the end of the plan year *(3.16)*, you have the same deadline to receive a distribution of your HFSA balance, but it does not have to be used to pay medical expenses.

CHAPTER 36

How To Treat Foreign Earned Income

There is a tax incentive for working abroad—in 2023 up to $120,000 of income earned abroad may escape U.S. income taxes and you may be entitled to an exclusion or deduction for certain housing costs. In measuring the economic value of this tax savings, consider the extra cost of living abroad. In some areas, the high cost of living and currency exchange rates will erode your tax savings.

The exclusion does not apply to investment income or to any other earned income that does not meet the exclusion tests.

To claim a foreign income exclusion you must satisfy a foreign residence or physical presence test (36.5).

Employees of the U.S. government may not claim an exclusion based on the government pay earned abroad.

If you keep income in a foreign bank or other financial accounts, you may have special reporting requirements for the accounts (4.12, 48.7).

36.1 Claiming the Foreign Earned Income Exclusion

If your tax home is in a foreign country and you meet either the foreign residence test or physical presence test *(36.3)*, you may exclude up to $120,000 of foreign earned income earned in 2023. You must file a U.S. return if your gross income exceeds the filing threshold for your personal status, even though all or part of your foreign earned income may be tax free. For years after 2023, the maximum $120,000 exclusion will likely be increased by an inflation adjustment; *see the e-Supplement* at *jklasser.com*.

The exclusion is not automatic; you must elect the exclusion. You elect the foreign earned income exclusion on Form 2555, which you attach to Form 1040 or 1040-SR. The housing cost exclusion *(36.4)* is also elected on Form 2555.

A separate exclusion is allowed for the value of meals and lodging received by employees living in qualified camps; *see 36.8*.

If you claim the foreign income exclusion of $120,000, you may not:

- Claim business deductions allocable to the excluded income;
- Make a deductible traditional IRA contribution, or a Roth IRA contribution, based on the excluded income; or
- Claim foreign taxes paid on excluded income as a credit or deduction.

In deciding whether to claim the exclusion, compare the overall tax (1) with the exclusion and (2) without the exclusion but with the full foreign tax credit and allocable deductions. Make your selection based on which tax filing gives you the lower tax; *see 36.3* and *36.6*.

Keep in mind, if you claim the exclusion, any taxable income not subject to the earned income and housing exclusions will be taxed at the same rates that would have applied had no exclusions been allowed. To apply this "stacking" rule, you must figure your regular tax liability using the Foreign Earned Income Tax Worksheet in the instructions to Form 1040 or 1040-SR. Also, to figure AMT liability, use the Foreign Earned Income Tax Worksheet in the instructions to Form 6251.

Election applies until revoked. Once you elect the exclusion, that election remains in effect for all future years unless you revoke it. If you revoke the election, you cannot elect the exclusion again during the next five years without IRS consent. A revocation is made in a statement attached to your return for the year you want it to take effect. The foreign earned income exclusion and the housing cost exclusion must be revoked separately.

The IRS may consent to a reinstatement of the exclusion following a revocation under the following circumstances: you return for a period of time to the United States, you move to another foreign country with different tax rates, you change employers, or there has been substantial change in the tax law of the foreign country of residence or physical presence.

> **EXAMPLE**
>
> A U.S. citizen living abroad asked the IRS if the declaration of a tax holiday by a foreign country in 1999 was a substantial change of law. Prior to 1996, while working abroad he had claimed the foreign income exclusion. But in 1996 and 1997, he revoked the election and claimed a foreign tax credit for taxes paid on his foreign earnings. In 1999, he wanted to resume claiming the income exclusion due to the declaration of a tax holiday in the country in which he was employed. The IRS ruled that he can claim the exclusion. The declaration of a tax holiday is considered a substantial change of law because he went from being taxed to being exempt from tax.

36.2 What Is Foreign Earned Income?

For exclusion purposes, foreign earned income includes salaries, wages, commissions, professional fees, and bonuses for personal services performed while your tax home is in a foreign country and you meet either the foreign residence test or the physical presence test; *see 36.3*. Earned income also includes allowances from your employer for housing or other expenses, as well as the value of housing or a car provided by the

Caution

Claiming Foreign Tax Credit Revokes Prior Election

If you have been claiming the exclusion and decide that it would be advantageous this year to forego the exclusion and instead claim the foreign tax credit for foreign earned income, be aware that claiming the credit is treated by the IRS as a revocation of the prior exclusion election. You may not claim an exclusion for the next five years unless the IRS allows you to reelect the exclusion.

Claiming a foreign tax credit also may revoke a prior election to claim the housing cost exclusion. Depending on the foreign earned income in the year the credit is claimed, the credit may be considered a revocation of a prior earned income exclusion election and also a prior housing cost exclusion election, or as a revocation of only one of the elections.

A good faith error in calculating foreign earned income that leads to claiming a foreign credit will not be treated as a revocation of prior elections.

employer. It may also include business profits, royalties, and rents, provided this income is tied to the performance of services. Earned income does not include pension or annuity income, payments for nonqualified employee trusts or nonqualified annuities, dividends, interest, capital gains, gambling winnings, alimony, or the value of tax-free meals or lodging under the rules in *3.13*.

Foreign earned income does not include amounts earned in countries subject to U.S. government travel restrictions.

Courts have agreed with the IRS that income earned in Antarctica, in international waters, and in international airspace is not earned in a foreign country and thus cannot qualify for the exclusion.

United States government pay ineligible. If you are an employee of the U.S. government or its agencies, you may not exclude any part of your pay from your government employer. Courts have agreed with the IRS that U.S. government workers were U.S. employees even though they were paid from sources other than Congressionally appropriated funds. If you are not an employee of the U.S. government or any of its agencies, your pay is excludable even if paid by a government source. You are not considered a U.S. government employee if you work for a private employer that has contracted with the government, provided you are under the employer's control and supervision, you are paid by the employer, and no U.S. government agency would be liable for your salary if your employer defaulted.

Under a special law, tax liability is waived for a civilian or military employee of the U.S. government killed in a military action overseas; *see 35.6*.

> ### EXAMPLES
>
> 1. A U.S. citizen resides in England. He invests in an English partnership that sells manufactured goods outside the U.S. He performs no services for the business. His share of net profits does not qualify as earned income.
>
> 2. Same facts as in Example 1, except he devotes his full time to the partnership business. Then up to 30% of his share of the net profits may qualify as earned income. Thus, if his share of profits is $50,000, earned income is $15,000 (30% of $50,000), assuming the value of his services is at least $15,000.
>
> 3. You and another person are consultants, operating as a partnership in Europe. Since capital is not an income-producing element, the entire gross income of the business is earned income.
>
>   The partnership agreement generally determines the tax status of partnership income in a U.S. partnership with a foreign branch. Thus, if the partnership agreement allocates foreign earnings to partners abroad, the allocation will be recognized unless it lacks substantial economic effect.

Profits from sole proprietorship or partnership. If your business consists solely of services (no capital investment), 100% of gross income is considered earned income. If services and capital are both income-producing factors, the value of your personal services, but no more than 30% of your share of the net profit, is considered earned income. Net profit is reduced by the deduction for the employer-equivalent portion of self-employment tax *(12.2)* before figuring your 30% share.

If you do not contribute any services to a business (for example, you are a "silent partner"), your share of the net profit is not earned income.

If you do not have a net profit, the portion of your gross profit that represents a reasonable allowance for personal services is considered earned income.

Fringe benefits. The value of fringe benefits, such as the right to use company property and facilities, is added to your compensation when figuring the amount of your earned income.

Royalties. Royalties from articles or books are earned income if you receive them for transferring all of your rights to your work, or you are contracted to write the articles or book for an amount in cash plus a royalty on sales.

Royalties from the leasing of oil and mineral lands and from patents are not earned income.

 *Caution*

Qualified Business Income Deduction Barred

The 20% deduction for qualified business income does not apply to foreign income. That deduction is limited to income effectively connected with the conduct of a trade or business within the U.S. and that is includible in taxable income.

Caution

Rental Income

Rental income is generally not earned income. However, if you perform personal services, for example as an owner-manager of a hotel or rooming house in a foreign country, then up to 30% of your net rents may be earned income.

Reimbursement of employee expenses. Do not include reimbursement of expenses as earned income to the extent they equal expenses that you adequately accounted for to your employer; *see 20.18*. If your expenses exceed reimbursements, the excess is allocated according to the rules in *36.6*. If reimbursements exceed expenses, the excess is treated as earned income.

Straight commission salespersons or other employees who arrange with their employers, for withholding purposes, to consider a percentage of their commissions as attributable to their expenses treat such amounts as earned income.

36.3 Qualifying for the Foreign Earned Income Exclusion

You may elect the exclusion for foreign earned income (*see 36.2*, including the rule that denies eligibility for U.S. government pay) only if your tax home is in a foreign country and you meet either the foreign residence test (residence for an entire tax year) or the foreign physical presence test (330 full days in 12-month period). The foreign residence and physical presence tests are discussed in *36.5*. Tax home is discussed at *20.6–20.8*. If your tax home is in the U.S., you may not claim the exclusion but may claim the foreign tax credit and your living expenses while away from home if you meet the rules in *20.9* for temporary assignments that are expected to last, and actually do last, for one year or less. Contractors and their employees who support U.S. Armed Forces in designated combat zones *(35.4)* are treated as meeting the foreign tax home test even if they have an abode in the United States.

Exclusion prorated on a daily basis. If you qualify under the foreign residence or physical presence test for only part of 2023, the $120,000 exclusion limit is reduced on a daily basis.

> **EXAMPLES**
>
> 1. You were a resident of France from February 20, 2021, until July 1, 2023. On July 2, 2023, you returned to the U.S. Since your period of foreign residency included all of 2022, thereby satisfying the foreign residence test *(36.5)*, you may claim a prorated exclusion for 2023. As you were abroad for 182 of the 365 days in 2023 (January 1 through July 1), you can exclude earnings up to $59,844 or 182/365 of the $120,000 maximum exclusion. If you earned more than $59,844, the exclusion is limited to $59,844.
>
> 2. You worked in France from June 1, 2022, through September 30, 2023. Your only days outside France were a 15-day vacation to the U.S. in December 2022. You do not qualify for an exclusion under the foreign residence test because you were not abroad for a full taxable year; you were not abroad for either the full year of 2022 or 2023. However, you do qualify under the physical presence test; you were physically present abroad for at least 330 full days during a 12-month period. The 12-month period giving you the largest 2022 exclusion is the 12-month period starting October 21, 2022, and ending October 20, 2023. See *36.5* for figuring the 12-month period. Since you were abroad for at least 330 full days during that 12-month period, you may claim an exclusion. In 2023, you were abroad for 293 days within the 12-month period (January 1 through October 20, 2023, is 293 days). Thus, you exclude earnings up to $96,336 ($120,000 × 293/365). Earnings exceeding $96,336 are not excludable.

Caution

Countries Subject to Travel Restrictions

You may not claim the foreign earned income exclusion, or the housing exclusion or deduction, if you work in a country subject to U.S. government travel restrictions, such as Cuba (not including non-government workers at Guantanamo Bay). You are not treated as a bona fide resident of, or as present in, a country subject to the travel ban. *See* Publication 54 and the Form 2555 instructions for a list of countries subject to travel restrictions.

If you are married and you and your spouse each have foreign earned income and meet the foreign residence or physical presence test, you may each claim a separate exclusion. If your permanent home is in a community property state, your earned income is not considered community property for purposes of the exclusion.

Foreign earnings from a prior year. Foreign income earned in a prior year but paid in 2023 does not qualify for the 2023 exclusion. However, if the income was attributable to foreign services performed in 2022, the pay is tax free in 2023 to the extent that you did not use the full 2022 exclusion of $112,000. Under another exception, payments received in 2023 for 2022 services are treated as 2023 income if the payment was within a normal payroll period of 16 days or less that included the last day of 2022. If the services were performed before 2022, no exclusion is available to shelter the pay. You cannot exclude income that you receive after the end of the year following the year in which you provide the services.

Income for services performed in the U.S. does not qualify for the exclusion, even though it is paid to you while you are abroad.

Foreign tax credit. Foreign taxes paid on tax-free foreign earned income do not qualify for a credit or deduction. If your foreign pay for 2023 exceeds $120,000, you may claim a foreign tax credit or deduction for the foreign taxes allocated to taxable income. The instructions to Form 1116 and IRS Publication 514 provide details for making the computation.

36.4 How To Treat Housing Costs

Employees and self-employed persons who meet the tests for the foreign earned income exclusion *(36.3)* are subject to different housing cost rules. Employees get a housing exclusion; self-employed persons get a deduction from taxable foreign earned income. If you live in a special camp provided by your employer, all housing costs are excluded; *see 36.8*.

Exclusion for employer-financed housing costs. The housing exclusion is the excess of the employer-financed reasonable housing expenses *(see below)* over a "base housing amount." The daily base housing amount is 16% of the maximum foreign earned income exclusion, prorated for the number of your qualifying days of foreign residence or presence for the year. Thus, for 2023, the base housing amount is $19,200 ($120,000 maximum foreign earned income exclusion × 16%) if you qualify under the foreign residence or physical presence test for the entire year. If you qualify under the residence or presence test for only part of the year, the $19,200 maximum base amount is prorated on a daily basis, so $52.60 ($19,200 ÷ 365) is allowed for each qualifying day in 2023.

In figuring housing expenses in excess of the base housing amount, there is a limit on the expenses that can be taken into account. Generally, the housing expenses cannot exceed 30% of the maximum earned income exclusion, prorated as applicable by the number of qualifying days of foreign residence or presence for the year. Thus, for 2023, the limit on housing expenses is generally $36,000 (30% × $120,000), or $98.63 per day, and the maximum housing exclusion is generally $16,800 ($36,000 – $19,200 maximum base amount). However, the expense limit, and the exclusion, may be significantly more than this if you work in a high cost locality. The IRS provides a higher annual limit for housing expenses in expensive foreign areas. The adjusted limits for high cost areas are provided in a table included in the instructions to Form 2555. In addition, when the IRS announces the high cost area limits for 2024 (in a notice likely to be released in March or April 2024), it is likely that it will allow taxpayers to use those 2024 limits to figure their housing exclusion for 2023 if the 2024 limit for housing expenses (full-year or daily) is higher than the amount allowed by the high cost area table in the 2023 Form 2555 instructions.

On Form 2555, your foreign earned income exclusion is limited to the excess of your foreign earned income (including employer-financed housing costs) over your housing exclusion.

Reasonable housing expenses. When calculating your housing expenses, include your rent, utilities other than telephone costs, insurance, parking, furniture rentals, and household repairs. The following expenses do not qualify: cost of purchasing a home, furniture, or accessories; pay television, home improvements; payments of mortgage principal; domestic labor; and depreciation on a home or on improvements to leased housing. Furthermore, interest and taxes that are otherwise deductible do not qualify for the exclusion.

You may include the costs of a separate household that you maintain outside the U.S. for your spouse and dependents because living conditions at your foreign home are adverse.

Self-employed persons. On Form 2555, self-employed individuals may claim a limited deduction (but not an exclusion) for housing costs exceeding the base housing amount. You may claim this deduction only to the extent it offsets taxable foreign earned income. The deduction is claimed "above the line" on Line 24j of Schedule 1 (Form 1040 or 1040-SR), even if you do not itemize deductions.

 *Filing Tip*

Claiming the Housing Exclusion

On Form 2555, you figure the housing exclusion before the foreign income exclusion. The income exclusion is limited to the excess of foreign earned income over the housing exclusion.

If your housing costs exceed your taxable foreign earned income, you may carry those expenses forward to the next year and deduct in that year to the extent of taxable foreign earned income. Only a one-year carryover is allowed. If you have a carryover from 2023 to 2024 that cannot be claimed for 2022, that amount is lost.

If you are an employee and self-employed during the same year. Housing expenses above the base amount are partly excludable and partly deductible. For example, if half of your foreign earned income is from services as an employee, half of the excess housing expenses over the base amount are excludable. The remaining excess housing costs are deductible to the extent you have taxable foreign earned income after reducing it by the total of your allowable earned income exclusion plus your housing exclusion. Follow the instructions to Form 2555.

Countries ineligible for tax benefits. Housing expenses incurred in a country subject to a U.S. government travel restriction are not eligible for the tax benefits explained in this section. *See* Form 2555 instructions for a list of countries to which travel restrictions apply.

36.5 Meeting the Foreign Residence or Physical Presence Test

To qualify for the foreign earned income exclusion, you must be (1) a U.S. citizen (or U.S. resident alien who is a citizen or national of a country with which the U.S. has a tax treaty) who meets the foreign residence test, or (2) a U.S. citizen or resident alien meeting the physical presence test in a foreign country. The following areas are not considered foreign countries: Puerto Rico, Virgin Islands, Guam, Commonwealth of the Northern Mariana Islands, American Samoa, or the Antarctic region. The Tax Court has held that income earned in international airspace (by a flight attendant, for example) or in international waters (by a ship officer, for example) is not earned in a foreign country and thus does not qualify for the foreign earned income exclusion.

If, by the due date of your 2023 return (April 15, 2024), you have not yet satisfied the foreign residence or physical presence test, but you expect to meet either test after the filing date, you may either file on the due date and report your earnings or ask for a filing extension under the rules at *36.7*.

> **EXAMPLE**
>
> You are a bona fide foreign resident from September 30, 2022, to March 25, 2024. The period includes your entire 2023 tax year. Therefore, up to $120,000 of your 2023 earnings is excludable. Your overseas earnings in 2022 and 2024 qualify for a proportionate part of the maximum exclusion allowed for those years.

Waiver of time test. If war or civil unrest prevented you from meeting the foreign residence or physical presence test, you may claim the exclusion for the period you actually were a resident or physically present abroad. The foreign locations and the time periods that qualify for the waiver of the 2023 residency and physical presence tests will be listed in the Internal Revenue Bulletin early in 2024; *see* the *e-Supplement* at *jklasser. com* for any update.

Foreign residence test. You must be a U.S. citizen who is a bona fide resident of a foreign country for an uninterrupted period that includes one full tax year; a full tax year is from January 1 through December 31 for individuals who file on a calendar-year basis. A U.S. resident alien who is a citizen or national of a country with which the U.S. has an income tax treaty and meets the full-year foreign residence test also qualifies. Business or vacation trips to the U.S. or another country will not disqualify you from satisfying the foreign residence test. If you are abroad more than one year but less than two, the entire period qualifies if it includes one full tax year.

To prove you are a foreign resident, you must show your intention to be a resident of the foreign country. Evidence tending to confirm your intention to stay in a foreign country includes: (1) your family accompanies you; (2) you buy a house or rent an apartment rather than a hotel room; (3) you participate in the foreign community activities; (4) you can speak the foreign language; (5) you have a permanent foreign address; (6) you join clubs there; or (7) you open charge accounts in stores in the foreign country.

Planning Reminder

Claiming Exemption From Withholding for Excludable Income

You can file Form 673 with your U.S. employer to claim an exemption from withholding on wages to the extent of your expected foreign earned income exclusion and foreign housing exclusion. You must certify, under penalty of perjury, that you have good reason to believe that you will qualify under the foreign residence or physical presence test and also must certify your estimated foreign housing costs.

You will not qualify if you take inconsistent positions toward your foreign residency. That is, you will not be treated as a bona fide resident of a foreign country if you have earned income from sources within that country, filed a statement with the authorities of that country that you are not a resident there, and have been held not subject to the income tax of that country. However, this rule does not prevent you from qualifying under the physical presence test.

If you cannot prove that you are a resident, check to determine if your stay qualifies under the physical presence test.

Physical presence test. To qualify under this test, you must show you were on foreign soil 330 full days (about 11 months) during a 12-month period. Whether you were a resident or a transient is of no importance. You have to show you were physically present in a foreign country or countries for 330 full days during any 12-consecutive-month period. The 330 qualifying days do not have to be consecutive. The 12-month period may begin with any day. There is no requirement that it begin with your first full day abroad. It may begin before or after arrival in a foreign country and may end before or after departure from a foreign country. A full day is from midnight to midnight (24 consecutive hours). You must spend each of the 330 days on foreign soil. In departing from U.S. soil to go directly to the foreign country, or in returning directly to the U.S. from a foreign country, the time you spend on or over international waters does not count toward the 330-day total.

EXAMPLES

1. On August 9, you fly from New York City to London. You arrive there at 10 a.m. August 10. Your first full qualifying day toward the 330-day period is August 11.
   You may count in your 330-day period:
2. Time spent traveling between foreign countries.
3. Time spent on a vacation in foreign countries. There is no requirement that the 330 days must be spent on a job.
4. Time spent in a foreign country while employed by the U.S. government counts towards the 330-day test, even though pay from the government does not qualify for the earned income exclusion.
5. Time in foreign countries, territorial waters, or travel in the air over a foreign country. However, you will lose qualifying days if any part of such travel is on or over international waters and takes 24 hours or more, or any part of such travel is within the U.S. or its possessions.
6. You depart from Naples, Italy, by ship on June 10 at 6:00 p.m. and arrive at Haifa, Israel, at 7:00 a.m. on June 14. The trip exceeded 24 hours and passed through international waters. Therefore, you lose as qualifying days June 10, 11, 12, 13, and 14. Assuming you remain in Haifa, Israel, the next qualifying day is June 15.

Choosing the 12-month period. You qualify under the physical presence test if you were on foreign soil 330 days during any period of 12 consecutive months. Since there may be several 12-month periods during which you meet the 330-day test, you should choose the 12-month period allowing you the largest possible exclusion if you qualify under the physical presence test for only part of 2022.

EXAMPLE

You worked in France from June 1, 2022, through September 30, 2023, and the next day you left the country. During this period, you left France only for a 15-day vacation to the U.S. during December 2022. You earned $100,000 for your work in France during 2023. Your maximum 2023 exclusion is figured as follows:

1. Start with your last full day, September 30, 2023, and count back 330 full days during which you were abroad. Not counting the 15 vacation days in the U.S., the 330th day is October 21, 2022. This is the first day of your 12-month period.
2. From October 21, 2022, count forward 12 months to October 20, 2023, which is the last day of your 12-month period.

 *Caution*

Residence or Domicile?

Residence does not have the same meaning as domicile. Your domicile is a permanent place of abode; it is the place to which you eventually plan to return wherever you go. You may have a residence in a place other than your domicile. Thus, you may go, say, to Amsterdam, and take up residence there and still intend to return to your domicile in the U.S. But leaving your domicile does not, by itself, establish a bona fide residence in a new place. You must intend to make a new place your residence.

3. Count the number of days in 2023 that fall within the 12-month period ending October 20, 2023. Here, the number of qualifying days is 293, from January 1 through October 20, 2023.

4. The maximum 2023 exclusion is $120,000 × 293/365, or $96,336. You may exclude $96,336, the lesser of the maximum exclusion or your actual earnings of $100,000.

36.6 Claiming Deductions

You may not deduct expenses that are allocable to the foreign earned income and housing exclusions. If you elect the earned income exclusion, you deduct expenses as follows:

Personal or nonbusiness deductions, such as medical expenses, mortgage interest, and real estate taxes paid on a personal residence, are deductible if you take advantage of the itemize deductions filing option. Business expenses from self-employment that are attributable to earning excludable income are not deductible. Job-related business expenses attributable to non-excludable earnings are in any case not deductible from 2018 through 2025 tax years due to the suspension of miscellaneous itemized deductions subject to the 2% of adjusted gross income floor.

If your foreign earnings exceed the exclusion ceiling, you allocate expenses between taxable and excludable income and deduct the amount allocated to taxable earned income; *see* Example 2 below.

EXAMPLES

1. You were a resident of Denmark and elect to exclude your self-employment earnings of $70,000 from income. You also incurred unreimbursed travel expenses of $2,000. You may not deduct the travel expenses, since the amount is attributable to the earning of tax-free income.

2. You have self-employment earnings of $140,000 in Germany and satisfy the physical presence test. Your unreimbursed travel expenses for 2023 are $5,000. If you elect the $120,000 exclusion (85% of your foreign earnings), 15% of the travel expenses, or $750, attributable to the taxable 15% of earnings, may be claimed as a business deduction on Schedule C.

If your job expenses are reimbursed and the expenses are adequately accounted for to your employer *(20.18)*, the reimbursements are not reported as income on your Form W-2. You may have to allocate state income taxes paid on your income.

If either you or your spouse elects the earned income or housing exclusion, you may not claim an IRA deduction based on excluded income.

If you were reimbursed by your employer under a non-accountable plan, or if the reimbursement is for expenses that you deducted in an earlier year, the reimbursement is considered earned income in the year of receipt and is added to other earned income before taking the exclusion and making the allocation.

Compulsory home leave. Foreign service officers stationed abroad must periodically return to the U.S. because the home leave is compulsory, foreign service officers may deduct their travel expenses; travel expenses of the officer's family are not deductible.

36.7 Exclusion Not Established When Your Return Is Due

When your 2023 return is due, you may not have been abroad long enough to qualify for the exclusion. If you expect to qualify under either the residence or physical presence test after the due date for your 2023 return, you may either (1) ask for an extension of time for filing your return on Form 2350 until after you qualify under either rule or (2) file your return on the due date, reporting the foreign income on the return, pay the full tax, and then file for a refund when you qualify.

If you will have tax to pay even after qualifying for the exclusion—for example, your earned income exceeds the exclusion—you may file for an extension to file but you will

Filing Tip

Extension of Time To File

If you are living and working abroad on April 15, 2024, you have an automatic extension to June 15, 2024, but you will owe interest on any tax not paid by April 15. For an additional four months, file Form 4868 by June 15, 2024, and pay the estimated tax to limit interest and late payment penalties. For a longer extension, in anticipation of owing no tax on your foreign income, you may file Form 2350 either with the Internal Revenue Service Center in Austin, TX 73301-0045, or with a local IRS representative. File Form 2350 by the due date for filing your 2023 return, which is June 15, 2024, if you are abroad and are on a calendar year. Generally, you will be granted an extension for a period ending 30 days after the date you reasonably expect to qualify for the foreign earned income exclusion.

owe interest on the tax due. To avoid interest charges on the tax, you may take one of the following steps:

1. File a timely return and pay the total tax due without the application of the exclusion. When you do qualify, make sure you file a timely *(47.2)* refund claim; or

2. Pay the estimated tax liability when you apply for the extension to file on Form 2350. If the extension is granted, the payment is applied to the tax shown on your return when you file.

36.8 Tax-Free Meals and Lodging for Workers in Camps

If you must live in a camp provided by your employer, you may exclude from income *(3.13)* the value of the lodging and meals furnished to you if the camp is (1) provided because you work in a remote area where satisfactory housing is not available; (2) located as near as is practical to the worksite; and (3) in an enclave that normally houses at least 10 employees and in which lodgings are not offered to the general public.

You also may qualify for the earned income exclusion; *see 36.1.*

36.9 U. S. Virgin Islands, Samoa, Guam, and Northern Marianas

The U.S. Virgin Islands, Puerto Rico, Guam, American Samoa, and the Commonwealth of the Northern Mariana Islands are U.S. possessions that have their own independent tax departments. Therefore, contact the particular tax authority for the proper treatment of your income and obtain a copy of IRS Publication 570, Tax Guide for Individuals With Income From U.S. Possessions, which provides phone, mail, and internet contact information.

Possession exclusion. A possession exclusion applies to bona fide residents of American Samoa for the entire year. On Form 4563, such residents may exclude for U.S. tax purposes their income from sources in American Samoa and income effectively connected with a business in American Samoa. The exclusion applies to amounts earned for services as an employee of the American Samoan government or its agencies but does not apply to pay as an employee, whether civilian or military, of the U.S. government or its agencies.

36.10 Earnings in Puerto Rico

If you are a U.S. citizen or resident alien who is also a resident of Puerto Rico for the entire year, you generally report all of your income on your Puerto Rico tax return. You report income from U.S. sources on the Puerto Rico tax return, and a credit against the Puerto Rico tax may be claimed for income taxes paid to the United States.

If you are not a resident of Puerto Rico, you report on a Puerto Rico return only income from Puerto Rico sources. Wages earned for services performed in Puerto Rico for the U.S. government or for private employers are treated as income from Puerto Rico sources.

United States· tax returns. As a U.S. citizen, you must file a U.S. tax return reporting income from all sources. If you are a bona fide resident of Puerto Rico for an entire tax year, you do not report on a U.S. tax return any income earned in Puerto Rico during your residence there, except amounts received for services performed in Puerto Rico as an employee of the U.S. government. Similar rules apply if you have been a bona fide resident of Puerto Rico for at least two years before changing your residence from Puerto Rico. On a U.S. tax return, you may not deduct expenses or claim tax credits allocable to the excludable income.

If you are not a bona fide resident of Puerto Rico for the entire tax year, or were not a bona fide resident for two years prior to the tax year, you report on your U.S. tax return all income you earned in Puerto Rico, as well as all income from other sources. If you are required to report income earned in Puerto Rico on your U.S. tax return, you may claim a credit for income tax paid to Puerto Rico. You figure the credit on Form 1116.

See IRS Publication 570, Tax Guide for Individuals With Income from U.S. Possessions, for further information on filing U.S. and Puerto Rico tax returns.

Caution

Form 8898 To Report Change of Residence

You generally must file Form 8898 for a tax year in which you have worldwide income of over $75,000 and in which you become or cease to be a bona fide resident of the U.S. Virgin Islands, Puerto Rico, Guam, American Samoa, or the Northern Mariana Islands. The test is for each person, so if you and your spouse each meet the test, each of you must file a Form 8898. A $1,000 penalty may be imposed for failure to file a required Form 8898.

Planning Reminder

Information for Puerto Rico Filing

Information on Puerto Rico tax returns may be obtained at www.hacienda.gobierno.pr. The phone number is 787-622-0123. Written requests may be sent to the Departamento de Hacienda, Negociado de Asistencia Contributiva, P.O. Box 9024140, San Juan, Puerto Rico, 00902-4140.

36.11 Tax Treaties With Foreign Countries

Tax treaties between the United States and foreign countries modify some of the rules discussed in this chapter. The purpose of the treaties is to avoid double taxation. Consult your tax advisor about the effect of these treaties on your income. IRS Publications 54 and 901 have information about the tax treaties the U.S. maintains with foreign countries; also find information at www.irs.gov/Businesses/International-Businesses/United-States-Income-Tax-Treaties — A-to-Z.

36.12 Exchange Rates and Blocked Currency

Income reported on your federal income tax return must be stated in U.S. dollars. When you are paid in foreign currency, you report your pay in U.S. dollars on the basis of the exchange rates prevailing at the time the income is actually or constructively received. You use the rate that most closely reflects the value of the foreign currency. Be prepared to justify the rate you use.

Fulbright grants. If 70% or more of a Fulbright grant is paid in nonconvertible foreign currency, U.S. tax may be paid in the foreign currency. *See* IRS Publication 54 for details.

Blocked currency. A citizen or resident alien may be paid in a foreign currency that cannot be converted into American dollars and removed from the foreign country. If your income is in blocked currency, you may elect to defer the reporting of that income until: (1) the currency becomes convertible into dollars, (2) you actually convert it into dollars, or (3) you use it for personal expenses. Purchase of a business or investment in the foreign country is not the kind of use that is treated as a conversion. (4) You make a gift of it or leave it in your will. (5) You are a resident alien and you give up your U.S. residence.

If you use this method to defer the income, you may not deduct the expenses of earning it until you report it. You must continue to use this method after you choose it. You may only change with permission of the IRS.

You do not defer the reporting of capital losses incurred in a country having a blocked currency.

There may be these disadvantages in deferring income:

- Many years' income may accumulate and all be taxed in one year.
- You have no control over the year in which the blocked income becomes taxable. You usually cannot control the events that cause the income to become unblocked.

You choose to defer income in blocked currency by filing a tentative tax return reporting your blocked taxable income and explaining that you are deferring the payment of income tax because your income is not in dollars or in property or currency that is readily convertible into dollars. You must attach to your tentative return a regular return, reporting any unblocked taxable income received during the year or taxable income that became unblocked during the year. When the currency finally becomes unblocked or convertible into a currency or property convertible to dollars, you pay tax on the earnings at the rate prevailing in the year the currency became unblocked or convertible. On the tentative return, note at the top: "Report of Deferrable Foreign Income, pursuant to Revenue Ruling 74-351." File separate returns for each country from which blocked currency is received. The election must be made by the due date for filing a return for the year in which an election is sought.

36.13 Foreign Tax Credit or Deduction for Foreign Taxes Paid

You do not have to live abroad to have paid foreign taxes; the taxes may result from having foreign investments. You may claim an itemized deduction (Line 6 of Schedule A, Form 1040 or 1040-SR) for qualified foreign income taxes or you may claim a foreign tax credit. You must file Form 1116 to compute your credit unless the *de minimis* exception applies; *see* below. You may not claim a foreign tax credit or deduction for taxes paid on income not subject to U.S. tax. If all of your foreign earned income is excluded, none of the foreign taxes paid on such income may be taken as a credit or deduction on your U.S. return. If you exclude only part of your foreign pay, you determine which foreign taxes are attributable to excluded income and thus barred as foreign tax credits by applying the fractional computation provided in the instructions to Form 1116 and IRS Publication 514.

Planning Reminder

Getting Paid in Cryptocurrency

If you are paid in virtual currency for services performed, either as an employee or self-employed person, you recognize ordinary income. This may still qualify for the foreign earned income exclusion.

Filing Tip

Choosing Foreign Tax Credit or Itemized Deduction

If you qualify for a credit or deduction for foreign income taxes, you will generally receive a larger tax reduction by claiming a tax credit rather than a deduction. A deduction is only a partial offset against your tax, whereas a credit is deducted in full from your tax. Also, taking a deduction may bar you from carrying back an excess credit from a later year. However, a deduction for foreign income taxes may give you a larger tax saving if the foreign tax is levied at a high rate and the proportion of foreign income to U.S. income is small. Compute your tax under both methods and choose the one providing the larger tax reduction.

For any tax year, you may not elect to deduct some foreign taxes and claim others as a credit. One method must be applied to all taxes paid or accrued during the tax year. If you are a cash-basis taxpayer, you may claim a credit for accrued foreign taxes, but you must consistently follow this method once elected.

Exemption from credit limit for *de minimis* foreign taxes. If you have $300 or less of creditable foreign taxes, $600 or less if married filing jointly, you may elect to be exempt from the overall limitation on the credit, provided that your only foreign source income is qualified passive income and all the income and any foreign taxes paid on it were reported to you on a qualified payee statement such as Form 1099-DIV, Form 1099-INT, Schedule K-1 of Form 1041, or Schedule K-3 of 1065, 1065-B, or 1120-S. If the election is made, a foreign tax credit may be claimed without filing Form 1116. *See* the instructions to Form 1116 for rules on making this election.

Credit disallowed. The credit may not be claimed if:
- You are a nonresident alien. However, under certain circumstances, if you are a bona fide resident for an entire taxable year in Puerto Rico you may be able to claim the credit. Also, a nonresident alien engaged in a U.S. trade or business may be able to claim a credit for foreign taxes paid on foreign source income effectively connected to that U.S. business.
- You are a citizen of a U.S. possession (except Puerto Rico) but not a U.S. citizen or resident.

No credit is allowed for taxes imposed by a country designated by the government as engaging in terroristic activities; *see* IRS Publication 514 for a list of these countries.

Taxes qualifying for the credit. The credit is allowed only for foreign income tax, excess profits taxes, and similar taxes in the nature of an income tax. It is not allowed for any taxes paid to foreign countries on sales, gross receipts, production, the privilege to do business, personal property, or export of capital. *See* the instructions to Form 1116 and IRS Publication 514 for other taxes that may qualify for the credit.

Reporting foreign income on your return. You report the gross amount of your foreign income in terms of United States currency. You also attach a schedule showing how you figured the foreign income in United States currency.

Limit on credit. Your credit for foreign income taxes paid or accrued is subject to a limitation on Form 1116 unless you qualify for and elect the exemption for *de minimis* taxes discussed above. The limitation is your total U.S. regular tax liability multiplied by a fraction: the numerator is your net foreign source taxable income (after required adjustments), and the denominator is your total taxable income from all sources. To determine the limit, you must separate your foreign source income into either the passive income category or the general income category. If you have both categories of foreign source income, you must figure the credit limit for each category on a separate Form 1116. If you have income from activities in sanctioned countries, or certain income re-sourced by treaty as foreign source income, or you paid taxes on a foreign source lump-sum distribution from a pension plan, a separate Form 1116 must be used to figure the limit for these categories as well. If you have more than one category of income, you combine the credits for the separate categories on Part IV of the Form 1116 with the largest credit. Part IV is not completed on the other Forms 1116, which are filed as attachments. *See* IRS Publication 514 and the instructions to Form 1116 for the details on these computations.

Carryback and carryover of excess foreign tax credit. If you are unable to claim all of the qualified foreign taxes paid or accrued during the year because of the limit on the credit, the balance may be carried back one year and then carried forward 10 years. For further details, *see* IRS Publication 514 and the instructions to Form 1116.

Caution

Foreign Accounts May Be Reportable

If you have foreign financial accounts, you may have to report them annually; *see 4.12, 48.7.*

CHAPTER 37

Planning Alimony and Marital Settlements

The tax treatment of alimony in 2023 for both the payer (the spouse making payments) and the payee (the spouse receiving payments) depends on when the divorce decree or separation agreement was finalized. Payments under decrees and agreements finalized before 2019 that meet the tax law tests for alimony are deductible if you pay them, and taxable if you receive them. Payments are not deductible by the payer unless taxable to the recipient. Payments under decrees and agreements finalized after 2018 are not deductible or taxable.

If alimony is deductible, you deduct the payments on Schedule 1 (Form 1040 or 1040-SR) even if you claim the standard deduction rather than itemizing deductions. You must enter the date of the original divorce or separation agreement and the Social Security number of your ex-spouse. Otherwise, your deduction may be disallowed and you may have to pay a $50 penalty. If you pay deductible alimony to more than one ex-spouse, enter the Social Security number of one of them and provide similar information for the others on a separate statement attached to your return.

If you receive taxable alimony, report the payments and enter the date of the divorce or separation agreement on Schedule 1 (Form 1040 or 1040-SR). You must give your ex-spouse your Social Security number and could be subject to a $50 penalty if you fail to do so.

Child support payments are not deductible by the parent who makes them or taxable to the parent who receives them, regardless of when the divorce occurred.

Transfers of property between spouses during marriage, as well as transfers incident to divorce, are generally treated as tax-free exchanges. The transferor-spouse does not realize gain or loss and the transferee takes the transferor's basis in the property *(6.6)*.

37.1 Rules for Post-2018 Divorce and Separation Agreements

If you have a divorce decree or separation agreement that is finalized after December 31, 2018, no deduction is allowed for alimony payments and the receipt of alimony payments is not taxable. There are no exceptions.

Modifications of earlier decrees. If you executed a divorce or separation instrument before January 1, 2019, but it is modified on or after this date, the above rules for post-2018 agreements apply only if the modification expressly states that alimony will not be deductible by the payer or taxable to the recipient. If the modification does not expressly state that the post-2018 rules apply to payments made after the date of the modification, the rules for pre-2019 agreements, discussed at *37.2–37.7*, continue to apply.

37.2 Rules for Pre-2019 Divorces or Separation Agreements

While the tax law has changed the treatment of alimony paid pursuant to post-2018 divorces and separation agreements *(37.1)*, the former tax treatment continues to apply to alimony paid under pre-2019 divorces and separation agreements.

Alimony requirements. For payments under a pre-2019 agreement to be alimony that is deductible by the payer and taxable to the recipient, separate returns must be filed if you are still married at the end of the year, and these rules must be met:

- The alimony must be paid under a decree of divorce or legal separation, a written separation agreement or decree of support *(37.3)*. Payments may be called alimony, spousal support, spousal maintenance, or another term required by local law.

- The agreement must provide for cash payments *(37.4)*. A noncash property settlement is not alimony. There is no minimum payout period for annual cash alimony payments. However, under a pre-2019 agreement, alimony deductions claimed in the first or second year had to be recaptured in the third year where payments within the first three years declined by more than $15,000 *(37.7)*.

- In providing for the support of children, a specific allocation to their support or the setting of certain contingencies disqualifies payments as alimony, so such payments are not deductible by the payer and not taxable to the recipient *(37.6)*.

- Divorced and legally separated parties must not live in the same household when payments are made. If they live in the same household, alimony payments are not deductible or taxable. However, there are these exceptions: A spouse who makes payments while preparing to leave the common residence may deduct payments made within one month before the departure. Also, where the spouses are separated under a written agreement, but not legally separated under a decree of divorce or separate maintenance, payments can be alimony even if they are members of the same household when the payments are made.

- The payer-spouse's liability to pay alimony must end on the death of the payee-spouse. The alimony agreement does not have to state expressly that payments end on death if liability ends under state law *(37.5)*.

Qualifying payments can be designated as "not alimony." You may specifically state in the decree or agreement that payments that otherwise would be alimony are not. A provision stating that the payments are neither taxable to the payee-spouse (under IRC Section 71) nor deductible by the payer-spouse (under IRC Section 215) effectively disqualifies the payments from alimony treatment. A copy of the agreement that contains the statement must be attached to the tax return of the payee-spouse for each year the statement is applicable.

Law Alert

Recipient's Legal Fees not Deductible

Legal fees allocable to the receipt of taxable alimony had been deductible before 2018 as a miscellaneous itemized deduction subject to the 2% of adjusted gross income floor. However, due to the suspension of this deduction for 2018 through 2025, write-offs can no longer be taken for legal fees related to marital settlements.

Filing Instruction

Reporting Alimony

If you paid alimony in 2023 meeting the deductible tests, you deduct the payment on Line 19a of Schedule 1 (Form 1040 or 1040-SR). You must report the recipient's Social Security number and the date of the original divorce or separation agreement on Lines 19b and 19c. If you received taxable alimony, report the income on Line 2a of Schedule 1 (Form 1040 or 1040-SR) and enter the date of the original divorce or separation agreement on Line 2b.

37.3 Decree or Agreement Required

To be deductible and taxable as alimony under pre-2019 divorces and separation agreements *(37.2)*, payments must be required by one of the following divorce or separation instruments: (1) a decree of divorce or legal separation; (2) a written separation agreement; or (3) a decree of support. Voluntary payments are not deductible or taxable.

When a decree of divorce or separate maintenance fails to mention alimony, payments qualify as long as they are made under a written agreement considered "incident to" the decree.

Payments made under an agreement amended after a divorce or legal separation may also qualify, if the amendment is considered "incident" to the divorce or separation. For example, the IRS agrees that a written amendment changing the amount of alimony payments is incident to the divorce where the legal obligation to support under the original agreement survived the divorce. However, payments under an amended agreement did not qualify where the original agreement settled all rights between the parties and made no provision for future support. The legal obligation to support the former spouse did not survive the divorce and could not be revived by the new agreement.

Divorced or legally separated. The obligation to pay alimony must be imposed by the decree of divorce or separate maintenance or a written agreement incident to the divorce or separation.

Alimony paid under a Mexican divorce decree qualifies. Payments under a Mexican or state decree declared invalid by another jurisdiction do not qualify according to the IRS. Two appeals courts have rejected the IRS position.

Support payments ordered by a court in a spouse's home state qualify as alimony, even though not provided for by an ex parte divorce decree obtained by the other spouse in another state. Similarly, payments qualified when a state court increased support originally ordered before the husband obtained an uncontested Mexican divorce.

Payments made under a separation approved by a Roman Catholic ecclesiastical board do not qualify.

Annulments. Payments made under an annulment decree qualify as deductible (and taxable) alimony.

Separated from spouse. Where spouses are separated and living apart, alimony is deductible by the payer-spouse and taxable to the payee-spouse provided it is paid under either a written separation agreement or decree of support.

A decree of support. Any court decree or order requiring support payments qualifies, including alimony pendente lite (temporary alimony while the action is pending) and an interlocutory (not final) divorce decree.

In certain community property states, payments under a decree of alimony pendente lite which do not exceed the spouse's interest in community income are neither deductible by one spouse nor taxable to the other spouse; payments exceeding a spouse's interest are taxable to that spouse and deductible by the other spouse.

37.4 Cash Payments Required

For purposes of pre-2019 divorces and separation agreements, only payments of cash, checks, and money orders payable on demand qualify as taxable and deductible alimony. Your cash payment to a third party for a spouse qualifies if made under the terms of a divorce decree or separation instrument. For example, as required by your divorce decree, you pay your former spouse's mortgage payments and real estate taxes on a home he or she owns, as well as his or her medical costs and tuition expenses. Assuming the other alimony tests *(37.2)* are met, you may deduct the payments as alimony and your former spouse must report them as alimony received. Your former spouse may deduct the real estate taxes, mortgage interest, medical and tuition costs as if he or she had paid them directly, subject to the regular deduction limits.

Planning Reminder

Property Transfers

A property transfer to a former spouse that is incident to a divorce is generally treated as a tax-free exchange *(6.6)*.

Planning Reminder

Payments to a Third Party

Cash payments to a third party may be deducted as alimony if they are under the terms of a pre-2019 divorce decree or separation instrument. You may also deduct as alimony payments made to a third party at the written request of the payee-spouse. For example, your former spouse asks you to make a cash donation to a charitable organization instead of paying alimony installments to her. Her request must be in writing and state that both she and you intend the payment to be treated as alimony. You must receive the written request before you file your return for the taxable year in which the payment was made. Your former spouse may deduct the payment as a charitable contribution if she claims itemized deductions.

You may not deduct payments to maintain property owned by you but used by your spouse. For example, you pay the mortgage expenses, real estate taxes, and insurance premiums for a house you own and in which your former spouse lives. You may not deduct those payments as alimony even if they are required by a decree or agreement.

Providing services or transferring or providing property does not qualify. For example, you may not deduct as alimony your note, the assignment of a third party note, or an annuity contract.

Premiums paid for term or whole life insurance on your life made under a divorce or separation instrument qualify as deductible alimony to the extent your former spouse owns the policy.

37.5 Payments Must Stop at Death

For alimony to be deductible by the payer-spouse and taxable to the payee-spouse under a pre-2019 divorce or separation agreement *(37.2)*, liability for a payment must end on the death of the payee-spouse. If all the payments must continue after the death of the payee-spouse, none of the payments, whether made before or after the payee's death, qualify as taxable (to payee-spouse) or deductible (by payer-spouse) alimony. If some payments must continue after the payee's death, that amount is not alimony regardless of when paid. The divorce decree or separation agreement does not have to specifically state that payments end at death, if under state law the liability to pay ends on the death of the payee-spouse.

Note that these rules do not just prevent a deduction for payments made to the payee-spouse's estate or heirs after the payee's death, but may also have the surprising result of disallowing an alimony deduction for otherwise qualifying payments actually made to the payee-spouse. The issue is a hypothetical one: would the payment have to be made after the payee-spouse's death? If the answer is yes, the payment is not deductible, regardless of when made.

EXAMPLES

1. Under the terms of a pre-2019 divorce decree, Smith is obligated to make annual alimony payments of $30,000, terminating on the earlier of the end of six years or the death of Mrs. Smith. She also is to keep custody of their two minor children. The decree also provides that if on her death the children are still minors, Smith is to pay annually $10,000 to a trust each year. The trust income and corpus are to be used for the children until the youngest child reaches the age of majority. Under these facts, Smith's possible liability to make annual $10,000 payments to the trust is treated as a substitute for $10,000 of the $30,000 annual payments. $10,000 of each of the $30,000 annual payments does not qualify as alimony.

2. Same facts as in Example 1, but the alimony is to end on the earlier of the expiration of 15 years or the death of Mrs. Smith. Further, if Mrs. Smith dies before the end of the 15-year period, Smith will pay her estate the difference between the total amount that he would have paid had she survived and the amount actually paid. For example, if she dies at the end of the tenth year, he will pay her estate $150,000 ($450,000 − $300,000). Under these facts, his liability to make a lump-sum payment to her estate is a substitute for the full amount of each of the annual $30,000 payments. Accordingly, none of the annual $30,000 payments qualify as alimony.

To the extent that one or more payments are to begin, increase in amount, or accelerate after the death of the payee-spouse, such payments may be viewed as a substitute for continuing payments after the death of the payee-spouse. Such substitute payments will be denied alimony treatment.

Attorneys' fees. Under the laws of many states, a court award of attorneys' fees remains enforceable after the death of the payee-spouse, thereby disqualifying a payer's alimony deduction for the payment and making it nontaxable to the payee-spouse. For example, a husband who was ordered by an Oklahoma court to pay his wife $154,000 for her attorneys' fees prior to the entry of a final divorce decree was unable to deduct his payment.

The Tax Court and the Tenth Circuit Court of Appeals agreed with the IRS that under Oklahoma law, the husband's liability to pay the attorneys' fees would not have ended, as a hypothetical matter, had the wife died before the final decree was entered. The policy reason for the state law is to assure that attorneys get paid for their services, which will enable indigent clients to retain counsel in divorce actions.

In this situation, the payer can obtain a deduction if the attorneys' fees remain the liability of the payee-spouse and the court decree increases the amount of cash alimony to cover the fees, rather than having them paid separately. The cash alimony would be taxable to the payee-spouse. The payee-spouse's payment of the fees to the attorneys were deductible for years before 2018 as a miscellaneous expense subject to the 2% of AGI floor, but this deduction has been suspended for 2018 through 2025.

37.6 Child Support Payments Are Not Alimony

A payment that is specifically designated as child support in a pre-2019 divorce or separation instrument *(37.3)* is not deductible by the payer or taxable as alimony to the payee.

Even if there is not a specific allocation to child support, a payment will be presumed by the IRS to be payable for child support if it is to be reduced on the happening of a contingency relating to the child, such as: the child reaches a specific age or income level, or the child leaves school, marries, leaves the parent's household, or begins to work.

If a divorce or separation instrument requires both alimony and child support payments, and child support payments for a prior year were missed, or current-year child support payments are less than the required amount, an expected alimony deduction for current-year payments can be lost because the payments are applied first to the child support obligations, including any arrearage. For example, a taxpayer paid $17,963 to his ex-spouse in 2004. His total child support obligation in 2004 for his two children was $23,147, of which $12,000 was for 2004 child support, $5,125 for past-due child support, and $6,022 to reimburse his ex-spouse for her payment of health insurance premiums and medical expenses for the children that he was obligated to pay. Since his total payments in 2004 of $17,963 were less than the total child support owed for 2004, the Tax Court held that all of the payments were allocable to the child support and not deductible as alimony.

Tax refund diversion for delinquent child support. The IRS can give your tax refund to a state that is paying support to your child if you fail to make support payments. The IRS will not notify you of the diversion until it is made to the state. However, the state agency must provide prior notice of the proposed offset and procedures for contesting it.

> **EXAMPLE**
>
> On March 1, 2017, Thomas and Tina were divorced when their children, John (born July 15, 2003), and Jane (born September 23, 2005), were ages 13 and 11. Under the divorce decree, Thomas is to make monthly alimony payments of $2,000. The monthly payments are to be reduced to $1,500 on January 1, 2024, and to $1,000 on January 1, 2028. On January 1, 2024, the date of the first reduction, John will be 20 years, 5 months, and 17 days old. On January 1, 2028, the date of the second reduction, Jane will be 22 years, 3 months, and 9 days old. As each reduction is to occur not more than one year before or after each child reaches the age of 21 years and four months, the IRS will presume that the reductions are associated with the happening of a contingency relating to the children. The two reductions total $1,000 per month and are treated as the amount fixed for the support of the children. Thus, $1,000 of the $2,000 monthly payment does not qualify as alimony. To avoid this result, Thomas must prove that the reductions were not related to the support of the children.

37.7 No Minimum Payment Period for Alimony

In the past, there was a recapture rule that applied if payments in the first three years dropped significantly. The purpose of the rule was to prevent front-loading of deductible alimony. However, because the first three years of payments under a pre-2019 agreement would have ended before 2022, the recapture rule cannot apply for 2023.

Caution

Alimony Reductions Tied to Child's Age

If a reduction in your payments is not specifically tied to your child's reaching majority age but the scheduled date for the reduction is within six months before or after your child reaches age 18 or 21 (or other age of majority under local law), the IRS holds that the reduction is tied to the child's age. The reduction amount will be treated as child support unless you can prove that the reduction is for some other purpose. The IRS makes the same presumption if you have more than one child and your alimony payments are to be reduced at least twice and each reduction is within one year of a different child's reaching a particular age between ages 18 and 24; *see* the Example in *37.6*.

CHAPTER 38

Other Taxes

The regular income tax figured on taxable income may not be the net amount of taxes you owe for the year. There are additional taxes that may apply to you. For example, if you employ a household worker, such as a nanny, you may owe employment taxes for this worker *(38.1–38.4)*.

Most additional taxes, including the alternative minimum tax *(23.1–23.5)*, are entered in Schedule 2 of Form 1040 or 1040-SR. Some of these other taxes are covered in this chapter; others are covered in chapters as noted in *Table 38-1*.

Estimated taxes *(27.1–27.5)* are not a separate tax liability; they are merely a way to pay taxes where income tax withholding does not cover the expected tax bill for the year.

38.1 Overview of Household Employment Taxes

If you hired someone to do household work in or around your home and you were able to control what work he or she did and how it was done, you had a household employee. This could include a babysitter, house cleaner, cook, nanny, yard worker, maid, driver, health aide, or private nurse. Unless an exception applies *(see below)*, such a worker is your employee regardless of whether the work is full or part time or whether you hired the worker through an agency or from a list provided by an agency or association. Also, it does not matter if the wages were paid for work done on an hourly, daily, weekly, or per-job basis.

If a worker is your household employee, you may have to withhold and pay Social Security and Medicare taxes (FICA) *38.2*, and pay federal unemployment tax (FUTA) *38.4*.

Workers who are not your employees. Workers you hire through an agency are not your employees if the agency is responsible for who does the work and how it is done. If you use a placement agency that exercises control over what work is done and how it is done, the worker is not your employee. Self-employed workers are also not your employees; in addition to maintaining control over how their work is done, self-employed workers usually provide their own tools and offer services to the general public. For example, you need work done on your lawn and you hire the self-employed owner of a lawn care business, who provides his own tools and supplies and hires and pays other workers as needed. He and his workers are not your household employees.

Notable exceptions to the household employee definition. You do not have to file a Schedule H and pay Social Security, Medicare, or federal unemployment taxes if the household employee was your spouse, your child who was under age 21, or, in most cases, your parent. However, for Social Security and Medicare tax *(38.2)* purposes, you must treat your parent as your household employee if he or she takes care of your child in your home for compensation and (1) the child is either under age 18 or has a physical or mental condition that requires personal care by a adult for at least four continuous weeks in a calendar quarter, and (2) you are divorced and not remarried, are widowed, or are living with a spouse whose physical or mental condition prevents him or her from caring for your child for at least four continuous weeks in a calendar quarter.

For Social Security and Medicare tax purposes, you do not have to include wages paid to an individual who is under age 18 at any point during the year so long as his or her principal occupation is not providing household services; a student under age 18 qualifies for this exception and is not considered a household employee.

Verifying employment status. It is unlawful to employ an alien who cannot legally work in the United States. If you hire a household employee to work for you on a regular basis, you and the employee must each complete part of the U.S. Citizenship and Immigration Services (USCIS) Form I-9, "Employment Eligibility Verification." By looking at documents the employee shows you, you must verify he or she is either a U.S. citizen or an alien who can legally work in the U.S. It is important to keep the Form I-9 for your records. The form and a USCIS Handbook for Employers can be obtained at www.uscis.gov or by calling (800) 870-3676. For answers to other questions about the employment eligibility verification process or other immigration-related matters, contact the USCIS Contact Center at (800) 375-5283.

Employee's Social Security number. You are required to get each employee's name and Social Security number and enter them on Form W-2. This applies to both resident and nonresident alien employees. You may not accept an individual taxpayer identification number (ITIN) in place of an SSN. An ITIN is only available to resident and nonresident aliens who are ineligible to work in the U.S. and need identification for tax purposes. You may verify up to 10 names and numbers by calling the Social Security Administration and registering for automated telephone access at (800) 772-6270, or by getting online access at SSA.gov/employer/ssnv.htm.

Table 38-1   Key to Other Taxes

Item—	Comments—
Alternative minimum tax	If you are able to reduce your regular tax bill through allowable deductions and other tax breaks, you may still owe tax through a shadow tax system called the alternative minimum tax (AMT). This applies when your income figured in a special way (with certain adjustments from the regular tax) exceeds an exemption based on your filing status *(23.1–23.5)*.
Household employment taxes	If you employ someone to care for your children or elderly parent in your home, clean your residence, cook, or provide personal services in or around your home, you may be obligated to pay and withhold Social Security and Medicare taxes, as well as federal unemployment (FUTA) taxes *(38.1–38.4)*.
Self-employment tax	If you have net earnings from an unincorporated business, such as a sole proprietorship, partnership, or limited liability company of $400 or more, you must figure Social Security and Medicare taxes on the net earnings; this is called self-employment tax *(45.1–45.6)*. If you also have wages and other taxable compensation, some or all of the Social Security portion of self-employment tax may be satisfied by FICA.
Additional tax on IRAs and other benefit plans	Certain actions with respect to various benefit plans results in a penalty. These include taking early distributions from IRAs and qualified retirement plans *(7.13, 7.17, 8.12)*, failing to take required minimum distributions (RMDs) from IRAs and qualified retirement plans *(7.11, 8.13)*, making contributions to IRAs and qualified retirement plans over allowable limits *(7.15, 8.7)*, taking withdrawals from health savings accounts for nonmedical purposes *(41.12)*, and taking distributions from Coverdell education savings accounts for nonqualified purposes *(33.11)*. These penalties are figured on Form 5329.
Kiddie tax	If you have a child under a certain age with investment income over $2,500 in 2023, you may have to figure the child's income tax using the parent's top marginal tax rate for such income over this threshold amount; the tax is imposed on the child. *(24.1–24.4)*.
Repayment of the first-time homebuyer credit	If you purchased a home in 2008 and qualified for the first-time homebuyer credit of up to $7,500, you must report 1/15th of the credit as an additional tax until it is fully recaptured *(25.17)*.
Additional Medicare tax on earned income	If you have earned income from a job or self-employment exceeding a threshold amount for your filing status, you must pay 0.9% on any excess earned income *(28.1–28.2)*.
Net Investment Income tax	If you have net investment income and your modified adjusted gross income is over a threshold amount for your filing status, you must pay 3.8% on the lesser of your net investment income or your MAGI over the threshold amount *(28.1 and 28.3)*.

38.2   Social Security and Medicare (FICA) Taxes for Household Employees

Income tax withholding is not required for a household employee *(38.3)*, but generally you must withhold Social Security and Medicare (FICA) taxes from the employee's cash wages and also pay the employer share of FICA yourself, unless the wages are below an annual threshold, which for 2023 is $2,600. You report and pay the FICA taxes on Schedule H, which you must attach to your Form 1040 or 1040-SR; *see 38.3*. If you pay the household employee cash wages of less than $2,600, the wages are not subject to FICA taxes.

Once payments to a household employee *(see 38.1 for employee exceptions)* equal or exceed $2,600 in 2023, the entire amount, including the first $2,600, is subject to FICA taxes. The $2,600 threshold may be increased for 2024 by an inflation adjustment.

Tax rates. If in 2023 you pay your household employee cash wages of $2,600 or more, you are liable for: (1) Social Security taxes at the rate of 12.4% (6.2% for you and also 6.2% for your employee) on wages up to the annual Social Security wage base, which for 2023 is $160,200, and (2) Medicare taxes at a rate of 2.9% (1.45% for each of you) on all wages with no limit.

Caution

W-2 Distribution Deadline

Even if you request an extension to file copies of Form W-2 with the Social Security Administration, you must still furnish Form W-2 for 2023 to each employee by January 31, 2024.

You are responsible for paying your employee's share of Social Security and Medicare taxes as well as your own share. You must either withhold your employee's share from his or her wages or pay it from your own funds. On Schedule H, you are liable for the total tax, both your share and the employee's share *(38.3)*. If you decide to pay the employee's share of the Social Security and Medicare taxes from your own funds rather than withholding the taxes from the employee's pay, you must treat your payment as additional wages when you report the employee's wages on his or her Form W-2, but the payment is not considered wages for purposes of figuring your FICA or FUTA liability on Schedule H; *see* the Example in *38.3*.

Withholding requirement for Additional Medicare Tax if employee paid over $200,000. In the unlikely situation where wages paid to a household employee exceed $200,000 for the year, you must withhold from your employee's pay, in addition to the 1.45% Medicare tax, the 0.9% Additional Medicare Tax from the wages exceeding $200,000 *(28.2)*. The 0.9% tax is imposed only on the employee; there is no separate employer share.

Estimated taxes. To cover the household employment taxes you owe, you may need to increase the federal income tax withheld from your pay or pay estimated taxes to avoid an estimated tax penalty *(27.1)*.

Reporting options for self-employed persons who have regular business employees as well as household employees. Self-employed persons who have business employees in addition to household employees may use one of the following reporting options:

1. Report FICA and FUTA taxes and any income tax withholding for household employees annually on Schedule H, and report FICA taxes and any income tax withholding for other employees quarterly on Form 941 and FUTA taxes annually on Form 940; or

2. Report FICA taxes and any income tax withholding for all employees (household employees as well as other employees) quarterly on Form 941 and report FUTA taxes annually on Form 940.

Small employers whose annual liability for Social Security, Medicare, and withheld federal income tax is $1,000 or less may be notified by the IRS that they must file Form 944 to report and pay the taxes only once a year, instead of quarterly on Form 941. If you are a new employer filing Form SS-4 to get an EIN *(38.3)* and expect to have $1,000 or less of employment tax liability, you may tell the IRS on the Form SS-4 that you would like to file Form 944. You may also make a request to use Form 944 if you have used Form 941 but expect to have employment tax liability of $1,000 or less for the upcoming calendar year; you must make the request by the deadline specified in the Form 944 instructions. If you receive a notification from the IRS that you must file Form 944, you may request a change to Form 941 filing; *see* the Form 944 instructions.

Employers of household employees must also give copies of Form W-2 ("Wage and Tax Statement") to each employee and to the Social Security Administration, as discussed in *38.3*.

38.3 Filing Schedule H To Report Household Employment Taxes

You must file Schedule H with your 2023 Form 1040 or 1040-SR if you paid any one household employee cash wages of $2,600 or more in 2023, or withheld federal income tax during 2023 for a household employee, or paid cash wages totaling $1,000 or more in any calendar quarter during 2022 or 2023 to all household employees. On Schedule H, you report the Social Security and Medicare taxes *(38.2)*, federal income taxes withheld, if any *(see below)*, and federal unemployment taxes *(38.4)* for your household employees. Total household employment taxes from Schedule H are entered on Line 9 of Schedule 2 (Form 1040 or 1040-SR).

If you get an extension to file your return, file Schedule H with the return by the extended due date. If you are not required to file a 2023 tax return, you may file Schedule H by itself by the filing deadline, April 15, 2024. The completed Schedule H should be mailed to the same address that you would use for filing a return, along with a check or money order for the total household employment taxes due.

Withholding federal income taxes. Income tax withholding is not required for a household employee, but if the employee requests withholding and you agree to do it, the employee must furnish you with a complete Form W-4, "Employee's Withholding Allowance Certificate." Use the income tax withholding tables in IRS Publication 15 (Circular E, Employer's Tax Guide), which has detailed instructions.

The Earned Income Credit (EIC). Copy B of Form W-2 has a notice about the EIC. If you do not give Copy B (or a substitute with similar EIC information) to your household employee by January 31, 2024, you must provide equivalent EIC notice on Notice 797 or your own written equivalent statement by the deadline. If you agreed to withhold federal income taxes from the employee's 2023 wages, but a Form W-2 is not required (under the Form W-2 instructions), the EIC notice should be given to the employee by February 7, 2024.

Fringe benefits. All or part of the value of certain fringe benefits is specifically excluded from a household employee's taxable wages. If you provide a household employee with lodging or meals on your premises, the benefits are not taxable if furnished for your convenience as a condition of employment. You may also provide tax-free transportation assistance to an employee. The tax-free limit for transportation fringe benefits in 2023 is $300 per month for transit passes you give to your household employee, and $300 per month for reimbursements you provide for your employee's parking costs near your home or near a mass transit location from which your employee commutes to your home.

EXAMPLE

On February 25, 2023, Nancy Nixon hired Eleanor Edwards to clean her house every Wednesday. She paid Eleanor $70 every Wednesday and did not withhold Eleanor's share of Social Security and Medicare (FICA) taxes from her wages. Instead, Nancy will pay Eleanor's share of Social Security and Medicare taxes out of pocket when she files Schedule H with her 2023 Form 1040. Nancy also did not withhold any federal income taxes because Eleanor did not give her a W-4 or in any other way request that income taxes be withheld. Nancy has never had any other household employee.

Eleanor worked for a total of 44 Wednesdays and received $3,080 (44 weeks × $70) in total cash wages from Nancy.

Eleanor's share of employment taxes paid by Nancy:
Social security tax $190.96 ($3,080 × 6.2%)
Medicare tax $44.66 ($3,080 × 1.45%)

Wages included in Box 1 of Eleanor's Form W-2 and Nancy's Form W-3:

Cash wages	$3,080
Eleanor's share of Social Security tax paid by Nancy	190.96
Eleanor's share of Medicare tax paid by Nancy	44.66
Total wages for Eleanor on Form W-2	$3,315.62

Although the taxable wages that Nancy reports for Eleanor in Box 1 of Form W-2 ($3,315.62) includes her payment of Eleanor's share of FICA taxes (Social Security and Medicare) in addition to the cash wages, only the cash wages of $3,080 are reported as Social Security and Medicare wages in Boxes 3 and 5 of Eleanor's Form W-2. When Nancy computes her liability for Social Security and Medicare taxes in Part I of Schedule H, she pays the combined employer/employee rate of 12.4% for Social Security and also the combined employer/employee Medicare rate of 2.9% on the cash wages of $3,080.

Nancy is not liable for FUTA tax *(38.4)* in Part II of Schedule H because she did not pay household employee wages of $1,000 or more in any quarter of 2022 (no household employees in 2022) or in any calendar quarter of 2023 to Eleanor.

Employer identification number (EIN). If you have a household employee, you will need an employer identification number (EIN) to report employment taxes on Schedule H. You can obtain an EIN by completing Form SS-4, Application for an Employer Identification Number. The number can be obtained immediately by phone, over the internet, or in four weeks if you apply by mail. If you applied for an EIN and are still waiting for it when filing Schedule H, do not enter your Social Security number as a substitute. Instead, enter "Applied For" and the date you applied for the EIN in the space provided for the number on Schedule H.

Forms W-2 and W-3. You need an EIN in order to properly file the necessary W-2 and W-3 forms. You must file a Form W-2 for each household employee to whom you paid $2,600 or more of cash wages in 2023 that are subject to Social Security and Medicare (FICA) taxes. You also must file Form W-2 for an employee whose wages were not subject to FICA taxes *(38.1)* but for whom you withheld income taxes. Furnish copies B, C, and 2 of Form W-2 to your household employee by January 31, 2024.

If you file one or more Forms W-2 for 2023, you must also file a Form W-3, Transmittal of Wage and Tax Statement. You must send Copy A of all Forms W-2 together with Form W-3 to the Social Security Administration (SSA) by January 31, 2024, whether you submit Forms W-2 and W-3 on paper or file electronically.

38.4 Federal Unemployment Taxes (FUTA) for Household Employees

As an employer, you are also liable for FUTA (federal unemployment taxes) for 2023 in Part II of Schedule H if you paid cash wages of $1,000 or more for household services (by all household employees) during any calendar quarter of 2023 or in any calendar quarter of 2022. Your employee is not liable for FUTA. You must pay it with your own funds. You do not pay FUTA on wages paid to your spouse, your parents, or your children under age 21. Schedule H is attached to your Form 1040 or 1040-SR. If you have regular business employees, *see 38.2* for more reporting options.

The FUTA rate is 6% of the first $7,000 of cash wages paid to each household employee in 2023. However, there is a credit of up to 5.4% for state unemployment taxes that reduces FUTA liability, resulting in a net tax of 0.6% where the full 5.4% credit is available. Only employers that pay all the required state unemployment fund contributions for 2023 by April 15, 2024, will receive the full credit; the credit for contributions made after this date, is limited to 90% of the pre-deadline credit.

In some years, employers in some states will not be entitled to the full 5.4% credit because the state owes money to the federal unemployment fund. A worksheet in the Schedule H instructions shows the reduced credit rate allowed in the affected states where applicable.

Caution

Check State Requirements for Employers

You may have to register and pay state unemployment tax for a household employee. Contact your state unemployment tax agency; IRS Publication 926 has contact information. You should also contact the state labor department to determine if you need to carry workers' compensation insurance or pay other state employment taxes.

Caution

Reduced Credit for Some States

If you are in a state that owes money to the federal unemployment fund, your FUTA credit for state unemployment taxes is reduced on Schedule H. Credit reduction states, if any, are listed in Schedule A of Form 940 and in the Schedule H instructions.

CHAPTER 39

Gift and Estate Tax Planning Basics

Gift planning can be an important part of estate planning. This chapter provides an overview of the federal gift tax and estate tax, which is separate and apart from income tax. Developing an estate plan for your assets requires professional assistance, but the basic guidelines in this chapter can help you begin to estimate your potential estate and start thinking about property transfers that may reduce or avoid the estate tax.

Relatively small gifts can completely avoid gift tax *(39.2)* because of the annual gift tax exclusion, which for 2023 is $17,000 per donee. Gifts to a spouse and certain gifts to pay educational or medical expenses also are not subject to the gift tax.

Gift tax *(39.4)* generally does not have to be paid even on substantial taxable gifts because the tax is offset by a tax credit that for 2023 effectively exempts up to $12.92 million of taxable gifts from the tax.

The credit for gift and estate taxes is unified, so the same exemption of $12.92 million applies to the estates of those dying in 2023, to the extent that the exemption was not used to offset lifetime taxable gifts. An unlimited estate tax marital deduction is allowed for transfers to a citizen spouse. The estate of a married individual can make a portability election that allows any portion of the decedent's unused exemption amount to pass to the surviving spouse.

Unless Congress acts, both the gift and estate tax exemptions will revert to $6.46 million as of January 1, 2026, as increased by inflation adjustments.

39.1 Gifts of Appreciated Property

Making a gift of appreciated property to a family member in advance of an anticipated sale can reduce the income tax liability for the family as a whole. By making a gift of interests in the property to several family members, it may be possible to spread the profit and the tax among a number of taxpayers in low tax brackets. Depending on the value of the property, you may or may not have to file a gift tax return *(39.2)*.

However, the tax benefit of making gifts of property to younger family members is limited by the "kiddie tax." The kiddie tax *(24.2)* also covers most 18-year-olds and college students age 19 to 23.

Do not make a gift of investment property such as stock that has decreased in value if you want a deduction for the loss. Once you give the property away, the loss deduction for income tax purposes is gone forever. Neither you nor your donee can ever take direct advantage of the loss. The better way is to first sell the property, get a loss deduction, and then make a gift from the proceeds of the sale.

Warning: The IRS may claim that the gift was never completed if, after sale by the donee, you control the sales proceeds or have the use of them.

39.2 Gift Tax Basics

You can make substantial gifts of cash or property without incurring gift tax liability because of exclusions allowed by the tax law. Even where a gift exceeds the available exclusions and is technically subject to the gift tax, liability computed on Form 709 can generally be avoided by applying the lifetime credit, which for 2023 effectively exempts up to $12.92 million of taxable gifts from the tax *(39.4)*.

The annual exclusion and other tax-free gifts. Gift tax liability may be avoided by making gifts that do not exceed the annual exclusion. The annual exclusion applies separately to each donee to whom you make gifts during a calendar year. For gifts made in 2023, the per-donee exclusion is $17,000, or $34,000 if your spouse consents on Form 709 to "split" your gifts. The annual exclusion is allowed only for cash gifts or gifts of present interests in property; gifts of future interests do not qualify. For gifts made in 2024, the annual exclusion might be increased above $17,000 by an inflation adjustment; *see* the *e-Supplement* at *jklasser.com* for an update.

Gifts to your spouse are completely tax free under the gift tax marital deduction if your spouse is a U.S. citizen at the time of the gift. For gifts to a spouse who is not a U.S. citizen, there is an annual exclusion, which for 2023 gifts is $175,000, provided that the $158,000 excess over the basic $17,000 annual exclusion otherwise qualifies for the marital deduction.

There is an unlimited gift tax exclusion for payments of another person's tuition or medical expenses, if you make the payment directly to the educational organization or care provider. The medical and educational exclusions are allowed without regard to the relationship between you and the donee for whom you are making the payments. The exclusion for directly paid educational expenses applies only to tuition, not to room and board, books, or supplies.

Contributions to a qualified tuition program (QTP; *see 33.5*) on behalf of a designated beneficiary do not qualify for the educational exclusion, but do qualify for an enhanced annual exclusion. You can elect to treat a QTP contribution over the basic annual exclusion as if it were made ratably over a five-year period, but only up to five times the annual exclusion. For example, a QTP contribution made in 2023 of up to $85,000 may be treated as if ⅕, or $17,000, had been contributed in 2023 and in each of the next four years. Thus, the entire gift up to $85,000 can avoid gift tax and if your spouse consents to split the gift on Form 709 *(39.3)* the exclusion increases to $170,000. If you make QTP contributions for more than one person in the same year, you can make the special QTP election for each of them.

Taxable gifts. If you make a gift that exceeds the allowable annual exclusion and which is not otherwise exempt from the gift tax, you must report the gift on Form 709 *(39.3)*. *Table 39-1 (39.9)* shows the tax rates applicable to taxable gifts made in 2023 and later years. However, the tax as computed using the rate table can be offset by the allowable credit *(39.4)*.

Planning Reminder

Annual Gift Tax Exclusion

For 2023, the annual gift tax exclusion *(39.2)* exempts from gift tax the first $17,000 of cash gifts and/or gifts of present interests made to each donee. If your spouse consents on Form 709 to split your 2023 gifts, the exclusion for each donee doubles to $34,000. Any change to the exclusion amount for gifts made in 2023 will be reported in the *e-Supplement* at *jklasser.com*.

If you make gifts of present interests in trust for more than one beneficiary, each beneficiary is treated separately for purposes of the annual exclusion. Also, if you give a present interest in property to more than one person as joint tenants, the annual exclusion can be claimed for each donee.

Caution

Gifts to ABLE Accounts not QTP Contributions

While contributions to a QTP qualify for five times the annual gift tax exclusion in one year, there is no comparable rule for contributions to ABLE accounts *(34.12)*; tax-free contributions in 2023 to ABLE accounts generally are limited to $17,000 (but can be higher through 2025 for contributions made by a designated beneficiary).

Basis for property received as gift. The basis for appreciated property received as a gift is generally the same as the donor's basis. If gift tax was paid by the donor, basis is increased. Gifts of property with a fair market value less than the donor's adjusted basis may trigger certain adjustments to basis, depending upon its value at the time of eventual disposition. The basis computation is explained in *5.17*.

39.3 Filing a Gift Tax Return

A gift tax return generally must be filed on Form 709 for a gift made during 2023 to an individual other than your spouse if it exceeds $17,000 or is a gift of a future interest (regardless of value). A return does not have to be filed for gifts qualifying for the tuition or medical expense exclusion discussed in *39.2*.

Married couples who want to split gifts of over $17,000 in 2023 to any one person must report the gifts to the IRS on Form 709 and the consenting spouse must sign the consent in Part I. No gift tax is due under the annual exclusion if the "split" gift is $34,000 or less.

Form 709 for 2023 generally must be filed by April 15, 2024. If you get a filing extension (Form 4868) for your income tax return, the extension also applies to the gift tax return. If you do not request an extension for your income tax return, you can use Form 8892 to request a filing extension for your gift tax return.

> **EXAMPLES**
>
> 1. On July 19, 2023, Randall Johnson makes a gift of publicly traded stock to his son, Philip. He gives Philip 1,000 shares of stock valued at $20,000 ($20 per share). His cost basis for the 1,000 shares was $16,000. On Randall's Form 709, Randall's wife, Claire, consents to split the gift, thereby doubling the $17,000 annual exclusion for the gift. Neither Randall nor Claire made any other gifts during 2023 and neither had made a taxable gift before 2023. As a result of the gift splitting, Randall and Claire are each considered to have made a gift of $10,000 that is offset by the annual exclusion for each of them. No gift tax is due.
>
> 2. Same facts as in Example 1 except that the value of the stock given to Philip was $40,000 instead of $20,000. After Claire consents to split Randall's gift, there is a taxable gift of $6,000 ($40,000 – $34,000 for two annual exclusions of $17,000), of which half, or $3,000, is attributed to each of them. They each must file their own Form 709. They will each figure a gift tax of $540 on their $3,000 gift *(Table 39-1)*, but no tax is due because it is offset by the credit *(39.4)*.

39.4 Gift Tax Credit

On Form 709, any gift tax that you otherwise would owe is eliminated or reduced by a tax credit. The credit applies to lifetime gifts, so any credit that was used to offset gift tax in prior years reduces the credit available for taxable gifts made in 2023 or later years. The amount of the gifts that can pass tax free depends on the applicable credit amount allowed for the year. For 2023, the maximum credit against taxable gifts is $5,113,800, unless it is increased for a surviving spouse because a portability election *(see below)* was made. The $5,113,800 applicable credit amount offsets the tax (figured under *Table 39-1*) on the basic exclusion amount for 2023 of $12.92 million ($12,920,000). The "exclusion amount" is often referred to as the "exemption" from tax. Since the basic exclusion amount (exemption) is subject to annual inflation increases and the credit is based on the basic exclusion amount, both amounts may increase for 2024; any increase will be in the *e-Supplement* at *jklasser.com*.

If your spouse died after 2010 and your spouse's estate made the "portability" election on a timely filed Form 706 to transfer to you his or her unused basic exclusion amount *(39.9)*, your maximum gift tax exclusion is increased by the unused exclusion amount from your spouse, thereby increasing your available tax credit; *see* the Form 709 instructions.

The basic exclusion amount and credit are "unified" for gift tax and estate tax purposes, so any basic exclusion amount/credit used to offset lifetime taxable gifts reduces the estate tax basic exclusion amount/credit that may be used by your estate *(39.9)*.

 *Caution*

Gift Disclosure Starts Running of Statute of Limitations

To begin the running of the statute of limitations on gift valuation, the gift must be adequately disclosed on Form 709 filed for the year of the gift. Follow the gift reporting instructions for Schedule A of Form 709. Given this statute of limitations consideration, even donors of property valued at under the annual exclusion ($17,000 for 2023) may want to report the gift on Form 709 in order to start the clock running on how long the IRS has to challenge valuation of the gift.

39.5 Custodial Accounts for Minors

A minor generally lacks the ability to manage property. You could create a formal trust, but this step may be costly. A practical alternative may be a custodial account under the Uniform Gifts to Minors Act (UGMA), or the Uniform Transfers to Minors Act (UTMA), which has replaced the UGMA in practically every state.

Custodial accounts set up in a bank, mutual fund, or brokerage firm can achieve income splitting; the tax consequences discussed below generally apply to such accounts. Trust accounts that are considered revocable under state law are ineffective in splitting income.

Although custodial accounts may be opened anywhere in the United States, the rules governing the accounts may vary from state to state. The differences between the laws of the states generally do not affect federal tax consequences.

There are limitations placed on the custodian. Proceeds from the sale of an investment or income from an investment may not be used to buy additional securities on margin. While a custodian should prudently seek reasonable income and capital preservation, he or she generally is not liable for losses unless they result from bad faith, intentional wrongdoing, or gross negligence.

When the minor reaches majority age (depending on state law), property in the custodial account is turned over to him or her. No formal accounting is required. The child, now an adult, may sign a simple release freeing the custodian from any liability. But on reaching majority, the child may request a formal accounting if there are any doubts as to the propriety of the custodian's actions while acting as custodian. For this reason, and also for tax recordkeeping purposes, a separate bank account should be opened in which proceeds from sales of investments and investment income are deposited pending reinvestment on behalf of the child. Such an account will furnish a convenient record of sales proceeds, investment income, and reinvestment of the same.

Income tax treatment of custodian account. Income from a custodian account is generally taxable to the child. However, if the "kiddie tax" applies *(24.2)*, taxable income from a custodial account in excess of the annual "kiddie" tax floor ($2,500 in 2023) is taxed to the child using the parent's top marginal rate.

If a parent is the donor of the custodial property or the custodian of the account and income from the account is used to discharge the parent's legal obligation to support the child, the account income is taxed to the parent.

Gift tax treatment of custodial account. When setting up a custodial account, you may have to pay a gift tax. A transfer of cash or securities to a custodial account is a gift. You are not subject to a gift tax if you properly plan the cash contributions or purchase of securities for your children's accounts. You may make gifts that are sheltered from gift tax by the annual exclusion. The exclusion applies each year to each person to whom you make a gift. If your spouse consents to join with you in the gift, the annual exclusion is doubled. For gifts in 2023, the per-donee exclusion is $17,000, $34,000 if your spouse consents to split the gift *(39.2)*.

If the custodial account is set up at the end of December, another tax-free transfer of up to the annual exclusion may be made in the first days of January of the following year. Assuming the annual exclusion in each year is $17,000, a total of $68,000 can be shifted within the two-month period with spousal consent.

Even if gifts exceeding the annual exclusion are made, gift tax liability may be offset by the unified credit *(39.4)*.

Estate tax treatment of custodial account. The value of a custodial account will be taxed in your estate if you die while acting as custodian of an account before your child reaches his or her majority. However, you may avoid the problem by naming someone other than yourself as custodian. If you should decide to act as custodian, taking the risk that the account will be taxed in your estate, remember that no estate tax is incurred if the tax on your estate is offset by the estate tax credit.

If you act as custodian and decide to terminate the custodianship, care should be taken to formally close the account. Otherwise, if you die while retaining power over the account, the IRS may try to tax the account in your estate.

Planning Reminder

529 Plans an Alternative to UTMAs

These education plans can be used in lieu of UTMAs to save money for children's education. UTMAs can be rolled into 529 plans *(33.6)*.

Planning Reminder

Custodial Securities Account

Purchase of securities through custodial accounts provides a practical method for making a gift of securities to a minor child, eliminating the need for a trust. The mechanics of opening a custodial account are simple. An adult opens a stock brokerage account for a minor child and registers the securities in the name of a custodian for the benefit of the child. The custodian may be a parent, a child's guardian, grandparent, brother, sister, uncle, or aunt. In some states, the custodian may be any adult or a bank or trust company. The custodian has the right to sell securities in the account and collect sales proceeds and investment income, and use them for the child's benefit or reinvestment. Tax treatment of custodial accounts is discussed in *39.5*.

39.6 Trusts in Family Planning

You establish a trust by transferring legal title to property to a trustee who manages the property for one or more beneficiaries. As the one who sets up the trust, you are called the grantor or settlor of the trust. The trustee may be one or more individuals or an institution such as a bank or a trust company.

You can create a trust during your lifetime or by your will. A trust created during your lifetime is called an inter vivos trust; one established in your will is a testamentary trust. An inter vivos trust can be revocable or irrevocable. An irrevocable trust does not allow for changes of heart; it requires a complete surrender of property. By conveying property irrevocably to a trust, you may relieve yourself of tax on the income from the trust principal. Furthermore, the property in trust usually is not subject to estate tax, although it may be subject to gift tax. A trust should be made irrevocable only if you are certain you will not need the trust property in a financial emergency.

Consult with an experienced tax professional if you are considering the use of a trust.

Trust income. When a child is a trust beneficiary, the child reports distributable net trust income as taxable income. Distributable net income may be subject to the "kiddie tax" *(24.2)*. Income that is accumulated for the benefit of a minor child is generally not taxable and, thus, not subject to the kiddie tax.

Grantor trusts. The grantor of a grantor trust is taxed on the income of the trust. A trust is treated as a grantor trust where the grantor has a reversionary interest (at the time of the transfer) of more than 5% of the value of the property transferred to the trust. Under an exception, a grantor is not treated as having a reversionary interest if that interest can take effect only upon the death before age 21 of a beneficiary who is a lineal descendant of the grantor. The beneficiary must have the entire present interest in the trust or trust portion for this exception to apply.

Given the highly compressed tax brackets for trust income, a grantor may intentionally retain an interest in the trust property so that he or she will be taxed under the grantor trust rules. By setting up such a "defective" grantor trust, trust income may be subject to lower tax at the grantor's tax bracket than under the trust rate schedule.

39.7 What is the Estate Tax?

The estate you built up may not be entirely yours to give away. If your estate is substantial enough, the federal government and, in most cases, at least one state government stand ready to claim their shares. The federal estate tax is a tax on the act of transferring property at death. It is not a tax on the right of the beneficiary to receive the property. If tax is due, the estate and the estate alone pays the tax, although the property passing to individual beneficiaries may be diminished by the tax.

You may not have to be concerned about a future federal estate tax liability because of the large exemption (also called the basic exclusion amount) allowed under the tax law. Current law allows a basic exclusion amount (exemption) of up to $12.92 million for 2023 estates *(39.9)*, and the basic exclusion amount will increase in future years with inflation adjustments (at least through 2025). However, your potential taxable estate may be larger than you realize. The estate includes not only your business interests, real estate holdings (foreign and domestic), bank accounts, retirement accounts, stocks and bonds, mutual funds, and personal property such as art objects, but can also include life insurance, your interest in trusts or jointly held property, and certain interests you have in other estates. *See* *39.8* for estimating the value of your potential estate.

You will need to consult with an experienced estate tax planning professional, who can explain the potential extent of estate tax costs and help you develop a plan that can avoid or reduce those costs.

 *Planning Reminder*

Revocable Trusts

In a revocable trust, you retain control over the property by reserving the right to revoke the trust. As such, it is considered an incomplete gift and offers no present income tax savings. Furthermore, the trust property will be included as part of your estate. But a revocable trust minimizes delay in passing property to beneficiaries if you die while the trust is in force. When you transfer property to a trust, the property is generally not subject to probate, administration expenses, delays attendant on distributions of estates, or claims of creditors. The interests of trust beneficiaries are generally more secure than those of heirs under a will because a will may be denied probate if found invalid.

Life Insurance

If you are buying a new policy with yourself as the insured, and you want to keep the proceeds out of your gross estate, set up an irrevocable trust to buy the policy or have the individual beneficiary buy the policy. For example, a daughter applies for a $1 million policy on her father's life and is the policy owner under the terms of the policy. If the father pays the premiums, his payments are treated as gifts, but the proceeds paid at his death are not subject to estate tax because he never had ownership rights in the policy.

If you have an existing policy, you may assign your ownership rights, such as the right to change beneficiaries, the right to surrender or cancel the policy, the right to assign it, and the right to borrow against it, but the assignment must occur more than three years before death to exclude the proceeds from your estate.

Executor Must Report Property Values to Heirs

If an estate tax return is required to be filed because the value of the gross estate is more than $12.92 million in 2023, the executor must tell the heirs (and the IRS) the estate tax value of the inherited property items. The estate tax value becomes the heirs' tax basis in the property for income tax purposes *(5.17)*.

39.8 Take Inventory and Estimate the Value of Your Potential Estate

The first step in estate tax planning requires taking inventory of all the assets you own. Your assets include your cash, real estate (domestic and international), securities, retirement accounts, mortgages, rights in property, trust accounts, personal effects, collections, and art works. Life insurance is includible if: (1) the policy is payable to your estate; (2) the policy is payable to others and you have kept "incidents of ownership" such as the right to change beneficiaries, surrender or assign the policy, or pledge the policy for a loan; or (3) you assign the policy and die within three years.

If you own property jointly with your spouse, your estate includes only one-half of the property's value.

If you had appraisals made of specially treasured items or collections, or property of substantial value, file such appraisals with your estate papers and then enter the value on your inventory.

Retirement benefits. The gross estate includes benefits payable at your death from any of the following retirement plans: corporate or self-employed pension and profit-sharing plans, traditional IRAs, Roth IRAs, or annuities. The fact that your account balance in an IRA, 401(k), or other retirement plan is a nonprobate asset that passes outside of the estate to the beneficiaries designated by the terms of the plan does not change the fact that these assets are included in the gross estate.

Estimating the value of your assets. When you have completed your inventory, assign to each asset what you consider to be its fair market value. This may be difficult to do for some assets. Resist the tendency to overvalue articles that arouse feelings of pride or sentiment and undervalue some articles of great intrinsic worth. For purposes of your initial estimate, it is better to err on the side of overvaluation. You can list ordinary personal effects at nominal value.

If you have a family business, your idea of the business's value and that of the IRS may vary greatly. Estate plans have been upset by the higher value placed on such a business by the IRS. You can protect your estate by anticipating this problem in consultation with your business associates and counselors.

If your business is owned by a closely held corporation, and there is no ready or open market in which the stock can be valued, get some factual basis for a figure that will be reported on the estate tax return. One of the ways to do this is by arranging a buy-sell agreement with a potential purchaser. This agreement must fix the value of the stock. Generally, an agreement that binds both the estate and the purchaser and restricts lifetime sales of the stock will effectively fix the value of the stock for estate tax purposes. Another option would be to make a gift of some shares to a family member and have value established in gift tax proceedings.

If a substantial part of your estate is real estate used in farming or a closely held business, your executor may be able to elect, with the consent of heirs having an interest in the property, to value the property on the basis of its farming or business use, rather than its highest and best use.

39.9 Estate Tax for 2023

The estate tax is figured by the executor on Form 706, "United States Estate (and Generation-Skipping Transfer) Tax Return." The executor must file Form 706 for the estate of an individual dying in 2023 if the gross estate, plus adjusted taxable gifts made after 1976, is more than $12.92 million ($12,920,000), the basic estate tax exclusion amount for 2023; the term "exemption" is often used interchangably with "exclusion amount". Form 706 also must be timely filed, regardless of the size of the decedent's gross estate, if the executor wants to make the portability election *(see below)* to permit the decedent's surviving spouse to use the decedent's unused basic exclusion amount. Form 706 must be filed within nine months after the date of death; an automatic six-month filing extension can be obtained by filing Form 4768.

On Form 706, the gross estate is reduced by allowable deductions. On the schedules of Form 706, deductions are allowed for funeral expenses, executor commissions, costs of preserving and distributing estate assets including attorney, accountant, and appraiser fees and court costs, debts owed by the decedent, bequests to a surviving spouse that qualify for the marital deduction, and charitable transfers. A deduction on Form 706 is also allowed for state death taxes (state estate, inheritance, legacy, or succession taxes) paid to any state or the District of Columbia on account of the decedent's death.

The estate tax rates from *Table 39-1* are applied to the taxable estate, the gross estate minus allowable deductions. If taxable gifts (over the annual gift tax exclusion) were made after 1976, the gifts are added to the taxable estate and the tax is figured on the total. The tentative tax from the rate table is reduced by the gift taxes paid or payable on the post-1976 gifts (*see* the Form 706 instructions). The practical effect of making the adjustments for prior taxable gifts is to reduce the basic exclusion amount and tax credit available to the estate by the basic exclusion amount and credit amounts used to offset the taxable gifts.

After making the required adjustments for lifetime gifts on Form 706, the resulting gross estate tax is then reduced by the applicable credit. The credit equals the tax on the basic exclusion amount (exemption). The basic exclusion amount for 2023 is $12.92 million, so the 2023 applicable credit is $5,113,800, the tax on a net estate of $12.92 million (*see Table 39-1*). The basic exclusion amount is increased above $12.92 million if the decedent is the surviving spouse of a predeceased spouse who died after 2010 and the executor of the earlier estate made the portability election on Form 706. If the basic exclusion amount is increased by the portability election, the applicable credit is also increased, so that it equals the tax on the increased basic exclusion amount.

If there is any estate tax due on Form 706 after subtracting the applicable credit (and any other available credits), the balance must be paid within nine months after the date of death, but if it is impossible or impractical to meet the deadline, a request for a payment extension may be made on Form 4768; a detailed explanation must be attached to justify the request.

Portability election. The estate of a married individual dying after 2010 can make a special portability election to benefit a surviving spouse. The election allows any part of the basic exclusion amount that was unused by the deceased spouse for gift or estate tax purposes to be left to the surviving spouse. The portable amount is called the "deceased spousal unused exclusion," or DSUE.

The estate of a 2023 decedent makes the portability election on Part 6 of Form 706. Generally, the election must be made on a timely filed and complete Form 706 (filed within nine months of the decedent's death or by the end of the six-month extension period if Form 4768 was filed). Form 706 must be filed to elect portability even if the assets of the estate are below the filing threshold ($12.92 million for 2023). However, if the executor was not otherwise required to file Form 706 (value of estate was below filing threshold), and the return was not timely filed solely to elect portability, Revenue Procedure 2022-32 allows an extension. The executor may file the Form 706 and elect portability on or before the fifth anniversary of the decedent's death. At the top of the Form 706, the executor should state that the return is "Filed Pursuant to Rev. Proc. 2022-32 to Elect Portability under section 2010(c)(5)(A)." For more information on this extension, *see* Rev. Proc. 2022-32 (2022-30 IRB 101).

If the executor of an estate of a decedent with a surviving spouse is required to file Form 706 and does not want to elect portability, check the box in Section A of Part 6 to opt out.

The surviving spouse on whose behalf the portability election is made may increase his or her lifetime gift tax exemption (basic exclusion amount) by the transferred DSUE, or it will increase the basic exclusion amount available to his or her estate. If the surviving spouse who received the DSUE from a predeceased spouse died in 2023, the basic exclusion amount allowed to his or her estate on Form 706 is increased by the DSUE that was not applied against lifetime gifts. On the 2023 Form 706, the available DSUE is entered on Line 9b of Part II, and is added to the basic exclusion amount of $12.92 million shown on Line 9a.

 *Caution*

Form 706 Must Be Filed for Small Estates to Get Portability

The estate of a deceased married person must file Form 706 to make a portability election for the surviving spouse. This is so even though Form 706 is not otherwise required to be filed where the value of the estate is below the filing threshold ($12.92 million for 2023).

39.10 Planning for a Potential Estate Tax

If you have substantial assets that forseeably may exceed the basic exclusion amount (exemption) available to your estate, there are general approaches that you can take to reduce or eliminate a potential estate tax.

You can make direct lifetime gifts. Any appreciation on the property transferred will be removed from your estate. Furthermore, each gift, to the extent of the annual per donee exclusion *(39.2)*, reduces your gross estate *(39.9)*. Life insurance can be assigned to avoid estate tax, provided the assignment takes place more than three years before death *(39.8)*. You can provide in your will for bequests that will qualify for the marital and charitable deductions.

The marital deduction. An unlimited marital deduction is available for property passing to a spouse who is a U.S. citizen. What should be done if you believe your spouse cannot manage property? The law permits you to put the property in certain trust arrangements that provide the surviving spouse with ownership rights sufficient to allow the marital deduction. An estate tax attorney can explain how you can protect your spouse's interest and qualify the trust property for the marital deduction.

Life insurance proceeds may qualify as marital deduction property. Name your spouse the unconditional beneficiary of the proceeds with unrestricted control over any unpaid proceeds. If your spouse is not given this control or general power of appointment, and there is no requirement that proceeds remaining on your spouse's death be payable to his or her estate, the insurance proceeds will not qualify for the marital deduction.

Marital deduction restrictions for noncitizen spouses. A marital deduction may not be claimed for property passing outright to a surviving spouse who is not a U.S. citizen. However, the marital deduction is allowed if the surviving spouse's interest is in a qualifying domestic trust (QDOT). At least one trustee must be an individual U.S. citizen or domestic corporation with power to withhold estate tax due from distributions of trust corpus. The trust must maintain sufficient assets as required by IRS regulations. For the marital deduction to apply, the executor must make an irrevocable election on the decedent's estate tax return. On Form 706-QDT, estate tax will apply to certain distributions of trust corpus made prior to the surviving spouse's death, and to the value of the QDOT property remaining at the surviving spouse's death. You should consult an experienced tax practitioner to set up a QDOT trust and plan for distribution provisions.

The estate of a nonresident alien is subject to estate tax only to the extent that the estate is located in the United States. A marital deduction may be claimed by the estate of a nonresident alien for property passing to a surviving spouse who is a U.S. citizen. If the surviving spouse is not a U.S. citizen, then the transferred interest must be in the form of a QDOT.

Periodically review your estate plan. No estate plan is ever really final. Economic conditions and inflation constantly change values. For this reason, your plan must be reviewed periodically as changes occur in your family and business, as when a birth or death occurs; when you receive a substantial increase or decrease in income; when you enter a new business venture or resign from an old one; or when you sell, retire from, or bring new persons into your business. A member of your family may no longer need any part of your estate, while others may need more. Material changes may occur in the health or life expectancy of one of your beneficiaries. Furthermore, tax law changes may require you to adjust your estate planning, Beginning on January 1, 2026, the gift and estate tax exemptions will fall to half of the 2023 or later years' exemption, or $6.46 million, adjusted for inflation since then, if Congress takes no action to extend the existing exemptions or otherwise change gift and estate tax rules. In connection with any post-2025 "sunset" amount, however, the IRS has reassured taxpayers (IR-2019-189) that it will not retroactively "claw back" gifts made while the higher exemption amount is in place. Also important in any estate and gift tax plan is the impact of any possible state estate or inheritance taxes that may be due, depending upon residency.

Caution

Generation-Skipping Transfer Tax

Tax may not be avoided by having a grandparent transfer property to a grandchild, skipping the child's generation. A special tax, called the generation-skipping transfer (GST) tax, may apply in this case (whether the transfer is made during life or at death). The GST exemption amount for 2023 is $12.92 million (the basic estate tax exclusion amount). The GST rules are complicated and you should consult an experienced tax professional if you are contemplating a generation-skipping transfer.

Table 39-1	Unified Estate and Gift Tax Schedule for 2022 and Later Years			
If taxable amount is: over—	But not over—	The tax is—	Plus %—	Of the amount over—
$0	$10,000	$0	18	$0
10,000	20,000	1,800	20	10,000
20,000	40,000	3,800	22	20,000
40,000	60,000	8,200	24	40,000
60,000	80,000	13,000	26	60,000
80,000	100,000	18,200	28	80,000
100,000	150,000	23,800	30	100,000
150,000	250,000	38,800	32	150,000
250,000	500,000	70,800	34	250,000
500,000	750,000	155,800	37	500,000
750,000	1,000,000	248,300	39	750,000
1,000,000		345,800	40	1,000,000

PART 6

Business Tax Planning

In this part, you will learn how to report your income from a business, profession, or other self-employed activity, and how to reduce your tax liability by claiming expense deductions. Pay special attention to—

- Reporting rules for income and expenses on Schedule C *(Chapter 40)*.
- Restrictions on deducting home office expenses. Your deduction may be limited by a restrictive income test *(Chapter 40)*.
- The 20% deduction for qualified business income (QBI) *(Chapter 40)*.
- SEP, and SIMPLE, and qualified retirement plan rules if you are self-employed. These plans offer tax deductions for contributions and tax-free accumulation of income within the plan *(Chapter 41)*.
- Health savings accounts and other medical plans *(Chapter 41)*.
- First-year expensing and depreciation write-offs for business assets *(Chapter 42)*.
- The IRS mileage allowance as an alternative to claiming actual expenses for your business automobile *(Chapter 43)*.
- Reporting sales of business property on Form 4797 *(Chapter 44)*.
- Computing and paying self-employment tax on self-employment earnings from a business or profession *(Chapter 45)*.

CHAPTER 40

Income or Loss From Your Business or Profession

As a self-employed person, you report income and expenses from your business or profession separately from your other income, such as income from wages. On Schedule C, you report your business income and itemize your expenses. Any net profit is subject to self-employment tax, as well as regular tax. A net profit can also be the basis of deductible contributions to a SEP or qualified retirement plan, as discussed in *Chapter 41*.

If you work out of your home, you may deduct home office expenses *(40.12)*.

If you claim a loss on Schedule C, be prepared to show that you regularly and substantially participate in the business. Otherwise, your loss may be considered a passive loss deductible only from passive income, as discussed in *Chapter 10*.

If you show a profit, you may be eligible for a personal deduction of 20% of qualified business income *(40.24)*. If you have a loss that you can't fully use on your 2023 return, you may be able to carry it forward to offset income in future years *(40.18)*.

Schedule F for Farming Business

If you are self-employed and your business involves farming, you report on Schedule F instead of Schedule C. However, much of the information contained in *Chapters 40 through 45* applies to you as well.

40.1 Forms of Doing Business

The legal form of your business determines the way you report business income and loss, the taxes you pay, the ability of the business to accumulate capital, the extent of your personal liability, and whether you qualify to take a 20% qualified business income (QBI) deduction off your taxable income. It is beyond the scope of this book to discuss the pros and cons of each form. The decision should be made with the services of a professional experienced in both the legal and tax consequences of doing business in a particular form as it applies to your current and future business prospects, especially in light of the 21% tax rate on regular corporations.

If you are going into business alone, your choices are: operating as a sole proprietor, incorporating, and forming a limited liability company (LLC). If you are going to operate with associates, you may choose to operate as a partnership, a corporation, or an LLC. If you are concerned with limiting your personal liability, your choice is between a corporation or an LLC. An LLC gives you the advantage of limited liability without having to incorporate.

As a sole proprietor, you report business profit or loss on your personal tax return, as explained in this chapter. If you are a partner, you report your share of partnership profit and loss as explained in *Chapter 11*. If you incorporate, the corporation pays tax on business income. You are taxed on salaries and dividends paid to you by the corporation. You may avoid this double corporate tax by making an S corporation election, which allows you to report corporate income and loss *(11.14)*.

If you operate through an LLC with no co-owners, you report income and loss as a sole proprietor. If you operate an LLC with associates, the LLC reports as a partnership and you report your share of income and loss. However, under check-the-box rules, the LLC may elect on Form 8832 to report as an association taxable as a corporation.

40.2 Reporting Self-Employed Income

You file a Schedule C along with Form 1040 or 1040-SR if you are a sole proprietor of a business or a professional in your own practice. If you do freelance work as an independent contractor, you are self-employed and use Schedule C. If you are an employee but have a sideline business (e.g., you work through a platform such as TaskRabbit, Fiverr or Upwork), report the self-employment income and expenses from that business on Schedule C. File a separate Schedule C for each different business you run (e.g., one for being a freelance writer and another for running a boutique). Do not file Schedule C if your business is operated through a partnership or corporation. *See* the guide to Schedule C in *40.6*.

On Schedule C, you deduct your allowable business expenses from your business income. Net business profit (or loss) figured on Schedule C is entered on Line 3, Schedule1 (Form 1040 or 1040-SR). Thus, business profit (or loss) is added to (or subtracted from) nonbusiness income on Form 1040 or 1040-SR to compute adjusted gross income. This procedure gives you the chance to deduct your business expenses, whether you claim itemized deductions on Schedule A, such as charitable contributions, state and local taxes up to $10,000, and medical expenses, or you claim the standard deduction where it exceeds your allowable itemized deductions *(13.2)*.

Passive loss restrictions. Pay special attention to the passive loss restrictions discussed in *Chapter 10*. Generally, if you do not regularly and substantially participate in your business, losses are considered passive and are deductible only against other passive income.

Recordkeeping. You are required to keep books and records for your business activities, tracking your income and expenses carefully so you can report them accurately on your return. You enter this information according to your method of accounting *(40.3)*.

The tax law does not determine the way in which you must keep these records; today most self-employed taxpayers use computer-based or cloud-based recordkeeping systems.

Tax ID number. As a sole proprietor, you usually do not need a separate tax ID number for Schedule C; you can use your Social Security number as your tax ID number. However, you must obtain an employer identification number if you have any employees and/or maintain a qualified retirement plan (you may also need one to open a business bank account). You can obtain your employer identification number online at https://www.irs.gov/businesses/small-businesses-self-employed/employer-id-numbers.

Spouses Can File on Schedule C for Jointly Owned Business

Instead of having to file a partnership return, spouses can elect qualified joint venture status and each file as sole proprietors on Schedule C if they are the sole owners of their business, they both materially participate in the business, and they file a joint return; *see 40.6* for details.

Table 40-1 Key to Reporting Business and Professional Income and Loss

Item—	Comments—
Tax return to file	If you are self-employed, prepare Schedule C to report business or professional income. If you are a farmer, use Schedule F. You attach Schedule C and/or F to Schedule 1 (Form 1040 or 1040-SR). If you operate as a partnership, use Form 1065; if you operate as a corporation, use Form 1120-S or Form 1120. If you are a one-member limited liability company that has not elected to be taxed as a corporation, file Schedule C.
Method of reporting income	The cash or accrual accounting rules determine when you report income and expenses. You must use the accrual basis if you sell a product that must be inventoried unless you meet a new gross receipts test. The cash-basis and accrual-basis methods are discussed at *40.3*.
Tax reporting year	There are two general tax reporting years: calendar years that end on December 31 and fiscal years that end on the last day of any month other than December. Your taxable year must be the same for both your business and nonbusiness income. Most business income must be reported on a calendar-year basis. If, as a self-employed person, you report your business income on a fiscal-year basis, you must also report your nonbusiness income on a fiscal-year basis. Use of a fiscal year is restricted for partnerships and S corporations.
Office in home	To claim home office expenses as a self-employed person, you must use the home area exclusively and on a regular basis either as a place of business to meet or deal with patients, clients, or customers in the normal course of your business or as your principal place of business *(40.12)*. You may claim a standard amount (simplified method) on Schedule C or use Form 8829 to compute the deduction based on actual expenses *(40.13)*.
Social Security coverage	If you have self-employment income, you may have to pay self-employment tax, which goes to financing Social Security and Medicare benefits; *see Chapter 45*.
Passive participation in a business	If you do not regularly, continuously, and substantially participate in the business, your business income or loss is subject to passive activity restrictions. A loss is deductible only against other passive activity income. The passive activity restrictions are discussed in detail in *Chapter 10*.
Self-employed retirement plan	You may set up a retirement plan based on business or professional income. Individuals who are self-employed may contribute to a self-employed retirement plan, according to the rules in *Chapter 41*.
Health insurance	You may deduct 100% of premiums paid for health insurance coverage for yourself, spouse, and dependents. This deduction is claimed directly from gross income on Schedule 1 (Form 1040 or 1040-SR). You may also take advantage of a health savings account; *see Chapter 41*.
Depreciation	Under the first-year expensing deduction, you generally may deduct up to $1,160,000 for equipment placed in service in 2023 *(42.3)*. Depreciation rules for assets not deducted under first-year expensing are in *Chapter 42*. Cars and trucks are subject to special depreciation limits; *see Chapter 43*.
Losses	A loss incurred in your profession or business is deducted from other income reported on Form 1040 or 1040-SR. If the loss exceeds income, the excess is carried forward to offset 80% of taxable income in future years until used up *(40.18)*. A current deduction for losses is limited if income is over a set amount, with any excess losses treated as net operating losses in the following year *(40.20)*.
Sideline business	You report business income of a sideline business following the rules that apply to full-time business. For example, if you are self-employed, you report business income on Schedule C. You may also have to pay self-employment tax on this income; *see Chapter 45*. You may also set up a self-employment retirement plan based on such income; *see Chapter 41*. If you incur losses over several years, the hobby loss rules *(40.10)* may bar any loss deduction.
Qualified business income deduction	If your business is profitable, you may qualify for a personal deduction of 20% of your profits (with certain adjustments) reported on Schedule C. The deduction does not reduce your business income; it is a subtraction from taxable income on Form 1040 or 1040-SR *(40.24)*.

Law Alert

Cash Method for Small Businesses

Businesses with average annual gross receipts in 2023 of $29 million or less in the three prior years are eligible to use a cash method ("gross receipts test").

Planning Reminder

Advantage of Cash Basis Accounting

The cash basis has this advantage over other accounting methods: You may defer reporting income by postponing the receipt of income. But make certain that you avoid the constructive receipt rule. For example, if 2023 is a high income year or you might drop to a lower tax bracket in 2024, you might delay mailing some of your customers' bills so they do not receive them until 2024. You may also postpone the payment of presently due expenses to a year in which the deduction gives you a greater tax savings.

Filing Tip

Changing to Cash Method

A change to the cash method under the gross receipts test is an automatic change in accounting method. *See* Rev. Proc. 2022-14.

40.3 Accounting Methods for Reporting Business Income

Business income is reported on either the accrual or cash basis. If you have more than one business, you may have a different accounting method for each business.

Inventories. Unless the gross receipts test *(discussed below)* applies, the IRS requires inventories at the beginning and end of every taxable year in which the production, purchase, or sale of merchandise is an income-producing factor. If you must keep inventories, you must use the accrual basis unless you meet the gross receipts test.

Cash method. You report income items in the taxable year in which they are received; you deduct all expenses in the taxable year in which they are paid. Under the cash method, income is also reported if it is "constructively" received. You have "constructively" received income when an amount is credited to your account, subject to your control, or set apart for you and may be drawn by you at any time. For example, in 2023 you receive a check in payment of services, but you do not cash it until 2024. You have constructively received the income in 2023, and it is taxable in 2023.

On the cash basis, you deduct expenses in the year of payment. Expenses paid by credit card are deducted in the year they are charged. Expenses paid through a "pay by phone" account with a bank are deducted in the year the bank sends the payment. This date is reported by the bank on your account statements.

Advance payments. Generally, no immediate deduction can be claimed for advance rent or premium covering charges of a later year. However, under a "12-month rule," you can claim an immediate deduction for prepayments that create rights or benefits that do not extend beyond the earlier of: (1) 12 months after the first date on which the taxpayer realizes rights or benefits attributable to the expenditure, or (2) the end of the taxable year following the taxable year in which the payment is made. However, prepayments of rent remain nondeductible for accrual-method taxpayers under the economic performance rules.

Cash method of accounting limited. Generally, the following may not use the cash method: a regular C corporation, a partnership with a C corporation as a partner, a tax shelter, or a tax-exempt trust with unrelated business income. However, in 2023, businesses with average annual gross receipts of $29 million or less in the three prior years ("gross receipts test") can use the cash method. This is so even if the business would otherwise have to account for inventories under the accrual method. A qualifying taxpayer may not deduct items purchased for resale to customers or used as raw materials for producing finished goods until the year the items are provided to customers if that is later than the year the items were purchased. A qualifying small business that used the accrual method in 2022 and wants to change to the cash method in 2023 must file for an accounting method change as explained in the instructions to Form 3115.

Accrual method. On the accrual method, report income that has been earned, whether or not received, unless your right to collect the income is unsure because a substantial contingency may prevent payment; *see* the Example below. In technical language, income for a business reporting on the accrual method is includible in gross income when all the events have occurred that fix the right to receive the income and the amount to be received can be determined with reasonable accuracy (the "all events test").

> **EXAMPLE**
>
> You report business income as a calendar-year accrual taxpayer. You sell several products on December 28, 2023, and bill the customer in January 2024. You report the sales income on your 2023 Schedule C, even though payment is not made until 2024. Under the accrual method, you are considered to earn the income when the products are sold and delivered to the customer.

Where you are prepaid for services to be performed in a later year, you usually can elect to defer income for only one year. However, this election does not apply to prepaid rents and certain other items. Expenses under the accrual method are deductible in the year your liability for payment is fixed, even though payment is made in a later year. To prevent manipulation of expense deductions, there are tax law tests for fixing the timing of accrual method expense deductions. The tests generally require that economic performance must occur before a deduction may be claimed, but there are exceptions, such as for "recurring expenses." These rules are discussed in IRS Publication 538.

Long-term contracts. Section 460 of the Internal Revenue Code has a special percentage of completion method of accounting for long-term construction contractors.

Capitalize costs of business property you produce or buy for resale. A complicated statute (Code Section 263A) generally requires manufacturers and builders to capitalize certain indirect costs (such as administrative costs, interest expenses, storage fees, and insurance), as well as direct production expenses, by including them in inventory costs; *see* IRS Publication 538, Form 3115, and the regulations to Code Section 263A.

Non-accrual experience method (NAE) for deferring service income. Taxpayers using the accrual method who either provide services in the fields of health, law, accounting, actuarial science, engineering, architecture, performing arts, or consulting, or who in 2023 meet the gross receipts test (the test is in "cash method" above), can use the non-accrual experience method (NAE). If you qualify, you do not have to accrue amounts that on the basis of your experience will not be collected. However, if interest or a penalty is charged for a failure to make a timely payment for the services, income is reported when the amount is billed. Furthermore, if discounts for early payments are offered, the full amount of the bill must be accrued; the discount for early payment is treated as an adjustment to income in the year payment is made.

Regulation Section 1.448(f) allows four safe harbor NAE methods.

Planning Reminder

Advantage of Accrual-Method Accounting

The accrual method has this advantage over the cash basis: It generally gives a more even and balanced financial report.

40.4 Tax Reporting Year for Self-Employed

Your taxable year must be the same for both your business and nonbusiness income. If you report your business income on a fiscal year basis, you must also report your nonbusiness income on a fiscal year basis.

Generally, you report the tax consequences of transactions that have occurred during a 12-month period. If the period ends on December 31, it is called a calendar year. If it ends on the last day of any month other than December, it is called a fiscal year. A reporting period, technically called a taxable year, can never be longer than 12 months unless you report on a 52-to-53-week fiscal year basis, details of which can be found in IRS Publication 538. A reporting period may be less than 12 months whenever you start or end your business in the middle of your regular taxable year, or change your taxable year.

To change from a calendar year to fiscal year reporting for self-employment income, you must ask the IRS for permission by filing Form 1128. Support your request with a business reason such as that the use of the fiscal year coincides with your business cycle. To use a fiscal year basis, you must keep your books and records following that fiscal year period.

Fiscal year restrictions. Restrictions on fiscal years for partnerships, personal service corporations, and S corporations are discussed in *11.11* and IRS Publication 538.

40.5 Reporting Certain Payments and Receipts to the IRS

In certain situations, you are required to report payments and receipts to the IRS. If you fail to comply with this reporting requirement, you can be penalized.

Payments to independent contractors. If you pay independent contractors, freelancers, or subcontractors a total of $600 or more within the year, you must report all payments to the IRS and the contractors on Form 1099-NEC. For 2023 payments, furnish the contractor with the form and provide a copy to the IRS by January 31, 2024, whether you file by paper or electronically.

The penalty for not filing or filing late depends on the extent of tardiness. For example, the penalty is only $60 per information return if you miss the due date but then file correctly within 30 days. The maximum penalty for 2023 returns filed in 2024 can go

 *Caution*

Reporting Requirements for Merchant Transactions

Banks and credit card processors report to the IRS all credit card and electronic payments (including PayPal, Google Checkout, and Amazon Pay) of merchants. Reporting is required if your total transactions for the calendar year exceed $600, regardless of the number of transactions. If you do receive Form 1099-K, you are not required to reconcile amounts reported on the form with your income. Report your gross receipts in the usual way, taking into account returns, allowances, and other adjustments (not reflected on Form 1099-K).

 *Filing Tip*

Penalty Relief Program for Form 5500-EZ Late Filers

Delinquent returns can be submitted without penalty, although there is an IRS $500 filing fee. Details are in Revenue Procedure 2015-32.

as high as $220,500 for a small business, which includes a self-employed individual with average annual gross receipts for three years of $5 million or less.

Receipts of cash payments over $10,000. If you are paid more than $10,000 in cash in one or more related transactions in the course of your business, you must report the transaction to the IRS. "Cash" includes currency, cashier's checks, money orders, bank drafts, and traveler's checks having a face amount of $10,000 or less received in a transaction used to avoid this reporting requirement. File Form 8300 with the IRS no later than the 15th day after the date the cash was received. For example, if you receive a $12,000 cash payment on May 1, 2023, you must report it by May 16, 2023.

You have until January 31 of the year following the year of the transaction to give a written statement to the party that paid you. In the Example above, this means giving the statement to the party that paid you on May 1, 2023, by January 31, 2024.

There can be civil and even criminal penalties for not filing this return.

Pension distributions to employees. If your business maintains a qualified retirement plan and makes distributions from the plan to you or any employee, you must report the distributions to the IRS on Form 1099-R and furnish a copy to the recipient.

Furnish each contractor and the IRS with a Form 1099-R by January 31, 2024, for 2023 payments.

The penalty is $60, $120, or $310 per return for late filing, depending on the lateness of the return (*see* the general instructions for Forms 1099).

Retirement plans. If you maintain a qualified retirement plan (other than a SEP or SIMPLE-IRA), you must file an annual information return with the Department of Labor unless your plan is exempt.

No return is required if you (or you and your spouse) are the only participant(s) and plan assets at the end of 2023 do not exceed $250,000. However, regardless of the amount of plan assets, a return is required in the final year of the plan.

File Form 5500-EZ if you (or you and your spouse) are the only participant(s). If your plan covers employees, file Form 5500. The form is an IRS form, but it is filed with the Employee Benefits Security Administration of the U.S. Department of Labor (DOL). The due date for the form is the last day of the seventh month after the close of the plan year (e.g., July 31, 2024, for 2023 calendar-year plans).

The IRS's late filing penalty is $250 per day (up to $150,000). In addition, there is a DOL penalty.

Small cash transactions. If you are in a business, such as a convenience store, liquor store, or gas station, that sells or redeems money orders or traveler's checks in excess of $1,000 per customer per day or issues your own value cards, the government asks that you report any suspicious transactions that exceed $2,000. While this filing isn't mandatory (there is no penalty for non-filing), the Treasury Department asks that you report when someone provides false or expired identification, buys multiple money orders in even hundred-dollar denominations or in unusual quantities, attempts to bribe or threaten you or your employee, or does anything else suspicious.

File FinCEN Form 109, "Suspicious Activity Report by Money Services Business," with the Treasury Department within 30 days of the suspicious activity (it is filed electronically by submitting a "Registration of Money Service Business (RMSB)" form through the BSA e-filing system at https://bsaefiling.fincen.treas.gov/main.html). Under federal law, you are protected from civil liability so the person you report cannot sue for damages.

Wages to employees. If you have any employees, including your spouse or child, you must report wages for the year to the Social Security Administration and the employee. Furnish the employee with Form W-2 and a copy plus a transmittal form with the Social Security Administration by January 31 of the year following the year in which the wages were paid.

40.6 Filing Schedule C

In this section are explanations of how a sole proprietor reports income and expenses on Schedule C, a sample of which is on the following pages. If you have more than one sole proprietorship, use a separate Schedule C for each business.

Statutory employees. Statutory employees report income and expenses on Schedule C. Thus, expenses may be deducted in full on Schedule C. Statutory employees are full-time life insurance salespersons, agent or commission drivers distributing certain foods and beverages, pieceworkers, and full-time traveling or city salespersons who solicit on behalf of and transmit to their principals orders from wholesalers and retailers for merchandise for resale or for supplies.

The term full time refers to an exclusive or principal business activity for a single company or person and not to the time spent on the job. If your principal activity is soliciting orders for one company, but you also solicit incidental orders for another company, you are a full-time salesperson for the primary company. Solicitations of orders are considered incidental to a principal business activity if you devote 20% or less of your time to the solicitation activity. A city or traveling salesperson is presumed to meet the principal business activity test in a calendar year in which he or she devotes 80% or more of working time to soliciting orders for one principal.

IRS regulations give this example: A salesperson's principal activity is getting orders from retail pharmacies for a wholesale drug company called Que Company. He occasionally takes orders for two other companies. He is a statutory employee only for Que Company.

If you are a statutory employee, your company checks Box 13 on Form W-2, identifying you as a statutory employee. Although a statutory employee may treat job expenses as business expenses, the employer withholds FICA (Social Security and Medicare) taxes on wages and commissions.

If you received a Form W-2 with "Statutory employee" checked in Box 13, include the income from Box 1 of the W-2 on Line 1 of Schedule C and check the box on that line. If you also have self-employment earnings from another business, you must report the self-employment earnings and statutory employee income on separate Schedules C. If both types of income are earned in the same business, allocate the expenses between the two activities on the separate schedules.

Gross receipts or sales on Schedule C. Your gross receipts are reported on Line 1 of Schedule C.

If you received business payments through merchant credit cards and third party networks such as PayPal, Amazon Pay, and Google Checkout, such payments should have been reported to you by banks and third party network payers in Box 1 of Form 1099-K if your total transactions are $600 or more for the year. No special reporting on Schedule C is required; report gross receipts as you would whether or not you receive Form 1099-K. As discussed above, "statutory employee" income from Form W-2 is entered on Line 1.

Do not report as receipts on Schedule C the following items:

- Gains or losses on the sale of property used in your business or profession. These transactions are reported on Schedule D and Form 4797.
- Dividends from stock held in the ordinary course of your business. These are reported as dividends from stocks that are held for investment.

Deductions on Schedule C. You can usually deduct most expenses incurred in your business, although there may be limits on the amount or timing of deductions. The basic requirement for deductibility is that expenses must be ordinary and necessary to your business. An ordinary expense is one that is common and accepted in your business; a necessary expense is one that is helpful and appropriate to your business.

Deductible business expenses are claimed in Part II; the descriptive breakdown of items is generally self-explanatory. However, note these points:

Car and truck expenses (Line 9): In the year you place a car in service, you may choose between the IRS mileage allowance and deducting actual expenses, plus depreciation. You must also attach Form 4562 to support a depreciation deduction; *see Chapter 43.*

Filing Tip

Spouses Can Elect Qualified Joint Venture Status for Their Business

Instead of having to file a partnership return, spouses can elect qualified joint venture status, which allows them to file as sole proprietors on Schedule C, provided they are the sole owners of their business, they both materially participate in the business, and they file a joint return.

To make the election, each spouse must file a separate Schedule C and report his or her respective share of the income and expenses from the business. For a rental real estate business, Schedule E is used instead of Schedule C.

If the election is made, each spouse's share of the net profit is considered to be his or her self-employment earnings for purposes of figuring self-employment tax *(45.1)* and for crediting Social Security and Medicare benefits.

Filing Tip

Health Insurance Premiums

As a sole proprietor, you do not deduct your health insurance premiums on Schedule C. Instead, you deduct 100% of health insurance costs for yourself, your spouse, and your dependents on Line 17 of Schedule 1 (Form 1040 or 1040-SR).

Claim health savings account contributions on Line 13 of Schedule 1 (Form 1040 or 1040-SR) *(41.11).*

Sample Schedule C—Profit or Loss From Business
(This sample is subject to change; see the e-Supplement at jklasser.com)

SCHEDULE C **(Form 1040)** Department of the Treasury Internal Revenue Service	**Profit or Loss From Business** (Sole Proprietorship) Attach to Form 1040, 1040-SR, 1040-SS, 1040-NR, or 1041; partnerships must generally file Form 1065. Go to *www.irs.gov/ScheduleC* for instructions and the latest information.	OMB No. 1545-0074 **2023** Attachment Sequence No. **09**

Name of proprietor | Social security number (SSN)

A Principal business or profession, including product or service (see instructions)

B Enter code from instructions

C Business name. If no separate business name, leave blank.

D Employer ID number (EIN) (see instr.)

E Business address (including suite or room no.)
City, town or post office, state, and ZIP code

F Accounting method: **(1)** ☐ Cash **(2)** ☐ Accrual **(3)** ☐ Other (specify)

G Did you "materially participate" in the operation of this business during 2023? If "No," see instructions for limit on losses   ☐ Yes ☐ No

H If you started or acquired this business during 2023, check here   ☐

I Did you make any payments in 2023 that would require you to file Form(s) 1099? See instructions   ☐ Yes ☐ No

J If "Yes," did you or will you file required Form(s) 1099?   ☐ Yes ☐ No

Part I   Income

1	Gross receipts or sales. See instructions for line 1 and check the box if this income was reported to you on Form W-2 and the "Statutory employee" box on that form was checked ☐	**1**
2	Returns and allowances	**2**
3	Subtract line 2 from line 1	**3**
4	Cost of goods sold (from line 42)	**4**
5	**Gross profit.** Subtract line 4 from line 3	**5**
6	Other income, including federal and state gasoline or fuel tax credit or refund (see instructions)	**6**
7	**Gross income.** Add lines 5 and 6	**7**

Part II   Expenses. Enter expenses for business use of your home **only** on line 30.

8	Advertising	**8**	**18**	Office expense (see instructions)	**18**
9	Car and truck expenses (see instructions)	**9**	**19**	Pension and profit-sharing plans	**19**
10	Commissions and fees	**10**	**20**	Rent or lease (see instructions):	
11	Contract labor (see instructions)	**11**	**a**	Vehicles, machinery, and equipment	**20a**
12	Depletion	**12**	**b**	Other business property	**20b**
13	Depreciation and section 179 expense deduction (not included in Part III) (see instructions)	**13**	**21**	Repairs and maintenance	**21**
			22	Supplies (not included in Part III)	**22**
			23	Taxes and licenses	**23**
			24	Travel and meals:	
14	Employee benefit programs (other than on line 19)	**14**	**a**	Travel	**24a**
15	Insurance (other than health)	**15**	**b**	Deductible meals (see instructions)	**24b**
16	Interest (see instructions):		**25**	Utilities	**25**
a	Mortgage (paid to banks, etc.)	**16a**	**26**	Wages (less employment credits)	**26**
b	Other	**16b**	**27a**	Other expenses (from line 48)	**27a**
17	Legal and professional services	**17**	**b**	Energy efficient commercial bldgs deduction (attach Form 7205)	**27b**

28	**Total expenses** before expenses for business use of home. Add lines 8 through 27b	**28**
29	Tentative profit or (loss). Subtract line 28 from line 7	**29**
30	Expenses for business use of your home. Do not report these expenses elsewhere. Attach Form 8829 unless using the simplified method. See instructions. **Simplified method filers only:** Enter the total square footage of (a) your home: _____ and (b) the part of your home used for business: _____ . Use the Simplified Method Worksheet in the instructions to figure the amount to enter on line 30	**30**
31	**Net profit or (loss).** Subtract line 30 from line 29. • If a profit, enter on both **Schedule 1 (Form 1040), line 3,** and on **Schedule SE, line 2.** (If you checked the box on line 1, see instructions.) Estates and trusts, enter on **Form 1041, line 3.** • If a loss, you **must** go to line 32.	**31**
32	If you have a loss, check the box that describes your investment in this activity. See instructions. • If you checked 32a, enter the loss on both **Schedule 1 (Form 1040), line 3,** and on **Schedule SE, line 2.** (If you checked the box on line 1, see the line 31 instructions.) Estates and trusts, enter on **Form 1041, line 3.** • If you checked 32b, you **must** attach **Form 6198.** Your loss may be limited.	**32a** ☐ All investment is at risk. **32b** ☐ Some investment is not at risk.

For Paperwork Reduction Act Notice, see the separate instructions.   Cat. No. 11334P   Schedule C (Form 1040) 2023

Sample Schedule C—Profit or Loss From Business
(This sample is subject to change; see the e-Supplement at jklasser.com)

Schedule C (Form 1040) 2023   Page **2**

Part III   **Cost of Goods Sold** (see instructions)

33   Method(s) used to
value closing inventory: **a** ☐ Cost   **b** ☐ Lower of cost or market   **c** ☐ Other (attach explanation)

34   Was there any change in determining quantities, costs, or valuations between opening and closing inventory?
If "Yes," attach explanation . . . . ☐ Yes   ☐ No

35	Inventory at beginning of year. If different from last year's closing inventory, attach explanation . . .	35	
36	Purchases less cost of items withdrawn for personal use	36	
37	Cost of labor. Do not include any amounts paid to yourself	37	
38	Materials and supplies	38	
39	Other costs	39	
40	Add lines 35 through 39	40	
41	Inventory at end of year	41	
42	**Cost of goods sold.** Subtract line 41 from line 40. Enter the result here and on line 4	42	

Part IV   **Information on Your Vehicle. Complete this part only if you are claiming car or truck expenses on line 9 and are not required to file Form 4562 for this business. See the instructions for line 13 to find out if you must file Form 4562.**

43   When did you place your vehicle in service for business purposes? (month/day/year) _____/_____/_____

44   Of the total number of miles you drove your vehicle during 2023, enter the number of miles you used your vehicle for:

a Business _____   **b** Commuting (see instructions) _____   **c** Other _____

45   Was your vehicle available for personal use during off-duty hours? . . . . ☐ Yes   ☐ No

46   Do you (or your spouse) have another vehicle available for personal use?. . . . . ☐ Yes   ☐ No

47a   Do you have evidence to support your deduction? . . . . ☐ Yes   ☐ No

    b   If "Yes," is the evidence written? . . . . ☐ Yes   ☐ No

Part V   **Other Expenses.** List below business expenses not included on lines 8–26, line 27b, or line 30.

---	
48 **Total other expenses.** Enter here and on line 27a	48	

Schedule C (Form 1040) 2023

Depreciation (Line 13): Enter here the amount of your annual depreciation deduction or Section 179 expensing. A complete discussion of depreciation may be found in *Chapter 42*. You must figure your deduction on Form 4562 for assets placed in service in 2023, or for cars or other "listed property," regardless of when the assets were placed in service.

Employee benefit programs including health insurance (Line 14): Enter your cost for the following programs you provide for your employees: accident or health plans; QSEHRAs, ICHRAs, and EBHRAs *(41.14)*; group-term life insurance; long-term care insurance coverage; wage continuation; dependent care assistance; educational assistance programs; supplemental unemployment benefits; and prepaid legal expenses. Retirement plan contributions for employees, such as to pension and profit-sharing plans, are reported separately on Line 19.

Insurance other than health insurance (Line 15): Insurance policy premiums for the protection of your business, such as accident, burglary, embezzlement, marine risks, plate glass, public liability, workers' compensation, fire, storm, or theft, and indemnity bonds upon employees, are deductible. State unemployment insurance payments are deducted here or as taxes if they are considered taxes under state law.

Premiums paid on an insurance policy on the life of an employee or one financially interested in a business, for the purpose of protecting you from loss in the event of the death of the insured, are not deductible.

Under a "12-month" rule, prepaid premiums can be deducted in the year paid if the coverage term does not extend more than 12 months beyond the first date coverage is received, and also does not extend beyond the taxable year following the year in which the premium is paid.

Premiums for disability insurance to cover loss of earnings when out ill or injured are nondeductible personal expenses. But you may deduct premiums covering business overhead expenses.

Interest (Line 16): While large businesses have a limitation on how much interest they can deduct, small businesses (the same $29 million gross receipts test in 2023 for using the cash method explained earlier on page 694) can deduct all business interest unless other limitations apply. Include interest on business debts, but prepaid interest that applies to future years is not deductible.

Interest on a loan against a life insurance policy on the life of a self-employed person or his or her employee is deductible only to the extent the loan is no more than $50,000.

Pension and profit-sharing plans (Line 19): SEP, SIMPLE, or qualified retirement plan contributions made for your employees are entered here; contributions made for your account are entered on Line 16 of Schedule 1 (Form 1040 or 1040-SR) as an adjustment to income. In addition, you may have to file an information return by the last day of the seventh month following the end of the plan year *(41.8)*.

Rent on business property (Line 20): Rent paid for the use of lofts, buildings, trucks, and other equipment is deductible. Prepaid rents can be deducted by cash-method taxpayers in the year of payment if the rent term does not extend more than 12 months beyond the first day of the lease and also not beyond the end of the taxable year following the taxable year in which the prepayment is made. However, the economic performance rules prevent accrual-method taxpayers from deducting prepaid rent; economic performance occurs only ratably over the lease term.

Taxes on leased property that you pay to the lessor are deductible as additional rent.

Repairs (Line 21): The cost of repairs and maintenance generally is deductible. Expenses of repairs or replacements that increase the value of property, make it more useful, or lengthen its life are capitalized and their cost recovered through depreciation unless safe harbors or *de minimis* rules under final repair regulations are used.

Taxes (Line 23): Deduct real estate and personal property taxes on business assets here. Also deduct your share of Social Security and Medicare taxes paid on behalf of employees and payments of federal unemployment tax. Federal highway use tax is deductible. Federal import duties and excise and stamp taxes normally not deductible as itemized deductions are deductible as business taxes if incurred by the business. Taxes on business property, such as an ad valorem tax, must be deducted here; they are not to be treated as itemized deductions. However, the IRS holds that you may not deduct

Caution

Interest on Business Tax Deficiency

Interest on a tax deficiency based on business income reported on Form 1040 or 1040-SR is not a deductible business expense; interest on a tax deficiency is always nondeductible personal interest.

Filing Tip

Tax Advice and Tax Preparation Costs

On Line 17 of Schedule C, you deduct the portion of tax preparation costs allocable to preparing Schedule C and related tax forms. Also deduct on Line 17 fees for tax advice related to the business.

state income taxes on business income as a business expense. Its reasoning: Income taxes are personal taxes even when paid on business income. As such, you may deduct state income tax only as an itemized deduction on Schedule A, subject to the $10,000 limit on personal state and local taxes *(16.1)*. The Tax Court supports the IRS rule on the grounds that it reflects Congressional intent toward the treatment of state income taxes in figuring taxable income.

For purposes of computing a net operating loss, state income tax on business income is treated as a business deduction.

If you pay or accrue sales tax on the purchase of nondepreciable business property, the sales tax is a deductible business expense. If the property is depreciable, add the sales tax to the cost basis for purposes of computing depreciation deductions.

Travel and meals (Line 24): Travel expenses (lodging and transportation) on overnight business trips while "away from home" *(20.5)* are claimed on Line 24a. All deductible meal expenses, including business meals on travel away from home, are claimed on Line 24b. The limit is 50% of cost incurred (80% for transportation industry workers subject to the Department of Transportation hours of service limits). Wining and dining customers, vendors and other business associates at a nondeductible entertainment event (e.g., a ballgame) is deductible, provided the meals are not lavish or extravagant under the circumstances, the cost of the meals is separately billed from the cost of the entertainment, and the owner or an employee is present *(20.14)*.

Self-employed persons may use the IRS meal allowance rates *(20.4)*, instead of claiming actual expenses. Recordkeeping requirements for travel expenses are discussed in *20.16*.

Utilities (Line 25): Deduct utilities such as gas, electric, and telephone expenses incurred in your business. However, if you have a home office *(40.12)*, you may not deduct the base rate (including taxes) of the first phone line into your home *(19.15)*.

Wages (Line 26): You do not deduct wages paid to yourself. You may deduct reasonable wages paid to family members who work for you. If you have an employee who works in your office and also in your home, such as a domestic worker, you deduct that part of the salary allocated to the work in your office. If you claim any employment-related tax credit *(40.26)*, the wage deduction is reduced by the credit.

Other expenses (Line 27): In Part V of Schedule C, you list deductible expenses not reported in Part II, such as amortizable business start-up costs *(40.11)*, business-related education *(33.15)*, subscriptions, and professional dues, energy-efficient commercial buildings, and enter the total on Line 27.

Home office deduction (Line 30): If you qualify for this deduction, it is first figured separately on Form 8829 if you use the actual expense method, or multiply your square footage (up to 300 square feet) by $5; the deductible amount is then entered here *(40.12)*.

Net profit (or loss) (Line 31): The net results of your entries on lines 1 through 30 will produce a profit (or loss). A profit, called net earnings from self-employment, is subject to self-employment tax *(45.1–45.6)*. It may also be subject to a 0.9% additional Medicare tax *(28.2)*. But a profit may entitle you to a 20% deduction *(40.24)*.

Limited deduction for business gifts. Your deduction for gifts to business customers and clients is limited to $25 per person per year. You and your spouse are treated as one person in figuring this limitation even if you do not file a joint return and even if you have separate business connections with the recipient. The $25 limitation also applies to partnerships; thus a gift by the partnership to one person may not exceed $25, regardless of the number of partners. Gifts not coming within the $25 limit are: (1) scholarships that are tax free under the rules in *Chapter 33*; (2) prizes and awards that are tax free under the rules in *11.1*; and (3) awards to employees, discussed below.

If you made a gift to the spouse of a business associate, it is considered as made to the associate. If the spouse has an independent bona fide business connection with you, the gift is not considered as made to the associate unless it is intended for the associate's eventual use. If you made a gift to a corporation or other business group intended for the personal use of an employee, stockholder, or other owner of the corporation, the gift generally is considered as made to that individual.

 *Caution*

Employment Tax Responsibilities

If you have employees, you must comply with employment tax responsibilities, such as collecting and paying to the government income tax withholding from employee wages. For details, *see* IRS Publication 15, Circular E, Employer's Tax Guide.

 *Filing Tip*

Deduction for Commercial Buildings

Owners and leaseholders of commercial buildings that are certified to meet certain energy-efficiency standards are able to qualify for a deduction for 2023 of up to $5.36 per square foot: *see* Form 7205 and its instructions.

Packaged food or drink given to a business associate is a gift if it is to be consumed at a later time. Theater or sporting event tickets given to business associates are entertainment, not gift, expenses if you accompany them; they are not deductible *(20.13)*. If you do not accompany them, you may treat the tickets as gifts, subject to the $25 limitation.

In figuring the $25 limitation to each business associate, do not include the following items:

1. A gift of a specialty advertising item that costs $4 or less on which your name is clearly and permanently imprinted. This exception saves you the trouble of having to keep records of such items as pens, desk sets, plastic bags, and cases on which you have your name imprinted for business promotion.

2. Signs, displays, racks, or other promotional material that is used on business premises by the person to whom you gave the material.

3. Incidental costs of wrapping, insuring, mailing, or delivering the gift. However, the cost of an ornamental basket or container must be included if it has a substantial value in relation to the goods it contains.

Deducting length of service or safety achievement awards to employees. There is an exception to the $25 gift deduction limitation for achievement awards of tangible personal property given to your employees in recognition of length of service or safety achievement, provided they are given as part of a presentation under circumstances indicating that they are not a form of disguised compensation. These rules do not apply to cash awards, gift cards, gift certificates (unless they entitle the employee to select from an approved employer list of items of tangible personal property), vacations, meals, lodging, tickets to sports or theater events, stocks, bonds, other securities, or similar items.

The amount of your deduction for the cost of a length of service or safety achievement award depends on whether it is considered a qualified plan award. To be a qualified plan award, the award must be given under an established written plan or program that does not discriminate in favor of highly compensated employees. The average cost of all awards under the plan for the year (to all employees) must not exceed $400. In determining this $400 average cost, awards of nominal value are not to be taken into account. You may deduct up to $1,600 for all qualified plan awards (safety and length of service) given to the same employee during the taxable year. If the award is not a qualified plan award, the annual deduction ceiling for each employee is $400. The $1,600 overall limit applies if the same employee receives some qualified plan awards and some non-qualified awards during the same year. Claim the deduction as a non-wage expense on your Schedule C. In a partnership, the deduction limitation applies to the partnership as well as to each partner.

A length of service award does not qualify as an employee achievement award if it is given during the employee's first five years or if another length of service was received in the current year or previous four years.

A safety award granted to managers, administrators, clerical employees, or professional employees are not considered employee achievement awards. Furthermore, if during the year more than 10% of other employees (not counting managers, administrators, clerical employees, or professional employees) previously received safety awards, none of the later awards are subject to the employee achievement award rules.

The amount that you deduct (up to the $400 or $1,600 limit) for an employee achievement award is tax free to the employee *(3.12)*. For example, you give a qualified plan award costing $2,000 to an employee. You may deduct only $1,600. The employee is not taxed on the award up to $1,600; the $400 balance is taxable.

40.7 Deductions for Professionals

The following expenses incurred by self-employed professionals in the course of their work are generally allowed as deductions from income when figuring profit (or loss) from their professional practices on Schedule C:

- Dues to professional societies.
- Operating expenses and repairs of car used on professional calls.
- Supplies.
- Subscriptions to professional journals.

 *Caution*

Employee Bonuses

Employee bonuses should not be labeled as gifts. An IRS agent examining your records may, with this description, limit the deduction to $25 unless you can prove the excess over $25 was compensation. By describing the payment as a gift, you are inviting an IRS disallowance of the excess over $25. This was the experience of an attorney who gave his secretary $200 at Christmas. The IRS disallowed $175 of his deduction. The Tax Court refused to reverse the IRS. The attorney could not prove that the payment was for services.

- Continuing education courses.
- Rent for office space.
- Cost of fuel, light, water, and telephone used in the office.
- Salaries of assistants.
- Malpractice insurance *(40.6)*.
- Cost of books, information services, professional instruments, and equipment with a useful life of one year or less. Professional libraries are depreciable if their value decreases with time. Depreciation rules are discussed in *42.1*.
- Fees paid to a tax preparer for preparing Schedule C and related business forms.

Professionals as employees. Professionals who are not in their own practice may not deduct professional expenses on Schedule C. Salaried professionals may not deduct professional expenses, which previously were claimed as miscellaneous itemized deductions on Schedule A, subject to the 2% of adjusted gross income (AGI) floor *(19.1)*, because this deduction has been suspended though 2025. However, "statutory" employees may use Schedule C *(40.6)*.

The cost of preparing for a profession. You may not deduct the cost of a professional education *(33.15)*.

The IRS does not allow a deduction for the cost of a license to practice. However, the Tax Court has allowed attorneys to amortize over their life expectancy bar admission fees paid to state authorities.

Payment of clients' expenses. An attorney may follow a practice of paying his or her clients' expenses in pending cases. The IRS will disallow a deduction claimed for these payments on the grounds that the expenses are those of the client, not the attorney. The courts agree with the IRS position where there is a net fee agreement. In a net fee agreement, expenses first reduce the recovery before the attorney takes a fee. However, where the attorney is paid under a gross fee agreement, an appeals court has reversed a Tax Court decision that disallowed the deduction of the attorney's payment of client expenses. Under a gross fee agreement, the attorney's fee is based on the gross award; the prior payment of expenses does not enter into the fee agreement and so is not reimbursed. Because he would not be reimbursed, an attorney claimed his payment of client expenses was deductible. An appeals court accepted this argument and allowed the deduction. The court allowed the deduction although California law disapproved of the practice of paying client expenses without a right of reimbursement. The court believed that there is no ethical difficulty with the practice and other jurisdictions approve of it. It is necessary for and it is the practice of personal injury firms to pay the costs of many of their clients.

If you are not allowed a current deduction for payment of clients' expenses, you may deduct your advance as a bad debt if the claim is worthless in another year *(40.6)*.

An attorney might deduct a payment to a client reimbursing the client for a bad investment recommended by the attorney. A court upheld the deduction on the grounds that the reimbursement was required to protect the reputation of an established law practice. However, no deduction is allowed when malpractice insurance reimbursement is available, but the attorney fails to make a claim.

40.8 Nondeductible Expense Items

Capital expenditures may not be deducted. Generally, the cost of acquiring an asset or of prolonging its life is a capital expenditure that must be amortized over its expected life. If the useful life of an item is less than a year, its cost, including sales tax on the purchase, is deductible. Otherwise, you generally may recover your cost only through depreciation except to the extent first-year expensing *(42.3)* or bonus depreciation *(42.30)* applies. IRS regulations provide safe harbors, including a "12-month" rule, for expenditures relating to intangible assets or benefits *(40.3)*.

Expenses while you are not in business. You are not allowed to deduct business expenses incurred during the time you are not engaged in your business or profession.

Filing Tip

Partners May Deduct Unreimbursed Business Expenses

Business expenses paid by partners (not reimbursed by the partnership) are deducted on Line 28 of Schedule E and noted as "UBE." *See 11.10*.

Caution

Penalties and Fines

Penalties or fines paid to a government agency because of a violation of any law are not deductible. You may deduct penalties imposed by a business contract for late performance or nonperformance.

Caution

No Deductions for Cannabis Businesses

Even though the sale of marijuana for medical or recreational purposes is legal in the majority of states, it remains contraband under federal law. As such, no business deductions are allowed because of Code Sec. 280E. However, the IRS allows cannabis businesses to take the cost of cannabis into account in figuring the cost of goods sold (Chief Counsel Memorandum 201504011).

Bribes and kickbacks. Bribes and kickbacks are not deductible if they are illegal under a federal or a generally enforced state law that subjects the payer to a criminal penalty or provides for the loss of license or privilege to engage in business. A kickback, even if not illegal, is not deductible by a physician or other person who has furnished items or services that are payable under the Medicare or Medicaid programs. A kickback includes payments for referral of a client, patient, or customer.

In one case, the IRS, with support from the Tax Court and a federal appeals court, disallowed a deduction for legal kickbacks paid by a subcontractor. The courts held that the kickbacks were not a "necessary" business expense because the contractor had obtained nearly all of its other contracts without paying kickbacks, including contracts from the same general contractor bribed here.

Sexual harassment settlements subject to confidentiality agreements. The cost of settlements, including legal fees, paid or incurred after December 31, 2017, are not deductible if subject to a nondisclosure agreement.

40.9 How Authors and Artists May Write Off Expenses

Self-employed authors, artists, photographers, and other qualifying creative professionals may write off business expenses as they are paid. The law (Code Section 263A) that requires expenses to be amortized over the period income is received does not apply to freelancers who personally create literary manuscripts, musical or dance scores, paintings, pictures, sculptures, drawings, cartoons, graphic designs, original print editions, photographs, or photographic negatives or transparencies. Furthermore, expenses of a personal service corporation do not have to be amortized if they directly relate to expenses of a qualifying author, artist, or photographer who owns (or whose relatives own) substantially all of the corporation's stock. This is so even if the gross receipts test *(40.3)* is not met.

Current deductions generally are not allowed for expenses relating to motion picture films, videotapes, printing, photographic plates, or similar items. However, bonus depreciation is allowed for film and television productions and live theatrical productions *(42.18)*.

An author or artist with expenses exceeding income may be barred by the IRS from claiming a loss under a profit motive test; in that case, the profit-presumption rule *(40.10)* may allow a deduction of the loss.

40.10 Deducting Expenses of a Sideline Business or Hobby

There is a one-way tax rule for hobbies: Income from a hobby is taxable as "other income" on Schedule 1 (Form 1040 or 1040-SR); expenses (other than amounts allowed without regard to whether the activity is engaged in for profit, such as mortgage interest) are not deductible. Before 2018, hobby expenses could be deducted as an itemized deduction to the extent of income from the activity, but the deduction for miscellaneous itemized deductions subject to the 2%-of-AGI floor has been suspended, so there are no such write-offs permitted through 2025. A profitable sale of a hobby collection or activity held long term is taxable as capital gain; losses are not deductible.

Presumption of profit-seeking motive. You are presumed to be engaged in an activity for profit if you can show a profit in at least three of the last five years, including the current year. If the activity is horse breeding, training, racing, or showing, the profit presumption applies if you show profits in two of the last seven (including current) years. The presumption does not necessarily mean that losses will automatically be allowed; the IRS may try to rebut the presumption. You would then have to prove a profit motive by showing these types of facts: You spend considerable time in the activity; you keep

Planning Reminder

Hobby or Sideline Business

The question of whether an activity, such as dog breeding or collecting and selling coins and stamps, is a hobby or sideline business arises when losses are incurred. As long as you show a profit, you may deduct the expenses of the activity. If your return is examined, you may be able to take advantage of a "profit presumption" *(40.10)*, or you may have to prove that you are engaged in the activity to make a profit. If you have more than one business activity, you may be able to aggregate them to show that you have an overall profit motive.

businesslike records; you have a written business plan showing how you plan to make a profit; you relied on expert advice; you expect the assets to appreciate in value; and losses are common in the start-up phase of your type of business.

Election postpones determination of profit presumption. If you have losses in the first few years of an activity and the IRS tries to disallow them as hobby losses, you have this option: You may make an election on Form 5213 to postpone the determination of whether the above profit presumption applies. The postponement is until after the end of the fourth taxable year (sixth year for a horse breeding, training, showing, or racing activity) following the first year of the activity. For example, if you enter a farming activity in 2023, you can elect to postpone the profit motive determination until after the end of 2027. Then, if you have realized profits in at least three of the five years (2023–2027), the profit presumption applies. When you make the election on Form 5213, you agree to waive the statute of limitations for all activity-related items in the taxable years involved. The waiver generally gives the IRS an additional two years after the filing due date for the last year in the presumption period to issue deficiencies related to the activity.

To make the election, you must file Form 5213 within three years of the due date of the return for the year you started the activity. If before the end of this three-year period you receive a deficiency notice from the IRS disallowing a loss from the activity and you have not yet made the election, you can still do so within 60 days of receiving the notice. These election rules apply to individuals, partnerships, and S corporations. An election by a partnership or S corporation is binding on all partners or S corporation shareholders holding interests during the presumption period.

40.11 Deducting Expenses of Looking for a New Business

When you are planning to invest in a business, you may incur preliminary expenses for traveling to look at the property and for legal or accounting advice. Expenses incurred during a general search or preliminary investigation of a business are not deductible, including expenses related to the decision whether or not to enter a transaction. However, when you go beyond a general search and actually go into business, you may elect to deduct or amortize your start-up costs.

Deductible or amortizable start-up costs. If you began your business in 2023, up to $5,000 of eligible start-up expenses is allowed. The limit is reduced by the amount of start-up costs exceeding $50,000. Start-up costs over the first-year deduction limit may be amortized over 15 years. An election to amortize is made by claiming the deduction on Form 4562, and it is then entered in Part V ("Other Expenses") of Schedule C.

Eligible costs include investigating and setting up the business, such as expenses of surveying potential markets, products, labor supply, and transportation facilities; travel and other expenses incurred in lining up prospective distributors, suppliers, or customers; salaries or fees paid to consultants or attorneys, and fees for similar professional services. The business may be one you acquire from someone else or a new business you create.

Organizational costs for a partnership or corporation. Costs incident to the creation of a partnership or corporation are also deductible or amortizable under the rules for start-up costs discussed above. For a partnership, qualifying expenses include legal fees for negotiating and preparing a partnership agreement, and management, consulting, or accounting fees in setting up the partnership. No deduction or amortization is allowed for syndication costs of issuing and marketing partnership interests such as brokerage and registration fees, fees of an underwriter, and costs of preparing a prospectus.

For a corporation, qualifying expenses include the cost of organizational meetings, incorporation fees, and accounting and legal fees for drafting corporate documents. Costs of selling stock or securities, such as commissions, do not qualify.

An election to amortize is made on Part VI of Form 4562 for the first year the partnership or corporation is in business. The election on Form 4562 and the required statement must be filed no later than the return due date, including extensions, for the year in which the business begins.

Filing Tip

Aggregating Activities

If you have two or more activities, they can be grouped together to determine an overall profit motive based on the degree of organization and economic interrelationship of the various undertakings, the business purpose of carrying them on together or separately, and the similarity of various undertakings.

Filing Tip

Remember Amortized Start-up Costs from Previous Years

If you started your business and did not fully deduct your start-up costs in your first year, you may have an amortized amount that is deductible on this year's return. Check prior tax returns for any unamortized amount that can be deducted in 2023.

Caution

Nonqualifying Costs

You may not deduct or amortize the expenses incurred in acquiring or selling securities or partnership interests such as securities registration expenses or underwriters' commissions.

Nonqualifying expenses. Deductible and amortizable expenses are restricted to expenses incurred in investigating the acquisition or creation of an active business, and setting up such an active business. They do not include taxes or interest. Research and experimental costs are not start-up costs, but are separately deductible or amortizable; *see* IRS Publication 535 and Code Section 174. For rental activities to qualify as an active business, there must be significant furnishing of services incident to the rentals. For example, the operation of an apartment complex, an office building, or a shopping center would generally be considered an active business.

If you do not elect to deduct or amortize qualifying start-up costs, you treat the expenses as follows:

- Costs connected with the acquisition of capital assets are capitalized and depreciated; and
- Costs related to assets with unlimited or indeterminable useful lives are recovered only on the future sale or liquidation of the business.

If the acquisition fails, and you have gone beyond a general search and have focused on the acquisition of a particular business, but the acquisition falls through, you may deduct the expenses as a capital loss.

EXAMPLES

1. In search of a business, you place newspaper advertisements and travel to investigate various prospective ventures. You pay for audits to evaluate the potential of some of the ventures. You then decide to purchase a specific business and hire a law firm to draft necessary documents. However, you change your mind and later abandon your plan to acquire the business. According to the IRS, you may not deduct the related expenses for advertisements, travel, and audits. These are considered investigatory. You may deduct the expense of hiring the law firm.

2. Domenie left his job to invest in a business. He advertised and was contacted by a party who wished to sell. He agreed to buy, hired an attorney, transferred funds to finance the business, and worked a month with the company manager to familiarize himself with the business. Discovering misrepresentations, he refused to buy the company and deducted over $5,000 for expenses, including travel and legal fees. The IRS disallowed the deduction as incurred in a business search. The Tax Court disagreed. Domenie thought he had found a business and acted as such in transferring funds and drawing legal papers for a takeover.

40.12 Home Office Deduction

If you operate your business from your home, using a room or other space as an office or area to assemble or prepare items for sale, you may be able to deduct expenses such as utilities, insurance, repairs, and depreciation allocated to your business use of the area. Collectively, these expenses are deducted as a single write-off, called the home office deduction. There are now two ways to figure the deduction: using your actual expenses or relying on an IRS-set standard amount *(40.13)*.

Exclusive and regular use. To deduct home office expenses, you must prove that you use the home area exclusively and on a regular basis either as:

1. A place of business to meet or deal with patients, clients, or customers in the normal course of your business (incidental or occasional meetings do not meet this test), or

2. Your principal place of business. Your home office will qualify as your principal place of business if you spend most of your working time there and most of your business income is attributable to your activities there.

Administrative (recordkeeping) activity. A home office meets the principal place of business test (Test 2), even if you spend most of your working time providing services at outside locations, if: (1) you use it regularly and exclusively for administrative or management activities of your business and (2) you have no other fixed location where you do a substantial amount of such administrative work. Self-employed persons are the beneficiaries of this administrative/management rule. Examples of administrative

Filing Tip

Incidental Personal Use of a Home Office

Merely walking through a home office area to get to personal use space in a small apartment or storing some personal papers in the home office does not violate the exclusive use test.

and management activities include billing customers, clients, or patients; keeping books and records; ordering supplies; setting up appointments; forwarding orders; and writing reports.

According to the IRS, performance of management or administrative activities under the following conditions do not disqualify a home office as a principal place of business:

- You have a company send out your bills from its place of business (*see* Example 1 below).
- You do administrative or management activities at times from a hotel or automobile (*see* Example 2 below).
- You occasionally conduct minimal administrative or management activities at a fixed location outside your home.
- You have suitable space to do administrative or management work outside your home but choose to use your home office for such activities (*see* Example 3 below).

EXAMPLES

1. A self-employed plumber does all of his repair and installation services outside of his home where he has a small office used to phone customers, order supplies, and keep his books. However, he uses a local bookkeeping service to bill his customers. He has no other fixed location for doing his administrative work. That he uses an outside billing service does not disqualify his home office as a principal place of business.

2. A self-employed sales representative for several products uses a home office to set up appointments and write up orders. When she is out of town, she writes up such orders from a hotel room. The occasional use of a hotel room to write up orders does not disqualify the home office as a principal place of business.

3. A self-employed anesthesiologist spends most of his professional time at three local hospitals. One of the hospitals provides him with a small shared office where he could do administrative and management work; however, he does not use this space. He uses his home as an office to: contact patients, surgeons, and hospitals regarding schedules; prepare presentations; keep billing records and patient logs; and read medical journals and books. His use of the home office for administrative activities satisfies the principal place of business test. His choice to use his home office instead of the one provided by one hospital does not disqualify his home office as the principal place of business.

If you work at home and also outside of your home at other locations and you do not meet the administrative/management rule, deductions of home office expenses should be supported by evidence that your activities at home are relatively more important or time consuming than those outside your home.

Exclusive and regular business use of home area required. If you use a room, such as a den, both for business and family purposes, be prepared to show that a specific section of the den is used exclusively as office space. For example, a real estate operator was not allowed to deduct the cost of a home office, on evidence that he also used the office area for nonbusiness purposes. A partition or other physical separation of the office area is helpful but not required.

Under the regular basis test, expenses attributable to incidental or occasional trade or business use are not deductible, even if the room is used for no other purpose but business.

Even if you meet these tests, your deduction for allocable office expenses may be substantially limited or barred by a restrictive rule that limits deductions to the income from the office activity. This computation is made on Form 8829 *(40.15)*.

Multiple business use of home office. If you use a home office for more than one business, make sure that the home office tests are met for all businesses before you claim deductions. If one business use qualifies and another use does not, the IRS will disallow deductions even for the qualifying use.

 *Caution*

Principal Place of Business Test

The tests for deducting office expenses will generally not present problems where the home area is the principal place of business or professional activity. For example, you are a doctor and *see* most of your patients at an office set aside in your home. A tax dispute may arise where you have a principal place of business elsewhere and use a part of your home for occasional work or administrative paperwork. Occasional use is not sufficient. If your deduction is questioned, you must prove that the area is used regularly and exclusively to meet with customers, clients, or patients or that the home office is the only place where administrative/management activities for the business are conducted. Have evidence that you have actual office facilities. Furnish the room as an office—with a desk, files, and a phone used only for business calls. Also keep a record of work done and business visitors.

Separate structure. If in your business you use a separate structure not attached to your home, such as a studio adjacent but unattached to your home, the expenses are generally deductible if you satisfy the exclusive use and regular basis tests discussed earlier. A separate structure does not have to qualify as your principal place of business or a place for meeting patients, clients, or customers.

However, an income limitation *(40.15)* applies. In one case, a taxpayer argued that an office located in a separate building in his backyard was not subject to either the exclusive and regular business use tests or the gross income limitation. However, the IRS and Tax Court held that it was. The office building was "appurtenant" to the home and thus part of it, based on these facts: The office building was 12 feet away from the house and within the same fenced-in residential area; it did not have a separate address; it was included in the same title and subject to the same mortgage as the house; and all taxes, utilities, and insurance were paid as a unit for both buildings.

Day-care services. The exclusive-use test does not have to be met for business use of a home to provide day-care services for children and handicapped persons, or persons age 65 or older, provided certain state licensing requirements are met. If part of your home is regularly but not exclusively used to provide day-care services, you may deduct an allocable part of your home expenses. You allocate expenses by multiplying the total costs by two fractions: (1) The total square footage in the home that is available for day-care use throughout each business day and regularly so used, divided by the total square footage for the home. (2) The total hours of business operation divided by the total number of hours in the year (8,760 in 2023).

If the area is exclusively used for day-care services, only fraction (1) applies.

> **EXAMPLE**
>
> In 2023, Alice Jones operates a day-care center at home from 7 a.m. to 6 p.m., five days a week for 50 weeks, for a total of 2,750 business-use hours during the year. Her family uses the area the rest of the time. Annual home expenses total $10,000 ($5,000 for interest and taxes; $4,000 for electricity, gas, water, trash collection, maintenance, and insurance; and $1,000 for depreciation). The total floor area of the home is 2,000 square feet; 1,500 square feet are used for day-care purposes. Alice multiplies her $10,000 of expenses by 75%, the part of the home used for day-care purposes (1,500 square feet ÷ 2,000 square feet), and also by 31.39%, the percentage of business-use time (2,750 hours ÷ 8,760 hours). Thus, she may deduct $2,354 ($10,000 × 75% × 31.39%). The full $2,354 is deductible only if net income generated from the day-care facility is at least that much.
>
> In one case, the Tax Court held that utility rooms, such as a laundry and storage room and garage, may be counted as part of the day-care business area. The IRS had argued that because the children were not allowed in these areas, the space could not be considered as used for business. The Tax Court disagreed. The laundry room was used to wash the children's clothes; the storage room and garage were used to store play items and equipment. Thus, the space was considered as used for child care even though the rooms were off limits to the children.

Storage space and inventory. If your home is the only location of a business selling products (wholesale or retail), you may deduct expenses allocated to space regularly used for inventory storage, including product samples, if the space is separately identifiable and suitable for storage. The space does not have to be used exclusively for business.

40.13 Write-Off Methods for Home Office Expenses

There are two ways in which you can figure your home office deduction: deduct your actual expenses or rely on an IRS-set standard deduction (simplified method). The two methods are explained below.

Simplified method. As long as the use of a portion of your home qualifies as a home office *(40.12)*, you can choose to use a standard home office deduction (safe harbor) amount. For 2023, the amount is $5 per square foot for up to 300 of square feet of office space (maximum deduction is $1,500). Figure the deduction using a worksheet in the instructions for line 30 of Schedule C.

Filing Tip

Mobile Offices

If you use a recreational vehicle (RV) as your office, you may be able to deduct some related costs, provided you can document business use.

Caution

No Home Office Deduction for Records Storage

The exception to the exclusive use test for storing inventory and supplies does not extend to storing records. This is so even if storage is required by state law and doing this in the home is the most convenient and least expensive option.

You can decide whether to use the safe harbor method from year to year. In making your choice, keep in mind that the portion of the safe harbor amount that is not deductible because of the gross income limit *(40.15)* cannot be carried over and is lost forever. However, if in 2021you deducted actual costs and switched to the simplified method for 2022 and for 2023 you are going back to deducting actual expenses, any unallowed expenses from 2021 may be deducted on your 2023 Form 8829.

When you opt for the safe harbor amount, no additional depreciation allowance can be claimed for that year (depreciation deduction is deemed to be zero). If, in a future year you deduct your actual costs, figure your depreciation deduction for that year based on the number of years the home office has been in service, disregarding the fact that the optional method was used in a prior year.

EXAMPLE

You started claiming a home office deduction in 2019 based on your actual expenses but decided to use the safe harbor allowance for 2022. In 2023, you again deduct your actual costs, including depreciation. For 2023, you are now in year 5 (2019, 2020, 2021, 2022, and 2023) and use the MACRS rate for year 5 to figure your depreciation deduction for 2023.

Actual expense method. For a qualifying home office *(40.12)* for which the actual expense method is used, deductible costs may include real estate taxes, mortgage interest, operating expenses (such as home insurance premiums and utility costs), and depreciation allocated to the area used for business. The deduction figured on Form 8829 may not exceed the net income derived from the business *(40.15)*.

The deduction from Form 8829 is entered on Line 30 of Schedule C.

Expenses that affect only the business part of your home, such as repairs or painting of the home office only, are entered on Form 8829 as "direct" expenses. Expenses for running the entire home, including mortgage interest, taxes, utilities, and insurance, are deductible as "indirect" expenses to the extent of your business-use percentage *(40.14)*.

Household expenses and repairs that do not benefit the office space are not deductible. However, a pro rata share of the cost of painting the outside of a house or repairing a roof is deductible. Costs of a new roof and landscaping are capital improvements according to the IRS, and so are not deductible immediately but may be recovered through depreciation.

Table 40-2   Nonresidential Real Property
(39 years—Property placed in service after May 12, 1993)

Use the column for the month of taxable year placed in service.

	1	2	3	4	5	6	7	8	9	10	11	12
	0	0	0	0	0	0	0	0	0	0	0	0
Year												
1	2.461%	2.247%	2.033%	1.819%	1.605%	1.391%	1.177%	0.963%	0.749%	0.535%	0.321%	0.107%
2–39	2.564	2.564	2.564	2.564	2.564	2.564	2.564	2.564	2.564	2.564	2.564	2.564
40	0.107	0.321	0.535	0.749	0.963	1.177	1.391	1.605	1.819	2.033	2.247	2.461

Filing Instruction

Form 8829

If using the actual expense method, you must report deductible home office expenses on Form 8829. Part I is used for showing the space allocated to business use *(40.14)*; Part II for reporting deductible expenses allocated to business use *(40.14)*; Part III for figuring depreciation on the business area *(40.13)*; and Part IV for carryover to 2024 of expenses not allowed in 2023 because of income limitations applied in Part II *(40.15)*. A sample copy of Form 8829 is on page 712.

Filing Instruction

When to Figure Depreciation on a Home Office Using 27.5 Year Recovery

While depreciation of a home office usually is figured using a 39-year recovery period *(Table 40-2)*, a 27.5 year recovery period can be used by an on-site landlord of a building in which at least one dwelling unit is rented out and 80% or more of the gross rental income is rental income from dwelling units within the building. In applying the 80% test, the rental value of the entire landlord's unit is treated as gross rental income and the rental value of the landlord's residential space (but not the home office) is treated as rental income from a dwelling unit.

For example, where a landlord lived in one unit of his eight-unit building and used a room in his unit for a home office, the IRS allowed the home office to be depreciated over 27.5 years as residential rental property.

If you install a security system for all your home's windows and doors, the portion of your monthly maintenance fee that is allocable to the office area is a deductible operating expense. Furthermore, the business portion of your cost for the system is depreciable. Thus, if the office takes up 20% of your home *(40.14)* you may deduct, subject to an income limitation *(40.15)*, 20% of the maintenance fee and a depreciation deduction for 20% of the cost.

EXAMPLE

In April 2023, you start to use one room in your single-family house exclusively and on a regular basis to meet with clients. This room is 10% of the square footage of your home. In 2008, you bought the property for $100,000, of which $90,000 was allocated to the house. The house has a fair market value of $385,000 in April 2023. You compute depreciation on the cost basis of $90,000, which is lower than the value. You multiply $90,000 by 10% (business-use percentage), which gives you $9,000 as the depreciable basis of the business part of the house. As you started business use in the fourth month of 2023 you multiply the depreciable basis of $9,000 by 1.819%. This percentage is listed for the fourth month in *Table 40-2*. Your depreciation deduction is $163.71 ($9,000 × 1.819%).

Figuring depreciation. Even though a home is a residence, depreciation on a home office usually is figured as if it were commercial property using a 39-year recovery period *(see Table 40-2)*. For depreciation purposes, the cost basis of the house is the lower of the fair market value of the house at the time you started to use a part of it for business or its adjusted basis, exclusive of the land. Only that part of the cost basis allocated to the office is depreciable. Form 8829 has a special section, Part III, for making this computation.

40.14 Allocating Expenses to Business Use

Allocate to home office use qualifying operating expenses *(40.13)* as follows: If the rooms are not equal or approximately equal in size, compare the number of square feet of space used for business with the total number of square feet in the home and then apply the resulting percentage to the total deductible expenses.

If all rooms in your home are approximately the same size, you may base the allocation on a comparison of the number of rooms used as an office to the total number of rooms.

EXAMPLE

A doctor rents the ground floor of a home and uses three rooms for his office and seven rooms for his residence. The rooms are not equal in size. The entire area has 2,000 square feet; the office has 600. He allocates 30% (600/2,000) of the following expenses to his office:

	Total	Office	Residence
Rent	$7,200	$2,160	$5,040
Light	600	180	420
Heat	1,000	300	700
Wages of domestic	2,000	600	1,400
	$10,800	$3,240	$7,560

The $3,240 of office expenses are deductible as indirect expenses on Form 8829, subject to an income limitation *(40.15)*.

40.15 Business Income May Limit Home Office Deductions

Even if your home business use satisfies the deduction tests *(40.12)*, your deduction may not exceed the income attributable to the office, as figured on Form 8829. If you do not realize income during the year, no deduction is allowed. For example, you are a full-time writer and use an office in your home. You do not sell any of your work this year or receive any advances or royalties. Therefore, you may not claim a home office deduction for this year. *See* also the rules for writers and artists earlier in this chapter *(40.9)*.

EXAMPLE

In April 2023, Samuel Brown starts to use a room in his single-family house regularly and exclusively as a home office for his sideline consulting business. The office space takes up 20% of the area of his home. His gross income in 2023 from consulting services is $12,400. He paid $7,600 for a photocopy machine and a computer, and had office telephone expenses of $600 and office supply costs of $800.

In addition, his home costs are:

Mortgage interest	$10,000
Real estate taxes	4,000
Insurance	1,200
Utilities	1,800

Samuel claims the standard deduction on his 2023 return.

On Schedule C he claims first-year expensing *(42.3)* for the copier and the computer, and also deducts the office phone costs and supplies. This gives a tentative profit of $3,400 ($12,400 − $9,000) on Line 29, Schedule C.

In Part I of Form 8829, he lists the total area of the home and the area used for business, showing 20% business use.

In Part II, he enters the mortgage interest, real estate taxes, insurance and utilities *(see above)*, on the appropriate lines of the form.

In Part III, Samuel figures depreciation on the cost basis of his home of $188,975 (excluding the land), as this is less than its value in April 2023 when his home office use began. Taking into account that the office is 20% of the home area, his depreciable basis is $37,795 (20% × $188,975), and using a depreciation rate of 1.819% for the fourth month of year 1 from *Table 40-2*, he figures depreciation allocated to business use of $687.

Samuel Brown's Form 8829 is on page 712. Here are the entries from the relevant lines of the Form 8829 to illustrate the computation of his home office deduction.

Form 8829, Part II, Line—

8 & 15	Tentative profit from Schedule C, Line 29	$3,400
16, column b.	Excess mortgage interest	10,000
17, column b.	Excess real estate taxes	4,000
18, column b	Insurance	1,200
21, column b.	Utilities	1,800
23, column b	Total of Lines 16-22	17,000
24 and 26	Business portion (20%) of Line 23b	3,400
27.	Smaller of Line 15 or Line 26 is allowable operating expenses	3,400
28	Remaining tentative profit	0

Home office expenses of $3,400 from Line 34 are allowed on Line 36 of Form 8829 and entered as a deduction on Line 30, Schedule C. No depreciation is deductible on Line 33 because there is no remaining business income (Line 28 is 0) and excess home office expenses may not generate a loss deduction. The depreciation of $687, shown on Lines 30 and 42 is carried over to 2024 on Line 44.

Form **8829**	**Expenses for Business Use of Your Home**	OMB No. 1545-0074
Department of the Treasury Internal Revenue Service	File only with Schedule C (Form 1040). Use a separate Form 8829 for each home you used for business during the year. Go to *www.irs.gov/Form8829* for instructions and the latest information.	**2023** Attachment Sequence No. **176**

Name(s) of proprietor(s)	Your social security number

Part I   Part of Your Home Used for Business

1	Area used regularly and exclusively for business, regularly for daycare, or for storage of inventory or product samples (see instructions)	**1**	
2	Total area of home	**2**	
3	Divide line 1 by line 2. Enter the result as a percentage	**3**	%

For daycare facilities not used exclusively for business, go to line 4. All others, go to line 7.

4	Multiply days used for daycare during year by hours used per day	**4**	hr.
5	If you started or stopped using your home for daycare during the year, see instructions; otherwise, enter 8,760	**5**	hr.
6	Divide line 4 by line 5. Enter the result as a decimal amount	**6**	.
7	Business percentage. For daycare facilities not used exclusively for business, multiply line 6 by line 3 (enter the result as a percentage). All others, enter the amount from line 3	**7**	%

Part II   Figure Your Allowable Deduction

8	Enter the amount from Schedule C, line 29, **plus** any gain derived from the business use of your home, **minus** any loss from the trade or business not derived from the business use of your home. See instructions.	**8**	

See instructions for columns (a) and (b) before completing lines 9–22.

		(a) Direct expenses	(b) Indirect expenses	
9	Casualty losses (see instructions)	**9**		
10	Deductible mortgage interest (see instructions)	**10**		
11	Real estate taxes (see instructions)	**11**		
12	Add lines 9, 10, and 11	**12**		
13	Multiply line 12, column (b), by line 7	**13**		
14	Add line 12, column (a), and line 13			**14**
15	Subtract line 14 from line 8. If zero or less, enter -0-			**15**
16	Excess mortgage interest (see instructions)	**16**		
17	Excess real estate taxes (see instructions)	**17**		
18	Insurance	**18**		
19	Rent	**19**		
20	Repairs and maintenance	**20**		
21	Utilities	**21**		
22	Other expenses (see instructions)	**22**		
23	Add lines 16 through 22	**23**		
24	Multiply line 23, column (b), by line 7	**24**		
25	Carryover of prior year operating expenses (see instructions)	**25**		
26	Add line 23, column (a), line 24, and line 25			**26**
27	Allowable operating expenses. Enter the **smaller** of line 15 or line 26			**27**
28	Limit on excess casualty losses and depreciation. Subtract line 27 from line 15			**28**
29	Excess casualty losses (see instructions)	**29**		
30	Depreciation of your home from line 42 below	**30**		
31	Carryover of prior year excess casualty losses and depreciation (see instructions)	**31**		
32	Add lines 29 through 31			**32**
33	Allowable excess casualty losses and depreciation. Enter the **smaller** of line 28 or line 32			**33**
34	Add lines 14, 27, and 33			**34**
35	Casualty loss portion, if any, from lines 14 and 33. Carry amount to **Form 4684**. See instructions			**35**
36	**Allowable expenses for business use of your home.** Subtract line 35 from line 34. Enter here and on Schedule C, line 30. If your home was used for more than one business, see instructions			**36**

Part III   Depreciation of Your Home

37	Enter the **smaller** of your home's adjusted basis or its fair market value. See instructions	**37**	
38	Value of land included on line 37	**38**	
39	Basis of building. Subtract line 38 from line 37	**39**	
40	Business basis of building. Multiply line 39 by line 7	**40**	
41	Depreciation percentage (see instructions)	**41**	%
42	Depreciation allowable (see instructions). Multiply line 40 by line 41. Enter here and on line 30 above	**42**	

Part IV   Carryover of Unallowed Expenses to 2024

43	Operating expenses. Subtract line 27 from line 26. If less than zero, enter -0-	**43**	
44	Excess casualty losses and depreciation. Subtract line 33 from line 32. If less than zero, enter -0-	**44**	

For Paperwork Reduction Act Notice, see your tax return instructions.   Cat. No. 13232M   Form **8829** (2023)

Part II of Form 8829 limits the deduction of home office expenses to net income derived from office use. You start with the tentative profit from Schedule C. If you sold your home during the year, increase the tentative profit by any net gain (or decrease tentative profit by any net loss) that is allocable to the office area and reported on Schedule D or Form 4797.

Expenses that are allocable to the home office reduce the Schedule C tentative profit in a particular order in Part II of Form 8829. If you itemize deductions on Schedule A, the Form 8829 instructions may require you to first reduce the income by the business portion of casualty losses attributable to federal disasters that damaged your residence, deductible mortgage interest, and deductible real estate taxes (Lines 9, 10, and 11 of Form 8829). If your itemized deduction for state and local taxes is subject to the SALT limitation *(16.1)*, you must use the "Line 11 Worksheet" in the instructions to figure how much, if any, of your real estate taxes to enter on Line 11.

Any mortgage interest and real estate taxes that do not reduce income at this first stage are entered later as "excess mortgage interest" (Line 16) and "excess real estate taxes" (Line 17) and then combined with operating expenses, such as home insurance premiums, repair and maintenance expenses, utility expenses, and rent (Lines 18-22). The total of these expenses is allowed to the extent there is income to offset (Line 27).

The last expenses taken into account are depreciation (Line 30) and "excess casualty losses" (Line 29), which are casualty losses not initially subtracted from income on Line 9.

Business expenses not related to the home are deducted on the appropriate lines of Schedule C. For example, a salary paid to a secretary is deducted on Line 26 of Schedule C; the cost of depreciable business equipment used in your home is deducted on Line 13 of Schedule C.

The amount of real estate taxes, mortgage interest, or federally-declared disaster losses not allocated to home office use may be claimed as itemized deductions on Schedule A.

40.16 Home Office for Sideline Business

You may have an occupation and also run a sideline business from an office in your home. The home office expenses for the sideline business are deductible on Form 8829 if the office is a principal place of operating the business or a place to meet with clients, customers, or patients. *See* the deduction tests *(40.12)* and the income limit computation *(40.15)* for home office deductions. Managing rental property may qualify as a business.

> **EXAMPLE**
>
> A doctor was employed full time by a hospital. He also owned six rental properties that he personally managed. He sought new tenants, supplied furnishings, and cleaned and prepared the units for tenants. He used one bedroom in his two-bedroom home exclusively as an office to manage the properties. The room was furnished with a desk, bookcase, filing cabinet, calculators, and answering service; furnishings and other materials for preparing rental units for tenants were stored there. According to the Tax Court, the doctor's efforts in managing the rental properties constituted a business; he could deduct expenses allocable to the home office.

Managing your own securities portfolio. Investors managing their own securities portfolios may find it difficult to convince a court that investment management is a business activity. According to Congressional committee reports, a home office deduction should be denied to an investor who uses a home office to read financial periodicals and reports, clip bond coupons, and perform similar activities. In one case, the Claims Court allowed a deduction to Moller, who spent about 40 hours a week at a home office managing a substantial stock portfolio. The Claims Court held these activities amounted to a business. However, an appeals court reversed the decision. According to the appeals court, the test is whether or not a person is a trader. A trader is in a business; an investor is not. A trader buys and sells frequently to catch daily market swings. An investor buys securities for capital appreciation and income without regard to daily market developments. Therefore, to be a trader, one's activities must be directed

Planning Reminder

Carryover Allowed

Expenses disallowed under the actual expense method because of the income limitation may be carried forward and treated as home office expenses in a later tax year (Part IV, Form 8829). The carryover, as well as the expenses of the later year, are subject to the income limitation of that year. For example, tentative profit for 2023 on Line 29 of Schedule C is $1,000. Expenses allocated to the home office are $2,000. Only $1,000 of the expenses are deductible on Form 8829; $1,000 is carried over to 2024.

Substantiating the Sideline Business

In claiming home office expenses of a sideline business, it is important to be ready to prove that you are actually in business *(40.10)*. In the case cited in the Example in *40.16*, the Tax Court held that the doctor's personal efforts in managing the six units for tenants were sufficiently systematic and continuous to put him in the rental real estate business. In some cases, the rental of even a single piece of real property may be a business if additional services are provided such as cleaning or maid service.

to short-term trading, not the long-term holding of investments. Here, Moller was an investor; he was primarily interested in the long-term growth potential of stock. He did not earn his income from the short-term turnovers of stocks. He had no significant trading profits. His interest and dividend incomes were 98% of his income. *See* the discussion of trader expenses in *30.15*.

40.17 Depreciation of Office in Cooperative Apartment

If your home office meets the tests discussed in *40.12*, you may deduct depreciation on your stock interest in the cooperative. The basis for depreciation may be your share of the cooperative corporation's basis for the building or an amount computed from the price you paid for the stock. The method you use depends on whether you are the first or a later owner of the stock.

You are the first owner. In figuring your depreciation, you start with the cooperative's depreciable basis of the building. You then take your share of depreciation according to the percentage of stock interest you own. The cooperative can provide the details needed for the computation.

If space in the building is rented to commercial tenants who do not have stock interests in the corporation, the total allowable depreciation is reduced by the amount allocated to the space used by the commercial tenants.

You are a later owner of the cooperative's stock. When you buy stock from a prior owner, your depreciable basis is determined by the price of your stock and your share of the co-op's outstanding mortgage, reduced by amounts allocable to land and to commercial space.

40.18 Net Operating Losses (NOLs)

A loss incurred in your profession or unincorporated business is deducted from other income reported on Form 1040 or 1040-SR. If the loss exceeds your other income, you may have a net operating loss (NOL). A loss incurred in your profession or unincorporated business is deducted from other income reported on Form 1040 or 1040-SR. If the loss exceeds your other income, you may have a net operating loss (NOL). An NOL can be used to offset taxable income in other years. More specifically, for NOLs arising in 2021 or later, you can carry the loss forward indefinitely to offset income until the NOL is used up. There is no carryback for a post-2020 NOL, although those engaged in farming (Schedule F filers) have a two-year carryback (which can be waived so the NOL is only carried forward).

80% offset. For NOLs in 2023, the carryover can offset only 80% of taxable income in the carryforward (or in the case of farming losses, the carryback) year.

Carryover of loss from prior year to 2023. If you had a net operating loss in an earlier year that is being carried forward to 2023, the loss carryover is reported as a minus figure on the line for "other income" on Schedule 1 (Form 1040 or 1040-SR). You must attach a detailed statement showing how you figured the carryover. It can only offset 80% of taxable income in 2023.

Change in marital status. If you incur a net operating loss while single but are married filing jointly in a carryback or carryforward year, the loss may be used only to offset your own income on the joint return.

If the net operating loss was claimed on a joint return and in the carryback or carryforward year you are not filing jointly with the same spouse, only your allocable share of the original loss may be claimed; *see* IRS Publication 536.

Passive activity limitation. Losses subject to passive activity rules of *Chapter 10* are not deductible as net operating losses. However, losses of rental operations coming within the $25,000 allowance *(10.2)* may be treated as net operating loss if the loss exceeds passive and other income.

Adjustment for Capital Losses

A net nonbusiness capital loss may not be included in a net operating loss. If nonbusiness capital losses exceed nonbusiness capital gains, the excess is an adjustment that reduces your loss on Schedule A of Form 1045. In figuring your loss, you may take into account business capital losses only up to the total of business capital gains plus any nonbusiness capital gains remaining after the adjustment for nonbusiness deductions.

Figuring an NOL. A net operating loss is generally the excess of deductible business expenses over business income. The net operating loss may also include the following losses and deductions:

- Your share of a partnership or S corporation operating loss.
- Loss on the sale of small business investment company (SBIC) stock.
- Loss incurred on Section 1244 stock.

An operating loss may not include:

- Net operating loss carryback or carryover from any year.
- Capital losses that exceed capital gain.
- Excess of nonbusiness deductions over nonbusiness income plus nonbusiness net capital gain.
- A self-employed person's contribution to a qualified retirement plan or SEP.
- An IRA deduction.

Income from other sources may eliminate or reduce your net operating loss.

> **EXAMPLE**
>
> You are self-employed and incur a business loss of $10,000. Your spouse earns a salary of $10,000. When you file a joint return, your business loss will be eliminated by your spouse's salary. Similarly, if you also had salary from another position, the salary would reduce your business loss.

40.19 How To Report a Net Operating Loss

You compute your net operating loss deduction on Schedule A of Form 1045 *(40.21)*. You start with adjusted gross income and personal deductions shown on your tax return. As these figures include items not allowed for net operating loss purposes, you follow the line-by-line steps of Schedule A (Form 1045) to eliminate them. That is, you reduce the loss by the nonallowed items such as deductions for personal exemptions, net capital loss, and nonbusiness deductions exceeding nonbusiness income. The Example at the end of this section illustrates the steps in the schedule.

Adjustment for nonbusiness deductions. Nonbusiness deductions that exceed nonbusiness income may not be included in a net operating loss deduction. Nonbusiness deductions include deductions for IRA and qualified retirement plans and itemized deductions such as charitable contributions, interest expense, state taxes, and medical expenses. Do not include in this non-allowed group deductible casualty and theft losses, which for net operating loss purposes are treated as business losses. If you do not claim itemized deductions in the year of the loss, you must treat the standard deduction as a nonbusiness deduction.

Nonbusiness income is income that is not from a trade or business—such as dividends, interest, and annuity income. The excess of nonbusiness capital gains over nonbusiness capital losses is also treated as part of nonbusiness income that offsets nonbusiness deductions.

> **EXAMPLE**
>
> Income from dividends and interest is $6,000 and nonbusiness deductions are $6,500. The excess deduction of $500 is an adjustment that reduces your loss on Form 1045.

At-risk loss limitations. The loss used to figure your net operating loss deduction is subject to the at-risk rules *(10.17)*. If part of your investment is in nonrecourse loans or is otherwise not at risk, you must compute your deductible loss on Form 6198, which you attach to Form 1040 or 1040-SR. The deductible loss from Form 6198 is reflected in the income and deduction figures you enter on the Form 1045 schedule to compute your net operating loss deduction.

EXAMPLE

You are single and in 2023 you have a salary of $3,000, interest of $1,200, a net business loss of $10,000 (income of $50,000 and expenses of $60,000), itemized Schedule A deductions of $15,000, and a net nonbusiness capital gain of $1,000. After the required addbacks and adjustments are made, your net operating loss is $7,000. The following computation approximates the steps of the computation on Schedule A, Form 1045.

Salary	$3,000
Interest	1,200
Capital gain income	1,000
Business loss	($10,000)
Adjusted gross income	($4,800)
Itemized deductions	(15,000)
	(19,800)
Adjustments:	
Excess nonbusiness deduction*	12,800
Net operating loss	($7,000)

*The excess nonbusiness expenses deduction was figured as follows:

Itemized deductions		$15,000
Net capital gain income	$1,000	
Interest income	1,200	2,200
Excess		$12,800

Reporting prior-year NOLs. NOLs carried forward from prior years are reported on line 8a of Schedule 1 (Form 1040 or 1040-SR) as a negative amount.

40.20 Excess Business Losses

Noncorporate taxpayers, such as Schedule C and Schedule F filers, have a special rule for losses after 2017 through 2028. Except for 2020 (due to the CARES Act), excess business losses cannot be claimed in the current year. They are treated as a net operating loss carryover *(40.18)*.

Excess business losses. For 2023, this is the excess, if any, of:
- Your aggregate deductions for your business, determined without regard to whether or not such deductions are disallowed for the year because of the excess business loss limitation, over
- The sum of (1) your gross income or gain from your trades or businesses, plus (2) $289,000 ($578,000 if you are married filing jointly).

The passive activity loss rules are taken into account before the excess business loss limitation.

The limitation on excess business losses is figured on Form 461, "Limitation on Business Losses."

EXAMPLE

In 2023, you are single and have gross income on Schedule C of $1 million and deductions from the business of $1.3 million. Your excess business loss is $11,000 ($1.3 million − [$1 million + $289,000]). The excess business loss of $11,000 is an NOL carryover to 2024.

40.21 Business Credits

You may be eligible to reduce your tax liability by credits related to your business. Unlike personal credits, however, many business-related credits are subject to a special limitation, called the general business credit. The general business credit is not a separate credit; it is a compilation of one or more separate business-related credits that are specifically included by law within the general business credit. Many of these credits are discrete and apply to a very small number of taxpayers. As such, a complete review of all of the credits falling under the general business credit are beyond the scope of this book. However, we find in practice the most common credits to include the following:

- **Investment credit on Form 3468, consisting of the rehabilitation property credit** *(31.8)*
  On Form 3468, you may claim a 20% credit for rehabilitating certified historic structures. To claim the credit, you must generally incur rehabilitation expenses that exceed the greater of $5,000 or your adjusted basis in the building.

- **Low-income housing credit on Form 8586** *(31.8)*
  Qualifying investors are allowed to claim a tax credit in annual installments over 10 years for qualifying newly constructed low-income housing and certain existing structures that are substantially rehabilitated. The amount of the credit depends on whether the building is new and whether federal subsidies are received.

- **Credit for small employer pension plan startup costs on Form 8881** *(41.6)*
  Employers with 100 or fewer employees that do not have a qualified retirement plan generally may claim a tax credit on Form 8881 for administrative costs of setting up a pension plan, profit-sharing plan, 401(k) plan, SEP, or SIMPLE plan. The plan must cover at least one non-highly-compensated employee.
  The maximum credit is 50% of startup costs up to the greater of (1) $500 or (2) the lesser of (a) $250 per non-highly-compensated employee eligible to participate or (b) $5,000.

- **Credit for employer-provided childcare facilities and services on Form 8882**
  Employers who provide childcare facilities, resources, and/or referral expenditures may make a claim for said expenditures.
  A 25% credit for qualified childcare facility expenditures may be claimed; the qualifying expenditures relate to amounts paid or incurred to acquire, construct, or expand a childcare facility.
  A 10% credit for qualified resources and referral expenditures may be claimed for expenses like wages paid to employees of the childcare facility, training expenses for the employees, and contract fees paid to another childcare facility to provide childcare to the employees of the taxpayer.
  The credit may be claimed any time within 3 years from the due date of the return on either the original or amended return. This credit is limited to $150,000 per tax year.

- **Credit for small employer health insurance premiums (Form 8941)** *(41.15)*
  If you pay at least half of the premiums for your staff and you meet eligibility requirements, you can claim a tax credit of 50% of your eligible payments on Form 8941.

- **Credit for paid family and medical leave (the income tax credit) on Form 8994**
  Paid family and medical leave is a program that an eligible employer can offer employees in the event an employee has to take time off work in order to care for an ill family member, a new child, or for themselves.
  An eligible employer may claim a credit between 12.5% and 25% of certain wages paid to a qualifying employee while the employee is on paid family and medical leave.
  An eligible employer is determined by having a written policy in place, and providing paid family and medical leave, while achieving minimum pay requirements.
  An eligible employee is one who has been employed by the employer for one year or more and whose wages for the prior year does not exceed 60% of $135,000 for compensation earned in 2022.

- **Work opportunity credit on Form 5884**

  The Work Opportunity Tax Credit (WOTC) is a credit that may be claimed by a taxpayer for wages paid to a certain individual who begins working on or before December 31, 2025, and who is an individual certified by a designated local agency as being a member of one of ten targeted groups. The targeted groups are as follows: Qualified IV-A Recipient; Qualified Veteran; Qualified Ex-Felon; Designated Community Resident; Vocational Rehabilitation Referral; Qualified Summer Youth Employee; Qualified Supplemental Nutrition Assistance Program (SNAP) Benefits Recipient; Qualified Supplemental Security Income (SSI) Recipient; Long-Term Family Assistance Recipient; and Qualified Long-Term Unemployment Recipient.

  If an new employee meets any of the above stated criteria, the taxpayer may claim a credit equal to 40% of the first $6,000 of wages paid to, or incurred by, an employee who: (1) is in their first year of employment; (2) is a certified member of a targeted group, and (3) performs at least 400 hours of services for that taxpayer. The maximum credit is generally $2,400 per eligible employee.

40.22 Filing Schedule F

The designation "farm" includes stock, dairy, poultry, fruit, and truck farms, plantations, ranches, and all lands used for farming operations. A fish farm where fish are specially fed and raised, and not just caught, is a farm. So too are animal breeding farms, such as mink, fox, and chinchilla farms.

A farmer who is a sole proprietor files Schedule F along with his or her Form 1040. This schedule is similar to Schedule C for sole proprietors other than farmers; it reports income and expenses related to farming activities.

The same rules for accounting, the reporting period, and for income and expenses to Schedule C apply for farmers filing Schedule F. However, there are some key exceptions designed to provide special breaks for farmers. Since most farmers report on the cash basis and use a calendar year for tax reporting, the following information is limited to these farmers.

Special income treatment. Certain types of farm-related income enjoy special tax treatment:

- Sales of livestock (including poultry) and produce can receive Section 1231 treatment. If crops are sold on a deferred payment contract, report the income when payment is received.

- Sales of livestock caused by drought, flood, or other weather conditions can be reported in the following year if you can show that the sale would not have occurred but for the weather condition and you are eligible for federal assistance because of the weather condition.

- Rents, including crop shares, are treated as rental income, rather than as farm income, and are not part of farm net income or loss.

40.23 Farming Expenses

Certain types of expenses related to farmers enjoy special tax treatment. Here are some key rules unique to farmers:

Depreciation. There are special recovery periods for certain farm animals and equipment, including farm buildings and agricultural structures (see IRS Publication 225).

Prepaid farm supplies. While cash method farmers usually can deduct expenses in the year they are paid, prepaid farm supplies must be deducted ratably over the period in which they are used. However, there is a special exception that allows them to be deducted in the year of payment if they do not exceed 50% of other deductible farm expenses (including depreciation and amortization); any prepaid expenses in excess of this limit are deductible in the following year.

Livestock feed. While the cost of feed usually is deductible in the year it is consumed, it can be deducted in the year of payment if:

1. The expense is a payment for the purchase of food (and not a deposit).
2. The prepayment has a business, and not merely a tax avoidance, purpose.
3. The deduction of feed costs does not result in a material distortion of income.

Filing Tip

Figuring Tax on Farm Income

Farmers and commercial fisherman can use income averaging to figure the tax on their business income *(22.6)*.

Planning Reminder

Farming NOLs Subject to a Carryback

Farmers who experience net operating losses *(40.18)* may carry them back to offset 80% of taxable income in the two previous years.

Breeding fees. A cash basis farmer can deduct breeding fees as a business expense; an accrual method farmer must capitalize the fees and allocate them to the cost basis of the calf, foal, or other animal to which they relate.

Fertilizer and lime. You can deduct the cost of fertilizer and lime in the year of payment or you can capitalize the cost and deduct a part of it each year in which the benefit lasts as long as the benefit lasts more than one year.

Soil and water conservation expenses. Usually, these expenses must be capitalized. However, you can elect to deduct them within limits (the deduction cannot be more than 25% of gross income from farming).

Reforestation expenses. You can deduct up to $5,000 ($10,000 if married filing jointly). Costs in excess of this dollar limit can be amortized over 84 months.

Conservation easement. Farmers and ranchers can claim a full deduction for a donation of a conservation easement without regard to their adjusted gross income *(14.10)*.

40.24 Qualified Business Income Deduction

If your business shows a profit on Schedule C, you may be eligible for a personal deduction of up to 20% of that profit (with some adjustments). The deduction rules are complicated. The deduction generally equals 20% of qualified business income (QBI), which is essentially an owner's share of profits with some adjustments (*see* the definition of QBI *below*). The deduction is subtracted from adjusted gross income (not from business income or as an adjustment to gross income) on Form 1040 or 1040-SR, but not as an itemized deduction, so the deduction is available to those claiming the standard deduction as well as those who itemize. If your taxable income in 2023 does not exceed $364,200 for married filing joint returns and $182,100 for all other returns, the deduction is 20% of QBI. You may also be entitled to add to the QBI deduction up to 20% of combined qualified REIT dividends *(4.4)* and qualified publicly traded partnership (PTP) income *(31.6)*.

QBI. Your qualified business income (QBI) is the net amount of items of income, gain, deduction, or loss from your business. It does not include any capital gain (including Section 1231 gain) or loss, dividends, or interest income (other than interest properly allocable to your business). It does not include any net operating loss carryovers (other than those attributable to excess business losses of noncorporate taxpayers as explained in *40.19*).

You must reduce QBI by the following deductions claimed as adjustments to income on Schedule 1 (Form 1040 or 1040-SR): (1) the deductible part of self-employment tax, (2) the self-employed health insurance deduction, and (3) deductible contributions to self-employed retirement plans.

Limitations. If your taxable income in 2023 is more than the taxable income limit above, special limitations to the 20% deduction apply. Your deduction is the lesser of (1) 20% of QBI or (2) the greater of (a) 50% of the total W-2 wages paid by the business to employees, or (b) 25% of W-2 wages plus 2.5% of the unadjusted basis immediately after acquisition (UBIA) of depreciable tangible property owned by the business. "Qualified property" is depreciable business property for which the "depreciable period" has not ended before the close of the year. The depreciable period is the period beginning on the date the property is placed in service and ends on the later of 10 years after this date or the last day of the full year of the applicable recovery period. The component of the deduction for REIT dividends and PTP income is not limited by W-2 wages or the UBIA of qualified property.

Specified service trade or business. If you are in "specified service trade or business" (SSTB) and your taxable income exceeds the applicable threshold for your filing status, the amount of qualified business income that can be taken into account for purposes of figuring the limitation on the deduction phases out over the first $100,000 of taxable income above the threshold for joint filers, or over the first $50,000 exceeding the threshold for others. Thus, doctors, lawyers, accountants, consultants, financial advisors,

Filing Tip

Livestock Sales Due to Drought Have 4-Year Replacement Period

Farmers and ranchers forced to sell livestock who are in areas specified by the IRS as eligible for special drought relief generally have four years in which to defer gain from the sale. The 4-year period can be extended in areas of persistent drought until the end of the taxpayer's first taxable year ending after the first drought-free year for the applicable region. This extension applies to farmers and ranchers whose 4-year replacement period was scheduled to expire at the end of August 2022 if their county is listed in IRS Notice 2022-43.

actuaries, athletes, and performing artists, as well as owners of other businesses where the reputation or skill of the employees is "the principal asset of the business," cannot claim any deduction once 2023 taxable income reaches $464,200 for married filing joint returns, and $232,100 for other filers.

If your taxable income is no more than the taxable income threshold ($364,200 or $182,100 for 2023), you figure the deduction using Form 8995, Qualified Business Income Deduction Simplified Computation.

If your taxable income is greater than the threshold, then use Form 8995-A, Qualified Business Income Deduction. There are several schedules accompanying this form:

Schedule A, Specified Service Trades or Businesses

Schedule B, Aggregation of Business Operations

Schedule C, Loss Netting and Carryforward

Schedule D, Special Rules for Patrons of Agricultural or Horticultural Cooperatives

Treatment of disallowed, limited, or suspended losses and deductions. If you have losses and deductions that couldn't be used in years after 2017 due to the at-risk limitation, the passive activity loss limitation, or other limitation but which are currently allowed, they are taken into account on first-in first-out (FIFO) basis (i.e., the oldest amounts that are now deductible are used first).

CHAPTER 41

Retirement and Medical Plans for Self-Employed

Self-employed persons and partners can take advantage of tax-sheltered retirement plans or simplified employee pension plans (SEPs) *(41.2)*.

Advantages flow from: (1) tax deductions allowed for contributions to the plan (a form of forced savings); (2) tax-free accumulations of income earned on assets held by the plan; and (3) in limited cases, special averaging for lump-sum benefits paid from a qualified retirement plan on retirement.

If you have employees, you must consider the cost of covering them when setting up your plan.

If you do not have any other retirement plan and have no more than 100 employees, you may set up a salary-reduction SIMPLE plan.

If you choose to set up a retirement plan covering at least one participant who isn't an owner or other highly-compensated employee, you may be eligible for a tax credit *(41.6)*. And if you include automatic enrollment, you may claim an additional tax credit *(41.6)*.

Sole proprietors who want to buy health coverage through a government exchange must use the Marketplace for individuals, rather than an agent for the SHOPs for small businesses. Self-employed persons can pay for their health coverage on a more tax advantageous basis than other individuals because an adjustment from income (above-the-line deduction) may be claimed for their coverage.

If you have employees and want to help them pay for the cost of their personal medical insurance, you may be able to use a qualified small employer health reimbursement arrangement (QSEHRA) or an individual coverage health reimbursement arrangement (ICHRA) *(41.14)*.

If you pay a certain amount for coverage of employees that's purchased from a SHOP, you may be entitled to a tax credit *(41.15)*.

Employees Who Are Self-Employed on the Side

If you are an employee who participates in a company retirement plan and you also carry on a self-employed enterprise or profession on the side, you may set up a qualified retirement plan for the sideline business. For example, you are employed by a company that has a qualified 401(k) plan to which you make salary deferrals. At the same time, you have a sideline consulting business. You may set up a retirement plan based on your consultant earnings. Each plan is independent of the other. As an alternative to a retirement plan, you may contribute to a simplified employee pension plan (SEP) *(41.3)* or a SIMPLE IRA *(41.9)*.

One-Person (Solo) 401(k) Plan

If you have no employees other than your spouse, you may want to consider a "solo" 401(k) plan, which allows you to contribute more than to a SEP. For example, for 2023, elective deferrals of up to $22,500 could be made, or $30,000 if age 50 or older during the year (up to $7,500 in "catch-up" contributions). Elective deferrals can be deductible or, if the plan allows, some or all of the deferrals can be nondeductible designated Roth contributions *(7.18)*. The annual income limit for Roth IRA contributions *(8.21)* does not apply to Roth 401(k) deferrals. If you make designated Roth contributions to your solo 401(k), they reduce the deductible elective deferral limit for the year. In addition to the deferrals, an "employer" contribution of up to 20% of net earnings (reduced by the deductible portion of self-employment tax liability *(41.4)*) can be made to your account, subject to the overall limit, which for 2023 is $66,000, or $73,500 if you are age 50 or older. Use *Worksheet 41-1* to figure your maximum deductible contribution for 2023.

41.1 Overview of Retirement and Medical Plans

Self-employed individuals can shelter income and obtain desired retirement savings and health coverage using various plans. While the plans are tied to being in business, the deductions for them are not business write-offs. Instead, deductions for the self-employed person's own coverage are claimed directly on Schedule 1(Form 1040 or 1040-SR). For example, a self-employed person's deductions for contributions to his or her own account in a qualified retirement plan *(41.2)*, SEP *(41.3)*, or SIMPLE IRA *(41.9)* are claimed on Line 15 of Schedule 1 (Form 1040 or 1040-SR). If the plans also cover employees of the self-employed person, deductions related to employees are claimed on Schedule C.

Self-employed individuals who obtain their own health insurance can deduct the premiums from gross income, rather than as an itemized medical expense *(12.2)*. They may be able to cut the high cost of health coverage by using a high-deductible health plan, combined with a health savings account (HSA) *(41.10)*. Contributions to the HSA are also deductible from gross income *(41.11)*. Alternatively, self-employed individuals who have previously set up Archer MSAs can continue to use these tax-advantaged accounts to pay for medical costs not covered by insurance *(41.13)*. If they have employees they may be able to reimburse them for their individual health coverage (up to a set dollar limit) using a qualified small employer health reimbursement arrangement (QSEHRA) or an individual coverage health reimbursement arrangement (ICHRA) and deduct the reimbursement as a business expense on Schedule C *(41.14)*.

41.2 Choosing a Qualified Retirement Plan

You may set up a self-employed retirement plan if you have net earnings (gross business or professional income less allowable business deductions) from your sole proprietorship or partnership for which the plan is established. If you are an inactive owner, such as a limited partner, you do not qualify to set up a qualified plan—unless you receive guaranteed payments for services that are treated as earnings from self-employment.

Deadline for setting up plan and making contributions. You can adopt a qualified plan after the close of a taxable year and make "employer" contributions for that year up until the due date (including extensions) for filing your return. However, if you want to make elective deferral contributions (including nondeductible designated Roth contributions) as well as employer contributions to a defined contribution plan, such as a solo 401(k) plan (*see* the "One-Person" Planning Reminder on this page), the plan must be adopted by the end of the taxable year. For example, if you are a calendar-year taxpayer and adopted a solo 401(k) plan by the end of 2023, and you obtain a filing extension for your 2023 return *(46.3)*, you can make deductible employer contributions and elective deferrals (deductible and/or Roth deferrals) for 2023 up until October 15, 2024, subject to the limits at *41.4*. If the plan was not set up by the end of 2023, you have until the extended filing due date to set up the plan, but only employer contributions, not elective deferrals, can be made for 2023.

Partnership plans. An individual partner or partners, although self-employed, may not set up a qualified plan. The plan must be established by the partnership. Partnership deductions for contributions to an individual partner's account are reported on the partner's Schedule K-1 (Form 1065) and deducted by the partner as an adjustment to income on Line 15 of Schedule 1 (Form 1040 or 1040-SR).

Including employees in your plan. You must include in your plan all employees who have reached age 21 with at least one year of service. An employee may be required to complete two years of service before participating if your plan provides for full and immediate vesting after no more than two years. You generally are not required to cover seasonal or part-time employees who work less than 1,000 hours during a 12-month period. A minimum coverage rule requires that a defined benefit plan must include at least 40% of all employees, or 50 employees if that is less.

Your plan may not exclude employees who are over a certain age.

A plan may not discriminate in favor of officers or other highly compensated personnel. Benefits must be for the employees and their beneficiaries, and their plan rights may not be subject to forfeiture. A plan may not allow any of its funds to be diverted for purposes other than pension benefits. Contributions made on your behalf may not exceed the ratio of contributions made on behalf of employees.

Types of qualified plans. There are two types of qualified plans: defined benefit plans and defined contribution plans, and different rules apply to each. A defined benefit plan provides in advance for a specific retirement benefit funded by quarterly contributions based on an IRS formula and actuarial assumptions. A defined contribution plan does not fix a specific retirement benefit, but rather sets the amount of annual contributions so that the amount of retirement benefits depends on contributions and income earned on those contributions. If contributions are geared to profits, the plan is a profit-sharing plan, but fixed annual contributions are not required. A plan that requires fixed contributions regardless of profits is a money purchase plan. If you have a profit-sharing plan, a 401(k) plan arrangement can be included to allow you (and other participants) to make elective deferral contributions of before-tax compensation to the plan.

A defined benefit plan may prove costly if you have older employees who also must be provided with proportionate defined benefits. Furthermore, a defined benefit plan requires you to contribute to their accounts even if you do not have profits. For 2023, the benefit limit is the lesser of (a) 100% of the participant's average compensation for the three consecutive years of highest compensation as an active participant or (b) $265,000. This dollar limit is reduced if benefits begin before age 62 and increased if benefits begin after age 65.

For defined contribution plans, the 2023 limit on annual contributions and other additions (excluding earnings) was the lesser of 100% of compensation or $66,000 ($73,500 for employees 50 years old by year-end).

41.3 Choosing a SEP

Under a SEP (simplified employee pension plan), you may contribute to a special type of IRA more than is allowed under the regular IRA rules *(41.4)*. The deadline for both setting up and contributing to a SEP is the due date for your return, including extensions. Contributions do not have to be made every year. When you do make contributions, they must be based on a written allocation formula and must not discriminate in favor of yourself, other owners with more than a 5% interest, or highly compensated employees. Coverage requirements for employees are in *8.15*. A salary-reduction arrangement for employees may be provided under a qualifying SEP established before 1997 or under a SIMPLE IRA plan established after 1996 *(8.17)*.

41.4 Deductible Contributions

The deductible limit for a qualified retirement plan depends on whether you have a defined contribution plan (solo 401(k), profit-sharing or money purchase pension plan) or a defined benefit plan. A SEP is treated as a profit-sharing plan subject to the defined contribution plan deduction limits explained below.

If you have a defined benefit plan, you generally may deduct contributions needed to produce the accrued benefits provided for by the plan, including any unfunded current liability. This is a complicated calculation requiring actuarial computations that call for the services of a pension expert.

Deductible contribution to a defined contribution qualified retirement plan or a SEP. Before figuring the deductible contribution you can make for 2023 to a solo 401(k), profit-sharing plan, or money purchase pension plan, or to a SEP account, you must first figure your self-employment tax liability on Schedule SE and your deduction for one-half of the self-employment tax to be claimed on Line 15 of Schedule 1 (Form 1040 or 1040-SR). In computing your deductible plan contribution, your net profit from Line 31 of Schedule C, or Line 34 of Schedule F is reduced by the deduction for one half of your self-employment tax; *see* the Example below.

 *Law Alert*

Roth 401(k) Employer Contributions

Individual Roth 401(k) employer contributions are allowed beginning in 2023.

 *Filing Tip*

Retirement Plan Contributions Reduce QBI

Deductions for contributions to qualified retirement plans for self-employed individuals reduce qualified business income (QBI) for purposes of figuring the 20% deduction *(40.24)*.

As a self-employed person, you are not allowed to figure the deductible contribution for yourself by applying the contribution rate stated in your plan. The rate must be reduced, as required by law, to reflect the reduction of net earnings by the deductible contribution itself. If your plan rate is a whole number, the reduced percentage is shown in the Rate Table for Self-Employed *(Table 41-1)* on page 726. If the plan rate is fractional, the reduced percentage is figured using the Fractional Rate Worksheet for Self-Employed *(Worksheet 41-2)*.

Figuring your maximum deductible contribution. After figuring your net earnings and reducing that amount by one-half of your self-employment tax liability, you multiply the balance by the reduced rate from *Table 41-1* or *Worksheet 41-2*. This is generally your maximum deductible contribution to a profit-sharing qualified retirement plan or SEP. However, the maximum deductible contribution cannot exceed the annual limit on additions to a defined contribution plan. The annual limit for 2023 is the lesser of (1) $66,000, or (2) $330,000 (maximum compensation that can be taken into account) multiplied by the stated plan contribution rate, not the reduced rate. *See* the Deduction Worksheet for Self-Employed *(Worksheet 41-1)* on the next page, which takes you through the steps of figuring your deductible contribution.

If elective deferrals were made during the year, extra steps are required to compute the maximum deductible contribution; *see* Step 9 of *Worksheet 41-1*, shown on page 725. Any "catch-up" contributions are entered in Step 17 of the Worksheet.

> ### EXAMPLE
>
> Maya, age 56, is a sole proprietor with no employees. She adopted a solo 401(k) plan several years ago that provides for a 25% contribution rate (the maximum for self-employed plan) and allows elective deferrals including designated Roth contributions. Under *Table 41-1* below, the maximum deductible rate is reduced to 20%. Maya's net self-employment earnings for 2023 from Line 31 of Schedule C are $150,000. She did not have wages in 2023. On Schedule SE, she figures self-employment tax liability *(45.3)* of $21,194 (Line 12 of Schedule SE), and one-half of this, or $10,597 (Line 13 of Schedule SE) is the allowable deduction for self-employment tax, which she claims on Line 15 of Schedule 1 (Form 1040 or 1040-SR).
>
> To figure her maximum deductible contribution for 2023, Maya completes *Worksheet 41-1 (see next page).* If she does not make any elective deferrals or catch-up contributions, her maximum deductible contribution, shown in Step 7 of the Worksheet, is $27,881. If Maya wants to maximize her deduction, she can complete Steps 9 through 21 of the Worksheet. She can make elective deferrals of $22,500, allowed in Step 15 of the Worksheet, plus catch-up contributions of $7,500 (since she is age 50 or over), allowed in Step 18 of the Worksheet. Thus, her maximum deductible contribution for 2023 is $57,881 ($27,881 + $22,500 + $7,500, in Step 19 of Worksheet).
>
> Maya could elect to reduce her deduction for elective deferrals by making designated Roth contributions (nondeductible). For example, if Maya made designated Roth contributions of $10,000, this would reduce her maximum deductible contribution to $47,881 in Steps 20 and 21 of the Worksheet.

Worksheet 41-1 Maximum 2023 Deduction for Self-Employed Defined Contribution Plan or SEP *(see Maya Example, page 724)*

Step 1   Enter your net profit from—
- line 31, Schedule C (Form 1040 or 1040-SR);
- line 34, Schedule F (Form 1040 or 1040-SR)*;
- or box 14, code A**, Schedule K1 (Form 1065)*.

For information on other income included in net profit from self-employment, *see* the Instructions for Schedule SE, Form 1040 or 1040-SR.

*Reduce this amount by any amount reported on Schedule SE (Form 1040 or 1040-SR), line 1b.

**General partners should reduce this amount by the same additional expenses subtracted from box 14, code A, to determine the amount on line 3 of Schedule SE. $ 150,000

Step 2   Enter your deduction for self-employment tax from line 15 of Schedule 1 (Form 1040 or 1040-SR)   2   10,597

Step 3   Net earnings from self-employment. Subtract step 2 from step 1.   3   139,403

Step 4   Enter your rate from the Rate Table for Self-Employed or Rate Worksheet for Self-Employed.   .20

Step 5   Multiply step 3 by step 4.   27,881

Step 6   Multiply $330,000 by your plan contribution rate (not the reduced rate).   82,500

Step 7   Enter the smaller of step 5 or step 6.   27,881

Step 8   Contribution dollar limit:
- If you made any elective deferrals to your self-employed plan, go to step 9.
- Otherwise, skip steps 9 through 20 and enter the smaller of step 7 or step 8 on step 21.   66,000

Step 9   Enter your allowable elective deferrals (including designated Roth contributions) made to your self-employed plan for the 2023 plan year. Do not enter more than $22,500.   22,500

Step 10   Subtract step 9 from step 8.   43,500

Step 11   Subtract step 9 from step 3.   95,903

Step 12   Enter one-half of step 11.   47,952

Step 13   Enter the smallest of steps 7, 10, or 12.   27,881

Step 14   Subtract step 13 from step 3.   111,522

Step 15   Enter the smaller of step 9 or step 14:
If you made catch-up contributions, go to step 16.
Otherwise, skip steps 16 through 18 and go to step 19.   22,500

Step 16   Subtract step 15 from step 14.   93,022

Step 17   Enter your catchup contributions (including designated Roth contributions), if any. Do not enter more than $7,500.   7,500

Step 18   Enter the smaller of step 16 or step 17.   7,500

Step 19   Add steps 13, 15, and 18.   57,881

Step 20   Enter the amount of designated Roth contributions included on lines 9 and 17.   0

Step 21   Subtract step 20 from step 19. This is your maximum deduction contribution. $ 57,881

Next: Enter your actual contribution, not to exceed your maximum deductible contribution, on line 16 of Schedule 1 (Form 1040 or 1040-SR).

Table 41-1   Rate Table for Self-Employed

If plan rate is—	Self-employed person's reduced rate is—
1 %	.009901
2	.019608
3	.029126
4	.038462
5	.047619
6	.056604
7	.065421
8	.074074
9	.082569
10	.090909
11	.099099
12	.107143
13	.115044
14	.122807
15	.130435
16	.137931
17	.145299
18	.152542
19	.159664
20	.166667
21	.173554
22	.180328
23	.186992
24	.193548
25*	.200000*

* The maximum deductible percentage for contributions (other than elective deferrals) to your own profit-sharing, money-purchase, or SEP is 20% and for your employees, 25%.

Worksheet 41-2   Fractional Rate Worksheet for Self-Employed

If the plan rate is fractional and thus not listed in the table above, figure your deductible percentage this way:

1. Write the plan rate as a decimal. For example, if the plan rate is 10.5%, write .105 as the decimal amount.   1. _____

2. Add 1 to the decimal rate. For example, if the rate is .105, the result is 1.105.   2. _____

3. Divide Step 1 by Step 2. This gives you the deductible percentage. If the plan rate is .105, the deductible percentage is .0950 (.105 ÷ 1.105).   3. _____

Contributions for your employees. The deduction complications that apply to your own contributions do not apply to contributions for employees. You make contributions for your employees at the rate specified in your plan, based upon their compensation, subject to the annual limit discussed above. Thus, if your plan contribution rate is 25%, you would contribute 25% of your employees' pay to the plan, even though your own contribution rate is reduced to 20% under the Rate Table for Self Employed shown above. You deduct contributions for employees when figuring your net earnings from self-employment on Schedule C or Schedule F before figuring your own deductible contribution using the steps shown in Worksheet 41-1.

Contributions allowed regardless of age. Attaining the full retirement age for Social Security benefits *(34.5)* has no impact on eligibility to contribute to a retirement plan. You may continue to make contributions for yourself to a qualified retirement plan or SEP as long as you have self-employment income. However, you must begin to receive required minimum distributions from a SEP by April 1 of the year following the year in which you reach age 73 *(8.13)*. This age 73 required distribution beginning date also applies to a qualified retirement plan if you are a more-than-5% owner of the business *(7.11)*.

Excess contributions. Contributions to a plan exceeding the deduction ceiling may be carried over and deducted in later years subject to the ceiling for those years. However, if contributions exceed the deductible amount, you are generally subject to a 10% penalty on nondeductible contributions that are not returned by the end of your tax year. The penalty is computed on Form 5330, which must be filed with the IRS by the end of the seventh month following the end of the tax year.

41.5 How To Qualify a Retirement Plan or SEP Plan

You may set up a qualified retirement plan and contribute to it without advance approval. But since advance approval is advisable, you may, in a determination letter, ask the IRS to review your plan. Approval requirements depend on whether you set up your own administered plan or join a master plan administered by a bank, insurance company, mutual fund, or a prototype plan sponsored by a trade or professional association. If you start your own individually designed plan, you pay the IRS a fee and request a determination letter; *see* IRS Publication 560.

If you join a master or prototype plan, the sponsoring organization applies to the IRS for approval of its plan. You should then be given a copy of the approved plan and copies of any subsequent amendments.

To set up a SEP with a bank, broker, or other financial institution, you do not need IRS approval. If you do not maintain any other qualified retirement plan apart from another SEP and other tests are met, a model SEP may be adopted using Form 5305-SEP.

41.6 Tax Credits for Setting Up a Retirement Plan

If you have no employees, there is no tax credit for choosing to set up a retirement plan for yourself. But if you have at least one employee who is not an owner or other highly-compensated employee, you may be eligible for tax credits.

Small employer credit for retirement plan startup costs. Employers with 100 or fewer employees that do not have a qualified retirement plan generally may claim a tax credit on Form 8881 for administrative costs of setting up a pension plan, profit-sharing plan, 401(k) plan, SEP, or SIMPLE plan. The plan must cover at least one non-highly-compensated employee.

The maximum credit is 50% of startup costs up to the greater of (1) $500 or (2) the lesser of (a) $250 per employee eligible to participate who is not highly compensated or (b) $5,000. The credit applies for three years. This means the credit can be claimed for the year that the plan begins plus the next two years. Alternatively, you can opt to claim the credit starting in the year before the year in which the plan begins, plus the next two years.

Credit for automatic enrollment plan. If you start an automatic enrollment plan, such as a 401(k) or SIMPLE-IRA, or you change your existing 401(k) plan to an automatic enrollment plan, you can take a tax credit of $500 per year to defray the costs associated with setting up or changing the plan. This credit can also be claimed for up to three years, and it can be taken in addition to the other startup credit.

Employer Contribution Tax Credit. SECURE 2.0 added a new tax credit providing up to $1,000 per eligible employee per year. The eligibility is based on the same eligible employer requirements as discussed in "Small employer credit for retirement plan startup costs" above. The maximum number of employees is 100; however, the credit is reduced by 2% for each employee over 50 employees earning less than $100,000 annually. The credit is available for five years and is capped at $1,000 per year per employee. The credit is applied as 100% of employer contributions for the first two years, 75% of employer contributions in year three, 50% of employer contributions in year four, and 25% of employer contributions in year five. Note: no deduction is allowed for contributions upon which the credit is based.

41.7 Annual Qualified Retirement Plan Reporting

If your retirement plan covers any employee other than yourself, your spouse, or a partner, you must file Form 5500 or 5500-SR. The return is due at the end of the 7th month after the close of the plan year (July 31 for a calendar year plan). For 2023 plans, the due date is July 31, 2023. You can obtain a filing extension; *see* the form instructions for filing electronically or when a paper form can be used.

Partial relief from one burdensome IRS paperwork requirement may be available if your pension or profit-sharing plan covers only yourself, or you and your spouse, or you and your business partners and the spouses of the partners. Such plans are treated as one-participant plans by the IRS.

A one-participant plan does not file the extensive annual Form 5500 information return. A one-participant plan either files Form 5500-EZ on paper, or if eligible, it may file the form electronically. If a sole proprietor has a plan for employees, file Form 5500-SF.

Under an exception for small one-participant plans, Form 5500-EZ does not have to be filed if the value of plan assets at the end of the year is not more than $250,000. The exception applies if you have two or more one-participant plans that together have not exceeded the $250,000 asset threshold. All one-participant plans must file a Form 5500-EZ for their final plan year even if the plan assets have always been below $250,000.

The IRS penalties for failure to file retirement plan returns have been greatly increased for returns required to be filed after 2019. However, the IRS and the U.S. Department of Labor have programs under which you can come into compliance with reduced penalties.

41.8 How Qualified Retirement Plan Distributions Are Taxed

Distributions from a qualified retirement plan generally may not be received without penalty before age 59½ unless you are disabled or meet the other exceptions listed in *7.13*. If you are a more-than-5% owner, you usually must begin to receive minimum required distributions (RMDs) by April 1 of the year following the year in which you reach age 73, even though you are not retired; penalties may apply if an insufficient distribution is received *(7.11)*.

A lump-sum and other eligible distributions *(7.5)* may be rolled over tax free to another employer plan or IRA. For participants born before January 2, 1936, 10-year averaging may be available *(7.3)*. Pension distributions from a defined benefit plan are taxed under the annuity rules discussed in *7.24–7.26*, but for purposes of figuring your cost investment, include only nondeductible voluntary contributions; deductible contributions made on your behalf are not part of your investment.

If you receive amounts in excess of the benefits provided for you under the plan formula and you own more than a 5% interest in the employer, the excess benefit is subject to a 10% penalty. The penalty also applies if you were a more-than-5% owner at any time during the five plan years preceding the plan year that ends within the year of an excess distribution.

 *Planning Reminder*

No Annual Filing for SEPs and SIMPLE IRAs

These plans do not have to file Form 5500-EZ or any other annual information return in the 5500 series.

Other rules discussed in *7.1–7.14* apply to self-employed qualified plans as well as qualified corporate plans.

Distributions to a surviving spouse can be rolled over to that spouse's IRA *(7.4)*. Distributions to non-spouse beneficiaries can be directly rolled over in a trustee-to-trustee transfer to an IRA that is treated as an inherited IRA from which required minimum distributions must be received according to applicable rules *(7.6, 8.14)*.

SEP distributions. Distributions from a SEP are subject to the IRA rules at *8.8*.

41.9 SIMPLE IRA Plans

If you do not maintain any other retirement plan and have 100 or fewer employees, you may set up a salary-reduction type of plan for yourself and your employees. The SIMPLE IRA contribution rules are discussed at *8.17*. A SIMPLE plan may also be made as part of a 401(k) plan *(7.15)*.

Under a SIMPLE IRA for 2023, you may contribute to your own account up to $15,500 of net earnings plus an additional $3,500 if age 50 or over by the end of the year. You may also make a "matching" contribution of up to 3% of your net earnings.

If you have employees, they generally could make elective salary-reduction contributions for 2023 up to $15,500 (plus $3,500 if age 50 or over). You must make a 3% matching contribution unless you choose to make a 2% non-elective contribution.

See *Chapter 8* for further details on SIMPLE IRAs *(8.18–8.19)*.

41.10 Health Savings Account (HSA) Basics

Health savings accounts (HSAs) can be used by individuals covered by a high-deductible health plan (HDHP) to save for health-care costs on a tax-free basis in an IRA-like account. HSAs are intended to supplant Archer MSAs; *see* the discussion of Archer MSA rules later in this Chapter *(41.13)*.

The HSA provides a tax-sheltered account for paying routine medical expenses that fall below the deductible set by the HDHP. To contribute to an HSA, you must not be enrolled in Medicare Part A or Part B and you must not be a dependent of another taxpayer.

A qualifying HDHP must have a minimum annual deductible and a maximum annual limit on out-of-pocket costs *(see below)*. However, a plan will not fail to be treated as an HDHP even though it provides certain benefits (e.g., preventive care; all medical care services received and items purchased associated with testing for and treatment of COVID-19) without requiring the deductible to be exhausted first.

Generally, contributions to an HSA are not allowed if the taxpayer has coverage under any health plan that does not meet the "high deductible" requirement of an HDHP, but there are exceptions. A plan that otherwise satisfies HDHP rules may provide preventive care benefits *(3.2)* without a deductible or with a deductible below the minimum annual deductible. Benefits may also be provided under certain types of "permitted" coverage and insurance before the deductible of the HDHP is satisfied. Permitted coverage includes coverage for vision, dental or long-term care, accidents, and disability. Permitted insurance includes per diem insurance while hospitalized, insurance for a specific disease or illness (such as cancer, diabetes, asthma, or heart failure), and insurance relating to workers' compensation liability, tort liability, or liabilities relating to owning or using a car or other property.

Qualifying HDHP for 2023. For 2023, the minimum annual HDHP deductible is $1,500 for self-only coverage and $3,000 for family coverage. The limit on out-of-pocket costs for 2023 is $7,500 for self-only coverage and $15,000 for family coverage. The limit applies to co-payments, deductibles, and other payments but not premiums.

41.11 Limits on Deductible HSA Contributions

If you are an eligible individual *(41.10)*, you can set up an HSA with an insurance company, bank, or other financial institution that has been approved by the IRS for this purpose. Contributions can be made up until the due date for filing your tax return

Planning Reminder

HSA Limits and HDHP Requirements for 2023

The HSA contribution limits for 2023 are $3,850 for self-only coverage and $7,750 for family coverage. If you are age 55 or older by the end of the year, you can contribute an additional $1,000, but the right to contribute ends once you enroll in Medicare.

The minimum HDHP deductible for 2023 is $1,500 for self-only coverage and $3,000 for family coverage. The limit on out-of-pocket costs for 2023 (excluding premiums) is $7,500 for self-only coverage and $15,000 for family coverage.

Filing Instruction

Report HSA Contributions and Distributions on Form 8889

Report your HSA contributions on Form 8889 and follow the instructions to figure any limitations on the amount you may deduct. Also use Form 8889 to report an HSA distribution and figure the amount, if any, that is taxable. Form 8889 must be attached to your Form 1040 or 1040-SR.

Filing Instruction

HSA Contributions Reduce QBI

Deductions for contributions to health savings accounts for self-employed individuals reduce qualified business income (QBI) for purposes of figuring the 20% deduction *(40.24)*.

(without extensions). Thus, HSA contributions for 2023 can be made through April 15, 2024. HSA contributions are reported to the IRS on Form 5498-SA.

Last-month rule. The full contribution limit for 2023 (depending on your coverage; *see below*) is available regardless of when during the year you became eligible *(41.10)* for an HSA, if you were eligible on December 1, 2023; you are treated as if you were enrolled in the December 1 plan for the entire year. However, if you do not remain eligible for the next 13 months (December 1, 2023, through December 31, 2024), and are not disabled, you have to recapture as income on your 2023 return the contribution that could not have been made without the 12-month rule and pay a 10% penalty; *see* Publication 969 and the Form 8889 instructions for details on this recapture rule. If the 12-month rule does not apply, the contribution limit is figured on a monthly basis.

For 2024, the maximum deductible contribution limit for an individual with self-only HDHP coverage is $3,850. For an individual with family coverage, the maximum deductible contribution for 2023 is $7,500. If a married couple has family HDHP coverage and both spouses are eligible for an HSA, they can decide between themselves how to allocate HSA contributions.

The contribution limit is increased for an account owner who is at least age 55 by the end of the year and who has not enrolled in Medicare. The "catch-up" contribution limit is $1,000. If both spouses are age 55 or older and not yet on Medicare, each must make this catch-up contribution to separate HSAs.

However, starting with the month that an individual enrolls in Medicare Part A, B, or Medicare Advantage (generally at age 65), no further contributions, including catch-up contributions, can be made to his or her HSA. For example, if you turned age 65 and enrolled in Medicare in September 2023 and had been contributing to a HDHP with self-only coverage, you can make an HSA contribution for the eight months preceding the month of Medicare enrollment. Given the full-year contribution limit for 2023 would be $4,850 ($3,850 for self-only HDHP plus $1,000 additional for being at least age 55), your contribution limit for eight months (January through August) is $3,233 ($4,850 × 8/12).

You may have more than one HSA, but the above maximum annual contribution limit applies to the aggregate contributions to all of the HSAs.

If you are an employee eligible to contribute and your employer contributes to an HSA on your behalf, employer contributions within the limit are excludable from your income *(3.2)*. If your employer's contribution is below the applicable limit, you may contribute to your HSA but the totals of all the contributions cannot exceed the applicable limit.

Contributions exceeding your applicable HSA limit are not deductible and are subject to a 6% excise tax, figured on Form 5329. Contributions by an employer to an employee's HSA in excess of the limit are includible in the employee's income and subject to the excise tax. However, if you make a timely withdrawal of the excess contributions and any allocable income, the contributions will be treated as if they had never been made; the excise tax does not apply and the distribution of the excess contribution is not taxed. Any withdrawn income must be included as "other income" on your return for the year in which you receive the withdrawn contributions and earnings. For an excess 2023 contribution, the withdrawal deadline is generally the filing due date for your 2023 return, or April 15, 2024 plus extensions. However, if you timely file without making the withdrawal, you may do so by October 15, 2024. In this case, file an amended return for 2023 and write at the top "Filed pursuant to section 301.9100-2." Attach an explanation of the withdrawal and make any necessary changes on the amended return; *see* the instructions to Form 5329 for further details.

Use Form 8889 to report your HSA contributions and figure your deduction. You must report your HSA contributions for 2023 and apply the deduction limits on Form 8889, which must be attached to Form 1040. The deduction from Form 8889 is entered on Line 13 of Schedule 1 (Form 1040 or 1040-SR), where it is deductible "above the line" from gross income.

41.12 Distributions From HSAs

Earnings accumulate tax free within an HSA, as with an IRA. Distributions from an HSA used exclusively to pay or reimburse qualified medical expenses of the account owner, his or her spouse, or dependents are not taxable. Distributions used for anything other than qualified medical expenses are taxable. Taxable distributions are also subject to a 20% penalty unless the distribution is made after the account owner becomes disabled, reaches age 65, or dies.

Distributions need not be taken in the year in which the expense is incurred to be tax free; they can be taken in the following year or in any later year. This may be necessary if there are insufficient funds to cover the expense at the time it is incurred. For example, an HSA account holder who incurs a $1,500 medical expense on December 1, 2023, can wait until 2024 (or later) when the account balance exceeds $1,500. The distribution is tax free so long as records are kept to show that the distribution was used to reimburse qualified medical expenses that were not covered by insurance or otherwise reimbursed and not claimed in a prior year as an itemized deduction. The HSA must have been set up before the expense was incurred.

For tax-free distribution purposes, a "qualified medical expense" is generally a non-reimbursed payment for medical care that would otherwise be eligible for an itemized deduction (17.2). In addition, over-the-counter medications and menstrual products are qualified medical expenses for HSA purposes although they are not eligible for an itemized deduction. Health-care premiums generally do not qualify for HSA purposes, but there are exceptions. An HSA can pay for premiums for long-term-care insurance, COBRA health-care continuation coverage, health coverage while an individual is receiving unemployment compensation, and for individuals over age 65, Medicare Part A, B, or D, Medicare Advantage, and the employee share of premiums for employer-sponsored health insurance including retiree health insurance. HSA distributions used to pay or reimburse long-term-care premiums are tax free only to the extent of the age-based deductible limit for such premiums (17.15). For example, if a person age 41 uses HSA funds to pay long-term-care premiums of $1,800 in 2023, only $850 (the deductible limit for those age 41 through 50 in 2023) is tax free. The balance of the distribution is taxable and subject to a 20% penalty for withdrawal of funds prior to age 65.

A qualified medical expense may be for the care of the account owner, his or her spouse, or dependents, without regard to whether they are eligible to make HSA contributions. In the case of a married couple where both spouses have HSAs, one spouse may use a distribution from his or her HSA to pay or reimburse the qualified medical costs of the other spouse. However, both HSAs may not reimburse the same expense.

If an HSA account holder mistakenly takes a distribution such as to reimburse an expense he or she reasonably but mistakenly believes is a qualified medical expense, the funds can be repaid to the HSA in order to avoid tax on the withdrawn amount, assuming the plan accepts a return of mistaken distributions. The funds must be returned by April 15 of the year following the first year that the account holder knew or should have known of the mistake.

Inherited HSAs. If the beneficiary of an HSA is the surviving spouse of the deceased account owner, the surviving spouse becomes the owner of the account and will be subject to tax only on distributions that are not used for qualified medical expenses. If the beneficiary is not the surviving spouse, the account ceases to be an HSA as of the date of the owner's death and the date-of-death value of the HSA assets must be included in the beneficiary's income. The beneficiary (other than the decedent's estate) may reduce the taxable amount by any HSA payments for the decedent's medical expenses made within one year after death. A beneficiary is not subject to the 20% penalty for taxable distributions.

Report HSA distributions on Form 8889. The HSA custodian or trustee will report a distribution to you and the IRS on Form 1099-SA. You must report an HSA distribution on Part II of Form 8889, which must be attached to Form 1040 or 1040-SR. A taxable distribution, if any, from Form 8889 is reported as "other income" on Line 8f of Schedule 1 (Form 1040 or 1040-SR). If there is a taxable distribution and no exception to the penalty is available, the 20% penalty is entered on Form 8889 and reported on Line 17c of Schedule 2 (Form 1040 or 1040-SR).

Law Alert

Eligible Expenses Now Include More

Eligible HSA expenses now include menstrual products and over-the-counter drugs without a prescription. However, vitamins and supplements are still not eligible expenses.

Caution

IRS Can Levy on HSAs

The IRS can levy on an HSA to recover taxed owed. If the HSA owner is under age 65, there is a 20% penalty (there is no exception from this penalty for an involuntary distribution such as an IRS levy).

Caution

Employer Contribution to Spouse's MSA

If you and your spouse are covered under a high-deductible health plan with family coverage, employer contributions to either of your Archer MSAs bar both of you from making Archer MSA contributions for that year. If you each have self-only coverage under a high-deductible health plan, employer contributions to one of your Archer MSAs do not prevent the other from making MSA contributions.

Planning Reminder

MSA Contribution Deadline

You have until April 15, 2024, to make a deductible contribution to an Archer MSA for 2023.

41.13 Archer MSAs

Archer MSAs (medical savings accounts) have largely been replaced by health savings accounts (HSAs) *(3.2, 41.10)*. The law authorizing the establishment of new Archer MSAs has expired. However, taxpayers who set up Archer MSAs before 2008 can continue to fund them.

An Archer MSA can be rolled over to an HSA. Contributions may not be made to an Archer MSA or to an HSA after you become entitled to Medicare benefits.

For 2023, a high-deductible health plan for self-only coverage must have a deductible of at least $2,650 and no more than $3,950. For family coverage, the deductible must be at least $5,300 and no more than $7,900. The high-deductible plan must limit out-of-pocket costs (other than premiums) for 2023 to $5,300 for self-only coverage and $9,650 for family coverage. You generally may not have any other coverage in addition to the high-deductible plan, but separate policies are allowed for disability, vision or dental care, long-term care, accidental injuries, specific diseases or illnesses, fixed payments during hospitalization, workers' compensation liability, tort liability, and liabilities arising from the ownership or use of property.

Deductible contribution limit. If you are self-employed, the maximum deductible contribution is 65% of the annual policy deductible if you have self-only coverage under a high-deductible plan, and 75% of the annual policy deductible if you have family coverage. To deduct the maximum amount, you must have the policy for the entire year. Otherwise one-twelfth of the limit may be deducted for each full month of coverage. The deduction may not exceed your net self-employment income from the business through which you have the high-deductible insurance.

If you are an employee of an MSA-participating employer and your employer makes any contributions to your Archer MSA, you are barred from making a deductible contribution; also *see* the Caution on employer contributions to a spouse's Archer MSA. Your employer's contribution to your Archer MSA is not taxable to you if it is within the 65%/75% limit discussed above *(3.2)*.

Report contributions to your Archer MSA on Form 8853, which must be attached to your Form 1040. The deductible contribution shown on Form 8853 is entered on Line 23 of Schedule 1 (Form 1040 or 1040-SR).

Report Archer MSA distributions on Form 8853. The MSA custodian or trustee will report the distribution to you and the IRS on Form 1099-SA. You must report the distribution on Form 8853, which must be attached to your Form 1040. Distributions used to pay for qualified medical expenses that are not reimbursable under your high-deductible plan are tax free. Qualifying expenses are the same as for HSAs *(41.12)*. Taxable MSA distributions are reported as "other income" on Line 8e of Schedule 1 (Form 1040 or 1040-SR). Taxable MSA distributions are also subject to a 20% penalty unless the distribution is made after you become disabled, reach age 65, or die. If applicable, the 20% penalty is entered on Form 8853 and reported on Line 17e of Schedule 2 (Form 1040 or 1040-SR).

41.14 Health Reimbursement Arrangements (HRAs)

If you have employees, you can reimburse them for their individual health coverage and other costs and benefits as long as you fit this within an allowable reimbursement arrangement. If so, then reimbursements are not taxable to employees but are deductible by you as the employer. HRAs cannot be used to cover costs for self-employed individuals.

Qualified Small Employer Health Reimbursement Arrangement (QSEHRA). If you are a "small employer," which means you have fewer than 50 full-time and full-time-equivalent employees so that you're not subject to the employer mandate under the Affordable Care Act, you can help employees pay for health coverage they buy on their own using a Qualified Small Employer Health Reimbursement Account (QSEHRA). This is not a group health plan, but you deduct the reimbursements you make for the year and employees are not taxed on them.

For a QSEHRA, all of the following conditions must be satisfied:

- The arrangement is funded entirely by employer contributions (no employee salary reduction contributions are allowed)
- Eligible employees must provide you (the employer) with proof of having minimum essential health coverage.
- Reimbursement for 2023 is limited to $5,850 for self-only coverage or $11,800 for family coverage. You can set a lower reimbursement amount.
- The arrangement is provided on a nondiscriminatory basis.

Individual Coverage Health Reimbursement Arrangement (ICHRA). This type of reimbursement arrangement allows an employer to decide how much to reimburse employees annually for the cost of their individually obtained health insurance on or off the Marketplace. Reimbursements must be nondiscriminatory, which means coverage is offered on the same terms to all individuals within a class of employees. ICHRAs cannot be offered to employees with a traditional group plan. For example, if full-time employees are covered by the company's group health plan, you can offer an ICHRA to part-time employees.

You must provide notice to employees about the plan and the impact that reimbursement has on eligibility for the premium tax credit if they buy coverage through the Marketplace. Employees must certify to you that they have coverage before receiving a reimbursement. Use a model notice and attestation forms from the IRS at *www.irs.gov/pub/irs-utl/health_reimbursement_arrangements_faqs.pdf*.

Excepted Benefit Health Reimbursement Arrangement (EBHRA). This type of reimbursement arrangement supplements, not supplants, basic health coverage. It is meant to cover costs not covered by insurance, whether obtained by an employee individually or through an employer's traditional group health plan, such as vision, dental, and hearing coverage, as well as certain out-of-pocket costs. An EBHRA must meet all of the following conditions:

- The maximum reimbursement in 2023 is $1,950 per employee.
- The EBHRA must be offered in conjunction with a traditional group health plan (whether or not an employee actually enrolls in it)
- Reimbursements cannot be used to pay individual or group health insurance premiums (other than COBRA), or Medicare premiums.
- The EBHRA must be uniformly available to all similarly situated employees

41.15 Small Employer Health Insurance Credit

If you pay at least half of the premiums for your staff and you meet eligibility requirements, you can claim a tax credit of 50% of your eligible payments on Form 8941. The credit is highly complex.

Eligibility. You must meet these four tests for a 2023 credit:

1. You have fewer than 25 full-time equivalent employees (FTEs) for the tax year. Add up the hours per year (but not more than 2,080 hours per employee) that employees (other than owners, relatives, and seasonal workers) work and divide by 2,080 to find the number of full-time equivalents.
2. The average annual wages of its employees for the year is less than about $62,000 per FTE. You must pay the premiums under a "qualifying arrangement."
3. You purchase the coverage through a government Marketplace (SHOP) via an agent. However, the IRS has provided relief to employers in counties that do not offer coverage; the credit can be claimed for coverage purchased directly outside of a SHOP (*see* Notice 2018-27).

Credit amount. A full credit applies if you have no more than 10 FTEs with average wages of $30,000 per FTE. The credit phases out for those with 10 to 25 FTEs and with wages of $30,000 to about $62,000.

The credit is based on the lesser of actual payments or the average premium for the small group market in the states where your employees work. The 2023 average premiums will be listed on a county-by-county basis for each state in the Form 8941 instructions.

 *Filing Tip*

QSEHRAs Reported on Form W-2

As an employer, you report the permitted benefit, not the actual reimbursement, on an employee's Form W-2 (box 12, Code FF). So, if your QSEHRA provides for reimbursement up to $4,000 and an employee receives reimbursement of $3,500, you enter $4,000 (the permitted benefit).

 *Caution*

No Credit for Self-Employed Premiums

You cannot take a tax credit on Form 8941 for premiums you pay to cover yourself, your spouse, or your dependents.

 *Planning Reminder*

Credit for 2023?

The small employer health insurance credit can only be claimed for two consecutive years, so if you claimed it for 2021 and 2022, you cannot do so in 2023.

CHAPTER 42

Claiming Depreciation Deductions

There are several methods of claiming expense deductions for your purchases in 2023 of equipment, fixtures, autos, and trucks used in your business:

- First-year expensing (Section 179 deduction), which allows a deduction of up to $1,160,000 (42.3).
- Bonus depreciation, which is another first-year deduction at 80% of cost for eligible property (42.18).
- Regular depreciation, which allows a prorated deduction over a period of years. Most business equipment is depreciable under MACRS (modified accelerated cost recovery system) over a six-year period. MACRS applies to new and used property. The objective of MACRS is to provide rapid depreciation and to eliminate disputes over useful life, salvage value, and depreciation methods. Useful life and depreciation methods are fixed by law; salvage value is treated as zero. If you do not want to use MACRS accelerated rates, you may elect the straight line method.

Capital investments in buildings are depreciable using the straight line method; residential buildings are depreciated over 27.5 years; nonresidential real property placed in service after May 12, 1993, is depreciated over 39 years (42.12). Specific annual rates for each class of property are provided by IRS tables.

Land is not depreciable.

42.1 What Property May Be Depreciated?

Depreciation deductions may be claimed only for property used in your business or other income-producing activity. If the primary purpose of the property is to produce income but it fails to yield any income, the property may still be depreciated.

Depreciation may not be claimed on property held for personal purposes such as a personal residence or pleasure car. If property, such as a car, is used both for business and pleasure, only the business portion may be depreciated.

EXAMPLES

1. An anesthesiologist suspended his practice indefinitely because of malpractice premium rate increases. He continued to maintain his professional competence by taking courses and keeping up his equipment. The IRS ruled that he could not take depreciation on his equipment. Since he was no longer practicing, the depreciation did not relate to a current trade or business.

2. An electrician spent $1,325 on a trailer to carry his tools and protective clothing. Based on a useful life of three years less salvage value of $25, annual depreciation deductions came to $433. However, the IRS claimed that he could not claim depreciation during the months he was not working and the trailer was not used. The Tax Court disagreed. Depreciation is allowed as long as the asset is held for use in a trade or business, even though the asset is idle or its use is temporarily suspended due to business conditions.

Nondepreciable assets. Not all assets used in your business or for the production of income may be depreciable. Land is not depreciable, but the cost of landscaping business property may be depreciated if the landscaping is so closely associated with a building that it would have to be destroyed if the building were replaced. Qualifying trees and bushes are depreciable over 15 years.

Property held primarily for sale to customers or property includible in inventory is not depreciable, regardless of its useful life.

Amortization for business intangibles. The cost of goodwill, going concern value, and other intangibles including covenants not to compete, information bases, customer lists, franchises, licenses, and trademarks is amortizable over a 15-year period.

The amortization rule generally applies to property acquired after August 10, 1993 *(42.17)*.

Residences. For depreciation of rented residences, *see 9.5*. For depreciation of a home office, *(40.13)*. For depreciation of a sublet cooperative apartment or one used in business, *(40.17)*.

Farm property. Farmland is not depreciable; farm machinery and buildings are. Livestock acquired for work, breeding, or dairy purposes and not included in inventory may also be depreciated. For a detailed explanation of the highly technical rules for depreciating farm property and livestock, *see* IRS Publication 225, Farmer's Tax Guide.

Relevance of useful life. According to the Tax Court, under current MACRS law (as under prior ACRS rules for assets placed in service 1981–1986), useful life is irrelevant for claiming depreciation if you can show that an asset is subject to exhaustion, wear and tear, or obsolescence. Thus, in the case of antique musical instruments played by professional musicians, depreciation is allowable because of wear and tear, even though the instruments have an indeterminable useful life. Two federal appeals courts agreed, allowing professional violinists to deduct ACRS depreciation for their instruments.

In a case involving exotic cars that were not used for transportation but for exhibition, MACRS depreciation was allowed because the owner showed that they were subject to obsolescence. The autos were purchased solely for exhibition. The three state-of-the-art autos were a 1987 Lotus Pantera costing $63,000, a Lotus Espirit costing $48,000, and a Ferrari Testarossa costing $290,453. Over a four-year period, the owner deducted depreciation of over $298,000 while reporting gross income from exhibition fees of $96,630. The IRS disallowed the depreciation because the cars had no determinable useful

Caution

Tangible Personal Property

If you use the *de minimis* rule to deduct the cost of tangible personal property up to $2,500 per item or invoice, you do not put the property on your balance sheet and you do not depreciate the cost. *See 9.3.*

Caution

Corrections to Prior Year Returns

If you did not deduct the correct amount of depreciation for a prior year, you may be able to make a correction by filing an amended return. However, if you did not deduct the correct amount of depreciation for two or more consecutive years, you must request an accounting method change; *see* IRS Publication 946 for details. Adjustments to basis for unclaimed depreciation taken in prior years are discussed in *5.20*.

life. The Tax Court allowed the depreciation because such cars are subject to obsolescence in the car-show business when new models appear with newer designs and high-tech features. One witness testified this could occur in some cases within a year.

The Tax Court warned that such exotic cars should not be confused with museum pieces. If they had been museum pieces, such as antique cars, no depreciation would have been allowed. In the case of art objects and antiques used as business assets, the useful life requirement remains relevant because such assets are not subject to exhaustion, wear or tear, or obsolescence.

The IRS may continue to dispute and litigate cases in which depreciation is claimed on assets with indeterminable useful lives. For example, in a private ruling, the IRS did not allow a developer to depreciate street improvements that had been turned over to a city. The improvements were an intangible asset that improved the developer's access to its real estate projects, but this asset had an unlimited life. There was no determinable useful life because the city had agreed to maintain and replace the improvements as necessary, and there was no evidence that the city would ever assess the developer for replacement costs.

Basis for depreciation. Generally, the basis of the property on which you figure depreciation is its adjusted basis, which usually is its cost. To determine basis when property is acquired other than by purchase, *see 5.16* through *5.20*.

If you convert property from personal to business use, the basis for depreciation purposes is the lower of its adjusted basis or its fair market value at the time of the conversion.

> **EXAMPLE**
>
> In 2021, you bought a laptop for $2,400 for personal use. In 2023, when it is worth $800, you convert the computer to business use. The basis for depreciation is $800, the fair market value of the computer, which is lower than its adjusted basis of $2,400.

42.2 Claiming Depreciation on Your Tax Return

If you report business or professional self-employed income, use Form 4562 for assets placed in service during 2023; enter the total deduction on Line 13, Schedule C. For claiming depreciation on "listed property" such as cars, you use Form 4562, regardless of the year placed in service. *See* the explanation of listed property in this chapter *(42.10)*. If your only depreciation deduction is for pre-2023 assets, none of which is listed property, you do not need to use Form 4562; figure the deduction on your own worksheet, and enter it on Line 13, Schedule C.

Employees are no longer allowed to claim depreciation or other unreimbursed job expenses as an itemized deduction *(19.2)*. Qualifying Armed Forces reservists, performing artists, and state or local officials paid on a fee basis may be allowed to claim auto expenses, including depreciation for a vehicle used for work, on Form 2106; the deduction is as an adjustment to income *(19.2)*; *see* the Form 2106 instructions.

If you claim a home office deduction using the actual expense method *(40.13)*, you must use Form 8829 to claim depreciation on the portion of your home used for business.

If you report rental income on Schedule E, you must use Form 4562 for claiming depreciation on buildings placed in service in 2023. For buildings placed in service before 2023, enter the depreciation deduction directly on Schedule E. If you have a rental loss on Schedule E, your deduction for depreciation and other expenses may have to be included on Form 8582 to figure net passive activity income or loss; *see Chapter 10*.

42.3 First-Year Expensing Deduction

The dollar limit on first-year expensing in 2023 is $1,160,000. The dollar limit is phased out if the cost of qualifying property placed in service during the year exceeds a set dollar limit ($2.89 million in 2023).

Costs eligible for expensing. You may elect first-year expensing for tangible personal property bought for business use, such as machinery, equipment, or a car, truck or computer, provided the property is acquired from a non-related party. Qualified improvement property and certain improvements to nonresidential real property (e.g., roofs; heating,

Planning Reminder

Allocating Basis between Land and Buildings

The allocation should be made by relying on your county assessor's assessments or a sound appraisal.

Planning Reminder

Computer Software

Software with a useful life of more than one year that's purchased "off the shelf" (*see* the Filing Tip in *42.16*) and used for business is eligible for first-year expensing *(42.3)* and also qualifies for bonus depreciation *(42.18)*. Alternatively, it may be depreciated using the straight line method over 36 months. If the useful life does not exceed one year (such as an annual tax program), the cost is deductible as a business expense for the year of purchase.

ventilation, and air-conditioning; fire protection and alarm systems; security systems) also qualify for expensing *(42.14)*. Expensing is not allowed for property held for investment.

To elect the expensing deduction for the cost of qualifying property for 2023, the qualifying property must have been purchased and placed in service in 2023. You may not elect first-year expensing for property purchased before 2023 if 2023 is the first year you use it for business. For example, if you bought a laptop for family use in 2022 and in 2023 you converted it to business use, expensing is not allowed on your 2023 return. Vehicles are subject to special dollar limits *(43.4)*.

The portion of cost not eligible for first-year expensing may be recovered by depreciation under the regular MACRS rules *(42.4, 42.5)*. The first-year expensing deduction is technically called the "Section 179 deduction."

Electing first-year expensing. You make the election simply by reporting on Form 4562 the assets for which the election applies. You are permitted to make an election or revoke an election (or change the amount of an election or the assets for which the election applies) on a timely filed amended return. You do not need IRS consent. A revocation, once made, is irrevocable.

Partial business use. If you use the equipment for both business and personal use, business use must exceed 50% in the year the equipment is first placed into service to claim a first-year expensing deduction. The expensing deduction may be claimed for the cost allocated to business use up to the dollar limit. For business vehicles, the deduction may not exceed the annual depreciation limit *(43.4)*.

To elect first-year expensing for "listed property" such as a car or van *(42.10)*, business use in the first year you use it must exceed 50%. If it does, you show the amount eligible for expensing in the section for "Listed Property" on Form 4562 and then transfer the amount to the part of Form 4562 where the expensing election is claimed.

Figuring the deduction. For business use of less than 100% (but more than 50%), the expensing deduction is limited to the business portion of the cost. As discussed below, the dollar limit may have to be reduced because your taxable income is lower than the applicable dollar limit ($1,160,000 in 2023), eligible purchases exceed a set dollar amount ($2.89 million), or you are married filing separately.

If you qualify for expensing, you do not have to claim the entire amount. If in 2023 you place in service more than one item of property, you may allocate the dollar limit between the items. If you placed in service only one item of qualifying property that cost less than the dollar limit, your deduction is limited to that cost.

If you acquire property in a trade-in, the cost eligible for expensing is limited to the cash you paid. You may not include the adjusted basis of the property traded in, although your basis for the new property includes that amount.

Limit reduced if taxable income is lower. Your expensing deduction may not exceed net income from all your active businesses; *see* the Caution on this page.

Limit reduced if qualifying purchases exceed threshold. If the total cost of qualifying property placed in service during 2023 exceeds the purchase limit of $2.89 million, the dollar limit on expensing is reduced dollar-for-dollar by the cost of qualifying property exceeding the limit. For example, if in 2023 you place in service machinery costing $2.95 million, the $1,160,000 limit is reduced by $60,000 ($2.95 million − $2.89 million). The reduced limit of $1,100,000 is shown on Form 4562 on Line 5 of Part I (labeled "Dollar limitation for tax year.") If the total cost is $4.05 million ($4,050,000) or more, no first-year expensing deduction is allowed for 2023.

Limit reduced if married filing separately. If you and your spouse file separate returns, the 2023 expensing limit for both of you is one-half the usual amount. Unless you agree to a different allocation, you are each allowed only one-half of the limit, or $580,000. The phaseout threshold for purchases also applies to both of you as a unit.

Partners and S corporation stockholders. For property bought by a partnership or an S corporation, the dollar limit and taxable income limit applies to the business, as well as the owners as individual taxpayers. The partnership or S corporation determines its expensing

Filing Tip

First-Year Expensing or Bonus Depreciation?

If the property you place in service in 2023 qualifies for both types of write-offs, you may simply use bonus depreciation *(42.18)* and not elect first-year expensing.

Caution

Losses and Low Income May Limit Expensing Deduction

The expensing deduction may not exceed the net taxable income from all businesses that you actively conduct. Net income from active businesses is figured without regard to expensing, the deduction for the employer portion of self-employment liability, or any net operating loss carryback or carryforward. You may include wage or salary income as active business income and if you are married filing jointly, also include your spouse's net taxable income.

If you have an overall net loss from all actively conducted businesses, you may not claim an expensing deduction for 2023. If net income is less than the cost of qualifying assets, expensing is limited to the income. However, the cost over the income limit is carried forward to 2024 on Form 4562 provided you complete the expensing section of Form 4562 for 2023. You do not get a carryover unless the deduction is claimed on the return for the first year the property is placed in service. An expensing deduction cannot be used to create or increase a net operating loss.

deduction subject to the limits and allocates the deduction, if any, among the partners or shareholders. The allocated deduction may not exceed the net taxable income of the partnership or S corporation from actively conducted businesses.

An individual partner's expensing deduction may not exceed the annual dollar limit, regardless of how many partnership interests he or she has. However, the partner must reduce the basis of each partnership interest by the full allocable share of each partnership's expensing deduction, even if that amount is not deductible because of the dollar limit.

Disqualified acquisitions from related parties. Property does not qualify for the expense election if:

1. It is acquired from a spouse, ancestor, or lineal descendant, or from non–family-related parties subject to the loss disallowance rule *(5.6)*. For purposes of the expensing election, a corporation is controlled by you and thus subject to the loss disallowance rule *(5.6)* if 50% or more of the stock is owned by you, your spouse, your ancestors, or your descendants.

2. The property is acquired by a member of the same controlled group (using a 50% control test).

3. The basis of the property is determined in whole or in part (a) by reference to the adjusted basis of the property of the person from whom you acquired it or (b) under the stepped-up basis rules for inherited property.

Recapture of expensing deduction. Recapture of the first-year expensing deduction may occur on a disposition of the asset or if business use falls to 50% or less. If business use falls to 50% or less after the year the property is placed in service but before the end of the depreciable recovery period *(42.4, 42.10)*, you must "recapture" the benefit from the first-year expensing deduction. The amount recaptured is the excess of the expensing deduction over the amount of depreciation that would have been claimed (through the year of recapture) without expensing *(42.10)*. Recaptured amounts are reported as ordinary income on Form 4797.

When you sell or dispose of the property, the first-year expensing deduction is treated as depreciation for purposes of the recapture rules *(44.3)* that treat gain as ordinary income to the extent of depreciation claimed.

42.4 MACRS Recovery Periods

Depreciable assets other than buildings fall within a three-, five-, seven-, 10-, 15-, or 20-year recovery period under the general depreciation system (GDS).

Straight line recovery for buildings is claimed over a period of 27.5 years for residential rental property or 39 years for nonresidential real property *(42.13)*.

Note: The actual write-off period of depreciation for an asset is one year longer than the class life because of the convention rules *(42.5–42.7)*.

Three-year property. This class includes property with a class life of four years or less, other than cars and light-duty trucks, which are in the five-year class.

This class includes: special handling devices for the manufacture of food and beverages; special tools and devices for the manufacture of rubber products; special tools for the manufacture of finished plastic products, fabricated metal products, or motor vehicles; and breeding hogs. By law, racehorses and other horses more than 12 years old when placed in service are also in the three-year class.

Five-year property. This class includes property with a class life of more than four years and less than 10 years such as computers *(42.10)*, typewriters, copiers, duplicating equipment, most farming equipment, heavy general-purpose trucks, trailers, cargo containers, and trailer-mounted containers. Also included by law in the five-year class are cars, light-duty trucks (actual unloaded weight less than 13,000 pounds), taxis, buses, computer-based telephone central office switching equipment, computer-related peripheral equipment, semiconductor manufacturing equipment, and property used in research and experimentation. These leasehold improvements eligible for a five-year recovery period must be depreciated using the straight line method.

Planning Reminder

Year-End Purchases

Equipment placed in service on the last day of the 2023 taxable year may qualify for the entire first-year expensing limit. You do not have to prorate the limit for the amount of time you held the property.

Planning Reminder

Recovery Periods

The depreciation recovery periods for different types of assets are generally fixed by law according to the rules on this and the next page.

Seven-year property. This class includes any property with a class life of 10 years or more but less than 16 years. This is also a catch-all category for assets with no class life that have not been assigned by law to another class. Included in the seven-year class are: office furniture and fixtures, such as desks, safes, and files; cellular phones; fax machines; refrigerators; dishwashers; motor sports entertainment complexes; and machines used to produce jewelry, musical instruments, toys, and sporting goods.

Ten-year property. This includes property with a class life of 16 years or more and less than 20 years, such as vessels, barges, tugs, and water transportation equipment, and assets used in petroleum refining or in the manufacture of tobacco products and certain food products. The 10-year class also includes single-purpose agricultural and horticultural structures, and trees or vines bearing fruit or nuts.

Fifteen-year property. This includes land improvements such as fences, sidewalks, docks, shrubbery, roads, and bridges as well as qualified improvement property (certain internal building improvements). It also includes other property with a class life of 20 years or more but less than 25 years, such as municipal sewage plants and telephone distribution plants. Gas station convenience stores are in the 15-year class if the property is no more than 1,400 square feet, or at least 50% of the floor space is devoted to selling petroleum products, or at least 50% of revenues are from petroleum sales. The owner of the gas station property does not have to be the operator of businesses on the property.

Twenty-year property. This class includes property with a class life of 25 years or more, such as farm buildings and municipal sewers, except that residential and nonresidential real estate is excluded *(42.13)*.

42.5 MACRS Rates

The MACRS rate under the general depreciation system depends on the recovery period *(42.4)* for the property and whether the half-year or mid-quarter convention applies. The 200% declining balance rate applies to three-year property, five-year property, seven-year property, and 10-year property. *See 42.8* for the 150% declining balance rate election. These rates are adjusted for the convention rules explained below. When the 200% declining balance rate provides a lower annual deduction than the straight line rate, the 200% declining balance rate is replaced by the straight line rate. The rates in *Table 42-1* incorporate the applicable convention and the change from the 200% declining balance rate to a straight line recovery. MACRS straight line rates are discussed later in this Chapter *(42.9)*.

Conventions. Under the half-year convention, all property acquired during the year, regardless of when acquired during the year, is treated as acquired in the middle of the year. As a result, only one-half of the full first-year depreciation is deductible and in the year after the last class life year, the balance of the depreciation is written off. Furthermore, in the year property is sold, only half of the full depreciation for that year is deductible *(42.6)*.

The half-year convention applies unless the total cost bases of depreciable assets placed in service during the last three months of the taxable year exceed 40% of the total bases of all property placed in service during the entire year. If this 40% test applies, you must use a mid-quarter convention to figure your annual depreciation deduction *(42.7)*.

Buildings are depreciated using a mid-month convention *(42.12)*.

Depreciation tables. *Table 42-1* provides year-by-year rates for property in the three, five-, and seven-year classes. The rates incorporate the adjustment for the half-year or mid-quarter convention and the switch from the 200% declining balance rate to the straight line method. Use the rate shown in the table under the convention for your asset. The rate is applied to original basis, minus any first-year expensing deduction *(42.3)* and bonus depreciation *(42.20)* you claimed. After applying the rate from the table to the basis, you claim the deduction on Form 4562, Part III, Section B, labeled "General Depreciation System" (GDS).

You use the tables for the entire recovery period unless you claim a deductible casualty loss that reduces your basis in the property. For the year of the casualty loss and later years, depreciation must be based on the adjusted basis of the property at the end of the year. The tables may no longer be used; *see* IRS Publication 946 for further details.

EXAMPLE

During June 2023, you place in business service a machine costing $20,000. It is your only acquisition in 2023. (Assume you do not elect to expense the cost and opt out of bonus depreciation for all 5-year property.) The machine is 5-year property and is subject to the half-year convention. The depreciation rate for the first year is 20% (*see Table 42-1* below for 5-year property). Your 2023 depreciation deduction is $4,000 ($20,000 × 20%). If you hold the machine for the entire 6-year recovery period, your total deduction for all years will equal your $20,000 cost.

Summary of Deductions

Year	Deduction
1 (2023)	$4,000
2 (2024)	6,400
3 (2025)	3,840
4 (2026)	2,304
5 (2027)	2,304
6 (2028)	1,152
Total	$20,000

Planning Reminder

Half-Year Convention

The half-year convention applies unless the total cost basis of depreciable assets placed in service during the last three months of the year exceeds 40% of the total basis of all property placed in service during the year.

Under the half-year convention, all assets placed in service during the year are treated as placed in service at the midpoint of the year.

42.6 Half-Year Convention for MACRS

The half-year convention treats all business equipment placed in service during a tax year as placed in service in the midpoint of that tax year. The same rule applies in the year in which the property is disposed of. The effect of this rule is as follows: A half-year of depreciation is allowed in the first year that property is placed in service, regardless of when the property is placed in service during the tax year. For each of the remaining years of the recovery period, a full year of depreciation is claimed. If you hold the property for the entire recovery period, a half-year of depreciation is claimed for the year following the end of the recovery period. If you dispose of the property before the end of the recovery period, a half-year of depreciation is allowable for the year of disposition.

See Table 42-1 for year-by-year rates under the half-year convention. Apply the rate from the table to the original basis, minus any first-year expensing (42.3) deduction and bonus depreciation (42.20) claimed. The Example in 42.5 shows the year-by-year deduction computation for five-year property under the half-year convention.

If you dispose of property before the end of its recovery period (42.5), your deduction for the year of disposition is one-half of the deduction that would be allowed for the full year using the rate shown in the table. For example, if you sell the machine in the Example in 42.5 in year three, the deduction is $1,920 (½ of $3,840).

Table 42-1   MACRS Depreciation Rates

| Year | Half-Year Convention | Mid-Quarter Convention | | | |
		1st (Quarter)	2nd (Quarter)	3rd (Quarter)	4th (Quarter)
		3-Year Property			
1	33.33%	58.33%	41.67%	25.00%	8.33%
2	44.45	27.78	38.89	50.00	61.11
3	14.81	12.35	14.14	16.67	20.37
4	7.41	1.54	5.30	8.33	10.19
		5-Year Property			
1	20.00%	35.00%	25.00%	15.00%	5.00%
2	32.00	26.00	30.00	34.00	38.00
3	19.20	15.60	18.00	20.40	22.80
4	11.52	11.01	11.37	12.24	13.68
5	11.52	11.01	11.37	11.30	10.94
6	5.76	1.38	4.26	7.06	9.58
		7-Year Property			
1	14.29%	25.00%	17.85%	10.71%	3.57%
2	24.49	21.43	23.47	25.51	27.55
3	17.49	15.31	16.76	18.22	19.68
4	12.49	10.93	11.97	13.02	14.06
5	8.93	8.75	8.87	9.30	10.04
6	8.92	8.74	8.87	8.85	8.73
7	8.93	8.75	8.87	8.86	8.73
8	4.46	1.09	3.33	5.53	7.64

42.7   Last Quarter Placements—Mid-Quarter Convention

A mid-quarter convention generally applies if the total cost basis of business equipment placed in service during the last three months of the tax year exceeds 40% of the total basis of all the property placed in service during the year. In applying the 40% rule, you do not count residential rental property, nonresidential realty, and assets that were placed in service and disposed of during the same year.

Under the mid-quarter convention, the first-year depreciation allowance for all property (other than nonresidential real property and residential rental property) placed in service during the year is based on the number of quarters that the asset was in service. Property placed in service at any time during a quarter is treated as having been placed in service in the middle of the quarter. The mid-quarter convention also applies to sales and disposals of property. The disposal is treated as occurring in the midpoint of the quarter.

> **EXAMPLE**
>
> During August 2023, you place in service office furniture costing $1,000, and in October, a computer costing $5,000. You are on the calendar year. The total basis of all property placed in service in 2023 is $6,000. As the $5,000 basis of the computer placed in service in the last quarter exceeds 40% of the total basis of all property placed in service during 2023, you must use the mid-quarter convention for the furniture and the computer. The office furniture, which is seven-year property, and the computer, which is five-year property, are depreciated using MACRS and a mid-quarter convention.
>
> You first multiply the $1,000 basis of the furniture by 10.71%—the first-year mid-quarter convention rate for seven-year property placed in service in the third quarter *(see Table 42-1)*. The depreciation deduction is $107. You then multiply the $5,000 basis of the computer by 5%—the five-year property mid-quarter convention rate for the fourth quarter of the first year *(see Table 42-1)*. The deduction is $250. Total depreciation is $357.

If you dispose of property before the end of its recovery period *(42.5)*, your deduction for the year is figured by multiplying a full year of depreciation by the percentage listed in the following chart for the quarter in which you disposed of the property.

Quarter	Percentage
First	12.5%
Second	37.5%
Third	62.5%
Fourth	87.5%

> **EXAMPLE**
>
> On November 1, 2020, you placed in service a machine costing $10,000 with a five-year recovery period. You used the mid-quarter convention because it was the only item placed in service during the year. In May 2023, you sell the machine.
>
> To determine depreciation for 2023, first figure the deduction for the full year *(see Table 42-1)*. This is $1,368 (13.68%, rate for fourth year, fourth quarter, of $10,000). May, the month of disposition, is in the second quarter of the year; thus you multiply $1,368 by 37.5% to figure your depreciation deduction for 2023 of $513.

42.8 150% Rate Election

Instead of using the 200% declining balance rate for property in the three-, five-, seven-, and 10-year classes, you may elect a 150% declining balance rate. You may prefer the 150% rate when you are subject to the alternative minimum tax (AMT). For AMT purposes, you must use the 150% rate and adjust your taxable income if the 200% rate was used for regular tax purposes *(23.2)*. If for regular tax purposes you elect to apply the 150% rate, use the same recovery period *(42.4)* you would have used if you had claimed the 200% declining balance rate. Thus, the recovery period is five years for cars and computers and seven years for office furniture and fixtures. If the half-year convention applies, the first-year rate for the five-year class is 15%, and 10.71% for the seven-year class; *see* the table *below*. Apply the rate from the table to your original basis, minus any first-year expensing deduction and bonus depreciation claimed. If you are subject to the mid-quarter convention, *see* IRS Publication 946 for the tables showing mid-quarter convention rates.

The election to use the 150% rate must be made for all property within a given class placed in service in the same year. The election is irrevocable.

Table 42-2 Half-Year Convention—150% Rate

	Recovery Period	
Year—	5-Year—	7-Year—
1	15.00%	10.71%
2	25.50	19.13
3	17.85	15.03
4	16.66	12.25
5	16.66	12.25
6	8.33	12.25
7		12.25
8		6.13

42.9 Straight Line Depreciation

You may not want an accelerated rate and may prefer to write off depreciation at an even pace. There are two straight line methods. You may make an irrevocable election to use the straight line method over the regular MACRS recovery period *(42.4)* under the general depreciation system (GDS). Alternatively, you may elect straight line recovery over the designated recovery period for the class life under the alternative depreciation system (ADS). For some assets, such as cars, the GDS and ADS recovery periods are the same (five years for a car). In most cases, the ADS recovery period is longer than the GDS recovery period. For example, the recovery period for office furniture and fixtures is seven years under GDS and 10 years under ADS.

Half-year and quarter-year conventions apply to both straight line methods *(42.6, 42.7)*. A mid-month convention applies under the straight line rule for buildings *(42.12)*.

Straight line over regular recovery period (GDS). You make this election on Form 4562, Part III, Section B, labeled "General Depreciation System". To elect this method for one asset, you must also use it for all other assets in the same class that are placed in service during the year. The straight line election is irrevocable.

Straight line under the alternative depreciation system (ADS). Under the alternative depreciation system (ADS), the straight line recovery period is generally the same as the "class life" of the asset as determined by the IRS; the ADS recovery periods are shown in IRS Publication 946. The ADS recovery period for cars, light trucks, and computers is five years, the same as under the GDS. For business office furniture and fixtures, the ADS straight line recovery period is 10 years. The ADS recovery period for personal property with no class life is 12 years. For nonresidential real property, the ADS recovery period is 40 years; for residential rental property, the ADS recovery period is 30 years for property placed in service after 2017 (40 years for older property). *See* IRS Publication 946 for other ADS class lives.

Except for real estate, the ADS election applies to all property within the same class placed in service during the taxable year. For real estate, the election to use the alternative depreciation method may be made on a property-by-property basis. The election is irrevocable. The deduction is claimed on Form 4562, Part III, Section C, labeled "Alternative Depreciation System,"

Straight line rate table. *Table 42-3 below* shows straight line rates for five-year, seven-year, and 10-year property under the half-year convention. As discussed earlier, the recovery period depends on whether the GDS or ADS straight line method is used. If you are subject to the mid-quarter convention *(42.7)*, *see* IRS Publication 946 for tables showing the applicable rates.

Filing Tip

Should You Elect Straight Line Recovery?
Accelerated rates of MACRS merely give you an opportunity to advance the time of taking your deduction. This may be a decided advantage where the higher deductions in the first few years will provide you with cash for working capital or for investments in other income-producing sources. That is, by accelerating the deductions, you defer the payment of taxes that would be due if you claimed smaller depreciation deductions, using more conservative straight line rates. The tax deferral lasts until the rapid method provides lower depreciation deductions than would the more conservative method. You are generally more likely to benefit from accelerated MACRS in an ongoing business.

If you are starting a new business in which you expect losses or low income at the start, accelerated MACRS may waste depreciation deductions that could be used in later years when your income increases. Therefore, before deciding to use accelerated MACRS rates, consider your income prospects.

Table 42-3 Half-Year Convention—Straight Line Rate

Year—	Recovery Period		
	5-Year—	7-Year—	10-Year—
1	10.00%	7.14%	5.00%
2	20.00	14.29	10.00
3	20.00	14.29	10.00
4	20.00	14.28	10.00
5	20.00	14.29	10.00
6	10.00	14.28	10.00
7		14.29	10.00
8		7.14	10.00
9			10.00
10			10.00
11			5.00

AMT depreciation. There is no AMT adjustment for depreciation if for regular tax purposes straight line depreciation is claimed on tangible personal property placed in service after 1998. Similarly, for real estate placed in service after 1998, the straight line depreciation deduction claimed for regular tax purposes does not have to be refigured for AMT. For real property placed in service before 1999, regular tax straight line depreciation is refigured for AMT purposes using the straight line method over 40 years.

Mandatory straight line depreciation. You are required to use the alternative depreciation system for automobiles *(43.3)* and certain computers *(42.10)* used 50% or less for business.

Alternative MACRS depreciation must also be used for:
* Figuring earnings and profits;
* Tangible property which, during the taxable year, is used predominantly outside the United States;
* Tax-exempt use property;
* Tax-exempt bond financed property; and
* Imported property covered by an executive order.

42.10 Listed Property

"Listed property" is a term applied to certain equipment that may be used for personal and business purposes. For such property, the law allows first-year expensing *(42.3)*, bonus depreciation *(42.20)*, or accelerated MACRS *(42.5)* deductions only if business use exceeds 50%. For business use of 50% or less, you must use ADS straight line depreciation *(42.9)*. Deductions for listed property are claimed on Part V of Form 4562. If the more-than-50%-business-use test is met in the first year and first-year expensing or accelerated MACRS is claimed, but business use of listed property falls to 50% or less during the ADS straight line recovery period *(42.9)*, you must "recapture" first-year expensing, bonus depreciation and accelerated MACRS deductions.

What is "listed property"? Listed property includes passenger autos and other transportation vehicles *(see* exceptions at *43.4)*, boats, airplanes, and any photographic, sound, or video recording equipment that could be used for entertainment or recreational purposes. However, there is an exception for photographic, phonographic, communications, or video equipment used exclusively and regularly in your business or at your regular business establishment. A home office that meets the requirements for deducting home office expenses *(40.12)* is considered a regular business establishment.

Deductions for listed property subject to recapture. If business use of listed property exceeds 50% in the first year but drops to 50% or less within the ADS recovery period *(Table 42-3)*, bonus depreciation, MACRS and any first-year expensing deduction are subject to "recapture." In the year in which business use drops to 50% or less, you recapture the excess of (1) the MACRS, bonus depreciation, and first-year expensing deductions claimed in prior years over (2) the deductions that would have been allowed using ADS straight line depreciation *(42.9)*. For the rest of the recovery period, you continue to use the alternative straight line rate.

Recapture is figured on Form 4797. The recapture computation follows the steps shown in *43.10* for recapture of excess depreciation on an automobile.

Leasing listed property. You may deduct the portion of your lease payments attributable to business use. However, if business use is 50% or less for any year, you must report as income an amount based on the fair market value of the unit, the percentage of business plus investment use, and percentages from two IRS tables shown in Publication 946. Special rules apply for leasing cars, light trucks, and vans *(43.12)*.

42.11 Assets in Service Before 1987

Assets placed in service before 1987 were depreciated under a different recovery system called ACRS. Most of the assets have already been fully depreciated, although some assets, such as certain real estate placed in service before 1987, continue to be governed by these rules *(42.15)*.

42.12 MACRS for Real Estate Placed in Service After 1986

The recovery period for residential rental property placed in service after December 31, 1986, is 27.5 years. The recovery period for nonresidential real property is either 39 years or 31.5 years, depending on when the property was placed in service.

The method of recovery for nonresidential or residential property is the straight line method using a mid-month convention. *See Table 42-4* for rate tables for each class of property.

For nonresidential real property placed in service after December 31, 1986, but before May 13, 1993, the depreciation recovery period is 31.5 years.

For nonresidential real property placed in service after May 12, 1993, the recovery period is 39 years. Under a transition rule, the 31.5-year recovery period rather than the 39-year recovery period applies to a building placed in service before 1994 if before May 13, 1993, you had entered into a binding, written contract to buy or build it, or if, before that date, you had begun construction. The transition rule also applies if you obtained the contract or property from someone else who satisfied the pre–May 13, 1993, contract or construction requirement, provided he or she never placed the building in service and you did so before 1994.

Table 42-4   MACRS Real Estate Depreciation

Residential Rental Property (27.5 years; see 42.12)
Use the column for the month of taxable year placed in service.

Year	Month property placed in service 1	2	3	4	5	6	7	8	9	10	11	12
1	3.485%	3.182%	2.879%	2.576%	2.273%	1.970%	1.667%	1.364%	1.061%	0.758%	0.455%	0.152%
2–9	3.636	3.636	3.636	3.636	3.636	3.636	3.636	3.636	3.636	3.636	3.636	3.636
10	3.637	3.637	3.637	3.637	3.637	3.637	3.636	3.636	3.636	3.636	3.636	3.636
11	3.636	3.636	3.636	3.636	3.636	3.636	3.637	3.637	3.637	3.637	3.637	3.637
12	3.637	3.637	3.637	3.637	3.637	3.637	3.636	3.636	3.636	3.636	3.636	3.636
13	3.636	3.636	3.636	3.636	3.636	3.636	3.637	3.637	3.637	3.637	3.637	3.637
14	3.637	3.637	3.637	3.637	3.637	3.637	3.636	3.636	3.636	3.636	3.636	3.636
15	3.636	3.636	3.636	3.636	3.636	3.636	3.637	3.637	3.637	3.637	3.637	3.637
16	3.637	3.637	3.637	3.637	3.637	3.637	3.636	3.636	3.636	3.636	3.636	3.636
17	3.636	3.636	3.636	3.636	3.636	3.636	3.637	3.637	3.637	3.637	3.637	3.637
18	3.637	3.637	3.637	3.637	3.637	3.637	3.636	3.636	3.636	3.636	3.636	3.636
19	3.636	3.636	3.636	3.636	3.636	3.636	3.637	3.637	3.637	3.637	3.637	3.637
20	3.637	3.637	3.637	3.637	3.637	3.637	3.636	3.636	3.636	3.636	3.636	3.636
21	3.636	3.636	3.636	3.636	3.636	3.636	3.637	3.637	3.637	3.637	3.637	3.637
22	3.637	3.637	3.637	3.637	3.637	3.637	3.636	3.636	3.636	3.636	3.636	3.636
23	3.636	3.636	3.636	3.636	3.636	3.636	3.637	3.637	3.637	3.637	3.637	3.637
24	3.637	3.637	3.637	3.637	3.637	3.637	3.636	3.636	3.636	3.636	3.636	3.636
25	3.636	3.636	3.636	3.636	3.636	3.636	3.637	3.637	3.637	3.637	3.637	3.637
26	3.637	3.637	3.637	3.637	3.637	3.637	3.636	3.636	3.636	3.636	3.636	3.636
27	3.636	3.636	3.636	3.636	3.636	3.636	3.637	3.637	3.637	3.637	3.637	3.637
28	1.97	2.273	2.576	2.879	3.182	3.485	3.636	3.636	3.636	3.636	3.636	3.636
29							0.152	0.455	0.758	1.061	1.364	1.667

Nonresidential Real Property (39 years—placed in service on or after May 13, 1993; see 42.12)
Use the column for the month of taxable year placed in service.

Year \ Month	1	2	3	4	5	6	7	8	9	10	11	12
1	2.461%	2.247%	2.033%	1.819%	1.605%	1.391%	1.177%	0.963%	0.749%	0.535%	0.321%	0.107%
2–39	2.564	2.564	2.564	2.564	2.564	2.564	2.564	2.564	2.564	2.564	2.564	2.564
40	0.107	0.321	0.535	0.749	0.963	1.177	1.391	1.605	1.819	2.033	2.247	2.461

Nonresidential Real Property (31.5 years—placed in service before May 13, 1993; see 42.12)
Use the column for the month of taxable year placed in service

Year \ Month	1	2	3	4	5	6	7	8	9	10	11	12
20	3.175	3.174	3.175	3.174	3.175	3.174	3.175	3.174	3.175	3.174	3.175	3.174
21	3.174	3.175	3.174	3.175	3.174	3.175	3.174	3.175	3.174	3.175	3.174	3.175
22	3.175	3.174	3.175	3.174	3.175	3.174	3.175	3.174	3.175	3.174	3.175	3.174
23	3.174	3.175	3.174	3.175	3.174	3.175	3.174	3.175	3.174	3.175	3.174	3.175
24	3.175	3.174	3.175	3.174	3.175	3.174	3.175	3.174	3.175	3.174	3.175	3.174
25	3.174	3.175	3.174	3.175	3.174	3.175	3.174	3.175	3.174	3.175	3.174	3.175
26	3.175	3.174	3.175	3.174	3.175	3.174	3.175	3.174	3.175	3.174	3.175	3.174
27	3.174	3.175	3.174	3.175	3.174	3.175	3.174	3.175	3.174	3.175	3.174	3.175
28	3.175	3.174	3.175	3.174	3.175	3.174	3.175	3.174	3.175	3.174	3.175	3.174
29	3.174	3.175	3.174	3.175	3.174	3.175	3.174	3.175	3.174	3.175	3.174	3.175
30	3.175	3.174	3.175	3.174	3.175	3.174	3.175	3.174	3.175	3.174	3.175	3.174
31	3.174	3.175	3.174	3.175	3.174	3.175	3.174	3.175	3.174	3.175	3.174	3.175
32	1.720	1.984	2.249	2.513	2.778	3.042	3.175	3.174	3.175	3.174	3.175	3.174
33							0.132	0.397	0.661	0.926	1.190	1.455

However, *see 42.14* for qualified improvement property.

Residential rental property subject to the 27.5 year recovery period is defined as a rental building or structure for which 80% or more of the gross rental income for the tax year is rental income from dwelling units. If you occupy any part of the building, the gross rental income includes the fair rental value of the part you occupy.

A dwelling unit is a house or an apartment used to provide living accommodations in a building or structure, but not a unit in a hotel, motel, inn, or other establishment where more than one-half of the units are used on a transient basis.

Mid-month convention. Under a mid-month convention, all residential rental property and nonresidential real property placed in service or disposed of during any month is treated as placed in service or disposed of at the midpoint of that month. You may determine the first-year deduction for your property by applying the percentage from *Table 42-4* to the original depreciable basis. In later years, use the same column of the table to figure your deduction. If the property is disposed of before the end of the recovery period, the deduction for the year of disposition is figured by prorating the full-year deduction for the months the property was in service, treating the month of disposition as one-half of a month of use.

> **EXAMPLES**
>
> 1. In February 2023, you buy an apartment building for $100,000 and place it in service. You use the calendar year. *Table 42-4* (page 746) gives a first-year depreciation rate of 3.182% for 27.5-year residential rental property placed in service during February. Applying this rate, you get a deduction of $3,182.
>   For 2024 (year 2), the rate will be 3.636%, for a deduction of $3,636.
>
> 2. Assume that you sell the apartment building in Example 1 on March 7, 2025. A full year of depreciation for 2025 is $3,636 (3.636% rate for year 3 × $100,000). You are treated as using the property for 2.5 months in 2025, so your deduction is $757.50 ($3,636 ÷ 12 × 2.5).

Additions or improvements to property. The depreciation deduction for any additions to, or improvement of, any property is figured in the same way as the deduction for the property would be figured if the property had been placed in service at the same time as the addition or improvement. However, *see 42.14* for qualified improvement property.

42.13 Demolishing a Building

When you buy improved property, the purchase price is allocated between the land and the building; only the building may be depreciated. The land may not *(42.1)*. If you later demolish the building, you may not deduct the cost of the demolition or the undepreciated basis of the building as a loss in the year of demolition. Expenses or losses in connection with the demolition of any structure, including certified historic structures, are not deductible. They must be capitalized and added to the basis of the land on which the structure is located.

Major rehabilitation. Where you are considering a major rehabilitation of a building that involves some demolition of the building, IRS guidelines may allow you to deduct the costs of demolition and a removal of part of the structure. Under the IRS rules, the costs of structural modification may avoid capitalization if 75% or more of the existing external walls are retained as internal or external walls and 75% or more of the existing internal framework is also retained. For certified historic structures, the modification must also be part of a certified rehabilitation.

42.14 Qualified Improvement Property

Qualified improvement property has a 15-year recovery period. As such, it qualifies for bonus depreciation. For 2023, bonus depreciation is 80%; *see 42.18*.

Filing Tip

Additions and Improvements

The MACRS class for an addition or improvement is generally determined by the MACRS class of the property to which the addition or improvement is made. For example, if you put an addition on a rental home that you are depreciating over 27.5 years, the addition is depreciated as 27.5-year residential rental property. The period for figuring depreciation begins on the date that the addition or improvement is placed in service, or, if later, the date that the property to which the addition or improvement was made is placed in service.

Qualified improvement property. Qualified improvement property is any improvement to an interior part of a building that is nonresidential realty and is made after the date the building was placed in service. However, any improvements for the enlargement of the building, an elevator or escalator, or changes to the internal framework of the building, are not qualified improvement property.

42.15 Depreciating Real Estate Placed in Service After 1980 and Before 1987

The ACRS recovery period of almost all buildings placed in service before 1987 has already ended. Some pre-1987 buildings are still being depreciated over a 35-year or 45-year period if the straight line election discussed in the next paragraph was made.

Election to use straight line depreciation. For 15-year, 18-year, or 19-year real property, you may have elected to use the straight line method over 35 or 45 years. An election of the straight line method for real property had to be made on a property-by-property basis, by the return due date, plus extensions, for the year the property was placed in service.

Rate of recovery. The rate of recovery is listed in Treasury tables that are available in IRS Publication 534.

Substantial improvements. Substantial improvements made after 1986 to an ACRS building are depreciable under MACRS *(42.13)*, not ACRS.

Recapture. *See 44.1* for recapture rules on the sale of ACRS property.

42.16 Amortizing Goodwill and Other Intangibles (Section 197)

The costs of intangibles coming within Section 197 are amortized over a 15-year period. The 15-year period applies regardless of the actual useful life of "Section 197 intangibles" that are held in connection with a business or income-producing activity.

Generally, the amount subject to amortization is cost. Annual amortization is reported on Form 4562. The 15-year period starts with the month the intangible was acquired.

A "Section 197 intangible" is: (1) goodwill; (2) going-concern value; (3) workforce in place; (4) information base; (5) know-how, but *see* exceptions below; (6) any customer-based intangible; (7) any supplier-based intangible; (8) any license, permit, or other right granted by a governmental unit or agency; (9) any covenant not to compete made in the acquisition of a business; and (10) any franchise, trademark, or trade name.

Goodwill. Goodwill is the value of a business attributable to the expectancy of continued customer patronage, due to the name or reputation of a business or any other factor.

Franchises, trademarks, and trade names. A franchise (excluding sports franchises), trademark, or trade name is a Section 197 intangible. Amounts, whether fixed or contingent, paid on the transfer of a trademark, trade name, or franchise are chargeable to capital account and must be ratably amortized over a 15-year period. The renewal of a franchise, trademark, or trade name is treated as an acquisition of the franchise, trademark, or trade name. Renewal costs are amortized over 15 years beginning in the month of renewal.

Know-how. A patent, copyright, formula, process, design, pattern, format, or similar item may be a Section 197 intangible. However, the following interests are not Section 197 intangibles unless acquired as part of the acquisition of a business: patents, copyrights, and interests in films, sound recordings, videotapes, books, or other similar property.

Customer-based intangibles. Customer-based intangibles include the portion of an acquired trade or business attributable to a customer base, circulation base, undeveloped market or market growth, insurance in force, investment management contracts, or other relationships with customers that involve the future provision of goods or services.

Supplier-based intangibles. The portion of the purchase price of an acquired business attributable to a favorable relationship with persons who provide distribution services, such as favorable shelf or display space at a retail outlet, the existence of a favorable credit rating, or the existence of favorable supply contracts, are Section 197 intangibles.

Going-concern value. This is the additional value that attaches to property because it is an integral part of a going concern. This includes the value attributable to the ability of a trade or business to continue to operate and generate sales without interruption in spite of a change in ownership.

Workforce in place. The portion of the purchase price of an acquired business attributable to a highly skilled workforce is amortizable over 15 years. Similarly, the cost of acquiring an existing employment contract is amortizable over 15 years.

Information base. This includes the cost of acquiring customer lists; subscription lists; insurance expirations; patient or client files; lists of newspaper, magazine, radio, or television advertisers; business books and records; and operating systems. The intangible value of technical manuals, training manuals or programs, data files, and accounting or inventory control systems is also a Section 197 intangible.

Self-created intangibles. A Section 197 intangible created by a taxpayer is generally not amortizable, unless created in connection with a transaction that involves the acquisition of assets of a business. However, this deduction bar for self-created intangibles does not apply to the following: (1) any license, permit, or other right granted by a governmental unit or agency; (2) a covenant not to compete entered into on the acquisition of a business; or (3) any franchise, trademark, or trade name. For example, the 15-year amortization period may apply to the capitalized costs of registering or developing a trademark or trade name.

A person who contracts for or renews a contract for the use of a Section 197 intangible may not be considered to have created that intangible. For example, a licensee who contracts for the use of know-how may amortize capitalized costs over 15 years.

The following intangible assets are not Section 197 intangibles. (1) interests in a corporation, partnership, trust, or estate; (2) interests under certain financial contracts; (3) interests in land; (4) certain computer software (*see* the Filing Tip on this page); (5) certain separately acquired rights and interests; (6) interests under existing leases of tangible property; (7) interests under existing indebtedness; (8) sports franchises; (9) certain residential mortgage servicing rights; and (10) certain corporate transaction costs. Loss limitations. A person who disposes of an amortizable Section 197 intangible at a loss and at the same time retains other Section 197 intangibles acquired in the same transaction may not deduct the loss. The disallowed loss is added to the basis of the retained Section 197 intangibles. The same rule applies if a Section 197 intangible is abandoned or becomes worthless and other Section 197 intangibles acquired in the same transaction are kept. The basis of the remaining intangibles is increased by the disallowed loss.

You may not treat a covenant not to compete as worthless any earlier than the disposition or worthlessness of the entire interest in a business.

Dispositions. An amortizable Section 197 intangible is not a capital asset. It is treated as depreciable property, and if held for more than one year, it will generally qualify as a Section 1231 asset *(44.1)*. Amortization claimed on a Section 197 intangible is subject to recapture under Section 1245 and gain on its sale to certain related persons is subject to ordinary income treatment under Section 1239.

Planning Reminder

Covenants Not to Compete

A covenant not to compete is a Section 197 intangible if paid for in connection with the acquisition of a business. Excessive compensation or rental paid to a former owner of a business for continuing to perform services or provide the use of property is considered an amount paid for a covenant not to compete if the services or property benefits the trade or business. But an amount paid under a covenant not to compete that actually represents additional consideration for corporate stock is not a Section 197 intangible and must be added to the basis of the acquired stock.

Filing Tip

Computer Software Not Considered a Section 197 Intangible

Computer software is not a Section 197 intangible if it is readily available to the general public, is not subject to an exclusive license and has not been substantially changed. If this test is met, business software is treated as "off the shelf" software that is eligible for first-year expensing *(42.3)* or bonus depreciation *(42.18)*, or it may be depreciated over 36 months using the straight line method if it has a useful life of over one year.

Even if the above test is not met, computer software is not a Section 197 intangible unless it is acquired in the acquisition of a business.

42.17 Amortizing Research and Experimentation Costs

If you have these costs, you must amortize them over a period of not less than five years (15 years for foreign expenditures). Before 2022, you could have elected to take a current deduction for the full amount of costs, but this option no longer applies.

You may be eligible for a tax credit for increasing your R&D costs *(40.26)*. However, you cannot take a deduction and a credit with respect to the same costs.

Planning Reminder

**Abandonment of
Leasehold Improvements**

Upon the termination of a lease, the adjusted basis of a lessee's leasehold improvements that are abandoned may be claimed as a loss. A lessor may follow the rule applied to lessees if the improvements are irrevocably disposed of or abandoned at the termination of the lease. The lessor may recognize loss for the remaining adjusted basis of the improvements.

See the Form 4562 instructions for further details.

Law Alert

**Bonus Depreciation for New and
Pre-Owned Property**

Bonus depreciation can be claimed for eligible property whether it is new or used.

42.18 Bonus Depreciation

Bonus depreciation is an additional first-year depreciation allowance equal to a set percentage of the adjusted basis of eligible property. The percentage for bonus depreciation for 2023 is 80%; however, bonus depreciation is fully deductible for alternative minimum tax purposes *(23.2)*; no adjustment is required.

Bonus depreciation (also called a Section 168(k) allowance and a special depreciation allowance) can be claimed in addition to any first-year expensing *(42.3)*, depending on the cost of the property. In figuring "adjusted basis" for purposes of bonus depreciation, any first-year expensing deduction is taken into account first. Then, you figure bonus depreciation on the depreciable cost (business portion) of the property minus the first-year expensing allowance.

Bonus depreciation cannot be claimed for property that must be depreciated under the ADS straight line method *(42.9)*. For example, it may not be used for listed property used 50% or less for business *(42.10)* since such property must be depreciated under ADS.

Bonus depreciation allows the first-year dollar limit on write-offs for vehicles weighing less than 6,000 pounds to be increased by a fixed dollar amount reflecting bonus depreciation, provided that business use exceeds 50%. The bonus allowance increases the total dollar limit for such vehicles placed in service during 2023 by $8,000 *(43.4)*.

Eligible property. Bonus depreciation can be claimed for any property with a recovery period of 20 years or less, computer software that is not a Section 197 intangible (*see* the Filing Tip in *42.16*), and buildings that replace or rehabilitate property damaged, destroyed, or condemned as a result of a federally declared disaster. Eligible property also includes the costs of television, film, and theatrical production and the cost of certain plants that are planted and grafted. And it includes qualified improvement property *(42.14)*.

Claiming bonus depreciation. You report bonus depreciation in Part II of Form 4562 labeled "Special Depreciation Allowance," unless the property is "listed property" *(42.10)*. For listed property, use Part V of Form 4562.

Election out of bonus depreciation. Unlike regular depreciation, you are not required to use bonus depreciation and have the option of electing out of its use. If eligible for bonus depreciation, you can elect not to use it. The election out is made on a per-asset-class basis. Thus, for example, you can opt out of bonus depreciation for all five-year property while claiming it for seven-year property. To make the election out of claiming bonus depreciation, attach a statement to your return specifying the class of property for which the election not to claim additional depreciation is being made.

If you fail to make an election not to claim bonus depreciation, then you are deemed to have claimed it (even though you did not) and must reduce the basis of the property by the amount of bonus depreciation that could have been claimed.

CHAPTER 43

Deducting Car and Truck Expenses

The costs of buying and operating a car, truck, or van for business are deductible under rules hedged with restrictions. Depreciation deductions for most cars, trucks, and vans are subject to annual ceilings, but for vehicles placed in service in 2023 and used 100% for business, bonus depreciation allows a first-year depreciation limit of $20,200 *(43.5)*. The cost of heavy SUVs used 100% for business that are placed in service in 2023 can be fully deducted in 2023.

To avoid accounting for actual vehicle expenses and depreciation, you may claim an IRS mileage allowance. The allowance is 65.5 cents per mile; keep a record of business trip mileage.

If you are self-employed, you deduct your vehicle expenses on Schedule C *(40.6)*. Use Form 4562 to compute depreciation if you claim actual operating costs instead of the IRS mileage allowance. If you are an employee, you cannot deduct your unreimbursed vehicle expenses because of the suspension of miscellaneous itemized deductions subject to the 2% of adjusted gross income floor through 2025 *(19.2)*.

If you bought an electric vehicle in 2023 for business and/or personal use, you may be eligible for a tax credit, depending on the manufacturer *(25.16)*.

43.1 Standard Mileage Rate

If you start to use your car for business in 2023, you have a choice of either deducting the actual operating costs of your car during business trips or deducting a flat IRS allowance. For 2023, the rate is 65.5 cents per mile. The mileage allowance also applies to business trips in a van or pickup or panel truck as if it were a car.

If you placed a car, van, pick-up, or panel truck in service before 2023 and have always used the IRS mileage allowance, you may apply the applicable cents-per-mile rate to your 2023 business mileage or deduct your actual operating costs plus straight line depreciation over the remaining estimated useful life of the vehicle (assuming the vehicle is not considered fully depreciated).

The rate may not be used to deduct the costs of a vehicle used for nonbusiness income-producing activities such as looking after investment property.

Allowance must be elected for the first year. The choice of the mileage allowance must be made in the first year you place the vehicle in service for business travel. If you do not use the allowance in the year you first use the vehicle for business, you may not use the allowance for that vehicle in any other year. Thus, if you bought a car for business in 2022 and on your 2022 return you deducted actual operating costs plus depreciation, you may not use the mileage allowance on your 2023 return or in any later year. The mileage allowance takes the place of fixed operating costs plus depreciation. If you claim the allowance, you cannot deduct your actual outlays for expenses such as gasoline (including state and local taxes), oil, repairs, license tags, or insurance, nor can you deduct depreciation (if you own the vehicle) or lease payments. Parking fees and tolls during business trips are deductible in addition to the mileage allowance. The IRS will not disallow a deduction based on the allowance even though it exceeds your actual vehicle costs. If you use more than one automobile in your business travel and elect the allowance, total the business mileage traveled in both cars.

Planning Reminder

First-Year Election Affects Later Years

In deciding whether to elect the allowance in the first year, consider not only whether you will get a bigger first-year deduction using the allowance, or deducting actual operating costs plus depreciation, but also project your mileage, operating expenses, and depreciation expenses over the years you expect to use the vehicle. If in the first year you elect to deduct actual costs, including bonus depreciation, first-year expensing, MACRS or straight line MACRS depreciation, you may not use the IRS auto allowance for that vehicle in a later year. On the other hand, claiming the IRS allowance in the first year you put a vehicle in service forfeits your privilege to use MACRS and first-year expensing. If you switch from the allowance to deducting actual expenses in later years, you may claim straight line depreciation over the remaining estimated useful life of the vehicle if the vehicle is not considered fully depreciated.

> ### EXAMPLES
>
> 1. You buy a car in 2023 and drive it on business trips. You keep a record of your business mileage. You traveled 30,000 miles for business during the year (assume you drove 2,500 miles each month). You may deduct $19,650 (30,000 x 65.5 cents). In addition to the $19,650 allowance, you may deduct your expenses for tolls and parking.
>
> 2. You use one car primarily for business and occasionally your spouse's car for business trips. In 2023, you drove your car on business trips 10,000 miles and your spouse's car 2,000 miles. Total business mileage is 12,000 miles for purposes of the IRS mileage allowance.

Records. You may decide to use the allowance if you do not keep accurate records of operating costs. However, you must keep a record of your business trips, dates, customers or clients visited, business purpose of the trips, your total mileage during the year, and the number of miles traveled on business. An IRS agent may attempt to verify mileage by asking for repair bills near the beginning and end of the year if the bills note mileage readings.

Mileage allowance for leased vehicle. The IRS mileage allowance is also available for leased cars, vans, and pick-up or panel trucks, but it must be used for the entire lease period or not at all. For example, if in 2022 you leased a car for business purposes and you claim the cents-per-mile allowance, you will also have to use it for the remainder of the lease period, including renewals.

Interest on a vehicle loan and taxes. The deduction rules are discussed in the following section *(43.2)*.

Mileage allowance disallowed. You may not claim the cents-per-mile allowance if:

- You have claimed depreciation, first-year expensing, or first-year bonus depreciation in the year the vehicle was placed in service.
- You use in your business five or more vehicles simultaneously, such as in a fleet operation.

Caution

No Standard Mileage Rate for Fleets

IRS policy has not allowed use of the standard mileage rate if you use five or more automobiles simultaneously (such as in fleet operations), whether you own or lease the vehicles. You must use the actual expense method for all the vehicles (i.e., deduct the actual operating costs of the vehicles). If you alternate use among five (or more) vehicles, so they are not used in your business at the same time, you may use the standard mileage rate for all the vehicles.

IRS allowance includes depreciation. When you use the IRS mileage allowance, you may not claim a separate depreciation deduction. The IRS mileage allowance includes an estimate for depreciation. For purposes of figuring gain or loss on a disposition, you must reduce the basis of the vehicle by the following depreciation amounts: 24 cents per mile in 2015 and 2016, 25 cents per mile in 2017 and 2018, 26 cents per mile in 2019, 27 cents per mile in 2020, 26 cents per mile in 2021, 26 cents per mile in 2022, and 28 cents per mile in 2023.

Depreciation when switching from allowance to actual costs. If you use the IRS mileage allowance in the first year, you may switch to the actual-cost method in a later year, but depreciation must be based on the straight line method over the remaining estimated useful life. However, no depreciation may be claimed if basis has been reduced to zero under the annual cents-per-mile reduction rule in the preceding paragraph.

43.2 Expense Allocations

If you do not claim the IRS mileage allowance, you may deduct car, truck, or van expenses on business trips such as the cost of gas and oil (including state and local taxes), repairs and maintenance (including car washes), parking, and tolls, in addition to depreciation for your car *(43.3– 43.5)*.

If you use your vehicle exclusively for business, all of your operating expenses are deductible.

Apportioning vehicle expenses between business and personal use. For a vehicle used for business and personal purposes, deduct only the expenses and depreciation allocated to your business use of the vehicle.

The business portion of vehicle expenses is determined by the percentage of mileage driven on business trips during the year.

Table 43-1 Deducting Car and Truck Expenses

Item—	Tax Rule—
IRS mileage allowance	You may avoid the trouble of keeping a record of actual vehicle expenses and calculating depreciation by electing the IRS mileage allowance for a car, van, or pick-up or panel truck. However, to claim the allowance, you must be ready to prove business use of the vehicle and keep a record of your mileage. The allowance may give you a larger deduction than your actual outlays plus depreciation. You must elect the allowance in the first year you use the vehicle for business. If you do not, you may not use the allowance for that vehicle in any other year If your actual operating costs plus depreciation exceed the allowance for the first year you place the vehicle in business service, you may claim your actual operating expenses and depreciation, but doing so will forfeit your right to elect the allowance for that vehicle in any later year.
Depreciation	If you claim actual operating expenses, such as gasoline, repairs, and insurance costs, you may also claim depreciation. There is a cap on the annual depreciation deduction. For a car placed in service in 2023, the first-year depreciation limit is $20,200 ($12,200, if bonus depreciation is not used). These limits must be reduced for personal use *(43.4)*. Electing first-year expensing or depreciation for a car, truck, or van placed in service in 2023 prevents you from using the IRS mileage allowance *(43.1)* for that car in later years. For cars, trucks, and vans placed in business service in 2023 that are used 50% or less for business, you must use straight line depreciation subject to the dollar limits *(43.6)*. If business use is initially over 50% but declines to 50% or less in a later year, prior year depreciation deductions, including bonus depreciation and first-year expensing, must be recaptured as income to the extent they exceeded straight line deductions *(43.10)*. For a vehicle placed in service before 2023, *see Tables 43-2* and *43-3* for the maximum depreciation you can claim for 2023.
Vehicle used for business and personal driving	You may deduct only the amount allocated to business mileage. For example, total mileage is 20,000 in 2023 and your business mileage is 15,000. You may claim only 75% of your deductible costs (15,000 ÷ 20,000).
Tax return reporting	As a self-employed individual, you deduct business costs on Schedule C and use Form 4562 to compute depreciation if you claim actual operating costs. Employees cannot take a deduction for business driving as a miscellaneous itemized deduction; this deduction is suspended for 2018 through 2025 *(19.2)*.

EXAMPLE

You have been deducting actual expenses plus depreciation each year for your car rather than the IRS mileage allowance. In 2023, you drove your car 15,000 miles. Of this, 12,000 miles was on business trips. The percentage of business use is 80%:

$$\frac{\text{business mileage}}{\text{total mileage}} = \frac{12,000}{15,000} = 80\%$$

If your actual car expenses (gas, oil, repairs, etc.) for the year were $3,000, $2,400 ($3,000 × 80%) is deductible plus 80% of allowable depreciation.

Interest on vehicle loan. If you are self-employed, the allocated business percentage of the interest is fully deductible on Schedule C; the personal percentage is not deductible. If you are an employee, all of the interest is considered personal interest and is not deductible even if you use the vehicle 100% of the time for your job.

Taxes paid on your car. The business portion of sales taxes paid on your vehicle is not deductible whether you are an employee or self-employed; the tax is added to the basis of the vehicle for depreciation purposes *(43.3)*.

If you are an employee, state and local vehicle registration and license fees may be deducted as personal property taxes if you itemize deductions on Schedule A, but only if they are based on the value of the vehicle *(16.8)* (and subject to the $10,000 cap on state and local taxes) *(16.1)*. If you are self-employed, deduct the business portion of the personal property taxes on Schedule C and the personal percentage on Schedule A if you itemize (subject to the $10,000 cap on state and local taxes).

Leased vehicle. If you lease a car, truck, or van for business use and do not claim the IRS mileage allowance *(43.1)*, you deduct the lease payments plus other costs of operating the vehicle. If the vehicle is also used for personal driving, the lease payments must be allocated between business and personal mileage. The rules requiring a reduction in the deduction for lease payments are discussed later in this chapter *(43.12)*.

43.3 Depreciation Restrictions on Cars, Trucks, and Vans

The law contains restrictions on so-called "listed property" that limit and, in some cases, deny depreciation deductions for a business car, truck, or van. Self-employed individuals must determine if they can use accelerated MACRS rates or must use straight line rates. Finally, regardless of which depreciation method is used, the annual deduction may not exceed a ceiling set by law for passenger cars and certain light trucks and vans; details on the annual ceilings are in *43.4*.

EXAMPLE

Theodore bought a light truck subject to the annual ceiling *(43.4)* on March 4, 2023, for $40,000, and uses it 100% for business. Theodore's MACRS deduction using the 200% declining balance method and the half-year convention under *Table 43-4* is $8,000 ($40,000 × .20 first-year rate). But bonus depreciation for 2023 increases the first-year deduction limit to $20,200, unless Theodore "elects out" of bonus depreciation *(43.5)*.

More-than-50%-business-use test for claiming expensing, bonus depreciation, or accelerated MACRS depreciation. Automobiles and other vehicles used to transport persons or goods are considered "listed property" *(42.10)*, but there are exceptions for ambulances, hearses, and trucks or vans that are qualified non-personal-use vehicles *(43.4)*. Unless the vehicle is excepted from the listed property rules, you must use the vehicle more than 50% of the time for business in the year you place it in service in order to claim bonus depreciation, first-year expensing or accelerated MACRS *(43.5)*. The annual ceiling, if applicable *(43.4)*, applies to the total of any bonus allowance, first-year expensing and MACRS depreciation.

If you meet the more-than-50%-business-use test in the year you place the vehicle in service but in a later year within the recovery period your business use falls to 50% or less, you must use straight line depreciation and recapture "excess" deductions for prior years; *see* the Caution on this page and *43.10*.

If business use is 50% or less in the year the vehicle is placed in service, bonus depreciation, first-year expensing and accelerated MACRS are barred; depreciation must be claimed over a six-year period under the straight line method. Technically, the recovery period is five years, but the period is extended to six years because, in the first year, a convention rule limits the deductible percentage. See *Table 43-6* and *Table 43-7 (43.6)*. The straight line method must be used for the entire recovery period, even if business use in the years after the first year exceeds 50%.

> **EXAMPLE**
>
> Jeremy bought a truck on March 4, 2023, for $40,000, but business use is 40%. His basis for depreciation is $10,000 ($40,000 × 40% business use). Jeremy cannot use bonus depreciation or accelerated MACRS depreciation. His depreciation allowance for 2023 under the straight line method *(43.6)* is $1,000 ($10,000 × .10 first-year rate).

If a vehicle is used for both business and investment purposes, only business use is considered in determining whether you meet the more-than-50%-business-use test and therefore qualify for MACRS. However, investment use is added to business use in determining your actual deduction.

Do your employees use the vehicle? In certain cases, an employer who provides a vehicle to employees as part of their compensation may be unable to count the employee's use as qualified business use, thereby preventing the employer from meeting the more-than-50%-business-use test for claiming MACRS. An employer is allowed to treat the employee's use as qualified business use only if: (1) the employee is not a relative and does not own more than 5% of the business and (2) the employer treats the fair market value of the employee's personal use of the vehicle as wage income and withholds tax on that amount. If such income is reported, all of the employee's use, including personal use, may be counted by an employer as qualified business use.

If an employee owning more than a 5% interest is allowed use of a company-owned vehicle as part of his or her compensation, the employer may not count that use as qualified business use, even if the personal use is reported as income. The same strict rule applies if the vehicle is provided to a person who is related to the employer.

43.4 Annual Ceilings on Depreciation

Annual ceilings limit the amount of depreciation you may deduct for passenger cars, light trucks, and vans; *see* below for affected vehicles and exceptions. The annual ceiling, if applicable, applies to the total of any bonus allowance, first-year expensing and MACRS depreciation. As a result of the ceilings, the actual write-off period for your car may be several years longer than the MACRS recovery period of six years *(43.5)*.

Year-by-year limits for vehicles placed in service in 2023 and prior years can be found in *Table 43-2* (cars) and *Table 43-3* (trucks and vans).

Annual ceilings generally apply to vehicles weighing 6,000 pounds or less (cars, trucks, or vans). The ceiling on depreciation for a vehicle placed in service in 2023 and used 50% or less for business is $12,200, reduced by personal use. If the vehicle is used more than 50% for business in 2023, the first-year dollar limit is increased by the bonus depreciation allowance to $20,200, reduced by personal use, unless you elect not to claim bonus depreciation for 2023 *(see* "election out," in *42.18)*, in which case the limit is $12,200, reduced by personal use.

The law applies the annual depreciation ceilings to a "passenger automobile," but this is defined as any four-wheeled vehicle that is manufactured primarily for use on public thoroughfares and that is weight-rated by the manufacturer at 6,000 pounds or less when

Caution

Recapture of MACRS Deductions

If you meet the more-than-50% test in the year the car or other vehicle is placed in service, which entitles you to claim bonus depreciation, first-year expensing, or accelerated MACRS, but business use falls to 50% or less in a later year within the recovery period, you become subject to straight line depreciation and recapture rules *(43.10)* apply.

Filing Tip

Claiming First-Year Expensing, Bonus Depreciation, or MACRS Depreciation for Your Car

First-year expensing, bonus depreciation, or MACRS depreciation (under the 200% or 150% declining balance method, or the straight line method) is claimed on Form 4562 and then entered on Schedule C (Form 1040 or 1040-SR) if you are self employed.

unloaded (without passengers or cargo), or, in the case of trucks or vans, 6,000 pounds or less gross vehicle weight. However, the following vehicles are not treated as passenger automobiles and are exempt from the annual depreciation limits: (1) an ambulance, hearse, or combination ambulance-hearse used directly in a business; (2) a vehicle such as a taxi cab used directly in the business of transporting persons or property for compensation or hire; and (3) qualified non-personal-use vehicles discussed below.

Qualified non-personal-use vehicles. The depreciation limits do not apply to trucks and vans that are qualified non-personal-use vehicles. These include moving vans, flatbed trucks, and delivery trucks with seating only for the driver (or driver seat plus folding jump seat). Also included are specially modified trucks and vans that are unlikely to be used more than a minimal amount for personal purposes. An example would be a van that has been painted to display advertising or the company's name and which has permanent shelving for carrying merchandise or equipment.

Heavy trucks, vans, and SUVs. Trucks, vans, and SUVs built on a truck chassis that are weight-rated by the manufacturer at more than 6,000 pounds gross vehicle weight are not subject to the annual depreciation ceilings. However, first-year expensing *(42.3)* for the vehicle may be limited to $28,900 rather than the general expensing limit, which for 2023 is $1,160,000 *(42.3)*. The vehicle must be used more than 50% for business to qualify for first-year expensing. If first-year expensing is not or cannot be elected *(42.3)*, a full depreciation deduction using the MACRS rate *(43.5)* is allowed with no dollar limit.

Further, if bought and placed in service in 2023 and used over 50% for business, bonus depreciation *(42.18)* of up to 80% can be used, thereby avoiding the $28,900 limit on first-year expensing. In effect, the cost of a heavy SUV bought and placed in service in 2023 can be fully deducted using bonus depreciation, assuming business use is 100%.

The $28,900 limit on first-year expensing applies to SUVs rated at more than 6,000 pounds but not more than 14,000 pounds gross vehicle weight. For purposes of the $28,900 expensing limit, an SUV means any four-wheeled vehicle primarily designed or which can be used to carry passengers over public thoroughfares. Trucks and vans as well as SUVs can be covered by this definition, but the law allows certain exceptions. The $28,900 limit does not apply for vehicles with seating for more than nine passengers behind the driver, for pickup trucks with an interior cargo bed at least six feet long that is an open area or is enclosed by a cap and not readily accessible to passengers, and cargo vans without rear seating and with no body sections protruding more than 30 inches ahead of the windshield. For these excepted vehicles, the $28,900 limit on first-year expensing does not apply.

43.5 MACRS Rates for Cars, Trucks, and Vans

Business autos, trucks, and vans are technically in a five-year MACRS class *(42.4)*, but because of the half-year or mid-quarter convention, the MACRS recovery period for five-year property is six years, and because of the annual deduction ceilings *(43.4*, and *Table 43-2* and *Table 43-3* below), the actual write-off period may be years longer.

First-year business use must exceed 50% to claim bonus depreciation or accelerated MACRS rates. To use accelerated MACRS rates, you must meet the more-than-50%-business-use test *(43.3)* in the year the vehicle is placed in business service. Generally, the accelerated MACRS rate is based on the 200% declining balance method, but as shown on *Table 43-4* (half-year convention) or *Table 43-5* (mid-quarter convention), a 150% declining balance rate may be elected, which may be advantageous when you are subject to the alternative minimum tax *(23.2)*.

If you do not meet the more-than-50%-business-use test in the year the vehicle is placed in service, you must compute your depreciation deductions using the straight line rates shown in *43.6*, subject to the first-year depreciation limit for vehicles that do not qualify for bonus depreciation.

Assuming business use of the vehicle exceeds 50% in the year it is placed in service, bonus depreciation increases the first-year depreciation ceiling to $8,000 more than would be allowed using the regular annual ceiling, unless you elect on your return not to claim bonus depreciation (see "election out," in *42.18*). For example, for a vehicle placed in service

Filing Tip

Capital Improvements

A capital improvement to a business vehicle is depreciable under MACRS in the year the improvement is made. The MACRS deductions for the improvement and the vehicle are considered as a unit for purposes of applying the limits on the annual MACRS depreciation deduction.

in 2023, the maximum depreciation deduction taking bonus depreciation into account is $20,200; *see Table 43-2* and *Table 43-3*. The $20,200 limit is the combined limit for first-year expensing, bonus depreciation, and regular MACRS depreciation. The maximum $20,200 deduction ceiling assumes 100% business use and must be reduced for personal use.

If business use for a vehicle placed in service in 2023 exceeds 50% but you elect out of bonus depreciation (*see* "election out," in *42.18*), the maximum depreciation deduction is $12,200, as shown in *Table 43-2* and *Table 43-3*, and the $12,200 limit must be reduced if business use is under 100%. However, your depreciation deduction for 2023 is limited to the lesser of the deduction figured using the first-year MACRS rate shown in *Table 43-4* or *Table 43-5*, or the $12,200 ceiling, as reduced for personal use.

Deductions for later years in the recovery period. For years two through six of the recovery period, the MACRS rate from *Table 43-4* or *Table 43-5* is used unless business use for a year falls to 50% or less *(43.10)*. However, the deduction figured under the MACRS table for years two through six is allowed only if it does not exceed the annual depreciation ceiling *(43.4)* shown in *Table 43-2* or *Table 43-3*; *see* the Bill Johnston Example on page 759. *See* below for details on using the MACRS tables.

Caution: Safe harbor if bonus depreciation used: If you used the 100% bonus depreciation rule for vehicles placed in service in 2021 to increase your first-year depreciation deduction, you must use an IRS safe harbor to figure your deductions starting in 2022 (the second recovery year), as explained in Revenue Procedure 2019-13. Under the safe harbor, depreciation for years two through six is the lesser of (1) the MACRS rate from *Table 43-4* or *Table 43-5*, whichever applies, multiplied by the basis that remains after the first year, or (2) the annual depreciation ceiling for the year from *Table 43-2* or *Table 43-3*. No special form or election statement is required to use this safe harbor, which applies to vehicles placed in service before 2023 (when bonus depreciation begins to phase out). Simply figure the appropriate safe harbor depreciation on your tax return for the first year following the year in which the vehicle is placed in service. *See* Revenue Procedure 2019-13 for safe harbor details.

Deduction for year of disposition. If you dispose of your vehicle before the end of the six-year MACRS recovery period, a partial-year deduction is allowed for the year of disposition under the half-year or mid-quarter convention *(43.7)*.

Use of vehicle after end of recovery period. If you continue to use the vehicle for business after the end of the recovery period, and the annual deduction ceilings prevented you from deducting your full unadjusted basis during the recovery period, you generally may deduct depreciation in the succeeding years up to the annual ceiling *(43.8)*.

Business use falls to 50% or less after the first year. What if business use exceeds 50% in the year the vehicle is placed in service but in a later year within the recovery period business use drops to 50% or lower? In that case, the right to use accelerated MACRS (200% or 150% declining balance method) terminates. You must use the straight line method and recapture the benefit of the accelerated deductions claimed for the prior years *(43.10)*.

Straight line election for vehicle if business use exceeds 50%. If business use of your vehicle exceeds 50% in the year you place it in service, you may elect to write off your cost under the straight line method *(43.6)* instead of using the regular MACRS 200% or 150% declining balance method *(43.5)*. The straight line deduction *(43.6)* is limited by the annual depreciation ceilings shown in *Table 43-2* and *Table 43-3*. By electing straight line depreciation, you avoid the recapture of excess MACRS deductions if business use drops to 50% or less in a later year *(43.10)*. If the election is made, you must also use the straight line method for all other five-year property placed in service during the same year as the vehicle.

Electing 150% declining balance method. Depreciation rates under the half-year and mid-quarter conventions are generally based on the 200% declining balance method. You may instead make an irrevocable election to apply the 150% declining balance method. The 150% method may be advantageous when you are subject to the alternative minimum tax. For alternative minimum tax (AMT) purposes *(23.2)*, vehicle depreciation is based on the 150% declining balance method unless you use the straight line method for regular tax purposes. If you are subject to AMT and use the 150% declining balance method instead of the 200% declining balance method for regular tax purposes, you do not have to report an AMT adjustment on Form 6251.

An election to use the 150% declining balance method is irrevocable and must be applied to all depreciable assets placed in service in the same year, except for nonresidential real and residential rental property.

MACRS Tables Applying the Half-Year Convention or Mid-Quarter Convention if Business Use Exceeds 50%

For the year you place the vehicle in service and the year (within the recovery period) you dispose of the property, you may not claim a full year's worth of MACRS depreciation. The deduction is limited by either the half-year convention or the mid-quarter convention, depending on the month in which the vehicle was placed in service and the other business assets, if any, placed in service during that year.

The applicable convention determines the rate table you will use to figure your depreciation deduction for the entire six-year recovery period, assuming that your business use each year exceeds 50%. The half-year and mid-quarter convention rates shown in *Table 43-4* or *Table 43-5* reflect the 200% or 150% declining balance method, with a switch to the straight line method when that method provides a larger deduction; the switch to straight line is built into the tables.

Rate applied to unadjusted basis. For each year in the recovery period, the rate from MACRS *Table 43-4* or *Table 43-5* is applied against the business use percentage of your unadjusted basis for the vehicle. The deduction figured using the table rate may be claimed to the extent that it does not exceed the annual depreciation ceiling *(Table 43-2* or *Table 43-3)*; *see* the Bill Johnston Example on the next page. Investment use may be added to the business use percentage, but keep in mind that the MACRS table may be used only if business use by itself exceeds 50% *(43.3)*.

Unadjusted basis is your cost minus any first-year expensing deduction as well as any special first-year bonus depreciation. The basis reduction for bonus depreciation applies if you were eligible for the special allowance, even if you did not claim it, unless on your return you "elected out" of the special allowance for the vehicle and all other five-year property placed in service during the same year *(42.18)*.

Basis for vehicle converted from personal to business use. The basis for depreciation is the lower of the fair market value of the vehicle at the time of conversion or its adjusted basis, which is your original cost plus any substantial improvements and minus any deductible casualty losses or diesel fuel tax credit claimed for the vehicle. In most cases, the value of the vehicle will be lower than adjusted basis, and thus the value will be your depreciable basis. For a vehicle converted to business use in 2023, the MACRS rate is applied to basis allocated to business travel. Unless you have mileage records for the entire year, you should base your business-use percentage on driving after the conversion. For example, in April 2023, you started to use your car for business and in the last nine months of the year you drove 10,000 miles, 8,000 of which were for business. This business percentage of 80% is multiplied by the fraction 9/12 (months used for business divided by 12) to give you a business-use percentage for the year of 60% (9/12 of 80%).

Determining whether the half-year convention or mid-quarter convention applies. If you bought a vehicle for use in your business in 2023 (the vehicle is "equipment" for purposes of the applicable convention), and it was the only business equipment placed in service during the year, then the half-year convention applies, unless you bought the vehicle in the last quarter of 2023 (October, November, or December). Under the half-year convention, the vehicle is treated as if it were placed in service in the middle of the year. Use *Table 43-4* below to determine your deduction under the half-year convention.

If the only business equipment bought in 2023 was a vehicle bought in the last quarter (October, November, or December), the mid-quarter convention applies. Under *Table 43-5* for the mid-quarter convention, a 5% rate applies under the 200% declining balance method for a vehicle purchased in the fourth quarter, subject to the deduction ceiling in 2023 (*Table 43-2* or *Table 43-3*).

If you bought other business equipment in addition to the vehicle, you must consider the total cost basis of property placed in service during the last quarter of 2023. If the total bases of such acquisitions (other than realty) exceed 40% of the total bases of all property placed in service during the year, then a mid-quarter rate applies to all of the property (other than realty). The mid-quarter rate for each asset then depends on the quarter the asset was placed in service, and that quarter determines the mid-quarter rates for each year of the recovery period; *see Table 43-5*. If the 40% test is not met, then the half-year convention *(Table 43-4)* applies to all the property acquisitions.

Deduction from MACRS Tables Cannot Exceed Annual Ceiling

If the deduction figured under the half-year or mid-quarter convention MACRS table *(Table 43-4* or *Table 43-5)*, or the straight line table *(Table 43-6* or *Table 43-7)*, exceeds the annual deduction ceiling *(Table 43-2* or *Table 43-3)*, your deduction is limited to the annual ceiling, reduced by the percentage of your personal use; *see* the Bill Johnston Example below.

Keep in mind that if you were eligible for the special first-year depreciation allowance (bonus depreciation) for a vehicle placed in service after September 10, 2001, and before January 1, 2005, and during 2008 through September 27, 2017, basis for MACRS purposes is reduced by the special allowance unless you elected on your return not to claim it.

Caution: If you used bonus depreciation for a vehicle placed in service after September 27, 2017, you cannot claim any deduction in years two through six unless you use an IRS safe harbor explained in Revenue Procedure 2019-13; *see* the text Caution: "Safe harbor if bonus depreciation used" on page 757.

EXAMPLE

On May 5, 2017, Bill Johnston placed in service a new car that cost $20,000, which he used 100% for business for the rest of 2017. He did not claim first-year expensing and "elected out" of bonus depreciation (which was a 50% limit at that time). Bill continued to use the car 100% for business through 2020. In 2021 and 2022, he uses it 75% of the time for business. Here is Bill's depreciation schedule for the six-year recovery period, using the 200% declining balance rate as limited by the annual ceilings.

For years after 2022, Bill can deduct his "unrecovered basis," but the amount of unrecovered basis is figured as if there had been 100% business use during the entire six-year recovery period *(43.8)*.

Year	Deduction from MACRS (Table 43-4)	Annual ceiling (Table 43-2)	Allowable deduction
2017	$ 4,000 (20% × $20,000)	$ 3,160	$ 3,160
2018	6,400 (32% × $20,000)	5,100	5,100
2019	3,840 (19.20% × $20,000)	3,050	3,050
2020	2,304 (11.52% × $20,000)	1,875	1,875
2021	1,728 (11.52% × $20,000 × 75%)	1,406 ($1,875 × 75%)	1,406
2022*	864 (5.76% × $20,000 × 75%)	1,406 ($1,875 × 75%)	864

*Note that for the first five years (2017 – 2021), the allowable deduction is limited to the annual ceiling but for year six (2022), the deduction is based on the MACRS rate table because $864 (5.76% × $20,000 × 75% business use) is less than the $1,406 annual ceiling ($1,875 × 75% business use).

Table 43-2   Maximum Depreciation Deduction for Cars
(Caution: The ceiling must be reduced for personal use.)

Year Placed In Service	1st Year	2nd Year	3rd Year	4th and Later Years
2023	$20,200[1]	$19,500	$11,700	$6,950
2022	$19,200[1]	18,000	10,800	6,460
2021	18,200[1]	16,400	9,800	5,860
2019 and 2020	18,100[1]	16,100	9,700	5,760

[1] $8,000 less if the car does not qualify for the bonus allowance, or if you elect not to claim bonus depreciation.

Table 43-3   Maximum Depreciation Deduction for Trucks and Vans
(Caution: The ceiling must be reduced for personal use.)

Year Placed In Service	1st Year	2nd Year	3rd Year	4th and Later Years
2023	$20,200[1]	$19,500	$11,700	$6,950
2022	19,200[1]	18,000	10,800	6,460
2021	18,200[1]	16,400	9,800	5,860
2019 and 2020	18,100[1]	16,100	9,700	5,760

[1] $8,000 less if the vehicle does not qualify for the bonus allowance, or if you elect not to claim bonus depreciation.

Table 43-4   MACRS Deduction: Half-Year Convention

Year	200% Rate	150% Rate
1	20.00%	15.00%
2	32.00	25.50
3	19.20	17.85
4	11.52	16.66
5	11.52	16.66
6	5.76	8.33

Table 43-5   MACRS Deduction: Mid-Quarter Convention

Placed in service in—

Year	First Quarter		Second Quarter		Third Quarter		Fourth Quarter	
	200% Rate	150% Rate	200% Rate	150% Rate	200% Rate	150% Rate	200% Rate	150% Rate
1	35.00%	26.25%	25.00%	18.75%	15.00%	11.25%	5.00%	3.75%
2	26.00	22.13	30.00	24.38	34.00	26.63	38.00	28.88
3	15.60	16.52	18.00	17.06	20.40	18.64	22.80	20.21
4	11.01	16.52	11.37	16.76	12.24	16.56	13.68	16.40
5	11.01	16.52	11.37	16.76	11.30	16.57	10.94	16.41
6	1.38	2.06	4.26	6.29	7.06	10.35	9.58	14.35

43.6 Straight Line Method

You may not use first-year expensing (Section 179 deduction), bonus depreciation, or accelerated MACRS *(43.5)* if your business use of your car, truck, or van is 50% or less in the year you place it in service; only business use is considered here, not investment use. Mandatory straight line recovery rates for business use of 50% or less using the half-year or mid-quarter convention are shown below. These straight line rates are also used if your business use exceeds 50% and you elect straight line recovery instead of the regular MACRS method. *See* the preceding section *(43.5)* for determining whether the half-year or mid-quarter convention applies.

For each year of the six-year recovery period, apply the straight line rate from the applicable table against your unadjusted basis, which is the business part of your cost minus any first-year expensing deduction or special bonus depreciation allowance *(43.5)*. Investment use may be added to the business use part of cost when figuring the straight line deduction for each year. The deduction from the table is allowed only to the extent that it does not exceed the annual deduction ceiling *(Table 43-2* or *Table 43-3)*.

If business use initially exceeds 50% and accelerated MACRS is claimed but business use drops to 50% or less before the end of the six-year recovery period, a recapture rule applies a straight line computation retroactively *(43.10)*.

Table 43-6 Straight Line Half-Year Convention*

Straight line year—	Half-year convention rate—
1	10%
2	20
3	20
4	20
5	20
6	10

*The deduction may not exceed the annual deduction ceiling *(Table 43-2* or *43-3)*.

EXAMPLE

In April 2023, you place in service a used automobile which cost $34,000. You used it 40% for business. The depreciable basis is $13,600 (40% of $34,000). The straight line depreciation deduction for 2023 is $1,360 (10% of $13,600) if the half-year convention applies. This is your deduction because it is less than the annual deduction ceiling of $4,880 (40% of the $12,200 first-year ceiling that applies for 2023 if business use does not exceed 50%, so bonus depreciation is not allowed); *see 43.5* and *Table 43-2*.

Table 43-7 Straight Line Mid-Quarter Convention*

Placed in service in—

Year	First Quarter	Second Quarter	Third Quarter	Fourth Quarter
1	17.50%	12.50%	7.50%	2.50%
2	20.00	20.00	20.00	20.00
3	20.00	20.00	20.00	20.00
4	20.00	20.00	20.00	20.00
5	20.00	20.00	20.00	20.00
6	2.50	7.50	12.50	17.50

*The deduction may not exceed the annual deduction ceiling *(Table 43-2 or 43-3)*.

> **EXAMPLE**
>
> In 2023, you place in service a car costing $25,000 that you used 40% for business. Assume the mid-quarter convention applies. Depending on the quarter placed in service, the deduction is listed below, figured on a basis of $10,000 ($25,000 × 40%). The first-year depreciation ceiling *(see 43.5* and *Table 43-2)* at 40% business use is $4,880 ($12,200 × 40%). The $4,880 ceiling does not apply because the mid-quarter rates provide a lower deduction.
>
> | Quarter | Deduction |
> |---------|-----------|
> | 1 | $1,750 ($10,000 × 17.5%) |
> | 2 | $1,250 ($10,000 × 12.5%) |
> | 3 | 750 ($10,000 × 7.5%) |
> | 4 | 250 ($10,000 × 2.5%) |

43.7 Depreciation for Year Vehicle Is Disposed Of

If you dispose of your car, truck, or van before the end of the six-year recovery period, you are allowed a partial depreciation deduction for the year of disposition. The deduction depends on the depreciation method and convention being used.

If you were depreciating the vehicle under the half-year convention *(43.5)*, you may claim for the year of disposition 50% of the deduction that would be allowed for the full year under the 200% or 150% declining balance method *(Table 43-4)*, or the straight line method *(Table 43-6)*.

If you were depreciating the vehicle under the mid-quarter convention *(43.5)*, your deduction for the year of disposition depends on the month of disposition. You deduct 87.5% of the full-year mid-quarter convention deduction (from *Table 43-5* or *Table 43-7*) if the disposition occurred in October–December. If the disposition is in July–September, 62.5% of the full year's deduction is allowed. Your deduction is 37.5% of the full-year deduction if the disposition is in April–June, or 12.5% of the full-year deduction if the disposition is in January–March.

> **EXAMPLE**
>
> In December 2019, you bought a used car costing $20,000 that you used exclusively for business until you sold it in April 2023. You depreciated the car under the mid-quarter convention and the 200% rate *(Table 43-5)*.
>
> For 2023, the year of disposition, the full-year deduction would be $5,760, the annual ceiling for the fifth year under *Table 43-2* for a car placed in service in 2019. The annual ceiling of $5,760 does not apply because it is more than the $2,188 deduction (10.94% × $20,000) allowed for the fifth year under the mid-quarter convention table *(Table 43-5)* for fourth quarter property using the 200% rate. Since the car was disposed of in April, you may deduct 37.5% of $2,188, or $821, on your 2023 return.

43.8 Depreciation After Recovery Period Ends

If your business use of a car, truck, or van throughout the six-year recovery period is 100% and your deductions are limited by the annual ceilings *(43.4* and *Table 43-2* and *Table 43-3)*, any remaining basis that was not deducted because of the ceilings, called "unrecovered basis," may be depreciated in the years after the end of the recovery period. The maximum you can deduct each year will be the deduction ceiling for that year multiplied by your business use percentage.

If the vehicle was used less than 100% for business during the recovery period, your "unrecovered basis" is deductible in later years, but to determine unrecovered basis, original basis must be reduced by the depreciation that would have been allowed had the vehicle been used 100% for business.

EXAMPLE

In January 2016, you bought a used car costing $28,600 that you used 100% for business every year from 2016 through 2021. You elected not to claim first-year expensing for 2016 and bonus depreciation was not available because the car was used. Your depreciation deductions for the six-year recovery period under the 200% declining balance method and half-year convention *(Table 43-4)* were limited because of the annual deduction ceilings *(Table 43-2)*. For 2016 through 2020, you deducted the annual ceiling amounts. For 2021, your deduction ($1,647) was based on the MACRS half-year convention rate table *(Table 43-4)* because this amount was less than the annual ceiling ($1,875). Total allowable depreciation deductions for 2016–2021 were $16,707 as shown below.

Year	200% rate deduction *(Table 43-4)*	Annual ceiling *(Table 43-2)*	Allowable deduction
2016	$5,720 (20% × $28,600)	$ 3,160	$ 3,160
2017	9,152 (32% × $28,600)	5,100	5,100
2018	5,491 (19.20% × $28,600)	3,050	3,050
2019	3,295 (11.52% × $28,600)	1,875	1,875
2020	3,295 (11.52% × $28,600)	1,875	1,875
2021	1,647 (5.76% × $28,600)	1,875	1,647

At the beginning of 2022, your unrecovered basis in the car is $11,893 (the original basis of $28,600 minus the $16,707 of depreciation deductions allowed from 2016 through 2021). If you continue to use the car 100% for business in 2022 and later years, you can deduct $1,875 in 2022 and also in later years until the $11,893 of unrecovered basis is used up. In years of partial business use, the deduction will be limited to $1,875 multiplied by the business-use percentage.

If your business use percentage was not 100% for the entire six-year recovery period, your unrecovered basis as of the beginning of 2022 would still be $11,893. That is because for purposes of figuring unrecovered basis, you must reduce original basis by the depreciation that would have been allowed based on 100% business use. Even if you actually deducted less than $16,707 from 2016 through 2021, you still must reduce your $28,600 basis by $16,707, leaving you with an unrecovered basis of $11,893 that can be depreciated starting in 2022.

43.9 Trade-in of Business Vehicle

For trade-ins before 2018, you were able to avoid recognition of gain, but this rule no longer applies. If you trade in your business vehicle in 2023, you must figure gain on the trade-in. In effect, whether you sell or trade in your old vehicle, the tax result is the same. Gain is the difference between what you receive (an allowance toward the purchase of a new vehicle) and the adjusted basis of the vehicle you trade in.

Example

In 2023, you trade in a truck that you bought for $32,000 for which you've claimed depreciation totaling $22,285. Your adjusted basis is $9,715 ($32,000 − $22,285). If the allowance toward the purchase of a new truck is $12,000, you must report a gain of $2,285 ($12,000 − $9,715).

43.10 Recapture of Deductions on Business Car, Truck, or Van

If you use your car, truck, or van more than 50% for business in the year you place it in service, you may use MACRS accelerated rates *(43.5)*. If business use drops to 50% or less in the second, third, fourth, fifth, or sixth year, earlier MACRS deductions must be recaptured and reported as ordinary income. As "listed property" *(42.10)*, cars, trucks,

Planning Reminder

Sell the vehicle rather than trade it in

You get the same tax treatment whether you sell the vehicle or trade it in. But you may be able to receive more through a sale to a third party than the trade-in allowance from a car dealer.

vans, and other vehicles used to transport persons or goods are subject to the more-than-50%-business-use test and recapture rule, but there are exceptions for ambulances, hearses, and other trucks and vans that are considered qualified non-personal-use vehicles *(43.4)*.

The recapture rules do not apply if you elected straight line recovery instead of applying accelerated MACRS rates.

In the year in which business use drops to 50% or less, you must recapture excess depreciation for all prior years. Excess depreciation is the difference between: (1) the MACRS deductions allowed in previous years, including the first-year expensing deduction and bonus first-year depreciation allowance *(43.4)*, if any, and (2) the amount of depreciation that would have been allowed if you claimed straight line depreciation *(43.6)* based on a six-year recovery period. *See* the Example below.

To compute depreciation for the year in which business use drops to 50% or less and for later years within the six-year, straight line recovery period, you apply the applicable straight line rate *(43.6)* to your original cost (unadjusted basis), multiplied by the business use percentage for that year, but the deduction may be limited by the annual ceiling for that year *(Table 43-2* or *Table 43-3)*; *see* the Example below.

Figuring and reporting recapture. Recapture is figured and reported on Part IV of Form 4797. The recaptured amount from Form 4797 is entered as other income on Schedule C (Line 6), assuming the original deductions were claimed on Schedule C. Schedule C and Form 4797 must be attached to Schedule 1 (Form 1040 or 1040-SR).

Any recaptured amount increases the adjusted basis of the property for purposes of figuring gain or loss when you dispose of the vehicle.

EXAMPLE

On June 28, 2019, you bought a used car for $11,000 that you used exclusively for business in 2019, 2020, 2021, and 2022. For 2019, you "elected out" of bonus depreciation. The half-year convention applied to your MACRS deductions *(43.5)*. The deductions figured under the half-year convention table *(Table 43-4)* were $2,200 for 2019 (20% rate), $3,520 for 2020 (32% rate), $2,112 for 2021 (19.20% rate), and $1,267 for 2022 (11.52% rate). These were the allowable amounts because they were less than the annual ceilings for those years. During 2023, you used the car 40% for business and 60% for personal purposes. As you did not meet the more-than-50%-business-use test in 2023, excess depreciation of $1,724 is recaptured and reported on Form 4797 for 2023:

Total MACRS depreciation claimed	$9,099
(2019–2022: $2,200 + $3,520 + $2,112 + $1,267)	
Total straight line depreciation *(Table 43-6 at 43.6)* allowable:	
2019—lesser of 10% of $11,000 or annual ceiling of $10,000 = $1,100	
2020—lesser of 20% of $11,000 or annual ceiling of $16,000 = $2,200	
2021—lesser of 20% of $11,000 or annual ceiling of $9,600 = $2,200	
2022—lesser of 20% of $11,000 or annual ceiling of $5,760 = $1,875	
	$7,375
Excess depreciation recaptured ($9,099 – $7,375)	$1,724

Your 2023 depreciation deduction is $880, the straight line deduction from *Table 43-6* ($11,000 × 20% straight line rate in fifth year × 40% business use in 2023). It is less than the reduced annual ceiling of $2,304 ($5,760 ceiling *(Table 43-2)* × 40% business use in 2023).

The amount of recaptured depreciation increases the adjusted basis for purposes of computing gain or loss on a disposition of the automobile.

43.11 Keeping Records of Business Use

Keep a log or diary or similar record of the business use of a car. You can also find an app for your smartphone or other mobile device to keep track of your business mileage. Record the purpose of the business trips and mileage covered for business travel. In the record book or electronic record, also note the odometer reading for the beginning and end of the taxable year. You need this data to prove business use. If you do not keep written records of business mileage and your return is examined, you will have to convince an IRS agent of your business mileage through oral testimony. Without written evidence, you may be unable to convince an IRS agent that you use the car for business travel or that you meet the business-use tests for claiming MACRS. You may also be subject to general negligence penalties for claiming deductions that you cannot prove you incurred.

Unless you are electing the standard mileage rate *(43.1)*, mileage records are not required for vehicles that are unlikely to be used for personal purposes, such as delivery trucks with seating only for the driver.

43.12 Leased Business Vehicles: Deductions and Income

If you lease rather than purchase a car, truck, or van for business use, you may deduct the lease charges as a business expense deduction if you use the vehicle exclusively for business. If you also use the vehicle for personal driving, you may deduct only the lease payments allocated to business travel. Also keep a record of business use; *see 43.11*.

Inclusion amount. If in 2023 you lease a vehicle for 30 days or more, you may have to reduce the deduction for the lease payment for an inclusion amount listed in an IRS table. This rule applies if you deduct the business portion of your lease payments plus other operating costs; it does not apply if you claim the standard mileage allowance *(43.1)*. On Schedule C (if self-employed), the inclusion amount reduces your deduction for lease payments similar to the way your depreciation deductions would have been limited if you had bought the vehicle outright. The income amount is reduced where you leased the vehicle for less than the entire year or business use is less than 100%. For vehicles first leased in 2023, there's no inclusion amount if the fair market value of the vehicle at the start of the lease is $60,000 or less.

The lease tables, which are in IRS Publication 463, show income amounts for each year of the lease. Publication 463 also has tables showing income amounts for vehicles leased before 2023. You can also *see* the inclusion amounts for vehicles first leased in 2023 in Rev. Proc. 2023-14.

Caution

Leased Vehicle

If in 2023 you leased a car, truck, or van for at least 30 days and you deduct the lease charges as a business expense *(43.12)*, you generally must reduce the deduction by an "income inclusion amount" based on an IRS table. If you claim the standard mileage allowance *(43.1)*, the income inclusion rule does not apply. *See* IRS Publication 463 for details.

Planning Pointer

Apps for Tracking Mileage

There are a number of free or low-cost apps for smartphones and tablets that can be used to record the necessary information for business driving.

CHAPTER 44

Sales of Business Property

On the sale of business assets, the tax treatment depends on the type of asset sold.

Inventory items: Profits are taxable as ordinary income; losses are fully deductible. Sales of merchandise are reported on Schedule C if you are self-employed or Schedule F if you are a farmer.

Depreciable property, such as buildings, machinery, and equipment: If you sell at a gain, the gain is taxable as ordinary income to the extent depreciation is recaptured *(44.1–44.2)*. Any remaining gain may be treated as capital gain or ordinary income, depending on the Section 1231 computation *(44.8)*. Losses may be deductible as ordinary losses *(44.8)*. Sales are reported on Form 4797. Depreciable business equipment subject to recapture is described as a Section 1245 asset. Depreciable livestock is also a Section 1245 asset. Depreciable realty is generally described as a Section 1250 asset.

Land: If used in your business, capital gain or ordinary income may be realized under the rules of Section 1231 *(44.8)*. If land owned by your business is held for investment, gain or loss is subject to capital gain treatment. Schedule D is used to report the sale of capital assets.

44.1 Depreciation Recaptured as Ordinary Income on Sale of Personal Property

On Form 4797, you report gain or loss on the sale of depreciable property. Gain realized on the sale of depreciable personal property (Section 1245 property) is treated as ordinary income to the extent the gain is attributed to depreciation deductions that reduced basis. In other words, the depreciation deductions are "recaptured" as ordinary income. If gain exceeds the amount of depreciation subject to recapture, the excess may be capital gain under Section 1231 *(44.8)*.

Gain on the sale of real estate placed in service before 1987 may be subject to depreciation recapture *(44.2)*.

Gain subject to recapture for Section 1245 property is limited to the lower of (1) the amount of gain on the sale (amount realized less adjusted basis) or (2) the depreciation allowed or allowable while you held the property. Generally, the depreciation deduction taken into account for each year is the amount allowed or allowable, whichever is greater. However, for purposes of figuring what portion of the gain is treated as ordinary income under the recapture rules (but not for purposes of figuring gain or loss), the depreciation taken into account for any year will be the amount actually "allowed" on your prior returns under a proper depreciation method, rather than the amount "allowable," if the allowed deduction is smaller and you can prove its amount.

The adjusted basis of personal property depreciable under ACRS, such as business equipment and machinery, is fixed as of the beginning of the year of disposition. However, property depreciated under MACRS is subject to the convention rules so that partial depreciation under the applicable convention is allowed in the year of sale; this year of sale depreciation reduces adjusted basis.

Caution

Dispositions Other Than Sales

Recapture rules affect gifts, charitable donations, and inheritances of depreciable property *(44.4)*, as well as like-kind exchanges and involuntary conversions *(44.5)*.

EXAMPLE

In March 2021, you bought and placed in service a pre-owned light truck (five-year property) at a cost of $10,000. You used the truck 100% for business. You deducted depreciation under the half-year convention of $2,000 for 2021 and $3,200 for 2022; *see* the MACRS and dollar limits on depreciation for light trucks in *43.4*. In January 2023, you sold the truck for $6,000. For 2023, you are allowed an MACRS deduction of one-half of the full year deduction, or $960 (19.20% × $10,000 ÷ 2). Your adjusted basis is $3,840 ($10,000 cost − $6,160 total depreciation). Your gain on the sale is $2,160 ($6,000 proceeds − $3,840 adjusted basis). You must recapture the entire $2,160 gain as ordinary income, as it is less than the $6,160 depreciation.

44.2 Depreciation Recaptured as Ordinary Income on Sale of Real Estate

All or part of a gain on the sale of depreciable real property may be attributable to depreciation deductions that reduced the basis of the property. On Form 4797, gain attributable to depreciation on Section 1250 realty placed in service before 1987 is subject to recapture as ordinary income unless straight-line depreciation was used. The amount of depreciation recapture depends on when the building was placed in service and whether it was residential or nonresidential; *see* below.

There is no ordinary income recapture for residential rental and nonresidential real property placed in service after 1986 because such properties are depreciated using the straight-line MACRS method *(42.13)*. Previously claimed bonus depreciation is subject to recapture.

To the extent depreciation is not subject to ordinary income recapture, the gain on the sale is subject to the Section 1231 netting rules *(44.8)*. If there is a net Section 1231 gain, the gain attributed to the depreciation is entered on the Unrecaptured Section 1250 Gain Worksheet in the Schedule D (Form 1040 or 1040-SR) instructions. The unrecaptured Section 1250 gain from that worksheet is subject to a top rate of 25% on the Schedule D Tax Worksheet included in the Schedule D instructions.

Recaptured depreciation. Ordinary income recapture may apply to Section 1250 realty placed in service before 1987. Section 1250 property includes buildings and structural components, except for elevators and escalators or other tangible property used as an integral part of manufacturing, production, or extraction, or of furnishing transportation, electrical energy, water, gas, sewage disposal services, or communications. Property may initially be Section 1250 property and then, on a change of use, become Section 1245 property *(44.1)*. Such property may not be reconverted to Section 1250 property.

Depreciation claimed on realty placed in service after 1980 and before 1987. For real property placed in service after 1980 and before 1987 that was subject to ACRS, adjusted basis for computing gain or loss is the adjusted basis at the start of the year reduced by the ACRS deduction, if any, allowed for the year of disposition (based on number of months the realty is in service in disposition year; *see 42.15*). The recapture rules distinguish between residential and nonresidential property.

If the prescribed accelerated method is used to recover the cost of nonresidential property, all gain on the disposition of the realty is recaptured as ordinary income to the extent of recovery allowances previously taken. Thus, nonresidential realty will be treated in the same way as personal property *(44.1)* for purposes of recapture if the accelerated recovery allowance was claimed. If the straight-line method was elected, there is no recapture; all gain is subject to the netting rules of Section 1231 *(44.8)*.

If accelerated cost recovery is used for a nonresidential building and straight-line depreciation is used for a substantial improvement to that building that you are allowed to depreciate separately *(42.15)*, all gain on a disposition of the entire building is treated as ordinary income to the extent of the accelerated cost recovery claimed. Remaining gain is subject to the rules for Section 1231 assets *(44.8)*.

For residential real estate, 100% of the excess depreciation claimed is subject to recapture. That is, if there is ordinary income recapture to the extent the depreciation allowed under the prescribed accelerated method exceeds the recovery that would have been allowable if the straight-line method over the ACRS recovery period had been used. If the straight-line method was elected, there is no recapture. All gain is subject to Section 1231 netting *(44.8)*.

For low-income rental housing, the percentage of excess depreciation (over straight-line) subject to recapture is 100% minus 1% for each full month the property was held over 100 months, so there is no recapture of cost recovery deductions once the property was held at least 200 months (16 years and 8 months). If you dispose of low-income housing with separate improvements, or with units placed in service at different times, the amount of excess depreciation must be computed separately for each element. *See* IRS Publication 544 for details on the recapture rules for low-income housing.

Different recapture rules applied to depreciation on realty placed in service before 1981.

44.3 Recapture of First-Year Expensing and Bonus Depreciation

On Form 4797, the first-year expensing deduction (Section 179 deduction; *see 42.3*) and bonus depreciation *(42.18)* are treated as depreciation for purposes of recapture. When depreciable property is sold or exchanged, gain is recaptured as ordinary income *(44.1)* to the extent of the first-year expense deduction plus MACRS deductions and bonus depreciation *(42.18)*, if any. If the entire cost of the property was deducted, adjusted basis will generally be reduced to zero, gain on a sale or exchange will equal the sales price (less expenses), and the entire gain will be recaptured as ordinary income.

The first-year expensing deduction is also subject to recapture if the property is not used more than 50% of the time for business in any year before the end of the recovery period. The amount recaptured is the excess of the first-year expensing deduction over the amount of depreciation that would have been claimed in prior years and in the recapture year without expensing *(42.3)*.

Caution

Installment Sale

If you sell property on the installment basis, any first-year expensing or bonus depreciation deduction claimed for the property is recaptured in the year of sale on Form 4797. An installment sale does not defer recapture of the deductions *(44.6)*.

Automobiles and other "listed property." If the more-than-50%-business-use test for a business automobile or other "listed property" *(42.10)* is not met in a year after the auto or other "listed property" is placed in service and before the end of the recovery period, any first-year expensing deduction, bonus depreciation, and MACRS deductions are subject to recapture on Form 4797; *see* the Example at *43.10*.

44.4 Gifts and Inheritances of Depreciable Property

Gifts and charitable donations of depreciable property may be affected by the recapture rules. On the gift of depreciable property, the ordinary income potential of the depreciation carries over into the hands of the donee (the person who received the gift). When the donee later sells the property at a profit, he or she will realize ordinary income *(44.1)*.

On the donation of depreciable property, the amount of the charitable contribution deduction is reduced by the amount that would be taxed as ordinary income had the donor sold the equipment at its fair market value.

The transfer of depreciable property to an heir through inheritance is not a taxable event for recapture purposes. The ordinary income potential does not carry over to the heir because his or her basis is usually fixed as of the date of the decedent's death.

Important: A gift of depreciable property subject to a mortgage may be taxed to the extent that the liability exceeds the basis of the property *(14.6, 31.15)*.

44.5 Involuntary Conversions and Tax-Free Exchanges

Involuntary conversions. Gain may be taxed as ordinary income in either of the following two cases: (1) you do not buy qualified replacement property or (2) you buy a qualified replacement, but the cost of the replacement is less than the amount realized on the conversion *(18.19)*. The amount taxable as ordinary income may not exceed the amount of gain that is normally taxed under involuntary conversion rules when the replacement cost is less than the amount realized on the conversion. Also, the amount of ordinary income is increased by the value of any nondepreciable property that is bought as qualified replacement property, such as the purchase of 80% or more of stock in a company that owns property similar to the converted property.

Distributions by a partnership to a partner. A distribution of depreciable property by a partnership to a partner does not result in ordinary income to the distributee at the time of the distribution. But the partner assumes the ordinary income potential of the depreciation deduction taken by the partnership on the property. When he or she later disposes of the property, ordinary income may be realized.

44.6 Installment Sale of Depreciable Property

All depreciation recapture income (including the first-year expensing deduction and bonus depreciation) is fully taxable in the year of sale, without regard to the time of payment. Recapture is figured on Form 4797. On Form 6252, the gain in excess of the recapture income is reported under the installment method *(5.21)*.

44.7 Sale of a Proprietorship

The sale of a sole proprietorship is not considered as the sale of a business unit but as sales of individual business assets. Each sale is reported separately on your tax return.

A purchase of a business involves the purchase of various individual business assets of the business. To force buyers and sellers to follow the same allocation rules, current law requires both the buyer and the seller to allocate the purchase price of a business among the transferred assets using a residual method formula. Allocations are based on the proportion of sales price to an asset's fair market value and they are made in a specific order set out on Form 8594.

 *Caution*

Tax–Free Exchanges

Ordinary income generally is not realized on a tax-free exchange (unless some gain is taxed because the exchange is accompanied by "boot" *(6.3)* such as money). The ordinary income potential is assumed in the basis of the new property. However, where depreciable realty acquired before 1987 is exchanged for land, the amount of any depreciation recapture is immediately taxable in the year of the exchange.

44.8 Property Used in a Business (Section 1231 Assets)

Form 4797 is used to report the sale or exchange of Section 1231 assets. The following properties used in a business are considered "Section 1231 assets":

- Depreciable assets such as buildings, machinery, and other equipment held more than one year. Depreciable rental property and royalty property fits in this category if held more than one year.
- Land (including growing crops and water rights underlying farmland) held more than one year.
- Timber, coal, or domestic iron ore subject to special capital gain treatment.
- Leaseholds held more than one year.
- An unharvested crop on farmlands, if the crop and land are sold, exchanged, or involuntarily converted at the same time and to the same person and the land has been held more than one year. Such property is not included here if you retain an option to reacquire the land.
- Cattle and horses held for draft, breeding, dairy, or sporting purposes for at least 24 months.
- Livestock (other than cattle and horses) held for draft, breeding, dairy, or sporting purposes for at least 12 months. Poultry is not treated as livestock for purposes of Section 1231.

Section 1231 netting. On Form 4797, you combine all losses and gains, except gains allocated to depreciation recapture, from:

- The sale of Section 1231 assets (*see* the bulleted list above).
- The involuntary conversion of Section 1231 assets and capital assets held for more than one year for business or investment purposes. You include casualty and theft losses incurred on business or investment property held for more than one year and condemnations of such property held over one year. However, there is an exception if losses exceed gains from casualties or thefts in one taxable year.
- Involuntary conversions of capital assets held for personal purposes are not subject to a Section 1231 computation. Gains and losses from casualties and thefts of personal-use property are reported on Form 4684; *see 18.9*.

Result of netting. A net gain on Section 1231 assets from Form 4797 is entered on Schedule D as a long-term capital gain unless the recapture rule (*see* the second Caution on this page) for net ordinary losses apply. A net loss on Section 1231 assets is treated as an ordinary loss that is combined on Form 4797 with ordinary income from depreciation recapture *(44.1)* and with ordinary gains and losses from the sale of business property that does not qualify for Section 1231 netting.

Installment sale. Gain realized on the installment sale of business or income-producing property held for more than a year may be capital gain one year and ordinary income another year. Actual treatment in each year depends on the net result of all sales, including installment payments received in that year *(44.6)*.

> **EXAMPLE**
>
> You suffer an uninsured fire loss of $2,000 on business equipment and gain of $1,000 on other insured investment property damaged by a storm. All of the property was held more than one year. Because loss exceeds gain, neither transaction enters into a Section 1231 computation. The gain is reported as ordinary income and the loss is deducted as an ordinary loss. The effect is a net $1,000 loss deduction. If the figures were reversed, that is, if the gain were $2,000 and the loss $1,000, both assets would be entered into the Section 1231 computation. If only the fire loss occurred, the loss would be treated as a casualty loss and would not be entered into the Section 1231 computation.

Losses exceed gains from casualties or thefts. On Form 4684, you must compute the net financial result from all involuntary conversions arising from fire, storm, or other casualty or

Caution

Capital Gain or Ordinary Loss

Profitable sales and involuntary conversions of Section 1231 assets are generally treated as capital gain, except for profits on equipment *(44.1)* and real estate allocated to recaptured depreciation *(44.2)*, and losses are deducted as ordinary loss. However, the exact tax result depends on the net profit and loss realized for all sales of such property made during the tax year. Under the netting rules *(44.8)*, the net result of these sales determines the tax treatment of each individual sale. In making the computation on Form 4797, you must also consider losses and gains from casualty, theft, and other involuntary conversions involving business and investment property held more than one year. Follow the Form 4797 instructions.

Caution

Recapture of Net Ordinary Losses

Net Section 1231 gain is not treated as capital gain but as ordinary income to the extent of net Section 1231 losses realized in the five most recent prior taxable years. Losses in the five preceding years that have not yet been applied against net Section 1231 gains are recaptured in chronological order on Line 8 of Form 4797. Losses that have already been "recaptured" under this rule in prior years are not taken into account.

theft of assets used in your business and capital assets held for business or income-producing purposes and held more than one year. The purpose of the computation is to determine whether these involuntary conversions enter into the above Section 1231 computation. If the net result is a gain, all of the assets enter into the Section 1231 computation. If the net result is a loss, then these assets do not enter into the computation; the losses are deducted separately as casualty losses, and the gains reported separately as ordinary income. If you incur only losses, the losses similarly do not enter into the Section 1231 computation.

44.9 Sale of Property Used for Business and Personal Purposes

One sale will be reported as two separate sales for tax purposes when you sell a car or any other equipment used for business and personal purposes, or in some cases where a sold residence *(29.7)* was used partly as a residence and partly as a place of business or to produce rent income.

You allocate the sales price and the basis of the property between the business portion and the personal portion. The allocation is based on use. For example, with a car, the allocation is based on mileage used in business and personal driving.

> ### EXAMPLE
>
> Two partners bought an airplane for about $54,000. They used approximately 75% of its flying time for personal flights and 25% for business flights. After using the plane for eight years, they sold it for about $35,000. Depreciation taken on the business part of the plane amounted to $13,000. The partners figured they incurred a loss of $6,000 on the sale. The IRS, allocating the proceeds and basis between business and personal use, claimed they realized a profit of $8,250 on the business part of the plane and a nondeductible loss of $14,250 on the personal part. The allocation was as follows:
>
> | | | IRS Position | |
> | --- | --- | --- | --- |
> | | Partners' claim | Business (25%) | Personal (75%) |
> | Original cost | $54,000 | $13,500 | $40,500 |
> | Depreciation | 13,000 | 13,000 | |
> | Adjusted basis | 41,000 | 500 | 40,500 |
> | Selling price | 35,000 | 8,750 | 26,250 |
> | Gain (Nondeductible loss) | ($6,000) | $8,250 | ($14,250) |
>
> The partners argued the IRS could not split the sale into two separate sales. They sold only one airplane and therefore there was only one sale. A federal district court and appeals court disagreed and held the IRS method of allocation is practical and fair.

44.10 Should You Trade in Business Equipment?

The purchase of new business equipment is often partially financed by trading in old equipment. For tax purposes, a trade-in of equipment in 2023, including business vehicles, is treated as a sale. Gain on the sale must be immediately recognized. It may be preferable to sell the equipment and then use the proceeds to buy new equipment if you can get more on this sale to a third party.

44.11 Corporate Liquidation

Liquidation of a corporation and distribution of its assets for your stock is generally subject to capital gain or loss treatment. For example, on a corporate liquidation, you receive property worth $10,000 from the corporation. Assume the basis of your shares, which you have held long term, is $6,000. You have realized a long-term gain of $4,000.

Note the basis of the distributed assets in the hands of the shareholder going forward will be the property's fair market value. Thus, while a gain may be recognized at distribution, subsequent gain or loss when the assets are sold will be based upon the property's fair market value (essentially reestablishing basis).

If you incur legal expenses in pressing payment of a claim, you treat the fee as a capital expense, according to the IRS. The Tax Court and an appeals court have held that the fee is an expense incurred to produce income and is deductible as a miscellaneous itemized deduction subject to the 2% of adjusted gross income (AGI) floor. However, the deduction cannot be claimed through 2025 due to the suspension of this deduction *(19.2)*.

If you recover a judgment against the liquidator of a corporation for misuse of corporate funds, the judgment is considered part of the amount you received on liquidation and gives you capital gain, not ordinary income.

If you paid a corporate debt after liquidation, the payment reduces the gain realized on the corporate liquidation in the earlier year; thus, in effect, it is a capital loss.

If the corporation distributes liquidating payments over a period of years, gain is not reported until the distributions exceed the adjusted basis of your stock.

44.12 Additional Taxes on Higher-Income Taxpayers

Self-employed individuals who sell business property and who have "high-income" may be subject to additional taxes that are intended to help pay for health care reform. If your income exceeds the applicable threshold for your filing status, you may be subject to either or both of these taxes:

- An additional 0.9% Medicare tax on net earnings from self-employment *(28.2)*.
- An additional 3.8% tax on net investment income (NII tax) *(28.3)*.

When are sales of business property treated as earned income (for the 0.9% tax) or investment income (for the 3.8% tax)? The following guidance should be applied to determine whether the additional taxes apply:

- *Active businesses.* Self-employed people who are active in their businesses do not treat gains from the sale of business assets as subject to either the 0.9% tax (the gains are not part of net earnings from self-employment) or the 3.8% tax (the gains are from a business, not an investment).
- *Passive activities.* Those who are not active in their businesses (i.e., they are passive investors) treat taxable gains from the sales of business property as investment income for purposes of the 3.8% tax. This assumes that the business is a passive activity because the self-employed person does not meet the material participation tests *(10.6)*; *see Chapter 10* for details on the passive activity rules.

 *Caution*

No Deduction for Additional Medicare Tax

While self-employed individuals can deduct one-half of the Medicare tax that applies to their net earnings from self employment *(45.3)*, no deduction is allowed for any portion of the 0.9% additional Medicare tax.

CHAPTER 45

Figuring Self-Employment Tax

Self-employment tax provides funds for Social Security and Medicare benefits. The self-employment tax is calculated on Schedule SE. You are required to prepare Schedule SE if you have self-employment net earnings of $400 or more in 2023, but you will not incur the tax unless your net self-employment earnings exceed $433.13. The tax is added to your income tax liability. When preparing your estimated tax liability, you must also include an estimate of self-employment tax; *see Chapter 27*.

On Schedule SE, self-employment income is reduced by a deduction reflected in the decimal of .9235 listed on the form. You also deduct one-half of the self-employment tax on Line 15 of Schedule 1 (Form 1040 or 1040-SR).

For 2023, the self-employment tax of 15.3% consists of the following two rates: 12.4% for Social Security and 2.9% for Medicare. After multiplying the net earnings by .9235, the combined 15.3% rate applies to a taxable earnings base of $160,200 or less; the 2.9% rate applies to all taxable earnings exceeding $160,200.

You are required to pay self-employment tax on self-employment income even after you retire and receive Social Security benefits.

Caution

Self-employment in Puerto Rico

Even though residents of Puerto Rico are exempt from federal income tax, self-employed individuals still owe self-employment tax on net earnings earned in Puerto Rico.

Caution

Freelancer Fees

Fees you earn for freelance work as an independent contractor are business earnings reportable on Schedule C, and if you have a net profit, they are subject to self-employment tax on Schedule SE.

Filing Tip

Real Estate Investor

The owner of one office building who holds it for investment (rather than for sale in the ordinary course of business) is not a real estate dealer, but a real estate investor. If the only tenant services provided are heat, light, water, and trash collection, report the rental income and expenses on Schedule E. The activity is not a Schedule C business subject to self-employment tax.

45.1 What Is Self-Employment Income?

On Schedule SE, you generally figure self-employment tax on the net profit from your business or profession whether you participate in its activities full or part time. Net profit is generally the amount shown on Line 31 of Schedule C if you are a sole proprietor. If you are a partner, net earnings subject to self-employment tax are taken from Box 14, Schedule K-1, of Form 1065. If you are a farmer, net farm profit is shown on Line 34, Schedule F.

If you have more than one self-employed operation, your net profit from all the operations is combined. A loss in one self-employed business will reduce the income from another business. You file separate Schedules C for each operation and one Schedule SE showing the combined income (less losses, if any).

For self-employment tax purposes, net earnings are not reduced by deductible contributions to your own SEP or self-employed qualified retirement plan (41.4).

Married couples. Where you and your spouse each have self-employment income, each spouse must figure separate self-employment income on a separate Schedule SE. Each pays the tax on the separate self-employment income. Both schedules are attached to the joint return.

If you live in a community property state, business income is not treated as community property for self-employment tax purposes. The spouse who is actually carrying on the business is subject to self-employment tax on the earnings. However, a qualified joint venture election by spouses may be made to the extent you and your spouse are the only members of the business that is jointly own and operate, you each materially participate in the business, and you file a joint return. Under these conditions a joint election to file as sole proprietors on Schedule C ("qualified joint venture election") instead of as a partnership may be made. You make the joint venture election by filing separate Schedule Cs on which each spouse reports the respective share (according to respective ownership interests) of the business income, gains, losses, deductions, and credits. If you make the election, each of you must file a separate Schedule SE to figure self-employment tax on your share of the joint venture income.

However, the reporting rule is different if you are making the election for a rental real estate business. In that case, use Schedule E instead of Schedule C. On one Schedule E, you each report your respective interests in the qualified joint venture and divide the income, gains, losses, deductions, and credits between you; check the "QJV" box on Schedule E and *see* the instructions. Given rental real estate income is generally not subject to self-employment tax (see exception 1 below), you do not have to file Schedule SE unless you have other income that is subject to self-employment tax.

Exceptions to self-employment tax. The following types of income or payments are not included as self-employment income on Schedule SE:

1. Rent from real estate is generally not self-employment income. However, self-employment tax applies to the business income of a real estate dealer or income in a rental business where substantial services are rendered to the occupant, as in the leasing of—

   - Rooms in a hotel or in a boarding house.

   - Apartments, but only if extra services for the occupants' convenience, such as maid service or changing linens, are provided.

   - Cabins or cabanas in tourist camps where you provide maid services, linens, utensils, and swimming, boating, fishing, and other facilities, for which you do not charge separately.

   - Farmland in which the landlord materially participates in the actual production of the farm or in the management of production. For purposes of "material participation," the activities of a landlord's agent are not counted, only the landlord's actual participation.

2. Capital gains are not self-employment income. Self-employment income does not include gains from the sale of property unless it is inventory or held for sale to customers in the ordinary course of business. Thus, traders in securities (30.14) who buy and sell securities for their own account do not treat net gains or losses from the sales as self-employment income or loss. Dealers in commodities and options are subject to self-employment tax *see Table 45-1.*

3. Dividends and interest. Generally, dividends and interest are not self-employment income. However, dividends earned by a dealer in securities and interest on accounts receivable are treated as self-employment income if the securities are not being held for investment. A dealer is one who buys stock as inventory to sell to customers.

4. Conservation Reserve Program payments received by farmers receiving Social Security retirement or disability benefits. These payments reduce net farm profit reported on Schedule SE.

Certain family-related compensation. Payments you receive from an insurance company or government program as a family caregiver are not treated as self-employment income unless you are in the trade or business of being a caregiver. Similarly, executor fees for handling an estate are not considered self-employment income unless you are in the business of regularly acting as an executor for estates.

Net operating loss deduction. A loss carryover from past years does not reduce business income for self-employment tax purposes.

Statutory employees. Wages of a statutory employee, such as a full-time life insurance salesperson *(40.6)*, are not subject to self-employment tax because Social Security and Medicare tax have been withheld.

Farmers. A share farmer's part of the profit from crops on land owned by another is self-employment income.

Business interruption proceeds. The IRS and the Tax Court disagree over whether business interruption insurance proceeds must be reported as earnings subject to self-employment tax. The Tax Court held that insurance payments made to a grocer as compensation for lost earnings due to a fire were not subject to self-employment tax because the payment was not for actual services. The IRS refuses to follow the decision, holding that such payments represented income that would have been earned had business operations not been interrupted.

 *Filing Tip*

Trader in Securities

If you are a trader in securities *(30.14)*, gains or losses from your trading business are not subject to self-employment tax.

45.2 Partners Pay Self-Employment Tax

A general partner includes his or her share of partnership income or loss in net earnings from self-employment, including guaranteed payments. If your personal tax year is different from the partnership's year, you include your share of partnership income or loss for the partnership tax year ending within 2023.

A limited partner is not subject to self-employment tax on his or her share of partnership income except for guaranteed payments for services performed, which are subject to the tax.

If a general partner dies within the partnership's tax year, self-employment income includes his or her distributive share of the income earned by the partnership through the end of the month in which the death occurs. This is true even though his or her heirs or estate succeeds to the partnership rights. For this purpose, partnership income for the year is considered to be earned ratably each month.

Retirement payments from partnership. Retirement payments you receive from your partnership are not subject to self-employment tax if the following conditions are met:

1. The payments are made under a qualified written plan providing for periodic payments on retirement of partners with payments to continue until death.

2. You rendered no services in any business conducted by the partnership during the tax year of the partnership ending within or with your tax year.

3. By the end of the partnership's tax year, your share in the partnership's capital has been paid to you in full, and there is no obligation from the other partners to you other than with respect to the retirement payments under the plan.

Limited liability company (LLC) members. Are LLC members treated as general or limited partners for purposes of self-employment tax? The matter is not completely settled, but it appears that members owe self-employment tax when they perform services for their business, participate in management activities, and are not mere investors.

45.3 Schedule SE

Self-employment tax for 2023 is figured on Part I of Schedule SE. As shown in the sample Schedule SE (next page), you reduce your net profit on Line 4a by .9235 to get your net earnings from self-employment. In other words, only 92.35% of the net earnings is subject to self-employment tax. The .9235 adjustment is the equivalent of a 7.65% reduction to net earnings, which, along with the income tax deduction for one-half of self-employment tax on Schedule 1 of Form 1040 or 1040-SR, attempts to place self-employed individuals on the same level as employees subject to FICA taxes.

After the .9235 adjustment is made, net earnings are subject to the 12.4% and 2.9% rates, assuming the resulting net earnings are $400 or more. For 2023, the 12.4% Social Security rate applies to the first $160,200 of net earnings and the 2.9% Medicare rate applies to all of the net earnings.

> **EXAMPLE**
>
> Kim Farr's 2023 net profit from Schedule C is $170,000. As shown in the Schedule SE on page 777, Kim's net earnings subject to self-employment tax are $156,995 after the .9235 adjustment. Kim's self-employment tax is $24,020, which she reports on Line 4 of Schedule 2 (Form 1040 or 1040-SR). She may deduct $12,010 of the tax on Line 15 of Schedule 1 (Form 1040 or 1040-SR).

45.4 How Wages Affect Self-Employment Tax

If you have both net earnings from self-employment and also wage and/or tip income subject to FICA taxes (Social Security and Medicare), the amount of such FICA earnings may affect your self-employment tax liability.

If your 2023 FICA wages or tips were $160,200 or over, your net self-employment earnings (after the .9235 adjustment) are subject only to the 2.9% Medicare rate. If the total of your 2023 FICA wages (and tips) and net self-employment earnings was $160,200 or less, all of your net earnings are subject to the 12.4% Social Security rate and the 2.9% Medicare rate.

If your 2023 FICA wages or tips were under $160,200 but the total of the wages and tips plus your 2023 net earnings was over the $160,200 limit for the 12.4% Social Security rate, the 12.4% rate applies to the lesser of: (1) Line 6 of Schedule SE, which shows your net self-employment earnings (after the .9235 adjustment), or (2) Line 9 of Schedule SE, which shows the excess of $160,200 over the FICA wages and tips. The 2.9% Medicare rate applies to the entire amount of net self-employment earnings. *See* the following Example and the filled-in Part I of Schedule SE on page 778.

> **EXAMPLE**
>
> Jay Lowe earned a salary of $93,000 in 2023 and had a net profit from Schedule C of $82,850. His earnings from self-employment on Line 6 of the Schedule SE shown on page 778 are $76,512 ($82,850 × .9235). The Line 9 amount is $67,200, the excess of the $160,200 maximum Social Security tax base over the $93,000 in wages. The 12.4% Social Security rate applies to the lesser of the Line 6 or Line 9 amounts, or $67,200. In other words, $67,200 of the $76,512 net earnings (after the .9235 adjustment) are subject to the 12.4% Social Security tax. The 2.9% Medicare rate applies to the entire net earnings.
>
> | | |
> |---|---|
> | 12.4% × $67,200 | $8,333 |
> | 2.9% × $76,512 | + 2,219 |
> | | $10,552 |
>
> Jay's self-employment tax liability of $10,552 is entered on Line 4 of Schedule 2 (Form 1040 or 1040-SR). One half of that, $5,276, is deductible on Line 15 of Schedule 1 (Form 1040 or 1040-SR).

⚠ *Caution*

Foreign Earned Income

If you are self employed and living outside the United States and qualify for the 2023 foreign earned income exclusion of up to $120,000 *(36.3)*, you are still subject to self-employment tax on all of your earnings, unless an exception is allowed under a social security agreement between the United States and the government of the country in which you are living.

Kim Farr's Sample Schedule SE (Form 1040)—Self-Employment Tax

(This sample is subject to change; see the e-Supplement at jklasser.com)

SCHEDULE SE
(Form 1040)

Department of the Treasury
Internal Revenue Service

Self-Employment Tax

Attach to Form 1040, 1040-SR, 1040-SS, or 1040-NR.
Go to www.irs.gov/ScheduleSE for instructions and the latest information.

OMB No. 1545-0074

2023

Attachment
Sequence No. **17**

Name of person with self-employment income (as shown on Form 1040, 1040-SR, 1040-SS, or 1040-NR)	Social security number of person with **self-employment** income	
Kim Farr		011-X1-0X01

Part I Self-Employment Tax

Note: If your only income subject to self-employment tax is **church employee income**, see instructions for how to report your income and the definition of church employee income.

A If you are a minister, member of a religious order, or Christian Science practitioner **and** you filed Form 4361, but you had $400 or more of **other** net earnings from self-employment, check here and continue with Part I . . . . ☐

Skip lines 1a and 1b if you use the farm optional method in Part II. See instructions.

1a	Net farm profit or (loss) from Schedule F, line 34, and farm partnerships, Schedule K-1 (Form 1065), box 14, code A	**1a**	
b	If you received social security retirement or disability benefits, enter the amount of Conservation Reserve Program payments included on Schedule F, line 4b, or listed on Schedule K-1 (Form 1065), box 20, code AQ	**1b**	( )

Skip line 2 if you use the nonfarm optional method in Part II. See instructions.

2	Net profit or (loss) from Schedule C, line 31; and Schedule K-1 (Form 1065), box 14, code A (other than farming). See instructions for other income to report or if you are a minister or member of a religious order	**2**	170,000
3	Combine lines 1a, 1b, and 2	**3**	170,000
4a	If line 3 is more than zero, multiply line 3 by 92.35% (0.9235). Otherwise, enter amount from line 3 .	**4a**	156,995
	Note: If line 4a is less than $400 due to Conservation Reserve Program payments on line 1b, see instructions.		
b	If you elect one or both of the optional methods, enter the total of lines 15 and 17 here	**4b**	
c	Combine lines 4a and 4b. If less than $400, **stop**; you don't owe self-employment tax. **Exception:** If less than $400 and you had **church employee income**, enter -0- and continue	**4c**	156,995
5a	Enter your **church employee income** from Form W-2. See instructions for definition of church employee income . . . . [**5a**]		
b	Multiply line 5a by 92.35% (0.9235). If less than $100, enter -0-	**5b**	
6	Add lines 4c and 5b	**6**	156,995
7	Maximum amount of combined wages and self-employment earnings subject to social security tax or the 6.2% portion of the 7.65% railroad retirement (tier 1) tax for 2023	**7**	*160,200*
8a	Total social security wages and tips (total of boxes 3 and 7 on Form(s) W-2) and railroad retirement (tier 1) compensation. If $160,200 or more, skip lines 8b through 10, and go to line 11 . . . . [**8a**]		
b	Unreported tips subject to social security tax from Form 4137, line 10 . . . [**8b**]		
c	Wages subject to social security tax from Form 8919, line 10 . . . . . . [**8c**]		
d	Add lines 8a, 8b, and 8c	**8d**	
9	Subtract line 8d from line 7. If zero or less, enter -0- here and on line 10 and go to line 11	**9**	160,200
10	Multiply the **smaller** of line 6 or line 9 by 12.4% (0.124)	**10**	19,467
11	Multiply line 6 by 2.9% (0.029)	**11**	4,553
12	**Self-employment tax.** Add lines 10 and 11. Enter here and on **Schedule 2 (Form 1040), line 4**, or **Form 1040-SS, Part I, line 3**	**12**	24,020
13	**Deduction for one-half of self-employment tax.** Multiply line 12 by 50% (0.50). Enter here and on **Schedule 1 (Form 1040), line 15** . . . . [**13**] 12,010		

For Paperwork Reduction Act Notice, see your tax return instructions. Cat. No. 11358Z Schedule SE (Form 1040) 2023

Jay Lowe's Sample Schedule SE (Form 1040)—Self-Employment Tax
(This sample is subject to change; see the e-Supplement at jklasser.com)

SCHEDULE SE **(Form 1040)** Department of the Treasury Internal Revenue Service	**Self-Employment Tax** Attach to Form 1040, 1040-SR, 1040-SS, or 1040-NR. Go to *www.irs.gov/ScheduleSE* for instructions and the latest information.

OMB No. 1545-0074

2023

Attachment Sequence No. **17**

Name of person with self-employment income (as shown on Form 1040, 1040-SR, 1040-SS, or 1040-NR) Jay Lowe	Social security number of person with **self-employment** income	1X0-01-X110

Part I Self-Employment Tax

Note: If your only income subject to self-employment tax is **church employee income**, see instructions for how to report your income and the definition of church employee income.

A If you are a minister, member of a religious order, or Christian Science practitioner **and** you filed Form 4361, but you had $400 or more of **other** net earnings from self-employment, check here and continue with Part I . . . . ☐

Skip lines 1a and 1b if you use the farm optional method in Part II. See instructions.

1a	Net farm profit or (loss) from Schedule F, line 34, and farm partnerships, Schedule K-1 (Form 1065), box 14, code A	**1a**	
b	If you received social security retirement or disability benefits, enter the amount of Conservation Reserve Program payments included on Schedule F, line 4b, or listed on Schedule K-1 (Form 1065), box 20, code AQ	**1b**	( )

Skip line 2 if you use the nonfarm optional method in Part II. See instructions.

2	Net profit or (loss) from Schedule C, line 31; and Schedule K-1 (Form 1065), box 14, code A (other than farming). See instructions for other income to report or if you are a minister or member of a religious order .	**2**	82,850
3	Combine lines 1a, 1b, and 2	**3**	82,850
4a	If line 3 is more than zero, multiply line 3 by 92.35% (0.9235). Otherwise, enter amount from line 3 .	**4a**	76,512
	Note: If line 4a is less than $400 due to Conservation Reserve Program payments on line 1b, see instructions.		
b	If you elect one or both of the optional methods, enter the total of lines 15 and 17 here	**4b**	
c	Combine lines 4a and 4b. If less than $400, **stop**; you don't owe self-employment tax. **Exception:** If less than $400 and you had **church employee income**, enter -0- and continue	**4c**	76,512
5a	Enter your **church employee income** from Form W-2. See instructions for definition of church employee income **5a**		
b	Multiply line 5a by 92.35% (0.9235). If less than $100, enter -0-	**5b**	
6	Add lines 4c and 5b	**6**	76,512
7	Maximum amount of combined wages and self-employment earnings subject to social security tax or the 6.2% portion of the 7.65% railroad retirement (tier 1) tax for 2023	**7**	160,200
8a	Total social security wages and tips (total of boxes 3 and 7 on Form(s) W-2) and railroad retirement (tier 1) compensation. If $160,200 or more, skip lines 8b through 10, and go to line 11 . . . . **8a**	93,000	
b	Unreported tips subject to social security tax from Form 4137, line 10 . . . **8b**		
c	Wages subject to social security tax from Form 8919, line 10 . . . . . . **8c**		
d	Add lines 8a, 8b, and 8c	**8d**	93,000
9	Subtract line 8d from line 7. If zero or less, enter -0- here and on line 10 and go to line 11	**9**	67,200
10	Multiply the **smaller** of line 6 or line 9 by 12.4% (0.124)	**10**	8,333
11	Multiply line 6 by 2.9% (0.029)	**11**	2,219
12	**Self-employment tax.** Add lines 10 and 11. Enter here and on **Schedule 2 (Form 1040), line 4,** or **Form 1040-SS, Part I, line 3**	**12**	10,552
13	**Deduction for one-half of self-employment tax.** Multiply line 12 by 50% (0.50). Enter here and on **Schedule 1 (Form 1040), line 15** **13**	5,276	

For Paperwork Reduction Act Notice, see your tax return instructions.   Cat. No. 11358Z   Schedule SE (Form 1040) 2023

45.5 Optional Method If 2023 Was a Low-Income or Loss Year

The law provides a small increased tax base for Social Security coverage if you have a low net profit or a net loss. The increased tax base is provided by an optional method and is figured in Part II of Schedule SE. One optional method is for nonfarm self-employment and another for farm income. You may not use the optional method to report an amount less than your actual net earnings from nonfarm self-employment.

Nonfarm optional method. You may use the nonfarm optional method for 2023 if you meet all the following tests:

1. Your net earnings (profit) from nonfarm self-employment are less than $6,560.
2. Your net nonfarm profits are less than 72.189% of your gross nonfarm income.
3. You had net earnings from self-employment of $400 or more in at least two of the following years: 2020, 2021, and 2022.
4. You have not previously used this method for more than four years. There is a five-year lifetime limit for use of the nonfarm optional base. The years do not have to be consecutive.

If your net profit from all nonfarm trades or businesses is less than $6,560 and also less than 72.189% of gross nonfarm income, and you have no gross farm income, you may report two-thirds of the gross income from your nonfarm business as net earnings from self-employment for 2023.

 *Filing Tip*

Optional Method

Electing the optional method to increase the base for Social Security coverage may also increase earned income for purposes of the dependent care credit, the additional child tax credit, and the Earned Income Credit.

EXAMPLES

1. Brown had net earnings from self-employment of $800 in 2021 and $900 in 2022 and so meets Test 3 above. In 2023, she has gross nonfarm self-employment income of $6,200 and net nonfarm self-employment earnings of $4,000. Net earnings from self-employment of $4,000 are less than $6,560 (Test 1 above) and also less than $4,476 (72.189% × $6,200) (Test 2). Brown may figure self-employment tax on $4,133 (²/₃ of $6,200).

2. Same facts as in Example 1, but Brown has a net self-employment loss of $700. She may elect to report $4,133 (²/₃ of $6,200) as net earnings under the optional method.

3. Smith had gross nonfarm income of $1,000 and net nonfarm self-employment earnings of $800. He may not use the optional method because net earnings of $800 are not less than 72.189% of $1,000 gross income, or $722.

4. Jones has gross nonfarm income of $525 and net nonfarm self-employment earnings of $175. Jones may not use the optional method because two-thirds of his gross income, or $350, is less than the minimum income of $400 required to be subject to the self-employment tax.

Optional farm method. If you have farming income (other than as a limited partner) you may use the farm optional method to figure your net earnings from farm self-employment.

You can use the farm optional method for 2023 only if your gross farm income was not more than $9,840 or your net farm profits were less than $6,560.

You may report the smaller of two-thirds of your gross income or $6,560 as your net earnings from farm self-employment.

Farm income includes income from cultivating the soil or harvesting any agricultural commodities. It also includes income from the operation of a livestock, dairy, poultry, bee, fish, fruit, or truck farm, or plantation, ranch, nursery, range, orchard, or oyster bed, as well as income in the form of crop shares if you materially participate in production or management of production.

45.6   Self-Employment Tax Rules for Certain Positions

Table 45-1   Self-Employed or Employee?

If you are—	Tax rule—
Babysitter	Where you perform services in your own home and determine the nature and manner of the services to be performed, you are considered to have self-employment income. However, where services are performed in the parent's home according to instructions by the parents, you are an employee of the parents and do not have self-employment earnings. In one case, the Tax Court held that grandparents who provided care only for their own grandchildren and received payments from a state-sponsored childcare assistance program had to pay income tax on the payments, but the payments were not subject to self-employment tax because the grandparents' primary purpose in providing the care was not to make a profit.
Clergy	If you are an ordained minister, priest, or rabbi, a member of a religious order who has not taken a vow of poverty, or a Christian Science practitioner, you are subject to self-employment tax, unless you elect not to be covered on the grounds of conscientious or religious objection to Social Security benefits. An application for exemption from Social Security coverage must be filed on Form 4361 by the due date, including extensions, of your income tax return for the second taxable year for which you have net earnings from services of $400 or more. An exemption, once granted, is irrevocable. Self-employment tax does not apply to the rental value of any parsonage or parsonage allowance provided after retirement. Other retirement benefits from a church plan are also exempted.
Consultant	The IRS generally takes the position that income earned by a consultant is subject to self-employment tax. The IRS has also held that a retired executive hired as a consultant by his former firm received self-employment income, even though he was subject to an agreement prohibiting him from giving advice to competing companies. According to the IRS, consulting for one firm is a business; it makes no difference that you act as a consultant only with your former company. The IRS has also imposed self-employment tax on consulting fees, although no services were performed for them. The courts have generally approved the IRS position.
Dealer in commodities and options	Registered options dealers and commodities dealers are subject to self-employment tax on net gains from trading in Section 1256 contracts, which include regulated futures contracts, foreign currency contracts, dealer equity options, and non-equity options. Self-employment tax also applies to net gains from trading property related to such contracts, like stock used to hedge options.
Director	You are taxed as a self-employed person if you are not an employee of the company. Fees for attendance at meetings are self-employment income. If the fees are not received until after the year you provide the services, you treat the fees as self-employment earnings in the year they are received.
Employee of foreign government or international organization	If you are a U.S. citizen and you work in the United States, Puerto Rico, the Virgin Islands, American Samoa, the Commonwealth of the Northern Mariana Islands, or Guam, for a foreign government or its wholly owned instrumentality, or an international organization, you pay self-employment tax on your earnings if Social Security and Medicare taxes are not withheld from your pay.
Executor or guardian	If you are a professional fiduciary, your fees will always be treated as self-employment income, regardless of the assets held by the estate. But if you serve as a nonprofessional executor or administrator for the estate of a deceased friend or relative, your fees will not be treated as self-employment income unless all of the following tests are met: (1) the estate includes a business; (2) you actively participate in the operation of the business; and (3) all or part of your fee is related to your operation of the business. The IRS applied similar business tests to deny self-employment treatment for a guardian who was appointed by a court to care for a disabled cousin. The guardian negotiated sales of the cousin's property and invested the proceeds, but these activities were not extensive enough to be considered management of a business.
Former insurance salespersons	Termination payments by a former insurance salesperson may be exempt from self-employment tax. They must be received from an insurance company after the termination of a services agreement. No services may be performed for the company after the agreement ends and before the end of the tax year. The payments must be conditioned on the salesperson's entering into a covenant not to compete with the company for at least one year after termination. The amount of the payment must be primarily based on policies sold by (or credited to) the salesperson during the last year of the services agreement or on the period for which such policies remain in force after the termination.

Table 45-1   Self-Employed or Employee? (continued)

If you are—	Tax rule—
Gig worker	Whether you are an employee or independent contractor depends on your worker classification for federal income tax purposes. If you are an independent contractor, then your net earnings from full-time, part-time, temporary, or sideline work is subject to self-employment tax, regardless of the form in which you are paid (e.g., cash, property, goods, virtual currency) and whether or not you receive an information return (e.g., Form 1099-NEC, Form 1099-MISC, Form 1099-K, etc).
Lecturer	You are not taxed as a self-employed person if you give only occasional lectures. If, however, you seek lecture engagements and get them with reasonable regularity, your lecture fees are treated as self-employment income.
Nonresident alien	You generally do not pay Social Security tax on your self-employment income derived from a trade, business, or profession in the United States. This is so even though you pay income tax. However, an international agreement between the United States and another country might provide that you are covered under the U.S. Social Security system, in which case, you are subject to self-employment tax. In the absence of such an agreement, you are exempt from self-employment tax even if your business in the United States is carried on by an agent, employee, or partnership of which you are a member. However, if you live in Puerto Rico, the Virgin Islands, American Samoa, the Commonwealth of the Northern Mariana Islands, or Guam, you are not considered a nonresident alien and are subject to self-employment tax.
Nurse	If you are a registered nurse or licensed practical nurse who is hired directly by clients for private nursing services, you are considered self-employed. You are an employee if hired directly by a hospital or a private physician and work for a salary following a strict routine during fixed hours, or if you provide primarily domestic services in the home of a client. Where registered or licensed practical nurses are assigned nursing jobs by an agency that pays them, the IRS, in several rulings, has treated such nurses as employees of the agency. Nurses' aides, domestics, and other unlicensed individuals who classify themselves as practical nurses are treated by the IRS as employees, regardless of whether they work for a medical institution, a private physician, or a private household.
Real estate agent or door-to-door salesperson	Licensed real estate agents are considered self-employed if they have a contract specifying that they are not to be treated as employees and if substantially all of their pay is related to sales rather than number of hours worked. The same rule also applies to door-to-door salespeople with similar contracts who work on a commission basis selling products in homes or other non-retail establishments.
Technical service contractor	Consulting engineers and computer technicians who receive assignments from technical service agencies are generally treated as employees and do not pay self-employment tax. The IRS distinguishes between (1) technicians who in three-party arrangements are assigned clients by a technical services agency and (2) those who directly enter into contracts with clients. Employee status covers only technicians in Group 1. Technical specialists who contract directly with clients may be classified as independent contractors by showing that they have been consistently treated as independent contractors by the client, and that other workers in similar positions have also been treated as independent contractors. Thus, they may treat their income as self-employment income. Firms that are treated as employers of technical specialists are responsible for withholding and payroll taxes.
Traders in securities	Gains and losses from a trading business are not subject to self-employment tax.
Writer	Royalties from writing books are self-employment income to a writer. Royalties on books by a professor employed by a university may also be self-employment income despite employment as a professor.

PART 7

Filing Your Return and the Process After You File

This part is designed to help you —

- Organize your tax data. First, gather and organize all your tax documents pertaining to the 2023 tax year.
- Understand how the IRS reviews your return and initiates audit procedures.
- Know how to avoid penalties for underpaying your tax *(48.6)*.
- Understand the factors that might lead to an audit *(48.1)*.
- Prepare for an audit. Advance preparations and knowing your rights can help support your position *(48.4)*.
- Know how to dispute adverse IRS determinations in an audit *(48.8)*.
- File a timely refund claim if you have overpaid your tax *(47.2)*.
- File an amended return if you omitted income or claimed excessive deductions on your original return *(47.8)*.

CHAPTER 46

Filing Your Return

Whether you prepare your return yourself or retain a professional preparer, you must first collect and organize your tax records. Organizing and compiling all necessary tax documents will help file an accurate tax return. Good records will help you figure your income, deductions, and credits and will serve as a written record to present to the IRS in the event that you are audited.

Review income statements from banks, employers, brokers, and governmental agencies on their respective income forms. When reviewing these income documents, look for miscalculations, additions, and omissions.

Survey *Chapters 12–20* of this book for deductions you can claim directly from gross income and itemized deductions you can claim on Schedule A of Form 1040 or 1040-SR.

Reviewing your tax return from prior years will help refresh your memory as to how you accounted for income and claimed expenses in prior years. This review will also remind you of deductions, carryover losses, and other items you might have otherwise overlooked that you could be eligible for. If you self-prepare your return using the same software or an online solution as in the prior year, it will display this information for your review, if you choose to elect the use of those features. If your prior year returns were prepared by a professional, he or she should be able to provide you with a copy of your returns, if you do not have copies. Otherwise, you may obtain copies of prior year tax returns by filing Form 4506 with the IRS for a fee.

In this chapter you will find a checklist of steps to take when preparing and checking your return. If you do not believe you will be able to file your 2023 tax return by April 15, 2024, and need to file for an extension, *see 46.3*.

IRS Alert

Getting a Copy of an Old Tax Return

You can obtain a copy of a prior year tax return from the IRS by filing Form 4506 and paying a $43 fee per return.

You can use Form 4506-T or 4506T-EZ to order free of charge a transcript of tax return information that provides line entries from tax returns for the three prior years and a transcript of data from Forms W-2 and 1099 for up to 10 years in some cases.

You can obtain a transcript online using the IRS service "Get Transcript" (irs.gov/individuals/get-transcript). This involves a registration process in order to view your tax transcript.

Planning Reminder

Keep Copies

Make a copy of your signed return if filing on paper or a printout of a return if filing electronically and keep it with copies of Form W-2 and other income statements, plus receipts, canceled checks, and other items to substantiate your deductions.

46.1   Keeping Tax Records

To maximize tax-savings opportunities, you must keep good records throughout the year. Good recordkeeping makes it easier to prepare your return, reduces errors, and provides a defense to any challenge from the IRS.

- Make a habit of keeping receipts or records of deductible items.
- Keep a calender or diary of expenses to record deductible items.
- Keep a file of bills and receipts. This will remind you of deductible items and provide you with supporting evidence to present to the IRS if audited.
- Use your credit card receipts, online account statements, and checkbook stubs as a record. If you own a business, you must keep a complete set of account books for the business.

IRA records. If you have made nondeductible contributions to a traditional IRA, keep a record of both your nondeductible and deductible contributions. This will help when you withdraw IRA money to figure the tax-free and taxable parts of the withdrawal *(8.9)*. Also keep records of contributions and conversions to Roth IRAs *(8.21–8.24)*. For these purposes, you should keep copies of Form 8606 and Form 5498 *(8.8)*.

Reinvested mutual fund or ETF distributions. Keep a record of mutual fund or ETF distributions that you have reinvested in additional fund shares. The reinvested amounts are part of your cost basis in the fund. When you redeem your shares, you need to know your basis to compute gain or loss *(32.10)*.

Passive losses. If you have losses that are suspended and carried forward to future years under the passive loss restrictions *(10.13)*, keep the worksheets to Form 8582 as a record of the carry-forward losses. Also, if you deducted passive losses from rental real estate as an active participant or a real estate professional, retain records, such as a diary, showing your participation in the rental activities.

Home mortgage interest. Keep your bank statements and canceled checks. If a loan secured by a first or second home is used to make substantial home improvements, keep records of the improvement costs to support your home interest deduction *(15.5)*.

How long should you keep your records? Your records should be kept for a minimum of three years after the year to which they are applicable, since the IRS generally has three years from the date your return is filed to audit your return. Some authorities advise keeping them for six years, since in some cases where income has not been reported, the IRS may go back as far as six years to question a tax return. In cases of suspected tax fraud, there is no time limitation at all.

Keep records of transactions relating to the basis of property for as long as they are important in figuring the basis of the original or replacement property. For example, records of the purchase of rental property or improvements must be held as long as you own the property.

As mentioned above, if you have made any nondeductible IRA contributions, records of IRA contributions and distributions must be kept until all funds have been withdrawn. Similarly, you should save confirmations from stock dividend reinvestment plans and mutual funds, or other records showing reinvested dividends and cash purchases of shares; these are part of your cost basis and will reduce taxable gain when you sell shares in the fund.

46.2   Getting Ready to File Your Return

You must collect your tax records before you can start the preparation of your return. Even if you employ a tax professional to prepare your return, organizing your tax data is essential.

You may obtain IRS forms and publications online at IRS.gov. You can obtain forms by phone from the IRS by calling (800) 829-3676.

Checking for possible errors. If you prepare a paper return, when you have completed your return, put it aside and postpone checking your completed return for several hours or even a day so that you can review the return in a fresh state of mind. If you prepare your return electronically, be sure to run "check errors" before filing. *See* below for common errors that might delay a refund or result in a tax deficiency and interest costs.

If filing electronically. To do this, you need your prior-year adjusted gross income (AGI) to validate your signature. If your return is rejected, read the explanation for rejection; this could help you find a starting point to fix the return. If you have further questions, call the IRS at (800) 829-1040. Find more information at E-File Options for Individuals at https://www.irs.gov/filing/e-file-options.

If mailing your return. If you are mailing your paper return to the IRS, first check it to ensure the following:

- Your arithmetic is correct.
- Your Social Security number, and that of your spouse if you are filing jointly, is recorded correctly on each form and schedule.
- You have filled in the proper boxes that state your filing status and your dependents, including their Social Security number and relationship to you *(21.8)*.
- You have claimed the full standard deduction you are entitled to if you are age 65 or older, or blind *(13.4)*.
- You have used the Tax Table, Tax Computation Worksheet, or special capital gain or foreign earned income worksheet applicable to your tax status. If you do not have net capital gain or qualified dividends, use the Tax Table if your taxable income is less than $100,000, or the Tax Computation Worksheet if your taxable income is $100,000 or more. *See 22.4* if you have net capital gain or qualified dividends. *See 22.5* if you claimed the foreign earned income exclusion or foreign housing exclusion.
- You have put the refund due you or your tax payable on the correct line.
- If you owe tax and are paying by check, your check should be made out to the "United States Treasury" for the correct amount due and your Social Security number should be on the check. Send payment voucher Form 1040-V along with your payment.
- You have signed your return and, if you are filing a joint return, your spouse has also signed *(1.4)*.
- You have attached the correct copy of your Form W-2 and all appropriate forms and schedules to your return.
- If you have elected to have your refund directly deposited into your personal account, verify that you have provided the IRS with the correct routing number and account number on Lines 35b, c, and d of Form 1040 or 1040-SR.
- You have correctly addressed the envelope and affixed proper postage.
- You use certified or registered mail or an IRS-specified private delivery service to prove that your return was postmarked on or before the filing date. *See* the adjacent Planning Reminder for more details.

46.3 Applying for an Extension

If you cannot file your return on time, apply by the due date of the return for an extension of time to file. Send the extension request on Form 4868 to the Internal Revenue Service office with which you file your return.

Automatic filing extension. You may get an extension without waiting for the IRS to act on your request. You receive an automatic six-month extension for your 2023 return if you file Form 4868 by April 15, 2024. The extension gives you until October 15, 2024, to file your 2023 return. A late filing penalty will not be imposed if you fail to submit a payment with Form 4868 provided you make a good faith estimate of your liability based upon available information at the time of filing. However, although the extension will be allowed without a payment, you will be subject to interest charges and possible penalties (discussed below) on 2023 taxes not paid by April 15, 2024.

You may e-file Form 4868 for free through the IRS Free File program (go to IRS. gov). You may also file Form 4868 electronically using tax preparation software or your tax preparer may file it electronically for you. To make a tax payment, you may use a credit card or debit card (a fee will be charged), you can authorize a payment from your savings or checking account through IRS Direct Pay at www.irs.gov/Payments/

Caution

Common Law "Mailbox Rule" Rejected

There had been an accepted practice called the "mailbox rule" that had allowed taxpayers to create a rebuttable presumption that a return was physically delivered to the IRS by showing through credible testimony that it was postmarked on time. The IRS eliminated this rule in 2011 with a regulation that requires a certified or registered mail receipt and an appellate court in 2019 (Baldwin v. U.S., 9th Circuit) upheld the IRS' authority to do so. The U.S. Supreme Court refused to hear the case, so the appellate court decision stands.

Planning Reminder

Use Special Mailing Services for Last Minute Filing

Last minute filers who do not e-file may use specified services from Federal Express, UPS, and DHL as well as the U.S. Postal Service. The IRS instructions to Form 1040 and 1040-SR have a list of the eligible private delivery services. If using the U.S. Postal Service, send the return certified (or registered) mail and keep the postmark receipt. If you use a private delivery service, keep a copy of the mailing label or obtain a receipt to verify a timely postmark. If your return is postmarked before or at any time on the filing due date (April 15, 2024, for 2023 returns), it is considered timely filed under a "timely-mailing-is-timely-filing" rule, even if the IRS receives it after the due date.

The timely mailing rule also applies if you obtain a filing extension and are mailing your return on or before the extended due date.

A timely foreign postmark for a return filed from abroad will also be accepted by the IRS as proof of a timely filing.

Planning Reminder

You Can Get a Six-Month Filing Extension

You can get an automatic six-month extension to file your 2023 return by filing Form 4868 by April 15, 2024. The extension is for filing only and does not extend the time to pay your taxes for 2023.

Filing Tip

Certain Refunds Delayed

No refund related to the Earned Income Tax Credit or the Child Tax Credit can be issued before February 15, no matter how early you file your return.

Direct-Pay, or you can make a payment through the Electronic Federal Tax Payment System (EFTPS); for details go to http://www.irs.gov/payments. When you make a payment with Direct Pay, a credit or debit card, or EFTPS, you get a confirmation number that you should keep for your records. You can pay cash using PayNearMe at a local 7-Eleven, CVS Pharmacy, Walgreens or other participating store, which requires you to obtain an online confirmation code from the IRS.

When you file your return within the extension period, you enter on the appropriate line of the return any tax payment that you sent with your extension request, and include the balance of the unpaid tax, if any.

While the extension is automatically obtained by a proper filing on Form 4868, the IRS may terminate the extension by mailing you a notice at least 10 days prior to the termination date designated in the notice.

Interest and penalty for late payment. You have to pay interest on any 2023 tax not paid by April 15, 2024, even if you obtain an extension. In addition, if the tax paid with Form 4868, plus withholdings and estimated tax payments for 2023, is less than 90% of the amount due, you will be subject to a late-payment penalty (usually one-half of 1% of the unpaid tax per month)—unless you can show reasonable cause.

Abroad on April 15, 2024. You do not get an automatic extension for filing and paying your tax merely because you are out of the country on the filing due date. If you plan to be traveling abroad on April 15, 2024, you must either request the automatic six-month filing extension on Form 4868, or request an extension along with a payment made by EFTPS, account withdrawal, credit card or debit card *(see above)*.

The only exception is for U.S. citizens or residents who live and have their main place of business outside the U.S. or Puerto Rico, or military personnel stationed outside the U.S. or Puerto Rico, on April 15, 2024. If you qualify, you are allowed an automatic two-month extension without having to request it, until June 17, 2024. The two-month extension is for filing your return and also paying any tax due. However, the IRS will charge interest from the original April 15th due date on any unpaid tax. If you cannot file within the two-month extension period, you can obtain an additional four-month extension by filing Form 4868 by June 17, 2024. This additional four-month extension is for filing only and not payment. In addition to interest, a late payment penalty may be imposed *(see above)* on any tax not paid by June 17, 2024.

If you are eligible for the two-month extension but expect to qualify for the foreign earned income exclusion *(36.3)* under the foreign residence or presence test after June 17, 2024, you can request on Form 2350 an extension until after the expected qualification date; *see 36.7*.

46.4 Getting Your Refund

If you show an overpayment of tax on your 2023 return, you can have a refund check mailed to you or have the IRS directly deposit the refund into as many as three bank, brokerage, or mutual fund accounts; *see* below. For a direct deposit you must provide the IRS with the correct routing information for your account. On your 2023 Form 1040 or 1040-SR, you can apply all or part of your refund to your 2024 estimated tax; this is an irrevocable election.

Direct-deposit refund option. If you want the IRS to directly deposit your refund into only one account, just give the IRS the appropriate routing and account numbers on the refund line of your return. If you want the refund to be directly deposited into two or three accounts, file Form 8888 with your Form 1040 or 1040-SR. You can have the refund directly deposited into a checking or savings account, an online Treasury Direct account, or even to a traditional IRA *(8.1)* Roth IRA *(8.21)*, or health savings account *(41.10)*. If you want the deposit to go into a traditional IRA or Roth IRA, you must establish the IRA before you request direct deposit. Make sure that you notify the IRA trustee if you want the deposit to count as an IRA contribution for 2023 (rather than for 2024 when the deposit is made). To count as a 2023 IRA contribution (traditional or Roth), the direct deposit must actually be made to the IRA by the April 15, 2024, due date for your 2023 return (extensions are disregarded).

You can also request on Form 8888 for your refund (or part of it) to be invested in up to $5,000 of paper series I bonds *(30.13)*.

If you file Form 8379 *(see below)* for a refund as an injured spouse, you cannot use Form 8888.

Checking refund status online or by phone. You can check the status of your refund online at IRS.gov (click on "Where's My Refund"). You will need to provide the Social Security number shown on the return (or the first Social Security number if you filed a joint return), your filing status, and the amount of the refund. You also can check the status of your refund by downloading the IRS2Go app, by calling the automated refund information phone number (800) 829-1954, or by calling (800) 829-1040.

Form 8379: Injured spouse may get refund that was withheld to pay spouse's debts. If a refund was due on a joint return that you filed with a spouse who owed child or spousal support, federal student loans, or state income tax, the Treasury Department's Bureau of the Fiscal Service may have withheld the refund to cover the obligations. If your spouse owed federal taxes, the refund may have been offset by the IRS. If you are not liable for the past-due payments, and your tax payments (withholdings or estimated tax installments) or refundable credits exceed your income reported on the joint return, you may file Form 8379 to get back your share of the refund.

Penalty for filing excessive refund claim. A 20% penalty can apply to an excessive claim for refund or credit on an original or amended return *(47.8)*. The penalty is 20% of the "excessive" amount, the excess of the refund or credit claimed over the amount allowed, unless there is a reasonable basis for the amount claimed.

The penalty does not apply to claims relating to the Earned Income Credit *(25.6)*. It also does not apply to any portion of the excess that is subject to the accuracy-related penalties (including the penalty for understatements due to reportable or listed transactions), or the fraud penalty *(48.6)*.

46.5 Paying Taxes Due

If you owe tax on a return that you are mailing to the IRS, you may pay by check, money order, credit card, or debit card. Payments can also be made by direct debit from your bank account, either by phone or online using the IRS' Direct Pay or Electronic Federal Tax Payment System (EFTPS). For those who do not have a bank account or credit card, payment can also be made in cash, although it is not sent to the IRS or Treasury, as explained below.

If paying by check or money order, make it payable to the "United States Treasury." Write your Social Security number on the check or money order. Attach Form 1040-V along with your payment.

A credit card or debit card payment can be made by phone or on the internet with a service provider that handles the transaction for the IRS. The service provider will impose a fee based on the amount you are paying. Go to www.irs.gov/payments. The IRS is now authorized to accept payments directly (not through a service provider), but details about this are not yet clear; *see* the *e-Supplement* at *jklasser.com* for any update.

IRS online or phone option for making payments. The IRS' Electronic Federal Tax Payment System (EFTPS) accepts online tax payments from individual as well as business taxpayers. You may use EFTPS to pay the balance due on your individual tax return or to pay estimated tax installments.

Payments are made by direct debit from an account that you designate when you enroll with EFTPS. Individual tax payments may be scheduled up to 365 days in advance and business taxes up to 120 days in advance. You can enroll online at www.eftps.gov.

Payments via EFTPS can also be made by phone after you enroll with EFTPS and set up a direct debit arrangement. Call (800) 555-4477 for enrollment information.

Caution

Direct Deposit of Joint Refund

If you are due a refund on a joint return, your financial institution may reject a request to have a direct deposit of the joint refund made to an individual account or IRA. If the direct deposit is rejected, the IRS will mail you a refund check.

Planning Reminder

Interest Not Paid on Most Refunds

If your 2023 return is filed on or before the April 15, 2024, filing deadline, the IRS does not have to pay interest if the refund is issued on or before May 30, 2024, which is the 45th day after April 15. If the return is filed after April 15, 2024, with or without an extension, no interest is due on refunds issued within 45 days after the actual filing date. If the overpayment is not refunded within 45 days, interest is paid from the date the tax was overpaid up to a date determined by the IRS that can be as much as 30 days before the date of the refund check.

Direct Pay. Instead of registering to use EFTPS.gov or paying a convenience fee to charge your taxes (as explained below), you can use the free IRS online payment system at www.irs.gov/Payments/Direct-Pay. You authorize the IRS to withdraw funds from your checking or savings account to pay your taxes, but bank account and other information is not stored.

Pay in cash. If you do not have a bank account or credit card to use for paying taxes, you can pay cash through the IRS' PayNearMe option at participating retailers, such as 7-Eleven stores, Family Dollar, CVS Pharmacies, Royal Farms and Speedway, among others. You must go to the Official Payments website and follow instructions to receive a confirmation of your information that will then be verified by the IRS. After you receive a payment code from the IRS via email, you can present it and make your payment in cash at your local store. This payment option costs $1.50 and is limited to $1,000 per day. Find details at https://www.irs.gov/payments/pay-with-cash-at-a-retail-partner.

Paying electronically. If you file electronically, you may pay your taxes by authorizing a direct debit from your checking or savings account, or by using a credit or debit card. If you use a credit/debit card, the processing company will charge you a fee.

Filing Tip

Voice Bots Used to Set Up Installment Agreements

The IRS now uses voice bots to verify your identity if you want to set up a payment plan.

Installment agreements. If you cannot pay the full amount due on your return when you file, but will be able to pay the full amount within 180 days, you may ask the IRS for a short-term extension by calling (800) 829-1040 or applying online. The IRS will not charge a fee for a 180-day extension, but interest will be charged and a late payment penalty *(46.9)* might be imposed. A short-term payment plan under an online application is limited to a balance due of less than $100,000 in combined tax, penalties, and interest.

If you need more than 180 days, you can request an installment agreement on Form 9465. If you owe $50,000 or less (tax, penalties and interest), you can apply online for a payment agreement instead of filing Form 9465; select "Payments" at IRS.gov. Even if the IRS agrees to an installment arrangement, you will be charged interest and may have to pay a late payment penalty *(46.9)* on any tax not paid by the due date.

If you owe $10,000 or less and agree to pay the full amount owed within three years, your request for an installment agreement cannot be turned down, provided that for the previous five years, you (and your spouse if currently filing jointly) timely filed and paid the taxes due and did not have an installment agreement during that period. Under such a "guaranteed installment agreement," you must timely file and pay any taxes due while the agreement is in effect.

If payments are not made under a three-year guaranteed installment agreement, you generally must pay the full balance due in no more than 72 monthly installments. If you owe over $25,000 but not over $50,000, you must disclose financial details to the IRS on Form 433-F ("Collection Information Statement") unless you agree to make payments by direct debit from your checking account or by payroll deduction. For individuals, balances of over $25,000 must be paid by Direct Debit. If you owe more than $50,000, you must complete Form 433-F as part of your application.

The IRS may approve a request to make installment payments for less than the full amount you owe, but only after a thorough review of your financial circumstances and after you have sold assets and used home equity to reduce the tax bill. If agreed to, the IRS will reevaluate a partial payment plan every two years.

The IRS will usually inform you within 30 days if your proposed payment plan is accepted. If the payment plan is accepted, you will have to pay a processing fee. If payments are made by direct debit from your checking account, the fee is $107 for agreements set up by phone or mail, but only $31 for direct debit agreements set up online. For payment plans of more than 120 days, the fee is $225, or $130 if set up online.

A reduced $43 fee generally applies for individuals whose income does not exceed 250% of the federal poverty guidelines, but this fee is waived if the taxpayer agrees to make direct debit payments from a checking account. If a taxpayer is unable to make direct debit payments and indicates this on the application (Line 13c of Form 9465), the $43 fee is reimbursed upon completion of the installment agreement. When you apply for an installment agreement, whether on Form 9465, online (at IRS.gov), by phone, or face-to-face with an IRS employee, the IRS will automatically review the income information from your return to determine eligibility for the reduced fee. If the IRS approves a monthly installment plan without granting a reduced user fee and you think you qualify, you can request the reduced fee by filing Form 13844 with the IRS within 30 days of receiving the IRS' acceptance notice.

If you are using an installment agreement to pay the tax due on a timely filed return (including extensions), the late payment penalty is reduced by half from .5% to .25% per month.

Offer in Compromise. If your financial circumstances are dire and you believe you will be unable to pay the tax l iability you owe even with an installment agreement, you may make an offer to settle your tax debt for less than the full amount due on Form 656 ("Offer in Compromise"), as discussed in *48.10*.

46.6   Handling Identity Theft

Identity theft continues to proliferate, and annually makes the IRS' list of Dirty Dozen Tax Scams. If you know your personal information has been compromised, or suspect that it has been, notify the IRS. File Form 14039, "Identity Theft Affidavit," at https://www.irs.gov/pub/irs-pdf/f14039.pdf, to put the IRS on alert immediately. Follow the instructions for mailing or faxing the form to the IRS. By filing this form, the IRS marks your tax account as "suspect." Unfortunately, this will not necessarily speed up the issuance of your tax refund, but it may ease filings going forward.

Special tax identification number. If someone else is using your Social Security number to file an illegitimate tax return, this will interfere with your filings. You can obtain an Identity Protection Personal Identification Number (IP PIN), a six-digit number, to use in place of your Social Security number on future tax returns.

You must obtain an IP PIN if:

- You lost an IRS notice (CP01A) sent to you with an IP PIN.
- You had an IP PIN before but didn't receive a new one.
- Your e-filed return was rejected because your IP PIN was missing or incorrect.

You can choose to obtain an IP PIN if you want one (e.g, as a protection against tax identity theft)

To obtain an IP PIN online, you must go through an authentication process called "Secure Access Steps." These steps are explained at the IRS' Secure Access page at https://www.irs.gov/individuals/secure-access-how-to-register-for-certain-online-self-help-tools.

Learning more about tax-related ID theft. Combating ID theft is a priority for the IRS, and the IRS has many resources to help you.

- https://www.irs.gov/individuals/how-irs-id-theft-victim-assistance-works
- Publication 4524, Security Awareness to Taxpayers.
- Taxes. Security. Together. This is a joint campaign by the IRS, state tax administrators, and the private-sector tax industry to encourage taxpayers to protect personal and financial data online and offline.
- Taxpayer Guide to Identity Theft, which is a landing page at https://www.irs.gov/uac/taxpayer-guide-to-identity-theft that contains information and links.

46.7   Notify the IRS of Address Changes

If the IRS does not have your current address, payment of a refund due you may be delayed. If you owe taxes, the IRS may enforce a deficiency notice sent to the address on your most recently filed tax return, even if you never receive the IRS notice.

To avoid these problems, you can call the IRS to update your address at (800) 829-1040. You also may file Form 8822 with the IRS to provide notice of an address change, or send a signed written statement to the IRS Service Center notifying the IRS of your new residence. The statement should state the new and old address, your full name, and your Social Security or employer identification number.

Planning Reminder

Greater Protection for Identity Theft

If you are a victim of tax identity theft, you'll be assigned one person in the IRS to deal with (a point of contact). Also, the IRS is now required to notify you if there is any suspected unauthorized use of your tax information (e.g., someone obtained a tax refund using your Social Security number).

If you and your spouse separate after filing a joint return, you should each notify the IRS of your current address.

If after you move you receive an IRS correspondence that has been forwarded by the Post Office, you may correct the address shown on the letter and mail it back to the IRS. Your correction is considered notice of an address change.

46.8   Interest on Tax Underpayments

You may be charged interest by the IRS if you have an underpaid tax liability. The interest rate, which equals the federal short-term rate plus 3%, is determined every quarter. Interest begins to accrue from the due date of the return. Interest is compounded daily except for estimated tax penalties. If you relied on IRS assistance in preparing a return, and taxes are owed because of a mathematical or clerical error, interest does not begin to accrue until 30 days from a formal demand by the IRS for the payment of additional taxes.

IRS interest rates on taxes owed are as follows:

Interest Rate on Underpayments		
From—	To—	Underpayment Rate—
7/1/2023	9/30/2023	7%
4/1/2023	6/30/2023	7%
1/1/2023	3/31/2023	7%
10/1/2022	12/31/2022	6%
7/1/2022	9/30/2022	5%
4/1/2022	6/30/2022	4%
7/1/2020	3/31/2022	3%
7/1/2019	6/30/2020	5%
1/1/2019	6/30/2019	6%

46.9   Tax Penalties for Late Filing and Late Payment

Late filing. If your return is filed after the due date, including extensions, without reasonable cause (illness, death in family, natural disaster, or other event beyond your control) and you owe tax, the IRS may impose a penalty of 5% of the net tax due for each month or part of a month that the return is late, up to five months (25% maximum); *see* the Note below.

If your return is more than 60 days late, there is a minimum penalty, which for 2023 returns is equal to the smaller of $450 and 100% of the tax due. In one case, the IRS tried to impose the minimum penalty on a taxpayer who did not owe any tax because her withholdings exceeded her liability. However, the Tax Court held that the minimum penalty does not apply unless tax is underpaid. The IRS has agreed to follow the decision.

If failure to file is fraudulent, the monthly penalty is 15% of the net tax due, with a maximum penalty of 75%.

Note: For months that you are subject to the 0.5% monthly penalty for late payment (described below) as well as the penalty for late filing, the combined penalty is 5% with the late filing penalty reduced by the late payment penalty, from 5% to 4.5% per month. Thus, the combined penalty for each of the first five months is 5% (4.5% + 0.5%), with the late filing penalty reaching its maximum of 22.5% in five months (4.5% × 5 = 22.5%). After five months, the 0.5% monthly late payment penalty can continue until the tax is paid but not beyond the 50th month when the 25% late payment limit is reached (0.5% × 50 = 25%)

Late payments. If you are late in paying your taxes, a monthly penalty of 0.5% (½ of 1%) may be imposed on the net amount of tax due and not paid by the regular due date (without extensions). The maximum penalty is 25% of the tax due. The penalty is in addition to the regular interest charge. This penalty does not apply to the estimated tax *(27.1)*. The late payment penalty does not apply if you can show that the failure to pay is due to reasonable cause and not to willful neglect.

A special reasonable cause rule applies if you obtain a filing extension. If by the original due date you paid at least 90% of your total tax liability through withholdings, estimated tax installments, or payment with your extension request, reasonable cause is presumed and the penalty does not apply for the period covered by the extension.

Unless reasonable cause is shown, the 0.5% monthly penalty also applies for failure to pay a tax deficiency within 21 calendar days of the date of notice and demand for payment if the tax due is less than $100,000. If the tax is $100,000 or more, the penalty-free payment period is 10 business days.

The monthly penalty may be doubled to 1%, if, after repeated requests to pay and a notice of levy, you do not pay. The increased penalty applies starting in the month that begins after the earlier of the following IRS notices: (1) a notice that the IRS will levy upon your assets within 10 days unless payment is made or (2) a notice demanding immediate payment where the IRS believes collection of the tax is in jeopardy. If the tax is not paid after such a demand for immediate payment, the IRS may levy upon your assets without waiting 10 days.

CHAPTER 47

Filing Refund Claims, and Amended Returns

You file a refund claim on Form 1040-X if you want to take advantage of a retroactive tax law change, if you overpaid taxes due to a failure in claiming allowable deductions or credits, or overstated your income. You may use Form 1040-X to correct your return if you underreported your income or improperly claimed deductions.

Filing a refund claim on time is a requirement to receive any refund. The time limits discussed in *47.2* must be strictly observed; otherwise, even if you file a valid refund claim, the claim will be denied due to late filing. By filing electronically, the processing of the return and receipt of refund is much quicker than paper filing.

You do not have to file a refund claim if you have overpaid your tax due to excessive withholding on your wages or salary, or if you have overpaid your estimated tax. You receive a refund of these overpayments by filing your tax return and requesting a refund for these amounts. You must file your return within three years from the time the tax was paid to get the refund *(47.2)*.

For a refund of overpaid FICA taxes, *see 26.8* for how to claim a refund on your tax return. If you are not required to file a tax return, you file a refund claim on Form 843.

If you are entitled to a refund due to the Earned Income Credit for certain low-income working families, you must file your tax return to receive the refund, even though your income and filing status would not otherwise require you to file a return. *See Chapter 25*.

47.1 Filing an Amended Return

You should file Form 1040-X (Amended U.S. Individual Income Tax Return) to revise a previously filed return, either to claim a refund *(see below)* or to report additional tax owed *(47.7)*. This can be done on a paper return or, for amended returns for 2019 and later, the return can be filed electronically.

As a refund claim, Form 1040-X can be filed if you overpaid your tax on your original return, such as where you failed to take allowable deductions or credits or overstated your income. You generally can use Form 1040-X to change your filing status, such as where you were entitled to head of household status but filed as a single taxpayer. You can change your filing status from married filing separately to married filing jointly, but you cannot switch from a joint return to separate returns after the due date for the return.

If you are entitled to a refund, the IRS will issue a check for any overpayment captured on an amended return. A refund on an amended return cannot be made by direct deposit to your bank account.

You do not have to file a refund claim if you have overpaid your tax due to excessive withholding of taxes on your wages or salary, or if you have overpaid your estimated tax. You will receive a refund on those overpayments by filing your tax return and requesting a refund at that time *(46.4)*.

Claiming an unwarranted refund can be costly. There is a 20% penalty for an excessive claim for refund or credit *(47.8)*.

Married or divorced taxpayers. If a joint return was filed for a year in which a refund is due, both spouses are entitled to recover jointly and both must file a joint refund claim. Where separate returns were filed, each spouse is a separate taxpayer and may not file a claim to recover a refund based on the other spouse's return, except if that spouse becomes the fiduciary when one spouse becomes incompetent or dies. If you are divorced and incur a net operating loss or credit that may be carried back to a year in which you were married, you may file a refund claim based on the carryback *(40.18)* with your signature alone and the refund check will be made out only to you.

47.2 When to File a Refund Claim

You may file a refund claim on Form 1040-X within three years from the time your original return was filed, or within two years from the time you paid your tax, whichever is later. However, a refund claim on a late-filed return may be barred under a three-year "look back" rule; *see* below. A return filed before its due date is treated as having been filed on the due date. If you filed an extension, but filed before the extension deadline, your return is considered filed on the actual filing date. The filing deadlines are suspended if you are unable to manage your financial affairs; *see* the Planning Reminder on the next page.

A refund claim based on a bad debt or worthless securities may be made within seven years of the original due date of the return (without extensions) for the year in which the debt or security became worthless.

The time for filing refund claims based on carrybacks of net operating losses or general business credits is within three years of the due date (including extensions) of the return for the year the loss or credit arose.

If you filed an agreement giving the IRS an extended period of time in which to assess a tax against you, you are allowed an additional period in which to file a claim for refund. The claim, up to certain amounts, may be filed through the extension period and for six months afterwards.

The Look-back rule may limit refund claims for withholdings and estimated tax payments on late-filed original return. A refund for withheld income taxes or estimated tax installments may be lost if you delay filing your original return for too long. The Supreme Court agrees with the IRS that the withholdings and estimated tax are considered to be paid on the original due date of the return. To obtain a refund of these withholdings or estimated tax installments, you must file the return within three years of the due date, or within three years plus any extension period, if an extension was filed for the year the taxes were withheld or paid. If the return is filed after the end of this three-year (plus extension) "look-back" period, the withholdings and estimated taxes cannot be refunded.

Caution

Time Limits Must Be Observed

Failure to file a timely refund claim is fatal, regardless of its merits. Even if you expect that your claim will have to be pursued in court, you must still file a timely refund claim with the IRS. Mailing a refund claim by registered or certified mail so that it is postmarked by the due date (including extensions) qualifies as a timely filing if you use the U.S. Postal Service. The timely mailing rule also applies to refund claims that are timely deposited with private delivery services that have been designated by the IRS.

Planning Reminder

Disability Suspends Limitation

The limitations period for filing a refund claim is suspended during any period in which a person is unable to manage his or her financial affairs due to a physical or mental impairment that has lasted or is expected to last for at least one year or to result in death. The suspension does not apply during a period in which a guardian is authorized to handle the individual's financial affairs.

For example, if taxes were withheld from your 2019 wages and you are due a refund but have not yet filed your 2019 return, you must do so by April 18, 2023, to obtain a refund of the withholdings. If you had obtained an extension until October 15, 2020, to file your 2019 return, and still have not filed, the deadline for doing so and claiming the refund for the 2019 taxes will be October 16, 2023. What if you claim the refund for the withheld 2019 taxes on an original 2019 return mailed and postmarked on or slightly before the last day of the "three years plus extension" period, namely, April 18, 2023, or October 16, 2023, if you had an extension for the 2019 return? Even if the mailing is not received until after the April 18 or October 16 deadline, the timely mailing/timely filing rule applies, and the IRS treats the claim as filed on the date of mailing for purposes of applying the "three years plus extension" look-back rule.

Armed Forces service members and veterans. In determining the time limits within which a refund claim may be filed, you disregard intervening periods of service in a combat zone or in a contingency operation, plus periods of continuous hospitalization outside the United States as a result of combat zone injury, and the next 180 days thereafter *(35.5)*.

Claiming refund for deceased taxpayer. If you are a surviving spouse filing an amended joint return to claim a refund for you and your deceased spouse, you only need to file Form 1040-X. A court-appointed personal representative must attach Form 1310 to Form 1040-X to claim the refund.

47.3 Stating the Reasons for Refund Claim

After entering changes to your original return on Form 1040-X, in Part III of the form you explain the changes made and tell the IRS why you are claiming a refund. Where appropriate, you should attach a statement explaining:

- All the facts that support the claim. Attach all supporting documents and tax forms reinforcing your claim for refund.
- All the grounds for the claim. If you are uncertain about the exact legal grounds, alternative and even inconsistent grounds may be given. For example: "The loss was incurred from an embezzlement; if not, from a bad debt." To protect against understating the amount of the claim, you might preface the claim with this phrase: "The following or such greater amounts as may be legally refunded."

If your refund claim is denied by the IRS, the claim may become the basis of a court suit. If you have not stated all the grounds on Form 1040-X, you may not be allowed to argue them in court.

47.4 Quick Refund Claims

Form 1045 may be used for filing refunds due to carrybacks from net operating losses, the general business credit, and net Section 1256 contract losses. Form 1045 also may be used for a quick refund based on a repayment exceeding $3,000 of income reported in an earlier year. Form 1045 generally must be filed within 12 months after the end of the year in which the loss, credit, or repayment claim arose; *see* the Form 1045 instructions. The IRS will generally process your claim within 90 days, or if later, 90 days after the end of the month in which your return is due. Payment of quick refund claims is not a final settlement of your return; the IRS may still audit and possibly disallow the refund claim if the claim is not accurate. Note that the filing of a quick refund, if rejected, may not be the basis of a suit for refund; a regular refund claim must be filed.

47.5 Interest Paid on Refund Claims

If a refund claim is filed within the time limits in *47.2* and the IRS pays the refund within 45 days, interest is paid from the date of overpayment to the date the claim was filed. If the refund is not made within the 45-day period, interest is paid from the date of overpayment to a date set by the IRS that is not more than 30 days before the date of the refund check.

The IRS does not have to pay interest on overpayments resulting from net operating loss carrybacks or business credit carrybacks if a refund is paid within 45 days of the filing of the refund claim. If a refund claim based on a loss or credit carryback is filed and subsequently a quick refund claim is filed on Form 1045 for the same refund, the 45-day period starts to run on the date Form 1045 is filed.

Interest rates applied to overpayments are as follows:

Refund for—	Overpayment rate is—
1/1/2023–9/30/2023	7
10/1/2022–12/31/2022	6
7/1/2022–9/30/2022	5
4/1/2022–6/30/2022	4
7/1/2020–3/31/2022	3
7/1/2019–6/30/2020	5
1/1/2019–6/30/2019	6
4/1/2018–12/31/2018	5

47.6 Refunds Withheld to Cover Debts

The IRS may withhold all or part of your refund if you owe federal taxes. Under the Treasury Offset Program (TOP), the IRS may withhold all or part of your refund if you owe child or spousal support or federal non-tax debts, such as student loans or state income taxes. If you file a joint return with a spouse who owes child support or federal debts, you may be able to obtain your share of a refund due on the joint return by filing Form 8379 (46.4).

47.7 Amended Returns Showing Additional Tax

If, after filing your 2022 return, you find that you did not report all of your income or claimed excessive deductions, you should file an amended return on Form 1040-X to limit interest charges and possible tax penalties.

If you filed early and then file an amended return by the filing due date (including any extensions) that shows additional tax due, you will not be charged interest or penalties based on the original return; the amended return is considered a substitute for the original.

You must pay the additional tax due as shown on Form 1040-X. Even if you expect a refund on your original return, the IRS will not reduce the refund check to cover the additional tax. You must pay the liability and you will receive the original refund separately.

47.8 Penalty for Filing Excessive Refund Claim

A 20% penalty can apply to an excessive claim for refund or credit that you claim on an original return (46.4) or amended (47.1) return. The penalty is 20% of the "excessive" amount, the excess of the refund or credit claimed over the amount allowed. For example, assume that you mailed your 2022 Form 1040 to the IRS on April 12, 2023, and included a $400 check to cover the tax due. On June 13, 2024, you file an amended return and claim a $2,000 refund based on an increase in itemized deductions. The IRS reduces the refund to $1,000. If you cannot show that you had reasonable cause for making the additional $1,000 claim, the IRS will assess a penalty of $200 (20% of the $1,000 excess).

The penalty does not apply if there is reasonable cause for making the excessive claim. It does not apply to claims relating to the Earned Income Credit (25.6) or to any portion of the excess that is subject to the accuracy-related penalties (including the penalty for understatements due to reportable or listed transactions), or the fraud penalty, discussed at 48.6.

 *Caution*

Refund Offset for Overdue State Taxes

If you owe state income taxes, the state can refer the debt to the Treasury Department's Bureau of the Fiscal Service (BFS), which administers the Treasury Offset Program. The BFS can offset your federal tax refund by the state tax if your address on the return is within the state seeking the offset. The state must give you written notice that the debt is being referred to the BFS and provide an opportunity for disputing the liability.

CHAPTER 48

If the IRS Examines Your Return

The IRS is only able to examine a low percentage of returns; therefore the IRS follows a policy of examining returns which, upon preliminary inspection, indicate the largest possible source of potential tax deficiency. Various weights are assigned to specific items on each tax return, thus permitting the ranking of returns for the greatest potential error.

This chapter discusses the items that may trigger an audit and how you can handle an audit if your return is selected for examination.

Also discussed in this chapter are various penalties the IRS can assess if you file an inaccurate return, and the penalties for not reporting your foreign financial accounts.

48.1 Odds of Being Audited

The odds are quite low that your return will be picked for an audit. The IRS 2022 Data Book for its 2022 fiscal year (October 2021 through September 2022) does not give statistics for 2022 (audit rates for tax years 2012 through 2020, for individuals averaged 0.49%). The audit rates are higher for taxpayers with large adjusted gross incomes and sole proprietors with substantial total gross receipts. There are a considerable number of audits on taxpayers claiming the earned income tax credit. Budget pressures on the IRS suggest that low audit rates will continue for most income groups for the foreseeable future, although budget increases under the Inflation Reduction Act of 2022 could lead to higher audit rates for the years ahead.

Audit odds vary depending on your income, profession, type of return, type of transactions reported, and where you live. Individual returns are classified by all income items on the return without regard to losses. Professional or business income reported on Schedule C and farm income reported on Schedule F is classified by total gross receipts, and corporate returns are classified by total assets.

Your return may command special IRS scrutiny because of your profession, the type of transactions reported, or the deductions claimed. The chances of being audited are greater under the following circumstances:

- Your information reported on the tax return does not match information received from third-party documentation, such as Forms 1099 and W-2.
- Your itemized deductions exceed IRS targets.
- You claim tax-shelter losses.
- You report complex investment or business transactions without clear explanations.
- You receive cash payments related to your work that the IRS feels are easy to conceal, such as cash fees received by doctors or tips received by cab drivers and waiters.
- Business expenses are excessive in relation to income.
- Cash contributions to charity are large in relation to income.
- You are a shareholder of a closely held corporation whose return has been examined.
- A prior audit resulted in a tax deficiency.
- An informer provides the IRS with information that leads the IRS to believe that you are omitting income from your return.

Itemized deductions. If your itemized deductions exceed target ranges set by the IRS, the chances of being audited increase. The IRS does not publicize its audit criteria for excessive deductions, but it does release statistics showing the average amount of deductions claimed according to reported income.

Taxpayer Bill of Rights. The "Taxpayer Bill of Rights" collectively refers to a series of laws that aim to protect taxpayers from mistreatment by IRS personnel and ensure that they are treated fairly, professionally, promptly, and with courtesy by the IRS and its employees:

1. The right to be informed
2. The right to quality service
3. The right to pay no more than the correct amount of tax
4. The right to challenge the IRS' position and be heard
5. The right to appeal an IRS decision in an independent forum
6. The right to finality
7. The right to privacy
8. The right to confidentiality
9. The right to retain representation
10. The right to a fair and just tax system

These rights are listed in the IRS instructions for Forms 1040 and 1040-SR and in IRS Publication 1.

If you have a dispute with the IRS, you should ask for an explanation of the procedural rules affecting your case, if these are not already included in the documents sent to you. For example, before the IRS may enforce a tax lien by seizing property by levy, the IRS must provide you with a notice of your right to a hearing before an appeals officer, an explanation of the levy procedures, the availability of administrative appeals and the appeals procedures, the alternatives to the proposed levy such as an installment agreement, and the rules for obtaining the release of a lien. *See* IRS Publication 1, Your Rights as a Taxpayer, IRS Publication 556, Examination of Returns, Appeal Rights, and Claims for Refund; IRS Publication 594, The IRS Collection Process; and IRS Publication 5, Your Appeal Rights and How to Prepare a Protest if You Don't Agree.

Taxpayer Advocate. The Taxpayer Advocate Service (TAS) is an independent office within the IRS. The function of the TAS is to assist taxpayers in resolving problems with the IRS, propose changes in administrative practices of the IRS, and identify potential legislative changes that may mitigate problems and improve the tax system.

You may be able to receive TAS assistance if you have unsuccessfully tried to resolve your problem with the IRS and have not had your calls or letters returned. However, due to the demand on its resources, the TAS is most likely to provide assistance if you face a significant hardship because of an impending IRS action or lack of IRS response to your problem. If you qualify, you will be assigned a personal advocate to try to resolve your problem. Contact the TAS at its homepage at https://taxpayeradvocate.irs.gov. From the website, you can access a state-by-state list of addresses and phone numbers for TAS offices. The list is also in IRS Publication 1546. You can contact the TAS by calling 1-877-777-4778, or you may apply for assistance by filing Form 911 ("Request for Taxpayer Advocate Service Assistance (And Application for Taxpayer Assistance Order)").

48.2 When the IRS Can Assess Additional Taxes

Three-year statute of limitations. The IRS has three years after the date on which your return is filed to assess additional taxes. When you file a return before the due date, however, the three-year period starts from the due date, generally April 15.

When the due date of a return falls on a Saturday, Sunday, or legal holiday, the due date is postponed to the next business day.

> **EXAMPLES**
>
> 1. You filed your 2023 return on February 9, 2024. The last day on which the IRS can make an assessment on your 2023 return is April 15, 2027.
> 2. You filed your 2019 return on May 15, 2020. The IRS had until May 15, 2023, to assess a deficiency.

Amended returns. If you file an amended return shortly before the three-year limitations period is about to expire and the return shows that you owe additional tax, the IRS has 60 days from the date it receives the return to assess the additional tax, even though the regular limitations period would expire before the 60-day period.

Six-year statute. When you fail to report an item of gross income which is more than 25% of the gross income reported on your return, the IRS has six years after the return is filed to assess additional taxes. An item that is adequately disclosed is not considered an omission. An overstatement of basis that minimizes gain is an "omission" of gross income in determining if the 25% test for triggering the six-year statute of limitations is met.

IRS request for audit extension. If the IRS cannot complete an audit within three years, it may request that you sign Form 872 to extend the time for assessing the tax. However, where an individual was "scared" into signing such an agreement, it was held invalid. *See* the following Example.

> **EXAMPLE**
>
> Robertson, a plumber, won $30,000 in a sweepstakes. An IRS agent asked him to sign an agreement to extend the tax assessment deadline. Robertson never had any prior dealings with the IRS, he did not know that his return was under examination, and he was not in touch with the lawyer who prepared the return on which his sweepstakes winnings were averaged.

Caution

No Limitation Period for Fraud

There is no limitation on when tax may be assessed where a false or fraudulent return is filed with intent to evade tax, or where no return is filed.

Robertson wanted to see his lawyer before signing Form 872, but the agent pressed hard for the signature, phoning him and his wife at home and at work 20 times in a week. The agent did not tell him the amount of additional tax that might be involved, or explain that if he refused to sign he would have an opportunity before the IRS and the courts to contest any additional tax. Instead, the agent's comments gave him the impression that his home could be confiscated if he refused to sign. Robertson signed and the IRS later increased his tax.

Robertson argued that the agreement was not valid. He signed under duress. The Tax Court agreed. He convinced the court that he really believed he could lose his house and property if he did not comply. No adequate explanation of the real consequences of refusal to sign was made, although Robertson asked. Since he signed Form 872 under duress, the IRS could not increase his tax after the three-year period.

48.3 Audit Overview

When you file your annual tax return, the IRS checks your return for computational accuracy and clerical errors, such as a missing signature or missing or inaccurate Social Security numbers. To check whether you have omitted income from your return, the IRS will match your return against the Forms W-2 and Forms 1099 it receives from employers, brokers, payers of interest and dividends, and others who have filed information returns reporting payments to you.

If an error is found, or you have not submitted required attachments, you will probably be advised by mail of the corrections and of additional tax due, or you may be asked to provide additional information to substantiate tax deductions or credits. If you disagree with an IRS assessment of additional tax, you may request an interview or submit additional information. For example, if you file your 2023 return early, then you are advised of an error, and you make the correction before April 15, 2024, interest is not charged.

If your refund is selected for a more thorough review, you will be notified by mail.

Types of audits. An examination may be held by correspondence, at a local IRS office, at your tax preparer's office or your place of business, office, or home. Correspondence audits are by far the most common type of audit. An examination at an IRS office is called a desk or office examination. An examination at your office or your preparer's office, or your place of business or home, is called a field examination. When you are contacted by the IRS, you should receive an explanation of the examination process.

In a correspondence audit, the IRS sends you a letter asking for additional information about an item on your return. For example, the IRS may ask you to document a claimed deduction for charitable contributions or medical expenses. If the IRS is not satisfied with your response, you may be called in for an office audit. The IRS also notifies you by letter of mathematical or clerical errors you have made on your return—for example, if you have failed to report income, such as interest or dividends, that are shown by payers on information returns and matched to taxpayer returns by IRS computers.

The IRS has a pilot audit program called the Security Messaging Taxpayer Digital Communication program which can be used in place of an audit through the mail. You communicate with an examiner through an online portal to respond to questions, attach requested documents, and resolve issues.

If the IRS wants to conduct an in-person audit, the complexity of the transactions reported on a return generally determines whether a return will be reviewed at an office or field examination.

Most in-person audits of individual returns, except for returns reporting self-employment income, are conducted at IRS offices. An office audit usually covers only a few specific issues which the IRS specifies in its notice to you.

Field audits generally involve business returns; they are more extensive and time-consuming than office audits and are handled by more experienced IRS agents. For self-employed individuals, most examinations are field audits at their place of business. It is advisable to have a tax professional go over the potential weak spots in your return and represent you at the examination.

Filing Tip

Authorize Someone to Represent You

Just above the signature section of your Form 1040 or 1040-SR, you may consent to contacts between the IRS and your designee to resolve return processing issues such as mathematical errors, missing return information, or questions about refunds or payments. The designee can be a friend or relative and need not be a tax professional. If you want to authorize someone to represent you at an audit or appeals procedure, or to handle collection notices, you must give that person a power of attorney on Form 2848. However, preparers who are not attorneys, CPAs, or enrolled agents cannot represent you before the IRS unless they participate in the IRS' Annual Filing Season Program.

48.4　Preparing for the Audit

After an office audit is scheduled, the first thing to do is look over your return to refresh your memory. Examine the items the IRS questioned in its notice of audit and organize your records accordingly. At this point, you should take a broad view of your return to anticipate problems you may encounter. Assume that the agent will assess additional tax, but establish the range you will consider reasonable. You can always change your mind, but giving some thought beforehand to possible settlement terms will help you later when settlements are actually discussed.

You may authorize an attorney, CPA, enrolled agent, or other individual recognized to practice before the IRS to represent you at the examination without you being present. To do so, give your representative authorization on Form 2848, Power of Attorney. An attorney or other representative authorized on Form 2848 can perform any acts that you could, including entering into a binding settlement agreement.

Caution: A preparer who is not an attorney, CPA or enrolled agent cannot represent you at an audit unless he or she has completed continuing education courses and received a Record of Completion as part of the IRS' Annual Filing Season Program (AFSP). Even with an AFSP Record of Completion, the preparer cannot represent you before IRS appeals or collection officers.

If you attend the audit, take only the records related to the items questioned in the IRS notice. If you are concerned that there may be a problem of fraud, *see* a qualified attorney before you come into contact with an IRS official. The attorney can put your actions in perspective and help protect your legal rights. Besides, what you tell an attorney is privileged information; he or she cannot divulge or be forced to divulge data you have provided, other than data used to prepare your tax return.

A field audit of your business return is likely to involve a comprehensive examination and requires careful preparation. Together with your tax adviser, go over your return for potential areas of weakness. The agent may suspect that a portion of these business deductions are actually nondeductible personal travel costs; be prepared to substantiate the business portion of your total mileage and operating expenses.

The IRS is generally required to hold an office audit at the office located nearest to your home. The IRS generally may not conduct a field audit at the site of a small business if the audit would essentially require the shutting down of the business, unless a direct visit is necessary to determine inventory or verify assets.

48.5　Handling the Audit

If you have authorized an individual to represent you at the examination, your representative may appear at the examination without you. If the IRS wants to question you, it must issue you an administrative summons. If you are present and questioned, you may stop the examination to consult with counsel, unless the examination is pursuant to an administrative summons.

The key to handling the audit is advance preparation. When you arrive at the IRS office, be prepared to produce your records quickly. Records should be organized by topic so that you do not waste time leafing through pages for a receipt or other document.

If the agent decides to question an item not mentioned in the notice of audit, refuse politely but firmly to answer the questions. Tell the agent that you must first review your records. If the agent insists on pursuing the matter, another meeting will have to be scheduled. The agent might decide it is not worth the time and drop the issue.

Common sense rules of courtesy should be your guide in your contacts with the agent. Avoid personality clashes; they can only interfere with a speedy and fair resolution of the examination. However, be firm in your approach and, if the agent appears to be unreasonable in his or her approach, make it clear that—if necessary—you will go all the way to court to win your point. A vacillating approach may weaken your position in reaching a settlement.

If the IRS has scheduled a field audit, ask that the examination be held at your representative's office. If you have not retained professional help and the examination takes place on your business premises, do not allow the agent free run of the area: Provide the agent with a comfortable work area for examining your records. If possible, the workplace

Planning Reminder

Audit Scheduling

Make sure that the examination is scheduled far enough in advance for you to get ready. Do not let the IRS hurry you into an examination until you are prepared. In some localities, particularly rural areas, the IRS may give short notice in scheduling a field audit. An agent may even appear at your place of business and try to begin the audit immediately. Resist this pressure and reschedule the meeting at your convenience.

should be isolated so that the agent can concentrate on the examination without being distracted by office operations that might spark questions. Tell your employees not to answer questions about your business or engage in small talk with the agent. As with an office audit, help speed along the field examination by having prepared your records so that requested information can be quickly produced.

Recording the examination. You have the right to make an audio recording of any interview with an IRS official. Video recordings are not permitted. No later than 10 calendar days before the interview, give written notice to the agent conducting the interview that you will make a recording. Later requests are at the discretion of the IRS. You must pay for all recording expenses and supply the equipment. The IRS may also make a recording of the interview, upon giving notice of at least 10 calendar days. However, IRS notice is not necessary if you have already submitted a request to make a recording. You have the right to obtain a transcript, at your own expense, of any recording made by the IRS. Generally, a request for a copy must be received by the IRS agent within 30 calendar days after the recording, although later requests may be honored.

48.6 Tax Penalties for Inaccurate Returns

As discussed in this section, an "accuracy-related" penalty applies to the portion of any tax underpayment attributable to any of the following: (1) negligence or disregard of IRS rules and regulations; (2) substantial understatement of tax liability; (3) overvaluation of property; (4) undervaluation of property on a gift tax or estate tax return; (5) claim of benefits from a transaction lacking economic substance, (6) an undisclosed foreign financial asset, or (7) claiming a basis for property in excess of the amount reported on an estate tax return. There is no stacking of penalties. Only one penalty can be imposed on a portion of an underpayment, even if that portion is attributable to more than one of the above types of prohibited conduct.

The above accuracy-related penalties generally may be avoided by showing that you acted in good faith and with reasonable cause in underpaying the tax. Reliance on a tax preparer may constitute reasonable cause and good faith, but the reliance on the preparer must be reasonable. The Tax Court has held that reliance on a preparer is not reasonable if the taxpayer does not provide the preparer with the documents necessary to make a professional conclusion, or if the preparer lacks sufficient expertise to justify reliance. A stricter reasonable cause exception applies to the penalty for overvaluing charitable donations or the basis of depreciable property; *see* below. There is no reasonable cause exception for penalties attributable to transactions lacking economic substance.

Also discussed below are penalties for (1) failing to disclose participation in "reportable" transactions, (2) understating tax liability on "listed" transactions or on other reportable transactions with a significant tax avoidance purpose, (3) filing an erroneous refund claim, and (4) filing a frivolous return.

Negligence or disregard of IRS rules or regulations. The 20% penalty applies to the portion of the underpayment attributable to negligence. Negligence is defined as failing to make a reasonable attempt to comply with the law. Failure to report income shown on an information return, such as interest or dividends, is considered strong evidence of negligence.

The 20% penalty may also apply if you take a position on a return which is contrary to IRS revenue rulings, notices, or regulations. This penalty for disregarding IRS rules or regulations may be avoided if you have a reasonable basis for your position and you disclose that position on Form 8275 or on Form 8275-R in the case of a good faith position contrary to a regulation. Thus, disclosure will not avoid a penalty for a position that does not have a reasonable basis.

Substantial understatement of tax. If you understate tax liability on a return by the greater of $5,000 or 10% of the proper tax, you may be subject to a penalty equal to 20% of the underpayment attributable to the understatement. If any QBI deduction *(40.24)* is claimed, the threshold is reduced from 10% to 5%.

 *Caution*

Too Good to Be True

If you claim a deduction, credit, or exclusion on your return that would seem, to a reasonable person, to be "too good to be true" under the circumstances, the IRS is likely to consider you negligent unless you show you made an attempt to verify the correctness of the position.

The penalty may be avoided if you have a reasonable basis for your position and you disclose the position to the IRS on Form 8275, or on Form 8275-R in the case of a position that is contrary to an IRS regulation.

The penalty also may be avoided if you can show that your position was supported by "substantial authority" such as statutes, court decisions, final, temporary, or proposed IRS regulations, IRS revenue rulings and procedures, and notices, announcements, and other administrative pronouncements published by the IRS in the weekly Internal Revenue Bulletin. You may also rely on IRS private letter rulings, technical advice memoranda, and FAQs as well as IRS actions on decisions and general counsel memoranda. However, according to the IRS, such rulings and internal IRS memoranda that are more than 10 years old should be accorded very little weight. Congressional committee reports and the tax law explanations prepared by Congress's Joint Committee on Taxation, known as the "Blue Book," may be relied on as authority for your position.

However, the exceptions for disclosed positions (with a reasonable basis) and substantial authority do not apply to items attributable to a tax shelter, which for this purpose means any arrangement that has tax avoidance or evasion as a significant purpose. An understatement of tax due to tax shelter positions may be subject to the understatement penalty for "reportable" transactions discussed below; if the understatement penalty for "reportable" transactions does apply, the 20% penalty discussed above for substantial understatements of tax does not apply to the same understatement.

Overvaluing donated property value or depreciable basis. If the claimed value of property donated to charity is 150% or more of the correct value, resulting in a tax underpayment exceeding $5,000, a penalty equal to 20% of the underpayment applies, and the penalty is doubled to 40% if the overvaluation is 200% or more. The same penalty thresholds and rates apply where the basis of depreciable property has been inflated. A reasonable cause exception to the 20% penalty is available (but not for the 40% penalty) if you relied on a qualified appraisal and you investigated the value of the property in good faith *(14.16)*.

Undervaluation on gift or estate tax return. If the value of property reported on a gift tax or estate tax return is 65% or less of the correct value, and the resulting tax underpayment from the undervaluation exceeds $5,000, the penalty is 20% of the underpayment. The penalty doubles to 40% of the underpayment if the claimed value of the property is 40% or less of the correct value.

Claiming benefits from transaction lacking economic substance. If you claim tax benefits from a transaction lacking economic substance, the penalty is 20% of the resulting underpayment. There is no reasonable cause exception for transactions lacking economic substance. The penalty doubles to 40% of the underpayment if the transaction is not adequately disclosed.

Understatement due to undisclosed foreign financial asset. A 40% accuracy-related penalty applies to the portion of a tax underpayment that is attributable to an undisclosed specified foreign financial asset. These are assets required to be reported on Form 8938, as discussed in *48.7*.

Claiming basis higher than estate tax value. As discussed in *5.17*, you are subject to a 20% penalty if you inherit property that increased the estate tax liability owed by the estate and you claim a basis for the property (such as when you sell or claim depreciation) that is higher than the estate tax value reported to you on Schedule A of Form 8971.

Penalties relating to reportable transactions. A penalty may be imposed on individuals and business entities who fail to adequately disclose a "reportable" transaction on Form 8886. This penalty is in addition to any other penalty that may be imposed. Some reportable transactions may fall into the category of "listed" transactions. The Form 8886 instructions explain the difference between listed transactions and other types of reportable transactions. The amount of the penalty for failure to disclose is generally 75% of the tax reduction claimed on the return as a result of the transaction, but there is a minimum penalty of $5,000 per reportable transaction (whether or not listed) for individuals ($10,000 for non-individual returns). There is also a maximum penalty: if the failure to disclose involves a reportable transaction that is not a listed transaction, the maximum penalty is $10,000 for individuals ($50,000 for non-individual returns). If the transaction is a listed transaction, the maximum penalty is $100,000 for individuals ($200,000 for non-individual returns).

There is a separate "accuracy-related" penalty for understating tax liability attributable to a listed transaction or to any reportable transaction (other than a listed transaction) with a significant tax avoidance purpose. The penalty is generally 20% of the understatement if the transaction was adequately disclosed on Form 8886. There is an exception for reasonable cause, but to qualify, stringent requirements must be met; *see* Code Section 6664(d). If the transaction was not adequately disclosed, the penalty increases to 30% of the understatement and there is no reasonable cause exception.

Fraud penalty. A 75% penalty applies to the portion of any tax underpayment due to fraud. If the IRS establishes that any part of an underpayment is due to fraud, the entire underpayment will be attributed to fraud, unless you prove otherwise.

Interest on penalties. A higher interest cost is imposed on individuals subject to the following penalties: failure to file a timely return *(46.9)*, negligence or fraud, overvaluation of property, undervaluation of gift or estate tax property, substantial understatement of tax liability, or understatements attributable to reportable transactions or undisclosed foreign financial assets. Interest starts to run on these penalties from the due date of the return (including extensions) until the date the penalty is paid. For other penalties, interest is imposed only if the penalty is not paid within 21 calendar days of an IRS demand for payment if the penalty is less than $100,000. The interest-free period is 10 business days after the IRS demand for payment if the penalty is $100,000 or more.

Penalty for filing erroneous refund claim or tax credit claim. A 20% penalty can apply to an erroneous tax credit or claim for refund on any original *(46.4)* or amended return *(47.8)*, but it does not apply to claims relating to the Earned Income Credit *(25.7)*. The penalty is 20% of the "excessive" amount, the excess of the refund or credit claimed over the amount allowed, unless there is a reasonable cause for the amount claimed. The penalty applies only where the IRS initially disallows part of the credit or refund at the time the return is processed. It does not apply to any portion of the excess that is subject to the accuracy-related penalties (including the penalty for understatements due to reportable or listed transactions), or the fraud penalty. If a refund is paid to a taxpayer and the IRS later determines that the refund was excessive, the accuracy-related or fraud penalty might apply, but the erroneous refund penalty would not apply since the IRS disallowance was after the issuance of the refund.

Penalty for frivolous tax return or submission. In addition to any other penalty, there is a $5,000 penalty for filing a frivolous tax return. A $5,000 penalty also applies to frivolous submissions, including requests for a collection due process hearing or an application for an installment agreement, offer-in-compromise, or Taxpayer Assistance Order based on a frivolous position. In Notice 2010-33, the IRS lists positions it considers frivolous. The IRS provides an in-depth rebuttal of frivolous positions at www.irs.gov/tax-professionals/the-truth-about-frivolous-tax-arguments-introduction.

Acting on wrong IRS advice. A penalty will not be imposed if you reasonably rely on erroneous advice provided in writing by IRS officials in response to your specific written request. It is necessary for you to show that you provided accurate information when asking for advice.

48.7 Penalties for Not Reporting Foreign Financial Accounts

If you have financial interests in foreign bank accounts or other foreign financial accounts or assets, you may be required to file a FBAR, Form 8938, or both. Depending on your holdings, you may be required to file both forms, so check the filing requirements for both. Failure to file a required form may result in substantial penalties.

FBAR. A Report of Foreign Bank and Financial Accounts, generally referred to as the "FBAR", must be filed if you have a financial interest in or signature authority over foreign bank or other financial accounts and the aggregate value of the accounts at any time during the year exceeds $10,000. The annual report is FinCEN Form 114, which is filed electronically with the Treasury Department. FinCEN is the Treasury's Financial Crimes Enforcement Network.

The FBAR, if required, is not filed with your income tax return. For 2023 foreign holdings, the FBAR report is due on April 15, 2024. The report is filed with the Treasury Department separately from the income tax return. There is an automatic 6-month filing extension for FinCEN Form 114; no form needs to be filed to obtain the extension.

In Part III of Schedule B (Form 1040 or 1040-SR) you must tell the IRS if you had a financial interest in or signature interest over a financial account located in a foreign country. If you answer yes, you are directed to the FBAR instructions to determine if you must file the form, and if you are required to file the FBAR, you are asked to enter the name of the foreign country where the financial account is located.

Penalties. If you are required to file a FBAR and fail to do so, a civil penalty of up to $10,000 per violation in 2023 (this amount is subject to inflation adjustments) may be imposed if the violation was not willful. The penalty may be waived if there was reasonable cause for the failure and a FBAR is properly filed. For a willful failure to file, the civil penalty per violation can be up to the greater of $100,000 in 2023 (this amount is subject to inflation adjustments) or 50% of the account balance at the time of the violation; criminal penalties may also apply.

Form 8938. Form 8938 must be filed with Form 1040 or 1040-SR if you have specified foreign financial assets (SFFAs) at the end of the year in excess of the applicable threshold. SFFAs include, in addition to financial accounts maintained by foreign financial institutions, foreign stocks and securities, financial instruments or contracts issued by a foreign party, and interests in certain foreign estates, trusts, and partnerships. The Form 8938 instructions have detailed definitions of SFFAs and exceptions.

The reporting threshold depends on whether you live in the U.S. or abroad and whether you are married filing jointly. For example, unmarried taxpayers living in the U.S., and married taxpayers filing separately and living in the U.S., must file Form 8938 with their 2023 Form 1040 (or 1040-SR) if the total value of their SFFAs on the last day of 2022 exceeded $50,000, or if the value exceeded $75,000 at any time in 2023. For married couples filing jointly and living in the U.S., reporting on Form 8938 is required if the year-end value of their SFFAs exceeded $100,000, or over $150,000 at any time during the year. For a U.S. citizen living abroad who has been a bona fide foreign resident for a full year or who meets a 330-day physical presence test, Form 8938 must be filed if the year-end value of SFFAs exceeded $200,000, or exceeded $300,000 at any time during the year; these thresholds are doubled to $400,000/$600,000 for married couples filing jointly. The Form 8938 instructions have examples of situations in which filing is and is not required.

Penalties. Failure to file Form 8938, or understating tax by omitting income attributable to an undisclosed SFFA, can result in substantial penalties.

There is a $10,000 penalty for not filing a complete and correct Form 8938 by the due date (including extensions) of your return, and a continuing failure to file within 90 days after receiving IRS notice to file may result in additional $10,000 penalties for each 30-day period, up to a maximum additional penalty of $50,000 (for a maximum penalty of $60,000). If you can show reasonable cause for not filing Form 8938 or not reporting one or more SFFAs, the penalty can be avoided.

As noted at *48.6*, an accuracy-related penalty may be imposed if you do not disclose an SFFA and income related to the undisclosed SFFA is not reported on your return. The penalty is 40% of the tax underpayment resulting from the omission of income. The penalty can be avoided if you can show reasonable cause for the underpayment. An underpayment due to fraud is subject to a 75% penalty.

Caution

Penalty Per Account or Per Form?

On February 28, 2023, the Federal courts decided the civil penalty for non-willful failure to file a required FBAR report is applied on a per form basis.

48.8 Agreeing to the Audit Changes

After the audit, the agent will discuss proposed changes either with you or your representative.

If you agree with the agent's proposed changes, you will be asked to sign a Form 870, which, when signed, permits an immediate assessment of a deficiency plus penalties and interest, if due. The Form 870 is called "Waiver of Restrictions on Assessment and Collection of Deficiency in Tax and Acceptance of Overassessment."

If you believe that you have done as well or better than expected regarding the proposed deficiency, you can bring the case to a close by signing the Form 870, but the agent's supervisor must also approve the assessment.

By signing the form, you limit the amount of interest charges added to the deficiency. A signed Form 870 does not prevent the IRS from reopening the case to assess an additional deficiency. If on review the deficiency is increased, you will receive a revised Form 870. You can refuse to sign the form. The signed first form has the effect of stopping the interest on the original deficiency. As a matter of practice, however, waivers of acceptances ordinarily result in closing of the case.

It is possible, although unlikely, that upon examining your return, the agent will determine that you are due a refund. In this situation, a signed Form 870 is considered a valid refund claim. You should file a protective refund claim even if you sign the Form 870 acknowledging the overpayment. Generally, the agent will process the refund, but if he or she fails to do so or the review staff puts it aside for some reason and the limitations period expires, the refund will be lost. The refund claim will protect you from such a mishap.

The payment of tax before the deficiency notice (90-day letter) is mailed is, in effect, a waiver of the restrictions on assessment and collection. If the payment satisfies your entire tax liability for that year, you cannot appeal to the Tax Court. You must sue for a refund in either federal district court or the Court of Federal Claims.

48.9 Disputing the Audit Changes

If you disagree with the agent and the examination takes place in an IRS office, you may ask for an immediate meeting with a supervisor to argue your side of the dispute. If an agreement is not reached at this meeting or the audit is at your office or home, the agent prepares a report of the proposed adjustments. You will receive a 30-day letter in which you are given the opportunity to request a conference. You may decide not to ask for a conference and await a formal notice of deficiency (90-day letter).

Appeals conference. If your examination was conducted as an office audit or by correspondence, or the disputed amount does not exceed $25,000, you do not have to prepare a written protest for a conference with the IRS Independent Office of Appeals. The written protest is a detailed presentation of your reasons for disagreeing with the agent's report. Even where a formal written protest is not required, you must provide a brief written statement indicating your reasons for disagreeing with the agent when you request an appeals conference; you can use Form 12203 (Request for Appeals Review).

At the conference you may appear for yourself or be represented by an attorney or other agent, and you may bring witnesses. The conference is held in an informal manner and you are given ample opportunity to present your case.

If you cannot reach a settlement, you will receive a Notice of Deficiency, commonly called a 90-day letter. In it, you are notified that at the end of 90 days from the date it was mailed, the government will assess the additional tax.

Interest abatement. An IRS delay in completing an audit increases the interest that you have to pay when a deficiency notice is eventually issued. You may ask the IRS on Form 843 for an abatement of interest charges that are attributable to unreasonable errors or delays by IRS employees in performing a ministerial or managerial act.

A ministerial act is defined as a procedural or mechanical act that does not involve the exercise of an IRS employee's discretion or judgment, such as the transfer of a taxpayer's case to a different IRS office after the transfer is approved by a group manager. A managerial act refers to the exercise of discretion or judgment by an IRS employee in managing personnel.

Caution

Waiving Your Right to Appeal

Before deciding whether to sign the Form 870, consider that, by signing, you are giving up your right of appeal to both the IRS Office of Appeals and the Tax Court. However, you may still file a refund suit in a federal district court or in the Court of Federal Claims unless you have agreed not to do so on the Form 870.

Caution

Penalty for Frivolous Tax Court Action

If you bring a case to the Tax Court that the Court concludes is frivolous or brought primarily for delay, or you unreasonably failed to pursue IRS administrative remedies, the Tax Court may impose a penalty of up to $25,000. Furthermore, if you appeal a Tax Court decision and the federal appeals court or the Supreme Court finds that the appeal was frivolous or brought primarily for delay, the Court may impose a penalty.

Caution

Don't Be Duped by OIC Mills

The IRS noted in its 2023 list of the Dirty Dozen Tax Scams the use of OIC mills. These promise the unwary that they'll escape tax debt for pennies on the dollar, while the mills collect fees and don't deliver on the promise.

Misplacing the taxpayer's case file is also a managerial act. General IRS administrative decisions, such as prioritizing the order of processing returns, or decisions on applying the tax law, that result in delay, are not ministerial or management acts for which interest abatement is available.

If you make a request on Form 843 for an abatement of interest and the IRS rejects your claim, you can petition the Tax Court within 180 days to review whether the IRS abused its discretion, provided that your net worth does not exceed $2 million ($7 million for businesses). The same net worth limit applies to recoveries of administrative and litigation costs; *see 48.10*. The Tax Court has exclusive jurisdiction to review the denial of the interest abatement request; an appeal of the IRS decision cannot be brought in a federal district court or the U.S. Court of Claims.

Going to court. Within 90 days from the date a 90-day letter (notice of deficiency) is mailed to you (150 days if it is addressed to you outside the United States), you may file a petition with the Tax Court without having to pay the tax. The Tax Court has a small tax case procedure for deficiencies of $50,000 or less. Such cases are handled expeditiously and informally. Cases may be heard by appointed special trial judges. A small claim case may be discontinued at any time before a decision, but the decision when made is final. No appeal may be taken by you or the IRS.

Instead of petitioning the Tax Court, you may pay the additional tax, file a refund claim for it, and—after the refund claim is denied—sue for a refund in a federal district court or the U.S. Court of Federal Claims.

You should consult with an experienced tax practitioner before deciding to litigate.

48.10 Offer in Compromise

If you are unable to pay a tax debt in full, you may be able to make an offer in compromise (OIC), but it should be considered a last resort. An OIC is an agreement between a taxpayer and the IRS in which the IRS accepts less than full payment of the outstanding tax liabilities as settlement of the tax debt.

However, the number of accepted offers has declined steadily, and the National Taxpayer Advocate believes that taxpayers are deterred from applying by the burdensome disclosure and other application requirements. There is generally a $205 application fee (some exceptions apply) that the IRS will keep unless the offer cannot be processed. There also is a requirement to submit a nonrefundable payment with the offer on Form 656, and this has been strongly criticized as a major reason for reducing access to the OIC program.

There are two payment options. You can make an up-front payment on Form 656 equal to 20% of a lump-sum offer, with the balance payable in five or fewer installments within five months of IRS acceptance. Alternatively, you may choose the periodic payment option, which requires you to submit the first proposed payment with Form 656 and pay the rest of your offer within 24 months. You must make regular payments in accordance with your proposed offer while the IRS considers your application. These upfront payments are not refundable even if you withdraw the offer prior to IRS acceptance or the IRS rejects the offer; they will be applied to your tax debt.

The only exceptions to the application fee and upfront payment requirements are for (1) low-income individuals who certify that their income is below poverty guidelines, and (2) taxpayers who file an offer on Form 656-L based on doubt as to liability. The IRS as well as the Treasury Department and Taxpayer Advocate have called on Congress for legislation to eliminate mandatory upfront payments.

Grounds for an Offer in Compromise. The IRS has authority to settle or "compromise" for one of the following reasons: Doubt as to liability, doubt as to collectibility, and effective tax administration. Doubt as to liability means that doubt exists concerning the correctness of the IRS' tax assessment. Doubt as to collectibility means that you may never be able to pay the full amount of tax owed. Even where there is no doubt that you owe the tax and you could manage full repayment, you can apply for an OIC on "effective tax administration" grounds if collection of the full tax would cause you economic hardship or there are exceptional circumstances that would make full collection unfair and inequitable.

Applying for an Offer in Compromise on Form 656 or 656-L. You must submit an OIC on Form 656 where the offer is based on doubt as to collectibility or effective tax administration (exceptional circumstances). The IRS will consider the OIC only after other payment options have been exhausted, including an installment agreement. An OIC based on doubt as to liability must be filed on Form 656-L; there is no application fee or upfront payment requirement for an offer made on Form 656-L.

When you submit an OIC on Form 656, you must make an upfront payment unless the exception for low-income taxpayers applies as discussed above. Form 656-B, the OIC booklet, includes an explanation of the OIC program and instructions for completing Form 656. The booklet also includes financial disclosure statements that must be attached to support an OIC based on doubt as to collectibility or effective tax administration. Wage earners and self-employed individuals must use Form 433-A, while partnerships and corporations use Form 433-B. In some cases, the IRS may request Form 433-A from corporate officers or individual partners. Form 656-B is available online at IRS.gov or can be obtained by calling (800) 829-3676.

If your offer is rejected, you will be given an opportunity to appeal the decision and to amend the offer.

Application fee. An application fee must be paid with Form 656 unless you certify in Section 1 of Form 656 that your total monthly income is at or below federal poverty guidelines (Section 1 has a table showing the monthly income limits based on family size). The fee is $205. No fee is required for an offer made on Form 656-L based on doubt as to liability.

Compliance conditions. If the IRS accepts an OIC, you must pay the agreed-to amount in accordance with the acceptance agreement and must timely file and pay all required taxes for a period of five years from the acceptance date, or until the accepted amount is paid in full, whichever is longer. You may also be asked as part of the agreement to pay a percentage of your future earnings to the IRS. A failure to comply with the agreement causes default of the OIC and the reinstatement of the original liability.

48.11 Recovering Costs of a Tax Dispute

In a tax dispute, you may believe that the IRS has taken an unreasonable position, forcing you to incur legal fees and other expenses to win your case. You may be able to recover all or part of—

1. Reasonable administrative costs of proceedings within the IRS, and
2. Reasonable litigation costs in a court proceeding.

A judgment for reasonable litigation costs will not be awarded in any court proceeding if you did not exhaust all IRS administrative remedies. A refusal by the taxpayer to agree to an extension of time for a tax assessment is not a bar to an award, but unreasonably delaying the proceedings is.

You may not recover costs if your net worth at the time the action begins exceeds $2 million. The $2 million net worth limit applies separately to each spouse in determining whether a married couple filing jointly is entitled to recover legal fees. No recovery is allowed to sole proprietors, partnerships, and corporations if their net worth exceeds $7 million or they have more than 500 employees.

To receive an award, you must "substantially prevail" as to the key issues in the case or the amount of tax involved. If you do, you will be entitled to a recovery unless the IRS proves that it was "substantially justified" in maintaining the position that it did. You may be treated as the prevailing party if a court determines that your liability is equal to or less than an amount that you offered in settlement. The offer must be considered a qualified offer made during a period that begins on the date of the first letter of proposed deficiency allowing for an IRS administrative appeal and ends 30 days before the date first set for trial.

The Tax Court and other courts have interpreted "substantially justified" to be a reasonableness standard. The IRS is presumed not to be "substantially justified" if it does not follow its own published regulations, revenue rulings, procedures, notices, announcements, or a private ruling issued to the taxpayer. The IRS may try to rebut the presumption. A court may also consider whether an IRS position has been rejected by federal courts of appeal of other circuits in determining whether the IRS position was substantially justified.

 *Filing Tip*

Appealing Rejected Offer

You can appeal a rejection within 30 days by filing Form 13711, "Request for Appeal of Offer in Compromise."

 *Planning Reminder*

Recovering Attorneys' Fees

Attorneys' fees include the fees paid by a taxpayer for the services of anyone who is authorized to practice before the Tax Court or IRS.

Reasonable administrative costs include IRS fees, reasonable fees for witnesses and experts, and attorneys' fees subject to the annual limit; *see* below. The IRS determines the amount of such an award, which may include costs incurred from the date the IRS sent its first letter of a proposed deficiency allowing you to ask for an administrative appeal. For an award of administrative costs, you must file an application with the IRS before the 91st day after the date on which the IRS mailed you its final decision. To appeal a denial of your application, you must petition the Tax Court within 90 days from the date the IRS mailed the denial.

Reasonable litigation costs include reasonable court costs, fees of witnesses and experts, and attorneys' fees. Fees of witnesses may not exceed the rate paid by the U.S. government. For attorneys' fees incurred in 2023, the limit is $250 per hour. For 2022, the limit was $220, and in 2020 and 2021, the limit was $210 per hour. The court may also increase the award for attorneys' fees to account for special factors, such as the difficulty of the issues and the availability of local tax expertise. However, an attorney's general expertise in tax law or experience in tax litigation is not in itself a special factor warranting a higher fee award.

You may not recover attorneys' fees if you represent yourself (pro se). However, you are still entitled to recover fees for witnesses and experts. If you represent a prevailing taxpayer on a pro bono basis or for a nominal fee, a court may award you or your employer reasonable attorneys' fees.

48.12 Suing the IRS for Unauthorized Collection

If an IRS employee or officer recklessly, intentionally, or negligently disregards the law or IRS regulations when taking a collection action, you may sue the IRS in federal district court for actual economic damages resulting from the IRS employee's misconduct, plus certain costs of bringing the action. The lawsuit must be filed within two years of the date that the unauthorized collection action was taken.

For negligent IRS collection activities, you may sue for damages of up to $100,000, and for reckless or intentional misconduct, the maximum damage award is $1 million. Administrative remedies must be exhausted to obtain an award.

According to IRS regulations, actual economic damages that may be recovered are monetary losses you suffer as a direct result of the IRS' action. For example, a business may lose loyal customers and suffer an actual cash loss if the IRS' action damages the business's reputation. Other actual expenses could include the cost of renting a house or a car if the IRS puts a lien on or seizes your property, or loss of income due to the garnishment of your paycheck. Damages from the IRS for loss of reputation, inconvenience, or emotional distress are allowed only to the extent that they result in such actual monetary loss.

The IRS defines "costs of action" that you may recover as (1) fees of the clerk and marshall; (2) fees of the court reporter; (3) fees and disbursements for printing and witnesses; (4) copying fees; (5) docket fees; and (6) compensation for court-appointed experts and interpreters.

Litigation costs and administrative proceeding costs are not treated as "costs of the action." However, if the IRS denies your administrative claim for damages and you successfully sue in federal district court, you are considered a "prevailing party" and may recover attorneys' fees, related litigation expenses, and administrative costs before the IRS as discussed in *48.11*.

Caution

Penalty for Frivolous Action

If you bring an action in federal district court for unauthorized collection activities that the court considers to be frivolous, it may impose a penalty of up to $10,000.

Planning Reminder

IRS Failure to Release Lien

A suit for damages may also be brought in federal district court against the IRS if IRS employees improperly fail to release a lien on your property. Before you sue, you must file an administrative claim for damages. The lawsuit must be filed within two years after your claim arose. You may sue for actual economic damages plus costs of the action; the types of damages that may be recovered are similar to those discussed for suing the IRS for unauthorized collection actions.

PART 8

2023 Tax Forms

In the following pages, you will find Form 1040, Form 1040-SR, and selected Schedules and Forms, which are subject to change. The final versions of these and other Forms and tax return-related materials will be available from the IRS website, IRS.gov, and in the *e-Supplement* at *jklasser.com*.

Form 1040 Department of the Treasury—Internal Revenue Service
U.S. Individual Income Tax Return **2023** OMB No. 1545-0074 IRS Use Only—Do not write or staple in this space.

For the year Jan. 1–Dec. 31, 2023, or other tax year beginning _____, 2023, ending _____, 20 _____ See separate instructions.

Your first name and middle initial	Last name	Your social security number

If joint return, spouse's first name and middle initial	Last name	Spouse's social security number

Home address (number and street). If you have a P.O. box, see instructions. | Apt. no.

City, town, or post office. If you have a foreign address, also complete spaces below. | State | ZIP code

Foreign country name | Foreign province/state/county | Foreign postal code

Presidential Election Campaign
Check here if you, or your spouse if filing jointly, want $3 to go to this fund. Checking a box below will not change your tax or refund.
☐ You ☐ Spouse

Filing Status
Check only one box.

☐ Single ☐ Head of household (HOH)
☐ Married filing jointly (even if only one had income)
☐ Married filing separately (MFS) ☐ Qualifying surviving spouse (QSS)

If you checked the MFS box, enter the name of your spouse. If you checked the HOH or QSS box, enter the child's name if the qualifying person is a child but not your dependent: _____

Digital Assets
At any time during 2023, did you: (a) receive (as a reward, award, or payment for property or services); or (b) sell, exchange, or otherwise dispose of a digital asset (or a financial interest in a digital asset)? (See instructions.) ☐ Yes ☐ No

Standard Deduction
Someone can claim: ☐ You as a dependent ☐ Your spouse as a dependent
☐ Spouse itemizes on a separate return or you were a dual-status alien

Age/Blindness **You:** ☐ Were born before January 2, 1959 ☐ Are blind **Spouse:** ☐ Was born before January 2, 1959 ☐ Is blind

Dependents (see instructions):
If more than four dependents, see instructions and check here ☐

(1) First name Last name	(2) Social security number	(3) Relationship to you	(4) Check the box if qualifies for (see instructions):	
			Child tax credit	Credit for other dependents
			☐	☐
			☐	☐
			☐	☐
			☐	☐

Income

Attach Form(s) W-2 here. Also attach Forms W-2G and 1099-R if tax was withheld.

If you did not get a Form W-2, see instructions.

1a	Total amount from Form(s) W-2, box 1 (see instructions)	1a
b	Household employee wages not reported on Form(s) W-2	1b
c	Tip income not reported on line 1a (see instructions)	1c
d	Medicaid waiver payments not reported on Form(s) W-2 (see instructions)	1d
e	Taxable dependent care benefits from Form 2441, line 26	1e
f	Employer-provided adoption benefits from Form 8839, line 29	1f
g	Wages from Form 8919, line 6	1g
h	Other earned income (see instructions)	1h
i	Nontaxable combat pay election (see instructions) . . . 1i	
z	Add lines 1a through 1h	1z

Attach Sch. B if required.

2a	Tax-exempt interest . . .	2a	b Taxable interest	2b
3a	Qualified dividends . . .	3a	b Ordinary dividends	3b
4a	IRA distributions . . .	4a	b Taxable amount	4b
5a	Pensions and annuities . .	5a	b Taxable amount	5b
6a	Social security benefits . .	6a	b Taxable amount	6b

Standard Deduction for—
• Single or Married filing separately, $13,850
• Married filing jointly or Qualifying surviving spouse, $27,700
• Head of household, $20,800
• If you checked any box under *Standard Deduction,* see instructions.

c	If you elect to use the lump-sum election method, check here (see instructions) ☐	
7	Capital gain or (loss). Attach Schedule D if required. If not required, check here ☐	7
8	Additional income from Schedule 1, line 10	8
9	Add lines 1z, 2b, 3b, 4b, 5b, 6b, 7, and 8. This is your **total income**	9
10	Adjustments to income from Schedule 1, line 26	10
11	Subtract line 10 from line 9. This is your **adjusted gross income**	11
12	Standard deduction or itemized deductions (from Schedule A)	12
13	Qualified business income deduction from Form 8995 or Form 8995-A	13
14	Add lines 12 and 13	14
15	Subtract line 14 from line 11. If zero or less, enter -0-. This is your **taxable income**	15

For Disclosure, Privacy Act, and Paperwork Reduction Act Notice, see separate instructions. Cat. No. 11320B Form **1040** (2023)

Form 1040 (2023)   Page **2**

Tax and Credits	16	**Tax** (see instructions). Check if any from Form(s): **1** ☐ 8814 **2** ☐ 4972 **3** ☐ _____	16
	17	Amount from Schedule 2, line 3	17
	18	Add lines 16 and 17	18
	19	Child tax credit or credit for other dependents from Schedule 8812	19
	20	Amount from Schedule 3, line 8	20
	21	Add lines 19 and 20	21
	22	Subtract line 21 from line 18. If zero or less, enter -0-	22
	23	Other taxes, including self-employment tax, from Schedule 2, line 21	23
	24	Add lines 22 and 23. This is your **total tax**	24

Payments	25	Federal income tax withheld from:		
	a	Form(s) W-2	25a	
	b	Form(s) 1099	25b	
	c	Other forms (see instructions)	25c	
	d	Add lines 25a through 25c		25d
If you have a qualifying child, attach Sch. EIC.	26	2023 estimated tax payments and amount applied from 2022 return		26
	27	Earned income credit (EIC)	27	
	28	Additional child tax credit from Schedule 8812	28	
	29	American opportunity credit from Form 8863, line 8	29	
	30	Reserved for future use	30	
	31	Amount from Schedule 3, line 15	31	
	32	Add lines 27, 28, 29, and 31. These are your **total other payments and refundable credits**		32
	33	Add lines 25d, 26, and 32. These are your **total payments**		33

Refund	34	If line 33 is more than line 24, subtract line 24 from line 33. This is the amount you **overpaid**		34
	35a	Amount of line 34 you want **refunded to you**. If Form 8888 is attached, check here ☐		35a
Direct deposit? See instructions.	b	Routing number	**c** Type: ☐ Checking ☐ Savings	
	d	Account number		
	36	Amount of line 34 you want **applied to your 2024 estimated tax**	36	

Amount You Owe	37	Subtract line 33 from line 24. This is the **amount you owe.** For details on how to pay, go to *www.irs.gov/Payments* or see instructions	37
	38	Estimated tax penalty (see instructions)	38

Third Party Designee

Do you want to allow another person to discuss this return with the IRS? See instructions . . . .   ☐ **Yes.** Complete below.   ☐ **No**

Designee's name _____   Phone no. _____   Personal identification number (PIN) ☐☐☐☐☐☐

Sign Here

Under penalties of perjury, I declare that I have examined this return and accompanying schedules and statements, and to the best of my knowledge and belief, they are true, correct, and complete. Declaration of preparer (other than taxpayer) is based on all information of which preparer has any knowledge.

Joint return? See instructions. Keep a copy for your records.

Your signature	Date	Your occupation	If the IRS sent you an Identity Protection PIN, enter it here (see inst.) ☐☐☐☐☐☐
Spouse's signature. If a joint return, **both** must sign.	Date	Spouse's occupation	If the IRS sent your spouse an Identity Protection PIN, enter it here (see inst.) ☐☐☐☐☐☐

Phone no. _____   Email address _____

Paid Preparer Use Only

Preparer's name	Preparer's signature	Date	PTIN	Check if: ☐ Self-employed
Firm's name			Phone no.	
Firm's address			Firm's EIN	

Go to *www.irs.gov/Form1040* for instructions and the latest information.   Form **1040** (2023)

Form **1040-SR**

Department of the Treasury—Internal Revenue Service
U.S. Tax Return for Seniors

2023 | OMB No. 1545-0074 | IRS Use Only—Do not write or staple in this space.

For the year Jan. 1–Dec. 31, 2023, or other tax year beginning _____, 2023, ending _____, 20_____ | See separate instructions.

Your first name and middle initial	Last name	Your social security number

If joint return, spouse's first name and middle initial	Last name	Spouse's social security number

Home address (number and street). If you have a P.O. box, see instructions. | Apt. no.

City, town, or post office. If you have a foreign address, also complete spaces below. | State | ZIP code

Foreign country name | Foreign province/state/county | Foreign postal code

Presidential Election Campaign
Check here if you, or your spouse if filing jointly, want $3 to go to this fund. Checking a box below will not change your tax or refund.
☐ You ☐ Spouse

Filing Status
Check only one box.

☐ Single   ☐ Married filing jointly (even if only one had income)   ☐ Married filing separately (MFS)
☐ Head of household (HOH)   ☐ Qualifying surviving spouse (QSS)

If you checked the MFS box, enter the name of your spouse. If you checked the HOH or QSS box, enter the child's name if the qualifying person is a child but not your dependent: _____

Digital Assets

At any time during 2023, did you: (a) receive (as a reward, award, or payment for property or services); or (b) sell, exchange, or otherwise dispose of a digital asset (or a financial interest in a digital asset)? (See instructions.) . . . . ☐ Yes ☐ No

Standard Deduction

Someone can claim: ☐ You as a dependent   ☐ Your spouse as a dependent
☐ Spouse itemizes on a separate return or you were a dual-status alien

Age/Blindness { **You:** ☐ Were born before January 2, 1959 ☐ Are blind
Spouse: ☐ Was born before January 2, 1959 ☐ Is blind

Dependents (see instructions):

(1) First name Last name	(2) Social security number	(3) Relationship to you	(4) Check the box if qualifies for (see instructions):	
			Child tax credit	Credit for other dependents
			☐	☐
			☐	☐
			☐	☐
			☐	☐

If more than four dependents, see instructions and check here ☐

Income

Attach Form(s) W-2 here. Also attach Forms W-2G and 1099-R if tax was withheld.

If you did not get a Form W-2, see instructions.

1a	Total amount from Form(s) W-2, box 1 (see instructions)	**1a**	
b	Household employee wages not reported on Form(s) W-2	**1b**	
c	Tip income not reported on line 1a (see instructions)	**1c**	
d	Medicaid waiver payments not reported on Form(s) W-2 (see instructions)	**1d**	
e	Taxable dependent care benefits from Form 2441, line 26	**1e**	
f	Employer-provided adoption benefits from Form 8839, line 29	**1f**	
g	Wages from Form 8919, line 6	**1g**	
h	Other earned income (see instructions)	**1h**	
i	Nontaxable combat pay election (see instructions) .	1i		
z	Add lines 1a through 1h	**1z**	

Attach Schedule B if required.

2a	Tax-exempt interest .	2a		**b** Taxable interest . .	**2b**
3a	Qualified dividends . .	3a		**b** Ordinary dividends .	**3b**
4a	IRA distributions . . .	4a		**b** Taxable amount . .	**4b**
5a	Pensions and annuities	5a		**b** Taxable amount . .	**5b**
6a	Social security benefits .	6a		**b** Taxable amount . .	**6b**
c	If you elect to use the lump-sum election method, check here (see instructions) . . . . ☐				

For Disclosure, Privacy Act, and Paperwork Reduction Act Notice, see separate instructions. | Cat. No. 71930F | Form **1040-SR** (2023)

Form 1040-SR

7	Capital gain or (loss). Attach Schedule D if required. If not required, check here . . . . ☐	**7**
8	Additional income from Schedule 1, line 10	**8**
9	Add lines 1z, 2b, 3b, 4b, 5b, 6b, 7, and 8. This is your **total income** . .	**9**
10	Adjustments to income from Schedule 1, line 26	**10**
11	Subtract line 10 from line 9. This is your **adjusted gross income** . . .	**11**
12	**Standard deduction or itemized deductions** (from Schedule A) . . .	**12**
13	Qualified business income deduction from Form 8995 or Form 8995-A .	**13**
14	Add lines 12 and 13	**14**
15	Subtract line 14 from line 11. If zero or less, enter -0-. This is your **taxable income**	**15**

Standard Deduction
See *Standard Deduction Chart* on the last page of this form.

Tax and Credits

16	**Tax** (see instructions). Check if any from:	
	1 ☐ Form(s) 8814 **2** ☐ Form(s) 4972 **3** ☐ _____	**16**
17	Amount from Schedule 2, line 3	**17**
18	Add lines 16 and 17	**18**
19	Child tax credit or credit for other dependents from Schedule 8812 . .	**19**
20	Amount from Schedule 3, line 8	**20**
21	Add lines 19 and 20	**21**
22	Subtract line 21 from line 18. If zero or less, enter -0-	**22**
23	Other taxes, including self-employment tax, from Schedule 2, line 21 . .	**23**
24	Add lines 22 and 23. This is your **total tax**	**24**

Payments

25	Federal income tax withheld from:		
a	Form(s) W-2	**25a**	
b	Form(s) 1099	**25b**	
c	Other forms (see instructions)	**25c**	
d	Add lines 25a through 25c		**25d**
26	2023 estimated tax payments and amount applied from 2022 return . .		**26**

If you have a qualifying child, attach Sch. EIC.

27	Earned income credit (EIC)	**27**	
28	Additional child tax credit from Schedule 8812 . . .	**28**	
29	American opportunity credit from Form 8863, line 8 .	**29**	
30	Reserved for future use	**30**	
31	Amount from Schedule 3, line 15	**31**	
32	Add lines 27, 28, 29, and 31. These are your **total other payments and refundable credits**		**32**
33	Add lines 25d, 26, and 32. These are your **total payments**		**33**

Go to *www.irs.gov/Form1040SR* for instructions and the latest information.   Form **1040-SR** (2023)

Refund	34	If line 33 is more than line 24, subtract line 24 from line 33. This is the amount you **overpaid**	**34**	
	35a	Amount of line 34 you want **refunded to you**. If Form 8888 is attached, check here . . . . ☐	**35a**	

Direct deposit? See instructions.

b Routing number | | | | | | | | | | | **c** Type: ☐ Checking ☐ Savings

d Account number | | | | | | | | | | | | | | | | |

	36	Amount of line 34 you want **applied to your 2024 estimated tax**	36		

Amount You Owe	37	Subtract line 33 from line 24. This is the **amount you owe**. For details on how to pay, go to *www.irs.gov/Payments* or see instructions	**37**	
	38	Estimated tax penalty (see instructions)	38		

Third Party Designee	Do you want to allow another person to discuss this return with the IRS? See instructions . . . . ☐ **Yes.** Complete below. ☐ **No**

Designee's name

Phone no.

Personal identification number (PIN) | | | | |

Sign Here	Under penalties of perjury, I declare that I have examined this return and accompanying schedules and statements, and to the best of my knowledge and belief, they are true, correct, and complete. Declaration of preparer (other than taxpayer) is based on all information of which preparer has any knowledge.

Joint return? See instructions. Keep a copy for your records.

Your signature	Date	Your occupation	If the IRS sent you an Identity Protection PIN, enter it here (see inst.)					
Spouse's signature. If a joint return, **both** must sign.	Date	Spouse's occupation	If the IRS sent your spouse an Identity Protection PIN, enter it here (see inst.)					
Phone no.		Email address						

Paid Preparer Use Only	Preparer's name	Preparer's signature	Date	PTIN	Check if: ☐ Self-employed
	Firm's name			Phone no.	
	Firm's address			Firm's EIN	

Go to *www.irs.gov/Form1040SR* for instructions and the latest information.

Form **1040-SR** (2023)

Form 1040-SR

Standard Deduction Chart*

Add the number of boxes checked in the "Age/Blindness" section of *Standard Deduction* on page 1 . . . . . .

IF your filing status is. . .	AND the number of boxes checked is. . .	THEN your standard deduction is. . .
Single	1	$15,700
	2	17,550
Married filing jointly	1	$29,200
	2	30,700
	3	32,200
	4	33,700
Qualifying surviving spouse	1	$29,200
	2	30,700
Head of household	1	$22,650
	2	24,500
Married filing separately**	1	$15,350
	2	16,850
	3	18,350
	4	19,850

*Don't use this chart if someone can claim you (or your spouse if filing jointly) as a dependent, your spouse itemizes on a separate return, or you were a dual-status alien. Instead, see instructions.

**You can check the boxes for your spouse if your filing status is married filing separately and your spouse had no income, isn't filing a return, and can't be claimed as a dependent on another person's return.

Go to *www.irs.gov/Form1040SR* for instructions and the latest information.   Form **1040-SR** (2023)

<table>
<tr><td>SCHEDULE 1
(Form 1040)

Department of the Treasury
Internal Revenue Service</td><td>**Additional Income and Adjustments to Income**

Attach to Form 1040, 1040-SR, or 1040-NR.
Go to *www.irs.gov/Form1040* for instructions and the latest information.</td><td>OMB No. 1545-0074
2023
Attachment
Sequence No. **01**</td></tr>
</table>

Name(s) shown on Form 1040, 1040-SR, or 1040-NR	Your social security number

Part I — Additional Income

1	Taxable refunds, credits, or offsets of state and local income taxes	**1**	
2a	Alimony received	**2a**	
b	Date of original divorce or separation agreement (see instructions): _____		
3	Business income or (loss). Attach Schedule C	**3**	
4	Other gains or (losses). Attach Form 4797	**4**	
5	Rental real estate, royalties, partnerships, S corporations, trusts, etc. Attach Schedule E .	**5**	
6	Farm income or (loss). Attach Schedule F	**6**	
7	Unemployment compensation	**7**	
8	Other income:		

a	Net operating loss	**8a** (	)
b	Gambling	**8b**	
c	Cancellation of debt	**8c**	
d	Foreign earned income exclusion from Form 2555	**8d** (	)
e	Income from Form 8853	**8e**	
f	Income from Form 8889	**8f**	
g	Alaska Permanent Fund dividends	**8g**	
h	Jury duty pay	**8h**	
i	Prizes and awards	**8i**	
j	Activity not engaged in for profit income	**8j**	
k	Stock options	**8k**	
l	Income from the rental of personal property if you engaged in the rental for profit but were not in the business of renting such property . . .	**8l**	
m	Olympic and Paralympic medals and USOC prize money (see instructions)	**8m**	
n	Section 951(a) inclusion (see instructions)	**8n**	
o	Section 951A(a) inclusion (see instructions)	**8o**	
p	Section 461(l) excess business loss adjustment	**8p**	
q	Taxable distributions from an ABLE account (see instructions) . . .	**8q**	
r	Scholarship and fellowship grants not reported on Form W-2 . . .	**8r**	
s	Nontaxable amount of Medicaid waiver payments included on Form 1040, line 1a or 1d	**8s** (	)
t	Pension or annuity from a nonqualifed deferred compensation plan or a nongovernmental section 457 plan	**8t**	
u	Wages earned while incarcerated	**8u**	
z	Other income. List type and amount: _____	**8z**	

9	Total other income. Add lines 8a through 8z	**9**	
10	Combine lines 1 through 7 and 9. This is your **additional income**. Enter here and on Form 1040, 1040-SR, or 1040-NR, line 8	**10**	

For Paperwork Reduction Act Notice, see your tax return instructions. Cat. No. 71479F **Schedule 1 (Form 1040) 2023**

Part II   Adjustments to Income

11	Educator expenses	**11**	
12	Certain business expenses of reservists, performing artists, and fee-basis government officials. Attach Form 2106	**12**	
13	Health savings account deduction. Attach Form 8889	**13**	
14	Moving expenses for members of the Armed Forces. Attach Form 3903	**14**	
15	Deductible part of self-employment tax. Attach Schedule SE	**15**	
16	Self-employed SEP, SIMPLE, and qualified plans	**16**	
17	Self-employed health insurance deduction	**17**	
18	Penalty on early withdrawal of savings	**18**	
19a	Alimony paid	**19a**	
b	Recipient's SSN		
c	Date of original divorce or separation agreement (see instructions): _____		
20	IRA deduction	**20**	
21	Student loan interest deduction	**21**	
22	Reserved for future use	**22**	
23	Archer MSA deduction	**23**	

24   Other adjustments:

a	Jury duty pay (see instructions)	**24a**	
b	Deductible expenses related to income reported on line 8l from the rental of personal property engaged in for profit	**24b**	
c	Nontaxable amount of the value of Olympic and Paralympic medals and USOC prize money reported on line 8m	**24c**	
d	Reforestation amortization and expenses	**24d**	
e	Repayment of supplemental unemployment benefits under the Trade Act of 1974	**24e**	
f	Contributions to section 501(c)(18)(D) pension plans	**24f**	
g	Contributions by certain chaplains to section 403(b) plans	**24g**	
h	Attorney fees and court costs for actions involving certain unlawful discrimination claims (see instructions)	**24h**	
i	Attorney fees and court costs you paid in connection with an award from the IRS for information you provided that helped the IRS detect tax law violations	**24i**	
j	Housing deduction from Form 2555	**24j**	
k	Excess deductions of section 67(e) expenses from Schedule K-1 (Form 1041)	**24k**	
z	Other adjustments. List type and amount: _____	**24z**	

25	Total other adjustments. Add lines 24a through 24z	**25**	
26	Add lines 11 through 23 and 25. These are your **adjustments to income**. Enter here and on Form 1040, 1040-SR, or 1040-NR, line 10	**26**	

SCHEDULE 2
(Form 1040)

Department of the Treasury
Internal Revenue Service

Additional Taxes

Attach to Form 1040, 1040-SR, or 1040-NR.
Go to *www.irs.gov/Form1040* for instructions and the latest information.

OMB No. 1545-0074

20**23**

Attachment
Sequence No. **02**

Name(s) shown on Form 1040, 1040-SR, or 1040-NR | Your social security number

Part I — Tax

1	Alternative minimum tax. Attach Form 6251	**1**	
2	Excess advance premium tax credit repayment. Attach Form 8962	**2**	
3	Add lines 1 and 2. Enter here and on Form 1040, 1040-SR, or 1040-NR, line 17 . .	**3**	

Part II — Other Taxes

4	Self-employment tax. Attach Schedule SE	**4**	
5	Social security and Medicare tax on unreported tip income. Attach Form 4137 . . . . **5**		
6	Uncollected social security and Medicare tax on wages. Attach Form 8919 . . . . **6**		
7	Total additional social security and Medicare tax. Add lines 5 and 6	**7**	
8	Additional tax on IRAs or other tax-favored accounts. Attach Form 5329 if required. If not required, check here . . . . ☐	**8**	
9	Household employment taxes. Attach Schedule H	**9**	
10	Repayment of first-time homebuyer credit. Attach Form 5405 if required	**10**	
11	Additional Medicare Tax. Attach Form 8959	**11**	
12	Net investment income tax. Attach Form 8960	**12**	
13	Uncollected social security and Medicare or RRTA tax on tips or group-term life insurance from Form W-2, box 12	**13**	
14	Interest on tax due on installment income from the sale of certain residential lots and timeshares	**14**	
15	Interest on the deferred tax on gain from certain installment sales with a sales price over $150,000	**15**	
16	Recapture of low-income housing credit. Attach Form 8611	**16**	

(continued on page 2)

For Paperwork Reduction Act Notice, see your tax return instructions.   Cat. No. 71478U   Schedule 2 (Form 1040) 2023

Part II	**Other Taxes** *(continued)*			

17 Other additional taxes:

a Recapture of other credits. List type, form number, and amount:

_____ **17a**

b Recapture of federal mortgage subsidy, if you sold your home see instructions **17b**

c Additional tax on HSA distributions. Attach Form 8889 . . . . **17c**

d Additional tax on an HSA because you didn't remain an eligible individual. Attach Form 8889 . . . . **17d**

e Additional tax on Archer MSA distributions. Attach Form 8853 . **17e**

f Additional tax on Medicare Advantage MSA distributions. Attach Form 8853 . . . . **17f**

g Recapture of a charitable contribution deduction related to a fractional interest in tangible personal property **17g**

h Income you received from a nonqualified deferred compensation plan that fails to meet the requirements of section 409A . . . **17h**

i Compensation you received from a nonqualified deferred compensation plan described in section 457A **17i**

j Section 72(m)(5) excess benefits tax **17j**

k Golden parachute payments **17k**

l Tax on accumulation distribution of trusts **17l**

m Excise tax on insider stock compensation from an expatriated corporation **17m**

n Look-back interest under section 167(g) or 460(b) from Form 8697 or 8866 . . . . **17n**

o Tax on non-effectively connected income for any part of the year you were a nonresident alien from Form 1040-NR **17o**

p Any interest from Form 8621, line 16f, relating to distributions from, and dispositions of, stock of a section 1291 fund **17p**

q Any interest from Form 8621, line 24 . . . . **17q**

z Any other taxes. List type and amount: _____

_____ **17z**

18 Total additional taxes. Add lines 17a through 17z **18**

19 Reserved for future use **19**

20 Section 965 net tax liability installment from Form 965-A . . . **20**

21 Add lines 4, 7 through 16, and 18. These are your **total other taxes.** Enter here and on Form 1040 or 1040-SR, line 23, or Form 1040-NR, line 23b **21**

Schedule 2 (Form 1040) 2023

SCHEDULE 3
(Form 1040)

Department of the Treasury
Internal Revenue Service

Additional Credits and Payments

Attach to Form 1040, 1040-SR, or 1040-NR.
Go to *www.irs.gov/Form1040* for instructions and the latest information.

OMB No. 1545-0074

2023

Attachment
Sequence No. **03**

Name(s) shown on Form 1040, 1040-SR, or 1040-NR

Your social security number

Part I Nonrefundable Credits

1	Foreign tax credit. Attach Form 1116 if required	**1**	
2	Credit for child and dependent care expenses from Form 2441, line 11. Attach Form 2441	**2**	
3	Education credits from Form 8863, line 19	**3**	
4	Retirement savings contributions credit. Attach Form 8880	**4**	
5a	Residential clean energy credit from Form 5695, line 15	**5a**	
b	Energy efficient home improvement credit from Form 5695, line 32	**5b**	
6	Other nonrefundable credits:		
a	General business credit. Attach Form 3800 — **6a**		
b	Credit for prior year minimum tax. Attach Form 8801 — **6b**		
c	Adoption credit. Attach Form 8839 — **6c**		
d	Credit for the elderly or disabled. Attach Schedule R — **6d**		
e	Reserved for future use — **6e**		
f	Clean vehicle credit. Attach Form 8936 — **6f**		
g	Mortgage interest credit. Attach Form 8396 — **6g**		
h	District of Columbia first-time homebuyer credit. Attach Form 8859 — **6h**		
i	Qualified electric vehicle credit. Attach Form 8834 — **6i**		
j	Alternative fuel vehicle refueling property credit. Attach Form 8911 — **6j**		
k	Credit to holders of tax credit bonds. Attach Form 8912 — **6k**		
l	Amount on Form 8978, line 14. See instructions — **6l**		
m	Credit for previously owned clean vehicles. Attach Form 8936 — **6m**		
z	Other nonrefundable credits. List type and amount: _____ — **6z**		
7	Total other nonrefundable credits. Add lines 6a through 6z	**7**	
8	Add lines 1 through 4, 5a, 5b, and 7. Enter here and on Form 1040, 1040-SR, or 1040-NR, line 20	**8**	

(continued on page 2)

For Paperwork Reduction Act Notice, see your tax return instructions.   Cat. No. 71480G   **Schedule 3 (Form 1040) 2023**

Part II	Other Payments and Refundable Credits		
9	Net premium tax credit. Attach Form 8962	9	
10	Amount paid with request for extension to file (see instructions)	10	
11	Excess social security and tier 1 RRTA tax withheld	11	
12	Credit for federal tax on fuels. Attach Form 4136	12	
13	Other payments or refundable credits:		
a	Form 2439 . . . . **13a**		
b	Credit for repayment of amounts included in income from earlier years **13b**		
c	Elective payment election amount from Form 3800, Part III, line 6, column (i) **13c**		
d	Deferred amount of net 965 tax liability (see instructions) . . . **13d**		
z	Other payments or refundable credits. List type and amount: _____ **13z**		
14	Total other payments or refundable credits. Add lines 13a through 13z	14	
15	Add lines 9 through 12 and 14. Enter here and on Form 1040, 1040-SR, or 1040-NR, line 31	15	

SCHEDULE A
(Form 1040)

Department of the Treasury
Internal Revenue Service

Itemized Deductions

Attach to Form 1040 or 1040-SR.
Go to *www.irs.gov/ScheduleA* **for instructions and the latest information.**

Caution: If you are claiming a net qualified disaster loss on Form 4684, see the instructions for line 16.

OMB No. 1545-0074

2023

Attachment
Sequence No. **07**

Name(s) shown on Form 1040 or 1040-SR

Your social security number

Medical and Dental Expenses		**Caution:** Do not include expenses reimbursed or paid by others.			
	1	Medical and dental expenses (see instructions)	**1**		
	2	Enter amount from Form 1040 or 1040-SR, line 11 **2**			
	3	Multiply line 2 by 7.5% (0.075)	**3**		
	4	Subtract line 3 from line 1. If line 3 is more than line 1, enter -0-		**4**	
Taxes You Paid	5	State and local taxes.			
	a	State and local income taxes or general sales taxes. You may include either income taxes or general sales taxes on line 5a, but not both. If you elect to include general sales taxes instead of income taxes, check this box ☐	**5a**		
	b	State and local real estate taxes (see instructions)	**5b**		
	c	State and local personal property taxes	**5c**		
	d	Add lines 5a through 5c	**5d**		
	e	Enter the smaller of line 5d or $10,000 ($5,000 if married filing separately)	**5e**		
	6	Other taxes. List type and amount: _____	**6**		
	7	Add lines 5e and 6		**7**	
Interest You Paid **Caution:** Your mortgage interest deduction may be limited. See instructions.	8	Home mortgage interest and points. If you didn't use all of your home mortgage loan(s) to buy, build, or improve your home, see instructions and check this box ☐			
	a	Home mortgage interest and points reported to you on Form 1098. See instructions if limited	**8a**		
	b	Home mortgage interest not reported to you on Form 1098. See instructions if limited. If paid to the person from whom you bought the home, see instructions and show that person's name, identifying no., and address	**8b**		
	c	Points not reported to you on Form 1098. See instructions for special rules	**8c**		
	d	Reserved for future use	**8d**		
	e	Add lines 8a through 8c	**8e**		
	9	Investment interest. Attach Form 4952 if required. See instructions	**9**		
	10	Add lines 8e and 9		**10**	
Gifts to Charity **Caution:** If you made a gift and got a benefit for it, see instructions.	11	Gifts by cash or check. If you made any gift of $250 or more, see instructions	**11**		
	12	Other than by cash or check. If you made any gift of $250 or more, see instructions. You **must** attach Form 8283 if over $500	**12**		
	13	Carryover from prior year	**13**		
	14	Add lines 11 through 13		**14**	
Casualty and Theft Losses	15	Casualty and theft loss(es) from a federally declared disaster (other than net qualified disaster losses). Attach Form 4684 and enter the amount from line 18 of that form. See instructions		**15**	
Other Itemized Deductions	16	Other—from list in instructions. List type and amount: _____		**16**	
Total Itemized Deductions	17	Add the amounts in the far right column for lines 4 through 16. Also, enter this amount on Form 1040 or 1040-SR, line 12		**17**	
	18	If you elect to itemize deductions even though they are less than your standard deduction, check this box ☐			

For Paperwork Reduction Act Notice, see the Instructions for Form 1040.   Cat. No. 17145C   **Schedule A (Form 1040) 2023**

SCHEDULE B
(Form 1040)

Department of the Treasury
Internal Revenue Service

Interest and Ordinary Dividends

Attach to Form 1040 or 1040-SR.
Go to www.irs.gov/ScheduleB for instructions and the latest information.

OMB No. 1545-0074

2023

Attachment
Sequence No. **08**

Name(s) shown on return | Your social security number

Part I **Interest**				Amount
(See instructions and the Instructions for Form 1040, line 2b.)	**1**	List name of payer. If any interest is from a seller-financed mortgage and the buyer used the property as a personal residence, see the instructions and list this interest first. Also, show that buyer's social security number and address:		
Note: If you received a Form 1099-INT, Form 1099-OID, or substitute statement from a brokerage firm, list the firm's name as the payer and enter the total interest shown on that form.			**1**	
	2	Add the amounts on line 1	**2**	
	3	Excludable interest on series EE and I U.S. savings bonds issued after 1989. Attach Form 8815	**3**	
	4	Subtract line 3 from line 2. Enter the result here and on Form 1040 or 1040-SR, line 2b	**4**	

Note: If line 4 is over $1,500, you must complete Part III.

Part II **Ordinary Dividends**				Amount
(See instructions and the Instructions for Form 1040, line 3b.)	**5**	List name of payer:		
Note: If you received a Form 1099-DIV or substitute statement from a brokerage firm, list the firm's name as the payer and enter the ordinary dividends shown on that form.			**5**	
	6	Add the amounts on line 5. Enter the total here and on Form 1040 or 1040-SR, line 3b	**6**	

Note: If line 6 is over $1,500, you must complete Part III.

Part III
Foreign Accounts and Trusts

Caution: If required, failure to file FinCEN Form 114 may result in substantial penalties. Additionally, you may be required to file Form 8938, Statement of Specified Foreign Financial Assets. See instructions.

You must complete this part if you (**a**) had over $1,500 of taxable interest or ordinary dividends; (**b**) had a foreign account; or (**c**) received a distribution from, or were a grantor of, or a transferor to, a foreign trust.

		Yes	No
7a	At any time during 2023, did you have a financial interest in or signature authority over a financial account (such as a bank account, securities account, or brokerage account) located in a foreign country? See instructions		
	If "Yes," are you required to file FinCEN Form 114, Report of Foreign Bank and Financial Accounts (FBAR), to report that financial interest or signature authority? See FinCEN Form 114 and its instructions for filing requirements and exceptions to those requirements		
b	If you are required to file FinCEN Form 114, list the name(s) of the foreign country(-ies) where the financial account(s) is (are) located:		
8	During 2023, did you receive a distribution from, or were you the grantor of, or transferor to, a foreign trust? If "Yes," you may have to file Form 3520. See instructions		

For Paperwork Reduction Act Notice, see your tax return instructions. Cat. No. 17146N **Schedule B (Form 1040) 2023**

SCHEDULE 8812
(Form 1040)

Department of the Treasury
Internal Revenue Service

Credits for Qualifying Children and Other Dependents

Attach to Form 1040, 1040-SR, or 1040-NR.

Go to *www.irs.gov/Schedule8812* for instructions and the latest information.

OMB No. 1545-0074

2023

Attachment
Sequence No. **47**

Name(s) shown on return | Your social security number

	Part I	**Child Tax Credit and Credit for Other Dependents**		
1	Enter the amount from line 11 of your Form 1040, 1040-SR, or 1040-NR		**1**	
2a	Enter income from Puerto Rico that you excluded	**2a**		
b	Enter the amounts from lines 45 and 50 of your Form 2555	**2b**		
c	Enter the amount from line 15 of your Form 4563	**2c**		
d	Add lines 2a through 2c		**2d**	
3	Add lines 1 and 2d		**3**	
4	Number of qualifying children under age 17 with the required social security number	**4**		
5	Multiply line 4 by $2,000		**5**	
6	Number of other dependents, including any qualifying children who are not under age 17 or who do not have the required social security number	**6**		
	Caution: Do not include yourself, your spouse, or anyone who is not a U.S. citizen, U.S. national, or U.S. resident alien. Also, do not include anyone you included on line 4.			
7	Multiply line 6 by $500		**7**	
8	Add lines 5 and 7		**8**	
9	Enter the amount shown below for your filing status. • Married filing jointly—$400,000 • All other filing statuses—$200,000		**9**	
10	Subtract line 9 from line 3. • If zero or less, enter -0-. • If more than zero and not a multiple of $1,000, enter the next multiple of $1,000. For example, if the result is $425, enter $1,000; if the result is $1,025, enter $2,000, etc.		**10**	
11	Multiply line 10 by 5% (0.05)		**11**	
12	Is the amount on line 8 more than the amount on line 11?		**12**	
	☐ **No. STOP.** You cannot take the child tax credit, credit for other dependents, or additional child tax credit. Skip Parts II-A and II-B. Enter -0- on lines 14 and 27.			
	☐ **Yes.** Subtract line 11 from line 8. Enter the result.			
13	Enter the amount from **Credit Limit Worksheet A**		**13**	
14	Enter the smaller of line 12 or line 13. **This is your child tax credit and credit for other dependents** . . .		**14**	
	Enter this amount on Form 1040, 1040-SR, or 1040-NR, line 19.			

If the amount on line 12 is more than the amount on line 14, you may be able to take the **additional child tax credit** on Form 1040, 1040-SR, or 1040-NR, line 28. Complete your Form 1040, 1040-SR, or 1040-NR through line 27 (also complete Schedule 3, line 11) before completing Part II-A.

For Paperwork Reduction Act Notice, see your tax return instructions.   Cat. No. 59761M   **Schedule 8812 (Form 1040) 2023**

Part II-A   Additional Child Tax Credit for All Filers

Caution: If you file Form 2555, you cannot claim the additional child tax credit.

15	Check this box if you **do not** want to claim the additional child tax credit. Skip Parts II-A and II-B. Enter -0- on line 27 . . . . ☐		
16a	Subtract line 14 from line 12. If zero, **stop here**; you cannot take the additional child tax credit. Skip Parts II-A and II-B. Enter -0- on line 27	**16a**	
b	Number of qualifying children under 17 with the required social security number: _____ x $1,600. Enter the result. If zero, **stop here**; you cannot claim the additional child tax credit. Skip Parts II-A and II-B. Enter -0- on line 27	**16b**	
	TIP: The number of children you use for this line is the same as the number of children you used for line 4.		
17	Enter the **smaller** of line 16a or line 16b	**17**	
18a	Earned income (see instructions)	**18a**	
b	Nontaxable combat pay (see instructions) **18b**		
19	Is the amount on line 18a more than $2,500?		
	☐ **No.** Leave line 19 blank and enter -0- on line 20.		
	☐ **Yes.** Subtract $2,500 from the amount on line 18a. Enter the result	**19**	
20	Multiply the amount on line 19 by 15% (0.15) and enter the result	**20**	
	Next. On line 16b, is the amount $4,800 or more?		
	☐ **No.** If you are a bona fide resident of Puerto Rico, go to line 21. Otherwise, skip Part II-B and enter the **smaller** of line 17 or line 20 on line 27.		
	☐ **Yes.** If line 20 is equal to or more than line 17, skip Part II-B and enter the amount from line 17 on line 27. Otherwise, go to line 21.		

Part II-B   Certain Filers Who Have Three or More Qualifying Children and Bona Fide Residents of Puerto Rico

21	Withheld social security, Medicare, and Additional Medicare taxes from Form(s) W-2, boxes 4 and 6. If married filing jointly, include your spouse's amounts with yours. If your employer withheld or you paid Additional Medicare Tax or tier 1 RRTA taxes, or if you are a bona fide resident of Puerto Rico, see instructions.	**21**	
22	Enter the total of the amounts from Schedule 1 (Form 1040), line 15; Schedule 2 (Form 1040), line 5; Schedule 2 (Form 1040), line 6; and Schedule 2 (Form 1040), line 13 .	**22**	
23	Add lines 21 and 22	**23**	
24	**1040 and**		
	1040-SR filers: Enter the total of the amounts from Form 1040 or 1040-SR, line 27, and Schedule 3 (Form 1040), line 11.		
	1040-NR filers: Enter the amount from Schedule 3 (Form 1040), line 11.	**24**	
25	Subtract line 24 from line 23. If zero or less, enter -0-	**25**	
26	Enter the **larger** of line 20 or line 25	**26**	
	Next, enter the **smaller** of line 17 or line 26 on line 27.		

Part II-C   Additional Child Tax Credit

27	**This is your additional child tax credit. Enter this amount on Form 1040, 1040-SR, or 1040-NR, line 28** . .	**27**	

Form **2441**

Department of the Treasury
Internal Revenue Service

Child and Dependent Care Expenses

Attach to Form 1040, 1040-SR, or 1040-NR.
Go to *www.irs.gov/Form2441* for instructions and the latest information.

OMB No. 1545-0074

2023

Attachment
Sequence No. **21**

Name(s) shown on return

Your social security number

A You can't claim a credit for child and dependent care expenses if your filing status is married filing separately unless you meet the requirements listed in the instructions under *Married Persons Filing Separately*. If you meet these requirements, check this box . . ☐

B If you or your spouse was a student or was disabled during 2023 and you're entering deemed income of $250 or $500 a month on Form 2441 based on the income rules listed in the instructions under *If You or Your Spouse Was a Student or Disabled*, check this box . ☐

Part I — Persons or Organizations Who Provided the Care—You **must** complete this part.

If you have more than three care providers, see the instructions and check this box . . . . ☐

1 (a) Care provider's name	(b) Address (number, street, apt. no., city, state, and ZIP code)	(c) Identifying number (SSN or EIN)	(d) Was the care provider your household employee in 2023? For example, this generally includes nannies but not daycare centers. (see instructions)	(e) Amount paid (see instructions)
			☐ Yes ☐ No	
			☐ Yes ☐ No	
			☐ Yes ☐ No	

Did you receive **dependent care benefits**?

— **No** ———— Complete only Part II below.

— **Yes** ———— Complete Part III on page 2 next.

Caution: If the care provider is your household employee, you may owe employment taxes. For details, see the Instructions for Schedule H (Form 1040). If you incurred care expenses in 2023 but didn't pay them until 2024, or if you prepaid in 2023 for care to be provided in 2024, don't include these expenses in column (d) of line 2 for 2023. See the instructions.

Part II — Credit for Child and Dependent Care Expenses

2 Information about your **qualifying person(s)**. If you have more than three qualifying persons, see the instructions and check this box ☐

(a) Qualifying person's name First	Last	(b) Qualifying person's social security number	(c) Check here if the qualifying person was over age 12 and was disabled. (see instructions)	(d) Qualified expenses you incurred and paid in 2023 for the person listed in column (a)
			☐	
			☐	
			☐	

3 Add the amounts in column (d) of line 2. **Don't** enter more than $3,000 if you had one qualifying person or $6,000 if you had two or more persons. If you completed Part III, enter the amount from line 31 . | **3** |

4 Enter your **earned income**. See instructions . . . . | **4** |

5 If married filing jointly, enter your spouse's earned income (if you or your spouse was a student or was disabled, see the instructions); **all others**, enter the amount from line 4 . . . . . . | **5** |

6 Enter the **smallest** of line 3, 4, or 5 . . . . | **6** |

7 Enter the amount from Form 1040, 1040-SR, or 1040-NR, line 11 . . . | **7** |

8 Enter on line 8 the decimal amount shown below that applies to the amount on line 7.

If line 7 is: Over	But not over	Decimal amount is	If line 7 is: Over	But not over	Decimal amount is	If line 7 is: Over	But not over	Decimal amount is
$0—15,000		.35	$25,000—27,000		.29	$37,000—39,000		.23
15,000—17,000		.34	27,000—29,000		.28	39,000—41,000		.22
17,000—19,000		.33	29,000—31,000		.27	41,000—43,000		.21
19,000—21,000		.32	31,000—33,000		.26	43,000—No limit		.20
21,000—23,000		.31	33,000—35,000		.25			
23,000—25,000		.30	35,000—37,000		.24			

8 | X**.**

9a Multiply line 6 by the decimal amount on line 8 . . . . | **9a** |

b If you paid 2022 expenses in 2023, complete Worksheet A in the instructions. Enter the amount from line 13 of the worksheet here. Otherwise, enter -0- on line 9b and go to line 9c . . . . | **9b** |

c Add lines 9a and 9b and enter the result . . . . | **9c** |

10 Tax liability limit. Enter the amount from the Credit Limit Worksheet in the instructions | **10** |

11 **Credit for child and dependent care expenses.** Enter the **smaller** of line 9c or line 10 here and on Schedule 3 (Form 1040), line 2 . . . . | **11** |

For Paperwork Reduction Act Notice, see your tax return instructions. Cat. No. 11862M Form **2441** (2023)

Part III	Dependent Care Benefits		

12	Enter the total amount of **dependent care benefits** you received in 2023. Amounts you received as an employee should be shown in box 10 of your Form(s) W-2. **Don't** include amounts reported as wages in box 1 of Form(s) W-2. If you were self-employed or a partner, include amounts you received under a dependent care assistance program from your sole proprietorship or partnership	**12**	
13	Enter the amount, if any, you carried over from 2022 and used in 2023 during the grace period. See instructions	**13**	
14	If you forfeited or carried over to 2024 any of the amounts reported on line 12 or 13, enter the amount. See instructions	**14**	( )
15	Combine lines 12 through 14. See instructions	**15**	
16	Enter the total amount of **qualified expenses** incurred in 2023 for the care of the **qualifying person(s)**	**16**	
17	Enter the **smaller** of line 15 or 16	**17**	
18	Enter your **earned income**. See instructions	**18**	
19	Enter the amount shown below that applies to you.		
	• If married filing jointly, enter your spouse's earned income (if you or your spouse was a student or was disabled, see the instructions for line 5).	**19**	
	• If married filing separately, see instructions.		
	• All others, enter the amount from line 18.		
20	Enter the **smallest** of line 17, 18, or 19	**20**	
21	Enter $5,000 ($2,500 if married filing separately **and** you were required to enter your spouse's earned income on line 19). However, don't enter more than the maximum amount allowed under your dependent care plan. See instructions	**21**	
22	Is any amount on line 12 or 13 from your sole proprietorship or partnership?		
	☐ **No.** Enter -0-.		
	☐ **Yes.** Enter the amount here	**22**	
23	Subtract line 22 from line 15	**23**	
24	**Deductible benefits.** Enter the **smallest** of line 20, 21, or 22. Also, include this amount on the appropriate line(s) of your return. See instructions	**24**	
25	**Excluded benefits.** If you checked "No" on line 22, enter the smaller of line 20 or line 21. Otherwise, subtract line 24 from the smaller of line 20 or line 21. If zero or less, enter -0- . .	**25**	
26	**Taxable benefits.** Subtract line 25 from line 23. If zero or less, enter -0-. Also, enter this amount on Form 1040, 1040-SR, or 1040-NR, line 1e	**26**	

To claim the child and dependent care credit,
complete lines 27 through 31 below.

27	Enter $3,000 ($6,000 if two or more qualifying persons)	**27**	
28	Add lines 24 and 25	**28**	
29	Subtract line 28 from line 27. If zero or less, **stop.** You can't take the credit. **Exception.** If you paid 2022 expenses in 2023, see the instructions for line 9b	**29**	
30	Complete line 2 on page 1 of this form. **Don't** include in column (d) any benefits shown on line 28 above. Then, add the amounts in column (d) and enter the total here	**30**	
31	Enter the **smaller** of line 29 or 30. Also, enter this amount on line 3 on page 1 of this form and complete lines 4 through 11	**31**	

Form **2441** (2023)

Form 8863

Department of the Treasury
Internal Revenue Service

Education Credits
(American Opportunity and Lifetime Learning Credits)

Attach to Form 1040 or 1040-SR.
Go to *www.irs.gov/Form8863* for instructions and the latest information.

OMB No. 1545-0074

2023

Attachment
Sequence No. **50**

Name(s) shown on return

Your social security number

> ⚠️ **CAUTION**
> *Complete a separate Part III on page 2 for each student for whom you're claiming either credit before you complete Parts I and II.*

Part I — Refundable American Opportunity Credit

1	After completing Part III for each student, enter the total of all amounts from all Parts III, line 30	**1**
2	Enter: $180,000 if married filing jointly; $90,000 if single, head of household, or qualifying surviving spouse — **2**	
3	Enter the amount from Form 1040 or 1040-SR, line 11. But if you're filing Form 2555 or 4563, or you're excluding income from Puerto Rico, see Pub. 970 for the amount to enter instead — **3**	
4	Subtract line 3 from line 2. If zero or less, **stop**; you can't take any education credit — **4**	
5	Enter: $20,000 if married filing jointly; $10,000 if single, head of household, or qualifying surviving spouse — **5**	
6	If line 4 is: • Equal to or more than line 5, enter 1.000 on line 6 • Less than line 5, divide line 4 by line 5. Enter the result as a decimal (rounded to at least three places)	**6**
7	Multiply line 1 by line 6. **Caution:** If you were under age 24 at the end of the year **and** meet the conditions described in the instructions, you **can't** take the refundable American opportunity credit; skip line 8, enter the amount from line 7 on line 9, and check this box ☐	**7**
8	**Refundable American opportunity credit.** Multiply line 7 by 40% (0.40). Enter the amount here and on Form 1040 or 1040-SR, line 29. Then go to line 9 below.	**8**

Part II — Nonrefundable Education Credits

9	Subtract line 8 from line 7. Enter here and on line 2 of the Credit Limit Worksheet (see instructions)	**9**
10	After completing Part III for each student, enter the total of all amounts from all Parts III, line 31. If zero, skip lines 11 through 17, enter -0- on line 18, and go to line 19	**10**
11	Enter the smaller of line 10 or $10,000	**11**
12	Multiply line 11 by 20% (0.20)	**12**
13	Enter: $180,000 if married filing jointly; $90,000 if single, head of household, or qualifying surviving spouse — **13**	
14	Enter the amount from Form 1040 or 1040-SR, line 11. But if you're filing Form 2555 or 4563, or you're excluding income from Puerto Rico, see Pub. 970 for the amount to enter instead — **14**	
15	Subtract line 14 from line 13. If zero or less, skip lines 16 and 17, enter -0- on line 18, and go to line 19 — **15**	
16	Enter: $20,000 if married filing jointly; $10,000 if single, head of household, or qualifying surviving spouse — **16**	
17	If line 15 is: • Equal to or more than line 16, enter 1.000 on line 17 and go to line 18 • Less than line 16, divide line 15 by line 16. Enter the result as a decimal (rounded to at least three places)	**17**
18	Multiply line 12 by line 17. Enter here and on line 1 of the Credit Limit Worksheet (see instructions)	**18**
19	**Nonrefundable education credits.** Enter the amount from line 7 of the Credit Limit Worksheet (see instructions) here and on Schedule 3 (Form 1040), line 3	**19**

For Paperwork Reduction Act Notice, see your tax return instructions.

Cat. No. 25379M

Form **8863** (2023)

Name(s) shown on return	Your social security number

> ⚠️ **CAUTION**
> **Complete Part III for each student for whom you're claiming either the American opportunity credit or lifetime learning credit. Use additional copies of page 2 as needed for each student.**

Part III	**Student and Educational Institution Information.** See instructions.

20 Student name (as shown on page 1 of your tax return)

21 Student social security number (as shown on page 1 of your tax return)

22 Educational institution information (see instructions)

a. Name of first educational institution	**b.** Name of second educational institution (if any)
(1) Address. Number and street (or P.O. box). City, town or post office, state, and ZIP code. If a foreign address, see instructions.	**(1)** Address. Number and street (or P.O. box). City, town or post office, state, and ZIP code. If a foreign address, see instructions.
(2) Did the student receive Form 1098-T from this institution for 2023? ☐ Yes ☐ No	**(2)** Did the student receive Form 1098-T from this institution for 2023? ☐ Yes ☐ No
(3) Did the student receive Form 1098-T from this institution for 2022 with box 7 checked? ☐ Yes ☐ No	**(3)** Did the student receive Form 1098-T from this institution for 2022 with box 7 checked? ☐ Yes ☐ No
(4) Enter the institution's employer identification number (EIN) if you're claiming the American opportunity credit or if you checked "Yes" in (**2**) or (**3**). You can get the EIN from Form 1098-T or from the institution.	**(4)** Enter the institution's employer identification number (EIN) if you're claiming the American opportunity credit or if you checked "Yes" in (**2**) or (**3**). You can get the EIN from Form 1098-T or from the institution.
— — – — — — — — — —	— — – — — — — — — —

23 Has the American opportunity credit been claimed for this student for any 4 prior tax years?
☐ Yes — **Stop!** Go to line 31 for this student. ☐ No — Go to line 24.

24 Was the student enrolled at least half-time for at least one academic period that began or is treated as having begun in 2023 at an eligible educational institution in a program leading towards a postsecondary degree, certificate, or other recognized postsecondary educational credential? See instructions.
☐ Yes — Go to line 25. ☐ No — **Stop!** Go to line 31 for this student.

25 Did the student complete the first 4 years of postsecondary education before 2023? See instructions.
☐ Yes — **Stop!** Go to line 31 for this student. ☐ No — Go to line 26.

26 Was the student convicted, before the end of 2023, of a felony for possession or distribution of a controlled substance?
☐ Yes — **Stop!** Go to line 31 for this student. ☐ No — Complete lines 27 through 30 for this student.

> ⚠️ **CAUTION**
> You **can't** take the American opportunity credit and the lifetime learning credit for the **same student** in the same year. If you complete lines 27 through 30 for this student, don't complete line 31.

American Opportunity Credit

27	Adjusted qualified education expenses (see instructions). **Don't enter more than $4,000**	**27**	
28	Subtract $2,000 from line 27. If zero or less, enter -0-	**28**	
29	Multiply line 28 by 25% (0.25)	**29**	
30	If line 28 is zero, enter the amount from line 27. Otherwise, add $2,000 to the amount on line 29 and enter the result. Skip line 31. Include the total of all amounts from all Parts III, line 30, on Part I, line 1 .	**30**	

Lifetime Learning Credit

31	Adjusted qualified education expenses (see instructions). Include the total of all amounts from all Parts III, line 31, on Part II, line 10	**31**	

Form **8863** (2023)

2023 Tax Table

CAUTION

See the instructions for line 16 to see if you must use the Tax Table below to figure your tax.

Example. A married couple are filing a joint return. Their taxable income on Form 1040, line 15, is $25,300. First, they find the $25,300-25,350 taxable income line. Next, they find the column for married filing jointly and read down the column. The amount shown where the taxable income line and filing status column meet is $2,599. This is the tax amount they should enter in the entry space on Form 1040, line 16.

Sample Table

At Least	But Less Than	Single	Married filing jointly*	Married filing separately	Head of a household
			Your tax is—		
25,200	25,250	2,807	2,587	2,807	2,713
25,250	25,300	2,813	2,593	2,813	2,719
25,300	25,350	2,819	(2,599)	2,819	2,725
25,350	25,400	2,825	2,605	2,825	2,731

If line 15 (taxable income) is— At least	But less than	And you are— Single	Married filing jointly*	Married filing separately	Head of a household
			Your tax is—		
0	5	0	0	0	0
5	15	1	1	1	1
15	25	2	2	2	2
25	50	4	4	4	4
50	75	6	6	6	6
75	100	9	9	9	9
100	125	11	11	11	11
125	150	14	14	14	14
150	175	16	16	16	16
175	200	19	19	19	19
200	225	21	21	21	21
225	250	24	24	24	24
250	275	26	26	26	26
275	300	29	29	29	29
300	325	31	31	31	31
325	350	34	34	34	34
350	375	36	36	36	36
375	400	39	39	39	39
400	425	41	41	41	41
425	450	44	44	44	44
450	475	46	46	46	46
475	500	49	49	49	49
500	525	51	51	51	51
525	550	54	54	54	54
550	575	56	56	56	56
575	600	59	59	59	59
600	625	61	61	61	61
625	650	64	64	64	64
650	675	66	66	66	66
675	700	69	69	69	69
700	725	71	71	71	71
725	750	74	74	74	74
750	775	76	76	76	76
775	800	79	79	79	79
800	825	81	81	81	81
825	850	84	84	84	84
850	875	86	86	86	86
875	900	89	89	89	89
900	925	91	91	91	91
925	950	94	94	94	94
950	975	96	96	96	96
975	1,000	99	99	99	99

1,000

At least	But less than	Single	Married filing jointly*	Married filing separately	Head of a household
1,000	1,025	101	101	101	101
1,025	1,050	104	104	104	104
1,050	1,075	106	106	106	106
1,075	1,100	109	109	109	109
1,100	1,125	111	111	111	111
1,125	1,150	114	114	114	114
1,150	1,175	116	116	116	116
1,175	1,200	119	119	119	119
1,200	1,225	121	121	121	121
1,225	1,250	124	124	124	124
1,250	1,275	126	126	126	126
1,275	1,300	129	129	129	129
1,300	1,325	131	131	131	131
1,325	1,350	134	134	134	134
1,350	1,375	136	136	136	136
1,375	1,400	139	139	139	139
1,400	1,425	141	141	141	141
1,425	1,450	144	144	144	144
1,450	1,475	146	146	146	146
1,475	1,500	149	149	149	149
1,500	1,525	151	151	151	151
1,525	1,550	154	154	154	154
1,550	1,575	156	156	156	156
1,575	1,600	159	159	159	159
1,600	1,625	161	161	161	161
1,625	1,650	164	164	164	164
1,650	1,675	166	166	166	166
1,675	1,700	169	169	169	169
1,700	1,725	171	171	171	171
1,725	1,750	174	174	174	174
1,750	1,775	176	176	176	176
1,775	1,800	179	179	179	179
1,800	1,825	181	181	181	181
1,825	1,850	184	184	184	184
1,850	1,875	186	186	186	186
1,875	1,900	189	189	189	189
1,900	1,925	191	191	191	191
1,925	1,950	194	194	194	194
1,950	1,975	196	196	196	196
1,975	2,000	199	199	199	199

2,000

At least	But less than	Single	Married filing jointly*	Married filing separately	Head of a household
2,000	2,025	201	201	201	201
2,025	2,050	204	204	204	204
2,050	2,075	206	206	206	206
2,075	2,100	209	209	209	209
2,100	2,125	211	211	211	211
2,125	2,150	214	214	214	214
2,150	2,175	216	216	216	216
2,175	2,200	219	219	219	219
2,200	2,225	221	221	221	221
2,225	2,250	224	224	224	224
2,250	2,275	226	226	226	226
2,275	2,300	229	229	229	229
2,300	2,325	231	231	231	231
2,325	2,350	234	234	234	234
2,350	2,375	236	236	236	236
2,375	2,400	239	239	239	239
2,400	2,425	241	241	241	241
2,425	2,450	244	244	244	244
2,450	2,475	246	246	246	246
2,475	2,500	249	249	249	249
2,500	2,525	251	251	251	251
2,525	2,550	254	254	254	254
2,550	2,575	256	256	256	256
2,575	2,600	259	259	259	259
2,600	2,625	261	261	261	261
2,625	2,650	264	264	264	264
2,650	2,675	266	266	266	266
2,675	2,700	269	269	269	269
2,700	2,725	271	271	271	271
2,725	2,750	274	274	274	274
2,750	2,775	276	276	276	276
2,775	2,800	279	279	279	279
2,800	2,825	281	281	281	281
2,825	2,850	284	284	284	284
2,850	2,875	286	286	286	286
2,875	2,900	289	289	289	289
2,900	2,925	291	291	291	291
2,925	2,950	294	294	294	294
2,950	2,975	296	296	296	296
2,975	3,000	299	299	299	299

(Continued)

* This column must also be used by a qualifying surviving spouse.

If line 15 (taxable income) is—		And you are—			
At least	But less than	Single	Married filing jointly *	Married filing separately	Head of a household
		Your tax is—			

3,000

At least	But less than	Single	MFJ *	MFS	HoH
3,000	3,050	303	303	303	303
3,050	3,100	308	308	308	308
3,100	3,150	313	313	313	313
3,150	3,200	318	318	318	318
3,200	3,250	323	323	323	323
3,250	3,300	328	328	328	328
3,300	3,350	333	333	333	333
3,350	3,400	338	338	338	338
3,400	3,450	343	343	343	343
3,450	3,500	348	348	348	348
3,500	3,550	353	353	353	353
3,550	3,600	358	358	358	358
3,600	3,650	363	363	363	363
3,650	3,700	368	368	368	368
3,700	3,750	373	373	373	373
3,750	3,800	378	378	378	378
3,800	3,850	383	383	383	383
3,850	3,900	388	388	388	388
3,900	3,950	393	393	393	393
3,950	4,000	398	398	398	398

4,000

At least	But less than	Single	MFJ *	MFS	HoH
4,000	4,050	403	403	403	403
4,050	4,100	408	408	408	408
4,100	4,150	413	413	413	413
4,150	4,200	418	418	418	418
4,200	4,250	423	423	423	423
4,250	4,300	428	428	428	428
4,300	4,350	433	433	433	433
4,350	4,400	438	438	438	438
4,400	4,450	443	443	443	443
4,450	4,500	448	448	448	448
4,500	4,550	453	453	453	453
4,550	4,600	458	458	458	458
4,600	4,650	463	463	463	463
4,650	4,700	468	468	468	468
4,700	4,750	473	473	473	473
4,750	4,800	478	478	478	478
4,800	4,850	483	483	483	483
4,850	4,900	488	488	488	488
4,900	4,950	493	493	493	493
4,950	5,000	498	498	498	498

5,000

At least	But less than	Single	MFJ *	MFS	HoH
5,000	5,050	503	503	503	503
5,050	5,100	508	508	508	508
5,100	5,150	513	513	513	513
5,150	5,200	518	518	518	518
5,200	5,250	523	523	523	523
5,250	5,300	528	528	528	528
5,300	5,350	533	533	533	533
5,350	5,400	538	538	538	538
5,400	5,450	543	543	543	543
5,450	5,500	548	548	548	548
5,500	5,550	553	553	553	553
5,550	5,600	558	558	558	558
5,600	5,650	563	563	563	563
5,650	5,700	568	568	568	568
5,700	5,750	573	573	573	573
5,750	5,800	578	578	578	578
5,800	5,850	583	583	583	583
5,850	5,900	588	588	588	588
5,900	5,950	593	593	593	593
5,950	6,000	598	598	598	598

6,000

At least	But less than	Single	MFJ *	MFS	HoH
6,000	6,050	603	603	603	603
6,050	6,100	608	608	608	608
6,100	6,150	613	613	613	613
6,150	6,200	618	618	618	618
6,200	6,250	623	623	623	623
6,250	6,300	628	628	628	628
6,300	6,350	633	633	633	633
6,350	6,400	638	638	638	638
6,400	6,450	643	643	643	643
6,450	6,500	648	648	648	648
6,500	6,550	653	653	653	653
6,550	6,600	658	658	658	658
6,600	6,650	663	663	663	663
6,650	6,700	668	668	668	668
6,700	6,750	673	673	673	673
6,750	6,800	678	678	678	678
6,800	6,850	683	683	683	683
6,850	6,900	688	688	688	688
6,900	6,950	693	693	693	693
6,950	7,000	698	698	698	698

7,000

At least	But less than	Single	MFJ *	MFS	HoH
7,000	7,050	703	703	703	703
7,050	7,100	706	708	708	708
7,100	7,150	713	713	713	713
7,150	7,200	718	718	718	718
7,200	7,250	723	723	723	723
7,250	7,300	728	728	728	728
7,300	7,350	733	733	733	733
7,350	7,400	738	738	738	738
7,400	7,450	743	743	743	743
7,450	7,500	748	748	748	748
7,500	7,550	753	753	753	753
7,550	7,600	758	758	758	758
7,600	7,650	763	763	763	763
7,650	7,700	768	768	768	768
7,700	7,750	773	773	773	773
7,750	7,800	778	778	778	778
7,800	7,850	783	783	783	783
7,850	7,900	786	788	788	788
7,900	7,950	793	793	793	793
7,950	8,000	798	798	798	798

8,000

At least	But less than	Single	MFJ *	MFS	HoH
8,000	8,050	803	803	803	803
8,050	8,100	808	808	808	808
8,100	8,150	813	813	813	813
8,150	8,200	818	818	818	818
8,200	8,250	823	823	823	823
8,250	8,300	828	828	828	828
8,300	8,350	833	833	833	833
8,350	8,400	838	838	838	838
8,400	8,450	843	843	843	843
8,450	8,500	848	848	848	848
8,500	8,550	853	853	853	853
8,550	8,600	858	858	858	858
8,600	8,650	863	863	863	863
8,650	8,700	868	868	868	868
8,700	8,750	873	873	873	873
8,750	8,800	878	878	878	878
8,800	8,850	883	883	883	883
8,850	8,900	888	888	888	888
8,900	8,950	893	893	893	893
8,950	9,000	898	898	898	898

9,000

At least	But less than	Single	MFJ *	MFS	HoH
9,000	9,050	903	903	903	903
9,050	9,100	908	908	908	908
9,100	9,150	913	913	913	913
9,150	9,200	918	918	918	918
9,200	9,250	923	923	923	923
9,250	9,300	928	928	928	928
9,300	9,350	933	933	933	933
9,350	9,400	938	938	938	938
9,400	9,450	943	943	943	943
9,450	9,500	948	948	948	948
9,500	9,550	953	953	953	953
9,550	9,600	958	958	958	958
9,600	9,650	963	963	963	963
9,650	9,700	968	968	968	968
9,700	9,750	973	973	973	973
9,750	9,800	978	978	978	978
9,800	9,850	983	983	983	983
9,850	9,900	988	988	988	988
9,900	9,950	993	993	993	993
9,950	10,000	998	998	998	998

10,000

At least	But less than	Single	MFJ *	MFS	HoH
10,000	10,050	1,003	1,003	1,003	1,003
10,050	10,100	1,008	1,008	1,008	1,008
10,100	10,150	1,013	1,013	1,013	1,013
10,150	10,200	1,018	1,018	1,018	1,018
10,200	10,250	1,023	1,023	1,023	1,023
10,250	10,300	1,028	1,028	1,028	1,028
10,300	10,350	1,033	1,033	1,033	1,033
10,350	10,400	1,038	1,038	1,038	1,038
10,400	10,450	1,043	1,043	1,043	1,043
10,450	10,500	1,048	1,048	1,048	1,048
10,500	10,550	1,053	1,053	1,053	1,053
10,550	10,600	1,058	1,058	1,058	1,058
10,600	10,650	1,063	1,063	1,063	1,063
10,650	10,700	1,068	1,068	1,068	1,068
10,700	10,750	1,073	1,073	1,073	1,073
10,750	10,800	1,078	1,078	1,078	1,078
10,800	10,850	1,083	1,083	1,083	1,083
10,850	10,900	1,088	1,088	1,088	1,088
10,900	10,950	1,093	1,093	1,093	1,093
10,950	11,000	1,098	1,098	1,098	1,098

11,000

At least	But less than	Single	MFJ *	MFS	HoH
11,000	11,050	1,103	1,103	1,103	1,103
11,050	11,100	1,109	1,108	1,109	1,108
11,100	11,150	1,115	1,113	1,115	1,113
11,150	11,200	1,121	1,118	1,121	1,118
11,200	11,250	1,127	1,123	1,127	1,123
11,250	11,300	1,133	1,128	1,133	1,128
11,300	11,350	1,139	1,133	1,139	1,133
11,350	11,400	1,145	1,138	1,145	1,138
11,400	11,450	1,151	1,143	1,151	1,143
11,450	11,500	1,157	1,148	1,157	1,148
11,500	11,550	1,163	1,153	1,163	1,153
11,550	11,600	1,169	1,158	1,169	1,158
11,600	11,650	1,175	1,163	1,175	1,163
11,650	11,700	1,181	1,168	1,181	1,168
11,700	11,750	1,187	1,173	1,187	1,173
11,750	11,800	1,193	1,178	1,193	1,178
11,800	11,850	1,199	1,183	1,199	1,183
11,850	11,900	1,205	1,188	1,205	1,188
11,900	11,950	1,211	1,193	1,211	1,193
11,950	12,000	1,217	1,198	1,217	1,198

* This column must also be used by a qualifying surviving spouse.

(Continued)

If line 15 (taxable income) is—		And you are—				If line 15 (taxable income) is—		And you are—				If line 15 (taxable income) is—		And you are—			
At least	But less than	Single	Married filing jointly *	Married filing separately	Head of a household	At least	But less than	Single	Married filing jointly *	Married filing separately	Head of a household	At least	But less than	Single	Married filing jointly *	Married filing separately	Head of a household
		Your tax is—						Your tax is—						Your tax is—			

12,000 / 15,000 / 18,000

At least	But less than	Single	MFJ	MFS	HoH	At least	But less than	Single	MFJ	MFS	HoH	At least	But less than	Single	MFJ	MFS	HoH
12,000	12,050	1,223	1,203	1,223	1,203	15,000	15,050	1,583	1,503	1,583	1,503	18,000	18,050	1,943	1,803	1,943	1,849
12,050	12,100	1,229	1,208	1,229	1,208	15,050	15,100	1,589	1,508	1,589	1,508	18,050	18,100	1,949	1,808	1,949	1,855
12,100	12,150	1,235	1,213	1,235	1,213	15,100	15,150	1,595	1,513	1,595	1,513	18,100	18,150	1,955	1,813	1,955	1,861
12,150	12,200	1,241	1,218	1,241	1,218	15,150	15,200	1,601	1,518	1,601	1,518	18,150	18,200	1,961	1,818	1,961	1,867
12,200	12,250	1,247	1,223	1,247	1,223	15,200	15,250	1,607	1,523	1,607	1,523	18,200	18,250	1,967	1,823	1,967	1,873
12,250	12,300	1,253	1,228	1,253	1,228	15,250	15,300	1,613	1,528	1,613	1,528	18,250	18,300	1,973	1,828	1,973	1,879
12,300	12,350	1,259	1,233	1,259	1,233	15,300	15,350	1,619	1,533	1,619	1,533	18,300	18,350	1,979	1,833	1,979	1,885
12,350	12,400	1,265	1,238	1,265	1,238	15,350	15,400	1,625	1,538	1,625	1,538	18,350	18,400	1,985	1,838	1,985	1,891
12,400	12,450	1,271	1,243	1,271	1,243	15,400	15,450	1,631	1,543	1,631	1,543	18,400	18,450	1,991	1,843	1,991	1,897
12,450	12,500	1,277	1,248	1,277	1,248	15,450	15,500	1,637	1,548	1,637	1,548	18,450	18,500	1,997	1,848	1,997	1,903
12,500	12,550	1,283	1,253	1,283	1,253	15,500	15,550	1,643	1,553	1,643	1,553	18,500	18,550	2,003	1,853	2,003	1,909
12,550	12,600	1,289	1,258	1,289	1,258	15,550	15,600	1,649	1,558	1,649	1,558	18,550	18,600	2,009	1,858	2,009	1,915
12,600	12,650	1,295	1,263	1,295	1,263	15,600	15,650	1,655	1,563	1,655	1,563	18,600	18,650	2,015	1,863	2,015	1,921
12,650	12,700	1,301	1,268	1,301	1,268	15,650	15,700	1,661	1,568	1,661	1,568	18,650	18,700	2,021	1,868	2,021	1,927
12,700	12,750	1,307	1,273	1,307	1,273	15,700	15,750	1,667	1,573	1,667	1,573	18,700	18,750	2,027	1,873	2,027	1,933
12,750	12,800	1,313	1,278	1,313	1,278	15,750	15,800	1,673	1,578	1,673	1,579	18,750	18,800	2,033	1,878	2,033	1,939
12,800	12,850	1,319	1,283	1,319	1,283	15,800	15,850	1,679	1,583	1,679	1,585	18,800	18,850	2,039	1,883	2,039	1,945
12,850	12,900	1,325	1,288	1,325	1,288	15,850	15,900	1,685	1,588	1,685	1,591	18,850	18,900	2,045	1,888	2,045	1,951
12,900	12,950	1,331	1,293	1,331	1,293	15,900	15,950	1,691	1,593	1,691	1,597	18,900	18,950	2,051	1,893	2,051	1,957
12,950	13,000	1,337	1,298	1,337	1,298	15,950	16,000	1,697	1,598	1,697	1,603	18,950	19,000	2,057	1,898	2,057	1,963

13,000 / 16,000 / 19,000

At least	But less than	Single	MFJ	MFS	HoH	At least	But less than	Single	MFJ	MFS	HoH	At least	But less than	Single	MFJ	MFS	HoH
13,000	13,050	1,343	1,303	1,343	1,303	16,000	16,050	1,703	1,603	1,703	1,609	19,000	19,050	2,063	1,903	2,063	1,969
13,050	13,100	1,349	1,308	1,349	1,308	16,050	16,100	1,709	1,608	1,709	1,615	19,050	19,100	2,069	1,908	2,069	1,975
13,100	13,150	1,355	1,313	1,355	1,313	16,100	16,150	1,715	1,613	1,715	1,621	19,100	19,150	2,075	1,913	2,075	1,981
13,150	13,200	1,361	1,318	1,361	1,318	16,150	16,200	1,721	1,618	1,721	1,627	19,150	19,200	2,081	1,918	2,081	1,987
13,200	13,250	1,367	1,323	1,367	1,323	16,200	16,250	1,727	1,623	1,727	1,633	19,200	19,250	2,087	1,923	2,087	1,993
13,250	13,300	1,373	1,328	1,373	1,328	16,250	16,300	1,733	1,628	1,733	1,639	19,250	19,300	2,093	1,928	2,093	1,999
13,300	13,350	1,379	1,333	1,379	1,333	16,300	16,350	1,739	1,633	1,739	1,645	19,300	19,350	2,099	1,933	2,099	2,005
13,350	13,400	1,385	1,338	1,385	1,338	16,350	16,400	1,745	1,638	1,745	1,651	19,350	19,400	2,105	1,938	2,105	2,011
13,400	13,450	1,391	1,343	1,391	1,343	16,400	16,450	1,751	1,643	1,751	1,657	19,400	19,450	2,111	1,943	2,111	2,017
13,450	13,500	1,397	1,348	1,397	1,348	16,450	16,500	1,757	1,648	1,757	1,663	19,450	19,500	2,117	1,948	2,117	2,023
13,500	13,550	1,403	1,353	1,403	1,353	16,500	16,550	1,763	1,653	1,763	1,669	19,500	19,550	2,123	1,953	2,123	2,029
13,550	13,600	1,409	1,358	1,409	1,358	16,550	16,600	1,769	1,658	1,769	1,675	19,550	19,600	2,129	1,958	2,129	2,035
13,600	13,650	1,415	1,363	1,415	1,363	16,600	16,650	1,775	1,663	1,775	1,681	19,600	19,650	2,135	1,963	2,135	2,041
13,650	13,700	1,421	1,368	1,421	1,368	16,650	16,700	1,781	1,668	1,781	1,687	19,650	19,700	2,141	1,968	2,141	2,047
13,700	13,750	1,427	1,373	1,427	1,373	16,700	16,750	1,787	1,673	1,787	1,693	19,700	19,750	2,147	1,973	2,147	2,053
13,750	13,800	1,433	1,378	1,433	1,378	16,750	16,800	1,793	1,678	1,793	1,699	19,750	19,800	2,153	1,978	2,153	2,059
13,800	13,850	1,439	1,383	1,439	1,383	16,800	16,850	1,799	1,683	1,799	1,705	19,800	19,850	2,159	1,983	2,159	2,065
13,850	13,900	1,445	1,388	1,445	1,388	16,850	16,900	1,805	1,688	1,805	1,711	19,850	19,900	2,165	1,988	2,165	2,071
13,900	13,950	1,451	1,393	1,451	1,393	16,900	16,950	1,811	1,693	1,811	1,717	19,900	19,950	2,171	1,993	2,171	2,077
13,950	14,000	1,457	1,398	1,457	1,398	16,950	17,000	1,817	1,698	1,817	1,723	19,950	20,000	2,177	1,998	2,177	2,083

14,000 / 17,000 / 20,000

At least	But less than	Single	MFJ	MFS	HoH	At least	But less than	Single	MFJ	MFS	HoH	At least	But less than	Single	MFJ	MFS	HoH
14,000	14,050	1,463	1,403	1,463	1,403	17,000	17,050	1,823	1,703	1,823	1,729	20,000	20,050	2,183	2,003	2,183	2,089
14,050	14,100	1,469	1,408	1,469	1,408	17,050	17,100	1,829	1,708	1,829	1,735	20,050	20,100	2,189	2,008	2,189	2,095
14,100	14,150	1,475	1,413	1,475	1,413	17,100	17,150	1,835	1,713	1,835	1,741	20,100	20,150	2,195	2,013	2,195	2,101
14,150	14,200	1,481	1,418	1,481	1,418	17,150	17,200	1,841	1,718	1,841	1,747	20,150	20,200	2,201	2,018	2,201	2,107
14,200	14,250	1,487	1,423	1,487	1,423	17,200	17,250	1,847	1,723	1,847	1,753	20,200	20,250	2,207	2,023	2,207	2,113
14,250	14,300	1,493	1,428	1,493	1,428	17,250	17,300	1,853	1,728	1,853	1,759	20,250	20,300	2,213	2,028	2,213	2,119
14,300	14,350	1,499	1,433	1,499	1,433	17,300	17,350	1,859	1,733	1,859	1,765	20,300	20,350	2,219	2,033	2,219	2,125
14,350	14,400	1,505	1,438	1,505	1,438	17,350	17,400	1,865	1,738	1,865	1,771	20,350	20,400	2,225	2,038	2,225	2,131
14,400	14,450	1,511	1,443	1,511	1,443	17,400	17,450	1,871	1,743	1,871	1,777	20,400	20,450	2,231	2,043	2,231	2,137
14,450	14,500	1,517	1,448	1,517	1,448	17,450	17,500	1,877	1,748	1,877	1,783	20,450	20,500	2,237	2,048	2,237	2,143
14,500	14,550	1,523	1,453	1,523	1,453	17,500	17,550	1,883	1,753	1,883	1,789	20,500	20,550	2,243	2,053	2,243	2,149
14,550	14,600	1,529	1,458	1,529	1,458	17,550	17,600	1,889	1,758	1,889	1,795	20,550	20,600	2,249	2,058	2,249	2,155
14,600	14,650	1,535	1,463	1,535	1,463	17,600	17,650	1,895	1,763	1,895	1,801	20,600	20,650	2,255	2,063	2,255	2,161
14,650	14,700	1,541	1,468	1,541	1,468	17,650	17,700	1,901	1,768	1,901	1,807	20,650	20,700	2,261	2,068	2,261	2,167
14,700	14,750	1,547	1,473	1,547	1,473	17,700	17,750	1,907	1,773	1,907	1,813	20,700	20,750	2,267	2,073	2,267	2,173
14,750	14,800	1,553	1,478	1,553	1,478	17,750	17,800	1,913	1,778	1,913	1,819	20,750	20,800	2,273	2,078	2,273	2,179
14,800	14,850	1,559	1,483	1,559	1,483	17,800	17,850	1,919	1,783	1,919	1,825	20,800	20,850	2,279	2,083	2,279	2,185
14,850	14,900	1,565	1,488	1,565	1,488	17,850	17,900	1,925	1,788	1,925	1,831	20,850	20,900	2,285	2,088	2,285	2,191
14,900	14,950	1,571	1,493	1,571	1,493	17,900	17,950	1,931	1,793	1,931	1,837	20,900	20,950	2,291	2,093	2,291	2,197
14,950	15,000	1,577	1,498	1,577	1,498	17,950	18,000	1,937	1,798	1,937	1,843	20,950	21,000	2,297	2,098	2,297	2,203

(Continued)

* This column must also be used by a qualifying surviving spouse.

21,000

At least	But less than	Single	Married filing jointly *	Married filing separately	Head of a household
21,000	21,050	2,303	2,103	2,303	2,209
21,050	21,100	2,309	2,108	2,309	2,215
21,100	21,150	2,315	2,113	2,315	2,221
21,150	21,200	2,321	2,118	2,321	2,227
21,200	21,250	2,327	2,123	2,327	2,233
21,250	21,300	2,333	2,128	2,333	2,239
21,300	21,350	2,339	2,133	2,339	2,245
21,350	21,400	2,345	2,138	2,345	2,251
21,400	21,450	2,351	2,143	2,351	2,257
21,450	21,500	2,357	2,148	2,357	2,263
21,500	21,550	2,363	2,153	2,363	2,269
21,550	21,600	2,369	2,158	2,369	2,275
21,600	21,650	2,375	2,163	2,375	2,281
21,650	21,700	2,381	2,168	2,381	2,287
21,700	21,750	2,387	2,173	2,387	2,293
21,750	21,800	2,393	2,178	2,393	2,299
21,800	21,850	2,399	2,183	2,399	2,305
21,850	21,900	2,405	2,188	2,405	2,311
21,900	21,950	2,411	2,193	2,411	2,317
21,950	22,000	2,417	2,198	2,417	2,323

22,000

At least	But less than	Single	Married filing jointly *	Married filing separately	Head of a household
22,000	22,050	2,423	2,203	2,423	2,329
22,050	22,100	2,429	2,209	2,429	2,335
22,100	22,150	2,435	2,215	2,435	2,341
22,150	22,200	2,441	2,221	2,441	2,347
22,200	22,250	2,447	2,227	2,447	2,353
22,250	22,300	2,453	2,233	2,453	2,359
22,300	22,350	2,459	2,239	2,459	2,365
22,350	22,400	2,465	2,245	2,465	2,371
22,400	22,450	2,471	2,251	2,471	2,377
22,450	22,500	2,477	2,257	2,477	2,383
22,500	22,550	2,483	2,263	2,483	2,389
22,550	22,600	2,489	2,269	2,489	2,395
22,600	22,650	2,495	2,275	2,495	2,401
22,650	22,700	2,501	2,281	2,501	2,407
22,700	22,750	2,507	2,287	2,507	2,413
22,750	22,800	2,513	2,293	2,513	2,419
22,800	22,850	2,519	2,299	2,519	2,425
22,850	22,900	2,525	2,305	2,525	2,431
22,900	22,950	2,531	2,311	2,531	2,437
22,950	23,000	2,537	2,317	2,537	2,443

23,000

At least	But less than	Single	Married filing jointly *	Married filing separately	Head of a household
23,000	23,050	2,543	2,323	2,543	2,449
23,050	23,100	2,549	2,329	2,549	2,455
23,100	23,150	2,555	2,335	2,555	2,461
23,150	23,200	2,561	2,341	2,561	2,467
23,200	23,250	2,567	2,347	2,567	2,473
23,250	23,300	2,573	2,353	2,573	2,479
23,300	23,350	2,579	2,359	2,579	2,485
23,350	23,400	2,585	2,365	2,585	2,491
23,400	23,450	2,591	2,371	2,591	2,497
23,450	23,500	2,597	2,377	2,597	2,503
23,500	23,550	2,603	2,383	2,603	2,509
23,550	23,600	2,609	2,389	2,609	2,515
23,600	23,650	2,615	2,395	2,615	2,521
23,650	23,700	2,621	2,401	2,621	2,527
23,700	23,750	2,627	2,407	2,627	2,533
23,750	23,800	2,633	2,413	2,633	2,539
23,800	23,850	2,639	2,419	2,639	2,545
23,850	23,900	2,645	2,425	2,645	2,551
23,900	23,950	2,651	2,431	2,651	2,557
23,950	24,000	2,657	2,437	2,657	2,563

24,000

At least	But less than	Single	Married filing jointly *	Married filing separately	Head of a household
24,000	24,050	2,663	2,443	2,663	2,569
24,050	24,100	2,669	2,449	2,669	2,575
24,100	24,150	2,675	2,455	2,675	2,581
24,150	24,200	2,681	2,461	2,681	2,587
24,200	24,250	2,687	2,467	2,687	2,593
24,250	24,300	2,693	2,473	2,693	2,599
24,300	24,350	2,699	2,479	2,699	2,605
24,350	24,400	2,705	2,485	2,705	2,611
24,400	24,450	2,711	2,491	2,711	2,617
24,450	24,500	2,717	2,497	2,717	2,623
24,500	24,550	2,723	2,503	2,723	2,629
24,550	24,600	2,729	2,509	2,729	2,635
24,600	24,650	2,735	2,515	2,735	2,641
24,650	24,700	2,741	2,521	2,741	2,647
24,700	24,750	2,747	2,527	2,747	2,653
24,750	24,800	2,753	2,533	2,753	2,659
24,800	24,850	2,759	2,539	2,759	2,665
24,850	24,900	2,765	2,545	2,765	2,671
24,900	24,950	2,771	2,551	2,771	2,677
24,950	25,000	2,777	2,557	2,777	2,683

25,000

At least	But less than	Single	Married filing jointly *	Married filing separately	Head of a household
25,000	25,050	2,783	2,563	2,783	2,689
25,050	25,100	2,789	2,569	2,789	2,695
25,100	25,150	2,795	2,575	2,795	2,701
25,150	25,200	2,801	2,581	2,801	2,707
25,200	25,250	2,807	2,587	2,807	2,713
25,250	25,300	2,813	2,593	2,813	2,719
25,300	25,350	2,819	2,599	2,819	2,725
25,350	25,400	2,825	2,605	2,825	2,731
25,400	25,450	2,831	2,611	2,831	2,737
25,450	25,500	2,837	2,617	2,837	2,743
25,500	25,550	2,843	2,623	2,843	2,749
25,550	25,600	2,849	2,629	2,849	2,755
25,600	25,650	2,855	2,635	2,855	2,761
25,650	25,700	2,861	2,641	2,861	2,767
25,700	25,750	2,867	2,647	2,867	2,773
25,750	25,800	2,873	2,653	2,873	2,779
25,800	25,850	2,879	2,659	2,879	2,785
25,850	25,900	2,885	2,665	2,885	2,791
25,900	25,950	2,891	2,671	2,891	2,797
25,950	26,000	2,897	2,677	2,897	2,803

26,000

At least	But less than	Single	Married filing jointly *	Married filing separately	Head of a household
26,000	26,050	2,903	2,683	2,903	2,809
26,050	26,100	2,909	2,689	2,909	2,815
26,100	26,150	2,915	2,695	2,915	2,821
26,150	26,200	2,921	2,701	2,921	2,827
26,200	26,250	2,927	2,707	2,927	2,833
26,250	26,300	2,933	2,713	2,933	2,839
26,300	26,350	2,939	2,719	2,939	2,845
26,350	26,400	2,945	2,725	2,945	2,851
26,400	26,450	2,951	2,731	2,951	2,857
26,450	26,500	2,957	2,737	2,957	2,863
26,500	26,550	2,963	2,743	2,963	2,869
26,550	26,600	2,969	2,749	2,969	2,875
26,600	26,650	2,975	2,755	2,975	2,881
26,650	26,700	2,981	2,761	2,981	2,887
26,700	26,750	2,987	2,767	2,987	2,893
26,750	26,800	2,993	2,773	2,993	2,899
26,800	26,850	2,999	2,779	2,999	2,905
26,850	26,900	3,005	2,785	3,005	2,911
26,900	26,950	3,011	2,791	3,011	2,917
26,950	27,000	3,017	2,797	3,017	2,923

27,000

At least	But less than	Single	Married filing jointly *	Married filing separately	Head of a household
27,000	27,050	3,023	2,803	3,023	2,929
27,050	27,100	3,029	2,809	3,029	2,935
27,100	27,150	3,035	2,815	3,035	2,941
27,150	27,200	3,041	2,821	3,041	2,947
27,200	27,250	3,047	2,827	3,047	2,953
27,250	27,300	3,053	2,833	3,053	2,959
27,300	27,350	3,059	2,839	3,059	2,965
27,350	27,400	3,065	2,845	3,065	2,971
27,400	27,450	3,071	2,851	3,071	2,977
27,450	27,500	3,077	2,857	3,077	2,983
27,500	27,550	3,083	2,863	3,083	2,989
27,550	27,600	3,089	2,869	3,089	2,995
27,600	27,650	3,095	2,875	3,095	3,001
27,650	27,700	3,101	2,881	3,101	3,007
27,700	27,750	3,107	2,887	3,107	3,013
27,750	27,800	3,113	2,893	3,113	3,019
27,800	27,850	3,119	2,899	3,119	3,025
27,850	27,900	3,125	2,905	3,125	3,031
27,900	27,950	3,131	2,911	3,131	3,037
27,950	28,000	3,137	2,917	3,137	3,043

28,000

At least	But less than	Single	Married filing jointly *	Married filing separately	Head of a household
28,000	28,050	3,143	2,923	3,143	3,049
28,050	28,100	3,149	2,929	3,149	3,055
28,100	28,150	3,155	2,935	3,155	3,061
28,150	28,200	3,161	2,941	3,161	3,067
28,200	28,250	3,167	2,947	3,167	3,073
28,250	28,300	3,173	2,953	3,173	3,079
28,300	28,350	3,179	2,959	3,179	3,085
28,350	28,400	3,185	2,965	3,185	3,091
28,400	28,450	3,191	2,971	3,191	3,097
28,450	28,500	3,197	2,977	3,197	3,103
28,500	28,550	3,203	2,983	3,203	3,109
28,550	28,600	3,209	2,989	3,209	3,115
28,600	28,650	3,215	2,995	3,215	3,121
28,650	28,700	3,221	3,001	3,221	3,127
28,700	28,750	3,227	3,007	3,227	3,133
28,750	28,800	3,233	3,013	3,233	3,139
28,800	28,850	3,239	3,019	3,239	3,145
28,850	28,900	3,245	3,025	3,245	3,151
28,900	28,950	3,251	3,031	3,251	3,157
28,950	29,000	3,257	3,037	3,257	3,163

29,000

At least	But less than	Single	Married filing jointly *	Married filing separately	Head of a household
29,000	29,050	3,263	3,043	3,263	3,169
29,050	29,100	3,269	3,049	3,269	3,175
29,100	29,150	3,275	3,055	3,275	3,181
29,150	29,200	3,281	3,061	3,281	3,187
29,200	29,250	3,287	3,067	3,287	3,193
29,250	29,300	3,293	3,073	3,293	3,199
29,300	29,350	3,299	3,079	3,299	3,205
29,350	29,400	3,305	3,085	3,305	3,211
29,400	29,450	3,311	3,091	3,311	3,217
29,450	29,500	3,317	3,097	3,317	3,223
29,500	29,550	3,323	3,103	3,323	3,229
29,550	29,600	3,329	3,109	3,329	3,235
29,600	29,650	3,335	3,115	3,335	3,241
29,650	29,700	3,341	3,121	3,341	3,247
29,700	29,750	3,347	3,127	3,347	3,253
29,750	29,800	3,353	3,133	3,353	3,259
29,800	29,850	3,359	3,139	3,359	3,265
29,850	29,900	3,365	3,145	3,365	3,271
29,900	29,950	3,371	3,151	3,371	3,277
29,950	30,000	3,377	3,157	3,377	3,283

(Continued)

* This column must also be used by a qualifying surviving spouse.

2023 Tax Table — *Continued*

If line 15 (taxable income) is — And you are — Your tax is—

At least	But less than	Single	Married filing jointly *	Married filing separately	Head of a household
30,000					
30,000	30,050	3,383	3,163	3,383	3,289
30,050	30,100	3,389	3,169	3,389	3,295
30,100	30,150	3,395	3,175	3,395	3,301
30,150	30,200	3,401	3,181	3,401	3,307
30,200	30,250	3,407	3,187	3,407	3,313
30,250	30,300	3,413	3,193	3,413	3,319
30,300	30,350	3,419	3,199	3,419	3,325
30,350	30,400	3,425	3,205	3,425	3,331
30,400	30,450	3,431	3,211	3,431	3,337
30,450	30,500	3,437	3,217	3,437	3,343
30,500	30,550	3,443	3,223	3,443	3,349
30,550	30,600	3,449	3,229	3,449	3,355
30,600	30,650	3,455	3,235	3,455	3,361
30,650	30,700	3,461	3,241	3,461	3,367
30,700	30,750	3,467	3,247	3,467	3,373
30,750	30,800	3,473	3,253	3,473	3,379
30,800	30,850	3,479	3,259	3,479	3,385
30,850	30,900	3,485	3,265	3,485	3,391
30,900	30,950	3,491	3,271	3,491	3,397
30,950	31,000	3,497	3,277	3,497	3,403
31,000					
31,000	31,050	3,503	3,283	3,503	3,409
31,050	31,100	3,509	3,289	3,509	3,415
31,100	31,150	3,515	3,295	3,515	3,421
31,150	31,200	3,521	3,301	3,521	3,427
31,200	31,250	3,527	3,307	3,527	3,433
31,250	31,300	3,533	3,313	3,533	3,439
31,300	31,350	3,539	3,319	3,539	3,445
31,350	31,400	3,545	3,325	3,545	3,451
31,400	31,450	3,551	3,331	3,551	3,457
31,450	31,500	3,557	3,337	3,557	3,463
31,500	31,550	3,563	3,343	3,563	3,469
31,550	31,600	3,569	3,349	3,569	3,475
31,600	31,650	3,575	3,355	3,575	3,481
31,650	31,700	3,581	3,361	3,581	3,487
31,700	31,750	3,587	3,367	3,587	3,493
31,750	31,800	3,593	3,373	3,593	3,499
31,800	31,850	3,599	3,379	3,599	3,505
31,850	31,900	3,605	3,385	3,605	3,511
31,900	31,950	3,611	3,391	3,611	3,517
31,950	32,000	3,617	3,397	3,617	3,523
32,000					
32,000	32,050	3,623	3,403	3,623	3,529
32,050	32,100	3,629	3,409	3,629	3,535
32,100	32,150	3,635	3,415	3,635	3,541
32,150	32,200	3,641	3,421	3,641	3,547
32,200	32,250	3,647	3,427	3,647	3,553
32,250	32,300	3,653	3,433	3,653	3,559
32,300	32,350	3,659	3,439	3,659	3,565
32,350	32,400	3,665	3,445	3,665	3,571
32,400	32,450	3,671	3,451	3,671	3,577
32,450	32,500	3,677	3,457	3,677	3,583
32,500	32,550	3,683	3,463	3,683	3,589
32,550	32,600	3,689	3,469	3,689	3,595
32,600	32,650	3,695	3,475	3,695	3,601
32,650	32,700	3,701	3,481	3,701	3,607
32,700	32,750	3,707	3,487	3,707	3,613
32,750	32,800	3,713	3,493	3,713	3,619
32,800	32,850	3,719	3,499	3,719	3,625
32,850	32,900	3,725	3,505	3,725	3,631
32,900	32,950	3,731	3,511	3,731	3,637
32,950	33,000	3,737	3,517	3,737	3,643

At least	But less than	Single	Married filing jointly *	Married filing separately	Head of a household
33,000					
33,000	33,050	3,743	3,523	3,743	3,649
33,050	33,100	3,749	3,529	3,749	3,655
33,100	33,150	3,755	3,535	3,755	3,661
33,150	33,200	3,761	3,541	3,761	3,667
33,200	33,250	3,767	3,547	3,767	3,673
33,250	33,300	3,773	3,553	3,773	3,679
33,300	33,350	3,779	3,559	3,779	3,685
33,350	33,400	3,785	3,565	3,785	3,691
33,400	33,450	3,791	3,571	3,791	3,697
33,450	33,500	3,797	3,577	3,797	3,703
33,500	33,550	3,803	3,583	3,803	3,709
33,550	33,600	3,809	3,589	3,809	3,715
33,600	33,650	3,815	3,595	3,815	3,721
33,650	33,700	3,821	3,601	3,821	3,727
33,700	33,750	3,827	3,607	3,827	3,733
33,750	33,800	3,833	3,613	3,833	3,739
33,800	33,850	3,839	3,619	3,839	3,745
33,850	33,900	3,845	3,625	3,845	3,751
33,900	33,950	3,851	3,631	3,851	3,757
33,950	34,000	3,857	3,637	3,857	3,763
34,000					
34,000	34,050	3,863	3,643	3,863	3,769
34,050	34,100	3,869	3,649	3,869	3,775
34,100	34,150	3,875	3,655	3,875	3,781
34,150	34,200	3,881	3,661	3,881	3,787
34,200	34,250	3,887	3,667	3,887	3,793
34,250	34,300	3,893	3,673	3,893	3,799
34,300	34,350	3,899	3,679	3,899	3,805
34,350	34,400	3,905	3,685	3,905	3,811
34,400	34,450	3,911	3,691	3,911	3,817
34,450	34,500	3,917	3,697	3,917	3,823
34,500	34,550	3,923	3,703	3,923	3,829
34,550	34,600	3,929	3,709	3,929	3,835
34,600	34,650	3,935	3,715	3,935	3,841
34,650	34,700	3,941	3,721	3,941	3,847
34,700	34,750	3,947	3,727	3,947	3,853
34,750	34,800	3,953	3,733	3,953	3,859
34,800	34,850	3,959	3,739	3,959	3,865
34,850	34,900	3,965	3,745	3,965	3,871
34,900	34,950	3,971	3,751	3,971	3,877
34,950	35,000	3,977	3,757	3,977	3,883
35,000					
35,000	35,050	3,983	3,763	3,983	3,889
35,050	35,100	3,989	3,769	3,989	3,895
35,100	35,150	3,995	3,775	3,995	3,901
35,150	35,200	4,001	3,781	4,001	3,907
35,200	35,250	4,007	3,787	4,007	3,913
35,250	35,300	4,013	3,793	4,013	3,919
35,300	35,350	4,019	3,799	4,019	3,925
35,350	35,400	4,025	3,805	4,025	3,931
35,400	35,450	4,031	3,811	4,031	3,937
35,450	35,500	4,037	3,817	4,037	3,943
35,500	35,550	4,043	3,823	4,043	3,949
35,550	35,600	4,049	3,829	4,049	3,955
35,600	35,650	4,055	3,835	4,055	3,961
35,650	35,700	4,061	3,841	4,061	3,967
35,700	35,750	4,067	3,847	4,067	3,973
35,750	35,800	4,073	3,853	4,073	3,979
35,800	35,850	4,079	3,859	4,079	3,985
35,850	35,900	4,085	3,865	4,085	3,991
35,900	35,950	4,091	3,871	4,091	3,997
35,950	36,000	4,097	3,877	4,097	4,003

At least	But less than	Single	Married filing jointly *	Married filing separately	Head of a household
36,000					
36,000	36,050	4,103	3,883	4,103	4,009
36,050	36,100	4,109	3,889	4,109	4,015
36,100	36,150	4,115	3,895	4,115	4,021
36,150	36,200	4,121	3,901	4,121	4,027
36,200	36,250	4,127	3,907	4,127	4,033
36,250	36,300	4,133	3,913	4,133	4,039
36,300	36,350	4,139	3,919	4,139	4,045
36,350	36,400	4,145	3,925	4,145	4,051
36,400	36,450	4,151	3,931	4,151	4,057
36,450	36,500	4,157	3,937	4,157	4,063
36,500	36,550	4,163	3,943	4,163	4,069
36,550	36,600	4,169	3,949	4,169	4,075
36,600	36,650	4,175	3,955	4,175	4,081
36,650	36,700	4,181	3,961	4,181	4,087
36,700	36,750	4,187	3,967	4,187	4,093
36,750	36,800	4,193	3,973	4,193	4,099
36,800	36,850	4,199	3,979	4,199	4,105
36,850	36,900	4,205	3,985	4,205	4,111
36,900	36,950	4,211	3,991	4,211	4,117
36,950	37,000	4,217	3,997	4,217	4,123
37,000					
37,000	37,050	4,223	4,003	4,223	4,129
37,050	37,100	4,229	4,009	4,229	4,135
37,100	37,150	4,235	4,015	4,235	4,141
37,150	37,200	4,241	4,021	4,241	4,147
37,200	37,250	4,247	4,027	4,247	4,153
37,250	37,300	4,253	4,033	4,253	4,159
37,300	37,350	4,259	4,039	4,259	4,165
37,350	37,400	4,265	4,045	4,265	4,171
37,400	37,450	4,271	4,051	4,271	4,177
37,450	37,500	4,277	4,057	4,277	4,183
37,500	37,550	4,283	4,063	4,283	4,189
37,550	37,600	4,289	4,069	4,289	4,195
37,600	37,650	4,295	4,075	4,295	4,201
37,650	37,700	4,301	4,081	4,301	4,207
37,700	37,750	4,307	4,087	4,307	4,213
37,750	37,800	4,313	4,093	4,313	4,219
37,800	37,850	4,319	4,099	4,319	4,225
37,850	37,900	4,325	4,105	4,325	4,231
37,900	37,950	4,331	4,111	4,331	4,237
37,950	38,000	4,337	4,117	4,337	4,243
38,000					
38,000	38,050	4,343	4,123	4,343	4,249
38,050	38,100	4,349	4,129	4,349	4,255
38,100	38,150	4,355	4,135	4,355	4,261
38,150	38,200	4,361	4,141	4,361	4,267
38,200	38,250	4,367	4,147	4,367	4,273
38,250	38,300	4,373	4,153	4,373	4,279
38,300	38,350	4,379	4,159	4,379	4,285
38,350	38,400	4,385	4,165	4,385	4,291
38,400	38,450	4,391	4,171	4,391	4,297
38,450	38,500	4,397	4,177	4,397	4,303
38,500	38,550	4,403	4,183	4,403	4,309
38,550	38,600	4,409	4,189	4,409	4,315
38,600	38,650	4,415	4,195	4,415	4,321
38,650	38,700	4,421	4,201	4,421	4,327
38,700	38,750	4,427	4,207	4,427	4,333
38,750	38,800	4,433	4,213	4,433	4,339
38,800	38,850	4,439	4,219	4,439	4,345
38,850	38,900	4,445	4,225	4,445	4,351
38,900	38,950	4,451	4,231	4,451	4,357
38,950	39,000	4,457	4,237	4,457	4,363

(Continued)

* This column must also be used by a qualifying surviving spouse.

39,000

At least	But less than	Single	Married filing jointly *	Married filing separately	Head of a household
39,000	39,050	4,463	4,243	4,463	4,369
39,050	39,100	4,469	4,249	4,469	4,375
39,100	39,150	4,475	4,255	4,475	4,381
39,150	39,200	4,481	4,261	4,481	4,387
39,200	39,250	4,487	4,267	4,487	4,393
39,250	39,300	4,493	4,273	4,493	4,399
39,300	39,350	4,499	4,279	4,499	4,405
39,350	39,400	4,505	4,285	4,505	4,411
39,400	39,450	4,511	4,291	4,511	4,417
39,450	39,500	4,517	4,297	4,517	4,423
39,500	39,550	4,523	4,303	4,523	4,429
39,550	39,600	4,529	4,309	4,529	4,435
39,600	39,650	4,535	4,315	4,535	4,441
39,650	39,700	4,541	4,321	4,541	4,447
39,700	39,750	4,547	4,327	4,547	4,453
39,750	39,800	4,553	4,333	4,553	4,459
39,800	39,850	4,559	4,339	4,559	4,465
39,850	39,900	4,565	4,345	4,565	4,471
39,900	39,950	4,571	4,351	4,571	4,477
39,950	40,000	4,577	4,357	4,577	4,483

40,000

At least	But less than	Single	Married filing jointly *	Married filing separately	Head of a household
40,000	40,050	4,583	4,363	4,583	4,489
40,050	40,100	4,589	4,369	4,589	4,495
40,100	40,150	4,595	4,375	4,595	4,501
40,150	40,200	4,601	4,381	4,601	4,507
40,200	40,250	4,607	4,387	4,607	4,513
40,250	40,300	4,613	4,393	4,613	4,519
40,300	40,350	4,619	4,399	4,619	4,525
40,350	40,400	4,625	4,405	4,625	4,531
40,400	40,450	4,631	4,411	4,631	4,537
40,450	40,500	4,637	4,417	4,637	4,543
40,500	40,550	4,643	4,423	4,643	4,549
40,550	40,600	4,649	4,429	4,649	4,555
40,600	40,650	4,655	4,435	4,655	4,561
40,650	40,700	4,661	4,441	4,661	4,567
40,700	40,750	4,667	4,447	4,667	4,573
40,750	40,800	4,673	4,453	4,673	4,579
40,800	40,850	4,679	4,459	4,679	4,585
40,850	40,900	4,685	4,465	4,685	4,591
40,900	40,950	4,691	4,471	4,691	4,597
40,950	41,000	4,697	4,477	4,697	4,603

41,000

At least	But less than	Single	Married filing jointly *	Married filing separately	Head of a household
41,000	41,050	4,703	4,483	4,703	4,609
41,050	41,100	4,709	4,489	4,709	4,615
41,100	41,150	4,715	4,495	4,715	4,621
41,150	41,200	4,721	4,501	4,721	4,627
41,200	41,250	4,727	4,507	4,727	4,633
41,250	41,300	4,733	4,513	4,733	4,639
41,300	41,350	4,739	4,519	4,739	4,645
41,350	41,400	4,745	4,525	4,745	4,651
41,400	41,450	4,751	4,531	4,751	4,657
41,450	41,500	4,757	4,537	4,757	4,663
41,500	41,550	4,763	4,543	4,763	4,669
41,550	41,600	4,769	4,549	4,769	4,675
41,600	41,650	4,775	4,555	4,775	4,681
41,650	41,700	4,781	4,561	4,781	4,687
41,700	41,750	4,787	4,567	4,787	4,693
41,750	41,800	4,793	4,573	4,793	4,699
41,800	41,850	4,799	4,579	4,799	4,705
41,850	41,900	4,805	4,585	4,805	4,711
41,900	41,950	4,811	4,591	4,811	4,717
41,950	42,000	4,817	4,597	4,817	4,723

42,000

At least	But less than	Single	Married filing jointly *	Married filing separately	Head of a household
42,000	42,050	4,823	4,603	4,823	4,729
42,050	42,100	4,829	4,609	4,829	4,735
42,100	42,150	4,835	4,615	4,835	4,741
42,150	42,200	4,841	4,621	4,841	4,747
42,200	42,250	4,847	4,627	4,847	4,753
42,250	42,300	4,853	4,633	4,853	4,759
42,300	42,350	4,859	4,639	4,859	4,765
42,350	42,400	4,865	4,645	4,865	4,771
42,400	42,450	4,871	4,651	4,871	4,777
42,450	42,500	4,877	4,657	4,877	4,783
42,500	42,550	4,883	4,663	4,883	4,789
42,550	42,600	4,889	4,669	4,889	4,795
42,600	42,650	4,895	4,675	4,895	4,801
42,650	42,700	4,901	4,681	4,901	4,807
42,700	42,750	4,907	4,687	4,907	4,813
42,750	42,800	4,913	4,693	4,913	4,819
42,800	42,850	4,919	4,699	4,919	4,825
42,850	42,900	4,925	4,705	4,925	4,831
42,900	42,950	4,931	4,711	4,931	4,837
42,950	43,000	4,937	4,717	4,937	4,843

43,000

At least	But less than	Single	Married filing jointly *	Married filing separately	Head of a household
43,000	43,050	4,943	4,723	4,943	4,849
43,050	43,100	4,949	4,729	4,949	4,855
43,100	43,150	4,955	4,735	4,955	4,861
43,150	43,200	4,961	4,741	4,961	4,867
43,200	43,250	4,967	4,747	4,967	4,873
43,250	43,300	4,973	4,753	4,973	4,879
43,300	43,350	4,979	4,759	4,979	4,885
43,350	43,400	4,985	4,765	4,985	4,891
43,400	43,450	4,991	4,771	4,991	4,897
43,450	43,500	4,997	4,777	4,997	4,903
43,500	43,550	5,003	4,783	5,003	4,909
43,550	43,600	5,009	4,789	5,009	4,915
43,600	43,650	5,015	4,795	5,015	4,921
43,650	43,700	5,021	4,801	5,021	4,927
43,700	43,750	5,027	4,807	5,027	4,933
43,750	43,800	5,033	4,813	5,033	4,939
43,800	43,850	5,039	4,819	5,039	4,945
43,850	43,900	5,045	4,825	5,045	4,951
43,900	43,950	5,051	4,831	5,051	4,957
43,950	44,000	5,057	4,837	5,057	4,963

44,000

At least	But less than	Single	Married filing jointly *	Married filing separately	Head of a household
44,000	44,050	5,063	4,843	5,063	4,969
44,050	44,100	5,069	4,849	5,069	4,975
44,100	44,150	5,075	4,855	5,075	4,981
44,150	44,200	5,081	4,861	5,081	4,987
44,200	44,250	5,087	4,867	5,087	4,993
44,250	44,300	5,093	4,873	5,093	4,999
44,300	44,350	5,099	4,879	5,099	5,005
44,350	44,400	5,105	4,885	5,105	5,011
44,400	44,450	5,111	4,891	5,111	5,017
44,450	44,500	5,117	4,897	5,117	5,023
44,500	44,550	5,123	4,903	5,123	5,029
44,550	44,600	5,129	4,909	5,129	5,035
44,600	44,650	5,135	4,915	5,135	5,041
44,650	44,700	5,141	4,921	5,141	5,047
44,700	44,750	5,147	4,927	5,147	5,053
44,750	44,800	5,158	4,933	5,158	5,059
44,800	44,850	5,169	4,939	5,169	5,065
44,850	44,900	5,180	4,945	5,180	5,071
44,900	44,950	5,191	4,951	5,191	5,077
44,950	45,000	5,202	4,957	5,202	5,083

45,000

At least	But less than	Single	Married filing jointly *	Married filing separately	Head of a household
45,000	45,050	5,213	4,963	5,213	5,089
45,050	45,100	5,224	4,969	5,224	5,095
45,100	45,150	5,235	4,975	5,235	5,101
45,150	45,200	5,246	4,981	5,246	5,107
45,200	45,250	5,257	4,987	5,257	5,113
45,250	45,300	5,268	4,993	5,268	5,119
45,300	45,350	5,279	4,999	5,279	5,125
45,350	45,400	5,290	5,005	5,290	5,131
45,400	45,450	5,301	5,011	5,301	5,137
45,450	45,500	5,312	5,017	5,312	5,143
45,500	45,550	5,323	5,023	5,323	5,149
45,550	45,600	5,334	5,029	5,334	5,155
45,600	45,650	5,345	5,035	5,345	5,161
45,650	45,700	5,356	5,041	5,356	5,167
45,700	45,750	5,367	5,047	5,367	5,173
45,750	45,800	5,378	5,053	5,378	5,179
45,800	45,850	5,389	5,059	5,389	5,185
45,850	45,900	5,400	5,065	5,400	5,191
45,900	45,950	5,411	5,071	5,411	5,197
45,950	46,000	5,422	5,077	5,422	5,203

46,000

At least	But less than	Single	Married filing jointly *	Married filing separately	Head of a household
46,000	46,050	5,433	5,083	5,433	5,209
46,050	46,100	5,444	5,089	5,444	5,215
46,100	46,150	5,455	5,095	5,455	5,221
46,150	46,200	5,466	5,101	5,466	5,227
46,200	46,250	5,477	5,107	5,477	5,233
46,250	46,300	5,488	5,113	5,488	5,239
46,300	46,350	5,499	5,119	5,499	5,245
46,350	46,400	5,510	5,125	5,510	5,251
46,400	46,450	5,521	5,131	5,521	5,257
46,450	46,500	5,532	5,137	5,532	5,263
46,500	46,550	5,543	5,143	5,543	5,269
46,550	46,600	5,554	5,149	5,554	5,275
46,600	46,650	5,565	5,155	5,565	5,281
46,650	46,700	5,576	5,161	5,576	5,287
46,700	46,750	5,587	5,167	5,587	5,293
46,750	46,800	5,598	5,173	5,598	5,299
46,800	46,850	5,609	5,179	5,609	5,305
46,850	46,900	5,620	5,185	5,620	5,311
46,900	46,950	5,631	5,191	5,631	5,317
46,950	47,000	5,642	5,197	5,642	5,323

47,000

At least	But less than	Single	Married filing jointly *	Married filing separately	Head of a household
47,000	47,050	5,653	5,203	5,653	5,329
47,050	47,100	5,664	5,209	5,664	5,335
47,100	47,150	5,675	5,215	5,675	5,341
47,150	47,200	5,686	5,221	5,686	5,347
47,200	47,250	5,697	5,227	5,697	5,353
47,250	47,300	5,708	5,233	5,708	5,359
47,300	47,350	5,719	5,239	5,719	5,365
47,350	47,400	5,730	5,245	5,730	5,371
47,400	47,450	5,741	5,251	5,741	5,377
47,450	47,500	5,752	5,257	5,752	5,383
47,500	47,550	5,763	5,263	5,763	5,389
47,550	47,600	5,774	5,269	5,774	5,395
47,600	47,650	5,785	5,275	5,785	5,401
47,650	47,700	5,796	5,281	5,796	5,407
47,700	47,750	5,807	5,287	5,807	5,413
47,750	47,800	5,818	5,293	5,818	5,419
47,800	47,850	5,829	5,299	5,829	5,425
47,850	47,900	5,840	5,305	5,840	5,431
47,900	47,950	5,851	5,311	5,851	5,437
47,950	48,000	5,862	5,317	5,862	5,443

(Continued)

* This column must also be used by a qualifying surviving spouse.

2023 Tax Table — *Continued*

If line 15 (taxable income) is—		And you are—			
At least	But less than	Single	Married filing jointly *	Married filing separately	Head of a household
		Your tax is—			

48,000

At least	But less than	Single	MFJ *	MFS	HoH
48,000	48,050	5,873	5,323	5,873	5,449
48,050	48,100	5,884	5,329	5,884	5,455
48,100	48,150	5,895	5,335	5,895	5,461
48,150	48,200	5,906	5,341	5,906	5,467
48,200	48,250	5,917	5,347	5,917	5,473
48,250	48,300	5,928	5,353	5,928	5,479
48,300	48,350	5,939	5,359	5,939	5,485
48,350	48,400	5,950	5,365	5,950	5,491
48,400	48,450	5,961	5,371	5,961	5,497
48,450	48,500	5,972	5,377	5,972	5,503
48,500	48,550	5,983	5,383	5,983	5,509
48,550	48,600	5,994	5,389	5,994	5,515
48,600	48,650	6,005	5,395	6,005	5,521
48,650	48,700	6,016	5,401	6,016	5,527
48,700	48,750	6,027	5,407	6,027	5,533
48,750	48,800	6,038	5,413	6,038	5,539
48,800	48,850	6,049	5,419	6,049	5,545
48,850	48,900	6,060	5,425	6,060	5,551
48,900	48,950	6,071	5,431	6,071	5,557
48,950	49,000	6,082	5,437	6,082	5,563

49,000

At least	But less than	Single	MFJ *	MFS	HoH
49,000	49,050	6,093	5,443	6,093	5,569
49,050	49,100	6,104	5,449	6,104	5,575
49,100	49,150	6,115	5,455	6,115	5,581
49,150	49,200	6,126	5,461	6,126	5,587
49,200	49,250	6,137	5,467	6,137	5,593
49,250	49,300	6,148	5,473	6,148	5,599
49,300	49,350	6,159	5,479	6,159	5,605
49,350	49,400	6,170	5,485	6,170	5,611
49,400	49,450	6,181	5,491	6,181	5,617
49,450	49,500	6,192	5,497	6,192	5,623
49,500	49,550	6,203	5,503	6,203	5,629
49,550	49,600	6,214	5,509	6,214	5,635
49,600	49,650	6,225	5,515	6,225	5,641
49,650	49,700	6,236	5,521	6,236	5,647
49,700	49,750	6,247	5,527	6,247	5,653
49,750	49,800	6,258	5,533	6,258	5,659
49,800	49,850	6,269	5,539	6,269	5,665
49,850	49,900	6,280	5,545	6,280	5,671
49,900	49,950	6,291	5,551	6,291	5,677
49,950	50,000	6,302	5,557	6,302	5,683

50,000

At least	But less than	Single	MFJ *	MFS	HoH
50,000	50,050	6,313	5,563	6,313	5,689
50,050	50,100	6,324	5,569	6,324	5,695
50,100	50,150	6,335	5,575	6,335	5,701
50,150	50,200	6,346	5,581	6,346	5,707
50,200	50,250	6,357	5,587	6,357	5,713
50,250	50,300	6,368	5,593	6,368	5,719
50,300	50,350	6,379	5,599	6,379	5,725
50,350	50,400	6,390	5,605	6,390	5,731
50,400	50,450	6,401	5,611	6,401	5,737
50,450	50,500	6,412	5,617	6,412	5,743
50,500	50,550	6,423	5,623	6,423	5,749
50,550	50,600	6,434	5,629	6,434	5,755
50,600	50,650	6,445	5,635	6,445	5,761
50,650	50,700	6,456	5,641	6,456	5,767
50,700	50,750	6,467	5,647	6,467	5,773
50,750	50,800	6,478	5,653	6,478	5,779
50,800	50,850	6,489	5,659	6,489	5,785
50,850	50,900	6,500	5,665	6,500	5,791
50,900	50,950	6,511	5,671	6,511	5,797
50,950	51,000	6,522	5,677	6,522	5,803

51,000

At least	But less than	Single	MFJ *	MFS	HoH
51,000	51,050	6,533	5,683	6,533	5,809
51,050	51,100	6,544	5,689	6,544	5,815
51,100	51,150	6,555	5,695	6,555	5,821
51,150	51,200	6,566	5,701	6,566	5,827
51,200	51,250	6,577	5,707	6,577	5,833
51,250	51,300	6,588	5,713	6,588	5,839
51,300	51,350	6,599	5,719	6,599	5,845
51,350	51,400	6,610	5,725	6,610	5,851
51,400	51,450	6,621	5,731	6,621	5,857
51,450	51,500	6,632	5,737	6,632	5,863
51,500	51,550	6,643	5,743	6,643	5,869
51,550	51,600	6,654	5,749	6,654	5,875
51,600	51,650	6,665	5,755	6,665	5,881
51,650	51,700	6,676	5,761	6,676	5,887
51,700	51,750	6,687	5,767	6,687	5,893
51,750	51,800	6,698	5,773	6,698	5,899
51,800	51,850	6,709	5,779	6,709	5,905
51,850	51,900	6,720	5,785	6,720	5,911
51,900	51,950	6,731	5,791	6,731	5,917
51,950	52,000	6,742	5,797	6,742	5,923

52,000

At least	But less than	Single	MFJ *	MFS	HoH
52,000	52,050	6,753	5,803	6,753	5,929
52,050	52,100	6,764	5,809	6,764	5,935
52,100	52,150	6,775	5,815	6,775	5,941
52,150	52,200	6,786	5,821	6,786	5,947
52,200	52,250	6,797	5,827	6,797	5,953
52,250	52,300	6,808	5,833	6,808	5,959
52,300	52,350	6,819	5,839	6,819	5,965
52,350	52,400	6,830	5,845	6,830	5,971
52,400	52,450	6,841	5,851	6,841	5,977
52,450	52,500	6,852	5,857	6,852	5,983
52,500	52,550	6,863	5,863	6,863	5,989
52,550	52,600	6,874	5,869	6,874	5,995
52,600	52,650	6,885	5,875	6,885	6,001
52,650	52,700	6,896	5,881	6,896	6,007
52,700	52,750	6,907	5,887	6,907	6,013
52,750	52,800	6,918	5,893	6,918	6,019
52,800	52,850	6,929	5,899	6,929	6,025
52,850	52,900	6,940	5,905	6,940	6,031
52,900	52,950	6,951	5,911	6,951	6,037
52,950	53,000	6,962	5,917	6,962	6,043

53,000

At least	But less than	Single	MFJ *	MFS	HoH
53,000	53,050	6,973	5,923	6,973	6,049
53,050	53,100	6,984	5,929	6,984	6,055
53,100	53,150	6,995	5,935	6,995	6,061
53,150	53,200	7,006	5,941	7,006	6,067
53,200	53,250	7,017	5,947	7,017	6,073
53,250	53,300	7,028	5,953	7,028	6,079
53,300	53,350	7,039	5,959	7,039	6,085
53,350	53,400	7,050	5,965	7,050	6,091
53,400	53,450	7,061	5,971	7,061	6,097
53,450	53,500	7,072	5,977	7,072	6,103
53,500	53,550	7,083	5,983	7,083	6,109
53,550	53,600	7,094	5,989	7,094	6,115
53,600	53,650	7,105	5,995	7,105	6,121
53,650	53,700	7,116	6,001	7,116	6,127
53,700	53,750	7,127	6,007	7,127	6,133
53,750	53,800	7,138	6,013	7,138	6,139
53,800	53,850	7,149	6,019	7,149	6,145
53,850	53,900	7,160	6,025	7,160	6,151
53,900	53,950	7,171	6,031	7,171	6,157
53,950	54,000	7,182	6,037	7,182	6,163

54,000

At least	But less than	Single	MFJ *	MFS	HoH
54,000	54,050	7,193	6,043	7,193	6,169
54,050	54,100	7,204	6,049	7,204	6,175
54,100	54,150	7,215	6,055	7,215	6,181
54,150	54,200	7,226	6,061	7,226	6,187
54,200	54,250	7,237	6,067	7,237	6,193
54,250	54,300	7,248	6,073	7,248	6,199
54,300	54,350	7,259	6,079	7,259	6,205
54,350	54,400	7,270	6,085	7,270	6,211
54,400	54,450	7,281	6,091	7,281	6,217
54,450	54,500	7,292	6,097	7,292	6,223
54,500	54,550	7,303	6,103	7,303	6,229
54,550	54,600	7,314	6,109	7,314	6,235
54,600	54,650	7,325	6,115	7,325	6,241
54,650	54,700	7,336	6,121	7,336	6,247
54,700	54,750	7,347	6,127	7,347	6,253
54,750	54,800	7,358	6,133	7,358	6,259
54,800	54,850	7,369	6,139	7,369	6,265
54,850	54,900	7,380	6,145	7,380	6,271
54,900	54,950	7,391	6,151	7,391	6,277
54,950	55,000	7,402	6,157	7,402	6,283

55,000

At least	But less than	Single	MFJ *	MFS	HoH
55,000	55,050	7,413	6,163	7,413	6,289
55,050	55,100	7,424	6,169	7,424	6,295
55,100	55,150	7,435	6,175	7,435	6,301
55,150	55,200	7,446	6,181	7,446	6,307
55,200	55,250	7,457	6,187	7,457	6,313
55,250	55,300	7,468	6,193	7,468	6,319
55,300	55,350	7,479	6,199	7,479	6,325
55,350	55,400	7,490	6,205	7,490	6,331
55,400	55,450	7,501	6,211	7,501	6,337
55,450	55,500	7,512	6,217	7,512	6,343
55,500	55,550	7,523	6,223	7,523	6,349
55,550	55,600	7,534	6,229	7,534	6,355
55,600	55,650	7,545	6,235	7,545	6,361
55,650	55,700	7,556	6,241	7,556	6,367
55,700	55,750	7,567	6,247	7,567	6,373
55,750	55,800	7,578	6,253	7,578	6,379
55,800	55,850	7,589	6,259	7,589	6,385
55,850	55,900	7,600	6,265	7,600	6,391
55,900	55,950	7,611	6,271	7,611	6,397
55,950	56,000	7,622	6,277	7,622	6,403

56,000

At least	But less than	Single	MFJ *	MFS	HoH
56,000	56,050	7,633	6,283	7,633	6,409
56,050	56,100	7,644	6,289	7,644	6,415
56,100	56,150	7,655	6,295	7,655	6,421
56,150	56,200	7,666	6,301	7,666	6,427
56,200	56,250	7,677	6,307	7,677	6,433
56,250	56,300	7,688	6,313	7,688	6,439
56,300	56,350	7,699	6,319	7,699	6,445
56,350	56,400	7,710	6,325	7,710	6,451
56,400	56,450	7,721	6,331	7,721	6,457
56,450	56,500	7,732	6,337	7,732	6,463
56,500	56,550	7,743	6,343	7,743	6,469
56,550	56,600	7,754	6,349	7,754	6,475
56,600	56,650	7,765	6,355	7,765	6,481
56,650	56,700	7,776	6,361	7,776	6,487
56,700	56,750	7,787	6,367	7,787	6,493
56,750	56,800	7,798	6,373	7,798	6,499
56,800	56,850	7,809	6,379	7,809	6,505
56,850	56,900	7,820	6,385	7,820	6,511
56,900	56,950	7,831	6,391	7,831	6,517
56,950	57,000	7,842	6,397	7,842	6,523

(Continued)

* This column must also be used by a qualifying surviving spouse.

If line 15 (taxable income) is—		And you are—				If line 15 (taxable income) is—		And you are—				If line 15 (taxable income) is—		And you are—			
At least	But less than	Single	Married filing jointly *	Married filing separately	Head of a household	At least	But less than	Single	Married filing jointly *	Married filing separately	Head of a household	At least	But less than	Single	Married filing jointly *	Married filing separately	Head of a household
		Your tax is—						Your tax is—						Your tax is—			

57,000 / 60,000 / 63,000

At least	But less than	Single	MFJ*	MFS	HoH	At least	But less than	Single	MFJ*	MFS	HoH	At least	But less than	Single	MFJ*	MFS	HoH
57,000	57,050	7,853	6,403	7,853	6,529	60,000	60,050	8,513	6,763	8,513	6,907	63,000	63,050	9,173	7,123	9,173	7,567
57,050	57,100	7,864	6,409	7,864	6,535	60,050	60,100	8,524	6,769	8,524	6,918	63,050	63,100	9,184	7,129	9,184	7,578
57,100	57,150	7,875	6,415	7,875	6,541	60,100	60,150	8,535	6,775	8,535	6,929	63,100	63,150	9,195	7,135	9,195	7,589
57,150	57,200	7,886	6,421	7,886	6,547	60,150	60,200	8,546	6,781	8,546	6,940	63,150	63,200	9,206	7,141	9,206	7,600
57,200	57,250	7,897	6,427	7,897	6,553	60,200	60,250	8,557	6,787	8,557	6,951	63,200	63,250	9,217	7,147	9,217	7,611
57,250	57,300	7,908	6,433	7,908	6,559	60,250	60,300	8,568	6,793	8,568	6,962	63,250	63,300	9,228	7,153	9,228	7,622
57,300	57,350	7,919	6,439	7,919	6,565	60,300	60,350	8,579	6,799	8,579	6,973	63,300	63,350	9,239	7,159	9,239	7,633
57,350	57,400	7,930	6,445	7,930	6,571	60,350	60,400	8,590	6,805	8,590	6,984	63,350	63,400	9,250	7,165	9,250	7,644
57,400	57,450	7,941	6,451	7,941	6,577	60,400	60,450	8,601	6,811	8,601	6,995	63,400	63,450	9,261	7,171	9,261	7,655
57,450	57,500	7,952	6,457	7,952	6,583	60,450	60,500	8,612	6,817	8,612	7,006	63,450	63,500	9,272	7,177	9,272	7,666
57,500	57,550	7,963	6,463	7,963	6,589	60,500	60,550	8,623	6,823	8,623	7,017	63,500	63,550	9,283	7,183	9,283	7,677
57,550	57,600	7,974	6,469	7,974	6,595	60,550	60,600	8,634	6,829	8,634	7,028	63,550	63,600	9,294	7,189	9,294	7,688
57,600	57,650	7,985	6,475	7,985	6,601	60,600	60,650	8,645	6,835	8,645	7,039	63,600	63,650	9,305	7,195	9,305	7,699
57,650	57,700	7,996	6,481	7,996	6,607	60,650	60,700	8,656	6,841	8,656	7,050	63,650	63,700	9,316	7,201	9,316	7,710
57,700	57,750	8,007	6,487	8,007	6,613	60,700	60,750	8,667	6,847	8,667	7,061	63,700	63,750	9,327	7,207	9,327	7,721
57,750	57,800	8,018	6,493	8,018	6,619	60,750	60,800	8,678	6,853	8,678	7,072	63,750	63,800	9,338	7,213	9,338	7,732
57,800	57,850	8,029	6,499	8,029	6,625	60,800	60,850	8,689	6,859	8,689	7,083	63,800	63,850	9,349	7,219	9,349	7,743
57,850	57,900	8,040	6,505	8,040	6,631	60,850	60,900	8,700	6,865	8,700	7,094	63,850	63,900	9,360	7,225	9,360	7,754
57,900	57,950	8,051	6,511	8,051	6,637	60,900	60,950	8,711	6,871	8,711	7,105	63,900	63,950	9,371	7,231	9,371	7,765
57,950	58,000	8,062	6,517	8,062	6,643	60,950	61,000	8,722	6,877	8,722	7,116	63,950	64,000	9,382	7,237	9,382	7,776

58,000 / 61,000 / 64,000

At least	But less than	Single	MFJ*	MFS	HoH	At least	But less than	Single	MFJ*	MFS	HoH	At least	But less than	Single	MFJ*	MFS	HoH
58,000	58,050	8,073	6,523	8,073	6,649	61,000	61,050	8,733	6,883	8,733	7,127	64,000	64,050	9,393	7,243	9,393	7,787
58,050	58,100	8,084	6,529	8,084	6,655	61,050	61,100	8,744	6,889	8,744	7,138	64,050	64,100	9,404	7,249	9,404	7,798
58,100	58,150	8,095	6,535	8,095	6,661	61,100	61,150	8,755	6,895	8,755	7,149	64,100	64,150	9,415	7,255	9,415	7,809
58,150	58,200	8,106	6,541	8,106	6,667	61,150	61,200	8,766	6,901	8,766	7,160	64,150	64,200	9,426	7,261	9,426	7,820
58,200	58,250	8,117	6,547	8,117	6,673	61,200	61,250	8,777	6,907	8,777	7,171	64,200	64,250	9,437	7,267	9,437	7,831
58,250	58,300	8,128	6,553	8,128	6,679	61,250	61,300	8,788	6,913	8,788	7,182	64,250	64,300	9,448	7,273	9,448	7,842
58,300	58,350	8,139	6,559	8,139	6,685	61,300	61,350	8,799	6,919	8,799	7,193	64,300	64,350	9,459	7,279	9,459	7,853
58,350	58,400	8,150	6,565	8,150	6,691	61,350	61,400	8,810	6,925	8,810	7,204	64,350	64,400	9,470	7,285	9,470	7,864
58,400	58,450	8,161	6,571	8,161	6,697	61,400	61,450	8,821	6,931	8,821	7,215	64,400	64,450	9,481	7,291	9,481	7,875
58,450	58,500	8,172	6,577	8,172	6,703	61,450	61,500	8,832	6,937	8,832	7,226	64,450	64,500	9,492	7,297	9,492	7,886
58,500	58,550	8,183	6,583	8,183	6,709	61,500	61,550	8,843	6,943	8,843	7,237	64,500	64,550	9,503	7,303	9,503	7,897
58,550	58,600	8,194	6,589	8,194	6,715	61,550	61,600	8,854	6,949	8,854	7,248	64,550	64,600	9,514	7,309	9,514	7,908
58,600	58,650	8,205	6,595	8,205	6,721	61,600	61,650	8,865	6,955	8,865	7,259	64,600	64,650	9,525	7,315	9,525	7,919
58,650	58,700	8,216	6,601	8,216	6,727	61,650	61,700	8,876	6,961	8,876	7,270	64,650	64,700	9,536	7,321	9,536	7,930
58,700	58,750	8,227	6,607	8,227	6,733	61,700	61,750	8,887	6,967	8,887	7,281	64,700	64,750	9,547	7,327	9,547	7,941
58,750	58,800	8,238	6,613	8,238	6,739	61,750	61,800	8,898	6,973	8,898	7,292	64,750	64,800	9,558	7,333	9,558	7,952
58,800	58,850	8,249	6,619	8,249	6,745	61,800	61,850	8,909	6,979	8,909	7,303	64,800	64,850	9,569	7,339	9,569	7,963
58,850	58,900	8,260	6,625	8,260	6,751	61,850	61,900	8,920	6,985	8,920	7,314	64,850	64,900	9,580	7,345	9,580	7,974
58,900	58,950	8,271	6,631	8,271	6,757	61,900	61,950	8,931	6,991	8,931	7,325	64,900	64,950	9,591	7,351	9,591	7,985
58,950	59,000	8,282	6,637	8,282	6,763	61,950	62,000	8,942	6,997	8,942	7,336	64,950	65,000	9,602	7,357	9,602	7,996

59,000 / 62,000 / 65,000

At least	But less than	Single	MFJ*	MFS	HoH	At least	But less than	Single	MFJ*	MFS	HoH	At least	But less than	Single	MFJ*	MFS	HoH
59,000	59,050	8,293	6,643	8,293	6,769	62,000	62,050	8,953	7,003	8,953	7,347	65,000	65,050	9,613	7,363	9,613	8,007
59,050	59,100	8,304	6,649	8,304	6,775	62,050	62,100	8,964	7,009	8,964	7,358	65,050	65,100	9,624	7,369	9,624	8,018
59,100	59,150	8,315	6,655	8,315	6,781	62,100	62,150	8,975	7,015	8,975	7,369	65,100	65,150	9,635	7,375	9,635	8,029
59,150	59,200	8,326	6,661	8,326	6,787	62,150	62,200	8,986	7,021	8,986	7,380	65,150	65,200	9,646	7,381	9,646	8,040
59,200	59,250	8,337	6,667	8,337	6,793	62,200	62,250	8,997	7,027	8,997	7,391	65,200	65,250	9,657	7,387	9,657	8,051
59,250	59,300	8,348	6,673	8,348	6,799	62,250	62,300	9,008	7,033	9,008	7,402	65,250	65,300	9,668	7,393	9,668	8,062
59,300	59,350	8,359	6,679	8,359	6,805	62,300	62,350	9,019	7,039	9,019	7,413	65,300	65,350	9,679	7,399	9,679	8,073
59,350	59,400	8,370	6,685	8,370	6,811	62,350	62,400	9,030	7,045	9,030	7,424	65,350	65,400	9,690	7,405	9,690	8,084
59,400	59,450	8,381	6,691	8,381	6,817	62,400	62,450	9,041	7,051	9,041	7,435	65,400	65,450	9,701	7,411	9,701	8,095
59,450	59,500	8,392	6,697	8,392	6,823	62,450	62,500	9,052	7,057	9,052	7,446	65,450	65,500	9,712	7,417	9,712	8,106
59,500	59,550	8,403	6,703	8,403	6,829	62,500	62,550	9,063	7,063	9,063	7,457	65,500	65,550	9,723	7,423	9,723	8,117
59,550	59,600	8,414	6,709	8,414	6,835	62,550	62,600	9,074	7,069	9,074	7,468	65,550	65,600	9,734	7,429	9,734	8,128
59,600	59,650	8,425	6,715	8,425	6,841	62,600	62,650	9,085	7,075	9,085	7,479	65,600	65,650	9,745	7,435	9,745	8,139
59,650	59,700	8,436	6,721	8,436	6,847	62,650	62,700	9,096	7,081	9,096	7,490	65,650	65,700	9,756	7,441	9,756	8,150
59,700	59,750	8,447	6,727	8,447	6,853	62,700	62,750	9,107	7,087	9,107	7,501	65,700	65,750	9,767	7,447	9,767	8,161
59,750	59,800	8,458	6,733	8,458	6,859	62,750	62,800	9,118	7,093	9,118	7,512	65,750	65,800	9,778	7,453	9,778	8,172
59,800	59,850	8,469	6,739	8,469	6,865	62,800	62,850	9,129	7,099	9,129	7,523	65,800	65,850	9,789	7,459	9,789	8,183
59,850	59,900	8,480	6,745	8,480	6,874	62,850	62,900	9,140	7,105	9,140	7,534	65,850	65,900	9,800	7,465	9,800	8,194
59,900	59,950	8,491	6,751	8,491	6,885	62,900	62,950	9,151	7,111	9,151	7,545	65,900	65,950	9,811	7,471	9,811	8,205
59,950	60,000	8,502	6,757	8,502	6,896	62,950	63,000	9,162	7,117	9,162	7,556	65,950	66,000	9,822	7,477	9,822	8,216

(Continued)

* This column must also be used by a qualifying surviving spouse.

2023 Tax Table — *Continued*

66,000

If line 15 (taxable income) is— At least	But less than	Single	Married filing jointly *	Married filing separately	Head of a household
66,000	66,050	9,833	7,483	9,833	8,227
66,050	66,100	9,844	7,489	9,844	8,238
66,100	66,150	9,855	7,495	9,855	8,249
66,150	66,200	9,866	7,501	9,866	8,260
66,200	66,250	9,877	7,507	9,877	8,271
66,250	66,300	9,888	7,513	9,888	8,282
66,300	66,350	9,899	7,519	9,899	8,293
66,350	66,400	9,910	7,525	9,910	8,304
66,400	66,450	9,921	7,531	9,921	8,315
66,450	66,500	9,932	7,537	9,932	8,326
66,500	66,550	9,943	7,543	9,943	8,337
66,550	66,600	9,954	7,549	9,954	8,348
66,600	66,650	9,965	7,555	9,965	8,359
66,650	66,700	9,976	7,561	9,976	8,370
66,700	66,750	9,987	7,567	9,987	8,381
66,750	66,800	9,998	7,573	9,998	8,392
66,800	66,850	10,009	7,579	10,009	8,403
66,850	66,900	10,020	7,585	10,020	8,414
66,900	66,950	10,031	7,591	10,031	8,425
66,950	67,000	10,042	7,597	10,042	8,436

67,000

At least	But less than	Single	Married filing jointly *	Married filing separately	Head of a household
67,000	67,050	10,053	7,603	10,053	8,447
67,050	67,100	10,064	7,609	10,064	8,458
67,100	67,150	10,075	7,615	10,075	8,469
67,150	67,200	10,086	7,621	10,086	8,480
67,200	67,250	10,097	7,627	10,097	8,491
67,250	67,300	10,108	7,633	10,108	8,502
67,300	67,350	10,119	7,639	10,119	8,513
67,350	67,400	10,130	7,645	10,130	8,524
67,400	67,450	10,141	7,651	10,141	8,535
67,450	67,500	10,152	7,657	10,152	8,546
67,500	67,550	10,163	7,663	10,163	8,557
67,550	67,600	10,174	7,669	10,174	8,568
67,600	67,650	10,185	7,675	10,185	8,579
67,650	67,700	10,196	7,681	10,196	8,590
67,700	67,750	10,207	7,687	10,207	8,601
67,750	67,800	10,218	7,693	10,218	8,612
67,800	67,850	10,229	7,699	10,229	8,623
67,850	67,900	10,240	7,705	10,240	8,634
67,900	67,950	10,251	7,711	10,251	8,645
67,950	68,000	10,262	7,717	10,262	8,656

68,000

At least	But less than	Single	Married filing jointly *	Married filing separately	Head of a household
68,000	68,050	10,273	7,723	10,273	8,667
68,050	68,100	10,284	7,729	10,284	8,678
68,100	68,150	10,295	7,735	10,295	8,689
68,150	68,200	10,306	7,741	10,306	8,700
68,200	68,250	10,317	7,747	10,317	8,711
68,250	68,300	10,328	7,753	10,328	8,722
68,300	68,350	10,339	7,759	10,339	8,733
68,350	68,400	10,350	7,765	10,350	8,744
68,400	68,450	10,361	7,771	10,361	8,755
68,450	68,500	10,372	7,777	10,372	8,766
68,500	68,550	10,383	7,783	10,383	8,777
68,550	68,600	10,394	7,789	10,394	8,788
68,600	68,650	10,405	7,795	10,405	8,799
68,650	68,700	10,416	7,801	10,416	8,810
68,700	68,750	10,427	7,807	10,427	8,821
68,750	68,800	10,438	7,813	10,438	8,832
68,800	68,850	10,449	7,819	10,449	8,843
68,850	68,900	10,460	7,825	10,460	8,854
68,900	68,950	10,471	7,831	10,471	8,865
68,950	69,000	10,482	7,837	10,482	8,876

69,000

At least	But less than	Single	Married filing jointly *	Married filing separately	Head of a household
69,000	69,050	10,493	7,843	10,493	8,887
69,050	69,100	10,504	7,849	10,504	8,898
69,100	69,150	10,515	7,855	10,515	8,909
69,150	69,200	10,526	7,861	10,526	8,920
69,200	69,250	10,537	7,867	10,537	8,931
69,250	69,300	10,548	7,873	10,548	8,942
69,300	69,350	10,559	7,879	10,559	8,953
69,350	69,400	10,570	7,885	10,570	8,964
69,400	69,450	10,581	7,891	10,581	8,975
69,450	69,500	10,592	7,897	10,592	8,986
69,500	69,550	10,603	7,903	10,603	8,997
69,550	69,600	10,614	7,909	10,614	9,008
69,600	69,650	10,625	7,915	10,625	9,019
69,650	69,700	10,636	7,921	10,636	9,030
69,700	69,750	10,647	7,927	10,647	9,041
69,750	69,800	10,658	7,933	10,658	9,052
69,800	69,850	10,669	7,939	10,669	9,063
69,850	69,900	10,680	7,945	10,680	9,074
69,900	69,950	10,691	7,951	10,691	9,085
69,950	70,000	10,702	7,957	10,702	9,096

70,000

At least	But less than	Single	Married filing jointly *	Married filing separately	Head of a household
70,000	70,050	10,713	7,963	10,713	9,107
70,050	70,100	10,724	7,969	10,724	9,118
70,100	70,150	10,735	7,975	10,735	9,129
70,150	70,200	10,746	7,981	10,746	9,140
70,200	70,250	10,757	7,987	10,757	9,151
70,250	70,300	10,768	7,993	10,768	9,162
70,300	70,350	10,779	7,999	10,779	9,173
70,350	70,400	10,790	8,005	10,790	9,184
70,400	70,450	10,801	8,011	10,801	9,195
70,450	70,500	10,812	8,017	10,812	9,206
70,500	70,550	10,823	8,023	10,823	9,217
70,550	70,600	10,834	8,029	10,834	9,228
70,600	70,650	10,845	8,035	10,845	9,239
70,650	70,700	10,856	8,041	10,856	9,250
70,700	70,750	10,867	8,047	10,867	9,261
70,750	70,800	10,878	8,053	10,878	9,272
70,800	70,850	10,889	8,059	10,889	9,283
70,850	70,900	10,900	8,065	10,900	9,294
70,900	70,950	10,911	8,071	10,911	9,305
70,950	71,000	10,922	8,077	10,922	9,316

71,000

At least	But less than	Single	Married filing jointly *	Married filing separately	Head of a household
71,000	71,050	10,933	8,083	10,933	9,327
71,050	71,100	10,944	8,089	10,944	9,338
71,100	71,150	10,955	8,095	10,955	9,349
71,150	71,200	10,966	8,101	10,966	9,360
71,200	71,250	10,977	8,107	10,977	9,371
71,250	71,300	10,988	8,113	10,988	9,382
71,300	71,350	10,999	8,119	10,999	9,393
71,350	71,400	11,010	8,125	11,010	9,404
71,400	71,450	11,021	8,131	11,021	9,415
71,450	71,500	11,032	8,137	11,032	9,426
71,500	71,550	11,043	8,143	11,043	9,437
71,550	71,600	11,054	8,149	11,054	9,448
71,600	71,650	11,065	8,155	11,065	9,459
71,650	71,700	11,076	8,161	11,076	9,470
71,700	71,750	11,087	8,167	11,087	9,481
71,750	71,800	11,098	8,173	11,098	9,492
71,800	71,850	11,109	8,179	11,109	9,503
71,850	71,900	11,120	8,185	11,120	9,514
71,900	71,950	11,131	8,191	11,131	9,525
71,950	72,000	11,142	8,197	11,142	9,536

72,000

At least	But less than	Single	Married filing jointly *	Married filing separately	Head of a household
72,000	72,050	11,153	8,203	11,153	9,547
72,050	72,100	11,164	8,209	11,164	9,558
72,100	72,150	11,175	8,215	11,175	9,569
72,150	72,200	11,186	8,221	11,186	9,580
72,200	72,250	11,197	8,227	11,197	9,591
72,250	72,300	11,208	8,233	11,208	9,602
72,300	72,350	11,219	8,239	11,219	9,613
72,350	72,400	11,230	8,245	11,230	9,624
72,400	72,450	11,241	8,251	11,241	9,635
72,450	72,500	11,252	8,257	11,252	9,646
72,500	72,550	11,263	8,263	11,263	9,657
72,550	72,600	11,274	8,269	11,274	9,668
72,600	72,650	11,285	8,275	11,285	9,679
72,650	72,700	11,296	8,281	11,296	9,690
72,700	72,750	11,307	8,287	11,307	9,701
72,750	72,800	11,318	8,293	11,318	9,712
72,800	72,850	11,329	8,299	11,329	9,723
72,850	72,900	11,340	8,305	11,340	9,734
72,900	72,950	11,351	8,311	11,351	9,745
72,950	73,000	11,362	8,317	11,362	9,756

73,000

At least	But less than	Single	Married filing jointly *	Married filing separately	Head of a household
73,000	73,050	11,373	8,323	11,373	9,767
73,050	73,100	11,384	8,329	11,384	9,778
73,100	73,150	11,395	8,335	11,395	9,789
73,150	73,200	11,406	8,341	11,406	9,800
73,200	73,250	11,417	8,347	11,417	9,811
73,250	73,300	11,428	8,353	11,428	9,822
73,300	73,350	11,439	8,359	11,439	9,833
73,350	73,400	11,450	8,365	11,450	9,844
73,400	73,450	11,461	8,371	11,461	9,855
73,450	73,500	11,472	8,377	11,472	9,866
73,500	73,550	11,483	8,383	11,483	9,877
73,550	73,600	11,494	8,389	11,494	9,888
73,600	73,650	11,505	8,395	11,505	9,899
73,650	73,700	11,516	8,401	11,516	9,910
73,700	73,750	11,527	8,407	11,527	9,921
73,750	73,800	11,538	8,413	11,538	9,932
73,800	73,850	11,549	8,419	11,549	9,943
73,850	73,900	11,560	8,425	11,560	9,954
73,900	73,950	11,571	8,431	11,571	9,965
73,950	74,000	11,582	8,437	11,582	9,976

74,000

At least	But less than	Single	Married filing jointly *	Married filing separately	Head of a household
74,000	74,050	11,593	8,443	11,593	9,987
74,050	74,100	11,604	8,449	11,604	9,998
74,100	74,150	11,615	8,455	11,615	10,009
74,150	74,200	11,626	8,461	11,626	10,020
74,200	74,250	11,637	8,467	11,637	10,031
74,250	74,300	11,648	8,473	11,648	10,042
74,300	74,350	11,659	8,479	11,659	10,053
74,350	74,400	11,670	8,485	11,670	10,064
74,400	74,450	11,681	8,491	11,681	10,075
74,450	74,500	11,692	8,497	11,692	10,086
74,500	74,550	11,703	8,503	11,703	10,097
74,550	74,600	11,714	8,509	11,714	10,108
74,600	74,650	11,725	8,515	11,725	10,119
74,650	74,700	11,736	8,521	11,736	10,130
74,700	74,750	11,747	8,527	11,747	10,141
74,750	74,800	11,758	8,533	11,758	10,152
74,800	74,850	11,769	8,539	11,769	10,163
74,850	74,900	11,780	8,545	11,780	10,174
74,900	74,950	11,791	8,551	11,791	10,185
74,950	75,000	11,802	8,557	11,802	10,196

(Continued)

* This column must also be used by a qualifying surviving spouse.

75,000

At least	But less than	Single	Married filing jointly *	Married filing separately	Head of a household
75,000	75,050	11,813	8,563	11,813	10,207
75,050	75,100	11,824	8,569	11,824	10,218
75,100	75,150	11,835	8,575	11,835	10,229
75,150	75,200	11,846	8,581	11,846	10,240
75,200	75,250	11,857	8,587	11,857	10,251
75,250	75,300	11,868	8,593	11,868	10,262
75,300	75,350	11,879	8,599	11,879	10,273
75,350	75,400	11,890	8,605	11,890	10,284
75,400	75,450	11,901	8,611	11,901	10,295
75,450	75,500	11,912	8,617	11,912	10,306
75,500	75,550	11,923	8,623	11,923	10,317
75,550	75,600	11,934	8,629	11,934	10,328
75,600	75,650	11,945	8,635	11,945	10,339
75,650	75,700	11,956	8,641	11,956	10,350
75,700	75,750	11,967	8,647	11,967	10,361
75,750	75,800	11,978	8,653	11,978	10,372
75,800	75,850	11,989	8,659	11,989	10,383
75,850	75,900	12,000	8,665	12,000	10,394
75,900	75,950	12,011	8,671	12,011	10,405
75,950	76,000	12,022	8,677	12,022	10,416

76,000

At least	But less than	Single	Married filing jointly *	Married filing separately	Head of a household
76,000	76,050	12,033	8,683	12,033	10,427
76,050	76,100	12,044	8,689	12,044	10,438
76,100	76,150	12,055	8,695	12,055	10,449
76,150	76,200	12,066	8,701	12,066	10,460
76,200	76,250	12,077	8,707	12,077	10,471
76,250	76,300	12,088	8,713	12,088	10,482
76,300	76,350	12,099	8,719	12,099	10,493
76,350	76,400	12,110	8,725	12,110	10,504
76,400	76,450	12,121	8,731	12,121	10,515
76,450	76,500	12,132	8,737	12,132	10,526
76,500	76,550	12,143	8,743	12,143	10,537
76,550	76,600	12,154	8,749	12,154	10,548
76,600	76,650	12,165	8,755	12,165	10,559
76,650	76,700	12,176	8,761	12,176	10,570
76,700	76,750	12,187	8,767	12,187	10,581
76,750	76,800	12,198	8,773	12,198	10,592
76,800	76,850	12,209	8,779	12,209	10,603
76,850	76,900	12,220	8,785	12,220	10,614
76,900	76,950	12,231	8,791	12,231	10,625
76,950	77,000	12,242	8,797	12,242	10,636

77,000

At least	But less than	Single	Married filing jointly *	Married filing separately	Head of a household
77,000	77,050	12,253	8,803	12,253	10,647
77,050	77,100	12,264	8,809	12,264	10,658
77,100	77,150	12,275	8,815	12,275	10,669
77,150	77,200	12,286	8,821	12,286	10,680
77,200	77,250	12,297	8,827	12,297	10,691
77,250	77,300	12,308	8,833	12,308	10,702
77,300	77,350	12,319	8,839	12,319	10,713
77,350	77,400	12,330	8,845	12,330	10,724
77,400	77,450	12,341	8,851	12,341	10,735
77,450	77,500	12,352	8,857	12,352	10,746
77,500	77,550	12,363	8,863	12,363	10,757
77,550	77,600	12,374	8,869	12,374	10,768
77,600	77,650	12,385	8,875	12,385	10,779
77,650	77,700	12,396	8,881	12,396	10,790
77,700	77,750	12,407	8,887	12,407	10,801
77,750	77,800	12,418	8,893	12,418	10,812
77,800	77,850	12,429	8,899	12,429	10,823
77,850	77,900	12,440	8,905	12,440	10,834
77,900	77,950	12,451	8,911	12,451	10,845
77,950	78,000	12,462	8,917	12,462	10,856

78,000

At least	But less than	Single	Married filing jointly *	Married filing separately	Head of a household
78,000	78,050	12,473	8,923	12,473	10,867
78,050	78,100	12,484	8,929	12,484	10,878
78,100	78,150	12,495	8,935	12,495	10,889
78,150	78,200	12,506	8,941	12,506	10,900
78,200	78,250	12,517	8,947	12,517	10,911
78,250	78,300	12,528	8,953	12,528	10,922
78,300	78,350	12,539	8,959	12,539	10,933
78,350	78,400	12,550	8,965	12,550	10,944
78,400	78,450	12,561	8,971	12,561	10,955
78,450	78,500	12,572	8,977	12,572	10,966
78,500	78,550	12,583	8,983	12,583	10,977
78,550	78,600	12,594	8,989	12,594	10,988
78,600	78,650	12,605	8,995	12,605	10,999
78,650	78,700	12,616	9,001	12,616	11,010
78,700	78,750	12,627	9,007	12,627	11,021
78,750	78,800	12,638	9,013	12,638	11,032
78,800	78,850	12,649	9,019	12,649	11,043
78,850	78,900	12,660	9,025	12,660	11,054
78,900	78,950	12,671	9,031	12,671	11,065
78,950	79,000	12,682	9,037	12,682	11,076

79,000

At least	But less than	Single	Married filing jointly *	Married filing separately	Head of a household
79,000	79,050	12,693	9,043	12,693	11,087
79,050	79,100	12,704	9,049	12,704	11,098
79,100	79,150	12,715	9,055	12,715	11,109
79,150	79,200	12,726	9,061	12,726	11,120
79,200	79,250	12,737	9,067	12,737	11,131
79,250	79,300	12,748	9,073	12,748	11,142
79,300	79,350	12,759	9,079	12,759	11,153
79,350	79,400	12,770	9,085	12,770	11,164
79,400	79,450	12,781	9,091	12,781	11,175
79,450	79,500	12,792	9,097	12,792	11,186
79,500	79,550	12,803	9,103	12,803	11,197
79,550	79,600	12,814	9,109	12,814	11,208
79,600	79,650	12,825	9,115	12,825	11,219
79,650	79,700	12,836	9,121	12,836	11,230
79,700	79,750	12,847	9,127	12,847	11,241
79,750	79,800	12,858	9,133	12,858	11,252
79,800	79,850	12,869	9,139	12,869	11,263
79,850	79,900	12,880	9,145	12,880	11,274
79,900	79,950	12,891	9,151	12,891	11,285
79,950	80,000	12,902	9,157	12,902	11,296

80,000

At least	But less than	Single	Married filing jointly *	Married filing separately	Head of a household
80,000	80,050	12,913	9,163	12,913	11,307
80,050	80,100	12,924	9,169	12,924	11,318
80,100	80,150	12,935	9,175	12,935	11,329
80,150	80,200	12,946	9,181	12,946	11,340
80,200	80,250	12,957	9,187	12,957	11,351
80,250	80,300	12,968	9,193	12,968	11,362
80,300	80,350	12,979	9,199	12,979	11,373
80,350	80,400	12,990	9,205	12,990	11,384
80,400	80,450	13,001	9,211	13,001	11,395
80,450	80,500	13,012	9,217	13,012	11,406
80,500	80,550	13,023	9,223	13,023	11,417
80,550	80,600	13,034	9,229	13,034	11,428
80,600	80,650	13,045	9,235	13,045	11,439
80,650	80,700	13,056	9,241	13,056	11,450
80,700	80,750	13,067	9,247	13,067	11,461
80,750	80,800	13,078	9,253	13,078	11,472
80,800	80,850	13,089	9,259	13,089	11,483
80,850	80,900	13,100	9,265	13,100	11,494
80,900	80,950	13,111	9,271	13,111	11,505
80,950	81,000	13,122	9,277	13,122	11,516

81,000

At least	But less than	Single	Married filing jointly *	Married filing separately	Head of a household
81,000	81,050	13,133	9,283	13,133	11,527
81,050	81,100	13,144	9,289	13,144	11,538
81,100	81,150	13,155	9,295	13,155	11,549
81,150	81,200	13,166	9,301	13,166	11,560
81,200	81,250	13,177	9,307	13,177	11,571
81,250	81,300	13,188	9,313	13,188	11,582
81,300	81,350	13,199	9,319	13,199	11,593
81,350	81,400	13,210	9,325	13,210	11,604
81,400	81,450	13,221	9,331	13,221	11,615
81,450	81,500	13,232	9,337	13,232	11,626
81,500	81,550	13,243	9,343	13,243	11,637
81,550	81,600	13,254	9,349	13,254	11,648
81,600	81,650	13,265	9,355	13,265	11,659
81,650	81,700	13,276	9,361	13,276	11,670
81,700	81,750	13,287	9,367	13,287	11,681
81,750	81,800	13,298	9,373	13,298	11,692
81,800	81,850	13,309	9,379	13,309	11,703
81,850	81,900	13,320	9,385	13,320	11,714
81,900	81,950	13,331	9,391	13,331	11,725
81,950	82,000	13,342	9,397	13,342	11,736

82,000

At least	But less than	Single	Married filing jointly *	Married filing separately	Head of a household
82,000	82,050	13,353	9,403	13,353	11,747
82,050	82,100	13,364	9,409	13,364	11,758
82,100	82,150	13,375	9,415	13,375	11,769
82,150	82,200	13,386	9,421	13,386	11,780
82,200	82,250	13,397	9,427	13,397	11,791
82,250	82,300	13,408	9,433	13,408	11,802
82,300	82,350	13,419	9,439	13,419	11,813
82,350	82,400	13,430	9,445	13,430	11,824
82,400	82,450	13,441	9,451	13,441	11,835
82,450	82,500	13,452	9,457	13,452	11,846
82,500	82,550	13,463	9,463	13,463	11,857
82,550	82,600	13,474	9,469	13,474	11,868
82,600	82,650	13,485	9,475	13,485	11,879
82,650	82,700	13,496	9,481	13,496	11,890
82,700	82,750	13,507	9,487	13,507	11,901
82,750	82,800	13,518	9,493	13,518	11,912
82,800	82,850	13,529	9,499	13,529	11,923
82,850	82,900	13,540	9,505	13,540	11,934
82,900	82,950	13,551	9,511	13,551	11,945
82,950	83,000	13,562	9,517	13,562	11,956

83,000

At least	But less than	Single	Married filing jointly *	Married filing separately	Head of a household
83,000	83,050	13,573	9,523	13,573	11,967
83,050	83,100	13,584	9,529	13,584	11,978
83,100	83,150	13,595	9,535	13,595	11,989
83,150	83,200	13,606	9,541	13,606	12,000
83,200	83,250	13,617	9,547	13,617	12,011
83,250	83,300	13,628	9,553	13,628	12,022
83,300	83,350	13,639	9,559	13,639	12,033
83,350	83,400	13,650	9,565	13,650	12,044
83,400	83,450	13,661	9,571	13,661	12,055
83,450	83,500	13,672	9,577	13,672	12,066
83,500	83,550	13,683	9,583	13,683	12,077
83,550	83,600	13,694	9,589	13,694	12,088
83,600	83,650	13,705	9,595	13,705	12,099
83,650	83,700	13,716	9,601	13,716	12,110
83,700	83,750	13,727	9,607	13,727	12,121
83,750	83,800	13,738	9,613	13,738	12,132
83,800	83,850	13,749	9,619	13,749	12,143
83,850	83,900	13,760	9,625	13,760	12,154
83,900	83,950	13,771	9,631	13,771	12,165
83,950	84,000	13,782	9,637	13,782	12,176

(Continued)

* This column must also be used by a qualifying surviving spouse.

84,000

If line 15 (taxable income) is—		And you are—			
At least	But less than	Single	Married filing jointly *	Married filing separately	Head of a household
		Your tax is—			
84,000	84,050	13,793	9,643	13,793	12,187
84,050	84,100	13,804	9,649	13,804	12,198
84,100	84,150	13,815	9,655	13,815	12,209
84,150	84,200	13,826	9,661	13,826	12,220
84,200	84,250	13,837	9,667	13,837	12,231
84,250	84,300	13,848	9,673	13,848	12,242
84,300	84,350	13,859	9,679	13,859	12,253
84,350	84,400	13,870	9,685	13,870	12,264
84,400	84,450	13,881	9,691	13,881	12,275
84,450	84,500	13,892	9,697	13,892	12,286
84,500	84,550	13,903	9,703	13,903	12,297
84,550	84,600	13,914	9,709	13,914	12,308
84,600	84,650	13,925	9,715	13,925	12,319
84,650	84,700	13,936	9,721	13,936	12,330
84,700	84,750	13,947	9,727	13,947	12,341
84,750	84,800	13,958	9,733	13,958	12,352
84,800	84,850	13,969	9,739	13,969	12,363
84,850	84,900	13,980	9,745	13,980	12,374
84,900	84,950	13,991	9,751	13,991	12,385
84,950	85,000	14,002	9,757	14,002	12,396

85,000

At least	But less than	Single	Married filing jointly *	Married filing separately	Head of a household
85,000	85,050	14,013	9,763	14,013	12,407
85,050	85,100	14,024	9,769	14,024	12,418
85,100	85,150	14,035	9,775	14,035	12,429
85,150	85,200	14,046	9,781	14,046	12,440
85,200	85,250	14,057	9,787	14,057	12,451
85,250	85,300	14,068	9,793	14,068	12,462
85,300	85,350	14,079	9,799	14,079	12,473
85,350	85,400	14,090	9,805	14,090	12,484
85,400	85,450	14,101	9,811	14,101	12,495
85,450	85,500	14,112	9,817	14,112	12,506
85,500	85,550	14,123	9,823	14,123	12,517
85,550	85,600	14,134	9,829	14,134	12,528
85,600	85,650	14,145	9,835	14,145	12,539
85,650	85,700	14,156	9,841	14,156	12,550
85,700	85,750	14,167	9,847	14,167	12,561
85,750	85,800	14,178	9,853	14,178	12,572
85,800	85,850	14,189	9,859	14,189	12,583
85,850	85,900	14,200	9,865	14,200	12,594
85,900	85,950	14,211	9,871	14,211	12,605
85,950	86,000	14,222	9,877	14,222	12,616

86,000

At least	But less than	Single	Married filing jointly *	Married filing separately	Head of a household
86,000	86,050	14,233	9,883	14,233	12,627
86,050	86,100	14,244	9,889	14,244	12,638
86,100	86,150	14,255	9,895	14,255	12,649
86,150	86,200	14,266	9,901	14,266	12,660
86,200	86,250	14,277	9,907	14,277	12,671
86,250	86,300	14,288	9,913	14,288	12,682
86,300	86,350	14,299	9,919	14,299	12,693
86,350	86,400	14,310	9,925	14,310	12,704
86,400	86,450	14,321	9,931	14,321	12,715
86,450	86,500	14,332	9,937	14,332	12,726
86,500	86,550	14,343	9,943	14,343	12,737
86,550	86,600	14,354	9,949	14,354	12,748
86,600	86,650	14,365	9,955	14,365	12,759
86,650	86,700	14,376	9,961	14,376	12,770
86,700	86,750	14,387	9,967	14,387	12,781
86,750	86,800	14,398	9,973	14,398	12,792
86,800	86,850	14,409	9,979	14,409	12,803
86,850	86,900	14,420	9,985	14,420	12,814
86,900	86,950	14,431	9,991	14,431	12,825
86,950	87,000	14,442	9,997	14,442	12,836

87,000

If line 15 (taxable income) is—		And you are—			
At least	But less than	Single	Married filing jointly *	Married filing separately	Head of a household
		Your tax is—			
87,000	87,050	14,453	10,003	14,453	12,847
87,050	87,100	14,464	10,009	14,464	12,858
87,100	87,150	14,475	10,015	14,475	12,869
87,150	87,200	14,486	10,021	14,486	12,880
87,200	87,250	14,497	10,027	14,497	12,891
87,250	87,300	14,508	10,033	14,508	12,902
87,300	87,350	14,519	10,039	14,519	12,913
87,350	87,400	14,530	10,045	14,530	12,924
87,400	87,450	14,541	10,051	14,541	12,935
87,450	87,500	14,552	10,057	14,552	12,946
87,500	87,550	14,563	10,063	14,563	12,957
87,550	87,600	14,574	10,069	14,574	12,968
87,600	87,650	14,585	10,075	14,585	12,979
87,650	87,700	14,596	10,081	14,596	12,990
87,700	87,750	14,607	10,087	14,607	13,001
87,750	87,800	14,618	10,093	14,618	13,012
87,800	87,850	14,629	10,099	14,629	13,023
87,850	87,900	14,640	10,105	14,640	13,034
87,900	87,950	14,651	10,111	14,651	13,045
87,950	88,000	14,662	10,117	14,662	13,056

88,000

At least	But less than	Single	Married filing jointly *	Married filing separately	Head of a household
88,000	88,050	14,673	10,123	14,673	13,067
88,050	88,100	14,684	10,129	14,684	13,078
88,100	88,150	14,695	10,135	14,695	13,089
88,150	88,200	14,706	10,141	14,706	13,100
88,200	88,250	14,717	10,147	14,717	13,111
88,250	88,300	14,728	10,153	14,728	13,122
88,300	88,350	14,739	10,159	14,739	13,133
88,350	88,400	14,750	10,165	14,750	13,144
88,400	88,450	14,761	10,171	14,761	13,155
88,450	88,500	14,772	10,177	14,772	13,166
88,500	88,550	14,783	10,183	14,783	13,177
88,550	88,600	14,794	10,189	14,794	13,188
88,600	88,650	14,805	10,195	14,805	13,199
88,650	88,700	14,816	10,201	14,816	13,210
88,700	88,750	14,827	10,207	14,827	13,221
88,750	88,800	14,838	10,213	14,838	13,232
88,800	88,850	14,849	10,219	14,849	13,243
88,850	88,900	14,860	10,225	14,860	13,254
88,900	88,950	14,871	10,231	14,871	13,265
88,950	89,000	14,882	10,237	14,882	13,276

89,000

At least	But less than	Single	Married filing jointly *	Married filing separately	Head of a household
89,000	89,050	14,893	10,243	14,893	13,287
89,050	89,100	14,904	10,249	14,904	13,298
89,100	89,150	14,915	10,255	14,915	13,309
89,150	89,200	14,926	10,261	14,926	13,320
89,200	89,250	14,937	10,267	14,937	13,331
89,250	89,300	14,948	10,273	14,948	13,342
89,300	89,350	14,959	10,279	14,959	13,353
89,350	89,400	14,970	10,285	14,970	13,364
89,400	89,450	14,981	10,291	14,981	13,375
89,450	89,500	14,992	10,300	14,992	13,386
89,500	89,550	15,003	10,311	15,003	13,397
89,550	89,600	15,014	10,322	15,014	13,408
89,600	89,650	15,025	10,333	15,025	13,419
89,650	89,700	15,036	10,344	15,036	13,430
89,700	89,750	15,047	10,355	15,047	13,441
89,750	89,800	15,058	10,366	15,058	13,452
89,800	89,850	15,069	10,377	15,069	13,463
89,850	89,900	15,080	10,388	15,080	13,474
89,900	89,950	15,091	10,399	15,091	13,485
89,950	90,000	15,102	10,410	15,102	13,496

90,000

If line 15 (taxable income) is—		And you are—			
At least	But less than	Single	Married filing jointly *	Married filing separately	Head of a household
		Your tax is—			
90,000	90,050	15,113	10,421	15,113	13,507
90,050	90,100	15,124	10,432	15,124	13,518
90,100	90,150	15,135	10,443	15,135	13,529
90,150	90,200	15,146	10,454	15,146	13,540
90,200	90,250	15,157	10,465	15,157	13,551
90,250	90,300	15,168	10,476	15,168	13,562
90,300	90,350	15,179	10,487	15,179	13,573
90,350	90,400	15,190	10,498	15,190	13,584
90,400	90,450	15,201	10,509	15,201	13,595
90,450	90,500	15,212	10,520	15,212	13,606
90,500	90,550	15,223	10,531	15,223	13,617
90,550	90,600	15,234	10,542	15,234	13,628
90,600	90,650	15,245	10,553	15,245	13,639
90,650	90,700	15,256	10,564	15,256	13,650
90,700	90,750	15,267	10,575	15,267	13,661
90,750	90,800	15,278	10,586	15,278	13,672
90,800	90,850	15,289	10,597	15,289	13,683
90,850	90,900	15,300	10,608	15,300	13,694
90,900	90,950	15,311	10,619	15,311	13,705
90,950	91,000	15,322	10,630	15,322	13,716

91,000

At least	But less than	Single	Married filing jointly *	Married filing separately	Head of a household
91,000	91,050	15,333	10,641	15,333	13,727
91,050	91,100	15,344	10,652	15,344	13,738
91,100	91,150	15,355	10,663	15,355	13,749
91,150	91,200	15,366	10,674	15,366	13,760
91,200	91,250	15,377	10,685	15,377	13,771
91,250	91,300	15,388	10,696	15,388	13,782
91,300	91,350	15,399	10,707	15,399	13,793
91,350	91,400	15,410	10,718	15,410	13,804
91,400	91,450	15,421	10,729	15,421	13,815
91,450	91,500	15,432	10,740	15,432	13,826
91,500	91,550	15,443	10,751	15,443	13,837
91,550	91,600	15,454	10,762	15,454	13,848
91,600	91,650	15,465	10,773	15,465	13,859
91,650	91,700	15,476	10,784	15,476	13,870
91,700	91,750	15,487	10,795	15,487	13,881
91,750	91,800	15,498	10,806	15,498	13,892
91,800	91,850	15,509	10,817	15,509	13,903
91,850	91,900	15,520	10,828	15,520	13,914
91,900	91,950	15,531	10,839	15,531	13,925
91,950	92,000	15,542	10,850	15,542	13,936

92,000

At least	But less than	Single	Married filing jointly *	Married filing separately	Head of a household
92,000	92,050	15,553	10,861	15,553	13,947
92,050	92,100	15,564	10,872	15,564	13,958
92,100	92,150	15,575	10,883	15,575	13,969
92,150	92,200	15,586	10,894	15,586	13,980
92,200	92,250	15,597	10,905	15,597	13,991
92,250	92,300	15,608	10,916	15,608	14,002
92,300	92,350	15,619	10,927	15,619	14,013
92,350	92,400	15,630	10,938	15,630	14,024
92,400	92,450	15,641	10,949	15,641	14,035
92,450	92,500	15,652	10,960	15,652	14,046
92,500	92,550	15,663	10,971	15,663	14,057
92,550	92,600	15,674	10,982	15,674	14,068
92,600	92,650	15,685	10,993	15,685	14,079
92,650	92,700	15,696	11,004	15,696	14,090
92,700	92,750	15,707	11,015	15,707	14,101
92,750	92,800	15,718	11,026	15,718	14,112
92,800	92,850	15,729	11,037	15,729	14,123
92,850	92,900	15,740	11,048	15,740	14,134
92,900	92,950	15,751	11,059	15,751	14,145
92,950	93,000	15,762	11,070	15,762	14,156

(Continued)

* This column must also be used by a qualifying surviving spouse.

If line 15 (taxable income) is—		And you are—			
At least	But less than	Single	Married filing jointly *	Married filing separately	Head of a household
		Your tax is—			

93,000

At least	But less than	Single	Married filing jointly *	Married filing separately	Head of a household
93,000	93,050	15,773	11,081	15,773	14,167
93,050	93,100	15,784	11,092	15,784	14,178
93,100	93,150	15,795	11,103	15,795	14,189
93,150	93,200	15,806	11,114	15,806	14,200
93,200	93,250	15,817	11,125	15,817	14,211
93,250	93,300	15,828	11,136	15,828	14,222
93,300	93,350	15,839	11,147	15,839	14,233
93,350	93,400	15,850	11,158	15,850	14,244
93,400	93,450	15,861	11,169	15,861	14,255
93,450	93,500	15,872	11,180	15,872	14,266
93,500	93,550	15,883	11,191	15,883	14,277
93,550	93,600	15,894	11,202	15,894	14,288
93,600	93,650	15,905	11,213	15,905	14,299
93,650	93,700	15,916	11,224	15,916	14,310
93,700	93,750	15,927	11,235	15,927	14,321
93,750	93,800	15,938	11,246	15,938	14,332
93,800	93,850	15,949	11,257	15,949	14,343
93,850	93,900	15,960	11,268	15,960	14,354
93,900	93,950	15,971	11,279	15,971	14,365
93,950	94,000	15,982	11,290	15,982	14,376

94,000

At least	But less than	Single	Married filing jointly *	Married filing separately	Head of a household
94,000	94,050	15,993	11,301	15,993	14,387
94,050	94,100	16,004	11,312	16,004	14,398
94,100	94,150	16,015	11,323	16,015	14,409
94,150	94,200	16,026	11,334	16,026	14,420
94,200	94,250	16,037	11,345	16,037	14,431
94,250	94,300	16,048	11,356	16,048	14,442
94,300	94,350	16,059	11,367	16,059	14,453
94,350	94,400	16,070	11,378	16,070	14,464
94,400	94,450	16,081	11,389	16,081	14,475
94,450	94,500	16,092	11,400	16,092	14,486
94,500	94,550	16,103	11,411	16,103	14,497
94,550	94,600	16,114	11,422	16,114	14,508
94,600	94,650	16,125	11,433	16,125	14,519
94,650	94,700	16,136	11,444	16,136	14,530
94,700	94,750	16,147	11,455	16,147	14,541
94,750	94,800	16,158	11,466	16,158	14,552
94,800	94,850	16,169	11,477	16,169	14,563
94,850	94,900	16,180	11,488	16,180	14,574
94,900	94,950	16,191	11,499	16,191	14,585
94,950	95,000	16,202	11,510	16,202	14,596

95,000

At least	But less than	Single	Married filing jointly *	Married filing separately	Head of a household
95,000	95,050	16,213	11,521	16,213	14,607
95,050	95,100	16,224	11,532	16,224	14,618
95,100	95,150	16,235	11,543	16,235	14,629
95,150	95,200	16,246	11,554	16,246	14,640
95,200	95,250	16,257	11,565	16,257	14,651
95,250	95,300	16,268	11,576	16,268	14,662
95,300	95,350	16,279	11,587	16,279	14,673
95,350	95,400	16,290	11,598	16,290	14,684
95,400	95,450	16,302	11,609	16,302	14,696
95,450	95,500	16,314	11,620	16,314	14,708
95,500	95,550	16,326	11,631	16,326	14,720
95,550	95,600	16,338	11,642	16,338	14,732
95,600	95,650	16,350	11,653	16,350	14,744
95,650	95,700	16,362	11,664	16,362	14,756
95,700	95,750	16,374	11,675	16,374	14,768
95,750	95,800	16,386	11,686	16,386	14,780
95,800	95,850	16,398	11,697	16,398	14,792
95,850	95,900	16,410	11,708	16,410	14,804
95,900	95,950	16,422	11,719	16,422	14,816
95,950	96,000	16,434	11,730	16,434	14,828

If line 15 (taxable income) is—		And you are—			
At least	But less than	Single	Married filing jointly *	Married filing separately	Head of a household
		Your tax is—			

96,000

At least	But less than	Single	Married filing jointly *	Married filing separately	Head of a household
96,000	96,050	16,446	11,741	16,446	14,840
96,050	96,100	16,458	11,752	16,458	14,852
96,100	96,150	16,470	11,763	16,470	14,864
96,150	96,200	16,482	11,774	16,482	14,876
96,200	96,250	16,494	11,785	16,494	14,888
96,250	96,300	16,506	11,796	16,506	14,900
96,300	96,350	16,518	11,807	16,518	14,912
96,350	96,400	16,530	11,818	16,530	14,924
96,400	96,450	16,542	11,829	16,542	14,936
96,450	96,500	16,554	11,840	16,554	14,948
96,500	96,550	16,566	11,851	16,566	14,960
96,550	96,600	16,578	11,862	16,578	14,972
96,600	96,650	16,590	11,873	16,590	14,984
96,650	96,700	16,602	11,884	16,602	14,996
96,700	96,750	16,614	11,895	16,614	15,008
96,750	96,800	16,626	11,906	16,626	15,020
96,800	96,850	16,638	11,917	16,638	15,032
96,850	96,900	16,650	11,928	16,650	15,044
96,900	96,950	16,662	11,939	16,662	15,056
96,950	97,000	16,674	11,950	16,674	15,068

97,000

At least	But less than	Single	Married filing jointly *	Married filing separately	Head of a household
97,000	97,050	16,686	11,961	16,686	15,080
97,050	97,100	16,698	11,972	16,698	15,092
97,100	97,150	16,710	11,983	16,710	15,104
97,150	97,200	16,722	11,994	16,722	15,116
97,200	97,250	16,734	12,005	16,734	15,128
97,250	97,300	16,746	12,016	16,746	15,140
97,300	97,350	16,758	12,027	16,758	15,152
97,350	97,400	16,770	12,038	16,770	15,164
97,400	97,450	16,782	12,049	16,782	15,176
97,450	97,500	16,794	12,060	16,794	15,188
97,500	97,550	16,806	12,071	16,806	15,200
97,550	97,600	16,818	12,082	16,818	15,212
97,600	97,650	16,830	12,093	16,830	15,224
97,650	97,700	16,842	12,104	16,842	15,236
97,700	97,750	16,854	12,115	16,854	15,248
97,750	97,800	16,866	12,126	16,866	15,260
97,800	97,850	16,878	12,137	16,878	15,272
97,850	97,900	16,890	12,148	16,890	15,284
97,900	97,950	16,902	12,159	16,902	15,296
97,950	98,000	16,914	12,170	16,914	15,308

98,000

At least	But less than	Single	Married filing jointly *	Married filing separately	Head of a household
98,000	98,050	16,926	12,181	16,926	15,320
98,050	98,100	16,938	12,192	16,938	15,332
98,100	98,150	16,950	12,203	16,950	15,344
98,150	98,200	16,962	12,214	16,962	15,356
98,200	98,250	16,974	12,225	16,974	15,368
98,250	98,300	16,986	12,236	16,986	15,380
98,300	98,350	16,998	12,247	16,998	15,392
98,350	98,400	17,010	12,258	17,010	15,404
98,400	98,450	17,022	12,269	17,022	15,416
98,450	98,500	17,034	12,280	17,034	15,428
98,500	98,550	17,046	12,291	17,046	15,440
98,550	98,600	17,058	12,302	17,058	15,452
98,600	98,650	17,070	12,313	17,070	15,464
98,650	98,700	17,082	12,324	17,082	15,476
98,700	98,750	17,094	12,335	17,094	15,488
98,750	98,800	17,106	12,346	17,106	15,500
98,800	98,850	17,118	12,357	17,118	15,512
98,850	98,900	17,130	12,368	17,130	15,524
98,900	98,950	17,142	12,379	17,142	15,536
98,950	99,000	17,154	12,390	17,154	15,548

If line 15 (taxable income) is—		And you are—			
At least	But less than	Single	Married filing jointly *	Married filing separately	Head of a household
		Your tax is—			

99,000

At least	But less than	Single	Married filing jointly *	Married filing separately	Head of a household
99,000	99,050	17,166	12,401	17,166	15,560
99,050	99,100	17,178	12,412	17,178	15,572
99,100	99,150	17,190	12,423	17,190	15,584
99,150	99,200	17,202	12,434	17,202	15,596
99,200	99,250	17,214	12,445	17,214	15,608
99,250	99,300	17,226	12,456	17,226	15,620
99,300	99,350	17,238	12,467	17,238	15,632
99,350	99,400	17,250	12,478	17,250	15,644
99,400	99,450	17,262	12,489	17,262	15,656
99,450	99,500	17,274	12,500	17,274	15,668
99,500	99,550	17,286	12,511	17,286	15,680
99,550	99,600	17,298	12,522	17,298	15,692
99,600	99,650	17,310	12,533	17,310	15,704
99,650	99,700	17,322	12,544	17,322	15,716
99,700	99,750	17,334	12,555	17,334	15,728
99,750	99,800	17,346	12,566	17,346	15,740
99,800	99,850	17,358	12,577	17,358	15,752
99,850	99,900	17,370	12,588	17,370	15,764
99,900	99,950	17,382	12,599	17,382	15,776
99,950	100,000	17,394	12,610	17,394	15,788

$100,000
or over
use the Tax
Computation
Worksheet

* This column must also be used by a qualifying surviving spouse.

2023 Tax Computation Worksheet—Line 16

See the instructions for line 16 to see if you must use the worksheet below to figure your tax.

Note. If you are required to use this worksheet to figure the tax on an amount from another form or worksheet, such as the Qualified Dividends and Capital Gain Tax Worksheet, the Schedule D Tax Worksheet, Schedule J, Form 8615, or the Foreign Earned Income Tax Worksheet, enter the amount from that form or worksheet in column (a) of the row that applies to the amount you are looking up. Enter the result on the appropriate line of the form or worksheet that you are completing.

Section A—Use if your filing status is **Single.** Complete the row below that applies to you.

Taxable income. If line 15 is—	(a) Enter the amount from line 15	(b) Multiplication amount	(c) Multiply (a) by (b)	(d) Subtraction amount	Tax. Subtract (d) from (c). Enter the result here and on the entry space on line 16.
At least $100,000 but not over $182,100	$	× 24% (0.24)	$	$ 6,600.00	$
Over $182,100 but not over $231,250	$	× 32% (0.32)	$	$ 21,168.00	$
Over $231,250 but not over $578,125	$	× 35% (0.35)	$	$ 28,105.50	$
Over $578,125	$	× 37% (0.37)	$	$ 39,668.00	$

Section B—Use if your filing status is **Married filing jointly** or **Qualifying surviving spouse.** Complete the row below that applies to you.

Taxable income. If line 15 is—	(a) Enter the amount from line 15	(b) Multiplication amount	(c) Multiply (a) by (b)	(d) Subtraction amount	Tax. Subtract (d) from (c). Enter the result here and on the entry space on line 16.
At least $100,000 but not over $190,750	$	× 22% (0.22)	$	$ 9,385.00	$
Over $190,750 but not over $364,200	$	× 24% (0.24)	$	$ 13,200.00	$
Over $364,200 but not over $462,500	$	× 32% (0.32)	$	$ 42,336.00	$
Over $462,500 but not over $693,750	$	× 35% (0.35)	$	$ 56,211.00	$
Over $693,750	$	× 37% (0.37)	$	$ 70,086.00	$

Section C—Use if your filing status is **Married filing separately.** Complete the row below that applies to you.

Taxable income. If line 15 is—	(a) Enter the amount from line 15	(b) Multiplication amount	(c) Multiply (a) by (b)	(d) Subtraction amount	Tax. Subtract (d) from (c). Enter the result here and on the entry space on line 16.
At least $100,000 but not over $182,100	$	× 24% (0.24)	$	$ 6,600.00	$
Over $182,100 but not over $231,250	$	× 32% (0.32)	$	$ 21,168.00	$
Over $231,250 but not over $346,875	$	× 35% (0.35)	$	$ 28,105.50	$
Over $346,875	$	× 37% (0.37)	$	$ 35,043.00	$

Section D—Use if your filing status is **Head of household.** Complete the row below that applies to you.

Taxable income. If line 15 is—	(a) Enter the amount from line 15	(b) Multiplication amount	(c) Multiply (a) by (b)	(d) Subtraction amount	Tax. Subtract (d) from (c). Enter the result here and on the entry space on line 16.
At least $100,000 but not over $182,100	$	× 24% (0.24)	$	$ 8,206.00	$
Over $182,100 but not over $231,250	$	× 32% (0.32)	$	$ 22,774.00	$
Over $231,250 but not over $578,100	$	× 35% (0.35)	$	$ 29,711.50	$
Over $578,100	$	× 37% (0.37)	$	$ 41,273.50	$

2023 Earned Income Credit (EIC) Table
Caution. This is **not** a tax table.

1. To find your credit, read down the "At least - But less than" columns and find the line that includes the amount you were told to look up from your EIC Worksheet.

2. Then, go to the column that includes your filing status and the number of qualifying children you have who have valid SSNs as defined earlier. Enter the credit from that column on your EIC Worksheet.

Example. If your filing status is single, you have one qualifying child who has a valid SSN, and the amount you are looking up from your EIC Worksheet is $2,455, you would enter $842.

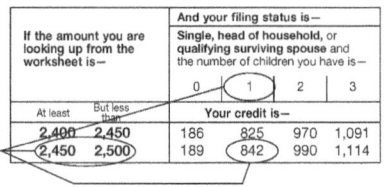

If the amount you are looking up from the worksheet is—	And your filing status is— Single, head of household, or qualifying surviving spouse and the number of children you have is—			
	0	1	2	3
At least / But less than	Your credit is—			
2,400 – 2,450	186	825	970	1,091
2,450 – 2,500	189	842	990	1,114

Left table

If the amount you are looking up from the worksheet is—		Single, head of household, or qualifying surviving spouse★ and you have—				Married filing jointly and you have—			
At least	But less than	0	1	2	3	0	1	2	3
		Your credit is—				Your credit is—			
1	50	2	9	10	11	2	9	10	11
50	100	6	26	30	34	6	26	30	34
100	150	10	43	50	56	10	43	50	56
150	200	13	60	70	79	13	60	70	79
200	250	17	77	90	101	17	77	90	101
250	300	21	94	110	124	21	94	110	124
300	350	25	111	130	146	25	111	130	146
350	400	29	128	150	169	29	128	150	169
400	450	33	145	170	191	33	145	170	191
450	500	36	162	190	214	36	162	190	214
500	550	40	179	210	236	40	179	210	236
550	600	44	196	230	259	44	196	230	259
600	650	48	213	250	281	48	213	250	281
650	700	52	230	270	304	52	230	270	304
700	750	55	247	290	326	55	247	290	326
750	800	59	264	310	349	59	264	310	349
800	850	63	281	330	371	63	281	330	371
850	900	67	298	350	394	67	298	350	394
900	950	71	315	370	416	71	315	370	416
950	1,000	75	332	390	439	75	332	390	439
1,000	1,050	78	349	410	461	78	349	410	461
1,050	1,100	82	366	430	484	82	366	430	484
1,100	1,150	86	383	450	506	86	383	450	506
1,150	1,200	90	400	470	529	90	400	470	529
1,200	1,250	94	417	490	551	94	417	490	551
1,250	1,300	98	434	510	574	98	434	510	574
1,300	1,350	101	451	530	596	101	451	530	596
1,350	1,400	105	468	550	619	105	468	550	619
1,400	1,450	109	485	570	641	109	485	570	641
1,450	1,500	113	502	590	664	113	502	590	664
1,500	1,550	117	519	610	686	117	519	610	686
1,550	1,600	120	536	630	709	120	536	630	709
1,600	1,650	124	553	650	731	124	553	650	731
1,650	1,700	128	570	670	754	128	570	670	754
1,700	1,750	132	587	690	776	132	587	690	776
1,750	1,800	136	604	710	799	136	604	710	799
1,800	1,850	140	621	730	821	140	621	730	821
1,850	1,900	143	638	750	844	143	638	750	844
1,900	1,950	147	655	770	866	147	655	770	866
1,950	2,000	151	672	790	889	151	672	790	889
2,000	2,050	155	689	810	911	155	689	810	911
2,050	2,100	159	706	830	934	159	706	830	934
2,100	2,150	163	723	850	956	163	723	850	956
2,150	2,200	166	740	870	979	166	740	870	979
2,200	2,250	170	757	890	1,001	170	757	890	1,001
2,250	2,300	174	774	910	1,024	174	774	910	1,024
2,300	2,350	178	791	930	1,046	178	791	930	1,046
2,350	2,400	182	808	950	1,069	182	808	950	1,069
2,400	2,450	186	825	970	1,091	186	825	970	1,091
2,450	2,500	189	842	990	1,114	189	842	990	1,114
2,500	2,550	193	859	1,010	1,136	193	859	1,010	1,136
2,550	2,600	197	876	1,030	1,159	197	876	1,030	1,159
2,600	2,650	201	893	1,050	1,181	201	893	1,050	1,181
2,650	2,700	205	910	1,070	1,204	205	910	1,070	1,204
2,700	2,750	208	927	1,090	1,226	208	927	1,090	1,226
2,750	2,800	212	944	1,110	1,249	212	944	1,110	1,249

Right table

If the amount you are looking up from the worksheet is—		Single, head of household, or qualifying surviving spouse★ and you have—				Married filing jointly and you have—			
At least	But less than	0	1	2	3	0	1	2	3
		Your credit is—				Your credit is—			
2,800	2,850	216	961	1,130	1,271	216	961	1,130	1,271
2,850	2,900	220	978	1,150	1,294	220	978	1,150	1,294
2,900	2,950	224	995	1,170	1,316	224	995	1,170	1,316
2,950	3,000	228	1,012	1,190	1,339	228	1,012	1,190	1,339
3,000	3,050	231	1,029	1,210	1,361	231	1,029	1,210	1,361
3,050	3,100	235	1,046	1,230	1,384	235	1,046	1,230	1,384
3,100	3,150	239	1,063	1,250	1,406	239	1,063	1,250	1,406
3,150	3,200	243	1,080	1,270	1,429	243	1,080	1,270	1,429
3,200	3,250	247	1,097	1,290	1,451	247	1,097	1,290	1,451
3,250	3,300	251	1,114	1,310	1,474	251	1,114	1,310	1,474
3,300	3,350	254	1,131	1,330	1,496	254	1,131	1,330	1,496
3,350	3,400	258	1,148	1,350	1,519	258	1,148	1,350	1,519
3,400	3,450	262	1,165	1,370	1,541	262	1,165	1,370	1,541
3,450	3,500	266	1,182	1,390	1,564	266	1,182	1,390	1,564
3,500	3,550	270	1,199	1,410	1,586	270	1,199	1,410	1,586
3,550	3,600	273	1,216	1,430	1,609	273	1,216	1,430	1,609
3,600	3,650	277	1,233	1,450	1,631	277	1,233	1,450	1,631
3,650	3,700	281	1,250	1,470	1,654	281	1,250	1,470	1,654
3,700	3,750	285	1,267	1,490	1,676	285	1,267	1,490	1,676
3,750	3,800	289	1,284	1,510	1,699	289	1,284	1,510	1,699
3,800	3,850	293	1,301	1,530	1,721	293	1,301	1,530	1,721
3,850	3,900	296	1,318	1,550	1,744	296	1,318	1,550	1,744
3,900	3,950	300	1,335	1,570	1,766	300	1,335	1,570	1,766
3,950	4,000	304	1,352	1,590	1,789	304	1,352	1,590	1,789
4,000	4,050	308	1,369	1,610	1,811	308	1,369	1,610	1,811
4,050	4,100	312	1,386	1,630	1,834	312	1,386	1,630	1,834
4,100	4,150	316	1,403	1,650	1,856	316	1,403	1,650	1,856
4,150	4,200	319	1,420	1,670	1,879	319	1,420	1,670	1,879
4,200	4,250	323	1,437	1,690	1,901	323	1,437	1,690	1,901
4,250	4,300	327	1,454	1,710	1,924	327	1,454	1,710	1,924
4,300	4,350	331	1,471	1,730	1,946	331	1,471	1,730	1,946
4,350	4,400	335	1,488	1,750	1,969	335	1,488	1,750	1,969
4,400	4,450	339	1,505	1,770	1,991	339	1,505	1,770	1,991
4,450	4,500	342	1,522	1,790	2,014	342	1,522	1,790	2,014
4,500	4,550	346	1,539	1,810	2,036	346	1,539	1,810	2,036
4,550	4,600	350	1,556	1,830	2,059	350	1,556	1,830	2,059
4,600	4,650	354	1,573	1,850	2,081	354	1,573	1,850	2,081
4,650	4,700	358	1,590	1,870	2,104	358	1,590	1,870	2,104
4,700	4,750	361	1,607	1,890	2,126	361	1,607	1,890	2,126
4,750	4,800	365	1,624	1,910	2,149	365	1,624	1,910	2,149
4,800	4,850	369	1,641	1,930	2,171	369	1,641	1,930	2,171
4,850	4,900	373	1,658	1,950	2,194	373	1,658	1,950	2,194
4,900	4,950	377	1,675	1,970	2,216	377	1,675	1,970	2,216
4,950	5,000	381	1,692	1,990	2,239	381	1,692	1,990	2,239
5,000	5,050	384	1,709	2,010	2,261	384	1,709	2,010	2,261
5,050	5,100	388	1,726	2,030	2,284	388	1,726	2,030	2,284
5,100	5,150	392	1,743	2,050	2,306	392	1,743	2,050	2,306
5,150	5,200	396	1,760	2,070	2,329	396	1,760	2,070	2,329
5,200	5,250	400	1,777	2,090	2,351	400	1,777	2,090	2,351
5,250	5,300	404	1,794	2,110	2,374	404	1,794	2,110	2,374
5,300	5,350	407	1,811	2,130	2,396	407	1,811	2,130	2,396
5,350	5,400	411	1,828	2,150	2,419	411	1,828	2,150	2,419
5,400	5,450	415	1,845	2,170	2,441	415	1,845	2,170	2,441
5,450	5,500	419	1,862	2,190	2,464	419	1,862	2,190	2,464
5,500	5,550	423	1,879	2,210	2,486	423	1,879	2,210	2,486
5,550	5,600	426	1,896	2,230	2,509	426	1,896	2,230	2,509

★ Use this column if your filing status is married filing separately and you qualify to claim the EIC. See the instructions for line 27.

(Continued)

Earned Income Credit (EIC) Table - *Continued*

(**Caution.** This is **not** a tax table.)

If the amount you are looking up from the worksheet is–		Single, head of household, or qualifying surviving spouse★ and you have–				Married filing jointly and you have–			
At least	But less than	0	1	2	3	0	1	2	3
		Your credit is–				Your credit is–			
5,600	5,650	430	1,913	2,250	2,531	430	1,913	2,250	2,531
5,650	5,700	434	1,930	2,270	2,554	434	1,930	2,270	2,554
5,700	5,750	438	1,947	2,290	2,576	438	1,947	2,290	2,576
5,750	5,800	442	1,964	2,310	2,599	442	1,964	2,310	2,599
5,800	5,850	446	1,981	2,330	2,621	446	1,981	2,330	2,621
5,850	5,900	449	1,998	2,350	2,644	449	1,998	2,350	2,644
5,900	5,950	453	2,015	2,370	2,666	453	2,015	2,370	2,666
5,950	6,000	457	2,032	2,390	2,689	457	2,032	2,390	2,689
6,000	6,050	461	2,049	2,410	2,711	461	2,049	2,410	2,711
6,050	6,100	465	2,066	2,430	2,734	465	2,066	2,430	2,734
6,100	6,150	469	2,083	2,450	2,756	469	2,083	2,450	2,756
6,150	6,200	472	2,100	2,470	2,779	472	2,100	2,470	2,779
6,200	6,250	476	2,117	2,490	2,801	476	2,117	2,490	2,801
6,250	6,300	480	2,134	2,510	2,824	480	2,134	2,510	2,824
6,300	6,350	484	2,151	2,530	2,846	484	2,151	2,530	2,846
6,350	6,400	488	2,168	2,550	2,869	488	2,168	2,550	2,869
6,400	6,450	492	2,185	2,570	2,891	492	2,185	2,570	2,891
6,450	6,500	495	2,202	2,590	2,914	495	2,202	2,590	2,914
6,500	6,550	499	2,219	2,610	2,936	499	2,219	2,610	2,936
6,550	6,600	503	2,236	2,630	2,959	503	2,236	2,630	2,959
6,600	6,650	507	2,253	2,650	2,981	507	2,253	2,650	2,981
6,650	6,700	511	2,270	2,670	3,004	511	2,270	2,670	3,004
6,700	6,750	514	2,287	2,690	3,026	514	2,287	2,690	3,026
6,750	6,800	518	2,304	2,710	3,049	518	2,304	2,710	3,049
6,800	6,850	522	2,321	2,730	3,071	522	2,321	2,730	3,071
6,850	6,900	526	2,338	2,750	3,094	526	2,338	2,750	3,094
6,900	6,950	530	2,355	2,770	3,116	530	2,355	2,770	3,116
6,950	7,000	534	2,372	2,790	3,139	534	2,372	2,790	3,139
7,000	7,050	537	2,389	2,810	3,161	537	2,389	2,810	3,161
7,050	7,100	541	2,406	2,830	3,184	541	2,406	2,830	3,184
7,100	7,150	545	2,423	2,850	3,206	545	2,423	2,850	3,206
7,150	7,200	549	2,440	2,870	3,229	549	2,440	2,870	3,229
7,200	7,250	553	2,457	2,890	3,251	553	2,457	2,890	3,251
7,250	7,300	557	2,474	2,910	3,274	557	2,474	2,910	3,274
7,300	7,350	560	2,491	2,930	3,296	560	2,491	2,930	3,296
7,350	7,400	564	2,508	2,950	3,319	564	2,508	2,950	3,319
7,400	7,450	568	2,525	2,970	3,341	568	2,525	2,970	3,341
7,450	7,500	572	2,542	2,990	3,364	572	2,542	2,990	3,364
7,500	7,550	576	2,559	3,010	3,386	576	2,559	3,010	3,386
7,550	7,600	579	2,576	3,030	3,409	579	2,576	3,030	3,409
7,600	7,650	583	2,593	3,050	3,431	583	2,593	3,050	3,431
7,650	7,700	587	2,610	3,070	3,454	587	2,610	3,070	3,454
7,700	7,750	591	2,627	3,090	3,476	591	2,627	3,090	3,476
7,750	7,800	595	2,644	3,110	3,499	595	2,644	3,110	3,499
7,800	7,850	600	2,661	3,130	3,521	600	2,661	3,130	3,521
7,850	7,900	600	2,678	3,150	3,544	600	2,678	3,150	3,544
7,900	7,950	600	2,695	3,170	3,566	600	2,695	3,170	3,566
7,950	8,000	600	2,712	3,190	3,589	600	2,712	3,190	3,589
8,000	8,050	600	2,729	3,210	3,611	600	2,729	3,210	3,611
8,050	8,100	600	2,746	3,230	3,634	600	2,746	3,230	3,634
8,100	8,150	600	2,763	3,250	3,656	600	2,763	3,250	3,656
8,150	8,200	600	2,780	3,270	3,679	600	2,780	3,270	3,679
8,200	8,250	600	2,797	3,290	3,701	600	2,797	3,290	3,701
8,250	8,300	600	2,814	3,310	3,724	600	2,814	3,310	3,724
8,300	8,350	600	2,831	3,330	3,746	600	2,831	3,330	3,746
8,350	8,400	600	2,848	3,350	3,769	600	2,848	3,350	3,769
8,400	8,450	600	2,865	3,370	3,791	600	2,865	3,370	3,791
8,450	8,500	600	2,882	3,390	3,814	600	2,882	3,390	3,814
8,500	8,550	600	2,899	3,410	3,836	600	2,899	3,410	3,836
8,550	8,600	600	2,916	3,430	3,859	600	2,916	3,430	3,859
8,600	8,650	600	2,933	3,450	3,881	600	2,933	3,450	3,881
8,650	8,700	600	2,950	3,470	3,904	600	2,950	3,470	3,904
8,700	8,750	600	2,967	3,490	3,926	600	2,967	3,490	3,926
8,750	8,800	600	2,984	3,510	3,949	600	2,984	3,510	3,949

If the amount you are looking up from the worksheet is–		Single, head of household, or qualifying surviving spouse★ and you have–				Married filing jointly and you have–			
At least	But less than	0	1	2	3	0	1	2	3
		Your credit is–				Your credit is–			
8,800	8,850	600	3,001	3,530	3,971	600	3,001	3,530	3,971
8,850	8,900	600	3,018	3,550	3,994	600	3,018	3,550	3,994
8,900	8,950	600	3,035	3,570	4,016	600	3,035	3,570	4,016
8,950	9,000	600	3,052	3,590	4,039	600	3,052	3,590	4,039
9,000	9,050	600	3,069	3,610	4,061	600	3,069	3,610	4,061
9,050	9,100	600	3,086	3,630	4,084	600	3,086	3,630	4,084
9,100	9,150	600	3,103	3,650	4,106	600	3,103	3,650	4,106
9,150	9,200	600	3,120	3,670	4,129	600	3,120	3,670	4,129
9,200	9,250	600	3,137	3,690	4,151	600	3,137	3,690	4,151
9,250	9,300	600	3,154	3,710	4,174	600	3,154	3,710	4,174
9,300	9,350	600	3,171	3,730	4,196	600	3,171	3,730	4,196
9,350	9,400	600	3,188	3,750	4,219	600	3,188	3,750	4,219
9,400	9,450	600	3,205	3,770	4,241	600	3,205	3,770	4,241
9,450	9,500	600	3,222	3,790	4,264	600	3,222	3,790	4,264
9,500	9,550	600	3,239	3,810	4,286	600	3,239	3,810	4,286
9,550	9,600	600	3,256	3,830	4,309	600	3,256	3,830	4,309
9,600	9,650	600	3,273	3,850	4,331	600	3,273	3,850	4,331
9,650	9,700	600	3,290	3,870	4,354	600	3,290	3,870	4,354
9,700	9,750	600	3,307	3,890	4,376	600	3,307	3,890	4,376
9,750	9,800	600	3,324	3,910	4,399	600	3,324	3,910	4,399
9,800	9,850	598	3,341	3,930	4,421	600	3,341	3,930	4,421
9,850	9,900	594	3,358	3,950	4,444	600	3,358	3,950	4,444
9,900	9,950	590	3,375	3,970	4,466	600	3,375	3,970	4,466
9,950	10,000	586	3,392	3,990	4,489	600	3,392	3,990	4,489
10,000	10,050	583	3,409	4,010	4,511	600	3,409	4,010	4,511
10,050	10,100	579	3,426	4,030	4,534	600	3,426	4,030	4,534
10,100	10,150	575	3,443	4,050	4,556	600	3,443	4,050	4,556
10,150	10,200	571	3,460	4,070	4,579	600	3,460	4,070	4,579
10,200	10,250	567	3,477	4,090	4,601	600	3,477	4,090	4,601
10,250	10,300	563	3,494	4,110	4,624	600	3,494	4,110	4,624
10,300	10,350	560	3,511	4,130	4,646	600	3,511	4,130	4,646
10,350	10,400	556	3,528	4,150	4,669	600	3,528	4,150	4,669
10,400	10,450	552	3,545	4,170	4,691	600	3,545	4,170	4,691
10,450	10,500	548	3,562	4,190	4,714	600	3,562	4,190	4,714
10,500	10,550	544	3,579	4,210	4,736	600	3,579	4,210	4,736
10,550	10,600	540	3,596	4,230	4,759	600	3,596	4,230	4,759
10,600	10,650	537	3,613	4,250	4,781	600	3,613	4,250	4,781
10,650	10,700	533	3,630	4,270	4,804	600	3,630	4,270	4,804
10,700	10,750	529	3,647	4,290	4,826	600	3,647	4,290	4,826
10,750	10,800	525	3,664	4,310	4,849	600	3,664	4,310	4,849
10,800	10,850	521	3,681	4,330	4,871	600	3,681	4,330	4,871
10,850	10,900	518	3,698	4,350	4,894	600	3,698	4,350	4,894
10,900	10,950	514	3,715	4,370	4,916	600	3,715	4,370	4,916
10,950	11,000	510	3,732	4,390	4,939	600	3,732	4,390	4,939
11,000	11,050	506	3,749	4,410	4,961	600	3,749	4,410	4,961
11,050	11,100	502	3,766	4,430	4,984	600	3,766	4,430	4,984
11,100	11,150	498	3,783	4,450	5,006	600	3,783	4,450	5,006
11,150	11,200	495	3,800	4,470	5,029	600	3,800	4,470	5,029
11,200	11,250	491	3,817	4,490	5,051	600	3,817	4,490	5,051
11,250	11,300	487	3,834	4,510	5,074	600	3,834	4,510	5,074
11,300	11,350	483	3,851	4,530	5,096	600	3,851	4,530	5,096
11,350	11,400	479	3,868	4,550	5,119	600	3,868	4,550	5,119
11,400	11,450	475	3,885	4,570	5,141	600	3,885	4,570	5,141
11,450	11,500	472	3,902	4,590	5,164	600	3,902	4,590	5,164
11,500	11,550	468	3,919	4,610	5,186	600	3,919	4,610	5,186
11,550	11,600	464	3,936	4,630	5,209	600	3,936	4,630	5,209
11,600	11,650	460	3,953	4,650	5,231	600	3,953	4,650	5,231
11,650	11,700	456	3,970	4,670	5,254	600	3,970	4,670	5,254
11,700	11,750	452	3,987	4,690	5,276	600	3,987	4,690	5,276
11,750	11,800	449	3,995	4,710	5,299	600	3,995	4,710	5,299
11,800	11,850	445	3,995	4,730	5,321	600	3,995	4,730	5,321
11,850	11,900	441	3,995	4,750	5,344	600	3,995	4,750	5,344
11,900	11,950	437	3,995	4,770	5,366	600	3,995	4,770	5,366
11,950	12,000	433	3,995	4,790	5,389	600	3,995	4,790	5,389

★ Use this column if your filing status is married filing separately and you qualify to claim the EIC. See the instructions for line 27.

(Continued)

Earned Income Credit (EIC) Table - *Continued* **(Caution.** This is **not** a tax table.)

If the amount you are looking up from the worksheet is–		Single, head of household, or qualifying surviving spouse★ and you have–				Married filing jointly and you have–			
At least	But less than	0	1	2	3	0	1	2	3
		Your credit is–				Your credit is–			
12,000	12,050	430	3,995	4,810	5,411	600	3,995	4,810	5,411
12,050	12,100	426	3,995	4,830	5,434	600	3,995	4,830	5,434
12,100	12,150	422	3,995	4,850	5,456	600	3,995	4,850	5,456
12,150	12,200	418	3,995	4,870	5,479	600	3,995	4,870	5,479
12,200	12,250	414	3,995	4,890	5,501	600	3,995	4,890	5,501
12,250	12,300	410	3,995	4,910	5,524	600	3,995	4,910	5,524
12,300	12,350	407	3,995	4,930	5,546	600	3,995	4,930	5,546
12,350	12,400	403	3,995	4,950	5,569	600	3,995	4,950	5,569
12,400	12,450	399	3,995	4,970	5,591	600	3,995	4,970	5,591
12,450	12,500	395	3,995	4,990	5,614	600	3,995	4,990	5,614
12,500	12,550	391	3,995	5,010	5,636	600	3,995	5,010	5,636
12,550	12,600	387	3,995	5,030	5,659	600	3,995	5,030	5,659
12,600	12,650	384	3,995	5,050	5,681	600	3,995	5,050	5,681
12,650	12,700	380	3,995	5,070	5,704	600	3,995	5,070	5,704
12,700	12,750	376	3,995	5,090	5,726	600	3,995	5,090	5,726
12,750	12,800	372	3,995	5,110	5,749	600	3,995	5,110	5,749
12,800	12,850	368	3,995	5,130	5,771	600	3,995	5,130	5,771
12,850	12,900	365	3,995	5,150	5,794	600	3,995	5,150	5,794
12,900	12,950	361	3,995	5,170	5,816	600	3,995	5,170	5,816
12,950	13,000	357	3,995	5,190	5,839	600	3,995	5,190	5,839
13,000	13,050	353	3,995	5,210	5,861	600	3,995	5,210	5,861
13,050	13,100	349	3,995	5,230	5,884	600	3,995	5,230	5,884
13,100	13,150	345	3,995	5,250	5,906	600	3,995	5,250	5,906
13,150	13,200	342	3,995	5,270	5,929	600	3,995	5,270	5,929
13,200	13,250	338	3,995	5,290	5,951	600	3,995	5,290	5,951
13,250	13,300	334	3,995	5,310	5,974	600	3,995	5,310	5,974
13,300	13,350	330	3,995	5,330	5,996	600	3,995	5,330	5,996
13,350	13,400	326	3,995	5,350	6,019	600	3,995	5,350	6,019
13,400	13,450	322	3,995	5,370	6,041	600	3,995	5,370	6,041
13,450	13,500	319	3,995	5,390	6,064	600	3,995	5,390	6,064
13,500	13,550	315	3,995	5,410	6,086	600	3,995	5,410	6,086
13,550	13,600	311	3,995	5,430	6,109	600	3,995	5,430	6,109
13,600	13,650	307	3,995	5,450	6,131	600	3,995	5,450	6,131
13,650	13,700	303	3,995	5,470	6,154	600	3,995	5,470	6,154
13,700	13,750	299	3,995	5,490	6,176	600	3,995	5,490	6,176
13,750	13,800	296	3,995	5,510	6,199	600	3,995	5,510	6,199
13,800	13,850	292	3,995	5,530	6,221	600	3,995	5,530	6,221
13,850	13,900	288	3,995	5,550	6,244	600	3,995	5,550	6,244
13,900	13,950	284	3,995	5,570	6,266	600	3,995	5,570	6,266
13,950	14,000	280	3,995	5,590	6,289	600	3,995	5,590	6,289
14,000	14,050	277	3,995	5,610	6,311	600	3,995	5,610	6,311
14,050	14,100	273	3,995	5,630	6,334	600	3,995	5,630	6,334
14,100	14,150	269	3,995	5,650	6,356	600	3,995	5,650	6,356
14,150	14,200	265	3,995	5,670	6,379	600	3,995	5,670	6,379
14,200	14,250	261	3,995	5,690	6,401	600	3,995	5,690	6,401
14,250	14,300	257	3,995	5,710	6,424	600	3,995	5,710	6,424
14,300	14,350	254	3,995	5,730	6,446	600	3,995	5,730	6,446
14,350	14,400	250	3,995	5,750	6,469	600	3,995	5,750	6,469
14,400	14,450	246	3,995	5,770	6,491	600	3,995	5,770	6,491
14,450	14,500	242	3,995	5,790	6,514	600	3,995	5,790	6,514
14,500	14,550	238	3,995	5,810	6,536	600	3,995	5,810	6,536
14,550	14,600	234	3,995	5,830	6,559	600	3,995	5,830	6,559
14,600	14,650	231	3,995	5,850	6,581	600	3,995	5,850	6,581
14,650	14,700	227	3,995	5,870	6,604	600	3,995	5,870	6,604
14,700	14,750	223	3,995	5,890	6,626	600	3,995	5,890	6,626
14,750	14,800	219	3,995	5,910	6,649	600	3,995	5,910	6,649
14,800	14,850	215	3,995	5,930	6,671	600	3,995	5,930	6,671
14,850	14,900	212	3,995	5,950	6,694	600	3,995	5,950	6,694
14,900	14,950	208	3,995	5,970	6,716	600	3,995	5,970	6,716
14,950	15,000	204	3,995	5,990	6,739	600	3,995	5,990	6,739
15,000	15,050	200	3,995	6,010	6,761	600	3,995	6,010	6,761
15,050	15,100	196	3,995	6,030	6,784	600	3,995	6,030	6,784
15,100	15,150	192	3,995	6,050	6,806	600	3,995	6,050	6,806
15,150	15,200	189	3,995	6,070	6,829	600	3,995	6,070	6,829

If the amount you are looking up from the worksheet is–		Single, head of household, or qualifying surviving spouse★ and you have–				Married filing jointly and you have–			
At least	But less than	0	1	2	3	0	1	2	3
		Your credit is–				Your credit is–			
15,200	15,250	185	3,995	6,090	6,851	600	3,995	6,090	6,851
15,250	15,300	181	3,995	6,110	6,874	600	3,995	6,110	6,874
15,300	15,350	177	3,995	6,130	6,896	600	3,995	6,130	6,896
15,350	15,400	173	3,995	6,150	6,919	600	3,995	6,150	6,919
15,400	15,450	169	3,995	6,170	6,941	600	3,995	6,170	6,941
15,450	15,500	166	3,995	6,190	6,964	600	3,995	6,190	6,964
15,500	15,550	162	3,995	6,210	6,986	600	3,995	6,210	6,986
15,550	15,600	158	3,995	6,230	7,009	600	3,995	6,230	7,009
15,600	15,650	154	3,995	6,250	7,031	600	3,995	6,250	7,031
15,650	15,700	150	3,995	6,270	7,054	600	3,995	6,270	7,054
15,700	15,750	146	3,995	6,290	7,076	600	3,995	6,290	7,076
15,750	15,800	143	3,995	6,310	7,099	600	3,995	6,310	7,099
15,800	15,850	139	3,995	6,330	7,121	600	3,995	6,330	7,121
15,850	15,900	135	3,995	6,350	7,144	600	3,995	6,350	7,144
15,900	15,950	131	3,995	6,370	7,166	600	3,995	6,370	7,166
15,950	16,000	127	3,995	6,390	7,189	600	3,995	6,390	7,189
16,000	16,050	124	3,995	6,410	7,211	600	3,995	6,410	7,211
16,050	16,100	120	3,995	6,430	7,234	600	3,995	6,430	7,234
16,100	16,150	116	3,995	6,450	7,256	600	3,995	6,450	7,256
16,150	16,200	112	3,995	6,470	7,279	600	3,995	6,470	7,279
16,200	16,250	108	3,995	6,490	7,301	600	3,995	6,490	7,301
16,250	16,300	104	3,995	6,510	7,324	600	3,995	6,510	7,324
16,300	16,350	101	3,995	6,530	7,346	600	3,995	6,530	7,346
16,350	16,400	97	3,995	6,550	7,369	600	3,995	6,550	7,369
16,400	16,450	93	3,995	6,570	7,391	596	3,995	6,570	7,391
16,450	16,500	89	3,995	6,590	7,414	592	3,995	6,590	7,414
16,500	16,550	85	3,995	6,604	7,430	588	3,995	6,604	7,430
16,550	16,600	81	3,995	6,604	7,430	584	3,995	6,604	7,430
16,600	16,650	78	3,995	6,604	7,430	580	3,995	6,604	7,430
16,650	16,700	74	3,995	6,604	7,430	576	3,995	6,604	7,430
16,700	16,750	70	3,995	6,604	7,430	573	3,995	6,604	7,430
16,750	16,800	66	3,995	6,604	7,430	569	3,995	6,604	7,430
16,800	16,850	62	3,995	6,604	7,430	565	3,995	6,604	7,430
16,850	16,900	59	3,995	6,604	7,430	561	3,995	6,604	7,430
16,900	16,950	55	3,995	6,604	7,430	557	3,995	6,604	7,430
16,950	17,000	51	3,995	6,604	7,430	553	3,995	6,604	7,430
17,000	17,050	47	3,995	6,604	7,430	550	3,995	6,604	7,430
17,050	17,100	43	3,995	6,604	7,430	546	3,995	6,604	7,430
17,100	17,150	39	3,995	6,604	7,430	542	3,995	6,604	7,430
17,150	17,200	36	3,995	6,604	7,430	538	3,995	6,604	7,430
17,200	17,250	32	3,995	6,604	7,430	534	3,995	6,604	7,430
17,250	17,300	28	3,995	6,604	7,430	531	3,995	6,604	7,430
17,300	17,350	24	3,995	6,604	7,430	527	3,995	6,604	7,430
17,350	17,400	20	3,995	6,604	7,430	523	3,995	6,604	7,430
17,400	17,450	16	3,995	6,604	7,430	519	3,995	6,604	7,430
17,450	17,500	13	3,995	6,604	7,430	515	3,995	6,604	7,430
17,500	17,550	9	3,995	6,604	7,430	511	3,995	6,604	7,430
17,550	17,600	5	3,995	6,604	7,430	508	3,995	6,604	7,430
17,600	17,650	*	3,995	6,604	7,430	504	3,995	6,604	7,430
17,650	17,700	0	3,995	6,604	7,430	500	3,995	6,604	7,430
17,700	17,750	0	3,995	6,604	7,430	496	3,995	6,604	7,430
17,750	17,800	0	3,995	6,604	7,430	492	3,995	6,604	7,430
17,800	17,850	0	3,995	6,604	7,430	488	3,995	6,604	7,430
17,850	17,900	0	3,995	6,604	7,430	485	3,995	6,604	7,430
17,900	17,950	0	3,995	6,604	7,430	481	3,995	6,604	7,430
17,950	18,000	0	3,995	6,604	7,430	477	3,995	6,604	7,430
18,000	18,050	0	3,995	6,604	7,430	473	3,995	6,604	7,430
18,050	18,100	0	3,995	6,604	7,430	469	3,995	6,604	7,430
18,100	18,150	0	3,995	6,604	7,430	466	3,995	6,604	7,430
18,150	18,200	0	3,995	6,604	7,430	462	3,995	6,604	7,430
18,200	18,250	0	3,995	6,604	7,430	458	3,995	6,604	7,430
18,250	18,300	0	3,995	6,604	7,430	454	3,995	6,604	7,430
18,300	18,350	0	3,995	6,604	7,430	450	3,995	6,604	7,430
18,350	18,400	0	3,995	6,604	7,430	446	3,995	6,604	7,430

★　Use this column if your filing status is married filing separately and you qualify to claim the EIC. See the instructions for line 27.

*　If the amount you are looking up from the worksheet is at least $17,600 but less than $17,640, and you have no qualifying children who have valid SSNs, your credit is $2.

If the amount you are looking up from the worksheet is $17,640 or more, and you have no qualifying children who have valid SSNs, you can't take the credit.

(Continued)

Earned Income Credit (EIC) Table - *Continued* (**Caution.** This is **not** a tax table.)

If the amount you are looking up from the worksheet is–		Single, head of household, or qualifying surviving spouse★ and you have–				Married filing jointly and you have–			
At least	But less than	0	1	2	3	0	1	2	3
		Your credit is–				Your credit is–			
18,400	18,450	0	3,995	6,604	7,430	443	3,995	6,604	7,430
18,450	18,500	0	3,995	6,604	7,430	439	3,995	6,604	7,430
18,500	18,550	0	3,995	6,604	7,430	435	3,995	6,604	7,430
18,550	18,600	0	3,995	6,604	7,430	431	3,995	6,604	7,430
18,600	18,650	0	3,995	6,604	7,430	427	3,995	6,604	7,430
18,650	18,700	0	3,995	6,604	7,430	423	3,995	6,604	7,430
18,700	18,750	0	3,995	6,604	7,430	420	3,995	6,604	7,430
18,750	18,800	0	3,995	6,604	7,430	416	3,995	6,604	7,430
18,800	18,850	0	3,995	6,604	7,430	412	3,995	6,604	7,430
18,850	18,900	0	3,995	6,604	7,430	408	3,995	6,604	7,430
18,900	18,950	0	3,995	6,604	7,430	404	3,995	6,604	7,430
18,950	19,000	0	3,995	6,604	7,430	400	3,995	6,604	7,430
19,000	19,050	0	3,995	6,604	7,430	397	3,995	6,604	7,430
19,050	19,100	0	3,995	6,604	7,430	393	3,995	6,604	7,430
19,100	19,150	0	3,995	6,604	7,430	389	3,995	6,604	7,430
19,150	19,200	0	3,995	6,604	7,430	385	3,995	6,604	7,430
19,200	19,250	0	3,995	6,604	7,430	381	3,995	6,604	7,430
19,250	19,300	0	3,995	6,604	7,430	378	3,995	6,604	7,430
19,300	19,350	0	3,995	6,604	7,430	374	3,995	6,604	7,430
19,350	19,400	0	3,995	6,604	7,430	370	3,995	6,604	7,430
19,400	19,450	0	3,995	6,604	7,430	366	3,995	6,604	7,430
19,450	19,500	0	3,995	6,604	7,430	362	3,995	6,604	7,430
19,500	19,550	0	3,995	6,604	7,430	358	3,995	6,604	7,430
19,550	19,600	0	3,995	6,604	7,430	355	3,995	6,604	7,430
19,600	19,650	0	3,995	6,604	7,430	351	3,995	6,604	7,430
19,650	19,700	0	3,995	6,604	7,430	347	3,995	6,604	7,430
19,700	19,750	0	3,995	6,604	7,430	343	3,995	6,604	7,430
19,750	19,800	0	3,995	6,604	7,430	339	3,995	6,604	7,430
19,800	19,850	0	3,995	6,604	7,430	335	3,995	6,604	7,430
19,850	19,900	0	3,995	6,604	7,430	332	3,995	6,604	7,430
19,900	19,950	0	3,995	6,604	7,430	328	3,995	6,604	7,430
19,950	20,000	0	3,995	6,604	7,430	324	3,995	6,604	7,430
20,000	20,050	0	3,995	6,604	7,430	320	3,995	6,604	7,430
20,050	20,100	0	3,995	6,604	7,430	316	3,995	6,604	7,430
20,100	20,150	0	3,995	6,604	7,430	313	3,995	6,604	7,430
20,150	20,200	0	3,995	6,604	7,430	309	3,995	6,604	7,430
20,200	20,250	0	3,995	6,604	7,430	305	3,995	6,604	7,430
20,250	20,300	0	3,995	6,604	7,430	301	3,995	6,604	7,430
20,300	20,350	0	3,995	6,604	7,430	297	3,995	6,604	7,430
20,350	20,400	0	3,995	6,604	7,430	293	3,995	6,604	7,430
20,400	20,450	0	3,995	6,604	7,430	290	3,995	6,604	7,430
20,450	20,500	0	3,995	6,604	7,430	286	3,995	6,604	7,430
20,500	20,550	0	3,995	6,604	7,430	282	3,995	6,604	7,430
20,550	20,600	0	3,995	6,604	7,430	278	3,995	6,604	7,430
20,600	20,650	0	3,995	6,604	7,430	274	3,995	6,604	7,430
20,650	20,700	0	3,995	6,604	7,430	270	3,995	6,604	7,430
20,700	20,750	0	3,995	6,604	7,430	267	3,995	6,604	7,430
20,750	20,800	0	3,995	6,604	7,430	263	3,995	6,604	7,430
20,800	20,850	0	3,995	6,604	7,430	259	3,995	6,604	7,430
20,850	20,900	0	3,995	6,604	7,430	255	3,995	6,604	7,430
20,900	20,950	0	3,995	6,604	7,430	251	3,995	6,604	7,430
20,950	21,000	0	3,995	6,604	7,430	247	3,995	6,604	7,430
21,000	21,050	0	3,995	6,604	7,430	244	3,995	6,604	7,430
21,050	21,100	0	3,995	6,604	7,430	240	3,995	6,604	7,430
21,100	21,150	0	3,995	6,604	7,430	236	3,995	6,604	7,430
21,150	21,200	0	3,995	6,604	7,430	232	3,995	6,604	7,430
21,200	21,250	0	3,995	6,604	7,430	228	3,995	6,604	7,430
21,250	21,300	0	3,995	6,604	7,430	225	3,995	6,604	7,430
21,300	21,350	0	3,995	6,604	7,430	221	3,995	6,604	7,430
21,350	21,400	0	3,995	6,604	7,430	217	3,995	6,604	7,430
21,400	21,450	0	3,995	6,604	7,430	213	3,995	6,604	7,430
21,450	21,500	0	3,995	6,604	7,430	209	3,995	6,604	7,430
21,500	21,550	0	3,995	6,604	7,430	205	3,995	6,604	7,430
21,550	21,600	0	3,995	6,604	7,430	202	3,995	6,604	7,430

If the amount you are looking up from the worksheet is–		Single, head of household, or qualifying surviving spouse★ and you have–				Married filing jointly and you have–			
At least	But less than	0	1	2	3	0	1	2	3
		Your credit is–				Your credit is–			
21,600	21,650	0	3,985	6,590	7,416	198	3,995	6,604	7,430
21,650	21,700	0	3,977	6,580	7,405	194	3,995	6,604	7,430
21,700	21,750	0	3,969	6,569	7,395	190	3,995	6,604	7,430
21,750	21,800	0	3,961	6,559	7,384	186	3,995	6,604	7,430
21,800	21,850	0	3,953	6,548	7,374	182	3,995	6,604	7,430
21,850	21,900	0	3,945	6,538	7,363	179	3,995	6,604	7,430
21,900	21,950	0	3,937	6,527	7,353	175	3,995	6,604	7,430
21,950	22,000	0	3,929	6,517	7,342	171	3,995	6,604	7,430
22,000	22,050	0	3,921	6,506	7,332	167	3,995	6,604	7,430
22,050	22,100	0	3,913	6,496	7,321	163	3,995	6,604	7,430
22,100	22,150	0	3,905	6,485	7,311	160	3,995	6,604	7,430
22,150	22,200	0	3,897	6,474	7,300	156	3,995	6,604	7,430
22,200	22,250	0	3,889	6,464	7,289	152	3,995	6,604	7,430
22,250	22,300	0	3,881	6,453	7,279	148	3,995	6,604	7,430
22,300	22,350	0	3,873	6,443	7,268	144	3,995	6,604	7,430
22,350	22,400	0	3,865	6,432	7,258	140	3,995	6,604	7,430
22,400	22,450	0	3,857	6,422	7,247	137	3,995	6,604	7,430
22,450	22,500	0	3,849	6,411	7,237	133	3,995	6,604	7,430
22,500	22,550	0	3,841	6,401	7,226	129	3,995	6,604	7,430
22,550	22,600	0	3,833	6,390	7,216	125	3,995	6,604	7,430
22,600	22,650	0	3,825	6,380	7,205	121	3,995	6,604	7,430
22,650	22,700	0	3,817	6,369	7,195	117	3,995	6,604	7,430
22,700	22,750	0	3,809	6,359	7,184	114	3,995	6,604	7,430
22,750	22,800	0	3,801	6,348	7,174	110	3,995	6,604	7,430
22,800	22,850	0	3,793	6,338	7,163	106	3,995	6,604	7,430
22,850	22,900	0	3,785	6,327	7,153	102	3,995	6,604	7,430
22,900	22,950	0	3,777	6,317	7,142	98	3,995	6,604	7,430
22,950	23,000	0	3,769	6,306	7,132	94	3,995	6,604	7,430
23,000	23,050	0	3,761	6,295	7,121	91	3,995	6,604	7,430
23,050	23,100	0	3,753	6,285	7,110	87	3,995	6,604	7,430
23,100	23,150	0	3,745	6,274	7,100	83	3,995	6,604	7,430
23,150	23,200	0	3,737	6,264	7,089	79	3,995	6,604	7,430
23,200	23,250	0	3,729	6,253	7,079	75	3,995	6,604	7,430
23,250	23,300	0	3,721	6,243	7,068	72	3,995	6,604	7,430
23,300	23,350	0	3,713	6,232	7,058	68	3,995	6,604	7,430
23,350	23,400	0	3,705	6,222	7,047	64	3,995	6,604	7,430
23,400	23,450	0	3,697	6,211	7,037	60	3,995	6,604	7,430
23,450	23,500	0	3,689	6,201	7,026	56	3,995	6,604	7,430
23,500	23,550	0	3,681	6,190	7,016	52	3,995	6,604	7,430
23,550	23,600	0	3,673	6,180	7,005	49	3,995	6,604	7,430
23,600	23,650	0	3,665	6,169	6,995	45	3,995	6,604	7,430
23,650	23,700	0	3,657	6,159	6,984	41	3,995	6,604	7,430
23,700	23,750	0	3,649	6,148	6,974	37	3,995	6,604	7,430
23,750	23,800	0	3,641	6,138	6,963	33	3,995	6,604	7,430
23,800	23,850	0	3,633	6,127	6,952	29	3,995	6,604	7,430
23,850	23,900	0	3,625	6,116	6,942	26	3,995	6,604	7,430
23,900	23,950	0	3,617	6,106	6,931	22	3,995	6,604	7,430
23,950	24,000	0	3,609	6,095	6,921	18	3,995	6,604	7,430
24,000	24,050	0	3,601	6,085	6,910	14	3,995	6,604	7,430
24,050	24,100	0	3,593	6,074	6,900	10	3,995	6,604	7,430
24,100	24,150	0	3,585	6,064	6,889	7	3,995	6,604	7,430
24,150	24,200	0	3,577	6,053	6,879	3	3,995	6,604	7,430
24,200	24,250	*	3,569	6,043	6,868	0	3,995	6,604	7,430
24,250	24,300	0	3,561	6,032	6,858	0	3,995	6,604	7,430
24,300	24,350	0	3,553	6,022	6,847	0	3,995	6,604	7,430
24,350	24,400	0	3,545	6,011	6,837	0	3,995	6,604	7,430
24,400	24,450	0	3,537	6,001	6,826	0	3,995	6,604	7,430
24,450	24,500	0	3,529	5,990	6,816	0	3,995	6,604	7,430
24,500	24,550	0	3,521	5,980	6,805	0	3,995	6,604	7,430
24,550	24,600	0	3,513	5,969	6,795	0	3,995	6,604	7,430
24,600	24,650	0	3,505	5,959	6,784	0	3,995	6,604	7,430
24,650	24,700	0	3,497	5,948	6,773	0	3,995	6,604	7,430
24,700	24,750	0	3,489	5,937	6,763	0	3,995	6,604	7,430
24,750	24,800	0	3,481	5,927	6,752	0	3,995	6,604	7,430

★ Use this column if your filing status is married filing separately and you qualify to claim the EIC. See the instructions for line 27.

* If the amount you are looking up from the worksheet is at least $24,200 but less than $24,210, and you have no qualifying children who have valid SSNs, your credit is $0.

If the amount you are looking up from the worksheet is at least $24,210 or more, and you have no qualifying children who have valid SSNs, you can't take the credit.

(Continued)

Earned Income Credit (EIC) Table - *Continued* (**Caution.** This is **not** a tax table.)

If the amount you are looking up from the worksheet is–		Single, head of household, or qualifying surviving spouse★ and you have–				Married filing jointly and you have–			
At least	But less than	0	1	2	3	0	1	2	3
		Your credit is–				Your credit is–			
24,800	24,850	0	3,473	5,916	6,742	0	3,995	6,604	7,430
24,850	24,900	0	3,465	5,906	6,731	0	3,995	6,604	7,430
24,900	24,950	0	3,457	5,895	6,721	0	3,995	6,604	7,430
24,950	25,000	0	3,449	5,885	6,710	0	3,995	6,604	7,430
25,000	25,050	0	3,441	5,874	6,700	0	3,995	6,604	7,430
25,050	25,100	0	3,433	5,864	6,689	0	3,995	6,604	7,430
25,100	25,150	0	3,425	5,853	6,679	0	3,995	6,604	7,430
25,150	25,200	0	3,417	5,843	6,668	0	3,995	6,604	7,430
25,200	25,250	0	3,409	5,832	6,658	0	3,995	6,604	7,430
25,250	25,300	0	3,401	5,822	6,647	0	3,995	6,604	7,430
25,300	25,350	0	3,393	5,811	6,637	0	3,995	6,604	7,430
25,350	25,400	0	3,385	5,801	6,626	0	3,995	6,604	7,430
25,400	25,450	0	3,377	5,790	6,616	0	3,995	6,604	7,430
25,450	25,500	0	3,369	5,780	6,605	0	3,995	6,604	7,430
25,500	25,550	0	3,361	5,769	6,594	0	3,995	6,604	7,430
25,550	25,600	0	3,353	5,758	6,584	0	3,995	6,604	7,430
25,600	25,650	0	3,345	5,748	6,573	0	3,995	6,604	7,430
25,650	25,700	0	3,337	5,737	6,563	0	3,995	6,604	7,430
25,700	25,750	0	3,329	5,727	6,552	0	3,995	6,604	7,430
25,750	25,800	0	3,321	5,716	6,542	0	3,995	6,604	7,430
25,800	25,850	0	3,313	5,706	6,531	0	3,995	6,604	7,430
25,850	25,900	0	3,305	5,695	6,521	0	3,995	6,604	7,430
25,900	25,950	0	3,297	5,685	6,510	0	3,995	6,604	7,430
25,950	26,000	0	3,289	5,674	6,500	0	3,995	6,604	7,430
26,000	26,050	0	3,281	5,664	6,489	0	3,995	6,604	7,430
26,050	26,100	0	3,274	5,653	6,479	0	3,995	6,604	7,430
26,100	26,150	0	3,266	5,643	6,468	0	3,995	6,604	7,430
26,150	26,200	0	3,258	5,632	6,458	0	3,995	6,604	7,430
26,200	26,250	0	3,250	5,622	6,447	0	3,995	6,604	7,430
26,250	26,300	0	3,242	5,611	6,437	0	3,995	6,604	7,430
26,300	26,350	0	3,234	5,600	6,426	0	3,995	6,604	7,430
26,350	26,400	0	3,226	5,590	6,415	0	3,995	6,604	7,430
26,400	26,450	0	3,218	5,579	6,405	0	3,995	6,604	7,430
26,450	26,500	0	3,210	5,569	6,394	0	3,995	6,604	7,430
26,500	26,550	0	3,202	5,558	6,384	0	3,995	6,604	7,430
26,550	26,600	0	3,194	5,548	6,373	0	3,995	6,604	7,430
26,600	26,650	0	3,186	5,537	6,363	0	3,995	6,604	7,430
26,650	26,700	0	3,178	5,527	6,352	0	3,995	6,604	7,430
26,700	26,750	0	3,170	5,516	6,342	0	3,995	6,604	7,430
26,750	26,800	0	3,162	5,506	6,331	0	3,995	6,604	7,430
26,800	26,850	0	3,154	5,495	6,321	0	3,995	6,604	7,430
26,850	26,900	0	3,146	5,485	6,310	0	3,995	6,604	7,430
26,900	26,950	0	3,138	5,474	6,300	0	3,995	6,604	7,430
26,950	27,000	0	3,130	5,464	6,289	0	3,995	6,604	7,430
27,000	27,050	0	3,122	5,453	6,279	0	3,995	6,604	7,430
27,050	27,100	0	3,114	5,443	6,268	0	3,995	6,604	7,430
27,100	27,150	0	3,106	5,432	6,258	0	3,995	6,604	7,430
27,150	27,200	0	3,098	5,421	6,247	0	3,995	6,604	7,430
27,200	27,250	0	3,090	5,411	6,236	0	3,995	6,604	7,430
27,250	27,300	0	3,082	5,400	6,226	0	3,995	6,604	7,430
27,300	27,350	0	3,074	5,390	6,215	0	3,995	6,604	7,430
27,350	27,400	0	3,066	5,379	6,205	0	3,995	6,604	7,430
27,400	27,450	0	3,058	5,369	6,194	0	3,995	6,604	7,430
27,450	27,500	0	3,050	5,358	6,184	0	3,995	6,604	7,430
27,500	27,550	0	3,042	5,348	6,173	0	3,995	6,604	7,430
27,550	27,600	0	3,034	5,337	6,163	0	3,995	6,604	7,430
27,600	27,650	0	3,026	5,327	6,152	0	3,995	6,604	7,430
27,650	27,700	0	3,018	5,316	6,142	0	3,995	6,604	7,430
27,700	27,750	0	3,010	5,306	6,131	0	3,995	6,604	7,430
27,750	27,800	0	3,002	5,295	6,121	0	3,995	6,604	7,430
27,800	27,850	0	2,994	5,285	6,110	0	3,995	6,604	7,430
27,850	27,900	0	2,986	5,274	6,100	0	3,995	6,604	7,430
27,900	27,950	0	2,978	5,264	6,089	0	3,995	6,604	7,430
27,950	28,000	0	2,970	5,253	6,079	0	3,995	6,604	7,430

If the amount you are looking up from the worksheet is–		Single, head of household, or qualifying surviving spouse★ and you have–				Married filing jointly and you have–			
At least	But less than	0	1	2	3	0	1	2	3
		Your credit is–				Your credit is–			
28,000	28,050	0	2,962	5,242	6,068	0	3,995	6,604	7,430
28,050	28,100	0	2,954	5,232	6,057	0	3,995	6,604	7,430
28,100	28,150	0	2,946	5,221	6,047	0	3,995	6,604	7,430
28,150	28,200	0	2,938	5,211	6,036	0	3,986	6,592	7,418
28,200	28,250	0	2,930	5,200	6,026	0	3,978	6,582	7,407
28,250	28,300	0	2,922	5,190	6,015	0	3,970	6,571	7,397
28,300	28,350	0	2,914	5,179	6,005	0	3,962	6,561	7,386
28,350	28,400	0	2,906	5,169	5,994	0	3,954	6,550	7,376
28,400	28,450	0	2,898	5,158	5,984	0	3,946	6,540	7,365
28,450	28,500	0	2,890	5,148	5,973	0	3,938	6,529	7,355
28,500	28,550	0	2,882	5,137	5,963	0	3,930	6,519	7,344
28,550	28,600	0	2,874	5,127	5,952	0	3,922	6,508	7,334
28,600	28,650	0	2,866	5,116	5,942	0	3,914	6,498	7,323
28,650	28,700	0	2,858	5,106	5,931	0	3,906	6,487	7,313
28,700	28,750	0	2,850	5,095	5,921	0	3,898	6,477	7,302
28,750	28,800	0	2,842	5,085	5,910	0	3,890	6,466	7,292
28,800	28,850	0	2,834	5,074	5,899	0	3,882	6,456	7,281
28,850	28,900	0	2,826	5,063	5,889	0	3,874	6,445	7,270
28,900	28,950	0	2,818	5,053	5,878	0	3,866	6,434	7,260
28,950	29,000	0	2,810	5,042	5,868	0	3,858	6,424	7,249
29,000	29,050	0	2,802	5,032	5,857	0	3,850	6,413	7,239
29,050	29,100	0	2,794	5,021	5,847	0	3,842	6,403	7,228
29,100	29,150	0	2,786	5,011	5,836	0	3,834	6,392	7,218
29,150	29,200	0	2,778	5,000	5,826	0	3,826	6,382	7,207
29,200	29,250	0	2,770	4,990	5,815	0	3,818	6,371	7,197
29,250	29,300	0	2,762	4,979	5,805	0	3,810	6,361	7,186
29,300	29,350	0	2,754	4,969	5,794	0	3,802	6,350	7,176
29,350	29,400	0	2,746	4,958	5,784	0	3,794	6,340	7,165
29,400	29,450	0	2,738	4,948	5,773	0	3,786	6,329	7,155
29,450	29,500	0	2,730	4,937	5,763	0	3,778	6,319	7,144
29,500	29,550	0	2,722	4,927	5,752	0	3,770	6,308	7,134
29,550	29,600	0	2,714	4,916	5,742	0	3,762	6,298	7,123
29,600	29,650	0	2,706	4,906	5,731	0	3,755	6,287	7,113
29,650	29,700	0	2,698	4,895	5,720	0	3,747	6,277	7,102
29,700	29,750	0	2,690	4,884	5,710	0	3,739	6,266	7,091
29,750	29,800	0	2,682	4,874	5,699	0	3,731	6,255	7,081
29,800	29,850	0	2,674	4,863	5,689	0	3,723	6,245	7,070
29,850	29,900	0	2,666	4,853	5,678	0	3,715	6,234	7,060
29,900	29,950	0	2,658	4,842	5,668	0	3,707	6,224	7,049
29,950	30,000	0	2,650	4,832	5,657	0	3,699	6,213	7,039
30,000	30,050	0	2,642	4,821	5,647	0	3,691	6,203	7,028
30,050	30,100	0	2,634	4,811	5,636	0	3,683	6,192	7,018
30,100	30,150	0	2,626	4,800	5,626	0	3,675	6,182	7,007
30,150	30,200	0	2,618	4,790	5,615	0	3,667	6,171	6,997
30,200	30,250	0	2,610	4,779	5,605	0	3,659	6,161	6,986
30,250	30,300	0	2,602	4,769	5,594	0	3,651	6,150	6,976
30,300	30,350	0	2,594	4,758	5,584	0	3,643	6,140	6,965
30,350	30,400	0	2,586	4,748	5,573	0	3,635	6,129	6,955
30,400	30,450	0	2,578	4,737	5,563	0	3,627	6,119	6,944
30,450	30,500	0	2,570	4,727	5,552	0	3,619	6,108	6,934
30,500	30,550	0	2,562	4,716	5,541	0	3,611	6,098	6,923
30,550	30,600	0	2,554	4,705	5,531	0	3,603	6,087	6,912
30,600	30,650	0	2,546	4,695	5,520	0	3,595	6,076	6,902
30,650	30,700	0	2,538	4,684	5,510	0	3,587	6,066	6,891
30,700	30,750	0	2,530	4,674	5,499	0	3,579	6,055	6,881
30,750	30,800	0	2,522	4,663	5,489	0	3,571	6,045	6,870
30,800	30,850	0	2,514	4,653	5,478	0	3,563	6,034	6,860
30,850	30,900	0	2,506	4,642	5,468	0	3,555	6,024	6,849
30,900	30,950	0	2,498	4,632	5,457	0	3,547	6,013	6,839
30,950	31,000	0	2,490	4,621	5,447	0	3,539	6,003	6,828
31,000	31,050	0	2,482	4,611	5,436	0	3,531	5,992	6,818
31,050	31,100	0	2,475	4,600	5,426	0	3,523	5,982	6,807
31,100	31,150	0	2,467	4,590	5,415	0	3,515	5,971	6,797
31,150	31,200	0	2,459	4,579	5,405	0	3,507	5,961	6,786

★ Use this column if your filing status is married filing separately and you qualify to claim the EIC. See the instructions for line 27.

(Continued)

Earned Income Credit (EIC) Table - *Continued*   (**Caution.** This is **not** a tax table.)

If the amount you are looking up from the worksheet is–		And your filing status is–							
		Single, head of household, or qualifying surviving spouse★ and you have–				Married filing jointly and you have–			
At least	But less than	0	1	2	3	0	1	2	3
		Your credit is–				Your credit is–			
31,200	31,250	0	2,451	4,569	5,394	0	3,499	5,950	6,776
31,250	31,300	0	2,443	4,558	5,384	0	3,491	5,940	6,765
31,300	31,350	0	2,435	4,547	5,373	0	3,483	5,929	6,755
31,350	31,400	0	2,427	4,537	5,362	0	3,475	5,918	6,744
31,400	31,450	0	2,419	4,526	5,352	0	3,467	5,908	6,733
31,450	31,500	0	2,411	4,516	5,341	0	3,459	5,897	6,723
31,500	31,550	0	2,403	4,505	5,331	0	3,451	5,887	6,712
31,550	31,600	0	2,395	4,495	5,320	0	3,443	5,876	6,702
31,600	31,650	0	2,387	4,484	5,310	0	3,435	5,866	6,691
31,650	31,700	0	2,379	4,474	5,299	0	3,427	5,855	6,681
31,700	31,750	0	2,371	4,463	5,289	0	3,419	5,845	6,670
31,750	31,800	0	2,363	4,453	5,278	0	3,411	5,834	6,660
31,800	31,850	0	2,355	4,442	5,268	0	3,403	5,824	6,649
31,850	31,900	0	2,347	4,432	5,257	0	3,395	5,813	6,639
31,900	31,950	0	2,339	4,421	5,247	0	3,387	5,803	6,628
31,950	32,000	0	2,331	4,411	5,236	0	3,379	5,792	6,618
32,000	32,050	0	2,323	4,400	5,226	0	3,371	5,782	6,607
32,050	32,100	0	2,315	4,390	5,215	0	3,363	5,771	6,597
32,100	32,150	0	2,307	4,379	5,205	0	3,355	5,761	6,586
32,150	32,200	0	2,299	4,368	5,194	0	3,347	5,750	6,576
32,200	32,250	0	2,291	4,358	5,183	0	3,339	5,739	6,565
32,250	32,300	0	2,283	4,347	5,173	0	3,331	5,729	6,554
32,300	32,350	0	2,275	4,337	5,162	0	3,323	5,718	6,544
32,350	32,400	0	2,267	4,326	5,152	0	3,315	5,708	6,533
32,400	32,450	0	2,259	4,316	5,141	0	3,307	5,697	6,523
32,450	32,500	0	2,251	4,305	5,131	0	3,299	5,687	6,512
32,500	32,550	0	2,243	4,295	5,120	0	3,291	5,676	6,502
32,550	32,600	0	2,235	4,284	5,110	0	3,283	5,666	6,491
32,600	32,650	0	2,227	4,274	5,099	0	3,275	5,655	6,481
32,650	32,700	0	2,219	4,263	5,089	0	3,267	5,645	6,470
32,700	32,750	0	2,211	4,253	5,078	0	3,259	5,634	6,460
32,750	32,800	0	2,203	4,242	5,068	0	3,251	5,624	6,449
32,800	32,850	0	2,195	4,232	5,057	0	3,243	5,613	6,439
32,850	32,900	0	2,187	4,221	5,047	0	3,235	5,603	6,428
32,900	32,950	0	2,179	4,211	5,036	0	3,227	5,592	6,418
32,950	33,000	0	2,171	4,200	5,026	0	3,219	5,582	6,407
33,000	33,050	0	2,163	4,189	5,015	0	3,211	5,571	6,397
33,050	33,100	0	2,155	4,179	5,004	0	3,203	5,560	6,386
33,100	33,150	0	2,147	4,168	4,994	0	3,195	5,550	6,375
33,150	33,200	0	2,139	4,158	4,983	0	3,187	5,539	6,365
33,200	33,250	0	2,131	4,147	4,973	0	3,179	5,529	6,354
33,250	33,300	0	2,123	4,137	4,962	0	3,171	5,518	6,344
33,300	33,350	0	2,115	4,126	4,952	0	3,163	5,508	6,333
33,350	33,400	0	2,107	4,116	4,941	0	3,155	5,497	6,323
33,400	33,450	0	2,099	4,105	4,931	0	3,147	5,487	6,312
33,450	33,500	0	2,091	4,095	4,920	0	3,139	5,476	6,302
33,500	33,550	0	2,083	4,084	4,910	0	3,131	5,466	6,291
33,550	33,600	0	2,075	4,074	4,899	0	3,123	5,455	6,281
33,600	33,650	0	2,067	4,063	4,889	0	3,115	5,445	6,270
33,650	33,700	0	2,059	4,053	4,878	0	3,107	5,434	6,260
33,700	33,750	0	2,051	4,042	4,868	0	3,099	5,424	6,249
33,750	33,800	0	2,043	4,032	4,857	0	3,091	5,413	6,239
33,800	33,850	0	2,035	4,021	4,846	0	3,083	5,403	6,228
33,850	33,900	0	2,027	4,010	4,836	0	3,075	5,392	6,217
33,900	33,950	0	2,019	4,000	4,825	0	3,067	5,381	6,207
33,950	34,000	0	2,011	3,989	4,815	0	3,059	5,371	6,196
34,000	34,050	0	2,003	3,979	4,804	0	3,051	5,360	6,186
34,050	34,100	0	1,995	3,968	4,794	0	3,043	5,350	6,175
34,100	34,150	0	1,987	3,958	4,783	0	3,035	5,339	6,165
34,150	34,200	0	1,979	3,947	4,773	0	3,027	5,329	6,154
34,200	34,250	0	1,971	3,937	4,762	0	3,019	5,318	6,144
34,250	34,300	0	1,963	3,926	4,752	0	3,011	5,308	6,133
34,300	34,350	0	1,955	3,916	4,741	0	3,003	5,297	6,123
34,350	34,400	0	1,947	3,905	4,731	0	2,995	5,287	6,112

If the amount you are looking up from the worksheet is–		And your filing status is–							
		Single, head of household, or qualifying surviving spouse★ and you have–				Married filing jointly and you have–			
At least	But less than	0	1	2	3	0	1	2	3
		Your credit is–				Your credit is–			
34,400	34,450	0	1,939	3,895	4,720	0	2,987	5,276	6,102
34,450	34,500	0	1,931	3,884	4,710	0	2,979	5,266	6,091
34,500	34,550	0	1,923	3,874	4,699	0	2,971	5,255	6,081
34,550	34,600	0	1,915	3,863	4,689	0	2,963	5,245	6,070
34,600	34,650	0	1,907	3,853	4,678	0	2,956	5,234	6,060
34,650	34,700	0	1,899	3,842	4,667	0	2,948	5,224	6,049
34,700	34,750	0	1,891	3,831	4,657	0	2,940	5,213	6,038
34,750	34,800	0	1,883	3,821	4,646	0	2,932	5,202	6,028
34,800	34,850	0	1,875	3,810	4,636	0	2,924	5,192	6,017
34,850	34,900	0	1,867	3,800	4,625	0	2,916	5,181	6,007
34,900	34,950	0	1,859	3,789	4,615	0	2,908	5,171	5,996
34,950	35,000	0	1,851	3,779	4,604	0	2,900	5,160	5,986
35,000	35,050	0	1,843	3,768	4,594	0	2,892	5,150	5,975
35,050	35,100	0	1,835	3,758	4,583	0	2,884	5,139	5,965
35,100	35,150	0	1,827	3,747	4,573	0	2,876	5,129	5,954
35,150	35,200	0	1,819	3,737	4,562	0	2,868	5,118	5,944
35,200	35,250	0	1,811	3,726	4,552	0	2,860	5,108	5,933
35,250	35,300	0	1,803	3,716	4,541	0	2,852	5,097	5,923
35,300	35,350	0	1,795	3,705	4,531	0	2,844	5,087	5,912
35,350	35,400	0	1,787	3,695	4,520	0	2,836	5,076	5,902
35,400	35,450	0	1,779	3,684	4,510	0	2,828	5,066	5,891
35,450	35,500	0	1,771	3,674	4,499	0	2,820	5,055	5,881
35,500	35,550	0	1,763	3,663	4,488	0	2,812	5,045	5,870
35,550	35,600	0	1,755	3,652	4,478	0	2,804	5,034	5,859
35,600	35,650	0	1,747	3,642	4,467	0	2,796	5,023	5,849
35,650	35,700	0	1,739	3,631	4,457	0	2,788	5,013	5,838
35,700	35,750	0	1,731	3,621	4,446	0	2,780	5,002	5,828
35,750	35,800	0	1,723	3,610	4,436	0	2,772	4,992	5,817
35,800	35,850	0	1,715	3,600	4,425	0	2,764	4,981	5,807
35,850	35,900	0	1,707	3,589	4,415	0	2,756	4,971	5,796
35,900	35,950	0	1,699	3,579	4,404	0	2,748	4,960	5,786
35,950	36,000	0	1,691	3,568	4,394	0	2,740	4,950	5,775
36,000	36,050	0	1,683	3,558	4,383	0	2,732	4,939	5,765
36,050	36,100	0	1,676	3,547	4,373	0	2,724	4,929	5,754
36,100	36,150	0	1,668	3,537	4,362	0	2,716	4,918	5,744
36,150	36,200	0	1,660	3,526	4,352	0	2,708	4,908	5,733
36,200	36,250	0	1,652	3,516	4,341	0	2,700	4,897	5,723
36,250	36,300	0	1,644	3,505	4,331	0	2,692	4,887	5,712
36,300	36,350	0	1,636	3,494	4,320	0	2,684	4,876	5,702
36,350	36,400	0	1,628	3,484	4,309	0	2,676	4,865	5,691
36,400	36,450	0	1,620	3,473	4,299	0	2,668	4,855	5,680
36,450	36,500	0	1,612	3,463	4,288	0	2,660	4,844	5,670
36,500	36,550	0	1,604	3,452	4,278	0	2,652	4,834	5,659
36,550	36,600	0	1,596	3,442	4,267	0	2,644	4,823	5,649
36,600	36,650	0	1,588	3,431	4,257	0	2,636	4,813	5,638
36,650	36,700	0	1,580	3,421	4,246	0	2,628	4,802	5,628
36,700	36,750	0	1,572	3,410	4,236	0	2,620	4,792	5,617
36,750	36,800	0	1,564	3,400	4,225	0	2,612	4,781	5,607
36,800	36,850	0	1,556	3,389	4,215	0	2,604	4,771	5,596
36,850	36,900	0	1,548	3,379	4,204	0	2,596	4,760	5,586
36,900	36,950	0	1,540	3,368	4,194	0	2,588	4,750	5,575
36,950	37,000	0	1,532	3,358	4,183	0	2,580	4,739	5,565
37,000	37,050	0	1,524	3,347	4,173	0	2,572	4,729	5,554
37,050	37,100	0	1,516	3,337	4,162	0	2,564	4,718	5,544
37,100	37,150	0	1,508	3,326	4,152	0	2,556	4,708	5,533
37,150	37,200	0	1,500	3,315	4,141	0	2,548	4,697	5,523
37,200	37,250	0	1,492	3,305	4,130	0	2,540	4,686	5,512
37,250	37,300	0	1,484	3,294	4,120	0	2,532	4,676	5,501
37,300	37,350	0	1,476	3,284	4,109	0	2,524	4,665	5,491
37,350	37,400	0	1,468	3,273	4,099	0	2,516	4,655	5,480
37,400	37,450	0	1,460	3,263	4,088	0	2,508	4,644	5,470
37,450	37,500	0	1,452	3,252	4,078	0	2,500	4,634	5,459
37,500	37,550	0	1,444	3,242	4,067	0	2,492	4,623	5,449
37,550	37,600	0	1,436	3,231	4,057	0	2,484	4,613	5,438

★ Use this column if your filing status is married filing separately and you qualify to claim the EIC. See the instructions for line 27.

(Continued)

Earned Income Credit (EIC) Table - *Continued* (**Caution.** This is **not** a tax table.)

If the amount you are looking up from the worksheet is–		Single, head of household, or qualifying surviving spouse★ and you have–				Married filing jointly and you have–			
At least	But less than	0	1	2	3	0	1	2	3
		Your credit is–				Your credit is–			
37,600	37,650	0	1,428	3,221	4,046	0	2,476	4,602	5,428
37,650	37,700	0	1,420	3,210	4,036	0	2,468	4,592	5,417
37,700	37,750	0	1,412	3,200	4,025	0	2,460	4,581	5,407
37,750	37,800	0	1,404	3,189	4,015	0	2,452	4,571	5,396
37,800	37,850	0	1,396	3,179	4,004	0	2,444	4,560	5,386
37,850	37,900	0	1,388	3,168	3,994	0	2,436	4,550	5,375
37,900	37,950	0	1,380	3,158	3,983	0	2,428	4,539	5,365
37,950	38,000	0	1,372	3,147	3,973	0	2,420	4,529	5,354
38,000	38,050	0	1,364	3,136	3,962	0	2,412	4,518	5,344
38,050	38,100	0	1,356	3,126	3,951	0	2,404	4,507	5,333
38,100	38,150	0	1,348	3,115	3,941	0	2,396	4,497	5,322
38,150	38,200	0	1,340	3,105	3,930	0	2,388	4,486	5,312
38,200	38,250	0	1,332	3,094	3,920	0	2,380	4,476	5,301
38,250	38,300	0	1,324	3,084	3,909	0	2,372	4,465	5,291
38,300	38,350	0	1,316	3,073	3,899	0	2,364	4,455	5,280
38,350	38,400	0	1,308	3,063	3,888	0	2,356	4,444	5,270
38,400	38,450	0	1,300	3,052	3,878	0	2,348	4,434	5,259
38,450	38,500	0	1,292	3,042	3,867	0	2,340	4,423	5,249
38,500	38,550	0	1,284	3,031	3,857	0	2,332	4,413	5,238
38,550	38,600	0	1,276	3,021	3,846	0	2,324	4,402	5,228
38,600	38,650	0	1,268	3,010	3,836	0	2,316	4,392	5,217
38,650	38,700	0	1,260	3,000	3,825	0	2,308	4,381	5,207
38,700	38,750	0	1,252	2,989	3,815	0	2,300	4,371	5,196
38,750	38,800	0	1,244	2,979	3,804	0	2,292	4,360	5,186
38,800	38,850	0	1,236	2,968	3,793	0	2,284	4,350	5,175
38,850	38,900	0	1,228	2,957	3,783	0	2,276	4,339	5,164
38,900	38,950	0	1,220	2,947	3,772	0	2,268	4,328	5,154
38,950	39,000	0	1,212	2,936	3,762	0	2,260	4,318	5,143
39,000	39,050	0	1,204	2,926	3,751	0	2,252	4,307	5,133
39,050	39,100	0	1,196	2,915	3,741	0	2,244	4,297	5,122
39,100	39,150	0	1,188	2,905	3,730	0	2,236	4,286	5,112
39,150	39,200	0	1,180	2,894	3,720	0	2,228	4,276	5,101
39,200	39,250	0	1,172	2,884	3,709	0	2,220	4,265	5,091
39,250	39,300	0	1,164	2,873	3,699	0	2,212	4,255	5,080
39,300	39,350	0	1,156	2,863	3,688	0	2,204	4,244	5,070
39,350	39,400	0	1,148	2,852	3,678	0	2,196	4,234	5,059
39,400	39,450	0	1,140	2,842	3,667	0	2,188	4,223	5,049
39,450	39,500	0	1,132	2,831	3,657	0	2,180	4,213	5,038
39,500	39,550	0	1,124	2,821	3,646	0	2,172	4,202	5,028
39,550	39,600	0	1,116	2,810	3,636	0	2,164	4,192	5,017
39,600	39,650	0	1,108	2,800	3,625	0	2,157	4,181	5,007
39,650	39,700	0	1,100	2,789	3,614	0	2,149	4,171	4,996
39,700	39,750	0	1,092	2,778	3,604	0	2,141	4,160	4,985
39,750	39,800	0	1,084	2,768	3,593	0	2,133	4,149	4,975
39,800	39,850	0	1,076	2,757	3,583	0	2,125	4,139	4,964
39,850	39,900	0	1,068	2,747	3,572	0	2,117	4,128	4,954
39,900	39,950	0	1,060	2,736	3,562	0	2,109	4,118	4,943
39,950	40,000	0	1,052	2,726	3,551	0	2,101	4,107	4,933
40,000	40,050	0	1,044	2,715	3,541	0	2,093	4,097	4,922
40,050	40,100	0	1,036	2,705	3,530	0	2,085	4,086	4,912
40,100	40,150	0	1,028	2,694	3,520	0	2,077	4,076	4,901
40,150	40,200	0	1,020	2,684	3,509	0	2,069	4,065	4,891
40,200	40,250	0	1,012	2,673	3,499	0	2,061	4,055	4,880
40,250	40,300	0	1,004	2,663	3,488	0	2,053	4,044	4,870
40,300	40,350	0	996	2,652	3,478	0	2,045	4,034	4,859
40,350	40,400	0	988	2,642	3,467	0	2,037	4,023	4,849
40,400	40,450	0	980	2,631	3,457	0	2,029	4,013	4,838
40,450	40,500	0	972	2,621	3,446	0	2,021	4,002	4,828
40,500	40,550	0	964	2,610	3,435	0	2,013	3,992	4,817
40,550	40,600	0	956	2,599	3,425	0	2,005	3,981	4,806
40,600	40,650	0	948	2,589	3,414	0	1,997	3,970	4,796
40,650	40,700	0	940	2,578	3,404	0	1,989	3,960	4,785
40,700	40,750	0	932	2,568	3,393	0	1,981	3,949	4,775
40,750	40,800	0	924	2,557	3,383	0	1,973	3,939	4,764

If the amount you are looking up from the worksheet is–		Single, head of household, or qualifying surviving spouse★ and you have–				Married filing jointly and you have–			
At least	But less than	0	1	2	3	0	1	2	3
		Your credit is–				Your credit is–			
40,800	40,850	0	916	2,547	3,372	0	1,965	3,928	4,754
40,850	40,900	0	908	2,536	3,362	0	1,957	3,918	4,743
40,900	40,950	0	900	2,526	3,351	0	1,949	3,907	4,733
40,950	41,000	0	892	2,515	3,341	0	1,941	3,897	4,722
41,000	41,050	0	884	2,505	3,330	0	1,933	3,886	4,712
41,050	41,100	0	877	2,494	3,320	0	1,925	3,876	4,701
41,100	41,150	0	869	2,484	3,309	0	1,917	3,865	4,691
41,150	41,200	0	861	2,473	3,299	0	1,909	3,855	4,680
41,200	41,250	0	853	2,463	3,288	0	1,901	3,844	4,670
41,250	41,300	0	845	2,452	3,278	0	1,893	3,834	4,659
41,300	41,350	0	837	2,441	3,267	0	1,885	3,823	4,649
41,350	41,400	0	829	2,431	3,256	0	1,877	3,812	4,638
41,400	41,450	0	821	2,420	3,246	0	1,869	3,802	4,627
41,450	41,500	0	813	2,410	3,235	0	1,861	3,791	4,617
41,500	41,550	0	805	2,399	3,225	0	1,853	3,781	4,606
41,550	41,600	0	797	2,389	3,214	0	1,845	3,770	4,596
41,600	41,650	0	789	2,378	3,204	0	1,837	3,760	4,585
41,650	41,700	0	781	2,368	3,193	0	1,829	3,749	4,575
41,700	41,750	0	773	2,357	3,183	0	1,821	3,739	4,564
41,750	41,800	0	765	2,347	3,172	0	1,813	3,728	4,554
41,800	41,850	0	757	2,336	3,162	0	1,805	3,718	4,543
41,850	41,900	0	749	2,326	3,151	0	1,797	3,707	4,533
41,900	41,950	0	741	2,315	3,141	0	1,789	3,697	4,522
41,950	42,000	0	733	2,305	3,130	0	1,781	3,686	4,512
42,000	42,050	0	725	2,294	3,120	0	1,773	3,676	4,501
42,050	42,100	0	717	2,284	3,109	0	1,765	3,665	4,491
42,100	42,150	0	709	2,273	3,099	0	1,757	3,655	4,480
42,150	42,200	0	701	2,262	3,088	0	1,749	3,644	4,470
42,200	42,250	0	693	2,252	3,077	0	1,741	3,633	4,459
42,250	42,300	0	685	2,241	3,067	0	1,733	3,623	4,448
42,300	42,350	0	677	2,231	3,056	0	1,725	3,612	4,438
42,350	42,400	0	669	2,220	3,046	0	1,717	3,602	4,427
42,400	42,450	0	661	2,210	3,035	0	1,709	3,591	4,417
42,450	42,500	0	653	2,199	3,025	0	1,701	3,581	4,406
42,500	42,550	0	645	2,189	3,014	0	1,693	3,570	4,396
42,550	42,600	0	637	2,178	3,004	0	1,685	3,560	4,385
42,600	42,650	0	629	2,168	2,993	0	1,677	3,549	4,375
42,650	42,700	0	621	2,157	2,983	0	1,669	3,539	4,364
42,700	42,750	0	613	2,147	2,972	0	1,661	3,528	4,354
42,750	42,800	0	605	2,136	2,962	0	1,653	3,518	4,343
42,800	42,850	0	597	2,126	2,951	0	1,645	3,507	4,333
42,850	42,900	0	589	2,115	2,941	0	1,637	3,497	4,322
42,900	42,950	0	581	2,105	2,930	0	1,629	3,486	4,312
42,950	43,000	0	573	2,094	2,920	0	1,621	3,476	4,301
43,000	43,050	0	565	2,083	2,909	0	1,613	3,465	4,291
43,050	43,100	0	557	2,073	2,898	0	1,605	3,454	4,280
43,100	43,150	0	549	2,062	2,888	0	1,597	3,444	4,269
43,150	43,200	0	541	2,052	2,877	0	1,589	3,433	4,259
43,200	43,250	0	533	2,041	2,867	0	1,581	3,423	4,248
43,250	43,300	0	525	2,031	2,856	0	1,573	3,412	4,238
43,300	43,350	0	517	2,020	2,846	0	1,565	3,402	4,227
43,350	43,400	0	509	2,010	2,835	0	1,557	3,391	4,217
43,400	43,450	0	501	1,999	2,825	0	1,549	3,381	4,206
43,450	43,500	0	493	1,989	2,814	0	1,541	3,370	4,196
43,500	43,550	0	485	1,978	2,804	0	1,533	3,360	4,185
43,550	43,600	0	477	1,968	2,793	0	1,525	3,349	4,175
43,600	43,650	0	469	1,957	2,783	0	1,517	3,339	4,164
43,650	43,700	0	461	1,947	2,772	0	1,509	3,328	4,154
43,700	43,750	0	453	1,936	2,762	0	1,501	3,318	4,143
43,750	43,800	0	445	1,926	2,751	0	1,493	3,307	4,133
43,800	43,850	0	437	1,915	2,740	0	1,485	3,297	4,122
43,850	43,900	0	429	1,904	2,730	0	1,477	3,286	4,111
43,900	43,950	0	421	1,894	2,719	0	1,469	3,275	4,101
43,950	44,000	0	413	1,883	2,709	0	1,461	3,265	4,090

★ Use this column if your filing status is married filing separately and you qualify to claim the EIC. See the instructions for line 27.

(Continued)

Earned Income Credit (EIC) Table - *Continued*

(Caution. This is **not** a tax table.)

At least	But less than	S 0	S 1	S 2	S 3	M 0	M 1	M 2	M 3
44,000	44,050	0	405	1,873	2,698	0	1,453	3,254	4,080
44,050	44,100	0	397	1,862	2,688	0	1,445	3,244	4,069
44,100	44,150	0	389	1,852	2,677	0	1,437	3,233	4,059
44,150	44,200	0	381	1,841	2,667	0	1,429	3,223	4,048
44,200	44,250	0	373	1,831	2,656	0	1,421	3,212	4,038
44,250	44,300	0	365	1,820	2,646	0	1,413	3,202	4,027
44,300	44,350	0	357	1,810	2,635	0	1,405	3,191	4,017
44,350	44,400	0	349	1,799	2,625	0	1,397	3,181	4,006
44,400	44,450	0	341	1,789	2,614	0	1,389	3,170	3,996
44,450	44,500	0	333	1,778	2,604	0	1,381	3,160	3,985
44,500	44,550	0	325	1,768	2,593	0	1,373	3,149	3,975
44,550	44,600	0	317	1,757	2,583	0	1,365	3,139	3,964
44,600	44,650	0	309	1,747	2,572	0	1,358	3,128	3,954
44,650	44,700	0	301	1,736	2,561	0	1,350	3,118	3,943
44,700	44,750	0	293	1,725	2,551	0	1,342	3,107	3,932
44,750	44,800	0	285	1,715	2,540	0	1,334	3,096	3,922
44,800	44,850	0	277	1,704	2,530	0	1,326	3,086	3,911
44,850	44,900	0	269	1,694	2,519	0	1,318	3,075	3,901
44,900	44,950	0	261	1,683	2,509	0	1,310	3,065	3,890
44,950	45,000	0	253	1,673	2,498	0	1,302	3,054	3,880
45,000	45,050	0	245	1,662	2,488	0	1,294	3,044	3,869
45,050	45,100	0	237	1,652	2,477	0	1,286	3,033	3,859
45,100	45,150	0	229	1,641	2,467	0	1,278	3,023	3,848
45,150	45,200	0	221	1,631	2,456	0	1,270	3,012	3,838
45,200	45,250	0	213	1,620	2,446	0	1,262	3,002	3,827
45,250	45,300	0	205	1,610	2,435	0	1,254	2,991	3,817
45,300	45,350	0	197	1,599	2,425	0	1,246	2,981	3,806
45,350	45,400	0	189	1,589	2,414	0	1,238	2,970	3,796
45,400	45,450	0	181	1,578	2,404	0	1,230	2,960	3,785
45,450	45,500	0	173	1,568	2,393	0	1,222	2,949	3,775
45,500	45,550	0	165	1,557	2,382	0	1,214	2,939	3,764
45,550	45,600	0	157	1,546	2,372	0	1,206	2,928	3,753
45,600	45,650	0	149	1,536	2,361	0	1,198	2,917	3,743
45,650	45,700	0	141	1,525	2,351	0	1,190	2,907	3,732
45,700	45,750	0	133	1,515	2,340	0	1,182	2,896	3,722
45,750	45,800	0	125	1,504	2,330	0	1,174	2,886	3,711
45,800	45,850	0	117	1,494	2,319	0	1,166	2,875	3,701
45,850	45,900	0	109	1,483	2,309	0	1,158	2,865	3,690
45,900	45,950	0	101	1,473	2,298	0	1,150	2,854	3,680
45,950	46,000	0	93	1,462	2,288	0	1,142	2,844	3,669
46,000	46,050	0	85	1,452	2,277	0	1,134	2,833	3,659
46,050	46,100	0	78	1,441	2,267	0	1,126	2,823	3,648
46,100	46,150	0	70	1,431	2,256	0	1,118	2,812	3,638
46,150	46,200	0	62	1,420	2,246	0	1,110	2,802	3,627
46,200	46,250	0	54	1,410	2,235	0	1,102	2,791	3,617
46,250	46,300	0	46	1,399	2,225	0	1,094	2,781	3,606
46,300	46,350	0	38	1,388	2,214	0	1,086	2,770	3,596
46,350	46,400	0	30	1,378	2,203	0	1,078	2,759	3,585
46,400	46,450	0	22	1,367	2,193	0	1,070	2,749	3,574
46,450	46,500	0	14	1,357	2,182	0	1,062	2,738	3,564
46,500	46,550	0	6	1,346	2,172	0	1,054	2,728	3,553
46,550	46,600	0	*	1,336	2,161	0	1,046	2,717	3,543
46,600	46,650	0	0	1,325	2,151	0	1,038	2,707	3,532
46,650	46,700	0	0	1,315	2,140	0	1,030	2,696	3,522
46,700	46,750	0	0	1,304	2,130	0	1,022	2,686	3,511
46,750	46,800	0	0	1,294	2,119	0	1,014	2,675	3,501
46,800	46,850	0	0	1,283	2,109	0	1,006	2,665	3,490
46,850	46,900	0	0	1,273	2,098	0	998	2,654	3,480
46,900	46,950	0	0	1,262	2,088	0	990	2,644	3,469
46,950	47,000	0	0	1,252	2,077	0	982	2,633	3,459
47,000	47,050	0	0	1,241	2,067	0	974	2,623	3,448
47,050	47,100	0	0	1,231	2,056	0	966	2,612	3,438
47,100	47,150	0	0	1,220	2,046	0	958	2,602	3,427
47,150	47,200	0	0	1,209	2,035	0	950	2,591	3,417
47,200	47,250	0	0	1,199	2,024	0	942	2,580	3,406
47,250	47,300	0	0	1,188	2,014	0	934	2,570	3,395
47,300	47,350	0	0	1,178	2,003	0	926	2,559	3,385
47,350	47,400	0	0	1,167	1,993	0	918	2,549	3,374
47,400	47,450	0	0	1,157	1,982	0	910	2,538	3,364
47,450	47,500	0	0	1,146	1,972	0	902	2,528	3,353
47,500	47,550	0	0	1,136	1,961	0	894	2,517	3,343
47,550	47,600	0	0	1,125	1,951	0	886	2,507	3,332
47,600	47,650	0	0	1,115	1,940	0	878	2,496	3,322
47,650	47,700	0	0	1,104	1,930	0	870	2,486	3,311
47,700	47,750	0	0	1,094	1,919	0	862	2,475	3,301
47,750	47,800	0	0	1,083	1,909	0	854	2,465	3,290
47,800	47,850	0	0	1,073	1,898	0	846	2,454	3,280
47,850	47,900	0	0	1,062	1,888	0	838	2,444	3,269
47,900	47,950	0	0	1,052	1,877	0	830	2,433	3,259
47,950	48,000	0	0	1,041	1,867	0	822	2,423	3,248
48,000	48,050	0	0	1,030	1,856	0	814	2,412	3,238
48,050	48,100	0	0	1,020	1,845	0	806	2,401	3,227
48,100	48,150	0	0	1,009	1,835	0	798	2,391	3,216
48,150	48,200	0	0	999	1,824	0	790	2,380	3,206
48,200	48,250	0	0	988	1,814	0	782	2,370	3,195
48,250	48,300	0	0	978	1,803	0	774	2,359	3,185
48,300	48,350	0	0	967	1,793	0	766	2,349	3,174
48,350	48,400	0	0	957	1,782	0	758	2,338	3,164
48,400	48,450	0	0	946	1,772	0	750	2,328	3,153
48,450	48,500	0	0	936	1,761	0	742	2,317	3,143
48,500	48,550	0	0	925	1,751	0	734	2,307	3,132
48,550	48,600	0	0	915	1,740	0	726	2,296	3,122
48,600	48,650	0	0	904	1,730	0	718	2,286	3,111
48,650	48,700	0	0	894	1,719	0	710	2,275	3,101
48,700	48,750	0	0	883	1,709	0	702	2,265	3,090
48,750	48,800	0	0	873	1,698	0	694	2,254	3,080
48,800	48,850	0	0	862	1,687	0	686	2,244	3,069
48,850	48,900	0	0	851	1,677	0	678	2,233	3,058
48,900	48,950	0	0	841	1,666	0	670	2,222	3,048
48,950	49,000	0	0	830	1,656	0	662	2,212	3,037
49,000	49,050	0	0	820	1,645	0	654	2,201	3,027
49,050	49,100	0	0	809	1,635	0	646	2,191	3,016
49,100	49,150	0	0	799	1,624	0	638	2,180	3,006
49,150	49,200	0	0	788	1,614	0	630	2,170	2,995
49,200	49,250	0	0	778	1,603	0	622	2,159	2,985
49,250	49,300	0	0	767	1,593	0	614	2,149	2,974
49,300	49,350	0	0	757	1,582	0	606	2,138	2,964
49,350	49,400	0	0	746	1,572	0	598	2,128	2,953
49,400	49,450	0	0	736	1,561	0	590	2,117	2,943
49,450	49,500	0	0	725	1,551	0	582	2,107	2,932
49,500	49,550	0	0	715	1,540	0	574	2,096	2,922
49,550	49,600	0	0	704	1,530	0	566	2,086	2,911
49,600	49,650	0	0	694	1,519	0	559	2,075	2,901
49,650	49,700	0	0	683	1,508	0	551	2,065	2,890
49,700	49,750	0	0	672	1,498	0	543	2,054	2,879
49,750	49,800	0	0	662	1,487	0	535	2,043	2,869
49,800	49,850	0	0	651	1,477	0	527	2,033	2,858
49,850	49,900	0	0	641	1,466	0	519	2,022	2,848
49,900	49,950	0	0	630	1,456	0	511	2,012	2,837
49,950	50,000	0	0	620	1,445	0	503	2,001	2,827
50,000	50,050	0	0	609	1,435	0	495	1,991	2,816
50,050	50,100	0	0	599	1,424	0	487	1,980	2,806
50,100	50,150	0	0	588	1,414	0	479	1,970	2,795
50,150	50,200	0	0	578	1,403	0	471	1,959	2,785
50,200	50,250	0	0	567	1,393	0	463	1,949	2,774
50,250	50,300	0	0	557	1,382	0	455	1,938	2,764
50,300	50,350	0	0	546	1,372	0	447	1,928	2,753
50,350	50,400	0	0	536	1,361	0	439	1,917	2,743

★ Use this column if your filing status is married filing separately and you qualify to claim the EIC. See the instructions for line 27.

* If the amount you are looking up from the worksheet is at least $46,550 but less than $46,560, and you have one qualifying child who has a valid SSN, your credit is $1.

If the amount you are looking up from the worksheet is $46,560 or more, and you have one qualifying child who has a valid SSN, you can't take the credit.

(Continued)

Earned Income Credit (EIC) Table - *Continued* (**Caution.** This is **not** a tax table.)

If the amount you are looking up from the worksheet is–		Single, head of household, or qualifying surviving spouse★ and you have–				Married filing jointly and you have–			
At least	But less than	0	1	2	3	0	1	2	3
		Your credit is–				Your credit is–			
50,400	50,450	0	0	525	1,351	0	431	1,907	2,732
50,450	50,500	0	0	515	1,340	0	423	1,896	2,722
50,500	50,550	0	0	504	1,329	0	415	1,886	2,711
50,550	50,600	0	0	493	1,319	0	407	1,875	2,700
50,600	50,650	0	0	483	1,308	0	399	1,864	2,690
50,650	50,700	0	0	472	1,298	0	391	1,854	2,679
50,700	50,750	0	0	462	1,287	0	383	1,843	2,669
50,750	50,800	0	0	451	1,277	0	375	1,833	2,658
50,800	50,850	0	0	441	1,266	0	367	1,822	2,648
50,850	50,900	0	0	430	1,256	0	359	1,812	2,637
50,900	50,950	0	0	420	1,245	0	351	1,801	2,627
50,950	51,000	0	0	409	1,235	0	343	1,791	2,616
51,000	51,050	0	0	399	1,224	0	335	1,780	2,606
51,050	51,100	0	0	388	1,214	0	327	1,770	2,595
51,100	51,150	0	0	378	1,203	0	319	1,759	2,585
51,150	51,200	0	0	367	1,193	0	311	1,749	2,574
51,200	51,250	0	0	357	1,182	0	303	1,738	2,564
51,250	51,300	0	0	346	1,172	0	295	1,728	2,553
51,300	51,350	0	0	335	1,161	0	287	1,717	2,543
51,350	51,400	0	0	325	1,150	0	279	1,706	2,532
51,400	51,450	0	0	314	1,140	0	271	1,696	2,521
51,450	51,500	0	0	304	1,129	0	263	1,685	2,511
51,500	51,550	0	0	293	1,119	0	255	1,675	2,500
51,550	51,600	0	0	283	1,108	0	247	1,664	2,490
51,600	51,650	0	0	272	1,098	0	239	1,654	2,479
51,650	51,700	0	0	262	1,087	0	231	1,643	2,469
51,700	51,750	0	0	251	1,077	0	223	1,633	2,458
51,750	51,800	0	0	241	1,066	0	215	1,622	2,448
51,800	51,850	0	0	230	1,056	0	207	1,612	2,437
51,850	51,900	0	0	220	1,045	0	199	1,601	2,427
51,900	51,950	0	0	209	1,035	0	191	1,591	2,416
51,950	52,000	0	0	199	1,024	0	183	1,580	2,406
52,000	52,050	0	0	188	1,014	0	175	1,570	2,395
52,050	52,100	0	0	178	1,003	0	167	1,559	2,385
52,100	52,150	0	0	167	993	0	159	1,549	2,374
52,150	52,200	0	0	156	982	0	151	1,538	2,364
52,200	52,250	0	0	146	971	0	143	1,527	2,353
52,250	52,300	0	0	135	961	0	135	1,517	2,342
52,300	52,350	0	0	125	950	0	127	1,506	2,332
52,350	52,400	0	0	114	940	0	119	1,496	2,321
52,400	52,450	0	0	104	929	0	111	1,485	2,311
52,450	52,500	0	0	93	919	0	103	1,475	2,300
52,500	52,550	0	0	83	908	0	95	1,464	2,290
52,550	52,600	0	0	72	898	0	87	1,454	2,279
52,600	52,650	0	0	62	887	0	79	1,443	2,269
52,650	52,700	0	0	51	877	0	71	1,433	2,258
52,700	52,750	0	0	41	866	0	63	1,422	2,248
52,750	52,800	0	0	30	856	0	55	1,412	2,237
52,800	52,850	0	0	20	845	0	47	1,401	2,227
52,850	52,900	0	0	9	835	0	39	1,391	2,216
52,900	52,950	0	0	*	824	0	31	1,380	2,206
52,950	53,000	0	0	0	814	0	23	1,370	2,195
53,000	53,050	0	0	0	803	0	15	1,359	2,185
53,050	53,100	0	0	0	792	0	7	1,348	2,174
53,100	53,150	0	0	0	782	0	**	1,338	2,163
53,150	53,200	0	0	0	771	0	0	1,327	2,153
53,200	53,250	0	0	0	761	0	0	1,317	2,142
53,250	53,300	0	0	0	750	0	0	1,306	2,132
53,300	53,350	0	0	0	740	0	0	1,296	2,121
53,350	53,400	0	0	0	729	0	0	1,285	2,111
53,400	53,450	0	0	0	719	0	0	1,275	2,100
53,450	53,500	0	0	0	708	0	0	1,264	2,090
53,500	53,550	0	0	0	698	0	0	1,254	2,079
53,550	53,600	0	0	0	687	0	0	1,243	2,069
53,600	53,650	0	0	0	677	0	0	1,233	2,058
53,650	53,700	0	0	0	666	0	0	1,222	2,048
53,700	53,750	0	0	0	656	0	0	1,212	2,037
53,750	53,800	0	0	0	645	0	0	1,201	2,027
53,800	53,850	0	0	0	634	0	0	1,191	2,016
53,850	53,900	0	0	0	624	0	0	1,180	2,005
53,900	53,950	0	0	0	613	0	0	1,169	1,995
53,950	54,000	0	0	0	603	0	0	1,159	1,984
54,000	54,050	0	0	0	592	0	0	1,148	1,974
54,050	54,100	0	0	0	582	0	0	1,138	1,963
54,100	54,150	0	0	0	571	0	0	1,127	1,953
54,150	54,200	0	0	0	561	0	0	1,117	1,942
54,200	54,250	0	0	0	550	0	0	1,106	1,932
54,250	54,300	0	0	0	540	0	0	1,096	1,921
54,300	54,350	0	0	0	529	0	0	1,085	1,911
54,350	54,400	0	0	0	519	0	0	1,075	1,900
54,400	54,450	0	0	0	508	0	0	1,064	1,890
54,450	54,500	0	0	0	498	0	0	1,054	1,879
54,500	54,550	0	0	0	487	0	0	1,043	1,869
54,550	54,600	0	0	0	477	0	0	1,033	1,858
54,600	54,650	0	0	0	466	0	0	1,022	1,848
54,650	54,700	0	0	0	455	0	0	1,012	1,837
54,700	54,750	0	0	0	445	0	0	1,001	1,826
54,750	54,800	0	0	0	434	0	0	990	1,816
54,800	54,850	0	0	0	424	0	0	980	1,805
54,850	54,900	0	0	0	413	0	0	969	1,795
54,900	54,950	0	0	0	403	0	0	959	1,784
54,950	55,000	0	0	0	392	0	0	948	1,774
55,000	55,050	0	0	0	382	0	0	938	1,763
55,050	55,100	0	0	0	371	0	0	927	1,753
55,100	55,150	0	0	0	361	0	0	917	1,742
55,150	55,200	0	0	0	350	0	0	906	1,732
55,200	55,250	0	0	0	340	0	0	896	1,721
55,250	55,300	0	0	0	329	0	0	885	1,711
55,300	55,350	0	0	0	319	0	0	875	1,700
55,350	55,400	0	0	0	308	0	0	864	1,690
55,400	55,450	0	0	0	298	0	0	854	1,679
55,450	55,500	0	0	0	287	0	0	843	1,669
55,500	55,550	0	0	0	276	0	0	833	1,658
55,550	55,600	0	0	0	266	0	0	822	1,647
55,600	55,650	0	0	0	255	0	0	811	1,637
55,650	55,700	0	0	0	245	0	0	801	1,626
55,700	55,750	0	0	0	234	0	0	790	1,616
55,750	55,800	0	0	0	224	0	0	780	1,605
55,800	55,850	0	0	0	213	0	0	769	1,595
55,850	55,900	0	0	0	203	0	0	759	1,584
55,900	55,950	0	0	0	192	0	0	748	1,574
55,950	56,000	0	0	0	182	0	0	738	1,563

★ Use this column if your filing status is married filing separately and you qualify to claim the EIC. See the instructions for line 27.

* If the amount you are looking up from the worksheet is at least $52,900 but less than $52,918, and you have two qualifying children who have valid SSNs, your credit is $2.

If the amount you are looking up from the worksheet is $52,918 or more, and you have two qualifying children who have valid SSNs, you can't take the credit.

** If the amount you are looking up from the worksheet is at least $53,100 but less than $53,120, and you have one qualifying child who has a valid SSN, your credit $2.

If the amount you are looking up from the worksheet is $53,120 or more, and you have one qualifying child who has a valid SSN, you can't take the credit.

(Continued)

Earned Income Credit (EIC) Table - Continued

(**Caution.** This is **not** a tax table.)

If the amount you are looking up from the worksheet is–		Single, head of household, or qualifying surviving spouse★ and you have–				Married filing jointly and you have–			
At least	But less than	0	1	2	3	0	1	2	3
		Your credit is–				Your credit is–			
56,000	56,050	0	0	0	171	0	0	727	1,553
56,050	56,100	0	0	0	161	0	0	717	1,542
56,100	56,150	0	0	0	150	0	0	706	1,532
56,150	56,200	0	0	0	140	0	0	696	1,521
56,200	56,250	0	0	0	129	0	0	685	1,511
56,250	56,300	0	0	0	119	0	0	675	1,500
56,300	56,350	0	0	0	108	0	0	664	1,490
56,350	56,400	0	0	0	97	0	0	653	1,479
56,400	56,450	0	0	0	87	0	0	643	1,468
56,450	56,500	0	0	0	76	0	0	632	1,458
56,500	56,550	0	0	0	66	0	0	622	1,447
56,550	56,600	0	0	0	55	0	0	611	1,437
56,600	56,650	0	0	0	45	0	0	601	1,426
56,650	56,700	0	0	0	34	0	0	590	1,416
56,700	56,750	0	0	0	24	0	0	580	1,405
56,750	56,800	0	0	0	13	0	0	569	1,395
56,800	56,850	0	0	0	*	0	0	559	1,384
56,850	56,900	0	0	0	0	0	0	548	1,374
56,900	56,950	0	0	0	0	0	0	538	1,363
56,950	57,000	0	0	0	0	0	0	527	1,353
57,000	57,050	0	0	0	0	0	0	517	1,342
57,050	57,100	0	0	0	0	0	0	506	1,332
57,100	57,150	0	0	0	0	0	0	496	1,321
57,150	57,200	0	0	0	0	0	0	485	1,311
57,200	57,250	0	0	0	0	0	0	474	1,300
57,250	57,300	0	0	0	0	0	0	464	1,289
57,300	57,350	0	0	0	0	0	0	453	1,279
57,350	57,400	0	0	0	0	0	0	443	1,268
57,400	57,450	0	0	0	0	0	0	432	1,258
57,450	57,500	0	0	0	0	0	0	422	1,247
57,500	57,550	0	0	0	0	0	0	411	1,237
57,550	57,600	0	0	0	0	0	0	401	1,226
57,600	57,650	0	0	0	0	0	0	390	1,216
57,650	57,700	0	0	0	0	0	0	380	1,205
57,700	57,750	0	0	0	0	0	0	369	1,195
57,750	57,800	0	0	0	0	0	0	359	1,184
57,800	57,850	0	0	0	0	0	0	348	1,174
57,850	57,900	0	0	0	0	0	0	338	1,163
57,900	57,950	0	0	0	0	0	0	327	1,153
57,950	58,000	0	0	0	0	0	0	317	1,142
58,000	58,050	0	0	0	0	0	0	306	1,132
58,050	58,100	0	0	0	0	0	0	295	1,121
58,100	58,150	0	0	0	0	0	0	285	1,110
58,150	58,200	0	0	0	0	0	0	274	1,100
58,200	58,250	0	0	0	0	0	0	264	1,089
58,250	58,300	0	0	0	0	0	0	253	1,079
58,300	58,350	0	0	0	0	0	0	243	1,068
58,350	58,400	0	0	0	0	0	0	232	1,058
58,400	58,450	0	0	0	0	0	0	222	1,047
58,450	58,500	0	0	0	0	0	0	211	1,037
58,500	58,550	0	0	0	0	0	0	201	1,026
58,550	58,600	0	0	0	0	0	0	190	1,016
58,600	58,650	0	0	0	0	0	0	180	1,005
58,650	58,700	0	0	0	0	0	0	169	995
58,700	58,750	0	0	0	0	0	0	159	984
58,750	58,800	0	0	0	0	0	0	148	974

If the amount you are looking up from the worksheet is–		Single, head of household, or qualifying surviving spouse★ and you have–				Married filing jointly and you have–			
At least	But less than	0	1	2	3	0	1	2	3
		Your credit is–				Your credit is–			
58,800	58,850	0	0	0	0	0	0	138	963
58,850	58,900	0	0	0	0	0	0	127	952
58,900	58,950	0	0	0	0	0	0	116	942
58,950	59,000	0	0	0	0	0	0	106	931
59,000	59,050	0	0	0	0	0	0	95	921
59,050	59,100	0	0	0	0	0	0	85	910
59,100	59,150	0	0	0	0	0	0	74	900
59,150	59,200	0	0	0	0	0	0	64	889
59,200	59,250	0	0	0	0	0	0	53	879
59,250	59,300	0	0	0	0	0	0	43	868
59,300	59,350	0	0	0	0	0	0	32	858
59,350	59,400	0	0	0	0	0	0	22	847
59,400	59,450	0	0	0	0	0	0	11	837
59,450	59,500	0	0	0	0	0	0	**	826
59,500	59,550	0	0	0	0	0	0	0	816
59,550	59,600	0	0	0	0	0	0	0	805
59,600	59,650	0	0	0	0	0	0	0	795
59,650	59,700	0	0	0	0	0	0	0	784
59,700	59,750	0	0	0	0	0	0	0	773
59,750	59,800	0	0	0	0	0	0	0	763
59,800	59,850	0	0	0	0	0	0	0	752
59,850	59,900	0	0	0	0	0	0	0	742
59,900	59,950	0	0	0	0	0	0	0	731
59,950	60,000	0	0	0	0	0	0	0	721
60,000	60,050	0	0	0	0	0	0	0	710
60,050	60,100	0	0	0	0	0	0	0	700
60,100	60,150	0	0	0	0	0	0	0	689
60,150	60,200	0	0	0	0	0	0	0	679
60,200	60,250	0	0	0	0	0	0	0	668
60,250	60,300	0	0	0	0	0	0	0	658
60,300	60,350	0	0	0	0	0	0	0	647
60,350	60,400	0	0	0	0	0	0	0	637
60,400	60,450	0	0	0	0	0	0	0	626
60,450	60,500	0	0	0	0	0	0	0	616
60,500	60,550	0	0	0	0	0	0	0	605
60,550	60,600	0	0	0	0	0	0	0	594
60,600	60,650	0	0	0	0	0	0	0	584
60,650	60,700	0	0	0	0	0	0	0	573
60,700	60,750	0	0	0	0	0	0	0	563
60,750	60,800	0	0	0	0	0	0	0	552
60,800	60,850	0	0	0	0	0	0	0	542
60,850	60,900	0	0	0	0	0	0	0	531
60,900	60,950	0	0	0	0	0	0	0	521
60,950	61,000	0	0	0	0	0	0	0	510
61,000	61,050	0	0	0	0	0	0	0	500
61,050	61,100	0	0	0	0	0	0	0	489
61,100	61,150	0	0	0	0	0	0	0	479
61,150	61,200	0	0	0	0	0	0	0	468
61,200	61,250	0	0	0	0	0	0	0	458
61,250	61,300	0	0	0	0	0	0	0	447
61,300	61,350	0	0	0	0	0	0	0	437
61,350	61,400	0	0	0	0	0	0	0	426
61,400	61,450	0	0	0	0	0	0	0	415
61,450	61,500	0	0	0	0	0	0	0	405
61,500	61,550	0	0	0	0	0	0	0	394
61,550	61,600	0	0	0	0	0	0	0	384

★ Use this column if your filing status is married filing separately and you qualify to claim the EIC. See the instructions for line 27.

* If the amount you are looking up from the worksheet is at least $56,800 but less than $56,838, and you have three qualifying children who have valid SSNs, your credit is $4.

If the amount you are looking up from the worksheet is $56,838 or more, and you have three qualifying children who have valid SSNs, you can't take the credit.

** If the amount you are looking up from the worksheet is at least $59,450 but less than $59,478, and you have two qualifying children who have valid SSNs, your credit is $3.

If the amount you are looking up from the worksheet is $59,478 or more, and you have two qualifying children who have valid SSNs, you can't take the credit.

(Continued)

Earned Income Credit (EIC) Table - *Continued*   (**Caution.** This is **not** a tax table.)

If the amount you are looking up from the worksheet is—		Single, head of household, or qualifying surviving spouse★ and you have—				Married filing jointly and you have—				If the amount you are looking up from the worksheet is—		Single, head of household, or qualifying surviving spouse★ and you have—				Married filing jointly and you have—			
At least	But less than	0	1	2	3	0	1	2	3	At least	But less than	0	1	2	3	0	1	2	3
		Your credit is—				Your credit is—						Your credit is—				Your credit is—			
61,600	61,650	0	0	0	0	0	0	0	373	62,800	62,850	0	0	0	0	0	0	0	121
61,650	61,700	0	0	0	0	0	0	0	363	62,850	62,900	0	0	0	0	0	0	0	110
61,700	61,750	0	0	0	0	0	0	0	352	62,900	62,950	0	0	0	0	0	0	0	100
61,750	61,800	0	0	0	0	0	0	0	342	62,950	63,000	0	0	0	0	0	0	0	89
61,800	61,850	0	0	0	0	0	0	0	331	63,000	63,050	0	0	0	0	0	0	0	79
61,850	61,900	0	0	0	0	0	0	0	321	63,050	63,100	0	0	0	0	0	0	0	68
61,900	61,950	0	0	0	0	0	0	0	310	63,100	63,150	0	0	0	0	0	0	0	57
61,950	62,000	0	0	0	0	0	0	0	300	63,150	63,200	0	0	0	0	0	0	0	47
62,000	62,050	0	0	0	0	0	0	0	289	63,200	63,250	0	0	0	0	0	0	0	36
62,050	62,100	0	0	0	0	0	0	0	279	63,250	63,300	0	0	0	0	0	0	0	26
62,100	62,150	0	0	0	0	0	0	0	268	63,300	63,350	0	0	0	0	0	0	0	15
62,150	62,200	0	0	0	0	0	0	0	258	63,350	63,400	0	0	0	0	0	0	0	*
62,200	62,250	0	0	0	0	0	0	0	247										
62,250	62,300	0	0	0	0	0	0	0	236										
62,300	62,350	0	0	0	0	0	0	0	226										
62,350	62,400	0	0	0	0	0	0	0	215										
62,400	62,450	0	0	0	0	0	0	0	205										
62,450	62,500	0	0	0	0	0	0	0	194										
62,500	62,550	0	0	0	0	0	0	0	184										
62,550	62,600	0	0	0	0	0	0	0	173										
62,600	62,650	0	0	0	0	0	0	0	163										
62,650	62,700	0	0	0	0	0	0	0	152										
62,700	62,750	0	0	0	0	0	0	0	142										
62,750	62,800	0	0	0	0	0	0	0	131										

★ Use this column if your filing status is married filing separately and you qualify to claim the EIC. See the instructions for line 27.

* If the amount you are looking up from the worksheet is at least $63,350 but less than $63,398, and you have three qualifying children who have valid SSNs, your credit is $5.

If the amount you are looking up from the worksheet is $63,398 or more, and you have three qualifying children who have valid SSNs, you can't take the credit.

PART 9

Tax Law Authorities

The federal income tax law is based on statutes passed by Congress. The statutes are organized into a Code, which is currently cited as the Internal Revenue Code of 1986.

Ideally, there should be no need for legal sources other than the Code. This may be true where a statute as passed by Congress is so clear and specific that no one doubts its application. However, in the many cases where the wording of a statute in the Code is general and may be interpreted in several ways, you must seek interpretations that may help you resolve a tax question or support your point of view in a tax dispute. Authoritative interpretations are made by the Treasury and the Internal Revenue Service in regulations and rulings and by federal courts in specific decisions. The relative authoritativeness of these sources is discussed in this part.

LEGISLATIVE AUTHORITIES

Internal Revenue Code

The 1986 Tax Act redesignated the Internal Revenue Code as the Internal Revenue Code of 1986. The prior designation date was 1954.

The title of the Code remains fixed with the date 1986, although sections of the Code may be amended every year. Structurally, the Code is divided into:

- Subtitles (for example, Subtitle A: Income Taxes; Subtitle B: Estate and Gift Taxes, etc.);
- Chapters (for example, Chapter I of Subtitle A: Normal Taxes and Surtaxes);
- Subchapters (for example, Subchapter A of Chapter 1: Determination of Tax Liability);
- Parts (for example, Part I of Subchapter A: Tax on Individuals); and
- Sections (for example, Section I of Part 1: Tax Imposed).

Sections run consecutively in the Code from Section 1 up to Section 9834. However, in the sequence, many numbers are missing to allow for further expansion. Each section itself is then broken down as follows:

- Lettered subsections: (a), (b), (c), etc.
- Numbered paragraphs: (1), (2), (3), etc.
- Capital-lettered subparagraphs: (A), (B), (C), etc.
- Roman-numbered sub-subparagraphs: (i), (ii), (iii), etc.

The Code is changed by Public Laws, which are designated by a P.L. number, such as P.L.117-169. The first number, 117, references the Congressional session in which the law was passed. The second number, 169, is the bill enacted during the session. In Part 10 of this book, we may reference the name of the Act and the P.L. number. Where there is no name for an Act, the P.L. number is referenced in Part 10. The following are the Acts referenced in Part 10:

- Inflation Reduction Act of 2022 *(P.L. 117-169, 8/16/2022)*
- Consolidated Appropriations Act, 2022 *(P.L. 117-103, 3/14/2022)*
- Infrastructure Investment and Jobs Act of 2021 *(P.L. 117-58, 11/15/2021)*
- Further Surface Transportation Extension Act of 2021 *(P.L. 117-52, 10/31/2021)*
- American Rescue Plan Act of 2021 *(P.L. 117-2, 3/11/2021)*
- Consolidated Appropriations Act, 2021 *(P.L. 2016-260, 12/27, 2020)*
- Coronavirus Aid, Relief, and Economic Security (CARES) Act of 2020 *(P.L. 116-136, 3/27/2020)*
- SECURE Act *(P.L. 116-94, 12/20/2019)*
- Taxpayer Certainty and Disaster Tax Relief Act of 2020 *(P.L. 116-260, 12/27/2020)*
- Taxpayer Certainty and Disaster Tax Relief Act of 2019 *(P.L. 116-94, 12/20/2019)*
- Bipartisan Budget Act of 2018 *(P.L. 115-123, 2/9/2018)*
- Tax Cuts and Jobs Act of 2017 *(P.L. 115-97, 12/22/2017)*
- Combat-Injured Veterans Tax Fairness Act of 2016, *(P.L. 114-292, 12/16/2016)*
- Taxpayer Certainty and Disaster Tax Relief Act of 2021 *(P.L. 114-255, 12/13/2016)*

- Trade Facilitation and Trade Enforcement Act of 2015, *(P.L. 114-125, 2/24/2016)*
- Bipartisan Budget Act of 2015 (BBA) *(P.L. 114-74, 2/19/2018)*
- Surface Transportation and Veterans Health Choice Improvement Act of 2015, *(P.L. 114-41, 7/31/2015)*
- P.L. 114-14 *(5/22/2015)*
- Achieving a Better Life Experience Act of 2014 *(P.L. 113-295. 12/19/2014)*
- Small Business Jobs Act of 2010 *(P.L. 111-240, 9/27/2010)*
- Tax Relief Act of 2010 *(P.L. 111-32, 12/17/10)*
- P.L. 106-170 *(12/17/1999)*
- P.L. 104-95 *(1/10/96)*
- Social Security Domestic Employment Reform Act of 1994 *(P.L. 103-387, 10/22/1994)*
- P.L. 103-465 *(12/8/1994)*
- Tax Reform Act of 1986 *(P.L. 99-514, 10/22/1986)*
- P.L. 98-21 *(4/20/1983)*

Congressional Committee Reports

The legislative history of a Code section may be found in the reports of the Congressional committee that wrote the section. Under the Constitution, tax bills originate in the House of Representatives, although in practice, the Senate has sometimes considered tax legislation before the House. In recent years, the House and Senate increasingly have moved tax bills towards enactment without following the traditional practice of having the House Ways and Means Committee and the Senate Finance Committee release formal written reports explaining the provisions in their respective Committee bills, prior to consideration by the full House and Senate. Where there are no formal Committee reports, each Committee typically prepares a bill summary, and the Joint Committee on Taxation issues a description of the provisions in the respective House and Senate bills.

Where the House and Senate approve different versions of a bill, the traditional means of settling the differences between the two versions is for House and Senate leaders to appoint a Conference Committee that prepares a compromise measure and a Conference Committee report that explains it. If the House and Senate both pass the compromise bill, it is sent to the President and becomes law after the President signs it. In recent years, House and Senate Conferees have often met informally, and at times there has been no Conference Report. The Joint Committee on Taxation typically releases an explanation of the Conference Agreement, commonly called the "Blue Book." The Joint Committee explanation cannot be cited as the official Conference Committee Report, but it may be given deference by a reviewing court if it supports an official House, Senate, or Conference report, or is not contradicted by an official report.

House, Senate, and Conference Committee reports are available online from the Library of Congress (www.loc.gov) and from the Government Publishing Office (www.gpo.gov). The Joint Committee on Taxation (www.jct.gov) has the Joint Committee explanations as well as links to the House Ways and Means Committee (waysandmeans.house.gov) and the Senate Finance Committee (www.finance.senate.gov).

ADMINISTRATIVE AUTHORITIES

Treasury Regulations

Regulations authorized by the Internal Revenue Code have the force and effect of law and may be relied upon as authority. Failure to comply with such a regulation can result in a negligence penalty.

The validity of a regulation can be questioned. Courts are not bound by regulations and can overrule them if they are unreasonable and plainly inconsistent with the Code.

Once a regulation has interpreted a Code provision, passage of a similar law with the exact wording is regarded by the courts as evidence that Congress is satisfied with the regulation and, thus, the regulation generally will not be overruled. If a regulation is disapproved by a court, the IRS can continue to enforce the regulation unless the regulation is reversed by the Supreme Court.

New regulations are generally first announced as proposed regulations. During a stated time limit, tax professionals and taxpayers are allowed to suggest changes or additions. Often, the IRS will hold special hearings to discuss the proposals, and then, after reviewing the suggestions, will issue final regulations as Treasury Decisions (TDs), which include a general explanation of the regulations and are published in the Federal Register and in the IRS Internal Revenue Bulletin. The IRS also issues some regulations as temporary regulations, which generally are effective upon publication and remain in effect until replaced by final regulations. Temporary regulations must be simultaneously issued as proposed regulations and may remain in effect for no more than three years after the date of issuance. Temporary regulations, like final regulations, are issued as Treasury Decisions (TDs). Tax services for professionals provide the text of proposed, temporary, and final regulations to their subscribers.

Each section of the regulations is preceded by the section, subsection, or paragraph of the Internal Revenue Code that it interprets. The sections of the regulations are distinguished from sections of the Code by the Arabic numeral 1, followed by a decimal point (1.) before the corresponding provision of the Internal Revenue Code. This designation is then followed by a dash (-) and a number further identifying a section of the regulation. With these numbers you can find regulations interpreting a Code provision. Thus, the regulation explaining IRC Section 301 is designated 1.301, and a section of that regulation is identified as 1.301-1.

Revenue Rulings

Revenue Rulings make up a large body of IRS interpretations of the tax law. They are generally official replies by the IRS National Office to specific problems raised by taxpayers. They are published to provide guidance in cases having similar facts to those presented in the rulings.

Revenue Rulings are published weekly in the Internal Revenue Bulletin. Every half-year, these rulings are republished in a book, called the Cumulative Bulletin, which is available to the public from the Government Printing Office. The weekly bulletins are available online from the IRS at apps.irs.gov/app/picklist/list/internalRevenueBulletins.html.

See below for references to Revenue Rulings appearing in the Internal Revenue Bulletin and the Cumulative Bulletin.

In the Weekly Internal Revenue Bulletin

Rev. Rul. 2023-15, 2023-35 IRB 152 means that the particular ruling is the 15th ruling for 2023, it appears in the 35th weekly bulletin for 2023, and can be found on page 152 of that bulletin.

In the Cumulative Bulletin

Rev. Rul. 94-43, 1994-2 CB 198—means that the ruling appears in the second semiannual Cumulative Bulletin for 1994 and, in that book, can be found on page 198.

Other IRS Rulings and Releases

After Revenue Rulings, there are several other IRS releases and rulings that are helpful in determining IRS policy.

Revenue procedures. These describe internal practices and procedures within the IRS and filing procedures for taxpayers. They are published in the Internal Revenue Bulletin. References to them are prefixed by the abbreviation "Rev. Proc." For example, Rev. Proc. 2023-38, 2023-45 IRB 445, means that the revenue procedure is the 38th procedure for 2023, it appears in the 45th weekly bulletin for 2023, and can be found on page 445 of that bulletin.

Notices and announcements. These describe current IRS policy toward a specific issue. They are primarily intended to provide IRS guidance on new tax law developments. The IRS used notices to update dollar limits, such as the annual mileage allowance, hi-low substantiation limits for business travel in the continental U.S., and contribution and benefit amounts for qualified retirement plans and IRAs. They may contain the advance text of Revenue Rulings. Announcements and Notices are published in the Internal Revenue Bulletin.

Letter rulings. These include private rulings, determination letters, and technical advice memoranda. Such rulings are not officially published and may not be cited as a precedent by any other taxpayer. However, they may be helpful, as they reflect the IRS' policy and interpretation of the law. In one case, the Supreme Court noted that private letter rulings are evidence of an IRS position, although they have no authoritative force. Virtually all letter rulings are open to public inspection after all information that could identify the taxpayer involved has been deleted.

General counsel memoranda, actions on decisions, technical memoranda. These are internal IRS documents that provide reasons for rulings, regulations, and acquiescences or nonacquiescences to court decisions. General Counsel Memoranda (GCMs) and Chief Counsel Advice (CCA) are legal opinions on proposed revenue rulings, private rulings, and technical advice memoranda. Actions on Decisions (AODs) recommend whether or not to appeal adverse court decisions. Technical Memoranda (TMs) indicate the legal and policy basis for proposed Treasury regulations. The documents are released by the IRS after deletions are made to remove identifying information.

Q&As and FAQs. These types of guidance are provided on IRS web pages only. The IRS has extensively used FAQs to quickly provide guidance on new tax legislation. In response to concerns that FAQs are not published in the Internal Revenue Bulletin and may not be cited as legal authority for purposes of penalty relief or litigation arguments, the IRS announced that a taxpayer who reasonably relies in good faith on a FAQ will have a "reasonable cause" defense against a negligence penalty or other accuracy-related penalty to the extent the reliance results in a tax underpayment.

JUDICIAL AUTHORITIES

A taxpayer who receives a notice of deficiency can appeal to the Tax Court without actually paying the deficiency. Alternatively, the deficiency can be paid and a claim for a refund filed with the IRS; if the refund claim is denied, a refund suit can be brought in Federal District Court. A refund suit may also be brought in the U.S. Court of Federal Claims. Appeals from these courts are heard by a Federal Court of Appeals.

Court Decisions

The authority of court decisions varies. When using court decisions, keep these points in mind:

- The IRS is not bound to follow a court decision in any case apart from the case in which the decision has been handed down. The only exception to this rule is a decision of the Supreme Court.
- Court decisions are not of equal weight. A decision of the Tax Court has substantially greater significance than a decision rendered by a Federal District Court and often by a Federal Court of Appeals, primarily because the Tax Court hears cases all over the nation and will apply its decisions on a nationwide basis.

    Federal District Courts are local federal courts and a Court of Appeals hears appeals only on a regional basis. So whereas one decision of the Tax Court will generally be applied throughout the United States, there may be several conflicting interpretations between district courts in various localities and Courts of Appeals in the various geographical regions. For example, a district court in California is not bound to follow a decision handed down by a district court in New York. And a Court of Appeals for one region is not bound to follow a decision of a Court of Appeals for another region. On the other hand, the precedent of a Tax Court decision rendered in New York is generally controlling authority in a Tax Court hearing held anywhere else in the United States. However, the Tax Court generally will follow a decision of the Court of Appeals to which the current case is appealable if that appeals court decision is squarely on point.

U.S. Tax Court

The Tax Court is a special court for taxpayers who appeal tax deficiencies imposed by the IRS for income, estate, or gift taxes. It is independent of the IRS and the Treasury department; its members are judges, and its decisions are subject to the same judicial review as that of any other federal court. They can be appealed at a Court of Appeals and then to the Supreme Court.

The IRS is not bound by a Tax Court decision except in the particular case in which the decision has been rendered. It can continue to litigate the same issue in other cases before the Tax Court and in other courts. However, in a tax dispute with a taxpayer involving the same issue that the Court decided against

the government, the IRS may be more inclined to negotiate a settlement than have the taxpayer bring a case before the Tax Court for another unfavorable decision against its position.

There are three types of Tax Court decisions:

Regular decisions. These are officially reported by the Tax Court and published in the United States Tax Court Reports by the U.S. Government Printing Office. Regular decisions are available on the Tax Court website, www.ustaxcourt.gov. They are also available from private tax publishers and online services. In Part 10 of this book, we reference regular decisions by decision number in the CCH Tax Court Reporter if a citation to the official reporter was not available.

Memorandum decisions. These are not reported by the Tax Court in official volumes, but are available on the Tax Court website, www.ustaxcourt.gov, and from private tax publishers and online services. In Part 10, memorandum decisions are referenced to the CCH Inc. series, Tax Court Memorandum Decisions, cited "TCM," where such a citation is available. Otherwise, citations are to decision number.

What is the court test for reporting a case as either a regular decision or as a memorandum decision? The Court says a memorandum decision involves no question of law, but merely facts that the Court believes are limited to a number of cases. If a memorandum decision does involve a question of law, the question is usually one that has been decided previously by the Tax Court and followed by the Court of Appeals. However, taxpayers can and do appeal memorandum decisions to the Court of Appeals as they can regular decisions.

Although these are considered by the Court as minor decisions, they are further examples of Tax Court policy toward a particular tax issue. Furthermore, memorandum decisions are often appealed and the decision of the appeals court in these cases may become important authority.

Current Tax Court policy in issues disputed by two or more Courts of Appeals is to follow the opinion of the Court to which the appeal may be taken, if that Court has ruled on the issue.

Summary opinions. These are cases decided under the Tax Court's small tax case procedure for deficiencies of $50,000 or less (IRC §7463). Such cases are handled expeditiously and informally. It is available at the option of the taxpayer if the Court concurs. Cases may be heard by appointed special trial judges. A small claim case can be discontinued at any time before a decision, but the decision, when made, is final. No appeal can be taken. A decision does not have precedential value. Summary opinions are available on the Tax Court website, www.ustaxcourt.gov, and from private tax publishers and online services.

IRS response to decision. The IRS may announce its acceptance of or disagreement with a Tax Court holding against a position held by the IRS in an officially reported decision. No policy statements are made for memorandum decisions. These announcements are made in the weekly Internal Revenue Bulletin, as acquiescences or nonacquiescences. The IRS cautions that an acquiescence of a particular decision merely signifies its acceptance of the Court's conclusion. It does not necessarily mean that it has accepted or approved of the Court's reasons for the conclusion, and it advises its officials to apply the rule of acquiesced cases only to cases that have substantially the same facts and circumstances as the acquiesced case. An acquiescence or nonacquiescence of a reported case can be recognized by the abbreviation (Acq.) or (Nonacq.) at the end of the case citation. However, if you are going to rely on an acquiesced case, try to find the exact terms of the IRS approval from the weekly Internal Revenue Bulletin or Cumulative Bulletin. Sometimes an acquiescence is limited only to one particular issue of a case. Finally, the IRS is free to withdraw an acquiescence or non-acquiescence.

Federal District Court

There is at least one Federal District Court for each state, with the more populous states having two or more district courts. A Federal District Court can hear only tax cases in which a taxpayer sues for a refund after his or her claim has been denied by the IRS.

Not all district court decisions are rendered in written form. But where they are in writing, they may be handed down as an Opinion, Findings of Fact and Conclusions of Law, or both. Generally, a district court opinion is not strong authority, primarily because of the local nature of a district court. However, a well-reasoned district court decision may be accepted by other courts and even the IRS, and in the absence of any other authority on a particular issue, a decision of a district court may prove helpful as presenting at least one published view of the problem.

District court decisions are referred in this book to their place in the Federal Supplement Series published by the West Publishing Company. For example, take the case Seymour Gale, 768 F. Supp. 1305 (N.D. IL. (1991)). Seymour Gale is the name of the case; 768 refers to the volume of the Federal Supplement Series, 1305 to the page within that volume, N.D. IL. to the Northern District of Illinois, and 1991 to the year of decision. District court decisions not cited to the Federal Supplement Series are cited to the U.S. Tax Cases published by CCH Inc. These citations are explained in the section on Court of Appeals decisions below.

U.S. Court of Federal Claims

The only tax cases heard by the U.S. Court of Federal Claims (formerly called the U.S. Claims Court) are those involving refunds of taxes. Decisions by the U.S. Court of Federal Claims on income tax questions have not had an important effect on the development of the income tax law. However, a favorable decision of the Court of Federal Claims on a particular issue that you may be disputing with the IRS may encourage you to choose that court to hear your case. A well-reasoned decision rendered by the Court of Federal Claims may be followed by the other courts. Appeals from the Court of Federal Claims decisions are heard by the Court of Appeals for the Federal Circuit.

Court of Federal Claims decisions are referred in this book to their place in the Federal Claims Reporter published by West Publishing Company. If citations to the Federal Claims Reporter are not available, Court of Federal Claims decisions are cited to the U.S. Tax Cases published by CCH Inc.

Court of Appeals Decisions

There are 12 Courts of Appeals that hear appeals taken either by taxpayers or the government from decisions rendered by the Tax Court or Federal District Court. Eleven of these are regional courts that hear cases arising within their regions, which are technically called "circuits"; the twelfth hears cases arising within the District of Columbia. The circuits and the states within each circuit are listed in the table below.

Appeals of tax refund decisions from the U.S. Court of Federal Claims are heard by a separate appeals court, the U.S. Court of Appeals for the Federal Circuit.

Court of Appeals decisions make up an important part of federal tax law. But the effectiveness of a particular decision may vary because of these factors:

- The IRS is not bound to follow any precedent set by an appeals court decision. The IRS will sometimes announce its decision to follow or not to follow a Court of Appeals decision.

- The Tax Court does not consider itself bound to follow any precedent set by an appeals court decision. The Tax Court view is that its nationwide jurisdiction cannot be restricted by the rules of the 12 different appeals courts. However, it will generally follow an appeals court decision in the circuit to which the case before it may be appealed.

- A Court of Appeals of one region is not bound to follow the precedent of a Court of Appeals in another region. Consequently, a decision of a particular appeals court is far stronger for taxpayers who can bring their appeals before that court than for taxpayers who must appeal to other appeals courts. A court will generally follow its own precedents unless it is overruled or later decides its original position was wrong.

Court of Appeals decisions are referred in this book to their place in the Federal Series reports published by the West Publishing Company. The first series is cited as "F.," the second series as "F.2d," and the third as "F.3d." For example, take the citation Albertson's, Inc., 12 F.3d 1529 (9th Cir. (1994)). Albertson's, Inc., is the name of the taxpayer, and the decision in 1994 by the 9th circuit appeals court appears on page 1529 of volume 12 of the third series of the Federal Series reports.

In some instances, citations may be reported in unofficial sources. For example, Nathaniel A. Carter, 2022-2 USTC ¶50,232 (11th Cir. 2022), may be found in U.S. Tax Cases published by CCH Inc. 2022-2 refers to the second volume of 2022; ¶50,232 is the paragraph at which the case is located.

Appeals court decisions may also be obtained from online services.

Supreme Court Decisions

Supreme Court decisions are the only decisions that the Internal Revenue Service and lower courts are required to follow. They have the same force as the Code and remain in force until Congress specifically changes the Court's interpretation or unless the Supreme Court in a later decision reverses its own position. Tax cases come before the Supreme Court when either a taxpayer or the government files a petition for a Writ of Certiorari, asking the Court to review the decision of a U.S. Court of Appeals. However, the Supreme Court generally limits its review of tax disputes to cases where there is a conflict of decisions among several U.S. Courts of Appeals on a specific interpretation of a tax law. An example of a reference to a Supreme Court decision is: Harold Davis, 495 U.S. 472 (1990). Harold Davis is the taxpayer, and the 1990 decision is found on page 472 of volume 495 of the official Supreme Court volumes.

The case can also be found in volumes published by private publishers that are released before the official Supreme Court volumes. For example, unofficial Supreme Court decisions may be found in the Supreme Court Reporter, put out by West Publishing Company, or in U.S. Tax Cases, published by CCH Inc. An example of a U.S. Tax Cases citation is: Boechler, P.C., 2022-1 USTC ¶50,142 (S.Ct. 2022).

States Within Court of Appeals Regions

FIRST CIRCUIT
Maine
Massachusetts
New Hampshire
Rhode Island
Puerto Rico

SECOND CIRCUIT
Connecticut
New York
Vermont

THIRD CIRCUIT
Delaware
New Jersey
Pennsylvania
Virgin Islands

FOURTH CIRCUIT
Maryland
North Carolina
South Carolina
Virginia
West Virginia

FIFTH CIRCUIT
Canal Zone
Louisiana
Mississippi
Texas

SIXTH CIRCUIT
Kentucky
Michigan
Ohio
Tennessee

SEVENTH CIRCUIT
Illinois
Indiana
Wisconsin

EIGHTH CIRCUIT
Arkansas
Iowa
Minnesota
Missouri
Nebraska
North Dakota
South Dakota

NINTH CIRCUIT
Alaska
Arizona
California
Hawaii
Idaho
Montana
Nevada
Oregon
Washington
Guam

TENTH CIRCUIT
Colorado
Kansas
New Mexico
Oklahoma
Utah
Wyoming

ELEVENTH CIRCUIT
Alabama
Florida
Georgia

CIRCUIT FOR THE DISTRICT OF COLUMBIA
Washington, D.C.

Citations of Authority

Part 10 contains the citations of authority for the text and material in *Parts 1–7*. You may use the Chapter Contents starting on page v or the Index starting on page 1023 to locate the tax topic you are interested in researching. After locating the topic, authority for the discussion can be found by locating the same number in this part. Regardless of where you find the number of your topic—from the text, the index, or the checklists—you will find the citation of authority under that number in this part. The tax information in the text of *Parts 1–7* is identified further by the use of italics under the identical number in this Part 10. For example, if you are interested in the tax law authorities for the discussion of tax-free employer accident and health plans at *3.1* on page 58 of the text, these may be found under *3.1* in *Part 10* on pages 872–873.

The references to law reviews, tax journal articles, and private letter rulings in this section are not cited as authority for any position taken in *Your Income Tax*. They are provided as a reference for your further study of the topics under which they are cited.

Key to Citations

Authority	Example
Internal Revenue Code of 1986	IRC §305(b)(2)
Treasury Regulation	Reg. §1.305-1
U.S. Tax Court	
Regular decision, in official court reporter	DeWayne Bond, 100 TC 32 (1993)
Regular decision, not in official court reporter	Michelle Delponte, 158 TC No. 7 (2022)
Memorandum opinion, in Tax Court Memorandum Decisions	Douglas Kemmerer, 66 TCM 550 (1993)
Memorandum opinion, not in Tax Court Memorandum Decisions	Mohamed H. Elbasha, TC Memo 2022-1
Summary opinion (the asterisk indicates that it may not be treated as precedent for any other case)	* Maribel Gonzalez, TC Summary Opinion 2022-13
Reversed or affirmed	George S. Nalle, III, 997 F.2d 1134 (5th Cir. 1993), rev'g 99 TC 187 (1992)
Board of Tax Appeals (predecessor to U.S. Tax Court)	
Regular opinion	Steven Smith, 30 BTA 49
Memorandum opinion	A.F.C. Oil Co., BTA Memo. Dec. 10, 958-F (1939)
IRS Acquiescence	Jones, 12 TC 49 (Acq.)
IRS Non-acquiescence	Smith, 13 TC 62 (Nonacq.)
Federal District Court	
Decision in Federal Supplement	Chester J. Maleszewski, 827 F. Supp. 1553 (D.C. FL 1993)
Decision not in Federal Supplement	Edwin H. Zimmerman, 2022-1 USTC ¶50,110 (D.C. PA)
U.S. Claims Court (renamed U.S. Court of Federal Claims, October 29, 1992)	Anthony Stack, 25 Ct. Cl. 634 (1992)
U.S. Court of Federal Claims	
Opinion, in Federal Claims Reporter	Robert P. Kliethermes, 27 Fed. Cl. 111 (1992)
Opinion, not in Federal Claims Reporter	Alan C. Dixon, 2022-1 USTC ¶50,106 (Ct. Fed Claims 2022)
U.S. Court of Appeals	
Opinion, in Federal Reporter	Mickey L. Worden, 2 F.3d 359 (10th Cir. 1993)
Opinion, not in Federal Reporter	Kirgizia I. Grajales, 2022-2 USTC ¶50,213 (2nd Cir. 2022)
U.S. Supreme Court	
Opinion, in official court reporter	Harvey F. Euge, 444 U.S. 707 (1980)
Opinion, not in official court reporter	Obergerfell v. Hodges, 2015-1 USTC ¶50,357 (Sup. Ct. 2015)

Revenue Rulings, Treasury Decisions, Releases, and Abbreviations

Revenue Ruling found in Cumulative Bulletin	Rev. Rul. 94-44,1994-2 CB 190
Revenue Ruling found in Internal Revenue Bulletin	Rev. Rul. 2022-13, 2022-30 IRB 99
Announcement found in Internal Revenue Bulletin	Announcement 2022-9, 2022-22 IRB 1153
Internal Revenue News Release	News Release IR-2022-188
Notice found in the Cumulative Bulletin	Notice 93-12, 1993-1 CB 298
Notice found in the Internal Revenue Bulletin	Notice 2022-55, 2022-45 IRB 443
Private Letter Ruling (the asterisk indicates that it may not be cited as authority)	* Letter Ruling 9530005 (pre-1999), 202244029 (post-1998)
Revenue Procedure found in Cumulative Bulletin	Rev. Proc. 93-26, 1993-1 CB 504
Revenue Procedure found in Internal Revenue Bulletin	Rev. Proc. 2022-35, 2022-40 IRB 270
Treasury Decision found in Internal Revenue Bulletin	T.D. 9963, 2022-34 IRB 145
Treasury Decision found in Federal Register	T.D. 9824, 82 F.R. 44925 (2017)

These cannot be cited as precedent.

Law Reviews and Periodicals

Articles are cited according to their title, author, and periodical title. The number before the periodical title is the volume number, and the number following is the page number, which is then followed by the year of publication.

Filing Basics

FILING TESTS

Filing thresholds for 2018 through 2025
IRC §6012 (f), added by the Tax Cuts and Jobs Act (P.L. 115-97, 12/22/2017)

Joint returns
IRC §6013

Reg. §1.6013-1(a)(1)

Determination of marital status
IRC §7703

Qualifying widow/widower
IRC §2(a)

Reg. §1.2-2

Spouse missing in action
IRC §2(a)(3)

Head of household
IRC §2(b)

Self-employment income
IRC §6017

Married, living apart
IRC §2(c)

IRC §7703(b)

Different tax years bar joint return
IRC §6013(a)(2)

Reg. §1.6013-1(c)

Different tax years before marriage
Frank E. Bertucci, 146 F. Supp. 949 (Ct. Cl. 1957)

Gross income
IRC §61

WHERE TO FILE
IRC §6091

Reg. §1.6091-2

Armed Forces
* IRS Publication 3

FILING DEADLINES (ON OR BEFORE)

April 15 due date for individuals
IRC §6072(a)

Reg. §1.6072-1

Due date falls on weekend or holiday
IRC §7503

Emancipation Day and Patriots' Day
Rev. Rul. 2015-13, 2015-22 IRB 1011

Timely mailing is timely filing
IRC §7502

Reg. §301.7502-1

Mailbox rule ended
Howard L. Baldwin, 921 F.3d 836 (9th Cir. 2019), cert. denied

Automatic six-month extension
Reg. §301.9100-2

Citizens/residents with tax home outside or in military outside U.S. and Puerto Rico
Reg. §1.6081-5(a)(5) and (6) (automatic two-month extension)

Reg. §1.6081-4T and -5T (may file for additional four-month extension)

Postage meter date ignored
Irving Fishman, 51 TC 869 (1969), aff'd per curiam, 420 F.2d 491 (2d Cir. 1970)

Combat zone
IRC §7508

IRC §112

Spouse traveling outside U.S.
Rev. Rul. 82-161, 1982-2 CB 379

1 FILING STATUS

1.1 WHICH FILING STATUS SHOULD YOU USE?

* IRS Publication 501

DOMA's denial of tax benefits for gay and lesbian partners held unconstitutional

Edith Schlain Windsor, 2013-2 USTC ¶50,400 (Sup. Ct. 2013)

IRS guidance for same-sex married couples

Notice 2015-86, 2015-52 IRB 887

Rev. Rul. 2013-17, 2013-38 IRB 201

Joint returns

IRC §6013

Qualifying widow/widower

IRC §2(a)

Reg. §1.2-2

Head of household

IRC §2(b)

Unmarried individuals

IRC §1(c)

1.2 TAX RATES BASED ON FILING STATUS

IRC §1(a)–1(d)

2023 inflation-adjusted tax brackets

Rev. Proc. 2022-38, 2022-38 IRC § 1(j)(2) (A)-(D)

1.3 FILING SEPARATELY INSTEAD OF JOINTLY

IRC §1(d)

Non-community-property states; joint accounts

Rev. Rul. 59-66, 1959-1 CB 60

Three years to elect joint return after separate returns

Reg. §1.6013-2

Alternative minimum tax exemption

IRC §55(d)

Standard deduction restriction

IRC §63(c)(6)(A)

Reduction of itemized deductions

IRC §68

Phaseout of exemptions on separate return

IRC §151(d)(3)(B)

IRC §151(d)(3)(C)(iv)

1.4 FILING A JOINT RETURN

Joint return requires two signatures

Bradley Reifler, TC Memo 2015-199

Unmarried couple can't file joint return

*Gabriel Mora, TC Summary Opinion 2010-60

IRS guidance for same-sex married couples

Notice 2015-86, 2015-52 IRB 887 Rev. Rul. 2013-17, 2013-38 IRB 201

Joint return with new spouse denied when state law invalidates prior Mexican divorce

A. Gersten, 267 F.2d 195 (9th Cir. 1957), aff'g in part 28 TC 756 (1957)

H.K. Lee, 64 TC 552, aff'd, 550 F.2d 1201 (9th Cir. 1977)

Interlocutory divorce decree

William F. Holcomb, 237 F.2d 502 (9th Cir. 1956)

J. R. Calhoun, Jr., 27 TC 115 (1956) (Acq.)

Joyce P. Lane, 26 TC 405 (1956) (Acq.)

Rev. Rul. 57-368, 1957-2 CB 896

Joint return with new spouse allowed although prior divorce decree declared invalid by state law

Harold E. Wondsel, 350 F.2d 339 (2d Cir. 1965), cert. denied, 383 U.S. 935

Herman Borax Est., 349 F.2d 666 (2d Cir. 1965), rev'g 40 TC 1001 (1963), cert. denied, 383 U.S. 935

Rev. Rul. 67-442, 1967-2 CB 65 (IRS will not follow Wondsel or Borax decisions)

No consent to file joint return disallowed

*Laura A. Brady, TC Summary Opinion 2010-107

Each spouse liable for tax

IRC §6013(d)(3)

Reg. §1.6013-4(b)

Vaughn C. Payne, 247 F.2d 481 (8th Cir. 1957), cert. denied, 355 U.S. 923

W. L. Kann, 210 F.2d 247 (3d Cir. 1954), cert. denied, 347 U.S. 967

Myrna S. Howell, 175 F.2d 240 (6th Cir. 1949)

Alma Helfrich, 25 TC 404 (1955) (Acq.)

Virginia M. Wilkins, 19 TC 752 (1953) (Acq.)

Eva M. Manton, 11 TC 831 (1948) (Acq.)

William W. Kellet, 5 TC 608 (1945) (Acq.)

Spouse relieved of joint return liability

IRC §6015

Notice 98-61, 1998-51 IRB 13

Divorce or legal separation

IRC §143(a)(2)

IRC §6013(d)

Reg. §1.6013-4(a)

Kenneth T. Sullivan, 256 F.2d 664 (4th Cir. 1958), aff'g 29 TC 71 (1957)

Executor disaffirms

IRC §6013(a)(3)

Reg. §1.6013-1(d)(5)

Dependent's joint return used as refund claim

Rev. Rul. 54-567, 1954-2 CB 108, affirmed by Rev. Rul. 65-34, 1965-1 CB 86

Sign as spouse's agent

Reg. §1.6013-1(a)(2)

Reg. §1.6012-1(a)(5)

Sick spouse

Rev. Rul. 70-216, 1970-1 CB 265

Intended joint return

Walter M. Ferguson, Jr., 14 TC 846 (1950) (Acq.)

Alfred E. Whitehouse Est., 14 TCM 501 (1955)

John Young, 11 TCM 239 (1952)

Jeremy H. Peirce, 43 TCM 400 (1982)

Frank Boyle, 67 TCM 294 (1994)

One spouse agreed to have other spouse handle tax matters

Muriel Heim, 251 F.2d 44 (8th Cir. 1958)

Myrna S. Howell, 10 TC 859 (1948), aff'd, 175 F.2d 240 (6th Cir. 1949)

Answers indicate intent

W. L. Kann, 210 F.2d 247 (3d Cir. 1954), cert. denied, 347 U.S. 967

Explain spouse's failure

Joyce P. Lane, 26 TC 405 (1956) (Acq.)

May elect joint return after separate return was filed

IRC §6013(b)(2)

After joint return filed may not elect separate returns after due date

Reg. §1.6013-1(a)(1)

Matthew L. Ladden, 38 TC 530 (1962) (Acq.)

Thomas J. Leger, 29 TCM 101 (1970)

IRS settlement with bankrupt husband does not protect wife

Carolyn S. Kroh, 98 TC 29 (1992)

1.5 NONRESIDENT ALIEN SPOUSE

Nonresident alien spouse generally bars joint return

IRC §6013(a)(1)

Reg. §1.6013-1(b)

Claim nonresident alien spouse as exemption

IRC §151

Reg. §1.151-1

Joint return under election

IRC §6013(g)

Special election where nonresident alien spouse becomes a resident during the year

IRC §6013(h)

1.6 COMMUNITY PROPERTY RULES

* IRS Publication 555

Community property rules do not apply where couple does not elect joint return

IRC §879

One-half vested interest

Aimee D. Bagur, 66 TC 817 (1976), rem'd, 603 F.2d 491 (5th Cir. 1979)

Community rules inapplicable to certain separated couples

IRC §66(a)

Community property rules for earned income disregarded—spouse not notified of income

IRC §66(b)

Community property rules disregarded—innocent spouse

IRC §66(c)

California registered domestic partners must split income

* Chief Counsel Memorandum 201021050

Spouse receiving temporary alimony

Charlotte J. Kimes, 55 TC 774 (1971)

Renunciation of interest

Anne G. Mitchell, 403 U.S. 190 (1971)

Self-employment tax for spouses

Rev. Rul. 82-39, 1982-1 CB 119

Intention to move to a community property state

George D. Hampton, Jr., 38 TC 131 (1962)

Dependency exemption on joint return

Thomas R. Jones, 38 TCM 599 (1977)

1.7 INNOCENT SPOUSE RULES

Final word on innocent spouse relief from Office of Chief Counsel DelPonte, 158 TC No. 7 (2022)

IRC §6015(b) (basic innocent spouse relief)

IRC §6015(c) (separate liability relief)

IRC §6015(f) (equitable relief)

Reg. §§ 1.6015-1 through 1.6015-9 (final regulations, T.D. 9003, 7/17/02)

Rev. Proc. 2013-34, 2013-43 IRB 397

* IRS Publication 971

Innocent spouse election

IRC §6015(b)

Reg. §1.6015-2

Tax Court appeal

IRC §6015(e)

Shielding of battered spouse who files for relief

IRS News Release IR-2001-23

Appeals rights for nonrequesting spouses

Andrew J. Young, TC Memo 2012-255

Rev. Proc. 2003-19, 2003-5 IRB 371

Knowledge or reason to know standard

IRC §6015(b)(1)(C)

Reg. §1.6015-2(c) (reason to know)

Reg. §1.6015-3(c)(2) (actual knowledge)

Kathryn Cheshire, 282 F.3d 326 (5th Cir. 2002), aff'g 115 TC 183 (2000) (knowledge of omitted income bars relief)

Knowledge of omitted income bars innocent spouse relief

Adetutu Canty, TC Memo 2016-169

*Joe Stewart, TC Summary Opinion 2010-31

Lack of knowledge standard — Pre-1998 Act

Bokum II, 94 TC 126 (1990), aff'd, 922 F.2d 1132 (1993)

Gwen Erdahl, 58 TCM 1532 (1990), rev'd and rem'd, 930 F.2d 585 (8th Cir. 1991)

Patricia A. Price, 887 F.2d 959 (9th Cir. 1989)

Janet Bliss, 59 F. 3d 374 (2d Cir., 1995), aff'g 66

TCM 522 (1993) (attorney's knowledge imputed to spouse)

Lucille E. Kistner, 18 F.3d 1521 (11th Cir. 1994)

1.8 SEPARATE LIABILITY RELIEF FOR FORMER SPOUSES

IRC §6015(c)

* IRS Publication 971

Innocent spouse allowed to introduce evidence outside administrative record

AOD-2012-07, June 4, 2013, in Karen Marie Wilson, 2013-1 USTC ¶50,147 (9th Cir. 2013)

Innocent spouse can recover attorneys' fees

Barbara A. Owen, TC Memo 2005-115

Helen E. Foy, TC Memo 2005-116

Separate liability election

IRC §6015(c)

Reg. §1.6015-3

Spouse's knowledge of omitted income

IRC §6015(c)

Reg. §1.6015-3(c)(2)(A)

Kathryn Cheshire, 282 F.3d 326 (5th Cir. 2002), aff'g 115 TC 183 (2000) (knowledge of omitted income bars relief)

Herbert L. Mitchell, 2002-2 USTC ¶50,475 (D.C. Cir. 2002) (follows Fifth Circuit's knowledge test analysis in Cheshire above)

Fredie Lynn Charlton, 114 TC 333 (2000) (relief where spouse does not know amount of omitted income)

Innocent spouse relief granted despite access to joint account

* Songie S. Milhouse, TC Summary Opinion 2011-12

Spouse's knowledge of erroneous deduction

Reg. §1.6015-3(c)(2)(B)

Isaac Baranowicz, TC Memo 2003-274

Patricia M. Mora, 117 TC 279 (2002)

Kathy A. King, 116 TC 198 (2001)

Tax Court appeal

IRC §6015(e)

Relief denied under tax benefit rule

Patricia M. Mora, 117 TC 279 (2002)

1.9 EQUITABLE RELIEF

Equitable relief allowed for penalties/interest on own income where misled by spouse

Joseph Patrick Boyle, TC Memo 2016-87

Requesting innocent spouse relief

Reg. § 1.6014-1.6015

Equitable relief

IRC §6015(f)

Reg. §1.6015-4

Rev. Proc. 2003-61, 2003-32 IRB 296 (criteria for relief)

IRS eases requirements for innocent spouse equitable relief

Notice 2012-8, 2012-4 IRB 309

IRS eliminates its two-year deadline for requesting relief

Notice 2011-70, 2011-32 IRB 135

Appellate courts uphold two-year rule

Denise Mannella, 631 F.3d 115 (3d Cir. 2011)

Cathy Marie Lantz, 2010-1 USTC ¶50,446 (7th Cir. 2010), rev'g 132 TC 131 (2009)

Tax Court remains opposed to two-year rule

Audrey Marie Hall, 135 TC 374 (2010)

Relief where other spouse fails to remit tax payment

Mitchell S. Wiest, TC Memo 2003-91

No relief for spouse with reason to know of income omission

Michael B. Butler, 114 TC 276 (2000)

Equitable relief granted for former spouse's theft of tax money

* Robby Goodale Gilbert, TC Summary Opinion 2007-16

Equitable relief denied to financially inexperienced spouse

Nancy A. Sjodin, TC Memo 2004-205

1.10 DEATH OF YOUR SPOUSE IN 2023

Joint return for decedent and survivor

IRC §6013(a)(3)

Reg. §1.6013-1(d)-3, -4

Remarriage

Reg. §1.6013-1(d)(2)

Change in accounting period

IRC §6013(a)(2)

IRC §443(a)(1)

Reg. §1.6013-1(d)(2)

Nonresident alien

IRC §6013(a)(1) and (g)(4)(B)

Reg. §1.6013-1(b)

Disaffirmance by executor

Reg. §1.6013-1(d)(5) and (6)

Co-executrix could not disaffirm

Frank J. Floyd Est., 51-2 USTC ¶9415 (Orphans' Ct., Del. County, Pa. 1951)

Treat as late return

Reg. §1.6013-1(d)(5) and (6)

Signing

IRC §6061

Reg. §1.6061-1

Reg. §1.6012-2(b)(1)

Reg. §1.6013-1(a)(2)

Privilege of treating survivor's return as joint return

IRC §2

Reg. §1.2-2

Reg. §1.6013-1(e)

Survivor bound to joint return liability

Maxine Ruzich, 47 TC 380 (1967)

1.11 QUALIFYING WIDOW/WIDOWER STATUS FOR 2023 IF YOUR SPOUSE DIED IN 2022 OR 2021

Qualifying widows or widowers

IRC §2(a)(1)(B)

1.12 QUALIFYING AS HEAD OF HOUSEHOLD

Head of household defined

IRC §2(b)

Qualifying children for tax years starting after 2004

IRC §2(b)(1)(A)(i)

Nonqualifying child or dependent

Jean Cowan, TC Memo 2015-85

* Edwin Davila Jr., TC Summary Opinion 2012-6

Special rule for parents

IRC §2(b)(1)(B)

Reg. §1.2-2(c)(2)

Maintaining household

IRC §2(b)(1)

IRC §1.2-2(c) and (d)

Interlocutory decree

Carole F. Brown, 31 TCM 194 (1972)

Support order pendente lite as interlocutory decree

Walter G. Brusey, 41 TCM 1223 (1981)

Separated spouse must live apart for last six months

Laurel Hopkins, 63 TCM 3113 (1992)

Status denied when children change residence after separation agreement

Fred J. Stanback, Jr., 77-1 USTC ¶9181

(D.N.C. 1977)

Parent in rest home

Rev. Rul. 70-279, 1970-1 CB 1

Taxpayer must reside in same home as dependent for substantial period

John C. Muse, 434 F.2d 349 (4th Cir. 1970)

Levon P. Biolchin, 433 F.2d 301 (7th Cir. 1970)

Relative resides in your household

IRC §2(b)(1)

Reg. §1.2-2(b)

Same residence for taxpayer and dependent

Reg. §1.2-2(c)

Rev. Rul. 72-43, 1972-1 CB 4

Sharon Stanford, 69 TCM 78 (1995)

Spouse living in separate residence not head of household

W. E. Grace, 51 TC 685 (1969), aff'd per curiam, 421 F.2d 165 (5th Cir. 170)

James A. Petrie, IV, 70 TCM 1566 (1995)

Old-age home

Rev. Rul. 57-307, 1957-2 CB 12

John Robinson, 51 TC 520 (1968) (Acq.), vacated and rem'd, 442 F.2d 873 (9th Cir. 1970)

Nonresident alien not a dependent

Rev. Rul. 55-711, 1955-2 CB 13, amplified by Rev. Rul. 74-370, 1974-2 CB 7

Two-family house

Jean F. Fleming Est., 33 TMC 619 (1974)

Mother is head of household for child living in different states

Clair Smith, 332 F.2d 671 (9th Cir. 1964)

Rev. Rul. 72-43, 1972-1 CB 4 (IRS nonacq. to Smith)

Can still get dependency credit

Katherine Atchison, 17 TCM 718 (1958)

Same person can qualify only once

Reg. §1.2-2(b)(2)

Illegitimate child

Rev. Rul. 54-498, 1954-2 CB 107

Can move household

Reg. §1.2-2(c)

Dependent confined in hospital

Reg. §1.2-2(c)

Abbie D. Reardon, 158 F. Supp. 745 (D.S. Dak. 1958)

Father's absence because of marital dispute

Walter Petlow, 34 TCM 51 (1975)

Probably never return

Harold K. Brehmer, 191 F. Supp. 421 (D. Minn. 1961)

Walter J. Hein, 28 TC 826 (1957) (Acq.)

Rev. Rul. 66-28, 1966-1 CB 31

Pay more than one-half of household costs

IRC §2(b)

Reg. §1.2-2(d)

Figuring household costs

Donald G. Teeling, 42 TC 671 (1964) (Acq.)

Need not be head of family

Rev. Rul. 57-415, 1957-2 CB 13

Custody decree has no effect where son in boarding school

Allan L. Blair, 63 TC 214 (1974) (Acq.), aff'd, 538 F.2d 155 (7th Cir. 1976)

Mother keeps separate house for mentally ill son

Lillie B. McDonald, 61 TCM 2764 (1991)

1.13 FILING FOR YOUR CHILD

Minor's earnings and deductions

IRC §73

Reg. §1.73-1

Filing requirement for dependent child

IRC §6012(a)(1)(C)

IRC §63(c)(5)

Reg. §1.73-1

Reg. §1.6012-1(a)(4)

Signing return

Rev. Rul. 82-206, 1982-2 CB 356

Social Security number of dependent

IRC §6109(e)

IRC §6724(d)(3)(D)

IRC §6723 ($50 penalty)

Deduction for pay to minor

Zeno J. Pucci, 10 TCM 529 (1951)

Samuel Rottenberg, 20 BTA 589 (Acq.)

Rev. Rul. 73-393, 1973-2 CB 33

Salary to young children

Nathaniel A. Denman, 48 TC 439 (1967)

Filing for Social Security self-employment tax

IRC §1401

IRC §1402

IRC §6017

Parental responsibility

IRC §6201(c)

Minors under age 18

IRC §1(g)

Child must pay penalties for parents' failure to file

Skye Bassett, 100 TC 41 (1993)

1.14 RETURN FOR DECEASED

* IRS Publication 559

Responsibility for filing

IRC §6012(b)

Reg. §1.6012-3(b)(1)

Reg. §1.6012-1(a)(2)(ii)

How reported

IRC §443

Reg. §1.443-1(a)(2)

IRC §451(b)

U.S. Savings Bonds—jointly owned

Rev. Rul. 58-435, 1958-2 CB 370, distinguished by Rev. Rul. 68-145, 1968-1 CB 203

Community property

R. D. Merrill, 211 F.2d 297 (9th Cir. 1954)

Hunt Henderson Est., 155 F.2d 310 (5th Cir. 1946)

Stella W. Bishop, 152 F.2d 389 (9th Cir. 1946)

Rev. Rul. 55-726, 1955-2 CB 24

Income received after death

IRC §691

Reg. §1.691(a)-1

Income accrued

IRC §451(b)

Reg. §1.451-1(b)

Returns

IRC §6012(b)(1) and (4)

Reg. §1.6012-3

Deduction for estate tax

IRC §691(b)

Reg. §1.691(a)-4

Reg. §1.691(c)-1

Marital status

IRC §143

Reg. §1.143-1

Exemptions

IRC §153

Reg. §1.153-1

No estimated tax for years ending before 2 years after decedent's death

IRC §6654(1)(2)

Due date

IRC §6072

Reg. §1.6071-1(b)

Reg. §1.6072-1(b)

Refund

Reg. §301.6402-2

Death before return filed for previous year

Reg. §1.6013-1(d)(3)

Request for prompt assessment

IRC §6501(d)

1.15 RETURN FOR AN INCOMPETENT PERSON

Guardian files

IRC §6012(b)(2)

Reg. §1.6012-3(b)(3)

Rev. Rul. 55-387, 1955-1 CB 131

Incompetency bars joint return

David Herman, 38 TCM 119, aff'd in unpublished opinion (3d Cir. Dec. 13, 1979)

Spouse may file

Rev. Rul. 55-387, 1955-1 CB 131 (joint return for missing spouse)

Rev. Rul. 56-22, 1956-1 CB 558, modified by Rev. Rul. 58-267, 1958-1 CB 327 (return for incompetent spouse)

1.16 HOW A NONRESIDENT ALIEN IS TAXED

IRC §871

* IRS Publication 519

Portion of non-resident golfer's endorsements taxable in U.S.

Sergio Garcia, 140 TC No. 6 (2013)

Resident taxed as U.S. citizen

Reg. §1.871-1

Prop. Reg. §1.871-1(a)

Tax on nonresident golfer's endorsements

Retief Goosen, 136 TC 574 (2011)

Nonresident subject to 30% tax

IRC §871(a)

Capital gains

IRC §871(a)(2)

Doing business

IRC §871(b)

1.17 HOW A RESIDENT ALIEN IS TAXED

* IRS Publication 519

Same as U.S. citizen

Reg. §1.871-1

Prop. Reg. §1.871-1(a)

Work for foreign government

IRC §893

Reg. §1.893-1

Joint return

IRC §6013(a)(1)

IRC §6013(g) and (h)

1.18 WHO IS A RESIDENT ALIEN?

* IRS Publication 519

IRC §7701(b)

Foreign students

U.S. Treasury Doc. No. 5588

Rev. Rul. 54-87, 1954-1 CB 155, amplified by Rev. Rul. 67-159, 1967-1 CB 280

1.19 CERTIFICATE OF TAX COMPLIANCE FOR ALIEN LEAVING THE UNITED STATES

* IRS Publication 519

1.20 EXPATRIATION TAX

IRC §877 (expatriation before June 17, 2008)

IRC §877 (expatriation on or after June 17, 2008)

Notification and reporting requirements

IRC §7701(n)

IRC §6039G

Notice 2005-36, 2005-19 IRB 1007 (Form 8854 required)

* IRS Publication 519

2 WAGES, SALARY, AND OTHER COMPENSATION

2.1 SALARY AND WAGE INCOME

IRC §61

Reg. §1.61-2

Mose Duberstein, 363 U.S. 278 (1960)

Lloyd M. Joshel, 296 F.2d 645 (10th Cir. 1962), aff'g 19 TCM 1349 (1960)

Thomas L. Johnson, 48 TC 636 (1967) (Acq.)

Hugh A. Brimm, 27 TCM 1148 (1968)

Abe A. Danish, 19 TCM 1349 (1960)

Moving expense reimbursements generally taxable for 2018 through 2025

IRC §132(g)(2), added by the Tax Cuts and Jobs Act (P.L. 115-97, 12/22/2017)

Notice 2018-75, 2018-41 IRB 556 (reimbursement received in 2018 for qualifying 2017 moving expenses not taxable)

Reasonableness of CEO's compensation

Menard, Inc. and John R. Menard, Jr., 2009-1 USTC ¶50,270 (7th Cir. 2009)

City's moral obligation to disabled employee

Rev. Rul. 73-346, 1973-2 CB 24

Gift of stock

Rev. Rul. 69-140, 1969-1 CB 46

Employee gifts and awards

IRC §274(b)

Ann. 82-7, 1982-3 IRB 48

NASA employee taxed

Robert Jones, 79 TC 1008 (1982)

Taxable severance pay sent by certified mail

Rev. Rul. 76-3, 1976-1 CB 114

Employee waiver does not make severance payment tax-free

Albert Taggi, 35 F.3d 93 (1994)

Chris Galligan, U.S. Dist. Ct. (E. Dist. of Pa. 1994)

Fees paid to controlled company

Terry Hardtke, 71 TCM 3220 (1996)

Contingent fee transfer

Richard Kochansky, 92 F.3d 357 (9th Cir. 1996)

Tip sharing

Kathleen Brown, 72 TCM 59 (1996)

Fee income held by a professional corporation

Carnation Y. L. Correa, D.C. Cir. (10/13/96)

Employee exclusion for donation to major disaster leave-sharing program

Notice 2006-59, 2006-28 IRB 60

Veteran not taxed on payments from compensated work therapy program

Roosevelt Wallace, 128 TC 132 (2007); Acq. IRB 2007-44

2.2 CONSTRUCTIVE RECEIPT OF YEAR-END PAYCHECKS

Employee not taxed on check received until following year

Beatrice Davis, 37 TCM 42 (1978)

Check received after bank closes on last day of year

C. F. Kahler, 18 TC 31 (1952)

Refused back pay check delivered by courier taxable when delivered

Diane Visco, TC Memo 2000-77

2.3 PAY RECEIVED IN PROPERTY IS TAXED

Reg. §1.61-1(a)

Reg. §1.61-2(d)(2)

Employer's note

Reg. §1.61-2(d)(4)

Samuel Segel, 24 TCM 1131 (1965)

Paul M. Potter, 5 TCM 116 (1946)

Debt canceled by employer

Fred E. Werner, 21 TCM 1435 (1962)

Prize points

Rev. Rul. 70-331, 1970-1 CB 14

Frequent flyer miles

Philip Charley, 91 F.3d 72 (9th Cir. 1996)

* Letter Ruling 9340007

2.4 COMMISSIONS TAXABLE WHEN CREDITED

Unearned commissions taxable when credited to account

Mary Rosenberg, 295 F. Supp. 820 (E.D. Mo. 1969), aff'd per curiam, 422 F.2d 341 (8th Cir. 1970)

Ada E. Sivley, 75 F.2d 916 (9th Cir. 1935)

C. E. Shockley, 6 TCM 1092 (1947)

Unearned commissions—income in year of advance despite repayment obligation

Rev. Rul. 79-311, 1979-2 CB 25

Rev. Proc. 83-4, 1983-1 CB 577

George Blood Enterprises, Inc., 35 TCM 436 (1976)

* Letter Ruling 9519002

Unearned commissions—no repayment required

James v. United States, 366 U.S. 213 (1961)

James J. Gales, 77 TCM 1316 (1999)

Write-off of advances

Rev. Rul. 69-465, 1969-2 CB 27

Repayment of commission when customer defaults

Rev. Rul. 72-78, 1972-1 CB 45

Commission on own purchase taxable

Kenneth W. Daehler, 281 F.2d 823 (5th Cir. 1960), rev'g 31 TC 722 (1959) (Nonacq.)

Sol Minzer, 279 F.2d 338 (5th Cir. 1960), rev'g 31 TC 1130 (1959) (Nonacq.)

J. E. Ostheimer, 264 F.2d 789 (3d Cir. 1959), cert. denied, 361 U.S. 818

Jack Williams, 64 TC 1085 (1975)

Commissions waived on policies sold to friends still taxed

Charles O. Mensik, 37 TC 703 (1962), aff'd, 328 F.2d 147 (7th Cir. 1964), cert. denied, 379 U.S. 827

Agent not taxed on rebated commissions

Mickey L. Worden, 2 F.3d 359 (10th Cir. 1993), rev'g 64 TCM 408 (1992)

Agent taxed on illegal rebate of commission

James Alex, 70 TC 322 (1978)

2.5 UNEMPLOYMENT BENEFITS

IRC §85

IRC §85(c) (exclusion for 2020 only)

Contribution from unemployment benefits

Donald Russell, 71 TCM 3184 (1996)

2.6 STRIKE PAY BENEFITS AND PENALTIES

Emergency benefits funded by federal government

Rev. Rul. 73-154, 1973-1 CB 40

Supplemental payments

News Release IR-156, May 29, 1956

Unemployment benefits from union fund

Halsey L. Williams, 37 TC 1099 (1962) (Acq.)

Strike benefits

Richard Osborne, 69 TCM 1895 (1995) (pilot's strike benefits taxable)

Allen Kaiser, 363 U.S. 299 (1960), aff'g 262 F.2d 367 (7th Cir. 1959)

James W. Godwin, 65-1 USTC ¶9121 (D. Tenn. 1965)

William A. Brown, 47 TC 399 (1967) (Acq.), aff'd per curiam, 398 F.2d 832 (6th Cir. 1968), cert. denied, 393 U.S. 1065

John N. Hagar, 43 TC 468 (1965)

Rev. Rul. 58-139, 1958-1 CB 14, modified by Rev. Rul. 61-136, 1961-2 CB 20

Rev. Rul. 57-1, 1957-1 CB 15

Pay penalty

Rev. Rul. 72-130, 1976-1 CB 16

2.7 NONQUALIFIED DEFERRED COMPENSATION

IRC §409A

Final Regulations: TD 9321, 2007-19 IRB 1123

Notice 2007-86, 2007-46 IRB 990 (transition relief generally extended through 2008), modifying Notice 2006-79, 2006-43 IRB 763

Divorce transfer of deferred compensation

Rev. Rul. 2002-22, 2002-19 IRB 849

Notice 2002-31, 2002-19 IRB 908

State or local government deferred pay plan

IRC §457

Qualified cash or deferred arrangement

IRC §401

IRC §401(k)

Model rabbi trust

Rev. Proc. 92-64, 1992-2 CB 214

2.8 DIID YOU RETURN WAGES RECEIVED IN A PRIOR YEAR?

IRC §1341

Reg. §1.1341-1

Return of embezzled funds — no claim of right computation

Rev. Rul. 65-254, 1965-2 CB 50

Return of unreasonable salary under agreement deductible

Rev. Rul. 69-115, 1969-1 CB 50

Author lacked unrestricted right to advanced royalties

Stewart H. Holbrook, 194 F. Supp. 252 (U.S. Dist. Ct. Ore. 1961)

No deduction where repayment not required

John G. Pahl, 67 TC 286 (1976)

Repayment of supplemental unemployment benefits—above-the-line deduction

IRC §62(a)(12)

Restitution payments may be deductible

Jess Kraft, et ux., 114 S. Ct. 467, cert. denied, 991 F.2d 292 (6th Cir. 1993)

Hedge agreement allows Section 1341 recalculation

Eugene Van Cleave, 718 F.2d 193 (6th Cir. 1983)

Escrow payment for contested liability deductible

Warnock Davies, 101 TC 282 (1993)

2.9 WAIVER OF EXECUTOR'S AND TRUSTEE'S COMMISSIONS

George M. Breidert, 50 TC 844 (1968) (Acq.)

Rev. Rul. 66-167, 1966-1 CB 20

Rev. Rul. 64-225, 1964-2 CB 15

Rev. Rul. 56-472, 1956-2 CB 21

2.10 LIFE INSURANCE BENEFITS

Final split-dollar insurance regulations

T.D. 9092, 2003-46 IRB 1055 (effective for split-dollar arrangements entered into or materially modified by September 17, 2003 and not materially modified thereafter)

Notice 2002-8, 2002-4 IRB 398 (guidance for split-dollar arrangements entered into before September 18, 2003)

Effect of Sect. 409A deferred compensation rules on split-dollar insurance

Notice 2007-34, 2007-17 IRB 996

Assignment of group policy

Rev. Rul. 76-490, 1976-2 CB 300

Rev. Rul. 68-334, 1968-1 CB 403

Permanent and paid-up insurance—taxed to employee

Reg. §1.61-2(d)(2)

* Letter Ruling 9604001

Frank D. Yuengling, 69 F.2d 971 (3d Cir. 1934)

W. F. Parker, 38 BTA 989

Rev. Rul. 56-400, 1956-2 CB 116

Rev. Rul. 78-420, 1978-2 CB 67

Rev. Rul. 64-328, 1964-2 CB 11, amplified by Rev. Rul. 66-110, 1966-1 CB 112

2.11 EDUCATIONAL BENEFITS FOR EMPLOYEES' CHILDREN

Grants by private foundations

Rev. Proc. 76-47, 1976-2 CB 670, amplified by Rev. Proc. 77-32, 1977-2 CB 541

* Letter Ruling 9018068 (scholarship plan approved)

Educational benefit trusts

Rev. Rul. 75-448, 1975-2 CB 55

Richard T. Armantrout, 67 TC 996 (1977), aff'd per curiam, 570 F.2d 210 (7th Cir. 1978)

Grant-Jacoby, Inc., 73 TC 700 (1980)

John C. Saunders, 720 F.2d 871 (5th Cir. 1983), aff'g 45 TCM 82 (1982)

Reg. §1.677(b)-1(f)

2.12 SICK PAY IS TAXABLE

IRC §61

Tax-free benefits from private insurance

IRC §104(a)(3)

2.13 WORKERS' COMPENSATION IS TAX FREE

IRC §104(a)(1)

Police officer's leave payments not excludable

Clarence William Speer, 144 TC No. 14 (2015)

Lump-sum settlement not treated as worker's compensation

Kathleen S. Simpson, 141 TC No. 10

Workers' compensation

IRC §104(a)(1)

Reg. §1.104-1(b)

Given to employer

Rev. Rul. 56-83, 1956-1 CB 79

N.Y.C. teacher under Board of Ed. regulations

Madeline G. Dyer, 71 TC 560 (1979) (Acq. in result only)

N.Y.C. retirees may exclude job-related disability pay

Rev. Rul. 83-91, 1983-1 CB 38

Civil Service Retirement Act payments not workers' compensation

Daniel S. Haar, 78 TC 864 (1982), aff'd per curiam, 709 F.2d 1207 (8th Cir. 1983)

Policeman's sick leave under labor contract not workers' compensation

William Rutter, 48 TCM 1269 (1984), aff'd per curiam, 760 F.2d 466 (2d Cir. 1985)

Los Angeles Sheriff's sick leave elected under workers' compensation statute is tax free

Donald Givens, 90 TC 1145 (1988)

(Nonacq.; 89-1 CB 1)

Policeman's disability amounts under state law not affected by PBA contract

James Fotis, 57 TCM 697 (1989)

Police officer's disability retirement pay partly taxable

Jay Sewards, 138 TC No.15 (2012)

Judge's medical disability tax free although same amount as regular retirement

Raymond J. Byrne, TC Memo 2002-319

New York City law change allows tax-free sick leave for police and firefighters

Local Law 87, 12/29/88

Local Law 78, 10/25/89

2.14 Disability Pay and Pensions

Military disability generally taxable

IRC §104(a)(4)

IRC §104(b)

Law allows refunds of improper withholding to disabled combat veterans

News Release IR-2019-125

Combat-Injured Veterans Tax Fairness Act of 2016, P.L. 114-292, 12/16/16

Benefits to public safety officers' survivors tax free

P.L. 114-14, adding Code Section 104(a)(6), signed into law 5/22/15

Combat-related injuries

IRC §104(b)(2)(C)

IRC §104(b)(3)

Injuries from terroristic or military actions

IRC §104(a)(5)

Social Security disability benefits taxable

William D. Reimels, 123 TC 243 aff'd 2006-1 USTC ¶50,147 (2d Cir. 2006) (Vietnam veteran)

Will L. Thomas, TC Memo 2001-120

Meat cutter taxed on disability pension from union plan

Roger W. Zardo, TC Memo 2011-7

2.15 Stock Appreciation Rights (SARs)

SARs not treated as nonqualified deferred compensation

Reg. §1.409A-1 (b) (5) (i) (B)

Notice 2005-1, 2005-2 IRB 274 (initial guidance preceding proposed regulations to IRC §409A)

Pre-2004 rules (prior to enactment of IRC §409A)

Rev. Rul. 80-300, 1980-2 CB 165 (no tax on receipt of SARs)

Rev. Rul. 82-121, 1982-1 CB 79 (no constructive receipt on SAR tied to stock option)

* Letter Ruling 8120103 (tax on expiration of SARs)

2.16 Stock Options

* "Tax-Efficient Strategies for Exercising Compensatory Stock Options," Sidney R. Finkel and Kelly G. Besaw, 71 Practical Tax Strategies 15 (July 2003)

Qualified statutory stock options

IRC §421

Incentive stock options

IRC §422

Temp. Reg. §14a.422A-1

Employee stock purchase plans

IRC §423

Nonqualified stock options

IRC §83

Reg. §1.83-7

Pagel, Inc., 91 TC 200 (1988) (upholding Reg. §1.83-7)

Mandatory W-2 reporting on exercising nonqualified option

Announcement 2002-108; 2002-49 IRB 952

Divorce transfer of nonqualified options

Rev. Rul. 2004-60, 2004-24 IRB 1051

Rev. Rul. 2002-22, 2002-19 IRB 849

Notice 2002-31, 2002-19 IRB 908

2.17 Election to Defer Income on Qualified Equity Grants from Private Companies (Section 83(i) Election)

*IRS Publication 525

Notice 2018-97. 2018-52 IRB 1062

2.18 Restricted Stock

Stock not substantially vested under an employment agreement

Larry E. Austin, 141 TC No. 18 (2013)

Sale treated as option

Reg. §1.83-3(a)(2)

Restricted stock

IRC §83(c)

Executive cannot deduct loss on sale of restricted stock to key employees

Henry C. Tilford, Jr., 75 TC 134 (1980), rev'd, 705 F.2d 828 (6th Cir. 1983)

Section 83(b) election—electing tax on unrestricted value within 30 days

Prop. Reg. Sec. 1.83-2(c), REG-135524-14, 7/7/15

IRC §83(b)

Making a Section 83(b) election for restricted stock(sample election language)

Rev. Proc. 2012-29, 2012-28 IRB 49

Revoking Section 83(b) election

Rev. Proc. 2006-31, 2006-27 IRB 32

Attorney taxed on income remitted to firm

* Letter Ruling 9514008

Lapsed restrictions disregarded

IRC §422A(e)(10)

3 FRINGE BENEFITS

3.1 Tax-Free Health and Accident Coverage Under Employer Plans

Wellness program payment taxable

Chief Counsel Memorandum 201622031

Identity theft protection following data breach is tax free

Announcement 2015-22, 2015-35 IRB 288

Health coverage election in cafeteria plans

Notice 2014-55, 2014-41 IRB

Employer-paid premiums not taxable

IRC §106(a)

Rev. Rul. 82-196, 1982-2 CB 53 (retired employee not taxed and deceased employee's survivors not taxed)

Rev. Rul. 85-121, 1985-2 CB 57 (laid-off employee not taxed)

* Letter Ruling 9409006

Rugby Productions, 100 TC 35 (1993)

Notice 94-103, 1994-51 IRB 10

Employee taxed on employer's reimbursement of premiums financed by pre-tax salary reduction

Rev. Rul. 2002-3, 2002-3 IRB 316, amplified by Rev. Rul. 2002-80, 2002-49 IRB 925

Employee taxed on "advance reimbursement" or "loan" intended to offset salary reduction

Rev. Rul. 2002-80, 2002-49 IRB 925, amplifying Rev. Rul. 2002-3, 2002-3 IRB 316

New dependent definition doesn't affect medical exclusion

Notice 2004-79, 2004-49 IRB 898

Employee taxed on coverage for domestic partner

* Letter Ruling 9717018

* Letter Ruling 9603011

* Letter Ruling 200108010

DOMA's denial of tax benefits for gay and lesbian partners held unconstitutional

Edith Schlain Windsor, 2013-2 USTC ¶50,400 (Sup. Ct. 2013)

Long-term-care coverage

IRC §7702(B) (generally tax-free)

IRC §106(c) (taxable if provided through FSA)

Archer MSA coverage not taxed to employee

IRC §106(b) (contributions up to deductible limit of IRC §220(b)(1))

Access and portability rules for group health plans

IRC §4980D (daily penalties on employers)

IRC §9801 (pre-existing condition exclusions)

IRC §9802 (health status discrimination prohibited)

IRC §9811 (mothers and newborns)

IRC §9812 (mental health benefits)

Continuing coverage required (COBRA)

IRC §4980B

Rev. Rul. 96-8, 1996-1 CB 286

COBRA coverage for spouse dropped before divorce

Rev. Rul. 2002-88, 2002-52 IRB 995

3.2 HEALTH SAVINGS ACCOUNTS (HSAs) AND ARCHER MSAs

IRS adds preventive care items as qualified expenses for HDHP

Notice 2019-45, 2019-32 IRB 593

HSA and HDHP inflation adjustment

Rev. Proc. 2022-24, 2022-20 IRB 1075 (2023 rules)

Rev. Proc. 2021-25, 2021-21 IRB 1161 (2022 rules)

Rev. Proc. 2020-32, 2020-24 IRB 930 (2021 rules)

Rev. Proc. 2019-25, 2019-22 IRB 1261 (2020 rules)

Rev. Proc. 2018-30, 2018-21 IRB 622 (2019 rules)

Employer contributions to employee's health savings accounts (HSAs)

IRC §106(d) (contributions up to deductible limit of IRC §223(b))

Notice 2004-2, 2004-2 IRB 269

IRS guidelines for HSAs

*Chief Counsel INFO Letter 2016-0014 (contribution limit for individual enrolling in Medicare)

*Chief Counsel INFO Letter 2016-0003 (husband and wife both enroll in Medicare in same year)

Notice 2004-50, 2004-33 IRB 196 (Q&A)

Rev. Rul. 2004-38, 2004-15 IRB 717 (prescription drug coverage)

Rev. Proc. 2004-22, 2004-15 IRB 727 (transition for prescription drugs)

Notice 2004-23, 2004-15 IRB 725 (preventive care)

Notice 2004-25, 2004-15 IRB 727 (transition for 2004 expenses)

Notice 2004-43, 2004-27 IRB 10 (state law mandates)

High-deductible health plan

IRC §223(c)(2)

HSA catch-up contribution limit

IRC §223(b)(3)

Limited use of FSA and HRA with HSAs

Rev. Rul. 2004-45, 2004-22 IRB 971

HSA contributions during FSA grace period

Notice 2005-86; 2005-49 IRB 1075

Medicare Advantage MSA

IRC §138

Employer contribution limit to Archer MSA

IRC §106(b) (contributions up to deductible limit of IRC §220(b)(1))

Rev. Proc. 2020-45, 2020-46 IRB 1016 (2021 rules)

3.3 REIMBURSEMENTS AND OTHER TAX-FREE PAYMENTS FROM EMPLOYER HEALTH AND ACCIDENT PLANS

Qualified Small Employer Health Reimbursement Arrangements (QSEHRAs)

IRC §9831(d), as added by P.L. 114-255, 12/13/2016

Specific reimbursements of medical expenses

IRC §105(b)

Reg. §1.105-2

Rev. Rul. 63-181, 1963-2 CB 74

Reimbursement of dependent's expenses

IRC §105(b)

Health reimbursement arrangements

Rev. Rul. 2002-41, 2002-28 IRB 75

Notice 2002-45, 2002-28 IRB 93

Direct transfer from HRA to HSA

IRC §106(e)

Limited use of FSA and HRA with HSAs

Rev. Rul. 2004-45, 2004-22 IRB 971

Cash option renders HRA taxable

Rev. Rul. 2005-24, 2005-16 IRB 892

Reimbursements taxed if beneficiaries could receive unreimbursed amounts

Rev. Rul. 2006-36, 2006-36 IRB 353

Medical costs reimbursed with debit, credit, or stored value cards

Notice 2006-69, 2006-31 IRB 107 Rev. Rul. 2003-43, 2003-21 IRB 935 (debit card)

Sole proprietor reimbursement plan covering spouse

Darwin J. Albers, TC Memo 2007-144 (spouse was bona fide employee but plan was not bona fide)

*Peter Speltz, TC Summary Opinion 2006-25 (spouse is bona fide employee)

Richard Haeder, TC Memo 2001-17 (spouse not a bona fide employee)

* James A. Poyda, TC Summary Opinion 2001-91 (spouse not a bona fide employee)

Self-insured medical reimbursement plans

IRC §105(h)

Reg. §1.105-11

Highly compensated under medical self-insured plans

IRC §105(h)(5)

IRC §401(k)(12)

Physicals may be given to executives only

Reg. §1.105-11(g)(1)

Permanent loss of use of part of body

IRC §105(c)

Reg. §1.105-3

Benefit must be based on injury

Randall Beisler, 814 F.2d 1304 (9th Cir. 1987)

Kenneth Rosen, 829 F.2d 506 (4th Cir. 1987)

Hypertension not loss of body function

Frank S. Watts, 82-1 USTC ¶9226 (D. Cal. 1982), aff'd, 83-1 USTC ¶9286 (9th Cir. 1983)

Pilot's heart attack not loss of body function

Oscar J. Hines, 72 TC 715 (1979)

Surgeon's nerve damage is loss of body function

Jon L. Stolte, TC Memo 1999-271

Meat cutter taxed on disability pension from union plan

Roger W. Zardo, TC Memo 2011-7

Taxable benefits under employer-paid coverage

IRC §105(a)

Reg. §1.105-1

Tax-free benefits under private policy

IRC §104(a)(3)

Reg. §1.104-1(d)

Disability payments from profit-sharing plan taxed

George H. Gordon, 88 TC 630 (1987)

Michael J. Berman, 58 TCM 919 (1989)

Close corporations

Alan B. Larkin, 48 TC 629 (1967), aff'd, 394 F.2d 494 (1st Cir. 1968)

Arthur R. Seidel, 30 TCM 1021 (1971)

Sanders & Sons, Inc., 26 TCM 671 (1967)

3.4 GROUP-TERM LIFE INSURANCE PREMIUMS

IRC §79

Reg. §1.79-0 through 3

Temp. Reg. §1.79-4T

IRS rate table

Temp. Reg. §1.79-3(d)(2)

Assignment of policy

Rev. Rul. 73-174, 1973-1 CB 43

Combination policies

Reg. §1.79-1(b)

Former employees

IRC §79(e)

Retire on disability

IRC §79(b)(1)

Key employees taxed under discriminatory plans

IRC §79(d)

Temp. Reg. §1.79-4T, question 6

Key employees defined

IRC §416(i)

IRC §79(d)(6) (includes retirees)

Separate discriminatory testing of active and retired employees

Reg. §1.79-4T, questions 7 and 8

Group-term insurance for dependents

Notice 89-110, 1989-49 IRB 17

3.5 DEPENDENT CARE ASSISTANCE

Dependent care services

IRC §129

IRC §129(a)(2)(D) (higher exclusion limit for 2021)

Identify employer provider of child care on return

IRC §129(e)(9)

COVID-19 related carryover rules

Notice 2021-26, 2021-21 IRB 1157

3.6 ADOPTION BENEFITS

Exclusion for employer benefits

IRC §137

Rev. Proc. 2020-45, 2020-46 IRB 1016 (exclusion for 2021)

* IRS Publication 968

Safe harbor for determining finality of foreign adoptions

Rev. Proc. 2010-31, 2010-40 IRB 413 (Hague convention countries)

Rev. Proc. 2005-31, 2005-1 CB 1374 (non-Hague convention countries)

3.7 EDUCATION ASSISTANCE PLANS

Education assistance exclusion

IRC §127

Tuition reductions

IRC §117(c) and (d)

* Letter Ruling 9040045 (faculty and staff)

Daniel Wolpaw, 47 F.3d 787 (6th Cir. 1995)

Working condition benefit

IRC §132(h)(9)

3.8 COMPANY CARS, PARKING, AND TRANSIT PASSES

IRC §132(a)(3) (working condition fringe benefits)

IRC §132(f) (qualified transportation fringe benefits: transit passes, van/bus employee commuting, parking benefits)

Reg. §1.132-9 (qualified transportation fringe benefits)

Suspension of exclusion for bicycle commuting reimbursements for 2018 through 2025

IRC §132(f)(8)

Permanent parity for transit benefits exclusion with parking

IRC §132(f)(2), as amended by the Protecting Americans from Tax Hikes Act of 2015 (PATH Act)

Rev. Proc. 2016-14, 2016-9 IRB 365

Bike share program is not excludable transportation benefit

* Chief Counsel Information Letter 2013-0032

Valuation of benefits

Reg. §1.61-21

Excludable non-personal-use vehicles

Temp. Reg. §1.274-5T(k)

Chauffeur bodyguard

Reg. §1.132-5(m)

100% inclusion rule for cars

Reg. §1.274-6T(c)

Transit passes, parking benefits, and bicycle commuting reimbursements

IRC §132(f)

Reg. §1.132-9

Parking at non-temporary location

* IRS Legal Memorandum 200105007

3.9 WORKING CONDITION FRINGE BENEFITS

IRC §132(d)

Reg. §1.132-5

Employees not taxed on employer-provided cell phones

Notice 2011-72, 2011-38 IRB 407

Job-placement assistance

Rev. Rul. 92-69, 1992-2 CB 51

Employee personal use of company airplane

IRC §274(e)(2) (overturning Sutherland decision below)

Sutherland Lumber-Southwest Inc., 255 F.3d 495 (8th Cir. 2001) (Acq.)

S Corp owners may deduct personally used plane

* Chief Counsel Advice 200344008

Unused commuting salary reductions cannot be refunded

* Chief Counsel Information Letter 2003-0244

Financial counseling

* Letter Ruling 199929043

Mandatory employer-provided tax-preparation services

* IRS Field Service Advice 200137039

Appeals court finds business purpose for fishing trips

Townsend Industries, Inc., 2003-2 ¶50,666 (8th Cir. 2003

Rev. Proc. 2001-56, IRB 2001-51 590

3.10 DE MINIMIS FRINGE BENEFITS

IRC §132(e)

Reg. §1.132-6

Occasional overtime meal money or cab fare

Reg. §1.132-6(d)(2)(i)

Commuting under unsafe circumstances

Reg. §1.132-6(d)(2)(iii) (outside normal hours)

Reg. §1.61-21(k) ($1.50 valuation rule for hourly employees)

3.11 EMPLOYER-PROVIDED RETIREMENT ADVICE

IRC §132(m)

3.12 EMPLOYEE ACHIEVEMENT AWARDS

IRC §74(c)

Taxable amount

Prop. Reg. §1.74-2

3.13 EMPLOYER-FURNISHED MEALS OR LODGING

Meals and lodging

IRC §119

Reg. §1.119-1

Maschmeyer's Nursery, Inc., 71 TMC 2188 (1996)

Boyd Gaming Corp., 117 F.3d 1096 (9th Cir. 1999)

Meals treated as furnished for employer's convenience

IRC §119(b)(4)

Remote camp in foreign country

* James A. Nielson, TC Summary Opinion 2007-53

IRC §119(c)(2)

Company cafeteria

Reg. §1.119-1(d)

Hotel manager or executive

Charles N. Anderson, 371 F.2d 59 (6th Cir. 1967), cert. denied, 387 U.S. 906

Jack B. Lindeman, 60 TC 609 (1973) (Acq.)

Atlanta Biltmore Hotel Corp., 22 TCM 1266 (1963), mod'd and aff'd, 349 F.2d 677 (5th Cir. 1965)

Adolph Coors Co., 27 TCM 1351 (1968)

State civil service employee

Reg. §1.119-1(d)

No exclusion for purchases at commissary

Michael A. Tougher, Jr., 51 TC 737 (1969), aff'd per curiam, 441 F.2d 1148 (9th Cir. 1971), cert. denied, 404 U.S. 856

Executive luncheon

Carlton R. Mabley, 24 TCM 1794 (1965)

Casino employees

Boyd Gaming Corp., 117 F.3d 1096 (9th Cir. 1999)

Waitress's day off

Reg. §1.119-1(d)

Restaurant employees

Reg. §1.119-1(d)

Emergency

Reg. §1.119-1(a)(2)(ii)(a)

Reg. §1.119-1(d)

Bank teller

Reg. §1.119-1(f)

School superintendent one block away

Virgil L. Erdelt, 715 F. Supp. 278 (D.C. N. Dak. 1989), aff'd, 909 F.2d 510 (8th Cir. 1990), IRS Action on Decision 1992-001

Short meal period

Reg. §1.119-1(a)(2)(ii)(A) and (d)

* Letter Ruling 9602001

Lodging off premises

Charles Anderson, 371 F.2d 59 (6th Cir. 1967), rev'g 42 TC 410 (1964), cert. denied, 387 U.S. 906

Gordon S. Dole, 351 F.2d 308 (1st Cir. 1965), aff'g per curiam 43 TC 697 (1964) (Acq.)

Harold T. Giesinger, 66 TC 6 (1976) (Acq.)

Jack B. Lindeman, 60 TC 609 (1973) (Acq.)

College president taxed on lodging four miles away

Richard D. Winchell, 564 F. Supp. 131 (D. C. Neb. 1983), aff'd without opinion, 725 F.2d 689 (8th Cir. 1983)

* Letter Ruling 9404005

Faculty housing

IRC §119(d)

Lodging for dorm parents and evening house is tax free

* Letter Ruling 9404005

Hospital lodging not a condition of employment where others live in apartments

* Letter Ruling 8938014

Employer gives cash allowance

Reg. §1.119-1

Employer deducts fixed amount from pay

IRC §119(b)

Reg. §1.119-1(a)(3)(ii)

Melvin J. Boykin, 260 F.2d 249 (8th Cir. 1958)

Rev. Rul. 59-307, 1959-2 CB 48

Utilities

Charles R. Considine, 68 TC 52 (1977)

Rev. Rul. 68-579, 1968-2 CB 61

Workers in remote area

Reg. §1.119-1(d)

William L. Olkjer, 32 TC 464 (1959) (Acq.)

Farm supervision

M. Caratan, 442 F.2d 606 (9th Cir. 1971)

Other employees

Lloyd N. Farnham, 6 TCM 1049 (1947)

Special Ruling, December 3, 1950

Insufficient eating facilities

Reg. §1.119-1(a)(2)(ii)(c)

Park employee

Robert L. Coyner, 344 F.2d 736 (3d Cir. 1965)

Partnerships

C. C. Wilson 376 F.2d 280 (Court of Claims 1967) (reimbursed food taxed)

Ann L. Armstrong, 394 F.2d 661 (5th Cir. 1968) (meals and lodging excludable)

Unprepared food

Walter Jacob, 493 F.2d 1294 (3d Cir. 1974)

Michael A. Tougher, Jr., 441 F.2d 1148 (9th Cir. 1971), cert. denied, 404 U.S. 856

Hotel partnership deductions

George A. Papineau, 16 TC 130 (1952) (Nonacq.)

Peace Corps volunteer

IRC §912

VISTA volunteer

Carol Goldstein, 73 TC 164 (1979)

3.14 MINISTER'S HOUSING OR HOUSING ALLOWANCE

IRC §107

Cash housing allowance (IRC §107(2)) held constitutional

Ann Laurie Gaylor, 919 F.3d 420 (CA-7, 2019), rev'g. Ann Laurie Gaylor, No.16-CV-215 (W.D. WI. 2017)

Tax-free allowance limited to fair rental value of house

IRC §107(2), as amended by the Clergy Housing Allowance Clarification Act of 2002, effectively reversing the holding in Richard D. Warren, 114 TC 343 (2000)

Appeals court disallows tax-free allowance for minister's second home

Philip A. Driscoll, 2012-1 USTC ¶50,187(11th Cir. 2012), rev'g 135 TC 557 (2010); cert. denied

Services performed by minister

Reg. §1.1402(c)-5

Allocation for minister with salary and self-employment income to determine deductible expenses

* Johnny J. Young, TC Summary Opinion 2005-76

Exclusion allowed for ordained executive directors of parochial schools

Rev. Rul. 62-171, 1962-2 CB 39

No deduction for ordained minister working for a nonreligious organization

Rev. Rul. 68-68, 1968-1 CB 51

Not allowed for unordained ministers

Rev. Rul. 59-270, 1959-2 CB 44

Unordained educational director

Robert D. Lawrence, 50 TC 494 (1968)

Cantors

Abraham A. Salkov, 46 TC 190 (1966) (Nonacq.)

Max Silverman, 253 F.2d 849 (8th Cir. 1958)

Rev. Rul. 78-301, 1978-2 CB 103

Traveling evangelist

Rev. Rul. 64-326, 1964-2 CB 37

Retired minister

Rev. Rul. 63-156, 1963-2 CB 79

Widow not entitled to exclusion

Rev. Rul. 72-249, 1972-1 CB 36

Anti-communist crusade

James D. Colbert, 61 TC 449 (1974)

Priest living as layman

Francis E. Kelley, 62 TC 131 (1974)

Not allowed for unordained executive of tax-exempt nonreligious organization

W. Astor Kirk, 425 F.2d 492 (D.C. Cir. 1970), cert. denied, 400 U.S. 853

Civilian chaplain at VA hospital

Rev. Rul. 72-462, 1972-2 CB 76

Administrator of nonreligious old-age home

Jesse A. Toavs, 67 TC 897 (1977)

Rev. Rul. 72-606, 1972-2 CB 78

No exclusion for rabbi as director of interreligious affairs

Marc H. Tanenbaum, 58 TC 1 (1972)

Exclusion for rabbi as UJA director

Melvin Libman, 44 TCM 371 (1982)

Minister teaching at church-related college

* Letter Ruling 9144047

3.15 CAFETERIA PLANS PROVIDE CHOICE OF BENEFITS

IRC §125

Notice 2014-55, 2014-41 IRB 672

Reg. §1.125-3 (effect of Family and Medical Leave Act)

Reg. §1.125-4 (permitted election changes)

Prop. Reg. §1.125-2 (general questions and answers)

IRS guidance on employee benefit plans for same-sex couples

Notice 2015-86, 2015-52 IRB 887

Key employees

IRC §125(b)(2)

3.16 FLEXIBLE SPENDING ARRANGEMENTS

IRC §125

Prop. Reg. §1.125-2 (general questions and answers)

Over-the-counter drugs and menstrual products qualify for health FSA reimbursement, Health flexible spending arrangements

Reg. §1.125-3 (effect of Family and Medical Leave Act)

Reg. §1.125-4 (permitted election changes)

Prop. Reg. §1.125-2

One-time FSA-to-HSA transfer

IRC §106(e)

Employer option to allow grace period extension to use-it-or-lose-it deadline

Notice 2005-42, 2005-23 IRB 1204

Medical costs reimbursed with debit, credit, or stored value cards

Notice 2006-69, 2006-31 IRB 107

Cost of doctor-prescribed herb can be reimbursed by FSA

* Chief Counsel Letter, INFO 2010-0080

Breastfeeding equipment is medical expense

Announcement 2011-14, 2011-9 IRB 532

3.17 COMPANY SERVICES PROVIDED AT NO ADDITIONAL COST

Mihalik v. Commr, TC Memo 2022-36

IRC §132(a)(1) (exclusion allowed)

IRC §132(b) ("no additional cost service" defined)

Reg. §1.132-2

Highly compensated employees

IRC §132(j)(1) (non-discrimination rule)

IRC §132(j)(6) (defined)

Line of business limitation

Reg. §1.132-4

Temp. Reg. §54.4977-1T (1985 election)

3.18 DISCOUNTS ON COMPANY PRODUCTS OR SERVICES

IRC §132(a)(2)(exclusion allowed)

IRC §132(c)(qualified employee discount defined)

Reg. §1.132-3

* Letter Ruling 9328016

Highly compensated employees

IRC §132(j)(1) (non-discrimination rule

IRC §132(j)(6) (defined)

4 DIVIDEND AND INTEREST INCOME

4.1 REPORTING DIVIDENDS AND MUTUAL-FUND DISTRIBUTIONS

* IRS Publication 564

Ordinary dividend portion

IRC §854(b)(2)

Reg. §1.854-2

Rev. Rul. 77-149, 1977-1 CB 82

Deferral of interest does not apply to tax-exempt obligations

IRC §1278(a)(1)(C)

Election to currently report discount

IRC §1278(b)

Partial principal payments

IRC §1276(a)(3)

4.21 Discount on Short-Term Obligations

Current inclusion required

IRC §1281

Tax-exempts excluded from inclusion rule

IRC §1283(a)(1)(B)

Deferred interest deduction

IRC §1282

4.22 Stripped Coupon Bonds and Stock

IRC §1286

Zero coupon bond (OID reported annually)

IRC §1272

Market discount bonds

IRC §1276

OID treatment for stripped preferred stock

IRC §305(e)

* IRS Publication 1212

4.23 Sale or Retirement of Bonds and Notes

IRC §1271

IRC §1272

* IRS Publication 550

* IRS Publication 1212

Registered form

IRC §1287

Retirement defined

Donald S. McClain, 311 U.S. 527 (1941)

Unearned original issue discount is capital gain

Ted Bolnick, 44 TC 245 (1965) (Acq.)

4.24 State and City Interest Generally Tax Exempt

* IRS Publication 550

State, city obligations

IRC §103(a)

Reg. §1.103-1

Rhode Island Hospital Trust Co., 8 BTA 555, vacated and remanded, 29 F.2d 339 (1st Cir. 1929)

Agreement of purchase and sale

Newlin Machinery Corp., 28 TC 837 (1957) (Acq.)

Sale of municipal certificates of indebtedness to municipality

Palm Beach Trust Co., 9 TC 1060 (1947), aff'd per curiam, 174 F.2d 527 (D.C. Cir. 1949), cert. denied, 338 U.S. 825

Qualified private activity bonds not taxed

IRC §141(e)

AMT exception for 2009/2010 private activity bonds

IRC §47(a)(5)(C)(vi)

4.25 Taxable State and City Interest

IRC §103(e)

Qualified private activity bonds not taxed

IRC §141(e)

Community open account purchases

Kurtz Bros., 42 BTA 561

Volunteer fire companies

Seagrave Corp., 38 TC 247 (1962)

Tax sale certificates

Charles H. Wiltsie, 3 F. Supp. 743 (Ct. Cl. 1933), cert. denied, 291 U.S. 664

Municipal bond in open market

Rev. Rul. 57-49, 1957-1 CB 62

Rev. Rul. 60-210, 1960-1 CB 38, modified by Rev. Rul. 60-376, 1960-2 CB 38

4.26 Tax-Exempt Bonds Bought at a Discount

IRC §1288

Bond bought at discount

Rev. Rul. 73-112, 1973-1 CB 47

Rev. Rul. 57-49, 1957-1 CB 62

Rev. Rul. 60-210, 1960-1 CB 38

Redeemed old bond at premium

Rev. Rul. 72-587, 1972-2 CB 74

District Bond Co., 1 TC 837 (1943)

Redemption of bonds issued after June 8, 1980

Rev. Rul. 80-143, 1980-1 CB 89, modifying Rev. Rul. 72-587, 1972-2 CB 74

Market discount rules do not apply to tax-exempt bonds

IRC §1278

Stripped tax-exempt obligations

IRC §1286(d)

4.27 Treasury Bills, Notes, and Bonds

Taxable interest

Reg. §1.61-7

Taxed at maturity

IRC §454(b)

Gain on sale of short-term obligations (ratable share of discount)

IRC §1271(a)(3)(D)

Acquisition discount currently taxed to accrual-basis taxpayers and dealers

IRC §1281

Interest deduction limitation

IRC §1281

IRC §1282

4.28 Interest on United States Savings Bonds

* IRS Publication 550

Annual increase in value

IRC §454

Reg. §1.454-1(c) (taxed in year of redemption or final maturity)

Election to report interest annually on timely return

Rev. Rul. 55-655, 1955-2 CB 253

Change in taxpayer's reporting method

Rev. Proc. 89-46, 1989-2 CB 597

4.29 Deferring United States Savings Bond Interest

* IRS Publication 550

Transferring to a revocable trust

*Chief Counsel Information Letter 2015-0027

Changing from annual reporting to deferral

Rev. Proc. 2002-9, 2002-3 IRB 327

Postpone tax during extended maturity period

IRC §454(c)

Reg. §1.454-1

Change form of registration of E bond

IRC §454(c)

Reg. §1.454-1

Rev. Rul. 55-278, 1955-1 CB 471

Rev. Rul. 54-327, 1954-2 CB 50

Correction of error in registration

Rev. Rul. 70-428, 1970-2 CB 5

Co-owners

Rev. Rul. 54-143, 1954-1 CB 12

Rev. Rul. 55-278, 1955-1 CB 471

Rev. Rul. 58-435, 1958-2 CB 370, distinguished by Rev. Rul. 68-145, 1968-1 CB 203

Transfer to charity

* Letter Ruling 8010082

Bonds transferred by gift without reissue

Edward G. Chandler, 410 U.S. 257 (1973), rev'g 460 F.2d 1281 (9th Cir. 1972)

Mae Elliott Est., 57 TC 152 (1971), aff'd per curiam, 474 F.2d 1008 (5th Cir. 1973)

Lyla C. Curry Est., 409 F.2d 671 (6th Cir. 1969)

Alice H. Silverman, 259 F.2d 731 (3d Cir. 1958)

Helen K. Chambless, 1970 WL 319 (DCSC) (1970)

Death of owner

Rev. Rul. 64-104, 1964-1 CB 223, distinguished by Rev. Rul. 68-145, 1968-1 CB 203

Election on decedent's return

Rev. Rul. 68-145, 1968-1 CB 203

4.30 MINIMUM INTEREST RULES

IRC §7872 (loans)

IRC §1274 and §483 (seller financing)

4.31 INTEREST-FREE OR BELOW-MARKET-INTEREST LOANS

IRC §7872

Prop. Reg. §1.7872-1 through §1.7872-14

Blended annual rate for demand loans

Rev. Rul. 2023-12, 2023-27 IRB 1111 (blended rate for 2023)

Rev. Rul. 2022-12, 2022-27 IRB 1 (blended rate for 2022)

Rev. Rul. 2021-12, 2021-27 IRB 1 (blended rate for 2021)

Rev. Rul. 2020-14, 2020-28 IRB 33 (blended rate for 2020)

Rev. Rul. 2019-16, 2018-28 IRB 96 (blended rate for 2019)

Rev. Rul. 86-17, 1986-1 CB 377 (IRS authorizes blended rate)

$10,000 gift loan exception

IRC §7872 (c)(2)

Prop. Reg. §1.7872-8(b)

$100,000 gift loan exception

IRC §7872(d)

Prop. Reg. §1.7872-8(c)

$10,000 compensation-related loan exception

IRC §7872(c)(3)

4.32 MINIMUM INTEREST ON SELLER-FINANCED SALES

IRC §1274

IRC §1275

IRC §483

Reg. §1.1274-1 through §1.1274.7

Reg. §1.483-1 through §1.483-5

* IRS Publication 537

General rate required

IRC §1274A

Definitions and special rules

IRC §1275

Minimum interest rules not applicable to buyer of personal-use property

IRC §1275(b)

Which AFR rate applies to sales

Reg. §1.1274-6(e)

Reg. §1.483-4(d)

Timing of reporting under §483

Reg. §1.483-2(a)(ii)

Cash method election

IRC §1274A(C)

Rev. Proc. 2022-38, 2022-45 IRB 445 (inflation adjusted amount for 2023)

Rev. Proc. 2021-45, 2021-48 IRB 764 (inflation adjusted amount for 2022)

Rev. Proc. 2020-45, 2020-46 IRB 1016 (inflation adjusted amount for 2021)

Rev. Proc. 2019-44, 2019-47 IRB 1093 (inflation adjusted amount for 2020)

Rev. Proc. 2018-57, 2018-49 IRB 827 (inflation adjusted amount for 2019)

6% rate for land sales between related parties

IRC §483(e)

9% safe harbor

IRC §1274A(b)

Reg. §1.1274A-1

Inflation adjustment to seller-financed amount for safe harbor

IRC §1274A(d)(2)

Rev. Proc. 2022-38, 2022-45 IRB 445 (inflation adjusted amount for 2023)

Rev. Proc. 2021-45, 2021-48 IRB 764 (inflation adjusted amount for 2022)

Rev. Proc. 2020-45, 2020-46 IRB 1016 (inflation adjusted amount for 2021)

Rev. Proc. 2019-44, 2019-47 IRB 1093 (inflation adjusted amount for 2020)

Rev. Proc. 2018-57, 2018-49 IRB 827 (inflation adjusted amount for 2019)

5 REPORTING PROPERTY SALES

5.1 GENERAL TAX RULES FOR PROPERTY SALES

IRC §1(h)

* IRS Publication 544

Bitcoin treated like property

Notice 2014-21, 2014-16 IRB 938

5.2 HOW PROPERTY SALES ARE CLASSIFIED AND TAXED

IRC §1(h)

IRC §1221(capital asset defined)

IRC §1222 (short-term, long-term, net capital gain defined)

* IRS Publication 544

Down payment's tax treatment when a sale falls through

CRI-Leslie, LLC, 147 TC No. 8 (2016)

Self-created musical works

IRC §1221(b)(3)

5.3 CAPITAL GAINS RATES AND HOLDING PERIODS

IRC §1(h)

IRC §1222 (long-term, short-term net capital gain defined)

IRC §1223 (holding period)

Zero rate starting in 2008

IRC §1(h)(1)(B)

5.4 CAPITAL LOSSES AND CARRYOVERS

IRC §1211

IRC §1212

IRC §1222(10)

Reg. §1.1222-1

Taking a capital loss on property you don't own

Pamela Lynn Brooks, TC Memo 2013-141

Carryover loss if taxable income is negative

IRC §1212(b)(2)(B)

Loss must be considered even if no tax benefit is realized

Rev. Rul. 76-177, 1976-1 CB 224

Not deductible as a business expense

Frank Lester, 70 TMC 77 (1995)

5.5 CAPITAL LOSSES OF MARRIED COUPLES

One capital loss deduction on joint return

John E. Ross, 37 TC 445 (1961)

Reg. §1.1211-1(d)

Reg. §1.1211-1(c)

Surviving spouse may not use deceased spouse's loss carryover

* Letter Ruling 8510053

5.6 LOSSES MAY BE DISALLOWED ON SALES TO RELATED PERSONS

Nondeductible losses

IRC §267

Reg. §1.267(a)-1(a)

Bona fide

Reg. §1.267(a)-1(c)

Nathan Blum, 5 TC 702 (1945)

Stock exchange

John P. McWilliams, 331 U.S. 694 (1947)

John B. Shethar, 28 TC 1222 (1957)

Foreclose mortgage

Thomas Zacek, 8 TC 1056 (1947)

Pledgee's sale

Charles E. Cooney, 1 TCM 55 (1942)

Members of family

IRC §267(b)(1) and (c)(4)

Reg. §1.267(c)-1(a)(4)

Nominee

Charles J. Stamler, 45 BTA 37

O. Phil Nordling, 166 F.2d 703 (9th Cir. 1948), cert. denied, 337 U.S. 938

Wife's relative

J. Henry DeBoer, 194 F.2d 989 (2d Cir. 1952), (Nonacq.)

Son-in-law

Fervel Topek, 9 TC 763 (1947)

* Letter Ruling 9017008

Family hostility may not be considered

David L. Miller, 75 TC 182 (1980)

Withdrawal from joint ventures and partnerships

T. N. Mauritz, 205 F.2d 135 (5th Cir. 1953)

Fritz Busche, 229 F.2d 437 (5th Cir. 1956)

Henry V. B. Smith, 5 TC 323 (1945)

Controlled corporation

IRC §267

Reg. §1.267(b)-1

Reg. §1.267(c)-1

Other losses disallowed

IRC §267

Reg. §1.267(b)-1

Partnership and controlling persons

IRC §707(b)(1)(A)

Related party's profitable resale

IRC §267(d)

5.7 SPECIAL TREATMENT OF GAIN ON SALE OF SMALL BUSINESS STOCK OR QUALIFIED OPPORTUNITY ZONE INVESTMENT

IRC §1045 (rollover of gain from small business stock)

IRC §1202 (exclusion of gain)

IRC §1397B (rollover of empowerment zone asset gain)

IRC §1400 Z-1 (designation of qualified opportunity zones)

IRC §1400 Z-2 (deferral and possible exclusion for capital gains reinvested in qualified opportunity zones)

Notice 2018-48, 2018-28 IRB 9 (list of population census tracts designated by Secretary of Treasury as qualified opportunity zones)

* IRS Publication 550

Election on return required for Section 1045 rollover

Ralph E. Holmes, TC Memo 2012-25

Section1202 exclusion percentages

IRC §1202(a)(1)(50% for stock acquired before 2/18/09)

IRC §1202(a)(3) (75% for stock acquired after 2/17/09 and before 9/28/10)

IRC §1202(a)(4) (100% for stock acquired after 9/27/10)

Section 1202 exclusion doesn't apply to options

Sivatharan Natkunanathan, 2012-2 USTC ¶50,456 (9th Cir. 2012), aff'g TC Memo. 2010-15

5.8 REPORTING CAPITAL ASSET SALES ON FORM 8949 AND ON SCHEDULE D

* IRS Publication 544

Reporting capital gains and losses

IRC §1(h)

IRC §1222

* IRS Publication 544

Short-term and long-term transactions

IRC §1222

Capital losses

IRC §1211(b) and 1212(b)

IRC §62(a)(3)

5.9 COUNTING THE MONTHS IN YOUR HOLDING PERIOD

Long- and short-term capital gain or loss

IRC §1222

IRC §1223

Reg. §1.1222-1

Reg. §1.1223-1(a)

Exclude day asset acquired

Lewis Caspe, 694 F. 2d 1116 (8th Cir. 1982), aff'g 80-1 USTC ¶9201 (D.C. IA. 1980)

Holding period rules

IRC §1222

Futures transactions

IRC §1222

5.10 HOLDING PERIOD FOR SECURITIES

Stock exchange transactions

Rev. Rul. 72-381, 1972-2 CB 233

Rev. Rul. 70-598, 1970-2 CB 168

Installment sale not allowed for publicly traded stock

IRC §453(k)(2)

Stock subscriptions

Mayme C. Sommers, Admtrx., 63 F.2d 551 (10th Cir. 1933)

William J. Wineberg, 20 TCM 1715 (1961), aff'd, 326 F.2d 157 (9th Cir. 1964)

Exercise of rights

IRC §1223(5)(6)

Reg. §1.1223-1(f)

Rev. Rul. 56-572, 1956-2, CB 182

Different lots

Reg. §1.1223-1(i)

Employee stock option

John H. Rolfe, 58 TC 361 (1972), aff'd per curiam, 488 F.2d 1092 (9th Cir. 1974)

Commodity satisfaction of futures contract

IRC §1223(8)

Reg. §1.1223-1(h)

"When issued" transactions
I.T. 3721, 1945 CB 164, as modified by Rev. Rul. 57-29, 1957-1 CB 519

Wash sales
IRC §1223(4)

Reg. §1.1223-1(d)

5.11 HOLDING PERIOD FOR REAL ESTATE
Rev. Rul. 54-607, 1954-2 CB 177

New construction
M. A. Paul, 206 F.2d 763 (3d Cir. 1953)

Fred Draper, 32 TC 545 (1959) (Acq.)

Portion of building constructed within long-term holding period
Rev. Rul. 75-524, 1975-2 CB 342

5.12 HOLDING PERIOD: GIFTS, INHERITANCES, AND OTHER PROPERTY

Gift after 1920
IRC §1223(2)

Reg. §1.1223-1(b)

Donee's sale at loss
Rev. Rul. 59-86, 1959-1 CB 209

Automatic holding period of over one year for property acquired from decedent
IRC §1223(11)

Property purchased by executors
Marjorie K. Campbell, 313 U.S. 15 (1941)

Richard Van Nest Gambrill, 313 U.S. 11 (1941)

Distribution in kind from partnership
IRC §735(b)

Reg. §1.735-1

Involuntary conversion
IRC §1223(1)(A)

Reg. §1.1223-1(a)

5.13 CALCULATING GAIN OR LOSS

Gain or loss
IRC §1001

Reg. §1.1001-1 (amount realized)

Property basis cannot be increased by unsubstantiated improvements
Jovita Diaz, TC Memo 2012-241

5.14 AMOUNT REALIZED IS THE TOTAL SELLING PRICE

Selling price
Reg. §1.1001

IRC §1001

Mortgage included in price
Beulah B. Crane, 331 U.S. 1 (1947)

Property valued at less than mortgage
John F. Tufts, 456 U.S. 960 (1983)

Legal fee—cost of sale
Fred W. Gunn, 49 TC 38 (1967)

5.15 FINDING YOUR COST

Unadjusted basis
IRC §1012

Reg. §1.1012-1

Improvements
IRC §1016

Reg. §1.016-2

Adjusted basis
IRC §1011

Reg. §1.1011-1

Improvements not covered by note
Glenda P. McCormick, 99-1 USTC ¶50,380 (D. Tenn. 1999)

5.16 UNADJUSTED BASIS OF YOUR PROPERTY
* IRS Publication 551

Basis is cash cost
IRC §1012

Reg. §1.1012-1

Property subject to mortgage
Beulah B. Crane, 331 U.S. 1 (1947)

Adjusted cost after depreciation allowed
IRC §1016

Reg. §1.1016-3

Rendering services
Reg. §1.61-2

W. H. Weaver, 25 TC 1067 (1956)

Lawrence S. Vadner, 14 TCM 866 (1955)

Taxable exchange of property
Philadelphia Park Amusement Co., 126 F. Supp. 184 (Ct. Cl. 1954)

Rev. Rul. 56-100, 1956-1 CB 624

Tax-free exchange of property
IRC §1031

Reg. §1.1031(d)-1

Life estate or remainder interest
Reg. §1.1014-5

Sale of life estate—zero basis
IRC §1001(e)

Property subject to lease
Harriet M. Bryant Trust, 11 TC 374 (1948) (Acq.)

Distribution to settle claim
Rev. Rul. 55-117, 1955-1 CB 233

Compulsory or involuntary conversion
IRC §1033(b)

Distribution on orders of SEC
IRC §1081

Reg. §1.1081

Prenuptial agreement
Doris Farid-es-Sultaneh, 160 F.2d 812 (2d Cir. 1947), rev'g 6 TC 652 (1946)

Basis of new residence after home sale deferral
IRC §1034(e)

Reg. §1.1034-1

Dividends in property
IRC §301

Reg. §1.301-1

5.17 BASIS OF PROPERTY YOU INHERITED OR RECEIVED AS A GIFT
* "Basis of Property Acquired by Gifts," Katherine D. Black and Jeffrey N. Barnes, 82 Taxes 41 (November 2004)

IRC §1014

Reg. §1.1014-1

Reg. §1.1014-2

Heirs must report basis consistent with value reported by executor on estate tax return filed after July 31, 2015
IRC §1014 (f) (consistency requirement for heirs, as added by Surface Transportation and Veterans Health Choice Improvement Act of 2015, P.L. 114-41, 7/31/15)

IRC §6035 (executor reporting requirement, as added by Surface Transportation and Veterans Health Choice Improvement Act of 2015, P.L. 114-41, 7/31/15)

IRC §§6662(b)(8) and (k) (penalty on heirs for claiming inconsistent basis, as added by Surface Transportation and Veterans Health Choice Improvement Act of 2015, P.L. 114-41, 7/31/15)

T.D. 9757, 2016-12 IRB 462 (proposed regulations provide guidance on executor reporting and basis consistency rules)

Notice 2016-27, 2016-15 IRB 576 (IRS delays executor reporting to June 30, 2016)

Carryover basis election on Form 8939

Notice 2011-66, 2011-35 IRB 184

Rev. Proc. 2011-41, 2011-35 IRB 188

Foreign property

Rev. Rul. 84-139, 1984-2 CB 168

Gift tax paid increases basis

IRC §1015(d)(6)

Gift after December 31, 1920

IRC §1015

Reg. §1.1015-1

Inheritance of property transferred to decedent within one year of death

IRC §1014(e)

Estate tax value questioned

Sam F. McIntosh, 26 TCM 1164 (1967)

Right to buy deceased's property

J. Gordon Mack, 3 TC 390 (1944), aff'd 148 F.2d 62 (3d Cir. 1945), cert. denied, 326 U.S. 719

Distributions from trust

IRC §1015

Reg. §1.1015-2

IRC §643(e)

5.18 Joint Tenancy Basis Rules for Surviving Tenants

IRC §1014

Reg. §1.1014-2

IRC §2040(b)

* IRS Publication 551

* IRS Publication 559

Figuring basis of property inherited from spouse who died after 1981

IRC §2040(b)

Spousal joint tenancies created before 1977

M. Lee Gallenstein, 975 F.2d 286 (6th Cir. 1992)

Joy B. Patten, 116 F.3d 1029 (4th Cir. 1997)

Therese Hahn, 110 TC 1040 (1998) (Acq.)

5.19 Allocating Cost Among Several Assets

Apportionment of cost

Frederick Leake, 140 F.2d 451 (6th Cir. 1944), cert. denied, 323 U.S. 722

Nathan Blum, 5 TC 702 (1945)

Johnson Lumber Corp., 12 TC 348 (1949) (Acq.)

Fairfield Plaza, Inc., 39 TC 706 (1963) (Acq.)

Apportion land

McDonald, BTA Memo, P-H 41,409

Harlan E. McGregor, 14 TCM 897 (1955)

Sale of stock first bought

Reg. §1.1012-1(c)

A. F. Mack, 31 BTA 1149

5.20 How To Find Adjusted Basis

Improvements and betterments to property

IRC §1016

Reg. §1.1016-2

Edgar S. Appleby Est., 123 F.2d 700 (2d Cir. 1941)

Basis cannot be increased by unsubstantiated improvements

Jovita Diaz, TC Memo 2012-241

Improvements covered by note not included in basis

John W. Owen, 34 F. Supp. 2d 1071 (W.D. Tenn. 1998)

Commissions on security sales

Adolph B. Spreckles, 315 U.S. 626 (1942)

Carrying charges

IRC §1016

Reg. §1.1016-2

Personal residence

Isaiah Megibow, 218 F.2d 687 (3d Cir. 1955)

Purchaser's share of real estate tax

IRC §164(d)

Reg. §1.164-6

Unharvested crops

IRC §1016(a)(11)

Reg. §1.1016-5(g)

Demolition cost

Reg. §1.165-3

Edgar S. Appleby Est., 123 F.2d 700 (2d Cir. 1941)

Deduction from basis

IRC §1016

Reg. §1.1016-1 through 8

Return of capital

IRC §1010(a)(4)

Reg. §1.1016-5(a)(1-2)

Casualty loss

IRC §1016(a)(1)

Pasquale Colabella, 17 TCM 704 (1958)

Wrap fees cannot be added to basis of securities

*Chief Counsel Advice 200721015

Depletion allowances

IRC §1016(a)(2)

Reg. §1.1016-3 and 4

Depreciation, amortization, obsolescence

IRC §1016(a)(2)

Reg. §1.1016-3 and 4

Rev. Proc. 97-37, 1997-33 IRB 18 (adjustment for unclaimed depreciation in a closed year)

5.21 Tax Advantage of Installment Sales

IRC §453

* IRS Publication 537

Depreciation recapture

IRC §453(i)

Not applicable to year-end sale of securities

IRC §453(k)(2)

Farmer who does not inventory

Temp. Reg. §15A.453-1(b)(4)

Not applicable to sale of inventory

Andrew A. Monaghan, 40 TC 680 (1963) (Acq.)

IRC §453(6)(2)(B)

Crispo Gallery Inc., 2nd Cir. (6/13/96)

Not applicable to building contractor

Rev. Rul. 73-438, 1973-2 CB 156

Dealers

IRC §453(b)(2)

Timeshares and residential lots

IRC §453(1)(2) and (1)(3)

5.22 Figuring the Taxable Part of Installment Payments

Selling price

Temp. Reg. §15A.453-1(b)(2)(ii)

Contract price

Temp. Reg. §15A.453-1(b)(2)(iii)

Payments received

Temp. Reg. §15A.453-1(b)(3)

Gross profit

Temp. Reg. §15A.453-1(b)(2)(v)

Wraparound mortgages

Temp. Reg. §15A.453-1(b)(3)(ii)

Tax Court rejects IRS wraparound regs.

Professional Equities, Inc., 89 TC 165 (1987) (Acq.)

5.33 Tax Consequences of Bad Debts

Non-business bad debt for unpaid business-related loans

Harry Robert Haury, No. 13–1780 (8th Cir., 2014)

Business bad debt

IRC §166

Reg. §1.166-1

* IRS Publication 535

Michael J. Burke, TC Memo 2018-18

Debt worthless after termination of business

IRC §166(d)(2)(A)

Reg. §1.166-5

Sell merchandise on credit

Reg. §1.166-6

No deduction for unpaid account receivable

Lawrence Washburn, 61 TCM 2529 (1991)

Business of investing or making loans

Allerton Cushman, 148 F. Supp. 880 (D. Ariz. 1956)

L. Washburn, 51 F.2d 949 (8th Cir. 1931)

Hyman R. Minkoff, 15 TCM 1404 (1956)

Morris H. Cone Estate, 13 TCM 512 (1954)

Sell your business

Reg. §1.166-5(d)(6)

Promoter

Vincent C. Campbell, 11 TC 510 (1948) (Acq.)

Loan to maintain business reputation

Wilfred J. Funk, 35 TC 42 (1960) (Acq.)

Stuart Bart, 21 TC 880 (1954) (Acq.)

Loan to insure merchandise delivery

Robert Haverty Est., 12 TCM 1295 (1953)

J. T. Dorminey, 26 TC 940 (1956) (Acq.)

Loan to controlled corporation to further business

Lawrence M. Weil Est., 29 TC 366 (1957) (Acq.)

Nonbusiness debt

IRC §166(d)

IRC §1211

Reg. §1.166-5

Reg. §1.1211-1

Guarantors

Reg. §1.166-9

Reg. §1.1211-1

Personal advances

Gifford A. Cochran, 14 TCM 206 (1955)

Attorney's loan to client

Robert H. McNeil, 251 F.2d 863 (4th Cir. 1958)

Payment of another's taxes

Albert Gersten, 28 TC 756 (1957) (Acq.), aff'd in part, rev'd in part on other issues, 267 F.2d 195 (9th Cir. 1959)

Payment of joint tax by spouse

Frank R. Haynes, 27 TCM 1531 (1968)

Loss of deposit

Rev. Rul. 69-457, 1969-2 CB 32

Dominant motive test

Edna Generes, 405 U.S. 93 (1972)

Loan by shareholder-employees to protect job

Edna Generes, 405 U.S. 93 (1972), rev'g 427 F.2d 279 (5th Cir. 1970)

Kenneth W. Graves, TC Memo 2004-140

Harry Litwin, 983 F.2d 997 (10th Cir. 1993)

Donald C. Niblock, Jr., 417 F.2d 1185 (7th Cir. 1969)

James O. Gould, 64 TC 132 (1975)

Odee Smith, 55 TC 260 (1970), vacated and rem'd per curiam, 457 F.2d 797 (5th Cir. 1972), on rem'd 60 TC 316 (1973) (Acq.)

Lawrence J. Doerfler, 36 TCM 789 (1977)

William G. Young, 33 TCM 397 (1974)

Loans to corporations

Charles Kadlec, 71 TCM 2399 (1996) (closely held corporation)

Donald C. Van Pelt, 191 F.2d 861 (6th Cir. 1951)

Janet McBride, 23 TC 926 (1955) (Acq.)

Weldon D. Smith, 17 TC 135 (1951), rev'd, 203 F.2d 310 (2d Cir. 1953), cert. denied, 346 U.S. 816

Sam Schaltzer, 13 TC 43 (1949) (Acq.), aff'd per curiam, 183 F.2d 70 (9th Cir. 1950), cert. denied, 340 U.S. 911

Rev. Rul. 60-48, 1960-1 CB 112

Unpaid stockholder loans to corporation

A. J. Whipple, 373 U.S. 193 (1963) (nonbusiness bad debt for payment to protect investment)

Stockholder loan to key employee deductible

Charles W. Carter, 39 TCM 456 (1979)

5.34 Four Rules To Prove a Bad Debt Deduction

Advances to insolvent corporation

W. F. Young, Inc., 120 F.2d 159 (1st Cir. 1941)

Advances repaid only if profit is shown

Lucia C. Ewing, 20 TC 216 (1953), aff'd, 213 F.2d 438 (2d Cir. 1954)

Usurious loan

William K. Harriman, 26 TCM 941 (1967)

Usurious loan as a business loss

Herbert E. Tharp, 31 TCM 22 (1972)

Debtor-creditor relationship

Kentucky Rock Asphalt Co., 108 F.2d 779 (6th Cir. 1940)

W. M. Robertson, 7 TCM 62 (1948)

Loan included in income

IRC §166

Reg. §1.166-1

Consulting engineer

Jack Shapiro, 20 TCM 579 (1961)

Worthless during year

IRC §166

Reg. §1.166-1

Bankruptcy by court order

Reg. §1.166-2(c)

Final liquidation dividend

Leedom & Worrall Co., 10 BTA 825

First National Bank of Los Angeles, 6 BTA 850 (Acq.)

Corporation liquidation resolution

Pantex Oil Corp., 8 TCM 1079 (1949)

Disappearance of debtor

Fridolin Pabst, 36 F.2d 614 (D.C. Cir. 1930)

Debtor's refusal to pay

Philip C. Hughes, 10 TCM 204 (1951)

Revocation of corporate charter

Leila S. Kirby, 35 BTA 578 (Acq. and nonacq.), aff'd in part, rev'd in part, 102 F.2d 115 (5th Cir. 1939)

Cancelled debt

Nathan Fink, 29 TC 1119 (1958) (Acq.)

No hope of later value

American Trust Co., 31 F.2d 47 (9th Cir. 1939), aff'g 10 BTA 490

Alemite Die Casting & Manufacturing Co., 1 BTA 548

Debt worthless before due

Clarence Bonynge, 117 F.2d 157 (2d Cir. 1941)

Statute of limitations has run

Ralph H. Cross, 54 F.2d 781 (9th Cir. 1932)

Leo Stein, 4 BTA 1016

Statute ran before death

Clara Burdette, 69 F.2d 410 (9th Cir. 1934)

Debt guaranteed by collateral

John Hubble, 42 TCM 1537 (1981)

Release an endorser

Reg. §1.166-8

Eleanor A. Bradford, 22 TC 1057 (1954), rev'd, 233 F.2d 935 (6th Cir. 1956)

Breach of contract

Zelma T. Kyle, 242 F.2d 825 (2d Cir. 1957)

Less than full payment

Edgar H. Gleason, Jr., 62 TCM 600 (1991)

Embezzled funds

Reg.§ 1.165-8

5.35 FAMILY BAD DEBTS

Reg. §1.166-1

Defaulted support payment

Carolyn Perry, 92 TC 470 (1989) (reaffirms Swenson)

Dale Swenson, 43 TC 897 (1965)

Shirley S. Imeson, 487 F.2d 319 (9th Cir. 1973), aff'g per curiam 28 TCM 899 (1969), cert. denied, 418 U.S. 917

Rev. Rul. 93-27, 1993 CB 32 (IRS rejects Ninth Circuit's possible deduction arguments)

M. J. Williford, 34 TCM 354 (1975)

Loans to family

Loy Bowman, 69 TCM 286 (1995)

Myer B. Barr, 77 TCM 1370 (1999)

6 TAX-FREE EXCHANGES OF PROPERTY

6.1 LIKE-KIND EXCHANGES OF REAL PROPERTY USED FOR INVESTMENT OR BUSINESS

IRC §1031(a) (1), as amended by the Tax Cuts and Jobs Act, limiting like-kind treatment to real estate for exchanges completed after 2017

* IRS Publication 544

What is real property?

T.D. 9935 (November 2020)

Personal use safe harbor for tax deferred exchange

Rev. Proc. 2008-16, 2008-10 IRB 547

Exchange solely for like-kind property

IRC §1031(a)

Reg. §1.1031(a)-1

Wittig, 70 TCM 824 (withdrawn 11/9/95)

Must be used in trade or business or for investment

IRC §1031(a)

Reg. §1.1031(a)-1

Depreciable equipment on which there is potential gain

IRC §1245(b)(3)

Farm for city property

L. M. Dyke, 1 BTA Memo 32-157

E. R. Braley, 14 BTA 1153 (Acq.)

Farms exchanged

Rev. Rul. 59-229, 1959-2 CB 180

Exchange of ownership interest in realty for 30-year leasehold

Reg. §1.1031(a)-1(c)

Rev. Rul. 78-72, 1978-1 CB 258

Land for water rights

Rev. Rul. 55-749, 1955-2 CB 295, distinguished by Rev. Rul. 67-255, 1967-2 CB 270

Exchange of partnership interests

IRC §1031(e)

Rollin E. Meyers, Sr., Est., 503 F.2d 556 (9th Cir. 1974), aff'g per curiam, 58 TC 311 (1972) (Nonacq.)

Reg. §1.1031(a)-1(a) and (e)

Timber rights

Oregon Lumber Co., 20 TC 192 (1953) (Acq.)

U.S. and foreign real estate not "like kind"

IRC §1031(h)

6.2 RECEIPT OF CASH AND OTHER PROPERTY—"BOOT"

Boot is taxed

IRC §1031(b)

Reg. §1.1031(b)-1

No loss recognized if boot given

IRC §1031(c) and (d)

Reg. §1.1031(c)-1 and (d)-1

Mortgage release is boot

Reg. §1031(d)-2

Beulah B. Crane, 331 U.S. 1 (1947)

Wittig, 70 TCM 824 (withdrawn 11/9/95)

Basis of property received

Reg. §1.1031(d)-2

Exclusion plus gain deferral on exchange of residence

Rev. Proc. 2005-14, 2005-7 IRB 528

6.3 TIME LIMITS AND SECURITY ARRANGEMENTS FOR DEFERRED EXCHANGES

Time limits

IRC §1031(a)(3)

Reg. §1.1031(k)-1(b)

Identifying replacement property

Reg. §1.1031(k)-1(c) and (d)

Safe harbors for security arrangements

Reg. §1.1031(k)-1(g)

Safe harbor if qualified intermediary defaults

Rev. Proc. 2010-14, 2010-12 IRB 456

Direct deed transfer

Rev. Rul. 90-34, 1990-1 CB 154

Like-kind exchange tax deferral allowed despite moving into replacement property

Patrick A. Reesink, TC Memo 2012-118

Escrow accounts—final regs

Reg. §1.7872-5 (b) (16)

Tax-deferred exchange fails without restrictive escrow account

*Ralph E. Crandall, TC Summary Opinion 2011-14

6.4 QUALIFIED EXCHANGE ACCOMMODATION ARRANGEMENTS (QEAAs) FOR REVERSE EXCHANGES

Safe-harbor tests for reverse exchanges

Rev. Proc. 2000-37, 2000-40 IRB 308

Restriction on "parking" safe harbor

Rev. Proc. 2004-51, 2004-33 IRB 294

6.5 EXCHANGES BETWEEN RELATED PARTIES

IRC §1031(f)

Two-year freeze on exchange with related party

IRC §1031(f)

Prearranged plans

IRC §1031(f)(4)

6.6 PROPERTY TRANSFERS BETWEEN SPOUSES AND EX-SPOUSES

IRC §1041

Temp. Reg. §1.041-IT

Sale of business interest to ex-spouse not taxable

Joseph R. Belot, TC Memo 2016-113

Final regulations: divorce-related stock redemptions

Reg. §1.1041-2 (tax-free treatment for transferor conditional on constructive distribution for non-transferor)

Divorce-related stock redemption is tax free

Joann C. Arnes, 981 F.2d 456 (9th Cir. 1993)

John A. Arnes, 102 TC 20 (1994)

Carol M. Read, 114 TC 14 (2000)

Linda Craven, 215 F.3d 1201 (11th Cir. 2000)

Divorce-related stock redemption is taxable

Gloria T. Blatt, 102 TC 5 (1994)

* Letter Ruling 9427009

Divorce transfer of nonqualified options

Rev. Rul. 2004-60, 2004-24 IRB 1051

Rev. Rul. 2002-22, 2002-19 IRB 849

Readjustment of property settlement

Louise F. Young, 2001-1 USTC ¶50,244 (4th Cir. 2001)

Cash paid for house transfer in property settlement

Michael J. Godlewski, 90 TC 200 (1988)

Nonresident spouses

IRC §1041(a)

Transfer of savings bonds

Rev. Rul. 87-112, 1987-2 CB 207

Gain realized on transfer in trust

IRC §1041(e)

Temp. Reg. §1.1041-1T

Divorce-related exchange of marital rights is tax free

* Letter Ruling 200442003

Tax-free transfer for relinquishment of community property right to retirement pay

Hazel E. Balding, 98 TC 368 (1992)

Divorced wife taxed on sale of business

Vincent Yonadi, 21 F.3d 1292 (1994)

6.7 TAX-FREE EXCHANGES OF STOCK IN SAME CORPORATION

Tax-free exchange of stock for stock in same company

IRC §1036

Reg. §1.1036-1

Recapitalization is a type of reorganization

IRC §368(a)(1)(E)

Reg. §1.368-2(e)

Stock dividends and stock rights

IRC §305(a)

6.8 JOINT OWNERSHIP INTERESTS

Exchange of tenants in common

Rev. Rul. 73-476, 1973-2 CB 300

Joint tenancy and tenancy in common

Rev. Rul. 56-437, 1956-2 CB 507

Boot not offset by assumption of liability

Rev. Rul. 79-44, 1979-1 CB 265

6.9 SETTING UP CLOSELY HELD CORPORATIONS

IRC §351

Securities as boot

IRC §351(a)

6.10 TAX-FREE EXCHANGES OF INSURANCE POLICIES

Tax-free exchanges

IRC §1035

Reg. §1.1035-1

Tax-free exchange of policy from financially troubled insurer

Rev. Proc. 92-44, 1992-1 CB 875, amplified by Rev. Proc. 92-44A

Partial tax-free exchange of annuity contracts

Rev. Proc. 2011-38, 2011-30 IRB 66 (transfers after 10-23-11)

Rev. Proc. 2008-24, 2008–1 C.B. 684 (transfers before 10-24-11)

Dona Conway, 111 TC 350 (1998), Acq. 1999-2 CB xvi

Tax-free exchange of key executive policy

Rev. Rul. 90-109, 1990-2 CB 191

Endorsement of annuity check for another annuity is taxable

Rev. Rul. 2007-24, 2007-21 IRB 1282

7 RETIREMENT AND ANNUITY INCOME

7.1 RETIREMENT DISTRIBUTIONS ON FORM 1099-R

* IRS Publication 575

Uncashed distribution check from qualified retirement plan is taxable

Rev. Proc. 2019-19, 2019-36 IRB 674

Companies may not limit ex-employees' investments

Rev. Rul. 96-47, 1996-2 CB 35

State's ability to tax pension income limited

P.L. 104-95 (1/10/96)

Waiver of pension benefits taxable

Alfred Gallade, 106 TC 20 (1996)

7.2 LUMP-SUM DISTRIBUTIONS

Sections 1122(h)(3) and (5) of the Tax Reform Act of 1986 (P.L. 99-514)

* IRS Publication 575

Qualified plans

IRC §401

Employer must withhold 20% tax on lump sum

IRC §3405(c)

Computation of averaging

Reg. §1.402(e)-2(d)

Five-year participation test for 10-year averaging

Reg. §1.402(e)-2(e)(3)

Averaging barred by post-2001 rollover to same plan

Section 641(f)(3) of EGTRRA 2001

7.3 LUMP-SUM OPTIONS IF YOU WERE BORN BEFORE JANUARY 2, 1936

Employer must withhold 20% tax on lump sum

IRC §3405(c)

Irrevocability of rollover election

Temp. Reg. §1.402(a)(5)-1T (Q&A-4)

Lump-sum treatment denied on retroactive revocation of plan qualification

John V. Fazi, 102 TC 31 (1994) (Tax Court will no longer follow its Baetens decision and will follow appeals courts)

Curtis B. Woodson, 73 TC 779 (1980), rev'd, 651 F.2d 1094 (5th Cir. 1981)

Theodore L. Baetens, 82 TC 152 (1984), rev'd, 777 F.2d 1160 (6th Cir. 1985)

Donald L. Benbow, 82 TC 941 (1984), rev'd, 774 F.2d 740 (7th Cir. 1985)

Partial lump-sum treatment on retroactive plan disqualification

Harold D. Greenwald, 366 F.2d 538 (2d Cir. 1982)

Making a partial rollover bars averaging

Sanford O. Barnes, Jr., 67 TCM 2341 (1994)

Averaging election must apply to all eligible lump sums received in same year

Robert O. Fowler, 98 TC 503 (1992)

10-year averaging if born before 1936

P.L. 99-514 (1986 Tax Reform Act), Act Section 1122(h)(3) and (h)(5)

One lifetime election for averaging

IRC §402(e)(4)(B)

Taxable portion

IRC §402(a)(1)

Prop. Reg. §1.402(a)-1(a)(9)(b)

IRC §402(e)(4)(D)

Prop. Reg. §1.402(c)-2(d)(2)

Community property

Prop. Reg. §1.402-2(e)(2)

Electing 20% capital gain treatment if born before 1936

P.L. 99-415 (1986 Tax Reform Act), Act Section 1122(h)(3) and (h)(6)

7.4 LUMP-SUM PAYMENTS RECEIVED BY BENEFICIARY

IRC §402(e)(4)(A)(i)

Richard Gunnison, 461 F.2d 496 (7th Cir. 1972), aff'g 54 TC 1766 (1970)

Robert A. Stefanowski Est., 63 TC 386 (1974)

Five-year participation of employee not required

Reg. §1.402(e)-2(e)(3)

Beneficiary does not have to meet age test but deceased employee does

Mary E. Cebula, 101 TC 5 (1993)

Capital gain treatment

Prop. Reg. §1.403(a)-2(b)

Reg. §1.402(e)-2(d)

Up-to-$5,000 death benefit exclusion

IRC §101(b)

Distribution to trust or estate

Reg. §1.402(c)-3

Reg. §1.402(e)-2(e)(6)

7.5 TAX-FREE ROLLOVERS FROM QUALIFIED PLANS

* IRS Publication 575

Rollover of distributions

IRC §402(c)

Plan may allow immediate distributions of segregated rollovers

Rev. Rul. 2004-12, 2004-7 IRB 478

20% withholding if plan does not make direct rollover

IRC §3405(c)

Tax-sheltered annuity rollover

IRC §403(b)(8)

IRC §408(d)(3)(A)(iii)

Employer required to explain options

IRC §402(f)

Reg. §1.402(f)-1

Notice 2002-3, 2002-2 IRB 289 (IRS model notice)

Rollover treatment disallowed for minimum required distributions

IRC §402(c)(4)(B)

IRC §408(d)(3)(E)

Hardship distributions from 401(k) or 403(b) plan cannot be rolled over

IRC §402(c)(4)(c)

IRC §403(b)(8)(B)

Distribution under qualified domestic relations order (QDRO) to spouse or ex-spouse may be rolled over

IRC §402(e)(1)

7.6 DIRECT ROLLOVER OR PERSONAL ROLLOVER

* IRS Publication 575

20% withholding if plan does not make direct rollover

IRC §3405(c)

Taxable rollover to Roth IRA

IRC §408A(e)

Conduit IRAs

IRC §408(d)(3)(A)(ii)

Plan may allow immediate distributions of segregated rollovers

Rev. Rul. 2004-12, 2004-7 IRB 478

Commingled IRA funds prevent conduit rollover treatment

* Letter Ruling 9604028

Waiver on equitable grounds of 60-day rollover deadline

Rev. Proc. 2016-47, 2016-37 IRB 346 (self-certification procedure for getting waiver)

Rev. Proc. 2003-16, 2003-4 IRB 359 (automatic waiver if institution error and letter ruling procedure for requesting waiver)

IRS refuses extension of 60-day IRA rollover period

* Letter Ruling 201227011

Distribution of life insurance

Rev. Rul. 81-275, 1981-2 CB 75

Extension of 60-day period for frozen assets

IRC §402(c)(7)

Rollover by surviving spouse

IRC §402(c)(9)

Section 641(f)(3) of EGTRRA 2001 (averaging barred for amounts rolled over by surviving spouse after 2001 to same plan)

Nonspouse beneficiary may make rollover to inherited IRA

IRC §402(c)(11)(A), as amended by the Worker, Retiree, and Employer Recovery Act of 2008

Diversification of rollover permitted

Rev. Rul. 79-265, 1979-2 CB 186

7.7 ROLLOVER OF PROCEEDS FROM SALE OF PROPERTY

Rollover of sales proceeds

IRC §402(a)(6)(D)

Designation of cash

IRC §402(a)(6)(D)(iii)(II)

Designation of employee contributions

IRC §402(a)(6)(D)(iii)(I)

Allocation methods

IR-2086, February 6, 1979

7.8 DISTRIBUTION OF EMPLOYER STOCK OR OTHER SECURITIES

* IRS Publication 575

Unrealized appreciation due to employee's contributions

IRC §402(e)(4)

Reg. §1.402(a)-1(b)

Reg. §1.402(a)-1(a)(9)(B)

Unrealized appreciation due to employer's contributions

IRC §402(e)(4)

Reg. §1.402(a)-1(b)

Reg. §1.402(a)-1(a)(9)(B)

Reg. §1.401(e)-2(d)(2)

Waiving tax-free treatment

IRC §402(e)(4)(B)

Shares valued below your cost

Rev. Rul. 71-251, 1971-1 CB 129, amplified by Rev. Rul. 72-15, 1972-1 CB 114

Worthless shares

Rev. Rul. 72-328, 1972-8 CB 224

Holding period

Reg. §1.402(a)-1(b)

Holding period for post-distribution appreciation

Rev. Rul. 81-122, 1981-1 CB 202

Distribution other than lump sum

Reg. §1.402(a)-1(b)(3)

Reg. §1.402(a)-1(a)(9)(b)

Unrealized appreciation affects pro rata recovery for non-lump sum

Notice 89-25, 1989-1 CB 662

NUA attributable to employee contributions immediately taxed on rollover of partial distributions

IRC §402(a)(5)(D)(iv)

Electing to include NUA in income

Notice 89-25, 1989-1 CB 662

7.9 SURVIVOR ANNUITY FOR SPOUSE

IRC §401(a)(11)(QJSA and QPSA are plan qualification requirements)

Temporary relief to permit remote signatures

Notice 2020-42, 2020-26 IRB 986

IRS guidance on employee benefit plans for same-sex couples

Notice 2015-86, 2015-52 IRB 887

Survivor annuity requirements

IRC §417

Reg. §1.417(e)-1

Reg. §1.401(a)-1(a) and §1.401(a)-

20 questions and answers

Notice 94-23, 1994-1 CB 340

Involuntary cashouts

IRC §417(e)

7.10 COURT DISTRIBUTIONS TO FORMER SPOUSE UNDER A QDRO

Ex-spouse taxed on 401(k) divorce distribution

Gina B. Weaver-Adams, TC Memo 2014-73

Employer plan distribution used for alimony subject to early distribution penalty

Charles L. Hartley, TC Memo 2012-311

Husband's workers' comp. exclusion not available to wife after divorce

Shannon L. Fernandez, 138 TC No. 20 (2012)

QDRO defined

IRC §414(p)

Averaging

IRC §402(d)(4)(J)

Spouse treated as payee

IRC §402(e)(1)(A)

Marcia Fraser, 56 F.3d 722 (6th Cir. 1995)

Rollover allowed by spouse

IRC §402(e)(1)(B)

Husband taxed on QDRO distribution

Robert L. Karem, 100 TC 34 (1993)

7.11 WHEN YOU MUST BEGIN RECEIVING REQUIRED MINIMUM DISTRIBUTIONS (RMDs)

IRC §401 (a) (9)

Reg. §§ 1.401(a)(9)-1 through (a)(9)-9 (pre-SECURE Act final regulations, T.D. 8987, 2002-19 IRB 852)

* IRS Publication 575

Waiver of required minimum distribution for 2020 (CARES Act)

IRC §401(a)(9) (I), added by Section 2203 (a) of the CARES Act

Notice 2020-51, 2020-29 IRB 73

Required beginning date age increased to 72 (SECURE Act)

IRC §401(a)(9)(C)(i) (I), as amended by Section 114 of the SECURE Act (Division O of P.L. 116-94, 12-20-2019)

Required beginning date age increased to 73 to 75 (SECURE 2.0 Act)

IRC §401(a)(9)(C)(i) (I), as amended by Section 302 of the SECURE 2.0 Act (P.L. 117-328, 12-29-2022)

All employees subject to 5% owner rule

Reg. §1.401(a)(9)-2 (Q&A-2(e))

Required beginning date for 403(b) annuities

IRC §403(b)(10)

Distribution methods

IRC §401(a)(9)(A) and (B)

Reg. §1.401(a)(9)-1, 5 and -9

Penalty for not receiving minimum distributions

IRC §4974(a), as amended by Section 107 of the SECURE 2.0 Act (P.L. 117-328, 12-29-2022)

Governmental and church plans

IRC §401(a)(9)(C)(iv)

No RMD required for active partner

* Letter Ruling 200524032

7.12 PAYOUTS TO BENEFICIARIES

IRC §401 (a) (9)

Reg. §1.401(a)(9)-4, -5, -8, and -9 (pre-SECURE Act)

* IRS Publication 575

Determining designated beneficiaries

Reg. §1.401(a)(9)-4

Distribution period for beneficiaries

Reg. §1.401(a)(9)-5 (Q&A-5)(pre-SECURE Act)

Beneficiaries of participants dying after 2019 (SECURE Act)

IRC §401 (a) (9) (H), added by Section 401 of the SECURE Act (Division O of P.L. 116-94, 12-20-2019)

Ex-spouse beneficiary gets 401(k) benefits

Donna Rae Egelhoff, U.S. Supreme Court, 3/21/01

Nonspouse beneficiary may make rollover to inherited IRA

IRC §402(c)(11)

7.13 PENALTY FOR DISTRIBUTIONS BEFORE AGE 59½

IRC §72(t)

Penalty exception for qualified birth or adoption distribution(SECURE Act)

IRC §72(t) (2) (H), added by Section 113 of the SECURE Act (Division O of P.L. 116-94, 12-20-19)

Notice 2020-68, 2020-38 IRB 567

Diabetes isn't disability for 10% penalty exception

*Charles D. Trainito, TC Summary Opinion 2015-37

Disabled retiree subject to early distribution penalty

Kathleen Susan Stipe, TC Memo 2011-92

Is the added tax cost of early distribution a penalty or a tax?

Ralim S. El, 144 TC No. 9 (2015)

Early retirement plan distribution costly

*David C. Matthews, TC Summary Opinion 2014-84

Unsubstantiated medical costs not sufficient to avoid an early distribution penalty

William K. McGraw, TC Memo 2013-152

Penalty exceptions

IRC §72(t)(2)

Penalty exception for qualified reservists

IRC §72(t)(2)(G)

Penalty exception for qualified public safety employees

IRC §72(t)(10)

No penalty exception for distribution after Hurricane Ike

*Jeffrey S. Carter, TC Summary Opinion, 2012-33

Long-term depression requiring hospitalization qualifies for disability exception

* Mary L. Coleman-Stephens, TC Summary Opinion 2003-91

Penalty exception for separating from service after age 55

*Gail Marie Watson, TC Summary Opinion 2011-113

Age 55 penalty exception not available after IRA rollover

Young Kim, 2012-1 USTC ¶50,340 (7th Cir. 2012)

No penalty exception for financial hardship

Eugene Dollander, TC Memo 2009-187

Candice Elaine, TC Memo 2017-

7.14 RESTRICTIONS ON LOANS FROM COMPANY PLANS

IRC §72(p)

Reg. §1.72(p)-1

COVID-19-related loans from company plans

Section 2202 (b) of the CARES Act (P.L. 116-136, 3-27-2020)

Notice 2020-50, 2020-28 IRB 35

Loan relief for victims of qualified disasters

Section 202 of the Taxpayer Certainty and Disaster Tax Relief Act of 2019 (Division Q of P.L. 116-94, 12-20-2019)

*IRS Publication 976

Extended rollover period for plan loan offset amounts

IRC §402(c)(3) (C), added by the Tax Cuts and Jobs Act (P.L. 115-97, 12/22/2017)

50% security cap

Labor Dept. Reg. 2550.408(b)-1

Demand loan taxed

Thomas Gray Estate, 70 TCM 556 (1995)

Balloon loan taxed

Clayton W. Plotkin, TC Memo 2001-71

Unpaid loan at separation from service

Notice 93-3, 1993-3 IRB 11

*Letter Ruling 200617037 (rollover of outstanding loan balance avoids taxable distribution)

Spousal consent

IRC §417(a)(4)

Notice 2021-40, 2021-28 IRB 15 (remote witnessing permitted through June 30, 2022)

Interest deduction limitations

IRC §72(p)(3)

Residence used as loan collateral

* Letter Ruling 8933018

7.15 TAX BENEFITS OF 401(K) PLANS

Automatic 401(k) enrollment

Rev. Proc. 2015-28, 2015-16 IRB 920 (self-correction program)

IRC §401(k)(13) (nondiscrimination tests)

Preapproved plan amendments for automatic enrollment

Notice 2009-65, 2009-39 IRB 413

Automatic annual increase of employee contributions

Rev. Rul. 2009-30, 2009-39 IRB 391

Plan qualification requirement: Plan must limit deferrals to 402(g) ceiling

IRC §401(a)(30)

Qualified cash or deferred arrangements

IRC §401(k)

Reg. §1.401(k)-1

Roth 401(k) option

IRC §402A

Reg. §1.401(k)-1(f) (Treasury Decision 9237, 12/30/05)

Reg. §§ 1.402 A-1, A-2 and A-10 (distributions)

Notice 2006-44, 2006-20 IRB 889 (IRS sample plan amendment)

IRS approves automatic 401(k) plan coverage

Rev. Rul. 98-30, 1998-25 IRB 8

Nondiscrimination rules

IRC §401(k)(3)

SIMPLE 401(k) satisfies nondiscrimination tests

IRC §401(k)(11)

Tax-exempt organizations may set up 401(k) plans

IRC §401(k)(4)(B)

Employees not taxed on contribution of excess vacation pay to 401(k) plan

* Letter Ruling 200311043

Partnership plans

Reg. §1.401(k)-1(a)(6)

Rev. Proc. 91-47, 1991-2 CB 757

7.16 LIMIT ON SALARY-REDUCTION DEFERRALS

Annual limits on elective deferrals and "catch-up" contributions

IRC §402(g)(1)

Notice 2022-55, 2022-45 IRB 443 (deferral limits for 2023)

Notice 2021-61, 2021-47 IRB 738 (deferral limits for 2022)

Notice 2020-79, 2020-46 IRB 1014 (deferral limits for 2021)

Notice 2019-59, 2019-47 IRB 1091 (deferral limits for 2020)

Notice 2018-83, 2018-47 IRB 774 (deferral limits for 2019)

"Catch-up" contributions if age 50 or older

IRC §414(v)

One-time election

Reg. §1.401(k)-1(a)(3)(iv)

Nondiscrimination rules

IRC §401(k)(3)

IRC §401(k)(12)

7.17 WITHDRAWALS FROM 401(K) PLANS RESTRICTED

IRC §401(k)(2)(B)

T.D. 9875, 2019-41 IRB 856 (final regulations on hardship distributions, effective 9/23/19)

Credit card debt as a hardship

* Chief Counsel INFO 2015-0003

Qualified reservist distributions

IRC §401(k)(2)(B)(i)(V)

Hardship distributions ineligible for rollover

IRC §402(c)(4)

IRS may not levy 401(k) account until employee retires

* IRS Legal Memorandum 200032004

7.18 DESIGNATED ROTH ACCOUNT WITHIN 401(K), 403(B), OR GOVERNMENTAL 457 PLANS

Roth 401(k) option

IRC §402A

Reg. §1.401(k)-1(f)

Reg. §1.403(b)-3(c)

Reg. §§ 1.402A-1, A-2 and A-10 (distributions)

Notice 2006-44, 2006-20 IRB 889 (IRS sample plan amendment)

In-plan rollover to designated Roth account

IRC §402A(c)(4), as added by the Small Business Jobs Act of 2010, P.L. 111-240, 9/27/10

Notice 2013-74, 2013-52 IRB 819

7.19 403(B) Plans (tax-sheltered annuity plans) for Employees of Tax-Exempts and Schools and Ministers

IRC §403(b)

* IRS Publication 571

Salary-reduction limit

IRC §402(g)(3)(c)

IRC §401(a)(30) (plan qualification requirement)

Notice 2022-55, 2022-45 IRB 443 (deferral limits for 2023)

Notice 2021-61, 2021-47 IRB 738 (deferral limits for 2022)

Notice 2020-79, 2020-46 IRB 1014 (deferral limits for 2021)

Notice 2019-59, 2019-47 IRB 1091 (deferral limits for 2020)

Notice 2018-83, 2018-47 IRB 774 (deferral limits for 2019)

Up-to-$3,000 annual exclusion for health insurance premiums of public safety officers

IRC §402(1)

Employer may automatically enroll employees in 403(b) plan

Rev. Rul. 2000-35, 2000-31 IRB 138

One-time election

IRC §402(g)(3)

Increased salary-reduction limit for 15-year employees

IRC §402(g)(7)

Rollovers

IRC §403(b)(8)

Contribution limit for year of separation from service

IRC §415(c)(4)(A)

7.20 Government and Exempt Organization Deferred Pay Plans

Federal thrift plans

IRC §7701(j)

Notice 2022-55, 2022-45 IRB 443 (deferral limits for 2023)

Notice 2021-61, 2021-47 IRB 738 (deferral limits for 2022)

Notice 2020-79, 2020-46 IRB 1014 (deferral limits for 2021)

Notice 2019-59, 2019-47 IRB 1091 (deferral limits for 2020)

Notice 2018-83, 2018-47 IRB 774 (deferral limits for 2019)

Section 457 plan elective deferrals

IRC §457(e)(15)(A)

Notice 2022-55, 2022-45 IRB 443 (deferral limits for 2023)

Notice 2021-61, 2021-47 IRB 738 (deferral limits for 2022)

Notice 2020-79, 2020-46 IRB 1014 (deferral limits for 2021)

Notice 2019-59, 2019-47 IRB 1091 (deferral limits for 2020)

Notice 2018-83, 2018-47 IRB 774 (deferral limits for 2019)

Up-to-$3,000 annual exclusion for health insurance premiums of public safety officers

IRC §402(1)

Employer may automatically enroll employees in Section 457 plan

Rev. Rul. 2000-33, 2000-31 IRB 142

Section 457 plan distributions

IRC §457(d)

Section 457(b) plan distribution taxed despite financial hardship

Herbert W.G. Clanton, 2012-2 USTC ¶50,508 (6th Cir. 2012)

Rollover options

IRC §457(e)(16)

Averaging for qualified plan distribution barred by post-2001 rollover from governmental 457 plan

Section 641(f)(3)

Unforeseen emergency: Section 457 plan withdrawals

Reg. §1.457-6(c)

7.21 Figuring the Taxable Part of Commercial Annuities

* IRS Publication 575

What is an annuity?

IRC §72

Payments before annuity starting date

IRC §72(e)

Edward N. Tobias, TC Memo 2015-164

Penalty for pre-59½ withdrawals from deferred annuity

IRC §72(q)

* Letter Ruling 200113022 (substantially equal payments exception to penalty)

Switch in pre-59½ payments schedule for owners of nonqualified annuities

Notice 2004-15, 2004-9 IRB 526

Increasing annuity payments triggers penalty

* Letter Ruling 201120011

Unisex actuarial tables

Reg. §1.72-9

Pre–July 1986 investment and post–June 1986 investment

Reg. §1.72-6(d)(8)

Annuity exclusion limited to investment

IRC §72(b)(2)

Investment

IRC §72(c)(1)

Reg. §1.72-6

Expected return

IRC §72(c)(3)

Reg. §1.72-5

Deduction on final return for unrecovered investment

IRC §72(b)(3) and (4)

Refund feature

IRC §72(c)(2)

Reg. §1.72-7

Exclusion ratio

IRC §72(b)

Reg. §1.72-4

Total receipts for year

Reg. §1.72-4

Single annuity

Reg. §1.72-5(a)

Reg. §1.72-9, Table I or Table V

Temporary annuity

Reg. §1.72-9, Table IV or Table VIII

Reg. §1.72-5(a)(3)

One annuitant-stepped down annuity

Reg. §1.72-9, Tables I and IV, or Tables V and VIII

Reg. §1.72-5(a)(4)

One annuitant-stepped up annuity

Reg. §1.72-9, Tables I and IV, or Tables V and VIII

Reg. §1.72-5(a)(5)

Uniform joint and survivor annuities

Reg. §1.72-5(b)

Reg. §1.72-9, Table II or VI

Variable joint and survivor annuities

Reg. §1.72-9, Tables I, II, and IIA, or Tables V, VI, and VIA

7.22 Life Expectancy Tables for Figuring Expected Return for Commercial Annuities

Reg. §1.72-6

* IRS Publication 939

Unisex actuarial tables

Reg. §1.72-9, Tables V, VI, VIA, VII, and VIII

7.23 WHEN YOU CONVERT YOUR ENDOWMENT POLICY

IRC §72(e) and (h)

Interest option

Henry L. Blum, 150 F.2d 471 (2nd Cir. 1945)

Sale of endowment contract

Percy W. Phillips, 30 TC 866 (1958) (Nonacq.), rev'd, 275 F.2d 33 (4th Cir. 1960)

Bolling Jones, 39 TC 404 (1962)

Sale of an annuity contract

Andrew Wineman Est., 163 F. Supp. 865 (Ct. Cl. 1958), cert. denied, 359 U.S. 943

First Nat'l Bank of Kansas City, 20 TCM 1411 (1961), aff'd, 309 F.2d 587 (8th Cir. 1962)

Harry Roff, 36 TC 818 (1961), aff'd, 304 F.2d 450 (3d Cir. 1962)

Sale of insurance policies

Gertrude H. Crocker Est., 37 TC 605 (1962)

7.24 REPORTING EMPLOYEE ANNUITIES

IRC §72(d)

* IRS Publications 575 and 721

IRA transfer to boost federal pension isn't a rollover

Dennis E. Bohner, 143 TC No. 11 (2014)

7.25 SIMPLIFIED METHOD FOR CALCULATING TAXABLE EMPLOYEE ANNUITY

IRC §72(d)(1)(B)

* IRS Publications 575 and 721

Amounts paid

IRC §72(b) and (e)

IRC §403

Reg. §1.403(a)

Reg. §1.72-8

Employer's payments

Reg. §1.72-8

Taxpayer's inflation adjustment not allowed

Kenneth L. Nordtvedt, 116 TC 165 (2001), aff'd unpublished opinion, 2001-2 USTC ¶50,772 (9th Cir. 2001)

7.26 WITHDRAWALS FROM EMPLOYER'S QUALIFIED RETIREMENT PLAN BEFORE ANNUITY STARTING DATE

IRC §72(e)(8)

Notice 87-13, 1987-1 CB 432

Employee contributions (and interest allocable) treated as separate contract

IRC §72(d)

IRC §414(k) (defined benefit plans)

Notice 87-13, 1987-1 CB 432 (Q & A 14)

Plans existing on May 5, 1986

IRC §72(e)(8)(D)

8 IRAS

8.1 STARTING A TRADITIONAL IRA

* IRS Publication 590-A

Longevity annuities in IRAs or 401(k)s

T.D. 9673, 2014-30 IRB 212

Attempted realty purchase by IRA is a taxable distribution

Guy M. Dabney, TC Memo 2014-108

Individual retirement account

IRC §408(a)

Reg. §1.408-2

Individual retirement annuity

IRC §408(b)

Reg. §1.408-3

Loss on surrender of IRA annuity nondeductible

Rev. Rul. 80-268, 1980-2 CB 141

Flexible premiums

IRC §408(b)(2)

Reg. §1.408-3(b)(6)

Endowment contract issued after November 6, 1978

Reg. §1.408-3(e)

Broker restrictions

Special Ruling, August 24, 1983

Tax treatment of distribution

IRC §408(d)

Reg. §1.408-4

Diversification of investment permitted

Rev. Rul. 79-265, 1979-2 CB 186

Collectibles investments restricted

IRC §408(m)(3)

Bullion investment allowed if in trustee's possession

IRC §408(m)(3)

* Letter Ruling 200217059

Time for making contributions

IRC §219(f)(3)

Prohibited transaction terminates an IRA

Lawrence F. Peek, 140 TC No. 12 (2013)

Bankruptcy protection for IRAs

In re: Richard L. Jones, U.S. Bankruptcy Ct. SD-IL, No. 18-31532, 4/15/19

Public Law 109-8, 4/20/05

Rousey v. Jacoway, Supreme Court, 4/4/05

8.2 CONTRIBUTION LIMIT FOR TRADITIONAL IRAS

IRC §219

* IRS Publication 590-A

Earned income limits IRA contributions

* Alex Halo, TC Summary Opinion 2014-92

Limit on deductible contributions

IRC §219(b)(5)(A)

IRC §219(b)(5)(B) (catch-up contributions if age 50 or older)

Notice 2022-55, 2022-45 IRB 444 (deductible limits for 2023)

Notice 2021-61, 2021-47 IRB 738 (deductible limits for 2022)

Notice 2020-79, 2020-46 IRB 1014 (deductible limits for 2021)

Notice 2019-59, 2019-47 IRB 1091 (deductible limits for 2020)

Notice 2018-83, 2018-47 IRB 774 (deductible limits for 2019)

Repeal of age limit for contributions (SECURE Act)

Section 107 of the SECURE Act (Division O of P.L. 116-94, 12-20-2019), repealing IRC §219(d)(1)

Time for making contribution

IRC §219(f)(3)

Higher contribution limit for 401(k) participants of certain bankrupt companies

IRC §219(b)(5)(C)

Compensatory damages for mismanaged IRA may be redeposited

* Letter Ruling 200852034

* Letter Ruling 200850054

Compensation defined

Reg. §1.219-1(c)(1)

Unemployment benefits

Donald G. Russell, 71 TCM 3184 (1996)

Earned income

IRC §219

IRC §401(c)(2)

IRC §1402(a)

Qualified Charitable Distributions (QCDs) if age 70½ or older

IRC §408(d)(8)

Qualified hurricane distributions

IRC §1400Q(a)

IRS levy of IRA is taxable distribution

M.E. Schroeder, 78 TCM 566 (1999)

Former spouse's garnishment of IRA for child support treated as distribution

Mark J. Vorwald, TC Memo 1997-15

Custodian's check to company for stock not a taxable distribution

Robert Ancira, 119 TC 135 (2002)

8.9 PARTIALLY TAX-FREE TRADITIONAL IRA DISTRIBUTIONS ALLOCABLE TO NONDEDUCTIBLE CONTRIBUTIONS

* IRS Publication 590-B

Figuring tax if nondeductible contributions have been made

IRC §408(d)(2)

Notice 87-16, 1987-1 CB 446 (loss allowed for unrecovered basis)

8.10 TAX-FREE DIRECT TRANSFER OR ROLLOVERS FROM ONE TRADITIONAL IRA TO ANOTHER

IRC §408(d)(3)

* IRS Publication 590-A

Rollover protects IRA funds in bankruptcy

In re: Richard L. Jones, U.S. Bankruptcy Ct. SD-IL, No. 18-31532, 4/15/19

IRA distributions from failed banks not subject to one-rollover limit

Information Letter, IRS-INFO-2017-0018, 6/30/2017

Only one IRA rollover each 12 months

Alvan L. Bobrow, TC Memo 2014-21

Announcement 2014-15, 2014-16 IRB 973

Direct transfer of account between trustees is not rollover

Rev. Rul. 78-406, 1978-2 CB 157

Rollover within 60 days not taxed

IRC §408(d)(3)(A)

60-day loan

* Letter Ruling 901007

IRS discretion to waive 60-day rollover deadline in hardship cases

IRC §408(d)(3)(I)

Rev. Proc. 2020-46, 2020-45 IRB 995; News Release IR-2016-113 (self-certification procedure for getting waiver)

Rev. Proc. 2003-16, 2003-4 IRB 359 (automatic waiver if institution error and letter ruling procedure for requesting waiver)

Rev. Proc. 2003-16, 2003-4 IRB 359 (IRS guidelines for granting waiver)

* Letter Ruling 201533023 (IRS denies extension when funds used as short-term loan)

* Letter Ruling 200327064 (IRS grants waiver when investment manager misappropriates funds)

* Letter Ruling 200422053 (IRS denies waivers for unemployed taxpayer's short-term loan)

* Letter Ruling 200634064 (IRS allows extension after online mixup)

* Letter Ruling 200921040 (extension allowed after failure to redeposit funds due to Parkinson's disease and memory loss)

* Letter Ruling 200921037 (extension allowed where medical condition impairs taxpayer's ability to manage financial affairs)

* Letter Ruling 200921038 (extension allowed where financial advisor fails to follow taxpayer's instructions)

* Letter Ruling 200914071 (extension denied financial institution fails to inform taxpayer of 60-day rollover period)

Rollover deadline extended where financial advisor misappropriates funds

* Letter Ruling 200922056
* Letter Ruling 200922057
* Letter Ruling 200922058
* Letter Ruling 200922059
* Letter Ruling 200922060

Extension denied where taxpayer believes rollover period to be 90 days

* Letter Ruling 200907049
* Letter Ruling 200919071

Extension granted for passive activity loss election

* Letter Ruling 201031008
* Letter Ruling 201031009

60-day period extended for frozen deposits

IRC §408(d)(3)(F)

* Letter Ruling 199933038

120-day rollover period for failed first home acquisition

IRC §72(t)(8)(E)

* Letter Ruling 200423033

Rollover treatment disallowed for minimum required distribution

IRC §408(d)(3)(E)

No IRS waiver of rollover deadline for short-term IRA loan

* Letter Ruling 201240031

Extension denied for loan to purchase home for disabled parent

* Letter Ruling 201118025

Stock bought with IRA distribution— no tax-free rollover

Albert Lemishaw, 110 TC 26 (1998)

Withdrawals following bank failure

Alan Aronson, 98 TC 283 (1992)

Beneficiary can authorize trustee-to-trustee transfer

* Letter Ruling 8716058

8.11 TRANSFER OF TRADITIONAL IRA TO SPOUSE AT DIVORCE

* IRS Publication 590-A

Transfer because of divorce

IRC §408(d)(6)

IRA transfer to ex-spouse

William Elias Rosenberg, TC Memo 2019-124 (transferred IRA funds taxable to recipient upon withdrawal)

John R. Kirkpatrick, TC Memo 2018-20 (indirect payment to spouse is taxable)

Stephen R. Jones, TC Memo 2000-19 (payment to spouse from closed-out account is taxable distribution)

QDRO

IRC §402(e)(1)(B)

IRC §402(d)(4)(J)

Rollover by surviving spouse

IRC §408(d)(3)(C)(ii)

IRC §408(a)(6)

8.12 PENALTY FOR TRADITIONAL IRA WITHDRAWALS BEFORE AGE 59½

IRC §72(t)

* IRS Publication 590-B

Penalty exception for qualified birth or adoption distribution (SECURE Act)

IRC §72(t) (2) (H), added by Section 113 of the SECURE Act (Division O of P.L. 116-94, 12-20-19)

Notice 2020-68, 2020-38 IRB 567

Financial hardship isn't a 10% penalty exception

Candace Elaine, TC Memo 2017-3

Kevin Cheves, TC Memo 2017-22

No penalty exception for paying income taxes

David D. and Barbara H. Pritchard, TC Memo 2017-136

No penalty exception for financial hardship

*Jeffrey S. Carter, TC Summary Opinion, 2012-33

No exception for distribution to pay medical expenses of non-dependent son

*Cheryl Lynn Ireland, TC Summary Opinion 2015-60

Exception for substantially equal payments

Notice 2022-6, 2022-5 IRB 460

IRC §72(t)(2)(A)(iv) and (t)(4)

Rev. Rul. 2002-62, 2002-42 IRB 710 (IRS allows one-time switch from fixed payment method to required minimum distribution method)

Interest charges added to penalty for adjusting annuity-type schedule

* Letter Ruling 9401040

Divorce may modify annuitized distribution schedule

* Letter Rulings 200052039 and 200050046

* Letter Ruling 200503036 (broker's error permits corrective distributions)

Pre-59½ withdrawals allowed for medical expenses

IRC §72(t)(2)(B)

Unemployed medical insurance exception

IRC §72(t)(2)(D)(iii)

Penalty-free qualified reservist distributions

IRC §72 (t)(2)(G)

Penalty exception for Hurricane Katrina, Rita, and Wilma victims

IRC §1400Q(a)(1)

Penalty exception for higher education expenses

IRC §72(t)(2)(E)

Watch timing of IRA withdrawals for education expenses

Roger F. Duronio, TC Memo 2007-90

Linda Louise Lodder-Beckert, TC Memo 2005-162

* Malia K. Ambata, TC Summary Opinion 2005-93

Computer not "qualified" college expense

* James M. Gorski, TC Summary Opinion 2005-112

Withdrawals for high school subject to penalty

David Brian Nolan, TC Memo 2007-306

Penalty exception for first-time homebuyer expenses

IRC §72(t)(2)(F)

* Jeffrey Thomas Olup, TC Summary Opinion 2005-183 (both spouses must meet first-time test)

* Vincent A. Suarez Jr., TC Summary Opinion 2005-71 (homeowner not eligible for penalty exception)

Disability exception

IRC §72(t)(2)(A)(iii)

Depression may be exception

Robert Dwyer, 106 TC 18 (1996) (no exception for stockholder who continues to work)

*Mary L. Coleman-Stephens, TC Summary Opinion 2003-91 (exception allowed for long-term depression preventing employment)

* Beverly Johnson, TC Summary Opinion 2006-62 (no exception for short-term depression)

* Brian P. Keeley, TC Summary Opinion 2003-53 (no exception for short-term depression)

No penalty for IRS levy of plan account

IRC §72(t)(2)(A)(vii)

No penalty exception for withdrawals to pay child support

* James K. Moyer, TC Summary Opinion 2006-189

8.13 REQUIRED MINIMUM DISTRIBUTIONS FROM A TRADITIONAL IRA

IRC §408(a)(6)

IRC §401(a)(9)

Reg. §§ 1.408-8, 1.401(a)(9)-1 through -9 (pre-SECURE Act final regulations, T.D. 8987, 2002-19 IRB 852)

REG-105954-20, 2022-11 IRB 828 (proposed SECURE Act regulations)

* IRS Publication 590-B

Required beginning date age increased to 72 (SECURE Act)

IRC §401(a)(9)(C)(i) (I), as amended by Section 114 of the SECURE Act (Division O of P.L. 116-94, 12-20-2019)

Required beginning date age increased to 73 to 75 (SECURE 2.0 Act)

IRC §401(a)(9)(C)(i) (I), as amended by Section 302 of the SECURE 2.0 Act (P.L. 117-328, 12-29-2022)

Waiver of required minimum distribution for 2020 (CARES Act)

IRC §401(a)(9) (I), added by Section 2203 (a) of the CARES Act

Notice 2020-51, 2020-29 IRB 73

Revised life expectancy tables take effect in 2022

Reg. §1.401(a)(9)-9, as revised by T.D. 9930, 85 F.R. 72472 (2020); 2020-49 IRB 1400

Insufficient distribution penalty

IRC §4974(b)

Distributions don't have to be from each account

Notice 88-38 1988-15 IRB 9

Waiver of penalty

Reg. §54.4974-2 (Q&A-7)

8.14 BENEFICIARIES OF TRADITIONAL IRA OWNERS WHO DIED BEFORE 2020

IRC §408(a)(6)

Reg. §§ 1.408-8, 1.401(a)(9)-4, -5, -8, and -9

* IRS Publication 590-B

Waiver of required minimum distribution for 2020 (CARES Act)

IRC §401(a)(9) (I), added by Section 2203 (a) of the CARES Act (P.L. 116-136, 3-27-2020)

Notice 2020-51, 2020-29 IRB 73

Successor beneficiaries subject to 10-year rule (SECURE Act)

Section 401(b)(5) of the SECURE Act (Division O of P.L. 116-94, 12-20-2019)

REG-105954-20, 2022-11 IRB 828 (proposed SECURE Act regulations)

Revised single life expectancy table takes effect in 2022

Reg. §1.401(a)(9)-9, as revised by T.D. 9930, 85 F.R. 72472 (2020); 2020-49 IRB 1400

Rollover by surviving spouse

IRC §408(d)(3)(C)(ii)

IRC §408(a)(6)

Inherited IRA not exempt in bankruptcy

Brandon C Clark, No. 13–299 (Sup. Ct. 2014)

Distributions from inherited IRAs not excludable from income

Mark William Murray, TC Memo 2012-213

Nonspouse beneficiary may make trustee-to-trustee transfer but not 60-day rollover

*Charles Grant Beech, TC Summary Opinion 2012-74

Required distributions to trust beneficiaries

* Letter Ruling 200329048

Trust named as IRA beneficiary in will not a designated beneficiary

* Letter Ruling 200849019

Qualified disclaimer after taking RMD

Rev. Rul. 2005-36, 2005-26 IRB 1368

8.15 BENEFICIARIES OF TRADITIONAL IRA OWNERS WHO DIED AFTER 2019

IRC §401 (a) (9) (H), added by Section 401 of the SECURE Act (Division O of P.L. 116-94, 12-20-2019)

REG-105954-20, 2022-11 IRB 828 (proposed SECURE Act regulations)

Notice 2022-53, 2022-45 IRB 437

* IRS Publication 590-B

Proposed SECURE Act regulations for beneficiaries

REG-105954-20, 2022-11 IRB 828

Notice 2022-53, 2022-45 IRB 437 (penalty waiver on certain missed 2021 or 2022 RMDs)

Definition of designated beneficiary

IRC §401 (a) (9) (E) (i), as added by Section 401 of the SECURE Act (Division O of P.L. 116-94, 12-20-2019)

Reg. § 1.401(a)(9)-4 (Q&A-1)

Eligible designated beneficiaries may use life expectancy method (SECURE Act)

IRC §401 (a) (9) (H) (ii), added by Section 401 of the SECURE Act (Division O of P.L. 116-94, 12-20-2019)

Definition of eligible designated beneficiary(SECURE Act)

IRC §401 (a) (9) (E) (ii), as added by Section 401 of the SECURE Act (Division O of P.L. 116-94, 12-20-2019)

10-year rule for noneligible designated beneficiaries (SECURE Act)

IRC §401 (a) (9) (H) (i), added by Section 401 of the SECURE Act (Division O of P.L. 116-94, 12-20-2019)

Revised single life expectancy table takes effect in 2022

Reg. §1.401(a)(9)-9, as revised by T.D. 9930, 85 F.R. 72472 (2020); 2020-49 IRB 1400

Successor beneficiaries of eligible designated beneficiaries (SECURE Act)

IRC §401 (a) (9) (H) (iii), added by Section 401 of the SECURE Act (Division O of P.L. 116-94, 12-20-2019)

Successor beneficiaries of noneligible designated beneficiaries (SECURE Act)

IRC §401(a) (9) (H) (i), added by Section 401 of the SECURE Act (Division O of P.L. 116-94, 12-20-2019)

8.16 SEP BASICS

IRC §219(b)(2)

IRC §404(h)

IRC §408(j), (k), and (l)

Reg. §1.219-1(d)(4) and -3

Reg. §1.404(h)-1

Reg. §1.408-7 through 9

* IRS Publication 560

Overall tax-free SEP contribution limit

IRC §402(h)(2)

Employer contribution limits

Notice 2022-55, 2022-45 IRB 443 (limits for 2023)

Notice 2021-61, 2021-47 IRB 738 (limits for 2022)

Notice 2020-79, 2020-46 IRB 1014 (limits for 2021)

Notice 2019-59, 2019-47 IRB 1091 (limits for 2020)

Notice 2018-83, 2018-47 IRB 774 (limits for 2019)

Salary-reduction SEP

IRC §408(k)(6)

Elective salary-reduction limit

IRC §402(g)(1)

Employer's deductible limit

IRC §404(h)(1)(c)

8.17 SALARY-REDUCTION SEP SET UP BEFORE 1997

* IRS Publications 560

Contribution limits

Notice 2022-55, 2022-45 IRB 443 (limits for 2023)

Notice 2021-61, 2021-47 IRB 738 (limits for 2022)

Notice 2020-79, 2020-46 IRB 1014 (limits for 2021)

Notice 2019-59, 2019-47 IRB 1091 (limits for 2020)

Notice 2018-83, 2018-47 IRB 774 (limits for 2019)

SEP

IRC §408(k)(6)

8.18 WHO IS ELIGIBLE FOR A SIMPLE IRA?

IRC §408(p)

SIMPLE salary-reduction limit

IRC §408 (p) (2) (E)

IRC §414 (v) (2) (B (ii)(catch-up contributions)

Notice 2022-55, 2022-45 IRB 443 (limits for 2023)

Notice 2021-61, 2021-47 IRB 738 (limit for 2022)

Notice 2020-79, 2020-46 IRB 1014 (limit for 2021)

Notice 2017-64, 2017-45 IRB 486 (limit for 2018)

Notice 2016-62, 2016-46 IRB 725 (limit for 2017)

Automatic enrollment for SIMPLE IRAs

Notice 2009-66, 2009-39 IRB 418

Notice 2009-67, 2009-39 IRB 420

8.19 SIMPLE IRA CONTRIBUTIONS AND DISTRIBUTIONS

IRC §408(p)

* IRS Publications 560 and 590-A

SIMPLE salary-reduction limits

IRC §408(p)(2)(E)

Notice 2022-55, 2022-45 IRB 443 (limits for 2023)

Notice 2021-61, 2021-47 IRB 738 (limits for 2022)

Notice 2020-79, 2020-46 IRB 1014 (limits for 2021)

Notice 2019-59, 2019-47 IRB 1091 (limits for 2020)

Notice 2018-83, 2018-47 IRB 774 (limits for 2019)

Penalty for distributions before age 59½

IRC §72(t)(6)

Rollover from SIMPLE to other plans

IRC §408 (d)(3)(G)

8.20 ROTH IRA ADVANTAGES

IRC §408A

* IRS Publications 590-A (contributions); 590-B (distributions)

Roth IRA guidelines

Reg. §1.408A-1 through A-9

Direct rollover from employer plan to Roth IRA

IRC §408A(e)

8.21 ANNUAL CONTRIBUTIONS TO A ROTH IRA

* IRS Publication 590-A

Good faith efforts allow relief to recharacterize Roth IRA

Letter Ruling 201603048

Banks not obliged to inform about rollover time limits

Letter Rulings 201339002 and 201339003

Annual contributions to Roth IRA

IRC §408A(c)(2) (limit keyed to deductible IRA limit)

IRC §408A(c)(3) (phaseout of contribution limit)

Reg. §1.408A-3

Contribution phaseout range

Notice 2022-55, 2022-45 IRB 443 (limits for 2023)

Notice 2021-61, 2021-47 IRB 738 (limit for 2022)

Notice 2020-79, 2020-46 IRB 1014 (limit for 2021)

Notice 2019-59, 2019-47 IRB 1091 (limit for 2020)

Notice 2018-83, 2018-47 IRB 774 (limit for 2019)

Excess contributions to Roth IRA

IRC §4973(f)

Roth IRA contributions based on tax-free combat pay

IRC §219(f)(7)

8.22 RECHARACTERIZING A TRADITIONAL IRA CONTRIBUTION TO A ROTH IRA AND VICE VERSA

* IRS Publication 590-A

Recharacterization deadline

Reg. §1.408A-5 (Q&A-6) (filing due date)

Extension to recharacterize Roth IRA after IRS audit

* Letter Ruling 200533025

8.23 CONVERTING A TRADITIONAL IRA TO A ROTH IRA

IRC §408A(d)(3)(A)

* IRS Publication 590-A

Conversion to Roth IRA

Reg. §1.408A-4 (Q&A)

News Release IR-2013-21

Two-year ratable income inclusion for conversion made in 2010

IRC §408A(d)(3)(A)(iii)

IRC §408A(d)(3)(E)

Annuity conversion to Roth IRA must be valued at fair market value

Rev. Proc. 2006-13, 2006-3 IRB 315

Temp. Reg. §1.408A-4T

Rollover from qualified retirement plan to Roth IRA

Notice 2009-75, 2009-39 IRB 436

8.24 CONVERSIONS MADE AFTER 2017 TO A ROTH IRA CANNOT BE RECHARACTERIZED

IRC §408A(d)(6)(B)(iii), added by the Tax Cuts and Jobs Act (P.L. 115-97, 12/22/2017)

* IRS Publication 590-A

Undoing a conversion (made before 2018) with recharacterization

IRC §408A(d)(6), prior to amendment by the Tax Cuts and Jobs Act (P.L. 115-97, 12/22/2017)

Reg. §1.408A-5

Recharacterization deadline (pre-2018 conversions)

Reg. §1.408A-5 (Q&A-6) (filing due date)

Extension of deadline for late recharacterization (pre-2018 conversions)

* Letter Rulings 200315027, 200317028, 200213030, 200116053, 200116057, and 200116059

Delay required before reconverting after recharacterizing (pre-2018 conversions)

Reg. §1.408A-5 (Q&A-9)

8.25 DISTRIBUTIONS FROM A ROTH IRA

IRC §408A(d)

Reg. §1.408A-6

* IRS Publication 590-B

8.26 DISTRIBUTIONS TO ROTH IRA BENEFICIARIES

Reg. §1.408A-6 (Q&A-7) (owner's five-year holding period for tax-free distributions applies to beneficiary)

Reg. §1.408A-6 (Q&A-11) (Roth IRA owner's death before end of five-year period)

* IRS Publication 590-B

Designated beneficiaries of owners dying before 2020

Reg. §1.408A-6 (Q&A-14) (beneficiary uses life expectancy method unless 5-year rule is elected)

Eligible designated beneficiaries of owners dying after 2019 may use life expectancy method(SECURE Act)

IRC §401 (a) (9) (H) (ii), added by Section 401 of the SECURE Act (Division O of P.L. 116-94, 12-20-2019)

10-year rule for noneligible designated beneficiaries of owners dying after 2019 (SECURE Act)

IRC §401 (a) (9) (H) (i), added by Section 401 of the SECURE Act (Division O of P.L. 116-94, 12-20-2019)

Proposed REG §1.408-8 (b) (1) (ii), REG-105954-20, 2022-11 IRB 828 (ROTH IRA

owners treated as dying before their required beginning date)

Revised single life expectancy table takes effect in 2022

Reg. §1.401(a)(9)-9, as revised by T.D. 9930, 85 F.R. 72472 (2020); 2020-49 IRB 1400

Successor beneficiaries of designated beneficiaries of owners dying before 2020 (SECURE Act)

Section 401(b)(5) of the SECURE Act (Division O of P.L. 116-94, 12-20-2019)

Successor beneficiaries of eligible designated beneficiaries of owners dying after 2019 (SECURE Act)

IRC §401 (a) (9) (H) (iii), added by Section 401 of the SECURE Act (Division O of P.L. 116-94, 12-20-2019)

Successor beneficiaries of noneligible designated beneficiaries of owners dying after 2019 (SECURE Act)

IRC §401 (a) (9) (H) (i), added by Section 401 of the SECURE Act (Division O of P.L. 116-94, 12-20-2019)

9 INCOME FROM REAL ESTATE RENTALS AND ROYALTIES

9.1 REPORTING RENTAL REAL ESTATE INCOME AND EXPENSES

IRC §61(a)(5) and (6)

IRC §469

Reg. §1.61-8

* IRS Publications 527 and 925

Minimal efforts to rent vacation home not a conversion to rental property

Robert I. Redisch, TC Memo 2015-95

Rents received

Reg. §1.61-8

Cash basis

Morris-Poston Coal Co., 42 F.2d 620 (6th Cir. 1930)

Andrew J. Pembroke, 23 BTA 1176, aff'd 70 F.2d 850 (D.C. Cir. 1935)

Jas. M. Butler, 18 BTA 718 (Acq.)

Accrual basis

Suffolk & Berks, 40 BTA 1121 (Acq.)

American Fork & Hoe Co., 33 BTA 1139

Oregon Terminals Co., 29 BTA 1332 (Nonacq.)

Advance rentals or bonuses

Reg. §1.61-8(b)

Hyde Park Realty, Inc., 211 F.2d 462 (2d Cir. 1954), aff'g 20 TC 43 (1953)

Chateau Frontenac, 147 F.2d 856 (6th Cir. 1945)

Clinton Hotel Realty Corp., 128 F.2d 968 (5th Cir. 1945)

Beach D. Lyon, 97 F.2d 70 (9th Cir. 1938)

Edward A. Renwick, 87 F.2d 123 (7th Cir. 1937)

R. L. Harcum, 164 F. Supp. 650 (E.D. Vir. 1958)

John Mantell, 17 TC 1143 (1952) (Acq.)

Advances transferred to new landlord

Hyde Park Realty, Inc., 211 F.2d 462 (2d Cir. 1954), aff'g 20 TC 43 (1953)

Security for performance

Astor Holding Co., 135 F.2d 47 (5th Cir. 1943)

Clinton Hotel Realty Corp., 128 F.2d 968 (5th Cir. 1942)

R. L. Harcum, 164 F. Supp. 650 (E.D. Vir. 1958)

Andrew J. Pembroke, 70 F.2d 850 (D.C. Cir. 1935)

John Mantell, 17 TC 1143 (1952) (Acq.)

Taxes, interest, etc. as rent

Reg. §1.61-8(c)

Insurance proceeds

John S. Mellinger, 228 F.2d 688 (5th Cir. 1956)

Oppenheim's Inc., 90 F. Supp. 107 (D. Mich. 1960)

Cancelled lease

Reg. §1.61-8(b)

Walter M. Hort, 313 U.S. 28 (1941)

Amortizing lease cancellation cost over term of old lease

Handlery Hotels, Inc., 663 F.2d 892 (9th Cir. 1981)

Improvement by tenant

IRC §109

Reg. §1.109-1

Personal holding companies

Char-Lil Corporation, 2000-2 USTC ¶50,827 (10th Cir. 2000), aff'g TC Memo 1998-457

9.2 CHECKLIST OF RENTAL DEDUCTIONS

* IRS Publication 527

Maintenance expenses

IRC §212

Reg. §1.212-1

Salaries and wages

IRC §212

Reg. §1.212-1

Travel expenses

E. M. Goodson, 5 TCM 648 (1946)

Legal expenses

Arthur T. Galt, 19 TC 892 (1953), aff'd in part, rev'd in part, 216 F.2d 41 (7th Cir. 1954), cert. denied, 348 U.S. 951

Louis F. Tucker, Sr., 9 TCM 956 (1950)

E. M. Godson, 5 TCM 648 (1946)

Interest on mortgages

IRC §163(c)

Reg. §1.163-1

Commissions to secure rental

Mary C. Young, 59 F.2d 691 (9th Cir. 1953), cert. denied, 287 U.S. 652, on remand, 14 TCM 869 (1955)

John Griffiths, 70 F.2d 946 (8th Cir. 1934)

Louis A. Meyran, 63 F.2d 986 (3d Cir. 1933)

Central Bank Block Assn., 57 F.2d 5 (5th Cir. 1932)

Commissions to acquire property

IRC §263

Reg. §1.263(a)-1 and 2

Abandonment loss

Reg. §1.167(a)-8

Belridge Oil Co., 11 BTA 127

I. G. Zumwalt, 25 BTA 566

Rev. Rul. 54-581, 1954-2 CB 112

Insurance premiums

Reg. §1.162-1

Year deductible

Reg. §1.461-1(a)(1)

Rev. Rul. 70-413, 1970-2 CB 103

Inherited lease

Mary Y. Moore, 207 F.2d 265 (9th Cir. 1953), cert. denied, 347 U.S. 942, on remand, 14 TCM 869 (1955)

Release from mortgage

Rev. Rul. 57-198, 1957-1 CB 94

Rent for less than fair value

Nicath Realty (Hummel), 25 TCM 1260 (1966)

Cost of canceling a lease

Handlery Hotels, Inc., 663 F.2d 892 (9th Cir. 1981)

Tenant in common

Elmer B. Boyd Est., 28 TC 564 (1957)

Payment of full tax by co-tenant deductible

Lulu Lung Powell, 26 TCM 161 (1967)

No deduction for co-tenant without proof of payment

Donald Peters, 29 TCM 1441 (1970)

9.3 DISTINGUISHING BETWEEN A REPAIR AND AN IMPROVEMENT

Capital improvements

IRC §263

Reg. §1.263(a)-1 and -2

Final regulations distinguishing repairs from improvements

T.D. 9636, 2013-43 IRB 331 Painting

Replacing roof-covering materials to prevent leaks is deductible repair

* Thomas J. Northen, Jr., TC Summary Opinion 2003-113

* Nevia Campbell, TC Summary Opinion 2002-117

Oberman Manufacturing Co., 47 TC 471 (1967)

General improvement program

Home News Publishing Co., 18 BTA 1008

Cowell, 18 BTA 997

Repairs and improvements unconnected

W. A. Stoeltzing, 266 F.2d 374 (3d Cir. 1959), aff'g 17 TCM 567 (1958)

Major hotel allowed deduction for maintenance during improvement plan

Jerome Moss, 831 F.2d 833 (9th Cir. 1987)

9.4 REPORTING RENTS FROM A MULTI-UNIT RESIDENCE

* IRS Publication 527

Three-way allocation

Rev. Rul. 76-287, 1976-2 CB 80

Rental of condo during slack market

Edward W. Andrews, 931 F.2d 132 (1st Cir., 1991)

9.5 DEPRECIATION ON CONVERTING A HOME TO RENTAL PROPERTY

* IRS Publication 527

Take depreciation

IRC §167(a)

Reg. §1.212-1(h)

Recapture of pre-MACRS depreciation

IRC §1250(d)(7)

Reg. §1.1250-3(g)

27½-year recovery

IRC §168(c)(1)

Lower of adjusted basis or value at conversion

Reg. §1.167(g)-1

J. Russell Parsons, 227 F.2d 437 (3d Cir. 1956)

Louise Biesek, 22 TCM 464 (1963)

Basis when you sell

Reg. §1.165-9(b)

Tindle and Union Trust Co., 276 U.S. 582 (1928)

Mary Louise Bok, 46 BTA 678 (Acq.), aff'd, 132 F.2d 365 (3d Cir. 1942)

Bert P. Newron, 11 TC 512 (1948) (Acq.)

Alan H. Colcord, 9 TCM 729 (1950)

Need of appraisal

Sam Perry Robinson, 19 TCM 1374 (1960)

Depreciation on vacant residence

Hulet P. Smith, 26 TCM 149 (1967), aff'd, 397 F.2d 804 (9th Cir. 1968)

George W. Mitchell, 47 TC 120 (1966) (Nonacq.)

Frank A. Newcombe, 54 TC 1298 (1970)

James J. Sherlock, 31 TCM 383 (1972)

Edward G. Lowry, Jr., 384 F. Supp. 257 (D. N.H. 1974)

9.6 RENTING A RESIDENCE TO A RELATIVE

IRC §280A(d)(2)(A)

IRC §280A(d)(3)

* IRS Publication 527

Son's rental of Florida condo to parents

Cedric R. Kotowicz, 62 TCM 1229 (1991)

Renting inherited home to relatives

Ronald P. Barranti, 76 TCM 957 (1998)

9.7 PERSONAL USE AND RENTAL OF A RESIDENCE DURING THE YEAR

IRC §280A(d)

* IRS Publication 527

Personally used (14-day/10%) residence exempt from passive activity rules

IRC §469(j)(10)

14-day or 10% personal-use tests

IRC §280A(d)(1)

No deductions for rental of home space to employer

IRC §280A(c)(6)

Rental for less than 15 days

IRC §280A(g)

No deductions for short-term rentals

Charles M. Akers, TC Memo 2010-85

"Mini motor home" as vacation home

Ronald L. Haberkorn, 75 TC 259 (1980)

Time spent on repairs not personal use

Robert J. Twohey, 66 TCM 1394 (1993)

B&B's mixed-use areas ineligible for hotel exception

Charles E. Anderson, TC Memo 2006-33

9.8 COUNTING PERSONAL-USE DAYS AND RENTAL DAYS FOR A RESIDENCE

IRC §280A(d)

Personal-use day defined

IRC §280A(d)(2)

Income limitation on deductions

IRC §280A(c)(5)

Shared-equity financing agreement

IRC §280A(d)(3)(C)

Prop. Reg. §1.280A-1(e)(3)

Son's rental of Florida condo to parents

Cedric R. Kotowicz, 62 TCM 1229 (1991)

Rental of personal residence

IRC §280A(d)(4)

Stephen Bolaris, 776 F.2d 1428 (9th Cir. 1985), rev'g 81 TC 840 (1983)

Rental pool arrangements

Prop. Reg. §1.280A-3(e)

Richard S. Fine, 493 F. Supp. 540 (D. Ill. 1980), aff'd, 647 F.2d 763 (7th Cir. 1981)

Kenneth G. Byers, Jr., 82 TC 919

Rental guarantee on Florida condo

Mehdi Razavi, 96-1 USTC ¶50,060 (6th Cir. 1996)

9.9 ALLOCATING EXPENSES OF A RESIDENCE TO RENTAL DAYS

* IRS Publication 527

IRS allocation method

Prop. Reg. §1.280A-3(d)(3)

Allocation method

Dorance D. Bolton, 77 TC 104 (1981), aff'd, 694 F.2d 556 (9th Cir. 1982)

Edith McKinney, 732 F.2d 414 (10th Cir. 1983), cert. denied (1984)

Interest expense

IRC §163(h)

IRC §469(j)(7)

9.10 IRS MAY CHALLENGE LOSS CLAIMED ON TEMPORARY RENTAL OF RESIDENCE BEFORE SALE

IRC §280A

IRC §183

Minimal efforts to rent vacation home not a conversion to rental property

Robert I. Redisch, TC Memo 2015-95

Showing profit motive defeats hobby loss rule

* John E. Morrissey, TC Summary Opinion 2005-86

Failure to charge fair rental value

Lawrence E. Colbert, 63 TCM 1818 (1992)

Mobile home not rented for profit

James E. Wittstruck, 645 F.2d 618 (8th Cir. 1981), aff'g per curiam 39 TCM 1168 (1980)

Temporary rental preceding sale

Stephen Bolaris, 776 F.2d 1428 (9th Cir. 1985), rev'g 81 TC 840 (1983)

Profit motive

Robert I. Redisch, TC Memo 2015-95

IRC §183

Terence D. Clancy, 37 TCM 400 (1978)

Marvin Eisenstein, 37 TCM 441 (1978)

Truett E. Allen, 72 TC 28 (1979) (Acq.)

Lester W. Lindow, 37 TCM 1257 (1978)

Richard H. Nelson, 37 TCM 1204 (1978)

Mark M. Vandeyacht, 62 TCM 2606 (1994)

9.11 REPORTING ROYALTY INCOME

License fees for use of patented article

Reg. §1.61-8(a)

Renting fees

Reg. §1.61-8(a)

Author's royalties

Reg. §1.61-8(a)

Rev. Rul. 60-31, 1960-1 CB 174, modified by Rev. Rul. 64-279, 1964-2 CB 121 and Rev. Rul. 70-435, 1970-2 CB 100

Works of art, etc.

Reg. §1.61-8(a)

Partial sale of rights

Reg. §1.61-8(a)

Lessee's payment of taxes

Wallin Coal Corp., 71 F.2d 521 (4th Cir. 1934)

Rev. Rul. 64-91, 1964-1 CB (Part I) 219

Royalty taxed as ordinary income

IRC §61(a)(6)

Reg. §1.61-8(a)

Royalty taxed as ordinary income

IRC §61(a)(6)

Reg. §1.61-8(a)

Depletion allowed

IRC §611

Reg. §1.611

Bonus payment

Reg. §1.612-3(a)(3)

Reg. §1.613-2(c)(5)

H. H. Weinert Est., 294 F.2d 740 (5th Cir. 1961)

Ann. 76-34, 1976-12 IRB 28

Rev. Rul. 73-537, 1973-2 CB 197

Percentage depletion allowed on advanced royalty

Fred Engle, 677 F.2d 564 (7th Cir. 1982), aff'd, 464 U.S. 206 (1984)

Ann. 84-59 1984-23 IRB 58

Local law

Henry Harmel, 287 U.S. 103 (1932)

Delay rental

Reg. §1.612-3(c)

Overriding royalty

Reg. §1.613-2 and 3(b)

E. G. Palmer v. Bender, 287 U.S. 551 (1933)

West Prod. Co., 121 F.2d 9 (5th Cir. 1941), cert. denied, 314 U.S. 682

H. R. Cullen, 118 F.2d 651 (5th Cir. 1941)

Production payments treated as loans

IRC §636

Oil payments

J. Steve Anderson, 310 U.S. 404 (1940)

Caldwell Oil Corp., 141 F.2d 559 (5th Cir. 1944)

Mamie S. Hammonds, 106 F.2d 420 (10th Cir. 1939)

Roy H. Laird, 97 F.2d 730 (5th Cir. 1938)

William Fleming, 82 F.2d 328 (5th Cir. 1936)

Chester Addison Jones, 82 F.2d 329 (5th Cir. 1936)

Elliott Petroleum Corp., 82 F.2d 193 (9th Cir. 1936)

Proof of oil payment

J. A. Morgan, 321 F.2d 781 (5th Cir. 1963), on remand, 245 F. Supp. 388 (D. Miss. 1965)

Both oil payment and overriding royalty

J. Steve Anderson, 310 U.S. 404 (1940)

E. G. Palmer v. Bender, 287 U.S. 551 (1933)

H. R. Cullen, 118 F.2d 651 (5th Cir. 1941), rev'g 41 BTA 1042

Marrs McLean, 120 F.2d 942 (5th Cir. 1941), cert. denied, 314 U.S. 670

Fred T. Hogan, 1 TCM 208 (1942), aff'd, 141 F.2d 92 (5th Cir. 1944), cert. denied, 323 U.S. 710

Net profits

Kirby Petroleum Co., 326 U.S. 599 (1946)

Thomas A. O'Donnell, 303 U.S. 370 (1938)

Carried interest

Abercrombie Co., 162 F.2d 338 (5th Cir. 1947), aff'g 7 TC 120 (1946) (Nonacq.)

Donald McMurray, 60 F.2d 843 (10th Cir. 1935), cert. denied, 287 U.S. 664

Carved-out oil payments

P. G. Lake, Inc., 356 U.S. 260 (1958)

Murphy J. Foster, 324 F.2d 702 (5th Cir. 1963)

9.12 PRODUCTION COSTS OF BOOKS AND CREATIVE PROPERTIES

IRC §263A

Exemption for freelance authors, artists, and playwrights

IRC §263A(h)

9.13 DEDUCTING THE COST OF PATENTS OR COPYRIGHTS

Patent and copyright

Reg. §1.167(a)-6(a)

Depreciation deduction

Associated Partners, Inc., 4 TC 979 (1945)

Rev. Rul. 67-136, 1967-1 CB 58

Inherited

IRC §1014

John L. Whitehurst, 12 BTA 1416 (Nonacq.)

Worthless interest

Robert S. Davis, 241 F.2d 701 (7th Cir. 1958)

James Petroleum Corp., 238 F.2d 678 (2d Cir. 1956), cert. denied, 353 U.S. 910

9.14 INTANGIBLE DRILLING COSTS

IRC §263(c)

Recapture of intangible drilling costs

IRC §1254

Prop. Reg. §1.1254

90-day "spudding"

IRC §461(i)(2)(A)

9.15 DEPLETION DEDUCTION

* IRS Publication 535

IRC §611 through §613

Reg. §1.611-1

Reg. §1.612-1

Reg. §1.613-1 and 2

9.16 OIL AND GAS PERCENTAGE DEPLETION

* IRS Publication 535

Percentage depletion for gas and oil wells

IRC §613A

No depletion for lease bonuses

IRC §613A(d)(5)

Reg. §1.613A-3(j)

Depletable gas quantity

Reg. §1.613A-5

Small-producer 75,000 barrel limit

IRC §613A(d)(4)

Retail sales less than $5 million

IRC §613A(d)(2)

Limit of 100% of taxable income from the property

IRC §613(a)

Limit of 65% of taxable income from all sources

IRC §613A(d)(1)

Depletion rate for marginal production

Notice 2022-17, 2022-18 IRB 1048

IRC §613A(c)(6)

IRC §613A(c)(6)(H) (suspension of taxable income limit)

9.17 QUALIFIED BUSINESS INCOME DEDUCTION FOR REAL ESTATE ACTIVITIES

Rev. Proc. 2019-38

IRC §199A

* IRS Publication 535

Safe harbor for rental real estate enterprises

Rev. Proc. 2019-38, 2019-42 IRB 942

10 LOSS RESTRICTIONS: PASSIVE ACTIVITIES AND AT-RISK LIMITS

10.1 RENTAL ACTIVITIES GENERALLY TREATED AS PASSIVE

IRC §469 (c)(2)

Reg §1.469-4

Limits on deductible losses for rental properties

* Jesse Burgain, TC Summary Opinion 2013-61

Exceptions from rental activity category

Reg §1.469-1T(e)(3)

Exception for rental of personal residence

IRC §469(j)(10)

Exception for extraordinary personal services

Assaf F. Al Assaf and Rehab Assaf, TC Memo 2005-14

Material participation tests not met for seven-days-or-less rentals

Theodore Chapin, 71 TCM 2027 (1996)

Arnold Mordkin, 71 TCM 2796 (1996)

Loss on short-term resort rental

George Pohoski, 75 TCM 1574 (1998)

No deductions for short-term rentals

Charles M. Akers, TC Memo 2010-85

Rental losses from LLC can't offset wages from C corp

Carlos A. Senra, TC Memo 2009-79

Gain on sale of non-rented buildings offsetsrental losses

Raymond Vandegrift, TC Memo 2012-14

10.2 RENTAL REAL ESTATE LOSS ALLOWANCE OF UP TO $25,000

IRC §469(i)

Phaseout of allowance

IRC §469(i)(3)(A)

Phaseout of low-income housing and rehabilitation credits

IRC §469(i)(3)(B)

Estates

IRC §469(i)(4)

10.3 REAL ESTATE PROFESSIONALS

IRC §469(c)(7)

Reg. §1.469-9

Mortgage broker not a real estate professional

Chief Counsel Memorandum 201504010

Home improvement hours don't necessarily count toward real estate professional status

* John Erwin Smith, TC Summary Opinion 2014-13

Employee's services not counted

Antonio Pungot, TC Memo 2000-60

Late election on amended return to aggregate real estate activities

Rev. Proc. 2011-34, 2011-24 IRB 875

Full-time tugboat pilot is a real estate professional

Tom Miller, TC Memo 2011-219

"On call" time not counted for real estate professional test

James F. Moss, 135 TC 365 (2010)

Specific election to aggregate required

Matti Kosonen, TC Memo 2000-107

Extension for aggregation election

* Letter Ruling 200044025

10.4 BUSINESS PARTICIPATION MAY AVOID PASSIVE LOSS RESTRICTIONS

Material participation

IRC §469 (h)

Active participation

IRC §469 (i)

Passive loss rule avoided by attorney-landlord

Assaf F. Al Assaf and Rehab Assaf, TC Memo 2005-14

10.5 CLASSIFYING BUSINESS ACTIVITIES AS ONE OR SEVERAL

Determining passive or nonpassive activity not always easy

Stephen P. Hardy, TC Memo 2017-16

Identifying and aggregating passive activities

Reg. §1.469-4

William A. Goshorn, 66 TCM 1499 (1993)

10.6 MATERIAL PARTICIPATION IN A BUSINESS

IRC §469(h)

Temp. Reg. §1.469-5T

A trust can be a real estate professional

Frank Aragona Trust, 142 TC No.9

Limited partner

Prop. Reg. 1.469-5(e)

IRC §469(h)(2)

LLC/LLP members not automatically passive investors

Paul D. Garnett, 132 TC 368 (2009)

Managing member of LLC avoids passive loss treatment

Lee E. Newell, TC Memo 2010-23

LLC owners can materially participate in activities

James R. Thompson, 2009-2 USTC ¶50,501 (Fed. Cl. 2009)

IRS concedes LLC interest not presumptively passive

Action On Decision Memorandum (acquiescence to Thompson decision result)

Material participation test—not met

Joseph Machado, 70 TCM 1165 (1995)

Charles M. Akers, TC Memo 2010-85

Lack of records prevents passive losses

Ben Bartlett, TC Memo 2013-182

10.7 TAX CREDITS OF PASSIVE ACTIVITIES LIMITED

IRC §469(a)(1)(B)

IRC §469(d)(2)

Phaseout of low-income and rehabilitation credit

IRC §469(i)(3)(B)

Basis adjustment for suspended credits

IRC §469(j)(9)

10.8 DETERMINING PASSIVE OR NONPASSIVE INCOME AND LOSS

Joseph Veriha et ux., 139 TC No. 3 (2012)

IRC §469(e)(1)

Compensation for personal services

IRC §469(e)(3)

Self-charged interest

Reg. §1.469-7, as amended by T.D. 9013, 2002-38 IRB 542

Self-charged management fees

David H. Hillman, 263 F.3d 338 (4th Cir. 2001), rev'g 114 TC 103 (2000) (no offset for self-charged management fees)

David H. Hillman, 118 TC 323 (2002) (alternative argument fails to avoid effect of Fourth Circuit decision cited above)

Covenant not to compete

William Schaefer, 105 TC 16 (1996)

10.9 PASSIVE INCOME RECHARACTERIZED AS NONPASSIVE INCOME

Significant participation

Temp. Reg. §1.469-2T(f)(2)

Temp. Reg. §1.469-5T(c)

Net interest income from passive equity-financed lending

Temp. Reg. §1.469-2T(f)(4)

Incidental rental of property by development activity

Reg. §1.469-2(f)(5)(i)

Rental property with an insubstantial depreciable basis

Reg. §1.469-2(f)(6)

Shirley M. Wiseman, 69 TCM 3144 (1994)

Property rented to business in which you materially participate (self-rentals)

Reg. §1.469-2(f)(6)

Gary Beecher, 2007-1 USTC ¶50,379 (9th Cir. 2007) (upholds constitutionality of self-rental rule)

Thomas P. Krukowski, 279 F.3d 547 (7th Cir. 2002), aff'g 114 TC 366 (2000) (upholds validity of recharacterization regulation)

Tony R. Carlos, 123 TC 275 (2004) (self-rental rule disallows loss offset despite grouping)

Larry Williams, TC Memo 2015-76(doctor's rental income from S corporation recharacterized as nonpassive

Licensing of intangible property

Temp. Reg. §1.469-2T(f)(7)

10.10 WORKING INTERESTS IN OIL AND GAS WELLS

IRC §469(c)(3)

Reg. §1.469-2(c)(6)

Temp. Reg. §1.469-1T(e)(4)

Working oil and gas interests outside of passive activity restrictions

IRC §469(c)(3)

10.11 PARTNERS AND MEMBERS OF LLCS AND LLPS

Limited partners

IRC §469(h)(2)

Prop. Reg. §1.469-5(e) (2011 proposed re-definition of limited partner), would replace Temp. Reg. §1.469-5T(e)(3)

LLC/LLP members not automatically passive investors

Paul D. Garnett, 132 TC 368 (2009)

Managing member of LLC avoids passive loss treatment

Lee E. Newell, TC Memo 2010-23

LLC owners can materially participate in activities

James R. Thompson, 2009-2 USTC ¶50,501 (Fed. Cl. 2009)

IRS concedes LLC interest not presumptively passive

Action On Decision Memorandum (acquiescence to Thompson decision result)

Retired partners

IRC §469(h)(3)

Publicly traded partnerships

IRC §469(k)

Notice 88-75, 1988-2 CB 386

Publicly traded partnerships treated as corporations

IRC §7704

Allocation on disposition

Temp. Reg. §1.469-2T(e)(3)(ii)

10.12 FORM 8582 AND OTHER TAX FORMS

* IRS Publication 925

10.13 SUSPENDED LOSSES ALLOWED ON DISPOSITION OF YOUR INTEREST

Chief Counsel Memorandum 201415002

IRC §469(g)

Carryover

IRC §469(b)

Gifts

IRC §469(j)(6)

Installment sales

IRC §469(g)(3)

10.14 SUSPENDED TAX CREDITS

Basis election for suspended credits

IRC §469(i)(9)

10.15 PERSONAL SERVICE AND CLOSELY HELD CORPORATIONS

Closely held corporations

IRC §469 (j)(1)

Personal service corporations

IRC §469(j)(2)

Material participation tests

IRC §469(h)(4)

Full-time manager or employees

IRC §465(c)(7)(C)

Passive losses offset net active income

IRC §469(e)(2)

10.16 SALES OF PROPERTY AND OF PASSIVE ACTIVITY INTERESTS

IRC §469(g)

Temp. Reg. §1.469-2T(c)

Installment sale

IRC §469(g)(3)

Substantially appreciated property formerly used in nonpassive activity

Reg. §1.469-2(c)(2)(iii)

Property used in more than one activity in a 12-month period preceding disposition

Temp. Reg. §1.469-2T(c)(2)(ii)

Partnership and S corporation interests

Temp. Reg. §1.469-2T(e)(3)

10.17 AT-RISK LIMITS

IRC §465

Prop. Reg. §1.465-1 through §95

Activities subject to at-risk rules

IRC §465(c)

Arnold Berger, 67 TCM 3144 (1994)

Active corporation

IRC §465(c)(7)(B)

Aggregation of partnership or S corporation activities until further notice

Notice 89-39, 1989-1 CB 681

10.18 WHAT IS AT RISK?

IRC §465(b)

Special at-risk rule for real estate

IRC §465(b)(6)

Lender's capital interest in loan after May 3, 2004

Reg. §1.465-8

Personal liability note to general partner not at risk

Rev. Rul. 80-327, 1980-2 CB 23

10.19 AMOUNTS NOT AT RISK

Borrowing from relatives

IRC §465(b)(3)(A)

Dispositions of interest in property used in at-risk activity

Prop. Reg. §1.465-68

Recourse not convertible to nonrecourse

Rev. Rul. 81-283, 1981-2 CB 115

TV film investment

Rev. Rul. 78-413, 1978-2 CB 167

Gold mine venture

Rev. Rul. 80-72, 1980-I CB 109

Prop. Reg. §1.465-41

Ernest J. Saviano, 80 TC 955 (1983)

Potential cash call

John Callahan, 98 TC 22 (1992)

Jerry Pritchett, et al., 85 TC 580 (1985), rev'd, 527 F.2d 644 (9th Cir. 1987)

10.20 AT-RISK INVESTMENT IN SEVERAL ACTIVITIES

Aggregation for actively managed businesses

IRC §465(c)(2)(B)(ii)

IRC §465(c)(3)(B)

Aggregation allowed for partnership or S corporation leasing of Section 1245 property

IRC §465(c)(2)(B)

10.21 CARRYOVER OF DISALLOWED LOSSES

IRC §465(a)(2)

10.22 RECAPTURE OF LOSSES WHERE AT RISK IS LESS THAN ZERO

IRC §465(e)

IRC §61

11 OTHER INCOME

11.1 PRIZES AND AWARDS

IRC §74(a)

Cash awards to winning Olympians generally tax free

IRC §74(d)

(Public Law 114-239, 10/7/16)

Rules governing, and types of, whistleblower awards

Whistleblower 21276-13W, 147 TC No. 4 (2016)

Redemption of bank rewards points

Parimal H. Shankar, 143 TC No. 5 (2014)

Prizes and awards

IRC §74

Reg. §1.74-1

Civic achievement award

Rev. Rul. 65-161, 1965-1 CB 38

Pulitzer prize

Reg. §1.74-1

Rev. Rul. 54-110, 1954-1 CB 28

Government award

Francis M. Rogallo, 474 F.2d 1 (4th Cir. 1974), rev'g 341 F. Supp. 998 (D. Va. 1972)

Door prize

Reg. §1.74-1

Essay contest

Arsham Amirkian, 197 F.2d 442 (4th Cir. 1952)

Herbert Stein, 14 TC 494 (1950)

Frederick V. Waugh, 9 TCM 309 (1950)

Lottery ticket

* Letter Ruling 9217004

Award under Incentive Awards Act

Hobart M. Griggs, 314 F. Supp. 515 (Ct. Cl. 1963)

Prize from employer

Reg. §1.74-1

NASA award taxable

Robert Jones, 79 TC 1008 (1982)

Manufacturer's trip prize to dealer

Bell Electric Co., 45 TC 158 (1965) (Acq.)

Prize of car to football player

Paul Hornung, 47 TC 428 (1967) (Acq.)

Radio or TV contest

Reg. §1.74-1(b)

Prize of merchandise

Reg. §1.74-1(a)(2)

Vacation trip

Nathan L. Wade, 55 TCM 413 (1988)

Steamship ticket

Reginald Turner, 13 TCM 462 (1954)

Car prize

Lawrence W. McCoy, 38 TC 841 (1962) (Acq. 1963-1 CB 4)

Script award

Rev. Rul. 70-331, 1970-1 CB 14

Taxable scholarship to Miss America

Rev. Rul. 68-20, 1968-1 CB 55

Treasure you find

Rev. Rul. 53-61, 1953-1 CB 17

Transfer to charity or governmental unit

IRC §74(b)

Rev. Proc. 87-54, 1987-2 CB 669

Employee achievement

IRC §74(c)

11.2 LOTTERY AND SWEEPSTAKE WINNINGS

Transfer of lottery prize to family S corporation is taxable gift

Tonda Lynn Dickerson, TC Memo 2012-60

Lump sum received for future lottery payments

George Lattera, 437 F.3d 399 (3rd Cir. 2006)

Peter U. Boehme, TC Memo 2003-81

James F. Davis, 119 TC 1 (2002)

US v. J. Michael Maginnis, 2002-2 USTC ¶50,494 (D.C. Or. 2002)

Lottery prize held by parents as custodians

Joseph Anastasio, 67 TC 814 (1977)

Prize taxed when received not won

Roy V. Thomas, 99-1 USTC ¶50,451

Raffle winnings

Diane M. Solomon, 25 TC 936 (1956)

H. Collings Downes, 30 TC 396 (1958)

Sweepstake winnings divided among family members

Henry Braunstein, 21 TCM 1132 (1962)

Couple's joint ownership agreement

* Letter Ruling 9217004

Ticket bought for foreign uncle

Alfonso Diaz, 58 TC 560 (1972) (Acq.)

Sweepstake winnings held by court

Rev. Rul. 67-203, 1967-1 CB 105

Agreement to share winnings

Samuel L. Huntington, 35 BTA 835 (Acq.)

Agreement to pool winnings

Christian H. Droge, 35 BTA 829 (Acq.)

Lump-sum option ignored if installments received

IRC §451(h)

11.3 GAMBLING WINNINGS AND LOSSES

IRC §165(d) (losses allowed only to extent of gains)

IRC §67(b)(3) (losses to extent of gains allowed as "other" itemized deduction)

Reg. §1.165-10

IRS drops proposals for electronically tracked slot winnings

T.D. 9807, 2017-5 IRB 573; Final Regulation Section 1.6041-10

Figuring gain/loss from electronically tracked slot machine transactions-- Proposed Safe Harbor

Notice 2015-21, 2015-12 IRB 765

Gambling addict enrolled in state plan not taxed

Chief Counsel Memorandum 201433015

No deduction for race track's "takeout"

Shiraz Noormohamed Lakhani, 142 TC No.8

Professional gambler's business expenses other than wagers, in addition to the actual wagers, limited to gambling winnings

IRC §165(d), effectively reversing the result in Ronald Andrew Mayo, 136 TC 81 (2011)

Poker tournament losses in excess of winnings not deductible

George E. Tschetschot, TC Memo 2007-38 (2007)

Full-time gambler is in business

Robert P. Groetzinger, 107 S. Ct. 980 (1987)

Gains and losses of casual slot machine gamblers

*Chief Counsel Advice 2009-011

Casual slot machine players can't net wins and losses

George D. Shollenberger, TC Memo 2009-306

David J. Crawford, TC Memo 2010-54

Diary supported loss deduction

Leon Faulkner, 40 TCM 1 (1980)

Tickets with sequential numbers supported loss deduction

Theodore L. Wolkomir, 40 TCM 1078 (1980)

Game-show contestant is not in business

Stanley Whitten, 70 TCM 1064 (1995)

"Comps" offset by gambling losses

Robert Libutti, 71 TCM 2343 (1996)

Casino debt

David Zarin, 90-2 USTC ¶50,530 (3rd Cir. 1990)

11.4 Gifts and Inheritances

Payments for participation in medical experiments not a gift

Daniel Hugh O'Connor, CA-9, unpublished opinion, 6/22/15 (affirming TC Memo 2012-317)

IRS can collect unpaid estate tax from heirs

Maureen G. Mangiardi, DC FL No. 9:13-cv-80256, 7/22/13

Gifts and inheritances exempt

IRC §102

Reg. §1.102-1

Incompetent's gift taxable

Carl Elmer Henry Bader, 23 TC 813 (1973)

No fixed rule to determine taxability of gifts

Mose Duberstein, 363 U.S. 278 (1960)

Will compromise

Munro L. Lyeth v. Hoey, 305 U.S. 188 (1938)

Sale of expected inheritance

Rev. Rul. 70-60, 1970-1 CB 11

Bequest to executor

Frederick L. Merriam, 263 U.S. 179

Bequest to attorney

Lee S. Jones, 23 TCM 235 (1964)

Victor R. Wolder, 493 F.2d 608 (2d Cir. 1974), aff'g 58 TC 974 (1972) (Nonacq.), cert. denied, 419 U.S. 828

Campaign contributions—when taxable

Rev. Rul. 68-19, 1968-1 CB 42

When beneficiary is taxed

IRC §652

When grantor is taxed

IRC §671

Adoption assistance from charity tax free

*Chief Counsel Information Letter 2006-0027

Hush money not a gift

* Milton D. Peebles, TC Summary Opinion 2006-61

11.5 Refunds of State and Local Tax Deductions

IRC §111

* IRS Publication 525

How tax benefit rule interacts with SALT deduction limit

Rev. Rul. 2019-11, 2019-17 IRB 1041

11.6 Other Recovered Deductions

IRC §111

Refundable part of state business tax credits taxable

David J. Maines, 144 TC No. 8 (2015)

Refund of adjustable rate mortgage interest

Rev. Rul. 92-91, 1992-2 CB 49

Donated property returned

Sidney W. Rosen, 611 F.2d 942 (1st Cir. 1979)

Reimbursement of loss absorbed by $100 floor not taxable

Rev. Rul. 80-65, 1980-1 CB 183

Debt forgiveness of accrual-basis debtor with carryover

IRC §111(c)

Annuity beneficiaries get IRD deduction

Rev. Rul. 2005-30, 2005-20 IRB 1015

11.7 How Legal Damages Are Taxed

IRC §104(a)(2)

Information Letter 2021-0012

Settlement payment for other than physical injury/sickness includible in gross income

Denise Celeste McMillan, TC Memo 2019-108

Back pay recovery can include tax consequences

Greg Allen, et. al., No. 1:02-cv-00902-RLY-TAB (D.C. Indiana, 4/18/17)

Employee's settlement not a capital gain

James Duffy, CA-Federal Circuit, 1/8/16

Damages for emotional distress not excludable

Debra Rose Theresa Barbato, TC Memo 2016-23

Payments for participation in medical experiments were taxable compensation for services

Daniel Hugh O'Connor, CA-9, unpublished opinion, 6/22/15 (affirming TC Memo 2012-317)

Fee for egg donation taxable, despite pain during procedures

Nichelle G. Perez, 144 TC No. 4 (2015)

Damages for suing advisor for bad advice not taxed

Garey A. Cosentino, TC Memo 2014-186

Payments to avoid possible future illness likely taxable

* Chief Counsel Information Letter INFO Letter 2014-0035

Settlement not treated as worker's compensation

Kathleen S. Simpson, 141 TC No. 10

Settlement of age discrimination claim subject to FICA

Chester Gerstenbluth v. Credit Suisse Securities (USA) LLC et al., CA-2, No. 12-4125 (8/27/13)

Recovery of damages from landlord is taxable

* Aster Tirfe, TC Summary Opinion 2013-42

Back pay award taxable in the year received

* Kenneth Michael Francis et ux; TC Summary Opinion 2012-79

Compensatory damages received on account of physical injury or sickness after August 20, 1996

IRC §104(a)(2)

* Letter Ruling 200041022 (emotional damages allocable to physical assault may not be taxed)

Tax on damages for emotional distress and injury to professional reputation not unconstitutional

Marrita Murphy, 2007-2, USTC ¶50,531 (Dist. Ct. D.C. 2007), aff'd 2006-2 USTC ¶50,476 (D.C. Cir. 2006), vacating 2005-1 USTC ¶50,237 (Dist. Ct., D.C. 2005)

No exclusion for punitive-only damages

Linda R. Benavides, 2007-2, USTC ¶50,638 (5th Cir. 2007)

Damages for emotional distress are usually taxable

Nancy J. Vincent, TC Memo 2005-95

Damages related to depression are taxable

M. Blackwood, TC Memo 2012-190

Partially tax-free settlement for discharged employee with MS

Julie Leigh Domeny, TC Memo 2010-9

Settlement for false imprisonment taxable

Daniel J. and Brenda J. Stadnyk, 2010-1 USTC ¶50,252 (6th Cir. 2010)

Employer discrimination settlement payment for emotional damages taxable

Justin W. Hansen, TC Memo 2009-87

Punitive damages received after August 20, 1996

IRC §104(a)(2)

IRC §104(c)

Holocaust reparations tax free after 1999

Public Law 107-358 (2002)

Supreme Court requires contingency fee to be included in gross income

John W. Banks II, 2005-1 USTC ¶50,155 (Sup. Ct. 2005)

Attorney fees under fee-shifting statute included in gross income

Nancy J. Vincent, TC Memo 2005-95 (issue not resolved by Supreme Court in Banks)

Above-the-line deduction for attorney fees in discrimination cases

IRC §62(a)(20)

IRC §62(e) (unlawful discrimination defined)

Deduction for attorney fees and other miscellaneous itemized deductions subject to 2% floor suspended for 2018 through 2025

IRC §67(g), as added by the Tax Cuts and Jobs Act (P.L. 115-97, 12/22/2017)

Loss of profit

Phoenix Coal Co., 231 F.2d 420 (2d Cir. 1956)

D. T. Longino Est., 32 TC 904 (1959)

Loss of wages

Bill McKay, 5th Cir. (4/10/96)

Slander or libel—state law governs

James E. Threlkeld, 87 TC 1294 (1986), aff'd 848 F.2d 81 (6th Cir. 1988)

Paul F. Roemer, Jr., 79 TC 398 (1982), rev'd 716 F.2d 693 (9th Cir. 1983) (Nonacq.) Rev. Rul. 85-143, 1985-2 CB 55

Defamation legal costs nondeductible to extent of tax-free damages

Wade E. Church, 80 TC 1104 (1983)

Taxes avoided on assigned damages

* Letter Ruling 200107019

Breach of promise to marry

Lyde McDonald, 9 BTA 1340 (Acq.)

Alienation of affection

C. A. Hawkins, 6 BTA 1023 (Acq.)

Rev. Rul. 74-77, 1974-1 CB 33

Support of children

IRC §71(b)

Reg. §1.71-1

Business reputation

Mason Knuckles, 23 TCM 182 (1964), aff'd 349 F.2d 610 (10th Cir. 1965)

Paul Draper, 26 TC 201 (1956) (Acq.)

Prejudgement interest includible in gross income

Chad Anthony Chamberlain et al., 2005-1 USTC ¶50,194 (5th Cir. 2005)

Charles Francisco, 267 F.2d 303 (2001)

Joseph Rozpad, 154 F.3d 1 (1st Cir. 1998)

John Brabson, 73 F.3d 1040 (10th Cir., 1996)

Goodwill

Farmers and Merchants Bank of Catlettsburg, Kentucky, 59 F.2d 912 (6th Cir. 1932)

William Basle, 16 TCM 745 (1957), aff'd per curiam, 256 F.2d 381 (3d Cir. 1958)

Embezzlement forgiven

Rev. Rul. 61-185, 1961-2 CB 9

Extortion

James Rutkin, 343 U.S. 130 (1952), aff'g 189 F.2d 431 (3d Cir. 1951)

James J. Moran, 236 F.2d 361 (2d Cir. 1956), cert. denied, 352 U.S. 909

Swindlers

James A. Akers, 167 F.2d 718 (5th Cir. 1948), cert. denied, 335 U.S. 823

Attorney receives payment

Thomas H. Hannaford, 19 TCM 409 (1960)

11.8 Cancellation of Debts You Owe

IRC §108

Exclusion for certain discharged debt

IRC §108

Canceled debts may be taxable

Reg. §1.61-12

Income from cancellation of home equity debt not excludible

Mary Bui, TC Memo 2019-54

Creditor's tardiness in filing Form 1099-INT gives taxpayer relief

Patricia D. Clark, TC Memo 2015-175

No cancellation of debt income exclusion on home equity loan

* Said H. Koriakos, TC Summary Opinion 2014-70

Car repossession

* Timothy W. Fuller, TC Summary Opinion 2009-91

Exclusion for discharge of qualified principal residence indebtedness

IRC §108(a)(1)(E), IRC §108(h)(2), as amended by the Consolidated Appropriations Act, 2021, P.L. 116-260, 12-27-20 (exclusion amount reduced; exclusion extended through 2025)

Reduction of tax attributes

IRC §108(b)

Reduce basis of depreciable property

IRC §108(b)(5)

IRC §108(c)

IRC §1017

S corp's discharged debt

IRC §108(d)(7)(A), overriding David A. Gitlitz, 121 S. Ct. 701 (2001)

Appreciated asset transferred to pay off debt taxable

James Gehl, 102 TC 37 (1994)

Loan cancelled by foundations

IRC §108(f)

Price adjustment not taxed

IRC §108(e)(5)

Special exclusion for student loan cancellations in 2021-2025

IRC §108(f)(5), as amended by the American Rescue Plan Act (P.L. 117-2, 3/11/2021)

Students working in certain areas in certain professions

IRC §108(f)(1)-(f)(4)

*John Joseph Martin Jr., TC Summary Opinion 2011-62

Credit card insurance is discharge of indebtedness

* Khen T. Huynh, TC Summary Opinion, 2001-131

* Gerald A. Bunker, TC Summary Opinion 2005-36

Income results from credit card settlement

Robert F. Melvin, TC Memo 2009-199

Income from debt forgiveness not avoided by divorce decree

Paul Neal Jensen, TC Memo 2010-77

Debtor taxed on reduction of nonrecourse mortgage debt

Rev. Rul. 91-31, 1991-1 CB19

Rev. Rul. 92-53,1992-2 CB 48 (effect of debt reduction on solvency)

Prepayment of mortgage at discount

Rev. Rul. 82-202, 1982-2 CB 35

Debt discharge income despite Agriculture Department's recapture rule

Dennis Jelle, 116 TC 63 (2001)

Insolvency of debtor

IRC §108(a)(1)(B)

George Aberl, 78 F.3d 241 (6th Cir., 1996)

Creditor-exempt assets included when determining insolvency

Roderick E. Carlson, 116 TC 87 (2001)

Insolvency determined at partnership level

IRC §108(d)(6)

D.B. Merkel, 99-2 USTC ¶50,848

Farm indebtedness

IRC §108(g)

Proceedings under Bankruptcy Act

Reg. §1.61-12

Reg. §1.1016-7

In re: James Bruner, 55 F.3d 195 (5th Cir. 1995)

In re: Bernice Haas, 48 F.2d 1153 (11th Cir. 1995)

Business real estate debt

IRC §108(8)(1)(D)

IRC §108(c)

Financial institution reporting of discharged debt

Reg. §1.6050P-1

Voluntary forgiveness by creditor

American Dental Co., 318 U.S. 322 (1943)

Creditor intended a gift

New York Creditmen's Adjustment Bureau, Inc., 110 F. Supp. 214 (D NY 1953)

Identify debt canceled

Lewis F. Jacobson, 336 U.S. 28 (1949)

Adjust purchase price

Des Moines Improvement Co., 7 BTA 279 (Nonacq.)

Sobel, Inc., 40 BTA 1263 (Nonacq.)

Decline in value of property

Kalman Hirsch, 115 F.2d 656 (7th Cir. 1940)

Borrow money

Manual A. Frank, 44 F. Supp. 729 (D. Pa. 1942), aff'd, 131 F.2d 864 (3d Cir.)

No legal obligation

Kern Co., 1 TC 249 (1942) (Acq.)

Hotel Astoria, Inc., 42 BTA 759 (Acq.)

Fulton Gold Corp., 31 BTA 519

Partial cancellation of indebtedness

Gehring Publishing Co., Inc., 1 TC 345 (1942) (Acq.)

Unauthorized sale of pledged stock is discharge of indebtedness

Regina A. Poczatek, 71 TC 371 (1978)

Inventory

Rev. Rul. 76-86, 1976-1 CB 37

11.9 SCHEDULE K-1

* IRS Publications 541 (partnership) and 559 (estate)

11.10 HOW PARTNERS REPORT PARTNERSHIP PROFIT AND LOSS

* IRS Publication 541

Final check-the-box regulations

Reg. §301.7701-1 through 301.7701-3

Partnership not taxed

IRC §701

Reg. §1.701-1

What is a partnership?

IRC §761

Reg. §1.761-1

Health insurance premiums

IRC §162(l)

Salary from partnership guaranteed

IRC §707(c)

Reg. §1.707-1(c)

Special allocations

IRC §704(b)

Substantial economic effect

Reg. §1.704-1(b)(2)

Mary Ogden, 84 TC 871 (1985)

Allocations to partners upon property contributions made after December 20, 1993

Reg. §1.704-3

No advance ruling of partnership provisions re substantial economic effect

Rev. Proc. 79-14, 1979-1 CB 496

Change of partnership interests during the year

IRC §706(d)

Passive loss limitations

IRC §469

IRS may allow unincorporated businesses to choose partnership of corporate taxation

Notice 95-14, 1995-14 IRB 7 (check-the-box initiative)

Failure to file information return

IRC §6698

Sales to controlled partnership

IRC §1239(b) and (c)

Partner reports

IRC §702

Reg. §1.702-1

Transferring partnership interests

IRC §6050K

Reg. §1.6050K-1

Composite 25 transfer rule

Reg. §1.6050K-1(a)(3)

Substantially appreciated inventory

IRC §751(d)(1)

Assignment of outside referral fees to partnership

Stephen B. Schneer, 97 TC 643 (1991)

Retroactive allocations

IRC §706(d)

Net operating loss

Reg. §1.702-2

Credits deductible

IRC §702(b)

Reg. §1.702-2

Partner's distributive share

Temp. Reg. §1.704-IT

P.L. 103-465 12/8/94

Partnership distribution of contributed property within two years

IRC §707(a)(2)(B)

Reg. §1.707-3 through §1.707-9

Recognition of gain by partner on distribution of contributed property
IRC §732

11.11 WHEN A PARTNER REPORTS INCOME OR LOSS

When a partnership reports income or loss
IRC §706
Reg. §1.706-1
Harry W. Lehman, 19 TC 659 (1953)

Fiscal year limitations
IRC §706(b)(1)

Fiscal year election
IRC §444
Temp. Reg. §1.444-1T

Limitations on electable fiscal years
Temp. Reg. §1.444-1T(b)(3)

Required payment
IRC §7519

Refund of required payments
IRC §7519(c)
Announcement 90-112, 1990-40 IRB 37

11.12 PARTNERSHIP LOSS LIMITATIONS

IRC §704
Reg. §1.704-1
F. A. Falconer, 40 TC 1011 (1963) (Acq.)

Limitation on losses
IRC §704(d)
IRC §465

Partners may not increase basis by accrued partnership liabilities
Rev. Rul. 88-77, 1988-2 CB 128

11.13 TAX AUDITS OF PARTNERSHIPS

IRC §§ 6221-6231
The Bipartisan Budget Act of 2015 (BBA) (P.L. 114-74) (new law generally effective for tax years beginning after 2017)

Election out of BBA rules
T.D. 9829, 2018-4 IRB 307

Partnership representative under BBA
T.D. 9839, 2018-35 IRB 325

11.14 STOCKHOLDER REPORTING OF S CORPORATION INCOME OR LOSS

IRC §1361 through 1379

Pass-through of income and losses
IRC §1366

Distributions
IRC §1368
IRC §1366(d)(1)(A)

Income must be included in return
IRC §1367(b)

Health insurance premiums
IRC §162(l)
IRC §1362(d)(3)
IRC §1366(f)(3)
IRC §1375

Relative treated as 2% S corporation shareholder
Richard E. and Mary Ann Hurst, 124 TC 16 (2005)

IRS previews family S corp guidance
Notice 2005-91, 2005-51 IRB 1164

Allocation for new and old shareholder
IRC §1377(a)

Family allocation
IRC §1366(e)

Appreciated property distribution
IRC §1363(d)
IRC §1362(a)
IRC §1362(b)

Effect of election on corporation
IRC §1363(e)

Invalid elections may be corrected
IRC §1362(b)(5) and 1362(f)

Built-in gains tax
IRC §1374
Rev. Rul. 86-141, 1986-2 CB 151
IRC §1362(d)

Inadvertent terminations
IRC §1362(f)

Treatment of termination year
IRC §1362(e)

Re-election following termination
IRC §1362(g)
IRC §1372

Waiver of tax
IRC §1375(d)
IRC §1374

IRS may approve invalid elections
IRC §1362(b)(5)
IRC §1362(f)

Agreement to terminate year
IRC §1377

Audit rules
IRC §§ 6241-6245 repealed (corporate level audit procedures)

IRC §6037(c) (shareholder must report consistently with S Corporation return)

Retroactive re-election
IRC §1362(g)

Adjustments before the loss limitation
IRC §1366(d)(1)(A)
IRC §1368(d)

Income in respect of a decedent
IRC §1367(b)(4)

11.15 HOW BENEFICIARIES REPORT ESTATE OR TRUST INCOME

IRC §652
Reg. §1.652(a) and (b)
* IRS Publication 559

Depreciation and depletion
IRC §167(g)
IRC §611(b)(3)

Net operating losses
IRC §642(d)
Reg. §1.642(h)-1
George W. Balkwill, 25 BTA 1147, aff'd, 77 F.2d 569 (6th Cir. 1935), cert. denied, 296 U.S. 609
George C. Reeves, 15 TCM 394 (1956)

When to report
IRC §652
Reg. §1.652(a)-1

Multiple trusts
IRC §643(f)

Consistent reporting by beneficiaries
IRC §6034A(c)
IRC §6048(d)

11.16 REPORTING INCOME IN RESPECT OF A DECEDENT (IRD)

* IRS Publication 559

Attorneys' fees
IRC §2053(a)
Reg. §20.2053-3(c)

Administration expenses
IRC §2053(b)
Reg. §20.2053-3(a)

Capital gain reduction
IRC §691(c)(4)

Lump-sum distributions
IRC §691(c)(5)

Valuation of short sale closed after death
* Letter Ruling 9436017

11.17 Deduction for Estate Tax Attributable to IRD

* IRS Publication 559

Deduction for estate tax paid
IRC §691(c)
Reg. §1.691(c)-1

No double deduction
IRC §2053
IRC §2054

Annuity beneficiaries get IRD deduction
Rev. Rul. 2005-30, 2005-20 IRB 1015

11.18 How Life Insurance Proceeds Are Taxed to a Beneficiary

IRC §101
IRC §7702
Reg. §1.101-1 to §1.101-4

Flexible premium policies issued before 1985
IRC §101(f)

Life insurance contract defined: policy issued after 1984
IRC §7702

Spouse's exclusion for interest: deaths before 12/23/86
IRC §101(d)(1)(B), prior to amendment by Tax Reform Act of 1986
Reg. §1.101-4(a)

Taxable interest on installment payments
IRC §101(c)
Reg. §1.101-3

No exclusion for combined insurance-annuity pre-1986 Tax Act
Rev. Rul. 65-57, 1965-1 CB 56

Remarriage does not affect interest exclusion pre-1986 Tax Act
Rev. Rul. 72-164, 1972-1 CB 28

Estate tax on life insurance
IRC §2042
Reg. §20.2042-1(c)

Policy transferred within three years of death included in taxable estate
IRC §2035
* Letter Ruling 9533001

Modified endowment contracts
IRC §7702A
IRC §72(e)(10)
IRC §72(v) (premature withdrawal penalty)

11.19 A Policy with a Family Income Rider

Reg. §1.101-4(h)

11.20 Selling or Surrendering Life Insurance Policy

Tax results of selling or surrendering policy
Rev. Rul. 2020-05, 2020-9 IRB 454, modifying Rev. Rul. 2009-13, 2009-21 IRB 1029

Endowment policies paid because of death
Reg. §1.101-1(a)

Policy transferred for valuable consideration
IRC §101(b)
Reg. §1.101-1(b)

Sale of policy to viatical company is income
* Letter Ruling 9443020

11.21 Jury Duty Fees

*IRS Publication 525

11.22 Foster Care Payments

IRC §131
*IRS Publication 525

Medicaid waiver payments are "difficulty of care" payments eligible for exclusion
Notice 2014-7, 2014-4 IRB 445

No exclusion for care services not provided in taxpayer's home
Jonathan E. Stromme, 138 TC No.9 (2012)

11.23 Virtual Currency

Economic Impact payments
IRC §6428B, added by the American Rescue Plan Act (P.L. 117-2, 3/11/2021)

12 DEDUCTIONS ALLOWED IN FIGURING ADJUSTED GROSS INCOME

12.1 Figuring Adjusted Gross Income (AGI)

Gross income
IRC §61

Adjusted gross income
IRC §62

Reg. §1.62-1

Taxable income
IRC §63

Interest on rental property
Isaac R. Wharton, 207 F. 2d 526 (5th Cir. 1953)

12.2 Claiming Deductions From Gross Income

IRC §62
Reg. §1.62-1

Tax Court can review whistleblower claims
Whistleblower 11332-13W, 142 TC No, 21 (2014)

Whistleblower can deduct legal fees
Richard D. Bagley, 2013-2 USTC 50,462 (D. Cal. 2013)

Educator expenses
IRC §62(a)(2)(D)
IRC §62(d)
Rev. Proc. 2021-15, 2021-8 IRB 891 (deduction for COVID-19-related classroom protective items)

Self-employed health insurance deduction
IRC §162(l)

Health insurance for self-employed not a Schedule C deduction
*Chief Counsel Advice 200623001

Tuition and fees deduction
IRC §222

Health savings account deduction
IRC §223

HSA inflation adjustments
Rev. Proc. 2022-24, 2022-20 IRB 1075 (2023 rules)
Rev. Proc. 2021-25, 2021-22 IRB 1161 (2022 rules)
Rev. Proc. 2020-32, 2020-24 IRB 930 (2021 rules)
Rev. Proc. 2019-25, 2019-22 IRB 1261 (2020 rules)
Rev. Proc. 2018-30, 2018-21 IRB 622 (2019 rules)

Reservists and National Guard Members
IRC §62(a)(2)(E)
IRC §162(p) (deemed away from home)

Attorneys' fees in unlawful discrimination cases
Kathleen S. Simpson, 141 TC No. 10 (2013)
IRC §§ 62(a)(20) and 62(e)

Performing artists

IRC §62(a)(2)(B)

IRC §62(b)

State and local officials paid on fee basis

IRC §62(a)(2)(C)

12.3 Moving Costs Are Deductible Only by Qualifying Members of the U.S. Armed Forces

IRC §217(k), as added by the Tax Cuts and Jobs Act for 2018 through 2025 (P.L. 115-97, 12/22/2017),

* IRS Publication 521

Moving wife's belongings not deductible

Jeffrey B. Palmer, TC Memo 2015-30

Mileage rates

Notice 2023-03, 2023-3 IRB 388 (mileage rates for 2023)

Notice 2022-3, 2022-2 IRB 308 (mileage rates for first half of 2022)

Announcement 2022-13, 2022-26 IRB 1185 (mileage rate for second half of 2022)

Notice 2021-2, 2021-3 IRB 478 (mileage rates for 2021)

Notice 2020-5, 2020-4 IRB 380 (mileage rates for 2020)

Notice 2019-02, 2019-02 IRB 281 (mileage rates for 2019)

Direct expenses

Reg. §1.217-2(b)(3), (4)

Cost of moving a pet deductible

Rev. Rul. 66-305, 1966-2 CB 102

Cost of moving car deductible

Rev. Rul. 65-309, 1965-2 CB 77

Depreciation not allowed

Rev. Rul. 70-656, 1970-2 CB 67

Cost of moving a boat nondeductible

William E. Aksomitas, 50 TC 679 (1968)

Cost of moving boat deductible

John R. Fogg, 89 TC 310 (1987)

Apartment lease cancellation fee not deductible

*Darren J. Newell, TC Summary Opinion 2012-57

Delay of family's move due to child's completing education

Rev. Rul. 78-200, 1978-1 CB 77

Reg. §1.217-2(a)(3)

* Letter Ruling 8346039

Furniture purchased en route

Rev. Rul. 70-625, 1970-2 CB 67

13 CLAIMING THE STANDARD DEDUCTION OR ITEMIZED DEDUCTIONS

IRC §63 (standard deduction)

13.1 Does Your Standard Deduction for 2023 Exceed Your Itemized Deductions?

Basic standard deduction increase for 2018 through 2025

IRC §63(c) (7), as added by the Tax Cuts and Jobs Act for 2018 through 2025 (P.L. 115-97, 12/22/2017)

*IRS Publication 5307, Tax Reform: Basics for Individuals and Families

* IRS Publication 501

When to itemize

IRC §63(e)

Changing an election

IRC §63(e)(3)

Taxable income

IRC §63(b)

Nonresident alien

IRC §63(c)(6)(B)

Estate or trust

IRC §63(c)(6)(D)

Short tax year

IRC §63(c)(6)(C)

13.2 Basic Standard Deduction

IRC §63(c) (7), as added by the Tax Cuts and Jobs Act for 2018 through 2025 (P.L. 115-97, 12/22/2017)

Rev. Proc 2022-38, 2022-45 IRS 445 (deduction for 2023)

Rev. Proc. 2021-45, 2021-48 IRB 764 (deduction for 2022)

Rev. Proc. 2020-45, 2020-46 IRB 1016 (deduction for 2021)

Rev. Proc. 2019-44, 2019-47 IRB 1093 (deduction for 2020)

Rev. Proc. 2018-57, 2018-49 IRB 827 (deduction for 2019)

* IRS Publication 501

Additional standard deduction for net disaster losses

Section 304(b)(1)(C) of the Taxpayer Certainty and Disaster Tax Relief Act of 2020 (Division EE of P.L. 116-260, 12-27-2020)

13.3 Spouses Filing Separate Returns

IRC §63(c)(6)(A) (zero standard deduction for spouses filing separately where either itemizes deductions)

Claiming itemized deductions when you are living apart from your spouse

IRC §63(g)

IRC §7703(b) (considered unmarried)

Head of household status when living apart from your spouse

IRC §7703(b) (considered unmarried)

IRC §2(b)(1) (maintain home for qualifying child or relative)

13.4 Standard Deduction If 65 or Older or Blind

IRC §63(c)(3)

Rev. Proc 2022-38, 2022-45 IRS 445 (deduction for 2023)

Rev. Proc. 2021-45, 2021-48 IRB 764 (deduction for 2022)

Rev. Proc. 2020-45, 2020-46 IRB 1016 (deduction for 2021)

Rev. Proc. 2019-44, 2019-47 IRB 1093 (deduction for 2020)

Rev. Proc. 2018-57, 2018-49 IRB 827 (additional amount for 2019)

* IRS Publication 501

Additional amount for age or blindness

IRC §63(f)(1) (age)

IRC §63(f)(2) (blindness)

IRC §63(f)(4) (blindness defined)

13.5 Standard Deduction for Dependents

* IRS Publication 501

IRC §63(c)(5)

Rev. Proc 2022-38, 2022-45 IRS 445 (deduction for 2023)

Rev. Proc. 2021-45, 2021-48 IRB 764 (deduction for 2022)

Rev. Proc. 2020-45, 2020-46 IRB 1016 (standard deduction for dependent for 2021)

Rev. Proc. 2019-44, 2019-47 IRB 1093 (deduction for 2020)

Rev. Proc. 2018-57, 2018-49 IRB 827 (standard deduction for dependent for 2019)

Dependent's standard deduction not reduced by business loss

* Allyson C. Briggs, TC Summary Opinion 2004-22

13.6 PREPAYING OR POSTPONING ITEMIZED EXPENSES

* Schedule A (Form 1040) instructions

13.7 ITEMIZED DEDUCTIONS NO LONGER REDUCED FOR HIGHER-INCOME TAXPAYERS

IRC §68 (f), added by the Tax Cuts and Jobs Act for 2018 through 2025 (P.L. 115-97, 12/22/2017)

14 CHARITABLE CONTRIBUTION DEDUCTIONS

14.1 DEDUCTIBLE CONTRIBUTIONS

IRC §170

IRC §501

IRC §508

* IRS Publication 526

Substantiation requirement for property contributions exceeding $500

IRC §170(f)(11)

* IRS Publication 526

Substantiation requirement for charitable contributions of $250 or more

IRC §170(f)(17)

Reg. §1.170A-13(f)

* IRS Publication 526

All cash donations must be substantiated by bank record or receipt from charity

IRC §170(f)(17)

Contribution by check

Reg. §1.170A-1(b)

Elie B. Witt Est., 160 F. Supp. 521 (D. Fla. 1956)

Estelle Broussard, 16 TC 23 (1951)

Modie J. Spiegel Est., 12 TC 524 (1949) (Acq.)

Rev. Rul. 54-465, 1954-2 CB 93

Direct distribution from IRA not deductible donation

IRC §408(d)(8(E)

Year-end mailing

Stanley G. Reedy, 42 TCM 1401 (1981)

Contribution of note

Sheldon B. Gurenj, 66 TC 118 (1976)

Norman Petty, 40 TC 521 (1963)

Credit cards

Rev. Rul. 78-38, 1978-1 CB 67

* Letter Ruling 9623035

Voluntary payroll deduction

Rev. Rul. 54-549, 1954-2 CB 94

Fund-raising agency

Rev. Rul. 55-192, 1955-1 CB 294; amplified by Rev. Rul. 86-25, 1986-1 CB 202

Religious

IRC §170(c)(2)(B)

IRC §501(c)(3)

Clarence Morey, 205 F. Supp. 918 (S.D. Cal. 1962)

Saint Germain Foundation, 26 TC 648 (1956) (Acq.)

Charitable

IRC §170(c)(2)(B)

IRC §501(c)(3)

IRC §509(a)

T. J. Moss Tie Co., 18 TC 188 (1952) (Nonacq.)

Isabel Peters, 21 TC 55 (1953) (Acq.)

William Waller, 39 TC 665 (1963) (Acq.)

Lorain Avenue Clinic, 31 TC 141 (1958)

Scientific, literary, and educational

IRC §170(c)(2)(B)

IRC §501(c)(3)

IRC §509(a)

Science and Research Foundation, Inc., 181 F. Supp. 526 (S.D. Ill. 1960)

Rev. Rul. 67-291, 1967-2 CB 184

Rev. Rul. 67-292, 1967-2 CB 184

Rev. Rul. 93-73, 1993-2 CB 75

Prevention of cruelty to children or animals

IRC §170(c)(2)(B)

IRC §501(c)(3)

John A. Mustard, Exr., 155 F. Supp. 325 (Ct. Cl. 1957)

Amateur athletic associations

IRC §170(c)(2)(B)

IRC §501(c)(3)

Domestic nonprofit veterans organizations

IRC §170(c)(3)

Rev. Rul. 57-327, 1957-2 CB 155

Rev. Rul. 59-151, 1959-1 CB 53

Domestic fraternal group

IRC §170(c)(4)

IRC §501(c)(8)

Nonprofit cemetery and burial companies

IRC §170(c)(5)

IRC §501(c)(13)

Rev. Rul. 58-190, 1958-1 CB 15

Foreign charities

IRC §170(c)(2)(A)

IRC §1.170-2(a)(1)

Dora A. Welti, 1 TC 905 (1943)

Louise K. Herter, 20 TCM 78 (1953)

Rev. Rul. 63-252, 1963-2 CB 101, amplified by Rev. Rul. 66-79, 1966-1 CB 48

Rev. Rul. 69-80, 1969-1 CB 65

Legal fees to preserve donation

Anne Archbold, 444 F.2d 1120 (Ct. Cl. 1971)

Organizations qualifying for deductible donations

IRC §170(c)

Rev. Rul. 54-243, 1954-1 CB 92

* IRS Publication 78 Cumulative List (online only)

United States, state, city, etc.

IRC §170(b)(1)(a)

IRC §170(c)(1)

Rev. Rul. 56-126, 1956-1 CB 56

Social Security system

Rev. Rul. 82-169, 1982-2 CB 72

Indian tribes

Rev. Rul. 74-179, 1974-1 CB 279

Land donated to municipality

Mary W. Toole (D. Fla. 1963), 63-1 USTC ¶9267 (D. Fla. 1963)

Citizens and Southern Nat'l Bank of S.C., 243 F. Supp. 900 (D.S. Car. 1965)

14.2 NONDEDUCTIBLE CONTRIBUTIONS

Disclosure of nondeductibility by political fund-raisers

IRC §6113

Lobbying

IRC §170(c)

IRC §501(c)(3)

IRC §501(h)

Alan B. Kuper, 332 F.2d 562 (3d Cir. 1964), aff'g 22 TCM 1208 (1963), cert. denied, 379 U.S. 920

Murray Seasongood, 227 F.2d 907 (6th Cir. 1956)

McClintock-Trunkey Co., 19 TC 297 (1952), rev'd on another issue, 217 F.2d 329 (9th Cir. 1955)

Mosby Hotel Co., 13 TCM 996 (1954)

Rev. Rul. 62-71, 1962-1 CB 85

Organization benefitting restricted groups

IRC §170(c)

Boston Safe Deposit & Trust Co., 30 BTA 679

Colonial Trust Co., Exr., 19 BTA 174 (Acq.)

Montgomery, 63 Ct. Cl. 588

Bar association donations

Rev. Rul. 77-232, 1977-2 CB 71, clarified by Rev. Rul. 78-129, 1978-1 CB 67

No deduction if bar association rates judicial candidates

Association of Bar of City of NY, 858 F.2d 876 (2d Cir. 1988), cert. denied, 109 S. Ct. 1768, rev'g 89 TC 599 (1987)

Communist organizations

IRC §170(k)

Sec. 11(a), Internal Security Act of 1950 (64 Stat. 996; 50 U.S.C. 790)

Reg. §1.501(e)-1

Benefit private individual

IRC §170(c)

IRC §501(c)(3)

Emanuel Kolkey, 27 TC 37 (1956) (Acq.), aff'd, 254 F.2d 51 (7th Cir. 1958)

Saint Germain Foundation, 26 TC 648 (1956) (Acq.)

Mark B. Lloyd, 29 TCM 453 (1970)

Purchase of church building bond

Rev. Rul. 75-112, 1975-1 CB 274

Rev. Rul. 58-262, 1958-1 CB 143

Blood donations

Rev. Rul. 162, 1953-2 CB 127

Foreign governments

R. Hess, 30 TCM 1043 (1971) (State of Israel)

Son's payment for mother's apartment

Ernest S. & Janet M. Klapperbach, 52 TCM 437 (1986)

Donation of services

Reg. §1.170A-1(g)

Rev. Rul. 67-236, 1967-2 CB 103

Rev. Rul. 57-462, 1957-2 CB 157

William W. Grant, 84 TC 809 (1985)

Value of use of property

IRC §170(f)(3)(A)

Reg. §1.170A-7(d)

No deduction for donated vacation home time

Rev. Rul. 89-51, 1989-1 CB 89

No deduction for payments to support Mormon missionary

Harold Davis, 110 S. Ct. 2014 (1990)

14.3 Contributions That Provide You With Benefits

* IRS Publication 526

Token benefits

Rev. Proc 2022-38, 2022-45 IRB 445 (token amounts disregarded for 2023 donations)

Rev. Proc. 2021-45, 2021-48 IRB 764 (token amounts disregarded for 2022 donations)

Rev. Proc. 2020-45, 2020-46 IRB 1016 (token amounts disregarded for 2021 donations)

Rev. Proc. 2019-44, 2019-47 IRB 1093 (token amounts disregarded for 2020 donations)

Rev. Proc. 90-12, 1990-1 CB 471, amplified by Rev. Proc. 92-49, 1992-1 CB 987

Deduction reduced for state and local contribution if state/local tax credits are received in "SALT" cap workaround

T.D.9907, 2020-38 IRB 559 (safe harbor)

T.D. 9864, 2019-27 IRB 6

Value in return for contribution

Katherine Channing, 67 F.2d 98 (1st Cir.), cert. denied, 291 U.S. 686

Morris N. Scharf, 32 TCM 124 (1973)

Albin J. Strandquist, 29 TCM 38 (1970)

Rev. Rul. 67-246, 1967-2 CB 104 distinguished by Rev. Rul. 74-348, 1974-2 CB 80

Rev. Rul. 58-303, 1958-1 CB 61

Tuition

Harold De Jong, 309 F.2d 373 (9th Cir. 1962), aff'g 36 TC 896 (1961)

Rev. Rul. 71-112, 1971-1 CB 93

Jacob Oppewal, 30 TCM 1177 (1971), aff'd, 468 F.2d 1000 (1st Cir. 1972)

Jewish day school courses not deductible despite IRS concession on Scientology courses

Michael Sklar, 2009-1 USTC ¶50,106 (9th Cir. 2008)

Michael Sklar, 279 F.3d 697 (9th Cir. 2002)

No deduction for Church of Scientology trainings

Robert L. Hernandez, 490 U.S. 680 (1989)

Rest home

O. J. Wardwell Est., 35 TC 443 (1960), rev'd, 301 F.2d 632 (8th Cir. 1962)

Deduction allowed for retirement community sponsorship gift

Ruth Dowell, 553 F.2d 1233 (10th Cir. 1977)

Deductible dues

Eunice A. Horne, 16 TCM 953 (1957)

Rev. Rul. 54-565, 1954-2 CB 95, modified by Rev. Rul. 68-432, 1968-2 CB 104

Rev. Rul. 55-192, 1955-1 CB 294, amplified by Rev. Rul. 86-25, 1986-1 CB 202

No deduction for house donated to fire department

Theodore R. Rolfs, 135 TC No. 24 (2010), aff'd, 668 F.3d 888 (7th Cir. 2012)

Upen G. Patel, 138 TC No. 23 (2012)

James Hendrix, DC Ohio, 2010-2 USTC ¶50,541

Benefit tickets

Rev. Rul. 74-348, 1974-2 CB 80

No deduction for regular price tickets even if not used

Charles F. Urbauer, 63 TCM 2492 (1992)

No deduction for payment giving right to buy athletic stadium tickets

IRC §170(l), as amended by the Tax Cuts and Jobs Act for contributions made after 2017 (P.L. 115-97, 12/22/2017)

Membership benefits

Reg. §1.170 A-13 (f)(8)(i)(B)

14.4 Unreimbursed Expenses of Volunteer Workers

Out-of-pocket costs deductible

Reg. §1.170 A-1 (g)

Substantiating expenses under $250

Jan Elizabeth Van Dusen, 136 TC No. 25 (2011)

Written acknowledgment of services required for expenses of $250 or more

Reg. §1.170 A-13 (f)(10)

Jan Elizabeth Van Dusen, 136 TC No. 25 (2011)

Mileage rate for unreimbursed charitable volunteers

Notice 2023-03, 2023-3 IRB 388 (mileage rates for 2023)

IRC §170(i) (14 cents per mile rate fixed by statute)

Travel expenses

Francois Louis, 25 TCM 1047 (1966)

Rev. Rul. 59-160, 1959-1 CB 59

Rev. Rul. 58-279, 1958-1 CB 145

Rev. Rul. 58-240, 1958-1 CB 141, clarified by Rev. Rul. 71-135, 1971-1 CB 94

Rev. Rul. 57-327, 1957-2 CB 155

Rev. Rul. 55-4, 1955-1 CB 291

No deduction for value of donated services

Reg. §1.170A-1(g)

William W. Grant, 84 TC 809 (1985)

Per diem allowances

Rev. Rul. 74-433, 1974-2 CB 92

Rev. Rul. 67-30, 1967-1 CB 9

Uniform costs

Rev. Rul. 56-508, 1956-2 CB 126

Delegate

Harris W. Seed, 57 TC 265 (1971)

John R. Wood, 57 TC 220 (1971), aff'd per curiam, 462 F.2d 691 (5th Cir. 1972)

Rev. Rul. 58-240, 1958-1 CB 141, clarified by Rev. Rul. 71-135, 1971-1 CB 94

* Letter Ruling 8242042

Services authorized

Russell Doty, Jr., 62 TC 587 (1974)

Travis Smith, 60 TC 988 (1973) (Acq.)

Replacing engine while doing volunteer work

Rev. Rul. 59-239, 1959-2 CB 100

Noncompensated minister deducts car expenses

Rev. Rul. 69-645, 1969-2 CB 37

CAP volunteer

Larry A. Miller, 34 TCM 1207 (1975)

Repairs attributable to charitable services deductible

John Orr, 343 F.2d 553 (5th Cir. 1965)

Rev. Rul. 58-279, 1958-1 CB 145

Babysitting costs

Rev. Rul. 73-597, 1973-2 CB 69

Foster care costs

Rev. Rul. 77-280, 1977-2 CB 14

Kingman Babcock, 71 TCM 2257 (1996)

No deduction for travel unless elements of personal pleasure absent

IRC §170(j)

Notice 87-23, 1987-1 CB 467, modified by Rev. Proc. 90-15, 1990-1 CB 476

14.5 Support of a Student in Your Home

IRC §170(g)

Reg. §1.170A-2

14.6 What Kind of Property Are You Donating?

* IRS Publication 526

Gift of property

IRC §170

Rev. Rul. 55-410, 1955-1 CB 297

Magnolia Development Corp., 19 TCM 934 (1960)

Stock donation to private foundation

IRC §170(e)(5)(D)(ii)

* Letter Ruling 200112002 (applying family aggregation rules)

No deduction if voting rights retained

Rev. Rul. 81-282, 1981-2 CB 78

Delivery of stock gift

Jack W. Londen, 45 TC 106 (1965)

Fair market value of property

Philip Kaplan, 43 TC 663 (1965) (Acq.)

Daniel S. McGuire, 44 TC 801 (1965) (Acq.)

Morris Schapiro, 27 TCM 205 (1968)

Alexia DuPont O. De Bie Est., 56 TC 876 (1971) (Acq.)

Lucky Stores, Inc., 105 TC 28 (1996)

Guidelines for valuations

Rev. Rul. 66-49, 1966-1 CB 36, amplified by Rev. Rul. 72-366, 1972-2 CB 91

Ordinary income property

IRC §170(e)(1)(A)

Reg. §1.170A-4(b)(1)

Leonard Greene, 13 F.3d 577 (2nd Cir. 1994)

Congressman's papers

James H. Morrison, 71 TC 683 (1979), aff'd per curiam, 611 F.2d 98 (5th Cir. 1980)

No charitable deduction for McVeigh trial papers

Sherrel and Leslie Stephen Jones, 2009-1 USTC ¶50,316 (10th Cir. 2009)

Partnership property

Rev. Rul. 96-11, 1996-4 IRB 28

Deduction limits for tangible personal property

IRC §170(e)(1)(B)

Reg. §1.170A-4(b)(3)(ii)(b) (reasonably anticipate related use)

Recapture of deduction without certification of exempt-use

IRC §170(e)(7)

Donating used car

IRC §170(f)(12) (for vehicles valued at over $500)

Notice 2005-44, 2005-25 IRB 1287

* IRS Publication 526

Partial interests

IRC §170(f)(3)(A) and (B)

Reg. §1.170A-7

Future interests in tangible personal property

IRC §170(a)(3)

Election to reduce appreciation

IRC §170(b)(1)(C)(iii)

Reg. §1.170A-8(d)(2)

Rev. Rul. 74-53, 1974-1 CB 60

Capital gain property donated to private foundation

IRC §170(b)(1)(D)

IRC §170(e)

Fair market value deduction for gift of publicly traded stock to private foundation

IRC §170(e)(5)

* Letter Ruling 200322005 (American Depositary Receipts)

John C. Todd, 118 TC 334 (2002)

Trust interests

IRC §170(f)(2)

Prepaid interest

IRC §170(f)(5)

Reg. §1.170A-3

Donation of remainder interests

IRC §664

Reg. §1.664-4

Gift of mortgaged property

Rev. Rul. 81-163, 1981-1 CB 433

Winston Guest, 77 TC 9 (1981) (Acq.)

Leo Ebben et al.,783 F.2d 906 (9th Cir. 1986)

Bargain sale

IRC §170(e)(2)

IRC §1011(b)

Reg. §1.170A-4(c)(2)

Leonard Greene, 13 F.3d 577 (2nd Cir. 1994)

Gift of depreciable mortgaged property

Aaron Levine Est., 634 F.2d 12 (2d Cir. 1980)

Teofilo Evangelista, 629 F.2d 1218 (7th Cir. 1980)

Donating intellectual property to charity

Code Sections 170(e)(1)(B)(iii) and 170(m) (allowable deduction)

Notice 2005-41, 2005-23 IRB 1203 (donor notification)

T.D. 9206, 2005-25 IRB 1283 (donee reporting regulations)

14.7 Cars, Clothing, and Other Property Valued Below Cost

* Publication 526

Used vehicles, boats, airplanes

IRC §170(f)(12)

Notice 2005-44, 2005-25 IRB 1287

* IRS Publication 526

Used clothing and household items

IRC §170 (f)(16)

Deduction limited to cost

LaVar Withers, 69 TC 900 (1978)

14.8 Bargain Sales of Appreciated Property

IRC §170(e)(2)

IRC §1011(b)

Reg. §1.170A-4(c)(2)

Reg. §1.1011-2

Fair market value disputed on bargain sale to charity

Bob R. Davis, TC Memo 2015-88

Appreciation reduction for contributed portion only

Estate of Pauline Bullard, 87 TC 261 (1986)

Basis allocation applies even if annual ceiling bars deduction

Warner W. Hodgdon, 98 TC 31 (1992)

Bargain sale under installment agreement

Kenneth L. Musgrave, TC Memo 2000-285

14.9 Art Objects

IRS Art Advisory Panel renewed

FR Doc. 2022-02101, at 87 FR 7847 (2-022022) (two-year renewal of Art Advisory Panel)

Rev. Proc. 2023-1, 2023-1 IRB 1 (Section 9 of Appendix A, user fee for SOV)

Art not used for tax-exempt purposes

IRC §170(e)(1)(B)(i)

Recapture of tax benefit on donated property not used for exempt purposes

IRC §170(e)(7)

Restrictions on contributions of fractional interests

IRC §170(o)

IRS statement of value

FR Doc. 2022-02101, at 87 FR 7847 (2-2-2022) (two-year renewal of Art Advisory Panel))

Rev. Proc. 2023-1, 2023-1 IRB 1 (Section 9 of Appendix A, user fee for SOV)

Rev. Proc. 96-15, 1996-3 IRB 41

Appraising contributions of art works

Adolph Posner, 35 TCM 943 (1976)

Edwin F. Gordon, 35 TCM 1227 (1976)

Appraisal fee an itemized expense

Rev. Rul. 67-461, 1967-1 CB 125

Family's allocation of portion of collection

Gifford M. Mast, 56 TCM 1523 (1989)

Deduction allowed despite lack of possession

James Winokur, 90 TC 733 (1988) (Acq.)

14.10 Interests in Real Estate

Settlement for syndicated conservation easements

IR-2020-130, 6/25/20

Conservation easement deduction requires strict adherence to requirements

15 West 17th Street LLC, TC No. 19 (2016)

Conservation easement deduction limited by terms of donation

Patrick J. Wachter, 142 TC No. 7 (2014)

Lawrence G. Graev, 140 TC No. 17 (2013)

Conservation Easement – Safe Harbor Language for Extinguishment and Boundary Line Adjustment Clause

Notice 2023-20, 2023-17 IRB 766

Ability to substitute easement property bars charitable deduction

B.V. Belk, 140 TC No.1 (2013)

Fractional transfers

IRC §170(f)(3)(B)(ii)

Rev. Rul. 58-261, 1958-1 CB 143

Remainder interests

IRC §170(f)(4)

Prop. Reg. §1.170A-12

Option on realty

Rev. Rul. 82-197, 1982-2 CB 72

Farms or residences

IRC §170(f)(3)(B)(i)

Rev. Rul. 76-357, 1976-2 CB 285

Partial interests donated for qualified conservation purposes

IRC §170(h)

Charles F. Glass, 2007-2 USTC ¶50,111 (6th Cir. 2006)

Conservation easement deduction denied for property subject to unsubordinated deed of trust

Ramona L. Mitchell, 138 TC No. 16 (2012)

Restrictions on contributions of facade easements on certified historic structures

IRC §170(h)(4)(B) and (C)

Mortgage does not bar charitable deduction for façade easement

Gordon Kaufman, 2012-2 USTC ¶50,472 (1st Cir. 2012), rev'g 134 TC No. 9 (2010)

Deduction allowed for facade easement

Dorothy Jean Simmonds, TC Memo 2009-208

No deduction for home donated to fire department

Upen G. Patel, 138 TC No. 23 (2012)

James Hendrix, DC Ohio, 2010-2 USTC ¶50,541

Theodore R. Rolfs, 135 TC No. 24 (2010), aff'd, 668 F.3d 888 (7th Cir. 2012)

Vacation use retained

Rev. Rul. 75-420, 1975-2 CB 78

Right to use of property

IRC §170(f)(3)(A)

Reg. §1.170A-7(d)

Charles M. Petgers, 35 TCM 770 (1976)

No deduction for airspace over historic building

J. Maurice Herman, TC Memo 2009-205

Waiver of grazing permit not a charitable donation

Otto Bischel, 2006-1 USTC ¶50,216 (DC, NV)

Donating use of vacation home

Rev. Rul. 89-51, 1989-1 CB 89

14.11 Life Insurance

Deductible if irrevocably assigned

Eppa Hunton, IV, 1 TC 821 (1943) (Acq.)

Premiums deductible if beneficiary a charity

Mortimer C. Adler, 5 BTA 1063

Rev. Rul. 58-372, 1958-2 CB 99

Charity's insurable interest

* Letter Ruling 9147040, revoking Letter Ruling 9110016

Contribution of cash surrender value not deductible

Rev. Rul. 76-143, 1976-1 CB 63

Rev. Rul. 76-1, 1976-1 CB 57

Split-dollar insurance

IRS Notice 99-36, 1999-26 IRB

14.12 Business Inventory

Corporate inventory

Reg. §1.170A-4(e)

Gifts at fair market value

IRC §170(e)

Charles N. Prothro, 209 F.2d 331 (5th Cir. 1954)

David C. Whitge, 104 F. Supp. 213 (D. Kan. 1952)

Rev. Rul. 55-138, 1955-1 CB 223

Crops

Clyde G. Tatum, 46 TC 736 (1966), aff'd, 400 F.2d 242 (5th Cir. 1968)

Certain corporate contributions for care of ill, needy, or infants

IRC §170(e)(3)

14.13 DONATIONS THROUGH TRUSTS

Income interests

IRC §170(f)(2)(B)

IRC §671

Abusive charitable lead trust transactions

Treasury Decision 8923, 1/5/01

Charitable remainder trusts

IRC §170(f)(2)(A)

IRC §170(f)(3)(B)

IRC §170(f)(4)

IRC §170(f)(7)

IRC §664

Treasury Decision 8926 (abusive remainder trust transactions)

Life income plans

IRC §170(f)(2)(A)

IRC §642(c)(5)

IRC §664

IRS valuation tables

Notice 89-60, 1989-1 CB 700

14.14 RECORDS NEEDED TO SUBSTANTIATE YOUR CONTRIBUTIONS

T.D. 9836, 2018-33 IRB 291 (final regulations on substantiating cash and noncash contributions

* IRS Publication 526

Lack of substantiation voids charitable deduction

David P. Durden, TC Memo 2012-140

Appraisals and documentation requirements

IRC §170(f)(11)

Definition of qualified appraisal and qualifed appraiser revised

IRC §170(f)(11)(E)

Acknowledgement requirement for vehicles, boats, or airplanes valued at over $500

IRC §170(f)(12)

Notice 2005-44, 2005-25 IRB 1287

Substantiation for cash donations

IRC §170(f)(17) (bank record or receipt from charity regardless of amount)

Charitable contributions by payroll deductions

Notice 2006-11, 2006-51 IRB 1127

Charity disclosure statement for donations exceeding $75

IRC §6115

Contribution by check

Reg. §1.170A-1(b)

Elie B. Witt Est., 160 F. Supp. 521 (D. Fla. 1956)

Estelle Broussard, 16 TC 23 (1951)

Modie J. Spiegel Est., 12 TC 524 (1949) (Acq.)

Rev. Rul. 54-465, 1954-2 CB 93

14.15 FORM 8283 AND WRITTEN APPRAISAL REQUIREMENTS FOR PROPERY DONATIONS

Qualified appraisals and qualified appraisers

IRC §170(f)(11)

Reg. §1.170A-17 (final regulation, in T.D. 9836, 2018-33 IRB 291)

Appraising wrong asset costs donor charitable deduction

Estate of Harvey Evenchik, TC Memo 2013-34

Appraisals and documentation requirements

IRC §170(f)(11)

* IRS Publication 526

Donor's self-appraisals not qualified; deduction completely disallowed

Joseph Mohamed, Sr., TC Memo 2012-152

Penalty for overvaluation

IRC §6662(e)(1)(A) (20% penalty)

IRC §6662(h)(2)(A) (40% penalty)

14.16 PENALTY FOR SUBSTANTIAL OVERVALUATION OF PROPERTY

20% penalty

IRC §6662 (e)(1)(A)

40% penalty

IRC §6662 (h)(2)(A)

Penalty for overstating the $300/$600 deduction for 2021 charitable cash contributions

IRC §6662(l), added by the Consolidated Appropriations Act, 2021 (P.L. 116-260, 12/27/2020)

Penalty and displinary action imposed on apprasiers for substantial or gross overvaluation

IRC §6695A

Reasonable cause reliance on appraisal

Reg. §1.6664.4 (g)

Professional appraiser subject to penalty

IRC §6701

14.17 CEILING ON CHARITABLE CONTRIBUTIONS

IRC §170(b)

* IRS Publication 526

60% of AGI limit for cash contributions to 50% limit organizations

IRC §170(b) (1) (G), added by the Tax Cuts and Jobs Act for 2018 through 2025 (P.L. 115-97, 12/22/2017),

Direct distribution from IRA not deductible donation

IRC §408(d)(8(E)

Higher deduction ceiling for qualified conservation contributions

IRC §170(b)(1)(E)

Organizations qualifying for 50% ceiling

IRC §170(b)(1)(A)

Reg. §1.170A-9

30% limit for capital gain property

IRC §170(b)(1)(C)

30% limit for non-operating foundations

IRC 170(b)(1)(B)

20% limit for certain capital gain property

IRC §170(b)(1)(D)

Donations by corporations

IRC §170(b)(2)

Order of taking deductions

IRC §170(b)(1)(C) and (D)

Reg. §1.170A-8(f)

14.18 CARRYOVER FOR EXCESS DONATIONS

Individuals

IRC §170(d)(1)

Sidney Rimmer, 69 TCM 2620 (1995)

Corporations

IRC §170(d)(2)

Donations to foundations

IRC §170(b)(1)(B)

IRC §170(b)(1)(D)

14.19 ELECTION TO REDUCE FAIR MARKET VALUE BY APPRECIATION

Reduction for appreciation

IRC §170(e)(1)

Electing 50% ceiling

IRC §170(b)(1)(C)(iii)

Reg. §1.170A-8(d)(2)

Election is irreversible

Orin Woodbury, 900 F.2d 1457 (10th Cir. 1990)

15 ITEMIZED DEDUCTION FOR INTEREST EXPENSES

15.1 DEDUCTION FOR HOME MORTGAGE INTEREST

IRC §163(h)

* IRS Publication 530

* IRS Publication 936

Mortgage interest deduction rules for 2018 through 2025 (Tax Cuts and Jobs Act)

IRC §163(h) (3) (F), as added by the Tax Cuts and Jobs Act (P.L. 115-97, 12/22/2017)

IRC §163(h) (3) (F) (i) (I) (no deduction for interest on home equity debt not otherwise qualifying as acquisition debt)

IRC §163(h) (3) (F) (i) (II) and (III) (limit on acquisition debt incurred after December 15, 2017 reduced to $750,000 ($375,000 if married filing separately)

IRC §163 (h) (3) (F) (i) (III) (prior law acquisition debt limit of $1 million ($500,000 if married filing separately) "grandfathered" for debt incurred on or before December 15, 2007)

IRC §163(h) (3) (F) (iii) (refinancing of "grandfathered" acquisition debt (acquisition debt incurred before 12/16/17) still subject to $1 million limit ($500,000 if married filing separately))

Two-residence test

IRC §163(h)(4)(A)

No mortgage payments deduction without proof of beneficial or equitable ownership

*James David Jackson, TC Summary Opinion 2016-33

Expanded lender reporting requirements for statements filed after 2016

IRC §6050 H, as amended by the Surface Transportation and Veterans Health Choice Improvement Act of 2015, P.L. 114-41, 7/31/15

Paying sibling's mortgage not deductible

Lourdes Puentes, TC Memo 2013-277

Married persons filing separate returns

IRC §163(h)(4)(A)(ii)(qualified residences)

Faina Bronstein, 138 TC No. 21 (2012) ($500,000 acquisition debt and $50,000 home equity debt limits apply under pre-2018 rules)

IRS safe harbor if assistance received from Hardest Hit Fund

Notice 2018-63, 2018-34 IRB 318

Home mortgage certificates

IRC §25

Temp. Reg. §1.25-1T through 8T

Qualified residence

H. Roger Lawler, 69 TCM 1699 (1995)

Safe harbor rules for homeowners receiving HAF funds

Rev. Proc. 2021-47

15.2 HOME ACQUISITION LOANS

Acquisition indebtedness defined

IRC §163(h)(3)(B)(i)

Home acquisition debt limits for 2018 through 2025 (Tax Cuts and Jobs Act)

IRC §163(h) (3) (F) (i) (II) and (III) (limit on acquisition debt incurred after December 15, 2017 reduced to $750,000 ($375,000 if married filing separately)

IRC §163 (h) (3) (F) (i) (III) (prior law acquisition debt limit of $1 million ($500,000 if married filing separately) "grandfathered" for debt incurred on or before December 15, 2007)

IRC §163(h) (3) (F) (iii) (refinancing of "grandfathered" acquisition debt (acquisition debt incurred before 12/16/17) still subject to $1 million limit ($500,000 if married filing separately))

Mortgage interest limit for unmarried co-owners

Bruce H. Voss, 796 F.3d 1051 (9th Cir. 2015)(interest limit applies per taxpayer); rev'g. Charles J. Sophy, 138 TC No. 8 (2012) (unmarried owners must allocate debt limit between them)

AOD 2016-02, 2016-31 IRB 193 (IRS acquiescence to 9th Circuit decision in Voss above)

* Chief Counsel Memorandum 200911007

Pre-2018 rule: up to $100,000 of home purchase loan over $1 million may be home equity debt

Rev. Rul. 2010-25, 2010-44 IRB 571

Beneficial owner can deduct interest on relative's mortgage

* Qui Van Phan, TC Summary Opinion 2015-1

*Conrad Y. Edosada, TC Summary Opinion 2012-17

Paul Trans Dang, TC Memo 1999-233

Saffet Uslu, TC Memo 1997-551

Seller's debt

Wendell Belden, 70 TCM 274 (1995)

Passive activity interest

IRC §469

Married persons filing separate returns

IRC §163(h)(4)(A)(ii)(qualified residences)

Faina Bronstein, 138 TC No. 21 (2012) ($500,000 acquisition debt and $50,000 home equity debt limits apply under pre-2018 rules)

Cooperatives

IRC §163(h)(4)(B)

Destroyed house rebuilt

Rev. Rul 96-32, 1996-25 IRB 4

15.3 HOME EQUITY LOANS

Rule for 2018 through 2025 (Tax Cuts and Jobs Act)

IRC §163(h) (3) (F) (i) (I) (no deduction for interest on home equity indebtedness not otherwise qualifying as acquisition debt)

IRC §163(h)(3)(C) (i) (definition of home equity indebtedness)

Pre-2018 rule: up to $100,000 of home purchase loan over $1 million may be home equity debt

Rev. Rul. 2010-25, 2010-44 IRB 571

Mortgage interest limit for unmarried co-owners

Bruce H. Voss, 796 F.3d 1051 (9th Cir. 2015) (interest limit applies per taxpayer); rev'g. Charles J. Sophy, 138 TC No. 8 (2012) (unmarried owners must allocate debt limit between them)

AOD 2016-02, 2016-31 IRB 193 (IRS acquiescence to 9th Circuit decision in Voss above)

* Chief Counsel Memorandum 200911007

15.4 HOME CONSTRUCTION LOANS

Residence under construction

Temp. Reg. §1.163-10T(p)(5)

Notice 88-74, 1988-2 CB 385

Mortgage interest deduction allowed for constructing house that never gets built

*Thomas G. Rose, TC Summary Opinion 2011-117

15.5 MORTGAGE INSURANCE PREMIUMS AND OTHER PAYMENT RULES

Deduction for payments of mortgage insurance premiums allowed through 2021

IRC §163(h)(3)(E)(iv), as amended by the Consolidated Appropriations Act, 2021 (P.L. 116-260,12/27/2020)

IRS safe harbor if assistance received from Hardest Hit Fund

Notice 2018-63, 2018-34 IRB 318

Home mortgage certificates

IRC §25

Temp. Reg. §1.25-1T through 8T

Joint obligor can deduct payment from own funds

Austin B. Ewell, Jr., TC Memo 1996-253

Barbara S. Finney, 35 TCM 1504 (1976)

Penalty for prepaying mortgage

Rev. Rul. 57-198, 1957-1 CB 94

Mortgage assistance payments under §235 of the National Housing Act not deductible

Reg. §1.163-1(d)

Rev. Rul. 75-271, 1975-2 CB 23

Delinquency charges not deductible

Robert G. West, 61 TCM 1694 (1991)

Graduated payment mortgages

* Letter Ruling 8031087

Reverse mortgage loan

Rev. Rul. 80-248, 1980-2 CB 164

Zero interest mortgages

Rev. Rul. 82-124, 1982-1 CB 89

Shared appreciation mortgage

Rev. Rul. 83-51, 1983-1 CB 48

H.U.D. interest reduction payments

Rev. Rul. 76-75, 1976-1 CB 14

Alvin V. Graff, 74 TC 743 (1980)

15.6 INTEREST ON REFINANCED LOANS

Refinancing

IRC §163(h)(3)(B)(i) (refinanced acquisition debt treated as acquisition debt)

IRC §163(h) (3) (F) (iii), as added by the Tax Cuts and Jobs Act (P.L. 115-97, 12/22/2017) (for 2018 through 2025, refinancing of "grandfathered" acquisition debt (acquisition debt incurred before 12/16/17) still subject to $1 million limit ($500,000 if married filing separately))

James R. Huntsman, 91 TC (1988), rev'd by 905 F.2d 1182 (8th Cir. 1990) (points on refinancing)

Rev. Rul. 87-22, 1987-1 CB 146 (points)

David A. Kelly, 62 TCM 401 (1991) (Huntsman 8th Circuit exception inapplicable)

15.7 "POINTS"

* IRS Publication 530

* IRS Publication 936

"Points" treated as prepaid interest

IRC §461(g)

IRS position on deducting points

Rev. Proc. 94-27, 1994-1 CB 613

Seller-paid points

Rev. Proc. 94-27, 1994-1 CB 613

Amortize points starting in second year

* Letter Ruling 199905033

VA and FHA loan origination fees deductible as points

Rev. Proc. 92-12A, 1992-1 CB 664

Loan fees amortized

Karl Von Muff, 46 TCM 1185 (1983)

Richard Goodwin, 75 TC 424 (1981)

Rev. Rul. 81-161, 1981-1 CB 313

Rev. Rul. 81-160, 1981-1 CB 312

Loan fees: prior law

Robert E. Stewart, 41 TCM 318 (1980)

Points withheld from principal not deductible

Roger A. Schubel, 77 TC 701 (1981)

Refinancing

James R. Huntsman, 91 TC (1988), rev'd by 905 F.2d 1182 (8th Cir. 1990)

Rev. Rul. 87-22, 1987-1 CB 146

Rev. Proc. 87-15, 1987-1 CB 624

David A. Kelly, 62 TCM 401 (1991)

(Huntsman 8th Circuit exception inapplicable)

15.8 COOPERATIVE AND CONDOMINIUM APARTMENTS

* IRS Publication 936

Cooperative apartments

IRC §163(h)(4)(B)

IRC §216

Reg. §1.216-1(c) and (d)

Rev. Rul. 73-15, 1973-1 CB 141

Rev. Rul. 59-257, 1959-2 CB 101

Rev. Rul. 53-120, 1953-2 CB 130

Holdover tenants do not jeopardize deductions to co-op owners

Rev. Rul. 80-299, 1980-2 CB 82

Condominiums

Rev. Rul. 64-31, 1964-1 (Pt. 1) CB 300

Raymond J. Wachter, 75-1 USTC ¶9172 (DC Wash. 1975)

15.9 INVESTMENT INTEREST LIMITATIONS

* IRS Publication 550

Investment interest

IRC §163(d)(3)

IRC §163(h)(2)(B)

Rev. Rul. 95-16, 1995-1 CB 9

Warren Halle, 83 F.3d 649 (4th Cir. 1996)

Passive activity interest

IRC §469

Net capital gain and qualified dividends excluded from investment income unless election made

IRC §163(d)(4)(B)

Capital loss carryover reduces investment income

* William Lenehan III, TC Summary Opinion 2002-124

Carryforward of disallowed interest

IRC §163(d)(2)

15.10 DEBTS TO CARRY TAX-EXEMPT OBLIGATIONS

Frank Batten, 322 F. Supp. 629 (E. D. Vir. 1971)

Amedeo Louis Marionenzi, 32 TCM 681 (1973), aff'd per curiam, 490 F.2d 92 (1st Cir. 1974)

Interest on borrowings to carry tax-exempt obligations

IRC §265

Reg. §1.265-2

Constance M. Bishop, 41 TC 154 (1963), aff'd, 342 F.2d 757 (6th Cir. 1965)

Rev. Proc. 72-18, 1972-1 CB 740, clarified by Rev. Proc. 74-8, 1974-1 CB 419

Interest on joint venture mortgage

Max R. Israelson, 367 F. Supp. 1104 (D. Md. 1974), aff'd per curiam, 75-1 USTC ¶9,131 (4th Cir. 1975)

Interest on loan to carry mutual-fund shares paying exempt-interest dividends

IRC §265(a)(4)

Short sales

IRC §265(a)(5)

15.11 EARMARKING USE OF LOAN PROCEEDS FOR INVESTMENT OR BUSINESS

Reg. §1.163-8T

Expenses within 30 days of depositing loan in account

Notice 89-35, 1989-1 CB 675

Pre-existing debt

Warren Halle, 83 F.3d 649 (4th Cir. 1996)

15.12 YEAR TO CLAIM AN INTEREST DEDUCTION

Promissory note is not payment of interest

Francis R. Hart, 54 F.2d 848 (1st Cir. 1932)

Increasing of loan

Julius I. Peyser, 1 TCM 807 (1943)

Fred W. Leadbetter, 39 BTA 629 (Nonacq.)

Life insurance loan

L. B. Hirsch, 42 BTA 566 (Acq.), aff'd, 124 F.2d 24 (9th Cir. 1941)

Arthur A. Beaudry, 1 TCM 838 (1943), modified and rem'd, 150 F.2d 20 (2d Cir. 1945), on remand, 5 TCM 61 (1946)

J. Simpson Dean, 35 TC 1083 (1961) (Nonacq.)

Margin account with broker

Rev. Rul. 70-221, 1970-1 CB 33

Contested note or obligation

Allegheny Steel Co., 18 F. Supp. 398 (Ct. Cl. 1937)

Shellabarger Grain Products Co., 2 TC 75 (1943) (Acq.), aff'd in part, rev'd in part, 146 F.2d 177 (7th Cir. 1944)

Partial payment of loan

McConway & Torley Corp., 2 TC 593 (1943)

Theodore R. Plunkett, 41 BTA 700 (Acq.), aff'd on other grounds, 118 F.2d 644 (1st Cir. 1941)

Paul N. Bowen Est., 2 TC 783 (1973)

George R. Newhouse, 59 TC 783 (1973)

John B. Ferenc, 33 TCM 136 (1974)

Full settlement of debt

William J. Petit, 8 TC 228 (1947) (Acq.)

Warner Co., 11 TC 419 (1948), aff'd per curiam, 181 F.2d 599 (3d Cir. 1950)

Using borrowed funds to pay interest

News Release IR-83-93, July 6, 1983

Barry L. Battelstein, 631 F.2d 1182 (5th Cir. 1980), cert. denied

Donald L. Wilkerson, 655 F.2d 980 (9th Cir. 1981)

Note that is renewed

S. E. Thomason, 33 BTA 576

David J. Secunda, 36 TCM 763 (1977)

Interest paid with a loan from lender

Charles Davison, 107 TC 4 (1996)

15.13 PREPAID INTEREST

IRC §461(g)

16 DEDUCTIONS FOR TAXES

16.1 OVERALL LIMIT ON DEDUCTIONS FOR STATE AND LOCAL TAXES

Overall deduction limit of $10,000($5,000 if married filing separately) for state and local taxes (Tax Cuts and Jobs Act)

IRC §164 (b) (6), as added by the Tax Cuts and Jobs Act (P.L. 115-97, 12/22/2017) for 2018 through 2025

Safe harbor if charitable contribution deduction reduced due to receipt of state/local tax credit

Notice 2019-12, 2019-27 IRB 57

SALT cap bypass by pass-through owners

Notice 2020-75, 2020-49 IRB 1453

Election to deduct general state and local sales taxes in lieu of state and local income taxes

IRC §164(b)(5)

16.2 NONDEDUCTIBLE TAXES

IRC §164

Reg. §1.164-1

Nondeductible taxes

IRC §275

Transfer taxes on securities sale reduce amount realized

Announcement 88-54, 1988-13 IRB 35

IRC §164(a)

Transfer taxes

Rev. Rul. 65-313, 1965-2 CB 47

Federal minimum tax not deductible

Rev. Rul. 77-396, 1977-2 CB 86

Cash basis

IRC §461

IRC §1.461-1(a)(1)

Joseph Shalleck, 1 TCM 292 (1942)

Borrowed funds

In re Barry L. Battelstein, 77-2 USTC ¶9516 (S.D. Tex. 1977)

Payment by bank

Frank J. Hradesky, 65 TC 87 (1975), aff'd per curiam, 540 F.2d 821 (5th Cir. 1976)

Rev. Rul. 78-103, 1978-1 CB 58

Water bills

Benjamin Mahler, 119 F.2d 869 (2d Cir. 1941), aff'g on the point BTA Memo., P-H 39,468, cert. denied, 314 U.S. 660

Rufus K. Steel, 7 TCM 558 (1948)

Assessments not deductible as taxes

Rev. Rul. 77-29, 1977-2 CB 538

Rev. Rul. 76-495, 1976-2 CB 43

Parking meter charges

Rev. Rul. 73-91, 1973-1 CB 71

Sewer fees

Louis M. Roth, 17 TC 1450 (1952) (Acq.)

Postage

Reg. §1.164-2

Turnpike or thruway tolls

Donald L. Cox, 41 TC 161 (1963)

16.3 STATE AND LOCAL INCOME TAXES OR GENERAL SALES TAXES

Overall deduction limit of $10,000($5,000 if married filing separately) for state and local taxes (Tax Cuts and Jobs Act)

IRC §164 (b) (6), as added by the Tax Cuts and Jobs Act (P.L. 115-97, 12/22/2017) for 2018 through 2025

Ban on state and local sales taxes on Internet access made permanent

Trade Facilitation and Trade Enforcement Act of 2015, P.L. 114-125, 2 /24/16

Supreme Court ends state's double tax

Maryland v. Wynne, Supreme Court, 5/18/15

Nonresident taxes on partnership income must be itemized

Matthew L. Cutler, TC Memo 2015-73

State and local income taxes

IRC §164(a)(3)

Election to deduct general state and local sales taxes in lieu of state and local income taxes

IRC §164(b)(5)

State tax paid before end of year

Rev. Rul. 74-140, 1974-1 CB 50

Rev. Rul. 82-208, 1982-2 CB 58

Accrual taxpayer contested liability

IRC §461(f)

Alabama unemployment tax deductible

Rev. Rul. 75-156, 1975-1 CB 66

Sales tax deduction on home purchase disallowed

* Jason Dewey, TC Summary Opinion 2010-38

* Carl D. Naso, TC Summary Opinion 2010-39

Rhode Island disability deductible

James R. McGowan, 67 TC 599 (1976)

News Release IR-1742 (1/28/77)

California disability deductible

Anthony Trujillo, 68 TC 56 (1977)

IR-1967, March 10, 1978

New York and New Jersey disability deductible

News Release IR-1967, March 10, 1978

16.4 DEDUCTING REAL ESTATE TAXES

Overall deduction limit of $10,000($5,000 if married filing separately) for state and local taxes (Tax Cuts and Jobs Act)

IRC §164 (b) (6), as added by the Tax Cuts and Jobs Act (P.L. 115-97, 12/22/2017) for 2018 through 2025

IRS safe harbor if assistance received from Hardest Hit Fund

Notice 2018-63, 2018-34 IRB 318

Fire prevention fee not a deductible tax

* Chief Counsel Memorandum 201310029

Payments to bank escrow account deductible when disbursed to tax authorities

Rev. Rul. 78-103, 1978-1 CB 58

Buyer of foreclosed property

* Letter Ruling 8207030

Beneficial owner

Paul Trans Dang, TC Memo 1999-233

Husband for his wife

William A. Colston, 59 F.2d 867 (D.C. Cir. 1932), aff'g 21 BTA 396, cert. denied, 287 U.S. 640

Charles F. Dean Est., 1 BTA 27

Daughter's deduction allowed for property taxes paid by mother

Judith F. Lang, TC Memo 2010-286

Mortgage required husband to pay

Eugene W. Small, 27 BTA 1219

Condominium apartment owner

Rev. Rul. 64-31, 1964-1 (Pt. 1) CB 300

Cooperative apartment owner

IRC §216

Life tenant

Cornelia C. F. Horsford, 2 TC 826 (1943) (Acq.)

Jointly and severally liable for tax

Rev. Rul. 72-79, 1972-1 CB 51

Tenancy by the entirety

Thomas D. Conroy, 17 TCM 21 (1958)

F. C. Nicodemus, Jr., 26 BTA 125 (Acq.)

Rev. Rul. 71-268, 1971-1 CB 58

Tenant in common

Lulu Lung Powell, 26 TCM 161 (1967)

Joseph James, 70 TCM 1420 (1995)

Mortgagee

John Hancock Mutual Life Ins. Co., 10 BTA 736 (Acq.)

Lucy S. Schiffelin Est., 44 BTA 137 (Acq.)

Tax on others' property

Albion D. T. Libby, 133 F.2d 203 (3d Cir. 1943), aff'g BTA Memo. P-H 42,252

J. Raymond Batcheller, 5 TCM 746 (1946)

Solomon N. Scale, 9 TCM 48 (1950)

Gordon W. Bonnette Est., 9 TCM 158 (1950)

Eugene W. Small, 27 BTA 1219 (1971)

Virginia N. Cramer, 55 TC 1125 (1971) (Acq.)

Gregory E. Macdonald, 35 TCM 346 (1976)

Have interest in property

Alfred J. Grosso, BTA Memo. P-H 41,581

A. J. Gilbert, 11 TCM 457 (1952)

Protection of beneficial interest

Rev. Rul. 67-21, 1967-1 CB 45

Trust for life of another

Herman A. Harper, 4 TCM 1097 (1945)

Robert C. Ligget, 4 TCM 598 (1945)

John H. Hord, 95 F.2d 179 (6th Cir. 1944), rev'g 33 BTA 342

Realty owned by parent

J. Raymond Batcheller, 5 TCM 746 (1946)

Stockholder property interest

Fred N. Acker, 258 F.2d 568 (6th Cir. 1958), aff'd, 361 U.S. 87 (1959)

16.5 ASSESSMENTS

Homeowner's association fees not deductible

Rev. Rul. 76-495, 1976-2 CB 43

Charges for local benefits

IRC §164(c)(1)

Reg. §1.164-4

16.6 TENANTS' PAYMENT OF TAXES

Deductible

Hawaii real property tax law:

Rev. Rul. 64-327, 1964-2 CB 56

California real property tax law:

Rev. Rul. 68-84, 1968-1 CB 71

Not deductible

Tax surcharge:

Rev. Rul. 75-301, 1975-2 CB 66

U.K. rates tax:

Maynard Waxenberg, 62 TC 594 (1974); Rev. Rul. 73-600, 1973-2 CB 47

Maryland-Prince George's County renters: Rev. Rul. 75-558, 1975-2 CB 67

New York: Rev. Rul. 79-180, 1979-1 CB 95

16.7 ALLOCATING TAXES WHEN YOU SELL OR BUY REALTY

IRC §164(d)

Reg. §1.164-6

Form 1099-S

IRC §6045(e)

Accrual-basis deduction

IRC §164(d)(2)(B)

Reg. §1.164-6(d)(6)

IRC §461(c) (ratable election)

Seller on cash basis

Reg. §1.164-6(d)(1)

Buyer's payment of seller's back taxes capitalized

Al S. Reinhardt, 75 TC 47 (1980)

16.8 AUTOMOBILE LICENSE FEES

Reg. §1.164-3(c)

Rev. Rul. 74-454, 1974-2 CB 57

16.9 TAXES DEDUCTIBLE AS BUSINESS EXPENSES

IRC §162

IRC §212

Reg §1.263A-2(a)

16.10 FOREIGN TAXES

IRC §164(a)(3)

17 MEDICAL AND DENTAL EXPENSE DEDUCTIONS

17.1 MEDICAL AND DENTAL EXPENSES MUST EXCEED AGI THRESHOLD

7.5% of AGI floor made permanent

IRC §213(a), as amended by the Consolidated Appropriations Act, 2021 (P.L. 116-260, 12/27/2020)

* IRS Publication 502

Loan as payment

William J. Granan, 55 TC 753 (1971)

Rev. Rul. 78-173, 1978-1 CB 73

Credit card charge

Rev. Rul. 78-39, 1978-1 CB 73

17.2 ALLOWABLE MEDICAL AND DENTAL CARE COSTS

IRC §213

Reg. §1.213-1

* IRS Publication 502

Deduction for COVID-19-related personal protective equipment

Announcement 2021-7, 2021-15 IRB 1061

Deduction for DNA collection kit

* Letter Ruling 201933005

Breastfeeding equipment is medical expense

Announcement 2011-14, 2011-9 IRB 532

Prescribed drugs and insulin

IRC §213(b)

IRC §213(d)(3) (definition of prescribed drug)

IRS position on special foods

Rev. Rul. 55-261, 1955-1 CB 307

Extra cost of health food

Theron G. Randolph, 67 TC 481 (1976)

Leona Von Kalb, 37 TCM 1511 (1978)

Warren L. Becher, 53 TCM 683 (1987) (taxpayer appeal pending)

Nonrefundable advance payment for lifetime care of disabled dependent

* IRS Publication 502

Rev. Rul. 75-303, 1975-2 CB 87, as clarified by Rev. Rul. 93-72, 1993-2 CB 77

Medical treatments

Reg. §1.213-1(e)(1)(ii)

Rev. Rul. 55-261, 1955-1 CB 307

Medical deduction for caregiver payments

Estate of Lillian Baral et al., 137 TC (2011)

Premiums

Reg. §1.213-1(e)(1)(i)

Premiums allocable to lost wages, loss of life or limbs

Reg. §1.213-1(e)(4)

Medicare by persons not automatically covered

Rev. Rul. 79-175, 1979-1 CB 117

Smoking cessation costs

Rev. Rul. 99-28, 1999-1CB 1269

Weight loss program for obesity or other specific disease deductible

Rev. Rul. 2002-19, 2002-16 IRB 778

Rev. Rul. 79-151, 1979-1 CB 116

Breast reconstruction and vision correction

Rev. Rul. 2003-57, 2003-22 IRB 959

Daughter's deduction allowed for medical costs paid by mother

Judith F. Lang, TC Memo 2010-286

Gym fees

*Office of Chief Counsel INFO Letter 2010-0175

Childbirth classes

* Letter Ruling 8919009

Chiropractor (lic.)

Rev. Rul. 55-261, 1955-1 CB 307

Christian Science practitioner

Rev. Rul. 55-261, 1955-1 CB 307

Dermatologist

Rev. Rul. 55-261, 1955-1 CB 307

Obstetrical services

Reg. §1.213-1(e)(1)(ii)

Osteopath (lic.)

Rev. Rul. 55-261, 1955-1 CB 307

Nurse

Reg. §1.213-1(e)(1)(ii)

Jacob Hentz, Jr., Est., 12 TCM 368 (1953)

George B. Wendell, 12 TC 161 (1949)

Rev. Rul. 58-339, 1958-2 CB 106

Rev. Rul. 55-261, 1955-1 CB 307

Psychiatrist

Rev. Rul. 53-143, 1953-2 CB 129, modified by Rev. Rul. 63-91, 1963-1 CB 54

Rev. Rul. 55-261, 1955-1 CB 307

Rev. Rul. 56-263, 1956-1 CB 135

Payments to unlicensed practitioners

Rev. Rul. 63-91, 1963-1 CB 54

Dental services

Reg. §1.213-1(e)(1)(ii)

Equipment and supplies

Reg. §1.213-1(e)(1)(ii)

Crutches, bandages and blood sugar test kits

Rev. Rul. 2003-58, 2003-22 IRB 959

Auto devices for handicapped

Rev. Rul. 66-80, 1966-1 CB 57

Modifications to van

David Henderson, TC Memo 2001-321

Elevator

Edna G. Hollander, 219 F.2d 934 (3d Cir. 1955), rev'g 22 TC 646 (1954)

James E. Berry, 174 F. Supp. 748 (D. Okla. 1958)

W. A. Post, 150 F. Supp. 299 (D. Ala. 1956)

W. E. Snellings, 149 F. Supp. 825 (E.D. Vir. 1956)

Rev. Rul. 59-411, 1959-2 CB 100

Laetrile

Rev. Rul. 78-325, 1978-2 CB 124

Contact lens replacement insurance protection

Rev. Rul. 74-429, 1974-2 CB 83

Fluoridation unit

Rev. Rul. 64-267, 1964-2 CB 69

Invalid chair

Rev. Rul. 58-155, 1958-1 CB 156

Rev. Rul. 66-80, 1966-1 CB 57

Rev. Rul. 67-76, 1967-1 CB 70

Wig

Rev. Rul. 62-189, 1962-2 CB 88

Elastic hosiery

Bessie Cohen, 10 TCM 29 (1951)

Lodging

* Letter Ruling 8516025

Special home construction costs deductible upon completion

Laurence S. Zipkin, 2000-2 USTC ¶50,863 (D.C. Minn. 2000)

Hospital services

Reg. §1.213-1(e)(1)(ii)

Rev. Rul. 55-261, 1955-1 CB 307

Alcoholic's inpatient care

Rev. Rul. 72-325, 1973-1 CB 75

Birth control pills

Rev. Rul. 73-200, 1973-1 CB 140

Clarinet lessons

Rev. Rul. 62-210, 1962-2 CB 89

Navajo sings

Raymond H. Tso, 40 TCM 1277 (1980)

Health institute

Rev. Rul. 55-261, 1955-1 CB 307

Drug center costs

Rev. Rul. 72-226, 1972-1 CB 96

Legal fees

Carl A. Gerstacker, 414 F.2d 448 (6th Cir. 1969)

Rev. Rul. 71-281, 1971-1 CB 121

Nurses' board and wages

Reg. §1.213-1(e)(1)(ii)

Federal Insurance Contributions Act
Rev. Rul. 57-489, 1957-2 CB 207

Remedial reading
Rev. Rul. 69-607, 1969-2 CB 40

Seeing-eye dog
Rev. Rul. 55-261, 1955-1 CB 307

Sex reassignment surgery is deductible medical expense
Rhiannon G. O'Donnabhain, 134 TC No. 4 (2010)(Acq.)

*Chief Counsel Advice 200603025 (IRS' pre-O'Donnabhain case position denying deduction)

Vasectomy
Rev. Rul. 73-201, 1973-1 CB 140

Sterilization
Rev. Rul. 73-603, 1973-2 CB 76

Egg donation costs
* Letter Ruling 200318017

Tuition fee
Rev. Rul. 54-457, 1954-2 CB 100

Wages of guide
Rev. Rul. 64-173, 1964-1 (Pt. 1) CB 121

Organ transplant costs
Rev. Rul. 68-452, 1968-2 CB 111

Telephone-teletype
Rev. Rul. 71-48, 1971-1 CB 99, amplified by Rev. Rul. 73-53, 1973-1 CB 139

Television adapter for closed caption service
Rev. Rul. 80-340, 1980-2 CB 81

Braille book
Rev. Rul. 75-318, 1975-2 CB 88

Personal protective equipment
Ann. 2021-7, 2021-15 IRB 1061

17.3 NONDEDUCTIBLE MEDICAL EXPENSES

Reg. §1.213-1

Cosmetic surgery
RC §213(d)(9)

Payroll withholding to cover Medicare A not deductible
Rev. Rul. 66-216, 1966-2 CB 100

Car insurance premiums not deductible
Rev. Rul. 73-483, 1973-2 CB 75

Infant formula not deductible
* Letter Ruling 200941003

Toothpaste
Reg. §1.213-1(e)(2)

Antiseptic diaper service and maternity clothes
Rev. Rul. 55-261, 1955-1 CB 307

Male cannot deduct in vitro fertilization expenses
William Magdalin, 2010-1 USTC ¶50,150 (1st Cir. 2010); cert. denied

Joseph F. Morrissey (DC FL, 12/22/16)

Monument
Carolyn W. Libby Est., 14 TCM 699 (1955)

No deduction for advance payment of services to be performed next year
R.M. Rose, 435 F.2d 149 (5th Cir. 1970)

Anticipated expenses not deductible
W.B. Andrews, 37 TCM 744 (1978)

Illegal operations, etc.
Reg. §1.213-1(e)(1)(ii)

Divorced wife
IRC §213(a)

Cost of oil furnace
Reg. §1.213-1(e)(1)(ii)

Special hospital room
Reg. §1.213-1(e)(i)(iv)

Specially designed car
Rev. Rul. 55-261, 1955-1 CB 307

Rev. Rul. 58-8, 1958-1 CB 154, amplified by Rev. Rul. 67-76, 1967-1 CB 70

Special food or beverages
Rev. Rul. 55-261, 1955-1 CB 307

Leo R. Cohn, 38 TC 387 (1962) (Nonacq.)

John R. Newman, 902 F.2d 159 (2nd Cir. 1990)

T. G. Randolph, 67 TC 481 (1976)

Organically grown food
Warren Becher, 53 TCM 683 (1987)

Bottled water
Rev. Rul. 56-19, 1956-1 CB 135

Health programs
Rev. Rul. 57-130, 1957-1 CB 108

Domestic help
Rev. Rul. 58-339, 1958-2 CB 106

Athletic club
Rev. Rul. 55-261, 1955-1 CB 307

Health spa
Jill Ford Murray, 43 TCM 1377 (1982)

Healthy child to boarding school
Samuel Ochs, 17 TC 130 (1951), aff'd, 195 F.2d 692 (2d Cir. 1952), cert. denied, 344 U.S. 827

Tuition for problem child
Gordon Pascal, 15 TCM 434 (1956)

Transportation costs
James Donnelly, 28 TC 1278 (1957), aff'd, 262 F.2d 411 (2d Cir. 1959)

Rev. Rul. 55-261, 1955-1 CB 307

Toiletries and sundries
Reg. §1.213-1(e)(2)

O. G. Russell, 12 TCM 1276 (1953)

Hotel costs
Reg. §1.213-1(e)(1)(iv)

Loren Wilks, 27 TCM 1086 (1968)

Living costs of outpatient
Harlin H. Lucas, 25 TCM 1312 (1966)

Look for new place to live
Gunnar E. Erickson, 13 TCM 1045 (1954)

Change of environment trip
Rev. Rul. 56-474, 1956-2 CB 157

Dance lessons
John J. Thoene, 33 TC 62 (1959)

Irving A. Adler, 22 TCM 965 (1963), aff'd, 330 F.2d 91 (9th Cir. 1964)

Rose France, 49 TCM 508 (1980), aff'd, 82-1 USTC 9225 (6th Cir. 1982)

Fallout shelter
Fred H. Daniels, 41 TC 324 (1963)

Travel to golf course
Leon S. Altman, 53 TC 487 (1969)

Scientology fees
Donald H. Brown, 62 TC 551 (1974), aff'd per curiam, 523 F.2d 365 (8th Cir. 1975)

Rev. Rul. 78-190, 1978-1 CB 74

Divorce costs
Joel H. Jacobs, 62 TC 813 (1974)

Marriage counseling fee
Rev. Rul. 75-319, 1975-2 CB 88

Hotel room for sex therapy
Rev. Rul. 75-187, 1975-1 CB 92

Veterinary fees
L. J. Schoen, 34 TCM 736 (1975)

Babysitter expenses
Rev. Rul. 78-266, 1978-2 CB 123

Tattooing and ear piercing
Rev. Rul. 82-111, 1982-1 CB 48

Moving from airport noise
Luke W. Findlay, Jr., 44 TCM 123 (1982)

17.4 REIMBURSEMENTS REDUCE DEDUCTIBLE EXPENSES

Reimbursements reduce deduction
IRC §213(a)

Reg. §1.213-1(g)

Failure to make claim

* Letter Ruling 8102010

Loss of earnings, etc.

Reg. §1.213-1(e)(4)(i)

Excess reimbursements

Rev. Rul. 69-154, 1969-1 CB 46

Injury awards treated as medical cost reimbursements

Benjamin D. Morgan, 55 TC 376 (1970)

Daniel T. Cooney, 30 TCM 845 (1971)

17.5 EXPENSES OF YOUR SPOUSE

Deduction allowed

IRC §213(a)

Reg. §1.213-1(a)(3)

Status at the time medical expense is incurred or paid

Reg. §1.213-1(e)(3)

17.6 EXPENSES OF YOUR DEPENDENTS

* IRS Publication 502

Dependents

IRC §213(a)

IRC §213(d)(5) (divorced or separated parents)

Must contribute half of support

IRC §152

Reg. §1.152-1 and 2

Not related at time of bill

Rev. Rul. 57-310, 1957-2 CB 206

Parent's welfare payments used to pay medical bills

Robert W. Hodge, 44 TC 186 (1965)

Adopted children

Benny L. Kilpatrick, 68 TC 469 (1977)

Rev. Rul. 60-255, 1960-2 CB 105

Multiple support

IRC §152(c)

Reg. §1.152-3

Loring P. Litchfield, 330 F.2d 509 (1st Cir. 1964)

17.7 DECEDENT'S MEDICAL EXPENSES

IRC §213(d)

Reg. §1.213-1(d)

Rev. Rul. 77-357, 1977-2 CB 328

17.8 PREMIUMS FOR HEALTH INSURANCE

IRC §213(d)(1)(C)

Policy for loss of life, limb, or sight— premium not deductible

Reg. §1.213-1(e)(4)

No deduction for policy guaranteeing specific amount for hospitalization

Rev. Rul. 68-451, 1968-2 CB 111

Self-employed health insurance deduction

IRC §162(l)(1)

* Letter Ruling 9409006

17.9 TRAVEL COSTS MAY BE MEDICAL DEDUCTIONS

Medical deduction for traveling expenses

IRC §213(d)(1)(B)

Reg. §1.213-1(e)(1)(iv)

Optional standard mileage rate

Notice 2023-03, 2023-3 IRB 388 (mileage rates for 2023)

Notice 2022-2, 2022-3 IRB 308 (mileage rates for first half of 2022)

Announcement 2022-13, 2022-26 IRB 1185 (mileage rate for second half of 2022)

Notice 2021-2, 2021-3 IRB 478 (mileage rates for 2021)

Notice 2020-5, 2020-4 IRB 380 (rate for 2020)

Notice 2019-02, 2019-02 IRB 281 (rate for 2019)

Trip to medical conference deductible

Rev. Rul. 2000-24, 2000-19 IRB 963

Relieve specific chronic ailments

Rev. Rul. 58-110, 1958-1 CB 155

Rev. Rul. 55-261, 1955-1 CB 307

Sally L. Bilder, 369 U.S. 499 (1963), rev'g 289 F.2d 291 (3d Cir. 1961)

Taxi fare

Rev. Rul. 98-63, 1998-52 IRB

Out-of-pocket auto expenses

Maurice S. Gordon, 37 TC 986 (1962)

Lodging — $50 daily allowance

IRC §213(d)(2)

* Letter Ruling 8516025

Transportation to Florida deductible but not $50 lodging allowance

Earlene Polyak, 94 TC 20 (1990)

Hotel costs for convalescent

Daniel S. W. Kelly, 440 F.2d 307 (7th Cir. 1971), rev'g 28 TCM 1208 (1969)

Nurse's fare

Rev. Rul. 58-110, 1958-1 CB 155

Parent's trip prescribed

Martin J. Lichterman, 37 TC 586 (1961) (Acq.) (to take child to school — deductible)

Rev. Rul. 58-533, 1958-2 CB 108 (to visit child—deductible)

Robert Rose, 52 TC 21 (1969) (taking child on trip for health reason — deductible)

* Letter Ruling 7813004 (picking up mentally disturbed son—transportation plus overnight food and lodging — deductible)

Visit specialist

Bertha M. Rodgers, 25 TC 254 (1955) (Acq.), aff'd, 241 F.2d 552 (8th Cir. 1957)

Treatment in distant city

Reg. §1.213-1(e)(1)(iv), contra:

Stanley D. Winderman, 32 TC 1197 (1959) (Acq.) (airfare to see trusted doctor deductible)

Escape bad climate

Reg. §1.213-1(e)(1)(iv)

L. Keever Stringham, 12 TC 580 (1949) (Acq.), aff'd, 183 F.2d 579 (6th Cir. 1950)

Rev. Rul. 53-261, 1955-1 CB 307

Alcoholics Anonymous

Rev. Rul. 63-273, 1963-2 CB 112

Disabled veteran's commuting

Sanford H. Weinzimer, 17 TCM 712 (1958)

Wife's trip to provide nursing care deductible

Daniel S. W. Kelly, 28 TCM 1208 (1969), rev'd on other grounds, 440 F.2d 307 (7th Cir. 1971)

Travel costs of kidney transplant donor or prospective donor

Rev. Rul. 73-189, 1973-1 CB 139

Driving as therapy

Michael R. Bordas, 29 TCM 458 (1970)

General improvement

Reg. §1.213-1(e)(1)(iv)

Margherita Diamond Est., 22 TCM 1073 (1963)

Annual trips south are personal expenses

Bertha M. Rodgers, 241 F.2d 552 (8th Cir. 1957), aff'g 25 TC 254 (1955) (Acq.)

Meals en route

Morris C. Montgomery, 428 F.2d 243 (6th Cir. 1970), aff'g 51 TC 410 (1968)

Meals and lodging (pre-1984 decisions)

Reg. §1.213-1(e)(1)(iv)

Max Carasso, 34 TC 1139 (1960), aff'd, 292 F.2d 367 (2d Cir. 1961), cert. denied, 369 U.S. 874

Sally L. Bilder, 369 U.S. 499 (1963), rev'g 289 F.2d 291 (3d Cir. 1961)

Extra cost of salt-free food

Leo Cohn, 38 TC 387 (1962) (Nonacq.)

Leo Cohn, 240 F. Supp. 786 (D. Ind. 1965)

Meals and lodging in transit deductible

Morris C. Montgomery, 428 F.2d 243 (6th Cir. 1970), aff'g 51 TC 410 (1968)

Spiritual aid

Vincent P. Ring, 23 TC 950 (1955)

Climate more suitable to ill wife's condition

Lawrence Prem, 21 TCM 873 (1962)

Moving household furnishings

C. Earle Phares, 21 TCM 1446 (1962)

Auto for leg condition

Benjamin Ginsberg, 237 F. Supp. 968 (S.D.N.Y. 1965)

Special vehicle

Rev. Rul. 55-261, 1955-1 CB 307

Rev. Rul. 66-80, 1966-1 CB 57

Rev. Rul. 70-606, 1970-2 CB 66

Convalescence cruise

Margherita Diamond Est., 22 TCM 1073 (1963)

Transporting invalid child to public school

Rev. Rul. 65-255, 1965-2 CB 76

Loss on sale of car

Robert K. Weary, 510 F.2d 435 (10th Cir. 1975), cert. denied, 423 U.S. 838

Patient on medical seminar cruise

Rev. Rul. 76-79, 1976-1 CB 70

17.10 SCHOOLING FOR THE MENTALLY OR PHYSICALLY DISABLED

Reg. §1.213-1(e)(1)(v)

Rev. Rul. 55-261, 1955-1 CB 307

Special education tuition for child's learning disability is deductible

* Letter Ruling 200521003

Private school with psychologists

C. Fink Fischer, 50 TC 164 (1968) (Acq.)

Hobart J. Hendrick, 35 TC 1223 (1960) (Acq.)

Boarding school recommended by therapist

John A. Dreifus, 36 TCM 368 (1977)

Hyperactive child in regular boarding school

Ernest M. Newkirk, 611 F.2d 373 (6th Cir. 1979)

Deduction for child's behavior therapy at school

Charles F. Urbauer, 63 TCM 2492 (1992)

Private military academy

H. Grant Atkinson, Jr., 44 TC 39 (1965) (Acq.)

Edward S. Enck, 26 TCM 314 (1967)

Rolland T. Olson, 23 TCM 2008 (1964)

Everett F. Glaze, 20 TCM 1276 (1961)

School in Arizona

Martin J. Lichterman, 37 TC 586 (1961) (Acq.)

Cost of college for deaf child (deductible)

Reuben A. Baer Est., 26 TCM 170 (1967)

Blind student at regular school

Arnold P. Grunwald, 51 TC 108 (F.2d 1968)

Halfway house

* Letter Ruling 7714016

Special public school class for retarded: cost of tuition and travel

Rev. Rul. 70-285, 1970-1 CB 52

Cost of remedial reading school

Paul H. Ripple, 54 TC 1442 (1970)

Cost of private school for epileptic

DeVora R. Shidler, 30 TCM 529 (1971)

17.11 NURSING HOMES

* IRS Publication 502)

Reg. §1.213-1(e)(1)(v)

Apartment rent

Sidney J. Ungar, 22 TCM 766 (1963)

17.12 NURSES' WAGES

Daughter acting as nurse

Myrtle P. Dodge Est., 20 TCM 811 (1961)

Working parents

Maurice Levy, Jr., 20 TCM 1534 (1961)

Domestic

John Frier, 30 TCM 345 (1971)

Rev. Rul. 58-339, 1958-2 CB 106

Allocation of medical and household services

Rev. Rul. 76-106, 1976-1 CB 71

Clerk's salary

Sidney J. Ungar, 22 TCM 766 (1963)

Nonprofessional therapy

Rev. Rul. 70-170, 1970-1 CB 51

Relative providing care

Walter D. Bye, 31 TCM 238 (1972)

17.13 HOME IMPROVEMENTS AS MEDICAL EXPENSES

Reg. §1.213-1(e)(1)(iii)

John Riach, 302 F.2d 374 (9th Cir. 1962)

Raymon Gerard, 37 TC 826 (1962) (Acq.)

Karlis A. Pols, 24 TCM 1140 (1965)

Air conditioning device

Rev. Rul. 55-261, 1955 CB 307

Removal of lead-based paint

Rev. Rul. 79-66, 1979-1 CB 114

Special bathroom in rented house

Rev. Rul. 70-395, 1970-2 CB 65

Swimming pool of osteoarthritis patient

Rev. Rul. 83-33, 1983-1 CB 70

Least expensive construction

Collins H. Ferris, 36 TCM 765 (1977), rev'd, 582 F.2d 1112 (7th Cir. 1978)

Buying house with pool

Paul A. Lerew, 44 TCM 918 (1982)

Pool of emphysema patient

Herbert Cherry, 46 TCM 1033 (1983)

Pool as personal convenience

C. W. Haines, 71 TC 257 (1979)

Operating costs

Reg. §1.213(e)(iii)

Handicap exception for ramps, etc.

Conference Committee Report to P.L. 99-514, Act Sec. 133, 1986-3 (vol. 4) CB 22

Rev. Rul. 87-106, 1987-2 CB 67

Modifications to van

David Henderson, TC Memo 2001-321

Special home construction costs deductible upon completion

Laurence S. Zipkin, 2002-2 USTC ¶50,863 (D. Minn. 2000)

17.14 COSTS DEDUCTIBLE AS BUSINESS EXPENSES

Medical checkup for job

Rev. Rul. 58-382, 1958-2 CB 59

Throat specialist fee

Rev. Rul. 71-45, 1971-1 CB 51

Services for physically handicapped

Rev. Rul. 75-317, 1975-2 CB 57

Psychoanalysis for social worker

Harry H. Voigt, 74 TC 82 (1980) (Nonacq.)

Therapy for psychiatrist

Kenneth Porter, 52 TCM 615 (1986)

17.15 Long-Term Care Premiums and Services

Long-term-care premiums

IRC §213(d)(1)(D)

IRC §213(d)(10)

Rev. Proc 2022-38, 2022-45 IRB 445 (deductible premiums for 2023)

Rev. Proc 2021-45, 2021-48 IRB 764 (deductible premiums for 2022)

Rev. Proc. 2020-45, 2020-46 IRB 1016 (deductible premiums for 2021)

Rev. Proc. 2017-58, 2017-45 IRB 489 (deductible premiums for 2018)

Rev. Proc. 2016-55, 2016-45 IRB 707 (deductible premiums for 2017)

Long-term care services

IRC §213(d)(1)(C)

IRC §7702B(c) (definition of qualified long-term care services)

Exclusion for payments from qualified contracts

IRC §7702 B(a)(2)

IRC §7702 B(d)(2) (per diem limit)

Rev. Proc 2022-38, 2022-45 IRB 445 (per diem exclusion for 2023)

Rev. Proc 2021-45, 2021-48 IRB 764 (per diem exclusion for 2022)

Rev. Proc. 2020-45, 2020-46 IRB 1016 (per diem exclusion for 2021)

Rev. Proc. 2017-58, 2017-45 IRB 489 (per diem exclusion for 2018)

Rev. Proc. 2016-55, 2016-45 IRB 707 (per diem exclusion for 2017)

17.16 Life Insurance Used by Chronically Ill or Terminally Ill Person

Terminally ill: tax-free accelerated benefits

IRC §101(g)(1)(A)

IRC §101(g)(4)(A)

Chronically ill: tax-free accelerated benefits

IRC §101(g)(1)(B)

IRC §101(g)(3)

IRC §101(g)(4)(B)

Viatical settlements

IRC §101(g)(2)

18 CASUALTY AND THEFT LOSSES AND INVOLUNTARY CONVERSIONS

18.1 Casualty or Theft Losses for Personal-Use Property Must Be Due to a Federally Declared Disaster

Casualty and theft loss deductions restricted for 2018 through 2025 (Tax Cuts and Jobs Act)

IRC §165 (h) (5) (A), as added by the Tax Cuts and Jobs Act (P.L. 115-97, 12/22/2017) (deduction for personal-use property must be attributable to federally declared disaster)

IRC §165 (h) (5) (B), as added by the Tax Cuts and Jobs Act (P.L. 115-97, 12/22/2017) (exception allows personal-use losses not attributable to federally declared disasters to offset personal casualty gains)

IRC §165(h)(3) (definitions of personal casualty gain and personal casualty loss)

*IRS Publication 547

Qualified disaster losses

Section 304(b) of the Taxpayer Certainty and Disaster Tax Relief Act of 2020 (Division EE of P.L. 116-260, 12-27-2020)

Relocation or demolition of house in disaster area treated as disaster loss

IRC §165(k)

Safe harbor deduction for repairing deteriorating home concrete foundation caused by the mineral pyrrhotite

Rev. Proc. 2017-60, 2017-50 IRB 559

Collapsed wall not a deductible casualty loss for co-op shareholder

Christina A. Alphonso, TC Memo 2016-130

State law violation doesn't block casualty loss deduction

Chief Counsel Memorandum ILM 201346009

Great Lakes high water level

Rev. Rul. 76-134, 1976-1 CB 54

Safe harbor deduction for repair of corrosive drywall

Rev. Proc. 2010-36, 2010-42 IRB 439

Intoxicated driver allowed casualty loss deduction

* Justin M. Rohrs, TC Summary Opinion 2009-190

Water damage to wallpaper

Rupert Stuart, 20 TCM 938 (1961)

Termites

E. G. Kilroe, 32 TC 1304 (1959) (Nonacq.)

Alan M. Winsor, 18 TCM 383 (1959), aff'd, 278 F.2d 634 (1st Cir. 1960)

Rev. Rul. 63-232, 1963-2 CB 97

Foreseeable damage

Jack R. Farber, 57 TC 714 (1972) (Acq.)

Harry Heyn, 46 TC 714 (1966) (Acq.)

Car towed away and destroyed

Abraham Hananel, 62 TCM 439 (1991)

Ring destroyed by disposal unit

William H. Carpenter, 25 TCM 965 (1966)

Ring destroyed by closing of door

John P. White, 48 TC 430 (1967) (Acq.)

Diamond unexplainedly lost

Theodore R. Kielts, 42 TCM 238 (1981)

Sinking ship from failure of pump

William D. Shields, 54 TCM 711 (1987)

Fire loss, damage, destruction

IRC §165

Reg. §1.165-7

Judgment paid by tenant

Rev. Rul. 73-41, 1973-1 CB 74

Automobile

Tracy V. Buckwalter, 20 BTA 1005, aff'd, 61 F.2d 571 (6th Cir. 1932)

Furniture and home

E. C. O'Rear, 80 F.2d 473 (6th Cir. 1935)

W. B. Brooks, 12 BTA 31, aff'd, 35 F.2d 178 (4th Cir. 1929)

* Francis N. Leonard, TC Summary Opinion 2005-114

Hurricane

Alfred M. Hickman, 207 F.2d 460 (4th Cir. 1953)

Willard T. Burkett, 10 TCM 948 (1951)

Tornado

Richard E. Stein, 14 TCM 191 (1955)

Heavy rains

Clarence E. Stewart, 12 TCM 921 (1953)

Lightning

S. F. Horn, 18 TCM 177 (1959)

Floods

W. M. Ferguson, 59 F.2d 893 (10th Cir. 1933)

E. T. Hutchings, 41-2 USTC ¶9673 (D. Ky. 1941)

Storms

Webb, 1 BTA 759

Robert B. Honeyman, Jr., BTA Memo. P-H 39,021

Landslides

W. K. Stowers, 169 F. Supp. 246 (D. Mass. 1959)

Smog

Rev. Rul. 71-560, 1971-2 CB 126

Drought

Jack M. Short, 55 TCM 54 (1988) (deduction claimed too late)

Frank Buttram, 87 F. Supp. 322 (D. Okl. 1943)

Rev. Rul. 66-303, 1966-2 CB 55

Rev. Rul. 54-85 1954-1 CB 58

Norman H. Ruecker, 41 TCM 1587 (1981)

Dust storms

R. F. Barry, 175 F. Supp. 308 (D. Okl. 1959)

Poor construction

Irving J. Hayutin, 31 TCM 509 (1972), aff'd, 508 F.2d 462 (10th Cir. 1975)

Shipwreck

IRC §165(c)(3)

Edward H. R. Green, 19 BTA 904

Sinking of land

Harry Johnston Grant, 30 BTA 1028 (Acq.)

Tidal wave

M. A. Ferst, 129 F. Supp. 606 (D. Ga. 1955)

Rev. Rul. 76-134, 1976-1 CB 54

Disturbances below earth's surface

Harry Johnston Grant, 30 BTA 1028 (Acq.)

Ice pressure

Paul E. Jackson, 13 TCM 1175 (1954)

Seward City Mills, 44 BTA 173

Underground water

Delbert P. Hesler, 13 TCM 972 (1954)

Car falling through ice

Rev. Rul. 69-88, 1969-1 CB 58

Ice damage

Sherman L. Whipple, 25 F.2d 520 (D. Mass. 1928)

Richard R. Hollington, 15 TCM 668 (1956)

Frederick H. Nash, 22 BTA 482 (Acq.)

Cave-ins

W. K. Stowers, 169 F. Supp. 246 (D. Miss. 1959)

Harry Johnston Grant, 30 BTA 1028 (Acq.)

Quarry blast

Ray Durden, 3 TC 1 (1944) (Acq.)

Severe winter blizzard

Emory M. Nourse, 73 F. Supp. 70 (D. Iowa 1947)

Vandals

Burrell E. Davis, 34 TC 586 (1960) (Acq.)

Rentals for temporary living quarters

Rev. Rul. 59-398, 1959-2 CB 76

Potential buyer's resistance

George W. Finkbohner Jr., 788 F.2d 723 (11th Cir. 1986)

Gerald Chamales, TC Memo 2000-33 (O.J. Simpson trial)

Michael N. Caan, 99-1 USTC ¶50,349 (C.D. Cal 1999) (O.J. Simpson trial)

Gordon Lund, 2000-1 USTC ¶50,234 (C.D. UT. 2000)

Harvey Pulvers, 48 TC 245 (1967), aff'd per curiam, 407 F.2d 838 (9th Cir. 1969)

Lewis F. Ford, 33 TCM 496 (1974)

Charles W. P. Kamanski, 29 TCM 1702 (1970), aff'd, 477 F.2d 452 (9th Cir. 1973)

Jointly owned property

J. H. Anderson, 7 TCM 811 (1948)

Life estate holder may deduct damage for wind storm

Katherine Bliss, 27 TC 770 (1957) (Acq.), rev'd, 256 F.2d 533 (2d Cir. 1958)

Latent effects not considered

Leonard J. Jenard, 20 TCM 346 (1961)

Decrease in value of land

Bessie Knapp, 23 TC 716 (1955) (Acq.)

Cost less depreciation

Edmund W. Cornelius, 56 TC 976 (1971) (Acq.)

Myron E. Cherry, 26 TCM 556 (1967)

Market value based on inventory

Loy L. Stone, 31 TCM 1042 (1972)

Damage to trees, shrubs, etc.

John M. Winters, Jr., 58-1 USTC ¶9205 (D. Okl. 1958), rev'd on other grounds, 261 F.2d 675 (10th Cir. 1959), cert. denied, 359 U.S. 943

Bessie Knapp, 23 TC 716 (1955) (Acq.)

Subsoil shrinkage during drought

Rev. Rul. 54-85, 1954-1 CB 58

Wreck caused by icy road

George L. Shearer, 16 F.2d 995 (2d Cir. 1927)

Collision caused by faulty driving

Reg. §1.165-7(a)(3)

Elwood J. Clark, 5 TCM 236 (1946), aff'd, 158 F.2d 851 (6th Cir. 1947)

Lawn damage caused by careless use of weed killer

Jack R. Farber, 57 TC 714 (1972) (Acq.)

Defending suit for damages

L. Oransky, 1 BTA 1239

Sonic boom

Rev. Rul. 60-329, 1960-2 CB 67

Property used by dependent

Thomas J. Draper, 15 TC 135 (1950)

Howard Scharf, 32 TCM 1281 (1973), rem'd per curiam, 535 F.2d 1250 (4th Cir. 1976)

High water levels

Rev. Rul. 75-134, 1975-1 CB 33

Preventative measures nondeductible

Cade L. Austin, 74 TC 1334 (1980)

Washing machine flood damage deduction

* Pamela S. Cooper, TC Summary Opinion 2003-168

18.2 WHEN TO DEDUCT A CASUALTY OR THEFT LOSS

Reg. §1.165-1(d)

* IRS Publication 547

Failure to prove insurance claim doesn't bar casualty deduction

Mark D. Ambrose, 2012-2 USTC ¶50,518 (U.S. Court of Federal Claims 2012)

Reimbursement expected

Reg. §1.165-1(d)

Arthur T. Davidson, 34 TCM 1010 (1975)

Year in which insurance company denies liability is not controlling

Louis Gale, 41 TC 269 (1963)

Flood loss deducted year claim settled

Earl Callan, 235 F.2d 190 (9th Cir. 1956)

Unseasonable blizzard

Emory M. Nourse, 73 F. Supp. 70 (DC Iowa 1947)

Hurricane damage

Willard T. Burkett, 10 TM 948 (1951)

Loss allowed in year of drought not later year of discovery

Alfred M. Cox, 24 TCM 23 (1965), aff'd per curiam, 354 F.2d 659 (3d Cir. 1966)

Swimming pool damages not deductible in later year

Donald H. Kunsman, 49 TC 62 (1967)

Subsequent recovery of insurance taxable

John E. Montgomery, 65 TC 511 (1975)

18.3 PRIOR-YEAR ELECTION FOR DISASTER LOSSES

IRC §165(i)

Reg. §1.165-11

IRS safe harbors for determining loss in value to personal-use residential property

Rev. Proc. 2018-8, 2018-2 IRB (safe harbor methods to figure loss in value to homes and personal belongings in any casualty or theft, plus additional safe harbors solely for federally-declared disasters)

Rev. Proc. 2018-9, 2018-2 IRB (loss in value to homes resulting from Hurricane and Tropical Storm Harvey, and Hurricanes Irma, and Maria)

News Release IR-2017-202

IRS extends period to elect/revoke disaster loss claim in prior year

T.D. 9789 (Temp. Reg. Sec. 1.165-11T), Rev. Proc. 2016-53, 2016-44 IRB 527

Rev. Proc. 2016-53, 2016-44 IRB 530 (procedures for making or revoking prior-year election under T.D. 9789)

Early election may be revoked up to filing due date

Chester Matheson, 74 TC 834 (1980) (Acq. in results only)

Relocation or demolition of house in disaster area treated as disaster loss

IRC §165(k)

18.4 Gain Realized From Insurance Proceeds for Damaged or Destroyed Principal Residence

IRC §165(h)(3)(A) (definition of personal casualty gain

* IRS Publication 547

Insurance reimbursements for unscheduled personal property are tax free

IRC §1033 (h)(1)(A)

Disaster relief payments not taxed

IRC §139

Flood mitigation grants not taxed

IRC §139(g)

Sale of land after disaster

Rev. Rul. 96-32, 1996-25 IRB 5

Disaster relief funds used to buy mobile home not taxed

News Release SD-2004-13

18.5 Who May Deduct a Casualty or Theft Loss

Separate return

Robert M. Loewenstein, 27 TCM 1112 (1968)

Rev. Rul. 75-347, 1975-2 CB 70

No deduction for cost of repairing rented car

J. Gill, 34 TCM 10 (1975)

Corporate shareholder

Drew Jensen, 39 TCM 163 (1979)

18.6 Proving a Casualty Loss

* IRS Publication 547

News Release IR-2012-60 (backup your records)

Cleanup expenses

Ralph Walton, 20 TCM 653 (1961)

Appraisal upheld

Doyle E. Collup, 21 TCM 128 (1962)

Auto bluebook

Gus S. Caras, 23 TCM 1103 (1964)

Dealer's estimate of trade-in not evidence

Gus S. Caras, 23 TCM 1103 (1964)

Fire damage

John Pfalzgraf, 67 TC 784 (1977) (Acq.)

Inventories of property destroyed by fire sustained loss

Loy L. Stone, 31 TCM 1042 (1972)

18.7 Theft Losses

Reg. §1.165-8

* IRS Publication 547

Theft loss deductions restricted for 2018 through 2025 (Tax Cuts and Jobs Act)

IRC §165 (h) (5) (A), as added by the Tax Cuts and Jobs Act (P.L. 115-97, 12/22/2017) (deduction for personal-use property must be attributable to federally declared disaster)

IRC §165 (h) (5) (B), as added by the Tax Cuts and Jobs Act (P.L. 115-97, 12/22/2017) (exception allows personal-use losses not attributable to federally declared disasters to offset personal casualty gains)

Estate gets theft loss deduction

Estate of Heller, 147 TC No. 11 (2016)

No theft loss in alleged patent infringement

Tim Sheridan, TC Memo 2015-25

No theft loss for funds used by ex-wife for couple's children

William L. West, TC Memo 2014-2

State law determines if theft committed

Arthur C. Bromberg, Exr., 232 F.2d 107 (5th Cir. 1956)

Necessity of proving cost

Jane V. Elliott, 40 TC 304 (1963) (Acq.)

Stanley J. Prescott, 28 TCM 435 (1969)

Must prove property was stolen

Paul Bakewell, Jr., 23 TC 803 (1955)

Mary F. Allen, 16 TC 163 (1951)

John L. Seymour, 14 TC 1111 (1950)

Edna M. Oatis, 6 TCM 569 (1947)

Corporate misconduct doesn't support theft loss deduction

Notice 2004-27, 2004-16 IRB 782

* Ronald C. Singerman, TC Summary Opinion 2005-4

Theft losses allowed to victims of Madoff and other Ponzi schemes

Rev. Proc. 2011-58, 2011-50 IRB 849 (expanded eligibility for safe harbor)

Rev. Rul. 2009-9, 2009-14 IRB 735

Rev. Rul. 2009-20, 2009-14 IRB 749 (optional safe harbor)

Chief Counsel Memorandum 2015-11018 (year of discovery for claiming deduction)

Estate gets theft loss deduction for LLC account invested with Madoff

Est. of Heller, 147 TC No. 11 (2016)

No theft loss for poor investment decision

Oscar C. Hawaii, TC Memo 2011-134

Theft of trees

Ella Gene Raberge, 20 TCM 1490 (1961)

Locked valuable pin in compartment

Warner L. Jones, 24 TC 525 (1955) (Acq.)

Report to police

James W. Thomas, 12 TCM 41 (1953)

Henrietta Sava-Goiu, 9 TCM 128 (1950)

Allowed even though not reported

Robert W. Jorg, 52 TC 288 (1969) (Acq.)

Frederick C. Moser, 18 TCM 116 (1959)

Year reported

Reg. §1.165-1(d)(3)

Reg. §1.165-8

Virginia M. Cramer, 55 TC 1125 (1971) (Acq.)

Deduction based on estimated recovery is premature

Aben E. Johnson, 2007-1 USTC ¶50,136 (Ct. Fed. Cl. 2006)

Cannot recover property

Henry Kraft Mercantile Co., 14 TCM 833 (1955)

Legal fee

Katherine Ander, 47 TC 592 (1967)

Appraisal value on stamp collection

Max P. Engel, 31 TCM 1223 (1972)

Building contractor absconded

Thomas Miller, 19 TC 1046 (1953) (Acq.)

Allen Hartley, 26 TCM 1281 (1977)

Contractor runs out of money

Otis B. Kent, 12 TCM 1491 (1953)

Additional money to correct defects

IRC §1016(a)(1)

Reg. §1.1016-2

Payments to subcontractor

Evelyn Nell Norton, 40 TC 500 (1963) (Acq.), aff'd, 333 F.2d 1005 (9th Cir. 1964)

Embezzlement losses

Mary O. Alsop, 34 TC 606 (1960), aff'd, 290 F.2d 726 (2d Cir. 1961)

Embezzlement not cause of bank depositor's loss

Rev. Rul. 77-383, 1977-2 CB 66

Worthless stock

Paul C. Vietzke, 37 TC 504 (1961) (Acq.)

Illegal sale of unregistered stock not a theft loss

Carroll J. Beilis, 61 TC 453 (1973), aff'd, 540 F.2d 448 (9th Cir. 1976)

Loss from tax avoidance scheme based on fraudulent statements of advisor

Perry A. Nichols et al., 43 TC 842 (1965) (Nonacq.)

Extortion and ransom payment

Rev. Rul. 72-112, 1972-1 CB 60

Expenses of recovering abducted child nondeductible

Ebrahim Otmishi, 41 TCM 237 (1980)

Fortune tellers

George John Kreiner, 60 TCM 1251 (1990)

Seizure of car by creditors

Robert V. Rafter, 489 F.2d 752 (2d Cir. 1974), cert. denied, 419 U.S. 826

Payment for forged divorce decree deductible

* Letter Ruling 8146030

Vandalism

Ann E. Lattimore, 353 F.2d 379 (9th Cir. 1966)

Charles Gutwirth, 40 TC 666 (1963) (Acq.)

Burrell E. Davis, 34 TC 586 (1960) (Acq.)

Riot damage

IRC §165(c)(3) and (e)

Perishable food discarded after civil disturbance

Rev. Rul. 69-354, 1969-1 CB 58

No deduction for confiscation by foreign government

William J. Powers, 36 TC 1191 (1961)

L.B.G. Farcasanu, 70-2 USTC ¶9753 (D.C. Cir. 1970)

H.W. Mongold, 43 TCM 117 (1981)

Swindled by friend

Nanette Holt Price, 94-1 USTC ¶50,160 (N.D. OK. 1994)

18.8 FLOORS FOR PERSONAL-USE PROPERTY LOSSES

Qualified disaster losses

Section 304(b) of the Taxpayer Certainty and Disaster Tax Relief Act of 2020 (Division EE of P.L. 116-260, 12-27-2020)

$100 floor

IRC §165(h)(1)

Reg. §1.165-7(b)(4)

10% AGI floor

IRC §165(h)(2)

18.9 FIGURING YOUR LOSS ON FORM 4684

* IRS Publication 547

Casualty and theft loss deductions restricted for 2018 through 2025 (Tax Cuts and Jobs Act)

IRC §165 (h) (5) (A), as added by the Tax Cuts and Jobs Act (P.L. 115-97, 12/22/2017) (deduction for personal-use property must be attributable to federally declared disaster)

IRC §165 (h) (5) (B), as added by the Tax Cuts and Jobs Act (P.L. 115-97, 12/22/2017) (exception allows personal-use losses not attributable to federally declared disasters to offset personal casualty gains)

IRS safe harbors for determining loss in value to personal-use residential property

Rev. Proc. 2018-8, 2018-2 IRB (safe harbor methods to figure loss in value to homes and personal belongings in any casualty or theft, plus additional safe harbors solely for federally-declared disasters)

News Release IR-2017-202

$100 floor

IRC §165(h)(1)

Reg. §1.165-7(b)(4)

10% adjusted gross income limit

Reg. §165(h)

Cost less depreciation method

E. W. Cornelius, 56 TC 976 (Acq. 1977-2 CBI)

Proof of cost

Donald Owens, 305 U.S. 468

Hal Millsap, Jr., 46 TC 751 (1966) (Acq.), aff'd 387 F.2d 420 (8th Cir. 1968)

Jay Beams, 67 TCM 3152 (1994)

Vitale, TC Memo 1999-272

Separate computation for each item

Rev. Rul. 66-50, 1966-1 CB 40

Community property damaged before divorce settlement

Armore L. Kamins, 54 TC 977 (1970)

Loss of records in fire no bar

John Pfalzgraf, Jr., 67 TC 784 (1977) (Acq.)

Appraisals for disaster relief

IRC §165(i)(4)

18.10 PERSONAL AND BUSINESS USE OF PROPERTY

IRC §165

Reg. §1.165-7(b)(4)(iv)

* IRS Publication 547

18.11 REPAIRS MAY BE A "MEASURE OF LOSS"

Cost of repairs

Reg. §1.165-7(a)(2)(ii)

S. P. Keith, Jr., 52 TC 41 (1969) (Acq.)

Estimated repairs not measure of loss

Claire E. Lamphere, 70 TC 391 (1978) (Acq.)

Venancio A. Bagnol, 37 TCM 1038 (1978)

Repairs, though not made, may affect post-casualty value

Paul Abrams, 41 TCM 1459 (1981)

Loss of value exceeds repair costs

George E. Conner, 439 F.2d 974 (5th Cir. 1971)

Anne Marie Hagerty, 34 TCM 356 (1975)

18.12 EXCESS LIVING COSTS PAID BY INSURANCE ARE NOT TAXABLE

IRC §123

Reg. §1.123-1

* IRS Publication 547

Taxable income determined at end of dislocation period

Rev. Rul. 93-43, 1993-2 CB 69

18.13 DO YOUR CASUALTY OR THEFT LOSSES EXCEED YOUR INCOME?

Carryback of losses

IRC §172

Reg. §1.172-1

Reg. §1.172-3(b)

18.14 DEFER GAIN FROM INVOLUNTARY CONVERSION BY REPLACING PROPERTY

IRC §1033

* IRS Publication 547

Home contractor's fraud is deductible theft loss

James M. Urtis, TC Memo 2013-66

Gain on business disaster grants

Rev. Rul. 2005-46, 2005-30 IRB 120

Temporary taking of real estate treated as lease not involuntary conversion

* Field Attorney Advice 20115101F

18.15 INVOLUNTARY CONVERSIONS QUALIFYING FOR TAX DEFERRAL

What is an involuntary conversion?

IRC §1033

Reg. §1.1033(a)-1

* IRS Publication 544

* IRS Publication 547

Deferral on preemptive sale of property in urban redevelopment area

* Letter Ruling 200145001

Threat of condemnation by government employee

Frank O. Maixner, 33 TC 191 (1959) (Acq.)

Carson Estate Co., 22 TCM 425 (1963)

Sale under hazard mitigation program

IRC §1033 (k)

Voluntary sale

Harry G. Masser, 30 TC 741 (1958) (Acq.)

Rev. Rul. 59-361, 1959-2 CB 183

Rev. Rul. 63-221, 1963-2 CB 332

Chemical contamination of home

* Chief Counsel Information Letter 2005-0013

Condemnation as unfit for habitation

Rev. Rul. 57-314, 1957-2 CB 523

Threat of building code violation not sufficient

Thorpe Glass Mfg. Corp., 51 TC 300 (1968)

Deferral relief for salvaged trees

Willamette Industries Inc., 118 TC 126 (2002)

Farmers—irrigation project

Reg. §1.1033(d)-1

Cattle diseased

IRC §1033(d)

Reg. §1.1033(e)-1

Livestock sales due to drought

IRC §1033(e)

Reg. §1.1033(f)-1

Sale to private party after governmental threat of conversion

Creative Solutions, Inc., 320 F.2d 809 (5th Cir. 1963)

Identity of threatening authority not disclosed

Rev. Rul. 74-8, 1974-2 CB 200

Tax sale

Rev. Rul. 77-370, 1977-2 CB 306

Gain on involuntary conversion

IRC §1033

Reg. §1.1033(a)-1 and 2

Russel C. Smith, 59 TC 107 (1972)

Pesticide crop damage

* Letter Ruling 9615041

House destroyed by a tornado

Rev. Rul. 96-32, 1996-1 CB 177

Contested award

Conlorez Corp., 51 TC 467 (1968) (Acq.)

Harry D. Aldridge, 51 TC 475 (1968)

Casalina Co., 60 TC 694 (1973) (Acq.), aff'd per curiam, 511 F.2d 1162 (4th Cir. 1975)

18.16 HOW TO ELECT TO DEFER GAIN

* IRS Publications 544 and 547

Dissolution of partnership not termination

Morton Fuchs, 80 TC 506 (1983)

18.17 TYPES OF QUALIFYING REPLACEMENT PROPERTY

Like-kind test

IRC §1033(g)

Reg. §1.1031(a)-1(b)

Related use

Liant Record Inc., 303 F.2d 326 (2d Cir. 1963), on rem'd, 22 TCM 203 (1963)

Clifton Investment Co., 312 F.2d 719 (6th Cir. 1963), cert. denied, 373 U.S. 921

Loco Realty Co., 306 F.2d 207 (8th Cir. 1962)

Thomas McCaffrey Jr., 275 F.2d 27 (2d Cir. 1960), cert. denied

Arnold L. Santucci, 32 TCM 840 (1973)

Rev. Rul. 64-237, 1964-2 CB 319

Replacement of rental house by residence does not qualify

Rev. Rul. 76-84, 1976-1 CB 219

Contract to buy does not qualify

Herrick L. Johnston Est., 51 TC 290 (1968), aff'd, 430 F.2d 1019 (6th Cir. 1970)

Purchase of leasehold of at least 30 years

Rev. Rul. 68-392, 1968-2 CB 338

Improvements to retained land

Rev. Rul. 67-255, 1967-2 CB 270

Rev. Rul. 67-255, 1967-2 CB 270

* Letter Ruling 9117030

* Letter Ruling 9118007

A.S. Davis, 589 F.2d 446 (9th Cir. 1979)

Business or investment property damaged in disaster area

IRC §1033(h)(2)

18.18 TIME PERIOD FOR BUYING REPLACEMENT PROPERTY

Four-year replacement period for livestock of drought-affected farmers and ranchers

IRC §1033(e)(2)(A)

IRC §1033(e)(2)(B)(IRS may extend four-year period on regional basis due to drought or other severe conditions)

Notice 2023-42, 2023-67 IRB 1074

Notice 2022-43, 2022-42 IRB 297 (IRS extends 4-year replacement period to listed counties facing severe drought in 12-month period ending 8/31/22)

Notice 2021-55, 2021-41 IRB 461 (IRS extends 4-year replacement period to listed counties facing severe drought in 12-month period ending 8/31/21)

Three-year replacement for condemned realty

IRC §1033(g)(4)

Four-year replacement period for principal residence involuntarily converted by disaster

IRC §1033 (h)(1)(B)

Election irrevocable

John McShain, 65 TC 686 (1976)

No substitution of replacement property

Rev. Rul. 83-39, 1983-1 CB 190

Environmental Protection Agency order

Rev. Rul. 89-2, 1989-1 CB 259

Advance payment of award starts replacement period

Stewart & Co., 57 TC 122 (1971)

Estate makes replacement

John E. Morris Est., 55 TC 636 (1971), aff'd per curiam, 454 F.2d 208 (4th Cir. 1972)

Isaac Goodman Est., 199 F.2d 895 (3d Cir. 1952)

Rev. Rul. 64-161, 1964-1 (Pt. 1) CB 298

Investment by widow

George W. Jayne Est., 61 TC 744 (1974)

Must report details of replacement

Reg. §1.1033(a)-2(c)(2)

Commute to nuclear power plant

John C. Banekatis, 56 TCM 376 (1988)

Electrician's commute to power plant

Philip D. Williams, 60 TCM 627 (1990)

Deductible travel from office in home

Thomas C. St. John, 29 TCM 1045 (1970)

Joe J. Adams, 43 TCM 1203 (1982) (repairman)

Thomas L. Wicker, 51 TCM 225 (1986)

Robert Leitch, 58 TCM 343 (1989)

Julio Mazzotta, 57 TC 427 (1971)

Musician driving from home office to restaurant

Leroy Kahuku, 58 TCM 1247 (1990)

20.3 OVERNIGHT-SLEEP TEST LIMITS DEDUCTION OF MEAL COSTS

Local lodging necessary to participate in employer business meeting

Notice 2007-47, 2007-24 IRB 1393

Sleep or rest rule

Homer O. Correll, 389 U.S. 299 (1968), rev'g 369 F.2d 87 (6th Cir. 1966)

Nap in parked car

Frederick J. Barry, 54 TC 1210 (1970), and per curiam, 435 F.2d 91 1290 (1st Cir. 1971)

Railroad personnel

Rev. Rul. 75-170, 1975-1 CB 60

Ferryboat captain's meals and incidentals

Marc G. Bissonnette, 127 TC 124 (2006)

Truck drivers

Rev. Rul. 75-168, 1975-1 CB 58

Meal costs during overtime not deductible

D. S. Courtney, 32 TC 334 (1959)

W. K. Liang, 34 TCM 1298 (1975)

20.4 IRS MEAL ALLOWANCE

Optional meal allowance based on federal meals and incidental expense (M&IE) rate

Notice 2022-42, 2022-41 IRB 276

* IRS Publication 463

Transportation industry M&IE rate

IRC §274(n)(3)

Notice 2023-68, 2023-41 IRB 1060 (business trips from October 1, 2023, to September 30, 2024)

Notice 2022-44, 2022-41 IRB 277 (business trips from October 1, 2022. to September 30, 2023)

Notice 2021-52, 2021-38 IRB 381 (business trips from October 1, 2021, to September 30, 2022)

Notice 2020-71, 2020-40 IRB 786 (business trips from October 1, 2020, to September 30, 2021)

Notice 2019-55, 2019-42 IRB 937 (business trips from October 1, 2019, to September 30, 2020)

Notice 2018-77, 2018-42 IRB 601 (business trips from October 1, 2018, to September 30, 2019)

20.5 BUSINESS TRIP DEDUCTIONS

Reg. §1.162-2(a)

* IRS Publication 463

Local lodging necessary to participate in employer business meeting

Notice 2007-47, 2007-24 IRB 1393

REG-137589-07 (Prop. Reg. §1.162-31; amendments to Reg. §1.262-1 (2012))

Laundry, cab fare

Rev. Rul. 63-145, 1963-2 CB 86

Lavish or extravagant

Rev. Rul. 63-144, 1963-2 CB 129

Double the highest per diem for cruise ship costs

IRC §274(m)(1)

Saturday-night stayover

* Letter Ruling 9237014

20.6 WHEN ARE YOU AWAY FROM HOME?

Limits to deducting temporary away-from-home expenses

* Roj Carl Snellman, TC Summary Opinion 2014-10

Place of business as tax home

Raymond K. Yeates, 55 TCM 1077 (1988)

J. N. Flowers, 326 U.S. 465 (1946)

Lee E. Daly, 72 TC 190 (1979), rev'd 631 F.2d 351 (4th Cir. 1980), aff'g Tax Court and rev'g after hearing en banc, 662 F.2d 253 (4th Cir. 1981)

Couple with shared residence and different tax homes

*Jac E. Baker, TC Summary Opinion 2011-95

Ethel Merman case

Robert F. Six, 450 F.2d 66 (2d Cir. 1971)

Robert Rosenspan, 438 F.2d 905 (2d Cir. 1971), cert. denied, 404 U.S. 864

Residence is tax home

Charles W. Rambo, 69 TC 920 (1978) (Acq. in result only)

Edward M. McKarzel, 30 TCM 366 (1971)

Eli F. McOimsey, 30 TCM 521 (1971)

Rev. Rul. 71-247, 1971-1 CB 54

Hotel after move to new job- not away from home

* Darren J. Newell, TC Summary Opinion 2012-57

Army officer at permanent duty port

H. A. Stidger, 386 U.S. 287 (1967)

Unmarried person

Robert Rosenspan, 438 F.2d 905 (2d Cir. 1971), cert. denied, 404 U.S. 864

Irving M. Sapson, 49 TC 636 (1968) (Acq.)

Max W. Tugel, 20 TCM 693 (1961)

Curtis L. Ralston, 27 TCM 1312 (1968)

Rev. Rul. 773-529, 1973-2 CB 37

Arthur Crossland, 33 TCM 1278 (1974), aff'd, 535 F.2d 1240 (2nd Cir. 1976)

Multiple short jobs at same locale

Thomas J. Mitchell, TC Memo 1999-283

Living with boyfriend doesn't create tax home

* Susan D. Thompson, TC Summary Opinion 2009-111

Edward W. Andrews, 60 TCM 277 (1990), rev'd, 931 F.2d 132 (1st Cir. 1991)

Francis Markey, 491 F.2d 1249 (6th Cir. 1974), rev'g 31 TCM 766 (1972)

Joseph Sherman, 16 TC 332 (1951) (Acq.)

Chong, TC Memo 1996-232

S. M. R. O'Hara, 6 TC 841 (1946)

Richard E. Benson, 27 TCM 1555 (1968)

John H. Webster, 9 TCM 550 (1950)

W. Edward Winterhalter, 10 TCM 268 (1951)

Vincent Treanor, 10 TCM 336 (1951)

Rev. Rul. 55-604, 1955-2 CB 49

Rev. Rul. 63-82, 1963-1 CB 33

Thomas J. Mitchell, TC Memo 1999-283

Baseball players, coaches, pilots, etc. might have other business

Rev. Rul. 54-147, 1954-1 CB 51

Tracy Stright, 66 TCM 1490 (1993)

Special Ruling, December 29, 1953

Maury Wills, 411 F.2d 537 (9th Cir. 1969)

20.7 TAX HOME OF MARRIED COUPLE WORKING IN DIFFERENT CITIES

Robert A. Coerver, 297 F.2d 837 (3d Cir. 1962), aff'g 36 TC 252 (1951)

Arthur B. Hammond, 213 F.2d 43 (5th Cir. 1954)

Virginia Foote, 67 TC 1 (1976)

George P. Leyland, 34 TCM 1502 (1975)

Charles J. Hundt, 20 TCM 369 (1961)

20.8 Deducting Living Costs on Temporary Assignment

* IRS Publication 463

Temporary assignments—one year or less

IRC §162 (a)

Rev. Rul. 93-86, 1993-2 CB 71 (IRS' realistic expectation test)

Family at temporary post

Emil J. Michaels, 53 TC 269 (1969) (Acq.)

Federal crime investigations

IRC §162(a)

Engineer on 20-month job

Philip Rolbin, 29 TCM 848 (1970)

Retired Florida stenographer

Virginia C. Avery, 29 TCM 1187 (1970)

Student's summer job

Saterios Hantzis, 38 TCM 1169 (1979), rev'd, 638 F.2d 248 (1st Cir. 1981), cert. denied, 101 S. Ct. 3112

Court rejection of one-year test

David L. Cowger, 25 TCM 513 (1966)

Ronald Brown, 30 TCM 41 (1971)

Louis R. Frederick, 457 F. Supp. 1274 (D.N. Dak. 1978), aff'd, 603 F.2d 1292 (8th Cir. 1979)

Recurrent summer job

Franklin C. Dilley, 58 TC 276 (1972)

State judge traveling to other circuits

Frank Fisher, 24 TC 269 (1955) (Acq.)

State judge who must live in district

James A. Emmert, 146 F. Supp. 322 (D. Ind. 1955)

Employed for test period

Richard C. Lipps, 21 TCM 358 (1962)

Rev. Rul. 60-314, 1960-2 CB 48

Employment for part of a year

James R. Whitaker, 24 TC 750 (1955)

George R. Lanning, 34 TCM 1366 (1975)

F. J. McGinley, Jr., 15 TCM 641 (1956)

Linesman working out of Oakland, California

Max W. Tugel, 20 TCM 693 (1961)

Baseball player's expenses

Rev. Rul. 54-147, 1954-1 CB 51

Professional football player

Ronald C. Gardin, 64 TC 1079 (1975)

Temporary assignment

James E. Peurifoy, 358 U.S. 59 (1958)

Michael Kuris, 15 TCM 854 (1956)

Robert K. Denning, 14 TCM 838 (1955)

Rev. Rul. 60-189, 1960-1 CB 60

Temporary becomes permanent

Hansel H. Johnson, Jr., 77 TCM 1966 (1999)

Itinerant worker

George H. James, 308 F.2d 204 (9th Cir. 1962), aff'g 176 F. Supp. 270 (D. Nev. 1959)

One-year test disregarded

Michael L. Hanna, 63 TCM 2917 (1992)

Ronald Brown, 30 TCM 41 (1971)

20.9 Business-Vacation Trips Within the United States

* IRS Publication 463

Reg. §1.274-4(e)(2)

IRC §274(c)(3)

Saturday night stayover deductible

* Letter Ruling 9237014

20.10 Business-Vacation Trips Outside the United States

IRC §274(c)

Control over trip, managing executive, related to employer

Reg. §1.274-4(f)(5)

Counting days outside U.S.

Reg. §1.274-4(c)

Allocation formula

Reg. §1.274-4(f)

No allocation necessary if not managing executive or self-employed

Reg. §1.274-4(f)(5)

20.11 Deducting Expenses of Business Conventions

* IRS Publication 463

Business or pleasure trip

Reg. §1.162-2(b)

Convention expenses

Reg. §1.162-2(d)

Rev. Rul. 63-266, 1963-2 CB 88

Connection with business

Rev. Rul. 59-316, 1959-2 CB 57, clarified by Rev. Rul. 63-266, 1963-2 CB 88

No deduction for investment seminars after 1986

IRC §274(h)

Lawyer's convention expenses

Wade H. Ellis, 50 F.2d 343 (D.C. Cir. 1931)

Legal secretary's convention expenses

Rita M. Callinan, 12 TCM 170 (1953)

Insurance agent

C. J. D. Rudolph, 291 F.2d 841 (5th Cir. 1961), aff'g 189 F. Supp. 2 (N.D. Tex. 1960), cert. dismissed, 370 U.S. 269 (1962)

Business convention in coastal resort

Rev. Rul. 56-168, 1956-1 CB 93

Reg. §1.162-2(b)(1)

Cruises

DeWitt N. Burnham, 17 TCM 240 (1958)

Reuben B. Hoover, 35 TC 566 (1961) (Acq.)

No deduction for Super Bowl weekend meetings

Danville Plywood Corp., 16 Cl. Ct. 584 (1989), aff'd, 899 F.2d 3 (Fed. Cir. 1990)

Fraternal organizations' conventions

Reg. §1.162-2(d)

20.12 Restrictions on Foreign Conventions and Cruises

Reasonableness of foreign location

IRC §274(h)

North American area

Rev. Rul. 2011-26, 2011-48 IRB

Cruise ship conventions

IRC §274(h)(2) ($2,000 limit)

IRC §274(h)(5) (recordkeeping)

20.13 Entertainment Expenses Generally Not Deductible

IRC §274 (a) (1)(A), as amended by the Tax Cuts and Jobs Act (P.L. 115-97, 12/22/2017) (repeal of exceptions for entertainment expenses paid or incurred after 2017)

* IRS Publication 463

Final regulations on disallowance rule for entertainment expenses

T.D. 9925, 85 F.R. 64026 (2020)

Exceptions to disallowance of entertainment expenses

IRC §274(e)

Prior law: Directly related and associated with tests for pre-2018 entertainment expenses (prior to repeal by the Tax Cuts and Jobs Act)

Reg. §1.274-2(c) (directly related entertainment)

Reg. §1.274-2(d) (associated with entertainment)

* IRS Publication 463 for 2017

20.14 Business Meals Are Generally Deductible

* IRS Publication 463

Final regulations on business meals
T.D. 9925, 85 F.R. 64026 (2020)

Definition of "restaurant"
Notice 2021-25, 2021-17 IRB 1118

Lavish and extravagant entertainment
IRC §274(k)

Reg. §1.274-1

Rev. Rul. 63-144, 1963-2 CB 129

Donald G. Harper, 23 TCM 461 (1964)

Townsend Industries, Inc., 2003-2 USTC
¶50,666 (8th Cir. 2003)

20.15 Limitation on Some Deductible Meals

* IRS Publication 463

Final regulations on business meals
T.D. 9925, 85 F.R. 64026 (2020)

General 50% limitation
IRC §274 (n)(1), as amended by the Tax Cuts
and Jobs Act (P.L. 115-97, 12/22/2017)

Exceptions to 50% limit
IRC §274(n)(2)(A-C), as amended by the Tax
Cuts and Jobs Act (P.L. 115-97, 12/22/2017)

**Exception for goods and services
sold to public by restaurants and
nightclubs**
IRC §274 (e)(8)

Exception for compensation paid
IRC §274(e)(2)

**80% limit for transportation industry
workers**
IRC §274(n)(3)

20.16 Substantiating Travel Expenses

Reg. §1.274-5(c)

Reg. §1.274-5T

* IRS Publication 463

Diary
Reg. §1.274-5(c)(2)(iii)

Joseph L. Weinfeld, 20 TCM 70 (1961)

Warren Cummings, 20 TCM 1699 (1961)

Travel receipt threshold raised to $75
Notice 95-50, 1995-2 CB 333

**Hotel bill not needed if per diem
allowance received**
Rev. Proc. 63-4, 1963-1 CB 494

Receipts
Reg. §1.274-5(c)(2)(iii)

Notice 95-50, 1992-2 CB 333

Sampling
Temp. Reg. §1.274-5T(c)(3)(ii)

* IRS Publication 463

Noting expense items
Reg. §1.274-5(c)

Reg. §1.274-5(c)(6)

Failure to show business purpose
Norman E. Kennelly, 56 TC 936 (1971), aff'd,
456 F.2d 1335 (2nd Cir. 1972)

Time limit for keeping records
Reg. §1.274-5(c)(2)(iv)

Credit cards
Reg. §1.274-5(e)(2)

Rev. Rul. 59-410 1959-2 CB 64

Excuses for inadequate records
Reg. §1.274-5(c)

**Attorney required to keep travel and
entertainment records**
William Andress, Jr., 51 TC 863 (1969), aff'd
per curiam, 423 F.2d 679 (5th Cir. 1970)

Loss of records
Lewis M. Bryan, 33 TCM 1188 (1974)

Bills but no other proof
Cam F. Dowell, Jr., 522 F.2d 708 (5th Cir.
1975), cert. denied, 26 U.S. 920

Loss due to eviction
Irvin A. Murray, 41 TCM 337 (1980)

**Loss due to destruction by estranged
wife**
Matthew J. Canfield, 41 TCM 461 (1980)

Loss of records due to fire
Robert Inzano, 76 TCM 231 (1998)

20.17 Employee Reporting of Unreimbursed Expenses

* IRS Publication 463

**Most employees barred from
deducting unreimbursed travel and
transportation costs starting in 2018
(Tax Cuts and Jobs Act)**
IRC §67(g), as added by the Tax Cuts and Jobs
Act (P.L. 115-97, 12/22/2017) (suspension for
2018 through 2025 of miscellaneous itemized
deduction for unreimbursed employee travel
and transportation costs)

**Prior law deduction rules for
employees (prior to Tax Cuts and Jobs
Act)**
IRC §67 (2% AGI floor for miscellaneous
itemized deductions including employee

expenses, prior to addition of IRC §67 (g) in
the Tax Cuts and Jobs Act)
IRC §274(n)(1)(50% limit for pre-2018
employee deductions for unreimbursed meals
and entertainment)

20.18 Are You Reimbursed Under an Accountable Plan?

IRC §62(c)

Reg. §1.62-2(c)(2) and (c)(4)

* IRS Publication 463

Reimbursement given to avoid FICA
* Letter Ruling 9504002

Failure to get reimbursed
Earl M. Coplon, 18 TCM 166 (1959), aff'd, 277
F.2d 534 (6th Cir. 1960)

Marvin A. Heidt, 18 TCM 149 (1959), aff'd,
274 F.2d 25 (7th Cir. 1960)

Eugene J. Rogers, 18 TCM 866 (1959)

Jack C. Morgan, 24 TCM 644 (1965)

**Frequent flyer allowance under
accountable plans**
* Letter Ruling 9547001

20.19 Per Diem Travel Allowance Under Accountable Plans

* IRS Publications 463

High-low reimbursement method
Notice 2023-68, 2023-41 IRB 1060 (business
trips from October 1, 2023, to September 30,
2024)

Notice 2022-44, 2022-41 IRB 277 (business
trips from October 1, 2022, to September 30,
2023)

Notice 2021-52, 2021-38 IRB 381 (business
trips from October 1, 2021, to September 30,
2022)

Notice 2020-71, 2020-40 IRB 786 (business
trips from October 1, 2020, to September 30,
2021)

Notice 2019- 55, 2019-42 IRB 937 (business
trips from October 1, 2019, to September 30,
2020)

Notice 2018- 77, 2018-42 IRB 601 (business
trips from October 1, 2018, to September 30,
2019)

20.20 Automobile Mileage Allowance

* IRS Publication 463

Mileage allowance
Notice 2023-03, 2023-3 IRB 388 (mileage
rates for 2023)

Notice 2022-3, 2022-2 IRB 308 (rate for first
half of 2022)

Announcement 2022-13, 2022-26 IRB 1185
(rate for second half of 2022)

Notice 2021-2, 2021-3 IRB 478 (2021 rate)

Notice 2020-05, 2020-04 IRB 380 (2020 rate)

Notice 2019-02, 2019-02 IRB 281 (2019 rate)

20.21 REIMBURSEMENTS UNDER NON-ACCOUNTABLE PLANS

Reg. §1.62-2(c)(3) and (c)(5)

* Letter Ruling 9443025

* IRS Publication 463

21   DEPENDENTS

21.1 NO EXEMPTION DEDUCTIONS ARE ALLOWED

IRC §151(d) (5) (A), as added by the Tax Cuts and Jobs Act (P.L. 115-97, 12/22/2017) for 2018 through 2025 (exemption amount is zero for 2018 through 2025)

* IRS Publication 501

21.2 HOW MANY DEPENDENTS DO YOU HAVE?

IRC §151

IRC §152

* IRS Publication 501

Definition of qualifying child

IRC §152(c)

Definition of qualifying relative

IRC §152(d)

Social Security numbers

IRC §151(e)

Spouses' Social Security numbers on joint returns

News Release IR-2000-68

Dependent can't claim dependents

IRC §152(b)(1)

21.3 QUALIFYING CHILDREN

IRC §152(c)

* IRS Publication 501

Qualifying child defined

IRC §152(c)

Descendants of child

IRC §152(c)(2)(A)

Sibling and sibling's descendants

IRC §152(c)(2)(B)

IRC §152(f)(4) (sibling by half-blood)

Adopted child

IRC §152(f)(1)(B)

Foster child

IRC §152(f)(1)(C)

Tax consequences when foster child status ends

Jean Cowan, TC Memo 2015-85

Principal place of abode test

IRC §152(c)(1)(B)

IRC §152(f)(6) (kidnapped children)

Grandparent's home meets principal bode test

*James Edward Roberts, TC Summary Opinion 2014-88

Age or student test

IRC §152(c)(3)

IRC §152(f)(2) (full-time students)

Tie-breaker rules

IRC §152(c)(4)

Can't provide over half of own support

IRC §152(c)(1)(D)

Infants born during tax year

Reg. §1.152-1(b)

Unborn child does not qualify

Andrea L. Cassman, 31 Fed Cl. 121 (1994)

Nieces

Oralia Pavia, TC Memo 2008-270

21.4 QUALIFYING RELATIVES

IRC §152(d)

* IRS Publication 501

Relationship test

IRC §152(d)(2)

Jean Cowan, TC Memo 2015-85

Can't be qualifying child

IRC §152(d)(1)(D)

Support test

IRC §152(d)(1)(C)

Gross income limit

IRC §152(d)(1)(B)

Rev. Proc. 2020-45, 2020-46 IRB 1016 (limit for 2021)

Notice 2018-70, 2018-38 IRB 441; reduction of exemption amount to zero for 2018-2025 not applicable for qualifying relative purposes)

Nephew, niece

IRC §152(d)(2)(E)

Oralia Pavia, TC Memo 2008-270

Uncle, aunt

IRC §152(d)(2)(F)

In-laws

IRC §152(d)(2)(G)

Cousin

IRC §152(d)(2)(H)(member of household test)

*Edwin Davila Jr., TC Summary Opinion 2012-6 (cousin's kids living in home only part of year)

21.5 MEETING THE SUPPORT TEST FOR A QUALIFYING RELATIVE

IRC §152(d)(1)(C)

* IRS Publication 501

Support includes board, lodging, etc., from all sources

Reg. §1.152-1(a)(2)

Scholarship for full-time student not counted as support

IRC §152(f)(5)

Cost of car and T.V. may be support items

Rev. Rul. 77-282, 1977-2 CB 52

Summer camp

Betty A. Shapiro, 54 TC 347 (1970) (Acq.)

Singing and drama lessons

Raymond McKay, 34 TC 1080 (1960)

Musical instrument

Virginia M. Cramer, 55 TC 1125 (1955) (Acq.)

Payment by insurance company

Rev. Rul. 64-223, 1964-2 CB 50

Social Security benefits used for own support

Reg. §1.152-1(a)(2)(ii)

Social Security to children

Rev. Rul. 74-543, 1974-2 CB 39

Rev. Rul. 74-115, 1974-1 CB 100

Rev. Rul. 57-344, 1957-2 CB 112

Medicare benefits not counted as support

Alfred H. Turecamo, 64 TC 720 (1975), aff'd, 554 F.2d 564 (2nd Cir. 1977) (Acq.)

Rev. Rul. 79-173, 1979-1 CB 86

Medicaid benefits not counted as support

Mary Archer, 73 TC 963 (1980)

Use of welfare payments

Rev. Rul. 71-468, 1971-2 CB 115

Norman Williams, 71 TCM 2423 (1996)

Eddie Carter, 55 TC 109 (1970) (Acq.)

Lodging fair rental value

Reg. §1.152-1(a)(2)(i)

* IRS Publication 501

Allocating Social Security benefits

Wilfred Abel, 21 TCM 1044 (1962)

Credit lost when foster child status ends

Jean Cowan, TC Memo 2015-85

Grandfather who meets abode test can claim credit

*James Edward Roberts, TC Summary Opinion 2014-88

25.3 FIGURING THE CHILD TAX CREDIT AND ADDITIONAL CHILD TAX CREDIT

IRC §24(i), added by the American Rescue Plan Act (P.L. 117-2, 3/11/2021) (credit rules for 2021 only)

IRC §24 (h), as added by the Tax Cuts and Jobs Act (P.L. 115-97, 12/22/2017) (child tax credit rules for 2018 through 2025)

* IRS Publication 972

Additional credit denied if foreign earned income exclusion is elected

IRC §24(d)(3)

25.4 CREDIT FOR OTHER DEPENDENTS

IRC §24 (h) (4), as added by the Tax Cuts and Jobs Act (P.L. 115-97, 12/22/2017) for 2018 through 2025)

* IRS Publication 972

25.5 CHILD AND DEPENDENT CARE CREDIT

IRC §21(g), added by the American Rescue Plan Act (P.L. 117-2, 3/11/2021) (for 2021 only)

* IRS Publication 503

No child tax credit for older disabled daughter

Robert Polsky, No. 15-2232, CA-3, 12/15/16

Dependent care credit denied if Social Security number of dependent is omitted

IRC §21(e)(1

Joint returns

IRC §21(e)(2)

No FICA for family

IRC §3121(b)

Paying babysitter's share of FICA qualifies for credit

Carolyn Perry, 92 TC 470 (1989)

Dependent care provider must be identified on return

IRC §21(e)(9)

Payments to relatives

IRC §21(e)(6)

Qualifying dependents

IRC §21(b)4

Reg. §1.44A-1(b)

Maintaining a household

IRC §21(e)(1)

Marital status

IRC §21(e)(3)

Spouse is not member of your household

IRC §21(e)(4)

Special rule if divorced or separated

IRC §21(e)(5)

Reg. §1.44A-1(b)(2)

25.6 FIGURING THE CHILD AND DEPENDENT CARE CREDIT

IRC §21

* IRS Publication 503

Credit percentage

IRC §21(a)

Eligible expenses limited to earned income

IRC §21(d)

Expenses qualifying for the dependent care credit

IRC §21(b)(2)

Prop. Reg. §1.21-1, -2, -3, -4

FICA tax

Rev. Rul. 74-176, 1974-1 CB 68

Least expensive alternative not required

Reg. §1.44A-1(c)(3)(ii)

Outside-the-home care

IRC §21(b)(2)(B)

No credit for overnight camp

IRC §21(b)(2)(A)

Summer camp

Edith W. Zoltan, 79 TC 490 (1982)

No deduction for travel to day-care center

Dorothy E. Warner, 69 TC 995 (1978)

Medical expense

Reg. §1.44A-4(b)

Allocation between qualifying/ nonqualifying service

Reg. §1.44A-1(c)(6)

Allocation of expenses on daily basis

Reg. §1.44A-1(c)(1)(ii)

Airplane transportation of children to grandparents ineligible

Caroline Perry, 92 TC 470 (1989)

Employer dependent care reduces credit base

IRC §21(c)

Dependent care provider must be identified on return

IRC §21(e)(9)

Spouse is student or disabled

IRC §21(d)(2)

Two or more families

Reg. §1.44A-1(d)(2)

25.7 QUALIFYING TESTS FOR EIC

IRC §32, as amended by the American Rescue Plan Act (P.L. 117-2, 3/11/2021)

* IRS Publication 596

Qualifying child

IRC §32(c)(3)

* James Edward Roberts, TC Summary Opinion 2014-88

Jean Cowan, TC Memo 2015-85

Oralia Pavia, TC Memo 2008-270 (nieces)

Eligible individual

IRC §32(c)(1)

Childless workers may qualify for the credit

IRC §32(c)(1)(A)(ii)

Rev. Proc. 2021-23, 2021-19 IRB 1153 (2021 amounts for childless workers, reflecting the American Rescue Plan Act (P.L. 117-2, 3/11/2021))

Childless EIC may be allowed in tiebreaker situation

Proposed Regulation Section 1.32-2 (c) (3); REG-137604-07, 2017-7 IRB 920

Social Security numbers required by due date of return

IRC §32(m)

Married must file jointly

IRC §32(d)

IRC §7703

Tax preparers must file EIC checklist with returns

Final Regulation 1.6695-2, as amended by Treasury Decision 9570, 12/20/11

*Form 8867 instructions

25.8 INCOME TESTS FOR EARNED INCOME CREDIT (EIC)

IRC §32(c)(2)(B) (determining earned income)

* IRS Publication 596

No earned income tax credit for disability income

Eva B. Vellai-Palotay, Ct. Fed. Cl., No: 1:16-cv-00125, 7/13/16

Inflation adjustments to earned income amount and phaseout threshold

IRC §32(j)

Rev. Proc 2022-38, 2022-45 IRB 445 (inflation adjustments for 2023)

Rev. Proc. 2021-45, 2021-48 IRB 764 (inflation adjustments for 2022)

Rev. Proc. 2020-45, 2020-46 IRB 1016 (inflation adjustments for 2021) (modified for childless workers by Rev. Proc. 2021-23, 2021-19 IRB 1153)

Rev. Proc. 2019-44, 2019-47 IRB 1093 (inflation adjustments for 2020)

Rev. Proc. 2018-57, 2018-49 IRB 827 (inflation adjustments for 2019)

Earned income eligible for credit

IRC §32(c)(2)(A)(i)

Election to treat tax-free combat pay as earned income

IRC §32(c)(2)(B)(vi)

Union paid strike benefits

Rev. Rul. 78-191, 1978-1 CB 8

Military housing allowance

Michael C. Neff, Ct. Cl., 5/25/99

Denial of credit if excessive investment income

IRC §32(i), as amended by the American Rescue Plan Act (P.L. 117-2, 3/11/2021)

Rev. Proc. 2021-45, 2021-48 IRB 764 (investment income limit for 2022)

Phaseout of credit

IRC §32(b)(2)

Credit determined by tables

IRC §32(f)

25.9 Qualifying for the Adoption Credit

IRC §23

Special needs adoption credit not automatic for biracial child

Joseph Lahmeyer (Dist. Ct. FL, 2014)

Joint return rule for adoption credit is constitutional

Nancy Louise Field v. Commissioner; TC Memo. 2013-111

25.10 Claiming the Adoption Credit on Form 8839

IRC §23

Inflation adjustments to credit amount and phaseout threshold

Rev. Proc 2022-38, 2022-45 IRB 445 (inflation adjustments for 2023)

Rev. Proc. 2021-45, 2021-48 IRB 764 (inflation adjustments for 2022)

Rev. Proc. 2020-45, 2020-46 IRB 1016 (inflation adjustments for 2021)

Rev. Proc. 2019-44, 2019-47 IRB 1093 (inflation adjustments for 2020)

Rev. Proc. 2018-57, 2018-49 IRB 827 (inflation adjustments for 2019)

Rev. Proc. 2018-18, 2018-10 IRB 392 (inflation adjustments for 2018)

Rev. Proc. 2016-55, 2016-45 IRB 707 (inflation adjustments for 2017)

When to claim the credit for foreign adoption

*General Counsel Advice 201509037

Safe harbor for determining finality of foreign adoptions

Rev. Proc. 2010-31, 2010-40 IRB 413 (finality of Hague Convention adoption)

Rev. Proc. 2005-31, 2005-26, IRB 1374

Announcement 2005-45, 2005-26 IRB 1377

Substantiating the adoption credit for 2010 and later years

Notice 2010-66, 2010-42 IRB 437

25.11 Eligibility for the Saver's Credit

IRC §25B (qualified retirement savings)

IRC §25B(b) (gross income limitations inflation indexing)

IRC §25B(h) (credit made permanent)

ABLE contributions by designated beneficiary

IRC §25B (d) (1)(D), as added by the Tax Cuts and Jobs Act (P.L. 115-97, 12/22/2017) for 2018 through 2025)

25.12 Figuring the Saver's Credit

Credit brackets

Notice 2022-53, 2022-45 IRB 443 (brackets for 2023)

Notice 2021-61, 2021-47 IRB 738 (brackets for 2022)

Notice 2020-79, 2020-46 IRB 1014 (brackets for 2021)

Notice 2019-59, 2019-47 IRB 1091 (brackets for 2020)

Notice 2018-83, 2018-47 IRB 774 (brackets for 2019)

25.13 Premium Tax Credit

IRC §36B, as amended by the American Rescue Plan Act (P.L. 117-2, 3/11/2021) and the Inflation Reduction Act of 2022 (P.L. 117-169, 8/16/2022)

400% FPL limit waived for 2021 through 2025

IRC §36B (b)(3)(A)(iii), IRC §36B (c)(1)(E), as amended by the Inflation Reduction Act of 2022 (P.L. 117-169, 8/16/2022)

Change in marital status may result in loss of premium tax credit

Timothy Todd Fisher, TC Memo 2019-44

Bankruptcy plan payments do not reduce household income for premium tax credit

Luis Palafox, TC Memo 2018-124

Final income may necessitate repayment of premium tax credit

* Carol Sue and Theodore Paul Walker, TC Summary Opinion 2017-50

No premium tax credit for non-marketplace coverage

David Lee and Cynthia Elizabeth Nelson, TC Order, 4/19/17

Supreme Court upholds credit for coverage from federal as well as state exchanges

David King v. Sylvia Mathews Burwell, 2015-1 USTC ¶50,356(Sup. Ct. 2015)

Supreme Court rejects constitutional challenge to ACA

Texas v. California (Sup. Ct. 6/17/21)

25.14 Mortgage Interest Credit

IRC §25 (qualified home mortgage certificates)

25.15 Residential Energy Credits

Notice 2023-65, 2023-42 IRB 1067 (Guidance on the new energy-efficient home credit)

Energy-efficient home improvement credit for 2022 (formerly the nonbusiness energy property credit)

IRC §25C (a) and (b), prior to amendment by the Inflation Reduction Act of 2022 (P.L. 117-169, 8/16/2022)

Residential clean energy credit (formerly the residential energy-efficient property credit)

IRC §25 D (solar panels, solar water heaters, geothermal heat pumps, wind turbines, fuel-cell property), as amended by the Consolidated Appropriations Act, 2021 (P.L. 116-260, 12/27/2020)

25.16 CLEAN VEHICLE CREDITS

Rev. Proc. 2023-33, 2023-43 IRB 1135

IRC §30D, as amended by the Inflation Reduction Act of 2022 (P.L. 117-169, 8/16/2022)

Final assembly requirement for vehicles sold after 8/16/2022

IRC §30D (d) (1) (G)

IRC §30D (d) (5) (definition of "final assembly")

Phaseout based on manufacturer's sales before 2023

IRC §30D (e), prior to elmination by the Inflation Reduction Act of 2022 (P.L. 117-169, 8/16/2022)

Notice 2018-96, 2018-52 IRB 1061(Tesla)

Notice 2019-22, 2019-14 IRB 931(General Motors)

25.17 REPAYMENT OF THE FIRST-TIME HOMEBUYER CREDIT

IRC §36, as amended by the Homebuyer Assistance and Improvement Act of 2010

Repayment of credit

IRC §36 (f)

Ex-spouse with full ownership must report annual repayment amount of the credit

Code Sec. 36(f)(4)(C)

Both spouses must qualify to claim credit

Robert D. Packard, CA-11, 3/27/14

Long-time resident homebuyer credit for married buyers

Robert D. Packard, 139 TC No. 15 (2012)

Allocation of first-time homebuyer credit between unmarried purchasers

Notice 2009-12, 2009-6 IRB 446

No credit for beneficiary purchasing from estate

* Chief Counsel Letter, INFO 2010-0071

*Cary Allen Nievinski, TC Summary Opinion 2011-10

No credit for child purchasing from a parent

* Chief Counsel Letter, INFO 2010-0073

No credit for home purchased from mother's estate

*Alice Schneider, TC Summary Opinion 2011-72

Three-year separation before divorce bars credit

* Chief Counsel Letter, INFO 2009-0135

Having co-signer doesn't block credit

* Chief Counsel Letter, INFO 2009-0101

* Chief Counsel Letter, INFO 2009-0171

26 TAX WITHHOLDINGS

26.1 WITHHOLDINGS SHOULD COVER ESTIMATED TAX

* IRS Publication 505

Form W-2

IRC §6051

Social Security maximum

IRC §31(b)(1)

Reg. §1.31-2

Graduated withholding rates

IRC §3402

Voluntary Social Security withholding

IRC §3402(p)

Indicate marital status on exemption certificate

IRC §3402(f)(1)

Allowable exemption on Form W-4

Reg. §31.3402(f)(1)-1

26.2 INCOME TAXES WITHHELD ON WAGES

Wages

IRC §3401(a)

Reg. §31.3401(a)-1

Fringe benefits

Temp. Reg. §31.3401(a)

Bonuses and supplemental wages—third lowest rate

Section 13273 of the Revenue Reconciliation Act of 1993

* IRS Publication 505

Payments other than wages (annuities, supplemental unemployment benefits)

IRC §3402(o)

Reg. §31.3402(o)-1

Withholding required for differential wages

IRC §3401(h), added by Heroes Earnings Assistance Tax Relief Act of 2008

Rev. Rul. 2009-11, 2009-18 IRB 896

Domestics

Reg. §31.3401(a)-3(b)

Agricultural workers

IRC §3401(a)(2)

Computer operators

* Letter Ruling 9534002

Ministers

Reg. §31.3401(A)(9)-1

Nonresident aliens

Reg. §31.3401(a)(6)-1

Public officials

Reg. §31.3401(a)-2(b)

Traveling advances

Reg. §31.3401(a)-1(b)(2)

Board, lodging, health benefits, etc.

Reg. §31.3401(a)(11)-1

Reg. §31.3401(a)-1(b)(9) and (10)

Foreign government pay

Reg. §31.3401(a)(5)-1

Foreign residents

Reg. §31.3401(a)(8)(A)-1

U.S. possessions

Reg. §31.3401(a)(8)(B)-1

No withholding on cancellation of employment contract

Rev. Rul. 58-301, 1958-1 CB 23, distinguished by Rev. Rul. 74-252, 1974-1 (withholding required on dismissal payments) CB 287 and Rev. Rul. 75-44, 1975-1 CB 15 (withholding on payment for relinquishment of seniority rights)

Terminated employee

IRC §6051(a)

Refund of employer overwithholding

Rev. Rul. 82-84, 1982-1 CB 208

26.3 LOW EARNERS MAY BE EXEMPT FROM WITHHOLDING

IRC §3402(i) and (p)

* IRS Publication 505

Electronic filing of W-4

Reg. §31.3402 (f)(5)-1(c)

Voluntary withholding on Social Security and other federal benefits

IRC §3402(p)

26.4 ARE YOU WITHHOLDING THE RIGHT AMOUNT?

IRC §3402(n)

IRC §3402(m)

Reg. §31.3402(m)-1

W-4 verification requirement dropped

Treasury Decision T.D. 9196, 2005-19 IRB 1000

26.5 VOLUNTARY WITHHOLDING ON GOVERNMENT PAYMENTS

IRC §3402(p)(1) and (2)

26.6 WHEN TIPS ARE SUBJECT TO WITHHOLDING

Tax withheld on tips

IRC §3402(k)

Reg. §31.3402(k)

Written report

IRC §6053

FICA tax

IRC §3101

IRC §3102

Rev. Rul. 95-7, 1995-1 CB 185

Tip allocation rules

IRC §6053(c)

Reg. §31.6053-3

Supreme Court approves IRS estimation method to assess employer FICA tax on tips

Fior D'Italia, Inc., 2002-1 USTC ¶50,549 (Sup. Ct. 2002)

26.7 WITHHOLDING ON GAMBLING WINNINGS

IRC §3402(q)(1)

* IRS Publication 505

26.8 FICA WITHHOLDINGS

IRC §3121

Severance pay subject to withholding

United States v. Quality Stores, 693 F.3d 605 (Sup. Ct., 2014)

Rate of tax

IRC §3101 (employee)

IRC §3111 (employer)

Withholding required for differential wages paid

IRC §3401(h), added by Heroes Earnings Assistance Tax Relief Act of 2008

Rev. Rul. 2009-11, 2009-18 IRB 896

"Wages" same as for income tax

Rowan Companies, Inc., 81-1 USTC ¶9479 (S. Ct. 1981)

Medical residents subject to FICA

Mayo Foundation for Medical Education and Research, Supreme Court, 1/11/2011

Responsible person for withholding

Edward Finley, 82 F.3d 966 (10th Cir., 1996)

Mary Phillips, 73 F.3d 939 (9th Cir., 1996)

Ellen L. Marino, 2004-1 USTC ¶50,262 (D. Fl. 2004)

Rev. Rul. 2004-41, IRB 2004-18, 845

Responsible person must be given written IRS notice before penalty

IRC §6672(b)

CFO escapes liability for trust fund taxes

Jose D. Salzillo, 2005-1 USTC ¶50,324 (Fed. Cl. 2005)

Deferred pay plans

Rev. Rul. 78-263, 1978-2 CB 253

Prop. Reg. §31.3121(v)(2)-1,2

Prop. Reg. §31.3306(r)(2)-1

Sick pay

IRC §3121(a)(2)

IRC §3231(e)

Spouse and children as employees

IRC §3121(b)(3)(A) and (B)

Back wages subject to FICA when paid

U.S. v. Cleveland Indians Baseball Co., 121 S. Ct. 1433 (2001)

Student employees

IRC §3121(b)(10)

Notice 2004-12, 2004-10 IRB 556 (proposed guidelines)

26.9 WITHHOLDING ON DISTRIBUTIONS FROM RETIREMENT PLANS AND COMMERCIAL ANNUITIES

IRC §3405

* IRS Publication 505

Withholding on payments outside U.S.

IRC §3405(e)(13)

20% withholding from employer plans

IRC §3405(c)

Notice 93-3, 1993-1 CB 293

26.10 BACKUP WITHHOLDING

IRC §3406(a)(1)

$50 penalty

IRC §6723 and §6724(d)(3)

27 ESTIMATED TAX PAYMENTS

27.1 DO YOU OWE AN ESTIMATED TAX PENALTY FOR 2023?

IRC §6654

* IRS Publication 505

$1,000 threshold

IRC §6654(e)(1)

90% threshold or prior year safe harbor

IRC §6654(d)

Late filers can use prior-year estimated tax safe harbor

Rev. Rul. 2003-23, 2003-8 IRB 511

Safe harbor percentage if adjusted gross income exceeds $150,000

IRC §6654(d)(1)(C)

No liability in prior tax year

IRC §6654(e)(2)

Rev. Rul. 57-185, 1957-1 CB 454

Rev. Rul. 58-369, 1958-2 CB 894

John A. Guglielmetti, 35 TC 668 (1961) (Acq.)

Penalty waiver for hardship, retirement, or disability

IRC §6654(e)(3)

Mental disorders not reasonable cause for failure to file

Austin Danne Hardin, TC Memo 2012-162

Farmers and fishermen

IRC §6654(i)

27.2 PLANNING ESTIMATED TAX PAYMENTS FOR 2024

* IRS Publication 505

$1,000 threshold

IRC §6654(e)(1)

90% or prior year safe harbor

IRC §6654(d)

Safe harbor percentage if adjusted gross income exceeds $150,000

IRC §6654(d)(1)(C)

Partners

Reg. §1.6654-2(d)(2)

Farmers and fishermen

IRC §6654(i)

27.3 DATES FOR PAYING ESTIMATED TAX INSTALLMENTS FOR 2024

* IRS Publication 505

Effect of Emancipation Day andt Patriots' Day on first installment due date

Rev. Rul. 2015-13, 2015-22 IRB 1011

Due dates for required installments

IRC §6654(c)

Return filed by January 31

IRC §6654(h)

Partial exclusion allowed after birth of second child

*Letter Ruling 201628002

September 11 terrorist attacks

Notice 2002-60, 2002-36 IRB 482

Being run out of town allows reduced exclusion

* Letter Ruling 200403049

Policeman's job change allows reduced exclusion

* Letter Ruling 200504012

Child adoption allows reduced exclusion

* Letter Ruling 200613009

Partial exclusion allowed for early move from retirement community

* Letter Ruling 200601023

Taking in paralyzed mother-in-law allows reduced exclusion

* Letter Ruling 200626024

Assaults in neighborhood allow reduced exclusion

* Letter Ruling 200630004 (crime exception)

* Letter Ruling 200601009 (crime exception)

Settlement proceeds for airplane noise eligible for exclusion

* Letter Ruling 200702032

Need for larger home following birth of another child is unforeseen circumstance

* Letter Ruling 200745011

29.5 FIGURING GAIN OR LOSS

* IRS Publication 523

Gain or loss

IRC §1001

Reg. §1.1001-1 (amount realized)

Selling price

Reg. §1.1001

IRC §1001

Mortgage included in price

Beulah B. Crane, 331 U.S. 1 (1947)

Home basis does not include furniture

R. John Forte, DC-UT, 6/21/21

Property valued at less than mortgage

John F. Tufts, 456 U.S. 960 (1983)

Reduce price by expenses

Seleths O. Thompson, 9 BTA 1342 (Acq.)

Samuel C. Chapin, 12 TC 235 (1949), aff'd, 180 F.2d 140 (8th Cir. 1950)

Legal fee—cost of sale

Fred W. Gunn, 49 TC 38 (1967)

29.6 FIGURING ADJUSTED BASIS

Unadjusted basis

IRC §1012

Reg. §1.1012-1

* IRS Publication 551

Improvements

IRC §1016

Reg. §1.016-2

Adjusted basis

IRC §1011

Reg. §1.1011-1

Improvements not covered by note

Glenda P. McCormick, 99-1 USTC ¶50,380

Basis is cash cost

IRC §1012

Reg. §1.1012-1

Adjusted cost after depreciation allowed

IRC §1016

Reg. §1.1016-3

Tax-free exchange of property

IRC §1031

Reg. §1.1031(d)-1

Basis of new residence after home sale deferral

IRC §1034(e)

Reg. §1.1034-1

Property subject to lease

Harriet M. Bryant Trust, 11 TC 374 (1948) (Acq.)

Property subject to mortgage

Beulah B. Crane, 331 U.S. 1 (1947)

Compulsory or involuntary conversion

IRC §1033(b)

29.7 PERSONAL AND BUSINESS USE OF A HOME

Reg. §1.121-1(e)

* IRS Publication 523

Post-2008 exclusion cut back for post-2008 nonqualified use

IRC 121(b)(5)

Exclusion plus gain deferral on exchange of residence

Rev. Proc. 2005-14, 2005-7 IRB 528

29.8 NO LOSS ALLOWED ON PERSONAL RESIDENCE

Reg. §1.165-9(a)

29.9 LOSS ON RESIDENCE CONVERTED TO RENTAL PROPERTY

IRC §165(c)(2)

Reg. §1.165-9(b)

90-day lease returning a profit with option to buy

Paul H. Rechnitzer, 26 TCM 298 (1967)

Rental loss on temporary rental before sale

Stephen Bolaris, 776 F.2d 1428 (9th Cir. 1985), rev'g 81 TC 840 (1983)

Ronald S. Adams, 69 TCM 2297 (1995)

No loss unless move out

Peter Seletos, 254 F.2d 794 (8th Cir. 1958)

Loss on rented vacation home

James B. Murtaugh, 74 TCM 75 (1997)

Annual rent

Austin F. Stillman, 9 TCM 425 (1950)

Conversion to business property

Reg. §1.165-9(b)

Isolated rental

Charles A. Foehl, Jr., 20 TCM 418 (1961)

Intent to sell at profit, loss allowed

Lucille H. Gaunt, 69 F. Supp. 747 (D. Ky.)

Albert W. Bassett, 35 TCM 40 (1976)

Vandalism

Elbert S. Tillotson, 12 TCM 171 (1953)

Architect

Leonard Hyatt, 20 TCM 1635 (1961), supplemented by 20 TCM 1712 (1961), aff'd, 325 F.2d 715 (5th Cir. 1964), cert. denied, 379 U.S. 832

Listing for sale or rent

George D. Morgan, 76 F.2d 390 (5th Cir. 1935), cert. denied, 296 U.S. 601

Walden E. Sweet, 68-2 USTC ¶9656 (N.D. Cal. 1968)

James J. Sherlock, 31 TCM 383 (1972)

Rental to buyer

Henry B. Dawson, Jr., 31 TCM 5 (1972)

Expenses of rental attempt

Paul F. Stutz, 24 TCM 888 (1965)

Deducting expense of vacant building put up for sale

George W. Mitchell, 47 TC 120 (1966) (Nonacq.)

Limit on expense deductions where house used for personal purposes during the year

IRC §280a

Widow allowed capital loss not rental loss

Victoria Balsamo, 54 TCM 608 (1987)

Stock in co-op apartment

Rev. Rul. 60-76, 1960-1 CB 296

Cecil P. Stewart, 5 TCM 229 (1946)

William M. Calder, Jr., 16 TC 144 (1951) (Acq.)

Sale of partly rented house

Virginia V. Gary, BTA Memo., P-H 32,174, December 1, 1932 (capital gain on rental part; nondeductible loss on personal part)

29.10 LOSS ON RESIDENCE ACQUIRED BY GIFT OR INHERITANCE

Residence acquired by gift or inheritance

IRC §165(c)(2)

N. Stuart Campbell, 5 TC 272 (1945) (Acq.)

Maria Assmann Est., 16 TC 632 (1951)

Reed A. Watkins, 32 TCM 1260 (1973)

George W. Carnrick, 9 TC 756 (1947) (Acq.)

Pauline Miller Est., 26 TCM 229 (1967)

30 TAX RULES FOR INVESTORS IN SECURITIES

30.1 PLANNING YEAR-END SECURITIES TRANSACTIONS

Capital gain holding period

IRC §1222

Capital loss deduction against ordinary income

IRC §1211(b)

Gain and loss recognized on trade date for year-end sale of publicly traded securities

IRC §453 (k)(2)

30.2 EARMARKING STOCK LOTS

Registered in own name

Reg. §1.1012-1(c)(5)

James E. Davidson, 305 U.S. 44 (1938)

Margin account registered in "street" name

James L. Rankin, Exr., 295 U.S. 123 (1936)

Laura M. Curtis, 101 F.2d 40 (2d Cir. 1939)

James L. Rankin, Exr. 84 F.2d 551 (3d Cir. 1936)

Recapitalization

Robert E. Ford, 33 BTA 1229 (Acq.)

Reorganization—identified

Amelia D. Bloch, 148 F.2d 452 (9th Cir. 1945)

Failure to show certificate numbers

Kluger Associates, 69 TC 925 (1978), aff'd, 617 F.2d 323 (2d Cir. 1980)

Reorganization—average cost

Christian W. Von Gunten, 76 F.2d 670 (6th Cir. 1935)

Harry M. Runkle, 39 BTA 458

Pio Crespi, 126 F.2d 699 (5th Cir. 1942)

Big Wolf Corp., 2 TC 751 (1943) (Acq.)

Split-up

Robert E. Ford, 33 BTA 1229 (Acq.)

Herbert H. Franklin, 37 BTA 471 (Acq.)

Solomon B. Kraus, 88 F.2d 616 (2d Cir. 1937)

Stock dividends

George Vawter, 83 F.2d 11 (10th Cir. 1936), cert. denied, 299 U.S. 578

Stock rights

Williams R. Perkins, 12 F. Supp. 481 (Ct. Cl. 1935), cert. denied, 297 U.S. 710

30.3 SALE OF STOCK DIVIDENDS

Holding period

IRC §1223

Reg. §1.1223-1

Public utility stock dividend

IRC §305(e)

30.4 STOCK RIGHTS

Stockholder rights expire

IRC §1223

IRC §307

Reg. §1.1223-1(e)

Reg. §1.307-1 and 2

Sidney Z. Mitchell, 18 BTA 994, aff'd, 48 F.2d 697 (2d Cir. 1931), cert. denied, 284 U.S. 646

Stock rights sold

IRC §1223(5)

Reg. §1.1223-1(e)

Stock rights exercised

IRC §1223(6)

Reg. §1.1223-1(f)

Rights purchased

IRC §1223

Reg. §1.1223-1

Figuring basis of stock rights

IRC §307

IRC §307(b)(1)(B) ("less than 15%" exception)

Reg. §1.307-1

Election

Reg. §1.307-2

30.5 SHORT SALES OF STOCK

* IRS Publication 550

Rev. Rul. 2002-44, 2002-28 IRB 84 (timing of gain or loss reporting)

Short sale closing

H. S. Richardson, 121 F.2d 1 (2d Cir. 1941), cert. denied, 314 U.S. 684

William P. Doyle, 286 F.2d 654 (7th Cir. 1961), rev'g 19 TCM 677 (1960)

* Letter Ruling 9436017

Appreciated financial position at year-end

IRC §1259

Rev. Rul. 2002-44, 2002-28 IRB 84

Husband and wife

Reg. §1.1233-1(d)(3)

Special short-sale rules

IRC §1233(b)

Reg. §1.1233-1(c)(2)

Special rule on short-sale losses

IRC §1233(d)

Reg. §1.1233-1(c)(4)

Time of loss

Walter Hendricks, 29 TCM 36 (1970), aff'd, 423 F.2d 485 (4th Cir. 1970)

Payment in lieu of dividends: 46-day rule

IRC §263(b)

Puts (options to sell)

IRC §1233(c)

Reg. §1.1233-1(c)(3)

Expenses of short sales; stock dividends

Rev. Rul. 72-521, 1972-2 CB 178

Cash dividends paid on stock sold short

IRC §263(h)

1955 Production Exposition, Inc., 41 TC 85 (1963)

Main Line Distributors, Inc., 37 TC 1090 (1962), aff'd, 321 F.2d 562 (6th Cir. 1963)

Compensation for use of collateral

IRC §263(h)(5)

Extraordinary dividends

IRC §263(h)(2)

IRC §263(h)(3)

Death before sale is closed

Rev. Rul. 73-524, 1973-2 CB 307

Wash sales

IRC §1091(e)

30.6 WASH SALES

* IRS Publication 550

Wash sales

IRC §1091

Reg. §1.1091-1 and 2

Rev. Rul. 2008-5, 2008-3, IRB 271 (replacement shares purchased in IRA)

Trader

Sol H. Morris, 38 BTA 265 (Acq.)

Richard S. Coulter, 32 BTA 617

IRC §1236

Reg. §1.471-5

Wilson, 76 F.2d 476 (10th Cir. 1935)

Walter Hirshon, 116 F. Supp. 135 (Ct. Cl. 1953)

L. B. Maytag, 32 TC 270 (1959)

Dealer

IRC §1091(a)

Donander Co., 29 BTA 312

Oral agreement

Estate of Maxwell J. Estroff, 47 TCM 234 (1983)

Substantially identical securities

Corn Products Refining Co., 215 F.2d 524 (2d Cir. 1954), aff'd, 350 U.S. 46 (1955)

Trenton Cotton Oil Co., 147 F.2d 33 (6th Cir. 1945), rehearing denied, 148 F.2d 208 (6th Cir. 1945)

Marie Hanlin, 197 F.2d 429 (3d Cir. 1939)

Sicanoff Vegetable Oil Co., 27 TC 1056 (1957)

Rev. Rul. 76-346, 1976-1 CB 247

Rev. Rul. 58-210, 1958-1 CB 523

Rev. Rul. 58-211, 1958-1 CB 529

Maturity dates

Marie Hanlin et al., 108 F.2d 429 (3d Cir. 1939)

Rev. Rul. 76-346, 1976-1 CB 247

Rev. Rul. 58-211, 1958-1 CB 259

Interest rates differed

Rev. Rul. 76-346, 1976-1 CB 247

Rev. Rul. 60-195, 1960-1 CB 300

Issue date and interest payments of bonds not material

Marjorie K. Campbell, 39 BTA 916 (Acq.), aff'd, 112, F.2d 530 (2d Cir. 1940), rev'd, 313 U.S. 15 (1941)

Warrants

Rev. Rul. 56-406, 1956-2 CB 523

Contract to sell stock

Rev. Rul. 59-418, 1959-2 CB 184

Short sales

Reg. §1.1091-1(g)

William P. Doyle, 286 F.2d 654 (7th Cir. 1961), rev'g 19 TCM 677 (1960)

Foreign currencies are not "securities"

Rev. Rul. 74-218, 1974-1 CB 202

Commodity futures

IRC §1092(b)

* Letter Ruling 8241006

30.7 CONVERTIBLE STOCKS AND BONDS

No gain or loss

Rev. Rul. 72-265, 1972-1 CB 222

Holding period

IRC §1223(1)

Split-holding period

Rev. Rul. 62-140, 1962-2 CB 181

Basis

IRC §358

30.8 STOCK OPTIONS

Options to buy or sell stock

IRC §1234

30.9 SOPHISTICATED FINANCIAL TRANSACTIONS

IRC §1234(b)

IRC §1256

Arbitrage transactions

IRC §1233(f)

Reg. §1.1233-1(f)

Capital gain

IRC §1234

Reg. §1234-1

Convert to long-term profits

Rev. Rul. 58-384, 1958-2 CB 410

Capital gain restricted on conversion transactions

IRC §1258

Constructive sales of appreciated financial positions

IRC §1259

Straddle losses

IRC §1092

IRC §1256

IRC §263(g)

Loss barred on identified straddle position

IRC §1092(a)(2)(A)

Carryback of net Section 1256 loss

IRC §1212(c)

Mixed straddle election to avoid marked-to-market rules

Temp. Reg. §1.1092(b)-3T and §4T

IRC §1258

30.10 INVESTING IN TAX-EXEMPTS

IRC §103

Qualified private activity bonds

IRC §141(e)

AMT exception for private activity bonds issued in 2009 and 2010

IRC §57(a)(5)(C)(vi)

Tax preference item

IRC §57(a)(5)

30.11 ORDINARY LOSS FOR SMALL BUSINESS STOCK (SECTION 1244)

IRC §1244

* IRS Publication 550

Record-keeping

Reg. §1.1244(e)-1(b)

30.12 SERIES EE BONDS

* IRS Publication 550

Reporting EE bond interest annually

IRC §454(c)

Reg. §1.454-1

Deduction for estate tax

Rev. Rul. 58-435, 1958-2 CB 370, distinguished by Rev. Rul. 68-145 1968-1 CB 203

Savings bond tuition plans

IRC §135

Transferring savings bonds to a revocable trust

* Chief Counsel Information Letter 2015-0027

EE bonds issued after April 2005 pay fixed interest

Treasury Department Press Release, 4/4/05

30.13 I BONDS

* IRS Publication 550

Taxation of Series I bonds

31 CFR Sec 359.9 (b)(1)

Transferring savings bonds to a revocable trust

* Chief Counsel Information Letter 2015-0027

30.14 TRADER, DEALER, OR INVESTOR?

* IRS Publication 550

Sporadic trading bars trader status

William G. Holsinger, TC Memo 2008-141

Frank Chen, TC Memo 2004-132

Henricus C. van der Lee, TC Memo 2011-234

Securities investor denied trader status

Frederick R. Mayer, TC Memo 1994-209

Home office deduction denied to investor

Joseph Moller, 721 F.2d 810 (CA-Fed. Cir. 1983)

30.15 MARK-TO-MARKET ELECTION FOR TRADERS

IRC §475(f)

Election procedure

Rev. Proc. 99-17, 1999-7 IRB 52

* IRS Publication 550

Deadline for mark-to-market election

Kazim Z. Acar, 2008-2 USTC ¶50,564 (9th Circuit 2008) (IRS deadline applies)

Ronald A. Lehrer, TC Memo 2005-167 (IRS deadline applies)

L.S. Vines, 126 TC 279 (2006) (extension allowed over IRS objection)

30.16 CRYPTOCURRENCY TRANSACTIONS

Notice 2014-21, 2014-16 IRB (cryptocurrency is treated as property)

Chief Counsel Advice 202114020 (income results from permanent hard split)

Rev. Rul. 2019-24, 2019-44 IRB 1004 (explains when hard fork does not result in income)

31 TAX SAVINGS FOR INVESTORS IN REAL ESTATE

31.1 REAL ESTATE VENTURES

Syndicates

Reg. §301.7701-1

Limited partnership not taxable as corporation

Phillip G. Larson, 66 TC 159 (1976) (Acq.)

Rev. Rul. 79-106, 1979-1 CB 448

IRS to study minimum capitalization requirement

Ann. 83-4, 1983-2 IRB 31

Publicly traded partnerships

IRC §7704

IRC §469

Real estate investment trusts

IRC §856

IRC §857

IRC §858

Reg. §1.856

Reg. §1.857

Reg. §1.858

REMICs

IRC §860A-860G

* IRS Publication 550

31.2 SALES OF SUBDIVIDED LAND— DEALER OR INVESTOR?

IRC §1237

Reg. §1.1237-1

Liquidation of business property—no capital gain

Morley v. Commr, 87 TC 1206 (1986)

John W. Kelley, 18 TCM 329 (1959), aff'd, 281 F.2d 527 (9th Cir. 1959)

No sales effort

Robert E. Austin, 263 F.2d 460 (9th Cir. 1959)

William T. Minor, Jr., 18 TCM 14 (1959)

James G. Hoover, 32 TC 618 (1959) (Acq.)

Allen Moore, 30 TC 1306 (1958) (Acq.)

Sam E. Broadhead Est., 32 TCM 1047 (1973)

Robert L. Adams, 60 TC 996 (1973) (Acq.)

Substantial improvements bar Section 1237 treatment

Jesse W. English, 65 TCM 2160 (1993)

Dealers may not use installment method

IRC §453(b)(2)(A)

IRC §453(l)

Sale to controlled corporation

Ralph E. Gordy, 36 TC 855 (1961) (Acq.)

Real estate dealer

Richard H. Pritchett, 63 TC 149 (1974) (Acq.)

Effect of condemnation

Thomas K. McManus, 65 TC 197 (1975)

Tri S. Corp., 400 F.2d 862 (10th Cir. 1968) (capital gains allowed)

Theodore H. Case, 633 F.2d 1240 (6th Cir. 1980) (capital gains denied)

Developer allowed capital gains on sale to city

Est. of Eileen Knudsen, 40 TCM 510 (1980)

Oscar Fraley, 66 TCM 100 (1993)

Developer not allowed capital gain on land sale

Robert P. Walsh, 67 TCM 3134 (1994)

31.3 EXCHANGING REAL ESTATE WITHOUT TAX

IRC §1031

"Like kind"

Reg. §1.1031(a)-1(b) and (c)

Rev. Rul. 59-229, 1959-2 CB 180

P. G. Lake, Inc., 356 U.S. 260 (1958)

Productive use in trade or business

IRC §1031

Reg. §1.1031(a)-1(a)

Personal-use safe harbor for tax deferred exchange

Rev. Proc. 2008-16, 2008-10 IRB 547

Time limits

IRC §1031(a)(3)

Reg. §1.1031(a)-3

"Parking" for a like-kind exchange is limited

Rev. Proc. 2004-51, 2004-33 IRB 294

Treasury Department News Release JS-1798, 7/20/04

Direct deed transfer

Rev. Rul. 90-34, 1990-1 CB 154

Two-year freeze on exchange with related party

IRC §1031(f)

Basis

IRC §1031(d)

Reg. §1.1031(d)-1 and -2

Dealer

IRC §1031

Reg. §1.1031(a)-1(a)

Luther A. Harr, 15 F. Supp. 1004 (D. Pa. 1936)

Resale

Ethel Black, 35 TC 90 (1960)

Exchanges of remainder and life interests

Rev. Rul. 72-601, 1972-2 CB 467

Boot

Reg. §1.1031(b)-1

Partially tax-free exchanges

IRC §1031(b)

Reg. §1.1031(b)-1

Receipt of cash contractually obligated to be applied against liabilities not boot

Earlene T. Barker, 74 TC 555 (1980)

Loss not recognized

IRC §1031(a)

Reg. §1.1031(a)-1

Planning tax-free exchange

Rev. Rul. 77-297, 1977-2 CB 304

99-year lease exchanged for fee interest is like-kind

Carl E. Koch, 71 TC 54 (1978) (Acq.)

Optional renewal periods added to initial lease terms

Century Electric, 192 F.2d 155 (8th Cir. 1951), cert. denied, 342 U.S. 954

No tax-free exchange treatment for vacation property

Barry E. Moore, TC Memo 2007-134

Like-kind exchange tax deferral allowed depsite moving into replacement property

Patrick A. Reesink, TC Memo 2012-118

31.4 TIMING YOUR REAL PROPERTY SALES

Installment sales

IRC §453

Tax in year of sale

Milton S. Yunker, 26 TC 161 (1956), rev'd on other issue, 256 F.2d 130 (6th Cir. 1958)

Title passes

Alfred M. Bedell, 30 F.2d 622 (2d Cir. 1929)

Completion of terms of contingent sale

E. F. Baertschi, 412 F.2d 494 (6th Cir. 1969), rev'g 49 TC 289 (1967)

Deliver deed and possession

William C. King, 10 BTA 308 (Acq.)

Big Western Oil & Gas Co., 9 BTA 427 (Acq.)

Possession this year, deed next year

J. T. Pittard, 5 BTA 929 (Acq.)

Standard Lumber Co., 28 BTA 352

Buyer in possession

Ted F. Merrill, 40 TC 66 (1963), and per curiam, 366 F.2d 771 (9th Cir. 1964)

Marshall E. Boykin, 344 F.2d 889 (5th Cir. 1965)

Property held in escrow

Arthur Long, 1 BTA 796

Harry C. Moir, 14 BTA 23 (Nonacq.), aff'd, 45 F.2d 356 (7th Cir. 1930)

Deed delivered

William F. Scruggs, 281 F.2d 900 (10th Cir. 1960)

Option to sell exercised next year

Samuel C. Chapin, 180 F.2d 140 (8th Cir. 1950)

Contract to sell

Rev. Rul. 69-93, 1969-1 CB 139

No fair market value

A. M. Nichols, 44 F.2d 157 (3d Cir. 1930)

Nina Ennis, 17 TC 465 (1951)

Purchase price held

George I. Bumbaugh, 10 BTA 672

R. M. Waggoner, 9 BTA 629 (Nonacq.)

Preston R. Bassett, 33 BTA 182, aff'd per curiam, 90 F.2d 1004 (2d Cir. 1950)

K. E. Merren, 18 BTA 156 (Acq.), aff'd, 51 F.2d 44 (5th Cir. 1931)

31.5 CANCELLATION OF A LEASE

IRC §1241

Reg. §1.1241-1

31.6 SALE OF AN OPTION

IRC §1234

Reg. §1.1234-1

31.7 GRANTING OF AN EASEMENT

David Fasten, 71 TC 650 (1979) (Acq.)

Inaja Land Co. Ltd., 9 TC 727 (1947) (Acq.)

Rev. Rul. 59-121, 1959-1 CB 212, clarified by Rev. Rul. 68-291, 1968-1 CB 351

Rev. Rul. 72-433, 1972-2 CB 470

Rev. Rul. 73-161, 1973-1 CB 366

Rev. Rul. 72-255, 1972-1 CB 221

Restrictive covenant released

Rev. Rul. 70-203, 1970-1 CB 171

31.8 SPECIAL TAX CREDITS FOR REAL ESTATE INVESTMENTS

Low-income housing credit permanently extended

IRC §42

Rehabilitating historic buildings

IRC §47, as amended by the Tax Cuts and Jobs Act (P.L. 115-97, 12/22/2017) (repealing 10% rehabilitation credit for pre-1936 buildings)

Recapture of rehabilitation credits

IRC §50(a)(i)

Substantial rehabilitation test applies to entire building

Karl R. Alexander III, 97 TC 244 (1991)

Credit allowed for relocated building

George Nalle, 997 F.2d 1134 (5th Cir., 1993)

Effect of charitable deduction on credit

Rome I, Ltd, 96 TC 697 (1991)

Higher credit for Gulf Opportunity Zone property

IRC §1400N(h)

31.9 FORECLOSURES, REPOSSESSIONS, SHORT SALES, AND VOLUNTARY CONVEYANCES TO CREDITORS

* IRS Publication 4681

National Mortgage Settlement (NMS) program payments

Rev. Rul. 2014-2, 2014-2 IRB 255

Sale or exchange requirement

IRC §1222

Exclusion for discharge of qualified principal residence indebtedness

IRC §108 (a)(1)(E), RC §108 (h)(2), as amended by the Consolidated Appropriations Act, 2021 (P.L. 116-260, 12/27/2020); exclusion amount reduced and exclusion extended through 2025

Capital asset treatment for lapse, cancellation, abandonment, etc., of commodity options

IRC §1234A

Property pledged as collateral

Morgan W. Jopling, 46 BTA 262

Voluntary conveyance of mortgaged property

Rev. Rul. 78-164, 1978-1 CB 264

Eugene L. Freeland, 74 TC 970 (1980)

Transfer by insolvent taxpayer

Rev. Rul. 90-16, 1990-1 CB 12

Foreclosure proceeds less than outstanding mortgage

Joseph Aizawa, 99 TC 197 (1992), aff'd. without published opinion, 29 F. 3d 630 (9th Cir. 1994)

Foreclosure bid price more than fair market value

Richard Frazier, 111 TC 243 (1998)

Business lease as 1231 asset

Rev. Rul. 72-85, 1972-1 CB 234

31.10 Restructuring Mortgage Debt

IRC §61(a)(12)

Exclusion for discharge of qualified principal residence indebtedness

IRC §108(a)(1)(E)

IRC 108(h)

Tax-free debt reductions

IRC §108(a)

Restructuring nonrecourse debt

Rev. Rul. 91-31, 1991-1 CB 19

IRS computation of insolvency

Rev. Rul. 92-53, 1992-2 CB 48

Relief for discharge of business real estate debt

IRC §108(a)(1)(D)

IRC §108(c)

31.11 Abandonments

Foreclosure of mortgage on abandoned property triggers gain

* Drucella T. Malonzo, TC Summary Opinion 2013-47

Abandonment treated as sale

Milledge L. Middleton, 77 TC 310 (1981), aff'd, 693 F.2d 124 (11th Cir., 1982)

James W. Yarbro, 45 TCM 170 (1982), aff'd, 737 F.2d 479 (5th Cir. 1984)

Abandonment of partnership interest

John C. Echols, 93 TC 553 (1989), rev'd by 950 F.2d 209 (5th Cir. 1991)

Philip Citron, 97 TC 200 (1991)

31.12 Seller's Repossession After Buyer's Default on Mortgage

IRC §1038

Reg. §1.1038-1 through 3

Recapture of home sale exclusion on repossession

Marvin E. DeBough, 142 TC No. 17 (2014)

End of holding period for depreciation recapture purposes where property foreclosed

IRC §1250(D)(10)

Personal residence

IRC §1038(e)

31.13 Foreclosure on Mortgages Other Than Purchase Money

You bid on property at foreclosure sale

Reg. §1.166-6(a)(1) and (b)(1)

Hadley Falls Trust Co., 110 F.2d 887 (1st Cir. 1940)

Unreported but accrued interest as income in foreclosure

Midland Mutual Life Ins. Co., 300 U.S. 216 (1937)

Bid price as fair market value

West Production Co., 121 F.2d 9 (5th Cir. 1941), cert. denied, 314 U.S. 682

Harold S. Weil, 111 F. Supp. 390 (D. La. 1953)

Must prove worthlessness of debt

Reg. §1.166-2

Property voluntarily conveyed in satisfaction of debt

Achilles H. Kohn, 197 F.2d 480 (2d Cir. 1952)

Nonrecourse debt is not protected by insolvency

Rev. Rul. 91-31, 1991-1 CB 19

Rev. Rul. 92-53, 1992-2 CB 48

James J. Gehl, 102 TC 37 (1994)

* Letter Ruling 9302001

Unreported but accrued interest as income in voluntary conveyance

Reserve Loan Life Ins. Co., 18 BTA 359 (Acq. and nonacq.)

Prudential Ins. Co. of America, 33 BTA 332 (Nonacq.)

Year deductible

Hadley Falls Trust Co., 110 F.2d 887 (1st Cir. 1940)

William C. Heinemann & Co., 40 BTA 1090

31.14 Foreclosure Sale to Third Party

* "Gain on Foreclosure Sales of Realty Need Not Be Recognized," Edward J. Schnee, 54 Taxation for Accountants 292 (May 1995)

Foreclosure expenses

Coeur d'Alene Hotel Inc., BTA Memo., Dec. 12,097-A

Bowles Lunch, Inc., 33 F. Supp. 235 (Ct. Cl. 1940)

Foreclosure sale at less than your mortgage

Reg. §1.166-6(a)(1)

Business bad debt is fully deductible

IRC §166(a)

Nonbusiness bad debt is a limited capital loss

IRC §166(d)

Partially worthless debts

IRC §166(a)(2) and (d)(1)(A)

Business and nonbusiness bad debt must be uncollectible

IRC §166(a)(1) and (d)

31.15 Transferring Mortgaged Realty

Corporation

IRC §351

IRC §357

F. W. Drybrough, 376 F.2d 350 (6th Cir. 1967)

Gifts

Est. of Aaron Levine, 634 F.2d 12 (2d Cir. 1980)

Teofilo Evangelista, 629 F. 2d 1218 (7th Cir. 1980)

31.16 QBI Deduction for REIT Dividends

IRC §199A, as added by the Tax Cuts and Jobs Act (P.L. 115-97, 12/22/2017) for 2018 through 2025

* IRS Publication 535

32 TAX RULES FOR INVESTORS IN MUTUAL FUNDS

32.1 Timing of Your Investment Can Affect Your Taxes

* IRS Publication 550

Capital gain

IRC §852(b)(3)

IRC §854(a)

Deferred annuities

Rev. Rul. 81-220, 1981-2 CB 175

Rev. Rul. 82-54, 1982-1 CB 11

Dividend declared in October, November, or December paid by following February

IRC §852(b)(7)

32.2 Reinvestment Plans

* IRS Publication 550

32.3 Mutual-Fund Distributions Reported on Form 1099-DIV

* IRS Publication 550

Qualified dividends taxed at capital gain rates

IRC §1(h)(11)

33.6 Distributions From Qualified Tuition Programs (Section 529 Plans)

Tax-free QTP distributions for qualified education expenses

IRC §529(c)(3)(B)(i) and (ii) (exclusion allowed for qualified higher education expenses)

IRC §529(e)(3)(definition of qualified higher education expenses)

IRC §529(c)(7) and §529(e)(3) (A), as added by the Tax Cuts and Jobs Act (P.L. 115-97, 12/22/2017) (elementary and secondary school tuition treated as qualified higher education expenses up to $10,000 per year for distributions made after 2017)

Definition of qualified expenses expanded (SECURE Act)

IRC §529(c)(8), as added by Section 302(a) of the SECURE Act (Division O of P.L.116-94, 12-20-2019) (certain apprenticeship program expenses)

IRC §529(c)(9), as added by Section 302(b) of the SECURE Act (Division O of P.L.116-94, 12-20-2019) (qualified education loan repayments)

Grantor trust rule if legal obligation to provide college education

Reg. §1.677(b)-1(f)

IRS allows changes in investment options

Notice 2001-58, 2001-39 IRB 299

33.7 Education Tax Credits

IRC §25A(a)

Reg. §§ 1.25A-1 through 1.25A-5

* IRS Publication 970

Form 1098-T required for education credit

IRC §25A(g)(8)

No Lifetime learning credit for amount not shown to be tuition

* Ann Marie Adams, TC Summary Opinion 2013-57

Refundable portion of American Opportunity Tax Credit

IRC §25A(i)

Who claims credit for expenses paid by dependent

Reg. §§ 1.25A-1(f) and 1.25A-5(a) (taxpayer claiming student as dependent gets credit)

Reg. §1.25A-5(b) (expenses paid by third party directly to college)

Reg. §1.25A-1(f)(2) (student eligible for credit if not claimed as dependent)

* IRS Legal Memorandum 200236001

Prepaid tuition allows credit only for year of payment

* Lucas Matthew McCarville, TC Summary Opinion 2016-14

* John Mark Ferm, TC Summary Opinion 2014-115 (American Opportunity credit)

* Jayesh B. Patel, TC Summary Opinion 2006-40 (Lifetime Learning credit)

33.8 American Opportunity Credit

IRC §25A(b) (amount of credit)

IRC §25A(d) (1) (A) (phaseout range; not subject to annual inflation adjustments)

IRC §25A(i) (40% refundable portion)

* IRS Publication 970

TIN needed by filer and student by return due date

IRC §25A (g) (1) (B)

Credit denial could lead to future disallowance

IRC §25A (b) (4) (B)

Veteran's GI benefits bar education credit

Johnny Lara, TC Memo 2016-96

Credit for pre-paid tuition applies only in the payment year

* John Mark Ferm, TC Summary Opinion 2014-115

Credit for expenses paid by dependent student

Reg. §§ 1.25A-1(f) and 1.25A-5(a) (taxpayer claiming student as dependent gets credit)

Reg. §1.25A-5(b) (expenses paid by third party directly to college)

Reg. §1.25A-1(f)(2) (student eligible for credit if not claimed as dependent)

* IRS Legal Memorandum 200236001

33.9 Lifetime Learning Credit

IRC §25A(c)

Reg. §1.25A-4

Phaseout threshold for credit

IRC §25A(d)(1), as amended by the Consolidated Appropriations Act, 2021 (P.L. 116-260, 12/27/2020) (aligned with phaseout for the American opportunity credit)

Prepaid tuition allows credit only for year of payment

* Jayesh B. Patel, TC Summary Opinion 2006-40

33.10 Contributing to a Coverdell Education Savings Account (ESA)

IRC §530

* IRS Publication 970

Contribution limit

IRC §530(b)(1)(A)(iii)

Phaseout of contribution limit

IRC §530(c)

33.11 Distributions From Coverdell ESAs

IRC §530(d)

* IRS Publication 970

Coordination with education credits and QTPs

IRC §530(d)(2)(C)

Exception to additional tax for Service Academy appointees

IRC §530 (d)(4)(B)(iv)

33.12 Tuition and Fees Deduction No Longer Allowed

IRC §222

Deduction repealed for years after 2020

IRC §222, repealed by the Consolidated Appropriations Act, 2021 (P.L. 116-260, 12/27/2020)

* IRS Publication 970

33.13 Student Loan Interest Deduction

IRC §221

IRC §221 (b) (1) (deduction limited to $2,500; not subject to annual inflation adjustments)

* IRS Publication 970

Phaseout of deduction

IRC §221(b)(2)(B) (inflation adjustments to phaseout ranges authorized)

Rev. Proc. 2022-38, 2022-45 IRB 445 (phaseout ranges for 2023 deduction)

Rev. Proc. 2021-45, 2021-48 IRB 764 (phaseout ranges for 2022 deduction)

Rev. Proc. 2020-45, 2020-46 IRB 1016 (phaseout ranges for 2021 deduction)

Rev. Proc. 2019-44, 2017-47 IRB 1093 (phaseout ranges for 2020 deduction)

Rev. Proc. 2018-57, 2018-49 IRB 827 (phaseout ranges for 2019 deduction)

33.14 Types of Deductible Work-Related Costs

Reg. §1.162-5

* IRS Publication 970

Employees barred from deducting work-related education costs for 2018 through 2025 (Tax Cuts and Jobs Act)

IRC §67(g), as added by the Tax Cuts and Jobs Act (P.L. 115-97, 12/22/2017) (suspension of miscellaneous itemized deductions for 2018 through 2025)

2% floor for employee miscellaneous itemized deductions (pre-2018)

IRC §67(a), prior to suspension of miscellaneous itemized deductions for 2018 through 2025 by the Tax Cuts and Jobs Act (P.L. 115-97, 12/22/2017)

Repaying a medical tuition grant may not be deductible

Tripp Dargie, 014 PTC 69 (6th Cir., 2014)

MBA costs can be deductible

Daniel R. Allemeier Jr., TC Memo 2005-207

33.15 WORK-RELATED TESTS FOR EDUCATION COSTS

Reg. §1.162-5

* IRS Publication 970

Employees barred from deducting work-related education costs for 2018 through 2025 (Tax Cuts and Jobs Act)

IRC §67(g), as added by the Tax Cuts and Jobs Act (P.L. 115-97, 12/22/2017) (suspension of miscellaneous itemized deductions for 2018 through 2025)

2% floor for employee miscellaneous itemized deductions (pre-2018)

IRC §67(a), prior to suspension of miscellaneous itemized deductions for 2018 through 2025 by the Tax Cuts and Jobs Act (P.L. 115-97, 12/22/2017)

Minimum job requirements

Reg. §1.162-5(b)(2)

Eduardo Antuna, 36 TCM 1778 (1977)

David Cooper, 37 TCM 529 (1978)

Maintain or improve skills

Reg. §1.162-5(c)(1)

Clark S. Marlor, 251 F.2d 615 (2d Cir. 1958)

Qualification for new business

Reg. §1.162-5(b)(3)

Teacher did not abandon profession

John C. Ford, 56 TC 1300 (1971), aff'd per curiam, 487 F.2d 1025 (9th Cir. 1973)

Prerequisites not deductible

Neal F. Krauss, 39 TCM 725 (1979)

MBA expenses deductible

* Tao Long, TC Summary Opinion 2016-88

Daniel R. Allemeier Jr., TC Memo 2005-207

Robert C. Beatty, 40 TCM 438 (1980)

Frank S. Blair, 41 TCM 289 (1980)

MBA expenses not deductible

Adam Edward Hart, TCM 289 (2013)

Ross L. Link, 90 TC 460 (1988)

Ronald T. Smith, 41 TCM 1186 (1981)

Eduardo Antuna, 36 TCM 1778 (1977)

Nurse can deduct cost of MBA

* Lori A. Singleton-Clarke, TC Summary Opinion 2009-182

Undergraduate courses not deductible by accountant

Diane Zimmer, 64 TCM 1388 (1992)

Undergraduate courses not deductible by financial planner

Judith Meredith, 65 TCM 2876 (1993)

Associate degree classes not deductible by golf instructor

* Edward M. Fields, TC Summary Opinion, 2001-35

Undergraduate courses not deductible by office manager

Theresa M. Malek, 50 TCM 792 (1985)

Undergraduate college costs not deductible by policeman

James A. Carroll, 51 TC 213 (1968), aff'd, 418 F.2d 91 (7th Cir. 1969)

Industrial psychologist

Cosimo A. Carlucci, 37 TC 695 (1962) (Acq.)

Engineering aide to maintain skills

Ralph A. Fattore, 22 TCM 1093 (1963)

Attorney attending graduate courses

Albert C. Ruehmann, 30 TCM 675 (1971)

Charles B. Johnson, 332 F. Supp. 906 (D. La. 1971)

Larry R. Adamson, 32 TCM 484 (1973)

Unemployed teacher

Edward J. P. Zimmerman, 71 TC 367 (1978), aff'd, 79-2 USTC ¶9617 (2nd Cir. 1979)

Engineer not established in his profession

Barry Reisine, 29 TCM 1429 (1970)

Thomas W. Gallery, 57 TC 257 (1971)

Orthodontic course

Rev. Rul. 74-78, 1974-1 CB 44

CPA review course not deductible

Rev. Rul. 69-282, 1969-1 CB 55

William D. Glenn, 62 TC 270 (1974)

Private tutoring in management

Walter G. Lage, 52 TC 119 (1969) (Acq.)

Bar admission fee not deductible

Arthur E. Ryman, Jr., 51 TC 799 (1969)

William J. Brennan, 22 TCM 1222 (1963)

Broker license cost not deductible

Robert Kersey, 50 F.3d 15 (9th Cir. 1995)

Music therapy courses not deductible

Herbert Hewett, 71 TCM 2350 (1996)

Flying lessons of freelance news photographer

Alan Aaronson, 29 TCM 786 (1970)

Flight school for NASA engineer not deductible

Ronald Z. Thompson, TC Memo 2007-174

Law school

Reg. §1.162-5(b)(2) and (3)

Colleen J. O'Connor and Mark Tracy, TC Memo 2015-155

Jeffrey S. Augen, 33 TCM 1022 (1974)

Robert J. Connelly, 72-1 USTC ¶9188 (1st Cir. 1972)

Charles M. Watkins, 59 TCM 467 (1990)

Tax law courses taken by lawyer

Joseph T. Booth, III, 35 TC 1144 (1961)

Business law teacher

Juanita Ardavany, 38 TCM 569 (1979)

Amortization of fees to state bar admission authorities

Joel Sharon, 591 F. 2d 1273 (9th Cir. 1978), aff'g 66 TC 515 (1976)

Costs to practice law in second state

Joseph J. Vetrick, 37 TCM 392 (1978), aff'd, 628 F.2d 885 (5th Cir. 1980)

Lawyer must practice profession

Albert C. Ruehmann, III, 30 TCM 675 (1971)

Richard M. Randick, 35 TCM 195 (1976)

Paul R. Wassenaar, 72 TC 1195 (1979)

David M. Kohen, 44 TCM 1518 (1982)

* Letter Ruling 9112003

Psychiatry courses

John S. Watson, 31 TC 1014 (1959) (Nonacq.)

Psychoanalytic courses

Ramon M. Greenberg, 367 F.2d 663 (1st Cir. 1966)

Psychiatrist's therapy by phone and cassette

Kenneth Porter, 51 TCM 481 (1986)

Cost of physician's assistant course

Matthew J. Reisinger, 71 TC 568 (1979)

Social worker denied deduction for education necessary for faculty position

Kenneth C. Davis, 65 TC 1014 (1976)

Teaching assistant denied deduction of graduate study costs

Arthur M. Jungreis, 55 TC 581 (1970)

Charitable deduction for sponsorship gift

Ruth Dowell, 553 F.2d 1233 (10th Cir. 1977)

No charitable deduction for donation that represents cost of apportionment

Ernest Klappenbach, 52 TCM 437 (1986)

Medical deduction for portion of entry fee to assisted living facility

John O. Finzer, Jr., 2007-2 USTC ¶50,591 (D. IL 2007)

Investment in community equivalent to home purchase

* Letter Ruling 8837022

Highland Farms, Inc., 106 TC 12 (1996)

Imputed interest exception for qualified continuing care facilities

IRC §7872(h)

34.10 MEDICARE PART B AND PART D PREMIUMS FOR 2024

Section 53114 of the Bipartisan Budget Act of 2018 (P.L. 115-123, 2/9/18) (adding fifth surcharge tier for Part B premiums starting in 2019)

Section 811 of the Medicare Prescription Drug, Improvement and Modernization Act of 2003 (authorizing Part B premium surcharges)

2024 premiums

Centers for Medicare & Medicaid Services Fact Sheet, 10/12/2023, https://www.cms.gov/newsroom/fact-sheets/2024-medicare-parts-b-premiums-and-deductibles

34.11 SPECIAL TAX RULES FOR INDIVIDUALS WITH A DISABILITY

* IRS Publication 907

34.12 ABLE ACCOUNTS

IRC §529A, added by 2014 Stephen Beck Jr. Achieving a Better Life Experience Act of 2014 (P.L. 113-295, 12/19/14)

Proposed regulations for ABLE accounts

REG-128246-18, 2019-44 IRB 1037

Increased contribution limit for beneficiaries with compensation (Tax Cuts and Jobs Act)

IRC §529A (b) (2) (B) (ii), as added by the Tax Cuts and Jobs Act (P.L. 115-97, 12/22/2017) for 2018 through 2025

IRC §529A (b) (7), as added by the Tax Cuts and Jobs Act (P.L. 115-97, 12/22/2017) (designated beneficiaries eligible for increased contribution limit for 2018 through 2025)

Notice 2018-62, 2018-34 IRB 316 (IRS guidance on contribution limits to ABLE accounts)

IRS News Release IR-2018-139 (6-15-18)

Rollover from qualified tuition plan to ABLE account (Tax Cuts and Jobs Act)

IRC §529 (c) (3) (C) (i) (III), as added by the Tax Cuts and Jobs Act (P.L. 115-97, 12/22/2017) for 2018 through 2025

Notice 2018-58, 2018-33 IRB 305 (IRS guidance on rollover from a QTP to an ABLE account)

35 MEMBERS OF THE ARMED FORCES

35.1 TAXABLE ARMED FORCES PAY AND BENEFITS

* IRS Publication 3

Regular pay, leave pay, enlistment bonuses taxable

Rev. Rul. 55-249, 1955-1 CB 21

Withholding required for differential wages paid after 2008

IRC §3401(h), added by Heroes Earnings Assistance Tax Relief Act of 2008

Rev. Rul. 2009-11, 2009-18 IRB 896

35.2 TAX BREAKS FOR ARMED FORCES MEMBERS

* IRS Publication 3

Tax-free combat pay

IRC §112

Exclusion for qualified military benefits

IRC §134

Exclusion for death gratuity payment

Section 1478(a) of Title 10, U.S. Code IRC §134(b)(3)(C)

Withholding required for differential wages paid after 2008

IRC §3401(h), added by Heroes Earnings Assistance Tax Relief Act of 2008

Rev. Rul. 2009-11, 2009-18 IRB 896

Subsistence allowance

Rev. Rul. 55-572, 1955-2 CB 45, distinguished by Rev. Rul. 63-64, 1963-1 CB 30

Subsistence payments

Veterans Administration Release, February 14, 1957

Allotments for dependents

Special Ruling, Jan. 10, 1946

Rev. Rul. 70-87, 1970-1 CB 29

Serviceman's Readjustment Act

Veterans Administration Release, February 14, 1957

Ephraim Banks, 17 TC 1386 (1952)

Family separation allowance

Clifford Jones, 60 Ct. Cl. 552

Rev. Rul. 70-281, 1970-1 CB 16

Moving and storage

IRC §217(g)

Mustering out pay

IRC §113

Reg. §1.113-1

Naval attaché expense money

Rev. Rul. 77-351, 1977-2 CB 23

Retirement pay reduction to provide survivor annuity

IRC §122

Return to active duty

Special Ruling, January 24, 1945

Travel expenses—permanent duty station

W. W. Bercaw, 165 F.2d 521 (4th Cir. 1948)

Rev. Rul. 55-571, 1955-2 CB 44

Uniforms, uniform allowances

Reg. §1.61-2(b)

Medical and pension benefit from Veteran's Administration

Rev. Rul. 72-605, 1972-2 CB 35

Injuries or sickness

Career Compensation Act of 1949, Sec. 402

Pay forfeited on court martial order

Armed Forces Fed. Income Tax, '77 ed.

Former prisoners of war

Rev. Rul. 55-132, 1955-1 CB 213

Rev. Rul. 56-462, 1956-2 CB 20

Bonuses

Rev. Rul. 56-610, 1956-2 CB 25

State bonus

Rev. Rul. 68-158, 1968-1 CB 47

Gratuity

Rev. Rul. 55-330, 1955-1 CB 236

Dividends on GI insurance

Special Ruling, February 3, 1947

Interest on VA life insurance dividends

Rev. Rul. 91-14, 1991-1 CB 18 revoking

Rev. Rul. 57-441, 1957-2 CB 45

Disability retirement pay

IRC §104(a)(4)

IRC §104(b)

Career Compensation Act of 1949, Sec. 402

Zebulon L. Strickland, Jr., 540 F.2d 1196 (4th Cir. 1976)

Rev. Rul. 78-161, 1978-1 CB 31

Veteran not taxed on payments from compensated work program

Roosevelt Wallace, 128 TC 132 (2007); Acq.

35.3 DEDUCTIONS FOR ARMED FORCES PERSONNEL

* IRS Publication 3

Armed Forces members barred from deducting unreimbursed costs after 2017 (Tax Cuts and Jobs Act)

IRC §67(g), as added by the Tax Cuts and Jobs Act (P.L. 115-97, 12/22/2017) (suspension of miscellaneous itemized deductions for 2018 through 2025)

Board and lodging costs

Rev. Rul. 55-571, 1955-2 CB 44, modified by Rev. Rul. 67-438, 1967-2 CB 82

Cost of insignia

Charles A. Harris, 12 TCM 42 (1953)

Contributions to "Company" fund

Rev. Rul. 73-296, 1973-2 CB 67

Rev. Rul. 55-201, 1955-1 CB 269

B. O. Mahaffey, 1 TC 176 (1942), rev'd, 140 F.2d 879 (8th Cir. 1944)

Morris Investment Corp., 156 F.2d 748 (3d Cir. 1946), cert. denied, 329 U.S. 788

Jacob Kaplan, 21 TC 134 (1953) (Acq.)

William F. Krahl, 9 TC 862 (1947)

Court martial expenses

Lindsay C. Howard, 202 F.2d 28 (9th Cir. 1953), aff'g 16 TC 157 (1951) (Acq.)

Professional societies

Rev. Rul. 55-250, 1955-1 CB 270

Increased retirement pay

IRC §212

Professional journals

Charles A. Harris, 12 TCM 42 (1953)

No away from home expenses for those at permanent duty station

Howe Stidger, 386 U.S. 287 (1967)

Travel status and duty expenses

Rev. Rul. 67-438, 1967-2 CB 82, modifying Rev. Rul. 55-571, 1955-2 CB 44

Charles A. Harris, 12 TCM 42 (1953)

Temporary lodging allowance

Rev. Rul. 76-2, 1976-1 CB 82

Fatigues

Rev. Rul. 67-1 15, 1967-1 CB 30

35.4 TAX-FREE PAY FOR SERVICE IN COMBAT ZONE

* IRS Publication 3

Combat pay exclusion

IRC §112

Reg. §1.112-1

Sinai Peninsula of Egypt is a qualified hazardous area treated the same as a combat zone (Tax Cuts and Jobs Act)

Section 11026 of the Tax Cuts and Jobs Act (P.L. 115-97, 12/22/2017), retroactively effective for taxable years beginning after June 9, 2015 and through 2025)

IRS News Release IR-2018-95 (4-13-18)

Civilian employees not eligible for combat zone exclusion

* Chief Counsel Memorandum AM 2009-003

Officers

IRC §112(b)

Severance pay not included

Ralph P. Waterman, 179 F.3d 123 (4th Cir. 1999), aff'g 110 T.C. 103 (1998)

Operation Iraqi Freedom

Notice 2003-21, 2003-17 IRB 817 (question and answer guidance on combat zone relief)

Executive Order No. 12744, 56 Fed. Reg. 2663 (1/23/91), designating the "Arabian Peninsula Areas" as a combat zone, continues to be in effect

Afghanistan

Executive Order No. 132-39, 66 Fed. Reg. 241 (12/14/01) (area designated as combat zone)

Notice 2002-17, 2002-9 IRB 567 (question and answer guidance on combat zone relief)

IRA contributions based on tax-free combat pay

IRC §219(f)(7), as added by Public Law 109-227, 5/29/06

News Release IR-2006-129 (HERO Act)

"Missing" status

IRC §112(d)

Joint return election by spouse of person MIA

IRC §6013(f)(1)

Waiver of tax

Rev. Rul. 68-393, 1968-2 CB 292

Rev. Rul. 72-169, 1972-1 CB 43

Hospitalized serviceman

IRC §112(a)(2)

35.5 TAX DEADLINES EXTENDED FOR COMBAT ZONE OR CONTINGENCY OPERATION SERVICE

* IRS Publication 3

IRC §7508(a)

Sinai Peninsula of Egypt is a qualified hazardous area treated the same as a combat zone (Tax Cuts and Jobs Act)

Section 11026 of the Tax Cuts and Jobs Act (P.L. 115-97, 12/22/2017), retroactively effective for taxable years beginning after June 9, 2015 and through 2025)

IRS News Release IR-2018-95 (4-13-18)

Filing extensions extended to contingency operations

IRC §7508(a)

Operation Iraqi Freedom

Notice 2003-21, 2003-17 IRB 817 (question and answer guidance on combat zone relief)

Executive Order No. 12744, 56 Fed. Reg. 2663 (1/23/91), designating the "Arabian Peninsula Areas" as a combat zone, continues to be in effect

Five-year test period for home sale exclusion suspended

IRC §121(d)(9)

Desert Shield personnel qualify for extension

IRC §7508(f)

Extensions available to spouse

IRC §7508(c)

35.6 TAX FORGIVENESS FOR COMBAT ZONE OR TERRORIST OR MILITARY ACTION DEATHS

Combat zone death

IRC §692

Sinai Peninsula of Egypt is a qualified hazardous area treated the same as a combat zone (Tax Cuts and Jobs Act)

Section 11026 of the Tax Cuts and Jobs Act (P.L. 115-97, 12/22/2017), retroactively effective for taxable years beginning after June 9, 2015 and through 2025)

IRS News Release IR-2018-95 (4-13-18)

Afghanistan

Executive Order No. 132-39, 66 Fed. Reg. 241 (12/14/01) (area designated as combat zone)

Notice 2002-17, 2002-9 IRB 567 (question and answer guidance on combat zone relief)

Terroristic or military actions

IRC §692(c)

MIAs

IRA §692(b)

Filing extension for refund claims if combat zone death

IRC §7508(b)

35.7 EXTENSION TO PAY YOUR TAX WHEN ENTERING THE SERVICE

* IRS Publication 3

Rev. Proc. 57-25, 1957-2 CB 1092

Soldiers' and Sailors' Civil Relief Act of 1940, Sec. 513

T.D. 5279, 1943 CB 952, amended by T.D.'s 5293, 5429, 5444, 5959

35.8 TAX INFORMATION FOR RESERVISTS

* IRS Publication 3

Reservists generally barred from deducting unreimbursed travel costs to reservist meetings after 2017 (Tax Cuts and Jobs Act)

IRC §67(g), as added by the Tax Cuts and Jobs Act (P.L. 115-97, 12/22/2017) (suspension of miscellaneous itemized deductions for 2018 through 2025)

Above-the-line deduction for overnight travel costs of National Guard and Reserve members if more than 100 miles from tax home

IRC §62 (a) (2) (E)

Penalty exception for qualified reservists

IRC §72(t)(2)(G)

Operation Iraqi Freedom

Notice 2003-21, 2003-17 IRB 817 (question and answer guidance on combat zone relief)

Executive Order No. 12744, 56 Fed. Reg. 2663 (1/23/91), designating the "Arabian Peninsula Areas" as a combat zone, continues to be in effect

Penalty exception for qualified reservists

IRC §72(t)(2)(G)

36 HOW TO TREAT FOREIGN EARNED INCOME

36.1 CLAIMING THE FOREIGN EARNED INCOME EXCLUSION

* IRS Publication 54

Foreign earned income exclusion

IRC §911

Exclusion amount adjusted for inflation

IRC §911(b)(2)(D)(ii) (inflation adjustments authorized)

Rev. Proc. 2020-45, 2020-46 IRB 1016 (exclusion for 2021

Must file return even if exclusion is available

Reg. §1.911-6

IRC §6012

Reg. §1.6012-1(a)(3)

William Faltesek, 92 TC 78 (1989)

Panama Canal Commission employees

1986 Tax Act Section 1232

36.2 WHAT IS FOREIGN EARNED INCOME?

IRC §911(b)

* IRS Publication 54

Reimbursed moving expenses

Rev. Rul. 75-84, 1975-1 CB 236, amplified by Rev. Rul. 76-162, 1976-1 CB 197

Clifford Dammers, 76 TC 835 (1981)

36.3 QUALIFYING FOR THE FOREIGN EARNED INCOME EXCLUSION

Foreign residence and foreign physical presence test

IRC §911(d)(1)

* IRS Publication 54

Foreign tax home

IRC §911(d)(1)

IRC §911(d)(3)

Contractors supporting U.S. Armed Forces in combat zone treated as having foreign tax home

IRC §911(d) (3), as amended by the Bipartisan Budget Act of 2018 (P.L. 115-123, 2/9/18) for tax years beginning after 2017)

IRS News Release IR-2018-173 (8-24-18)

International airspace not a foreign country

William D. Rogers, TC Memo 2009-111

Exclusion allowed in year services performed

IRC §911(b)(2)(B)

Prorating exclusion on daily basis

IRC §911(b)(2)

Exclusion must be elected

IRC §911(a)

No foreign tax credit on excluded income

IRC §911(d)(6)

No exclusion for countries under U.S. travel ban

IRC §911(d)(8)

Workers paid with nonappropriated funds

David Matthews, 907 F.2d 1173 (DC Cir. 1990), aff'g 92 TC 351 (1989)

Professor on sabbatical does not have foreign tax home

Lynn W. Gelhar, 63 TCM 2466

36.4 HOW TO TREAT HOUSING COSTS

* IRS Publication 54

Exclusion for employer-financed housing

IRC §911(a)

IRC §911(c)

Basic limitation on housing expenses

IRC §911(c)(1)-(2)

Larger foreign housing cost limits for major cities

Notice 2023-26, 2023-13 IRB 577 (amounts for 2023; 2023 limits may be applied to 2022 returns if advantageous)

Notice 2022-10, 2022-10 IRB 815 (amounts for 2022; 2022 limits may be applied to 2021 returns if advantageous)

Notice 2021-18, 2021-11 IRB 911 (amounts for 2021; 2021 limits may be applied to 2020 returns if advantageous)

Notice 2020-13, 2020-11 IRB 502 (amounts for 2020; 2020 limits may be applied to 2019 return if advantageous)

Deduction for housing costs not paid for by employer

IRC §911(c)(3)

36.5 MEETING THE FOREIGN RESIDENCE OR PHYSICAL PRESENCE TEST

No Foreign earned income exclusion for worker in Afghanistan and Iraq

James F. Daly, TC Memo 2013-147

Bona fide residence test

IRC §911(d)(1)(A)

IRC §911(d)(5)

Waiver of time tests due to war or civil unrest

IRC §911(d)(4)

International airspace not a foreign country

William D. Rogers, TC Memo 2009-111

Physical presence test—330-day/12-month requirement

IRC §911(d)(1)(B)

Reinstatement of exclusion after tax holiday

* Letter Ruling 200025019

36.6 CLAIMING DEDUCTIONS

No deduction for expenses attributable to excluded income

IRC §911(d)(6)

Employee expenses attributable to non-excludable earnings not deductible after 2017 (Tax Cuts and Jobs Act)

IRC §67(g), as added by the Tax Cuts and Jobs Act (P.L. 115-97, 12/22/2017) (suspension of miscellaneous itemized deductions for 2018 through 2025)

36.7 EXCLUSION NOT ESTABLISHED WHEN YOUR RETURN IS DUE

IRS Form 2350

36.8 TAX-FREE MEALS AND LODGING FOR WORKERS IN CAMPS

IRC §119(c)

36.9 U.S. VIRGIN ISLANDS, SAMOA, GUAM, AND NORTHERN MARIANAS

* IRS Publication 570

Guam, Samoa, N. Mariana Islands

IRC §931

Virgin Islands

IRC §932

IRC §934

U.S. or agencies

IRC §931(d)

Rev. Rul. 54-612, 1954-2 CB 169

36.10 EARNINGS IN PUERTO RICO

IRC §933

Reg. §1.933-1

Rev. Rul. 56-585, 1956-2 CB 166

* IRS Publication 570

Moving expenses allocable to tax-exempt income from Puerto Rico not deductible

Alberto Roque, 65 TC 920 (1976)

36.11 TAX TREATIES WITH FOREIGN COUNTRIES

IRC §894

Reg. §1.894-1

IRC §7852(d)

* IRS Publication 570

36.12 EXCHANGE RATES AND BLOCKED CURRENCY

* IRS Publication 54

Foreign currency gains and losses

IRC §988

Euro conversion

TD 8776; Reg. Sec. §1.985-8T

36.13 FOREIGN TAX CREDIT OR DEDUCTION FOR FOREIGN TAXES PAID

* IRS Publication 514

Foreign tax credit

IRC §901(a)

Reg. §1.901-1 and 2

Rev. Rul. 2016-8, 2016-11 IRB 426 (Cuba removed from restricted list)

Deduction in lieu of credit

IRC §164(a)

De minimis credit

IRC §904(j)

Overall limitation

IRC §904(a)

Separate credit limitation categories

IRC §904(d)

Recapture of overall foreign loss

IRC §904(f)

Capital gains

IRC §904(b)(2)

Carryback and carryover

IRC §904(c)

37 PLANNING ALIMONY AND MARITAL SETTLEMENTS

37.1 RULES FOR POST-2018 DIVORCE AND SEPARATION AGREEMENTS

* IRS Publication 504

Alimony rules repealed for divorce and separation instruments executed after 2018 (Tax Cuts and Jobs Act)

IRC §62(a)(10), IRC §71, and IRC §215 repealed by the Tax Cuts and Jobs Act (P.L. 115-97, 12/22/2017) (alimony paid no longer deductible and alimony received no longer taxed)

IRC §682, repealed by the Tax Cuts and Jobs Act (P.L. 115-97, 12/22/2017)

Modification after 2018 of divorce and separation instruments executed before 2019 (Tax Cuts and Jobs Act)

Act Section 11051 (c) of the Tax Cuts and Jobs Act (P.L. 115-97, 12/22/2017) (pre-2019 rules continue to apply unless post-2018 modification expressly states that the Tax Cuts and Jobs Act repeal rules shall apply)

Legal fees allocable to receipt of taxable alimony not deductible after 2017 (Tax Cuts and Jobs Act)

IRC §67(g), as added by the Tax Cuts and Jobs Act (P.L. 115-97, 12/22/2017) (suspension of miscellaneous itemized deductions for 2018 through 2025)

37.2 RULES FOR PRE-2019 DIVORCES OR SEPARATION AGREEMENTS

* IRS Publication 504

Alimony paid deductible from gross income

IRC §62(a)(10)(above-the-line deduction)

IRC §215 (deduction allowed if payments qualify as alimony taxable to recipient)

IRC §1.215-1

Treasury Inspector General for Tax Administration (TIGTA) report, TIGTA 2014-40-022

Alimony received included in gross income

IRC §71 (alimony requirements)

Reg. §1.71

Treasury Inspector General for Tax Administration (TIGTA) report, TIGTA 2014-40-022

Pre-2018 deduction allowed to recipient for legal fees attributable to arranging receipt of taxable alimony

Reg. §1.262-1(b)(7)

Barbara B. LeMond, 13 TC 670 (1949) (Acq.)

Ruth K. Wild, 42 TC 706 (1964) (Acq.)

Jimmie T. Jernigen, 34 TCM 615 (1975)

No deduction if paid by another

Reg. §1.215-1(b)

Same household rule

IRC §71(b)(1)(c)

Bertram Coltman, Jr., 980 F.2d 1134 (7th Cir. 1992)

Spouses may designate nonqualifying payments

IRC §71(b)(1)(B)

Temp. Reg. §1.71-1T (Q-8)

Income from alimony trust taxed to payee spouse and not deductible by payor spouse

IRC §682 (payee spouse treated as trust beneficiary rather than alimony recipient)

Payment of ex-spouse's student loan claimed as alimony deduction

*Jeremy Adam Vanderhal, TC Summary Opinion 2018-41

Pretrial order support payments are alimony

Barry Maurice Anderson, TC Memo 2016-47

Health insurance payments for ex-spouse not alimony

*James Alston Tucker, TC Summary Opinion 2013-94

Health insurance premiums paid from cafeteria plan were deductible alimony

Charles H. Leyh, 157 TC No. 7 (2021)

Payments under written separation agreement deductible despite common household

Thomas Benham, TC Memo 2000-165

Husband not taxed on payments from transferred property

IRC §71(d)

Paying off ex-spouse's mortgage not alimony

James F. Moore, TC Memo 2011-200

Alimony payments to nonresident alien

* IRS Publication 504

Wife not taxed on tax-exempt interest from alimony trust

Mary C. Ellis, 416 F.2d 894 (6th Cir. 1969)

Alimony trusts

IRC §682

Voluntary payment

Natalia D. Murray, 174 F.2d 816 (2d Cir. 1949)

Benjamin B. Cox, 176 F.2d 226 (3d Cir. 1949), aff'g 10 TC 955 (1948)

Permanent alimony after remarriage

Allen Hoffman, 54 TC 1607 (1971), aff'd, 455 F.2d 161 (7th Cir. 1972)

Alfredo Mass, 81 TC 112 (1983)

Voluntary payments after court order denies temporary alimony

Sylvia E. Taylor, 55 TC 1134 (1971)

Payments from oil lease are alimony

Ronald Prater, 55 F.3d 527 (10th Cir. 1995)

Payments recommended by state domestic relations master are not deductible

Eugene E. Deyette, 36 TCM 1343 (1977)

Wife taxable on voluntary alimony

Rev. Rul. 81-8, 1981-1 CB 42

Excess payments are voluntary

George H. Moore, 449 F. Supp. 163 (D. Tex. 1978)

Gift tax on voluntary payments

Rev. Rul. 79-118, 1979-1 CB 315

Post-remarriage payments not alimony

Martha K. Brown, 415 F.2d 310 (4th Cir. 1969)

Allen Hoffman, 54 TC 1607 (1970) (Acq.), aff'd per curiam, 455 F.2d 161 (7th Cir. 1972)

Deduction for estate

Homer Laughlin Est., 167 F.2d 828 (9th Cir. 1948)

Daniel G. Reid Est., 15 TC 573 (1950), aff'd, 193 F.2d 625 (2d Cir. 1952)

37.3 DECREE OR AGREEMENT REQUIRED

* IRS Publication 504

Decree or separation agreement required—Post-1984 law

IRC §71(b)(1)(A)

IRC §71(b)(2)

Decree required—Pre-1985 law

IRC §71(a)(1)

Reg. §1.71-1(b)(1)

Alimony deduction based on spousal support affidavit

*Timothy Owen Micek, TC Summary Opinion 2011-45

State decree declared invalid by another state: IRS view disallowing alimony deduction

Rev. Rul. 67-442, 1967-2 CB 65

Harold K. Lee, 550 F.2d 1201 (9th Cir. 1977)

State decree declared invalid by another state

Harold E. Wondsel, 350 F.2d 339 (2d Cir. 1965), cert. denied, 383 U.S. 935

Est. of Herman Borax, 349 F.2d 666 (2d Cir. 1965)

George J. Feinberg, 198 F.2d 260 (3d Cir. 1952)

Local support order after out-of-state divorce

Rev. Rul. 70-61, 1970-1 CB 18

Local support order before Mexican decree

Rev. Rul. 71-390, 1971-2 CB 82

Roman Catholic ecclesiastical board

Harold L. Clark, 40 TC 57 (1965)

Sample clauses for alimony agreements

Rev. Proc. 82-53, 1982-2 CB 842

Amendment of written agreement after divorce or legal separation

Rev. Rul. 60-140, 1960-1 CB 31

Rev. Rul. 60-141, 1960-1 CB 33

Rev. Rul. 58-152, 1958-1 CB 32

Agreement not incident

Rev. Rul. 60-142, 1960-1 CB 34

Annulment

Andrew M. Newburger, 61 TC 457 (1974) (Acq.)

George F. Reisman, 49 TC 570 (1968) (Acq.)

Anne S. Laster, 48 TC 178 (1967) (Acq.)

Written separation agreement

Howard Bogard, 59 TC 97 (1972) (Acq.)

Oral modification not valid

Eugene H. Bishop, 46 TCM 15

Reference to agreement not sufficient

Welford E. Garner, Jr., 32 TCM 353 (1973)

Support decree

Rev. Rul. 59-248, 1959-2 CB 31

Support decree valid after divorce

Joanne S. Knobler, 59 TC 261 (1972)

Support decree not valid after divorce

Benjamin Wolman, 64 TC 883 (1975)

37.4 CASH PAYMENTS REQUIRED

IRC §71(b)(1)

* IRS Publication 504

Payments to third party

Temp. Reg. §1.71-1T (Q-6 to 7)

37.5 PAYMENTS MUST STOP AT DEATH

IRC §71(b)(1)(D)

* IRS Publication 504

McNeill Stokes, 68 TCM 705 (1994)

Richard E. Hoover, 102 F. 3d 846 (6th Cir. 1996)

No deduction for fixed sum that is vested under state law

H. Michael Muniz, TC Memo 2015-125

No deduction for payments that could survive death of payee-spouse

David LaPoint, TC Memo 2012-107

No deduction for attorneys' fees

Thomas D. Berry, 2002-1 USTC ¶50,453 (10th Cir. 2002)

* Leonard Salesky, TC Summary Opinion 2006-162

Deduction allowed for unallocated support

* Michael Robert Peterson, TC Summary Opinion 2003-122 (no post-death obligation under New Jersey law)

No deduction for unallocated support

John H. Lovejoy, 2002-2 USTC ¶50,473 (10th Cir. 2002)

37.6 CHILD SUPPORT PAYMENTS ARE NOT ALIMONY

IRC §71(c)

Reg. §301.6402-5

Temp. Reg. §1.71-1T (Q-15, 16, 17, 18)

* IRS Publication 504

Change in homeschooling doesn't reduce alimony deduction

* Joshua Henry Wish, TC Summary Opinion 2015-25

Payments allocable to unpaid child support not deductible

Gregory H. Haubrich, TC Memo 2008-299

Refund diversion for delinquent child support

IRC §6402(c)

Reg. §301.3402-5(b)

Payments treated as nondeductible child support despite state court allocation to alimony

* Eric S. Knoedler, TC Summary Opinion 2011-18

Payments ending in six years taxed as alimony; not contingency related to child

Sharon F. Schilling, TC Memo 2012-256

Federal Court must provide notice

Elinor Nelson, 731 F.2d 105 (2nd Cir. 1984)

Kenneth Marcello, 574 F. Supp. 586 (D.C., RI. 1984)

Interest on overdue child support is taxable income

* Chief Counsel Memorandum 200444026

37.7 NO MINIMUM PAYMENT PERIOD FOR ALIMONY

IRC §71(f) (repealed by the Tax Cuts and Jobs Act (P.L. 115-97, 12/22/2017)

Notice 87-9, 1987-1 CB 421

* IRS Publication 504

38 OTHER TAXES

38.1 OVERVIEW OF HOUSEHOLD EMPLOYMENT TAXES

IRC §3121(d) (general definition of employee)

IRC §3121(b)(3)(B) (exceptions for relative)

IRC §3121(b)(21) (exception for part-time employee under age 18)

* IRS Publication 926

38.2 SOCIAL SECURITY AND MEDICARE (FICA) TAXES FOR HOUSEHOLD EMPLOYEES

* IRS Publication 926

FICA withholding under Social Security Domestic Employment Reform Act of 1994

IRC §3121(a)(7)(B) (exclusion for wages below annual threshold)

IRC §3121(x) (inflation adjustments to threshold)

IRC §3510 (payment with income tax return)

FICA exemption for parent, child, spouse

IRC §3121(b)(3)

38.3 FILING SCHEDULE H TO REPORT HOUSEHOLD EMPLOYMENT TAXES

* IRS Publication 926

The Social Security Domestic Employment Reform Act of 1994 (P.L. 103-387, 10/22/94)

Annual employment tax filing for small employers

T.D. 9239, 2006-6 IRB 401

38.4 FEDERAL UNEMPLOYMENT TAXES (FUTA) FOR HOUSEHOLD EMPLOYEES

* IRS Publication 926

FUTA on household wages over $1,000

IRC §3306(a)(3)

39 GIFT AND ESTATE TAX PLANNING BASICS

39.1 GIFTS OF APPRECIATED PROPERTY

Trust transfers to family members with Crummey right of withdrawal avoid gift tax

Israel Mikel, TC Memo 2015-64

Gift planning opportunities

IRC §1(h)

Give appreciated property

W. G. Farrier Est., 15 TC 277 (1950) (Acq.)

Charles N. Prothro, 209 F.2d 331 (5th Cir. 1954)

Elsie Sorelle, 22 TC 459 (1954) (Acq.)

Marvin Berry, 11 TCM 301 (1952)

Emily J. Haley, 381 F. Supp. 3431 (M.D. Ga. 1974)

Rev. Rul. 55-531, 1955-2 CB 520, distinguished by Rev. Rul. 63-66, 1963-1 CB 13, as modified by Rev. Rul. 75-11, 1975-1 CB 27

Avoid claim that gift not completed

William R. Tracy, 70 F.2d 93 (6th Cir. 1934)

Rev. Rul. 58-337, 1958-2 CB 13

Richard G. Shafto, 246 F.2d 338 (4th Cir. 1957)

Jeannette W. FitzGibbon, 19 TC 78 (1952)

Get loss deduction by selling first

Reg. §1.165-1(b)

Private annuities—gain reported ratably over life expectancy

Rev. Rul. 69-74, 1969-1 CB 43

Gain immediately taxed on secured private annuity

Bell Est., 60 TC 469 (1973)

212 Corp., 70 TC 788 (1978)

Recovery of basis defers gain in private annuity

Esther LaFargue, 689 F.2d 845 (9th Cir. 1982)

No interest deduction for annuity payments

Rebecca Bell, 76 TC 233 (1981), aff'd per curiam, 668 F.2d 448 (8th Cir. 1982)

39.2 GIFT TAX BASICS

IRC §2001(c) (gift tax rates)

IRC §2 503 (taxable gifts)

IRC §2505 (unified credit)

IRC §2522 (charitable deduction)

Annual gift tax exclusion

IRC §2503(b)

Rev. Proc. 2022-38, 2022-45 IRB 445 ($17,000 per donee exclusion for 2023; $175,000 exclusion for 2023 gifts to spouse who is not a U.S. citizen)

Rev. Proc. 2021-45, 2021-48 IRB 764 ($16,000 per donee exclusion for 2022; $164,000 exclusion for 2022 gifts to spouse who is not a U.S. citizen)

Lifetime exemption amount

IRC §2505(a)(1) (applying the estate tax credit under IRC §2010(c))

Marital deduction

IRC §2523

* Letter Ruling 9606008

Gifting employee stock options

* Letter Ruling 9514017

Exclusion for educational or medical expenses

IRC §2503(e)

Qualified tuition program contributions

IRC §529(c)(2)(B)

Pre-paid tuition

* Letter Ruling 199941013

Valuation of life insurance contracts

Reg. §25.2512-6

Trust transfers to family members with Crummey right of withdrawal avoid gift tax

Israel Mikel, TC Memo 2015-64

Gift tax exclusion for contingent trust beneficiaries

Est. of Maria Cristofani, 97 TC 74 (1991)

IRS Action on Decision 1992-09 (IRS does not concede Cristofani issue)

* Letter Ruling 9141008 (IRS denies exclusion for contingent trust interests)

Loans to relatives taxable

IRC §7872

Esther C. Dickman, 465 U.S. 330 (1984)

Elizabeth Miller, 71 TCM 1674 (1996)

Cannot assign income

Paul R. G. Horst, 311 U.S. 112 (1940)

Guy C. Earl, 281 U.S. 11 (1930)

Edward T. Blair, 300 U.S. 5 (1937)

Donees liable for gift tax

Kirkman O'Neal, II, 102 TC 28 (1994)

Art donations valued by IRS

Rev. Proc. 96-15, 1996-1 CB 627

Assignment of licensing agreement by inventor

Lewis R. Heim, 262 F.2d 887 (2d Cir. 1959)

"Incomplete" gifts made by personal check included

Robert Rosano, 2001-1 USTC ¶60,401 (2d Cir. 2001)

Power of attorney must explicitly authorize gifts

Estate of Silvia S. Swanson, Court of Appeals for the Federal Circuit, 5/25/01

Transfer of lottery prize to family S corporation is taxable gift

Tonda Lynn Dickerson, TC Memo 2012-60

39.3 FILING A GIFT TAX RETURN

IRC §2503

*IRS instructions to Form 709 (United States Gift (and Generation-Skipping Transfer) Tax Return)

Late filing in gift tax return penalized despite health problems

Margaret V. Stine, U.S. Court of Federal Claims,10/23/12

39.4 GIFT TAX CREDIT

IRC §2505(a) (applying the estate tax credit under IRC §2010(c))

Gift tax and estate tax exclusion for 2018 through 2025 (Tax Cuts and Jobs Act)

IRC §2010 (c) (3) (C), as added by the Tax Cuts and Jobs Act (P.L. 115-97, 12/22/2017) for 2018 through 2025 (doubling estate tax basic exclusion amount to $10 million, prior to inflation adjustments)

Inflation-adjusted gift tax and estate tax exclusion amounts

Rev. Proc. 2022-38, 2022-45 IRB 445 (inflation-adjusted exclusion amount of $12.92 million for 2023)

Rev. Proc. 2021-45, 2021-48 IRB 764 (inflation-adjusted exclusion amount of $12.06 million for 2022)

Rev. Proc. 2020-45, 2020-46 IRB 1016 (inflation-adjusted exclusion amount of $11.7 million for 2021)

39.5 CUSTODIAL ACCOUNTS FOR MINORS

Investment income of children subject to kiddie tax

IRC §1(g)

Income taxed to child

Rev. Rul. 55-469, 1955-2 CB 519

Rev. Rul. 56-484, 1956-2 CB 23

Rev. Rul. 59-357, 1959-2 CB 212

Trust accounts ineffective to split interest income

Roy K. Heintz, 41 TCM 429 (1980)

Child remains dependent and exemption allowed

IRC §151(e)

Reg. §1.151-2

Gift tax

IRC §2501

IRC §2503

Reg. §25.2503-3

Reg. §25.2503-4

IRC §2505

IRC §2513

Rev. Rul. 56-86, 1956-1 CB 449

Trust for child under 21

IRC §2503(c)

Invalid custodian account

John Dubisky, 1994 USTC ¶13745 (N. Dist. of Ill.), rehearing denied (7th Cir. 1995)

Estate tax

IRC §2001(c) (estate tax rates)

IRC §2010 (unified credit)

No estate tax where securities purchased with jointly owned funds in which deceased custodian had no interest

Estate of Jack F. Chrysler, 361 F.2d 508 (2d Cir. 1966)

No estate tax on estate of deceased spouse who was custodian and agreed to gift splitting

Rev. Rul. 74-556, 1974-2 CB 300

No estate tax where custodian made gift of custodial securities before death

Antonia B. Vogel Est., 36 TCM 875 (1977)

39.6 TRUSTS IN FAMILY PLANNING

SECURE Act reinstates Kiddie Tax computation based on parent's tax rate

Section 501 of the SECURE Act (Division O of P.L. 116-94, 12-20-2019), which repealed IRC §1 (j) (4), as added by the Tax Cuts and Jobs Act (P.L. 115-97, 12/22/2017)

5% grantor trust rule

IRC §673(a)

Minor lineal descendants

IRC §673(b)

Grantor trusts: spouse's interest

IRC §672(e)

Tax rates for trusts and estates

IRC §1(e)

Rev. Proc. 96-59, 1996-2 CB 392 (1997 rates)

Division of income

T. N. Mauritz, 206 F.2d 135 (5th Cir. 1953)

Estelle Morris Trusts, 51 TC 20 (1968), aff'd per curiam, 427 F.2d 1361 (9th Cir. 1970)

Trust for spouse may be taxed to creator

IRC §677(a)

"Apocalypse" family trust

Rev. Rul. 75-257, 1975-2 CB 251

Rev. Rul. 75-258, 1975-2 CB 503

Rev. Rul. 75-259, 1975-2 CB 361

Rev. Rul. 75-260, 1975-2 CB 376

Family trust for earned income is tax avoidance scheme

Richard L. Wesenberg, 69 TC 1005 (1978) (Nonacq.)

Family trust materials not deductible

Louis P. Contini, 76 TC 447 (1981) (Acq.)

Rev. Rul. 79-324, 1979-2 CB 119

Trust sale of appreciated property within two years

IRC §644

Escape estate tax

IRC §2038

Green Estate, 68 F.3d 151 (6th Cir. 1995) (identical trusts)

Gift tax

IRC §2511

Reg. §1.2511-1

Revocable trust—no tax savings

IRC §676

IRC §2038

Testamentary trust—estate tax

IRC §2037

Accumulation trust

IRC §665 through 667

Foreign trusts with U.S. beneficiaries

IRC §643

IRC §668

IRC §679

Generation-skipping transfers

IRC §§ 2601 through 2622

39.7 WHAT IS THE ESTATE TAX?

Imposition and rate of estate tax

IRC §2001

Unified credit

IRC §2010

Gross estate defined

IRC §2031

39.8 TAKE INVENTORY AND ESTIMATE THE VALUE OF YOUR POTENTIAL ESTATE

Gross estate defined

IRC §2031

Property in which decedent had interest

IRC §2033

Transfers with retained life estate

IRC §2036

Failure to use safe harbor language for power of appointment not fatal

Est. of Norman H. Vissering, 990 F.2d 578 (10th Cir. 1993), rev'g and rem'g 96 TC 749 (1991)

Life insurance

IRC §2042

IRC §2035(d)(2) (gifts within three years of death)

IRS concedes policy is excluded from estate where insured held no incidents of ownership

IRS Action on Decision 1991-012

Estate of Eddie L. Headrick, 918 F.2d 1263 (6th Cir. 1990), aff'g 93 TC 171 (1989)

Estate of Joseph Leder, 893 F.2d 237 (10th Cir. 1989), aff'g 89 TC 235 (1987)

Estate of Frank Martin Perry, 927 F.2d 209 (5th Cir. 1991), aff'g 59 TCM 67 (1990)

Estate of Samuel Ard, Jr., 59 TCM 869 (1990)

Assignment of group-term policy

Rev. Rul. 84-147, 1984-2 CB 201

Son paid premiums

Morris R. Silverman Est., 61 TC 338 (1974) (Acq.), aff'd, 521 F.2d 574 (2d Cir. 1975)

Exclusion for certain retirement benefits

Rev. Rul. 92-22, 1992-1 CB 313

Temp. Reg. §20.2039-1T

"Incomplete gifts" made by personal check

Robert Rosano, 2001-1 USTC ¶60,401 (2d Cir. 2001)

Power of attorney must explicitly authorize gifts

Estate of Sylvia S. Swanson, Court of Appeals for the Federal Circuit, 05/25/01

Special farming or business use valuation

IRC §2032A

Estate freeze restrictions

IRC §2036(c)

Notice 89-99, 1989-2 CB 422

IRS evaluation of art donations

Rev. Proc. 96-15, 1996-3 IRB 41

Value of pending lawsuit

Estate of Davis, 66 TCM 542 (1993)

Value of lottery winnings

* Letter Ruling 9616004

Estate of Paul C. Gribauskas, 342 F. 3d 85 (2d Cir. 2003)

Estate of Gladys J. Cook, 2003-2 USTC ¶60,471 (5th Cir. 2003)

39.9 ESTATE TAX FOR 2023

Imposition and rate of estate tax

IRC §2001

Unified credit

IRC §2010(c)(1) and (2) (credit equals the tax imposed on the basic exclusion amount plus the deceased spousal unused exclusion subject to portability election if applicable)

Estate tax basic exclusion amount for 2018 through 2025 (Tax Cuts and Jobs Act)

IRC §2010 (c) (3) (C), as added by the Tax Cuts and Jobs Act (P.L. 115-97, 12/22/2017) for 2018 through 2025 (doubling estate tax basic exclusion amount to $10 million, prior to inflation adjustments)

Rev. Proc. 2020-45, 2020-46 IRB 1016 (inflation adjustment to basic exclusion amount for 2021 to $11.7 million)

Rev. Proc. 2019-44, 2019-47 IRB 1093 (inflation adjustment to basic exclusion amount for 2020 to $11.58 million)

Gross estate defined

IRC §2031

Portability election allows surviving spouse to claim deceased spouse's unused exclusion (DSUE)

Rev. Proc. 2022-32, 2022-30 IRB 101 (extension to file estate tax return to elect portability of DSUE where return not otherwise required)

IRC §2010(c)(4)-(5)

Rev. Proc. 2017-34, 2017-26 IRB 1282 (extension to file estate tax return to elect portability of DSUE where return not otherwise required)

Estate gets theft loss deduction for LLC account invested with Madoff

Est. of Heller, 147 TC No. 11 (2016)

Late filing fee

Peter Knappe, Executor, CA-9, No. 10-56904; cert. denied, 10/15/13

Special option for estate of person who died in 2010

Act Section 301(c) of the Tax Relief Act of 2010 (P.L. 111-32, 12/17/10)

Notice 2011-76, 2011-40 IRB (475)

39.10 PLANNING FOR A POTENTIAL ESTATE TAX

Annual gift tax exclusion
IRC §2503(b)

Marital deduction
IRC §2056

Accumulation clause defeats QTIP marital deduction
Estate of Ellingson, 96 TC 34 (1991)

Son's disclaimer declared valid
Quinto DePaoli, Jr., 62 F.3d 1259 (10th Cir. 1995)

Compensation for son's care not deductible by mother's estate
Est. of Emilia W. Olivo et al., TC Memo 2011-163

Marital deduction disallowed for property surrendered in family settlement
Harry D. Schroeder, 924 F.2d 1547

(10th Cir. 1991)

Disclaimer disallowed
Estate of Monroe, 104 TC 16 (1994)

Conditional bequest loses marital deduction
Edwin L. Bond, 104 TC 31 (1995)

40 INCOME OR LOSS FROM YOUR BUSINESS OR PROFESSION

40.1 FORMS OF DOING BUSINESS

Check-the-box election
Reg. §§301.7701-1 through 301.7701-3

Changing a partnership to an LLC
Rev. Rul. 95-37, 1995-1 CB 150

Rev. Rul. 95-55, 1995-2 CB 313

Electing LLC status
News Release IR 95-29 (3/29/95)

Employment taxes
* Legal Memorandum ILM 199922053

40.2 REPORTING SELF-EMPLOYED INCOME

* IRS Publication 334

*https://www.irs.gov/businesses/small-businesses-self-employed/sharing-economy-tax-center

Election for husband and wife sole owners
IRC 761(f)

Health insurance deduction for self-employed
IRC §162(l)

Passive losses
IRC §469

Professor's expenses not deductible
* Vladimir Shpilrain, TC Summary Opinion 2010-133

Adjunct is an employee
William Edward Schramm, TC Memo 2011-212

40.3 ACCOUNTING METHODS FOR REPORTING BUSINESS INCOME

* IRS Publication 538

Permissible methods
IRC §446(c)

IRC §446(d) (more than one business)

Reg. §1.446-1

Change to cash method under the gross receipts test
Rev. Proc. 2022-14, 2022-7 IRB 502

Limits on use of cash method
IRC §448

Cash method safe harbor for small businesses (Tax Cuts and Jobs Act)
IRC §448 (b) (3) and (c) (1), as amended by the Tax Cuts and Jobs Act (P.L. 115-97, 12/22/2017) for tax years beginning after 2017; $25 million average annual gross receipts test)

IRC §448 (c) (4) (inflation adjustment to $25 million average annual gross receipts amount for years after 2018), as added by the Tax Cuts and Jobs Act (P.L. 115-97, 12/22/2017)

Rev. Proc. 2020-45, 2020-46 IRB 1016 (inflation adjustment for 2021 remains at $26 million)

Election for accrual-method taxpayer to defer inclusion of advance payments (Tax Cuts and Jobs Act)
IRC §451(c), as added by the Tax Cuts and Jobs Act (P.L. 115-97, 12/22/2017)

Advance payments—12-month rule
Reg. §1.263(a)-4(f)

Change from cash to accrual method
IRC §446(e) and (f)

Rev. Proc. 67-10, 1967-1 CB 585, amplified by Rev. Proc. 72-52, 1972-2 CB 833

Constructive receipt
Reg. §1.451-2

Deductions—generally
IRC §461

Reg. §1.461-1(a)

3½ month test for services or goods
Reg. §1.461-4(d)(6)

Taxes
Reg. §1.461-4(g)(6)

8½ month test
Reg. §1.461-5(b)(ii)

Payment through "pay by phone" account
Rev. Rul. 80-335, 1980-2 CB 170

Cash-basis tax shelters
IRC §461(i)

All events test—economic performance test
IRC §461(h)

Reg. §1.461-4

Economic performance—recurring item exception
IRC §461(h)(3)

Prop. Reg. §1.461-5

Reporting accrual income from disputed shipments
Rev. Rul. 2003-10, 2003-3 IRB 288

Payment to related cash-basis taxpayer of salary and interest
IRC §267(a)(2)

Long-term contracts
IRC §460

Advance interest payments ("paid or accrued")
IRC §163

Advance tax payments ("paid or accrued")
IRC §164

Accrual-effect of contingency
Safety Car Heating Co., 297 U.S. 88 (1936)

Continental Tie & Lumber Co., 286 U.S. 290 (1932)

American Code Co., 280 U.S. 445 (1930)

Deferred payments for use of property or services
IRC §467

Income not deferred by agent
Rev. Rul. 70-294, 1970-1 CB 13

Income deferred on wheat sale
Rev. Rul. 58-162, 1958-1 CB 234, distinguished by Rev. Rul. 70-294, 1970-1 CB 13

Non-accrual experience (NAE) method of deferring accrued income from services

IRC §448(d)(5)

Reg. §1.448-2T(b)

40.4 TAX REPORTING YEAR FOR SELF-EMPLOYED

Taxable year

IRC §441(b)

Reg. §1.441-1(b)

* IRS Publication 538

Calendar year

IRC §441(d)

Fiscal year

IRC §441(e)

Personal service corporation year

IRC §441(i)

Partnership year

IRC §706(b)

S corporation year

IRC §1378(b)

52–53 weeks

IRC §441(f)

Reg. §1.441-2

Period of less than 12 months

IRC §443

Reg. §1.443-1

Sole proprietor's tax year

Rev. Rul. 58-389, 1957-2 CB 298, modified by Rev. Rul. 77-293, 1977-2 CB 91

Change of accounting period

IRC §442

Reg. §1.442-1(b)

40.5 REPORTING CERTAIN PAYMENTS AND RECEIPTS TO THE IRS

IRC §6050 I

Reg. §1.6050 I-1

Reg. §1.6050 I-2

Penalty for failure to file correct information return

IRC §6721

Rev. Proc. 2022-38, 2022-45 IRB 445 (inflation adjusted penalty amounts for 2023 information returns)

Rev. Proc. 2021-45, 2021-48 IRB 764 (inflation adjusted penalty amounts for 2022 information returns)

Rev. Proc. 2020-45, 2020-46 IRB 1016 (inflation adjusted penalty amounts for 2021 information returns)

Rev. Proc. 2019-44, 2019-47 IRB 1093 (inflation adjusted penalty amounts for 2020 information returns)

Attorneys must identify clients paying over $10,000

News Release IR-93-113 (intentional disregard penalties may be imposed)

Goldberger and Dubin, 935 F.2d 501 (2d Cir. 1991)

Richard H. Sindel, 53 F.3d 874 (8th Cir. 1995) (disclosure of client identity not required if it would reveal confidential communications)

Attorney not required to identify client paying over $10,000 where IRS does not follow summons procedure

Nancy Gertner, 65 F.3d 963 (1st Cir.,1995)

Failure to report business car over $10,000

Announcement 90-142, 1990-53 IRB 63

Cash equivalents under $10,000

Reg. §1.6050I-1(c)(1)(ii)

$3,000 cash log requirement dropped

Treasury Regulations Bank Secretary Act §103.29

News Release IR 95-37

Cash bail over $10,000

Reg. §1.6050 I-2

40.6 FILING SCHEDULE C

* IRS Publication 535

Deducting length of service or safety achievement awards to employees (Tax Cuts and Jobs Act)

IRC §274(j)

IRC §274(j)(3)(A) (ii), as added by the Tax Cuts and Jobs Act (P.L. 115-97, 12/22/2017) for amounts paid or incurred after 2017 (definition of tangible personal property)

Nonresident taxes on partnership income must be itemized

Matthew L. Cutler, TC Memo 2015-73

When employing your children doesn't result in a deduction

* Patricia Diane Ross, TC Summary Opinion 2014-68

IRS checking compliance with business receipts shown on Form 1099-K

http://www.irs.gov/Businesses/Small-Businesses-&-Self-Employed/New-Notices-Related-to-Form-1099-K

Qualified joint venture election for spouses who are sole owners

IRC 761(f)

Statutory employees

IRC §3121(d)(3)

Reg. §31.3121(d)-1(d)(3)(IV)

Business expenses—adjusted gross income

IRC §62

Business expenses—in general

IRC §162

Reg. §1.162-1

Deductible repair or capital improvement to tangible property

T.D. 9636 (9/13/13)

No business deduction for personal expenses

William J. Dunn, TC Memo 2010-198

Restitution for fraudulent billings is deductible business expense

Peter D. Cavaretta, TC Memo 2010-4

Unreasonable business expense

Palo Alto Town & Country Village, Inc., 32 TCM 1048 (1973), aff'd in part, rev'd in part and rem'd, 565 F.2d 1388 (9th Cir. 1978)

No depreciation for B&B's mixed-use areas

Charles E. Anderson, TC Memo 2006-33

Inventory losses

Reg. §1.165-7(a)(4)

Reg. §1.471-2(c)

National Home Products, 71 TC 501 (1979)

Bad debts

IRC §166

Michael J. Burke, TC Memo 2018-18

Family day-care providers may use standard meal allowance

Rev. Proc. 2003-22, 2003-10 IRB 577

Workers' compensation

Harvey R. Otten, 68 TCM 1342 (1994)

Insurance premiums

Reg. §1.162-1

Disability insurance

Marvin J. Blaess, 28 TC 710 (1957)

Rev. Rul. 58-480, 1958-2 CB 62

Termination payments

Robert E. Milligan, 38 F.3d 1094 (9th Cir. 1994)

Advance payments—IRS proposes 12-month rule for created intangibles

Prop. Reg. §1.263(a)-4(f)

Prepaid premiums

Waldheim Realty & Investment, 245 F.2d 823 (8th Cir. 1957)

Boylston Market Ass'n, 131 F.2d 966 (1st Cir. 1942)

Premiums for disability insurance

Rev. Rul. 55-331, 1955-1 CB 271, modified by Rev. Rul. 68-212, 1968-1 CB 91

Health insurance for self-employed

IRC §162(1) (100% above-the-line deduction)

* Chief Counsel Advice 200623001

Premium for malpractice insurance

Rev. Rul. 60-365, 1960-2 CB 49

Non-practicing malpractice insurance

Merlin A. Steger, 113 TC 227 (1999)

Malpractice premiums to physician-owned carrier

Rev. Rul. 80-120, 1980-1 CB 41

Physicians may not deduct cost of setting up insurance carrier

Carl Herman, et al., 84 TC 120 (1985)

No imputed expense deduction for developing website

* Richard Mondello, TC Summary Opinion 2011-97

Policies for business overhead expenses

Rev. Rul. 55-264, 1955-1 CB 11

Interest

IRC §163

Reg. §1.163-1

Interest deduction limited to $50,000 on employee life insurance

IRC §264(a)(4)

Interest on deferred pay accounts

Albertson's, Inc., 12 F.3d 1539 (9th Cir. 1994)

No deduction for interest owed on business tax deficiency

Edward A. Robinson III, 119 TC 44 (2002) (Tax Court sides with IRS and appeals courts in disallowing deduction)

David Miller, 65 F.3d 687 (8th Cir. 1995), aff'g 841 F. Supp. 305 (N.D. 1993) (interest never deductible)

Richard R. Allen, Sr., 99-1 USTC ¶50,470 (4th Cir. 1999)

Nick Kikalos, 99-2 USTC ¶50,823 (7th Cir. 1999)

Interest on funds used in personal affairs

Ebb. J. Ford, Jr., 29 TC 499 (1957)

Payments before title passes treated as interest

Warren Halle, 83 F.3d 649 (4th Cir. 1996)

Rents

Reg. §1.162-1

Reg. §1.162-11

Rev. Rul. 74-209 1974-1 CB 46

Advance rents

Martin J. Zaninovich, 616 F.2d 429 (9th Cir. 1980)

No deduction of prepaid rent without substantial business purpose

Howard Howe, TC Memo 2000-291

Repairs

Reg. §1.162-4

Louise Kingsley, 11 BTA 296 (Acq.)

Incidental repairs deductible

Indopco, Inc., 112 S. Ct. 1039 (1992), aff'g 918 F. 2d 426 (2nd Cir. 1991)

Rev. Rul. 94-12, 1994-1 CB 36

Taxes

IRC §164

Reg. §1.164

State income taxes not a business deduction

D.H. Tanner, 363 F.2d 36 (4th Cir. 1966)

State income taxes for net operating loss

Rev. Rul. 70-40, 1970-1 CB 50

Business property tax

E. W. Brown, Jr., 439 F.2d 1065 (5th Cir. 1954)

Salaries and wages

IRC §162(a)(1)

Reg. §1.162-7(a)

Legal fees

Rev. Rul. 74-392, 1974-2 CB 10

Rev. Rul. 71-470, 1971-2 CB 12

Deduction for legal fee of unsuccessful defense of criminal charge arising out of business

Walter F. Tellier, 383 U.S. 687 (1966)

Litigation expense of retired officer's rank

Rev. Rul. 72-169, 1972-1 CB 43

Expenses of discontinued business

Rev. Rul. 67-12, 1967-1 CB 29

Wages to your children deductible

Walt E. Eller, 77 TC 934 (1981)

James A. Moriarty, 48 TCM 59 (1984)

Cell phone expenses

* George W. Moss, TC Summary Opinion 2004-56

40.7 DEDUCTIONS FOR PROFESSIONALS

Repaying a medical tuition grant may not be deductible

Tripp Dargie, 014 PTC 69 (6th Cir., 2014)

Bogus management fees aren't deductible

Wiley M. Elick, TC Memo 2013-139

IRS list of deductible professional expenses

Reg. §1.162-6

Cost of establishing professional reputation

Miron Kroyt, 20 TCM 1665 (1961)

Amortization of bar admission costs

Joel A. Sharon, 66 TC 515 (1976), aff'd, 591 F.2d 1273 (9th Cir. 1978), cert. denied

Doctor may amortize patient's records

Los Angeles Central Animal Hospital, Inc., 58 TC 269 (1977) (Acq.)

Payment for hospital rights

S. M. Howard, 39 TC 833 (1963)

E. Vance Walters, 383 F.2d 922 (6th Cir. 1967)

Amortizing cost of right to practice in a hospital

Rev. Rul. 70-171, 1970-1 CB 55

Payment of client's expenses

Reginald G. Hearn, 36 TC 672 (1961), aff'd, 309 F.2d 431 (9th Cir. 1962), cert. denied, 373 U.S. 909

C. Doris Pepper, 36 TC 886 (1961) (Acq.)

Advances to client deductible/not deductible

Warren Burnett, 356 F.2d 755 (5th Cir. 1966), cert. denied, 385 U.S. 832

James Boccard, 95-1 USTC §50,284 (9th Cir. 1995)

Professionals not in own practice

Wesley J. Rogers, 20 TCM 1515 (1961)

No deduction if failed to make malpractice claim

Rev. Rul. 78-141, 1978-1 CB 380

Extracurricular teaching costs

Samuel F. Patterson, 30 TCM 1003 (1971), on remand from 436 F.2d 359 (9th Cir.), rev'g and rem'g 27 TCM 640 (1968)

Seymour Feinstein, 29 TCM 1338 (1970)

Earl T. Jefferson, 74-1 USTC ¶9205 (N.D. Ga. 1974)

Adjunct professor must itemize expenses

* George A. Beitel, TC Summary Opinion 2001-101

Luncheon discussion

John D. Moss, Jr., 758 F.2d 211 (7th Cir. 1985), cert. denied, 474 U.S. 979 (1985)

Richard R. Hankenson, 47 TCM 1567 (1984)

Myron W. Mizell, et al., 55 TCM 169 (1988)

Asbestos removal from office building is ordinary business expense

Cinergy Corp., 55 Fed. Cl. 489 (2003)

40.8 NONDEDUCTIBLE EXPENSE ITEMS

Capital expenditures

IRC §263

Reg. §1.263(a)

Uniform capitalization rules

IRC §263A

Temp. Reg. Sec. §1.263A-1T

Bonuses paid to shareholder-employees partly nondeductible

Pediatric Surgical Associates, P.C., TC Memo 2001-81

New roof on building

George W. Ritter, 163 F.2d 1019 (6th Cir. 1947)

Oberman Mfg., 47 TC 471 (1967) (Acq.)

Thomas J. Locke, 8 BTA 534 (Acq.)

Georgia Car and Locomotive Co., 2 BTA 986 (Nonacq.)

Personal expenses paid with business funds

IRC §262

Reg. §1.262-1

Expenses while not in business

Henry G. Owen, 23 TC 377 (1955)

Deductible repair or capital improvement to tangible property

T.D. 9564, 76 F.R. 81060-81127 (2011 temporary regulations)

Payment of fines

IRC §162(f)

Hoover Motor Express Co., Inc., 356 U.S. 38 (1958)

Tank Truck Rentals, Inc., 356 U.S. 30 (1958)

Herbert Davis, 26 TC 49 (1956) (Acq.)

Harry Wiedetz, 2 TC 1262 (1943)

Kickback

IRC §162(c)

Reg. §1.162-1(c)

Subcontractor's legal kickback not deductible

Car-Ron Asphalt Paving Co., Inc., 758 F.2d 1132 (6th Cir. 1985), aff'g 46 TCM 1314 (1983)

Contributions to campaigns

IRC §162(e)

Expenses from illegal medical marijuana dispensary not deductible due to Code Sec. 280E

Martin Olive, 139 TC No. 2 (2012) Northern California Small Business Assistants Inc., 154 TC No. 4 (2019)

Standing Akimro, LLC, S.Ct. (6/28/21)

40.9 HOW AUTHORS AND ARTISTS MAY WRITE OFF EXPENSES

IRC §263A(h)

Notice 89-67, 1988-1 CB 55

* IRS Publication 538

40.10 DEDUCTING EXPENSES OF A SIDELINE BUSINESS OR HOBBY

IRC §183

* IRS Publication 535

Expenses of hobby activity not deductible for 2018 through 2025 (Tax Cuts and Jobs Act)

IRC §67(g), as added by the Tax Cuts and Jobs Act (P.L. 115-97, 12/22/2017) (suspension of miscellaneous itemized deductions for 2018 through 2025)

Horse business denied deduction for lack of a horse

Denise Celeste McMillan, TC Memo 2019-108

Hobby loss rule doesn't apply to C corporations

Jeff M Potter and Marsha R. Potter, TC Memo 2018-153

Model airplane supply store meets profit motive for loss deduction

Cheryl R. Savello, TC Memo 2015-24

Investigating father's death does not result in hobby/sideline business loss deduction

Herb Vest, TC Memo 2016-187

Horse breeder had profit motive in some years

Merrill C. Roberts, TC Memo 2014-74

Writer's Travel deductions disallowed and penalty imposed

* Sal A. Westrich, TC Summary Opinion 2013-35

Coach's profit motive upheld despite steady losses

* John Dalton Parks III, TC Summary Opinion 2012-105

Order of claiming hobby deductions

Reg. §1.183-1(b)

Election to postpone determination of profit presumption

Temp. Reg. §12.9

Waiver of statute of limitations—items affected

IRC §183(e)(4)

Determining presumption period

Rev. Rul. 78-22, 1978-1 CB 72

Presumption period ends with death

Rev. Rul. 79-204, 1979-2 CB 111

Manner business conducted

Robert Schwartz, TC Memo 2003-86

James Jasienski, 64 TCM 1369 (1992)

Robert Matlock, 63 TCM 3108 (1992)

Leonard F. Barcus, 32 TCM 660 (1973), aff'd, 492 F.2d 1237 (2d Cir. 1974)

C. West Churchman, 68 TC 696 (1977)

Lester R. Westphal, 68 TCM 1038 (1994)

Danny Eldridge, 70 TCM 380 (1995)

History of income/losses from activity

Warren T. Brown, 280 F. Supp. 854 (D.N. Mex., 1968)

Henry P. White, 23 TC 90 (1954), aff'd per curiam, 227 F.2d 779 (6th Cir. 1956), cert. denied, 351 U.S. 939

Leonard P. Sasso, 20 TCM 1068 (1961)

Charles D. Eggert, 16 TCM 1010 (1957)

Lawrence Hoyle, 68 TCM 1321 (1994)

Anthony Ranciato, 52 F.3d 23 (2nd Cir. 1995)

* John E. Morrissey, TC Summary Opinion 2005-86

Profit motive can be based on aggregate of business activities

Peter Morton, Fed. Cl., 4/27/2011

Sideline charter boat

John R. Zwicky, 48 TCM 1025 (1984)

Douglas C. Heppe, 70 TCM 63 (1995)

Jet charter business not a hobby

Leonard Rabinowitz, TC Memo 2005-188

X-ray technician not a professional gambler

Randy L. Moore, TC Memo 2011-173

Drag racer not allowed business expense deduction

Ronald J. Zenzen, TC Memo 2011-167

Horse activity not a hobby

Maria Trescott Helmick, TC Memo 2009-220

Consulting activity not a business

Estate of Roger E. Stangeland et al., TC Memo 2010-185

Elements of personal pleasure/recreation

Valentine Howell, 41 TC 13 (1963), aff'd per curiam, 332 F.2d 428 (3d Cir. 1964)

Charles H. Carter, 37 TCM 859 (1978)

Peter Hurd, 37 TCM 499 (1978)

Norman D. Demler, 25 TCM 620 (1966)

Tolbert Wilkinson, 71 TCM 1959 (1996)

Aspiring authors

Paul Snyder, 674 F.2d 1359 (10th Cir. 1982) (allowed)

Maurice Dreicer, 78 TC 642 (1982) (disallowed), aff'd in unpublished opinion (D.C. Cir. 2/22/83)

Partnerships subject to IRC §183

Rev. Rul. 77-320, 1977-2 CB 78

40.11 DEDUCTING EXPENSES OF LOOKING FOR A NEW BUSINESS

* IRS Publication 334

Election to deduct business start-up costs

IRC §195(b)(1)

Election to deduct organization costs of corporation

IRC §248(a)

Election to deduct organization costs of partnership

IRC §709(b)

Partnership syndication costs not amortizable

Rev. Rul. 89-11, 1989-1 CB 179

Expenses of getting a savings and loan charter; loss deduction is allowed

Harris W. Seed, 52 TC 880 (1969) (Acq.)

Funds advanced for mining

Charles T. Parker, 1 TC 709 (1943) (Acq.)

Investigating new business which is not entered into

Frank B. Polachek, 22 TC 858 (1954)

Morton Frank, 20 TC 511 (1953)

Johan Domenie, 34 TCM 469 (1975)

Rev. Rul. 77-254, 1977-2 CB 63

Search for car agency not deductible

William E. Day, 15 TCM 1303 (1956)

40.12 HOME OFFICE DEDUCTION

IRC §280A

Prop. Reg. §1.280A-1 through 3

* IRS Publication 587

Minimal personal use doesn't kill home office deduction

* Lauren Elizabeth Miller, TC Summary Opinion 2014-74

IRS safe harbor (simplified method) for home office expenses starting in 2013

Rev. Proc. 2013-13, 2013-6 IRB 478

Administrative office in home

IRC §280A(c)(1), overturning result of Supreme Court's decision in Soliman

Supreme Court sets principal place of business tests—prior to amendment of IRC §280A(c)(i)

Nader Soliman, 113 S. Ct. 701 (1993)

Rev. Rul. 94-24, 1994-1 CB 87 (IRS examples applying Soliman tests)

Principal place of business (before Supreme Court's Soliman decision)

Rudolph Baie, 74 TC 105 (1980) (road stand)

Ernest Drucker, 79 TC 605 (1982) (musician), rev'd 715 F.2d 67 (2d Cir. 1983)

David J. Weissman, 751 F.2d 512 (2d Cir. 1985) (college professor)

Stanley Pomerantz, 860 F.2d 960 (9th Cir. 1988) (emergency room physician)

No home office deduction for hallway and bathroom

Luis Bulas, TC Memo 2011-201

Violinist's home practice area

Katia V. Popov, 2001-1 USTC ¶50,353 (9th Cir. 2001) (deduction allowed under Soliman)

Multiple use of home office

Alfred Hamacher, 94 TC 348 (1990)

Deduction denied for area minimally used by family

Jeffrey L. Rayden, TC Memo 2011-1

Inventory storage and product samples

IRC §280A(c)(2)

Portion of room as office

* Jack Chien Ching Huang, TC Summary Opinion 2002-93 (part of bedroom studio qualifies for deduction)

George H. Weightman, 42 TCM 104 (1981) (allowed); 45 TCM 167 (1982) (disallowed for following year on other grounds)

Reg. §1.280A-2(g)(1) (no partition required—follows Weightman case)

Practicing medicine at home—no deduction

Joon Chong, 71 TCM 3035 (1996)

Backyard office is "appurtenant"

Charles A. Scott, 84 TC 683 (1985)

Art gallery in home

Joseph Cunningham, 71 TCM 2527 (1996)

Day-care in home

IRC §280A(c)(4)

Brian Uphus, 67 TCM 2229 (1994)

Rev. Rul. 92-3, 1992-1 CB 141

40.13 WRITE-OFF METHODS FOR HOME OFFICE EXPENSES

IRS safe harbor (simplified method) for home office expenses starting in 2013

Rev. Proc. 2013-13, 2013-6 IRB 478

Actual expense method

IRC §280A

Lawn care not deductible

Tom E. Butz, 35 TCM 532 (1976)

Home security system

Rev. Rul. 86-148, 1986-2 CB 43

Depreciation

IRC §168(c) (residential rental or nonresidential real property)

* IRS Publication 587

On-site landlord's home office depreciation

* Chief Counsel Advice 200526002

40.14 ALLOCATING EXPENSES TO BUSINESS USE

Any reasonable method accepted

Rev. Rul. 62-180, 1962-2 CB 52

Joseph Cunningham, 71 TCM 2527 (1996)

40.15 BUSINESS INCOME MAY LIMIT HOME OFFICE DEDUCTIONS

IRC §280A(c)(5)

Prop. Reg. §1.280A-2(i) and 2(iii)

* Letter Ruling 8347012

40.16 HOME OFFICE FOR SIDELINE BUSINESS

Doctor with rental properties

Edwin R. Curphey, 73 TC 766 (1980)

Investors carrying on business

Joseph Moller, 721 F.2d 810 (CA-Fed. Cir. 1983)

40.17 DEPRECIATION OF OFFICE IN COOPERATIVE APARTMENT

IRC §216(c)

Reg. §1.216-2

40.18 Net Operating Losses (NOLs)

IRC §172

Reg. §1.172

* IRS Publication 536

Carryback eliminated for NOLs arising in tax years ending after 2017; unlimited carryforward allowed (Tax Cuts and Jobs Act)

IRC §172(b)(1) (A), as amended by the Tax Cuts and Jobs Act (P.L. 115-97, 12/22/2017)

Two-year carryback for farming losses (Tax Cuts and Jobs Act)

IRC §172(b)(1) (B), as added by the Tax Cuts and Jobs Act (P.L. 115-97, 12/22/2017)

Theft losses allowed to victims of Madoff and other Ponzi schemes

Rev. Rul. 2009-9, 2009-14 IRB 735

Rev. Rul. 2009-20, 2009-14 IRB 149

40.19 How To Report a Net Operating Loss

IRC §172

* IRS Publication 536

40.20 Excess Business Losses

*IRS Publication 536

Excess business losses not allowed for 2018 through 2026; treated as NOL carryover (Tax Cuts and Jobs Act)

IRC §461(l), as added by the Tax Cuts and Jobs Actand the American Opportunity Tax Act

Rev. Proc. 2020-45, 2020-46 IRB 1016 (2021 threshold for excess losses)

40.21 Business Credits

Small business health insurance exchange (SHOP)

Posting on November 27, 2013; www.hhs. gov/healthcare/facts/blog/2013/11/direct-newpath-to-shop-marketplace.html

General business credit

IRC §38

Small business health tax credit

IRC §45R

Notice 2010-44, 2010-22 IRB 717

Small employer credit for retirement plan startup costs

IRC §45E

Employer-provided child-care credit

IRC §45 F

Work Opportunity Tax Credit

IRC §51

Investment credit

IRC §46 through 48

Investment credit transition property

IRC §49(e)

Rev. Rul. 87-113, 1987-2 CB 33

Investment credit carryovers

IRC §49(c) (35% reduction)

IRC §39(d)

Recapture of investment credit

IRC §47(a)(1)

Reg. §1.47-1

Investment credit recapture for automobiles and other listed property

Temp. Reg. §1.280F-3T

When recapture does not apply

IRC §47(b)

Rehabilitation investment credit

IRC §48(g)

IRC §46(b)(4)

Business energy credit

IRC §46(b)

Alcohol fuels credit

IRC §40

Research credit

IRC §41

Low-income housing credit

IRC §42

Disabled access credit

IRC §44

David B. Hubbard, TC Memo 2003-245 (credit for general use equipment accommodating disabled and non-disabled patients)

Empowerment zone employment credit

IRC §1396(a)

Indian employment credit

IRC §45A

Employer Social Security credit on tips

IRC §45B(a)

Community development corporations credit

Section 13311 of the 1993 Revenue

Reconciliation Act

No disposition under Bankruptcy Act

IRC §1017(c)(2), as amended by §2(b) of the Bankruptcy Tax Act

Transfer from private practice to professional corporation requires recapture

Rev. Rul. 76-514, 1976-2 CB 11

Diesel vehicles

IRC §6427(g)

Federal gasoline and oil tax credit

* IRS Publication 510

IRC §34

Alternative fuel production credit

IRC §29

Enhanced oil recovery credit

IRC §43

Renewable electricity production credit

IRC §45

40.22 Filing Schedule F

* IRS Publication 225

40.23 Farming Expenses

* IRS Publication 225

40.24 Qualified Business Income Deduction

IRC §199A, as added by the Tax Cuts and Jobs Act (P.L. 115-97, 12/22/2017) for tax years beginning after 2017

Rev. Proc. 2022-38, 2022-45 IRB 445 (taxable income thresholds for 2023, above which QBI deduction limitations apply)

Rev. Proc. 2021-45, 2021-48 IRB 764 (taxable income thresholds for 2022, above which QBI deduction limitations apply)

Rev. Proc. 2020-45, 2020-46 IRB 1016 (taxable income thresholds for 2021, above which QBI deduction limitations apply)

Rev. Proc. 2019-44, 2019-47 IRB 1093 (taxable income thresholds for 2020, above which QBI deduction limitations apply)

Rev. Proc. 2019-38, IRB 2019-42 942 (Rental real estat safe harbor for the QBI deduction)

Rev. Proc. 2018-57, 2018-49 IRB 827 (taxable income thresholds for 2019, above which QBI deduction limitations apply)

Notice 2018-64, 2018-35 IRB 347 (methods of calculating W-2 wages for purposes of QBI deduction)

News Release IR 2018-162, 2018-35 IRB 347 (announcing release of proposed regulations)

* IRS Publication 535

41 RETIREMENT AND MEDICAL PLANS FOR SELF-EMPLOYED

* IRS Publication 560

41.1 OVERVIEW OF RETIREMENT AND MEDICAL PLANS

IRC §45 E (small employer credit for retirement plan startup costs)

IRC §401(d)

IRC §401(c)

Reg. §1.401-11

* IRS Publication 560

Earnings from more than one trade or business

Reg. §1.401-10(b)(2)

Reg. §1.401-10(c)

Controlled businesses

Reg. §1.401-12(1), (2), and (3)

S corporation shareholder may not set up a Keogh plan

Antonio Durando, 70 F.3d 584 (9th Cir. 1995)

Including employees in the plan

IRC §410

Minimum participation requirement for defined benefit plan

IRC §401(a)(26)

Contributions based on compensation

IRC §1.401-10

IRC §1.401-11

41.2 CHOOSING A QUALIFIED RETIREMENT PLAN

IRC §401

Reg. §401(e)

25% of compensation limit

IRC §402(h)(2)(A)

Integration with Social Security

IRC §401(1)

41.3 CHOOSING A SEP

SEP defined

IRC §408(k)

Working for foreign consulate doesn't make a taxpayer an employee

Michael Rosenfeld, CA-9, 7/9/13, affirming TC Memo 2011-110

Overall limit on employer SEP contributions

IRC §402(h)(2)

Deduction limit of 25% for SEP contributions

IRC §404(h)(1)(C)

Deductible SEP contributions up to filing date plus extensions

IRC §404(h)(1)(B)

Prop. Reg. §1.408-7(b)

State Department worker may contribute to SEP

Lisa Beth Levine, TC Memo 2005-86

41.4 DEDUCTIBLE CONTRIBUTIONS

IRC §404

Reg. §1.404(a)-I

* IRS Publication 560

Deductible contribution limits for defined contribution plans and SEPs

Notice 2022-55, 2022-45 IRB 443 (for 2023)

Notice 2021-61, 2021-47 IRB 738 (for 2022)

Notice 2020-79, 2020-46 IRB 1014 (for 2021)

Notice 2019-59, 2019-47 IRB 1091 (for 2020)

Notice 2018-83, 2018-47 IRB 774 (for 2019)

Limit on annual additions to defined contribution plans

IRC §415(c)(1)

Benefit limit for defined benefit plans

IRC §415(b)

Earned income reduced by deductible contributions(reducing deductible rate)

IRC §401(c)(2)(A)(v)

IRC §404(a)(8)

Compensation limit

IRC §401(a)(17)

Deduction limit of 25% for profit-sharing plans

IRC §404(a)(3)(A)(i)(I)

10% penalty for nondeductible contributions

IRC §4972

Time for making contributions

Temp. Reg. §11.40(a)(6)-I

Contributions for owner do not reduce self-employment income

Seymour L. Gale, 91-2 USTC ¶50,356 (D., Ill. 1991)

Deductible contributions up to due date of return

IRC §404(a)(6)

41.5 HOW TO QUALIFY A RETIREMENT PLAN OR SEP PLAN

IRC §401

IRC §404

IRC §405

Failure to set up written plan

Nelson H. Jones, 51 TC 651 (1969)

Correction of defects made more affordable

Rev. Proc. 94-16, 1994-1 CB 576

41.6 TAX CREDITS FOR SETTING UP A RETIREMENT PLAN

Credit for startup costsl

IRC §45E(b), as amended by Section 104 of the SECURE Act (Division O of P.L. 116-94, 12-20-2019)

Credit for automatic enrollment plans

IRC §45T, as added by Section 105 of the SECURE Act (Division O of P.L. 116-94, 12-20-2019)

41.7 ANNUAL QUALIFIED RETIREMENT PLAN REPORTING

* IRS Publication 560

Filing requirement for one-participant plans

§1103 of the Pension Protection Act of 2006

41.8 HOW QUALIFIED RETIREMENT PLAN DISTRIBUTIONS ARE TAXED

* IRS Publication 560

Lump-sum averaging

Sections 1122(h)(3)-(6) of 1986 Tax Reform Act (P.L. 99-514)

10% penalty for excess benefits under plan formula

IRC §72(m)(5)(A)

Disqualification of plan completely bars tax-free rollover

Reg. §1.402(a)-1(a)(i)

John U. Fazi, 102 TC 31 (1994)

41.9 SIMPLE IRA PLANS

IRC §408(p)

* IRS Publication 560

Contribution limits

Notice 2022-55, 2022-45 IRB 443 (for 2023)

Notice 2021-61, 2021-47 IRB 738 (for 2022)

Notice 2020-79, 2020-46 IRB 1014 (for 2021)

Notice 2019-59, 2019-47 IRB 1091 (for 2020)

Notice 2018-83, 2018-47 IRB 774 (for 2019)

Limit on elective deferrals

IRC §408(p)(2)(E)

IRC §414(v)(2)(B)(ii)

41.10 HEALTH SAVINGS ACCOUNT (HSA) BASICS

IRC §223

* IRS Publication 969

Prorated contribution limit for year an individual enrolls in Medicare

Chief Counsel INFO Letter 2016-0014 (contribution limit for individual enrolling in Medicare)

Chief Counsel INFO Letter 2016-0003 (husband and wife both enroll in Medicare in same year)

Veterans receiving VA medical care eligible for HSA after 2015

IRC §223(c)(1)(C), added by P.L. 114-41 (7/31/15)

No HSA for carryover medical FSA

Chief Counsel Memorandum 201413005

Deductible limit

IRC §223

IRS guidelines for HSAs

Notice 2004-50, 2004-33 IRB 196 (Q&A)

Rev. Rul. 2004-38, 2004-15 IRB 717 (prescription drug coverage)

Rev. Proc. 2004-22, 2004-15 IRB 727 (transition for prescription drugs)

Notice 2004-23, 2004-15 IRB 725 (preventive care)

High-deductible health plan

IRC §223(c)(2)

Coverage may be in name of self-employed owner

* Chief Counsel Advice 200524001

Annually adjusted minimum HDHP deductible and out-of-pocket maximum, and HSA contribution limit

Rev. Proc. 2022-24, 2022-20 IRB 1075 (for 2023)

Rev. Proc. 2021-25, 2021-21 IRB 1161 (for 2022)

Rev. Proc. 2020-32, 2020-24 IRB 930 (for 2021)

Rev. Proc. 2019-25, 2019-22 IRB 1261 (for 2020)

HSA catch-up contribution limit

IRC §223(b)(3)

HSA contributions for spouses

Rev. Rul. 2005-25, 2005-18 IRB 971

41.11 Limits on Deductible HSA Contributions

IRC §223

* IRS Publication 969

IRS adds preventive care items as qualified expenses for HDHPs

Notice 2019-45, 2019-32 IRB 593

HSA and HDHP inflation adjustments

Notice 2022-55, 2022-45 IRB 443 (for 2023)

Notice 2021-61, 2021-47 IRB 738 (for 2022)

Rev. Proc. 2020-32, 2020-24 IRB 930 (for 2021)

Rev. Proc. 2019-25, 2019-22 IRB 1261 (for 2020)

41.12 Distributions From HSAs

IRC §223(f)

* IRS Publication 969

Over-the-counter drugs and menstrual products qualify as medical expenses(CARES Act)

IRC §223(d)(2)(A), as amended by Section 3702 of the CARES Act (P.L.116-136, 3-27-2020)

COVID-19-related personal protective equipment qualfies as medical expense

Announcement 2021-7, 2021-15 IRB 1061

41.13 Archer MSAs

* IRS Publication 969

Archer MSA deductibles and out-of-pocket limits

Rev. Proc. 2022-38, 2022-45 IRB 452 (for 2023)

Rev. Proc. 2021-45, 2021-48 IRB 764 (for 2022)

Rev. Proc. 2020-45, 2020-46 IRB 1016 (for 2021)

Rev. Proc. 2019-44, 2019-47 IRB 1093(for 2020)

Rev. Proc. 2018-57, 2018-49 IRB 827(for 2019)

Archer MSA deductions

IRC §220

Employer contributions

IRC §106 (contributions up to deductible limit of IRC §220(b)(i))

IRS guidelines on Archer MSAs

Notice 96-53, 1996-51 IRB 5

41.14 Health Reimbursement Arrangements (HRAs)

QSEHRAs

IRC §9831(d)

Rev. Proc. 2022-38, 2022-45 IRB 415 (reimbursement limit for 2023)

Rev. Proc. 2021-45, 2021-48 IRB 764 (reimbursement limit for 2022)

Rev. Proc. 2020-45, 2020-46 IRB 1016 (reimbursement limit for 2021)

Rev. Proc. 2019-44, 2019-47 IRB 1093(reimbursement limit for 2020)

Rev. Proc. 2018-57, 2018-49 IRB 827(reimbursement limit for 2019)

ICHRAs

T.D. 9867, 2019-28 IRB 98

EBHRAs

T.D. 9867, 2019-28 IRB 98

Reg. §54.9831-1(c) (3) (viii) (B) ($1,800 reimbursement limit for 2021)

41.15 Small Employer Health Insurance Credit

IRC §45R

REG-113792-13

Average wage amount for determining eligibility for credit

Rev. Proc. 2022-38, 2022-45 IRB 415 (for 2023)

Rev. Proc. 2021-45, 2021-48 IRB 764 (for 2022)

Rev. Proc. 2020-45, 2020-46 IRB 1016 (for 2021)

42 CLAIMING DEPRECIATION DEDUCTIONS

42.1 What Property May Be Depreciated?

IRC §168

* IRS Publication 946

Nonproducing property

Reg. §1.212-1(b)

George W. Mitchell, 47 TC 120 (1966) (Nonacq.)

Maurice H. Connell, 11 TCM 771 (1952)

Charles D. Gallagher, 39 TCM 291 (1979)

Depreciation on residence put up for sale

Hulet P. Smith, 26 TCM 149 (1967), aff'd per curiam, 397 F.2d 804 (9th Cir. 1968)

Depreciation not allowed on idle ranch residence held by business

John T. Steen, 61 TC 298 (1973), aff'd per curiam, 508 F.2d 268 (5th Cir. 1975)

Cohan rule no basis for depreciation deduction

Tyson Foods, Inc., TC Memo 2007-188

Car partly for business

IRC §280F

J. R. James, 2 BTA 1071 (Acq.)

Kenneth Branchard, 12 TCM 550 (1953)

Paul McWilliams, 9 TCM (1950)

W. H. Wilson, 5 TCM 592 (1946), aff'd, 161 F.2d 556 (4th Cir. 1947), cert. denied, 332 U.S. 769

Depreciation not allowed on equipment in suspended medical practice

Rev. Rul. 77-32, 1977-1 CB 38

Depreciation allowed on equipment while owner unemployed

Charles D. Gallagher, 39 TCM 291 (1979)

Land

Reg. §1.167(a)-2

Clarence D. Hawkins, 14 TCM 382 (1955), rev'd on another issue, 234 F.2d 359 (6th Cir. 1956)

Cost of education not depreciable

Nathaniel A. Denman, 48 TC 439 (1967) (Acq.)

Goodwill, customer lists, agreements not to compete, and other intangibles

IRC §197

Election to apply amortization of intangibles retroactively

Revenue Reconciliation Act of 1993, Act Sec. 13261(g)(2)-(3)

One year or less

W. H. Tompkins Co., 47 BTA 292

International Shoe Co., 38 BTA 81 (Acq.)

Rev. Rul. 59-249, 1959-2 CB 55

Farm property

Reg. §1.167(a)(6)

When depreciation is claimed

Reg. §1.167(a)-10

Depreciation allowed on violin

Richard Simon, 68 F.3d 41 (2nd Cir., 1995), aff'g, 103 TC 15 (1994)

Brian P. Liddle, 65 F.3d 329 (3rd Cir. 1995), aff'g 103 TC 285 (1994)

Depreciation allowed on exotic cars

Bruce Selig, TC Memo 1995-519

Work of art not depreciable

Rev. Rul. 68-232, 1968-1 CB 79

Depreciating paintings in office

D. Joseph Judge, 35 TCM 1264 (1976)

Cannot accumulate depreciation

Fort Orange Paper Co., 1 BTA 1230 (Acq.)

First National Bank of Thompson, Iowa, 2 BTA 735

Morris & Bailey Steel Co., 9 BTA 205 (Acq.)

42.2 CLAIMING DEPRECIATION ON YOUR TAX RETURN

IRC §168

* IRS Publication 946

42.3 FIRST-YEAR EXPENSING DEDUCTION

IRC §179

* IRS Publication 946

Expensing limit and reduction threshold

Rev. Proc. 2022-38, 2022-45 IRB 445 (2023 expensing limit and reduction threshold)

Rev. Proc. 2021-45, 2021-48 IRB 764 (2022 expensing limit and reduction threshold)

Rev. Proc. 2020-45, 2020-46 IRB 1016 (2021 expensing limit and reduction threshold)

Rev. Proc. 2019-44, 2019-47 IRB 1093 (2020 expensing limit and reduction threshold

Election to expense qualified real property

IRC §179(d)(1) (B), as amended by the Tax Cuts and Jobs Act (P.L. 115-97, 12/22/2017) for tax years beginning after 2017 (election to claim expensing for qualified real property)

Computer software eligible for expensing

IRC §179(d)(1)(A)(ii)

Changing expensing elections without IRS consent

IRC §179(c)(2)

50% business-use test for automobiles, and other listed property

IRC §280F(b)

IRC §280F(d)(4)

Temp. Reg. §1.280F-6T(b)

Timing of expensing deduction for equipment components

*Courtney A. Brown, TC Summary Opinion 2009-171

Expensed assets should have been depreciated

Alacare Home Health Services, TC Memo 2001-149

Furniture bought in year before business begins—no expensing deduction

Kenneth A. Baratelle, TC Memo 2000-359

Expensing election cannot be increased after audit

Sam H. Patton, 116 TC 206 (2001)

Rental fleet motor home qualifies for first-year expensing

Robert D. Shirley, TC Memo 2004-188

Partners with more than one expensing deduction

Rev. Rul. 89-7, 1989-1 CB 178

Recapture of deduction if business use drops

IRC §179(d)(10)

42.4 MACRS RECOVERY PERIODS

IRC §168(e)

* IRS Publication 946

42.5 MACRS RATES

IRC §168(b)

42.6 HALF-YEAR CONVENTION FOR MACRS

IRC §168(d)(1)

42.7 LAST QUARTER PLACEMENTS— MID-QUARTER CONVENTION

IRC §168(d)(3)

Disregard real estate and property disposed of during year

IRC §168(d)(3)(B)

42.8 150% RATE ELECTION

IRC §168(b)(2)

42.9 STRAIGHT LINE DEPRECIATION

IRC §168(g)

42.10 LISTED PROPERTY

* IRS Publication 946

Listed property defined

IRC §280F(d)(4)

Computers and peripheral equipment no longer treated as "listed" property (Tax Cuts and Jobs Act)

IRC §280F(d)(4)(A), as amended by the Tax Cuts and Jobs Act (P.L. 115-97, 12/22/2017), for property placed in service after 2017

Computers and peripheral equipment placed in service before 2018

IRC §280F(d)(4)(A) (iv) (general rule treating computers as listed property, prior to repeal by the Tax Cuts and Jobs Act)

IRC §280F(d)(4)(B)(exception for computer in regular business establishment, prior to repeal by the Tax Cuts and Jobs Act)

Cell phones no longer listed property

IRC §280F(d)(4), as amended by Small Business Jobs Act of 2010, P.L. 111-240

Cell phone expenses-pre-2010 substantiation rule

* George W. Moss, TC Summary Opinion 2004-56

Straight-line depreciation required if business use is 50% or less

IRC §280F(b)(1)

Recapture of excess depreciation if business use drops to 50% or less

IRC §280F(b)(2)

Reg. §1.280F-3T(d)

Income inclusion for leases

Reg. §1.280F-5T(f)(2)

* IRS Publication 946

42.11 ASSETS IN SERVICE BEFORE 1987

IRC §168(c) prior to 1986 Tax Act

IRC §168(b)(1)(A) prior to 1986 Tax Act (straight-line recovery)

* IRS Publication 534

Depreciation of automobiles and home computers

IRC §280F

42.12 MACRS FOR REAL ESTATE PLACED IN SERVICE AFTER 1986

* IRS Publication 946

Residential rental property and nonresidential real property defined

IRC §168(e)(2)

Recovery periods

IRC §168(c)

15-year recovery for qualified leasehold improvement property

IRC §168(e)(3)(E)(iv)

IRC §168(e)(6) (qualified property defined)

15-year recovery for qualified restaurant property

IRC §168(e)(3)(E)(v)

IRC §168(e)(7) (qualified property defined)

42.13 DEMOLISHING A BUILDING

Capitalization required

IRC §280B

Test for partial demolition costs

Rev. Proc. 95-27, 1995-1 CB 704

Pre-1984 decisions

Donald S. Levinson, 59 TC 676 (1973)

John A. Lemm, 32 TCM 515 (1973)

J. Alfred Rider, 30 TCM 188 (1971)

Yates Motor Co., 561 F.2d 15 (6th Cir. 1977), rev'g 34 TCM 1235 (1975)

Rossel M. Hightower, 463 F.2d 182 (5th Cir. 1972)

Mayer Feldman, 335 F.2d 264 (9th Cir. 1964)

Herman Landerman, 454 F.2d 338 (7th Cir. 1972), cert. denied, 406 U.S. 967

Thomas P. Foltz, 458 F.2d 600 (8th Cir. 1972)

Ivan Grossman, 74 TC 1147 (1980) (Nonacq.)

42.14 QUALIFIED IMPROVEMENT PROPERTY

Qualified improvement property retroactively eligible for bonus depreciation (CARES Act)

IRC §168(e)(3)(E)(vii), added by Section 2307 of the CARES Act (P.L.116-136, 3-27-2020)

Rev. Proc. 2020-25, IRB 2020-19 IRB 785(refund opportunity for 2018 or 2019)

Qualified improvement property eligible for first-year expensing (Tax Cuts and Jobs Act)

IRC §179(f)(1), as amended by the Tax Cuts and Jobs Act (P.L. 115-97, 12/22/2017, for tax years beginning after 2017)

Expensing leasehold, restaurant and retail improvements---property placed in service before 2018

IRC §179(f)(2), prior to amendment by the Tax Cuts and Jobs Act (P.L. 115-97, 12/22/2017)

Lessor's disposition or abandonment of improvements

IRC §168(i)(8)

42.15 DEPRECIATING REAL ESTATE PLACED IN SERVICE AFTER 1980 AND BEFORE 1987

* IRS Publication 534

(The following citations are to Code sections before 1986 Tax Act)

Recovery period

IRC §168(c)(2)(D)

Low-income housing

IRC §168(b)(4)

IRC §168(c)(2)(F)

Treasury tables

Notice 81-16, 1981-2 CB 545

Election to use straight-line depreciation

IRC §168(b)(3)

Rate of recovery

IRC §168(b)(2)

Separate depreciation for components not allowed

IRC §168(f)(1)

Components added after March 15, 1984

IRC §168(f)(1)(B)

IRC §168(g)(4)

42.16 AMORTIZING GOODWILL AND OTHER INTANGIBLES (SECTION 197)

IRC §197

15-year amortization required for covenant not to compete

Recovery Group, Inc., TC Memo 2010-76

15-year amortization for non-compete agreement in business acquisition

Frontier Chevrolet Co., 116 TC 289 (2001), aff'g 2003-1 USTC ¶50,490 (9th Cir. 2003)

Computer software not treated as Section 197 intangible

IRC §197 (e) (3)

42.17 AMORTIZING RESEARCH AND EXPERIMENTATION COSTS

IRC §174 (b)

* IRS Publication 535

42.18 BONUS DEPRECIATION

IRC 168(k), as amended by the Tax Cuts and Jobs Act (P.L. 115-97, 12/22/2017)

* IRS Publication 946

Safe harbor for vehicles qualifying for 80% bonus depreciation and subject to annual depreciation ceiling

Rev. Proc. 2023-14, 2023-03 IRB 388

Bonus depreciation percentage decreased to 80% (Tax Cuts and Jobs Act)

IRC §168(k)(6)(A), as amended by the Tax Cuts and Jobs Act (P.L. 115-97, 12/22/2017)

Used as well as new property can qualify for bonus depreciation (Tax Cuts and Jobs Act)

IRC §168(k)(2)(A) (ii), and §168(k)(2)(E) (ii), as amended by the Tax Cuts and Jobs Act (P.L. 115-97, 12/22/2017, for property acquired and placed in service after September 27, 2017)(property must not be acquired from related party)

43 DEDUCTING CAR AND TRUCK EXPENSES

43.1 STANDARD MILEAGE RATE

* IRS Publication 463

Annual standard mileage rates

Notice 2023-3, 2023-3 IRB 388 (for 2023)

Notice 2022-3, 2022-2 IRB 308 (mileage rates for first half of 2022)

Announcement 2022-13, 2022-26 IRB 1185 (mileage rate for second half of 2022)

Notice 2021-2, 2021-3 IRB 478 (for 2021)

Notice 2020-5, 2020-4 IRB 380 (for 2020)

Notice 2019-02, 2019-02 IRB 281 (for 2019)

Allowance for rural delivery mail carriers

IRC §162(o)(2)

Two cars used at one time

Carroll H. West, 63 TC 252 (1974)

Married couple's separately owned cars

* Letter Ruling 8343005

Diary record of business mileage

John E. Frankel, 27 TCM 817 (1968)

Lack of mileage record results in denial of deduction for vehicle costs

Duncan Bass, TC Memo 2018-19

Allowance for driving to distant research library

* Richard Orin Berge, TC Summary Opinion 2006-29

Interest

IRC §163(h)(2)(A)

IRC §163(d)(6)

Useful life: prior law

Rev. Proc. 75-3, 1975-1 CB 643

60,000 miles as useful life: prior law

Rev. Proc. 81-54, 1981-2 CB 649

43.2 EXPENSE ALLOCATIONS

* IRS Publication 463

No "Double-dipping" for vehicle expenses

* Jody Eldred and Pamela Eldred, TC Summary Opinion 2018-49

Allocation based on miles

Reg. Sec. 1.280F-6(e)

Some car expenses capitalized

Doris Jones, 11 TCM 529 (1952)

Apportioning car expense between business and personal use

IRC §163(h)(2)(A)

Lawrence Au, 40 TC 264 (1963), aff'd per curiam, 330 F.2d 1008 (9th Cir. 1964), cert. denied, 379 U.S. 960

Clarence J. Sapp, 309 F.2d 143 (5th Cir. 1962), aff'g 36 TC 852 91 (1961) (Acq.)

43.3 DEPRECIATION RESTRICTIONS ON CARS, TRUCKS, AND VANS

IRC §280F

IRC §168(k)

* IRS Publication 463

Employer convenience test (for pre-2018 employee deductions)

IRC §280F(d)(3)

More than 50% business-use test

Temp. Reg. §280F(b)

Temp. Reg. §1.280F-6T(d)(4)

Business-investment percentage

Temp. Reg. §1.280F-6T(d)(3)

Temp. Reg. §1.280F-2T(i)

Vehicles other than cars

IRC §280F(d)(4)

Temp. Reg. §1.280F-6T(b)

Vehicles exempted from more-than-50%-business-use test

Temp. Reg. §1.280F-6T(b)

Temp. Reg. §1.274-5T(k)

Transportation for hire

IRC §280F(d)(4)(C)

Employee use of company car (for pre-2018 employee deductions)

IRC §280F(d)(6)

Temp. Reg. §1.280F-6T(d)(2)

43.4 ANNUAL CEILINGS ON DEPRECIATION

IRC §280F(a) (1) (A), as amended by the Tax Cuts and Jobs Act (P.L. 115-97, 12/22/2017)

* IRS Publication 463

IRS safe harbor if 100% bonus depreciation claimed for vehicle placed in service after 9/27/17 and subject to annual ceilings

Rev. Proc. 2019-13, IRB 2019-09 744

Depreciation limits increased for vehicles placed in service after 2017

IRC §280F(a)(1)(A), as amended by the Tax Cuts and Jobs Act (P.L. 115-97, 12/22/2017)

Rev. Proc. 2023-14, 2023-06 IRB 466 (depreciation limits for vehicles leased in 2023)

Rev. Proc. 2022-17, 2022-13 IRB 930 (depreciation limits for vehicles leased in 2022)

Rev. Proc. 2021-31, 2021-34 IRB 324 (depreciation limits for vehicles placed in service in 2021)

Rev. Proc. 2020-37, 2020-33 IRB 381 (depreciation limits for vehicles placed in service in 2020)

Rev. Proc. 2019-26, 2019-24 IRB 1323 (depreciation limits for vehicles placed in service in 2019)

Bonus depreciation increases first-year ceiling by $8,000

IRC §168(k)(2)(F) (i)

Annual limit on depreciation (pre-2018)

IRC §280F(a)(1)(A), prior to amendment by the Tax Cuts and Jobs Act (P.L. 115-97, 12/22/2017)

* IRS Publication 463

Rev. Proc. 2017-29, 2017-14 IRB 1065 (depreciation limits for vehicles placed in service in 2017)

Rev. Proc. 2016-23, 2016-16 IRB 581 (depreciation limits for vehicles placed in service in 2016; revised depreciation limits for 2015 to reflect PATH Act)

Passenger automobile defined

IRC §280F(d)(5)

T. D. 9069, 2003-37 IRB 525 (qualified non-personal-use vehicles not considered passenger automobiles

First-year expensing limitation

IRC §280F(d)(1)

First-year expensing limit for SUVs

IRC §179(b)(5) and (6)

Rev. Proc. 2023-14, 2023-06 IRB 466 (SUVs placed in service during 2023)

Rev. Proc. 2022-17, 2022-13 IRB 930 (SUVs placed in service during 2022)

Rev. Proc. 2021-31, 2021-34 IRB 324 (SUVs placed in service during 2021)

Rev. Proc. 2020-37, 2020-33 IRB 381 (SUVs placed in service during 2020)

Rev. Proc. 2019-26, 2019-24 IRB 1323 (SUVs placed in service during 2019)

Personal-use percentage reduces ceiling

IRC §280F(a)(2)

Temp. Reg. §1.280F-2T(i)

43.5 MACRS RATES FOR CARS, TRUCKS, AND VANS

* IRS Publication 463

IRC §168(e)(3)(B)(i)

IRC §168(b)

IRC §168(c)

Annual deduction limits

IRC §280F(a) (1) (A), as amended by the Tax Cuts and Jobs Act (P.L. 115-97, 12/22/2017)

Rev. Proc. 2023-14, 2023-06 IRB 466 (vehicles placed in service during 2023)

Rev. Proc. 2022-17, 2022-13 IRB 930 (vehicles placed in service during 2022)

Rev. Proc. 2021-31, 2021-34 IRB 324 (vehicles placed in service during 2021)

Rev. Proc. 2020-37, 2020-33 IRB 381 (vehicles placed in service during 2020)

Rev. Proc. 2019-26, 2019-24 IRB 1323 (vehicles placed in service during 2019)

IRS safe harbor if 100% bonus depreciation claimed for vehicle placed in service after 9/27/17 and subject to annual ceilings

Rev. Proc. 2019-13, IRB 2019-09 744

Conventions

IRC §168(d)

Basis reduction for personal use

Temp. Reg. §1.280F-2T(g)

IRS safe harbor if 100% bonus allowance claimed for vehicle purchased after September 8, 2010 and placed in service before 2012

Rev. Proc. 2011-26, 2011-16 IRB 664

43.6 STRAIGHT LINE METHOD

Mandatory straight-line recovery

IRC §280F(b)(2) and (b)(4)

Temp. Reg. §1.280F-3T(c) and (e)

Optional straight-line recovery if business use exceeds 50%

IRC §168(f)(2)(c)

Prop. Reg. §1.168-2(c)

43.7 DEPRECIATION FOR YEAR VEHICLE IS DISPOSED OF

* IRS Publication 463

* IRS Publication 946

IRC §280F

IRC §168(d) (applicable convention)

43.8 DEPRECIATION AFTER RECOVERY PERIOD ENDS

IRC §280F(a) (1) (B), as amended by the Tax Cuts and Jobs Act (P.L. 115-97, 12/22/2017)

* IRS Publication 463

Converting a pleasure car to business use

Prop. Reg. §1.168-2(j)(1)

Increase in business use after recovery period

Prop. Reg. §1.168-2(j)(2) (Pre-6/18/84 cars)

43.9 TRADE-IN OF BUSINESS VEHICLE

IRC §1031 (a) (1), as amended by the Tax Cuts and Jobs Act (P.L. 115-97, 12/22/2017) (gain must be recognized on trade-in of business vehicle after 2017; like-kind exchange treatment no longer allowed)

* IRS Publication 463

Trade-in before 2018 (prior to Tax Cuts and Jobs Act)

Reg. §1.168(i)-6

* IRS Publication 463

43.10 RECAPTURE OF DEDUCTIONS ON BUSINESS CAR, TRUCK, OR VAN

Business use drops to 50% or less

IRC §280F(b)(2)

IRC §280F(b)(3)

Temp. Reg. §1.280F-3T(c)(2)

43.11 KEEPING RECORDS OF BUSINESS USE

* IRS Publication 463

Record-keeping requirements

IRC §274(d)

Temp. Reg. §1.274-5T

Vehicles exempted from record-keeping requirements

IRC §274(d)(4)

Temp. Reg. §1.274-5T(k)

Written company policy restricting personal use

Temp. Reg. §1.274-6T

Control employees, owners and highly compensated

Reg. §1.274-6T(a)(3)(i)(E)

Reg. §1.61-2T(f)(5) and (f)(6)

Poor mileage log prevents deduction for car expenses

*Willie J. Moore et ux., TC Summary Opinion 2010-102

43.12 LEASED BUSINESS VEHICLES: DEDUCTIONS AND INCOME

IRC §280F(c)

* IRS Publication 463

Fair market value threshold for income inclusion

Rev. Proc. 2023-14, 2023-6 IRB 466 (leased in 2023)

Rev. Proc. 2022-17, 2022-13 IRB 930 (leased in 2022)

Rev. Proc. 2021-31, 2021-34 IRB 324 (leased in 2021)

Rev. Proc. 2020-37, 2020-33 IRB 381 (leased in 2020)

Rev. Proc. 2019-26, 2019-24 IRB 1323 (leased in 2019)

Rev. Proc. 2018-25, 2018-18 IRB 543 (leased in 2018; reflecting the Tax Cuts and Jobs Act (P.L. 115-97, 12/22/2017)

44 SALES OF BUSINESS PROPERTY

44.1 DEPRECIATION RECAPTURED AS ORDINARY INCOME ON SALE OF PERSONAL PROPERTY

* IRS Publication 544

IRC §1245(a)

IRC §1250

44.2 DEPRECIATION RECAPTURED AS ORDINARY INCOME ON SALE OF REAL ESTATE

IRC §1250

* IRS Publication 544

25% tax rate for unrecaptured Section 1250 gain

IRC §1(h)(1)(D)

Computing excess over straight line

Reg. §1.1250(b)(1)

Holding period where property is foreclosed

IRC §1250 (d)(10)

Reg. §1.1250-1 through 5

Recapture for GO Zone property

IRC §1400N(d)(5)

44.3 RECAPTURE OF FIRST-YEAR EXPENSING AND BONUS DEPRECIATION

* IRS Publication 544

IRC §179(d)(10)

44.4 GIFTS AND INHERITANCES OF DEPRECIABLE PROPERTY

IRC §1245(a)

Tax not imposed at time of gift or inheritance

IRC §1245(b)(1), (2), and (3)

Reg. §1.1245-4

44.5 INVOLUNTARY CONVERSIONS AND TAX-FREE EXCHANGES

* IRS Publication 544

IRC §1245(b)(4)

IRC §1250(d)(4)

Reg. §1.704-4

Reg. §1.737-1-5 (gain/loss recognition on partnership distributions of contributed property)

44.6 INSTALLMENT SALE OF DEPRECIABLE PROPERTY

Reg. §1.1245-6(d)

Sales after June 6, 1984

IRC §453(i)

44.7 SALE OF A PROPRIETORSHIP

Amortization of goodwill, customer lists, agreements not to compete, and other intangibles

IRC §197

Individual proprietorship

IRC §1231

Reg. §1.1231-1

Aaron F. Williams, 152 F.2d 570 (2d Cir. 1946)

IRC §1060

Rev. Rul. 55-79, 1955-1 CB 370

44.8 PROPERTY USED IN A BUSINESS (SECTION 1231 ASSETS)

IRC §1231

Reg. §1.1231-1 and 2

* IRS Publication 544

Down payment's tax treatment when a sale falls through

CRI-Leslie, LLC, 147 TC No. 8 (2016)

12 months for livestock

IRC §1231(b)(3)

Recapture of ordinary loss

IRC §1231(c)

44.9 SALE OF PROPERTY USED FOR BUSINESS AND PERSONAL PURPOSES

Sale of airplane

Hugh Sharp, Jr., 199 F. Supp. 743 (D. Del. 1961), aff'd, 303 F.2d 783 (3d Cir. 1962)

44.10 SHOULD YOU TRADE IN BUSINESS EQUIPMENT?

IRC §1031 (a) (1), as amended by the Tax Cuts and Jobs Act (P.L. 115-97, 12/22/2017) (gain must be recognized on trade-in of equipment after 2017)

* IRS Publication 463

Loss on trade-in

National Outdoor Advertising Bureau, Inc., 89 F.2d 878 (2d Cir. 1937), on remand, BTA Dec. 10,072-C, 6/24/38

Sale to dealer

Rev. Rul. 61-119, 1961-1 CB 395

44.11 CORPORATE LIQUIDATION

IRC §331

Louis Greenspan, 229 F.2d 947 (8th Cir. 1956)

Susan J. Carter, 170 F.2d 911 (2d Cir. 1948)

L. M. Graves, 11 TCM 467 (1952)

Rev. Rul. 59-228, 1959-2 CB 89

Legal expenses of collecting claim

Otto C. Doering, Jr., 335 F.2d 738 (2d Cir. 1964)

44.12 ADDITIONAL TAXES ON HIGHER-INCOME TAXPAYERS

IRC §3101(b)(2) (Additional 0.9% tax)

IRC §1411(Additional 3.8% tax)

45 FIGURING SELF-EMPLOYMENT TAX

45.1 WHAT IS SELF-EMPLOYMENT INCOME?

IRC §1402

IRC §6017

Reg. §1.6017-1(b)

Reg. §1.1402(a)-1

Reg. §1.1402(b)-1

* IRS Publication 334

LLC members are not limited partners exempt from self-employment tax

* Chief Counsel Advice 201436049

Health insurance for self-employed not a schedule C deduction

* Chief Counsel Advice 200623001

Qualified joint venture election for husband and wife owners

IRC §761(f)

Husband and wife

Donald R. Fitch, TC Memo 2013-244

IRC §6017

Grandparents' childcare income not subject to self-employment tax

* Derrolyn Steele, TC Summary Opinion 2009-45

Rents

Reg. §1.1402(a)-4

Capital gains and losses

Reg. §1.1402(a)-6

Dividends and interest

Reg. §1.1402(a)-5

Net operating loss carryover

IRC §1402(a)(4) and (5)

Business interruption insurance proceeds not self-employment income

Max G. Newberry, 76 TC 441 (1981)

Illegal employment

Rev. Rul. 60-77, 1960-1 CB 386

Employee can be independent contractor for Keogh purposes

James S. Reece, 63 TCM 3129 (1992)

Insurance agent subject to SE tax

Bruce Isom, 70 TCM 376 (1996)

Extended earnings

Herbert Gump, Federal Cir. (6/12/96)

Robert Schelbe, 71 TCM 3166 (1996)

Frequent real estate sales: ordinary income or capital gains?

Patricia A. and Donald J. Flood, TC Memo 2012-243

45.2 PARTNERS PAY SELF-EMPLOYMENT TAX

IRC §701

Reg. §1.701-12

Reg. §1.702-1

Limited (LLC) member-managers subject to self-employment tax

Vincent J. and Marie Castigliola et. al., TC Memo 2017-62

Limited partner not subject to self-employment tax

IRC §1402(a)(13)

Partner dying during taxable year

Reg. §1.1402(f)-1

Retirement payments for partnerships

IRC §1402(a)(10)

Rev. Rul. 79-34, 1979-1 CB 285

Restricting partnership status of foreign consultant does not avoid self-employment tax

Atef A. Gamal-Eldin, 55 TCM 582 (1988), aff'd in unpublished opinion 876 F.2d 896 (9th Cir. 1989)

45.3 SCHEDULE SE

Social Security changes for 2023

Social Security Administration News Release and Fact Sheet, 10/13/22 https://www.ssa.gov/news/press/releases/2022/#10-2022-2

Social Security changes for 2022

Social Security Administration News Release and Fact Sheet, 10/13/21 https://www.ssa.gov/news/press/releases/2021/#10-2021-2

Social Security changes for 2021

Social Security Administration News Release and Fact Sheet, 10/13/20 https://www.ssa.gov/news/press/releases/2020/#10-2020-1

Income tax deduction for 50% of self-employment tax

IRC §164(f)

45.4 HOW WAGES AFFECT SELF-EMPLOYMENT TAX

Effect of wages on self-employment tax rates

IRC §1402(b)

Notice 2007-92, 2007-47 IRB 1036

Social Security tax base

For 2023-Social Security Administration News Release and Fact Sheet, 10/13/22 https://www.ssa.gov/news/press/releases/2022/#10-2022-2

For 2022-Social Security Administration News Release and Fact Sheet, 10/13/21 https://www.ssa.gov/news/press/releases/2021/#10-2021-2

For 2021-Social Security Administration News Release and Fact Sheet, 10/13/20 https://www.ssa.gov/news/press/releases/2020/#10-2020-1

45.5 OPTIONAL METHOD IF 2023 WAS A LOW-INCOME OR LOSS YEAR

IRC §1402(a)(15)

IRC §1402(l)

* IRS Publication 334

45.6 SELF-EMPLOYMENT TAX RULES FOR CERTAIN POSITIONS

Self-employed

IRC §1401

IRC §1402

IRC §1403

Reg. §1.1401-1

Reg. §1.1402(a)-1

Reg. §1.1402(b)-1

Reg. §1.1402(c)-1

Babysitter

Rev. Rul. 77-279, 1977-2 CB 12

Clergy

IRC §1402(e)

Temp. Reg. §1.1402(e)-5T

James B. Hall, 30 F.3d 1304 (10th Cir. 1994)

Ministers who elected out of Social Security coverage may re-elect coverage

Section 403 of P.L. 106-170 (1999)

Consulting

Rev. Rul. 82-210, 1982-2 CB 203

Grosswald v. Schweicker, 653 F.2d 58 (2d Cir. 1981)

Steffens v. United States, 707 F.2d 478 (11th Cir. 1983)

James M. Hornaday, 81 TC 830 (1983) (fees received without services)

Dealers in commodities and options

IRC §1402(i)

Independent contractor

Dan P. Butts, 49 F.3d 713 (11th Cir. 1995)

LLC members

Prop. Regs. §§ 1.1402 (a)-18

Rev. Proc. 95-10, 1995-1 CB 501

Insurance agent treated as independent contractor

Dan P. Butts, 49 F. 3d 713 (11th Cir. 1995)

Director's fees

IRC §1402(a)

Rev. Rul. 68-595, 1968-2 CB 378

Drivers

Boles Trucking, Inc., 8th Cir. (2/12/96)

Adult entertainers

303 West 42nd Street Enterprises, Inc., NY District Court (2/28/96)

Used car salesmen

Martin Springfield, 9th Cir. (7/3/96)

Employees of foreign government or international organization

Reg. §1.1402(c)-3(d)

Jessica M. Smart, 222 F. Supp. 65 (S.D.N.Y. 1963)

Fees as executor

Cresence E. Clarke, 27 TC 861 (1957)

Rev. Rul. 58-5, 1958-1 CB 322, distinguished by Rev. Rul. 72-86, 1972-1 CB 273

Nonprofessional executor or administrator

Rev. Rul. 58-5, 1958-1 CB 322, distinguished by Rev. Rul. 72-86, 1972-1 CB 273

Guardian for disabled cousin

* Letter Ruling 8845025

Trust beneficiaries not self-employed

Reg. §1.1402(a)-2(b)

Fee for occasional speech

Rev. Rul. 55-431, 1955-2 CB 312

PIK payments to farmers

Pub. L. No. 98-4

Announcement 83-43, 1983-10 IRB 29

Nonresident alien

IRC §1402(b)

Nurses: IRS traditional tests

Rev. Rul. 75-101, 1975-1 CB 318

Rev. Rul. 61-96, 1961-2 CB 155

* Letter Ruling 8845049

Nurses obtaining job through agency

Rev. Rul. 75-41, 1975-1 CB 323

Rev. Rul. 75-101, 1975-1 CB 318

* Letter Ruling 8913002

* Letter Ruling 8839073

* Letter Ruling 8904033

Hospital Resource Personnel, Inc., 68 F.3d 421 (11th Cir. 1995)

Payroll taxes withheld from practical nurse's wages

* Letter Ruling 9123005

Gambling income not subject to self-employment tax

Alfred A. Gentile, 6 TC 1 (1946)

Public official

IRC §1402(c)

Reg. §1.402(c)-2

Technical specialists

Section 1706 of 1986 Tax Reform Act

Rev. Rul. 87-41, 1987-1 CB 296

Writer

Rev. Rul. 68-498, 1968-2 CB 377

Rev. Rul. 79-390, 1972-2 CB 308

Rev. Rul. 55-385, 1955-1 CB 100 (professor's writing as self-employment income)

Real estate salesman and door-to-door salesman

IRC §3508(a)

Rev. Rul. 85-63, 1985-1 CB 292

46 FILING YOUR RETURN

46.1 KEEPING TAX RECORDS

News Release IR-2021-217

* IRS Publication 5027 (identity theft information for taxpayers and victims)

* News Release IR-2012-60 (backing up records in case of natural disaster)

46.2 GETTING READY TO FILE YOUR RETURN

News Release IR-2021-217

Private postage meter cannot establish date of timely filing

Robert H. Tilden, CA-7, 1/13/17, reversing TC Memo 2015-188

IRS-designated private delivery services

Notice 2016-30, 2016-18 IRB 676 (IRS adds to list of designated services)

Voluntary continuing education and testing for unenrolled preparers

American Institute of Certified Public Accountants v. IRS (CA-DC, 8/14/18)

Rev. Proc. 2014-42, 2014-29 IRB 192

Timely mailing treated as timely filing

IRC §7502(a)

Reg. §301.7502-1, as amended by T.D. 9543, 2011-40 IRB 470

Reg. §301.7502-1(e)(2) (registered and certified mail and designated private delivery service are exclusive means to establish prima facie evidence of delivery to IRS)

Common law "mailbox rule" rejected

Howard L. Baldwin, 921 F.3d 836 (9th Cir. 2019)

Foreign postmarks

Rev. Rul. 2002-23, 2002-18 IRB 811

Snow day in District of Columbia extends filing deadline for Tax Court petition

Felix Guralnik, Tax Court Order, 8/24/15

Using wrong delivery service for Tax Court petition

Marcius J. Scaggs, TC Memo 2012-258

46.3 APPLYING FOR AN EXTENSION

* IRS Form 4868

Extension of time to file return

IRC §6081

Reg. §1.6081-4

Automatic six-month filing extensions

Temp. Regs. §1.6081-4T (T.D. 9229, 70 Federal Register 67356, 11/7/05)

IRS may terminate on 10 days notice

Reg. §1.6081-4(c)

Extension of time to pay tax

IRC §6161

Reg. §1.616-1 (undue hardship required)

IRC §6601(b)(1) (interest on underpayment applies from original due date)

IRS-designated private delivery services

IRC §7502(f)

Notice 2016-30, 2016-18 IRB 676 (IRS adds to list of designated private delivery services)

Filing and payment extension until June 15 for being out of the country

Reg. §1.6081-5

Temp. Reg. 1.6081-5T (T.D. 9229, 70 Federal Register 67356, 11/7/05)

Penalty for late payment—90% exception for taxpayer with automatic extension

IRC §6651(a)(2)

Reg. §301.6651-1(c)(3)

46.4 GETTING YOUR REFUND

* IRS Publication 17

* IRS Instructions to Forms 1040 and 1040-SRZ

Offers in compromise

IRC §7122

Buying Savings Bonds with refund

IRS Fact Sheet FS-2011-06

46.5 PAYING TAXES DUE

Installment agreement with IRS to cost more

News Release IR-2016-108

REG-108792-16, 2016-36 IRB 320

PayNearMe payment option

News Release IR-2016-56

IRS direct pay

News Release IR-2014-67

IRS can disregard tithing & college expenses in figuring installment payments

George Thompson, 140 TC No. 4 (2013)

Paying tax in installments

IRC §6159

REG-144990-12

Online payment agreement

News Release IR-2006-159

IRS offers split-refund option to direct depositors

News Release IR-2006-85

46.6 HANDLING IDENTITY THEFT

IRS and tax industry fighting identity theft

*https://www.irs.gov./identity-theft-central

* IRS Publication 5027 (identity theft information for taxpayers and victims)

* IRS Publication 4524 (security awareness for taxpayers)

News Release IR-2023-71 (recap of 2023 Dirty Dozen tax scams)

News Release IR-2022-113, IR-2022-117, IR-2022-119, IR-2022-122, IR-2022-125 (recap of 2022 Dirty Dozen tax scams)

News Release IR-2021-135 (recap of 2021 Dirty Dozen tax scams)

46.7 NOTIFY THE IRS OF ADDRESS CHANGES

Last known address rule for deficiency notices

Rev. Proc. 90-18, 1990-1 CB 491

Barbara Abeles, 91 TC 1019 (1988) (acq. 1989-31 IRB4)

Nancy J. Bayer, 98 TC 19 (1991)

46.8 INTEREST ON TAX UNDERPAYMENTS

IRC §6601

IRC §6621

IRS interest rates through December 31, 2023

IR2023-154

Rev. Rul. 2023-17, 2023-37 IRB 798

Same interest rate for deficiencies and refunds

IRC §6621(a)

Quarterly interest rates based on short-term federal rate

Notice 88-59, 1988-1 CB 546

Quarterly rates after 1986

IRC §6621(b)

Interest runs from due date without extensions to date paid

IRC §6601(a)

IRC §6601(b)(1)

Deposit suspends interest accrual on potential underpayment

IRC §6603

Rev. Proc. 2005-18, 2005-13 IRB 798

Interest and dividend information disclosed to government agencies

IRC §6103(1)(7)

46.9 TAX PENALTIES FOR LATE FILING AND LATE PAYMENT

Monthly penalty for late filing

IRC §6651(a)(1)

Minimum late filing penalty increased to $435 (SECURE Act)

IRC §6651(a), as amended by Section 402 of the SECURE Act (Division O of P.L.116-94, 12-20-2019)

Rev. Proc. 2020-45, 2020-46 IRB 1016 (minimum payment remains $435 dollars for 2021 return)

No tax due, no late filing penalty

Christine Patronik-Holder, 100 TC 374 (1993) (acq. 1993-38 IRB 4)

Reliance on preparer to file extension no excuse for late filing

Anthony Tesoriero, TC Memo 2012-261

Reasonable cause/not reasonable cause for failure to file

Elizabeth Gravett, 67 TCM 2651 (1994)

Douglas D. Kemmerer, 66 TCM 550 (1993)

ADHD and other psychological problems not reasonable cause for not filing

Austin Danne Hardin, TC Memo 2012-162

Mental illness may be reaonable cause for late filing

*Chief Counsel Advice 201637012

Veteran's anxiety no excuse for not filing

Manuel Verduzco, TC Memo 2010-278

Late filing in gift tax return penalized despite health problmes

Margaret V. Stine, U.S. Court of Federal Claims,10/23/12

Monthly penalty for late payment

IRC §6651(a)(2)

47 FILING REFUND CLAIMS, AND AMENDED RETURNS

47.1 FILING AN AMENDED RETURN

Filing for disabled persons

Rev. Proc. 99-21, 1997-17 IRB

47.2 WHEN TO FILE A REFUND CLAIM

Refund for overpayment

IRC §6401

IRC §6402

Reg. §301.6401-1

Reg. §301.6402-2(c) and -3

Three-year and two-year rule for filing refund claim

IRC 6511(a)

Withholdings and estimated tax considered paid on original due date

David H. Baral, 120 S. Ct. 1006 (2000)

Refunds of withholdings and estimated taxes on late-filed original return

Astrid E.A. Omohundro, 2002-2 USTC ¶50,590 (9th Cir. 2002) (siding with T. D. 8932 and Weisbart decision)

T. D. 8932, 2001-11 IRB 813, amending Reg. §301.7502-1(f) to reflect IRS acquiescence to Weisbart, 222 F.3d (2d Cir. 2000)

Emanuel Weisbart, 222 F.3d 93 (2d Cir. 2000) (Acq; 2000-48 IRB)

Faye Anastasoff, 235 F.3d 1054 (8th Cir. 2000), vacating original decision at 223 F.3d 898 (8th Cir. 2000)

Tax Court refunds for delinquent filers

IRC §6512 (b)(3) (allowing three-year lookback period barred under 1996 Supreme Court Lundy decision)

Robert Lundy, 116 S. Ct. 647 (1996)

Suspension of limitations period during period of disability

IRC §6511(h)(1) (reverses effect of Supreme Court's Brockamp decision in certain cases)

Marian Brockamp, 117 S. Ct. 849 (1997)

Financial disability standard not met

Matthias Haller, TC Memo 2010-147

Richard J. Pleconis Sr., D.C.N.J. 8/10/2011

Bad debt and worthless securities

IRC §6511(d)(1)

Divorce and net operating loss carryback

Rev. Rul. 75-368, 1975-2 CB 480

Net operating loss carryback

IRC §6511(d)(2)

Credit against future estimated tax liability

IRC §6402(b)

Refund diversion for overdue child support

IRC §6402(c)

Refund withheld if debt owed federal agency

IRC §6402(d)

Extension for Armed Forces combat zone service

IRC §7508

Payment with request for extension of time to file

Troy W. Ott, 98-1 USTC ¶50,331 (9th Cir. 1998)

47.3 STATING THE REASONS FOR REFUND CLAIM

Reg. §301.6402-2(b)

Form 1040-X

47.4 QUICK REFUND CLAIMS

IRC §6411

Reg. §1.6411-1(a)

Tax-shelter refunds

Rev. Proc. 84-84, 1984-2 CB 782

47.5 INTEREST PAID ON REFUND CLAIMS

IRC §6611

IRS interest rates through December 31, 2023

IR 2023-154

Rev. Rul. 2023-17, 2023-37 IRB 798

Same interest rate for deficiencies and refunds

IRC §6621(a)

Interest from date of overpayment

Reg. §301.6611-1(a)

Interest to 30 days before date of refund check

IRC §6611(b)(2)

Interest on net operating loss carryback

IRC §6611(f)

Reg. §301.6611-1(e)

45-day rule for original returns

IRC §6611(e)(1)

IRC §6664(d) (reasonable cause exception to penalty)

Relying on professional advice not always a penalty excuse

Terry L. Wright, TC Memo 2014-175

Hector Sanchez, TC Memo 2014-174

How the accuracy-related penalty is figured

Yltzchok D. Rand, 141 TC No. 12 (2013)

Penalty for failure to disclose reportable transactions

IRC §6707A, as amended by Small Business Jobs Act of 2010, P.L. 111-240, 9/27/10

To avoid negligence penalties, reasonable reliance

Herbert T. Cobey, Jr., 67 TCM 24 (1994)

Negligence or disregard of rules or regulations

IRC §6662(b)(1) and (c)

Reg. §1.6662-3

Negligence penalty applies to entire underpayment: prior law

Asphalt Products Co. Inc., 482 U.S. 117 (1987)

Disclosure prevents penalties

Emmanuel Fellouzis, 95-1 USTC ¶50,287 (D. Fl. 1995)

Information returns

IRC §6721-6724

Reasonable cause exception for accuracy-related penalties

IRC §6664(c)

Reg. §1.6664-4

Reasonable basis required for disclosed position on return

IRC §6662(d)(2)(B)(ii)

Temp. Reg. §1.6662-7T

Reg. §1.6664-4

Proposed Regulation §1.6664-4

Substantial understatement of tax

IRC §6662(d) (1) (A) (general rule)

IRC §6662(d)(1) (C) (threshold reduced to 5% if any QBI deduction claimed)

Shiraz Noormohamed Lakhani, 142 TC No.8 (2014) (CPA subject to penalty for claiming gambling losses)

Anthony J. Pasqualini, et al., 68 TCM 89 (1994)

Substantial understatement

William Woods II, 91 TC 11 (1988)

Isolated error transcribing data entry to tax software-reasonable cause for substantial understatement

*Kurt C. Olsen, TC Summary Opinion 2011-131

Substantial valuation misstatement

IRC §6662(e)

Reg. §1.6662-5

Fraud penalty

Mark W. May, 137 TC No. 11 (2011)

IRC §6663

Frivolous return penalty

IRC §6702

Martin Bradley, 817 F.2d 1400 (9th Cir. 1987)

Criminal fraud and false statements

IRC §7206

Criminal willful evasion

IRC §7201

Criminal penalty for willful failure to pay or file

IRC §7203

Failure to file partnership return

IRC §6698

Failure to report Social Security number of dependents

IRC §6724(d)(3)(D)

Bad check

IRC §6657

Reg. §301.6657-1

Interest on penalties

IRC §6601(e)(2)(A)

Higher interest on certain penalties

IRC §6601(e)(2)(B)

Reliance on erroneous written IRS advice

IRC §6404(f)

Undervaluation on gift or estate tax return

IRC §6662(g) (20% penalty)

IRC §6662(h)(2)(C) (40% penalty)

48.7 PENALTIES FOR NOT REPORTING FOREIGN FINANCIAL ACCOUNTS

Instructions to Form TD F 90-22.1 (FBAR) and Form 8938 (Statement of Specified Foreign Financial Assets)

Offshore Voluntary Compliance Program (OVDP) ended 9-28-18

News Release IR-2018-176

Filing deadline change for FBAR reporting

Section 2006(b)(11) of the Surface Transportation and Veterans Health Choice Improvement Act of 2015, P.L. 114-41, 7/31/15

Treasury Announcement, 12-16-16,

https://www.fincen.gov/news/news-releases/new-due-date-fbars-0 (April 15 due date for FBARs)

Foreign online gambling accounts and FBAR reporting

John C. Hom, CA-9, 7/26/16, at http://cdn.ca9.uscourts.gov/datastore/memoranda/2016/07/26/14-16214.pdf

IRS simplifies reporting for taxpayers with Canadian retirement plans

Rev. Proc. 2014-55, 2014-44 IRB 753

Civil penalties for not filing FBAR

31 U.S.C. Section 5321 (a) (5)

Penalty for failure to file Form 8938

IRC §6038D(d)

Penalty for underpaying tax related to undisclosed specified foreign financial asset

IRC §6662(j)(3)

48.8 AGREEING TO THE AUDIT CHANGES

Waiver of restrictions on assessment

IRC §6213(d)

48.9 DISPUTING THE AUDIT CHANGES

* IRS Publication 5

Fast Track Settlement (FTS) for self-employed

Rev. Proc. 2017-25, 2017-14 IRB 1039

IRS not barred from challenge because of prior inaction

* James Ramone Taylor, TC Summary Opinion 2017-4

Telephone conversation qualifies as hearing

Scott William Katz, 115 TC No. 26 (2000)

Petition to Tax Court

IRC §6213

IRC §741-7465

IRS failure to specify deadline for Tax Court petition

Virgil B. Elings, 324 F.3d 1110 (9th Cir. 2003)

James Rochelle, 293 F.3d 740 (5th Cir. 2002), aff'g per curiam 116 TC 356 (2001)

Eric E. Smith, 275 F.3d 912 (10th Cir. 2001)

Using wrong delivery service for Tax Court petition misses deadline

Marcius J. Scaggs, TC Memo 2012-258

Small tax cases ($50,000 or less)

IRC §7463

Civil action for refund

IRC §7422

IRS provides mediation option

Rev. Proc. 2014-63, 2014-53 IRB 1014

Supreme Court says IRS lien overrides tenancy by the entirety

U.S. v. Sandra L. Craft, 2002-1 USTC ¶50,361 (Sup. Ct. 2002)

Howard D. and Sheila A. Popky, Third Circuit, 5/17/05, affirming Pennsylvania District Court, 6/15/04

Lien on commissions

Jefferson-Pilot Life Insurance Co., 37 F.3d 1495 (4th Cir., 1994)

Penalty on taxpayer for frivolous Tax Court action

IRC §6673(a)(1)

Nis Family Trust, 115 TC No. 523 (2000)

Ronald W. Davenport, TC Memo 2009-248

Mary Lynn Collard, 2009-2 USTC ¶50,746 (5th Cir. 2009)

W. James Kubon, TC Memo 2011-41

Scott Ray Holmes, TC Memo 2011-31

Penalty on attorney for Tax Court delay

IRC §6673(a)(2)

Nis Family Trust, 115 TC 523 (2000)

Appeals court penalty where appeal from Tax court is frivolous or intended to delay

IRC §7482(c)(4)

Federal district court penalizes attorney for frivolous tax-protestor arguments

Donald Zimmerman, District Court, Eastern District of California, 2001-1 USTC ¶50,107, adopting findings at ¶50,106

IRS can reopen an estate audit despite closing letter

IRC §6404(e)

Robert A. Strang, TC Memo 2001-104 (no interest abatement for IRS delay due to workload)

Estate of Bommer, 69 TCM 2541 (1995)

IRS may abate interest charges

IRC §6404(e)(i)(B)

Reg. §301.6404-2

48.10 Offer in Compromise

IRC §7122

Reg. §301.7122-1(c)(3) (economic hardship)

* Form 656-B (Offer in Compromise Booklet)

OIC pre-qualifier (online tool)

https://irs.treasury.gov/oic_pre_qualifier/

Post-appeal mediation program for OIC

Rev. Proc. 2014-63, 2014-53 IRB 1014

IRS not required to re-open OIC

Tom Reed, 141 TC No. 7 (2013)

Partial payments required with submission

IRC §7122(c)

Notice 2006-68, 2006-31 IRB 105

Offers deemed accepted if not rejected within a certain period

IRC §7122(f)

48.11 Recovering Costs of a Tax Dispute

IRC §7430

Limit on attorney fee awards

Rev. Proc. 2022-38, 2022-45 IRB 445 (for 2023)

Rev. Proc. 2021-45, 2021-48 IRB 764 (for 2022)

Rev. Proc. 2020-45, 2020-46 IRB 1016 (for 2021)

Rev. Proc. 2019-44, 2019-47 IRB 1093 (for 2020)

Rev. Proc. 2018-57, 2018-49 IRB 827 (for 2019)

Attorney can't sue IRS for fees

David B. Greenberg, 147 TC No. 13 (2016)

Net worth limitation in recovery of legal fees

IRC §7430(c)(4)(D)

Expenses of administrative proceedings

IRC 7430(c)(2) and (c)(7)

Exhausting administrative remedies

Reg. §301.7430-1

Substantially justified same as reasonableness test

Ronald Sokol, 92 TC 760 (1989)

Tax expertise does not support increased award

Walter J. Levy, 63 TCM 2927 (1992)

Robert T. Cozean, 109 TC 227 (1997)

Higher attorneys' fees not awarded for tax law competency

Caspian Consulting Group, Inc., TC Memo 2006-85

Winning the dispute does not guarantee legal fees

Benjamin Harrison, 69 TCM 1969 (1995)

Legal fees disallowed

Walker B. Fite, 67 TCM 2794 (1994) (IRS position held justified)

Laura E. Austin, TC Memo 1997-157

Legal fee award for excessive IRS penalties

David Heasley, 967 F.2d 116 (5th Cir. 1992), rev'g 61 TCM 2503 (1991)

Penalty for bringing frivolous suit against the IRS

IRC §6673(b)(1)

IRS concession no guarantee of award

Ronald Sokol, 92 TC 760 (1989)

Pre-1986 cases: IRS pre-litigation position considered

Comer Family Trust, 856 F.2d 775 (6th Cir. 1988)

Sylvia Sliva, 839 F.2d 602 (9th Cir. 1988)

David Kaufman, 758 F.2d 1 (1st Cir. 1985)

David Powell, 791 F.2d 385 (5th Cir. 1986)

Pre-1986 cases: Only IRS litigating position considered

Robert Baker, 83 TC 822 (1984), aff'd 787 F.2d 637 (D.C. Cir. 1986)

Eva Wickert, 842 F.2d 1005 (8th Cir. 1988)

Ewing and Thomas, P.A., 803 F.2d 613 (11th Cir. 1986)

Balanced Financial Management Inc., 769 F.2d 1440 (10th Cir. 1985)

Refund of third party's tax payment allowed

Lori Williams, 115 S. Ct. 1611 aff'g 24 F.3d 1143 (9th Cir. 1995)

48.12 Suing the IRS for Unauthorized Collection

IRC 7433

Reg. §301.7433-1

Sovereign immunity does not preclude award of emotional distress damages for IRS' willful violation of automatic bankruptcy stay

Jonathan Eldon Hunsaker, Case No. 16-35991 (9th. Cir; 8/30/2018)

Suing the IRS for wrongfully failing to release

IRC 7432

Unauthorized IRS sales

Carole Marshall, 921 F. Supp. 641 (D. Minn. 1996)

Commissions paid to independent contractor subject to continuous wage levy

Jefferson-Pilot Life Insurance Co., 49 F.3d 1020 (4th Cir. 1995), aff'g 95-1 USTC ¶50,263 (1994)

PART 11

Practice Before the IRS

Due to the IRS's inability to examine *every* return, the policy of examining returns is determined by a preliminary inspection, specifically looking for indications of the highly possible source of potential tax deficiency.

Returns are rated for audit according to a mathematical formula called the discriminant function system (DIF). In recent years, the IRS has audited fewer returns overall, but has increased audits of high-income taxpayers, Schedule C filers, S corporation and tax-shelter investors.

Taxpayers selected for an audit are advised of their right to be represented by a certified public accountant, attorney, or enrolled agent. Once the taxpayer has chosen a representative, the IRS may not interview the taxpayer alone, unless consent is given.

In the first IRS notice of proposed tax deficiency, 32198, the IRS will show the filing discrepancies, and provide the taxpayer a clear and complete explanation of the administrative process, from examination to petitioning the Tax Court.

The IRS's protocols to examine tax returns and to respond to preliminary and follow-up requests from taxpayer or their advisor are set forth by strict rules governing audits and collection. The IRS is restricted in it's ability to conduct audits and collect taxes due by the available resources at the time of the audit. The Inflation Reduction Act of 2022 allocated an additional $80 billion to the IRS over a ten-year period, in part to address growing taxpayer and tax practitioner frustration regarding the responsiveness of the IRS to general tax matters.

HOW RETURNS ARE EXAMINED

Preliminary Examination

Correspondence notices are used to correct the following types of obvious errors spotted at IRS Service Centers: medical expenses under the applicable adjusted gross income limitation; limits on disaster losses; auto mileage rates for business transportation in excess of the IRS mileage allowance; and income on Form W-2, Form 1099, or Schedule K-1 incorrectly reported on a tax return. Taxpayers are advised by mail of the corrections and if additional tax is due. The taxpayer may request an interview or submit additional information if he or she disagrees with the adjustments. If the corrections are made and the additional tax is paid before the due date of the return, the taxpayer may avoid interest charges.

If an underpayment of tax results from a mathematical or clerical error, the IRS may use a summary assessment procedure. However, the IRS must give the taxpayer an explanation of the error, and time to file a request for the abatement of the assessment. The IRS must honor that request (IRC §6213(b)(2)). After the IRS has provided the taxpayer with an explanation of error, normal deficiency procedures must be followed. These summary procedures are used for the following types of mathematical and clerical errors: (1) arithmetic errors (addition, subtraction, multiplication, or division); (2) errors in transferring amounts on the tax forms; (3) missing schedules or forms; (4) incorrect use of any Treasury table; and (5) entries that exceed statutory limitations. Summary procedures also apply to the omission of a correct Social Security number by a taxpayer claiming the dependent care tax credit, child tax credit, higher education credits, or the earned income credit (IRC §6213 (g)(2)).

Where an arithmetic error is made by an IRS representative who is helping a taxpayer prepare their return, the IRS may abate any interest due on the underpayment of tax for any period ending on or before the 30th day following the date of notice and demand for payment of the deficiency (IRC §6404(d)).

Interest Abatement Due to IRS Delay

The IRS may abate interest charges attributable to IRS procedural or mechanical errors that unreasonably delay processing of a deficiency, such as delays resulting from the loss of records, IRS personnel transfers, or extended training, illness, or leave of IRS personnel (IRC §6404(e)(1)(A)). Interest is not eligible for abatement if a delay is related to general administrative decisions including IRS work priorities, discretionary judgments, or decisions concerning the application of the tax laws. An abatement request is made on Form 843.

The Tax Court may review whether the IRS has abused its discretion in failing to abate interest if the taxpayer meets the net worth and size requirements for recovering attorneys' fees (IRC §6404(h)). An eligible taxpayer must file a petition and pay a $60 filing fee (unless hardship is shown); *see* Tax Court Rule 281 for petition details.

Types of Personal Examinations

A specific examination of a tax return may be by correspondence, at a local IRS office, or at the taxpayer's place of business, office, or home. An examination at an IRS office or by correspondence is called a desk or office examination; an examination at a place of business or home is called a field examination. The complexity of the transactions reported on a return generally determines whether a return will be subject to an office or field examination.

An office examination is initiated by a letter of notification listing the items to be examined. The agent will ordinarily not go beyond these items. However, the agent may, in his or her discretion, extend an office examination to other items reported on the tax filing, or open the scope of the examination to other tax filing years. A field examination may involve a review of the entire return.

A correspondence examination is used to question simple individual returns. The taxpayer is asked to explain a particular item or to send supporting evidence regarding the specific item. A correspondence examination may end up as an interview type of office examination or a field examination. A taxpayer can keep a correspondence examination from turning into a office or field examination by providing satisfactory answers to correspondence. If you feel that a correspondence examination is impractical to handle the concerns or that it places you at a disadvantage, request an office examination conference. Practitioners generally feel that the absence of personal contact and discussion is a disadvantage.

You may request a transfer of a case from an office examination to a field examination. Requests for transfers have been granted in cases of voluminous records or physical incapacity. A request will be denied if it is clear that you have no legitimate reason for the transfer.

A field examination may be shifted to the office of the taxpayer's representative if he or she has the client's records and it is more convenient to hold the examination there. It may be possible to use videoconferencing instead of meeting in person; however a request for videoconferencing must be granted to large businesses, as yet there is no similar mandate for individuals.

An individual taxpayer may appear at an examination in his or her own behalf, and a corporation may be represented by an officer. The preparer of a tax return may, if authorized, represent the client before an agent in connection with the return, although the preparer is not enrolled to practice before the IRS. An attorney, enrolled agent, or CPA may also represent a taxpayer before the IRS.

If you represent a taxpayer, file IRS Form 2848, power of attorney. Indicate on Form 2848 that you would like to receive all correspondence involving the examination. In your correspondence with the IRS, always reference the IRS code symbols found on the IRS's letter. Before the examination, review not only the return in question but also the records of prior examinations of the client's return. The agent has reviewed these records and will use them as a starting point for the present examination.

Restrictions on IRS Examinations of Books

The IRS may not make more than one examination of a taxpayer's books of accounts for any taxable period unless the taxpayer requests otherwise, or the IRS, after investigation, notifies the taxpayer in writing that an additional inspection is necessary (IRC §7605(b)). However, this restriction does not bar the IRS from examining public records or bank accounts. Nor does it bar examination of the books of a third party, such as the taxpayer's corporation, unless the identities of the taxpayer and his or her corporation are so inextricable that the examination of the books of one constitutes an examination of the books of the other.

A taxpayer may protest a second examination by refusing to give the agent access to his books. The IRS may then issue a summons. If the taxpayer still refuses access, the IRS may seek enforcement of the summons in district court. The taxpayer then has the opportunity to present the lack of neccesity for a second examination in front of the district court.

The IRS tries to avoid examining the same items appearing on a taxpayer's returns for more than one year, such as the treatment of installment sale payments. Take, for example, where the taxpayer's return was examined in either of the two years prior to the current examination for the same items, and that examination resulted in no change in tax liability. In a situation like this, the IRS will suspend the current examination, upon the taxpayer's notifying the appointment clerk or the examiner, pending a review of its files to determine whether the examination should proceed. If the IRS decides to proceed with the examination, the taxpayer has no recourse.

The IRS may not conduct audits based on financial status or "economic reality" to determine if income was omitted from a return unless there is a reasonable likelihood that income has not been reported (IRC §7602(e)).

Administrative Appeal Procedures Applicable to an Examined Return

It is important to follow IRS administrative appeal procedures to lay a basis for recovering from the IRS litigation costs and for shifting the burden of proof in a later noncriminal court case. If the IRS takes an unreasonable position at an audit and the dispute goes to court, you may not recover an award for litigation costs unless you have exhausted administrative remedies within the IRS (IRC §7430(b)(1)).

Similarly, you may not shift the burden of proof to the IRS if you did not exhaust all administrative appeals. In tax litigation, there is a presumption in favor of the IRS' determination of tax liability. This requires a taxpayer to come forward with evidence to disprove the IRS' determinations by a "preponderance of the evidence." A taxpayer may in a court action shift the burden of proof to the IRS with respect to factual issues relevant in determining tax liability. However, before the burden is shifted, the taxpayer must show: (1) compliance with substantiation and record-keeping requirements imposed by the Code or IRS regulations; and (2) cooperation with reasonable requests by the IRS for meetings, information, and access to witnesses, as well as exhaustion of all IRS administrative appeals (IRC §7491).

How to Handle the Examination

Common sense rules of courtesy should be your guide in regards to your contacts with the agent, whether in person or remotely. Avoid personality clashes; they can only interfere with a speedy and fair resolution of the examination. However, be firm in your approach and, if the agent appears to be unreasonable, make it clear that, if necessary, you will go all the way to court to prove your point. A vacillating approach may weaken your position in reaching a settlement.

If a taxpayer authorizes a practitioner to handle the audit, the taxpayer should not be present during discussions with the agent. The taxpayer can add nothing to the discussion that the practitioner does not already know after becoming thoroughly acquainted with the return. The taxpayer may damage the case by volunteering information harmful to his or her position.

In a field audit, the agent will want to review original books and records. If the agent also wants supporting secondary records, ask him or her to give you a list of needs, which you can then present as a unit.

Original records should not be taken out of your client's office; give copies of relevant records to the agent. Do not volunteer data. The agent will ask for any addititonal information needed. Try to provide an adequate area for the agent to work in.

After the review and before the audit report is prepared, the agent will discuss his or her findings and recommendations. At this stage, disputes generally involve questions of fact. The agent will readily use discretion in compromising issues of fact where, for example, there are inadequate primary records but there is other convincing evidence that the taxpayer has made a valid claim. As for conflicting interpretations of law, the agent will abide by well-defined IRS policy. The agent will not lean to an interpretation conflicting with or not covered by IRS policy. Compromises involving open issues or conflicts between IRS and court positions are possible at a higher level conference in the Appeals office. Occasionally, a disputed point in an examination may be resolved by asking the IRS for technical advice.

In some instances, you may be asked by the agent to submit a legal memorandum. This may be a signal that the agent is not sure of the legal issues involved in your case and wants your help. You are not required to do this and may refuse where the memo might reveal more of your case than you would care to divulge. However, where the facts are not in dispute and you feel a clarification of the law might expedite the case, a memo may be advisable. Keep in mind that any documentation submitted to the agent becomes part of the record that will pass through the levels of the IRS review.

Also be alert to the possibility that the agent may be developing a fraud issue. If you suspect such a possibility, consider whether you should allow the agent to *see* further records that may be incriminating. Also consider contacting a practitioner experienced in tax fraud issues.

Your readiness to compromise will depend on the extent of the agent's examination and the amount of the proposed deficiency or refund. Sometimes an agent will pick up one point but fail to develop another that could lead to a substantial deficiency. Here, it may be tactically advisable to accept the proposal. Pursuing the case beyond this point might lead to the possibility of opening the audit to other items on the return.

If You Agree with the Examiner

When you agree to the agent's proposed changes, your client generally will be asked to sign a Form 4549, "Income Tax Examination Changes," (or Form 4549-A, "Income Tax Examination Changes (Unagreed and Excepted Agreed)" or Form 4549-E, "Income Tax Discrepancy Adjustments") and a Form 870, "Waiver of Restrictions on Assessment and Collection of Deficiency in Tax and Acceptance of Overassessment," or other appropriate agreement form. When signed, the agreement permits an immediate assessment of a deficiency.

The only advantage in signing is to stop interest accruing on the tax deficiency within 30 days after the date the waiver is filed. In an overassessment, that is, where a refund is due, a signed waiver is merely an acknowledgment of the overassessment.

A signed Form 870 does not prevent the IRS from reopening the case to assess an additional deficiency. If on review the deficiency is increased, you will receive a revised Form 870. Your client can refuse to sign the form. The signed first form has the effect of stopping the interest on the original deficiency. As a matter of practice, however, waivers or acceptances ordinarily result in a closing of the case.

If your client signs a Form 870 after a formal deficiency notice (90-day letter) has been mailed, his or her right to appeal to the Tax Court is retained. However, if Form 870 is signed before a deficiency notice has been mailed, your client loses the right to appeal to the Tax Court. An appeal to the Tax Court may not be made, but a suit for a refund may still be filed unless your client agrees on the form not to seek a refund.

The payment of the tax before the deficiency notice is mailed is, in effect, a waiver of the restrictions on assessment and collection. If the payment satisfies your client's entire tax liability for that year, an appeal cannot be made to the Tax Court. The taxpayer's only recourse is to sue for a refund in either the district court or U.S. Court of Federal Claims.

If a refund is due and a Form 870 is signed, you may file a protective refund claim. Generally, an agent will process the refund, but if he or she fails to do so or the review staff puts it aside for some reason and the limitation period expires, the refund will be lost. The refund claim will protect your client from such a mishap.

An Agreed Case Is Always Reviewed

Once a Form 4549 and Form 870 are signed, the agent prepares the audit report, which is reviewed by the agent's supervisor. While the agent's report is approved in most cases, do not assume that this review is a mere formality. Agreed cases receive closer review than unagreed cases. Once approved, an agreed case has, except for isolated cases, "reached the end of the line." A reviewer thus realizes that he or she has a greater responsibility in checking the agreed case than in an unagreed case where the facts and law may be reviewed several times as the case proceeds through administrative channels. The reviewer will check the following points:

Facts appearing in the agent's report and in the return filed by the taxpayer. The reviewer may find facts that the agent overlooked or emphasize facts that did not appear important to the agent.

Agent's Interpretation And Application of the Code's Provisions to the Facts in the Case

Agent's judgment. The taxpayer might not have substantiated all of the deductions claimed with primary evidence, but the agent allowed a portion of the deduction based on secondary evidence. The reviewer may question the judgment of the agent or believe that the agent was too lenient. The agent may try to justify his or her position, but if the reviewer and agent cannot agree, the chief reviewer will resolve the problem.

Other tax returns. Where an individual's return shows income from an estate, trust, or partnership, the reviewer will usually ask the agent to check the estate, trust, or partnership return, or to transfer the case to an agent who may be examining one of these returns.

Tax returns of prior tax years. The agent may be required to examine the facts on prior returns. The inquiry may result in the development of new facts that may widen the scope of the audit. The number of ways in which a reviewer may develop new facts depends only on his or her ingenuity, experience, and zeal. Therefore, remember that even after an agreement is signed (Form 870), the agent may ask for additional facts, and confront you with new interpretations.

You will not be allowed to argue your case directly with the reviewer. You may be sure that the initial auditing-agent will present your case in the best light if for no other reason than to justify his or her own judgment.

What to Do If You Disagree with the Agent

If you disagree with the agent at an office examination, the agent is required to explain the adjustments and available appeal rights. If you desire an immediate conference with the agent's supervisor, it will be granted if practicable. In most cases, mediation may be requested through the IRS' Fast Track Mediation process to help resolve the dispute. You may withdraw from mediation at any time and either party may reject the mediator's proposals; see IRS Publication 3605, Fast Track Mediation—Collection: A Process for Prompt Resolution of Tax Issues.

If no agreement can be reached, you will receive a copy of the examination report and a 30-day letter providing the following alternatives: (1) You can agree to the proposed adjustments and sign enclosed Forms 4549 and 870; (2) you can request an Appeals office conference by written protest or small case request; or (3) you may ignore the letter, in which case you will eventually receive a statutory notice of deficiency (90-day letter).

If you disagree with the agent at the field examination, he or she will prepare a complete examination report fully explaining the proposed adjustments. The agent will then send it to the review staff for a technical and procedural review. If the review staff agrees with the agent, you will receive a 30-day letter, as in the case of the office examination. The 30-day letter is accompanied by a copy of the examination report and a detailed explanation of the available appeal procedures, with a request that you inform the IRS of your choice of action. You have the following alternatives:

1. Sign a Form 4549 and a Form 870 (which preclude appeal to the Tax Court);

2. Request an Appeals office conference by written protest or small case request;

3. Ignore the 30-day letter and wait for the statutory notice of deficiency (90-day letter); or

4. Pay the tax and file a claim for refund.

A 30-day letter is not required by the Code and, if the IRS wants to, it may choose to send you the 90-day letter. The 30-day letter is merely an additional attempt by the IRS to settle the case without going to trial. If necessary, you may get additional time to file your protest or a small case request. However, if the limitation period for the assessment of tax is running out on the tax year in question, you will get neither a 30-day letter nor an extension unless you sign a waiver extending the limitation period.

Should You Ask for a Conference?

The answer lies in the nature of your disagreement with the auditing agent. You may feel his or her authority to accept proposals for settlement is too limited. You may believe the agent has overemphasized certain facts or has disregarded or failed to give proper weight to other facts. Perhaps he or she has misinterpreted applicable tax law or misapplied it to your case. The agent may even have ignored law that supports your claim.

The very existence of the conference procedure is in itself a recognition that your objection to the agent's decision may be right. If the IRS were convinced that the auditing agent was always correct, there would be no purpose to the conferences.

It is usually advisable to take your case to the Appeals office. The chances of a settlement are favorable. Most cases are settled in conference. Although before going ahead, consider these points:

1. When the IRS has an established policy regarding the disputed issue, taking a case further in the IRS usually gains nothing. All IRS personnel are bound by the same rules.

2. Interest continues to accrue. It does not stop unless you make a cash deposit.

3. The IRS will find out your position on all issues. If the case comes to trial, there can be no element of surprise.

4. The IRS can always find additional issues.

Appealing Your Case

You start an appeal by filing either a written protest or a small case request.

You can make a small case request if the total amount of the IRS' proposed change in tax, penalties, and interest for a tax year is $25,000 or less. You can use Form 12203 to make a small case request, or you can simply send in a letter asking for a review of the IRS' proposed changes, noting the changes to which you object and your reasons. However, no small case requests are allowed for tax disputes of any amount involving partnerships, S corporations, employee plans, and exempt organizations.

When the total in dispute for any tax year (tax, interest, and penalties) exceeds $25,000, you must file a formal written protest. There is no special form for the protest. The important thing is to include information and arguments that will present your case in the best light to the appeals officer.

Seven specific points must be included in the protest:

1. Taxpayer's name, address, and daytime telephone number.

2. Date and symbols on the 30-day letter transmitting the proposed adjustments.

3. Years covered and the amounts of tax liability in dispute for each year. List here only the amount of the proposed deficiency with which you disagree. This is often less than the entire proposed deficiency.

4. An itemized schedule of the agent's findings with which you disagree. Make sure you cover every item contested. Where more than one finding is involved, list each separately and number it.

5. A statements of the facts supporting your position for each of the items named in (4). Use separate numbered paragraphs for each issue; make sure the number of each paragraph corresponds with the number of the item in (4) that it covers.

6. A statement of the law on which you rely for each of the items listed in (4); use separate paragraphs, numbered to correspond with the items in (4).

7. A request for a hearing with the Appeals office. You must make such request in the protest. Otherwise, you will get no hearing and the case will be decided on the basis of what you submit as your protest.

The most important part of the protest is the presentation of your arguments. These you divide into three parts: (1) Give the arguments in summary form, numbered. (2) Provide a statement of facts covering the disputed items. (3) Develop each argument and support it by citations of authority.

- Separate protests do not have to be filed if more than one tax year is involved. All the tax years covered in the 30-day letter may be covered in one protest.

- An original and a copy of the protest must be filed.

- Stress the equities of your case. A case that shows that a decision against you would be unfair may be stronger than one where you have the technicalities on your side.

- Write the facts so that they can be understood. They should be clear and accurate. List them in the order in which they happened.

- Do not omit the facts that seem to be against you. When explained, they may not be as detrimental to your case as they first appear.

- Substantiate the facts with exhibits, affidavits, or any other proof.

- Try to avoid unimportant facts that are not relevant to the issue. Make sure you understand the principles of law affecting any fact you state. Otherwise, the argument you will later make may be weak.

- Discuss the issues in the order of their importance. Leave the least important for last. Say what and who is involved.

- Write short descriptive headings before each issue. Repeat important facts if they help your argument.

- Summarize your point and show how it applies to your case.

- Sometimes a short quotation from a leading case is effective if you can relate the case to your facts.

- Be sure that every case you cite stands for what you say it does.
- Try to put yourself in the place of the conferee who is going to read the protest. Ask yourself what you would want to know in order to answer the questions, and then try to supply the information.
- Take the time to write a well-organized, succinct, and interesting protest.
- Consider the appearance of the letter. Give it eye appeal. Use side heads to break up solid pages of type. Sometimes graphs, photographs, charts, and other illustrations help make your point in an attractive manner.

How the protest is signed. The taxpayer must certify, under penalty of perjury, that the statements of facts in the protest are true. Add the following signed statement to the protest: "Under penalties of perjury, I declare that the facts stated in this protest and in any accompanying documents are true, correct, and complete to the best of my knowledge and belief."

If you as the taxpayer's representative submit the protest, a substitute declaration may be used, stating that you prepared the protest and indicating whether you personally know that the statements of facts are true and correct. A power of attorney should be attached to the protest, if not previously filed.

If, after reading a protest, a reviewer believes that there is a basis for settlement, he or she will refer the case back for settlement. For this reason, make sure that your protest presents your case well so that a reviewer can have a basis for such a decision.

How the Appeals Office Operates

The 2019 Taxpayer First Act established the Internal Revenue Service Independent Office of Appeals (IRC §7803 (e)). The 2019 Act renamed the IRS Office of Appeals to include "Independent" to stress its impartiality; it also included some additional taxpayer protections Appeals' role is to settle disputes in a fair and impartial manner that favors neither the government nor the taxpayer. It attempts to resolve cases after IRS compliance functions (Accounts Management, Collection, and Examination) have made a determination with which the taxpayer disagrees. It does not perform compliance actions. More information about the Independent Office of Appeals is in FAQs at https://www.irs.gov/pub/irs-utl/office_of_appeals_faqs.pdf.

In the Appeals office, your case is assigned to an appeals officer. After he or she becomes acquainted with your case, the officer sets the time of the conference. If it is inconvenient, you may ask for another date or time. The IRS Independent Office of Appeals' initial contact letter, as revised in 2022, advises that taxpayers and representatives can choose a conference with Appeals through telephone, video, or in person. Contacts with Appeals are also permitted through the mail or secure electronic messaging. The initial contact letter also now provides the name and phone number of the Appeals officer's manager, "in the rare instance additional help is needed."

An immediate hearing may be granted if you have some unusual reason for it. The hearing may be held in a regional Appeals office, a local branch of the Service, or "on circuit" (Appeals officers sometimes travel to outlying districts to save taxpayers the expense and time involved in a trip to a metropolitan area).

The Appeals office is separated functionally from the Examination Division. The major purpose of the separation is to provide an appellate procedure that, organizationally at least, will tend to produce free and unbiased opinions. An officer in the Appeals office is not responsible to the Revenue Agent and his or her supervisor. Thus, the officer is less likely to be unduly influenced by the conclusions reached in that office and more likely to reach decisions objectively. The officer does not need, and does not seek, the approval of the Revenue Agent or the agent's supervisor for any decisions made.

To ensure the independence of the Appeals process, the IRS by law must prohibit ex parte communications between Appeals employees and other IRS personnel to the extent that such communications appear to compromise Appeals' independence (Section 1001(a) of the IRS Restructuring Act of 1998, P.L.105-206).

When you protest the conclusions reached in the Examination Division, the entire case file is sent to the Appeals office, and the Examination Division's control over the case ceases.

A primary concern of the Appeals office is the statute of limitations. If not much time is available, the case may not be transmitted to an Appeals office unless at least 120 days remain before the limitations period expires. As a condition to appellate review, a taxpayer may be asked to sign either a Form 872, "Consent to Extend the Time to Assess Tax" or a Form 872-A, "Special Consent to Extend the Time to Assess Tax."

In the majority of cases, neither the agent nor any other representative of the Examination Division will attend your conference with the appeals officer. If, in a few situations, the agent does attend a conference, it will be at the invitation of the Appeals office and only for the purpose of establishing the facts. Since you are appealing from the recommendations of the agent, do not re-argue the case with him or her. Your sole problem will be to convince the appeals officer. In all cases, however, you should remember that the officer has a copy of the agent's recommendations and confidential report, which you never see.

Cases that reach the Appeals office after the 90-day letter has been issued are known as "90-day cases." Conferences at this stage are not easily granted. You must generally show that you have not had a previous conference for reasons beyond your control, and there is a reasonable expectation that a settlement will be reached.

The settlement authority in the Appeals office is broader than in the Examination Division. The Appeals office may trade or split issues where substantial uncertainties exist either in law or in fact, or in both, as to the correct application of the law. They may also settle issues based on their judgment as to the hazards of litigation. The agents have no authority to consider litigation hazards. One explanation for the reluctance of district office personnel to close a case is that they realize there is another administrative step following theirs. If they have any doubts about the acceptability of a settlement proposal, they can resolve their doubts by recommending that the case be considered by the Appeals office. The appeals officer thinks in terms of the cost and possible result of extended litigation. Cases are generally settled on the "merit approach." That is, the merits of each issue are considered, regardless of the amount of tax involved. A second, less preferred method of settlement is on the basis of a flat sum or percentage of the dollars involved. This second method is limited in use and may not be used, for example, where an issue will recur in subsequent years or where the issue is present in other similar cases, unless they are all to be disposed of together upon the same basis.

Settlement authority of appeals officers may also depend on whether or not the issue is on an IRS appeals coordinated issue list. If the issue is on the list, the officer does not have independent settlement authority; he or she must submit the proposed settlement to a person within the regional office who is in charge of reviewing issues placed on the coordination list. If this person does not agree to the settlement, the appeals officer may present the dispute to an appeals director in the region for a decision. You will not be given the chance to argue your position at this stage because the appeal coordination list procedure is an internal administration measure through which the IRS attempts to provide a consistent national settlement policy on certain issues that involve large numbers of taxpayers.

How To Handle the Conference

The conference is held in an informal manner. No stenographic record is made. Testimony under oath is not taken. Your approach to the conference will vary, depending on whether your client wishes to settle, whether the issues in dispute are factual or legal, and how strong you feel your case is on a specific issue.

You can assume the conferee:

- **Has the agent's recitation of the facts, opinions, and recommendations**—all of which appear in a transmittal memo that you do not receive. He or she also has a record of the informal conference and copies of reports covering examinations of prior years.
- **Has read your protest** with your version of the facts and your arguments. He or she will read the cases you cite. When you cite a case, make sure that it is on point. If you cite it for the dicta incorporated in the opinion, indicate that fact. There is nothing more discouraging than wading through a case only to find that it is not on point. The appeals officer may well conclude that you do not understand the issue, that you think the conferee does not understand the issue, or that you believe the conferee is careless enough to accept citations without reading the cases. A conclusio like this will affect you adversely.
- **Knows the strengths and weaknesses of your position** and what you would settle for. If your case is the type that should be settled, the appeals officer has thought of possible settlements. As a general proposition, an officer would rather settle cases than send them to the Tax Court. Rarely is he or she more anxious to settle than you are.

You may bring witnesses. However, do not plan on using witnesses unless they are absolutely necessary and you are sure they will not testify beyond your objectives. Instead, you may want to present their statements in affidavit form. Facts brought up for the first time will be referred back to the Examination Division for reconsideration.

Sufficient time is given to present your side of the case. Additional hearings are granted as needed.

An attorney may become aware that his or her client has no hope of winning but is stalling the date of actual payment of the deficiency by going through the various appellate procedures. This tactic violates IRS rules of practice and professional canons of ethics.

Does It Pay to Settle Your Tax Dispute with the IRS?

Here are some approaches followed by practitioners:

- **If you want rapid settlement** of the dispute, consider using the Fast Track Settlement Program if you are a self-employed individual, which can resolve matters within 60 days of acceptance into the program. If you cannot use the program or do not want to and cannot convince the IRS of your position, consider paying the deficiency—then suing for refund in the District Court or Court of Federal Claims. But first check the docket of the District Court where you will sue. Some District Courts are as overloaded as the Tax Court.
- **In a dispute involving a difference of opinion over the facts,** accept a fair offer from the IRS. You may not do any better before the Tax Court. If the IRS refuses to accept any settlement offer, you may take your case to court. You will have to wait for a hearing, but you stand a good chance of getting a better break.
- **In a complicated case or one involving a difficult point of law,** the Tax Court is favored over the District Court. There is less risk of judicial misinterpretation of the tax law since the Tax Court judges are more familiar with the intricacies of the Code.
- **Where you have a question of fact** and your position is appealing to the average person, pay the deficiency and then sue for a refund in the District Court where a jury will determine the facts. In the Tax Court, the facts are determined by judges who may be less sympathetic to you than a jury might be. You are not entitled to a jury trial in Tax Court. Your case is also decided by a judge if you pay the deficiency and sue for a refund in the Court of Federal Claims.

What Happens When You Propose a Settlement

Settlement proposals are generally made orally but more complicated proposals may be in writing. If your proposal is accepted, you are asked to sign either a Form 870 or 870-AD. Form 870 is signed for a settlement based on a complete agreement with the changes originally recommended by the agent. In situations where the IRS makes concessions in reaching a settlement in the Appeals office, a conditional consent, Form 870-AD, is signed. Form 870-AD contains pledges against reopening; the Form 870 does not. This means that once a Form 870-AD is executed, the IRS may not make an additional assessment. If Form 870 is executed, it acts as a waiver of restriction on assessment when received whereas Form 870-AD is not effective until it is signed by the Commissioner of Internal Revenue or his or her delegate.

Form 870-AD has been called an informal closing agreement. It is an agreement not to file a claim for refund, except for overassessments shown on the agreement form and amounts attributed to a net operating loss carryback deduction. Similarly, the IRS agrees not to assert further deficiencies for the year in question, except where there is fraud, malfeasance, concealment, or misrepresentation of a material fact, an important mathematical error, an excessive tentative allowance of a net operating loss carryback or investment credit carryback, or deficiencies determined at a partnership-level audit or S corporation–level audit.

The effect of an 870-AD is one-sided. The taxpayer agrees to an immediate assessment of the deficiency, whereas the IRS does not agree to pay an immediate refund as, for example, where the agreement covers two years, and one year involves an overassessment. It may, therefore, be advisable to file a protective claim for refund at the same time as the Form 870-AD is signed, or at least before the expiration of the refund period for the year in question. The refund claim should be accompanied by a letter explaining that the purpose of the claim is to protect the taxpayer against an unfavorable disposition of the waiver issue, and that the claim will be withdrawn upon the IRS' favorable action on the waiver.

Whether or not Form 870-AD is binding to the IRS and the taxpayer as a closing agreement has been litigated. The decisions present conflicting opinions on the issue.

Filing a Form 870-AD does not automatically stop the accrual of interest. Interest stops 30 days after the date the IRS accepts the form. In any event, the accumulation of interest can be avoided by prepaying the deficiency.

After Form 870-AD is signed, the appeals officer presents the report to a reviewing officer, such as an Associate Chief. If the official approves the proposed settlement, he or she will accept the agreement and the case is then ready for closing.

What if the settlement on review is rejected by the Associate Chief or other official? He or she will then discuss the case with the appeals officer. If the case remains unapproved, you may ask for a hearing before the reviewer who turned down the settlement.

What if you do not submit a settlement or the appeals officer rejects your proposal? The officer then prepares the report together with a proposed statutory notice of deficiency. The report is sent to an Associate Chief or other official for review. If the official approves the report, the case is then reviewed by the Chief Appeals Officer. The statutory notice of deficiency is checked by the Regional Counsel. After final approval by both offices, a 90-day letter is then mailed to your client.

Cash Deposit Stops Interest Accrual on Potential Deficiency

An individual who faces a potentially large interest charge on a tax deficiency may cut off the accrual of interest by making a cash deposit (not actually in cash despite the name of the deposit) against a potential deficiency. Under Code Section 6603, a taxpayer can make a deposit with the IRS in order to suspend the accrual of interest on a potential underpayment of income, gift, estate, or generation-skipping transfer tax that has not yet been assessed by the IRS.

Under IRS guidelines provided in Rev. Proc. 2005-18, 2005-13 IRB 798, a deposit is made by submitting a check or money order, accompanied by a written statement that designates the remittance as a Section 6603 deposit, specifies the type of tax (e.g., income tax) and the tax year or years, and describes the amount and nature of the "disputable" tax. Without the required designation and statement, a deposit will be treated as a tax payment and applied toward any outstanding tax liability, starting with the earliest year for which there is a liability.

If the IRS ultimately assesses tax on a proposed deficiency and a Section 6603 deposit is applied against the assessed liability, the suspension of the accrual of interest is effective as of the date that the IRS received the deposit, not when the liability is later assessed or the deposit is actually applied to the liability.

The taxpayer can request a return of a Section 6603 deposit at any time unless the money has been used to pay a tax or the IRS believes payment is in jeopardy. The request must be made in writing and include the date and amount of the original deposit, the type of tax to which the deposit was intended to apply, and the tax years involved. Interest is payable on a returned deposit to the extent it is attributable to a disputable tax. Interest is figured at the applicable federal short-term rate, compounded daily, from the date of deposit to a date that is no more than 30 days before the date of the check paying the return of the deposit.

What to Do After Receiving a 90-Day Letter

Before the IRS can assess a deficiency, it must send by registered or certified mail a statutory notice of deficiency (IRC §6212(a)). This notice is called a "90-day letter." It gives your client the chance, within 90 days from the date of its mailing, to file a petition to the Tax Court of the United States. If the notice is mailed to an address outside the United States, you are allowed 150 days. In the event the 90th or 150th day falls on a Saturday or Sunday, or on a legal holiday in the District of Columbia, you have until the next business day to file a petition with the Tax Court (IRC §6213(a)).

The IRS must specifically note on deficiency notices when the 90-day period ends (IRC §6213(a)).

Your client receives a 90-day letter at the end of the period allowed in the 30-day letter if he or she has not signed a Form 870 or filed a formal protest, or after an Appeals office conference. At the end of the 90 (or 150) days, the deficiency is assessed.

On receipt of the 90-day letter, you can do one of the following:

- File a petition with the Tax Court. No assessment can be made until its decision (which includes all appeals) becomes final. For a timely Tax Court petition, the Tax Court must receive the petition no later than the 90th day after the IRS' mailing of the deficiency notice. A petition postmarked by the U.S. Post Office by the 90th day is considered timely even if received by the Tax Court after the 90th day (IRC §7502(a)).

  A dated receipt from an IRS-approved private delivery service also qualifies under the "timely-mailing-is-timely-filing" rule (IRC §7502(f)). Specific services from DHL, Federal Express, and United Parcel Service have been approved (Notice 2016-30, 2016-18 IRB 676); the current Form 1040 and 1040-SR instructions also have the list.

- Do nothing and wait for the assessment of the deficiency. Sign the Form 870. This limits the interest on the deficiency. Your client can still take his or her case to the Tax Court or pay the disputed deficiency and file a refund claim. When it is rejected, your client can sue for a refund in a Federal District Court or the U.S. Court of Federal Claims.

An assessment may only be made if a notice of deficiency is sent to the taxpayer's last known address. Generally, a taxpayer's address is the address shown on his most recently filed return.

For a deficiency involving a joint return, the 90-day letter is mailed as a single joint notice. So, where a husband and wife have separated, notify the IRS of their separate addresses to insure receipt of the notice. The IRS will then send a duplicate original of the joint notice to both the husband and wife.

The IRS may issue more than one 90-day letter for the same year before the earliest of the following events: (1) expiration of the assessment period; (2) execution of a final closing agreement or compromise; or (3) filing of a timely petition to the Tax Court.

When a 90-Day Letter Is Not Necessary

The 90-day letter is the only notice of deficiency that the law requires the IRS to send. Without it, you cannot petition the Tax Court to litigate your matter. However, there are situations in which the 90-day letter is not required and you have no recourse to the Tax Court.

1. A 90-day letter is not sent where a mathematical error has been made in your return. Taking an excessive credit on your tax liability for taxes withheld or for estimated taxes paid is considered a mathematical error.

2. A voluntary payment "paid as a tax or in respect of a tax" eliminates any deficiency, allowing the IRS to assess without the issuance of a 90-day letter.

3. An immediate assessment may be made without issuance of a 90-day letter whenever the IRS believes that assessment or collection will be jeopardized by delay. For example, if the IRS finds out that a taxpayer is leaving the country with all assets before paying his or her tax liability, it is not necessary to send a 90-day letter and then wait 90 days before assessment.

4. In the case of bankruptcy or receivership, an assessment may be made before a 90-day letter is sent.

5. If you sign a Form 870 before a 90-day letter is sent, you are not thereafter entitled to a 90-day letter.

Getting a Settlement After Filing a Petition with the Tax Court

You may still be able to come to a settlement even after you have filed a petition in the Tax Court. If you have brought your case to the Tax Court without first appealing to the Appeals office for a conference to settle the dispute, you will be asked to discuss a settlement with the Appeals office.

Even if you have filed a Tax Court petition after an unsuccessful conference in the Appeals office, your case will still be referred back to the Appeals office for settlement unless the Counsel determines that there is little likelihood of a settlement. The Appeals office may enter into a binding settlement. If the case is returned to the Counsel's office, it determines whether to settle or proceed to trial.

AUDIT RULES FOR PARTNERSHIPS

The IRS determines the tax treatment of partnership items at the partnership level in a centralized audit regime (referred to as the BBA regime because it was created by the Bipartisan Budget Act of 2015) for partnership tax years beginning after 2017 (IRC §6221(a)). Under the BBA regime, partnerships may be taxed on adjustments, including penalties and interest, resulting from an audit. The tax is assessed at the highest federal marginal rate for individuals or corporations for the tax year being audited (IRC §6225(b)(1)). Note: Different rules applied for partnership audits of returns filed for partnership taxable years beginning before 2018.

Overview. Under the unified audit regime created by the Tax Equity and Fiscal Responsibility Act of 1982 (TEFRA), partnerships other than small partnerships (10 or fewer partners) were subject to audit, although any changes in the partnership return creating adjustments for partners meant that the IRS had to seek recovery from each partner. This has been changed by the BBA regime, where partnerships are liable for any tax resulting from audit adjustments unless they elect to push out the adjustments to the partners.

Partnerships with 100 or fewer partners all of whom are "eligible partners" can elect out of the BBA regime (IRC §6221(b)). If spouses are a partnership, they are counted as two partners. The election is generally irrevocable. An "eligible partner" is any individual, C corporation, "eligible foreign entity," S corporation, or estate of a deceased partner. The election out of the BBA regime must be made on a timely filed partnership return (including extensions) for the year to which the election relates. Thus, the election out must be made annually. The partnership must provide each partner's name, TIN (including any foreign partner), and tax classification (e.g., S corporation). The partnership must also notify each partner of the election within 30 days in a manner set by the partnership.

Partnership representative. Under TEFRA, the partnership representative was a "tax matters partner." Under the BBA regime, there is a partnership representative (PR). The PR has broad authority to bind the partnership, including extending the statute of limitations and pursuing litigation; no communication with partners during the audit process is required. This PR does not have to be a partner (in contrast to this requirement for being a tax matters partner). It can be an individual or entity who has a "substantial presence in the U.S" (i.e., having the ability to meet in person with the IRS at a reasonable time and place). If there is no PR designation, the IRS can choose one.

Treatment of audit adjustments. Instead of having the partnership pay any resulting tax adjustments, the partnership can make an election under the BBA rules to push out adjustments to the partners (IRC §6226(a)-(b)). The push-out election must be made within 45 days after a Notice of Final Partnership Adjustment (FPA). If the election is made, the partnership must provide a written statement to the IRS and to each partner listing the partner's allocable share of the partnership adjustments of income, gain, loss, deduction, and/or credit, plus any penalties. The cost for making the push-out election is the imposition of a higher interest rate charged to each partner on an underpayment; the interest rate is two percentage points greater than the normal interest rate applicable to an underpayment (IRC §6226(c)(2)(C)).

S corporations. S corporation shareholders are audited on a shareholder-by-shareholder basis. Shareholders must report S corporation items consistent with the treatment on the corporation's Form 1120-S unless the shareholder identifies the inconsistency in a statement to the IRS (IRC §6037(c)).

THE TIME LIMITS WITHIN WHICH THE IRS MUST ACT FOR ADDITIONAL TAXES

The Three-Year Rule

Generally, the IRS has three years after the date on which your tax return is filed to proceed against you with a tax assessment (IRC §6501(a)). However, when you file a return before the due date, the period does not start from the filing date but from the day after the due date. To illustrate, instead of filing your last quarterly estimated tax payment on January 15, you file a final return on January 31. The limitation period on the final return begins the day after April 15, the date the final return is due, not on January 31, the date the return is filed.

To start the running of the statute of limitations, the IRS must receive your return. In any controversy concerning the statute, you must prove that you filed a return. If you fail to do this, there is no limit on the time during which the government may make an assessment against you. Similarly, filing a return containing insufficient information of your tax liability does not start the running of the statute.

What Is the Starting Date for the Limitation Period?

Amended return. The statute starts running when the original return was filed. If an amended return is filed within the last 60 days of the regular limitations period, the IRS has 60 days from the date the amended return is received to assess additional tax (IRC §6501(c)(7)).

Incorrect return form. The statute starts running when you file (or from the due date if later), if the return has all of the information on which the correct tax liability can be figured.

Tax information on a form other than a return. The statute starts running when you file the information (or from the due date if later), if it contains the information on which your tax liability can be figured. If you claim you do not have to pay a tax, notify the IRS of your claim and the basis for it. A tentative return does not start the period running since it does not specifically state the items of gross income and deductions.

Improperly executed return. The statute starts running when the return is properly executed. Example: A corporate return must be signed by one of the corporation's officers. Filing a return signed by an unauthorized person does not start the running of the statute.

Sometimes, a taxpayer or a group of taxpayers may operate as a trust or as a partnership without knowing that the organization under the tax law is really a corporation, and so must file a corporate return rather than a trust or partnership return. Even though a partnership or trust return is filed, this filing can be treated as the filing of a corporate return for purposes of starting the statute. To obtain this result, the taxpayer(s) must prove that the determination of the trust or partnership status was made in good faith.

A similar rule covers a situation where a taxpayer, in good faith, determines that it is an exempt organization. In such cases, the filing of a return for an exempt organization starts the statute—even though it is later held to be a taxable corporation for that tax year.

Fraud and other special situations. There are several exceptions to the general rule that the filing of a return starts the running of the statutory period:

- Where a false or fraudulent return is filed with intent to evade tax, tax may be assessed at any time (IRC §6501(c)(1)). The Supreme Court has held (*Badaracco*, 464 U.S. 386 (1984)) that a later filing of an amended nonfraudulent return does not start the running of the three-year period of limitations.

- Where a willful attempt in any manner is made to defeat or evade the tax, tax may be assessed at any time (IRC §6501(c)(2)).

- Where a return is executed by the IRS (IRC §6501(b)(3)), the statute does not run with the making of the return.

- Where no return is filed (IRC §6501(c)(3)), the tax may be assessed at any time, but the subsequent filing of a nonfraudulent return starts the running of the three-year limitation period.

If More Than 25% of Gross Income Is Omitted

If you omit an amount that is more than 25% of the gross income shown on your return, the IRS may make an assessment within six years after the return is filed rather than three years (IRC §6501(e)(1)(A)). For example, on a 2017 return filed on April 17, 2018 (Emancipation Day was celebrated on Monday, April 16, 2018, so the due date was extended to Tuesday, April 17), gross income of $50,000 was reported. But a $20,000 gain from the sale of a vacation home was omitted. In this case, the IRS has until April 17, 2024, to assess a deficiency on the 2017 return. The reason: The omitted $20,000 gain is more than 25% of the gross income reported on the return (25% of $50,000, or $12,500). However, if gross income of $100,000 is reported, the three-year statute applies rather than the six-year statute because the omission is not more than 25% of the reported gross income (25% of $100,000, or $25,000).

To apply the six-year statute, the IRS has the burden of proving that there is an omission and that it exceeds 25% of the reported gross income. If it fails to sustain its claim, the three-year statute applies. To be successful against such a claim, you must then show that the items were not omitted, for example, that the item was tax free or not taxable in the particular year, or that the IRS' valuation is incorrect. You cannot base your defense on a plea of an honest mistake or the use of an incorrect method of accounting, or that the omission was reduced to less than 25% by an amended return. The statute runs from the filing of the original return. It is not affected by the filing of an amended return.

In determining whether capital gains omitted from a return are "gross income" under the 25%-of-gross-income test, treat the gains as gross income, without regard to capital losses that may have been used to figure the net gain or loss shown on the return. Where you are in business, gross income means gross receipts, that is, the total amount received from the sale of goods or services unreduced by the cost of such goods or services. Gross income of a partner's share of partnership income means the partner's share of the partnership gross income, not partnership net income.

An overstatement of basis that results in an understatement of income is treated as an omission from gross income for purposes of the 25%-of-gross-income test (IRC §6501(e)(1)(B)(ii)).

The Tax Court has made it clear that when capital gains have been omitted from gross income, it is the amount of the omitted gains and not the entire amounts realized that must be taken into account for purposes of determining whether the six-year statute of limitations applies (*G. Douglas Barkett*, 143 TC No. 6 (2014)).

Adequate Disclosure. If you omit a questionable item from gross income, you may prevent an extension of the statute by adequately disclosing the facts of the omission. If the disclosure adequately tells the IRS of the nature and amount of the item omitted, that item will not be counted in determining whether there has been an omission of more than 25% of gross income.

The following are examples of adequate disclosure: (1) sales receipts were fully stated, but claimed deductions were excessive; (2) opening inventory was overstated, resulting in understated profits; (3) total income was revealed by a schedule attached to the return; and (4) total income was disclosed on the return, but was erroneously claimed as exempt.

There was not an adequate disclosure where the taxpayer liquidated his real estate corporation, attaching a statement of depreciation on the liquidation property, but failed to report gain realized on the liquidation.

When the Limitation Period May Be Reduced

To expedite the closings of income tax cases of estates and of liquidated corporations, the statutory period may be reduced to 18 months (IRC §6501(d)). After you have filed a return reporting income received by a decedent in his or her lifetime, an estate during administration, or a corporation being liquidated, send the Commissioner a letter specifically asking for a prompt assessment on the return in the following 18 months. Make this request after the return is filed, or it will not be effective. Send your letter in a separate envelope. Do not mail it with the return.

When the request is made for a corporation, you must notify the Commissioner that liquidation is contemplated within 18 months, begin the liquidation in good faith within that time, and complete the liquidation.

When you request a prompt assessment for an estate, also send evidence of your authority to act for the estate.

The receipt of the filing of the request for prompt assessment starts the 18-month period. The shortened limitation period will not apply if more than 25% of gross income is omitted from the return or if there is a fraudulent or willful attempt to evade tax.

Limitation Rules for Carryback

Net operating loss or capital loss carryback. A deficiency resulting from an erroneous carryback may be assessed within the statutory period of the loss year in which the carryback originated (IRC §6501(h)). For example, a net operating loss in 2019 carried back five years (IRC §172(b)(1)) to 2014 results in a refund of $5,000; in an audit of the 2019 return, the carryback is reduced and it is determined that the refund should have been $1,000. The IRS has until April 18, 2023, to recover $4,000 of the refund attributed to the carryback to 2014. (Note: there is no carryback for a post-2020 NOL, except for certain farming losses; only carryforwards are allowed.)Foreign tax credit carryback. A deficiency resulting from an improper carryback of the foreign tax credit may be assessed within one year after the period for assessment for the year producing the excess foreign tax credit (IRC §6501(i)).

Investment credit or other general business credit carryback. A deficiency resulting from an erroneous carryback may be assessed within the statutory period of the year producing the credit (IRC §6501(j)).

Where a quick refund was elected, the IRS has an extended time to audit the year to which the carryback was made (except in the case of foreign tax credit). The IRS may assess within the statutory period for the year that produced the carryback a tax deficiency not to exceed the amount of the refund or credit arising from the carryback (IRC §6501(k)).

EXAMPLES

1. A sole proprietor files a quick refund claim for 2019 based on an unused general business credit of $50,000 arising in 2020 and receives a refund of $50,000. In 2021, the IRS reduces the general business credit from $50,000 to $30,000. The taxpayer filed her 2020 return on May 17, 2021, so the period for assessing the excess $20,000 does not expire until May 17, 2024.

2. Same facts as in Example 1, but the IRS also finds that the taxpayer owes $40,000 of additional tax for 2019 because of her failure to report certain income for that year. On or before May 17, 2024, the IRS may assess a deficiency not in excess of $30,000.

Other Limitation Rules for Married Couples

Where separate returns were originally filed and later a joint return is filed, the period of limitations must extend to at least one year after the time the joint return was actually filed. The regular limitation periods are figured from the following deemed filing dates for the joint return, but if these limitations periods would expire before one year after the joint return was filed, then the period is extended until the end of that one year (IRC §6013(b)(4)).

Where both spouses previously filed separate returns, the regular limitation period begins on the last date that either spouse could have filed a separate return (IRC §6013(b)(3)(A)(i)).

Where only one spouse filed a separate return because the other had gross income under the requirement for filing a return, the regular limitation period begins on the last date the spouse who filed could have filed his or her separate return (IRC §6013(b)(3)(A)(ii)).

Where only one spouse filed a separate return, even though the other had gross income requiring the filing of a return, the regular limitation period begins when they file the joint return (IRC §6013(b)(3)(A)(iii).

Limitation Periods Where Recognition of Gain Is Deferred

Where an involuntary conversion has occurred, tax on the gain may be deferred by investing the proceeds in similar property. When tax is deferred, the three-year period starts when the IRS is notified that the property has been replaced or that no replacement has been or will be made (IRC §1033(a)(2)(C)).

If a replacement is made before the beginning of the last year in which any part of the gain is received on the conversion, then the limitation period for any year before that year (during which the election to replace was in effect) ends when the limitation period for the last year ends (IRC §1033(a)(2)(D)).

Warning: Failure to notify the IRS prevents the statute of limitation from closing.

Waiving the Limitation Period

If a return is being examined during a time close to the expiration of the statutory period for assessing deficiencies, the IRS may ask for a waiver of the statute of limitations on a Form 872. An IRS request that you agree to an extension of the limitations period for tax assessments must include a notice that you have the right to refuse an extension or to limit an extension to certain issues or a particular period (IRC §6501(c)(4)(B)).

Should a Waiver Extending the Statute Be Signed?

A return is subject to a possible deficiency assessment for at least three years. An extension of the statute of limitations may be an advantage because the time to file refund claims is extended by the extension period plus six months. However, taxpayers generally regard an extension as a disadvantage. They assume the IRS, in making the request, has become suspicious of the return after a preliminary examination and a more thorough examination is likely to lead to a deficiency assessment.

It is advisable to agree to the consent if it is anticipated that disputed items may be amicably compromised.

If consent is refused, the statute of limitations binds both the taxpayer and the Commissioner. Neither party is obliged to agree to an extension.

What is the practical result of a refusal to consent? If the refusal comes:

- Before the agent has had the opportunity to make an examination, he or she can recommend the disallowance of every claimed deduction. A statutory notice of deficiency (90-day letter) can be sent on that basis. Since the refusal to an extension prevented any reasonable determination, the agent is forced to do this to protect the government's interest. The agent can, in appropriate cases, also recommend a jeopardy assessment. If a 90-day letter is issued without an audit, the IRS' action may be attacked as arbitrary.

- Before the agent has completed the examination, or before he or she has time to consider the merits of your position, the agent's recommendations will be based on the assumption that there is no merit to your position.

- When your case is in the Appeals office and before the Appeals officer has an opportunity to consider the merits of your position, the agent's recommendations might be sustained.

In all of these situations, the case may have to go to court. There will be delay and expense. Give all these facts thought before you object to signing a Form 872.

You may stipulate on the Form 872 how long the statute of limitations is to be extended.

Form 872-A permits flexibility by extending the statute of limitations until 90 days after you are mailed a deficiency notice, or 90 days after you terminate or the IRS terminates the agreement (by filing Form 872-T).

When the Running of the Statute Is Suspended

The limitation period is automatically suspended in the following cases:

When a 90-day letter is sent, the period of limitations is automatically suspended for 150 days. (Technically, this includes the 90-day period during which the IRS cannot assess a deficiency, plus an additional 60 days.) However, if the period would have expired during the suspended period, the IRS cannot assess an additional deficiency after that time, though it can still assess the original deficiency (IRC §6503(a)(1)).

If you file a timely petition in the Tax Court, the limitation period is extended until the Tax Court decision (including all appeals) becomes final and for 60 days afterwards (IRC §6503(a)(1)).

Where a Title 11 bankruptcy case has commenced, a notice of deficiency may be mailed but assessment by the IRS is barred until 60 days after the termination of the case, or, if earlier, 60 days after the stay on assessment is lifted by the bankruptcy court (IRC §6503(h)).

Where assets are in the custody or control of a court, the period of limitation for collection after assessment is suspended for the period in which the assets are in the hands of the court and for six months thereafter (IRC §6503(b)).

When a taxpayer is out of the country for a continuous period of six months or more, the limitation period is suspended during the absence. The period of limitation does not expire until six months after he or she returns to the United States (IRC §6503(c)).

Where property of a third party is wrongfully seized by the government, the limitation period for collection after assessment is suspended. The suspension begins when the property is wrongfully seized or received and ends 30 days after the IRS determines the levy was wrongful and returns the property. If the third party goes to court, the suspension ends 30 days after entry of a final judgment that the levy was wrongful (IRC §6503(f)).

If the IRS is attempting to obtain records from a third party and a dispute over the records is not solved within six months after the IRS issues an administrative summons, the period is suspended until the issue is resolved. Further, if you intervene in a dispute between the IRS and the third-party record keeper, the limitation period is suspended from that date until the entire dispute is resolved (IRC §7609(e)).

Mitigating the Effect of the Limitation Period to Avoid Double Tax

Suppose income that should have been reported on a 2020 return is reported on a 2019 return. In March 2024, after the limitation period for filing a refund claim for 2019 has expired, the IRS asserts a deficiency on this item for 2020. You take the case to the Tax Court, but it upholds the government's position.

Can you get a refund for the tax paid on this item for 2019 even though the statute has run out on that year?

The answer is yes. In this and in certain other cases, the limitation period is lifted, not only to prevent double taxation of the taxpayer, but also to protect the government in cases where an item of income might otherwise escape taxation (IRC §1311).

EXAMPLES

1. Jones and his son were partners. Each was entitled to one-half of partnership profits. On his 2019 return, Jones Sr. included the entire partnership profits. In early 2023, he filed a timely refund claim for that portion of tax he paid on his son's share for the year 2019. In 2024, a Federal District Court approves the claim. This allows the IRS to assess a deficiency against the son for that portion of the 2019 profits on which he did not pay tax.

2. Howe assigned his salary in 2016 to his spouse. She reported it on her return for 2017. In 2019, the IRS assessed a deficiency against Howe for the omission of the salary in 2016. In 2021, the Tax Court upheld the IRS' position. Mrs. Howe was then entitled to a refund on the tax she paid on her husband's salary for 2016, even though the statute had expired for that year.

When a Closed Year May Be Reopened

Before the limitation period can be lifted, the taxpayer or the IRS must show there has been a final determination that requires an adjustment specifically covered by the relief statute. A final determination (IRC §1313(a)) may be a:

Closing agreement. It is considered final when the agreement is approved.

Decision of the Tax Court or other competent court. It is considered final at the end of the time allowed for taking an appeal if no appeal has been taken.

Final disposition of a refund claim. It is considered final as to:
- Allowed items either on the date of the allowance of the refund or the credit or on the date of mailing a notice of disallowance. The last situation arises when the allowed items are offset by other items.
- Disallowed items when time for filing a refund suit expires (unless a suit is started before that time). This rule covers items disallowed in whole or in part, or items that have reduced a refund.
- Informal agreement signed by the taxpayer and the IRS.

Situations when a closed year may be reopened. A closed year may be reopened for an adjustment only in limited cases (IRC §1312). The law allows for a reopening in the following seven situations (an eighth situation involving affiliated companies is not discussed here). In the first five situations, there must have been an inconsistent position.

1. The determination includes in gross income an item that was erroneously included in the taxpayer's gross income or in the gross income of a related taxpayer in a tax year that is now closed (IRC §1312(1)).

   Example: Smith, who keeps his books on the cash basis, included in his 2019 return an item of accrued rent. In 2023, after the limitation period for 2019 has expired, the IRS claims that the rent was received in 2021, and asserts a deficiency. The deficiency for 2021 is upheld by the Tax Court. Smith can get a refund for tax paid on the rent on his 2019 return.

2. The determination allows a deduction or a credit that was erroneously allowed to the taxpayer or to a related taxpayer in a tax year now closed (IRC §1312(2)).

   Example: Green claimed and was allowed a casualty loss deduction on his 2018 return for the destruction of his house by a federally declared disaster that occurred in 2019. After the end of the period of limitations for the assessment of a deficiency for 2018, Green files a refund claim for 2019 based upon a deduction for the casualty loss in that year. The refund claim is allowed for 2019, and the IRS may make an assessment for the deduction taken for 2018.

3. The determination excludes from gross income an item on which the taxpayer paid a tax or that was included in a filed return (whether or not he paid a tax on it). However, in a closed year, the item was erroneously excluded or omitted from the taxpayer's gross income or from the gross income of a related taxpayer (IRC §1312(3)(A)).

   Example: Brown, in 2019, received under a contract payments that were included in his 2019 return. In 2022, he filed a refund claim for 2019, asserting he was on the accrual basis, and since the payments had accrued in 2018, they should have been taxed then. The refund claim is allowed in 2023. An assessment may be made for 2018 even though the statute of limitations has run out on that year.

4. The determination involves the correction of a deduction or income item of an estate or a trust, or beneficiaries of either. An adjustment to the closed year is allowed where a determination requires the disallowance of an estate or trust deduction of an amount erroneously included in the income of a beneficiary or heir, or where a determination allows an estate or trust deduction for an amount that was erroneously omitted from income of a beneficiary or heir (IRC §1312(5)).

   Example: A trustee claimed in a trust's return for 2018 a deduction for income distributed to the beneficiary. The beneficiary reported the distribution as income for 2018. In 2022, the IRS asserted a deficiency against the trust for 2018 on the ground that the amount given to the beneficiary was corpus, not income. In 2023, the deficiency is sustained by the Tax Court. Even though the period for filing claims for a refund by the beneficiary for 2018 has expired, the refund may still be allowed.

5. The determination fixes the basis of property for any purpose, and the adjustment affects either an error made in the treatment of a transaction that the basis depends on or an error made in treating the transaction as one involving

the basis in the first place (IRC §1312(7)). In applying this rule, the following two tests have to be met:

a. This error has to be either an erroneous:

- Inclusion in or omission from gross income;
- Recognition or nonrecognition of gain or loss;
- Deduction of an item that should have been charged to a capital account; or
- Charge to a capital account that should have been deducted from income.

b. Before any one of the above mistakes may be corrected in a closed year the taxpayer or the IRS must show that a determination was made in:

- The taxpayer's case; or
- A tax case of a party who received title to the property from the taxpayer after it was acquired in a transaction in which he or she treated improperly the basis of the property; or
- A tax case of a party who received title from the taxpayer by gift after erroneously treating a transaction that affected the basis of the donated property. Note that the improperly treated transaction does not have to be the one in which the taxpayer acquired the property. Compare this with the above rule in which the transaction is required to be the one in which the party acquired title.

Example: In 2017, Stone transferred property that had cost him $5,000 to A Co. in exchange for an original issue of stock worth $10,000. On his 2017 return, he treated the exchange as tax free.

In 2021, A Co. claims that gain should have been recognized and so the property should have a $10,000 basis. If its argument is sustained, there can be no adjustment in the 2017 tax of A Co. There was no erroneous inclusion in or omission from its gross income by A Co. or an erroneous recognition or nonrecognition of gain or loss. Nor was there an erroneous deduction of an item that should have been charged to a capital account or a charge to a capital account that should have been deducted from income. As for Stone, the determination on A Co.'s basis did not affect his tax. Nor does the determination relate to a transaction in which he acquired the property. It applies to the property A Co. acquired.

In 2022, Stone sells A Co. stock and claims that since gain should have been recognized on the exchange in 2017, the basis for figuring gain or loss should be $10,000. If his claim is allowed, an adjustment will be made to his 2017 tax. The basis for computing gain on the sale depends on the 2017 transactions. Here there was an erroneous nonrecognition of gain to Stone. He was the taxpayer for whom the determination was made.

Assume Stone does not sell the stock but gives it to his son, who later sells it and claims the $10,000 basis. A closing agreement sustains his claim. Stone's 2017 tax will be adjusted. The basis for computing gain or loss on the sale by his son depends on the 2017 transaction where there was an erroneous nonrecognition of gain. Stone is deemed the person who acquired title in the transaction and from whom his son derived title subsequent to the transaction.

6. The determination disallows a deduction or a credit that should have been allowed to, but was not allowed to, the taxpayer or to a related taxpayer in a tax year now closed (IRC §1312(4)).

Important: Here, a refund or a credit is allowed only if the deduction was not barred at the time the taxpayer first claimed it in writing, that is, where he or she files a return, a refund claim, or a petition to the Tax Court (IRC §1311(b)(2)(B)).

Example: Burns reports on the accrual basis. For 2018, he deducted an expense item that he paid in that year. (At the time he filed his 2018 return, the statute had not expired for 2017.) Later, the IRS claimed that the item should have been accrued in 2017. In 2022, the Tax Court disallowed the deduction for 2018. But Burns can get an adjustment for 2017 even though it is now a closed year. The reason: When he took the 2018 deduction, 2017 was still an open year. (Note: Suppose the liability should have been accrued in 2014 instead of 2017—Burns could not get an adjustment if a refund or credit for the year 2014 was already barred when he took the deduction by error for 2018.)

7. The determination rejects an IRS deficiency for an item of income that the taxpayer did not report or pay tax for, but holds that the income should have been reported in the taxpayer's gross income or in the gross income of a related taxpayer in a different tax year now closed (IRC §1312(3)(B)).

Important: Here, an adjustment is allowed only if a deficiency assessment was not barred at the time the IRS first claimed, either in a deficiency notice or before the Tax Court, that the item should be reported for the tax year to which the determination relates (IRC §1311(b)(2)(A)).

Example: Jones reports on the accrual basis. In 2017, he did some work for A Co. He got paid in 2017 and 2018. He did not report the 2018 payment in either year. In 2020, the IRS sent him a deficiency notice for 2017, claiming he should have reported all the payments then. Jones contested the deficiency notice on the basis that in 2017 he had no accruable right to the payments received in 2018. In 2023, the Tax Court agrees with him. But the IRS can assess a deficiency for 2018, even though it is now a closed year. The reason: A deficiency assessment for 2018 was not barred in 2020 when the deficiency notice for 2017 was sent.

Inconsistent Positions Requirement

In the first five situations previously discussed that allow the lifting of the statute of limitations, the taxpayer or the IRS must have maintained an inconsistent position in the determination (IRC §1311(b)(1)). This means that either party would benefit unfairly if the closed year was not reopened for an adjustment (either for a refund or an assessment of a deficiency). Here is how the rule works:

For an additional assessment: The taxpayer—not the IRS—must have maintained an inconsistent position.

Example: Adam, on his 2017 return, claimed and was allowed a deduction for a charitable contribution. In 2022, he filed a refund claim for the year 2018, claiming that the charitable contribution was made in 2018. The claim was later allowed. Adam maintained a position inconsistent with the allowance of the deduction for 2017 by filing a refund claim for 2018 based on the same deduction. So the Commissioner may assert an additional assessment for 2017.

For a refund or credit: The Commissioner—not the taxpayer—must have maintained an inconsistent position.

> Example: Evans, in his 2019 return, erroneously included an item of income which should have been reported on his 2020 return. After the limitation period for 2019 has expired, the Commissioner asserts a deficiency for the year 2020 on this item. The Tax Court sustains the deficiency. Here, the Commissioner has maintained an inconsistent position. The Commissioner got Evans's tax for both 2019 and 2020. Evans may get a refund for the year 2019.

Related taxpayers. Where a taxpayer maintained an inconsistent position, a deficiency adjustment may not affect a related taxpayer unless his or her relationship to the taxpayer was maintained when the inconsistent position was taken in a return, in a refund claim, or in a Tax Court petition (IRC §1311(b)(3)). If a taxpayer does not hold an inconsistent position, then the relationship must be fixed at the time of the final determination. These rules do not apply to situation No. 7 above, which is not subject to the inconsistent position rule.

Only the following are considered "related taxpayers" (IRC §1313(c)):

- Spouses
- Grantor and fiduciary
- Grantor and beneficiary
- Decedent and decedent's estate
- Partners
- Fiduciary and legatee, heir, or beneficiary
- Members of an affiliated group of corporations

If the Statute Is Lifted

If there is an additional assessment for any of the adjustments described in the preceding pages, you will receive a statutory notice of deficiency (90-day letter). You can pay the deficiency and sue for a refund, or appeal to the Tax Court. The IRS must send a deficiency notice within one year from the date of the determination (IRC §1314(b)).

If entitled to a refund or credit, you must file a refund claim within one year from the date of the determination, unless the IRS makes the refund without a claim (IRC §1314(b)). If the claim is turned down, you can sue for a refund.

An informal agreement involving a closed year can be revoked or altered. When this happens, a later readjustment is treated in the same way as the original adjustment was treated.

Where the adjustment results in an additional assessment by the IRS, you will be charged with interest and penalties. Where the adjustment results in a refund to you, the IRS will pay interest. However, the adjustment that is made by lifting the statute of limitations is not affected by any item other than the one that is the subject of the adjustment.

FILING REFUND CLAIMS

The technical rules outlined in this chapter should be strictly observed. Often, refunds are denied because of a taxpayer's failure to comply with a technical rule. Moreover, the filing of a refund claim is the first step that must be taken before suing the government. Unless a proper claim has been filed, a suit will be dismissed.

But before you decide to file a refund claim, carefully review the return involved for accuracy. A refund claim opens the return to a thorough investigation in which the IRS may find errors that reduce or completely eliminate the refund claim, and may even lead to the assessment of a deficiency.

Some practitioners wait until the end of the limitation period to file refund claims. If the IRS, after the limitation period, finds a deficiency, it can use the deficiency only to offset the claimed refund.

If, in good faith, you accept an erroneous refund and the IRS later discovers its mistake, repay the refund promptly. Otherwise, you will be liable for interest.

File Timely Refund Claims

A refund claim for income taxes must meet a time limitation and a dollar limitation.

Time limitation for refund. A refund claim for income tax must be filed within three years from the time the return was filed or two years from the time the tax was paid, whichever period ends later (IRC §6511(a)). For purposes of determining the three-year period, a return that is filed before the original due date is deemed to have been filed on the due date. For example, a return due on April 15 but filed April 1 is deemed filed on April 15, the due date. However, where an extension for filing is obtained, a return filed before the extended due date is deemed to have been filed on the actual date of filing and not on the extended due date. For example, if your due date for filing is April 15 but you get an extension to October 15 and actually file the return on October 1, your return is deemed to have been filed on October 1.

Where the last day for filing falls on a Saturday, Sunday, or legal holiday, the return is treated as timely filed if the return is filed or postmarked on the next work day. A legal holiday includes a legal holiday in the District of Columbia, as well as a legal holiday in the state in which you have to file the claim (IRC §7503).

You may file a protective refund claim when a particular issue is being litigated by other taxpayers and you want to await the outcome. This type of claim is generally accompanied by a cover letter to the IRS explaining its nature. Filing the protective refund claim preserves your right to sue for a refund. A suit must be brought before the expiration of two years from the date that the notice of disallowance of your claim was mailed.

With agreement of the IRS, Form 907 may be used to extend the two-year period for filing suit. The two-year period may not be extended once it has run out.

File your refund claim with the IRS Service Center serving the district in which the tax was paid. Where circumstances have forced you to wait until the last minute to file a refund claim, make sure that you meet the filing deadline. If you timely mail the claim or obtain a timely electronic postmark, the claim is deemed to be timely filed even if it is not received by the IRS until after the filing deadline. For an electronically filed claim, an electronic postmark means a record of the date and time (in the taxpayer's time zone) that an authorized electronic return transmitter receives the claim on its host system (Reg. §301.7502-1(d)).

To be considered timely mailed, a document must be enclosed in an envelope that is properly addressed with postage prepaid and postmarked by the U.S. Postal Service on or before the last day of the statutory period (IRC §7502(a)). A postmark by a private postage meter does not establish the date of mailing (it only indicates the date that the postage was purchased). The IRS may designate certain types of service of a private delivery service (PDS) as being equivalent to the U.S. Postal Service for purposes of the postmark rule (IRC §7502(f); Reg. §301.7502-1(c)(3)).

Proof of registered mail or a certified mail receipt with evidence that the envelope was properly addressed is deemed to be "prima facie evidence" that the document was actually delivered to the IRS (Reg. §301.7502-1(e)(2)(i)). The IRS may extend the "prima facie" delivery rule to a service of a designated private delivery service (PDS) where the IRS determines such service to be substantially equivalent to United States registered or certified mail (Reg. §301.7502-1(e)(2)(ii)). Unless the return is actually delivered to the IRS by the applicable deadline, the exclusive means of establishing prima facie evidence of delivery of a document to the IRS is proof of proper use of registered or certified mail, or of equivalent PDS services that have been designated by the IRS (designated PDS services are listed in Notice 2016-30, 2016-18 IRB 676). No other evidence of a postmark or of mailing will be prima facie evidence of delivery or raise a presumption that the document was delivered (Reg. §301.7502-1(e)(2)(i)). The old "mailbox rule" that had allowed other proof of timely filing (e.g., testimony) can no longer be used.

Refund claim for bad debt or worthless security. If you fail to claim a bad debt deduction or worthless security deduction on the return for the year in which the debt or security became worthless, you may file a refund claim to claim the deduction within seven years from the due date (without extensions) of the return for the year of the loss (IRC §6511(d)(1)).

Disability suspends limitations period for refund claims. The statute of limitations is suspended for refund claims made during any period in which a person is unable to manage financial affairs because of a physical or mental impairment that may be expected to result in death or to last for a period of not less than 12 months (IRC §6511(h)). This rule does not apply, however, if a party is authorized to act on the disabled person's behalf in financial matters.

Dollar limitation for refund. Under a "look-back" rule, the amount of a refund may be limited. If the refund claim is filed within three years from the time the return was filed (thereby meeting the time limitation of Section 6511(a), a refund is allowed for taxes paid within the three-year period, plus any extension of time for filing, preceding the filing of the refund claim (IRC §6511(b)(2)(A)). If the refund claim is not filed within three years of the filing of the return, a refund may not exceed the amount of tax paid within the two-year period preceding the filing of the claim (IRC §6511(b)(2)(B)). A taxpayer has no absolute right to the refund

of an overpayment. The Commissioner may credit the amount of an overpayment against any tax liability of the taxpayer.

> Example: Smith's 2018 return was due on April 15, 2019. He obtained an extension for filing until October 15, 2019. His return was actually filed on October 6, 2019, and he remitted a check with his return for a tax liability of $2,000. On October 3, 2022, Smith files a claim for a refund for $1,000 on his 2018 return. The claim is timely filed since he meets the time limitation (within three years of the actual date of filing, October 6, 2019) and the amount limitation (tax paid within the three years preceding the filing of the refund claim).

If no return was filed, the refund claim must be made within two years from the time the tax was paid, and the amount of the refund cannot be more than the tax paid during the two years immediately preceding the filing of the claim.

Refund of withheld taxes and estimated tax payments. All estimated taxes and taxes withheld by an employer are deemed to have been paid on the "15th day of the fourth month" following the close of the taxable year for which the return is due (IRC §6513(b); *David H. Baral*, 120 S. Ct. 1006 (2000)). For example, your 2018 return was due by April 15, 2019, but you received a six-month extension until October 15, 2019. You filed the return on October 6, 2019. Your 2018 withholding taxes and estimated tax payments for 2018 are deemed paid on April 15, 2019, and not on the October 6 filing date. Now suppose you file a claim for a refund of a portion of the estimated or withholding tax on July 13, 2022. The claim is timely, even though the estimated or withholding tax is deemed paid on April 15, 2019, or more than three years prior to the claim for refund. You meet the time limitation since the claim was filed within three years of the date the return was filed, October 6, 2019. Also, the refund is allowed under the dollar limitation since the refund claim is filed (July 13, 2022) within three years, plus any extensions of time for filing the return, from the date the estimated or withholding tax is deemed paid, or April 15, 2019. The last day for filing a refund claim under the "three years plus extension" look-back period would be October 15, 2022 (three years from the April 15, 2019, deemed payment date plus a six-month extension).

Where a refund is claimed on an original return mailed and postmarked (U.S. Postal Service or private delivery service designated by the IRS) on or slightly before the last day of the "three years plus extension" period, the IRS will allow the refund claim (Reg. §301.7502-1(f)).The IRS treats refund claims included on delinquent original returns as filed on the date of mailing for purposes of applying the "three years plus extension" look-back rule of Section 6511(b)(2)(A).

Extended assessment and refund period. When you agree with the IRS to extend the time during which it can assess your tax, you may file a refund claim during this extended period plus an additional six months afterwards (IRC §6511(c)(1)). A refund made during this time includes the refund you would have received if you had filed a claim at the time the extension was signed, plus the tax paid after the agreement was signed but before you filed your claim (IRC §6511(c)(2)). These extension period rules do not apply to refunds of estate taxes. Where your claim is filed more than six months after the end of the extended period, the refunded amount cannot be more than the tax paid during the two years before the filing of the claim (IRC §6511(c)(3)(B)).

> Example: A 2018 return, filed on April 15, 2019, is under audit. On January 12, 2022, an agreement is made to extend the statutory period of assessment to July 12, 2022. But for this extension, the deadline for filing a refund claim for 2018 would have been April 18, 2022 (the April 15th deadline is extended because of Emancipation Day in D.C.). With the extension (six months after July 12, 2022), you now have until January 12, 2023, to file a refund claim on your 2018 return.

Refund lookback period for nonfilers. If no return is filed, a refund claim must be made within two years from when the tax was paid, and the amount of the refund cannot exceed the tax paid during the two years immediately preceding the filing of the claim (Reg. §301.6511(b)-1(b)(1)(iii)).

If the IRS mails the deficiency notice in the third year after the return due date, but before a return has been filed, a refund may be obtained in the Tax Court for taxes paid within the three years preceding the date of the deficiency notice (IRC §6512(b)(3)).

What Refund Form to Use

Refund claims should be filed on Form 1040-X (for an individual who originally filed on Form 1040, Form 1040-SR, Form 1040A, or Form 1040EZ) or on Form 1120-X (for a corporation that filed Form 1120). Where an income tax form other than Form 1040, Form 1040-SR, Form 1040A, Form 1040EZ, or Form 1120 was filed, a refund claim is generally made on an amended return. However, a partner in a TEFRA partnership must use Form 8082 to make a refund claim in the form of an administrative adjustment request (AAR) of partnership items for a partnership tax year beginning before January 1, 2018. Form 843 may be used for claiming refunds for estate, gift, and employment taxes or certain excise taxes.

To correct an error on a return filed before its due date, you can file a corrected return on or before its due date. This return is not considered an amended return. However, a corrected return filed after the due date is an amended return and acts as a refund claim.

Letters to the IRS are usually held by the courts as not satisfying the requirements for an adequate refund claim.

Overwithheld taxes. You need not file a formal claim for overpayment of personal income tax resulting from excessive withholding of taxes on wages or excessive estimated tax payments. In these two cases, a tax return requesting a refund of the overpayment acts as a claim for refund. But there is one exception. On the death of an individual who has overpaid tax, the administrator or executor of the estate files a refund claim on Form 1310.

Generally, refunds for excessive withholding or estimating of tax are made soon after a tax return is filed. However, a return may be subject to a "pre-refund" audit, especially where the income shown on the return is less than $10,000 or there are large deductions or many exemptions that require substantiation.

Preparing Your Refund Claim

The most important part of a refund claim is stating the "reasons" for the refund. A general claim where you just note an overpayment, without supporting facts and grounds, is not sufficient. If a claim is denied by the IRS, it may become the basis of a court suit. If you have not stated all the grounds, you may not be allowed to show them in court. The courts have limited taxpayers to the exact claim shown on the form. Make a full claim and show:

- All the facts that support the claim. You may attach to the form as much evidence as is helpful. Be sure your facts are simply and fully stated.
- All the grounds for the claim. You may hedge if you are uncertain about the exact grounds; alternate and even inconsistent grounds may be given. For example:

The loss was incurred from an embezzlement; if not, it was incurred from a bad debt.

The gain from the sale is entitled to capital gain treatment as the property sold was a capital asset; if not, it was depreciable property used in business.

The loss was due to a loss on the acquisition of real estate and from a partial bad debt (where the claim arose from the extinguishing of a mortgage by a deed in lieu of a foreclosure).

While it is necessary to be complete and precise in specifying the facts and reasons for your claim, you are not required to present your evidence; you must merely inform the IRS of the basis for your claim.

To protect against your understating the amount of your claim, it may be advisable to preface the claim with this phrase: "The following or such greater amounts as may be legally refunded." However, neither this nor any other "protective clause" will allow you to support your refund claim on grounds other than those mentioned in the original claim or in amendments made before the period of limitations has expired.

A separate claim must be made for each year in which a refund is claimed. It must be made in duplicate and signed under oath by the taxpayer or the duly authorized agent. If an agent signs, he or she must attach to the claim evidence of authority. If the claim is based on a joint return, it must be signed by both spouses.

A refund claim filed before there is an overpayment is invalid, unless the IRS waives the defect.

When you file a petition to the Tax Court, thus giving that court jurisdiction over your case, you may no longer file a refund claim for any part of the tax for the taxable year in question.

Submitting a Refund Claim

Refund claims for 2020, 2021 and 2022 on Form 1040-X can be e-filed. Currently, refund claims for tax years before 2020 must be submitted on paper. *See* the *e-Supplement* at *jklasser.com* for any update.

Amending the Refund Claim

You may generally amend your refund claim before the occurrence of either of the following events: (1) expiration of the period for filing the original claim (generally two years after paying the tax or three years after filing the return, whichever is later), and (2) final action taken by the IRS on the refund claim. After the expiration of the time limitation, you may not raise new issues or grounds in an amended refund claim, even though the original claim was timely.

Regardless of the time limitations above, file your amended claim immediately upon discovering the need for the amendment. Make certain that your amended claim meets all the technical standards discussed in the previous paragraphs.

Filing an Informal Claim

There is no advantage in filing an informal claim for refund. An informal claim must meet the same requirements as a formal claim made on the official IRS form (Form 1040-X, Form 1120-X, or Form 843). Although some informal claims have been allowed, many more have been denied and have not been permitted to be the basis of refund suits. For example, you may not base a refund suit on an informal claim that is limited to a:

- Letter suggesting a change in tax computation;
- Request for a ruling stating the facts and grounds for a refund; or
- Sworn statement that states the facts and grounds for a refund but does not include a demand for one.

Refunds based on informal claims have been allowed where an informal claim was accompanied by a brief that gave the basis of the claim or where, as a result of a conference, letters and memoranda stating the taxpayer's position were filed and a general claim referring to these papers was later filed.

Getting a Partial Refund in a Contested Case

The IRS, in three situations, may allow partial refunds in cases where contested issues still remain to be settled.

1. Two or more refund issues where some issues are settled and others are still contested. Here, a refund may be allowed on the settled issues.

   Example: You file a refund claim based on two issues. The first one, which would result in a $1,000 refund, is settled. The second one, which would result in a $500 refund, is contested. The IRS may give you a partial refund of $1,000.

2. Two or more issues where some issues will result in a refund and the others in a deficiency, but the overall netting results in a refund.

   Example: A case involves a refund issue that is not contested and a deficiency issue that is contested. The allowance of the refund issue would result in a net overassessment of $5,000 after offsetting the deficiency issue. A $5,000 refund may be allowed, even though the contested issue is still pending.

3. Two or more years are under examination. In one year, there is a contested proposed deficiency. In the other year, there is an agreement on an overassessment that is greater than the proposed deficiency.

   Example: For year 2021, the IRS proposes a deficiency of $4,000 that you contest. But for 2022, the IRS agrees that it owes you a refund of $7,000. A partial refund of not more than $3,000 may be made.

Note: The IRS will not give partial refunds in cases where there may be an overall deficiency, even though there is no dispute on the tax refunding issue.

If the refund differs from the amount you sought, you usually get a notice of adjustment explaining the difference before receiving the refund. But sometimes the refund is received without prior explanation. In that case, the IRS recommends this action: If the refund is smaller than you claimed, cash the check and write to your IRS Service Center asking why the refund was less than the amount claimed. If the refund exceeds your claim, return the check to the Service Center with a request for an explanation.

After a Refund Claim Is Filed

No matter how small a refund claim is, it is thoroughly scrutinized by the IRS.

The examination procedure is like the one used in examining your return. It provides for an agent's examination in a desk examination or in the field, and if the agent disputes your claim you may ask for a conference at a higher level.

If your claim is finally turned down, you are notified by certified or registered mail. A disallowed claim may not be amended. Sometimes the IRS will reconsider a denied claim. But this reopening cannot extend the time in which you can sue for a refund. Of course, you may file a new claim so long as the limitation period within which a claim may be filed has not expired, but it must be on new grounds.

A refund suit may not be filed in a Federal District Court on in the U.S. Court of Federal Claims until six months after the date the refund claim is filed with the IRS, or, if earlier, the date of the IRS' denial of the claim. The deadline for commencing the court suit is two years from the date the IRS mails the notice of disallowance by certified or registered mail (IRC §6532(a)).

If a claim is allowed, you receive a Certificate of Overassessment. Check it for accuracy. The IRS does not have to pay interest for the period after the filing of the claim if the refund is paid by the 45th day after the claim is filed (IRC §6611(e)(2)). If the refund is not paid within the 45-day period, interest is calculated from the date of overpayment to a date preceding the date of the check by no more than 30 days (IRC §6611(b)(2)).

Before the check is mailed, the IRS investigates to *see* that no taxes are owed by the taxpayer for other years. If the taxpayer's record is clear, the check is mailed. If not, the check is held up until payment of the taxes, or it is credited against the outstanding balance.

Refunds in Excess of Two Million Dollars Checked by Congress

A tax refund or credit over $2 million may not be made until 30 days after a report is made ($5 million for C corporation) to Congress' Joint Committee on Taxation (IRC §6405). This provision of the law does not apply to refunds or credits resulting from tentative carryback adjustments. Where the refund claim is for the prior taxable year under the special disaster area loss election (IRC §165(i)), the IRS has discretion to allow the refund without regard to the 30-day rule, and to make a later report to the Joint Committee (IRC §6405(c)).

These cases do not require greater documentation and are not subject to closer examination than regular cases. The right to appeal within the IRS is the same as in other cases. If a protest is not made and no Tax Court petition is filed, the report to the Joint Committee will be prepared by regional specialists in the Examination Division, called Joint Committee Coordinators. If a protest is made, the report is prepared either by an appeals officer or counsel attorney. The report contains:

- The name of the person to whom the refund or credit is to be made;
- The amount of the refund or credit;
- A summary of the facts of the case; and
- The decision of the Commissioner.

Quick Refund for Carryback Items

You may file an application for a tentative carryback adjustment of prior years' taxes due to a carryback of unused general business credit, corporate capital loss, or a previously reported income item under claim of right. If accepted, you may receive a quick refund without extensive audit procedures (IRC §6411). Net operating losses (NOLs) arising in 2021 or later can be carried forward indefinitely to offset 80% of taxable income until the NOL is used up. No carryback is allowed for post-2020 NOLs (with the exception of a two-year carryback for farmers filing Schedule F).

The application, on Form 1045 (Form 1139 for corporations), must be filed within 12 months from the end of the taxable year in which the loss or unused credit occurs. The IRS must act on your application within 90 days of filing or 90 days from the last day of the month in which your return is due, whichever is later. In the case of a quick refund based on a claim of right under IRC §1341(b)(1), the IRS must act within 90 days from the date on which the application is filed or the date of overpayment (the last day for the payment of tax for the year in which a deduction is allowed for the restoration of income held under a claim of right), whichever is later. (IRC §6411(d)).

The IRS may refuse your application if there are computational errors or material omissions that cannot be corrected within the 90-day period. Further, quick refund claims attributable to questionable tax-shelter losses may be withheld by the IRS.

The application does not act as a claim for refund. You may file a separate claim for refund before, at the same time, or after you file your application.

Even though the IRS allows the carryback adjustments according to your application and refunds prior taxes to you, it is not barred from later assessing a deficiency. The purpose of the quick refund procedure is to give you cash immediately when you most likely need it.

HOW TO ARRANGE CLOSING AGREEMENTS AND COMPROMISES

A closing agreement may be used to correct the final tax liability of a taxable period or to determine the tax consequences of specific items without settling the final tax liability of that period (IRC §7121).

A closing agreement is the only statutorily authorized method for entering into an agreement binding on both the service and a taxpayer. Section 7121 permits but does not require the IRS to enter into a closing agreement. As a result, the IRS has the discretion to decide whether and under what conditions a closing agreement is executed.

You may want a closing agreement, even though no tax is due for the period to which the agreement relates. You may enter into a series of agreements relating to the tax liability of a single period. To cover these and other situations, the IRS provides the following closing agreement forms:

Form 866, which covers liability for any past period.

Form 906, which closes specific items of tax liability for either past, current, or future periods (Reg §601.202(b)).

Procedures for entering into closing agreements are also detailed in IRS Rev. Proc. 68-16, 1968-1 CB 770, as modified by Rev. Proc. 94-67, 1994-2 CB 800.

Before entering into a closing agreement, make sure that you understand all of its consequences. After both you and the IRS sign, you cannot change your position. A closing agreement is final on the matter expressly stated in the agreement, unless there is a showing of fraud, malfeasance, or misrepresentation of a material fact. It cannot be modified, set aside, or disregarded in a later suit, action, or proceeding.

Why Use a Closing Agreement?

The main object of a closing agreement is to protect the individual against the reopening of an agreed matter at some later date by the IRS. It also stops an individual from suing or filing other claims for refund. A closing agreement also may be used to fix tax liability for a year barred or arguably barred by the statute of limitations.

You may want a closing agreement for recurring transactions. Cost, fair market value, or adjusted basis as of a given date in the past may be established.

Establishing tax liability may facilitate a transaction such as the sale of stock.

A corporation in the process of liquidation or dissolution may want an agreement to wind up its affairs.

In estate tax proceedings, a closing agreement can assure the fiduciary that the estate is closed for federal tax purposes.

When Is Form 866 Used?

Form 866, "Agreement as to Final Determination of Tax Liability," is used for tax periods ending before the agreement. It closes the total liability of the individual for those periods. It is used where the tax period for which the agreement is asked has ended, and tax liability for the period has been determined.

The total tax liability determined has to be separated into tax periods and types of taxes. Also, the exact section of the law under which each tax covered was imposed must be noted.

Whenever Form 866 is used, the tax liability stated for each period shown in the agreement has to be the total tax liability determined for each period, without any penalty or interest. But the government may want the closing agreement to include ad valorem penalties that have been incurred. Then the tax and penalty are described in the agreement. Three copies of Form 866 must be completed.

When Is Form 906 Used?

Closing agreements on specific items are made on Form 906. This is so whether they are related to past, current, or future periods. A closing agreement of a year ending after the agreement is always made on Form 906. It relates only to a specific item or items affecting tax liability. It cannot attempt to conclude total tax liability for any period. Specific items on past periods that it may cover are items such as:

- Amount of gross income, deductions for losses, depreciation, or depletion;
- Year for which an item of income is to be included in gross income;
- Year for which an item of loss is to be deducted; and
- Value of property on a specified date.

Combined Agreements

Neither Form 866 nor Form 906 is designed to determine both tax liability and tax consequences of specific items. Instead, a combined agreement may be used. The format is shown in Rev. Proc. 68-16, 1968-1 CB 770. The main reason for a combined agreement is that a determination of liability does not fix the amount of income or deductions taken into account in reaching liability. Later, you may be able to prove a net operating loss for the year liability was determined, even though the tax was based on facts showing taxable income. In such a case, while the tax liability has been fixed, the effect of transactions of that year on other years has not. If agreed, the problem may be avoided by a combined agreement determining taxable income for such year and any carryovers from the year.

How to Apply for Closing Agreements

To apply for a closing agreement, send your request to the Director with audit jurisdiction over the returns, or to the Appeals office if your request relates to a case pending before it.

A request is only an offer. It may be withdrawn any time before it is accepted. The closing agreement may be prepared by the taxpayer or the examining agent, but in most cases collaboration is preferable. The taxpayer executes the agreement first, but may withdraw prior to the signing on behalf of the Commissioner.

If it covers a joint return, both spouses have to sign. When an attorney or agent signs, he or she has to include papers proving the authority to sign. Specific instructions for the preparation of closing agreements are contained in Rev. Proc. 68-16, 1968-1 CB 770.

When preparing a closing agreement:

- Fill in the required number of forms. All copies have to be exactly the same. Avoid erasures or corrections; do not switch typewriters.
- Include a statement of how you want the liability fixed and your reasons.
- Use words describing the kind of tax liability involved, such as "Federal income tax."

- Mention all statutes, regulations, and decisions supporting your case, and show how they apply to your facts.
- Describe the taxes involved.
- Include anything else that will help the IRS decide the case.

When a closing agreement is submitted either on Form 866 or Form 906, the taxpayer is asked to sign a Form 870. This permits the immediate assessment and collection of the agreed deficiency. But it may be conditioned on the approval of the final closing agreement. The IRS will insert a paragraph stating this.

IRS Policy on Closing Agreements

The policy is to enter into a closing agreement in any case in which you can show:

- An advantage in having the case permanently closed, as, for example, where, in the settlement of disputed issues, you and the government have made mutual concessions.
- Good and sufficient reasons for desiring a closing agreement, and that the government will suffer no disadvantage if the agreement is entered into.
- The purpose is to mitigate the effect of the statute of limitations or to allow a deficiency dividend.
- Properly executed amended returns have been filed, after the expiration of the period in which assessments might have been made, and no fraud was involved.

A request for a closing agreement is reviewed much more closely than a request for a ruling. The very fact that the IRS is being asked to enter into a binding agreement often makes it suspicious of your motives. Because of the involved nature of the procedure connected with a closing agreement, the IRS is not anxious to use this form. It prefers the much simpler rulings procedure.

There is no assurance in the case of a closing agreement that the Commissioner will agree to it. But no application for a closing agreement can or will be rejected solely because it gives no apparent advantage to the IRS.

Offers in Compromise

The IRS may compromise any civil or criminal case (IRC §7122) unless the case has already been referred to the Department of Justice for prosecution or defense. Once the referral takes place, the Attorney General has the final authority to compromise.

An offer in compromise is a proposal by the taxpayer to pay a sum in full satisfaction of the unpaid tax liability, including interest, penalties, and other additions. When an offer has been accepted and the taxpayer has been notified by letter of the acceptance, the compromise is a legally enforceable contract between the IRS and the taxpayer. All questions of tax liability for the years in question are conclusively and finally settled. Neither the taxpayer nor the IRS may reopen the case except for the showing of falsification, concealment, or mutual mistake of a material fact.

The compromise of a tax liability may rest upon: (1) doubtful liability, (2) doubtful collectibility, or (3) economic hardship or exceptional circumstances. An offer in compromise will be accepted by the IRS if the amount offered reasonably reflects collection potential.

An offer in compromise is filed on Form 656, except for offers based on doubt as to liability, which must be submitted on Form 656-L.

A $205 application fee must accompany Form 656, except for qualifying low-income taxpayers and for taxpayers who have submitted an offer on Form 656-L based on doubt as to liability.

A taxpayer qualifies for low-income certification if the adjusted gross income on his or her most recently filed tax return, or his or her gross monthly income, is no more than the amount shown in a chart in Section 1 of Form 656 based on family size. Qualifying taxpayers can certify their eligibility for the fee-payment exception by checking a box in Section 1.

When an offer is based on doubtful collectibility, economic hardship or exceptional circumstances, Form 656 must be accompanied by either Form 433-A (individuals) or Form 433-B (businesses), which are statements of financial condition.

Before rejecting a proposed offer, the IRS must provide for independent administrative review and if an offer is rejected, you must be notified of the right to appeal to the IRS Appeals office.

An offer is deemed to be accepted by the IRS if the IRS does not reject it within 24 months of the submission date, disregarding periods that tax liability is in dispute in a judicial proceeding (IRC §7122(f)).

Economic hardship or exceptional circumstances. Where there is no doubt as to liability or collectibility, the IRS may agree to a compromise to promote effective tax administration on the grounds of economic hardship or exceptional circumstances. The IRS will consider all the facts and circumstances, including the taxpayer's overall record of tax compliance, in considering the offer. An offer will not be accepted by the IRS if the taxpayer is involved in an open bankruptcy proceeding or if all required federal tax returns have not been filed.

The following are treated as economic hardship situations: (1) long-term illness or disability of the taxpayer or the taxpayer's dependent makes it likely that the taxpayer's financial resources will be exhausted, or (2) liquidation of the taxpayer's assets would prevent the taxpayer from meeting basic living expenses. An example of an exceptional circumstance may be erroneous advice from an IRS employee that results in additional tax liability and penalties (Reg. §301.7122-1(c)(3)(iv)(Example 2)).

Partial payments required. Upfront payments are required (IRC §7122(c)). For a lump-sum offer, which means offers to pay in five or fewer installments, the taxpayer must include with the offer an upfront payment of 20% of the offer amount. For periodic payment offers, the taxpayer must submit the first proposed installment with the application. The upfront payment is in addition to the regular user fee, but the fee will be credited to the outstanding tax liability.

The IRS will waive the partial payment requirement (as well as the application fee) for low-income taxpayers who have certified their status on Form 656, and for taxpayers who have submitted an offer on Form 656-L based on doubt as to liability.

HOW TO GET THE IRS' OPINION ON A TAX PROBLEM

The IRS provides an invaluable service in giving, through letter rulings and determination letters, opinions on tax questions asked by taxpayers. Any taxpayer may ask for an opinion, and requesting one is often a necessary step in making business decisions. Not every tax problem may be satisfactorily resolved, and where an adverse tax holding might disrupt a planned transaction, requesting an IRS opinion before undertaking the proposed move is advisable. However, a fee must be paid to the IRS with your ruling request and the fee may be substantial.

An IRS opinion may also be requested for a closed transaction to determine how to report it on a tax return.

The IRS' discretion to rule on taxpayers' problems is broad. As a matter of policy, it does not give opinions in certain areas and also distinguishes between the type of opinions that can be given by IRS personnel. A letter ruling is issued by the appropriate Office of Associate Chief Counsel in Washington and is in response to questions involving prospective transactions or completed transactions before a return is filed. A determination letter is issued by a Director in response to questions involving completed transactions. As for prospective transactions, determination letters are issued for determining the qualification of proposed pension or profit-sharing plans, or the exempt status of certain organizations. A determination letter is issued only if the questions presented can be specifically answered by clearly established rules in statutes, regulations, or IRS rulings and court decisions published in the Internal Revenue Bulletin.

Revenue rulings are generally modifications of letter rulings that have been selected because of their importance or interest for publication in the Internal Revenue Bulletin.

Procedures for requesting rulings and determination letters are detailed in Rev. Proc. 2022-1, 2022-1 IRB 1. *See* the e-Supplement at jklasser.com for any update.

Should You Ask for an IRS Ruling?

Before requesting a ruling, it is advisable to carefully research the tax law applying to your problem. If your review shows that IRS policy is against your position, do not ask for a ruling. If you proceed without a ruling, there is always the chance that, if the transaction is examined, a settlement might be reached at that time.

Ask for a ruling if you have a fair chance of receiving a favorable ruling or have an alternative plan if you receive an unfavorable reply. Even if the request is turned down, at least you know that you will encounter possible litigation if you proceed with the transaction. This knowledge may also be important in planning and executing the transaction.

User Fee for Ruling

You must pay the IRS a fee for handling a ruling request. The amount of the fee depends on the specific type of ruling involved.

The user fee schedule can be found in Appendix A of Rev. Proc. 2022-1. Taxpayers requesting letter rulings, closing agreements, and rulings using Forms 1128, 2553, 3115 or 8716, must pay the fee electronically at Pay.gov (Section 15.08 of Rev. Proc. 2022-1; News Release IR-2017-102).

Getting Advice for Future Transactions

If your question involves a prospective transaction, then only the appropriate Office of Associate Chief Counsel in Washington has the authority to answer in a letter ruling. Unless the law or regulations specifically provide otherwise, the issuance of an answer is a matter that rests within the discretion of Associate Chief Counsel.

If the question is about the qualification of proposed pension, profit-sharing, or stock bonus plans, then a determination letter may be obtained under the rules in Rev. Proc. 2022-4, 2021-1 IRB 161.

Getting Advice on Closed Transactions

A problem concerning a completed transaction may be answered by the appropriate Office of Associate Chief Counsel in a ruling if no return has been filed, and the answer requires the interpretation of the tax laws.

If the answer to the question requires simply the routine application of established principles and policies, the appropriate IRS Director may answer in a determination letter.

In a particular case, it may be difficult to draw the line between a novel or routine problem. If you are not sure of your position, you can send your question to the appropriate Office of Associate Chief Counsel in Washington. The final decision on whether a question is routine or novel, simple or complex, rests with the IRS. If you send a question to an IRS Director on the theory that the matter is routine, he or she may decide that it is novel and refer the question to Associate Chief Counsel. You will be notified of the change.

You Cannot Get a Ruling for . . .

- Hypothetical transactions.
- Questions of fact involving: market value of property; reasonableness of compensation; accumulated earnings penalty.
- Matters involving a court decision adverse to IRS policy and the IRS has not decided whether to follow or litigate the issue.
- An issue that is identical to an issue involved in a return filed by the taxpayer for an earlier year and that issue is under examination or has been examined by an Area Director or has been considered by an Appeals office, and the statute of limitations has not yet expired.
- Questions involved in pending tax cases—if the government's position would be hurt by giving you a ruling.
- Tax avoidance schemes (you must have a legitimate business purpose in carrying out your transaction).
- Questions that the IRS thinks it cannot properly settle by rulings.
- An issue that is expected to be covered by imminent legislation.
- Questions on replacing involuntarily converted property, even though replacement has not been made, if a return has been filed for the year in which the property was converted. An Area Director can give a determination letter on this issue.

A listing of the areas for which the IRS will not issue rulings or determination letters is published from time to time in the Internal Revenue Bulletin. *See* Section 6 of Rev. Proc. 2022-1, 2022-1 IRB 1 for a general discussion of no-ruling areas and Section 3 of Rev. Proc. 2022-3, 2022-1 IRB 144 for a list of specific questions and problems for which rulings and determination letters will not be issued. The list is not all-inclusive since the IRS may decline to issue rulings or determination letters on other questions whenever warranted by the facts or circumstances of a particular case. Finally, when there has been new legislation, the IRS hesitates to rule on issues involving Code sections for which regulations have not been made final.

You cannot, by court action, force the IRS to give you a ruling or to apply a ruling in your favor.

Generally, rulings are not issued to business, trade, or industrial associations or to other similar groups relating to the application of the tax laws to members of the groups. However, rulings may be issued to such groups or associations relating to their own tax status or liability.

How To Request a Ruling

Your request must be in writing. The IRS does not issue rulings or determination letters upon oral requests. IRS employees ordinarily will not discuss a substantive tax issue prior to the receipt of a written request for a ruling. If they do, their oral opinions are not binding upon the IRS. This should not discourage an inquiry on whether the IRS will rule on a particular question or a discussion on the procedure for submitting a request for a ruling.

Conference to discuss letter ruling issues. Sometimes, it is helpful to ask for a conference before submitting a letter ruling request relating to a proposed transaction. The Associate Chief Counsel has discretion as to whether a pre-submission conference is held. The taxpayer's identity must be provided, the taxpayer must actually intend to submit a ruling request, and the request must involve a matter on which a letter ruling is ordinarily issued. Before a conference is scheduled, you will be asked to provide a draft of your ruling request or other written statement explaining the proposed transaction, the tax issues involved, and your legal analysis. Note that if a pre-submission conference is held, any discussion of substantive issues is merely advisory. It does not bind the IRS. *See* Section 10.07 of Rev. Proc. 2022-1 for details on scheduling a pre-submission conference.

If you submit a ruling request and want to have a conference on the issues involved, request the conference in writing when filing the request or soon thereafter; *see* Section 10 of Rev. Proc. 2022-1 for conference scheduling details.

Making a ruling request. Appendix B of Rev. Proc. 2022-1, 2022-1 IRB 1 has a sample format for a letter ruling request. To ensure that your request is in order so the IRS can respond quickly, complete the checklist in Appendix C of Rev. Proc. 2022-1, sign and date it, and attach it to the top of your request.

The following rules are highlighted in Appendix B and C:

1. A declaration under penalties of perjury that the facts presented are true, correct, and complete must be signed by the person on whose behalf the request is made; *see* the required language in Section 7.01(16) of Rev. Proc. 2022-1, 2022-1 IRB 1, and in the sample format shown in Appendix B.

2. Mark your package "RULING REQUEST SUBMISSION" and mail it to the appropriate Associate Chief Counsel, as shown in checklist item 56 in Appendix C of Rev. Proc. 2022-1.

Submit the original and one copy of the request. If multiple issues are presented in the request and you want separate letter rulings for each issue, make this clear in the request and submit the original and at least two copies of the request, with an additional copy for each additional separate letter ruling requested. Submit the original and two copies of the request if a closing agreement is requested on the issue presented (Sections 7.04(1) and 7.02(1) of Rev. Proc. 2022-1).

Alternatively, you may submit a letter ruling request electronically, either by secure electronic facsimile (encouraged by IRS) or by encrypted email (considered riskier) (Sections 7.04(2) and (3) of Rev. Proc. 2022-1). An electronic submission must include an image of a signature (scanned or photographed) or a digital signature (Sec. 7.01(13) of Rev. Proc. 2022-1).

3. Do not submit alternative plans in requests for a ruling.

4. Be sure to include:
   - Complete facts.
   - Names, addresses, and taxpayer account numbers of all interested parties.
   - Copies, not originals, of all pertinent documents. The copies should be attested to be the same as the originals. Do not send originals, as they become part of the IRS file and are not returned.

   The balance sheet nearest the date of the transaction, if a corporate reorganization, distribution, or similar transaction is involved.

   If documents are submitted, they must be accompanied by an analysis of their relevancy to the issue.

5. Give the business reason for the transaction (favorable rulings often depend upon the existence of a bona fide business reason for the transaction).

6. Give the grounds for your stand and your supporting authority and specify what ruling or rulings you want. If you want a particular determination, explain the basis for your contentions, together with a statement of relevant authorities. Even if you do not urge a particular determination, you must give your view of the tax result, supported by a statement of relevant authorities such as statutes and regulations. All requests must include a statement of whether the applicable law is uncertain and whether the issue is adequately addressed by relevant authorities (Section 7.01(9) of Rev. Proc. 2022-1).

7. The IRS encourages the disclosure of any legislation, regulations, revenue rulings, or revenue procedures contrary to the taxpayer's position. The IRS believes that disclosure will lead to more rapid action. Technically, the IRS encourages but does not require the statement of contrary authorities. However, if contrary authorities are not provided, the IRS wants the ruling request to include a statement that there are no contrary authorities. If the taxpayer does not take either action and refuses a subsequent request of the IRS to do so, the IRS may refuse to issue a ruling (Section 7.01(10) of Rev. Proc. 2022-1). The IRS specifically requires that any relevant pending legislation be identified in the ruling request. The IRS must also be notified if legislation is introduced after the request is filed but before a ruling is issued (Section 7.01(11) of Rev. Proc. 2022-1).

8. If a conference on the issues is desired, ask for one in the ruling request or soon afterwards in writing (Section 7.02(6) of Rev. Proc. 2022-1).

9. Sign the request. If you are representing a taxpayer, include your power of attorney and if you are an enrolled agent, show evidence of enrollment. The ruling request is signed by the taxpayer or by an authorized representative who is (1) an attorney who has filed a written declaration that he or she is currently qualified as an attorney and is authorized to represent the taxpayer; (2) a certified public accountant who files with the IRS written declaration that he or she is currently qualified as a certified public accountant and is authorized to represent the taxpayer; (3) a person, other than an attorney or certified public accountant, enrolled to practice before the Service; or (4) any other person who has received a Letter of Authorization from the IRS Director of the Office of Professional Responsibility to represent the taxpayer in this particular matter (Sections 7.01(13-15) of Rev. Proc. 2022-1).

10. Submit payment of user fee. Each ruling request must be accompanied by the appropriate fee. For specific payment instructions, *see* Section 15 and Appendix A of Rev. Proc. 2022-1. Pay.gov is the only permissible payment method for the following rulings described in Rev. Proc. 2022-1: private letter rulings, closing agreements, and rulings using Forms 1128, 2553, 3115 or 8716.

User fees for employee plans and exempt organizations are in Section 30 and Appendix A of Rev. Proc. 2022-4, 2022-1 IRB 161.

Requests that do not comply with the above requirements will be acknowledged, and the requirements that have not been met will be pointed out. If the missing information is not supplied within 21 days, and an extension is not granted, the IRS will notify you in writing that the ruling request has been closed (Section 8.05(1) of Rev. Proc. 2022-1). If you supply the missing information after the closing letter is mailed, your request will be reopened and treated as a new request as of the date of the receipt of the information, but a new user fee must be paid (Section 8.05(3) of Rev. Proc. 2022-1).

The IRS has an alternate two-part procedure to expedite the processing of ruling requests for proposed transactions (Sections 7.02(3) and (4) of Rev. Proc. 2022-1). Under the procedure, you may submit, together with the detailed statement of facts, documents and other required information, a summary statement of the controlling facts that support your request. If the Office of Associate Chief Counsel finds your summary satisfactory, the ruling will be based on these facts. This procedure has the advantage of eliminating many of the facts that the reviewer must assess. In addition, it removes some of the subjectivity exercised by the reviewer in determining whether the transaction was carried out substantially as proposed and whether minor deviations are material. On the other hand, this procedure poses the problem of what is a sufficient statement of the facts.

Withdrawing your request. You may withdraw your request for a ruling or a determination letter at any time prior to the signing of the letter of reply. However, this may prove futile. The Office of Associate Chief Counsel may give its views on your request to the appropriate official with examination jurisdiction of the return. The information you submitted with your request will be considered in a later audit or examination of your return. Even though you withdraw your request, all correspondence and exhibits are retained by the IRS and are not returned to you.

Your Ruling Will Be Open to Public Inspection

Code §6110 requires the IRS to open to public inspection virtually all letter rulings, determination letters, and technical advice memoranda (called "written determinations") and related background files. Before your ruling is made public, it must be "sanitized" by deleting the following information:

1. Identifying details, such as names, addresses, Social Security numbers, and any other information that would identify any person (other than certain third parties who communicate with the IRS regarding the determination). Identifying details include information that would permit a person in the appropriate community (such as an industry or geographic location) to identify any person.

2. Information specifically authorized to be kept secret in the interest of national defense or foreign policy.

3. Information exempt from disclosure under other laws.

4. Trade secrets and privileged or confidential commercial or financial information.

5. Information the disclosure of which would constitute a clearly unwarranted invasion of personal privacy. This would include, for example, details not yet made public of a pending divorce or of medical treatment.

6. Information concerning the agency regulation of financial institutions.

7. Geological and geophysical information and data, including maps concerning wells.

Requesting deletions from written determination. When you request a determination letter, ruling, or technical advice memorandum, you must also submit a separate statement of proposed deletions (Section 7.01(12) of Rev. Proc. 2022-1). At the same time the letter ruling or determination letter on your case is issued, you will receive a notice that it will be disclosed to the public. You will also receive a copy of the text the IRS proposes to disclose on which is indicated the material the IRS proposes to delete, any substitutions, and any third-party communications. (In the case of a background file or written determination that is disclosed only on written request for disclosure, the disclosure notice will be mailed to you within a reasonable time after the IRS received its first request for disclosure.) You then have 20 days after the notice is mailed to submit a written statement identifying those items that you believe should be deleted but were not. You must also submit a copy of the proposed IRS text and indicate by brackets further deletions that you want the IRS to make. Generally, the IRS will not delete any material that you had not earlier proposed be deleted. The IRS will mail to you its final administrative conclusions regarding deletions within 20 days of receiving your response (Section 7.01(12)(e) of Rev. Proc.

2022-1). The IRS will attempt to resolve the differences, but will not grant a conference specifically for that purpose. However, you may discuss issues involving deletions at any conference that has been otherwise scheduled with respect to the requested ruling or determination letter.

Court remedies when you and the IRS do not agree on deletions. If you are still not satisfied with the deletions proposed by the IRS, you may file a petition in the Tax Court (anonymously, if appropriate) within 60 days after the date on which the IRS mailed the disclosure notice (IRC §6110(f)(3)). You must have exhausted your remedies within the IRS prior to petitioning the Tax Court. If your request for deletions has not been responded to by the IRS within 50 days of the mailing of the disclosure notice, this is considered an exhaustion of administrative remedies allowing a filing of a petition in the Tax Court (Reg. §301.6110-5(b)(3)).

Within 15 days, the IRS will notify by registered or certified mail any other person identified by name and address in the written determination or background file that a petition has been filed in the Tax Court. Such person may intervene in the Tax Court action (anonymously, if appropriate) (IRC §6110(f)(3)(B)).

The Tax Court will make a decision as soon as possible on the extent of deletions and may close its proceedings on the issue to the public (IRC §6110(f)(5) and (6)).

When Written Determinations Are Open to Public Inspection

Generally, written determinations and background files will be open to public inspection no earlier than 75 days and no later than 90 days after the IRS mailed you the disclosure notice. If you sued in the Tax Court regarding deletions, the written determination or background file will be open to the public within 30 days after the court order becomes final, although the court may extend the 30-day period to give the IRS time to comply with its order (IRC §6110(g)).

Request for Delay of Disclosure

Where the transaction that is the subject of the written determination is not complete when the determination is issued, you may request that the IRS postpone disclosure until 15 days after the transaction is completed. However, disclosure generally must occur within 180 days after the IRS mailed you the disclosure notice (IRC §6110 (g)(3)). If the transaction is still not completed within the 180-day period, and disclosure would interfere with the transaction, you may again request a postponement until 15 days after the transaction. Overall, postponement may not exceed 360 days after the IRS mailing of the disclosure notice (IRC §6110 (g)(4); Reg. §301.6110-5(c)(2)(ii)(B)).

Your request for postponement must be in writing and state the date on which you expect to complete the transaction. To get the first postponement, send your request so that the IRS receives it within 60 days after the disclosure notice. To get the second postponement, send your request so that the IRS receives it within 15 days before the date you stated you expected to complete the transaction (Reg. §301.6110-5(c)(2)(ii)(C)).

You must notify the IRS when you complete the transaction if that happens earlier than you expected. The written determination will be open to public inspection 30 days after notice of completion or on the date originally scheduled for disclosure, whichever date is earlier (Reg. §301.6110-5(c)(2)(ii)(D)).

What to Do When the IRS Fails to Meet the Time Limitations or Fails to Make Deletions

Where the IRS fails to meet the time limitations, such as disclosing before 75 days after the disclosure notice was mailed to you or failing to postpone disclosure pursuant to your request, you may sue the government in the U.S. Court of Federal Claims. You or any other person identified in the determination may sue the government in the U.S. Court of Federal Claims if the IRS fails to make deletions as required by its own agreement or by court order. Where the court determines that any employee of the IRS intentionally or willfully failed to make a deletion or failed to act within the time limits, you may recover your actual damages (but not less than $1,000) plus costs and reasonable attorneys' fees for bringing the action (IRC §6110(j)(2)).

How Soon May You Receive an Answer?

Letter rulings and determination letters are issued on a first-come-first-served basis. You may get a preference by showing a compelling need for a faster consideration but the IRS will grant expedited handling only in rare and unusual cases (for details, *see* Section 7.02(4) of Rev. Proc. 2022-1). Even if the IRS decides to grant expedited handling, it will not assure you that your request will be processed by the date you request.

You may request that the IRS fax or email you or your representative a copy of the letter ruling, but the ruling is not considered "issued" until it is mailed (Section 7.02(5) of Rev. Proc. 2022-1).

To learn the status of a tax ruling, contact the representative indicated on the IRS acknowledgment of your request.

You May Get an Information Letter

Even though you request a ruling or a determination letter, you may receive an information letter. This is a statement issued either by the Office of Associate Chief Counsel or by a Director. It does no more than call attention to a well-established interpretation or principle of tax law without applying it to a specific set of facts. You may receive an information letter if your request seeks general information or does not meet all the requirements for a ruling or determination letter (Section 2.04 of Rev. Proc. 2022-1).

Can You Rely on a Letter Ruling?

You can usually rely on a letter ruling sent to you, although the IRS has the power to revoke the ruling retroactively. However, the IRS only under rare circumstances exercises this power. If the ruling is changed or revoked, the effect is almost always prospective. Be sure, in applying a ruling to the actual transaction, that the facts of the transaction are as you had stated them in your request and that the law has not changed in the meantime (Section 11.03 of Rev. Proc. 2022-1).

When preparing the return for the year in which the transaction involved takes place, attach a copy of the ruling or letter to the return. IRS personnel compare the facts reported on the return with the representations upon which the ruling was based. They do this to determine whether there has been a misstatement or omission of a material fact, or if the transaction upon which the ruling was based was actually carried out in a manner materially different from that represented.

When you receive a ruling, the IRS will generally audit the return reporting the transaction that is the subject of the ruling.

You may not rely on a letter ruling issued to another taxpayer, although the ruling may be helpful in discerning the IRS position on a particular issue. The law specifically states that written determinations may not be cited as precedent by either the IRS or taxpayers unless the IRS provides otherwise in regulations (IRC §6110(k)(3)). The Supreme Court has stated that although the law bars the use of private rulings as precedents, they are nonetheless "evidence" of IRS views. The IRS may designate in a widely circulated official government publication (such as the Internal Revenue Bulletin) that a determination will be used as precedent.

You may rely on Revenue Rulings published in the Internal Revenue Bulletin in determining the rule applicable to your own case if the facts and circumstances of your transaction are substantially the same as in the published ruling.

Review and Revocation of Determination Letters

Determination letters involving income taxes are not generally reviewed by the Office of Associate Chief Counsel, as they merely repeat a position previously established in a regulation, ruling, or court decision published in the Internal Revenue Bulletin. If you believe a determination letter to be in error, you may ask the appropriate Director to reconsider the matter. You may also ask the Director to request technical advice from the Associate Office of Chief Counsel (Section 12.06 of Rev. Proc. 2022-1).

A Director may revoke a determination letter on re-examination of the issue or on an audit of the taxpayer's return. The revocation is generally retroactive because the letter was issued for a completed transaction (so you did not rely upon the letter when entering into the transaction). A Director does not have authority under IRC § 7805(b) to limit the revocation or modification of the determination letter, but if the Field office proposes to revoke or modify the letter, you may ask the Director that issued the determination letter to seek technical advice from the Associate office that would limit the retroactive effect of the revocation or modification (Section 13.02 of Rev. Proc. 2022-1).

The revocation of a determination letter on the status of pension and profit-sharing plans and exempt organizations, however, is generally prospective in effect.

How Letter Rulings Become Revenue Rulings

Revenue Rulings are often revised letter rulings that the IRS believes have value as precedents or guides for taxpayers and IRS personnel. Although it is on the same subject matter, a Revenue

Ruling differs from a letter ruling. When a letter ruling is edited for publication as a Revenue Ruling, the taxpayers' names and identifying facts are deleted. However, the ruling retains relevant facts with modifications to fit within the IRS' intention to propound a general rule. Finally, Revenue Rulings are subject to higher review, whereas many letter rulings are issued with no review above the branch level.

Requesting Technical Advice From the National Office

IRS field office personnel determine whether to request a technical advice memorandum (TAM) from the Office of Associate Chief Counsel when an issue is raised during an audit or conference as to the proper application of the Internal Revenue Code or IRS rules to a specific set of facts. A TAM may not be requested for prospective or hypothetical transactions (Section 3.01 of Rev. Proc. 2022-2, 2022-1 IRB 120). Before requesting technical advice, the field office must coordinate with field counsel and all requests for technical advice must be approved in writing by an IRS Director (Section 5.01 of Rev. Proc. 2022-2).

You may request that the IRS Director refer an issue on a closed transaction to the Office of Associate Chief Counsel for a TAM (Section 5.02 of Rev. Proc. 2022-2). You may do this on the grounds that the issue has not been handled by the IRS in a uniform manner, or the issue, because of its complexity or unusualness, warrants consideration by the Associate Chief Counsel. Request for technical advice should be made as early as possible. If you wait until the case is in the Appeals office, the request for technical advice may be made before the Appeals office conference.

Your request for technical advice should be directed to the field office, either orally or in writing (Section 5.02 of Rev. Proc. 2022-2). The field office will notify you if it decides that your request for technical advice is unwarranted, and you may appeal the decision within 30 days of the notification by submitting to the field office a written statement of the reasons why the matter should be referred to the appropriate Office of Associate Chief Counsel (Section 5.03 of Rev. Proc. 2022-2). The statement should describe the pertinent facts and legal authorities and explain your position and the need for technical advice. The statement, along with the field office's statement of why technical advice is not needed, will be forwarded to the appropriate Compliance Director or territory manager for a decision. No conference will be held with you or your representative. If the Director proposes to deny the request, you will be sent a written explanation. You may not appeal a proposed denial, but at your request the Director will review the file and make a decision solely on the basis of the written record; no conference will be held. The reviewing Director will notify the field office of its decision within 45 days of receiving the information and then the field office will notify you (Section 5.04 of Rev. Proc. 2022-2).

If the field office intends to request technical advice, it will arrange a pre-submission conference to frame the issues and prepare the documents that must be included with the request (Section 6 of Rev. Proc. 2022-2). The pre-submission conference is generally conducted by telephone but may be conducted in person if the parties so choose (Section 6.07 of Rev. Proc. 2022-2).

You will be informed if the Associate Chief Counsel proposes to issue a TAM that is adverse to you, and a conference will be held, generally in person within 10 days unless you waive the right to the conference (Sections 9.01-9.02 of Rev. Proc. 2022-2). Generally, you should attempt to provide all documents and arguments in writing well in advance of the conference, but if at the conference it appears that new information may be helpful, the new information should be provided within 10 days after the conference. Extensions of the 10-day period must be requested in writing and are not typically granted by the Associate Chief Counsel (Section 9.06 of Rev. Proc. 2022-2).

A TAM contains: (1) a statement of the issues; (2) a statement of the facts pertinent to the issues; (3) the conclusions of the Associate Chief Counsel; (4) a discussion of the laws, regulations, rulings, and court decisions; and (5) a discussion of the rationale supporting the conclusions reached by the Associate Chief Counsel. The conclusions give direct answers, whenever possible, to the specific issues raised by the field office (Section 10.01 of Rev. Proc. 2021-2).

Accompanying the TAM is a notice under IRC §6110(f)(1) to disclose a TAM, including a copy of the version proposed to be open to public inspection. Before issuing the TAM, the Associate Chief Counsel will inform you if the IRS has decided to include in the TAM any of the material that you asked to be deleted. In that case, you have 10 days to submit further arguments supporting your proposed deletions (Section 10.09 of Rev. Proc. 2022-2).

After the Associate Chief Counsel provides a copy of the final TAM to the field office, the field office generally gives you a copy of the issued TAM, along with a copy of the version proposed to be open to public inspection (Sections 10.07–10.10 of Rev. Proc. 2022-2). However, a copy of the TAM will not be given to you if your case involved a criminal or civil fraud investigation, or a jeopardy or termination assessment, until all of the proceedings in the investigation or assessment are complete (Section 10.12 of Rev. Proc. 2022-2).

Effect of technical advice. A technical advice memorandum represents the IRS' views of the law, applied to the facts of your specific case. Generally, a technical advice memorandum has the same effect as a ruling on a closed and completed transaction. It usually disposes of the matter in which it was requested and usually applies retroactively (Section 13 of Rev. Proc. 2022-2). But note: (1) Technical advice is not binding in a subsequent year, even though it is not revoked. (2) The IRS office handling your case may raise an issue in any taxable period, even though it has received technical advice concerning the same issue in another taxable period.

You may not rely on a TAM issued by the IRS for another taxpayer (IRC §6110(k)(3); (Section 13.04 of Rev. Proc. 2022-2).

Technical advice memoranda often form the basis for revenue rulings.

Note: Other details on the furnishing of technical advice are in Rev. Proc. 2022-2, 2022-1 IRB 120.

How to Get Written Determinations Issued to Other Taxpayers

While you may not use letter rulings, determination letters, or technical advice memoranda issued to other taxpayers as precedent, they may be helpful as they reflect IRS policy and interpretation of the law. Written determinations are available from subscription services and in government reading rooms as discussed in the following section; background files are open to inspection only on written request.

Disclosure is not required of any technical advice memorandum (and its related background file) where the case involves civil fraud, criminal investigation, jeopardy, or termination assessment, until any action relating to the investigation or assessment is completed. Furthermore, a determination relating to IRS approval of the adoption or change in accounting method or period, qualified retirement plan funding method or plan year, or taxable year of a partner or partnership need not be open to public inspection, although the IRS must honor a written request for inspection.

Where You May Inspect Written Determinations

Some private publishing firms, such as Tax Analysts, Research Institute of America, and Commerce Clearing House, regularly publish rulings and technical advice memoranda.

The IRS makes letter rulings and technical advice memoranda available in its FOIA Library; go to the section for "Non-precedential Rulings and Advice" at https://www.irs.gov./privacy-disclosure/foia-library.

Rulings and technical advice memoranda are also available for inspection and copying in the IRS Freedom of Information Reading Room located at 1111 Constitution Avenue, N.W., Washington D.C. 20224.

Actions To Obtain Additional Disclosure

You may seek disclosure of additional information on any written determination or background file open to public inspection (IRC §6110(f)(4)). You must request the additional disclosure from the Internal Revenue Office that issued the written determination, specifying the deleted information that you believe should be disclosed and why. The IRS says it will not disclose names, addresses, or identifying numbers. The IRS will notify all people identified by name and address in the determination or background file that additional disclosure is sought. If all agree to the additional disclosure within 20 days, the determination or background file will be revised to reflect the additional disclosure. If anyone objects, the IRS will deny your request (Reg. §301.6110-5(d)(1)).

If your request is denied, you may file a petition in Tax Court or the District Court for the District of Columbia for the additional disclosure. The IRS will notify anyone identified by name and address in the determination or background file of the suit within 15 days by registered or certified mail, and such person may intervene in the suit (anonymously, if appropriate) (Reg. §301.6110-5(d)(2)-(5)).

CIRCULAR 230: PRACTICE BEFORE THE IRS

The requirements, privileges, and duties of persons qualified to practice before the IRS are described in Treasury Department Circular No. 230. The IRS Office of Professional Responsibility (OPR) may impose sanctions *(discussed below)* on practitioners who violate the Circular standards.

You can access Circular 230 (with a revision date of June 2014; this is the latest revision at the time this book was completed) and related tax practice information at the Circular 230 Tax Professionals Home page: https://www.irs.gov/tax-professionals/circular-230-tax-professionals.

Practitioners subject to Circular 230. The provisions of Circular 230 apply to attorneys, certified public accountants, enrolled agents, enrolled retirement plan agents, and enrolled actuaries. Other individuals are subject to Circular 230 to the extent they (1) have "limited representation rights", allowing them to represent taxpayers only before IRS examination, customer service and similar personnel (including the Taxpayer Advocate Service) in connection with returns they prepared and signed (see "Preparer representation rights before the IRS" on this page), (2) represent others pursuant to the limited practice regulations (see text below at "Limited Practice in Special Cases"), or (3) they give written advice concerning transactions, arrangements or entities that the IRS determines to have a tax avoidance or evasion purpose.

The attempt by the IRS to subject "unenrolled" tax return preparers (preparers other than attorneys, CPAs, or enrolled agents) to the practice rules of Circular 230 was rejected in 2014 by the Court of Appeals for the District of Columbia Circuit (*Loving v. IRS*, 742 F.3d 1013 (D.C. Cir. 2014)). The D.C. Circuit held that the IRS lacked the statutory authority to issue the 2011 regulations (T.D. 9527, 2011-27 IRB 1) that treated tax return preparers as engaged in "practice" before the IRS and which required preparers who were not attorneys, CPAs, or enrolled agents to qualify as "registered tax return preparers" (RTRPs) by passing a minimum competency test, undergoing a tax compliance check and background suitability check, and taking continuing education courses. According to the D.C. Circuit, the statute that allows the IRS to regulate individuals who "practice" before it (31 U.S.C. Sec. 330) does not cover those who merely prepare tax returns, as Congress intended "practice" to mean the representation of a taxpayer in a contested proceeding during the examination and appeals stages before the IRS.

Note that the D.C. Circuit decision in *Loving* has no impact on the statutory requirement that all paid tax return preparers must have a PTIN (see discussion below) and enter it on their clients' tax returns (Code Section 6109(a)(4)).

Although the regulations on "registered tax return preparers" (RTRPs) were invalidated by the D.C. Circuit's decision in *Loving*, those regulations were still in the version of Circular 230 posted on IRS.gov at the time this book was completed (Reg. §§10.3(f), 10.4(c), and 10.5 of the June 2014 revision of Circular 230).

Annual Filing Season Program was adopted by IRS in response to the *Loving* decision. In response to the D.C. Circuit decision in *Loving (see above)*, the IRS has implemented a voluntary program of continuing education and testing for unenrolled preparers, which it calls the "Annual Filing Season Program". The requirements for the Annual Filing Season Program and benefits of participation for unenrolled preparers are discussed below.

Preparer representation rights before the IRS. The only tax professionals with unlimited representation rights before the IRS are attorneys, CPAs, and enrolled agents. These credentialed practitioners may represent clients on all matters before the IRS, including audits, payments, collections, and appeals.

Non-credentialed preparers (not CPAs, enrolled agents or attorneys) who have received a Record of Completion under the Annual Filing Season Program (AFSP, *see* below) for both the year they prepared and signed the return and the year in which representation occurs have "limited representation rights" with respect to returns they prepared and signed after 2015. Having limited representation rights means that the AFSP participant may represent a taxpayer whose tax return he or she prepared and signed during an audit of that return, but only before IRS revenue agents, customer service representatives, and similar IRS employees, including the Taxpayer Advocate Service. Non-credentialed preparers are not allowed to represent the taxpayer before appeals or collections officers even if they have a Record of Completion under the Annual Filing Season Program.

Non-credentialed preparers who do not complete the Annual Filing Season Program may not represent taxpayers before the IRS in any way with respect to returns and refund claims prepared and signed after 2015 (News Release IR-2015-123; Rev. Proc. 2014-42, 2014-29 IRB 192). With respect to returns they prepared and signed before 2016, all non-credentialed preparers have "limited representation rights", as described above.

The IRS Return Preparer Office (RPO). The IRS Return Preparer Office administers (1) the PTIN application and renewal system for paid preparers, (2) continuing education for tax professionals, and (3) the Annual Filing Season Program *(see below)*. The RPO also manages the enrollment programs for enrolled agents, enrolled actuaries, and enrolled retirement agents. For enrolled agents, this includes (1) applications for enrollment, the tax competency test, preliminary suitability and tax compliance determinations, and (2) enrolled agent renewals, including the continuing education requirements.

The Office of Professional Responsibility (OPR). The Office of Professional Responsibility (OPR) enforces the Circular 230 standards of practitioner conduct and discipline, including instituting disciplinary proceedings and pursuing sanctions.

PTINs are Mandatory and Must Be Renewed Annually by Paid Tax Return Preparers

Anyone who receives compensation to prepare all or substantially all of a federal tax return or refund claim must obtain a preparer tax identification number (PTIN) from the IRS. A paid preparer must include a valid PTIN on federal returns he or she prepares or be subject to penalties (IRC §6695(c)). The penalty for 2022 returns or refund claims filed in 2023 is $55 per return/refund claim, up to a maximum of $28,000.

The PTIN requirement applies to non-credentialed preparers, as well as to attorneys, certified public accountants, enrolled retirement plan agents, and enrolled actuaries if for compensation they prepare or help prepare any tax return or refund claim. All enrolled agents must have a valid PTIN regardless of whether they prepare tax returns.

Supervised preparers (non-signing preparers who work under the supervision of an attorney, CPA, or enrolled agent, actuary, or retirement plan agent) and preparers who do not prepare Form 1040 series forms must obtain a PTIN and renew it annually. This is true even though the returns they prepare (or assist in preparing) are reviewed and signed by a supervisor.

The IRS ruled that enrolled retirement plan agents are not required to obtain a PTIN prior to applying for enrollment or renewing enrollment if they prepare only Form 5300 series returns or Form 5500 series returns (Notice 2011-91, 2011-47 IRB 792).

PTINs are issued for a specific calendar year and must be renewed by the end of a year for the following year. The PTIN "open season" for obtaining or renewing a PTIN for the following year normally begins in mid-October of the prior year. Preparers with 2023 PTINs must renew their PTINs for 2024 by December 31, 2023 (News Release IR-2022-190).

Preparers are urged to sign up for or renew a PTIN online at https://www.irs.gov/tax-professionals/ptin-requirements-for-tax-return-preparers. A paper application for obtaining or renewing a PTIN can also be made on Form W-12 (IRS Paid Preparer Tax Identification Number Application), but processing will take 4-6 weeks.

Fee to obtain or renew a PTIN. After years of litigation (see the next paragraph), the IRS reinstituted user fees for obtaining or renewing a PTIN in 2020 final regulations (T.D. 9903, 2020-32 IRB 235). There was no fee for 2018-2020. The fee for a PTIN for 2021 and 2022 was $35.95 (same as for 2021), of which $21 is the IRS user fee to cover the costs of administering the PTIN program (the $21 per application or renewal is fixed in the regulations), and the balance ($14.95) was payable to a third-party contractor for processing PTIN applications and operating a call center. For the 2023 filing season, the fee is $30.75. The fee is non-refundable.

The 2020 regulations followed years of litigation over the authority of the IRS to charge a user fee for obtaining or renewing a PTIN. A federal district court held in 2017 that the IRS lacked the statutory to charge a PTIN user fee and enjoined the IRS from imposing one (*Steele*, 260 F. Supp.3d 52 (D.D.C. 2017), but this decision was reversed in 2019 by the D.C. Circuit (*Montrois v. United States*, 916 F.3d 1056 (D.C.Cir. 2019)). The D.C. Circuit held that the IRS acted within its authority under the Independent Offices Appropriations Act in charging tax-return preparers a fee to obtain and renew PTINs, because a federal agency that provides a specific service to identifiable individuals rather than the public at large may charge the identifiable individuals a fee for the service. A PTIN is a specific service provided to tax return preparers by the IRS, which incurs substantial costs to maintain the program. The PTIN program confers a specific benefit to preparers by enabling them to enter the PTIN on the returns they prepare, rather than their Social Security number.

The IRS' Annual Filing Season Program for Non-Credentialed Preparers

After the D.C. Circuit decision in *Loving* struck down mandatory testing and continuing education for non-credentialed tax preparers, the IRS put into place the "Annual Filing Season Program (AFSP)", starting with the 2015 tax filing season (Rev. Proc. 2014-42, 2014-29 IRB 192). The AFSP is intended to encourage non-credentialed tax preparers (preparers other than attorneys, CPAs, enrolled agents, enrolled actuaries, and enrolled retirement plan agents) to voluntarily undergo annual continuing education and take a tax competency exam (unless exempt) so that they can enhance their credibility with potential clients. The IRS provides an overview of the AFSP at www.irs.gov/Tax-Professionals/Annual-Filing-Season-Program. There are links to details on the CE courses and test requirements, the test exemptions, frequently asked questions, and other AFSP rules.

The IRS' authority to establish the AFSP was challenged in the federal courts by the AICPA, but the D.C. Circuit Court of Appeals held in 2018 that the IRS had statutory authority under 31 U.S.C. Sec. 330 (a) to establish and operate the AFSP. That statute authorizes the IRS to regulate the practice of representatives and to admit to practice only individuals with good character and with the necessary qualifications and competence. The IRS uses the education, testing, and certification portions of the AFSP to ensure that non-credentialed preparers who participate demonstrate the qualifications and competence necessary to represent a taxpayer before it during an examination. In addition, the IRS has the authority to publish the AFSP under Section 7803(a)(2)(A) of the Internal Revenue Code (giving the IRS Commissioner power to administer the execution and application of the internal revenue laws or related statutes) (*American Institute of Certified Public Accountants v. IRS*, 2018-2 USTC ¶50,375 (D.C. Cir. 2018).

Completing the AFSP allows listing on IRS directory of preparers. Non-credentialed preparers who meet the AFSP continuing education and other requirements (*see below*) receive a "Record of Completion" from the IRS and are included in a searchable directory of tax preparers that taxpayers can access at https://irs.treasury.gov/rpo/rpo.jsf. On the directory, which is updated regularly, attorneys, CPAs, enrolled agents, enrolled actuaries, and enrolled retirement plan agents with valid PTINs are recognized as having professional credentials. Preparers that have obtained an AFSP Record of Completion (*see* requirements below) are not called "credentialed" preparers on the directory but are identified separately as having an "other qualification". The IRS allows non-credentialed preparers with an AFSP Record of Completion to state (in advertising and otherwise) only that they have met the IRS requirements for receiving the Record of Completion. They may not state or imply that the IRS has "endorsed", "certified", "enrolled", or "licensed" them.

Continuing education required to obtain AFSP Record of Completion. Generally, 18 hours of continuing education (CE) must be completed by the end of the year to obtain an AFSP Record of Completion for the upcoming tax season. The CE must be from IRS-Approved CE Providers. Unless the preparer has

an exemption (*see below*), the 18 hours must include a six-hour federal tax refresher course followed by a tax comprehension examination. Preparers with an exemption from the refresher course and the test must still complete 15 hours of continuing education. CE providers determine course fees; the IRS does not charge a fee for participating in the AFSP.

For those who are not exempt from the refresher course and testing, the 18 hours of CE must include the following:

1. the six-hour annual tax refresher course (AFTR course) covering filing season and tax law updates, followed by a comprehension examination on the tax topics covered by the AFTR course. The test as well as the AFTR course is designed and administered by the CE provider and not the IRS. The IRS provides a course outline and test parameters that CE providers must follow. For example, the test must have 100 multiple choice questions, of which at least 70% must be answered correctly.

2. 10 hours of additional federal tax law topics in addition to the AFTR, and

3. two hours of ethics.

If the preparer is exempt (see next paragraph) from the AFTR course and examination, the preparer must complete 15 hours of CE as follows:

1. 10 hours of federal tax law topics

2. three hours of federal tax law updates, and

3. two hours of ethics.

Exemption from tax refresher course and test. Non-credentialed preparers who have taken other recognized tax competency tests can obtain the AFSP Record of Completion without taking the AFSP refresher course and examination. Preparers qualifying for an exemption must still take 15 hours of CE as shown above. Exempted from the refresher course and examination are preparers who passed the IRS' Registered Tax Return Preparer test between November 2011 and January 2013 (prior to the Loving decision), and preparers in California, Oregon, and Maryland who are currently subject to state-based testing. The full list of exemptions is at https://www.irs.gov/tax-professionals/reduced-requirements-for-exempt-individuals-for-the-annual-filing-season-program-record-of-completion.

Preparer must have valid PTIN and consent to certain Circular 230 provisions to obtain AFSP Record of Completion. In addition to completing the required CE, a preparer must consent to be bound by the tax practice obligations in Subpart B of Circular 230 (Reg. Sections 10.20-10.38) and in Section 10.51, (which is in Subpart C of Circular 230) and must have an active PTIN for the upcoming tax year to receive the Record of Completion. Once preparers have completed their CE requirements and obtained or renewed their PTIN for the upcoming year, they will receive an email from "TaxPros @ ptin.irs.gov" with instructions on how to consent to the Circular 230 practice requirements, after which they will receive their Record of Completion certificate in their online secure mailbox. Preparers without an online PTIN account will receive a letter with instructions for completing the application process and obtaining their Record of Completion.

Limited representation rights. As noted earlier (see above at "Preparer representation rights before the IRS"), for tax returns prepared and signed after 2015, a non-credentialed preparer with an AFSP Record of Completion has limited representation rights, meaning that they can represent the taxpayer during an audit of the return (including a refund claim), but only before IRS revenue agents, customer service representatives, and similar IRS employees, including the Taxpayer Advocate Service. The preparer must have had an AFSP Record of Completion for the year in which the return was prepared and signed and also must have an AFSP Record of Completion for the year or years in which the representation occurs.

Attorneys and CPAs, Enrolled Agents, Enrolled Retirement Plan Agents, and Enrolled Actuaries

If you are an attorney, a certified public accountant, or enrolled agent in good standing with the IRS (not under suspension or disbarment from practice), you may practice before the IRS by submitting a properly completed Form 2848 signed by you and your client, which serves as a power of attorney and as your declaration that you are currently qualified to practice under Circular 230 and that you are authorized to represent the taxpayer in the tax matters specified on Form 2848 (Reg. §10.3(a), (b), and (c), Circular 230). The IRS may approve a substitute Form 2848; see the Form 2848 instructions.

Enrolled actuary. If you are enrolled as an actuary by the Joint Board for the Enrollment of Actuaries, and if you complete an application for enrollment on Form 5434 and pay the IRS' application fee, currently $250, you may practice before the IRS (assuming you are not under suspension or disbarment by IRS) by representing taxpayers with respect to issues involving specified statutory provisions (such as those related to qualified employee plans).

To represent a taxpayer, you must have a power of attorney and file a declaration attesting to your enrolled actuary status. Form 2848 can satisfy both requirements. The issues for which representation is allowed are listed in Reg. §10.3(d), Circular 230. For further information on the enrolled actuary program, see https://www.irs.gov/tax-professionals/enrolled-actuaries/enrolled-actuary-information.

Enrollment must be renewed every three years after completing continuing education. The renewal application for enrollment for the April 1, 2023, to March 31, 2026, period will be available in early January 2023. To timely renew your enrollment, you must complete continuing professional education (CPE) requirements by December 31, 2022, and submit a completed Form 5434-A and renewal fee by March 1, 2023. The renewal fee is the same amount as the initial application fee, $250. If you miss either of the above deadlines and do not receive an official renewal notice prior to April 1, 2023, you will be treated as "inactive" beginning April 1, 2023, until the date the Joint Board mails your official renewal notice. Depending on your initial enrollment date, there may be an increased continuing education requirement in order to apply for a return to active status from inactive status; see https://

www.irs.gov/tax-professionals/enrolled-actuaries/news-from-the-joint-board.

Enrolled retirement plan agent. The IRS is no longer accepting applications by individuals to become an enrolled retirement plan agent (ERPA). After February 12, 2016, the IRS stopped offering the special competency examination (ERPA SEE) and also stopped granting enrollment by virtue of past service and technical retirement plan experience within the IRS. Individuals who passed the ERPA SEE by February 12, 2016, and who became enrolled retirement plan agents, or who were granted ERPA enrollment by that date based on prior IRS employment, can maintain their enrollment by completing 72 hours of continuing professional education every three years and applying for renewal on Form 8554-EP. The renewal fee is $140 (T.D. 9966, 2022-44 IRB 380); see Form 8554-EP for details.

Enrolled Agents

To become an enrolled agent, a PTIN must be obtained and a three-part special enrollment examination (SEE; see below) must be passed to demonstrate technical competence in tax matters. Certain former IRS employees may apply for enrollment without examination, as discussed below. In addition to having a PTIN, an applicant for enrollment must not have engaged in conduct that would justify suspension or disbarment under the Circular 230 rules (Reg. §10.4(a), Circular 230).

Enrolled agents, like attorneys and certified public accountants (CPAs), are unrestricted as to which taxpayers they can represent, what types of tax matters they can handle, and which IRS offices they can practice before.

The IRS homepage for the Enrolled Agent Program has links to details on becoming an enrolled agent and maintaining enrolled status, including frequently asked questions; see https://www.irs.gov/tax-professionals/enrolled-agents.

Special Enrollment Examination (SEE). The test for individuals who want to become Enrolled Agents, the Special Enrollment Examination, is administered by a private company, Prometric. The three parts of the SEE may be taken on the same day or on separate days in any order. Each examination part may be taken up to four times during each test window (May 1 through the following February).

There is a non-refundable testing fee for each part of the SEE that is payable when an appointment to take the examination is scheduled (Form 2587). For the examination period beginning May 1, 2023, and ending February 28, 2024, the total testing fee is $206 for each part of the examination, of which $99 is the IRS user fee and $107 is Prometric's fee.

Generally, a candidate who passes a part of the SEE can carry over the passing grade for up to two years; see the Prometric website at https://www.prometric.com/test-takers/search/irs.

The IRS has questions and answers on the SEE at: https://www.irs.gov/tax-professionals/enrolled-agents/enrolled-agents-frequently-asked-questions. Here, the IRS provides links to the Prometric website, including the Candidate Information Bulletin prepared by Prometric on all aspects of the examination.

Former IRS employees. You may be admitted to practice before the IRS without taking the SEE if you apply for enrollment within three years from the date you separated from service with the IRS. You generally must have had at least five years of continuous service with the IRS, and, during those five years, you must have been regularly engaged in applying and interpreting the provisions of the Internal Revenue Code and regulations. The permission to practice may, at the discretion of the IRS, be limited to certain areas (Reg. §10.4(d), Circular 230). For further details, go to: https://www.irs.gov/tax-professionals/enrolled-agents/enrolled-agent-information-for-former-irs-employees.

Application for enrollment. After passing all three parts of the SEE or if you are an eligible former IRS employee, you must apply for enrollment on Form 23 (Reg. §10.5(a) of Circular 230). You must have a PTIN and enter it on Form 23. The $140 fee must be paid to the IRS with Form 23 and is nonrefundable. In the process of evaluating your application, the IRS Office of Professional Responsibility (OPR) will conduct a background check that includes your record of tax compliance (https://www.irs.gov/tax-professionals/enrolled-agents/enrolled-agents-frequently-asked-questions#enrollment; Reg. §10.5(d), Circular 230).

Upon receipt of a properly executed application, the IRS may grant you temporary recognition to practice pending a determination as to whether permanent enrollment should be granted, but this is done only in unusual circumstances (Reg. §10.5(e), Circular 230).

If your application is denied, you will be informed of the reasons for the denial in writing and within 30 days after receipt of the notice of denial, you may file a written protest (Reg. §10.5(f), Circular 230).

Continuing education required to renew enrollment. You must renew enrollment status every three years. Renewal my be either online at Pay.gov. Form 8554, or on paper using Form 8554. You must renew your PTIN each year (between mid-October and December 31) and complete tax-related courses as a requirement for renewal. Renewal periods for enrollment status are staggered, depending on the last digit of your Social Security number (Reg. §10.6(d)(2), Circular 230), and your Form 8554 renewal application must be submitted between November 1 and January 31 prior to April 1 of the year in which your next renewal cycle begins. See Form 8554 and Publication 5186 for when your next renewal cycle begins (https://www.irs.gov/pub/irs-pdf/p5186.pdf). A renewal fee (nonrefundable) of $140 (same fee as for initial enrollment; *see* above) must be paid with Form 8554.

Generally, you must complete a minimum of 72 hours of continuing education during each three-year cycle, and during each enrollment year, a minimum of 16 hours must be completed, of which two hours is on ethics or professional conduct. However, individuals whose initial enrollment occurs during an enrollment cycle must complete two hours of qualifying CE credit per month and two hours of ethics/professional conduct per year for the rest of that enrollment cycle. When the new enrollment cycle begins, the full 72-hour CE requirement must be satisfied (https://www.irs.gov/pub/irs-pdf/p5186.pdf; Reg. §10.6(e)(2), Circular 230). Qualifying courses include federal tax subjects or tax-related matters such as data security and identity theft. Credit cannot be received for authoring publications (Reg. §10.6(f), Circular 230).

Details on the continuing education requirements are posted on the IRS website at https://www.irs.gov/tax-professionals/faqs-enrolled-agent-continuing-education-requirements.

Limited Practice in Special Cases

Even if you are not authorized to practice before the IRS, you may represent yourself or members of your immediate family provided you have their authorization. You may also represent a taxpayer in the following cases where you have authorization: (1) You represent your regular full-time employer or a partnership in which you are a partner or full-time employee. (2) You are an officer or regular full-time employee representing a corporation, trust, estate, association, or organized group. (3) You are a fiduciary or full-time employee, representing a trust, receivership, guardianship, or estate. (4) You are an officer or regular employee in the course of your official business, representing a governmental unit, agency, or authority. (5) You are serving as a representative of any individual or entity outside of the United States before personnel of the IRS. The Director of the Office of Professional Responsibility may also authorize any person to represent another without enrollment for the purpose of a particular matter (Reg. §10.7, Circular 230).

Standards for Signing Returns and Advising Clients on Tax Return Positions

The practice standards under Section 10.34 of Circular 230 generally are consistent with the penalty standards for tax return preparers in Code Section 6694 while also providing broader professional ethics standards.

Signing returns. A practitioner may not willfully, recklessly, or through gross incompetence sign a tax return or refund claim that he or she knows or reasonably should know contains a position that either (1) lacks a reasonable basis, (2) is unreasonable under the preparer penalty rules of Code Section 6694(a)(2) (understatement due to unreasonable positions), or (3) is a willful attempt by the practitioner to understate tax liability or recklessly or intentionally disregard IRS rules (subject to the Code Section 6694(b)(2) penalty) (Regulation §10.34(a)(1)(i)). The IRS will take into account a practitioner's pattern of conduct in determining whether the practitioner has acted willfully, recklessly, or through gross incompetence (Regulation §10.34(a)(2)).

Special due diligence requirements. Special requirements apply for paid preparers when clients claim the earned income credit, the American opportunity credit, the child tax credit (including the additional child tax credit and the credit for other dependents), and/or head of household status (IRC §6695(g). Paid preparers must complete Form 8867, Paid Preparer's Due Diligence Checklist, which requires the preparer to certify that all the answers on the form are, to the best of his or her knowledge, true, correct, and complete (*see* page 1015 for further details). The form must be filed with the client's return or amended return.

Advice on tax return positions. The standards for client advice mirror the above rules for signing returns. A practitioner may not willfully, recklessly, or through gross incompetence advise a client to take a position on a tax return or refund claim, or prepare a portion of a return containing a position, that either (1) lacks a reasonable basis, (2) is unreasonable under the Code Section 6694(a)(2) penalty rules, or (3) is a willful attempt by the practitioner to understate tax liability or intentionally disregard IRS rules under the Code Section 6694(b)(2) penalty rules (Regulation §10.34(a)(1)(ii)).

Differences between practice standards on tax return positions and preparer penalties. A practitioner is subject to discipline under Regulation §10.52 (*see* "Sanctions" below) for a violation of Regulation §10.34(a) only after willful, reckless, or grossly incompetent conduct, whereas a preparer penalty under Code Section 6694 may be imposed without such a showing. The fact that a practitioner is assessed a penalty under Code Section 6694 does not automatically mean that the practitioner will be subject to discipline under Regulation §10.34 for willful, reckless, or grossly incompetent conduct; an independent determination will be made. Also note that a practitioner may be subject to discipline because a position taken on a return violates Regulation §10.34(a) even if other positions on the return eliminate any tax understatement, whereas a preparer penalty must be abated (Code Section 6694(d)) if there is a final determination that the taxpayer did not understate tax liability.

Standards for Written Tax Advice

In 2014 the IRS eliminated the much criticized "covered" opinion rules (in prior Regulation §10.35, Circular 230) and replaced them with more flexible standards for written tax advice in a revised Regulation §10.37 (T.D. 9668, 2014-27 IRB 1).

Regulation §10.37 requires practitioners to base all written tax advice on reasonable factual and legal assumptions, to exercise reasonable reliance, and consider all relevant facts that the practitioner knows or should know. Reasonable efforts must be made to ascertain the facts relevant to the written advice. Reliance on statements or representations of the taxpayer or any other person, or agreements, findings, appraisals, or financial forecasts of another person, must be reasonable (Regulation §10.37(a)(2)(iv)). Reliance on the advice of another tax practitioner or of any other person (such as an appraiser or other professional) must be reasonable and in good faith; reliance is not reasonable if a practitioner knows or should know that the other practitioner has a conflict of interest, is not competent to give the advice, or otherwise is not giving reliable advice (Regulation §10.37(b)).

In evaluating a federal tax matter, a practitioner must not take into account the possibility that the IRS will not audit the return or raise the issue on audit (Regulation §10.37(a)(2)(vi)). On the other hand, a practitioner providing written advice may take into account the possibility that an issue may be settled, as there may be an obligation to inform the client as to the likelihood of a settlement.

The IRS will apply a "reasonable practitioner" standard, taking into account all facts and circumstances, in evaluating whether written advice meets the standards of Regulation §10.37. In the case of a written opinion that the practitioner knows or has reason to know will be used to market or promote an investment plan that has tax avoidance or evasion as a significant purpose, the IRS will take into account the "additional risk caused by the practitioner's lack of knowledge of the taxpayer's particular circumstances," in applying the reasonable practitioner standard (Regulation §10.37(c)(2)).

Under Regulation §10.37, a practitioner does not have to provide (as was required by former Regulation §10.35) a detailed account of the relevant facts (including assumptions and representations), or apply the law to those facts along with his or her conclusions. Whether these should be provided in written advice will depend on the type and specificity of advice sought by the client along with other appropriate facts and circumstances.

The IRS intended the elimination of the covered opinion rules and the amendments to Regulation §10.37 to remove the need for disclaimers by practitioners in their written communications to clients. The revised rules do not prohibit the use of disclaimers, but practitioners have been warned against stating that a disclaimer is required by the IRS or by Circular 230.

Firm Managers Must Have Procedures to Ensure Compliance with Circular 230

Managers of a firm who have principal authority and responsibility for overseeing the firm's tax practice (governed by Subpart B of Circular 230) must take reasonable steps to ensure that the firm has procedures in place for ensuring compliance with Circular 230. The procedures must ensure compliance not only with the provisions of Subpart B of Circular 230 (duties and restrictions relating to practice), but also with Subparts A (authority to practice) and C (sanctions for violations) (Reg. §10.36, Circular 230, as amended by T.D. 9668, 2014-27 IRB 1).

The responsibility for these procedures falls on the principal firm managers who are themselves practitioners subject to Circular 230. In the event that there is no Circular 230 practitioner with principal authority over the firm's tax practice, the IRS may identify a Circular 230 practitioner who will be held responsible for ensuring that there are compliance procedures (Regulation §10.36(a)).

Sanctions *(see below)* may be imposed on such a manager if a firm member or employee engages in a pattern or practice of not complying with Circular 230 and the manager, through willfulness, recklessness, or gross incompetence, fails to ensure that compliance procedures are in place or that firm procedures are properly followed. Sanctions may also be imposed on managers who know or should know that members or employees have engaged in noncompliant activities and who, through willfulness, recklessness, or gross incompetence, fail to promptly take action to correct the noncompliance (Regulation §10.36(b)).

Advertising and Solicitation

A practitioner must avoid misleading or deceptive statements or claims in public communications or private solicitations. Solicitation of employment in matters related to the IRS is prohibited if the solicitation violates a federal or state rule, such as state licensing rules for attorneys. Fee information may be communicated in emails, mailings, professional lists, telephone directories, print media, radio and television. In describing their professional designation, practitioners may not use the term "certified" or imply an employer/employee relationship with the IRS. Details on solicitation and advertising restrictions are in Regulation §10.30 of Circular 230. A solicitation of employment that violates Regulation §10.30 is considered "disreputable" conduct subject to sanctions; *see* below.

Contingent Fees

Under Reg. §10.27 of Circular 230, a practitioner may charge a contingency fee only in specified circumstances. A contingency fee is allowed for services rendered in connection with an IRS examination of, or challenge to, (1) an original return, or (2) to an amended return or refund claim filed before receiving written notice of the examination or challenge to the original return, or no later than 120 days after receiving such notice (Notice 2008-43, 2008-15 IRB 748, clarifying Reg. §10.27 (b) (2) (ii), Circular 230).

A contingency fee may also be charged in connection with reviews of interest and penalty assessments, and services connected with tax-related judicial proceedings (Reg. §10.27(b), Circular 230), and in connection with whistleblower claims under Code Section 7623 (Notice 2008-43, 2008-15 IRB 748).

However, the U.S. District Court for the District of Columbia, relying on the D.C. Circuit's decision in *Loving v. IRS* (discussed earlier), held that the IRS lacks authority to prohibit contingency fees for the preparation and filing of "ordinary refund claims"; that is, refund claims filed by a practitioner after the taxpayer files his or her original return but before the IRS initiates an audit of the return (*Gerald Ridgely, Jr.*, 2014-2 USTC ¶50,359 (D.D.C. 2014)). The District Court agreed with Ridgely, a CPA, that preparing and filing ordinary refund claims does not constitute "practice" before the IRS and thus it is not subject to the Circular 230 prohibition against contingency fees.

The IRS did not file an appeal of the *Ridgely* decision with the D.C. Circuit (which had ruled against the IRS in *Loving*). However, Reg. §10.27 had not been changed to reflect the *Ridgely* decision at the time this book was completed.

The AICPA has reminded its members that the association's Code of Professional Conduct contains a prohibition of contingency fees similar to the prohibition in Reg. §10.27 that was successfully challenged in the *Ridgely* decision.

Reg. §10.27(a) bars a practitioner from charging an unconscionable fee. Former OPR Director Hawkins stated that the Ridgely decision does not affect this prohibition, and that OPR still has jurisdiction over unconscionable fees whether they are contingency based or hourly based.

Negotiating Client's Refund Check

Regulation §10.31 prohibits any individual who is subject to the practice rules of Circular 230 (not just tax return preparers) from directing by electronic or any other means a check issued by the IRS to a client into an account owned or controlled by the practitioner or any associate of the practitioner (Reg. §10.31, Circular 230).

To endorse or otherwise negotiate a client's refund check not only violates Reg. §10.31, but also gives rise to a penalty under Code Section 6695(f) as discussed below (under "Preparer Penalties for Not Meeting Disclosure and Record-Keeping Requirements").

The Office of Professional Responsibility (OPR) has focused on preparers who take their fee out of part of a client's refund, such as by using Form 8888 to take part of a refund by setting up a split direct deposit. Splitting the refund is prohibited even if the preparer has the client's permission.

Sanctions

Any practitioner may be censured (publicly reprimanded), disbarred, or suspended from practice before the IRS for incompetence, willfully violating any of the practice regulations, or engaging in "disreputable" conduct (Reg. §10.50, Circular 230). Examples of disreputable conduct include giving false or misleading information to the IRS, engaaging in a prohibited solicitation of employment, willfully assisting or encouraging a client to violate any federal tax law, willfully preparing or signing a return without having a valid PTIN, willfully representing a taxpayer before the IRS without authority under Circular 230, and willfully failing to electronically file income tax returns when required to do so (Reg. §10.51, Circular 230).

A violation of the Section 10.34 rules on tax return positions, the Section 10.36 rules for ensuring a firm's compliance, and the Section 10.37 rules on giving written advice, are subject to sanction if the violation results from willfulness, recklessness, or gross incompetence (Reg. §10.52(a)(2), Circular 230). Similarly, sanctions may be imposed (under Reg. §10.52) on a practitioner who through reckless behavior or gross incompetence violates the general standard of competence in Reg. §10.35 (competent practice requires the appropriate level of knowledge, skill, thoroughness, and preparation necessary for the matter for which the practitioner is engaged).

Expedited suspension procedures may be applied by OPR if a practitioner has engaged in serious misconduct as specified in Reg. §10.82. This includes practitioners who have demonstrated willful disreputable conduct by failing to meet their own tax filing obligations. Failure to file income tax returns in four of the five years preceding the initiation of a suspension proceeding can trigger the expedited suspension procedures, as can failure to file returns required more frequently than annually (employment/excise tax returns) in five of the seven tax years preceding the initiation of a suspension proceeding (Reg. §10.82(b)(5)).

A monetary penalty may be imposed in addition to or in lieu of any suspension, censure, or disbarment. The amount may be up to the gross income derived (or to be derived) from the conduct giving rise to the penalty. A separate monetary penalty may be imposed on the employer of an offending practitioner, or firm on whose behalf the practitioner was acting, if the employer or firm knew or reasonably should have known of the practitioner's conduct (Reg. §10.50(c), Circular 230).

Further, Code Section 6701 allows a $1,000 penalty ($10,000 with respect to corporate returns) to be imposed on a representative who presents a return or other document (such as an affidavit) at an IRS examination knowing that it understates tax.

Practice by Former Government Employees

If you are a former government employee, you may not represent a client in a matter on which you previously worked as a government employee (Reg. §10.25(b)(2)). The matter may have involved a decision, a finding, a letter ruling, technical advice, or approval or disapproval of a contract. You are considered to have participated in a matter if you were substantially involved in making decisions, or if you prepared or reviewed documents (with or without the right to exercise a judgment of approval or disapproval), participated in conferences or investigations, or gave substantial advice.

Where you had official responsibilities for a particular matter within a period of one year before you left government service, you may not within two years after your government employment ended represent or assist in that matter any person who is or was a specific party to that matter (Reg. §10.25(b)(3)).

Within one year after leaving government service, you may not appear before, or communicate with the intent to influence, the IRS in a matter involving the publication, withdrawal, amendment, modification, or interpretation of a rule if you participated in its development or, within a period of one year prior to the termination of your government employment, you had official responsibility for the rule. However, you may appear on your own behalf or represent a client in a transaction involving the application or interpretation of the rule provided you do not use or disclose any confidential information you acquired in the development of the rule (Reg. §10.25(b)(4), Circular 230). A rule includes Treasury Regulations, whether issued or under preparation for issuance as Notices of Proposed Rule Making or as Treasury Decisions, and revenue rulings and revenue procedures published in the Internal Revenue Bulletin (Reg. §10.25(a)(5), Circular 230).

Firm representation. A firm of which you are a member may not represent or knowingly assist a person who was or is a specific party in any particular matter in which you substantially participated as a government employee, unless the firm isolates you in such a way that you do not assist in the representation. You and another member of your firm acting on behalf of your firm must sign a statement under oath that you will be isolated from participating in the transaction, and the statement must be provided by the firm, upon request, to the IRS Office of Professional Responsibility (OPR) (Reg. §10.25(c), Circular 230).

Tax Information Authorization

If you do not file a power of attorney (Form 2848 or equivalent substitute), you have to file a tax information authorization in order to inspect or receive certain confidential tax information of your client, such as his or her tax return, and to receive notices and other written communications from the IRS concerning his or her liability. The tax information authorization is signed by the taxpayer and specifies the particular authorization given. IRS Form 8821 may be used. The authorization only includes the right to receive information and does not allow you to represent the taxpayer before the IRS; representation requires a power of attorney.

No tax information authorization is required where: (1) a power of attorney has already been filed for the same matter, or (2) the taxpayer is present, such as at a conference, when the information is divulged, or (3) the receipt of notices and other matters are not of a confidential nature.

Practitioner Priority Service. The Practitioner Priority Service (PPS) is available to all tax practitioners with valid third-party authorizations, i.e., Forms 2848, 8821, and/or 8655. The IRS advises that the PPS is "the tax practitioner's first point of contact for account-related issues," with "a professional support line staffed by IRS customer service representatives specially trained to handle practitioners' accounts questions." PPS is reached at 866-860-4259 (toll free). The IRS admitted in early Fall 2022 that such service continues to fall short of its goal because of major access issues] but that improvements are on the way. The PPS phone line's wait times have been long, both because of the lack of IRS personnel and because robocall services have "jammed-up the lines," allowing some practitioners to gain priority over others. In late 2022, the IRS announced two steps to alleviate the problem in anticipation of the 2023 tax filing season:

- A pilot program that requires PPS callers to repeat phrases before being transferred to an IRS assister. Speech recognition will be used to help ensure a live person is calling and not a mechanical device (IR-2022-191, October 27, 2022).
- The IRS also announced that it recently hired 4,000 new customer service representatives to help answer phones and provide other services. The inference is that at least some of them will be allocated to PPS.

PPS is limited to tax practitioners who provide tax advice, prepare income tax returns, or act on the taxpayer's behalf (for example, obtaining transcripts, preparing and filing documents, or corresponding and communicating with the IRS regarding tax matters). Tax practitioners also have other avenues to access information:

Transcript Delivery Service. If you are registered with the IRS for e-Services and have a valid third-party authorization recorded on the Centralized Authorization File (CAF), you do not need to contact PPS to obtain a transcript. Transcripts are available through e-Services. Only through an approved e-file application can tax professionals, who are Electronic Return Originators (EROs), Circular 230 Practitioners, or Reporting Agents (RAs), gain access to the Transcript Delivery System. For EROs to qualify, they must have successfully submitted five accepted e-file returns in the current or prior year. The IRS advises that, if you have specific questions related to e-Services registration, you should contact the e-Services help desk at 866-255-0654.

Taxpayer Digital Communications. In an effort to improve customer service and "the taxpayer experience," the IRS launched the Taxpayer Digital Communications (TDC) platform in 2016. The platform, developed and maintained by eGain Corp, is designed to enable faster communication as well as offer taxpayers and their authorized representatives the ability to securely send and receive electronic messages and documents to and from IRS agents and customer service representatives.

TAX RETURN PREPARER PENALTIES

Preparers are subject to penalties under the Internal Revenue Code for negligent or fraudulent preparation of returns and for violation of specific disclosure and record requirements. Therefore, the rules discussed in this chapter deserve careful consideration by all tax practitioners.

Who Is a Preparer Subject to Penalties?

Anyone who prepares or employs another to prepare all or a substantial part of any income tax return or refund claim for compensation is considered a tax return preparer (IRC §7701(a)(36)(A)).

A person may be considered a preparer regardless of educational qualifications or professional status (Reg. §301.7701-15(d)). But an IRS employee performing his or her official duties is not considered an income tax preparer (Reg. §301.7701-15(f)(1)).

You are not a preparer if you perform only the following services (Reg. §301.7701-15(f)):

- Merely type or reproduce returns; or
- Prepare a return or refund claim for your employer, an officer of your employer, a fellow employee, or a general partner in a partnership in which you are a general partner or an employee. An employee of a subsidiary corporation is also considered an employee of the parent corporation; or
- Prepare a return as fiduciary; or
- Prepare a claim for refund in response to a notice of deficiency issued to the taxpayer or a waiver of restriction after initiation of an audit of the taxpayer or another taxpayer, or a determination whether the audit of that other taxpayer affects the liability of the taxpayer for tax.
- Prepare a return for a friend, a relative, or neighbor with no implicit or explicit agreement for compensation, even though you receive a gift or return service or favor.

Signing and nonsigning preparers. Final regulations provide separate definitions for signing and nonsigning preparers. A signing preparer is the individual preparer with primary responsibility for the overall substantive accuracy of the return or refund claim (Reg. §301.7701-15 (b)(1)). A nonsigning preparer is a preparer other than a signing preparer who prepares all or a substantial portion (*discussed below*) of a return or refund claim with respect to events that have occurred at the time the advice is given. A preparer who provides written or oral advice to a taxpayer or other preparer is a nonsigning preparer where the advice leads to a position or entry that is a substantial portion of the return (Reg. §301.7701-15 (b)(2)). If you provide advice with respect to a proposed transaction but do not provide advice after it is completed, you are not considered a preparer because the advice was not rendered with respect to events that have occurred. Time spent on advice given after events occur may be ignored in determining whether a person is a nonsigning preparer if such time is less than 5% of the time spent providing advice on a position, but there is an anti-abuse exception to this rule (Reg. §301.7701-15 (b)(2)).

See "Preparer Penalties for Understatements of Taxpayer Liability" *below* for application of the Section 6694 penalties to signing and nonsigning preparers.

Substantial portion. Only a person who prepares all or a substantial portion of a return or refund claim is considered to be a preparer of the return or claim. You are considered the preparer of an entry on a return or refund claim if you rendered advice that is directly relevant to the determination of the existence, characterization, or amount of that entry (Reg. §301.7701-15 (b)(3)). Whether the entry is a substantial portion of the return or refund claim depends on whether you knew or reasonably should have known that the tax attributable to the schedule, entry or other portion is a substantial portion of the tax required to be shown on the return or refund claim. The IRS will take into account the size and complexity of the item relative to the taxpayer's gross income and the size of the understatement attributable to the item compared to the tax liability reported by the taxpayer.

A *de minimis* rule may apply to a person who otherwise would be considered a nonsigning preparer. A schedule, entry or other portion is not considered a substantial portion if it involves gross income, deductions, or amounts on which credits are based that are either (1) less than $10,000, or (2) less than $400,000 and also less than 20% of a taxpayer's adjusted gross income, or for non-individual taxpayers, 20% of the gross income shown on the return or refund claim. Where more than one schedule or other portion is involved, the amounts are aggregated (Reg. §301.7701-15(b)(3)(ii).

> ### *Example:*
> You prepare for a taxpayer a Schedule B (Form 1040 or 1040-SR) that reports $4,000 in dividend income and also give advice about Schedule A (Form 1040 or 1040-SR) that results in a claimed medical expense deduction of $5,000. You do not sign the return. Under the *de minimis* rule, you are not considered a nonsigning preparer because the total amount of the deductions is less than $10,000.

Even though entries on a return you prepare affect entries on the return of another taxpayer, you are not the preparer of the other return, unless the entries on the return you prepared are directly reflected on that other return and constitute a substantial portion of that return. For example, if you prepare a partnership return, you are not the preparer of a partner's return, unless the entries on the partnership return reportable on the partner's return constitute a substantial portion (*as discussed above*) of the return (Reg. §301.7701-15(b)(3)(iii)).

Preparer Penalties for Understatements of Taxpayer Liability

Section 6694 penalties. There is a "first-tier" penalty under Code Section 6694(a) for understatements due to unreasonable positions and a "second-tier" penalty for willful or reckless conduct under Code Section 6694(b). These penalties apply not only to income tax return preparers, but also to preparers of estate and gift tax, employment tax, and excise tax returns, and returns of exempt organizations.

If there is a signing preparer (*discussed above*) within a firm, he or she is generally considered the person primarily responsible for all of the positions on the return or refund claim giving rise to an understatement of liability, and thus is subject to a penalty under Section 6694. However, if the IRS concludes based on credible information that a nonsigning preparer *(discussed above)* within the same firm is primarily responsible for a position giving rise to an understatement, that nonsigning partner is subject to the Section 6694 penalty (Reg. §1.6694-1(b)(2)). If the IRS finds that both a signing and nonsigning preparer within a firm are responsible for a position giving rise to an understatement, the IRS will determine which of them is primarily responsible and the Section 6694 penalty will be assessed only against that primarily responsible preparer (Reg. §1.6694-1(b)(4)).

If preparers from different firms provide advice with respect to a position that gives rise to an understatement, and the IRS determines that both are primarily responsible for the position, both can be penalized (Reg. §1.6694-1(b)(1)). A firm that employs a preparer who is subject to a penalty under Section 6694 may also be subject to a penalty if the management participated in or knew about the conduct giving rise to the penalty, or if procedures for reviewing return positions were not provided or were willfully or recklessly disregarded (Regs. §1.6694-2(a)(2) and 1.6694-3(a)(2)).

First-tier penalty (Code Section 6694(a)). The first-tier penalty in Code Section 6694(a) applies to a tax return preparer who knew or reasonably should have known of an "unreasonable" position to which an understatement of liability is due. The amount of the first-tier penalty is the greater of $1,000 or 50% of the return preparer's compensation derived from the return or refund claim (Reg. §1.6694-1(a)(1)). The maximum penalty based on 50% of compensation refers to the compensation that the preparer receives or expects to receive with respect to the position on the return or refund claim that gave rise to the understatement (Reg. §1.6694-1(f)(1)). For purposes of calculating the penalty, only compensation for tax advice that is given with respect to events that have occurred at the time the advice is rendered and that relates to the position giving rise to the understatement is taken into account (Reg. §1.6694-1(f)(2)(ii)).

What is an unreasonable position? An undisclosed position that is not attributable to a tax shelter or reportable transaction is considered unreasonable unless there was substantial authority for the position taken on the return (IRC §6694(a)(2)(A)). A disclosed position that is not attributable to a tax shelter or a reportable transaction is unreasonable unless there was a reasonable basis for it (IRC §6694(a)(2)(B)). However, for positions relating to either tax shelters (under Code Section 6662(d)(2)(C)(ii)) or reportable transactions (under Code Section 6662A)), the penalty applies unless the preparer had a reasonable belief that the position would more likely than not be sustained on its merits, whether or not the position was disclosed (IRC §6694(a)(2)(C)).

There is an exception to the first-tier penalty if the preparer acted in good faith and can show reasonable cause for the understatement (IRC §6694(a)(3)).

The standard for determining whether there is "substantial authority" for a position unrelated to a tax shelter or reportable transaction is not spelled out in Code Section 6694(a) or in Reg.

§1.6694-2. However, under Notice 2009-5 (2009-3 IRB 309), which was still in effect at the time this book was completed, the "substantial authority" rules of Section 6662(d) (taxpayer penalty for substantial understatement of tax) apply for purposes of the Section 6694(a) preparer penalty. Specifically, Notice 2009-5 provides that a preparer may consider the authorities listed in Reg. §1.6662-4(d)(3)(iii), and the weight to be accorded those authorities in determining whether there is substantial authority for a position should be based on the analysis required by Reg. §§1.6662-4(d)(3)(i) and (ii).

For tax shelter (IRC §6694(d)(2)(c)(ii)) or reportable transaction (Code Section 6662A) positions, Reg. §1.6694-2(b) provides that in determining whether it is "reasonable to believe that a position would more likely than not be sustained on its merits," a preparer should consider the authorities listed in Reg. §1.6662-4(d)(3)(iii) and those authorities should be weighed using the analysis in Reg. §1.6662-4(d)(3)(ii). Notice 2009-5 also provides that a position with respect to a tax shelter will not be deemed unreasonable for purposes of the Section 6694(a) preparer penalty if there was substantial authority for the position and the preparer advises the taxpayer in writing that if the position is deemed to have a significant purpose of tax avoidance or evasion, the taxpayer will be subject to a penalty under Section 6662(d) for a substantial understatement of tax (if otherwise applicable) unless the taxpayer has a reasonable belief that the tax treatment was more likely than not correct.

Second-tier penalty (Code Section 6694(b)). The second-tier penalty in Code Section 6694(b) applies to a tax return if an understatement of liability on the return is due to the preparer's willful attempt to understate the liability or the preparer's reckless or intentional disregard of IRS rules. The second-tier penalty is the greater of $5,000 or 75% of the preparer's compensation. For this purpose, "compensation" is defined as discussed earlier under "First-tier penalty." The second-tier penalty is reduced by the amount of any first-tier penalty paid with respect to the return (IRC § 6694(b)(3)).

Aiding and abetting understatements. The IRS may impose on a preparer a $1,000 penalty ($10,000 for corporate returns) for aiding and abetting the understatement of tax liability on a tax return or other document (IRC §6701). The Section 6701 penalty is in lieu of a penalty under Section 6694(a) or 6694(b) (IRC §6701(f)(2)).

The $1,000/$10,000 penalty may be imposed on a person who (1) knows or has "reason to believe" that a return or document that he or she has helped prepare will be used in connection with tax matters, and (2) knows that tax liability will be understated on that return or document (IRC §6701(a)). The penalty can apply regardless of whether the taxpayer knows about the understatement (Code Section 6701(d)). A supervisor who does not actually prepare a return or document is subject to the penalty if he or she orders or causes a subordinate to take actions subject to the penalty, or if the supervisor knows of such an act by a subordinate but does not attempt to prevent it (IRC §6701(c)).

Preparer Penalties for Not Meeting Disclosure and Record-Keeping Requirements

Under Code Section 6695, tax return preparers may be penalized for failure to satisfy recordkeeping or disclosure requirements or not providing required information when preparing returns. The Section 6695 penalties apply not only to income tax return preparers, but also to preparers of all other returns (estate and gift, employment and excise tax returns, and returns of exempt organizations).

Each of the Section 6695 penalties has a per return (or refund claim) penalty amount and most have a maximum annual penalty amount. The per return and maximum amounts are subject to annual inflation adjustments (IRC §6695(h)). For returns and refund claims filed in 2022, the penalty amounts shown below are in Rev. Proc. 2020-45; for returns and refund claims filed in 2023, the penalty amounts shown below are in Rev. Proc. 2021-45; for returns and refund claims filed in 2024, the penalty amounts may be found in Rev. Proc. 2022-38.

Failure to retain records on preparers. A person who employs one or more signing preparers must retain a record of the name, Social Security number, and place of work of each employed preparer (IRC §6060). The records must be retained for a three-year period following the close of the return period (defined as a 12-month period beginning on July 1 of each year), and the records must be made available for inspection upon request by the IRS (Reg. §1.6060-1(a)). Each failure to retain and make available a proper record and each failure to include a required item in the record is subject to a penalty, unless it is shown that there was reasonable cause for the failure (IRC §6695(e)). For returns or refund claims filed in 2022, there is a $50 penalty for each such failure, subject to a maximum penalty of $27,000; for returns or refund claims filed in 2023, the penalty amounts are $55 and $28,000, respectively.

Failure to sign returns. For a return or refund claim that is not electronically signed, a preparer considered to be a signing preparer must sign the return or claim after it is completed and before it is presented to the taxpayer for signature (IRC §6695(b); Reg. §1.6695-1(b)(1)). If more than one person worked on the return, the person primarily responsible for the overall accuracy of the return (Reg. §301.7701-15(b)(1)) must sign the return in order to avoid a penalty under IRC §6695(a). If the preparer required to sign is unavailable to sign the return, another preparer must so advise the client, review the entire preparation of the return or claim, and then sign it (Reg. §1.6695-1(b)(1)).

The information on an electronically signed return must be provided to the taxpayer contemporaneously with furnishing Form 8879, "IRS e-file Signature Authorization" (Reg. §1.6695-1(b)(2)).

For returns or refund claims filed in 2022, the penalty for failing to sign is $50 per return/refund claim unless reasonable cause is shown; the maximum penalty is $27,000; for returns or refund claims filed in 2023, the penalty amounts are $55 and $28,000, respectively.

Failure to furnish PTIN on return. A preparer considered to be a signing preparer *(discussed above)* must include his or her PTIN (preparer tax identification number) on each return or refund claim (IRC §6109(a)(4); PTIN requirement at Reg. §1.6109-2(a)

(2)(ii)). Each failure to include the PTIN is subject to a penalty unless it is shown that there was reasonable cause for the failure (IRC §6695(c); Reg. §1.6695-1(c)). For returns or refund claims filed in 2023, the per return/refund claim penalty is $55, subject to a maximum penalty of $28,000.

Failure to furnish client with copy of return or refund claim. A preparer considered to be a signing preparer *(discussed above)* must furnish a completed copy of the return or refund claim to the taxpayer no later than when it is presented to the taxpayer for signature (IRC §6107(a); Reg. §1.6107-1 (a)(1)). The copy may be provided in any media, including electronic media, that is acceptable to both the taxpayer and the preparer (Reg. §1.6107-1(a)(2)). Where two or more persons are considered preparers with respect to the same return, and there is an employment relationship between them, the employer is responsible for furnishing the copy; where there is a partnership relationship, the partnership must furnish the copy (Reg. §1.6107-1(c)).

A penalty applies to each failure to furnish a copy unless it can be shown that failure was due to reasonable cause and not due to willful neglect (IRC §6695(a); Reg. §1.6695-1(a)(1)). For returns or refund claims filed in 2023, the penalty for each failure is $55, subject to a maximum penalty of $28,000.

The preparer may request a receipt as proof of having satisfied this requirement (Reg. §1.6107-1(a)(1)).

Failure to retain copy or list. A signing preparer *(see above)* must keep for three years and make available for IRS inspection copies of all returns and refund claims he or she prepares or a list of the taxpayers for whom returns were prepared, including each name, taxpayer identification number, taxable year of the taxpayer for whom the return or refund claim was prepared, and the type of return or refund claim prepared (IRC §6107(b); Reg. §1.6107-1(b)).

A penalty may be imposed for each failure unless reasonable cause for the failure is shown (IRC §6695(d);Reg. §1.6695-1(d)). For returns or refund claims filed in 2023, the penalty for each failure is $55, subject to a maximum penalty of $28,000.

Where there is an employment relationship or a partnership relationship between two or more preparers, the employer must retain the required records, and in the case of a partnership arrangement, the partnership must keep the records (Reg. §1.6107-1(c)).

If the preparer is a corporation or partnership that goes out of business before the end of the three-year period, the person who is responsible for winding up the affairs of the corporation or partnership under state law must retain the records until the three-year period ends. If state law does not specify who is responsible for winding up, the directors or general partners are subject to the record-retention rules and they will be jointly and severally liable for the Section 6695(d) penalty ($55 per failure and $28,000 maximum penalty for returns and refund claims filed in 2023) if the records are not retained (Reg. §1.6107-1(b)(2); 5.

Negotiation of refund checks prohibited. A preparer is subject to a penalty for each endorsement or negotiation of a refund check (including an electronic version of a check) resulting from a return that he or she prepared (IRC §6695(f)). The penalty is $560 with respect to each refund check for a return or refund claim filed in 2023; for returns or refund claims filed in 2024.{XXXXDoes this sentence need information for 2024?}

The penalty does not apply to a preparer-bank (a preparer that is also a financial institution) that has not made a refund anticipation loan to the taxpayer if the full amount of the refund check is deposited to the taxpayer's account or the check is cashed and the cash remitted to the taxpayer (IRC §6695(f); Reg. §1.6695-1(f)(2)).

If the preparer obtains authorization from the taxpayer to affix the taxpayer's name to a refund check for the purpose of depositing it in the taxpayer's account, or in an account held jointly with anyone excluding the preparer, the penalty does not apply (Reg. §1.6695-1 (f)(1)).

Failure to be diligent in determining earned income credit, American Opportunity credit, the child tax credit, the credit for other dependents, and head of household status. A paid tax return preparer is subject to a penalty for failing to meet IRS due diligence requirements in determining a taxpayer's eligibility for, or the amount of, the earned income credit (EIC), American Opportunity tax credit (AOTC), the child tax credit and/or additional child tax credit (CTC/ACTC), the credit for other dependents (ODC), and head of household (HOH) filing status (IRC §6695(g)).

For each credit for which the due diligence requirements are not met, the penalty with respect to returns or refund claims filed in 2023 is $560 per credit per return. There is no limit on this penalty.

Preparers are required to file Form 8867 (Paid Preparer's Due Diligence Checklist) with the taxpayer's return (or amended return) claiming the EIC, the AOTC, the CTC/ACTC, the ODC credit, and/or HOH filing status, in order to document that they have met the due diligence requirements for each credit claimed.

If the actions described on the Form 8867 checklist and detailed in the Form 8867 instructions were completed by the preparer for each credit claimed, such as asking the client adequate questions and obtaining sufficient information to determine eligibility for and the amount of the credit, and the Form 8867 is truthfully and accurately completed, the due diligence tests are considered met, provided that specified records are kept for three years. In addition to a copy of Form 8867, the records that must be retained for three years are:

1. The applicable IRS worksheets for the credits claimed or the preparer's own worksheets that provide equivalent information,

2. Copies of taxpayer documents that were relied upon to determine eligibility for and the amount of the credits,

3. A record detailing how, when, and from whom the information used to prepare the relevant worksheets and Form 8867 was obtained, and

4. A record of any additional questions that were asked of the taxpayer to determine eligibility for and the amount of the credits, and the taxpayer's answers.

The three-year retention period begins on whichever of these dates is latest: (1) the due date for the return or refund claim, without extensions, (2) the date a signing preparer files it electronically or presents the return to the taxpayer for signature if the taxpayer is filing it, or (3) for a nonsigning preparer, the date that the part of the return for which he or she was responsible is submitted to the signing preparer (Reg. §1.6695-2(b)(4)(ii)).

In certain cases, firms as well as individual paid preparers may be subject to the penalty for failure to exercise due diligence. A firm can be penalized if management participated in the failure or knew prior to the filing of the return that an employed preparer had failed to comply with the rules. If management became aware of the failure after the return was filed, the firm is subject to the penalty if it lacked reasonable procedures to ensure compliance, or it had such procedures but willfully, recklessly or with gross indifference disregarded them when preparing the return or refund claim (Reg. §1.6695-2(c)).

An individual preparer, but not a firm, may be able to avoid a penalty by convincing the IRS that he or she has reasonable office procedures that are routinely followed to ensure compliance with the due diligence requirements, and the failure to meet the rules for a particular tax return or refund claim was isolated and inadvertent (Reg. §1.6695-2(d)).

Preparer Penalty Assessment Procedures

Penalties under IRC §6694(a) for understatements of tax or the penalties under IRC §6695 for failure to meet the disclosure and record-keeping requirements, must be assessed within three years after a return or refund claim is filed; no court proceeding for collection of the penalty without assessment may be begun after the three-year period. Penalties for willful or reckless understatements of tax liability under IRC §6694(b) may be assessed, or court proceedings for collection without assessment may begin, at any time (IRC §6696(d)(1)).

The IRS will issue a preparer a 30-day letter notifying the preparer of a proposed penalty and offering an opportunity to pursue administrative remedies prior to assessment of a penalty under Section 6694(a) or (b). If the preparer appeals an IRS penalty determination, the IRS cannot assess the penalties until after a final determination adverse to the taxpayer is made (Reg. §1.6694-4(a)(2)).

If a penalty for understatement of tax under either Section 6694(a) or (b) is assessed and the preparer does not pursue an administrative remedy or pursues such a remedy but receives an adverse final administrative determination from the IRS, the preparer has two alternatives (Reg. §1.6694-4(a)(4)):

1. Pay the entire amount assessed within 30 days of the IRS' statement of notice and demand and then file a claim for refund of the amount paid not later than three years from the date the penalty is paid, which if denied may be appealed in court; or

2. Pay 15% or more of the penalty within 30 days of the IRS' statement of notice and demand for payment and file a claim for refund of the amount paid within the same 30-day period. Form 6118 is used to claim the refund.

If under alternative (2) a preparer timely pays at least 15% of the penalty and files a refund claim, the IRS has six months to act on the claim. During that period, the IRS may not seek collection of the remaining 85% of the penalty (Reg. §1.6694-4(a)(5)). If the IRS denies the refund claim, the preparer may bring an action for refund in a Federal District Court within 30 days of the date of denial.

The action must be brought within the 30-day period to postpone or avoid collection measures by the IRS as to the remaining 85% of the penalty under the second alternative above. If the IRS does not deny a claim for refund by the end of six months after the claim is made, the preparer may bring an action in federal district court within 30 days after the expiration of the six-month period to determine liability for the penalty. If such an action is not brought, the IRS may pursue collection of the remaining 85% of the penalty (Reg. §1.6694-4(b)). If such an action is brought, the IRS may counterclaim for the balance of the penalty (Reg. §1.6694-4(a)(6)).

IRS May Seek Injunction Against Preparer

The IRS may seek an injunction in a federal district court to prohibit improper conduct by any tax return preparer (IRC §7407). An injunction may be sought regardless of whether penalties have been or may be assessed against the preparer. An injunction may be issued where the court finds that the preparer has:

- Engaged in conduct subject to the disclosure and record-keeping requirement penalties (IRC §6695) or the understatement of taxpayer liability penalties (IRC §6694);
- Engaged in conduct subject to criminal penalties under the Internal Revenue Code;
- Misrepresented his or her eligibility to practice before the IRS or his or her experience or education as a tax return preparer;
- Guaranteed payment of any tax refund or the allowance of any tax credit; or
- Engaged in other fraudulent or deceptive conduct that interferes with administration of the tax laws.

A court may also enjoin the person from acting as a preparer if it finds that the person has repeatedly engaged in any of the above practices and an injunction prohibiting specified conduct would not be sufficient (IRC §7407(b)).

A

ABLE account. An account for a person who became disabled before age 26. Nondeductible annual contributions can be made up to a specified limit and distributions are tax free if used to pay qualified disability expenses; *see 34.12.*

Accelerated cost recovery system (ACRS). A statutory method –of depreciation allowing accelerated rates for most types of property used in business and income-producing activities during the years 1981 through 1986. It has been superseded by the modified accelerated cost recovery system (MACRS) for assets placed in service after 1986; *see 42.4* and *42.12.*

Accelerated depreciation. Depreciation methods that allow faster write-offs than straight-line rates in the earlier periods of the useful life of an asset. For example, in the first few years of recovery, MACRS allows a 200% double declining balance write-off, twice the straight-line rate; *see 42.5–42.8.*

Accountable reimbursement plan. An employer reimbursement or allowance arrangement that requires you to adequately substantiate business expenses to your employer, and to return any excess reimbursement; *see 20.18.*

Accrual method of accounting. A business method of accounting requiring income to be reported when earned and expenses to be deducted when incurred. However, deductions generally may not be claimed until economic performance has occurred; *see 40.3.*

Acquisition debt. Debt used to buy, build, or construct a principal residence or second home and that generally qualifies for a full interest expense deduction; *see 15.2.*

Active participation. Test for determining deductibility of IRA deductions. Active participants in employer retirement plans are subject to IRA deduction phaseout rules if adjusted gross income exceeds certain thresholds; *see 8.4.*

Adjusted basis. A statutory term describing the cost used to determine your profit or loss from a sale or exchange of property. It is generally your original cost, increased by capital improvements, and decreased by depreciation, depletion, and other capital write-offs; *see 5.20.*

Adjusted gross income (AGI). Gross income less allowable adjustments, such as deductions for IRAs, alimony, and self-employed retirement plans. AGI determines whether various tax benefits are phased out, such as the child tax credit, the Earned Income Credit, and the rental loss allowance; *see 12.1* and modified adjusted gross income (MAGI).

Alimony. Payments made to a separated or divorced spouse as required by a decree or agreement. Qualifying payments are deductible by the payor and taxable to the payee; *see Chapter 37.*

Alternative minimum tax (AMT). A tax triggered if certain tax benefits reduce your regular income tax below the tax computed on Form 6251 for AMT purposes; *see Chapter 23.*

Amended return. On Form 1040-X, you may file an amended return within a three-year period to claim a refund or correct a mistake made on an original or previously amended return; *see Chapter 47.*

Amortizable bond premium. The additional amount paid over the face amount of an obligation that may be deducted under the rules in *4.17.*

Amortization of intangibles. Writing off an investment in intangible assets over a specified period; *see 42.17–42.19.*

Amount realized. A statutory term used to figure your profit or loss on a sale or exchange. Generally, it is sales proceeds plus mortgages assumed or taken subject to, less transaction expenses, such as commissions and legal costs; *see 5.14.*

Amount recognized. The amount of gain reportable and subject to tax. On certain tax-free exchanges of property, gain is not recognized in the year it is realized; *see 6.1.*

Annualized rate. A rate for a period of less than a year computed as though for a full year.

Annuity. An annual payment of money by a company or individual to a person called the annuitant. Payment is for a fixed period or the life of the annuitant. Tax consequences depend on the type of contract and funding; *see 7.21–7.26.*

Applicable federal rate. Interest rate fixed by the Treasury for determining imputed interest; *see 4.30–4.32.*

Appreciation in value. Increase in value of property due to market conditions. When you sell appreciated property, you pay tax on the appreciation since the date of purchase. When you donate appreciated property held long term, you may generally deduct the appreciated value; *see 14.8.*

Archer Medical Savings Account (MSA). A type of medical plan combining high deductible medical insurance protection with an IRA-type savings account fund to pay unreimbursed medical expenses; *see 41.13.*

Assessment. The IRS action of fixing tax liability that sets in motion collection procedures, such as charging interest, imposing penalties, and, if necessary, seizing property; *see 48.2.*

Assignment. The legal transfer of property, rights, or interest to another person called an assignee. You cannot avoid tax on income by assigning the income to another person.

At-risk rules. Rules limiting loss deductions to cash investments and personal liability notes. An exception for real estate treats certain nonrecourse commercial loans as amounts "at risk"; *see 10.18.*

Audit. An IRS examination of your tax return, generally limited to a three-year period after you file; *see Chapter 48.*

Away from home. A tax requirement for deducting travel expenses on a business trip. Sleeping arrangements are required for at least one night before returning home; *see 20.3* and *20.5–20.7.*

B

Balloon. A final payment on a loan in one lump sum.

Basis. Generally, the amount paid for property. You need to know your basis to figure gain or loss on a sale; *see 5.16.*

Bonus depreciation. An additional first-year depreciation allowance (80% for 2023) for qualifying property; *see 42.18.*

Boot. Generally, the receipt of cash or its equivalent accompanying an exchange of property. In a tax-free exchange, boot is subject to immediate tax; *see 6.3.*

C

Cancellation of debt. Release of a debt without consideration by a creditor. Cancellations of debt are generally taxable; *see 11.8.*

Capital. The excess of assets over liabilities.

Capital asset. Property subject to capital gain or loss treatment. Almost all assets you own are considered capital assets except for certain business assets or works you created; *see 5.2.*

Capital expenses. Costs that are not currently deductible and that are added to the basis of property. A capital expense generally increases the value of property. When added to depreciable property, the cost is deductible over the life of the asset.

Capital gain or loss. The difference between amount realized and adjusted basis on the sale or exchange of capital assets. Long-term capital gains are taxed favorably, as explained in *Chapter 5.* Capital losses are deducted first against capital gains, and then again up to $3,000 of other income; *see 5.1–5.5.*

Capital gain distribution. A mutual fund distribution allocated to gains realized on the sale of fund portfolio assets. You report the distribution as long-term capital gain even if you held the fund shares short term; *see 32.3–32.4.*

Capital loss carryover. A capital loss that is not deductible because it exceeds the annual $3,000 capital loss ceiling. A carryover loss may be deducted from capital gains of later years plus up to $3,000 of ordinary income; *see 5.4.*

Capitalization. Adding a cost or expense to the basis of the property.

Carryforward. A tax technique of applying a loss or credit from a current year to a later year. For example, a business net operating loss may be carried forward indefinitely; *see 40.18.*

Cash method of accounting. Reporting income when actually or constructively received and deducting expenses when paid. Certain businesses may not use the cash method; *see 40.3.*

Casualty loss. Loss from an unforeseen and sudden event that in the case of personal-use property is deductible only if attributable to a federally declared disaster, subject to a $100 per event floor and an overall 10% income floor; *see 18.1.*

Child and dependent care credit. A credit ranging up to 35% of certain care expenses incurred to allow you to work; *see 25.4.*

Child tax credit. A tax credit up to $2,000 per child under age 17, with a potential refundable amount of $1,500. A $500 nonrefundable credit applies for other dependents; *see 25.2.–25.4.*

Community income. Income earned by persons domiciled in community property states and treated as belonging equally to husband and wife; *see 1.6.*

Condemnation. The seizure of property by a public authority for a public purpose. Tax on gain realized on many conversions may be deferred; *see 18.19–18.20.*

Constructive receipt. A tax rule that taxes income that is not received by you but that you may draw upon; *see 2.2.*

Consumer interest. Interest incurred on personal debt and consumer credit. Consumer interest is not deductible.

Convention. Rule for determining MACRS depreciation in the year property is placed in service. Either a half-year convention, mid-quarter convention, or mid-month convention applies; *see 42.5–42.7, 42.12.*

Coverdell Education Savings Account. A special account set up to fund education expenses of a student; *see 33.10–33.11.*

Credit. A tax credit directly reduces tax liability, as opposed to a deduction that reduces income subject to tax.

D

Declining balance method. A rapid depreciation method determined by a constant percentage based on useful life and applied to the adjusted basis of the property; *see 42.5* and *42.8.*

Deductions. Items directly reducing income. Personal deductions such as for mortgage interest, state and local taxes, and charitable contributions are allowed only if deductions are itemized on Schedule A of form 1040 or 1040-SR, but deductions such as for alimony, capital losses, business losses, student loan interest, the deductible part of self-employment tax, and traditional IRA and self-employed retirement plan contributions are deducted from gross income even if itemized deductions are not claimed; *see Chapter 12.*

Deferral. The postponement of tax. Examples of deferral include certain income (e.g., deferred compensation at *2.7*) and certain gains (e.g., gain on like-kind exchange at *6.1*).

Deferred compensation. A portion of earnings withheld by an employer or put into a retirement plan for distribution to the employee at a later date. If certain legal requirements are met, the deferred amount is not taxable until actually paid, for example, after retirement; *see 2.7.*

Deficiency. The excess of the tax assessed by the IRS over the amount reported on your return; *see 48.8.*

Defined benefit plan. A retirement plan that pays fixed benefits based on actuarial projections; *see 41.2.*

Defined contribution plan. A retirement plan that pays benefits based on contributions to individual accounts, plus accumulated earnings. Contributions are generally based on a percentage of salary or earned income; *see 41.2.*

Dependent. A relative or household member for whom various tax benefits may be claimed; *see Chapter 21.*

Depletion. Deduction claimed for the use of mineral resources; *see 9.15.*

Depreciable property. A business or income-producing asset with a useful life exceeding one year; *see 42.1.*

Depreciation. Writing off the cost of depreciable property over a period of years, usually its class life or recovery period specified in the tax law; *see 42.4.*

Depreciation recapture. An amount of gain on the sale of certain depreciable property that is treated as ordinary income in the case of personal property. Recapture is computed on Form 4797; *see 44.1.* For recapture on the sale of realty, *see 44.2.*

Disaster losses. Casualty losses such as from a hurricane or severe flooding, in areas declared by the President to warrant federal assistance. An election may be made to deduct the loss in the year before the loss or the year of the loss; *see 18.3.*

Dividend. A distribution made by a corporation to its shareholders generally of company earnings or surplus. Most dividends are taxable but exceptions are explained in *Chapter 4.*

E

Earned income. Compensation for performing personal services. You must have earned income for a deductible IRA, *see 8.2,* or to claim the Earned Income Credit, *see 25.7.*

Earned income credit. A credit allowed to taxpayers with earned income or adjusted gross income (AGI) below certain thresholds; *see 25.7.*

Education IRA. *See* Coverdell Education Savings Account and *33.10–33.11.*

Electronic Federal Tax Payment System (EFTPS). An online and phone tax payment system available 24 hours a day. For enrollment information, call (800) 555-4477, or go to www.eftps.gov.

Estimated tax. Advance payment of current tax liability based either on wage withholdings or installment payments of your estimated tax liability. To avoid penalties, you generally must pay to the IRS either 90% of your final tax liability, or either 100% or 110% of the prior year's tax liability, depending on your adjusted gross income; *see Chapter 27*.

Expected contribution. The amount a taxpayer must contribute toward premiums for health coverage bought through a government Marketplace, based on a sliding scale according to household income.

F

Fair market value. What a willing buyer would pay to a willing seller when neither is under any compulsion to buy or sell.

Fiduciary. A person or corporation such as a trustee, executor, or guardian who manages property for another person.

Final assembly requirement. A condition for claiming the clean vehicle credit for an electric vehicle placed in service on or after August 16, 2022; *see 25.16*.

First-year expensing (or Section 179 deduction). A deduction of the cost of business equipment in the year placed in service; *see 42.3* for limitations.

Fiscal year. A 12-month period ending on the last day of any month other than December. Partnerships, S corporations, and personal service corporations are limited in their choice of fiscal years and face special restrictions.

Flexible spending arrangement. A salary reduction plan that allows employees to pay for enhanced medical coverage or dependent care expenses on a tax-free basis; *see 3.16*.

Foreign earned income exclusion. For 2023, up to $120,000 of foreign earned income is exempt from tax if a foreign residence or physical presence test is met; *see 36.1–36.2*.

Foreign tax credit. A credit for income taxes paid to a foreign country or U.S. possession; *see 36.13*.

401(k) plan. A deferred pay plan, authorized by Section 401(k) of the Internal Revenue Code, under which a percentage of an employee's salary is withheld and placed in a savings account or the company's profit-sharing plan. Income accumulates on the deferred amount until withdrawn by the employee after reaching age 59½ or when the employee retires or leaves the company; *see 7.15*.

G

General business credit. An overall limit on business credits that offset income tax; it is not a separate credit. *See 40.21*.

Gift tax. Gifts in excess of an per-donee annual exclusion ($17,000 for 2023) are subject to gift tax, but the tax may be offset by a gift tax credit; *see 39.2*.

Grantor trust rules. Tax rules that tax the grantor of a trust on the trust income; *see 39.6*.

Gross income. The total amount of income received from all sources before exclusions and deductions.

Gross receipts. Total business receipts reported on Schedule C before deducting adjustments for returns and allowances and cost of goods sold; *see 40.6*.

Group-term life insurance. Employees are not taxed on up to $50,000 of group-term coverage; *see 3.4*.

H

Head of household. Generally, an unmarried person who maintains a household for dependents and is allowed to compute his or her tax based on head of household rates, which are more favorable than single person rates; *see 1.12*.

Health reimbursement arrangement (HRA). An employer-established account that provides tax-free reimbursements to employees for deductibles and other medical expenses that could be taken as itemized deductions; *see 3.3*.

Health savings account. For calendar year 2023, taxpayers covered by an HDHP may contribute up to $3,850 ($7,750 for family coverage) plus $1,000 extra if age 55 or older and not enrolled in Medicare; *see 3.2* and *41.11*.

High deductible health plan (HDHP). For 2023, a high deductible health plan is a health plan with an annual deductible that is not less than $1,500 for self-only coverage or $3,000 for family coverage, and with annual out-of-pocket expenses that do not exceed $7,500 or $15,000, respectively.

Hobby loss. Hobby expenses are deductible only up to income from the activity; loss deductions are not allowed; *see 40.10*.

Holding period. The length of time that an asset is owned and that generally determines long- or short-term capital gain treatment; *see 5.3* and *5.9–5.12*.

Household income. This amount is used to determine eligibility for the premium tax credit *(25.13)*. It is AGI increased by excluded foreign income and tax-exempt interest.

I

Imputed interest. Interest deemed earned on seller-financed sales or low-interest loans, where the parties' stated interest rate is below the applicable IRS federal rate; *see 4.31* and *4.32*.

Incentive stock option. Option meeting tax law tests that defers tax on the option transaction until the obtained stock is sold; *see 2.16*.

Inclusion amount for leased cars. Based on an IRS table, an amount that reduces a business deduction taken for payments on an auto leased for a minimum of 30 days; *see 43.12*.

Income in respect of a decedent (IRD). Income earned by a person before death but taxable to an estate or heir who receives it; *see 1.14* and *11.16*.

Independent contractor. One who controls his or her own work and reports as a self-employed person; *see Chapters 40* and *45*.

Individual retirement account (IRA). A retirement account to which up to $6,500 (or $7,500 if you are 50 or over) may be contributed for 2023, but deductions for contributions to a traditional IRA are restricted if you are covered by a company retirement plan. Earnings accumulate tax free; *see Chapter 8*.

Installment payment agreement. A formal arrangement with the IRS to pay taxes over time; *see 46.5*.

Installment sale. A sale of property that allows for tax deferment if at least one payment is received after the end of the tax year in which the sale occurs. The installment method does not apply to year-end sales of publicly traded securities. Dealers may not use the installment method. Investors with very large installment balances could face a special tax; *see 5.21*.

Intangible assets. Intangible assets that come within Section 197, such as goodwill, are amortizable over a 15-year period; *see 42.17*.

Inter vivos or lifetime trust. A trust created during the lifetime of the person who created the trust. If irrevocable, income on the trust principal is generally shifted to the trust beneficiaries; *see 39.6*.

Investment in the contract. The total cost investment in an annuity. When annuity payments are made, the portion allocable to the cost investment is tax free; *see 7.21* and *7.24–7.26*.

Investment interest. Interest on debt used to carry investments, but not including interest expense from a passive activity. Deductions are limited to net investment income; *see 15.9.*

Involuntary conversion. Forced disposition of property due to condemnation, theft, or casualty. Tax on gain from involuntary conversions may be deferred if replacement property is purchased; *see 18.14–18.19.*

Itemized deductions. Items, such as interest, state and local income and sales taxes, charitable contributions, and medical deductions, claimed on Schedule A of Form 1040 or 1040-SR. Itemized deductions are subtracted from adjusted gross income to arrive at taxable income; *see Chapter 13.*

J

Joint return. A return filed by a married couple reporting their combined income and deductions. Joint return status provides tax savings to many couples; *see 1.4.*

Joint tenants. Ownership of property by two persons. When one dies, the decedent's interest passes to the survivor; *see 5.18.*

K

Kiddie tax. The tax on the investment income in excess of an annual floor ($2,500 for 2023) of a child under age 18, and many children age 18–23. The tax is based on the parent's top marginal rate and computed on Form 8615; *see 24.2.*

L

Legally separated. Spouses who are required to live apart from each other by the terms of a decree of separate maintenance. Payments under the decree are deductible by the payor and taxable to the payee as alimony; *see 37.2.*

Like-kind exchange. An exchange of similar assets used in a business or held for investment on which gain may be deferred; *see 6.1.*

Lump-sum distribution. Payments within one tax year of the entire amount due to a participant in a qualified retirement plan. Qualifying lump sums may be directly rolled over tax free. For participants born before January 2, 1936, a lump sum may be eligible for current tax under a favorable averaging method; *see 7.2.*

M

Marital deduction. An estate tax and gift tax deduction for assets passing to a spouse. It allows estate and gift transfers completely free of tax; *see 39.10.*

Market discount. The difference between face value of a bond and lower market price, attributable to rising interest rates. On a sale, gain on the bond is generally taxed as ordinary income to the extent of the discount; *see 4.20.*

Material participation tests. Rules for determining whether a person is active in a business activity for passive activity rule purposes. Unless the tests are met, passive loss limits apply; *see 10.6.*

Modified ACRS (MACRS). Depreciation methods applied to assets placed in service after 1986.

Modified adjusted gross income (MAGI). This is generally adjusted gross income increased by certain items such as tax-free foreign earned income. MAGI usually is used to determine phaseouts of certain deductions and credits.

Mortgage insurance. An amount charged when a lender buys a home with less than a 20% down payment. Mortgage insurance premiums are not deductible after 2021; *see 15.5.*

Mortgage interest. Interest on acquisition debt for up to two residences that is fully deductible if within debt ceilings; *see 15.1.*

N

Net operating loss. A business loss that may be carried forward as a deduction from future income until eliminated; *see 40.18–40.20.*

Nonperiodic distributions. A 20% withholding rule applies to nonperiodic distributions, such as lump-sum distributions, paid directly to employees from an employer plan; *see 7.6* and *26.9.*

Nonrecourse financing. Debt on which a person is not personally liable. In case of nonpayment, the creditor must foreclose on property securing the debt. At-risk rules generally bar losses where there is nonrecourse financing, but an exception applies to certain nonrecourse financing for real estate; *see 10.18.*

O

Offer in compromise (OIC). A proposal to the IRS that, if accepted, allows a taxpayer to pay less than the full amount of tax owed; *see 48.10.*

Ordinary and necessary. A statutory requirement for the deductibility of a business expense.

Ordinary income. Income other than long-term capital gains or qualified dividends that are taxed the same as long-term capital gains; *see 5.3.*

Ordinary loss. A loss other than a capital loss.

Original issue discount (OID). The difference between the face value of a bond and its original issue price. OID is reported on an annual basis as interest income; *see 4.19.*

P

Partnership. An unincorporated business or income-producing entity organized by two or more persons. A partnership is not subject to tax but passes through to the partners all income, deductions, and credits, according to the terms of the partnership agreement; *see 11.9–11.13.*

Passive activity loss rules. Rules that limit the deduction of losses from passive activities to income from other passive activities. Passive activities include investment rental operations or businesses in which you do not materially participate; *see 10.1.*

Patronage dividend. A taxable distribution made by a cooperative to its members or patrons.

Percentage depletion. A deduction method that applies a fixed percentage to the gross income generated by mineral property; *see 9.15.*

Personal interest. Tax term for interest on personal loans and consumer purchases. Interest on personal loans other than home mortgages and student loans is not deductible.

Placed in service. The time when a depreciable asset is ready to be used. The date fixes the beginning of the depreciation period.

Points. Charges to the homeowner at the time of the loan. A point is equal to 1 percent. Depending on the type of loan, points may be currently deductible or amortized over the life of the loan; *see 15.7.*

Premature distributions. Withdrawals before age 59½ from qualified retirement plans are subject to penalties unless specific exceptions are met; *see 7.13* and *8.12.*

Principal residence. On a sale of a principal residence, you may avoid tax under the rules explained in *Chapter 29.*

Private letter ruling. A written determination issued to a taxpayer by the IRS that interprets and applies the tax laws to the taxpayer's specific set of facts. A letter ruling advises the taxpayer regarding the tax treatment that can be expected from the IRS in the circumstances specified by the ruling. It may not be used or cited as precedent by another taxpayer.

Probate estate. Property held in a decedent's name passing by will; *see 39.7.*

Profit-sharing plan. A defined contribution plan under which the amount contributed to the employees' accounts is based on a percentage of the employer's profits; *see 7.15* and *41.2.*

Provisional income. If your provisional income exceeds a base amount, part of your Social Security benefits may be subject to tax. To figure provisional income, *see 34.3.*

PTIN. A preparer tax identification number required for tax professionals to prepare tax returns for compensation.

Q

Qualified business income deduction. A deduction for 20% of qualified business income, subject to income limitations; *see 40.24*

Qualified charitable distribution (QCD). A transfer from an IRA to a charity up to $100,000 per year by someone age 70½ or older; *see 8.8.*

Qualified charitable organization. A nonprofit philanthropic organization that is approved by the U.S. Treasury to receive charitable contribution deductions; *see 14.1.*

Qualified dividends. Dividends that are taxed at the long-term capital gain rate; *see 4.2.*

Qualified domestic relations order (QDRO). A specialized domestic relations court order that conforms to IRS regulations and provides instructions to pension plan administrators and IRA custodians as to how to pay benefits to a divorced spouse; *see 7.10* and *8.11.*

Qualified Longevity Annuity Contract (QLAC). An annuity purchased with IRA funds to defer required minimum distributions, but not past age 85: *see 8.13.*

Qualified plan. A retirement plan that meets tax law tests and allows for tax deferment and tax-free accumulation of income until benefits are withdrawn. Pension, profit-sharing, stock bonus, employee stock ownership, and IRAs may be qualified plans; *see Chapters 7, 8,* and *41.*

Qualifying Survivng Spouse. A filing status entitling the taxpayer with dependents to use joint tax rates for up to two tax years after the death of a spouse. This filing status is fomerly known as Qualifying Widow/Widower; *see 1.11.*

Qualified tuition program (QTP). A state-sponsored college savings plan or prepayment plan, or a prepayment plan established by a private college; *see 33.5.*

R

Real estate investment trust (REIT). An entity that invests primarily in real estate and mortgages and passes through income to investors; *see 31.1.*

Real estate professional. An individual who, because of his or her real estate activity, qualifies to deduct rental losses from nonpassive income; *see 10.3.*

Real property. Land and the buildings on land. Buildings are depreciable; *see 42.12* and *42.15.*

Recognized gain or loss. The amount of gain or loss to be reported on a tax return. Gain may not be recognized on certain exchanges of property; *see 6.1.*

Recovery property. Tangible depreciable property placed in service after 1980 and before 1987 and depreciable under ACRS; *see 42.11* and *42.15.*

Refundable tax credit. A credit that entitles you to a refund even if you owe no tax for the year.

Required Minimum Distributions (RMDs). Distributions that must be taken annually to avoid an IRS penalty by a traditional IRA account owner starting with the year of attaining a specified age. For qualified plan participants the starting date may be delayed for employees working beyond the required starting date. Minimum distribution rules also apply to beneficiaries of qualified plans, traditional IRAs, and Roth IRAs. *See 7.10–7.11, 8.13–8.15,* and *8.26.*

Residence interest. Term for deductible mortgage interest on a principal residence and a second home; *see 15.1–15.2.*

Residential rental property. Real property in which 80% or more of the gross income is from dwelling units. Under MACRS, depreciation is claimed over *27.5* years under the straight-line method; *see 42.12.*

Retirement savers credit. Eligible taxpayers may claim a tax credit for 10%, 20%, or 50% of up to $2,000 of retirement plan contributions; *see 25.11-25.12.*

Return of capital. A distribution of your investment that is not subject to tax unless the distribution exceeds your investment; *see 4.11.*

Revenue ruling. A revenue ruling is the Commissioner's "official interpretation of the interpretation of the law" and generally is binding on revenue agents and other IRS officials. Taxpayers generally may rely on published revenue rulings in determining the tax treatment of their own transactions that arise out of similar facts and circumstances.

Revocable trust. A trust that may be changed or terminated by its creator or another person. Such trusts do not provide an income tax savings to the creator; *see 39.6.*

Rollover. A tax-free reinvestment of a distribution from a qualified retirement plan into an IRA or other qualified plan, or from one IRA to another, within 60 days of the distribution; *see 7.2, 7.6,* and *8.10.*

Roth IRA. A nondeductible contributory IRA that allows for tax-free accumulation of income. Qualifying distributions are completely tax free. See *8.19–8.25.*

S

Salvage value. The estimated value of an asset at the end of its useful life. Salvage value is ignored by ACRS and MACRS rules.

S corporation. A corporation that elects S status in order to receive tax treatment similar to that of a partnership; *see Chapter 11.*

Section 179 deduction (or First-year expensing). A deduction allowed for investments in depreciable business equipment in the year the property is placed in service; *see 42.3* for limitations.

Section 457 plan. Deferred compensation plan set up by a state or local government, or tax-exempt organization, which allows tax-free deferrals of salary; *see 7.20.*

Section 1231 property. Depreciable property used in a trade or business and held for more than a year. All Section 1231 gains and losses are netted; a net gain is treated as capital gain, a net loss as an ordinary loss; *see 44.8.*

Section 1244 stock. Stock in a closely-held corporation for which losses up to a dollar limit are treated as ordinary rather than capital losses; *see 30.11.*

Self-employed person. An individual who operates a business or profession as a proprietor or independent contractor and reports self-employment income on Schedule C; *see Chapters 40* and *45.*

Self-employment tax. Tax paid by self-employed persons to finance Social Security and Medicare coverage. For 2023, there are two rates. A 12.4% rate (for Social Security) applies to a taxable earnings base of $160,200 or less and a 2.9% rate (for Medicare) applies to all net earnings; see *Chapter 45*.

Separate return. Return filed by a married person who does not file a joint return. Filing separately may save taxes where each spouse has separate deductions, but certain tax benefits require a joint return; see *1.3*.

Short sale. Sale of borrowed securities made to freeze a paper profit or to gain from a declining market; see *30.5*.

Short tax year. A tax year of less than 12 months. May occur with the startup of a business or change in accounting method.

Short-term capital gain or loss. Gain or loss on the sale or exchange of a capital asset held one year or less; see *5.1*, *5.3*, and *5.10*.

Simplified employee plan (SEP). IRA-type plan set up by an employer, rather than the employee. Salary-reduction contributions may be allowed to plans of small employers set up before 1997; see *8.15–8.16*.

Standard deduction. A fixed deduction allowed to taxpayers who do not itemize deductions, based on filing status, plus an additional amount for those age 65 or older or blind; see *13.1*.

Standard mileage rate. A fixed rate allowed by the IRS for business auto expenses in place of deducting actual expenses; see *43.1*.

Statutory employees. Certain employees, such as full-time life insurance salespersons, who may report income and deductions on Schedule C, rather than on Schedule A as miscellaneous itemized deductions; see *40.6*.

Stock dividend. A distribution of additional shares of a corporation's stock to its shareholders; see *4.6*.

Stock option. A right to buy stock at a fixed price.

Straddle. Taking an offsetting investment position to reduce the risk of loss in a similar investment; see *30.9*.

Straight-line method. A method of depreciating the cost of a depreciable asset on a pro rata basis over its cost recovery period; see *42.9*, *42.12*, *42.15*.

T

Tangible personal property. Movable property, such as desks, computers, machinery, and autos, depreciable over a five-year or seven-year period; see *42.4*.

Taxable income. Net income after claiming all deductions from gross income and adjusted gross income, such as IRA deductions, itemized deductions or the standard deduction, and the qualified business income deduction; see *22.1*.

Tax attributes. When debts are canceled in bankruptcy cases, the canceled amount is excluded from gross income. Tax attributes are certain losses, credits, and property basis that must be reduced to the extent of the exclusion; see *11.8*.

Tax benefit rule. A requirement to include in gross income an item deducted in a prior year to the extent it reduced tax liability that year; see *11.5*.

Tax deferral. Shifting income to a later year, such as where you defer taxable interest to the following year by purchasing a T-bill or savings certificate maturing after the end of the current year; see *Chapter 4.* Investments in qualified retirement plans provide tax deferral (*Chapters 7, 8,* and *41*).

Tax home. The area of your principal place of business or employment. You must be away from your tax home on a business trip to deduct travel expenses; see *20.6*.

Tax identification number. For an individual, his or her Social Security number; for businesses, fiduciaries, and other non-individual taxpayers, the employer identification number.

Tax preference items. Items that may subject a taxpayer to the alternative minimum tax (AMT); see *23.2*.

Tax-sheltered annuity. A type of retirement annuity offered to employees of charitable organizations and educational systems, generally funded by employee salary-reduction contributions; see *7.19*.

Tax year. A period (generally 12 months) for reporting income and expenses; see *40.4*.

Tenancy by the entireties. A joint tenancy in real property in the name of both husband and wife. On the death of one tenant, the survivor receives entire interest.

Tenants in common. Two or more persons who have undivided ownership rights in property. Upon death of a tenant, his or her share passes to his or her estate, rather than to the surviving tenants.

Testamentary trust. A trust established under a will.

Total income. *See* gross income.

Total tax liability. The amount of federal income tax owed by a taxpayer to the federal government.

Trust. An arrangement under which one person transfers legal ownership of assets to another person or corporation (the trustee) for the benefit of one or more third persons (beneficiaries).

U

Unrecaptured Section 1250 gain. Long-term gain realized on the sale of depreciable realty attributed to depreciation deductions and subject to a 25% capital gain rate; see *5.3* and *44.2*.

Useful life. For property not depreciated under ACRS or MACRS, the estimate of time in which a depreciable asset will be used.

W

Wash sales. Sales on which losses are disallowed because you recover your market position within a 61-day period; see *30.6*.

Withholding. An amount taken from income as a prepayment of an individual's tax liability for the year. In the case of wages, the employer withholds part of every wage payment. Backup withholding from dividend or interest income is required if you do not provide the payer with a correct taxpayer identification number. Withholding on pensions and IRAs is automatic unless you elect to waive withholding; see *Chapter 26*.

Q